A2 ALTITUDE CORRECTION TABLES 10°-90°—SUN, STARS, PLANETS

OCT.—MAR. SUN APR.—SEPT.

App. Alt.	Lower Limb	Upper Limb	App. Alt.	Lower Limb	Upper Limb
° ′	′	′	° ′	′	′
9 33	+10.8	−21.5	9 39	+10.6	−21.2
9 45	+10.9	−21.4	9 50	+10.7	−21.1
9 56	+11.0	−21.3	10 02	+10.8	−21.0
10 08	+11.1	−21.2	10 14	+10.9	−20.9
10 20	+11.2	−21.1	10 27	+11.0	−20.8
10 33	+11.3	−21.0	10 40	+11.1	−20.7
10 46	+11.4	−20.9	10 53	+11.2	−20.6
11 00	+11.5	−20.8	11 07	+11.3	−20.5
11 15	+11.6	−20.7	11 22	+11.4	−20.4
11 30	+11.7	−20.6	11 37	+11.5	−20.3
11 45	+11.8	−20.5	11 53	+11.6	−20.2
12 01	+11.9	−20.4	12 10	+11.7	−20.1
12 18	+12.0	−20.3	12 27	+11.8	−20.0
12 36	+12.1	−20.2	12 45	+11.9	−19.9
12 54	+12.2	−20.1	13 04	+12.0	−19.8
13 14	+12.3	−20.0	13 24	+12.1	−19.7
13 34	+12.4	−19.9	13 44	+12.2	−19.6
13 55	+12.5	−19.8	14 06	+12.3	−19.5
14 17	+12.6	−19.7	14 29	+12.4	−19.4
14 41	+12.7	−19.6	14 53	+12.5	−19.3
15 05	+12.8	−19.5	15 18	+12.6	−19.2
15 31	+12.9	−19.4	15 45	+12.7	−19.1
15 59	+13.0	−19.3	16 13	+12.8	−19.0
16 27	+13.1	−19.2	16 43	+12.9	−18.9
16 58	+13.2	−19.1	17 14	+13.0	−18.8
17 30	+13.3	−19.0	17 47	+13.1	−18.7
18 05	+13.4	−18.9	18 23	+13.2	−18.6
18 41	+13.5	−18.8	19 00	+13.3	−18.5
19 20	+13.6	−18.7	19 41	+13.4	−18.4
20 02	+13.7	−18.6	20 24	+13.5	−18.3
20 46	+13.8	−18.5	21 10	+13.6	−18.2
21 34	+13.9	−18.4	21 59	+13.7	−18.1
22 25	+14.0	−18.3	22 52	+13.8	−18.0
23 20	+14.1	−18.2	23 49	+13.9	−17.9
24 20	+14.2	−18.1	24 51	+14.0	−17.8
25 24	+14.3	−18.0	25 58	+14.1	−17.7
26 34	+14.4	−17.9	27 11	+14.2	−17.6
27 50	+14.5	−17.8	28 31	+14.3	−17.5
29 13	+14.6	−17.7	29 58	+14.4	−17.4
30 44	+14.7	−17.6	31 33	+14.5	−17.3
32 24	+14.8	−17.5	33 18	+14.6	−17.2
34 15	+14.9	−17.4	35 15	+14.7	−17.1
36 17	+15.0	−17.3	37 24	+14.8	−17.0
38 34	+15.1	−17.2	39 48	+14.9	−16.9
41 06	+15.2	−17.1	42 28	+15.0	−16.8
43 56	+15.3	−17.0	45 29	+15.1	−16.7
47 07	+15.4	−16.9	48 52	+15.2	−16.6
50 43	+15.5	−16.8	52 41	+15.3	−16.5
54 46	+15.6	−16.7	56 59	+15.4	−16.4
59 21	+15.7	−16.6	61 50	+15.5	−16.3
64 28	+15.8	−16.5	67 15	+15.6	−16.2
70 10	+15.9	−16.4	73 14	+15.7	−16.1
76 24	+16.0	−16.3	79 42	+15.8	−16.0
83 05	+16.1	−16.2	86 31	+15.9	−15.9
90 00			90 00		

STARS AND PLANETS

App. Alt.	Corrn	App. Alt.	Additional Corrn
° ′	′	**2015**	
9 55	−5.3	**VENUS**	
10 07	−5.2	Jan. 1–May 3	
10 20	−5.1	Dec. 4–Dec. 31	
10 32	−5.0	° ′	
10 46	−4.9	60	+0.1
10 59	−4.8		
11 14	−4.7	May 4–June 22	
11 29	−4.6	Oct. 13–Dec. 3	
11 44	−4.5	° ′	
12 00	−4.4	41	+0.2
12 17	−4.3	76	+0.1
12 35	−4.2		
12 53	−4.1	June 23–July 14	
13 12	−4.0	Sept. 19–Oct. 12	
13 32	−3.9	° ′	
13 53	−3.8	34	+0.3
14 16	−3.7	60	+0.2
14 39	−3.6	80	+0.1
15 03	−3.5		
15 29	−3.4	July 15–July 30	
15 56	−3.3	Sept. 2–Sept. 18	
16 25	−3.2	° ′	
16 55	−3.1	29	+0.4
17 27	−3.0	51	+0.3
18 01	−2.9	68	+0.2
18 37	−2.8	83	+0.1
19 16	−2.7		
19 56	−2.6	July 31–Sept. 1	
20 40	−2.5	° ′	
21 27	−2.4	26	+0.5
22 17	−2.3	46	+0.4
23 11	−2.2	60	+0.3
24 09	−2.1	73	+0.2
25 12	−2.0	84	+0.1
26 20	−1.9		
27 34	−1.8	**MARS**	
28 54	−1.7	Jan. 1–Dec. 31	
30 22	−1.6	° ′	
31 58	−1.5	60	+0.1
33 43	−1.4		
35 38	−1.3		
37 45	−1.2		
40 06	−1.1		
42 42	−1.0		
45 34	−0.9		
48 45	−0.8		
52 16	−0.7		
56 09	−0.6		
60 26	−0.5		
65 06	−0.4		
70 09	−0.3		
75 32	−0.2		
81 12	−0.1		
87 03	0.0		
90 00			

DIP

Ht. of Eye	Corrn	Ht. of Eye	Ht. of Eye	Corrn
m	′	ft.	m	′
2.4	−2.8	8.0	1.0	− 1.8
2.6	−2.9	8.6	1.5	− 2.2
2.8	−3.0	9.2	2.0	− 2.5
3.0	−3.1	9.8	2.5	− 2.8
3.2	−3.2	10.5	3.0	− 3.0
3.4	−3.3	11.2	See table ←	
3.6	−3.4	11.9		
3.8	−3.5	12.6	m	′
4.0	−3.6	13.3	20	− 7.9
4.3	−3.7	14.1	22	− 8.3
4.5	−3.8	14.9	24	− 8.6
4.7	−3.9	15.7	26	− 9.0
5.0	−4.0	16.5	28	− 9.3
5.2	−4.1	17.4		
5.5	−4.2	18.3	30	− 9.6
5.8	−4.3	19.1	32	− 10.0
6.1	−4.4	20.1	34	− 10.3
6.3	−4.5	21.0	36	− 10.6
6.6	−4.6	22.0	38	− 10.8
6.9	−4.7	22.9		
7.2	−4.8	23.9	40	− 11.1
7.5	−4.9	24.9	42	− 11.4
7.9	−5.0	26.0	44	− 11.7
8.2	−5.1	27.1	46	− 11.9
8.5	−5.2	28.1	48	− 12.2
8.8	−5.3	29.2		
9.2	−5.4	30.4	ft.	
9.5	−5.5	31.5	2	− 1.4
9.9	−5.6	32.7	4	− 1.9
10.3	−5.7	33.9	6	− 2.4
10.6	−5.8	35.1	8	− 2.7
11.0	−5.9	36.3	10	− 3.1
11.4	−6.0	37.6	See table ←	
11.8	−6.1	38.9		
12.2	−6.2	40.1	ft.	′
12.6	−6.3	41.5	70	− 8.1
13.0	−6.4	42.8	75	− 8.4
13.4	−6.5	44.2	80	− 8.7
13.8	−6.6	45.5	85	− 8.9
14.2	−6.7	46.9	90	− 9.2
14.7	−6.8	48.4	95	− 9.5
15.1	−6.9	49.8		
15.5	−7.0	51.3	100	− 9.7
16.0	−7.1	52.8	105	− 9.9
16.5	−7.2	54.3	110	− 10.2
16.9	−7.3	55.8	115	− 10.4
17.4	−7.4	57.4	120	− 10.6
17.9	−7.5	58.9	125	− 10.8
18.4	−7.6	60.5		
18.8	−7.7	62.1	130	− 11.1
19.3	−7.8	63.8	135	− 11.3
19.8	−7.9	65.4	140	− 11.5
20.4	−8.0	67.1	145	− 11.7
20.9	−8.1	68.8	150	− 11.9
21.4		70.5	155	− 12.1

App. Alt. = Apparent altitude = Sextant altitude corrected for index error and dip.

App. Alt.	OCT.—MAR. SUN Lower Limb	Upper Limb	APR.—SEPT. SUN Lower Limb	Upper Limb	STARS PLANETS	App. Alt.	OCT.—MAR. SUN Lower Limb	Upper Limb	APR.—SEPT. SUN Lower Limb	Upper Limb	STARS PLANETS
° ′	′	′	′	′	′	° ′	′	′	′	′	′
0 00	− 17·5	− 49·8	− 17·8	− 49·6	− 33·8	3 30	+ 3·4	− 28·9	+ 3·1	− 28·7	− 12·9
0 03	16·9	49·2	17·2	49·0	33·2	3 35	3·6	28·7	3·3	28·5	12·7
0 06	16·3	48·6	16·6	48·4	32·6	3 40	3·8	28·5	3·6	28·2	12·5
0 09	15·7	48·0	16·0	47·8	32·0	3 45	4·0	28·3	3·8	28·0	12·3
0 12	15·2	47·5	15·4	47·2	31·5	3 50	4·2	28·1	4·0	27·8	12·1
0 15	14·6	46·9	14·8	46·6	30·9	3 55	4·4	27·9	4·1	27·7	11·9
0 18	− 14·1	− 46·4	− 14·3	− 46·1	− 30·4	4 00	+ 4·6	− 27·7	+ 4·3	− 27·5	− 11·7
0 21	13·5	45·8	13·8	45·6	29·8	4 05	4·8	27·5	4·5	27·3	11·5
0 24	13·0	45·3	13·3	45·1	29·3	4 10	4·9	27·4	4·7	27·1	11·4
0 27	12·5	44·8	12·8	44·6	28·8	4 15	5·1	27·2	4·9	26·9	11·2
0 30	12·0	44·3	12·3	44·1	28·3	4 20	5·3	27·0	5·0	26·8	11·0
0 33	11·6	43·9	11·8	43·6	27·9	4 25	5·4	26·9	5·2	26·6	10·9
0 36	− 11·1	− 43·4	− 11·3	− 43·1	− 27·4	4 30	+ 5·6	− 26·7	+ 5·3	− 26·5	− 10·7
0 39	10·6	42·9	10·9	42·7	26·9	4 35	5·7	26·6	5·5	26·3	10·6
0 42	10·2	42·5	10·5	42·3	26·5	4 40	5·9	26·4	5·6	26·2	10·4
0 45	9·8	42·1	10·0	41·8	26·1	4 45	6·0	26·3	5·8	26·0	10·3
0 48	9·4	41·7	9·6	41·4	25·7	4 50	6·2	26·1	5·9	25·9	10·1
0 51	9·0	41·3	9·2	41·0	25·3	4 55	6·3	26·0	6·1	25·7	10·0
0 54	− 8·6	− 40·9	− 8·8	− 40·6	− 24·9	5 00	+ 6·4	− 25·9	+ 6·2	− 25·6	− 9·8
0 57	8·2	40·5	8·4	40·2	24·5	5 05	6·6	25·7	6·3	25·5	9·7
1 00	7·8	40·1	8·0	39·8	24·1	5 10	6·7	25·6	6·5	25·3	9·6
1 03	7·4	39·7	7·7	39·5	23·7	5 15	6·8	25·5	6·6	25·2	9·5
1 06	7·1	39·4	7·3	39·1	23·4	5 20	7·0	25·3	6·7	25·1	9·3
1 09	6·7	39·0	7·0	38·8	23·0	5 25	7·1	25·2	6·8	25·0	9·2
1 12	− 6·4	− 38·7	− 6·6	− 38·4	− 22·7	5 30	+ 7·2	− 25·1	+ 6·9	− 24·9	− 9·1
1 15	6·0	38·3	6·3	38·1	22·3	5 35	7·3	25·0	7·1	24·7	9·0
1 18	5·7	38·0	6·0	37·8	22·0	5 40	7·4	24·9	7·2	24·6	8·9
1 21	5·4	37·7	5·7	37·5	21·7	5 45	7·5	24·8	7·3	24·5	8·8
1 24	5·1	37·4	5·3	37·1	21·4	5 50	7·6	24·7	7·4	24·4	8·7
1 27	4·8	37·1	5·0	36·8	21·1	5 55	7·7	24·6	7·5	24·3	8·6
1 30	− 4·5	− 36·8	− 4·7	− 36·5	− 20·8	6 00	+ 7·8	− 24·5	+ 7·6	− 24·2	− 8·5
1 35	4·0	36·3	4·3	36·1	20·3	6 10	8·0	24·3	7·8	24·0	8·3
1 40	3·6	35·9	3·8	35·6	19·9	6 20	8·2	24·1	8·0	23·8	8·1
1 45	3·1	35·4	3·4	35·2	19·4	6 30	8·4	23·9	8·2	23·6	7·9
1 50	2·7	35·0	2·9	34·7	19·0	6 40	8·6	23·7	8·3	23·5	7·7
1 55	2·3	34·6	2·5	34·3	18·6	6 50	8·7	23·6	8·5	23·3	7·6
2 00	− 1·9	− 34·2	− 2·1	− 33·9	− 18·2	7 00	+ 8·9	− 23·4	+ 8·7	− 23·1	− 7·4
2 05	1·5	33·8	1·7	33·5	17·8	7 10	9·1	23·2	8·8	23·0	7·2
2 10	1·1	33·4	1·4	33·2	17·4	7 20	9·2	23·1	9·0	22·8	7·1
2 15	0·8	33·1	1·0	32·8	17·1	7 30	9·3	23·0	9·1	22·7	6·9
2 20	0·4	32·7	0·7	32·5	16·7	7 40	9·5	22·8	9·2	22·6	6·8
2 25	− 0·1	32·4	− 0·3	32·1	16·4	7 50	9·6	22·7	9·4	22·4	6·7
2 30	+ 0·2	− 32·1	0·0	− 31·8	− 16·1	8 00	+ 9·7	− 22·6	+ 9·5	− 22·3	− 6·6
2 35	0·5	31·8	+ 0·3	31·5	15·8	8 10	9·9	22·4	9·6	22·2	6·4
2 40	0·8	31·5	0·6	31·2	15·4	8 20	10·0	22·3	9·7	22·1	6·3
2 45	1·1	31·2	0·9	30·9	15·2	8 30	10·1	22·2	9·9	21·9	6·2
2 50	1·4	30·9	1·2	30·6	14·9	8 40	10·2	22·1	10·0	21·8	6·1
2 55	1·7	30·6	1·4	30·4	14·6	8 50	10·3	22·0	10·1	21·7	6·0
3 00	+ 2·0	− 30·3	+ 1·7	− 30·1	− 14·3	9 00	+ 10·4	− 21·9	+ 10·2	− 21·6	− 5·9
3 05	2·2	30·1	2·0	29·8	14·1	9 10	10·5	21·8	10·3	21·5	5·8
3 10	2·5	29·8	2·2	29·6	13·8	9 20	10·6	21·7	10·4	21·4	5·7
3 15	2·7	29·6	2·5	29·3	13·6	9 30	10·7	21·6	10·5	21·3	5·6
3 20	2·9	29·4	2·7	29·1	13·4	9 40	10·8	21·5	10·6	21·2	5·5
3 25	3·2	29·1	2·9	28·9	13·1	9 50	10·9	21·4	10·6	21·2	5·4
3 30	+ 3·4	− 28·9	+ 3·1	− 28·7	− 12·9	10 00	+ 11·0	− 21·3	+ 10·7	− 21·1	− 5·3

Additional corrections for temperature and pressure are given on the following page.

For bubble sextant observations ignore dip and use the star corrections for Sun, planets and stars.

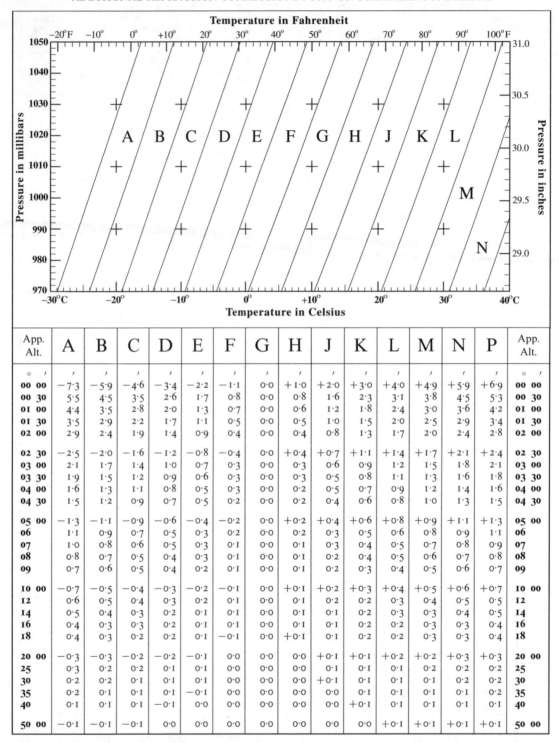

App. Alt.	A	B	C	D	E	F	G	H	J	K	L	M	N	P	App. Alt.
° ′	′	′	′	′	′	′	′	′	′	′	′	′	′	′	° ′
00 00	−7·3	−5·9	−4·6	−3·4	−2·2	−1·1	0·0	+1·0	+2·0	+3·0	+4·0	+4·9	+5·9	+6·9	00 00
00 30	5·5	4·5	3·5	2·6	1·7	0·8	0·0	0·8	1·6	2·3	3·1	3·8	4·5	5·3	00 30
01 00	4·4	3·5	2·8	2·0	1·3	0·7	0·0	0·6	1·2	1·8	2·4	3·0	3·6	4·2	01 00
01 30	3·5	2·9	2·2	1·7	1·1	0·5	0·0	0·5	1·0	1·5	2·0	2·5	2·9	3·4	01 30
02 00	2·9	2·4	1·9	1·4	0·9	0·4	0·0	0·4	0·8	1·3	1·7	2·0	2·4	2·8	02 00
02 30	−2·5	−2·0	−1·6	−1·2	−0·8	−0·4	0·0	+0·4	+0·7	+1·1	+1·4	+1·7	+2·1	+2·4	02 30
03 00	2·1	1·7	1·4	1·0	0·7	0·3	0·0	0·3	0·6	0·9	1·2	1·5	1·8	2·1	03 00
03 30	1·9	1·5	1·2	0·9	0·6	0·3	0·0	0·3	0·5	0·8	1·1	1·3	1·6	1·8	03 30
04 00	1·6	1·3	1·1	0·8	0·5	0·3	0·0	0·2	0·5	0·7	0·9	1·2	1·4	1·6	04 00
04 30	1·5	1·2	0·9	0·7	0·5	0·2	0·0	0·2	0·4	0·6	0·8	1·0	1·3	1·5	04 30
05 00	−1·3	−1·1	−0·9	−0·6	−0·4	−0·2	0·0	+0·2	+0·4	+0·6	+0·8	+0·9	+1·1	+1·3	05 00
06	1·1	0·9	0·7	0·5	0·3	0·2	0·0	0·2	0·3	0·5	0·6	0·8	0·9	1·1	06
07	1·0	0·8	0·6	0·5	0·3	0·1	0·0	0·1	0·3	0·4	0·5	0·7	0·8	0·9	07
08	0·8	0·7	0·5	0·4	0·3	0·1	0·0	0·1	0·2	0·4	0·5	0·6	0·7	0·8	08
09	0·7	0·6	0·5	0·4	0·2	0·1	0·0	0·1	0·2	0·3	0·4	0·5	0·6	0·7	09
10 00	−0·7	−0·5	−0·4	−0·3	−0·2	−0·1	0·0	+0·1	+0·2	+0·3	+0·4	+0·5	+0·6	+0·7	10 00
12	0·6	0·5	0·4	0·3	0·2	0·1	0·0	0·1	0·2	0·2	0·3	0·4	0·5	0·5	12
14	0·5	0·4	0·3	0·2	0·1	0·1	0·0	0·1	0·1	0·2	0·3	0·3	0·4	0·5	14
16	0·4	0·3	0·3	0·2	0·1	0·1	0·0	0·1	0·1	0·2	0·2	0·3	0·3	0·4	16
18	0·4	0·3	0·2	0·2	0·1	−0·1	0·0	+0·1	0·1	0·2	0·2	0·3	0·3	0·4	18
20 00	−0·3	−0·3	−0·2	−0·2	−0·1	0·0	0·0	0·0	+0·1	+0·1	+0·2	+0·2	+0·3	+0·3	20 00
25	0·3	0·2	0·2	0·1	0·1	0·0	0·0	0·0	0·1	0·1	0·1	0·2	0·2	0·2	25
30	0·2	0·2	0·1	0·1	0·1	0·0	0·0	0·0	+0·1	0·1	0·1	0·1	0·2	0·2	30
35	0·2	0·1	0·1	0·1	−0·1	0·0	0·0	0·0	0·0	0·1	0·1	0·1	0·1	0·2	35
40	0·1	0·1	0·1	−0·1	0·0	0·0	0·0	0·0	+0·1	0·1	0·1	0·1	0·1		40
50 00	−0·1	−0·1	−0·1	0·0	0·0	0·0	0·0	0·0	0·0	0·0	+0·1	+0·1	+0·1	+0·1	50 00

The graph is entered with arguments temperature and pressure to find a zone letter; using as arguments this zone letter and apparent altitude (sextant altitude corrected for index error and dip), a correction is taken from the table. This correction is to be applied to the sextant altitude in addition to the corrections for standard conditions (for the Sun, stars and planets from page A2-A3 and for the Moon from pages xxxiv and xxxv).

2015
Nautical Almanac
COMMERCIAL EDITION

PUBLISHED BY:

Paradise Cay Publications, Inc.
Post Office Box 29
Arcata, CA 95518-0029
Tel: 1-707-822-9063
Fax: 1-707-822-9163
www.paracay.com

ISBN: 978-1-937196-15-8

Printed and distributed with permission by Paradise Cay Publications, Inc.

NOTE

Every care is taken to prevent errors in the production of this publication. As a final precaution it is recommended that the sequence of pages in this copy be examined on receipt. If faulty, it should be returned for replacement.

PREFACE

The first three sections of this book are a complete and accurate duplication from *The Nautical Almanac* produced jointly by Her Majesty's Nautical Almanac Office, United Kingdom Hydrographic Office, Admiralty Way, Taunton, Somerset, TA1 2DN, United Kingdom and the Nautical Almanac Office of the US Naval Observatory.

Copyright for *The Nautical Almanac* is held by the United Kingdom Hydrographic Office, and is protected by international copyright law. All rights reserved. No part of this publication may be reproduced, stored in a retrieval system or transmitted in any form or by any means, electronic, mechanical, photocopying, recording or otherwise without prior permission of HM Nautical Almanac Office, United Kingdom Hydrographic Office, Admiralty Way, Taunton, Somerset, TA1 2DN, United Kingdom.

The following United States government work is excepted from the above notice and no copyright is claimed for it in the United States: pages 6 and 7, and pages 286-315.

We gratefully acknowledge the United Kingdom Hydrographic Office and the United States Naval Observatory for permission to use the material contained in the almanac sections of this publication.

The 2015 Nautical Almanac
Commercial Edition

RELIGIOUS CALENDARS

Epiphany	Jan. 6	Low Sunday	Apr. 12
Septuagesima Sunday	Feb. 1	Rogation Sunday	May 10
Quinquagesima Sunday	Feb. 15	Ascension Day—Holy Thursday	May 14
Ash Wednesday	Feb. 18	Whit Sunday—Pentecost	May 24
Quadragesima Sunday	Feb. 22	Trinity Sunday	May 31
Palm Sunday	Mar. 29	Corpus Christi	June 4
Good Friday	Apr. 3	First Sunday in Advent	Nov. 29
Easter Day	Apr. 5	Christmas Day (Friday)	Dec. 25
First Day of Passover (Pesach)	Apr. 4	Day of Atonement (Yom Kippur)	Sept. 23
Feast of Weeks (Shavuot)	May 24	First day of Tabernacles (Succoth)	Sept. 28
Jewish New Year 5776 (Rosh Hashanah)	Sept. 14		
Ramadân, First day of (tabular)	June 18	Islamic New Year (1437)	Oct. 15

The Jewish and Islamic dates above are tabular dates, which begin at sunset on the previous evening and end at sunset on the date tabulated. In practice, the dates of Islamic fasts and festivals are determined by an actual sighting of the appropriate new moon.

CIVIL CALENDAR—UNITED KINGDOM

Accession of Queen Elizabeth II	Feb. 6	Birthday of Prince Philip, Duke of Edinburgh	June 10
St David (Wales)	Mar. 1		
Commonwealth Day	Mar. 9	The Queen's Official Birthday†	June 13
St Patrick (Ireland)	Mar. 17	Remembrance Sunday	Nov. 8
Birthday of Queen Elizabeth II	Apr. 21	Birthday of the Prince of Wales	Nov. 14
St George (England)	Apr. 23	St Andrew (Scotland)	Nov. 30
Coronation Day	June 2		

PUBLIC HOLIDAYS

England and Wales—Jan. 1†, Apr. 3, Apr. 6, May 4†, May 25, Aug. 31, Dec. 25, Dec. 28

Northern Ireland—Jan. 1†, Mar. 17, Apr. 3, Apr. 6, May 4†, May 25, July 13†, Aug. 31, Dec. 25, Dec. 28

Scotland—Jan. 1, Jan. 2, Apr. 3, May 4, May 25†, Aug. 3, Dec. 25, Dec. 28†

CIVIL CALENDAR—UNITED STATES OF AMERICA

New Year's Day	Jan. 1	Labor Day	Sept. 7
Martin Luther King's Birthday	Jan. 19	Columbus Day	Oct. 12
Washington's Birthday	Feb. 16	Election Day (in certain States)	Nov. 3
Memorial Day	May 25	Veterans Day	Nov. 11
Independence Day	July 4	Thanksgiving Day	Nov. 26

†Dates subject to confirmation

PHASES OF THE MOON

New Moon			First Quarter			Full Moon			Last Quarter		
	d	h m		d	h m		d	h m		d	h m
						Jan.	5	04 53	Jan.	13	09 46
Jan.	20	13 14	Jan.	27	04 48	Feb.	3	23 09	Feb.	12	03 50
Feb.	18	23 47	Feb.	25	17 14	Mar.	5	18 05	Mar.	13	17 48
Mar.	20	09 36	Mar.	27	07 43	Apr.	4	12 06	Apr.	12	03 44
Apr.	18	18 57	Apr.	25	23 55	May	4	03 42	May	11	10 36
May	18	04 13	May	25	17 19	June	2	16 19	June	9	15 42
June	16	14 05	June	24	11 03	July	2	02 20	July	8	20 24
July	16	01 24	July	24	04 04	July	31	10 43	Aug.	7	02 03
Aug.	14	14 53	Aug.	22	19 31	Aug.	29	18 35	Sept.	5	09 54
Sept.	13	06 41	Sept.	21	08 59	Sept.	28	02 50	Oct.	4	21 06
Oct.	13	00 06	Oct.	20	20 31	Oct.	27	12 05	Nov.	3	12 24
Nov.	11	17 47	Nov.	19	06 27	Nov.	25	22 44	Dec.	3	07 40
Dec.	11	10 29	Dec.	18	15 14	Dec.	25	11 11			

DAYS OF THE WEEK AND DAYS OF THE YEAR

Day	JAN. Wk Yr	FEB. Wk Yr	MAR. Wk Yr	APR. Wk Yr	MAY Wk Yr	JUNE Wk Yr	JULY Wk Yr	AUG. Wk Yr	SEPT. Wk Yr	OCT. Wk Yr	NOV. Wk Yr	DEC. Wk Yr
1	Th. 1	Su. 32	Su. 60	W. 91	F. 121	M. 152	W. 182	Sa. 213	Tu. 244	Th. 274	Su. 305	Tu. 335
2	F. 2	M. 33	M. 61	Th. 92	Sa. 122	Tu. 153	Th. 183	Su. 214	W. 245	F. 275	M. 306	W. 336
3	Sa. 3	Tu. 34	Tu. 62	F. 93	Su. 123	W. 154	F. 184	M. 215	Th. 246	Sa. 276	Tu. 307	Th. 337
4	Su. 4	W. 35	W. 63	Sa. 94	M. 124	Th. 155	Sa. 185	Tu. 216	F. 247	Su. 277	W. 308	F. 338
5	M. 5	Th. 36	Th. 64	Su. 95	Tu. 125	F. 156	Su. 186	W. 217	Sa. 248	M. 278	Th. 309	Sa. 339
6	Tu. 6	F. 37	F. 65	M. 96	W. 126	Sa. 157	M. 187	Th. 218	Su. 249	Tu. 279	F. 310	Su. 340
7	W. 7	Sa. 38	Sa. 66	Tu. 97	Th. 127	Su. 158	Tu. 188	F. 219	M. 250	W. 280	Sa. 311	M. 341
8	Th. 8	Su. 39	Su. 67	W. 98	F. 128	M. 159	W. 189	Sa. 220	Tu. 251	Th. 281	Su. 312	Tu. 342
9	F. 9	M. 40	M. 68	Th. 99	Sa. 129	Tu. 160	Th. 190	Su. 221	W. 252	F. 282	M. 313	W. 343
10	Sa. 10	Tu. 41	Tu. 69	F. 100	Su. 130	W. 161	F. 191	M. 222	Th. 253	Sa. 283	Tu. 314	Th. 344
11	Su. 11	W. 42	W. 70	Sa. 101	M. 131	Th. 162	Sa. 192	Tu. 223	F. 254	Su. 284	W. 315	F. 345
12	M. 12	Th. 43	Th. 71	Su. 102	Tu. 132	F. 163	Su. 193	W. 224	Sa. 255	M. 285	Th. 316	Sa. 346
13	Tu. 13	F. 44	F. 72	M. 103	W. 133	Sa. 164	M. 194	Th. 225	Su. 256	Tu. 286	F. 317	Su. 347
14	W. 14	Sa. 45	Sa. 73	Tu. 104	Th. 134	Su. 165	Tu. 195	F. 226	M. 257	W. 287	Sa. 318	M. 348
15	Th. 15	Su. 46	Su. 74	W. 105	F. 135	M. 166	W. 196	Sa. 227	Tu. 258	Th. 288	Su. 319	Tu. 349
16	F. 16	M. 47	M. 75	Th. 106	Sa. 136	Tu. 167	Th. 197	Su. 228	W. 259	F. 289	M. 320	W. 350
17	Sa. 17	Tu. 48	Tu. 76	F. 107	Su. 137	W. 168	F. 198	M. 229	Th. 260	Sa. 290	Tu. 321	Th. 351
18	Su. 18	W. 49	W. 77	Sa. 108	M. 138	Th. 169	Sa. 199	Tu. 230	F. 261	Su. 291	W. 322	F. 352
19	M. 19	Th. 50	Th. 78	Su. 109	Tu. 139	F. 170	Su. 200	W. 231	Sa. 262	M. 292	Th. 323	Sa. 353
20	Tu. 20	F. 51	F. 79	M. 110	W. 140	Sa. 171	M. 201	Th. 232	Su. 263	Tu. 293	F. 324	Su. 354
21	W. 21	Sa. 52	Sa. 80	Tu. 111	Th. 141	Su. 172	Tu. 202	F. 233	M. 264	W. 294	Sa. 325	M. 355
22	Th. 22	Su. 53	Su. 81	W. 112	F. 142	M. 173	W. 203	Sa. 234	Tu. 265	Th. 295	Su. 326	Tu. 356
23	F. 23	M. 54	M. 82	Th. 113	Sa. 143	Tu. 174	Th. 204	Su. 235	W. 266	F. 296	M. 327	W. 357
24	Sa. 24	Tu. 55	Tu. 83	F. 114	Su. 144	W. 175	F. 205	M. 236	Th. 267	Sa. 297	Tu. 328	Th. 358
25	Su. 25	W. 56	W. 84	Sa. 115	M. 145	Th. 176	Sa. 206	Tu. 237	F. 268	Su. 298	W. 329	F. 359
26	M. 26	Th. 57	Th. 85	Su. 116	Tu. 146	F. 177	Su. 207	W. 238	Sa. 269	M. 299	Th. 330	Sa. 360
27	Tu. 27	F. 58	F. 86	M. 117	W. 147	Sa. 178	M. 208	Th. 239	Su. 270	Tu. 300	F. 331	Su. 361
28	W. 28	Sa. 59	Sa. 87	Tu. 118	Th. 148	Su. 179	Tu. 209	F. 240	M. 271	W. 301	Sa. 332	M. 362
29	Th. 29		Su. 88	W. 119	F. 149	M. 180	W. 210	Sa. 241	Tu. 272	Th. 302	Su. 333	Tu. 363
30	F. 30		M. 89	Th. 120	Sa. 150	Tu. 181	Th. 211	Su. 242	W. 273	F. 303	M. 334	W. 364
31	Sa. 31		Tu. 90		Su. 151		F. 212	M. 243		Sa. 304		Th. 365

ECLIPSES

There are two eclipses of the Sun and two of the Moon.

1. *A total eclipse of the Sun,* March 20. See map on page 6. The eclipse begins at $07^h\ 41^m$ and ends at $11^h\ 50^m$; the total phase begins at $09^h\ 10^m$ and ends at $10^h\ 21^m$. The maximum duration of totality is $2^m\ 50^s$.

2. *A total eclipse of the Moon,* April 4. The umbral eclipse begins at $10^h\ 15^m$ and ends at $13^h\ 45^m$. Totality lasts from $11^h\ 54^m$ to $12^h\ 06^m$. It is visible from the western half on North America, Oceania, Australasia and Eastern Asia.

3. *A partial eclipse of the Sun,* September 13. See map on page 7. The eclipse begins at $04^h\ 42^m$ and ends at $09^h\ 06^m$. The time of greatest eclipse is $06^h\ 54^m$, when 0·79 of the Sun's diameter is obscured.

4. *A total eclipse of the Moon,* September 28. The umbral eclipse begins at $01^h\ 07^m$ and ends at $04^h\ 27^m$. Totality lasts from $02^h\ 11^m$ to $03^h\ 24^m$. It is visible from western Asia, Africa, Europe and the Americas excluding the western half of Alaska.

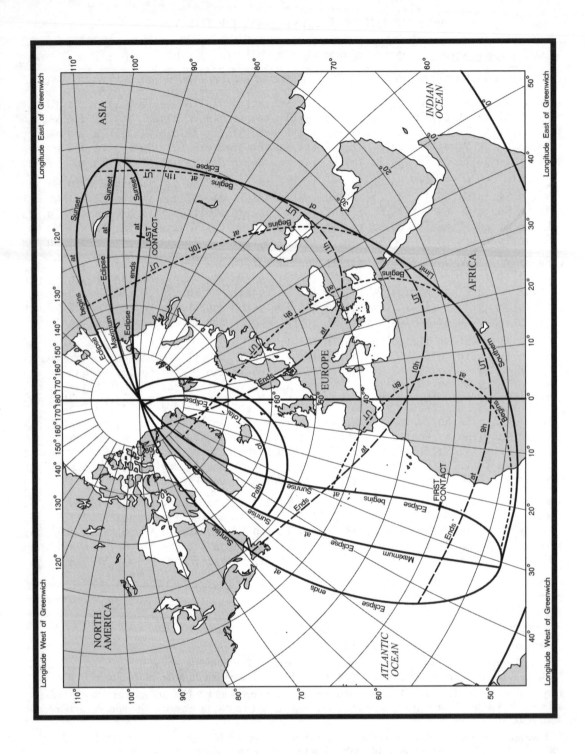

SOLAR ECLIPSE DIAGRAMS

The principal features shown on the above diagrams are: the paths of
total and annular eclipses; the northern and southern limits of partial
eclipse; the sunrise and sunset curves; dashed lines which show the
times of beginning and end of partial eclipse at hourly intervals.

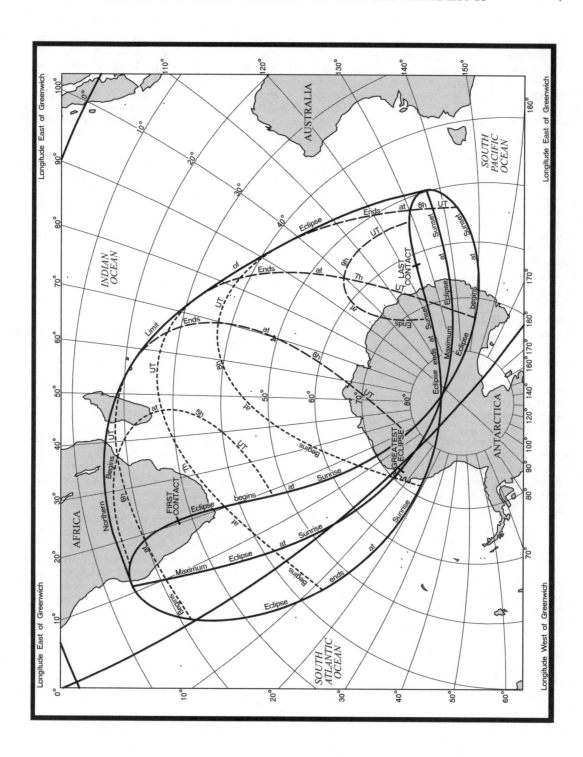

SOLAR ECLIPSE DIAGRAMS

Further details of the paths and times of central eclipse are given in
The Astronomical Almanac.

VISIBILITY OF PLANETS

VENUS is a brilliant object in the evening sky until in the second week of Aug. it becomes too close to the Sun for observation. From the end of the third week of Aug. it reappears in the morning sky where it stays until the end of the year. Venus is in conjunction with Mercury on Aug. 5, with Mars on Feb. 21, Aug. 29 and Nov. 3 and with Jupiter on July 1, July 31 and Oct. 26.

MARS is visible as a reddish object in Capricornus in the evening sky at the start of the year. Its eastward elongation decreases as it moves through Aquarius from early Jan., Pisces from mid-Feb., briefly into Cetus in early March, then into Pisces again and into Aries in late March. It becomes too close to the Sun for observation in mid-April. It reappears in the morning sky during the first week of Aug. in Gemini and then moves into Cancer in early Aug., Leo from early Sept. (passing 0°8 N. of *Regulus* on Sept. 24) and into Virgo early in Nov., where it remains for the rest of the year (passing 4° N. of *Spica* on Dec. 21). Mars is in conjunction with Venus on Feb. 21, Aug. 29 and Nov. 3 and with Jupiter on Oct. 17.

JUPITER can be seen for most of the night in Leo at the start of the year. Its westward elongation gradually increases, passes into Cancer in early Feb., and is at opposition on Feb. 6. Its eastward elongation then decreases and from mid-May can be seen only in the evening sky. It passes into Leo in the second week of June (passing 0°4 N. of *Regulus* on Aug. 10). In mid-Aug. it becomes too close to the Sun for observation until in the second week of Sept. it reappears in the morning sky in Leo where it remains for the rest of the year. Its westward elongation increases and by mid-Dec. it can be seen for more than half the night. Jupiter is in conjunction with Venus on July 1, July 31 and Oct. 26, with Mercury on Aug. 7 and with Mars on Oct. 17.

SATURN rises well before sunrise at the start of the year in Libra and moves into Scorpius in mid-Jan. It returns to Libra in the second week of May, is at opposition on May 23, and in mid-Oct. returns to Scorpius. From mid-Aug. until mid-Nov. it can only be seen in the evening sky and then becomes too close to the Sun for observation. It reappears in mid-Dec. in Ophiuchus and is visible only in the morning sky for the rest of the year.

MERCURY can only be seen low in the east before sunrise, or low in the west after sunset (about the time of beginning or end of civil twilight). It is visible in the mornings between the following approximate dates: Feb. 6 (+2·0) to Apr. 1 (−1·1), June 9 (+3·1) to July 16 (−1·5) and Oct. 7 (+1·9) to Nov. 3 (−1·0); the planet is brighter at the end of each period. It is visible in the evenings between the following approximate dates: Jan. 1 (−0·8) to Jan. 24 (+1·4), Apr. 18 (−1·5) to May 21 (+3·0), Aug. 1 (−1·2) to Sept. 24 (+2·4) and Dec. 5 (−0·7) to Dec. 31 (−0·5); the planet is brighter at the beginning of each period. The figures in parentheses are the magnitudes.

PLANET DIAGRAM

General Description. The diagram on the opposite page shows, in graphical form for any date during the year, the local mean time of meridian passage of the Sun, of the five planets Mercury, Venus, Mars, Jupiter, and Saturn, and of each 30° of SHA; intermediate lines corresponding to particular stars, may be drawn in by the user if desired. It is intended to provide a general picture of the availability of planets and stars for observation.

On each side of the line marking the time of meridian passage of the Sun a band, 45^m wide, is shaded to indicate that planets and most stars crossing the meridian within 45^m of the Sun are too close to the Sun for observation.

Method of use and interpretation. For any date the diagram provides immediately the local mean times of meridian passage of the Sun, planets and stars, and thus the following information:

    (a) whether a planet or star is too close to the Sun for observation;

    (b) some indication of its position in the sky, especially during twilight;

    (c) the proximity of other planets.

When the meridian passage of an outer planet occurs at midnight the body is in opposition to the Sun and is visible all night; a planet may then be observable during both morning and evening twilights. As the time of meridian passage decreases, the body eventually ceases to be observable in the morning, but its altitude above the eastern horizon at sunset gradually increases; this continues until the body is on the meridian during evening twilight. From then onwards the body is observable above the western horizon and its altitude at sunset gradually decreases; eventually the body becomes too close to the Sun for observation. When the body again becomes visible it is seen low in the east during morning twilight; its altitude at sunrise increases until meridian passage occurs during morning twilight. Then, as the time of meridian passage decreases to 0^h, the body is observable in the west during morning twilight with a gradually decreasing altitude, until it once again reaches opposition.

DO NOT CONFUSE

Venus with Mercury in the first three weeks of January, with Mars in mid-February to early March and again in late October to mid-November and with Jupiter in late June to mid-July and again in late October; on all occasions Venus is the brighter object.

Jupiter with Mercury in early August and with Mars in October after the first week; on both occasions Jupiter is the brighter object.

LOCAL MEAN TIME OF MERIDIAN PASSAGE

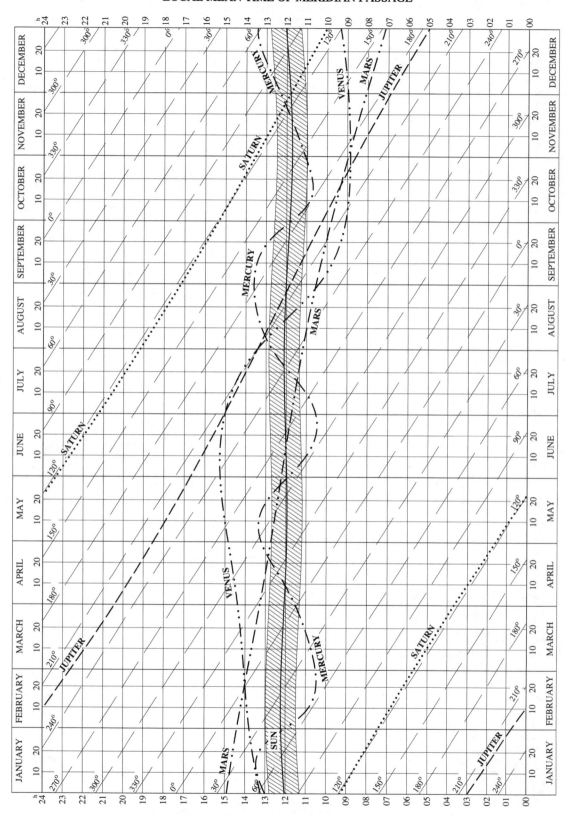

LOCAL MEAN TIME OF MERIDIAN PASSAGE

UT	ARIES	VENUS −3.9		MARS +1.1		JUPITER −2.5		SATURN +0.6		STARS		
	GHA	GHA	Dec	GHA	Dec	GHA	Dec	GHA	Dec	Name	SHA	Dec
d h	° ′	° ′	° ′	° ′	° ′	° ′	° ′	° ′	° ′		° ′	° ′
1 00	100 19.9	161 17.9	S22 08.4	136 31.0	S15 33.3	315 54.9	N15 03.6	221 11.3	S18 26.3	Acamar	315 17.3	S40 15.0
01	115 22.3	176 17.0	07.8	151 31.5	32.6	330 57.6	03.7	236 13.5	26.4	Achernar	335 26.0	S57 10.0
02	130 24.8	191 16.1	07.3	166 32.1	32.0	346 00.2	03.7	251 15.7	26.4	Acrux	173 07.8	S63 10.7
03	145 27.2	206 15.3 ..	06.7	181 32.6 ..	31.3	1 02.9 ..	03.8	266 17.9 ..	26.5	Adhara	255 11.3	S28 59.8
04	160 29.7	221 14.4	06.2	196 33.2	30.7	16 05.5	03.9	281 20.1	26.5	Aldebaran	290 47.8	N16 32.2
05	175 32.2	236 13.5	05.6	211 33.7	30.0	31 08.1	03.9	296 22.3	26.6			
06	190 34.6	251 12.7	S22 05.1	226 34.3	S15 29.3	46 10.8	N15 04.0	311 24.5	S18 26.6	Alioth	166 19.9	N55 52.4
07	205 37.1	266 11.8	04.5	241 34.8	28.7	61 13.4	04.1	326 26.7	26.7	Alkaid	152 58.3	N49 14.1
T 08	220 39.6	281 11.0	03.9	256 35.4	28.0	76 16.1	04.1	341 28.9	26.7	Al Na'ir	27 42.8	S46 53.4
H 09	235 42.0	296 10.1 ..	03.4	271 35.9 ..	27.4	91 18.7 ..	04.2	356 31.1 ..	26.8	Alnilam	275 45.0	S 1 11.8
U 10	250 44.5	311 09.2	02.8	286 36.5	26.7	106 21.4	04.3	11 33.3	26.8	Alphard	217 54.8	S 8 43.6
R 11	265 47.0	326 08.4	02.3	301 37.0	26.1	121 24.0	04.4	26 35.5	26.9			
S 12	280 49.4	341 07.5	S22 01.7	316 37.6	S15 25.4	136 26.6	N15 04.4	41 37.8	S18 26.9	Alphecca	126 10.4	N26 39.9
D 13	295 51.9	356 06.7	01.1	331 38.1	24.8	151 29.3	04.5	56 40.0	27.0	Alpheratz	357 42.4	N29 10.6
A 14	310 54.4	11 05.8	00.6	346 38.7	24.1	166 31.9	04.6	71 42.2	27.0	Altair	62 07.5	N 8 54.7
Y 15	325 56.8	26 04.9	22 00.0	1 39.2 ..	23.5	181 34.6 ..	04.6	86 44.4 ..	27.1	Ankaa	353 14.8	S42 13.7
16	340 59.3	41 04.1	21 59.4	16 39.8	22.8	196 37.2	04.7	101 46.6	27.1	Antares	112 25.3	S26 27.7
17	356 01.7	56 03.2	58.9	31 40.3	22.2	211 39.9	04.8	116 48.8	27.2			
18	11 04.2	71 02.4	S21 58.3	46 40.9	S15 21.5	226 42.5	N15 04.8	131 51.0	S18 27.2	Arcturus	145 54.9	N19 06.2
19	26 06.7	86 01.5	57.7	61 41.4	20.9	241 45.2	04.9	146 53.2	27.3	Atria	107 26.6	S69 02.9
20	41 09.1	101 00.7	57.1	76 42.0	20.2	256 47.8	05.0	161 55.4	27.3	Avior	234 16.9	S59 33.5
21	56 11.6	115 59.8 ..	56.6	91 42.5 ..	19.5	271 50.5 ..	05.1	176 57.6 ..	27.3	Bellatrix	278 30.5	N 6 21.6
22	71 14.1	130 59.0	56.0	106 43.1	18.9	286 53.1	05.1	191 59.8	27.4	Betelgeuse	270 59.8	N 7 24.3
23	86 16.5	145 58.1	55.4	121 43.6	18.2	301 55.8	05.2	207 02.0	27.4			
2 00	101 19.0	160 57.2	S21 54.8	136 44.2	S15 17.6	316 58.4	N15 05.3	222 04.2	S18 27.5	Canopus	263 55.1	S52 42.5
01	116 21.5	175 56.4	54.3	151 44.7	16.9	332 01.1	05.3	237 06.4	27.5	Capella	280 32.4	N46 00.6
02	131 23.9	190 55.5	53.7	166 45.3	16.3	347 03.7	05.4	252 08.6	27.6	Deneb	49 31.1	N45 20.3
03	146 26.4	205 54.7 ..	53.1	181 45.9 ..	15.6	2 06.3 ..	05.5	267 10.8 ..	27.6	Denebola	182 32.5	N14 29.1
04	161 28.9	220 53.8	52.5	196 46.4	14.9	17 09.0	05.5	282 13.0	27.7	Diphda	348 54.8	S17 54.4
05	176 31.3	235 53.0	51.9	211 47.0	14.3	32 11.6	05.6	297 15.2	27.7			
06	191 33.8	250 52.1	S21 51.3	226 47.5	S15 13.6	47 14.3	N15 05.7	312 17.4	S18 27.8	Dubhe	193 50.3	N61 39.8
07	206 36.2	265 51.3	50.8	241 48.1	13.0	62 16.9	05.8	327 19.6	27.8	Elnath	278 10.9	N28 37.0
08	221 38.7	280 50.4	50.2	256 48.6	12.3	77 19.6	05.8	342 21.9	27.9	Eltanin	90 46.2	N51 29.3
F 09	236 41.2	295 49.6 ..	49.6	271 49.2 ..	11.7	92 22.2 ..	05.9	357 24.1 ..	27.9	Enif	33 46.3	N 9 56.8
R 10	251 43.6	310 48.7	49.0	286 49.7	11.0	107 24.9	06.0	12 26.3	28.0	Fomalhaut	15 23.0	S29 32.6
I 11	266 46.1	325 47.9	48.4	301 50.3	10.3	122 27.5	06.0	27 28.5	28.0			
D 12	281 48.6	340 47.0	S21 47.8	316 50.8	S15 09.7	137 30.2	N15 06.1	42 30.7	S18 28.1	Gacrux	171 59.5	S57 11.6
A 13	296 51.0	355 46.2	47.2	331 51.4	09.0	152 32.8	06.2	57 32.9	28.1	Gienah	175 51.1	S17 37.5
Y 14	311 53.5	10 45.4	46.6	346 52.0	08.4	167 35.5	06.3	72 35.1	28.2	Hadar	148 46.5	S60 26.4
15	326 56.0	25 44.5 ..	46.0	1 52.5 ..	07.7	182 38.2 ..	06.3	87 37.3 ..	28.2	Hamal	327 59.4	N23 32.0
16	341 58.4	40 43.7	45.4	16 53.1	07.0	197 40.8	06.4	102 39.5	28.3	Kaus Aust.	83 42.8	S34 22.4
17	357 00.9	55 42.8	44.8	31 53.6	06.4	212 43.5	06.5	117 41.7	28.3			
18	12 03.4	70 42.0	S21 44.2	46 54.2	S15 05.7	227 46.1	N15 06.5	132 43.9	S18 28.3	Kochab	137 20.9	N74 05.4
19	27 05.8	85 41.1	43.6	61 54.7	05.0	242 48.8	06.6	147 46.1	28.4	Markab	13 37.4	N15 17.3
20	42 08.3	100 40.3	43.0	76 55.3	04.4	257 51.4	06.7	162 48.3	28.4	Menkar	314 13.7	N 4 08.8
21	57 10.7	115 39.4 ..	42.4	91 55.8 ..	03.7	272 54.1 ..	06.8	177 50.5 ..	28.5	Menkent	148 06.4	S36 26.4
22	72 13.2	130 38.6	41.8	106 56.4	03.1	287 56.7	06.8	192 52.7	28.5	Miaplacidus	221 38.5	S69 46.7
23	87 15.7	145 37.8	41.2	121 57.0	02.4	302 59.4	06.9	207 55.0	28.6			
3 00	102 18.1	160 36.9	S21 40.6	136 57.5	S15 01.7	318 02.0	N15 07.0	222 57.2	S18 28.6	Mirfak	308 38.4	N49 54.9
01	117 20.6	175 36.1	40.0	151 58.1	01.1	333 04.7	07.0	237 59.4	28.7	Nunki	75 57.4	S26 16.5
02	132 23.1	190 35.2	39.4	166 58.6	15 00.4	348 07.3	07.1	253 01.6	28.7	Peacock	53 18.2	S56 41.1
03	147 25.5	205 34.4 ..	38.8	181 59.2	14 59.7	3 10.0 ..	07.2	268 03.8 ..	28.8	Pollux	243 26.1	N27 59.1
04	162 28.0	220 33.6	38.2	196 59.7	59.1	18 12.7	07.3	283 06.0	28.8	Procyon	244 58.3	N 5 10.9
05	177 30.5	235 32.7	37.6	212 00.3	58.4	33 15.3	07.3	298 08.2	28.9			
06	192 32.9	250 31.9	S21 37.0	227 00.9	S14 57.8	48 18.0	N15 07.4	313 10.4	S18 28.9	Rasalhague	96 05.8	N12 33.1
07	207 35.4	265 31.0	36.4	242 01.4	57.1	63 20.6	07.5	328 12.6	29.0	Regulus	207 42.2	N11 53.4
S 08	222 37.9	280 30.2	35.7	257 02.0	56.4	78 23.3	07.6	343 14.8	29.0	Rigel	281 10.7	S 8 11.3
A 09	237 40.3	295 29.4 ..	35.1	272 02.5 ..	55.8	93 25.9 ..	07.6	358 17.0 ..	29.1	Rigil Kent.	139 50.5	S60 53.4
T 10	252 42.8	310 28.5	34.5	287 03.1	55.1	108 28.6	07.7	13 19.2	29.1	Sabik	102 11.6	S15 44.4
U 11	267 45.2	325 27.7	33.9	302 03.7	54.4	123 31.3	07.8	28 21.4	29.1			
R 12	282 47.7	340 26.9	S21 33.3	317 04.2	S14 53.8	138 33.9	N15 07.9	43 23.7	S18 29.2	Schedar	349 39.2	N56 37.4
D 13	297 50.2	355 26.0	32.7	332 04.8	53.1	153 36.6	07.9	58 25.9	29.2	Shaula	96 20.9	S37 06.6
A 14	312 52.6	10 25.2	32.0	347 05.3	52.4	168 39.2	08.0	73 28.1	29.3	Sirius	258 32.4	S16 44.5
Y 15	327 55.1	25 24.3 ..	31.4	2 05.9 ..	51.8	183 41.9 ..	08.1	88 30.3 ..	29.3	Spica	158 30.2	S11 14.3
16	342 57.6	40 23.5	30.8	17 06.5	51.1	198 44.5	08.1	103 32.5	29.4	Suhail	222 51.2	S43 29.6
17	358 00.0	55 22.7	30.2	32 07.0	50.4	213 47.2	08.2	118 34.7	29.4			
18	13 02.5	70 21.8	S21 29.5	47 07.6	S14 49.8	228 49.9	N15 08.3	133 36.9	S18 29.5	Vega	80 38.7	N38 48.0
19	28 05.0	85 21.0	28.9	62 08.1	49.1	243 52.5	08.4	148 39.1	29.5	Zuben'ubi	137 04.4	S16 06.1
20	43 07.4	100 20.2	28.3	77 08.7	48.4	258 55.2	08.4	163 41.3	29.6		SHA	Mer. Pass.
21	58 09.9	115 19.4 ..	27.7	92 09.3 ..	47.8	273 57.8 ..	08.5	178 43.5 ..	29.6		° ′	h m
22	73 12.3	130 18.5	27.0	107 09.8	47.1	289 00.5	08.6	193 45.7	29.7	Venus	59 38.2	13 17
23	88 14.8	145 17.7	26.4	122 10.4	46.4	304 03.2	08.7	208 48.0	29.7	Mars	35 25.2	14 53
	h m									Jupiter	215 39.4	2 52
Mer. Pass. 17 11.9		v −0.8	d 0.6	v 0.6	d 0.7	v 2.7	d 0.1	v 2.2	d 0.0	Saturn	120 45.2	9 10

UT	SUN GHA	SUN Dec	MOON GHA	v	MOON Dec	d	HP
d h	° ′	° ′	° ′	′	° ′	′	′
1 00	179 12.0	S23 02.4	51 21.2	9.9	N15 06.3	6.3	57.2
01	194 11.7	02.2	65 50.1	9.9	15 12.6	6.2	57.1
02	209 11.4	02.0	80 20.0	9.8	15 18.8	6.1	57.1
03	224 11.1	01.8	94 47.8	9.9	15 24.9	6.0	57.1
04	239 10.8	01.6	109 16.7	9.8	15 30.9	5.9	57.1
05	254 10.5	01.4	123 45.5	9.8	15 36.8	5.9	57.1
06	269 10.2	S23 01.2	138 14.3	9.8	N15 42.7	5.7	57.0
07	284 10.0	01.0	152 43.1	9.8	15 48.4	5.7	57.0
08	299 09.7	00.8	167 11.9	9.8	15 54.1	5.6	57.0
09	314 09.4	00.6	181 40.7	9.8	15 59.7	5.5	57.0
10	329 09.1	00.4	196 09.5	9.7	16 05.2	5.4	57.0
11	344 08.8	00.2	210 38.2	9.8	16 10.6	5.3	56.9
12	359 08.5	S23 00.0	225 07.0	9.7	N16 15.9	5.2	56.9
13	14 08.2	22 59.8	239 35.7	9.8	16 21.1	5.1	56.9
14	29 07.9	59.6	254 04.5	9.7	16 26.2	5.0	56.9
15	44 07.6	59.4	268 33.2	9.8	16 31.2	5.0	56.9
16	59 07.3	59.2	283 02.0	9.7	16 36.2	4.8	56.8
17	74 07.0	59.0	297 30.7	9.7	16 41.0	4.8	56.8
18	89 06.7	S22 58.8	311 59.4	9.7	N16 45.8	4.6	56.8
19	104 06.4	58.6	326 28.1	9.7	16 50.4	4.6	56.8
20	119 06.1	58.4	340 56.8	9.7	16 55.0	4.4	56.7
21	134 05.8	58.2	355 25.5	9.7	16 59.4	4.4	56.7
22	149 05.5	57.9	9 54.2	9.7	17 03.8	4.3	56.7
23	164 05.3	57.7	24 22.9	9.7	17 08.1	4.2	56.7
2 00	179 05.0	S22 57.5	38 51.6	9.7	N17 12.3	4.1	56.7
01	194 04.7	57.3	53 20.3	9.6	17 16.4	3.9	56.6
02	209 04.4	57.1	67 48.9	9.7	17 20.3	3.9	56.6
03	224 04.1	56.9	82 17.6	9.7	17 24.2	3.8	56.6
04	239 03.8	56.6	96 46.3	9.7	17 28.0	3.7	56.6
05	254 03.5	56.4	111 15.0	9.7	17 31.7	3.6	56.6
06	269 03.2	S22 56.2	125 43.7	9.6	N17 35.3	3.5	56.5
07	284 02.9	56.0	140 12.3	9.7	17 38.8	3.4	56.5
08	299 02.6	55.8	154 41.0	9.7	17 42.2	3.3	56.5
09	314 02.3	55.6	169 09.7	9.7	17 45.5	3.2	56.5
10	329 02.0	55.3	183 38.4	9.6	17 48.7	3.1	56.5
11	344 01.8	55.1	198 07.0	9.7	17 51.8	3.0	56.4
12	359 01.5	S22 54.9	212 35.7	9.7	N17 54.8	3.0	56.4
13	14 01.2	54.7	227 04.4	9.7	17 57.8	2.8	56.4
14	29 00.9	54.4	241 33.1	9.7	18 00.6	2.7	56.4
15	44 00.6	54.2	256 01.8	9.7	18 03.3	2.6	56.4
16	59 00.3	54.0	270 30.5	9.7	18 05.9	2.5	56.3
17	74 00.0	53.8	284 59.2	9.7	18 08.4	2.4	56.3
18	88 59.7	S22 53.5	299 27.9	9.7	N18 10.8	2.3	56.3
19	103 59.4	53.3	313 56.6	9.7	18 13.1	2.3	56.3
20	118 59.1	53.1	328 25.3	9.7	18 15.4	2.1	56.3
21	133 58.9	52.8	342 54.0	9.7	18 17.5	2.0	56.2
22	148 58.6	52.6	357 22.7	9.8	18 19.5	1.9	56.2
23	163 58.3	52.4	11 51.5	9.7	18 21.4	1.8	56.2
3 00	178 58.0	S22 52.1	26 20.2	9.8	N18 23.2	1.7	56.2
01	193 57.7	51.9	40 49.0	9.8	18 24.9	1.7	56.2
02	208 57.4	51.7	55 17.8	9.8	18 26.6	1.5	56.1
03	223 57.1	51.4	69 46.6	9.8	18 28.1	1.4	56.1
04	238 56.8	51.2	84 15.4	9.8	18 29.5	1.3	56.1
05	253 56.5	51.0	98 44.2	9.8	18 30.8	1.2	56.1
06	268 56.3	S22 50.7	113 13.0	9.8	N18 32.0	1.2	56.1
07	283 56.0	50.5	127 41.8	9.9	18 33.2	1.0	56.0
08	298 55.7	50.2	142 10.7	9.8	18 34.2	0.9	56.0
09	313 55.4	50.0	156 39.5	9.9	18 35.1	0.8	56.0
10	328 55.1	49.8	171 08.4	9.9	18 35.9	0.8	56.0
11	343 54.8	49.6	185 37.3	9.9	18 36.7	0.6	56.0
12	358 54.5	S22 49.3	200 06.2	9.9	N18 37.3	0.5	55.9
13	13 54.2	49.0	214 35.1	10.0	18 37.8	0.4	55.9
14	28 54.0	48.8	229 04.1	10.0	18 38.2	0.4	55.9
15	43 53.7	48.5	243 33.1	9.9	18 38.6	0.2	55.9
16	58 53.4	48.3	258 02.0	10.1	18 38.8	0.1	55.9
17	73 53.1	48.1	272 31.1	10.0	18 38.9	0.1	55.9
18	88 52.8	S22 47.8	287 00.1	10.0	N18 39.0	0.1	55.8
19	103 52.5	47.6	301 29.1	10.1	18 38.9	0.2	55.8
20	118 52.2	47.3	315 58.2	10.1	18 38.7	0.2	55.8
21	133 52.0	47.1	330 27.3	10.1	18 38.5	0.4	55.8
22	148 51.7	46.8	344 56.4	10.2	18 38.1	0.4	55.8
23	163 51.4	46.6	359 25.6	10.1	N18 37.7	0.6	55.7
	SD 16.3	d 0.2	SD 15.5		15.4		15.2

(Column note: d/h — THURSDAY; FRIDAY; SATURDAY)

Moonrise

Lat.	Twilight Naut.	Twilight Civil	Sunrise	Moonrise 1	2	3	4
°	h m	h m	h m	h m	h m	h m	h m
N 72	08 23	10 40	■	10 48	10 28	□	□
N 70	08 04	09 48	■	11 29	11 42	12 12	13 12
68	07 49	09 16	■	11 57	12 20	12 58	13 55
66	07 37	08 52	10 26	12 18	12 46	13 27	14 23
64	07 26	08 34	09 49	12 35	13 07	13 50	14 45
62	07 17	08 18	09 22	12 49	13 23	14 08	15 03
60	07 09	08 05	09 02	13 01	13 37	14 23	15 17
N 58	07 02	07 54	08 45	13 11	13 49	14 35	15 29
56	06 55	07 44	08 31	13 20	14 00	14 46	15 40
54	06 50	07 35	08 19	13 28	14 09	14 56	15 49
52	06 44	07 28	08 08	13 35	14 17	15 04	15 58
50	06 39	07 21	07 58	13 42	14 24	15 12	16 05
45	06 28	07 05	07 38	13 56	14 40	15 29	16 21
N 40	06 18	06 52	07 22	14 07	14 53	15 42	16 35
35	06 09	06 40	07 08	14 17	15 04	15 54	16 46
30	06 00	06 30	06 56	14 26	15 14	16 04	16 56
20	05 44	06 11	06 35	14 41	15 30	16 21	17 12
N 10	05 28	05 54	06 17	14 54	15 45	16 36	17 27
0	05 12	05 38	06 00	15 07	15 58	16 50	17 41
S 10	04 53	05 20	05 43	15 19	16 12	17 04	17 55
20	04 31	05 00	05 24	15 32	16 27	17 19	18 09
30	04 02	04 36	05 03	15 48	16 44	17 37	18 26
35	03 44	04 21	04 50	15 57	16 53	17 47	18 36
40	03 22	04 03	04 35	16 07	17 05	17 58	18 47
45	02 52	03 41	04 18	16 19	17 18	18 12	19 00
S 50	02 08	03 12	03 56	16 33	17 34	18 29	19 16
52	01 42	02 57	03 45	16 40	17 42	18 36	19 24
54	01 03	02 40	03 33	16 48	17 50	18 45	19 32
56	////	02 19	03 20	16 56	18 00	18 55	19 41
58	////	01 51	03 04	17 06	18 10	19 06	19 52
S 60	////	01 08	02 44	17 17	18 23	19 19	20 04

Moonset

Lat.	Sunset	Twilight Civil	Twilight Naut.	Moonset 1	2	3	4
°	h m	h m	h m	h m	h m	h m	h m
N 72	■	13 28	15 45	06 47	08 56	□	□
N 70	■	14 20	16 04	06 08	07 42	09 00	09 47
68	■	14 52	16 19	05 41	07 05	08 15	09 04
66	13 42	15 16	16 31	05 20	06 39	07 45	08 35
64	14 19	15 34	16 42	05 04	06 19	07 23	08 13
62	14 46	15 50	16 51	04 50	06 02	07 05	07 55
60	15 06	16 03	16 59	04 39	05 49	06 50	07 41
N 58	15 23	16 14	17 06	04 29	05 37	06 37	07 28
56	15 37	16 24	17 13	04 20	05 27	06 26	07 17
54	15 49	16 33	17 18	04 12	05 18	06 17	07 08
52	16 00	16 40	17 24	04 05	05 10	06 08	06 59
50	16 10	16 48	17 29	03 59	05 03	06 01	06 52
45	16 30	17 03	17 40	03 46	04 47	05 44	06 35
N 40	16 46	17 16	17 50	03 35	04 35	05 31	06 22
35	17 00	17 28	17 59	03 26	04 24	05 19	06 11
30	17 12	17 38	18 08	03 18	04 15	05 09	06 01
20	17 33	17 56	18 24	03 03	03 59	04 52	05 44
N 10	17 51	18 13	18 40	02 51	03 45	04 37	05 29
0	18 08	18 30	18 56	02 40	03 31	04 23	05 15
S 10	18 25	18 48	19 15	02 28	03 18	04 09	05 01
20	18 43	19 08	19 37	02 16	03 04	03 54	04 46
30	19 05	19 32	20 05	02 02	02 48	03 37	04 28
35	19 17	19 47	20 23	01 54	02 39	03 27	04 18
40	19 32	20 05	20 46	01 44	02 28	03 16	04 07
45	19 50	20 27	21 15	01 34	02 16	03 02	03 53
S 50	20 11	20 55	21 59	01 21	02 01	02 46	03 37
52	20 22	21 10	22 24	01 15	01 53	02 38	03 29
54	20 34	21 27	23 03	01 08	01 46	02 30	03 20
56	20 47	21 48	////	01 01	01 37	02 20	03 10
58	21 03	22 15	////	00 52	01 27	02 09	02 59
S 60	21 23	22 57	////	00 43	01 15	01 56	02 46

SUN / MOON

Day	SUN Eqn. of Time 00ʰ	SUN Eqn. of Time 12ʰ	SUN Mer. Pass.	MOON Mer. Pass. Upper	MOON Mer. Pass. Lower	Age	Phase
d	m s	m s	h m	h m	h m	d	%
1	03 11	03 25	12 03	21 19	08 53	10	86
2	03 40	03 54	12 04	22 11	09 45	11	93
3	04 07	04 21	12 04	23 02	10 37	12	97

UT	ARIES	VENUS −3.9		MARS +1.1		JUPITER −2.5		SATURN +0.6		STARS		
	GHA	GHA	Dec	GHA	Dec	GHA	Dec	GHA	Dec	Name	SHA	Dec
d h	° ′	° ′	° ′	° ′	° ′	° ′	° ′	° ′	° ′		° ′	° ′
4 00	103 17.3	160 16.9	S21 25.8	137 11.0	S14 45.8	319 05.8	N15 08.7	223 50.2	S18 29.8	Acamar	315 17.3	S40 15.0
01	118 19.7	175 16.0	25.1	152 11.5	45.1	334 08.5	08.8	238 52.4	29.8	Achernar	335 26.0	S57 10.0
02	133 22.2	190 15.2	24.5	167 12.1	44.4	349 11.2	08.9	253 54.6	29.8	Acrux	173 07.8	S63 10.7
03	148 24.7	205 14.4	.. 23.9	182 12.6	.. 43.7	4 13.8	.. 09.0	268 56.8	.. 29.9	Adhara	255 11.3	S28 59.8
04	163 27.1	220 13.6	23.2	197 13.2	43.1	19 16.5	09.0	283 59.0	29.9	Aldebaran	290 47.8	N16 32.2
05	178 29.6	235 12.7	22.6	212 13.8	42.4	34 19.1	09.1	299 01.2	30.0			
06	193 32.1	250 11.9	S21 22.0	227 14.3	S14 41.7	49 21.8	N15 09.2	314 03.4	S18 30.0	Alioth	166 19.9	N55 52.4
07	208 34.5	265 11.1	21.3	242 14.9	41.1	64 24.5	09.3	329 05.6	30.1	Alkaid	152 58.3	N49 14.1
08	223 37.0	280 10.2	20.7	257 15.5	40.4	79 27.1	09.3	344 07.8	30.1	Al Na'ir	27 42.8	S46 53.4
S 09	238 39.5	295 09.4	.. 20.0	272 16.0	.. 39.7	94 29.8	.. 09.4	359 10.1	.. 30.2	Alnilam	275 45.0	S 1 11.8
U 10	253 41.9	310 08.6	19.4	287 16.6	39.1	109 32.5	09.5	14 12.3	30.2	Alphard	217 54.8	S 8 43.6
N 11	268 44.4	325 07.8	18.7	302 17.1	38.4	124 35.1	09.6	29 14.5	30.3			
D 12	283 46.8	340 06.9	S21 18.1	317 17.7	S14 37.7	139 37.8	N15 09.6	44 16.7	S18 30.3	Alphecca	126 10.4	N26 39.9
A 13	298 49.3	355 06.1	17.5	332 18.3	37.0	154 40.5	09.7	59 18.9	30.4	Alpheratz	357 42.4	N29 10.6
Y 14	313 51.8	10 05.3	16.8	347 18.8	36.4	169 43.1	09.8	74 21.1	30.4	Altair	62 07.5	N 8 54.7
15	328 54.2	25 04.5	.. 16.2	2 19.4	.. 35.7	184 45.8	.. 09.9	89 23.3	.. 30.4	Ankaa	353 14.8	S42 13.7
16	343 56.7	40 03.7	15.5	17 20.0	35.0	199 48.5	09.9	104 25.5	30.5	Antares	112 25.2	S26 27.7
17	358 59.2	55 02.8	14.9	32 20.5	34.3	214 51.1	10.0	119 27.7	30.5			
18	14 01.6	70 02.0	S21 14.2	47 21.1	S14 33.7	229 53.8	N15 10.1	134 30.0	S18 30.6	Arcturus	145 54.9	N19 06.2
19	29 04.1	85 01.2	13.6	62 21.7	33.0	244 56.5	10.2	149 32.2	30.6	Atria	107 26.5	S69 02.9
20	44 06.6	100 00.4	12.9	77 22.2	32.3	259 59.1	10.3	164 34.4	30.7	Avior	234 16.9	S59 33.5
21	59 09.0	114 59.6	.. 12.3	92 22.8	.. 31.7	275 01.8	.. 10.3	179 36.6	.. 30.7	Bellatrix	278 30.5	N 6 21.6
22	74 11.5	129 58.7	11.6	107 23.4	31.0	290 04.5	10.4	194 38.8	30.8	Betelgeuse	270 59.8	N 7 24.3
23	89 14.0	144 57.9	10.9	122 23.9	30.3	305 07.1	10.5	209 41.0	30.8			
5 00	104 16.4	159 57.1	S21 10.3	137 24.5	S14 29.6	320 09.8	N15 10.6	224 43.2	S18 30.9	Canopus	263 55.1	S52 42.5
01	119 18.9	174 56.3	09.6	152 25.1	29.0	335 12.5	10.6	239 45.4	30.9	Capella	280 32.4	N46 00.6
02	134 21.3	189 55.5	09.0	167 25.6	28.3	350 15.1	10.7	254 47.6	30.9	Deneb	49 31.1	N45 20.3
03	149 23.8	204 54.7	.. 08.3	182 26.2	.. 27.6	5 17.8	.. 10.8	269 49.9	.. 31.0	Denebola	182 32.5	N14 29.1
04	164 26.3	219 53.8	07.6	197 26.8	26.9	20 20.5	10.9	284 52.1	31.0	Diphda	348 54.9	S17 54.4
05	179 28.7	234 53.0	07.0	212 27.3	26.3	35 23.1	10.9	299 54.3	31.1			
06	194 31.2	249 52.2	S21 06.3	227 27.9	S14 25.6	50 25.8	N15 11.0	314 56.5	S18 31.1	Dubhe	193 50.2	N61 39.8
07	209 33.7	264 51.4	05.6	242 28.5	24.9	65 28.5	11.1	329 58.7	31.2	Elnath	278 10.9	N28 37.0
08	224 36.1	279 50.6	05.0	257 29.0	24.2	80 31.1	11.2	345 00.9	31.2	Eltanin	90 46.2	N51 29.3
M 09	239 38.6	294 49.8	.. 04.3	272 29.6	.. 23.5	95 33.8	.. 11.3	0 03.1	.. 31.3	Enif	33 46.3	N 9 56.8
O 10	254 41.1	309 49.0	03.6	287 30.2	22.9	110 36.5	11.3	15 05.3	31.3	Fomalhaut	15 23.0	S29 32.6
N 11	269 43.5	324 48.2	03.0	302 30.7	22.2	125 39.2	11.4	30 07.6	31.4			
D 12	284 46.0	339 47.3	S21 02.3	317 31.3	S14 21.5	140 41.8	N15 11.5	45 09.8	S18 31.4	Gacrux	171 59.5	S57 11.6
A 13	299 48.5	354 46.5	01.6	332 31.9	20.8	155 44.5	11.6	60 12.0	31.4	Gienah	175 51.1	S17 37.5
Y 14	314 50.9	9 45.7	01.0	347 32.4	20.2	170 47.2	11.6	75 14.2	31.5	Hadar	148 46.4	S60 26.4
15	329 53.4	24 44.9	21 00.3	2 33.0	.. 19.5	185 49.8	.. 11.7	90 16.4	.. 31.5	Hamal	327 59.4	N23 32.0
16	344 55.8	39 44.1	20 59.6	17 33.6	18.8	200 52.5	11.8	105 18.6	31.6	Kaus Aust.	83 42.8	S34 22.4
17	359 58.3	54 43.3	58.9	32 34.2	18.1	215 55.2	11.9	120 20.8	31.6			
18	15 00.8	69 42.5	S20 58.3	47 34.7	S14 17.4	230 57.9	N15 12.0	135 23.1	S18 31.7	Kochab	137 20.9	N74 05.4
19	30 03.2	84 41.7	57.6	62 35.3	16.8	246 00.5	12.0	150 25.3	31.7	Markab	13 37.4	N15 17.3
20	45 05.7	99 40.9	56.9	77 35.9	16.1	261 03.2	12.1	165 27.5	31.8	Menkar	314 13.7	N 4 08.8
21	60 08.2	114 40.1	.. 56.2	92 36.4	.. 15.4	276 05.9	.. 12.2	180 29.7	.. 31.8	Menkent	148 06.4	S36 26.4
22	75 10.6	129 39.3	55.5	107 37.0	14.7	291 08.6	12.3	195 31.9	31.9	Miaplacidus	221 38.5	S69 46.7
23	90 13.1	144 38.5	54.9	122 37.6	14.1	306 11.2	12.3	210 34.1	31.9			
6 00	105 15.6	159 37.7	S20 54.2	137 38.1	S14 13.4	321 13.9	N15 12.4	225 36.3	S18 31.9	Mirfak	308 38.4	N49 54.9
01	120 18.0	174 36.8	53.5	152 38.7	12.7	336 16.6	12.5	240 38.5	32.0	Nunki	75 57.4	S26 16.5
02	135 20.5	189 36.0	52.8	167 39.3	12.0	351 19.3	12.6	255 40.8	32.0	Peacock	53 18.2	S56 41.1
03	150 23.0	204 35.2	.. 52.1	182 39.9	.. 11.3	6 21.9	.. 12.7	270 43.0	.. 32.1	Pollux	243 26.1	N27 59.1
04	165 25.4	219 34.4	51.4	197 40.4	10.6	21 24.6	12.7	285 45.2	32.1	Procyon	244 58.3	N 5 10.9
05	180 27.9	234 33.6	50.7	212 41.0	10.0	36 27.3	12.8	300 47.4	32.2			
06	195 30.3	249 32.8	S20 50.1	227 41.6	S14 09.3	51 30.0	N15 12.9	315 49.6	S18 32.2	Rasalhague	96 05.8	N12 33.1
07	210 32.8	264 32.0	49.4	242 42.1	08.6	66 32.6	13.0	330 51.8	32.3	Regulus	207 42.2	N11 53.4
08	225 35.3	279 31.2	48.7	257 42.7	07.9	81 35.3	13.1	345 54.0	32.3	Rigel	281 10.7	S 8 11.3
T 09	240 37.7	294 30.4	.. 48.0	272 43.3	.. 07.2	96 38.0	.. 13.1	0 56.3	.. 32.3	Rigil Kent.	139 50.4	S60 53.4
U 10	255 40.2	309 29.6	47.3	287 43.9	06.6	111 40.7	13.2	15 58.5	32.4	Sabik	102 11.6	S15 44.4
E 11	270 42.7	324 28.8	46.6	302 44.4	05.9	126 43.4	13.3	31 00.7	32.4			
S 12	285 45.1	339 28.0	S20 45.9	317 45.0	S14 05.2	141 46.0	N15 13.4	46 02.9	S18 32.5	Schedar	349 39.2	N56 37.4
D 13	300 47.6	354 27.2	45.2	332 45.6	04.5	156 48.7	13.5	61 05.1	32.5	Shaula	96 20.9	S37 06.6
A 14	315 50.1	9 26.4	44.5	347 46.2	03.8	171 51.4	13.5	76 07.3	32.6	Sirius	258 32.4	S16 44.5
Y 15	330 52.5	24 25.6	.. 43.8	2 46.7	.. 03.1	186 54.1	.. 13.6	91 09.6	.. 32.6	Spica	158 30.1	S11 14.3
16	345 55.0	39 24.8	43.1	17 47.3	02.5	201 56.7	13.7	106 11.8	32.7	Suhail	222 51.2	S43 29.7
17	0 57.4	54 24.1	42.4	32 47.9	01.8	216 59.4	13.8	121 14.0	32.7			
18	15 59.9	69 23.3	S20 41.7	47 48.5	S14 01.1	232 02.1	N15 13.9	136 16.2	S18 32.7	Vega	80 38.7	N38 48.0
19	31 02.4	84 22.5	41.0	62 49.0	14 00.4	247 04.8	13.9	151 18.4	32.8	Zuben'ubi	137 04.4	S16 06.1
20	46 04.8	99 21.7	40.3	77 49.6	13 59.7	262 07.5	14.0	166 20.6	32.8		SHA	Mer. Pass.
21	61 07.3	114 20.9	.. 39.6	92 50.2	.. 59.0	277 10.1	.. 14.1	181 22.9	.. 32.9		° ′	h m
22	76 09.8	129 20.1	38.9	107 50.8	58.3	292 12.8	14.2	196 25.1	32.9	Venus	55 40.7	13 21
23	91 12.2	144 19.3	38.2	122 51.3	57.7	307 15.5	14.3	211 27.3	33.0	Mars	33 08.1	14 50
	h m									Jupiter	215 53.4	2 39
Mer. Pass. 17 00.1		v −0.8	d 0.7	v 0.6	d 0.7	v 2.7	d 0.1	v 2.2	d 0.0	Saturn	120 26.8	9 00

UT	SUN GHA	SUN Dec	MOON GHA	v	Dec	d	HP
d h	° ′	° ′	° ′	′	° ′	′	′
4 00	178 51.1	S22 46.3	13 54.7	10.2	N18 37.1	0.6	55.7
01	193 50.8	46.0	28 23.9	10.2	18 36.5	0.8	55.7
02	208 50.5	45.8	42 53.1	10.3	18 35.7	0.8	55.7
03	223 50.2 ..	45.5	57 22.4	10.2	18 34.9	1.0	55.7
04	238 50.0	45.3	71 51.6	10.3	18 33.9	1.0	55.6
05	253 49.7	45.0	86 20.9	10.4	18 32.9	1.1	55.6
06	268 49.4	S22 44.8	100 50.3	10.3	N18 31.8	1.2	55.6
07	283 49.1	44.5	115 19.6	10.4	18 30.6	1.3	55.6
08	298 48.8	44.3	129 49.0	10.4	18 29.3	1.5	55.6
09	313 48.5 ..	44.0	144 18.4	10.4	18 27.8	1.5	55.6
10	328 48.3	43.7	158 47.8	10.5	18 26.3	1.6	55.5
11	343 48.0	43.5	173 17.3	10.5	18 24.7	1.7	55.5
12	358 47.7	S22 43.2	187 46.8	10.6	N18 23.0	1.7	55.5
13	13 47.4	43.0	202 16.4	10.5	18 21.3	1.9	55.5
14	28 47.1	42.7	216 45.9	10.6	18 19.4	2.0	55.5
15	43 46.9 ..	42.4	231 15.5	10.7	18 17.4	2.0	55.4
16	58 46.6	42.2	245 45.2	10.6	18 15.4	2.2	55.4
17	73 46.3	41.9	260 14.8	10.7	18 13.2	2.2	55.4
18	88 46.0	S22 41.6	274 44.5	10.8	N18 11.0	2.4	55.4
19	103 45.7	41.4	289 14.3	10.7	18 08.6	2.4	55.4
20	118 45.4	41.1	303 44.0	10.8	18 06.2	2.5	55.4
21	133 45.2 ..	40.8	318 13.8	10.9	18 03.7	2.6	55.3
22	148 44.9	40.6	332 43.7	10.9	18 01.1	2.7	55.3
23	163 44.6	40.3	347 13.6	10.9	17 58.4	2.8	55.3
5 00	178 44.3	S22 40.0	1 43.5	10.9	N17 55.6	2.9	55.3
01	193 44.0	39.7	16 13.4	11.0	17 52.7	2.9	55.3
02	208 43.8	39.5	30 43.4	11.1	17 49.8	3.1	55.2
03	223 43.5 ..	39.2	45 13.5	11.0	17 46.7	3.1	55.2
04	238 43.2	38.9	59 43.5	11.2	17 43.6	3.2	55.2
05	253 42.9	38.7	74 13.7	11.1	17 40.4	3.3	55.2
06	268 42.6	S22 38.4	88 43.8	11.2	N17 37.1	3.4	55.2
07	283 42.4	38.1	103 14.0	11.2	17 33.7	3.5	55.2
08	298 42.1	37.8	117 44.2	11.3	17 30.2	3.5	55.1
09	313 41.8 ..	37.5	132 14.5	11.3	17 26.7	3.7	55.1
10	328 41.5	37.3	146 44.8	11.4	17 23.0	3.7	55.1
11	343 41.2	37.0	161 15.2	11.3	17 19.3	3.8	55.1
12	358 41.0	S22 36.7	175 45.5	11.5	N17 15.5	3.9	55.1
13	13 40.7	36.4	190 16.0	11.5	17 11.6	3.9	55.1
14	28 40.4	36.1	204 46.5	11.5	17 07.7	4.1	55.0
15	43 40.1 ..	35.9	219 17.0	11.5	17 03.6	4.1	55.0
16	58 39.9	35.6	233 47.5	11.7	16 59.5	4.2	55.0
17	73 39.6	35.3	248 18.2	11.6	16 55.3	4.3	55.0
18	88 39.3	S22 35.0	262 48.8	11.7	N16 51.0	4.4	55.0
19	103 39.0	34.7	277 19.5	11.7	16 46.6	4.4	55.0
20	118 38.7	34.4	291 50.2	11.8	16 42.2	4.5	54.9
21	133 38.5 ..	34.1	306 21.0	11.8	16 37.7	4.6	54.9
22	148 38.2	33.9	320 51.8	11.9	16 33.1	4.7	54.9
23	163 37.9	33.6	335 22.7	11.9	16 28.4	4.7	54.9
6 00	178 37.6	S22 33.3	349 53.6	12.0	N16 23.7	4.9	54.9
01	193 37.4	33.0	4 24.6	12.0	16 18.8	4.8	54.9
02	208 37.1	32.7	18 55.6	12.0	16 14.0	5.0	54.9
03	223 36.8 ..	32.4	33 26.6	12.1	16 09.0	5.1	54.8
04	238 36.5	32.1	47 57.7	12.1	16 03.9	5.1	54.8
05	253 36.3	31.8	62 28.8	12.2	15 58.8	5.2	54.8
06	268 36.0	S22 31.5	77 00.0	12.2	N15 53.6	5.2	54.8
07	283 35.7	31.2	91 31.2	12.3	15 48.4	5.4	54.8
08	298 35.4	30.9	106 02.5	12.3	15 43.0	5.4	54.8
09	313 35.2 ..	30.6	120 33.8	12.4	15 37.6	5.4	54.8
10	328 34.9	30.3	135 05.2	12.4	15 32.2	5.6	54.7
11	343 34.6	30.0	149 36.6	12.4	15 26.6	5.6	54.7
12	358 34.3	S22 29.7	164 08.0	12.5	N15 21.0	5.7	54.7
13	13 34.1	29.4	178 39.5	12.6	15 15.3	5.7	54.7
14	28 33.8	29.1	193 11.1	12.6	15 09.6	5.8	54.7
15	43 33.5 ..	28.8	207 42.7	12.6	15 03.8	5.9	54.7
16	58 33.2	28.5	222 14.3	12.7	14 57.9	5.9	54.7
17	73 33.0	28.2	236 46.0	12.7	14 52.0	6.0	54.6
18	88 32.7	S22 27.9	251 17.7	12.8	N14 46.0	6.1	54.6
19	103 32.4	27.6	265 49.5	12.8	14 39.9	6.1	54.6
20	118 32.2	27.3	280 21.3	12.8	14 33.8	6.2	54.6
21	133 31.9 ..	27.0	294 53.1	12.9	14 27.6	6.3	54.6
22	148 31.6	26.7	309 25.0	13.0	14 21.3	6.3	54.6
23	163 31.3	26.4	323 57.0	13.0	N14 15.0	6.4	54.6
	SD 16.3	d 0.3	SD 15.1		15.0		14.9

(Day labels: SUNDAY — 4, MONDAY — 5, TUESDAY — 6)

Lat.	Naut.	Civil	Sunrise	Moonrise 4	5	6	7
°	h m	h m	h m	h m	h m	h m	h m
N 72	08 20	10 31	■■■	▭	13 37	15 30	17 13
N 70	08 02	09 43	■■■	13 12	14 34	16 04	17 35
68	07 47	09 12	11 31	13 55	15 07	16 28	17 52
66	07 35	08 50	10 20	14 23	15 32	16 47	18 06
64	07 25	08 32	09 45	14 45	15 50	17 02	18 17
62	07 16	08 17	09 20	15 03	16 06	17 15	18 26
60	07 08	08 04	09 00	15 17	16 19	17 25	18 35
N 58	07 01	07 53	08 44	15 29	16 30	17 35	18 42
56	06 55	07 43	08 30	15 40	16 40	17 43	18 48
54	06 49	07 35	08 18	15 49	16 48	17 50	18 54
52	06 44	07 27	08 07	15 58	16 56	17 56	18 59
50	06 39	07 20	07 58	16 05	17 03	18 02	19 03
45	06 28	07 05	07 38	16 21	17 17	18 15	19 13
N 40	06 18	06 52	07 22	16 35	17 29	18 25	19 21
35	06 09	06 41	07 08	16 46	17 40	18 34	19 28
30	06 01	06 31	06 57	16 56	17 49	18 42	19 35
20	05 45	06 12	06 36	17 12	18 04	18 55	19 45
N 10	05 29	05 56	06 18	17 27	18 18	19 07	19 55
0	05 13	05 39	06 02	17 41	18 30	19 18	20 03
S 10	04 55	05 22	05 45	17 55	18 43	19 29	20 12
20	04 33	05 02	05 26	18 09	18 56	19 40	20 21
30	04 05	04 38	05 05	18 26	19 12	19 53	20 32
35	03 47	04 23	04 53	18 36	19 21	20 01	20 38
40	03 25	04 06	04 38	18 47	19 31	20 10	20 45
45	02 56	03 44	04 21	19 00	19 43	20 20	20 53
S 50	02 13	03 16	03 59	19 16	19 57	20 32	21 02
52	01 48	03 01	03 49	19 24	20 04	20 38	21 07
54	01 12	02 45	03 37	19 32	20 11	20 44	21 12
56	////	02 24	03 24	19 41	20 20	20 51	21 17
58	////	01 58	03 08	19 52	20 29	20 59	21 23
S 60	////	01 18	02 49	20 04	20 40	21 08	21 30

Lat.	Sunset	Civil	Naut.	Moonset 4	5	6	7
°	h m	h m	h m	h m	h m	h m	h m
N 72	■■■	13 40	15 51	▭	11 05	10 52	10 44
N 70	■■■	14 28	16 09	09 47	10 08	10 17	10 21
68	12 40	14 58	16 24	09 04	09 34	09 52	10 03
66	13 51	15 21	16 36	08 35	09 09	09 33	09 49
64	14 26	15 39	16 46	08 13	08 50	09 17	09 37
62	14 51	15 54	16 55	07 55	08 34	09 04	09 26
60	15 11	16 07	17 03	07 41	08 21	08 53	09 18
N 58	15 27	16 18	17 10	07 28	08 10	08 43	09 10
56	15 41	16 27	17 16	07 17	08 00	08 34	09 03
54	15 53	16 36	17 22	07 08	07 51	08 27	08 57
52	16 03	16 44	17 27	06 59	07 43	08 20	08 51
50	16 13	16 51	17 32	06 52	07 36	08 14	08 46
45	16 33	17 06	17 43	06 35	07 21	08 01	08 36
N 40	16 49	17 19	17 53	06 22	07 08	07 50	08 27
35	17 02	17 30	18 02	06 11	06 58	07 40	08 19
30	17 14	17 40	18 10	06 01	06 48	07 32	08 12
20	17 34	17 58	18 26	05 44	06 32	07 18	08 00
N 10	17 52	18 15	18 41	05 29	06 18	07 05	07 50
0	18 09	18 31	18 57	05 15	06 05	06 53	07 40
S 10	18 26	18 49	19 16	05 01	05 52	06 41	07 30
20	18 44	19 08	19 37	04 46	05 37	06 29	07 19
30	19 05	19 32	20 05	04 28	05 21	06 14	07 07
35	19 18	19 47	20 23	04 18	05 11	06 06	07 00
40	19 32	20 05	20 45	04 07	05 01	05 56	06 52
45	19 49	20 26	21 14	03 53	04 48	05 45	06 43
S 50	20 11	20 54	21 56	03 37	04 32	05 31	06 31
52	20 21	21 08	22 21	03 29	04 25	05 24	06 26
54	20 33	21 25	22 56	03 20	04 17	05 17	06 20
56	20 46	21 45	////	03 10	04 07	05 09	06 14
58	21 01	22 11	////	02 59	03 57	05 00	06 06
S 60	21 20	22 50	////	02 46	03 45	04 50	05 58

	SUN			MOON			
Day	Eqn. of Time 00h	12h	Mer. Pass.	Mer. Pass. Upper	Lower	Age	Phase
d	m s	m s	h m	h m	h m	d	%
4	04 35	04 49	12 05	23 53	11 28	13	99
5	05 02	05 16	12 05	24 42	12 18	14	100
6	05 29	05 42	12 06	00 42	13 06	15	98

UT	ARIES GHA	VENUS −3.9 GHA	VENUS Dec	MARS +1.1 GHA	MARS Dec	JUPITER −2.5 GHA	JUPITER Dec	SATURN +0.6 GHA	SATURN Dec	Star Name	SHA	Dec
7 00	106 14.7	159 18.5	S20 37.5	137 51.9	S13 57.0	322 18.2	N15 14.3	226 29.5	S18 33.0	Acamar	315 17.4	S40 15.0
01	121 17.2	174 17.7	36.7	152 52.5	56.3	337 20.9	14.4	241 31.7	33.1	Achernar	335 26.0	S57 10.0
02	136 19.6	189 16.9	36.0	167 53.1	55.6	352 23.5	14.5	256 33.9	33.1	Acrux	173 07.8	S63 10.7
03	151 22.1	204 16.1 ..	35.3	182 53.6 ..	54.9	7 26.2 ..	14.6	271 36.2 ..	33.1	Adhara	255 11.3	S28 59.8
04	166 24.6	219 15.3	34.6	197 54.2	54.2	22 28.9	14.7	286 38.4	33.2	Aldebaran	290 47.8	N16 32.2
05	181 27.0	234 14.5	33.9	212 54.8	53.5	37 31.6	14.7	301 40.6	33.2			
W 06	196 29.5	249 13.8	S20 33.2	227 55.4	S13 52.9	52 34.3	N15 14.8	316 42.8	S18 33.3	Alioth	166 19.8	N55 52.4
E 07	211 31.9	264 13.0	32.5	242 55.9	52.2	67 37.0	14.9	331 45.0	33.3	Alkaid	152 58.2	N49 14.1
D 08	226 34.4	279 12.2	31.7	257 56.5	51.5	82 39.6	15.0	346 47.2	33.4	Al Na'ir	27 42.8	S46 53.4
N 09	241 36.9	294 11.4 ..	31.0	272 57.1 ..	50.8	97 42.3 ..	15.1	1 49.5 ..	33.4	Alnilam	275 45.0	S 1 11.8
E 10	256 39.3	309 10.6	30.3	287 57.7	50.1	112 45.0	15.1	16 51.7	33.5	Alphard	217 54.7	S 8 43.6
S 11	271 41.8	324 09.8	29.6	302 58.2	49.4	127 47.7	15.2	31 53.9	33.5			
D 12	286 44.3	339 09.0	S20 28.9	317 58.8	S13 48.7	142 50.4	N15 15.3	46 56.1	S18 33.5	Alphecca	126 10.3	N26 39.8
A 13	301 46.7	354 08.3	28.1	332 59.4	48.0	157 53.1	15.4	61 58.3	33.6	Alpheratz	357 42.4	N29 10.6
Y 14	316 49.2	9 07.5	27.4	348 00.0	47.3	172 55.8	15.5	77 00.5	33.6	Altair	62 07.5	N 8 54.7
15	331 51.7	24 06.7 ..	26.7	3 00.6 ..	46.7	187 58.4 ..	15.6	92 02.8 ..	33.7	Ankaa	353 14.8	S42 13.7
16	346 54.1	39 05.9	26.0	18 01.1	46.0	203 01.1	15.6	107 05.0	33.7	Antares	112 25.2	S26 27.7
17	1 56.6	54 05.1	25.2	33 01.7	45.3	218 03.8	15.7	122 07.2	33.8			
18	16 59.1	69 04.3	S20 24.5	48 02.3	S13 44.6	233 06.5	N15 15.8	137 09.4	S18 33.8	Arcturus	145 54.9	N19 06.2
19	32 01.5	84 03.6	23.8	63 02.9	43.9	248 09.2	15.9	152 11.6	33.9	Atria	107 26.5	S69 02.9
20	47 04.0	99 02.8	23.1	78 03.4	43.2	263 11.9	16.0	167 13.8	33.9	Avior	234 16.9	S59 33.6
21	62 06.4	114 02.0 ..	22.3	93 04.0 ..	42.5	278 14.6 ..	16.0	182 16.1 ..	33.9	Bellatrix	278 30.5	N 6 21.6
22	77 08.9	129 01.2	21.6	108 04.6	41.8	293 17.2	16.1	197 18.3	34.0	Betelgeuse	270 59.8	N 7 24.3
23	92 11.4	144 00.4	20.9	123 05.2	41.1	308 19.9	16.2	212 20.5	34.0			
8 00	107 13.8	158 59.7	S20 20.1	138 05.8	S13 40.4	323 22.6	N15 16.3	227 22.7	S18 34.1	Canopus	263 55.1	S52 42.5
01	122 16.3	173 58.9	19.4	153 06.3	39.7	338 25.3	16.4	242 24.9	34.1	Capella	280 32.4	N46 00.6
02	137 18.8	188 58.1	18.7	168 06.9	39.1	353 28.0	16.5	257 27.2	34.2	Deneb	49 31.1	N45 20.3
03	152 21.2	203 57.3 ..	17.9	183 07.5 ..	38.4	8 30.7 ..	16.5	272 29.4 ..	34.2	Denebola	182 32.5	N14 29.1
04	167 23.7	218 56.5	17.2	198 08.1	37.7	23 33.4	16.6	287 31.6	34.2	Diphda	348 54.9	S17 54.4
05	182 26.2	233 55.8	16.4	213 08.7	37.0	38 36.1	16.7	302 33.8	34.3			
T 06	197 28.6	248 55.0	S20 15.7	228 09.2	S13 36.3	53 38.7	N15 16.8	317 36.0	S18 34.3	Dubhe	193 50.2	N61 39.8
H 07	212 31.1	263 54.2	15.0	243 09.8	35.6	68 41.4	16.9	332 38.3	34.4	Elnath	278 10.9	N28 37.0
U 08	227 33.6	278 53.4	14.2	258 10.4	34.9	83 44.1	17.0	347 40.5	34.4	Eltanin	90 46.2	N51 29.3
R 09	242 36.0	293 52.7 ..	13.5	273 11.0 ..	34.2	98 46.8 ..	17.0	2 42.7 ..	34.5	Enif	33 46.3	N 9 56.8
S 10	257 38.5	308 51.9	12.7	288 11.6	33.5	113 49.5	17.1	17 44.9	34.5	Fomalhaut	15 23.0	S29 32.6
D 11	272 40.9	323 51.1	12.0	303 12.2	32.8	128 52.2	17.2	32 47.1	34.5			
A 12	287 43.4	338 50.4	S20 11.2	318 12.7	S13 32.1	143 54.9	N15 17.3	47 49.4	S18 34.6	Gacrux	171 59.5	S57 11.6
Y 13	302 45.9	353 49.6	10.5	333 13.3	31.4	158 57.6	17.4	62 51.6	34.6	Gienah	175 51.1	S17 37.5
14	317 48.3	8 48.8	09.8	348 13.9	30.7	174 00.3	17.5	77 53.8	34.7	Hadar	148 46.4	S60 26.4
15	332 50.8	23 48.0 ..	09.0	3 14.5 ..	30.0	189 03.0 ..	17.5	92 56.0 ..	34.7	Hamal	327 59.4	N23 32.0
16	347 53.3	38 47.3	08.3	18 15.1	29.3	204 05.7	17.6	107 58.2	34.8	Kaus Aust.	83 42.8	S34 22.4
17	2 55.7	53 46.5	07.5	33 15.6	28.7	219 08.3	17.7	123 00.5	34.8			
18	17 58.2	68 45.7	S20 06.7	48 16.2	S13 28.0	234 11.0	N15 17.8	138 02.7	S18 34.8	Kochab	137 20.8	N74 05.4
19	33 00.7	83 45.0	06.0	63 16.8	27.3	249 13.7	17.9	153 04.9	34.9	Markab	13 37.4	N15 17.3
20	48 03.1	98 44.2	05.2	78 17.4	26.6	264 16.4	18.0	168 07.1	34.9	Menkar	314 13.7	N 4 08.8
21	63 05.6	113 43.4 ..	04.5	93 18.0 ..	25.9	279 19.1 ..	18.0	183 09.3 ..	35.0	Menkent	148 06.3	S36 26.4
22	78 08.0	128 42.7	03.7	108 18.6	25.2	294 21.8	18.1	198 11.6	35.0	Miaplacidus	221 38.4	S69 46.7
23	93 10.5	143 41.9	03.0	123 19.1	24.5	309 24.5	18.2	213 13.8	35.1			
9 00	108 13.0	158 41.1	S20 02.2	138 19.7	S13 23.8	324 27.2	N15 18.3	228 16.0	S18 35.1	Mirfak	308 38.4	N49 54.9
01	123 15.4	173 40.4	01.5	153 20.3	23.1	339 29.9	18.4	243 18.2	35.1	Nunki	75 57.4	S26 16.5
02	138 17.9	188 39.6	20 00.7	168 20.9	22.4	354 32.6	18.5	258 20.4	35.2	Peacock	53 18.2	S56 41.1
03	153 20.4	203 38.8	19 59.9	183 21.5 ..	21.7	9 35.3 ..	18.5	273 22.7 ..	35.2	Pollux	243 26.1	N27 59.1
04	168 22.8	218 38.1	59.2	198 22.1	21.0	24 38.0	18.6	288 24.9	35.3	Procyon	244 58.3	N 5 10.9
05	183 25.3	233 37.3	58.4	213 22.7	20.3	39 40.7	18.7	303 27.1	35.3			
F 06	198 27.8	248 36.6	S19 57.6	228 23.2	S13 19.6	54 43.4	N15 18.8	318 29.3	S18 35.4	Rasalhague	96 05.8	N12 33.1
R 07	213 30.2	263 35.8	56.9	243 23.8	18.9	69 46.1	18.9	333 31.6	35.4	Regulus	207 42.1	N11 53.4
I 08	228 32.7	278 35.0	56.1	258 24.4	18.2	84 48.8	19.0	348 33.8	35.4	Rigel	281 10.7	S 8 11.3
D 09	243 35.2	293 34.3 ..	55.3	273 25.0 ..	17.5	99 51.5 ..	19.1	3 36.0 ..	35.5	Rigil Kent.	139 50.4	S60 53.4
A 10	258 37.6	308 33.5	54.6	288 25.6	16.8	114 54.1	19.1	18 38.2	35.5	Sabik	102 11.6	S15 44.4
Y 11	273 40.1	323 32.7	53.8	303 26.2	16.1	129 56.8	19.2	33 40.4	35.6			
12	288 42.5	338 32.0	S19 53.0	318 26.8	S13 15.4	144 59.5	N15 19.3	48 42.7	S18 35.6	Schedar	349 39.2	N56 37.4
13	303 45.0	353 31.2	52.3	333 27.3	14.7	160 02.2	19.4	63 44.9	35.7	Shaula	96 20.8	S37 06.6
14	318 47.5	8 30.5	51.5	348 27.9	14.0	175 04.9	19.5	78 47.1	35.7	Sirius	258 32.4	S16 44.5
15	333 49.9	23 29.7 ..	50.7	3 28.5 ..	13.3	190 07.6 ..	19.6	93 49.3 ..	35.7	Spica	158 30.1	S11 14.3
16	348 52.4	38 29.0	50.0	18 29.1	12.6	205 10.3	19.7	108 51.6	35.8	Suhail	222 51.2	S43 29.7
17	3 54.9	53 28.2	49.2	33 29.7	11.9	220 13.0	19.7	123 53.8	35.8			
18	18 57.3	68 27.4	S19 48.4	48 30.3	S13 11.2	235 15.7	N15 19.8	138 56.0	S18 35.9	Vega	80 38.6	N38 48.0
19	33 59.8	83 26.7	47.6	63 30.9	10.5	250 18.4	19.9	153 58.2	35.9	Zuben'ubi	137 04.4	S16 06.1
20	49 02.3	98 25.9	46.8	78 31.5	09.8	265 21.1	20.0	169 00.5	36.0		SHA	Mer.Pass.
21	64 04.7	113 25.2 ..	46.1	93 32.0 ..	09.1	280 23.8 ..	20.1	184 02.7 ..	36.0	Venus	51 45.8	h m 13 25
22	79 07.2	128 24.4	45.3	108 32.6	08.4	295 26.5	20.2	199 04.9	36.0	Mars	30 51.9	14 47
23	94 09.7	143 23.7	44.5	123 33.2	07.7	310 29.2	20.3	214 07.1	36.1	Jupiter	216 08.8	2 26
Mer.Pass. 16 48.3		v −0.8	d 0.7	v 0.6	d 0.7	v 2.7	d 0.1	v 2.2	d 0.0	Saturn	120 08.9	8 49

UT	SUN GHA	Dec	MOON GHA	v	Dec	d	HP
d h	° ′	° ′	° ′	′	° ′	′	′
7 00	178 31.1	S22 26.1	338 29.0	13.0	N14 08.6	6.4	54.5
01	193 30.8	25.8	353 01.0	13.1	14 02.2	6.5	54.5
02	208 30.5	25.5	7 33.1	13.1	13 55.7	6.6	54.5
03	223 30.3	.. 25.2	22 05.2	13.2	13 49.1	6.6	54.5
04	238 30.0	24.9	36 37.4	13.2	13 42.5	6.7	54.5
05	253 29.7	24.6	51 09.6	13.3	13 35.8	6.7	54.5
06	268 29.5	S22 24.2	65 41.9	13.3	N13 29.1	6.8	54.5
W 07	283 29.2	23.9	80 14.2	13.3	13 22.3	6.8	54.5
E 08	298 28.9	23.6	94 46.5	13.4	13 15.5	6.9	54.5
D 09	313 28.6	.. 23.3	109 18.9	13.4	13 08.6	7.0	54.4
N 10	328 28.4	23.0	123 51.3	13.5	13 01.6	7.0	54.4
E 11	343 28.1	22.7	138 23.8	13.5	12 54.6	7.0	54.4
S 12	358 27.8	S22 22.3	152 56.3	13.6	N12 47.6	7.1	54.4
D 13	13 27.6	22.0	167 28.9	13.6	12 40.5	7.2	54.4
A 14	28 27.3	21.7	182 01.5	13.6	12 33.3	7.2	54.4
Y 15	43 27.0	.. 21.4	196 34.1	13.7	12 26.1	7.3	54.4
16	58 26.8	21.1	211 06.8	13.7	12 18.8	7.3	54.4
17	73 26.5	20.7	225 39.5	13.8	12 11.5	7.3	54.4
18	88 26.2	S22 20.4	240 12.3	13.8	N12 04.2	7.5	54.3
19	103 26.0	20.1	254 45.1	13.8	11 56.7	7.4	54.3
20	118 25.7	19.8	269 17.9	13.9	11 49.3	7.5	54.3
21	133 25.4	.. 19.5	283 50.8	13.9	11 41.8	7.6	54.3
22	148 25.2	19.1	298 23.7	14.0	11 34.2	7.6	54.3
23	163 24.9	18.8	312 56.7	14.0	11 26.6	7.6	54.3
8 00	178 24.6	S22 18.5	327 29.7	14.0	N11 19.0	7.7	54.3
01	193 24.4	18.2	342 02.7	14.1	11 11.3	7.8	54.3
02	208 24.1	17.8	356 35.8	14.1	11 03.5	7.7	54.3
03	223 23.8	.. 17.5	11 08.9	14.1	10 55.8	7.9	54.3
04	238 23.6	17.2	25 42.0	14.2	10 47.9	7.8	54.3
05	253 23.3	16.8	40 15.2	14.2	10 40.1	7.9	54.2
06	268 23.0	S22 16.5	54 48.4	14.3	N10 32.2	8.0	54.2
T 07	283 22.8	16.2	69 21.7	14.3	10 24.2	8.0	54.2
H 08	298 22.5	15.8	83 55.0	14.3	10 16.2	8.0	54.2
U 09	313 22.2	.. 15.5	98 28.3	14.4	10 08.2	8.1	54.2
R 10	328 22.0	15.2	113 01.7	14.4	10 00.1	8.1	54.2
S 11	343 21.7	14.8	127 35.1	14.4	9 52.0	8.1	54.2
D 12	358 21.4	S22 14.5	142 08.5	14.5	N 9 43.9	8.2	54.2
A 13	13 21.2	14.2	156 42.0	14.5	9 35.7	8.2	54.2
Y 14	28 20.9	13.8	171 15.5	14.5	9 27.5	8.3	54.2
15	43 20.7	.. 13.5	185 49.0	14.6	9 19.2	8.3	54.2
16	58 20.4	13.2	200 22.6	14.6	9 10.9	8.3	54.2
17	73 20.1	12.8	214 56.2	14.6	9 02.6	8.4	54.2
18	88 19.9	S22 12.5	229 29.8	14.6	N 8 54.2	8.4	54.2
19	103 19.6	12.1	244 03.4	14.7	8 45.8	8.4	54.2
20	118 19.3	11.8	258 37.1	14.7	8 37.4	8.5	54.1
21	133 19.1	.. 11.4	273 10.8	14.8	8 28.9	8.4	54.1
22	148 18.8	11.1	287 44.6	14.8	8 20.5	8.6	54.1
23	163 18.6	10.8	302 18.4	14.7	8 11.9	8.5	54.1
9 00	178 18.3	S22 10.4	316 52.1	14.9	N 8 03.4	8.6	54.1
01	193 18.0	10.1	331 26.0	14.8	7 54.8	8.6	54.1
02	208 17.8	09.7	345 59.8	14.9	7 46.2	8.7	54.1
03	223 17.5	.. 09.4	0 33.7	14.9	7 37.5	8.7	54.1
04	238 17.3	09.0	15 07.6	14.9	7 28.8	8.7	54.1
05	253 17.0	08.7	29 41.5	15.0	7 20.1	8.7	54.1
06	268 16.7	S22 08.3	44 15.5	15.0	N 7 11.4	8.8	54.1
07	283 16.5	08.0	58 49.5	15.0	7 02.6	8.8	54.1
F 08	298 16.2	07.6	73 23.5	15.0	6 53.8	8.8	54.1
R 09	313 16.0	.. 07.3	87 57.5	15.0	6 45.0	8.8	54.1
I 10	328 15.7	06.9	102 31.5	15.1	6 36.2	8.9	54.1
D 11	343 15.4	06.6	117 05.6	15.1	6 27.3	8.9	54.1
A 12	358 15.2	S22 06.2	131 39.7	15.1	N 6 18.4	8.9	54.1
Y 13	13 14.9	05.9	146 13.8	15.1	6 09.5	8.9	54.1
14	28 14.7	05.5	160 47.9	15.2	6 00.6	9.0	54.1
15	43 14.4	.. 05.2	175 22.1	15.1	5 51.6	9.0	54.1
16	58 14.2	04.8	189 56.2	15.2	5 42.6	9.0	54.1
17	73 13.9	04.4	204 30.4	15.2	5 33.6	9.0	54.1
18	88 13.6	S22 04.1	219 04.6	15.2	N 5 24.6	9.0	54.1
19	103 13.4	03.7	233 38.8	15.3	5 15.6	9.1	54.1
20	118 13.1	03.4	248 13.1	15.2	5 06.5	9.1	54.1
21	133 12.9	.. 03.0	262 47.3	15.3	4 57.4	9.1	54.1
22	148 12.6	02.6	277 21.6	15.3	4 48.3	9.1	54.1
23	163 12.4	02.3	291 55.9	15.3	N 4 39.2	9.2	54.1
	SD 16.3	d 0.3	SD 14.8		14.8		14.7

Lat.	Twilight Naut.	Civil	Sunrise	Moonrise 7	8	9	10
°	h m	h m	h m	h m	h m	h m	h m
N 72	08 15	10 20	■■	17 13	18 51	20 26	21 59
N 70	07 58	09 37	■■	17 35	19 05	20 33	22 01
68	07 44	09 08	11 11	17 52	19 16	20 39	22 02
66	07 33	08 46	10 13	18 06	19 25	20 44	22 03
64	07 23	08 29	09 40	18 17	19 33	20 48	22 04
62	07 14	08 14	09 16	18 26	19 39	20 52	22 04
60	07 07	08 02	08 57	18 35	19 45	20 55	22 05
N 58	07 00	07 51	08 41	18 42	19 50	20 58	22 06
56	06 54	07 42	08 28	18 48	19 54	21 00	22 06
54	06 48	07 34	08 16	18 54	19 58	21 02	22 06
52	06 43	07 26	08 06	18 59	20 01	21 04	22 07
50	06 38	07 19	07 57	19 03	20 05	21 06	22 07
45	06 28	07 04	07 38	19 13	20 12	21 10	22 08
N 40	06 18	06 52	07 22	19 21	20 17	21 13	22 09
35	06 09	06 41	07 09	19 28	20 22	21 16	22 09
30	06 01	06 31	06 57	19 35	20 27	21 18	22 10
20	05 46	06 13	06 37	19 45	20 34	21 23	22 11
N 10	05 31	05 57	06 19	19 55	20 41	21 27	22 12
0	05 15	05 41	06 03	20 03	20 47	21 30	22 12
S 10	04 57	05 23	05 46	20 12	20 53	21 34	22 13
20	04 35	05 04	05 28	20 21	21 00	21 37	22 14
30	04 07	04 40	05 07	20 32	21 08	21 42	22 15
35	03 50	04 26	04 55	20 38	21 12	21 44	22 15
40	03 28	04 09	04 41	20 45	21 17	21 47	22 16
45	03 00	03 48	04 24	20 53	21 23	21 50	22 17
S 50	02 19	03 20	04 03	21 02	21 29	21 54	22 18
52	01 55	03 06	03 53	21 07	21 32	21 56	22 18
54	01 21	02 50	03 42	21 12	21 36	21 58	22 18
56	////	02 30	03 28	21 17	21 40	22 00	22 19
58	////	02 05	03 13	21 23	21 44	22 02	22 19
S 60	////	01 29	02 55	21 30	21 48	22 05	22 20

Lat.	Sunset	Twilight Civil	Naut.	Moonset 7	8	9	10
°	h m	h m	h m	h m	h m	h m	h m
N 72	■■	13 54	15 58	10 44	10 38	10 32	10 26
N 70	■■	14 37	16 16	10 21	10 23	10 23	10 23
68	13 03	15 06	16 29	10 03	10 10	10 16	10 20
66	14 00	15 27	16 41	09 49	10 00	10 09	10 17
64	14 33	15 45	16 51	09 37	09 52	10 04	10 15
62	14 57	15 59	16 59	09 26	09 44	09 59	10 13
60	15 16	16 11	17 07	09 18	09 38	09 55	10 11
N 58	15 32	16 22	17 14	09 10	09 32	09 52	10 10
56	15 46	16 31	17 20	09 03	09 27	09 49	10 08
54	15 57	16 40	17 25	08 57	09 23	09 46	10 07
52	16 07	16 47	17 30	08 51	09 19	09 43	10 06
50	16 16	16 54	17 35	08 46	09 15	09 41	10 05
45	16 36	17 09	17 46	08 36	09 07	09 36	10 02
N 40	16 51	17 22	17 55	08 27	09 00	09 31	10 01
35	17 05	17 33	18 04	08 19	08 54	09 27	09 59
30	17 16	17 42	18 12	08 12	08 49	09 24	09 57
20	17 36	18 00	18 27	08 00	08 40	09 18	09 55
N 10	17 54	18 16	18 43	07 50	08 32	09 13	09 53
0	18 10	18 33	18 59	07 40	08 25	09 08	09 50
S 10	18 27	18 50	19 17	07 30	08 17	09 03	09 48
20	18 45	19 09	19 38	07 19	08 09	08 58	09 46
30	19 05	19 33	20 05	07 07	08 00	08 52	09 43
35	19 18	19 47	20 23	07 00	07 55	08 48	09 42
40	19 32	20 04	20 45	06 52	07 48	08 44	09 40
45	19 49	20 25	21 13	06 43	07 41	08 40	09 38
S 50	20 10	20 52	21 53	06 31	07 33	08 34	09 35
52	20 20	21 06	22 17	06 26	07 29	08 32	09 34
54	20 31	21 22	22 49	06 20	07 24	08 29	09 33
56	20 44	21 42	////	06 14	07 20	08 26	09 32
58	20 59	22 07	////	06 06	07 14	08 22	09 30
S 60	21 17	22 42	////	05 58	07 08	08 18	09 28

	SUN			MOON			
Day	Eqn. of Time 00h	12h	Mer. Pass.	Mer. Pass. Upper	Lower	Age	Phase
d	m s	m s	h m	h m	h m	d	%
7	05 55	06 08	12 06	01 29	13 52	16	95
8	06 21	06 34	12 07	02 14	14 36	17	90
9	06 46	06 59	12 07	02 58	15 19	18	84

UT	ARIES GHA	VENUS −3.9 GHA	VENUS Dec	MARS +1.1 GHA	MARS Dec	JUPITER −2.5 GHA	JUPITER Dec	SATURN +0.6 GHA	SATURN Dec	STARS Name	SHA	Dec
d h	° ′	° ′	° ′	° ′	° ′	° ′	° ′	° ′	° ′		° ′	° ′
10 00	109 12.1	158 22.9	S19 43.7	138 33.8	S13 07.0	325 31.9	N15 20.3	229 09.3	S18 36.1	Acamar	315 17.4	S40 15.0
01	124 14.6	173 22.2	42.9	153 34.4	06.3	340 34.6	20.4	244 11.6	36.2	Achernar	335 26.0	S57 10.0
02	139 17.0	188 21.4	42.2	168 35.0	05.6	355 37.3	20.5	259 13.8	36.2	Acrux	173 07.7	S63 10.7
03	154 19.5	203 20.7 ..	41.4	183 35.6 ..	04.9	10 40.0 ..	20.6	274 16.0 ..	36.3	Adhara	255 11.3	S28 59.8
04	169 22.0	218 19.9	40.6	198 36.2	04.2	25 42.7	20.7	289 18.2	36.3	Aldebaran	290 47.8	N16 32.2
05	184 24.4	233 19.2	39.8	213 36.8	03.5	40 45.4	20.8	304 20.5	36.3			
06	199 26.9	248 18.4	S19 39.0	228 37.3	S13 02.8	55 48.1	N15 20.9	319 22.7	S18 36.4	Alioth	166 19.8	N55 52.4
S 07	214 29.4	263 17.7	38.2	243 37.9	02.1	70 50.8	20.9	334 24.9	36.4	Alkaid	152 58.2	N49 14.1
A 08	229 31.8	278 16.9	37.4	258 38.5	01.4	85 53.5	21.0	349 27.1	36.5	Al Na'ir	27 42.8	S46 53.4
T 09	244 34.3	293 16.2 ..	36.6	273 39.1 ..	00.7	100 56.2 ..	21.1	4 29.4 ..	36.5	Alnilam	275 45.0	S 1 11.8
U 10	259 36.8	308 15.4	35.8	288 39.7	13 00.0	115 58.9	21.2	19 31.6	36.5	Alphard	217 54.7	S 8 43.6
R 11	274 39.2	323 14.7	35.1	303 40.3	12 59.3	131 01.6	21.3	34 33.8	36.6			
D 12	289 41.7	338 13.9	S19 34.3	318 40.9	S12 58.6	146 04.3	N15 21.4	49 36.0	S18 36.6	Alphecca	126 10.3	N26 39.8
A 13	304 44.1	353 13.2	33.5	333 41.5	57.9	161 07.0	21.5	64 38.3	36.7	Alpheratz	357 42.4	N29 10.5
Y 14	319 46.6	8 12.5	32.7	348 42.1	57.1	176 09.8	21.6	79 40.5	36.7	Altair	62 07.5	N 8 54.6
15	334 49.1	23 11.7 ..	31.9	3 42.7 ..	56.4	191 12.5 ..	21.6	94 42.7 ..	36.8	Ankaa	353 14.8	S42 13.7
16	349 51.5	38 11.0	31.1	18 43.2	55.7	206 15.2	21.7	109 44.9	36.8	Antares	112 25.2	S26 27.7
17	4 54.0	53 10.2	30.3	33 43.8	55.0	221 17.9	21.8	124 47.2	36.8			
18	19 56.5	68 09.5	S19 29.5	48 44.4	S12 54.3	236 20.6	N15 21.9	139 49.4	S18 36.9	Arcturus	145 54.9	N19 06.2
19	34 58.9	83 08.7	28.7	63 45.0	53.6	251 23.3	22.0	154 51.6	36.9	Atria	107 26.5	S69 02.9
20	50 01.4	98 08.0	27.9	78 45.6	52.9	266 26.0	22.1	169 53.8	37.0	Avior	234 16.8	S59 33.6
21	65 03.9	113 07.3 ..	27.1	93 46.2 ..	52.2	281 28.7 ..	22.2	184 56.1 ..	37.0	Bellatrix	278 30.5	N 6 21.6
22	80 06.3	128 06.5	26.3	108 46.8	51.5	296 31.4	22.2	199 58.3	37.0	Betelgeuse	270 59.8	N 7 24.3
23	95 08.8	143 05.8	25.5	123 47.4	50.8	311 34.1	22.3	215 00.5	37.1			
11 00	110 11.3	158 05.0	S19 24.7	138 48.0	S12 50.1	326 36.8	N15 22.4	230 02.7	S18 37.1	Canopus	263 55.1	S52 42.5
01	125 13.7	173 04.3	23.9	153 48.6	49.4	341 39.5	22.5	245 05.0	37.2	Capella	280 32.4	N46 00.6
02	140 16.2	188 03.6	23.0	168 49.2	48.7	356 42.2	22.6	260 07.2	37.2	Deneb	49 31.1	N45 20.3
03	155 18.6	203 02.8 ..	22.2	183 49.8 ..	48.0	11 44.9 ..	22.7	275 09.4 ..	37.3	Denebola	182 32.4	N14 29.1
04	170 21.1	218 02.1	21.4	198 50.4	47.3	26 47.6	22.8	290 11.7	37.3	Diphda	348 54.9	S17 54.4
05	185 23.6	233 01.4	20.6	213 50.9	46.5	41 50.3	22.9	305 13.9	37.3			
06	200 26.0	248 00.6	S19 19.8	228 51.5	S12 45.8	56 53.0	N15 23.0	320 16.1	S18 37.4	Dubhe	193 50.1	N61 39.8
07	215 28.5	262 59.9	19.0	243 52.1	45.1	71 55.7	23.0	335 18.3	37.4	Elnath	278 10.9	N28 37.0
08	230 31.0	277 59.1	18.2	258 52.7	44.4	86 58.5	23.1	350 20.6	37.5	Eltanin	90 46.1	N51 29.3
S 09	245 33.4	292 58.4 ..	17.4	273 53.3 ..	43.7	102 01.2 ..	23.2	5 22.8 ..	37.5	Enif	33 46.3	N 9 56.8
U 10	260 35.9	307 57.7	16.6	288 53.9	43.0	117 03.9	23.3	20 25.0	37.5	Fomalhaut	15 23.1	S29 32.6
N 11	275 38.4	322 56.9	15.7	303 54.5	42.3	132 06.6	23.4	35 27.2	37.6			
D 12	290 40.8	337 56.2	S19 14.9	318 55.1	S12 41.6	147 09.3	N15 23.5	50 29.5	S18 37.6	Gacrux	171 59.4	S57 11.6
A 13	305 43.3	352 55.5	14.1	333 55.7	40.9	162 12.0	23.6	65 31.7	37.7	Gienah	175 51.1	S17 37.5
Y 14	320 45.7	7 54.8	13.3	348 56.3	40.2	177 14.7	23.7	80 33.9	37.7	Hadar	148 46.3	S60 26.4
15	335 48.2	22 54.0 ..	12.5	3 56.9 ..	39.5	192 17.4 ..	23.8	95 36.2 ..	37.7	Hamal	327 59.4	N23 32.0
16	350 50.7	37 53.3	11.6	18 57.5	38.7	207 20.1	23.8	110 38.4	37.8	Kaus Aust.	83 42.8	S34 22.4
17	5 53.1	52 52.6	10.8	33 58.1	38.0	222 22.8	23.9	125 40.6	37.8			
18	20 55.6	67 51.8	S19 10.0	48 58.7	S12 37.3	237 25.5	N15 24.0	140 42.8	S18 37.9	Kochab	137 20.8	N74 05.4
19	35 58.1	82 51.1	09.2	63 59.3	36.6	252 28.3	24.1	155 45.1	37.9	Markab	13 37.4	N15 17.3
20	51 00.5	97 50.4	08.4	78 59.9	35.9	267 31.0	24.2	170 47.3	37.9	Menkar	314 13.8	N 4 08.8
21	66 03.0	112 49.7 ..	07.5	94 00.5 ..	35.2	282 33.7 ..	24.3	185 49.5 ..	38.0	Menkent	148 06.3	S36 26.4
22	81 05.5	127 48.9	06.7	109 01.1	34.5	297 36.4	24.4	200 51.8	38.0	Miaplacidus	221 38.4	S69 46.7
23	96 07.9	142 48.2	05.9	124 01.7	33.8	312 39.1	24.5	215 54.0	38.1			
12 00	111 10.4	157 47.5	S19 05.0	139 02.3	S12 33.1	327 41.8	N15 24.6	230 56.2	S18 38.1	Mirfak	308 38.4	N49 54.9
01	126 12.9	172 46.8	04.2	154 02.9	32.3	342 44.5	24.6	245 58.4	38.2	Nunki	75 57.4	S26 16.5
02	141 15.3	187 46.0	03.4	169 03.5	31.6	357 47.2	24.7	261 00.7	38.2	Peacock	53 18.2	S56 41.1
03	156 17.8	202 45.3 ..	02.6	184 04.0 ..	30.9	12 50.0 ..	24.8	276 02.9 ..	38.2	Pollux	243 26.1	N27 59.1
04	171 20.2	217 44.6	01.7	199 04.6	30.2	27 52.7	24.9	291 05.1	38.3	Procyon	244 58.3	N 5 10.9
05	186 22.7	232 43.9	00.9	214 05.2	29.5	42 55.4	25.0	306 07.4	38.3			
06	201 25.2	247 43.1	S19 00.1	229 05.8	S12 28.8	57 58.1	N15 25.1	321 09.6	S18 38.4	Rasalhague	96 05.8	N12 33.1
07	216 27.6	262 42.4	18 59.2	244 06.4	28.1	73 00.8	25.2	336 11.8	38.4	Regulus	207 42.1	N11 53.4
08	231 30.1	277 41.7	58.4	259 07.0	27.4	88 03.5	25.3	351 14.0	38.4	Rigel	281 10.7	S 8 11.3
M 09	246 32.6	292 41.0 ..	57.5	274 07.6 ..	26.6	103 06.2 ..	25.4	6 16.3 ..	38.5	Rigil Kent.	139 50.3	S60 53.4
O 10	261 35.0	307 40.3	56.7	289 08.2	25.9	118 08.9	25.5	21 18.5	38.5	Sabik	102 11.6	S15 44.4
N 11	276 37.5	322 39.5	55.9	304 08.8	25.2	133 11.7	25.5	36 20.7	38.6			
D 12	291 40.0	337 38.8	S18 55.0	319 09.4	S12 24.5	148 14.4	N15 25.6	51 23.0	S18 38.6	Schedar	349 39.2	N56 37.4
A 13	306 42.4	352 38.1	54.2	334 10.0	23.8	163 17.1	25.7	66 25.2	38.6	Shaula	96 20.8	S37 06.6
Y 14	321 44.9	7 37.4	53.3	349 10.6	23.1	178 19.8	25.8	81 27.4	38.7	Sirius	258 32.4	S16 44.5
15	336 47.4	22 36.7 ..	52.5	4 11.2 ..	22.4	193 22.5 ..	25.9	96 29.7 ..	38.7	Spica	158 30.1	S11 14.3
16	351 49.8	37 36.0	51.7	19 11.8	21.6	208 25.2	26.0	111 31.9	38.8	Suhail	222 51.2	S43 29.7
17	6 52.3	52 35.2	50.8	34 12.4	20.9	223 28.0	26.1	126 34.1	38.8			
18	21 54.7	67 34.5	S18 50.0	49 13.0	S12 20.2	238 30.7	N15 26.2	141 36.3	S18 38.8	Vega	80 38.6	N38 48.0
19	36 57.2	82 33.8	49.1	64 13.6	19.5	253 33.4	26.3	156 38.6	38.9	Zuben'ubi	137 04.3	S16 06.1
20	51 59.7	97 33.1	48.3	79 14.2	18.8	268 36.1	26.4	171 40.8	38.9		SHA	Mer. Pass.
21	67 02.1	112 32.4 ..	47.4	94 14.8 ..	18.1	283 38.8 ..	26.4	186 43.0 ..	39.0		° ′	h m
22	82 04.6	127 31.7	46.6	109 15.4	17.3	298 41.5	26.5	201 45.3	39.0	Venus	47 53.8	13 28
23	97 07.1	142 31.0	45.7	124 16.0	16.6	313 44.2	26.6	216 47.5	39.0	Mars	28 36.7	14 44
	h m									Jupiter	216 25.5	2 13
Mer. Pass. 16 36.5	v −0.7 d 0.8			v 0.6 d 0.7		v 2.7 d 0.1		v 2.2 d 0.0		Saturn	119 51.5	8 39

UT	SUN GHA	SUN Dec	MOON GHA	v	Dec	d	HP
d h	° ′	° ′	° ′	′	° ′	′	′
10 00	178 12.1	S22 01.9	306 30.2	15.3	N 4 30.0	9.1	54.1
01	193 11.8	01.6	321 04.5	15.3	4 20.9	9.2	54.1
02	208 11.6	01.2	335 38.8	15.3	4 11.7	9.2	54.1
03	223 11.3	.. 00.8	350 13.1	15.4	4 02.5	9.2	54.1
04	238 11.1	00.5	4 47.5	15.3	3 53.3	9.2	54.1
05	253 10.8	22 00.1	19 21.8	15.4	3 44.1	9.3	54.1
06	268 10.6	S21 59.7	33 56.2	15.3	N 3 34.8	9.2	54.1
07	283 10.3	59.4	48 30.5	15.4	3 25.6	9.3	54.1
S 08	298 10.1	59.0	63 04.9	15.4	3 16.3	9.2	54.1
A 09	313 09.8	.. 58.6	77 39.3	15.4	3 07.1	9.3	54.1
T 10	328 09.6	58.3	92 13.7	15.4	2 57.8	9.3	54.1
U 11	343 09.3	57.9	106 48.1	15.4	2 48.5	9.4	54.1
R 12	358 09.1	S21 57.5	121 22.5	15.4	N 2 39.1	9.3	54.1
D 13	13 08.8	57.1	135 56.9	15.4	2 29.8	9.3	54.1
A 14	28 08.5	56.8	150 31.3	15.4	2 20.5	9.3	54.1
Y 15	43 08.3	.. 56.4	165 05.7	15.4	2 11.1	9.3	54.1
16	58 08.0	56.0	179 40.1	15.4	2 01.8	9.4	54.1
17	73 07.8	55.6	194 14.5	15.4	1 52.4	9.4	54.2
18	88 07.5	S21 55.3	208 48.9	15.5	N 1 43.0	9.3	54.2
19	103 07.3	54.9	223 23.4	15.4	1 33.7	9.4	54.2
20	118 07.0	54.5	237 57.8	15.4	1 24.3	9.4	54.2
21	133 06.8	.. 54.1	252 32.2	15.4	1 14.9	9.4	54.2
22	148 06.5	53.8	267 06.6	15.4	1 05.5	9.4	54.2
23	163 06.3	53.4	281 41.0	15.4	0 56.1	9.5	54.2
11 00	178 06.0	S21 53.0	296 15.4	15.4	N 0 46.6	9.4	54.2
01	193 05.8	52.6	310 49.8	15.4	0 37.2	9.4	54.2
02	208 05.5	52.2	325 24.2	15.4	0 27.8	9.4	54.2
03	223 05.3	.. 51.8	339 58.6	15.4	0 18.4	9.5	54.2
04	238 05.0	51.5	354 33.0	15.4	N 0 08.9	9.4	54.2
05	253 04.8	51.1	9 07.4	15.4	S 0 00.5	9.4	54.2
06	268 04.5	S21 50.7	23 41.8	15.3	S 0 09.9	9.5	54.3
07	283 04.3	50.3	38 16.1	15.4	0 19.4	9.4	54.3
S 08	298 04.0	49.9	52 50.5	15.3	0 28.8	9.4	54.3
U 09	313 03.8	.. 49.5	67 24.8	15.4	0 38.2	9.5	54.3
N 10	328 03.6	49.1	81 59.2	15.3	0 47.7	9.4	54.3
D 11	343 03.3	48.8	96 33.5	15.3	0 57.1	9.5	54.3
A 12	358 03.1	S21 48.4	111 07.8	15.3	S 1 06.6	9.4	54.3
Y 13	13 02.8	48.0	125 42.1	15.3	1 16.0	9.4	54.3
14	28 02.6	47.6	140 16.4	15.3	1 25.4	9.5	54.3
15	43 02.3	.. 47.2	154 50.7	15.2	1 34.9	9.4	54.3
16	58 02.1	46.8	169 24.9	15.3	1 44.3	9.4	54.4
17	73 01.8	46.4	183 59.2	15.2	1 53.7	9.5	54.4
18	88 01.6	S21 46.0	198 33.4	15.2	S 2 03.2	9.4	54.4
19	103 01.3	45.6	213 07.6	15.2	2 12.6	9.4	54.4
20	118 01.1	45.2	227 41.8	15.2	2 22.0	9.4	54.4
21	133 00.8	.. 44.8	242 16.0	15.1	2 31.4	9.4	54.4
22	148 00.6	44.4	256 50.1	15.2	2 40.8	9.4	54.4
23	163 00.4	44.0	271 24.2	15.1	2 50.2	9.4	54.5
12 00	178 00.1	S21 43.6	285 58.3	15.1	S 2 59.6	9.4	54.5
01	192 59.9	43.2	300 32.4	15.1	3 09.0	9.3	54.5
02	207 59.6	42.8	315 06.5	15.0	3 18.3	9.4	54.5
03	222 59.4	.. 42.4	329 40.5	15.0	3 27.7	9.4	54.5
04	237 59.1	42.0	344 14.5	15.0	3 37.1	9.3	54.5
05	252 58.9	41.6	358 48.5	15.0	3 46.4	9.3	54.5
06	267 58.7	S21 41.2	13 22.5	14.9	S 3 55.7	9.4	54.6
07	282 58.4	40.8	27 56.4	14.9	4 05.1	9.3	54.6
08	297 58.2	40.4	42 30.3	14.9	4 14.4	9.3	54.6
M 09	312 57.9	.. 40.0	57 04.2	14.9	4 23.7	9.3	54.6
O 10	327 57.7	39.6	71 38.1	14.8	4 33.0	9.2	54.6
N 11	342 57.4	39.2	86 11.9	14.8	4 42.2	9.3	54.6
D 12	357 57.2	S21 38.8	100 45.7	14.7	S 4 51.5	9.2	54.7
A 13	12 57.0	38.4	115 19.4	14.8	5 00.7	9.3	54.7
Y 14	27 56.7	38.0	129 53.2	14.7	5 10.0	9.2	54.7
15	42 56.5	.. 37.6	144 26.9	14.6	5 19.2	9.2	54.7
16	57 56.2	37.2	159 00.5	14.7	5 28.4	9.2	54.7
17	72 56.0	36.8	173 34.2	14.6	5 37.6	9.1	54.8
18	87 55.8	S21 36.3	188 07.8	14.5	S 5 46.7	9.2	54.8
19	102 55.5	35.9	202 41.3	14.5	5 55.9	9.1	54.8
20	117 55.3	35.5	217 14.8	14.5	6 05.0	9.1	54.8
21	132 55.0	.. 35.1	231 48.3	14.5	6 14.1	9.1	54.8
22	147 54.8	34.7	246 21.8	14.4	6 23.2	9.0	54.9
23	162 54.6	34.3	260 55.2	14.3	S 6 32.3	9.0	54.9
	SD 16.3	d 0.4	SD 14.7		14.8		14.9

Lat.	Twilight Naut.	Civil	Sunrise	Moonrise 10	11	12	13
°	h m	h m	h m	h m	h m	h m	h m
N 72	08 10	10 09	■	21 59	23 33	25 08	01 08
N 70	07 54	09 30	■	22 01	23 28	24 58	00 58
68	07 40	09 02	10 54	22 02	23 25	24 49	00 49
66	07 29	08 42	10 05	22 03	23 22	24 42	00 42
64	07 20	08 25	09 35	22 04	23 20	24 37	00 37
62	07 12	08 11	09 12	22 04	23 17	24 31	00 31
60	07 05	08 00	08 54	22 05	23 16	24 27	00 27
N 58	06 58	07 49	08 39	22 06	23 14	24 23	00 23
56	06 52	07 40	08 26	22 06	23 12	24 20	00 20
54	06 47	07 32	08 14	22 06	23 11	24 17	00 17
52	06 42	07 25	08 04	22 07	23 10	24 14	00 14
50	06 37	07 18	07 55	22 07	23 09	24 11	00 11
45	06 27	07 04	07 37	22 08	23 07	24 06	00 06
N 40	06 18	06 51	07 21	22 09	23 05	24 01	00 01
35	06 09	06 41	07 08	22 09	23 03	23 57	24 53
30	06 01	06 31	06 57	22 10	23 01	23 54	24 48
20	05 46	06 14	06 37	22 11	22 59	23 48	24 38
N 10	05 32	05 58	06 20	22 12	22 57	23 43	24 30
0	05 16	05 42	06 04	22 12	22 55	23 38	24 23
S 10	04 58	05 25	05 48	22 13	22 53	23 33	24 15
20	04 37	05 06	05 30	22 14	22 50	23 28	24 07
30	04 10	04 43	05 10	22 15	22 48	23 22	23 58
35	03 53	04 29	04 58	22 15	22 47	23 19	23 53
40	03 32	04 12	04 44	22 16	22 45	23 15	23 47
45	03 04	03 51	04 28	22 17	22 43	23 11	23 40
S 50	02 25	03 24	04 07	22 18	22 41	23 06	23 32
52	02 02	03 11	03 57	22 18	22 40	23 03	23 29
54	01 32	02 55	03 46	22 18	22 39	23 01	23 25
56	00 28	02 36	03 34	22 19	22 38	22 58	23 20
58	////	02 13	03 19	22 19	22 37	22 55	23 15
S 60	////	01 40	03 01	22 20	22 35	22 51	23 09

Lat.	Sunset	Twilight Civil	Naut.	Moonset 10	11	12	13
°	h m	h m	h m	h m	h m	h m	h m
N 72	■	14 08	16 06	10 26	10 21	10 15	10 10
N 70	■	14 47	16 23	10 23	10 22	10 22	10 22
68	13 22	15 14	16 36	10 20	10 23	10 27	10 32
66	14 11	15 34	16 47	10 17	10 24	10 31	10 40
64	14 41	15 51	16 56	10 15	10 25	10 35	10 47
62	15 04	16 05	17 04	10 13	10 26	10 39	10 53
60	15 22	16 17	17 11	10 11	10 26	10 41	10 58
N 58	15 37	16 27	17 18	10 10	10 27	10 44	11 03
56	15 50	16 36	17 24	10 08	10 27	10 46	11 07
54	16 02	16 44	17 29	10 07	10 27	10 48	11 11
52	16 12	16 51	17 34	10 06	10 28	10 50	11 14
50	16 20	16 58	17 39	10 05	10 28	10 52	11 17
45	16 39	17 12	17 49	10 02	10 29	10 56	11 24
N 40	16 54	17 24	17 58	10 01	10 29	10 59	11 30
35	17 07	17 35	18 06	09 59	10 30	11 02	11 35
30	17 19	17 45	18 14	09 57	10 30	11 04	11 39
20	17 38	18 02	18 29	09 55	10 31	11 08	11 46
N 10	17 55	18 18	18 44	09 53	10 32	11 12	11 53
0	18 11	18 34	19 00	09 50	10 33	11 15	11 59
S 10	18 28	18 50	19 17	09 48	10 33	11 19	12 05
20	18 45	19 09	19 38	09 46	10 34	11 22	12 12
30	19 05	19 32	20 05	09 43	10 35	11 27	12 20
35	19 17	19 46	20 22	09 42	10 35	11 29	12 24
40	19 31	20 03	20 43	09 40	10 36	11 32	12 29
45	19 48	20 24	21 11	09 38	10 36	11 35	12 35
S 50	20 08	20 50	21 50	09 35	10 37	11 39	12 42
52	20 18	21 04	22 12	09 34	10 37	11 40	12 45
54	20 29	21 19	22 41	09 33	10 37	11 42	12 48
56	20 41	21 38	23 37	09 32	10 38	11 45	12 52
58	20 56	22 01	////	09 30	10 38	11 47	12 57
S 60	21 13	22 33	////	09 28	10 39	11 50	13 01

Day	SUN Eqn. of Time 00h	12h	Mer. Pass.	MOON Mer. Pass. Upper	Lower	Age	Phase
d	m s	m s	h m	h m	h m	d %	
10	07 11	07 23	12 07	03 40	16 01	19 76	
11	07 35	07 47	12 08	04 22	16 44	20 68	
12	07 59	08 11	12 08	05 05	17 27	21 59	

2015 JANUARY 13, 14, 15 (TUES., WED., THURS.)

UT	ARIES	VENUS −3.9		MARS +1.1		JUPITER −2.5		SATURN +0.6		STARS		
	GHA	GHA	Dec	GHA	Dec	GHA	Dec	GHA	Dec	Name	SHA	Dec
d h	° ′	° ′	° ′	° ′	° ′	° ′	° ′	° ′	° ′		° ′	° ′
13 00	112 09.5	157 30.2	S18 44.9	139 16.6	S12 15.9	328 47.0	N15 26.7	231 49.7	S18 39.1	Acamar	315 17.4	S40 15.0
01	127 12.0	172 29.5	44.0	154 17.2	15.2	343 49.7	26.8	246 52.0	39.1	Achernar	335 26.1	S57 10.0
02	142 14.5	187 28.8	43.2	169 17.8	14.5	358 52.4	26.9	261 54.2	39.2	Acrux	173 07.7	S63 10.7
03	157 16.9	202 28.1	.. 42.3	184 18.4	.. 13.8	13 55.1	.. 27.0	276 56.4	.. 39.2	Adhara	255 11.3	S28 59.8
04	172 19.4	217 27.4	41.5	199 19.0	13.0	28 57.8	27.1	291 58.7	39.2	Aldebaran	290 47.9	N16 32.2
05	187 21.8	232 26.7	40.6	214 19.6	12.3	44 00.6	27.2	307 00.9	39.3			
06	202 24.3	247 26.0	S18 39.8	229 20.2	S12 11.6	59 03.3	N15 27.3	322 03.1	S18 39.3	Alioth	166 19.8	N55 52.4
07	217 26.8	262 25.3	38.9	244 20.8	10.9	74 06.0	27.4	337 05.4	39.4	Alkaid	152 58.2	N49 14.1
08	232 29.2	277 24.6	38.0	259 21.4	10.2	89 08.7	27.4	352 07.6	39.4	Al Na'ir	27 42.8	S46 53.4
09	247 31.7	292 23.9	.. 37.2	274 22.0	.. 09.5	104 11.4	.. 27.5	7 09.8	.. 39.4	Alnilam	275 45.0	S 1 11.8
10	262 34.2	307 23.2	36.3	289 22.7	08.7	119 14.2	27.6	22 12.1	39.5	Alphard	217 54.7	S 8 43.6
11	277 36.6	322 22.5	35.5	304 23.3	08.0	134 16.9	27.7	37 14.3	39.5			
12	292 39.1	337 21.8	S18 34.6	319 23.9	S12 07.3	149 19.6	N15 27.8	52 16.5	S18 39.6	Alphecca	126 10.3	N26 39.8
13	307 41.6	352 21.0	33.7	334 24.5	06.6	164 22.3	27.9	67 18.8	39.6	Alpheratz	357 42.4	N29 10.5
14	322 44.0	7 20.3	32.9	349 25.1	05.9	179 25.0	28.0	82 21.0	39.6	Altair	62 07.5	N 8 54.6
15	337 46.5	22 19.6	.. 32.0	4 25.7	.. 05.1	194 27.8	.. 28.1	97 23.2	.. 39.7	Ankaa	353 14.8	S42 13.7
16	352 49.0	37 18.9	31.1	19 26.3	04.4	209 30.5	28.2	112 25.5	39.7	Antares	112 25.2	S26 27.7
17	7 51.4	52 18.2	30.3	34 26.9	03.7	224 33.2	28.3	127 27.7	39.8			
18	22 53.9	67 17.5	S18 29.4	49 27.5	S12 03.0	239 35.9	N15 28.4	142 29.9	S18 39.8	Arcturus	145 54.8	N19 06.2
19	37 56.3	82 16.8	28.5	64 28.1	02.3	254 38.6	28.5	157 32.2	39.8	Atria	107 26.4	S69 02.9
20	52 58.8	97 16.1	27.7	79 28.7	01.5	269 41.4	28.6	172 34.4	39.9	Avior	234 16.8	S59 33.6
21	68 01.3	112 15.4	.. 26.8	94 29.3	.. 00.8	284 44.1	.. 28.6	187 36.6	.. 39.9	Bellatrix	278 30.5	N 6 21.5
22	83 03.7	127 14.7	25.9	109 29.9	12 00.1	299 46.8	28.7	202 38.9	39.9	Betelgeuse	270 59.8	N 7 24.3
23	98 06.2	142 14.0	25.1	124 30.5	11 59.4	314 49.5	28.8	217 41.1	40.0			
14 00	113 08.7	157 13.3	S18 24.2	139 31.1	S11 58.7	329 52.3	N15 28.9	232 43.3	S18 40.0	Canopus	263 55.1	S52 42.5
01	128 11.1	172 12.6	23.3	154 31.7	57.9	344 55.0	29.0	247 45.6	40.1	Capella	280 32.4	N46 00.7
02	143 13.6	187 11.9	22.4	169 32.3	57.2	359 57.7	29.1	262 47.8	40.1	Deneb	49 31.1	N45 20.3
03	158 16.1	202 11.2	.. 21.6	184 32.9	.. 56.5	15 00.4	.. 29.2	277 50.0	.. 40.1	Denebola	182 32.4	N14 29.1
04	173 18.5	217 10.6	20.7	199 33.5	55.8	30 03.1	29.3	292 52.3	40.2	Diphda	348 54.9	S17 54.4
05	188 21.0	232 09.9	19.8	214 34.1	55.1	45 05.9	29.4	307 54.5	40.2			
06	203 23.5	247 09.2	S18 18.9	229 34.7	S11 54.3	60 08.6	N15 29.5	322 56.7	S18 40.3	Dubhe	193 50.1	N61 39.8
07	218 25.9	262 08.5	18.1	244 35.3	53.6	75 11.3	29.6	337 59.0	40.3	Elnath	278 10.9	N28 37.0
08	233 28.4	277 07.8	17.2	259 36.0	52.9	90 14.0	29.7	353 01.2	40.3	Eltanin	90 46.1	N51 29.3
09	248 30.8	292 07.1	.. 16.3	274 36.6	.. 52.2	105 16.8	.. 29.8	8 03.4	.. 40.4	Enif	33 46.3	N 9 56.8
10	263 33.3	307 06.4	15.4	289 37.2	51.4	120 19.5	29.9	23 05.7	40.4	Fomalhaut	15 23.1	S29 32.6
11	278 35.8	322 05.7	14.5	304 37.8	50.7	135 22.2	29.9	38 07.9	40.5			
12	293 38.2	337 05.0	S18 13.6	319 38.4	S11 50.0	150 24.9	N15 30.0	53 10.1	S18 40.5	Gacrux	171 59.4	S57 11.6
13	308 40.7	352 04.3	12.8	334 39.0	49.3	165 27.7	30.1	68 12.4	40.5	Gienah	175 51.0	S17 37.5
14	323 43.2	7 03.6	11.9	349 39.6	48.5	180 30.4	30.2	83 14.6	40.6	Hadar	148 46.3	S60 26.4
15	338 45.6	22 02.9	.. 11.0	4 40.2	.. 47.8	195 33.1	.. 30.3	98 16.9	.. 40.6	Hamal	327 59.4	N23 32.0
16	353 48.1	37 02.3	10.1	19 40.8	47.1	210 35.9	30.4	113 19.1	40.6	Kaus Aust.	83 42.8	S34 22.4
17	8 50.6	52 01.6	09.2	34 41.4	46.4	225 38.6	30.5	128 21.3	40.7			
18	23 53.0	67 00.9	S18 08.3	49 42.0	S11 45.6	240 41.3	N15 30.6	143 23.6	S18 40.7	Kochab	137 20.7	N74 05.4
19	38 55.5	82 00.2	07.4	64 42.6	44.9	255 44.0	30.7	158 25.8	40.8	Markab	13 37.4	N15 17.3
20	53 57.9	96 59.5	06.5	79 43.2	44.2	270 46.8	30.8	173 28.0	40.8	Menkar	314 13.8	N 4 08.8
21	69 00.4	111 58.8	.. 05.7	94 43.8	.. 43.5	285 49.5	.. 30.9	188 30.3	.. 40.8	Menkent	148 06.3	S36 26.4
22	84 02.9	126 58.1	04.8	109 44.5	42.7	300 52.2	31.0	203 32.5	40.9	Miaplacidus	221 38.4	S69 46.8
23	99 05.3	141 57.4	03.9	124 45.1	42.0	315 54.9	31.1	218 34.7	40.9			
15 00	114 07.8	156 56.8	S18 03.0	139 45.7	S11 41.3	330 57.7	N15 31.2	233 37.0	S18 41.0	Mirfak	308 38.5	N49 54.9
01	129 10.3	171 56.1	02.1	154 46.3	40.6	346 00.4	31.3	248 39.2	41.0	Nunki	75 57.4	S26 16.5
02	144 12.7	186 55.4	01.2	169 46.9	39.8	1 03.1	31.3	263 41.5	41.0	Peacock	53 18.2	S56 41.1
03	159 15.2	201 54.7	18 00.3	184 47.5	.. 39.1	16 05.9	.. 31.4	278 43.7	.. 41.1	Pollux	243 26.0	N27 59.1
04	174 17.7	216 54.0	17 59.4	199 48.1	38.4	31 08.6	31.5	293 45.9	41.1	Procyon	244 58.3	N 5 10.9
05	189 20.1	231 53.3	58.5	214 48.7	37.7	46 11.3	31.6	308 48.2	41.1			
06	204 22.6	246 52.7	S17 57.6	229 49.3	S11 36.9	61 14.0	N15 31.7	323 50.4	S18 41.2	Rasalhague	96 05.7	N12 33.1
07	219 25.1	261 52.0	56.7	244 49.9	36.2	76 16.8	31.8	338 52.6	41.2	Regulus	207 42.1	N11 53.4
08	234 27.5	276 51.3	55.8	259 50.6	35.5	91 19.5	31.9	353 54.9	41.3	Rigel	281 10.7	S 8 11.3
09	249 30.0	291 50.6	.. 54.9	274 51.2	.. 34.8	106 22.2	.. 32.0	8 57.1	.. 41.3	Rigil Kent.	139 50.3	S60 53.4
10	264 32.4	306 50.0	54.0	289 51.8	34.0	121 25.0	32.1	23 59.4	41.3	Sabik	102 11.6	S15 44.4
11	279 34.9	321 49.3	53.1	304 52.4	33.3	136 27.7	32.2	39 01.6	41.4			
12	294 37.4	336 48.6	S17 52.2	319 53.0	S11 32.6	151 30.4	N15 32.3	54 03.8	S18 41.4	Schedar	349 39.3	N56 37.4
13	309 39.8	351 47.9	51.3	334 53.6	31.8	166 33.2	32.4	69 06.1	41.5	Shaula	96 20.8	S37 06.6
14	324 42.3	6 47.2	50.4	349 54.2	31.1	181 35.9	32.5	84 08.3	41.5	Sirius	258 32.4	S16 44.5
15	339 44.8	21 46.6	.. 49.5	4 54.8	.. 30.4	196 38.6	.. 32.6	99 10.5	.. 41.5	Spica	158 30.1	S11 14.3
16	354 47.2	36 45.9	48.5	19 55.4	29.7	211 41.4	32.7	114 12.8	41.6	Suhail	222 51.2	S43 29.7
17	9 49.7	51 45.2	47.6	34 56.1	28.9	226 44.1	32.8	129 15.0	41.6			
18	24 52.2	66 44.5	S17 46.7	49 56.7	S11 28.2	241 46.8	N15 32.9	144 17.3	S18 41.6	Vega	80 38.6	N38 48.0
19	39 54.6	81 43.9	45.8	64 57.3	27.5	256 49.5	33.0	159 19.5	41.7	Zuben'ubi	137 04.3	S16 06.1
20	54 57.1	96 43.2	44.9	79 57.9	26.7	271 52.3	33.1	174 21.7	41.7		SHA	Mer.Pass.
21	69 59.6	111 42.5	.. 44.0	94 58.5	.. 26.0	286 55.0	.. 33.1	189 24.0	.. 41.7		° ′	h m
22	85 02.0	126 41.9	43.1	109 59.1	25.3	301 57.7	33.2	204 26.2	41.8	Venus	44 04.7	13 32
23	100 04.5	141 41.2	42.2	124 59.7	24.6	317 00.5	33.3	219 28.5	41.8	Mars	26 22.4	14 41
	h m									Jupiter	216 43.6	2 00
Mer.Pass. 16 24.7		v −0.7	d 0.9	v 0.6	d 0.7	v 2.7	d 0.1	v 2.2	d 0.0	Saturn	119 34.7	8 28

Day markers: 13 — TUESDAY; 14 — WEDNESDAY; 15 — THURSDAY

UT	SUN GHA	SUN Dec	MOON GHA	v	MOON Dec	d	HP
d h	° ′	° ′	° ′	′	° ′	′	′
13 00	177 54.3	S21 33.9	275 28.5	14.3	S 6 41.3	9.0	54.9
01	192 54.1	33.4	290 01.8	14.3	6 50.3	9.0	54.9
02	207 53.9	33.0	304 35.1	14.3	6 59.3	9.0	55.0
03	222 53.6	.. 32.6	319 08.4	14.2	7 08.3	9.0	55.0
04	237 53.4	32.2	333 41.6	14.1	7 17.3	8.9	55.0
05	252 53.2	31.8	348 14.7	14.1	7 26.2	8.9	55.0
06	267 52.9	S21 31.4	2 47.8	14.1	S 7 35.1	8.9	55.1
07	282 52.7	30.9	17 20.9	14.0	7 44.0	8.9	55.1
T 08	297 52.4	30.5	31 53.9	14.0	7 52.9	8.8	55.1
U 09	312 52.2	.. 30.1	46 26.9	13.9	8 01.7	8.8	55.1
E 10	327 52.0	29.7	60 59.8	13.9	8 10.5	8.8	55.1
S 11	342 51.7	29.2	75 32.7	13.8	8 19.3	8.7	55.2
D 12	357 51.5	S21 28.8	90 05.5	13.8	S 8 28.0	8.7	55.2
A 13	12 51.3	28.4	104 38.3	13.7	8 36.7	8.7	55.2
Y 14	27 51.0	28.0	119 11.0	13.7	8 45.4	8.7	55.2
15	42 50.8	.. 27.5	133 43.7	13.6	8 54.1	8.6	55.3
16	57 50.6	27.1	148 16.3	13.6	9 02.7	8.6	55.3
17	72 50.3	26.7	162 48.9	13.5	9 11.3	8.5	55.3
18	87 50.1	S21 26.3	177 21.4	13.5	S 9 19.8	8.5	55.4
19	102 49.9	25.8	191 53.9	13.4	9 28.4	8.5	55.4
20	117 49.6	25.4	206 26.3	13.4	9 36.9	8.4	55.4
21	132 49.4	.. 25.0	220 58.7	13.3	9 45.3	8.4	55.5
22	147 49.2	24.5	235 31.0	13.2	9 53.8	8.3	55.5
23	162 48.9	24.1	250 03.2	13.2	10 02.1	8.4	55.5
14 00	177 48.7	S21 23.7	264 35.4	13.1	S10 10.5	8.3	55.5
01	192 48.5	23.2	279 07.5	13.1	10 18.8	8.3	55.5
02	207 48.2	22.8	293 39.6	13.0	10 27.1	8.2	55.6
03	222 48.0	.. 22.4	308 11.6	13.0	10 35.3	8.2	55.6
04	237 47.8	21.9	322 43.6	12.9	10 43.5	8.2	55.6
05	252 47.6	21.5	337 15.5	12.8	10 51.7	8.1	55.7
06	267 47.3	S21 21.1	351 47.3	12.8	S10 59.8	8.0	55.7
W 07	282 47.1	20.6	6 19.1	12.7	11 07.8	8.1	55.7
E 08	297 46.9	20.2	20 50.8	12.6	11 15.9	7.9	55.7
D 09	312 46.6	.. 19.7	35 22.4	12.6	11 23.8	8.0	55.8
N 10	327 46.4	19.3	49 54.0	12.5	11 31.8	7.9	55.8
E 11	342 46.2	18.9	64 25.5	12.4	11 39.7	7.8	55.8
S 12	357 46.0	S21 18.4	78 56.9	12.4	S11 47.5	7.8	55.9
D 13	12 45.7	18.0	93 28.3	12.3	11 55.3	7.8	55.9
A 14	27 45.5	17.5	107 59.6	12.3	12 03.1	7.7	55.9
Y 15	42 45.3	.. 17.1	122 30.9	12.2	12 10.8	7.6	56.0
16	57 45.0	16.6	137 02.1	12.1	12 18.4	7.6	56.0
17	72 44.8	16.2	151 33.2	12.1	12 26.0	7.6	56.0
18	87 44.6	S21 15.7	166 04.3	11.9	S12 33.6	7.5	56.1
19	102 44.4	15.3	180 35.2	11.9	12 41.1	7.4	56.1
20	117 44.1	14.9	195 06.1	11.9	12 48.5	7.4	56.1
21	132 43.9	.. 14.4	209 37.0	11.8	12 55.9	7.4	56.2
22	147 43.7	14.0	224 07.8	11.7	13 03.3	7.3	56.2
23	162 43.5	13.5	238 38.5	11.6	13 10.6	7.2	56.2
15 00	177 43.2	S21 13.1	253 09.1	11.5	S13 17.8	7.2	56.3
01	192 43.0	12.6	267 39.6	11.5	13 25.0	7.1	56.3
02	207 42.8	12.2	282 10.1	11.4	13 32.1	7.0	56.3
03	222 42.6	.. 11.7	296 40.5	11.4	13 39.1	7.0	56.4
04	237 42.3	11.2	311 10.9	11.2	13 46.1	7.0	56.4
05	252 42.1	10.8	325 41.1	11.2	13 53.1	6.9	56.4
06	267 41.9	S21 10.3	340 11.3	11.1	S14 00.0	6.8	56.5
T 07	282 41.7	09.9	354 41.4	11.1	14 06.8	6.7	56.5
H 08	297 41.4	09.4	9 11.5	11.0	14 13.5	6.7	56.5
U 09	312 41.2	.. 09.0	23 41.5	10.9	14 20.2	6.6	56.6
R 10	327 41.0	08.5	38 11.4	10.8	14 26.8	6.6	56.6
S 11	342 40.8	08.1	52 41.2	10.7	14 33.4	6.5	56.6
D 12	357 40.6	S21 07.6	67 10.9	10.7	S14 39.9	6.4	56.7
A 13	12 40.3	07.1	81 40.6	10.6	14 46.3	6.3	56.7
Y 14	27 40.1	06.7	96 10.2	10.5	14 52.6	6.3	56.8
15	42 39.9	.. 06.2	110 39.7	10.4	14 58.9	6.2	56.8
16	57 39.7	05.8	125 09.1	10.4	15 05.1	6.2	56.8
17	72 39.5	05.3	139 38.5	10.3	15 11.3	6.1	56.9
18	87 39.2	S21 04.8	154 07.8	10.2	S15 17.4	5.9	56.9
19	102 39.0	04.4	168 37.0	10.1	15 23.3	6.0	56.9
20	117 38.8	03.9	183 06.1	10.0	15 29.3	5.8	57.0
21	132 38.6	.. 03.4	197 35.1	10.0	15 35.1	5.8	57.0
22	147 38.4	03.0	212 04.1	9.9	15 40.9	5.7	57.1
23	162 38.1	02.5	226 33.0	9.8	S15 46.6	5.6	57.1
	SD 16.3	d 0.4	SD 15.0		15.2		15.4

Twilight / Sunrise / Moonrise

Lat.	Naut.	Civil	Sunrise	Moonrise 13	14	15	16
°	h m	h m	h m	h m	h m	h m	h m
N 72	08 04	09 57	■	01 08	02 49	04 36	06 35
N 70	07 48	09 21	■	00 58	02 31	04 07	05 46
68	07 36	08 56	10 39	00 49	02 16	03 45	05 15
66	07 26	08 37	09 57	00 42	02 05	03 29	04 52
64	07 17	08 21	09 28	00 37	01 55	03 15	04 34
62	07 09	08 08	09 07	00 31	01 47	03 03	04 19
60	07 02	07 56	08 50	00 27	01 40	02 54	04 07
N 58	06 56	07 47	08 35	00 23	01 34	02 45	03 56
56	06 50	07 38	08 23	00 20	01 28	02 38	03 47
54	06 45	07 30	08 12	00 17	01 23	02 31	03 39
52	06 40	07 23	08 02	00 14	01 19	02 25	03 31
50	06 36	07 17	07 54	00 11	01 15	02 20	03 25
45	06 26	07 03	07 35	00 06	01 06	02 08	03 11
N 40	06 17	06 51	07 20	00 01	00 59	01 59	02 59
35	06 09	06 40	07 08	24 53	00 53	01 50	02 49
30	06 01	06 31	06 57	24 48	00 48	01 43	02 40
20	05 47	06 14	06 38	24 38	00 38	01 31	02 26
N 10	05 33	05 59	06 21	24 30	00 30	01 20	02 13
0	05 17	05 43	06 05	24 23	00 23	01 10	02 01
S 10	05 00	05 27	05 49	24 15	00 15	01 00	01 49
20	04 40	05 08	05 32	24 07	00 07	00 50	01 36
30	04 13	04 46	05 12	23 58	24 38	00 38	01 21
35	03 56	04 32	05 01	23 53	24 31	00 31	01 13
40	03 36	04 15	04 47	23 47	24 23	00 23	01 03
45	03 09	03 55	04 31	23 40	24 14	00 14	00 52
S 50	02 31	03 29	04 11	23 32	24 03	00 03	00 39
52	02 10	03 16	04 02	23 29	23 58	24 32	00 32
54	01 42	03 01	03 51	23 25	23 52	24 25	00 25
56	00 55	02 43	03 39	23 20	23 46	24 18	00 18
58	////	02 21	03 25	23 15	23 39	24 09	00 09
S 60	////	01 51	03 08	23 09	23 31	23 59	24 36

Sunset / Twilight / Moonset

Lat.	Sunset	Civil	Naut.	Moonset 13	14	15	16
°	h m	h m	h m	h m	h m	h m	h m
N 72	■	14 22	16 15	10 10	10 03	09 55	09 42
N 70	■	14 57	16 30	10 22	10 22	10 25	10 32
68	13 39	15 22	16 43	10 32	10 38	10 47	11 03
66	14 22	15 42	16 53	10 40	10 50	11 05	11 27
64	14 50	15 58	17 02	10 47	11 01	11 20	11 45
62	15 11	16 11	17 09	10 53	11 10	11 32	12 01
60	15 29	16 22	17 16	10 58	11 18	11 42	12 13
N 58	15 43	16 32	17 22	11 03	11 25	11 51	12 24
56	15 56	16 41	17 28	11 07	11 31	11 59	12 34
54	16 06	16 48	17 33	11 11	11 36	12 06	12 43
52	16 16	16 55	17 38	11 14	11 41	12 12	12 50
50	16 25	17 02	17 42	11 17	11 46	12 18	12 57
45	16 43	17 16	17 52	11 24	11 55	12 31	13 12
N 40	16 58	17 27	18 01	11 30	12 03	12 41	13 24
35	17 10	17 38	18 09	11 35	12 10	12 50	13 34
30	17 21	17 47	18 17	11 39	12 16	12 58	13 44
20	17 40	18 04	18 31	11 46	12 27	13 11	13 59
N 10	17 57	18 19	18 45	11 53	12 36	13 23	14 13
0	18 13	18 35	19 01	11 59	12 45	13 34	14 26
S 10	18 28	18 51	19 18	12 05	12 54	13 45	14 39
20	18 45	19 10	19 38	12 12	13 03	13 57	14 53
30	19 05	19 32	20 04	12 20	13 14	14 10	15 08
35	19 17	19 46	20 21	12 24	13 20	14 18	15 17
40	19 30	20 02	20 42	12 29	13 27	14 27	15 28
45	19 46	20 22	21 08	12 35	13 36	14 38	15 40
S 50	20 06	20 48	21 45	12 42	13 46	14 51	15 55
52	20 15	21 00	22 06	12 45	13 50	14 56	16 02
54	20 26	21 15	22 33	12 48	13 55	15 03	16 10
56	20 38	21 33	23 17	12 52	14 01	15 10	16 19
58	20 52	21 55	////	12 57	14 07	15 19	16 29
S 60	21 08	22 24	////	13 01	14 15	15 28	16 40

SUN / MOON

Day	SUN Eqn. of Time 00ʰ	12ʰ	Mer. Pass.	MOON Mer. Pass. Upper	Lower	Age	Phase
d	m s	m s	h m	h m	h m	d	%
13	08 22	08 34	12 09	05 48	18 11	22	49
14	08 45	08 56	12 09	06 34	18 58	23	39
15	09 07	09 17	12 09	07 22	19 47	24	30

UT	ARIES GHA	VENUS −3.9 GHA	Dec	MARS +1.2 GHA	Dec	JUPITER −2.5 GHA	Dec	SATURN +0.5 GHA	Dec	STARS Name	SHA	Dec
16 00	115 06.9	156 40.5	S17 41.3	140 00.3	S11 23.8	332 03.2	N15 33.4	234 30.7	S18 41.9	Acamar	315 17.4	S40 15.0
01	130 09.4	171 39.8	40.3	155 01.0	23.1	347 05.9	33.5	249 32.9	41.9	Achernar	335 26.1	S57 10.0
02	145 11.9	186 39.2	39.4	170 01.6	22.4	2 08.7	33.6	264 35.2	41.9	Acrux	173 07.6	S63 10.7
03	160 14.3	201 38.5	.. 38.5	185 02.2	.. 21.6	17 11.4	.. 33.7	279 37.4	.. 42.0	Adhara	255 11.3	S28 59.8
04	175 16.8	216 37.8	37.6	200 02.8	20.9	32 14.1	33.8	294 39.7	42.0	Aldebaran	290 47.9	N16 32.2
05	190 19.3	231 37.2	36.7	215 03.4	20.2	47 16.9	33.9	309 41.9	42.1			
06	205 21.7	246 36.5	S17 35.7	230 04.0	S11 19.4	62 19.6	N15 34.0	324 44.1	S18 42.1	Alioth	166 19.7	N55 52.4
07	220 24.2	261 35.8	34.8	245 04.6	18.7	77 22.4	34.1	339 46.4	42.1	Alkaid	152 58.1	N49 14.1
08	235 26.7	276 35.2	33.9	260 05.3	18.0	92 25.1	34.2	354 48.6	42.2	Al Na'ir	27 42.8	S46 53.3
F 09	250 29.1	291 34.5	.. 33.0	275 05.9	.. 17.2	107 27.8	.. 34.3	9 50.9	.. 42.2	Alnilam	275 45.0	S 1 11.8
R 10	265 31.6	306 33.8	32.1	290 06.5	16.5	122 30.6	34.4	24 53.1	42.2	Alphard	217 54.7	S 8 43.6
I 11	280 34.1	321 33.2	31.1	305 07.1	15.8	137 33.3	34.5	39 55.3	42.3			
D 12	295 36.5	336 32.5	S17 30.2	320 07.7	S11 15.1	152 36.0	N15 34.6	54 57.6	S18 42.3	Alphecca	126 10.3	N26 39.8
A 13	310 39.0	351 31.9	29.3	335 08.3	14.3	167 38.8	34.7	69 59.8	42.4	Alpheratz	357 42.5	N29 10.5
Y 14	325 41.4	6 31.2	28.4	350 08.9	13.6	182 41.5	34.8	85 02.1	42.4	Altair	62 07.5	N 8 54.6
15	340 43.9	21 30.5	.. 27.4	5 09.6	.. 12.9	197 44.2	.. 34.9	100 04.3	.. 42.4	Ankaa	353 14.8	S42 13.7
16	355 46.4	36 29.9	26.5	20 10.2	12.1	212 47.0	35.0	115 06.6	42.5	Antares	112 25.1	S26 27.7
17	10 48.8	51 29.2	25.6	35 10.8	11.4	227 49.7	35.1	130 08.8	42.5			
18	25 51.3	66 28.5	S17 24.6	50 11.4	S11 10.7	242 52.4	N15 35.2	145 11.0	S18 42.5	Arcturus	145 54.8	N19 06.2
19	40 53.8	81 27.9	23.7	65 12.0	09.9	257 55.2	35.3	160 13.3	42.6	Atria	107 26.4	S69 02.9
20	55 56.2	96 27.2	22.8	80 12.6	09.2	272 57.9	35.4	175 15.5	42.6	Avior	234 16.8	S59 33.6
21	70 58.7	111 26.6	.. 21.8	95 13.3	.. 08.5	288 00.7	.. 35.4	190 17.8	.. 42.7	Bellatrix	278 30.5	N 6 21.5
22	86 01.2	126 25.9	20.9	110 13.9	07.7	303 03.4	35.5	205 20.0	42.7	Betelgeuse	270 59.8	N 7 24.3
23	101 03.6	141 25.3	20.0	125 14.5	07.0	318 06.1	35.6	220 22.2	42.7			
17 00	116 06.1	156 24.6	S17 19.0	140 15.1	S11 06.3	333 08.9	N15 35.7	235 24.5	S18 42.8	Canopus	263 55.1	S52 42.5
01	131 08.5	171 23.9	18.1	155 15.7	05.5	348 11.6	35.8	250 26.7	42.8	Capella	280 32.4	N46 00.7
02	146 11.0	186 23.3	17.2	170 16.3	04.8	3 14.4	35.9	265 29.0	42.8	Deneb	49 31.1	N45 20.2
03	161 13.5	201 22.6	.. 16.2	185 17.0	.. 04.0	18 17.1	.. 36.0	280 31.2	.. 42.9	Denebola	182 32.4	N14 29.1
04	176 15.9	216 22.0	15.3	200 17.6	03.3	33 19.8	36.1	295 33.5	42.9	Diphda	348 54.9	S17 54.4
05	191 18.4	231 21.3	14.3	215 18.2	02.5	48 22.6	36.2	310 35.7	43.0			
06	206 20.9	246 20.7	S17 13.4	230 18.8	S11 01.8	63 25.3	N15 36.3	325 37.9	S18 43.0	Dubhe	193 50.1	N61 39.8
07	221 23.3	261 20.0	12.5	245 19.4	01.1	78 28.1	36.4	340 40.2	43.0	Elnath	278 10.9	N28 37.0
S 08	236 25.8	276 19.4	11.5	260 20.0	11 00.4	93 30.8	36.5	355 42.4	43.1	Eltanin	90 46.1	N51 29.3
A 09	251 28.3	291 18.7	.. 10.6	275 20.7	10 59.6	108 33.5	.. 36.6	10 44.7	.. 43.1	Enif	33 46.3	N 9 56.8
T 10	266 30.7	306 18.1	09.6	290 21.3	58.9	123 36.3	36.7	25 46.9	43.1	Fomalhaut	15 23.1	S29 32.6
U 11	281 33.2	321 17.4	08.7	305 21.9	58.2	138 39.0	36.8	40 49.2	43.2			
R 12	296 35.7	336 16.8	S17 07.7	320 22.5	S10 57.4	153 41.8	N15 36.9	55 51.4	S18 43.2	Gacrux	171 59.3	S57 11.6
D 13	311 38.1	351 16.1	06.8	335 23.1	56.7	168 44.5	37.0	70 53.7	43.2	Gienah	175 51.0	S17 37.5
A 14	326 40.6	6 15.5	05.9	350 23.8	56.0	183 47.2	37.1	85 55.9	43.3	Hadar	148 46.3	S60 26.4
Y 15	341 43.0	21 14.8	.. 04.9	5 24.4	.. 55.2	198 50.0	.. 37.2	100 58.1	.. 43.3	Hamal	327 59.4	N23 32.0
16	356 45.5	36 14.2	04.0	20 25.0	54.5	213 52.7	37.3	116 00.4	43.4	Kaus Aust.	83 42.7	S34 22.4
17	11 48.0	51 13.5	03.0	35 25.6	53.7	228 55.5	37.4	131 02.6	43.4			
18	26 50.4	66 12.9	S17 02.1	50 26.2	S10 53.0	243 58.2	N15 37.5	146 04.9	S18 43.4	Kochab	137 20.6	N74 05.4
19	41 52.9	81 12.2	01.1	65 26.9	52.3	259 00.9	37.6	161 07.1	43.5	Markab	13 37.4	N15 17.3
20	56 55.4	96 11.6	17 00.2	80 27.5	51.5	274 03.7	37.7	176 09.4	43.5	Menkar	314 13.8	N 4 08.7
21	71 57.8	111 10.9	16 59.2	95 28.1	.. 50.8	289 06.4	.. 37.8	191 11.6	.. 43.5	Menkent	148 06.3	S36 26.4
22	87 00.3	126 10.3	58.2	110 28.7	50.1	304 09.2	37.9	206 13.9	43.6	Miaplacidus	221 38.4	S69 46.8
23	102 02.8	141 09.6	57.3	125 29.3	49.3	319 11.9	38.0	221 16.1	43.6			
18 00	117 05.2	156 09.0	S16 56.3	140 30.0	S10 48.6	334 14.7	N15 38.1	236 18.3	S18 43.6	Mirfak	308 38.5	N49 54.9
01	132 07.7	171 08.4	55.4	155 30.6	47.8	349 17.4	38.2	251 20.6	43.7	Nunki	75 57.3	S26 16.5
02	147 10.2	186 07.7	54.4	170 31.2	47.1	4 20.1	38.3	266 22.8	43.7	Peacock	53 18.2	S56 41.1
03	162 12.6	201 07.1	.. 53.5	185 31.8	.. 46.4	19 22.9	.. 38.4	281 25.1	.. 43.8	Pollux	243 26.0	N27 59.1
04	177 15.1	216 06.4	52.5	200 32.4	45.6	34 25.6	38.5	296 27.3	43.8	Procyon	244 58.3	N 5 10.9
05	192 17.5	231 05.8	51.5	215 33.1	44.9	49 28.4	38.6	311 29.6	43.8			
06	207 20.0	246 05.2	S16 50.6	230 33.7	S10 44.1	64 31.1	N15 38.7	326 31.8	S18 43.9	Rasalhague	96 05.7	N12 33.1
07	222 22.5	261 04.5	49.6	245 34.3	43.4	79 33.9	38.8	341 34.1	43.9	Regulus	207 42.1	N11 53.4
08	237 24.9	276 03.9	48.7	260 34.9	42.7	94 36.6	38.9	356 36.3	43.9	Rigel	281 10.7	S 8 11.4
S 09	252 27.4	291 03.2	.. 47.7	275 35.5	.. 41.9	109 39.4	.. 39.0	11 38.6	.. 44.0	Rigil Kent.	139 50.3	S60 53.4
U 10	267 29.9	306 02.6	46.7	290 36.2	41.2	124 42.1	39.1	26 40.8	44.0	Sabik	102 11.6	S15 44.4
N 11	282 32.3	321 02.0	45.8	305 36.8	40.4	139 44.8	39.2	41 43.1	44.0			
D 12	297 34.8	336 01.3	S16 44.8	320 37.4	S10 39.7	154 47.6	N15 39.3	56 45.3	S18 44.1	Schedar	349 39.3	N56 37.4
A 13	312 37.3	351 00.7	43.8	335 38.0	39.0	169 50.3	39.4	71 47.5	44.1	Shaula	96 20.8	S37 06.6
Y 14	327 39.7	6 00.1	42.9	350 38.7	38.2	184 53.1	39.4	86 49.8	44.1	Sirius	258 32.4	S16 44.5
15	342 42.2	20 59.4	.. 41.9	5 39.3	.. 37.5	199 55.8	.. 39.5	101 52.0	.. 44.2	Spica	158 30.1	S11 14.3
16	357 44.7	35 58.8	40.9	20 39.9	36.7	214 58.6	39.6	116 54.3	44.2	Suhail	222 51.1	S43 29.7
17	12 47.1	50 58.2	40.0	35 40.5	36.0	230 01.3	39.7	131 56.5	44.3			
18	27 49.6	65 57.5	S16 39.0	50 41.2	S10 35.3	245 04.1	N15 39.8	146 58.8	S18 44.3	Vega	80 38.6	N38 48.0
19	42 52.0	80 56.9	38.0	65 41.8	34.5	260 06.8	39.9	162 01.0	44.3	Zuben'ubi	137 04.3	S16 06.1
20	57 54.5	95 56.3	37.1	80 42.4	33.8	275 09.6	40.0	177 03.3	44.4		SHA	Mer.Pass.
21	72 57.0	110 55.6	.. 36.1	95 43.0	.. 33.0	290 12.3	.. 40.1	192 05.5	.. 44.4	Venus	40 18.5	13 35
22	87 59.4	125 55.0	35.1	110 43.7	32.3	305 15.1	40.2	207 07.8	44.4	Mars	24 09.0	14 38
23	103 01.9	140 54.4	34.1	125 44.3	31.6	320 17.8	40.3	222 10.0	44.5	Jupiter	217 02.8	1 47
Mer.Pass. 16 12.9		v −0.6 d 0.9		v 0.6 d 0.7		v 2.7 d 0.1		v 2.2 d 0.0		Saturn	119 18.4	8 17

UT	SUN GHA	SUN Dec	MOON GHA	v	MOON Dec	d	HP
16 00	177 37.9	S21 02.0	241 01.8	9.7	S15 52.2	5.5	57.1
01	192 37.7	01.6	255 30.5	9.7	15 57.7	5.5	57.2
02	207 37.5	01.1	269 59.2	9.6	16 03.2	5.4	57.2
03	222 37.3	.. 00.6	284 27.8	9.5	16 08.6	5.3	57.2
04	237 37.1	21 00.2	298 56.3	9.4	16 13.9	5.2	57.3
05	252 36.8	20 59.7	313 24.7	9.3	16 19.1	5.1	57.3
06	267 36.6	S20 59.2	327 53.0	9.3	S16 24.2	5.1	57.4
07	282 36.4	58.7	342 21.3	9.2	16 29.3	4.9	57.4
F 08	297 36.2	58.3	356 49.5	9.1	16 34.2	4.9	57.4
R 09	312 36.0	.. 57.8	11 17.6	9.0	16 39.1	4.8	57.5
I 10	327 35.8	57.3	25 45.6	9.0	16 43.9	4.7	57.5
D 11	342 35.5	56.9	40 13.6	8.9	16 48.6	4.6	57.6
A 12	357 35.3	S20 56.4	54 41.5	8.8	S16 53.2	4.5	57.6
Y 13	12 35.1	55.9	69 09.3	8.7	16 57.7	4.4	57.6
14	27 34.9	55.4	83 37.0	8.6	17 02.1	4.4	57.7
15	42 34.7	.. 54.9	98 04.6	8.6	17 06.5	4.2	57.7
16	57 34.5	54.5	112 32.2	8.5	17 10.7	4.2	57.7
17	72 34.3	54.0	126 59.7	8.4	17 14.9	4.0	57.8
18	87 34.0	S20 53.5	141 27.1	8.4	S17 18.9	4.0	57.8
19	102 33.8	53.0	155 54.5	8.2	17 22.9	3.8	57.9
20	117 33.6	52.5	170 21.7	8.2	17 26.7	3.8	57.9
21	132 33.4	.. 52.1	184 48.9	8.1	17 30.5	3.7	57.9
22	147 33.2	51.6	199 16.0	8.1	17 34.2	3.5	58.0
23	162 33.0	51.1	213 43.1	7.9	17 37.7	3.5	58.0
17 00	177 32.8	S20 50.6	228 10.0	7.9	S17 41.2	3.4	58.1
01	192 32.6	50.1	242 36.9	7.8	17 44.6	3.2	58.1
02	207 32.4	49.6	257 03.7	7.8	17 47.8	3.2	58.1
03	222 32.1	.. 49.2	271 30.5	7.7	17 51.0	3.0	58.2
04	237 31.9	48.7	285 57.2	7.6	17 54.0	3.0	58.2
05	252 31.7	48.2	300 23.8	7.5	17 57.0	2.8	58.3
06	267 31.5	S20 47.7	314 50.3	7.5	S17 59.8	2.8	58.3
07	282 31.3	47.2	329 16.8	7.4	18 02.6	2.6	58.3
S 08	297 31.1	46.7	343 43.2	7.3	18 05.2	2.5	58.4
A 09	312 30.9	.. 46.2	358 09.5	7.2	18 07.7	2.4	58.4
T 10	327 30.7	45.7	12 35.7	7.2	18 10.1	2.4	58.4
U 11	342 30.5	45.3	27 01.9	7.2	18 12.5	2.1	58.5
R 12	357 30.3	S20 44.8	41 28.1	7.0	S18 14.6	2.1	58.5
D 13	12 30.1	44.3	55 54.1	7.0	18 16.7	2.0	58.6
A 14	27 29.8	43.8	70 20.1	6.9	18 18.7	1.9	58.6
Y 15	42 29.6	.. 43.3	84 46.0	6.9	18 20.6	1.7	58.6
16	57 29.4	42.8	99 11.9	6.8	18 22.3	1.6	58.7
17	72 29.2	42.3	113 37.7	6.7	18 23.9	1.6	58.7
18	87 29.0	S20 41.8	128 03.4	6.7	S18 25.5	1.4	58.8
19	102 28.8	41.3	142 29.1	6.6	18 26.9	1.3	58.8
20	117 28.6	40.8	156 54.7	6.6	18 28.2	1.1	58.8
21	132 28.4	.. 40.3	171 20.3	6.5	18 29.3	1.1	58.9
22	147 28.2	39.8	185 45.8	6.5	18 30.4	0.9	58.9
23	162 28.0	39.3	200 11.3	6.3	18 31.3	0.8	58.9
18 00	177 27.8	S20 38.8	214 36.6	6.4	S18 32.1	0.7	59.0
01	192 27.6	38.3	229 02.0	6.3	18 32.8	0.6	59.0
02	207 27.4	37.8	243 27.3	6.2	18 33.4	0.5	59.1
03	222 27.2	.. 37.3	257 52.5	6.2	18 33.9	0.3	59.1
04	237 27.0	36.8	272 17.7	6.1	18 34.2	0.2	59.1
05	252 26.8	36.3	286 42.8	6.1	18 34.4	0.1	59.2
06	267 26.6	S20 35.8	301 07.9	6.0	S18 34.5	0.0	59.2
07	282 26.4	35.3	315 32.9	6.0	18 34.5	0.2	59.2
08	297 26.2	34.8	329 57.9	5.9	18 34.3	0.3	59.3
S 09	312 26.0	.. 34.3	344 22.8	5.9	18 34.0	0.4	59.3
U 10	327 25.8	33.8	358 47.7	5.8	18 33.6	0.5	59.3
N 11	342 25.6	33.3	13 12.5	5.8	18 33.1	0.6	59.4
D 12	357 25.4	S20 32.7	27 37.3	5.8	S18 32.5	0.8	59.4
A 13	12 25.2	32.2	42 02.1	5.7	18 31.7	0.9	59.5
Y 14	27 25.0	31.7	56 26.8	5.7	18 30.8	1.0	59.5
15	42 24.8	.. 31.2	70 51.5	5.6	18 29.8	1.2	59.5
16	57 24.6	30.7	85 16.1	5.6	18 28.6	1.3	59.6
17	72 24.4	30.2	99 40.7	5.6	18 27.3	1.4	59.6
18	87 24.2	S20 29.7	114 05.3	5.6	S18 25.9	1.5	59.6
19	102 24.0	29.2	128 29.9	5.5	18 24.4	1.6	59.7
20	117 23.8	28.7	142 54.4	5.4	18 22.8	1.8	59.7
21	132 23.6	.. 28.1	157 18.8	5.5	18 21.0	1.9	59.7
22	147 23.4	27.6	171 43.3	5.4	18 19.1	2.1	59.8
23	162 23.2	27.1	186 07.7	5.4	S18 17.0	2.2	59.8
	SD 16.3	d 0.5	SD 15.7		15.9		16.2

Twilight — Sunrise — Moonrise

Lat.	Naut.	Civil	Sunrise	Moonrise 16	17	18	19
N 72	07 56	09 44	■■	06 35	■■	■■	10 38
N 70	07 42	09 13	11 48	05 46	07 22	08 36	09 12
68	07 31	08 49	10 25	05 15	06 39	07 48	08 33
66	07 21	08 31	09 48	04 52	06 11	07 17	08 05
64	07 13	08 16	09 22	04 34	05 49	06 54	07 44
62	07 06	08 03	09 01	04 19	05 32	06 35	07 27
60	06 59	07 53	08 45	04 07	05 17	06 20	07 13
N 58	06 53	07 43	08 31	03 56	05 05	06 07	07 01
56	06 48	07 35	08 19	03 47	04 54	05 56	06 50
54	06 43	07 28	08 09	03 39	04 45	05 46	06 41
52	06 39	07 21	08 00	03 31	04 36	05 38	06 33
50	06 34	07 15	07 51	03 25	04 29	05 30	06 26
45	06 25	07 01	07 34	03 11	04 13	05 13	06 09
N 40	06 16	06 50	07 19	02 59	04 00	05 00	05 56
35	06 09	06 40	07 07	02 49	03 49	04 48	05 45
30	06 01	06 31	06 56	02 40	03 39	04 38	05 35
20	05 47	06 14	06 38	02 26	03 22	04 20	05 18
N 10	05 33	05 59	06 22	02 13	03 08	04 05	05 04
0	05 18	05 44	06 06	02 01	02 54	03 51	04 50
S 10	05 02	05 28	05 51	01 49	02 41	03 37	04 36
20	04 42	05 10	05 34	01 36	02 26	03 22	04 22
30	04 16	04 48	05 15	01 21	02 10	03 05	04 05
35	04 00	04 35	05 04	01 13	02 01	02 55	03 55
40	03 40	04 19	04 51	01 03	01 50	02 43	03 44
45	03 14	04 00	04 35	00 52	01 37	02 30	03 31
S 50	02 38	03 35	04 16	00 39	01 22	02 13	03 15
52	02 18	03 22	04 07	00 32	01 14	02 06	03 07
54	01 52	03 08	03 56	00 25	01 06	01 57	02 59
56	01 13	02 51	03 45	00 18	00 57	01 48	02 50
58	////	02 30	03 31	00 09	00 47	01 37	02 39
S 60	////	02 02	03 15	24 36	00 36	01 24	02 27

Sunset — Twilight — Moonset

Lat.	Sunset	Civil	Naut.	Moonset 16	17	18	19
N 72	■■	14 36	16 25	09 42	■■	■■	11 38
N 70	12 33	15 08	16 39	10 32	10 49	11 35	13 03
68	13 56	15 32	16 50	11 03	11 32	12 13	13 42
66	14 33	15 50	17 00	11 27	12 01	12 54	14 09
64	14 59	16 05	17 08	11 45	12 23	13 17	14 29
62	15 19	16 17	17 15	12 01	12 41	13 35	14 46
60	15 36	16 28	17 22	12 13	12 55	13 50	15 00
N 58	15 49	16 37	17 27	12 24	13 08	14 03	15 12
56	16 01	16 45	17 33	12 34	13 18	14 14	15 22
54	16 12	16 53	17 37	12 43	13 28	14 24	15 31
52	16 21	17 00	17 42	12 50	13 37	14 33	15 39
50	16 29	17 06	17 46	12 57	13 44	14 41	15 47
45	16 47	17 19	17 55	13 12	14 00	14 57	16 02
N 40	17 01	17 31	18 04	13 24	14 14	15 11	16 15
35	17 13	17 41	18 12	13 34	14 25	15 22	16 26
30	17 24	17 50	18 19	13 44	14 35	15 33	16 35
20	17 42	18 06	18 33	13 59	14 52	15 50	16 51
N 10	17 58	18 21	18 47	14 13	15 07	16 05	17 05
0	18 14	18 36	19 01	14 26	15 21	16 19	17 18
S 10	18 29	18 52	19 18	14 39	15 35	16 33	17 32
20	18 46	19 09	19 38	14 53	15 50	16 48	17 45
30	19 05	19 31	20 03	15 08	16 07	17 05	18 01
35	19 16	19 45	20 20	15 17	16 17	17 15	18 10
40	19 29	20 00	20 40	15 28	16 28	17 26	18 21
45	19 44	20 20	21 05	15 40	16 42	17 40	18 33
S 50	20 03	20 44	21 41	15 55	16 58	17 56	18 48
52	20 12	20 57	22 00	16 02	17 05	18 04	18 55
54	20 22	21 11	22 25	16 10	17 14	18 12	19 03
56	20 34	21 28	23 02	16 19	17 23	18 22	19 11
58	20 47	21 48	////	16 29	17 34	18 32	19 21
S 60	21 03	22 15	////	16 40	17 47	18 45	19 32

SUN and MOON

Day	Eqn. of Time 00h	Eqn. of Time 12h	Mer. Pass.	Mer. Pass. Upper	Mer. Pass. Lower	Age	Phase
16	09 28	09 38	12 10	08 13	20 40	25	21
17	09 48	09 59	12 10	09 08	21 36	26	13
18	10 08	10 18	12 10	10 05	22 34	27	6

UT	ARIES	VENUS −3.9		MARS +1.2		JUPITER −2.5		SATURN +0.5		STARS		
	GHA	GHA	Dec	GHA	Dec	GHA	Dec	GHA	Dec	Name	SHA	Dec
d h	° ′	° ′	° ′	° ′	° ′	° ′	° ′	° ′	° ′		° ′	° ′
19 00	118 04.4	155 53.7	S16 33.2	140 44.9	S10 30.8	335 20.6	N15 40.4	237 12.3	S18 44.5	Acamar	315 17.4	S40 15.0
01	133 06.8	170 53.1	32.2	155 45.5	30.1	350 23.3	40.5	252 14.5	44.5	Achernar	335 26.1	S57 10.0
02	148 09.3	185 52.5	31.2	170 46.1	29.3	5 26.0	40.6	267 16.8	44.6	Acrux	173 07.6	S63 10.7
03	163 11.8	200 51.9	.. 30.2	185 46.8	.. 28.6	20 28.8	.. 40.7	282 19.0	.. 44.6	Adhara	255 11.3	S28 59.9
04	178 14.2	215 51.2	29.3	200 47.4	27.8	35 31.5	40.8	297 21.3	44.6	Aldebaran	290 47.9	N16 32.2
05	193 16.7	230 50.6	28.3	215 48.0	27.1	50 34.3	40.9	312 23.5	44.7			
06	208 19.2	245 50.0	S16 27.3	230 48.7	S10 26.4	65 37.0	N15 41.0	327 25.8	S18 44.7	Alioth	166 19.7	N55 52.4
07	223 21.6	260 49.4	26.3	245 49.3	25.6	80 39.8	41.1	342 28.0	44.8	Alkaid	152 58.1	N49 14.0
M 08	238 24.1	275 48.7	25.3	260 49.9	24.9	95 42.5	41.2	357 30.3	44.8	Al Na'ir	27 42.8	S46 53.3
O 09	253 26.5	290 48.1	.. 24.4	275 50.5	.. 24.1	110 45.3	.. 41.3	12 32.5	.. 44.8	Alnilam	275 45.0	S 1 11.8
N 10	268 29.0	305 47.5	23.4	290 51.2	23.4	125 48.0	41.4	27 34.8	44.9	Alphard	217 54.7	S 8 43.6
D 11	283 31.5	320 46.9	22.4	305 51.8	22.6	140 50.8	41.5	42 37.0	44.9			
A 12	298 33.9	335 46.2	S16 21.4	320 52.4	S10 21.9	155 53.5	N15 41.6	57 39.3	S18 44.9	Alphecca	126 10.3	N26 39.8
Y 13	313 36.4	350 45.6	20.4	335 53.0	21.2	170 56.3	41.7	72 41.5	45.0	Alpheratz	357 42.5	N29 10.5
14	328 38.9	5 45.0	19.4	350 53.7	20.4	185 59.0	41.8	87 43.8	45.0	Altair	62 07.5	N 8 54.6
15	343 41.3	20 44.4	.. 18.5	5 54.3	.. 19.7	201 01.8	.. 41.9	102 46.0	.. 45.0	Ankaa	353 14.8	S42 13.7
16	358 43.8	35 43.7	17.5	20 54.9	18.9	216 04.5	42.0	117 48.3	45.1	Antares	112 25.1	S26 27.7
17	13 46.3	50 43.1	16.5	35 55.5	18.2	231 07.3	42.1	132 50.5	45.1			
18	28 48.7	65 42.5	S16 15.5	50 56.2	S10 17.4	246 10.0	N15 42.2	147 52.8	S18 45.1	Arcturus	145 54.8	N19 06.2
19	43 51.2	80 41.9	14.5	65 56.8	16.7	261 12.8	42.3	162 55.0	45.2	Atria	107 26.3	S69 02.9
20	58 53.6	95 41.3	13.5	80 57.4	15.9	276 15.5	42.4	177 57.3	45.2	Avior	234 16.8	S59 33.6
21	73 56.1	110 40.7	.. 12.5	95 58.1	.. 15.2	291 18.3	.. 42.5	192 59.5	.. 45.2	Bellatrix	278 30.5	N 6 21.5
22	88 58.6	125 40.0	11.5	110 58.7	14.4	306 21.1	42.6	208 01.8	45.3	Betelgeuse	270 59.8	N 7 24.3
23	104 01.0	140 39.4	10.5	125 59.3	13.7	321 23.8	42.7	223 04.0	45.3			
20 00	119 03.5	155 38.8	S16 09.5	140 59.9	S10 13.0	336 26.6	N15 42.8	238 06.3	S18 45.3	Canopus	263 55.1	S52 42.6
01	134 06.0	170 38.2	08.6	156 00.6	12.2	351 29.3	42.9	253 08.5	45.4	Capella	280 32.4	N46 00.7
02	149 08.4	185 37.6	07.6	171 01.2	11.5	6 32.1	43.0	268 10.8	45.4	Deneb	49 31.1	N45 20.2
03	164 10.9	200 37.0	.. 06.6	186 01.8	.. 10.7	21 34.8	.. 43.1	283 13.0	.. 45.5	Denebola	182 30.4	N14 29.1
04	179 13.4	215 36.3	05.6	201 02.4	10.0	36 37.6	43.2	298 15.3	45.5	Diphda	348 54.9	S17 54.4
05	194 15.8	230 35.7	04.6	216 03.1	09.2	51 40.3	43.3	313 17.5	45.5			
06	209 18.3	245 35.1	S16 03.6	231 03.7	S10 08.5	66 43.1	N15 43.4	328 19.8	S18 45.6	Dubhe	193 50.0	N61 39.8
07	224 20.8	260 34.5	02.6	246 04.3	07.7	81 45.8	43.5	343 22.0	45.6	Elnath	278 10.9	N28 37.0
T 08	239 23.2	275 33.9	01.6	261 05.0	07.0	96 48.6	43.6	358 24.3	45.6	Eltanin	90 46.1	N51 29.2
U 09	254 25.7	290 33.3	16 00.6	276 05.6	.. 06.2	111 51.3	.. 43.7	13 26.5	.. 45.7	Enif	33 46.3	N 9 56.8
E 10	269 28.1	305 32.7	15 59.6	291 06.2	05.5	126 54.1	43.8	28 28.8	45.7	Fomalhaut	15 23.1	S29 32.6
S 11	284 30.6	320 32.1	58.6	306 06.9	04.7	141 56.8	43.9	43 31.0	45.7			
D 12	299 33.1	335 31.5	S15 57.6	321 07.5	S10 04.0	156 59.6	N15 44.0	58 33.3	S18 45.8	Gacrux	171 59.3	S57 11.6
A 13	314 35.5	350 30.8	56.6	336 08.1	03.2	172 02.3	44.1	73 35.5	45.8	Gienah	175 51.0	S17 37.5
Y 14	329 38.0	5 30.2	55.6	351 08.7	02.5	187 05.1	44.2	88 37.8	45.8	Hadar	148 46.2	S60 26.4
15	344 40.5	20 29.6	.. 54.6	6 09.4	.. 01.7	202 07.9	.. 44.3	103 40.1	.. 45.9	Hamal	327 59.4	N23 32.0
16	359 42.9	35 29.0	53.6	21 10.0	01.0	217 10.6	44.4	118 42.3	45.9	Kaus Aust.	83 42.7	S34 22.4
17	14 45.4	50 28.4	52.5	36 10.6	10 00.3	232 13.4	44.5	133 44.6	45.9			
18	29 47.9	65 27.8	S15 51.5	51 11.3	S 9 59.5	247 16.1	N15 44.6	148 46.8	S18 46.0	Kochab	137 20.6	N74 05.4
19	44 50.3	80 27.2	50.5	66 11.9	58.8	262 18.9	44.7	163 49.1	46.0	Markab	13 37.4	N15 17.3
20	59 52.8	95 26.6	49.5	81 12.5	58.0	277 21.6	44.8	178 51.3	46.0	Menkar	314 13.8	N 4 08.7
21	74 55.3	110 26.0	.. 48.5	96 13.2	.. 57.3	292 24.4	.. 44.9	193 53.6	.. 46.1	Menkent	148 06.2	S36 26.4
22	89 57.7	125 25.4	47.5	111 13.8	56.5	307 27.1	45.0	208 55.8	46.1	Miaplacidus	221 38.4	S69 46.8
23	105 00.2	140 24.8	46.5	126 14.4	55.8	322 29.9	45.1	223 58.1	46.1			
21 00	120 02.6	155 24.2	S15 45.5	141 15.1	S 9 55.0	337 32.7	N15 45.2	239 00.3	S18 46.2	Mirfak	308 38.5	N49 54.9
01	135 05.1	170 23.6	44.5	156 15.7	54.3	352 35.4	45.3	254 02.6	46.2	Nunki	75 57.3	S26 16.5
02	150 07.6	185 23.0	43.5	171 16.3	53.5	7 38.2	45.4	269 04.9	46.2	Peacock	53 18.2	S56 41.1
03	165 10.0	200 22.4	.. 42.4	186 17.0	.. 52.8	22 40.9	.. 45.5	284 07.1	.. 46.3	Pollux	243 26.0	N27 59.1
04	180 12.5	215 21.8	41.4	201 17.6	52.0	37 43.7	45.7	299 09.4	46.3	Procyon	244 58.2	N 5 10.9
05	195 15.0	230 21.2	40.4	216 18.2	51.3	52 46.4	45.8	314 11.6	46.3			
06	210 17.4	245 20.6	S15 39.4	231 18.9	S 9 50.5	67 49.2	N15 45.9	329 13.9	S18 46.4	Rasalhague	96 05.7	N12 33.0
W 07	225 19.9	260 20.0	38.4	246 19.5	49.8	82 52.0	46.0	344 16.1	46.4	Regulus	207 42.1	N11 53.4
E 08	240 22.4	275 19.4	37.4	261 20.1	49.0	97 54.7	46.1	359 18.4	46.4	Rigel	281 10.7	S 8 11.4
D 09	255 24.8	290 18.8	.. 36.3	276 20.8	.. 48.3	112 57.5	.. 46.2	14 20.6	.. 46.5	Rigil Kent.	139 50.2	S60 53.4
N 10	270 27.3	305 18.2	35.3	291 21.4	47.5	128 00.2	46.3	29 22.9	46.5	Sabik	102 11.5	S15 44.4
E 11	285 29.8	320 17.6	34.3	306 22.0	46.8	143 03.0	46.4	44 25.1	46.5			
S 12	300 32.2	335 17.0	S15 33.3	321 22.7	S 9 46.0	158 05.7	N15 46.5	59 27.4	S18 46.6	Schedar	349 39.3	N56 37.4
D 13	315 34.7	350 16.4	32.3	336 23.3	45.3	173 08.5	46.6	74 29.7	46.6	Shaula	96 20.7	S37 06.6
A 14	330 37.1	5 15.8	31.2	351 23.9	44.5	188 11.3	46.7	89 31.9	46.6	Sirius	258 32.4	S16 44.5
Y 15	345 39.6	20 15.2	.. 30.2	6 24.6	.. 43.8	203 14.0	.. 46.8	104 34.2	.. 46.7	Spica	158 30.0	S11 14.3
16	0 42.1	35 14.6	29.2	21 25.2	43.0	218 16.8	46.9	119 36.4	46.7	Suhail	222 51.1	S43 29.7
17	15 44.5	50 14.0	28.2	36 25.8	42.2	233 19.5	47.0	134 38.7	46.7			
18	30 47.0	65 13.4	S15 27.2	51 26.5	S 9 41.5	248 22.3	N15 47.1	149 40.9	S18 46.8	Vega	80 38.6	N38 47.9
19	45 49.5	80 12.8	26.1	66 27.1	40.7	263 25.1	47.2	164 43.2	46.8	Zuben'ubi	137 04.3	S16 06.1
20	60 51.9	95 12.3	25.1	81 27.7	40.0	278 27.8	47.3	179 45.5	46.8		SHA	Mer. Pass.
21	75 54.4	110 11.7	.. 24.1	96 28.4	.. 39.2	293 30.6	.. 47.4	194 47.7	.. 46.9		° ′	h m
22	90 56.9	125 11.1	23.0	111 29.0	38.5	308 33.3	47.5	209 50.0	46.9	Venus	36 35.3	13 38
23	105 59.3	140 10.5	22.0	126 29.6	37.7	323 36.1	47.6	224 52.2	46.9	Mars	21 56.4	14 35
	h m									Jupiter	217 23.0	1 34
Mer. Pass.	16 01.1	v −0.6	d 1.0	v 0.6	d 0.7	v 2.8	d 0.1	v 2.3	d 0.0	Saturn	119 02.8	8 06

SUN and MOON

UT	SUN GHA	Dec	MOON GHA	v	Dec	d	HP
d h	° ′	° ′	° ′	′	° ′	′	′
19 00	177 23.0	S20 26.6	200 32.1	5.4	S18 14.8	2.2	59.8
01	192 22.8	26.1	214 56.5	5.3	18 12.6	2.5	59.8
02	207 22.6	25.6	229 20.8	5.3	18 10.1	2.5	59.9
03	222 22.4	.. 25.0	243 45.1	5.3	18 07.6	2.7	59.9
04	237 22.2	24.5	258 09.4	5.3	18 04.9	2.8	59.9
05	252 22.0	24.0	272 33.7	5.2	18 02.1	2.9	60.0
06	267 21.8	S20 23.5	286 57.9	5.3	S17 59.2	3.1	60.0
M 07	282 21.6	23.0	301 22.2	5.2	17 56.1	3.2	60.0
O 08	297 21.4	22.4	315 46.4	5.2	17 52.9	3.3	60.1
N 09	312 21.2	.. 21.9	330 10.6	5.2	17 49.6	3.4	60.1
D 10	327 21.0	21.4	344 34.8	5.2	17 46.2	3.6	60.1
A 11	342 20.8	20.9	358 59.0	5.1	17 42.6	3.7	60.1
Y 12	357 20.7	S20 20.3	13 23.1	5.2	S17 38.9	3.8	60.2
13	12 20.5	19.8	27 47.3	5.2	17 35.1	4.0	60.2
14	27 20.3	19.3	42 11.5	5.1	17 31.1	4.0	60.2
15	42 20.1	.. 18.8	56 35.6	5.1	17 27.1	4.2	60.2
16	57 19.9	18.2	70 59.7	5.2	17 22.9	4.4	60.3
17	72 19.7	17.7	85 23.9	5.1	17 18.5	4.4	60.3
18	87 19.5	S20 17.2	99 48.0	5.1	S17 14.1	4.6	60.3
19	102 19.3	16.7	114 12.1	5.2	17 09.5	4.7	60.4
20	117 19.1	16.1	128 36.3	5.1	17 04.8	4.8	60.4
21	132 18.9	.. 15.6	143 00.4	5.1	17 00.0	4.9	60.4
22	147 18.7	15.1	157 24.5	5.1	16 55.1	5.1	60.4
23	162 18.6	14.5	171 48.7	5.1	16 50.0	5.2	60.4
20 00	177 18.4	S20 14.0	186 12.8	5.2	S16 44.8	5.3	60.5
01	192 18.2	13.5	200 37.0	5.1	16 39.5	5.4	60.5
02	207 18.0	12.9	215 01.1	5.2	16 34.1	5.6	60.5
03	222 17.8	.. 12.4	229 25.3	5.2	16 28.5	5.6	60.5
04	237 17.6	11.9	243 49.5	5.1	16 22.9	5.8	60.6
05	252 17.4	11.3	258 13.6	5.2	16 17.1	5.9	60.6
06	267 17.2	S20 10.8	272 37.8	5.3	S16 11.2	6.1	60.6
T 07	282 17.1	10.3	287 02.1	5.2	16 05.1	6.1	60.6
U 08	297 16.9	09.7	301 26.3	5.2	15 59.0	6.3	60.6
E 09	312 16.7	.. 09.2	315 50.5	5.3	15 52.7	6.3	60.6
S 10	327 16.5	08.6	330 14.8	5.3	15 46.4	6.5	60.7
D 11	342 16.3	08.1	344 39.1	5.3	15 39.9	6.6	60.7
A 12	357 16.1	S20 07.6	359 03.4	5.3	S15 33.3	6.7	60.7
Y 13	12 15.9	07.0	13 27.7	5.3	15 26.6	6.8	60.7
14	27 15.8	06.5	27 52.0	5.4	15 19.8	7.0	60.7
15	42 15.6	.. 05.9	42 16.4	5.3	15 12.8	7.0	60.7
16	57 15.4	05.4	56 40.7	5.5	15 05.8	7.2	60.8
17	72 15.2	04.8	71 05.2	5.4	14 58.6	7.2	60.8
18	87 15.0	S20 04.3	85 29.6	5.4	S14 51.4	7.4	60.8
19	102 14.8	03.8	99 54.0	5.5	14 44.0	7.5	60.8
20	117 14.7	03.2	114 18.5	5.5	14 36.5	7.6	60.8
21	132 14.5	.. 02.7	128 43.0	5.6	14 28.9	7.6	60.8
22	147 14.3	02.1	143 07.6	5.5	14 21.3	7.8	60.8
23	162 14.1	01.6	157 32.1	5.6	14 13.5	7.9	60.9
21 00	177 13.9	S20 01.0	171 56.7	5.7	S14 05.6	8.0	60.9
01	192 13.7	20 00.5	186 21.4	5.6	13 57.6	8.1	60.9
02	207 13.6	19 59.9	200 46.0	5.7	13 49.5	8.2	60.9
03	222 13.4	.. 59.4	215 10.7	5.8	13 41.3	8.2	60.9
04	237 13.2	58.8	229 35.5	5.7	13 33.1	8.4	60.9
05	252 13.0	58.3	244 00.2	5.8	13 24.7	8.5	60.9
06	267 12.8	S19 57.7	258 25.0	5.9	S13 16.2	8.6	60.9
W 07	282 12.7	57.2	272 49.9	5.8	13 07.6	8.6	60.9
E 08	297 12.5	56.6	287 14.7	5.9	12 59.0	8.8	60.9
D 09	312 12.3	.. 56.1	301 39.6	6.0	12 50.2	8.8	60.9
N 10	327 12.1	55.5	316 04.6	6.0	12 41.4	8.9	60.9
E 11	342 12.0	54.9	330 29.6	6.0	12 32.5	9.1	60.9
S 12	357 11.8	S19 54.4	344 54.6	6.1	S12 23.4	9.1	61.0
D 13	12 11.6	53.8	359 19.7	6.1	12 14.3	9.1	61.0
A 14	27 11.4	53.3	13 44.8	6.1	12 05.2	9.3	61.0
Y 15	42 11.2	.. 52.7	28 09.9	6.2	11 55.9	9.4	61.0
16	57 11.1	52.2	42 35.1	6.2	11 46.5	9.4	61.0
17	72 10.9	51.6	57 00.3	6.3	11 37.1	9.5	61.0
18	87 10.7	S19 51.0	71 25.6	6.3	S11 27.6	9.6	61.0
19	102 10.5	50.5	85 50.9	6.3	11 18.0	9.7	61.0
20	117 10.4	49.9	100 16.2	6.4	11 08.3	9.7	61.0
21	132 10.2	.. 49.4	114 41.6	6.5	10 58.6	9.8	61.0
22	147 10.0	48.8	129 07.1	6.4	10 48.8	9.9	61.0
23	162 09.8	48.2	143 32.5	6.6	S10 38.9	10.0	61.0
	SD 16.3	d 0.5	SD 16.4		16.5		16.6

Moonrise

Lat.	Naut.	Civil	Sunrise	19	20	21	22
°	h m	h m	h m	h m	h m	h m	h m
N 72	07 49	09 32	■■	10 38	10 05	09 54	09 47
N 70	07 36	09 03	11 08	09 12	09 26	09 31	09 33
68	07 25	08 42	10 11	08 33	08 58	09 13	09 22
66	07 16	08 25	09 38	08 05	08 37	08 58	09 13
64	07 08	08 11	09 14	07 44	08 20	08 46	09 06
62	07 01	07 59	08 55	07 27	08 07	08 36	08 59
60	06 55	07 49	08 40	07 13	07 55	08 27	08 53
N 58	06 50	07 40	08 27	07 01	07 44	08 19	08 48
56	06 45	07 32	08 15	06 50	07 35	08 13	08 44
54	06 40	07 25	08 05	06 41	07 27	08 06	08 39
52	06 36	07 18	07 57	06 33	07 20	08 01	08 36
50	06 32	07 12	07 49	06 25	07 14	07 56	08 32
45	06 23	06 59	07 32	06 09	07 00	07 45	08 25
N 40	06 15	06 48	07 18	05 56	06 48	07 36	08 19
35	06 08	06 39	07 06	05 45	06 39	07 28	08 13
30	06 01	06 30	06 56	05 35	06 30	07 21	08 09
20	05 47	06 14	06 38	05 18	06 15	07 09	08 01
N 10	05 34	06 00	06 22	05 04	06 02	06 59	07 53
0	05 20	05 45	06 07	04 50	05 50	06 49	07 47
S 10	05 03	05 30	05 52	04 36	05 38	06 39	07 40
20	04 44	05 12	05 36	04 22	05 24	06 29	07 33
30	04 19	04 51	05 18	04 05	05 09	06 17	07 24
35	04 03	04 38	05 07	03 55	05 01	06 10	07 20
40	03 44	04 23	04 54	03 44	04 51	06 02	07 14
45	03 19	04 04	04 39	03 31	04 39	05 52	07 08
S 50	02 45	03 40	04 21	03 15	04 25	05 41	07 00
52	02 26	03 28	04 12	03 07	04 18	05 36	06 57
54	02 02	03 14	04 02	02 59	04 11	05 30	06 53
56	01 29	02 58	03 51	02 50	04 03	05 24	06 49
58	////	02 39	03 38	02 39	03 54	05 17	06 44
S 60	////	02 13	03 23	02 27	03 43	05 08	06 38

Moonset

Lat.	Sunset	Civil	Naut.	19	20	21	22
°	h m	h m	h m	h m	h m	h m	h m
N 72	■■	14 51	16 34	11 38	14 15	16 29	18 36
N 70	13 15	15 20	16 47	13 03	14 54	16 51	18 48
68	14 12	15 41	16 58	13 42	15 20	17 08	18 57
66	14 44	15 58	17 07	14 09	15 41	17 21	19 04
64	15 08	16 12	17 14	14 29	15 57	17 33	19 11
62	15 27	16 24	17 21	14 46	16 10	17 42	19 16
60	15 43	16 34	17 27	15 00	16 21	17 50	19 21
N 58	15 56	16 43	17 32	15 12	16 31	17 57	19 25
56	16 07	16 51	17 37	15 22	16 40	18 03	19 29
54	16 17	16 58	17 42	15 31	16 47	18 09	19 32
52	16 26	17 04	17 46	15 39	16 54	18 14	19 35
50	16 34	17 10	17 50	15 47	17 00	18 18	19 38
45	16 51	17 23	17 59	16 02	17 13	18 28	19 44
N 40	17 04	17 34	18 07	16 15	17 24	18 36	19 49
35	17 16	17 43	18 14	16 26	17 33	18 43	19 53
30	17 26	17 52	18 21	16 35	17 41	18 49	19 56
20	17 44	18 08	18 35	16 51	17 55	18 59	20 03
N 10	18 00	18 22	18 48	17 05	18 07	19 08	20 08
0	18 15	18 37	19 02	17 18	18 18	19 17	20 13
S 10	18 29	18 52	19 18	17 32	18 29	19 25	20 18
20	18 45	19 09	19 37	17 45	18 41	19 34	20 24
30	19 04	19 30	20 02	18 01	18 54	19 44	20 30
35	19 15	19 43	20 18	18 10	19 02	19 49	20 33
40	19 27	19 58	20 37	18 21	19 11	19 56	20 37
45	19 42	20 17	21 02	18 33	19 21	20 03	20 42
S 50	20 00	20 41	21 36	18 48	19 33	20 12	20 47
52	20 09	20 53	21 54	18 55	19 39	20 17	20 49
54	20 19	21 06	22 17	19 03	19 45	20 21	20 52
56	20 30	21 22	22 49	19 11	19 52	20 26	20 55
58	20 42	21 44	////	19 21	20 00	20 32	20 58
S 60	20 57	22 06	////	19 32	20 09	20 38	21 02

SUN and MOON

Day	Eqn. of Time 00h	12h	Mer. Pass.	Mer. Pass. Upper	Lower	Age	Phase
d	m s	m s	h m	h m	h m	d	%
19	10 28	10 37	12 11	11 04	23 34	28	2
20	10 46	10 55	12 11	12 04	24 34	29	0
21	11 04	11 13	12 11	13 03	00 34	01	1 ●

UT	ARIES GHA	VENUS −3.9 GHA	Dec	MARS +1.2 GHA	Dec	JUPITER −2.5 GHA	Dec	SATURN +0.5 GHA	Dec	STARS Name	SHA	Dec
22 00	121 01.8	155 09.9	S15 21.0	141 30.3	S 9 37.0	338 38.9	N15 47.7	239 54.5	S18 47.0	Acamar	315 17.4	S40 15.0
01	136 04.2	170 09.3	20.0	156 30.9	36.2	353 41.6	47.8	254 56.7	47.0	Achernar	335 26.1	S57 10.0
02	151 06.7	185 08.7	18.9	171 31.5	35.5	8 44.4	47.9	269 59.0	47.0	Acrux	173 07.6	S63 10.7
03	166 09.2	200 08.1	.. 17.9	186 32.2	.. 34.7	23 47.1	.. 48.0	285 01.3	.. 47.1	Adhara	255 11.3	S28 59.9
04	181 11.6	215 07.5	16.9	201 32.8	34.0	38 49.9	48.1	300 03.5	47.1	Aldebaran	290 47.9	N16 32.2
05	196 14.1	230 07.0	15.8	216 33.5	33.2	53 52.7	48.2	315 05.8	47.1			
06	211 16.6	245 06.4	S15 14.8	231 34.1	S 9 32.5	68 55.4	N15 48.3	330 08.0	S18 47.2	Alioth	166 19.7	N55 52.4
07	226 19.0	260 05.8	13.8	246 34.7	31.7	83 58.2	48.4	345 10.3	47.2	Alkaid	152 58.1	N49 14.0
T 08	241 21.5	275 05.2	12.7	261 35.4	31.0	99 01.0	48.5	0 12.6	47.2	Al Na'ir	27 42.8	S46 53.3
H 09	256 24.0	290 04.6	.. 11.7	276 36.0	.. 30.2	114 03.7	.. 48.6	15 14.8	.. 47.3	Alnilam	275 45.0	S 1 11.8
U 10	271 26.4	305 04.0	10.7	291 36.6	29.4	129 06.5	48.7	30 17.1	47.3	Alphard	217 54.7	S 8 43.6
R 11	286 28.9	320 03.5	09.6	306 37.3	28.7	144 09.2	48.8	45 19.3	47.3			
S 12	301 31.4	335 02.9	S15 08.6	321 37.9	S 9 27.9	159 12.0	N15 48.9	60 21.6	S18 47.4	Alphecca	126 10.2	N26 39.8
D 13	316 33.8	350 02.3	07.5	336 38.5	27.2	174 14.8	49.0	75 23.8	47.4	Alpheratz	357 42.5	N29 10.5
A 14	331 36.3	5 01.7	06.5	351 39.2	26.4	189 17.5	49.1	90 26.1	47.4	Altair	62 07.5	N 8 54.6
Y 15	346 38.7	20 01.1	.. 05.5	6 39.8	.. 25.7	204 20.3	.. 49.2	105 28.4	.. 47.5	Ankaa	353 14.9	S42 13.7
16	1 41.2	35 00.5	04.4	21 40.5	24.9	219 23.0	49.3	120 30.6	47.5	Antares	112 25.1	S26 27.7
17	16 43.7	50 00.0	03.4	36 41.1	24.2	234 25.8	49.4	135 32.9	47.5			
18	31 46.1	64 59.4	S15 02.3	51 41.7	S 9 23.4	249 28.6	N15 49.5	150 35.1	S18 47.6	Arcturus	145 54.8	N19 06.1
19	46 48.6	79 58.8	01.3	66 42.4	22.6	264 31.3	49.6	165 37.4	47.6	Atria	107 26.3	S69 02.9
20	61 51.1	94 58.2	15 00.3	81 43.0	21.9	279 34.1	49.7	180 39.7	47.6	Avior	234 16.8	S59 33.7
21	76 53.5	109 57.7	14 59.2	96 43.7	.. 21.1	294 36.9	.. 49.8	195 41.9	.. 47.7	Bellatrix	278 30.5	N 6 21.5
22	91 56.0	124 57.1	58.2	111 44.3	20.4	309 39.6	49.9	210 44.2	47.7	Betelgeuse	270 59.8	N 7 24.3
23	106 58.5	139 56.5	57.1	126 44.9	19.6	324 42.4	50.0	225 46.4	47.7			
23 00	122 00.9	154 55.9	S14 56.1	141 45.6	S 9 18.9	339 45.2	N15 50.1	240 48.7	S18 47.8	Canopus	263 55.1	S52 42.6
01	137 03.4	169 55.3	55.0	156 46.2	18.1	354 47.9	50.3	255 51.0	47.8	Capella	280 32.4	N46 00.7
02	152 05.9	184 54.8	54.0	171 46.8	17.4	9 50.7	50.4	270 53.2	47.8	Deneb	49 31.1	N45 20.2
03	167 08.3	199 54.2	.. 52.9	186 47.5	.. 16.6	24 53.5	.. 50.5	285 55.5	.. 47.9	Denebola	182 32.4	N14 29.1
04	182 10.8	214 53.6	51.9	201 48.1	15.8	39 56.2	50.6	300 57.8	47.9	Diphda	348 54.9	S17 54.4
05	197 13.2	229 53.1	50.8	216 48.8	15.1	54 59.0	50.7	316 00.0	47.9			
06	212 15.7	244 52.5	S14 49.8	231 49.4	S 9 14.3	70 01.7	N15 50.8	331 02.3	S18 48.0	Dubhe	193 50.0	N61 39.9
07	227 18.2	259 51.9	48.7	246 50.0	13.6	85 04.5	50.9	346 04.5	48.0	Elnath	278 10.9	N28 37.0
08	242 20.6	274 51.3	47.7	261 50.7	12.8	100 07.3	51.0	1 06.8	48.0	Eltanin	90 46.1	N51 29.2
F 09	257 23.1	289 50.8	.. 46.6	276 51.3	.. 12.1	115 10.0	.. 51.1	16 09.1	.. 48.1	Enif	33 46.3	N 9 56.7
R 10	272 25.6	304 50.2	45.6	291 52.0	11.3	130 12.8	51.2	31 11.3	48.1	Fomalhaut	15 23.1	S29 32.6
I 11	287 28.0	319 49.6	44.5	306 52.6	10.5	145 15.6	51.3	46 13.6	48.1			
D 12	302 30.5	334 49.1	S14 43.5	321 53.3	S 9 09.8	160 18.3	N15 51.4	61 15.8	S18 48.2	Gacrux	171 59.3	S57 11.6
A 13	317 33.0	349 48.5	42.4	336 53.9	09.0	175 21.1	51.5	76 18.1	48.2	Gienah	175 51.0	S17 37.5
Y 14	332 35.4	4 47.9	41.4	351 54.5	08.3	190 23.9	51.6	91 20.4	48.2	Hadar	148 46.2	S60 26.4
15	347 37.9	19 47.3	.. 40.3	6 55.2	.. 07.5	205 26.6	.. 51.7	106 22.6	.. 48.2	Hamal	327 59.5	N23 32.0
16	2 40.3	34 46.8	39.2	21 55.8	06.8	220 29.4	51.8	121 24.9	48.3	Kaus Aust.	83 42.7	S34 22.4
17	17 42.8	49 46.2	38.2	36 56.5	06.0	235 32.2	51.9	136 27.2	48.3			
18	32 45.3	64 45.6	S14 37.1	51 57.1	S 9 05.2	250 34.9	N15 52.0	151 29.4	S18 48.3	Kochab	137 20.5	N74 05.4
19	47 47.7	79 45.1	36.1	66 57.7	04.5	265 37.7	52.1	166 31.7	48.4	Markab	13 37.4	N15 17.3
20	62 50.2	94 44.5	35.0	81 58.4	03.7	280 40.5	52.2	181 34.0	48.4	Menkar	314 13.8	N 4 08.7
21	77 52.7	109 44.0	.. 34.0	96 59.0	.. 03.0	295 43.2	.. 52.3	196 36.2	.. 48.4	Menkent	148 06.2	S36 26.4
22	92 55.1	124 43.4	32.9	111 59.7	02.2	310 46.0	52.4	211 38.5	48.5	Miaplacidus	221 38.3	S69 46.8
23	107 57.6	139 42.8	31.8	127 00.3	01.4	325 48.8	52.5	226 40.7	48.5			
24 00	123 00.1	154 42.3	S14 30.8	142 01.0	S 9 00.7	340 51.5	N15 52.6	241 43.0	S18 48.5	Mirfak	308 38.5	N49 54.9
01	138 02.5	169 41.7	29.7	157 01.6	8 59.9	355 54.3	52.7	256 45.3	48.6	Nunki	75 57.3	S26 16.5
02	153 05.0	184 41.1	28.6	172 02.2	59.2	10 57.1	52.8	271 47.5	48.6	Peacock	53 18.2	S56 41.1
03	168 07.5	199 40.6	.. 27.6	187 02.9	.. 58.4	25 59.8	.. 52.9	286 49.8	.. 48.6	Pollux	243 26.0	N27 59.1
04	183 09.9	214 40.0	26.5	202 03.5	57.6	41 02.6	53.0	301 52.1	48.7	Procyon	244 58.2	N 5 10.9
05	198 12.4	229 39.5	25.4	217 04.2	56.9	56 05.4	53.1	316 54.3	48.7			
06	213 14.8	244 38.9	S14 24.4	232 04.8	S 8 56.1	71 08.1	N15 53.3	331 56.6	S18 48.7	Rasalhague	96 05.7	N12 33.0
07	228 17.3	259 38.3	23.3	247 05.5	55.4	86 10.9	53.4	346 58.9	48.8	Regulus	207 42.1	N11 53.4
08	243 19.8	274 37.8	22.2	262 06.1	54.6	101 13.7	53.5	2 01.1	48.8	Rigel	281 10.7	S 8 11.4
S 09	258 22.2	289 37.2	.. 21.2	277 06.7	.. 53.8	116 16.5	.. 53.6	17 03.4	.. 48.8	Rigil Kent.	139 50.2	S60 53.4
A 10	273 24.7	304 36.7	20.1	292 07.4	53.1	131 19.2	53.7	32 05.7	48.8	Sabik	102 11.5	S15 44.4
T 11	288 27.2	319 36.1	19.0	307 08.0	52.3	146 22.0	53.8	47 07.9	48.9			
U 12	303 29.6	334 35.6	S14 18.0	322 08.7	S 8 51.6	161 24.8	N15 53.9	62 10.2	S18 48.9	Schedar	349 39.3	N56 37.4
R 13	318 32.1	349 35.0	16.9	337 09.3	50.8	176 27.5	54.0	77 12.4	48.9	Shaula	96 20.7	S37 06.6
D 14	333 34.6	4 34.4	15.8	352 10.0	50.0	191 30.3	54.1	92 14.7	49.0	Sirius	258 32.4	S16 44.5
A 15	348 37.0	19 33.9	.. 14.7	7 10.6	.. 49.3	206 33.1	.. 54.2	107 17.0	.. 49.0	Spica	158 30.0	S11 14.4
Y 16	3 39.5	34 33.3	13.7	22 11.3	48.5	221 35.8	54.3	122 19.2	49.0	Suhail	222 51.1	S43 29.8
17	18 42.0	49 32.8	12.6	37 11.9	47.8	236 38.6	54.4	137 21.5	49.1			
18	33 44.4	64 32.2	S14 11.5	52 12.6	S 8 47.0	251 41.4	N15 54.5	152 23.8	S18 49.1	Vega	80 38.6	N38 47.9
19	48 46.9	79 31.7	10.5	67 13.2	46.2	266 44.2	54.6	167 26.0	49.1	Zuben'ubi	137 04.2	S16 06.1
20	63 49.3	94 31.1	09.4	82 13.8	45.5	281 46.9	54.7	182 28.3	49.2		SHA	Mer. Pass.
21	78 51.8	109 30.6	.. 08.3	97 14.5	.. 44.7	296 49.7	.. 54.8	197 30.6	.. 49.2			
22	93 54.3	124 30.0	07.2	112 15.1	43.9	311 52.5	54.9	212 32.8	49.2	Venus	32 55.0	13 41
23	108 56.7	139 29.5	06.1	127 15.8	43.2	326 55.2	55.0	227 35.1	49.3	Mars	19 44.6	14 32
										Jupiter	217 44.2	1 21
Mer.Pass. 15 49.3		v −0.6	d 1.1	v 0.6	d 0.8	v 2.8	d 0.1	v 2.3	d 0.0	Saturn	118 47.8	7 56

UT	SUN GHA	SUN Dec	MOON GHA	v	Dec	d	HP
d h	° ′	° ′	° ′	′	° ′	′	′
22 00	177 09.7	S19 47.7	157 58.1	6.5	S10 28.9	10.0	61.0
01	192 09.5	47.1	172 23.6	6.6	10 18.9	10.1	61.0
02	207 09.3	46.5	186 49.2	6.7	10 08.8	10.1	61.0
03	222 09.2	.. 46.0	201 14.9	6.7	9 58.7	10.3	61.0
04	237 09.0	45.4	215 40.6	6.7	9 48.4	10.3	61.0
05	252 08.8	44.8	230 06.3	6.8	9 38.1	10.3	60.9
06	267 08.6	S19 44.3	244 32.1	6.9	S 9 27.8	10.4	60.9
T 07	282 08.5	43.7	258 58.0	6.8	9 17.4	10.5	60.9
H 08	297 08.3	43.1	273 23.8	7.0	9 06.9	10.5	60.9
U 09	312 08.1	.. 42.6	287 49.8	6.9	8 56.4	10.6	60.9
R 10	327 08.0	42.0	302 15.7	7.0	8 45.8	10.6	60.9
S 11	342 07.8	41.4	316 41.7	7.1	8 35.2	10.7	60.9
D 12	357 07.6	S19 40.9	331 07.8	7.1	S 8 24.5	10.8	60.9
A 13	12 07.5	40.3	345 33.9	7.1	8 13.7	10.8	60.9
Y 14	27 07.3	39.7	0 00.0	7.2	8 02.9	10.8	60.9
15	42 07.1	.. 39.1	14 26.2	7.3	7 52.1	10.9	60.9
16	57 06.9	38.6	28 52.5	7.3	7 41.2	11.0	60.9
17	72 06.8	38.0	43 18.8	7.3	7 30.2	10.9	60.9
18	87 06.6	S19 37.4	57 45.1	7.4	S 7 19.3	11.1	60.8
19	102 06.4	36.8	72 11.5	7.4	7 08.2	11.0	60.8
20	117 06.3	36.3	86 37.9	7.4	6 57.2	11.1	60.8
21	132 06.1	.. 35.7	101 04.3	7.5	6 46.1	11.2	60.8
22	147 05.9	35.1	115 30.8	7.6	6 34.9	11.2	60.8
23	162 05.8	34.5	129 57.4	7.6	6 23.7	11.2	60.8
23 00	177 05.6	S19 34.0	144 24.0	7.6	S 6 12.5	11.2	60.8
01	192 05.5	33.4	158 50.6	7.7	6 01.3	11.3	60.8
02	207 05.3	32.8	173 17.3	7.7	5 50.0	11.3	60.7
03	222 05.1	.. 32.2	187 44.0	7.8	5 38.7	11.4	60.7
04	237 05.0	31.6	202 10.8	7.8	5 27.3	11.3	60.7
05	252 04.8	31.1	216 37.6	7.9	5 16.0	11.4	60.7
06	267 04.6	S19 30.5	231 04.5	7.9	S 5 04.6	11.5	60.7
F 07	282 04.5	29.9	245 31.4	7.9	4 53.1	11.4	60.7
R 08	297 04.3	29.3	259 58.3	8.0	4 41.7	11.5	60.7
I 09	312 04.1	.. 28.7	274 25.3	8.0	4 30.2	11.5	60.6
D 10	327 04.0	28.1	288 52.3	8.1	4 18.7	11.5	60.6
A 11	342 03.8	27.5	303 19.4	8.1	4 07.2	11.5	60.6
Y 12	357 03.7	S19 27.0	317 46.5	8.1	S 3 55.7	11.6	60.6
13	12 03.5	26.4	332 13.6	8.2	3 44.1	11.6	60.6
14	27 03.3	25.8	346 40.8	8.3	3 32.6	11.6	60.5
15	42 03.2	.. 25.2	1 08.1	8.2	3 21.0	11.6	60.5
16	57 03.0	24.6	15 35.3	8.3	3 09.4	11.6	60.5
17	72 02.9	24.0	30 02.6	8.4	2 57.8	11.6	60.5
18	87 02.7	S19 23.4	44 30.0	8.3	S 2 46.2	11.6	60.5
19	102 02.5	22.8	58 57.3	8.5	2 34.6	11.6	60.4
20	117 02.4	22.2	73 24.8	8.4	2 23.0	11.7	60.4
21	132 02.2	.. 21.7	87 52.2	8.5	2 11.3	11.6	60.4
22	147 02.1	21.1	102 19.7	8.5	1 59.7	11.6	60.4
23	162 01.9	20.5	116 47.2	8.6	1 48.1	11.7	60.4
24 00	177 01.8	S19 19.9	131 14.8	8.6	S 1 36.4	11.6	60.3
01	192 01.6	19.3	145 42.4	8.6	1 24.8	11.6	60.3
02	207 01.4	18.7	160 10.0	8.7	1 13.2	11.7	60.3
03	222 01.3	.. 18.1	174 37.7	8.7	1 01.5	11.6	60.3
04	237 01.1	17.5	189 05.4	8.7	0 49.9	11.6	60.2
05	252 01.0	16.9	203 33.1	8.8	0 38.3	11.6	60.2
06	267 00.8	S19 16.3	218 00.9	8.8	S 0 26.7	11.6	60.2
S 07	282 00.7	15.7	232 28.7	8.9	0 15.1	11.6	60.2
A 08	297 00.5	15.1	246 56.6	8.8	S 0 03.5	11.6	60.1
T 09	312 00.4	.. 14.5	261 24.4	8.9	N 0 08.1	11.6	60.1
U 10	327 00.2	13.9	275 52.3	9.0	0 19.7	11.6	60.1
R 11	342 00.1	13.3	290 20.3	8.9	0 31.3	11.5	60.1
D 12	356 59.9	S19 12.7	304 48.2	9.0	N 0 42.8	11.5	60.0
A 13	11 59.7	12.1	319 16.2	9.0	0 54.3	11.6	60.0
Y 14	26 59.6	11.5	333 44.2	9.1	1 05.9	11.5	60.0
15	41 59.4	.. 10.9	348 12.3	9.0	1 17.4	11.4	60.0
16	56 59.3	10.3	2 40.3	9.1	1 28.8	11.5	59.9
17	71 59.1	09.7	17 08.4	9.2	1 40.3	11.4	59.9
18	86 59.0	S19 09.1	31 36.6	9.1	N 1 51.7	11.5	59.9
19	101 58.8	08.5	46 04.7	9.2	2 03.2	11.3	59.8
20	116 58.7	07.9	60 32.9	9.2	2 14.5	11.4	59.8
21	131 58.5	.. 07.3	75 01.1	9.2	2 25.9	11.4	59.8
22	146 58.4	06.7	89 29.3	9.3	2 37.3	11.3	59.8
23	161 58.2	06.0	103 57.6	9.3	N 2 48.6	11.3	59.7
SD	16.3	d 0.6	SD 16.6		16.5		16.4

Lat.	Twilight Naut.	Civil	Sunrise	Moonrise 22	23	24	25
°	h m	h m	h m	h m	h m	h m	h m
N 72	07 40	09 19	■■■	09 47	09 40	09 35	09 29
N 70	07 28	08 53	10 43	09 33	09 34	09 35	09 35
68	07 19	08 33	09 58	09 22	09 29	09 35	09 40
66	07 10	08 18	09 28	09 13	09 25	09 35	09 45
64	07 03	08 05	09 06	09 06	09 21	09 35	09 49
62	06 57	07 53	08 49	08 59	09 18	09 35	09 52
60	06 51	07 44	08 34	08 53	09 15	09 35	09 55
N 58	06 46	07 35	08 22	08 48	09 13	09 35	09 57
56	06 42	07 28	08 11	08 44	09 11	09 35	10 00
54	06 37	07 21	08 01	08 39	09 09	09 35	10 02
52	06 34	07 15	07 53	08 36	09 07	09 35	10 03
50	06 30	07 09	07 45	08 32	09 05	09 35	10 05
45	06 21	06 57	07 29	08 25	09 01	09 36	10 09
N 40	06 14	06 47	07 16	08 19	08 58	09 36	10 12
35	06 07	06 38	07 05	08 13	08 56	09 36	10 15
30	06 00	06 29	06 55	08 09	08 53	09 36	10 17
20	05 47	06 14	06 38	08 01	08 49	09 36	10 22
N 10	05 35	06 00	06 22	07 53	08 46	09 36	10 25
0	05 21	05 46	06 08	07 47	08 42	09 36	10 29
S 10	05 05	05 31	05 54	07 40	08 39	09 37	10 33
20	04 46	05 14	05 38	07 33	08 35	09 37	10 37
30	04 22	04 54	05 20	07 24	08 31	09 37	10 41
35	04 07	04 41	05 10	07 20	08 29	09 37	10 44
40	03 48	04 27	04 58	07 14	08 26	09 37	10 47
45	03 24	04 09	04 43	07 08	08 23	09 38	10 50
S 50	02 52	03 46	04 26	07 00	08 20	09 38	10 54
52	02 34	03 34	04 17	06 57	08 18	09 38	10 56
54	02 13	03 21	04 08	06 53	08 16	09 38	10 58
56	01 43	03 06	03 57	06 49	08 14	09 38	11 01
58	00 52	02 48	03 45	06 44	08 12	09 39	11 03
S 60	////	02 24	03 31	06 38	08 09	09 39	11 06

Lat.	Sunset	Twilight Civil	Naut.	Moonset 22	23	24	25
°	h m	h m	h m	h m	h m	h m	h m
N 72	■■■	15 05	16 45	18 36	20 38	22 35	24 30
N 70	13 42	15 31	16 56	18 48	20 41	22 31	24 19
68	14 27	15 51	17 06	18 57	20 44	22 28	24 10
66	14 56	16 07	17 14	19 04	20 46	22 26	24 02
64	15 18	16 20	17 21	19 11	20 48	22 24	23 56
62	15 36	16 31	17 27	19 16	20 50	22 22	23 51
60	15 50	16 40	17 33	19 21	20 51	22 20	23 46
N 58	16 02	16 49	17 38	19 25	20 53	22 19	23 42
56	16 13	16 56	17 42	19 29	20 54	22 17	23 38
54	16 23	17 03	17 47	19 32	20 55	22 16	23 35
52	16 31	17 09	17 51	19 35	20 56	22 15	23 32
50	16 39	17 15	17 54	19 38	20 57	22 14	23 29
45	16 55	17 27	18 03	19 44	20 59	22 12	23 24
N 40	17 08	17 37	18 10	19 49	21 00	22 11	23 19
35	17 19	17 46	18 17	19 53	21 02	22 09	23 15
30	17 29	17 55	18 24	19 56	21 03	22 08	23 11
20	17 46	18 09	18 36	20 03	21 05	22 05	23 05
N 10	18 01	18 23	18 49	20 08	21 07	22 03	22 59
0	18 15	18 37	19 03	20 13	21 08	22 01	22 54
S 10	18 30	18 52	19 18	20 18	21 10	21 59	22 48
20	18 45	19 09	19 37	20 24	21 11	21 57	22 43
30	19 03	19 29	20 01	20 30	21 13	21 55	22 37
35	19 13	19 42	20 16	20 33	21 14	21 54	22 33
40	19 25	19 56	20 34	20 37	21 15	21 52	22 29
45	19 40	20 14	20 58	20 42	21 17	21 50	22 24
S 50	19 57	20 37	21 30	20 47	21 18	21 48	22 18
52	20 05	20 48	21 47	20 49	21 19	21 47	22 16
54	20 15	21 01	22 08	20 52	21 20	21 46	22 13
56	20 25	21 16	22 36	20 55	21 21	21 45	22 10
58	20 37	21 34	23 23	20 58	21 22	21 44	22 06
S 60	20 51	21 56	////	21 02	21 23	21 42	22 02

Day	SUN Eqn. of Time 00h	12h	Mer. Pass.	MOON Mer. Pass. Upper	Lower	Age	Phase
d	m s	m s	h m	h m	h m	d	%
22	11 21	11 29	12 11	14 00	01 32	02	6
23	11 37	11 45	12 12	14 55	02 28	03	13
24	11 53	12 00	12 12	15 49	03 22	04	21

UT	ARIES	VENUS −3.9		MARS +1.2		JUPITER −2.6		SATURN +0.5		STARS		
	GHA	GHA	Dec	GHA	Dec	GHA	Dec	GHA	Dec	Name	SHA	Dec
d h	° ′	° ′	° ′	° ′	° ′	° ′	° ′	° ′	° ′		° ′	° ′
25 00	123 59.2	154 28.9	S14 05.1	142 16.4	S 8 42.4	341 58.0	N15 55.1	242 37.4	S18 49.3	Acamar	315 17.5	S40 15.1
01	139 01.7	169 28.4	04.0	157 17.1	41.7	357 00.8	55.2	257 39.6	49.3	Achernar	335 26.2	S57 10.0
02	154 04.1	184 27.8	02.9	172 17.7	40.9	12 03.5	55.3	272 41.9	49.3	Acrux	173 07.5	S63 10.7
03	169 06.6	199 27.3	. . 01.8	187 18.4	. . 40.1	27 06.3	. . 55.4	287 44.2	. . 49.4	Adhara	255 11.3	S28 59.9
04	184 09.1	214 26.7	14 00.7	202 19.0	39.4	42 09.1	55.5	302 46.4	49.4	Aldebaran	290 47.9	N16 32.2
05	199 11.5	229 26.2	13 59.7	217 19.7	38.6	57 11.9	55.6	317 48.7	49.4			
06	214 14.0	244 25.6	S13 58.6	232 20.3	S 8 37.8	72 14.6	N15 55.8	332 51.0	S18 49.5	Alioth	166 19.6	N55 52.4
07	229 16.4	259 25.1	57.5	247 21.0	37.1	87 17.4	55.9	347 53.3	49.5	Alkaid	152 58.0	N49 14.0
08	244 18.9	274 24.5	56.4	262 21.6	36.3	102 20.2	56.0	2 55.5	49.5	Al Na'ir	27 42.8	S46 53.3
S 09	259 21.4	289 24.0	. . 55.3	277 22.3	. . 35.6	117 22.9	. . 56.1	17 57.8	. . 49.6	Alnilam	275 45.0	S 1 11.8
U 10	274 23.8	304 23.4	54.2	292 22.9	34.8	132 25.7	56.2	33 00.1	49.6	Alphard	217 54.7	S 8 43.7
N 11	289 26.3	319 22.9	53.2	307 23.5	34.0	147 28.5	56.3	48 02.3	49.6			
D 12	304 28.8	334 22.4	S13 52.1	322 24.2	S 8 33.3	162 31.3	N15 56.4	63 04.6	S18 49.7	Alphecca	126 10.2	N26 39.8
A 13	319 31.2	349 21.8	51.0	337 24.8	32.5	177 34.0	56.5	78 06.9	49.7	Alpheratz	357 42.5	N29 10.5
Y 14	334 33.7	4 21.3	49.9	352 25.5	31.7	192 36.8	56.6	93 09.1	49.7	Altair	62 07.5	N 8 54.6
15	349 36.2	19 20.7	. . 48.8	7 26.1	. . 31.0	207 39.6	. . 56.7	108 11.4	. . 49.7	Ankaa	353 14.9	S42 13.7
16	4 38.6	34 20.2	47.7	22 26.8	30.2	222 42.4	56.8	123 13.7	49.8	Antares	112 25.1	S26 27.7
17	19 41.1	49 19.6	46.6	37 27.4	29.4	237 45.1	56.9	138 15.9	49.8			
18	34 43.6	64 19.1	S13 45.5	52 28.1	S 8 28.7	252 47.9	N15 57.0	153 18.2	S18 49.8	Arcturus	145 54.7	N19 06.1
19	49 46.0	79 18.6	44.5	67 28.7	27.9	267 50.7	57.1	168 20.5	49.9	Atria	107 26.2	S69 02.8
20	64 48.5	94 18.0	43.4	82 29.4	27.2	282 53.4	57.2	183 22.8	49.9	Avior	234 16.8	S59 33.7
21	79 50.9	109 17.5	. . 42.3	97 30.0	. . 26.4	297 56.2	. . 57.3	198 25.0	. . 49.9	Bellatrix	278 30.6	N 6 21.5
22	94 53.4	124 17.0	41.2	112 30.7	25.6	312 59.0	57.4	213 27.3	50.0	Betelgeuse	270 59.8	N 7 24.3
23	109 55.9	139 16.4	40.1	127 31.3	24.9	328 01.8	57.5	228 29.6	50.0			
26 00	124 58.3	154 15.9	S13 39.0	142 32.0	S 8 24.1	343 04.5	N15 57.6	243 31.8	S18 50.0	Canopus	263 55.1	S52 42.6
01	140 00.8	169 15.3	37.9	157 32.6	23.3	358 07.3	57.7	258 34.1	50.0	Capella	280 32.4	N46 00.7
02	155 03.3	184 14.8	36.8	172 33.3	22.6	13 10.1	57.8	273 36.4	50.1	Deneb	49 31.1	N45 20.2
03	170 05.7	199 14.3	. . 35.7	187 33.9	. . 21.8	28 12.9	. . 58.0	288 38.6	. . 50.1	Denebola	182 32.3	N14 29.1
04	185 08.2	214 13.7	34.6	202 34.6	21.0	43 15.6	58.1	303 40.9	50.1	Diphda	348 54.9	S17 54.4
05	200 10.7	229 13.2	33.5	217 35.2	20.3	58 18.4	58.2	318 43.2	50.2			
06	215 13.1	244 12.7	S13 32.4	232 35.9	S 8 19.5	73 21.2	N15 58.3	333 45.5	S18 50.2	Dubhe	193 50.0	N61 39.9
07	230 15.6	259 12.1	31.3	247 36.5	18.7	88 24.0	58.4	348 47.7	50.2	Elnath	278 10.9	N28 37.0
08	245 18.0	274 11.6	30.2	262 37.2	18.0	103 26.7	58.5	3 50.0	50.3	Eltanin	90 46.1	N51 29.2
M 09	260 20.5	289 11.1	. . 29.1	277 37.8	. . 17.2	118 29.5	. . 58.6	18 52.3	. . 50.3	Enif	33 46.3	N 9 56.7
O 10	275 23.0	304 10.5	28.0	292 38.5	16.4	133 32.3	58.7	33 54.5	50.3	Fomalhaut	15 23.1	S29 32.6
N 11	290 25.4	319 10.0	26.9	307 39.1	15.7	148 35.1	58.8	48 56.8	50.3			
D 12	305 27.9	334 09.5	S13 25.8	322 39.8	S 8 14.9	163 37.8	N15 58.9	63 59.1	S18 50.4	Gacrux	171 59.2	S57 11.6
A 13	320 30.4	349 08.9	24.7	337 40.4	14.1	178 40.6	59.0	79 01.4	50.4	Gienah	175 50.9	S17 37.5
Y 14	335 32.8	4 08.4	23.6	352 41.1	13.4	193 43.4	59.1	94 03.6	50.4	Hadar	148 46.1	S60 26.4
15	350 35.3	19 07.9	. . 22.5	7 41.8	. . 12.6	208 46.2	. . 59.2	109 05.9	. . 50.5	Hamal	327 59.5	N23 32.0
16	5 37.8	34 07.4	21.4	22 42.4	11.8	223 48.9	59.3	124 08.2	50.5	Kaus Aust.	83 42.7	S34 22.4
17	20 40.2	49 06.8	20.3	37 43.1	11.1	238 51.7	59.4	139 10.5	50.5			
18	35 42.7	64 06.3	S13 19.2	52 43.7	S 8 10.3	253 54.5	N15 59.5	154 12.7	S18 50.6	Kochab	137 20.4	N74 05.4
19	50 45.2	79 05.8	18.1	67 44.4	09.5	268 57.3	59.6	169 15.0	50.6	Markab	13 37.4	N15 17.2
20	65 47.6	94 05.2	17.0	82 45.0	08.8	284 00.0	59.7	184 17.3	50.6	Menkar	314 13.8	N 4 08.7
21	80 50.1	109 04.7	. . 15.9	97 45.7	. . 08.0	299 02.8	15 59.8	199 19.5	. . 50.6	Menkent	148 06.2	S36 26.4
22	95 52.5	124 04.2	14.8	112 46.3	07.2	314 05.6	16 00.0	214 21.8	50.7	Miaplacidus	221 38.3	S69 46.8
23	110 55.0	139 03.7	13.7	127 47.0	06.5	329 08.4	00.1	229 24.1	50.7			
27 00	125 57.5	154 03.1	S13 12.5	142 47.6	S 8 05.7	344 11.2	N16 00.2	244 26.4	S18 50.7	Mirfak	308 38.5	N49 54.9
01	140 59.9	169 02.6	11.4	157 48.3	04.9	359 13.9	00.3	259 28.6	50.8	Nunki	75 57.3	S26 16.5
02	156 02.4	184 02.1	10.3	172 48.9	04.2	14 16.7	00.4	274 30.9	50.8	Peacock	53 18.2	S56 41.0
03	171 04.9	199 01.6	. . 09.2	187 49.6	. . 03.4	29 19.5	. . 00.5	289 33.2	. . 50.8	Pollux	243 26.0	N27 59.1
04	186 07.3	214 01.0	08.1	202 50.2	02.6	44 22.3	00.6	304 35.5	50.8	Procyon	244 58.2	N 5 10.9
05	201 09.8	229 00.5	07.0	217 50.9	01.9	59 25.0	00.7	319 37.7	50.9			
06	216 12.3	244 00.0	S13 05.9	232 51.5	S 8 01.1	74 27.8	N16 00.8	334 40.0	S18 50.9	Rasalhague	96 05.7	N12 33.0
07	231 14.7	258 59.5	04.8	247 52.2	8 00.3	89 30.6	00.9	349 42.3	50.9	Regulus	207 42.0	N11 53.4
08	246 17.2	273 59.0	03.7	262 52.9	7 59.6	104 33.4	01.0	4 44.6	51.0	Rigel	281 10.7	S 8 11.4
T 09	261 19.7	288 58.4	. . 02.5	277 53.5	. . 58.8	119 36.1	. . 01.1	19 46.8	. . 51.0	Rigil Kent.	139 50.1	S60 53.4
U 10	276 22.1	303 57.9	01.4	292 54.2	58.0	134 38.9	01.2	34 49.1	51.0	Sabik	102 11.5	S15 44.4
E 11	291 24.6	318 57.4	13 00.3	307 54.8	57.2	149 41.7	01.3	49 51.4	51.0			
S 12	306 27.0	333 56.9	S12 59.2	322 55.5	S 7 56.5	164 44.5	N16 01.4	64 53.7	S18 51.1	Schedar	349 39.3	N56 37.4
D 13	321 29.5	348 56.4	58.1	337 56.1	55.7	179 47.3	01.5	79 55.9	51.1	Shaula	96 20.7	S37 06.6
A 14	336 32.0	3 55.8	57.0	352 56.8	54.9	194 50.0	01.6	94 58.2	51.1	Sirius	258 32.4	S16 44.5
Y 15	351 34.4	18 55.3	. . 55.8	7 57.4	. . 54.2	209 52.8	. . 01.7	110 00.5	. . 51.2	Spica	158 30.0	S11 14.4
16	6 36.9	33 54.8	54.7	22 58.1	53.4	224 55.6	01.9	125 02.8	51.2	Suhail	222 51.1	S43 29.8
17	21 39.4	48 54.3	53.6	37 58.8	52.6	239 58.4	02.0	140 05.0	51.2			
18	36 41.8	63 53.8	S12 52.5	52 59.4	S 7 51.9	255 01.2	N16 02.1	155 07.3	S18 51.3	Vega	80 38.6	N38 47.9
19	51 44.3	78 53.3	51.4	68 00.1	51.1	270 03.9	02.2	170 09.6	51.3	Zuben'ubi	137 04.2	S16 06.1
20	66 46.8	93 52.8	50.2	83 00.7	50.3	285 06.7	02.3	185 11.9	51.3		SHA	Mer. Pass.
21	81 49.2	108 52.2	. . 49.1	98 01.4	. . 49.5	300 09.5	. . 02.4	200 14.1	. . 51.3		° ′	h m
22	96 51.7	123 51.7	48.0	113 02.0	48.8	315 12.3	02.5	215 16.4	51.4	Venus	29 17.5	13 43
23	111 54.1	138 51.2	46.9	128 02.7	48.0	330 15.0	02.6	230 18.7	51.4	Mars	17 33.6	14 29
	h m									Jupiter	218 06.2	1 07
Mer. Pass. 15 37.5		v −0.5	d 1.1	v 0.7	d 0.8	v 2.8	d 0.1	v 2.3	d 0.0	Saturn	118 33.5	7 45

UT	SUN GHA	SUN Dec	MOON GHA	v	MOON Dec	d	HP
d h	° ′	° ′	° ′	′	° ′	′	′
25 00	176 58.1	S19 05.4	118 25.9	9.3	N 2 59.9	11.2	59.7
01	191 57.9	04.8	132 54.2	9.3	3 11.1	11.2	59.7
02	206 57.8	04.2	147 22.5	9.4	3 22.3	11.2	59.6
03	221 57.7	.. 03.6	161 50.9	9.3	3 33.5	11.2	59.6
04	236 57.5	03.0	176 19.2	9.4	3 44.7	11.1	59.6
05	251 57.4	02.4	190 47.6	9.4	3 55.8	11.1	59.6
06	266 57.2	S19 01.8	205 16.0	9.5	N 4 06.9	11.1	59.5
07	281 57.1	01.2	219 44.5	9.4	4 18.0	11.0	59.5
08	296 56.9	19 00.6	234 12.9	9.5	4 29.0	11.0	59.5
S 09	311 56.8	18 59.9	248 41.4	9.5	4 40.0	10.9	59.4
U 10	326 56.6	59.3	263 09.9	9.5	4 50.9	10.9	59.4
N 11	341 56.5	58.7	277 38.4	9.5	5 01.8	10.9	59.4
D 12	356 56.3	S18 58.1	292 06.9	9.6	N 5 12.7	10.8	59.3
A 13	11 56.2	57.5	306 35.5	9.5	5 23.5	10.7	59.3
Y 14	26 56.1	56.9	321 04.0	9.6	5 34.2	10.8	59.3
15	41 55.9	.. 56.2	335 32.6	9.6	5 45.0	10.7	59.3
16	56 55.8	55.6	350 01.2	9.6	5 55.7	10.6	59.2
17	71 55.6	55.0	4 29.8	9.6	6 06.3	10.6	59.2
18	86 55.5	S18 54.4	18 58.4	9.7	N 6 16.9	10.5	59.2
19	101 55.3	53.8	33 27.1	9.6	6 27.4	10.5	59.1
20	116 55.2	53.1	47 55.7	9.7	6 37.9	10.5	59.1
21	131 55.1	.. 52.5	62 24.4	9.7	6 48.4	10.4	59.1
22	146 54.9	51.9	76 53.1	9.7	6 58.8	10.3	59.0
23	161 54.8	51.3	91 21.8	9.7	7 09.1	10.3	59.0
26 00	176 54.6	S18 50.7	105 50.5	9.7	N 7 19.4	10.2	59.0
01	191 54.5	50.0	120 19.2	9.7	7 29.6	10.2	58.9
02	206 54.4	49.4	134 47.9	9.8	7 39.8	10.1	58.9
03	221 54.2	.. 48.8	149 16.7	9.7	7 49.9	10.1	58.9
04	236 54.1	48.2	163 45.4	9.8	8 00.0	10.0	58.8
05	251 53.9	47.5	178 14.2	9.7	8 10.0	10.0	58.8
06	266 53.8	S18 46.9	192 42.9	9.8	N 8 20.0	9.9	58.8
07	281 53.7	46.3	207 11.7	9.8	8 29.9	9.8	58.8
08	296 53.5	45.7	221 40.5	9.8	8 39.7	9.8	58.7
M 09	311 53.4	.. 45.0	236 09.3	9.8	8 49.5	9.7	58.7
O 10	326 53.3	44.4	250 38.1	9.8	8 59.2	9.7	58.7
N 11	341 53.1	43.8	265 06.9	9.8	9 08.9	9.5	58.6
D 12	356 53.0	S18 43.1	279 35.7	9.8	N 9 18.4	9.6	58.6
A 13	11 52.8	42.5	294 04.5	9.9	9 28.0	9.4	58.6
Y 14	26 52.7	41.9	308 33.4	9.8	9 37.4	9.4	58.5
15	41 52.6	.. 41.2	323 02.2	9.9	9 46.8	9.4	58.5
16	56 52.4	40.6	337 31.1	9.8	9 56.2	9.2	58.5
17	71 52.3	40.0	351 59.9	9.9	10 05.4	9.2	58.4
18	86 52.2	S18 39.3	6 28.8	9.8	N10 14.6	9.2	58.4
19	101 52.0	38.7	20 57.6	9.9	10 23.8	9.0	58.4
20	116 51.9	38.1	35 26.5	9.8	10 32.8	9.0	58.3
21	131 51.8	.. 37.4	49 55.3	9.9	10 41.8	9.0	58.3
22	146 51.6	36.8	64 24.2	9.9	10 50.8	8.8	58.3
23	161 51.5	36.2	78 53.1	9.9	10 59.6	8.8	58.2
27 00	176 51.4	S18 35.5	93 22.0	9.9	N11 08.4	8.7	58.2
01	191 51.3	34.9	107 50.9	9.9	11 17.1	8.6	58.2
02	206 51.1	34.3	122 19.8	9.8	11 25.7	8.6	58.1
03	221 51.0	.. 33.6	136 48.6	9.9	11 34.3	8.5	58.1
04	236 50.9	33.0	151 17.5	9.9	11 42.8	8.4	58.1
05	251 50.7	32.3	165 46.4	9.9	11 51.2	8.4	58.0
06	266 50.6	S18 31.7	180 15.3	9.9	N11 59.6	8.2	58.0
07	281 50.5	31.1	194 44.2	9.9	12 07.8	8.2	58.0
08	296 50.3	30.4	209 13.1	9.9	12 16.0	8.1	58.0
T 09	311 50.2	.. 29.8	223 42.0	9.9	12 24.1	8.1	57.9
U 10	326 50.1	29.1	238 10.9	9.9	12 32.2	7.9	57.9
E 11	341 50.0	28.5	252 39.8	10.0	12 40.1	7.9	57.9
S 12	356 49.8	S18 27.8	267 08.8	9.9	N12 48.0	7.8	57.8
D 13	11 49.7	27.2	281 37.7	9.9	12 55.8	7.7	57.8
A 14	26 49.6	26.5	296 06.6	9.9	13 03.5	7.7	57.8
Y 15	41 49.5	.. 25.9	310 35.5	9.9	13 11.2	7.5	57.7
16	56 49.3	25.3	325 04.4	9.9	13 18.7	7.5	57.7
17	71 49.2	24.6	339 33.3	9.9	13 26.2	7.4	57.7
18	86 49.1	S18 24.0	354 02.2	9.9	N13 33.6	7.3	57.6
19	101 49.0	23.3	8 31.1	10.0	13 40.9	7.3	57.6
20	116 48.8	22.7	23 00.1	9.9	13 48.2	7.1	57.6
21	131 48.7	.. 22.0	37 29.0	9.9	13 55.3	7.1	57.5
22	146 48.6	21.4	51 57.9	9.9	14 02.4	7.0	57.5
23	161 48.5	20.7	66 26.8	9.9	N14 09.4	6.9	57.5
	SD 16.3	d 0.6	SD 16.2		16.0		15.8

Lat.	Twilight Naut.	Twilight Civil	Sunrise	Moonrise 25	26	27	28
°	h m	h m	h m	h m	h m	h m	h m
N 72	07 31	09 06	11 46	09 29	09 23	09 17	09 10
N 70	07 20	08 43	10 22	09 35	09 36	09 39	09 44
68	07 11	08 25	09 45	09 40	09 47	09 55	10 08
66	07 04	08 10	09 18	09 45	09 56	10 09	10 27
64	06 58	07 58	08 58	09 49	10 03	10 20	10 42
62	06 52	07 48	08 42	09 52	10 10	10 30	10 55
60	06 47	07 39	08 28	09 55	10 15	10 39	11 06
N 58	06 42	07 31	08 16	09 57	10 20	10 46	11 16
56	06 38	07 24	08 06	10 00	10 25	10 52	11 24
54	06 34	07 17	07 57	10 02	10 29	10 58	11 31
52	06 30	07 12	07 49	10 03	10 32	11 03	11 38
50	06 27	07 06	07 42	10 05	10 36	11 08	11 44
45	06 19	06 55	07 27	10 09	10 43	11 19	11 57
N 40	06 12	06 45	07 14	10 12	10 49	11 27	12 08
35	06 06	06 36	07 03	10 15	10 54	11 35	12 17
30	05 59	06 28	06 54	10 17	10 59	11 41	12 26
20	05 47	06 14	06 37	10 22	11 07	11 53	12 40
N 10	05 35	06 00	06 23	10 25	11 14	12 03	12 52
0	05 22	05 47	06 09	10 29	11 21	12 12	13 04
S 10	05 07	05 33	05 55	10 33	11 28	12 22	13 16
20	04 49	05 17	05 40	10 37	11 35	12 32	13 28
30	04 25	04 57	05 23	10 41	11 43	12 44	13 43
35	04 11	04 45	05 13	10 44	11 48	12 51	13 51
40	03 53	04 31	05 01	10 47	11 54	12 59	14 01
45	03 30	04 13	04 47	10 50	12 00	13 08	14 12
S 50	02 59	03 51	04 31	10 54	12 08	13 19	14 26
52	02 43	03 41	04 23	10 56	12 12	13 24	14 32
54	02 23	03 28	04 14	10 58	12 16	13 30	14 39
56	01 57	03 13	04 04	11 01	12 20	13 36	14 47
58	01 17	02 57	03 52	11 03	12 25	13 43	14 56
S 60	////	02 36	03 39	11 06	12 30	13 51	15 06

Lat.	Sunset	Twilight Civil	Twilight Naut.	Moonset 25	26	27	28
°	h m	h m	h m	h m	h m	h m	h m
N 72	12 40	15 20	16 56	24 30	00 30	02 24	04 19
N 70	14 04	15 43	17 06	24 19	00 19	02 04	03 46
68	14 41	16 01	17 15	24 10	00 10	01 48	03 23
66	15 08	16 16	17 22	24 02	00 02	01 36	03 04
64	15 28	16 28	17 28	23 56	25 25	01 25	02 50
62	15 44	16 38	17 34	23 51	25 16	01 16	02 37
60	15 58	16 47	17 39	23 46	25 09	01 09	02 27
N 58	16 09	16 55	17 43	23 42	25 02	01 02	02 18
56	16 19	17 02	17 48	23 38	24 56	00 56	02 10
54	16 28	17 08	17 52	23 35	24 51	00 51	02 03
52	16 36	17 14	17 55	23 32	24 46	00 46	01 57
50	16 43	17 19	17 59	23 29	24 42	00 42	01 51
45	16 59	17 31	18 06	23 24	24 33	00 33	01 39
N 40	17 11	17 40	18 13	23 19	24 25	00 25	01 29
35	17 22	17 49	18 20	23 15	24 18	00 18	01 20
30	17 32	17 57	18 26	23 11	24 12	00 12	01 12
20	17 48	18 11	18 38	23 05	24 02	00 02	00 59
N 10	18 02	18 25	18 50	22 59	23 54	24 48	00 48
0	18 16	18 38	19 03	22 54	23 45	24 37	00 37
S 10	18 30	18 52	19 18	22 48	23 37	24 26	00 26
20	18 45	19 08	19 36	22 43	23 29	24 15	00 15
30	19 02	19 28	19 59	22 37	23 19	24 02	00 02
35	19 12	19 40	20 14	22 33	23 13	23 54	24 38
40	19 23	19 54	20 31	22 29	23 06	23 46	24 28
45	19 37	20 11	20 54	22 24	22 59	23 36	24 16
S 50	19 53	20 32	21 24	22 18	22 50	23 24	24 02
52	20 01	20 43	21 40	22 16	22 46	23 18	23 55
54	20 10	20 55	22 00	22 13	22 41	23 12	23 48
56	20 20	21 09	22 25	22 10	22 36	23 05	23 40
58	20 31	21 26	23 02	22 06	22 30	22 58	23 30
S 60	20 44	21 47	////	22 02	22 24	22 49	23 20

Day	SUN Eqn. of Time 00ʰ	SUN Eqn. of Time 12ʰ	SUN Mer. Pass.	MOON Mer. Pass. Upper	MOON Mer. Pass. Lower	Age	Phase
d	m s	m s	h m	h m	h m	d	%
25	12 07	12 14	12 12	16 41	04 15	05	32
26	12 21	12 28	12 12	17 33	05 07	06	42
27	12 34	12 40	12 13	18 25	05 59	07	53

UT	ARIES GHA	VENUS −3.9 GHA	Dec	MARS +1.2 GHA	Dec	JUPITER −2.6 GHA	Dec	SATURN +0.5 GHA	Dec	STARS Name	SHA	Dec
28 00	126 56.6	153 50.7	S12 45.8	143 03.3	S 7 47.2	345 17.8	N16 02.7	245 21.0	S18 51.4	Acamar	315 17.5	S40 15.1
01	141 59.1	168 50.2	44.6	158 04.0	46.5	0 20.6	02.8	260 23.3	51.5	Achernar	335 26.2	S57 10.0
02	157 01.5	183 49.7	43.5	173 04.7	45.7	15 23.4	02.9	275 25.5	51.5	Acrux	173 07.5	S63 10.8
03	172 04.0	198 49.2	.. 42.4	188 05.3	.. 44.9	30 26.2	.. 03.0	290 27.8	.. 51.5	Adhara	255 11.3	S28 59.9
04	187 06.5	213 48.7	41.3	203 06.0	44.2	45 28.9	03.1	305 30.1	51.5	Aldebaran	290 47.9	N16 32.2
05	202 08.9	228 48.1	40.1	218 06.6	43.4	60 31.7	03.2	320 32.4	51.6			
06	217 11.4	243 47.6	S12 39.0	233 07.3	S 7 42.6	75 34.5	N16 03.3	335 34.6	S18 51.6	Alioth	166 19.6	N55 52.4
W 07	232 13.9	258 47.1	37.9	248 07.9	41.8	90 37.3	03.4	350 36.9	51.6	Alkaid	152 58.0	N49 14.0
E 08	247 16.3	273 46.6	36.8	263 08.6	41.1	105 40.1	03.5	5 39.2	51.7	Al Na'ir	27 42.8	S46 53.3
D 09	262 18.8	288 46.1	.. 35.6	278 09.3	.. 40.3	120 42.8	.. 03.7	20 41.5	.. 51.7	Alnilam	275 45.0	S 1 11.8
N 10	277 21.3	303 45.6	34.5	293 09.9	39.5	135 45.6	03.8	35 43.8	51.7	Alphard	217 54.7	S 8 43.7
E 11	292 23.7	318 45.1	33.4	308 10.6	38.8	150 48.4	03.9	50 46.0	51.7			
S 12	307 26.2	333 44.6	S12 32.2	323 11.2	S 7 38.0	165 51.2	N16 04.0	65 48.3	S18 51.8	Alphecca	126 10.2	N26 39.8
D 13	322 28.6	348 44.1	31.1	338 11.9	37.2	180 54.0	04.1	80 50.6	51.8	Alpheratz	357 42.5	N29 10.5
A 14	337 31.1	3 43.6	30.0	353 12.6	36.4	195 56.7	04.2	95 52.9	51.8	Altair	62 07.5	N 8 54.6
Y 15	352 33.6	18 43.1	.. 28.8	8 13.2	.. 35.7	210 59.5	.. 04.3	110 55.1	.. 51.8	Ankaa	353 14.9	S42 13.7
16	7 36.0	33 42.6	27.7	23 13.9	34.9	226 02.3	04.4	125 57.4	51.9	Antares	112 25.0	S26 27.7
17	22 38.5	48 42.1	26.6	38 14.5	34.1	241 05.1	04.5	140 59.7	51.9			
18	37 41.0	63 41.6	S12 25.4	53 15.2	S 7 33.4	256 07.9	N16 04.6	156 02.0	S18 51.9	Arcturus	145 54.7	N19 06.1
19	52 43.4	78 41.1	24.3	68 15.9	32.6	271 10.7	04.7	171 04.3	52.0	Atria	107 26.2	S69 02.8
20	67 45.9	93 40.6	23.2	83 16.5	31.8	286 13.4	04.8	186 06.5	52.0	Avior	234 16.8	S59 33.7
21	82 48.4	108 40.1	.. 22.0	98 17.2	.. 31.0	301 16.2	.. 04.9	201 08.8	.. 52.0	Bellatrix	278 30.6	N 6 21.5
22	97 50.8	123 39.6	20.9	113 17.8	30.3	316 19.0	05.0	216 11.1	52.0	Betelgeuse	270 59.8	N 7 24.3
23	112 53.3	138 39.1	19.8	128 18.5	29.5	331 21.8	05.1	231 13.4	52.1			
29 00	127 55.8	153 38.6	S12 18.6	143 19.2	S 7 28.7	346 24.6	N16 05.2	246 15.7	S18 52.1	Canopus	263 55.2	S52 42.6
01	142 58.2	168 38.1	17.5	158 19.8	27.9	1 27.3	05.4	261 17.9	52.1	Capella	280 32.4	N46 00.7
02	158 00.7	183 37.6	16.4	173 20.5	27.2	16 30.1	05.5	276 20.2	52.2	Deneb	49 31.1	N45 20.2
03	173 03.1	198 37.1	.. 15.2	188 21.1	.. 26.4	31 32.9	.. 05.6	291 22.5	.. 52.2	Denebola	182 32.3	N14 29.1
04	188 05.6	213 36.6	14.1	203 21.8	25.6	46 35.7	05.7	306 24.8	52.2	Diphda	348 54.9	S17 54.4
05	203 08.1	228 36.1	12.9	218 22.5	24.9	61 38.5	05.8	321 27.1	52.2			
06	218 10.5	243 35.6	S12 11.8	233 23.1	S 7 24.1	76 41.3	N16 05.9	336 29.4	S18 52.3	Dubhe	193 49.9	N61 39.9
T 07	233 13.0	258 35.1	10.7	248 23.8	23.3	91 44.0	06.0	351 31.6	52.3	Elnath	278 10.9	N28 37.0
H 08	248 15.5	273 34.6	09.5	263 24.4	22.5	106 46.8	06.1	6 33.9	52.3	Eltanin	90 46.0	N51 29.2
U 09	263 17.9	288 34.1	.. 08.4	278 25.1	.. 21.8	121 49.6	.. 06.2	21 36.2	.. 52.3	Enif	33 46.3	N 9 56.7
R 10	278 20.4	303 33.6	07.2	293 25.8	21.0	136 52.4	06.3	36 38.5	52.4	Fomalhaut	15 23.1	S29 32.6
S 11	293 22.9	318 33.1	06.1	308 26.4	20.2	151 55.2	06.4	51 40.8	52.4			
D 12	308 25.3	333 32.6	S12 04.9	323 27.1	S 7 19.4	166 57.9	N16 06.5	66 43.0	S18 52.5	Gacrux	171 59.2	S57 11.7
A 13	323 27.8	348 32.1	03.8	338 27.7	18.7	182 00.7	06.6	81 45.3	52.5	Gienah	175 50.9	S17 37.6
Y 14	338 30.3	3 31.6	02.7	353 28.4	17.9	197 03.5	06.7	96 47.6	52.5	Hadar	148 46.1	S60 26.4
15	353 32.7	18 31.1	.. 01.5	8 29.1	.. 17.1	212 06.3	.. 06.8	111 49.9	.. 52.5	Hamal	327 59.5	N23 32.0
16	8 35.2	33 30.6	12 00.4	23 29.7	16.3	227 09.1	06.9	126 52.2	52.5	Kaus Aust.	83 42.7	S34 22.4
17	23 37.6	48 30.1	11 59.2	38 30.4	15.6	242 11.9	07.1	141 54.5	52.6			
18	38 40.1	63 29.6	S11 58.1	53 31.1	S 7 14.8	257 14.6	N16 07.2	156 56.7	S18 52.6	Kochab	137 20.4	N74 05.4
19	53 42.6	78 29.1	56.9	68 31.7	14.0	272 17.4	07.3	171 59.0	52.6	Markab	13 37.5	N15 17.2
20	68 45.0	93 28.6	55.8	83 32.4	13.2	287 20.2	07.4	187 01.3	52.6	Menkar	314 13.8	N 4 08.7
21	83 47.5	108 28.2	.. 54.6	98 33.0	.. 12.5	302 23.0	.. 07.5	202 03.6	.. 52.7	Menkent	148 06.2	S36 26.4
22	98 50.0	123 27.7	53.5	113 33.7	11.7	317 25.8	07.6	217 05.9	52.7	Miaplacidus	221 38.3	S69 46.9
23	113 52.4	138 27.2	52.3	128 34.4	10.9	332 28.6	07.7	232 08.2	52.7			
30 00	128 54.9	153 26.7	S11 51.2	143 35.0	S 7 10.1	347 31.3	N16 07.8	247 10.4	S18 52.8	Mirfak	308 38.5	N49 54.9
01	143 57.4	168 26.2	50.0	158 35.7	09.4	2 34.1	07.9	262 12.7	52.8	Nunki	75 57.3	S26 16.5
02	158 59.8	183 25.7	48.9	173 36.4	08.6	17 36.9	08.0	277 15.0	52.8	Peacock	53 18.2	S56 41.0
03	174 02.3	198 25.2	.. 47.7	188 37.0	.. 07.8	32 39.7	.. 08.1	292 17.3	.. 52.8	Pollux	243 26.0	N27 59.1
04	189 04.7	213 24.7	46.6	203 37.7	07.0	47 42.5	08.2	307 19.6	52.9	Procyon	244 58.2	N 5 10.9
05	204 07.2	228 24.3	45.4	218 38.4	06.3	62 45.3	08.3	322 21.9	52.9			
06	219 09.7	243 23.8	S11 44.3	233 39.0	S 7 05.5	77 48.1	N16 08.4	337 24.1	S18 52.9	Rasalhague	96 05.7	N12 33.0
07	234 12.1	258 23.3	43.1	248 39.7	04.7	92 50.8	08.5	352 26.4	52.9	Regulus	207 42.0	N11 53.4
F 08	249 14.6	273 22.8	42.0	263 40.3	03.9	107 53.6	08.7	7 28.7	53.0	Rigel	281 10.8	S 8 11.4
R 09	264 17.1	288 22.3	.. 40.8	278 41.0	.. 03.2	122 56.4	.. 08.8	22 31.0	.. 53.0	Rigil Kent.	139 50.1	S60 53.4
I 10	279 19.5	303 21.8	39.7	293 41.7	02.4	137 59.2	08.9	37 33.3	53.0	Sabik	102 11.5	S15 44.4
D 11	294 22.0	318 21.3	38.5	308 42.3	01.6	153 02.0	09.0	52 35.6	53.1			
A 12	309 24.5	333 20.9	S11 37.3	323 43.0	S 7 00.8	168 04.8	N16 09.1	67 37.9	S18 53.1	Schedar	349 39.4	N56 37.4
Y 13	324 26.9	348 20.4	36.2	338 43.7	7 00.1	183 07.5	09.2	82 40.1	53.1	Shaula	96 20.7	S37 06.6
14	339 29.4	3 19.9	35.0	353 44.3	6 59.3	198 10.3	09.3	97 42.4	53.1	Sirius	258 32.4	S16 44.6
15	354 31.9	18 19.4	.. 33.9	8 45.0	.. 58.5	213 13.1	.. 09.4	112 44.7	.. 53.2	Spica	158 30.0	S11 14.4
16	9 34.3	33 18.9	32.7	23 45.7	57.7	228 15.9	09.5	127 47.0	53.2	Suhail	222 51.1	S43 29.8
17	24 36.8	48 18.5	31.6	38 46.3	57.0	243 18.7	09.6	142 49.3	53.2			
18	39 39.2	63 18.0	S11 30.4	53 47.0	S 6 56.2	258 21.5	N16 09.7	157 51.6	S18 53.2	Vega	80 38.6	N38 47.9
19	54 41.7	78 17.5	29.2	68 47.7	55.4	273 24.3	09.8	172 53.9	53.3	Zuben'ubi	137 04.2	S16 06.1
20	69 44.2	93 17.0	28.1	83 48.3	54.6	288 27.0	09.9	187 56.2	53.3		SHA	Mer. Pass.
21	84 46.6	108 16.5	.. 26.9	98 49.0	.. 53.8	303 29.8	.. 10.0	202 58.4	.. 53.3		° '	h m
22	99 49.1	123 16.1	25.7	113 49.7	53.1	318 32.6	10.1	218 00.7	53.3	Venus	25 42.8	13 46
23	114 51.6	138 15.6	24.6	128 50.3	52.3	333 35.4	10.3	233 03.0	53.4	Mars	15 23.4	14 26
Mer. Pass.	h m 15 25.7	v −0.5	d 1.1	v 0.7	d 0.8	v 2.8	d 0.1	v 2.3	d 0.0	Jupiter	218 28.8	0 54
										Saturn	118 19.9	7 34

INDEX TO SELECTED STARS, 2015

Name	No	Mag	SHA	Dec		No	Name	Mag	SHA	Dec
			°	°					°	°
Acamar	7	3·2	315	S 40		1	Alpheratz	2·1	358	N 29
Achernar	5	0·5	335	S 57		2	Ankaa	2·4	353	S 42
Acrux	30	1·3	173	S 63		3	Schedar	2·2	350	N 57
Adhara	19	1·5	255	S 29		4	Diphda	2·0	349	S 18
Aldebaran	10	0·9	291	N 17		5	Achernar	0·5	335	S 57
Alioth	32	1·8	166	N 56		6	Hamal	2·0	328	N 24
Alkaid	34	1·9	153	N 49		7	Acamar	3·2	315	S 40
Al Na'ir	55	1·7	28	S 47		8	Menkar	2·5	314	N 4
Alnilam	15	1·7	276	S 1		9	Mirfak	1·8	309	N 50
Alphard	25	2·0	218	S 9		10	Aldebaran	0·9	291	N 17
Alphecca	41	2·2	126	N 27		11	Rigel	0·1	281	S 8
Alpheratz	1	2·1	358	N 29		12	Capella	0·1	281	N 46
Altair	51	0·8	62	N 9		13	Bellatrix	1·6	279	N 6
Ankaa	2	2·4	353	S 42		14	Elnath	1·7	278	N 29
Antares	42	1·0	112	S 26		15	Alnilam	1·7	276	S 1
Arcturus	37	0·0	146	N 19		16	Betelgeuse	Var.*	271	N 7
Atria	43	1·9	107	S 69		17	Canopus	−0·7	264	S 53
Avior	22	1·9	234	S 60		18	Sirius	−1·5	259	S 17
Bellatrix	13	1·6	279	N 6		19	Adhara	1·5	255	S 29
Betelgeuse	16	Var.*	271	N 7		20	Procyon	0·4	245	N 5
Canopus	17	−0·7	264	S 53		21	Pollux	1·1	243	N 28
Capella	12	0·1	281	N 46		22	Avior	1·9	234	S 60
Deneb	53	1·3	50	N 45		23	Suhail	2·2	223	S 43
Denebola	28	2·1	183	N 14		24	Miaplacidus	1·7	222	S 70
Diphda	4	2·0	349	S 18		25	Alphard	2·0	218	S 9
Dubhe	27	1·8	194	N 62		26	Regulus	1·4	208	N 12
Elnath	14	1·7	278	N 29		27	Dubhe	1·8	194	N 62
Eltanin	47	2·2	91	N 51		28	Denebola	2·1	183	N 14
Enif	54	2·4	34	N 10		29	Gienah	2·6	176	S 18
Fomalhaut	56	1·2	15	S 30		30	Acrux	1·3	173	S 63
Gacrux	31	1·6	172	S 57		31	Gacrux	1·6	172	S 57
Gienah	29	2·6	176	S 18		32	Alioth	1·8	166	N 56
Hadar	35	0·6	149	S 60		33	Spica	1·0	158	S 11
Hamal	6	2·0	328	N 24		34	Alkaid	1·9	153	N 49
Kaus Australis	48	1·9	84	S 34		35	Hadar	0·6	149	S 60
Kochab	40	2·1	137	N 74		36	Menkent	2·1	148	S 36
Markab	57	2·5	14	N 15		37	Arcturus	0·0	146	N 19
Menkar	8	2·5	314	N 4		38	Rigil Kentaurus	−0·3	140	S 61
Menkent	36	2·1	148	S 36		39	Zubenelgenubi	2·8	137	S 16
Miaplacidus	24	1·7	222	S 70		40	Kochab	2·1	137	N 74
Mirfak	9	1·8	309	N 50		41	Alphecca	2·2	126	N 27
Nunki	50	2·0	76	S 26		42	Antares	1·0	112	S 26
Peacock	52	1·9	53	S 57		43	Atria	1·9	107	S 69
Pollux	21	1·1	243	N 28		44	Sabik	2·4	102	S 16
Procyon	20	0·4	245	N 5		45	Shaula	1·6	96	S 37
Rasalhague	46	2·1	96	N 13		46	Rasalhague	2·1	96	N 13
Regulus	26	1·4	208	N 12		47	Eltanin	2·2	91	N 51
Rigel	11	0·1	281	S 8		48	Kaus Australis	1·9	84	S 34
Rigil Kentaurus	38	−0·3	140	S 61		49	Vega	0·0	81	N 39
Sabik	44	2·4	102	S 16		50	Nunki	2·0	76	S 26
Schedar	3	2·2	350	N 57		51	Altair	0·8	62	N 9
Shaula	45	1·6	96	S 37		52	Peacock	1·9	53	S 57
Sirius	18	−1·5	259	S 17		53	Deneb	1·3	50	N 45
Spica	33	1·0	158	S 11		54	Enif	2·4	34	N 10
Suhail	23	2·2	223	S 43		55	Al Na'ir	1·7	28	S 47
Vega	49	0·0	81	N 39		56	Fomalhaut	1·2	15	S 30
Zubenelgenubi	39	2·8	137	S 16		57	Markab	2·5	14	N 15

*0·1 — 1·2

ALTITUDE CORRECTION TABLES 10°–90°—SUN, STARS, PLANETS

OCT.–MAR. SUN APR.–SEPT.

App. Alt.	Lower Limb	Upper Limb	App. Alt.	Lower Limb	Upper Limb
9 33	+10·8	−21·5	9 39	+10·6	−21·2
9 45	+10·9	−21·4	9 50	+10·7	−21·1
9 56	+11·0	−21·3	10 02	+10·8	−21·0
10 08	+11·1	−21·2	10 14	+10·9	−20·9
10 20	+11·2	−21·1	10 27	+11·0	−20·8
10 33	+11·3	−21·0	10 40	+11·1	−20·7
10 46	+11·4	−20·9	10 53	+11·2	−20·6
11 00	+11·5	−20·8	11 07	+11·3	−20·5
11 15	+11·6	−20·7	11 22	+11·4	−20·4
11 30	+11·7	−20·6	11 37	+11·5	−20·3
11 45	+11·8	−20·5	11 53	+11·6	−20·2
12 01	+11·9	−20·4	12 10	+11·7	−20·1
12 18	+12·0	−20·3	12 27	+11·8	−20·0
12 36	+12·1	−20·2	12 45	+11·9	−19·9
12 54	+12·2	−20·1	13 04	+12·0	−19·8
13 14	+12·3	−20·0	13 24	+12·1	−19·7
13 34	+12·4	−19·9	13 44	+12·2	−19·6
13 55	+12·5	−19·8	14 06	+12·3	−19·5
14 17	+12·6	−19·7	14 29	+12·4	−19·4
14 41	+12·7	−19·6	14 53	+12·5	−19·3
15 05	+12·8	−19·5	15 18	+12·6	−19·2
15 31	+12·9	−19·4	15 45	+12·7	−19·1
15 59	+13·0	−19·3	16 13	+12·8	−19·0
16 27	+13·1	−19·2	16 43	+12·9	−18·9
16 58	+13·2	−19·1	17 14	+13·0	−18·8
17 30	+13·3	−19·0	17 47	+13·1	−18·7
18 05	+13·4	−18·9	18 23	+13·2	−18·6
18 41	+13·5	−18·8	19 00	+13·3	−18·5
19 20	+13·6	−18·7	19 41	+13·4	−18·4
20 02	+13·7	−18·6	20 24	+13·5	−18·3
20 46	+13·8	−18·5	21 10	+13·6	−18·2
21 34	+13·9	−18·4	21 59	+13·7	−18·1
22 25	+14·0	−18·3	22 52	+13·8	−18·0
23 20	+14·1	−18·2	23 49	+13·9	−17·9
24 20	+14·2	−18·1	24 51	+14·0	−17·8
25 24	+14·3	−18·0	25 58	+14·1	−17·7
26 34	+14·4	−17·9	27 11	+14·2	−17·6
27 50	+14·5	−17·8	28 31	+14·3	−17·5
29 13	+14·6	−17·7	29 58	+14·4	−17·4
30 44	+14·7	−17·6	31 33	+14·5	−17·3
32 24	+14·8	−17·5	33 18	+14·6	−17·2
34 15	+14·9	−17·4	35 15	+14·7	−17·1
36 17	+15·0	−17·3	37 24	+14·8	−17·0
38 34	+15·1	−17·2	39 48	+14·9	−16·9
41 06	+15·2	−17·1	42 28	+15·0	−16·8
43 56	+15·3	−17·0	45 29	+15·1	−16·7
47 07	+15·4	−16·9	48 52	+15·2	−16·6
50 43	+15·5	−16·8	52 41	+15·3	−16·5
54 46	+15·6	−16·7	56 59	+15·4	−16·4
59 21	+15·7	−16·6	61 50	+15·5	−16·3
64 28	+15·8	−16·5	67 15	+15·6	−16·2
70 10	+15·9	−16·4	73 14	+15·7	−16·1
76 24	+16·0	−16·3	79 42	+15·8	−16·0
83 05	+16·1	−16·2	86 31	+15·9	−15·9
90 00			90 00		

STARS AND PLANETS

App Alt	Corrn
9 55	−5·3
10 07	−5·2
10 20	−5·1
10 32	−5·0
10 46	−4·9
10 59	−4·8
11 14	−4·7
11 29	−4·6
11 44	−4·5
12 00	−4·4
12 17	−4·3
12 35	−4·2
12 53	−4·1
13 12	−4·0
13 32	−3·9
13 53	−3·8
14 16	−3·7
14 39	−3·6
15 03	−3·5
15 29	−3·4
15 56	−3·3
16 25	−3·2
16 55	−3·1
17 27	−3·0
18 01	−2·9
18 37	−2·8
19 16	−2·7
19 56	−2·6
20 40	−2·5
21 27	−2·4
22 17	−2·3
23 11	−2·2
24 09	−2·1
25 12	−2·0
26 20	−1·9
27 34	−1·8
28 54	−1·7
30 22	−1·6
31 58	−1·5
33 43	−1·4
35 38	−1·3
37 45	−1·2
40 06	−1·1
42 42	−1·0
45 34	−0·9
48 45	−0·8
52 16	−0·7
56 09	−0·6
60 26	−0·5
65 06	−0·4
70 09	−0·3
75 32	−0·2
81 12	−0·1
87 03	0·0
90 00	

App. Alt. Additional Corrn

2015

VENUS

Jan. 1–May 3
Dec. 4–Dec. 31

App. Alt.	Additional Corrn
60	+0·1

May 4–June 22
Oct. 13–Dec. 3

App. Alt.	Additional Corrn
41	+0·2
76	+0·1

June 23–July 14
Sept. 19–Oct. 12

App. Alt.	Additional Corrn
34	+0·3
60	+0·2
80	+0·1

July 15–July 30
Sept. 2–Sept. 18

App. Alt.	Additional Corrn
29	+0·4
51	+0·3
68	+0·2
83	+0·1

July 31–Sept. 1

App. Alt.	Additional Corrn
26	+0·5
46	+0·4
60	+0·3
73	+0·2
84	+0·1

MARS

Jan. 1–Dec. 31

App. Alt.	Additional Corrn
60	+0·1

DIP

Ht. of Eye (m)	Corrn	Ht. of Eye (ft.)	Ht. of Eye	Corrn
2·4	−2·8	8·0	1·0	− 1·8
2·6	−2·9	8·6	1·5	− 2·2
2·8	−3·0	9·2	2·0	− 2·5
3·0	−3·1	9·8	2·5	− 2·8
3·2	−3·2	10·5	3·0	− 3·0
3·4	−3·3	11·2	See table ←	
3·6	−3·4	11·9	m	
3·8	−3·5	12·6	20	− 7·9
4·0	−3·6	13·3	22	− 8·3
4·3	−3·7	14·1	24	− 8·6
4·5	−3·8	14·9	26	− 9·0
4·7	−3·9	15·7	28	− 9·3
5·0	−4·0	16·5		
5·2	−4·1	17·4	30	− 9·6
5·5	−4·2	18·3	32	− 10·0
5·8	−4·3	19·1	34	− 10·3
6·1	−4·4	20·1	36	− 10·6
6·3	−4·5	21·0	38	− 10·8
6·6	−4·6	22·0		
6·9	−4·7	22·9	40	− 11·1
7·2	−4·8	23·9	42	− 11·4
7·5	−4·9	24·9	44	− 11·7
7·9	−5·0	26·0	46	− 11·9
8·2	−5·1	27·1	48	− 12·2
8·5	−5·2	28·1	ft.	
8·8	−5·3	29·2	2	− 1·4
9·2	−5·4	30·4	4	− 1·9
9·5	−5·5	31·5	6	− 2·4
9·9	−5·6	32·7	8	− 2·7
10·3	−5·7	33·9	10	− 3·1
10·6	−5·8	35·1	See table ←	
11·0	−5·9	36·3	ft.	
11·4	−6·0	37·6	70	− 8·1
11·8	−6·1	38·9	75	− 8·4
12·2	−6·2	40·1	80	− 8·7
12·6	−6·3	41·5	85	− 8·9
13·0	−6·4	42·8	90	− 9·2
13·4	−6·5	44·2	95	− 9·5
13·8	−6·6	45·5	100	− 9·7
14·2	−6·7	46·9	105	− 9·9
14·7	−6·8	48·4	110	− 10·2
15·1	−6·9	49·8	115	− 10·4
15·5	−7·0	51·3	120	− 10·6
16·0	−7·1	52·8	125	− 10·8
16·5	−7·2	54·3	130	− 11·1
16·9	−7·3	55·8	135	− 11·3
17·4	−7·4	57·4	140	− 11·5
17·9	−7·5	58·9	145	− 11·7
18·4	−7·6	60·5	150	− 11·9
18·8	−7·7	62·1	155	− 12·1
19·3	−7·8	63·8		
19·8	−7·9	65·4		
20·4	−8·0	67·1		
20·9	−8·1	68·8		
21·4		70·5		

App. Alt. = Apparent altitude = Sextant altitude corrected for index error and dip.

SUN and MOON

UT	SUN GHA	SUN Dec	MOON GHA	v	MOON Dec	d	HP
d h	° ′	° ′	° ′	′	° ′	′	′
28 00	176 48.3	S18 20.1	80 55.7	9.9	N14 16.3	6.8	57.5
01	191 48.2	19.4	95 24.6	9.9	14 23.1	6.7	57.4
02	206 48.1	18.8	109 53.5	10.0	14 29.8	6.6	57.4
03	221 48.0	.. 18.1	124 22.5	9.9	14 36.4	6.6	57.4
04	236 47.8	17.5	138 51.4	9.9	14 43.0	6.4	57.3
05	251 47.7	16.8	153 20.3	9.9	14 49.4	6.4	57.3
06	266 47.6	S18 16.1	167 49.2	9.9	N14 55.8	6.3	57.3
W 07	281 47.5	15.5	182 18.1	10.0	15 02.1	6.2	57.2
E 08	296 47.4	14.8	196 47.1	9.9	15 08.3	6.1	57.2
D 09	311 47.2	.. 14.2	211 16.0	9.9	15 14.4	6.1	57.2
N 10	326 47.1	13.5	225 44.9	9.9	15 20.5	5.9	57.2
E 11	341 47.0	12.9	240 13.8	10.0	15 26.4	5.8	57.1
S 12	356 46.9	S18 12.2	254 42.8	9.9	N15 32.2	5.8	57.1
D 13	11 46.8	11.6	269 11.7	9.9	15 38.0	5.7	57.1
A 14	26 46.7	10.9	283 40.6	9.9	15 43.7	5.5	57.0
Y 15	41 46.5	.. 10.2	298 09.5	10.0	15 49.2	5.5	57.0
16	56 46.4	09.6	312 38.5	9.9	15 54.7	5.4	57.0
17	71 46.3	08.9	327 07.4	9.9	16 00.1	5.3	57.0
18	86 46.2	S18 08.3	341 36.3	10.0	N16 05.4	5.2	56.9
19	101 46.1	07.6	356 05.3	9.9	16 10.6	5.1	56.9
20	116 46.0	06.9	10 34.2	9.9	16 15.7	5.1	56.9
21	131 45.8	.. 06.3	25 03.1	10.0	16 20.8	4.9	56.8
22	146 45.7	05.6	39 32.1	9.9	16 25.7	4.8	56.8
23	161 45.6	04.9	54 01.0	10.0	16 30.5	4.8	56.8
29 00	176 45.5	S18 04.3	68 30.0	9.9	N16 35.3	4.6	56.8
01	191 45.4	03.6	82 58.9	10.0	16 39.9	4.6	56.7
02	206 45.3	02.9	97 27.9	9.9	16 44.5	4.5	56.7
03	221 45.2	.. 02.3	111 56.8	10.0	16 49.0	4.3	56.7
04	236 45.0	01.6	126 25.8	10.0	16 53.3	4.3	56.7
05	251 44.9	00.9	140 54.8	9.9	16 57.6	4.2	56.6
06	266 44.8	S18 00.3	155 23.7	10.0	N17 01.8	4.1	56.6
T 07	281 44.7	17 59.6	169 52.7	10.0	17 05.9	4.0	56.6
H 08	296 44.6	58.9	184 21.7	10.0	17 09.9	3.9	56.5
U 09	311 44.5	.. 58.3	198 50.7	10.0	17 13.8	3.8	56.5
R 10	326 44.4	57.6	213 19.7	10.0	17 17.6	3.7	56.5
S 11	341 44.3	56.9	227 48.7	10.0	17 21.3	3.6	56.5
D 12	356 44.2	S17 56.3	242 17.7	10.0	N17 24.9	3.5	56.4
A 13	11 44.0	55.6	256 46.7	10.0	17 28.4	3.4	56.4
Y 14	26 43.9	54.9	271 15.7	10.0	17 31.8	3.3	56.4
15	41 43.8	.. 54.2	285 44.7	10.0	17 35.1	3.3	56.4
16	56 43.7	53.6	300 13.7	10.1	17 38.4	3.1	56.3
17	71 43.6	52.9	314 42.8	10.0	17 41.5	3.0	56.3
18	86 43.5	S17 52.2	329 11.8	10.1	N17 44.5	3.0	56.3
19	101 43.4	51.5	343 40.9	10.0	17 47.5	2.8	56.3
20	116 43.3	50.9	358 09.9	10.1	17 50.3	2.8	56.2
21	131 43.2	.. 50.2	12 39.0	10.1	17 53.1	2.6	56.2
22	146 43.1	49.5	27 08.1	10.1	17 55.7	2.6	56.2
23	161 43.0	48.8	41 37.2	10.1	17 58.3	2.4	56.2
30 00	176 42.9	S17 48.2	56 06.3	10.1	N18 00.7	2.4	56.1
01	191 42.8	47.5	70 35.4	10.1	18 03.1	2.2	56.1
02	206 42.7	46.8	85 04.5	10.2	18 05.3	2.2	56.1
03	221 42.5	.. 46.1	99 33.7	10.1	18 07.5	2.1	56.1
04	236 42.4	45.4	114 02.8	10.2	18 09.6	1.9	56.0
05	251 42.3	44.8	128 32.0	10.2	18 11.5	1.9	56.0
06	266 42.2	S17 44.1	143 01.2	10.2	N18 13.4	1.8	56.0
07	281 42.1	43.4	157 30.4	10.2	18 15.2	1.7	56.0
08	296 42.0	42.7	171 59.6	10.2	18 16.9	1.5	56.0
F 09	311 41.9	.. 42.0	186 28.8	10.2	18 18.4	1.5	55.9
R 10	326 41.8	41.3	200 58.0	10.2	18 19.9	1.4	55.9
I 11	341 41.7	40.7	215 27.2	10.3	18 21.3	1.3	55.9
D 12	356 41.6	S17 40.0	229 56.5	10.3	N18 22.6	1.2	55.9
A 13	11 41.5	39.3	244 25.8	10.3	18 23.8	1.1	55.8
Y 14	26 41.4	38.6	258 55.1	10.3	18 24.9	1.0	55.8
15	41 41.3	.. 37.9	273 24.4	10.3	18 25.9	0.9	55.8
16	56 41.2	37.2	287 53.7	10.4	18 26.8	0.8	55.8
17	71 41.1	36.5	302 23.1	10.3	18 27.6	0.7	55.8
18	86 41.0	S17 35.9	316 52.4	10.4	N18 28.3	0.7	55.7
19	101 40.9	35.2	331 21.8	10.4	18 29.0	0.5	55.7
20	116 40.8	34.5	345 51.2	10.4	18 29.5	0.4	55.7
21	131 40.7	.. 33.8	0 20.6	10.5	18 29.9	0.3	55.7
22	146 40.6	33.1	14 50.1	10.4	18 30.2	0.3	55.6
23	161 40.5	32.4	29 19.5	10.5	N18 30.5	0.1	55.6
SD	16.3	d 0.7	SD	15.6	15.4		15.2

Twilight / Sunrise / Moonrise

Lat.	Naut.	Civil	Sunrise	Moonrise 28	29	30	31
°	h m	h m	h m	h m	h m	h m	h m
N 72	07 21	08 53	10 58	09 10	08 59	☐	☐
N 70	07 12	08 32	10 04	09 44	09 54	10 18	11 05
68	07 04	08 16	09 32	10 08	10 28	11 00	11 49
66	06 57	08 02	09 08	10 27	10 52	11 28	12 18
64	06 52	07 51	08 49	10 42	11 11	11 50	12 40
62	06 46	07 41	08 34	10 55	11 27	12 07	12 57
60	06 42	07 33	08 21	11 06	11 40	12 22	13 12
N 58	06 38	07 26	08 11	11 16	11 51	12 34	13 24
56	06 34	07 19	08 01	11 24	12 01	12 45	13 35
54	06 30	07 13	07 53	11 31	12 10	12 54	13 44
52	06 27	07 08	07 45	11 38	12 18	13 02	13 53
50	06 24	07 03	07 38	11 44	12 25	13 10	14 01
45	06 17	06 52	07 24	11 57	12 40	13 26	14 17
N 40	06 10	06 43	07 12	12 08	12 52	13 39	14 30
35	06 04	06 34	07 01	12 17	13 03	13 51	14 41
30	05 58	06 27	06 52	12 26	13 12	14 01	14 51
20	05 47	06 13	06 36	12 40	13 28	14 18	15 08
N 10	05 35	06 01	06 23	12 52	13 42	14 32	15 23
0	05 22	05 48	06 10	13 04	13 55	14 46	15 37
S 10	05 08	05 34	05 56	13 16	14 09	15 00	15 51
20	04 51	05 19	05 42	13 28	14 23	15 15	16 05
30	04 29	05 00	05 26	13 43	14 39	15 32	16 22
35	04 14	04 48	05 16	13 51	14 48	15 42	16 32
40	03 57	04 35	05 05	14 01	14 59	15 54	16 44
45	03 35	04 18	04 52	14 12	15 12	16 07	16 57
S 50	03 06	03 57	04 36	14 26	15 28	16 24	17 13
52	02 51	03 47	04 28	14 32	15 35	16 31	17 21
54	02 32	03 35	04 20	14 39	15 43	16 40	17 29
56	02 09	03 22	04 10	14 47	15 52	16 50	17 39
58	01 37	03 06	04 00	14 56	16 03	17 01	17 49
S 60	////	02 46	03 47	15 06	16 15	17 13	18 02

Sunset / Twilight / Moonset

Lat.	Sunset	Civil	Naut.	Moonset 28	29	30	31
°	h m	h m	h m	h m	h m	h m	h m
N 72	13 29	15 34	17 07	04 19	06 17	☐	☐
N 70	14 23	15 55	17 16	03 46	05 23	06 46	07 44
68	14 56	16 12	17 23	03 23	04 50	06 04	07 00
66	15 19	16 25	17 30	03 04	04 26	05 36	06 31
64	15 38	16 36	17 36	02 50	04 07	05 14	06 09
62	15 53	16 46	17 41	02 37	03 52	04 57	05 51
60	16 05	16 54	17 45	02 27	03 39	04 43	05 37
N 58	16 16	17 01	17 49	02 18	03 28	04 31	05 24
56	16 26	17 08	17 53	02 10	03 18	04 20	05 13
54	16 34	17 13	17 57	02 03	03 10	04 11	05 04
52	16 42	17 19	18 00	01 57	03 03	04 02	04 55
50	16 48	17 24	18 03	01 51	02 56	03 55	04 48
45	17 03	17 35	18 10	01 39	02 41	03 39	04 31
N 40	17 15	17 44	18 16	01 29	02 29	03 26	04 18
35	17 25	17 52	18 22	01 20	02 19	03 15	04 07
30	17 34	17 59	18 28	01 12	02 10	03 05	03 57
20	17 50	18 13	18 40	00 59	01 55	02 48	03 40
N 10	18 04	18 26	18 51	00 48	01 41	02 34	03 25
0	18 17	18 38	19 04	00 37	01 29	02 20	03 11
S 10	18 30	18 52	19 18	00 26	01 16	02 06	02 57
20	18 44	19 07	19 35	00 15	01 03	01 52	02 42
30	19 00	19 26	19 57	00 02	00 47	01 35	02 25
35	19 10	19 37	20 11	24 38	00 38	01 25	02 14
40	19 21	19 51	20 28	24 28	00 28	01 14	02 03
45	19 34	20 07	20 50	24 16	00 16	01 01	01 50
S 50	19 49	20 28	21 18	24 02	00 02	00 45	01 33
52	19 57	20 38	21 33	23 55	24 37	00 37	01 25
54	20 05	20 49	21 51	23 48	24 29	00 29	01 17
56	20 14	21 02	22 14	23 40	24 20	00 20	01 07
58	20 25	21 18	22 45	23 30	24 09	00 09	00 56
S 60	20 37	21 37	23 46	23 20	23 57	24 43	00 43

SUN / MOON

Day	Eqn. of Time 00h	Eqn. of Time 12h	Mer. Pass.	Mer. Pass. Upper	Mer. Pass. Lower	Age	Phase
d	m s	m s	h m	h m	h m	d	%
28	12 46	12 52	12 13	19 16	06 50	08	64
29	12 58	13 03	12 13	20 08	07 42	09	73
30	13 08	13 13	12 13	20 59	08 33	10	82

UT	ARIES GHA	VENUS −3.9 GHA	Dec	MARS +1.2 GHA	Dec	JUPITER −2.6 GHA	Dec	SATURN +0.5 GHA	Dec	STARS Name	SHA	Dec
31 00	129 54.0	153 15.1	S11 23.4	143 51.0	S 6 51.5	348 38.2	N16 10.4	248 05.3	S18 53.4	Acamar	315 17.5	S40 15.1
01	144 56.5	168 14.6	22.3	158 51.7	50.7	3 41.0	10.5	263 07.6	53.4	Achernar	335 26.2	S57 10.0
02	159 59.0	183 14.2	21.1	173 52.3	50.0	18 43.8	10.6	278 09.9	53.4	Acrux	173 07.4	S63 10.8
03	175 01.4	198 13.7	.. 19.9	188 53.0	.. 49.2	33 46.5	.. 10.7	293 12.2	.. 53.5	Adhara	255 11.3	S28 59.9
04	190 03.9	213 13.2	18.8	203 53.7	48.4	48 49.3	10.8	308 14.5	53.5	Aldebaran	290 47.9	N16 32.2
05	205 06.4	228 12.7	17.6	218 54.3	47.6	63 52.1	10.9	323 16.7	53.5			
06	220 08.8	243 12.2	S11 16.4	233 55.0	S 6 46.9	78 54.9	N16 11.0	338 19.0	S18 53.6	Alioth	166 19.6	N55 52.4
07	235 11.3	258 11.8	15.3	248 55.7	46.1	93 57.7	11.1	353 21.3	53.6	Alkaid	152 58.0	N49 14.0
S 08	250 13.7	273 11.3	14.1	263 56.3	45.3	109 00.5	11.2	8 23.6	53.6	Al Na'ir	27 42.8	S46 53.3
A 09	265 16.2	288 10.8	.. 12.9	278 57.0	.. 44.5	124 03.3	.. 11.3	23 25.9	.. 53.6	Alnilam	275 45.0	S 1 11.8
T 10	280 18.7	303 10.4	11.8	293 57.7	43.7	139 06.0	11.4	38 28.2	53.7	Alphard	217 54.6	S 8 43.7
U 11	295 21.1	318 09.9	10.6	308 58.3	43.0	154 08.8	11.5	53 30.5	53.7			
R 12	310 23.6	333 09.4	S11 09.4	323 59.0	S 6 42.2	169 11.6	N16 11.6	68 32.8	S18 53.7	Alphecca	126 10.2	N26 39.8
D 13	325 26.1	348 08.9	08.3	338 59.7	41.4	184 14.4	11.7	83 35.0	53.7	Alpheratz	357 42.5	N29 10.5
A 14	340 28.5	3 08.5	07.1	354 00.3	40.6	199 17.2	11.9	98 37.3	53.8	Altair	62 07.5	N 8 54.6
Y 15	355 31.0	18 08.0	.. 05.9	9 01.0	.. 39.8	214 20.0	.. 12.0	113 39.6	.. 53.8	Ankaa	353 14.9	S42 13.7
16	10 33.5	33 07.5	04.8	24 01.7	39.1	229 22.8	12.1	128 41.9	53.8	Antares	112 25.0	S26 27.7
17	25 35.9	48 07.1	03.6	39 02.3	38.3	244 25.6	12.2	143 44.2	53.8			
18	40 38.4	63 06.6	S11 02.4	54 03.0	S 6 37.5	259 28.3	N16 12.3	158 46.5	S18 53.9	Arcturus	145 54.7	N19 06.1
19	55 40.9	78 06.1	01.2	69 03.7	36.7	274 31.1	12.4	173 48.8	53.9	Atria	107 26.1	S69 02.8
20	70 43.3	93 05.7	11 00.1	84 04.3	36.0	289 33.9	12.5	188 51.1	53.9	Avior	234 16.8	S59 33.7
21	85 45.8	108 05.2	10 58.9	99 05.0	.. 35.2	304 36.7	.. 12.6	203 53.4	.. 53.9	Bellatrix	278 30.6	N 6 21.5
22	100 48.2	123 04.7	57.7	114 05.7	34.4	319 39.5	12.7	218 55.7	54.0	Betelgeuse	270 59.8	N 7 24.3
23	115 50.7	138 04.3	56.5	129 06.4	33.6	334 42.3	12.8	233 58.0	54.0			
1 00	130 53.2	153 03.8	S10 55.4	144 07.0	S 6 32.8	349 45.1	N16 12.9	249 00.2	S18 54.0	Canopus	263 55.2	S52 42.6
01	145 55.6	168 03.3	54.2	159 07.7	32.1	4 47.8	13.0	264 02.5	54.0	Capella	280 32.4	N46 00.7
02	160 58.1	183 02.9	53.0	174 08.4	31.3	19 50.6	13.1	279 04.8	54.1	Deneb	49 31.1	N45 20.2
03	176 00.6	198 02.4	.. 51.8	189 09.0	.. 30.5	34 53.4	.. 13.2	294 07.1	.. 54.1	Denebola	182 32.3	N14 29.1
04	191 03.0	213 01.9	50.7	204 09.7	29.7	49 56.2	13.4	309 09.4	54.1	Diphda	348 54.9	S17 54.4
05	206 05.5	228 01.5	49.5	219 10.4	28.9	64 59.0	13.5	324 11.7	54.1			
06	221 08.0	243 01.0	S10 48.3	234 11.0	S 6 28.2	80 01.8	N16 13.6	339 14.0	S18 54.2	Dubhe	193 49.9	N61 39.9
07	236 10.4	258 00.5	47.1	249 11.7	27.4	95 04.6	13.7	354 16.3	54.2	Elnath	278 10.9	N28 37.0
S 08	251 12.9	273 00.1	46.0	264 12.4	26.6	110 07.4	13.8	9 18.6	54.2	Eltanin	90 46.0	N51 29.2
U 09	266 15.3	287 59.6	.. 44.8	279 13.1	.. 25.8	125 10.2	.. 13.9	24 20.9	.. 54.2	Enif	33 46.3	N 9 56.7
N 10	281 17.8	302 59.2	43.6	294 13.7	25.0	140 12.9	14.0	39 23.2	54.3	Fomalhaut	15 23.1	S29 32.6
D 11	296 20.3	317 58.7	42.4	309 14.4	24.3	155 15.7	14.1	54 25.5	54.3			
A 12	311 22.7	332 58.2	S10 41.2	324 15.1	S 6 23.5	170 18.5	N16 14.2	69 27.7	S18 54.3	Gacrux	171 59.2	S57 11.7
Y 13	326 25.2	347 57.8	40.1	339 15.7	22.7	185 21.3	14.3	84 30.0	54.3	Gienah	175 50.9	S17 37.6
14	341 27.7	2 57.3	38.9	354 16.4	21.9	200 24.1	14.4	99 32.3	54.4	Hadar	148 46.0	S60 26.4
15	356 30.1	17 56.8	.. 37.7	9 17.1	.. 21.1	215 26.9	.. 14.5	114 34.6	.. 54.4	Hamal	327 59.5	N23 32.0
16	11 32.6	32 56.4	36.5	24 17.8	20.4	230 29.7	14.6	129 36.9	54.4	Kaus Aust.	83 42.6	S34 22.4
17	26 35.1	47 55.9	35.3	39 18.4	19.6	245 32.5	14.7	144 39.2	54.4			
18	41 37.5	62 55.5	S10 34.1	54 19.1	S 6 18.8	260 35.2	N16 14.8	159 41.5	S18 54.5	Kochab	137 20.3	N74 05.4
19	56 40.0	77 55.0	33.0	69 19.8	18.0	275 38.0	15.0	174 43.8	54.5	Markab	13 37.5	N15 17.2
20	71 42.5	92 54.6	31.8	84 20.4	17.2	290 40.8	15.1	189 46.1	54.5	Menkar	314 13.8	N 4 08.7
21	86 44.9	107 54.1	.. 30.6	99 21.1	.. 16.5	305 43.6	.. 15.2	204 48.4	.. 54.5	Menkent	148 06.1	S36 26.4
22	101 47.4	122 53.6	29.4	114 21.8	15.7	320 46.4	15.3	219 50.7	54.6	Miaplacidus	221 38.3	S69 46.9
23	116 49.8	137 53.2	28.2	129 22.5	14.9	335 49.2	15.4	234 53.0	54.6			
2 00	131 52.3	152 52.7	S10 27.0	144 23.1	S 6 14.1	350 52.0	N16 15.5	249 55.3	S18 54.6	Mirfak	308 38.5	N49 54.9
01	146 54.8	167 52.3	25.8	159 23.8	13.3	5 54.8	15.6	264 57.6	54.6	Nunki	75 57.3	S26 16.5
02	161 57.2	182 51.8	24.7	174 24.5	12.6	20 57.6	15.7	279 59.9	54.7	Peacock	53 18.1	S56 41.0
03	176 59.7	197 51.4	.. 23.5	189 25.1	.. 11.8	36 00.3	.. 15.8	295 02.2	.. 54.7	Pollux	243 26.0	N27 59.1
04	192 02.2	212 50.9	22.3	204 25.8	11.0	51 03.1	15.9	310 04.4	54.7	Procyon	244 58.2	N 5 10.9
05	207 04.6	227 50.5	21.1	219 26.5	10.2	66 05.9	16.0	325 06.7	54.7			
06	222 07.1	242 50.0	S10 19.9	234 27.2	S 6 09.4	81 08.7	N16 16.1	340 09.0	S18 54.8	Rasalhague	96 05.6	N12 33.0
07	237 09.6	257 49.6	18.7	249 27.8	08.6	96 11.5	16.2	355 11.3	54.8	Regulus	207 42.0	N11 53.4
08	252 12.0	272 49.1	17.5	264 28.5	07.9	111 14.3	16.3	10 13.6	54.8	Rigel	281 10.8	S 8 11.4
M 09	267 14.5	287 48.7	.. 16.3	279 29.2	.. 07.1	126 17.1	.. 16.5	25 15.9	.. 54.8	Rigil Kent.	139 50.0	S60 53.5
O 10	282 17.0	302 48.2	15.1	294 29.9	06.3	141 19.9	16.6	40 18.2	54.9	Sabik	102 11.4	S15 44.4
N 11	297 19.4	317 47.8	13.9	309 30.5	05.5	156 22.7	16.7	55 20.5	54.9			
D 12	312 21.9	332 47.3	S10 12.8	324 31.2	S 6 04.7	171 25.4	N16 16.8	70 22.8	S18 54.9	Schedar	349 39.4	N56 37.4
A 13	327 24.3	347 46.9	11.6	339 31.9	04.0	186 28.2	16.9	85 25.1	54.9	Shaula	96 20.7	S37 06.6
Y 14	342 26.8	2 46.4	10.4	354 32.6	03.2	201 31.0	17.0	100 27.4	55.0	Sirius	258 32.4	S16 44.6
15	357 29.3	17 46.0	.. 09.2	9 33.2	.. 02.4	216 33.8	.. 17.1	115 29.7	.. 55.0	Spica	158 29.9	S11 14.4
16	12 31.7	32 45.5	08.0	24 33.9	01.6	231 36.6	17.2	130 32.0	55.0	Suhail	222 51.1	S43 29.8
17	27 34.2	47 45.1	06.8	39 34.6	00.8	246 39.4	17.3	145 34.3	55.0			
18	42 36.7	62 44.6	S10 05.6	54 35.3	S 6 00.0	261 42.2	N16 17.4	160 36.6	S18 55.1	Vega	80 38.5	N38 47.9
19	57 39.1	77 44.2	04.4	69 35.9	5 59.3	276 45.0	17.5	175 38.9	55.1	Zuben'ubi	137 04.2	S16 06.1
20	72 41.6	92 43.7	03.2	84 36.6	58.5	291 47.8	17.6	190 41.2	55.1		SHA	Mer.Pass.
21	87 44.1	107 43.3	.. 02.0	99 37.3	.. 57.7	306 50.6	.. 17.7	205 43.5	.. 55.1			h m
22	102 46.5	122 42.8	10 00.8	114 38.0	56.9	321 53.3	17.8	220 45.8	55.2	Venus	22 10.6	13 48
23	117 49.0	137 42.4	S 9 59.6	129 38.6	56.1	336 56.1	18.0	235 48.1	55.2	Mars	13 13.9	14 23
Mer.Pass.	h m 15 14.0	v −0.5	d 1.2	v 0.7	d 0.8	v 2.8	d 0.1	v 2.3	d 0.0	Jupiter	218 51.9	0 41
										Saturn	118 07.1	7 23

UT	SUN GHA	SUN Dec	MOON GHA	v	Dec	d	HP
	° ′	° ′	° ′	′	° ′	′	′
31 00	176 40.4	S17 31.7	43 49.0	10.5	N18 30.6	0.1	55.6
01	191 40.3	31.0	58 18.5	10.5	18 30.7	0.1	55.6
02	206 40.2	30.3	72 48.0	10.6	18 30.6	0.1	55.6
03	221 40.1 ..	29.6	87 17.6	10.5	18 30.5	0.3	55.5
04	236 40.1	29.0	101 47.1	10.6	18 30.2	0.3	55.5
05	251 40.0	28.3	116 16.7	10.6	18 29.9	0.4	55.5
06	266 39.9	S17 27.6	130 46.3	10.7	N18 29.5	0.5	55.5
S 07	281 39.8	26.9	145 16.0	10.6	18 29.0	0.6	55.5
A 08	296 39.7	26.2	159 45.6	10.7	18 28.4	0.8	55.4
T 09	311 39.6 ..	25.5	174 15.3	10.7	18 27.6	0.7	55.4
U 10	326 39.5	24.8	188 45.0	10.8	18 26.9	0.9	55.4
R 11	341 39.4	24.1	203 14.8	10.7	18 26.0	1.0	55.4
D 12	356 39.3	S17 23.4	217 44.5	10.8	N18 25.0	1.1	55.4
A 13	11 39.2	22.7	232 14.3	10.8	18 23.9	1.2	55.3
Y 14	26 39.1	22.0	246 44.1	10.9	18 22.7	1.2	55.3
15	41 39.0 ..	21.3	261 14.0	10.9	18 21.5	1.4	55.3
16	56 38.9	20.6	275 43.9	10.8	18 20.1	1.4	55.3
17	71 38.8	19.9	290 13.7	11.0	18 18.7	1.6	55.3
18	86 38.8	S17 19.2	304 43.7	10.9	N18 17.1	1.6	55.3
19	101 38.7	18.5	319 13.6	11.0	18 15.5	1.7	55.2
20	116 38.6	17.8	333 43.6	11.0	18 13.8	1.8	55.2
21	131 38.5 ..	17.1	348 13.6	11.1	18 12.0	1.9	55.2
22	146 38.4	16.4	2 43.7	11.0	18 10.1	2.0	55.2
23	161 38.3	15.7	17 13.7	11.1	18 08.1	2.0	55.2
1 00	176 38.2	S17 15.0	31 43.8	11.2	N18 06.1	2.2	55.1
01	191 38.1	14.3	46 14.0	11.1	18 03.9	2.2	55.1
02	206 38.0	13.6	60 44.1	11.2	18 01.7	2.3	55.1
03	221 38.0 ..	12.9	75 14.3	11.3	17 59.3	2.4	55.1
04	236 37.9	12.2	89 44.6	11.2	17 56.9	2.5	55.1
05	251 37.8	11.4	104 14.8	11.3	17 54.4	2.6	55.1
06	266 37.7	S17 10.7	118 45.1	11.3	N17 51.8	2.7	55.0
S 07	281 37.6	10.0	133 15.4	11.4	17 49.1	2.8	55.0
U 08	296 37.5	09.3	147 45.8	11.4	17 46.3	2.8	55.0
N 09	311 37.4 ..	08.6	162 16.2	11.4	17 43.5	2.9	55.0
D 10	326 37.4	07.9	176 46.6	11.5	17 40.6	3.1	55.0
A 11	341 37.3	07.2	191 17.1	11.5	17 37.5	3.1	55.0
Y 12	356 37.2	S17 06.5	205 47.6	11.5	N17 34.4	3.2	54.9
13	11 37.1	05.8	220 18.1	11.5	17 31.2	3.2	54.9
14	26 37.0	05.1	234 48.6	11.6	17 28.0	3.4	54.9
15	41 36.9 ..	04.4	249 19.2	11.7	17 24.6	3.4	54.9
16	56 36.9	03.6	263 49.9	11.6	17 21.2	3.5	54.9
17	71 36.8	02.9	278 20.5	11.7	17 17.7	3.6	54.9
18	86 36.7	S17 02.2	292 51.2	11.8	N17 14.1	3.7	54.9
19	101 36.6	01.5	307 22.0	11.8	17 10.4	3.8	54.8
20	116 36.5	00.8	321 52.8	11.8	17 06.6	3.8	54.8
21	131 36.4	17 00.1	336 23.6	11.8	17 02.8	3.9	54.8
22	146 36.4	16 59.4	350 54.4	11.9	16 58.9	4.0	54.8
23	161 36.3	58.6	5 25.3	11.9	16 54.9	4.1	54.8
2 00	176 36.2	S16 57.9	19 56.2	12.0	N16 50.8	4.2	54.8
01	191 36.1	57.2	34 27.2	12.0	16 46.6	4.2	54.7
02	206 36.0	56.5	48 58.2	12.0	16 42.4	4.3	54.7
03	221 36.0 ..	55.8	63 29.2	12.1	16 38.1	4.4	54.7
04	236 35.9	55.1	78 00.3	12.1	16 33.7	4.5	54.7
05	251 35.8	54.3	92 31.4	12.2	16 29.2	4.5	54.7
06	266 35.7	S16 53.6	107 02.6	12.2	N16 24.7	4.6	54.7
M 07	281 35.7	52.9	121 33.8	12.2	16 20.1	4.7	54.7
O 08	296 35.6	52.2	136 05.0	12.3	16 15.4	4.8	54.7
N 09	311 35.5 ..	51.5	150 36.3	12.3	16 10.6	4.8	54.6
D 10	326 35.4	50.7	165 07.6	12.3	16 05.8	4.9	54.6
A 11	341 35.4	50.0	179 38.9	12.4	16 00.9	5.0	54.6
Y 12	356 35.3	S16 49.3	194 10.3	12.4	N15 55.9	5.0	54.6
13	11 35.2	48.6	208 41.7	12.5	15 50.9	5.1	54.6
14	26 35.1	47.8	223 13.2	12.5	15 45.8	5.2	54.6
15	41 35.1 ..	47.1	237 44.7	12.5	15 40.6	5.3	54.6
16	56 35.0	46.4	252 16.2	12.6	15 35.3	5.3	54.6
17	71 34.9	45.7	266 47.8	12.6	15 30.0	5.4	54.5
18	86 34.8	S16 44.9	281 19.4	12.6	N15 24.6	5.5	54.5
19	101 34.8	44.2	295 51.0	12.7	15 19.1	5.5	54.5
20	116 34.7	43.5	310 22.7	12.7	15 13.6	5.6	54.5
21	131 34.6 ..	42.8	324 54.5	12.7	15 08.0	5.7	54.5
22	146 34.5	42.0	339 26.2	12.9	15 02.3	5.7	54.5
23	161 34.5	41.3	353 58.1	12.8	N14 56.6	5.8	54.5
	SD 16.3	d 0.7	SD 15.1		15.0		14.9

Twilight / Sunrise / Moonrise

Lat.	Naut.	Civil	Sunrise	31	1	2	3
°	h m	h m	h m	h m	h m	h m	h m
N 72	07 11	08 40	10 30	☐	11 10	13 05	14 49
N 70	07 03	08 21	09 47	11 05	12 18	13 45	15 15
68	06 56	08 06	09 19	11 49	12 55	14 12	15 34
66	06 50	07 54	08 57	12 18	13 21	14 33	15 50
64	06 45	07 44	08 40	12 40	13 40	14 49	16 02
62	06 41	07 35	08 26	12 57	13 57	15 03	16 13
60	06 36	07 27	08 15	13 12	14 10	15 14	16 22
N 58	06 33	07 20	08 04	13 24	14 22	15 24	16 30
56	06 29	07 14	07 55	13 35	14 32	15 33	16 37
54	06 26	07 09	07 48	13 44	14 40	15 41	16 43
52	06 23	07 04	07 40	13 53	14 48	15 47	16 49
50	06 20	06 59	07 34	14 01	14 55	15 54	16 54
45	06 14	06 49	07 20	14 17	15 11	16 07	17 05
N 40	06 08	06 40	07 09	14 30	15 23	16 18	17 14
35	06 02	06 32	06 59	14 41	15 34	16 27	17 23
30	05 57	06 25	06 51	14 51	15 43	16 36	17 28
20	05 46	06 13	06 36	15 08	15 59	16 50	17 40
N 10	05 35	06 01	06 22	15 23	16 13	17 02	17 50
0	05 23	05 48	06 10	15 37	16 26	17 14	18 00
S 10	05 10	05 35	05 57	15 51	16 39	17 25	18 09
20	04 53	05 21	05 44	16 05	16 53	17 38	18 19
30	04 32	05 02	05 28	16 22	17 09	17 52	18 31
35	04 18	04 51	05 19	16 32	17 18	18 00	18 38
40	04 02	04 39	05 09	16 44	17 29	18 09	18 45
45	03 41	04 23	04 56	16 57	17 41	18 20	18 54
S 50	03 13	04 03	04 41	17 13	17 56	18 33	19 05
52	02 59	03 53	04 34	17 21	18 03	18 39	19 10
54	02 42	03 42	04 26	17 29	18 11	18 46	19 15
56	02 21	03 30	04 17	17 39	18 19	18 53	19 21
58	01 53	03 15	04 07	17 49	18 29	19 01	19 28
S 60	01 07	02 57	03 55	18 02	18 41	19 11	19 35

Sunset / Twilight / Moonset

Lat.	Sunset	Civil	Naut.	31	1	2	3
°	h m	h m	h m	h m	h m	h m	h m
N 72	13 59	15 49	17 18	☐	09 22	09 08	09 00
N 70	14 41	16 07	17 26	07 44	08 13	08 27	08 33
68	15 10	16 22	17 32	07 00	07 37	07 59	08 13
66	15 31	16 34	17 38	06 31	07 11	07 38	07 56
64	15 48	16 44	17 43	06 09	06 50	07 21	07 43
62	16 02	16 53	17 48	05 51	06 34	07 07	07 32
60	16 13	17 01	17 52	05 37	06 20	06 55	07 22
N 58	16 23	17 07	17 55	05 24	06 08	06 44	07 14
56	16 32	17 13	17 59	05 13	05 58	06 35	07 06
54	16 40	17 19	18 02	05 04	05 49	06 27	07 00
52	16 47	17 24	18 05	04 55	05 41	06 20	06 54
50	16 54	17 29	18 07	04 48	05 34	06 14	06 48
45	17 07	17 39	18 14	04 31	05 18	06 00	06 36
N 40	17 19	17 47	18 20	04 18	05 06	05 48	06 27
35	17 28	17 55	18 25	04 07	04 55	05 38	06 18
30	17 37	18 02	18 31	03 57	04 45	05 30	06 11
20	17 52	18 15	18 41	03 40	04 29	05 15	05 58
N 10	18 05	18 27	18 52	03 25	04 14	05 02	05 47
0	18 17	18 39	19 04	03 11	04 01	04 49	05 36
S 10	18 29	18 52	19 17	02 57	03 47	04 37	05 25
20	18 43	19 06	19 34	02 42	03 33	04 23	05 14
30	18 58	19 24	19 55	02 25	03 16	04 08	05 01
35	19 07	19 35	20 08	02 14	03 06	03 59	04 53
40	19 18	19 48	20 24	02 03	02 55	03 49	04 45
45	19 30	20 03	20 45	01 50	02 42	03 37	04 35
S 50	19 45	20 23	21 12	01 33	02 26	03 23	04 22
52	19 52	20 32	21 26	01 25	02 19	03 16	04 16
54	20 00	20 43	21 42	01 17	02 10	03 09	04 10
56	20 09	20 55	22 03	01 07	02 01	03 00	04 03
58	20 18	21 10	22 30	00 56	01 50	02 51	03 55
S 60	20 30	21 27	23 11	00 43	01 38	02 40	03 46

SUN / MOON

Day	Eqn. of Time 00ʰ	Eqn. of Time 12ʰ	Mer. Pass.	Mer. Pass. Upper	Mer. Pass. Lower	Age	Phase
d	m s	m s	h m	h m	h m	d	%
31	13 18	13 23	12 13	21 49	09 24	11	89
1	13 27	13 31	12 14	22 38	10 13	12	94
2	13 35	13 39	12 14	23 25	11 01	13	98

UT	ARIES GHA	VENUS −3.9 GHA	Dec	MARS +1.2 GHA	Dec	JUPITER −2.6 GHA	Dec	SATURN +0.5 GHA	Dec	STARS Name	SHA	Dec
d h	° ′	° ′	° ′	° ′	° ′	° ′	° ′	° ′	° ′		° ′	° ′
3 00	132 51.5	152 41.9	S 9 58.4	144 39.3	S 5 55.4	351 58.9	N16 18.1	250 50.4	S18 55.2	Acamar	315 17.5	S40 15.1
01	147 53.9	167 41.5	57.2	159 40.0	54.6	7 01.7	18.2	265 52.7	55.2	Achernar	335 26.2	S57 10.0
02	162 56.4	182 41.0	56.0	174 40.7	53.8	22 04.5	18.3	280 55.0	55.2	Acrux	173 07.4	S63 10.8
03	177 58.8	197 40.6 ..	54.8	189 41.3 ..	53.0	37 07.3 ..	18.4	295 57.3 ..	55.3	Adhara	255 11.3	S28 59.9
04	193 01.3	212 40.2	53.6	204 42.0	52.2	52 10.1	18.5	310 59.6	55.3	Aldebaran	290 47.9	N16 32.2
05	208 03.8	227 39.7	52.4	219 42.7	51.4	67 12.9	18.6	326 01.9	55.3			
06	223 06.2	242 39.3	S 9 51.2	234 43.4	S 5 50.7	82 15.7	N16 18.7	341 04.2	S18 55.3	Alioth	166 19.5	N55 52.4
07	238 08.7	257 38.8	50.0	249 44.0	49.9	97 18.5	18.8	356 06.5	55.4	Alkaid	152 57.9	N49 14.0
08	253 11.2	272 38.4	48.8	264 44.7	49.1	112 21.2	18.9	11 08.8	55.4	Al Na'ir	27 42.8	S46 53.3
09	268 13.6	287 37.9 ..	47.6	279 45.4 ..	48.3	127 24.0 ..	19.0	26 11.1 ..	55.4	Alnilam	275 45.0	S 1 11.8
10	283 16.1	302 37.5	46.4	294 46.1	47.5	142 26.8	19.1	41 13.4	55.4	Alphard	217 54.6	S 8 43.7
11	298 18.6	317 37.1	45.2	309 46.7	46.7	157 29.6	19.2	56 15.7	55.5			
12	313 21.0	332 36.6	S 9 44.0	324 47.4	S 5 46.0	172 32.4	N16 19.3	71 18.0	S18 55.5	Alphecca	126 10.1	N26 39.7
13	328 23.5	347 36.2	42.8	339 48.1	45.2	187 35.2	19.4	86 20.3	55.5	Alpheratz	357 42.5	N29 10.5
14	343 25.9	2 35.8	41.6	354 48.8	44.4	202 38.0	19.6	101 22.6	55.5	Altair	62 07.4	N 8 54.6
15	358 28.4	17 35.3 ..	40.4	9 49.5 ..	43.6	217 40.8 ..	19.7	116 24.9 ..	55.6	Ankaa	353 14.9	S42 13.7
16	13 30.9	32 34.9	39.2	24 50.1	42.8	232 43.6	19.8	131 27.2	55.6	Antares	112 25.0	S26 27.7
17	28 33.3	47 34.4	38.0	39 50.8	42.0	247 46.4	19.9	146 29.5	55.6			
18	43 35.8	62 34.0	S 9 36.8	54 51.5	S 5 41.3	262 49.2	N16 20.0	161 31.8	S18 55.6	Arcturus	145 54.7	N19 06.1
19	58 38.3	77 33.6	35.6	69 52.2	40.5	277 51.9	20.1	176 34.1	55.6	Atria	107 26.0	S69 02.8
20	73 40.7	92 33.1	34.4	84 52.8	39.7	292 54.7	20.2	191 36.4	55.7	Avior	234 16.8	S59 33.7
21	88 43.2	107 32.7 ..	33.2	99 53.5 ..	38.9	307 57.5 ..	20.3	206 38.7 ..	55.7	Bellatrix	278 30.6	N 6 21.5
22	103 45.7	122 32.3	32.0	114 54.2	38.1	323 00.3	20.4	221 41.0	55.7	Betelgeuse	270 59.8	N 7 24.3
23	118 48.1	137 31.8	30.8	129 54.9	37.3	338 03.1	20.5	236 43.3	55.7			
4 00	133 50.6	152 31.4	S 9 29.5	144 55.6	S 5 36.5	353 05.9	N16 20.6	251 45.6	S18 55.8	Canopus	263 55.2	S52 42.6
01	148 53.1	167 30.9	28.3	159 56.2	35.8	8 08.7	20.7	266 47.9	55.8	Capella	280 32.5	N46 00.7
02	163 55.5	182 30.5	27.1	174 56.9	35.0	23 11.5	20.8	281 50.2	55.8	Deneb	49 31.1	N45 20.2
03	178 58.0	197 30.1 ..	25.9	189 57.6 ..	34.2	38 14.3 ..	20.9	296 52.5 ..	55.8	Denebola	182 32.3	N14 29.1
04	194 00.4	212 29.6	24.7	204 58.3	33.4	53 17.1	21.0	311 54.8	55.9	Diphda	348 54.9	S17 54.4
05	209 02.9	227 29.2	23.5	219 58.9	32.6	68 19.9	21.2	326 57.1	55.9			
06	224 05.4	242 28.8	S 9 22.3	234 59.6	S 5 31.8	83 22.6	N16 21.3	341 59.4	S18 55.9	Dubhe	193 49.9	N61 39.9
07	239 07.8	257 28.3	21.1	250 00.3	31.1	98 25.4	21.4	357 01.7	55.9	Elnath	278 10.9	N28 37.0
08	254 10.3	272 27.9	19.9	265 01.0	30.3	113 28.2	21.5	12 04.0	55.9	Eltanin	90 46.0	N51 29.2
09	269 12.8	287 27.5 ..	18.7	280 01.7 ..	29.5	128 31.0 ..	21.6	27 06.3 ..	56.0	Enif	33 46.3	N 9 56.7
10	284 15.2	302 27.1	17.4	295 02.3	28.7	143 33.8	21.7	42 08.6	56.0	Fomalhaut	15 23.1	S29 32.6
11	299 17.7	317 26.6	16.2	310 03.0	27.9	158 36.6	21.8	57 10.9	56.0			
12	314 20.2	332 26.2	S 9 15.0	325 03.7	S 5 27.1	173 39.4	N16 21.9	72 13.2	S18 56.0	Gacrux	171 59.1	S57 11.7
13	329 22.6	347 25.8	13.8	340 04.4	26.3	188 42.2	22.0	87 15.5	56.1	Gienah	175 50.9	S17 37.6
14	344 25.1	2 25.3	12.6	355 05.1	25.6	203 45.0	22.1	102 17.8	56.1	Hadar	148 46.0	S60 26.4
15	359 27.6	17 24.9 ..	11.4	10 05.7 ..	24.8	218 47.8 ..	22.2	117 20.1 ..	56.1	Hamal	327 59.5	N23 32.0
16	14 30.0	32 24.5	10.2	25 06.4	24.0	233 50.6	22.3	132 22.4	56.1	Kaus Aust.	83 42.6	S34 22.4
17	29 32.5	47 24.1	08.9	40 07.1	23.2	248 53.3	22.4	147 24.7	56.2			
18	44 34.9	62 23.6	S 9 07.7	55 07.8	S 5 22.4	263 56.1	N16 22.5	162 27.0	S18 56.2	Kochab	137 20.3	N74 05.4
19	59 37.4	77 23.2	06.5	70 08.5	21.6	278 58.9	22.7	177 29.3	56.2	Markab	13 37.5	N15 17.2
20	74 39.9	92 22.8	05.3	85 09.1	20.8	294 01.7	22.8	192 31.6	56.2	Menkar	314 13.8	N 4 08.7
21	89 42.3	107 22.3 ..	04.1	100 09.8 ..	20.1	309 04.5 ..	22.9	207 33.9 ..	56.2	Menkent	148 06.1	S36 26.4
22	104 44.8	122 21.9	02.9	115 10.5	19.3	324 07.3	23.0	222 36.3	56.3	Miaplacidus	221 38.3	S69 46.9
23	119 47.3	137 21.5	01.7	130 11.2	18.5	339 10.1	23.1	237 38.6	56.3			
5 00	134 49.7	152 21.1	S 9 00.4	145 11.9	S 5 17.7	354 12.9	N16 23.2	252 40.9	S18 56.3	Mirfak	308 38.6	N49 54.9
01	149 52.2	167 20.6	8 59.2	160 12.5	16.9	9 15.7	23.3	267 43.2	56.3	Nunki	75 57.2	S26 16.5
02	164 54.7	182 20.2	58.0	175 13.2	16.1	24 18.5	23.4	282 45.5	56.4	Peacock	53 18.1	S56 41.0
03	179 57.1	197 19.8 ..	56.8	190 13.9 ..	15.3	39 21.3 ..	23.5	297 47.8 ..	56.4	Pollux	243 26.0	N27 59.1
04	194 59.6	212 19.4	55.6	205 14.6	14.6	54 24.1	23.6	312 50.1	56.4	Procyon	244 58.2	N 5 10.9
05	210 02.0	227 18.9	54.3	220 15.3	13.8	69 26.9	23.7	327 52.4	56.4			
06	225 04.5	242 18.5	S 8 53.1	235 16.0	S 5 13.0	84 29.6	N16 23.8	342 54.7	S18 56.4	Rasalhague	96 05.6	N12 33.0
07	240 07.0	257 18.1	51.9	250 16.6	12.2	99 32.4	23.9	357 57.0	56.5	Regulus	207 42.0	N11 53.4
08	255 09.4	272 17.7	50.7	265 17.3	11.4	114 35.2	24.0	12 59.3	56.5	Rigel	281 10.8	S 8 11.4
09	270 11.9	287 17.3 ..	49.5	280 18.0 ..	10.6	129 38.0 ..	24.1	28 01.6 ..	56.5	Rigil Kent.	139 50.0	S60 53.5
10	285 14.4	302 16.8	48.2	295 18.7	09.8	144 40.8	24.2	43 03.9	56.5	Sabik	102 11.4	S15 44.4
11	300 16.8	317 16.4	47.0	310 19.4	09.1	159 43.6	24.4	58 06.2	56.6			
12	315 19.3	332 16.0	S 8 45.8	325 20.0	S 5 08.3	174 46.4	N16 24.5	73 08.5	S18 56.6	Schedar	349 39.4	N56 37.4
13	330 21.8	347 15.6	44.6	340 20.7	07.5	189 49.2	24.6	88 10.8	56.6	Shaula	96 20.6	S37 06.6
14	345 24.2	2 15.2	43.3	355 21.4	06.7	204 52.0	24.7	103 13.2	56.6	Sirius	258 32.4	S16 44.6
15	0 26.7	17 14.7 ..	42.1	10 22.1 ..	05.9	219 54.8 ..	24.8	118 15.5 ..	56.6	Spica	158 29.9	S11 14.4
16	15 29.2	32 14.3	40.9	25 22.8	05.1	234 57.6	24.9	133 17.8	56.7	Suhail	222 51.1	S43 29.8
17	30 31.6	47 13.9	39.7	40 23.5	04.3	250 00.4	25.0	148 20.1	56.7			
18	45 34.1	62 13.5	S 8 38.4	55 24.1	S 5 03.6	265 03.1	N16 25.1	163 22.4	S18 56.7	Vega	80 38.5	N38 47.9
19	60 36.5	77 13.1	37.2	70 24.8	02.8	280 05.9	25.2	178 24.7	56.7	Zuben'ubi	137 04.1	S16 06.1
20	75 39.0	92 12.6	36.0	85 25.5	02.0	295 08.7	25.3	193 27.0	56.7		SHA	Mer.Pass.
21	90 41.5	107 12.2 ..	34.8	100 26.2 ..	01.2	310 11.5 ..	25.4	208 29.3 ..	56.8		° ′	h m
22	105 43.9	122 11.8	33.5	115 26.9	5 00.4	325 14.3	25.5	223 31.6	56.8	Venus	18 40.8	13 50
23	120 46.4	137 11.4	32.3	130 27.6	S 4 59.6	340 17.1	25.6	238 33.9	56.8	Mars	11 05.0	14 20
	h m									Jupiter	219 15.3	0 28
Mer. Pass. 15 02.2	*v* −0.4 *d* 1.2	*v* 0.7 *d* 0.8		*v* 2.8 *d* 0.1		*v* 2.3 *d* 0.0				Saturn	117 55.0	7 12

UT	SUN GHA	SUN Dec	MOON GHA	v	MOON Dec	d	HP
d h	° ′	° ′	° ′	′	° ′	′	′
3 00	176 34.4	S16 40.6	8 29.9	12.9	N14 50.8	5.9	54.5
01	191 34.3	39.9	23 01.8	12.9	14 44.9	5.9	54.4
02	206 34.3	39.1	37 33.7	13.0	14 39.0	6.0	54.4
03	221 34.2	.. 38.4	52 05.7	13.0	14 33.0	6.1	54.4
04	236 34.1	37.7	66 37.7	13.0	14 26.9	6.1	54.4
05	251 34.1	36.9	81 09.7	13.1	14 20.8	6.2	54.4
06	266 34.0	S16 36.2	95 41.8	13.1	N14 14.6	6.2	54.4
07	281 33.9	35.5	110 13.9	13.2	14 08.4	6.3	54.4
T 08	296 33.8	34.7	124 46.1	13.2	14 02.1	6.4	54.4
U 09	311 33.8	.. 34.0	139 18.3	13.2	13 55.7	6.4	54.4
E 10	326 33.7	33.3	153 50.5	13.3	13 49.3	6.5	54.4
S 11	341 33.6	32.5	168 22.8	13.3	13 42.8	6.5	54.3
D 12	356 33.6	S16 31.8	182 55.1	13.4	N13 36.3	6.6	54.3
A 13	11 33.5	31.1	197 27.5	13.4	13 29.7	6.7	54.3
Y 14	26 33.4	30.3	211 59.9	13.4	13 23.0	6.7	54.3
15	41 33.4	.. 29.6	226 32.3	13.5	13 16.3	6.7	54.3
16	56 33.3	28.9	241 04.8	13.5	13 09.6	6.9	54.3
17	71 33.2	28.1	255 37.3	13.5	13 02.7	6.8	54.3
18	86 33.2	S16 27.4	270 09.8	13.6	N12 55.9	7.0	54.3
19	101 33.1	26.6	284 42.4	13.6	12 48.9	7.0	54.3
20	116 33.1	25.9	299 15.0	13.7	12 41.9	7.0	54.3
21	131 33.0	.. 25.2	313 47.7	13.7	12 34.9	7.1	54.2
22	146 32.9	24.4	328 20.4	13.7	12 27.8	7.1	54.2
23	161 32.9	23.7	342 53.1	13.7	12 20.7	7.2	54.2
4 00	176 32.8	S16 22.9	357 25.8	13.8	N12 13.5	7.3	54.2
01	191 32.7	22.2	11 58.6	13.9	12 06.2	7.3	54.2
02	206 32.7	21.5	26 31.5	13.8	11 58.9	7.3	54.2
03	221 32.6	.. 20.7	41 04.3	13.9	11 51.6	7.4	54.2
04	236 32.6	20.0	55 37.2	14.0	11 44.2	7.4	54.2
05	251 32.5	19.2	70 10.2	14.0	11 36.8	7.5	54.2
06	266 32.4	S16 18.5	84 43.2	14.0	N11 29.3	7.5	54.2
W 07	281 32.4	17.7	99 16.2	14.0	11 21.8	7.6	54.2
E 08	296 32.3	17.0	113 49.2	14.1	11 14.2	7.6	54.2
D 09	311 32.3	.. 16.3	128 22.3	14.1	11 06.6	7.7	54.2
N 10	326 32.2	15.5	142 55.4	14.1	10 58.9	7.7	54.1
E 11	341 32.1	14.8	157 28.5	14.2	10 51.2	7.8	54.1
S 12	356 32.1	S16 14.0	172 01.7	14.2	N10 43.4	7.8	54.1
D 13	11 32.0	13.3	186 34.9	14.3	10 35.6	7.8	54.1
A 14	26 32.0	12.5	201 08.2	14.2	10 27.8	7.9	54.1
Y 15	41 31.9	.. 11.8	215 41.4	14.3	10 19.9	7.9	54.1
16	56 31.8	11.0	230 14.7	14.4	10 12.0	8.0	54.1
17	71 31.8	10.3	244 48.1	14.3	10 04.0	8.0	54.1
18	86 31.7	S16 09.5	259 21.4	14.4	N 9 56.0	8.1	54.1
19	101 31.7	08.8	273 54.8	14.5	9 47.9	8.0	54.1
20	116 31.6	08.0	288 28.3	14.4	9 39.9	8.2	54.1
21	131 31.6	.. 07.3	303 01.7	14.5	9 31.7	8.1	54.1
22	146 31.5	06.5	317 35.2	14.5	9 23.6	8.2	54.1
23	161 31.5	05.8	332 08.7	14.6	9 15.4	8.3	54.1
5 00	176 31.4	S16 05.0	346 42.3	14.5	N 9 07.1	8.2	54.1
01	191 31.3	04.3	1 15.8	14.6	8 58.9	8.3	54.1
02	206 31.3	03.5	15 49.4	14.7	8 50.6	8.4	54.1
03	221 31.2	.. 02.8	30 23.1	14.6	8 42.2	8.4	54.1
04	236 31.2	02.0	44 56.7	14.7	8 33.8	8.4	54.0
05	251 31.1	01.3	59 30.4	14.7	8 25.4	8.4	54.0
06	266 31.1	S16 00.5	74 04.1	14.7	N 8 17.0	8.5	54.0
07	281 31.0	15 59.7	88 37.8	14.8	8 08.5	8.5	54.0
T 08	296 31.0	59.0	103 11.6	14.8	8 00.0	8.5	54.0
H 09	311 30.9	.. 58.2	117 45.4	14.8	7 51.5	8.6	54.0
U 10	326 30.9	57.5	132 19.2	14.8	7 42.9	8.6	54.0
R 11	341 30.8	56.7	146 53.0	14.9	7 34.3	8.6	54.0
S 12	356 30.8	S15 56.0	161 26.9	14.9	N 7 25.7	8.7	54.0
D 13	11 30.7	55.2	176 00.8	14.9	7 17.0	8.7	54.0
A 14	26 30.7	54.4	190 34.7	14.9	7 08.3	8.7	54.0
Y 15	41 30.6	.. 53.7	205 08.6	14.9	6 59.6	8.7	54.0
16	56 30.6	52.9	219 42.5	15.0	6 50.9	8.8	54.0
17	71 30.5	52.2	234 16.5	15.0	6 42.1	8.8	54.0
18	86 30.5	S15 51.4	248 50.5	15.0	N 6 33.3	8.8	54.0
19	101 30.4	50.6	263 24.5	15.0	6 24.5	8.8	54.0
20	116 30.4	49.9	277 58.5	15.1	6 15.7	8.9	54.0
21	131 30.3	.. 49.1	292 32.6	15.1	6 06.8	8.9	54.0
22	146 30.3	48.3	307 06.7	15.1	5 57.9	8.9	54.0
23	161 30.3	47.6	321 40.8	15.1	N 5 49.0	8.9	54.0
	SD 16.3	d 0.7	SD 14.8		14.7		14.7

Twilight / Moonrise

Lat.	Naut.	Civil	Sunrise	3	4	5	6
°	h m	h m	h m	h m	h m	h m	h m
N 72	07 00	08 26	10 06	14 49	16 28	18 03	19 37
N 70	06 53	08 10	09 31	15 15	16 44	18 13	19 40
68	06 47	07 56	09 06	15 34	16 57	18 21	19 43
66	06 42	07 45	08 47	15 50	17 08	18 27	19 46
64	06 38	07 36	08 31	16 02	17 17	18 33	19 48
62	06 34	07 28	08 18	16 13	17 25	18 37	19 50
60	06 31	07 21	08 07	16 22	17 31	18 41	19 51
N 58	06 27	07 15	07 58	16 30	17 37	18 45	19 53
56	06 24	07 09	07 50	16 37	17 42	18 48	19 54
54	06 22	07 04	07 42	16 43	17 47	18 51	19 55
52	06 19	06 59	07 36	16 49	17 51	18 54	19 56
50	06 16	06 55	07 30	16 54	17 55	18 56	19 57
45	06 11	06 46	07 17	17 05	18 03	19 01	19 59
N 40	06 05	06 38	07 06	17 14	18 10	19 05	20 01
35	06 00	06 30	06 57	17 21	18 15	19 09	20 02
30	05 55	06 24	06 49	17 28	18 20	19 12	20 04
20	05 45	06 12	06 35	17 40	18 29	19 18	20 06
N 10	05 35	06 00	06 22	17 50	18 37	19 23	20 08
0	05 24	05 49	06 10	18 00	18 44	19 28	20 10
S 10	05 11	05 36	05 58	18 09	18 51	19 32	20 12
20	04 55	05 22	05 46	18 19	18 59	19 37	20 14
30	04 35	05 05	05 31	18 31	19 08	19 43	20 16
35	04 22	04 55	05 22	18 38	19 13	19 46	20 18
40	04 06	04 43	05 12	18 45	19 19	19 49	20 19
45	03 46	04 28	05 01	18 54	19 25	19 54	20 21
S 50	03 20	04 09	04 46	19 05	19 33	19 59	20 23
52	03 07	04 00	04 40	19 10	19 37	20 01	20 24
54	02 52	03 50	04 32	19 15	19 41	20 04	20 25
56	02 33	03 38	04 24	19 21	19 45	20 06	20 26
58	02 08	03 24	04 14	19 28	19 50	20 09	20 27
S 60	01 32	03 08	04 04	19 35	19 55	20 13	20 29

Sunset / Twilight / Moonset

Lat.	Sunset	Civil	Naut.	3	4	5	6
°	h m	h m	h m	h m	h m	h m	h m
N 72	14 23	16 03	17 30	09 00	08 54	08 48	08 43
N 70	14 58	16 19	17 36	08 33	08 36	08 37	08 37
68	15 23	16 33	17 42	08 13	08 22	08 28	08 32
66	15 42	16 44	17 47	07 56	08 10	08 20	08 28
64	15 58	16 53	17 51	07 43	08 00	08 13	08 25
62	16 10	17 01	17 55	07 32	07 52	08 08	08 22
60	16 21	17 08	17 58	07 22	07 44	08 03	08 19
N 58	16 31	17 14	18 01	07 14	07 38	07 58	08 17
56	16 39	17 19	18 04	07 06	07 32	07 55	08 15
54	16 46	17 24	18 07	07 00	07 27	07 51	08 13
52	16 53	17 29	18 09	06 54	07 22	07 48	08 11
50	16 59	17 33	18 12	06 48	07 18	07 45	08 09
45	17 12	17 43	18 18	06 36	07 09	07 39	08 06
N 40	17 22	17 51	18 23	06 27	07 01	07 33	08 03
35	17 31	17 58	18 28	06 18	06 55	07 29	08 01
30	17 39	18 04	18 33	06 11	06 49	07 25	07 59
20	17 53	18 16	18 43	05 58	06 39	07 17	07 55
N 10	18 06	18 28	18 53	05 47	06 30	07 11	07 51
0	18 17	18 39	19 04	05 36	06 21	07 05	07 48
S 10	18 29	18 51	19 17	05 25	06 13	06 59	07 45
20	18 42	19 05	19 32	05 14	06 04	06 53	07 41
30	18 56	19 22	19 52	05 01	05 54	06 46	07 37
35	19 05	19 32	20 05	04 53	05 47	06 41	07 35
40	19 15	19 44	20 21	04 45	05 41	06 37	07 32
45	19 26	19 59	20 40	04 35	05 33	06 31	07 29
S 50	19 40	20 18	21 06	04 22	05 23	06 24	07 25
52	19 47	20 26	21 19	04 16	05 18	06 21	07 24
54	19 54	20 37	21 34	04 10	05 14	06 18	07 22
56	20 02	20 48	21 52	04 03	05 08	06 14	07 20
58	20 12	21 02	22 16	03 55	05 02	06 10	07 17
S 60	20 22	21 17	22 49	03 46	04 55	06 05	07 15

SUN / MOON

Day	Eqn. of Time 00ʰ	Eqn. of Time 12ʰ	Mer. Pass.	Mer. Pass. Upper	Mer. Pass. Lower	Age	Phase
d	m s	m s	h m	h m	h m	d	%
3	13 42	13 46	12 14	24 11	11 48	14	100
4	13 49	13 52	12 14	00 11	12 33	15	100
5	13 54	13 57	12 14	00 55	13 16	16	98

○

UT	ARIES GHA	VENUS −3.9 GHA	Dec	MARS +1.2 GHA	Dec	JUPITER −2.6 GHA	Dec	SATURN +0.5 GHA	Dec	Name	SHA	Dec
d h 6 00	135 48.9	152 11.0	S 8 31.1	145 28.2	S 4 58.8	355 19.9	N16 25.7	253 36.2	S18 56.8	Acamar	315 17.5	S40 15.1
01	150 51.3	167 10.6	29.9	160 28.9	58.0	10 22.7	25.8	268 38.5	56.9	Achernar	335 26.3	S57 10.0
02	165 53.8	182 10.1	28.6	175 29.6	57.3	25 25.5	26.0	283 40.9	56.9	Acrux	173 07.4	S63 10.8
03	180 56.3	197 09.7	.. 27.4	190 30.3	.. 56.5	40 28.3	.. 26.1	298 43.2	.. 56.9	Adhara	255 11.3	S28 59.9
04	195 58.7	212 09.3	26.2	205 31.0	55.7	55 31.1	26.2	313 45.5	56.9	Aldebaran	290 47.9	N16 32.2
05	211 01.2	227 08.9	24.9	220 31.7	54.9	70 33.9	26.3	328 47.8	56.9			
06	226 03.6	242 08.5	S 8 23.7	235 32.3	S 4 54.1	85 36.7	N16 26.4	343 50.1	S18 57.0	Alioth	166 19.5	N55 52.4
07	241 06.1	257 08.1	22.5	250 33.0	53.3	100 39.4	26.5	358 52.4	57.0	Alkaid	152 57.9	N49 14.0
08	256 08.6	272 07.7	21.3	265 33.7	52.5	115 42.2	26.6	13 54.7	57.0	Al Na'ir	27 42.8	S46 53.3
F 09	271 11.0	287 07.3	.. 20.0	280 34.4	.. 51.7	130 45.0	.. 26.7	28 57.0	.. 57.0	Alnilam	275 45.0	S 1 11.9
R 10	286 13.5	302 06.8	18.8	295 35.1	51.0	145 47.8	26.8	43 59.3	57.0	Alphard	217 54.6	S 8 43.7
I 11	301 16.0	317 06.4	17.6	310 35.8	50.2	160 50.6	26.9	59 01.6	57.1			
D 12	316 18.4	332 06.0	S 8 16.3	325 36.5	S 4 49.4	175 53.4	N16 27.0	74 04.0	S18 57.1	Alphecca	126 10.1	N26 39.7
A 13	331 20.9	347 05.6	15.1	340 37.1	48.6	190 56.2	27.1	89 06.3	57.1	Alpheratz	357 42.5	N29 10.5
Y 14	346 23.4	2 05.2	13.9	355 37.8	47.8	205 59.0	27.2	104 08.6	57.1	Altair	62 07.4	N 8 54.6
15	1 25.8	17 04.8	.. 12.6	10 38.5	.. 47.0	221 01.8	.. 27.3	119 10.9	.. 57.2	Ankaa	353 14.9	S42 13.7
16	16 28.3	32 04.4	11.4	25 39.2	46.2	236 04.6	27.4	134 13.2	57.2	Antares	112 25.0	S26 27.7
17	31 30.8	47 04.0	10.2	40 39.9	45.4	251 07.4	27.5	149 15.5	57.2			
18	46 33.2	62 03.6	S 8 08.9	55 40.6	S 4 44.7	266 10.2	N16 27.7	164 17.8	S18 57.2	Arcturus	145 54.6	N19 06.1
19	61 35.7	77 03.2	07.7	70 41.3	43.9	281 13.0	27.8	179 20.1	57.2	Atria	107 26.0	S69 02.8
20	76 38.1	92 02.7	06.5	85 41.9	43.1	296 15.7	27.9	194 22.4	57.3	Avior	234 16.8	S59 33.7
21	91 40.6	107 02.3	.. 05.2	100 42.6	.. 42.3	311 18.5	.. 28.0	209 24.8	.. 57.3	Bellatrix	278 30.6	N 6 21.5
22	106 43.1	122 01.9	04.0	115 43.3	41.5	326 21.3	28.1	224 27.1	57.3	Betelgeuse	270 59.8	N 7 24.3
23	121 45.5	137 01.5	02.8	130 44.0	40.7	341 24.1	28.2	239 29.4	57.3			
7 00	136 48.0	152 01.1	S 8 01.5	145 44.7	S 4 39.9	356 26.9	N16 28.3	254 31.7	S18 57.3	Canopus	263 55.2	S52 42.6
01	151 50.5	167 00.7	8 00.3	160 45.4	39.1	11 29.7	28.4	269 34.0	57.4	Capella	280 32.5	N46 00.7
02	166 52.9	182 00.3	7 59.0	175 46.1	38.3	26 32.5	28.5	284 36.3	57.4	Deneb	49 31.1	N45 20.1
03	181 55.4	196 59.9	.. 57.8	190 46.7	.. 37.6	41 35.3	.. 28.6	299 38.6	.. 57.4	Denebola	182 32.3	N14 29.1
04	196 57.9	211 59.5	56.6	205 47.4	36.8	56 38.1	28.7	314 41.0	57.4	Diphda	348 55.0	S17 54.4
05	212 00.3	226 59.1	55.3	220 48.1	36.0	71 40.9	28.8	329 43.3	57.4			
06	227 02.8	241 58.7	S 7 54.1	235 48.8	S 4 35.2	86 43.7	N16 28.9	344 45.6	S18 57.5	Dubhe	193 49.9	N61 39.9
07	242 05.3	256 58.3	52.9	250 49.5	34.4	101 46.5	29.0	359 47.9	57.5	Elnath	278 10.9	N28 37.0
S 08	257 07.7	271 57.9	51.6	265 50.2	33.6	116 49.3	29.1	14 50.2	57.5	Eltanin	90 46.5	N51 29.2
A 09	272 10.2	286 57.5	.. 50.4	280 50.9	.. 32.8	131 52.0	.. 29.2	29 52.5	.. 57.5	Enif	33 46.3	N 9 56.7
T 10	287 12.6	301 57.1	49.1	295 51.5	32.0	146 54.8	29.3	44 54.8	57.5	Fomalhaut	15 23.1	S29 32.6
U 11	302 15.1	316 56.7	47.9	310 52.2	31.3	161 57.6	29.5	59 57.1	57.6			
R 12	317 17.6	331 56.3	S 7 46.7	325 52.9	S 4 30.5	177 00.4	N16 29.6	74 59.5	S18 57.6	Gacrux	171 59.1	S57 11.7
D 13	332 20.0	346 55.9	45.4	340 53.6	29.7	192 03.2	29.7	90 01.8	57.6	Gienah	175 50.9	S17 37.6
A 14	347 22.5	1 55.5	44.2	355 54.3	28.9	207 06.0	29.8	105 04.1	57.6	Hadar	148 46.0	S60 26.4
Y 15	2 25.0	16 55.1	.. 42.9	10 55.0	.. 28.1	222 08.8	.. 29.9	120 06.4	.. 57.7	Hamal	327 59.5	N23 32.0
16	17 27.4	31 54.7	41.7	25 55.7	27.3	237 11.6	30.0	135 08.7	57.7	Kaus Aust.	83 42.6	S34 22.4
17	32 29.9	46 54.2	40.5	40 56.4	26.5	252 14.4	30.1	150 11.0	57.7			
18	47 32.4	61 53.8	S 7 39.2	55 57.0	S 4 25.7	267 17.2	N16 30.2	165 13.4	S18 57.7	Kochab	137 20.2	N74 05.4
19	62 34.8	76 53.4	38.0	70 57.7	24.9	282 20.0	30.3	180 15.7	57.7	Markab	13 37.5	N15 17.2
20	77 37.3	91 53.0	36.7	85 58.4	24.2	297 22.8	30.4	195 18.0	57.8	Menkar	314 13.8	N 4 08.7
21	92 39.7	106 52.6	.. 35.5	100 59.1	.. 23.4	312 25.6	.. 30.5	210 20.3	.. 57.8	Menkent	148 06.1	S36 26.5
22	107 42.2	121 52.3	34.2	115 59.8	22.6	327 28.4	30.6	225 22.6	57.8	Miaplacidus	221 38.3	S69 46.9
23	122 44.7	136 51.9	33.0	131 00.5	21.8	342 31.1	30.7	240 24.9	57.8			
8 00	137 47.1	151 51.5	S 7 31.7	146 01.2	S 4 21.0	357 33.9	N16 30.8	255 27.3	S18 57.8	Mirfak	308 38.6	N49 54.9
01	152 49.6	166 51.1	30.5	161 01.9	20.2	12 36.7	30.9	270 29.6	57.9	Nunki	75 57.2	S26 16.5
02	167 52.1	181 50.7	29.3	176 02.6	19.4	27 39.5	31.0	285 31.9	57.9	Peacock	53 18.1	S56 41.0
03	182 54.5	196 50.3	.. 28.0	191 03.2	.. 18.6	42 42.3	.. 31.1	300 34.2	.. 57.9	Pollux	243 26.0	N27 59.1
04	197 57.0	211 49.9	26.8	206 03.9	17.8	57 45.1	31.2	315 36.5	57.9	Procyon	244 58.2	N 5 10.9
05	212 59.5	226 49.5	25.5	221 04.6	17.0	72 47.9	31.4	330 38.8	57.9			
06	228 01.9	241 49.1	S 7 24.3	236 05.3	S 4 16.3	87 50.7	N16 31.5	345 41.2	S18 58.0	Rasalhague	96 05.6	N12 33.0
07	243 04.4	256 48.7	23.0	251 06.0	15.5	102 53.5	31.6	0 43.5	58.0	Regulus	207 42.0	N11 53.4
08	258 06.9	271 48.3	21.8	266 06.7	14.7	117 56.3	31.7	15 45.8	58.0	Rigel	281 10.8	S 8 11.4
S 09	273 09.3	286 47.9	.. 20.5	281 07.4	.. 13.9	132 59.1	.. 31.8	30 48.1	.. 58.0	Rigil Kent.	139 50.0	S60 53.5
U 10	288 11.8	301 47.5	19.3	296 08.1	13.1	148 01.9	31.9	45 50.4	58.0	Sabik	102 11.4	S15 44.4
N 11	303 14.2	316 47.1	18.0	311 08.8	12.3	163 04.7	32.0	60 52.7	58.0			
D 12	318 16.7	331 46.7	S 7 16.8	326 09.5	S 4 11.5	178 07.4	N16 32.1	75 55.1	S18 58.1	Schedar	349 39.4	N56 37.4
A 13	333 19.2	346 46.3	15.5	341 10.1	10.7	193 10.2	32.2	90 57.4	58.1	Shaula	96 20.6	S37 06.6
Y 14	348 21.6	1 45.9	14.3	356 10.8	09.9	208 13.0	32.3	105 59.7	58.1	Sirius	258 32.4	S16 44.6
15	3 24.1	16 45.5	.. 13.0	11 11.5	.. 09.2	223 15.8	.. 32.4	121 02.0	.. 58.1	Spica	158 29.9	S11 14.4
16	18 26.6	31 45.1	11.8	26 12.2	08.4	238 18.6	32.5	136 04.3	58.1	Suhail	222 51.1	S43 29.8
17	33 29.0	46 44.7	10.5	41 12.9	07.6	253 21.4	32.6	151 06.7	58.2			
18	48 31.5	61 44.3	S 7 09.3	56 13.6	S 4 06.8	268 24.2	N16 32.7	166 09.0	S18 58.2	Vega	80 38.5	N38 47.9
19	63 34.0	76 43.9	08.0	71 14.3	06.0	283 27.0	32.8	181 11.3	58.2	Zuben'ubi	137 04.1	S16 06.2
20	78 36.4	91 43.6	06.8	86 15.0	05.2	298 29.8	32.9	196 13.6	58.2		SHA	Mer.Pass.
21	93 38.9	106 43.2	.. 05.5	101 15.7	.. 04.4	313 32.6	.. 33.0	211 15.9	.. 58.2		° ′	h m
22	108 41.3	121 42.8	04.3	116 16.4	03.6	328 35.4	33.1	226 18.3	58.3	Venus	15 13.1	13 52
23	123 43.8	136 42.4	03.0	131 17.0	02.8	343 38.2	33.3	241 20.6	58.3	Mars	8 56.7	14 16
Mer.Pass.	h m 14 50.4	v −0.4	d 1.2	v 0.7	d 0.8	v 2.8	d 0.1	v 2.3	d 0.0	Jupiter	219 38.9	0 14
										Saturn	117 43.7	7 01

UT	SUN GHA	SUN Dec	MOON GHA	v	MOON Dec	d	HP
d h	° ′	° ′	° ′	′	° ′	′	′
6 00	176 30.2	S15 46.8	336 14.9	15.1	N 5 40.1	9.0	54.0
01	191 30.2	46.1	350 49.0	15.1	5 31.1	8.9	54.0
02	206 30.1	45.3	5 23.1	15.2	5 22.2	9.0	54.0
03	221 30.1 ..	44.5	19 57.3	15.2	5 13.2	9.0	54.0
04	236 30.0	43.8	34 31.5	15.1	5 04.2	9.1	54.0
05	251 30.0	43.0	49 05.6	15.3	4 55.1	9.0	54.0
F 06	266 29.9	S15 42.2	63 39.9	15.2	N 4 46.1	9.1	54.0
R 07	281 29.9	41.5	78 14.1	15.2	4 37.0	9.1	54.0
I 08	296 29.9	40.7	92 48.3	15.2	4 27.9	9.1	54.0
D 09	311 29.8 ..	39.9	107 22.5	15.3	4 18.8	9.1	54.0
A 10	326 29.8	39.2	121 56.8	15.3	4 09.7	9.2	54.0
Y 11	341 29.7	38.4	136 31.1	15.3	4 00.5	9.1	54.0
12	356 29.7	S15 37.6	151 05.4	15.2	N 3 51.4	9.2	54.0
13	11 29.6	36.8	165 39.6	15.4	3 42.2	9.2	54.0
14	26 29.6	36.1	180 14.0	15.3	3 33.0	9.2	54.0
15	41 29.6 ..	35.3	194 48.3	15.3	3 23.8	9.2	54.0
16	56 29.5	34.5	209 22.6	15.3	3 14.6	9.2	54.0
17	71 29.5	33.8	223 56.9	15.4	3 05.4	9.2	54.0
18	86 29.4	S15 33.0	238 31.3	15.3	N 2 56.2	9.3	54.0
19	101 29.4	32.2	253 05.6	15.4	2 46.9	9.2	54.0
20	116 29.4	31.4	267 40.0	15.3	2 37.7	9.3	54.0
21	131 29.3 ..	30.7	282 14.3	15.4	2 28.4	9.3	54.0
22	146 29.3	29.9	296 48.7	15.4	2 19.1	9.3	54.0
23	161 29.2	29.1	311 23.1	15.3	2 09.8	9.2	54.0
7 00	176 29.2	S15 28.4	325 57.4	15.4	N 2 00.6	9.4	54.0
01	191 29.2	27.6	340 31.8	15.3	1 51.2	9.3	54.0
02	206 29.1	26.8	355 06.2	15.4	1 41.9	9.3	54.0
03	221 29.1 ..	26.0	9 40.6	15.4	1 32.6	9.3	54.0
04	236 29.1	25.2	24 15.0	15.4	1 23.3	9.3	54.0
05	251 29.0	24.5	38 49.4	15.4	1 14.0	9.4	54.0
S 06	266 29.0	S15 23.7	53 23.8	15.4	N 1 04.6	9.3	54.0
A 07	281 29.0	22.9	67 58.2	15.4	0 55.3	9.3	54.0
T 08	296 28.9	22.1	82 32.6	15.4	0 46.0	9.4	54.0
U 09	311 28.9 ..	21.4	97 07.0	15.3	0 36.6	9.3	54.1
R 10	326 28.9	20.6	111 41.3	15.4	0 27.3	9.4	54.1
D 11	341 28.8	19.8	126 15.7	15.4	0 17.9	9.4	54.1
A 12	356 28.8	S15 19.0	140 50.1	15.4	N 0 08.5	9.3	54.1
Y 13	11 28.8	18.2	155 24.5	15.4	S 0 00.8	9.4	54.1
14	26 28.7	17.5	169 58.9	15.4	0 10.2	9.3	54.1
15	41 28.7 ..	16.7	184 33.3	15.3	0 19.5	9.4	54.1
16	56 28.7	15.9	199 07.6	15.4	0 28.9	9.3	54.1
17	71 28.6	15.1	213 42.0	15.4	0 38.2	9.4	54.1
18	86 28.6	S15 14.3	228 16.4	15.3	S 0 47.6	9.3	54.1
19	101 28.6	13.5	242 50.7	15.4	0 56.9	9.4	54.1
20	116 28.5	12.8	257 25.1	15.3	1 06.3	9.3	54.1
21	131 28.5 ..	12.0	271 59.4	15.4	1 15.6	9.4	54.1
22	146 28.5	11.2	286 33.7	15.4	1 25.0	9.3	54.1
23	161 28.4	10.4	301 08.1	15.3	1 34.3	9.4	54.1
8 00	176 28.4	S15 09.6	315 42.4	15.3	S 1 43.7	9.3	54.2
01	191 28.4	08.8	330 16.7	15.3	1 53.0	9.3	54.2
02	206 28.4	08.0	344 51.0	15.2	2 02.3	9.3	54.2
03	221 28.3 ..	07.3	359 25.2	15.3	2 11.6	9.3	54.2
04	236 28.3	06.5	13 59.5	15.2	2 20.9	9.3	54.2
05	251 28.3	05.7	28 33.7	15.3	2 30.2	9.3	54.2
S 06	266 28.2	S15 04.9	43 08.0	15.2	S 2 39.5	9.3	54.2
U 07	281 28.2	04.1	57 42.2	15.2	2 48.8	9.3	54.2
N 08	296 28.2	03.3	72 16.4	15.2	2 58.1	9.3	54.2
D 09	311 28.2 ..	02.5	86 50.6	15.2	3 07.4	9.2	54.2
A 10	326 28.1	01.7	101 24.8	15.1	3 16.6	9.3	54.2
Y 11	341 28.1	00.9	115 58.9	15.2	3 25.9	9.2	54.3
12	356 28.1	S15 00.2	130 33.1	15.1	S 3 35.1	9.2	54.3
13	11 28.1	14 59.4	145 07.2	15.1	3 44.3	9.2	54.3
14	26 28.0	58.6	159 41.3	15.1	3 53.5	9.2	54.3
15	41 28.0 ..	57.8	174 15.4	15.0	4 02.7	9.2	54.3
16	56 28.0	57.0	188 49.4	15.1	4 11.9	9.2	54.3
17	71 28.0	56.2	203 23.5	15.0	4 21.1	9.2	54.3
18	86 27.9	S14 55.4	217 57.5	15.0	S 4 30.3	9.1	54.3
19	101 27.9	54.6	232 31.5	14.9	4 39.4	9.1	54.4
20	116 27.9	53.8	247 05.4	15.0	4 48.5	9.1	54.4
21	131 27.9 ..	53.0	261 39.4	14.9	4 57.6	9.1	54.4
22	146 27.8	52.2	276 13.3	14.9	5 06.7	9.1	54.4
23	161 27.8	51.4	290 47.2	14.9	S 5 15.8	9.0	54.4
	SD 16.2	d 0.8	SD 14.7		14.7		14.8

Lat.	Twilight Naut.	Civil	Sunrise	Moonrise 6	7	8	9
°	h m	h m	h m	h m	h m	h m	h m
N 72	06 48	08 13	09 45	19 37	21 09	22 43	24 19
N 70	06 43	07 58	09 15	19 40	21 07	22 35	24 05
68	06 38	07 46	08 53	19 43	21 06	22 29	23 53
66	06 34	07 36	08 36	19 46	21 04	22 24	23 44
64	06 31	07 28	08 22	19 48	21 03	22 19	23 36
62	06 27	07 21	08 10	19 50	21 02	22 15	23 29
60	06 24	07 14	08 00	19 51	21 02	22 12	23 23
N 58	06 22	07 09	07 51	19 53	21 01	22 09	23 18
56	06 19	07 03	07 44	19 54	21 00	22 07	23 14
54	06 17	06 59	07 37	19 55	21 00	22 04	23 09
52	06 15	06 55	07 31	19 56	20 59	22 02	23 06
50	06 12	06 51	07 25	19 57	20 59	22 00	23 02
45	06 07	06 42	07 13	19 59	20 57	21 56	22 55
N 40	06 02	06 35	07 03	20 01	20 57	21 53	22 49
35	05 58	06 28	06 54	20 02	20 56	21 50	22 44
30	05 53	06 22	06 47	20 04	20 55	21 47	22 39
20	05 44	06 11	06 33	20 06	20 54	21 42	22 32
N 10	05 35	06 00	06 22	20 08	20 53	21 38	22 25
0	05 24	05 49	06 11	20 10	20 52	21 35	22 18
S 10	05 12	05 38	05 59	20 12	20 51	21 31	22 12
20	04 57	05 24	05 47	20 14	20 50	21 27	22 05
30	04 38	05 08	05 33	20 16	20 49	21 23	21 58
35	04 25	04 58	05 25	20 18	20 49	21 20	21 53
40	04 11	04 47	05 16	20 19	20 48	21 18	21 48
45	03 52	04 32	05 05	20 21	20 47	21 14	21 43
S 50	03 28	04 15	04 52	20 23	20 46	21 10	21 36
52	03 15	04 06	04 45	20 24	20 46	21 09	21 33
54	03 01	03 57	04 38	20 25	20 46	21 07	21 29
56	02 43	03 46	04 31	20 26	20 45	21 05	21 26
58	02 22	03 33	04 22	20 27	20 44	21 02	21 21
S 60	01 52	03 18	04 12	20 29	20 44	21 00	21 17

Lat.	Sunset	Twilight Civil	Naut.	Moonset 6	7	8	9
°	h m	h m	h m	h m	h m	h m	h m
N 72	14 45	16 17	17 42	08 43	08 38	08 33	08 28
N 70	15 14	16 32	17 47	08 37	08 37	08 37	08 37
68	15 36	16 43	17 51	08 32	08 37	08 41	08 45
66	15 53	16 53	17 55	08 28	08 36	08 43	08 52
64	16 07	17 01	17 59	08 25	08 36	08 46	08 57
62	16 19	17 09	18 02	08 22	08 35	08 48	09 02
60	16 29	17 15	18 05	08 19	08 35	08 50	09 06
N 58	16 38	17 20	18 07	08 17	08 34	08 52	09 10
56	16 45	17 26	18 10	08 15	08 34	08 53	09 13
54	16 52	17 30	18 12	08 13	08 34	08 55	09 16
52	16 58	17 34	18 14	08 11	08 34	08 55	09 19
50	17 04	17 38	18 17	08 10	08 33	08 57	09 22
45	17 16	17 47	18 22	08 06	08 33	09 00	09 27
N 40	17 26	17 54	18 26	08 03	08 33	09 02	09 32
35	17 34	18 01	18 31	08 01	08 32	09 03	09 36
30	17 42	18 07	18 35	07 59	08 32	09 05	09 39
20	17 55	18 18	18 44	07 55	08 31	09 08	09 45
N 10	18 07	18 28	18 53	07 51	08 31	09 10	09 51
0	18 18	18 39	19 04	07 48	08 30	09 13	09 56
S 10	18 29	18 50	19 16	07 45	08 30	09 15	10 01
20	18 41	19 04	19 31	07 41	08 29	09 17	10 06
30	18 54	19 20	19 50	07 37	08 29	09 20	10 12
35	19 02	19 29	20 02	07 35	08 28	09 22	10 16
40	19 12	19 41	20 17	07 32	08 28	09 24	10 20
45	19 22	19 55	20 35	07 29	08 27	09 26	10 24
S 50	19 35	20 12	20 59	07 25	08 27	09 28	10 30
52	19 42	20 20	21 11	07 24	08 26	09 29	10 33
54	19 48	20 30	21 25	07 22	08 26	09 31	10 35
56	19 56	20 41	21 42	07 20	08 26	09 32	10 38
58	20 05	20 53	22 03	07 17	08 25	09 33	10 42
S 60	20 14	21 08	22 31	07 15	08 25	09 35	10 46

Day	SUN Eqn. of Time 00h	12h	SUN Mer. Pass.	MOON Mer. Pass. Upper	Lower	Age	Phase
d	m s	m s	h m	h m	h m	d	%
6	13 59	14 01	12 14	01 38	13 59	17	94
7	14 03	14 05	12 14	02 20	14 41	18	89
8	14 06	14 08	12 14	03 02	15 24	19	83

UT	ARIES GHA	VENUS −3.9 GHA	Dec	MARS +1.2 GHA	Dec	JUPITER −2.6 GHA	Dec	SATURN +0.5 GHA	Dec
MONDAY 9									
00	138 46.3	151 42.0	S 7 01.8	146 17.7	S 4 02.0	358 41.0	N16 33.4	256 22.9	S18 58.3
01	153 48.7	166 41.6	7 00.5	161 18.4	01.2	13 43.7	33.5	271 25.2	58.3
02	168 51.2	181 41.2	6 59.3	176 19.1	4 00.5	28 46.5	33.6	286 27.5	58.3
03	183 53.7	196 40.8	.. 58.0	191 19.8	3 59.7	43 49.3	.. 33.7	301 29.9	.. 58.4
04	198 56.1	211 40.4	56.8	206 20.5	58.9	58 52.1	33.8	316 32.2	58.4
05	213 58.6	226 40.0	55.5	221 21.2	58.1	73 54.9	33.9	331 34.5	58.4
06	229 01.1	241 39.7	S 6 54.3	236 21.9	S 3 57.3	88 57.7	N16 34.0	346 36.8	S18 58.4
07	244 03.5	256 39.3	53.0	251 22.6	56.5	104 00.5	34.1	1 39.1	58.4
08	259 06.0	271 38.9	51.7	266 23.3	55.7	119 03.3	34.2	16 41.5	58.5
09	274 08.5	286 38.5	.. 50.5	281 24.0	.. 54.9	134 06.1	.. 34.3	31 43.8	.. 58.5
10	289 10.9	301 38.1	49.2	296 24.6	54.1	149 08.9	34.4	46 46.1	58.5
11	304 13.4	316 37.7	48.0	311 25.3	53.3	164 11.7	34.5	61 48.4	58.5
12	319 15.8	331 37.3	S 6 46.7	326 26.0	S 3 52.6	179 14.5	N16 34.6	76 50.7	S18 58.5
13	334 18.3	346 37.0	45.5	341 26.7	51.8	194 17.3	34.7	91 53.1	58.5
14	349 20.8	1 36.6	44.2	356 27.4	51.0	209 20.0	34.8	106 55.4	58.6
15	4 23.2	16 36.2	.. 43.0	11 28.1	.. 50.2	224 22.8	.. 34.9	121 57.7	.. 58.6
16	19 25.7	31 35.8	41.7	26 28.8	49.4	239 25.6	35.0	137 00.0	58.6
17	34 28.2	46 35.4	40.4	41 29.5	48.6	254 28.4	35.1	152 02.4	58.6
18	49 30.6	61 35.0	S 6 39.2	56 30.2	S 3 47.8	269 31.2	N16 35.2	167 04.7	S18 58.6
19	64 33.1	76 34.6	37.9	71 30.9	47.0	284 34.0	35.3	182 07.0	58.7
20	79 35.6	91 34.3	36.7	86 31.6	46.2	299 36.8	35.5	197 09.3	58.7
21	94 38.0	106 33.9	.. 35.4	101 32.3	.. 45.4	314 39.6	.. 35.6	212 11.7	.. 58.7
22	109 40.5	121 33.5	34.1	116 33.0	44.6	329 42.4	35.7	227 14.0	58.7
23	124 43.0	136 33.1	32.9	131 33.7	43.9	344 45.2	35.8	242 16.3	58.7
TUESDAY 10									
00	139 45.4	151 32.7	S 6 31.6	146 34.3	S 3 43.1	359 48.0	N16 35.9	257 18.6	S18 58.8
01	154 47.9	166 32.3	30.4	161 35.0	42.3	14 50.8	36.0	272 21.0	58.8
02	169 50.3	181 32.0	29.1	176 35.7	41.5	29 53.6	36.1	287 23.3	58.8
03	184 52.8	196 31.6	.. 27.8	191 36.4	.. 40.7	44 56.3	.. 36.2	302 25.6	.. 58.8
04	199 55.3	211 31.2	26.6	206 37.1	39.9	59 59.1	36.3	317 27.9	58.8
05	214 57.7	226 30.8	25.3	221 37.8	39.1	75 01.9	36.4	332 30.3	58.8
06	230 00.2	241 30.4	S 6 24.1	236 38.5	S 3 38.3	90 04.7	N16 36.5	347 32.6	S18 58.9
07	245 02.7	256 30.1	22.8	251 39.2	37.5	105 07.5	36.6	2 34.9	58.9
08	260 05.1	271 29.7	21.5	266 39.9	36.7	120 10.3	36.7	17 37.2	58.9
09	275 07.6	286 29.3	.. 20.3	281 40.6	.. 35.9	135 13.1	.. 36.8	32 39.6	.. 58.9
10	290 10.1	301 28.9	19.0	296 41.3	35.2	150 15.9	36.9	47 41.9	58.9
11	305 12.5	316 28.5	17.8	311 42.0	34.4	165 18.7	37.0	62 44.2	59.0
12	320 15.0	331 28.2	S 6 16.5	326 42.7	S 3 33.6	180 21.5	N16 37.1	77 46.5	S18 59.0
13	335 17.4	346 27.8	15.2	341 43.4	32.8	195 24.3	37.2	92 48.9	59.0
14	350 19.9	1 27.4	14.0	356 44.1	32.0	210 27.1	37.3	107 51.2	59.0
15	5 22.4	16 27.0	.. 12.7	11 44.8	.. 31.2	225 29.8	.. 37.4	122 53.5	.. 59.0
16	20 24.8	31 26.6	11.4	26 45.4	30.4	240 32.6	37.5	137 55.8	59.0
17	35 27.3	46 26.3	10.2	41 46.1	29.6	255 35.4	37.6	152 58.2	59.1
18	50 29.8	61 25.9	S 6 08.9	56 46.8	S 3 28.8	270 38.2	N16 37.7	168 00.5	S18 59.1
19	65 32.2	76 25.5	07.6	71 47.5	28.0	285 41.0	37.9	183 02.8	59.1
20	80 34.7	91 25.1	06.4	86 48.2	27.2	300 43.8	38.0	198 05.1	59.1
21	95 37.2	106 24.8	.. 05.1	101 48.9	.. 26.4	315 46.6	.. 38.1	213 07.5	.. 59.1
22	110 39.6	121 24.4	03.8	116 49.6	25.7	330 49.4	38.2	228 09.8	59.1
23	125 42.1	136 24.0	02.6	131 50.3	24.9	345 52.2	38.3	243 12.1	59.2
WEDNESDAY 11									
00	140 44.6	151 23.6	S 6 01.3	146 51.0	S 3 24.1	0 55.0	N16 38.4	258 14.5	S18 59.2
01	155 47.0	166 23.3	6 00.0	161 51.7	23.3	15 57.8	38.5	273 16.8	59.2
02	170 49.5	181 22.9	5 58.8	176 52.4	22.5	31 00.5	38.6	288 19.1	59.2
03	185 51.9	196 22.5	.. 57.5	191 53.1	.. 21.7	46 03.3	.. 38.7	303 21.4	.. 59.2
04	200 54.4	211 22.1	56.2	206 53.8	20.9	61 06.1	38.8	318 23.8	59.3
05	215 56.9	226 21.8	55.0	221 54.5	20.1	76 08.9	38.9	333 26.1	59.3
06	230 59.3	241 21.4	S 5 53.7	236 55.2	S 3 19.3	91 11.7	N16 39.0	348 28.4	S18 59.3
07	246 01.8	256 21.0	52.4	251 55.9	18.5	106 14.5	39.1	3 30.8	59.3
08	261 04.3	271 20.6	51.2	266 56.6	17.7	121 17.3	39.2	18 33.1	59.3
09	276 06.7	286 20.3	.. 49.9	281 57.3	.. 16.9	136 20.1	.. 39.3	33 35.4	.. 59.3
10	291 09.2	301 19.9	48.6	296 58.0	16.2	151 22.9	39.4	48 37.7	59.4
11	306 11.7	316 19.5	47.4	311 58.7	15.4	166 25.7	39.5	63 40.1	59.4
12	321 14.1	331 19.2	S 5 46.1	326 59.4	S 3 14.6	181 28.5	N16 39.6	78 42.4	S18 59.4
13	336 16.6	346 18.8	44.8	342 00.1	13.8	196 31.2	39.7	93 44.7	59.4
14	351 19.1	1 18.4	43.6	357 00.8	13.0	211 34.0	39.8	108 47.1	59.4
15	6 21.5	16 18.0	.. 42.3	12 01.4	.. 12.2	226 36.8	.. 39.9	123 49.4	.. 59.4
16	21 24.0	31 17.7	41.0	27 02.1	11.4	241 39.6	40.0	138 51.7	59.5
17	36 26.4	46 17.3	39.7	42 02.8	10.6	256 42.4	40.1	153 54.1	59.5
18	51 28.9	61 16.9	S 5 38.5	57 03.5	S 3 09.8	271 45.2	N16 40.2	168 56.4	S18 59.5
19	66 31.4	76 16.6	37.2	72 04.2	09.0	286 48.0	40.3	183 58.7	59.5
20	81 33.8	91 16.2	35.9	87 04.9	08.2	301 50.8	40.4	199 01.1	59.5
21	96 36.3	106 15.8	.. 34.7	102 05.6	.. 07.4	316 53.6	.. 40.5	214 03.4	.. 59.5
22	111 38.8	121 15.5	33.4	117 06.3	06.6	331 56.4	40.7	229 05.7	59.6
23	126 41.2	136 15.1	32.1	132 07.0	05.9	346 59.2	40.8	244 08.0	59.6
Mer. Pass. 14 38.6		v −0.4	d 1.3	v 0.7	d 0.8	v 2.8	d 0.1	v 2.3	d 0.0

STARS

Name	SHA	Dec
Acamar	315 17.5	S40 15.1
Achernar	335 26.3	S57 10.0
Acrux	173 07.3	S63 10.8
Adhara	255 11.3	S28 59.9
Aldebaran	290 47.9	N16 32.2
Alioth	166 19.5	N55 52.4
Alkaid	152 57.9	N49 14.0
Al Na'ir	27 42.8	S46 53.3
Alnilam	275 45.0	S 1 11.9
Alphard	217 54.6	S 8 43.7
Alphecca	126 10.1	N26 39.7
Alpheratz	357 42.5	N29 10.5
Altair	62 07.4	N 8 54.6
Ankaa	353 14.9	S42 13.7
Antares	112 25.0	S26 27.7
Arcturus	145 54.6	N19 06.1
Atria	107 25.9	S69 02.8
Avior	234 16.8	S59 33.8
Bellatrix	278 30.6	N 6 21.5
Betelgeuse	270 59.8	N 7 24.3
Canopus	263 55.2	S52 42.7
Capella	280 32.5	N46 00.7
Deneb	49 31.1	N45 20.1
Denebola	182 32.3	N14 29.1
Diphda	348 55.0	S17 54.4
Dubhe	193 49.8	N61 39.9
Elnath	278 11.0	N28 37.0
Eltanin	90 45.9	N51 29.1
Enif	33 46.3	N 9 56.7
Fomalhaut	15 23.1	S29 32.6
Gacrux	171 59.1	S57 11.7
Gienah	175 50.9	S17 35.4
Hadar	148 45.9	S60 26.4
Hamal	327 59.5	N23 32.0
Kaus Aust.	83 42.6	S34 22.4
Kochab	137 20.1	N74 05.4
Markab	13 37.5	N15 17.2
Menkar	314 13.9	N 4 08.7
Menkent	148 06.0	S36 26.5
Miaplacidus	221 38.3	S69 46.9
Mirfak	308 38.6	N49 54.9
Nunki	75 57.2	S26 16.5
Peacock	53 18.1	S56 41.0
Pollux	243 26.0	N27 59.1
Procyon	244 58.2	N 5 10.9
Rasalhague	96 05.6	N12 33.0
Regulus	207 42.0	N11 53.4
Rigel	281 10.8	S 8 11.4
Rigil Kent.	139 49.9	S60 53.5
Sabik	102 11.4	S15 44.4
Schedar	349 39.5	N56 37.4
Shaula	96 20.6	S37 06.6
Sirius	258 32.4	S16 44.6
Spica	158 29.9	S11 14.4
Suhail	222 51.1	S43 29.9
Vega	80 38.5	N38 47.8
Zuben'ubi	137 04.1	S16 06.2

	SHA	Mer. Pass.
Venus	11 47.3	13 54
Mars	6 48.9	14 13
Jupiter	220 02.6	0 01
Saturn	117 33.2	6 50

UT	SUN GHA	SUN Dec	MOON GHA	v	Dec	d	HP
d h	° '	° '	° '	'	° '	'	'
9 00	176 27.8	S14 50.6	305 21.1	14.8	S 5 24.8	9.1	54.4
01	191 27.8	49.8	319 54.9	14.8	5 33.9	9.0	54.4
02	206 27.8	49.0	334 28.7	14.8	5 42.9	9.0	54.4
03	221 27.7 ..	48.2	349 02.5	14.8	5 51.9	9.0	54.5
04	236 27.7	47.4	3 36.3	14.7	6 00.9	8.9	54.5
05	251 27.7	46.6	18 10.0	14.7	6 09.8	9.0	54.5
06	266 27.7	S14 45.8	32 43.7	14.7	S 6 18.8	8.9	54.5
07	281 27.7	45.0	47 17.4	14.7	6 27.7	8.9	54.5
08	296 27.6	44.2	61 51.1	14.6	6 36.6	8.8	54.5
M 09	311 27.6 ..	43.4	76 24.7	14.5	6 45.4	8.9	54.6
O 10	326 27.6	42.6	90 58.2	14.6	6 54.3	8.8	54.6
N 11	341 27.6	41.8	105 31.8	14.5	7 03.1	8.8	54.6
D 12	356 27.6	S14 41.0	120 05.3	14.5	S 7 11.9	8.8	54.6
A 13	11 27.6	40.2	134 38.8	14.4	7 20.7	8.7	54.6
Y 14	26 27.5	39.4	149 12.2	14.4	7 29.4	8.7	54.6
15	41 27.5 ..	38.6	163 45.6	14.4	7 38.1	8.7	54.7
16	56 27.5	37.8	178 19.0	14.3	7 46.8	8.6	54.7
17	71 27.5	37.0	192 52.3	14.3	7 55.4	8.7	54.7
18	86 27.5	S14 36.2	207 25.6	14.3	S 8 04.1	8.6	54.7
19	101 27.5	35.4	221 58.9	14.2	8 12.7	8.5	54.7
20	116 27.4	34.6	236 32.1	14.2	8 21.2	8.6	54.7
21	131 27.4 ..	33.8	251 05.3	14.1	8 29.8	8.5	54.8
22	146 27.4	33.0	265 38.4	14.1	8 38.3	8.5	54.8
23	161 27.4	32.2	280 11.5	14.1	8 46.8	8.4	54.8
10 00	176 27.4	S14 31.4	294 44.6	14.0	S 8 55.2	8.4	54.8
01	191 27.4	30.6	309 17.6	13.9	9 03.6	8.4	54.8
02	206 27.4	29.8	323 50.5	14.0	9 12.0	8.3	54.9
03	221 27.4 ..	29.0	338 23.5	13.9	9 20.3	8.3	54.9
04	236 27.3	28.1	352 56.4	13.8	9 28.6	8.3	54.9
05	251 27.3	27.3	7 29.2	13.8	9 36.9	8.2	54.9
06	266 27.3	S14 26.5	22 02.0	13.7	S 9 45.1	8.2	54.9
07	281 27.3	25.7	36 34.7	13.7	9 53.3	8.2	55.0
T 08	296 27.3	24.9	51 07.4	13.7	10 01.5	8.1	55.0
U 09	311 27.3 ..	24.1	65 40.1	13.6	10 09.6	8.1	55.0
E 10	326 27.3	23.3	80 12.7	13.6	10 17.7	8.0	55.0
S 11	341 27.3	22.5	94 45.3	13.5	10 25.7	8.0	55.1
D 12	356 27.3	S14 21.7	109 17.8	13.4	S10 33.7	8.0	55.1
A 13	11 27.3	20.9	123 50.2	13.4	10 41.7	7.9	55.1
Y 14	26 27.2	20.0	138 22.6	13.4	10 49.6	7.9	55.1
15	41 27.2 ..	19.2	152 55.0	13.3	10 57.5	7.8	55.2
16	56 27.2	18.4	167 27.3	13.3	11 05.3	7.8	55.2
17	71 27.2	17.6	181 59.6	13.2	11 13.1	7.8	55.2
18	86 27.2	S14 16.8	196 31.8	13.1	S11 20.9	7.7	55.2
19	101 27.2	16.0	211 03.9	13.1	11 28.6	7.6	55.3
20	116 27.2	15.2	225 36.0	13.1	11 36.2	7.6	55.3
21	131 27.2 ..	14.3	240 08.1	12.9	11 43.8	7.6	55.3
22	146 27.2	13.5	254 40.0	13.0	11 51.4	7.5	55.3
23	161 27.2	12.7	269 12.0	12.9	11 58.9	7.5	55.4
11 00	176 27.2	S14 11.9	283 43.9	12.8	S12 06.4	7.4	55.4
01	191 27.2	11.1	298 15.7	12.7	12 13.8	7.3	55.4
02	206 27.2	10.3	312 47.4	12.7	12 21.1	7.4	55.4
03	221 27.2 ..	09.4	327 19.1	12.7	12 28.5	7.2	55.5
04	236 27.2	08.6	341 50.8	12.6	12 35.7	7.2	55.5
05	251 27.2	07.8	356 22.4	12.5	12 42.9	7.2	55.5
06	266 27.1	S14 07.0	10 53.9	12.5	S12 50.1	7.1	55.5
07	281 27.1	06.2	25 25.4	12.4	12 57.2	7.1	55.6
W 08	296 27.1	05.3	39 56.8	12.4	13 04.3	7.0	55.6
E 09	311 27.1 ..	04.5	54 28.2	12.3	13 11.3	6.9	55.6
D 10	326 27.1	03.7	68 59.5	12.2	13 18.2	6.9	55.7
N 11	341 27.1	02.9	83 30.7	12.2	13 25.1	6.8	55.7
E 12	356 27.1	S14 02.1	98 01.9	12.1	S13 31.9	6.8	55.7
S 13	11 27.1	01.2	112 33.0	12.0	13 38.7	6.7	55.7
D 14	26 27.1	14 00.4	127 04.0	12.0	13 45.4	6.6	55.8
A 15	41 27.1	13 59.6	141 35.0	11.9	13 52.0	6.6	55.8
Y 16	56 27.1	58.8	156 05.9	11.9	13 58.6	6.5	55.8
17	71 27.1	57.9	170 36.8	11.8	14 05.1	6.5	55.9
18	86 27.1	S13 57.1	185 07.6	11.7	S14 11.6	6.4	55.9
19	101 27.1	56.3	199 38.3	11.7	14 18.0	6.4	55.9
20	116 27.1	55.5	214 09.0	11.6	14 24.4	6.2	56.0
21	131 27.1 ..	54.6	228 39.6	11.5	14 30.6	6.2	56.0
22	146 27.1	53.8	243 10.1	11.4	14 36.8	6.2	56.0
23	161 27.1	53.0	257 40.5	11.5	S14 43.0	6.1	56.0
	SD 16.2	d 0.8	SD 14.9		15.0		15.2

Lat.	Twilight Naut.	Twilight Civil	Sunrise	Moonrise 9	Moonrise 10	Moonrise 11	Moonrise 12
°	h m	h m	h m	h m	h m	h m	h m
N 72	06 37	07 59	09 26	24 19	00 19	02 00	03 48
N 70	06 32	07 46	09 00	24 05	00 05	01 37	03 12
68	06 29	07 36	08 40	23 53	25 19	01 19	02 46
66	06 26	07 27	08 25	23 44	25 05	01 05	02 26
64	06 23	07 19	08 12	23 36	24 53	00 53	02 11
62	06 20	07 13	08 02	23 29	24 43	00 43	01 57
60	06 18	07 07	07 52	23 23	24 35	00 35	01 46
N 58	06 16	07 02	07 44	23 18	24 28	00 28	01 37
56	06 14	06 58	07 37	23 14	24 21	00 21	01 28
54	06 12	06 53	07 31	23 09	24 15	00 15	01 21
52	06 10	06 50	07 25	23 06	24 10	00 10	01 14
50	06 08	06 46	07 20	23 02	24 05	00 05	01 08
45	06 04	06 38	07 09	22 55	23 55	24 56	00 56
N 40	05 59	06 31	06 59	22 49	23 47	24 45	00 45
35	05 55	06 25	06 51	22 44	23 39	24 36	00 36
30	05 51	06 20	06 44	22 39	23 33	24 28	00 28
20	05 43	06 09	06 32	22 32	23 22	24 14	00 14
N 10	05 34	05 59	06 21	22 25	23 13	24 03	00 03
0	05 25	05 49	06 11	22 18	23 04	23 51	24 42
S 10	05 13	05 39	06 00	22 12	22 55	23 40	24 29
20	04 59	05 26	05 49	22 05	22 46	23 29	24 16
30	04 41	05 11	05 36	21 58	22 35	23 15	24 00
35	04 29	05 01	05 28	21 53	22 29	23 08	23 51
40	04 15	04 50	05 20	21 48	22 22	22 59	23 41
45	03 57	04 37	05 09	21 43	22 14	22 49	23 29
S 50	03 34	04 21	04 57	21 36	22 04	22 37	23 15
52	03 23	04 13	04 51	21 33	22 00	22 31	23 08
54	03 10	04 04	04 45	21 29	21 55	22 25	23 01
56	02 54	03 54	04 38	21 26	21 49	22 18	22 52
58	02 34	03 42	04 29	21 21	21 43	22 10	22 43
S 60	02 09	03 28	04 20	21 17	21 37	22 01	22 32

Lat.	Sunset	Twilight Civil	Twilight Naut.	Moonset 9	Moonset 10	Moonset 11	Moonset 12
°	h m	h m	h m	h m	h m	h m	h m
N 72	15 04	16 31	17 54	08 28	08 22	08 16	08 07
N 70	15 30	16 44	17 58	08 37	08 38	08 40	08 45
68	15 49	16 54	18 01	08 45	08 51	08 59	09 12
66	16 05	17 03	18 04	08 52	09 01	09 14	09 32
64	16 17	17 10	18 07	08 57	09 10	09 26	09 48
62	16 28	17 16	18 09	09 02	09 18	09 37	10 02
60	16 37	17 22	18 12	09 06	09 24	09 46	10 13
N 58	16 45	17 27	18 14	09 10	09 30	09 54	10 23
56	16 52	17 32	18 16	09 13	09 36	10 01	10 32
54	16 58	17 36	18 18	09 16	09 40	10 07	10 40
52	17 04	17 40	18 19	09 19	09 44	10 13	10 47
50	17 09	17 43	18 21	09 22	09 48	10 18	10 53
45	17 20	17 51	18 25	09 27	09 57	10 29	11 07
N 40	17 29	17 57	18 29	09 32	10 04	10 39	11 18
35	17 37	18 04	18 33	09 36	10 10	10 47	11 28
30	17 44	18 09	18 37	09 39	10 15	10 54	11 36
20	17 57	18 19	18 45	09 45	10 24	11 06	11 51
N 10	18 07	18 29	18 54	09 51	10 32	11 16	12 03
0	18 18	18 39	19 04	09 56	10 40	11 26	12 15
S 10	18 28	18 50	19 15	10 01	10 48	11 36	12 27
20	18 39	19 02	19 29	10 06	10 56	11 47	12 40
30	18 52	19 17	19 47	10 12	11 05	11 59	12 55
35	18 59	19 26	19 59	10 16	11 10	12 06	13 03
40	19 08	19 37	20 12	10 20	11 17	12 14	13 13
45	19 18	19 50	20 30	10 24	11 24	12 24	13 24
S 50	19 30	20 06	20 52	10 30	11 32	12 35	13 38
52	19 36	20 14	21 03	10 33	11 36	12 41	13 45
54	19 42	20 23	21 16	10 35	11 41	12 46	13 52
56	19 49	20 33	21 32	10 38	11 46	12 53	14 00
58	19 57	20 44	21 51	10 42	11 51	13 00	14 09
S 60	20 06	20 58	22 15	10 46	11 57	13 09	14 19

	SUN			MOON			
Day	Eqn. of Time 00h	Eqn. of Time 12h	Mer. Pass.	Mer. Pass. Upper	Mer. Pass. Lower	Age	Phase
d	m s	m s	h m	h m	h m	d	%
9	14 09	14 10	12 14	03 45	16 07	20	75
10	14 10	14 11	12 14	04 29	16 52	21	66
11	14 11	14 11	12 14	05 15	17 39	22	57

UT	ARIES GHA	VENUS −3.9 GHA	VENUS Dec	MARS +1.2 GHA	MARS Dec	JUPITER −2.6 GHA	JUPITER Dec	SATURN +0.5 GHA	SATURN Dec	STARS Name	SHA	Dec
12 00	141 43.7	151 14.7	S 5 30.8	147 07.7	S 3 05.1	2 01.9	N16 40.9	259 10.4	S18 59.6	Acamar	315 17.6	S40 15.1
01	156 46.2	166 14.4	29.6	162 08.4	04.3	17 04.7	41.0	274 12.7	59.6	Achernar	335 26.3	S57 10.0
02	171 48.6	181 14.0	28.3	177 09.1	03.5	32 07.5	41.1	289 15.0	59.6	Acrux	173 07.3	S63 10.8
03	186 51.1	196 13.6	.. 27.0	192 09.8	.. 02.7	47 10.3	.. 41.2	304 17.4	.. 59.6	Adhara	255 11.3	S29 00.0
04	201 53.5	211 13.3	25.7	207 10.5	01.9	62 13.1	41.3	319 19.7	59.7	Aldebaran	290 47.9	N16 32.2
05	216 56.0	226 12.9	24.5	222 11.2	01.1	77 15.9	41.4	334 22.0	59.7			
06	231 58.5	241 12.5	S 5 23.2	237 11.9	S 3 00.3	92 18.7	N16 41.5	349 24.4	S18 59.7	Alioth	166 19.4	N55 52.4
T 07	247 00.9	256 12.2	21.9	252 12.6	2 59.5	107 21.5	41.6	4 26.7	59.7	Alkaid	152 57.9	N49 14.0
H 08	262 03.4	271 11.8	20.6	267 13.3	58.7	122 24.3	41.7	19 29.0	59.7	Al Na'ir	27 42.8	S46 53.3
U 09	277 05.9	286 11.4	.. 19.4	282 14.0	.. 57.9	137 27.1	.. 41.8	34 31.4	.. 59.7	Alnilam	275 45.0	S 1 11.9
R 10	292 08.3	301 11.1	18.1	297 14.7	57.1	152 29.8	41.9	49 33.7	59.8	Alphard	217 54.6	S 8 43.7
S 11	307 10.8	316 10.7	16.8	312 15.4	56.3	167 32.6	42.0	64 36.0	59.8			
D 12	322 13.3	331 10.3	S 5 15.5	327 16.1	S 2 55.6	182 35.4	N16 42.1	79 38.4	S18 59.8	Alphecca	126 10.1	N26 39.7
A 13	337 15.7	346 10.0	14.3	342 16.8	54.8	197 38.2	42.2	94 40.7	59.8	Alpheratz	357 42.5	N29 10.5
Y 14	352 18.2	1 09.6	13.0	357 17.5	54.0	212 41.0	42.3	109 43.0	59.8	Altair	62 07.4	N 8 54.6
15	7 20.7	16 09.2	.. 11.7	12 18.2	.. 53.2	227 43.8	.. 42.4	124 45.4	.. 59.8	Ankaa	353 14.9	S42 13.7
16	22 23.1	31 08.9	10.4	27 18.9	52.4	242 46.6	42.5	139 47.7	59.9	Antares	112 24.9	S26 27.7
17	37 25.6	46 08.5	09.2	42 19.6	51.6	257 49.4	42.6	154 50.0	59.9			
18	52 28.0	61 08.1	S 5 07.9	57 20.3	S 2 50.8	272 52.2	N16 42.7	169 52.4	S18 59.9	Arcturus	145 54.6	N19 06.1
19	67 30.5	76 07.8	06.6	72 21.0	50.0	287 55.0	42.8	184 54.7	59.9	Atria	107 25.9	S69 02.8
20	82 33.0	91 07.4	05.3	87 21.7	49.2	302 57.7	42.9	199 57.1	59.9	Avior	234 16.9	S59 33.8
21	97 35.4	106 07.1	.. 04.1	102 22.4	.. 48.4	318 00.5	.. 43.0	214 59.4	18 59.9	Bellatrix	278 30.6	N 6 21.5
22	112 37.9	121 06.7	02.8	117 23.1	47.6	333 03.3	43.1	230 01.7	19 00.0	Betelgeuse	270 59.9	N 7 24.3
23	127 40.4	136 06.3	01.5	132 23.8	46.8	348 06.1	43.2	245 04.1	00.0			
13 00	142 42.8	151 06.0	S 5 00.2	147 24.5	S 2 46.0	3 08.9	N16 43.3	260 06.4	S19 00.0	Canopus	263 55.2	S52 42.7
01	157 45.3	166 05.6	4 58.9	162 25.2	45.2	18 11.7	43.4	275 08.7	00.0	Capella	280 32.5	N46 00.7
02	172 47.8	181 05.2	57.7	177 25.9	44.5	33 14.5	43.5	290 11.1	00.0	Deneb	49 31.1	N45 20.1
03	187 50.2	196 04.9	.. 56.4	192 26.6	.. 43.7	48 17.3	.. 43.6	305 13.4	.. 00.0	Denebola	182 32.2	N14 29.1
04	202 52.7	211 04.5	55.1	207 27.3	42.9	63 20.1	43.7	320 15.7	00.1	Diphda	348 55.0	S17 54.4
05	217 55.2	226 04.2	53.8	222 28.0	42.1	78 22.8	43.8	335 18.1	00.1			
06	232 57.6	241 03.8	S 4 52.5	237 28.7	S 2 41.3	93 25.6	N16 43.9	350 20.4	S19 00.1	Dubhe	193 49.8	N61 39.9
07	248 00.1	256 03.4	51.3	252 29.4	40.5	108 28.4	44.0	5 22.7	00.1	Elnath	278 11.0	N28 37.0
F 08	263 02.5	271 03.1	50.0	267 30.1	39.7	123 31.2	44.1	20 25.1	00.1	Eltanin	90 45.9	N51 29.1
R 09	278 05.0	286 02.7	.. 48.7	282 30.8	.. 38.9	138 34.0	.. 44.2	35 27.4	.. 00.1	Enif	33 46.3	N 9 56.7
I 10	293 07.5	301 02.4	47.4	297 31.5	38.1	153 36.8	44.3	50 29.8	00.1	Fomalhaut	15 23.1	S29 32.6
D 11	308 09.9	316 02.0	46.1	312 32.2	37.3	168 39.6	44.4	65 32.1	00.2			
A 12	323 12.4	331 01.6	S 4 44.9	327 32.9	S 2 36.5	183 42.4	N16 44.5	80 34.4	S19 00.2	Gacrux	171 59.1	S57 11.7
Y 13	338 14.9	346 01.3	43.6	342 33.6	35.7	198 45.1	44.7	95 36.8	00.2	Gienah	175 50.8	S17 37.6
14	353 17.3	1 00.9	42.3	357 34.3	34.9	213 47.9	44.8	110 39.1	00.2	Hadar	148 45.9	S60 26.5
15	8 19.8	16 00.6	.. 41.0	12 35.0	.. 34.1	228 50.7	.. 44.9	125 41.5	.. 00.2	Hamal	327 59.5	N23 32.0
16	23 22.3	31 00.2	39.7	27 35.7	33.4	243 53.5	45.0	140 43.8	00.2	Kaus Aust.	83 42.6	S34 22.4
17	38 24.7	45 59.9	38.4	42 36.4	32.6	258 56.3	45.1	155 46.1	00.3			
18	53 27.2	60 59.5	S 4 37.2	57 37.1	S 2 31.8	273 59.1	N16 45.2	170 48.5	S19 00.3	Kochab	137 20.1	N74 05.4
19	68 29.6	75 59.1	35.9	72 37.8	31.0	289 01.9	45.3	185 50.8	00.3	Markab	13 37.5	N15 17.2
20	83 32.1	90 58.8	34.6	87 38.5	30.2	304 04.7	45.4	200 53.1	00.3	Menkar	314 13.9	N 4 08.7
21	98 34.6	105 58.4	.. 33.3	102 39.2	.. 29.4	319 07.5	.. 45.5	215 55.5	.. 00.3	Menkent	148 06.0	S36 26.5
22	113 37.0	120 58.1	32.0	117 39.9	28.6	334 10.2	45.6	230 57.8	00.3	Miaplacidus	221 38.3	S69 47.0
23	128 39.5	135 57.7	30.7	132 40.6	27.8	349 13.0	45.7	246 00.2	00.4			
14 00	143 42.0	150 57.4	S 4 29.5	147 41.3	S 2 27.0	4 15.8	N16 45.8	261 02.5	S19 00.4	Mirfak	308 38.6	N49 54.9
01	158 44.4	165 57.0	28.2	162 42.0	26.2	19 18.6	45.9	276 04.8	00.4	Nunki	75 57.2	S26 16.5
02	173 46.9	180 56.6	26.9	177 42.7	25.4	34 21.4	46.0	291 07.2	00.4	Peacock	53 18.1	S56 41.0
03	188 49.4	195 56.3	.. 25.6	192 43.4	.. 24.6	49 24.2	.. 46.1	306 09.5	.. 00.4	Pollux	243 26.0	N27 59.1
04	203 51.8	210 55.9	24.3	207 44.1	23.8	64 27.0	46.2	321 11.9	00.4	Procyon	244 58.2	N 5 10.9
05	218 54.3	225 55.6	23.0	222 44.8	23.0	79 29.8	46.3	336 14.2	00.4			
06	233 56.8	240 55.2	S 4 21.8	237 45.5	S 2 22.3	94 32.5	N16 46.4	351 16.5	S19 00.5	Rasalhague	96 05.6	N12 33.0
07	248 59.2	255 54.9	20.5	252 46.2	21.5	109 35.3	46.5	6 18.9	00.5	Regulus	207 42.0	N11 53.3
S 08	264 01.7	270 54.5	19.2	267 46.9	20.7	124 38.1	46.6	21 21.2	00.5	Rigel	281 10.8	S 8 11.4
A 09	279 04.1	285 54.2	.. 17.9	282 47.6	.. 19.9	139 40.9	.. 46.7	36 23.6	.. 00.5	Rigil Kent.	139 49.9	S60 53.5
T 10	294 06.6	300 53.8	16.6	297 48.3	19.1	154 43.7	46.8	51 25.9	00.5	Sabik	102 11.4	S15 44.4
U 11	309 09.1	315 53.5	15.3	312 49.0	18.3	169 46.5	46.9	66 28.3	00.5			
R 12	324 11.5	330 53.1	S 4 14.0	327 49.7	S 2 17.5	184 49.3	N16 47.0	81 30.6	S19 00.5	Schedar	349 39.5	N56 37.4
D 13	339 14.0	345 52.8	12.8	342 50.4	16.7	199 52.1	47.1	96 32.9	00.6	Shaula	96 20.6	S37 06.6
A 14	354 16.5	0 52.4	11.5	357 51.1	15.9	214 54.8	47.2	111 35.3	00.6	Sirius	258 32.4	S16 44.6
Y 15	9 18.9	15 52.1	.. 10.2	12 51.8	.. 15.1	229 57.6	.. 47.3	126 37.6	.. 00.6	Spica	158 29.9	S11 14.4
16	24 21.4	30 51.7	08.9	27 52.5	14.3	245 00.4	47.4	141 40.0	00.6	Suhail	222 51.1	S43 29.9
17	39 23.9	45 51.3	07.6	42 53.2	13.5	260 03.2	47.5	156 42.3	00.6			
18	54 26.3	60 51.0	S 4 06.3	57 53.9	S 2 12.7	275 06.0	N16 47.6	171 44.7	S19 00.6	Vega	80 38.5	N38 47.8
19	69 28.8	75 50.6	05.0	72 54.6	11.9	290 08.8	47.7	186 47.0	00.7	Zuben'ubi	137 04.1	S16 06.2
20	84 31.3	90 50.3	03.7	87 55.3	11.1	305 11.6	47.8	201 49.3	00.7		SHA	Mer. Pass.
21	99 33.7	105 49.9	.. 02.5	102 56.0	.. 10.4	320 14.3	.. 47.9	216 51.7	.. 00.7			h m
22	114 36.2	120 49.6	4 01.2	117 56.7	09.6	335 17.1	48.0	231 54.0	00.7	Venus	8 23.1	13 56
23	129 38.6	135 49.2	S 3 59.9	132 57.4	08.8	350 19.9	48.1	246 56.4	00.7	Mars	4 41.7	14 10
Mer. Pass.	h m 14 26.8	v −0.4	d 1.3	v 0.7	d 0.8	v 2.8	d 0.1	v 2.3	d 0.0	Jupiter	220 26.1	23 43
										Saturn	117 23.6	6 39

UT	SUN GHA	SUN Dec	MOON GHA	MOON v	MOON Dec	MOON d	MOON HP
d h	° '	° '	° '	'	° '	'	'
12 00	176 27.1	S13 52.2	272 11.0	11.3	S14 49.1	6.0	56.1
01	191 27.1	51.3	286 41.3	11.3	14 55.1	5.9	56.1
02	206 27.1	50.5	301 11.6	11.2	15 01.0	5.9	56.1
03	221 27.1 ..	49.7	315 41.8	11.1	15 06.9	5.8	56.2
04	236 27.2	48.9	330 11.9	11.1	15 12.7	5.8	56.2
05	251 27.2	48.0	344 42.0	10.9	15 18.5	5.6	56.2
T 06	266 27.2	S13 47.2	359 11.9	11.0	S15 24.1	5.6	56.3
H 07	281 27.2	46.4	13 41.9	10.8	15 29.7	5.5	56.3
U 08	296 27.2	45.5	28 11.7	10.8	15 35.2	5.5	56.3
R 09	311 27.2 ..	44.7	42 41.5	10.8	15 40.7	5.3	56.4
S 10	326 27.2	43.9	57 11.3	10.6	15 46.0	5.3	56.4
D 11	341 27.2	43.0	71 40.9	10.6	15 51.3	5.3	56.4
A 12	356 27.2	S13 42.2	86 10.5	10.5	S15 56.6	5.1	56.5
Y 13	11 27.2	41.4	100 40.0	10.5	16 01.7	5.1	56.5
14	26 27.2	40.6	115 09.5	10.3	16 06.8	5.0	56.5
15	41 27.2 ..	39.7	129 38.8	10.4	16 11.8	4.9	56.6
16	56 27.2	38.9	144 08.2	10.2	16 16.7	4.8	56.6
17	71 27.2	38.1	158 37.4	10.2	16 21.5	4.8	56.7
18	86 27.2	S13 37.2	173 06.6	10.1	S16 26.3	4.6	56.7
19	101 27.2	36.4	187 35.7	10.0	16 30.9	4.6	56.7
20	116 27.3	35.6	202 04.7	9.9	16 35.5	4.5	56.8
21	131 27.3 ..	34.7	216 33.6	9.9	16 40.0	4.4	56.8
22	146 27.3	33.9	231 02.5	9.9	16 44.4	4.4	56.8
23	161 27.3	33.0	245 31.4	9.7	16 48.8	4.2	56.9
13 00	176 27.3	S13 32.2	260 00.1	9.7	S16 53.0	4.2	56.9
01	191 27.3	31.4	274 28.8	9.6	16 57.2	4.0	56.9
02	206 27.3	30.5	288 57.4	9.5	17 01.2	4.0	57.0
03	221 27.3 ..	29.7	303 25.9	9.5	17 05.2	3.9	57.0
04	236 27.3	28.9	317 54.4	9.4	17 09.1	3.8	57.1
05	251 27.3	28.0	332 22.8	9.3	17 12.9	3.7	57.1
06	266 27.4	S13 27.2	346 51.1	9.3	S17 16.6	3.7	57.1
F 07	281 27.4	26.3	1 19.4	9.2	17 20.3	3.5	57.2
R 08	296 27.4	25.5	15 47.6	9.1	17 23.8	3.4	57.2
I 09	311 27.4 ..	24.7	30 15.7	9.1	17 27.2	3.4	57.3
D 10	326 27.4	23.8	44 43.8	9.0	17 30.6	3.2	57.3
A 11	341 27.4	23.0	59 11.8	8.9	17 33.8	3.2	57.3
Y 12	356 27.4	S13 22.1	73 39.7	8.8	S17 37.0	3.1	57.4
13	11 27.5	21.3	88 07.5	8.8	17 40.1	2.9	57.4
14	26 27.5	20.5	102 35.3	8.7	17 43.0	2.9	57.4
15	41 27.5 ..	19.6	117 03.0	8.7	17 45.9	2.8	57.5
16	56 27.5	18.8	131 30.7	8.5	17 48.7	2.6	57.5
17	71 27.5	17.9	145 58.2	8.6	17 51.3	2.6	57.6
18	86 27.5	S13 17.1	160 25.8	8.4	S17 53.9	2.5	57.6
19	101 27.5	16.3	174 53.2	8.4	17 56.4	2.3	57.6
20	116 27.6	15.4	189 20.6	8.3	17 58.7	2.3	57.7
21	131 27.6 ..	14.6	203 47.9	8.3	18 01.0	2.2	57.7
22	146 27.6	13.7	218 15.2	8.1	18 03.2	2.0	57.8
23	161 27.6	12.9	232 42.3	8.2	18 05.2	2.0	57.8
14 00	176 27.6	S13 12.0	247 09.5	8.0	S18 07.2	1.8	57.8
01	191 27.6	11.2	261 36.5	8.0	18 09.0	1.8	57.9
02	206 27.7	10.3	276 03.5	7.9	18 10.8	1.6	57.9
03	221 27.7 ..	09.5	290 30.4	7.9	18 12.4	1.6	58.0
04	236 27.7	08.6	304 57.3	7.8	18 14.0	1.4	58.0
05	251 27.7	07.8	319 24.1	7.8	18 15.4	1.3	58.0
S 06	266 27.7	S13 07.0	333 50.9	7.6	S18 16.7	1.2	58.1
A 07	281 27.8	06.1	348 17.5	7.7	18 17.9	1.1	58.1
T 08	296 27.8	05.3	2 44.2	7.5	18 19.0	1.0	58.2
U 09	311 27.8 ..	04.4	17 10.7	7.5	18 20.0	0.9	58.2
R 10	326 27.8	03.6	31 37.2	7.5	18 20.9	0.8	58.2
D 11	341 27.8	02.7	46 03.7	7.4	18 21.7	0.6	58.3
A 12	356 27.9	S13 01.9	60 30.1	7.3	S18 22.3	0.6	58.3
Y 13	11 27.9	01.0	74 56.4	7.3	18 22.9	0.4	58.4
14	26 27.9	13 00.2	89 22.7	7.2	18 23.3	0.3	58.4
15	41 27.9	12 59.3	103 48.9	7.2	18 23.6	0.2	58.4
16	56 28.0	58.5	118 15.1	7.1	18 23.8	0.1	58.5
17	71 28.0	57.6	132 41.2	7.1	18 23.9	0.0	58.5
18	86 28.0	S12 56.8	147 07.3	7.0	S18 23.9	0.2	58.6
19	101 28.0	55.9	161 33.3	6.9	18 23.7	0.2	58.6
20	116 28.0	55.1	175 59.2	6.9	18 23.5	0.4	58.7
21	131 28.1 ..	54.2	190 25.1	6.9	18 23.1	0.5	58.7
22	146 28.1	53.3	204 51.0	6.8	18 22.6	0.6	58.7
23	161 28.1	52.5	219 16.8	6.7	S18 22.0	0.7	58.8
	SD 16.2	d 0.8	SD 15.4		15.6		15.9

Twilight / Sunrise / Moonrise

Lat.	Twilight Naut.	Twilight Civil	Sunrise	Moonrise 12	13	14	15
°	h m	h m	h m	h m	h m	h m	h m
N 72	06 24	07 45	09 07	03 48	05 51	■	■
N 70	06 21	07 34	08 45	03 12	04 46	06 10	07 05
68	06 19	07 25	08 28	02 46	04 10	05 25	06 21
66	06 17	07 17	08 14	02 26	03 45	04 56	05 52
64	06 15	07 11	08 03	02 11	03 25	04 33	05 30
62	06 13	07 05	07 53	01 57	03 09	04 16	05 12
60	06 11	07 00	07 44	01 46	02 56	04 01	04 58
N 58	06 09	06 56	07 37	01 37	02 45	03 48	04 45
56	06 08	06 51	07 31	01 28	02 35	03 37	04 34
54	06 06	06 48	07 25	01 21	02 26	03 28	04 25
52	06 05	06 44	07 20	01 14	02 18	03 19	04 16
50	06 03	06 41	07 15	01 08	02 11	03 12	04 08
45	06 00	06 34	07 04	00 56	01 56	02 55	03 52
N 40	05 56	06 28	06 56	00 45	01 44	02 42	03 39
35	05 53	06 22	06 48	00 36	01 33	02 31	03 27
30	05 49	06 17	06 42	00 28	01 24	02 21	03 17
20	05 42	06 08	06 30	00 14	01 08	02 04	03 00
N 10	05 34	05 59	06 19	00 03	00 55	01 49	02 45
0	05 25	05 49	06 11	24 42	00 42	01 35	02 32
S 10	05 14	05 39	06 01	24 29	00 29	01 22	02 18
20	05 01	05 28	05 51	24 16	00 16	01 07	02 03
30	04 44	05 13	05 38	24 00	00 00	00 50	01 46
35	04 33	05 05	05 31	23 51	24 41	00 41	01 36
40	04 19	04 54	05 23	23 41	24 29	00 29	01 25
45	04 03	04 42	05 14	23 29	24 16	00 16	01 11
S 50	03 41	04 26	05 02	23 15	24 01	00 01	00 55
52	03 31	04 19	04 57	23 08	23 53	24 48	00 48
54	03 18	04 11	04 51	23 01	23 45	24 39	00 39
56	03 04	04 01	04 44	22 52	23 36	24 30	00 30
58	02 46	03 51	04 37	22 43	23 25	24 19	00 19
S 60	02 24	03 38	04 29	22 32	23 13	24 07	00 07

Sunset / Twilight / Moonset

Lat.	Sunset	Twilight Civil	Twilight Naut.	Moonset 12	13	14	15
°	h m	h m	h m	h m	h m	h m	h m
N 72	15 23	16 45	18 06	08 07	07 51	■	■
N 70	15 45	16 56	18 09	08 45	08 57	09 26	10 29
68	16 02	17 05	18 11	09 12	09 33	10 10	11 12
66	16 16	17 12	18 13	09 32	09 59	10 40	11 41
64	16 27	17 19	18 15	09 48	10 19	11 02	12 03
62	16 37	17 24	18 17	10 02	10 35	11 20	12 21
60	16 45	17 29	18 18	10 13	10 49	11 35	12 35
N 58	16 52	17 34	18 20	10 23	11 00	11 48	12 48
56	16 59	17 38	18 22	10 32	11 10	11 59	12 58
54	17 04	17 41	18 23	10 40	11 19	12 08	13 08
52	17 10	17 45	18 24	10 47	11 27	12 17	13 16
50	17 14	17 48	18 26	10 53	11 35	12 25	13 24
45	17 24	17 55	18 29	11 07	11 50	12 41	13 40
N 40	17 33	18 01	18 33	11 18	12 03	12 54	13 53
35	17 40	18 06	18 36	11 28	12 14	13 06	14 04
30	17 47	18 11	18 40	11 36	12 23	13 16	14 14
20	17 58	18 21	18 47	11 51	12 40	13 33	14 31
N 10	18 08	18 30	18 55	12 03	12 54	13 48	14 45
0	18 18	18 39	19 04	12 15	13 07	14 02	14 59
S 10	18 27	18 49	19 14	12 27	13 21	14 16	15 13
20	18 38	19 00	19 24	12 40	13 35	14 31	15 27
30	18 49	19 14	19 44	12 55	13 51	14 48	15 44
35	18 56	19 23	19 55	13 03	14 01	14 58	15 53
40	19 04	19 33	20 08	13 13	14 12	15 09	16 04
45	19 14	19 45	20 24	13 24	14 24	15 22	16 17
S 50	19 25	20 01	20 45	13 38	14 40	15 39	16 33
52	19 30	20 08	20 56	13 45	14 47	15 46	16 40
54	19 36	20 16	21 08	13 52	14 55	15 55	16 48
56	19 43	20 25	21 22	14 00	15 04	16 04	16 57
58	19 50	20 36	21 39	14 09	15 15	16 15	17 07
S 60	19 58	20 48	22 00	14 19	15 26	16 27	17 19

Day	SUN Eqn. of Time 00h	SUN Eqn. of Time 12h	SUN Mer. Pass.	MOON Mer. Pass. Upper	MOON Mer. Pass. Lower	Age	Phase
d	m s	m s	h m	h m	h m	d	%
12	14 11	14 11	12 14	06 03	18 29	23	47
13	14 11	14 10	12 14	06 55	19 21	24	36
14	14 10	14 09	12 14	07 49	20 17	25	26

UT	ARIES	VENUS −3.9		MARS +1.2		JUPITER −2.6		SATURN +0.5		STARS		
d h	GHA	GHA	Dec	GHA	Dec	GHA	Dec	GHA	Dec	Name	SHA	Dec
15 00	144 41.1	150 48.9 S 3 58.6		147 58.1 S 2 08.0		5 22.7 N16 48.2		261 58.7 S19 00.7		Acamar	315 17.6	S40 15.1
01	159 43.6	165 48.5	57.3	162 58.8	07.2	20 25.5	48.3	277 01.1	00.7	Achernar	335 26.3	S57 09.9
02	174 46.0	180 48.2	56.0	177 59.5	06.4	35 28.3	48.4	292 03.4	00.8	Acrux	173 07.3	S63 10.8
03	189 48.5	195 47.8 ..	54.7	193 00.2 ..	05.6	50 31.1 ..	48.5	307 05.7 ..	00.8	Adhara	255 11.3	S29 00.0
04	204 51.0	210 47.5	53.4	208 01.0	04.8	65 33.8	48.6	322 08.1	00.8	Aldebaran	290 48.0	N16 32.2
05	219 53.4	225 47.1	52.1	223 01.7	04.0	80 36.6	48.7	337 10.4	00.8			
06	234 55.9	240 46.8 S 3 50.9		238 02.4 S 2 03.2		95 39.4 N16 48.8		352 12.8 S19 00.8		Alioth	166 19.4	N55 52.4
07	249 58.4	255 46.4	49.6	253 03.1	02.4	110 42.2	48.9	7 15.1	00.8	Alkaid	152 57.8	N49 14.0
S 08	265 00.8	270 46.1	48.3	268 03.8	01.6	125 45.0	49.0	22 17.5	00.8	Al Na'ir	27 42.8	S46 53.2
U 09	280 03.3	285 45.8 ..	47.0	283 04.5 ..	00.8	140 47.8 ..	49.1	37 19.8 ..	00.9	Alnilam	275 45.0	S 1 11.9
N 10	295 05.8	300 45.4	45.7	298 05.2	2 00.0	155 50.6	49.2	52 22.2	00.9	Alphard	217 54.6	S 8 43.7
D 11	310 08.2	315 45.1	44.4	313 05.9	1 59.2	170 53.3	49.3	67 24.5	00.9			
A 12	325 10.7	330 44.7 S 3 43.1		328 06.6 S 1 58.5		185 56.1 N16 49.4		82 26.9 S19 00.9		Alphecca	126 10.0	N26 39.7
Y 13	340 13.1	345 44.4	41.8	343 07.3	57.7	200 58.9	49.5	97 29.2	00.9	Alpheratz	357 42.5	N29 10.5
14	355 15.6	0 44.0	40.5	358 08.0	56.9	216 01.7	49.6	112 31.5	00.9	Altair	62 07.4	N 8 54.6
15	10 18.1	15 43.7 ..	39.2	13 08.7 ..	56.1	231 04.5 ..	49.7	127 33.9 ..	00.9	Ankaa	353 14.9	S42 13.6
16	25 20.5	30 43.3	38.0	28 09.4	55.3	246 07.3	49.8	142 36.2	01.0	Antares	112 24.9	S26 27.7
17	40 23.0	45 43.0	36.7	43 10.1	54.5	261 10.1	49.9	157 38.6	01.0			
18	55 25.5	60 42.6 S 3 35.4		58 10.8 S 1 53.7		276 12.8 N16 50.0		172 40.9 S19 01.0		Arcturus	145 54.6	N19 06.1
19	70 27.9	75 42.3	34.1	73 11.5 *	52.9	291 15.6	50.1	187 43.3	01.0	Atria	107 25.8	S69 02.8
20	85 30.4	90 41.9	32.8	88 12.2	52.1	306 18.4	50.2	202 45.6	01.0	Avior	234 16.9	S59 33.8
21	100 32.9	105 41.6 ..	31.5	103 12.9 ..	51.3	321 21.2 ..	50.3	217 48.0 ..	01.0	Bellatrix	278 30.6	N 6 21.5
22	115 35.3	120 41.2	30.2	118 13.6	50.5	336 24.0	50.4	232 50.3	01.0	Betelgeuse	270 59.9	N 7 24.3
23	130 37.8	135 40.9	28.9	133 14.3	49.7	351 26.8	50.5	247 52.7	01.0			
16 00	145 40.2	150 40.6 S 3 27.6		148 15.0 S 1 48.9		6 29.5 N16 50.6		262 55.0 S19 01.1		Canopus	263 55.3	S52 42.7
01	160 42.7	165 40.2	26.3	163 15.7	48.1	21 32.3	50.7	277 57.4	01.1	Capella	280 32.5	N46 00.7
02	175 45.2	180 39.9	25.0	178 16.4	47.4	36 35.1	50.8	292 59.7	01.1	Deneb	49 31.1	N45 20.1
03	190 47.6	195 39.5 ..	23.7	193 17.1 ..	46.6	51 37.9 ..	50.9	308 02.1 ..	01.1	Denebola	182 32.2	N14 29.1
04	205 50.1	210 39.2	22.4	208 17.8	45.8	66 40.7	51.0	323 04.4	01.1	Diphda	348 55.0	S17 54.4
05	220 52.6	225 38.8	21.2	223 18.6	45.0	81 43.5	51.1	338 06.8	01.1			
06	235 55.0	240 38.5 S 3 19.9		238 19.3 S 1 44.2		96 46.2 N16 51.2		353 09.1 S19 01.1		Dubhe	193 49.8	N61 39.9
07	250 57.5	255 38.1	18.6	253 20.0	43.4	111 49.0	51.3	8 11.5	01.2	Elnath	278 11.0	N28 37.0
M 08	266 00.0	270 37.8	17.3	268 20.7	42.6	126 51.8	51.4	23 13.8	01.2	Eltanin	90 45.9	N51 29.1
O 09	281 02.4	285 37.5 ..	16.0	283 21.4 ..	41.8	141 54.6 ..	51.5	38 16.2 ..	01.2	Enif	33 46.3	N 9 56.7
N 10	296 04.9	300 37.1	14.7	298 22.1	41.0	156 57.4	51.6	53 18.5	01.2	Fomalhaut	15 23.1	S29 32.6
D 11	311 07.4	315 36.8	13.4	313 22.8	40.2	172 00.2	51.7	68 20.9	01.2			
A 12	326 09.8	330 36.4 S 3 12.1		328 23.5 S 1 39.4		187 02.9 N16 51.8		83 23.2 S19 01.2		Gacrux	171 59.0	S57 11.8
Y 13	341 12.3	345 36.1	10.8	343 24.2	38.6	202 05.7	51.9	98 25.6	01.2	Gienah	175 50.8	S17 37.6
14	356 14.7	0 35.7	09.5	358 24.9	37.8	217 08.5	52.0	113 27.9	01.3	Hadar	148 45.8	S60 26.5
15	11 17.2	15 35.4 ..	08.2	13 25.6 ..	37.0	232 11.3 ..	52.1	128 30.3 ..	01.3	Hamal	327 59.6	N23 32.0
16	26 19.7	30 35.1	06.9	28 26.3	36.2	247 14.1	52.2	143 32.6	01.3	Kaus Aust.	83 42.5	S34 22.4
17	41 22.1	45 34.7	05.6	43 27.0	35.5	262 16.9	52.3	158 35.0	01.3			
18	56 24.6	60 34.4 S 3 04.3		58 27.7 S 1 34.7		277 19.6 N16 52.4		173 37.3 S19 01.3		Kochab	137 20.0	N74 05.4
19	71 27.1	75 34.0	03.0	73 28.4	33.9	292 22.4	52.5	188 39.7	01.3	Markab	13 37.5	N15 17.2
20	86 29.5	90 33.7	01.7	88 29.1	33.1	307 25.2	52.6	203 42.0	01.3	Menkar	314 13.9	N 4 08.7
21	101 32.0	105 33.4 3 00.4		103 29.8 ..	32.3	322 28.0 ..	52.7	218 44.4 ..	01.3	Menkent	148 06.0	S36 26.5
22	116 34.5	120 33.0 2 59.1		118 30.5	31.5	337 30.8	52.8	233 46.7	01.4	Miaplacidus	221 38.3	S69 47.0
23	131 36.9	135 32.7	57.8	133 31.3	30.7	352 33.6	52.9	248 49.1	01.4			
17 00	146 39.4	150 32.3 S 2 56.5		148 32.0 S 1 29.9		7 36.3 N16 53.0		263 51.4 S19 01.4		Mirfak	308 38.7	N49 54.9
01	161 41.9	165 32.0	55.2	163 32.7	29.1	22 39.1	53.1	278 53.8	01.4	Nunki	75 57.2	S26 16.5
02	176 44.3	180 31.7	54.0	178 33.4	28.3	37 41.9	53.2	293 56.1	01.4	Peacock	53 18.1	S56 41.0
03	191 46.8	195 31.3 ..	52.7	193 34.1 ..	27.5	52 44.7 ..	53.3	308 58.5 ..	01.4	Pollux	243 26.0	N27 59.1
04	206 49.2	210 31.0	51.4	208 34.8	26.7	67 47.5	53.4	324 00.8	01.4	Procyon	244 58.2	N 5 10.9
05	221 51.7	225 30.6	50.1	223 35.5	25.9	82 50.2	53.5	339 03.2	01.4			
06	236 54.2	240 30.3 S 2 48.8		238 36.2 S 1 25.1		97 53.0 N16 53.6		354 05.5 S19 01.5		Rasalhague	96 05.5	N12 33.0
07	251 56.6	255 30.0	47.5	253 36.9	24.3	112 55.8	53.7	9 07.9	01.5	Regulus	207 42.0	N11 53.3
T 08	266 59.1	270 29.6	46.2	268 37.6	23.6	127 58.6	53.8	24 10.2	01.5	Rigel	281 10.8	S 8 11.4
U 09	282 01.6	285 29.3 ..	44.9	283 38.3 ..	22.8	143 01.4 ..	53.9	39 12.6 ..	01.5	Rigil Kent.	139 49.8	S60 53.5
E 10	297 04.0	300 28.9	43.6	298 39.0	22.0	158 04.2	54.0	54 14.9	01.5	Sabik	102 11.3	S15 44.4
S 11	312 06.5	315 28.6	42.3	313 39.7	21.2	173 06.9	54.1	69 17.3	01.5			
D 12	327 09.0	330 28.3 S 2 41.0		328 40.4 S 1 20.4		188 09.7 N16 54.2		84 19.7 S19 01.5		Schedar	349 39.5	N56 37.3
A 13	342 11.4	345 27.9	39.7	343 41.1	19.6	203 12.5	54.3	99 22.0	01.5	Shaula	96 20.5	S37 06.6
Y 14	357 13.9	0 27.6	38.4	358 41.9	18.8	218 15.3	54.3	114 24.4	01.6	Sirius	258 32.5	S16 44.6
15	12 16.4	15 27.3 ..	37.1	13 42.6 ..	18.0	233 18.1 ..	54.4	129 26.7 ..	01.6	Spica	158 29.8	S11 14.4
16	27 18.8	30 26.9	35.8	28 43.3	17.2	248 20.8	54.5	144 29.1	01.6	Suhail	222 51.1	S43 29.9
17	42 21.3	45 26.6	34.5	43 44.0	16.4	263 23.6	54.6	159 31.4	01.6			
18	57 23.7	60 26.2 S 2 33.2		58 44.7 S 1 15.6		278 26.4 N16 54.7		174 33.8 S19 01.6		Vega	80 38.5	N38 47.8
19	72 26.2	75 25.9	31.9	73 45.4	14.8	293 29.2	54.8	189 36.1	01.6	Zuben'ubi	137 04.0	S16 06.2
20	87 28.7	90 25.6	30.6	88 46.1	14.0	308 32.0	54.9	204 38.5	01.6		SHA	Mer. Pass.
21	102 31.1	105 25.2 ..	29.3	103 46.8 ..	13.2	323 34.7 ..	55.0	219 40.9 ..	01.6		° '	h m
22	117 33.6	120 24.9	28.0	118 47.5	12.5	338 37.5	55.1	234 43.2	01.7	Venus	5 00.3	13 58
23	132 36.1	135 24.6	26.7	133 48.2	11.7	353 40.3	55.2	249 45.6	01.7	Mars	2 34.8	14 06
	h m									Jupiter	220 49.3	23 30
Mer. Pass. 14 15.0		v −0.3	d 1.3	v 0.7	d 0.8	v 2.8	d 0.1	v 2.4	d 0.0	Saturn	117 14.8	6 27

UT	SUN GHA	SUN Dec	MOON GHA	v	MOON Dec	d	HP
d h	° ′	° ′	° ′	′	° ′	′	′
15 00	176 28.1	S12 51.6	233 42.5	6.8	S18 21.3	0.9	58.8
01	191 28.2	50.8	248 08.3	6.6	18 20.4	0.9	58.9
02	206 28.2	49.9	262 33.9	6.6	18 19.5	1.1	58.9
03	221 28.2	.. 49.1	276 59.5	6.6	18 18.4	1.2	58.9
04	236 28.2	48.2	291 25.1	6.5	18 17.2	1.3	59.0
05	251 28.3	47.4	305 50.6	6.5	18 15.9	1.5	59.0
06	266 28.3	S12 46.5	320 16.1	6.5	S18 14.4	1.5	59.1
07	281 28.3	45.6	334 41.6	6.4	18 12.9	1.7	59.1
08	296 28.4	44.8	349 07.0	6.3	18 11.2	1.8	59.1
S 09	311 28.4	.. 43.9	3 32.3	6.4	18 09.4	1.9	59.2
U 10	326 28.4	43.1	17 57.7	6.2	18 07.5	2.1	59.2
N 11	341 28.4	42.2	32 22.9	6.3	18 05.4	2.1	59.3
D 12	356 28.5	S12 41.4	46 48.2	6.2	S18 03.3	2.3	59.3
A 13	11 28.5	40.5	61 13.4	6.2	18 01.0	2.4	59.3
Y 14	26 28.5	39.6	75 38.6	6.1	17 58.6	2.6	59.4
15	41 28.6	.. 38.8	90 03.7	6.1	17 56.0	2.6	59.4
16	56 28.6	37.9	104 28.8	6.1	17 53.4	2.8	59.4
17	71 28.6	37.1	118 53.9	6.1	17 50.6	2.9	59.5
18	86 28.6	S12 36.2	133 19.0	6.0	S17 47.7	3.0	59.5
19	101 28.7	35.3	147 44.0	6.0	17 44.7	3.2	59.6
20	116 28.7	34.5	162 09.0	5.9	17 41.5	3.2	59.6
21	131 28.7	.. 33.6	176 33.9	5.9	17 38.3	3.4	59.6
22	146 28.8	32.8	190 58.8	5.9	17 34.9	3.5	59.7
23	161 28.8	31.9	205 23.7	5.9	17 31.4	3.7	59.7
16 00	176 28.8	S12 31.1	219 48.6	5.9	S17 27.7	3.7	59.7
01	191 28.9	30.2	234 13.5	5.8	17 24.0	3.9	59.8
02	206 28.9	29.3	248 38.3	5.8	17 20.1	4.0	59.8
03	221 28.9	.. 28.4	263 03.1	5.8	17 16.1	4.1	59.9
04	236 29.0	27.6	277 27.9	5.8	17 12.0	4.3	59.9
05	251 29.0	26.7	291 52.7	5.7	17 07.7	4.3	59.9
06	266 29.0	S12 25.9	306 17.4	5.8	S17 03.4	4.5	60.0
07	281 29.1	25.0	320 42.2	5.7	16 58.9	4.6	60.0
08	296 29.1	24.1	335 06.9	5.7	16 54.3	4.8	60.0
M 09	311 29.1	.. 23.3	349 31.6	5.7	16 49.5	4.8	60.1
O 10	326 29.2	22.4	3 56.3	5.7	16 44.7	5.0	60.1
N 11	341 29.2	21.5	18 21.0	5.6	16 39.7	5.1	60.1
D 12	356 29.3	S12 20.7	32 45.6	5.7	S16 34.6	5.2	60.2
A 13	11 29.3	19.8	47 10.3	5.6	16 29.4	5.3	60.2
Y 14	26 29.3	18.9	61 34.9	5.6	16 24.1	5.4	60.2
15	41 29.4	.. 18.1	75 59.5	5.7	16 18.7	5.6	60.3
16	56 29.4	17.2	90 24.2	5.6	16 13.1	5.7	60.3
17	71 29.4	16.3	104 48.8	5.6	16 07.4	5.8	60.3
18	86 29.5	S12 15.4	119 13.4	5.6	S16 01.6	5.9	60.4
19	101 29.5	14.6	133 38.0	5.6	15 55.7	6.0	60.4
20	116 29.5	13.7	148 02.6	5.6	15 49.7	6.2	60.4
21	131 29.6	.. 12.8	162 27.2	5.6	15 43.5	6.2	60.5
22	146 29.6	12.0	176 51.8	5.6	15 37.3	6.4	60.5
23	161 29.7	11.1	191 16.4	5.6	15 30.9	6.5	60.5
17 00	176 29.7	S12 10.2	205 41.0	5.6	S15 24.4	6.6	60.6
01	191 29.7	09.4	220 05.6	5.6	15 17.8	6.7	60.6
02	206 29.8	08.5	234 30.2	5.6	15 11.1	6.9	60.6
03	221 29.8	.. 07.6	248 54.8	5.6	15 04.2	6.9	60.6
04	236 29.9	06.7	263 19.4	5.6	14 57.3	7.1	60.7
05	251 29.9	05.9	277 44.0	5.6	14 50.2	7.1	60.7
06	266 30.0	S12 05.0	292 08.6	5.6	S14 43.1	7.3	60.7
07	281 30.0	04.1	306 33.2	5.6	14 35.8	7.4	60.7
08	296 30.0	03.2	320 57.8	5.7	14 28.4	7.5	60.8
T 09	311 30.1	.. 02.4	335 22.5	5.6	14 20.9	7.6	60.8
U 10	326 30.1	01.5	349 47.1	5.6	14 13.3	7.7	60.8
E 11	341 30.2	12 00.6	4 11.7	5.7	14 05.6	7.8	60.9
S 12	356 30.2	S11 59.8	18 36.4	5.7	S13 57.8	7.9	60.9
D 13	11 30.3	58.9	33 01.1	5.6	13 49.9	8.0	60.9
A 14	26 30.3	58.0	47 25.7	5.7	13 41.9	8.1	60.9
Y 15	41 30.3	.. 57.1	61 50.4	5.7	13 33.8	8.2	60.9
16	56 30.4	56.2	76 15.1	5.8	13 25.6	8.3	61.0
17	71 30.4	55.4	90 39.9	5.7	13 17.3	8.4	61.0
18	86 30.5	S11 54.5	105 04.6	5.8	S13 08.9	8.5	61.0
19	101 30.5	53.6	119 29.4	5.7	13 00.4	8.6	61.0
20	116 30.6	52.7	133 54.1	5.8	12 51.8	8.7	61.1
21	131 30.6	.. 51.9	148 18.9	5.8	12 43.1	8.8	61.1
22	146 30.7	51.0	162 43.7	5.8	12 34.3	8.9	61.1
23	161 30.7	50.1	177 08.5	5.9	S12 25.4	9.0	61.1
	SD 16.2	d 0.9	SD 16.2		16.4		16.6

Lat.	Twilight Naut.	Twilight Civil	Sunrise	Moonrise 15	16	17	18
°	h m	h m	h m	h m	h m	h m	h m
N 72	06 12	07 31	08 50	■■■	08 23	08 10	08 03
N 70	06 10	07 22	08 30	07 05	07 29	07 40	07 44
68	06 09	07 14	08 15	06 21	06 56	07 17	07 30
66	06 08	07 08	08 03	05 52	06 32	06 59	07 18
64	06 06	07 02	07 53	05 30	06 13	06 44	07 08
62	06 05	06 57	07 44	05 12	05 57	06 32	06 59
60	06 04	06 53	07 36	04 58	05 44	06 22	06 52
N 58	06 03	06 49	07 30	04 45	05 33	06 13	06 45
56	06 02	06 45	07 24	04 34	05 23	06 05	06 39
54	06 01	06 42	07 19	04 25	05 15	05 57	06 34
52	05 59	06 39	07 14	04 16	05 07	05 51	06 29
50	05 58	06 36	07 09	04 08	05 00	05 45	06 25
45	05 56	06 30	07 00	03 52	04 45	05 33	06 16
N 40	05 53	06 24	06 52	03 39	04 32	05 22	06 08
35	05 50	06 19	06 45	03 27	04 22	05 13	06 01
30	05 47	06 15	06 39	03 17	04 13	05 05	05 55
20	05 40	06 06	06 29	03 00	03 57	04 52	05 45
N 10	05 33	05 58	06 20	02 45	03 43	04 40	05 35
0	05 25	05 49	06 11	02 32	03 30	04 29	05 27
S 10	05 15	05 40	06 02	02 18	03 17	04 17	05 19
20	05 03	05 29	05 52	02 03	03 03	04 05	05 10
30	04 46	05 16	05 41	01 46	02 47	03 52	04 59
35	04 36	05 08	05 34	01 36	02 37	03 44	04 53
40	04 24	04 58	05 27	01 25	02 27	03 35	04 46
45	04 08	04 47	05 18	01 11	02 14	03 24	04 38
S 50	03 48	04 32	05 08	00 55	01 59	03 11	04 29
52	03 38	04 25	05 03	00 48	01 52	03 05	04 24
54	03 27	04 18	04 57	00 39	01 44	02 59	04 19
56	03 14	04 09	04 51	00 30	01 35	02 51	04 14
58	02 58	03 59	04 44	00 19	01 25	02 43	04 08
S 60	02 38	03 47	04 37	00 07	01 14	02 33	04 01

Lat.	Sunset	Twilight Civil	Twilight Naut.	Moonset 15	16	17	18
°	h m	h m	h m	h m	h m	h m	h m
N 72	15 40	16 59	18 19	■■■	11 14	13 30	15 40
N 70	15 59	17 08	18 20	10 29	12 06	13 59	15 57
68	16 14	17 15	18 21	11 12	12 39	14 21	16 10
66	16 26	17 22	18 22	11 41	13 03	14 38	16 20
64	16 37	17 27	18 23	12 03	13 21	14 52	16 29
62	16 45	17 32	18 24	12 21	13 36	15 03	16 37
60	16 53	17 37	18 25	12 35	13 49	15 13	16 43
N 58	16 59	17 40	18 26	12 48	14 00	15 22	16 49
56	17 05	17 44	18 27	12 58	14 09	15 29	16 54
54	17 10	17 47	18 29	13 08	14 18	15 36	16 59
52	17 15	17 50	18 30	13 16	14 25	15 42	17 03
50	17 19	17 53	18 31	13 24	14 32	15 47	17 07
45	17 29	17 59	18 33	13 40	14 46	15 59	17 15
N 40	17 37	18 04	18 36	13 53	14 58	16 08	17 21
35	17 43	18 09	18 39	14 04	15 08	16 16	17 27
30	17 49	18 14	18 42	14 14	15 17	16 24	17 32
20	18 00	18 22	18 48	14 31	15 32	16 36	17 40
N 10	18 09	18 30	18 55	14 45	15 45	16 47	17 48
0	18 17	18 39	19 03	14 59	15 58	16 56	17 55
S 10	18 26	18 48	19 13	15 13	16 10	17 06	18 02
20	18 36	18 59	19 25	15 27	16 23	17 17	18 09
30	18 47	19 12	19 41	15 44	16 38	17 29	18 17
35	18 53	19 20	19 51	15 53	16 46	17 36	18 22
40	19 01	19 29	20 03	16 04	16 56	17 43	18 27
45	19 09	19 40	20 19	16 17	17 07	17 52	18 33
S 50	19 19	19 55	20 38	16 33	17 21	18 03	18 41
52	19 24	20 01	20 48	16 40	17 27	18 08	18 44
54	19 30	20 09	20 59	16 48	17 34	18 14	18 48
56	19 36	20 17	21 12	16 57	17 42	18 20	18 52
58	19 42	20 27	21 28	17 07	17 51	18 27	18 56
S 60	19 50	20 38	21 47	17 19	18 01	18 34	19 01

Day	SUN Eqn. of Time 00h	SUN Eqn. of Time 12h	SUN Mer. Pass.	MOON Mer. Pass. Upper	MOON Mer. Pass. Lower	Age	Phase
d	m s	m s	h m	h m	h m	d	%
15	14 07	14 06	12 14	08 45	21 14	26	17
16	14 05	14 03	12 14	09 44	22 13	27	9
17	14 01	13 59	12 14	10 43	23 12	28	4

UT	ARIES	VENUS −3.9		MARS +1.3		JUPITER −2.5		SATURN +0.5		STARS		
	GHA	GHA	Dec	GHA	Dec	GHA	Dec	GHA	Dec	Name	SHA	Dec
d h	° ′	° ′	° ′	° ′	° ′	° ′	° ′	° ′	° ′		° ′	° ′
18 00	147 38.5	150 24.2	S 2 25.4	148 48.9	S 1 10.9	8 43.1	N16 55.3	264 47.9	S19 01.7	Acamar	315 17.6	S40 15.0
01	162 41.0	165 23.9	24.1	163 49.6	10.1	23 45.9	55.4	279 50.3	01.7	Achernar	335 26.3	S57 09.9
02	177 43.5	180 23.6	22.8	178 50.3	09.3	38 48.6	55.5	294 52.6	01.7	Acrux	173 07.3	S63 10.9
03	192 45.9	195 23.2	.. 21.5	193 51.0	.. 08.5	53 51.4	.. 55.6	309 55.0	.. 01.7	Adhara	255 11.3	S29 00.0
04	207 48.4	210 22.9	20.2	208 51.8	07.7	68 54.2	55.7	324 57.3	01.7	Aldebaran	290 48.0	N16 32.2
05	222 50.8	225 22.6	18.9	223 52.5	06.9	83 57.0	55.8	339 59.7	01.7			
06	237 53.3	240 22.2	S 2 17.6	238 53.2	S 1 06.1	98 59.8	N16 55.9	355 02.1	S19 01.8	Alioth	166 19.4	N55 52.4
W 07	252 55.8	255 21.9	16.3	253 53.9	05.3	114 02.5	56.0	10 04.4	01.8	Alkaid	152 57.8	N49 14.0
E 08	267 58.2	270 21.6	15.0	268 54.6	04.5	129 05.3	56.1	25 06.8	01.8	Al Na'ir	27 42.8	S46 53.2
D 09	283 00.7	285 21.2	.. 13.7	283 55.3	.. 03.7	144 08.1	.. 56.2	40 09.1	.. 01.8	Alnilam	275 45.0	S 1 11.9
N 10	298 03.2	300 20.9	12.4	298 56.0	02.9	159 10.9	56.3	55 11.5	01.8	Alphard	217 54.6	S 8 43.7
E 11	313 05.6	315 20.6	11.1	313 56.7	02.1	174 13.6	56.4	70 13.8	01.8			
S 12	328 08.1	330 20.2	S 2 09.8	328 57.4	S 1 01.4	189 16.4	N16 56.5	85 16.2	S19 01.8	Alphecca	126 10.0	N26 39.7
D 13	343 10.6	345 19.9	08.5	343 58.1	1 00.6	204 19.2	56.6	100 18.6	01.8	Alpheratz	357 42.5	N29 10.5
A 14	358 13.0	0 19.6	07.2	358 58.8	0 59.8	219 22.0	56.7	115 20.9	01.8	Altair	62 07.4	N 8 54.6
Y 15	13 15.5	15 19.2	.. 05.9	13 59.5	.. 59.0	234 24.8	.. 56.8	130 23.3	.. 01.9	Ankaa	353 15.0	S42 13.6
16	28 18.0	30 18.9	04.6	29 00.3	58.2	249 27.5	56.9	145 25.6	01.9	Antares	112 24.9	S26 27.7
17	43 20.4	45 18.6	03.3	44 01.0	57.4	264 30.3	57.0	160 28.0	01.9			
18	58 22.9	60 18.2	S 2 02.0	59 01.7	S 0 56.6	279 33.1	N16 57.1	175 30.4	S19 01.9	Arcturus	145 54.6	N19 06.1
19	73 25.3	75 17.9	2 00.7	74 02.4	55.8	294 35.9	57.2	190 32.7	01.9	Atria	107 25.8	S69 02.8
20	88 27.8	90 17.6	1 59.4	89 03.1	55.0	309 38.6	57.3	205 35.1	01.9	Avior	234 16.9	S59 33.8
21	103 30.3	105 17.2	.. 58.1	104 03.8	.. 54.2	324 41.4	.. 57.4	220 37.4	.. 01.9	Bellatrix	278 30.6	N 6 21.5
22	118 32.7	120 16.9	56.8	119 04.5	53.4	339 44.2	57.5	235 39.8	01.9	Betelgeuse	270 59.9	N 7 24.3
23	133 35.2	135 16.6	55.5	134 05.2	52.6	354 47.0	57.6	250 42.2	02.0			
19 00	148 37.7	150 16.2	S 1 54.2	149 05.9	S 0 51.8	9 49.8	N16 57.6	265 44.5	S19 02.0	Canopus	263 55.3	S52 42.7
01	163 40.1	165 15.9	52.9	164 06.6	51.1	24 52.5	57.7	280 46.9	02.0	Capella	280 32.5	N46 00.7
02	178 42.6	180 15.6	51.6	179 07.3	50.3	39 55.3	57.8	295 49.2	02.0	Deneb	49 31.1	N45 20.1
03	193 45.1	195 15.2	.. 50.3	194 08.1	.. 49.5	54 58.1	.. 57.9	310 51.6	.. 02.0	Denebola	182 32.2	N14 29.0
04	208 47.5	210 14.9	49.0	209 08.8	48.7	70 00.9	58.0	325 54.0	02.0	Diphda	348 55.0	S17 54.4
05	223 50.0	225 14.6	47.7	224 09.5	47.9	85 03.6	58.1	340 56.3	02.0			
06	238 52.5	240 14.2	S 1 46.4	239 10.2	S 0 47.1	100 06.4	N16 58.2	355 58.7	S19 02.0	Dubhe	193 49.8	N61 39.9
T 07	253 54.9	255 13.9	45.1	254 10.9	46.3	115 09.2	58.3	11 01.0	02.0	Elnath	278 11.0	N28 37.0
H 08	268 57.4	270 13.6	43.8	269 11.6	45.5	130 12.0	58.4	26 03.4	02.1	Eltanin	90 45.9	N51 29.1
U 09	283 59.8	285 13.2	.. 42.5	284 12.3	.. 44.7	145 14.7	.. 58.5	41 05.8	.. 02.1	Enif	33 46.3	N 9 56.7
R 10	299 02.3	300 12.9	41.1	299 13.0	43.9	160 17.5	58.6	56 08.1	02.1	Fomalhaut	15 23.1	S29 32.6
S 11	314 04.8	315 12.6	39.8	314 13.7	43.1	175 20.3	58.7	71 10.5	02.1			
D 12	329 07.2	330 12.3	S 1 38.5	329 14.4	S 0 42.3	190 23.1	N16 58.8	86 12.9	S19 02.1	Gacrux	171 59.0	S57 11.8
A 13	344 09.7	345 11.9	37.2	344 15.2	41.5	205 25.8	58.9	101 15.2	02.1	Gienah	175 50.8	S17 37.6
Y 14	359 12.2	0 11.6	35.9	359 15.9	40.8	220 28.6	59.0	116 17.6	02.1	Hadar	148 45.8	S60 26.5
15	14 14.6	15 11.3	.. 34.6	14 16.6	.. 40.0	235 31.4	.. 59.1	131 19.9	.. 02.1	Hamal	327 59.6	N23 32.0
16	29 17.1	30 10.9	33.3	29 17.3	39.2	250 34.2	59.2	146 22.3	02.1	Kaus Aust.	83 42.5	S34 22.4
17	44 19.6	45 10.6	32.0	44 18.0	38.4	265 36.9	59.3	161 24.7	02.2			
18	59 22.0	60 10.3	S 1 30.7	59 18.7	S 0 37.6	280 39.7	N16 59.4	176 27.0	S19 02.2	Kochab	137 19.9	N74 05.4
19	74 24.5	75 10.0	29.4	74 19.4	36.8	295 42.5	59.5	191 29.4	02.2	Markab	13 37.5	N15 17.2
20	89 26.9	90 09.6	28.1	89 20.1	36.0	310 45.3	59.6	206 31.8	02.2	Menkar	314 13.9	N 4 08.7
21	104 29.4	105 09.3	.. 26.8	104 20.8	.. 35.2	325 48.0	.. 59.7	221 34.1	.. 02.2	Menkent	148 06.0	S36 26.5
22	119 31.9	120 09.0	25.5	119 21.5	34.4	340 50.8	59.8	236 36.5	02.2	Miaplacidus	221 38.4	S69 47.0
23	134 34.3	135 08.6	24.2	134 22.3	33.6	355 53.6	59.8	251 38.9	02.2			
20 00	149 36.8	150 08.3	S 1 22.9	149 23.0	S 0 32.8	10 56.4	N16 59.9	266 41.2	S19 02.2	Mirfak	308 38.7	N49 54.9
01	164 39.3	165 08.0	21.6	164 23.7	32.0	25 59.1	17 00.0	281 43.6	02.2	Nunki	75 57.1	S26 16.5
02	179 41.7	180 07.7	20.3	179 24.4	31.2	41 01.9	00.1	296 46.0	02.2	Peacock	53 18.0	S56 40.9
03	194 44.2	195 07.3	.. 19.0	194 25.1	.. 30.5	56 04.7	.. 00.2	311 48.3	.. 02.3	Pollux	243 26.0	N27 59.1
04	209 46.7	210 07.0	17.7	209 25.8	29.7	71 07.5	00.3	326 50.7	02.3	Procyon	244 58.3	N 5 10.9
05	224 49.1	225 06.7	16.4	224 26.5	28.9	86 10.2	00.4	341 53.0	02.3			
06	239 51.6	240 06.3	S 1 15.1	239 27.2	S 0 28.1	101 13.0	N17 00.5	356 55.4	S19 02.3	Rasalhague	96 05.5	N12 33.0
07	254 54.1	255 06.0	13.8	254 27.9	27.3	116 15.8	00.6	11 57.8	02.3	Regulus	207 42.0	N11 53.3
08	269 56.5	270 05.7	12.5	269 28.7	26.5	131 18.6	00.7	27 00.1	02.3	Rigel	281 10.8	S 8 11.4
F 09	284 59.0	285 05.4	.. 11.2	284 29.4	.. 25.7	146 21.3	.. 00.8	42 02.5	.. 02.3	Rigil Kent.	139 49.8	S60 53.5
R 10	300 01.4	300 05.0	09.9	299 30.1	24.9	161 24.1	00.9	57 04.9	02.3	Sabik	102 11.3	S15 44.4
I 11	315 03.9	315 04.7	08.5	314 30.8	24.1	176 26.9	01.0	72 07.2	02.3			
D 12	330 06.4	330 04.4	S 1 07.2	329 31.5	S 0 23.3	191 29.6	N17 01.1	87 09.6	S19 02.4	Schedar	349 39.5	N56 37.3
A 13	345 08.8	345 04.1	05.9	344 32.2	22.5	206 32.4	01.2	102 12.0	02.4	Shaula	96 20.5	S37 06.6
Y 14	0 11.3	0 03.7	04.6	359 32.9	21.7	221 35.2	01.3	117 14.3	02.4	Sirius	258 32.5	S16 44.6
15	15 13.8	15 03.4	.. 03.3	14 33.6	.. 21.0	236 38.0	.. 01.4	132 16.7	.. 02.4	Spica	158 29.8	S11 14.4
16	30 16.2	30 03.1	02.0	29 34.3	20.2	251 40.7	01.5	147 19.1	02.4	Suhail	222 51.1	S43 29.9
17	45 18.7	45 02.8	1 00.7	44 35.1	19.4	266 43.5	01.5	162 21.4	02.4			
18	60 21.2	60 02.4	S 0 59.4	59 35.8	S 0 18.6	281 46.3	N17 01.6	177 23.8	S19 02.4	Vega	80 38.4	N38 47.8
19	75 23.6	75 02.1	58.1	74 36.5	17.8	296 49.0	01.7	192 26.2	02.4	Zuben'ubi	137 04.0	S16 06.2
20	90 26.1	90 01.8	56.8	89 37.2	17.0	311 51.8	01.8	207 28.5	02.4		SHA	Mer. Pass.
21	105 28.5	105 01.5	.. 55.5	104 37.9	.. 16.2	326 54.6	.. 01.9	222 30.9	.. 02.4		° ′	h m
22	120 31.0	120 01.1	54.2	119 38.6	15.4	341 57.4	02.0	237 33.3	02.5	Venus	1 38.6	13 59
23	135 33.5	135 00.8	52.9	134 39.3	14.6	357 00.1	02.1	252 35.7	02.5	Mars	0 28.3	14 03
	h m									Jupiter	221 12.1	23 16
Mer. Pass. 14 03.2		v −0.3	d 1.3	v 0.7	d 0.8	v 2.8	d 0.1	v 2.4	d 0.0	Saturn	117 06.9	6 16

UT	SUN GHA	SUN Dec	MOON GHA	v	MOON Dec	d	HP
18 00	176 30.8	S11 49.2	191 33.4	5.8	S12 16.4	9.1	61.1
01	191 30.8	48.3	205 58.2	5.9	12 07.3	9.1	61.1
02	206 30.8	47.5	220 23.1	5.9	11 58.2	9.3	61.2
03	221 30.9	46.6	234 48.0	5.9	11 48.9	9.3	61.2
04	236 30.9	45.7	249 12.9	5.9	11 39.6	9.4	61.2
05	251 31.0	44.8	263 37.8	6.0	11 30.2	9.5	61.2
W 06	266 31.0	S11 43.9	278 02.8	6.0	S11 20.7	9.6	61.2
E 07	281 31.1	43.1	292 27.8	6.0	11 11.1	9.7	61.2
D 08	296 31.1	42.2	306 52.8	6.0	11 01.4	9.8	61.3
N 09	311 31.2	41.3	321 17.8	6.1	10 51.6	9.8	61.3
E 10	326 31.2	40.4	335 42.9	6.1	10 41.8	9.9	61.3
S 11	341 31.3	39.5	350 08.0	6.1	10 31.9	10.0	61.3
D 12	356 31.3	S11 38.7	4 33.1	6.1	S10 21.9	10.0	61.3
A 13	11 31.4	37.8	18 58.2	6.1	10 11.9	10.2	61.3
Y 14	26 31.4	36.9	33 23.3	6.2	10 01.7	10.2	61.3
15	41 31.5	36.0	47 48.5	6.2	9 51.5	10.3	61.3
16	56 31.5	35.1	62 13.7	6.2	9 41.2	10.3	61.4
17	71 31.6	34.2	76 38.9	6.3	9 30.9	10.4	61.4
18	86 31.6	S11 33.4	91 04.2	6.3	S 9 20.5	10.5	61.4
19	101 31.7	32.5	105 29.5	6.3	9 10.0	10.6	61.4
20	116 31.8	31.6	119 54.8	6.3	8 59.4	10.6	61.4
21	131 31.8	30.7	134 20.1	6.4	8 48.8	10.7	61.4
22	146 31.9	29.8	148 45.5	6.4	8 38.1	10.7	61.4
23	161 31.9	28.9	163 10.9	6.4	8 27.4	10.8	61.4
19 00	176 32.0	S11 28.0	177 36.3	6.5	S 8 16.6	10.9	61.4
01	191 32.0	27.2	192 01.8	6.5	8 05.7	10.9	61.4
02	206 32.1	26.3	206 27.3	6.5	7 54.8	11.0	61.4
03	221 32.1	25.4	220 52.8	6.5	7 43.8	11.0	61.4
04	236 32.2	24.5	235 18.3	6.6	7 32.8	11.0	61.4
05	251 32.2	23.6	249 43.9	6.6	7 21.8	11.2	61.4
T 06	266 32.3	S11 22.7	264 09.5	6.6	S 7 10.6	11.1	61.4
H 07	281 32.4	21.8	278 35.1	6.6	6 59.5	11.3	61.4
U 08	296 32.4	20.9	293 00.7	6.7	6 48.2	11.2	61.4
R 09	311 32.5	20.0	307 26.4	6.7	6 37.0	11.3	61.4
S 10	326 32.5	19.2	321 52.1	6.8	6 25.7	11.4	61.4
D 11	341 32.6	18.3	336 17.9	6.8	6 14.3	11.4	61.4
A 12	356 32.6	S11 17.4	350 43.7	6.8	S 6 02.9	11.4	61.4
Y 13	11 32.7	16.5	5 09.5	6.8	5 51.5	11.5	61.4
14	26 32.8	15.6	19 35.3	6.9	5 40.0	11.5	61.4
15	41 32.8	14.7	34 01.2	6.9	5 28.5	11.5	61.4
16	56 32.9	13.8	48 27.1	6.9	5 17.0	11.6	61.4
17	71 32.9	12.9	62 53.0	6.9	5 05.4	11.6	61.4
18	86 33.0	S11 12.0	77 18.9	7.0	S 4 53.8	11.7	61.4
19	101 33.0	11.1	91 44.9	7.0	4 42.1	11.6	61.4
20	116 33.1	10.2	106 10.9	7.0	4 30.5	11.7	61.4
21	131 33.2	09.4	120 36.9	7.1	4 18.8	11.7	61.4
22	146 33.2	08.5	135 03.0	7.1	4 07.1	11.8	61.4
23	161 33.3	07.6	149 29.1	7.1	3 55.3	11.8	61.4
20 00	176 33.3	S11 06.7	163 55.2	7.2	S 3 43.5	11.7	61.3
01	191 33.4	05.8	178 21.4	7.2	3 31.8	11.8	61.3
02	206 33.5	04.9	192 47.6	7.2	3 20.0	11.9	61.3
03	221 33.5	04.0	207 13.8	7.2	3 08.1	11.8	61.3
04	236 33.6	03.1	221 40.0	7.3	2 56.3	11.8	61.3
05	251 33.7	02.2	236 06.3	7.3	2 44.5	11.9	61.3
F 06	266 33.7	S11 01.3	250 32.6	7.3	S 2 32.6	11.9	61.3
R 07	281 33.8	11 00.4	264 58.9	7.4	2 20.7	11.9	61.3
I 08	296 33.8	10 59.5	279 25.3	7.4	2 08.8	11.9	61.2
D 09	311 33.9	58.6	293 51.7	7.4	1 56.9	11.9	61.2
A 10	326 34.0	57.7	308 18.1	7.4	1 45.0	11.9	61.2
Y 11	341 34.0	56.8	322 44.5	7.5	1 33.1	11.9	61.2
12	356 34.1	S10 55.9	337 11.0	7.4	S 1 21.2	11.9	61.2
13	11 34.2	55.0	351 37.4	7.6	1 09.3	11.9	61.2
14	26 34.2	54.1	6 04.0	7.5	0 57.4	11.9	61.2
15	41 34.3	53.2	20 30.5	7.6	0 45.5	11.9	61.1
16	56 34.4	52.3	34 57.1	7.6	0 33.6	11.9	61.1
17	71 34.4	51.4	49 23.7	7.6	0 21.7	11.9	61.1
18	86 34.5	S10 50.5	63 50.3	7.6	S 0 09.8	11.9	61.1
19	101 34.6	49.6	78 16.9	7.7	N 0 02.1	11.8	61.1
20	116 34.6	48.7	92 43.6	7.7	0 13.9	11.9	61.0
21	131 34.7	47.8	107 10.3	7.7	0 25.8	11.9	61.0
22	146 34.8	46.9	121 37.0	7.8	0 37.7	11.8	61.0
23	161 34.8	46.0	136 03.8	7.7	N 0 49.5	11.8	61.0
	SD 16.2	d 0.9	SD 16.7		16.7		16.7

Lat.	Twilight Naut.	Twilight Civil	Sunrise	Moonrise 18	Moonrise 19	Moonrise 20	Moonrise 21
N 72	05 59	07 17	08 33	08 03	07 57	07 51	07 46
N 70	05 58	07 09	08 16	07 44	07 47	07 48	07 49
68	05 58	07 03	08 03	07 30	07 39	07 45	07 52
66	05 58	06 57	07 52	07 18	07 32	07 43	07 54
64	05 58	06 53	07 43	07 08	07 26	07 41	07 56
62	05 57	06 49	07 35	06 59	07 21	07 40	07 58
60	05 57	06 45	07 28	06 52	07 16	07 38	07 59
N 58	05 56	06 42	07 22	06 45	07 13	07 37	08 00
56	05 55	06 39	07 17	06 39	07 09	07 36	08 02
54	05 55	06 36	07 12	06 34	07 06	07 35	08 03
52	05 54	06 33	07 08	06 29	07 03	07 34	08 04
50	05 53	06 31	07 04	06 25	07 00	07 33	08 04
45	05 51	06 25	06 55	06 16	06 55	07 31	08 06
N 40	05 49	06 21	06 48	06 08	06 50	07 30	08 08
35	05 47	06 16	06 42	06 01	06 46	07 28	08 09
30	05 44	06 12	06 37	05 55	06 42	07 27	08 11
20	05 39	06 05	06 27	05 45	06 36	07 25	08 13
N 10	05 32	05 57	06 19	05 36	06 30	07 23	08 15
0	05 25	05 49	06 10	05 27	06 25	07 22	08 17
S 10	05 16	05 41	06 02	05 19	06 20	07 20	08 19
20	05 04	05 31	05 53	05 10	06 14	07 18	08 21
30	04 49	05 18	05 43	04 59	06 08	07 16	08 23
35	04 40	05 11	05 37	04 53	06 04	07 15	08 25
40	04 28	05 02	05 30	04 46	06 00	07 14	08 26
45	04 13	04 51	05 22	04 38	05 55	07 12	08 28
S 50	03 55	04 38	05 13	04 29	05 49	07 11	08 31
52	03 46	04 32	05 08	04 24	05 47	07 10	08 32
54	03 35	04 25	05 03	04 19	05 44	07 09	08 33
56	03 23	04 17	04 58	04 14	05 41	07 08	08 34
58	03 08	04 07	04 52	04 08	05 37	07 07	08 36
S 60	02 51	03 57	04 45	04 01	05 33	07 06	08 37

Lat.	Sunset	Twilight Civil	Twilight Naut.	Moonset 18	Moonset 19	Moonset 20	Moonset 21
N 72	15 57	17 12	18 31	15 40	17 46	19 49	21 49
N 70	16 13	17 20	18 31	15 57	17 54	19 49	21 41
68	16 26	17 26	18 31	16 10	18 00	19 49	21 35
66	16 37	17 32	18 31	16 20	18 05	19 49	21 30
64	16 46	17 36	18 32	16 29	18 09	19 49	21 26
62	16 54	17 40	18 32	16 37	18 13	19 49	21 22
60	17 01	17 44	18 32	16 43	18 16	19 49	21 19
N 58	17 07	17 47	18 33	16 49	18 19	19 49	21 16
56	17 12	17 50	18 33	16 54	18 21	19 49	21 14
54	17 16	17 53	18 34	16 59	18 24	19 49	21 12
52	17 21	17 55	18 35	17 03	18 26	19 49	21 10
50	17 25	17 58	18 35	17 07	18 28	19 49	21 08
45	17 33	18 03	18 37	17 15	18 32	19 48	21 04
N 40	17 40	18 08	18 39	17 21	18 35	19 48	21 00
35	17 46	18 12	18 41	17 27	18 38	19 48	20 57
30	17 51	18 16	18 44	17 32	18 40	19 48	20 55
20	18 01	18 23	18 49	17 40	18 45	19 48	20 50
N 10	18 09	18 31	18 55	17 48	18 48	19 48	20 47
0	18 17	18 38	19 03	17 55	18 52	19 48	20 43
S 10	18 25	18 47	19 12	18 02	18 55	19 48	20 39
20	18 34	18 57	19 23	18 09	18 59	19 48	20 35
30	18 44	19 09	19 38	18 17	19 03	19 47	20 31
35	18 50	19 16	19 47	18 22	19 06	19 47	20 28
40	18 57	19 25	19 59	18 27	19 08	19 47	20 25
45	19 04	19 35	20 13	18 33	19 11	19 47	20 22
S 50	19 14	19 48	20 31	18 41	19 15	19 47	20 18
52	19 18	19 55	20 40	18 44	19 16	19 47	20 16
54	19 23	20 02	20 51	18 48	19 18	19 46	20 14
56	19 28	20 09	21 02	18 52	19 20	19 46	20 12
58	19 34	20 18	21 16	18 56	19 22	19 46	20 09
S 60	19 41	20 29	21 33	19 01	19 25	19 46	20 07

Day	SUN Eqn. of Time 00h	SUN Eqn. of Time 12h	SUN Mer. Pass.	MOON Mer. Pass. Upper	MOON Mer. Pass. Lower	Age	Phase
18	13 57	13 55	12 14	11 41	24 10	29	0
19	13 52	13 50	12 14	12 39	00 10	01	0
20	13 47	13 44	12 14	13 35	01 07	02	3

UT	ARIES GHA	VENUS −3.9 GHA	Dec	MARS +1.3 GHA	Dec	JUPITER −2.5 GHA	Dec	SATURN +0.5 GHA	Dec	STARS Name	SHA	Dec
d h	° ′	° ′	° ′	° ′	° ′	° ′	° ′	° ′	° ′		° ′	° ′
21 00	150 35.9	150 00.5	S 0 51.6	149 40.0	S 0 13.8	12 02.9	N17 02.2	267 38.0	S19 02.5	Acamar	315 17.6	S40 15.0
01	165 38.4	165 00.2	50.3	164 40.7	13.0	27 05.7	02.3	282 40.4	02.5	Achernar	335 26.4	S57 09.9
02	180 40.9	179 59.8	49.0	179 41.5	12.2	42 08.4	02.4	297 42.8	02.5	Acrux	173 07.2	S63 10.9
03	195 43.3	194 59.5	.. 47.7	194 42.2	.. 11.5	57 11.2	.. 02.5	312 45.1	.. 02.5	Adhara	255 11.3	S29 00.0
04	210 45.8	209 59.2	46.4	209 42.9	10.7	72 14.0	02.6	327 47.5	02.5	Aldebaran	290 48.0	N16 32.2
05	225 48.3	224 58.9	45.0	224 43.6	09.9	87 16.8	02.7	342 49.9	02.5			
S 06	240 50.7	239 58.5	S 0 43.7	239 44.3	S 0 09.1	102 19.5	N17 02.8	357 52.2	S19 02.5	Alioth	166 19.4	N55 52.4
A 07	255 53.2	254 58.2	42.4	254 45.0	08.3	117 22.3	02.9	12 54.6	02.5	Alkaid	152 57.8	N49 14.0
T 08	270 55.7	269 57.9	41.1	269 45.7	07.5	132 25.1	03.0	27 57.0	02.5	Al Na'ir	27 42.8	S46 53.2
U 09	285 58.1	284 57.6	.. 39.8	284 46.4	.. 06.7	147 27.8	.. 03.0	42 59.3	.. 02.6	Alnilam	275 45.1	S 1 11.9
R 10	301 00.6	299 57.2	38.5	299 47.2	05.9	162 30.6	03.1	58 01.7	02.6	Alphard	217 54.6	S 8 43.7
D 11	316 03.0	314 56.9	37.2	314 47.9	05.1	177 33.4	03.2	73 04.1	02.6			
A 12	331 05.5	329 56.6	S 0 35.9	329 48.6	S 0 04.3	192 36.1	N17 03.3	88 06.5	S19 02.6	Alphecca	126 10.0	N26 39.7
Y 13	346 08.0	344 56.3	34.6	344 49.3	03.5	207 38.9	03.4	103 08.8	02.6	Alpheratz	357 42.6	N29 10.4
14	1 10.4	359 55.9	33.3	359 50.0	02.8	222 41.7	03.5	118 11.2	02.6	Altair	62 07.4	N 8 54.5
15	16 12.9	14 55.6	.. 32.0	14 50.7	.. 02.0	237 44.5	.. 03.6	133 13.6	.. 02.6	Ankaa	353 15.0	S42 13.6
16	31 15.4	29 55.3	30.7	29 51.4	01.2	252 47.2	03.7	148 15.9	02.6	Antares	112 24.8	S26 27.7
17	46 17.8	44 55.0	29.4	44 52.1	S 00.4	267 50.0	03.8	163 18.3	02.6			
18	61 20.3	59 54.6	S 0 28.1	59 52.9	N 0 00.4	282 52.8	N17 03.9	178 20.7	S19 02.6	Arcturus	145 54.5	N19 06.1
19	76 22.8	74 54.3	26.8	74 53.6	01.2	297 55.5	04.0	193 23.1	02.7	Atria	107 25.7	S69 02.8
20	91 25.2	89 54.0	25.5	89 54.3	02.0	312 58.3	04.1	208 25.4	02.7	Avior	234 16.9	S59 33.8
21	106 27.7	104 53.7	.. 24.1	104 55.0	.. 02.8	328 01.1	.. 04.2	223 27.8	.. 02.7	Bellatrix	278 30.6	N 6 21.5
22	121 30.1	119 53.4	22.8	119 55.7	03.6	343 03.8	04.3	238 30.2	02.7	Betelgeuse	270 59.9	N 7 24.3
23	136 32.6	134 53.0	21.5	134 56.4	04.4	358 06.6	04.3	253 32.6	02.7			
22 00	151 35.1	149 52.7	S 0 20.2	149 57.1	N 0 05.2	13 09.4	N17 04.4	268 34.9	S19 02.7	Canopus	263 55.3	S52 42.7
01	166 37.5	164 52.4	18.9	164 57.9	05.9	28 12.1	04.5	283 37.3	02.7	Capella	280 32.6	N46 00.7
02	181 40.0	179 52.1	17.6	179 58.6	06.7	43 14.9	04.6	298 39.7	02.7	Deneb	49 31.1	N45 20.1
03	196 42.5	194 51.7	.. 16.3	194 59.3	.. 07.5	58 17.7	.. 04.7	313 42.0	.. 02.7	Denebola	182 32.2	N14 29.0
04	211 44.9	209 51.4	15.0	210 00.0	08.3	73 20.4	04.8	328 44.4	02.7	Diphda	348 55.0	S17 54.4
05	226 47.4	224 51.1	13.7	225 00.7	09.1	88 23.2	04.9	343 46.8	02.7			
06	241 49.9	239 50.8	S 0 12.4	240 01.4	N 0 09.9	103 26.0	N17 05.0	358 49.2	S19 02.7	Dubhe	193 49.8	N61 39.9
07	256 52.3	254 50.5	11.1	255 02.1	10.7	118 28.7	05.1	13 51.5	02.8	Elnath	278 11.0	N28 37.0
08	271 54.8	269 50.1	09.8	270 02.8	11.5	133 31.5	05.2	28 53.9	02.8	Eltanin	90 45.8	N51 29.1
S 09	286 57.3	284 49.8	.. 08.5	285 03.6	.. 12.3	148 34.3	.. 05.3	43 56.3	.. 02.8	Enif	33 46.3	N 9 56.7
U 10	301 59.7	299 49.5	07.2	300 04.3	13.1	163 37.0	05.4	58 58.7	02.8	Fomalhaut	15 23.1	S29 32.6
N 11	317 02.2	314 49.2	05.8	315 05.0	13.8	178 39.8	05.4	74 01.0	02.8			
D 12	332 04.6	329 48.9	S 0 04.5	330 05.7	N 0 14.6	193 42.6	N17 05.5	89 03.4	S19 02.8	Gacrux	171 59.0	S57 11.8
A 13	347 07.1	344 48.5	03.2	345 06.4	15.4	208 45.3	05.6	104 05.8	02.8	Gienah	175 50.8	S17 37.6
Y 14	2 09.6	359 48.2	01.9	0 07.1	16.2	223 48.1	05.7	119 08.2	02.8	Hadar	148 45.8	S60 26.5
15	17 12.0	14 47.9	S 00.6	15 07.8	.. 17.0	238 50.9	.. 05.8	134 10.5	.. 02.8	Hamal	327 59.6	N23 32.0
16	32 14.5	29 47.6	N 00.7	30 08.6	17.8	253 53.6	05.9	149 12.9	02.8	Kaus Aust.	83 42.5	S34 22.4
17	47 17.0	44 47.3	02.0	45 09.3	18.6	268 56.4	06.0	164 15.3	02.8			
18	62 19.4	59 46.9	N 0 03.3	60 10.0	N 0 19.4	283 59.2	N17 06.1	179 17.7	S19 02.9	Kochab	137 19.9	N74 05.4
19	77 21.9	74 46.6	04.6	75 10.7	20.2	299 01.9	06.2	194 20.0	02.9	Markab	13 37.5	N15 17.2
20	92 24.4	89 46.3	05.9	90 11.4	21.0	314 04.7	06.3	209 22.4	02.9	Menkar	314 13.9	N 4 08.7
21	107 26.8	104 46.0	.. 07.2	105 12.1	.. 21.7	329 07.4	.. 06.4	224 24.8	.. 02.9	Menkent	148 05.9	S36 26.5
22	122 29.3	119 45.7	08.5	120 12.8	22.5	344 10.2	06.4	239 27.2	02.9	Miaplacidus	221 38.4	S69 47.0
23	137 31.8	134 45.3	09.8	135 13.6	23.3	359 13.0	06.5	254 29.6	02.9			
23 00	152 34.2	149 45.0	N 0 11.1	150 14.3	N 0 24.1	14 15.7	N17 06.6	269 31.9	S19 02.9	Mirfak	308 38.7	N49 54.9
01	167 36.7	164 44.7	12.5	165 15.0	24.9	29 18.5	06.7	284 34.3	02.9	Nunki	75 57.1	S26 16.5
02	182 39.1	179 44.4	13.8	180 15.7	25.7	44 21.3	06.8	299 36.7	02.9	Peacock	53 18.0	S56 40.9
03	197 41.6	194 44.1	.. 15.1	195 16.4	.. 26.5	59 24.0	.. 06.9	314 39.1	.. 02.9	Pollux	243 26.0	N27 59.1
04	212 44.1	209 43.7	16.4	210 17.1	27.3	74 26.8	07.0	329 41.4	02.9	Procyon	244 58.3	N 5 10.9
05	227 46.5	224 43.4	17.7	225 17.8	28.1	89 29.6	07.1	344 43.8	02.9			
06	242 49.0	239 43.1	N 0 19.0	240 18.6	N 0 28.9	104 32.3	N17 07.2	359 46.2	S19 03.0	Rasalhague	96 05.5	N12 33.0
07	257 51.5	254 42.8	20.3	255 19.3	29.6	119 35.1	07.3	14 48.6	03.0	Regulus	207 42.0	N11 53.3
08	272 53.9	269 42.5	21.6	270 20.0	30.4	134 37.8	07.4	29 51.0	03.0	Rigel	281 10.8	S 8 11.4
M 09	287 56.4	284 42.1	.. 22.9	285 20.7	.. 31.2	149 40.6	.. 07.4	44 53.3	.. 03.0	Rigil Kent.	139 49.8	S60 53.5
O 10	302 58.9	299 41.8	24.2	300 21.4	32.0	164 43.4	07.5	59 55.7	03.0	Sabik	102 11.3	S15 44.4
N 11	318 01.3	314 41.5	25.5	315 22.1	32.8	179 46.1	07.6	74 58.1	03.0			
D 12	333 03.8	329 41.2	N 0 26.8	330 22.8	N 0 33.6	194 48.9	N17 07.7	90 00.5	S19 03.0	Schedar	349 39.5	N56 37.3
A 13	348 06.2	344 40.9	28.1	345 23.6	34.4	209 51.7	07.8	105 02.9	03.0	Shaula	96 20.5	S37 06.6
Y 14	3 08.7	359 40.5	29.4	0 24.3	35.2	224 54.4	07.9	120 05.2	03.0	Sirius	258 32.5	S16 44.6
15	18 11.2	14 40.2	.. 30.8	15 25.0	.. 36.0	239 57.2	.. 08.0	135 07.6	.. 03.0	Spica	158 29.8	S11 14.4
16	33 13.6	29 39.9	32.1	30 25.7	36.7	254 59.9	08.1	150 10.0	03.0	Suhail	222 51.1	S43 29.9
17	48 16.1	44 39.6	33.4	45 26.4	37.5	270 02.7	08.2	165 12.4	03.0			
18	63 18.6	59 39.3	N 0 34.7	60 27.1	N 0 38.3	285 05.5	N17 08.3	180 14.8	S19 03.0	Vega	80 38.4	N38 47.8
19	78 21.0	74 39.0	36.0	75 27.9	39.1	300 08.2	08.3	195 17.1	03.1	Zuben'ubi	137 04.0	S16 06.2
20	93 23.5	89 38.6	37.3	90 28.6	39.9	315 11.0	08.4	210 19.5	03.1		SHA	Mer. Pass.
21	108 26.0	104 38.3	.. 38.6	105 29.3	.. 40.7	330 13.7	.. 08.5	225 21.9	.. 03.1		° ′	h m
22	123 28.4	119 38.0	39.9	120 30.0	41.5	345 16.5	08.6	240 24.3	03.1	Venus	358 17.6	14 01
23	138 30.9	134 37.7	41.2	135 30.7	42.3	0 19.3	08.7	255 26.7	03.1	Mars	358 22.1	14 00
	h m									Jupiter	221 34.3	23 03
Mer. Pass. 13 51.4	v −0.3 d 1.3	v 0.7 d 0.8		v 2.8 d 0.1		v 2.4 d 0.0				Saturn	116 59.8	6 05

UT	SUN GHA	SUN Dec	MOON GHA	v	MOON Dec	d	HP
d h	° ′	° ′	° ′	′	° ′	′	′
21 00	176 34.9	S10 45.1	150 30.5	7.8	N 1 01.3	11.8	61.0
01	191 35.0	44.2	164 57.3	7.8	1 13.1	11.8	60.9
02	206 35.0	43.3	179 24.1	7.9	1 24.9	11.8	60.9
03	221 35.1	.. 42.4	193 51.0	7.8	1 36.7	11.8	60.9
04	236 35.2	41.5	208 17.8	7.9	1 48.5	11.7	60.9
05	251 35.2	40.6	222 44.7	7.9	2 00.2	11.7	60.8
S 06	266 35.3	S10 39.7	237 11.6	8.0	N 2 11.9	11.7	60.8
A 07	281 35.4	38.8	251 38.6	7.9	2 23.6	11.6	60.8
T 08	296 35.5	37.9	266 05.5	8.0	2 35.2	11.7	60.8
U 09	311 35.5	.. 37.0	280 32.5	8.0	2 46.9	11.6	60.7
R 10	326 35.6	36.1	294 59.5	8.0	2 58.5	11.5	60.7
D 11	341 35.7	35.2	309 26.5	8.0	3 10.0	11.6	60.7
A 12	356 35.7	S10 34.3	323 53.5	8.1	N 3 21.6	11.5	60.7
Y 13	11 35.8	33.4	338 20.6	8.1	3 33.1	11.4	60.6
14	26 35.9	32.5	352 47.7	8.1	3 44.5	11.5	60.6
15	41 36.0	.. 31.6	7 14.8	8.1	3 56.0	11.4	60.6
16	56 36.0	30.7	21 41.9	8.1	4 07.4	11.3	60.5
17	71 36.1	29.8	36 09.0	8.2	4 18.7	11.4	60.5
18	86 36.2	S10 28.9	50 36.2	8.1	N 4 30.1	11.2	60.5
19	101 36.2	28.0	65 03.3	8.2	4 41.3	11.3	60.4
20	116 36.3	27.1	79 30.5	8.3	4 52.6	11.2	60.4
21	131 36.4	.. 26.1	93 57.8	8.2	5 03.8	11.1	60.4
22	146 36.5	25.2	108 25.0	8.2	5 14.9	11.1	60.4
23	161 36.5	24.3	122 52.2	8.3	5 26.0	11.1	60.3
22 00	176 36.6	S10 23.4	137 19.5	8.3	N 5 37.1	11.0	60.3
01	191 36.7	22.5	151 46.8	8.3	5 48.1	11.0	60.3
02	206 36.8	21.6	166 14.1	8.3	5 59.1	10.9	60.2
03	221 36.8	.. 20.7	180 41.4	8.3	6 10.0	10.8	60.2
04	236 36.9	19.8	195 08.7	8.4	6 20.8	10.7	60.1
05	251 37.0	18.9	209 36.1	8.3	6 31.7	10.7	60.1
S 06	266 37.1	S10 18.0	224 03.4	8.4	N 6 42.4	10.7	60.1
U 07	281 37.2	17.1	238 30.8	8.4	6 53.1	10.7	60.1
N 08	296 37.2	16.2	252 58.2	8.4	7 03.8	10.6	60.0
D 09	311 37.3	.. 15.2	267 25.6	8.5	7 14.4	10.5	60.0
A 10	326 37.4	14.3	281 53.1	8.4	7 24.9	10.5	60.0
Y 11	341 37.5	13.4	296 20.5	8.5	7 35.4	10.4	59.9
12	356 37.5	S10 12.5	310 48.0	8.4	N 7 45.8	10.3	59.9
13	11 37.6	11.6	325 15.4	8.5	7 56.1	10.3	59.9
14	26 37.7	10.7	339 42.9	8.5	8 06.4	10.2	59.8
15	41 37.8	.. 09.8	354 10.4	8.5	8 16.6	10.2	59.8
16	56 37.9	08.9	8 37.9	8.6	8 26.8	10.1	59.8
17	71 37.9	08.0	23 05.5	8.5	8 36.9	10.0	59.7
18	86 38.0	S10 07.0	37 33.0	8.6	N 8 46.9	10.0	59.7
19	101 38.1	06.1	52 00.6	8.5	8 56.9	9.9	59.6
20	116 38.2	05.2	66 28.1	8.6	9 06.8	9.8	59.6
21	131 38.3	.. 04.3	80 55.7	8.6	9 16.6	9.8	59.6
22	146 38.3	03.4	95 23.3	8.6	9 26.4	9.7	59.5
23	161 38.4	02.5	109 50.9	8.6	9 36.1	9.6	59.5
23 00	176 38.5	S10 01.6	124 18.5	8.7	N 9 45.7	9.6	59.5
01	191 38.6	10 00.6	138 46.2	8.6	9 55.3	9.4	59.4
02	206 38.7	9 59.7	153 13.8	8.7	10 04.7	9.5	59.4
03	221 38.7	.. 58.8	167 41.5	8.7	10 14.2	9.3	59.3
04	236 38.8	57.9	182 09.2	8.6	10 23.5	9.2	59.3
05	251 38.9	57.0	196 36.8	8.7	10 32.7	9.2	59.3
M 06	266 39.0	S 9 56.1	211 04.5	8.7	N10 41.9	9.1	59.2
O 07	281 39.1	55.2	225 32.2	8.8	10 51.0	9.0	59.2
N 08	296 39.2	54.2	240 00.0	8.7	11 00.0	9.0	59.2
D 09	311 39.2	.. 53.3	254 27.7	8.8	11 09.0	8.9	59.1
A 10	326 39.3	52.4	268 55.4	8.8	11 17.9	8.7	59.1
Y 11	341 39.4	51.5	283 23.2	8.8	11 26.6	8.8	59.0
12	356 39.5	S 9 50.6	297 51.0	8.7	N11 35.4	8.6	59.0
13	11 39.6	49.7	312 18.7	8.8	11 44.0	8.5	59.0
14	26 39.7	48.7	326 46.5	8.8	11 52.5	8.5	58.9
15	41 39.8	.. 47.8	341 14.3	8.8	12 01.0	8.4	58.9
16	56 39.8	46.9	355 42.1	8.8	12 09.4	8.3	58.9
17	71 39.9	46.0	10 09.9	8.9	12 17.7	8.2	58.8
18	86 40.0	S 9 45.1	24 37.8	8.8	N12 25.9	8.1	58.8
19	101 40.1	44.1	39 05.6	8.9	12 34.0	8.1	58.7
20	116 40.2	43.2	53 33.5	8.9	12 42.1	7.9	58.7
21	131 40.3	.. 42.3	68 01.4	8.8	12 50.0	7.9	58.7
22	146 40.4	41.4	82 29.2	8.9	12 57.9	7.8	58.6
23	161 40.4	40.5	96 57.1	8.9	N13 05.7	7.7	58.6
SD	16.2	d 0.9	16.5		16.3		16.1

Twilight / Moonrise

Lat.	Twilight Naut.	Twilight Civil	Sunrise	Moonrise 21	22	23	24
°	h m	h m	h m	h m	h m	h m	h m
N 72	05 45	07 03	08 16	07 46	07 41	07 36	07 30
N 70	05 46	06 57	08 02	07 49	07 50	07 53	07 58
68	05 47	06 52	07 50	07 52	07 58	08 07	08 19
66	05 48	06 47	07 41	07 54	08 05	08 18	08 35
64	05 48	06 43	07 33	07 56	08 11	08 28	08 49
62	05 49	06 40	07 26	07 58	08 16	08 36	09 00
60	05 49	06 37	07 20	07 59	08 20	08 43	09 10
N 58	05 49	06 34	07 14	08 00	08 24	08 50	09 19
56	05 49	06 32	07 10	08 02	08 27	08 55	09 26
54	05 48	06 29	07 05	08 03	08 31	09 00	09 33
52	05 48	06 27	07 02	08 04	08 33	09 05	09 39
50	05 48	06 25	06 58	08 04	08 36	09 09	09 45
45	05 47	06 21	06 50	08 06	08 42	09 18	09 57
N 40	05 45	06 17	06 44	08 08	08 46	09 26	10 07
35	05 43	06 13	06 39	08 09	08 50	09 32	10 15
30	05 42	06 09	06 34	08 11	08 54	09 38	10 23
20	05 37	06 03	06 25	08 13	09 00	09 48	10 36
N 10	05 31	05 56	06 17	08 15	09 06	09 57	10 47
0	05 25	05 49	06 10	08 17	09 11	10 05	10 58
S 10	05 16	05 41	06 03	08 19	09 17	10 14	11 09
20	05 06	05 32	05 55	08 21	09 22	10 23	11 21
30	04 52	05 21	05 45	08 23	09 29	10 33	11 34
35	04 43	05 14	05 40	08 25	09 33	10 39	11 42
40	04 32	05 06	05 34	08 26	09 37	10 46	11 51
45	04 19	04 56	05 27	08 28	09 42	10 54	12 01
S 50	04 01	04 44	05 18	08 31	09 49	11 03	12 14
52	03 53	04 38	05 14	08 32	09 51	11 08	12 20
54	03 43	04 31	05 10	08 33	09 55	11 13	12 27
56	03 32	04 24	05 05	08 34	09 58	11 18	12 34
58	03 19	04 16	04 59	08 36	10 02	11 25	12 42
S 60	03 03	04 06	04 53	08 37	10 06	11 32	12 51

Sunset / Twilight / Moonset

Lat.	Sunset	Twilight Civil	Twilight Naut.	Moonset 21	22	23	24
°	h m	h m	h m	h m	h m	h m	h m
N 72	16 13	17 26	18 44	21 49	23 47	25 45	01 45
N 70	16 27	17 32	18 43	21 41	23 32	25 18	01 18
68	16 38	17 37	18 42	21 35	23 19	24 58	00 58
66	16 48	17 41	18 41	21 30	23 09	24 43	00 43
64	16 56	17 45	18 40	21 26	23 00	24 30	00 30
62	17 03	17 48	18 40	21 22	22 53	24 19	00 19
60	17 08	17 51	18 40	21 19	22 47	24 10	00 10
N 58	17 14	17 54	18 39	21 16	22 41	24 02	00 02
56	17 18	17 56	18 40	21 14	22 36	23 54	25 07
54	17 22	17 59	18 40	21 12	22 32	23 48	24 59
52	17 26	18 01	18 40	21 10	22 28	23 43	24 52
50	17 30	18 03	18 40	21 08	22 24	23 37	24 46
45	17 37	18 07	18 41	21 04	22 17	23 26	24 32
N 40	17 43	18 11	18 42	21 00	22 10	23 17	24 21
35	17 49	18 15	18 44	20 57	22 05	23 09	24 11
30	17 54	18 18	18 46	20 55	22 00	23 02	24 03
20	18 02	18 24	18 50	20 50	21 51	22 51	23 48
N 10	18 10	18 31	18 56	20 47	21 44	22 40	23 35
0	18 17	18 38	19 02	20 43	21 37	22 31	23 24
S 10	18 24	18 45	19 10	20 39	21 30	22 21	23 12
20	18 32	18 54	19 21	20 35	21 23	22 11	22 59
30	18 41	19 06	19 35	20 31	21 14	21 59	22 45
35	18 46	19 12	19 43	20 28	21 10	21 52	22 36
40	18 52	19 20	19 54	20 25	21 04	21 44	22 27
45	18 59	19 30	20 07	20 22	20 58	21 35	22 16
S 50	19 08	19 42	20 24	20 18	20 50	21 25	22 02
52	19 12	19 48	20 33	20 16	20 47	21 20	21 56
54	19 16	19 54	20 42	20 14	20 43	21 14	21 49
56	19 21	20 01	20 53	20 12	20 39	21 08	21 41
58	19 26	20 09	21 06	20 09	20 34	21 01	21 33
S 60	19 32	20 19	21 21	20 07	20 29	20 54	21 23

SUN and MOON

Day	SUN Eqn. of Time 00h	SUN Eqn. of Time 12h	SUN Mer. Pass.	MOON Mer. Pass. Upper	MOON Mer. Pass. Lower	Age	Phase
d	m s	m s	h m	h m	h m	d	%
21	13 41	13 37	12 14	14 30	02 02	03	9
22	13 34	13 30	12 13	15 24	02 57	04	17
23	13 26	13 22	12 13	16 18	03 51	05	27

UT	ARIES GHA	VENUS −3.9 GHA	Dec	MARS +1.3 GHA	Dec	JUPITER −2.5 GHA	Dec	SATURN +0.5 GHA	Dec	STARS Name	SHA	Dec
24 00	153 33.4	149 37.4	N 0 42.5	150 31.4	N 0 43.1	15 22.0	N17 08.8	270 29.0	S19 03.1	Acamar	315 17.6	S40 15.0
01	168 35.8	164 37.0	43.8	165 32.1	43.8	30 24.8	08.9	285 31.4	03.1	Achernar	335 26.4	S57 09.9
02	183 38.3	179 36.7	45.1	180 32.9	44.6	45 27.5	09.0	300 33.8	03.1	Acrux	173 07.2	S63 10.9
03	198 40.7	194 36.4	.. 46.4	195 33.6	.. 45.4	60 30.3	.. 09.1	315 36.2	.. 03.1	Adhara	255 11.4	S29 00.0
04	213 43.2	209 36.1	47.8	210 34.3	46.2	75 33.1	09.1	330 38.6	03.1	Aldebaran	290 48.0	N16 32.2
05	228 45.7	224 35.8	49.1	225 35.0	47.0	90 35.8	09.2	345 40.9	03.1			
06	243 48.1	239 35.5	N 0 50.4	240 35.7	N 0 47.8	105 38.6	N17 09.3	0 43.3	S19 03.1	Alioth	166 19.3	N55 52.4
T 07	258 50.6	254 35.1	51.7	255 36.4	48.6	120 41.3	09.4	15 45.7	03.1	Alkaid	152 57.8	N49 14.0
U 08	273 53.1	269 34.8	53.0	270 37.2	49.4	135 44.1	09.5	30 48.1	03.1	Al Na'ir	27 42.8	S46 53.2
E 09	288 55.5	284 34.5	.. 54.3	285 37.9	.. 50.2	150 46.9	.. 09.6	45 50.5	.. 03.2	Alnilam	275 45.1	S 1 11.9
S 10	303 58.0	299 34.2	55.6	300 38.6	50.9	165 49.6	09.7	60 52.9	03.2	Alphard	217 54.6	S 8 43.7
D 11	319 00.5	314 33.9	56.9	315 39.3	51.7	180 52.4	09.8	75 55.2	03.2			
A 12	334 02.9	329 33.6	N 0 58.2	330 40.0	N 0 52.5	195 55.1	N17 09.9	90 57.6	S19 03.2	Alphecca	126 10.0	N26 39.7
Y 13	349 05.4	344 33.2	0 59.5	345 40.7	53.3	210 57.9	09.9	106 00.0	03.2	Alpheratz	357 42.6	N29 10.4
14	4 07.8	359 32.9	1 00.8	0 41.5	54.1	226 00.7	10.0	121 02.4	03.2	Altair	62 07.3	N 8 54.5
15	19 10.3	14 32.6	.. 02.1	15 42.2	.. 54.9	241 03.4	.. 10.1	136 04.8	.. 03.2	Ankaa	353 15.0	S42 13.6
16	34 12.8	29 32.3	03.4	30 42.9	55.7	256 06.2	10.2	151 07.2	03.2	Antares	112 24.8	S26 27.7
17	49 15.2	44 32.0	04.7	45 43.6	56.5	271 08.9	10.3	166 09.5	03.2			
18	64 17.7	59 31.7	N 1 06.1	60 44.3	N 0 57.2	286 11.7	N17 10.4	181 11.9	S19 03.2	Arcturus	145 54.5	N19 06.1
19	79 20.2	74 31.3	07.4	75 45.0	58.0	301 14.4	10.5	196 14.3	03.2	Atria	107 25.6	S69 02.8
20	94 22.6	89 31.0	08.7	90 45.7	58.8	316 17.2	10.6	211 16.7	03.2	Avior	234 16.9	S59 33.8
21	109 25.1	104 30.7	.. 10.0	105 46.5	0 59.6	331 20.0	.. 10.6	226 19.1	.. 03.2	Bellatrix	278 30.7	N 6 21.5
22	124 27.6	119 30.4	11.3	120 47.2	1 00.4	346 22.7	10.7	241 21.5	03.2	Betelgeuse	270 59.9	N 7 24.3
23	139 30.0	134 30.1	12.6	135 47.9	01.2	1 25.5	10.8	256 23.9	03.3			
25 00	154 32.5	149 29.8	N 1 13.9	150 48.6	N 1 02.0	16 28.2	N17 10.9	271 26.2	S19 03.3	Canopus	263 55.3	S52 42.7
01	169 35.0	164 29.4	15.2	165 49.3	02.8	31 31.0	11.0	286 28.6	03.3	Capella	280 32.6	N46 00.7
02	184 37.4	179 29.1	16.5	180 50.0	03.5	46 33.7	11.1	301 31.0	03.3	Deneb	49 31.0	N45 20.1
03	199 39.9	194 28.8	.. 17.8	195 50.8	.. 04.3	61 36.5	.. 11.2	316 33.4	.. 03.3	Denebola	182 32.2	N14 29.0
04	214 42.3	209 28.5	19.1	210 51.5	05.1	76 39.2	11.3	331 35.8	03.3	Diphda	348 55.0	S17 54.4
05	229 44.8	224 28.2	20.4	225 52.2	05.9	91 42.0	11.3	346 38.2	03.3			
06	244 47.3	239 27.9	N 1 21.7	240 52.9	N 1 06.7	106 44.8	N17 11.4	1 40.6	S19 03.3	Dubhe	193 49.8	N61 40.0
W 07	259 49.7	254 27.6	23.0	255 53.6	07.5	121 47.5	11.5	16 43.0	03.3	Elnath	278 11.0	N28 37.0
E 08	274 52.2	269 27.2	24.3	270 54.4	08.3	136 50.3	11.6	31 45.3	03.3	Eltanin	90 45.8	N51 29.1
D 09	289 54.7	284 26.9	.. 25.7	285 55.1	.. 09.1	151 53.0	.. 11.7	46 47.7	.. 03.3	Enif	33 46.3	N 9 56.7
N 10	304 57.1	299 26.6	27.0	300 55.8	09.8	166 55.8	11.8	61 50.1	03.3	Fomalhaut	15 23.1	S29 32.6
E 11	319 59.6	314 26.3	28.3	315 56.5	10.6	181 58.5	11.9	76 52.5	03.3			
S 12	335 02.1	329 26.0	N 1 29.6	330 57.2	N 1 11.4	197 01.3	N17 12.0	91 54.9	S19 03.3	Gacrux	171 59.0	S57 11.8
D 13	350 04.5	344 25.7	30.9	345 57.9	12.2	212 04.0	12.0	106 57.3	03.3	Gienah	175 50.8	S17 37.6
A 14	5 07.0	359 25.3	32.2	0 58.7	13.0	227 06.8	12.1	121 59.7	03.3	Hadar	148 45.7	S60 26.5
Y 15	20 09.5	14 25.0	.. 33.5	15 59.4	.. 13.8	242 09.5	.. 12.2	137 02.1	.. 03.4	Hamal	327 59.6	N23 31.9
16	35 11.9	29 24.7	34.8	31 00.1	14.6	257 12.3	12.3	152 04.4	03.4	Kaus Aust.	83 42.5	S34 22.4
17	50 14.4	44 24.4	36.1	46 00.8	15.4	272 15.1	12.4	167 06.8	03.4			
18	65 16.8	59 24.1	N 1 37.4	61 01.5	N 1 16.1	287 17.8	N17 12.5	182 09.2	S19 03.4	Kochab	137 19.8	N74 05.4
19	80 19.3	74 23.8	38.7	76 02.2	16.9	302 20.6	12.6	197 11.6	03.4	Markab	13 37.5	N15 17.2
20	95 21.8	89 23.5	40.0	91 03.0	17.7	317 23.3	12.6	212 14.0	03.4	Menkar	314 13.9	N 4 08.7
21	110 24.2	104 23.1	.. 41.3	106 03.7	.. 18.5	332 26.1	.. 12.7	227 16.4	.. 03.4	Menkent	148 05.9	S36 26.5
22	125 26.7	119 22.8	42.6	121 04.4	19.3	347 28.8	12.8	242 18.8	03.4	Miaplacidus	221 38.4	S69 47.0
23	140 29.2	134 22.5	43.9	136 05.1	20.1	2 31.6	12.9	257 21.2	03.4			
26 00	155 31.6	149 22.2	N 1 45.2	151 05.8	N 1 20.9	17 34.3	N17 13.0	272 23.6	S19 03.4	Mirfak	308 38.7	N49 54.9
01	170 34.1	164 21.9	46.5	166 06.5	21.6	32 37.1	13.1	287 25.9	03.4	Nunki	75 57.1	S26 16.5
02	185 36.6	179 21.6	47.9	181 07.3	22.4	47 39.8	13.2	302 28.3	03.4	Peacock	53 18.0	S56 40.9
03	200 39.0	194 21.2	.. 49.2	196 08.0	.. 23.2	62 42.6	.. 13.3	317 30.7	.. 03.4	Pollux	243 26.0	N27 59.1
04	215 41.5	209 20.9	50.5	211 08.7	24.0	77 45.3	13.3	332 33.1	03.4	Procyon	244 58.3	N 5 10.9
05	230 44.0	224 20.6	51.8	226 09.4	24.8	92 48.1	13.4	347 35.5	03.4			
06	245 46.4	239 20.3	N 1 53.1	241 10.1	N 1 25.6	107 50.8	N17 13.5	2 37.9	S19 03.4	Rasalhague	96 05.5	N12 33.0
T 07	260 48.9	254 20.0	54.4	256 10.9	26.4	122 53.6	13.6	17 40.3	03.4	Regulus	207 42.0	N11 53.3
H 08	275 51.3	269 19.7	55.7	271 11.6	27.1	137 56.3	13.7	32 42.7	03.5	Rigel	281 10.9	S 8 11.4
U 09	290 53.8	284 19.4	.. 57.0	286 12.3	.. 27.9	152 59.1	.. 13.8	47 45.1	.. 03.5	Rigil Kent.	139 49.7	S60 53.5
R 10	305 56.3	299 19.0	58.2	301 13.0	28.7	168 01.8	13.9	62 47.5	03.5	Sabik	102 11.3	S15 44.4
S 11	320 58.7	314 18.7	1 59.6	316 13.7	29.5	183 04.6	13.9	77 49.9	03.5			
D 12	336 01.2	329 18.4	N 2 00.9	331 14.4	N 1 30.3	198 07.3	N17 14.0	92 52.3	S19 03.5	Schedar	349 39.5	N56 37.3
A 13	351 03.7	344 18.1	02.2	346 15.2	31.1	213 10.1	14.1	107 54.6	03.5	Shaula	96 20.4	S37 06.6
Y 14	6 06.1	359 17.8	03.5	1 15.9	31.9	228 12.8	14.2	122 57.0	03.5	Sirius	258 32.5	S16 44.6
15	21 08.6	14 17.5	.. 04.8	16 16.6	.. 32.6	243 15.6	.. 14.3	137 59.4	.. 03.5	Spica	158 29.8	S11 14.5
16	36 11.1	29 17.2	06.1	31 17.3	33.4	258 18.3	14.4	153 01.8	03.5	Suhail	222 51.1	S43 29.9
17	51 13.5	44 16.8	07.4	46 18.0	34.2	273 21.1	14.4	168 04.2	03.5			
18	66 16.0	59 16.5	N 2 08.7	61 18.8	N 1 35.0	288 23.8	N17 14.5	183 06.6	S19 03.5	Vega	80 38.4	N38 47.8
19	81 18.4	74 16.2	10.0	76 19.5	35.8	303 26.6	14.6	198 09.0	03.5	Zuben'ubi	137 04.5	S16 06.2
20	96 20.9	89 15.9	11.3	91 20.2	36.6	318 29.3	14.7	213 11.4	03.5			
21	111 23.4	104 15.6	.. 12.7	106 20.9	.. 37.4	333 32.1	.. 14.8	228 13.8	.. 03.5		SHA	Mer. Pass.
22	126 25.8	119 15.3	14.0	121 21.6	38.1	348 34.8	14.9	243 16.2	03.5	Venus	354 57.3	14 02
23	141 28.3	134 15.0	15.3	136 22.3	38.9	3 37.6	15.0	258 18.6	03.5	Mars	356 16.1	13 56
	h m									Jupiter	221 55.7	22 50
Mer. Pass. 13 39.6	v −0.3	d 1.3		v 0.7	d 0.8	v 2.8	d 0.1	v 2.4	d 0.0	Saturn	116 53.8	5 53

UT	SUN GHA	SUN Dec	MOON GHA	MOON v	MOON Dec	MOON d	MOON HP
d h	° '	° '	° '	'	° '	'	'
24 00	176 40.5	S 9 39.5	111 25.0	8.9	N13 13.4	7.6	58.5
01	191 40.6	38.6	125 52.9	9.0	13 21.0	7.5	58.5
02	206 40.7	37.7	140 20.9	8.9	13 28.5	7.4	58.5
03	221 40.8	.. 36.8	154 48.8	8.9	13 35.9	7.4	58.4
04	236 40.9	35.9	169 16.7	9.0	13 43.3	7.2	58.4
05	251 41.0	34.9	183 44.7	9.0	13 50.5	7.2	58.3
06	266 41.1	S 9 34.0	198 12.7	9.0	N13 57.7	7.0	58.3
07	281 41.2	33.1	212 40.7	9.0	14 04.7	7.0	58.3
08	296 41.3	32.2	227 08.7	9.0	14 11.7	6.9	58.2
09	311 41.3	.. 31.2	241 36.7	9.0	14 18.6	6.8	58.2
10	326 41.4	30.3	256 04.7	9.0	14 25.4	6.7	58.2
11	341 41.5	29.4	270 32.7	9.1	14 32.1	6.6	58.1
12	356 41.6	S 9 28.5	285 00.8	9.0	N14 38.7	6.5	58.1
13	11 41.7	27.6	299 28.8	9.1	14 45.2	6.5	58.0
14	26 41.8	26.6	313 56.9	9.1	14 51.7	6.3	58.0
15	41 41.9	.. 25.7	328 25.0	9.1	14 58.0	6.2	58.0
16	56 42.0	24.8	342 53.1	9.1	15 04.2	6.2	57.9
17	71 42.1	23.9	357 21.2	9.1	15 10.4	6.0	57.9
18	86 42.2	S 9 22.9	11 49.3	9.2	N15 16.4	6.0	57.8
19	101 42.3	22.0	26 17.5	9.1	15 22.4	5.8	57.8
20	116 42.4	21.1	40 45.6	9.2	15 28.2	5.8	57.8
21	131 42.4	.. 20.2	55 13.8	9.1	15 34.0	5.6	57.7
22	146 42.5	19.2	69 41.9	9.2	15 39.6	5.6	57.7
23	161 42.6	18.3	84 10.1	9.2	15 45.2	5.5	57.7
25 00	176 42.7	S 9 17.4	98 38.3	9.3	N15 50.7	5.3	57.6
01	191 42.8	16.5	113 06.6	9.2	15 56.0	5.3	57.6
02	206 42.9	15.5	127 34.8	9.3	16 01.3	5.2	57.5
03	221 43.0	.. 14.6	142 03.1	9.2	16 06.5	5.1	57.5
04	236 43.1	13.7	156 31.3	9.3	16 11.6	4.9	57.5
05	251 43.2	12.7	170 59.6	9.3	16 16.5	4.9	57.4
06	266 43.3	S 9 11.8	185 27.9	9.3	N16 21.4	4.8	57.4
07	281 43.4	10.9	199 56.2	9.4	16 26.2	4.7	57.4
08	296 43.5	10.0	214 24.6	9.3	16 30.9	4.6	57.3
09	311 43.6	.. 09.0	228 52.9	9.4	16 35.5	4.5	57.3
10	326 43.7	08.1	243 21.3	9.4	16 40.0	4.4	57.3
11	341 43.8	07.2	257 49.7	9.4	16 44.4	4.3	57.2
12	356 43.9	S 9 06.2	272 18.1	9.4	N16 48.7	4.2	57.2
13	11 44.0	05.3	286 46.5	9.4	16 52.9	4.1	57.1
14	26 44.1	04.4	301 14.9	9.5	16 57.0	4.0	57.1
15	41 44.2	.. 03.5	315 43.4	9.4	17 01.0	3.9	57.1
16	56 44.3	02.5	330 11.8	9.5	17 04.9	3.8	57.0
17	71 44.4	01.6	344 40.3	9.5	17 08.7	3.7	57.0
18	86 44.5	S 9 00.7	359 08.8	9.6	N17 12.4	3.6	57.0
19	101 44.6	8 59.7	13 37.4	9.5	17 16.0	3.5	56.9
20	116 44.7	58.8	28 05.9	9.6	17 19.5	3.4	56.9
21	131 44.8	.. 57.9	42 34.5	9.6	17 22.9	3.3	56.9
22	146 44.9	56.9	57 03.1	9.6	17 26.2	3.2	56.8
23	161 45.0	56.0	71 31.7	9.6	17 29.4	3.1	56.8
26 00	176 45.1	S 8 55.1	86 00.3	9.7	N17 32.5	3.0	56.8
01	191 45.2	54.1	100 29.0	9.6	17 35.5	2.9	56.7
02	206 45.3	53.2	114 57.6	9.7	17 38.4	2.8	56.7
03	221 45.4	.. 52.3	129 26.3	9.7	17 41.2	2.7	56.7
04	236 45.5	51.4	143 55.0	9.8	17 43.9	2.6	56.6
05	251 45.6	50.4	158 23.8	9.7	17 46.5	2.5	56.6
06	266 45.7	S 8 49.5	172 52.5	9.8	N17 49.0	2.4	56.6
07	281 45.8	48.6	187 21.3	9.8	17 51.4	2.4	56.5
08	296 45.9	47.6	201 50.1	9.9	17 53.8	2.2	56.5
09	311 46.0	.. 46.7	216 19.0	9.8	17 56.0	2.1	56.5
10	326 46.1	45.7	230 47.8	9.9	17 58.1	2.0	56.4
11	341 46.2	44.8	245 16.7	9.9	18 00.1	1.9	56.4
12	356 46.3	S 8 43.9	259 45.6	9.9	N18 02.0	1.8	56.4
13	11 46.4	42.9	274 14.5	10.0	18 03.8	1.8	56.3
14	26 46.5	42.0	288 43.5	10.0	18 05.6	1.6	56.3
15	41 46.6	.. 41.1	303 12.5	10.0	18 07.2	1.5	56.3
16	56 46.7	40.1	317 41.5	10.0	18 08.7	1.4	56.2
17	71 46.8	39.2	332 10.5	10.1	18 10.1	1.4	56.2
18	86 46.9	S 8 38.3	346 39.6	10.0	N18 11.5	1.2	56.2
19	101 47.0	37.3	1 08.6	10.1	18 12.7	1.1	56.1
20	116 47.1	36.4	15 37.7	10.2	18 13.8	1.1	56.1
21	131 47.2	.. 35.5	30 06.9	10.2	18 14.9	0.9	56.1
22	146 47.4	34.5	44 36.1	10.2	18 15.8	0.9	56.1
23	161 47.5	33.6	59 05.3	10.2	N18 16.7	0.7	56.0
	SD 16.2	d 0.9	SD 15.8		15.6		15.4

Left day labels: TUESDAY, WEDNESDAY, THURSDAY.

Moonrise

Lat.	Twilight Naut.	Twilight Civil	Sunrise	Moonrise 24	25	26	27
°	h m	h m	h m	h m	h m	h m	h m
N 72	05 31	06 49	08 00	07 30	07 23	07 11	▭
N 70	05 34	06 44	07 48	07 58	08 07	08 26	09 05
68	05 36	06 40	07 38	08 19	08 36	09 04	09 48
66	05 38	06 37	07 29	08 35	08 58	09 31	10 16
64	05 39	06 34	07 22	08 49	09 16	09 51	10 38
62	05 40	06 31	07 16	09 00	09 30	10 08	10 55
60	05 41	06 29	07 11	09 10	09 42	10 22	11 10
N 58	05 41	06 27	07 06	09 19	09 53	10 34	11 22
56	05 42	06 25	07 02	09 26	10 02	10 44	11 33
54	05 42	06 23	06 59	09 33	10 11	10 53	11 42
52	05 42	06 21	06 55	09 39	10 18	11 02	11 50
50	05 42	06 19	06 52	09 45	10 25	11 09	11 58
45	05 42	06 16	06 46	09 57	10 39	11 25	12 14
N 40	05 41	06 13	06 40	10 07	10 51	11 37	12 28
35	05 40	06 09	06 35	10 15	11 01	11 48	12 38
30	05 39	06 07	06 31	10 23	11 10	11 58	12 48
20	05 35	06 01	06 23	10 36	11 25	12 15	13 05
N 10	05 30	05 55	06 16	10 47	11 38	12 29	13 20
0	05 24	05 49	06 10	10 58	11 51	12 43	13 34
S 10	05 17	05 42	06 03	11 09	12 04	12 57	13 48
20	05 07	05 34	05 56	11 21	12 17	13 11	14 02
30	04 54	05 23	05 48	11 34	12 33	13 28	14 19
35	04 46	05 17	05 43	11 42	12 42	13 38	14 29
40	04 36	05 09	05 37	11 51	12 52	13 49	14 41
45	04 24	05 00	05 31	12 01	13 05	14 02	14 54
S 50	04 07	04 49	05 23	12 14	13 19	14 18	15 10
52	04 00	04 44	05 20	12 20	13 26	14 26	15 18
54	03 51	04 38	05 16	12 27	13 34	14 34	15 26
56	03 41	04 31	05 11	12 34	13 43	14 44	15 36
58	03 29	04 23	05 06	12 42	13 53	14 54	15 46
S 60	03 14	04 15	05 01	12 51	14 04	15 07	15 59

Moonset

Lat.	Sunset	Twilight Civil	Twilight Naut.	Moonset 24	25	26	27
°	h m	h m	h m	h m	h m	h m	h m
N 72	16 28	17 39	18 58	01 45	03 42	05 44	▭
N 70	16 40	17 44	18 55	01 18	02 59	04 29	05 36
68	16 50	17 48	18 52	00 58	02 31	03 51	04 54
66	16 58	17 51	18 50	00 43	02 09	03 25	04 25
64	17 05	17 54	18 49	00 30	01 52	03 04	04 04
62	17 11	17 56	18 48	00 19	01 38	02 48	03 46
60	17 16	17 59	18 47	00 10	01 26	02 34	03 32
N 58	17 21	18 01	18 46	00 02	01 16	02 22	03 19
56	17 25	18 03	18 46	25 07	01 07	02 12	03 09
54	17 28	18 04	18 45	24 59	00 59	02 03	02 59
52	17 32	18 06	18 45	24 52	00 52	01 55	02 51
50	17 35	18 07	18 45	24 46	00 46	01 48	02 43
45	17 41	18 11	18 45	24 32	00 32	01 33	02 27
N 40	17 47	18 14	18 46	24 21	00 21	01 20	02 14
35	17 52	18 17	18 47	24 11	00 11	01 09	02 03
30	17 56	18 20	18 48	24 03	00 03	01 00	01 53
20	18 03	18 26	18 51	23 48	24 43	00 43	01 36
N 10	18 10	18 31	18 56	23 35	24 29	00 29	01 21
0	18 16	18 37	19 02	23 24	24 16	00 16	01 08
S 10	18 23	18 44	19 09	23 12	24 03	00 03	00 54
20	18 30	18 52	19 18	22 59	23 49	24 39	00 39
30	18 38	19 02	19 31	22 45	23 32	24 22	00 22
35	18 43	19 09	19 39	22 36	23 23	24 12	00 12
40	18 48	19 16	19 49	22 27	23 12	24 01	00 01
45	18 54	19 25	20 01	22 16	23 00	23 47	24 39
S 50	19 02	19 36	20 17	22 02	22 44	23 31	24 23
52	19 05	19 41	20 25	21 56	22 37	23 24	24 15
54	19 09	19 47	20 34	21 49	22 29	23 15	24 07
56	19 14	19 53	20 43	21 41	22 20	23 06	23 57
58	19 18	20 01	20 55	21 33	22 10	22 55	23 47
S 60	19 24	20 09	21 09	21 23	21 59	22 42	23 34

SUN and MOON

Day	SUN Eqn. of Time 00h	SUN Eqn. of Time 12h	SUN Mer. Pass.	MOON Mer. Pass. Upper	MOON Mer. Pass. Lower	Age	Phase
	m s	m s	h m	h m	h m	d	%
24	13 18	13 14	12 13	11 44	04 44	06	37
25	13 09	13 05	12 13	18 04	05 37	07	48
26	13 00	12 55	12 13	18 55	06 30	08	58

UT	ARIES GHA	VENUS −3.9 GHA	Dec	MARS +1.3 GHA	Dec	JUPITER −2.5 GHA	Dec	SATURN +0.5 GHA	Dec	STARS Name	SHA	Dec
27 00	156 30.8	149 14.6	N 2 16.6	151 23.1	N 1 39.7	18 40.3	N17 15.0	273 21.0	S19 03.5	Acamar	315 17.7	S40 15.0
01	171 33.2	164 14.3	17.9	166 23.8	40.5	33 43.1	15.1	288 23.4	03.5	Achernar	335 26.4	S57 09.9
02	186 35.7	179 14.0	19.2	181 24.5	41.3	48 45.8	15.2	303 25.8	03.5	Acrux	173 07.2	S63 10.9
03	201 38.2	194 13.7	.. 20.5	196 25.2	.. 42.1	63 48.6	.. 15.3	318 28.2	.. 03.6	Adhara	255 11.4	S29 00.0
04	216 40.6	209 13.4	21.8	211 25.9	42.8	78 51.3	15.4	333 30.6	03.6	Aldebaran	290 48.0	N16 32.2
05	231 43.1	224 13.1	23.1	226 26.7	43.6	93 54.0	15.5	348 32.9	03.6			
06	246 45.6	239 12.8	N 2 24.4	241 27.4	N 1 44.4	108 56.8	N17 15.5	3 35.3	S19 03.6	Alioth	166 19.3	N55 52.4
07	261 48.0	254 12.5	25.7	256 28.1	45.2	123 59.5	15.6	18 37.7	03.6	Alkaid	152 57.7	N49 14.0
08	276 50.5	269 12.1	27.0	271 28.8	46.0	139 02.3	15.7	33 40.1	03.6	Al Na'ir	27 42.8	S46 53.2
F 09	291 52.9	284 11.8	.. 28.3	286 29.5	.. 46.8	154 05.0	.. 15.8	48 42.5	.. 03.6	Alnilam	275 45.1	S 1 11.9
R 10	306 55.4	299 11.5	29.6	301 30.2	47.6	169 07.8	15.9	63 44.9	03.6	Alphard	217 54.6	S 8 43.8
I 11	321 57.9	314 11.2	30.9	316 31.0	48.3	184 10.5	16.0	78 47.3	03.6			
D 12	337 00.3	329 10.9	N 2 32.2	331 31.7	N 1 49.1	199 13.3	N17 16.0	93 49.7	S19 03.6	Alphecca	126 09.9	N26 39.7
A 13	352 02.8	344 10.6	33.5	346 32.4	49.9	214 16.0	16.1	108 52.1	03.6	Alpheratz	357 42.6	N29 10.4
Y 14	7 05.3	359 10.3	34.8	1 33.1	50.7	229 18.8	16.2	123 54.5	03.6	Altair	62 07.3	N 8 54.5
15	22 07.7	14 09.9	.. 36.1	16 33.8	.. 51.5	244 21.5	.. 16.3	138 56.9	.. 03.6	Ankaa	353 15.0	S42 13.6
16	37 10.2	29 09.6	37.4	31 34.6	52.3	259 24.2	16.4	153 59.3	03.6	Antares	112 24.8	S26 27.7
17	52 12.7	44 09.3	38.7	46 35.3	53.0	274 27.0	16.5	169 01.7	03.6			
18	67 15.1	59 09.0	N 2 40.0	61 36.0	N 1 53.8	289 29.7	N17 16.5	184 04.1	S19 03.6	Arcturus	145 54.5	N19 06.1
19	82 17.6	74 08.7	41.3	76 36.7	54.6	304 32.5	16.6	199 06.5	03.6	Atria	107 25.6	S69 02.8
20	97 20.1	89 08.4	42.6	91 37.4	55.4	319 35.2	16.7	214 08.9	03.6	Avior	234 16.9	S59 33.9
21	112 22.5	104 08.1	.. 43.9	106 38.2	.. 56.2	334 38.0	.. 16.8	229 11.3	.. 03.6	Bellatrix	278 30.7	N 6 21.5
22	127 25.0	119 07.7	45.2	121 38.9	57.0	349 40.7	16.9	244 13.7	03.6	Betelgeuse	270 59.9	N 7 24.3
23	142 27.4	134 07.4	46.5	136 39.6	57.7	4 43.5	17.0	259 16.1	03.6			
28 00	157 29.9	149 07.1	N 2 47.8	151 40.3	N 1 58.5	19 46.2	N17 17.0	274 18.5	S19 03.7	Canopus	263 55.4	S52 42.7
01	172 32.4	164 06.8	49.1	166 41.0	1 59.3	34 48.9	17.1	289 20.9	03.7	Capella	280 32.6	N46 00.7
02	187 34.8	179 06.5	50.4	181 41.8	2 00.1	49 51.7	17.2	304 23.3	03.7	Deneb	49 31.0	N45 20.0
03	202 37.3	194 06.2	.. 51.7	196 42.5	.. 00.9	64 54.4	.. 17.3	319 25.7	.. 03.7	Denebola	182 32.2	N14 29.0
04	217 39.8	209 05.9	53.1	211 43.2	01.7	79 57.2	17.4	334 28.1	03.7	Diphda	348 55.0	S17 54.4
05	232 42.2	224 05.5	54.4	226 43.9	02.4	94 59.9	17.5	349 30.5	03.7			
06	247 44.7	239 05.2	N 2 55.7	241 44.6	N 2 03.2	110 02.6	N17 17.5	4 32.9	S19 03.7	Dubhe	193 49.7	N61 40.0
07	262 47.2	254 04.9	57.0	256 45.4	04.0	125 05.4	17.6	19 35.3	03.7	Elnath	278 11.0	N28 37.0
S 08	277 49.6	269 04.6	58.3	271 46.1	04.8	140 08.1	17.7	34 37.7	03.7	Eltanin	90 45.8	N51 29.1
A 09	292 52.1	284 04.3	2 59.6	286 46.8	.. 05.6	155 10.9	.. 17.8	49 40.1	.. 03.7	Enif	33 46.3	N 9 56.7
T 10	307 54.5	299 04.0	3 00.9	301 47.5	06.4	170 13.6	17.9	64 42.5	03.7	Fomalhaut	15 23.1	S29 32.6
U 11	322 57.0	314 03.7	02.2	316 48.2	07.1	185 16.4	17.9	79 44.9	03.7			
R 12	337 59.5	329 03.4	N 3 03.5	331 49.0	N 2 07.9	200 19.1	N17 18.0	94 47.3	S19 03.7	Gacrux	171 59.0	S57 11.8
D 13	353 01.9	344 03.0	04.8	346 49.7	08.7	215 21.8	18.1	109 49.7	03.7	Gienah	175 50.8	S17 37.7
A 14	8 04.4	359 02.7	06.1	1 50.4	09.5	230 24.6	18.2	124 52.1	03.7	Hadar	148 45.7	S60 26.5
Y 15	23 06.9	14 02.4	.. 07.4	16 51.1	.. 10.3	245 27.3	.. 18.3	139 54.5	.. 03.7	Hamal	327 59.6	N23 31.9
16	38 09.3	29 02.1	08.7	31 51.8	11.1	260 30.1	18.4	154 56.9	03.7	Kaus Aust.	83 42.4	S34 22.4
17	53 11.8	44 01.8	10.0	46 52.6	11.8	275 32.8	18.4	169 59.3	03.7			
18	68 14.3	59 01.5	N 3 11.3	61 53.3	N 2 12.6	290 35.5	N17 18.5	185 01.7	S19 03.7	Kochab	137 19.8	N74 05.4
19	83 16.7	74 01.2	12.6	76 54.0	13.4	305 38.3	18.6	200 04.1	03.7	Markab	13 37.5	N15 17.2
20	98 19.2	89 00.8	13.9	91 54.7	14.2	320 41.0	18.7	215 06.5	03.7	Menkar	314 13.9	N 4 08.7
21	113 21.7	104 00.5	.. 15.2	106 55.4	.. 15.0	335 43.8	.. 18.8	230 08.9	.. 03.7	Menkent	148 05.9	S36 26.5
22	128 24.1	119 00.2	16.5	121 56.2	15.7	350 46.5	18.8	245 11.3	03.7	Miaplacidus	221 38.4	S69 47.0
23	143 26.6	133 59.9	17.8	136 56.9	16.5	5 49.2	18.9	260 13.7	03.7			
1 00	158 29.0	148 59.6	N 3 19.1	151 57.6	N 2 17.3	20 52.0	N17 19.0	275 16.1	S19 03.7	Mirfak	308 38.7	N49 54.9
01	173 31.5	163 59.3	20.4	166 58.3	18.1	35 54.7	19.1	290 18.5	03.8	Nunki	75 57.1	S26 16.5
02	188 34.0	178 59.0	21.7	181 59.0	18.9	50 57.4	19.2	305 20.9	03.8	Peacock	53 18.0	S56 40.9
03	203 36.4	193 58.6	.. 23.0	196 59.8	.. 19.7	66 00.2	.. 19.2	320 23.3	.. 03.8	Pollux	243 26.0	N27 59.1
04	218 38.9	208 58.3	24.3	212 00.5	20.4	81 02.9	19.3	335 25.7	03.8	Procyon	244 58.3	N 5 10.9
05	233 41.4	223 58.0	25.6	227 01.2	21.2	96 05.7	19.4	350 28.1	03.8			
06	248 43.8	238 57.7	N 3 26.9	242 01.9	N 2 22.0	111 08.4	N17 19.5	5 30.5	S19 03.8	Rasalhague	96 05.5	N12 33.0
07	263 46.3	253 57.4	28.2	257 02.6	22.8	126 11.1	19.6	20 32.9	03.8	Regulus	207 42.0	N11 53.3
08	278 48.8	268 57.1	29.5	272 03.4	23.6	141 13.9	19.7	35 35.3	03.8	Rigel	281 10.9	S 8 11.4
S 09	293 51.2	283 56.8	.. 30.8	287 04.1	.. 24.3	156 16.6	.. 19.7	50 37.8	.. 03.8	Rigil Kent.	139 49.7	S60 53.5
U 10	308 53.7	298 56.5	32.1	302 04.8	25.1	171 19.3	19.8	65 40.2	03.8	Sabik	102 11.2	S15 44.5
N 11	323 56.2	313 56.1	33.4	317 05.5	25.9	186 22.1	19.9	80 42.6	03.8			
D 12	338 58.6	328 55.8	N 3 34.7	332 06.2	N 2 26.7	201 24.8	N17 20.0	95 45.0	S19 03.8	Schedar	349 39.5	N56 37.3
A 13	354 01.1	343 55.5	36.0	347 07.0	27.5	216 27.5	20.1	110 47.4	03.8	Shaula	96 20.4	S37 06.6
Y 14	9 03.5	358 55.2	37.2	2 07.7	28.2	231 30.3	20.1	125 49.8	03.8	Sirius	258 32.5	S16 44.6
15	24 06.0	13 54.9	.. 38.5	17 08.4	.. 29.0	246 33.0	.. 20.2	140 52.2	.. 03.8	Spica	158 29.8	S11 14.5
16	39 08.5	28 54.6	39.8	32 09.1	29.8	261 35.7	20.3	155 54.6	03.8	Suhail	222 51.1	S43 29.9
17	54 10.9	43 54.3	41.1	47 09.8	30.6	276 38.5	20.4	170 57.0	03.8			
18	69 13.4	58 53.9	N 3 42.4	62 10.6	N 2 31.4	291 41.2	N17 20.5	185 59.4	S19 03.8	Vega	80 38.4	N38 47.8
19	84 15.9	73 53.6	43.7	77 11.3	32.1	306 44.0	20.5	201 01.8	03.8	Zuben'ubi	137 04.0	S16 06.2
20	99 18.3	88 53.3	45.0	92 12.0	32.9	321 46.7	20.6	216 04.2	03.8		SHA	Mer.Pass.
21	114 20.8	103 53.0	.. 46.3	107 12.7	.. 33.7	336 49.4	.. 20.7	231 06.6	.. 03.8	Venus	351 37.2	14 04
22	129 23.3	118 52.7	47.6	122 13.4	34.5	351 52.2	20.8	246 09.0	03.8	Mars	354 10.4	13 53
23	144 25.7	133 52.4	48.9	137 14.2	35.3	6 54.9	20.8	261 11.4	03.8	Jupiter	222 16.3	22 37
Mer. Pass. 13 27.8	v −0.3 d 1.3	v −0.3	d 1.3	v 0.7 d 0.8		v 2.7 d 0.1		v 2.4 d 0.0		Saturn	116 48.6	5 42

UT	SUN GHA	Dec	MOON GHA	v	Dec	d	HP
d h	° '	° '	° '	'	° '	'	'
27 00	176 47.6	S 8 32.6	73 34.5	10.2	N18 17.4	0.7	56.0
01	191 47.7	31.7	88 03.7	10.3	18 18.1	0.5	56.0
02	206 47.8	30.8	102 33.0	10.3	18 18.6	0.5	55.9
03	221 47.9	.. 29.8	117 02.3	10.4	18 19.1	0.3	55.9
04	236 48.0	28.9	131 31.7	10.3	18 19.4	0.5	55.9
05	251 48.1	28.0	146 01.0	10.4	18 19.7	0.2	55.9
06	266 48.2	S 8 27.0	160 30.4	10.5	N18 19.9	0.1	55.8
07	281 48.3	26.1	174 59.9	10.4	18 20.0	0.1	55.8
F 08	296 48.4	25.1	189 29.3	10.5	18 19.9	0.1	55.8
R 09	311 48.5	.. 24.2	203 58.8	10.5	18 19.8	0.2	55.7
I 10	326 48.6	23.3	218 28.3	10.6	18 19.6	0.3	55.7
D 11	341 48.8	22.3	232 57.9	10.6	18 19.3	0.4	55.7
A 12	356 48.9	S 8 21.4	247 27.5	10.6	N18 18.9	0.5	55.7
Y 13	11 49.0	20.4	261 57.1	10.7	18 18.4	0.5	55.6
14	26 49.1	19.5	276 26.8	10.6	18 17.9	0.7	55.6
15	41 49.2	.. 18.6	290 56.4	10.8	18 17.2	0.8	55.6
16	56 49.3	17.6	305 26.2	10.7	18 16.4	0.8	55.6
17	71 49.4	16.7	319 55.9	10.8	18 15.6	1.0	55.5
18	86 49.5	S 8 15.7	334 25.7	10.8	N18 14.6	1.0	55.5
19	101 49.6	14.8	348 55.5	10.9	18 13.6	1.1	55.5
20	116 49.8	13.9	3 25.4	10.9	18 12.5	1.3	55.5
21	131 49.9	.. 12.9	17 55.3	10.9	18 11.2	1.3	55.4
22	146 50.0	12.0	32 25.2	10.9	18 09.9	1.4	55.4
23	161 50.1	11.0	46 55.1	11.0	18 08.5	1.5	55.4
28 00	176 50.2	S 8 10.1	61 25.1	11.1	N18 07.0	1.5	55.4
01	191 50.3	09.1	75 55.2	11.0	18 05.5	1.7	55.3
02	206 50.4	08.2	90 25.2	11.1	18 03.8	1.8	55.3
03	221 50.5	.. 07.3	104 55.3	11.1	18 02.0	1.8	55.3
04	236 50.7	06.3	119 25.4	11.2	18 00.2	2.1	55.2
05	251 50.8	05.4	133 55.6	11.2	17 58.3	2.1	55.2
06	266 50.9	S 8 04.4	148 25.8	11.3	N17 56.2	2.1	55.2
07	281 51.0	03.5	162 56.1	11.2	17 54.1	2.2	55.2
S 08	296 51.1	02.5	177 26.3	11.4	17 51.9	2.2	55.2
A 09	311 51.2	.. 01.6	191 56.7	11.3	17 49.7	2.4	55.2
T 10	326 51.3	8 00.7	206 27.0	11.4	17 47.3	2.4	55.1
U 11	341 51.5	7 59.7	220 57.4	11.4	17 44.9	2.6	55.1
R 12	356 51.6	S 7 58.8	235 27.8	11.5	N17 42.3	2.6	55.1
D 13	11 51.7	57.8	249 58.3	11.5	17 39.7	2.7	55.1
A 14	26 51.8	56.9	264 28.8	11.5	17 37.0	2.8	55.1
Y 15	41 51.9	.. 55.9	278 59.3	11.6	17 34.2	2.9	55.0
16	56 52.0	55.0	293 29.9	11.6	17 31.3	2.9	55.0
17	71 52.2	54.0	308 00.5	11.7	17 28.4	3.0	55.0
18	86 52.3	S 7 53.1	322 31.2	11.7	N17 25.4	3.2	55.0
19	101 52.4	52.1	337 01.9	11.7	17 22.2	3.2	54.9
20	116 52.5	51.2	351 32.6	11.8	17 19.0	3.2	54.9
21	131 52.6	.. 50.3	6 03.4	11.8	17 15.8	3.4	54.9
22	146 52.7	49.3	20 34.2	11.8	17 12.4	3.4	54.9
23	161 52.9	48.4	35 05.0	11.9	17 09.0	3.6	54.9
1 00	176 53.0	S 7 47.4	49 35.9	11.9	N17 05.4	3.6	54.9
01	191 53.1	46.5	64 06.8	12.0	17 01.8	3.6	54.8
02	206 53.2	45.5	78 37.8	12.0	16 58.2	3.8	54.8
03	221 53.3	.. 44.6	93 08.8	12.0	16 54.4	3.8	54.8
04	236 53.4	43.6	107 39.8	12.1	16 50.6	3.9	54.8
05	251 53.6	42.7	122 10.9	12.1	16 46.7	4.0	54.8
06	266 53.7	S 7 41.7	136 42.0	12.2	N16 42.7	4.1	54.7
07	281 53.8	40.8	151 13.2	12.2	16 38.6	4.1	54.7
S 08	296 53.9	39.8	165 44.4	12.2	16 34.5	4.2	54.7
U 09	311 54.0	.. 38.9	180 15.6	12.3	16 30.3	4.3	54.7
N 10	326 54.2	37.9	194 46.9	12.3	16 26.0	4.4	54.7
D 11	341 54.3	37.0	209 18.2	12.4	16 21.6	4.4	54.7
A 12	356 54.4	S 7 36.0	223 49.6	12.3	N16 17.2	4.6	54.6
Y 13	11 54.5	35.1	238 20.9	12.5	16 12.6	4.5	54.6
14	26 54.7	34.1	252 52.4	12.4	16 08.1	4.7	54.6
15	41 54.8	.. 33.2	267 23.8	12.6	16 03.4	4.8	54.6
16	56 54.9	32.2	281 55.4	12.6	15 58.7	4.8	54.6
17	71 55.0	31.3	296 26.9	12.6	15 53.9	4.9	54.6
18	86 55.1	S 7 30.3	310 58.5	12.6	N15 49.0	4.9	54.6
19	101 55.3	29.4	325 30.1	12.7	15 44.1	5.0	54.5
20	116 55.4	28.4	340 01.8	12.7	15 39.1	5.1	54.5
21	131 55.5	.. 27.5	354 33.5	12.7	15 34.0	5.2	54.5
22	146 55.6	26.5	9 05.2	12.8	15 28.8	5.2	54.5
23	161 55.8	25.6	23 37.0	12.8	N15 23.6	5.3	54.5
	SD 16.2	d 0.9	SD 15.2		15.0		14.9

Lat.	Twilight Naut.	Twilight Civil	Sunrise	Moonrise 27	28	1	2
°	h m	h m	h m	h m	h m	h m	h m
N 72	05 17	06 34	07 44	▭	08 53	10 46	12 30
N 70	05 21	06 31	07 33	09 05	10 10	11 31	12 59
68	05 24	06 28	07 25	09 48	10 48	12 01	13 21
66	05 27	06 26	07 18	10 16	11 14	12 23	13 38
64	05 29	06 24	07 12	10 38	11 35	12 40	13 51
62	05 31	06 22	07 07	10 55	11 51	12 55	14 03
60	05 33	06 20	07 02	11 10	12 05	13 07	14 13
N 58	05 34	06 19	06 58	11 22	12 17	13 17	14 21
56	05 35	06 18	06 55	11 33	12 27	13 26	14 29
54	05 35	06 16	06 52	11 42	12 36	13 34	14 36
52	05 36	06 15	06 49	11 50	12 44	13 42	14 42
50	05 36	06 14	06 46	11 58	12 51	13 48	14 47
45	05 37	06 11	06 40	12 14	13 07	14 02	14 59
N 40	05 37	06 08	06 35	12 27	13 19	14 13	15 08
35	05 36	06 06	06 31	12 38	13 30	14 23	15 17
30	05 36	06 03	06 27	12 48	13 40	14 32	15 24
20	05 33	05 59	06 21	13 05	13 56	14 46	15 36
N 10	05 29	05 54	06 15	13 20	14 10	14 59	15 47
0	05 24	05 48	06 09	13 34	14 23	15 11	15 57
S 10	05 17	05 42	06 03	13 48	14 37	15 23	16 08
20	05 09	05 35	05 57	14 02	14 51	15 36	16 18
30	04 57	05 26	05 50	14 19	15 07	15 51	16 31
35	04 49	05 20	05 46	14 29	15 16	15 59	16 38
40	04 40	05 13	05 41	14 41	15 27	16 09	16 46
45	04 28	05 05	05 35	14 54	15 40	16 20	16 56
S 50	04 14	04 55	05 28	15 10	15 55	16 34	17 07
52	04 06	04 50	05 25	15 18	16 02	16 40	17 12
54	03 58	04 44	05 22	15 26	16 10	16 47	17 18
56	03 49	04 38	05 18	15 36	16 19	16 55	17 25
58	03 38	04 32	05 14	15 46	16 29	17 04	17 32
S 60	03 25	04 24	05 09	15 59	16 41	17 14	17 40

Lat.	Sunset	Twilight Civil	Twilight Naut.	Moonset 27	28	1	2
°	h m	h m	h m	h m	h m	h m	h m
N 72	16 43	17 53	19 11	▭	07 32	07 19	07 13
N 70	16 53	17 56	19 07	05 36	06 15	06 34	06 43
68	17 02	17 59	19 03	04 54	05 37	06 04	06 20
66	17 09	18 01	19 00	04 25	05 10	05 41	06 03
64	17 14	18 03	18 58	04 04	04 49	05 23	05 48
62	17 19	18 04	18 56	03 46	04 33	05 09	05 36
60	17 24	18 06	18 54	03 32	04 19	04 56	05 26
N 58	17 28	18 07	18 53	03 19	04 07	04 45	05 17
56	17 31	18 09	18 52	03 09	03 57	04 36	05 09
54	17 34	18 10	18 51	02 59	03 47	04 28	05 02
52	17 37	18 11	18 50	02 51	03 39	04 21	04 55
50	17 40	18 12	18 50	02 43	03 32	04 14	04 50
45	17 45	18 15	18 49	02 27	03 16	03 59	04 37
N 40	17 50	18 17	18 49	02 14	03 03	03 47	04 27
35	17 54	18 20	18 49	02 03	02 52	03 37	04 18
30	17 58	18 22	18 50	01 53	02 43	03 28	04 10
20	18 05	18 27	18 52	01 36	02 26	03 13	03 57
N 10	18 10	18 32	18 56	01 21	02 11	02 59	03 45
0	18 16	18 37	19 01	01 08	01 58	02 47	03 34
S 10	18 22	18 43	19 07	00 54	01 44	02 34	03 23
20	18 28	18 50	19 16	00 39	01 30	02 20	03 11
30	18 35	18 59	19 28	00 22	01 13	02 05	02 57
35	18 39	19 05	19 35	00 12	01 03	01 55	02 49
40	18 44	19 11	19 44	00 01	00 52	01 45	02 40
45	18 49	19 19	19 56	24 39	00 39	01 33	02 29
S 50	18 56	19 29	20 10	24 23	00 23	01 18	02 16
52	18 59	19 34	20 17	24 15	00 15	01 11	02 10
54	19 02	19 39	20 25	24 07	00 07	01 03	02 03
56	19 06	19 45	20 34	23 57	24 54	00 54	01 56
58	19 10	19 52	20 45	23 47	24 45	00 45	01 47
S 60	19 15	19 59	20 57	23 34	24 33	00 33	01 38

Day	SUN Eqn. of Time 00h	12h	Mer. Pass.	MOON Mer. Pass. Upper	Lower	Age	Phase
d	m s	m s	h m	h m	h m	d	%
27	12 50	12 45	12 13	19 46	07 21	09	68
28	12 39	12 34	12 13	20 35	08 11	10	77
1	12 28	12 23	12 12	21 22	08 59	11	84 ◗

UT	ARIES GHA	VENUS −3.9 GHA	Dec	MARS +1.3 GHA	Dec	JUPITER −2.5 GHA	Dec	SATURN +0.4 GHA	Dec
d h	° ′	° ′	° ′	° ′	° ′	° ′	° ′	° ′	° ′
2 00	159 28.2	148 52.1	N 3 50.2	152 14.9	N 2 36.0	21 57.6	N17 20.9	276 13.8	S19 03.8
01	174 30.7	163 51.7	51.5	167 15.6	36.8	37 00.4	21.0	291 16.2	03.8
02	189 33.1	178 51.4	52.8	182 16.3	37.6	52 03.1	21.1	306 18.7	03.8
03	204 35.6	193 51.1	.. 54.1	197 17.0	.. 38.4	67 05.8	.. 21.1	321 21.1	.. 03.8
04	219 38.0	208 50.8	55.4	212 17.8	39.2	82 08.6	21.2	336 23.5	03.8
05	234 40.5	223 50.5	56.7	227 18.5	39.9	97 11.3	21.3	351 25.9	03.8
06	249 43.0	238 50.2	N 3 58.0	242 19.2	N 2 40.7	112 14.0	N17 21.4	6 28.3	S19 03.8
07	264 45.4	253 49.9	3 59.3	257 19.9	41.5	127 16.7	21.5	21 30.7	03.8
08	279 47.9	268 49.5	4 00.6	272 20.7	42.3	142 19.5	21.6	36 33.1	03.8
M 09	294 50.4	283 49.2	.. 01.9	287 21.4	.. 43.1	157 22.2	.. 21.6	51 35.5	.. 03.8
O 10	309 52.8	298 48.9	03.2	302 22.1	43.8	172 24.9	21.7	66 37.9	03.9
N 11	324 55.3	313 48.6	04.5	317 22.8	44.6	187 27.7	21.8	81 40.3	03.9
D 12	339 57.8	328 48.3	N 4 05.8	332 23.5	N 2 45.4	202 30.4	N17 21.9	96 42.7	S19 03.9
A 13	355 00.2	343 48.0	07.1	347 24.3	46.2	217 33.1	22.0	111 45.2	03.9
Y 14	10 02.7	358 47.7	08.4	2 25.0	47.0	232 35.9	22.0	126 47.6	03.9
15	25 05.1	13 47.3	.. 09.7	17 25.7	.. 47.7	247 38.6	.. 22.1	141 50.0	.. 03.9
16	40 07.6	28 47.0	10.9	32 26.4	48.5	262 41.3	22.2	156 52.4	03.9
17	55 10.1	43 46.7	12.2	47 27.1	49.3	277 44.1	22.3	171 54.8	03.9
18	70 12.5	58 46.4	N 4 13.5	62 27.9	N 2 50.1	292 46.8	N17 22.3	186 57.2	S19 03.9
19	85 15.0	73 46.1	14.8	77 28.6	50.9	307 49.5	22.4	201 59.6	03.9
20	100 17.5	88 45.8	16.1	92 29.3	51.6	322 52.2	22.5	217 02.0	03.9
21	115 19.9	103 45.5	.. 17.4	107 30.0	.. 52.4	337 55.0	.. 22.6	232 04.4	.. 03.9
22	130 22.4	118 45.1	18.7	122 30.7	53.2	352 57.7	22.7	247 06.8	03.9
23	145 24.9	133 44.8	20.0	137 31.5	54.0	8 00.4	22.7	262 09.3	03.9
3 00	160 27.3	148 44.5	N 4 21.3	152 32.2	N 2 54.7	23 03.2	N17 22.8	277 11.7	S19 03.9
01	175 29.8	163 44.2	22.6	167 32.9	55.5	38 05.9	22.9	292 14.1	03.9
02	190 32.3	178 43.9	23.9	182 33.6	56.3	53 08.6	23.0	307 16.5	03.9
03	205 34.7	193 43.6	.. 25.2	197 34.4	.. 57.1	68 11.3	.. 23.0	322 18.9	.. 03.9
04	220 37.2	208 43.2	26.5	212 35.1	57.9	83 14.1	23.1	337 21.3	03.9
05	235 39.6	223 42.9	27.8	227 35.8	58.6	98 16.8	23.2	352 23.7	03.9
06	250 42.1	238 42.6	N 4 29.1	242 36.5	N 2 59.4	113 19.5	N17 23.3	7 26.1	S19 03.9
07	265 44.6	253 42.3	30.3	257 37.2	3 00.2	128 22.2	23.3	22 28.6	03.9
08	280 47.0	268 42.0	31.6	272 38.0	01.0	143 25.0	23.4	37 31.0	03.9
T 09	295 49.5	283 41.7	.. 32.9	287 38.7	.. 01.7	158 27.7	.. 23.5	52 33.4	.. 03.9
U 10	310 52.0	298 41.4	34.2	302 39.4	02.5	173 30.4	23.6	67 35.8	03.9
E 11	325 54.4	313 41.0	35.5	317 40.1	03.3	188 33.1	23.7	82 38.2	03.9
S 12	340 56.9	328 40.7	N 4 36.8	332 40.9	N 3 04.1	203 35.9	N17 23.7	97 40.6	S19 03.9
D 13	355 59.4	343 40.4	38.1	347 41.6	04.9	218 38.6	23.8	112 43.0	03.9
A 14	11 01.8	358 40.1	39.4	2 42.3	05.6	233 41.3	23.9	127 45.5	03.9
Y 15	26 04.3	13 39.8	.. 40.7	17 43.0	.. 06.4	248 44.0	.. 24.0	142 47.9	.. 03.9
16	41 06.7	28 39.5	42.0	32 43.7	07.2	263 46.8	24.0	157 50.3	03.9
17	56 09.2	43 39.1	43.3	47 44.5	08.0	278 49.5	24.1	172 52.7	03.9
18	71 11.7	58 38.8	N 4 44.5	62 45.2	N 3 08.7	293 52.2	N17 24.2	187 55.1	S19 03.9
19	86 14.1	73 38.5	45.8	77 45.9	09.5	308 54.9	24.3	202 57.5	03.9
20	101 16.6	88 38.2	47.1	92 46.6	10.3	323 57.7	24.3	217 59.9	03.9
21	116 19.1	103 37.9	.. 48.4	107 47.3	.. 11.1	339 00.4	.. 24.4	233 02.4	.. 03.9
22	131 21.5	118 37.6	49.7	122 48.1	11.8	354 03.1	24.5	248 04.8	03.9
23	146 24.0	133 37.2	51.0	137 48.8	12.6	9 05.8	24.6	263 07.2	03.9
4 00	161 26.5	148 36.9	N 4 52.3	152 49.5	N 3 13.4	24 08.6	N17 24.6	278 09.6	S19 03.9
01	176 28.9	163 36.6	53.6	167 50.2	14.2	39 11.3	24.7	293 12.0	03.9
02	191 31.4	178 36.3	54.9	182 51.0	14.9	54 14.0	24.8	308 14.4	03.9
03	206 33.9	193 36.0	.. 56.1	197 51.7	.. 15.7	69 16.7	.. 24.9	323 16.9	.. 03.9
04	221 36.3	208 35.7	57.4	212 52.4	16.5	84 19.5	24.9	338 19.3	03.9
05	236 38.8	223 35.3	4 58.7	227 53.1	17.3	99 22.2	25.0	353 21.7	03.9
06	251 41.2	238 35.0	N 5 00.0	242 53.8	N 3 18.0	114 24.9	N17 25.1	8 24.1	S19 03.9
07	266 43.7	253 34.7	01.3	257 54.6	18.8	129 27.6	25.2	23 26.5	03.9
08	281 46.2	268 34.4	02.6	272 55.3	19.6	144 30.3	25.2	38 28.9	03.9
W 09	296 48.6	283 34.1	.. 03.9	287 56.0	.. 20.4	159 33.1	.. 25.3	53 31.4	.. 03.9
E 10	311 51.1	298 33.8	05.2	302 56.7	21.1	174 35.8	25.4	68 33.8	03.9
D 11	326 53.6	313 33.4	06.4	317 57.5	21.9	189 38.5	25.5	83 36.2	03.9
N 12	341 56.0	328 33.1	N 5 07.7	332 58.2	N 3 22.7	204 41.2	N17 25.5	98 38.6	S19 03.9
E 13	356 58.5	343 32.8	09.0	347 58.9	23.5	219 43.9	25.6	113 41.0	03.9
S 14	12 01.0	358 32.5	10.3	2 59.6	24.2	234 46.7	25.7	128 43.5	03.9
D 15	27 03.4	13 32.2	.. 11.6	18 00.3	.. 25.0	249 49.4	.. 25.8	143 45.9	.. 03.9
A 16	42 05.9	28 31.9	12.9	33 01.1	25.8	264 52.1	25.8	158 48.3	03.9
Y 17	57 08.4	43 31.5	14.2	48 01.8	26.6	279 54.8	25.9	173 50.7	03.9
18	72 10.8	58 31.2	N 5 15.5	63 02.5	N 3 27.3	294 57.5	N17 26.0	188 53.1	S19 03.9
19	87 13.3	73 30.9	16.7	78 03.2	28.1	310 00.3	26.1	203 55.5	03.9
20	102 15.7	88 30.6	18.0	93 04.0	28.9	325 03.0	26.1	218 58.0	03.9
21	117 18.2	103 30.3	.. 19.3	108 04.7	.. 29.7	340 05.7	.. 26.2	234 00.4	.. 03.9
22	132 20.7	118 30.0	20.6	123 05.4	30.4	355 08.4	26.3	249 02.8	03.9
23	147 23.2	133 29.6	21.9	138 06.1	31.2	10 11.1	26.4	264 05.2	03.9
Mer. Pass.	h m 13 16.0	v −0.3	d 1.3	v 0.7	d 0.8	v 2.7	d 0.1	v 2.4	d 0.0

STARS

Name	SHA	Dec
Acamar	315 17.7	S40 15.0
Achernar	335 26.4	S57 09.9
Acrux	173 07.2	S63 10.9
Adhara	255 11.4	S29 00.0
Aldebaran	290 48.0	N16 32.2
Alioth	166 19.3	N55 52.4
Alkaid	152 57.7	N49 14.1
Al Na'ir	27 42.8	S46 53.2
Alnilam	275 45.1	S 1 11.9
Alphard	217 54.6	S 8 43.8
Alphecca	126 09.9	N26 39.7
Alpheratz	357 42.6	N29 10.4
Altair	62 07.3	N 8 54.5
Ankaa	353 15.0	S42 13.6
Antares	112 24.8	S26 27.7
Arcturus	145 54.5	N19 06.1
Atria	107 25.5	S69 02.8
Avior	234 17.0	S59 33.9
Bellatrix	278 30.7	N 6 21.5
Betelgeuse	270 59.9	N 7 24.3
Canopus	263 55.4	S52 42.7
Capella	280 32.6	N46 00.7
Deneb	49 31.0	N45 20.0
Denebola	182 32.2	N14 29.0
Diphda	348 55.0	S17 54.4
Dubhe	193 49.7	N61 40.0
Elnath	278 11.0	N28 37.0
Eltanin	90 45.8	N51 29.1
Enif	33 46.3	N 9 56.7
Fomalhaut	15 23.1	S29 32.6
Gacrux	171 58.9	S57 11.8
Gienah	175 50.8	S17 37.7
Hadar	148 45.7	S60 26.5
Hamal	327 59.6	N23 31.9
Kaus Aust.	83 42.4	S34 22.4
Kochab	137 19.7	N74 05.4
Markab	13 37.5	N15 17.2
Menkar	314 13.9	N 4 08.7
Menkent	148 05.9	S36 26.5
Miaplacidus	221 38.4	S69 47.1
Mirfak	308 38.8	N49 54.9
Nunki	75 57.1	S26 16.4
Peacock	53 17.9	S56 40.9
Pollux	243 26.1	N27 59.2
Procyon	244 58.3	N 5 10.9
Rasalhague	96 05.4	N12 32.9
Regulus	207 42.0	N11 53.3
Rigel	281 10.9	S 8 11.4
Rigil Kent.	139 49.7	S60 53.5
Sabik	102 11.2	S15 44.5
Schedar	349 39.5	N56 37.3
Shaula	96 20.4	S37 06.6
Sirius	258 32.5	S16 44.6
Spica	158 29.7	S11 14.5
Suhail	222 51.1	S43 30.0
Vega	80 38.3	N38 47.8
Zuben'ubi	137 03.9	S16 06.2

	SHA	Mer. Pass.
	° ′	h m
Venus	348 17.2	14 05
Mars	352 04.9	13 49
Jupiter	222 35.8	22 24
Saturn	116 44.3	5 30

UT	SUN GHA	SUN Dec	MOON GHA	v	MOON Dec	d	HP
d h	° ′	° ′	° ′		° ′	′	′
2 00	176 55.9	S 7 24.6	38 08.8	12.9	N15 18.3	5.3	54.5
01	191 56.0	23.7	52 40.7	12.9	15 13.0	5.4	54.5
02	206 56.1	22.7	67 12.6	12.9	15 07.6	5.5	54.4
03	221 56.3	.. 21.8	81 44.5	13.0	15 02.1	5.6	54.4
04	236 56.4	20.8	96 16.5	13.0	14 56.5	5.6	54.4
05	251 56.5	19.9	110 48.5	13.0	14 50.9	5.7	54.4
06	266 56.6	S 7 18.9	125 20.5	13.1	N14 45.2	5.7	54.4
07	281 56.8	18.0	139 52.6	13.1	14 39.5	5.8	54.4
08	296 56.9	17.0	154 24.7	13.2	14 33.7	5.9	54.4
09	311 57.0	.. 16.1	168 56.9	13.2	14 27.8	5.9	54.4
10	326 57.1	15.1	183 29.1	13.2	14 21.9	6.0	54.3
11	341 57.3	14.1	198 01.3	13.3	14 15.9	6.1	54.3
12	356 57.4	S 7 13.2	212 33.6	13.3	N14 09.8	6.1	54.3
13	11 57.5	12.2	227 05.9	13.3	14 03.7	6.1	54.3
14	26 57.6	11.3	241 38.2	13.4	13 57.6	6.3	54.3
15	41 57.8	.. 10.3	256 10.6	13.4	13 51.3	6.3	54.3
16	56 57.9	09.4	270 43.0	13.5	13 45.0	6.3	54.3
17	71 58.0	08.4	285 15.5	13.5	13 38.7	6.4	54.3
18	86 58.1	S 7 07.5	299 48.0	13.5	N13 32.3	6.5	54.3
19	101 58.3	06.5	314 20.5	13.6	13 25.8	6.5	54.2
20	116 58.4	05.6	328 53.1	13.6	13 19.3	6.6	54.2
21	131 58.5	.. 04.6	343 25.7	13.6	13 12.7	6.6	54.2
22	146 58.7	03.6	357 58.3	13.7	13 06.1	6.7	54.2
23	161 58.8	02.7	12 31.0	13.7	12 59.4	6.8	54.2
3 00	176 58.9	S 7 01.7	27 03.7	13.7	N12 52.6	6.8	54.2
01	191 59.0	7 00.8	41 36.4	13.8	12 45.8	6.8	54.2
02	206 59.2	6 59.8	56 09.2	13.8	12 39.0	6.9	54.2
03	221 59.3	.. 58.9	70 42.0	13.8	12 32.1	7.0	54.2
04	236 59.4	57.9	85 14.8	13.9	12 25.1	7.0	54.2
05	251 59.6	57.0	99 47.7	13.9	12 18.1	7.1	54.2
06	266 59.7	S 6 56.0	114 20.6	13.9	N12 11.0	7.1	54.1
07	281 59.8	55.0	128 53.5	14.0	12 03.9	7.1	54.1
08	296 59.9	54.1	143 26.5	14.0	11 56.8	7.2	54.1
09	312 00.1	.. 53.1	157 59.5	14.0	11 49.6	7.3	54.1
10	327 00.2	52.2	172 32.5	14.1	11 42.3	7.3	54.1
11	342 00.3	51.2	187 05.6	14.0	11 35.0	7.4	54.1
12	357 00.5	S 6 50.3	201 38.6	14.2	N11 27.6	7.4	54.1
13	12 00.6	49.3	216 11.8	14.1	11 20.2	7.4	54.1
14	27 00.7	48.3	230 44.9	14.2	11 12.8	7.5	54.1
15	42 00.9	.. 47.4	245 18.1	14.2	11 05.3	7.6	54.1
16	57 01.0	46.4	259 51.3	14.3	10 57.7	7.6	54.1
17	72 01.1	45.5	274 24.6	14.2	10 50.1	7.6	54.1
18	87 01.3	S 6 44.5	288 57.8	14.3	N10 42.5	7.7	54.1
19	102 01.4	43.5	303 31.1	14.4	10 34.8	7.7	54.1
20	117 01.5	42.6	318 04.5	14.3	10 27.1	7.7	54.1
21	132 01.7	.. 41.6	332 37.8	14.4	10 19.4	7.8	54.1
22	147 01.8	40.7	347 11.2	14.4	10 11.6	7.9	54.0
23	162 01.9	39.7	1 44.6	14.5	10 03.7	7.9	54.0
4 00	177 02.1	S 6 38.7	16 18.1	14.5	N 9 55.8	7.9	54.0
01	192 02.2	37.8	30 51.6	14.4	9 47.9	8.0	54.0
02	207 02.3	36.8	45 25.0	14.6	9 39.9	8.0	54.0
03	222 02.5	.. 35.9	59 58.6	14.5	9 31.9	8.0	54.0
04	237 02.6	34.9	74 32.1	14.6	9 23.9	8.1	54.0
05	252 02.7	33.9	89 05.7	14.6	9 15.8	8.1	54.0
06	267 02.9	S 6 33.0	103 39.3	14.6	N 9 07.7	8.2	54.0
07	282 03.0	32.0	118 12.9	14.7	8 59.5	8.2	54.0
08	297 03.1	31.1	132 46.6	14.6	8 51.3	8.2	54.0
09	312 03.3	.. 30.1	147 20.2	14.7	8 43.1	8.3	54.0
10	327 03.4	29.1	161 53.9	14.7	8 34.8	8.3	54.0
11	342 03.6	28.2	176 27.6	14.8	8 26.5	8.3	54.0
12	357 03.7	S 6 27.2	191 01.4	14.8	N 8 18.2	8.4	54.0
13	12 03.8	26.3	205 35.2	14.7	8 09.8	8.4	54.0
14	27 04.0	25.3	220 08.9	14.8	8 01.4	8.4	54.0
15	42 04.1	.. 24.3	234 42.7	14.9	7 53.0	8.5	54.0
16	57 04.2	23.4	249 16.6	14.8	7 44.5	8.4	54.0
17	72 04.4	22.4	263 50.4	14.9	7 36.1	8.6	54.0
18	87 04.5	S 6 21.4	278 24.3	14.9	N 7 27.5	8.5	54.0
19	102 04.6	20.5	292 58.2	14.9	7 19.0	8.6	54.0
20	117 04.8	19.5	307 32.1	14.9	7 10.4	8.6	54.0
21	132 04.9	.. 18.6	322 06.0	15.0	7 01.8	8.7	54.0
22	147 05.1	17.6	336 40.0	14.9	6 53.1	8.6	54.0
23	162 05.2	16.6	351 13.9	15.0	N 6 44.5	8.7	54.0
	SD 16.2	d 1.0	SD 14.8		14.7		14.7

Left row labels: M O N D A Y (March 2), T U E S D A Y (March 3), W E D N E S D A Y (March 4)

Moonrise

Lat.	Twilight Naut.	Twilight Civil	Sunrise	2	3	4	5
°	h m	h m	h m	h m	h m	h m	h m
N 72	05 02	06 20	07 28	12 30	14 09	15 44	17 18
N 70	05 08	06 18	07 20	12 59	14 28	15 56	17 23
68	05 12	06 17	07 13	13 21	14 43	16 06	17 28
66	05 16	06 15	07 07	13 38	14 55	16 13	17 32
64	05 19	06 14	07 02	13 51	15 05	16 20	17 35
62	05 22	06 13	06 57	14 03	15 14	16 26	17 38
60	05 24	06 12	06 54	14 13	15 21	16 31	17 40
N 58	05 26	06 11	06 50	14 21	15 28	16 35	17 43
56	05 27	06 10	06 47	14 29	15 33	16 39	17 44
54	05 29	06 09	06 45	14 36	15 38	16 42	17 46
52	05 30	06 08	06 42	14 42	15 43	16 45	17 48
50	05 30	06 08	06 40	14 47	15 47	16 48	17 49
45	05 32	06 06	06 35	14 59	15 56	16 54	17 52
N 40	05 33	06 04	06 31	15 08	16 04	16 59	17 55
35	05 33	06 02	06 27	15 17	16 10	17 04	17 57
30	05 33	06 00	06 24	15 24	16 16	17 08	17 59
20	05 31	05 56	06 19	15 36	16 26	17 14	18 03
N 10	05 28	05 52	06 14	15 47	16 34	17 20	18 05
0	05 24	05 48	06 09	15 57	16 42	17 26	18 08
S 10	05 18	05 43	06 04	16 08	16 50	17 31	18 11
20	05 10	05 36	05 58	16 18	16 59	17 37	18 14
30	04 59	05 28	05 52	16 31	17 08	17 44	18 18
35	04 52	05 23	05 48	16 38	17 14	17 48	18 20
40	04 44	05 17	05 44	16 46	17 20	17 52	18 22
45	04 33	05 09	05 39	16 56	17 28	17 57	18 25
S 50	04 20	05 00	05 33	17 07	17 36	18 03	18 28
52	04 13	04 56	05 31	17 12	17 40	18 06	18 29
54	04 06	04 51	05 28	17 18	17 45	18 09	18 31
56	03 57	04 45	05 24	17 25	17 50	18 12	18 32
58	03 47	04 39	05 21	17 32	17 55	18 16	18 34
S 60	03 36	04 32	05 16	17 40	18 01	18 20	18 36

Moonset

Lat.	Sunset	Twilight Civil	Twilight Naut.	2	3	4	5
°	h m	h m	h m	h m	h m	h m	h m
N 72	16 58	18 07	19 25	07 13	07 07	07 02	06 58
N 70	17 06	18 08	19 19	06 43	06 47	06 49	06 50
68	17 13	18 09	19 14	06 20	06 31	06 38	06 44
66	17 19	18 10	19 10	06 03	06 18	06 29	06 39
64	17 24	18 11	19 06	05 48	06 07	06 22	06 34
62	17 28	18 12	19 04	05 36	05 58	06 15	06 30
60	17 31	18 13	19 01	05 26	05 50	06 09	06 27
N 58	17 35	18 14	19 00	05 17	05 42	06 04	06 24
56	17 38	18 15	18 58	05 09	05 36	06 00	06 21
54	17 40	18 16	18 57	05 02	05 31	05 56	06 19
52	17 43	18 16	18 56	04 55	05 26	05 52	06 16
50	17 45	18 17	18 55	04 50	05 21	05 49	06 14
45	17 50	18 19	18 53	04 37	05 11	05 41	06 10
N 40	17 54	18 21	18 52	04 27	05 03	05 35	06 06
35	17 57	18 22	18 52	04 18	04 55	05 30	06 03
30	18 00	18 24	18 52	04 10	04 49	05 25	06 00
20	18 06	18 28	18 53	03 57	04 38	05 17	05 55
N 10	18 11	18 32	18 56	03 45	04 28	05 10	05 51
0	18 15	18 36	19 00	03 34	04 19	05 03	05 46
S 10	18 20	18 41	19 06	03 23	04 10	04 57	05 42
20	18 25	18 48	19 14	03 11	04 00	04 49	05 38
30	18 31	18 56	19 24	02 57	03 49	04 41	05 33
35	18 35	19 01	19 31	02 49	03 42	04 36	05 30
40	18 39	19 07	19 41	02 40	03 35	04 31	05 26
45	18 44	19 14	19 50	02 29	03 26	04 24	05 22
S 50	18 50	19 23	20 03	02 16	03 16	04 16	05 17
52	18 52	19 27	20 09	02 10	03 11	04 13	05 15
54	18 55	19 32	20 17	02 03	03 06	04 09	05 13
56	18 58	19 37	20 25	01 56	03 00	04 05	05 10
58	19 02	19 43	20 35	01 47	02 53	04 00	05 07
S 60	19 06	19 50	20 46	01 38	02 45	03 54	05 04

	SUN Eqn. of Time 00h	SUN Eqn. of Time 12h	SUN Mer. Pass.	MOON Mer. Pass. Upper	MOON Mer. Pass. Lower	Age	Phase
Day	m s	m s	h m	h m	h m	d	%
2	12 17	12 11	12 12	22 08	09 46	12	91
3	12 05	11 58	12 12	22 53	10 31	13	95
4	11 52	11 46	12 12	23 36	11 15	14	99

UT	ARIES GHA	VENUS −3.9 GHA	VENUS Dec	MARS +1.3 GHA	MARS Dec	JUPITER −2.5 GHA	JUPITER Dec	SATURN +0.4 GHA	SATURN Dec	STARS Name	SHA	Dec
THURSDAY												
5 00	162 25.6	148 29.3	N 5 23.2	153 06.8	N 3 32.0	25 13.8	N17 26.4	279 07.6	S19 03.9	Acamar	315 17.7	S40 15.0
01	177 28.1	163 29.0	24.4	168 07.6	32.8	40 16.6	26.5	294 10.1	03.9	Achernar	335 26.4	S57 09.9
02	192 30.5	178 28.7	25.7	183 08.3	33.5	55 19.3	26.6	309 12.5	03.9	Acrux	173 07.2	S63 11.0
03	207 33.0	193 28.4 ..	27.0	198 09.0 ..	34.3	70 22.0 ..	26.7	324 14.9 ..	03.9	Adhara	255 11.4	S29 00.0
04	222 35.5	208 28.0	28.3	213 09.7	35.1	85 24.7	26.7	339 17.3	03.9	Aldebaran	290 48.0	N16 32.2
05	237 37.9	223 27.7	29.6	228 10.5	35.9	100 27.4	26.8	354 19.8	03.9			
06	252 40.4	238 27.4	N 5 30.9	243 11.2	N 3 36.6	115 30.1	N17 26.9	9 22.2	S19 03.9	Alioth	166 19.3	N55 52.5
07	267 42.8	253 27.1	32.1	258 11.9	37.4	130 32.9	26.9	24 24.6	03.9	Alkaid	152 57.7	N49 14.1
08	282 45.3	268 26.8	33.4	273 12.6	38.2	145 35.6	27.0	39 27.0	03.9	Al Na'ir	27 42.8	S46 53.2
09	297 47.8	283 26.5 ..	34.7	288 13.3 ..	39.0	160 38.3 ..	27.1	54 29.4 ..	03.9	Alnilam	275 45.1	S 1 11.9
10	312 50.2	298 26.1	36.0	303 14.1	39.7	175 41.0	27.2	69 31.9	03.9	Alphard	217 54.6	S 8 43.8
11	327 52.7	313 25.8	37.3	318 14.8	40.5	190 43.7	27.2	84 34.3	03.9			
12	342 55.2	328 25.5	N 5 38.6	333 15.5	N 3 41.3	205 46.4	N17 27.3	99 36.7	S19 03.9	Alphecca	126 09.9	N26 39.7
13	357 57.6	343 25.2	39.8	348 16.2	42.0	220 49.1	27.4	114 39.1	03.9	Alpheratz	357 42.6	N29 10.4
14	13 00.1	358 24.9	41.1	3 17.0	42.8	235 51.9	27.5	129 41.6	03.9	Altair	62 07.3	N 8 54.5
15	28 02.6	13 24.5 ..	42.4	18 17.7 ..	43.6	250 54.6 ..	27.5	144 44.0 ..	03.9	Ankaa	353 15.0	S42 13.6
16	43 05.0	28 24.2	43.7	33 18.4	44.4	265 57.3	27.6	159 46.4	03.9	Antares	112 24.7	S26 27.7
17	58 07.5	43 23.9	45.0	48 19.1	45.1	281 00.0	27.7	174 48.8	03.9			
18	73 10.0	58 23.6	N 5 46.2	63 19.8	N 3 45.9	296 02.7	N17 27.7	189 51.2	S19 03.9	Arcturus	145 54.5	N19 06.1
19	88 12.4	73 23.3	47.5	78 20.6	46.7	311 05.4	27.8	204 53.7	03.9	Atria	107 25.5	S69 02.8
20	103 14.9	88 22.9	48.8	93 21.3	47.5	326 08.1	27.9	219 56.1	03.9	Avior	234 17.0	S59 33.9
21	118 17.3	103 22.6 ..	50.1	108 22.0 ..	48.2	341 10.9 ..	28.0	234 58.5 ..	03.9	Bellatrix	278 30.7	N 6 21.5
22	133 19.8	118 22.3	51.4	123 22.7	49.0	356 13.6	28.0	250 00.9	03.9	Betelgeuse	270 59.9	N 7 24.3
23	148 22.3	133 22.0	52.6	138 23.5	49.8	11 16.3	28.1	265 03.4	03.9			
FRIDAY												
6 00	163 24.7	148 21.7	N 5 53.9	153 24.2	N 3 50.5	26 19.0	N17 28.2	280 05.8	S19 03.9	Canopus	263 55.4	S52 42.7
01	178 27.2	163 21.3	55.2	168 24.9	51.3	41 21.7	28.2	295 08.2	03.9	Capella	280 32.6	N46 00.7
02	193 29.7	178 21.0	56.5	183 25.6	52.1	56 24.4	28.3	310 10.6	03.9	Deneb	49 31.0	N45 20.0
03	208 32.1	193 20.7 ..	57.8	198 26.4 ..	52.9	71 27.1 ..	28.4	325 13.1 ..	03.9	Denebola	182 32.2	N14 29.0
04	223 34.6	208 20.4	5 59.0	213 27.1	53.6	86 29.8	28.5	340 15.5	03.9	Diphda	348 55.0	S17 54.4
05	238 37.1	223 20.1	6 00.3	228 27.8	54.4	101 32.5	28.5	355 17.9	03.9			
06	253 39.5	238 19.7	N 6 01.6	243 28.5	N 3 55.2	116 35.3	N17 28.6	10 20.3	S19 03.9	Dubhe	193 49.7	N61 40.0
07	268 42.0	253 19.4	02.9	258 29.2	55.9	131 38.0	28.7	25 22.8	03.9	Elnath	278 11.1	N28 37.0
08	283 44.4	268 19.1	04.2	273 30.0	56.7	146 40.7	28.7	40 25.2	03.9	Eltanin	90 45.7	N51 29.1
09	298 46.9	283 18.8 ..	05.4	288 30.7 ..	57.5	161 43.4 ..	28.8	55 27.6 ..	03.9	Enif	33 46.3	N 9 56.7
10	313 49.4	298 18.5	06.7	303 31.4	58.3	176 46.1	28.9	70 30.1	03.9	Fomalhaut	15 23.1	S29 32.5
11	328 51.8	313 18.1	08.0	318 32.1	59.0	191 48.8	29.0	85 32.5	03.9			
12	343 54.3	328 17.8	N 6 09.3	333 32.9	N 3 59.8	206 51.5	N17 29.0	100 34.9	S19 03.9	Gacrux	171 58.9	S57 11.8
13	358 56.8	343 17.5	10.5	348 33.6	4 00.6	221 54.2	29.1	115 37.3	03.9	Gienah	175 50.7	S17 37.7
14	13 59.2	358 17.2	11.8	3 34.3	01.3	236 56.9	29.2	130 39.8	03.9	Hadar	148 45.7	S60 26.5
15	29 01.7	13 16.8 ..	13.1	18 35.0 ..	02.1	251 59.6 ..	29.2	145 42.2 ..	03.9	Hamal	327 59.6	N23 31.9
16	44 04.2	28 16.5	14.4	33 35.7	02.9	267 02.3	29.3	160 44.6	03.9	Kaus Aust.	83 42.4	S34 22.4
17	59 06.6	43 16.2	15.6	48 36.5	03.6	282 05.1	29.4	175 47.0	03.9			
18	74 09.1	58 15.9	N 6 16.9	63 37.2	N 4 04.4	297 07.8	N17 29.5	190 49.5	S19 03.9	Kochab	137 19.6	N74 05.4
19	89 11.6	73 15.6	18.2	78 37.9	05.2	312 10.5	29.5	205 51.9	03.9	Markab	13 37.5	N15 17.2
20	104 14.0	88 15.2	19.5	93 38.6	06.0	327 13.2	29.6	220 54.3	03.9	Menkar	314 14.0	N 4 08.7
21	119 16.5	103 14.9 ..	20.7	108 39.4 ..	06.7	342 15.9 ..	29.7	235 56.8 ..	03.9	Menkent	148 05.9	S36 26.6
22	134 18.9	118 14.6	22.0	123 40.1	07.5	357 18.6	29.7	250 59.2	03.9	Miaplacidus	221 38.5	S69 47.1
23	149 21.4	133 14.3	23.3	138 40.8	08.3	12 21.3	29.8	266 01.6	03.9			
SATURDAY												
7 00	164 23.9	148 13.9	N 6 24.6	153 41.5	N 4 09.0	27 24.0	N17 29.9	281 04.0	S19 03.9	Mirfak	308 38.8	N49 54.9
01	179 26.3	163 13.6	25.8	168 42.3	09.8	42 26.7	29.9	296 06.5	03.9	Nunki	75 57.0	S26 16.4
02	194 28.8	178 13.3	27.1	183 43.0	10.6	57 29.4	30.0	311 08.9	03.9	Peacock	53 17.9	S56 40.9
03	209 31.3	193 13.0 ..	28.4	198 43.7 ..	11.3	72 32.1 ..	30.1	326 11.3 ..	03.9	Pollux	243 26.1	N27 59.2
04	224 33.7	208 12.7	29.7	213 44.4	12.1	87 34.8	30.2	341 13.8	03.9	Procyon	244 58.3	N 5 10.9
05	239 36.2	223 12.3	30.9	228 45.1	12.9	102 37.5	30.2	356 16.2	03.9			
06	254 38.7	238 12.0	N 6 32.2	243 45.9	N 4 13.6	117 40.2	N17 30.3	11 18.6	S19 03.9	Rasalhague	96 05.4	N12 32.9
07	269 41.1	253 11.7	33.5	258 46.6	14.4	132 42.9	30.4	26 21.1	03.9	Regulus	207 42.0	N11 53.3
08	284 43.6	268 11.4	34.7	273 47.3	15.2	147 45.6	30.4	41 23.5	03.9	Rigel	281 10.9	S 8 11.4
09	299 46.0	283 11.0 ..	36.0	288 48.0 ..	16.0	162 48.3 ..	30.5	56 25.9 ..	03.9	Rigil Kent.	139 49.6	S60 53.6
10	314 48.5	298 10.7	37.3	303 48.8	16.7	177 51.0	30.6	71 28.3	03.9	Sabik	102 11.2	S15 44.5
11	329 51.0	313 10.4	38.6	318 49.5	17.5	192 53.8	30.6	86 30.8	03.9			
12	344 53.4	328 10.1	N 6 39.8	333 50.2	N 4 18.3	207 56.5	N17 30.7	101 33.2	S19 03.9	Schedar	349 39.6	N56 37.3
13	359 55.9	343 09.7	41.1	348 50.9	19.0	222 59.2	30.8	116 35.6	03.9	Shaula	96 20.4	S37 06.6
14	14 58.4	358 09.4	42.4	3 51.6	19.8	238 01.9	30.8	131 38.1	03.9	Sirius	258 32.5	S16 44.6
15	30 00.8	13 09.1 ..	43.6	18 52.4 ..	20.6	253 04.6 ..	30.9	146 40.5 ..	03.9	Spica	158 29.7	S11 14.5
16	45 03.3	28 08.8	44.9	33 53.1	21.3	268 07.3	31.0	161 42.9	03.9	Suhail	222 51.1	S43 30.0
17	60 05.8	43 08.4	46.2	48 53.8	22.1	283 10.0	31.0	176 45.4	03.9			
18	75 08.2	58 08.1	N 6 47.5	63 54.5	N 4 22.9	298 12.7	N17 31.1	191 47.8	S19 03.9	Vega	80 38.3	N38 47.8
19	90 10.7	73 07.8	48.7	78 55.3	23.6	313 15.4	31.2	206 50.2	03.9	Zuben'ubi	137 03.9	S16 06.2
20	105 13.2	88 07.5	50.0	93 56.0	24.4	328 18.1	31.3	221 52.7	03.9		SHA	Mer. Pass.
21	120 15.6	103 07.1 ..	51.3	108 56.7 ..	25.2	343 20.8 ..	31.3	236 55.1 ..	03.9	Venus	344 56.9	14 07
22	135 18.1	118 06.8	52.5	123 57.4	25.9	358 23.5	31.4	251 57.5	03.9	Mars	349 59.4	13 46
23	150 21.3	133 06.5	53.8	138 58.2	26.7	13 26.2	31.5	267 00.0	03.9	Jupiter	222 54.3	22 11
Mer. Pass. 13 04.2		v −0.3 d 1.3		v 0.7 d 0.8		v 2.7 d 0.1		v 2.4 d 0.0		Saturn	116 41.1	5 19

SUN and MOON

UT	SUN GHA	SUN Dec	MOON GHA	v	MOON Dec	d	HP
d h	° ′	° ′	° ′	′	° ′	′	′
5 00	177 05.3	S 6 15.7	5 47.9	15.0	N 6 35.8	8.8	54.0
01	192 05.5	14.7	20 21.9	15.0	6 27.0	8.7	54.0
02	207 05.6	13.7	34 55.9	15.0	6 18.3	8.8	54.0
03	222 05.8 ..	12.8	49 29.9	15.1	6 09.5	8.8	54.0
04	237 05.9	11.8	64 04.0	15.0	6 00.7	8.8	54.0
05	252 06.0	10.8	78 38.0	15.1	5 51.9	8.8	54.0
06	267 06.2	S 6 09.9	93 12.1	15.1	N 5 43.1	8.9	54.0
07	282 06.3	08.9	107 46.2	15.1	5 34.2	8.9	54.0
T 08	297 06.5	07.9	122 20.3	15.1	5 25.3	8.9	54.0
H 09	312 06.6 ..	07.0	136 54.4	15.2	5 16.4	9.0	54.0
U 10	327 06.7	06.0	151 28.6	15.1	5 07.4	8.9	54.0
R 11	342 06.9	05.1	166 02.7	15.2	4 58.5	9.0	54.0
S 12	357 07.0	S 6 04.1	180 36.9	15.1	N 4 49.5	9.0	54.0
D 13	12 07.2	03.1	195 11.0	15.2	4 40.5	9.0	54.0
A 14	27 07.3	02.2	209 45.2	15.2	4 31.5	9.0	54.0
Y 15	42 07.4 ..	01.2	224 19.4	15.2	4 22.5	9.1	54.0
16	57 07.6	6 00.2	238 53.6	15.2	4 13.4	9.1	54.0
17	72 07.7	5 59.3	253 27.8	15.2	4 04.3	9.1	54.0
18	87 07.9	S 5 58.3	268 02.0	15.2	N 3 55.2	9.1	54.0
19	102 08.0	57.3	282 36.2	15.3	3 46.1	9.1	54.0
20	117 08.1	56.4	297 10.5	15.2	3 37.0	9.1	54.0
21	132 08.3 ..	55.4	311 44.7	15.2	3 27.9	9.2	54.0
22	147 08.4	54.4	326 18.9	15.3	3 18.7	9.1	54.0
23	162 08.6	53.5	340 53.2	15.3	3 09.6	9.2	54.0
6 00	177 08.7	S 5 52.5	355 27.5	15.2	N 3 00.4	9.2	54.0
01	192 08.9	51.5	10 01.7	15.3	2 51.2	9.2	54.0
02	207 09.0	50.6	24 36.0	15.3	2 42.0	9.2	54.0
03	222 09.1 ..	49.6	39 10.3	15.2	2 32.8	9.2	54.0
04	237 09.3	48.6	53 44.5	15.3	2 23.6	9.2	54.0
05	252 09.4	47.7	68 18.8	15.3	2 14.4	9.3	54.0
06	267 09.6	S 5 46.7	82 53.1	15.3	N 2 05.1	9.2	54.0
07	282 09.7	45.7	97 27.4	15.3	1 55.9	9.3	54.0
08	297 09.9	44.7	112 01.7	15.3	1 46.6	9.3	54.0
F 09	312 10.0 ..	43.8	126 36.0	15.3	1 37.3	9.2	54.0
R 10	327 10.2	42.8	141 10.3	15.3	1 28.1	9.3	54.0
I 11	342 10.3	41.8	155 44.6	15.3	1 18.8	9.3	54.0
D 12	357 10.4	S 5 40.9	170 18.9	15.2	N 1 09.5	9.3	54.0
A 13	12 10.6	39.9	184 53.1	15.3	1 00.2	9.3	54.0
Y 14	27 10.7	38.9	199 27.4	15.3	0 50.9	9.3	54.0
15	42 10.9 ..	38.0	214 01.7	15.3	0 41.6	9.3	54.0
16	57 11.0	37.0	228 36.0	15.3	0 32.3	9.3	54.0
17	72 11.2	36.0	243 10.3	15.3	0 23.0	9.3	54.0
18	87 11.3	S 5 35.1	257 44.6	15.2	N 0 13.7	9.4	54.0
19	102 11.5	34.1	272 18.8	15.3	N 0 04.3	9.3	54.0
20	117 11.6	33.1	286 53.1	15.3	S 0 05.0	9.3	54.1
21	132 11.8 ..	32.2	301 27.4	15.3	0 14.3	9.3	54.1
22	147 11.9	31.2	316 01.7	15.2	0 23.6	9.3	54.1
23	162 12.1	30.2	330 35.9	15.3	0 32.9	9.3	54.1
7 00	177 12.2	S 5 29.2	345 10.2	15.2	S 0 42.2	9.4	54.1
01	192 12.4	28.3	359 44.4	15.2	0 51.6	9.3	54.1
02	207 12.5	27.3	14 18.6	15.3	1 00.9	9.3	54.1
03	222 12.6 ..	26.3	28 52.9	15.2	1 10.2	9.3	54.1
04	237 12.8	25.4	43 27.1	15.2	1 19.5	9.3	54.1
05	252 12.9	24.4	58 01.3	15.2	1 28.8	9.3	54.1
06	267 13.1	S 5 23.4	72 35.5	15.2	S 1 38.1	9.3	54.1
07	282 13.2	22.4	87 09.7	15.1	1 47.4	9.3	54.1
S 08	297 13.4	21.5	101 43.8	15.2	1 56.7	9.3	54.1
A 09	312 13.5 ..	20.5	116 18.0	15.2	2 06.0	9.2	54.1
T 10	327 13.7	19.5	130 52.2	15.1	2 15.2	9.3	54.1
U 11	342 13.8	18.6	145 26.3	15.1	2 24.5	9.3	54.2
R 12	357 14.0	S 5 17.6	160 00.4	15.2	S 2 33.8	9.2	54.2
D 13	12 14.1	16.6	174 34.6	15.1	2 43.0	9.3	54.2
A 14	27 14.3	15.6	189 08.7	15.0	2 52.3	9.2	54.2
Y 15	42 14.4 ..	14.7	203 42.7	15.1	3 01.5	9.2	54.2
16	57 14.6	13.7	218 16.8	15.1	3 10.7	9.3	54.2
17	72 14.7	12.7	232 50.9	15.0	3 20.0	9.2	54.2
18	87 14.9	S 5 11.8	247 24.9	15.0	S 3 29.2	9.2	54.2
19	102 15.0	10.8	261 58.9	15.0	3 38.4	9.1	54.2
20	117 15.2	09.8	276 32.9	15.0	3 47.5	9.2	54.2
21	132 15.3 ..	08.8	291 06.9	15.0	3 56.7	9.1	54.2
22	147 15.5	07.9	305 40.9	15.0	4 05.8	9.1	54.2
23	162 15.6	06.9	320 14.9	14.9	S 4 15.0	9.1	54.3
	SD 16.1	d 1.0	SD 14.7		14.7		14.8

Twilight / Sunrise / Moonrise

Lat.	Twilight Naut.	Twilight Civil	Sunrise	Moonrise 5	Moonrise 6	Moonrise 7	Moonrise 8
°	h m	h m	h m	h m	h m	h m	h m
N 72	04 46	06 05	07 12	17 18	18 50	20 24	21 58
N 70	04 54	06 05	07 06	17 23	18 50	20 18	21 47
68	05 00	06 04	07 00	17 28	18 50	20 13	21 37
66	05 05	06 04	06 55	17 32	18 50	20 09	21 29
64	05 09	06 04	06 51	17 35	18 50	20 06	21 22
62	05 12	06 04	06 48	17 38	18 50	20 03	21 17
60	05 15	06 03	06 45	17 40	18 51	20 01	21 12
N 58	05 18	06 03	06 42	17 43	18 51	19 59	21 07
56	05 20	06 03	06 40	17 44	18 51	19 57	21 04
54	05 21	06 02	06 38	17 46	18 51	19 55	21 00
52	05 23	06 02	06 36	17 48	18 51	19 54	20 57
50	05 24	06 02	06 34	17 49	18 51	19 52	20 54
45	05 27	06 01	06 30	17 52	18 51	19 49	20 48
N 40	05 28	05 59	06 26	17 55	18 51	19 47	20 43
35	05 29	05 58	06 23	17 57	18 51	19 44	20 39
30	05 29	05 57	06 21	17 59	18 51	19 42	20 35
20	05 29	05 54	06 16	18 03	18 51	19 39	20 28
N 10	05 27	05 51	06 12	18 06	18 51	19 36	20 22
0	05 23	05 47	06 08	18 08	18 51	19 33	20 17
S 10	05 18	05 43	06 04	18 11	18 51	19 31	20 11
20	05 11	05 37	05 59	18 14	18 51	19 28	20 06
30	05 02	05 30	05 54	18 18	18 51	19 25	19 59
35	04 55	05 25	05 51	18 20	18 51	19 23	19 55
40	04 47	05 20	05 47	18 22	18 51	19 21	19 51
45	04 38	05 13	05 43	18 25	18 51	19 18	19 46
S 50	04 25	05 05	05 38	18 28	18 52	19 16	19 41
52	04 19	05 01	05 36	18 29	18 52	19 14	19 38
54	04 13	04 57	05 34	18 31	18 52	19 13	19 35
56	04 05	04 52	05 31	18 32	18 52	19 11	19 32
58	03 56	04 47	05 28	18 34	18 52	19 10	19 28
S 60	03 46	04 41	05 24	18 36	18 52	19 08	19 24

Sunset / Twilight / Moonset

Lat.	Sunset	Twilight Civil	Twilight Naut.	Moonset 5	Moonset 6	Moonset 7	Moonset 8
°	h m	h m	h m	h m	h m	h m	h m
N 72	17 12	18 20	19 40	06 58	06 53	06 48	06 43
N 70	17 19	18 20	19 32	06 50	06 50	06 51	06 51
68	17 24	18 20	19 25	06 44	06 48	06 53	06 57
66	17 29	18 20	19 20	06 39	06 47	06 54	07 02
64	17 33	18 20	19 16	06 34	06 45	06 56	07 07
62	17 36	18 20	19 12	06 30	06 44	06 57	07 11
60	17 39	18 21	19 09	06 27	06 43	06 58	07 14
N 58	17 42	18 21	19 06	06 24	06 42	06 59	07 17
56	17 44	18 21	19 04	06 21	06 41	07 00	07 20
54	17 46	18 21	19 02	06 19	06 40	07 01	07 22
52	17 48	18 22	19 01	06 16	06 39	07 02	07 25
50	17 50	18 22	18 59	06 14	06 38	07 02	07 27
45	17 54	18 23	18 57	06 10	06 37	07 04	07 31
N 40	17 57	18 24	18 55	06 06	06 36	07 05	07 35
35	18 00	18 25	18 54	06 03	06 35	07 06	07 38
30	18 02	18 26	18 54	06 00	06 34	07 07	07 41
20	18 07	18 29	18 54	05 55	06 32	07 09	07 46
N 10	18 11	18 32	18 56	05 51	06 30	07 10	07 50
0	18 15	18 35	18 59	05 46	06 29	07 11	07 54
S 10	18 19	18 40	19 04	05 42	06 27	07 13	07 58
20	18 23	18 45	19 11	05 38	06 26	07 14	08 03
30	18 28	18 52	19 20	05 33	06 24	07 16	08 08
35	18 31	18 57	19 27	05 30	06 23	07 17	08 11
40	18 34	19 02	19 34	05 26	06 22	07 18	08 14
45	18 38	19 08	19 44	05 22	06 20	07 19	08 17
S 50	18 43	19 16	19 56	05 17	06 19	07 20	08 22
52	18 45	19 20	20 02	05 15	06 18	07 21	08 24
54	18 48	19 24	20 08	05 13	06 17	07 22	08 26
56	18 51	19 29	20 16	05 10	06 16	07 22	08 29
58	18 54	19 34	20 25	05 07	06 15	07 23	08 32
S 60	18 57	19 40	20 35	05 04	06 14	07 24	08 35

SUN and MOON

Day	SUN Eqn. of Time 00h	SUN Eqn. of Time 12h	SUN Mer. Pass.	MOON Mer. Pass. Upper	MOON Mer. Pass. Lower	Age	Phase
d	m s	m s	h m	h m	h m	d	%
5	11 39	11 32	12 12	24 19	11 57	15	100
6	11 25	11 18	12 11	00 19	12 40	16	99
7	11 11	11 04	12 11	01 01	13 22	17	97

UT	ARIES	VENUS −3.9		MARS +1.3		JUPITER −2.5		SATURN +0.4		STARS		
	GHA	GHA	Dec	GHA	Dec	GHA	Dec	GHA	Dec	Name	SHA	Dec
d h	° ′	° ′	° ′	° ′	° ′	° ′	° ′	° ′	° ′		° ′	° ′
8 00	165 23.0	148 06.2 N 6 55.1		153 58.9 N 4 27.5		28 28.9 N17 31.5		282 02.4 S19 03.9		Acamar	315 17.7	S40 15.0
01	180 25.5	163 05.8	56.3	168 59.6	28.2	43 31.6	31.6	297 04.8	03.9	Achernar	335 26.5	S57 09.9
02	195 27.9	178 05.5	57.6	184 00.3	29.0	58 34.3	31.7	312 07.3	03.9	Acrux	173 07.1	S63 11.0
03	210 30.4	193 05.2	6 58.9	199 01.0 . .	29.8	73 37.0 . .	31.7	327 09.7 . .	03.9	Adhara	255 11.4	S29 00.0
04	225 32.9	208 04.9	7 00.1	214 01.8	30.5	88 39.7	31.8	342 12.1	03.9	Aldebaran	290 48.1	N16 32.2
05	240 35.3	223 04.5	01.4	229 02.5	31.3	103 42.4	31.9	357 14.6	03.9			
06	255 37.8	238 04.2 N 7 02.7		244 03.2 N 4 32.1		118 45.1 N17 31.9		12 17.0 S19 03.9		Alioth	166 19.3	N55 52.5
07	270 40.3	253 03.9	03.9	259 03.9	32.8	133 47.8	32.0	27 19.4	03.9	Alkaid	152 57.7	N49 14.1
08	285 42.7	268 03.6	05.2	274 04.7	33.6	148 50.5	32.1	42 21.9	03.9	Al Na'ir	27 42.8	S46 53.2
S 09	300 45.2	283 03.2 . .	06.5	289 05.4 . .	34.4	163 53.2 . .	32.1	57 24.3 . .	03.9	Alnilam	275 45.1	S 1 11.9
U 10	315 47.6	298 02.9	07.7	304 06.1	35.1	178 55.9	32.2	72 26.7	03.9	Alphard	217 54.6	S 8 43.8
N 11	330 50.1	313 02.6	09.0	319 06.8	35.9	193 58.6	32.3	87 29.2	03.9			
D 12	345 52.6	328 02.2 N 7 10.3		334 07.6 N 4 36.7		209 01.3 N17 32.3		102 31.6 S19 03.9		Alphecca	126 09.9	N26 39.7
A 13	0 55.0	343 01.9	11.5	349 08.3	37.4	224 03.9	32.4	117 34.1	03.9	Alpheratz	357 42.6	N29 10.4
Y 14	15 57.5	358 01.6	12.8	4 09.0	38.2	239 06.6	32.5	132 36.5	03.9	Altair	62 07.3	N 8 54.5
15	31 00.0	13 01.3 . .	14.1	19 09.7 . .	39.0	254 09.3 . .	32.5	147 38.9 . .	03.9	Ankaa	353 15.0	S42 13.6
16	46 02.4	28 00.9	15.3	34 10.4	39.7	269 12.0	32.6	162 41.4	03.9	Antares	112 24.7	S26 27.7
17	61 04.9	43 00.6	16.6	49 11.2	40.5	284 14.7	32.7	177 43.8	03.9			
18	76 07.4	58 00.3 N 7 17.8		64 11.9 N 4 41.3		299 17.4 N17 32.7		192 46.2 S19 03.9		Arcturus	145 54.4	N19 06.1
19	91 09.8	73 00.0	19.1	79 12.6	42.0	314 20.1	32.8	207 48.7	03.9	Atria	107 25.4	S69 02.8
20	106 12.3	87 59.6	20.4	94 13.3	42.8	329 22.8	32.9	222 51.1	03.9	Avior	234 17.0	S59 33.9
21	121 14.8	102 59.3 . .	21.6	109 14.1 . .	43.5	344 25.5 . .	32.9	237 53.5 . .	03.9	Bellatrix	278 30.7	N 6 21.5
22	136 17.2	117 59.0	22.9	124 14.8	44.3	359 28.2	33.0	252 56.0	03.9	Betelgeuse	271 00.0	N 7 24.3
23	151 19.7	132 58.6	24.2	139 15.5	45.1	14 30.9	33.1	267 58.4	03.9			
9 00	166 22.1	147 58.3 N 7 25.4		154 16.2 N 4 45.8		29 33.6 N17 33.1		283 00.9 S19 03.9		Canopus	263 55.4	S52 42.7
01	181 24.6	162 58.0	26.7	169 17.0	46.6	44 36.3	33.2	298 03.3	03.8	Capella	280 32.7	N46 00.7
02	196 27.1	177 57.7	27.9	184 17.7	47.4	59 39.0	33.3	313 05.7	03.8	Deneb	49 31.0	N45 20.0
03	211 29.5	192 57.3 . .	29.2	199 18.4 . .	48.1	74 41.7 . .	33.3	328 08.2 . .	03.8	Denebola	182 32.2	N14 29.1
04	226 32.0	207 57.0	30.5	214 19.1	48.9	89 44.4	33.4	343 10.6	03.8	Diphda	348 55.0	S17 54.4
05	241 34.5	222 56.7	31.7	229 19.8	49.7	104 47.1	33.5	358 13.1	03.8			
06	256 36.9	237 56.3 N 7 33.0		244 20.6 N 4 50.4		119 49.8 N17 33.5		13 15.5 S19 03.8		Dubhe	193 49.7	N61 40.0
07	271 39.4	252 56.0	34.2	259 21.3	51.2	134 52.4	33.6	28 17.9	03.8	Elnath	278 11.1	N28 37.0
08	286 41.9	267 55.7	35.5	274 22.0	52.0	149 55.1	33.6	43 20.4	03.8	Eltanin	90 45.7	N51 29.1
M 09	301 44.3	282 55.3 . .	36.8	289 22.7 . .	52.7	164 57.8 . .	33.7	58 22.8 . .	03.8	Enif	33 46.2	N 9 56.7
O 10	316 46.8	297 55.0	38.0	304 23.5	53.5	180 00.5	33.8	73 25.2	03.8	Fomalhaut	15 23.1	S29 32.5
N 11	331 49.3	312 54.7	39.3	319 24.2	54.2	195 03.2	33.8	88 27.7	03.8			
D 12	346 51.7	327 54.4 N 7 40.5		334 24.9 N 4 55.0		210 05.9 N17 33.9		103 30.1 S19 03.8		Gacrux	171 58.9	S57 11.9
A 13	1 54.2	342 54.0	41.8	349 25.6	55.8	225 08.6	34.0	118 32.6	03.8	Gienah	175 50.7	S17 37.7
Y 14	16 56.6	357 53.7	43.0	4 26.4	56.5	240 11.3	34.0	133 35.0	03.8	Hadar	148 45.6	S60 26.6
15	31 59.1	12 53.4 . .	44.3	19 27.1 . .	57.3	255 14.0 . .	34.1	148 37.5 . .	03.8	Hamal	327 59.6	N23 31.9
16	47 01.6	27 53.0	45.6	34 27.8	58.1	270 16.7	34.2	163 39.9	03.8	Kaus Aust.	83 42.4	S34 22.4
17	62 04.0	42 52.7	46.8	49 28.5	58.8	285 19.4	34.2	178 42.3	03.8			
18	77 06.5	57 52.4 N 7 48.1		64 29.2 N 4 59.6		300 22.0 N17 34.3		193 44.8 S19 03.8		Kochab	137 19.6	N74 05.4
19	92 09.0	72 52.0	49.3	79 30.0	5 00.3	315 24.7	34.4	208 47.2	03.8	Markab	13 37.5	N15 17.2
20	107 11.4	87 51.7	50.6	94 30.7	01.1	330 27.4	34.4	223 49.7	03.8	Menkar	314 14.0	N 4 08.7
21	122 13.9	102 51.4 . .	51.8	109 31.4 . .	01.9	345 30.1 . .	34.5	238 52.1 . .	03.8	Menkent	148 05.8	S36 26.6
22	137 16.4	117 51.0	53.1	124 32.1	02.6	0 32.8	34.6	253 54.5	03.8	Miaplacidus	221 38.5	S69 47.1
23	152 18.8	132 50.7	54.3	139 32.9	03.4	15 35.5	34.6	268 57.0	03.8			
10 00	167 21.3	147 50.4 N 7 55.6		154 33.6 N 5 04.2		30 38.2 N17 34.7		283 59.4 S19 03.8		Mirfak	308 38.8	N49 54.9
01	182 23.7	162 50.0	56.9	169 34.3	04.9	45 40.9	34.7	299 01.9	03.8	Nunki	75 57.0	S26 16.4
02	197 26.2	177 49.7	58.1	184 35.0	05.7	60 43.6	34.8	314 04.3	03.8	Peacock	53 17.9	S56 40.9
03	212 28.7	192 49.4	7 59.4	199 35.7 . .	06.4	75 46.2 . .	34.9	329 06.8 . .	03.8	Pollux	243 26.1	N27 59.2
04	227 31.1	207 49.0	8 00.6	214 36.5	07.2	90 48.9	34.9	344 09.2	03.8	Procyon	244 58.3	N 5 10.8
05	242 33.6	222 48.7	01.9	229 37.2	08.0	105 51.6	35.0	359 11.6	03.8			
06	257 36.1	237 48.4 N 8 03.1		244 37.9 N 5 08.7		120 54.3 N17 35.1		14 14.1 S19 03.8		Rasalhague	96 05.4	N12 32.9
07	272 38.5	252 48.0	04.4	259 38.6	09.5	135 57.0	35.1	29 16.5	03.8	Regulus	207 42.0	N11 53.3
08	287 41.0	267 47.7	05.6	274 39.4	10.2	150 59.7	35.2	44 19.0	03.8	Rigel	281 10.9	S 8 11.4
T 09	302 43.5	282 47.4 . .	06.9	289 40.1 . .	11.0	166 02.4 . .	35.2	59 21.4 . .	03.8	Rigil Kent.	139 49.6	S60 53.6
U 10	317 45.9	297 47.0	08.1	304 40.8	11.8	181 05.0	35.3	74 23.9	03.7	Sabik	102 11.2	S15 44.5
E 11	332 48.4	312 46.7	09.4	319 41.5	12.5	196 07.7	35.4	89 26.3	03.7			
S 12	347 50.9	327 46.4 N 8 10.6		334 42.3 N 5 13.3		211 10.4 N17 35.4		104 28.7 S19 03.7		Schedar	349 39.6	N56 37.3
D 13	2 53.3	342 46.0	11.9	349 43.0	14.0	226 13.1	35.5	119 31.2	03.7	Shaula	96 20.3	S37 06.6
A 14	17 55.8	357 45.7	13.1	4 43.7	14.8	241 15.8	35.6	134 33.6	03.7	Sirius	258 32.5	S16 44.6
Y 15	32 58.2	12 45.4 . .	14.4	19 44.4 . .	15.6	256 18.5 . .	35.6	149 36.1 . .	03.7	Spica	158 29.7	S11 14.5
16	48 00.7	27 45.0	15.6	34 45.1	16.3	271 21.1	35.7	164 38.5	03.7	Suhail	222 51.1	S43 30.0
17	63 03.2	42 44.7	16.9	49 45.9	17.1	286 23.8	35.7	179 41.0	03.7			
18	78 05.6	57 44.4 N 8 18.1		64 46.6 N 5 17.8		301 26.5 N17 35.8		194 43.4 S19 03.7		Vega	80 38.3	N38 47.8
19	93 08.1	72 44.0	19.4	79 47.3	18.6	316 29.2	35.9	209 45.9	03.7	Zuben'ubi	137 03.9	S16 06.2
20	108 10.6	87 43.7	20.6	94 48.0	19.4	331 31.9	35.9	224 48.3	03.7		SHA	Mer.Pass.
21	123 13.0	102 43.3 . .	21.9	109 48.8 . .	20.1	346 34.6 . .	36.0	239 50.8 . .	03.7		° ′	h m
22	138 15.5	117 43.0	23.1	124 49.5	20.9	1 37.2	36.1	254 53.2	03.7	Venus	341 36.2	14 08
23	153 18.0	132 42.7	24.4	139 50.2	21.6	16 39.9	36.1	269 55.7	03.7	Mars	347 54.1	13 42
	h m									Jupiter	223 11.5	21 58
Mer. Pass. 12 52.4		v −0.3 d 1.3		v 0.7 d 0.8		v 2.7 d 0.1		v 2.4 d 0.0		Saturn	116 38.7	5 07

UT	SUN GHA	SUN Dec	MOON GHA	v	MOON Dec	d	HP
d h	° '	° '	° '	'	° '	'	'
8 00	177 15.8	S 5 05.9	334 48.8	14.9	S 4 24.1	9.1	54.3
01	192 15.9	04.9	349 22.7	14.9	4 33.2	9.1	54.3
02	207 16.1	04.0	3 56.6	14.9	4 42.3	9.1	54.3
03	222 16.2	.. 03.0	18 30.5	14.8	4 51.4	9.0	54.3
04	237 16.4	02.0	33 04.3	14.8	5 00.4	9.1	54.3
05	252 16.6	01.0	47 38.1	14.8	5 09.5	9.0	54.3
S 06	267 16.7	S 5 00.1	62 11.9	14.8	S 5 18.5	9.0	54.3
U 07	282 16.9	4 59.1	76 45.7	14.8	5 27.5	9.0	54.3
N 08	297 17.0	58.1	91 19.5	14.7	5 36.5	8.9	54.3
D 09	312 17.2	.. 57.2	105 53.2	14.7	5 45.4	9.0	54.4
A 10	327 17.3	56.2	120 26.9	14.7	5 54.4	8.9	54.4
Y 11	342 17.5	55.2	135 00.6	14.6	6 03.3	8.9	54.4
12	357 17.6	S 4 54.2	149 34.2	14.7	S 6 12.2	8.8	54.4
13	12 17.8	53.3	164 07.9	14.6	6 21.0	8.9	54.4
14	27 17.9	52.3	178 41.5	14.6	6 29.9	8.8	54.4
15	42 18.1	.. 51.3	193 15.1	14.5	6 38.7	8.8	54.4
16	57 18.2	50.3	207 48.6	14.5	6 47.5	8.8	54.4
17	72 18.4	49.4	222 22.1	14.5	6 56.3	8.7	54.5
18	87 18.5	S 4 48.4	236 55.6	14.5	S 7 05.0	8.8	54.5
19	102 18.7	47.4	251 29.1	14.4	7 13.8	8.6	54.5
20	117 18.9	46.4	266 02.5	14.4	7 22.4	8.7	54.5
21	132 19.0	.. 45.5	280 35.9	14.4	7 31.1	8.6	54.5
22	147 19.2	44.5	295 09.3	14.3	7 39.7	8.7	54.5
23	162 19.3	43.5	309 42.6	14.3	7 48.4	8.5	54.5
9 00	177 19.5	S 4 42.5	324 15.9	14.3	S 7 56.9	8.6	54.5
01	192 19.6	41.5	338 49.2	14.2	8 05.5	8.5	54.6
02	207 19.8	40.6	353 22.4	14.2	8 14.0	8.5	54.6
03	222 19.9	.. 39.6	7 55.6	14.2	8 22.5	8.4	54.6
04	237 20.1	38.6	22 28.8	14.1	8 30.9	8.4	54.6
05	252 20.3	37.6	37 01.9	14.1	8 39.3	8.4	54.6
M 06	267 20.4	S 4 36.7	51 35.0	14.1	S 8 47.7	8.4	54.6
O 07	282 20.6	35.7	66 08.1	14.0	8 56.1	8.3	54.6
N 08	297 20.7	34.7	80 41.1	14.0	9 04.4	8.3	54.7
D 09	312 20.9	.. 33.7	95 14.1	14.0	9 12.7	8.2	54.7
A 10	327 21.0	32.8	109 47.1	13.9	9 20.9	8.2	54.7
Y 11	342 21.2	31.8	124 20.0	13.9	9 29.1	8.2	54.7
12	357 21.4	S 4 30.8	138 52.9	13.8	S 9 37.3	8.1	54.7
13	12 21.5	29.8	153 25.7	13.8	9 45.4	8.1	54.7
14	27 21.7	28.8	167 58.5	13.8	9 53.5	8.1	54.8
15	42 21.8	.. 27.9	182 31.3	13.7	10 01.6	8.0	54.8
16	57 22.0	26.9	197 04.0	13.7	10 09.6	8.0	54.8
17	72 22.1	25.9	211 36.7	13.6	10 17.6	7.9	54.8
18	87 22.3	S 4 24.9	226 09.3	13.6	S10 25.5	7.9	54.8
19	102 22.5	24.0	240 41.9	13.6	10 33.4	7.8	54.8
20	117 22.6	23.0	255 14.5	13.5	10 41.2	7.8	54.9
21	132 22.8	.. 22.0	269 47.0	13.5	10 49.0	7.8	54.9
22	147 22.9	21.0	284 19.5	13.4	10 56.8	7.7	54.9
23	162 23.1	20.0	298 51.9	13.4	11 04.5	7.7	54.9
10 00	177 23.2	S 4 19.1	313 24.3	13.3	S11 12.2	7.6	54.9
01	192 23.4	18.1	327 56.6	13.3	11 19.8	7.6	54.9
02	207 23.6	17.1	342 28.9	13.3	11 27.4	7.5	55.0
03	222 23.7	.. 16.1	357 01.2	13.2	11 34.9	7.5	55.0
04	237 23.9	15.2	11 33.4	13.2	11 42.4	7.4	55.0
05	252 24.0	14.2	26 05.6	13.1	11 49.8	7.4	55.0
T 06	267 24.2	S 4 13.2	40 37.7	13.0	S11 57.2	7.4	55.0
U 07	282 24.4	12.2	55 09.7	13.1	12 04.6	7.2	55.1
E 08	297 24.5	11.2	69 41.8	12.9	12 11.8	7.3	55.1
S 09	312 24.7	.. 10.3	84 13.7	13.0	12 19.1	7.1	55.1
D 10	327 24.8	09.3	98 45.7	12.9	12 26.2	7.2	55.1
A 11	342 25.0	08.3	113 17.6	12.8	12 33.4	7.1	55.1
Y 12	357 25.2	S 4 07.3	127 49.4	12.8	S12 40.5	7.0	55.2
13	12 25.3	06.3	142 21.2	12.7	12 47.5	6.9	55.2
14	27 25.5	05.4	156 52.9	12.7	12 54.4	6.9	55.2
15	42 25.6	.. 04.4	171 24.6	12.6	13 01.3	6.9	55.2
16	57 25.8	03.4	185 56.2	12.6	13 08.2	6.8	55.2
17	72 26.0	02.4	200 27.8	12.6	13 15.0	6.7	55.3
18	87 26.1	S 4 01.4	214 59.4	12.5	S13 21.7	6.7	55.3
19	102 26.3	4 00.5	229 30.9	12.4	13 28.4	6.7	55.3
20	117 26.5	3 59.5	244 02.3	12.4	13 35.1	6.5	55.3
21	132 26.6	.. 58.5	258 33.7	12.3	13 41.6	6.5	55.4
22	147 26.8	57.5	273 05.0	12.3	13 48.1	6.5	55.4
23	162 26.9	56.5	287 36.3	12.2	S13 54.6	6.3	55.4
	SD 16.1	d 1.0	SD 14.8		14.9		15.0

Twilight / Sunrise / Moonrise

Lat.	Naut.	Civil	Sunrise	Moonrise 8	9	10	11
°	h m	h m	h m	h m	h m	h m	h m
N 72	04 30	05 50	06 57	21 58	23 37	25 20	01 20
N 70	04 40	05 51	06 52	21 47	23 17	24 49	00 49
68	04 47	05 52	06 47	21 37	23 02	24 27	00 27
66	04 53	05 53	06 44	21 29	22 49	24 10	00 10
64	04 58	05 54	06 41	21 22	22 39	23 56	25 10
62	05 03	05 54	06 38	21 17	22 30	23 44	24 55
60	05 06	05 55	06 36	21 12	22 23	23 34	24 43
N 58	05 09	05 55	06 34	21 07	22 16	23 25	24 32
56	05 12	05 55	06 32	21 04	22 11	23 17	24 23
54	05 14	05 55	06 30	21 00	22 05	23 11	24 15
52	05 16	05 55	06 29	20 57	22 01	23 04	24 07
50	05 18	05 55	06 27	20 54	21 57	22 59	24 01
45	05 21	05 55	06 24	20 48	21 47	22 47	23 46
N 40	05 23	05 55	06 22	20 43	21 40	22 37	23 35
35	05 25	05 54	06 19	20 39	21 33	22 29	23 25
30	05 26	05 54	06 17	20 35	21 28	22 22	23 16
20	05 26	05 52	06 14	20 28	21 18	22 09	23 01
N 10	05 25	05 49	06 11	20 22	21 09	21 58	22 48
0	05 22	05 47	06 07	20 17	21 01	21 48	22 36
S 10	05 18	05 43	06 04	20 11	20 53	21 37	22 24
20	05 12	05 38	06 00	20 06	20 45	21 27	22 11
30	05 04	05 32	05 56	19 59	20 35	21 14	21 57
35	04 58	05 28	05 54	19 55	20 30	21 07	21 48
40	04 51	05 23	05 51	19 51	20 24	20 59	21 39
45	04 42	05 18	05 47	19 46	20 16	20 50	21 27
S 50	04 31	05 10	05 43	19 41	20 08	20 38	21 14
52	04 26	05 07	05 41	19 38	20 04	20 33	21 08
54	04 19	05 03	05 39	19 35	20 00	20 27	21 01
56	04 12	04 59	05 37	19 32	19 55	20 21	20 53
58	04 04	04 54	05 35	19 28	19 49	20 14	20 44
S 60	03 55	04 49	05 32	19 24	19 43	20 06	20 34

Sunset / Twilight / Moonset

Lat.	Sunset	Civil	Naut.	Moonset 8	9	10	11
°	h m	h m	h m	h m	h m	h m	h m
N 72	17 26	18 34	19 55	06 43	06 38	06 33	06 27
N 70	17 31	18 32	19 45	06 51	06 52	06 54	06 58
68	17 35	18 31	19 37	06 57	07 03	07 10	07 21
66	17 39	18 30	19 30	07 02	07 12	07 24	07 39
64	17 42	18 29	19 25	07 07	07 19	07 35	07 54
62	17 44	18 28	19 20	07 11	07 26	07 44	08 07
60	17 46	18 28	19 16	07 14	07 32	07 52	08 17
N 58	17 48	18 28	19 13	07 17	07 37	07 59	08 26
56	17 50	18 27	19 11	07 20	07 41	08 06	08 34
54	17 52	18 27	19 08	07 22	07 46	08 11	08 42
52	17 53	18 27	19 06	07 25	07 49	08 17	08 48
50	17 55	18 27	19 04	07 27	07 53	08 21	08 54
45	17 58	18 27	19 01	07 31	08 00	08 31	09 07
N 40	18 00	18 27	18 58	07 35	08 06	08 40	09 17
35	18 02	18 27	18 57	07 38	08 11	08 47	09 26
30	18 04	18 28	18 56	07 41	08 16	08 53	09 34
20	18 08	18 30	18 55	07 46	08 24	09 05	09 48
N 10	18 11	18 32	18 56	07 50	08 31	09 14	10 00
0	18 14	18 35	18 59	07 54	08 38	09 23	10 11
S 10	18 17	18 38	19 03	07 58	08 45	09 33	10 23
20	18 21	18 43	19 08	08 03	08 52	09 42	10 34
30	18 25	18 49	19 17	08 08	09 00	09 53	10 48
35	18 27	18 52	19 22	08 10	09 05	10 00	10 56
40	18 30	18 57	19 29	08 14	09 10	10 07	11 05
45	18 33	19 03	19 38	08 17	09 16	10 16	11 15
S 50	18 37	19 10	19 49	08 22	09 24	10 26	11 28
52	18 39	19 13	19 54	08 24	09 27	10 31	11 34
54	18 41	19 17	20 00	08 26	09 31	10 36	11 41
56	18 43	19 21	20 07	08 29	09 36	10 42	11 48
58	18 45	19 25	20 15	08 32	09 40	10 49	11 57
S 60	18 48	19 31	20 24	08 35	09 46	10 57	12 06

SUN / MOON

Day	SUN Eqn. of Time 00h	12h	Mer. Pass.	MOON Mer. Pass. Upper	Lower	Age	Phase
d	m s	m s	h m	h m	h m	d	%
8	10 57	10 50	12 11	01 44	14 05	18	93
9	10 42	10 35	12 11	02 28	14 50	19	88
10	10 27	10 20	12 10	03 12	15 35	20	81

UT	ARIES	VENUS −3.9		MARS +1.3		JUPITER −2.5		SATURN +0.4		STARS		
	GHA	GHA	Dec	GHA	Dec	GHA	Dec	GHA	Dec	Name	SHA	Dec
d h	° ′	° ′	° ′	° ′	° ′	° ′	° ′	° ′	° ′		° ′	° ′
11 00	168 20.4	147 42.3	N 8 25.6	154 50.9	N 5 22.4	31 42.6	N17 36.2	284 58.1	S19 03.7	Acamar	315 17.7	S40 15.0
01	183 22.9	162 42.0	26.9	169 51.7	23.2	46 45.3	36.2	300 00.5	03.7	Achernar	335 26.5	S57 09.9
02	198 25.3	177 41.7	28.1	184 52.4	23.9	61 48.0	36.3	315 03.0	03.7	Acrux	173 07.1	S63 11.0
03	213 27.8	192 41.3	.. 29.3	199 53.1	.. 24.7	76 50.7	.. 36.4	330 05.4	.. 03.7	Adhara	255 11.4	S29 00.0
04	228 30.3	207 41.0	30.6	214 53.8	25.4	91 53.3	36.4	345 07.9	03.7	Aldebaran	290 48.1	N16 32.2
05	243 32.7	222 40.7	31.8	229 54.5	26.2	106 56.0	36.5	0 10.3	03.7			
06	258 35.2	237 40.3	N 8 33.1	244 55.3	N 5 27.0	121 58.7	N17 36.5	15 12.8	S19 03.7	Alioth	166 19.2	N55 52.5
W 07	273 37.7	252 40.0	34.3	259 56.0	27.7	137 01.4	36.6	30 15.2	03.7	Alkaid	152 57.6	N49 14.1
E 08	288 40.1	267 39.6	35.6	274 56.7	28.5	152 04.1	36.7	45 17.7	03.7	Al Na'ir	27 42.8	S46 53.1
D 09	303 42.6	282 39.3	.. 36.8	289 57.4	.. 29.2	167 06.7	.. 36.7	60 20.1	.. 03.7	Alnilam	275 45.1	S 1 11.9
N 10	318 45.1	297 39.0	38.1	304 58.2	30.0	182 09.4	36.8	75 22.6	03.7	Alphard	217 54.6	S 8 43.8
E 11	333 47.5	312 38.6	39.3	319 58.9	30.7	197 12.1	36.9	90 25.0	03.7			
S 12	348 50.0	327 38.3	N 8 40.5	334 59.6	N 5 31.5	212 14.8	N17 36.9	105 27.5	S19 03.6	Alphecca	126 09.9	N26 39.7
D 13	3 52.5	342 37.9	41.8	350 00.3	32.3	227 17.4	37.0	120 29.9	03.6	Alpheratz	357 42.6	N29 10.4
A 14	18 54.9	357 37.6	43.0	5 01.0	33.0	242 20.1	37.0	135 32.4	03.6	Altair	62 07.3	N 8 54.5
Y 15	33 57.4	12 37.3	.. 44.3	20 01.8	.. 33.8	257 22.8	.. 37.1	150 34.8	.. 03.6	Ankaa	353 15.0	S42 13.6
16	48 59.8	27 36.9	45.5	35 02.5	34.5	272 25.5	37.2	165 37.3	03.6	Antares	112 24.7	S26 27.7
17	64 02.3	42 36.6	46.8	50 03.2	35.3	287 28.2	37.2	180 39.7	03.6			
18	79 04.8	57 36.2	N 8 48.0	65 03.9	N 5 36.0	302 30.8	N17 37.3	195 42.2	S19 03.6	Arcturus	145 54.4	N19 06.1
19	94 07.2	72 35.9	49.2	80 04.7	36.8	317 33.5	37.3	210 44.6	03.6	Atria	107 25.4	S69 02.8
20	109 09.7	87 35.6	50.5	95 05.4	37.6	332 36.2	37.4	225 47.1	03.6	Avior	234 17.0	S59 33.9
21	124 12.2	102 35.2	.. 51.7	110 06.1	.. 38.3	347 38.9	.. 37.5	240 49.5	.. 03.6	Bellatrix	278 30.7	N 6 21.5
22	139 14.6	117 34.9	53.0	125 06.8	39.1	2 41.5	37.5	255 52.0	03.6	Betelgeuse	271 00.0	N 7 24.3
23	154 17.1	132 34.5	54.2	140 07.5	39.8	17 44.2	37.6	270 54.4	03.6			
12 00	169 19.6	147 34.2	N 8 55.4	155 08.3	N 5 40.6	32 46.9	N17 37.6	285 56.9	S19 03.6	Canopus	263 55.5	S52 42.7
01	184 22.0	162 33.9	56.7	170 09.0	41.3	47 49.6	37.7	300 59.3	03.6	Capella	280 32.7	N46 00.7
02	199 24.5	177 33.5	57.9	185 09.7	42.1	62 52.2	37.8	316 01.8	03.6	Deneb	49 31.0	N45 20.0
03	214 27.0	192 33.2	8 59.1	200 10.4	.. 42.9	77 54.9	.. 37.8	331 04.2	.. 03.6	Denebola	182 32.2	N14 29.1
04	229 29.4	207 32.8	9 00.4	215 11.2	43.6	92 57.6	37.9	346 06.7	03.6	Diphda	348 55.0	S17 54.4
05	244 31.9	222 32.5	01.6	230 11.9	44.4	108 00.3	37.9	1 09.1	03.6			
06	259 34.3	237 32.2	N 9 02.9	245 12.6	N 5 45.1	123 02.9	N17 38.0	16 11.6	S19 03.6	Dubhe	193 49.7	N61 40.0
T 07	274 36.8	252 31.8	04.1	260 13.3	45.9	138 05.6	38.0	31 14.0	03.6	Elnath	278 11.1	N28 37.0
H 08	289 39.3	267 31.5	05.3	275 14.1	46.6	153 08.3	38.1	46 16.5	03.6	Eltanin	90 45.7	N51 29.1
U 09	304 41.7	282 31.1	.. 06.6	290 14.8	.. 47.4	168 11.0	.. 38.2	61 18.9	.. 03.5	Enif	33 46.2	N 9 56.7
R 10	319 44.2	297 30.8	07.8	305 15.5	48.1	183 13.6	38.2	76 21.4	03.5	Fomalhaut	15 23.1	S29 32.5
S 11	334 46.7	312 30.4	09.0	320 16.2	48.9	198 16.3	38.3	91 23.9	03.5			
D 12	349 49.1	327 30.1	N 9 10.3	335 16.9	N 5 49.7	213 19.0	N17 38.3	106 26.3	S19 03.5	Gacrux	171 58.9	S57 11.9
A 13	4 51.6	342 29.7	11.5	350 17.7	50.4	228 21.6	38.4	121 28.8	03.5	Gienah	175 50.7	S17 37.7
Y 14	19 54.1	357 29.4	12.7	5 18.4	51.2	243 24.3	38.5	136 31.2	03.5	Hadar	148 45.6	S60 26.6
15	34 56.5	12 29.1	.. 14.0	20 19.1	.. 51.9	258 27.0	.. 38.5	151 33.7	.. 03.5	Hamal	327 59.6	N23 31.9
16	49 59.0	27 28.7	15.2	35 19.8	52.7	273 29.7	38.6	166 36.1	03.5	Kaus Aust.	83 42.3	S34 22.4
17	65 01.4	42 28.4	16.4	50 20.6	53.4	288 32.3	38.6	181 38.6	03.5			
18	80 03.9	57 28.0	N 9 17.7	65 21.3	N 5 54.2	303 35.0	N17 38.7	196 41.0	S19 03.5	Kochab	137 19.5	N74 05.4
19	95 06.4	72 27.7	18.9	80 22.0	54.9	318 37.7	38.7	211 43.5	03.5	Markab	13 37.5	N15 17.2
20	110 08.8	87 27.3	20.1	95 22.7	55.7	333 40.3	38.8	226 45.9	03.5	Menkar	314 14.0	N 4 08.7
21	125 11.3	102 27.0	.. 21.4	110 23.4	.. 56.4	348 43.0	.. 38.9	241 48.4	.. 03.5	Menkent	148 05.8	S36 26.6
22	140 13.8	117 26.6	22.6	125 24.2	57.2	3 45.7	38.9	256 50.8	03.5	Miaplacidus	221 38.5	S69 47.1
23	155 16.2	132 26.3	23.8	140 24.9	57.9	18 48.3	39.0	271 53.3	03.5			
13 00	170 18.7	147 26.0	N 9 25.1	155 25.6	N 5 58.7	33 51.0	N17 39.0	286 55.8	S19 03.5	Mirfak	308 38.8	N49 54.9
01	185 21.2	162 25.6	26.3	170 26.3	5 59.5	48 53.7	39.1	301 58.2	03.5	Nunki	75 57.0	S26 16.4
02	200 23.6	177 25.3	27.5	185 27.1	6 00.2	63 56.3	39.2	317 00.7	03.5	Peacock	53 17.9	S56 40.9
03	215 26.1	192 24.9	.. 28.7	200 27.8	.. 01.0	78 59.0	.. 39.2	332 03.1	.. 03.5	Pollux	243 26.1	N27 59.2
04	230 28.6	207 24.6	30.0	215 28.5	01.7	94 01.7	39.3	347 05.6	03.4	Procyon	244 58.3	N 5 10.8
05	245 31.0	222 24.2	31.2	230 29.2	02.5	109 04.3	39.3	2 08.0	03.4			
06	260 33.5	237 23.9	N 9 32.4	245 29.9	N 6 03.2	124 07.0	N17 39.4	17 10.5	S19 03.4	Rasalhague	96 05.4	N12 32.9
07	275 35.9	252 23.5	33.7	260 30.7	04.0	139 09.7	39.4	32 13.0	03.4	Regulus	207 42.0	N11 53.3
08	290 38.4	267 23.2	34.9	275 31.4	04.7	154 12.3	39.5	47 15.4	03.4	Rigel	281 10.9	S 8 11.4
F 09	305 40.9	282 22.8	.. 36.1	290 32.1	.. 05.5	169 15.0	.. 39.5	62 17.9	.. 03.4	Rigil Kent.	139 49.6	S60 53.6
R 10	320 43.3	297 22.5	37.3	305 32.8	06.2	184 17.7	39.6	77 20.3	03.4	Sabik	102 11.2	S15 44.5
I 11	335 45.8	312 22.1	38.6	320 33.5	07.0	199 20.3	39.7	92 22.8	03.4			
D 12	350 48.3	327 21.8	N 9 39.8	335 34.3	N 6 07.7	214 23.0	N17 39.7	107 25.2	S19 03.4	Schedar	349 39.6	N56 37.2
A 13	5 50.7	342 21.4	41.0	350 35.0	08.5	229 25.7	39.8	122 27.7	03.4	Shaula	96 20.3	S37 06.6
Y 14	20 53.2	357 21.1	42.2	5 35.7	09.2	244 28.3	39.8	137 30.2	03.4	Sirius	258 32.6	S16 44.6
15	35 55.7	12 20.7	.. 43.5	20 36.4	.. 10.0	259 31.0	.. 39.9	152 32.6	.. 03.4	Spica	158 29.7	S11 14.5
16	50 58.1	27 20.4	44.7	35 37.2	10.7	274 33.7	39.9	167 35.1	03.4	Suhail	222 51.2	S43 30.0
17	66 00.6	42 20.0	45.9	50 37.9	11.5	289 36.3	40.0	182 37.5	03.4			
18	81 03.1	57 19.7	N 9 47.1	65 38.6	N 6 12.2	304 39.0	N17 40.1	197 40.0	S19 03.4	Vega	80 38.3	N38 47.8
19	96 05.5	72 19.3	48.4	80 39.3	13.0	319 41.7	40.1	212 42.5	03.4	Zuben'ubi	137 03.9	S16 06.2
20	111 08.0	87 19.0	49.6	95 40.0	13.7	334 44.3	40.2	227 44.9	03.4			
21	126 10.4	102 18.6	.. 50.8	110 40.8	.. 14.5	349 47.0	.. 40.2	242 47.4	.. 03.3		SHA	Mer.Pass.
22	141 12.9	117 18.3	52.0	125 41.5	15.2	4 49.6	40.3	257 49.8	03.3	Venus	338 14.6	14 10
23	156 15.4	132 17.9	53.2	140 42.2	16.0	19 52.3	40.3	272 52.3	03.3	Mars	345 48.7	13 19
	h m									Jupiter	223 27.3	21 45
Mer.Pass. 12 40.6		v −0.3	d 1.2	v 0.7	d 0.8	v 2.7	d 0.1	v 2.5	d 0.0	Saturn	116 37.3	4 55

UT	SUN GHA	SUN Dec	MOON GHA	v	Dec	d	HP
d h	° ′	° ′	° ′	′	° ′	′	′
11 00	177 27.1	S 3 55.6	302 07.5	12.2	S14 00.9	6.4	55.4
01	192 27.3	54.6	316 38.7	12.1	14 07.3	6.2	55.4
02	207 27.4	53.6	331 09.8	12.1	14 13.5	6.2	55.5
03	222 27.6	.. 52.6	345 40.9	12.0	14 19.7	6.1	55.5
04	237 27.8	51.6	0 11.9	12.0	14 25.8	6.1	55.5
05	252 27.9	50.7	14 42.9	11.9	14 31.9	6.0	55.5
06	267 28.1	S 3 49.7	29 13.8	11.9	S14 37.9	5.9	55.6
W 07	282 28.2	48.7	43 44.7	11.8	14 43.8	5.9	55.6
E 08	297 28.4	47.7	58 15.5	11.7	14 49.7	5.8	55.6
D 09	312 28.6	.. 46.7	72 46.2	11.7	14 55.5	5.7	55.6
N 10	327 28.7	45.7	87 16.9	11.6	15 01.2	5.7	55.7
E 11	342 28.9	44.8	101 47.5	11.6	15 06.9	5.6	55.7
S 12	357 29.1	S 3 43.8	116 18.1	11.6	S15 12.5	5.5	55.7
D 13	12 29.2	42.8	130 48.7	11.4	15 18.0	5.5	55.7
A 14	27 29.4	41.8	145 19.1	11.5	15 23.5	5.3	55.8
Y 15	42 29.6	.. 40.8	159 49.6	11.3	15 28.8	5.4	55.8
16	57 29.7	39.9	174 19.9	11.3	15 34.2	5.2	55.8
17	72 29.9	38.9	188 50.2	11.3	15 39.4	5.1	55.8
18	87 30.0	S 3 37.9	203 20.5	11.2	S15 44.5	5.1	55.9
19	102 30.2	36.9	217 50.7	11.1	15 49.6	5.0	55.9
20	117 30.4	35.9	232 20.8	11.1	15 54.6	5.0	55.9
21	132 30.5	.. 34.9	246 50.9	11.0	15 59.6	4.8	56.0
22	147 30.7	34.0	261 20.9	11.0	16 04.4	4.8	56.0
23	162 30.9	33.0	275 50.9	10.9	16 09.2	4.7	56.0
12 00	177 31.0	S 3 32.0	290 20.8	10.9	S16 13.9	4.6	56.0
01	192 31.2	31.0	304 50.7	10.8	16 18.5	4.6	56.1
02	207 31.4	30.0	319 20.5	10.8	16 23.1	4.4	56.1
03	222 31.5	.. 29.1	333 50.3	10.7	16 27.5	4.4	56.1
04	237 31.7	28.1	348 20.0	10.6	16 31.9	4.3	56.1
05	252 31.9	27.1	2 49.6	10.6	16 36.2	4.3	56.2
06	267 32.0	S 3 26.1	17 19.2	10.5	S16 40.5	4.1	56.2
T 07	282 32.2	25.1	31 48.7	10.5	16 44.6	4.1	56.2
H 08	297 32.4	24.1	46 18.2	10.4	16 48.7	3.9	56.3
U 09	312 32.5	.. 23.2	60 47.6	10.3	16 52.6	3.9	56.3
R 10	327 32.7	22.2	75 16.9	10.3	16 56.5	3.8	56.3
S 11	342 32.9	21.2	89 46.2	10.3	17 00.3	3.7	56.4
D 12	357 33.0	S 3 20.2	104 15.5	10.2	S17 04.0	3.7	56.4
A 13	12 33.2	19.2	118 44.7	10.1	17 07.7	3.5	56.4
Y 14	27 33.4	18.2	133 13.8	10.1	17 11.2	3.5	56.4
15	42 33.5	.. 17.3	147 42.9	10.0	17 14.7	3.3	56.5
16	57 33.7	16.3	162 11.9	10.0	17 18.0	3.3	56.5
17	72 33.9	15.3	176 40.9	9.9	17 21.3	3.2	56.5
18	87 34.0	S 3 14.3	191 09.8	9.8	S17 24.5	3.1	56.6
19	102 34.2	13.3	205 38.6	9.8	17 27.6	3.0	56.6
20	117 34.4	12.3	220 07.4	9.8	17 30.6	2.9	56.6
21	132 34.5	.. 11.3	234 36.2	9.7	17 33.5	2.8	56.7
22	147 34.7	10.4	249 04.9	9.6	17 36.3	2.8	56.7
23	162 34.9	09.4	263 33.5	9.6	17 39.1	2.6	56.7
13 00	177 35.0	S 3 08.4	278 02.1	9.5	S17 41.7	2.5	56.8
01	192 35.2	07.4	292 30.6	9.5	17 44.2	2.5	56.8
02	207 35.4	06.4	306 59.1	9.4	17 46.7	2.3	56.8
03	222 35.5	.. 05.4	321 27.5	9.4	17 49.0	2.3	56.9
04	237 35.7	04.5	335 55.9	9.3	17 51.3	2.2	56.9
05	252 35.9	03.5	350 24.2	9.3	17 53.5	2.0	56.9
06	267 36.0	S 3 02.5	4 52.5	9.2	S17 55.5	2.0	57.0
07	282 36.2	01.5	19 20.7	9.2	17 57.5	1.8	57.0
08	297 36.4	3 00.5	33 48.9	9.1	17 59.3	1.8	57.0
F 09	312 36.6	2 59.5	48 17.0	9.0	18 01.1	1.7	57.1
R 10	327 36.7	58.5	62 45.0	9.0	18 02.8	1.6	57.1
I 11	342 36.9	57.6	77 13.0	9.0	18 04.4	1.4	57.1
D 12	357 37.1	S 2 56.6	91 41.0	8.9	S18 05.8	1.4	57.2
A 13	12 37.2	55.6	106 08.9	8.9	18 07.2	1.3	57.2
Y 14	27 37.4	54.6	120 36.8	8.8	18 08.5	1.1	57.2
15	42 37.6	.. 53.6	135 04.6	8.7	18 09.6	1.1	57.3
16	57 37.7	52.6	149 32.3	8.7	18 10.7	1.0	57.3
17	72 37.9	51.7	164 00.0	8.7	18 11.7	0.8	57.3
18	87 38.1	S 2 50.7	178 27.7	8.6	S18 12.5	0.8	57.4
19	102 38.3	49.7	192 55.3	8.6	18 13.3	0.6	57.4
20	117 38.4	48.7	207 22.9	8.5	18 13.9	0.6	57.4
21	132 38.6	.. 47.7	221 50.4	8.5	18 14.5	0.4	57.5
22	147 38.8	46.7	236 17.9	8.4	18 14.9	0.3	57.5
23	162 38.9	45.7	250 45.3	8.4	S18 15.2	0.3	57.5
	SD 16.1	d 1.0	SD 15.2		15.4		15.6

Lat.	Twilight Naut.	Civil	Sunrise	Moonrise 11	12	13	14
°	h m	h m	h m	h m	h m	h m	h m
N 72	04 13	05 34	06 41	01 20	03 11	■	■
N 70	04 25	05 37	06 38	00 49	02 22	03 48	04 54
68	04 34	05 40	06 35	00 27	01 51	03 08	04 10
66	04 41	05 42	06 33	00 10	01 28	02 40	03 40
64	04 48	05 43	06 30	25 10	01 10	02 19	03 18
62	04 53	05 45	06 29	24 55	00 55	02 02	03 01
60	04 57	05 45	06 27	24 43	00 43	01 48	02 46
N 58	05 01	05 47	06 26	24 32	00 32	01 36	02 33
56	05 04	05 47	06 24	24 23	00 23	01 25	02 23
54	05 07	05 48	06 23	24 15	00 15	01 16	02 13
52	05 09	05 48	06 22	24 07	00 07	01 08	02 05
50	05 11	05 49	06 21	24 01	00 01	01 00	01 57
45	05 16	05 50	06 19	23 46	24 45	00 45	01 41
N 40	05 19	05 50	06 17	23 35	24 32	00 32	01 27
35	05 21	05 50	06 15	23 25	24 21	00 21	01 16
30	05 22	05 50	06 14	23 16	24 11	00 11	01 06
20	05 24	05 49	06 11	23 01	23 55	24 49	00 49
N 10	05 24	05 48	06 09	22 48	23 41	24 34	00 34
0	05 22	05 46	06 07	22 36	23 27	24 20	00 20
S 10	05 19	05 43	06 04	22 24	23 14	24 07	00 07
20	05 13	05 39	06 01	22 11	23 00	23 52	24 48
30	05 06	05 34	05 58	21 57	22 43	23 35	24 31
35	05 01	05 31	05 56	21 48	22 34	23 25	24 22
40	04 55	05 27	05 54	21 39	22 23	23 14	24 11
45	04 47	05 22	05 51	21 27	22 11	23 01	23 58
S 50	04 37	05 16	05 48	21 14	21 56	22 45	23 42
52	04 32	05 13	05 47	21 08	21 48	22 37	23 35
54	04 26	05 09	05 45	21 01	21 40	22 29	23 27
56	04 20	05 06	05 43	20 53	21 32	22 20	23 18
58	04 13	05 01	05 41	20 44	21 22	22 09	23 08
S 60	04 04	04 57	05 39	20 34	21 10	21 57	22 56

Lat.	Sunset	Twilight Civil	Naut.	Moonset 11	12	13	14
°	h m	h m	h m	h m	h m	h m	h m
N 72	17 40	18 48	20 10	06 27	06 18	■	■
N 70	17 44	18 45	19 58	06 58	07 07	07 28	08 14
68	17 46	18 42	19 48	07 21	07 39	08 09	08 58
66	17 49	18 40	19 41	07 39	08 02	08 37	09 27
64	17 51	18 38	19 34	07 54	08 21	08 58	09 49
62	17 52	18 37	19 29	08 07	08 36	09 15	10 07
60	17 54	18 35	19 24	08 17	08 49	09 29	10 22
N 58	17 55	18 34	19 20	08 26	09 00	09 42	10 34
56	17 56	18 34	19 17	08 34	09 09	09 52	10 45
54	17 58	18 33	19 14	08 42	09 18	10 01	10 54
52	17 59	18 32	19 11	08 48	09 25	10 10	11 03
50	17 59	18 32	19 09	08 54	09 32	10 17	11 11
45	18 01	18 31	19 05	09 07	09 47	10 33	11 27
N 40	18 03	18 30	19 02	09 17	09 59	10 46	11 40
35	18 05	18 30	18 59	09 26	10 09	10 58	11 51
30	18 06	18 30	18 58	09 34	10 18	11 07	12 01
20	18 09	18 31	18 56	09 48	10 34	11 24	12 18
N 10	18 11	18 32	18 56	10 00	10 48	11 39	12 33
0	18 13	18 34	18 58	10 11	11 00	11 52	12 47
S 10	18 15	18 36	19 01	10 22	11 13	12 06	13 00
20	18 18	18 40	19 06	10 34	11 27	12 21	13 15
30	18 21	18 45	19 13	10 48	11 43	12 38	13 32
35	18 23	18 48	19 18	10 56	11 52	12 47	13 41
40	18 25	18 52	19 24	11 05	12 02	12 58	13 53
45	18 27	18 57	19 32	11 15	12 14	13 11	14 06
S 50	18 30	19 03	19 42	11 28	12 29	13 27	14 21
52	18 32	19 06	19 47	11 34	12 36	13 35	14 29
54	18 33	19 09	19 52	11 41	12 44	13 43	14 37
56	18 35	19 13	19 58	11 48	12 52	13 52	14 46
58	18 37	19 17	20 05	11 57	13 02	14 03	14 57
S 60	18 39	19 21	20 13	12 06	13 13	14 15	15 09

Day	SUN Eqn. of Time 00h	12h	Mer. Pass.	MOON Mer. Pass. Upper	Lower	Age	Phase
d	m s	m s	h m	h m	h m	d %	
11	10 12	10 04	12 10	03 59	16 23	21 72	
12	09 56	09 48	12 10	04 48	17 14	22 63	
13	09 40	09 32	12 10	05 40	18 06	23 53	◑

UT	ARIES	VENUS −3.9		MARS +1.3		JUPITER −2.4		SATURN +0.4		STARS		
	GHA	GHA	Dec	GHA	Dec	GHA	Dec	GHA	Dec	Name	SHA	Dec
d h	° ′	° ′	° ′	° ′	° ′	° ′	° ′	° ′	° ′		° ′	° ′
14 00	171 17.8	147 17.6	N 9 54.5	155 42.9	N 6 16.7	34 55.0	N17 40.4	287 54.7	S19 03.3	Acamar	315 17.7	S40 15.0
01	186 20.3	162 17.2	55.7	170 43.7	17.5	49 57.6	40.4	302 57.2	03.3	Achernar	335 26.5	S57 09.8
02	201 22.8	177 16.9	56.9	185 44.4	18.2	65 00.3	40.5	317 59.7	03.3	Acrux	173 07.1	S63 11.0
03	216 25.2	192 16.5	.. 58.1	200 45.1	.. 19.0	80 03.0	.. 40.6	333 02.1	.. 03.3	Adhara	255 11.4	S29 00.0
04	231 27.7	207 16.2	9 59.4	215 45.8	19.7	95 05.6	40.6	348 04.6	03.3	Aldebaran	290 48.1	N16 32.2
05	246 30.2	222 15.8	10 00.6	230 46.5	20.5	110 08.3	40.7	3 07.1	03.3			
06	261 32.6	237 15.5	N10 01.8	245 47.3	N 6 21.2	125 10.9	N17 40.7	18 09.5	S19 03.3	Alioth	166 19.2	N55 52.5
07	276 35.1	252 15.1	03.0	260 48.0	22.0	140 13.6	40.8	33 12.0	03.3	Alkaid	152 57.6	N49 14.1
S 08	291 37.6	267 14.8	04.2	275 48.7	22.7	155 16.3	40.8	48 14.4	03.3	Al Na'ir	27 42.7	S46 53.1
A 09	306 40.0	282 14.4	.. 05.4	290 49.4	.. 23.5	170 18.9	.. 40.9	63 16.9	.. 03.3	Alnilam	275 45.2	S 1 11.9
T 10	321 42.5	297 14.1	06.7	305 50.1	24.2	185 21.6	40.9	78 19.4	03.3	Alphard	217 54.6	S 8 43.8
U 11	336 44.9	312 13.7	07.9	320 50.9	25.0	200 24.2	41.0	93 21.8	03.3			
R 12	351 47.4	327 13.3	N10 09.1	335 51.6	N 6 25.7	215 26.9	N17 41.0	108 24.3	S19 03.3	Alphecca	126 09.8	N26 39.7
D 13	6 49.9	342 13.0	10.3	350 52.3	26.5	230 29.5	41.1	123 26.7	03.2	Alpheratz	357 42.6	N29 10.4
A 14	21 52.3	357 12.6	11.5	5 53.0	27.2	245 32.2	41.2	138 29.2	03.2	Altair	62 07.2	N 8 54.5
Y 15	36 54.8	12 12.3	.. 12.7	20 53.8	.. 28.0	260 34.9	.. 41.2	153 31.7	.. 03.2	Ankaa	353 15.0	S42 13.5
16	51 57.3	27 11.9	14.0	35 54.5	28.7	275 37.5	41.3	168 34.1	03.2	Antares	112 24.7	S26 27.7
17	66 59.7	42 11.6	15.2	50 55.2	29.5	290 40.2	41.3	183 36.6	03.2			
18	82 02.2	57 11.2	N10 16.4	65 55.9	N 6 30.2	305 42.8	N17 41.4	198 39.1	S19 03.2	Arcturus	145 54.4	N19 06.1
19	97 04.7	72 10.9	17.6	80 56.6	31.0	320 45.5	41.4	213 41.5	03.2	Atria	107 25.3	S69 02.8
20	112 07.1	87 10.5	18.8	95 57.4	31.7	335 48.1	41.5	228 44.0	03.2	Avior	234 17.0	S59 33.9
21	127 09.6	102 10.2	.. 20.0	110 58.1	.. 32.5	350 50.8	.. 41.5	243 46.5	.. 03.2	Bellatrix	278 30.7	N 6 21.5
22	142 12.0	117 09.8	21.2	125 58.8	33.2	5 53.5	41.6	258 48.9	03.2	Betelgeuse	271 00.0	N 7 24.3
23	157 14.5	132 09.4	22.5	140 59.5	34.0	20 56.1	41.6	273 51.4	03.2			
15 00	172 17.0	147 09.1	N10 23.7	156 00.2	N 6 34.7	35 58.8	N17 41.7	288 53.8	S19 03.2	Canopus	263 55.5	S52 42.7
01	187 19.4	162 08.7	24.9	171 01.0	35.4	51 01.4	41.7	303 56.3	03.2	Capella	280 32.7	N46 00.7
02	202 21.9	177 08.4	26.1	186 01.7	36.2	66 04.1	41.8	318 58.8	03.2	Deneb	49 30.9	N45 20.0
03	217 24.4	192 08.0	.. 27.3	201 02.4	.. 36.9	81 06.7	.. 41.8	334 01.2	.. 03.2	Denebola	182 32.1	N14 29.1
04	232 26.8	207 07.7	28.5	216 03.1	37.7	96 09.4	41.9	349 03.7	03.1	Diphda	348 55.0	S17 54.4
05	247 29.3	222 07.3	29.7	231 03.9	38.4	111 12.0	42.0	4 06.2	03.1			
06	262 31.8	237 06.9	N10 30.9	246 04.6	N 6 39.2	126 14.7	N17 42.0	19 08.6	S19 03.1	Dubhe	193 49.7	N61 40.0
07	277 34.2	252 06.6	32.1	261 05.3	39.9	141 17.3	42.1	34 11.1	03.1	Elnath	278 11.1	N28 37.0
S 08	292 36.7	267 06.2	33.3	276 06.0	40.7	156 20.0	42.1	49 13.6	03.1	Eltanin	90 45.6	N51 29.1
U 09	307 39.2	282 05.9	.. 34.5	291 06.7	.. 41.4	171 22.7	.. 42.2	64 16.0	.. 03.1	Enif	33 46.2	N 9 56.7
N 10	322 41.6	297 05.5	35.8	306 07.5	42.2	186 25.3	42.2	79 18.5	03.1	Fomalhaut	15 23.1	S29 32.5
D 11	337 44.1	312 05.1	37.0	321 08.2	42.9	201 28.0	42.3	94 21.0	03.1			
A 12	352 46.5	327 04.8	N10 38.2	336 08.9	N 6 43.7	216 30.6	N17 42.3	109 23.4	S19 03.1	Gacrux	171 58.9	S57 11.9
Y 13	7 49.0	342 04.4	39.4	351 09.6	44.4	231 33.3	42.4	124 25.9	03.1	Gienah	175 50.7	S17 37.7
14	22 51.5	357 04.1	40.6	6 10.3	45.1	246 35.9	42.4	139 28.4	03.1	Hadar	148 45.6	S60 26.6
15	37 53.9	12 03.7	.. 41.8	21 11.1	.. 45.9	261 38.6	.. 42.5	154 30.8	.. 03.1	Hamal	327 59.6	N23 31.9
16	52 56.4	27 03.3	43.0	36 11.8	46.6	276 41.2	42.5	169 33.3	03.1	Kaus Aust.	83 42.3	S34 22.4
17	67 58.9	42 03.0	44.2	51 12.5	47.4	291 43.9	42.6	184 35.8	03.1			
18	83 01.3	57 02.6	N10 45.4	66 13.2	N 6 48.1	306 46.5	N17 42.6	199 38.2	S19 03.0	Kochab	137 19.5	N74 05.4
19	98 03.8	72 02.3	46.6	81 13.9	48.9	321 49.2	42.7	214 40.7	03.0	Markab	13 37.4	N15 17.2
20	113 06.3	87 01.9	47.8	96 14.7	49.6	336 51.8	42.7	229 43.2	03.0	Menkar	314 14.0	N 4 08.7
21	128 08.7	102 01.5	.. 49.0	111 15.4	.. 50.4	351 54.5	.. 42.8	244 45.6	.. 03.0	Menkent	148 05.8	S36 26.6
22	143 11.2	117 01.2	50.2	126 16.1	51.1	6 57.1	42.8	259 48.1	03.0	Miaplacidus	221 38.5	S69 47.1
23	158 13.7	132 00.8	51.4	141 16.8	51.8	21 59.8	42.9	274 50.6	03.0			
16 00	173 16.1	147 00.4	N10 52.6	156 17.6	N 6 52.6	37 02.4	N17 42.9	289 53.0	S19 03.0	Mirfak	308 38.8	N49 54.9
01	188 18.6	162 00.1	53.8	171 18.3	53.3	52 05.1	43.0	304 55.5	03.0	Nunki	75 57.0	S26 16.4
02	203 21.0	176 59.7	55.0	186 19.0	54.1	67 07.7	43.0	319 58.0	03.0	Peacock	53 17.8	S56 40.9
03	218 23.5	191 59.4	.. 56.2	201 19.7	.. 54.8	82 10.3	.. 43.1	335 00.5	.. 03.0	Pollux	243 26.1	N27 59.2
04	233 26.0	206 59.0	57.4	216 20.4	55.6	97 13.0	43.1	350 02.9	03.0	Procyon	244 58.3	N 5 10.8
05	248 28.4	221 58.6	58.6	231 21.2	56.3	112 15.6	43.2	5 05.4	03.0			
06	263 30.9	236 58.3	N10 59.8	246 21.9	N 6 57.0	127 18.3	N17 43.2	20 07.9	S19 03.0	Rasalhague	96 05.3	N12 32.9
07	278 33.4	251 57.9	11 01.0	261 22.6	57.8	142 20.9	43.3	35 10.3	02.9	Regulus	207 42.0	N11 53.3
08	293 35.8	266 57.5	02.2	276 23.3	58.5	157 23.6	43.3	50 12.8	02.9	Rigel	281 10.9	S 8 11.4
M 09	308 38.3	281 57.2	.. 03.4	291 24.0	6 59.3	172 26.2	.. 43.4	65 15.3	.. 02.9	Rigil Kent.	139 49.5	S60 53.6
O 10	323 40.8	296 56.8	04.6	306 24.8	7 00.0	187 28.9	43.4	80 17.7	02.9	Sabik	102 11.1	S15 44.5
N 11	338 43.2	311 56.4	05.8	321 25.5	00.8	202 31.5	43.5	95 20.2	02.9			
D 12	353 45.7	326 56.1	N11 07.0	336 26.2	N 7 01.5	217 34.2	N17 43.5	110 22.7	S19 02.9	Schedar	349 39.6	N56 37.2
A 13	8 48.1	341 55.7	08.2	351 26.9	02.2	232 36.8	43.6	125 25.2	02.9	Shaula	96 20.3	S37 06.6
Y 14	23 50.6	356 55.3	09.4	6 27.6	03.0	247 39.4	43.6	140 27.6	02.9	Sirius	258 32.6	S16 44.6
15	38 53.1	11 55.0	.. 10.6	21 28.4	.. 03.7	262 42.1	.. 43.7	155 30.1	.. 02.9	Spica	158 29.7	S11 14.5
16	53 55.5	26 54.6	11.8	36 29.1	04.5	277 44.7	43.7	170 32.6	02.9	Suhail	222 51.2	S43 30.0
17	68 58.0	41 54.2	13.0	51 29.8	05.2	292 47.4	43.8	185 35.0	02.9			
18	84 00.5	56 53.9	N11 14.2	66 30.5	N 7 05.9	307 50.0	N17 43.8	200 37.5	S19 02.9	Vega	80 38.2	N38 47.8
19	99 02.9	71 53.5	15.4	81 31.2	06.7	322 52.7	43.9	215 40.0	02.9	Zuben'ubi	137 03.9	S16 06.2
20	114 05.4	86 53.1	16.6	96 32.0	07.4	337 55.3	43.9	230 42.5	02.8		SHA	Mer.Pass.
21	129 07.9	101 52.8	.. 17.8	111 32.7	.. 08.2	352 57.9	.. 44.0	245 44.9	.. 02.8		° ′	h m
22	144 10.3	116 52.4	18.9	126 33.4	08.9	8 00.6	44.0	260 47.4	02.8	Venus	334 52.1	14 12
23	159 12.8	131 52.0	20.1	141 34.1	09.7	23 03.2	44.1	275 49.9	02.8	Mars	343 43.3	13 35
	h m									Jupiter	223 41.8	21 32
Mer. Pass. 12 28.8		v −0.4	d 1.2	v 0.7	d 0.7	v 2.7	d 0.1	v 2.5	d 0.0	Saturn	116 36.9	4 44

UT	SUN GHA	SUN Dec	MOON GHA	v	MOON Dec	d	HP
d h	° ′	° ′	° ′	′	° ′	′	′
14 00	177 39.1	S 2 44.8	265 12.7	8.3	S18 15.5	0.1	57.6
01	192 39.3	43.8	279 40.0	8.3	18 15.6	0.0	57.6
02	207 39.4	42.8	294 07.3	8.3	18 15.6	0.1	57.6
03	222 39.6	.. 41.8	308 34.6	8.2	18 15.5	0.2	57.7
04	237 39.8	40.8	323 01.8	8.1	18 15.3	0.3	57.7
05	252 40.0	39.8	337 28.9	8.1	18 15.0	0.4	57.8
06	267 40.1	S 2 38.8	351 56.0	8.1	S18 14.6	0.5	57.8
S 07	282 40.3	37.9	6 23.1	8.1	18 14.1	0.7	57.8
A 08	297 40.5	36.9	20 50.2	8.0	18 13.4	0.7	57.9
T 09	312 40.7	.. 35.9	35 17.2	7.9	18 12.7	0.9	57.9
U 10	327 40.8	34.9	49 44.1	7.9	18 11.8	0.9	57.9
R 11	342 41.0	33.9	64 11.0	7.9	18 11.0	1.1	58.0
D 12	357 41.2	S 2 32.9	78 37.9	7.9	S18 09.8	1.2	58.0
A 13	12 41.3	31.9	93 04.8	7.8	18 08.6	1.3	58.0
Y 14	27 41.5	30.9	107 31.6	7.7	18 07.3	1.4	58.1
15	42 41.7	.. 30.0	121 58.3	7.8	18 05.9	1.5	58.1
16	57 41.9	29.0	136 25.1	7.7	18 04.4	1.6	58.2
17	72 42.0	28.0	150 51.8	7.6	18 02.8	1.8	58.2
18	87 42.2	S 2 27.0	165 18.4	7.6	S18 01.0	1.8	58.2
19	102 42.4	26.0	179 45.0	7.6	17 59.2	2.0	58.3
20	117 42.5	25.0	194 11.6	7.6	17 57.2	2.1	58.3
21	132 42.7	.. 24.0	208 38.2	7.5	17 55.1	2.2	58.3
22	147 42.9	23.1	223 04.7	7.5	17 52.9	2.3	58.4
23	162 43.1	22.1	237 31.2	7.5	17 50.6	2.4	58.4
15 00	177 43.2	S 2 21.1	251 57.7	7.4	S17 48.2	2.5	58.4
01	192 43.4	20.1	266 24.1	7.4	17 45.7	2.6	58.5
02	207 43.6	19.1	280 50.5	7.4	17 43.1	2.8	58.5
03	222 43.8	.. 18.1	295 16.9	7.3	17 40.3	2.9	58.6
04	237 43.9	17.1	309 43.2	7.3	17 37.4	3.0	58.6
05	252 44.1	16.1	324 09.5	7.3	17 34.4	3.0	58.6
06	267 44.3	S 2 15.2	338 35.8	7.3	S17 31.4	3.3	58.7
07	282 44.5	14.2	353 02.1	7.2	17 28.1	3.3	58.7
08	297 44.6	13.2	7 28.3	7.2	17 24.8	3.4	58.7
S 09	312 44.8	.. 12.2	21 54.5	7.2	17 21.4	3.6	58.8
U 10	327 45.0	11.2	36 20.7	7.2	17 17.8	3.6	58.8
N 11	342 45.2	10.2	50 46.9	7.1	17 14.2	3.8	58.9
D 12	357 45.3	S 2 09.2	65 13.0	7.2	S17 10.4	3.9	58.9
A 13	12 45.5	08.3	79 39.2	7.0	17 06.5	4.0	58.9
Y 14	27 45.7	07.3	94 05.2	7.1	17 02.5	4.1	59.0
15	42 45.9	.. 06.3	108 31.3	7.1	16 58.4	4.2	59.0
16	57 46.0	05.3	122 57.4	7.0	16 54.2	4.4	59.0
17	72 46.2	04.3	137 23.4	7.0	16 49.8	4.4	59.1
18	87 46.4	S 2 03.3	151 49.4	7.0	S16 45.4	4.6	59.1
19	102 46.6	02.3	166 15.4	7.0	16 40.8	4.7	59.1
20	117 46.7	01.3	180 41.4	7.0	16 36.1	4.8	59.2
21	132 46.9	2 00.4	195 07.4	6.9	16 31.3	4.9	59.2
22	147 47.1	1 59.4	209 33.3	6.9	16 26.4	5.0	59.3
23	162 47.3	58.4	223 59.2	7.0	16 21.4	5.1	59.3
16 00	177 47.4	S 1 57.4	238 25.2	6.9	S16 16.3	5.3	59.3
01	192 47.6	56.4	252 51.1	6.9	16 11.0	5.3	59.4
02	207 47.8	55.4	267 17.0	6.8	16 05.7	5.5	59.4
03	222 48.0	.. 54.4	281 42.8	6.9	16 00.2	5.5	59.4
04	237 48.1	53.4	296 08.7	6.8	15 54.7	5.7	59.5
05	252 48.3	52.4	310 34.5	6.9	15 49.0	5.8	59.5
06	267 48.5	S 1 51.5	325 00.4	6.8	S15 43.2	5.9	59.5
07	282 48.7	50.5	339 26.2	6.8	15 37.3	6.0	59.6
08	297 48.8	49.5	353 52.0	6.8	15 31.3	6.1	59.6
M 09	312 49.0	.. 48.5	8 17.8	6.8	15 25.2	6.2	59.6
O 10	327 49.2	47.5	22 43.6	6.8	15 19.0	6.4	59.7
N 11	342 49.4	46.5	37 09.4	6.8	15 12.6	6.4	59.7
D 12	357 49.5	S 1 45.5	51 35.2	6.8	S15 06.2	6.5	59.8
A 13	12 49.7	44.5	66 01.0	6.8	14 59.7	6.7	59.8
Y 14	27 49.9	43.6	80 26.8	6.7	14 53.0	6.7	59.8
15	42 50.1	.. 42.6	94 52.5	6.8	14 46.3	6.9	59.9
16	57 50.2	41.6	109 18.3	6.7	14 39.4	7.0	59.9
17	72 50.4	40.6	123 44.0	6.8	14 32.4	7.0	59.9
18	87 50.6	S 1 39.6	138 09.8	6.7	S14 25.4	7.2	60.0
19	102 50.8	38.6	152 35.5	6.8	14 18.2	7.3	60.0
20	117 51.0	37.6	167 01.3	6.7	14 10.9	7.3	60.0
21	132 51.1	.. 36.6	181 27.0	6.8	14 03.6	7.5	60.0
22	147 51.3	35.7	195 52.8	6.7	13 56.1	7.6	60.1
23	162 51.5	34.7	210 18.5	6.7	S13 48.5	7.6	60.1
	SD 16.1	d 1.0	SD 15.8		16.0		16.3

Lat.	Twilight Naut.	Twilight Civil	Sunrise	Moonrise 14	Moonrise 15	Moonrise 16	Moonrise 17
°	h m	h m	h m	h m	h m	h m	h m
N 72	03 55	05 19	06 26	■■	06 39	06 24	06 17
N 70	04 09	05 24	06 24	04 54	05 29	05 45	05 53
68	04 20	05 27	06 22	04 10	04 52	05 18	05 35
66	04 29	05 30	06 21	03 40	04 26	04 58	05 20
64	04 36	05 33	06 20	03 18	04 06	04 41	05 08
62	04 43	05 35	06 19	03 01	03 49	04 27	04 57
60	04 48	05 37	06 18	02 46	03 35	04 16	04 48
N 58	04 52	05 38	06 17	02 33	03 24	04 05	04 40
56	04 56	05 40	06 16	02 23	03 13	03 57	04 33
54	04 59	05 41	06 16	02 13	03 04	03 49	04 27
52	05 02	05 42	06 15	02 05	02 56	03 42	04 21
50	05 05	05 42	06 15	01 57	02 49	03 35	04 16
45	05 11	05 44	06 13	01 41	02 33	03 21	04 05
N 40	05 14	05 45	06 11	01 27	02 20	03 10	03 56
35	05 17	05 46	06 11	01 16	02 09	03 00	03 48
30	05 19	05 47	06 10	01 06	02 00	02 52	03 41
20	05 21	05 47	06 09	00 49	01 43	02 37	03 29
N 10	05 22	05 46	06 07	00 34	01 29	02 24	03 19
0	05 21	05 45	06 06	00 20	01 16	02 12	03 09
S 10	05 19	05 43	06 04	00 07	01 02	02 00	02 59
20	05 15	05 40	06 02	24 48	00 48	01 47	02 48
30	05 08	05 36	06 00	24 31	00 31	01 32	02 36
35	05 04	05 33	05 59	24 22	00 22	01 23	02 29
40	04 58	05 30	05 57	24 11	00 11	01 14	02 21
45	04 51	05 26	05 55	23 58	25 02	01 02	02 12
S 50	04 42	05 21	05 53	23 42	24 48	00 48	02 01
52	04 38	05 18	05 52	23 35	24 42	00 42	01 55
54	04 33	05 15	05 51	23 27	24 34	00 34	01 50
56	04 27	05 12	05 50	23 18	24 26	00 26	01 43
58	04 20	05 09	05 48	23 08	24 17	00 17	01 36
S 60	04 13	05 05	05 47	22 56	24 07	00 07	01 28

Lat.	Sunset	Twilight Civil	Twilight Naut.	Moonset 14	Moonset 15	Moonset 16	Moonset 17
°	h m	h m	h m	h m	h m	h m	h m
N 72	17 54	19 02	20 26	■■	08 25	10 39	12 45
N 70	17 56	18 57	20 12	08 14	09 34	11 16	13 08
68	17 57	18 53	20 01	08 58	10 11	11 43	13 25
66	17 59	18 50	19 51	09 27	10 37	12 03	13 39
64	18 00	18 47	19 44	09 49	10 57	12 19	13 50
62	18 01	18 45	19 37	10 07	11 13	12 32	14 00
60	18 01	18 43	19 32	10 22	11 27	12 43	14 08
N 58	18 02	18 41	19 27	10 34	11 38	12 53	14 15
56	18 03	18 40	19 23	10 45	11 48	13 01	14 21
54	18 03	18 39	19 20	10 54	11 57	13 09	14 27
52	18 04	18 37	19 17	11 03	12 05	13 15	14 32
50	18 04	18 37	19 14	11 11	12 12	13 21	14 36
45	18 05	18 35	19 09	11 27	12 27	13 34	14 46
N 40	18 06	18 33	19 05	11 40	12 40	13 45	14 55
35	18 07	18 32	19 02	11 51	12 50	13 54	15 02
30	18 08	18 32	19 00	12 01	13 00	14 02	15 08
20	18 09	18 31	18 57	12 18	13 16	14 16	15 18
N 10	18 11	18 32	18 56	12 33	13 29	14 28	15 27
0	18 12	18 33	18 57	12 47	13 42	14 39	15 36
S 10	18 14	18 35	18 59	13 00	13 55	14 50	15 44
20	18 15	18 37	19 03	13 15	14 09	15 02	15 53
30	18 18	18 41	19 09	13 32	14 25	15 15	16 04
35	18 19	18 44	19 14	13 41	14 34	15 23	16 10
40	18 20	18 47	19 19	13 53	14 44	15 32	16 16
45	18 22	18 51	19 26	14 06	14 56	15 42	16 24
S 50	18 24	18 56	19 35	14 21	15 11	15 54	16 33
52	18 25	18 59	19 39	14 29	15 17	16 00	16 37
54	18 26	19 01	19 44	14 37	15 25	16 06	16 42
56	18 27	19 04	19 49	14 46	15 33	16 13	16 47
58	18 28	19 08	19 56	14 57	15 43	16 21	16 53
S 60	18 30	19 12	20 03	15 09	15 54	16 30	16 59

	SUN			MOON			
Day	Eqn. of Time 00h	Eqn. of Time 12h	Mer. Pass.	Mer. Pass. Upper	Mer. Pass. Lower	Age	Phase
d	m s	m s	h m	h m	h m	d	%
14	09 24	09 16	12 09	06 33	19 01	24	42
15	09 07	08 59	12 09	07 29	19 57	25	31
16	08 51	08 42	12 09	08 26	20 54	26	21

2015 MARCH 17, 18, 19 (TUES., WED., THURS.)

UT	ARIES GHA	VENUS −4.0 GHA	VENUS Dec	MARS +1.3 GHA	MARS Dec	JUPITER −2.4 GHA	JUPITER Dec	SATURN +0.4 GHA	SATURN Dec	Name	SHA	Dec
17 00	174 15.3	146 51.7	N11 21.3	156 34.8	N 7 10.4	38 05.9	N17 44.1	290 52.4	S19 02.8	Acamar	315 17.7	S40 15.0
01	189 17.7	161 51.3	22.5	171 35.6	11.1	53 08.5	44.2	305 54.8	02.8	Achernar	335 26.5	S57 09.8
02	204 20.2	176 50.9	23.7	186 36.3	11.9	68 11.2	44.2	320 57.3	02.8	Acrux	173 07.1	S63 11.0
03	219 22.6	191 50.6 ..	24.9	201 37.0 ..	12.6	83 13.8 ..	44.3	335 59.8 ..	02.8	Adhara	255 11.5	S29 00.0
04	234 25.1	206 50.2	26.1	216 37.7	13.4	98 16.4	44.3	351 02.2	02.8	Aldebaran	290 48.1	N16 32.2
05	249 27.6	221 49.8	27.3	231 38.4	14.1	113 19.1	44.4	6 04.7	02.8			
06	264 30.0	236 49.4	N11 28.5	246 39.2	N 7 14.8	128 21.7	N17 44.4	21 07.2	S19 02.8	Alioth	166 19.2	N55 52.5
07	279 32.5	251 49.1	29.7	261 39.9	15.6	143 24.3	44.5	36 09.7	02.8	Alkaid	152 57.6	N49 14.1
T 08	294 35.0	266 48.7	30.8	276 40.6	16.3	158 27.0	44.5	51 12.1	02.7	Al Na'ir	27 42.7	S46 53.1
U 09	309 37.4	281 48.3 ..	32.0	291 41.3 ..	17.0	173 29.6 ..	44.6	66 14.6 ..	02.7	Alnilam	275 45.2	S 1 11.9
E 10	324 39.9	296 48.0	33.2	306 42.0	17.8	188 32.3	44.6	81 17.1	02.7	Alphard	217 54.6	S 8 43.8
S 11	339 42.4	311 47.6	34.4	321 42.8	18.5	203 34.9	44.7	96 19.6	02.7			
D 12	354 44.8	326 47.2	N11 35.6	336 43.5	N 7 19.3	218 37.5	N17 44.7	111 22.0	S19 02.7	Alphecca	126 09.8	N26 39.7
A 13	9 47.3	341 46.8	36.8	351 44.2	20.0	233 40.2	44.8	126 24.5	02.7	Alpheratz	357 42.6	N29 10.4
Y 14	24 49.8	356 46.5	38.0	6 44.9	20.7	248 42.8	44.8	141 27.0	02.7	Altair	62 07.2	N 8 54.5
15	39 52.2	11 46.1 ..	39.1	21 45.6 ..	21.5	263 45.4 ..	44.8	156 29.5 ..	02.7	Ankaa	353 15.0	S42 13.5
16	54 54.7	26 45.7	40.3	36 46.4	22.2	278 48.1	44.9	171 32.0	02.7	Antares	112 24.7	S26 27.7
17	69 57.1	41 45.3	41.5	51 47.1	23.0	293 50.7	44.9	186 34.4	02.7			
18	84 59.6	56 45.0	N11 42.7	66 47.8	N 7 23.7	308 53.4	N17 45.0	201 36.9	S19 02.7	Arcturus	145 54.4	N19 06.1
19	100 02.1	71 44.6	43.9	81 48.5	24.4	323 56.0	45.0	216 39.4	02.7	Atria	107 25.2	S69 02.8
20	115 04.5	86 44.2	45.1	96 49.2	25.2	338 58.6	45.1	231 41.9	02.6	Avior	234 17.1	S59 33.9
21	130 07.0	101 43.9 ..	46.2	111 50.0 ..	25.9	354 01.3 ..	45.1	246 44.3 ..	02.6	Bellatrix	278 30.7	N 6 21.5
22	145 09.5	116 43.5	47.4	126 50.7	26.6	9 03.9	45.2	261 46.8	02.6	Betelgeuse	271 00.0	N 7 24.3
23	160 11.9	131 43.1	48.6	141 51.4	27.4	24 06.5	45.2	276 49.3	02.6			
18 00	175 14.4	146 42.7	N11 49.8	156 52.1	N 7 28.1	39 09.2	N17 45.3	291 51.8	S19 02.6	Canopus	263 55.5	S52 42.7
01	190 16.9	161 42.3	51.0	171 52.8	28.8	54 11.8	45.3	306 54.2	02.6	Capella	280 32.7	N46 00.7
02	205 19.3	176 42.0	52.1	186 53.6	29.6	69 14.4	45.4	321 56.7	02.6	Deneb	49 30.9	N45 20.0
03	220 21.8	191 41.6 ..	53.3	201 54.3 ..	30.3	84 17.1 ..	45.4	336 59.2 ..	02.6	Denebola	182 32.1	N14 29.1
04	235 24.2	206 41.2	54.5	216 55.0	31.1	99 19.7	45.5	352 01.7	02.6	Diphda	348 55.0	S17 54.4
05	250 26.7	221 40.8	55.7	231 55.7	31.8	114 22.3	45.5	7 04.2	02.6			
06	265 29.2	236 40.5	N11 56.8	246 56.4	N 7 32.5	129 25.0	N17 45.5	22 06.6	S19 02.6	Dubhe	193 49.7	N61 40.0
W 07	280 31.6	251 40.1	58.0	261 57.1	33.3	144 27.6	45.6	37 09.1	02.5	Elnath	278 11.1	N28 37.0
E 08	295 34.1	266 39.7	11 59.2	276 57.9	34.0	159 30.2	45.6	52 11.6	02.5	Eltanin	90 45.6	N51 29.1
D 09	310 36.6	281 39.3	12 00.4	291 58.6 ..	34.7	174 32.9 ..	45.7	67 14.1 ..	02.5	Enif	33 46.2	N 9 56.7
N 10	325 39.0	296 39.0	01.6	306 59.3	35.5	189 35.5	45.7	82 16.6	02.5	Fomalhaut	15 23.1	S29 32.5
E 11	340 41.5	311 38.6	02.7	322 00.0	36.2	204 38.1	45.8	97 19.0	02.5			
S 12	355 44.0	326 38.2	N12 03.9	337 00.7	N 7 36.9	219 40.7	N17 45.8	112 21.5	S19 02.5	Gacrux	171 58.9	S57 11.9
D 13	10 46.4	341 37.8	05.1	352 01.5	37.7	234 43.4	45.9	127 24.0	02.5	Gienah	175 50.7	S17 37.7
A 14	25 48.9	356 37.4	06.3	7 02.2	38.4	249 46.0	45.9	142 26.5	02.5	Hadar	148 45.5	S60 26.6
Y 15	40 51.4	11 37.1 ..	07.4	22 02.9 ..	39.1	264 48.6 ..	46.0	157 29.0 ..	02.5	Hamal	327 59.7	N23 31.9
16	55 53.8	26 36.7	08.6	37 03.6	39.9	279 51.3	46.0	172 31.4	02.5	Kaus Aust.	83 42.3	S34 22.4
17	70 56.3	41 36.3	09.8	52 04.3	40.6	294 53.9	46.0	187 33.9	02.4			
18	85 58.7	56 35.9	N12 10.9	67 05.1	N 7 41.3	309 56.5	N17 46.1	202 36.4	S19 02.4	Kochab	137 19.4	N74 05.4
19	101 01.2	71 35.5	12.1	82 05.8	42.1	324 59.2	46.1	217 38.9	02.4	Markab	13 37.4	N15 17.2
20	116 03.7	86 35.2	13.3	97 06.5	42.8	340 01.8	46.2	232 41.4	02.4	Menkar	314 14.0	N 4 08.7
21	131 06.1	101 34.8 ..	14.5	112 07.2 ..	43.5	355 04.4 ..	46.2	247 43.8 ..	02.4	Menkent	148 05.8	S36 26.6
22	146 08.6	116 34.4	15.6	127 07.9	44.3	10 07.0	46.3	262 46.3	02.4	Miaplacidus	221 38.6	S69 47.1
23	161 11.1	131 34.0	16.8	142 08.6	45.0	25 09.7	46.3	277 48.8	02.4			
19 00	176 13.5	146 33.6	N12 18.0	157 09.4	N 7 45.7	40 12.3	N17 46.4	292 51.3	S19 02.4	Mirfak	308 38.9	N49 54.9
01	191 16.0	161 33.2	19.1	172 10.1	46.5	55 14.9	46.4	307 53.8	02.4	Nunki	75 56.9	S26 16.4
02	206 18.5	176 32.9	20.3	187 10.8	47.2	70 17.5	46.4	322 56.3	02.4	Peacock	53 17.8	S56 40.8
03	221 20.9	191 32.5 ..	21.5	202 11.5 ..	47.9	85 20.2 ..	46.5	337 58.7 ..	02.4	Pollux	243 26.1	N27 59.2
04	236 23.4	206 32.1	22.6	217 12.2	48.7	100 22.8	46.5	353 01.2	02.3	Procyon	244 58.3	N 5 10.8
05	251 25.9	221 31.7	23.8	232 13.0	49.4	115 25.4	46.6	8 03.7	02.3			
06	266 28.3	236 31.3	N12 25.0	247 13.7	N 7 50.1	130 28.0	N17 46.6	23 06.2	S19 02.3	Rasalhague	96 05.3	N12 32.9
07	281 30.8	251 30.9	26.1	262 14.4	50.9	145 30.7	46.7	38 08.7	02.3	Regulus	207 42.0	N11 53.3
T 08	296 33.2	266 30.6	27.3	277 15.1	51.6	160 33.3	46.7	53 11.2	02.3	Rigel	281 10.9	S 8 11.4
H 09	311 35.7	281 30.2 ..	28.5	292 15.8 ..	52.3	175 35.9 ..	46.8	68 13.6 ..	02.3	Rigil Kent.	139 49.5	S60 53.6
U 10	326 38.2	296 29.8	29.6	307 16.5	53.1	190 38.5	46.8	83 16.1	02.3	Sabik	102 11.1	S15 44.5
R 11	341 40.6	311 29.4	30.8	322 17.3	53.8	205 41.2	46.8	98 18.6	02.3			
S 12	356 43.1	326 29.0	N12 31.9	337 18.0	N 7 54.5	220 43.8	N17 46.9	113 21.1	S19 02.3	Schedar	349 39.6	N56 37.2
D 13	11 45.6	341 28.6	33.1	352 18.7	55.3	235 46.4	46.9	128 23.6	02.3	Shaula	96 20.3	S37 06.6
A 14	26 48.0	356 28.2	34.3	7 19.4	56.0	250 49.0	47.0	143 26.1	02.2	Sirius	258 32.6	S16 44.6
Y 15	41 50.5	11 27.9 ..	35.4	22 20.1 ..	56.7	265 51.7 ..	47.0	158 28.5 ..	02.2	Spica	158 29.7	S11 14.5
16	56 53.0	26 27.5	36.6	37 20.9	57.5	280 54.3	47.1	173 31.0	02.2	Suhail	222 51.2	S43 30.0
17	71 55.4	41 27.1	37.7	52 21.6	58.2	295 56.9	47.1	188 33.5	02.2			
18	86 57.9	56 26.7	N12 38.9	67 22.3	N 7 58.9	310 59.5	N17 47.1	203 36.0	S19 02.2	Vega	80 38.2	N38 47.8
19	102 00.3	71 26.3	40.1	82 23.0	7 59.6	326 02.1	47.2	218 38.5	02.2	Zuben'ubi	137 03.8	S16 06.2
20	117 02.8	86 25.9	41.2	97 23.7	8 00.4	341 04.8	47.2	233 41.0	02.2		SHA	Mer. Pass.
21	132 05.3	101 25.5 ..	42.4	112 24.4 ..	01.1	356 07.4 ..	47.3	248 43.5 ..	02.2	Venus	331 28.3	14 14
22	147 07.7	116 25.1	43.5	127 25.2	01.8	11 10.0	47.3	263 45.9	02.2	Mars	341 37.7	13 32
23	162 10.2	131 24.8	44.7	142 25.9	02.6	26 12.6	47.4	278 48.4	02.1	Jupiter	223 54.8	21 20
Mer. Pass.	h m 12 17.0	v −0.4	d 1.2	v 0.7	d 0.7	v 2.6	d 0.0	v 2.5	d 0.0	Saturn	116 37.4	4 32

UT	SUN		MOON				Lat.	Twilight		Sunrise	Moonrise			
								Naut.	Civil		17	18	19	20
	GHA	Dec	GHA	v	Dec	d	HP							
d h	° ′	° ′	° ′	′	° ′	′	′	°	h m	h m	h m	h m	h m	h m	h m
17 00	177 51.7	S 1 33.7	224 44.2	6.8	S13 40.9	7.8	60.1	N 72	03 37	05 03	06 11	06 17	06 11	06 06	06 01
01	192 51.8	32.7	239 10.0	6.7	13 33.1	7.9	60.2	N 70	03 53	05 09	06 10	05 53	05 57	05 59	06 00
02	207 52.0	31.7	253 35.7	6.7	13 25.2	8.0	60.2	68	04 06	05 14	06 10	05 35	05 45	05 53	06 00
03	222 52.2	.. 30.7	268 01.4	6.8	13 17.2	8.0	60.2	66	04 17	05 19	06 10	05 20	05 36	05 49	06 00
04	237 52.4	29.7	282 27.2	6.7	13 09.2	8.2	60.3	64	04 25	05 22	06 09	05 08	05 28	05 45	06 00
05	252 52.6	28.7	296 52.9	6.7	13 01.0	8.2	60.3	62	04 32	05 25	06 09	04 57	05 21	05 41	06 00
06	267 52.7	S 1 27.7	311 18.6	6.8	S12 52.8	8.4	60.3	60	04 38	05 28	06 09	04 48	05 15	05 38	06 00
T 07	282 52.9	26.8	325 44.4	6.7	12 44.4	8.4	60.4	N 58	04 43	05 30	06 09	04 40	05 10	05 35	06 00
U 08	297 53.1	25.8	340 10.1	6.8	12 36.0	8.5	60.4	56	04 48	05 32	06 09	04 33	05 05	05 33	05 59
E 09	312 53.3	.. 24.8	354 35.9	6.7	12 27.5	8.7	60.4	54	04 52	05 33	06 08	04 27	05 01	05 31	05 59
S 10	327 53.4	23.8	9 01.6	6.8	12 18.8	8.7	60.4	52	04 55	05 35	06 08	04 21	04 57	05 29	05 59
D 11	342 53.6	22.8	23 27.4	6.7	12 10.1	8.8	60.5	50	04 58	05 36	06 08	04 16	04 53	05 27	05 59
A 12	357 53.8	S 1 21.8	37 53.1	6.8	S12 01.3	8.9	60.5	45	05 04	05 39	06 08	04 05	04 46	05 23	05 59
Y 13	12 54.0	20.8	52 18.9	6.8	11 52.4	8.9	60.5	N 40	05 09	05 40	06 07	03 56	04 39	05 20	05 59
14	27 54.2	19.8	66 44.7	6.7	11 43.5	9.1	60.6	35	05 13	05 42	06 07	03 48	04 34	05 17	05 59
15	42 54.3	.. 18.8	81 10.4	6.8	11 34.4	9.2	60.6	30	05 15	05 43	06 07	03 41	04 29	05 14	05 59
16	57 54.5	17.9	95 36.2	6.8	11 25.2	9.2	60.6	20	05 19	05 44	06 06	03 29	04 20	05 10	05 59
17	72 54.7	16.9	110 02.0	6.8	11 16.0	9.3	60.6	N 10	05 20	05 45	06 06	03 19	04 13	05 06	05 59
18	87 54.9	S 1 15.9	124 27.8	6.8	S11 06.7	9.4	60.7	0	05 20	05 44	06 05	03 09	04 06	05 02	05 59
19	102 55.1	14.9	138 53.6	6.8	10 57.3	9.5	60.7	S 10	05 19	05 43	06 04	02 59	03 59	04 59	05 59
20	117 55.2	13.9	153 19.4	6.8	10 47.8	9.6	60.7	20	05 15	05 41	06 03	02 48	03 51	04 55	05 59
21	132 55.4	.. 12.9	167 45.2	6.8	10 38.2	9.6	60.7	30	05 10	05 38	06 02	02 36	03 43	04 51	05 59
22	147 55.6	11.9	182 11.0	6.8	10 28.6	9.7	60.8	35	05 06	05 36	06 01	02 29	03 38	04 48	05 59
23	162 55.8	10.9	196 36.8	6.8	10 18.9	9.8	60.8	40	05 01	05 33	06 00	02 21	03 32	04 45	05 59
18 00	177 56.0	S 1 09.9	211 02.6	6.9	S10 09.1	9.9	60.8	45	04 55	05 30	05 59	02 12	03 26	04 42	05 59
01	192 56.1	09.0	225 28.5	6.8	9 59.2	9.9	60.8	S 50	04 47	05 26	05 58	02 01	03 18	04 38	05 59
02	207 56.3	08.0	239 54.3	6.9	9 49.3	10.0	60.8	52	04 43	05 23	05 57	01 55	03 14	04 36	05 59
03	222 56.5	.. 07.0	254 20.2	6.8	9 39.3	10.1	60.9	54	04 39	05 21	05 57	01 50	03 10	04 34	05 59
04	237 56.7	06.0	268 46.0	6.9	9 29.2	10.2	60.9	56	04 34	05 19	05 56	01 43	03 06	04 32	05 59
05	252 56.9	05.0	283 11.9	6.9	9 19.0	10.2	60.9	58	04 28	05 16	05 55	01 36	03 01	04 29	05 59
06	267 57.0	S 1 04.0	297 37.8	6.8	S 9 08.8	10.3	60.9	S 60	04 22	05 12	05 54	01 28	02 55	04 27	05 59

UT	SUN		MOON				Lat.	Sunset	Twilight		Moonset			
	GHA	Dec	GHA	v	Dec	d	HP			Civil	Naut.	17	18	19	20
W 07	282 57.2	03.0	312 03.6	6.9	8 58.5	10.4	60.9	°	h m	h m	h m	h m	h m	h m	h m
E 08	297 57.4	02.0	326 29.5	6.9	8 48.1	10.4	61.0	N 72	18 08	19 16	20 44	12 45	14 50	16 53	18 56
D 09	312 57.6	.. 01.0	340 55.4	6.9	8 37.7	10.5	61.0	N 70	18 08	19 09	20 27	13 08	15 02	16 58	18 52
N 10	327 57.8	1 00.1	355 21.3	7.0	8 27.2	10.6	61.0	68	18 08	19 04	20 13	13 25	15 12	17 01	18 50
E 11	342 57.9	0 59.1	9 47.3	6.9	8 16.6	10.6	61.0	66	18 08	19 00	20 02	13 39	15 20	17 04	18 47
S 12	357 58.1	S 0 58.1	24 13.2	6.9	S 8 06.0	10.7	61.0	64	18 09	18 56	19 54	13 50	15 27	17 06	18 45
D 13	12 58.3	57.1	38 39.1	7.0	7 55.3	10.7	61.1	62	18 09	18 53	19 46	14 00	15 33	17 08	18 44
A 14	27 58.5	56.1	53 05.1	6.9	7 44.6	10.8	61.1	60	18 09	18 50	19 40	14 08	15 38	17 10	18 42
Y 15	42 58.7	.. 55.1	67 31.0	7.0	7 33.8	10.9	61.1	N 58	18 09	18 48	19 35	14 15	15 42	17 11	18 41
16	57 58.8	54.1	81 57.0	7.0	7 22.9	10.9	61.1	56	18 09	18 46	19 30	14 21	15 46	17 13	18 40
17	72 59.0	53.1	96 23.0	7.0	7 12.0	11.0	61.1	54	18 09	18 44	19 26	14 27	15 49	17 14	18 39
18	87 59.2	S 0 52.2	110 49.0	7.0	S 7 01.0	11.0	61.1	52	18 09	18 43	19 22	14 32	15 52	17 15	18 38
19	102 59.4	51.2	125 15.0	7.0	6 50.0	11.1	61.1	50	18 09	18 41	19 19	14 36	15 55	17 16	18 37
20	117 59.6	50.2	139 41.0	7.0	6 38.9	11.1	61.2	45	18 09	18 39	19 13	14 46	16 01	17 18	18 35
21	132 59.7	.. 49.2	154 07.0	7.0	6 27.8	11.2	61.2	N 40	18 10	18 37	19 08	14 55	16 07	17 20	18 33
22	147 59.9	48.2	168 33.0	7.1	6 16.6	11.2	61.2	35	18 10	18 35	19 04	15 02	16 11	17 22	18 32
23	163 00.1	47.2	182 59.0	7.1	6 05.4	11.2	61.2	30	18 10	18 34	19 02	15 08	16 15	17 23	18 31
19 00	178 00.3	S 0 46.2	197 25.1	7.0	S 5 54.2	11.3	61.2	20	18 10	18 32	18 58	15 18	16 22	17 25	18 29
01	193 00.5	45.2	211 51.1	7.1	5 42.9	11.4	61.2	N 10	18 11	18 32	18 56	15 27	16 27	17 27	18 27
02	208 00.6	44.2	226 17.2	7.1	5 31.5	11.4	61.2	0	18 11	18 32	18 56	15 36	16 33	17 29	18 25
03	223 00.8	.. 43.3	240 43.3	7.1	5 20.1	11.4	61.2	S 10	18 12	18 33	18 57	15 44	16 38	17 31	18 23
04	238 01.0	42.3	255 09.4	7.1	5 08.7	11.5	61.3	20	18 13	18 35	19 00	15 53	16 44	17 33	18 21
05	253 01.2	41.3	269 35.5	7.1	4 57.2	11.5	61.3	30	18 14	18 38	19 06	16 04	16 50	17 35	18 19
06	268 01.4	S 0 40.3	284 01.6	7.1	S 4 45.7	11.5	61.3	35	18 15	18 40	19 09	16 10	16 54	17 36	18 18
T 07	283 01.6	39.3	298 27.7	7.1	4 34.2	11.6	61.3	40	18 15	18 42	19 14	16 16	16 58	17 38	18 17
H 08	298 01.7	38.3	312 53.8	7.1	4 22.6	11.6	61.3	45	18 16	18 46	19 20	16 24	17 03	17 39	18 15
U 09	313 01.9	.. 37.3	327 19.9	7.2	4 11.0	11.6	61.3	S 50	18 17	18 50	19 28	16 33	17 08	17 41	18 13
R 10	328 02.1	36.3	341 46.1	7.1	3 59.4	11.7	61.3	52	18 18	18 52	19 32	16 37	17 11	17 42	18 12
S 11	343 02.3	35.3	356 12.2	7.2	3 47.7	11.7	61.3	54	18 18	18 54	19 36	16 42	17 14	17 43	18 11
D 12	358 02.5	S 0 34.4	10 38.4	7.1	S 3 36.0	11.7	61.3	56	18 19	18 56	19 41	16 47	17 17	17 44	18 10
A 13	13 02.6	33.4	25 04.5	7.2	3 24.3	11.7	61.3	58	18 20	18 59	19 46	16 53	17 20	17 45	18 09
Y 14	28 02.8	32.4	39 30.7	7.2	3 12.6	11.8	61.3	S 60	18 21	19 02	19 53	16 59	17 24	17 46	18 07
15	43 03.0	.. 31.4	53 56.9	7.2	3 00.8	11.8	61.3								
16	58 03.2	30.4	68 23.1	7.2	2 49.0	11.8	61.3								
17	73 03.4	29.4	82 49.3	7.2	2 37.2	11.8	61.3								

									SUN			MOON			
18	88 03.6	S 0 28.4	97 15.5	7.3	S 2 25.4	11.9	61.3	Day	Eqn. of Time		Mer.	Mer. Pass.		Age	Phase
19	103 03.7	27.4	111 41.8	7.2	2 13.5	11.8	61.3		00h	12h	Pass.	Upper	Lower		
20	118 03.9	26.4	126 08.0	7.2	2 01.7	11.9	61.3	d	m s	m s	h m	h m	h m	d	%
21	133 04.1	.. 25.5	140 34.2	7.3	1 49.8	11.9	61.3	17	08 34	08 25	12 08	09 22	21 51	27	12
22	148 04.3	24.5	155 00.5	7.2	1 37.9	11.8	61.3	18	08 17	08 08	12 08	10 19	22 48	28	6
23	163 04.5	23.5	169 26.7	7.3	S 1 26.1	11.9	61.3	19	07 59	07 51	12 08	11 16	23 44	29	1
	SD 16.1	d 1.0	SD 16.5		16.6		16.7									

UT (d h)	ARIES GHA	VENUS −4.0 GHA	VENUS Dec	MARS +1.3 GHA	MARS Dec	JUPITER −2.4 GHA	JUPITER Dec	SATURN +0.4 GHA	SATURN Dec	STARS Name	SHA	Dec
20 00	177 12.7	146 24.4	N12 45.9	157 26.6	N 8 03.3	41 15.2	N17 47.4	293 50.9	S19 02.1	Acamar	315 17.8	S40 15.0
01	192 15.1	161 24.0	47.0	172 27.3	04.0	56 17.9	47.4	308 53.4	02.1	Achernar	335 26.5	S57 09.8
02	207 17.6	176 23.6	48.2	187 28.0	04.8	71 20.5	47.5	323 55.9	02.1	Acrux	173 07.1	S63 11.0
03	222 20.1	191 23.2	. . 49.3	202 28.8	. . 05.5	86 23.1	. . 47.5	338 58.4	. . 02.1	Adhara	255 11.5	S29 00.0
04	237 22.5	206 22.8	50.5	217 29.5	06.2	101 25.7	47.6	354 00.9	02.1	Aldebaran	290 48.1	N16 32.2
05	252 25.0	221 22.4	51.6	232 30.2	06.9	116 28.3	47.6	9 03.3	02.1			
06	267 27.5	236 22.0	N12 52.8	247 30.9	N 8 07.7	131 30.9	N17 47.6	24 05.8	S19 02.1	Alioth	166 19.2	N55 52.5
07	282 29.9	251 21.6	53.9	262 31.6	08.4	146 33.6	47.7	39 08.3	02.1	Alkaid	152 57.6	N49 14.1
08	297 32.4	266 21.2	55.1	277 32.3	09.1	161 36.2	47.7	54 10.8	02.1	Al Na'ir	27 42.7	S46 53.1
F 09	312 34.8	281 20.9	. . 56.2	292 33.1	. . 09.9	176 38.8	. . 47.8	69 13.3	. . 02.0	Alnilam	275 45.2	S 1 11.9
R 10	327 37.3	296 20.5	57.4	307 33.8	10.6	191 41.4	47.8	84 15.8	02.0	Alphard	217 54.7	S 8 43.8
I 11	342 39.8	311 20.1	58.5	322 34.5	11.3	206 44.0	47.8	99 18.3	02.0			
D 12	357 42.2	326 19.7	N12 59.7	337 35.2	N 8 12.0	221 46.6	N17 47.9	114 20.8	S19 02.0	Alphecca	126 09.8	N26 39.7
A 13	12 44.7	341 19.3	13 00.8	352 35.9	12.8	236 49.3	47.9	129 23.3	02.0	Alpheratz	357 42.6	N29 10.4
Y 14	27 47.2	356 18.9	02.0	7 36.6	13.5	251 51.9	48.0	144 25.7	02.0	Altair	62 07.2	N 8 54.5
15	42 49.6	11 18.5	. . 03.1	22 37.4	. . 14.2	266 54.5	. . 48.0	159 28.2	. . 02.0	Ankaa	353 15.0	S42 13.5
16	57 52.1	26 18.1	04.3	37 38.1	14.9	281 57.1	48.1	174 30.7	02.0	Antares	112 24.6	S26 27.7
17	72 54.6	41 17.7	05.4	52 38.8	15.7	296 59.7	48.1	189 33.2	02.0			
18	87 57.0	56 17.3	N13 06.6	67 39.5	N 8 16.4	312 02.3	N17 48.1	204 35.7	S19 01.9	Arcturus	145 54.4	N19 06.1
19	102 59.5	71 16.9	07.7	82 40.2	17.1	327 04.9	48.2	219 38.2	01.9	Atria	107 25.2	S69 02.9
20	118 01.9	86 16.5	08.9	97 40.9	17.8	342 07.6	48.2	234 40.7	01.9	Avior	234 17.1	S59 33.9
21	133 04.4	101 16.1	. . 10.0	112 41.7	. . 18.6	357 10.2	. . 48.3	249 43.2	. . 01.9	Bellatrix	278 30.8	N 6 21.5
22	148 06.9	116 15.7	11.2	127 42.4	19.3	12 12.8	48.3	264 45.7	01.9	Betelgeuse	271 00.0	N 7 24.3
23	163 09.3	131 15.3	12.3	142 43.1	20.0	27 15.4	48.3	279 48.2	01.9			
21 00	178 11.8	146 14.9	N13 13.5	157 43.8	N 8 20.8	42 18.0	N17 48.4	294 50.6	S19 01.9	Canopus	263 55.6	S52 42.7
01	193 14.3	161 14.5	14.6	172 44.5	21.5	57 20.6	48.4	309 53.1	01.9	Capella	280 32.7	N46 00.7
02	208 16.7	176 14.1	15.7	187 45.2	22.2	72 23.2	48.5	324 55.6	01.9	Deneb	49 30.9	N45 20.0
03	223 19.2	191 13.7	. . 16.9	202 46.0	. . 22.9	87 25.8	. . 48.5	339 58.1	. . 01.8	Denebola	182 32.1	N14 29.1
04	238 21.7	206 13.3	18.0	217 46.7	23.7	102 28.4	48.5	355 00.6	01.8	Diphda	348 55.0	S17 54.4
05	253 24.1	221 12.9	19.2	232 47.4	24.4	117 31.1	48.6	10 03.1	01.8			
06	268 26.6	236 12.6	N13 20.3	247 48.1	N 8 25.1	132 33.7	N17 48.6	25 05.6	S19 01.8	Dubhe	193 49.7	N61 40.1
07	283 29.1	251 12.2	21.4	262 48.8	25.8	147 36.3	48.6	40 08.1	01.8	Elnath	278 11.1	N28 37.0
08	298 31.5	266 11.8	22.6	277 49.5	26.5	162 38.9	48.7	55 10.6	01.8	Eltanin	90 45.6	N51 29.1
S 09	313 34.0	281 11.4	. . 23.7	292 50.3	. . 27.3	177 41.5	. . 48.7	70 13.1	. . 01.8	Enif	33 46.2	N 9 56.7
A 10	328 36.4	296 11.0	24.9	307 51.0	28.0	192 44.1	48.8	85 15.6	01.8	Fomalhaut	15 23.0	S29 32.5
T 11	343 38.9	311 10.6	26.0	322 51.7	28.7	207 46.7	48.8	100 18.1	01.8			
U 12	358 41.4	326 10.2	N13 27.1	337 52.4	N 8 29.4	222 49.3	N17 48.8	115 20.5	S19 01.7	Gacrux	171 58.9	S57 11.9
R 13	13 43.8	341 09.8	28.3	352 53.1	30.2	237 51.9	48.9	130 23.0	01.7	Gienah	175 50.7	S17 37.7
D 14	28 46.3	356 09.4	29.4	7 53.8	30.9	252 54.5	48.9	145 25.5	01.7	Hadar	148 45.5	S60 26.6
A 15	43 48.8	11 09.0	. . 30.6	22 54.6	. . 31.6	267 57.1	. . 49.0	160 28.0	. . 01.7	Hamal	327 59.7	N23 31.9
Y 16	58 51.2	26 08.6	31.7	37 55.3	32.3	282 59.8	49.0	175 30.5	01.7	Kaus Aust.	83 42.3	S34 22.4
17	73 53.7	41 08.1	32.8	52 56.0	33.1	298 02.4	49.0	190 33.0	01.7			
18	88 56.2	56 07.7	N13 34.0	67 56.7	N 8 33.8	313 05.0	N17 49.1	205 35.5	S19 01.7	Kochab	137 19.4	N74 05.4
19	103 58.6	71 07.3	35.1	82 57.4	34.5	328 07.6	49.1	220 38.0	01.7	Markab	13 37.4	N15 17.1
20	119 01.1	86 06.9	36.2	97 58.1	35.2	343 10.2	49.1	235 40.5	01.7	Menkar	314 14.0	N 4 08.7
21	134 03.5	101 06.5	. . 37.4	112 58.9	. . 35.9	358 12.8	. . 49.2	250 43.0	. . 01.6	Menkent	148 05.8	S36 26.6
22	149 06.0	116 06.1	38.5	127 59.6	36.7	13 15.4	49.2	265 45.5	01.6	Miaplacidus	221 38.6	S69 47.2
23	164 08.5	131 05.7	39.6	143 00.3	37.4	28 18.0	49.3	280 48.0	01.6			
22 00	179 10.9	146 05.3	N13 40.7	158 01.0	N 8 38.1	43 20.6	N17 49.3	295 50.5	S19 01.6	Mirfak	308 38.9	N49 54.9
01	194 13.4	161 04.9	41.9	173 01.7	38.8	58 23.2	49.3	310 53.0	01.6	Nunki	75 56.9	S26 16.4
02	209 15.9	176 04.5	43.0	188 02.4	39.6	73 25.8	49.4	325 55.5	01.6	Peacock	53 17.8	S56 40.8
03	224 18.3	191 04.1	. . 44.1	203 03.2	. . 40.3	88 28.4	. . 49.4	340 58.0	. . 01.6	Pollux	243 26.1	N27 59.2
04	239 20.8	206 03.7	45.3	218 03.9	41.0	103 31.0	49.4	356 00.5	01.6	Procyon	244 58.4	N 5 10.8
05	254 23.3	221 03.3	46.4	233 04.6	41.7	118 33.6	49.5	11 03.0	01.5			
06	269 25.7	236 02.9	N13 47.5	248 05.3	N 8 42.4	133 36.2	N17 49.5	26 05.5	S19 01.5	Rasalhague	96 05.3	N12 32.9
07	284 28.2	251 02.5	48.7	263 06.0	43.2	148 38.8	49.6	41 07.9	01.5	Regulus	207 42.0	N11 53.3
08	299 30.7	266 02.1	49.8	278 06.7	43.9	163 41.4	49.6	56 10.4	01.5	Rigel	281 11.0	S 8 11.4
S 09	314 33.1	281 01.7	. . 50.9	293 07.4	. . 44.6	178 44.0	. . 49.6	71 12.9	. . 01.5	Rigil Kent.	139 49.5	S60 53.6
U 10	329 35.6	296 01.3	52.0	308 08.2	45.3	193 46.6	49.7	86 15.4	01.5	Sabik	102 11.1	S15 44.5
N 11	344 38.0	311 00.9	53.2	323 08.9	46.0	208 49.2	49.7	101 17.9	01.5			
D 12	359 40.5	326 00.5	N13 54.3	338 09.6	N 8 46.8	223 51.8	N17 49.7	116 20.4	S19 01.5	Schedar	349 39.6	N56 37.2
A 13	14 43.0	341 00.0	55.4	353 10.3	47.5	238 54.4	49.8	131 22.9	01.4	Shaula	96 20.2	S37 06.6
Y 14	29 45.4	355 59.6	56.5	8 11.0	48.2	253 57.0	49.8	146 25.4	01.4	Sirius	258 32.6	S16 44.6
15	44 47.9	10 59.2	. . 57.6	23 11.7	. . 48.9	268 59.6	. . 49.8	161 27.9	. . 01.4	Spica	158 29.7	S11 14.5
16	59 50.4	25 58.8	58.8	38 12.5	49.6	284 02.2	49.9	176 30.4	01.4	Suhail	222 51.2	S43 30.0
17	74 52.8	40 58.4	13 59.9	53 13.2	50.4	299 04.8	49.9	191 32.9	01.4			
18	89 55.3	55 58.0	N14 01.0	68 13.9	N 8 51.1	314 07.4	N17 50.0	206 35.4	S19 01.4	Vega	80 38.2	N38 47.8
19	104 57.8	70 57.6	02.1	83 14.6	51.8	329 10.0	50.0	221 37.9	01.4	Zuben'ubi	137 03.8	S16 06.2
20	120 00.2	85 57.2	03.3	98 15.3	52.5	344 12.6	50.0	236 40.4	01.4		SHA	Mer. Pass.
21	135 02.7	100 56.8	. . 04.4	113 16.0	. . 53.2	359 15.2	. . 50.1	251 42.9	. . 01.3		o ′	h m
22	150 05.1	115 56.4	05.5	128 16.7	53.9	14 17.8	50.1	266 45.4	01.3	Venus	328 03.1	14 15
23	165 07.6	130 56.0	06.6	143 17.5	54.7	29 20.4	50.1	281 47.9	01.3	Mars	339 32.0	13 28
	h m									Jupiter	224 06.2	21 07
Mer. Pass.	12 05.2	v −0.4	d 1.1	v 0.7	d 0.7	v 2.6	d 0.0	v 2.5	d 0.0	Saturn	116 38.8	4 20

UT	SUN GHA	SUN Dec	MOON GHA	v	MOON Dec	d	HP
d h	° ′	° ′	° ′	′	° ′	′	′
20 00	178 04.6	S 0 22.5	183 53.0	7.3	S 1 14.2	12.0	61.3
01	193 04.8	21.5	198 19.3	7.2	1 02.2	11.9	61.3
02	208 05.0	20.5	212 45.5	7.3	0 50.3	11.9	61.3
03	223 05.2	.. 19.5	227 11.8	7.3	0 38.4	11.9	61.3
04	238 05.4	18.5	241 38.1	7.3	0 26.5	11.9	61.3
05	253 05.6	17.5	256 04.4	7.3	S 0 14.6	11.9	61.3
06	268 05.7	S 0 16.6					
07	283 05.9	15.6					
08	298 06.1	14.6	A total eclipse of				
F 09	313 06.3	.. 13.6	the Sun occurs on this				
R 10	328 06.5	12.6	date. See page 5.				
I 11	343 06.7	11.6					
D 12	358 06.8	S 0 10.6	357 08.7	7.4	N 1 08.8	11.8	61.2
A 13	13 07.0	09.6	11 35.1	7.3	1 20.6	11.9	61.2
Y 14	28 07.2	08.6	26 01.4	7.4	1 32.5	11.9	61.2
15	43 07.4	.. 07.7	40 27.8	7.4	1 44.4	11.8	61.2
16	58 07.6	06.7	54 54.2	7.4	1 56.2	11.8	61.2
17	73 07.8	05.7	69 20.6	7.3	2 08.0	11.8	61.2
18	88 07.9	S 0 04.7	83 46.9	7.4	N 2 19.8	11.8	61.2
19	103 08.1	03.7	98 13.3	7.4	2 31.6	11.7	61.2
20	118 08.3	02.7	112 39.7	7.4	2 43.3	11.7	61.2
21	133 08.5	.. 01.7	127 06.1	7.4	2 55.0	11.7	61.1
22	148 08.7	S 00.7	141 32.5	7.5	3 06.7	11.7	61.1
23	163 08.9	N 00.2	155 59.0	7.4	3 18.4	11.7	61.1
21 00	178 09.1	N 0 01.2	170 25.4	7.4	N 3 30.1	11.6	61.1
01	193 09.2	02.2	184 51.8	7.4	3 41.7	11.6	61.1
02	208 09.4	03.2	199 18.2	7.5	3 53.3	11.5	61.1
03	223 09.6	.. 04.2	213 44.6	7.5	4 04.8	11.5	61.0
04	238 09.8	05.2	228 11.1	7.4	4 16.3	11.5	61.0
05	253 10.0	06.2	242 37.5	7.5	4 27.8	11.5	61.0
06	268 10.2	N 0 07.2	257 04.0	7.4	N 4 39.3	11.4	61.0
S 07	283 10.3	08.1	271 30.4	7.5	4 50.7	11.4	61.0
A 08	298 10.5	09.1	285 56.9	7.4	5 02.1	11.3	60.9
T 09	313 10.7	.. 10.1	300 23.3	7.5	5 13.4	11.3	60.9
U 10	328 10.9	11.1	314 49.8	7.4	5 24.7	11.2	60.9
R 11	343 11.1	12.1	329 16.2	7.5	5 35.9	11.2	60.9
D 12	358 11.3	N 0 13.1	343 42.7	7.5	N 5 47.1	11.2	60.9
A 13	13 11.4	14.1	358 09.2	7.5	5 58.3	11.1	60.8
Y 14	28 11.6	15.1	12 35.7	7.4	6 09.4	11.0	60.8
15	43 11.8	.. 16.1	27 02.1	7.5	6 20.4	11.0	60.8
16	58 12.0	17.0	41 28.6	7.5	6 31.4	11.0	60.8
17	73 12.2	18.0	55 55.1	7.5	6 42.4	10.9	60.7
18	88 12.4	N 0 19.0	70 21.6	7.5	N 6 53.3	10.8	60.7
19	103 12.6	20.0	84 48.1	7.5	7 04.1	10.8	60.7
20	118 12.7	21.0	99 14.6	7.5	7 14.9	10.8	60.7
21	133 12.9	.. 22.0	113 41.1	7.5	7 25.7	10.6	60.6
22	148 13.1	23.0	128 07.6	7.5	7 36.3	10.7	60.6
23	163 13.3	24.0	142 34.1	7.5	7 47.0	10.5	60.6
22 00	178 13.5	N 0 24.9	157 00.6	7.5	N 7 57.5	10.5	60.6
01	193 13.7	25.9	171 27.1	7.6	8 08.0	10.4	60.5
02	208 13.9	26.9	185 53.7	7.5	8 18.4	10.4	60.5
03	223 14.0	.. 27.9	200 20.2	7.5	8 28.8	10.3	60.5
04	238 14.2	28.9	214 46.7	7.5	8 39.1	10.2	60.4
05	253 14.4	29.9	229 13.2	7.6	8 49.3	10.2	60.4
06	268 14.6	N 0 30.9	243 39.8	7.5	N 8 59.5	10.1	60.4
07	283 14.8	31.9	258 06.3	7.6	9 09.6	10.0	60.4
08	298 15.0	32.8	272 32.9	7.5	9 19.6	10.0	60.3
S 09	313 15.2	.. 33.8	286 59.4	7.6	9 29.6	9.9	60.3
U 10	328 15.3	34.8	301 26.0	7.5	9 39.5	9.8	60.3
N 11	343 15.5	35.8	315 52.5	7.6	9 49.3	9.7	60.2
D 12	358 15.7	N 0 36.8	330 19.1	7.6	N 9 59.0	9.7	60.2
A 13	13 15.9	37.8	344 45.7	7.6	10 08.7	9.6	60.2
Y 14	28 16.1	38.8	359 12.3	7.5	10 18.3	9.5	60.1
15	43 16.3	.. 39.7	13 38.8	7.6	10 27.8	9.4	60.1
16	58 16.5	40.7	28 05.4	7.6	10 37.2	9.4	60.1
17	73 16.6	41.7	42 32.0	7.6	10 46.6	9.3	60.0
18	88 16.8	N 0 42.7	56 58.6	7.6	N10 55.9	9.2	60.0
19	103 17.0	43.7	71 25.2	7.6	11 05.1	9.1	60.0
20	118 17.2	44.7	85 51.8	7.6	11 14.2	9.0	59.9
21	133 17.4	.. 45.7	100 18.4	7.7	11 23.2	8.9	59.9
22	148 17.6	46.7	114 45.1	7.6	11 32.1	8.9	59.9
23	163 17.8	47.6	129 11.7	7.6	N11 41.0	8.8	59.8
	SD 16.1	d 1.0	SD 16.7		16.6		16.4

Lat.	Twilight Naut.	Twilight Civil	Sunrise	Moonrise 20	21	22	23
°	h m	h m	h m	h m	h m	h m	h m
N 72	03 17	04 47	05 55	06 01	05 56	05 51	05 46
N 70	03 37	04 55	05 56	06 00	06 02	06 04	06 08
68	03 52	05 01	05 57	06 00	06 07	06 15	06 26
66	04 03	05 07	05 58	06 00	06 11	06 24	06 40
64	04 13	05 11	05 59	06 00	06 15	06 32	06 51
62	04 21	05 15	05 59	06 00	06 18	06 38	07 01
60	04 28	05 18	06 00	06 00	06 21	06 44	07 10
N 58	04 34	05 21	06 00	06 00	06 23	06 49	07 17
56	04 39	05 24	06 01	05 59	06 26	06 53	07 24
54	04 44	05 26	06 01	05 59	06 28	06 57	07 30
52	04 48	05 28	06 01	05 59	06 30	07 01	07 35
50	04 51	05 29	06 02	05 59	06 31	07 04	07 40
45	04 59	05 33	06 02	05 59	06 35	07 12	07 51
N 40	05 04	05 36	06 03	05 59	06 38	07 18	08 00
35	05 08	05 38	06 03	05 59	06 41	07 23	08 07
30	05 12	05 39	06 03	05 59	06 43	07 28	08 14
20	05 16	05 42	06 04	05 59	06 47	07 36	08 26
N 10	05 19	05 43	06 04	05 59	06 51	07 43	08 36
0	05 19	05 43	06 04	05 59	06 54	07 50	08 46
S 10	05 19	05 43	06 04	05 59	06 58	07 57	08 55
20	05 16	05 42	06 04	05 59	07 02	08 04	09 06
30	05 12	05 40	06 04	05 59	07 06	08 13	09 18
35	05 09	05 38	06 04	05 59	07 09	08 18	09 25
40	05 05	05 36	06 03	05 59	07 12	08 23	09 33
45	04 59	05 34	06 03	05 59	07 15	08 30	09 42
S 50	04 52	05 30	06 03	05 59	07 19	08 38	09 53
52	04 49	05 29	06 03	05 59	07 21	08 42	09 59
54	04 45	05 27	06 02	05 59	07 23	08 46	10 04
56	04 41	05 25	06 02	05 59	07 26	08 50	10 11
58	04 36	05 23	06 02	05 59	07 28	08 55	10 18
S 60	04 30	05 20	06 01	05 59	07 31	09 01	10 26

Lat.	Sunset	Twilight Civil	Twilight Naut.	Moonset 20	21	22	23
°	h m	h m	h m	h m	h m	h m	h m
N 72	18 22	19 31	21 02	18 56	20 57	22 58	24 59
N 70	18 20	19 22	20 42	18 52	20 46	22 38	24 25
68	18 19	19 15	20 26	18 50	20 37	22 22	24 01
66	18 18	19 10	20 14	18 47	20 30	22 09	23 42
64	18 17	19 05	20 04	18 45	20 23	21 58	23 27
62	18 17	19 01	19 55	18 44	20 18	21 49	23 15
60	18 16	18 58	19 48	18 42	20 13	21 41	23 04
N 58	18 16	18 55	19 42	18 41	20 09	21 35	22 55
56	18 15	18 52	19 37	18 40	20 06	21 29	22 47
54	18 15	18 50	19 32	18 39	20 02	21 23	22 39
52	18 14	18 48	19 28	18 38	19 59	21 18	22 33
50	18 14	18 46	19 24	18 37	19 57	21 14	22 27
45	18 13	18 43	19 17	18 35	19 51	21 05	22 15
N 40	18 13	18 40	19 11	18 33	19 46	20 57	22 04
35	18 12	18 37	19 07	18 32	19 42	20 50	21 55
30	18 12	18 36	19 04	18 31	19 38	20 44	21 48
20	18 11	18 33	18 59	18 29	19 32	20 34	21 34
N 10	18 11	18 32	18 56	18 27	19 26	20 25	21 23
0	18 11	18 31	18 55	18 25	19 21	20 17	21 12
S 10	18 10	18 31	18 56	18 23	19 16	20 08	21 01
20	18 10	18 32	18 58	18 21	19 10	19 59	20 49
30	18 10	18 34	19 02	18 19	19 04	19 49	20 36
35	18 10	18 36	19 05	18 18	19 00	19 43	20 28
40	18 10	18 37	19 09	18 17	18 56	19 37	20 20
45	18 11	18 40	19 14	18 15	18 51	19 29	20 09
S 50	18 11	18 43	19 21	18 13	18 45	19 20	19 57
52	18 11	18 45	19 24	18 12	18 43	19 16	19 52
54	18 11	18 46	19 28	18 11	18 40	19 11	19 45
56	18 11	18 48	19 32	18 10	18 37	19 06	19 38
58	18 11	18 51	19 37	18 09	18 33	19 00	19 31
S 60	18 12	18 53	19 43	18 07	18 29	18 53	19 22

	SUN			MOON			
Day	Eqn. of Time 00ʰ	12ʰ	Mer. Pass.	Mer. Pass. Upper	Lower	Age	Phase
d	m s	m s	h m	h m	h m	d	%
20	07 42	07 33	12 08	12 12	24 40	00	0
21	07 24	07 15	12 07	13 08	00 40	01	2
22	07 06	06 58	12 07	14 03	01 36	02	6

UT	ARIES	VENUS −4.0		MARS +1.4		JUPITER −2.4		SATURN +0.3		STARS		
d h	GHA	GHA	Dec	GHA	Dec	GHA	Dec	GHA	Dec	Name	SHA	Dec
	° ′	° ′	° ′	° ′	° ′	° ′	° ′	° ′	° ′		° ′	° ′
23 00	180 10.1	145 55.5	N14 07.7	158 18.2	N 8 55.4	44 23.0	N17 50.2	296 50.4	S19 01.3	Acamar	315 17.8	S40 15.0
01	195 12.5	160 55.1	08.8	173 18.9	56.1	59 25.6	50.2	311 52.9	01.3	Achernar	335 26.5	S57 09.8
02	210 15.0	175 54.7	10.0	188 19.6	56.8	74 28.2	50.2	326 55.4	01.3	Acrux	173 07.1	S63 11.1
03	225 17.5	190 54.3 ..	11.1	203 20.3 ..	57.5	89 30.8 ..	50.3	341 57.9 ..	01.3	Adhara	255 11.5	S29 00.0
04	240 19.9	205 53.9	12.2	218 21.0	58.2	104 33.4	50.3	357 00.4	01.3	Aldebaran	290 48.1	N16 32.1
05	255 22.4	220 53.5	13.3	233 21.8	59.0	119 36.0	50.3	12 02.9	01.2			
M 06	270 24.9	235 53.1	N14 14.4	248 22.5	N 8 59.7	134 38.6	N17 50.4	27 05.4	S19 01.2	Alioth	166 19.2	N55 52.5
O 07	285 27.3	250 52.6	15.5	263 23.2	9 00.4	149 41.2	50.4	42 07.9	01.2	Alkaid	152 57.6	N49 14.1
N 08	300 29.8	265 52.2	16.6	278 23.9	01.1	164 43.8	50.4	57 10.4	01.2	Al Na'ir	27 42.7	S46 53.1
D 09	315 32.3	280 51.8 ..	17.8	293 24.6 ..	01.8	179 46.4 ..	50.5	72 12.9 ..	01.2	Alnilam	275 45.2	S 1 11.9
A 10	330 34.7	295 51.4	18.9	308 25.3	02.5	194 49.0	50.5	87 15.4	01.2	Alphard	217 54.7	S 8 43.8
Y 11	345 37.2	310 51.0	20.0	323 26.0	03.3	209 51.5	50.5	102 17.9	01.2			
12	0 39.6	325 50.6	N14 21.1	338 26.8	N 9 04.0	224 54.1	N17 50.6	117 20.4	S19 01.2	Alphecca	126 09.8	N26 39.7
13	15 42.1	340 50.2	22.2	353 27.5	04.7	239 56.7	50.6	132 22.9	01.1	Alpheratz	357 42.6	N29 10.4
14	30 44.6	355 49.7	23.3	8 28.2	05.4	254 59.3	50.6	147 25.4	01.1	Altair	62 07.2	N 8 54.5
15	45 47.0	10 49.3 ..	24.4	23 28.9 ..	06.1	270 01.9 ..	50.7	162 27.9 ..	01.1	Ankaa	353 15.0	S42 13.5
16	60 49.5	25 48.9	25.5	38 29.6	06.8	285 04.5	50.7	177 30.4	01.1	Antares	112 24.6	S26 27.7
17	75 52.0	40 48.5	26.6	53 30.3	07.5	300 07.1	50.7	192 32.9	01.1			
18	90 54.4	55 48.1	N14 27.7	68 31.0	N 9 08.3	315 09.7	N17 50.8	207 35.4	S19 01.1	Arcturus	145 54.4	N19 06.1
19	105 56.9	70 47.7	28.8	83 31.8	09.0	330 12.3	50.8	222 37.9	01.1	Atria	107 25.1	S69 02.9
20	120 59.4	85 47.2	30.0	98 32.5	09.7	345 14.9	50.8	237 40.4	01.1	Avior	234 17.1	S59 34.0
21	136 01.8	100 46.8 ..	31.1	113 33.2 ..	10.4	0 17.5 ..	50.9	252 42.9 ..	01.0	Bellatrix	278 30.8	N 6 21.5
22	151 04.3	115 46.4	32.2	128 33.9	11.1	15 20.0	50.9	267 45.4	01.0	Betelgeuse	271 00.0	N 7 24.3
23	166 06.8	130 46.0	33.3	143 34.6	11.8	30 22.6	50.9	282 48.0	01.0			
24 00	181 09.2	145 45.6	N14 34.4	158 35.3	N 9 12.5	45 25.2	N17 51.0	297 50.5	S19 01.0	Canopus	263 55.6	S52 42.7
01	196 11.7	160 45.1	35.5	173 36.0	13.3	60 27.8	51.0	312 53.0	01.0	Capella	280 32.8	N46 00.7
02	211 14.1	175 44.7	36.6	188 36.8	14.0	75 30.4	51.0	327 55.5	01.0	Deneb	49 30.9	N45 20.0
03	226 16.6	190 44.3 ..	37.7	203 37.5 ..	14.7	90 33.0 ..	51.1	342 58.0 ..	01.0	Denebola	182 32.1	N14 29.1
04	241 19.1	205 43.9	38.8	218 38.2	15.4	105 35.6	51.1	358 00.5	00.9	Diphda	348 55.0	S17 54.3
05	256 21.5	220 43.5	39.9	233 38.9	16.1	120 38.2	51.1	13 03.0	00.9			
T 06	271 24.0	235 43.0	N14 41.0	248 39.6	N 9 16.8	135 40.8	N17 51.2	28 05.5	S19 00.9	Dubhe	193 49.7	N61 40.1
U 07	286 26.5	250 42.6	42.1	263 40.3	17.5	150 43.3	51.2	43 08.0	00.9	Elnath	278 11.2	N28 37.0
E 08	301 28.9	265 42.2	43.2	278 41.0	18.2	165 45.9	51.2	58 10.5	00.9	Eltanin	90 45.5	N51 29.1
S 09	316 31.4	280 41.8 ..	44.3	293 41.8 ..	19.0	180 48.5 ..	51.3	73 13.0 ..	00.9	Enif	33 46.2	N 9 56.7
D 10	331 33.9	295 41.4	45.4	308 42.5	19.7	195 51.1	51.3	88 15.5	00.9	Fomalhaut	15 23.0	S29 32.5
A 11	346 36.3	310 40.9	46.5	323 43.2	20.4	210 53.7	51.3	103 18.0	00.9			
Y 12	1 38.8	325 40.5	N14 47.6	338 43.9	N 9 21.1	225 56.3	N17 51.4	118 20.5	S19 00.8	Gacrux	171 58.9	S57 11.9
13	16 41.2	340 40.1	48.7	353 44.6	21.8	240 58.9	51.4	133 23.0	00.8	Gienah	175 50.7	S17 37.7
14	31 43.7	355 39.7	49.8	8 45.3	22.5	256 01.4	51.4	148 25.5	00.8	Hadar	148 45.5	S60 26.6
15	46 46.2	10 39.2 ..	50.8	23 46.0 ..	23.2	271 04.0 ..	51.5	163 28.0 ..	00.8	Hamal	327 59.7	N23 31.9
16	61 48.6	25 38.8	51.9	38 46.7	23.9	286 06.6	51.5	178 30.5	00.8	Kaus Aust.	83 42.2	S34 22.4
17	76 51.1	40 38.4	53.0	53 47.5	24.6	301 09.2	51.5	193 33.0	00.8			
18	91 53.6	55 38.0	N14 54.1	68 48.2	N 9 25.4	316 11.8	N17 51.6	208 35.6	S19 00.8	Kochab	137 19.4	N74 05.4
19	106 56.0	70 37.5	55.2	83 48.9	26.1	331 14.4	51.6	223 38.1	00.7	Markab	13 37.4	N15 17.1
20	121 58.5	85 37.1	56.3	98 49.6	26.8	346 16.9	51.6	238 40.6	00.7	Menkar	314 14.0	N 4 08.7
21	137 01.0	100 36.7 ..	57.4	113 50.3 ..	27.5	1 19.5 ..	51.6	253 43.1 ..	00.7	Menkent	148 05.8	S36 26.6
22	152 03.4	115 36.3	58.5	128 51.0	28.2	16 22.1	51.7	268 45.6	00.7	Miaplacidus	221 38.6	S69 47.2
23	167 05.9	130 35.8	14 59.6	143 51.7	28.9	31 24.7	51.7	283 48.1	00.7			
25 00	182 08.4	145 35.4	N15 00.7	158 52.5	N 9 29.6	46 27.3	N17 51.7	298 50.6	S19 00.7	Mirfak	308 38.9	N49 54.8
01	197 10.8	160 35.0	01.8	173 53.2	30.3	61 29.9	51.7	313 53.1	00.7	Nunki	75 56.9	S26 16.4
02	212 13.3	175 34.5	02.8	188 53.9	31.0	76 32.4	51.8	328 55.6	00.6	Peacock	53 17.7	S56 40.8
03	227 15.7	190 34.1 ..	03.9	203 54.6 ..	31.7	91 35.0 ..	51.8	343 58.1 ..	00.6	Pollux	243 26.2	N27 59.2
04	242 18.2	205 33.7	05.0	218 55.3	32.4	106 37.6	51.9	359 00.6	00.6	Procyon	244 58.4	N 5 10.8
05	257 20.7	220 33.3	06.1	233 56.0	33.2	121 40.2	51.9	14 03.1	00.6			
W 06	272 23.1	235 32.8	N15 07.2	248 56.7	N 9 33.9	136 42.7	N17 51.9	29 05.7	S19 00.6	Rasalhague	96 05.3	N12 32.9
E 07	287 25.6	250 32.4	08.3	263 57.4	34.6	151 45.3	51.9	44 08.2	00.6	Regulus	207 42.0	N11 53.4
D 08	302 28.1	265 32.0	09.4	278 58.2	35.3	166 47.9	52.0	59 10.7	00.6	Rigel	281 11.0	S 8 11.4
N 09	317 30.5	280 31.5 ..	10.4	293 58.9 ..	36.0	181 50.5 ..	52.0	74 13.2 ..	00.6	Rigil Kent.	139 49.5	S60 53.6
E 10	332 33.0	295 31.1	11.5	308 59.6	36.7	196 53.1	52.0	89 15.7	00.5	Sabik	102 11.1	S15 44.5
S 11	347 35.5	310 30.7	12.6	324 00.3	37.4	211 55.6	52.1	104 18.2	00.5			
D 12	2 37.9	325 30.2	N15 13.7	339 01.0	N 9 38.1	226 58.2	N17 52.1	119 20.7	S19 00.5	Schedar	349 39.6	N56 37.2
A 13	17 40.4	340 29.8	14.8	354 01.7	38.8	242 00.8	52.1	134 23.2	00.5	Shaula	96 20.2	S37 06.6
Y 14	32 42.9	355 29.4	15.8	9 02.4	39.5	257 03.4	52.2	149 25.7	00.5	Sirius	258 32.6	S16 44.6
15	47 45.3	10 29.0 ..	16.9	24 03.1 ..	40.2	272 05.9 ..	52.2	164 28.2 ..	00.5	Spica	158 29.7	S11 14.5
16	62 47.8	25 28.5	18.0	39 03.9	40.9	287 08.5	52.2	179 30.8	00.5	Suhail	222 51.2	S43 30.0
17	77 50.2	40 28.1	19.1	54 04.6	41.6	302 11.1	52.2	194 33.3	00.4			
18	92 52.7	55 27.7	N15 20.2	69 05.3	N 9 42.3	317 13.7	N17 52.3	209 35.8	S19 00.4	Vega	80 38.2	N38 47.8
19	107 55.2	70 27.2	21.2	84 06.0	43.0	332 16.2	52.3	224 38.3	00.4	Zuben'ubi	137 03.8	S16 06.2
20	122 57.6	85 26.8	22.3	99 06.7	43.8	347 18.8	52.3	239 40.8	00.4		SHA	Mer.Pass.
21	138 00.1	100 26.4 ..	23.4	114 07.4 ..	44.5	2 21.4 ..	52.4	254 43.3 ..	00.4		° ′	h m
22	153 02.6	115 25.9	24.5	129 08.1	45.2	17 24.0	52.4	269 45.8	00.4	Venus	324 36.3	14 17
23	168 05.0	130 25.5	25.5	144 08.8	45.9	32 26.5	52.4	284 48.3	00.3	Mars	337 26.1	13 25
	h m									Jupiter	224 16.0	20 55
Mer.Pass. 11 53.4	v −0.4 d 1.1		v 0.7 d 0.7		v 2.6 d 0.0		v 2.5 d 0.0			Saturn	116 41.2	4 08

UT	SUN GHA	SUN Dec	MOON GHA	v	MOON Dec	d	HP
d h	° '	° '	° '	'	° '	'	'
23 00	178 17.9	N 0 48.6	143 38.3	7.7	N11 49.8	8.7	59.8
01	193 18.1	49.6	158 05.0	7.6	11 58.5	8.6	59.8
02	208 18.3	50.6	172 31.6	7.7	12 07.1	8.5	59.7
03	223 18.5 ..	51.6	186 58.3	7.6	12 15.6	8.4	59.7
04	238 18.7	52.6	201 24.9	7.7	12 24.0	8.4	59.6
05	253 18.9	53.6	215 51.6	7.7	12 32.4	8.2	59.6
06	268 19.1	N 0 54.5	230 18.3	7.7	N12 40.6	8.2	59.6
07	283 19.3	55.5	244 45.0	7.7	12 48.8	8.0	59.5
08	298 19.4	56.5	259 11.7	7.7	12 56.8	8.0	59.5
M 09	313 19.6 ..	57.5	273 38.4	7.7	13 04.8	7.9	59.5
O 10	328 19.8	58.5	288 05.1	7.7	13 12.7	7.8	59.4
N 11	343 20.0	0 59.5	302 31.8	7.8	13 20.5	7.7	59.4
D 12	358 20.2	N 1 00.5	316 58.6	7.7	N13 28.2	7.6	59.3
A 13	13 20.4	01.4	331 25.3	7.8	13 35.8	7.5	59.3
Y 14	28 20.6	02.4	345 52.1	7.8	13 43.3	7.4	59.3
15	43 20.7 ..	03.4	0 18.9	7.8	13 50.7	7.3	59.2
16	58 20.9	04.4	14 45.7	7.8	13 58.0	7.2	59.2
17	73 21.1	05.4	29 12.5	7.8	14 05.2	7.1	59.2
18	88 21.3	N 1 06.4	43 39.3	7.8	N14 12.3	7.0	59.1
19	103 21.5	07.4	58 06.1	7.8	14 19.3	7.0	59.1
20	118 21.7	08.3	72 32.9	7.9	14 26.3	6.8	59.0
21	133 21.9 ..	09.3	86 59.8	7.8	14 33.1	6.7	59.0
22	148 22.1	10.3	101 26.6	7.9	14 39.8	6.6	59.0
23	163 22.2	11.3	115 53.5	7.9	14 46.4	6.6	58.9
24 00	178 22.4	N 1 12.3	130 20.4	7.9	N14 53.0	6.4	58.9
01	193 22.6	13.3	144 47.3	7.9	14 59.4	6.3	58.9
02	208 22.8	14.3	159 14.2	8.0	15 05.7	6.2	58.8
03	223 23.0 ..	15.2	173 41.2	7.9	15 11.9	6.1	58.8
04	238 23.2	16.2	188 08.1	8.0	15 18.0	6.1	58.7
05	253 23.4	17.2	202 35.1	8.0	15 24.1	5.9	58.7
06	268 23.6	N 1 18.2	217 02.1	8.0	N15 30.0	5.8	58.6
07	283 23.7	19.2	231 29.1	8.0	15 35.8	5.7	58.6
T 08	298 23.9	20.2	245 56.1	8.1	15 41.5	5.6	58.6
U 09	313 24.1 ..	21.2	260 23.2	8.0	15 47.1	5.5	58.5
E 10	328 24.3	22.1	274 50.2	8.1	15 52.6	5.4	58.5
S 11	343 24.5	23.1	289 17.3	8.1	15 58.0	5.3	58.4
D 12	358 24.7	N 1 24.1	303 44.4	8.2	N16 03.3	5.2	58.4
A 13	13 24.9	25.1	318 11.6	8.1	16 08.5	5.1	58.4
Y 14	28 25.1	26.1	332 38.7	8.2	16 13.6	5.0	58.3
15	43 25.2 ..	27.1	347 05.9	8.2	16 18.6	4.8	58.3
16	58 25.4	28.0	1 33.1	8.2	16 23.4	4.8	58.2
17	73 25.6	29.0	16 00.3	8.2	16 28.2	4.7	58.2
18	88 25.8	N 1 30.0	30 27.5	8.3	N16 32.9	4.5	58.2
19	103 26.0	31.0	44 54.8	8.2	16 37.4	4.5	58.1
20	118 26.2	32.0	59 22.0	8.3	16 41.9	4.3	58.1
21	133 26.4 ..	33.0	73 49.3	8.4	16 46.2	4.3	58.0
22	148 26.6	34.0	88 16.7	8.3	16 50.5	4.1	58.0
23	163 26.7	34.9	102 44.0	8.4	16 54.6	4.0	57.9
25 00	178 26.9	N 1 35.9	117 11.4	8.4	N16 58.6	4.0	57.9
01	193 27.1	36.9	131 38.8	8.4	17 02.6	3.8	57.9
02	208 27.3	37.9	146 06.2	8.5	17 06.4	3.7	57.8
03	223 27.5 ..	38.9	160 33.7	8.5	17 10.1	3.6	57.8
04	238 27.7	39.9	175 01.2	8.5	17 13.7	3.5	57.7
05	253 27.9	40.8	189 28.7	8.6	17 17.2	3.4	57.7
06	268 28.1	N 1 41.8	203 56.3	8.5	N17 20.6	3.3	57.7
W 07	283 28.2	42.8	218 23.8	8.6	17 23.9	3.2	57.6
E 08	298 28.4	43.8	232 51.4	8.7	17 27.1	3.1	57.6
D 09	313 28.6 ..	44.8	247 19.1	8.6	17 30.2	3.0	57.5
N 10	328 28.8	45.8	261 46.7	8.7	17 33.2	2.8	57.5
E 11	343 29.0	46.7	276 14.4	8.7	17 36.0	2.8	57.5
S 12	358 29.2	N 1 47.7	290 42.1	8.8	N17 38.8	2.7	57.4
D 13	13 29.4	48.7	305 09.9	8.8	17 41.5	2.5	57.4
A 14	28 29.6	49.7	319 37.7	8.8	17 44.0	2.5	57.4
Y 15	43 29.8 ..	50.7	334 05.5	8.9	17 46.5	2.3	57.3
16	58 29.9	51.6	348 33.4	8.9	17 48.8	2.2	57.3
17	73 30.1	52.6	3 01.3	8.9	17 51.0	2.2	57.2
18	88 30.3	N 1 53.6	17 29.2	9.0	N17 53.2	2.0	57.2
19	103 30.5	54.6	31 57.2	8.9	17 55.2	1.9	57.2
20	118 30.7	55.6	46 25.1	9.1	17 57.1	1.9	57.1
21	133 30.9 ..	56.6	60 53.2	9.0	17 59.0	1.7	57.1
22	148 31.1	57.5	75 21.2	9.1	18 00.7	1.6	57.0
23	163 31.3	58.5	89 49.3	9.2	N18 02.3	1.5	57.0
	SD 16.1	d 1.0	SD 16.2		15.9		15.6

Lat.	Twilight Naut.	Twilight Civil	Sunrise	Moonrise 23	Moonrise 24	Moonrise 25	Moonrise 26
°	h m	h m	h m	h m	h m	h m	h m
N 72	02 55	04 30	05 40	05 46	05 41	05 35	▭
N 70	03 19	04 40	05 42	06 08	06 16	06 31	07 03
68	03 36	04 48	05 45	06 26	06 41	07 05	07 44
66	03 50	04 55	05 47	06 40	07 01	07 30	08 12
64	04 01	05 00	05 48	06 51	07 16	07 49	08 33
62	04 10	05 05	05 50	07 01	07 30	08 05	08 50
60	04 18	05 09	05 51	07 10	07 41	08 18	09 04
N 58	04 25	05 12	05 52	07 17	07 50	08 30	09 16
56	04 31	05 16	05 53	07 24	07 59	08 40	09 27
54	04 36	05 18	05 54	07 30	08 07	08 49	09 36
52	04 40	05 21	05 54	07 35	08 13	08 56	09 45
50	04 44	05 23	05 55	07 40	08 20	09 03	09 52
45	04 53	05 27	05 57	07 51	08 33	09 19	10 08
N 40	04 59	05 31	05 58	08 00	08 44	09 31	10 21
35	05 04	05 33	05 59	08 07	08 53	09 42	10 32
30	05 08	05 36	06 00	08 14	09 02	09 51	10 42
20	05 13	05 39	06 01	08 26	09 16	10 07	10 59
N 10	05 17	05 41	06 02	08 36	09 29	10 21	11 14
0	05 18	05 42	06 03	08 46	09 41	10 35	11 27
S 10	05 19	05 43	06 04	08 55	09 52	10 48	11 41
20	05 17	05 43	06 05	09 06	10 05	11 02	11 56
30	05 14	05 42	06 06	09 18	10 20	11 19	12 13
35	05 11	05 41	06 06	09 25	10 29	11 28	12 23
40	05 08	05 39	06 06	09 33	10 38	11 39	12 34
45	05 03	05 38	06 07	09 42	10 50	11 52	12 47
S 50	04 57	05 35	06 07	09 53	11 04	12 08	13 04
52	04 54	05 34	06 08	09 59	11 10	12 15	13 11
54	04 51	05 33	06 08	10 04	11 18	12 23	13 20
56	04 47	05 31	06 08	10 11	11 26	12 32	13 29
58	04 43	05 29	06 09	10 18	11 35	12 43	13 40
S 60	04 38	05 27	06 09	10 26	11 45	12 55	13 52

Lat.	Sunset	Twilight Civil	Twilight Naut.	Moonset 23	Moonset 24	Moonset 25	Moonset 26
°	h m	h m	h m	h m	h m	h m	h m
N 72	18 36	19 46	21 23	24 59	00 59	03 00	▭
N 70	18 33	19 35	20 58	24 25	00 25	02 04	03 23
68	18 30	19 27	20 40	24 01	00 01	01 30	02 43
66	18 28	19 20	20 26	23 42	25 06	01 06	02 15
64	18 26	19 14	20 14	23 27	24 47	00 47	01 54
62	18 25	19 10	20 05	23 15	24 31	00 31	01 37
60	18 23	19 05	19 56	23 04	24 18	00 18	01 22
N 58	18 22	19 02	19 49	22 55	24 07	00 07	01 10
56	18 21	18 59	19 43	22 47	23 58	25 00	01 00
54	18 20	18 56	19 38	22 39	23 49	24 50	00 50
52	18 19	18 53	19 34	22 33	23 41	24 42	00 42
50	18 19	18 51	19 30	22 27	23 35	24 35	00 35
45	18 17	18 46	19 21	22 15	23 20	24 19	00 19
N 40	18 16	18 43	19 15	22 04	23 08	24 06	00 06
35	18 15	18 40	19 10	21 55	22 57	23 55	24 47
30	18 14	18 38	19 05	21 48	22 48	23 45	24 37
20	18 12	18 34	19 00	21 34	22 33	23 28	24 21
N 10	18 11	18 32	18 56	21 23	22 19	23 14	24 06
0	18 10	18 30	18 54	21 12	22 07	23 00	23 52
S 10	18 09	18 30	18 54	21 01	21 54	22 47	23 39
20	18 08	18 30	18 55	20 49	21 40	22 32	23 24
30	18 07	18 31	18 58	20 36	21 25	22 15	23 07
35	18 06	18 31	19 01	20 28	21 16	22 05	22 57
40	18 06	18 33	19 04	20 20	21 06	21 54	22 46
45	18 05	18 34	19 08	20 09	20 54	21 41	22 33
S 50	18 04	18 36	19 14	19 57	20 39	21 25	22 16
52	18 04	18 38	19 17	19 52	20 32	21 18	22 09
54	18 04	18 39	19 20	19 45	20 25	21 10	22 00
56	18 03	18 40	19 24	19 38	20 16	21 00	21 51
58	18 03	18 42	19 28	19 31	20 07	20 50	21 40
S 60	18 03	18 44	19 33	19 22	19 56	20 38	21 28

Day	SUN Eqn. of Time 00h	SUN Eqn. of Time 12h	SUN Mer. Pass.	MOON Mer. Pass. Upper	MOON Mer. Pass. Lower	Age	Phase
d	m s	m s	h m	h m	h m	d	%
23	06 49	06 40	12 07	14 59	02 31	03	13
24	06 31	06 22	12 07	15 54	03 26	04	22
25	06 13	06 04	12 06	16 47	04 21	05	32

UT	ARIES	VENUS −4.0		MARS +1.4		JUPITER −2.4		SATURN +0.3		STARS		
d h	GHA	GHA	Dec	GHA	Dec	GHA	Dec	GHA	Dec	Name	SHA	Dec
26 00	183 07.5	145 25.0	N15 26.6	159 09.5	N 9 46.6	47 29.1	N17 52.4	299 50.8	S19 00.3	Acamar	315 17.8	S40 15.0
01	198 10.0	160 24.6	27.7	174 10.3	47.3	62 31.7	52.5	314 53.4	00.3	Achernar	335 26.5	S57 09.8
02	213 12.4	175 24.2	28.8	189 11.0	48.0	77 34.3	52.5	329 55.9	00.3	Acrux	173 07.1	S63 11.1
03	228 14.9	190 23.7 ..	29.8	204 11.7 ..	48.7	92 36.8 ..	52.5	344 58.4 ..	00.3	Adhara	255 11.5	S29 00.0
04	243 17.4	205 23.3	30.9	219 12.4	49.4	107 39.4	52.6	0 00.9	00.3	Aldebaran	290 48.1	N16 32.1
05	258 19.8	220 22.9	32.0	234 13.1	50.1	122 42.0	52.6	15 03.4	00.3			
06	273 22.3	235 22.4	N15 33.0	249 13.8	N 9 50.8	137 44.6	N17 52.6	30 05.9	S19 00.2	Alioth	166 19.2	N55 52.5
07	288 24.7	250 22.0	34.1	264 14.5	51.5	152 47.1	52.6	45 08.4	00.2	Alkaid	152 57.6	N49 14.1
T 08	303 27.2	265 21.6	35.2	279 15.2	52.2	167 49.7	52.7	60 11.0	00.2	Al Na'ir	27 42.7	S46 53.1
H 09	318 29.7	280 21.1 ..	36.2	294 16.0 ..	52.9	182 52.3 ..	52.7	75 13.5 ..	00.2	Alnilam	275 45.2	S 1 11.9
U 10	333 32.1	295 20.7	37.3	309 16.7	53.6	197 54.8	52.7	90 16.0	00.2	Alphard	217 54.7	S 8 43.8
R 11	348 34.6	310 20.2	38.4	324 17.4	54.3	212 57.4	52.7	105 18.5	00.2			
S 12	3 37.1	325 19.8	N15 39.4	339 18.1	N 9 55.0	228 00.0	N17 52.8	120 21.0	S19 00.2	Alphecca	126 09.8	N26 39.7
D 13	18 39.5	340 19.4	40.5	354 18.8	55.7	243 02.5	52.8	135 23.5	00.1	Alpheratz	357 42.6	N29 10.4
A 14	33 42.0	355 18.9	41.6	9 19.5	56.4	258 05.1	52.8	150 26.0	00.1	Altair	62 07.2	N 8 54.5
Y 15	48 44.5	10 18.5 ..	42.6	24 20.2 ..	57.1	273 07.7 ..	52.9	165 28.6 ..	00.1	Ankaa	353 15.0	S42 13.5
16	63 46.9	25 18.0	43.7	39 20.9	57.8	288 10.3	52.9	180 31.1	00.1	Antares	112 24.6	S26 27.7
17	78 49.4	40 17.6	44.8	54 21.6	58.5	303 12.8	52.9	195 33.6	00.1			
18	93 51.8	55 17.2	N15 45.8	69 22.4	N 9 59.2	318 15.4	N17 52.9	210 36.1	S19 00.1	Arcturus	145 54.4	N19 06.1
19	108 54.3	70 16.7	46.9	84 23.1	59.9	333 18.0	53.0	225 38.6	00.1	Atria	107 25.1	S69 02.9
20	123 56.8	85 16.3	47.9	99 23.8	10 00.6	348 20.5	53.0	240 41.1	00.0	Avior	234 17.2	S59 34.0
21	138 59.2	100 15.8 ..	49.0	114 24.5 ..	01.3	3 23.1 ..	53.0	255 43.6 ..	00.0	Bellatrix	278 30.8	N 6 21.5
22	154 01.7	115 15.4	50.1	129 25.2	02.0	18 25.7	53.0	270 46.2	00.0	Betelgeuse	271 00.0	N 7 24.3
23	169 04.2	130 14.9	51.1	144 25.9	02.7	33 28.2	53.1	285 48.7	00.0			
27 00	184 06.6	145 14.5	N15 52.2	159 26.6	N10 03.4	48 30.8	N17 53.1	300 51.2	S19 00.0	Canopus	263 55.6	S52 42.7
01	199 09.1	160 14.1	53.2	174 27.3	04.1	63 33.4	53.1	315 53.7	19 00.0	Capella	280 32.8	N46 00.7
02	214 11.6	175 13.6	54.3	189 28.0	04.8	78 35.9	53.1	330 56.2	18 59.9	Deneb	49 30.9	N45 20.0
03	229 14.0	190 13.2 ..	55.4	204 28.8 ..	05.5	93 38.5 ..	53.2	345 58.7 ..	59.9	Denebola	182 32.1	N14 29.1
04	244 16.5	205 12.7	56.4	219 29.5	06.2	108 41.0	53.2	1 01.3	59.9	Diphda	348 55.0	S17 54.3
05	259 19.0	220 12.3	57.5	234 30.2	06.9	123 43.6	53.2	16 03.8	59.9			
06	274 21.4	235 11.8	N15 58.5	249 30.9	N10 07.6	138 46.2	N17 53.2	31 06.3	S18 59.9	Dubhe	193 49.7	N61 40.1
07	289 23.9	250 11.4	15 59.6	264 31.6	08.3	153 48.7	53.3	46 08.8	59.9	Elnath	278 11.2	N28 37.0
08	304 26.3	265 10.9	16 00.6	279 32.3	09.0	168 51.3	53.3	61 11.3	59.9	Eltanin	90 45.5	N51 29.1
F 09	319 28.8	280 10.5 ..	01.7	294 33.0 ..	09.7	183 53.9 ..	53.3	76 13.9 ..	59.8	Enif	33 46.2	N 9 56.7
R 10	334 31.3	295 10.0	02.7	309 33.7	10.4	198 56.4	53.3	91 16.4	59.8	Fomalhaut	15 23.0	S29 32.5
I 11	349 33.7	310 09.6	03.8	324 34.4	11.1	213 59.0	53.4	106 18.9	59.8			
D 12	4 36.2	325 09.1	N16 04.8	339 35.1	N10 11.8	229 01.5	N17 53.4	121 21.4	S18 59.8	Gacrux	171 58.8	S57 12.0
A 13	19 38.7	340 08.7	05.9	354 35.9	12.5	244 04.1	53.4	136 23.9	59.8	Gienah	175 50.7	S17 37.7
Y 14	34 41.1	355 08.3	06.9	9 36.6	13.2	259 06.7	53.4	151 26.4	59.8	Hadar	148 45.5	S60 26.6
15	49 43.6	10 07.8 ..	08.0	24 37.3 ..	13.9	274 09.2 ..	53.5	166 29.0 ..	59.7	Hamal	327 59.7	N23 31.9
16	64 46.1	25 07.4	09.0	39 38.0	14.6	289 11.8	53.5	181 31.5	59.7	Kaus Aust.	83 42.2	S34 22.4
17	79 48.5	40 06.9	10.1	54 38.7	15.3	304 14.4	53.5	196 34.0	59.7			
18	94 51.0	55 06.5	N16 11.1	69 39.4	N10 16.0	319 16.9	N17 53.5	211 36.5	S18 59.7	Kochab	137 19.3	N74 05.5
19	109 53.5	70 06.0	12.2	84 40.1	16.7	334 19.5	53.6	226 39.0	59.7	Markab	13 37.4	N15 17.1
20	124 55.9	85 05.6	13.2	99 40.8	17.4	349 22.0	53.6	241 41.6	59.7	Menkar	314 14.0	N 4 08.7
21	139 58.4	100 05.1 ..	14.3	114 41.5 ..	18.1	4 24.6 ..	53.6	256 44.1 ..	59.7	Menkent	148 05.7	S36 26.6
22	155 00.8	115 04.7	15.3	129 42.2	18.8	19 27.1	53.6	271 46.6	59.6	Miaplacidus	221 38.7	S69 47.2
23	170 03.3	130 04.2	16.3	144 43.0	19.5	34 29.7	53.7	286 49.1	59.6			
28 00	185 05.8	145 03.7	N16 17.4	159 43.7	N10 20.2	49 32.3	N17 53.7	301 51.6	S18 59.6	Mirfak	308 38.9	N49 54.8
01	200 08.2	160 03.3	18.4	174 44.4	20.9	64 34.8	53.7	316 54.2	59.6	Nunki	75 56.9	S26 16.4
02	215 10.7	175 02.8	19.5	189 45.1	21.6	79 37.4	53.7	331 56.7	59.6	Peacock	53 17.7	S56 40.8
03	230 13.2	190 02.4 ..	20.5	204 45.8 ..	22.3	94 39.9 ..	53.7	346 59.2 ..	59.6	Pollux	243 26.2	N27 59.2
04	245 15.6	205 01.9	21.5	219 46.5	23.0	109 42.5	53.8	2 01.7	59.5	Procyon	244 58.4	N 5 10.8
05	260 18.1	220 01.5	22.6	234 47.2	23.6	124 45.0	53.8	17 04.2	59.5			
06	275 20.6	235 01.0	N16 23.6	249 47.9	N10 24.3	139 47.6	N17 53.8	32 06.8	S18 59.5	Rasalhague	96 05.3	N12 32.9
07	290 23.0	250 00.6	24.7	264 48.6	25.0	154 50.2	53.8	47 09.3	59.5	Regulus	207 42.0	N11 53.4
S 08	305 25.5	265 00.1	25.7	279 49.3	25.7	169 52.7	53.9	62 11.8	59.5	Rigel	281 11.0	S 8 11.4
A 09	320 27.9	279 59.7 ..	26.7	294 50.1 ..	26.4	184 55.3 ..	53.9	77 14.3 ..	59.5	Rigil Kent.	139 49.4	S60 53.6
T 10	335 30.4	294 59.2	27.8	309 50.8	27.1	199 57.8	53.9	92 16.9	59.4	Sabik	102 11.0	S15 44.5
U 11	350 32.9	309 58.8	28.8	324 51.5	27.8	215 00.4	53.9	107 19.4	59.4			
R 12	5 35.3	324 58.3	N16 29.8	339 52.2	N10 28.5	230 02.9	N17 54.0	122 21.9	S18 59.4	Schedar	349 39.6	N56 37.2
D 13	20 37.8	339 57.8	30.9	354 52.9	29.2	245 05.5	54.0	137 24.4	59.4	Shaula	96 20.2	S37 06.6
A 14	35 40.3	354 57.4	31.9	9 53.6	29.9	260 08.0	54.0	152 26.9	59.4	Sirius	258 32.6	S16 44.6
Y 15	50 42.7	9 56.9 ..	32.9	24 54.3 ..	30.6	275 10.6 ..	54.0	167 29.5 ..	59.4	Spica	158 29.7	S11 14.5
16	65 45.2	24 56.5	34.0	39 55.0	31.3	290 13.1	54.0	182 32.0	59.3	Suhail	222 51.2	S43 30.1
17	80 47.7	39 56.0	35.0	54 55.7	32.0	305 15.7	54.1	197 34.5	59.3			
18	95 50.1	54 55.6	N16 36.0	69 56.4	N10 32.7	320 18.2	N17 54.1	212 37.0	S18 59.3	Vega	80 38.1	N38 47.8
19	110 52.6	69 55.1	37.1	84 57.1	33.4	335 20.8	54.1	227 39.6	59.3	Zuben'ubi	137 03.8	S16 06.3
20	125 55.1	84 54.6	38.1	99 57.9	34.0	350 23.4	54.1	242 42.1	59.3		SHA	Mer. Pass.
21	140 57.5	99 54.2 ..	39.1	114 58.6 ..	34.7	5 25.9 ..	54.2	257 44.6 ..	59.3		° '	h m
22	156 00.0	114 53.7	40.1	129 59.3	35.4	20 28.5	54.2	272 47.1	59.3	Venus	321 07.9	14 19
23	171 02.4	129 53.3	41.2	145 00.0	36.1	35 31.0	54.2	287 49.7	59.2	Mars	335 20.0	13 22
	h m									Jupiter	224 24.2	20 42
Mer. Pass.	11 41.6	v −0.4	d 1.0	v 0.7	d 0.7	v 2.6	d 0.0	v 2.5	d 0.0	Saturn	116 44.6	3 56

SUN and MOON

UT	SUN GHA	SUN Dec	MOON GHA	v	MOON Dec	d	HP
d h	° '	° '	° '	'	° '	'	'
26 00	178 31.5	N 1 59.5	104 17.5	9.2	N18 03.8	1.4	57.0
01	193 31.6	2 00.5	118 45.7	9.2	18 05.2	1.3	56.9
02	208 31.8	01.5	133 13.9	9.2	18 06.5	1.2	56.9
03	223 32.0	.. 02.5	147 42.1	9.3	18 07.7	1.1	56.9
04	238 32.2	03.4	162 10.4	9.3	18 08.8	1.1	56.8
05	253 32.4	04.4	176 38.7	9.4	18 09.9	0.9	56.8
06	268 32.6	N 2 05.4	191 07.1	9.4	N18 10.8	0.8	56.7
07	283 32.8	06.4	205 35.5	9.5	18 11.6	0.6	56.7
08	298 33.0	07.4	220 04.0	9.4	18 12.2	0.6	56.7
09	313 33.1	.. 08.3	234 32.4	9.6	18 12.8	0.5	56.6
10	328 33.3	09.3	249 01.0	9.5	18 13.3	0.4	56.6
11	343 33.5	10.3	263 29.5	9.7	18 13.7	0.3	56.6
12	358 33.7	N 2 11.3	277 58.2	9.6	N18 14.0	0.2	56.5
13	13 33.9	12.3	292 26.8	9.7	18 14.2	0.1	56.5
14	28 34.1	13.2	306 55.5	9.7	18 14.3	0.0	56.5
15	43 34.3	.. 14.2	321 24.2	9.8	18 14.3	0.1	56.4
16	58 34.5	15.2	335 53.0	9.8	18 14.2	0.2	56.4
17	73 34.7	16.2	350 21.8	9.9	18 14.0	0.2	56.4
18	88 34.8	N 2 17.2	4 50.7	9.9	N18 13.8	0.4	56.3
19	103 35.0	18.2	19 19.6	10.0	18 13.4	0.5	56.3
20	118 35.2	19.1	33 48.6	10.0	18 12.9	0.6	56.3
21	133 35.4	.. 20.1	48 17.6	10.0	18 12.3	0.7	56.2
22	148 35.6	21.1	62 46.6	10.1	18 11.6	0.8	56.2
23	163 35.8	22.1	77 15.7	10.1	18 10.8	0.8	56.2
27 00	178 36.0	N 2 23.1	91 44.8	10.2	N18 10.0	1.0	56.1
01	193 36.2	24.0	106 14.0	10.2	18 09.0	1.0	56.1
02	208 36.4	25.0	120 43.2	10.3	18 08.0	1.2	56.1
03	223 36.5	.. 26.0	135 12.5	10.3	18 06.8	1.2	56.0
04	238 36.7	27.0	149 41.8	10.4	18 05.6	1.4	56.0
05	253 36.9	28.0	164 11.2	10.4	18 04.2	1.4	56.0
06	268 37.1	N 2 28.9	178 40.6	10.4	N18 02.8	1.5	55.9
07	283 37.3	29.9	193 10.0	10.5	18 01.3	1.6	55.9
08	298 37.5	30.9	207 39.5	10.6	17 59.7	1.7	55.9
09	313 37.7	.. 31.9	222 09.1	10.6	17 58.0	1.8	55.8
10	328 37.9	32.8	236 38.7	10.6	17 56.2	1.9	55.8
11	343 38.1	33.8	251 08.3	10.7	17 54.3	2.0	55.8
12	358 38.2	N 2 34.8	265 38.0	10.7	N17 52.3	2.1	55.7
13	13 38.4	35.8	280 07.7	10.8	17 50.2	2.1	55.7
14	28 38.6	36.8	294 37.5	10.8	17 48.1	2.2	55.7
15	43 38.8	.. 37.7	309 07.3	10.9	17 45.9	2.4	55.7
16	58 39.0	38.7	323 37.2	10.9	17 43.5	2.4	55.6
17	73 39.2	39.7	338 07.1	11.0	17 41.1	2.5	55.6
18	88 39.4	N 2 40.7	352 37.1	11.0	N17 38.6	2.6	55.6
19	103 39.6	41.7	7 07.1	11.1	17 36.0	2.6	55.5
20	118 39.8	42.6	21 37.2	11.1	17 33.4	2.8	55.5
21	133 39.9	.. 43.6	36 07.3	11.2	17 30.6	2.8	55.5
22	148 40.1	44.6	50 37.5	11.2	17 27.8	3.0	55.5
23	163 40.3	45.6	65 07.7	11.3	17 24.8	3.0	55.4
28 00	178 40.5	N 2 46.5	79 38.0	11.3	N17 21.8	3.1	55.4
01	193 40.7	47.5	94 08.3	11.3	17 18.7	3.1	55.4
02	208 40.9	48.5	108 38.6	11.4	17 15.6	3.3	55.3
03	223 41.1	.. 49.5	123 09.0	11.5	17 12.3	3.3	55.3
04	238 41.3	50.5	137 39.5	11.5	17 09.0	3.4	55.3
05	253 41.5	51.4	152 10.0	11.6	17 05.6	3.5	55.3
06	268 41.6	N 2 52.4	166 40.6	11.6	N17 02.1	3.6	55.2
07	283 41.8	53.4	181 11.2	11.6	16 58.5	3.7	55.2
08	298 42.0	54.4	195 41.8	11.7	16 54.8	3.7	55.2
09	313 42.2	.. 55.3	210 12.5	11.8	16 51.1	3.8	55.2
10	328 42.4	56.3	224 43.3	11.8	16 47.3	3.9	55.1
11	343 42.6	57.3	239 14.1	11.8	16 43.4	4.0	55.1
12	358 42.8	N 2 58.3	253 44.9	11.9	N16 39.4	4.0	55.1
13	13 43.0	2 59.2	268 15.8	11.9	16 35.4	4.1	55.1
14	28 43.2	3 00.2	282 46.7	12.0	16 31.3	4.2	55.1
15	43 43.3	.. 01.2	297 17.7	12.1	16 27.1	4.3	55.0
16	58 43.5	02.2	311 48.8	12.0	16 22.8	4.3	55.0
17	73 43.7	03.2	326 19.8	12.2	16 18.5	4.5	55.0
18	88 43.9	N 3 04.1	340 51.0	12.1	N16 14.0	4.5	55.0
19	103 44.1	05.1	355 22.1	12.3	16 09.5	4.5	54.9
20	118 44.3	06.1	9 53.4	12.2	16 05.0	4.7	54.9
21	133 44.5	.. 07.1	24 24.6	12.4	16 00.3	4.7	54.9
22	148 44.7	08.0	38 56.0	12.3	15 55.6	4.7	54.9
23	163 44.9	09.0	53 27.3	12.4	N15 50.9	4.9	54.9
	SD 16.1	d 1.0	SD 15.4		15.2		15.0

Twilight, Sunrise and Moonrise

Lat.	Naut.	Civil	Sunrise	Moonrise 26	27	28	29
°	h m	h m	h m	h m	h m	h m	h m
N 72	02 32	04 13	05 24	▢	06 28	08 25	10 10
N 70	03 00	04 25	05 28	07 03	08 00	09 17	10 43
68	03 20	04 35	05 32	07 44	08 39	09 49	11 07
66	03 36	04 43	05 35	08 12	09 06	10 13	11 26
64	03 49	04 49	05 38	08 33	09 27	10 31	11 41
62	03 59	04 55	05 40	08 50	09 44	10 46	11 53
60	04 08	05 00	05 42	09 04	09 58	10 59	12 04
N 58	04 16	05 04	05 43	09 16	10 10	11 09	12 13
56	04 22	05 07	05 45	09 27	10 20	11 19	12 21
54	04 28	05 11	05 46	09 36	10 30	11 27	12 28
52	04 33	05 13	05 47	09 45	10 38	11 35	12 34
50	04 37	05 16	05 49	09 52	10 45	11 41	12 40
45	04 47	05 21	05 51	10 08	11 01	11 56	12 52
N 40	04 54	05 26	05 53	10 21	11 14	12 08	13 03
35	05 00	05 29	05 55	10 32	11 25	12 18	13 11
30	05 04	05 32	05 56	10 42	11 34	12 27	13 19
20	05 11	05 36	05 58	10 59	11 51	12 42	13 32
N 10	05 15	05 39	06 00	11 14	12 05	12 55	13 44
0	05 17	05 42	06 02	11 27	12 19	13 08	13 55
S 10	05 19	05 43	06 04	11 41	12 32	13 20	14 05
20	05 18	05 44	06 06	11 56	12 46	13 33	14 17
30	05 16	05 44	06 07	12 13	13 03	13 48	14 30
35	05 14	05 43	06 08	12 23	13 13	13 57	14 38
40	05 11	05 43	06 10	12 34	13 24	14 07	14 46
45	05 07	05 41	06 11	12 47	13 36	14 19	14 56
S 50	05 02	05 40	06 12	13 04	13 52	14 33	15 09
52	05 00	05 39	06 13	13 11	13 59	14 40	15 14
54	04 57	05 38	06 14	13 20	14 08	14 47	15 20
56	04 54	05 37	06 14	13 29	14 17	14 55	15 27
58	04 50	05 36	06 15	13 40	14 27	15 05	15 35
S 60	04 46	05 35	06 16	13 52	14 39	15 15	15 44

Sunset, Twilight and Moonset

Lat.	Sunset	Civil	Naut.	Moonset 26	27	28	29
°	h m	h m	h m	h m	h m	h m	h m
N 72	18 50	20 01	21 46	▢	05 45	05 32	05 26
N 70	18 45	19 49	21 16	03 23	04 14	04 39	04 51
68	18 41	19 39	20 55	02 43	03 34	04 07	04 27
66	18 38	19 31	20 38	02 15	03 07	03 43	04 08
64	18 35	19 24	20 25	01 54	02 46	03 24	03 52
62	18 33	19 18	20 14	01 37	02 29	03 09	03 39
60	18 31	19 13	20 05	01 22	02 15	02 56	03 28
N 58	18 29	19 09	19 57	01 10	02 03	02 45	03 19
56	18 27	19 05	19 50	01 00	01 52	02 35	03 10
54	18 26	19 02	19 44	00 50	01 43	02 27	03 03
52	18 25	18 59	19 39	00 42	01 35	02 19	02 56
50	18 24	18 56	19 35	00 35	01 27	02 12	02 50
45	18 21	18 50	19 25	00 19	01 11	01 57	02 37
N 40	18 19	18 46	19 18	00 06	00 58	01 45	02 26
35	18 17	18 42	19 12	24 47	00 47	01 34	02 17
30	18 15	18 39	19 07	24 37	00 37	01 25	02 09
20	18 13	18 35	19 01	24 21	00 21	01 09	01 55
N 10	18 11	18 32	18 56	24 06	00 06	00 55	01 42
0	18 09	18 29	18 53	23 52	24 42	00 42	01 31
S 10	18 07	18 28	18 52	23 39	24 29	00 29	01 19
20	18 05	18 27	18 53	23 24	24 15	00 15	01 06
30	18 03	18 27	18 55	23 07	23 59	24 52	00 52
35	18 02	18 27	18 56	22 57	23 50	24 44	00 44
40	18 01	18 28	18 59	22 46	23 39	24 34	00 34
45	17 59	18 28	19 03	22 33	23 27	24 23	00 23
S 50	17 58	18 30	19 07	22 16	23 11	24 09	00 09
52	17 57	18 31	19 10	22 09	23 04	24 03	00 03
54	17 56	18 31	19 13	22 00	22 56	23 56	24 57
56	17 55	18 32	19 16	21 51	22 47	23 48	24 51
58	17 55	18 33	19 19	21 40	22 37	23 39	24 44
S 60	17 53	18 35	19 24	21 28	22 25	23 29	24 35

SUN and MOON

Day	Eqn. of Time 00h	12h	Mer. Pass.	Mer. Pass. Upper	Lower	Age	Phase
d	m s	m s	h m	h m	h m	d	%
26	05 55	05 46	12 06	17 40	05 14	06	42
27	05 36	05 27	12 06	18 31	06 05	07	52
28	05 18	05 09	12 05	19 19	06 55	08	62

UT	ARIES GHA	VENUS −4.0 GHA	Dec	MARS +1.4 GHA	Dec	JUPITER −2.3 GHA	Dec	SATURN +0.3 GHA	Dec	STARS Name	SHA	Dec
29 00	186 04.9	144 52.8	N16 42.2	160 00.7	N10 36.8	50 33.6	N17 54.2	302 52.2	S18 59.2	Acamar	315 17.8	S40 15.0
01	201 07.4	159 52.3	43.2	175 01.4	37.5	65 36.1	54.2	317 54.7	59.2	Achernar	335 26.5	S57 09.8
02	216 09.8	174 51.9	44.2	190 02.1	38.2	80 38.7	54.3	332 57.2	59.2	Acrux	173 07.1	S63 11.1
03	231 12.3	189 51.4 · ·	45.3	205 02.8 · ·	38.9	95 41.2 · ·	54.3	347 59.8 · ·	59.2	Adhara	255 11.5	S29 00.0
04	246 14.8	204 51.0	46.3	220 03.5	39.6	110 43.8	54.3	3 02.3	59.2	Aldebaran	290 48.1	N16 32.1
05	261 17.2	219 50.5	47.3	235 04.2	40.3	125 46.3	54.3	18 04.8	59.1			
06	276 19.7	234 50.0	N16 48.3	250 04.9	N10 40.9	140 48.8	N17 54.3	33 07.3	S18 59.1	Alioth	166 19.2	N55 52.6
07	291 22.2	249 49.6	49.3	265 05.6	41.6	155 51.4	54.4	48 09.9	59.1	Alkaid	152 57.6	N49 14.1
08	306 24.6	264 49.1	50.4	280 06.4	42.3	170 53.9	54.4	63 12.4	59.1	Al Na'ir	27 42.6	S46 53.1
S 09	321 27.1	279 48.6 · ·	51.4	295 07.1 · ·	43.0	185 56.5 · ·	54.4	78 14.9 · ·	59.1	Alnilam	275 45.2	S 1 11.9
U 10	336 29.6	294 48.2	52.4	310 07.8	43.7	200 59.0	54.4	93 17.4	59.1	Alphard	217 54.7	S 8 43.8
N 11	351 32.0	309 47.7	53.4	325 08.5	44.4	216 01.6	54.4	108 20.0	59.0			
D 12	6 34.5	324 47.3	N16 54.4	340 09.2	N10 45.1	231 04.1	N17 54.5	123 22.5	S18 59.0	Alphecca	126 09.7	N26 39.7
A 13	21 36.9	339 46.8	55.5	355 09.9	45.8	246 06.7	54.5	138 25.0	59.0	Alpheratz	357 42.6	N29 10.4
Y 14	36 39.4	354 46.3	56.5	10 10.6	46.5	261 09.2	54.5	153 27.6	59.0	Altair	62 07.1	N 8 54.5
15	51 41.9	9 45.9 · ·	57.5	25 11.3 · ·	47.1	276 11.8 · ·	54.5	168 30.1 · ·	59.0	Ankaa	353 15.0	S42 13.5
16	66 44.3	24 45.4	58.5	40 12.0	47.8	291 14.3	54.5	183 32.6	59.0	Antares	112 24.6	S26 27.8
17	81 46.8	39 44.9	16 59.5	55 12.7	48.5	306 16.9	54.6	198 35.1	58.9			
18	96 49.3	54 44.5	N17 00.5	70 13.4	N10 49.2	321 19.4	N17 54.6	213 37.7	S18 58.9	Arcturus	145 54.3	N19 06.1
19	111 51.7	69 44.0	01.5	85 14.1	49.9	336 21.9	54.6	228 40.2	58.9	Atria	107 25.0	S69 02.9
20	126 54.2	84 43.5	02.6	100 14.8	50.6	351 24.5	54.6	243 42.7	58.9	Avior	234 17.2	S59 34.0
21	141 56.7	99 43.1 · ·	03.6	115 15.5 · ·	51.3	6 27.0 · ·	54.6	258 45.2 · ·	58.9	Bellatrix	278 30.8	N 6 21.5
22	156 59.1	114 42.6	04.6	130 16.3	52.0	21 29.6	54.7	273 47.8	58.8	Betelgeuse	271 00.0	N 7 24.3
23	172 01.6	129 42.1	05.6	145 17.0	52.6	36 32.1	54.7	288 50.3	58.8			
30 00	187 04.0	144 41.6	N17 06.6	160 17.7	N10 53.3	51 34.7	N17 54.7	303 52.8	S18 58.8	Canopus	263 55.6	S52 42.7
01	202 06.5	159 41.2	07.6	175 18.4	54.0	66 37.2	54.7	318 55.4	58.8	Capella	280 32.8	N46 00.7
02	217 09.0	174 40.7	08.6	190 19.1	54.7	81 39.7	54.7	333 57.9	58.8	Deneb	49 30.8	N45 20.0
03	232 11.4	189 40.2 · ·	09.6	205 19.8 · ·	55.4	96 42.3 · ·	54.8	349 00.4 · ·	58.8	Denebola	182 32.1	N14 29.1
04	247 13.9	204 39.8	10.6	220 20.5	56.1	111 44.8	54.8	4 03.0	58.7	Diphda	348 55.0	S17 54.3
05	262 16.4	219 39.3	11.6	235 21.2	56.8	126 47.4	54.8	19 05.5	58.7			
06	277 18.8	234 38.8	N17 12.6	250 21.9	N10 57.4	141 49.9	N17 54.8	34 08.0	S18 58.7	Dubhe	193 49.8	N61 40.1
07	292 21.3	249 38.4	13.6	265 22.6	58.1	156 52.4	54.8	49 10.5	58.7	Elnath	278 11.2	N28 37.0
08	307 23.8	264 37.9	14.6	280 23.3	58.8	171 55.0	54.8	64 13.1	58.7	Eltanin	90 45.5	N51 29.1
M 09	322 26.2	279 37.4 · ·	15.6	295 24.0	10 59.5	186 57.5 · ·	54.9	79 15.6 · ·	58.7	Enif	33 46.1	N 9 56.7
O 10	337 28.7	294 36.9	16.6	310 24.7	11 00.2	202 00.1	54.9	94 18.1	58.6	Fomalhaut	15 23.0	S29 32.5
N 11	352 31.2	309 36.5	17.6	325 25.4	00.9	217 02.6	54.9	109 20.7	58.6			
D 12	7 33.6	324 36.0	N17 18.6	340 26.2	N11 01.5	232 05.1	N17 54.9	124 23.2	S18 58.6	Gacrux	171 58.8	S57 12.0
A 13	22 36.1	339 35.5	19.6	355 26.9	02.2	247 07.7	54.9	139 25.7	58.6	Gienah	175 50.7	S17 37.7
Y 14	37 38.5	354 35.1	20.6	10 27.6	02.9	262 10.2	55.0	154 28.3	58.6	Hadar	148 45.4	S60 26.7
15	52 41.0	9 34.6 · ·	21.6	25 28.3 · ·	03.6	277 12.7 · ·	55.0	169 30.8 · ·	58.6	Hamal	327 59.7	N23 31.9
16	67 43.5	24 34.1	22.6	40 29.0	04.3	292 15.3	55.0	184 33.3	58.5	Kaus Aust.	83 42.2	S34 22.4
17	82 45.9	39 33.6	23.6	55 29.7	05.0	307 17.8	55.0	199 35.9	58.5			
18	97 48.4	54 33.2	N17 24.6	70 30.4	N11 05.6	322 20.4	N17 55.0	214 38.4	S18 58.5	Kochab	137 19.3	N74 05.5
19	112 50.9	69 32.7	25.6	85 31.1	06.3	337 22.9	55.0	229 40.9	58.5	Markab	13 37.4	N15 17.1
20	127 53.3	84 32.2	26.6	100 31.8	07.0	352 25.4	55.1	244 43.4	58.5	Menkar	314 14.0	N 4 08.7
21	142 55.8	99 31.7 · ·	27.6	115 32.5 · ·	07.7	7 28.0 · ·	55.1	259 46.0 · ·	58.4	Menkent	148 05.7	S36 26.6
22	157 58.3	114 31.2	28.6	130 33.2	08.4	22 30.5	55.1	274 48.5	58.4	Miaplacidus	221 38.7	S69 47.2
23	173 00.7	129 30.8	29.6	145 33.9	09.1	37 33.0	55.1	289 51.0	58.4			
31 00	188 03.2	144 30.3	N17 30.6	160 34.6	N11 09.7	52 35.6	N17 55.1	304 53.6	S18 58.4	Mirfak	308 38.9	N49 54.8
01	203 05.7	159 29.8	31.6	175 35.3	10.4	67 38.1	55.1	319 56.1	58.4	Nunki	75 56.8	S26 16.4
02	218 08.1	174 29.3	32.6	190 36.0	11.1	82 40.6	55.2	334 58.6	58.4	Peacock	53 17.7	S56 40.8
03	233 10.6	189 28.9 · ·	33.5	205 36.7 · ·	11.8	97 43.2 · ·	55.2	350 01.2 · ·	58.3	Pollux	243 26.2	N27 59.2
04	248 13.0	204 28.4	34.5	220 37.4	12.5	112 45.7	55.2	5 03.7	58.3	Procyon	244 58.4	N 5 10.8
05	263 15.5	219 27.9	35.5	235 38.2	13.1	127 48.2	55.2	20 06.2	58.3			
06	278 18.0	234 27.4	N17 36.5	250 38.9	N11 13.8	142 50.8	N17 55.2	35 08.8	S18 58.3	Rasalhague	96 05.2	N12 32.9
07	293 20.4	249 26.9	37.5	265 39.6	14.5	157 53.3	55.2	50 11.3	58.3	Regulus	207 42.0	N11 53.4
08	308 22.9	264 26.5	38.5	280 40.3	15.2	172 55.8	55.3	65 13.8	58.3	Rigel	281 11.0	S 8 11.4
T 09	323 25.4	279 26.0 · ·	39.5	295 41.0 · ·	15.9	187 58.4 · ·	55.3	80 16.4 · ·	58.2	Rigil Kent.	139 49.4	S60 53.7
U 10	338 27.8	294 25.5	40.4	310 41.7	16.5	203 00.9	55.3	95 18.9	58.2	Sabik	102 11.0	S15 44.5
E 11	353 30.3	309 25.0	41.4	325 42.4	17.2	218 03.4	55.3	110 21.5	58.2			
S 12	8 32.8	324 24.5	N17 42.4	340 43.1	N11 17.9	233 06.0	N17 55.3	125 24.0	S18 58.2	Schedar	349 39.6	N56 37.2
D 13	23 35.2	339 24.1	43.4	355 43.8	18.6	248 08.5	55.3	140 26.5	58.2	Shaula	96 20.1	S37 06.6
A 14	38 37.7	354 23.6	44.4	10 44.5	19.2	263 11.0	55.3	155 29.1	58.1	Sirius	258 32.6	S16 44.6
Y 15	53 40.1	9 23.1 · ·	45.4	25 45.2 · ·	19.9	278 13.5 · ·	55.4	170 31.6 · ·	58.1	Spica	158 29.6	S11 14.5
16	68 42.6	24 22.6	46.3	40 45.9	20.6	293 16.1	55.4	185 34.1	58.1	Suhail	222 51.2	S43 30.1
17	83 45.1	39 22.1	47.3	55 46.6	21.3	308 18.6	55.4	200 36.7	58.1			
18	98 47.5	54 21.6	N17 48.3	70 47.3	N11 22.0	323 21.1	N17 55.4	215 39.2	S18 58.1	Vega	80 38.1	N38 47.8
19	113 50.0	69 21.2	49.3	85 48.0	22.6	338 23.7	55.4	230 41.7	58.1	Zuben'ubi	137 03.8	S16 06.3
20	128 52.5	84 20.7	50.2	100 48.7	23.3	353 26.2	55.4	245 44.3	58.0		SHA	Mer. Pass.
21	143 54.9	99 20.2 · ·	51.2	115 49.4 · ·	24.0	8 28.7 · ·	55.5	260 46.8 · ·	58.0		° '	h m
22	158 57.4	114 19.7	52.2	130 50.1	24.7	23 31.2	55.5	275 49.3	58.0	Venus	317 37.6	14 22
23	173 59.9	129 19.2	53.2	145 50.8	25.3	38 33.8	55.5	290 51.9	58.0	Mars	333 13.6	13 18
Mer. Pass.	h m 11 29.8	v −0.5	d 1.0	v 0.7	d 0.7	v 2.5	d 0.0	v 2.5	d 0.0	Jupiter	224 30.6	20 30
										Saturn	116 48.8	3 44

UT	SUN GHA	SUN Dec	MOON GHA	MOON v	MOON Dec	MOON d	MOON HP
d h	° ′	° ′	° ′	′	° ′	′	′
29 00	178 45.0	N 3 10.0	67 58.7	12.5	N15 46.0	4.9	54.8
01	193 45.2	11.0	82 30.2	12.5	15 41.1	5.0	54.8
02	208 45.4	11.9	97 01.7	12.5	15 36.1	5.0	54.8
03	223 45.6 ··	12.9	111 33.2	12.6	15 31.1	5.2	54.8
04	238 45.8	13.9	126 04.8	12.7	15 25.9	5.2	54.8
05	253 46.0	14.9	140 36.5	12.7	15 20.7	5.2	54.7
06	268 46.2	N 3 15.8	155 08.2	12.7	N15 15.5	5.4	54.7
07	283 46.4	16.8	169 39.9	12.8	15 10.1	5.3	54.7
08	298 46.5	17.8	184 11.7	12.8	15 04.8	5.5	54.7
S 09	313 46.7 ··	18.8	198 43.5	12.9	14 59.3	5.5	54.7
U 10	328 46.9	19.7	213 15.4	12.9	14 53.8	5.6	54.6
N 11	343 47.1	20.7	227 47.3	12.9	14 48.2	5.7	54.6
D 12	358 47.3	N 3 21.7	242 19.2	13.0	N14 42.5	5.7	54.6
A 13	13 47.5	22.7	256 51.2	13.1	14 36.8	5.7	54.6
Y 14	28 47.7	23.6	271 23.3	13.1	14 31.1	5.9	54.6
15	43 47.9 ··	24.6	285 55.4	13.1	14 25.2	5.9	54.5
16	58 48.1	25.6	300 27.5	13.2	14 19.3	5.9	54.5
17	73 48.2	26.5	314 59.7	13.2	14 13.4	6.1	54.5
18	88 48.4	N 3 27.5	329 31.9	13.2	N14 07.3	6.0	54.5
19	103 48.6	28.5	344 04.1	13.3	14 01.3	6.2	54.5
20	118 48.8	29.5	358 36.4	13.4	13 55.1	6.2	54.5
21	133 49.0 ··	30.4	13 08.8	13.4	13 48.9	6.2	54.5
22	148 49.2	31.4	27 41.2	13.4	13 42.7	6.4	54.4
23	163 49.4	32.4	42 13.6	13.4	13 36.3	6.3	54.4
30 00	178 49.6	N 3 33.4	56 46.0	13.5	N13 30.0	6.5	54.4
01	193 49.8	34.3	71 18.5	13.6	13 23.5	6.4	54.4
02	208 49.9	35.3	85 51.1	13.6	13 17.1	6.6	54.4
03	223 50.1 ··	36.3	100 23.7	13.6	13 10.5	6.6	54.4
04	238 50.3	37.2	114 56.3	13.6	13 03.9	6.6	54.4
05	253 50.5	38.2	129 28.9	13.7	12 57.3	6.7	54.3
06	268 50.7	N 3 39.2	144 01.6	13.8	N12 50.6	6.8	54.3
07	283 50.9	40.2	158 34.4	13.7	12 43.8	6.8	54.3
08	298 51.1	41.1	173 07.1	13.8	12 37.0	6.8	54.3
M 09	313 51.3 ··	42.1	187 39.9	13.9	12 30.2	7.0	54.3
O 10	328 51.4	43.1	202 12.8	13.9	12 23.2	6.9	54.3
N 11	343 51.6	44.0	216 45.7	13.9	12 16.3	7.0	54.3
D 12	358 51.8	N 3 45.0	231 18.6	13.9	N12 09.3	7.1	54.3
A 13	13 52.0	46.0	245 51.5	14.0	12 02.2	7.1	54.3
Y 14	28 52.2	47.0	260 24.5	14.0	11 55.1	7.2	54.2
15	43 52.4 ··	47.9	274 57.5	14.1	11 47.9	7.2	54.2
16	58 52.6	48.9	289 30.6	14.1	11 40.7	7.2	54.2
17	73 52.8	49.9	304 03.7	14.1	11 33.5	7.3	54.2
18	88 53.0	N 3 50.8	318 36.8	14.2	N11 26.2	7.4	54.2
19	103 53.1	51.8	333 10.0	14.2	11 18.8	7.4	54.2
20	118 53.3	52.8	347 43.2	14.2	11 11.4	7.4	54.2
21	133 53.5 ··	53.8	2 16.4	14.2	11 04.0	7.5	54.2
22	148 53.7	54.7	16 49.6	14.3	10 56.5	7.6	54.2
23	163 53.9	55.7	31 22.9	14.3	10 48.9	7.5	54.2
31 00	178 54.1	N 3 56.7	45 56.2	14.4	N10 41.4	7.7	54.2
01	193 54.3	57.6	60 29.6	14.4	10 33.7	7.6	54.1
02	208 54.5	58.6	75 03.0	14.4	10 26.1	7.7	54.1
03	223 54.6	3 59.6	89 36.4	14.4	10 18.4	7.8	54.1
04	238 54.8	4 00.5	104 09.8	14.5	10 10.6	7.8	54.1
05	253 55.0	01.5	118 43.3	14.5	10 02.8	7.8	54.1
06	268 55.2	N 4 02.5	133 16.8	14.5	N 9 55.0	7.9	54.1
07	283 55.4	03.4	147 50.3	14.5	9 47.1	7.9	54.1
08	298 55.6	04.4	162 23.8	14.6	9 39.2	7.9	54.1
T 09	313 55.8 ··	05.4	176 57.4	14.6	9 31.3	8.0	54.1
U 10	328 56.0	06.4	191 31.0	14.6	9 23.3	8.0	54.1
E 11	343 56.1	07.3	206 04.6	14.7	9 15.3	8.1	54.1
S 12	358 56.3	N 4 08.3	220 38.3	14.6	N 9 07.2	8.1	54.1
D 13	13 56.5	09.3	235 11.9	14.7	8 59.1	8.1	54.1
A 14	28 56.7	10.2	249 45.6	14.8	8 51.0	8.2	54.1
Y 15	43 56.9 ··	11.2	264 19.4	14.7	8 42.8	8.2	54.1
16	58 57.1	12.2	278 53.1	14.8	8 34.6	8.2	54.1
17	73 57.3	13.1	293 26.9	14.8	8 26.4	8.3	54.0
18	88 57.5	N 4 14.1	308 00.7	14.8	N 8 18.1	8.3	54.0
19	103 57.6	15.1	322 34.5	14.8	8 09.8	8.4	54.0
20	118 57.8	16.0	337 08.3	14.9	8 01.4	8.3	54.0
21	133 58.0 ··	17.0	351 42.2	14.9	7 53.1	8.4	54.0
22	148 58.2	18.0	6 16.1	14.9	7 44.7	8.5	54.0
23	163 58.4	18.9	20 50.0	14.9	N 7 36.2	8.4	54.0
	SD 16.0	d 1.0	SD 14.9		14.8		14.7

Twilight / Sunrise / Moonrise

Lat.	Twilight Naut.	Twilight Civil	Sunrise	Moonrise 29	Moonrise 30	Moonrise 31	Moonrise 1
°	h m	h m	h m	h m	h m	h m	h m
N 72	02 04	03 56	05 08	10 10	11 50	13 26	14 59
N 70	02 39	04 10	05 14	10 43	12 12	13 40	15 07
68	03 03	04 21	05 19	11 07	12 29	13 51	15 13
66	03 21	04 30	05 23	11 26	12 42	14 00	15 18
64	03 36	04 38	05 27	11 41	12 53	14 08	15 23
62	03 48	04 45	05 30	11 53	13 03	14 14	15 26
60	03 58	04 50	05 33	12 04	13 11	14 20	15 30
N 58	04 06	04 55	05 35	12 13	13 18	14 25	15 32
56	04 13	04 59	05 37	12 21	13 25	14 30	15 35
54	04 20	05 03	05 39	12 28	13 30	14 34	15 37
52	04 25	05 06	05 40	12 34	13 35	14 37	15 39
50	04 30	05 09	05 42	12 40	13 40	14 40	15 41
45	04 41	05 16	05 45	12 52	13 50	14 47	15 45
N 40	04 49	05 21	05 48	13 03	13 58	14 53	15 49
35	04 55	05 25	05 50	13 11	14 05	14 58	15 52
30	05 00	05 28	05 52	13 19	14 11	15 03	15 54
20	05 08	05 34	05 56	13 32	14 22	15 11	15 59
N 10	05 13	05 38	05 59	13 44	14 31	15 17	16 03
0	05 17	05 41	06 01	13 55	14 40	15 24	16 07
S 10	05 18	05 43	06 04	14 05	14 49	15 30	16 10
20	05 19	05 44	06 06	14 17	14 58	15 37	16 14
30	05 18	05 45	06 09	14 30	15 09	15 44	16 19
35	05 16	05 46	06 11	14 38	15 15	15 49	16 21
40	05 14	05 46	06 13	14 46	15 22	15 54	16 24
45	05 11	05 45	06 15	14 56	15 30	16 00	16 28
S 50	05 07	05 45	06 17	15 09	15 39	16 07	16 32
52	05 05	05 44	06 18	15 14	15 44	16 10	16 34
54	05 03	05 44	06 19	15 20	15 49	16 13	16 36
56	05 00	05 43	06 20	15 27	15 54	16 17	16 38
58	04 57	05 43	06 22	15 35	16 00	16 21	16 40
S 60	04 53	05 42	06 23	15 44	16 07	16 26	16 43

Sunset / Twilight / Moonset

Lat.	Sunset	Twilight Civil	Twilight Naut.	Moonset 29	Moonset 30	Moonset 31	Moonset 1
°	h m	h m	h m	h m	h m	h m	h m
N 72	19 04	20 17	22 13	05 26	05 21	05 16	05 11
N 70	18 57	20 03	21 36	04 51	04 57	05 00	05 02
68	18 52	19 51	21 10	04 27	04 40	04 48	04 54
66	18 48	19 41	20 51	04 08	04 25	04 38	04 48
64	18 44	19 33	20 36	03 52	04 13	04 29	04 42
62	18 41	19 27	20 24	03 39	04 03	04 22	04 38
60	18 38	19 21	20 14	03 28	03 54	04 15	04 33
N 58	18 36	19 16	20 05	03 19	03 46	04 10	04 30
56	18 33	19 11	19 57	03 10	03 40	04 04	04 26
54	18 31	19 07	19 51	03 03	03 34	04 00	04 23
52	18 30	19 04	19 45	02 56	03 28	03 56	04 21
50	18 28	19 01	19 40	02 50	03 23	03 52	04 18
45	18 25	18 54	19 29	02 37	03 12	03 44	04 13
N 40	18 22	18 49	19 21	02 26	03 03	03 37	04 08
35	18 19	18 45	19 15	02 17	02 56	03 31	04 04
30	18 17	18 41	19 09	02 09	02 49	03 26	04 01
20	18 14	18 36	19 02	01 55	02 37	03 17	03 55
N 10	18 11	18 32	18 56	01 42	02 27	03 09	03 50
0	18 08	18 29	18 53	01 31	02 17	03 01	03 45
S 10	18 05	18 26	18 51	01 19	02 07	02 54	03 39
20	18 02	18 24	18 50	01 06	01 56	02 46	03 34
30	17 59	18 23	18 51	00 52	01 44	02 36	03 28
35	17 58	18 23	18 52	00 44	01 37	02 31	03 24
40	17 56	18 23	18 54	00 34	01 29	02 25	03 20
45	17 54	18 23	18 57	00 23	01 20	02 18	03 15
S 50	17 51	18 23	19 01	00 09	01 09	02 09	03 10
52	17 50	18 24	19 03	00 03	01 03	02 05	03 07
54	17 49	18 24	19 05	24 57	00 57	02 00	03 04
56	17 48	18 25	19 08	24 51	00 51	01 56	03 01
58	17 46	18 25	19 11	24 44	00 44	01 50	02 57
S 60	17 44	18 26	19 14	24 35	00 35	01 44	02 53

SUN / MOON

Day	SUN Eqn. of Time 00h	SUN Eqn. of Time 12h	SUN Mer. Pass.	MOON Mer. Pass. Upper	MOON Mer. Pass. Lower	Age	Phase
d	m s	m s	h m	h m	h m	d	%
29	05 00	04 51	12 05	20 06	07 43	09	71
30	04 42	04 33	12 05	20 51	08 28	10	79
31	04 24	04 15	12 04	21 34	09 13	11	86

UT	ARIES	VENUS −4.0		MARS +1.4		JUPITER −2.3		SATURN +0.3		STARS		
	GHA	GHA	Dec	GHA	Dec	GHA	Dec	GHA	Dec	Name	SHA	Dec
d h	° ′	° ′	° ′	° ′	° ′	° ′	° ′	° ′	° ′		° ′	° ′
1 00	189 02.3	144 18.7	N17 54.1	160 51.6	N11 26.0	53 36.3	N17 55.5	305 54.4	S18 58.0	Acamar	315 17.8	S40 14.9
01	204 04.8	159 18.2	55.1	175 52.3	26.7	68 38.8	55.5	320 57.0	57.9	Achernar	335 26.5	S57 09.8
02	219 07.3	174 17.8	56.1	190 53.0	27.4	83 41.3	55.5	335 59.5	57.9	Acrux	173 07.1	S63 11.1
03	234 09.7	189 17.3 ..	57.1	205 53.7 ..	28.0	98 43.9 ..	55.5	351 02.0 ..	57.9	Adhara	255 11.6	S29 00.0
04	249 12.2	204 16.8	58.0	220 54.4	28.7	113 46.4	55.6	6 04.6	57.9	Aldebaran	290 48.2	N16 32.1
05	264 14.6	219 16.3	17 59.0	235 55.1	29.4	128 48.9	55.6	21 07.1	57.9			
06	279 17.1	234 15.8	N18 00.0	250 55.8	N11 30.1	143 51.4	N17 55.6	36 09.6	S18 57.9	Alioth	166 19.2	N55 52.6
W 07	294 19.6	249 15.3	00.9	265 56.5	30.7	158 54.0	55.6	51 12.2	57.8	Alkaid	152 57.5	N49 14.2
E 08	309 22.0	264 14.8	01.9	280 57.2	31.4	173 56.5	55.6	66 14.7	57.8	Al Na'ir	27 42.6	S46 53.1
D 09	324 24.5	279 14.3 ..	02.9	295 57.9 ..	32.1	188 59.0 ..	55.6	81 17.3 ..	57.8	Alnilam	275 45.2	S 1 11.9
N 10	339 27.0	294 13.9	03.8	310 58.6	32.8	204 01.5	55.6	96 19.8	57.8	Alphard	217 54.7	S 8 43.8
E 11	354 29.4	309 13.4	04.8	325 59.3	33.4	219 04.1	55.7	111 22.3	57.8			
S 12	9 31.9	324 12.9	N18 05.8	341 00.0	N11 34.1	234 06.6	N17 55.7	126 24.9	S18 57.7	Alphecca	126 09.7	N26 39.7
D 13	24 34.4	339 12.4	06.7	356 00.7	34.8	249 09.1	55.7	141 27.4	57.7	Alpheratz	357 42.5	N29 10.3
A 14	39 36.8	354 11.9	07.7	11 01.4	35.5	264 11.6	55.7	156 30.0	57.7	Altair	62 07.1	N 8 54.5
Y 15	54 39.3	9 11.4 ..	08.6	26 02.1 ..	36.1	279 14.1 ..	55.7	171 32.5 ..	57.7	Ankaa	353 15.0	S42 13.5
16	69 41.7	24 10.9	09.6	41 02.8	36.8	294 16.7	55.7	186 35.0	57.7	Antares	112 24.5	S26 27.8
17	84 44.2	39 10.4	10.6	56 03.5	37.5	309 19.2	55.7	201 37.6	57.6			
18	99 46.7	54 09.9	N18 11.5	71 04.2	N11 38.2	324 21.7	N17 55.7	216 40.1	S18 57.6	Arcturus	145 54.3	N19 06.1
19	114 49.1	69 09.4	12.5	86 04.9	38.8	339 24.2	55.8	231 42.7	57.6	Atria	107 25.9	S69 02.9
20	129 51.6	84 08.9	13.4	101 05.6	39.5	354 26.7	55.8	246 45.2	57.6	Avior	234 17.2	S59 34.0
21	144 54.1	99 08.4 ..	14.4	116 06.3 ..	40.2	9 29.3 ..	55.8	261 47.7 ..	57.6	Bellatrix	278 30.8	N 6 21.5
22	159 56.5	114 08.0	15.4	131 07.0	40.8	24 31.8	55.8	276 50.3	57.5	Betelgeuse	271 00.1	N 7 24.3
23	174 59.0	129 07.5	16.3	146 07.7	41.5	39 34.3	55.8	291 52.8	57.5			
2 00	190 01.5	144 07.0	N18 17.3	161 08.4	N11 42.2	54 36.8	N17 55.8	306 55.4	S18 57.5	Canopus	263 55.7	S52 42.7
01	205 03.9	159 06.5	18.2	176 09.1	42.9	69 39.3	55.8	321 57.9	57.5	Capella	280 32.8	N46 00.7
02	220 06.4	174 06.0	19.2	191 09.8	43.5	84 41.9	55.8	337 00.4	57.5	Deneb	49 30.8	N45 20.0
03	235 08.9	189 05.5 ..	20.1	206 10.5 ..	44.2	99 44.4 ..	55.9	352 03.0 ..	57.5	Denebola	182 32.1	N14 29.1
04	250 11.3	204 05.0	21.1	221 11.3	44.9	114 46.9	55.9	7 05.5	57.4	Diphda	348 55.0	S17 54.3
05	265 13.8	219 04.5	22.0	236 12.0	45.5	129 49.4	55.9	22 08.1	57.4			
06	280 16.2	234 04.0	N18 23.0	251 12.7	N11 46.2	144 51.9	N17 55.9	37 10.6	S18 57.4	Dubhe	193 49.8	N61 40.1
T 07	295 18.7	249 03.5	23.9	266 13.4	46.9	159 54.4	55.9	52 13.2	57.4	Elnath	278 11.2	N28 37.0
H 08	310 21.2	264 03.0	24.9	281 14.1	47.5	174 57.0	55.9	67 15.7	57.4	Eltanin	90 45.5	N51 29.1
U 09	325 23.6	279 02.5 ..	25.8	296 14.8 ..	48.2	189 59.5 ..	55.9	82 18.2 ..	57.3	Enif	33 46.1	N 9 56.7
R 10	340 26.1	294 02.0	26.8	311 15.5	48.9	205 02.0	55.9	97 20.8	57.3	Fomalhaut	15 23.0	S29 32.5
S 11	355 28.6	309 01.5	27.7	326 16.2	49.5	220 04.5	55.9	112 23.3	57.3			
D 12	10 31.0	324 01.0	N18 28.7	341 16.9	N11 50.2	235 07.0	N17 56.0	127 25.9	S18 57.3	Gacrux	171 58.8	S57 12.0
A 13	25 33.5	339 00.5	29.6	356 17.6	50.9	250 09.5	56.0	142 28.4	57.3	Gienah	175 50.7	S17 37.7
Y 14	40 36.0	354 00.0	30.5	11 18.3	51.6	265 12.0	56.0	157 30.9	57.2	Hadar	148 45.4	S60 26.7
15	55 38.4	8 59.5 ..	31.5	26 19.0 ..	52.2	280 14.6 ..	56.0	172 33.5 ..	57.2	Hamal	327 59.7	N23 31.9
16	70 40.9	23 59.0	32.4	41 19.7	52.9	295 17.1	56.0	187 36.0	57.2	Kaus Aust.	83 42.2	S34 22.4
17	85 43.3	38 58.5	33.4	56 20.4	53.6	310 19.6	56.0	202 38.6	57.2			
18	100 45.8	53 58.0	N18 34.3	71 21.1	N11 54.2	325 22.1	N17 56.0	217 41.1	S18 57.2	Kochab	137 19.2	N74 05.5
19	115 48.3	68 57.5	35.3	86 21.8	54.9	340 24.6	56.0	232 43.7	57.1	Markab	13 37.4	N15 17.1
20	130 50.7	83 57.0	36.2	101 22.5	55.6	355 27.1	56.0	247 46.2	57.1	Menkar	314 14.0	N 4 08.7
21	145 53.2	98 56.5 ..	37.1	116 23.2 ..	56.2	10 29.6 ..	56.0	262 48.8 ..	57.1	Menkent	148 05.7	S36 26.6
22	160 55.7	113 56.0	38.1	131 23.9	56.9	25 32.1	56.1	277 51.3	57.1	Miaplacidus	221 38.7	S69 47.2
23	175 58.1	128 55.5	39.0	146 24.6	57.6	40 34.7	56.1	292 53.8	57.1			
3 00	191 00.6	143 55.0	N18 39.9	161 25.3	N11 58.2	55 37.2	N17 56.1	307 56.4	S18 57.0	Mirfak	308 38.9	N49 54.8
01	206 03.1	158 54.5	40.9	176 26.0	58.9	70 39.7	56.1	322 58.9	57.0	Nunki	75 56.8	S26 16.4
02	221 05.5	173 54.0	41.8	191 26.7	11 59.6	85 42.2	56.1	338 01.5	57.0	Peacock	53 17.6	S56 40.8
03	236 08.0	188 53.5 ..	42.7	206 27.4	12 00.2	100 44.7 ..	56.1	353 04.0 ..	57.0	Pollux	243 26.2	N27 59.2
04	251 10.5	203 53.0	43.7	221 28.1	00.9	115 47.2	56.1	8 06.6	57.0	Procyon	244 58.4	N 5 10.8
05	266 12.9	218 52.5	44.6	236 28.8	01.5	130 49.7	56.1	23 09.1	56.9			
06	281 15.4	233 52.0	N18 45.5	251 29.5	N12 02.2	145 52.2	N17 56.1	38 11.7	S18 56.9	Rasalhague	96 05.2	N12 32.9
07	296 17.8	248 51.5	46.5	266 30.2	02.9	160 54.7	56.1	53 14.2	56.9	Regulus	207 42.0	N11 53.4
F 08	311 20.3	263 50.9	47.4	281 30.9	03.5	175 57.2	56.2	68 16.8	56.9	Rigel	281 11.0	S 8 11.4
R 09	326 22.8	278 50.4 ..	48.3	296 31.6 ..	04.2	190 59.7 ..	56.2	83 19.3 ..	56.9	Rigil Kent.	139 49.4	S60 53.7
I 10	341 25.2	293 49.9	49.3	311 32.3	04.9	206 02.3	56.2	98 21.8	56.8	Sabik	102 11.0	S15 44.5
D 11	356 27.7	308 49.4	50.2	326 33.0	05.5	221 04.8	56.2	113 24.4	56.8			
A 12	11 30.2	323 48.9	N18 51.1	341 33.7	N12 06.2	236 07.3	N17 56.2	128 26.9	S18 56.8	Schedar	349 39.6	N56 37.2
Y 13	26 32.6	338 48.4	52.0	356 34.4	06.9	251 09.8	56.2	143 29.5	56.8	Shaula	96 20.1	S37 06.6
14	41 35.1	353 47.9	53.0	11 35.1	07.5	266 12.3	56.2	158 32.0	56.8	Sirius	258 32.7	S16 44.6
15	56 37.6	8 47.4 ..	53.9	26 35.8 ..	08.2	281 14.8 ..	56.2	173 34.6 ..	56.7	Spica	158 29.6	S11 14.5
16	71 40.0	23 46.9	54.8	41 36.5	08.8	296 17.3	56.2	188 37.1	56.7	Suhail	222 51.3	S43 30.1
17	86 42.5	38 46.4	55.7	56 37.2	09.5	311 19.8	56.2	203 39.7	56.7			
18	101 44.9	53 45.9	N18 56.6	71 37.9	N12 10.2	326 22.3	N17 56.2	218 42.2	S18 56.7	Vega	80 38.1	N38 47.8
19	116 47.4	68 45.4	57.6	86 38.6	10.8	341 24.8	56.2	233 44.8	56.7	Zuben'ubi	137 03.8	S16 06.3
20	131 49.9	83 44.8	58.5	101 39.3	11.5	356 27.3	56.3	248 47.3	56.6		SHA	Mer. Pass.
21	146 52.3	98 44.3	18 59.4	116 40.0 ..	12.2	11 29.8 ..	56.3	263 49.9 ..	56.6		° ′	h m
22	161 54.8	113 43.8	19 00.3	131 40.7	12.8	26 32.3	56.3	278 52.4	56.6	Venus	314 05.5	14 24
23	176 57.3	128 43.3	N19 01.2	146 41.4	13.5	41 34.8	56.3	293 55.0	56.6	Mars	331 07.0	13 15
	h m									Jupiter	224 35.4	20 18
Mer. Pass. 11 18.0		v −0.5	d 0.9	v 0.7	d 0.7	v 2.5	d 0.0	v 2.5	d 0.0	Saturn	116 53.9	3 32

UT	SUN GHA	SUN Dec	MOON GHA	v	MOON Dec	d	HP
d h	° ′	° ′	° ′	′	° ′	′	′
1 00	178 58.6	N 4 19.9	35 23.9	14.9	N 7 27.8	8.5	54.0
01	193 58.8	20.9	49 57.8	15.0	7 19.3	8.6	54.0
02	208 59.0	21.8	64 31.8	14.9	7 10.7	8.5	54.0
03	223 59.1	.. 22.8	79 05.7	15.0	7 02.2	8.6	54.0
04	238 59.3	23.8	93 39.7	15.0	6 53.6	8.6	54.0
05	253 59.5	24.7	108 13.7	15.0	6 45.0	8.7	54.0
06	268 59.7	N 4 25.7	122 47.7	15.1	N 6 36.3	8.7	54.0
W 07	283 59.9	26.7	137 21.8	15.0	6 27.6	8.7	54.0
E 08	299 00.1	27.6	151 55.8	15.1	6 18.9	8.7	54.0
D 09	314 00.3	.. 28.6	166 29.9	15.1	6 10.2	8.7	54.0
N 10	329 00.4	29.6	181 04.0	15.1	6 01.5	8.8	54.0
E 11	344 00.6	30.5	195 38.1	15.1	5 52.7	8.8	54.0
S 12	359 00.8	N 4 31.5	210 12.2	15.1	N 5 43.9	8.8	54.0
D 13	14 01.0	32.4	224 46.3	15.1	5 35.1	8.9	54.0
A 14	29 01.2	33.4	239 20.4	15.2	5 26.2	8.8	54.0
Y 15	44 01.4	.. 34.4	253 54.6	15.1	5 17.4	8.9	54.0
16	59 01.6	35.3	268 28.7	15.2	5 08.5	8.9	54.0
17	74 01.7	36.3	283 02.9	15.2	4 59.6	9.0	54.0
18	89 01.9	N 4 37.3	297 37.1	15.1	N 4 50.6	8.9	54.0
19	104 02.1	38.2	312 11.2	15.2	4 41.7	9.0	54.0
20	119 02.3	39.2	326 45.4	15.2	4 32.7	9.0	54.0
21	134 02.5	.. 40.2	341 19.6	15.2	4 23.7	9.0	54.0
22	149 02.7	41.1	355 53.8	15.2	4 14.7	9.0	54.0
23	164 02.9	42.1	10 28.0	15.3	4 05.7	9.1	54.0
2 00	179 03.1	N 4 43.0	25 02.3	15.2	N 3 56.6	9.0	54.0
01	194 03.2	44.0	39 36.5	15.2	3 47.6	9.1	54.0
02	209 03.4	45.0	54 10.7	15.3	3 38.5	9.1	54.0
03	224 03.6	.. 45.9	68 45.0	15.2	3 29.4	9.1	54.0
04	239 03.8	46.9	83 19.2	15.2	3 20.3	9.2	54.0
05	254 04.0	47.9	97 53.4	15.3	3 11.1	9.1	54.0
06	269 04.2	N 4 48.8	112 27.7	15.2	N 3 02.0	9.2	54.0
T 07	284 04.4	49.8	127 01.9	15.3	2 52.8	9.1	54.0
H 08	299 04.5	50.7	141 36.2	15.3	2 43.7	9.2	54.0
U 09	314 04.7	.. 51.7	156 10.5	15.2	2 34.5	9.2	54.0
R 10	329 04.9	52.7	170 44.7	15.3	2 25.3	9.2	54.0
S 11	344 05.1	53.6	185 19.0	15.2	2 16.1	9.3	54.1
D 12	359 05.3	N 4 54.6	199 53.2	15.3	N 2 06.8	9.2	54.1
A 13	14 05.5	55.6	214 27.5	15.2	1 57.6	9.2	54.1
Y 14	29 05.7	56.5	229 01.7	15.3	1 48.4	9.3	54.1
15	44 05.8	.. 57.5	243 36.0	15.2	1 39.1	9.2	54.1
16	59 06.0	58.4	258 10.2	15.3	1 29.9	9.3	54.1
17	74 06.2	4 59.4	272 44.5	15.2	1 20.6	9.3	54.1
18	89 06.4	N 5 00.4	287 18.7	15.3	N 1 11.3	9.3	54.1
19	104 06.6	01.3	301 53.0	15.2	1 02.0	9.2	54.1
20	119 06.8	02.3	316 27.2	15.3	0 52.8	9.3	54.1
21	134 06.9	.. 03.2	331 01.5	15.2	0 43.5	9.3	54.1
22	149 07.1	04.2	345 35.7	15.2	0 34.2	9.3	54.1
23	164 07.3	05.2	0 09.9	15.2	0 24.9	9.3	54.1
3 00	179 07.5	N 5 06.1	14 44.1	15.2	N 0 15.6	9.4	54.1
01	194 07.7	07.1	29 18.3	15.2	N 0 06.2	9.3	54.1
02	209 07.9	08.0	43 52.5	15.2	S 0 03.1	9.3	54.1
03	224 08.1	.. 09.0	58 26.7	15.2	0 12.4	9.3	54.1
04	239 08.2	10.0	73 00.9	15.2	0 21.7	9.3	54.1
05	254 08.4	10.9	87 35.1	15.1	0 31.0	9.3	54.2
06	269 08.6	N 5 11.9	102 09.2	15.2	S 0 40.3	9.4	54.2
07	284 08.8	12.8	116 43.4	15.1	0 49.7	9.3	54.2
08	299 09.0	13.8	131 17.5	15.2	0 59.0	9.3	54.2
F 09	314 09.2	.. 14.7	145 51.7	15.1	1 08.3	9.3	54.2
R 10	329 09.3	15.7	160 25.8	15.1	1 17.6	9.3	54.2
I 11	344 09.5	16.7	174 59.9	15.1	1 26.9	9.4	54.2
D 12	359 09.7	N 5 17.6	189 34.0	15.1	S 1 36.3	9.3	54.2
A 13	14 09.9	18.6	204 08.1	15.0	1 45.6	9.3	54.2
Y 14	29 10.1	19.5	218 42.1	15.1	1 54.9	9.3	54.2
15	44 10.3	.. 20.5	233 16.2	15.0	2 04.2	9.3	54.2
16	59 10.4	21.4	247 50.2	15.1	2 13.5	9.3	54.2
17	74 10.6	22.4	262 24.2	15.1	2 22.8	9.2	54.2
18	89 10.8	N 5 23.4	276 58.3	14.9	S 2 32.0	9.3	54.3
19	104 11.0	24.3	291 32.2	15.0	2 41.3	9.3	54.3
20	119 11.2	25.3	306 06.2	15.0	2 50.6	9.2	54.3
21	134 11.4	.. 26.2	320 40.2	14.9	2 59.8	9.3	54.3
22	149 11.5	27.2	335 14.1	14.9	3 09.1	9.2	54.3
23	164 11.7	28.1	349 48.0	14.9	S 3 18.3	9.3	54.3
	SD 16.0	d 1.0	SD 14.7		14.7		14.8

Lat.	Twilight Naut.	Twilight Civil	Sunrise	Moonrise 1	Moonrise 2	Moonrise 3	Moonrise 4
°	h m	h m	h m	h m	h m	h m	h m
N 72	01 30	03 37	04 53	14 59	16 32	18 05	19 40
N 70	02 16	03 54	05 00	15 07	16 34	18 01	19 30
68	02 45	04 07	05 07	15 13	16 35	17 58	19 22
66	03 06	04 18	05 12	15 18	16 37	17 56	19 15
64	03 22	04 27	05 16	15 23	16 38	17 53	19 10
62	03 36	04 34	05 20	15 26	16 39	17 52	19 05
60	03 47	04 41	05 23	15 30	16 39	17 50	19 01
N 58	03 56	04 46	05 26	15 32	16 40	17 49	18 57
56	04 05	04 51	05 29	15 35	16 41	17 47	18 54
54	04 12	04 55	05 31	15 37	16 41	17 46	18 51
52	04 18	04 59	05 34	15 39	16 42	17 45	18 49
50	04 23	05 03	05 35	15 41	16 42	17 44	18 46
45	04 35	05 10	05 40	15 45	16 44	17 42	18 41
N 40	04 44	05 16	05 43	15 49	16 44	17 40	18 37
35	04 51	05 21	05 46	15 52	16 45	17 39	18 33
30	04 56	05 25	05 49	15 54	16 46	17 38	18 30
20	05 05	05 31	05 53	15 59	16 47	17 35	18 24
N 10	05 11	05 36	05 57	16 03	16 48	17 33	18 19
0	05 16	05 40	06 00	16 07	16 49	17 32	18 15
S 10	05 18	05 43	06 04	16 10	16 50	17 30	18 10
20	05 20	05 45	06 07	16 14	16 51	17 28	18 06
30	05 19	05 47	06 11	16 19	16 52	17 26	18 00
35	05 19	05 48	06 13	16 21	16 53	17 25	17 57
40	05 17	05 49	06 16	16 24	16 54	17 23	17 54
45	05 15	05 49	06 18	16 28	16 55	17 22	17 50
S 50	05 12	05 49	06 22	16 32	16 56	17 20	17 45
52	05 10	05 49	06 23	16 34	16 56	17 19	17 43
54	05 08	05 49	06 25	16 36	16 57	17 18	17 40
56	05 06	05 49	06 26	16 38	16 58	17 17	17 37
58	05 04	05 49	06 28	16 40	16 58	17 16	17 35
S 60	05 01	05 49	06 31	16 43	16 59	17 15	17 31

Lat.	Sunset	Twilight Civil	Twilight Naut.	Moonset 1	Moonset 2	Moonset 3	Moonset 4
°	h m	h m	h m	h m	h m	h m	h m
N 72	19 18	20 34	22 50	05 11	05 07	05 02	04 57
N 70	19 10	20 17	21 58	05 02	05 03	05 03	05 03
68	19 03	20 03	21 27	04 54	04 59	05 04	05 08
66	18 58	19 52	21 05	04 48	04 56	05 04	05 12
64	18 53	19 43	20 48	04 42	04 54	05 05	05 16
62	18 49	19 35	20 34	04 38	04 52	05 05	05 19
60	18 45	19 29	20 23	04 33	04 50	05 05	05 21
N 58	18 42	19 23	20 13	04 30	04 48	05 06	05 24
56	18 40	19 18	20 05	04 26	04 47	05 06	05 26
54	18 37	19 13	19 57	04 23	04 45	05 06	05 28
52	18 35	19 09	19 51	04 21	04 44	05 07	05 29
50	18 33	19 06	19 45	04 18	04 43	05 07	05 31
45	18 28	18 58	19 34	04 13	04 40	05 07	05 34
N 40	18 25	18 52	19 25	04 08	04 38	05 08	05 37
35	18 22	18 47	19 17	04 04	04 36	05 08	05 40
30	18 19	18 43	19 11	04 01	04 35	05 08	05 42
20	18 14	18 37	19 02	03 55	04 32	05 09	05 46
N 10	18 11	18 32	18 56	03 50	04 30	05 09	05 49
0	18 07	18 28	18 52	03 45	04 27	05 10	05 52
S 10	18 03	18 24	18 49	03 39	04 25	05 10	05 56
20	18 00	18 22	18 47	03 34	04 22	05 10	05 59
30	17 56	18 20	18 47	03 28	04 19	05 11	06 03
35	17 54	18 19	18 48	03 24	04 18	05 11	06 05
40	17 51	18 18	18 49	03 20	04 16	05 11	06 08
45	17 48	18 18	18 51	03 15	04 13	05 12	06 10
S 50	17 45	18 17	18 54	03 10	04 11	05 12	06 14
52	17 43	18 17	18 56	03 07	04 09	05 12	06 16
54	17 42	18 17	18 58	03 04	04 08	05 12	06 17
56	17 40	18 17	19 00	03 01	04 07	05 13	06 19
58	17 38	18 17	19 02	02 57	04 05	05 13	06 21
S 60	17 35	18 17	19 05	02 53	04 03	05 13	06 24

	SUN Eqn. of Time 00ʰ	SUN Eqn. of Time 12ʰ	SUN Mer. Pass.	MOON Mer. Pass. Upper	MOON Mer. Pass. Lower	MOON Age	MOON Phase
Day							
d	m s	m s	h m	h m	h m	d	%
1	04 06	03 57	12 04	22 17	09 56	12	92
2	03 48	03 39	12 04	22 59	10 38	13	96
3	03 30	03 22	12 03	23 42	11 21	14	99

UT	ARIES	VENUS −4.0		MARS +1.4		JUPITER −2.3		SATURN +0.3		STARS		
	GHA	GHA	Dec	GHA	Dec	GHA	Dec	GHA	Dec	Name	SHA	Dec
d h	° ′	° ′	° ′	° ′	° ′	° ′	° ′	° ′	° ′		° ′	° ′
4 00	191 59.7	143 42.8	N19 02.2	161 42.1	N12 14.1	56 37.3	N17 56.3	308 57.5	S18 56.6	Acamar	315 17.8	S40 14.9
01	207 02.2	158 42.3	03.1	176 42.8	14.8	71 39.8	56.3	324 00.1	56.5	Achernar	335 26.5	S57 09.7
02	222 04.7	173 41.8	04.0	191 43.5	15.5	86 42.3	56.3	339 02.6	56.5	Acrux	173 07.1	S63 11.1
03	237 07.1	188 41.3 ..	04.9	206 44.2 ..	16.1	101 44.8 ..	56.3	354 05.2 ..	56.5	Adhara	255 11.6	S29 00.0
04	252 09.6	203 40.8	05.8	221 44.9	16.8	116 47.3	56.3	9 07.7	56.5	Aldebaran	290 48.2	N16 32.1
05	267 12.1	218 40.2	06.7	236 45.6	17.4	131 49.8	56.3	24 10.3	56.5			
S 06	282 14.5	233 39.7	N19 07.6	251 46.3	N12 18.1	146 52.3	N17 56.3	39 12.8	S18 56.4	Alioth	166 19.2	N55 52.6
A 07	297 17.0	248 39.2	08.5	266 47.0	18.8	161 54.8	56.3	54 15.4	56.4	Alkaid	152 57.5	N49 14.2
T 08	312 19.4	263 38.7	09.5	281 47.7	19.4	176 57.3	56.3	69 17.9	56.4	Al Na'ir	27 42.6	S46 53.0
U 09	327 21.9	278 38.2 ..	10.4	296 48.4 ..	20.1	191 59.8 ..	56.3	84 20.5 ..	56.4	Alnilam	275 45.3	S 1 11.9
R 10	342 24.4	293 37.7	11.3	311 49.1	20.7	207 02.3	56.4	99 23.0	56.4	Alphard	217 54.7	S 8 43.8
D 11	357 26.8	308 37.1	12.2	326 49.8	21.4	222 04.8	56.4	114 25.6	56.3			
A 12	12 29.3	323 36.6	N19 13.1	341 50.5	N12 22.0	237 07.3	N17 56.4	129 28.1	S18 56.3	Alphecca	126 09.7	N26 39.7
Y 13	27 31.8	338 36.1	14.0	356 51.2	22.7	252 09.8	56.4	144 30.7	56.3	Alpheratz	357 42.5	N29 10.3
14	42 34.2	353 35.6	14.9	11 51.9	23.4	267 12.3	56.4	159 33.2	56.3	Altair	62 07.1	N 8 54.5
15	57 36.7	8 35.1 ..	15.8	26 52.6 ..	24.0	282 14.8 ..	56.4	174 35.8 ..	56.3	Ankaa	353 15.0	S42 13.5
16	72 39.2	23 34.6	16.7	41 53.3	24.7	297 17.3	56.4	189 38.3	56.2	Antares	112 24.5	S26 27.8
17	87 41.6	38 34.0	17.6	56 54.0	25.3	312 19.8	56.4	204 40.9	56.2			
18	102 44.1	53 33.5	N19 18.5	71 54.7	N12 26.0	327 22.3	N17 56.4	219 43.4	S18 56.2	Arcturus	145 54.3	N19 06.1
19	117 46.6	68 33.0	19.4	86 55.4	26.6	342 24.8	56.4	234 46.0	56.2	Atria	107 24.9	S69 02.9
20	132 49.0	83 32.5	20.3	101 56.1	27.3	357 27.3	56.4	249 48.5	56.2	Avior	234 17.2	S59 34.0
21	147 51.5	98 32.0 ..	21.2	116 56.8 ..	28.0	12 29.8 ..	56.4	264 51.1 ..	56.1	Bellatrix	278 30.8	N 6 21.5
22	162 53.9	113 31.5	22.1	131 57.5	28.6	27 32.3	56.4	279 53.6	56.1	Betelgeuse	271 00.1	N 7 24.3
23	177 56.4	128 30.9	23.0	146 58.2	29.3	42 34.8	56.4	294 56.2	56.1			
5 00	192 58.9	143 30.4	N19 23.9	161 58.9	N12 29.9	57 37.3	N17 56.4	309 58.7	S18 56.1	Canopus	263 55.7	S52 42.7
01	208 01.3	158 29.9	24.8	176 59.6	30.6	72 39.8	56.4	325 01.3	56.1	Capella	280 32.8	N46 00.7
02	223 03.8	173 29.4	25.7	192 00.3	31.2	87 42.3	56.4	340 03.8	56.0	Deneb	49 30.8	N45 19.9
03	238 06.3	188 28.8 ..	26.6	207 01.0 ..	31.9	102 44.8 ..	56.5	355 06.4 ..	56.0	Denebola	182 32.1	N14 29.1
04	253 08.7	203 28.3	27.5	222 01.7	32.5	117 47.3	56.5	10 09.0	56.0	Diphda	348 55.0	S17 54.3
05	268 11.2	218 27.8	28.4	237 02.4	33.2	132 49.7	56.5	25 11.5	56.0			
S 06	283 13.7	233 27.3	N19 29.3	252 03.1	N12 33.9	147 52.2	N17 56.5	40 14.1	S18 55.9	Dubhe	193 49.8	N61 40.1
U 07	298 16.1	248 26.8	30.2	267 03.8	34.5	162 54.7	56.5	55 16.6	55.9	Elnath	278 11.2	N28 37.0
N 08	313 18.6	263 26.2	31.0	282 04.5	35.2	177 57.2	56.5	70 19.2	55.9	Eltanin	90 45.4	N51 29.1
D 09	328 21.0	278 25.7 ..	31.9	297 05.2 ..	35.8	192 59.7 ..	56.5	85 21.7 ..	55.9	Enif	33 46.1	N 9 56.7
A 10	343 23.5	293 25.2	32.8	312 05.9	36.5	208 02.2	56.5	100 24.3	55.9	Fomalhaut	15 23.0	S29 32.4
Y 11	358 26.0	308 24.7	33.7	327 06.6	37.1	223 04.7	56.5	115 26.8	55.8			
12	13 28.4	323 24.1	N19 34.6	342 07.3	N12 37.8	238 07.2	N17 56.5	130 29.4	S18 55.8	Gacrux	171 58.8	S57 12.0
13	28 30.9	338 23.6	35.5	357 08.0	38.4	253 09.7	56.5	145 31.9	55.8	Gienah	175 50.7	S17 37.7
14	43 33.4	353 23.1	36.4	12 08.7	39.1	268 12.2	56.5	160 34.5	55.8	Hadar	148 45.4	S60 26.7
15	58 35.8	8 22.6 ..	37.3	27 09.4 ..	39.7	283 14.7 ..	56.5	175 37.0 ..	55.8	Hamal	327 59.7	N23 31.9
16	73 38.3	23 22.0	38.1	42 10.1	40.4	298 17.1	56.5	190 39.6	55.7	Kaus Aust.	83 42.1	S34 22.3
17	88 40.8	38 21.5	39.0	57 10.7	41.0	313 19.6	56.5	205 42.2	55.7			
18	103 43.2	53 21.0	N19 39.9	72 11.4	N12 41.7	328 22.1	N17 56.5	220 44.7	S18 55.7	Kochab	137 19.2	N74 05.5
19	118 45.7	68 20.5	40.8	87 12.1	42.3	343 24.6	56.5	235 47.3	55.7	Markab	13 37.4	N15 17.1
20	133 48.2	83 19.9	41.7	102 12.8	43.0	358 27.1	56.5	250 49.8	55.7	Menkar	314 14.0	N 4 08.7
21	148 50.6	98 19.4 ..	42.5	117 13.5 ..	43.6	13 29.6 ..	56.5	265 52.4 ..	55.6	Menkent	148 05.7	S36 26.7
22	163 53.1	113 18.9	43.4	132 14.2	44.3	28 32.1	56.5	280 54.9	55.6	Miaplacidus	221 38.8	S69 47.2
23	178 55.5	128 18.3	44.3	147 14.9	44.9	43 34.6	56.5	295 57.5	55.6			
6 00	193 58.0	143 17.8	N19 45.2	162 15.6	N12 45.6	58 37.0	N17 56.5	311 00.1	S18 55.6	Mirfak	308 38.9	N49 54.8
01	209 00.5	158 17.3	46.0	177 16.3	46.2	73 39.5	56.5	326 02.6	55.5	Nunki	75 56.8	S26 16.4
02	224 02.9	173 16.8	46.9	192 17.0	46.9	88 42.0	56.5	341 05.2	55.5	Peacock	53 17.6	S56 40.8
03	239 05.4	188 16.2 ..	47.8	207 17.7 ..	47.5	103 44.5 ..	56.5	356 07.7 ..	55.5	Pollux	243 26.2	N27 59.2
04	254 07.9	203 15.7	48.7	222 18.4	48.2	118 47.0	56.5	11 10.3	55.5	Procyon	244 58.4	N 5 10.8
05	269 10.3	218 15.2	49.5	237 19.1	48.8	133 49.5	56.5	26 12.8	55.5			
M 06	284 12.8	233 14.6	N19 50.4	252 19.8	N12 49.5	148 52.0	N17 56.5	41 15.4	S18 55.4	Rasalhague	96 05.2	N12 32.9
O 07	299 15.3	248 14.1	51.3	267 20.5	50.1	163 54.4	56.6	56 18.0	55.4	Regulus	207 42.0	N11 53.4
N 08	314 17.7	263 13.6	52.1	282 21.2	50.8	178 56.9	56.6	71 20.5	55.4	Rigel	281 11.0	S 8 11.4
D 09	329 20.2	278 13.0 ..	53.0	297 21.9 ..	51.4	193 59.4 ..	56.6	86 23.1 ..	55.4	Rigil Kent.	139 49.4	S60 53.7
A 10	344 22.6	293 12.5	53.9	312 22.6	52.1	209 01.9	56.6	101 25.6	55.4	Sabik	102 11.0	S15 44.5
Y 11	359 25.1	308 12.0	54.8	327 23.3	52.7	224 04.4	56.6	116 28.2	55.3			
12	14 27.6	323 11.4	N19 55.6	342 24.0	N12 53.4	239 06.9	N17 56.6	131 30.7	S18 55.3	Schedar	349 39.6	N56 37.1
13	29 30.0	338 10.9	56.5	357 24.7	54.0	254 09.3	56.6	146 33.3	55.3	Shaula	96 20.1	S37 06.6
14	44 32.5	353 10.4	57.3	12 25.4	54.7	269 11.8	56.6	161 35.9	55.3	Sirius	258 32.7	S16 44.6
15	59 35.0	8 09.8 ..	58.2	27 26.1 ..	55.3	284 14.3 ..	56.6	176 38.4 ..	55.2	Spica	158 29.6	S11 14.5
16	74 37.4	23 09.3	59.1	42 26.8	55.9	299 16.8	56.6	191 41.0	55.2	Suhail	222 51.3	S43 30.1
17	89 39.9	38 08.8	19 59.9	57 27.5	56.6	314 19.3	56.6	206 43.5	55.2			
18	104 42.4	53 08.2	N20 00.8	72 28.2	N12 57.2	329 21.8	N17 56.6	221 46.1	S18 55.2	Vega	80 38.1	N38 47.8
19	119 44.8	68 07.7	01.7	87 28.9	57.9	344 24.2	56.6	236 48.7	55.2	Zuben'ubi	137 03.8	S16 06.3
20	134 47.3	83 07.2	02.5	102 29.5	58.5	359 26.7	56.6	251 51.2	55.1		SHA	Mer. Pass.
21	149 49.8	98 06.6 ..	03.4	117 30.2 ..	59.2	14 29.2 ..	56.6	266 53.8 ..	55.1		° ′	h m
22	164 52.2	113 06.1	04.2	132 30.9	12 59.8	29 31.7	56.6	281 56.3	55.1	Venus	310 31.5	14 26
23	179 54.7	128 05.5	05.1	147 31.6	N13 00.5	44 34.2	56.6	296 58.9	55.1	Mars	329 00.0	13 11
	h m									Jupiter	224 38.4	20 06
Mer. Pass. 11 06.3	v −0.5 d 0.9		v 0.7 d 0.7		v 2.5 d 0.0		v 2.6 d 0.0		Saturn	116 59.9	3 20

SUN and MOON

UT	SUN GHA	SUN Dec	MOON GHA	v	MOON Dec	d	HP
d h	° ′	° ′	° ′	′	° ′	′	′
4 00	179 11.9	N 5 29.1	4 21.9	14.9	S 3 27.6	9.2	54.3
01	194 12.1	30.0	18 55.8	14.9	3 36.8	9.2	54.3
02	209 12.3	31.0	33 29.7	14.8	3 46.0	9.2	54.3
03	224 12.5	.. 32.0	48 03.5	14.8	3 55.2	9.2	54.3
04	239 12.6	32.9	62 37.3	14.8	4 04.4	9.1	54.3
05	254 12.8	33.9	77 11.1	14.8	4 13.5	9.2	54.4
06	269 13.0	N 5 34.8	91 44.9	14.7	S 4 22.7	9.1	54.4
07	284 13.2	35.8	106 18.6	14.7	4 31.8	9.2	54.4
08	299 13.4	36.7	120 52.3	14.7	4 41.0	9.1	54.4
09	314 13.6	.. 37.7	135 26.0	14.7	4 50.1	9.1	54.4
10	329 13.7	38.6	149 59.7	14.7	4 59.2	9.0	54.4
11	344 13.9	39.6	164 33.4	14.6	5 08.2	9.1	54.4
12	359 14.1	N 5 40.5	179 07.0	14.6	S 5 17.3	9.0	54.4
13	14 14.3	41.5	193 40.6	14.6	5 26.3	9.1	54.4
14	29 14.5	42.4	208 14.2	14.5	5 35.4	9.0	54.5
15	44 14.7	.. 43.4	222 47.7	14.5	5 44.4	8.9	54.5
16	59 14.8	44.4	237 21.2	14.5	5 53.3	9.0	54.5
17	74 15.0	45.3	251 54.7	14.5	6 02.3	8.9	54.5
18	89 15.2	N 5 46.3	266 28.2	14.4	S 6 11.2	9.0	54.5
19	104 15.4	47.2	281 01.6	14.4	6 20.2	8.8	54.5
20	119 15.6	48.2	295 35.0	14.4	6 29.0	8.9	54.5
21	134 15.7	.. 49.1	310 08.4	14.4	6 37.9	8.9	54.5
22	149 15.9	50.1	324 41.8	14.3	6 46.8	8.8	54.6
23	164 16.1	51.0	339 15.1	14.3	6 55.6	8.8	54.6
5 00	179 16.3	N 5 52.0	353 48.4	14.2	S 7 04.4	8.7	54.6
01	194 16.5	52.9	8 21.6	14.2	7 13.1	8.8	54.6
02	209 16.7	53.9	22 54.8	14.2	7 21.9	8.7	54.6
03	224 16.8	.. 54.8	37 28.0	14.2	7 30.6	8.7	54.6
04	239 17.0	55.8	52 01.2	14.1	7 39.3	8.6	54.6
05	254 17.2	56.7	66 34.3	14.1	7 47.9	8.7	54.6
06	269 17.4	N 5 57.7	81 07.4	14.0	S 7 56.6	8.5	54.7
07	284 17.6	58.6	95 40.4	14.1	8 05.1	8.6	54.7
08	299 17.7	5 59.6	110 13.5	14.0	8 13.7	8.5	54.7
09	314 17.9	6 00.5	124 46.5	13.9	8 22.2	8.5	54.7
10	329 18.1	01.5	139 19.4	13.9	8 30.7	8.5	54.7
11	344 18.3	02.4	153 52.3	13.9	8 39.2	8.4	54.7
12	359 18.5	N 6 03.4	168 25.2	13.8	S 8 47.6	8.4	54.7
13	14 18.6	04.3	182 58.0	13.8	8 56.0	8.4	54.7
14	29 18.8	05.3	197 30.8	13.8	9 04.4	8.3	54.8
15	44 19.0	.. 06.2	212 03.6	13.7	9 12.7	8.3	54.8
16	59 19.2	07.2	226 36.3	13.7	9 21.0	8.3	54.8
17	74 19.4	08.1	241 09.0	13.7	9 29.3	8.2	54.8
18	89 19.5	N 6 09.1	255 41.7	13.6	S 9 37.5	8.2	54.8
19	104 19.7	10.0	270 14.3	13.6	9 45.7	8.1	54.8
20	119 19.9	11.0	284 46.9	13.5	9 53.8	8.1	54.8
21	134 20.1	.. 11.9	299 19.4	13.5	10 01.9	8.1	54.9
22	149 20.3	12.9	313 51.9	13.5	10 10.0	8.0	54.9
23	164 20.4	13.8	328 24.4	13.4	10 18.0	7.9	54.9
6 00	179 20.6	N 6 14.7	342 56.8	13.4	S10 25.9	8.0	54.9
01	194 20.8	15.7	357 29.2	13.3	10 33.9	7.9	54.9
02	209 21.0	16.6	12 01.5	13.3	10 41.8	7.8	54.9
03	224 21.2	.. 17.6	26 33.8	13.2	10 49.6	7.8	55.0
04	239 21.3	18.5	41 06.0	13.2	10 57.4	7.8	55.0
05	254 21.5	19.5	55 38.2	13.2	11 05.2	7.7	55.0
06	269 21.7	N 6 20.4	70 10.4	13.1	S11 12.9	7.6	55.0
07	284 21.9	21.4	84 42.5	13.1	11 20.5	7.6	55.0
08	299 22.1	22.3	99 14.6	13.0	11 28.1	7.6	55.0
09	314 22.2	.. 23.3	113 46.6	13.0	11 35.7	7.5	55.1
10	329 22.4	24.2	128 18.6	13.0	11 43.2	7.5	55.1
11	344 22.6	25.2	142 50.6	12.9	11 50.7	7.4	55.1
12	359 22.8	N 6 26.1	157 22.5	12.8	S11 58.1	7.4	55.1
13	14 23.0	27.0	171 54.3	12.8	12 05.5	7.3	55.1
14	29 23.1	28.0	186 26.1	12.8	12 12.8	7.2	55.1
15	44 23.3	.. 28.9	200 57.9	12.7	12 20.0	7.2	55.2
16	59 23.5	29.9	215 29.6	12.7	12 27.2	7.2	55.2
17	74 23.7	30.8	230 01.3	12.7	12 34.4	7.1	55.2
18	89 23.8	N 6 31.8	244 33.0	12.5	S12 41.5	7.0	55.2
19	104 24.0	32.7	259 04.5	12.6	12 48.5	7.0	55.2
20	119 24.2	33.6	273 36.1	12.5	12 55.5	7.0	55.2
21	134 24.4	.. 34.6	288 07.6	12.4	13 02.5	6.8	55.3
22	149 24.6	35.5	302 39.0	12.4	13 09.3	6.8	55.3
23	164 24.7	36.5	317 10.4	12.4	S13 16.1	6.8	55.3
	SD 16.0	d 0.9	SD 14.8		14.9		15.0

Days marked: S A T U R D A Y (04–23 of 4th); S U N D A Y (5th); M O N D A Y (6th).

Twilight, Sunrise, Moonrise

Lat.	Naut.	Civil	Sunrise	Moonrise 4	5	6	7
°	h m	h m	h m	h m	h m	h m	h m
N 72	00 30	03 18	04 37	19 40	21 17	22 59	24 48
N 70	01 49	03 38	04 46	19 30	21 00	22 33	24 06
68	02 25	03 53	04 54	19 22	20 47	22 13	23 38
66	02 50	04 05	05 00	19 15	20 36	21 57	23 17
64	03 09	04 15	05 06	19 10	20 27	21 44	23 00
62	03 24	04 24	05 10	19 05	20 19	21 33	22 46
60	03 36	04 31	05 14	19 01	20 13	21 24	22 34
N 58	03 46	04 37	05 18	18 57	20 07	21 16	22 24
56	03 55	04 43	05 21	18 54	20 02	21 09	22 15
54	04 03	04 48	05 24	18 51	19 57	21 03	22 07
52	04 10	04 52	05 27	18 49	19 53	20 57	22 01
50	04 16	04 56	05 29	18 46	19 49	20 52	21 54
45	04 29	05 04	05 34	18 41	19 41	20 41	21 41
N 40	04 38	05 11	05 38	18 37	19 34	20 32	21 30
35	04 46	05 16	05 42	18 33	19 28	20 24	21 20
30	04 53	05 21	05 45	18 30	19 23	20 17	21 12
20	05 02	05 28	05 51	18 24	19 14	20 05	20 58
N 10	05 10	05 34	05 55	18 19	19 07	19 55	20 45
0	05 15	05 39	05 59	18 15	18 59	19 46	20 34
S 10	05 18	05 43	06 04	18 10	18 52	19 36	20 22
20	05 20	05 46	06 08	18 06	18 45	19 26	20 10
30	05 21	05 49	06 13	18 00	18 36	19 14	19 56
35	05 21	05 50	06 16	17 57	18 31	19 08	19 48
40	05 20	05 51	06 19	17 54	18 26	19 00	19 39
45	05 19	05 53	06 22	17 50	18 19	18 52	19 28
S 50	05 16	05 54	06 26	17 45	18 11	18 41	19 15
52	05 15	05 54	06 28	17 43	18 08	18 36	19 09
54	05 14	05 55	06 30	17 40	18 04	18 31	19 02
56	05 12	05 55	06 32	17 37	18 00	18 25	18 55
58	05 10	05 56	06 35	17 35	17 55	18 18	18 47
S 60	05 08	05 56	06 38	17 31	17 50	18 11	18 37

Sunset, Twilight, Moonset

Lat.	Sunset	Civil	Naut.	Moonset 4	5	6	7
°	h m	h m	h m	h m	h m	h m	h m
N 72	19 32	20 52	////	04 57	04 53	04 47	04 42
N 70	19 22	20 32	22 25	05 03	05 04	05 06	05 09
68	19 14	20 16	21 46	05 08	05 13	05 20	05 30
66	19 07	20 03	21 20	05 12	05 21	05 32	05 47
64	19 02	19 53	21 00	05 16	05 28	05 42	06 00
62	18 57	19 44	20 45	05 19	05 34	05 51	06 12
60	18 53	19 36	20 32	05 21	05 38	05 58	06 22
N 58	18 49	19 30	20 21	05 24	05 43	06 05	06 30
56	18 46	19 24	20 12	05 26	05 47	06 10	06 38
54	18 43	19 19	20 04	05 28	05 50	06 16	06 44
52	18 40	19 15	19 57	05 29	05 54	06 20	06 50
50	18 38	19 11	19 51	05 31	05 57	06 24	06 56
45	18 32	19 02	19 38	05 34	06 03	06 34	07 08
N 40	18 28	18 55	19 28	05 37	06 08	06 41	07 18
35	18 24	18 50	19 20	05 40	06 13	06 48	07 26
30	18 21	18 45	19 13	05 42	06 17	06 54	07 34
20	18 15	18 37	19 03	05 46	06 24	07 04	07 47
N 10	18 10	18 32	18 56	05 49	06 30	07 13	07 58
0	18 06	18 27	18 51	05 52	06 36	07 21	08 08
S 10	18 02	18 23	18 47	05 56	06 42	07 30	08 19
20	17 57	18 19	18 45	05 59	06 48	07 39	08 30
30	17 52	18 16	18 44	06 03	06 56	07 49	08 43
35	17 50	18 15	18 44	06 05	07 00	07 55	08 51
40	17 46	18 13	18 45	06 08	07 04	08 02	09 00
45	17 43	18 12	18 46	06 10	07 10	08 10	09 10
S 50	17 38	18 11	18 48	06 14	07 16	08 19	09 22
52	17 37	18 10	18 49	06 16	07 19	08 24	09 27
54	17 34	18 10	18 51	06 17	07 23	08 28	09 34
56	17 32	18 09	18 52	06 19	07 26	08 34	09 41
58	17 29	18 09	18 54	06 21	07 31	08 40	09 48
S 60	17 27	18 08	18 56	06 24	07 35	08 47	09 57

SUN and MOON

Day	Eqn. of Time 00ʰ	12ʰ	Mer. Pass.	Mer. Pass. Upper	Lower	Age	Phase
d	m s	m s	h m	h m	h m	d	%
4	03 13	03 04	12 03	24 04	12 04	15	100
5	02 55	02 47	12 03	00 26	12 48	16	99
6	02 38	02 29	12 02	01 10	13 33	17	96

UT	ARIES GHA	VENUS −4.0 GHA	Dec	MARS +1.4 GHA	Dec	JUPITER −2.3 GHA	Dec	SATURN +0.3 GHA	Dec	STARS Name	SHA	Dec
7 00	194 57.1	143 05.0	N20 05.9	162 32.3	N13 01.1	59 36.6	N17 56.6	312 01.5	S18 55.0	Acamar	315 17.8	S40 14.9
01	209 59.6	158 04.5	06.8	177 33.0	01.8	74 39.1	56.6	327 04.0	55.0	Achernar	335 26.6	S57 09.7
02	225 02.1	173 03.9	07.7	192 33.7	02.4	89 41.6	56.6	342 06.6	55.0	Acrux	173 07.1	S63 11.1
03	240 04.5	188 03.4 ..	08.5	207 34.4 ..	03.0	104 44.1 ..	56.6	357 09.1 ..	55.0	Adhara	255 11.6	S29 00.0
04	255 07.0	203 02.9	09.4	222 35.1	03.7	119 46.5	56.6	12 11.7	55.0	Aldebaran	290 48.2	N16 32.1
05	270 09.5	218 02.3	10.2	237 35.8	04.3	134 49.0	56.6	27 14.3	54.9			
06	285 11.9	233 01.8	N20 11.1	252 36.5	N13 05.0	149 51.5	N17 56.6	42 16.8	S18 54.9	Alioth	166 19.2	N55 52.6
07	300 14.4	248 01.2	11.9	267 37.2	05.6	164 54.0	56.6	57 19.4	54.9	Alkaid	152 57.5	N49 14.2
T 08	315 16.9	263 00.7	12.8	282 37.9	06.3	179 56.4	56.6	72 21.9	54.9	Al Na'ir	27 42.6	S46 53.0
U 09	330 19.3	278 00.2 ..	13.6	297 38.6 ..	06.9	194 58.9 ..	56.6	87 24.5 ..	54.8	Alnilam	275 45.3	S 1 11.9
E 10	345 21.8	292 59.6	14.4	312 39.3	07.5	210 01.4	56.6	102 27.1	54.8	Alphard	217 54.7	S 8 43.8
S 11	0 24.3	307 59.1	15.3	327 40.0	08.2	225 03.9	56.6	117 29.6	54.8			
D 12	15 26.7	322 58.5	N20 16.1	342 40.7	N13 08.8	240 06.4	N17 56.6	132 32.2	S18 54.8	Alphecca	126 09.7	N26 39.8
A 13	30 29.2	337 58.0	17.0	357 41.4	09.5	255 08.8	56.6	147 34.8	54.8	Alpheratz	357 42.5	N29 10.3
Y 14	45 31.6	352 57.4	17.8	12 42.0	10.1	270 11.3	56.6	162 37.3	54.7	Altair	62 07.1	N 8 54.5
15	60 34.1	7 56.9 ..	18.7	27 42.7 ..	10.7	285 13.8 ..	56.6	177 39.9 ..	54.7	Ankaa	353 15.0	S42 13.4
16	75 36.6	22 56.4	19.5	42 43.4	11.4	300 16.2	56.6	192 42.4	54.7	Antares	112 24.5	S26 27.8
17	90 39.0	37 55.8	20.4	57 44.1	12.0	315 18.7	56.6	207 45.0	54.7			
18	105 41.5	52 55.3	N20 21.2	72 44.8	N13 12.7	330 21.2	N17 56.6	222 47.6	S18 54.6	Arcturus	145 54.3	N19 06.1
19	120 44.0	67 54.7	22.0	87 45.5	13.3	345 23.7	56.6	237 50.1	54.6	Atria	107 24.9	S69 02.9
20	135 46.4	82 54.2	22.9	102 46.2	13.9	0 26.1	56.6	252 52.7	54.6	Avior	234 17.3	S59 34.0
21	150 48.9	97 53.6 ..	23.7	117 46.9 ..	14.6	15 28.6 ..	56.6	267 55.3 ..	54.6	Bellatrix	278 30.8	N 6 21.5
22	165 51.4	112 53.1	24.5	132 47.6	15.2	30 31.1	56.6	282 57.8	54.6	Betelgeuse	271 00.1	N 7 24.3
23	180 53.8	127 52.6	25.4	147 48.3	15.9	45 33.6	56.6	298 00.4	54.5			
8 00	195 56.3	142 52.0	N20 26.2	162 49.0	N13 16.5	60 36.0	N17 56.6	313 03.0	S18 54.5	Canopus	263 55.7	S52 42.7
01	210 58.7	157 51.5	27.0	177 49.7	17.1	75 38.5	56.6	328 05.5	54.5	Capella	280 32.9	N46 00.7
02	226 01.2	172 50.9	27.9	192 50.4	17.8	90 41.0	56.6	343 08.1	54.5	Deneb	49 30.8	N45 19.9
03	241 03.7	187 50.4 ..	28.7	207 51.1 ..	18.4	105 43.4 ..	56.6	358 10.6 ..	54.4	Denebola	182 32.1	N14 29.1
04	256 06.1	202 49.8	29.5	222 51.8	19.1	120 45.9	56.6	13 13.2	54.4	Diphda	348 55.0	S17 54.3
05	271 08.6	217 49.3	30.4	237 52.4	19.7	135 48.4	56.6	28 15.8	54.4			
06	286 11.1	232 48.7	N20 31.2	252 53.1	N13 20.3	150 50.8	N17 56.6	43 18.3	S18 54.4	Dubhe	193 49.8	N61 40.1
W 07	301 13.5	247 48.2	32.0	267 53.8	21.0	165 53.3	56.5	58 20.9	54.4	Elnath	278 11.2	N28 37.0
E 08	316 16.0	262 47.6	32.9	282 54.5	21.6	180 55.8	56.5	73 23.5	54.3	Eltanin	90 45.4	N51 29.1
D 09	331 18.5	277 47.1 ..	33.7	297 55.2 ..	22.2	195 58.2 ..	56.5	88 26.0 ..	54.3	Enif	33 46.1	N 9 56.7
N 10	346 20.9	292 46.5	34.5	312 55.9	22.9	211 00.7	56.5	103 28.6	54.3	Fomalhaut	15 23.0	S29 32.4
E 11	1 23.4	307 46.0	35.3	327 56.6	23.5	226 03.2	56.5	118 31.2	54.3			
S 12	16 25.9	322 45.4	N20 36.2	342 57.3	N13 24.1	241 05.6	N17 56.5	133 33.7	S18 54.2	Gacrux	171 58.8	S57 12.0
D 13	31 28.3	337 44.9	37.0	357 58.0	24.8	256 08.1	56.5	148 36.3	54.2	Gienah	175 50.7	S17 37.7
A 14	46 30.8	352 44.3	37.8	12 58.7	25.4	271 10.6	56.5	163 38.9	54.2	Hadar	148 45.4	S60 26.7
Y 15	61 33.2	7 43.8 ..	38.6	27 59.4 ..	26.1	286 13.0 ..	56.5	178 41.4 ..	54.2	Hamal	327 59.7	N23 31.9
16	76 35.7	22 43.2	39.4	43 00.1	26.7	301 15.5	56.5	193 44.0	54.1	Kaus Aust.	83 42.1	S34 22.3
17	91 38.2	37 42.7	40.3	58 00.8	27.3	316 18.0	56.5	208 46.6	54.1			
18	106 40.6	52 42.1	N20 41.1	73 01.4	N13 28.0	331 20.4	N17 56.5	223 49.1	S18 54.1	Kochab	137 19.2	N74 05.5
19	121 43.1	67 41.6	41.9	88 02.1	28.6	346 22.9	56.5	238 51.7	54.1	Markab	13 37.4	N15 17.1
20	136 45.6	82 41.0	42.7	103 02.8	29.2	1 25.4	56.5	253 54.3	54.1	Menkar	314 14.1	N 4 08.7
21	151 48.0	97 40.5 ..	43.5	118 03.5 ..	29.9	16 27.8 ..	56.5	268 56.8 ..	54.0	Menkent	148 05.7	S36 26.7
22	166 50.5	112 39.9	44.3	133 04.2	30.5	31 30.3	56.5	283 59.4	54.0	Miaplacidus	221 38.8	S69 47.2
23	181 53.0	127 39.4	45.2	148 04.9	31.1	46 32.8	56.5	299 02.0	54.0			
9 00	196 55.4	142 38.8	N20 46.0	163 05.6	N13 31.8	61 35.2	N17 56.5	314 04.5	S18 54.0	Mirfak	308 39.0	N49 54.8
01	211 57.9	157 38.2	46.8	178 06.3	32.4	76 37.7	56.5	329 07.1	53.9	Nunki	75 56.8	S26 16.4
02	227 00.4	172 37.7	47.6	193 07.0	33.0	91 40.2	56.5	344 09.7	53.9	Peacock	53 17.6	S56 40.8
03	242 02.8	187 37.1 ..	48.4	208 07.7 ..	33.7	106 42.6 ..	56.5	359 12.2 ..	53.9	Pollux	243 26.2	N27 59.2
04	257 05.3	202 36.6	49.2	223 08.4	34.3	121 45.1	56.5	14 14.8	53.9	Procyon	244 58.4	N 5 10.8
05	272 07.7	217 36.0	50.0	238 09.1	34.9	136 47.5	56.5	29 17.4	53.8			
06	287 10.2	232 35.5	N20 50.8	253 09.7	N13 35.6	151 50.0	N17 56.5	44 19.9	S18 53.8	Rasalhague	96 05.2	N12 33.0
07	302 12.7	247 34.9	51.6	268 10.4	36.2	166 52.5	56.5	59 22.5	53.8	Regulus	207 42.0	N11 53.4
T 08	317 15.1	262 34.4	52.4	283 11.1	36.8	181 54.9	56.5	74 25.1	53.8	Rigel	281 11.0	S 8 11.4
H 09	332 17.6	277 33.8 ..	53.2	298 11.8 ..	37.4	196 57.4 ..	56.5	89 27.7 ..	53.8	Rigil Kent.	139 49.3	S60 53.7
U 10	347 20.1	292 33.2	54.1	313 12.5	38.1	211 59.8	56.5	104 30.2	53.7	Sabik	102 11.0	S15 44.5
R 11	2 22.5	307 32.7	54.9	328 13.2	38.7	227 02.3	56.4	119 32.8	53.7			
S 12	17 25.0	322 32.1	N20 55.7	343 13.9	N13 39.3	242 04.8	N17 56.4	134 35.4	S18 53.7	Schedar	349 39.6	N56 37.1
D 13	32 27.5	337 31.6	56.5	358 14.6	40.0	257 07.2	56.4	149 37.9	53.7	Shaula	96 20.1	S37 06.6
A 14	47 29.9	352 31.0	57.3	13 15.3	40.6	272 09.7	56.4	164 40.5	53.6	Sirius	258 32.7	S16 44.6
Y 15	62 32.4	7 30.4 ..	58.1	28 16.0 ..	41.2	287 12.1 ..	56.4	179 43.1 ..	53.6	Spica	158 29.6	S11 14.5
16	77 34.8	22 29.9	58.9	43 16.6	41.9	302 14.6	56.4	194 45.6	53.6	Suhail	222 51.3	S43 30.1
17	92 37.3	37 29.3	20 59.7	58 17.3	42.5	317 17.0	56.4	209 48.2	53.6			
18	107 39.8	52 28.8	N21 00.5	73 18.0	N13 43.1	332 19.5	N17 56.4	224 50.8	S18 53.5	Vega	80 38.0	N38 47.8
19	122 42.2	67 28.2	01.2	88 18.7	43.7	347 22.0	56.4	239 53.4	53.5	Zuben'ubi	137 03.7	S16 06.3
20	137 44.7	82 27.6	02.0	103 19.4	44.4	2 24.4	56.4	254 55.9	53.5			
21	152 47.2	97 27.1 ..	02.8	118 20.1 ..	45.0	17 26.9 ..	56.4	269 58.5 ..	53.5		SHA	Mer.Pass.
22	167 49.6	112 26.5	03.6	133 20.8	45.6	32 29.3	56.4	285 01.1	53.4	Venus	306 55.7	14 29
23	182 52.3	127 26.0	04.4	148 21.5	46.3	47 31.8	56.4	300 03.6	53.4	Mars	326 52.7	13 08
Mer. Pass.	10 54.5	v −0.6	d 0.8	v 0.7	d 0.6	v 2.5	d 0.0	v 2.6	d 0.0	Jupiter	224 39.7	19 54
										Saturn	117 06.7	3 07

SUN / MOON

UT	SUN GHA	SUN Dec	MOON GHA	v	MOON Dec	d	HP
d h	° ′	° ′	° ′	′	° ′	′	′
7 00	179 24.9	N 6 37.4	331 41.8	12.3	S13 22.9	6.7	55.3
01	194 25.1	38.4	346 13.1	12.2	13 29.6	6.6	55.3
02	209 25.3	39.3	0 44.3	12.3	13 36.2	6.6	55.3
03	224 25.4	.. 40.2	15 15.6	12.1	13 42.8	6.5	55.4
04	239 25.6	41.2	29 46.7	12.1	13 49.3	6.5	55.4
05	254 25.8	42.1	44 17.8	12.1	13 55.8	6.4	55.4
T 06	269 26.0	N 6 43.1	58 48.9	12.0	S14 02.2	6.3	55.4
U 07	284 26.1	44.0	73 19.9	12.0	14 08.5	6.2	55.4
E 08	299 26.3	45.0	87 50.9	11.9	14 14.7	6.2	55.5
S 09	314 26.5	.. 45.9	102 21.8	11.9	14 20.9	6.2	55.5
D 10	329 26.7	46.8	116 52.7	11.8	14 27.1	6.0	55.5
A 11	344 26.9	47.8	131 23.5	11.8	14 33.1	6.0	55.5
Y 12	359 27.0	N 6 48.7	145 54.3	11.8	S14 39.1	5.9	55.5
13	14 27.2	49.7	160 25.1	11.6	14 45.0	5.9	55.6
14	29 27.4	50.6	174 55.7	11.7	14 50.9	5.8	55.6
15	44 27.6	.. 51.5	189 26.4	11.6	14 56.7	5.7	55.6
16	59 27.7	52.5	203 57.0	11.5	15 02.4	5.7	55.6
17	74 27.9	53.4	218 27.5	11.5	15 08.1	5.5	55.6
18	89 28.1	N 6 54.3	232 58.0	11.4	S15 13.6	5.5	55.6
19	104 28.3	55.3	247 28.4	11.4	15 19.1	5.5	55.7
20	119 28.4	56.2	261 58.8	11.4	15 24.6	5.3	55.7
21	134 28.6	.. 57.2	276 29.2	11.3	15 29.9	5.3	55.7
22	149 28.8	58.1	290 59.5	11.2	15 35.2	5.2	55.7
23	164 29.0	6 59.0	305 29.7	11.2	15 40.4	5.2	55.8
8 00	179 29.1	N 7 00.0	319 59.9	11.2	S15 45.6	5.0	55.8
01	194 29.3	00.9	334 30.1	11.1	15 50.6	5.0	55.8
02	209 29.5	01.9	349 00.2	11.1	15 55.6	4.9	55.8
03	224 29.7	.. 02.8	3 30.3	11.0	16 00.5	4.8	55.8
04	239 29.8	03.7	18 00.3	10.9	16 05.3	4.8	55.9
05	254 30.0	04.7	32 30.2	10.9	16 10.1	4.7	55.9
W 06	269 30.2	N 7 05.6	47 00.1	10.9	S16 14.8	4.6	55.9
E 07	284 30.4	06.5	61 30.0	10.8	16 19.4	4.5	55.9
D 08	299 30.5	07.5	75 59.8	10.8	16 23.9	4.4	55.9
N 09	314 30.7	.. 08.4	90 29.6	10.7	16 28.3	4.4	56.0
E 10	329 30.9	09.3	104 59.3	10.7	16 32.7	4.2	56.0
S 11	344 31.1	10.3	119 29.0	10.6	16 36.9	4.2	56.0
D 12	359 31.2	N 7 11.2	133 58.6	10.6	S16 41.1	4.1	56.0
A 13	14 31.4	12.1	148 28.2	10.5	16 45.2	4.0	56.0
Y 14	29 31.6	13.1	162 57.7	10.5	16 49.2	4.0	56.1
15	44 31.8	.. 14.0	177 27.2	10.5	16 53.2	3.8	56.1
16	59 31.9	15.0	191 56.7	10.4	16 57.0	3.8	56.1
17	74 32.1	15.9	206 26.1	10.3	17 00.8	3.6	56.1
18	89 32.3	N 7 16.8	220 55.4	10.3	S17 04.4	3.6	56.2
19	104 32.4	17.8	235 24.7	10.3	17 08.0	3.5	56.2
20	119 32.6	18.7	249 54.0	10.2	17 11.5	3.4	56.2
21	134 32.8	.. 19.6	264 23.2	10.2	17 14.9	3.4	56.2
22	149 33.0	20.6	278 52.4	10.1	17 18.3	3.2	56.3
23	164 33.1	21.5	293 21.5	10.1	17 21.5	3.1	56.3
9 00	179 33.3	N 7 22.4	307 50.6	10.0	S17 24.6	3.1	56.3
01	194 33.5	23.4	322 19.6	10.0	17 27.7	3.0	56.3
02	209 33.7	24.3	336 48.6	9.9	17 30.7	2.8	56.3
03	224 33.8	.. 25.2	351 17.5	10.0	17 33.5	2.8	56.4
04	239 34.0	26.1	5 46.5	9.8	17 36.3	2.7	56.4
05	254 34.2	27.1	20 15.3	9.8	17 39.0	2.6	56.4
T 06	269 34.3	N 7 28.0	34 44.1	9.8	S17 41.6	2.5	56.4
H 07	284 34.5	28.9	49 12.9	9.8	17 44.1	2.4	56.5
U 08	299 34.7	29.9	63 41.7	9.7	17 46.5	2.3	56.5
R 09	314 34.9	.. 30.8	78 10.4	9.6	17 48.8	2.2	56.5
S 10	329 35.0	31.7	92 39.0	9.6	17 51.0	2.2	56.5
D 11	344 35.2	32.7	107 07.6	9.6	17 53.2	2.0	56.6
A 12	359 35.4	N 7 33.6	121 36.2	9.5	S17 55.2	1.9	56.6
Y 13	14 35.5	34.5	136 04.7	9.5	17 57.1	1.8	56.6
14	29 35.7	35.5	150 33.2	9.5	17 58.9	1.8	56.6
15	44 35.9	.. 36.4	165 01.7	9.4	18 00.7	1.6	56.7
16	59 36.1	37.3	179 30.1	9.4	18 02.3	1.6	56.7
17	74 36.2	38.2	193 58.5	9.4	18 03.9	1.4	56.7
18	89 36.4	N 7 39.2	208 26.9	9.3	S18 05.3	1.3	56.7
19	104 36.6	40.1	222 55.2	9.2	18 06.6	1.3	56.8
20	119 36.7	41.0	237 23.4	9.3	18 07.9	1.1	56.8
21	134 36.9	.. 42.0	251 51.7	9.2	18 09.0	1.1	56.8
22	149 37.1	42.9	266 19.9	9.1	18 10.1	0.9	56.8
23	164 37.2	43.8	280 48.0	9.2	S18 11.0	0.9	56.9
	SD 16.0	d 0.9	SD 15.1		15.3		15.4

Twilight / Sunrise / Moonrise

Lat.	Twilight Naut.	Twilight Civil	Sunrise	Moonrise 7	8	9	10
°	h m	h m	h m	h m	h m	h m	h m
N 72	////	02 57	04 20	24 48	00 48	02 49	■■
N 70	01 14	03 21	04 32	24 06	00 06	01 35	02 48
68	02 03	03 38	04 41	23 38	24 57	00 57	02 04
66	02 32	03 52	04 49	23 17	24 31	00 31	01 35
64	02 54	04 04	04 55	23 00	24 11	00 11	01 13
62	03 11	04 13	05 01	22 46	23 54	24 55	00 55
60	03 25	04 21	05 05	22 34	23 41	24 41	00 41
N 58	03 36	04 28	05 10	22 24	23 29	24 28	00 28
56	03 46	04 35	05 13	22 15	23 19	24 17	00 17
54	03 55	04 40	05 17	22 07	23 10	24 08	00 08
52	04 02	04 45	05 20	22 01	23 02	23 59	24 52
50	04 09	04 49	05 23	21 54	22 55	23 52	24 44
45	04 23	04 59	05 29	21 41	22 39	23 36	24 28
N 40	04 33	05 06	05 34	21 30	22 27	23 22	24 15
35	04 42	05 12	05 38	21 20	22 16	23 11	24 04
30	04 49	05 17	05 42	21 12	22 07	23 01	23 54
20	05 00	05 26	05 48	20 58	21 51	22 44	23 38
N 10	05 08	05 32	05 54	20 45	21 37	22 30	23 23
0	05 14	05 38	05 59	20 34	21 24	22 16	23 09
S 10	05 18	05 42	06 04	20 22	21 11	22 02	22 56
20	05 21	05 47	06 09	20 10	20 57	21 47	22 41
30	05 23	05 51	06 15	19 56	20 41	21 31	22 24
35	05 23	05 52	06 18	19 48	20 32	21 21	22 15
40	05 23	05 54	06 22	19 39	20 22	21 10	22 03
45	05 22	05 56	06 26	19 28	20 09	20 57	21 50
S 50	05 21	05 58	06 31	19 15	19 55	20 41	21 35
52	05 20	05 59	06 33	19 09	19 48	20 33	21 27
54	05 19	06 00	06 36	19 02	19 40	20 25	21 19
56	05 18	06 01	06 38	18 55	19 31	20 16	21 10
58	05 17	06 02	06 42	18 47	19 22	20 05	20 59
S 60	05 15	06 03	06 45	18 37	19 11	19 53	20 47

Sunset / Twilight / Moonset

Lat.	Sunset	Twilight Civil	Twilight Naut.	Moonset 7	8	9	10
°	h m	h m	h m	h m	h m	h m	h m
N 72	19 47	21 12	////	04 42	04 34	04 18	■■
N 70	19 35	20 47	23 03	05 09	05 17	05 33	06 09
68	19 25	20 29	22 08	05 30	05 45	06 11	06 52
66	19 17	20 15	21 36	05 47	06 07	06 37	07 22
64	19 11	20 03	21 13	06 00	06 24	06 58	07 44
62	19 05	19 53	20 56	06 12	06 39	07 14	08 01
60	19 00	19 44	20 42	06 22	06 51	07 28	08 16
N 58	18 56	19 37	20 30	06 30	07 01	07 40	08 28
56	18 52	19 31	20 19	06 38	07 10	07 50	08 39
54	18 48	19 25	20 11	06 44	07 19	08 00	08 49
52	18 45	19 21	20 03	06 50	07 26	08 08	08 57
50	18 42	19 16	19 56	06 56	07 32	08 15	09 05
45	18 36	19 06	19 42	07 08	07 46	08 31	09 21
N 40	18 31	18 59	19 31	07 18	07 58	08 44	09 34
35	18 27	18 52	19 23	07 26	08 08	08 54	09 46
30	18 23	18 47	19 16	07 34	08 17	09 04	09 56
20	18 16	18 38	19 04	07 47	08 32	09 21	10 13
N 10	18 10	18 32	18 56	07 58	08 45	09 35	10 27
0	18 05	18 26	18 50	08 08	08 57	09 48	10 41
S 10	18 00	18 21	18 46	08 19	09 10	10 02	10 55
20	17 55	18 17	18 43	08 30	09 23	10 16	11 10
30	17 49	18 13	18 41	08 43	09 38	10 33	11 27
35	17 45	18 11	18 40	08 51	09 47	10 42	11 36
40	17 42	18 09	18 40	09 00	09 57	10 53	11 48
45	17 37	18 07	18 41	09 10	10 09	11 06	12 01
S 50	17 32	18 05	18 42	09 22	10 23	11 22	12 17
52	17 30	18 04	18 43	09 27	10 30	11 29	12 24
54	17 27	18 03	18 43	09 34	10 37	11 37	12 33
56	17 24	18 02	18 45	09 41	10 46	11 47	12 42
58	17 21	18 01	18 46	09 48	10 55	11 57	12 52
S 60	17 18	17 59	18 47	09 57	11 06	12 09	13 05

SUN / MOON

Day	SUN Eqn. of Time 00ʰ	SUN Eqn. of Time 12ʰ	SUN Mer. Pass.	MOON Mer. Pass. Upper	MOON Mer. Pass. Lower	Age	Phase
d	m s	m s	h m	h m	h m	d	%
7	02 21	02 12	12 02	01 57	14 21	18	92
8	02 04	01 55	12 02	02 46	15 11	19	85
9	01 47	01 39	12 02	03 36	16 02	20	77

UT	ARIES	VENUS −4.0		MARS +1.4		JUPITER −2.3		SATURN +0.2		STARS		
	GHA	GHA	Dec	GHA	Dec	GHA	Dec	GHA	Dec	Name	SHA	Dec
d h	° ′	° ′	° ′	° ′	° ′	° ′	° ′	° ′	° ′		° ′	° ′
10 00	197 54.6	142 25.4	N21 05.2	163 22.2	N13 46.9	62 34.2	N17 56.4	315 06.2	S18 53.4	Acamar	315 17.8	S40 14.9
01	212 57.0	157 24.8	06.0	178 22.9	47.5	77 36.7	56.4	330 08.8	53.4	Achernar	335 26.6	S57 09.7
02	227 59.5	172 24.3	06.8	193 23.5	48.1	92 39.1	56.4	345 11.3	53.4	Acrux	173 07.1	S63 11.6
03	243 02.0	187 23.7 ..	07.6	208 24.2 ..	48.8	107 41.6 ..	56.4	0 13.9 ..	53.3	Adhara	255 11.6	S29 00.0
04	258 04.4	202 23.1	08.4	223 24.9	49.4	122 44.1	56.3	15 16.5	53.3	Aldebaran	290 48.2	N16 32.1
05	273 06.9	217 22.6	09.2	238 25.6	50.0	137 46.5	56.3	30 19.1	53.3			
06	288 09.3	232 22.0	N21 09.9	253 26.3	N13 50.6	152 49.0	N17 56.3	45 21.6	S18 53.3	Alioth	166 19.2	N55 52.6
07	303 11.8	247 21.5	10.7	268 27.0	51.3	167 51.4	56.3	60 24.2	53.2	Alkaid	152 57.5	N49 14.2
08	318 14.3	262 20.9	11.5	283 27.7	51.9	182 53.9	56.3	75 26.8	53.2	Al Na'ir	27 42.6	S46 53.0
F 09	333 16.7	277 20.3 ..	12.3	298 28.4 ..	52.5	197 56.3 ..	56.3	90 29.4 ..	53.2	Alnilam	275 45.3	S 1 11.9
R 10	348 19.2	292 19.8	13.1	313 29.1	53.1	212 58.8	56.3	105 31.9	53.2	Alphard	217 54.7	S 8 43.8
I 11	3 21.7	307 19.2	13.9	328 29.7	53.8	228 01.2	56.3	120 34.5	53.1			
D 12	18 24.1	322 18.6	N21 14.6	343 30.4	N13 54.4	243 03.7	N17 56.3	135 37.1	S18 53.1	Alphecca	126 09.7	N26 39.8
A 13	33 26.6	337 18.1	15.4	358 31.1	55.0	258 06.1	56.3	150 39.6	53.1	Alpheratz	357 42.5	N29 10.3
Y 14	48 29.1	352 17.5	16.2	13 31.8	55.6	273 08.6	56.3	165 42.2	53.1	Altair	62 07.1	N 8 54.5
15	63 31.5	7 16.9 ..	17.0	28 32.5 ..	56.3	288 11.0 ..	56.3	180 44.8 ..	53.0	Ankaa	353 15.6	S42 13.4
16	78 34.0	22 16.4	17.7	43 33.2	56.9	303 13.5	56.3	195 47.4	53.0	Antares	112 24.5	S26 27.8
17	93 36.5	37 15.8	18.5	58 33.9	57.5	318 15.9	56.3	210 49.9	53.0			
18	108 38.9	52 15.2	N21 19.3	73 34.6	N13 58.1	333 18.4	N17 56.2	225 52.5	S18 53.0	Arcturus	145 54.3	N19 06.1
19	123 41.4	67 14.7	20.1	88 35.2	58.8	348 20.8	56.2	240 55.1	52.9	Atria	107 24.8	S69 02.9
20	138 43.8	82 14.1	20.8	103 35.9	13 59.4	3 23.3	56.2	255 57.7	52.9	Avior	234 17.3	S59 34.0
21	153 46.3	97 13.5 ..	21.6	118 36.6	14 00.0	18 25.7 ..	56.2	271 00.2 ..	52.9	Bellatrix	278 30.9	N 6 21.5
22	168 48.8	112 12.9	22.4	133 37.3	00.6	33 28.2	56.2	286 02.8	52.9	Betelgeuse	271 00.1	N 7 24.3
23	183 51.2	127 12.4	23.1	148 38.0	01.2	48 30.6	56.2	301 05.4	52.8			
11 00	198 53.7	142 11.8	N21 23.9	163 38.7	N14 01.9	63 33.1	N17 56.2	316 08.0	S18 52.8	Canopus	263 55.7	S52 42.7
01	213 56.2	157 11.2	24.7	178 39.4	02.5	78 35.5	56.2	331 10.5	52.8	Capella	280 32.9	N46 00.7
02	228 58.6	172 10.7	25.5	193 40.1	03.1	93 38.0	56.2	346 13.1	52.8	Deneb	49 30.7	N45 19.9
03	244 01.1	187 10.1 ..	26.2	208 40.8 ..	03.7	108 40.4 ..	56.2	1 15.7 ..	52.8	Denebola	182 32.1	N14 29.1
04	259 03.6	202 09.5	27.0	223 41.4	04.3	123 42.8	56.2	16 18.3	52.7	Diphda	348 55.0	S17 54.3
05	274 06.0	217 09.0	27.7	238 42.1	05.0	138 45.3	56.2	31 20.8	52.7			
06	289 08.5	232 08.4	N21 28.5	253 42.8	N14 05.6	153 47.7	N17 56.1	46 23.4	S18 52.7	Dubhe	193 49.8	N61 40.2
07	304 11.0	247 07.8	29.3	268 43.5	06.2	168 50.2	56.1	61 26.0	52.7	Elnath	278 11.2	N28 37.0
S 08	319 13.4	262 07.2	30.0	283 44.2	06.8	183 52.6	56.1	76 28.6	52.6	Eltanin	90 45.4	N51 29.1
A 09	334 15.9	277 06.7 ..	30.8	298 44.9 ..	07.4	198 55.1 ..	56.1	91 31.1 ..	52.6	Enif	33 46.1	N 9 56.7
T 10	349 18.3	292 06.1	31.6	313 45.6	08.1	213 57.5	56.1	106 33.7	52.6	Fomalhaut	15 23.0	S29 32.4
U 11	4 20.8	307 05.5	32.3	328 46.2	08.7	229 00.0	56.1	121 36.3	52.6			
R 12	19 23.3	322 04.9	N21 33.1	343 46.9	N14 09.3	244 02.4	N17 56.1	136 38.9	S18 52.5	Gacrux	171 58.8	S57 12.0
D 13	34 25.7	337 04.4	33.8	358 47.6	09.9	259 04.8	56.1	151 41.5	52.5	Gienah	175 50.7	S17 37.8
A 14	49 28.2	352 03.8	34.6	13 48.3	10.5	274 07.3	56.1	166 44.0	52.5	Hadar	148 45.4	S60 26.7
Y 15	64 30.7	7 03.2 ..	35.3	28 49.0 ..	11.2	289 09.7 ..	56.1	181 46.6 ..	52.5	Hamal	327 59.7	N23 31.9
16	79 33.1	22 02.6	36.1	43 49.7	11.8	304 12.2	56.0	196 49.2	52.4	Kaus Aust.	83 42.1	S34 22.3
17	94 35.6	37 02.1	36.8	58 50.4	12.4	319 14.6	56.0	211 51.8	52.4			
18	109 38.1	52 01.5	N21 37.6	73 51.0	N14 13.0	334 17.1	N17 56.0	226 54.3	S18 52.4	Kochab	137 19.2	N74 05.5
19	124 40.5	67 00.9	38.3	88 51.7	13.6	349 19.5	56.0	241 56.9	52.4	Markab	13 37.4	N15 17.1
20	139 43.0	82 00.3	39.1	103 52.4	14.2	4 21.9	56.0	256 59.5	52.3	Menkar	314 14.1	N 4 08.7
21	154 45.4	96 59.8 ..	39.8	118 53.1 ..	14.9	19 24.4 ..	56.0	272 02.1 ..	52.3	Menkent	148 05.7	S36 26.7
22	169 47.9	111 59.2	40.6	133 53.8	15.5	34 26.8	56.0	287 04.7	52.3	Miaplacidus	221 38.9	S69 47.2
23	184 50.4	126 58.6	41.3	148 54.5	16.1	49 29.3	56.0	302 07.2	52.3			
12 00	199 52.8	141 58.0	N21 42.1	163 55.2	N14 16.7	64 31.7	N17 56.0	317 09.8	S18 52.2	Mirfak	308 39.0	N49 54.8
01	214 55.3	156 57.4	42.8	178 55.9	17.3	79 34.1	56.0	332 12.4	52.2	Nunki	75 56.8	S26 16.4
02	229 57.8	171 56.9	43.6	193 56.5	17.9	94 36.6	56.0	347 15.0	52.2	Peacock	53 17.5	S56 40.8
03	245 00.2	186 56.3 ..	44.3	208 57.2 ..	18.5	109 39.0 ..	55.9	2 17.5 ..	52.2	Pollux	243 26.2	N27 59.2
04	260 02.7	201 55.7	45.1	223 57.9	19.2	124 41.5	55.9	17 20.1	52.1	Procyon	244 58.4	N 5 10.8
05	275 05.2	216 55.1	45.8	238 58.6	19.8	139 43.9	55.9	32 22.7	52.1			
06	290 07.6	231 54.6	N21 46.5	253 59.3	N14 20.4	154 46.3	N17 55.9	47 25.3	S18 52.1	Rasalhague	96 05.2	N12 33.0
07	305 10.1	246 54.0	47.3	269 00.0	21.0	169 48.8	55.9	62 27.9	52.1	Regulus	207 42.0	N11 53.4
08	320 12.6	261 53.4	48.0	284 00.6	21.6	184 51.2	55.9	77 30.4	52.0	Rigel	281 11.1	S 8 11.4
S 09	335 15.0	276 52.8 ..	48.8	299 01.3 ..	22.2	199 53.6 ..	55.9	92 33.0 ..	52.0	Rigil Kent.	139 49.3	S60 53.7
U 10	350 17.5	291 52.2	49.5	314 02.0	22.8	214 56.1	55.9	107 35.6	52.0	Sabik	102 10.9	S15 44.5
N 11	5 19.9	306 51.6	50.2	329 02.7	23.5	229 58.5	55.8	122 38.2	52.0			
D 12	20 22.4	321 51.1	N21 51.0	344 03.4	N14 24.1	245 00.9	N17 55.8	137 40.8	S18 51.9	Schedar	349 39.6	N56 37.1
A 13	35 24.9	336 50.5	51.7	359 04.1	24.7	260 03.4	55.8	152 43.3	51.9	Shaula	96 20.0	S37 06.6
Y 14	50 27.3	351 49.9	52.4	14 04.8	25.3	275 05.8	55.8	167 45.9	51.9	Sirius	258 32.7	S16 44.6
15	65 29.8	6 49.3 ..	53.2	29 05.4 ..	25.9	290 08.2 ..	55.8	182 48.5 ..	51.9	Spica	158 29.6	S11 14.5
16	80 32.3	21 48.7	53.9	44 06.1	26.5	305 10.7	55.8	197 51.1	51.8	Suhail	222 51.3	S43 30.1
17	95 34.7	36 48.2	54.6	59 06.8	27.1	320 13.1	55.8	212 53.7	51.8			
18	110 37.2	51 47.6	N21 55.3	74 07.5	N14 27.7	335 15.5	N17 55.8	227 56.2	S18 51.8	Vega	80 38.0	N38 47.8
19	125 39.7	66 47.0	56.1	89 08.2	28.3	350 18.0	55.8	242 58.8	51.8	Zuben'ubi	137 03.7	S16 06.3
20	140 42.1	81 46.4	56.8	104 08.9	29.0	5 20.4	55.7	258 01.4	51.7		SHA	Mer. Pass.
21	155 44.6	96 45.8 ..	57.5	119 09.5 ..	29.6	20 22.8 ..	55.7	273 04.0 ..	51.7		° ′	h m
22	170 47.1	111 45.2	58.2	134 10.2	30.2	35 25.3	55.7	288 06.6	51.7	Venus	303 18.1	14 32
23	185 49.5	126 44.6	59.0	149 10.9	30.8	50 27.7	55.7	303 09.2	51.7	Mars	324 45.0	13 05
	h m									Jupiter	224 39.4	19 43
Mer. Pass. 10 42.7		v −0.6	d 0.8	v 0.7	d 0.6	v 2.4	d 0.0	v 2.6	d 0.0	Saturn	117 14.3	2 55

UT	SUN GHA	SUN Dec	MOON GHA	MOON v	MOON Dec	MOON d	MOON HP
d h	° ′	° ′	° ′	′	° ′	′	′
10 00	179 37.4	N 7 44.7	295 16.2	9.1	S18 11.9	0.7	56.9
01	194 37.6	45.7	309 44.3	9.0	18 12.6	0.6	56.9
02	209 37.8	46.6	324 12.3	9.0	18 13.2	0.6	56.9
03	224 37.9 ..	47.5	338 40.3	9.0	18 13.8	0.4	57.0
04	239 38.1	48.4	353 08.3	9.0	18 14.2	0.4	57.0
05	254 38.3	49.4	7 36.3	8.9	18 14.6	0.2	57.0
06	269 38.4	N 7 50.3	22 04.2	8.9	S18 14.8	0.1	57.0
07	284 38.6	51.2	36 32.1	8.9	18 14.9	0.0	57.1
08	299 38.8	52.1	51 00.0	8.9	18 14.9	0.0	57.1
F 09	314 38.9 ..	53.1	65 27.8	8.8	18 14.9	0.2	57.1
R 10	329 39.1	54.0	79 55.6	8.8	18 14.7	0.3	57.2
I 11	344 39.3	54.9	94 23.4	8.8	18 14.4	0.4	57.2
D 12	359 39.4	N 7 55.8	108 51.2	8.7	S18 14.0	0.5	57.2
A 13	14 39.6	56.8	123 18.9	8.7	18 13.5	0.6	57.2
Y 14	29 39.8	57.7	137 46.6	8.7	18 12.9	0.7	57.3
15	44 39.9 ..	58.6	152 14.3	8.6	18 12.2	0.8	57.3
16	59 40.1	7 59.5	166 41.9	8.6	18 11.4	0.9	57.3
17	74 40.3	8 00.5	181 09.5	8.6	18 10.5	1.0	57.3
18	89 40.4	N 8 01.4	195 37.1	8.6	S18 09.5	1.2	57.4
19	104 40.6	02.3	210 04.7	8.5	18 08.3	1.2	57.4
20	119 40.8	03.2	224 32.2	8.5	18 07.1	1.3	57.4
21	134 40.9 ..	04.2	238 59.7	8.5	18 05.8	1.5	57.5
22	149 41.1	05.1	253 27.2	8.5	18 04.3	1.5	57.5
23	164 41.3	06.0	267 54.7	8.4	18 02.8	1.7	57.5
11 00	179 41.4	N 8 06.9	282 22.1	8.5	S18 01.1	1.8	57.5
01	194 41.6	07.8	296 49.6	8.4	17 59.3	1.8	57.6
02	209 41.8	08.8	311 17.0	8.4	17 57.5	2.0	57.6
03	224 41.9 ..	09.7	325 44.4	8.3	17 55.5	2.1	57.6
04	239 42.1	10.6	340 11.7	8.4	17 53.4	2.2	57.7
05	254 42.3	11.5	354 39.1	8.3	17 51.2	2.3	57.7
06	269 42.4	N 8 12.4	9 06.4	8.3	S17 48.9	2.4	57.7
S 07	284 42.6	13.4	23 33.7	8.3	17 46.5	2.5	57.7
A 08	299 42.8	14.3	38 01.0	8.3	17 44.0	2.6	57.8
T 09	314 42.9 ..	15.2	52 28.3	8.3	17 41.4	2.8	57.8
U 10	329 43.1	16.1	66 55.6	8.2	17 38.6	2.8	57.8
R 11	344 43.3	17.0	81 22.8	8.2	17 35.8	2.9	57.9
D 12	359 43.4	N 8 18.0	95 50.0	8.2	S17 32.9	3.1	57.9
A 13	14 43.6	18.9	110 17.2	8.2	17 29.8	3.1	57.9
Y 14	29 43.8	19.8	124 44.4	8.2	17 26.7	3.3	57.9
15	44 43.9 ..	20.7	139 11.6	8.2	17 23.4	3.4	58.0
16	59 44.1	21.6	153 38.8	8.2	17 20.0	3.4	58.0
17	74 44.3	22.6	168 06.0	8.1	17 16.6	3.6	58.0
18	89 44.4	N 8 23.5	182 33.1	8.2	S17 13.0	3.7	58.1
19	104 44.6	24.4	197 00.2	8.2	17 09.3	3.8	58.1
20	119 44.8	25.3	211 27.4	8.1	17 05.5	3.9	58.1
21	134 44.9 ..	26.2	225 54.5	8.1	17 01.6	4.0	58.1
22	149 45.1	27.1	240 21.6	8.1	16 57.6	4.1	58.2
23	164 45.2	28.1	254 48.7	8.1	16 53.5	4.2	58.2
12 00	179 45.4	N 8 29.0	269 15.8	8.0	S16 49.3	4.3	58.2
01	194 45.6	29.9	283 42.8	8.1	16 45.0	4.5	58.3
02	209 45.7	30.8	298 09.9	8.1	16 40.5	4.5	58.3
03	224 45.9 ..	31.7	312 37.0	8.0	16 36.0	4.6	58.3
04	239 46.1	32.6	327 04.0	8.1	16 31.4	4.8	58.3
05	254 46.2	33.6	341 31.1	8.0	16 26.6	4.8	58.4
06	269 46.4	N 8 34.5	355 58.1	8.1	S16 21.8	4.9	58.4
07	284 46.5	35.4	10 25.1	8.1	16 16.9	5.1	58.4
08	299 46.7	36.3	24 52.2	8.0	16 11.8	5.1	58.5
S 09	314 46.9 ..	37.2	39 19.2	8.0	16 06.7	5.3	58.5
U 10	329 47.0	38.1	53 46.2	8.0	16 01.4	5.3	58.5
N 11	344 47.2	39.0	68 13.2	8.0	15 56.1	5.5	58.6
D 12	359 47.4	N 8 39.9	82 40.2	8.0	S15 50.6	5.6	58.6
A 13	14 47.5	40.9	97 07.2	8.0	15 45.0	5.6	58.6
Y 14	29 47.7	41.8	111 34.2	8.0	15 39.4	5.8	58.6
15	44 47.8 ..	42.7	126 01.2	8.0	15 33.6	5.9	58.7
16	59 48.0	43.6	140 28.2	8.0	15 27.7	5.9	58.7
17	74 48.2	44.5	154 55.2	8.0	15 21.8	6.1	58.7
18	89 48.3	N 8 45.4	169 22.2	8.0	S15 15.7	6.1	58.8
19	104 48.5	46.3	183 49.2	8.0	15 09.6	6.3	58.8
20	119 48.6	47.2	198 16.2	8.0	15 03.3	6.4	58.8
21	134 48.8 ..	48.2	212 43.2	8.0	14 56.9	6.4	58.8
22	149 49.0	49.1	227 10.2	7.9	14 50.5	6.6	58.9
23	164 49.1	50.0	241 37.1	8.0	S14 43.9	6.6	58.9
SD 16.0	d 0.9		SD 15.6		15.8		16.0

Twilight / Moonrise

Lat.	Naut.	Civil	Sunrise	Moonrise 10	11	12	13
°	h m	h m	h m	h m	h m	h m	h m
N 72	////	02 35	04 04	■■■	05 11	04 40	04 31
N 70	////	03 03	04 17	02 48	03 32	03 53	04 03
68	01 37	03 23	04 28	02 04	02 52	03 22	03 41
66	02 13	03 39	04 37	01 35	02 24	03 00	03 24
64	02 39	03 52	04 44	01 13	02 03	02 42	03 10
62	02 58	04 02	04 51	00 55	01 46	02 27	02 58
60	03 13	04 12	04 56	00 41	01 32	02 14	02 48
N 58	03 26	04 19	05 01	00 28	01 20	02 03	02 39
56	03 37	04 26	05 06	00 17	01 09	01 54	02 32
54	03 46	04 32	05 10	00 08	01 00	01 45	02 25
52	03 55	04 38	05 13	24 52	00 52	01 38	02 18
50	04 02	04 43	05 16	24 44	00 44	01 31	02 13
45	04 17	04 53	05 23	24 28	00 28	01 17	02 01
N 40	04 28	05 01	05 29	24 15	00 15	01 05	01 50
35	04 37	05 08	05 34	24 04	00 04	00 54	01 42
30	04 45	05 14	05 38	23 54	24 45	00 45	01 34
20	04 57	05 23	05 46	23 38	24 30	00 30	01 21
N 10	05 06	05 31	05 52	23 23	24 16	00 16	01 09
0	05 13	05 37	05 58	23 09	24 04	00 04	00 58
S 10	05 18	05 42	06 04	22 56	23 51	24 48	00 48
20	05 22	05 47	06 10	22 41	23 37	24 36	00 36
30	05 25	05 52	06 16	22 24	23 22	24 23	00 23
35	05 25	05 55	06 20	22 15	23 13	24 15	00 15
40	05 26	05 57	06 25	22 03	23 03	24 06	00 06
45	05 26	06 00	06 30	21 50	22 51	23 56	25 06
S 50	05 25	06 03	06 35	21 35	22 36	23 44	24 56
52	05 25	06 04	06 38	21 27	22 29	23 38	24 52
54	05 25	06 06	06 41	21 19	22 21	23 31	24 47
56	05 24	06 07	06 44	21 10	22 13	23 24	24 42
58	05 23	06 08	06 48	20 59	22 03	23 16	24 36
S 60	05 22	06 10	06 52	20 47	21 52	23 07	24 29

Moonset

Lat.	Sunset	Twilight Civil	Naut.	Moonset 10	11	12	13
°	h m	h m	h m	h m	h m	h m	h m
N 72	20 02	21 33	////	■■■	05 38	08 03	10 06
N 70	19 48	21 04	////	06 09	07 16	08 49	10 34
68	19 37	20 43	22 34	06 52	07 56	09 19	10 54
66	19 27	20 26	21 54	07 22	08 23	09 41	11 10
64	19 20	20 13	21 27	07 44	08 44	09 59	11 24
62	19 13	20 02	21 07	08 01	09 01	10 13	11 35
60	19 07	19 53	20 52	08 16	09 15	10 25	11 44
N 58	19 02	19 44	20 38	08 28	09 27	10 36	11 53
56	18 58	19 37	20 27	08 39	09 38	10 45	12 00
54	18 54	19 31	20 18	08 49	09 47	10 53	12 06
52	18 50	19 26	20 09	08 57	09 55	11 00	12 12
50	18 47	19 21	20 02	09 05	10 02	11 07	12 17
45	18 40	19 10	19 47	09 21	10 18	11 21	12 28
N 40	18 34	19 02	19 35	09 34	10 31	11 32	12 38
35	18 29	18 55	19 25	09 46	10 42	11 42	12 46
30	18 25	18 49	19 18	09 56	10 51	11 51	12 53
20	18 17	18 39	19 05	10 13	11 08	12 05	13 04
N 10	18 10	18 32	18 56	10 27	11 22	12 18	13 15
0	18 04	18 25	18 50	10 41	11 35	12 30	13 25
S 10	17 59	18 20	18 44	10 55	11 48	12 42	13 34
20	17 52	18 15	18 40	11 10	12 03	12 54	13 44
30	17 45	18 09	18 37	11 27	12 19	13 09	13 56
35	17 41	18 07	18 36	11 36	12 28	13 17	14 03
40	17 37	18 04	18 36	11 48	12 39	13 26	14 10
45	17 32	18 01	18 35	12 01	12 51	13 37	14 19
S 50	17 26	17 58	18 36	12 17	13 06	13 51	14 30
52	17 23	17 57	18 36	12 24	13 13	13 57	14 35
54	17 20	17 56	18 37	12 33	13 21	14 03	14 40
56	17 17	17 54	18 37	12 42	13 30	14 11	14 46
58	17 13	17 53	18 38	12 52	13 40	14 20	14 52
S 60	17 09	17 51	18 39	13 05	13 51	14 29	15 00

SUN / MOON

Day	SUN Eqn. of Time 00ʰ	12ʰ	Mer. Pass.	MOON Mer. Pass. Upper	Lower	Age	Phase
d	m s	m s	h m	h m	h m	d	%
10	01 31	01 23	12 01	04 28	16 55	21	68
11	01 15	01 07	12 01	05 22	17 49	22	57
12	00 59	00 51	12 01	06 17	18 44	23	46

UT	ARIES GHA	VENUS −4.1 GHA	Dec	MARS +1.4 GHA	Dec	JUPITER −2.2 GHA	Dec	SATURN +0.2 GHA	Dec	STARS Name	SHA	Dec
13 00	200 52.0	141 44.1	N21 59.7	164 11.6	N14 31.4	65 30.1	N17 55.7	318 11.7	S18 51.6	Acamar	315 17.8	S40 14.9
01	215 54.4	156 43.5	22 00.4	179 12.3	32.0	80 32.6	55.7	333 14.3	51.6	Achernar	335 26.5	S57 09.7
02	230 56.9	171 42.9	01.1	194 13.0	32.6	95 35.0	55.7	348 16.9	51.6	Acrux	173 07.1	S63 11.2
03	245 59.4	186 42.3	.. 01.9	209 13.6	.. 33.2	110 37.4	.. 55.7	3 19.5	.. 51.6	Adhara	255 11.6	S29 00.0
04	261 01.8	201 41.7	02.6	224 14.3	33.8	125 39.9	55.6	18 22.1	51.5	Aldebaran	290 48.2	N16 32.1
05	276 04.3	216 41.1	03.3	239 15.0	34.4	140 42.3	55.6	33 24.7	51.5			
M 06	291 06.8	231 40.5	N22 04.0	254 15.7	N14 35.0	155 44.7	N17 55.6	48 27.2	S18 51.5	Alioth	166 19.2	N55 52.6
O 07	306 09.2	246 40.0	04.7	269 16.4	35.7	170 47.2	55.6	63 29.8	51.5	Alkaid	152 57.5	N49 14.2
N 08	321 11.7	261 39.4	05.4	284 17.1	36.3	185 49.6	55.6	78 32.4	51.4	Al Na'ir	27 42.5	S46 53.0
D 09	336 14.2	276 38.8	.. 06.2	299 17.7	.. 36.9	200 52.0	.. 55.6	93 35.0	.. 51.4	Alnilam	275 45.3	S 1 11.9
A 10	351 16.6	291 38.2	06.9	314 18.4	37.5	215 54.4	55.6	108 37.6	51.4	Alphard	217 54.7	S 8 43.8
Y 11	6 19.1	306 37.6	07.6	329 19.1	38.1	230 56.9	55.5	123 40.2	51.4			
12	21 21.5	321 37.0	N22 08.3	344 19.8	N14 38.7	245 59.3	N17 55.5	138 42.7	S18 51.3	Alphecca	126 09.7	N26 39.8
13	36 24.0	336 36.4	09.0	359 20.5	39.3	261 01.7	55.5	153 45.3	51.3	Alpheratz	357 42.5	N29 10.3
14	51 26.5	351 35.8	09.7	14 21.2	39.9	276 04.1	55.5	168 47.9	51.3	Altair	62 07.0	N 8 54.5
15	66 28.9	6 35.2	.. 10.4	29 21.8	.. 40.5	291 06.6	.. 55.5	183 50.5	.. 51.3	Ankaa	353 15.0	S42 13.4
16	81 31.4	21 34.7	11.1	44 22.5	41.1	306 09.0	55.5	198 53.1	51.2	Antares	112 24.5	S26 27.8
17	96 33.9	36 34.1	11.8	59 23.2	41.7	321 11.4	55.5	213 55.7	51.2			
18	111 36.3	51 33.5	N22 12.5	74 23.9	N14 42.3	336 13.9	N17 55.4	228 58.2	S18 51.2	Arcturus	145 54.3	N19 06.1
19	126 38.8	66 32.9	13.2	89 24.6	42.9	351 16.3	55.4	244 00.8	51.2	Atria	107 24.8	S69 02.9
20	141 41.3	81 32.3	13.9	104 25.2	43.5	6 18.7	55.4	259 03.4	51.1	Avior	234 17.3	S59 34.0
21	156 43.7	96 31.7	.. 14.6	119 25.9	.. 44.1	21 21.1	.. 55.4	274 06.0	.. 51.1	Bellatrix	278 30.9	N 6 21.5
22	171 46.2	111 31.1	15.4	134 26.6	44.7	36 23.6	55.4	289 08.6	51.1	Betelgeuse	271 00.1	N 7 24.3
23	186 48.7	126 30.5	16.1	149 27.3	45.5	51 26.0	55.4	304 11.2	51.0			
14 00	201 51.1	141 29.9	N22 16.8	164 28.0	N14 45.9	66 28.4	N17 55.4	319 13.8	S18 51.0	Canopus	263 55.8	S52 42.7
01	216 53.6	156 29.3	17.4	179 28.7	46.5	81 30.8	55.3	334 16.3	51.0	Capella	280 32.9	N46 00.7
02	231 56.0	171 28.7	18.1	194 29.3	47.1	96 33.2	55.3	349 18.9	51.0	Deneb	49 30.7	N45 19.9
03	246 58.5	186 28.1	.. 18.8	209 30.0	.. 47.7	111 35.7	.. 55.3	4 21.5	.. 50.9	Denebola	182 32.1	N14 29.1
04	262 01.0	201 27.5	19.5	224 30.7	48.3	126 38.1	55.3	19 24.1	50.9	Diphda	348 55.0	S17 54.3
05	277 03.4	216 26.9	20.2	239 31.4	49.0	141 40.5	55.3	34 26.7	50.9			
T 06	292 05.9	231 26.4	N22 20.9	254 32.1	N14 49.6	156 42.9	N17 55.3	49 29.3	S18 50.9	Dubhe	193 49.8	N61 40.2
U 07	307 08.4	246 25.8	21.6	269 32.7	50.2	171 45.4	55.2	64 31.9	50.8	Elnath	278 11.3	N28 37.0
E 08	322 10.8	261 25.2	22.3	284 33.4	50.8	186 47.8	55.2	79 34.4	50.8	Eltanin	90 45.3	N51 29.1
S 09	337 13.3	276 24.6	.. 23.0	299 34.1	.. 51.4	201 50.2	.. 55.2	94 37.0	.. 50.8	Enif	33 46.1	N 9 56.7
D 10	352 15.8	291 24.0	23.7	314 34.8	52.0	216 52.6	55.2	109 39.6	50.8	Fomalhaut	15 22.9	S29 32.4
A 11	7 18.2	306 23.4	24.4	329 35.5	52.6	231 55.0	55.2	124 42.2	50.7			
Y 12	22 20.7	321 22.8	N22 25.1	344 36.1	N14 53.2	246 57.5	N17 55.2	139 44.8	S18 50.7	Gacrux	171 58.8	S57 12.1
13	37 23.2	336 22.2	25.8	359 36.8	53.8	261 59.9	55.2	154 47.4	50.7	Gienah	175 50.7	S17 37.8
14	52 25.6	351 21.6	26.4	14 37.5	54.4	277 02.3	55.1	169 50.0	50.7	Hadar	148 45.4	S60 26.7
15	67 28.1	6 21.0	.. 27.1	29 38.2	.. 55.0	292 04.7	.. 55.1	184 52.6	.. 50.6	Hamal	327 59.7	N23 31.9
16	82 30.5	21 20.4	27.8	44 38.8	55.6	307 07.1	55.1	199 55.1	50.6	Kaus Aust.	83 42.1	S34 22.3
17	97 33.0	36 19.8	28.5	59 39.5	56.2	322 09.6	55.1	214 57.7	50.6			
18	112 35.5	51 19.2	N22 29.2	74 40.2	N14 56.8	337 12.0	N17 55.1	230 00.3	S18 50.6	Kochab	137 19.1	N74 05.5
19	127 37.9	66 18.6	29.8	89 40.9	57.4	352 14.4	55.1	245 02.9	50.5	Markab	13 37.3	N15 17.1
20	142 40.4	81 18.0	30.5	104 41.6	57.9	7 16.8	55.0	260 05.5	50.5	Menkar	314 14.1	N 4 08.7
21	157 42.9	96 17.4	.. 31.2	119 42.3	.. 58.5	22 19.2	.. 55.0	275 08.1	.. 50.5	Menkent	148 05.7	S36 26.7
22	172 45.3	111 16.8	31.9	134 42.9	59.1	37 21.6	55.0	290 10.7	50.5	Miaplacidus	221 38.9	S69 47.2
23	187 47.8	126 16.2	32.6	149 43.6	14 59.7	52 24.1	55.0	305 13.3	50.4			
15 00	202 50.3	141 15.6	N22 33.2	164 44.3	N15 00.3	67 26.5	N17 55.0	320 15.8	S18 50.4	Mirfak	308 39.0	N49 54.8
01	217 52.7	156 15.0	33.9	179 45.0	00.9	82 28.9	54.9	335 18.4	50.4	Nunki	75 56.7	S26 16.4
02	232 55.2	171 14.4	34.6	194 45.7	01.5	97 31.3	54.9	350 21.0	50.3	Peacock	53 17.5	S56 40.8
03	247 57.6	186 13.8	.. 35.3	209 46.3	.. 02.1	112 33.7	.. 54.9	5 23.6	.. 50.3	Pollux	243 26.3	N27 59.2
04	263 00.1	201 13.2	35.9	224 47.0	02.7	127 36.1	54.9	20 26.2	50.3	Procyon	244 58.5	N 5 10.9
05	278 02.6	216 12.6	36.6	239 47.7	03.3	142 38.5	54.9	35 28.8	50.3			
W 06	293 05.0	231 12.0	N22 37.3	254 48.4	N15 03.9	157 41.0	N17 54.9	50 31.4	S18 50.2	Rasalhague	96 05.1	N12 33.0
E 07	308 07.5	246 11.4	37.9	269 49.1	04.5	172 43.4	54.8	65 34.0	50.2	Regulus	207 42.0	N11 53.4
D 08	323 10.0	261 10.8	38.6	284 49.7	05.1	187 45.8	54.8	80 36.6	50.2	Rigel	281 11.1	S 8 11.4
N 09	338 12.4	276 10.2	.. 39.3	299 50.4	.. 05.7	202 48.2	.. 54.8	95 39.2	.. 50.2	Rigil Kent.	139 49.3	S60 53.7
E 10	353 14.9	291 09.6	39.9	314 51.1	06.3	217 50.6	54.8	110 41.7	50.1	Sabik	102 10.9	S15 44.5
S 11	8 17.4	306 09.0	40.6	329 51.8	06.9	232 53.0	54.8	125 44.3	50.1			
D 12	23 19.8	321 08.4	N22 41.3	344 52.5	N15 07.5	247 55.4	N17 54.8	140 46.9	S18 50.1	Schedar	349 39.5	N56 37.1
A 13	38 22.3	336 07.8	41.9	359 53.1	08.1	262 57.8	54.7	155 49.5	50.1	Shaula	96 20.0	S37 06.6
Y 14	53 24.8	351 07.2	42.6	14 53.8	08.7	278 00.3	54.7	170 52.1	50.0	Sirius	258 32.7	S16 44.6
15	68 27.2	6 06.6	.. 43.2	29 54.5	.. 09.3	293 02.7	.. 54.7	185 54.7	.. 50.0	Spica	158 29.6	S11 14.5
16	83 29.7	21 06.0	43.9	44 55.2	09.9	308 05.1	54.7	200 57.3	50.0	Suhail	222 51.3	S43 30.1
17	98 32.1	36 05.4	44.6	59 55.8	10.4	323 07.5	54.7	215 59.9	49.9			
18	113 34.6	51 04.8	N22 45.2	74 56.5	N15 11.0	338 09.9	N17 54.6	231 02.5	S18 49.9	Vega	80 38.0	N38 47.8
19	128 37.1	66 04.2	45.9	89 57.2	11.6	353 12.3	54.6	246 05.1	49.9	Zuben'ubi	137 03.7	S16 06.3
20	143 39.5	81 03.6	46.5	104 57.9	12.2	8 14.7	54.6	261 07.7	49.9			
21	158 42.0	96 02.9	.. 47.2	119 58.6	.. 12.8	23 17.1	.. 54.6	276 10.2	.. 49.8		SHA	Mer.Pass.
22	173 44.5	111 02.3	47.8	134 59.2	13.4	38 19.5	54.6	291 12.8	49.8	Venus	299 38.8	14 35
23	188 46.9	126 01.7	48.5	149 59.9	14.0	53 21.9	54.5	306 15.4	49.8	Mars	322 36.9	13 02
Mer. Pass.	h m 10 30.9	v −0.6	d 0.7	v 0.7	d 0.6	v 2.4	d 0.0	v 2.6	d 0.0	Jupiter	224 37.3	19 31
										Saturn	117 22.6	2 43

UT	SUN GHA	SUN Dec	MOON GHA	v	MOON Dec	d	HP
d h	° ′	° ′	° ′	′	° ′	′	′
13 00	179 49.3	N 8 50.9	256 04.1	8.0	S14 37.3	6.8	58.9
01	194 49.4	51.8	270 31.1	8.0	14 30.5	6.8	59.0
02	209 49.6	52.7	284 58.1	8.0	14 23.7	6.9	59.0
03	224 49.8	.. 53.6	299 25.1	8.0	14 16.8	7.1	59.0
04	239 49.9	54.5	313 52.1	8.0	14 09.7	7.1	59.0
05	254 50.1	55.4	328 19.1	8.0	14 02.6	7.2	59.1
06	269 50.2	N 8 56.3	342 46.1	8.0	S13 55.4	7.3	59.1
07	284 50.4	57.3	357 13.1	8.0	13 48.1	7.4	59.1
08	299 50.6	58.2	11 40.1	8.0	13 40.7	7.5	59.2
M 09	314 50.7	8 59.1	26 07.1	8.0	13 33.2	7.6	59.2
O 10	329 50.9	9 00.0	40 34.1	8.0	13 25.6	7.7	59.2
N 11	344 51.0	00.9	55 01.1	8.0	13 17.9	7.7	59.2
D 12	359 51.2	N 9 01.8	69 28.1	8.0	S13 10.2	7.9	59.3
A 13	14 51.4	02.7	83 55.1	8.0	13 02.3	7.9	59.3
Y 14	29 51.5	03.6	98 22.1	8.0	12 54.4	8.1	59.3
15	44 51.7	.. 04.5	112 49.1	8.1	12 46.3	8.1	59.4
16	59 51.8	05.4	127 16.2	8.0	12 38.2	8.2	59.4
17	74 52.0	06.3	141 43.2	8.0	12 30.0	8.3	59.4
18	89 52.1	N 9 07.2	156 10.2	8.1	S12 21.7	8.4	59.4
19	104 52.3	08.1	170 37.3	8.0	12 13.3	8.4	59.5
20	119 52.5	09.0	185 04.3	8.0	12 04.9	8.5	59.5
21	134 52.6	.. 09.9	199 31.3	8.1	11 56.4	8.7	59.5
22	149 52.8	10.8	213 58.4	8.1	11 47.7	8.7	59.5
23	164 52.9	11.7	228 25.4	8.1	11 39.0	8.7	59.6
14 00	179 53.1	N 9 12.7	242 52.5	8.0	S11 30.3	8.9	59.6
01	194 53.2	13.6	257 19.5	8.1	11 21.4	8.9	59.6
02	209 53.4	14.5	271 46.6	8.1	11 12.5	9.1	59.6
03	224 53.6	.. 15.4	286 13.7	8.0	11 03.4	9.1	59.7
04	239 53.7	16.3	300 40.7	8.1	10 54.3	9.1	59.7
05	254 54.0	17.2	315 07.8	8.1	10 45.2	9.3	59.7
06	269 54.0	N 9 18.1	329 34.9	8.1	S10 35.9	9.3	59.7
07	284 54.2	19.0	344 02.0	8.0	10 26.6	9.4	59.8
T 08	299 54.3	19.9	358 29.0	8.1	10 17.2	9.5	59.8
U 09	314 54.5	.. 20.8	12 56.1	8.1	10 07.7	9.5	59.8
E 10	329 54.6	21.7	27 23.2	8.1	9 58.2	9.6	59.8
S 11	344 54.8	22.6	41 50.3	8.1	9 48.6	9.7	59.9
D 12	359 55.0	N 9 23.5	56 17.4	8.1	S 9 38.9	9.7	59.9
A 13	14 55.1	24.4	70 44.5	8.1	9 29.2	9.8	59.9
Y 14	29 55.3	25.3	85 11.6	8.2	9 19.4	9.9	59.9
15	44 55.4	.. 26.2	99 38.8	8.1	9 09.5	10.0	60.0
16	59 55.6	27.1	114 05.9	8.1	8 59.5	10.0	60.0
17	74 55.7	28.0	128 33.0	8.1	8 49.5	10.0	60.0
18	89 55.9	N 9 28.9	143 00.1	8.1	S 8 39.5	10.2	60.0
19	104 56.0	29.8	157 27.2	8.2	8 29.3	10.2	60.1
20	119 56.2	30.7	171 54.4	8.1	8 19.1	10.2	60.1
21	134 56.3	.. 31.6	186 21.5	8.1	8 08.9	10.3	60.1
22	149 56.5	32.5	200 48.6	8.2	7 58.6	10.4	60.1
23	164 56.6	33.4	215 15.8	8.1	7 48.2	10.4	60.1
15 00	179 56.8	N 9 34.3	229 42.9	8.1	S 7 37.8	10.5	60.2
01	194 57.0	35.2	244 10.0	8.2	7 27.3	10.6	60.2
02	209 57.1	36.1	258 37.2	8.2	7 16.7	10.6	60.2
03	224 57.3	.. 37.0	273 04.3	8.2	7 06.1	10.6	60.2
04	239 57.4	37.9	287 31.5	8.1	6 55.5	10.7	60.2
05	254 57.6	38.7	301 58.6	8.2	6 44.8	10.7	60.3
06	269 57.7	N 9 39.6	316 25.8	8.1	S 6 34.1	10.8	60.3
07	284 57.9	40.5	330 52.9	8.2	6 23.3	10.9	60.3
W 08	299 58.0	41.4	345 20.1	8.1	6 12.4	10.9	60.3
E 09	314 58.2	.. 42.3	359 47.2	8.2	6 01.5	10.9	60.3
D 10	329 58.3	43.2	14 14.4	8.1	5 50.6	11.0	60.4
N 11	344 58.5	44.1	28 41.5	8.2	5 39.6	11.0	60.4
E 12	359 58.6	N 9 45.0	43 08.7	8.1	S 5 28.6	11.1	60.4
S 13	14 58.8	45.9	57 35.8	8.2	5 17.5	11.1	60.4
D 14	29 58.9	46.8	72 03.0	8.1	5 06.4	11.1	60.4
A 15	44 59.1	.. 47.7	86 30.1	8.2	4 55.3	11.2	60.4
Y 16	59 59.2	48.6	100 57.3	8.1	4 44.1	11.2	60.5
17	74 59.4	49.5	115 24.4	8.2	4 32.9	11.3	60.5
18	89 59.5	N 9 50.4	129 51.6	8.1	S 4 21.6	11.3	60.5
19	104 59.7	51.3	144 18.7	8.2	4 10.3	11.3	60.5
20	119 59.8	52.2	158 45.9	8.1	3 59.0	11.3	60.5
21	135 00.0	.. 53.0	173 13.0	8.1	3 47.7	11.4	60.5
22	150 00.1	53.9	187 40.1	8.2	3 36.3	11.4	60.5
23	165 00.3	54.8	202 07.3	8.1	S 3 24.9	11.4	60.5
	SD 16.0	d 0.9	SD 16.1		16.3		16.5

Moonrise

Lat.	Twilight Naut.	Twilight Civil	Sunrise	Moonrise 13	14	15	16
°	h m	h m	h m	h m	h m	h m	h m
N 72	////	02 10	03 47	04 31	04 25	04 20	04 15
N 70	////	02 44	04 03	04 03	04 07	04 10	04 12
68	01 02	03 07	04 15	03 41	03 53	04 02	04 09
66	01 52	03 25	04 25	03 24	03 41	03 55	04 06
64	02 22	03 40	04 34	03 10	03 32	03 49	04 04
62	02 44	03 52	04 41	02 58	03 23	03 44	04 02
60	03 02	04 02	04 48	02 48	03 16	03 39	04 01
N 58	03 16	04 11	04 53	02 39	03 09	03 36	03 59
56	03 28	04 18	04 58	02 32	03 04	03 32	03 58
54	03 38	04 25	05 02	02 25	02 59	03 29	03 57
52	03 47	04 31	05 06	02 18	02 54	03 26	03 56
50	03 54	04 36	05 10	02 13	02 50	03 23	03 55
45	04 11	04 47	05 18	02 01	02 41	03 18	03 53
N 40	04 23	04 56	05 24	01 50	02 33	03 13	03 51
35	04 33	05 04	05 30	01 42	02 26	03 09	03 50
30	04 41	05 10	05 35	01 34	02 21	03 05	03 49
20	04 54	05 21	05 43	01 21	02 10	02 59	03 46
N 10	05 04	05 29	05 50	01 09	02 02	02 53	03 44
0	05 12	05 36	05 57	00 58	01 53	02 48	03 43
S 10	05 18	05 42	06 04	00 48	01 45	02 43	03 41
20	05 23	05 48	06 10	00 36	01 36	02 37	03 39
30	05 26	05 54	06 18	00 23	01 26	02 31	03 37
35	05 28	05 57	06 23	00 15	01 20	02 27	03 35
40	05 29	06 00	06 28	00 06	01 13	02 23	03 34
45	05 30	06 04	06 33	25 06	01 06	02 18	03 32
S 50	05 30	06 07	06 40	24 56	00 56	02 12	03 30
52	05 30	06 09	06 43	24 52	00 52	02 09	03 29
54	05 30	06 11	06 47	24 47	00 47	02 07	03 28
56	05 30	06 13	06 50	24 42	00 42	02 03	03 27
58	05 29	06 15	06 55	24 36	00 36	02 00	03 26
S 60	05 29	06 17	06 59	24 29	00 29	01 55	03 25

Moonset

Lat.	Sunset	Twilight Civil	Twilight Naut.	Moonset 13	14	15	16
°	h m	h m	h m	h m	h m	h m	h m
N 72	20 17	21 58	////	10 06	12 07	14 06	16 05
N 70	20 01	21 22	////	10 34	12 23	14 14	16 06
68	19 48	20 57	23 14	10 54	12 36	14 20	16 06
66	19 38	20 39	22 15	11 10	12 46	14 25	16 06
64	19 29	20 24	21 43	11 24	12 55	14 30	16 07
62	19 21	20 11	21 20	11 35	13 02	14 34	16 07
60	19 15	20 01	21 02	11 44	13 09	14 37	16 07
N 58	19 09	19 52	20 47	11 53	13 15	14 40	16 07
56	19 04	19 44	20 35	12 00	13 20	14 42	16 07
54	18 59	19 37	20 25	12 06	13 24	14 45	16 07
52	18 55	19 31	20 16	12 12	13 28	14 47	16 07
50	18 52	19 26	20 08	12 17	13 32	14 49	16 08
45	18 44	19 14	19 51	12 28	13 40	14 53	16 08
N 40	18 37	19 05	19 39	12 38	13 46	14 56	16 08
35	18 31	18 57	19 28	12 46	13 52	14 59	16 08
30	18 26	18 51	19 20	12 53	13 57	15 02	16 08
20	18 18	18 40	19 07	13 04	14 05	15 06	16 08
N 10	18 10	18 32	18 57	13 15	14 12	15 10	16 08
0	18 04	18 25	18 49	13 25	14 19	15 14	16 08
S 10	17 57	18 18	18 43	13 34	14 26	15 17	16 09
20	17 50	18 12	18 38	13 44	14 33	15 21	16 09
30	17 42	18 06	18 34	13 56	14 41	15 25	16 09
35	17 38	18 03	18 33	14 03	14 46	15 28	16 09
40	17 33	18 00	18 31	14 10	14 51	15 30	16 09
45	17 27	17 56	18 30	14 19	14 58	15 34	16 09
S 50	17 20	17 52	18 30	14 30	15 05	15 37	16 09
52	17 17	17 51	18 30	14 35	15 08	15 39	16 09
54	17 13	17 49	18 30	14 40	15 12	15 41	16 09
56	17 09	17 47	18 30	14 46	15 16	15 43	16 09
58	17 05	17 45	18 30	14 52	15 20	15 45	16 09
S 60	17 00	17 43	18 31	15 00	15 25	15 48	16 09

	SUN	SUN	SUN	MOON	MOON	MOON	MOON
Day	Eqn. of Time 00h	Eqn. of Time 12h	Mer. Pass.	Mer. Pass. Upper	Mer. Pass. Lower	Age	Phase
d	m s	m s	h m	h m	h m	d	%
13	00 43	00 36	12 01	07 12	19 39	24	35
14	00 28	00 20	12 00	08 06	20 34	25	25
15	00 13	00 06	12 00	09 01	21 28	26	15

UT	ARIES GHA	VENUS −4.1 GHA	Dec	MARS +1.4 GHA	Dec	JUPITER −2.2 GHA	Dec	SATURN +0.2 GHA	Dec	STARS Name	SHA	Dec
d h	° ′	° ′	° ′	° ′	° ′	° ′	° ′	° ′	° ′		° ′	° ′
16 00	203 49.4	141 01.1	N22 49.1	165 00.6	N15 14.6	68 24.4	N17 54.5	321 18.0	S18 49.8	Acamar	315 17.9	S40 14.9
01	218 51.9	156 00.5	49.8	180 01.3	15.2	83 26.8	54.5	336 20.6	49.7	Achernar	335 26.5	S57 09.7
02	233 54.3	170 59.9	50.4	195 01.9	15.8	98 29.2	54.5	351 23.2	49.7	Acrux	173 07.1	S63 11.2
03	248 56.8	185 59.3 ..	51.1	210 02.6 ..	16.4	113 31.6 ..	54.5	6 25.8 ..	49.7	Adhara	255 11.6	S29 00.0
04	263 59.2	200 58.7	51.7	225 03.3	16.9	128 34.0	54.4	21 28.4	49.7	Aldebaran	290 48.2	N16 32.1
05	279 01.7	215 58.1	52.4	240 04.0	17.5	143 36.4	54.4	36 31.0	49.6			
T 06	294 04.2	230 57.5	N22 53.0	255 04.6	N15 18.1	158 38.8	N17 54.4	51 33.6	S18 49.6	Alioth	166 19.2	N55 52.6
H 07	309 06.6	245 56.9	53.7	270 05.3	18.7	173 41.2	54.4	66 36.2	49.6	Alkaid	152 57.5	N49 14.2
U 08	324 09.1	260 56.3	54.3	285 06.0	19.3	188 43.6	54.4	81 38.8	49.5	Al Na'ir	27 42.5	S46 53.0
R 09	339 11.6	275 55.7 ..	55.0	300 06.7 ..	19.9	203 46.0 ..	54.3	96 41.4 ..	49.5	Alnilam	275 45.3	S 1 11.9
S 10	354 14.0	290 55.0	55.6	315 07.4	20.5	218 48.4	54.3	111 44.0	49.5	Alphard	217 54.7	S 8 43.8
D 11	9 16.5	305 54.4	56.2	330 08.0	21.1	233 50.8	54.3	126 46.5	49.5			
A 12	24 19.0	320 53.8	N22 56.9	345 08.7	N15 21.7	248 53.2	N17 54.3	141 49.1	S18 49.4	Alphecca	126 09.7	N26 39.8
Y 13	39 21.4	335 53.2	57.5	0 09.4	22.2	263 55.6	54.3	156 51.7	49.4	Alpheratz	357 42.5	N29 10.3
14	54 23.9	350 52.6	58.2	15 10.1	22.8	278 58.0	54.2	171 54.3	49.4	Altair	62 07.0	N 8 54.5
15	69 26.4	5 52.0 ..	58.8	30 10.7 ..	23.4	294 00.4 ..	54.2	186 56.9 ..	49.4	Ankaa	353 14.9	S42 13.4
16	84 28.8	20 51.4	22 59.4	45 11.4	24.0	309 02.8	54.2	201 59.5	49.3	Antares	112 24.4	S26 27.8
17	99 31.3	35 50.8	23 00.1	60 12.1	24.6	324 05.2	54.2	217 02.1	49.3			
18	114 33.7	50 50.2	N23 00.7	75 12.8	N15 25.2	339 07.6	N17 54.2	232 04.7	S18 49.3	Arcturus	145 54.3	N19 06.1
19	129 36.2	65 49.6	01.3	90 13.4	25.8	354 10.0	54.1	247 07.3	49.2	Atria	107 24.7	S69 02.9
20	144 38.7	80 48.9	02.0	105 14.1	26.3	9 12.4	54.1	262 09.9	49.2	Avior	234 17.4	S59 34.0
21	159 41.1	95 48.3 ..	02.6	120 14.8 ..	26.9	24 14.9 ..	54.1	277 12.5 ..	49.2	Bellatrix	278 30.9	N 6 21.5
22	174 43.6	110 47.7	03.2	135 15.5	27.5	39 17.3	54.1	292 15.1	49.2	Betelgeuse	271 00.1	N 7 24.3
23	189 46.1	125 47.1	03.8	150 16.1	28.1	54 19.7	54.0	307 17.7	49.1			
17 00	204 48.5	140 46.5	N23 04.5	165 16.8	N15 28.7	69 22.1	N17 54.0	322 20.3	S18 49.1	Canopus	263 55.8	S52 42.7
01	219 51.0	155 45.9	05.1	180 17.5	29.3	84 24.5	54.0	337 22.9	49.1	Capella	280 32.9	N46 00.7
02	234 53.5	170 45.3	05.7	195 18.2	29.9	99 26.9	54.0	352 25.5	49.1	Deneb	49 30.7	N45 19.9
03	249 55.9	185 44.7 ..	06.3	210 18.8 ..	30.4	114 29.3 ..	54.0	7 28.1 ..	49.0	Denebola	182 32.1	N14 29.1
04	264 58.4	200 44.0	07.0	225 19.5	31.0	129 31.7	53.9	22 30.7	49.0	Diphda	348 55.0	S17 54.3
05	280 00.8	215 43.4	07.6	240 20.2	31.6	144 34.0	53.9	37 33.3	49.0			
06	295 03.3	230 42.8	N23 08.2	255 20.9	N15 32.2	159 36.4	N17 53.9	52 35.9	S18 48.9	Dubhe	193 49.8	N61 40.2
07	310 05.8	245 42.2	08.8	270 21.5	32.8	174 38.8	53.9	67 38.5	48.9	Elnath	278 11.3	N28 37.0
F 08	325 08.2	260 41.6	09.4	285 22.2	33.3	189 41.2	53.9	82 41.0	48.9	Eltanin	90 45.3	N51 29.1
R 09	340 10.7	275 41.0 ..	10.1	300 22.9 ..	33.9	204 43.6 ..	53.8	97 43.6 ..	48.9	Enif	33 46.0	N 9 56.7
I 10	355 13.2	290 40.4	10.7	315 23.6	34.5	219 46.0	53.8	112 46.2	48.8	Fomalhaut	15 22.9	S29 32.4
D 11	10 15.6	305 39.7	11.3	330 24.2	35.1	234 48.4	53.8	127 48.8	48.8			
A 12	25 18.1	320 39.1	N23 11.9	345 24.9	N15 35.7	249 50.8	N17 53.8	142 51.4	S18 48.8	Gacrux	171 58.8	S57 12.1
Y 13	40 20.6	335 38.5	12.5	0 25.6	36.3	264 53.2	53.7	157 54.0	48.8	Gienah	175 50.7	S17 37.8
14	55 23.0	350 37.9	13.1	15 26.3	36.8	279 55.6	53.7	172 56.6	48.7	Hadar	148 45.4	S60 26.7
15	70 25.5	5 37.3 ..	13.7	30 26.9 ..	37.4	294 58.0 ..	53.7	187 59.2 ..	48.7	Hamal	327 59.7	N23 31.9
16	85 28.0	20 36.7	14.4	45 27.6	38.0	310 00.4	53.7	203 01.8	48.7	Kaus Aust.	83 42.0	S34 22.3
17	100 30.4	35 36.0	15.0	60 28.3	38.6	325 02.8	53.6	218 04.4	48.6			
18	115 32.9	50 35.4	N23 15.6	75 29.0	N15 39.2	340 05.2	N17 53.6	233 07.0	S18 48.6	Kochab	137 19.1	N74 05.6
19	130 35.3	65 34.8	16.2	90 29.6	39.7	355 07.6	53.6	248 09.6	48.6	Markab	13 37.3	N15 17.1
20	145 37.8	80 34.2	16.8	105 30.3	40.3	10 10.0	53.6	263 12.2	48.6	Menkar	314 14.1	N 4 08.7
21	160 40.3	95 33.6 ..	17.4	120 31.0 ..	40.9	25 12.4 ..	53.6	278 14.8 ..	48.5	Menkent	148 05.7	S36 26.7
22	175 42.7	110 33.0	18.0	135 31.7	41.5	40 14.8	53.5	293 17.4	48.5	Miaplacidus	221 39.0	S69 47.2
23	190 45.2	125 32.3	18.6	150 32.3	42.0	55 17.2	53.5	308 20.0	48.5			
18 00	205 47.7	140 31.7	N23 19.2	165 33.0	N15 42.6	70 19.6	N17 53.5	323 22.6	S18 48.5	Mirfak	308 39.0	N49 54.8
01	220 50.1	155 31.1	19.8	180 33.7	43.2	85 22.0	53.5	338 25.2	48.4	Nunki	75 56.7	S26 16.4
02	235 52.6	170 30.5	20.4	195 34.3	43.8	100 24.3	53.4	353 27.8	48.4	Peacock	53 17.5	S56 40.8
03	250 55.1	185 29.9 ..	21.0	210 35.0 ..	44.4	115 26.7 ..	53.4	8 30.4 ..	48.4	Pollux	243 26.3	N27 59.2
04	265 57.5	200 29.2	21.6	225 35.7	44.9	130 29.1	53.4	23 33.0	48.3	Procyon	244 58.5	N 5 10.9
05	281 00.0	215 28.6	22.2	240 36.4	45.5	145 31.5	53.4	38 35.6	48.3			
06	296 02.5	230 28.0	N23 22.8	255 37.0	N15 46.1	160 33.9	N17 53.3	53 38.2	S18 48.3	Rasalhague	96 05.1	N12 33.0
S 07	311 04.9	245 27.4	23.4	270 37.7	46.7	175 36.3	53.3	68 40.8	48.3	Regulus	207 42.0	N11 53.4
A 08	326 07.4	260 26.8	24.0	285 38.4	47.2	190 38.7	53.3	83 43.4	48.2	Rigel	281 11.1	S 8 11.4
T 09	341 09.8	275 26.1 ..	24.6	300 39.1 ..	47.8	205 41.1 ..	53.3	98 46.0 ..	48.2	Rigil Kent.	139 49.3	S60 53.7
U 10	356 12.3	290 25.5	25.2	315 39.7	48.4	220 43.5	53.2	113 48.6	48.2	Sabik	102 10.9	S15 44.5
R 11	11 14.8	305 24.9	25.8	330 40.4	49.0	235 45.9	53.2	128 51.2	48.1			
D 12	26 17.2	320 24.3	N23 26.3	345 41.1	N15 49.5	250 48.3	N17 53.2	143 53.8	S18 48.1	Schedar	349 39.5	N56 37.1
A 13	41 19.7	335 23.7	26.9	0 41.7	50.1	265 50.6	53.2	158 56.4	48.1	Shaula	96 20.0	S37 06.6
Y 14	56 22.2	350 23.0	27.5	15 42.4	50.7	280 53.0	53.1	173 59.0	48.1	Sirius	258 32.7	S16 44.6
15	71 24.6	5 22.4 ..	28.1	30 43.1 ..	51.3	295 55.4 ..	53.1	189 01.6 ..	48.0	Spica	158 29.6	S11 14.5
16	86 27.1	20 21.8	28.7	45 43.8	51.8	310 57.8	53.1	204 04.2	48.0	Suhail	222 51.3	S43 30.1
17	101 29.6	35 21.2	29.3	60 44.4	52.4	326 00.2	53.1	219 06.8	48.0			
18	116 32.0	50 20.6	N23 29.9	75 45.1	N15 53.0	341 02.6	N17 53.0	234 09.4	S18 47.9	Vega	80 38.0	N38 47.8
19	131 34.5	65 19.9	30.4	90 45.8	53.6	356 05.0	53.0	249 12.0	47.9	Zuben'ubi	137 03.7	S16 06.3
20	146 36.9	80 19.3	31.0	105 46.4	54.1	11 07.3	53.0	264 14.6	47.9			
21	161 39.4	95 18.7 ..	31.6	120 47.1 ..	54.7	26 09.7 ..	53.0	279 17.2 ..	47.9		SHA	Mer. Pass.
22	176 41.9	110 18.1	32.2	135 47.8	55.3	41 12.1	52.9	294 19.8	47.8	Venus	295 58.0	14 38
23	191 44.7	125 17.4	32.8	150 48.5	55.8	56 14.5	52.9	309 22.4	47.8	Mars	320 28.3	12 58
	h m									Jupiter	224 33.5	19 19
Mer. Pass. 10 19.1	v −0.6 d 0.6			v 0.7 d 0.6		v 2.4 d 0.0		v 2.6 d 0.0		Saturn	117 31.7	2 30

UT	SUN GHA	SUN Dec	MOON GHA	v	Dec	d	HP
d h	° ′	° ′	° ′	′	° ′	′	′
16 00	180 00.4	N 9 55.7	216 34.4	8.1	S 3 13.5	11.5	60.6
01	195 00.6	56.6	231 01.5	8.1	3 02.0	11.5	60.6
02	210 00.7	57.5	245 28.6	8.2	2 50.5	11.5	60.6
03	225 00.9 ..	58.4	259 55.8	8.1	2 39.0	11.5	60.6
04	240 01.0	9 59.3	274 22.9	8.1	2 27.5	11.6	60.6
05	255 01.2	10 00.2	288 50.0	8.1	2 15.9	11.5	60.6
06	270 01.3	N10 01.1	303 17.1	8.1	S 2 04.4	11.6	60.6
T 07	285 01.5	01.9	317 44.2	8.1	1 52.8	11.6	60.6
H 08	300 01.6	02.8	332 11.3	8.1	1 41.2	11.7	60.6
U 09	315 01.8 ..	03.7	346 38.4	8.1	1 29.5	11.6	60.7
R 10	330 01.9	04.6	1 05.5	8.0	1 17.9	11.6	60.7
S 11	345 02.0	05.5	15 32.5	8.1	1 06.3	11.7	60.7
D 12	0 02.2	N10 06.4	29 59.6	8.1	S 0 54.6	11.7	60.7
A 13	15 02.3	07.3	44 26.7	8.0	0 42.9	11.6	60.7
Y 14	30 02.5	08.2	58 53.7	8.1	0 31.3	11.7	60.7
15	45 02.6 ..	09.0	73 20.8	8.0	0 19.6	11.7	60.7
16	60 02.8	09.9	87 47.8	8.1	S 0 07.9	11.7	60.7
17	75 02.9	10.8	102 14.9	8.0	N 0 03.8	11.7	60.7
18	90 03.1	N10 11.7	116 41.9	8.0	N 0 15.5	11.7	60.7
19	105 03.2	12.6	131 08.9	8.0	0 27.2	11.6	60.7
20	120 03.4	13.5	145 35.9	8.0	0 38.9	11.6	60.7
21	135 03.5 ..	14.4	160 02.9	8.0	0 50.5	11.7	60.7
22	150 03.7	15.2	174 29.9	8.0	1 02.2	11.7	60.7
23	165 03.8	16.1	188 56.9	7.9	1 13.9	11.7	60.7
17 00	180 03.9	N10 17.0	203 23.8	8.0	N 1 25.6	11.7	60.7
01	195 04.1	17.9	217 50.8	7.9	1 37.3	11.6	60.7
02	210 04.2	18.8	232 17.7	8.0	1 48.9	11.7	60.7
03	225 04.4 ..	19.7	246 44.7	7.9	2 00.6	11.6	60.7
04	240 04.5	20.5	261 11.6	7.9	2 12.2	11.6	60.7
05	255 04.6	21.4	275 38.5	7.9	2 23.8	11.6	60.7
06	270 04.8	N10 22.3	290 05.4	7.9	N 2 35.4	11.6	60.7
07	285 05.0	23.2	304 32.3	7.9	2 47.0	11.6	60.7
F 08	300 05.1	24.1	318 59.2	7.9	2 58.6	11.5	60.7
R 09	315 05.2 ..	25.0	333 26.1	7.9	3 10.1	11.6	60.7
I 10	330 05.4	25.8	347 53.0	7.8	3 21.7	11.5	60.7
D 11	345 05.5	26.7	2 19.8	7.8	3 33.2	11.5	60.7
A 12	0 05.7	N10 27.6	16 46.6	7.9	N 3 44.7	11.4	60.7
Y 13	15 05.8	28.5	31 13.5	7.8	3 56.1	11.5	60.7
14	30 06.0	29.4	45 40.3	7.8	4 07.6	11.4	60.7
15	45 06.1 ..	30.2	60 07.1	7.8	4 19.0	11.4	60.7
16	60 06.2	31.1	74 33.9	7.7	4 30.4	11.3	60.7
17	75 06.4	32.0	89 00.6	7.8	4 41.7	11.3	60.7
18	90 06.5	N10 32.9	103 27.4	7.7	N 4 53.0	11.3	60.7
19	105 06.7	33.8	117 54.1	7.8	5 04.3	11.3	60.7
20	120 06.8	34.6	132 20.9	7.7	5 15.6	11.2	60.7
21	135 07.0 ..	35.5	146 47.6	7.7	5 26.8	11.1	60.7
22	150 07.1	36.4	161 14.3	7.7	5 37.9	11.2	60.7
23	165 07.2	37.3	175 41.0	7.7	5 49.1	11.1	60.6
18 00	180 07.4	N10 38.1	190 07.7	7.6	N 6 00.2	11.0	60.6
01	195 07.5	39.0	204 34.3	7.7	6 11.2	11.0	60.6
02	210 07.7	39.9	219 01.0	7.6	6 22.2	11.0	60.6
03	225 07.8 ..	40.8	233 27.6	7.6	6 33.2	10.9	60.6
04	240 07.9	41.6	247 54.2	7.7	6 44.1	10.9	60.6
05	255 08.1	42.5	262 20.9	7.6	6 55.0	10.8	60.6
06	270 08.2	N10 43.4	276 47.5	7.5	N 7 05.8	10.8	60.6
07	285 08.4	44.3	291 14.0	7.6	7 16.6	10.7	60.6
S 08	300 08.5	45.1	305 40.6	7.6	7 27.3	10.7	60.5
A 09	315 08.6 ..	46.0	320 07.2	7.5	7 38.0	10.6	60.5
T 10	330 08.8	46.9	334 33.7	7.5	7 48.6	10.6	60.5
U 11	345 08.9	47.8	349 00.2	7.6	7 59.2	10.5	60.5
R 12	0 09.1	N10 48.6	3 26.8	7.5	N 8 09.7	10.4	60.5
D 13	15 09.2	49.5	17 53.3	7.4	8 20.1	10.4	60.5
A 14	30 09.3	50.4	32 19.7	7.5	8 30.5	10.3	60.5
Y 15	45 09.5 ..	51.2	46 46.2	7.5	8 40.8	10.3	60.4
16	60 09.6	52.1	61 12.7	7.4	8 51.1	10.2	60.4
17	75 09.7	53.0	75 39.1	7.5	9 01.3	10.1	60.4
18	90 09.9	N10 53.9	90 05.6	7.4	N 9 11.4	10.1	60.4
19	105 10.0	54.7	104 32.0	7.4	9 21.5	10.0	60.4
20	120 10.2	55.6	118 58.4	7.4	9 31.5	9.9	60.4
21	135 10.3 ..	56.5	133 24.8	7.4	9 41.4	9.9	60.3
22	150 10.4	57.3	147 51.2	7.4	9 51.3	9.8	60.3
23	165 10.6	58.2	162 17.6	7.3	N10 01.1	9.7	60.3
	SD 16.0	d 0.9	SD 16.5		16.5		16.5

Lat.	Twilight Naut.	Twilight Civil	Sunrise	Moonrise 16	17	18	19
°	h m	h m	h m	h m	h m	h m	h m
N 72	////	01 41	03 30	04 15	04 10	04 05	04 01
N 70	////	02 23	03 48	04 12	04 13	04 15	04 18
68	////	02 51	04 02	04 09	04 15	04 22	04 31
66	01 27	03 11	04 14	04 06	04 17	04 29	04 43
64	02 05	03 28	04 23	04 04	04 19	04 34	04 52
62	02 30	03 41	04 32	04 02	04 20	04 39	05 00
60	02 49	03 52	04 39	04 01	04 22	04 43	05 07
N 58	03 05	04 02	04 45	03 59	04 23	04 47	05 14
56	03 18	04 10	04 51	03 58	04 24	04 50	05 19
54	03 29	04 17	04 55	03 57	04 25	04 53	05 24
52	03 39	04 24	05 00	03 56	04 26	04 56	05 29
50	03 47	04 30	05 04	03 55	04 26	04 58	05 33
45	04 05	04 42	05 13	03 53	04 28	05 04	05 42
N 40	04 18	04 52	05 20	03 51	04 29	05 08	05 49
35	04 29	05 00	05 26	03 50	04 31	05 12	05 56
30	04 38	05 07	05 32	03 49	04 32	05 16	06 01
20	04 52	05 18	05 41	03 46	04 34	05 22	06 11
N 10	05 03	05 27	05 49	03 44	04 36	05 27	06 20
0	05 11	05 35	05 56	03 43	04 37	05 32	06 28
S 10	05 18	05 42	06 04	03 41	04 39	05 38	06 37
20	05 23	05 49	06 11	03 39	04 41	05 43	06 46
30	05 28	05 56	06 20	03 37	04 43	05 50	06 56
35	05 30	05 59	06 25	03 35	04 44	05 53	07 02
40	05 32	06 03	06 31	03 34	04 46	05 58	07 09
45	05 33	06 07	06 37	03 32	04 47	06 03	07 17
S 50	05 34	06 12	06 45	03 30	04 49	06 08	07 26
52	05 35	06 14	06 48	03 29	04 50	06 11	07 31
54	05 35	06 16	06 52	03 28	04 51	06 14	07 36
56	05 35	06 18	06 56	03 27	04 52	06 18	07 41
58	05 35	06 21	07 01	03 26	04 54	06 21	07 47
S 60	05 35	06 24	07 07	03 25	04 55	06 26	07 54

Lat.	Sunset	Twilight Civil	Twilight Naut.	Moonset 16	17	18	19
°	h m	h m	h m	h m	h m	h m	h m
N 72	20 34	22 28	////	16 05	18 05	20 06	22 09
N 70	20 15	21 42	////	16 06	17 58	19 51	21 42
68	20 00	21 13	////	16 06	17 53	19 39	21 23
66	19 48	20 51	22 40	16 06	17 48	19 29	21 07
64	19 38	20 34	22 00	16 07	17 44	19 20	20 54
62	19 29	20 21	21 33	16 07	17 40	19 13	20 43
60	19 22	20 09	21 13	16 07	17 38	19 07	20 34
N 58	19 16	19 59	20 57	16 07	17 35	19 02	20 26
56	19 10	19 51	20 43	16 07	17 33	18 57	20 19
54	19 05	19 43	20 32	16 07	17 30	18 53	20 13
52	19 00	19 37	20 22	16 07	17 28	18 49	20 07
50	18 56	19 31	20 13	16 08	17 27	18 45	20 02
45	18 47	19 18	19 56	16 08	17 23	18 38	19 51
N 40	18 40	19 08	19 42	16 08	17 20	18 31	19 42
35	18 34	19 00	19 31	16 08	17 17	18 26	19 34
30	18 28	18 53	19 22	16 08	17 15	18 21	19 27
20	18 19	18 41	19 08	16 08	17 11	18 13	19 15
N 10	18 11	18 32	18 57	16 08	17 07	18 06	19 05
0	18 03	18 24	18 48	16 08	17 03	17 59	18 55
S 10	17 55	18 17	18 41	16 09	17 00	17 52	18 45
20	17 48	18 10	18 36	16 09	16 56	17 45	18 35
30	17 39	18 03	18 31	16 09	16 52	17 37	18 23
35	17 34	17 59	18 29	16 09	16 50	17 32	18 16
40	17 28	17 56	18 27	16 09	16 47	17 27	18 09
45	17 22	17 51	18 25	16 09	16 44	17 20	18 00
S 50	17 14	17 47	18 24	16 09	16 40	17 13	17 49
52	17 10	17 45	18 24	16 09	16 38	17 10	17 44
54	17 06	17 42	18 23	16 09	16 36	17 06	17 39
56	17 02	17 40	18 23	16 09	16 34	17 02	17 32
58	16 57	17 37	18 23	16 09	16 32	16 57	17 26
S 60	16 52	17 34	18 23	16 09	16 29	16 52	17 18

Day	SUN Eqn. of Time 00h	SUN Eqn. of Time 12h	SUN Mer. Pass.	MOON Mer. Pass. Upper	MOON Mer. Pass. Lower	Age	Phase
d	m s	m s	h m	h m	h m	d	%
16	00 01	00 08	12 00	09 55	22 23	27	8
17	00 15	00 22	12 00	10 50	23 18	28	2
18	00 29	00 36	11 59	11 46	24 14	29	0

UT (d h)	ARIES GHA	VENUS −4.1 GHA	Dec	MARS +1.4 GHA	Dec	JUPITER −2.2 GHA	Dec	SATURN +0.2 GHA	Dec	STARS Name	SHA	Dec
19 00	206 46.8	140 16.8	N23 33.3	165 49.1	N15 56.4	71 16.9	N17 52.9	324 25.0	S18 47.8	Acamar	315 17.9	S40 14.9
01	221 49.3	155 16.2	33.9	180 49.8	57.0	86 19.3	52.9	339 27.6	47.7	Achernar	335 26.5	S57 09.6
02	236 51.7	170 15.6	34.5	195 50.5	57.6	101 21.7	52.8	354 30.2	47.7	Acrux	173 07.1	S63 11.2
03	251 54.2	185 14.9 ..	35.1	210 51.1 ..	58.1	116 24.0 ..	52.8	9 32.8 ..	47.7	Adhara	255 11.7	S29 00.0
04	266 56.7	200 14.3	35.6	225 51.8	58.7	131 26.4	52.8	24 35.4	47.7	Aldebaran	290 48.2	N16 32.1
05	281 59.1	215 13.7	36.2	240 52.5	59.3	146 28.8	52.7	39 38.0	47.6			
06	297 01.6	230 13.1	N23 36.8	255 53.2	N15 59.8	161 31.2	N17 52.7	54 40.6	S18 47.6	Alioth	166 19.2	N55 52.7
07	312 04.1	245 12.4	37.3	270 53.8	16 00.4	176 33.6	52.7	69 43.2	47.6	Alkaid	152 57.5	N49 14.2
08	327 06.5	260 11.8	37.9	285 54.5	01.0	191 36.0	52.7	84 45.8	47.6	Al Na'ir	27 42.5	S46 53.0
S 09	342 09.0	275 11.2 ..	38.5	300 55.2 ..	01.5	206 38.3 ..	52.6	99 48.4 ..	47.5	Alnilam	275 45.3	S 1 11.9
U 10	357 11.4	290 10.6	39.0	315 55.8	02.1	221 40.7	52.6	114 51.0	47.5	Alphard	217 54.8	S 8 43.8
N 11	12 13.9	305 09.9	39.6	330 56.5	02.7	236 43.1	52.6	129 53.6	47.5			
D 12	27 16.4	320 09.3	N23 40.2	345 57.2	N16 03.2	251 45.5	N17 52.5	144 56.3	S18 47.4	Alphecca	126 09.7	N26 39.8
A 13	42 18.8	335 08.7	40.7	0 57.9	03.8	266 47.9	52.5	159 58.9	47.4	Alpheratz	357 42.5	N29 10.3
Y 14	57 21.3	350 08.1	41.3	15 58.5	04.4	281 50.2	52.5	175 01.5	47.4	Altair	62 07.0	N 8 54.6
15	72 23.8	5 07.4 ..	41.9	30 59.2 ..	04.9	296 52.6 ..	52.5	190 04.1 ..	47.4	Ankaa	353 14.9	S42 13.4
16	87 26.2	20 06.8	42.4	45 59.9	05.5	311 55.0	52.4	205 06.7	47.3	Antares	112 24.4	S26 27.8
17	102 28.7	35 06.2	43.0	61 00.5	06.1	326 57.4	52.4	220 09.3	47.3			
18	117 31.2	50 05.5	N23 43.5	76 01.2	N16 06.6	341 59.8	N17 52.4	235 11.9	S18 47.2	Arcturus	145 54.3	N19 06.2
19	132 33.6	65 04.9	44.1	91 01.9	07.2	357 02.1	52.4	250 14.5	47.2	Atria	107 24.7	S69 02.9
20	147 36.1	80 04.3	44.6	106 02.5	07.8	12 04.5	52.3	265 17.1	47.2	Avior	234 17.4	S59 34.0
21	162 38.5	95 03.7 ..	45.2	121 03.2 ..	08.3	27 06.9 ..	52.3	280 19.7 ..	47.2	Bellatrix	278 30.9	N 6 21.5
22	177 41.0	110 03.0	45.7	136 03.9	08.9	42 09.3	52.3	295 22.3	47.2	Betelgeuse	271 00.1	N 7 24.3
23	192 43.5	125 02.4	46.3	151 04.5	09.5	57 11.7	52.3	310 24.9	47.1			
20 00	207 45.9	140 01.8	N23 46.9	166 05.2	N16 10.0	72 14.0	N17 52.2	325 27.5	S18 47.1	Canopus	263 55.8	S52 42.7
01	222 48.4	155 01.2	47.4	181 05.9	10.6	87 16.4	52.2	340 30.1	47.1	Capella	280 32.9	N46 00.7
02	237 50.9	170 00.5	48.0	196 06.6	11.2	102 18.8	52.2	355 32.7	47.0	Deneb	49 30.6	N45 19.9
03	252 53.3	184 59.9 ..	48.5	211 07.2 ..	11.7	117 21.2 ..	52.1	10 35.3 ..	47.0	Denebola	182 32.2	N14 29.1
04	267 55.8	199 59.3	49.0	226 07.9	12.3	132 23.5	52.1	25 37.9	47.0	Diphda	348 55.0	S17 54.3
05	282 58.3	214 58.6	49.6	241 08.6	12.9	147 25.9	52.1	40 40.5	47.0			
06	298 00.7	229 58.0	N23 50.1	256 09.2	N16 13.4	162 28.3	N17 52.1	55 43.1	S18 46.9	Dubhe	193 49.9	N61 40.2
07	313 03.2	244 57.4	50.7	271 09.9	14.0	177 30.7	52.0	70 45.7	46.9	Elnath	278 11.3	N28 37.0
08	328 05.7	259 56.7	51.2	286 10.6	14.5	192 33.0	52.0	85 48.3	46.9	Eltanin	90 45.3	N51 29.1
M 09	343 08.1	274 56.1 ..	51.8	301 11.2 ..	15.1	207 35.4 ..	52.0	100 50.9 ..	46.8	Enif	33 46.0	N 9 56.7
O 10	358 10.6	289 55.5	52.3	316 11.9	15.7	222 37.8	51.9	115 53.6	46.8	Fomalhaut	15 22.9	S29 32.4
N 11	13 13.0	304 54.9	52.8	331 12.6	16.2	237 40.2	51.9	130 56.2	46.8			
D 12	28 15.5	319 54.2	N23 53.4	346 13.2	N16 16.8	252 42.5	N17 51.9	145 58.8	S18 46.7	Gacrux	171 58.9	S57 12.1
A 13	43 18.0	334 53.6	53.9	1 13.9	17.4	267 44.9	51.8	161 01.4	46.7	Gienah	175 50.7	S17 37.8
Y 14	58 20.4	349 53.0	54.5	16 14.6	17.9	282 47.3	51.8	176 04.0	46.7	Hadar	148 45.4	S60 26.8
15	73 22.9	4 52.3 ..	55.0	31 15.2 ..	18.5	297 49.7 ..	51.8	191 06.6 ..	46.7	Hamal	327 59.7	N23 31.9
16	88 25.4	19 51.7	55.5	46 15.9	19.0	312 52.0	51.8	206 09.2	46.6	Kaus Aust.	83 42.0	S34 22.3
17	103 27.8	34 51.1	56.1	61 16.6	19.6	327 54.4	51.7	221 11.8	46.6			
18	118 30.3	49 50.4	N23 56.6	76 17.2	N16 20.2	342 56.8	N17 51.7	236 14.4	S18 46.6	Kochab	137 19.1	N74 05.6
19	133 32.8	64 49.8	57.1	91 17.9	20.7	357 59.1	51.7	251 17.0	46.6	Markab	13 37.3	N15 17.1
20	148 35.2	79 49.2	57.7	106 18.6	21.3	13 01.5	51.6	266 19.6	46.5	Menkar	314 14.1	N 4 08.7
21	163 37.7	94 48.5 ..	58.2	121 19.2 ..	21.8	28 03.9 ..	51.6	281 22.2 ..	46.5	Menkent	148 05.7	S36 26.7
22	178 40.2	109 47.9	58.7	136 19.9	22.4	43 06.3	51.6	296 24.8	46.5	Miaplacidus	221 39.0	S69 47.3
23	193 42.6	124 47.3	59.2	151 20.6	22.9	58 08.6	51.5	311 27.4	46.4			
21 00	208 45.1	139 46.6	N23 59.8	166 21.2	N16 23.5	73 11.0	N17 51.5	326 30.1	S18 46.4	Mirfak	308 39.0	N49 54.8
01	223 47.5	154 46.0	24 00.3	181 21.9	24.1	88 13.4	51.5	341 32.7	46.4	Nunki	75 56.7	S26 16.4
02	238 50.0	169 45.4	00.8	196 22.6	24.6	103 15.7	51.5	356 35.3	46.3	Peacock	53 17.4	S56 40.8
03	253 52.5	184 44.7 ..	01.3	211 23.3 ..	25.2	118 18.1 ..	51.4	11 37.9 ..	46.3	Pollux	243 26.3	N27 59.2
04	268 54.9	199 44.1	01.8	226 23.9	25.7	133 20.5	51.4	26 40.5	46.3	Procyon	244 58.5	N 5 10.9
05	283 57.4	214 43.5	02.4	241 24.6	26.3	148 22.8	51.4	41 43.1	46.3			
06	298 59.9	229 42.8	N24 02.9	256 25.3	N16 26.8	163 25.2	N17 51.3	56 45.7	S18 46.2	Rasalhague	96 05.1	N12 33.0
07	314 02.3	244 42.2	03.4	271 25.9	27.4	178 27.6	51.3	71 48.3	46.2	Regulus	207 42.1	N11 53.4
08	329 04.8	259 41.6	03.9	286 26.6	28.0	193 29.9	51.3	86 50.9	46.2	Rigel	281 11.1	S 8 11.4
T 09	344 07.3	274 40.9 ..	04.4	301 27.3 ..	28.5	208 32.3 ..	51.2	101 53.5 ..	46.1	Rigil Kent.	139 49.3	S60 53.8
U 10	359 09.7	289 40.3	05.0	316 27.9	29.1	223 34.7	51.2	116 56.1	46.1	Sabik	102 10.9	S15 44.5
E 11	14 12.2	304 39.7	05.5	331 28.6	29.6	238 37.0	51.2	131 58.7	46.1			
S 12	29 14.7	319 39.0	N24 06.0	346 29.2	N16 30.2	253 39.4	N17 51.1	147 01.4	S18 46.0	Schedar	349 39.5	N56 37.1
D 13	44 17.1	334 38.4	06.5	1 29.9	30.7	268 41.8	51.1	162 04.0	46.0	Shaula	96 20.0	S37 06.6
A 14	59 19.6	349 37.8	07.0	16 30.6	31.3	283 44.1	51.1	177 06.6	46.0	Sirius	258 32.7	S16 44.6
Y 15	74 22.0	4 37.1 ..	07.5	31 31.2 ..	31.8	298 46.5 ..	51.0	192 09.2 ..	46.0	Spica	158 29.6	S11 14.5
16	89 24.5	19 36.5	08.0	46 31.9	32.4	313 48.9	51.0	207 11.8	45.9	Suhail	222 51.4	S43 30.1
17	104 27.0	34 35.9	08.5	61 32.6	32.9	328 51.2	51.0	222 14.4	45.9			
18	119 29.4	49 35.2	N24 09.0	76 33.2	N16 33.5	343 53.6	N17 51.0	237 17.0	S18 45.9	Vega	80 38.0	N38 47.8
19	134 31.9	64 34.6	09.5	91 33.9	34.1	358 56.0	50.9	252 19.6	45.8	Zuben'ubi	137 03.7	S16 06.3
20	149 34.3	79 33.9	10.0	106 34.6	34.6	13 58.3	50.9	267 22.2	45.8			
21	164 36.8	94 33.3 ..	10.5	121 35.2 ..	35.2	29 00.7 ..	50.9	282 24.8 ..	45.8		SHA	Mer.Pass.
22	179 39.3	109 32.7	11.0	136 35.9	35.7	44 03.0	50.8	297 27.5	45.8	Venus	292 15.8	14 41
23	194 41.8	124 32.0	11.5	151 36.6	36.3	59 05.4	50.8	312 30.1	45.7	Mars	318 19.3	12 55
Mer.Pass.	10 07.3	v −0.6	d 0.5	v 0.7	d 0.6	v 2.4	d 0.0	v 2.6	d 0.0	Jupiter	224 28.1	19 08
										Saturn	117 41.6	2 18

©Copyright United Kingdom Hydrographic Office 2014

UT	SUN GHA	SUN Dec	MOON GHA	v	MOON Dec	d	HP
d h	° ′	° ′	° ′	′	° ′	′	′
19 00	180 10.7	N10 59.1	176 43.9	7.4	N10 10.8	9.7	60.3
01	195 10.8	11 00.0	191 10.3	7.3	10 20.5	9.5	60.3
02	210 11.0	00.8	205 36.6	7.3	10 30.0	9.6	60.2
03	225 11.1 ..	01.7	220 02.9	7.4	10 39.6	9.4	60.2
04	240 11.3	02.6	234 29.3	7.3	10 49.0	9.3	60.2
05	255 11.4	03.4	248 55.6	7.3	10 58.3	9.3	60.2
06	270 11.5	N11 04.3	263 21.9	7.2	N11 07.6	9.2	60.1
S 07	285 11.7	05.2	277 48.1	7.3	11 16.8	9.1	60.1
U 08	300 11.8	06.0	292 14.4	7.3	11 25.9	9.0	60.1
N 09	315 11.9 ..	06.9	306 40.7	7.3	11 34.9	9.0	60.1
D 10	330 12.1	07.8	321 07.0	7.2	11 43.9	8.9	60.0
A 11	345 12.2	08.6	335 33.2	7.3	11 52.8	8.8	60.0
Y 12	0 12.3	N11 09.5	349 59.5	7.2	N12 01.6	8.6	60.0
13	15 12.5	10.4	4 25.7	7.2	12 10.2	8.7	60.0
14	30 12.6	11.2	18 51.9	7.2	12 18.9	8.5	59.9
15	45 12.7 ..	12.1	33 18.1	7.3	12 27.4	8.4	59.9
16	60 12.9	12.9	47 44.4	7.2	12 35.8	8.4	59.9
17	75 13.0	13.8	62 10.6	7.2	12 44.2	8.2	59.9
18	90 13.1	N11 14.7	76 36.8	7.2	N12 52.4	8.2	59.8
19	105 13.3	15.5	91 03.0	7.2	13 00.6	8.1	59.8
20	120 13.4	16.4	105 29.2	7.2	13 08.7	8.0	59.8
21	135 13.5 ..	17.3	119 55.4	7.1	13 16.7	7.8	59.8
22	150 13.7	18.1	134 21.5	7.2	13 24.5	7.8	59.7
23	165 13.8	19.0	148 47.7	7.2	13 32.3	7.7	59.7
20 00	180 13.9	N11 19.9	163 13.9	7.2	N13 40.0	7.6	59.7
01	195 14.1	20.7	177 40.1	7.2	13 47.6	7.5	59.6
02	210 14.2	21.6	192 06.3	7.2	13 55.1	7.5	59.6
03	225 14.3 ..	22.4	206 32.5	7.1	14 02.6	7.3	59.6
04	240 14.5	23.3	220 58.6	7.2	14 09.9	7.2	59.5
05	255 14.6	24.2	235 24.8	7.2	14 17.1	7.1	59.5
06	270 14.7	N11 25.0	249 51.0	7.2	N14 24.2	7.0	59.5
07	285 14.9	25.9	264 17.2	7.2	14 31.2	6.9	59.5
M 08	300 15.0	26.7	278 43.4	7.1	14 38.1	6.9	59.4
O 09	315 15.1 ..	27.6	293 09.5	7.2	14 45.0	6.7	59.4
N 10	330 15.3	28.4	307 35.7	7.2	14 51.7	6.6	59.4
D 11	345 15.4	29.3	322 01.9	7.2	14 58.3	6.5	59.3
A 12	0 15.5	N11 30.2	336 28.1	7.2	N15 04.8	6.4	59.3
Y 13	15 15.7	31.0	350 54.3	7.2	15 11.2	6.3	59.3
14	30 15.8	31.9	5 20.5	7.3	15 17.5	6.2	59.2
15	45 15.9 ..	32.7	19 46.8	7.2	15 23.7	6.1	59.2
16	60 16.0	33.6	34 13.0	7.2	15 29.8	6.0	59.2
17	75 16.2	34.4	48 39.2	7.2	15 35.8	5.8	59.1
18	90 16.3	N11 35.3	63 05.4	7.3	N15 41.6	5.8	59.1
19	105 16.4	36.2	77 31.7	7.3	15 47.4	5.7	59.1
20	120 16.6	37.0	91 58.0	7.2	15 53.1	5.5	59.0
21	135 16.7 ..	37.9	106 24.2	7.3	15 58.6	5.5	59.0
22	150 16.8	38.7	120 50.5	7.3	16 04.1	5.3	59.0
23	165 16.9	39.6	135 16.8	7.3	16 09.4	5.3	58.9
21 00	180 17.1	N11 40.4	149 43.1	7.3	N16 14.7	5.1	58.9
01	195 17.2	41.3	164 09.4	7.4	16 19.8	5.0	58.8
02	210 17.3	42.1	178 35.8	7.3	16 24.8	4.9	58.8
03	225 17.5 ..	43.0	193 02.1	7.4	16 29.7	4.8	58.8
04	240 17.6	43.8	207 28.5	7.4	16 34.5	4.7	58.7
05	255 17.7	44.7	221 54.9	7.4	16 39.2	4.6	58.7
06	270 17.8	N11 45.5	236 21.3	7.4	N16 43.8	4.5	58.7
07	285 18.0	46.4	250 47.7	7.5	16 48.3	4.3	58.6
T 08	300 18.1	47.2	265 14.2	7.4	16 52.6	4.3	58.6
U 09	315 18.2 ..	48.1	279 40.6	7.5	16 56.9	4.1	58.6
E 10	330 18.4	48.9	294 07.1	7.5	17 01.0	4.0	58.5
S 11	345 18.5	49.8	308 33.6	7.5	17 05.0	4.0	58.5
D 12	0 18.6	N11 50.6	323 00.1	7.6	N17 09.0	3.8	58.4
A 13	15 18.7	51.5	337 26.7	7.6	17 12.8	3.7	58.4
Y 14	30 18.9	52.3	351 53.3	7.6	17 16.5	3.5	58.4
15	45 19.0 ..	53.2	6 19.9	7.6	17 20.0	3.5	58.3
16	60 19.1	54.0	20 46.5	7.6	17 23.5	3.4	58.3
17	75 19.2	54.9	35 13.1	7.7	17 26.9	3.2	58.3
18	90 19.4	N11 55.7	49 39.8	7.7	N17 30.1	3.2	58.2
19	105 19.5	56.6	64 06.5	7.7	17 33.3	3.0	58.2
20	120 19.6	57.4	78 33.2	7.8	17 36.3	2.9	58.1
21	135 19.7 ..	58.3	93 00.0	7.8	17 39.2	2.8	58.1
22	150 19.9	11 59.1	107 26.8	7.8	17 42.0	2.7	58.1
23	165 20.0	N12 00.0	121 53.6	7.9	N17 44.7	2.6	58.0
	SD 15.9	d 0.9	SD 16.3	16.2			15.9

Lat.	Twilight Naut.	Twilight Civil	Sunrise	Moonrise 19	20	21	22
°	h m	h m	h m	h m	h m	h m	h m
N 72	////	01 02	03 12	04 01	03 55	03 50	03 38
N 70	////	02 00	03 33	04 18	04 23	04 34	04 57
68	////	02 33	03 49	04 31	04 44	05 04	05 35
66	00 53	02 57	04 02	04 43	05 01	05 26	06 02
64	01 45	03 15	04 13	04 52	05 14	05 44	06 23
62	02 15	03 30	04 22	05 00	05 26	05 58	06 40
60	02 37	03 42	04 30	05 07	05 36	06 11	06 54
N 58	02 54	03 53	04 37	05 14	05 44	06 21	07 06
56	03 08	04 02	04 43	05 19	05 52	06 31	07 16
54	03 21	04 10	04 49	05 24	05 59	06 39	07 25
52	03 31	04 17	04 53	05 29	06 05	06 47	07 34
50	03 40	04 23	04 58	05 33	06 11	06 53	07 41
45	03 59	04 37	05 08	05 42	06 23	07 08	07 57
N 40	04 13	04 47	05 16	05 49	06 33	07 20	08 10
35	04 25	04 56	05 22	05 56	06 41	07 30	08 21
30	04 34	05 04	05 28	06 01	06 49	07 39	08 31
20	04 49	05 16	05 39	06 11	07 02	07 54	08 47
N 10	05 01	05 26	05 47	06 20	07 14	08 08	09 02
0	05 10	05 35	05 56	06 28	07 24	08 20	09 16
S 10	05 18	05 42	06 04	06 37	07 35	08 33	09 29
20	05 24	05 50	06 12	06 46	07 47	08 47	09 44
30	05 30	05 58	06 22	06 56	08 01	09 03	10 01
35	05 32	06 02	06 27	07 02	08 08	09 12	10 11
40	05 34	06 06	06 34	07 09	08 17	09 22	10 22
45	05 37	06 11	06 41	07 17	08 28	09 35	10 35
S 50	05 39	06 16	06 49	07 26	08 41	09 50	10 51
52	05 39	06 19	06 53	07 31	08 47	09 57	10 59
54	05 40	06 21	06 58	07 36	08 53	10 05	11 07
56	05 41	06 24	07 02	07 41	09 01	10 13	11 17
58	05 41	06 27	07 08	07 47	09 09	10 23	11 28
S 60	05 42	06 30	07 14	07 54	09 18	10 35	11 40

Lat.	Sunset	Twilight Civil	Twilight Naut.	Moonset 19	20	21	22
°	h m	h m	h m	h m	h m	h m	h m
N 72	20 51	23 14	////	22 09	24 13	00 13	02 20
N 70	20 29	22 05	////	21 42	23 29	25 02	01 02
68	20 12	21 29	////	21 23	23 00	24 24	00 24
66	19 58	21 05	23 20	21 07	22 38	23 57	24 59
64	19 47	20 46	22 19	20 54	22 21	23 36	24 37
62	19 38	20 30	21 47	20 43	22 07	23 20	24 20
60	19 30	20 18	21 24	20 34	21 55	23 06	24 05
N 58	19 23	20 07	21 06	20 26	21 44	22 54	23 53
56	19 16	19 58	20 52	20 19	21 35	22 44	23 43
54	19 11	19 50	20 39	20 13	21 27	22 35	23 33
52	19 06	19 42	20 29	20 07	21 20	22 27	23 25
50	19 01	19 36	20 19	20 02	21 14	22 19	23 17
45	18 51	19 22	20 00	19 51	21 00	22 04	23 01
N 40	18 43	19 12	19 46	19 42	20 49	21 51	22 48
35	18 36	19 03	19 34	19 34	20 39	21 40	22 37
30	18 30	18 55	19 24	19 27	20 30	21 31	22 27
20	18 20	18 42	19 09	19 15	20 16	21 15	22 10
N 10	18 11	18 32	18 57	19 05	20 03	21 00	21 55
0	18 02	18 23	18 48	18 55	19 51	20 47	21 41
S 10	17 54	18 15	18 40	18 45	19 39	20 34	21 28
20	17 45	18 08	18 34	18 35	19 27	20 19	21 13
30	17 36	18 00	18 28	18 23	19 12	20 03	20 56
35	17 30	17 56	18 25	18 16	19 04	19 53	20 46
40	17 24	17 51	18 23	18 09	18 54	19 43	20 34
45	17 17	17 47	18 21	18 00	18 43	19 30	20 21
S 50	17 08	17 41	18 19	17 49	18 29	19 14	20 05
52	17 04	17 38	18 18	17 44	18 23	19 07	19 57
54	16 59	17 36	18 17	17 39	18 16	18 59	19 49
56	16 55	17 33	18 16	17 32	18 08	18 50	19 39
58	16 49	17 30	18 15	17 26	17 59	18 40	19 28
S 60	16 43	17 26	18 15	17 18	17 49	18 28	19 16

	SUN Eqn. of Time 00h	12h	SUN Mer. Pass.	MOON Mer. Pass. Upper	Lower	Age	Phase
Day	m s	m s	h m	h m	h m	d	%
19	00 43	00 49	11 59	12 42	00 14	01	1
20	00 56	01 02	11 59	13 38	01 10	02	4
21	01 08	01 14	11 59	14 34	02 06	03	10

UT	ARIES	VENUS −4.1		MARS +1.4		JUPITER −2.2		SATURN +0.2		STARS		
	GHA	GHA	Dec	GHA	Dec	GHA	Dec	GHA	Dec	Name	SHA	Dec
d h	° ′	° ′	° ′	° ′	° ′	° ′	° ′	° ′	° ′		° ′	° ′
22 00	209 44.2	139 31.4	N24 12.0	166 37.2	N16 36.8	74 07.8	N17 50.8	327 32.7	S18 45.7	Acamar	315 17.9	S40 14.9
01	224 46.7	154 30.8	12.5	181 37.9	37.4	89 10.1	50.7	342 35.3	45.7	Achernar	335 26.5	S57 09.6
02	239 49.1	169 30.1	13.0	196 38.6	37.9	104 12.5	50.7	357 37.9	45.6	Acrux	173 07.1	S63 11.2
03	254 51.6	184 29.5 . .	13.5	211 39.2 . .	38.5	119 14.9 . .	50.7	12 40.5 . .	45.6	Adhara	255 11.7	S29 00.0
04	269 54.1	199 28.9	14.0	226 39.9	39.0	134 17.2	50.6	27 43.1	45.6	Aldebaran	290 48.2	N16 32.1
05	284 56.5	214 28.2	14.5	241 40.6	39.6	149 19.6	50.6	42 45.7	45.5			
06	299 59.0	229 27.6	N24 15.0	256 41.2	N16 40.1	164 21.9	N17 50.6	57 48.3	S18 45.5	Alioth	166 19.2	N55 52.7
W 07	315 01.5	244 26.9	15.5	271 41.9	40.7	179 24.3	50.5	72 51.0	45.5	Alkaid	152 57.5	N49 14.2
E 08	330 03.9	259 26.3	16.0	286 42.6	41.2	194 26.7	50.5	87 53.6	45.5	Al Na'ir	27 42.5	S46 53.0
D 09	345 06.4	274 25.7 . .	16.5	301 43.2 . .	41.8	209 29.0 . .	50.5	102 56.2 . .	45.4	Alnilam	275 45.3	S 1 11.9
N 10	0 08.9	289 25.0	17.0	316 43.9	42.3	224 31.4	50.4	117 58.8	45.4	Alphard	217 54.8	S 8 43.8
E 11	15 11.3	304 24.4	17.5	331 44.5	42.9	239 33.7	50.4	133 01.4	45.4			
S 12	30 13.8	319 23.7	N24 18.0	346 45.2	N16 43.4	254 36.1	N17 50.4	148 04.0	S18 45.3	Alphecca	126 09.6	N26 39.8
D 13	45 16.3	334 23.1	18.4	1 45.9	43.9	269 38.4	50.3	163 06.6	45.3	Alpheratz	357 42.5	N29 10.3
A 14	60 18.7	349 22.5	18.9	16 46.5	44.5	284 40.8	50.3	178 09.2	45.3	Altair	62 07.0	N 8 54.6
Y 15	75 21.2	4 21.8 . .	19.4	31 47.2 . .	45.0	299 43.2 . .	50.3	193 11.9 . .	45.3	Ankaa	353 14.9	S42 13.4
16	90 23.6	19 21.2	19.9	46 47.9	45.6	314 45.5	50.2	208 14.5	45.2	Antares	112 24.4	S26 27.8
17	105 26.1	34 20.6	20.4	61 48.5	46.1	329 47.9	50.2	223 17.1	45.2			
18	120 28.6	49 19.9	N24 20.8	76 49.2	N16 46.7	344 50.2	N17 50.2	238 19.7	S18 45.2	Arcturus	145 54.3	N19 06.2
19	135 31.0	64 19.3	21.3	91 49.9	47.2	359 52.6	50.1	253 22.3	45.1	Atria	107 24.6	S69 02.9
20	150 33.5	79 18.6	21.8	106 50.5	47.8	14 54.9	50.1	268 24.9	45.1	Avior	234 17.4	S59 34.0
21	165 36.0	94 18.0 . .	22.3	121 51.2 . .	48.3	29 57.3 . .	50.1	283 27.5 . .	45.1	Bellatrix	278 30.9	N 6 21.5
22	180 38.4	109 17.4	22.8	136 51.8	48.9	44 59.7	50.0	298 30.1	45.0	Betelgeuse	271 00.1	N 7 24.3
23	195 40.9	124 16.7	23.2	151 52.5	49.4	60 02.0	50.0	313 32.8	45.0			
23 00	210 43.4	139 16.1	N24 23.7	166 53.2	N16 50.0	75 04.4	N17 49.9	328 35.4	S18 45.0	Canopus	263 55.8	S52 42.7
01	225 45.8	154 15.4	24.2	181 53.8	50.5	90 06.7	49.9	343 38.0	45.0	Capella	280 32.9	N46 00.7
02	240 48.3	169 14.8	24.6	196 54.5	51.0	105 09.1	49.9	358 40.6	44.9	Deneb	49 30.6	N45 20.0
03	255 50.8	184 14.2 . .	25.1	211 55.2 . .	51.6	120 11.4 . .	49.8	13 43.2 . .	44.9	Denebola	182 32.2	N14 29.1
04	270 53.2	199 13.5	25.6	226 55.8	52.1	135 13.8	49.8	28 45.8	44.9	Diphda	348 55.0	S17 54.3
05	285 55.7	214 12.9	26.1	241 56.5	52.7	150 16.1	49.8	43 48.4	44.8			
06	300 58.1	229 12.2	N24 26.5	256 57.1	N16 53.2	165 18.5	N17 49.7	58 51.1	S18 44.8	Dubhe	193 49.9	N61 40.2
T 07	316 00.6	244 11.6	27.0	271 57.8	53.8	180 20.8	49.7	73 53.7	44.8	Elnath	278 11.3	N28 37.0
H 08	331 03.1	259 11.0	27.5	286 58.5	54.3	195 23.2	49.7	88 56.3	44.7	Eltanin	90 45.3	N51 29.1
U 09	346 05.5	274 10.3 . .	27.9	301 59.1 . .	54.8	210 25.5 . .	49.6	103 58.9 . .	44.7	Enif	33 46.0	N 9 56.7
R 10	1 08.0	289 09.7	28.4	316 59.8	55.4	225 27.9	49.6	119 01.5	44.7	Fomalhaut	15 22.9	S29 32.4
S 11	16 10.5	304 09.0	28.8	332 00.5	55.9	240 30.2	49.6	134 04.1	44.7			
D 12	31 12.9	319 08.4	N24 29.3	347 01.1	N16 56.5	255 32.6	N17 49.5	149 06.7	S18 44.6	Gacrux	171 58.9	S57 12.1
A 13	46 15.4	334 07.8	29.8	2 01.8	57.0	270 34.9	49.5	164 09.4	44.6	Gienah	175 50.7	S17 37.8
Y 14	61 17.9	349 07.1	30.2	17 02.4	57.5	285 37.3	49.5	179 12.0	44.6	Hadar	148 45.3	S60 26.8
15	76 20.3	4 06.5 . .	30.7	32 03.1 . .	58.1	300 39.6 . .	49.4	194 14.6 . .	44.5	Hamal	327 59.7	N23 31.9
16	91 22.8	19 05.8	31.1	47 03.8	58.6	315 42.0	49.4	209 17.2	44.5	Kaus Aust.	83 42.0	S34 22.3
17	106 25.3	34 05.2	31.6	62 04.4	59.2	330 44.3	49.3	224 19.8	44.5			
18	121 27.7	49 04.5	N24 32.0	77 05.1	N16 59.7	345 46.7	N17 49.3	239 22.4	S18 44.4	Kochab	137 19.1	N74 05.6
19	136 30.2	64 03.9	32.5	92 05.8	17 00.2	0 49.0	49.3	254 25.0	44.4	Markab	13 37.3	N15 17.1
20	151 32.6	79 03.3	32.9	107 06.4	00.8	15 51.4	49.2	269 27.7	44.4	Menkar	314 14.1	N 4 08.7
21	166 35.1	94 02.6 . .	33.4	122 07.1 . .	01.3	30 53.7 . .	49.2	284 30.3 . .	44.4	Menkent	148 05.7	S36 26.7
22	181 37.6	109 02.0	33.8	137 07.7	01.9	45 56.1	49.2	299 32.9	44.3	Miaplacidus	221 39.0	S69 47.3
23	196 40.0	124 01.3	34.3	152 08.4	02.4	60 58.4	49.1	314 35.5	44.3			
24 00	211 42.5	139 00.7	N24 34.7	167 09.1	N17 02.9	76 00.8	N17 49.1	329 38.1	S18 44.3	Mirfak	308 39.0	N49 54.8
01	226 45.0	154 00.0	35.2	182 09.7	03.5	91 03.1	49.0	344 40.7	44.2	Nunki	75 56.7	S26 16.4
02	241 47.4	168 59.4	35.6	197 10.4	04.0	106 05.5	49.0	359 43.4	44.2	Peacock	53 17.4	S56 40.7
03	256 49.9	183 58.8 . .	36.1	212 11.0 . .	04.5	121 07.8 . .	49.0	14 46.0 . .	44.2	Pollux	243 26.3	N27 59.2
04	271 52.4	198 58.1	36.5	227 11.7	05.1	136 10.2	48.9	29 48.6	44.1	Procyon	244 58.5	N 5 10.9
05	286 54.8	213 57.5	36.9	242 12.4	05.6	151 12.5	48.9	44 51.2	44.1			
06	301 57.3	228 56.8	N24 37.4	257 13.0	N17 06.1	166 14.9	N17 48.9	59 53.8	S18 44.1	Rasalhague	96 05.1	N12 33.0
07	316 59.7	243 56.2	37.8	272 13.7	06.7	181 17.2	48.8	74 56.4	44.0	Regulus	207 42.1	N11 53.4
08	332 02.2	258 55.5	38.3	287 14.3	07.2	196 19.6	48.8	89 59.1	44.0	Rigel	281 11.1	S 8 11.4
F 09	347 04.7	273 54.9 . .	38.7	302 15.0 . .	07.7	211 21.9 . .	48.8	105 01.7 . .	44.0	Rigil Kent.	139 49.3	S60 53.8
R 10	2 07.1	288 54.3	39.1	317 15.7	08.3	226 24.2	48.7	120 04.3	44.0	Sabik	102 10.9	S15 44.5
I 11	17 09.6	303 53.6	39.6	332 16.3	08.8	241 26.6	48.7	135 06.9	43.9			
D 12	32 12.1	318 53.0	N24 40.0	347 17.0	N17 09.3	256 28.9	N17 48.6	150 09.5	S18 43.9	Schedar	349 39.5	N56 37.1
A 13	47 14.5	333 52.3	40.4	2 17.6	09.9	271 31.3	48.6	165 12.1	43.9	Shaula	96 20.0	S37 06.6
Y 14	62 17.0	348 51.7	40.9	17 18.3	10.4	286 33.6	48.6	180 14.8	43.8	Sirius	258 32.8	S16 44.6
15	77 19.5	3 51.0 . .	41.3	32 19.0 . .	10.9	301 36.0 . .	48.5	195 17.4 . .	43.8	Spica	158 29.6	S11 14.5
16	92 21.9	18 50.4	41.7	47 19.6	11.5	316 38.3	48.5	210 20.0	43.8	Suhail	222 51.4	S43 30.1
17	107 24.4	33 49.8	42.2	62 20.3	12.0	331 40.6	48.4	225 22.6	43.7			
18	122 26.9	48 49.1	N24 42.6	77 20.9	N17 12.5	346 43.0	N17 48.4	240 25.2	S18 43.7	Vega	80 37.9	N38 47.8
19	137 29.3	63 48.5	43.0	92 21.6	13.1	1 45.3	48.4	255 27.9	43.7	Zuben'ubi	137 03.7	S16 06.3
20	152 31.8	78 47.8	43.4	107 22.3	13.6	16 47.7	48.3	270 30.5	43.7		SHA	Mer. Pass.
21	167 34.2	93 47.2 . .	43.9	122 22.9 . .	14.1	31 50.0 . .	48.3	285 33.1 . .	43.6		° ′	h m
22	182 36.7	108 46.5	44.3	137 23.6	14.7	46 52.3	48.3	300 35.7	43.6	Venus	288 32.7	14 44
23	197 39.2	123 45.9	44.7	152 24.2	15.2	61 54.7	48.2	315 38.3	43.6	Mars	316 09.8	12 52
	h m									Jupiter	224 21.0	18 57
Mer. Pass.	9 55.5	v −0.6	d 0.5	v 0.7	d 0.5	v 2.4	d 0.0	v 2.6	d 0.0	Saturn	117 52.0	2 05

UT	SUN GHA	SUN Dec	MOON GHA	v	MOON Dec	d	HP
d h	° ′	° ′	° ′	′	° ′	′	′
22 00	180 20.1	N12 00.8	136 20.5	7.8	N17 47.3	2.5	58.0
01	195 20.2	01.7	150 47.3	8.0	17 49.8	2.4	58.0
02	210 20.3	02.5	165 14.3	7.9	17 52.2	2.2	57.9
03	225 20.5 ..	03.4	179 41.2	8.0	17 54.4	2.2	57.9
04	240 20.6	04.2	194 08.2	8.0	17 56.6	2.0	57.8
05	255 20.7	05.0	208 35.2	8.1	17 58.6	1.9	57.8
06	270 20.8	N12 05.9	223 02.3	8.1	N18 00.5	1.9	57.8
W 07	285 21.0	06.7	237 29.4	8.1	18 02.4	1.7	57.7
E 08	300 21.1	07.6	251 56.5	8.1	18 04.1	1.6	57.7
D 09	315 21.2 ..	08.4	266 23.6	8.3	18 05.7	1.5	57.7
N 10	330 21.3	09.3	280 50.9	8.2	18 07.2	1.3	57.6
E 11	345 21.4	10.1	295 18.1	8.3	18 08.5	1.3	57.6
S 12	0 21.6	N12 10.9	309 45.4	8.3	N18 09.8	1.2	57.5
D 13	15 21.7	11.8	324 12.7	8.4	18 11.0	1.0	57.5
A 14	30 21.8	12.6	338 40.1	8.4	18 12.0	1.0	57.5
Y 15	45 21.9 ..	13.5	353 07.5	8.4	18 13.0	0.8	57.4
16	60 22.1	14.3	7 34.9	8.5	18 13.8	0.8	57.4
17	75 22.2	15.1	22 02.4	8.5	18 14.6	0.6	57.4
18	90 22.3	N12 16.0	36 29.9	8.6	N18 15.2	0.5	57.3
19	105 22.4	16.8	50 57.5	8.6	18 15.7	0.4	57.3
20	120 22.5	17.7	65 25.1	8.7	18 16.1	0.3	57.2
21	135 22.7 ..	18.5	79 52.8	8.7	18 16.4	0.2	57.2
22	150 22.8	19.3	94 20.5	8.8	18 16.6	0.1	57.2
23	165 22.9	20.2	108 48.3	8.8	18 16.7	0.0	57.1
23 00	180 23.0	N12 21.0	123 16.1	8.9	N18 16.7	0.1	57.1
01	195 23.1	21.8	137 44.0	8.9	18 16.6	0.2	57.1
02	210 23.3	22.7	152 11.9	8.9	18 16.4	0.3	57.0
03	225 23.4 ..	23.5	166 39.8	9.0	18 16.1	0.4	57.0
04	240 23.5	24.4	181 07.8	9.1	18 15.7	0.5	57.0
05	255 23.6	25.2	195 35.9	9.1	18 15.2	0.6	56.9
06	270 23.7	N12 26.0	210 04.0	9.1	N18 14.6	0.8	56.9
T 07	285 23.8	26.9	224 32.1	9.2	18 13.8	0.8	56.8
H 08	300 24.0	27.7	239 00.3	9.3	18 13.0	0.9	56.8
U 09	315 24.1 ..	28.5	253 28.6	9.3	18 12.1	1.0	56.8
R 10	330 24.2	29.4	267 56.9	9.3	18 11.1	1.1	56.7
S 11	345 24.3	30.2	282 25.2	9.4	18 10.0	1.2	56.7
D 12	0 24.4	N12 31.0	296 53.6	9.5	N18 08.8	1.4	56.7
A 13	15 24.6	31.9	311 22.1	9.5	18 07.4	1.4	56.6
Y 14	30 24.7	32.7	325 50.6	9.6	18 06.0	1.5	56.6
15	45 24.8 ..	33.5	340 19.2	9.6	18 04.5	1.6	56.6
16	60 24.9	34.4	354 47.8	9.7	18 02.9	1.7	56.5
17	75 25.0	35.2	9 16.5	9.7	18 01.2	1.8	56.5
18	90 25.1	N12 36.0	23 45.2	9.8	N17 59.4	1.9	56.5
19	105 25.2	36.8	38 14.0	9.8	17 57.5	2.0	56.4
20	120 25.4	37.7	52 42.8	9.9	17 55.5	2.0	56.4
21	135 25.5 ..	38.5	67 11.7	10.0	17 53.5	2.2	56.4
22	150 25.6	39.3	81 40.7	10.0	17 51.3	2.3	56.3
23	165 25.7	40.2	96 09.7	10.0	17 49.0	2.3	56.3
24 00	180 25.8	N12 41.0	110 38.7	10.2	N17 46.7	2.5	56.3
01	195 25.9	41.8	125 07.9	10.1	17 44.2	2.5	56.2
02	210 26.1	42.6	139 37.0	10.3	17 41.7	2.6	56.2
03	225 26.2 ..	43.5	154 06.3	10.3	17 39.1	2.8	56.2
04	240 26.3	44.3	168 35.6	10.3	17 36.3	2.8	56.1
05	255 26.4	45.1	183 04.9	10.4	17 33.5	2.8	56.1
06	270 26.5	N12 46.0	197 34.3	10.5	N17 30.7	3.0	56.1
F 07	285 26.6	46.8	212 03.8	10.5	17 27.7	3.1	56.0
R 08	300 26.7	47.6	226 33.3	10.6	17 24.6	3.1	56.0
I 09	315 26.9 ..	48.4	241 02.9	10.6	17 21.5	3.3	56.0
D 10	330 27.0	49.3	255 32.5	10.7	17 18.2	3.3	55.9
A 11	345 27.1	50.1	270 02.2	10.7	17 14.9	3.4	55.9
Y 12	0 27.2	N12 50.9	284 31.9	10.8	N17 11.5	3.5	55.9
13	15 27.3	51.7	299 01.7	10.9	17 08.0	3.6	55.8
14	30 27.4	52.6	313 31.6	10.9	17 04.4	3.6	55.8
15	45 27.5 ..	53.4	328 01.5	11.0	17 00.8	3.8	55.8
16	60 27.6	54.2	342 31.5	11.0	16 57.0	3.8	55.8
17	75 27.7	55.0	357 01.5	11.1	16 53.2	3.9	55.7
18	90 27.9	N12 55.8	11 31.6	11.2	N16 49.3	4.0	55.7
19	105 28.0	56.7	26 01.8	11.2	16 45.3	4.0	55.7
20	120 28.1	57.5	40 32.0	11.3	16 41.3	4.2	55.7
21	135 28.2 ..	58.3	55 02.3	11.3	16 37.1	4.2	55.6
22	150 28.3	59.1	69 32.6	11.4	16 32.9	4.3	55.6
23	165 28.4	59.9	84 03.0	11.4	N16 28.6	4.4	55.6
	SD 15.9	d 0.8	SD 15.7		15.4		15.2

Twilight / Sunrise / Moonrise

Lat.	Naut.	Civil	Sunrise	Moonrise 22	23	24	25
°	h m	h m	h m	h m	h m	h m	h m
N 72	////	////	02 53	03 38	▭	05 50	07 41
N 70	////	01 33	03 17	04 57	05 43	06 55	08 21
68	////	02 14	03 36	05 35	06 24	07 31	08 48
66	////	02 42	03 50	06 02	06 53	07 56	09 09
64	01 21	03 02	04 02	06 23	07 14	08 16	09 25
62	01 58	03 19	04 13	06 40	07 31	08 32	09 39
60	02 24	03 32	04 21	06 54	07 46	08 45	09 50
N 58	02 43	03 44	04 29	07 06	07 58	08 57	10 00
56	02 59	03 54	04 36	07 16	08 09	09 07	10 09
54	03 12	04 02	04 42	07 25	08 18	09 15	10 16
52	03 23	04 10	04 47	07 34	08 26	09 23	10 23
50	03 33	04 17	04 52	07 41	08 34	09 30	10 29
45	03 53	04 31	05 03	07 57	08 50	09 45	10 43
N 40	04 08	04 43	05 11	08 10	09 03	09 58	10 54
35	04 21	04 52	05 19	08 21	09 14	10 08	11 03
30	04 31	05 00	05 25	08 31	09 24	10 18	11 11
20	04 47	05 14	05 36	08 47	09 41	10 33	11 25
N 10	04 59	05 24	05 46	09 02	09 55	10 47	11 38
0	05 09	05 34	05 55	09 16	10 09	11 00	11 49
S 10	05 18	05 42	06 04	09 29	10 23	11 13	12 01
20	05 25	05 51	06 13	09 44	10 38	11 27	12 13
30	05 31	05 59	06 24	10 01	10 54	11 43	12 27
35	05 34	06 04	06 30	10 11	11 04	11 52	12 35
40	05 37	06 09	06 37	10 22	11 15	12 03	12 44
45	05 40	06 14	06 44	10 35	11 29	12 15	12 55
S 50	05 43	06 21	06 54	10 51	11 45	12 30	13 08
52	05 44	06 23	06 58	10 59	11 52	12 37	13 14
54	05 45	06 26	07 03	11 07	12 01	12 45	13 21
56	05 46	06 30	07 08	11 17	12 10	12 53	13 29
58	05 47	06 33	07 14	11 28	12 21	13 03	13 37
S 60	05 48	06 37	07 21	11 40	12 33	13 14	13 46

Sunset / Twilight / Moonset

Lat.	Sunset	Civil	Naut.	Moonset 22	23	24	25
°	h m	h m	h m	h m	h m	h m	h m
N 72	21 09	////	////	02 20	▭	03 49	03 41
N 70	20 43	22 32	////	01 02	02 08	02 44	03 01
68	20 24	21 48	////	00 24	01 27	02 08	02 33
66	20 09	21 19	////	24 59	00 59	01 42	02 12
64	19 57	20 57	22 43	24 37	00 37	01 23	01 55
62	19 46	20 40	22 03	24 20	00 20	01 06	01 41
60	19 37	20 27	21 37	24 05	00 05	00 53	01 29
N 58	19 29	20 15	21 17	23 53	24 41	00 41	01 19
56	19 22	20 05	21 00	23 43	24 31	00 31	01 10
54	19 16	19 56	20 47	23 33	24 22	00 22	01 02
52	19 11	19 48	20 35	23 25	24 14	00 14	00 55
50	19 06	19 41	20 25	23 17	24 07	00 07	00 48
45	18 55	19 27	20 05	23 01	23 51	24 35	00 35
N 40	18 46	19 15	19 49	22 48	23 39	24 23	00 23
35	18 39	19 05	19 37	22 37	23 28	24 13	00 13
30	18 32	18 57	19 26	22 27	23 18	24 05	00 05
20	18 21	18 43	19 10	22 10	23 02	23 50	24 34
N 10	18 11	18 32	18 58	21 55	22 47	23 36	24 23
0	18 02	18 23	18 48	21 41	22 34	23 24	24 12
S 10	17 53	18 14	18 39	21 28	22 20	23 12	24 01
20	17 43	18 06	18 32	21 13	22 06	22 59	23 50
30	17 33	17 57	18 25	20 56	21 49	22 43	23 37
35	17 27	17 52	18 22	20 46	21 40	22 34	23 29
40	17 20	17 47	18 19	20 34	21 29	22 24	23 21
45	17 12	17 42	18 16	20 21	21 16	22 12	23 10
S 50	17 02	17 35	18 13	20 05	21 00	21 58	22 58
52	16 58	17 33	18 12	19 57	20 52	21 51	22 52
54	16 53	17 30	18 11	19 49	20 44	21 44	22 46
56	16 47	17 26	18 10	19 39	20 35	21 35	22 39
58	16 41	17 23	18 08	19 28	20 24	21 26	22 31
S 60	16 35	17 19	18 07	19 16	20 12	21 15	22 22

SUN / MOON

Day	Eqn. of Time 00ʰ	Eqn. of Time 12ʰ	Mer. Pass.	Mer. Pass. Upper	Mer. Pass. Lower	Age	Phase
d	m s	m s	h m	h m	h m	d	%
22	01 20	01 26	11 59	15 29	03 01	04	17
23	01 32	01 38	11 58	16 22	03 55	05	26
24	01 43	01 49	11 58	17 12	04 47	06	36

UT (d h)	ARIES GHA	VENUS −4.1 GHA	VENUS Dec	MARS +1.4 GHA	MARS Dec	JUPITER −2.1 GHA	JUPITER Dec	SATURN +0.2 GHA	SATURN Dec	STARS Name	SHA	Dec
25 00	212 41.6	138 45.2	N24 45.1	167 24.9	N17 15.7	76 57.0	N17 48.2	330 40.9	S18 43.5	Acamar	315 17.9	S40 14.8
01	227 44.1	153 44.6	45.5	182 25.6	16.3	91 59.4	48.1	345 43.6	43.5	Achernar	335 26.5	S57 09.6
02	242 46.6	168 44.0	46.0	197 26.2	16.8	107 01.7	48.1	0 46.2	43.5	Acrux	173 07.1	S63 11.2
03	257 49.0	183 43.3	.. 46.4	212 26.9	.. 17.3	122 04.0	.. 48.1	15 48.8	.. 43.4	Adhara	255 11.7	S29 00.0
04	272 51.5	198 42.7	46.8	227 27.5	17.8	137 06.4	48.0	30 51.4	43.4	Aldebaran	290 48.2	N16 32.1
05	287 54.0	213 42.0	47.2	242 28.2	18.4	152 08.7	48.0	45 54.0	43.4			
06	302 56.4	228 41.4	N24 47.6	257 28.9	N17 18.9	167 11.1	N17 47.9	60 56.7	S18 43.3	Alioth	166 19.2	N55 52.7
S 07	317 58.9	243 40.7	48.0	272 29.5	19.4	182 13.4	47.9	75 59.3	43.3	Alkaid	152 57.5	N49 14.3
A 08	333 01.4	258 40.1	48.4	287 30.2	20.0	197 15.7	47.9	91 01.9	43.3	Al Na'ir	27 42.4	S46 53.0
T 09	348 03.8	273 39.4	.. 48.9	302 30.8	.. 20.5	212 18.1	.. 47.8	106 04.5	.. 43.3	Alnilam	275 45.3	S 1 11.9
U 10	3 06.3	288 38.8	49.3	317 31.5	21.0	227 20.4	47.8	121 07.1	43.2	Alphard	217 54.8	S 8 43.8
R 11	18 08.7	303 38.2	49.7	332 32.1	21.5	242 22.7	47.7	136 09.8	43.2			
D 12	33 11.2	318 37.5	N24 50.1	347 32.8	N17 22.1	257 25.1	N17 47.7	151 12.4	S18 43.2	Alphecca	126 09.6	N26 39.8
A 13	48 13.7	333 36.9	50.5	2 33.5	22.6	272 27.4	47.7	166 15.0	43.1	Alpheratz	357 42.5	N29 10.3
Y 14	63 16.1	348 36.2	50.9	17 34.1	23.1	287 29.8	47.6	181 17.6	43.1	Altair	62 07.0	N 8 54.6
15	78 18.6	3 35.6	.. 51.3	32 34.8	.. 23.6	302 32.1	.. 47.6	196 20.2	.. 43.1	Ankaa	353 14.9	S42 13.3
16	93 21.1	18 34.9	51.7	47 35.4	24.2	317 34.4	47.5	211 22.9	43.0	Antares	112 24.4	S26 27.8
17	108 23.5	33 34.3	52.1	62 36.1	24.7	332 36.8	47.5	226 25.5	43.0			
18	123 26.0	48 33.6	N24 52.5	77 36.7	N17 25.2	347 39.1	N17 47.5	241 28.1	S18 43.0	Arcturus	145 54.3	N19 06.2
19	138 28.5	63 33.0	52.9	92 37.4	25.7	2 41.4	47.4	256 30.7	42.9	Atria	107 24.6	S69 02.9
20	153 30.9	78 32.3	53.3	107 38.1	26.3	17 43.8	47.4	271 33.3	42.9	Avior	234 17.5	S59 34.0
21	168 33.4	93 31.7	.. 53.7	122 38.7	.. 26.8	32 46.1	.. 47.3	286 36.0	.. 42.9	Bellatrix	278 30.9	N 6 21.5
22	183 35.8	108 31.1	54.1	137 39.4	27.3	47 48.4	47.3	301 38.6	42.8	Betelgeuse	271 00.1	N 7 24.3
23	198 38.3	123 30.4	54.5	152 40.0	27.8	62 50.8	47.3	316 41.2	42.8			
26 00	213 40.8	138 29.8	N24 54.9	167 40.7	N17 28.4	77 53.1	N17 47.2	331 43.8	S18 42.8	Canopus	263 55.9	S52 42.7
01	228 43.2	153 29.1	55.3	182 41.3	28.9	92 55.4	47.2	346 46.5	42.8	Capella	280 32.9	N46 00.7
02	243 45.7	168 28.5	55.6	197 42.0	29.4	107 57.8	47.1	1 49.1	42.7	Deneb	49 30.6	N45 20.0
03	258 48.2	183 27.8	.. 56.0	212 42.7	.. 29.9	123 00.1	.. 47.1	16 51.7	.. 42.7	Denebola	182 32.2	N14 29.1
04	273 50.6	198 27.2	56.4	227 43.3	30.5	138 02.4	47.0	31 54.3	42.7	Diphda	348 55.0	S17 54.2
05	288 53.1	213 26.5	56.8	242 44.0	31.0	153 04.7	47.0	46 56.9	42.6			
06	303 55.6	228 25.9	N24 57.2	257 44.6	N17 31.5	168 07.1	N17 47.0	61 59.6	S18 42.6	Dubhe	193 49.9	N61 40.2
S 07	318 58.0	243 25.2	57.6	272 45.3	32.0	183 09.4	46.9	77 02.2	42.6	Elnath	278 11.3	N28 37.0
U 08	334 00.5	258 24.6	58.0	287 45.9	32.5	198 11.7	46.9	92 04.8	42.5	Eltanin	90 45.2	N51 29.1
N 09	349 03.0	273 24.0	.. 58.4	302 46.6	.. 33.1	213 14.1	.. 46.8	107 07.4	.. 42.5	Enif	33 46.0	N 9 56.7
D 10	4 05.4	288 23.3	58.7	317 47.3	33.6	228 16.4	46.8	122 10.1	42.5	Fomalhaut	15 22.9	S29 32.4
A 11	19 07.9	303 22.7	59.1	332 47.9	34.1	243 18.7	46.8	137 12.7	42.4			
Y 12	34 10.3	318 22.0	N24 59.5	347 48.6	N17 34.6	258 21.1	N17 46.7	152 15.3	S18 42.4	Gacrux	171 58.9	S57 12.1
13	49 12.8	333 21.4	24 59.9	2 49.2	35.1	273 23.4	46.7	167 17.9	42.4	Gienah	175 50.7	S17 37.8
14	64 15.3	348 20.7	25 00.3	17 49.9	35.7	288 25.7	46.6	182 20.5	42.4	Hadar	148 45.3	S60 26.8
15	79 17.7	3 20.1	.. 00.6	32 50.5	.. 36.2	303 28.0	.. 46.6	197 23.2	.. 42.3	Hamal	327 59.7	N23 31.9
16	94 20.2	18 19.4	01.0	47 51.2	36.7	318 30.4	46.5	212 25.8	42.3	Kaus Aust.	83 42.0	S34 22.3
17	109 22.7	33 18.8	01.4	62 51.9	37.2	333 32.7	46.5	227 28.4	42.3			
18	124 25.1	48 18.1	N25 01.8	77 52.5	N17 37.7	348 35.0	N17 46.5	242 31.0	S18 42.2	Kochab	137 19.1	N74 05.6
19	139 27.6	63 17.5	02.1	92 53.2	38.3	3 37.4	46.4	257 33.7	42.2	Markab	13 37.3	N15 17.1
20	154 30.1	78 16.8	02.5	107 53.8	38.8	18 39.7	46.4	272 36.3	42.2	Menkar	314 14.1	N 4 08.7
21	169 32.5	93 16.2	.. 02.9	122 54.5	.. 39.3	33 42.0	.. 46.3	287 38.9	.. 42.1	Menkent	148 05.6	S36 26.7
22	184 35.0	108 15.6	03.2	137 55.1	39.8	48 44.3	46.3	302 41.5	42.1	Miaplacidus	221 39.1	S69 47.3
23	199 37.5	123 14.9	03.6	152 55.8	40.3	63 46.7	46.2	317 44.2	42.1			
27 00	214 39.9	138 14.3	N25 04.0	167 56.4	N17 40.8	78 49.0	N17 46.2	332 46.8	S18 42.0	Mirfak	308 39.0	N49 54.7
01	229 42.4	153 13.6	04.3	182 57.1	41.3	93 51.3	46.2	347 49.4	42.0	Nunki	75 56.6	S26 16.4
02	244 44.8	168 13.0	04.7	197 57.7	41.9	108 53.6	46.1	2 52.0	42.0	Peacock	53 17.3	S56 40.7
03	259 47.3	183 12.3	.. 05.1	212 58.4	.. 42.4	123 56.0	.. 46.1	17 54.6	.. 41.9	Pollux	243 26.3	N27 59.2
04	274 49.8	198 11.7	05.4	227 59.1	42.9	138 58.3	46.0	32 57.3	41.9	Procyon	244 58.5	N 5 10.9
05	289 52.2	213 11.0	05.8	242 59.7	43.4	154 00.6	46.0	47 59.9	41.9			
06	304 54.7	228 10.4	N25 06.1	258 00.4	N17 43.9	169 02.9	N17 45.9	63 02.5	S18 41.8	Rasalhague	96 05.1	N12 33.0
07	319 57.2	243 09.7	06.5	273 01.0	44.4	184 05.3	45.9	78 05.1	41.8	Regulus	207 42.1	N11 53.4
08	334 59.6	258 09.1	06.9	288 01.7	44.9	199 07.6	45.9	93 07.8	41.8	Rigel	281 11.1	S 8 11.4
M 09	350 02.1	273 08.4	.. 07.2	303 02.3	.. 45.5	214 09.9	.. 45.8	108 10.4	.. 41.8	Rigil Kent.	139 49.2	S60 53.8
O 10	5 04.6	288 07.8	07.6	318 03.0	46.0	229 12.2	45.8	123 13.0	41.7	Sabik	102 10.8	S15 44.5
N 11	20 07.0	303 07.2	07.9	333 03.6	46.5	244 14.5	45.7	138 15.6	41.7			
D 12	35 09.5	318 06.5	N25 08.3	348 04.3	N17 47.0	259 16.9	N17 45.7	153 18.3	S18 41.7	Schedar	349 39.5	N56 37.1
A 13	50 11.9	333 05.9	08.6	3 04.9	47.5	274 19.2	45.6	168 20.9	41.6	Shaula	96 19.9	S37 06.6
Y 14	65 14.4	348 05.2	09.0	18 05.6	48.0	289 21.5	45.6	183 23.5	41.6	Sirius	258 32.8	S16 44.6
15	80 16.9	3 04.6	.. 09.3	33 06.3	.. 48.5	304 23.8	.. 45.5	198 26.1	.. 41.6	Spica	158 29.6	S11 14.5
16	95 19.3	18 03.9	09.7	48 06.9	49.0	319 26.1	45.5	213 28.8	41.5	Suhail	222 51.4	S43 30.1
17	110 21.8	33 03.3	10.0	63 07.6	49.6	334 28.5	45.5	228 31.4	41.5			
18	125 24.3	48 02.6	N25 10.4	78 08.2	N17 50.1	349 30.8	N17 45.4	243 34.0	S18 41.5	Vega	80 37.9	N38 47.8
19	140 26.7	63 02.0	10.7	93 08.9	50.6	4 33.1	45.4	258 36.6	41.4	Zuben'ubi	137 03.7	S16 06.3
20	155 29.2	78 01.3	11.1	108 09.5	51.1	19 35.4	45.3	273 39.3	41.4		SHA	Mer. Pass.
21	170 31.7	93 00.7	.. 11.4	123 10.2	.. 51.6	34 37.7	.. 45.3	288 41.9	.. 41.4	Venus	284 49.0	14 47
22	185 34.1	108 00.0	11.7	138 10.8	52.1	49 40.1	45.2	303 44.5	41.3	Mars	313 59.9	12 49
23	200 36.6	122 59.4	12.1	153 11.5	52.6	64 42.4	45.2	318 47.2	41.3	Jupiter	224 12.3	18 46
Mer. Pass.	h m 9 43.7	v −0.6	d 0.4	v 0.7	d 0.5	v 2.3	d 0.0	v 2.6	d 0.0	Saturn	118 03.1	1 53

UT	SUN GHA	SUN Dec	MOON GHA	v	MOON Dec	d	HP
d h	° ′	° ′	° ′	′	° ′	′	′
25 00	180 28.5	N13 00.8	98 33.4	11.5	N16 24.2	4.4	55.5
01	195 28.6	01.6	113 03.9	11.6	16 19.8	4.5	55.5
02	210 28.7	02.4	127 34.5	11.6	16 15.3	4.6	55.5
03	225 28.9 ..	03.2	142 05.1	11.7	16 10.7	4.7	55.4
04	240 29.0	04.0	156 35.8	11.7	16 06.0	4.8	55.4
05	255 29.1	04.9	171 06.5	11.8	16 01.2	4.8	55.4
06	270 29.2	N13 05.7	185 37.3	11.8	N15 56.4	4.9	55.4
07	285 29.3	06.5	200 08.1	11.9	15 51.5	4.9	55.3
08	300 29.4	07.3	214 39.0	11.9	15 46.6	5.1	55.3
09	315 29.5 ..	08.1	229 09.9	12.1	15 41.5	5.1	55.3
10	330 29.6	08.9	243 41.0	12.0	15 36.4	5.1	55.3
11	345 29.7	09.8	258 12.0	12.1	15 31.3	5.3	55.2
12	0 29.8	N13 10.6	272 43.1	12.2	N15 26.0	5.3	55.2
13	15 29.9	11.4	287 14.3	12.2	15 20.7	5.4	55.2
14	30 30.0	12.2	301 45.5	12.3	15 15.3	5.4	55.2
15	45 30.1 ..	13.0	316 16.8	12.4	15 09.9	5.5	55.1
16	60 30.3	13.8	330 48.2	12.3	15 04.4	5.6	55.1
17	75 30.4	14.6	345 19.5	12.5	14 58.8	5.6	55.1
18	90 30.5	N13 15.5	359 51.0	12.5	N14 53.2	5.7	55.1
19	105 30.6	16.3	14 22.5	12.5	14 47.5	5.8	55.0
20	120 30.7	17.1	28 54.0	12.6	14 41.7	5.8	55.0
21	135 30.8 ..	17.9	43 25.6	12.7	14 35.9	5.9	55.0
22	150 30.9	18.7	57 57.3	12.7	14 30.0	6.0	55.0
23	165 31.0	19.5	72 29.0	12.8	14 24.0	6.0	55.0
26 00	180 31.1	N13 20.3	87 00.8	12.8	N14 18.0	6.1	54.9
01	195 31.2	21.1	101 32.6	12.8	14 11.9	6.1	54.9
02	210 31.3	21.9	116 04.4	13.0	14 05.8	6.2	54.9
03	225 31.4 ..	22.8	130 36.4	12.9	13 59.6	6.3	54.9
04	240 31.5	23.6	145 08.3	13.0	13 53.3	6.3	54.8
05	255 31.6	24.4	159 40.3	13.1	13 47.0	6.4	54.8
06	270 31.7	N13 25.2	174 12.4	13.1	N13 40.6	6.4	54.8
07	285 31.8	26.0	188 44.5	13.2	13 34.2	6.5	54.8
08	300 31.9	26.8	203 16.7	13.2	13 27.7	6.6	54.8
09	315 32.0 ..	27.6	217 48.9	13.2	13 21.1	6.6	54.7
10	330 32.1	28.4	232 21.1	13.3	13 14.5	6.6	54.7
11	345 32.2	29.2	246 53.4	13.4	13 07.9	6.7	54.7
12	0 32.4	N13 30.0	261 25.8	13.4	N13 01.2	6.8	54.7
13	15 32.5	30.8	275 58.2	13.4	12 54.4	6.8	54.7
14	30 32.6	31.6	290 30.6	13.5	12 47.6	6.9	54.7
15	45 32.7 ..	32.4	305 03.1	13.6	12 40.7	6.9	54.6
16	60 32.8	33.2	319 35.7	13.6	12 33.8	7.0	54.6
17	75 32.9	34.0	334 08.3	13.6	12 26.8	7.0	54.6
18	90 33.0	N13 34.9	348 40.9	13.6	N12 19.8	7.1	54.6
19	105 33.1	35.7	3 13.5	13.8	12 12.7	7.1	54.6
20	120 33.2	36.5	17 46.3	13.7	12 05.6	7.2	54.6
21	135 33.3 ..	37.3	32 19.0	13.8	11 58.4	7.2	54.5
22	150 33.4	38.1	46 51.8	13.8	11 51.2	7.2	54.5
23	165 33.5	38.9	61 24.6	13.9	11 44.0	7.3	54.5
27 00	180 33.6	N13 39.7	75 57.5	13.9	N11 36.7	7.4	54.5
01	195 33.7	40.5	90 30.4	14.0	11 29.3	7.4	54.5
02	210 33.8	41.3	105 03.4	14.0	11 21.9	7.5	54.5
03	225 33.9 ..	42.1	119 36.4	14.0	11 14.4	7.5	54.5
04	240 34.0	42.9	134 09.4	14.1	11 06.9	7.5	54.4
05	255 34.1	43.7	148 42.5	14.1	10 59.4	7.6	54.4
06	270 34.2	N13 44.5	163 15.6	14.2	N10 51.8	7.6	54.4
07	285 34.3	45.3	177 48.8	14.2	10 44.2	7.7	54.4
08	300 34.4	46.1	192 22.0	14.2	10 36.5	7.7	54.4
09	315 34.5 ..	46.9	206 55.2	14.3	10 28.8	7.7	54.4
10	330 34.6	47.7	221 28.5	14.3	10 21.1	7.8	54.4
11	345 34.7	48.5	236 01.8	14.3	10 13.3	7.9	54.4
12	0 34.8	N13 49.3	250 35.1	14.4	N10 05.4	7.8	54.3
13	15 34.9	50.0	265 08.5	14.4	9 57.6	8.0	54.3
14	30 34.9	50.8	279 41.9	14.4	9 49.6	7.9	54.3
15	45 35.0 ..	51.6	294 15.3	14.5	9 41.7	8.0	54.3
16	60 35.1	52.4	308 48.8	14.5	9 33.7	8.0	54.3
17	75 35.2	53.2	323 22.3	14.5	9 25.7	8.1	54.3
18	90 35.3	N13 54.0	337 55.8	14.5	N9 17.6	8.1	54.3
19	105 35.4	54.8	352 29.3	14.6	9 09.5	8.1	54.3
20	120 35.5	55.6	7 02.9	14.6	9 01.4	8.2	54.3
21	135 35.6 ..	56.4	21 36.5	14.7	8 53.2	8.2	54.3
22	150 35.7	57.2	36 10.2	14.7	8 45.0	8.2	54.2
23	165 35.8	58.0	50 43.9	14.7	N8 36.8	8.3	54.2
	SD 15.9	d 0.8	SD 15.0		14.9		14.8

S A T U R D A Y (25), **S U N D A Y** (26), **M O N D A Y** (27)

Lat.	Twilight Naut.	Twilight Civil	Sunrise	Moonrise 25	26	27	28
°	h m	h m	h m	h m	h m	h m	h m
N 72	////	////	02 33	07 41	09 25	11 03	12 37
N 70	////	00 58	03 01	08 21	09 50	11 19	12 47
68	////	01 54	03 22	08 48	10 10	11 33	12 55
66	////	02 26	03 39	09 09	10 25	11 44	13 02
64	00 50	02 49	03 52	09 25	10 38	11 53	13 08
62	01 40	03 08	04 03	09 39	10 49	12 00	13 12
60	02 10	03 23	04 13	09 50	10 58	12 07	13 16
N 58	02 31	03 35	04 21	10 00	11 06	12 13	13 20
56	02 49	03 46	04 29	10 09	11 13	12 18	13 23
54	03 03	03 55	04 35	10 16	11 19	12 23	13 26
52	03 15	04 03	04 41	10 23	11 25	12 27	13 29
50	03 26	04 11	04 46	10 29	11 30	12 31	13 31
45	03 47	04 26	04 58	10 43	11 41	12 39	13 37
N 40	04 03	04 38	05 07	10 54	11 50	12 46	13 41
35	04 17	04 49	05 15	11 03	11 57	12 51	13 45
30	04 27	04 57	05 22	11 11	12 04	12 56	13 48
20	04 45	05 11	05 34	11 25	12 16	13 05	13 54
N 10	04 58	05 23	05 45	11 38	12 26	13 13	13 59
0	05 09	05 33	05 54	11 49	12 36	13 20	14 04
S 10	05 18	05 43	06 04	12 01	12 45	13 28	14 08
20	05 26	05 52	06 14	12 13	12 56	13 35	14 13
30	05 33	06 01	06 26	12 27	13 07	13 44	14 19
35	05 36	06 06	06 32	12 35	13 14	13 49	14 22
40	05 40	06 12	06 40	12 44	13 22	13 55	14 26
45	05 43	06 18	06 48	12 55	13 30	14 02	14 30
S 50	05 47	06 25	06 58	13 08	13 41	14 10	14 36
52	05 48	06 28	07 03	13 14	13 46	14 13	14 38
54	05 50	06 31	07 09	13 21	13 51	14 17	14 40
56	05 51	06 35	07 14	13 29	13 57	14 22	14 43
58	05 53	06 39	07 21	13 37	14 04	14 27	14 46
S 60	05 55	06 44	07 28	13 46	14 12	14 32	14 50

Lat.	Sunset	Twilight Civil	Twilight Naut.	Moonset 25	26	27	28
°	h m	h m	h m	h m	h m	h m	h m
N 72	21 28	////	////	03 41	03 36	03 31	03 26
N 70	20 59	23 14	////	03 01	03 09	03 13	03 14
68	20 37	22 08	////	02 33	02 48	02 58	03 05
66	20 20	21 34	////	02 12	02 32	02 46	02 57
64	20 06	21 09	23 19	01 55	02 19	02 37	02 51
62	19 54	20 51	22 21	01 41	02 08	02 28	02 45
60	19 45	20 35	21 50	01 29	01 58	02 21	02 40
N 58	19 36	20 23	21 27	01 19	01 49	02 14	02 35
56	19 28	20 12	21 09	01 10	01 42	02 09	02 31
54	19 22	20 02	20 55	01 02	01 35	02 03	02 28
52	19 16	19 54	20 42	00 55	01 29	01 59	02 25
50	19 10	19 46	20 31	00 48	01 24	01 54	02 22
45	18 59	19 31	20 10	00 35	01 12	01 45	02 15
N 40	18 49	19 18	19 53	00 23	01 02	01 38	02 10
35	18 41	19 08	19 40	00 13	00 54	01 31	02 05
30	18 34	18 59	19 29	00 05	00 47	01 25	02 01
20	18 22	18 45	19 11	24 34	00 34	01 15	01 54
N 10	18 11	18 33	18 58	24 23	00 23	01 06	01 47
0	18 01	18 22	18 47	24 12	00 12	00 58	01 41
S 10	17 52	18 13	18 38	24 01	00 01	00 49	01 35
20	17 41	18 04	18 30	23 50	24 40	00 40	01 29
30	17 30	17 54	18 22	23 37	24 30	00 30	01 21
35	17 23	17 49	18 19	23 29	24 23	00 23	01 17
40	17 16	17 44	18 15	23 21	24 17	00 17	01 12
45	17 07	17 37	18 12	23 10	24 09	00 09	01 07
S 50	16 57	17 30	18 08	22 58	23 59	25 00	01 00
52	16 52	17 27	18 07	22 52	23 54	24 57	00 57
54	16 46	17 23	18 05	22 46	23 49	24 53	00 53
56	16 41	17 20	18 03	22 39	23 44	24 49	00 49
58	16 34	17 16	18 02	22 31	23 38	24 45	00 45
S 60	16 27	17 11	18 00	22 22	23 31	24 40	00 40

	SUN			MOON			
Day	Eqn. of Time 00h	Eqn. of Time 12h	Mer. Pass.	Mer. Pass. Upper	Lower	Age	Phase
d	m s	m s	h m	h m	h m	d	%
25	01 54	01 59	11 58	18 01	05 37	07	45
26	02 04	02 09	11 58	18 47	06 24	08	55
27	02 14	02 19	11 58	19 31	07 09	09	64

UT	ARIES GHA	VENUS −4.1 GHA	VENUS Dec	MARS +1.4 GHA	MARS Dec	JUPITER −2.1 GHA	JUPITER Dec	SATURN +0.1 GHA	SATURN Dec
28 00	215 39.1	137 58.7	N25 12.4	168 12.1	N17 53.1	79 44.7	N17 45.1	333 49.8	S18 41.3
01	230 41.5	152 58.1	12.8	183 12.8	53.6	94 47.0	45.1	348 52.4	41.2
02	245 44.0	167 57.5	13.1	198 13.4	54.1	109 49.3	45.0	3 55.0	41.2
03	260 46.4	182 56.8 ..	13.4	213 14.1 ..	54.6	124 51.7 ..	45.0	18 57.7 ..	41.2
04	275 48.9	197 56.2	13.8	228 14.7	55.2	139 54.0	45.0	34 00.3	41.2
05	290 51.4	212 55.5	14.1	243 15.4	55.7	154 56.3	44.9	49 02.9	41.1
T 06	305 53.8	227 54.9	N25 14.4	258 16.1	N17 56.2	169 58.6	N17 44.9	64 05.5	S18 41.1
U 07	320 56.3	242 54.2	14.8	273 16.7	56.7	185 00.9	44.8	79 08.2	41.1
E 08	335 58.8	257 53.6	15.1	288 17.4	57.2	200 03.2	44.8	94 10.8	41.0
S 09	351 01.2	272 52.9 ..	15.4	303 18.0 ..	57.7	215 05.6 ..	44.7	109 13.4 ..	41.0
D 10	6 03.7	287 52.3	15.7	318 18.7	58.2	230 07.9	44.7	124 16.0	41.0
A 11	21 06.2	302 51.6	16.1	333 19.3	58.7	245 10.2	44.6	139 18.7	40.9
Y 12	36 08.6	317 51.0	N25 16.4	348 20.0	N17 59.2	260 12.5	N17 44.6	154 21.3	S18 40.9
13	51 11.1	332 50.3	16.7	3 20.6	17 59.7	275 14.8	44.5	169 23.9	40.9
14	66 13.6	347 49.7	17.0	18 21.3	18 00.2	290 17.1	44.5	184 26.6	40.8
15	81 16.0	2 49.1 ..	17.4	33 21.9 ..	00.7	305 19.4 ..	44.4	199 29.2 ..	40.8
16	96 18.5	17 48.4	17.7	48 22.6	01.2	320 21.8	44.4	214 31.8	40.8
17	111 20.9	32 47.8	18.0	63 23.2	01.7	335 24.1	44.4	229 34.4	40.7
18	126 23.4	47 47.1	N25 18.3	78 23.9	N18 02.2	350 26.4	N17 44.3	244 37.1	S18 40.7
19	141 25.9	62 46.5	18.6	93 24.5	02.7	5 28.7	44.3	259 39.7	40.7
20	156 28.3	77 45.8	19.0	108 25.2	03.2	20 31.0	44.2	274 42.3	40.6
21	171 30.8	92 45.2 ..	19.3	123 25.8 ..	03.7	35 33.3 ..	44.2	289 45.0 ..	40.6
22	186 33.3	107 44.5	19.6	138 26.5	04.2	50 35.6	44.1	304 47.6	40.6
23	201 35.7	122 43.9	19.9	153 27.1	04.7	65 37.9	44.1	319 50.2	40.5
29 00	216 38.2	137 43.2	N25 20.2	168 27.8	N18 05.2	80 40.2	N17 44.0	334 52.8	S18 40.5
01	231 40.7	152 42.6	20.5	183 28.4	05.7	95 42.6	44.0	349 55.5	40.5
02	246 43.1	167 42.0	20.8	198 29.1	06.2	110 44.9	43.9	4 58.1	40.4
03	261 45.6	182 41.3 ..	21.1	213 29.7 ..	06.7	125 47.2 ..	43.9	20 00.7 ..	40.4
04	276 48.0	197 40.7	21.4	228 30.4	07.2	140 49.5	43.8	35 03.4	40.4
05	291 50.5	212 40.0	21.7	243 31.0	07.7	155 51.8	43.8	50 06.0	40.4
W 06	306 53.0	227 39.4	N25 22.1	258 31.7	N18 08.2	170 54.1	N17 43.7	65 08.6	S18 40.3
E 07	321 55.4	242 38.7	22.4	273 32.3	08.7	185 56.4	43.7	80 11.2	40.3
D 08	336 57.9	257 38.1	22.7	288 33.0	09.2	200 58.7	43.6	95 13.9	40.3
N 09	352 00.4	272 37.4 ..	23.0	303 33.6 ..	09.7	216 01.0 ..	43.6	110 16.5 ..	40.2
E 10	7 02.8	287 36.8	23.3	318 34.3	10.2	231 03.3	43.6	125 19.1	40.2
S 11	22 05.3	302 36.1	23.6	333 34.9	10.7	246 05.7	43.5	140 21.8	40.2
D 12	37 07.8	317 35.5	N25 23.9	348 35.6	N18 11.2	261 08.0	N17 43.5	155 24.4	S18 40.1
A 13	52 10.2	332 34.9	24.2	3 36.2	11.7	276 10.3	43.4	170 27.0	40.1
Y 14	67 12.7	347 34.2	24.4	18 36.9	12.2	291 12.6	43.4	185 29.6	40.1
15	82 15.2	2 33.6 ..	24.7	33 37.5 ..	12.7	306 14.9 ..	43.3	200 32.3 ..	40.0
16	97 17.6	17 32.9	25.0	48 38.2	13.2	321 17.2	43.3	215 34.9	40.0
17	112 20.1	32 32.3	25.3	63 38.8	13.7	336 19.5	43.2	230 37.5	40.0
18	127 22.5	47 31.6	N25 25.6	78 39.5	N18 14.2	351 21.8	N17 43.1	245 40.2	S18 39.9
19	142 25.0	62 31.0	25.9	93 40.1	14.7	6 24.1	43.1	260 42.8	39.9
20	157 27.5	77 30.3	26.2	108 40.8	15.2	21 26.4	43.1	275 45.4	39.9
21	172 29.9	92 29.7 ..	26.5	123 41.4 ..	15.7	36 28.7 ..	43.0	290 48.1 ..	39.8
22	187 32.4	107 29.1	26.8	138 42.1	16.2	51 31.0	43.0	305 50.7	39.8
23	202 34.9	122 28.4	27.1	153 42.7	16.7	66 33.3	42.9	320 53.3	39.8
30 00	217 37.3	137 27.8	N25 27.3	168 43.4	N18 17.2	81 35.6	N17 42.9	335 56.0	S18 39.7
01	232 39.8	152 27.1	27.6	183 44.0	17.7	96 37.9	42.8	350 58.6	39.7
02	247 42.3	167 26.5	27.9	198 44.7	18.2	111 40.2	42.8	6 01.2	39.7
03	262 44.7	182 25.8 ..	28.2	213 45.3 ..	18.7	126 42.5 ..	42.7	21 03.8 ..	39.6
04	277 47.2	197 25.2	28.5	228 46.0	19.2	141 44.8	42.7	36 06.5	39.6
05	292 49.6	212 24.6	28.7	243 46.6	19.7	156 47.1	42.6	51 09.1	39.6
T 06	307 52.1	227 23.9	N25 29.0	258 47.3	N18 20.1	171 49.4	N17 42.6	66 11.7	S18 39.5
H 07	322 54.6	242 23.3	29.3	273 47.9	20.6	186 51.7	42.5	81 14.4	39.5
U 08	337 57.0	257 22.6	29.6	288 48.6	21.1	201 54.0	42.5	96 17.0	39.5
R 09	352 59.5	272 22.0 ..	29.8	303 49.2 ..	21.6	216 56.4 ..	42.4	111 19.6 ..	39.4
S 10	8 02.0	287 21.3	30.1	318 49.9	22.1	231 58.7	42.4	126 22.3	39.4
D 11	23 04.4	302 20.7	30.4	333 50.5	22.6	247 01.0	42.3	141 24.9	39.4
A 12	38 06.9	317 20.0	N25 30.7	348 51.2	N18 23.1	262 03.3	N17 42.3	156 27.5	S18 39.3
Y 13	53 09.4	332 19.4	30.9	3 51.8	23.6	277 05.6	42.2	171 30.2	39.3
14	68 11.8	347 18.8	31.2	18 52.5	24.1	292 07.9	42.2	186 32.8	39.3
15	83 14.3	2 18.1 ..	31.5	33 53.1 ..	24.5	307 10.2 ..	42.1	201 35.4 ..	39.3
16	98 16.8	17 17.5	31.7	48 53.8	25.0	322 12.5	42.1	216 38.1	39.2
17	113 19.2	32 16.8	32.0	63 54.4	25.5	337 14.8	42.0	231 40.7	39.2
18	128 21.7	47 16.2	N25 32.3	78 55.1	N18 26.0	352 17.1	N17 42.0	246 43.3	S18 39.2
19	143 24.1	62 15.5	32.5	93 55.7	26.5	7 19.4	41.9	261 46.0	39.1
20	158 26.6	77 14.9	32.8	108 56.4	27.0	22 21.6	41.9	276 48.6	39.1
21	173 29.1	92 14.3 ..	33.0	123 57.0 ..	27.5	37 23.9 ..	41.8	291 51.2 ..	39.1
22	188 31.5	107 13.6	33.3	138 57.6	28.0	52 26.2	41.8	306 53.9	39.0
23	203 34.0	122 13.0	33.6	153 58.3	28.5	67 28.5	41.7	321 56.5	39.0
Mer.Pass.	h m 9 31.9	v −0.6 d 0.3		v 0.7 d 0.5		v 2.3 d 0.0		v 2.6 d 0.0	

STARS

Name	SHA	Dec
Acamar	315 17.9	S40 14.8
Achernar	335 26.5	S57 09.6
Acrux	173 07.1	S63 11.2
Adhara	255 11.7	S29 00.0
Aldebaran	290 48.2	N16 32.1
Alioth	166 19.2	N55 52.7
Alkaid	152 57.5	N49 14.3
Al Na'ir	27 42.4	S46 52.9
Alnilam	275 45.3	S 1 11.9
Alphard	217 54.8	S 8 43.8
Alphecca	126 09.6	N26 39.8
Alpheratz	357 42.4	N29 10.3
Altair	62 06.9	N 8 54.6
Ankaa	353 14.9	S42 13.3
Antares	112 24.4	S26 27.8
Arcturus	145 54.3	N19 06.2
Atria	107 24.6	S69 03.0
Avior	234 17.5	S59 34.0
Bellatrix	278 30.9	N 6 21.5
Betelgeuse	271 00.2	N 7 24.3
Canopus	263 55.9	S52 42.7
Capella	280 32.9	N46 00.6
Deneb	49 30.6	N45 20.0
Denebola	182 32.2	N14 29.1
Diphda	348 54.9	S17 54.2
Dubhe	193 49.9	N61 40.2
Elnath	278 11.3	N28 37.0
Eltanin	90 45.2	N51 29.2
Enif	33 46.0	N 9 56.7
Fomalhaut	15 22.8	S29 32.4
Gacrux	171 58.9	S57 12.1
Gienah	175 50.7	S17 37.8
Hadar	148 45.3	S60 26.8
Hamal	327 59.7	N23 31.9
Kaus Aust.	83 41.9	S34 22.3
Kochab	137 19.1	N74 05.6
Markab	13 37.3	N15 17.2
Menkar	314 14.1	N 4 08.7
Menkent	148 05.6	S36 26.7
Miaplacidus	221 39.1	S69 47.3
Mirfak	308 39.0	N49 54.7
Nunki	75 56.6	S26 16.4
Peacock	53 17.3	S56 40.7
Pollux	243 26.3	N27 59.2
Procyon	244 58.5	N 5 10.9
Rasalhague	96 05.0	N12 33.0
Regulus	207 42.1	N11 53.4
Rigel	281 11.1	S 8 11.4
Rigil Kent.	139 49.2	S60 53.8
Sabik	102 10.8	S15 44.5
Schedar	349 39.5	N56 37.1
Shaula	96 19.9	S37 06.6
Sirius	258 32.8	S16 44.6
Spica	158 29.6	S11 14.5
Suhail	222 51.4	S43 30.1
Vega	80 37.9	N38 47.8
Zuben'ubi	137 03.7	S16 06.3

	SHA	Mer.Pass.
	° ′	h m
Venus	281 05.1	14 50
Mars	311 49.6	12 46
Jupiter	224 02.1	18 34
Saturn	118 14.6	1 40

SUN and MOON

UT (d h)	SUN GHA	SUN Dec	MOON GHA	v	MOON Dec	d	HP
28 00	180 35.9	N13 58.8	65 17.6	14.7	N 8 28.5	8.3	54.2
01	195 36.0	13 59.6	79 51.3	14.8	8 20.2	8.4	54.2
02	210 36.1	14 00.4	94 25.1	14.7	8 11.8	8.3	54.2
03	225 36.2	.. 01.2	108 58.8	14.8	8 03.5	8.4	54.2
04	240 36.3	01.9	123 32.6	14.9	7 55.1	8.5	54.2
05	255 36.4	02.7	138 06.5	14.8	7 46.6	8.4	54.2
06	270 36.5	N14 03.5	152 40.3	14.9	N 7 38.2	8.5	54.2
07	285 36.6	04.3	167 14.2	14.9	7 29.7	8.6	54.2
08	300 36.7	05.1	181 48.1	14.9	7 21.1	8.5	54.2
09	315 36.8	.. 05.9	196 22.0	15.0	7 12.6	8.6	54.2
10	330 36.9	06.7	210 56.0	14.9	7 04.0	8.6	54.2
11	345 36.9	07.5	225 29.9	15.0	6 55.4	8.7	54.2
12	0 37.0	N14 08.2	240 03.9	15.0	N 6 46.7	8.6	54.2
13	15 37.1	09.0	254 37.9	15.0	6 38.1	8.7	54.2
14	30 37.2	09.8	269 11.9	15.1	6 29.4	8.7	54.2
15	45 37.3	.. 10.6	283 46.0	15.0	6 20.7	8.8	54.2
16	60 37.4	11.4	298 20.0	15.1	6 11.9	8.8	54.1
17	75 37.5	12.2	312 54.1	15.1	6 03.1	8.8	54.1
18	90 37.6	N14 13.0	327 28.2	15.1	N 5 54.3	8.8	54.1
19	105 37.7	13.7	342 02.3	15.1	5 45.5	8.8	54.1
20	120 37.8	14.5	356 36.4	15.2	5 36.7	8.9	54.1
21	135 37.9	.. 15.3	11 10.6	15.1	5 27.8	8.9	54.1
22	150 38.0	16.1	25 44.7	15.2	5 18.9	8.9	54.1
23	165 38.0	16.9	40 18.9	15.2	5 10.0	8.9	54.1
29 00	180 38.1	N14 17.7	54 53.1	15.2	N 5 01.1	9.0	54.1
01	195 38.2	18.4	69 27.3	15.2	4 52.1	8.9	54.1
02	210 38.3	19.2	84 01.5	15.2	4 43.2	9.0	54.1
03	225 38.4	.. 20.0	98 35.7	15.2	4 34.2	9.0	54.1
04	240 38.5	20.8	113 09.9	15.2	4 25.2	9.1	54.1
05	255 38.6	21.6	127 44.1	15.3	4 16.1	9.0	54.1
06	270 38.7	N14 22.3	142 18.4	15.2	N 4 07.1	9.1	54.1
07	285 38.8	23.1	156 52.6	15.2	3 58.0	9.0	54.1
08	300 38.8	23.9	171 26.8	15.3	3 49.0	9.1	54.1
09	315 38.9	.. 24.7	186 01.1	15.3	3 39.9	9.2	54.1
10	330 39.0	25.5	200 35.4	15.2	3 30.7	9.1	54.1
11	345 39.1	26.2	215 09.6	15.3	3 21.6	9.1	54.1
12	0 39.2	N14 27.0	229 43.9	15.3	N 3 12.5	9.2	54.1
13	15 39.3	27.8	244 18.2	15.3	3 03.3	9.2	54.1
14	30 39.4	28.6	258 52.5	15.3	2 54.1	9.2	54.1
15	45 39.5	.. 29.3	273 26.8	15.2	2 44.9	9.2	54.1
16	60 39.5	30.1	288 01.0	15.3	2 35.7	9.2	54.1
17	75 39.6	30.9	302 35.3	15.3	2 26.5	9.2	54.2
18	90 39.7	N14 31.7	317 09.6	15.3	N 2 17.3	9.2	54.2
19	105 39.8	32.4	331 43.9	15.3	2 08.1	9.3	54.2
20	120 39.9	33.2	346 18.2	15.3	1 58.8	9.2	54.2
21	135 40.0	.. 34.0	0 52.5	15.3	1 49.6	9.3	54.2
22	150 40.1	34.8	15 26.8	15.2	1 40.3	9.3	54.2
23	165 40.1	35.5	30 01.0	15.3	1 31.0	9.2	54.2
30 00	180 40.2	N14 36.3	44 35.3	15.3	N 1 21.8	9.3	54.2
01	195 40.3	37.1	59 09.6	15.3	1 12.5	9.3	54.2
02	210 40.4	37.8	73 43.9	15.2	1 03.2	9.3	54.2
03	225 40.5	.. 38.6	88 18.1	15.3	0 53.9	9.4	54.2
04	240 40.6	39.4	102 52.4	15.2	0 44.5	9.3	54.2
05	255 40.6	40.2	117 26.6	15.3	0 35.2	9.3	54.2
06	270 40.7	N14 40.9	132 00.9	15.2	N 0 25.9	9.3	54.2
07	285 40.8	41.7	146 35.1	15.3	0 16.6	9.4	54.2
08	300 40.9	42.5	161 09.4	15.2	N 0 07.2	9.3	54.2
09	315 41.0	.. 43.2	175 43.6	15.2	S 0 02.1	9.3	54.2
10	330 41.1	44.0	190 17.8	15.2	0 11.4	9.4	54.2
11	345 41.1	44.8	204 52.0	15.2	0 20.8	9.3	54.2
12	0 41.2	N14 45.5	219 26.2	15.2	S 0 30.1	9.4	54.3
13	15 41.3	46.3	234 00.4	15.1	0 39.5	9.3	54.3
14	30 41.4	47.1	248 34.5	15.2	0 48.8	9.4	54.3
15	45 41.5	.. 47.8	263 08.7	15.1	0 58.2	9.3	54.3
16	60 41.6	48.6	277 42.8	15.1	1 07.5	9.4	54.3
17	75 41.6	49.4	292 16.9	15.2	1 16.9	9.3	54.3
18	90 41.7	N14 50.1	306 51.1	15.1	S 1 26.2	9.4	54.3
19	105 41.8	50.9	321 25.2	15.0	1 35.6	9.3	54.3
20	120 41.9	51.7	335 59.2	15.1	1 44.9	9.3	54.3
21	135 42.0	.. 52.4	350 33.3	15.0	1 54.2	9.4	54.3
22	150 42.0	53.2	5 07.3	15.1	2 03.6	9.3	54.3
23	165 42.1	53.9	19 41.4	15.0	S 2 12.9	9.3	54.3
	SD 15.9	d 0.8	SD 14.8		14.8		14.8

Column indicators for Tuesday (T U E S D A Y), Wednesday (W E D N E S D A Y), Thursday (T H U R S D A Y).

Moonrise / Twilight

Lat.	Twilight Naut.	Twilight Civil	Sunrise	Moonrise 28	29	30	1
N 72	////	////	02 11	12 37	14 10	15 43	17 17
N 70	////	////	02 45	12 47	14 14	15 42	17 10
68	////	01 30	03 08	12 55	14 18	15 40	17 04
66	////	02 09	03 27	13 02	14 20	15 39	16 59
64	////	02 36	03 42	13 08	14 23	15 38	16 55
62	01 19	02 56	03 54	13 12	14 25	15 37	16 51
60	01 55	03 13	04 05	13 16	14 26	15 37	16 48
N 58	02 20	03 26	04 14	13 20	14 28	15 36	16 45
56	02 39	03 38	04 22	13 23	14 29	15 35	16 42
54	02 54	03 48	04 29	13 26	14 30	15 35	16 40
52	03 07	03 57	04 35	13 29	14 32	15 34	16 38
50	03 19	04 05	04 41	13 31	14 33	15 34	16 36
45	03 41	04 21	04 53	13 37	14 35	15 33	16 32
N 40	03 59	04 34	05 03	13 41	14 37	15 32	16 29
35	04 13	04 45	05 12	13 45	14 38	15 32	16 26
30	04 24	04 54	05 19	13 48	14 40	15 31	16 23
20	04 42	05 09	05 32	13 54	14 42	15 30	16 19
N 10	04 56	05 22	05 44	13 59	14 44	15 29	16 15
0	05 08	05 33	05 54	14 04	14 46	15 29	16 12
S 10	05 18	05 43	06 04	14 08	14 48	15 28	16 08
20	05 26	05 52	06 15	14 13	14 50	15 27	16 04
30	05 34	06 03	06 27	14 19	14 53	15 26	16 00
35	05 38	06 08	06 35	14 22	14 54	15 26	15 58
40	05 42	06 14	06 43	14 26	14 56	15 25	15 55
45	05 47	06 21	06 52	14 30	14 58	15 25	15 52
S 50	05 51	06 29	07 03	14 36	15 00	15 24	15 48
52	05 53	06 33	07 08	14 38	15 01	15 23	15 46
54	05 55	06 36	07 14	14 40	15 02	15 23	15 45
56	05 57	06 41	07 20	14 43	15 03	15 23	15 43
58	05 59	06 45	07 27	14 46	15 05	15 22	15 40
S 60	06 01	06 50	07 35	14 50	15 06	15 22	15 38

Moonset / Twilight

Lat.	Sunset	Twilight Civil	Twilight Naut.	Moonset 28	29	30	1
N 72	21 50	////	////	03 26	03 21	03 17	03 12
N 70	21 15	////	////	03 14	03 15	03 16	03 16
68	20 50	22 33	////	03 05	03 10	03 15	03 19
66	20 31	21 50	////	02 57	03 06	03 14	03 22
64	20 15	21 22	////	02 51	03 03	03 13	03 24
62	20 03	21 01	22 42	02 45	02 59	03 13	03 26
60	19 52	20 44	22 04	02 40	02 57	03 12	03 28
N 58	19 43	20 30	21 38	02 35	02 54	03 12	03 30
56	19 35	20 19	21 19	02 31	02 52	03 12	03 31
54	19 27	20 08	21 03	02 28	02 50	03 11	03 32
52	19 21	19 59	20 49	02 25	02 48	03 11	03 34
50	19 15	19 51	20 38	02 22	02 47	03 11	03 35
45	19 03	19 35	20 15	02 15	02 43	03 10	03 37
N 40	18 52	19 21	19 57	02 10	02 40	03 10	03 39
35	18 43	19 10	19 43	02 05	02 38	03 09	03 41
30	18 36	19 01	19 31	02 01	02 35	03 09	03 42
20	18 23	18 46	19 13	01 54	02 31	03 08	03 45
N 10	18 11	18 33	18 59	01 47	02 28	03 07	03 47
0	18 01	18 22	18 47	01 41	02 24	03 07	03 49
S 10	17 50	18 12	18 37	01 35	02 21	03 06	03 51
20	17 39	18 02	18 28	01 29	02 17	03 05	03 54
30	17 27	17 52	18 20	01 21	02 13	03 04	03 56
35	17 20	17 46	18 16	01 17	02 11	03 04	03 58
40	17 12	17 40	18 12	01 12	02 08	03 03	03 59
45	17 02	17 33	18 08	01 07	02 05	03 03	04 01
S 50	16 51	17 25	18 03	01 00	02 01	03 02	04 04
52	16 46	17 21	18 01	00 57	01 59	03 02	04 05
54	16 40	17 18	17 59	00 51	01 57	03 01	04 06
56	16 34	17 13	17 57	00 49	01 55	03 01	04 07
58	16 27	17 09	17 55	00 45	01 53	03 00	04 09
S 60	16 19	17 04	17 53	00 40	01 50	03 00	04 10

SUN and MOON

Day	SUN Eqn. of Time 00h	SUN Eqn. of Time 12h	SUN Mer. Pass.	MOON Mer. Pass. Upper	MOON Mer. Pass. Lower	Age	Phase
d	m s	m s	h m	h m	h m	d	%
28	02 23	02 28	11 58	20 14	07 53	10	73
29	02 32	02 37	11 57	20 56	08 35	11	81
30	02 41	02 45	11 57	21 39	09 18	12	88

UT	ARIES	VENUS −4.2		MARS +1.4		JUPITER −2.1		SATURN +0.1		STARS		
	GHA	GHA	Dec	GHA	Dec	GHA	Dec	GHA	Dec	Name	SHA	Dec
d h	° ′	° ′	° ′	° ′	° ′	° ′	° ′	° ′	° ′		° ′	° ′
1 00	218 36.5	137 12.3	N25 33.8	168 58.9	N18 28.9	82 30.8	N17 41.7	336 59.1	S18 39.0	Acamar	315 17.9	S40 14.8
01	233 38.9	152 11.7	34.1	183 59.6	29.4	97 33.1	41.6	352 01.8	38.9	Achernar	335 26.5	S57 09.6
02	248 41.4	167 11.1	34.3	199 00.2	29.9	112 35.4	41.6	7 04.4	38.9	Acrux	173 07.1	S63 11.3
03	263 43.9	182 10.4 . .	34.6	214 00.9 . .	30.4	127 37.7 . .	41.5	22 07.0 . .	38.9	Adhara	255 11.7	S29 00.0
04	278 46.3	197 09.8	34.8	229 01.5	30.9	142 40.0	41.5	37 09.7	38.8	Aldebaran	290 48.2	N16 32.1
05	293 48.8	212 09.1	35.1	244 02.2	31.4	157 42.3	41.4	52 12.3	38.8			
06	308 51.2	227 08.5	N25 35.3	259 02.8	N18 31.8	172 44.6	N17 41.4	67 14.9	S18 38.8	Alioth	166 19.2	N55 52.7
07	323 53.7	242 07.8	35.6	274 03.5	32.3	187 46.9	41.3	82 17.6	38.7	Alkaid	152 57.5	N49 14.3
08	338 56.2	257 07.2	35.8	289 04.1	32.8	202 49.2	41.2	97 20.2	38.7	Al Na'ir	27 42.4	S46 52.9
F 09	353 58.6	272 06.6 . .	36.1	304 04.8 . .	33.3	217 51.5 . .	41.2	112 22.8 . .	38.7	Alnilam	275 45.3	S 1 11.8
R 10	9 01.1	287 05.9	36.3	319 05.4	33.8	232 53.8	41.1	127 25.5	38.6	Alphard	217 54.8	S 8 43.8
I 11	24 03.6	302 05.3	36.6	334 06.1	34.3	247 56.1	41.1	142 28.1	38.6			
D 12	39 06.0	317 04.6	N25 36.8	349 06.7	N18 34.8	262 58.4	N17 41.0	157 30.7	S18 38.6	Alphecca	126 09.6	N26 39.8
A 13	54 08.5	332 04.0	37.0	4 07.3	35.2	278 00.7	41.0	172 33.4	38.5	Alpheratz	357 42.4	N29 10.3
Y 14	69 11.0	347 03.4	37.3	19 08.0	35.7	293 03.0	40.9	187 36.0	38.5	Altair	62 06.9	N 8 54.6
15	84 13.4	2 02.7 . .	37.5	34 08.6 . .	36.2	308 05.3 . .	40.9	202 38.6 . .	38.5	Ankaa	353 14.9	S42 13.3
16	99 15.9	17 02.1	37.8	49 09.3	36.7	323 07.6	40.8	217 41.3	38.4	Antares	112 24.4	S26 27.8
17	114 18.4	32 01.4	38.0	64 09.9	37.2	338 09.8	40.8	232 43.9	38.4			
18	129 20.8	47 00.8	N25 38.2	79 10.6	N18 37.6	353 12.1	N17 40.7	247 46.5	S18 38.4	Arcturus	145 54.3	N19 06.2
19	144 23.3	62 00.2	38.5	94 11.2	38.1	8 14.4	40.7	262 49.2	38.3	Atria	107 24.5	S69 03.0
20	159 25.7	76 59.5	38.7	109 11.9	38.6	23 16.7	40.6	277 51.8	38.3	Avior	234 17.5	S59 34.0
21	174 28.2	91 58.9 . .	38.9	124 12.5 . .	39.1	38 19.0 . .	40.6	292 54.4 . .	38.3	Bellatrix	278 30.9	N 6 21.5
22	189 30.7	106 58.2	39.2	139 13.2	39.6	53 21.3	40.5	307 57.1	38.2	Betelgeuse	271 00.2	N 7 24.3
23	204 33.1	121 57.6	39.4	154 13.8	40.0	68 23.6	40.5	322 59.7	38.2			
2 00	219 35.6	136 57.0	N25 39.6	169 14.5	N18 40.5	83 25.9	N17 40.4	338 02.3	S18 38.2	Canopus	263 55.9	S52 42.7
01	234 38.1	151 56.3	39.9	184 15.1	41.0	98 28.2	40.4	353 05.0	38.1	Capella	280 33.0	N46 00.6
02	249 40.5	166 55.7	40.1	199 15.7	41.5	113 30.5	40.3	8 07.6	38.1	Deneb	49 30.5	N45 20.0
03	264 43.0	181 55.1 . .	40.3	214 16.4 . .	42.0	128 32.8 . .	40.2	23 10.2 . .	38.1	Denebola	182 32.2	N14 29.1
04	279 45.5	196 54.4	40.5	229 17.0	42.4	143 35.0	40.2	38 12.9	38.0	Diphda	348 54.9	S17 54.2
05	294 47.9	211 53.8	40.8	244 17.7	42.9	158 37.3	40.1	53 15.5	38.0			
06	309 50.4	226 53.1	N25 41.0	259 18.3	N18 43.4	173 39.6	N17 40.1	68 18.1	S18 38.0	Dubhe	193 50.0	N61 40.2
07	324 52.9	241 52.5	41.2	274 19.0	43.9	188 41.9	40.0	83 20.8	37.9	Elnath	278 11.3	N28 37.0
S 08	339 55.3	256 51.9	41.4	289 19.6	44.3	203 44.2	40.0	98 23.4	37.9	Eltanin	90 45.2	N51 29.2
A 09	354 57.8	271 51.2 . .	41.6	304 20.3 . .	44.8	218 46.5 . .	39.9	113 26.1 . .	37.9	Enif	33 45.9	N 9 56.7
T 10	10 00.2	286 50.6	41.9	319 20.9	45.3	233 48.8	39.9	128 28.7	37.8	Fomalhaut	15 22.8	S29 32.3
U 11	25 02.7	301 49.9	42.1	334 21.5	45.8	248 51.1	39.8	143 31.3	37.8			
R 12	40 05.2	316 49.3	N25 42.3	349 22.2	N18 46.2	263 53.3	N17 39.8	158 34.0	S18 37.8	Gacrux	171 58.9	S57 12.1
D 13	55 07.6	331 48.7	42.5	4 22.8	46.7	278 55.6	39.7	173 36.6	37.7	Gienah	175 50.7	S17 37.8
A 14	70 10.1	346 48.0	42.7	19 23.5	47.2	293 57.9	39.6	188 39.2	37.7	Hadar	148 45.3	S60 26.8
Y 15	85 12.6	1 47.4 . .	42.9	34 24.1 . .	47.7	309 00.2 . .	39.6	203 41.9 . .	37.7	Hamal	327 59.7	N23 31.9
16	100 15.0	16 46.8	43.1	49 24.8	48.1	324 02.5	39.5	218 44.5	37.6	Kaus Aust.	83 41.9	S34 22.3
17	115 17.5	31 46.1	43.4	64 25.4	48.6	339 04.8	39.5	233 47.1	37.6			
18	130 20.0	46 45.5	N25 43.6	79 26.1	N18 49.1	354 07.1	N17 39.4	248 49.8	S18 37.6	Kochab	137 19.1	N74 05.6
19	145 22.4	61 44.9	43.8	94 26.7	49.6	9 09.3	39.4	263 52.4	37.5	Markab	13 37.2	N15 17.2
20	160 24.9	76 44.2	44.0	109 27.3	50.0	24 11.6	39.3	278 55.1	37.5	Menkar	314 14.1	N 4 08.7
21	175 27.3	91 43.6 . .	44.2	124 28.0 . .	50.5	39 13.9 . .	39.3	293 57.7 . .	37.5	Menkent	148 05.6	S36 26.7
22	190 29.8	106 42.9	44.4	139 28.6	51.0	54 16.2	39.2	309 00.3	37.4	Miaplacidus	221 39.2	S69 47.3
23	205 32.3	121 42.3	44.6	154 29.3	51.4	69 18.5	39.2	324 03.0	37.4			
3 00	220 34.7	136 41.7	N25 44.8	169 29.9	N18 51.9	84 20.8	N17 39.1	339 05.6	S18 37.4	Mirfak	308 39.0	N49 54.7
01	235 37.2	151 41.0	45.0	184 30.6	52.4	99 23.0	39.0	354 08.2	37.3	Nunki	75 56.6	S26 16.4
02	250 39.7	166 40.4	45.2	199 31.2	52.9	114 25.3	39.0	9 10.9	37.3	Peacock	53 17.3	S56 40.7
03	265 42.1	181 39.8 . .	45.4	214 31.8 . .	53.3	129 27.6 . .	38.9	24 13.5 . .	37.3	Pollux	243 26.3	N27 59.2
04	280 44.6	196 39.1	45.6	229 32.5	53.8	144 29.9	38.9	39 16.1	37.2	Procyon	244 58.5	N 5 10.9
05	295 47.1	211 38.5	45.8	244 33.1	54.3	159 32.2	38.8	54 18.8	37.2			
06	310 49.5	226 37.9	N25 46.0	259 33.8	N18 54.7	174 34.5	N17 38.8	69 21.4	S18 37.2	Rasalhague	96 05.0	N12 33.0
07	325 52.0	241 37.2	46.2	274 34.4	55.2	189 36.7	38.7	84 24.1	37.1	Regulus	207 42.1	N11 53.4
08	340 54.5	256 36.6	46.4	289 35.1	55.7	204 39.0	38.7	99 26.7	37.1	Rigel	281 11.1	S 8 11.4
S 09	355 56.9	271 36.0 . .	46.5	304 35.7 . .	56.1	219 41.3 . .	38.6	114 29.3 . .	37.1	Rigil Kent.	139 49.2	S60 53.8
U 10	10 59.4	286 35.3	46.7	319 36.3	56.6	234 43.6	38.5	129 32.0	37.0	Sabik	102 10.8	S15 44.5
N 11	26 01.8	301 34.7	46.9	334 37.0	57.1	249 45.9	38.5	144 34.6	37.0			
D 12	41 04.3	316 34.1	N25 47.1	349 37.6	N18 57.5	264 48.1	N17 38.4	159 37.2	S18 37.0	Schedar	349 39.4	N56 37.0
A 13	56 06.8	331 33.4	47.3	4 38.3	58.0	279 50.4	38.4	174 39.9	36.9	Shaula	96 19.9	S37 06.6
Y 14	71 09.2	346 32.8	47.5	19 38.9	58.5	294 52.7	38.3	189 42.5	36.9	Sirius	258 32.8	S16 44.6
15	86 11.7	1 32.2 . .	47.7	34 39.6 . .	58.9	309 55.0 . .	38.3	204 45.2 . .	36.9	Spica	158 29.6	S11 14.5
16	101 14.2	16 31.5	47.9	49 40.2	59.4	324 57.3	38.2	219 47.8	36.8	Suhail	222 51.4	S43 30.1
17	116 16.6	31 30.9	48.0	64 40.8	18 59.9	339 59.5	38.1	234 50.4	36.8			
18	131 19.1	46 30.3	N25 48.2	79 41.5	N19 00.3	355 01.8	N17 38.1	249 53.1	S18 36.8	Vega	80 37.9	N38 47.8
19	146 21.6	61 29.6	48.4	94 42.1	00.8	10 04.1	38.0	264 55.7	36.7	Zuben'ubi	137 03.7	S16 06.3
20	161 24.0	76 29.0	48.6	109 42.8	01.3	25 06.4	38.0	279 58.4	36.7		SHA	Mer.Pass.
21	176 26.5	91 28.4 . .	48.7	124 43.4 . .	01.7	40 08.7 . .	37.9	295 01.0 . .	36.7		° ′	h m
22	191 29.0	106 27.7	48.9	139 44.0	02.2	55 10.9	37.9	310 03.6	36.6	Venus	277 21.4	14 53
23	206 31.4	121 27.1	49.1	154 44.7	02.7	70 13.2	37.8	325 06.3	36.6	Mars	309 38.8	12 42
	h m									Jupiter	223 50.3	18 23
Mer.Pass. 9 20.1		v −0.6	d 0.2	v 0.6	d 0.5	v 2.3	d 0.1	v 2.6	d 0.0	Saturn	118 26.7	1 28

SUN / MOON

UT	SUN GHA	SUN Dec	MOON GHA	v	MOON Dec	d	HP
d h	° ′	° ′	° ′	′	° ′	′	′
1 00	180 42.2	N14 54.7	34 15.4	15.0	S 2 22.2	9.4	54.4
01	195 42.3	55.5	48 49.4	15.0	2 31.6	9.3	54.4
02	210 42.4	56.2	63 23.4	14.9	2 40.9	9.3	54.4
03	225 42.4 ..	57.0	77 57.3	14.9	2 50.2	9.3	54.4
04	240 42.5	57.7	92 31.2	14.9	2 59.5	9.3	54.4
05	255 42.6	58.5	107 05.1	14.9	3 08.8	9.2	54.4
06	270 42.7	N14 59.3	121 39.0	14.9	S 3 18.0	9.3	54.4
07	285 42.7	15 00.0	136 12.9	14.8	3 27.3	9.3	54.4
08	300 42.8	00.8	150 46.7	14.9	3 36.6	9.3	54.4
F 09	315 42.9 ..	01.5	165 20.6	14.8	3 45.8	9.3	54.5
R 10	330 43.0	02.3	179 54.4	14.7	3 55.1	9.2	54.5
I 11	345 43.1	03.1	194 28.1	14.8	4 04.3	9.2	54.5
D 12	0 43.1	N15 03.8	209 01.9	14.7	S 4 13.5	9.3	54.5
A 13	15 43.2	04.6	223 35.6	14.7	4 22.8	9.1	54.5
Y 14	30 43.3	05.3	238 09.3	14.6	4 31.9	9.2	54.5
15	45 43.4 ..	06.1	252 42.9	14.7	4 41.1	9.2	54.5
16	60 43.4	06.8	267 16.6	14.6	4 50.3	9.1	54.5
17	75 43.5	07.6	281 50.2	14.6	4 59.4	9.2	54.6
18	90 43.6	N15 08.3	296 23.8	14.5	S 5 08.6	9.1	54.6
19	105 43.7	09.1	310 57.3	14.5	5 17.7	9.1	54.6
20	120 43.7	09.9	325 30.8	14.5	5 26.8	9.1	54.6
21	135 43.8 ..	10.6	340 04.3	14.5	5 35.9	9.0	54.6
22	150 43.9	11.4	354 37.8	14.4	5 44.9	9.1	54.6
23	165 44.0	12.1	9 11.2	14.4	5 54.0	9.0	54.6
2 00	180 44.0	N15 12.9	23 44.6	14.4	S 6 03.0	9.0	54.6
01	195 44.1	13.6	38 18.0	14.3	6 12.0	9.0	54.7
02	210 44.2	14.4	52 51.3	14.3	6 21.0	9.0	54.7
03	225 44.3 ..	15.1	67 24.6	14.2	6 30.0	8.9	54.7
04	240 44.3	15.9	81 57.8	14.3	6 38.9	8.9	54.7
05	255 44.4	16.6	96 31.1	14.2	6 47.8	8.9	54.7
06	270 44.5	N15 17.4	111 04.3	14.1	S 6 56.7	8.9	54.7
S 07	285 44.5	18.1	125 37.4	14.1	7 05.6	8.8	54.7
A 08	300 44.6	18.9	140 10.5	14.1	7 14.4	8.9	54.8
T 09	315 44.7 ..	19.6	154 43.6	14.1	7 23.3	8.7	54.8
U 10	330 44.8	20.4	169 16.7	14.0	7 32.0	8.8	54.8
R 11	345 44.8	21.1	183 49.7	13.9	7 40.8	8.7	54.8
D 12	0 44.9	N15 21.8	198 22.6	14.0	S 7 49.5	8.8	54.8
A 13	15 45.0	22.6	212 55.6	13.9	7 58.3	8.6	54.8
Y 14	30 45.0	23.3	227 28.5	13.8	8 06.9	8.6	54.9
15	45 45.1 ..	24.1	242 01.3	13.8	8 15.6	8.6	54.9
16	60 45.2	24.8	256 34.1	13.8	8 24.2	8.6	54.9
17	75 45.3	25.6	271 06.9	13.7	8 32.8	8.5	54.9
18	90 45.4	N15 26.3	285 39.6	13.7	S 8 41.3	8.6	54.9
19	105 45.4	27.1	300 12.3	13.7	8 49.9	8.4	54.9
20	120 45.5	27.8	314 45.0	13.6	8 58.3	8.5	54.9
21	135 45.5 ..	28.5	329 17.6	13.5	9 06.8	8.4	55.0
22	150 45.6	29.3	343 50.1	13.5	9 15.2	8.4	55.0
23	165 45.7	30.0	358 22.6	13.5	9 23.6	8.3	55.0
3 00	180 45.7	N15 30.8	12 55.1	13.4	S 9 31.9	8.4	55.0
01	195 45.8	31.5	27 27.5	13.4	9 40.3	8.2	55.0
02	210 45.9	32.2	41 59.9	13.4	9 48.5	8.3	55.0
03	225 45.9 ..	33.0	56 32.3	13.3	9 56.8	8.2	55.1
04	240 46.0	33.7	71 04.6	13.2	10 05.0	8.1	55.1
05	255 46.1	34.5	85 36.8	13.2	10 13.1	8.1	55.1
06	270 46.1	N15 35.2	100 09.0	13.2	S10 21.2	8.1	55.1
07	285 46.2	35.9	114 41.2	13.1	10 29.3	8.0	55.1
08	300 46.3	36.7	129 13.3	13.1	10 37.3	8.0	55.2
S 09	315 46.3 ..	37.4	143 45.4	13.0	10 45.3	7.9	55.2
U 10	330 46.4	38.1	158 17.4	13.0	10 53.2	7.9	55.2
N 11	345 46.5	38.9	172 49.4	12.9	11 01.1	7.9	55.2
D 12	0 46.5	N15 39.6	187 21.3	12.9	S11 09.0	7.8	55.2
A 13	15 46.6	40.4	201 53.2	12.8	11 16.8	7.8	55.2
Y 14	30 46.7	41.1	216 25.0	12.8	11 24.6	7.7	55.3
15	45 46.7 ..	41.8	230 56.8	12.7	11 32.3	7.6	55.3
16	60 46.8	42.6	245 28.5	12.7	11 39.9	7.7	55.3
17	75 46.9	43.3	260 00.2	12.6	11 47.6	7.5	55.3
18	90 46.9	N15 44.0	274 31.8	12.6	S11 55.1	7.5	55.3
19	105 47.0	44.8	289 03.4	12.6	12 02.6	7.5	55.4
20	120 47.1	45.5	303 35.0	12.5	12 10.1	7.4	55.4
21	135 47.1 ..	46.2	318 06.5	12.4	12 17.5	7.4	55.4
22	150 47.2	47.0	332 37.9	12.4	12 24.9	7.3	55.4
23	165 47.2	47.7	347 09.3	12.3	S12 32.2	7.2	55.4
	SD 15.9	d 0.7	SD 14.8		14.9		15.0

Twilight / Sunrise / Moonrise

Lat.	Naut.	Civil	Sunrise	Moonrise 1	2	3	4
°	h m	h m	h m	h m	h m	h m	h m
N 72	////	////	01 47	17 17	18 55	20 36	22 24
N 70	////	////	02 27	17 10	18 40	20 13	21 48
68	////	01 00	02 54	17 04	18 29	19 56	21 23
66	////	01 51	03 15	16 59	18 20	19 42	21 03
64	////	02 22	03 31	16 55	18 12	19 30	20 48
62	00 53	02 45	03 45	16 51	18 05	19 20	20 35
60	01 39	03 03	03 56	16 48	18 00	19 12	20 24
N 58	02 07	03 18	04 06	16 45	17 55	19 05	20 14
56	02 29	03 30	04 15	16 42	17 50	18 58	20 06
54	02 45	03 41	04 22	16 40	17 46	18 53	19 59
52	03 00	03 50	04 29	16 38	17 42	18 47	19 52
50	03 12	03 59	04 35	16 36	17 39	18 43	19 46
45	03 36	04 16	04 49	16 32	17 32	18 33	19 33
N 40	03 54	04 30	04 59	16 29	17 26	18 24	19 23
35	04 09	04 42	05 09	16 26	17 21	18 17	19 14
30	04 21	04 51	05 17	16 23	17 17	18 11	19 06
20	04 40	05 07	05 31	16 19	17 09	18 00	18 52
N 10	04 55	05 21	05 42	16 15	17 02	17 51	18 41
0	05 07	05 32	05 54	16 12	16 56	17 42	18 30
S 10	05 18	05 43	06 05	16 08	16 50	17 33	18 19
20	05 27	05 53	06 16	16 04	16 43	17 24	18 07
30	05 36	06 05	06 29	16 00	16 35	17 13	17 54
35	05 41	06 11	06 37	15 58	16 31	17 07	17 46
40	05 45	06 17	06 45	15 55	16 26	17 00	17 38
45	05 50	06 25	06 55	15 52	16 21	16 52	17 27
S 50	05 55	06 33	07 07	15 48	16 14	16 43	17 15
52	05 57	06 37	07 13	15 46	16 11	16 38	17 10
54	05 59	06 41	07 19	15 45	16 08	16 33	17 03
56	06 02	06 46	07 26	15 43	16 04	16 28	16 57
58	06 04	06 51	07 34	15 40	16 00	16 22	16 49
S 60	06 07	06 57	07 42	15 38	15 55	16 15	16 40

Sunset / Twilight / Moonset

Lat.	Sunset	Civil	Naut.	Moonset 1	2	3	4
°	h m	h m	h m	h m	h m	h m	h m
N 72	22 15	////	////	03 12	03 07	03 02	02 56
N 70	21 31	////	////	03 16	03 16	03 17	03 20
68	21 03	23 07	////	03 19	03 24	03 30	03 38
66	20 42	22 08	////	03 22	03 30	03 40	03 53
64	20 25	21 35	////	03 24	03 36	03 49	04 06
62	20 11	21 12	23 13	03 26	03 40	03 57	04 16
60	19 59	20 54	22 20	03 28	03 45	04 03	04 25
N 58	19 49	20 38	21 50	03 30	03 48	04 09	04 33
56	19 41	20 26	21 28	03 31	03 51	04 14	04 40
54	19 33	20 15	21 11	03 32	03 54	04 19	04 46
52	19 26	20 05	20 56	03 34	03 57	04 23	04 52
50	19 20	19 57	20 44	03 35	04 00	04 27	04 57
45	19 06	19 39	20 19	03 37	04 05	04 35	05 08
N 40	18 55	19 25	20 01	03 39	04 09	04 42	05 17
35	18 46	19 13	19 46	03 41	04 13	04 48	05 25
30	18 38	19 03	19 34	03 42	04 17	04 53	05 32
20	18 24	18 47	19 14	03 45	04 23	05 02	05 44
N 10	18 12	18 34	18 59	03 47	04 28	05 10	05 55
0	18 00	18 22	18 47	03 49	04 33	05 18	06 05
S 10	17 49	18 11	18 36	03 51	04 38	05 25	06 14
20	17 38	18 00	18 27	03 54	04 43	05 33	06 25
30	17 24	17 49	18 18	03 56	04 49	05 43	06 37
35	17 17	17 43	18 13	03 58	04 52	05 48	06 44
40	17 08	17 36	18 08	03 59	04 56	05 54	06 52
45	16 58	17 29	18 04	04 01	05 01	06 01	07 02
S 50	16 46	17 20	17 58	04 04	05 06	06 09	07 13
52	16 40	17 16	17 56	04 05	05 09	06 13	07 18
54	16 34	17 12	17 54	04 06	05 12	06 18	07 24
56	16 27	17 07	17 52	04 07	05 15	06 23	07 31
58	16 19	17 02	17 49	04 09	05 18	06 28	07 38
S 60	16 11	16 56	17 46	04 10	05 22	06 34	07 46

SUN / MOON

Day	SUN Eqn. of Time 00h	SUN Eqn. of Time 12h	SUN Mer. Pass.	MOON Mer. Pass. Upper	MOON Mer. Pass. Lower	Age	Phase
d	m s	m s	h m	h m	h m	d	%
1	02 49	02 52	11 57	22 22	10 00	13	93
2	02 56	02 59	11 57	23 07	10 44	14	97
3	03 03	03 06	11 57	23 53	11 30	15	100

UT	ARIES GHA	VENUS −4.2 GHA	Dec	MARS +1.4 GHA	Dec	JUPITER −2.1 GHA	Dec	SATURN +0.1 GHA	Dec	STARS Name	SHA	Dec
4 00	221 33.9	136 26.5	N25 49.3	169 45.3	N19 03.1	85 15.5	N17 37.7	340 08.9	S18 36.6	Acamar	315 17.9	S40 14.8
01	236 36.3	151 25.8	49.4	184 46.0	03.6	100 17.8	37.7	355 11.5	36.5	Achernar	335 26.5	S57 09.6
02	251 38.8	166 25.2	49.6	199 46.6	04.1	115 20.0	37.6	10 14.2	36.5	Acrux	173 07.1	S63 11.3
03	266 41.3	181 24.6 ..	49.8	214 47.2 ..	04.5	130 22.3 ..	37.6	25 16.8 ..	36.5	Adhara	255 11.7	S29 00.0
04	281 43.7	196 24.0	50.0	229 47.9	05.0	145 24.6	37.5	40 19.5	36.4	Aldebaran	290 48.2	N16 32.1
05	296 46.2	211 23.3	50.1	244 48.5	05.4	160 26.9	37.5	55 22.1	36.4			
06	311 48.7	226 22.7	N25 50.3	259 49.2	N19 05.9	175 29.1	N17 37.4	70 24.7	S18 36.4	Alioth	166 19.2	N55 52.7
07	326 51.1	241 22.1	50.5	274 49.8	06.4	190 31.4	37.3	85 27.4	36.3	Alkaid	152 57.5	N49 14.3
M 08	341 53.6	256 21.4	50.6	289 50.5	06.8	205 33.7	37.3	100 30.0	36.3	Al Na'ir	27 42.4	S46 52.9
O 09	356 56.1	271 20.8 ..	50.8	304 51.1 ..	07.3	220 36.0 ..	37.2	115 32.7 ..	36.3	Alnilam	275 45.3	S 1 11.8
N 10	11 58.5	286 20.2	50.9	319 51.7	07.7	235 38.2	37.2	130 35.3	36.2	Alphard	217 54.8	S 8 43.8
D 11	27 01.0	301 19.5	51.1	334 52.4	08.2	250 40.5	37.1	145 37.9	36.2			
A 12	42 03.4	316 18.9	N25 51.3	349 53.0	N19 08.7	265 42.8	N17 37.0	160 40.6	S18 36.2	Alphecca	126 09.6	N26 39.8
Y 13	57 05.9	331 18.3	51.4	4 53.7	09.1	280 45.1	37.0	175 43.2	36.1	Alpheratz	357 42.4	N29 10.3
14	72 08.4	346 17.7	51.6	19 54.3	09.6	295 47.3	36.9	190 45.9	36.1	Altair	62 06.9	N 8 54.6
15	87 10.8	1 17.0 ..	51.7	34 54.9 ..	10.0	310 49.6 ..	36.9	205 48.5 ..	36.1	Ankaa	353 14.9	S42 13.3
16	102 13.3	16 16.4	51.9	49 55.6	10.5	325 51.9	36.8	220 51.1	36.0	Antares	112 24.4	S26 27.8
17	117 15.8	31 15.8	52.1	64 56.2	11.0	340 54.1	36.8	235 53.8	36.0			
18	132 18.2	46 15.2	N25 52.2	79 56.9	N19 11.4	355 56.4	N17 36.7	250 56.4	S18 36.0	Arcturus	145 54.3	N19 06.2
19	147 20.7	61 14.5	52.4	94 57.5	11.9	10 58.7	36.6	265 59.1	35.9	Atria	107 24.5	S69 03.0
20	162 23.2	76 13.9	52.5	109 58.1	12.3	26 01.0	36.6	281 01.7	35.9	Avior	234 17.5	S59 34.0
21	177 25.6	91 13.3 ..	52.7	124 58.8 ..	12.8	41 03.2 ..	36.5	296 04.3 ..	35.9	Bellatrix	278 30.9	N 6 21.5
22	192 28.1	106 12.6	52.8	139 59.4	13.2	56 05.5	36.5	311 07.0	35.8	Betelgeuse	271 00.2	N 7 24.3
23	207 30.6	121 12.0	53.0	155 00.1	13.7	71 07.8	36.4	326 09.6	35.8			
5 00	222 33.0	136 11.4	N25 53.1	170 00.7	N19 14.2	86 10.0	N17 36.3	341 12.3	S18 35.8	Canopus	263 55.9	S52 42.7
01	237 35.5	151 10.8	53.2	185 01.3	14.6	101 12.3	36.3	356 14.9	35.7	Capella	280 33.0	N46 00.6
02	252 37.9	166 10.1	53.4	200 02.0	15.1	116 14.6	36.2	11 17.5	35.7	Deneb	49 30.5	N45 20.0
03	267 40.4	181 09.5 ..	53.5	215 02.6 ..	15.5	131 16.9 ..	36.2	26 20.2 ..	35.7	Denebola	182 32.2	N14 29.1
04	282 42.9	196 08.9	53.7	230 03.2	16.0	146 19.1	36.1	41 22.8	35.6	Diphda	348 54.9	S17 54.2
05	297 45.3	211 08.3	53.8	245 03.9	16.4	161 21.4	36.0	56 25.5	35.6			
06	312 47.8	226 07.6	N25 54.0	260 04.5	N19 16.9	176 23.7	N17 36.0	71 28.1	S18 35.6	Dubhe	193 50.0	N61 40.2
07	327 50.3	241 07.0	54.1	275 05.2	17.3	191 25.9	35.9	86 30.7	35.5	Elnath	278 11.3	N28 37.0
T 08	342 52.7	256 06.4	54.2	290 05.8	17.8	206 28.2	35.9	101 33.4	35.5	Eltanin	90 45.2	N51 29.2
U 09	357 55.2	271 05.8 ..	54.4	305 06.4 ..	18.3	221 30.5 ..	35.8	116 36.0 ..	35.5	Enif	33 45.9	N 9 56.7
E 10	12 57.7	286 05.1	54.5	320 07.1	18.7	236 32.7	35.7	131 38.7	35.4	Fomalhaut	15 22.8	S29 32.3
S 11	28 00.1	301 04.5	54.6	335 07.7	19.2	251 35.0	35.7	146 41.3	35.4			
D 12	43 02.6	316 03.9	N25 54.8	350 08.4	N19 19.6	266 37.3	N17 35.6	161 44.0	S18 35.4	Gacrux	171 58.9	S57 12.1
A 13	58 05.1	331 03.3	54.9	5 09.0	20.1	281 39.5	35.6	176 46.6	35.3	Gienah	175 50.7	S17 37.8
Y 14	73 07.5	346 02.7	55.0	20 09.6	20.5	296 41.8	35.5	191 49.2	35.3	Hadar	148 45.3	S60 26.8
15	88 10.0	1 02.0 ..	55.2	35 10.3 ..	21.0	311 44.1 ..	35.4	206 51.9 ..	35.3	Hamal	327 59.6	N23 31.9
16	103 12.4	16 01.4	55.3	50 10.9	21.4	326 46.3	35.4	221 54.5	35.2	Kaus Aust.	83 41.9	S34 22.3
17	118 14.9	31 00.8	55.4	65 11.5	21.9	341 48.6	35.3	236 57.2	35.2			
18	133 17.4	46 00.2	N25 55.5	80 12.2	N19 22.3	356 50.9	N17 35.3	251 59.8	S18 35.2	Kochab	137 19.1	N74 05.7
19	148 19.8	60 59.5	55.7	95 12.8	22.8	11 53.1	35.2	267 02.4	35.1	Markab	13 37.2	N15 17.2
20	163 22.3	75 58.9	55.8	110 13.5	23.2	26 55.4	35.1	282 05.1	35.1	Menkar	314 14.1	N 4 08.7
21	178 24.8	90 58.3 ..	55.9	125 14.1 ..	23.7	41 57.7 ..	35.1	297 07.7 ..	35.1	Menkent	148 05.6	S36 26.7
22	193 27.2	105 57.7	56.0	140 14.7	24.1	56 59.9	35.0	312 10.4	35.0	Miaplacidus	221 39.2	S69 47.3
23	208 29.7	120 57.1	56.1	155 15.4	24.6	72 02.2	35.0	327 13.0	35.0			
6 00	223 32.2	135 56.4	N25 56.3	170 16.0	N19 25.0	87 04.4	N17 34.9	342 15.7	S18 35.0	Mirfak	308 39.0	N49 54.7
01	238 34.6	150 55.8	56.4	185 16.7	25.5	102 06.7	34.8	357 18.3	34.9	Nunki	75 56.6	S26 16.4
02	253 37.1	165 55.2	56.5	200 17.3	25.9	117 09.0	34.8	12 20.9	34.9	Peacock	53 17.2	S56 40.7
03	268 39.5	180 54.6 ..	56.6	215 17.9 ..	26.3	132 11.2 ..	34.7	27 23.6 ..	34.9	Pollux	243 26.4	N27 59.2
04	283 42.0	195 54.0	56.7	230 18.6	26.8	147 13.5	34.6	42 26.2	34.8	Procyon	244 58.5	N 5 10.9
05	298 44.5	210 53.3	56.8	245 19.2	27.2	162 15.8	34.6	57 28.9	34.8			
06	313 46.9	225 52.7	N25 56.9	260 19.8	N19 27.7	177 18.0	N17 34.5	72 31.5	S18 34.8	Rasalhague	96 05.0	N12 33.0
W 07	328 49.4	240 52.1	57.1	275 20.5	28.1	192 20.3	34.5	87 34.2	34.7	Regulus	207 42.1	N11 53.4
E 08	343 51.9	255 51.5	57.2	290 21.1	28.6	207 22.5	34.4	102 36.8	34.7	Rigel	281 11.1	S 8 11.4
D 09	358 54.3	270 50.9 ..	57.3	305 21.7 ..	29.0	222 24.8 ..	34.3	117 39.4 ..	34.6	Rigil Kent.	139 49.2	S60 53.8
N 10	13 56.8	285 50.3	57.4	320 22.4	29.5	237 27.1	34.3	132 42.1	34.6	Sabik	102 10.8	S15 44.5
E 11	28 59.3	300 49.6	57.5	335 23.0	29.9	252 29.3	34.2	147 44.7	34.6			
S 12	44 01.7	315 49.0	N25 57.6	350 23.7	N19 30.4	267 31.6	N17 34.1	162 47.4	S18 34.5	Schedar	349 39.4	N56 37.0
D 13	59 04.2	330 48.4	57.7	5 24.3	30.8	282 33.8	34.1	177 50.0	34.5	Shaula	96 19.9	S37 06.6
A 14	74 06.7	345 47.8	57.8	20 24.9	31.2	297 36.1	34.0	192 52.7	34.5	Sirius	258 32.8	S16 44.6
Y 15	89 09.1	0 47.2 ..	57.9	35 25.6 ..	31.7	312 38.4 ..	34.0	207 55.3 ..	34.4	Spica	158 29.6	S11 14.5
16	104 11.6	15 46.6	58.0	50 26.2	32.1	327 40.6	33.9	222 57.9	34.4	Suhail	222 51.5	S43 30.1
17	119 14.0	30 45.9	58.1	65 26.8	32.6	342 42.9	33.8	238 00.6	34.4			
18	134 16.5	45 45.3	N25 58.2	80 27.5	N19 33.0	357 45.1	N17 33.8	253 03.2	S18 34.3	Vega	80 37.8	N38 47.8
19	149 19.0	60 44.7	58.3	95 28.1	33.5	12 47.4	33.7	268 05.9	34.3	Zuben'ubi	137 03.7	S16 06.3
20	164 21.4	75 44.1	58.4	110 28.7	33.9	27 49.7	33.7	283 08.5	34.3		SHA	Mer.Pass.
21	179 23.9	90 43.5 ..	58.5	125 29.4 ..	34.3	42 51.9 ..	33.6	298 11.2 ..	34.2		° '	h m
22	194 26.4	105 42.9	58.6	140 30.0	34.8	57 54.2	33.5	313 13.8	34.2	Venus	273 38.4	14 56
23	209 28.8	120 42.3	58.7	155 30.7	35.2	72 56.4	33.5	328 16.5	34.2	Mars	307 27.7	12 39
Mer.Pass.	h m 9 08.3	v −0.6	d 0.1	v 0.6	d 0.5	v 2.3	d 0.1	v 2.6	d 0.0	Jupiter	223 37.0	18 13
										Saturn	118 39.2	1 15

UT	SUN GHA	SUN Dec	MOON GHA	v	MOON Dec	d	HP
d h	° ′	° ′	° ′	′	° ′	′	′
4 00	180 47.3	N15 48.4	1 40.6	12.3	S12 39.4	7.2	55.4
01	195 47.4	49.1	16 11.9	12.2	12 46.6	7.1	55.5
02	210 47.4	49.9	30 43.1	12.2	12 53.7	7.1	55.5
03	225 47.5	.. 50.6	45 14.3	12.1	13 00.8	7.1	55.5
04	240 47.6	51.3	59 45.4	12.1	13 07.9	6.9	55.5
05	255 47.6	52.1	74 16.5	12.1	13 14.8	6.9	55.5
06	270 47.7	N15 52.8	88 47.6	11.9	S13 21.7	6.9	55.6
07	285 47.7	53.5	103 18.5	12.0	13 28.6	6.8	55.6
08	300 47.8	54.2	117 49.5	11.8	13 35.4	6.7	55.6
09	315 47.9	.. 55.0	132 20.3	11.9	13 42.1	6.6	55.6
10	330 47.9	55.7	146 51.2	11.7	13 48.7	6.6	55.6
11	345 48.0	56.4	161 21.9	11.7	13 55.3	6.6	55.7
12	0 48.0	N15 57.1	175 52.6	11.7	S14 01.9	6.5	55.7
13	15 48.1	57.9	190 23.3	11.6	14 08.4	6.4	55.7
14	30 48.2	58.6	204 53.9	11.6	14 14.8	6.3	55.7
15	45 48.2	15 59.3	219 24.5	11.5	14 21.1	6.3	55.7
16	60 48.3	16 00.0	233 55.0	11.5	14 27.4	6.2	55.8
17	75 48.3	00.8	248 25.5	11.4	14 33.6	6.1	55.8
18	90 48.4	N16 01.5	262 55.9	11.3	S14 39.7	6.1	55.8
19	105 48.5	02.2	277 26.2	11.3	14 45.8	6.0	55.8
20	120 48.5	02.9	291 56.5	11.3	14 51.8	5.9	55.8
21	135 48.6	.. 03.6	306 26.8	11.2	14 57.7	5.9	55.9
22	150 48.6	04.4	320 57.0	11.1	15 03.6	5.8	55.9
23	165 48.7	05.1	335 27.1	11.1	15 09.4	5.7	55.9
5 00	180 48.7	N16 05.8	349 57.2	11.1	S15 15.1	5.6	55.9
01	195 48.8	06.5	4 27.3	11.0	15 20.7	5.6	55.9
02	210 48.8	07.2	18 57.3	10.9	15 26.3	5.5	56.0
03	225 48.9	.. 07.9	33 27.2	10.9	15 31.8	5.4	56.0
04	240 49.0	08.7	47 57.1	10.9	15 37.2	5.4	56.0
05	255 49.0	09.4	62 27.0	10.7	15 42.6	5.2	56.0
06	270 49.1	N16 10.1	76 56.7	10.8	S15 47.8	5.2	56.0
07	285 49.1	10.8	91 26.5	10.7	15 53.0	5.1	56.1
08	300 49.2	11.5	105 56.2	10.6	15 58.1	5.0	56.1
09	315 49.2	.. 12.2	120 25.8	10.6	16 03.1	5.0	56.1
10	330 49.3	13.0	134 55.4	10.5	16 08.1	4.9	56.1
11	345 49.3	13.7	149 24.9	10.5	16 13.0	4.7	56.1
12	0 49.4	N16 14.4	163 54.4	10.5	S16 17.7	4.8	56.2
13	15 49.5	15.1	178 23.9	10.4	16 22.5	4.6	56.2
14	30 49.5	15.8	192 53.3	10.3	16 27.1	4.5	56.2
15	45 49.6	.. 16.5	207 22.6	10.3	16 31.6	4.5	56.2
16	60 49.6	17.2	221 51.9	10.3	16 36.1	4.3	56.2
17	75 49.7	17.9	236 21.2	10.2	16 40.4	4.3	56.3
18	90 49.7	N16 18.7	250 50.4	10.1	S16 44.7	4.2	56.3
19	105 49.8	19.4	265 19.5	10.1	16 48.9	4.2	56.3
20	120 49.8	20.1	279 48.6	10.1	16 53.1	4.0	56.3
21	135 49.9	.. 20.8	294 17.7	10.0	16 57.1	3.9	56.3
22	150 49.9	21.5	308 46.7	10.0	17 01.0	3.9	56.4
23	165 50.0	22.2	323 15.7	9.9	17 04.9	3.7	56.4
6 00	180 50.0	N16 22.9	337 44.6	9.9	S17 08.6	3.7	56.4
01	195 50.1	23.6	352 13.5	9.8	17 12.3	3.6	56.4
02	210 50.1	24.3	6 42.3	9.8	17 15.9	3.5	56.4
03	225 50.2	.. 25.0	21 11.1	9.7	17 19.4	3.4	56.5
04	240 50.2	25.7	35 39.8	9.7	17 22.8	3.3	56.5
05	255 50.3	26.4	50 08.5	9.7	17 26.1	3.2	56.5
06	270 50.3	N16 27.1	64 37.2	9.6	S17 29.3	3.1	56.5
07	285 50.4	27.9	79 05.8	9.6	17 32.4	3.1	56.5
08	300 50.4	28.6	93 34.4	9.5	17 35.5	2.9	56.6
09	315 50.5	.. 29.3	108 02.9	9.5	17 38.4	2.8	56.6
10	330 50.5	30.0	122 31.4	9.5	17 41.2	2.8	56.6
11	345 50.6	30.7	136 59.9	9.4	17 44.0	2.6	56.6
12	0 50.6	N16 31.4	151 28.3	9.4	S17 46.6	2.6	56.6
13	15 50.7	32.1	165 56.7	9.3	17 49.2	2.5	56.7
14	30 50.7	32.8	180 25.0	9.3	17 51.7	2.3	56.7
15	45 50.8	.. 33.5	194 53.3	9.2	17 54.0	2.3	56.7
16	60 50.8	34.2	209 21.5	9.3	17 56.3	2.1	56.7
17	75 50.9	34.9	223 49.8	9.1	17 58.4	2.1	56.8
18	90 50.9	N16 35.6	238 17.9	9.2	S18 00.5	2.0	56.8
19	105 50.9	36.3	252 46.1	9.1	18 02.5	1.8	56.8
20	120 51.0	37.0	267 14.2	9.1	18 04.3	1.8	56.8
21	135 51.0	.. 37.7	281 42.3	9.0	18 06.1	1.7	56.8
22	150 51.1	38.4	296 10.3	9.1	18 07.8	1.5	56.9
23	165 51.1	39.1	310 38.4	8.9	S18 09.3	1.5	56.9
	SD 15.9	d 0.7	SD 15.2		15.3		15.4

Left margin day labels: M O N D A Y (4); T U E S D A Y (5); W E D N E S D A Y (6)

Twilight / Sunrise / Moonrise

Lat.	Twilight Naut.	Twilight Civil	Sunrise	Moonrise 4	5	6	7
°	h m	h m	h m	h m	h m	h m	h m
N 72	////	////	01 18	22 24	24 23	00 23	■
N 70	////	////	02 09	21 48	23 21	24 43	00 43
68	////	////	02 40	21 23	22 46	23 59	24 54
66	////	01 31	03 03	21 03	22 21	23 30	24 25
64	////	02 08	03 21	20 48	22 02	23 08	24 03
62	////	02 33	03 36	20 35	21 46	22 51	23 46
60	01 21	02 53	03 48	20 24	21 33	22 36	23 31
N 58	01 54	03 09	03 59	20 14	21 22	22 24	23 19
56	02 18	03 22	04 08	20 06	21 12	22 13	23 08
54	02 37	03 34	04 16	19 59	21 03	22 04	22 58
52	02 52	03 44	04 24	19 52	20 55	21 55	22 50
50	03 05	03 53	04 30	19 46	20 48	21 48	22 42
45	03 31	04 11	04 44	19 33	20 33	21 31	22 26
N 40	03 50	04 26	04 56	19 23	20 21	21 18	22 13
35	04 05	04 38	05 06	19 14	20 11	21 07	22 01
30	04 18	04 49	05 14	19 06	20 02	20 57	21 51
20	04 38	05 06	05 29	18 52	19 46	20 40	21 34
N 10	04 53	05 20	05 41	18 41	19 33	20 26	21 19
0	05 07	05 32	05 53	18 30	19 20	20 12	21 06
S 10	05 18	05 43	06 05	18 19	19 07	19 58	20 52
20	05 28	05 54	06 17	18 07	18 54	19 44	20 37
30	05 38	06 06	06 31	17 54	18 38	19 27	20 20
35	05 43	06 13	06 39	17 46	18 30	19 17	20 10
40	05 48	06 20	06 48	17 38	18 19	19 06	19 59
45	05 53	06 28	06 59	17 27	18 08	18 53	19 46
S 50	05 59	06 37	07 12	17 15	17 53	18 38	19 30
52	06 01	06 42	07 18	17 10	17 47	18 30	19 22
54	06 04	06 46	07 25	17 03	17 39	18 22	19 14
56	06 07	06 51	07 32	16 57	17 31	18 13	19 04
58	06 09	06 57	07 40	16 49	17 22	18 03	18 53
S 60	06 13	07 03	07 50	16 40	17 11	17 51	18 41

Sunset / Twilight / Moonset

Lat.	Sunset	Twilight Civil	Twilight Naut.	Moonset 4	5	6	7
°	h m	h m	h m	h m	h m	h m	h m
N 72	22 46	////	////	02 56	02 48	02 35	■
N 70	21 50	////	////	03 20	03 25	03 37	04 04
68	21 17	////	////	03 38	03 51	04 12	04 48
66	20 53	22 29	////	03 53	04 11	04 38	05 17
64	20 35	21 50	////	04 06	04 27	04 58	05 39
62	20 20	21 23	////	04 16	04 41	05 14	05 57
60	20 07	21 03	22 38	04 25	04 52	05 27	06 12
N 58	19 56	20 46	22 03	04 33	05 02	05 39	06 24
56	19 47	20 33	21 38	04 40	05 11	05 49	06 35
54	19 38	20 21	21 19	04 46	05 19	05 58	06 45
52	19 31	20 11	21 03	04 52	05 26	06 06	06 53
50	19 24	20 02	20 50	04 57	05 32	06 13	07 01
45	19 10	19 43	20 24	05 08	05 45	06 28	07 17
N 40	18 58	19 28	20 04	05 17	05 57	06 41	07 30
35	18 48	19 16	19 49	05 25	06 06	06 52	07 42
30	18 40	19 05	19 36	05 32	06 14	07 01	07 52
20	18 25	18 48	19 15	05 44	06 29	07 17	08 09
N 10	18 12	18 34	19 00	05 55	06 42	07 31	08 24
0	18 00	18 22	18 47	06 05	06 54	07 45	08 38
S 10	17 48	18 10	18 35	06 14	07 05	07 58	08 51
20	17 36	17 59	18 25	06 25	07 18	08 12	09 06
30	17 22	17 47	18 15	06 37	07 33	08 28	09 23
35	17 14	17 40	18 10	06 44	07 41	08 38	09 33
40	17 05	17 33	18 05	06 52	07 51	08 49	09 44
45	16 54	17 25	18 00	07 02	08 02	09 01	09 58
S 50	16 41	17 15	17 54	07 13	08 16	09 17	10 14
52	16 35	17 11	17 51	07 18	08 22	09 24	10 21
54	16 28	17 07	17 49	07 24	08 29	09 32	10 30
56	16 21	17 01	17 46	07 31	08 37	09 41	10 39
58	16 13	16 56	17 43	07 38	08 46	09 51	10 50
S 60	16 03	16 50	17 40	07 46	08 57	10 03	11 02

SUN / MOON

Day	SUN Eqn. of Time 00h	12h	Mer. Pass.	MOON Mer. Pass. Upper	Lower	Age	Phase
d	m s	m s	h m	h m	h m	d	%
4	03 09	03 12	11 57	24 42	12 17	16	100
5	03 15	03 17	11 57	00 42	13 07	17	98
6	03 20	03 22	11 57	01 32	13 58	18	94

UT	ARIES GHA	VENUS −4.2 GHA	VENUS Dec	MARS +1.5 GHA	MARS Dec	JUPITER −2.1 GHA	JUPITER Dec	SATURN +0.1 GHA	SATURN Dec	STARS Name	SHA	Dec
d h	° ′	° ′	° ′	° ′	° ′	° ′	° ′	° ′	° ′		° ′	° ′
7 00	224 31.3	135 41.6 N25 58.8		170 31.3 N19 35.7		87 58.7 N17 33.4		343 19.1 S18 34.1		Acamar	315 17.9	S40 14.8
01	239 33.8	150 41.0	58.8	185 31.9	36.1	103 00.9	33.3	358 21.7	34.1	Achernar	335 26.5	S57 09.5
02	254 36.2	165 40.4	58.9	200 32.6	36.5	118 03.2	33.3	13 24.4	34.1	Acrux	173 07.1	S63 11.3
03	269 38.7	180 39.8 ..	59.0	215 33.2 ..	37.0	133 05.5 ..	33.2	28 27.0 ..	34.0	Adhara	255 11.7	S29 00.0
04	284 41.2	195 39.2	59.1	230 33.8	37.4	148 07.7	33.1	43 29.7	34.0	Aldebaran	290 48.2	N16 32.1
05	299 43.6	210 38.6	59.2	245 34.5	37.9	163 10.0	33.1	58 32.3	34.0			
06	314 46.1	225 38.0 N25 59.3		260 35.1 N19 38.3		178 12.2 N17 33.0		73 35.0 S18 33.9		Alioth	166 19.2	N55 52.7
07	329 48.5	240 37.4	59.4	275 35.7	38.7	193 14.5	33.0	88 37.6	33.9	Alkaid	152 57.5	N49 14.3
08	344 51.0	255 36.7	59.4	290 36.4	39.2	208 16.7	32.9	103 40.2	33.9	Al Na'ir	27 42.3	S46 52.9
09	359 53.5	270 36.1 ..	59.5	305 37.0 ..	39.6	223 19.0 ..	32.8	118 42.9 ..	33.8	Alnilam	275 45.4	S 1 11.8
10	14 55.9	285 35.5	59.6	320 37.6	40.1	238 21.2	32.8	133 45.5	33.8	Alphard	217 54.8	S 8 43.8
11	29 58.4	300 34.9	59.7	335 38.3	40.5	253 23.5	32.7	148 48.2	33.8			
12	45 00.9	315 34.3 N25 59.7		350 38.9 N19 40.9		268 25.7 N17 32.6		163 50.8 S18 33.7		Alphecca	126 09.6	N26 39.9
13	60 03.3	330 33.7	59.8	5 39.5	41.4	283 28.0	32.6	178 53.5	33.7	Alpheratz	357 42.4	N29 10.3
14	75 05.8	345 33.1 25 59.9		20 40.2	41.8	298 30.3	32.5	193 56.1	33.7	Altair	62 06.9	N 8 54.6
15	90 08.3	0 32.5 26 00.0		35 40.8 ..	42.2	313 32.5 ..	32.4	208 58.8 ..	33.6	Ankaa	353 14.8	S42 13.3
16	105 10.7	15 31.9	00.1	50 41.4	42.7	328 34.8	32.4	224 01.4	33.6	Antares	112 24.3	S26 27.8
17	120 13.2	30 31.3	00.1	65 42.1	43.1	343 37.0	32.3	239 04.1	33.6			
18	135 15.7	45 30.6 N26 00.2		80 42.7 N19 43.5		358 39.3 N17 32.2		254 06.7 S18 33.5		Arcturus	145 54.3	N19 06.2
19	150 18.1	60 30.0	00.3	95 43.3	44.0	13 41.5	32.2	269 09.3	33.5	Atria	107 24.5	S69 03.0
20	165 20.6	75 29.4	00.3	110 44.0	44.4	28 43.8	32.1	284 12.0	33.5	Avior	234 17.6	S59 34.0
21	180 23.0	90 28.8 ..	00.4	125 44.6 ..	44.8	43 46.0 ..	32.1	299 14.6 ..	33.4	Bellatrix	278 30.9	N 6 21.5
22	195 25.5	105 28.2	00.5	140 45.2	45.3	58 48.3	32.0	314 17.3	33.4	Betelgeuse	271 00.2	N 7 24.3
23	210 28.0	120 27.6	00.5	155 45.9	45.7	73 50.5	31.9	329 19.9	33.4			
8 00	225 30.4	135 27.0 N26 00.6		170 46.5 N19 46.1		88 52.8 N17 31.9		344 22.6 S18 33.3		Canopus	263 55.9	S52 42.7
01	240 32.9	150 26.4	00.7	185 47.1	46.6	103 55.0	31.8	359 25.2	33.3	Capella	280 33.0	N46 00.6
02	255 35.4	165 25.8	00.7	200 47.8	47.0	118 57.3	31.7	14 27.9	33.2	Deneb	49 30.5	N45 20.0
03	270 37.8	180 25.2 ..	00.8	215 48.4 ..	47.4	133 59.5 ..	31.7	29 30.5 ..	33.2	Denebola	182 32.2	N14 29.1
04	285 40.3	195 24.6	00.8	230 49.0	47.9	149 01.8	31.6	44 33.2	33.2	Diphda	348 54.9	S17 54.2
05	300 42.8	210 24.0	00.9	245 49.7	48.3	164 04.0	31.5	59 35.8	33.1			
06	315 45.2	225 23.4 N26 01.0		260 50.3 N19 48.7		179 06.3 N17 31.5		74 38.4 S18 33.1		Dubhe	193 50.0	N61 40.2
07	330 47.7	240 22.8	01.0	275 50.9	49.2	194 08.5	31.4	89 41.1	33.1	Elnath	278 11.3	N28 37.0
08	345 50.1	255 22.2	01.1	290 51.6	49.6	209 10.8	31.3	104 43.7	33.0	Eltanin	90 45.1	N51 29.2
09	0 52.6	270 21.6 ..	01.1	305 52.2 ..	50.0	224 13.0 ..	31.3	119 46.4 ..	33.0	Enif	33 45.9	N 9 56.7
10	15 55.1	285 21.0	01.2	320 52.8	50.4	239 15.3	31.2	134 49.0	33.0	Fomalhaut	15 22.8	S29 32.3
11	30 57.5	300 20.4	01.2	335 53.5	50.9	254 17.5	31.1	149 51.7	32.9			
12	46 00.0	315 19.8 N26 01.3		350 54.1 N19 51.3		269 19.8 N17 31.1		164 54.3 S18 32.9		Gacrux	171 58.9	S57 12.2
13	61 02.5	330 19.2	01.3	5 54.7	51.7	284 22.0	31.0	179 57.0	32.9	Gienah	175 50.7	S17 37.8
14	76 04.9	345 18.5	01.4	20 55.4	52.2	299 24.3	30.9	194 59.6	32.8	Hadar	148 45.3	S60 26.8
15	91 07.4	0 17.9 ..	01.4	35 56.0 ..	52.6	314 26.5 ..	30.9	210 02.3 ..	32.8	Hamal	327 59.6	N23 31.9
16	106 09.9	15 17.3	01.5	50 56.6	53.0	329 28.7	30.8	225 04.9	32.8	Kaus Aust.	83 41.9	S34 22.3
17	121 12.3	30 16.7	01.5	65 57.3	53.4	344 31.0	30.7	240 07.6	32.7			
18	136 14.8	45 16.1 N26 01.5		80 57.9 N19 53.9		359 33.2 N17 30.7		255 10.2 S18 32.7		Kochab	137 19.1	N74 05.7
19	151 17.3	60 15.5	01.6	95 58.5	54.3	14 35.5	30.6	270 12.8	32.7	Markab	13 37.2	N15 17.2
20	166 19.7	75 14.9	01.6	110 59.2	54.7	29 37.7	30.5	285 15.5	32.6	Menkar	314 14.0	N 4 08.7
21	181 22.2	90 14.3 ..	01.7	125 59.8 ..	55.1	44 40.0 ..	30.5	300 18.1 ..	32.6	Menkent	148 05.6	S36 26.7
22	196 24.6	105 13.7	01.7	141 00.4	55.6	59 42.2	30.4	315 20.8	32.6	Miaplacidus	221 39.3	S69 47.3
23	211 27.1	120 13.1	01.7	156 01.1	56.0	74 44.5	30.3	330 23.4	32.5			
9 00	226 29.6	135 12.6 N26 01.8		171 01.7 N19 56.4		89 46.7 N17 30.3		345 26.1 S18 32.5		Mirfak	308 39.0	N49 54.7
01	241 32.0	150 12.0	01.8	186 02.3	56.8	104 48.9	30.2	0 28.7	32.5	Nunki	75 56.5	S26 16.4
02	256 34.5	165 11.4	01.9	201 03.0	57.3	119 51.2	30.1	15 31.4	32.4	Peacock	53 17.2	S56 40.7
03	271 37.0	180 10.8 ..	01.9	216 03.6 ..	57.7	134 53.4 ..	30.1	30 34.0 ..	32.4	Pollux	243 26.4	N27 59.2
04	286 39.4	195 10.2	01.9	231 04.2	58.1	149 55.7	30.0	45 36.7	32.4	Procyon	244 58.6	N 5 10.9
05	301 41.9	210 09.6	01.9	246 04.9	58.5	164 57.9	29.9	60 39.3	32.3			
06	316 44.4	225 09.0 N26 02.0		261 05.5 N19 59.0		180 00.2 N17 29.9		75 42.0 S18 32.3		Rasalhague	96 05.0	N12 33.0
07	331 46.8	240 08.4	02.0	276 06.1	59.4	195 02.4	29.8	90 44.6	32.3	Regulus	207 42.1	N11 53.4
08	346 49.3	255 07.8	02.0	291 06.7 19 59.8		210 04.6	29.7	105 47.3	32.2	Rigel	281 11.1	S 8 11.4
09	1 51.8	270 07.2 ..	02.0	306 07.4 20 00.2		225 06.9 ..	29.7	120 49.9 ..	32.2	Rigil Kent.	139 49.2	S60 53.8
10	16 54.2	285 06.6	02.1	321 08.0	00.6	240 09.1	29.6	135 52.6	32.1	Sabik	102 10.8	S15 44.5
11	31 56.7	300 06.0	02.1	336 08.6	01.0	255 11.4	29.5	150 55.2	32.1			
12	46 59.1	315 05.4 N26 02.1		351 09.3 N20 01.5		270 13.6 N17 29.5		165 57.8 S18 32.1		Schedar	349 39.4	N56 37.0
13	62 01.6	330 04.8	02.1	6 09.9	01.9	285 15.9	29.4	181 00.5	32.0	Shaula	96 19.8	S37 06.6
14	77 04.1	345 04.2	02.2	21 10.5	02.3	300 18.1	29.3	196 03.1	32.0	Sirius	258 32.8	S16 44.6
15	92 06.5	0 03.6 ..	02.2	36 11.2 ..	02.7	315 20.3 ..	29.3	211 05.8 ..	32.0	Spica	158 29.6	S11 14.5
16	107 09.0	15 03.0	02.2	51 11.8	03.2	330 22.6	29.2	226 08.4	31.9	Suhail	222 51.5	S43 30.1
17	122 11.5	30 02.4	02.2	66 12.4	03.6	345 24.8	29.1	241 11.1	31.9			
18	137 13.9	45 01.8 N26 02.2		81 13.1 N20 04.0		0 27.1 N17 29.0		256 13.7 S18 31.9		Vega	80 37.8	N38 47.9
19	152 16.4	60 01.3	02.2	96 13.7	04.4	15 29.3	29.0	271 16.4	31.8	Zuben'ubi	137 03.7	S16 06.3
20	167 18.9	75 00.7	02.3	111 14.3	04.8	30 31.5	28.9	286 19.0	31.8		SHA	Mer.Pass.
21	182 21.3	90 00.1 ..	02.3	126 14.9 ..	05.3	45 33.8 ..	28.8	301 21.7 ..	31.8		° ′	h m
22	197 23.8	104 59.5	02.3	141 15.6	05.7	60 36.0	28.8	316 24.3	31.7	Venus	269 56.6	14 59
23	212 26.3	119 58.9	02.3	156 16.2	06.1	75 38.2	28.7	331 27.0	31.7	Mars	305 16.1	12 36
	h m									Jupiter	223 22.3	18 02
Mer.Pass.	8 56.5	v −0.6 d 0.0		v 0.6 d 0.4		v 2.2 d 0.1		v 2.6 d 0.0		Saturn	118 52.1	1 02

UT	SUN GHA	SUN Dec	MOON GHA	MOON v	MOON Dec	MOON d	MOON HP
d h	° ′	° ′	° ′	′	° ′	′	′
7 00	180 51.2	N16 39.8	325 06.3	9.0	S18 10.8	1.4	56.9
01	195 51.2	40.5	339 34.3	8.9	18 12.2	1.2	56.9
02	210 51.3	41.1	354 02.2	8.9	18 13.4	1.2	56.9
03	225 51.3 ..	41.8	8 30.1	8.8	18 14.6	1.1	57.0
04	240 51.4	42.5	22 57.9	8.9	18 15.7	0.9	57.0
05	255 51.4	43.2	37 25.8	8.8	18 16.6	0.9	57.0
06	270 51.4	N16 43.9	51 53.6	8.7	S18 17.5	0.7	57.0
07	285 51.5	44.6	66 21.3	8.8	18 18.2	0.7	57.0
08	300 51.5	45.3	80 49.1	8.7	18 18.9	0.5	57.1
T 09	315 51.6 ..	46.0	95 16.8	8.7	18 19.4	0.4	57.1
H 10	330 51.6	46.7	109 44.5	8.6	18 19.8	0.4	57.1
U 11	345 51.7	47.4	124 12.1	8.7	18 20.2	0.2	57.1
R 12	0 51.7	N16 48.1	138 39.8	8.6	S18 20.4	0.1	57.1
S 13	15 51.7	48.8	153 07.4	8.6	18 20.5	0.0	57.2
D 14	30 51.8	49.5	167 35.0	8.6	18 20.5	0.1	57.2
A 15	45 51.8 ..	50.1	182 02.6	8.5	18 20.4	0.2	57.2
Y 16	60 51.9	50.8	196 30.1	8.5	18 20.2	0.3	57.2
17	75 51.9	51.5	210 57.6	8.6	18 19.9	0.4	57.3
18	90 51.9	N16 52.2	225 25.2	8.4	S18 19.5	0.5	57.3
19	105 52.0	52.9	239 52.6	8.5	18 19.0	0.6	57.3
20	120 52.0	53.6	254 20.1	8.5	18 18.4	0.7	57.3
21	135 52.1 ..	54.3	268 47.6	8.4	18 17.7	0.9	57.3
22	150 52.1	55.0	283 15.0	8.4	18 16.8	0.9	57.4
23	165 52.1	55.6	297 42.4	8.4	18 15.9	1.0	57.4
8 00	180 52.2	N16 56.3	312 09.8	8.4	S18 14.9	1.2	57.4
01	195 52.2	57.0	326 37.2	8.4	18 13.7	1.3	57.4
02	210 52.3	57.7	341 04.6	8.3	18 12.4	1.3	57.4
03	225 52.3 ..	58.4	355 31.9	8.4	18 11.1	1.5	57.5
04	240 52.3	59.1	9 59.3	8.3	18 09.6	1.6	57.5
05	255 52.4	16 59.7	24 26.6	8.3	18 08.0	1.7	57.5
06	270 52.4	N17 00.4	38 53.9	8.3	S18 06.3	1.8	57.5
07	285 52.4	01.1	53 21.2	8.3	18 04.5	1.9	57.5
08	300 52.5	01.8	67 48.5	8.3	18 02.6	2.0	57.6
F 09	315 52.5 ..	02.5	82 15.8	8.3	18 00.6	2.1	57.6
R 10	330 52.6	03.1	96 43.1	8.3	17 58.5	2.2	57.6
I 11	345 52.6	03.8	111 10.4	8.3	17 56.3	2.4	57.6
D 12	0 52.6	N17 04.5	125 37.7	8.2	S17 53.9	2.4	57.6
A 13	15 52.7	05.2	140 04.9	8.3	17 51.5	2.5	57.7
Y 14	30 52.7	05.9	154 32.2	8.2	17 49.0	2.7	57.7
15	45 52.7 ..	06.5	168 59.4	8.3	17 46.3	2.7	57.7
16	60 52.8	07.2	183 26.7	8.2	17 43.6	2.9	57.7
17	75 52.8	07.9	197 53.9	8.2	17 40.7	3.0	57.7
18	90 52.8	N17 08.6	212 21.1	8.3	S17 37.7	3.0	57.8
19	105 52.9	09.2	226 48.4	8.2	17 34.7	3.2	57.8
20	120 52.9	09.9	241 15.6	8.2	17 31.5	3.3	57.8
21	135 52.9 ..	10.6	255 42.8	8.3	17 28.2	3.4	57.8
22	150 53.0	11.3	270 10.1	8.2	17 24.8	3.5	57.8
23	165 53.0	11.9	284 37.3	8.2	17 21.3	3.6	57.9
9 00	180 53.0	N17 12.6	299 04.5	8.3	S17 17.7	3.7	57.9
01	195 53.1	13.3	313 31.8	8.2	17 14.0	3.8	57.9
02	210 53.1	14.0	327 59.0	8.2	17 10.2	3.9	57.9
03	225 53.1 ..	14.6	342 26.2	8.3	17 06.3	4.1	57.9
04	240 53.2	15.3	356 53.5	8.2	17 02.2	4.1	58.0
05	255 53.2	16.0	11 20.7	8.2	16 58.1	4.2	58.0
06	270 53.2	N17 16.6	25 47.9	8.3	S16 53.9	4.3	58.0
07	285 53.3	17.3	40 15.2	8.2	16 49.6	4.5	58.0
08	300 53.3	18.0	54 42.4	8.3	16 45.1	4.5	58.1
S 09	315 53.3 ..	18.6	69 09.7	8.3	16 40.6	4.6	58.1
A 10	330 53.4	19.3	83 37.0	8.2	16 36.0	4.8	58.1
T 11	345 53.4	20.0	98 04.2	8.3	16 31.2	4.8	58.1
U 12	0 53.4	N17 20.6	112 31.5	8.3	S16 26.4	5.0	58.1
R 13	15 53.4	21.3	126 58.8	8.3	16 21.4	5.0	58.2
D 14	30 53.5	22.0	141 26.1	8.3	16 16.4	5.1	58.2
A 15	45 53.5 ..	22.6	155 53.4	8.3	16 11.3	5.3	58.2
Y 16	60 53.5	23.3	170 20.7	8.3	16 06.0	5.3	58.2
17	75 53.6	24.0	184 48.0	8.3	16 00.7	5.4	58.2
18	90 53.6	N17 24.6	199 15.3	8.4	S15 55.3	5.6	58.3
19	105 53.6	25.3	213 42.7	8.3	15 49.7	5.6	58.3
20	120 53.6	26.0	228 10.0	8.4	15 44.1	5.7	58.3
21	135 53.7 ..	26.6	242 37.4	8.3	15 38.4	5.9	58.3
22	150 53.7	27.3	257 04.7	8.4	15 32.5	5.9	58.3
23	165 53.7	28.0	271 32.1	8.4	S15 26.6	6.0	58.4
	SD 15.9	d 0.7	SD 15.6		15.7		15.8

Lat.	Twilight Naut.	Twilight Civil	Sunrise	Moonrise 7	Moonrise 8	Moonrise 9	Moonrise 10
°	h m	h m	h m	h m	h m	h m	h m
N 72	////	////	00 34	■■	■■	03 01	02 49
N 70	////	////	01 49	00 43	01 38	02 04	02 15
68	////	////	02 26	24 54	00 54	01 29	01 51
66	////	01 07	02 51	24 25	00 25	01 05	01 31
64	////	01 53	03 11	24 03	00 03	00 45	01 16
62	////	02 21	03 27	23 46	24 29	00 29	01 03
60	00 59	02 43	03 40	23 31	24 16	00 16	00 52
N 58	01 41	03 01	03 52	23 19	24 05	00 05	00 42
56	02 08	03 15	04 02	23 08	23 55	24 34	00 34
54	02 28	03 27	04 10	22 58	23 46	24 27	00 27
52	02 44	03 38	04 18	22 50	23 38	24 20	00 20
50	02 58	03 47	04 25	22 42	23 31	24 14	00 14
45	03 25	04 07	04 40	22 26	23 16	24 01	00 01
N 40	03 46	04 22	04 52	22 13	23 03	23 50	24 32
35	04 02	04 35	05 03	22 01	22 53	23 40	24 25
30	04 15	04 46	05 12	21 51	22 43	23 32	24 19
20	04 36	05 04	05 27	21 34	22 27	23 18	24 07
N 10	04 53	05 19	05 41	21 19	22 13	23 06	23 57
0	05 06	05 31	05 53	21 06	22 00	22 54	23 48
S 10	05 18	05 43	06 05	20 52	21 47	22 43	23 39
20	05 29	05 55	06 18	20 37	21 33	22 30	23 29
30	05 39	06 08	06 33	20 20	21 17	22 16	23 18
35	05 45	06 15	06 42	20 10	21 07	22 08	23 11
40	05 50	06 23	06 51	19 59	20 57	21 58	23 03
45	05 56	06 31	07 03	19 46	20 44	21 47	22 55
S 50	06 03	06 41	07 16	19 30	20 29	21 34	22 44
52	06 05	06 46	07 23	19 22	20 22	21 28	22 39
54	06 08	06 51	07 30	19 14	20 14	21 21	22 34
56	06 11	06 56	07 38	19 04	20 05	21 13	22 28
58	06 15	07 02	07 46	18 53	19 55	21 04	22 21
S 60	06 18	07 09	07 57	18 41	19 43	20 55	22 13

Lat.	Sunset	Twilight Civil	Twilight Naut.	Moonset 7	Moonset 8	Moonset 9	Moonset 10
°	h m	h m	h m	h m	h m	h m	h m
N 72	□	□	□	■■	■■	05 32	07 38
N 70	22 10	////	////	04 04	05 02	06 29	08 11
68	21 31	////	////	04 48	05 45	07 03	08 35
66	21 05	22 55	////	05 17	06 14	07 27	08 53
64	20 44	22 05	////	05 39	06 36	07 46	09 08
62	20 28	21 35	////	05 57	06 53	08 02	09 20
60	20 14	21 12	23 02	06 12	07 08	08 15	09 30
N 58	20 03	20 55	22 16	06 24	07 20	08 26	09 40
56	19 53	20 40	21 48	06 35	07 31	08 36	09 47
54	19 44	20 27	21 27	06 45	07 40	08 44	09 55
52	19 36	20 16	21 11	06 53	07 49	08 52	10 01
50	19 29	20 07	20 56	07 01	07 56	08 59	10 07
45	19 14	19 47	20 29	07 17	08 12	09 13	10 19
N 40	19 01	19 31	20 08	07 30	08 26	09 25	10 29
35	18 51	19 18	19 52	07 42	08 37	09 36	10 38
30	18 42	19 07	19 38	07 52	08 47	09 45	10 45
20	18 26	18 49	19 17	08 09	09 03	10 00	10 58
N 10	18 13	18 35	19 00	08 24	09 18	10 13	11 09
0	18 00	18 22	18 47	08 38	09 32	10 26	11 20
S 10	17 48	18 09	18 35	08 51	09 45	10 38	11 31
20	17 34	17 57	18 24	09 06	10 00	10 52	11 42
30	17 20	17 45	18 13	09 23	10 16	11 07	11 54
35	17 11	17 38	18 08	09 33	10 26	11 15	12 02
40	17 01	17 30	18 02	09 44	10 37	11 25	12 10
45	16 50	17 21	17 56	09 58	10 50	11 37	12 20
S 50	16 36	17 11	17 50	10 14	11 05	11 51	12 31
52	16 30	17 06	17 47	10 21	11 13	11 58	12 36
54	16 23	17 01	17 44	10 30	11 21	12 05	12 42
56	16 15	16 56	17 41	10 39	11 30	12 13	12 49
58	16 06	16 50	17 37	10 50	11 40	12 22	12 56
S 60	15 56	16 43	17 34	11 02	11 52	12 32	13 05

Day	SUN Eqn. of Time 00h	SUN Eqn. of Time 12h	SUN Mer. Pass.	MOON Mer. Pass. Upper	MOON Mer. Pass. Lower	Age	Phase
d	m s	m s	h m	h m	h m	d	%
7	03 25	03 27	11 57	02 25	14 52	19	88
8	03 29	03 30	11 56	03 19	15 46	20	81
9	03 32	03 34	11 56	04 13	16 40	21	71

UT	ARIES GHA	VENUS −4.2 GHA	Dec	MARS +1.5 GHA	Dec	JUPITER −2.0 GHA	Dec	SATURN +0.1 GHA	Dec	STARS Name	SHA	Dec
d h	° ′	° ′	° ′	° ′	° ′	° ′	° ′	° ′	° ′		° ′	° ′
10 00	227 28.7	134 58.3	N26 02.3	171 16.8	N20 06.5	90 40.5	N17 28.6	346 29.6	S18 31.7	Acamar	315 17.8	S40 14.8
01	242 31.2	149 57.7	02.3	186 17.5	06.9	105 42.7	28.6	1 32.3	31.6	Achernar	335 26.5	S57 09.5
02	257 33.6	164 57.1	02.3	201 18.1	07.3	120 45.0	28.5	16 34.9	31.6	Acrux	173 07.2	S63 11.3
03	272 36.1	179 56.5 ..	02.3	216 18.7 ..	07.8	135 47.2 ..	28.4	31 37.6 ..	31.6	Adhara	255 11.7	S29 00.0
04	287 38.6	194 56.0	02.3	231 19.4	08.2	150 49.4	28.4	46 40.2	31.5	Aldebaran	290 48.2	N16 32.1
05	302 41.0	209 55.4	02.3	246 20.0	08.6	165 51.7	28.3	61 42.9	31.5			
06	317 43.5	224 54.8	N26 02.3	261 20.6	N20 09.0	180 53.9	N17 28.2	76 45.5	S18 31.5	Alioth	166 19.2	N55 52.7
07	332 46.0	239 54.2	02.3	276 21.2	09.4	195 56.1	28.1	91 48.2	31.4	Alkaid	152 57.5	N49 14.3
08	347 48.4	254 53.6	02.3	291 21.9	09.8	210 58.4	28.1	106 50.8	31.4	Al Na'ir	27 42.3	S46 52.9
S 09	2 50.9	269 53.0 ..	02.3	306 22.5 ..	10.2	226 00.6 ..	28.0	121 53.5 ..	31.4	Alnilam	275 45.4	S 1 11.8
U 10	17 53.4	284 52.4	02.3	321 23.1	10.7	241 02.8	27.9	136 56.1	31.3	Alphard	217 54.8	S 8 43.8
N 11	32 55.8	299 51.8	02.3	336 23.8	11.1	256 05.1	27.9	151 58.8	31.3			
D 12	47 58.3	314 51.3	N26 02.3	351 24.4	N20 11.5	271 07.3	N17 27.8	167 01.4	S18 31.2	Alphecca	126 09.6	N26 39.9
A 13	63 00.7	329 50.7	02.3	6 25.0	11.9	286 09.6	27.7	182 04.1	31.2	Alpheratz	357 42.4	N29 10.3
Y 14	78 03.2	344 50.1	02.3	21 25.6	12.3	301 11.8	27.7	197 06.7	31.2	Altair	62 06.8	N 8 54.6
15	93 05.7	359 49.5 ..	02.3	36 26.3 ..	12.7	316 14.0 ..	27.6	212 09.4 ..	31.1	Ankaa	353 14.8	S42 13.3
16	108 08.1	14 48.9	02.3	51 26.9	13.1	331 16.3	27.5	227 12.0	31.1	Antares	112 24.3	S26 27.8
17	123 10.6	29 48.3	02.3	66 27.5	13.5	346 18.5	27.4	242 14.7	31.1			
18	138 13.1	44 47.8	N26 02.3	81 28.2	N20 13.9	1 20.7	N17 27.4	257 17.3	S18 31.0	Arcturus	145 54.3	N19 06.2
19	153 15.5	59 47.2	02.2	96 28.8	14.4	16 23.0	27.3	272 20.0	31.0	Atria	107 24.4	S69 03.0
20	168 18.0	74 46.6	02.2	111 29.4	14.8	31 25.2	27.2	287 22.6	31.0	Avior	234 17.6	S59 34.0
21	183 20.5	89 46.0 ..	02.2	126 30.0 ..	15.2	46 27.4 ..	27.2	302 25.2 ..	30.9	Bellatrix	278 30.9	N 6 21.5
22	198 22.9	104 45.4	02.2	141 30.7	15.6	61 29.7	27.1	317 27.9	30.9	Betelgeuse	271 00.2	N 7 24.3
23	213 25.4	119 44.9	02.2	156 31.3	16.0	76 31.9	27.0	332 30.5	30.9			
11 00	228 27.9	134 44.3	N26 02.1	171 31.9	N20 16.4	91 34.1	N17 27.0	347 33.2	S18 30.8	Canopus	263 56.0	S52 42.7
01	243 30.3	149 43.7	02.1	186 32.6	16.8	106 36.3	26.9	2 35.8	30.8	Capella	280 33.0	N46 00.6
02	258 32.8	164 43.1	02.1	201 33.2	17.2	121 38.6	26.8	17 38.5	30.8	Deneb	49 30.5	N45 20.0
03	273 35.2	179 42.5 ..	02.1	216 33.8 ..	17.6	136 40.8 ..	26.7	32 41.1 ..	30.7	Denebola	182 32.2	N14 29.1
04	288 37.7	194 42.0	02.1	231 34.4	18.0	151 43.0	26.7	47 43.8	30.7	Diphda	348 54.9	S17 54.2
05	303 40.2	209 41.4	02.1	246 35.1	18.4	166 45.3	26.6	62 46.4	30.7			
06	318 42.6	224 40.8	N26 02.0	261 35.7	N20 18.8	181 47.5	N17 26.5	77 49.1	S18 30.6	Dubhe	193 50.0	N61 40.3
07	333 45.1	239 40.2	02.0	276 36.3	19.2	196 49.7	26.5	92 51.7	30.6	Elnath	278 11.3	N28 37.0
08	348 47.6	254 39.7	02.0	291 36.9	19.7	211 52.0	26.4	107 54.4	30.6	Eltanin	90 45.1	N51 29.2
M 09	3 50.0	269 39.1 ..	01.9	306 37.6 ..	20.1	226 54.2 ..	26.3	122 57.0 ..	30.5	Enif	33 45.9	N 9 56.7
O 10	18 52.5	284 38.5	01.9	321 38.2	20.5	241 56.4	26.2	137 59.7	30.5	Fomalhaut	15 22.8	S29 32.3
N 11	33 55.0	299 37.9	01.9	336 38.8	20.9	256 58.6	26.2	153 02.3	30.4			
D 12	48 57.4	314 37.4	N26 01.9	351 39.5	N20 21.3	272 00.9	N17 26.1	168 05.0	S18 30.4	Gacrux	171 58.9	S57 12.2
A 13	63 59.9	329 36.8	01.8	6 40.1	21.7	287 03.1	26.0	183 07.6	30.4	Gienah	175 50.7	S17 37.8
Y 14	79 02.4	344 36.2	01.8	21 40.7	22.1	302 05.3	26.0	198 10.3	30.3	Hadar	148 45.3	S60 26.9
15	94 04.8	359 35.6 ..	01.8	36 41.3 ..	22.5	317 07.6 ..	25.9	213 12.9 ..	30.3	Hamal	327 59.6	N23 31.9
16	109 07.3	14 35.1	01.7	51 42.0	22.9	332 09.8	25.8	228 15.6	30.3	Kaus Aust.	83 41.8	S34 22.3
17	124 09.7	29 34.5	01.7	66 42.6	23.3	347 12.0	25.7	243 18.2	30.2			
18	139 12.2	44 33.9	N26 01.6	81 43.2	N20 23.7	2 14.2	N17 25.7	258 20.9	S18 30.2	Kochab	137 19.1	N74 05.7
19	154 14.7	59 33.3	01.6	96 43.8	24.1	17 16.5	25.6	273 23.5	30.2	Markab	13 37.2	N15 17.2
20	169 17.1	74 32.8	01.6	111 44.5	24.5	32 18.7	25.5	288 26.2	30.1	Menkar	314 14.0	N 4 08.8
21	184 19.6	89 32.2 ..	01.5	126 45.1 ..	24.9	47 20.9 ..	25.4	303 28.9 ..	30.1	Menkent	148 05.6	S36 26.8
22	199 22.1	104 31.6	01.5	141 45.7	25.3	62 23.1	25.4	318 31.5	30.1	Miaplacidus	221 39.3	S69 47.3
23	214 24.5	119 31.1	01.4	156 46.3	25.7	77 25.4	25.3	333 34.2	30.0			
12 00	229 27.0	134 30.5	N26 01.4	171 47.0	N20 26.1	92 27.6	N17 25.2	348 36.8	S18 30.0	Mirfak	308 39.0	N49 54.7
01	244 29.5	149 29.9	01.3	186 47.6	26.5	107 29.8	25.2	3 39.5	30.0	Nunki	75 56.5	S26 16.4
02	259 31.9	164 29.4	01.3	201 48.2	26.9	122 32.0	25.1	18 42.1	29.9	Peacock	53 17.2	S56 40.7
03	274 34.4	179 28.8 ..	01.2	216 48.9 ..	27.3	137 34.3 ..	25.0	33 44.8 ..	29.9	Pollux	243 26.4	N27 59.2
04	289 36.8	194 28.2	01.2	231 49.5	27.7	152 36.5	24.9	48 47.4	29.9	Procyon	244 58.6	N 5 10.9
05	304 39.3	209 27.7	01.1	246 50.1	28.1	167 38.7	24.9	63 50.1	29.8			
06	319 41.8	224 27.1	N26 01.1	261 50.7	N20 28.5	182 40.9	N17 24.8	78 52.7	S18 29.8	Rasalhague	96 05.0	N12 33.0
07	334 44.2	239 26.5	01.0	276 51.4	28.9	197 43.2	24.7	93 55.4	29.8	Regulus	207 42.1	N11 53.4
08	349 46.7	254 26.0	01.0	291 52.0	29.3	212 45.4	24.6	108 58.0	29.7	Rigel	281 11.1	S 8 11.4
T 09	4 49.2	269 25.4 ..	00.9	306 52.6 ..	29.7	227 47.6 ..	24.6	124 00.7 ..	29.7	Rigil Kent.	139 49.2	S60 53.9
U 10	19 51.6	284 24.8	00.9	321 53.2	30.1	242 49.8	24.5	139 03.3	29.6	Sabik	102 10.8	S15 44.5
E 11	34 54.1	299 24.3	00.8	336 53.9	30.5	257 52.1	24.4	154 06.0	29.6			
S 12	49 56.6	314 23.7	N26 00.7	351 54.5	N20 30.9	272 54.3	N17 24.3	169 08.6	S18 29.6	Schedar	349 39.4	N56 37.0
D 13	64 59.0	329 23.1	00.7	6 55.1	31.3	287 56.5	24.3	184 11.3	29.5	Shaula	96 19.8	S37 06.6
A 14	80 01.5	344 22.6	00.6	21 55.7	31.7	302 58.7	24.2	199 13.9	29.5	Sirius	258 32.8	S16 44.6
Y 15	95 04.0	359 22.0 ..	00.6	36 56.4 ..	32.1	318 00.9 ..	24.1	214 16.6 ..	29.5	Spica	158 29.6	S11 14.5
16	110 06.4	14 21.4	00.5	51 57.0	32.5	333 03.2	24.1	229 19.2	29.4	Suhail	222 51.5	S43 30.1
17	125 08.9	29 20.9	00.4	66 57.6	32.9	348 05.4	24.0	244 21.9	29.4			
18	140 11.3	44 20.3	N26 00.4	81 58.2	N20 33.3	3 07.6	N17 23.9	259 24.5	S18 29.4	Vega	80 37.8	N38 47.9
19	155 13.8	59 19.8	00.3	96 58.9	33.6	18 09.8	23.8	274 27.2	29.3	Zuben'ubi	137 03.6	S16 06.3
20	170 16.3	74 19.2	00.2	111 59.5	34.0	33 12.0	23.8	289 29.8	29.3		SHA	Mer.Pass.
21	185 18.7	89 18.6 ..	00.2	127 00.1 ..	34.4	48 14.3 ..	23.7	304 32.5 ..	29.3		° ′	h m
22	200 21.2	104 18.1	00.1	142 00.7	34.8	63 16.5	23.6	319 35.1	29.2	Venus	266 16.4	15 02
23	215 25.4	119 17.5	00.0	157 01.4	35.2	78 18.7	23.5	334 37.8	29.2	Mars	303 04.1	12 33
Mer.Pass.	**h m** 8 44.7	v −0.6	d 0.0	v 0.6	d 0.4	v 2.2	d 0.1	v 2.7	d 0.0	Jupiter	223 06.3	17 51
										Saturn	119 05.3	0 50

UT	SUN GHA	SUN Dec	MOON GHA	v	MOON Dec	d	HP
d h	° ′	° ′	° ′	′	° ′	′	′
10 00	180 53.8	N17 28.6	285 59.5	8.4	S15 20.6	6.1	58.4
01	195 53.8	29.3	300 26.9	8.4	15 14.5	6.2	58.4
02	210 53.8	29.9	314 54.3	8.4	15 08.3	6.3	58.4
03	225 53.8 ..	30.6	329 21.7	8.5	15 02.0	6.4	58.4
04	240 53.9	31.3	343 49.2	8.4	14 55.6	6.5	58.4
05	255 53.9	31.9	358 16.6	8.5	14 49.1	6.6	58.5
06	270 53.9	N17 32.6	12 44.1	8.5	S14 42.5	6.7	58.5
07	285 53.9	33.2	27 11.6	8.5	14 35.8	6.7	58.5
08	300 54.0	33.9	41 39.1	8.5	14 29.1	6.9	58.5
S 09	315 54.0 ..	34.5	56 06.6	8.5	14 22.2	6.9	58.5
U 10	330 54.0	35.2	70 34.1	8.5	14 15.3	7.0	58.6
N 11	345 54.0	35.8	85 01.6	8.6	14 08.3	7.2	58.6
D 12	0 54.1	N17 36.5	99 29.2	8.5	S14 01.1	7.2	58.6
A 13	15 54.1	37.2	113 56.7	8.6	13 53.9	7.3	58.6
Y 14	30 54.1	37.8	128 24.3	8.6	13 46.6	7.3	58.6
15	45 54.1 ..	38.5	142 51.9	8.6	13 39.3	7.5	58.7
16	60 54.1	39.1	157 19.5	8.6	13 31.8	7.6	58.7
17	75 54.2	39.8	171 47.1	8.7	13 24.2	7.6	58.7
18	90 54.2	N17 40.4	186 14.8	8.6	S13 16.6	7.7	58.7
19	105 54.2	41.1	200 42.4	8.7	13 08.9	7.8	58.7
20	120 54.2	41.7	215 10.1	8.7	13 01.1	7.9	58.8
21	135 54.3 ..	42.4	229 37.8	8.7	12 53.2	8.0	58.8
22	150 54.3	43.0	244 05.5	8.7	12 45.2	8.0	58.8
23	165 54.3	43.7	258 33.2	8.7	12 37.2	8.1	58.8
11 00	180 54.3	N17 44.3	273 00.9	8.8	S12 29.1	8.2	58.8
01	195 54.3	45.0	287 28.7	8.7	12 20.9	8.3	58.8
02	210 54.4	45.6	301 56.4	8.8	12 12.6	8.4	58.9
03	225 54.4 ..	46.3	316 24.2	8.8	12 04.2	8.4	58.9
04	240 54.4	46.9	330 52.0	8.8	11 55.8	8.5	58.9
05	255 54.4	47.6	345 19.8	8.8	11 47.3	8.6	58.9
06	270 54.4	N17 48.2	359 47.6	8.9	S11 38.7	8.7	58.9
07	285 54.5	48.8	14 15.5	8.8	11 30.0	8.7	59.0
08	300 54.5	49.5	28 43.3	8.9	11 21.3	8.8	59.0
M 09	315 54.5 ..	50.1	43 11.2	8.9	11 12.5	8.9	59.0
O 10	330 54.5	50.8	57 39.1	8.9	11 03.6	8.9	59.0
N 11	345 54.5	51.4	72 07.0	8.9	10 54.7	9.1	59.0
D 12	0 54.5	N17 52.1	86 34.9	8.9	S10 45.6	9.0	59.0
A 13	15 54.6	52.7	101 02.8	8.9	10 36.6	9.2	59.1
Y 14	30 54.6	53.3	115 30.7	9.0	10 27.4	9.2	59.1
15	45 54.6 ..	54.0	129 58.7	9.0	10 18.2	9.3	59.1
16	60 54.6	54.6	144 26.7	8.9	10 08.9	9.4	59.1
17	75 54.6	55.3	158 54.6	9.0	9 59.5	9.4	59.1
18	90 54.6	N17 55.9	173 22.6	9.0	S 9 50.1	9.5	59.1
19	105 54.7	56.5	187 50.6	9.1	9 40.6	9.5	59.2
20	120 54.7	57.2	202 18.7	9.0	9 31.1	9.6	59.2
21	135 54.7 ..	57.8	216 46.7	9.0	9 21.5	9.7	59.2
22	150 54.7	58.5	231 14.7	9.1	9 11.8	9.7	59.2
23	165 54.7	59.1	245 42.8	9.1	9 02.1	9.8	59.2
12 00	180 54.7	N17 59.7	260 10.9	9.0	S 8 52.3	9.8	59.2
01	195 54.8	18 00.4	274 38.9	9.1	8 42.5	9.9	59.3
02	210 54.8	01.0	289 07.0	9.1	8 32.6	10.0	59.3
03	225 54.8 ..	01.6	303 35.1	9.1	8 22.6	10.0	59.3
04	240 54.8	02.3	318 03.2	9.2	8 12.6	10.1	59.3
05	255 54.8	02.9	332 31.4	9.1	8 02.5	10.1	59.3
06	270 54.8	N18 03.5	346 59.5	9.1	S 7 52.4	10.2	59.3
07	285 54.8	04.2	1 27.6	9.2	7 42.2	10.2	59.4
T 08	300 54.8	04.8	15 55.8	9.1	7 32.0	10.3	59.4
U 09	315 54.9 ..	05.4	30 23.9	9.2	7 21.7	10.3	59.4
E 10	330 54.9	06.1	44 52.1	9.2	7 11.4	10.4	59.4
S 11	345 54.9	06.7	59 20.3	9.2	7 01.0	10.4	59.4
D 12	0 54.9	N18 07.3	73 48.5	9.1	S 6 50.6	10.4	59.4
A 13	15 54.9	08.0	88 16.6	9.2	6 40.2	10.6	59.4
Y 14	30 54.9	08.6	102 44.8	9.2	6 29.6	10.5	59.5
15	45 54.9 ..	09.2	117 13.0	9.3	6 19.1	10.6	59.5
16	60 54.9	09.8	131 41.3	9.2	6 08.5	10.6	59.5
17	75 54.9	10.5	146 09.5	9.2	5 57.9	10.7	59.5
18	90 54.9	N18 11.1	160 37.7	9.2	S 5 47.2	10.7	59.5
19	105 55.0	11.7	175 05.9	9.3	5 36.5	10.8	59.5
20	120 55.0	12.3	189 34.2	9.2	5 25.7	10.8	59.5
21	135 55.0 ..	13.0	204 02.4	9.3	5 14.9	10.8	59.5
22	150 55.0	13.6	218 30.6	9.3	5 04.1	10.9	59.6
23	165 55.0	14.2	232 58.9	9.2	S 4 53.2	10.9	59.6
	SD 15.9	d 0.6	SD 16.0		16.1		16.2

Lat.	Twilight Naut.	Twilight Civil	Sunrise	Moonrise 10	11	12	13
°	h m	h m	h m	h m	h m	h m	h m
N 72	□	□	□	02 49	02 42	02 36	02 30
N 70	////	////	01 26	02 15	02 20	02 23	02 24
68	////	////	02 10	01 51	02 04	02 13	02 20
66	////	00 31	02 39	01 31	01 50	02 04	02 15
64	////	01 36	03 01	01 16	01 39	01 57	02 12
62	////	02 09	03 19	01 03	01 29	01 50	02 09
60	00 27	02 33	03 33	00 52	01 21	01 45	02 06
N 58	01 26	02 52	03 45	00 42	01 14	01 40	02 04
56	01 57	03 08	03 56	00 34	01 07	01 36	02 01
54	02 19	03 21	04 05	00 27	01 01	01 32	01 59
52	02 37	03 32	04 13	00 20	00 56	01 28	01 58
50	02 52	03 42	04 21	00 14	00 51	01 25	01 56
45	03 20	04 03	04 36	00 01	00 41	01 18	01 53
N 40	03 42	04 19	04 49	24 32	00 32	01 12	01 50
35	03 59	04 32	05 00	24 25	00 25	01 07	01 47
30	04 13	04 44	05 10	24 19	00 19	01 02	01 45
20	04 35	05 02	05 26	24 07	00 07	00 55	01 41
N 10	04 52	05 18	05 40	23 57	24 48	00 48	01 37
0	05 06	05 31	05 53	23 48	24 41	00 41	01 34
S 10	05 18	05 44	06 06	23 39	24 35	00 35	01 31
20	05 30	05 56	06 19	23 29	24 28	00 28	01 27
30	05 41	06 10	06 35	23 18	24 20	00 20	01 24
35	05 47	06 17	06 44	23 11	24 16	00 16	01 21
40	05 53	06 25	06 54	23 03	24 10	00 10	01 19
45	05 59	06 35	07 06	22 55	24 04	00 04	01 16
S 50	06 06	06 45	07 21	22 44	23 57	25 12	01 12
52	06 09	06 50	07 27	22 39	23 54	25 11	01 11
54	06 13	06 56	07 35	22 34	23 50	25 09	01 09
56	06 16	07 01	07 43	22 28	23 46	25 07	01 07
58	06 20	07 08	07 53	22 21	23 42	25 05	01 05
S 60	06 24	07 15	08 03	22 13	23 37	25 02	01 02

Lat.	Sunset	Twilight Civil	Twilight Naut.	Moonset 10	11	12	13
°	h m	h m	h m	h m	h m	h m	h m
N 72	□	□	□	07 38	09 37	11 34	13 29
N 70	22 34	////	////	08 11	09 57	11 45	13 33
68	21 46	////	////	08 35	10 13	11 53	13 36
66	21 16	23 51	////	08 53	10 25	12 01	13 38
64	20 54	22 22	////	09 08	10 35	12 07	13 40
62	20 36	21 47	////	09 20	10 44	12 12	13 41
60	20 22	21 22	23 52	09 30	10 52	12 16	13 43
N 58	20 09	21 03	22 31	09 40	10 58	12 20	13 44
56	19 58	20 47	21 59	09 47	11 04	12 24	13 45
54	19 49	20 33	21 36	09 55	11 09	12 27	13 46
52	19 41	20 22	21 18	10 01	11 14	12 30	13 47
50	19 33	20 12	21 03	10 07	11 18	12 33	13 48
45	19 17	19 51	20 34	10 19	11 27	12 38	13 50
N 40	19 04	19 34	20 12	10 29	11 35	12 43	13 52
35	18 53	19 21	19 55	10 38	11 42	12 47	13 53
30	18 44	19 10	19 41	10 45	11 47	12 50	13 54
20	18 27	18 51	19 18	10 58	11 57	12 56	13 56
N 10	18 13	18 35	19 01	11 09	12 06	13 02	13 58
0	18 00	18 22	18 47	11 20	12 14	13 07	13 59
S 10	17 47	18 09	18 34	11 31	12 21	13 11	14 01
20	17 33	17 56	18 23	11 42	12 30	13 17	14 02
30	17 17	17 43	18 11	11 54	12 39	13 22	14 04
35	17 08	17 35	18 06	12 02	12 45	13 26	14 05
40	16 58	17 27	18 00	12 10	12 51	13 29	14 06
45	16 46	17 18	17 53	12 20	12 58	13 34	14 08
S 50	16 32	17 07	17 46	12 31	13 07	13 39	14 09
52	16 25	17 02	17 43	12 36	13 11	13 41	14 10
54	16 17	16 57	17 39	12 42	13 15	13 44	14 11
56	16 09	16 51	17 36	12 49	13 20	13 47	14 11
58	15 59	16 44	17 32	12 56	13 25	13 50	14 12
S 60	15 49	16 37	17 28	13 05	13 31	13 53	14 13

Day	SUN Eqn. of Time 00h	12h	Mer. Pass.	MOON Mer. Pass. Upper	Lower	Age	Phase
d	m s	m s	h m	h m	h m	d	%
10	03 35	03 36	11 56	05 07	17 34	22	61
11	03 37	03 38	11 56	06 01	18 27	23	49
12	03 39	03 40	11 56	06 54	19 20	24	38

UT	ARIES GHA	VENUS −4.2 GHA	Dec	MARS +1.5 GHA	Dec	JUPITER −2.0 GHA	Dec	SATURN +0.1 GHA	Dec	STARS Name	SHA	Dec
13 00	230 26.1	134 17.0	N26 00.0	172 02.0	N20 35.6	93 20.9	N17 23.5	349 40.4	S18 29.2	Acamar	315 17.8	S40 14.7
01	245 28.6	149 16.4	25 59.9	187 02.6	36.0	108 23.1	23.4	4 43.1	29.1	Achernar	335 26.5	S57 09.5
02	260 31.1	164 15.9	59.8	202 03.2	36.4	123 25.4	23.3	19 45.7	29.1	Acrux	173 07.2	S63 11.3
03	275 33.5	179 15.3	.. 59.7	217 03.9	.. 36.8	138 27.6	.. 23.2	34 48.4	.. 29.1	Adhara	255 11.8	S29 00.0
04	290 36.0	194 14.7	59.6	232 04.5	37.2	153 29.8	23.2	49 51.0	29.0	Aldebaran	290 48.2	N16 32.1
05	305 38.5	209 14.2	59.6	247 05.1	37.6	168 32.0	23.1	64 53.7	29.0			
W 06	320 40.9	224 13.6	N25 59.5	262 05.7	N20 38.0	183 34.2	N17 23.0	79 56.3	S18 28.9	Alioth	166 19.3	N55 52.8
E 07	335 43.4	239 13.1	59.4	277 06.3	38.3	198 36.5	22.9	94 59.0	28.9	Alkaid	152 57.5	N49 14.3
D 08	350 45.8	254 12.5	59.3	292 07.0	38.7	213 38.7	22.9	110 01.7	28.9	Al Na'ir	27 42.3	S46 52.9
N 09	5 48.3	269 12.0	.. 59.2	307 07.6	.. 39.1	228 40.9	.. 22.8	125 04.3	.. 28.8	Alnilam	275 45.4	S 1 11.8
E 10	20 50.8	284 11.4	59.2	322 08.2	39.5	243 43.1	22.7	140 07.0	28.8	Alphard	217 54.8	S 8 43.8
S 11	35 53.2	299 10.9	59.1	337 08.8	39.9	258 45.3	22.6	155 09.6	28.8			
D 12	50 55.7	314 10.3	N25 59.0	352 09.5	N20 40.3	273 47.5	N17 22.6	170 12.3	S18 28.7	Alphecca	126 09.6	N26 39.9
A 13	65 58.2	329 09.8	58.9	7 10.1	40.7	288 49.8	22.5	185 14.9	28.7	Alpheratz	357 42.3	N29 10.3
Y 14	81 00.6	344 09.2	58.8	22 10.7	41.1	303 52.0	22.4	200 17.6	28.7	Altair	62 06.8	N 8 54.6
15	96 03.1	359 08.7	.. 58.7	37 11.3	.. 41.5	318 54.2	.. 22.3	215 20.2	.. 28.6	Ankaa	353 14.8	S42 13.3
16	111 05.6	14 08.1	58.6	52 12.0	41.8	333 56.4	22.3	230 22.9	28.6	Antares	112 24.3	S26 27.8
17	126 08.0	29 07.6	58.5	67 12.6	42.2	348 58.6	22.2	245 25.5	28.6			
18	141 10.5	44 07.0	N25 58.5	82 13.2	N20 42.6	4 00.8	N17 22.1	260 28.2	S18 28.5	Arcturus	145 54.3	N19 06.2
19	156 12.9	59 06.5	58.4	97 13.8	43.0	19 03.0	22.0	275 30.8	28.5	Atria	107 24.4	S69 03.0
20	171 15.4	74 05.9	58.3	112 14.5	43.4	34 05.3	21.9	290 33.5	28.5	Avior	234 17.6	S59 34.0
21	186 17.9	89 05.4	.. 58.2	127 15.1	.. 43.8	49 07.5	.. 21.9	305 36.1	.. 28.4	Bellatrix	278 30.9	N 6 21.5
22	201 20.3	104 04.8	58.1	142 15.7	44.2	64 09.7	21.8	320 38.8	28.4	Betelgeuse	271 00.2	N 7 24.3
23	216 22.8	119 04.3	58.0	157 16.3	44.5	79 11.9	21.7	335 41.4	28.4			
14 00	231 25.3	134 03.7	N25 57.9	172 16.9	N20 44.9	94 14.1	N17 21.6	350 44.1	S18 28.3	Canopus	263 56.0	S52 42.6
01	246 27.7	149 03.2	57.8	187 17.6	45.3	109 16.3	21.6	5 46.7	28.3	Capella	280 33.0	N46 00.6
02	261 30.2	164 02.6	57.7	202 18.2	45.7	124 18.5	21.5	20 49.4	28.2	Deneb	49 30.4	N45 20.0
03	276 32.7	179 02.1	.. 57.6	217 18.8	.. 46.1	139 20.7	.. 21.4	35 52.1	.. 28.2	Denebola	182 32.2	N14 29.1
04	291 35.1	194 01.5	57.5	232 19.4	46.5	154 23.0	21.3	50 54.7	28.2	Diphda	348 54.9	S17 54.2
05	306 37.6	209 01.0	57.4	247 20.1	46.8	169 25.2	21.3	65 57.4	28.1			
T 06	321 40.1	224 00.5	N25 57.3	262 20.7	N20 47.2	184 27.4	N17 21.2	81 00.0	S18 28.1	Dubhe	193 50.1	N61 40.3
H 07	336 42.5	238 59.9	57.2	277 21.3	47.6	199 29.6	21.1	96 02.7	28.1	Elnath	278 11.3	N28 37.0
U 08	351 45.0	253 59.4	57.2	292 21.9	48.0	214 31.8	21.0	111 05.3	28.0	Eltanin	90 45.1	N51 29.2
R 09	6 47.4	268 58.8	.. 56.9	307 22.5	.. 48.4	229 34.0	.. 20.9	126 08.0	.. 28.0	Enif	33 45.9	N 9 56.7
S 10	21 49.9	283 58.3	56.8	322 23.2	48.7	244 36.2	20.9	141 10.6	28.0	Fomalhaut	15 22.7	S29 32.3
D 11	36 52.4	298 57.7	56.7	337 23.8	49.1	259 38.4	20.8	156 13.3	27.9			
A 12	51 54.8	313 57.2	N25 56.6	352 24.4	N20 49.5	274 40.6	N17 20.7	171 15.9	S18 27.9	Gacrux	171 58.9	S57 12.2
Y 13	66 57.3	328 56.7	56.5	7 25.0	49.9	289 42.9	20.6	186 18.6	27.9	Gienah	175 50.7	S17 37.8
14	81 59.8	343 56.1	56.4	22 25.7	50.3	304 45.1	20.6	201 21.2	27.8	Hadar	148 45.3	S60 26.9
15	97 02.2	358 55.6	.. 56.3	37 26.3	.. 50.6	319 47.3	.. 20.5	216 23.9	.. 27.8	Hamal	327 59.6	N23 31.9
16	112 04.7	13 55.0	56.1	52 26.9	51.0	334 49.5	20.4	231 26.5	27.8	Kaus Aust.	83 41.8	S34 22.3
17	127 07.2	28 54.5	56.0	67 27.5	51.4	349 51.7	20.3	246 29.2	27.7			
18	142 09.6	43 54.0	N25 55.9	82 28.1	N20 51.8	4 53.9	N17 20.2	261 31.8	S18 27.7	Kochab	137 19.1	N74 05.7
19	157 12.1	58 53.4	55.8	97 28.8	52.1	19 56.1	20.2	276 34.5	27.6	Markab	13 37.2	N15 17.2
20	172 14.5	73 52.9	55.7	112 29.4	52.5	34 58.3	20.1	291 37.2	27.6	Menkar	314 14.0	N 4 08.8
21	187 17.0	88 52.4	.. 55.5	127 30.0	.. 52.9	50 00.5	.. 20.0	306 39.8	.. 27.6	Menkent	148 05.6	S36 26.8
22	202 19.5	103 51.8	55.4	142 30.6	53.3	65 02.7	19.9	321 42.5	27.5	Miaplacidus	221 39.4	S69 47.3
23	217 21.9	118 51.3	55.3	157 31.2	53.7	80 04.9	19.9	336 45.1	27.5			
15 00	232 24.4	133 50.8	N25 55.2	172 31.9	N20 54.0	95 07.2	N17 19.8	351 47.8	S18 27.5	Mirfak	308 39.0	N49 54.7
01	247 26.9	148 50.2	55.0	187 32.5	54.4	110 09.4	19.7	6 50.4	27.4	Nunki	75 56.5	S26 16.4
02	262 29.3	163 49.7	54.9	202 33.1	54.8	125 11.6	19.6	21 53.1	27.4	Peacock	53 17.1	S56 40.7
03	277 31.8	178 49.2	.. 54.8	217 33.7	.. 55.2	140 13.8	.. 19.5	36 55.7	.. 27.4	Pollux	243 26.4	N27 59.2
04	292 34.3	193 48.6	54.7	232 34.3	55.5	155 16.0	19.5	51 58.4	27.3	Procyon	244 58.6	N 5 10.9
05	307 36.7	208 48.1	54.5	247 35.0	55.9	170 18.2	19.4	67 01.0	27.3			
F 06	322 39.2	223 47.6	N25 54.4	262 35.6	N20 56.3	185 20.4	N17 19.3	82 03.7	S18 27.3	Rasalhague	96 05.0	N12 33.0
R 07	337 41.7	238 47.0	54.3	277 36.2	56.7	200 22.6	19.2	97 06.3	27.2	Regulus	207 42.1	N11 53.4
I 08	352 44.1	253 46.5	54.1	292 36.8	57.0	215 24.8	19.1	112 09.0	27.2	Rigel	281 11.1	S 8 11.3
D 09	7 46.6	268 46.0	.. 54.0	307 37.5	.. 57.4	230 27.0	.. 19.1	127 11.7	.. 27.2	Rigil Kent.	139 49.2	S60 53.9
A 10	22 49.0	283 45.5	53.9	322 38.1	57.8	245 29.2	19.0	142 14.3	27.1	Sabik	102 10.7	S15 44.5
Y 11	37 51.5	298 44.9	53.7	337 38.7	58.1	260 31.4	18.9	157 17.0	27.1			
12	52 54.0	313 44.4	N25 53.6	352 39.3	N20 58.5	275 33.6	N17 18.8	172 19.6	S18 27.1	Schedar	349 39.3	N56 37.0
13	67 56.4	328 43.9	53.4	7 39.9	58.9	290 35.8	18.8	187 22.3	27.0	Shaula	96 19.8	S37 06.6
14	82 58.9	343 43.3	53.3	22 40.6	59.3	305 38.0	18.7	202 24.9	27.0	Sirius	258 32.8	S16 44.6
15	98 01.4	358 42.8	.. 53.2	37 41.2	20 59.6	320 40.2	.. 18.6	217 27.6	.. 26.9	Spica	158 29.6	S11 14.5
16	113 03.8	13 42.3	53.0	52 41.8	21 00.0	335 42.4	18.5	232 30.2	26.9	Suhail	222 51.5	S43 30.1
17	128 06.3	28 41.8	52.9	67 42.4	00.4	350 44.6	18.4	247 32.9	26.9			
18	143 08.8	43 41.3	N25 52.7	82 43.0	N21 00.7	5 46.8	N17 18.4	262 35.5	S18 26.8	Vega	80 37.8	N38 47.9
19	158 11.2	58 40.7	52.6	97 43.6	01.1	20 49.0	18.3	277 38.2	26.8	Zuben'ubi	137 03.6	S16 06.3
20	173 13.7	73 40.2	52.4	112 44.3	01.5	35 51.2	18.2	292 40.9	26.8			
21	188 16.2	88 39.7	.. 52.3	127 44.9	.. 01.8	50 53.4	.. 18.1	307 43.5	.. 26.7			
22	203 18.6	103 39.2	52.1	142 45.5	02.2	65 55.6	18.0	322 46.2	26.7			
23	218 21.1	118 38.6	52.0	157 46.1	02.6	80 57.8	18.0	337 48.8	26.7			

										Name	SHA	Mer. Pass.
										Venus	262 38.4	15 04
										Mars	300 51.7	12 30
										Jupiter	222 48.8	17 40
Mer. Pass.	8 32.9	v −0.5 d 0.1		v 0.6 d 0.4		v 2.2 d 0.1		v 2.7 d 0.0		Saturn	119 18.8	0 37

UT	SUN GHA	SUN Dec	MOON GHA	MOON v	MOON Dec	MOON d	MOON HP
d h	° ′	° ′	° ′	′	° ′	′	′
13 00	180 55.0	N18 14.8	247 27.1	9.3	S 4 42.3	10.9	59.6
01	195 55.0	15.5	261 55.4	9.2	4 31.4	11.0	59.6
02	210 55.0	16.1	276 23.6	9.2	4 20.4	11.0	59.6
03	225 55.0 ..	16.7	290 51.8	9.3	4 09.4	11.0	59.6
04	240 55.0	17.3	305 20.1	9.2	3 58.4	11.0	59.6
05	255 55.0	18.0	319 48.3	9.3	3 47.4	11.1	59.6
W 06	270 55.0	N18 18.6	334 16.6	9.2	S 3 36.3	11.1	59.7
E 07	285 55.1	19.2	348 44.8	9.3	3 25.2	11.1	59.7
D 08	300 55.1	19.8	3 13.1	9.2	3 14.1	11.2	59.7
N 09	315 55.1 ..	20.4	17 41.3	9.3	3 02.9	11.2	59.7
E 10	330 55.1	21.0	32 09.6	9.2	2 51.7	11.2	59.7
S 11	345 55.1	21.7	46 37.8	9.3	2 40.5	11.2	59.7
D 12	0 55.1	N18 22.3	61 06.1	9.2	S 2 29.3	11.3	59.7
A 13	15 55.1	22.9	75 34.3	9.2	2 18.1	11.3	59.7
Y 14	30 55.1	23.5	90 02.5	9.3	2 06.8	11.2	59.7
15	45 55.1 ..	24.1	104 30.8	9.2	1 55.6	11.3	59.7
16	60 55.1	24.7	118 59.0	9.2	1 44.3	11.3	59.8
17	75 55.1	25.4	133 27.2	9.2	1 33.0	11.4	59.8
18	90 55.1	N18 26.0	147 55.4	9.2	S 1 21.6	11.3	59.8
19	105 55.1	26.6	162 23.6	9.2	1 10.3	11.3	59.8
20	120 55.1	27.2	176 51.8	9.2	0 59.0	11.4	59.8
21	135 55.1 ..	27.8	191 20.0	9.2	0 47.6	11.3	59.8
22	150 55.1	28.4	205 48.2	9.2	0 36.3	11.4	59.8
23	165 55.1	29.0	220 16.4	9.1	0 24.9	11.4	59.8
14 00	180 55.1	N18 29.6	234 44.5	9.2	S 0 13.5	11.3	59.8
01	195 55.1	30.3	249 12.7	9.1	S 0 02.2	11.4	59.8
02	210 55.1	30.9	263 40.8	9.2	N 0 09.2	11.4	59.8
03	225 55.1 ..	31.5	278 09.0	9.1	0 20.6	11.4	59.8
04	240 55.1	32.1	292 37.1	9.1	0 32.0	11.4	59.8
05	255 55.1	32.7	307 05.2	9.1	0 43.4	11.4	59.9
06	270 55.1	N18 33.3	321 33.3	9.1	N 0 54.8	11.3	59.9
T 07	285 55.1	33.9	336 01.4	9.1	1 06.1	11.4	59.9
H 08	300 55.1	34.5	350 29.5	9.0	1 17.5	11.4	59.9
U 09	315 55.1 ..	35.1	4 57.5	9.1	1 28.9	11.3	59.9
R 10	330 55.1	35.7	19 25.6	9.0	1 40.2	11.4	59.9
S 11	345 55.1	36.3	33 53.6	9.0	1 51.6	11.4	59.9
D 12	0 55.1	N18 36.9	48 21.6	9.1	N 2 03.0	11.3	59.9
A 13	15 55.1	37.5	62 49.7	8.9	2 14.3	11.3	59.9
Y 14	30 55.1	38.1	77 17.6	9.0	2 25.6	11.3	59.9
15	45 55.1 ..	38.7	91 45.6	9.0	2 36.9	11.3	59.9
16	60 55.1	39.3	106 13.6	8.9	2 48.2	11.3	59.9
17	75 55.1	39.9	120 41.5	9.0	2 59.5	11.3	59.9
18	90 55.1	N18 40.5	135 09.5	8.9	N 3 10.8	11.2	59.9
19	105 55.1	41.1	149 37.4	8.9	3 22.0	11.3	59.9
20	120 55.1	41.7	164 05.3	8.8	3 33.3	11.2	59.9
21	135 55.1 ..	42.3	178 33.1	8.9	3 44.5	11.2	59.9
22	150 55.1	42.9	193 01.0	8.8	3 55.7	11.2	59.9
23	165 55.1	43.5	207 28.8	8.9	4 06.9	11.1	59.9
15 00	180 55.1	N18 44.1	221 56.7	8.8	N 4 18.0	11.1	59.9
01	195 55.1	44.7	236 24.5	8.7	4 29.1	11.1	59.9
02	210 55.1	45.3	250 52.2	8.8	4 40.2	11.1	59.9
03	225 55.1 ..	45.9	265 20.0	8.7	4 51.3	11.0	59.9
04	240 55.1	46.5	279 47.7	8.8	5 02.3	11.0	59.9
05	255 55.1	47.1	294 15.5	8.7	5 13.3	11.0	59.9
06	270 55.1	N18 47.7	308 43.2	8.6	N 5 24.3	11.0	59.9
F 07	285 55.1	48.3	323 10.8	8.7	5 35.3	10.9	59.9
R 08	300 55.1	48.9	337 38.5	8.6	5 46.2	10.8	59.9
I 09	315 55.0 ..	49.5	352 06.1	8.6	5 57.0	10.9	59.9
D 10	330 55.0	50.1	6 33.7	8.6	6 07.9	10.8	59.9
A 11	345 55.0	50.7	21 01.3	8.6	6 18.7	10.7	59.9
Y 12	0 55.0	N18 51.3	35 28.9	8.5	N 6 29.4	10.8	59.9
13	15 55.0	51.9	49 56.4	8.6	6 40.2	10.6	59.9
14	30 55.0	52.4	64 24.0	8.5	6 50.8	10.7	59.9
15	45 55.0 ..	53.0	78 51.5	8.4	7 01.5	10.6	59.9
16	60 55.0	53.6	93 18.9	8.5	7 12.1	10.5	59.9
17	75 55.0	54.2	107 46.4	8.4	7 22.6	10.5	59.9
18	90 55.0	N18 54.8	122 13.8	8.4	N 7 33.1	10.5	59.9
19	105 55.0	55.4	136 41.2	8.4	7 43.6	10.4	59.9
20	120 55.0	56.0	151 08.6	8.4	7 54.0	10.3	59.8
21	135 54.9 ..	56.6	165 36.0	8.3	8 04.3	10.4	59.8
22	150 54.9	57.1	180 03.3	8.3	8 14.7	10.2	59.8
23	165 54.9	57.7	194 30.6	8.3	N 8 24.9	10.2	59.8
	SD 15.9 d 0.6		SD 16.3		16.3		16.3

Lat.	Twilight Naut.	Twilight Civil	Sunrise	Moonrise 13	Moonrise 14	Moonrise 15	Moonrise 16
°	h m	h m	h m	h m	h m	h m	h m
N 72	☐	☐	☐	02 30	02 25	02 20	02 15
N 70	////	////	00 58	02 24	02 25	02 27	02 28
68	////	////	01 55	02 20	02 26	02 32	02 39
66	////	////	02 28	02 15	02 26	02 36	02 48
64	////	01 18	02 51	02 12	02 26	02 40	02 56
62	////	01 57	03 10	02 09	02 26	02 43	03 02
60	////	02 24	03 26	02 06	02 26	02 46	03 08
N 58	01 10	02 44	03 39	02 04	02 26	02 48	03 13
56	01 46	03 01	03 50	02 01	02 26	02 51	03 17
54	02 10	03 15	04 00	01 59	02 26	02 53	03 21
52	02 29	03 27	04 08	01 58	02 26	02 55	03 25
50	02 45	03 37	04 16	01 56	02 26	02 56	03 28
45	03 16	03 59	04 33	01 53	02 26	03 00	03 36
N 40	03 38	04 16	04 46	01 50	02 26	03 03	03 42
35	03 56	04 30	04 58	01 47	02 26	03 06	03 47
30	04 10	04 41	05 08	01 45	02 26	03 08	03 52
20	04 33	05 01	05 24	01 41	02 27	03 13	04 00
N 10	04 51	05 17	05 39	01 37	02 27	03 16	04 07
0	05 06	05 31	05 53	01 34	02 27	03 20	04 14
S 10	05 19	05 44	06 06	01 31	02 27	03 24	04 21
20	05 31	05 57	06 21	01 27	02 27	03 28	04 28
30	05 43	06 12	06 37	01 24	02 28	03 32	04 37
35	05 49	06 19	06 46	01 21	02 28	03 35	04 42
40	05 55	06 28	06 57	01 19	02 28	03 38	04 47
45	06 02	06 38	07 10	01 16	02 28	03 41	04 54
S 50	06 10	06 49	07 25	01 12	02 28	03 45	05 02
52	06 14	06 54	07 32	01 11	02 29	03 47	05 05
54	06 17	07 00	07 40	01 09	02 29	03 49	05 10
56	06 21	07 06	07 49	01 07	02 29	03 52	05 14
58	06 25	07 13	07 59	01 05	02 29	03 54	05 19
S 60	06 29	07 21	08 10	01 02	02 29	03 57	05 25

Lat.	Sunset	Twilight Civil	Twilight Naut.	Moonset 13	Moonset 14	Moonset 15	Moonset 16
°	h m	h m	h m	h m	h m	h m	h m
N 72	☐	☐	☐	13 29	15 25	17 22	19 22
N 70	23 06	////	////	13 33	15 21	17 11	19 01
68	22 03	////	////	13 36	15 18	17 02	18 45
66	21 28	////	////	13 38	15 16	16 55	18 32
64	21 04	22 41	////	13 40	15 14	16 48	18 22
62	20 44	21 59	////	13 41	15 12	16 43	18 13
60	20 29	21 32	////	13 43	15 10	16 38	18 05
N 58	20 15	21 11	22 49	13 44	15 09	16 34	17 58
56	20 04	20 54	22 10	13 45	15 08	16 30	17 52
54	19 54	20 40	21 45	13 46	15 07	16 27	17 47
52	19 45	20 27	21 25	13 47	15 06	16 24	17 42
50	19 37	20 17	21 09	13 48	15 05	16 21	17 37
45	19 21	19 55	20 38	13 50	15 03	16 16	17 28
N 40	19 07	19 38	20 15	13 52	15 01	16 11	17 20
35	18 56	19 24	19 58	13 53	14 59	16 07	17 13
30	18 46	19 12	19 43	13 54	14 58	16 03	17 08
20	18 28	18 52	19 20	13 56	14 56	15 56	16 57
N 10	18 14	18 36	19 02	13 58	14 54	15 51	16 48
0	18 00	18 22	18 47	13 59	14 52	15 46	16 40
S 10	17 46	18 08	18 34	14 01	14 50	15 40	16 32
20	17 32	17 55	18 22	14 02	14 48	15 35	16 23
30	17 15	17 41	18 10	14 04	14 46	15 28	16 13
35	17 06	17 33	18 03	14 05	14 44	15 25	16 07
40	16 55	17 24	17 57	14 06	14 43	15 21	16 00
45	16 43	17 14	17 50	14 08	14 41	15 16	15 53
S 50	16 27	17 03	17 42	14 09	14 39	15 10	15 43
52	16 20	16 58	17 39	14 10	14 38	15 07	15 39
54	16 12	16 52	17 35	14 11	14 37	15 04	15 35
56	16 03	16 46	17 31	14 11	14 36	15 01	15 29
58	15 53	16 39	17 27	14 12	14 35	14 58	15 24
S 60	15 42	16 31	17 23	14 13	14 33	14 54	15 17

Day	SUN Eqn. of Time 00h	SUN Eqn. of Time 12h	SUN Mer. Pass.	MOON Mer. Pass. Upper	MOON Mer. Pass. Lower	Age	Phase
d	m s	m s	h m	h m	h m	d	%
13	03 40	03 40	11 56	07 47	20 13	25	27
14	03 40	03 41	11 56	08 39	21 06	26	17
15	03 40	03 40	11 56	09 33	22 00	27	9

UT	ARIES	VENUS −4.3		MARS +1.5		JUPITER −2.0		SATURN +0.0		STARS		
	GHA	GHA	Dec	GHA	Dec	GHA	Dec	GHA	Dec	Name	SHA	Dec
d h	° ′	° ′	° ′	° ′	° ′	° ′	° ′	° ′	° ′		° ′	° ′
16 00	233 23.5	133 38.1	N25 51.8	172 46.7	N21 02.9	96 00.0	N17 17.9	352 51.5	S18 26.6	Acamar	315 17.8	S40 14.7
01	248 26.0	148 37.6	51.7	187 47.4	03.3	111 02.2	17.8	7 54.1	26.6	Achernar	335 26.4	S57 09.5
02	263 28.5	163 37.1	51.5	202 48.0	03.7	126 04.4	17.7	22 56.8	26.6	Acrux	173 07.2	S63 11.3
03	278 30.9	178 36.6 ..	51.4	217 48.6 ..	04.0	141 06.6 ..	17.6	37 59.4 ..	26.5	Adhara	255 11.8	S29 00.0
04	293 33.4	193 36.0	51.2	232 49.2	04.4	156 08.8	17.6	53 02.1	26.5	Aldebaran	290 48.2	N16 32.1
05	308 35.9	208 35.5	51.1	247 49.8	04.8	171 11.0	17.5	68 04.7	26.5			
S 06	323 38.3	223 35.0	N25 50.9	262 50.5	N21 05.1	186 13.2	N17 17.4	83 07.4	S18 26.4	Alioth	166 19.3	N55 52.8
A 07	338 40.8	238 34.5	50.7	277 51.1	05.5	201 15.4	17.3	98 10.1	26.4	Alkaid	152 57.5	N49 14.4
T 08	353 43.3	253 34.0	50.6	292 51.7	05.9	216 17.6	17.2	113 12.7	26.3	Al Na'ir	27 42.2	S46 52.9
U 09	8 45.7	268 33.5 ..	50.4	307 52.3 ..	06.2	231 19.8 ..	17.1	128 15.4 ..	26.3	Alnilam	275 45.4	S 1 11.8
R 10	23 48.2	283 33.0	50.2	322 52.9	06.6	246 22.0	17.1	143 18.0	26.3	Alphard	217 54.9	S 8 43.8
D 11	38 50.6	298 32.4	50.1	337 53.6	07.0	261 24.2	17.0	158 20.7	26.2			
A 12	53 53.1	313 31.9	N25 49.9	352 54.2	N21 07.3	276 26.4	N17 16.9	173 23.3	S18 26.2	Alphecca	126 09.6	N26 39.9
Y 13	68 55.6	328 31.4	49.8	7 54.8	07.7	291 28.6	16.8	188 26.0	26.2	Alpheratz	357 42.3	N29 10.3
14	83 58.0	343 30.9	49.6	22 55.4	08.1	306 30.8	16.7	203 28.6	26.1	Altair	62 06.8	N 8 54.6
15	99 00.5	358 30.4 ..	49.3	37 56.0 ..	08.4	321 33.0 ..	16.7	218 31.3 ..	26.1	Ankaa	353 14.8	S42 13.2
16	114 03.0	13 29.9	49.3	52 56.6	08.8	336 35.2	16.6	233 33.9	26.1	Antares	112 24.3	S26 27.8
17	129 05.4	28 29.4	49.1	67 57.3	09.1	351 37.4	16.5	248 36.6	26.0			
18	144 07.9	43 28.9	N25 48.9	82 57.9	N21 09.5	6 39.6	N17 16.4	263 39.3	S18 26.0	Arcturus	145 54.3	N19 06.2
19	159 10.4	58 28.3	48.7	97 58.5	09.9	21 41.8	16.3	278 41.9	26.0	Atria	107 24.4	S69 03.0
20	174 12.8	73 27.8	48.6	112 59.1	10.2	36 44.0	16.3	293 44.6	25.9	Avior	234 17.7	S59 34.0
21	189 15.3	88 27.3 ..	48.4	127 59.7 ..	10.6	51 46.2 ..	16.2	308 47.2 ..	25.9	Bellatrix	278 30.9	N 6 21.5
22	204 17.8	103 26.8	48.2	143 00.4	10.9	66 48.4	16.1	323 49.9	25.9	Betelgeuse	271 00.2	N 7 24.3
23	219 20.2	118 26.3	48.0	158 01.0	11.3	81 50.6	16.0	338 52.5	25.8			
17 00	234 22.7	133 25.8	N25 47.9	173 01.6	N21 11.7	96 52.8	N17 15.9	353 55.2	S18 25.8	Canopus	263 56.0	S52 42.6
01	249 25.1	148 25.3	47.7	188 02.2	12.0	111 55.0	15.8	8 57.8	25.7	Capella	280 33.0	N46 00.6
02	264 27.6	163 24.8	47.5	203 02.8	12.4	126 57.2	15.8	24 00.5	25.7	Deneb	49 30.4	N45 20.0
03	279 30.1	178 24.3 ..	47.3	218 03.4 ..	12.7	141 59.4 ..	15.7	39 03.2 ..	25.7	Denebola	182 32.2	N14 29.1
04	294 32.5	193 23.8	47.1	233 04.1	13.1	157 01.6	15.6	54 05.8	25.6	Diphda	348 54.9	S17 54.2
05	309 35.0	208 23.3	47.0	248 04.7	13.4	172 03.8	15.5	69 08.5	25.6			
S 06	324 37.5	223 22.8	N25 46.8	263 05.3	N21 13.8	187 06.0	N17 15.4	84 11.1	S18 25.6	Dubhe	193 50.1	N61 40.3
U 07	339 39.9	238 22.3	46.6	278 05.9	14.2	202 08.2	15.3	99 13.8	25.5	Elnath	278 11.3	N28 37.0
N 08	354 42.4	253 21.8	46.4	293 06.5	14.5	217 10.4	15.3	114 16.4	25.5	Eltanin	90 45.1	N51 29.2
D 09	9 44.9	268 21.3 ..	46.2	308 07.1 ..	14.9	232 12.5 ..	15.2	129 19.1 ..	25.5	Enif	33 45.8	N 9 56.7
A 10	24 47.3	283 20.8	46.0	323 07.8	15.2	247 14.7	15.1	144 21.7	25.4	Fomalhaut	15 22.7	S29 32.3
Y 11	39 49.8	298 20.3	45.8	338 08.4	15.6	262 16.9	15.0	159 24.4	25.4			
12	54 52.3	313 19.8	N25 45.6	353 09.0	N21 15.9	277 19.1	N17 14.9	174 27.1	S18 25.4	Gacrux	171 58.9	S57 12.2
13	69 54.7	328 19.3	45.5	8 09.6	16.3	292 21.3	14.8	189 29.7	25.3	Gienah	175 50.7	S17 37.8
14	84 57.2	343 18.8	45.3	23 10.2	16.7	307 23.5	14.8	204 32.4	25.3	Hadar	148 45.3	S60 26.9
15	99 59.6	358 18.3 ..	45.1	38 10.8 ..	17.0	322 25.7 ..	14.7	219 35.0 ..	25.3	Hamal	327 59.6	N23 31.9
16	115 02.1	13 17.8	44.9	53 11.5	17.4	337 27.9	14.6	234 37.7	25.2	Kaus Aust.	83 41.8	S34 22.3
17	130 04.6	28 17.3	44.7	68 12.1	17.7	352 30.1	14.5	249 40.3	25.2			
18	145 07.0	43 16.8	N25 44.5	83 12.7	N21 18.1	7 32.3	N17 14.4	264 43.0	S18 25.1	Kochab	137 19.1	N74 05.7
19	160 09.5	58 16.3	44.3	98 13.3	18.4	22 34.5	14.3	279 45.6	25.1	Markab	13 37.1	N15 17.2
20	175 12.0	73 15.8	44.1	113 13.9	18.8	37 36.7	14.3	294 48.3	25.1	Menkar	314 14.0	N 4 08.8
21	190 14.4	88 15.3 ..	43.9	128 14.5 ..	19.1	52 38.8 ..	14.2	309 51.0 ..	25.0	Menkent	148 05.6	S36 26.8
22	205 16.9	103 14.8	43.7	143 15.2	19.5	67 41.0	14.1	324 53.6	25.0	Miaplacidus	221 39.4	S69 47.3
23	220 19.4	118 14.3	43.5	158 15.8	19.8	82 43.2	14.0	339 56.3	25.0			
18 00	235 21.8	133 13.9	N25 43.3	173 16.4	N21 20.2	97 45.4	N17 13.9	354 58.9	S18 24.9	Mirfak	308 38.9	N49 54.7
01	250 24.3	148 13.4	43.1	188 17.0	20.5	112 47.6	13.8	10 01.6	24.9	Nunki	75 56.5	S26 16.4
02	265 26.7	163 12.9	42.9	203 17.6	20.9	127 49.8	13.8	25 04.2	24.9	Peacock	53 17.1	S56 40.7
03	280 29.2	178 12.4 ..	42.7	218 18.2 ..	21.2	142 52.0 ..	13.7	40 06.9 ..	24.8	Pollux	243 26.4	N27 59.2
04	295 31.7	193 11.9	42.4	233 18.9	21.6	157 54.2	13.6	55 09.5	24.8	Procyon	244 58.6	N 5 10.9
05	310 34.1	208 11.4	42.2	248 19.5	21.9	172 56.4	13.5	70 12.2	24.8			
M 06	325 36.6	223 10.9	N25 42.0	263 20.1	N21 22.3	187 58.6	N17 13.4	85 14.9	S18 24.7	Rasalhague	96 05.0	N12 33.0
O 07	340 39.1	238 10.4	41.8	278 20.7	22.6	203 00.7	13.3	100 17.5	24.7	Regulus	207 42.2	N11 53.4
N 08	355 41.5	253 10.0	41.6	293 21.3	23.0	218 02.9	13.3	115 20.2	24.7	Rigel	281 11.1	S 8 11.3
D 09	10 44.0	268 09.5 ..	41.4	308 21.9 ..	23.3	233 05.1 ..	13.2	130 22.8 ..	24.6	Rigil Kent.	139 49.2	S60 53.9
A 10	25 46.5	283 09.0	41.2	323 22.6	23.7	248 07.3	13.1	145 25.5	24.6	Sabik	102 10.7	S15 44.5
Y 11	40 48.9	298 08.5	41.0	338 23.2	24.0	263 09.5	13.0	160 28.1	24.5			
12	55 51.4	313 08.0	N25 40.8	353 23.8	N21 24.4	278 11.7	N17 12.9	175 30.8	S18 24.5	Schedar	349 39.3	N56 37.0
13	70 53.9	328 07.5	40.5	8 24.4	24.7	293 13.9	12.8	190 33.4	24.5	Shaula	96 19.8	S37 06.6
14	85 56.3	343 07.1	40.3	23 25.0	25.0	308 16.0	12.7	205 36.1	24.4	Sirius	258 32.8	S16 44.6
15	100 58.8	358 06.6 ..	40.1	38 25.6 ..	25.4	323 18.2 ..	12.7	220 38.8 ..	24.4	Spica	158 29.6	S11 14.5
16	116 01.2	13 06.1	39.9	53 26.3	25.7	338 20.4	12.6	235 41.4	24.4	Suhail	222 51.5	S43 30.1
17	131 03.7	28 05.6	39.7	68 26.9	26.1	353 22.6	12.5	250 44.1	24.3			
18	146 06.2	43 05.1	N25 39.4	83 27.5	N21 26.4	8 24.8	N17 12.4	265 46.7	S18 24.3	Vega	80 37.8	N38 47.9
19	161 08.6	58 04.7	39.2	98 28.1	26.8	23 27.0	12.3	280 49.4	24.3	Zuben'ubi	137 03.6	S16 06.3
20	176 11.1	73 04.2	39.0	113 28.7	27.1	38 29.2	12.2	295 52.0	24.2		SHA	Mer.Pass.
21	191 13.6	88 03.7 ..	38.8	128 29.3 ..	27.5	53 31.3 ..	12.1	310 54.7 ..	24.2		° ′	h m
22	206 16.0	103 03.2	38.5	143 29.9	27.8	68 33.5	12.1	325 57.3	24.2	Venus	259 03.1	15 07
23	221 18.5	118 02.7	38.3	158 30.6	28.1	83 35.7	12.0	341 00.0	24.1	Mars	298 38.9	12 27
	h m									Jupiter	222 30.1	17 30
Mer.Pass. 8 21.1		v −0.5	d 0.2	v 0.6	d 0.4	v 2.2	d 0.1	v 2.7	d 0.0	Saturn	119 32.5	0 24

UT	SUN GHA	SUN Dec	MOON GHA	v	MOON Dec	d	HP
d h	° ′	° ′	° ′	′	° ′	′	′
16 00	180 54.9	N18 58.3	208 57.9	8.3	N 8 35.1	10.1	59.8
01	195 54.9	58.9	223 25.2	8.2	8 45.2	10.1	59.8
02	210 54.9	18 59.5	237 52.4	8.2	8 55.3	10.1	59.8
03	225 54.9	19 00.1	252 19.6	8.2	9 05.4	9.9	59.8
04	240 54.9	00.6	266 46.8	8.2	9 15.3	9.9	59.8
05	255 54.9	01.2	281 14.0	8.1	9 25.2	9.9	59.8
06	270 54.9	N19 01.8	295 41.1	8.1	N 9 35.1	9.8	59.8
07	285 54.8	02.4	310 08.2	8.1	9 44.9	9.7	59.8
08	300 54.8	03.0	324 35.3	8.1	9 54.6	9.7	59.7
09	315 54.8	.. 03.5	339 02.4	8.0	10 04.3	9.6	59.7
10	330 54.8	04.1	353 29.4	8.0	10 13.9	9.5	59.7
11	345 54.8	04.7	7 56.4	8.0	10 23.4	9.5	59.7
12	0 54.8	N19 05.3	22 23.4	8.0	N10 32.9	9.3	59.7
13	15 54.8	05.9	36 50.4	7.9	10 42.2	9.4	59.7
14	30 54.8	06.4	51 17.3	8.0	10 51.6	9.2	59.7
15	45 54.7	.. 07.0	65 44.3	7.9	11 00.8	9.2	59.7
16	60 54.7	07.6	80 11.2	7.8	11 10.0	9.1	59.6
17	75 54.7	08.2	94 38.0	7.9	11 19.1	9.0	59.6
18	90 54.7	N19 08.7	109 04.9	7.8	N11 28.1	9.0	59.6
19	105 54.7	09.3	123 31.7	7.8	11 37.1	8.9	59.6
20	120 54.7	09.9	137 58.5	7.8	11 46.0	8.8	59.6
21	135 54.7	.. 10.5	152 25.3	7.8	11 54.8	8.7	59.6
22	150 54.6	11.0	166 52.1	7.7	12 03.5	8.6	59.6
23	165 54.6	11.6	181 18.8	7.7	12 12.1	8.6	59.5
17 00	180 54.6	N19 12.2	195 45.5	7.7	N12 20.7	8.5	59.5
01	195 54.6	12.7	210 12.2	7.7	12 29.2	8.4	59.5
02	210 54.6	13.3	224 38.9	7.7	12 37.6	8.3	59.5
03	225 54.6	.. 13.9	239 05.6	7.6	12 45.9	8.2	59.5
04	240 54.5	14.4	253 32.2	7.6	12 54.1	8.2	59.5
05	255 54.5	15.0	267 58.8	7.6	13 02.3	8.0	59.4
06	270 54.5	N19 15.6	282 25.4	7.6	N13 10.3	8.0	59.4
07	285 54.5	16.2	296 52.0	7.6	13 18.3	7.9	59.4
08	300 54.5	16.7	311 18.6	7.5	13 26.2	7.8	59.4
09	315 54.4	.. 17.3	325 45.1	7.5	13 34.0	7.7	59.4
10	330 54.4	17.8	340 11.6	7.6	13 41.7	7.6	59.4
11	345 54.4	18.4	354 38.2	7.5	13 49.3	7.5	59.3
12	0 54.4	N19 19.0	9 04.7	7.4	N13 56.8	7.5	59.3
13	15 54.4	19.5	23 31.1	7.5	14 04.3	7.3	59.3
14	30 54.4	20.1	37 57.6	7.4	14 11.6	7.2	59.3
15	45 54.3	.. 20.7	52 24.0	7.5	14 18.8	7.2	59.3
16	60 54.3	21.2	66 50.5	7.4	14 26.0	7.0	59.2
17	75 54.3	21.8	81 16.9	7.4	14 33.0	7.0	59.2
18	90 54.3	N19 22.4	95 43.3	7.4	N14 40.0	6.9	59.2
19	105 54.3	22.9	110 09.7	7.4	14 46.9	6.7	59.2
20	120 54.2	23.5	124 36.1	7.4	14 53.6	6.7	59.2
21	135 54.2	.. 24.0	139 02.5	7.3	15 00.3	6.5	59.1
22	150 54.2	24.6	153 28.8	7.4	15 06.8	6.5	59.1
23	165 54.2	25.1	167 55.2	7.3	15 13.3	6.4	59.1
18 00	180 54.1	N19 25.7	182 21.5	7.4	N15 19.7	6.2	59.1
01	195 54.1	26.3	196 47.9	7.3	15 25.9	6.2	59.0
02	210 54.1	26.8	211 14.2	7.3	15 32.1	6.0	59.0
03	225 54.1	.. 27.4	225 40.5	7.3	15 38.1	6.0	59.0
04	240 54.1	27.9	240 06.8	7.3	15 44.1	5.8	59.0
05	255 54.0	28.5	254 33.1	7.4	15 49.9	5.8	58.9
06	270 54.0	N19 29.0	268 59.5	7.3	N15 55.7	5.6	58.9
07	285 54.0	29.6	283 25.8	7.3	16 01.3	5.6	58.9
08	300 54.0	30.1	297 52.1	7.3	16 06.9	5.4	58.9
09	315 53.9	.. 30.7	312 18.4	7.2	16 12.3	5.3	58.8
10	330 53.9	31.2	326 44.6	7.3	16 17.6	5.2	58.8
11	345 53.9	31.8	341 10.9	7.3	16 22.8	5.1	58.8
12	0 53.9	N19 32.3	355 37.2	7.3	N16 27.9	5.0	58.8
13	15 53.8	32.9	10 03.5	7.3	16 32.9	4.9	58.7
14	30 53.8	33.4	24 29.8	7.3	16 37.8	4.8	58.7
15	45 53.8	.. 34.0	38 56.1	7.3	16 42.6	4.7	58.7
16	60 53.8	34.5	53 22.4	7.3	16 47.3	4.5	58.7
17	75 53.7	35.1	67 48.7	7.4	16 51.8	4.5	58.6
18	90 53.7	N19 35.6	82 15.1	7.3	N16 56.3	4.4	58.6
19	105 53.7	36.2	96 41.4	7.3	17 00.7	4.2	58.6
20	120 53.7	36.7	111 07.7	7.3	17 04.9	4.1	58.6
21	135 53.6	.. 37.3	125 34.0	7.4	17 09.0	4.0	58.5
22	150 53.6	37.8	140 00.4	7.3	17 13.0	3.9	58.5
23	165 53.6	38.4	154 26.7	7.4	N17 16.9	3.8	58.5
	SD 15.8	d 0.6	SD 16.3		16.2		16.0

Left day labels: **S A T U R D A Y** (16), **S U N D A Y** (17), **M O N D A Y** (18)

Moonrise

Lat.	Twilight Naut.	Twilight Civil	Sunrise	Moonrise 16	17	18	19
°	h m	h m	h m	h m	h m	h m	h m
N 72	☐	☐	☐	02 15	02 10	02 04	01 54
N 70	☐	☐	☐	02 28	02 32	02 39	02 54
68	////	////	01 38	02 39	02 49	03 04	03 29
66	////	////	02 16	02 48	03 03	03 24	03 54
64	////	00 55	02 42	02 56	03 15	03 40	04 14
62	////	01 44	03 02	03 02	03 25	03 53	04 30
60	////	02 14	03 19	03 08	03 33	04 04	04 43
N 58	00 50	02 36	03 32	03 13	03 41	04 14	04 54
56	01 34	02 54	03 44	03 17	03 47	04 23	05 05
54	02 02	03 09	03 55	03 21	03 53	04 30	05 13
52	02 22	03 21	04 04	03 25	03 59	04 37	05 21
50	02 39	03 32	04 12	03 28	04 04	04 43	05 29
45	03 11	03 55	04 29	03 36	04 14	04 57	05 45
N 40	03 34	04 13	04 43	03 42	04 23	05 08	05 57
35	03 53	04 27	04 55	03 47	04 31	05 17	06 07
30	04 08	04 39	05 06	03 52	04 37	05 26	06 17
20	04 32	05 00	05 23	04 00	04 49	05 40	06 33
N 10	04 50	05 16	05 39	04 07	04 59	05 53	06 47
0	05 05	05 31	05 53	04 14	05 09	06 05	07 01
S 10	05 19	05 45	06 07	04 21	05 19	06 17	07 14
20	05 32	05 59	06 22	04 28	05 29	06 30	07 29
30	05 44	06 13	06 39	04 37	05 41	06 45	07 45
35	05 51	06 22	06 49	04 42	05 48	06 53	07 55
40	05 58	06 31	07 00	04 47	05 56	07 03	08 06
45	06 05	06 41	07 13	04 54	06 06	07 15	08 19
S 50	06 13	06 53	07 29	05 02	06 17	07 29	08 35
52	06 17	06 58	07 36	05 05	06 22	07 35	08 42
54	06 21	07 04	07 45	05 10	06 28	07 43	08 50
56	06 25	07 11	07 54	05 14	06 35	07 51	09 00
58	06 29	07 18	08 05	05 19	06 42	08 00	09 10
S 60	06 34	07 27	08 17	05 25	06 50	08 11	09 22

Moonset

Lat.	Sunset	Twilight Civil	Twilight Naut.	Moonset 16	17	18	19
°	h m	h m	h m	h m	h m	h m	h m
N 72	☐	☐	☐	19 22	21 25	23 31	☐
N 70	☐	☐	☐	19 01	20 50	22 32	23 55
68	22 20	////	////	18 45	20 26	21 58	23 13
66	21 40	////	////	18 32	20 07	21 33	22 45
64	21 13	23 06	////	18 22	19 52	21 14	22 23
62	20 53	22 12	////	18 13	19 39	20 58	22 06
60	20 36	21 42	////	18 05	19 28	20 45	21 51
N 58	20 22	21 19	23 11	17 58	19 19	20 34	21 39
56	20 10	21 01	22 22	17 52	19 11	20 24	21 28
54	19 59	20 46	21 54	17 47	19 04	20 15	21 19
52	19 50	20 33	21 32	17 42	18 57	20 07	21 11
50	19 42	20 22	21 15	17 37	18 51	20 00	21 03
45	19 24	19 59	20 43	17 28	18 39	19 46	20 47
N 40	19 10	19 41	20 19	17 20	18 28	19 33	20 34
35	18 58	19 26	20 01	17 13	18 19	19 23	20 23
30	18 47	19 14	19 45	17 08	18 12	19 14	20 13
20	18 30	18 53	19 21	16 57	17 58	18 58	19 56
N 10	18 14	18 37	19 03	16 48	17 47	18 44	19 41
0	18 00	18 22	18 47	16 40	17 36	18 32	19 27
S 10	17 46	18 08	18 34	16 32	17 25	18 19	19 13
20	17 31	17 54	18 21	16 23	17 13	18 05	18 59
30	17 14	17 39	18 08	16 13	17 00	17 49	18 42
35	17 04	17 31	18 02	16 07	16 52	17 40	18 32
40	16 53	17 22	17 55	16 00	16 43	17 30	18 21
45	16 39	17 11	17 47	15 53	16 33	17 18	18 07
S 50	16 23	16 59	17 39	15 43	16 21	17 03	17 51
52	16 16	16 54	17 35	15 39	16 15	16 56	17 44
54	16 08	16 48	17 31	15 35	16 09	16 49	17 35
56	15 58	16 41	17 27	15 29	16 02	16 40	17 26
58	15 48	16 34	17 23	15 24	15 54	16 31	17 15
S 60	15 35	16 25	17 18	15 17	15 45	16 20	17 03

Day	SUN Eqn. of Time 00h	12h	Mer. Pass.	MOON Mer. Pass. Upper	Lower	Age	Phase
d	m s	m s	h m	h m	h m	d	%
16	03 40	03 39	11 56	10 27	22 55	28	4
17	03 38	03 38	11 56	11 22	23 50	29	1
18	03 37	03 35	11 56	12 18	24 46	00	0

UT	ARIES	VENUS −4.3		MARS +1.5		JUPITER −2.0		SATURN +0.0		STARS		
d h	GHA	GHA	Dec	GHA	Dec	GHA	Dec	GHA	Dec	Name	SHA	Dec
	° ′	° ′	° ′	° ′	° ′	° ′	° ′	° ′	° ′		° ′	° ′
19 00	236 21.0	133 02.3	N25 38.1	173 31.2	N21 28.5	98 37.9	N17 11.9	356 02.7	S18 24.1	Acamar	315 17.8	S40 14.7
01	251 23.4	148 01.8	37.8	188 31.8	28.8	113 40.1	11.8	11 05.3	24.1	Achernar	335 26.4	S57 09.5
02	266 25.9	163 01.3	37.6	203 32.4	29.2	128 42.3	11.7	26 08.0	24.0	Acrux	173 07.2	S63 11.3
03	281 28.4	178 00.9 ..	37.4	218 33.0 ..	29.5	143 44.4 ..	11.6	41 10.6 ..	24.0	Adhara	255 11.8	S29 00.0
04	296 30.8	193 00.4	37.2	233 33.6	29.9	158 46.6	11.5	56 13.3	23.9	Aldebaran	290 48.2	N16 32.1
05	311 33.3	207 59.9	36.9	248 34.2	30.2	173 48.8	11.5	71 15.9	23.9			
06	326 35.7	222 59.4	N25 36.7	263 34.9	N21 30.5	188 51.0	N17 11.4	86 18.6	S18 23.9	Alioth	166 19.3	N55 52.8
07	341 38.2	237 59.0	36.4	278 35.5	30.9	203 53.2	11.3	101 21.3	23.8	Alkaid	152 57.5	N49 14.4
T 08	356 40.7	252 58.5	36.2	293 36.1	31.2	218 55.4	11.2	116 23.9	23.8	Al Na'ir	27 42.2	S46 52.9
U 09	11 43.1	267 58.0 ..	36.0	308 36.7 ..	31.5	233 57.5 ..	11.1	131 26.6 ..	23.8	Alnilam	275 45.4	S 1 11.8
E 10	26 45.6	282 57.6	35.7	323 37.3	31.9	248 59.7	11.0	146 29.2	23.7	Alphard	217 54.9	S 8 43.8
S 11	41 48.1	297 57.1	35.5	338 37.9	32.2	264 01.9	10.9	161 31.9	23.7			
D 12	56 50.5	312 56.6	N25 35.2	353 38.5	N21 32.6	279 04.1	N17 10.9	176 34.5	S18 23.7	Alphecca	126 09.6	N26 39.9
A 13	71 53.0	327 56.2	35.0	8 39.2	32.9	294 06.3	10.8	191 37.2	23.6	Alpheratz	357 42.3	N29 10.3
Y 14	86 55.5	342 55.7	34.8	23 39.8	33.2	309 08.4	10.7	206 39.8	23.6	Altair	62 06.8	N 8 54.6
15	101 57.9	357 55.2 ..	34.5	38 40.4 ..	33.6	324 10.6 ..	10.6	221 42.5 ..	23.6	Ankaa	353 14.8	S42 13.2
16	117 00.4	12 54.8	34.3	53 41.0	33.9	339 12.8	10.5	236 45.2	23.5	Antares	112 24.3	S26 27.8
17	132 02.9	27 54.3	34.0	68 41.6	34.2	354 15.0	10.4	251 47.8	23.5			
18	147 05.3	42 53.8	N25 33.8	83 42.2	N21 34.6	9 17.2	N17 10.3	266 50.5	S18 23.5	Arcturus	145 54.3	N19 06.2
19	162 07.8	57 53.4	33.5	98 42.8	34.9	24 19.3	10.2	281 53.1	23.4	Atria	107 24.3	S69 03.0
20	177 10.2	72 52.9	33.3	113 43.5	35.3	39 21.5	10.2	296 55.8	23.4	Avior	234 17.7	S59 34.0
21	192 12.7	87 52.5 ..	33.0	128 44.1 ..	35.6	54 23.7 ..	10.1	311 58.4 ..	23.3	Bellatrix	278 30.9	N 6 21.5
22	207 15.2	102 52.0	32.8	143 44.7	35.9	69 25.9	10.0	327 01.1	23.3	Betelgeuse	271 00.2	N 7 24.3
23	222 17.6	117 51.5	32.5	158 45.3	36.3	84 28.1	09.9	342 03.8	23.3			
20 00	237 20.1	132 51.1	N25 32.3	173 45.9	N21 36.6	99 30.2	N17 09.8	357 06.4	S18 23.2	Canopus	263 56.0	S52 42.6
01	252 22.6	147 50.6	32.0	188 46.5	36.9	114 32.4	09.7	12 09.1	23.2	Capella	280 33.0	N46 00.6
02	267 25.0	162 50.2	31.8	203 47.1	37.3	129 34.6	09.6	27 11.7	23.2	Deneb	49 30.4	N45 20.0
03	282 27.5	177 49.7 ..	31.5	218 47.8 ..	37.6	144 36.8 ..	09.5	42 14.4 ..	23.1	Denebola	182 32.2	N14 29.2
04	297 30.0	192 49.3	31.2	233 48.4	37.9	159 38.9	09.5	57 17.0	23.1	Diphda	348 54.8	S17 54.2
05	312 32.4	207 48.8	31.0	248 49.0	38.3	174 41.1	09.4	72 19.7	23.1			
06	327 34.9	222 48.3	N25 30.7	263 49.6	N21 38.6	189 43.3	N17 09.3	87 22.4	S18 23.0	Dubhe	193 50.1	N61 40.3
W 07	342 37.4	237 47.9	30.5	278 50.2	38.9	204 45.5	09.2	102 25.0	23.0	Elnath	278 11.3	N28 37.0
E 08	357 39.8	252 47.4	30.2	293 50.8	39.3	219 47.7	09.1	117 27.7	23.0	Eltanin	90 45.1	N51 29.2
D 09	12 42.3	267 47.0 ..	29.9	308 51.4 ..	39.6	234 49.8 ..	09.0	132 30.3 ..	22.9	Enif	33 45.8	N 9 56.7
N 10	27 44.7	282 46.5	29.7	323 52.0	39.9	249 52.0	08.9	147 33.0	22.9	Fomalhaut	15 22.7	S29 32.3
E 11	42 47.2	297 46.1	29.4	338 52.7	40.2	264 54.2	08.8	162 35.6	22.9			
S 12	57 49.7	312 45.6	N25 29.1	353 53.3	N21 40.6	279 56.4	N17 08.7	177 38.3	S18 22.8	Gacrux	171 58.9	S57 12.2
D 13	72 52.1	327 45.2	28.9	8 53.9	40.9	294 58.5	08.7	192 41.0	22.8	Gienah	175 50.7	S17 37.8
A 14	87 54.6	342 44.7	28.6	23 54.5	41.2	310 00.7	08.6	207 43.6	22.8	Hadar	148 45.3	S60 26.9
Y 15	102 57.1	357 44.3 ..	28.3	38 55.1 ..	41.6	325 02.9 ..	08.5	222 46.3 ..	22.7	Hamal	327 59.6	N23 31.9
16	117 59.5	12 43.9	28.1	53 55.7	41.9	340 05.1	08.4	237 48.9	22.7	Kaus Aust.	83 41.8	S34 22.3
17	133 02.0	27 43.4	27.8	68 56.3	42.2	355 07.2	08.3	252 51.6	22.6			
18	148 04.5	42 43.0	N25 27.5	83 56.9	N21 42.5	10 09.4	N17 08.2	267 54.2	S18 22.6	Kochab	137 19.1	N74 05.7
19	163 06.9	57 42.5	27.3	98 57.6	42.9	25 11.6	08.1	282 56.9	22.6	Markab	13 37.1	N15 17.2
20	178 09.4	72 42.1	27.0	113 58.2	43.2	40 13.8	08.0	297 59.5	22.5	Menkar	314 14.0	N 4 08.8
21	193 11.8	87 41.6 ..	26.7	128 58.8 ..	43.5	55 15.9 ..	07.9	313 02.2 ..	22.5	Menkent	148 05.6	S36 26.8
22	208 14.3	102 41.2	26.4	143 59.4	43.8	70 18.1	07.9	328 04.9	22.5	Miaplacidus	221 39.4	S69 47.3
23	223 16.8	117 40.7	26.2	159 00.0	44.2	85 20.3	07.8	343 07.5	22.4			
21 00	238 19.2	132 40.3	N25 25.9	174 00.6	N21 44.5	100 22.4	N17 07.7	358 10.2	S18 22.4	Mirfak	308 38.9	N49 54.7
01	253 21.7	147 39.9	25.6	189 01.2	44.8	115 24.6	07.6	13 12.8	22.4	Nunki	75 56.5	S26 16.4
02	268 24.2	162 39.4	25.3	204 01.8	45.1	130 26.8	07.5	28 15.5	22.3	Peacock	53 17.0	S56 40.7
03	283 26.6	177 39.0 ..	25.0	219 02.5 ..	45.5	145 29.0 ..	07.4	43 18.1 ..	22.3	Pollux	243 26.4	N27 59.2
04	298 29.1	192 38.5	24.8	234 03.1	45.8	160 31.1	07.3	58 20.8	22.3	Procyon	244 58.6	N 5 10.9
05	313 31.6	207 38.1	24.5	249 03.7	46.1	175 33.3	07.2	73 23.5	22.2			
06	328 34.0	222 37.7	N25 24.2	264 04.3	N21 46.4	190 35.5	N17 07.1	88 26.1	S18 22.2	Rasalhague	96 04.9	N12 33.1
07	343 36.5	237 37.2	23.9	279 04.9	46.8	205 37.6	07.1	103 28.8	22.2	Regulus	207 42.2	N11 53.4
T 08	358 39.0	252 36.8	23.6	294 05.5	47.1	220 39.8	07.0	118 31.4	22.1	Rigel	281 11.1	S 8 11.3
H 09	13 41.4	267 36.4 ..	23.3	309 06.1 ..	47.4	235 42.0 ..	06.9	133 34.1 ..	22.1	Rigil Kent.	139 49.2	S60 53.9
U 10	28 43.9	282 35.9	23.0	324 06.7	47.8	250 44.2	06.8	148 36.7	22.0	Sabik	102 10.7	S15 44.5
R 11	43 46.3	297 35.5	22.7	339 07.4	48.1	265 46.3	06.7	163 39.4	22.0			
S 12	58 48.8	312 35.1	N25 22.5	354 08.0	N21 48.4	280 48.5	N17 06.6	178 42.1	S18 22.0	Schedar	349 39.3	N56 37.0
D 13	73 51.3	327 34.6	22.2	9 08.6	48.7	295 50.7	06.5	193 44.7	21.9	Shaula	96 19.8	S37 06.6
A 14	88 53.7	342 34.2	21.9	24 09.2	49.0	310 52.8	06.4	208 47.4	21.9	Sirius	258 32.8	S16 44.6
Y 15	103 56.2	357 33.8 ..	21.6	39 09.8 ..	49.3	325 55.0 ..	06.3	223 50.0 ..	21.9	Spica	158 29.6	S11 14.5
16	118 58.7	12 33.4	21.3	54 10.4	49.7	340 57.2	06.2	238 52.7	21.8	Suhail	222 51.5	S43 30.1
17	134 01.1	27 32.9	21.0	69 11.0	50.0	355 59.3	06.2	253 55.3	21.8			
18	149 03.6	42 32.5	N25 20.7	84 11.6	N21 50.3	11 01.5	N17 06.1	268 58.0	S18 21.8	Vega	80 37.7	N38 47.9
19	164 06.1	57 32.1	20.4	99 12.2	50.6	26 03.7	06.0	284 00.7	21.7	Zuben'ubi	137 03.6	S16 06.3
20	179 08.5	72 31.7	20.1	114 12.9	50.9	41 05.9	05.9	299 03.3	21.7		SHA	Mer. Pass.
21	194 11.0	87 31.2 ..	19.8	129 13.5 ..	51.2	56 08.0 ..	05.8	314 06.0 ..	21.7		° ′	h m
22	209 13.5	102 30.8	19.5	144 14.1	51.6	71 10.2	05.7	329 08.6	21.6	Venus	255 31.0	15 09
23	224 15.9	117 30.4	19.2	159 14.7	51.9	86 12.4	05.6	344 11.3	21.6	Mars	296 25.8	12 24
	h m									Jupiter	222 10.1	17 19
Mer. Pass.	8 09.3	v −0.4	d 0.3	v 0.6	d 0.3	v 2.2	d 0.1	v 2.7	d 0.0	Saturn	119 46.3	0 12

UT	SUN GHA	SUN Dec	MOON GHA	v	MOON Dec	d	HP
d h	° ′	° ′	° ′	′	° ′	′	′
19 00	180 53.5	N19 38.9	168 53.1	7.4	N17 20.7	3.7	58.4
01	195 53.5	39.4	183 19.5	7.4	17 24.4	3.6	58.4
02	210 53.5	40.0	197 45.9	7.4	17 28.0	3.4	58.4
03	225 53.5 ..	40.5	212 12.3	7.4	17 31.4	3.4	58.4
04	240 53.4	41.1	226 38.7	7.4	17 34.8	3.2	58.3
05	255 53.4	41.6	241 05.1	7.5	17 38.0	3.2	58.3
06	270 53.4	N19 42.2	255 31.6	7.5	N17 41.2	3.0	58.3
07	285 53.3	42.7	269 58.1	7.4	17 44.2	2.9	58.2
T 08	300 53.3	43.2	284 24.5	7.5	17 47.1	2.8	58.2
U 09	315 53.3 ..	43.8	298 51.0	7.6	17 49.9	2.6	58.2
E 10	330 53.3	44.3	313 17.6	7.5	17 52.5	2.6	58.1
S 11	345 53.2	44.8	327 44.1	7.6	17 55.1	2.4	58.1
D 12	0 53.2	N19 45.4	342 10.7	7.6	N17 57.5	2.4	58.1
A 13	15 53.2	45.9	356 37.3	7.6	17 59.9	2.2	58.1
Y 14	30 53.1	46.5	11 03.9	7.6	18 02.1	2.1	58.0
15	45 53.1 ..	47.0	25 30.5	7.7	18 04.2	2.0	58.0
16	60 53.1	47.5	39 57.2	7.7	18 06.2	1.9	58.0
17	75 53.0	48.1	54 23.9	7.7	18 08.1	1.8	57.9
18	90 53.0	N19 48.6	68 50.6	7.7	N18 09.9	1.7	57.9
19	105 53.0	49.1	83 17.3	7.8	18 11.6	1.5	57.9
20	120 52.9	49.7	97 44.1	7.8	18 13.1	1.5	57.8
21	135 52.9 ..	50.2	112 10.9	7.9	18 14.6	1.3	57.8
22	150 52.9	50.7	126 37.8	7.8	18 15.9	1.2	57.8
23	165 52.8	51.2	141 04.6	7.9	18 17.1	1.1	57.7
20 00	180 52.8	N19 51.8	155 31.5	8.0	N18 18.2	1.0	57.7
01	195 52.8	52.3	169 58.5	7.9	18 19.2	0.9	57.7
02	210 52.7	52.8	184 25.4	8.0	18 20.1	0.8	57.7
03	225 52.7 ..	53.4	198 52.4	8.1	18 20.9	0.7	57.6
04	240 52.7	53.9	213 19.5	8.1	18 21.6	0.5	57.6
05	255 52.6	54.4	227 46.6	8.1	18 22.1	0.5	57.6
06	270 52.6	N19 54.9	242 13.7	8.1	N18 22.6	0.3	57.5
W 07	285 52.6	55.5	256 40.8	8.2	18 22.9	0.3	57.5
E 08	300 52.5	56.0	271 08.0	8.3	18 23.2	0.1	57.5
D 09	315 52.5 ..	56.5	285 35.3	8.2	18 23.3	0.0	57.4
N 10	330 52.5	57.0	300 02.5	8.3	18 23.3	0.1	57.4
E 11	345 52.4	57.6	314 29.8	8.4	18 23.2	0.1	57.4
S 12	0 52.4	N19 58.1	328 57.2	8.4	N18 23.1	0.4	57.3
D 13	15 52.4	58.6	343 24.6	8.5	18 22.7	0.4	57.3
A 14	30 52.3	59.1	357 52.1	8.4	18 22.3	0.5	57.3
Y 15	45 52.3	19 59.6	12 19.5	8.6	18 21.8	0.6	57.2
16	60 52.2	20 00.2	26 47.1	8.6	18 21.2	0.7	57.2
17	75 52.2	00.7	41 14.7	8.6	18 20.5	0.8	57.2
18	90 52.2	N20 01.2	55 42.3	8.7	N18 19.7	1.0	57.1
19	105 52.1	01.7	70 10.0	8.7	18 18.7	1.0	57.1
20	120 52.1	02.2	84 37.7	8.8	18 17.7	1.1	57.1
21	135 52.1 ..	02.8	99 05.5	8.8	18 16.6	1.3	57.1
22	150 52.0	03.3	113 33.3	8.9	18 15.3	1.3	57.0
23	165 52.0	03.8	128 01.2	8.9	18 14.0	1.5	57.0
21 00	180 51.9	N20 04.3	142 29.1	9.0	N18 12.5	1.5	56.9
01	195 51.9	04.8	156 57.1	9.0	18 11.0	1.6	56.9
02	210 51.9	05.3	171 25.1	9.1	18 09.4	1.8	56.9
03	225 51.8 ..	05.8	185 53.2	9.1	18 07.6	1.8	56.9
04	240 51.8	06.4	200 21.3	9.2	18 05.8	2.0	56.8
05	255 51.7	06.9	214 49.5	9.2	18 03.8	2.0	56.8
06	270 51.7	N20 07.4	229 17.7	9.3	N18 01.8	2.1	56.8
T 07	285 51.7	07.9	243 46.0	9.4	17 59.7	2.3	56.7
H 08	300 51.6	08.4	258 14.4	9.4	17 57.4	2.3	56.7
U 09	315 51.6 ..	08.9	272 42.8	9.4	17 55.1	2.4	56.7
R 10	330 51.5	09.4	287 11.2	9.5	17 52.7	2.6	56.6
S 11	345 51.5	09.9	301 39.7	9.6	17 50.1	2.6	56.6
D 12	0 51.5	N20 10.4	316 08.3	9.6	N17 47.5	2.7	56.6
A 13	15 51.4	10.9	330 36.9	9.7	17 44.8	2.8	56.5
Y 14	30 51.4	11.5	345 05.6	9.8	17 42.0	2.9	56.5
15	45 51.3 ..	12.0	359 34.4	9.8	17 39.1	3.0	56.5
16	60 51.3	12.5	14 03.2	9.8	17 36.1	3.0	56.4
17	75 51.2	13.0	28 32.0	9.9	17 33.1	3.2	56.4
18	90 51.2	N20 13.5	43 00.9	10.0	N17 29.9	3.3	56.4
19	105 51.2	14.0	57 29.9	10.1	17 26.6	3.3	56.4
20	120 51.1	14.5	71 59.0	10.0	17 23.3	3.4	56.3
21	135 51.1 ..	15.0	86 28.0	10.2	17 19.9	3.5	56.3
22	150 51.0	15.5	100 57.2	10.2	17 16.4	3.7	56.3
23	165 51.0	16.0	115 26.4	10.3	N17 12.7	3.7	56.2
	SD 15.8	d 0.5	SD 15.8		15.6		15.4

Lat.	Twilight Naut.	Twilight Civil	Sunrise	Moonrise 19	20	21	22
°	h m	h m	h m	h m	h m	h m	h m
N 72	☐	☐	☐	01 54	☐	☐	05 01
N 70	☐	☐	☐	02 54	03 27	04 28	05 51
68	////	////	01 19	03 29	04 09	05 08	06 23
66	////	////	02 04	03 54	04 37	05 36	06 46
64	////	00 21	02 33	04 14	04 59	05 57	07 04
62	////	01 31	02 54	04 30	05 16	06 14	07 19
60	////	02 04	03 12	04 43	05 31	06 28	07 32
N 58	00 18	02 28	03 27	04 54	05 43	06 40	07 43
56	01 22	02 47	03 39	05 05	05 54	06 50	07 52
54	01 53	03 03	03 50	05 13	06 03	07 00	08 00
52	02 15	03 16	04 00	05 21	06 12	07 08	08 08
50	02 33	03 28	04 08	05 29	06 19	07 15	08 15
45	03 07	03 51	04 26	05 44	06 36	07 31	08 29
N 40	03 31	04 10	04 41	05 57	06 49	07 44	08 41
35	03 50	04 25	04 53	06 07	07 00	07 55	08 51
30	04 06	04 38	05 04	06 17	07 10	08 05	09 00
20	04 34	04 59	05 22	06 33	07 27	08 21	09 15
N 10	04 49	05 16	05 38	06 47	07 42	08 36	09 28
0	05 05	05 31	05 53	07 01	07 56	08 49	09 40
S 10	05 20	05 45	06 08	07 14	08 10	09 03	09 53
20	05 33	06 00	06 23	07 29	08 25	09 17	10 06
30	05 46	06 15	06 41	07 45	08 42	09 34	10 21
35	05 53	06 24	06 51	07 55	08 52	09 44	10 30
40	06 00	06 33	07 02	08 06	09 03	09 55	10 40
45	06 08	06 44	07 16	08 19	09 17	10 08	10 51
S 50	06 17	06 57	07 33	08 35	09 33	10 23	11 05
52	06 21	07 02	07 41	08 42	09 41	10 31	11 12
54	06 25	07 09	07 49	08 50	09 49	10 39	11 19
56	06 29	07 16	07 59	09 00	09 59	10 48	11 27
58	06 34	07 23	08 10	09 10	10 10	10 58	11 37
S 60	06 39	07 32	08 23	09 22	10 23	11 10	11 47

Lat.	Sunset	Twilight Civil	Twilight Naut.	Moonset 19	20	21	22
°	h m	h m	h m	h m	h m	h m	h m
N 72	☐	☐	☐	☐	☐	☐	02 02
N 70	☐	☐	☐	23 55	24 46	00 46	01 10
68	22 40	////	////	23 13	24 06	00 06	00 38
66	21 53	////	////	22 45	23 38	24 14	00 14
64	21 23	////	////	22 23	23 17	23 56	24 24
62	21 00	22 26	////	22 06	23 00	23 40	24 11
60	20 43	21 51	////	21 51	22 45	23 28	24 00
N 58	20 28	21 27	////	21 39	22 33	23 17	23 51
56	20 15	21 07	22 35	21 28	22 23	23 07	23 43
54	20 04	20 52	22 03	21 19	22 13	22 58	23 35
52	19 54	20 38	21 40	21 10	22 05	22 51	23 29
50	19 46	20 26	21 21	21 03	21 57	22 44	23 23
45	19 27	20 02	20 47	20 47	21 41	22 29	23 10
N 40	19 13	19 44	20 23	20 34	21 28	22 17	22 59
35	19 00	19 29	20 03	20 23	21 17	22 06	22 50
30	18 49	19 16	19 48	20 13	21 07	21 57	22 42
20	18 31	18 55	19 23	19 56	20 50	21 41	22 28
N 10	18 15	18 37	19 04	19 41	20 36	21 27	22 16
0	18 00	18 22	18 48	19 27	20 22	21 14	22 04
S 10	17 45	18 08	18 33	19 13	20 08	21 01	21 52
20	17 30	17 53	18 20	18 59	19 53	20 47	21 40
30	17 12	17 38	18 07	18 42	19 36	20 31	21 26
35	17 02	17 29	18 00	18 32	19 26	20 22	21 18
40	16 50	17 20	17 53	18 21	19 15	20 11	21 08
45	16 36	17 09	17 45	18 07	19 01	19 58	20 57
S 50	16 20	16 56	17 36	17 51	18 45	19 43	20 43
52	16 12	16 50	17 32	17 44	18 37	19 36	20 37
54	16 03	16 44	17 28	17 35	18 29	19 28	20 30
56	15 53	16 37	17 23	17 26	18 19	19 19	20 22
58	15 42	16 29	17 18	17 15	18 08	19 09	20 14
S 60	15 29	16 20	17 13	17 03	17 56	18 57	20 04

Day	SUN Eqn. of Time 00h	12h	SUN Mer. Pass.	MOON Mer. Pass. Upper	Lower	Age	Phase
d	m s	m s	h m	h m	h m	d	%
19	03 34	03 33	11 56	13 14	00 46	01	2
20	03 31	03 30	11 57	14 09	01 42	02	7
21	03 28	03 26	11 57	15 02	02 36	03	13

2015 MAY 22, 23, 24 (FRI., SAT., SUN.)

UT	ARIES	VENUS −4.3		MARS +1.5		JUPITER −2.0		SATURN +0.0		STARS		
	GHA	GHA	Dec	GHA	Dec	GHA	Dec	GHA	Dec	Name	SHA	Dec
d h	° ′	° ′	° ′	° ′	° ′	° ′	° ′	° ′	° ′		° ′	° ′
22 00	239 18.4	132 30.0	N25 18.9	174 15.3	N21 52.2	101 14.5	N17 05.5	359 13.9	S18 21.6	Acamar	315 17.8	S40 14.7
01	254 20.8	147 29.5	18.6	189 15.9	52.5	116 16.7	05.4	14 16.6	21.5	Achernar	335 26.4	S57 09.5
02	269 23.3	162 29.1	18.3	204 16.5	52.8	131 18.9	05.3	29 19.3	21.5	Acrux	173 07.2	S63 11.3
03	284 25.8	177 28.7 ..	18.0	219 17.1 ..	53.1	146 21.0 ..	05.2	44 21.9 ..	21.5	Adhara	255 11.8	S29 00.0
04	299 28.2	192 28.3	17.7	234 17.7	53.5	161 23.2	05.1	59 24.6	21.4	Aldebaran	290 48.2	N16 32.1
05	314 30.7	207 27.9	17.4	249 18.4	53.8	176 25.4	05.1	74 27.2	21.4			
06	329 33.2	222 27.4	N25 17.1	264 19.0	N21 54.1	191 27.5	N17 05.0	89 29.9	S18 21.3	Alioth	166 19.3	N55 52.8
07	344 35.6	237 27.0	16.7	279 19.6	54.4	206 29.7	04.9	104 32.5	21.3	Alkaid	152 57.6	N49 14.4
08	359 38.1	252 26.6	16.4	294 20.2	54.7	221 31.9	04.8	119 35.2	21.3	Al Na'ir	27 42.2	S46 52.9
F 09	14 40.6	267 26.2 ..	16.1	309 20.8 ..	55.0	236 34.0 ..	04.7	134 37.9 ..	21.2	Alnilam	275 45.4	S 1 11.8
R 10	29 43.0	282 25.8	15.8	324 21.4	55.3	251 36.2	04.6	149 40.5	21.2	Alphard	217 54.9	S 8 43.8
I 11	44 45.5	297 25.4	15.5	339 22.0	55.7	266 38.3	04.5	164 43.2	21.2			
D 12	59 48.0	312 25.0	N25 15.2	354 22.6	N21 56.0	281 40.5	N17 04.4	179 45.8	S18 21.1	Alphecca	126 09.6	N26 39.9
A 13	74 50.4	327 24.5	14.9	9 23.2	56.3	296 42.7	04.3	194 48.5	21.1	Alpheratz	357 42.3	N29 10.3
Y 14	89 52.9	342 24.1	14.5	24 23.9	56.6	311 44.8	04.2	209 51.1	21.1	Altair	62 06.8	N 8 54.6
15	104 55.3	357 23.7 ..	14.2	39 24.5	56.9	326 47.0 ..	04.1	224 53.8 ..	21.0	Ankaa	353 14.7	S42 13.2
16	119 57.8	12 23.3	13.9	54 25.1	57.2	341 49.2	04.0	239 56.5	21.0	Antares	112 24.3	S26 27.8
17	135 00.3	27 22.9	13.6	69 25.7	57.5	356 51.3	04.0	254 59.1	21.0			
18	150 02.7	42 22.5	N25 13.3	84 26.3	N21 57.8	11 53.5	N17 03.9	270 01.8	S18 20.9	Arcturus	145 54.3	N19 06.2
19	165 05.2	57 22.1	12.9	99 26.9	58.1	26 55.7	03.8	285 04.4	20.9	Atria	107 24.3	S69 03.1
20	180 07.7	72 21.7	12.6	114 27.5	58.5	41 57.8	03.7	300 07.1	20.9	Avior	234 17.7	S59 34.0
21	195 10.1	87 21.3 ..	12.3	129 28.1 ..	58.8	57 00.0 ..	03.6	315 09.7 ..	20.8	Bellatrix	278 30.9	N 6 21.5
22	210 12.6	102 20.9	12.0	144 28.7	59.1	72 02.1	03.5	330 12.4	20.8	Betelgeuse	271 00.2	N 7 24.3
23	225 15.1	117 20.5	11.7	159 29.3	59.4	87 04.3	03.4	345 15.1	20.8			
23 00	240 17.5	132 20.1	N25 11.3	174 30.0	N21 59.7	102 06.5	N17 03.3	0 17.7	S18 20.7	Canopus	263 56.0	S52 42.6
01	255 20.0	147 19.7	11.0	189 30.6	22 00.0	117 08.6	03.2	15 20.4	20.7	Capella	280 33.0	N46 00.6
02	270 22.4	162 19.3	10.7	204 31.2	00.3	132 10.8	03.1	30 23.0	20.6	Deneb	49 30.3	N45 20.0
03	285 24.9	177 18.9 ..	10.3	219 31.8 ..	00.6	147 13.0 ..	03.0	45 25.7 ..	20.6	Denebola	182 32.2	N14 29.2
04	300 27.4	192 18.5	10.0	234 32.4	00.9	162 15.1	02.9	60 28.3	20.6	Diphda	348 54.8	S17 54.1
05	315 29.8	207 18.1	09.7	249 33.0	01.2	177 17.3	02.8	75 31.0	20.5			
06	330 32.3	222 17.7	N25 09.3	264 33.6	N22 01.5	192 19.4	N17 02.7	90 33.7	S18 20.5	Dubhe	193 50.1	N61 40.3
07	345 34.8	237 17.3	09.0	279 34.2	01.8	207 21.6	02.7	105 36.3	20.5	Elnath	278 11.3	N28 37.0
S 08	0 37.2	252 16.9	08.7	294 34.8	02.1	222 23.8	02.6	120 39.0	20.4	Eltanin	90 45.1	N51 29.3
A 09	15 39.7	267 16.5 ..	08.3	309 35.4 ..	02.5	237 25.9 ..	02.5	135 41.6 ..	20.4	Enif	33 45.8	N 9 56.7
T 10	30 42.2	282 16.1	08.0	324 36.1	02.8	252 28.1	02.4	150 44.3	20.4	Fomalhaut	15 22.7	S29 32.3
U 11	45 44.6	297 15.7	07.7	339 36.7	03.1	267 30.2	02.3	165 46.9	20.3			
R 12	60 47.1	312 15.3	N25 07.3	354 37.3	N22 03.4	282 32.4	N17 02.2	180 49.6	S18 20.3	Gacrux	171 59.0	S57 12.2
D 13	75 49.6	327 14.9	07.0	9 37.9	03.7	297 34.6	02.1	195 52.3	20.3	Gienah	175 50.8	S17 37.8
A 14	90 52.0	342 14.5	06.7	24 38.5	04.0	312 36.7	02.0	210 54.9	20.2	Hadar	148 45.3	S60 26.9
Y 15	105 54.5	357 14.1 ..	06.3	39 39.1 ..	04.3	327 38.9 ..	01.9	225 57.6 ..	20.2	Hamal	327 59.6	N23 31.9
16	120 56.9	12 13.7	06.0	54 39.7	04.6	342 41.0	01.8	241 00.2	20.2	Kaus Aust.	83 41.8	S34 22.3
17	135 59.4	27 13.3	05.6	69 40.3	04.9	357 43.2	01.7	256 02.9	20.1			
18	151 01.9	42 12.9	N25 05.3	84 40.9	N22 05.2	12 45.3	N17 01.6	271 05.5	S18 20.1	Kochab	137 19.2	N74 05.8
19	166 04.3	57 12.6	04.9	99 41.5	05.5	27 47.5	01.5	286 08.2	20.1	Markab	13 37.1	N15 17.2
20	181 06.8	72 12.2	04.6	114 42.2	05.8	42 49.7	01.4	301 10.8	20.0	Menkar	314 14.0	N 4 08.8
21	196 09.3	87 11.8 ..	04.2	129 42.8 ..	06.1	57 51.8 ..	01.3	316 13.5 ..	20.0	Menkent	148 05.6	S36 26.8
22	211 11.7	102 11.4	03.9	144 43.4	06.4	72 54.0	01.2	331 16.2	19.9	Miaplacidus	221 39.5	S69 47.3
23	226 14.2	117 11.0	03.5	159 44.0	06.7	87 56.1	01.2	346 18.8	19.9			
24 00	241 16.7	132 10.6	N25 03.2	174 44.6	N22 07.0	102 58.3	N17 01.1	1 21.5	S18 19.9	Mirfak	308 38.9	N49 54.7
01	256 19.1	147 10.3	02.8	189 45.2	07.3	118 00.4	01.0	16 24.1	19.8	Nunki	75 56.4	S26 16.4
02	271 21.6	162 09.9	02.5	204 45.8	07.6	133 02.6	00.9	31 26.8	19.8	Peacock	53 17.0	S56 40.7
03	286 24.1	177 09.5 ..	02.1	219 46.4 ..	07.9	148 04.8 ..	00.8	46 29.4 ..	19.8	Pollux	243 26.4	N27 59.2
04	301 26.5	192 09.1	01.8	234 47.0	08.2	163 06.9	00.7	61 32.1	19.7	Procyon	244 58.6	N 5 10.9
05	316 29.0	207 08.7	01.4	249 47.6	08.5	178 09.1	00.6	76 34.8	19.7			
06	331 31.4	222 08.4	N25 01.1	264 48.2	N22 08.8	193 11.2	N17 00.5	91 37.4	S18 19.7	Rasalhague	96 04.9	N12 33.1
07	346 33.9	237 08.0	00.7	279 48.8	09.1	208 13.4	00.4	106 40.1	19.6	Regulus	207 42.2	N11 53.4
08	1 36.4	252 07.6	00.4	294 49.5	09.4	223 15.5	00.3	121 42.7	19.6	Rigel	281 11.1	S 8 11.3
S 09	16 38.8	267 07.2	25 00.0	309 50.1 ..	09.7	238 17.7 ..	00.2	136 45.4 ..	19.6	Rigil Kent.	139 49.2	S60 53.9
U 10	31 41.3	282 06.9	24 59.6	324 50.7	10.0	253 19.8	00.1	151 48.0	19.5	Sabik	102 10.7	S15 44.4
N 11	46 43.8	297 06.5	59.3	339 51.3	10.3	268 22.0	17 00.0	166 50.7	19.5			
D 12	61 46.2	312 06.1	N24 58.9	354 51.9	N22 10.5	283 24.1	N16 59.9	181 53.4	S18 19.5	Schedar	349 39.2	N56 37.0
A 13	76 48.7	327 05.7	58.6	9 52.5	10.8	298 26.3	59.8	196 56.0	19.4	Shaula	96 19.7	S37 06.6
Y 14	91 51.2	342 05.4	58.2	24 53.1	11.1	313 28.5	59.7	211 58.7	19.4	Sirius	258 32.8	S16 44.6
15	106 53.6	357 05.0 ..	57.8	39 53.7 ..	11.4	328 30.6 ..	59.6	227 01.3 ..	19.4	Spica	158 29.6	S11 14.5
16	121 56.1	12 04.6	57.5	54 54.3	11.7	343 32.8	59.5	242 04.0	19.3	Suhail	222 51.6	S43 30.1
17	136 58.6	27 04.3	57.1	69 54.9	12.0	358 34.9	59.4	257 06.6	19.3			
18	152 01.0	42 03.9	N24 56.7	84 55.5	N22 12.3	13 37.1	N16 59.3	272 09.3	S18 19.3	Vega	80 37.7	N38 47.9
19	167 03.5	57 03.5	56.4	99 56.2	12.6	28 39.2	59.2	287 12.0	19.2	Zuben'ubi	137 03.6	S16 06.3
20	182 05.9	72 03.2	56.0	114 56.8	12.9	43 41.4	59.1	302 14.6	19.2			
21	197 08.4	87 02.8 ..	55.6	129 57.4 ..	13.2	58 43.5 ..	59.1	317 17.3 ..	19.1		SHA	Mer. Pass.
22	212 10.9	102 02.4	55.2	144 58.0	13.5	73 45.7	59.0	332 19.9	19.1	Venus	252 02.5	15 11
23	227 13.3	117 02.1	54.9	159 58.6	13.8	88 47.8	58.9	347 22.6	19.1	Mars	294 12.4	12 22
	h m									Jupiter	221 48.9	17 09
Mer. Pass. 7 57.5		v −0.4	d 0.3	v 0.6	d 0.3	v 2.2	d 0.1	v 2.7	d 0.0	Saturn	120 00.2	23 55

UT	SUN GHA	SUN Dec	MOON GHA	v	MOON Dec	d	HP
d h	° ′	° ′	° ′	′	° ′	′	′
22 00	180 50.9	N20 16.5	129 55.7	10.3	N17 09.0	3.7	56.2
01	195 50.9	17.0	144 25.0	10.4	17 05.3	3.9	56.2
02	210 50.9	17.5	158 54.4	10.5	17 01.4	3.9	56.1
03	225 50.8	.. 18.0	173 23.9	10.5	16 57.5	4.1	56.1
04	240 50.8	18.5	187 53.4	10.6	16 53.4	4.1	56.1
05	255 50.7	19.0	202 23.0	10.6	16 49.3	4.2	56.1
06	270 50.7	N20 19.5	216 52.6	10.7	N16 45.1	4.3	56.0
07	285 50.6	20.0	231 22.3	10.8	16 40.8	4.3	56.0
08	300 50.6	20.5	245 52.1	10.8	16 36.5	4.5	56.0
F 09	315 50.5	.. 21.0	260 21.9	10.9	16 32.0	4.5	55.9
R 10	330 50.5	21.5	274 51.8	10.9	16 27.5	4.6	55.9
I 11	345 50.4	22.0	289 21.7	11.0	16 22.9	4.7	55.9
D 12	0 50.4	N20 22.4	303 51.7	11.1	N16 18.2	4.7	55.9
A 13	15 50.3	22.9	318 21.8	11.1	16 13.5	4.8	55.8
Y 14	30 50.3	23.4	332 51.9	11.2	16 08.7	4.9	55.8
15	45 50.3	.. 23.9	347 22.1	11.2	16 03.8	5.0	55.8
16	60 50.2	24.4	1 52.3	11.3	15 58.8	5.1	55.7
17	75 50.2	24.9	16 22.6	11.4	15 53.7	5.1	55.7
18	90 50.1	N20 25.4	30 53.0	11.4	N15 48.6	5.2	55.7
19	105 50.1	25.9	45 23.4	11.5	15 43.4	5.3	55.7
20	120 50.0	26.4	59 53.9	11.6	15 38.1	5.3	55.6
21	135 50.0	.. 26.9	74 24.5	11.6	15 32.8	5.4	55.6
22	150 49.9	27.4	88 55.1	11.7	15 27.4	5.5	55.6
23	165 49.9	27.8	103 25.8	11.7	15 21.9	5.6	55.6
23 00	180 49.8	N20 28.3	117 56.5	11.8	N15 16.3	5.6	55.5
01	195 49.8	28.8	132 27.3	11.9	15 10.7	5.7	55.5
02	210 49.7	29.3	146 58.2	11.9	15 05.0	5.7	55.5
03	225 49.7	.. 29.8	161 29.1	11.9	14 59.3	5.8	55.4
04	240 49.6	30.3	176 00.0	12.1	14 53.5	5.9	55.4
05	255 49.6	30.7	190 31.1	12.1	14 47.6	6.0	55.4
06	270 49.5	N20 31.2	205 02.2	12.1	N14 41.6	6.0	55.4
S 07	285 49.5	31.7	219 33.3	12.2	14 35.6	6.1	55.4
A 08	300 49.4	32.2	234 04.5	12.3	14 29.5	6.1	55.3
T 09	315 49.4	.. 32.7	248 35.8	12.3	14 23.4	6.2	55.3
U 10	330 49.3	33.2	263 07.1	12.4	14 17.2	6.3	55.3
R 11	345 49.3	33.6	277 38.5	12.4	14 10.9	6.3	55.3
D 12	0 49.2	N20 34.1	292 09.9	12.5	N14 04.6	6.4	55.2
A 13	15 49.2	34.6	306 41.4	12.6	13 58.2	6.5	55.2
Y 14	30 49.1	35.1	321 13.0	12.6	13 51.7	6.5	55.2
15	45 49.0	.. 35.5	335 44.6	12.6	13 45.2	6.5	55.2
16	60 49.0	36.0	350 16.2	12.7	13 38.7	6.7	55.1
17	75 48.9	36.5	4 47.9	12.8	13 32.0	6.6	55.1
18	90 48.9	N20 37.0	19 19.7	12.8	N13 25.4	6.8	55.1
19	105 48.8	37.4	33 51.5	12.9	13 18.6	6.8	55.1
20	120 48.8	37.9	48 23.4	13.0	13 11.8	6.8	55.1
21	135 48.7	.. 38.4	62 55.4	12.9	13 05.0	6.9	55.0
22	150 48.7	38.9	77 27.3	13.1	12 58.1	6.9	55.0
23	165 48.6	39.3	91 59.4	13.1	12 51.2	7.1	55.0
24 00	180 48.6	N20 39.8	106 31.5	13.1	N12 44.1	7.0	55.0
01	195 48.5	40.3	121 03.6	13.2	12 37.1	7.1	54.9
02	210 48.5	40.8	135 35.8	13.3	12 30.0	7.2	54.9
03	225 48.4	.. 41.2	150 08.1	13.3	12 22.8	7.2	54.9
04	240 48.3	41.7	164 40.4	13.3	12 15.6	7.2	54.9
05	255 48.3	42.2	179 12.7	13.4	12 08.4	7.3	54.9
06	270 48.2	N20 42.6	193 45.1	13.5	N12 01.1	7.4	54.9
07	285 48.2	43.1	208 17.6	13.5	11 53.7	7.4	54.8
08	300 48.1	43.6	222 50.1	13.5	11 46.3	7.4	54.8
S 09	315 48.1	.. 44.0	237 22.6	13.6	11 38.9	7.5	54.8
U 10	330 48.0	44.5	251 55.2	13.6	11 31.4	7.6	54.8
N 11	345 47.9	45.0	266 27.8	13.7	11 23.8	7.6	54.8
D 12	0 47.9	N20 45.4	281 00.5	13.7	N11 16.2	7.6	54.7
A 13	15 47.8	45.9	295 33.2	13.8	11 08.6	7.7	54.7
Y 14	30 47.8	46.3	310 06.0	13.8	11 00.9	7.7	54.7
15	45 47.7	.. 46.8	324 38.8	13.9	10 53.2	7.7	54.7
16	60 47.7	47.3	339 11.7	13.9	10 45.5	7.8	54.7
17	75 47.6	47.7	353 44.6	14.0	10 37.7	7.9	54.7
18	90 47.5	N20 48.2	8 17.6	14.0	N10 29.8	7.8	54.6
19	105 47.5	48.7	22 50.6	14.0	10 22.0	8.0	54.6
20	120 47.4	49.1	37 23.6	14.1	10 14.0	7.9	54.6
21	135 47.4	.. 49.6	51 56.7	14.1	10 06.1	8.0	54.6
22	150 47.3	50.0	66 29.8	14.1	9 58.1	8.1	54.6
23	165 47.2	50.5	81 02.9	14.2	N 9 50.0	8.0	54.6
	SD 15.8	d 0.5	SD 15.2	15.0			14.9

Lat.	Twilight Naut.	Twilight Civil	Sunrise	Moonrise 22	23	24	25
°	h m	h m	h m	h m	h m	h m	h m
N 72	☐	☐	☐	05 01	06 50	08 33	10 10
N 70	☐	☐	☐	05 51	07 22	08 54	10 23
68	////	////	00 57	06 23	07 45	09 10	10 33
66	////	////	01 51	06 46	08 03	09 22	10 42
64	////	////	02 24	07 04	08 18	09 33	10 49
62	////	01 16	02 47	07 19	08 30	09 42	10 55
60	////	01 55	03 06	07 32	08 40	09 50	11 00
N 58	////	02 21	03 21	07 43	08 49	09 57	11 05
56	01 09	02 41	03 34	07 52	08 57	10 03	11 09
54	01 44	02 58	03 46	08 00	09 04	10 08	11 13
52	02 09	03 12	03 56	08 08	09 10	10 13	11 16
50	02 28	03 24	04 05	08 15	09 16	10 17	11 19
45	03 03	03 48	04 23	08 29	09 28	10 27	11 26
N 40	03 28	04 07	04 39	08 41	09 38	10 35	11 31
35	03 48	04 23	04 51	08 51	09 46	10 42	11 36
30	04 04	04 36	05 03	09 00	09 54	10 47	11 40
20	04 29	04 58	05 22	09 15	10 07	10 58	11 47
N 10	04 49	05 15	05 38	09 28	10 18	11 07	11 53
0	05 05	05 31	05 53	09 40	10 29	11 15	11 59
S 10	05 20	05 46	06 08	09 53	10 39	11 23	12 05
20	05 34	06 01	06 24	10 06	10 51	11 32	12 11
30	05 47	06 17	06 42	10 21	11 04	11 42	12 18
35	05 55	06 26	06 53	10 30	11 11	11 48	12 23
40	06 02	06 35	07 05	10 40	11 19	11 55	12 27
45	06 11	06 47	07 19	10 51	11 29	12 03	12 32
S 50	06 20	07 00	07 37	11 05	11 41	12 12	12 39
52	06 24	07 06	07 45	11 12	11 47	12 16	12 42
54	06 28	07 13	07 54	11 19	11 53	12 21	12 45
56	06 33	07 20	08 04	11 27	11 59	12 26	12 49
58	06 38	07 28	08 16	11 37	12 07	12 32	12 53
S 60	06 44	07 37	08 29	11 47	12 16	12 38	12 57

Lat.	Sunset	Twilight Civil	Twilight Naut.	Moonset 22	23	24	25
°	h m	h m	h m	h m	h m	h m	h m
N 72	☐	☐	☐	02 02	01 54	01 48	01 43
N 70	☐	☐	☐	01 10	01 21	01 26	01 28
68	23 05	////	////	00 38	00 57	01 09	01 17
66	22 06	////	////	00 14	00 39	00 55	01 07
64	21 32	////	////	24 24	00 24	00 44	00 59
62	21 08	22 42	////	24 11	00 11	00 34	00 52
60	20 49	22 01	////	24 00	00 00	00 26	00 46
N 58	20 34	21 35	////	23 51	24 18	00 18	00 41
56	20 20	21 14	22 49	23 43	24 12	00 12	00 36
54	20 09	20 57	22 12	23 35	24 06	00 06	00 32
52	19 59	20 43	21 47	23 29	24 00	00 00	00 28
50	19 50	20 31	21 27	23 23	23 56	24 24	00 24
45	19 31	20 06	20 52	23 10	23 45	24 17	00 17
N 40	19 15	19 47	20 26	22 59	23 37	24 10	00 10
35	19 02	19 31	20 00	22 50	23 29	24 05	00 05
30	18 51	19 18	19 50	22 42	23 22	24 00	00 00
20	18 32	18 56	19 24	22 28	23 11	23 51	24 29
N 10	18 16	18 38	19 05	22 16	23 01	23 44	24 25
0	18 00	18 22	18 48	22 04	22 51	23 37	24 20
S 10	17 45	18 08	18 33	21 52	22 42	23 29	24 15
20	17 29	17 53	18 20	21 40	22 32	23 22	24 11
30	17 11	17 36	18 06	21 26	22 20	23 13	24 05
35	17 00	17 28	17 59	21 18	22 13	23 08	24 02
40	16 48	17 18	17 51	21 08	22 05	23 02	23 58
45	16 34	17 06	17 43	20 57	21 56	22 55	23 54
S 50	16 16	16 53	17 33	20 43	21 45	22 47	23 48
52	16 08	16 47	17 29	20 37	21 40	22 43	23 46
54	15 59	16 40	17 25	20 30	21 34	22 39	23 43
56	15 49	16 33	17 20	20 22	21 28	22 34	23 41
58	15 37	16 25	17 15	20 14	21 21	22 29	23 37
S 60	15 24	16 15	17 09	20 04	21 13	22 23	23 34

Day	SUN Eqn. of Time 00h	SUN Eqn. of Time 12h	SUN Mer. Pass.	MOON Mer. Pass. Upper	MOON Mer. Pass. Lower	Age	Phase
d	m s	m s	h m	h m	h m	d	%
22	03 24	03 22	11 57	15 52	03 27	04	21
23	03 19	03 17	11 57	16 40	04 17	05	29
24	03 14	03 12	11 57	17 26	05 03	06	39

UT	ARIES GHA	VENUS −4.3 GHA	Dec	MARS +1.5 GHA	Dec	JUPITER −2.0 GHA	Dec	SATURN +0.0 GHA	Dec	STARS Name	SHA	Dec
25 00	242 15.8	132 01.7	N24 54.5	174 59.2	N22 14.1	103 50.0	N16 58.8	2 25.2	S18 19.0	Acamar	315 17.8	S40 14.7
01	257 18.3	147 01.3	54.1	189 59.8	14.4	118 52.1	58.7	17 27.9	19.0	Achernar	335 26.4	S57 09.4
02	272 20.7	162 01.0	53.8	205 00.4	14.6	133 54.3	58.6	32 30.6	19.0	Acrux	173 07.3	S63 11.3
03	287 23.2	177 00.6 ..	53.4	220 01.0 ..	14.9	148 56.4 ..	58.5	47 33.2 ..	18.9	Adhara	255 11.8	S28 59.9
04	302 25.7	192 00.3	53.0	235 01.6	15.2	163 58.6	58.4	62 35.9	18.9	Aldebaran	290 48.2	N16 32.1
05	317 28.1	206 59.9	52.6	250 02.2	15.5	179 00.7	58.3	77 38.5	18.9			
06	332 30.6	221 59.5	N24 52.2	265 02.8	N22 15.8	194 02.9	N16 58.2	92 41.2	S18 18.8	Alioth	166 19.3	N55 52.8
M 07	347 33.0	236 59.2	51.9	280 03.4	16.1	209 05.0	58.1	107 43.8	18.8	Alkaid	152 57.6	N49 14.4
O 08	2 35.5	251 58.8	51.5	295 04.1	16.4	224 07.2	58.0	122 46.5	18.8	Al Na'ir	27 42.1	S46 52.9
N 09	17 38.0	266 58.5 ..	51.1	310 04.7 ..	16.7	239 09.3 ..	57.9	137 49.2 ..	18.7	Alnilam	275 45.4	S 1 11.8
D 10	32 40.4	281 58.1	50.7	325 05.3	16.9	254 11.5	57.8	152 51.8	18.7	Alphard	217 54.9	S 8 43.8
A 11	47 42.9	296 57.8	50.3	340 05.9	17.2	269 13.6	57.7	167 54.5	18.7			
Y 12	62 45.4	311 57.4	N24 49.9	355 06.5	N22 17.5	284 15.8	N16 57.6	182 57.1	S18 18.6	Alphecca	126 09.6	N26 39.9
13	77 47.8	326 57.1	49.6	10 07.1	17.8	299 17.9	57.5	197 59.8	18.6	Alpheratz	357 42.3	N29 10.3
14	92 50.3	341 56.7	49.2	25 07.7	18.1	314 20.1	57.4	213 02.4	18.6	Altair	62 06.7	N 8 54.6
15	107 52.8	356 56.4 ..	48.8	40 08.3 ..	18.4	329 22.2 ..	57.3	228 05.1 ..	18.5	Ankaa	353 14.7	S42 13.2
16	122 55.2	11 56.0	48.4	55 08.9	18.7	344 24.4	57.2	243 07.8	18.5	Antares	112 24.3	S26 27.8
17	137 57.7	26 55.7	48.0	70 09.5	19.0	359 26.5	57.1	258 10.4	18.5			
18	153 00.2	41 55.3	N24 47.6	85 10.1	N22 19.2	14 28.7	N16 57.0	273 13.1	S18 18.4	Arcturus	145 54.3	N19 06.3
19	168 02.6	56 55.0	47.2	100 10.7	19.5	29 30.8	56.9	288 15.7	18.4	Atria	107 24.3	S69 03.1
20	183 05.1	71 54.6	46.8	115 11.3	19.8	44 33.0	56.8	303 18.4	18.3	Avior	234 17.7	S59 34.0
21	198 07.5	86 54.3 ..	46.4	130 12.0 ..	20.1	59 35.1 ..	56.7	318 21.0 ..	18.3	Bellatrix	278 30.9	N 6 21.5
22	213 10.0	101 53.9	46.0	145 12.6	20.4	74 37.3	56.6	333 23.7	18.3	Betelgeuse	271 00.2	N 7 24.3
23	228 12.5	116 53.6	45.7	160 13.2	20.7	89 39.4	56.5	348 26.3	18.2			
26 00	243 14.9	131 53.3	N24 45.3	175 13.8	N22 20.9	104 41.5	N16 56.4	3 29.0	S18 18.2	Canopus	263 56.0	S52 42.6
01	258 17.4	146 52.9	44.9	190 14.4	21.2	119 43.7	56.3	18 31.7	18.2	Capella	280 33.0	N46 00.6
02	273 19.9	161 52.6	44.5	205 15.0	21.5	134 45.8	56.2	33 34.3	18.1	Deneb	49 30.3	N45 20.0
03	288 22.3	176 52.2 ..	44.1	220 15.6 ..	21.8	149 48.0 ..	56.1	48 37.0 ..	18.1	Denebola	182 32.2	N14 29.2
04	303 24.8	191 51.9	43.7	235 16.2	22.1	164 50.1	56.0	63 39.6	18.1	Diphda	348 54.8	S17 54.1
05	318 27.3	206 51.6	43.3	250 16.8	22.3	179 52.3	55.9	78 42.3	18.0			
06	333 29.7	221 51.2	N24 42.9	265 17.4	N22 22.6	194 54.4	N16 55.8	93 44.9	S18 18.0	Dubhe	193 50.2	N61 40.3
T 07	348 32.2	236 50.9	42.5	280 18.0	22.9	209 56.6	55.7	108 47.6	18.0	Elnath	278 11.3	N28 37.0
U 08	3 34.6	251 50.6	42.1	295 18.6	23.2	224 58.7	55.6	123 50.3	17.9	Eltanin	90 45.0	N51 29.3
E 09	18 37.1	266 50.2 ..	41.7	310 19.2 ..	23.5	240 00.9 ..	55.5	138 52.9 ..	17.9	Enif	33 45.8	N 9 56.8
S 10	33 39.6	281 49.9	41.2	325 19.8	23.7	255 03.0	55.4	153 55.6	17.9	Fomalhaut	15 22.6	S29 32.3
D 11	48 42.0	296 49.6	40.8	340 20.5	24.0	270 05.1	55.3	168 58.2	17.8			
A 12	63 44.5	311 49.2	N24 40.4	355 21.1	N22 24.3	285 07.3	N16 55.3	184 00.9	S18 17.8	Gacrux	171 59.0	S57 12.2
Y 13	78 47.0	326 48.9	40.0	10 21.7	24.6	300 09.4	55.2	199 03.5	17.8	Gienah	175 50.8	S17 37.8
14	93 49.4	341 48.6	39.6	25 22.3	24.8	315 11.6	55.1	214 06.2	17.7	Hadar	148 45.3	S60 26.9
15	108 51.9	356 48.3 ..	39.2	40 22.9 ..	25.1	330 13.7 ..	55.0	229 08.8 ..	17.7	Hamal	327 59.5	N23 31.9
16	123 54.4	11 47.9	38.8	55 23.5	25.4	345 15.9	54.9	244 11.5	17.7	Kaus Aust.	83 41.7	S34 22.4
17	138 56.8	26 47.6	38.4	70 24.1	25.7	0 18.0	54.8	259 14.2	17.6			
18	153 59.3	41 47.3	N24 38.0	85 24.7	N22 25.9	15 20.1	N16 54.7	274 16.8	S18 17.6	Kochab	137 19.2	N74 05.8
19	169 01.8	56 47.0	37.6	100 25.3	26.2	30 22.3	54.6	289 19.5	17.6	Markab	13 37.1	N15 17.2
20	184 04.2	71 46.6	37.1	115 25.9	26.5	45 24.4	54.5	304 22.1	17.5	Menkar	314 14.0	N 4 08.8
21	199 06.7	86 46.3 ..	36.7	130 26.5 ..	26.8	60 26.6 ..	54.4	319 24.8 ..	17.5	Menkent	148 05.6	S36 26.8
22	214 09.1	101 46.0	36.3	145 27.1	27.0	75 28.7	54.3	334 27.4	17.4	Miaplacidus	221 39.5	S69 47.3
23	229 11.6	116 45.7	35.9	160 27.7	27.3	90 30.8	54.2	349 30.1	17.4			
27 00	244 14.1	131 45.4	N24 35.5	175 28.3	N22 27.6	105 33.0	N16 54.1	4 32.8	S18 17.4	Mirfak	308 38.9	N49 54.7
01	259 16.5	146 45.0	35.1	190 28.9	27.9	120 35.1	54.0	19 35.4	17.3	Nunki	75 56.4	S26 16.4
02	274 19.0	161 44.7	34.6	205 29.6	28.1	135 37.3	53.9	34 38.1	17.3	Peacock	53 17.0	S56 40.7
03	289 21.5	176 44.4 ..	34.2	220 30.2 ..	28.4	150 39.4 ..	53.8	49 40.7 ..	17.3	Pollux	243 26.4	N27 59.2
04	304 23.9	191 44.1	33.8	235 30.8	28.7	165 41.6	53.7	64 43.4	17.2	Procyon	244 58.6	N 5 10.9
05	319 26.4	206 43.8	33.4	250 31.4	29.0	180 43.7	53.6	79 46.0	17.2			
06	334 28.9	221 43.5	N24 32.9	265 32.0	N22 29.2	195 45.8	N16 53.5	94 48.7	S18 17.2	Rasalhague	96 04.9	N12 33.1
W 07	349 31.3	236 43.2	32.5	280 32.6	29.5	210 48.0	53.4	109 51.3	17.1	Regulus	207 42.2	N11 53.4
E 08	4 33.8	251 42.8	32.1	295 33.2	29.8	225 50.1	53.3	124 54.0	17.1	Rigel	281 11.1	S 8 11.3
D 09	19 36.3	266 42.5 ..	31.7	310 33.8 ..	30.0	240 52.3 ..	53.2	139 56.7 ..	17.1	Rigil Kent.	139 49.2	S60 53.9
N 10	34 38.7	281 42.2	31.2	325 34.4	30.3	255 54.4	53.1	154 59.3	17.0	Sabik	102 10.7	S15 44.4
E 11	49 41.2	296 41.9	30.8	340 35.0	30.6	270 56.5	53.0	170 02.0	17.0			
S 12	64 43.6	311 41.6	N24 30.4	355 35.6	N22 30.8	285 58.7	N16 52.9	185 04.6	S18 17.0	Schedar	349 39.2	N56 37.0
D 13	79 46.1	326 41.3	30.0	10 36.2	31.1	301 00.8	52.8	200 07.3	16.9	Shaula	96 19.7	S37 06.6
A 14	94 48.6	341 41.0	29.5	25 36.8	31.4	316 02.9	52.7	215 09.9	16.9	Sirius	258 32.9	S16 44.6
Y 15	109 51.0	356 40.7 ..	29.1	40 37.4 ..	31.7	331 05.1 ..	52.6	230 12.6 ..	16.9	Spica	158 29.6	S11 14.5
16	124 53.5	11 40.4	28.7	55 38.0	31.9	346 07.2	52.5	245 15.3	16.8	Suhail	222 51.6	S43 30.1
17	139 56.0	26 40.1	28.2	70 38.6	32.2	1 09.4	52.4	260 17.9	16.8			
18	154 58.4	41 39.8	N24 27.8	85 39.3	N22 32.5	16 11.5	N16 52.3	275 20.6	S18 16.8	Vega	80 37.7	N38 47.9
19	170 00.9	56 39.5	27.4	100 39.9	32.7	31 13.6	52.2	290 23.2	16.7	Zuben'ubi	137 03.6	S16 06.3
20	185 03.4	71 39.2	26.9	115 40.5	33.0	46 15.8	52.0	305 25.9	16.7			
21	200 05.8	86 38.9 ..	26.5	130 41.1 ..	33.3	61 17.9 ..	51.9	320 28.5 ..	16.7			
22	215 08.3	101 38.8	26.0	145 41.7	33.5	76 20.0	51.8	335 31.2	16.6			
23	230 10.7	116 38.3	25.6	160 42.3	33.8	91 22.2	51.7	350 33.8	16.6			

											SHA	Mer. Pass.
Mer. Pass.	h m 7 45.7	v −0.3	d 0.4	v 0.6	d 0.3	v 2.1	d 0.1	v 2.7	d 0.0	Venus	248 38.3	15 13
										Mars	291 58.8	12 19
										Jupiter	221 26.6	16 59
										Saturn	120 14.1	23 42

UT	SUN GHA	SUN Dec	MOON GHA	v	MOON Dec	d	HP
d h	° ′	° ′	° ′	′	° ′	′	′
25 00	180 47.2	N20 50.9	95 36.1	14.3	N 9 42.0	8.2	54.6
01	195 47.1	51.4	110 09.4	14.3	9 33.8	8.1	54.5
02	210 47.1	51.9	124 42.7	14.3	9 25.7	8.2	54.5
03	225 47.0 ..	52.3	139 16.0	14.3	9 17.5	8.2	54.5
04	240 46.9	52.8	153 49.3	14.4	9 09.3	8.3	54.5
05	255 46.9	53.2	168 22.7	14.4	9 01.0	8.2	54.5
06	270 46.8	N20 53.7	182 56.1	14.5	N 8 52.8	8.4	54.5
07	285 46.8	54.1	197 29.6	14.5	8 44.4	8.3	54.5
08	300 46.7	54.6	212 03.1	14.5	8 36.1	8.4	54.5
M 09	315 46.6 ..	55.0	226 36.6	14.6	8 27.7	8.4	54.4
O 10	330 46.6	55.5	241 10.2	14.5	8 19.3	8.5	54.4
N 11	345 46.5	55.9	255 43.7	14.7	8 10.8	8.5	54.4
D 12	0 46.5	N20 56.4	270 17.4	14.6	N 8 02.3	8.5	54.4
A 13	15 46.4	56.8	284 51.0	14.7	7 53.8	8.5	54.4
Y 14	30 46.3	57.3	299 24.7	14.7	7 45.3	8.6	54.4
15	45 46.3 ..	57.7	313 58.4	14.8	7 36.7	8.6	54.4
16	60 46.2	58.2	328 32.2	14.7	7 28.1	8.6	54.4
17	75 46.1	58.6	343 05.9	14.8	7 19.5	8.7	54.4
18	90 46.1	N20 59.1	357 39.7	14.9	N 7 10.8	8.6	54.4
19	105 46.0	59.5	12 13.6	14.8	7 02.2	8.7	54.4
20	120 45.9	20 59.9	26 47.4	14.9	6 53.5	8.8	54.3
21	135 45.9	21 00.4	41 21.3	14.9	6 44.7	8.7	54.3
22	150 45.8	00.8	55 55.2	14.9	6 36.0	8.8	54.3
23	165 45.8	01.3	70 29.1	15.0	6 27.2	8.8	54.3
26 00	180 45.7	N21 01.7	85 03.1	14.9	N 6 18.4	8.9	54.3
01	195 45.6	02.2	99 37.0	15.0	6 09.5	8.8	54.3
02	210 45.6	02.6	114 11.0	15.0	6 00.7	8.9	54.3
03	225 45.5 ..	03.0	128 45.0	15.1	5 51.8	8.9	54.3
04	240 45.4	03.5	143 19.1	15.0	5 42.9	8.9	54.3
05	255 45.4	03.9	157 53.1	15.1	5 34.0	9.0	54.3
06	270 45.3	N21 04.3	172 27.2	15.1	N 5 25.0	8.9	54.3
07	285 45.2	04.8	187 01.3	15.1	5 16.1	9.0	54.3
T 08	300 45.2	05.2	201 35.4	15.2	5 07.1	9.0	54.3
U 09	315 45.1 ..	05.7	216 09.6	15.1	4 58.1	9.0	54.3
E 10	330 45.0	06.1	230 43.7	15.2	4 49.1	9.1	54.3
S 11	345 45.0	06.5	245 17.9	15.1	4 40.0	9.0	54.3
D 12	0 44.9	N21 07.0	259 52.0	15.2	N 4 31.0	9.1	54.3
A 13	15 44.8	07.4	274 26.2	15.2	4 21.9	9.1	54.3
Y 14	30 44.8	07.8	289 00.4	15.3	4 12.8	9.1	54.3
15	45 44.7 ..	08.3	303 34.7	15.2	4 03.7	9.1	54.3
16	60 44.6	08.7	318 08.9	15.2	3 54.6	9.2	54.2
17	75 44.6	09.1	332 43.1	15.3	3 45.4	9.1	54.2
18	90 44.5	N21 09.6	347 17.4	15.2	N 3 36.3	9.2	54.2
19	105 44.4	10.0	1 51.6	15.3	3 27.1	9.2	54.2
20	120 44.4	10.4	16 25.9	15.3	3 17.9	9.2	54.2
21	135 44.3 ..	10.8	31 00.2	15.3	3 08.7	9.2	54.2
22	150 44.2	11.3	45 34.5	15.3	2 59.5	9.2	54.2
23	165 44.1	11.7	60 08.8	15.3	2 50.3	9.3	54.2
27 00	180 44.1	N21 12.1	74 43.1	15.3	N 2 41.0	9.2	54.2
01	195 44.0	12.5	89 17.4	15.3	2 31.8	9.3	54.2
02	210 43.9	13.0	103 51.7	15.3	2 22.5	9.2	54.2
03	225 43.9 ..	13.4	118 26.0	15.3	2 13.3	9.3	54.2
04	240 43.8	13.8	133 00.3	15.3	2 04.0	9.3	54.2
05	255 43.7	14.2	147 34.6	15.4	1 54.7	9.3	54.2
06	270 43.7	N21 14.7	162 09.0	15.3	N 1 45.4	9.3	54.3
W 07	285 43.6	15.1	176 43.3	15.3	1 36.1	9.3	54.3
E 08	300 43.5	15.5	191 17.6	15.3	1 26.8	9.3	54.3
D 09	315 43.4 ..	15.9	205 51.9	15.3	1 17.5	9.4	54.3
N 10	330 43.4	16.3	220 26.2	15.4	1 08.1	9.3	54.3
E 11	345 43.3	16.8	235 00.6	15.3	0 58.8	9.4	54.3
S 12	0 43.2	N21 17.2	249 34.9	15.3	N 0 49.5	9.4	54.3
D 13	15 43.2	17.6	264 09.2	15.3	0 40.1	9.3	54.3
A 14	30 43.1	18.0	278 43.5	15.3	0 30.8	9.4	54.3
Y 15	45 43.0 ..	18.4	293 17.8	15.3	0 21.4	9.3	54.3
16	60 42.9	18.9	307 52.1	15.3	0 12.1	9.4	54.3
17	75 42.9	19.3	322 26.4	15.3	N 0 02.7	9.4	54.3
18	90 42.8	N21 19.7	337 00.7	15.3	S 0 06.7	9.3	54.3
19	105 42.7	20.1	351 35.0	15.2	0 16.0	9.4	54.3
20	120 42.6	20.5	6 09.2	15.3	0 25.4	9.4	54.3
21	135 42.6 ..	20.9	20 43.5	15.2	0 34.8	9.3	54.3
22	150 42.5	21.3	35 17.7	15.3	0 44.1	9.4	54.3
23	165 42.4	21.7	49 52.0	15.2	S 0 53.5	9.4	54.3
	SD 15.8	d 0.4	SD 14.8		14.8		14.8

Lat.	Twilight Naut.	Twilight Civil	Sunrise	Moonrise 25	Moonrise 26	Moonrise 27	Moonrise 28
°	h m	h m	h m	h m	h m	h m	h m
N 72	▭	▭	▭	10 10	11 45	13 17	14 51
N 70	▭	▭	▭	10 23	11 51	13 18	14 46
68	////	////	00 24	10 33	11 56	13 19	14 42
66	////	////	01 39	10 42	12 01	13 19	14 38
64	////	////	02 15	10 49	12 04	13 20	14 36
62	////	01 00	02 40	10 55	12 08	13 20	14 33
60	////	01 45	03 00	11 00	12 10	13 20	14 31
N 58	////	02 14	03 16	11 05	12 13	13 21	14 29
56	00 55	02 35	03 30	11 09	12 15	13 21	14 27
54	01 36	02 53	03 42	11 13	12 17	13 21	14 26
52	02 02	03 07	03 52	11 16	12 19	13 21	14 25
50	02 22	03 20	04 01	11 19	12 20	13 22	14 23
45	02 59	03 45	04 21	11 26	12 24	13 22	14 21
N 40	03 26	04 05	04 37	11 31	12 27	13 22	14 18
35	03 46	04 21	04 50	11 36	12 29	13 23	14 17
30	04 02	04 35	05 01	11 40	12 32	13 23	14 15
20	04 28	04 57	05 21	11 47	12 35	13 24	14 12
N 10	04 49	05 15	05 38	11 53	12 39	13 24	14 09
0	05 05	05 31	05 53	11 59	12 42	13 24	14 07
S 10	05 21	05 46	06 09	12 05	12 45	13 25	14 05
20	05 35	06 02	06 25	12 11	12 49	13 25	14 02
30	05 49	06 18	06 44	12 18	12 53	13 26	13 59
35	05 56	06 28	06 55	12 23	12 55	13 26	13 58
40	06 04	06 38	07 08	12 27	12 57	13 27	13 56
45	06 13	06 49	07 22	12 32	13 00	13 27	13 54
S 50	06 23	07 03	07 40	12 39	13 04	13 28	13 51
52	06 27	07 10	07 49	12 42	13 05	13 28	13 50
54	06 32	07 16	07 58	12 45	13 07	13 28	13 49
56	06 37	07 24	08 09	12 49	13 09	13 28	13 48
58	06 42	07 33	08 21	12 53	13 11	13 29	13 46
S 60	06 48	07 42	08 35	12 57	13 14	13 29	13 45

Lat.	Sunset	Twilight Civil	Twilight Naut.	Moonset 25	Moonset 26	Moonset 27	Moonset 28
°	h m	h m	h m	h m	h m	h m	h m
N 72	▭	▭	▭	01 43	01 38	01 33	01 28
N 70	▭	▭	▭	01 28	01 29	01 30	01 30
68	▭	▭	▭	01 17	01 23	01 27	01 31
66	22 19	////	////	01 07	01 17	01 25	01 32
64	21 42	////	////	00 59	01 12	01 23	01 33
62	21 16	22 59	////	00 52	01 08	01 21	01 34
60	20 55	22 11	////	00 46	01 04	01 20	01 35
N 58	20 39	21 42	////	00 41	01 01	01 19	01 36
56	20 25	21 20	23 04	00 36	00 58	01 17	01 37
54	20 13	21 03	22 21	00 32	00 55	01 16	01 37
52	20 03	20 48	21 54	00 28	00 53	01 15	01 38
50	19 53	20 35	21 33	00 24	00 50	01 15	01 38
45	19 34	20 09	20 56	00 17	00 46	01 13	01 39
N 40	19 18	19 50	20 29	00 10	00 41	01 11	01 40
35	19 05	19 33	20 09	00 05	00 38	01 10	01 41
30	18 53	19 20	19 52	00 00	00 35	01 08	01 42
20	18 33	18 57	19 26	24 29	00 29	01 06	01 43
N 10	18 16	18 39	19 06	24 25	00 25	01 04	01 44
0	18 01	18 23	18 49	24 20	00 20	01 03	01 45
S 10	17 45	18 07	18 33	24 15	00 15	01 01	01 46
20	17 28	17 52	18 19	24 11	00 11	00 59	01 47
30	17 10	17 35	18 05	24 05	00 05	00 56	01 48
35	16 59	17 26	17 57	24 02	00 02	00 55	01 49
40	16 46	17 16	17 49	23 58	24 54	00 54	01 49
45	16 31	17 04	17 41	23 54	24 52	00 52	01 50
S 50	16 13	16 50	17 31	23 48	24 50	00 50	01 51
52	16 05	16 44	17 26	23 46	24 49	00 49	01 52
54	15 55	16 37	17 22	23 43	24 48	00 48	01 52
56	15 45	16 29	17 17	23 41	24 47	00 47	01 53
58	15 33	16 21	17 11	23 37	24 45	00 45	01 53
S 60	15 18	16 11	17 05	23 34	24 44	00 44	01 54

	SUN			MOON			
Day	Eqn. of Time 00h	Eqn. of Time 12h	Mer. Pass.	Mer. Pass. Upper	Mer. Pass. Lower	Age	Phase
d	m s	m s	h m	h m	h m	d	%
25	03 09	03 06	11 57	18 10	05 48	07	48
26	03 03	03 00	11 57	18 52	06 31	08	57
27	02 56	02 53	11 57	19 35	07 13	09	67

UT	ARIES GHA	VENUS −4.4 GHA	Dec	MARS +1.5 GHA	Dec	JUPITER −1.9 GHA	Dec	SATURN +0.1 GHA	Dec	STARS Name	SHA	Dec
d h	° ′	° ′	° ′	° ′	° ′	° ′	° ′	° ′	° ′		° ′	° ′
28 00	245 13.2	131 38.0	N24 25.2	175 42.9	N22 34.0	106 24.3	N16 51.6	5 36.5	S18 16.6	Acamar	315 17.8	S40 14.7
01	260 15.7	146 37.7	24.7	190 43.5	34.3	121 26.5	51.5	20 39.2	16.5	Achernar	335 26.4	S57 09.4
02	275 18.1	161 37.4	24.3	205 44.1	34.6	136 28.6	51.4	35 41.8	16.5	Acrux	173 07.3	S63 11.3
03	290 20.6	176 37.1	.. 23.8	220 44.7	.. 34.8	151 30.7	.. 51.3	50 44.5	.. 16.5	Adhara	255 11.8	S28 59.9
04	305 23.1	191 36.8	23.4	235 45.3	35.1	166 32.9	51.2	65 47.1	16.4	Aldebaran	290 48.2	N16 32.1
05	320 25.5	206 36.5	22.9	250 45.9	35.4	181 35.0	51.1	80 49.8	16.4			
06	335 28.0	221 36.2	N24 22.5	265 46.5	N22 35.6	196 37.1	N16 51.0	95 52.4	S18 16.3	Alioth	166 19.3	N55 52.8
07	350 30.5	236 36.0	22.1	280 47.1	35.9	211 39.3	50.9	110 55.1	16.3	Alkaid	152 57.6	N49 14.4
T 08	5 32.9	251 35.7	21.6	295 47.7	36.2	226 41.4	50.8	125 57.7	16.3	Al Na'ir	27 42.1	S46 52.9
H 09	20 35.4	266 35.4	.. 21.2	310 48.3	.. 36.4	241 43.5	.. 50.7	141 00.4	.. 16.2	Alnilam	275 45.4	S 1 11.8
U 10	35 37.9	281 35.1	20.7	325 48.9	36.7	256 45.7	50.6	156 03.1	16.2	Alphard	217 54.9	S 8 43.8
R 11	50 40.3	296 34.8	20.3	340 49.5	36.9	271 47.8	50.5	171 05.7	16.2			
S 12	65 42.8	311 34.5	N24 19.8	355 50.2	N22 37.2	286 49.9	N16 50.4	186 08.4	S18 16.1	Alphecca	126 09.6	N26 39.9
D 13	80 45.2	326 34.2	19.4	10 50.8	37.5	301 52.1	50.3	201 11.0	16.1	Alpheratz	357 42.2	N29 10.3
A 14	95 47.7	341 34.0	18.9	25 51.4	37.7	316 54.2	50.2	216 13.7	16.1	Altair	62 06.7	N 8 54.7
Y 15	110 50.2	356 33.7	.. 18.5	40 52.0	.. 38.0	331 56.3	.. 50.1	231 16.3	.. 16.0	Ankaa	353 14.7	S42 13.2
16	125 52.6	11 33.4	18.0	55 52.6	38.2	346 58.5	50.0	246 19.0	16.0	Antares	112 24.3	S26 27.8
17	140 55.1	26 33.1	17.5	70 53.2	38.5	2 00.6	49.9	261 21.6	16.0			
18	155 57.6	41 32.8	N24 17.1	85 53.8	N22 38.7	17 02.7	N16 49.8	276 24.3	S18 15.9	Arcturus	145 54.3	N19 06.3
19	171 00.0	56 32.6	16.6	100 54.4	39.0	32 04.9	49.7	291 27.0	15.9	Atria	107 24.3	S69 03.1
20	186 02.5	71 32.3	16.2	115 55.0	39.3	47 07.0	49.6	306 29.6	15.9	Avior	234 17.8	S59 34.0
21	201 05.0	86 32.0	.. 15.7	130 55.6	.. 39.5	62 09.1	.. 49.5	321 32.3	.. 15.8	Bellatrix	278 30.9	N 6 21.5
22	216 07.4	101 31.7	15.3	145 56.2	39.8	77 11.3	49.4	336 34.9	15.8	Betelgeuse	271 00.2	N 7 24.3
23	231 09.9	116 31.5	14.8	160 56.8	40.0	92 13.4	49.3	351 37.6	15.8			
29 00	246 12.4	131 31.2	N24 14.3	175 57.4	N22 40.3	107 15.5	N16 49.2	6 40.2	S18 15.7	Canopus	263 56.0	S52 42.6
01	261 14.8	146 30.9	13.9	190 58.0	40.5	122 17.7	49.1	21 42.9	15.7	Capella	280 33.0	N46 00.6
02	276 17.3	161 30.7	13.4	205 58.6	40.8	137 19.8	49.0	36 45.5	15.7	Deneb	49 30.3	N45 20.0
03	291 19.7	176 30.4	.. 12.9	220 59.2	.. 41.1	152 21.9	.. 48.9	51 48.2	.. 15.6	Denebola	182 32.2	N14 29.2
04	306 22.2	191 30.1	12.5	235 59.8	41.3	167 24.0	48.8	66 50.9	15.6	Diphda	348 54.8	S17 54.1
05	321 24.7	206 29.8	12.0	251 00.4	41.6	182 26.2	48.7	81 53.5	15.6			
06	336 27.1	221 29.6	N24 11.5	266 01.0	N22 41.8	197 28.3	N16 48.6	96 56.2	S18 15.5	Dubhe	193 50.2	N61 40.3
07	351 29.6	236 29.3	11.1	281 01.7	42.1	212 30.4	48.5	111 58.8	15.5	Elnath	278 11.3	N28 37.0
08	6 32.1	251 29.1	10.6	296 02.3	42.3	227 32.6	48.4	127 01.5	15.5	Eltanin	90 45.0	N51 29.3
F 09	21 34.5	266 28.8	.. 10.1	311 02.9	.. 42.6	242 34.7	.. 48.3	142 04.1	.. 15.4	Enif	33 45.7	N 9 56.8
R 10	36 37.0	281 28.5	09.7	326 03.5	42.8	257 36.8	48.2	157 06.8	15.4	Fomalhaut	15 22.6	S29 32.2
I 11	51 39.5	296 28.3	09.2	341 04.1	43.1	272 39.0	48.1	172 09.4	15.4			
D 12	66 41.9	311 28.0	N24 08.7	356 04.7	N22 43.3	287 41.1	N16 47.9	187 12.1	S18 15.3	Gacrux	171 59.0	S57 12.2
A 13	81 44.4	326 27.8	08.3	11 05.3	43.6	302 43.2	47.8	202 14.7	15.3	Gienah	175 50.8	S17 37.8
Y 14	96 46.8	341 27.5	07.8	26 05.9	43.8	317 45.3	47.7	217 17.4	15.3	Hadar	148 45.3	S60 26.9
15	111 49.3	356 27.2	.. 07.3	41 06.5	.. 44.1	332 47.5	.. 47.6	232 20.1	.. 15.2	Hamal	327 59.5	N23 31.9
16	126 51.8	11 27.0	06.8	56 07.1	44.3	347 49.6	47.5	247 22.7	15.2	Kaus Aust.	83 41.7	S34 22.4
17	141 54.2	26 26.7	06.4	71 07.7	44.6	2 51.7	47.4	262 25.4	15.2			
18	156 56.7	41 26.5	N24 05.9	86 08.3	N22 44.8	17 53.9	N16 47.3	277 28.0	S18 15.1	Kochab	137 19.2	N74 05.8
19	171 59.2	56 26.2	05.4	101 08.9	45.1	32 56.0	47.2	292 30.7	15.1	Markab	13 37.0	N15 17.2
20	187 01.6	71 26.0	04.9	116 09.5	45.3	47 58.1	47.1	307 33.3	15.1	Menkar	314 14.0	N 4 08.8
21	202 04.1	86 25.7	.. 04.4	131 10.1	.. 45.6	63 00.2	.. 47.0	322 36.0	.. 15.0	Menkent	148 05.6	S36 26.8
22	217 06.6	101 25.5	04.0	146 10.7	45.8	78 02.4	46.9	337 38.6	15.0	Miaplacidus	221 39.6	S69 47.3
23	232 09.0	116 25.2	03.5	161 11.3	46.1	93 04.5	46.8	352 41.3	15.0			
30 00	247 11.5	131 25.0	N24 03.0	176 11.9	N22 46.3	108 06.6	N16 46.7	7 43.9	S18 14.9	Mirfak	308 38.9	N49 54.7
01	262 14.0	146 24.7	02.5	191 12.5	46.6	123 08.7	46.6	22 46.6	14.9	Nunki	75 56.4	S26 16.4
02	277 16.4	161 24.5	02.0	206 13.1	46.8	138 10.9	46.5	37 49.3	14.8	Peacock	53 16.9	S56 40.7
03	292 18.9	176 24.2	.. 01.5	221 13.7	.. 47.1	153 13.0	.. 46.4	52 51.9	.. 14.8	Pollux	243 26.4	N27 59.2
04	307 21.3	191 24.0	01.1	236 14.3	47.3	168 15.1	46.3	67 54.6	14.8	Procyon	244 58.6	N 5 10.9
05	322 23.8	206 23.7	00.6	251 15.0	47.5	183 17.2	46.2	82 57.2	14.7			
06	337 26.3	221 23.5	N24 00.1	266 15.6	N22 47.8	198 19.4	N16 46.1	97 59.9	S18 14.7	Rasalhague	96 04.9	N12 33.1
07	352 28.7	236 23.3	23 59.6	281 16.2	48.0	213 21.5	46.0	113 02.5	14.7	Regulus	207 42.2	N11 53.4
S 08	7 31.2	251 23.0	59.1	296 16.8	48.3	228 23.6	45.9	128 05.2	14.6	Rigel	281 11.1	S 8 11.3
A 09	22 33.7	266 22.8	.. 58.6	311 17.4	.. 48.5	243 25.7	.. 45.8	143 07.8	.. 14.6	Rigil Kent.	139 49.2	S60 53.9
T 10	37 36.1	281 22.5	58.1	326 18.0	48.8	258 27.9	45.6	158 10.5	14.6	Sabik	102 10.7	S15 44.4
U 11	52 38.6	296 22.3	57.6	341 18.6	49.0	273 30.0	45.5	173 13.1	14.5			
R 12	67 41.1	311 22.1	N23 57.1	356 19.2	N22 49.3	288 32.1	N16 45.4	188 15.8	S18 14.5	Schedar	349 39.2	N56 37.0
D 13	82 43.5	326 21.8	56.6	11 19.8	49.5	303 34.2	45.3	203 18.5	14.5	Shaula	96 19.7	S37 06.6
A 14	97 46.0	341 21.6	56.2	26 20.4	49.7	318 36.4	45.2	218 21.1	14.4	Sirius	258 32.9	S16 44.6
Y 15	112 48.4	356 21.4	.. 55.7	41 21.0	.. 50.0	333 38.5	.. 45.1	233 23.8	.. 14.4	Spica	158 29.6	S11 14.5
16	127 50.9	11 21.1	55.2	56 21.6	50.2	348 40.6	45.0	248 26.4	14.4	Suhail	222 51.6	S43 30.1
17	142 53.4	26 20.9	54.7	71 22.2	50.5	3 42.7	44.9	263 29.1	14.3			
18	157 55.8	41 20.7	N23 54.2	86 22.8	N22 50.7	18 44.9	N16 44.8	278 31.7	S18 14.3	Vega	80 37.7	N38 47.9
19	172 58.3	56 20.5	53.7	101 23.4	50.9	33 47.0	44.7	293 34.4	14.3	Zuben'ubi	137 03.6	S16 06.3
20	188 00.8	71 20.2	53.2	116 24.0	51.2	48 49.1	44.6	308 37.0	14.2			
21	203 03.2	86 20.0	.. 52.7	131 24.6	.. 51.4	63 51.2	.. 44.5	323 39.7	.. 14.2			
22	218 05.7	101 19.8	52.2	146 25.2	51.7	78 53.4	44.4	338 42.3	14.2			
23	233 08.2	116 19.6	51.7	161 25.8	51.9	93 55.5	44.3	353 45.0	14.1			

											SHA	Mer. Pass.
											° ′	h m
										Venus	245 18.8	15 14
										Mars	289 45.1	12 16
										Jupiter	221 03.2	16 49
										Saturn	120 27.9	23 29

	Mer. Pass. h m	v	d	v	d	v	d	v	d
	7 33.9	−0.3	0.5	0.6	0.3	2.1	0.1	2.7	0.0

UT	SUN GHA	Dec	MOON GHA	v	Dec	d	HP
d h	° ′	° ′	° ′	′	° ′	′	′
28 00	180 42.3	N21 22.2	64 26.2	15.2	S 1 02.9	9.3	54.3
01	195 42.3	22.6	79 00.4	15.2	1 12.2	9.4	54.3
02	210 42.2	23.0	93 34.6	15.2	1 21.6	9.4	54.4
03	225 42.1 ..	23.4	108 08.8	15.2	1 31.0	9.3	54.4
04	240 42.0	23.8	122 43.0	15.1	1 40.3	9.4	54.4
05	255 42.0	24.2	137 17.1	15.2	1 49.7	9.3	54.4
06	270 41.9	N21 24.6	151 51.3	15.1	S 1 59.0	9.4	54.4
T 07	285 41.8	25.0	166 25.4	15.1	2 08.4	9.3	54.4
H 08	300 41.7	25.4	180 59.5	15.1	2 17.7	9.4	54.4
U 09	315 41.7 ..	25.8	195 33.6	15.1	2 27.1	9.3	54.4
R 10	330 41.6	26.2	210 07.7	15.0	2 36.4	9.3	54.4
S 11	345 41.5	26.6	224 41.7	15.1	2 45.7	9.3	54.4
D 12	0 41.4	N21 27.0	239 15.8	15.0	S 2 55.0	9.4	54.4
A 13	15 41.4	27.4	253 49.8	15.0	3 04.4	9.3	54.5
Y 14	30 41.3	27.8	268 23.8	14.9	3 13.7	9.3	54.5
15	45 41.2 ..	28.2	282 57.7	15.0	3 23.0	9.2	54.5
16	60 41.1	28.6	297 31.7	14.9	3 32.2	9.3	54.5
17	75 41.1	29.0	312 05.6	14.9	3 41.5	9.3	54.5
18	90 41.0	N21 29.4	326 39.5	14.9	S 3 50.8	9.3	54.5
19	105 40.9	29.8	341 13.4	14.8	4 00.1	9.2	54.5
20	120 40.8	30.2	355 47.2	14.9	4 09.3	9.2	54.5
21	135 40.7 ..	30.6	10 21.1	14.8	4 18.5	9.2	54.5
22	150 40.7	31.0	24 54.9	14.7	4 27.7	9.3	54.6
23	165 40.6	31.4	39 28.6	14.8	4 37.0	9.1	54.6
29 00	180 40.5	N21 31.8	54 02.4	14.7	S 4 46.1	9.2	54.6
01	195 40.4	32.2	68 36.1	14.6	4 55.3	9.2	54.6
02	210 40.3	32.6	83 09.7	14.7	5 04.5	9.1	54.6
03	225 40.3 ..	33.0	97 43.4	14.6	5 13.6	9.2	54.6
04	240 40.2	33.4	112 17.0	14.6	5 22.8	9.1	54.6
05	255 40.1	33.8	126 50.6	14.6	5 31.9	9.1	54.7
06	270 40.0	N21 34.2	141 24.2	14.5	S 5 41.0	9.1	54.7
07	285 39.9	34.6	155 57.7	14.5	5 50.1	9.0	54.7
08	300 39.9	35.0	170 31.2	14.4	5 59.1	9.1	54.7
F 09	315 39.8 ..	35.4	185 04.6	14.4	6 08.2	9.0	54.7
R 10	330 39.7	35.7	199 38.0	14.4	6 17.2	9.0	54.7
I 11	345 39.6	36.1	214 11.4	14.4	6 26.2	9.0	54.7
D 12	0 39.5	N21 36.5	228 44.8	14.3	S 6 35.2	8.9	54.8
A 13	15 39.5	36.9	243 18.1	14.2	6 44.1	9.0	54.8
Y 14	30 39.4	37.3	257 51.3	14.3	6 53.1	8.9	54.8
15	45 39.3 ..	37.7	272 24.6	14.2	7 02.0	8.9	54.8
16	60 39.2	38.1	286 57.8	14.1	7 10.9	8.8	54.8
17	75 39.1	38.5	301 30.9	14.1	7 19.7	8.9	54.8
18	90 39.1	N21 38.8	316 04.0	14.1	S 7 28.6	8.8	54.9
19	105 39.0	39.2	330 37.1	14.1	7 37.4	8.7	54.9
20	120 38.9	39.6	345 10.2	13.9	7 46.1	8.8	54.9
21	135 38.8 ..	40.0	359 43.1	14.1	7 54.9	8.7	54.9
22	150 38.7	40.4	14 16.1	13.9	8 03.6	8.7	54.9
23	165 38.6	40.7	28 49.0	13.9	8 12.3	8.7	55.0
30 00	180 38.6	N21 41.1	43 21.9	13.8	S 8 21.0	8.7	55.0
01	195 38.5	41.5	57 54.7	13.8	8 29.7	8.6	55.0
02	210 38.4	41.9	72 27.5	13.7	8 38.3	8.5	55.0
03	225 38.3 ..	42.3	87 00.2	13.7	8 46.8	8.6	55.0
04	240 38.2	42.6	101 32.9	13.6	8 55.4	8.5	55.0
05	255 38.1	43.0	116 05.5	13.6	9 03.9	8.5	55.1
06	270 38.1	N21 43.4	130 38.1	13.5	S 9 12.4	8.4	55.1
07	285 38.0	43.8	145 10.6	13.5	9 20.8	8.5	55.1
S 08	300 37.9	44.1	159 43.1	13.5	9 29.3	8.3	55.1
A 09	315 37.8 ..	44.5	174 15.6	13.4	9 37.6	8.4	55.1
T 10	330 37.7	44.9	188 48.0	13.3	9 46.0	8.3	55.2
U 11	345 37.6	45.3	203 20.3	13.3	9 54.3	8.2	55.2
R 12	0 37.5	N21 45.6	217 52.6	13.3	S10 02.5	8.3	55.2
D 13	15 37.5	46.0	232 24.9	13.2	10 10.8	8.2	55.2
A 14	30 37.4	46.4	246 57.1	13.1	10 19.0	8.1	55.2
Y 15	45 37.3 ..	46.7	261 29.2	13.1	10 27.1	8.1	55.3
16	60 37.2	47.1	276 01.3	13.1	10 35.2	8.1	55.3
17	75 37.1	47.5	290 33.4	13.0	10 43.3	8.0	55.3
18	90 37.0	N21 47.8	305 05.4	12.9	S10 51.3	8.0	55.3
19	105 36.9	48.2	319 37.3	12.9	10 59.3	7.9	55.3
20	120 36.8	48.6	334 09.2	12.8	11 07.2	7.9	55.4
21	135 36.8 ..	48.9	348 41.0	12.8	11 15.1	7.9	55.4
22	150 36.7	49.3	3 12.8	12.7	11 23.0	7.8	55.4
23	165 36.6	49.7	17 44.5	12.7	S11 30.8	7.7	55.4
	SD 15.8	d 0.4	SD 14.8	14.9			15.0

Lat.	Twilight Naut.	Civil	Sunrise	Moonrise 28	29	30	31
°	h m	h m	h m	h m	h m	h m	h m
N 72	☐	☐	☐	14 51	16 26	18 06	19 53
N 70	☐	☐	☐	14 46	16 15	17 47	19 23
68	☐	☐	☐	14 42	16 06	17 33	19 01
66	////	////	01 27	14 38	15 59	17 21	18 43
64	////	////	02 07	14 36	15 53	17 11	18 29
62	////	00 41	02 34	14 33	15 47	17 02	18 18
60	////	01 36	02 55	14 31	15 43	16 55	18 08
N 58	////	02 07	03 12	14 29	15 38	16 49	17 59
56	00 37	02 30	03 26	14 27	15 35	16 43	17 52
54	01 27	02 48	03 38	14 26	15 32	16 38	17 45
52	01 56	03 03	03 49	14 25	15 29	16 33	17 39
50	02 18	03 16	03 59	14 23	15 26	16 29	17 33
45	02 56	03 43	04 19	14 21	15 20	16 20	17 22
N 40	03 23	04 03	04 35	14 18	15 15	16 13	17 12
35	03 44	04 20	04 49	14 17	15 11	16 07	17 04
30	04 01	04 33	05 00	14 15	15 07	16 01	16 56
20	04 28	04 56	05 20	14 12	15 01	15 52	16 44
N 10	04 48	05 15	05 38	14 09	14 56	15 43	16 33
0	05 06	05 32	05 54	14 07	14 50	15 36	16 23
S 10	05 21	05 47	06 10	14 05	14 45	15 28	16 13
20	05 36	06 03	06 27	14 02	14 40	15 20	16 02
30	05 50	06 20	06 46	13 59	14 34	15 10	15 50
35	05 58	06 29	06 57	13 58	14 30	15 05	15 43
40	06 06	06 40	07 10	13 56	14 26	14 59	15 35
45	06 15	06 52	07 25	13 54	14 22	14 52	15 26
S 50	06 26	07 06	07 44	13 51	14 16	14 44	15 14
52	06 30	07 13	07 52	13 50	14 14	14 40	15 09
54	06 35	07 20	08 02	13 49	14 11	14 36	15 04
56	06 40	07 28	08 13	13 48	14 08	14 31	14 57
58	06 46	07 37	08 26	13 46	14 05	14 26	14 50
S 60	06 52	07 47	08 41	13 45	14 01	14 20	14 42

Lat.	Sunset	Twilight Civil	Naut.	Moonset 28	29	30	31
°	h m	h m	h m	h m	h m	h m	h m
N 72	☐	☐	☐	01 28	01 23	01 17	01 11
N 70	☐	☐	☐	01 30	01 30	01 30	01 32
68	☐	☐	☐	01 31	01 35	01 41	01 48
66	22 32	////	////	01 32	01 40	01 49	02 01
64	21 50	////	////	01 33	01 44	01 57	02 11
62	21 23	23 21	////	01 34	01 48	02 03	02 21
60	21 01	22 21	////	01 35	01 51	02 08	02 29
N 58	20 44	21 49	////	01 36	01 54	02 13	02 36
56	20 30	21 26	23 24	01 37	01 56	02 18	02 42
54	20 17	21 08	22 30	01 37	01 59	02 22	02 47
52	20 06	20 52	22 00	01 38	02 01	02 25	02 52
50	19 57	20 39	21 38	01 38	02 02	02 28	02 57
45	19 37	20 13	21 00	01 39	02 07	02 35	03 07
N 40	19 20	19 52	20 32	01 40	02 10	02 41	03 15
35	19 07	19 36	20 11	01 41	02 13	02 46	03 22
30	18 55	19 22	19 54	01 42	02 16	02 51	03 29
20	18 34	18 59	19 27	01 43	02 20	02 59	03 39
N 10	18 17	18 40	19 07	01 44	02 24	03 05	03 49
0	18 01	18 23	18 49	01 45	02 28	03 12	03 58
S 10	17 45	18 08	18 34	01 46	02 32	03 18	04 07
20	17 28	17 52	18 19	01 47	02 36	03 25	04 17
30	17 09	17 35	18 04	01 48	02 40	03 33	04 28
35	16 57	17 25	17 56	01 49	02 43	03 38	04 34
40	16 45	17 14	17 48	01 49	02 46	03 43	04 41
45	16 29	17 02	17 39	01 50	02 49	03 49	04 50
S 50	16 11	16 48	17 29	01 51	02 53	03 56	05 00
52	16 02	16 41	17 24	01 52	02 55	03 59	05 05
54	15 52	16 34	17 19	01 52	02 57	04 03	05 10
56	15 41	16 26	17 14	01 53	03 00	04 07	05 16
58	15 28	16 17	17 08	01 53	03 02	04 12	05 22
S 60	15 14	16 07	17 02	01 54	03 05	04 17	05 29

Day	SUN Eqn. of Time 00h	12h	Mer. Pass.	MOON Mer. Pass. Upper	Lower	Age	Phase
d	m s	m s	h m	h m	h m	d	%
28	02 50	02 46	11 57	20 17	07 56	10	75
29	02 42	02 38	11 57	21 01	08 39	11	83
30	02 34	02 30	11 57	21 47	09 24	12	90

UT	ARIES GHA	VENUS −4.4 GHA	Dec	MARS +1.5 GHA	Dec	JUPITER −1.9 GHA	Dec	SATURN +0.1 GHA	Dec	STARS Name	SHA	Dec
31 00	248 10.6	131 19.3	N23 51.2	176 26.4	N22 52.1	108 57.6	N16 44.2	8 47.7	S18 14.1	Acamar	315 17.8	S40 14.7
01	263 13.1	146 19.1	50.7	191 27.0	52.4	123 59.7	44.1	23 50.3	14.1	Achernar	335 26.3	S57 09.4
02	278 15.6	161 18.9	50.2	206 27.6	52.6	139 01.8	44.0	38 53.0	14.0	Acrux	173 07.3	S63 11.3
03	293 18.0	176 18.7 ..	49.7	221 28.2 ..	52.8	154 04.0 ..	43.8	53 55.6 ..	14.0	Adhara	255 11.8	S28 59.9
04	308 20.5	191 18.5	49.1	236 28.8	53.1	169 06.1	43.7	68 58.3	14.0	Aldebaran	290 48.2	N16 32.1
05	323 22.9	206 18.2	48.6	251 29.5	53.3	184 08.2	43.6	84 00.9	13.9			
S 06	338 25.4	221 18.0	N23 48.1	266 30.1	N22 53.6	199 10.3	N16 43.5	99 03.6	S18 13.9	Alioth	166 19.4	N55 52.8
U 07	353 27.9	236 17.8	47.6	281 30.7	53.8	214 12.4	43.4	114 06.2	13.9	Alkaid	152 57.6	N49 14.4
N 08	8 30.3	251 17.6	47.1	296 31.3	54.0	229 14.6	43.3	129 08.9	13.8	Al Na'ir	27 42.1	S46 52.9
D 09	23 32.8	266 17.4 ..	46.6	311 31.9 ..	54.3	244 16.7 ..	43.2	144 11.5 ..	13.8	Alnilam	275 45.4	S 1 11.8
A 10	38 35.3	281 17.2	46.1	326 32.5	54.5	259 18.8	43.1	159 14.2	13.8	Alphard	217 54.9	S 8 43.8
Y 11	53 37.7	296 17.0	45.6	341 33.1	54.7	274 20.9	43.0	174 16.8	13.7			
12	68 40.2	311 16.7	N23 45.1	356 33.7	N22 55.0	289 23.0	N16 42.9	189 19.5	S18 13.7	Alphecca	126 09.6	N26 39.9
13	83 42.7	326 16.5	44.6	11 34.3	55.2	304 25.2	42.8	204 22.1	13.7	Alpheratz	357 42.2	N29 10.3
14	98 45.1	341 16.3	44.0	26 34.9	55.4	319 27.3	42.7	219 24.8	13.6	Altair	62 06.7	N 8 54.7
15	113 47.6	356 16.1 ..	43.5	41 35.5 ..	55.7	334 29.4 ..	42.6	234 27.5 ..	13.6	Ankaa	353 14.7	S42 13.2
16	128 50.1	11 15.9	43.0	56 36.1	55.9	349 31.5	42.5	249 30.1	13.6	Antares	112 24.2	S26 27.8
17	143 52.5	26 15.7	42.5	71 36.7	56.1	4 33.6	42.3	264 32.8	13.5			
18	158 55.0	41 15.5	N23 42.0	86 37.3	N22 56.4	19 35.8	N16 42.2	279 35.4	S18 13.5	Arcturus	145 54.3	N19 06.3
19	173 57.4	56 15.3	41.5	101 37.9	56.6	34 37.9	42.1	294 38.1	13.5	Atria	107 24.3	S69 03.1
20	188 59.9	71 15.1	40.9	116 38.5	56.8	49 40.0	42.0	309 40.7	13.4	Avior	234 17.8	S59 34.0
21	204 02.4	86 14.9 ..	40.4	131 39.1 ..	57.1	64 42.1 ..	41.9	324 43.4 ..	13.4	Bellatrix	278 30.9	N 6 21.6
22	219 04.8	101 14.7	39.9	146 39.7	57.3	79 44.2	41.8	339 46.0	13.4	Betelgeuse	271 00.2	N 7 24.3
23	234 07.3	116 14.5	39.4	161 40.3	57.5	94 46.3	41.7	354 48.7	13.3			
1 00	249 09.8	131 14.3	N23 38.9	176 40.9	N22 57.7	109 48.5	N16 41.6	9 51.3	S18 13.3	Canopus	263 56.1	S52 42.6
01	264 12.2	146 14.1	38.3	191 41.5	58.0	124 50.6	41.5	24 54.0	13.3	Capella	280 33.0	N46 00.6
02	279 14.7	161 13.9	37.8	206 42.1	58.2	139 52.7	41.4	39 56.6	13.2	Deneb	49 30.3	N45 20.1
03	294 17.2	176 13.7 ..	37.3	221 42.7 ..	58.4	154 54.8 ..	41.3	54 59.3 ..	13.2	Denebola	182 32.3	N14 29.2
04	309 19.6	191 13.5	36.8	236 43.3	58.7	169 56.9	41.2	70 01.9	13.2	Diphda	348 54.8	S17 54.1
05	324 22.1	206 13.3	36.2	251 43.9	58.9	184 59.0	41.0	85 04.6	13.1			
M 06	339 24.6	221 13.2	N23 35.7	266 44.5	N22 59.1	200 01.2	N16 40.9	100 07.3	S18 13.1	Dubhe	193 50.2	N61 40.3
O 07	354 27.0	236 13.0	35.2	281 45.1	59.3	215 03.3	40.8	115 09.9	13.1	Elnath	278 11.3	N28 37.0
N 08	9 29.5	251 12.8	34.6	296 45.7	59.5	230 05.4	40.7	130 12.6	13.0	Eltanin	90 45.0	N51 29.3
D 09	24 31.9	266 12.6 ..	34.1	311 46.3	22 59.8	245 07.5 ..	40.5	145 15.2 ..	13.0	Enif	33 45.7	N 9 56.8
A 10	39 34.4	281 12.4	33.6	326 47.0	23 00.0	260 09.6	40.5	160 17.9	13.0	Fomalhaut	15 22.6	S29 32.2
Y 11	54 36.9	296 12.2	33.0	341 47.6	00.2	275 11.7	40.4	175 20.5	12.9			
12	69 39.3	311 12.0	N23 32.5	356 48.2	N23 00.5	290 13.9	N16 40.3	190 23.2	S18 12.9	Gacrux	171 59.0	S57 12.2
13	84 41.8	326 11.9	32.0	11 48.8	00.7	305 16.0	40.2	205 25.8	12.9	Gienah	175 50.8	S17 37.8
14	99 44.3	341 11.7	31.4	26 49.4	00.9	320 18.1	40.1	220 28.5	12.8	Hadar	148 45.4	S60 26.9
15	114 46.7	356 11.5 ..	30.9	41 50.0 ..	01.1	335 20.2 ..	40.0	235 31.1 ..	12.8	Hamal	327 59.5	N23 31.9
16	129 49.2	11 11.3	30.4	56 50.6	01.4	350 22.3	39.9	250 33.8	12.8	Kaus Aust.	83 41.7	S34 22.4
17	144 51.7	26 11.1	29.8	71 51.2	01.6	5 24.4	39.7	265 36.4	12.7			
18	159 54.1	41 11.0	N23 29.3	86 51.8	N23 01.8	20 26.5	N16 39.6	280 39.1	S18 12.7	Kochab	137 19.2	N74 05.8
19	174 56.6	56 10.8	28.8	101 52.4	02.0	35 28.7	39.5	295 41.7	12.7	Markab	13 37.0	N15 17.2
20	189 59.0	71 10.6	28.2	116 53.0	02.3	50 30.8	39.4	310 44.4	12.6	Menkar	314 14.0	N 4 08.8
21	205 01.5	86 10.4 ..	27.7	131 53.6 ..	02.5	65 32.9 ..	39.3	325 47.0 ..	12.6	Menkent	148 05.6	S36 26.8
22	220 04.0	101 10.3	27.1	146 54.2	02.7	80 35.0	39.2	340 49.7	12.6	Miaplacidus	221 39.6	S69 47.3
23	235 06.4	116 10.1	26.6	161 54.8	02.9	95 37.1	39.1	355 52.3	12.5			
2 00	250 08.9	131 09.9	N23 26.1	176 55.4	N23 03.1	110 39.2	N16 39.0	10 55.0	S18 12.5	Mirfak	308 38.9	N49 54.6
01	265 11.4	146 09.7	25.5	191 56.0	03.4	125 41.3	38.9	25 57.6	12.5	Nunki	75 56.4	S26 16.4
02	280 13.8	161 09.6	25.0	206 56.6	03.6	140 43.4	38.8	41 00.3	12.4	Peacock	53 16.9	S56 40.7
03	295 16.3	176 09.4 ..	24.4	221 57.2 ..	03.8	155 45.6 ..	38.6	56 03.0 ..	12.4	Pollux	243 26.4	N27 59.2
04	310 18.8	191 09.2	23.9	236 57.8	04.0	170 47.7	38.5	71 05.6	12.4	Procyon	244 58.6	N 5 10.9
05	325 21.2	206 09.1	23.3	251 58.4	04.2	185 49.8	38.4	86 08.3	12.3			
T 06	340 23.7	221 08.9	N23 22.8	266 59.0	N23 04.5	200 51.9	N16 38.3	101 10.9	S18 12.3	Rasalhague	96 04.9	N12 33.1
U 07	355 26.2	236 08.8	22.2	281 59.6	04.7	215 54.0	38.2	116 13.6	12.3	Regulus	207 42.2	N11 53.4
E 08	10 28.6	251 08.6	21.7	297 00.2	04.9	230 56.1	38.1	131 16.2	12.2	Rigel	281 11.1	S 8 11.3
S 09	25 31.1	266 08.4 ..	21.2	312 00.8 ..	05.1	245 58.2 ..	38.0	146 18.9 ..	12.2	Rigil Kent.	139 49.2	S60 53.9
D 10	40 33.5	281 08.3	20.6	327 01.4	05.3	261 00.3	37.9	161 21.5	12.2	Sabik	102 10.7	S15 44.4
A 11	55 36.0	296 08.1	20.1	342 02.0	05.5	276 02.4	37.8	176 24.2	12.1			
Y 12	70 38.5	311 08.0	N23 19.5	357 02.6	N23 05.8	291 04.6	N16 37.7	191 26.8	S18 12.1	Schedar	349 39.2	N56 37.0
13	85 40.9	326 07.8	18.9	12 03.2	06.0	306 06.7	37.5	206 29.5	12.1	Shaula	96 19.7	S37 06.7
14	100 43.4	341 07.6	18.4	27 03.8	06.2	321 08.8	37.4	221 32.1	12.0	Sirius	258 32.9	S16 44.5
15	115 45.9	356 07.5 ..	17.8	42 04.4 ..	06.4	336 10.9 ..	37.3	236 34.8 ..	12.0	Spica	158 29.6	S11 14.5
16	130 48.3	11 07.3	17.3	57 05.0	06.6	351 13.0	37.2	251 37.4	12.0	Suhail	222 51.6	S43 30.1
17	145 50.8	26 07.2	16.7	72 05.6	06.8	6 15.1	37.1	266 40.1	11.9			
18	160 53.3	41 07.0	N23 16.2	87 06.3	N23 07.0	21 17.2	N16 37.0	281 42.7	S18 11.9	Vega	80 37.7	N38 48.0
19	175 55.7	56 06.9	15.6	102 06.9	07.3	36 19.3	36.9	296 45.4	11.9	Zuben'ubi	137 03.6	S16 06.3
20	190 58.2	71 06.7	15.0	117 07.5	07.5	51 21.4	36.8	311 48.0	11.8		SHA	Mer.Pass.
21	206 00.7	86 06.6 ..	14.5	132 08.1 ..	07.7	66 23.5 ..	36.7	326 50.7 ..	11.8			
22	221 03.1	101 06.5	13.9	147 08.7	07.9	81 25.6	36.6	341 53.3	11.8	Venus	242 04.5	15 15
23	236 05.6	116 06.3	13.4	162 09.3	08.1	96 27.8	36.4	356 56.0	11.7	Mars	287 31.2	12 13
Mer.Pass.	h m 7 22.1	v −0.2	d 0.5	v 0.6	d 0.2	v 2.1	d 0.1	v 2.7	d 0.0	Jupiter	220 38.7	16 38
										Saturn	120 41.6	23 16

SUN and MOON

UT	SUN GHA	SUN Dec	MOON GHA	v	Dec	d	HP
31 00	180 36.5	N21 50.0	32 16.2	12.6	S11 38.5	7.7	55.5
01	195 36.4	50.4	46 47.8	12.6	11 46.2	7.7	55.5
02	210 36.3	50.8	61 19.4	12.5	11 53.9	7.6	55.5
03	225 36.2 ..	51.1	75 50.9	12.4	12 01.5	7.6	55.5
04	240 36.1	51.5	90 22.3	12.4	12 09.1	7.5	55.5
05	255 36.1	51.9	104 53.7	12.4	12 16.6	7.4	55.6
S 06	270 36.0	N21 52.2	119 25.1	12.3	S12 24.0	7.4	55.6
U 07	285 35.9	52.6	133 56.4	12.2	12 31.4	7.4	55.6
N 08	300 35.8	52.9	148 27.6	12.1	12 38.8	7.3	55.6
D 09	315 35.7 ..	53.3	162 58.7	12.1	12 46.1	7.2	55.7
A 10	330 35.6	53.6	177 29.8	12.1	12 53.3	7.2	55.7
Y 11	345 35.5	54.0	192 00.9	12.0	13 00.5	7.1	55.7
12	0 35.4	N21 54.4	206 31.9	11.9	S13 07.6	7.1	55.7
13	15 35.3	54.7	221 02.8	11.9	13 14.7	7.0	55.7
14	30 35.3	55.1	235 33.7	11.8	13 21.7	7.0	55.8
15	45 35.2 ..	55.4	250 04.5	11.8	13 28.7	6.9	55.8
16	60 35.1	55.8	264 35.3	11.6	13 35.6	6.8	55.8
17	75 35.0	56.1	279 05.9	11.7	13 42.4	6.8	55.8
18	90 34.9	N21 56.5	293 36.6	11.6	S13 49.2	6.7	55.9
19	105 34.8	56.8	308 07.2	11.5	13 55.9	6.7	55.9
20	120 34.7	57.2	322 37.7	11.4	14 02.6	6.6	55.9
21	135 34.6 ..	57.5	337 08.1	11.4	14 09.2	6.5	55.9
22	150 34.5	57.9	351 38.5	11.4	14 15.7	6.4	56.0
23	165 34.4	58.2	6 08.9	11.2	14 22.1	6.4	56.0
1 00	180 34.3	N21 58.6	20 39.1	11.3	S14 28.5	6.4	56.0
01	195 34.3	58.9	35 09.4	11.1	14 34.9	6.2	56.0
02	210 34.2	59.3	49 39.5	11.1	14 41.1	6.2	56.1
03	225 34.1	21 59.6	64 09.6	11.1	14 47.3	6.1	56.1
04	240 34.0	22 00.0	78 39.7	10.9	14 53.4	6.1	56.1
05	255 33.9	00.3	93 09.6	11.0	14 59.5	5.9	56.1
M 06	270 33.8	N22 00.7	107 39.6	10.8	S15 05.4	5.9	56.2
O 07	285 33.7	01.0	122 09.4	10.8	15 11.3	5.9	56.2
N 08	300 33.6	01.3	136 39.2	10.7	15 17.2	5.7	56.2
D 09	315 33.5 ..	01.7	151 08.9	10.7	15 22.9	5.7	56.2
A 10	330 33.4	02.0	165 38.6	10.6	15 28.6	5.6	56.3
Y 11	345 33.3	02.4	180 08.2	10.6	15 34.2	5.6	56.3
12	0 33.2	N22 02.7	194 37.8	10.5	S15 39.8	5.4	56.3
13	15 33.1	03.0	209 07.3	10.4	15 45.2	5.4	56.3
14	30 33.0	03.4	223 36.7	10.4	15 50.6	5.3	56.4
15	45 32.9 ..	03.7	238 06.1	10.4	15 55.9	5.2	56.4
16	60 32.8	04.1	252 35.5	10.2	16 01.1	5.2	56.4
17	75 32.8	04.4	267 04.7	10.2	16 06.3	5.0	56.4
18	90 32.7	N22 04.7	281 33.9	10.2	S16 11.3	5.0	56.4
19	105 32.6	05.1	296 03.1	10.1	16 16.3	4.9	56.5
20	120 32.5	05.4	310 32.2	10.0	16 21.2	4.8	56.5
21	135 32.4 ..	05.7	325 01.2	10.0	16 26.0	4.8	56.5
22	150 32.3	06.1	339 30.2	9.9	16 30.8	4.6	56.5
23	165 32.2	06.4	353 59.1	9.9	16 35.4	4.6	56.6
2 00	180 32.1	N22 06.7	8 28.0	9.8	S16 40.0	4.5	56.6
01	195 32.0	07.1	22 56.8	9.7	16 44.5	4.4	56.6
02	210 31.9	07.4	37 25.5	9.7	16 48.9	4.3	56.6
03	225 31.8 ..	07.7	51 54.2	9.6	16 53.2	4.2	56.7
04	240 31.7	08.1	66 22.8	9.6	16 57.4	4.1	56.7
05	255 31.6	08.4	80 51.4	9.6	17 01.5	4.0	56.7
T 06	270 31.5	N22 08.7	95 20.0	9.4	S17 05.5	4.0	56.7
U 07	285 31.4	09.0	109 48.4	9.5	17 09.5	3.8	56.8
E 08	300 31.3	09.4	124 16.9	9.3	17 13.3	3.8	56.8
S 09	315 31.2 ..	09.7	138 45.2	9.3	17 17.1	3.7	56.8
D 10	330 31.1	10.0	153 13.5	9.3	17 20.8	3.5	56.8
A 11	345 31.0	10.3	167 41.8	9.2	17 24.3	3.5	56.9
Y 12	0 30.9	N22 10.7	182 10.0	9.2	S17 27.8	3.4	56.9
13	15 30.8	11.0	196 38.2	9.1	17 31.2	3.3	56.9
14	30 30.7	11.3	211 06.3	9.1	17 34.5	3.2	56.9
15	45 30.6 ..	11.6	225 34.4	9.0	17 37.7	3.1	57.0
16	60 30.5	12.0	240 02.4	8.9	17 40.8	3.0	57.0
17	75 30.4	12.3	254 30.3	9.0	17 43.8	2.9	57.0
18	90 30.3	N22 12.6	268 58.3	8.8	S17 46.7	2.8	57.0
19	105 30.2	12.9	283 26.1	8.9	17 49.5	2.7	57.1
20	120 30.1	13.2	297 54.0	8.7	17 52.2	2.6	57.1
21	135 30.0 ..	13.6	312 21.7	8.8	17 54.8	2.6	57.1
22	150 29.9	13.9	326 49.5	8.7	17 57.4	2.4	57.1
23	165 29.8	14.2	341 17.2	8.6	S17 59.8	2.3	57.2
SD	15.8	d 0.3	15.2		15.3		15.5

Twilight and Moonrise

Lat.	Naut.	Civil	Sunrise	Moonrise 31	1	2	3
N 72	□	□	□	19 53	21 48	■■	■■
N 70	□	□	□	19 23	20 59	22 29	23 38
68	□	□	□	19 01	20 28	21 48	22 52
66	////	////	01 14	18 43	20 05	21 20	22 22
64	////	////	01 59	18 29	19 47	20 58	21 59
62	////	00 08	02 28	18 18	19 32	20 41	21 41
60	////	01 27	02 50	18 08	19 19	20 27	21 26
N 58	////	02 01	03 08	17 59	19 09	20 14	21 14
56	00 07	02 25	03 22	17 52	18 59	20 04	21 03
54	01 19	02 44	03 35	17 45	18 51	19 55	20 53
52	01 51	03 00	03 46	17 39	18 44	19 46	20 44
50	02 13	03 14	03 56	17 33	18 37	19 39	20 37
45	02 53	03 41	04 17	17 22	18 23	19 23	20 20
N 40	03 21	04 01	04 33	17 12	18 11	19 10	20 07
35	03 42	04 18	04 47	17 04	18 01	18 59	19 55
30	04 00	04 32	04 59	16 56	17 53	18 49	19 45
20	04 27	04 56	05 20	16 44	17 38	18 33	19 28
N 10	04 48	05 15	05 38	16 33	17 25	18 18	19 13
0	05 06	05 32	05 54	16 23	17 13	18 05	18 59
S 10	05 22	05 48	06 10	16 13	17 01	17 51	18 45
20	05 37	06 04	06 28	16 02	16 48	17 37	18 30
30	05 52	06 21	06 47	15 50	16 33	17 21	18 13
35	06 00	06 31	06 59	15 43	16 25	17 11	18 03
40	06 08	06 42	07 12	15 35	16 15	17 00	17 52
45	06 18	06 54	07 28	15 26	16 04	16 48	17 38
S 50	06 28	07 09	07 47	15 14	15 50	16 32	17 22
52	06 33	07 16	07 56	15 09	15 44	16 25	17 15
54	06 38	07 23	08 06	15 04	15 37	16 17	17 06
56	06 44	07 32	08 17	14 57	15 29	16 08	16 57
58	06 49	07 41	08 30	14 50	15 20	15 58	16 46
S 60	06 56	07 51	08 46	14 42	15 10	15 47	16 34

Sunset, Twilight and Moonset

Lat.	Sunset	Civil	Naut.	Moonset 31	1	2	3
N 72	□	□	□	01 11	01 04	00 53	■■
N 70	□	□	□	01 32	01 35	01 43	02 02
68	□	□	□	01 48	01 58	02 15	02 44
66	22 46	////	////	02 01	02 16	02 38	03 12
64	21 59	////	////	02 11	02 31	02 57	03 34
62	21 29	////	////	02 21	02 43	03 12	03 51
60	21 07	22 31	////	02 29	02 53	03 25	04 06
N 58	20 49	21 56	////	02 36	03 02	03 36	04 18
56	20 34	21 32	////	02 42	03 10	03 46	04 29
54	20 21	21 12	22 39	02 47	03 18	03 54	04 38
52	20 10	20 56	22 06	02 52	03 24	04 02	04 47
50	20 00	20 43	21 43	02 57	03 30	04 09	04 54
45	19 39	20 16	21 03	03 07	03 43	04 23	05 11
N 40	19 22	19 55	20 35	03 15	03 53	04 36	05 24
35	19 08	19 38	20 14	03 22	04 02	04 46	05 35
30	18 56	19 23	19 56	03 29	04 10	04 55	05 45
20	18 36	19 00	19 29	03 39	04 23	05 11	06 02
N 10	18 18	18 41	19 08	03 49	04 35	05 25	06 17
0	18 01	18 24	18 50	03 58	04 46	05 37	06 31
S 10	17 45	18 08	18 34	04 07	04 58	05 50	06 44
20	17 28	17 51	18 19	04 17	05 10	06 04	06 59
30	17 08	17 34	18 04	04 28	05 23	06 20	07 16
35	16 56	17 24	17 55	04 34	05 31	06 29	07 26
40	16 43	17 13	17 47	04 41	05 40	06 39	07 37
45	16 28	17 01	17 38	04 50	05 51	06 52	07 50
S 50	16 09	16 46	17 27	05 00	06 04	07 07	08 06
52	16 00	16 39	17 22	05 05	06 10	07 14	08 14
54	15 49	16 32	17 12	05 10	06 16	07 21	08 22
56	15 38	16 24	17 12	05 16	06 24	07 30	08 32
58	15 25	16 14	17 06	05 22	06 32	07 40	08 43
S 60	15 09	16 04	16 59	05 29	06 42	07 51	08 55

SUN and MOON

Day	Eqn. of Time 00h	Eqn. of Time 12h	Mer. Pass.	Mer. Pass. Upper	Mer. Pass. Lower	Age	Phase
	m s	m s	h m	h m	h m	d	%
31	02 26	02 22	11 58	22 35	10 10	13	95
1	02 18	02 13	11 58	23 25	10 59	14	98
2	02 09	02 04	11 58	24 18	11 51	15	100 ○

UT	ARIES GHA	VENUS −4.4 GHA	VENUS Dec	MARS +1.5 GHA	MARS Dec	JUPITER −1.9 GHA	JUPITER Dec	SATURN +0.1 GHA	SATURN Dec
3 00	251 08.0	131 06.2	N23 12.8	177 09.9	N23 08.3	111 29.9	N16 36.3	11 58.6	S18 11.7
01	266 10.5	146 06.0	12.3	192 10.5	08.5	126 32.0	36.2	27 01.3	11.7
02	281 13.0	161 05.9	11.7	207 11.1	08.7	141 34.1	36.1	42 03.9	11.6
03	296 15.4	176 05.7 ..	11.1	222 11.7 ..	09.0	156 36.2 ..	36.0	57 06.6 ..	11.6
04	311 17.9	191 05.6	10.6	237 12.3	09.2	171 38.3	35.9	72 09.2	11.6
05	326 20.4	206 05.5	10.0	252 12.9	09.4	186 40.4	35.8	87 11.9	11.5
W 06	341 22.8	221 05.3	N23 09.4	267 13.5	N23 09.6	201 42.5	N16 35.7	102 14.5	S18 11.5
E 07	356 25.3	236 05.2	08.9	282 14.1	09.8	216 44.6	35.5	117 17.2	11.5
D 08	11 27.8	251 05.1	08.3	297 14.7	10.0	231 46.7	35.4	132 19.8	11.5
N 09	26 30.2	266 04.9 ..	07.7	312 15.3 ..	10.2	246 48.8 ..	35.3	147 22.5 ..	11.4
E 10	41 32.7	281 04.8	07.2	327 15.9	10.4	261 50.9	35.2	162 25.1	11.4
S 11	56 35.2	296 04.7	06.6	342 16.5	10.6	276 53.0	35.1	177 27.8	11.4
D 12	71 37.6	311 04.5	N23 06.0	357 17.1	N23 10.8	291 55.1	N16 35.0	192 30.4	S18 11.3
A 13	86 40.1	326 04.4	05.5	12 17.7	11.0	306 57.3	34.9	207 33.1	11.3
Y 14	101 42.5	341 04.3	04.9	27 18.3	11.2	321 59.4	34.8	222 35.7	11.3
15	116 45.0	356 04.1 ..	04.3	42 18.9 ..	11.5	337 01.5 ..	34.7	237 38.4 ..	11.2
16	131 47.5	11 04.0	03.7	57 19.5	11.7	352 03.6	34.5	252 41.0	11.2
17	146 49.9	26 03.9	03.2	72 20.1	11.9	7 05.7	34.4	267 43.7	11.2
18	161 52.4	41 03.8	N23 02.6	87 20.7	N23 12.1	22 07.8	N16 34.3	282 46.3	S18 11.1
19	176 54.9	56 03.7	02.0	102 21.3	12.3	37 09.9	34.2	297 49.0	11.1
20	191 57.3	71 03.5	01.4	117 21.9	12.5	52 12.0	34.1	312 51.6	11.1
21	206 59.8	86 03.4 ..	00.9	132 22.5 ..	12.7	67 14.1 ..	34.0	327 54.3 ..	11.0
22	222 02.3	101 03.3	23 00.3	147 23.1	12.9	82 16.2	33.9	342 56.9	11.0
23	237 04.7	116 03.2	22 59.7	162 23.7	13.1	97 18.3	33.8	357 59.6	11.0
4 00	252 07.2	131 03.1	N22 59.1	177 24.3	N23 13.3	112 20.4	N16 33.6	13 02.2	S18 10.9
01	267 09.6	146 03.0	58.6	192 24.9	13.5	127 22.5	33.5	28 04.9	10.9
02	282 12.1	161 02.8	58.0	207 25.5	13.7	142 24.6	33.4	43 07.5	10.9
03	297 14.6	176 02.7 ..	57.4	222 26.1 ..	13.9	157 26.7 ..	33.3	58 10.2 ..	10.8
04	312 17.0	191 02.6	56.8	237 26.7	14.1	172 28.8	33.2	73 12.8	10.8
05	327 19.5	206 02.5	56.2	252 27.3	14.3	187 30.9	33.1	88 15.5	10.8
T 06	342 22.0	221 02.4	N22 55.6	267 27.9	N23 14.5	202 33.0	N16 33.0	103 18.1	S18 10.7
H 07	357 24.4	236 02.3	55.1	282 28.5	14.7	217 35.1	32.8	118 20.8	10.7
U 08	12 26.9	251 02.2	54.5	297 29.1	14.9	232 37.2	32.7	133 23.4	10.7
R 09	27 29.4	266 02.1 ..	53.9	312 29.8 ..	15.1	247 39.3 ..	32.6	148 26.1 ..	10.6
S 10	42 31.8	281 02.0	53.3	327 30.4	15.3	262 41.4	32.5	163 28.7	10.6
D 11	57 34.3	296 01.9	52.7	342 31.0	15.5	277 43.5	32.4	178 31.4	10.6
A 12	72 36.8	311 01.8	N22 52.1	357 31.6	N23 15.7	292 45.6	N16 32.3	193 34.0	S18 10.5
Y 13	87 39.2	326 01.7	51.5	12 32.2	15.9	307 47.7	32.2	208 36.7	10.5
14	102 41.7	341 01.6	50.9	27 32.8	16.1	322 49.8	32.1	223 39.3	10.5
15	117 44.1	356 01.5 ..	50.4	42 33.4 ..	16.3	337 51.9 ..	31.9	238 42.0 ..	10.4
16	132 46.6	11 01.4	49.8	57 34.0	16.5	352 54.0	31.8	253 44.6	10.4
17	147 49.1	26 01.3	49.2	72 34.6	16.7	7 56.1	31.7	268 47.3	10.4
18	162 51.5	41 01.2	N22 48.6	87 35.2	N23 16.9	22 58.2	N16 31.6	283 49.9	S18 10.3
19	177 54.0	56 01.1	48.0	102 35.8	17.1	38 00.3	31.5	298 52.6	10.3
20	192 56.5	71 01.0	47.4	117 36.4	17.3	53 02.4	31.4	313 55.2	10.3
21	207 58.9	86 00.9 ..	46.8	132 37.0 ..	17.5	68 04.5 ..	31.3	328 57.9 ..	10.2
22	223 01.4	101 00.8	46.2	147 37.6	17.7	83 06.6	31.1	344 00.5	10.2
23	238 03.9	116 00.7	45.6	162 38.2	17.9	98 08.7	31.0	359 03.2	10.2
5 00	253 06.3	131 00.6	N22 45.0	177 38.8	N23 18.0	113 10.8	N16 30.9	14 05.8	S18 10.2
01	268 08.8	146 00.6	44.4	192 39.4	18.2	128 12.9	30.8	29 08.5	10.1
02	283 11.3	161 00.5	43.8	207 40.0	18.4	143 15.0	30.7	44 11.1	10.1
03	298 13.7	176 00.4 ..	43.2	222 40.6 ..	18.6	158 17.1 ..	30.6	59 13.8 ..	10.1
04	313 16.2	191 00.3	42.6	237 41.2	18.8	173 19.2	30.5	74 16.4	10.0
05	328 18.6	206 00.2	42.0	252 41.8	19.0	188 21.3	30.3	89 19.1	10.0
F 06	343 21.1	221 00.1	N22 41.4	267 42.4	N23 19.2	203 23.4	N16 30.2	104 21.7	S18 10.0
R 07	358 23.6	236 00.1	40.8	282 43.0	19.4	218 25.5	30.1	119 24.4	09.9
I 08	13 26.0	251 00.0	40.2	297 43.6	19.6	233 27.6	30.0	134 27.0	09.9
D 09	28 28.5	265 59.9 ..	39.6	312 44.2 ..	19.8	248 29.7 ..	29.9	149 29.7 ..	09.9
A 10	43 31.0	280 59.8	39.0	327 44.8	20.0	263 31.8	29.8	164 32.3	09.8
Y 11	58 33.4	295 59.8	38.4	342 45.4	20.2	278 33.9	29.7	179 35.0	09.8
12	73 35.9	310 59.7	N22 37.8	357 46.0	N23 20.3	293 36.0	N16 29.5	194 37.6	S18 09.8
13	88 38.4	325 59.6	37.2	12 46.6	20.5	308 38.1	29.4	209 40.3	09.7
14	103 40.8	340 59.5	36.6	27 47.2	20.7	323 40.2	29.3	224 42.9	09.7
15	118 43.3	355 59.5 ..	36.0	42 47.8 ..	20.9	338 42.3 ..	29.2	239 45.6 ..	09.7
16	133 45.8	10 59.4	35.4	57 48.4	21.1	353 44.4	29.1	254 48.2	09.6
17	148 48.2	25 59.3	34.8	72 49.0	21.3	8 46.5	29.0	269 50.9	09.6
18	163 50.7	40 59.3	N22 34.1	87 49.6	N23 21.5	23 48.6	N16 28.8	284 53.5	S18 09.6
19	178 53.1	55 59.2	33.5	102 50.2	21.7	38 50.7	28.7	299 56.2	09.5
20	193 55.6	70 59.1	32.9	117 50.8	21.8	53 52.8	28.6	314 58.8	09.5
21	208 58.1	85 59.1 ..	32.3	132 51.4 ..	22.0	68 54.9 ..	28.5	330 01.4 ..	09.5
22	224 00.5	100 59.0	31.7	147 52.0	22.2	83 57.0	28.4	345 04.1	09.4
23	239 03.0	115 59.0	31.1	162 52.6	22.4	98 59.1	28.3	0 06.7	09.4
Mer. Pass.	h m 7 10.3	v −0.1	d 0.6	v 0.6	d 0.2	v 2.1	d 0.1	v 2.6	d 0.0

STARS

Name	SHA	Dec
Acamar	315 17.8	S40 14.6
Achernar	335 26.3	S57 09.4
Acrux	173 07.3	S63 11.4
Adhara	255 11.8	S28 59.9
Aldebaran	290 48.2	N16 32.2
Alioth	166 19.4	N55 52.8
Alkaid	152 57.6	N49 14.4
Al Na'ir	27 42.1	S46 52.8
Alnilam	275 45.4	S 1 11.8
Alphard	217 54.9	S 8 43.8
Alphecca	126 09.6	N26 40.0
Alpheratz	357 42.2	N29 10.3
Altair	62 06.7	N 8 54.7
Ankaa	353 14.6	S42 13.2
Antares	112 24.2	S26 27.8
Arcturus	145 54.3	N19 06.3
Atria	107 24.2	S69 03.1
Avior	234 17.8	S59 33.9
Bellatrix	278 30.9	N 6 21.6
Betelgeuse	271 00.2	N 7 24.3
Canopus	263 56.1	S52 42.6
Capella	280 33.0	N46 00.6
Deneb	49 30.2	N45 20.1
Denebola	182 32.3	N14 29.2
Diphda	348 54.7	S17 54.1
Dubhe	193 50.2	N61 40.3
Elnath	278 11.3	N28 37.0
Eltanin	90 45.0	N51 29.3
Enif	33 45.7	N 9 56.8
Fomalhaut	15 22.6	S29 32.2
Gacrux	171 59.0	S57 12.2
Gienah	175 50.8	S17 37.8
Hadar	148 45.4	S60 26.9
Hamal	327 59.5	N23 31.9
Kaus Aust.	83 41.7	S34 22.4
Kochab	137 19.3	N74 05.8
Markab	13 37.0	N15 17.2
Menkar	314 14.0	N 4 08.8
Menkent	148 05.6	S36 26.8
Miaplacidus	221 39.6	S69 47.3
Mirfak	308 38.9	N49 54.6
Nunki	75 56.4	S26 16.4
Peacock	53 16.9	S56 40.7
Pollux	243 26.4	N27 59.2
Procyon	244 58.6	N 5 10.9
Rasalhague	96 04.9	N12 33.1
Regulus	207 42.2	N11 53.4
Rigel	281 11.1	S 8 11.3
Rigil Kent.	139 49.2	S60 53.9
Sabik	102 10.7	S15 44.4
Schedar	349 39.1	N56 37.0
Shaula	96 19.7	S37 06.7
Sirius	258 32.9	S16 44.5
Spica	158 29.6	S11 14.5
Suhail	222 51.6	S43 30.1
Vega	80 37.7	N38 48.0
Zuben'ubi	137 03.6	S16 06.3

	SHA	Mer. Pass.
Venus	238 55.9	15 16
Mars	285 17.1	12 10
Jupiter	220 13.2	16 28
Saturn	120 55.1	23 04

UT	SUN GHA	SUN Dec	MOON GHA	v	Dec	d	HP
d h	° '	° '	° '	'	° '	'	'
3 00	180 29.7	N22 14.5	355 44.8	8.6	S18 02.1	2.2	57.2
01	195 29.6	14.8	10 12.4	8.6	18 04.3	2.1	57.2
02	210 29.5	15.1	24 40.0	8.5	18 06.4	2.0	57.2
03	225 29.4	.. 15.5	39 07.5	8.5	18 08.4	1.9	57.2
04	240 29.3	15.8	53 35.0	8.4	18 10.3	1.8	57.3
05	255 29.2	16.1	68 02.4	8.4	18 12.1	1.7	57.3
06	270 29.1	N22 16.4	82 29.8	8.3	S18 13.8	1.6	57.3
W 07	285 29.0	16.7	96 57.1	8.4	18 15.4	1.4	57.3
E 08	315 28.9	17.0	111 24.5	8.2	18 16.8	1.4	57.4
D 09	315 28.8	.. 17.3	125 51.7	8.3	18 18.2	1.3	57.4
N 10	330 28.7	17.6	140 19.0	8.2	18 19.5	1.1	57.4
E 11	345 28.6	17.9	154 46.2	8.2	18 20.6	1.1	57.4
S 12	0 28.5	N22 18.2	169 13.4	8.1	S18 21.7	0.9	57.5
D 13	15 28.4	18.6	183 40.5	8.1	18 22.6	0.9	57.5
A 14	30 28.3	18.9	198 07.6	8.1	18 23.5	0.7	57.5
Y 15	45 28.2	.. 19.2	212 34.7	8.1	18 24.2	0.6	57.5
16	60 28.1	19.5	227 01.8	8.0	18 24.8	0.6	57.5
17	75 28.0	19.8	241 28.8	8.0	18 25.4	0.4	57.6
18	90 27.9	N22 20.1	255 55.8	7.9	S18 25.8	0.3	57.6
19	105 27.8	20.4	270 22.7	8.0	18 26.1	0.2	57.6
20	120 27.7	20.7	284 49.7	7.9	18 26.3	0.0	57.6
21	135 27.6	.. 21.0	299 16.6	7.9	18 26.3	0.0	57.7
22	150 27.5	21.3	313 43.5	7.8	18 26.3	0.1	57.7
23	165 27.4	21.6	328 10.3	7.8	18 26.2	0.3	57.7
4 00	180 27.3	N22 21.9	342 37.1	7.9	S18 25.9	0.4	57.7
01	195 27.2	22.2	357 04.0	7.7	18 25.5	0.4	57.7
02	210 27.1	22.5	11 30.7	7.8	18 25.1	0.6	57.8
03	225 27.0	.. 22.8	25 57.5	7.8	18 24.5	0.7	57.8
04	240 26.9	23.1	40 24.3	7.7	18 23.8	0.8	57.8
05	255 26.8	23.4	54 51.0	7.7	18 23.0	0.9	57.8
06	270 26.7	N22 23.7	69 17.7	7.7	S18 22.1	1.1	57.8
T 07	285 26.6	24.0	83 44.4	7.7	18 21.0	1.1	57.9
H 08	300 26.4	24.3	98 11.1	7.6	18 19.9	1.3	57.9
U 09	315 26.3	.. 24.6	112 37.7	7.7	18 18.6	1.3	57.9
R 10	330 26.2	24.9	127 04.4	7.6	18 17.3	1.5	57.9
S 11	345 26.1	25.1	141 31.0	7.6	18 15.8	1.6	57.9
D 12	0 26.0	N22 25.4	155 57.6	7.7	S18 14.2	1.7	58.0
A 13	15 25.9	25.7	170 24.3	7.6	18 12.5	1.8	58.0
Y 14	30 25.8	26.0	184 50.9	7.6	18 10.7	1.9	58.0
15	45 25.7	.. 26.3	199 17.5	7.5	18 08.8	2.1	58.0
16	60 25.6	26.6	213 44.0	7.6	18 06.7	2.1	58.0
17	75 25.5	26.9	228 10.6	7.6	18 04.6	2.3	58.1
18	90 25.4	N22 27.2	242 37.2	7.5	S18 02.3	2.4	58.1
19	105 25.3	27.5	257 03.7	7.6	17 59.9	2.4	58.1
20	120 25.2	27.7	271 30.3	7.6	17 57.5	2.6	58.1
21	135 25.1	.. 28.0	285 56.9	7.5	17 54.9	2.7	58.1
22	150 25.0	28.3	300 23.4	7.6	17 52.2	2.8	58.2
23	165 24.9	28.6	314 50.0	7.5	17 49.4	3.0	58.2
5 00	180 24.7	N22 28.9	329 16.5	7.6	S17 46.4	3.0	58.2
01	195 24.6	29.2	343 43.1	7.5	17 43.4	3.2	58.2
02	210 24.5	29.4	358 09.6	7.6	17 40.2	3.2	58.2
03	225 24.4	.. 29.7	12 36.2	7.5	17 37.0	3.4	58.2
04	240 24.3	30.0	27 02.7	7.6	17 33.6	3.4	58.3
05	255 24.2	30.3	41 29.3	7.5	17 30.2	3.6	58.3
06	270 24.1	N22 30.6	55 55.8	7.6	S17 26.6	3.7	58.3
07	285 24.0	30.8	70 22.4	7.6	17 22.9	3.8	58.3
08	300 23.9	31.1	84 49.0	7.5	17 19.1	3.9	58.3
F 09	315 23.8	.. 31.4	99 15.5	7.6	17 15.2	4.0	58.3
R 10	330 23.7	31.7	113 42.1	7.6	17 11.2	4.2	58.4
I 11	345 23.6	32.0	128 08.7	7.6	17 07.0	4.2	58.4
D 12	0 23.4	N22 32.2	142 35.3	7.6	S17 02.8	4.3	58.4
A 13	15 23.3	32.5	157 01.9	7.7	16 58.5	4.5	58.4
Y 14	30 23.2	32.8	171 28.6	7.6	16 54.0	4.5	58.4
15	45 23.1	.. 33.1	185 55.2	7.6	16 49.5	4.7	58.4
16	60 23.0	33.3	200 21.8	7.7	16 44.8	4.8	58.5
17	75 22.9	33.6	214 48.5	7.7	16 40.0	4.8	58.5
18	90 22.8	N22 33.9	229 15.2	7.7	S16 35.2	5.0	58.5
19	105 22.7	34.1	243 41.9	7.7	16 30.2	5.1	58.5
20	120 22.6	34.4	258 08.6	7.7	16 25.1	5.1	58.5
21	135 22.5	.. 34.7	272 35.3	7.7	16 20.0	5.3	58.5
22	150 22.3	34.9	287 02.0	7.7	16 14.7	5.4	58.6
23	165 22.2	35.2	301 28.7	7.8	S16 09.3	5.5	58.6
	SD 15.8	d 0.3	SD 15.7		15.8		15.9

Lat.	Twilight Naut.	Twilight Civil	Sunrise	Moonrise 3	4	5	6
°	h m	h m	h m	h m	h m	h m	h m
N 72	☐	☐	☐	■■	■■	01 34	01 10
N 70	☐	☐	☐	23 38	24 14	00 14	00 29
68	☐	☐	☐	22 52	23 35	24 00	00 00
66	////	////	01 01	22 22	23 08	23 39	24 00
64	////	////	01 52	21 59	22 47	23 22	23 47
62	////	////	02 23	21 41	22 30	23 08	23 37
60	////	01 19	02 46	21 26	22 16	22 56	23 27
N 58	////	01 55	03 04	21 14	22 04	22 45	23 19
56	////	02 21	03 19	21 03	21 54	22 36	23 12
54	01 12	02 41	03 33	20 53	21 44	22 28	23 05
52	01 46	02 57	03 44	20 44	21 36	22 21	23 00
50	02 09	03 11	03 54	20 37	21 29	22 15	22 54
45	02 51	03 39	04 15	20 20	21 13	22 01	22 43
N 40	03 19	04 00	04 32	20 07	21 00	21 49	22 33
35	03 41	04 17	04 47	19 55	20 49	21 39	22 25
30	03 59	04 32	04 59	19 45	20 39	21 30	22 18
20	04 27	04 55	05 20	19 28	20 23	21 15	22 06
N 10	04 48	05 15	05 38	19 13	20 08	21 02	21 55
0	05 06	05 32	05 55	18 59	19 54	20 50	21 45
S 10	05 22	05 49	06 11	18 45	19 41	20 38	21 35
20	05 38	06 05	06 29	18 30	19 26	20 24	21 24
30	05 53	06 23	06 49	18 13	19 10	20 09	21 11
35	06 01	06 33	07 01	18 03	19 00	20 01	21 04
40	06 10	06 44	07 14	17 52	18 49	19 51	20 56
45	06 20	06 57	07 30	17 38	18 36	19 39	20 46
S 50	06 31	07 12	07 50	17 22	18 20	19 25	20 34
52	06 36	07 19	07 59	17 15	18 13	19 18	20 29
54	06 41	07 26	08 09	17 06	18 04	19 11	20 23
56	06 46	07 35	08 21	16 57	17 55	19 02	20 16
58	06 53	07 44	08 34	16 46	17 44	18 53	20 09
S 60	06 59	07 55	08 50	16 34	17 32	18 42	20 00

Lat.	Sunset	Twilight Civil	Twilight Naut.	Moonset 3	4	5	6
°	h m	h m	h m	h m	h m	h m	h m
N 72	☐	☐	☐	■■	■■	02 47	05 08
N 70	☐	☐	☐	02 02	02 47	04 07	05 48
68	☐	☐	☐	02 44	03 33	04 46	06 15
66	23 00	////	////	03 12	04 03	05 12	06 36
64	22 07	////	////	03 34	04 26	05 33	06 52
62	21 35	////	////	03 51	04 44	05 49	07 06
60	21 12	22 40	////	04 06	04 59	06 03	07 18
N 58	20 53	22 03	////	04 18	05 11	06 15	07 27
56	20 38	21 37	////	04 29	05 22	06 25	07 36
54	20 25	21 17	22 47	04 38	05 32	06 34	07 44
52	20 13	21 00	22 12	04 47	05 40	06 42	07 51
50	20 03	20 46	21 48	04 54	05 48	06 49	07 57
45	19 42	20 18	21 06	05 11	06 05	07 05	08 10
N 40	19 25	19 57	20 38	05 24	06 18	07 18	08 21
35	19 10	19 40	20 16	05 35	06 29	07 28	08 30
30	18 58	19 25	19 58	05 45	06 39	07 38	08 39
20	18 37	19 01	19 30	06 02	06 57	07 54	08 53
N 10	18 19	18 42	19 08	06 17	07 11	08 08	09 05
0	18 02	18 24	18 50	06 31	07 25	08 21	09 16
S 10	17 45	18 08	18 34	06 44	07 39	08 34	09 28
20	17 28	17 51	18 19	06 59	07 54	08 48	09 40
30	17 07	17 34	18 03	07 16	08 11	09 04	09 53
35	16 56	17 24	17 55	07 26	08 21	09 13	10 01
40	16 42	17 12	17 46	07 37	08 32	09 23	10 10
45	16 26	17 00	17 36	07 50	08 45	09 36	10 21
S 50	16 07	16 45	17 26	08 06	09 01	09 50	10 33
52	15 57	16 38	17 21	08 14	09 09	09 57	10 39
54	15 47	16 30	17 15	08 22	09 17	10 05	10 45
56	15 35	16 21	17 10	08 32	09 27	10 14	10 53
58	15 22	16 12	17 04	08 43	09 37	10 23	11 01
S 60	15 06	16 01	16 57	08 55	09 50	10 34	11 10

	SUN			MOON			
Day	Eqn. of Time 00h	12h	Mer. Pass.	Mer. Pass. Upper	Lower	Age	Phase
d	m s	m s	h m	h m	h m	d	%
3	01 59	01 54	11 58	00 18	12 45	16	99
4	01 49	01 44	11 58	01 12	13 40	17	96
5	01 39	01 34	11 58	02 08	14 35	18	91

UT	ARIES GHA	VENUS −4.4 GHA	Dec	MARS +1.5 GHA	Dec	JUPITER −1.9 GHA	Dec	SATURN +0.1 GHA	Dec
6 00	254 05.5	130 58.9	N22 30.5	177 53.2	N23 22.6	114 01.2	N16 28.1	15 09.4	S18 09.4
01	269 07.9	145 58.8	29.9	192 53.8	22.8	129 03.3	28.0	30 12.0	09.4
02	284 10.4	160 58.8	29.2	207 54.4	23.0	144 05.4	27.9	45 14.7	09.3
03	299 12.9	175 58.7 ..	28.6	222 55.0 ..	23.1	159 07.5 ..	27.8	60 17.3 ..	09.3
04	314 15.3	190 58.7	28.0	237 55.6	23.3	174 09.5	27.7	75 20.0	09.3
05	329 17.8	205 58.6	27.4	252 56.2	23.5	189 11.6	27.6	90 22.6	09.2
S 06	344 20.3	220 58.6	N22 26.8	267 56.8	N23 23.7	204 13.7	N16 27.5	105 25.3	S18 09.2
A 07	359 22.7	235 58.5	26.1	282 57.5	23.9	219 15.8	27.3	120 27.9	09.2
T 08	14 25.2	250 58.5	25.5	297 58.1	24.1	234 17.9	27.2	135 30.6	09.1
U 09	29 27.6	265 58.4 ..	24.9	312 58.7 ..	24.2	249 20.0 ..	27.1	150 33.2 ..	09.1
R 10	44 30.1	280 58.4	24.3	327 59.3	24.4	264 22.1	27.0	165 35.9	09.1
D 11	59 32.6	295 58.3	23.7	342 59.9	24.6	279 24.2	26.9	180 38.5	09.0
A 12	74 35.0	310 58.3	N22 23.0	358 00.5	N23 24.8	294 26.3	N16 26.8	195 41.2	S18 09.0
Y 13	89 37.5	325 58.2	22.4	13 01.1	25.0	309 28.4	26.6	210 43.8	09.0
14	104 40.0	340 58.2	21.8	28 01.7	25.1	324 30.5	26.5	225 46.5	08.9
15	119 42.4	355 58.2 ..	21.2	43 02.3 ..	25.3	339 32.6 ..	26.4	240 49.1 ..	08.9
16	134 44.9	10 58.1	20.5	58 02.9	25.5	354 34.7	26.3	255 51.7	08.9
17	149 47.4	25 58.1	19.9	73 03.5	25.7	9 36.8	26.2	270 54.4	08.8
18	164 49.8	40 58.0	N22 19.3	88 04.1	N23 25.9	24 38.8	N16 26.1	285 57.0	S18 08.8
19	179 52.3	55 58.0	18.7	103 04.7	26.0	39 40.9	25.9	300 59.7	08.8
20	194 54.7	70 58.0	18.0	118 05.3	26.2	54 43.0	25.8	316 02.3	08.8
21	209 57.2	85 57.9 ..	17.4	133 05.9 ..	26.4	69 45.1 ..	25.7	331 05.0 ..	08.7
22	224 59.7	100 57.9	16.8	148 06.5	26.6	84 47.2	25.6	346 07.6	08.7
23	240 02.1	115 57.9	16.1	163 07.1	26.7	99 49.3	25.5	1 10.3	08.7
7 00	255 04.6	130 57.9	N22 15.5	178 07.7	N23 26.9	114 51.4	N16 25.3	16 12.9	S18 08.6
01	270 07.1	145 57.8	14.9	193 08.3	27.1	129 53.5	25.2	31 15.6	08.6
02	285 09.5	160 57.8	14.3	208 08.9	27.3	144 55.6	25.1	46 18.2	08.6
03	300 12.0	175 57.8 ..	13.6	223 09.5 ..	27.4	159 57.7 ..	25.0	61 20.9 ..	08.5
04	315 14.5	190 57.7	13.0	238 10.1	27.6	174 59.8	24.9	76 23.5	08.5
05	330 16.9	205 57.7	12.4	253 10.7	27.8	190 01.8	24.8	91 26.1	08.5
S 06	345 19.4	220 57.7	N22 11.7	268 11.3	N23 28.0	205 03.9	N16 24.6	106 28.8	S18 08.4
U 07	0 21.9	235 57.7	11.1	283 11.9	28.1	220 06.0	24.5	121 31.4	08.4
N 08	15 24.3	250 57.7	10.4	298 12.5	28.3	235 08.1	24.4	136 34.1	08.4
D 09	30 26.8	265 57.6 ..	09.8	313 13.1 ..	28.5	250 10.2 ..	24.3	151 36.7 ..	08.3
A 10	45 29.2	280 57.6	09.2	328 13.7	28.7	265 12.3	24.2	166 39.4	08.3
Y 11	60 31.7	295 57.6	08.5	343 14.3	28.8	280 14.4	24.1	181 42.0	08.3
12	75 34.2	310 57.6	N22 07.9	358 14.9	N23 29.0	295 16.5	N16 23.9	196 44.7	S18 08.3
13	90 36.6	325 57.6	07.3	13 15.5	29.2	310 18.6	23.8	211 47.3	08.2
14	105 39.1	340 57.6	06.6	28 16.1	29.3	325 20.7	23.7	226 50.0	08.2
15	120 41.6	355 57.6 ..	06.0	43 16.7 ..	29.5	340 22.7 ..	23.6	241 52.6 ..	08.2
16	135 44.0	10 57.6	05.3	58 17.3	29.7	355 24.8	23.5	256 55.3	08.1
17	150 46.5	25 57.5	04.7	73 17.9	29.9	10 26.9	23.4	271 57.9	08.1
18	165 49.0	40 57.5	N22 04.0	88 18.5	N23 30.0	25 29.0	N16 23.2	287 00.5	S18 08.1
19	180 51.4	55 57.5	03.4	103 19.1	30.2	40 31.1	23.1	302 03.2	08.0
20	195 53.9	70 57.5	02.8	118 19.7	30.4	55 33.2	23.0	317 05.8	08.0
21	210 56.4	85 57.5 ..	02.1	133 20.3 ..	30.5	70 35.3 ..	22.9	332 08.5 ..	08.0
22	225 58.8	100 57.5	01.5	148 20.9	30.7	85 37.4	22.7	347 11.1	07.9
23	241 01.3	115 57.5	00.8	163 21.5	30.9	100 39.4	22.6	2 13.8	07.9
8 00	256 03.7	130 57.5	N22 00.2	178 22.1	N23 31.0	115 41.5	N16 22.5	17 16.4	S18 07.9
01	271 06.2	145 57.5	21 59.5	193 22.7	31.2	130 43.6	22.4	32 19.1	07.8
02	286 08.7	160 57.5	58.9	208 23.3	31.4	145 45.7	22.3	47 21.7	07.8
03	301 11.1	175 57.5 ..	58.2	223 23.9 ..	31.5	160 47.8 ..	22.2	62 24.3 ..	07.8
04	316 13.6	190 57.5	57.6	238 24.5	31.7	175 49.9	22.0	77 27.0	07.8
05	331 16.1	205 57.5	56.9	253 25.1	31.9	190 52.0	21.9	92 29.6	07.7
M 06	346 18.5	220 57.6	N21 56.3	268 25.7	N23 32.0	205 54.0	N16 21.8	107 32.3	S18 07.7
O 07	1 21.0	235 57.6	55.6	283 26.3	32.2	220 56.1	21.7	122 34.9	07.7
N 08	16 23.5	250 57.6	55.0	298 27.0	32.4	235 58.2	21.6	137 37.6	07.6
D 09	31 25.9	265 57.6 ..	54.3	313 27.6 ..	32.5	251 00.3 ..	21.4	152 40.2 ..	07.6
A 10	46 28.4	280 57.6	53.7	328 28.2	32.7	266 02.4	21.3	167 42.9	07.6
Y 11	61 30.9	295 57.6	53.0	343 28.8	32.8	281 04.5	21.2	182 45.5	07.5
12	76 33.3	310 57.6	N21 52.4	358 29.4	N23 33.0	296 06.6	N16 21.1	197 48.1	S18 07.5
13	91 35.8	325 57.6	51.7	13 30.0	33.2	311 08.6	21.0	212 50.8	07.5
14	106 38.2	340 57.7	51.1	28 30.6	33.3	326 10.7	20.8	227 53.4	07.4
15	121 40.7	355 57.7 ..	50.4	43 31.2 ..	33.5	341 12.8 ..	20.7	242 56.1 ..	07.4
16	136 43.2	10 57.7	49.7	58 31.8	33.7	356 14.9	20.6	257 58.7	07.4
17	151 45.6	25 57.7	49.1	73 32.4	33.8	11 17.0	20.5	273 01.4	07.4
18	166 48.1	40 57.8	N21 48.4	88 33.0	N23 34.0	26 19.1	N16 20.4	288 04.0	S18 07.3
19	181 50.6	55 57.8	47.8	103 33.6	34.1	41 21.1	20.2	303 06.7	07.3
20	196 53.0	70 57.8	47.1	118 34.2	34.3	56 23.2	20.1	318 09.3	07.3
21	211 55.5	85 57.8 ..	46.4	133 34.8 ..	34.5	71 25.3 ..	20.0	333 11.9 ..	07.2
22	226 58.0	100 57.9	45.8	148 35.4	34.6	86 27.4	19.9	348 14.6	07.2
23	242 00.4	115 57.9	45.1	163 36.0	34.8	101 29.5	19.8	3 17.2	07.2
Mer. Pass.	h m 6 58.5	v 0.0	d 0.6	v 0.6	d 0.2	v 2.1	d 0.1	v 2.6	d 0.0

STARS

Name	SHA	Dec
Acamar	315 17.8	S40 14.6
Achernar	335 26.3	S57 09.4
Acrux	173 07.3	S63 11.4
Adhara	255 11.8	S28 59.9
Aldebaran	290 48.2	N16 32.2
Alioth	166 19.4	N55 52.8
Alkaid	152 57.6	N49 14.4
Al Na'ir	27 42.0	S46 52.8
Alnilam	275 45.3	S 1 11.8
Alphard	217 54.9	S 8 43.8
Alphecca	126 09.6	N26 40.0
Alpheratz	357 42.2	N29 10.4
Altair	62 06.7	N 8 54.7
Ankaa	353 14.6	S42 13.2
Antares	112 24.2	S26 27.8
Arcturus	145 54.3	N19 06.3
Atria	107 24.2	S69 03.1
Avior	234 17.8	S59 33.9
Bellatrix	278 30.9	N 6 21.6
Betelgeuse	271 00.2	N 7 24.3
Canopus	263 56.1	S52 42.5
Capella	280 32.9	N46 00.6
Deneb	49 30.2	N45 20.1
Denebola	182 32.3	N14 29.2
Diphda	348 54.7	S17 54.1
Dubhe	193 50.3	N61 40.3
Elnath	278 11.3	N28 37.0
Eltanin	90 45.0	N51 29.3
Enif	33 45.7	N 9 56.8
Fomalhaut	15 22.5	S29 32.2
Gacrux	171 59.0	S57 12.2
Gienah	175 50.8	S17 37.8
Hadar	148 45.4	S60 27.0
Hamal	327 59.5	N23 31.9
Kaus Aust.	83 41.7	S34 22.4
Kochab	137 19.3	N74 05.8
Markab	13 37.0	N15 17.2
Menkar	314 13.9	N 4 08.8
Menkent	148 05.6	S36 26.8
Miaplacidus	221 39.7	S69 47.3
Mirfak	308 38.8	N49 54.6
Nunki	75 56.3	S26 16.4
Peacock	53 16.8	S56 40.7
Pollux	243 26.4	N27 59.2
Procyon	244 58.6	N 5 10.9
Rasalhague	96 04.9	N12 33.1
Regulus	207 42.2	N11 53.4
Rigel	281 11.1	S 8 11.3
Rigil Kent.	139 49.2	S60 54.0
Sabik	102 10.7	S15 44.4
Schedar	349 39.1	N56 37.0
Shaula	96 19.7	S37 06.7
Sirius	258 32.9	S16 44.5
Spica	158 29.6	S11 14.5
Suhail	222 51.6	S43 30.1
Vega	80 37.6	N38 48.0
Zuben'ubi	137 03.6	S16 06.3

	SHA	Mer. Pass.
		h m
Venus	235 53.2	15 16
Mars	283 03.1	12 07
Jupiter	219 46.8	16 18
Saturn	121 08.3	22 51

UT	SUN GHA	SUN Dec	MOON GHA	v	MOON Dec	d	HP
d h	° ′	° ′	° ′	′	° ′	′	′
6 00	180 22.1	N22 35.5	315 55.5	7.8	S16 03.8	5.5	58.6
01	195 22.0	35.7	330 22.3	7.8	15 58.3	5.7	58.6
02	210 21.9	36.0	344 49.1	7.8	15 52.6	5.8	58.6
03	225 21.8	36.3	359 15.9	7.9	15 46.8	5.9	58.6
04	240 21.7	36.5	13 42.8	7.9	15 40.9	6.0	58.6
05	255 21.6	36.8	28 09.6	7.9	15 34.9	6.0	58.7
S 06	270 21.5	N22 37.1	42 36.5	7.9	S15 28.9	6.2	58.7
A 07	285 21.3	37.3	57 03.4	7.9	15 22.7	6.3	58.7
T 08	300 21.2	37.6	71 30.3	8.0	15 16.4	6.3	58.7
U 09	315 21.1	37.9	85 57.3	7.9	15 10.1	6.5	58.7
R 10	330 21.0	38.1	100 24.2	8.0	15 03.6	6.5	58.7
D 11	345 20.9	38.4	114 51.2	8.0	14 57.1	6.7	58.7
A 12	0 20.8	N22 38.6	129 18.2	8.1	S14 50.4	6.7	58.7
Y 13	15 20.7	38.9	143 45.3	8.1	14 43.7	6.9	58.8
14	30 20.6	39.1	158 12.3	8.1	14 36.8	6.9	58.8
15	45 20.4	39.4	172 39.4	8.1	14 29.9	7.0	58.8
16	60 20.3	39.7	187 06.5	8.1	14 22.9	7.1	58.8
17	75 20.2	39.9	201 33.6	8.2	14 15.8	7.2	58.8
18	90 20.1	N22 40.2	216 00.8	8.2	S14 08.6	7.3	58.8
19	105 20.0	40.4	230 28.0	8.2	14 01.3	7.3	58.8
20	120 19.9	40.7	244 55.2	8.2	13 54.0	7.5	58.8
21	135 19.8	40.9	259 22.4	8.3	13 46.5	7.5	58.9
22	150 19.6	41.2	273 49.7	8.3	13 39.0	7.6	58.9
23	165 19.5	41.4	288 17.0	8.3	13 31.4	7.7	58.9
7 00	180 19.4	N22 41.7	302 44.3	8.3	S13 23.7	7.8	58.9
01	195 19.3	41.9	317 11.6	8.4	13 15.9	7.9	58.9
02	210 19.2	42.2	331 39.0	8.4	13 08.0	7.9	58.9
03	225 19.1	42.4	346 06.4	8.4	13 00.1	8.1	58.9
04	240 19.0	42.7	0 33.8	8.5	12 52.0	8.1	58.9
05	255 18.8	42.9	15 01.3	8.5	12 43.9	8.2	58.9
S 06	270 18.7	N22 43.2	29 28.8	8.5	S12 35.7	8.2	59.0
U 07	285 18.6	43.4	43 56.3	8.5	12 27.5	8.4	59.0
N 08	300 18.5	43.7	58 23.8	8.6	12 19.1	8.4	59.0
D 09	315 18.4	43.9	72 51.4	8.6	12 10.7	8.6	59.0
A 10	330 18.3	44.2	87 19.0	8.6	12 02.2	8.6	59.0
Y 11	345 18.1	44.4	101 46.6	8.6	11 53.6	8.6	59.0
12	0 18.0	N22 44.6	116 14.2	8.7	S11 45.0	8.7	59.0
13	15 17.9	44.9	130 41.9	8.7	11 36.3	8.8	59.0
14	30 17.8	45.1	145 09.6	8.7	11 27.5	8.9	59.0
15	45 17.7	45.4	159 37.3	8.8	11 18.6	8.9	59.0
16	60 17.6	45.6	174 05.1	8.8	11 09.7	9.0	59.0
17	75 17.5	45.8	188 32.9	8.8	11 00.7	9.1	59.1
18	90 17.3	N22 46.1	203 00.7	8.8	S10 51.6	9.1	59.1
19	105 17.2	46.3	217 28.5	8.9	10 42.5	9.2	59.1
20	120 17.1	46.5	231 56.4	8.9	10 33.3	9.2	59.1
21	135 17.0	46.8	246 24.3	8.9	10 24.1	9.4	59.1
22	150 16.9	47.0	260 52.2	8.9	10 14.7	9.4	59.1
23	165 16.7	47.3	275 20.1	9.0	10 05.3	9.4	59.1
8 00	180 16.6	N22 47.5	289 48.1	9.0	S 9 55.9	9.5	59.1
01	195 16.5	47.7	304 16.1	9.0	9 46.4	9.6	59.1
02	210 16.4	48.0	318 44.1	9.1	9 36.8	9.6	59.1
03	225 16.3	48.2	333 12.2	9.1	9 27.2	9.7	59.1
04	240 16.2	48.4	347 40.3	9.1	9 17.5	9.7	59.1
05	255 16.0	48.6	2 08.4	9.1	9 07.8	9.8	59.1
M 06	270 15.9	N22 48.9	16 36.5	9.1	S 8 58.0	9.9	59.2
O 07	285 15.8	49.1	31 04.6	9.2	8 48.1	9.9	59.2
N 08	300 15.7	49.3	45 32.8	9.2	8 38.2	9.9	59.2
D 09	315 15.6	49.6	60 01.0	9.2	8 28.3	10.0	59.2
A 10	330 15.4	49.8	74 29.2	9.3	8 18.3	10.1	59.2
Y 11	345 15.3	50.0	88 57.5	9.3	8 08.2	10.1	59.2
12	0 15.2	N22 50.2	103 25.8	9.2	S 7 58.1	10.1	59.2
13	15 15.1	50.5	117 54.0	9.4	7 48.0	10.2	59.2
14	30 15.0	50.7	132 22.4	9.3	7 37.8	10.3	59.2
15	45 14.9	50.9	146 50.7	9.4	7 27.5	10.3	59.2
16	60 14.7	51.1	161 19.1	9.3	7 17.2	10.3	59.2
17	75 14.6	51.4	175 47.4	9.4	7 06.9	10.4	59.2
18	90 14.5	N22 51.6	190 15.8	9.5	S 6 56.5	10.4	59.2
19	105 14.4	51.8	204 44.3	9.4	6 46.1	10.5	59.2
20	120 14.3	52.0	219 12.7	9.5	6 35.6	10.5	59.2
21	135 14.1	52.2	233 41.2	9.4	6 25.1	10.5	59.2
22	150 14.0	52.5	248 09.6	9.5	6 14.6	10.6	59.2
23	165 13.9	52.7	262 38.1	9.5	S 6 04.0	10.6	59.2
	SD 15.8	d 0.2	SD 16.0		16.1		16.1

Lat.	Twilight Naut.	Twilight Civil	Sunrise	Moonrise 6	7	8	9
°	h m	h m	h m	h m	h m	h m	h m
N 72	□	□	□	01 10	01 00	00 53	00 47
N 70	□	□	□	00 29	00 35	00 38	00 39
68	□	□	□	00 00	00 16	00 25	00 33
66	////	////	00 47	24 00	00 00	00 15	00 27
64	////	////	01 45	23 47	24 07	00 07	00 22
62	////	////	02 18	23 37	23 59	24 18	00 18
60	////	01 11	02 42	23 27	23 53	24 14	00 14
N 58	////	01 51	03 01	23 19	23 47	24 11	00 11
56	////	02 17	03 17	23 12	23 42	24 08	00 08
54	01 04	02 38	03 30	23 05	23 37	24 05	00 05
52	01 41	02 55	03 42	23 00	23 33	24 03	00 03
50	02 06	03 09	03 53	22 54	23 29	24 01	00 01
45	02 49	03 37	04 14	22 43	23 21	23 56	24 29
N 40	03 18	03 59	04 31	22 33	23 14	23 52	24 28
35	03 40	04 17	04 46	22 25	23 08	23 49	24 27
30	03 58	04 31	04 58	22 18	23 03	23 46	24 27
20	04 26	04 55	05 20	22 06	22 54	23 40	24 25
N 10	04 48	05 15	05 38	21 55	22 46	23 36	24 24
0	05 07	05 33	05 55	21 45	22 39	23 31	24 23
S 10	05 23	05 49	06 12	21 35	22 31	23 27	24 22
20	05 39	06 06	06 30	21 24	22 23	23 22	24 21
30	05 54	06 24	06 50	21 11	22 14	23 17	24 20
35	06 03	06 34	07 02	21 04	22 09	23 14	24 19
40	06 12	06 46	07 16	20 56	22 03	23 10	24 18
45	06 22	06 59	07 32	20 46	21 56	23 06	24 17
S 50	06 33	07 14	07 52	20 34	21 47	23 01	24 16
52	06 38	07 21	08 02	20 29	21 43	22 59	24 16
54	06 43	07 29	08 12	20 23	21 39	22 57	24 15
56	06 49	07 38	08 24	20 16	21 34	22 54	24 15
58	06 55	07 47	08 38	20 09	21 29	22 51	24 14
S 60	07 02	07 58	08 55	20 00	21 23	22 48	24 13

Lat.	Sunset	Twilight Civil	Twilight Naut.	Moonset 6	7	8	9
°	h m	h m	h m	h m	h m	h m	h m
N 72	□	□	□	05 08	07 11	09 09	11 04
N 70	□	□	□	05 48	07 35	09 23	11 10
68	□	□	□	06 15	07 53	09 34	11 15
66	23 16	////	////	06 36	08 08	09 43	11 19
64	22 14	////	////	06 52	08 20	09 50	11 22
62	21 41	////	////	07 06	08 30	09 57	11 25
60	21 16	22 49	////	07 18	08 38	10 02	11 28
N 58	20 57	22 08	////	07 27	08 46	10 07	11 30
56	20 41	21 41	////	07 36	08 52	10 12	11 32
54	20 28	21 21	22 55	07 44	08 58	10 15	11 34
52	20 16	21 04	22 18	07 51	09 04	10 19	11 35
50	20 06	20 49	21 52	07 57	09 08	10 22	11 37
45	19 44	20 21	21 09	08 10	09 19	10 29	11 40
N 40	19 26	19 59	20 40	08 21	09 27	10 35	11 43
35	19 12	19 41	20 18	08 30	09 35	10 40	11 45
30	18 59	19 27	20 00	08 39	09 41	10 44	11 47
20	18 38	19 02	19 31	08 53	09 52	10 51	11 50
N 10	18 20	18 42	19 09	09 05	10 02	10 58	11 53
0	18 02	18 25	18 51	09 16	10 11	11 04	11 56
S 10	17 46	18 08	18 33	09 28	10 19	11 10	11 59
20	17 28	17 51	18 19	09 40	10 29	11 16	12 01
30	17 07	17 33	18 03	09 53	10 40	11 23	12 05
35	16 55	17 23	17 55	10 01	10 46	11 27	12 07
40	16 41	17 12	17 46	10 10	10 53	11 32	12 09
45	16 25	16 59	17 36	10 21	11 01	11 37	12 11
S 50	16 05	16 43	17 24	10 33	11 10	11 43	12 14
52	15 56	16 36	17 19	10 39	11 15	11 46	12 15
54	15 45	16 28	17 14	10 45	11 20	11 49	12 16
56	15 33	16 20	17 08	10 53	11 25	11 53	12 18
58	15 19	16 10	17 02	11 01	11 31	11 57	12 20
S 60	15 03	15 59	16 55	11 10	11 38	12 01	12 22

Day	SUN Eqn. of Time 00ʰ	SUN Eqn. of Time 12ʰ	SUN Mer. Pass.	MOON Mer. Pass. Upper	MOON Mer. Pass. Lower	Age	Phase
d	m s	m s	h m	h m	h m	d	%
6	01 29	01 23	11 59	03 03	15 30	19	83
7	01 18	01 12	11 59	03 58	16 25	20	74
8	01 07	01 01	11 59	04 51	17 17	21	63

UT	ARIES GHA	VENUS −4.5 GHA	VENUS Dec	MARS +1.5 GHA	MARS Dec	JUPITER −1.9 GHA	JUPITER Dec	SATURN +0.1 GHA	SATURN Dec
d h	° ′	° ′	° ′	° ′	° ′	° ′	° ′	° ′	° ′
9 00	257 02.9	130 57.9	N21 44.5	178 36.6	N23 34.9	116 31.6	N16 19.6	18 19.9	S18 07.1
01	272 05.3	145 58.0	43.8	193 37.2	35.1	131 33.6	19.5	33 22.5	07.1
02	287 07.8	160 58.0	43.1	208 37.8	35.2	146 35.7	19.4	48 25.2	07.1
03	302 10.3	175 58.0 ..	42.5	223 38.4 ..	35.4	161 37.8 ..	19.3	63 27.8 ..	07.0
04	317 12.7	190 58.1	41.8	238 39.0	35.6	176 39.9	19.2	78 30.4	07.0
05	332 15.2	205 58.1	41.1	253 39.6	35.7	191 42.0	19.0	93 33.1	07.0
06	347 17.7	220 58.1	N21 40.5	268 40.2	N23 35.9	206 44.0	N16 18.9	108 35.7	S18 07.0
T 07	2 20.1	235 58.2	39.8	283 40.8	36.0	221 46.1	18.8	123 38.4	06.9
U 08	17 22.6	250 58.2	39.1	298 41.4	36.2	236 48.2	18.7	138 41.0	06.9
E 09	32 25.1	265 58.3 ..	38.5	313 42.0 ..	36.3	251 50.3 ..	18.5	153 43.7 ..	06.9
S 10	47 27.5	280 58.3	37.8	328 42.6	36.5	266 52.4	18.4	168 46.3	06.8
D 11	62 30.0	295 58.4	37.1	343 43.2	36.6	281 54.5	18.3	183 48.9	06.8
A 12	77 32.5	310 58.4	N21 36.5	358 43.8	N23 36.8	296 56.5	N16 18.2	198 51.6	S18 06.8
Y 13	92 34.9	325 58.4	35.8	13 44.4	37.0	311 58.6	18.1	213 54.2	06.7
14	107 37.4	340 58.5	35.1	28 45.0	37.1	327 00.7	17.9	228 56.9	06.7
15	122 39.8	355 58.5 ..	34.4	43 45.6 ..	37.3	342 02.8 ..	17.7	243 59.5 ..	06.7
16	137 42.3	10 58.6	33.8	58 46.2	37.4	357 04.9	17.7	259 02.2	06.6
17	152 44.8	25 58.7	33.1	73 46.8	37.6	12 06.9	17.6	274 04.8	06.6
18	167 47.2	40 58.7	N21 32.4	88 47.4	N23 37.7	27 09.0	N16 17.5	289 07.4	S18 06.6
19	182 49.7	55 58.8	31.7	103 48.0	37.9	42 11.1	17.3	304 10.1	06.6
20	197 52.2	70 58.8	31.1	118 48.6	38.0	57 13.2	17.2	319 12.7	06.5
21	212 54.6	85 58.9 ..	30.4	133 49.2 ..	38.2	72 15.2 ..	17.1	334 15.4 ..	06.5
22	227 57.1	100 58.9	29.7	148 49.8	38.3	87 17.3	17.0	349 18.0	06.5
23	242 59.6	115 59.0	29.0	163 50.4	38.5	102 19.4	16.8	4 20.6	06.4
10 00	258 02.0	130 59.1	N21 28.4	178 51.0	N23 38.6	117 21.5	N16 16.7	19 23.3	S18 06.4
01	273 04.5	145 59.1	27.7	193 51.6	38.8	132 23.6	16.6	34 25.9	06.4
02	288 06.9	160 59.2	27.0	208 52.2	38.9	147 25.6	16.5	49 28.6	06.3
03	303 09.4	175 59.3 ..	26.3	223 52.8 ..	39.1	162 27.7 ..	16.4	64 31.2 ..	06.3
04	318 11.9	190 59.3	25.7	238 53.4	39.2	177 29.8	16.2	79 33.9	06.3
05	333 14.3	205 59.4	25.0	253 54.0	39.4	192 31.9	16.1	94 36.5	06.3
06	348 16.8	220 59.5	N21 24.3	268 54.6	N23 39.5	207 34.0	N16 16.0	109 39.1	S18 06.2
W 07	3 19.3	235 59.5	23.6	283 55.3	39.6	222 36.0	15.9	124 41.8	06.2
E 08	18 21.7	250 59.6	22.9	298 55.9	39.8	237 38.1	15.7	139 44.4	06.2
D 09	33 24.2	265 59.7 ..	22.2	313 56.5 ..	39.9	252 40.2 ..	15.6	154 47.1 ..	06.1
N 10	48 26.7	280 59.8	21.6	328 57.1	40.1	267 42.3	15.5	169 49.7	06.1
E 11	63 29.1	295 59.8	20.9	343 57.7	40.2	282 44.3	15.4	184 52.3	06.1
S 12	78 31.6	310 59.9	N21 20.2	358 58.3	N23 40.4	297 46.4	N16 15.3	199 55.0	S18 06.0
D 13	93 34.1	326 00.0	19.5	13 58.9	40.5	312 48.5	15.1	214 57.6	06.0
A 14	108 36.5	341 00.1	18.8	28 59.5	40.7	327 50.6	15.0	230 00.3	06.0
Y 15	123 39.0	356 00.2 ..	18.1	44 00.1 ..	40.8	342 52.6 ..	14.9	245 02.9 ..	06.0
16	138 41.4	11 00.2	17.4	59 00.7	41.0	357 54.7	14.8	260 05.5	05.9
17	153 43.9	26 00.3	16.8	74 01.3	41.1	12 56.8	14.6	275 08.2	05.9
18	168 46.4	41 00.4	N21 16.1	89 01.9	N23 41.2	27 58.9	N16 14.5	290 10.8	S18 05.9
19	183 48.8	56 00.5	15.4	104 02.5	41.4	43 00.9	14.4	305 13.5	05.8
20	198 51.3	71 00.6	14.7	119 03.1	41.5	58 03.0	14.3	320 16.1	05.8
21	213 53.8	86 00.7 ..	14.0	134 03.7 ..	41.7	73 05.1 ..	14.1	335 18.8 ..	05.8
22	228 56.2	101 00.8	13.3	149 04.3	41.8	88 07.2	14.0	350 21.4	05.7
23	243 58.7	116 00.9	12.6	164 04.9	41.9	103 09.2	13.9	5 24.0	05.7
11 00	259 01.2	131 01.0	N21 11.9	179 05.5	N23 42.1	118 11.3	N16 13.8	20 26.7	S18 05.7
01	274 03.6	146 01.1	11.2	194 06.1	42.2	133 13.4	13.7	35 29.3	05.7
02	289 06.1	161 01.1	10.5	209 06.7	42.4	148 15.5	13.5	50 32.0	05.6
03	304 08.6	176 01.2 ..	09.8	224 07.3 ..	42.5	163 17.5 ..	13.4	65 34.6 ..	05.6
04	319 11.0	191 01.3	09.2	239 07.9	42.6	178 19.6	13.3	80 37.2	05.6
05	334 13.5	206 01.4	08.5	254 08.5	42.8	193 21.7	13.2	95 39.9	05.5
06	349 15.9	221 01.6	N21 07.8	269 09.1	N23 42.9	208 23.8	N16 13.0	110 42.5	S18 05.5
T 07	4 18.4	236 01.7	07.1	284 09.7	43.1	223 25.8	12.9	125 45.1	05.5
H 08	19 20.9	251 01.8	06.4	299 10.3	43.2	238 27.9	12.8	140 47.8	05.4
U 09	34 23.3	266 01.9 ..	05.7	314 10.9 ..	43.3	253 30.0 ..	12.7	155 50.4 ..	05.4
R 10	49 25.8	281 02.0	05.0	329 11.5	43.5	268 32.1	12.5	170 53.1	05.4
S 11	64 28.3	296 02.1	04.3	344 12.1	43.6	283 34.1	12.4	185 55.7	05.4
D 12	79 30.7	311 02.2	N21 03.6	359 12.7	N23 43.7	298 36.2	N16 12.3	200 58.3	S18 05.3
A 13	94 33.2	326 02.3	02.9	14 13.3	43.9	313 38.3	12.2	216 01.0	05.3
Y 14	109 35.7	341 02.4	02.2	29 13.9	44.0	328 40.3	12.0	231 03.6	05.3
15	124 38.1	356 02.5 ..	01.5	44 14.5 ..	44.1	343 42.4 ..	11.9	246 06.3 ..	05.2
16	139 40.6	11 02.6	00.8	59 15.1	44.3	358 44.5	11.8	261 08.9	05.2
17	154 43.0	26 02.8	21 00.1	74 15.7	44.4	13 46.6	11.7	276 11.5	05.2
18	169 45.5	41 02.9	N20 59.4	89 16.3	N23 44.5	28 48.6	N16 11.5	291 14.2	S18 05.1
19	184 48.0	56 03.0	58.7	104 16.9	44.7	43 50.7	11.4	306 16.8	05.1
20	199 50.4	71 03.1	58.0	119 17.5	44.8	58 52.8	11.3	321 19.5	05.1
21	214 52.9	86 03.2 ..	57.3	134 18.1 ..	44.9	73 54.8 ..	11.2	336 22.1 ..	05.1
22	229 55.4	101 03.4	56.6	149 18.8	45.1	88 56.9	11.0	351 24.7	05.0
23	244 57.8	116 03.5	55.9	164 19.4	45.2	103 59.0	10.9	6 27.4	05.0
Mer. Pass.	h m 6 46.8	v 0.1	d 0.7	v 0.6	d 0.1	v 2.1	d 0.1	v 2.6	d 0.0

STARS

Name	SHA	Dec
Acamar	315 17.7	S40 14.6
Achernar	335 26.3	S57 09.4
Acrux	173 07.4	S63 11.4
Adhara	255 11.8	S28 59.9
Aldebaran	290 48.2	N16 32.2
Alioth	166 19.4	N55 52.8
Alkaid	152 57.6	N49 14.4
Al Na'ir	27 42.0	S46 52.8
Alnilam	275 45.3	S 1 11.8
Alphard	217 54.9	S 8 43.7
Alphecca	126 09.6	N26 40.0
Alpheratz	357 42.1	N29 10.4
Altair	62 06.7	N 8 54.7
Ankaa	353 14.6	S42 13.1
Antares	112 24.2	S26 27.8
Arcturus	145 54.3	N19 06.3
Atria	107 24.2	S69 03.1
Avior	234 17.8	S59 33.9
Bellatrix	278 30.9	N 6 21.6
Betelgeuse	271 00.2	N 7 24.3
Canopus	263 56.1	S52 42.5
Capella	280 32.9	N46 00.5
Deneb	49 30.2	N45 20.1
Denebola	182 32.3	N14 29.2
Diphda	348 54.7	S17 54.1
Dubhe	193 50.3	N61 40.3
Elnath	278 11.3	N28 37.0
Eltanin	90 45.0	N51 29.4
Enif	33 45.7	N 9 56.8
Fomalhaut	15 22.5	S29 32.2
Gacrux	171 59.1	S57 12.2
Gienah	175 50.8	S17 37.8
Hadar	148 45.4	S60 27.0
Hamal	327 59.5	N23 31.9
Kaus Aust.	83 41.6	S34 22.4
Kochab	137 19.3	N74 05.8
Markab	13 36.9	N15 17.2
Menkar	314 13.9	N 4 08.8
Menkent	148 05.6	S36 26.8
Miaplacidus	221 39.7	S69 47.2
Mirfak	308 38.8	N49 54.6
Nunki	75 56.3	S26 16.4
Peacock	53 16.8	S56 40.7
Pollux	243 26.4	N27 59.2
Procyon	244 58.6	N 5 10.9
Rasalhague	96 04.9	N12 33.1
Regulus	207 42.2	N11 53.4
Rigel	281 11.1	S 8 11.3
Rigil Kent.	139 49.3	S60 54.0
Sabik	102 10.6	S15 44.4
Schedar	349 39.1	N56 37.0
Shaula	96 19.7	S37 06.7
Sirius	258 32.9	S16 44.5
Spica	158 29.6	S11 14.5
Suhail	222 51.6	S43 30.1
Vega	80 37.6	N38 48.0
Zuben'ubi	137 03.6	S16 06.3

	SHA	Mer. Pass.
	° ′	h m
Venus	232 57.0	15 16
Mars	280 49.0	12 04
Jupiter	219 19.5	16 08
Saturn	121 21.3	22 38

UT	SUN GHA	SUN Dec	MOON GHA	v	MOON Dec	d	HP
9 00	180 13.8	N22 52.9	277 06.6	9.6	S 5 53.4	10.7	59.3
01	195 13.7	53.1	291 35.2	9.5	5 42.7	10.6	59.3
02	210 13.5	53.3	306 03.7	9.6	5 32.1	10.8	59.3
03	225 13.4 ..	53.5	320 32.3	9.6	5 21.3	10.7	59.3
04	240 13.3	53.8	335 00.9	9.6	5 10.6	10.8	59.3
05	255 13.2	54.0	349 29.5	9.6	4 59.8	10.8	59.3
T 06	270 13.0	N22 54.2	3 58.1	9.6	S 4 49.0	10.8	59.3
U 07	285 12.9	54.4	18 26.7	9.7	4 38.2	10.9	59.3
E 08	300 12.8	54.6	32 55.4	9.7	4 27.3	10.9	59.3
S 09	315 12.7 ..	54.8	47 24.0	9.7	4 16.4	10.9	59.3
D 10	330 12.6	55.0	61 52.7	9.7	4 05.5	11.0	59.3
A 11	345 12.4	55.2	76 21.4	9.7	3 54.5	10.9	59.3
Y 12	0 12.3	N22 55.4	90 50.1	9.7	S 3 43.6	11.0	59.3
13	15 12.2	55.7	105 18.8	9.7	3 32.6	11.0	59.3
14	30 12.1	55.9	119 47.5	9.7	3 21.6	11.0	59.3
15	45 11.9 ..	56.1	134 16.2	9.8	3 10.6	11.1	59.3
16	60 11.8	56.3	148 45.0	9.7	2 59.5	11.1	59.3
17	75 11.7	56.5	163 13.7	9.8	2 48.4	11.0	59.3
18	90 11.6	N22 56.7	177 42.5	9.7	S 2 37.4	11.1	59.3
19	105 11.5	56.9	192 11.2	9.8	2 26.3	11.2	59.3
20	120 11.3	57.1	206 40.0	9.8	2 15.1	11.1	59.3
21	135 11.2 ..	57.3	221 08.8	9.8	2 04.0	11.1	59.3
22	150 11.1	57.5	235 37.6	9.7	1 52.9	11.2	59.3
23	165 11.0	57.7	250 06.3	9.8	1 41.7	11.1	59.3
10 00	180 10.8	N22 57.9	264 35.1	9.8	S 1 30.6	11.2	59.3
01	195 10.7	58.1	279 03.9	9.8	1 19.4	11.2	59.3
02	210 10.6	58.3	293 32.7	9.9	1 08.2	11.2	59.3
03	225 10.5 ..	58.5	308 01.6	9.8	0 57.0	11.2	59.3
04	240 10.3	58.7	322 30.4	9.8	0 45.8	11.2	59.3
05	255 10.2	58.9	336 59.2	9.8	0 34.6	11.2	59.3
W 06	270 10.1	N22 59.1	351 28.0	9.8	S 0 23.4	11.2	59.3
E 07	285 10.0	59.3	5 56.8	9.8	0 12.2	11.2	59.3
D 08	300 09.9	59.5	20 25.6	9.8	S 0 01.0	11.2	59.3
N 09	315 09.7 ..	59.7	34 54.4	9.9	N 0 10.2	11.2	59.3
E 10	330 09.6	22 59.9	49 23.3	9.8	0 21.4	11.0	59.3
S 11	345 09.5	23 00.1	63 52.1	9.8	0 32.6	11.2	59.3
D 12	0 09.4	N23 00.2	78 20.9	9.8	N 0 43.8	11.2	59.3
A 13	15 09.2	00.4	92 49.7	9.8	0 55.0	11.2	59.3
Y 14	30 09.1	00.6	107 18.5	9.8	1 06.2	11.1	59.3
15	45 09.0 ..	00.8	121 47.3	9.8	1 17.3	11.2	59.3
16	60 08.9	01.0	136 16.1	9.8	1 28.5	11.2	59.3
17	75 08.7	01.2	150 44.9	9.8	1 39.7	11.1	59.3
18	90 08.6	N23 01.4	165 13.7	9.8	N 1 50.8	11.2	59.3
19	105 08.5	01.6	179 42.5	9.7	2 02.0	11.1	59.3
20	120 08.4	01.8	194 11.2	9.8	2 13.1	11.1	59.3
21	135 08.2 ..	01.9	208 40.0	9.8	2 24.2	11.1	59.3
22	150 08.1	02.1	223 08.8	9.7	2 35.3	11.1	59.3
23	165 08.0	02.3	237 37.5	9.8	2 46.4	11.1	59.3
11 00	180 07.8	N23 02.5	252 06.3	9.7	N 2 57.5	11.1	59.3
01	195 07.7	02.7	266 35.0	9.7	3 08.6	11.0	59.3
02	210 07.6	02.9	281 03.7	9.7	3 19.6	11.0	59.3
03	225 07.5 ..	03.0	295 32.4	9.7	3 30.6	11.0	59.3
04	240 07.3	03.2	310 01.1	9.7	3 41.6	11.0	59.3
05	255 07.2	03.4	324 29.8	9.7	3 52.6	10.9	59.3
T 06	270 07.1	N23 03.6	338 58.5	9.7	N 4 03.5	11.0	59.3
H 07	285 07.0	03.8	353 27.2	9.6	4 14.5	10.9	59.3
U 08	300 06.8	03.9	7 55.8	9.7	4 25.4	10.8	59.3
R 09	315 06.7 ..	04.1	22 24.5	9.6	4 36.2	10.9	59.2
S 10	330 06.6	04.3	36 53.1	9.6	4 47.1	10.8	59.2
D 11	345 06.5	04.5	51 21.7	9.6	4 57.9	10.8	59.2
A 12	0 06.3	N23 04.6	65 50.3	9.6	N 5 08.7	10.8	59.2
Y 13	15 06.2	04.8	80 18.9	9.6	5 19.5	10.7	59.2
14	30 06.1	05.0	94 47.5	9.5	5 30.2	10.7	59.2
15	45 05.9 ..	05.2	109 16.0	9.6	5 40.9	10.6	59.2
16	60 05.8	05.3	123 44.6	9.5	5 51.5	10.7	59.2
17	75 05.7	05.5	138 13.1	9.5	6 02.2	10.6	59.2
18	90 05.6	N23 05.7	152 41.6	9.5	N 6 12.8	10.5	59.2
19	105 05.4	05.8	167 10.1	9.4	6 23.3	10.5	59.2
20	120 05.3	06.0	181 38.5	9.5	6 33.8	10.5	59.2
21	135 05.2 ..	06.2	196 07.0	9.4	6 44.3	10.4	59.2
22	150 05.1	06.3	210 35.4	9.4	6 54.7	10.4	59.2
23	165 04.9	06.5	225 03.8	9.4	N 7 05.1	10.4	59.2
	SD 15.8	d 0.2	SD 16.2		16.2		16.1

Twilight / Sunrise / Moonrise

Lat.	Naut.	Civil	Sunrise	Moonrise 9	10	11	12
N 72	□	□	□	00 47	00 42	00 37	00 32
N 70	□	□	□	00 39	00 40	00 41	00 42
68	□	□	□	00 33	00 38	00 44	00 50
66	////	////	00 31	00 27	00 37	00 47	00 57
64	////	////	01 40	00 22	00 36	00 49	01 03
62	////	////	02 15	00 18	00 35	00 51	01 09
60	////	01 03	02 39	00 14	00 34	00 53	01 13
N 58	////	01 46	02 59	00 11	00 33	00 55	01 17
56	////	02 14	03 15	00 08	00 32	00 56	01 21
54	00 58	02 35	03 29	00 05	00 32	00 57	01 24
52	01 38	02 53	03 41	00 03	00 31	00 59	01 27
50	02 04	03 07	03 51	00 01	00 30	01 00	01 30
45	02 47	03 36	04 13	24 29	00 29	01 02	01 36
N 40	03 17	03 58	04 31	24 28	00 28	01 04	01 41
35	03 40	04 16	04 46	24 27	00 27	01 06	01 45
30	03 58	04 31	04 58	24 27	00 27	01 07	01 49
20	04 26	04 54	05 20	24 25	00 25	01 10	01 55
N 10	04 48	05 15	05 38	24 24	00 24	01 12	02 01
0	05 07	05 33	05 56	24 23	00 23	01 15	02 07
S 10	05 24	05 50	06 13	24 22	00 22	01 17	02 13
20	05 40	06 07	06 31	24 21	00 21	01 20	02 19
30	05 56	06 25	06 52	24 20	00 20	01 23	02 26
35	06 04	06 36	07 04	24 19	00 19	01 24	02 30
40	06 13	06 47	07 18	24 18	00 18	01 26	02 34
45	06 23	07 00	07 34	24 17	00 17	01 28	02 39
S 50	06 35	07 16	07 54	24 16	00 16	01 31	02 46
52	06 40	07 23	08 04	24 16	00 16	01 32	02 49
54	06 45	07 31	08 15	24 15	00 15	01 34	02 52
56	06 51	07 40	08 27	24 15	00 15	01 35	02 56
58	06 58	07 50	08 41	24 14	00 14	01 37	03 00
S 60	07 05	08 01	08 58	24 13	00 13	01 39	03 04

Sunset / Twilight / Moonset

Lat.	Sunset	Civil	Naut.	Moonset 9	10	11	12
N 72	□	□	□	11 04	12 58	14 52	16 47
N 70	□	□	□	11 10	12 57	14 43	16 31
68	□	□	□	11 15	12 56	14 37	16 18
66	23 35	////	////	11 19	12 55	14 31	16 07
64	22 20	////	////	11 22	12 54	14 27	15 58
62	21 45	////	////	11 25	12 54	14 23	15 51
60	21 20	22 58	////	11 28	12 53	14 19	15 44
N 58	21 00	22 13	////	11 30	12 53	14 16	15 38
56	20 44	21 45	////	11 32	12 53	14 13	15 33
54	20 30	21 24	23 03	11 34	12 52	14 11	15 29
52	20 18	21 07	22 22	11 35	12 52	14 09	15 25
50	20 08	20 52	21 56	11 37	12 52	14 07	15 21
45	19 46	20 23	21 12	11 40	12 51	14 02	15 13
N 40	19 28	20 01	20 42	11 43	12 51	13 59	15 06
35	19 13	19 43	20 19	11 45	12 50	13 55	15 01
30	19 01	19 28	20 01	11 47	12 50	13 53	14 56
20	18 39	19 03	19 33	11 50	12 49	13 48	14 47
N 10	18 20	18 43	19 10	11 53	12 48	13 44	14 39
0	18 03	18 26	18 52	11 56	12 48	13 40	14 32
S 10	17 46	18 09	18 35	11 59	12 47	13 36	14 25
20	17 28	17 52	18 19	12 01	12 46	13 31	14 17
30	17 07	17 33	18 03	12 05	12 45	13 26	14 09
35	16 55	17 23	17 54	12 07	12 45	13 24	14 04
40	16 41	17 11	17 45	12 09	12 44	13 21	13 58
45	16 24	16 58	17 35	12 11	12 44	13 17	13 52
S 50	16 04	16 42	17 24	12 14	12 43	13 13	13 44
52	15 55	16 35	17 19	12 15	12 43	13 11	13 40
54	15 44	16 27	17 13	12 16	12 42	13 08	13 36
56	15 31	16 18	17 07	12 18	12 42	13 06	13 32
58	15 17	16 08	17 01	12 20	12 41	13 03	13 27
S 60	15 00	15 57	16 53	12 22	12 41	13 00	13 22

SUN / MOON

Day	Eqn. of Time 00h	Eqn. of Time 12h	Mer. Pass.	Mer. Pass. Upper	Mer. Pass. Lower	Age	Phase
	m s	m s	h m	h m	h m	d	%
9	00 55	00 50	11 59	05 44	18 10	22	52
10	00 44	00 38	11 59	06 35	19 01	23	40
11	00 32	00 26	12 00	07 27	19 53	24	30

2015 JUNE 12, 13, 14 (FRI., SAT., SUN.)

UT	ARIES	VENUS −4.5		MARS +1.5		JUPITER −1.9		SATURN +0.1		STARS		
	GHA	GHA	Dec	GHA	Dec	GHA	Dec	GHA	Dec	Name	SHA	Dec
d h	° ′	° ′	° ′	° ′	° ′	° ′	° ′	° ′	° ′		° ′	° ′
12 00	260 00.3	131 03.6	N20 55.2	179 20.0	N23 45.3	119 01.1	N16 10.8	21 30.0	S18 05.0	Acamar	315 17.7	S40 14.6
01	275 02.8	146 03.8	54.4	194 20.6	45.5	134 03.1	10.7	36 32.6	04.9	Achernar	335 26.2	S57 09.4
02	290 05.2	161 03.9	53.7	209 21.2	45.6	149 05.2	10.5	51 35.3	04.9	Acrux	173 07.4	S63 11.4
03	305 07.7	176 04.0 . .	53.0	224 21.8 . .	45.7	164 07.3 . .	10.4	66 37.9 . .	04.9	Adhara	255 11.8	S28 59.9
04	320 10.2	191 04.1	52.3	239 22.4	45.9	179 09.3	10.3	81 40.6	04.9	Aldebaran	290 48.2	N16 32.2
05	335 12.6	206 04.3	51.6	254 23.0	46.0	194 11.4	10.2	96 43.2	04.8			
06	350 15.1	221 04.4	N20 50.9	269 23.6	N23 46.1	209 13.5	N16 10.0	111 45.8	S18 04.8	Alioth	166 19.4	N55 52.9
07	5 17.5	236 04.5	50.2	284 24.2	46.3	224 15.5	09.9	126 48.5	04.8	Alkaid	152 57.6	N49 14.5
08	20 20.0	251 04.7	49.5	299 24.8	46.4	239 17.6	09.8	141 51.1	04.7	Al Na'ir	27 42.0	S46 52.8
F 09	35 22.5	266 04.8 . .	48.8	314 25.4 . .	46.5	254 19.7 . .	09.7	156 53.8 . .	04.7	Alnilam	275 45.3	S 1 11.8
R 10	50 24.9	281 05.0	48.1	329 26.0	46.6	269 21.8	09.5	171 56.4	04.7	Alphard	217 54.9	S 8 43.7
I 11	65 27.4	296 05.1	47.4	344 26.6	46.8	284 23.8	09.4	186 59.0	04.6			
D 12	80 29.9	311 05.3	N20 46.6	359 27.2	N23 46.9	299 25.9	N16 09.3	202 01.7	S18 04.6	Alphecca	126 09.6	N26 40.0
A 13	95 32.3	326 05.4	45.9	14 27.8	47.0	314 28.0	09.2	217 04.3	04.6	Alpheratz	357 42.1	N29 10.4
Y 14	110 34.8	341 05.5	45.2	29 28.4	47.1	329 30.0	09.0	232 06.9	04.6	Altair	62 06.6	N 8 54.7
15	125 37.3	356 05.7 . .	44.5	44 29.0 . .	47.3	344 32.1 . .	08.9	247 09.6 . .	04.5	Ankaa	353 14.6	S42 13.1
16	140 39.7	11 05.8	43.8	59 29.6	47.4	359 34.2	08.8	262 12.2	04.5	Antares	112 24.2	S26 27.8
17	155 42.2	26 06.0	43.1	74 30.2	47.5	14 36.2	08.7	277 14.8	04.5			
18	170 44.7	41 06.1	N20 42.4	89 30.8	N23 47.6	29 38.3	N16 08.5	292 17.5	S18 04.4	Arcturus	145 54.3	N19 06.3
19	185 47.1	56 06.3	41.6	104 31.4	47.8	44 40.4	08.4	307 20.1	04.4	Atria	107 24.2	S69 03.1
20	200 49.6	71 06.4	40.9	119 32.0	47.9	59 42.4	08.3	322 22.8	04.4	Avior	234 17.9	S59 33.9
21	215 52.0	86 06.6 . .	40.2	134 32.6 . .	48.0	74 44.5 . .	08.2	337 25.4 . .	04.4	Bellatrix	278 30.9	N 6 21.6
22	230 54.5	101 06.8	39.5	149 33.2	48.1	89 46.6	08.0	352 28.0	04.3	Betelgeuse	271 00.2	N 7 24.3
23	245 57.0	116 06.9	38.8	164 33.8	48.3	104 48.6	07.9	7 30.7	04.3			
13 00	260 59.4	131 07.1	N20 38.1	179 34.4	N23 48.4	119 50.7	N16 07.8	22 33.3	S18 04.3	Canopus	263 56.1	S52 42.5
01	276 01.9	146 07.2	37.3	194 35.0	48.5	134 52.8	07.6	37 35.9	04.2	Capella	280 32.9	N46 00.5
02	291 04.4	161 07.4	36.6	209 35.6	48.6	149 54.8	07.5	52 38.6	04.2	Deneb	49 30.2	N45 20.1
03	306 06.8	176 07.6 . .	35.9	224 36.2 . .	48.7	164 56.9 . .	07.4	67 41.2 . .	04.2	Denebola	182 32.3	N14 29.2
04	321 09.3	191 07.7	35.2	239 36.8	48.9	179 59.0	07.3	82 43.8	04.2	Diphda	348 54.7	S17 54.1
05	336 11.8	206 07.9	34.4	254 37.4	49.0	195 01.0	07.1	97 46.5	04.1			
06	351 14.2	221 08.1	N20 33.7	269 38.1	N23 49.1	210 03.1	N16 07.0	112 49.1	S18 04.1	Dubhe	193 50.3	N61 40.3
07	6 16.7	236 08.2	33.0	284 38.7	49.2	225 05.2	06.9	127 51.8	04.1	Elnath	278 11.3	N28 37.0
S 08	21 19.1	251 08.4	32.3	299 39.3	49.4	240 07.2	06.8	142 54.4	04.0	Eltanin	90 45.0	N51 29.4
A 09	36 21.6	266 08.6 . .	31.6	314 39.9 . .	49.5	255 09.3 . .	06.6	157 57.0 . .	04.0	Enif	33 45.6	N 9 56.8
T 10	51 24.1	281 08.8	30.8	329 40.5	49.6	270 11.4	06.5	172 59.7	04.0	Fomalhaut	15 22.5	S29 32.2
U 11	66 26.5	296 08.9	30.1	344 41.1	49.7	285 13.4	06.4	188 02.3	04.0			
R 12	81 29.0	311 09.1	N20 29.4	359 41.7	N23 49.8	300 15.5	N16 06.2	203 04.9	S18 03.9	Gacrux	171 59.1	S57 12.2
D 13	96 31.5	326 09.3	28.7	14 42.3	49.9	315 17.6	06.1	218 07.6	03.9	Gienah	175 50.8	S17 37.8
A 14	111 33.9	341 09.5	27.9	29 42.9	50.1	330 19.6	06.0	233 10.2	03.9	Hadar	148 45.4	S60 27.0
Y 15	126 36.4	356 09.6 . .	27.2	44 43.5 . .	50.2	345 21.7 . .	05.9	248 12.8 . .	03.8	Hamal	327 59.4	N23 31.9
16	141 38.9	11 09.8	26.5	59 44.1	50.3	0 23.8	05.7	263 15.5	03.8	Kaus Aust.	83 41.6	S34 22.4
17	156 41.3	26 10.0	25.8	74 44.7	50.4	15 25.8	05.6	278 18.1	03.8			
18	171 43.8	41 10.2	N20 25.0	89 45.3	N23 50.5	30 27.9	N16 05.5	293 20.7	S18 03.8	Kochab	137 19.4	N74 05.8
19	186 46.3	56 10.4	24.3	104 45.9	50.6	45 29.9	05.4	308 23.4	03.7	Markab	13 36.9	N15 17.3
20	201 48.7	71 10.6	23.6	119 46.5	50.8	60 32.0	05.2	323 26.0	03.7	Menkar	314 13.9	N 4 08.8
21	216 51.2	86 10.8 . .	22.8	134 47.1 . .	50.9	75 34.1 . .	05.1	338 28.6 . .	03.7	Menkent	148 05.7	S36 26.8
22	231 53.6	101 10.9	22.1	149 47.7	51.0	90 36.1	05.0	353 31.3	03.6	Miaplacidus	221 39.8	S69 47.2
23	246 56.1	116 11.1	21.4	164 48.3	51.1	105 38.2	04.8	8 33.9	03.6			
14 00	261 58.6	131 11.3	N20 20.6	179 48.9	N23 51.2	120 40.3	N16 04.7	23 36.6	S18 03.6	Mirfak	308 38.8	N49 54.6
01	277 01.0	146 11.5	19.9	194 49.5	51.3	135 42.3	04.6	38 39.2	03.6	Nunki	75 56.3	S26 16.4
02	292 03.5	161 11.7	19.2	209 50.1	51.4	150 44.4	04.5	53 41.8	03.5	Peacock	53 16.8	S56 40.7
03	307 06.0	176 11.9 . .	18.4	224 50.7 . .	51.6	165 46.4 . .	04.3	68 44.5 . .	03.5	Pollux	243 26.4	N27 59.2
04	322 08.4	191 12.1	17.7	239 51.3	51.7	180 48.5	04.2	83 47.1	03.5	Procyon	244 58.6	N 5 10.9
05	337 10.9	206 12.3	17.0	254 51.9	51.8	195 50.6	04.1	98 49.7	03.4			
06	352 13.4	221 12.5	N20 16.2	269 52.5	N23 51.9	210 52.6	N16 03.9	113 52.4	S18 03.4	Rasalhague	96 04.9	N12 33.1
07	7 15.8	236 12.7	15.5	284 53.1	52.0	225 54.7	03.8	128 55.0	03.4	Regulus	207 42.2	N11 53.4
08	22 18.3	251 12.9	14.8	299 53.7	52.1	240 56.8	03.7	143 57.6	03.4	Rigel	281 11.1	S 8 11.3
S 09	37 20.8	266 13.1 . .	14.0	314 54.4 . .	52.2	255 58.8 . .	03.6	159 00.3 . .	03.3	Rigil Kent.	139 49.3	S60 54.0
U 10	52 23.2	281 13.3	13.3	329 55.0	52.3	271 00.9	03.4	174 02.9	03.3	Sabik	102 10.6	S15 44.4
N 11	67 25.7	296 13.6	12.6	344 55.6	52.4	286 02.9	03.3	189 05.5	03.3			
D 12	82 28.1	311 13.8	N20 11.8	359 56.2	N23 52.5	301 05.0	N16 03.2	204 08.2	S18 03.2	Schedar	349 39.0	N56 37.0
A 13	97 30.6	326 14.0	11.1	14 56.8	52.7	316 07.1	03.0	219 10.8	03.2	Shaula	96 19.7	S37 06.7
Y 14	112 33.1	341 14.2	10.4	29 57.4	52.8	331 09.1	02.9	234 13.4	03.2	Sirius	258 32.9	S16 44.5
15	127 35.5	356 14.4 . .	09.6	44 58.0 . .	52.9	346 11.2 . .	02.8	249 16.1 . .	03.2	Spica	158 29.6	S11 14.5
16	142 38.0	11 14.6	08.9	59 58.6	53.0	1 13.2	02.7	264 18.7	03.1	Suhail	222 51.7	S43 30.0
17	157 40.5	26 14.8	08.1	74 59.2	53.1	16 15.3	02.5	279 21.3	03.1			
18	172 42.9	41 15.1	N20 07.4	89 59.8	N23 53.2	31 17.4	N16 02.4	294 24.0	S18 03.1	Vega	80 37.6	N38 48.0
19	187 45.4	56 15.3	06.7	105 00.4	53.3	46 19.4	02.3	309 26.6	03.0	Zuben'ubi	137 03.6	S16 06.3
20	202 47.9	71 15.5	05.9	120 01.0	53.4	61 21.5	02.1	324 29.2	03.0		SHA	Mer.Pass.
21	217 50.3	86 15.7 . .	05.2	135 01.6 . .	53.5	76 23.5 . .	02.0	339 31.9 . .	03.0		° ′	h m
22	232 52.8	101 15.9	04.4	150 02.2	53.6	91 25.6	01.9	354 34.5	03.0	Venus	230 07.6	15 15
23	247 55.3	116 16.2	03.7	165 02.8	53.7	106 27.7	01.8	9 37.1	02.9	Mars	278 35.0	12 01
	h m									Jupiter	218 51.3	15 58
Mer. Pass. 6 35.0		v 0.2	d 0.7	v 0.6	d 0.1	v 2.1	d 0.1	v 2.6	d 0.0	Saturn	121 33.9	22 26

SUN and MOON

UT	SUN GHA	SUN Dec	MOON GHA	v	MOON Dec	d	HP
d h	° '	° '	° '	'	° '	'	'
12 00	180 04.8	N23 06.7	239 32.2	9.4	N 7 15.5	10.3	59.2
01	195 04.7	06.8	254 00.6	9.3	7 25.8	10.2	59.2
02	210 04.5	07.0	268 28.9	9.3	7 36.0	10.2	59.2
03	225 04.4	.. 07.2	282 57.2	9.3	7 46.2	10.2	59.1
04	240 04.3	07.3	297 25.5	9.3	7 56.4	10.1	59.1
05	255 04.2	07.5	311 53.8	9.3	8 06.5	10.1	59.1
06	270 04.0	N23 07.7	326 22.1	9.2	N 8 16.6	10.0	59.1
07	285 03.9	07.8	340 50.3	9.2	8 26.6	10.0	59.1
08	300 03.8	08.0	355 18.5	9.2	8 36.6	9.9	59.1
F 09	315 03.6	.. 08.2	9 46.7	9.2	8 46.5	9.8	59.1
R 10	330 03.5	08.3	24 14.9	9.1	8 56.3	9.9	59.1
I 11	345 03.4	08.5	38 43.0	9.2	9 06.2	9.7	59.1
D 12	0 03.3	N23 08.6	53 11.2	9.1	N 9 15.9	9.7	59.1
A 13	15 03.1	08.8	67 39.3	9.0	9 25.6	9.6	59.1
Y 14	30 03.0	08.9	82 07.3	9.1	9 35.2	9.6	59.1
15	45 02.9	.. 09.1	96 35.4	9.0	9 44.8	9.5	59.0
16	60 02.7	09.3	111 03.4	9.0	9 54.3	9.5	59.0
17	75 02.6	09.4	125 31.4	9.0	10 03.8	9.4	59.0
18	90 02.5	N23 09.6	139 59.4	8.9	N10 13.2	9.3	59.0
19	105 02.3	09.7	154 27.3	9.0	10 22.5	9.3	59.0
20	120 02.2	09.9	168 55.3	8.9	10 31.8	9.2	59.0
21	135 02.1	.. 10.0	183 23.2	8.9	10 41.0	9.1	59.0
22	150 02.0	10.2	197 51.1	8.8	10 50.1	9.1	59.0
23	165 01.8	10.3	212 18.9	8.9	10 59.2	9.0	59.0
13 00	180 01.7	N23 10.5	226 46.8	8.8	N11 08.2	8.9	59.0
01	195 01.6	10.6	241 14.6	8.7	11 17.1	8.9	58.9
02	210 01.4	10.8	255 42.3	8.8	11 26.0	8.8	58.9
03	225 01.3	.. 10.9	270 10.1	8.7	11 34.8	8.7	58.9
04	240 01.2	11.1	284 37.8	8.7	11 43.5	8.7	58.9
05	255 01.0	11.2	299 05.5	8.7	11 52.2	8.6	58.9
06	270 00.9	N23 11.4	313 33.2	8.7	N12 00.8	8.5	58.9
S 07	285 00.8	11.5	328 00.9	8.6	12 09.3	8.4	58.9
A 08	300 00.6	11.6	342 28.5	8.6	12 17.7	8.3	58.9
T 09	315 00.5	.. 11.8	356 56.1	8.6	12 26.0	8.3	58.8
U 10	330 00.4	11.9	11 23.7	8.6	12 34.3	8.2	58.8
R 11	345 00.3	12.1	25 51.3	8.5	12 42.5	8.1	58.8
D 12	0 00.1	N23 12.2	40 18.8	8.5	N12 50.6	8.1	58.8
A 13	15 00.0	12.3	54 46.3	8.5	12 58.7	7.9	58.8
Y 14	29 59.9	12.5	69 13.8	8.5	13 06.6	7.9	58.8
15	44 59.7	.. 12.6	83 41.3	8.4	13 14.5	7.8	58.8
16	59 59.6	12.8	98 08.7	8.4	13 22.3	7.7	58.7
17	74 59.5	12.9	112 36.1	8.4	13 30.0	7.7	58.7
18	89 59.3	N23 13.0	127 03.5	8.4	N13 37.7	7.5	58.7
19	104 59.2	13.2	141 30.9	8.3	13 45.2	7.5	58.7
20	119 59.1	13.3	155 58.2	8.4	13 52.7	7.3	58.7
21	134 58.9	.. 13.4	170 25.6	8.3	14 00.0	7.3	58.7
22	149 58.8	13.6	184 52.9	8.3	14 07.3	7.2	58.7
23	164 58.7	13.7	199 20.2	8.2	14 14.5	7.1	58.6
14 00	179 58.5	N23 13.8	213 47.4	8.3	N14 21.6	7.0	58.6
01	194 58.4	14.0	228 14.7	8.2	14 28.6	6.9	58.6
02	209 58.3	14.1	242 41.9	8.2	14 35.5	6.9	58.6
03	224 58.1	.. 14.2	257 09.1	8.2	14 42.4	6.7	58.6
04	239 58.0	14.4	271 36.3	8.1	14 49.1	6.7	58.6
05	254 57.9	14.5	286 03.4	8.2	14 55.8	6.5	58.5
06	269 57.7	N23 14.6	300 30.6	8.1	N15 02.3	6.5	58.5
07	284 57.6	14.8	314 57.7	8.1	15 08.8	6.4	58.5
08	299 57.5	14.9	329 24.8	8.1	15 15.2	6.2	58.5
S 09	314 57.3	.. 15.0	343 51.9	8.1	15 21.4	6.2	58.5
U 10	329 57.2	15.1	358 19.0	8.1	15 27.6	6.1	58.5
N 11	344 57.1	15.3	12 46.1	8.0	15 33.7	6.0	58.4
D 12	359 56.9	N23 15.4	27 13.1	8.0	N15 39.7	5.9	58.4
A 13	14 56.8	15.5	41 40.1	8.1	15 45.6	5.8	58.4
Y 14	29 56.7	15.6	56 07.2	8.0	15 51.4	5.7	58.4
15	44 56.5	.. 15.7	70 34.2	8.0	15 57.1	5.5	58.4
16	59 56.4	15.9	85 01.2	7.9	16 02.6	5.5	58.4
17	74 56.3	16.0	99 28.1	8.0	16 08.1	5.4	58.3
18	89 56.1	N23 16.1	113 55.1	8.0	N16 13.5	5.3	58.3
19	104 56.0	16.2	128 22.1	7.9	16 18.8	5.2	58.3
20	119 55.9	16.3	142 49.0	7.9	16 24.0	5.1	58.3
21	134 55.7	.. 16.5	157 15.9	8.0	16 29.1	5.0	58.3
22	149 55.6	16.6	171 42.9	7.9	16 34.1	4.8	58.2
23	164 55.5	16.7	186 09.8	7.9	N16 38.9	4.8	58.2
	SD 15.8	d 0.1	SD 16.1		16.0		15.9

Twilight, Sunrise and Moonrise

Lat.	Twilight Naut.	Twilight Civil	Sunrise	Moonrise 12	Moonrise 13	Moonrise 14	Moonrise 15
°	h m	h m	h m	h m	h m	h m	h m
N 72	▭	▭	▭	00 32	00 26	00 20	⟨00 12 / 23 45⟩
N 70	▭	▭	▭	00 42	00 44	00 49	00 58
68	▭	▭	▭	00 50	00 58	01 10	01 29
66	▭	▭	▭	00 57	01 10	01 27	01 52
64	////	////	01 36	01 03	01 20	01 41	02 10
62	////	////	02 12	01 09	01 29	01 53	02 25
60	////	00 57	02 37	01 13	01 36	02 03	02 37
N 58	////	01 43	02 57	01 17	01 43	02 12	02 48
56	////	02 12	03 14	01 21	01 48	02 20	02 58
54	00 52	02 34	03 28	01 24	01 53	02 27	03 06
52	01 35	02 51	03 40	01 27	01 58	02 33	03 14
50	02 02	03 06	03 51	01 30	02 02	02 39	03 21
45	02 46	03 36	04 13	01 36	02 12	02 51	03 35
N 40	03 16	03 58	04 31	01 41	02 19	03 01	03 47
35	03 39	04 16	04 45	01 45	02 26	03 10	03 57
30	03 58	04 31	04 58	01 49	02 32	03 18	04 07
20	04 26	04 56	05 20	01 55	02 42	03 31	04 22
N 10	04 49	05 16	05 39	02 01	02 51	03 43	04 36
0	05 08	05 34	05 56	02 07	03 00	03 54	04 49
S 10	05 24	05 51	06 14	02 13	03 09	04 05	05 02
20	05 40	06 08	06 32	02 19	03 18	04 17	05 16
30	05 57	06 27	06 53	02 26	03 28	04 31	05 31
35	06 05	06 37	07 05	02 30	03 35	04 39	05 41
40	06 15	06 49	07 19	02 34	03 42	04 48	05 51
45	06 25	07 02	07 36	02 39	03 50	04 58	06 04
S 50	06 36	07 18	07 56	02 46	04 00	05 11	06 19
52	06 42	07 25	08 06	02 49	04 04	05 17	06 26
54	06 47	07 33	08 17	02 52	04 09	05 24	06 34
56	06 53	07 42	08 29	02 56	04 15	05 32	06 43
58	07 00	07 52	08 44	03 00	04 21	05 40	06 53
S 60	07 07	08 04	09 01	03 04	04 29	05 50	07 05

Sunset, Twilight and Moonset

Lat.	Sunset	Twilight Civil	Twilight Naut.	Moonset 12	Moonset 13	Moonset 14	Moonset 15
°	h m	h m	h m	h m	h m	h m	h m
N 72	▭	▭	▭	16 47	18 45	20 48	23 10
N 70	▭	▭	▭	16 31	18 18	20 02	21 35
68	▭	▭	▭	16 18	17 57	19 32	20 55
66	▭	▭	▭	16 07	17 41	19 10	20 28
64	22 25	////	////	15 58	17 28	18 52	20 07
62	21 49	////	////	15 51	17 16	18 37	19 50
60	21 23	23 05	////	15 44	17 07	18 25	19 36
N 58	21 03	22 17	////	15 38	16 59	18 15	19 24
56	20 47	21 48	////	15 33	16 51	18 06	19 13
54	20 33	21 27	23 09	15 29	16 45	17 58	19 04
52	20 20	21 09	22 26	15 25	16 39	17 50	18 56
50	20 10	20 54	21 59	15 21	16 34	17 44	18 49
45	19 47	20 25	21 14	15 13	16 23	17 30	18 33
N 40	19 30	20 02	20 44	15 06	16 13	17 18	18 20
35	19 15	19 44	20 21	15 01	16 05	17 08	18 09
30	19 02	19 29	20 02	14 56	15 58	17 00	17 59
20	18 40	19 04	19 34	14 47	15 46	16 45	17 43
N 10	18 21	18 44	19 11	14 39	15 35	16 32	17 29
0	18 04	18 26	18 52	14 32	15 26	16 20	17 15
S 10	17 46	18 09	18 35	14 25	15 16	16 08	17 02
20	17 28	17 52	18 19	14 17	15 05	15 55	16 47
30	17 07	17 33	18 03	14 09	14 53	15 40	16 31
35	16 55	17 23	17 54	14 04	14 46	15 32	16 21
40	16 41	17 11	17 45	13 58	14 38	15 22	16 10
45	16 24	16 58	17 35	13 52	14 29	15 11	15 57
S 50	16 04	16 42	17 23	13 44	14 18	14 57	15 42
52	15 54	16 35	17 18	13 40	14 13	14 51	15 34
54	15 43	16 27	17 13	13 36	14 07	14 44	15 26
56	15 30	16 18	17 07	13 32	14 01	14 36	15 17
58	15 16	16 07	17 00	13 27	13 54	14 27	15 07
S 60	14 59	15 56	16 52	13 22	13 46	14 17	14 55

SUN and MOON

Day	SUN Eqn. of Time 00h	SUN Eqn. of Time 12h	SUN Mer. Pass.	MOON Mer. Pass. Upper	MOON Mer. Pass. Lower	Age	Phase
d	m s	m s	h m	h m	h m	d %	
12	00 19	00 13	12 00	08 19	20 46	25 20	
13	00 07	00 01	12 00	09 13	21 40	26 12	
14	00 06	00 12	12 00	10 07	22 34	27 5	◐

2015 JUNE 15, 16, 17 (MON., TUES., WED.)

UT	ARIES GHA	VENUS −4.5 GHA	Dec	MARS +1.5 GHA	Dec	JUPITER −1.9 GHA	Dec	SATURN +0.2 GHA	Dec	STARS Name	SHA	Dec
15 00	262 57.7	131 16.4	N20 02.9	180 03.4	N23 53.8	121 29.7	N16 01.6	24 39.8	S18 02.9	Acamar	315 17.7	S40 14.6
01	278 00.2	146 16.6	02.2	195 04.0	53.9	136 31.8	01.5	39 42.4	02.9	Achernar	335 26.2	S57 09.3
02	293 02.6	161 16.9	01.5	210 04.6	54.0	151 33.8	01.4	54 45.0	02.8	Acrux	173 07.4	S63 11.4
03	308 05.1	176 17.1 ..	00.7	225 05.2 ..	54.1	166 35.9 ..	01.2	69 47.6 ..	02.8	Adhara	255 11.8	S28 59.9
04	323 07.6	191 17.3	20 00.0	240 05.8	54.2	181 38.0	01.1	84 50.3	02.8	Aldebaran	290 48.2	N16 32.2
05	338 10.0	206 17.6	19 59.2	255 06.4	54.3	196 40.0	01.0	99 52.9	02.8			
06	353 12.5	221 17.8	N19 58.5	270 07.0	N23 54.4	211 42.1	N16 00.8	114 55.5	S18 02.7	Alioth	166 19.4	N55 52.9
07	8 15.0	236 18.0	57.7	285 07.7	54.5	226 44.1	00.7	129 58.2	02.7	Alkaid	152 57.7	N49 14.5
08	23 17.4	251 18.3	57.0	300 08.3	54.6	241 46.2	00.6	145 00.8	02.7	Al Na'ir	27 41.9	S46 52.8
M 09	38 19.9	266 18.5 ..	56.2	315 08.9 ..	54.7	256 48.3 ..	00.5	160 03.4 ..	02.7	Alnilam	275 45.3	S 1 11.8
O 10	53 22.4	281 18.8	55.5	330 09.5	54.9	271 50.3	00.3	175 06.1	02.6	Alphard	217 54.9	S 8 43.7
N 11	68 24.8	296 19.0	54.7	345 10.1	55.0	286 52.4	00.2	190 08.7	02.6			
D 12	83 27.3	311 19.3	N19 54.0	0 10.7	N23 55.1	301 54.4	N16 00.1	205 11.3	S18 02.5	Alphecca	126 09.6	N26 40.0
A 13	98 29.7	326 19.5	53.2	15 11.3	55.2	316 56.5	15 59.9	220 14.0	02.5	Alpheratz	357 42.1	N29 10.4
Y 14	113 32.2	341 19.7	52.5	30 11.9	55.2	331 58.5	59.8	235 16.6	02.5	Altair	62 06.6	N 8 54.7
15	128 34.7	356 20.0 ..	51.7	45 12.5 ..	55.3	347 00.6 ..	59.7	250 19.2 ..	02.5	Ankaa	353 14.5	S42 13.1
16	143 37.1	11 20.3	51.0	60 13.1	55.4	2 02.7	59.5	265 21.9	02.5	Antares	112 24.2	S26 27.8
17	158 39.6	26 20.5	50.2	75 13.7	55.5	17 04.7	59.4	280 24.5	02.4			
18	173 42.1	41 20.8	N19 49.5	90 14.3	N23 55.6	32 06.8	N15 59.3	295 27.1	S18 02.4	Arcturus	145 54.3	N19 06.3
19	188 44.5	56 21.0	48.7	105 14.9	55.7	47 08.8	59.2	310 29.8	02.4	Atria	107 24.2	S69 03.2
20	203 47.0	71 21.3	48.0	120 15.5	55.8	62 10.9	59.0	325 32.4	02.3	Avior	234 17.9	S59 33.9
21	218 49.5	86 21.5 ..	47.2	135 16.1 ..	55.9	77 12.9 ..	58.9	340 35.0 ..	02.3	Bellatrix	278 30.9	N 6 21.6
22	233 51.9	101 21.8	46.5	150 16.7	56.0	92 15.0	58.8	355 37.6	02.3	Betelgeuse	271 00.2	N 7 24.4
23	248 54.4	116 22.1	45.7	165 17.3	56.1	107 17.0	58.6	10 40.3	02.3			
16 00	263 56.9	131 22.3	N19 45.0	180 17.9	N23 56.2	122 19.1	N15 58.5	25 42.9	S18 02.2	Canopus	263 56.1	S52 42.5
01	278 59.3	146 22.6	44.2	195 18.5	56.3	137 21.2	58.4	40 45.5	02.2	Capella	280 32.9	N46 00.5
02	294 01.8	161 22.8	43.5	210 19.1	56.4	152 23.2	58.2	55 48.2	02.2	Deneb	49 30.1	N45 20.1
03	309 04.2	176 23.1 ..	42.7	225 19.8 ..	56.5	167 25.3 ..	58.1	70 50.8 ..	02.2	Denebola	182 32.3	N14 29.2
04	324 06.7	191 23.4	41.9	240 20.4	56.6	182 27.3	58.0	85 53.4	02.1	Diphda	348 54.7	S17 54.1
05	339 09.2	206 23.7	41.2	255 21.0	56.7	197 29.4	57.8	100 56.1	02.1			
06	354 11.6	221 23.9	N19 40.4	270 21.6	N23 56.8	212 31.4	N15 57.7	115 58.7	S18 02.1	Dubhe	193 50.3	N61 40.3
07	9 14.1	236 24.2	39.7	285 22.2	56.9	227 33.5	57.6	131 01.3	02.0	Elnath	278 11.3	N28 37.0
T 08	24 16.6	251 24.5	38.9	300 22.8	57.0	242 35.5	57.4	146 03.9	02.0	Eltanin	90 45.0	N51 29.4
U 09	39 19.0	266 24.8 ..	38.2	315 23.4 ..	57.1	257 37.6 ..	57.3	161 06.6 ..	02.0	Enif	33 45.6	N 9 56.8
E 10	54 21.5	281 25.0	37.4	330 24.0	57.2	272 39.7	57.2	176 09.2	02.0	Fomalhaut	15 22.5	S29 32.2
S 11	69 24.0	296 25.3	36.6	345 24.6	57.2	287 41.7	57.1	191 11.8	01.9			
D 12	84 26.4	311 25.6	N19 35.9	0 25.2	N23 57.3	302 43.8	N15 56.9	206 14.5	S18 01.9	Gacrux	171 59.1	S57 12.2
A 13	99 28.9	326 25.9	35.1	15 25.8	57.4	317 45.8	56.8	221 17.1	01.9	Gienah	175 50.8	S17 37.8
Y 14	114 31.4	341 26.2	34.4	30 26.4	57.5	332 47.9	56.7	236 19.7	01.9	Hadar	148 45.4	S60 27.0
15	129 33.8	356 26.4 ..	33.6	45 27.0 ..	57.6	347 49.9 ..	56.5	251 22.3 ..	01.8	Hamal	327 59.4	N23 31.9
16	144 36.3	11 26.7	32.8	60 27.6	57.7	2 52.0	56.4	266 25.0	01.8	Kaus Aust.	83 41.6	S34 22.4
17	159 38.7	26 27.0	32.1	75 28.2	57.8	17 54.0	56.3	281 27.6	01.8			
18	174 41.2	41 27.3	N19 31.3	90 28.8	N23 57.9	32 56.1	N15 56.1	296 30.2	S18 01.7	Kochab	137 19.4	N74 05.9
19	189 43.7	56 27.6	30.6	105 29.4	58.0	47 58.1	56.0	311 32.9	01.7	Markab	13 36.9	N15 17.3
20	204 46.1	71 27.9	29.8	120 30.1	58.1	63 00.2	55.9	326 35.5	01.7	Menkar	314 13.9	N 4 08.8
21	219 48.6	86 28.2 ..	29.0	135 30.7 ..	58.1	78 02.2 ..	55.7	341 38.1 ..	01.7	Menkent	148 05.7	S36 26.8
22	234 51.1	101 28.5	28.3	150 31.3	58.2	93 04.3	55.6	356 40.7	01.6	Miaplacidus	221 39.8	S69 47.2
23	249 53.5	116 28.8	27.5	165 31.9	58.3	108 06.3	55.5	11 43.4	01.6			
17 00	264 56.0	131 29.1	N19 26.7	180 32.5	N23 58.4	123 08.4	N15 55.3	26 46.0	S18 01.6	Mirfak	308 38.8	N49 54.6
01	279 58.5	146 29.4	26.0	195 33.1	58.5	138 10.4	55.2	41 48.6	01.6	Nunki	75 56.3	S26 16.4
02	295 00.9	161 29.7	25.2	210 33.7	58.6	153 12.5	55.1	56 51.3	01.5	Peacock	53 16.7	S56 40.7
03	310 03.4	176 30.0 ..	24.4	225 34.3 ..	58.7	168 14.5 ..	54.9	71 53.9 ..	01.5	Pollux	243 26.4	N27 59.2
04	325 05.9	191 30.3	23.7	240 34.9	58.7	183 16.6	54.8	86 56.5	01.5	Procyon	244 58.6	N 5 10.9
05	340 08.3	206 30.6	22.9	255 35.5	58.8	198 18.7	54.7	101 59.1	01.5			
06	355 10.8	221 30.9	N19 22.1	270 36.1	N23 58.9	213 20.7	N15 54.5	117 01.8	S18 01.4	Rasalhague	96 04.9	N12 33.1
W 07	10 13.2	236 31.2	21.4	285 36.7	59.0	228 22.8	54.4	132 04.4	01.4	Regulus	207 42.2	N11 53.4
E 08	25 15.7	251 31.5	20.6	300 37.3	59.1	243 24.8	54.3	147 07.0	01.4	Rigel	281 11.1	S 8 11.3
D 09	40 18.2	266 31.8 ..	19.8	315 37.9 ..	59.2	258 26.9 ..	54.1	162 09.6 ..	01.3	Rigil Kent.	139 49.3	S60 54.0
N 10	55 20.6	281 32.2	19.1	330 38.5	59.3	273 28.9	54.0	177 12.3	01.3	Sabik	102 10.6	S15 44.4
E 11	70 23.1	296 32.5	18.3	345 39.1	59.3	288 31.0	53.9	192 14.9	01.3			
S 12	85 25.6	311 32.8	N19 17.5	0 39.8	N23 59.4	303 33.0	N15 53.7	207 17.5	S18 01.2	Schedar	349 39.0	N56 37.0
D 13	100 28.0	326 33.1	16.7	15 40.4	59.5	318 35.1	53.6	222 20.2	01.2	Shaula	96 19.6	S37 06.7
A 14	115 30.5	341 33.4	16.0	30 41.0	59.6	333 37.1	53.5	237 22.8	01.2	Sirius	258 32.9	S16 44.5
Y 15	130 33.0	356 33.8 ..	15.2	45 41.6 ..	59.7	348 39.2 ..	53.3	252 25.4 ..	01.2	Spica	158 29.7	S11 14.5
16	145 35.4	11 34.1	14.4	60 42.2	59.7	3 41.2	53.2	267 28.0	01.2	Suhail	222 51.7	S43 30.0
17	160 37.9	26 34.4	13.7	75 42.8	59.8	18 43.3	53.1	282 30.7	01.1			
18	175 40.4	41 34.7	N19 12.9	90 43.4	N23 59.9	33 45.3	N15 52.9	297 33.3	S18 01.1	Vega	80 37.6	N38 48.0
19	190 42.8	56 35.1	12.1	105 44.0	24 00.0	48 47.4	52.8	312 35.9	01.1	Zuben'ubi	137 03.6	S16 06.3
20	205 45.3	71 35.4	11.3	120 44.6	00.1	63 49.4	52.7	327 38.5	01.1			
21	220 47.7	86 35.7 ..	10.6	135 45.2 ..	00.1	78 51.5 ..	52.5	342 41.2 ..	01.0		SHA	Mer. Pass.
22	235 50.2	101 36.1	09.8	150 45.8	00.2	93 53.5	52.4	357 43.8	01.0	Venus	227 25.5	15 14
23	250 52.7	116 36.4	09.0	165 46.4	00.3	108 55.6	52.3	12 46.4	01.0	Mars	276 21.1	11 58
Mer. Pass.	h m 6 23.2	v 0.3	d 0.8	v 0.6	d 0.1	v 2.1	d 0.1	v 2.6	d 0.0	Jupiter	218 22.2	15 49
										Saturn	121 46.0	22 13

SUN / MOON

UT	SUN GHA	SUN Dec	MOON GHA	v	Dec	d	HP
d h	° ′	° ′	° ′	′	° ′	′	′
15 00	179 55.3	N23 16.8	200 36.7	7.9	N16 43.7	4.7	58.2
01	194 55.2	16.9	215 03.6	7.9	16 48.4	4.6	58.2
02	209 55.1	17.0	229 30.5	7.9	16 53.0	4.4	58.2
03	224 54.9	.. 17.2	243 57.4	7.9	16 57.4	4.4	58.1
04	239 54.8	17.3	258 24.3	7.9	17 01.8	4.2	58.1
05	254 54.7	17.4	272 51.2	7.8	17 06.0	4.2	58.1
06	269 54.5	N23 17.5	287 18.0	7.9	N17 10.2	4.0	58.1
07	284 54.4	17.6	301 44.9	7.9	17 14.2	3.9	58.1
08	299 54.3	17.7	316 11.8	7.9	17 18.1	3.9	58.0
M 09	314 54.1	.. 17.8	330 38.7	7.9	17 22.0	3.7	58.0
O 10	329 54.0	17.9	345 05.6	7.8	17 25.7	3.6	58.0
N 11	344 53.9	18.0	359 32.4	7.9	17 29.3	3.5	58.0
D 12	359 53.7	N23 18.1	13 59.3	7.9	N17 32.8	3.4	58.0
A 13	14 53.6	18.2	28 26.2	7.9	17 36.2	3.3	57.9
Y 14	29 53.5	18.4	42 53.1	7.9	17 39.5	3.2	57.9
15	44 53.3	.. 18.5	57 20.0	7.9	17 42.7	3.0	57.9
16	59 53.2	18.6	71 46.9	7.9	17 45.7	3.0	57.9
17	74 53.1	18.7	86 13.8	7.9	17 48.7	2.9	57.8
18	89 52.9	N23 18.8	100 40.7	7.9	N17 51.6	2.7	57.8
19	104 52.8	18.9	115 07.6	7.9	17 54.3	2.6	57.8
20	119 52.7	19.0	129 34.5	8.0	17 56.9	2.6	57.8
21	134 52.5	.. 19.1	144 01.5	7.9	17 59.5	2.4	57.8
22	149 52.4	19.2	158 28.4	8.0	18 01.9	2.3	57.7
23	164 52.3	19.3	172 55.4	7.9	18 04.2	2.2	57.7
16 00	179 52.1	N23 19.4	187 22.3	8.0	N18 06.4	2.1	57.7
01	194 52.0	19.5	201 49.3	8.0	18 08.5	2.0	57.7
02	209 51.9	19.6	216 16.3	8.0	18 10.5	1.8	57.6
03	224 51.7	.. 19.7	230 43.3	8.1	18 12.3	1.8	57.6
04	239 51.6	19.8	245 10.4	8.0	18 14.1	1.6	57.6
05	254 51.4	19.9	259 37.4	8.1	18 15.7	1.6	57.6
06	269 51.3	N23 19.9	274 04.5	8.1	N18 17.3	1.4	57.5
07	284 51.2	20.0	288 31.6	8.1	18 18.7	1.3	57.5
T 08	299 51.0	20.1	302 58.7	8.1	18 20.0	1.2	57.5
U 09	314 50.9	.. 20.2	317 25.8	8.1	18 21.2	1.1	57.5
E 10	329 50.8	20.3	331 52.9	8.2	18 22.3	1.0	57.5
S 11	344 50.6	20.4	346 20.1	8.2	18 23.3	0.9	57.4
D 12	359 50.5	N23 20.5	0 47.3	8.2	N18 24.2	0.8	57.4
A 13	14 50.4	20.6	15 14.5	8.3	18 25.0	0.7	57.4
Y 14	29 50.2	20.7	29 41.8	8.2	18 25.7	0.5	57.4
15	44 50.1	.. 20.8	44 09.0	8.3	18 26.2	0.5	57.3
16	59 50.0	20.8	58 36.3	8.3	18 26.7	0.3	57.3
17	74 49.8	20.9	73 03.6	8.4	18 27.0	0.3	57.3
18	89 49.7	N23 21.0	87 31.0	8.4	N18 27.3	0.1	57.3
19	104 49.5	21.1	101 58.4	8.4	18 27.4	0.0	57.2
20	119 49.4	21.2	116 25.8	8.4	18 27.4	0.1	57.2
21	134 49.3	.. 21.3	130 53.2	8.5	18 27.3	0.1	57.2
22	149 49.1	21.4	145 20.7	8.5	18 27.2	0.3	57.2
23	164 49.0	21.4	159 48.2	8.5	18 26.9	0.4	57.1
17 00	179 48.9	N23 21.5	174 15.7	8.6	N18 26.5	0.5	57.1
01	194 48.7	21.6	188 43.3	8.6	18 26.0	0.7	57.1
02	209 48.6	21.7	203 10.9	8.7	18 25.3	0.7	57.1
03	224 48.5	.. 21.8	217 38.6	8.6	18 24.6	0.8	57.0
04	239 48.3	21.8	232 06.2	8.8	18 23.8	0.9	57.0
05	254 48.2	21.9	246 34.0	8.7	18 22.9	1.0	57.0
06	269 48.1	N23 22.0	261 01.7	8.8	N18 21.9	1.2	57.0
W 07	284 47.9	22.1	275 29.5	8.9	18 20.7	1.2	56.9
E 08	299 47.8	22.1	289 57.4	8.8	18 19.5	1.4	56.9
D 09	314 47.6	.. 22.2	304 25.2	9.0	18 18.1	1.4	56.9
N 10	329 47.5	22.3	318 53.2	8.9	18 16.7	1.5	56.8
E 11	344 47.4	22.4	333 21.1	9.0	18 15.2	1.7	56.8
S 12	359 47.2	N23 22.4	347 49.1	9.1	N18 13.5	1.7	56.8
D 13	14 47.1	22.5	2 17.2	9.1	18 11.8	1.9	56.8
A 14	29 47.0	22.6	16 45.3	9.1	18 09.9	1.9	56.7
Y 15	44 46.8	.. 22.6	31 13.4	9.2	18 08.0	2.0	56.7
16	59 46.7	22.7	45 41.6	9.2	18 06.0	2.2	56.7
17	74 46.6	22.8	60 09.8	9.3	18 03.8	2.2	56.7
18	89 46.4	N23 22.9	74 38.1	9.3	N18 01.6	2.4	56.6
19	104 46.3	22.9	89 06.4	9.4	17 59.2	2.4	56.6
20	119 46.1	23.0	103 34.8	9.4	17 56.8	2.5	56.6
21	134 46.0	.. 23.1	118 03.2	9.5	17 54.3	2.6	56.6
22	149 45.9	23.1	132 31.7	9.5	17 51.7	2.8	56.5
23	164 45.7	23.2	147 00.2	9.5	N17 48.9	2.8	56.5
	SD 15.8	d 0.1	SD 15.8		15.6		15.5

Twilight / Sunrise / Moonrise

Lat.	Twilight Naut.	Twilight Civil	Sunrise	Moonrise 15	16	17	18
°	h m	h m	h m	h m	h m	h m	h m
N 72	▭	▭	▭	00 12 / 23 45	▭	▭	02 12
N 70	▭	▭	▭	00 58	01 20	02 06	03 21
68	▭	▭	▭	01 29	02 00	02 50	03 58
66	▭	▭	▭	01 52	02 28	03 19	04 24
64	////	////	01 33	02 10	02 49	03 41	04 44
62	////	////	02 10	02 25	03 06	03 58	05 00
60	////	00 52	02 36	02 37	03 20	04 13	05 14
N 58	////	01 41	02 56	02 48	03 32	04 25	05 25
56	////	02 11	03 13	02 58	03 43	04 36	05 35
54	00 48	02 33	03 27	03 06	03 52	04 45	05 44
52	01 33	02 51	03 39	03 14	04 01	04 54	05 52
50	02 00	03 06	03 50	03 21	04 08	05 01	05 59
45	02 46	03 35	04 13	03 35	04 24	05 18	06 15
N 40	03 16	03 58	04 31	03 47	04 37	05 31	06 27
35	03 39	04 16	04 46	03 57	04 48	05 42	06 38
30	03 58	04 31	04 59	04 07	04 58	05 52	06 47
20	04 27	04 56	05 21	04 22	05 15	06 09	07 03
N 10	04 49	05 16	05 39	04 36	05 30	06 24	07 17
0	05 08	05 34	05 57	04 49	05 44	06 38	07 30
S 10	05 25	05 52	06 14	05 02	05 58	06 52	07 43
20	05 41	06 09	06 33	05 16	06 12	07 07	07 57
30	05 58	06 28	06 54	05 31	06 29	07 24	08 13
35	06 06	06 38	07 06	05 41	06 39	07 34	08 23
40	06 16	06 50	07 20	05 51	06 51	07 45	08 33
45	06 26	07 03	07 37	06 04	07 04	07 58	08 46
S 50	06 38	07 19	07 58	06 19	07 21	08 15	09 01
52	06 43	07 27	08 08	06 26	07 28	08 22	09 08
54	06 49	07 35	08 19	06 34	07 37	08 31	09 16
56	06 55	07 44	08 31	06 43	07 46	08 40	09 24
58	07 02	07 54	08 46	06 53	07 57	08 51	09 34
S 60	07 09	08 06	09 03	07 05	08 10	09 04	09 45

Sunset / Twilight / Moonset

Lat.	Sunset	Twilight Civil	Twilight Naut.	Moonset 15	16	17	18
°	h m	h m	h m	h m	h m	h m	h m
N 72	▭	▭	▭	23 10	▭	▭	00 27
N 70	▭	▭	▭	21 35	22 42	23 17	23 33
68	▭	▭	▭	20 55	21 59	22 40	23 05
66	▭	▭	▭	20 28	21 30	22 14	22 44
64	22 29	////	////	20 07	21 08	21 54	22 26
62	21 52	////	////	19 50	20 50	21 37	22 12
60	21 26	23 10	////	19 36	20 36	21 23	22 00
N 58	21 05	22 21	////	19 24	20 23	21 12	21 50
56	20 49	21 51	////	19 13	20 12	21 01	21 41
54	20 34	21 29	23 14	19 04	20 03	20 52	21 33
52	20 22	21 11	22 29	18 56	19 54	20 44	21 26
50	20 11	20 56	22 01	18 49	19 47	20 37	21 19
45	19 49	20 26	21 16	18 33	19 30	20 21	21 05
N 40	19 31	20 04	20 45	18 20	19 17	20 08	20 54
35	19 16	19 45	20 22	18 09	19 06	19 57	20 44
30	19 03	19 30	20 04	17 59	18 56	19 48	20 35
20	18 41	19 05	19 35	17 43	18 39	19 31	20 20
N 10	18 22	18 45	19 12	17 29	18 24	19 17	20 07
0	18 04	18 27	18 53	17 15	18 10	19 03	19 55
S 10	17 47	18 10	18 36	17 02	17 56	18 50	19 42
20	17 28	17 52	18 20	16 47	17 41	18 35	19 29
30	17 07	17 34	18 03	16 31	17 24	18 18	19 14
35	16 55	17 23	17 55	16 21	17 14	18 08	19 05
40	16 41	17 11	17 45	16 10	17 02	17 57	18 54
45	16 24	16 58	17 35	15 57	16 49	17 44	18 42
S 50	16 03	16 42	17 23	15 42	16 32	17 28	18 28
52	15 54	16 34	17 18	15 34	16 24	17 21	18 21
54	15 42	16 26	17 12	15 26	16 16	17 12	18 14
56	15 30	16 17	17 06	15 17	16 06	17 03	18 05
58	15 15	16 07	17 00	15 07	15 55	16 52	17 55
S 60	14 58	15 55	16 52	14 55	15 42	16 40	17 44

SUN / MOON

Day	SUN Eqn. of Time 00ʰ	SUN Eqn. of Time 12ʰ	Mer. Pass.	MOON Mer. Pass. Upper	MOON Mer. Pass. Lower	Age	Phase
d	m s	m s	h m	h m	h m	d	%
15	00 18	00 25	12 00	11 02	23 29	28	2
16	00 31	00 38	12 01	11 57	24 24	29	0
17	00 44	00 51	12 01	12 51	00 24	01	1

Phase: ● (New Moon)

UT	ARIES	VENUS −4.5		MARS +1.5		JUPITER −1.8		SATURN +0.2		STARS		
	GHA	GHA	Dec	GHA	Dec	GHA	Dec	GHA	Dec	Name	SHA	Dec
d h	° ′	° ′	° ′	° ′	° ′	° ′	° ′	° ′	° ′		° ′	° ′
18 00	265 55.1	131 36.7	N19 08.3	180 47.0	N24 00.4	123 57.6	N15 52.1	27 49.0	S18 01.0	Acamar	315 17.7	S40 14.6
01	280 57.6	146 37.1	07.5	195 47.6	00.5	138 59.6	52.0	42 51.7	00.9	Achernar	335 26.2	S57 09.3
02	296 00.1	161 37.4	06.7	210 48.2	00.5	154 01.7	51.9	57 54.3	00.9	Acrux	173 07.4	S63 11.4
03	311 02.5	176 37.7 . .	05.9	225 48.9 . .	00.6	169 03.7 . .	51.7	72 56.9 . .	00.9	Adhara	255 11.8	S28 59.9
04	326 05.0	191 38.1	05.1	240 49.5	00.7	184 05.8	51.6	87 59.5	00.8	Aldebaran	290 48.1	N16 32.2
05	341 07.5	206 38.4	04.4	255 50.1	00.8	199 07.8	51.5	103 02.2	00.8			
06	356 09.9	221 38.8	N19 03.6	270 50.7	N24 00.8	214 09.9	N15 51.3	118 04.8	S18 00.8	Alioth	166 19.5	N55 52.9
07	11 12.4	236 39.1	02.8	285 51.3	00.9	229 11.9	51.2	133 07.4	00.8	Alkaid	152 57.7	N49 14.5
T 08	26 14.9	251 39.5	02.0	300 51.9	01.0	244 14.0	51.1	148 10.0	00.7	Al Na'ir	27 41.9	S46 52.8
H 09	41 17.3	266 39.8 . .	01.3	315 52.5 . .	01.1	259 16.0 . .	50.9	163 12.7 . .	00.7	Alnilam	275 45.3	S 1 11.8
U 10	56 19.8	281 40.2	19 00.5	330 53.1	01.1	274 18.1	50.8	178 15.3	00.7	Alphard	217 54.9	S 8 43.7
R 11	71 22.2	296 40.5	18 59.7	345 53.7	01.2	289 20.1	50.7	193 17.9	00.7			
S 12	86 24.7	311 40.9	N18 58.9	0 54.3	N24 01.3	304 22.2	N15 50.5	208 20.5	S18 00.6	Alphecca	126 09.6	N26 40.0
D 13	101 27.2	326 41.2	58.1	15 54.9	01.4	319 24.2	50.4	223 23.2	00.6	Alpheratz	357 42.1	N29 10.4
A 14	116 29.6	341 41.6	57.4	30 55.5	01.4	334 26.3	50.3	238 25.8	00.6	Altair	62 06.6	N 8 54.7
Y 15	131 32.1	356 42.0 . .	56.6	45 56.1 . .	01.5	349 28.3 . .	50.1	253 28.4 . .	00.6	Ankaa	353 14.5	S42 13.1
16	146 34.6	11 42.3	55.8	60 56.8	01.6	4 30.4	50.0	268 31.0	00.5	Antares	112 24.2	S26 27.8
17	161 37.0	26 42.7	55.0	75 57.4	01.6	19 32.4	49.9	283 33.7	00.5			
18	176 39.5	41 43.0	N18 54.2	90 58.0	N24 01.7	34 34.4	N15 49.7	298 36.3	S18 00.5	Arcturus	145 54.3	N19 06.3
19	191 42.0	56 43.4	53.5	105 58.6	01.8	49 36.5	49.6	313 38.9	00.5	Atria	107 24.2	S69 03.2
20	206 44.4	71 43.8	52.7	120 59.2	01.9	64 38.5	49.5	328 41.5	00.4	Avior	234 17.5	S59 33.9
21	221 46.9	86 44.1 . .	51.9	135 59.8 . .	01.9	79 40.6 . .	49.3	343 44.2 . .	00.4	Bellatrix	278 30.9	N 6 21.6
22	236 49.3	101 44.5	51.1	151 00.4	02.0	94 42.6	49.2	358 46.8	00.4	Betelgeuse	271 00.2	N 7 24.4
23	251 51.8	116 44.9	50.3	166 01.0	02.1	109 44.7	49.1	13 49.4	00.4			
19 00	266 54.3	131 45.3	N18 49.5	181 01.6	N24 02.1	124 46.7	N15 48.9	28 52.0	S18 00.3	Canopus	263 56.1	S52 42.5
01	281 56.7	146 45.6	48.8	196 02.2	02.2	139 48.8	48.8	43 54.7	00.3	Capella	280 32.9	N46 00.5
02	296 59.2	161 46.0	48.0	211 02.8	02.3	154 50.8	48.6	58 57.3	00.3	Deneb	49 30.1	N45 20.1
03	312 01.7	176 46.4 . .	47.2	226 03.4 . .	02.3	169 52.9 . .	48.5	73 59.9 . .	00.2	Denebola	182 32.3	N14 29.2
04	327 04.1	191 46.8	46.4	241 04.1	02.4	184 54.9	48.4	89 02.5	00.2	Diphda	348 54.6	S17 54.0
05	342 06.6	206 47.2	45.6	256 04.7	02.5	199 56.9	48.2	104 05.1	00.2			
06	357 09.1	221 47.5	N18 44.8	271 05.3	N24 02.5	214 59.0	N15 48.1	119 07.8	S18 00.2	Dubhe	193 50.4	N61 40.3
07	12 11.5	236 47.9	44.0	286 05.9	02.6	230 01.0	48.0	134 10.4	00.1	Elnath	278 11.3	N28 37.0
08	27 14.0	251 48.3	43.3	301 06.5	02.7	245 03.1	47.8	149 13.0	00.1	Eltanin	90 45.0	N51 29.4
F 09	42 16.5	266 48.7 . .	42.5	316 07.1 . .	02.7	260 05.1 . .	47.7	164 15.6 . .	00.1	Enif	33 45.6	N 9 56.8
R 10	57 18.9	281 49.1	41.7	331 07.7	02.8	275 07.2	47.6	179 18.3	00.1	Fomalhaut	15 22.4	S29 32.2
I 11	72 21.4	296 49.5	40.9	346 08.3	02.9	290 09.2	47.4	194 20.9	00.0			
D 12	87 23.8	311 49.9	N18 40.1	1 08.9	N24 02.9	305 11.3	N15 47.3	209 23.5	S18 00.0	Gacrux	171 59.1	S57 12.2
A 13	102 26.3	326 50.3	39.3	16 09.5	03.0	320 13.3	47.2	224 26.1	00.0	Gienah	175 50.8	S17 37.8
Y 14	117 28.8	341 50.7	38.5	31 10.1	03.1	335 15.3	47.0	239 28.7	18 00.0	Hadar	148 45.4	S60 27.0
15	132 31.2	356 51.1 . .	37.7	46 10.7 . .	03.1	350 17.4 . .	46.9	254 31.4	17 59.9	Hamal	327 59.4	N23 31.9
16	147 33.7	11 51.5	37.0	61 11.4	03.2	5 19.4	46.7	269 34.0	59.9	Kaus Aust.	83 41.6	S34 22.4
17	162 36.2	26 51.9	36.2	76 12.0	03.3	20 21.5	46.6	284 36.6	59.9			
18	177 38.6	41 52.3	N18 35.4	91 12.6	N24 03.3	35 23.5	N15 46.5	299 39.2	S17 59.9	Kochab	137 19.4	N74 05.9
19	192 41.1	56 52.7	34.6	106 13.2	03.4	50 25.6	46.3	314 41.9	59.8	Markab	13 36.9	N15 17.3
20	207 43.6	71 53.1	33.8	121 13.8	03.4	65 27.6	46.2	329 44.5	59.8	Menkar	314 13.9	N 4 08.8
21	222 46.0	86 53.5 . .	33.0	136 14.4 . .	03.5	80 29.6 . .	46.1	344 47.1 . .	59.8	Menkent	148 05.7	S36 26.8
22	237 48.5	101 53.9	32.2	151 15.0	03.6	95 31.7	45.9	359 49.7	59.8	Miaplacidus	221 39.8	S69 47.2
23	252 51.0	116 54.3	31.4	166 15.6	03.6	110 33.7	45.8	14 52.3	59.7			
20 00	267 53.4	131 54.7	N18 30.6	181 16.2	N24 03.7	125 35.8	N15 45.7	29 55.0	S17 59.7	Mirfak	308 38.7	N49 54.6
01	282 55.9	146 55.1	29.8	196 16.8	03.7	140 37.8	45.5	44 57.6	59.7	Nunki	75 56.3	S26 16.4
02	297 58.3	161 55.5	29.0	211 17.5	03.8	155 39.8	45.4	60 00.2	59.7	Peacock	53 16.7	S56 40.7
03	313 00.8	176 56.0 . .	28.2	226 18.1 . .	03.9	170 41.9 . .	45.2	75 02.8 . .	59.6	Pollux	243 26.4	N27 59.2
04	328 03.3	191 56.4	27.4	241 18.7	03.9	185 43.9	45.1	90 05.4	59.6	Procyon	244 58.6	N 5 10.9
05	343 05.7	206 56.8	26.7	256 19.3	04.0	200 46.0	45.0	105 08.1	59.6			
06	358 08.2	221 57.2	N18 25.9	271 19.9	N24 04.0	215 48.0	N15 44.9	120 10.7	S17 59.6	Rasalhague	96 04.8	N12 33.2
07	13 10.7	236 57.6	25.1	286 20.5	04.1	230 50.1	44.7	135 13.3	59.5	Regulus	207 42.2	N11 53.4
S 08	28 13.1	251 58.1	24.3	301 21.1	04.1	245 52.1	44.6	150 15.9	59.5	Rigel	281 11.1	S 8 11.2
A 09	43 15.6	266 58.5 . .	23.5	316 21.7 . .	04.2	260 54.1 . .	44.4	165 18.5 . .	59.5	Rigil Kent.	139 49.3	S60 54.0
T 10	58 18.1	281 58.9	22.7	331 22.3	04.3	275 56.2	44.5	180 21.2	59.5	Sabik	102 10.6	S15 44.4
U 11	73 20.5	296 59.4	21.9	346 22.9	04.3	290 58.2	44.1	195 23.8	59.4			
R 12	88 23.0	311 59.8	N18 21.1	1 23.5	N24 04.4	306 00.3	N15 44.0	210 26.4	S17 59.4	Schedar	349 38.9	N56 37.0
D 13	103 25.5	327 00.2	20.3	16 24.2	04.4	321 02.3	43.9	225 29.0	59.4	Shaula	96 19.6	S37 06.7
A 14	118 27.9	342 00.7	19.5	31 24.8	04.5	336 04.3	43.7	240 31.6	59.4	Sirius	258 32.9	S16 44.5
Y 15	133 30.4	357 01.1 . .	18.7	46 25.4 . .	04.5	351 06.4 . .	43.6	255 34.3 . .	59.3	Spica	158 29.7	S11 14.5
16	148 32.8	12 01.5	17.9	61 26.0	04.6	6 08.4	43.5	270 36.9	59.3	Suhail	222 51.7	S43 30.0
17	163 35.3	27 02.0	17.1	76 26.6	04.6	21 10.5	43.3	285 39.5	59.3			
18	178 37.8	42 02.4	N18 16.3	91 27.2	N24 04.7	36 12.5	N15 43.2	300 42.1	S17 59.3	Vega	80 37.6	N38 48.1
19	193 40.2	57 02.9	15.5	106 27.8	04.8	51 14.5	43.1	315 44.7	59.2	Zuben'ubi	137 03.6	S16 06.3
20	208 42.7	72 03.3	14.7	121 28.4	04.8	66 16.6	42.9	330 47.4	59.2		SHA	Mer. Pass.
21	223 45.2	87 03.8 . .	13.9	136 29.0 . .	04.9	81 18.6 . .	42.8	345 50.0 . .	59.2		° ′	h m
22	238 47.6	102 04.2	13.1	151 29.7	04.9	96 20.6	42.6	0 52.6	59.2	Venus	224 51.0	15 13
23	253 50.2	117 04.7	12.3	166 30.3	05.0	111 22.7	42.5	15 55.2	59.1	Mars	274 07.3	11 55
	h m									Jupiter	217 52.4	15 39
Mer. Pass.	6 11.4	v 0.4	d 0.8	v 0.6	d 0.1	v 2.0	d 0.1	v 2.6	d 0.0	Saturn	121 57.8	22 01

UT	SUN GHA	SUN Dec	MOON GHA	MOON v	MOON Dec	MOON d	MOON HP
d h	° ′	° ′	° ′	′	° ′	′	′
18 00	179 45.6	N23 23.2	161 28.7	9.7	N17 46.1	2.9	56.5
01	194 45.5	23.3	175 57.4	9.6	17 43.2	3.0	56.5
02	209 45.3	23.4	190 26.0	9.7	17 40.2	3.1	56.4
03	224 45.2 ..	23.4	204 54.7	9.8	17 37.1	3.1	56.4
04	239 45.1	23.5	219 23.5	9.8	17 34.0	3.3	56.4
05	254 44.9	23.6	233 52.3	9.9	17 30.7	3.4	56.4
06	269 44.8 N23	23.6	248 21.2	9.9	N17 27.3	3.4	56.3
07	284 44.6	23.7	262 50.1	10.0	17 23.9	3.6	56.3
T 08	299 44.5	23.7	277 19.1	10.1	17 20.3	3.6	56.3
H 09	314 44.4 ..	23.8	291 48.2	10.1	17 16.7	3.7	56.3
U 10	329 44.2	23.8	306 17.3	10.1	17 13.0	3.9	56.2
R 11	344 44.1	23.9	320 46.4	10.2	17 09.1	3.9	56.2
S 12	359 44.0 N23	24.0	335 15.6	10.3	N17 05.2	3.9	56.2
D 13	14 43.8	24.0	349 44.9	10.3	17 01.3	4.1	56.2
A 14	29 43.7	24.1	4 14.2	10.3	16 57.2	4.2	56.1
Y 15	44 43.5 ..	24.1	18 43.5	10.5	16 53.0	4.2	56.1
16	59 43.4	24.2	33 13.0	10.4	16 48.8	4.3	56.1
17	74 43.3	24.2	47 42.4	10.6	16 44.5	4.4	56.1
18	89 43.1 N23	24.3	62 12.0	10.6	N16 40.1	4.5	56.0
19	104 43.0	24.3	76 41.6	10.6	16 35.6	4.6	56.0
20	119 42.9	24.4	91 11.2	10.7	16 31.0	4.6	56.0
21	134 42.7 ..	24.4	105 40.9	10.8	16 26.4	4.7	56.0
22	149 42.6	24.5	120 10.7	10.8	16 21.7	4.8	55.9
23	164 42.5	24.5	134 40.5	10.9	16 16.9	4.9	55.9
19 00	179 42.3 N23	24.6	149 10.4	11.0	N16 12.0	5.0	55.9
01	194 42.2	24.6	163 40.4	11.0	16 07.0	5.0	55.9
02	209 42.0	24.7	178 10.4	11.0	16 02.0	5.1	55.8
03	224 41.9 ..	24.7	192 40.4	11.1	15 56.9	5.2	55.8
04	239 41.8	24.7	207 10.5	11.2	15 51.7	5.3	55.8
05	254 41.6	24.8	221 40.7	11.2	15 46.4	5.3	55.8
06	269 41.5 N23	24.8	236 10.9	11.3	N15 41.1	5.4	55.7
07	284 41.4	24.9	250 41.2	11.4	15 35.7	5.5	55.7
F 08	299 41.2	24.9	265 11.6	11.4	15 30.2	5.6	55.7
R 09	314 41.1 ..	25.0	279 42.0	11.4	15 24.6	5.6	55.7
I 10	329 40.9	25.0	294 12.4	11.6	15 19.0	5.7	55.6
D 11	344 40.8	25.0	308 43.0	11.5	15 13.3	5.8	55.6
A 12	359 40.7 N23	25.1	323 13.5	11.7	N15 07.5	5.8	55.6
Y 13	14 40.5	25.1	337 44.2	11.7	15 01.7	5.9	55.6
14	29 40.4	25.1	352 14.9	11.7	14 55.8	6.0	55.5
15	44 40.3 ..	25.2	6 45.6	11.8	14 49.8	6.0	55.5
16	59 40.1	25.2	21 16.4	11.9	14 43.8	6.1	55.5
17	74 40.0	25.3	35 47.3	11.9	14 37.7	6.2	55.5
18	89 39.9 N23	25.3	50 18.2	12.0	N14 31.5	6.2	55.4
19	104 39.7	25.3	64 49.2	12.1	14 25.3	6.3	55.4
20	119 39.6	25.4	79 20.3	12.1	14 19.0	6.3	55.4
21	134 39.4 ..	25.4	93 51.4	12.1	14 12.7	6.5	55.4
22	149 39.3	25.4	108 22.5	12.3	14 06.2	6.4	55.4
23	164 39.2	25.4	122 53.8	12.2	13 59.8	6.6	55.3
20 00	179 39.0 N23	25.5	137 25.0	12.3	N13 53.2	6.6	55.3
01	194 38.9	25.5	151 56.3	12.4	13 46.6	6.6	55.3
02	209 38.8	25.5	166 27.7	12.5	13 40.0	6.8	55.3
03	224 38.6 ..	25.6	180 59.2	12.5	13 33.2	6.7	55.3
04	239 38.5	25.6	195 30.7	12.5	13 26.5	6.9	55.2
05	254 38.3	25.6	210 02.2	12.6	13 19.6	6.9	55.2
06	269 38.2 N23	25.7	224 33.8	12.7	N13 12.7	6.9	55.2
07	284 38.1	25.7	239 05.5	12.7	13 05.8	7.0	55.2
S 08	299 37.9	25.7	253 37.2	12.8	12 58.8	7.0	55.1
A 09	314 37.8 ..	25.7	268 09.0	12.8	12 51.8	7.2	55.1
T 10	329 37.7	25.7	282 40.8	12.9	12 44.6	7.1	55.1
U 11	344 37.5	25.8	297 12.7	12.9	12 37.5	7.2	55.1
R 12	359 37.4 N23	25.8	311 44.6	13.0	N12 30.3	7.3	55.1
D 13	14 37.2	25.8	326 16.6	13.0	12 23.0	7.3	55.0
A 14	29 37.1	25.8	340 48.6	13.1	12 15.7	7.4	55.0
Y 15	44 37.0 ..	25.8	355 20.7	13.1	12 08.3	7.4	55.0
16	59 36.8	25.9	9 52.8	13.2	12 00.9	7.4	55.0
17	74 36.7	25.9	24 25.0	13.3	11 53.5	7.5	55.0
18	89 36.6 N23	25.9	38 57.3	13.2	N11 46.0	7.6	55.0
19	104 36.4	25.9	53 29.5	13.4	11 38.4	7.6	54.9
20	119 36.3	25.9	68 01.9	13.4	11 30.8	7.6	54.9
21	134 36.2 ..	25.9	82 34.3	13.4	11 23.2	7.7	54.9
22	149 36.0	25.9	97 06.7	13.5	11 15.5	7.8	54.9
23	164 35.9	26.0	111 39.2	13.5	N11 07.7	7.7	54.9
SD 15.8	d 0.0		SD 15.3		15.1		15.0

Moonrise

Lat.	Twilight Naut.	Twilight Civil	Sunrise	18	19	20	21
°	h m	h m	h m	h m	h m	h m	h m
N 72	□	□	□	02 12	04 11	05 59	07 39
N 70	□	□	□	03 21	04 51	06 24	07 56
68	□	□	□	03 58	05 19	06 43	08 09
66	□	□	□	04 24	05 39	06 59	08 19
64	////	////	01 31	04 44	05 56	07 11	08 28
62	////	////	02 09	05 00	06 09	07 22	08 35
60	////	00 50	02 36	05 14	06 21	07 31	08 42
N 58	////	01 40	02 56	05 25	06 31	07 39	08 48
56	////	02 10	03 13	05 35	06 39	07 46	08 53
54	00 46	02 33	03 27	05 44	06 47	07 52	08 57
52	01 32	02 51	03 39	05 52	06 54	07 57	09 01
50	02 00	03 06	03 50	05 59	07 00	08 03	09 05
45	02 46	03 35	04 13	06 15	07 14	08 13	09 13
N 40	03 16	03 58	04 31	06 27	07 25	08 22	09 19
35	03 39	04 16	04 46	06 38	07 34	08 30	09 25
30	03 58	04 32	04 59	06 47	07 42	08 37	09 30
20	04 27	04 56	05 21	07 03	07 56	08 48	09 39
N 10	04 50	05 17	05 40	07 17	08 09	08 59	09 46
0	05 09	05 35	05 58	07 30	08 20	09 08	09 54
S 10	05 26	05 52	06 15	07 43	08 32	09 18	10 01
20	05 42	06 10	06 34	07 57	08 44	09 28	10 08
30	05 58	06 28	06 55	08 13	08 58	09 39	10 17
35	06 07	06 39	07 07	08 23	09 06	09 46	10 22
40	06 17	06 51	07 21	08 33	09 16	09 53	10 27
45	06 27	07 04	07 38	08 46	09 27	10 02	10 34
S 50	06 39	07 20	07 59	09 01	09 40	10 13	10 42
52	06 44	07 28	08 09	09 08	09 46	10 18	10 45
54	06 50	07 36	08 20	09 16	09 52	10 23	10 49
56	06 56	07 45	08 33	09 24	10 00	10 29	10 53
58	07 03	07 55	08 47	09 34	10 08	10 36	10 58
S 60	07 10	08 07	09 05	09 45	10 18	10 43	11 04

Moonset

Lat.	Sunset	Twilight Civil	Twilight Naut.	18	19	20	21
°	h m	h m	h m	h m	h m	h m	h m
N 72	□	□	□	00 27	00 14	00 06	(00 01 / 23 55)
N 70	□	□	□	23 33	23 40	23 43	23 44
68	□	□	□	23 05	23 19	23 29	23 35
66	□	□	□	22 44	23 03	23 17	23 28
64	22 32	////	////	22 26	22 50	23 08	23 21
62	21 54	////	////	22 12	22 39	22 59	23 16
60	21 27	23 13	////	22 00	22 29	22 52	23 11
N 58	21 07	22 22	////	21 50	22 21	22 46	23 07
56	20 50	21 52	////	21 41	22 13	22 40	23 03
54	20 36	21 30	23 18	21 33	22 07	22 35	23 00
52	20 23	21 13	22 31	21 26	22 01	22 30	22 56
50	20 12	20 57	22 03	21 19	21 55	22 26	22 53
45	19 50	20 27	21 17	21 05	21 44	22 17	22 47
N 40	19 32	20 05	20 46	20 54	21 34	22 10	22 42
35	19 17	19 46	20 23	20 44	21 26	22 03	22 38
30	19 04	19 31	20 04	20 35	21 18	21 57	22 34
20	18 42	19 06	19 35	20 20	21 05	21 47	22 27
N 10	18 23	18 46	19 13	20 07	20 54	21 39	22 21
0	18 05	18 28	18 54	19 55	20 44	21 30	22 15
S 10	17 48	18 10	18 37	19 42	20 33	21 22	22 09
20	17 29	17 53	18 20	19 29	20 22	21 13	22 03
30	17 08	17 34	18 04	19 14	20 09	21 03	21 56
35	16 55	17 24	17 55	19 05	20 01	20 57	21 51
40	16 41	17 12	17 46	18 54	19 52	20 50	21 47
45	16 24	16 58	17 35	18 42	19 42	20 42	21 41
S 50	16 04	16 42	17 24	18 28	19 30	20 32	21 35
52	15 54	16 35	17 18	18 21	19 24	20 28	21 32
54	15 43	16 26	17 13	18 14	19 18	20 23	21 28
56	15 30	16 17	17 06	18 05	19 11	20 18	21 24
58	15 15	16 07	17 00	17 55	19 03	20 11	21 20
S 60	14 58	15 55	16 52	17 44	18 54	20 05	21 16

Day	SUN Eqn. of Time 00h	SUN Eqn. of Time 12h	SUN Mer. Pass.	MOON Mer. Pass. Upper	MOON Mer. Pass. Lower	Age	Phase
d	m s	m s	h m	h m	h m	d	%
18	00 57	01 04	12 01	13 42	01 17	02	4
19	01 10	01 17	12 01	14 32	02 08	03	9
20	01 24	01 30	12 02	15 19	02 56	04	16

UT	ARIES GHA	VENUS −4.6 GHA	Dec	MARS +1.5 GHA	Dec	JUPITER −1.8 GHA	Dec	SATURN +0.2 GHA	Dec	STARS Name	SHA	Dec
d h	° ′	° ′	° ′	° ′	° ′	° ′	° ′	° ′	° ′		° ′	° ′
21 00	268 52.6	132 05.1	N18 11.5	181 30.9	N24 05.0	126 24.7	N15 42.4	30 57.8	S17 59.1	Acamar	315 17.7	S40 14.5
01	283 55.0	147 05.6	10.7	196 31.5	05.1	141 26.8	42.2	46 00.4	59.1	Achernar	335 26.1	S57 09.3
02	298 57.5	162 06.0	09.9	211 32.1	05.1	156 28.8	42.1	61 03.1	59.1	Acrux	173 07.5	S63 11.4
03	313 59.9	177 06.5 ..	09.1	226 32.7 ..	05.2	171 30.8 ..	41.9	76 05.7 ..	59.0	Adhara	255 11.8	S28 59.8
04	329 02.4	192 06.9	08.3	241 33.3	05.2	186 32.9	41.8	91 08.3	59.0	Aldebaran	290 48.1	N16 32.2
05	344 04.9	207 07.4	07.5	256 33.9	05.3	201 34.9	41.7	106 10.9	59.0			
06	359 07.3	222 07.9	N18 06.7	271 34.5	N24 05.3	216 37.0	N15 41.5	121 13.5	S17 59.0	Alioth	166 19.5	N55 52.9
07	14 09.8	237 08.3	05.9	286 35.2	05.4	231 39.0	41.4	136 16.2	58.9	Alkaid	152 57.7	N49 14.5
08	29 12.3	252 08.8	05.1	301 35.8	05.4	246 41.0	41.3	151 18.8	58.9	Al Na'ir	27 41.9	S46 52.8
S 09	44 14.7	267 09.2 ..	04.3	316 36.4 ..	05.5	261 43.1 ..	41.1	166 21.4 ..	58.9	Alnilam	275 45.3	S 1 11.7
U 10	59 17.2	282 09.7	03.5	331 37.0	05.5	276 45.1	41.0	181 24.0	58.9	Alphard	217 54.9	S 8 43.7
N 11	74 19.7	297 10.2	02.7	346 37.6	05.6	291 47.1	40.8	196 26.6	58.9			
D 12	89 22.1	312 10.7	N18 01.9	1 38.2	N24 05.6	306 49.2	N15 40.7	211 29.2	S17 58.8	Alphecca	126 09.6	N26 40.0
A 13	104 24.6	327 11.1	01.1	16 38.8	05.6	321 51.2	40.6	226 31.9	58.8	Alpheratz	357 42.0	N29 10.4
Y 14	119 27.1	342 11.6	18 00.3	31 39.4	05.7	336 53.3	40.4	241 34.5	58.8	Altair	62 06.6	N 8 54.7
15	134 29.5	357 12.1	17 59.5	46 40.0 ..	05.7	351 55.3 ..	40.3	256 37.1 ..	58.8	Ankaa	353 14.5	S42 13.1
16	149 32.0	12 12.6	58.7	61 40.7	05.8	6 57.3	40.1	271 39.7	58.7	Antares	112 24.2	S26 27.8
17	164 34.4	27 13.0	57.9	76 41.3	05.8	21 59.4	40.0	286 42.3	58.7			
18	179 36.9	42 13.5	N17 57.1	91 41.9	N24 05.9	37 01.4	N15 39.9	301 44.9	S17 58.7	Arcturus	145 54.3	N19 06.3
19	194 39.4	57 14.0	56.2	106 42.5	05.9	52 03.4	39.7	316 47.6	58.7	Atria	107 24.2	S69 03.2
20	209 41.8	72 14.5	55.4	121 43.1	06.0	67 05.5	39.6	331 50.2	58.6	Avior	234 17.9	S59 33.9
21	224 44.3	87 15.0 ..	54.6	136 43.7 ..	06.0	82 07.5 ..	39.5	346 52.8 ..	58.6	Bellatrix	278 30.9	N 6 21.6
22	239 46.8	102 15.5	53.8	151 44.3	06.0	97 09.5	39.3	1 55.4	58.6	Betelgeuse	271 00.2	N 7 24.4
23	254 49.2	117 16.0	53.0	166 44.9	06.1	112 11.6	39.2	16 58.0	58.6			
22 00	269 51.7	132 16.5	N17 52.2	181 45.6	N24 06.1	127 13.6	N15 39.0	32 00.6	S17 58.5	Canopus	263 56.1	S52 42.5
01	284 54.2	147 17.0	51.4	196 46.2	06.2	142 15.6	38.9	47 03.2	58.5	Capella	280 32.9	N46 00.5
02	299 56.6	162 17.4	50.6	211 46.8	06.2	157 17.7	38.8	62 05.9	58.5	Deneb	49 30.1	N45 20.2
03	314 59.1	177 17.9 ..	49.8	226 47.4 ..	06.3	172 19.7 ..	38.6	77 08.5 ..	58.5	Denebola	182 32.3	N14 29.2
04	330 01.6	192 18.4	49.0	241 48.0	06.3	187 21.8	38.5	92 11.1	58.4	Diphda	348 54.6	S17 54.0
05	345 04.0	207 18.9	48.2	256 48.6	06.3	202 23.8	38.3	107 13.7	58.4			
06	0 06.5	222 19.4	N17 47.4	271 49.2	N24 06.4	217 25.8	N15 38.2	122 16.3	S17 58.4	Dubhe	193 50.4	N61 40.3
07	15 08.9	237 20.0	46.6	286 49.8	06.4	232 27.9	38.1	137 18.9	58.4	Elnath	278 11.3	N28 37.0
08	30 11.4	252 20.5	45.7	301 50.5	06.5	247 29.9	37.9	152 21.6	58.3	Eltanin	90 45.0	N51 29.4
M 09	45 13.9	267 21.0 ..	44.9	316 51.1 ..	06.5	262 31.9 ..	37.8	167 24.2 ..	58.3	Enif	33 45.6	N 9 56.8
O 10	60 16.3	282 21.5	44.1	331 51.7	06.5	277 34.0	37.6	182 26.8	58.3	Fomalhaut	15 22.4	S29 32.2
N 11	75 18.8	297 22.0	43.3	346 52.3	06.6	292 36.0	37.5	197 29.4	58.3			
D 12	90 21.3	312 22.5	N17 42.5	1 52.9	N24 06.6	307 38.0	N15 37.4	212 32.0	S17 58.2	Gacrux	171 59.1	S57 12.2
A 13	105 23.7	327 23.0	41.7	16 53.5	06.7	322 40.1	37.2	227 34.6	58.2	Gienah	175 50.8	S17 37.8
Y 14	120 26.2	342 23.5	40.9	31 54.1	06.7	337 42.1	37.1	242 37.2	58.2	Hadar	148 45.4	S60 27.0
15	135 28.7	357 24.1 ..	40.1	46 54.7 ..	06.7	352 44.1 ..	36.9	257 39.9 ..	58.2	Hamal	327 59.4	N23 31.9
16	150 31.1	12 24.6	39.3	61 55.4	06.8	7 46.2	36.8	272 42.5	58.2	Kaus Aust.	83 41.6	S34 22.4
17	165 33.6	27 25.1	38.5	76 56.0	06.8	22 48.2	36.7	287 45.1	58.1			
18	180 36.0	42 25.6	N17 37.6	91 56.6	N24 06.8	37 50.2	N15 36.5	302 47.7	S17 58.1	Kochab	137 19.5	N74 05.9
19	195 38.5	57 26.1	36.8	106 57.2	06.9	52 52.3	36.4	317 50.3	58.1	Markab	13 36.9	N15 17.3
20	210 41.0	72 26.7	36.0	121 57.8	06.9	67 54.3	36.2	332 52.9	58.1	Menkar	314 13.9	N 4 08.9
21	225 43.4	87 27.2 ..	35.2	136 58.4 ..	06.9	82 56.3 ..	36.1	347 55.5 ..	58.0	Menkent	148 05.7	S36 26.8
22	240 45.9	102 27.7	34.4	151 59.0	07.0	97 58.4	36.0	2 58.1	58.0	Miaplacidus	221 39.9	S69 47.2
23	255 48.4	117 28.3	33.6	166 59.6	07.0	113 00.4	35.8	18 00.8	58.0			
23 00	270 50.8	132 28.8	N17 32.8	182 00.3	N24 07.0	128 02.4	N15 35.7	33 03.4	S17 58.0	Mirfak	308 38.7	N49 54.6
01	285 53.3	147 29.3	31.9	197 00.9	07.1	143 04.5	35.5	48 06.0	57.9	Nunki	75 56.3	S26 16.4
02	300 55.8	162 29.9	31.1	212 01.5	07.1	158 06.5	35.4	63 08.6	57.9	Peacock	53 16.7	S56 40.7
03	315 58.2	177 30.4 ..	30.3	227 02.1 ..	07.1	173 08.5 ..	35.3	78 11.2 ..	57.9	Pollux	243 26.4	N27 59.2
04	331 00.7	192 30.9	29.5	242 02.7	07.2	188 10.5	35.1	93 13.8	57.9	Procyon	244 58.6	N 5 10.9
05	346 03.2	207 31.5	28.7	257 03.3	07.2	203 12.6	35.0	108 16.4	57.9			
06	1 05.6	222 32.0	N17 27.9	272 03.9	N24 07.2	218 14.6	N15 34.8	123 19.0	S17 57.8	Rasalhague	96 04.8	N12 33.2
07	16 08.1	237 32.6	27.1	287 04.6	07.3	233 16.6	34.7	138 21.7	57.8	Regulus	207 42.2	N11 53.4
T 08	31 10.5	252 33.1	26.2	302 05.2	07.3	248 18.7	34.5	153 24.3	57.8	Rigel	281 11.1	S 8 11.2
U 09	46 13.0	267 33.7 ..	25.4	317 05.8 ..	07.3	263 20.7 ..	34.4	168 26.9 ..	57.8	Rigil Kent.	139 49.3	S60 54.0
E 10	61 15.5	282 34.2	24.6	332 06.4	07.4	278 22.7	34.3	183 29.5	57.7	Sabik	102 10.6	S15 44.4
S 11	76 17.9	297 34.8	23.8	347 07.0	07.4	293 24.8	34.1	198 32.1	57.7			
D 12	91 20.4	312 35.3	N17 23.0	2 07.6	N24 07.4	308 26.8	N15 34.0	213 34.7	S17 57.7	Schedar	349 38.9	N56 37.0
A 13	106 22.9	327 35.9	22.2	17 08.2	07.4	323 28.8	33.8	228 37.3	57.7	Shaula	96 19.6	S37 06.7
Y 14	121 25.3	342 36.5	21.3	32 08.9	07.5	338 30.9	33.7	243 39.9	57.6	Sirius	258 32.9	S16 44.5
15	136 27.8	357 37.0 ..	20.5	47 09.5 ..	07.5	353 32.9 ..	33.6	258 42.6 ..	57.6	Spica	158 29.7	S11 14.5
16	151 30.3	12 37.6	19.7	62 10.1	07.5	8 34.9	33.4	273 45.2	57.6	Suhail	222 51.7	S43 30.0
17	166 32.7	27 38.1	18.9	77 10.7	07.6	23 36.9	33.3	288 47.8	57.6			
18	181 35.2	42 38.7	N17 18.1	92 11.3	N24 07.6	38 39.0	N15 33.1	303 50.4	S17 57.6	Vega	80 37.6	N38 48.1
19	196 37.6	57 39.3	17.3	107 11.9	07.6	53 41.0	33.0	318 53.0	57.5	Zuben'ubi	137 03.6	S16 06.3
20	211 40.1	72 39.8	16.4	122 12.6	07.6	68 43.0	32.9	333 55.6	57.5		**SHA**	**Mer. Pass.**
21	226 42.6	87 40.4 ..	15.6	137 13.2 ..	07.7	83 45.1 ..	32.7	348 58.2 ..	57.5		° ′	h m
22	241 45.0	102 41.0	14.8	152 13.8	07.7	98 47.1	32.6	4 00.8	57.5	Venus	222 24.8	15 10
23	256 47.5	117 41.6	14.0	167 14.4	07.7	113 49.1	32.4	19 03.4	57.4	Mars	271 53.9	11 52
Mer. Pass.	h m 5 59.6	v 0.5 d 0.8		v 0.6 d 0.0		v 2.0 d 0.1		v 2.6 d 0.0		Jupiter	217 21.9	15 29
										Saturn	122 08.9	21 48

UT	SUN GHA	SUN Dec	MOON GHA	MOON v	MOON Dec	MOON d	MOON HP
d h	° ′	° ′	° ′	′	° ′	′	′
21 00	179 35.7	N23 26.0	126 11.7	13.6	N11 00.0	7.9	54.8
01	194 35.6	26.0	140 44.3	13.6	10 52.1	7.8	54.8
02	209 35.5	26.0	155 16.9	13.7	10 44.3	7.9	54.8
03	224 35.3	. . 26.0	169 49.6	13.7	10 36.4	8.0	54.8
04	239 35.2	26.0	184 22.3	13.8	10 28.4	8.0	54.8
05	254 35.1	26.0	198 55.1	13.8	10 20.4	8.0	54.8
S 06	269 34.9	N23 26.0	213 27.9	13.9	N10 12.4	8.0	54.7
U 07	284 34.8	26.0	228 00.8	13.9	10 04.4	8.2	54.7
N 08	299 34.6	26.0	242 33.7	13.9	9 56.2	8.1	54.7
D 09	314 34.5	. . 26.1	257 06.6	14.0	9 48.1	8.2	54.7
A 10	329 34.4	26.1	271 39.6	14.0	9 39.9	8.2	54.7
Y 11	344 34.2	26.1	286 12.6	14.1	9 31.7	8.2	54.7
12	359 34.1	N23 26.1	300 45.7	14.1	N 9 23.5	8.3	54.7
13	14 34.0	26.1	315 18.8	14.1	9 15.2	8.3	54.6
14	29 33.8	26.1	329 51.9	14.2	9 06.9	8.4	54.6
15	44 33.7	. . 26.1	344 25.1	14.3	8 58.5	8.4	54.6
16	59 33.6	26.1	358 58.4	14.2	8 50.1	8.4	54.6
17	74 33.4	26.1	13 31.6	14.3	8 41.7	8.5	54.6
18	89 33.3	N23 26.1	28 04.9	14.4	N 8 33.2	8.4	54.6
19	104 33.1	26.1	42 38.3	14.4	8 24.8	8.6	54.6
20	119 33.0	26.1	57 11.7	14.4	8 16.2	8.5	54.5
21	134 32.9	. . 26.1	71 45.1	14.4	8 07.7	8.6	54.5
22	149 32.7	26.1	86 18.5	14.5	7 59.1	8.6	54.5
23	164 32.6	26.1	100 52.0	14.5	7 50.5	8.6	54.5
22 00	179 32.5	N23 26.1	115 25.6	14.5	N 7 41.9	8.7	54.5
01	194 32.3	26.0	129 59.1	14.6	7 33.2	8.7	54.5
02	209 32.2	26.0	144 32.7	14.6	7 24.5	8.7	54.5
03	224 32.1	. . 26.0	159 06.3	14.7	7 15.8	8.7	54.5
04	239 31.9	26.0	173 40.0	14.7	7 07.1	8.8	54.5
05	254 31.8	26.0	188 13.7	14.7	6 58.3	8.8	54.4
M 06	269 31.6	N23 26.0	202 47.4	14.7	N 6 49.5	8.8	54.4
O 07	284 31.5	26.0	217 21.1	14.8	6 40.7	8.8	54.4
N 08	299 31.4	26.0	231 54.9	14.8	6 31.9	8.9	54.4
D 09	314 31.2	. . 26.0	246 28.7	14.8	6 23.0	8.9	54.4
A 10	329 31.1	26.0	261 02.5	14.9	6 14.1	8.9	54.4
Y 11	344 31.0	26.0	275 36.4	14.9	6 05.2	8.9	54.4
12	359 30.8	N23 25.9	290 10.3	14.9	N 5 56.3	9.0	54.4
13	14 30.7	25.9	304 44.2	14.9	5 47.3	8.9	54.4
14	29 30.6	25.9	319 18.1	15.0	5 38.4	9.0	54.4
15	44 30.4	. . 25.9	333 52.1	15.0	5 29.4	9.0	54.4
16	59 30.3	25.9	348 26.1	15.0	5 20.4	9.0	54.4
17	74 30.2	25.9	3 00.1	15.0	5 11.4	9.1	54.3
18	89 30.0	N23 25.8	17 34.1	15.1	N 5 02.3	9.1	54.3
19	104 29.9	25.8	32 08.2	15.0	4 53.2	9.0	54.3
20	119 29.7	25.8	46 42.2	15.1	4 44.2	9.1	54.3
21	134 29.6	. . 25.8	61 16.3	15.1	4 35.1	9.1	54.3
22	149 29.5	25.8	75 50.4	15.2	4 26.0	9.2	54.3
23	164 29.3	25.7	90 24.6	15.1	4 16.8	9.1	54.3
23 00	179 29.2	N23 25.7	104 58.7	15.2	N 4 07.7	9.2	54.3
01	194 29.1	25.7	119 32.9	15.2	3 58.5	9.2	54.3
02	209 28.9	25.7	134 07.1	15.2	3 49.3	9.1	54.3
03	224 28.8	. . 25.7	148 41.3	15.2	3 40.2	9.2	54.3
04	239 28.7	25.6	163 15.5	15.2	3 31.0	9.3	54.3
05	254 28.5	25.6	177 49.7	15.2	3 21.7	9.2	54.3
T 06	269 28.4	N23 25.6	192 23.9	15.3	N 3 12.5	9.2	54.3
U 07	284 28.3	25.5	206 58.2	15.3	3 03.3	9.3	54.3
E 08	299 28.1	25.5	221 32.5	15.2	2 54.0	9.2	54.3
S 09	314 28.0	. . 25.5	236 06.7	15.3	2 44.8	9.3	54.3
D 10	329 27.8	25.5	250 41.0	15.3	2 35.5	9.3	54.3
A 11	344 27.7	25.4	265 15.3	15.3	2 26.2	9.2	54.3
Y 12	359 27.6	N23 25.4	279 49.6	15.4	N 2 17.0	9.3	54.3
13	14 27.4	25.4	294 24.0	15.3	2 07.7	9.3	54.3
14	29 27.3	25.3	308 58.3	15.3	1 58.4	9.3	54.3
15	44 27.2	. . 25.3	323 32.6	15.3	1 49.1	9.4	54.3
16	59 27.0	25.3	338 06.9	15.4	1 39.7	9.3	54.3
17	74 26.9	25.2	352 41.3	15.3	1 30.4	9.3	54.3
18	89 26.8	N23 25.2	7 15.6	15.4	N 1 21.1	9.3	54.3
19	104 26.6	25.2	21 50.0	15.3	1 11.8	9.4	54.3
20	119 26.5	25.1	36 24.3	15.4	1 02.4	9.3	54.3
21	134 26.4	. . 25.1	50 58.7	15.4	0 53.1	9.4	54.3
22	149 26.2	25.1	65 33.1	15.3	0 43.7	9.3	54.3
23	164 26.1	25.0	80 07.4	15.4	N 0 34.4	9.4	54.3
SD	15.8	d 0.0	SD 14.9		14.8		14.8

Moonrise / Twilight

Lat.	Twilight Naut.	Twilight Civil	Sunrise	Moonrise 21	22	23	24
°	h m	h m	h m	h m	h m	h m	h m
N 72	☐	☐	☐	07 39	09 16	10 49	12 22
N 70	☐	☐	☐	07 56	09 25	10 53	12 20
68	☐	☐	☐	08 09	09 33	10 56	12 18
66	☐	☐	☐	08 19	09 39	10 58	12 17
64	////	////	01 31	08 28	09 44	11 00	12 15
62	////	////	02 09	08 35	09 49	11 01	12 14
60	////	00 49	02 36	08 42	09 53	11 03	12 13
N 58	////	01 41	02 56	08 48	09 56	11 04	12 12
56	////	02 11	03 13	08 53	09 59	11 05	12 12
54	00 45	02 33	03 28	08 57	10 02	11 06	12 11
52	01 32	02 51	03 40	09 01	10 04	11 07	12 10
50	02 00	03 06	03 51	09 05	10 07	11 08	12 10
45	02 46	03 36	04 13	09 13	10 12	11 10	12 08
N 40	03 17	03 59	04 31	09 19	10 16	11 12	12 07
35	03 40	04 17	04 47	09 25	10 19	11 13	12 07
30	03 59	04 32	05 00	09 30	10 23	11 14	12 06
20	04 28	04 57	05 22	09 39	10 28	11 16	12 04
N 10	04 50	05 18	05 41	09 46	10 33	11 18	12 03
0	05 09	05 36	05 58	09 54	10 37	11 20	12 02
S 10	05 27	05 53	06 16	10 01	10 42	11 22	12 01
20	05 43	06 10	06 34	10 08	10 47	11 24	12 00
30	05 59	06 29	06 56	10 17	10 52	11 26	11 59
35	06 08	06 40	07 08	10 22	10 55	11 27	11 58
40	06 17	06 52	07 22	10 27	10 59	11 28	11 57
45	06 28	07 05	07 39	10 34	11 03	11 30	11 56
S 50	06 40	07 21	08 00	10 42	11 07	11 32	11 55
52	06 45	07 29	08 10	10 45	11 10	11 33	11 55
54	06 51	07 37	08 21	10 49	11 12	11 34	11 54
56	06 57	07 46	08 33	10 53	11 15	11 35	11 54
58	07 04	07 56	08 48	10 58	11 18	11 36	11 53
S 60	07 11	08 08	09 06	11 04	11 21	11 37	11 52

Lat.	Sunset	Twilight Civil	Twilight Naut.	Moonset 21	22	23	24
°	h m	h m	h m	h m	h m	h m	h m
N 72	☐	☐	☐	{ 00 01 / 23 55 }	23 50	23 45	23 40
N 70	☐	☐	☐	23 44	23 45	23 45	23 45
68	☐	☐	☐	23 35	23 40	23 44	23 48
66	☐	☐	☐	23 28	23 36	23 44	23 52
64	22 32	////	////	23 21	23 33	23 44	23 54
62	21 54	////	////	23 16	23 30	23 43	23 57
60	21 28	23 14	////	23 11	23 28	23 43	23 59
N 58	21 07	22 23	////	23 07	23 25	23 43	24 00
56	20 51	21 53	////	23 03	23 24	23 43	24 02
54	20 36	21 31	23 18	23 00	23 22	23 43	24 03
52	20 24	21 13	22 31	22 56	23 20	23 42	24 05
50	20 13	20 58	22 03	22 54	23 19	23 42	24 06
45	19 50	20 28	21 18	22 47	23 15	23 42	24 09
N 40	19 32	20 05	20 47	22 42	23 13	23 42	24 11
35	19 17	19 47	20 24	22 38	23 10	23 42	24 13
30	19 04	19 32	20 05	22 34	23 08	23 41	24 15
20	18 42	19 07	19 36	22 27	23 04	23 41	24 18
N 10	18 23	18 46	19 13	22 21	23 01	23 41	24 20
0	18 06	18 28	18 54	22 15	22 58	23 40	24 23
S 10	17 48	18 11	18 37	22 09	22 55	23 40	24 25
20	17 30	17 54	18 21	22 03	22 51	23 40	24 28
30	17 08	17 35	18 05	21 56	22 48	23 39	24 31
35	16 56	17 24	17 56	21 51	22 45	23 39	24 32
40	16 42	17 12	17 46	21 47	22 43	23 39	24 34
45	16 25	16 59	17 36	21 41	22 40	23 38	24 37
S 50	16 04	16 43	17 24	21 35	22 36	23 38	24 39
52	15 54	16 35	17 19	21 32	22 35	23 38	24 40
54	15 43	16 27	17 13	21 28	22 33	23 37	24 42
56	15 30	16 18	17 07	21 24	22 31	23 37	24 43
58	15 16	16 08	17 00	21 20	22 29	23 37	24 45
S 60	14 58	15 56	16 53	21 16	22 26	23 36	24 47

SUN / MOON

Day	SUN Eqn. of Time 00h	SUN Eqn. of Time 12h	SUN Mer. Pass.	MOON Mer. Pass. Upper	MOON Mer. Pass. Lower	Age	Phase
d	m s	m s	h m	h m	h m	d	%
21	01 37	01 43	12 02	16 04	03 42	05	23
22	01 50	01 56	12 02	16 48	04 26	06	32
23	02 03	02 09	12 02	17 30	05 09	07	41

UT	ARIES	VENUS −4.6		MARS +1.5		JUPITER −1.8		SATURN +0.2		STARS		
	GHA	GHA	Dec	GHA	Dec	GHA	Dec	GHA	Dec	Name	SHA	Dec
d h	° ′	° ′	° ′	° ′	° ′	° ′	° ′	° ′	° ′		° ′	° ′
24 00	271 50.0	132 42.1	N17 13.2	182 15.0	N24 07.7	128 51.2	N15 32.3	34 06.1	S17 57.4	Acamar	315 17.6	S40 14.5
01	286 52.4	147 42.7	12.3	197 15.6	07.8	143 53.2	32.1	49 08.7	57.4	Achernar	335 26.1	S57 09.3
02	301 54.9	162 43.3	11.5	212 16.2	07.8	158 55.2	32.0	64 11.3	57.4	Acrux	173 07.5	S63 11.4
03	316 57.4	177 43.9 ..	10.7	227 16.9 ..	07.8	173 57.2 ..	31.9	79 13.9 ..	57.4	Adhara	255 11.8	S28 59.8
04	331 59.8	192 44.5	09.9	242 17.5	07.8	188 59.3	31.7	94 16.5	57.3	Aldebaran	290 48.1	N16 32.2
05	347 02.3	207 45.0	09.1	257 18.1	07.9	204 01.3	31.6	109 19.1	57.3			
W 06	2 04.8	222 45.6	N17 08.2	272 18.7	N24 07.9	219 03.3	N15 31.4	124 21.7	S17 57.3	Alioth	166 19.5	N55 52.9
E 07	17 07.2	237 46.2	07.4	287 19.3	07.9	234 05.4	31.3	139 24.3	57.3	Alkaid	152 57.7	N49 14.5
D 08	32 09.7	252 46.8	06.6	302 19.9	07.9	249 07.4	31.1	154 26.9	57.2	Al Na'ir	27 41.8	S46 52.8
N 09	47 12.1	267 47.4 ..	05.8	317 20.6 ..	07.9	264 09.4 ..	31.0	169 29.5 ..	57.2	Alnilam	275 45.3	S 1 11.7
E 10	62 14.6	282 48.0	05.0	332 21.2	08.0	279 11.4	30.9	184 32.1	57.2	Alphard	217 55.0	S 8 43.7
S 11	77 17.1	297 48.6	04.1	347 21.8	08.0	294 13.5	30.7	199 34.8	57.2			
D 12	92 19.5	312 49.2	N17 03.3	2 22.4	N24 08.0	309 15.5	N15 30.6	214 37.4	S17 57.2	Alphecca	126 09.6	N26 40.0
A 13	107 22.0	327 49.8	02.5	17 23.0	08.0	324 17.5	30.4	229 40.0	57.1	Alpheratz	357 42.0	N29 10.4
Y 14	122 24.5	342 50.4	01.7	32 23.6	08.1	339 19.5	30.3	244 42.6	57.1	Altair	62 06.6	N 8 54.7
15	137 26.9	357 51.0 ..	00.9	47 24.2 ..	08.1	354 21.6 ..	30.2	259 45.2 ..	57.1	Ankaa	353 14.4	S42 13.1
16	152 29.4	12 51.6	17 00.0	62 24.9	08.1	9 23.6	30.0	274 47.8	57.1	Antares	112 24.2	S26 27.8
17	167 31.9	27 52.2	16 59.2	77 25.5	08.1	24 25.6	29.9	289 50.4	57.0			
18	182 34.3	42 52.8	N16 58.4	92 26.1	N24 08.1	39 27.7	N15 29.7	304 53.0	S17 57.0	Arcturus	145 54.3	N19 06.3
19	197 36.8	57 53.4	57.6	107 26.7	08.1	54 29.7	29.6	319 55.6	57.0	Atria	107 24.2	S69 03.2
20	212 39.3	72 54.0	56.7	122 27.3	08.2	69 31.7	29.4	334 58.2	57.0	Avior	234 17.9	S59 33.9
21	227 41.7	87 54.7 ..	55.9	137 27.9 ..	08.2	84 33.7 ..	29.3	350 00.8 ..	57.0	Bellatrix	278 30.9	N 6 21.6
22	242 44.2	102 55.3	55.1	152 28.6	08.2	99 35.8	29.2	5 03.4	56.9	Betelgeuse	271 00.2	N 7 24.4
23	257 46.6	117 55.9	54.3	167 29.2	08.2	114 37.8	29.0	20 06.1	56.9			
25 00	272 49.1	132 56.5	N16 53.4	182 29.8	N24 08.2	129 39.8	N15 28.9	35 08.7	S17 56.9	Canopus	263 56.1	S52 42.4
01	287 51.6	147 57.1	52.6	197 30.4	08.2	144 41.8	28.7	50 11.3	56.9	Capella	280 32.9	N46 00.5
02	302 54.0	162 57.8	51.8	212 31.0	08.3	159 43.9	28.6	65 13.9	56.8	Deneb	49 30.1	N45 20.2
03	317 56.5	177 58.4 ..	51.0	227 31.7 ..	08.3	174 45.9 ..	28.4	80 16.5 ..	56.8	Denebola	182 32.3	N14 29.2
04	332 59.0	192 59.0	50.1	242 32.3	08.3	189 47.9	28.3	95 19.1	56.8	Diphda	348 54.6	S17 54.0
05	348 01.4	207 59.6	49.3	257 32.9	08.3	204 49.9	28.1	110 21.7	56.8			
T 06	3 03.9	223 00.3	N16 48.5	272 33.5	N24 08.3	219 52.0	N15 28.0	125 24.3	S17 56.8	Dubhe	193 50.4	N61 40.3
H 07	18 06.4	238 00.9	47.7	287 34.1	08.3	234 54.0	27.9	140 26.9	56.7	Elnath	278 11.3	N28 37.0
U 08	33 08.8	253 01.5	46.8	302 34.7	08.3	249 56.0	27.7	155 29.5	56.7	Eltanin	90 45.0	N51 29.4
R 09	48 11.3	268 02.2 ..	46.0	317 35.4 ..	08.4	264 58.0 ..	27.6	170 32.1 ..	56.7	Enif	33 45.6	N 9 56.9
S 10	63 13.7	283 02.8	45.2	332 36.0	08.4	280 00.1	27.4	185 34.7	56.7	Fomalhaut	15 22.4	S29 32.2
11	78 16.2	298 03.5	44.4	347 36.6	08.4	295 02.1	27.3	200 37.3	56.6			
D 12	93 18.7	313 04.1	N16 43.5	2 37.2	N24 08.4	310 04.1	N15 27.1	215 39.9	S17 56.6	Gacrux	171 59.2	S57 12.2
A 13	108 21.1	328 04.7	42.7	17 37.8	08.4	325 06.1	27.0	230 42.5	56.6	Gienah	175 50.9	S17 37.8
Y 14	123 23.6	343 05.4	41.9	32 38.4	08.4	340 08.2	26.9	245 45.2	56.6	Hadar	148 45.5	S60 27.0
15	138 26.1	358 06.0 ..	41.1	47 39.1 ..	08.4	355 10.2 ..	26.7	260 47.8 ..	56.6	Hamal	327 59.3	N23 31.9
16	153 28.5	13 06.7	40.2	62 39.7	08.4	10 12.2	26.6	275 50.4	56.5	Kaus Aust.	83 41.6	S34 22.4
17	168 31.0	28 07.3	39.4	77 40.3	08.4	25 14.2	26.4	290 53.0	56.5			
18	183 33.5	43 08.0	N16 38.6	92 40.9	N24 08.5	40 16.3	N15 26.3	305 55.6	S17 56.5	Kochab	137 19.5	N74 05.9
19	198 35.9	58 08.7	37.8	107 41.5	08.5	55 18.3	26.1	320 58.2	56.5	Markab	13 36.8	N15 17.3
20	213 38.4	73 09.3	36.9	122 42.2	08.5	70 20.3	26.0	336 00.8	56.5	Menkar	314 13.8	N 4 08.9
21	228 40.9	88 10.0 ..	36.1	137 42.8 ..	08.5	85 22.3 ..	25.8	351 03.4 ..	56.4	Menkent	148 05.7	S36 26.8
22	243 43.3	103 10.6	35.3	152 43.4	08.5	100 24.4	25.7	6 06.0	56.4	Miaplacidus	221 39.9	S69 47.2
23	258 45.8	118 11.3	34.4	167 44.0	08.5	115 26.4	25.6	21 08.6	56.4			
26 00	273 48.2	133 12.0	N16 33.6	182 44.6	N24 08.5	130 28.4	N15 25.4	36 11.2	S17 56.4	Mirfak	308 38.7	N49 54.6
01	288 50.7	148 12.6	32.8	197 45.2	08.5	145 30.4	25.3	51 13.8	56.3	Nunki	75 56.3	S26 16.4
02	303 53.2	163 13.3	32.0	212 45.9	08.5	160 32.5	25.1	66 16.4	56.3	Peacock	53 16.7	S56 40.8
03	318 55.6	178 14.0 ..	31.1	227 46.5 ..	08.5	175 34.5 ..	25.0	81 19.0 ..	56.3	Pollux	243 26.4	N27 59.2
04	333 58.1	193 14.6	30.3	242 47.1	08.5	190 36.5	24.8	96 21.6	56.3	Procyon	244 58.6	N 5 10.9
05	349 00.6	208 15.3	29.5	257 47.7	08.5	205 38.5	24.7	111 24.2	56.3			
06	4 03.0	223 16.0	N16 28.6	272 48.3	N24 08.5	220 40.5	N15 24.5	126 26.8	S17 56.2	Rasalhague	96 04.8	N12 33.2
07	19 05.5	238 16.7	27.8	287 49.0	08.5	235 42.6	24.4	141 29.4	56.2	Regulus	207 42.3	N11 53.4
F 08	34 08.0	253 17.3	27.0	302 49.6	08.6	250 44.6	24.3	156 32.0	56.2	Rigel	281 11.1	S 8 11.2
R 09	49 10.4	268 18.0 ..	26.2	317 50.2 ..	08.6	265 46.6 ..	24.1	171 34.6 ..	56.2	Rigil Kent.	139 49.3	S60 54.0
I 10	64 12.9	283 18.7	25.3	332 50.8	08.6	280 48.6	24.0	186 37.2	56.2	Sabik	102 10.6	S15 44.4
D 11	79 15.4	298 19.4	24.5	347 51.4	08.6	295 50.7	23.8	201 39.8	56.1			
A 12	94 17.8	313 20.1	N16 23.7	2 52.1	N24 08.6	310 52.7	N15 23.7	216 42.4	S17 56.1	Schedar	349 38.9	N56 37.0
Y 13	109 20.3	328 20.8	22.8	17 52.7	08.6	325 54.7	23.5	231 45.1	56.1	Shaula	96 19.6	S37 06.7
14	124 22.7	343 21.5	22.0	32 53.3	08.6	340 56.7	23.4	246 47.7	56.1	Sirius	258 32.9	S16 44.5
15	139 25.2	358 22.2 ..	21.2	47 53.9 ..	08.6	355 58.7 ..	23.2	261 50.3 ..	56.1	Spica	158 29.7	S11 14.5
16	154 27.7	13 22.8	20.4	62 54.5	08.6	11 00.8	23.1	276 52.9	56.0	Suhail	222 51.7	S43 30.0
17	169 30.1	28 23.5	19.5	77 55.2	08.6	26 02.8	22.9	291 55.5	56.0			
18	184 32.6	43 24.2	N16 18.7	92 55.8	N24 08.6	41 04.8	N15 22.8	306 58.1	S17 56.0	Vega	80 37.6	N38 48.1
19	199 35.1	58 24.9	17.9	107 56.4	08.6	56 06.8	22.7	322 00.7	56.0	Zuben'ubi	137 03.7	S16 06.3
20	214 37.5	73 25.6	17.0	122 57.0	08.6	71 08.8	22.4	337 03.3	55.9		SHA	Mer.Pass.
21	229 40.0	88 26.4 ..	16.2	137 57.6 ..	08.6	86 10.9 ..	22.4	352 05.9 ..	55.9		° ′	h m
22	244 42.5	103 27.1	15.4	152 58.3	08.6	101 12.9	22.2	7 08.5	55.9	Venus	220 07.4	15 08
23	259 44.9	118 27.8	14.5	167 58.9	08.6	116 14.9	22.1	22 11.1	55.9	Mars	269 40.7	11 50
	h m									Jupiter	216 50.7	15 19
Mer. Pass. 5 47.8		v 0.6	d 0.8	v 0.6	d 0.0	v 2.0	d 0.1	v 2.6	d 0.0	Saturn	122 19.6	21 36

UT	SUN GHA	SUN Dec	MOON GHA	v	MOON Dec	d	HP
d h	° ′	° ′	° ′	′	° ′	′	′
24 00	179 26.0	N23 25.0	94 41.8	15.3	N 0 25.0	9.3	54.3
01	194 25.8	24.9	109 16.1	15.4	0 15.7	9.4	54.3
02	209 25.7	24.9	123 50.5	15.3	N 0 06.3	9.3	54.3
03	224 25.6 ..	24.9	138 24.8	15.4	S 0 03.0	9.4	54.3
04	239 25.4	24.8	152 59.2	15.3	0 12.4	9.3	54.3
05	254 25.3	24.8	167 33.5	15.4	0 21.7	9.4	54.3
W 06	269 25.2	N23 24.7	182 07.9	15.3	S 0 31.1	9.3	54.3
E 07	284 25.0	24.7	196 42.2	15.4	0 40.4	9.4	54.3
D 08	299 24.9	24.6	211 16.6	15.3	0 49.8	9.4	54.3
N 09	314 24.7 ..	24.6	225 50.9	15.3	0 59.2	9.3	54.3
E 10	329 24.6	24.5	240 25.2	15.3	1 08.5	9.4	54.3
S 11	344 24.5	24.5	254 59.5	15.3	1 17.9	9.3	54.3
D 12	359 24.3	N23 24.5	269 33.8	15.3	S 1 27.2	9.3	54.3
A 13	14 24.2	24.4	284 08.1	15.3	1 36.5	9.4	54.3
Y 14	29 24.1	24.4	298 42.4	15.3	1 45.9	9.3	54.3
15	44 23.9 ..	24.3	313 16.7	15.2	1 55.2	9.3	54.3
16	59 23.8	24.3	327 50.9	15.3	2 04.5	9.3	54.3
17	74 23.7	24.2	342 25.2	15.2	2 13.8	9.4	54.3
18	89 23.5	N23 24.2	356 59.4	15.2	S 2 23.2	9.3	54.4
19	104 23.4	24.1	11 33.6	15.2	2 32.5	9.3	54.4
20	119 23.3	24.0	26 07.8	15.2	2 41.8	9.3	54.4
21	134 23.1 ..	24.0	40 42.0	15.2	2 51.1	9.2	54.4
22	149 23.0	23.9	55 16.2	15.1	3 00.3	9.3	54.4
23	164 22.9	23.9	69 50.3	15.1	3 09.6	9.3	54.4
25 00	179 22.7	N23 23.8	84 24.4	15.3	S 3 18.9	9.2	54.4
01	194 22.6	23.8	98 58.6	15.0	3 28.1	9.3	54.4
02	209 22.5	23.7	113 32.6	15.1	3 37.4	9.2	54.4
03	224 22.3 ..	23.6	128 06.7	15.1	3 46.6	9.2	54.4
04	239 22.2	23.6	142 40.8	15.0	3 55.8	9.2	54.4
05	254 22.1	23.5	157 14.8	15.0	4 05.0	9.2	54.5
T 06	269 21.9	N23 23.5	171 48.8	15.0	S 4 14.2	9.2	54.5
H 07	284 21.8	23.4	186 22.8	15.0	4 23.4	9.2	54.5
U 08	299 21.7	23.3	200 56.8	14.9	4 32.6	9.1	54.5
R 09	314 21.5 ..	23.3	215 30.7	14.9	4 41.7	9.2	54.5
S 10	329 21.4	23.2	230 04.6	14.9	4 50.9	9.1	54.5
D 11	344 21.3	23.2	244 38.5	14.8	5 00.0	9.1	54.5
A 12	359 21.1	N23 23.1	259 12.3	14.9	S 5 09.1	9.1	54.5
Y 13	14 21.0	23.0	273 46.2	14.8	5 18.2	9.0	54.5
14	29 20.9	23.0	288 20.0	14.7	5 27.2	9.1	54.6
15	44 20.7 ..	22.9	302 53.7	14.8	5 36.3	9.0	54.6
16	59 20.6	22.8	317 27.5	14.7	5 45.3	9.1	54.6
17	74 20.5	22.8	332 01.2	14.7	5 54.4	9.0	54.6
18	89 20.3	N23 22.7	346 34.9	14.6	S 6 03.4	8.9	54.6
19	104 20.2	22.6	1 08.5	14.6	6 12.3	9.0	54.6
20	119 20.1	22.5	15 42.1	14.6	6 21.3	8.9	54.6
21	134 20.0 ..	22.5	30 15.7	14.5	6 30.2	8.9	54.7
22	149 19.8	22.4	44 49.2	14.6	6 39.1	8.9	54.7
23	164 19.7	22.3	59 22.8	14.4	6 48.0	8.9	54.7
26 00	179 19.6	N23 22.3	73 56.2	14.5	S 6 56.9	8.8	54.7
01	194 19.4	22.2	88 29.7	14.4	7 05.7	8.9	54.7
02	209 19.3	22.1	103 03.1	14.3	7 14.6	8.8	54.7
03	224 19.2 ..	22.0	117 36.4	14.3	7 23.4	8.7	54.8
04	239 19.0	22.0	132 09.7	14.3	7 32.1	8.8	54.8
05	254 18.9	21.9	146 43.0	14.3	7 40.9	8.7	54.8
F 06	269 18.8	N23 21.8	161 16.3	14.2	S 7 49.6	8.7	54.8
R 07	284 18.6	21.7	175 49.5	14.1	7 58.3	8.6	54.8
I 08	299 18.5	21.6	190 22.6	14.2	8 06.9	8.7	54.8
D 09	314 18.4 ..	21.6	204 55.8	14.0	8 15.6	8.6	54.9
A 10	329 18.2	21.5	219 28.8	14.1	8 24.2	8.5	54.9
Y 11	344 18.1	21.4	234 01.9	14.0	8 32.7	8.6	54.9
12	359 18.0	N23 21.3	248 34.9	13.9	S 8 41.3	8.5	54.9
13	14 17.8	21.2	263 07.8	13.9	8 49.8	8.5	54.9
14	29 17.7	21.1	277 40.7	13.9	8 58.3	8.4	55.0
15	44 17.6 ..	21.1	292 13.6	13.8	9 06.7	8.4	55.0
16	59 17.5	21.0	306 46.4	13.7	9 15.1	8.4	55.0
17	74 17.3	20.9	321 19.1	13.7	9 23.5	8.4	55.0
18	89 17.2	N23 20.8	335 51.8	13.7	S 9 31.9	8.3	55.0
19	104 17.1	20.7	350 24.5	13.6	9 40.2	8.2	55.1
20	119 16.9	20.6	4 57.1	13.6	9 48.4	8.3	55.1
21	134 16.8 ..	20.5	19 29.7	13.5	9 56.7	8.2	55.1
22	149 16.7	20.5	34 02.2	13.5	10 04.9	8.2	55.1
23	164 16.5	20.4	48 34.7	13.4	S10 13.1	8.1	55.1
SD	15.8	d 0.1	SD 14.8		14.9		15.0

Moonrise

Lat.	Twilight Naut.	Civil	Sunrise	24	25	26	27
°	h m	h m	h m	h m	h m	h m	h m
N 72	▢	▢	▢	12 22	13 56	15 33	17 15
N 70	▢	▢	▢	12 20	13 48	15 18	16 51
68	▢	▢	▢	12 18	13 41	15 06	16 33
66	▢	▢	▢	12 17	13 36	14 56	16 18
64	////	////	01 33	12 15	13 31	14 48	16 06
62	////	////	02 11	12 14	13 27	14 41	15 56
60	////	00 52	02 37	12 13	13 24	14 35	15 48
N 58	////	01 42	02 58	12 12	13 21	14 30	15 40
56	////	02 12	03 14	12 12	13 18	14 25	15 33
54	00 47	02 34	03 29	12 11	13 16	14 21	15 27
52	01 34	02 52	03 41	12 10	13 13	14 17	15 22
50	02 02	03 07	03 52	12 10	13 11	14 14	15 17
45	02 47	03 37	04 14	12 08	13 07	14 06	15 07
N 40	03 18	03 59	04 32	12 07	13 03	14 00	14 58
35	03 41	04 18	04 47	12 07	13 00	13 55	14 51
30	04 00	04 33	05 00	12 06	12 58	13 50	14 44
20	04 29	04 58	05 22	12 04	12 53	13 42	14 33
N 10	04 51	05 18	05 41	12 03	12 49	13 35	14 24
0	05 10	05 36	05 59	12 02	12 45	13 29	14 15
S 10	05 27	05 54	06 16	12 01	12 41	13 22	14 06
20	05 43	06 11	06 35	12 00	12 37	13 15	13 56
30	06 00	06 30	06 56	11 59	12 32	13 08	13 45
35	06 09	06 40	07 08	11 58	12 30	13 03	13 39
40	06 18	06 52	07 23	11 57	12 27	12 58	13 32
45	06 28	07 06	07 39	11 56	12 23	12 52	13 24
S 50	06 40	07 22	08 00	11 55	12 19	12 45	13 14
52	06 45	07 29	08 10	11 55	12 18	12 42	13 09
54	06 51	07 37	08 21	11 54	12 16	12 38	13 04
56	06 57	07 46	08 34	11 54	12 13	12 35	12 59
58	07 04	07 57	08 48	11 53	12 11	12 30	12 53
S 60	07 11	08 08	09 06	11 52	12 08	12 25	12 46

Moonset

Lat.	Sunset	Twilight Civil	Naut.	24	25	26	27
°	h m	h m	h m	h m	h m	h m	h m
N 72	▢	▢	▢	23 40	23 35	23 29	23 23
N 70	▢	▢	▢	23 45	23 45	23 46	23 48
68	▢	▢	▢	23 48	23 53	23 59	24 07
66	▢	▢	▢	23 52	24 00	00 00	00 10
64	22 32	////	////	23 54	24 05	00 05	00 19
62	21 54	////	////	23 57	24 11	00 11	00 27
60	21 28	23 13	////	23 59	24 15	00 15	00 33
N 58	21 07	22 23	////	24 00	00 00	00 19	00 39
56	20 51	21 53	////	24 02	00 02	00 22	00 45
54	20 36	21 31	23 17	24 03	00 03	00 25	00 49
52	20 24	21 13	22 31	24 05	00 05	00 28	00 54
50	20 13	20 58	22 03	24 06	00 06	00 31	00 58
45	19 51	20 28	21 18	24 09	00 09	00 36	01 06
N 40	19 33	20 06	20 47	24 11	00 11	00 41	01 13
35	19 18	19 47	20 24	24 13	00 13	00 45	01 20
30	19 05	19 32	20 06	24 15	00 15	00 49	01 25
20	18 43	19 07	19 37	24 18	00 18	00 55	01 34
N 10	18 24	18 47	19 14	24 20	00 20	01 01	01 43
0	18 06	18 29	18 55	24 23	00 23	01 06	01 51
S 10	17 49	18 12	18 38	24 25	00 25	01 11	02 00
20	17 30	17 54	18 22	24 28	00 28	01 17	02 07
30	17 09	17 36	18 05	24 31	00 31	01 23	02 16
35	16 57	17 25	17 57	24 32	00 32	01 27	02 22
40	16 43	17 13	17 47	24 34	00 34	01 31	02 28
45	16 26	17 00	17 37	24 37	00 37	01 35	02 35
S 50	16 05	16 44	17 25	24 39	00 39	01 41	02 44
52	15 55	16 36	17 20	24 40	00 40	01 44	02 48
54	15 44	16 28	17 14	24 42	00 42	01 47	02 53
56	15 31	16 19	17 08	24 43	00 43	01 50	02 58
58	15 17	16 09	17 01	24 45	00 45	01 54	03 03
S 60	14 59	15 57	16 54	24 47	00 47	01 58	03 09

Day	SUN Eqn. of Time 00h	12h	Mer. Pass.	MOON Mer. Pass. Upper	Lower	Age	Phase
d	m s	m s	h m	h m	h m	d	%
24	02 16	02 22	12 02	18 12	05 51	08	51
25	02 29	02 35	12 03	18 55	06 34	09	60
26	02 42	02 48	12 03	19 40	07 17	10	69

UT	ARIES GHA	VENUS −4.6 GHA	VENUS Dec	MARS +1.6 GHA	MARS Dec	JUPITER −1.8 GHA	JUPITER Dec	SATURN +0.2 GHA	SATURN Dec	Star Name	SHA	Dec
27 00	274 47.4	133 28.5	N16 13.7	182 59.5	N24 08.6	131 16.9	N15 21.9	37 13.7	S17 55.9	Acamar	315 17.6	S40 14.5
01	289 49.8	148 29.2	12.9	198 00.1	08.6	146 18.9	21.8	52 16.3	55.8	Achernar	335 26.1	S57 09.3
02	304 52.3	163 29.9	12.0	213 00.7	08.6	161 21.0	21.6	67 18.9	55.8	Acrux	173 07.5	S63 11.4
03	319 54.8	178 30.6	.. 11.2	228 01.4	.. 08.6	176 23.0	.. 21.5	82 21.5	.. 55.8	Adhara	255 11.8	S28 59.8
04	334 57.2	193 31.3	10.4	243 02.0	08.6	191 25.0	21.3	97 24.1	55.8	Aldebaran	290 48.1	N16 32.2
05	349 59.7	208 32.1	09.5	258 02.6	08.6	206 27.0	21.2	112 26.7	55.8			
06	5 02.2	223 32.8	N16 08.7	273 03.2	N24 08.6	221 29.0	N15 21.1	127 29.3	S17 55.7	Alioth	166 19.5	N55 52.9
07	20 04.6	238 33.5	07.9	288 03.9	08.6	236 31.1	20.9	142 31.9	55.7	Alkaid	152 57.7	N49 14.5
S 08	35 07.1	253 34.2	07.0	303 04.5	08.5	251 33.1	20.8	157 34.5	55.7	Al Na'ir	27 41.8	S46 52.8
A 09	50 09.6	268 35.0	.. 06.2	318 05.1	.. 08.5	266 35.1	.. 20.6	172 37.1	.. 55.7	Alnilam	275 45.3	S 1 11.7
T 10	65 12.0	283 35.7	05.4	333 05.7	08.5	281 37.1	20.5	187 39.7	55.7	Alphard	217 55.0	S 8 43.7
U 11	80 14.5	298 36.4	04.6	348 06.3	08.5	296 39.1	20.3	202 42.3	55.6			
R 12	95 17.0	313 37.2	N16 03.7	3 07.0	N24 08.5	311 41.2	N15 20.2	217 44.9	S17 55.6	Alphecca	126 09.6	N26 40.0
D 13	110 19.4	328 37.9	02.9	18 07.6	08.5	326 43.2	20.0	232 47.5	55.6	Alpheratz	357 42.0	N29 10.4
A 14	125 21.9	343 38.6	02.1	33 08.2	08.5	341 45.2	19.9	247 50.1	55.6	Altair	62 06.6	N 8 54.8
Y 15	140 24.3	358 39.4	.. 01.2	48 08.8	.. 08.5	356 47.2	.. 19.7	262 52.7	.. 55.6	Ankaa	353 14.4	S42 13.1
16	155 26.8	13 40.1	16 00.4	63 09.4	08.5	11 49.2	19.6	277 55.3	55.5	Antares	112 24.2	S26 27.8
17	170 29.3	28 40.9	15 59.6	78 10.1	08.5	26 51.3	19.4	292 57.9	55.5			
18	185 31.7	43 41.6	N15 58.7	93 10.7	N24 08.5	41 53.3	N15 19.3	308 00.5	S17 55.5	Arcturus	145 54.3	N19 06.3
19	200 34.2	58 42.3	57.9	108 11.3	08.5	56 55.3	19.1	323 03.1	55.5	Atria	107 24.2	S69 03.2
20	215 36.7	73 43.1	57.1	123 11.9	08.5	71 57.3	19.0	338 05.7	55.5	Avior	234 17.9	S59 33.9
21	230 39.1	88 43.8	.. 56.2	138 12.6	.. 08.5	86 59.3	.. 18.9	353 08.3	.. 55.4	Bellatrix	278 30.9	N 6 21.6
22	245 41.6	103 44.6	55.4	153 13.2	08.5	102 01.3	18.7	8 10.9	55.4	Betelgeuse	271 00.1	N 7 24.4
23	260 44.1	118 45.4	54.6	168 13.8	08.4	117 03.4	18.6	23 13.5	55.4			
28 00	275 46.5	133 46.1	N15 53.7	183 14.4	N24 08.4	132 05.4	N15 18.4	38 16.1	S17 55.4	Canopus	263 56.1	S52 42.4
01	290 49.0	148 46.9	52.9	198 15.0	08.4	147 07.4	18.3	53 18.7	55.4	Capella	280 32.9	N46 00.5
02	305 51.5	163 47.6	52.0	213 15.7	08.4	162 09.4	18.1	68 21.3	55.3	Deneb	49 30.1	N45 20.2
03	320 53.9	178 48.4	.. 51.2	228 16.3	.. 08.4	177 11.4	.. 18.0	83 23.9	.. 55.3	Denebola	182 32.3	N14 29.2
04	335 56.4	193 49.2	50.4	243 16.9	08.4	192 13.5	17.8	98 26.5	55.3	Diphda	348 54.6	S17 54.0
05	350 58.8	208 49.9	49.5	258 17.5	08.4	207 15.5	17.7	113 29.1	55.3			
06	6 01.3	223 50.7	N15 48.7	273 18.2	N24 08.4	222 17.5	N15 17.5	128 31.7	S17 55.3	Dubhe	193 50.4	N61 40.3
07	21 03.8	238 51.5	47.9	288 18.8	08.4	237 19.5	17.4	143 34.3	55.2	Elnath	278 11.2	N28 37.0
S 08	36 06.2	253 52.2	47.0	303 19.4	08.3	252 21.5	17.2	158 36.9	55.2	Eltanin	90 45.0	N51 29.5
U 09	51 08.7	268 53.0	.. 46.2	318 20.0	.. 08.3	267 23.5	.. 17.1	173 39.5	.. 55.2	Enif	33 45.5	N 9 56.9
N 10	66 11.2	283 53.8	45.4	333 20.7	08.3	282 25.6	16.9	188 42.1	55.2	Fomalhaut	15 22.4	S29 32.2
D 11	81 13.6	298 54.6	44.5	348 21.3	08.3	297 27.6	16.8	203 44.7	55.2			
A 12	96 16.1	313 55.4	N15 43.7	3 21.9	N24 08.3	312 29.6	N15 16.6	218 47.2	S17 55.1	Gacrux	171 59.2	S57 12.2
Y 13	111 18.6	328 56.1	42.9	18 22.5	08.3	327 31.6	16.5	233 49.8	55.1	Gienah	175 50.9	S17 37.8
14	126 21.0	343 56.9	42.0	33 23.2	08.3	342 33.6	16.3	248 52.4	55.1	Hadar	148 45.5	S60 27.0
15	141 23.5	358 57.7	.. 41.2	48 23.8	.. 08.2	357 35.6	.. 16.2	263 55.0	.. 55.1	Hamal	327 59.3	N23 31.9
16	156 25.9	13 58.5	40.4	63 24.4	08.2	12 37.6	16.1	278 57.6	55.1	Kaus Aust.	83 41.6	S34 22.4
17	171 28.4	28 59.3	39.5	78 25.0	08.2	27 39.7	15.9	294 00.2	55.0			
18	186 30.9	44 00.1	N15 38.7	93 25.6	N24 08.2	42 41.7	N15 15.8	309 02.8	S17 55.0	Kochab	137 19.6	N74 05.9
19	201 33.3	59 00.9	37.9	108 26.3	08.2	57 43.7	15.6	324 05.4	55.0	Markab	13 36.8	N15 17.3
20	216 35.8	74 01.7	37.0	123 26.9	08.2	72 45.7	15.5	339 08.0	55.0	Menkar	314 13.8	N 4 08.9
21	231 38.3	89 02.5	.. 36.2	138 27.5	.. 08.1	87 47.7	.. 15.3	354 10.6	.. 55.0	Menkent	148 05.7	S36 26.8
22	246 40.7	104 03.3	35.4	153 28.1	08.1	102 49.7	15.2	9 13.2	54.9	Miaplacidus	221 39.9	S69 47.2
23	261 43.2	119 04.1	34.5	168 28.8	08.1	117 51.8	15.0	24 15.8	54.9			
29 00	276 45.7	134 04.9	N15 33.7	183 29.4	N24 08.1	132 53.8	N15 14.9	39 18.4	S17 54.9	Mirfak	308 38.7	N49 54.6
01	291 48.1	149 05.7	32.8	198 30.0	08.1	147 55.8	14.7	54 21.0	54.9	Nunki	75 56.2	S26 16.4
02	306 50.6	164 06.5	32.0	213 30.6	08.0	162 57.8	14.6	69 23.6	54.9	Peacock	53 16.6	S56 40.8
03	321 53.1	179 07.3	.. 31.2	228 31.3	.. 08.0	177 59.8	.. 14.4	84 26.2	.. 54.9	Pollux	243 26.4	N27 59.2
04	336 55.5	194 08.1	30.3	243 31.9	08.0	193 01.8	14.3	99 28.8	54.8	Procyon	244 58.6	N 5 10.9
05	351 58.0	209 09.0	29.5	258 32.5	08.0	208 03.8	14.1	114 31.4	54.8			
06	7 00.4	224 09.8	N15 28.7	273 33.1	N24 08.0	223 05.9	N15 14.0	129 34.0	S17 54.8	Rasalhague	96 04.8	N12 33.2
07	22 02.9	239 10.6	27.8	288 33.8	07.9	238 07.9	13.8	144 36.6	54.8	Regulus	207 42.3	N11 53.4
08	37 05.4	254 11.4	27.0	303 34.4	07.9	253 09.9	13.7	159 39.2	54.8	Rigel	281 11.1	S 8 11.2
M 09	52 07.8	269 12.2	.. 26.2	318 35.0	.. 07.9	268 11.9	.. 13.5	174 41.8	.. 54.7	Rigil Kent.	139 49.3	S60 54.0
O 10	67 10.3	284 13.1	25.3	333 35.6	07.9	283 13.9	13.4	189 44.3	54.7	Sabik	102 10.6	S15 44.4
N 11	82 12.8	299 13.9	24.5	348 36.3	07.9	298 15.9	13.2	204 46.9	54.7			
D 12	97 15.2	314 14.7	N15 23.6	3 36.9	N24 07.8	313 17.9	N15 13.1	219 49.5	S17 54.7	Schedar	349 38.8	N56 37.0
A 13	112 17.7	329 15.6	22.8	18 37.5	07.8	328 20.0	12.9	234 52.1	54.7	Shaula	96 19.6	S37 06.7
Y 14	127 20.2	344 16.4	22.0	33 38.1	07.8	343 22.0	12.8	249 54.7	54.6	Sirius	258 32.9	S16 44.5
15	142 22.6	359 17.2	.. 21.1	48 38.8	.. 07.8	358 24.0	.. 12.6	264 57.3	.. 54.6	Spica	158 29.7	S11 14.5
16	157 25.1	14 18.1	20.3	63 39.4	07.7	13 26.0	12.5	279 59.9	54.6	Suhail	222 51.7	S43 30.0
17	172 27.6	29 18.9	19.5	78 40.0	07.7	28 28.0	12.3	295 02.5	54.6			
18	187 30.0	44 19.7	N15 18.6	93 40.7	N24 07.7	43 30.0	N15 12.2	310 05.1	S17 54.6	Vega	80 37.6	N38 48.1
19	202 32.5	59 20.6	17.8	108 41.3	07.7	58 32.0	12.0	325 07.7	54.5	Zuben'ubi	137 03.7	S16 06.3
20	217 34.9	74 21.4	17.0	123 41.9	07.6	73 34.0	11.9	340 10.3	54.5		SHA	Mer. Pass.
21	232 37.4	89 22.3	.. 16.1	138 42.5	.. 07.6	88 36.1	.. 11.7	355 12.9	.. 54.5	Venus	217 56.9	15 04
22	247 39.9	104 23.1	15.3	153 43.2	07.6	103 38.1	11.6	10 15.5	54.5	Mars	267 27.9	11 47
23	262 42.3	119 24.0	14.4	168 43.8	07.6	118 40.1	11.4	25 18.1	54.5	Jupiter	216 18.9	15 10
Mer. Pass.	5 36.0	v 0.8	d 0.8	v 0.6	d 0.0	v 2.0	d 0.1	v 2.6	d 0.0	Saturn	122 29.6	21 23

UT	SUN GHA	SUN Dec	MOON GHA	v	MOON Dec	d	HP
27 00	179 16.4	N23 20.3	63 07.1	13.3	S10 21.2	8.1	55.2
01	194 16.3	20.2	77 39.4	13.3	10 29.3	8.0	55.2
02	209 16.1	20.1	92 11.7	13.3	10 37.3	8.0	55.2
03	224 16.0	.. 20.0	106 44.0	13.2	10 45.3	8.0	55.2
04	239 15.9	19.9	121 16.2	13.2	10 53.3	7.9	55.3
05	254 15.8	19.8	135 48.4	13.0	11 01.2	7.9	55.3
06	269 15.6	N23 19.7	150 20.4	13.1	S11 09.1	7.8	55.3
S 07	284 15.5	19.6	164 52.5	13.0	11 16.9	7.8	55.3
A 08	299 15.4	19.5	179 24.5	12.9	11 24.7	7.7	55.3
T 09	314 15.2	.. 19.4	193 56.4	12.9	11 32.4	7.7	55.4
U 10	329 15.1	19.3	208 28.3	12.8	11 40.1	7.7	55.4
R 11	344 15.0	19.2	223 00.1	12.7	11 47.8	7.6	55.4
D 12	359 14.9	N23 19.1	237 31.8	12.7	S11 55.4	7.6	55.4
A 13	14 14.7	19.0	252 03.5	12.7	12 03.0	7.5	55.5
Y 14	29 14.6	18.9	266 35.2	12.5	12 10.5	7.4	55.5
15	44 14.5	.. 18.8	281 06.7	12.6	12 17.9	7.4	55.5
16	59 14.3	18.7	295 38.3	12.4	12 25.3	7.4	55.5
17	74 14.2	18.6	310 09.7	12.4	12 32.7	7.3	55.6
18	89 14.1	N23 18.5	324 41.1	12.4	S12 40.0	7.3	55.6
19	104 13.9	18.4	339 12.5	12.2	12 47.3	7.2	55.6
20	119 13.8	18.3	353 43.7	12.2	12 54.5	7.1	55.6
21	134 13.7	.. 18.2	8 14.9	12.2	13 01.6	7.1	55.7
22	149 13.6	18.1	22 46.1	12.1	13 08.7	7.0	55.7
23	164 13.4	18.0	37 17.2	12.0	13 15.7	7.0	55.7
28 00	179 13.3	N23 17.9	51 48.2	12.0	S13 22.7	6.9	55.8
01	194 13.2	17.8	66 19.2	11.9	13 29.6	6.9	55.8
02	209 13.1	17.7	80 50.1	11.8	13 36.5	6.8	55.8
03	224 12.9	.. 17.6	95 20.9	11.8	13 43.3	6.7	55.8
04	239 12.8	17.4	109 51.7	11.7	13 50.0	6.7	55.9
05	254 12.7	17.3	124 22.4	11.7	13 56.7	6.6	55.9
06	269 12.5	N23 17.2	138 53.1	11.5	S14 03.3	6.6	55.9
S 07	284 12.4	17.1	153 23.6	11.6	14 09.9	6.5	55.9
U 08	299 12.3	17.0	167 54.2	11.4	14 16.4	6.4	56.0
N 09	314 12.2	.. 16.9	182 24.6	11.4	14 22.8	6.4	56.0
D 10	329 12.0	16.8	196 55.0	11.3	14 29.2	6.3	56.0
A 11	344 11.9	16.7	211 25.3	11.3	14 35.5	6.3	56.1
Y 12	359 11.8	N23 16.5	225 55.6	11.2	S14 41.8	6.1	56.1
13	14 11.6	16.4	240 25.8	11.1	14 47.9	6.1	56.1
14	29 11.5	16.3	254 55.9	11.1	14 54.0	6.1	56.1
15	44 11.4	.. 16.2	269 26.0	10.9	15 00.1	5.9	56.2
16	59 11.3	16.1	283 55.9	11.0	15 06.0	5.9	56.2
17	74 11.1	15.9	298 25.9	10.8	15 11.9	5.8	56.2
18	89 11.0	N23 15.8	312 55.7	10.8	S15 17.7	5.8	56.3
19	104 10.9	15.7	327 25.5	10.7	15 23.5	5.7	56.3
20	119 10.8	15.6	341 55.2	10.7	15 29.2	5.6	56.3
21	134 10.6	.. 15.5	356 24.9	10.6	15 34.8	5.5	56.3
22	149 10.5	15.3	10 54.5	10.5	15 40.3	5.5	56.4
23	164 10.4	15.2	25 24.0	10.5	15 45.8	5.3	56.4
29 00	179 10.3	N23 15.1	39 53.5	10.4	S15 51.1	5.3	56.4
01	194 10.1	15.0	54 22.9	10.3	15 56.4	5.3	56.5
02	209 10.0	14.8	68 52.2	10.3	16 01.7	5.1	56.5
03	224 09.9	.. 14.7	83 21.5	10.2	16 06.8	5.1	56.5
04	239 09.7	14.6	97 50.7	10.1	16 11.9	4.9	56.6
05	254 09.6	14.4	112 19.8	10.1	16 16.8	4.9	56.6
06	269 09.5	N23 14.3	126 48.9	10.0	S16 21.7	4.9	56.6
M 07	284 09.4	14.2	141 17.9	9.9	16 26.6	4.7	56.6
O 08	299 09.2	14.1	155 46.8	9.9	16 31.3	4.7	56.7
N 09	314 09.1	.. 13.9	170 15.7	9.8	16 36.0	4.5	56.7
D 10	329 09.0	13.8	184 44.5	9.7	16 40.5	4.5	56.7
A 11	344 08.9	13.7	199 13.2	9.7	16 45.0	4.4	56.8
Y 12	359 08.7	N23 13.5	213 41.9	9.6	S16 49.4	4.3	56.8
13	14 08.6	13.4	228 10.5	9.5	16 53.7	4.3	56.8
14	29 08.5	13.3	242 39.0	9.5	16 58.0	4.1	56.9
15	44 08.4	.. 13.1	257 07.5	9.4	17 02.1	4.0	56.9
16	59 08.2	13.0	271 35.9	9.4	17 06.1	4.0	56.9
17	74 08.1	12.9	286 04.3	9.3	17 10.1	3.9	57.0
18	89 08.0	N23 12.7	300 32.6	9.2	S17 14.0	3.7	57.0
19	104 07.9	12.6	315 00.8	9.1	17 17.7	3.7	57.0
20	119 07.7	12.4	329 28.9	9.2	17 21.4	3.6	57.0
21	134 07.6	.. 12.3	343 57.1	9.0	17 25.0	3.5	57.1
22	149 07.5	12.2	358 25.1	9.0	17 28.5	3.4	57.1
23	164 07.4	12.0	12 53.1	8.9	S17 31.9	3.3	57.1
SD	15.8	d 0.1	SD 15.1		15.3		15.5

Twilight / Moonrise

Lat.	Naut.	Civil	Sunrise	27	28	29	30
N 72	□	□	□	17 15	19 05	21 12	■
N 70	□	□	□	16 51	18 27	20 02	21 25
68	□	□	□	16 33	18 00	19 25	20 39
66	□	□	□	16 18	17 40	18 59	20 09
64	////	////	01 36	16 06	17 24	18 39	19 47
62	////	////	02 13	15 56	17 11	18 23	19 29
60	////	00 56	02 39	15 48	17 00	18 09	19 14
N 58	////	01 44	02 59	15 40	16 50	17 58	19 01
56	////	02 14	03 16	15 33	16 41	17 48	18 50
54	00 52	02 36	03 30	15 27	16 34	17 39	18 41
52	01 36	02 54	03 42	15 22	16 27	17 31	18 32
50	02 03	03 09	03 53	15 17	16 21	17 24	18 24
45	02 49	03 38	04 15	15 07	16 08	17 09	18 08
N 40	03 19	04 01	04 33	14 58	15 57	16 56	17 55
35	03 42	04 19	04 48	14 51	15 48	16 46	17 43
30	04 01	04 34	05 01	14 44	15 40	16 37	17 33
20	04 29	04 59	05 23	14 33	15 26	16 21	17 16
N 10	04 52	05 19	05 42	14 24	15 14	16 07	17 02
0	05 11	05 37	06 00	14 15	15 03	15 54	16 48
S 10	05 28	05 54	06 17	14 06	14 52	15 41	16 34
20	05 44	06 11	06 35	13 56	14 40	15 27	16 19
30	06 00	06 30	06 56	13 45	14 26	15 12	16 02
35	06 09	06 41	07 09	13 39	14 18	15 03	15 52
40	06 18	06 52	07 23	13 32	14 10	14 52	15 41
45	06 28	07 06	07 39	13 24	13 59	14 40	15 28
S 50	06 40	07 22	08 00	13 14	13 47	14 26	15 12
52	06 45	07 29	08 10	13 09	13 41	14 19	15 05
54	06 51	07 37	08 21	13 04	13 35	14 11	14 56
56	06 57	07 46	08 33	12 59	13 28	14 03	14 47
58	07 04	07 56	08 48	12 53	13 20	13 53	14 37
S 60	07 11	08 08	09 05	12 46	13 11	13 43	14 24

Sunset / Twilight / Moonset

Lat.	Sunset	Civil	Naut.	27	28	29	30
N 72	□	□	□	23 23	23 14	22 55	■
N 70	□	□	□	23 48	23 53	24 05	00 05
68	□	□	□	24 07	00 07	00 20	00 42
66	□	□	□	00 10	00 23	00 41	01 09
64	22 29	////	////	00 19	00 35	00 58	01 29
62	21 53	////	////	00 27	00 46	01 11	01 46
60	21 27	23 09	////	00 33	00 55	01 23	01 59
N 58	21 07	22 21	////	00 39	01 04	01 33	02 11
56	20 50	21 52	////	00 45	01 11	01 42	02 22
54	20 36	21 30	23 13	00 49	01 17	01 50	02 31
52	20 24	21 12	22 30	00 54	01 23	01 57	02 39
50	20 13	20 58	22 02	00 58	01 28	02 04	02 46
45	19 51	20 28	21 18	01 06	01 39	02 17	03 02
N 40	19 33	20 06	20 47	01 13	01 49	02 29	03 14
35	19 18	19 48	20 24	01 20	01 57	02 39	03 25
30	19 05	19 32	20 06	01 25	02 04	02 47	03 35
20	18 43	19 08	19 37	01 34	02 16	03 02	03 51
N 10	18 24	18 47	19 14	01 43	02 27	03 15	04 06
0	18 07	18 29	18 56	01 51	02 37	03 27	04 19
S 10	17 50	18 12	18 39	01 58	02 48	03 39	04 33
20	17 31	17 55	18 23	02 07	02 58	03 52	04 47
30	17 10	17 36	18 06	02 16	03 11	04 07	05 04
35	16 58	17 26	17 58	02 22	03 18	04 16	05 13
40	16 44	17 14	17 48	02 28	03 26	04 25	05 24
45	16 27	17 01	17 38	02 35	03 36	04 37	05 37
S 50	16 06	16 45	17 26	02 44	03 48	04 51	05 53
52	15 57	16 37	17 21	02 48	03 53	04 58	06 00
54	15 47	16 29	17 16	02 53	03 59	05 05	06 08
56	15 33	16 20	17 09	02 58	04 06	05 13	06 17
58	15 19	16 10	17 03	03 03	04 13	05 22	06 28
S 60	15 01	15 59	16 55	03 09	04 22	05 33	06 40

SUN and MOON

Day	SUN Eqn. of Time 00h	SUN Eqn. of Time 12h	SUN Mer. Pass.	MOON Mer. Pass. Upper	MOON Mer. Pass. Lower	Age	Phase
d	m s	m s	h m	h m	h m	d	%
27	02 54	03 00	12 03	20 26	08 02	11	78
28	03 07	03 13	12 03	21 15	08 50	12	86
29	03 19	03 25	12 03	22 07	09 40	13	92

UT	ARIES GHA	VENUS −4.6 GHA	Dec	MARS +1.6 GHA	Dec	JUPITER −1.8 GHA	Dec	SATURN +0.2 GHA	Dec	STARS Name	SHA	Dec
30 00	277 44.8	134 24.8	N15 13.6	183 44.4	N24 07.5	133 42.1	N15 11.3	40 20.7	S17 54.5	Acamar	315 17.6	S40 14.5
01	292 47.3	149 25.7	12.8	198 45.0	07.5	148 44.1	11.1	55 23.2	54.4	Achernar	335 26.0	S57 09.3
02	307 49.7	164 26.6	11.9	213 45.7	07.5	163 46.1	11.0	70 25.8	54.4	Acrux	173 07.5	S63 11.4
03	322 52.2	179 27.4 ..	11.1	228 46.3 ..	07.4	178 48.1 ..	10.8	85 28.4 ..	54.4	Adhara	255 11.8	S28 59.8
04	337 54.7	194 28.3	10.3	243 46.9	07.4	193 50.1	10.7	100 31.0	54.4	Aldebaran	290 48.1	N16 32.2
05	352 57.1	209 29.2	09.4	258 47.5	07.4	208 52.2	10.5	115 33.6	54.4			
T 06	7 59.6	224 30.0	N15 08.6	273 48.2	N24 07.4	223 54.2	N15 10.4	130 36.2	S17 54.3	Alioth	166 19.6	N55 52.9
U 07	23 02.1	239 30.9	07.8	288 48.8	07.3	238 56.2	10.2	145 38.8	54.3	Alkaid	152 57.7	N49 14.5
E 08	38 04.5	254 31.8	06.9	303 49.4	07.3	253 58.2	10.1	160 41.4	54.3	Al Na'ir	27 41.8	S46 52.8
S 09	53 07.0	269 32.6 ..	06.1	318 50.1 ..	07.3	269 00.2 ..	09.9	175 44.0 ..	54.3	Alnilam	275 45.3	S 1 11.7
D 10	68 09.4	284 33.5	05.2	333 50.7	07.2	284 02.2	09.8	190 46.6	54.3	Alphard	217 55.0	S 8 43.7
A 11	83 11.9	299 34.4	04.4	348 51.3	07.2	299 04.2	09.6	205 49.2	54.3			
Y 12	98 14.4	314 35.3	N15 03.6	3 51.9	N24 07.2	314 06.2	N15 09.5	220 51.8	S17 54.2	Alphecca	126 09.6	N26 40.0
13	113 16.8	329 36.2	02.7	18 52.6	07.1	329 08.2	09.3	235 54.3	54.2	Alpheratz	357 42.0	N29 10.4
14	128 19.3	344 37.0	01.9	33 53.2	07.1	344 10.3	09.2	250 56.9	54.2	Altair	62 06.6	N 8 54.8
15	143 21.8	359 37.9 ..	01.1	48 53.8 ..	07.1	359 12.3 ..	09.0	265 59.5 ..	54.2	Ankaa	353 14.4	S42 13.1
16	158 24.2	14 38.8	15 00.2	63 54.5	07.0	14 14.3	08.9	281 02.1	54.2	Antares	112 24.2	S26 27.8
17	173 26.7	29 39.7	14 59.4	78 55.1	07.0	29 16.3	08.7	296 04.7	54.1			
18	188 29.2	44 40.6	N14 58.6	93 55.7	N24 07.0	44 18.3	N15 08.6	311 07.3	S17 54.1	Arcturus	145 54.3	N19 06.3
19	203 31.6	59 41.5	57.7	108 56.3	06.9	59 20.3	08.4	326 09.9	54.1	Atria	107 24.2	S69 03.2
20	218 34.1	74 42.4	56.9	123 57.0	06.9	74 22.3	08.3	341 12.5	54.1	Avior	234 18.0	S59 33.8
21	233 36.6	89 43.3 ..	56.0	138 57.6 ..	06.9	89 24.3 ..	08.1	356 15.1 ..	54.1	Bellatrix	278 30.8	N 6 21.6
22	248 39.0	104 44.2	55.2	153 58.2	06.8	104 26.3	08.0	11 17.7	54.1	Betelgeuse	271 00.1	N 7 24.4
23	263 41.5	119 45.1	54.4	168 58.9	06.8	119 28.3	07.8	26 20.2	54.0			
1 00	278 43.9	134 46.0	N14 53.5	183 59.5	N24 06.8	134 30.4	N15 07.7	41 22.8	S17 54.0	Canopus	263 56.1	S52 42.4
01	293 46.4	149 46.9	52.7	199 00.1	06.7	149 32.4	07.5	56 25.4	54.0	Capella	280 32.8	N46 00.5
02	308 48.9	164 47.8	51.9	214 00.7	06.7	164 34.4	07.4	71 28.0	54.0	Deneb	49 30.1	N45 20.2
03	323 51.3	179 48.7 ..	51.0	229 01.4 ..	06.6	179 36.4 ..	07.2	86 30.6 ..	54.0	Denebola	182 32.3	N14 29.2
04	338 53.8	194 49.6	50.2	244 02.0	06.6	194 38.4	07.1	101 33.2	54.0	Diphda	348 54.5	S17 54.0
05	353 56.3	209 50.6	49.3	259 02.6	06.6	209 40.4	06.9	116 35.8	53.9			
W 06	8 58.7	224 51.5	N14 48.5	274 03.3	N24 06.5	224 42.4	N15 06.8	131 38.4	S17 53.9	Dubhe	193 50.5	N61 40.3
E 07	24 01.2	239 52.4	47.7	289 03.9	06.5	239 44.4	06.6	146 41.0	53.9	Elnath	278 11.2	N28 37.0
D 08	39 03.7	254 53.3	46.8	304 04.5	06.5	254 46.4	06.5	161 43.5	53.9	Eltanin	90 45.5	N51 29.5
N 09	54 06.1	269 54.2 ..	46.0	319 05.1 ..	06.4	269 48.4 ..	06.3	176 46.1 ..	53.9	Enif	33 45.5	N 9 56.9
E 10	69 08.6	284 55.2	45.2	334 05.8	06.4	284 50.4	06.2	191 48.7	53.8	Fomalhaut	15 22.3	S29 32.2
S 11	84 11.0	299 56.1	44.3	349 06.4	06.3	299 52.5	06.0	206 51.3	53.8			
D 12	99 13.5	314 57.0	N14 43.5	4 07.0	N24 06.3	314 54.5	N15 05.9	221 53.9	S17 53.8	Gacrux	171 59.2	S57 12.2
A 13	114 16.0	329 58.0	42.7	19 07.7	06.3	329 56.5	05.7	236 56.5	53.8	Gienah	175 50.9	S17 37.8
Y 14	129 18.4	344 58.9	41.8	34 08.3	06.2	344 58.5	05.6	251 59.1	53.8	Hadar	148 45.5	S60 27.0
15	144 20.9	359 59.8 ..	41.0	49 08.9 ..	06.2	0 00.5 ..	05.4	267 01.7 ..	53.8	Hamal	327 59.3	N23 31.9
16	159 23.4	15 00.8	40.1	64 09.6	06.1	15 02.5	05.3	282 04.2	53.7	Kaus Aust.	83 41.6	S34 22.4
17	174 25.8	30 01.7	39.3	79 10.2	06.1	30 04.5	05.1	297 06.8	53.7			
18	189 28.3	45 02.7	N14 38.5	94 10.8	N24 06.1	45 06.5	N15 05.0	312 09.4	S17 53.7	Kochab	137 19.6	N74 05.9
19	204 30.8	60 03.6	37.6	109 11.4	06.0	60 08.5	04.8	327 12.0	53.7	Markab	13 36.8	N15 17.3
20	219 33.2	75 04.6	36.8	124 12.1	06.0	75 10.5	04.7	342 14.6	53.7	Menkar	314 13.8	N 4 08.9
21	234 35.7	90 05.5 ..	36.0	139 12.7 ..	05.9	90 12.5 ..	04.5	357 17.2 ..	53.7	Menkent	148 05.7	S36 26.8
22	249 38.2	105 06.5	35.1	154 13.3	05.9	105 14.5	04.4	12 19.8	53.6	Miaplacidus	221 39.9	S69 47.2
23	264 40.6	120 07.4	34.3	169 14.0	05.8	120 16.5	04.2	27 22.3	53.6			
2 00	279 43.1	135 08.4	N14 33.5	184 14.6	N24 05.8	135 18.6	N15 04.1	42 24.9	S17 53.6	Mirfak	308 38.6	N49 54.6
01	294 45.5	150 09.3	32.6	199 15.2	05.7	150 20.6	03.9	57 27.5	53.6	Nunki	75 56.2	S26 16.4
02	309 48.0	165 10.3	31.8	214 15.9	05.7	165 22.6	03.7	72 30.1	53.6	Peacock	53 16.6	S56 40.8
03	324 50.5	180 11.3 ..	30.9	229 16.5 ..	05.7	180 24.6 ..	03.6	87 32.7 ..	53.6	Pollux	243 26.4	N27 59.2
04	339 52.9	195 12.2	30.1	244 17.1	05.6	195 26.6	03.4	102 35.3	53.5	Procyon	244 58.6	N 5 10.9
05	354 55.4	210 13.2	29.3	259 17.8	05.6	210 28.6	03.3	117 37.9	53.5			
T 06	9 57.9	225 14.2	N14 28.4	274 18.4	N24 05.5	225 30.6	N15 03.1	132 40.4	S17 53.5	Rasalhague	96 04.8	N12 33.2
H 07	25 00.3	240 15.2	27.6	289 19.0	05.5	240 32.6	03.0	147 43.0	53.5	Regulus	207 42.3	N11 53.4
U 08	40 02.8	255 16.1	26.8	304 19.7	05.4	255 34.6	02.8	162 45.6	53.5	Rigel	281 11.0	S 8 11.2
R 09	55 05.3	270 17.1 ..	25.9	319 20.3 ..	05.4	270 36.6 ..	02.7	177 48.2 ..	53.5	Rigil Kent.	139 49.4	S60 54.0
S 10	70 07.7	285 18.1	25.1	334 20.9	05.3	285 38.6	02.5	192 50.8	53.4	Sabik	102 10.6	S15 44.4
D 11	85 10.2	300 19.1	24.3	349 21.6	05.3	300 40.6	02.4	207 53.4	53.4			
A 12	100 12.7	315 20.0	N14 23.4	4 22.2	N24 05.2	315 42.6	N15 02.2	222 56.0	S17 53.4	Schedar	349 38.8	N56 37.0
Y 13	115 15.1	330 21.0	22.6	19 22.8	05.2	330 44.6	02.1	237 58.5	53.4	Shaula	96 19.6	S37 06.7
14	130 17.6	345 22.0	21.8	34 23.5	05.1	345 46.6	01.9	253 01.1	53.4	Sirius	258 32.8	S16 44.4
15	145 20.0	0 23.0 ..	20.9	49 24.1 ..	05.1	0 48.6 ..	01.8	268 03.7 ..	53.4	Spica	158 29.7	S11 14.5
16	160 22.5	15 24.0	20.1	64 24.7	05.0	15 50.7	01.6	283 06.3	53.3	Suhail	222 51.7	S43 30.0
17	175 25.0	30 25.0	19.3	79 25.3	05.0	30 52.7	01.5	298 08.9	53.3			
18	190 27.4	45 26.0	N14 18.4	94 26.0	N24 04.9	45 54.7	N15 01.3	313 11.5	S17 53.3	Vega	80 37.6	N38 48.1
19	205 29.9	60 27.0	17.6	109 26.6	04.9	60 56.7	01.2	328 14.0	53.3	Zuben'ubi	137 03.7	S16 06.3
20	220 32.4	75 28.0	16.7	124 27.2	04.8	75 58.7	01.0	343 16.6	53.3		SHA	Mer.Pass.
21	235 34.8	90 29.0 ..	15.9	139 27.9 ..	04.8	91 00.7 ..	00.8	358 19.2 ..	53.3	Venus	216 02.1	15 00
22	250 37.3	105 30.0	15.1	154 28.5	04.7	106 02.7	00.7	13 21.8	53.2	Mars	265 15.5	11 44
23	265 39.3	120 31.0	14.2	169 29.1	04.7	121 04.7	00.5	28 24.4	53.2	Jupiter	215 46.4	15 00
Mer. Pass.	h m 5 24.2	v 0.9	d 0.8	v 0.6	d 0.0	v 2.0	d 0.2	v 2.6	d 0.0	Saturn	122 38.9	21 11

UT	SUN GHA	SUN Dec	MOON GHA	v	MOON Dec	d	HP
d h	° ′	° ′	° ′	′	° ′	′	′
30 00	179 07.3	N23 11.9	27 21.0	8.9	S17 35.2	3.2	57.2
01	194 07.1	11.7	41 48.9	8.8	17 38.4	3.1	57.2
02	209 07.0	11.6	56 16.7	8.7	17 41.5	3.0	57.2
03	224 06.9	.. 11.4	70 44.4	8.7	17 44.5	2.9	57.3
04	239 06.8	11.3	85 12.1	8.6	17 47.4	2.9	57.3
05	254 06.6	11.2	99 39.7	8.6	17 50.3	2.7	57.3
06	269 06.5	N23 11.0	114 07.3	8.5	S17 53.0	2.6	57.3
07	284 06.4	10.9	128 34.8	8.5	17 55.6	2.5	57.4
08	299 06.3	10.7	143 02.3	8.4	17 58.1	2.4	57.4
09	314 06.1	.. 10.6	157 29.7	8.3	18 00.5	2.3	57.4
10	329 06.0	10.4	171 57.0	8.3	18 02.8	2.3	57.5
11	344 05.9	10.3	186 24.3	8.2	18 05.1	2.1	57.5
12	359 05.8	N23 10.1	200 51.5	8.2	S18 07.2	2.0	57.5
13	14 05.7	10.0	215 18.7	8.2	18 09.2	1.9	57.6
14	29 05.5	09.8	229 45.9	8.0	18 11.1	1.8	57.6
15	44 05.4	.. 09.7	244 12.9	8.1	18 12.9	1.6	57.6
16	59 05.3	09.5	258 40.0	8.0	18 14.5	1.6	57.7
17	74 05.2	09.4	273 07.0	7.9	18 16.1	1.5	57.7
18	89 05.0	N23 09.2	287 33.9	7.9	S18 17.6	1.4	57.7
19	104 04.9	09.0	302 00.8	7.8	18 19.0	1.2	57.7
20	119 04.8	08.9	316 27.6	7.8	18 20.2	1.2	57.8
21	134 04.7	.. 08.7	330 54.4	7.8	18 21.4	1.0	57.8
22	149 04.6	08.6	345 21.2	7.7	18 22.4	0.9	57.8
23	164 04.4	08.4	359 47.9	7.7	18 23.3	0.8	57.9
1 00	179 04.3	N23 08.3	14 14.6	7.6	S18 24.1	0.6	57.9
01	194 04.2	08.1	28 41.2	7.6	18 24.9	0.5	57.9
02	209 04.1	07.9	43 07.8	7.5	18 25.4	0.5	57.9
03	224 03.9	.. 07.8	57 34.3	7.5	18 25.9	0.4	58.0
04	239 03.8	07.5	72 00.8	7.5	18 26.3	0.3	58.0
05	254 03.7	07.5	86 27.3	7.4	18 26.6	0.1	58.0
06	269 03.6	N23 07.3	100 53.7	7.4	S18 26.7	0.1	58.1
07	284 03.5	07.1	115 20.1	7.3	18 26.8	0.1	58.1
08	299 03.3	07.0	129 46.4	7.3	18 26.7	0.2	58.1
09	314 03.2	.. 06.8	144 12.7	7.3	18 26.5	0.3	58.1
10	329 03.1	06.6	158 39.0	7.3	18 26.2	0.4	58.2
11	344 03.0	06.5	173 05.3	7.2	18 25.8	0.6	58.2
12	359 02.9	N23 06.3	187 31.5	7.2	S18 25.2	0.6	58.2
13	14 02.7	06.1	201 57.7	7.1	18 24.6	0.8	58.3
14	29 02.6	06.0	216 23.8	7.2	18 23.8	0.9	58.3
15	44 02.5	.. 05.8	230 50.0	7.1	18 22.9	1.0	58.3
16	59 02.4	05.6	245 16.1	7.0	18 21.9	1.1	58.3
17	74 02.3	05.5	259 42.1	7.1	18 20.8	1.2	58.4
18	89 02.1	N23 05.3	274 08.2	7.0	S18 19.6	1.3	58.4
19	104 02.0	05.1	288 34.2	7.0	18 18.3	1.5	58.4
20	119 01.9	04.9	303 00.2	7.0	18 16.8	1.6	58.4
21	134 01.8	.. 04.8	317 26.2	7.0	18 15.2	1.7	58.5
22	149 01.7	04.6	331 52.2	6.9	18 13.5	1.8	58.5
23	164 01.6	04.4	346 18.1	6.9	18 11.7	1.9	58.5
2 00	179 01.4	N23 04.2	0 44.0	6.9	S18 09.8	2.0	58.5
01	194 01.3	04.1	15 09.9	6.9	18 07.8	2.2	58.6
02	209 01.2	03.9	29 35.8	6.9	18 05.6	2.3	58.6
03	224 01.1	.. 03.7	44 01.7	6.8	18 03.3	2.3	58.6
04	239 01.0	03.5	58 27.5	6.9	18 01.0	2.6	58.6
05	254 00.8	03.4	72 53.4	6.8	17 58.4	2.6	58.7
06	269 00.7	N23 03.2	87 19.2	6.8	S17 55.8	2.7	58.7
07	284 00.6	03.0	101 45.0	6.8	17 53.1	2.9	58.7
08	299 00.5	02.8	116 10.8	6.8	17 50.2	2.9	58.7
09	314 00.4	.. 02.6	130 36.6	6.8	17 47.3	3.1	58.8
10	329 00.3	02.5	145 02.4	6.8	17 44.2	3.2	58.8
11	344 00.1	02.3	159 28.2	6.8	17 41.0	3.3	58.8
12	359 00.0	N23 02.1	173 54.0	6.8	S17 37.7	3.5	58.8
13	13 59.9	01.9	188 19.8	6.7	17 34.2	3.5	58.9
14	28 59.8	01.7	202 45.5	6.8	17 30.7	3.7	58.9
15	43 59.7	.. 01.5	217 11.3	6.8	17 27.0	3.7	58.9
16	58 59.5	01.3	231 37.1	6.7	17 23.3	3.9	58.9
17	73 59.4	01.2	246 02.8	6.8	17 19.4	4.0	58.9
18	88 59.3	N23 01.0	260 28.6	6.8	S17 15.4	4.2	59.0
19	103 59.2	00.8	274 54.4	6.7	17 11.2	4.2	59.0
20	118 59.1	00.6	289 20.1	6.8	17 07.0	4.3	59.0
21	133 59.0	.. 00.4	303 45.9	6.8	17 02.7	4.5	59.0
22	148 58.9	00.2	318 11.7	6.8	16 58.2	4.5	59.0
23	163 58.7	00.0	332 37.5	6.7	S16 53.7	4.7	59.1
	SD 15.8	d 0.2	SD 15.7		15.9		16.0

Days marked: TUESDAY (30), WEDNESDAY (1), THURSDAY (2).

Moonrise

Lat.	Twilight Naut.	Twilight Civil	Sunrise	Moonrise 30	1	2	3
°	h m	h m	h m	h m	h m	h m	h m
N 72	□	□	□	■	■	23 32	23 19
N 70	□	□	□	21 25	22 16	22 39	22 48
68	□	□	□	20 39	21 33	22 06	22 26
66	////	////	00 16	20 09	21 04	21 42	22 08
64	////	////	01 41	19 47	20 42	21 23	21 53
62	////	////	02 16	19 29	20 24	21 08	21 41
60	////	01 02	02 42	19 14	20 09	20 55	21 30
N 58	////	01 48	03 02	19 01	19 57	20 43	21 21
56	////	02 17	03 18	18 50	19 46	20 34	21 13
54	00 57	02 38	03 32	18 41	19 36	20 25	21 06
52	01 39	02 56	03 44	18 32	19 28	20 17	20 59
50	02 06	03 11	03 55	18 24	19 20	20 10	20 54
45	02 50	03 42	04 17	18 08	19 04	19 55	20 41
N 40	03 21	04 02	04 35	17 55	18 51	19 43	20 31
35	03 43	04 20	04 50	17 43	18 39	19 32	20 22
30	04 02	04 35	05 02	17 33	18 29	19 23	20 14
20	04 30	05 00	05 24	17 16	18 12	19 07	20 00
N 10	04 53	05 20	05 43	17 02	17 57	18 53	19 48
0	05 11	05 38	06 00	16 48	17 43	18 40	19 37
S 10	05 28	05 55	06 17	16 34	17 29	18 27	19 26
20	05 44	06 12	06 36	16 19	17 15	18 13	19 14
30	06 00	06 30	06 57	16 02	16 58	17 57	19 00
35	06 09	06 41	07 09	15 52	16 48	17 48	18 52
40	06 18	06 52	07 23	15 41	16 36	17 38	18 43
45	06 28	07 06	07 39	15 28	16 23	17 25	18 32
S 50	06 40	07 21	08 00	15 12	16 07	17 10	18 20
52	06 45	07 29	08 09	15 05	15 59	17 03	18 14
54	06 51	07 37	08 20	14 56	15 51	16 55	18 07
56	06 57	07 46	08 33	14 47	15 41	16 46	18 00
58	07 03	07 56	08 47	14 37	15 31	16 36	17 51
S 60	07 11	08 07	09 04	14 24	15 18	16 25	17 42

Moonset

Lat.	Sunset	Twilight Civil	Twilight Naut.	Moonset 30	1	2	3
°	h m	h m	h m	h m	h m	h m	h m
N 72	□	□	□	■	■	■	02 25
N 70	□	□	□	00 05	00 36	01 41	03 17
68	□	□	□	00 42	01 21	02 24	03 49
66	23 42	////	////	01 09	01 51	02 53	04 13
64	22 26	////	////	01 29	02 14	03 15	04 31
62	21 50	////	////	01 46	02 32	03 32	04 46
60	21 25	23 03	////	01 59	02 47	03 47	04 59
N 58	21 05	22 19	////	02 11	02 59	03 59	05 10
56	20 49	21 50	////	02 22	03 10	04 10	05 19
54	20 35	21 29	23 08	02 31	03 20	04 19	05 28
52	20 23	21 11	22 27	02 39	03 29	04 28	05 35
50	20 13	20 57	22 01	02 46	03 36	04 35	05 42
45	19 50	20 28	21 17	03 02	03 53	04 51	05 56
N 40	19 33	20 05	20 47	03 14	04 06	05 05	06 08
35	19 18	19 48	20 24	03 25	04 18	05 16	06 18
30	19 05	19 33	20 06	03 35	04 28	05 26	06 27
20	18 43	19 08	19 37	03 51	04 45	05 42	06 42
N 10	18 25	18 48	19 15	04 06	05 00	05 57	06 55
0	18 07	18 30	18 56	04 19	05 14	06 11	07 07
S 10	17 50	18 13	18 39	04 33	05 28	06 24	07 20
20	17 32	17 56	18 23	04 47	05 43	06 39	07 33
30	17 11	17 37	18 07	05 04	06 00	06 55	07 47
35	16 59	17 27	17 59	05 13	06 10	07 05	07 56
40	16 45	17 15	17 49	05 24	06 21	07 16	08 06
45	16 29	17 02	17 39	05 37	06 35	07 28	08 17
S 50	16 08	16 46	17 28	05 53	06 51	07 44	08 30
52	15 58	16 39	17 23	06 00	06 59	07 51	08 37
54	15 48	16 31	17 17	06 08	07 07	07 59	08 44
56	15 35	16 22	17 11	06 17	07 17	08 08	08 52
58	15 21	16 12	17 05	06 28	07 27	08 18	09 00
S 60	15 04	16 01	16 57	06 40	07 40	08 30	09 10

SUN / MOON

Day	SUN Eqn. of Time 00h	SUN Eqn. of Time 12h	SUN Mer. Pass.	MOON Mer. Pass. Upper	MOON Mer. Pass. Lower	Age	Phase
d	m s	m s	h m	h m	h m	d	%
30	03 31	03 37	12 04	23 01	10 33	14	97
1	03 43	03 48	12 04	23 57	11 29	15	99
2	03 54	04 00	12 04	24 54	12 25	16	100 ○

UT	ARIES	VENUS −4.7		MARS +1.6		JUPITER −1.8		SATURN +0.3		STARS		
	GHA	GHA	Dec	GHA	Dec	GHA	Dec	GHA	Dec	Name	SHA	Dec
d h	° ′	° ′	° ′	° ′	° ′	° ′	° ′	° ′	° ′		° ′	° ′
3 00	280 42.2	135 32.0	N14 13.4	184 29.8	N24 04.6	136 06.7	N15 00.4	43 27.0	S17 53.2	Acamar	315 17.6	S40 14.5
01	295 44.7	150 33.0	12.6	199 30.4	04.6	151 08.7	00.2	58 29.5	53.2	Achernar	335 26.0	S57 09.3
02	310 47.2	165 34.1	11.7	214 31.0	04.5	166 10.7	15 00.1	73 32.1	53.2	Acrux	173 07.6	S63 11.4
03	325 49.6	180 35.1 ..	10.9	229 31.7 ..	04.5	181 12.7	14 59.9	88 34.7 ..	53.2	Adhara	255 11.8	S28 59.8
04	340 52.1	195 36.1	10.1	244 32.3	04.4	196 14.7	59.8	103 37.3	53.1	Aldebaran	290 48.1	N16 32.2
05	355 54.5	210 37.1	09.2	259 33.0	04.3	211 16.7	59.6	118 39.9	53.1			
06	10 57.0	225 38.2	N14 08.4	274 33.6	N24 04.3	226 18.7	N14 59.5	133 42.5	S17 53.1	Alioth	166 19.6	N55 52.9
07	25 59.5	240 39.2	07.6	289 34.2	04.2	241 20.7	59.3	148 45.0	53.1	Alkaid	152 57.7	N49 14.5
08	41 01.9	255 40.2	06.7	304 34.9	04.2	256 22.7	59.2	163 47.6	53.1	Al Na'ir	27 41.8	S46 52.8
F 09	56 04.4	270 41.2 ..	05.9	319 35.5 ..	04.1	271 24.7 ..	59.0	178 50.2 ..	53.1	Alnilam	275 45.3	S 1 11.7
R 10	71 06.9	285 42.3	05.1	334 36.1	04.1	286 26.7	58.9	193 52.8	53.0	Alphard	217 55.0	S 8 43.7
I 11	86 09.3	300 43.3	04.2	349 36.8	04.0	301 28.7	58.7	208 55.4	53.0			
D 12	101 11.8	315 44.3	N14 03.4	4 37.4	N24 04.0	316 30.7	N14 58.5	223 57.9	S17 53.0	Alphecca	126 09.6	N26 40.1
A 13	116 14.3	330 45.4	02.6	19 38.0	03.9	331 32.7	58.4	239 00.5	53.0	Alpheratz	357 41.9	N29 10.4
Y 14	131 16.7	345 46.4	01.7	34 38.7	03.8	346 34.7	58.2	254 03.1	53.0	Altair	62 06.5	N 8 54.8
15	146 19.2	0 47.5 ..	00.9	49 39.3 ..	03.8	1 36.7 ..	58.1	269 05.7 ..	53.0	Ankaa	353 14.4	S42 13.1
16	161 21.7	15 48.5	14 00.1	64 39.9	03.7	16 38.8	57.9	284 08.3	53.0	Antares	112 24.2	S26 27.8
17	176 24.1	30 49.6	13 59.2	79 40.6	03.7	31 40.8	57.8	299 10.8	52.9			
18	191 26.6	45 50.6	N13 58.4	94 41.2	N24 03.6	46 42.8	N14 57.6	314 13.4	S17 52.9	Arcturus	145 54.3	N19 06.3
19	206 29.0	60 51.7	57.6	109 41.8	03.5	61 44.8	57.5	329 16.0	52.9	Atria	107 24.2	S69 03.2
20	221 31.5	75 52.7	56.7	124 42.5	03.5	76 46.8	57.3	344 18.6	52.9	Avior	234 18.0	S59 33.8
21	236 34.0	90 53.8 ..	55.9	139 43.1 ..	03.4	91 48.8 ..	57.2	359 21.2 ..	52.9	Bellatrix	278 30.8	N 6 21.6
22	251 36.4	105 54.9	55.1	154 43.7	03.4	106 50.8	57.0	14 23.7	52.9	Betelgeuse	271 00.1	N 7 24.4
23	266 38.9	120 55.9	54.2	169 44.4	03.3	121 52.8	56.9	29 26.3	52.8			
4 00	281 41.4	135 57.0	N13 53.4	184 45.0	N24 03.2	136 54.8	N14 56.7	44 28.9	S17 52.8	Canopus	263 56.1	S52 42.4
01	296 43.8	150 58.1	52.6	199 45.7	03.2	151 56.8	56.5	59 31.5	52.8	Capella	280 32.8	N46 00.5
02	311 46.3	165 59.1	51.7	214 46.3	03.1	166 58.8	56.4	74 34.1	52.8	Deneb	49 30.0	N45 20.2
03	326 48.8	181 00.2 ..	50.9	229 46.9 ..	03.1	182 00.8 ..	56.2	89 36.6 ..	52.8	Denebola	182 32.3	N14 29.2
04	341 51.2	196 01.3	50.1	244 47.6	03.0	197 02.8	56.1	104 39.2	52.8	Diphda	348 54.5	S17 54.0
05	356 53.7	211 02.4	49.3	259 48.2	02.9	212 04.8	55.9	119 41.8	52.8			
06	11 56.1	226 03.4	N13 48.4	274 48.8	N24 02.9	227 06.8	N14 55.8	134 44.4	S17 52.7	Dubhe	193 50.5	N61 40.3
07	26 58.6	241 04.5	47.6	289 49.5	02.8	242 08.8	55.6	149 47.0	52.7	Elnath	278 11.2	N28 37.0
08	42 01.1	256 05.6	46.8	304 50.1	02.7	257 10.8	55.5	164 49.5	52.7	Eltanin	90 45.5	N51 29.5
S 09	57 03.5	271 06.7 ..	45.9	319 50.7 ..	02.7	272 12.8 ..	55.3	179 52.1 ..	52.7	Enif	33 45.5	N 9 56.9
A 10	72 06.0	286 07.8	45.1	334 51.4	02.6	287 14.8	55.2	194 54.7	52.7	Fomalhaut	15 22.3	S29 32.2
T 11	87 08.5	301 08.9	44.3	349 52.0	02.5	302 16.8	55.0	209 57.3	52.7			
U 12	102 10.9	316 10.0	N13 43.4	4 52.7	N24 02.5	317 18.8	N14 54.8	224 59.8	S17 52.6	Gacrux	171 59.2	S57 12.2
R 13	117 13.4	331 11.1	42.6	19 53.3	02.4	332 20.8	54.7	240 02.4	52.6	Gienah	175 50.9	S17 37.8
D 14	132 15.9	346 12.2	41.8	34 53.9	02.3	347 22.8	54.5	255 05.0	52.6	Hadar	148 45.5	S60 27.0
A 15	147 18.3	1 13.3 ..	40.9	49 54.6 ..	02.3	2 24.8 ..	54.4	270 07.6 ..	52.6	Hamal	327 59.3	N23 31.9
Y 16	162 20.8	16 14.4	40.1	64 55.2	02.2	17 26.8	54.2	285 10.2	52.6	Kaus Aust.	83 41.6	S34 22.4
17	177 23.3	31 15.5	39.3	79 55.8	02.1	32 28.8	54.1	300 12.7	52.6			
18	192 25.7	46 16.6	N13 38.5	94 56.5	N24 02.1	47 30.8	N14 53.9	315 15.3	S17 52.6	Kochab	137 19.7	N74 05.9
19	207 28.2	61 17.7	37.6	109 57.1	02.0	62 32.8	53.8	330 17.9	52.5	Markab	13 36.8	N15 17.3
20	222 30.6	76 18.8	36.8	124 57.8	01.9	77 34.8	53.6	345 20.5	52.5	Menkar	314 13.8	N 4 08.9
21	237 33.1	91 19.9 ..	36.0	139 58.4 ..	01.9	92 36.8 ..	53.4	0 23.0 ..	52.5	Menkent	148 05.7	S36 26.8
22	252 35.6	106 21.0	35.1	154 59.0	01.8	107 38.8	53.3	15 25.6	52.5	Miaplacidus	221 40.0	S69 47.2
23	267 38.0	121 22.1	34.3	169 59.7	01.7	122 40.8	53.1	30 28.2	52.5			
5 00	282 40.5	136 23.3	N13 33.5	185 00.3	N24 01.7	137 42.8	N14 53.0	45 30.8	S17 52.5	Mirfak	308 38.6	N49 54.6
01	297 43.0	151 24.4	32.7	200 00.9	01.6	152 44.8	52.8	60 33.3	52.5	Nunki	75 56.2	S26 16.4
02	312 45.4	166 25.5	31.8	215 01.6	01.5	167 46.8	52.7	75 35.9	52.4	Peacock	53 16.6	S56 40.8
03	327 47.9	181 26.7 ..	31.0	230 02.2 ..	01.4	182 48.8 ..	52.5	90 38.5 ..	52.4	Pollux	243 26.4	N27 59.2
04	342 50.4	196 27.8	30.2	245 02.9	01.4	197 50.8	52.4	105 41.1	52.4	Procyon	244 58.6	N 5 10.9
05	357 52.8	211 28.9	29.3	260 03.5	01.3	212 52.8	52.2	120 43.6	52.4			
06	12 55.3	226 30.1	N13 28.5	275 04.1	N24 01.2	227 54.8	N14 52.0	135 46.2	S17 52.4	Rasalhague	96 04.8	N12 33.2
07	27 57.8	241 31.2	27.7	290 04.8	01.2	242 56.8	51.9	150 48.8	52.4	Regulus	207 42.3	N11 53.4
08	43 00.2	256 32.3	26.9	305 05.4	01.1	257 58.8	51.7	165 51.4	52.4	Rigel	281 11.0	S 8 11.2
S 09	58 02.7	271 33.5 ..	26.0	320 06.1 ..	01.0	273 00.8 ..	51.6	180 53.9 ..	52.3	Rigil Kent.	139 49.4	S60 54.0
U 10	73 05.1	286 34.6	25.2	335 06.7	00.9	288 02.8	51.4	195 56.5	52.3	Sabik	102 10.6	S15 44.4
N 11	88 07.6	301 35.8	24.4	350 07.3	00.9	303 04.8	51.3	210 59.1	52.3			
D 12	103 10.1	316 36.9	N13 23.6	5 08.0	N24 00.8	318 06.8	N14 51.1	226 01.7	S17 52.3	Schedar	349 38.8	N56 37.0
A 13	118 12.5	331 38.1	22.7	20 08.6	00.7	333 08.8	51.0	241 04.2	52.3	Shaula	96 19.6	S37 06.7
Y 14	133 15.0	346 39.2	21.9	35 09.3	00.6	348 10.8	50.8	256 06.8	52.3	Sirius	258 32.8	S16 44.4
15	148 17.5	1 40.4 ..	21.1	50 09.9 ..	00.6	3 12.8 ..	50.6	271 09.4 ..	52.2	Spica	158 29.7	S11 14.5
16	163 19.9	16 41.5	20.2	65 10.5	00.5	18 14.8	50.5	286 12.0	52.2	Suhail	222 51.7	S43 30.0
17	178 22.4	31 42.7	19.4	80 11.2	00.4	33 16.8	50.3	301 14.5	52.2			
18	193 24.9	46 43.9	N13 18.6	95 11.8	N24 00.3	48 18.8	N14 50.2	316 17.1	S17 52.2	Vega	80 37.6	N38 48.1
19	208 27.3	61 45.0	17.8	110 12.5	00.3	63 20.8	50.0	331 19.7	52.2	Zuben'ubi	137 03.7	S16 06.3
20	223 29.8	76 46.2	16.9	125 13.1	00.2	78 22.8	49.9	346 22.3	52.2		SHA	Mer. Pass.
21	238 32.3	91 47.4 ..	16.1	140 13.7 ..	00.1	93 24.8 ..	49.7	1 24.8 ..	52.2		° ′	h m
22	253 34.7	106 48.6	15.3	155 14.4	00.0	108 26.8	49.5	16 27.4	52.2	Venus	214 15.6	14 55
23	268 37.2	121 49.7	14.5	170 15.0	00.0	123 28.8	49.4	31 30.0	52.1	Mars	263 03.6	11 41
	h m									Jupiter	215 13.4	14 50
Mer. Pass.	5 12.4	v 1.1	d 0.8	v 0.6	d 0.1	v 2.0	d 0.2	v 2.6	d 0.0	Saturn	122 47.5	20 58

UT	SUN GHA	SUN Dec	MOON GHA	MOON v	MOON Dec	MOON d	MOON HP
d h	° ′	° ′	° ′	′	° ′	′	′
3 00	178 58.6	N22 59.8	347 03.2	6.8	S16 49.0	4.8	59.1
01	193 58.5	59.6	1 29.0	6.8	16 44.2	4.9	59.1
02	208 58.4	59.4	15 54.8	6.9	16 39.3	5.0	59.1
03	223 58.3 . .	59.2	30 20.7	6.8	16 34.3	5.1	59.1
04	238 58.2	59.0	44 46.5	6.8	16 29.2	5.3	59.2
05	253 58.0	58.9	59 12.3	6.9	16 23.9	5.3	59.2
06	268 57.9	N22 58.7	73 38.2	6.8	S16 18.6	5.4	59.2
07	283 57.8	58.5	88 04.0	6.9	16 13.2	5.6	59.2
08	298 57.7	58.3	102 29.9	6.9	16 07.6	5.6	59.2
F 09	313 57.6 . .	58.1	116 55.8	6.9	16 02.0	5.8	59.2
R 10	328 57.5	57.9	131 21.7	6.9	15 56.2	5.9	59.3
I 11	343 57.4	57.7	145 47.6	6.9	15 50.3	5.9	59.3
D 12	358 57.2	N22 57.5	160 13.5	7.0	S15 44.4	6.1	59.3
A 13	13 57.1	57.3	174 39.5	7.0	15 38.3	6.2	59.3
Y 14	28 57.0	57.1	189 05.5	6.9	15 32.1	6.3	59.3
15	43 56.9 . .	56.9	203 31.4	7.1	15 25.8	6.4	59.3
16	58 56.8	56.7	217 57.5	7.0	15 19.4	6.4	59.4
17	73 56.7	56.4	232 23.5	7.0	15 13.0	6.6	59.4
18	88 56.6	N22 56.2	246 49.5	7.1	S15 06.4	6.7	59.4
19	103 56.4	56.0	261 15.6	7.1	14 59.7	6.8	59.4
20	118 56.3	55.8	275 41.7	7.1	14 52.9	6.9	59.4
21	133 56.2 . .	55.6	290 07.8	7.2	14 46.0	7.0	59.4
22	148 56.1	55.4	304 34.0	7.1	14 39.0	7.0	59.4
23	163 56.0	55.2	319 00.1	7.2	14 32.0	7.2	59.5
4 00	178 55.9	N22 55.0	333 26.3	7.2	S14 24.8	7.3	59.5
01	193 55.8	54.8	347 52.5	7.3	14 17.5	7.3	59.5
02	208 55.7	54.6	2 18.8	7.3	14 10.2	7.5	59.5
03	223 55.5 . .	54.4	16 45.1	7.3	14 02.7	7.5	59.5
04	238 55.4	54.2	31 11.4	7.3	13 55.2	7.6	59.5
05	253 55.3	53.9	45 37.7	7.3	13 47.6	7.8	59.5
06	268 55.2	N22 53.7	60 04.0	7.4	S13 39.8	7.8	59.5
07	283 55.1	53.5	74 30.4	7.4	13 32.0	7.9	59.5
S 08	298 55.0	53.3	88 56.8	7.5	13 24.1	8.0	59.6
A 09	313 54.9 . .	53.1	103 23.3	7.5	13 16.1	8.0	59.6
T 10	328 54.8	52.9	117 49.8	7.5	13 08.1	8.2	59.6
U 11	343 54.6	52.7	132 16.3	7.5	12 59.9	8.2	59.6
R 12	358 54.5	N22 52.4	146 42.8	7.6	S12 51.7	8.4	59.6
D 13	13 54.4	52.2	161 09.4	7.6	12 43.3	8.4	59.6
A 14	28 54.3	52.0	175 36.0	7.6	12 34.9	8.5	59.6
Y 15	43 54.2 . .	51.8	190 02.6	7.6	12 26.4	8.5	59.6
16	58 54.1	51.6	204 29.2	7.7	12 17.9	8.7	59.6
17	73 54.0	51.3	218 55.9	7.7	12 09.2	8.7	59.6
18	88 53.9	N22 51.1	233 22.6	7.8	S12 00.5	8.8	59.6
19	103 53.8	50.9	247 49.4	7.8	11 51.7	8.9	59.7
20	118 53.7	50.7	262 16.2	7.8	11 42.8	8.9	59.7
21	133 53.5 . .	50.5	276 43.0	7.9	11 33.9	9.0	59.7
22	148 53.4	50.2	291 09.9	7.8	11 24.9	9.1	59.7
23	163 53.3	50.0	305 36.7	8.0	11 15.8	9.2	59.7
5 00	178 53.2	N22 49.8	320 03.7	7.9	S11 06.6	9.3	59.7
01	193 53.1	49.6	334 30.6	8.0	10 57.3	9.3	59.7
02	208 53.0	49.3	348 57.6	8.0	10 48.0	9.3	59.7
03	223 52.9 . .	49.1	3 24.6	8.1	10 38.7	9.5	59.7
04	238 52.8	48.9	17 51.7	8.1	10 29.2	9.5	59.7
05	253 52.7	48.6	32 18.8	8.1	10 19.7	9.6	59.7
06	268 52.6	N22 48.4	46 45.9	8.1	S10 10.1	9.6	59.7
07	283 52.5	48.2	61 13.0	8.2	10 00.5	9.7	59.7
08	298 52.3	47.9	75 40.2	8.2	9 50.8	9.7	59.7
S 09	313 52.2 . .	47.7	90 07.4	8.3	9 41.1	9.9	59.7
U 10	328 52.1	47.5	104 34.7	8.3	9 31.2	9.8	59.7
N 11	343 52.0	47.3	119 02.0	8.3	9 21.4	10.0	59.7
D 12	358 51.9	N22 47.0	133 29.3	8.4	S 9 11.4	10.0	59.7
A 13	13 51.8	46.8	147 56.7	8.3	9 01.4	10.0	59.7
Y 14	28 51.7	46.5	162 24.0	8.5	8 51.4	10.1	59.7
15	43 51.6 . .	46.3	176 51.5	8.4	8 41.3	10.2	59.7
16	58 51.5	46.1	191 18.9	8.5	8 31.1	10.2	59.7
17	73 51.4	45.8	205 46.4	8.5	8 20.9	10.2	59.7
18	88 51.3	N22 45.6	220 13.9	8.6	S 8 10.7	10.3	59.7
19	103 51.2	45.4	234 41.5	8.5	8 00.4	10.4	59.7
20	118 51.1	45.1	249 09.0	8.7	7 50.0	10.4	59.7
21	133 50.9 . .	44.9	263 36.7	8.6	7 39.6	10.4	59.7
22	148 50.8	44.6	278 04.3	8.7	7 29.2	10.5	59.7
23	163 50.7	44.4	292 32.0	8.7	S 7 18.7	10.5	59.7
	SD 15.8	d 0.2	SD 16.2	16.2			16.3

Lat.	Twilight Naut.	Twilight Civil	Sunrise	Moonrise 3	Moonrise 4	Moonrise 5	Moonrise 6
°	h m	h m	h m	h m	h m	h m	h m
N 72	☐	☐	☐	23 19	23 11	23 05	23 00
N 70	☐	☐	☐	22 48	22 52	22 54	22 55
68	☐	☐	☐	22 26	22 38	22 46	22 52
66	////	////	00 39	22 08	22 25	22 38	22 49
64	////	////	01 46	21 53	22 15	22 32	22 47
62	////	////	02 21	21 41	22 06	22 27	22 44
60	////	01 10	02 45	21 30	21 59	22 22	22 43
N 58	////	01 53	03 05	21 21	21 52	22 18	22 41
56	////	02 20	03 21	21 13	21 46	22 14	22 39
54	01 04	02 41	03 34	21 06	21 41	22 11	22 38
52	01 44	02 58	03 46	20 59	21 36	22 08	22 37
50	02 09	03 13	03 57	20 54	21 31	22 05	22 36
45	02 53	03 42	04 19	20 41	21 22	21 59	22 33
N 40	03 22	04 04	04 36	20 31	21 14	21 54	22 31
35	03 45	04 21	04 51	20 22	21 07	21 49	22 29
30	04 03	04 36	05 04	20 14	21 01	21 45	22 28
20	04 32	05 01	05 25	20 00	20 51	21 39	22 25
N 10	04 54	05 21	05 44	19 48	20 41	21 33	22 23
0	05 12	05 38	06 01	19 37	20 33	21 27	22 20
S 10	05 29	05 55	06 18	19 26	20 24	21 22	22 18
20	05 44	06 12	06 36	19 14	20 15	21 16	22 16
30	06 00	06 30	06 56	19 00	20 04	21 09	22 13
35	06 09	06 40	07 09	18 52	19 58	21 05	22 11
40	06 18	06 52	07 22	18 43	19 51	21 00	22 10
45	06 28	07 05	07 39	18 32	19 43	20 55	22 08
S 50	06 39	07 21	07 59	18 20	19 33	20 49	22 05
52	06 44	07 28	08 08	18 14	19 29	20 46	22 04
54	06 50	07 36	08 19	18 07	19 24	20 43	22 03
56	06 56	07 44	08 31	18 00	19 18	20 40	22 01
58	07 02	07 54	08 45	17 51	19 12	20 36	22 00
S 60	07 09	08 05	09 02	17 42	19 05	20 31	21 58

Lat.	Sunset	Twilight Civil	Twilight Naut.	Moonset 3	Moonset 4	Moonset 5	Moonset 6
°	h m	h m	h m	h m	h m	h m	h m
N 72	☐	☐	☐	02 25	04 36	06 40	08 38
N 70	☐	☐	☐	03 17	05 06	06 57	08 47
68	☐	☐	☐	03 49	05 28	07 10	08 54
66	23 24	////	////	04 13	05 45	07 21	08 59
64	22 21	////	////	04 31	05 58	07 31	09 04
62	21 47	////	////	04 46	06 10	07 38	09 09
60	21 23	22 56	////	04 59	06 20	07 45	09 12
N 58	21 03	22 15	////	05 10	06 28	07 51	09 15
56	20 47	21 48	////	05 19	06 36	07 56	09 18
54	20 34	21 27	23 02	05 28	06 43	08 01	09 21
52	20 22	21 10	22 24	05 35	06 49	08 05	09 23
50	20 12	20 55	21 59	05 42	06 54	08 09	09 25
45	19 50	20 27	21 15	05 56	07 06	08 17	09 30
N 40	19 32	20 05	20 46	06 08	07 15	08 24	09 33
35	19 18	19 47	20 24	06 18	07 23	08 30	09 37
30	19 05	19 32	20 05	06 27	07 31	08 35	09 39
20	18 44	19 08	19 37	06 42	07 43	08 44	09 44
N 10	18 25	18 48	19 15	06 55	07 54	08 52	09 49
0	18 08	18 30	18 57	07 07	08 04	08 59	09 53
S 10	17 51	18 14	18 40	07 20	08 14	09 06	09 56
20	17 33	17 57	18 24	07 33	08 24	09 14	10 01
30	17 12	17 39	18 08	07 47	08 36	09 22	10 05
35	17 00	17 28	18 00	07 56	08 43	09 27	10 08
40	16 47	17 17	17 51	08 06	08 51	09 32	10 11
45	16 30	17 04	17 41	08 17	09 00	09 39	10 14
S 50	16 10	16 48	17 30	08 30	09 11	09 46	10 18
52	16 01	16 41	17 25	08 37	09 16	09 50	10 20
54	15 50	16 33	17 19	08 44	09 22	09 54	10 22
56	15 38	16 25	17 13	08 52	09 28	09 58	10 25
58	15 24	16 15	17 07	09 00	09 35	10 03	10 27
S 60	15 07	16 04	17 00	09 10	09 42	10 08	10 30

	SUN Eqn. of Time 00h	SUN Eqn. of Time 12h	SUN Mer. Pass.	MOON Mer. Pass. Upper	MOON Mer. Pass. Lower	Age	Phase
Day	m s	m s	h m	h m	h m	d	%
d							
3	04 05	04 11	12 04	00 54	13 22	17	97
4	04 16	04 22	12 04	01 50	14 18	18	92
5	04 27	04 32	12 05	02 46	15 13	19	85

UT	ARIES GHA	VENUS −4.7 GHA	Dec	MARS +1.6 GHA	Dec	JUPITER −1.8 GHA	Dec	SATURN +0.3 GHA	Dec	STARS Name	SHA	Dec
d h	° ′	° ′	° ′	° ′	° ′	° ′	° ′	° ′	° ′		° ′	° ′
6 00	283 39.6	136 50.9	N13 13.6	185 15.7	N23 59.9	138 30.8	N14 49.2	46 32.6	S17 52.1	Acamar	315 17.6	S40 14.5
01	298 42.1	151 52.1	12.8	200 16.3	59.8	153 32.8	49.1	61 35.1	52.1	Achernar	335 26.0	S57 09.3
02	313 44.6	166 53.3	12.0	215 16.9	59.7	168 34.7	48.9	76 37.7	52.1	Acrux	173 07.6	S63 11.4
03	328 47.0	181 54.5 . .	11.2	230 17.6 . .	59.6	183 36.7 . .	48.8	91 40.3 . .	52.1	Adhara	255 11.8	S28 59.8
04	343 49.5	196 55.7	10.4	245 18.2	59.6	198 38.7	48.6	106 42.8	52.1	Aldebaran	290 48.0	N16 32.2
05	358 52.0	211 56.9	09.5	260 18.9	59.5	213 40.7	48.4	121 45.4	52.1			
06	13 54.4	226 58.1	N13 08.7	275 19.5	N23 59.4	228 42.7	N14 48.3	136 48.0	S17 52.0	Alioth	166 19.6	N55 52.9
07	28 56.9	241 59.2	07.9	290 20.1	59.3	243 44.7	48.1	151 50.6	52.0	Alkaid	152 57.8	N49 14.5
08	43 59.4	257 00.4	07.1	305 20.8	59.2	258 46.7	48.0	166 53.1	52.0	Al Na'ir	27 41.7	S46 52.8
M 09	59 01.8	272 01.6 . .	06.2	320 21.4 . .	59.2	273 48.7 . .	47.8	181 55.7 . .	52.0	Alnilam	275 45.3	S 1 11.7
O 10	74 04.3	287 02.9	05.4	335 22.1	59.1	288 50.7	47.7	196 58.3	52.0	Alphard	217 55.0	S 8 43.7
N 11	89 06.7	302 04.1	04.6	350 22.7	59.0	303 52.7	47.5	212 00.8	52.0			
D 12	104 09.2	317 05.3	N13 03.8	5 23.4	N23 58.9	318 54.7	N14 47.3	227 03.4	S17 52.0	Alphecca	126 09.6	N26 40.1
A 13	119 11.7	332 06.5	02.9	20 24.0	58.8	333 56.7	47.2	242 06.0	52.0	Alpheratz	357 41.9	N29 10.4
Y 14	134 14.1	347 07.7	02.1	35 24.6	58.7	348 58.7	47.0	257 08.6	51.9	Altair	62 06.5	N 8 54.8
15	149 16.6	2 08.9 . .	01.3	50 25.3 . .	58.7	4 00.7 . .	46.9	272 11.1 . .	51.9	Ankaa	353 14.3	S42 13.1
16	164 19.1	17 10.1	13 00.5	65 25.9	58.6	19 02.7	46.7	287 13.7	51.9	Antares	112 24.2	S26 27.8
17	179 21.5	32 11.4	12 59.7	80 26.6	58.5	34 04.7	46.6	302 16.3	51.9			
18	194 24.0	47 12.6	N12 58.8	95 27.2	N23 58.4	49 06.7	N14 46.4	317 18.8	S17 51.9	Arcturus	145 54.4	N19 06.3
19	209 26.5	62 13.8	58.0	110 27.8	58.3	64 08.7	46.2	332 21.4	51.9	Atria	107 24.2	S69 03.2
20	224 28.9	77 15.0	57.2	125 28.5	58.2	79 10.7	46.1	347 24.0	51.9	Avior	234 18.0	S59 33.8
21	239 31.4	92 16.3 . .	56.4	140 29.1 . .	58.1	94 12.7 . .	45.9	2 26.5 . .	51.8	Bellatrix	278 30.8	N 6 21.6
22	254 33.9	107 17.5	55.6	155 29.8	58.1	109 14.7	45.8	17 29.1	51.8	Betelgeuse	271 00.1	N 7 24.4
23	269 36.3	122 18.7	54.7	170 30.4	58.0	124 16.7	45.6	32 31.7	51.8			
7 00	284 38.8	137 20.0	N12 53.9	185 31.1	N23 57.9	139 18.7	N14 45.5	47 34.3	S17 51.8	Canopus	263 56.1	S52 42.4
01	299 41.2	152 21.2	53.1	200 31.7	57.8	154 20.7	45.3	62 36.8	51.8	Capella	280 32.8	N46 00.5
02	314 43.7	167 22.5	52.3	215 32.4	57.7	169 22.7	45.1	77 39.4	51.8	Deneb	49 30.0	N45 20.2
03	329 46.2	182 23.7 . .	51.5	230 33.0 . .	57.6	184 24.6 . .	45.0	92 42.0 . .	51.8	Denebola	182 32.4	N14 29.2
04	344 48.6	197 25.0	50.6	245 33.6	57.5	199 26.6	44.8	107 44.5	51.8	Diphda	348 54.5	S17 54.0
05	359 51.1	212 26.2	49.8	260 34.3	57.4	214 28.6	44.7	122 47.1	51.7			
06	14 53.6	227 27.5	N12 49.0	275 34.9	N23 57.4	229 30.6	N14 44.5	137 49.7	S17 51.7	Dubhe	193 50.5	N61 40.2
07	29 56.0	242 28.7	48.2	290 35.6	57.3	244 32.6	44.3	152 52.2	51.7	Elnath	278 11.2	N28 37.0
08	44 58.5	257 30.0	47.4	305 36.2	57.2	259 34.6	44.2	167 54.8	51.7	Eltanin	90 45.0	N51 29.5
T 09	60 01.0	272 31.2 . .	46.6	320 36.9 . .	57.1	274 36.6 . .	44.0	182 57.4 . .	51.7	Enif	33 45.5	N 9 56.9
U 10	75 03.4	287 32.5	45.7	335 37.5	57.0	289 38.6	43.9	197 59.9	51.7	Fomalhaut	15 22.3	S29 32.2
E 11	90 05.9	302 33.8	44.9	350 38.1	56.9	304 40.6	43.7	213 02.5	51.7			
S 12	105 08.3	317 35.0	N12 44.1	5 38.8	N23 56.8	319 42.6	N14 43.6	228 05.1	S17 51.7	Gacrux	171 59.2	S57 12.2
D 13	120 10.8	332 36.3	43.3	20 39.4	56.7	334 44.6	43.4	243 07.6	51.6	Gienah	175 50.9	S17 37.7
A 14	135 13.3	347 37.6	42.5	35 40.1	56.6	349 46.6	43.2	258 10.2	51.6	Hadar	148 45.5	S60 27.0
Y 15	150 15.7	2 38.9 . .	41.7	50 40.7 . .	56.5	4 48.6 . .	43.1	273 12.8 . .	51.6	Hamal	327 59.2	N23 31.9
16	165 18.2	17 40.1	40.8	65 41.4	56.5	19 50.6	42.9	288 15.3	51.6	Kaus Aust.	83 41.6	S34 22.4
17	180 20.7	32 41.4	40.0	80 42.0	56.4	34 52.6	42.8	303 17.9	51.6			
18	195 23.1	47 42.7	N12 39.2	95 42.7	N23 56.3	49 54.6	N14 42.6	318 20.5	S17 51.6	Kochab	137 19.7	N74 05.9
19	210 25.6	62 44.0	38.4	110 43.3	56.2	64 56.6	42.4	333 23.0	51.6	Markab	13 36.7	N15 17.3
20	225 28.1	77 45.3	37.6	125 44.0	56.1	79 58.5	42.3	348 25.6	51.6	Menkar	314 13.8	N 4 08.9
21	240 30.5	92 46.6 . .	36.8	140 44.6 . .	56.0	95 00.5 . .	42.1	3 28.2 . .	51.5	Menkent	148 05.7	S36 26.8
22	255 33.0	107 47.9	36.0	155 45.2	55.9	110 02.5	42.0	18 30.7	51.5	Miaplacidus	221 40.0	S69 47.2
23	270 35.5	122 49.2	35.1	170 45.9	55.8	125 04.5	41.8	33 33.3	51.5			
8 00	285 37.9	137 50.5	N12 34.3	185 46.5	N23 55.7	140 06.5	N14 41.7	48 35.9	S17 51.5	Mirfak	308 38.6	N49 54.6
01	300 40.4	152 51.8	33.5	200 47.2	55.6	155 08.5	41.5	63 38.4	51.5	Nunki	75 56.2	S26 16.4
02	315 42.8	167 53.1	32.7	215 47.8	55.5	170 10.5	41.3	78 41.0	51.5	Peacock	53 16.6	S56 40.8
03	330 45.3	182 54.4 . .	31.9	230 48.5 . .	55.4	185 12.5 . .	41.2	93 43.6 . .	51.5	Pollux	243 26.4	N27 59.2
04	345 47.8	197 55.7	31.1	245 49.1	55.3	200 14.5	41.0	108 46.1	51.5	Procyon	244 58.6	N 5 10.9
05	0 50.2	212 57.0	30.3	260 49.8	55.2	215 16.5	40.9	123 48.7	51.4			
06	15 52.7	227 58.3	N12 29.5	275 50.4	N23 55.1	230 18.5	N14 40.7	138 51.3	S17 51.4	Rasalhague	96 04.8	N12 33.2
W 07	30 55.2	242 59.6	28.6	290 51.1	55.0	245 20.5	40.5	153 53.8	51.4	Regulus	207 42.3	N11 53.4
E 08	45 57.6	258 01.0	27.8	305 51.7	54.9	260 22.5	40.4	168 56.4	51.4	Rigel	281 11.0	S 8 11.2
D 09	61 00.1	273 02.3 . .	27.0	320 52.4 . .	54.8	275 24.4 . .	40.2	183 59.0 . .	51.4	Rigil Kent.	139 49.4	S60 54.0
N 10	76 02.6	288 03.6	26.2	335 53.0	54.7	290 26.4	40.1	199 01.5	51.4	Sabik	102 10.6	S15 44.4
E 11	91 05.0	303 04.9	25.4	350 53.7	54.6	305 28.4	39.9	214 04.1	51.4			
S 12	106 07.5	318 06.3	N12 24.6	5 54.3	N23 54.5	320 30.4	N14 39.7	229 06.7	S17 51.4	Schedar	349 38.7	N56 37.1
D 13	121 10.0	333 07.6	23.8	20 54.9	54.4	335 32.4	39.6	244 09.2	51.3	Shaula	96 19.6	S37 06.7
A 14	136 12.4	348 08.9	23.0	35 55.6	54.3	350 34.4	39.4	259 11.8	51.3	Sirius	258 32.8	S16 44.4
Y 15	151 14.9	3 10.3 . .	22.2	50 56.2 . .	54.2	5 36.4 . .	39.3	274 14.3 . .	51.3	Spica	158 29.7	S11 14.5
16	166 17.3	18 11.6	21.4	65 56.9	54.1	20 38.4	39.1	289 16.9	51.3	Suhail	222 51.7	S43 30.0
17	181 19.8	33 13.0	20.6	80 57.5	54.0	35 40.4	38.9	304 19.5	51.3			
18	196 22.3	48 14.3	N12 19.7	95 58.2	N23 53.9	50 42.4	N14 38.8	319 22.0	S17 51.3	Vega	80 37.6	N38 48.1
19	211 24.7	63 15.7	18.9	110 58.8	53.8	65 44.4	38.6	334 24.6	51.3	Zuben'ubi	137 03.7	S16 06.3
20	226 27.2	78 17.0	18.1	125 59.5	53.7	80 46.4	38.5	349 27.2	51.3		SHA	Mer.Pass.
21	241 29.7	93 18.4 . .	17.3	141 00.1 . .	53.6	95 48.3 . .	38.3	4 29.7 . .	51.2		° ′	h m
22	256 32.1	108 19.7	16.5	156 00.8	53.5	110 50.3	38.1	19 32.3	51.2	Venus	212 41.2	14 49
23	271 34.6	123 21.1	15.7	171 01.4	53.4	125 52.3	38.0	34 34.8	51.2	Mars	260 52.3	11 37
	h m									Jupiter	214 39.9	14 41
Mer.Pass.	5 00.6	v 1.3	d 0.8	v 0.6	d 0.1	v 2.0	d 0.2	v 2.6	d 0.0	Saturn	122 55.5	20 46

UT	SUN GHA	SUN Dec	MOON GHA	MOON v	MOON Dec	MOON d	MOON HP	Lat.	Twilight Naut.	Twilight Civil	Sunrise	Moonrise 6	Moonrise 7	Moonrise 8	Moonrise 9
d h	° ′	° ′	° ′	′	° ′	′	′	°	h m	h m	h m	h m	h m	h m	h m
6 00	178 50.6	N22 44.2	306 59.7	8.7	S 7 08.2	10.6	59.7	N 72	▭	▭	▭	23 00	22 54	22 49	22 44
01	193 50.5	43.9	321 27.4	8.8	6 57.6	10.6	59.7	N 70	▭	▭	▭	22 55	22 56	22 57	22 59
02	208 50.4	43.7	335 55.2	8.8	6 47.0	10.7	59.7	68	▭	▭	00 56	22 52	22 58	23 04	23 11
03	223 50.3 ..	43.4	350 23.0	8.8	6 36.3	10.7	59.7	66	////	////	01 53	22 49	22 59	23 09	23 21
04	238 50.2	43.2	4 50.8	8.9	6 25.6	10.7	59.7	64	////	////	02 26	22 47	23 00	23 14	23 29
05	253 50.1	42.9	19 18.7	8.8	6 14.9	10.7	59.7	62	////	////	02 26	22 44	23 01	23 18	23 37
06	268 50.0	N22 42.7	33 46.5	8.9	S 6 04.2	10.8	59.7	60	////	01 19	02 49	22 43	23 02	23 22	23 43
07	283 49.9	42.4	48 14.4	9.0	5 53.4	10.9	59.7	N 58	////	01 58	03 08	22 41	23 03	23 25	23 49
08	298 49.8	42.2	62 42.4	9.0	5 42.5	10.8	59.7	56	////	02 24	03 24	22 39	23 03	23 28	23 54
M 09	313 49.7 ..	42.0	77 10.4	9.0	5 31.7	10.9	59.7	54	01 12	02 45	03 37	22 38	23 04	23 30	23 58
O 10	328 49.6	41.7	91 38.4	9.0	5 20.8	11.0	59.7	52	01 48	03 01	03 49	22 37	23 05	23 33	24 02
N 11	343 49.5	41.5	106 06.4	9.0	5 09.8	10.9	59.7	50	02 13	03 16	03 59	22 36	23 05	23 35	24 06
D 12	358 49.4	N22 41.2	120 34.4	9.1	S 4 58.9	11.0	59.7	45	02 55	03 40	04 21	22 33	23 06	23 39	24 14
A 13	13 49.3	41.0	135 02.5	9.1	4 47.9	11.0	59.7	N 40	03 25	04 06	04 38	22 31	23 07	23 43	24 21
Y 14	28 49.2	40.7	149 30.6	9.1	4 36.9	11.0	59.7	35	03 47	04 23	04 52	22 29	23 08	23 47	24 27
15	43 49.1 ..	40.4	163 58.7	9.2	4 25.9	11.1	59.7	30	04 05	04 38	05 05	22 28	23 09	23 50	24 32
16	58 48.9	40.2	178 26.9	9.2	4 14.8	11.1	59.7	20	04 33	05 02	05 26	22 25	23 11	23 55	24 41
17	73 48.8	39.9	192 55.1	9.1	4 03.7	11.1	59.7	N 10	04 54	05 21	05 44	22 23	23 11	24 00	00 00
18	88 48.7	N22 39.7	207 23.2	9.3	S 3 52.6	11.1	59.7	0	05 13	05 39	06 01	22 20	23 12	24 04	00 04
19	103 48.6	39.4	221 51.5	9.3	3 41.5	11.1	59.7	S 10	05 29	05 55	06 18	22 18	23 14	24 09	00 09
20	118 48.5	39.2	236 19.7	9.3	3 30.4	11.2	59.7	20	05 45	06 12	06 36	22 16	23 15	24 14	00 14
21	133 48.4 ..	38.9	250 48.0	9.3	3 19.2	11.1	59.6	30	06 00	06 30	06 56	22 13	23 16	24 19	00 19
22	148 48.3	38.7	265 16.3	9.3	3 08.1	11.2	59.6	35	06 09	06 40	07 08	22 11	23 17	24 22	00 22
23	163 48.2	38.4	279 44.6	9.3	2 56.9	11.2	59.6	40	06 18	06 51	07 22	22 10	23 18	24 26	00 26
7 00	178 48.1	N22 38.1	294 12.9	9.4	S 2 45.7	11.2	59.6	45	06 27	07 04	07 38	22 08	23 19	24 30	00 30
01	193 48.0	37.9	308 41.3	9.3	2 34.5	11.3	59.6	S 50	06 38	07 19	07 57	22 05	23 21	24 35	00 35
02	208 47.9	37.6	323 09.6	9.4	2 23.2	11.2	59.6	52	06 43	07 27	08 07	22 04	23 21	24 38	00 38
03	223 47.8 ..	37.4	337 38.0	9.5	2 12.0	11.2	59.6	54	06 49	07 34	08 17	22 03	23 22	24 40	00 40
04	238 47.7	37.1	352 06.5	9.4	2 00.8	11.3	59.6	56	06 54	07 43	08 29	22 01	23 23	24 43	00 43
05	253 47.6	36.8	6 34.9	9.4	1 49.5	11.3	59.6	58	07 01	07 52	08 43	22 00	23 24	24 47	00 47
06	268 47.5	N22 36.6	21 03.3	9.5	S 1 38.2	11.2	59.6	S 60	07 08	08 03	08 59	21 58	23 25	24 50	00 50
07	283 47.4	36.3	35 31.8	9.5	1 27.0	11.3	59.6	Lat.	Sunset	Twilight Civil	Twilight Naut.	Moonset 6	Moonset 7	Moonset 8	Moonset 9
08	298 47.3	36.1	50 00.3	9.5	1 15.7	11.3	59.6								
T 09	313 47.2 ..	35.8	64 28.8	9.5	1 04.4	11.2	59.6	°	h m	h m	h m	h m	h m	h m	h m
U 10	328 47.1	35.5	78 57.3	9.5	0 53.2	11.3	59.5	N 72	▭	▭	▭	08 38	10 34	12 28	14 21
E 11	343 47.0	35.3	93 25.8	9.6	0 41.9	11.3	59.5	N 70	▭	▭	▭	08 47	10 35	12 22	14 08
S 12	358 46.9	N22 35.0	107 54.4	9.5	S 0 30.6	11.3	59.5	68	▭	▭	▭	08 54	10 36	12 17	13 58
D 13	13 46.8	34.7	122 22.9	9.6	0 19.3	11.2	59.5	66	23 09	////	////	08 59	10 37	12 14	13 49
A 14	28 46.7	34.5	136 51.5	9.6	S 0 08.1	11.3	59.5	64	22 15	////	////	09 04	10 38	12 10	13 41
Y 15	43 46.6 ..	34.2	151 20.1	9.6	N 0 03.2	11.3	59.5	62	21 43	////	////	09 09	10 38	12 08	13 35
16	58 46.5	33.9	165 48.7	9.6	0 14.5	11.2	59.5	60	21 19	22 49	////	09 12	10 39	12 05	13 30
17	73 46.4	33.6	180 17.3	9.6	0 25.7	11.3	59.5	N 58	21 01	22 10	////	09 15	10 40	12 03	13 25
18	88 46.3	N22 33.4	194 45.9	9.6	N 0 37.0	11.2	59.5	56	20 45	21 44	////	09 18	10 40	12 01	13 21
19	103 46.2	33.1	209 14.5	9.7	0 48.2	11.3	59.5	54	20 32	21 24	22 55	09 21	10 40	11 59	13 17
20	118 46.1	32.8	223 43.2	9.6	0 59.5	11.2	59.4	52	20 20	21 08	22 20	09 23	10 41	11 58	13 13
21	133 45.9 ..	32.6	238 11.8	9.7	1 10.7	11.2	59.4	50	20 10	20 53	21 56	09 25	10 41	11 56	13 10
22	148 45.9	32.3	252 40.5	9.6	1 21.9	11.2	59.4	45	19 49	20 25	21 14	09 30	10 42	11 53	13 04
23	163 45.8	32.0	267 09.1	9.7	1 33.1	11.2	59.4	N 40	19 32	20 04	20 45	09 33	10 42	11 51	12 58
8 00	178 45.7	N22 31.7	281 37.8	9.7	N 1 44.3	11.2	59.4	35	19 17	19 47	20 23	09 37	10 43	11 48	12 53
01	193 45.6	31.5	296 06.5	9.7	1 55.5	11.1	59.4	30	19 05	19 32	20 05	09 39	10 43	11 46	12 49
02	208 45.5	31.2	310 35.2	9.7	2 06.6	11.2	59.4	20	18 44	19 08	19 37	09 44	10 44	11 43	12 42
03	223 45.4 ..	30.9	325 03.9	9.7	2 17.8	11.1	59.4	N 10	18 25	18 48	19 15	09 49	10 45	11 40	12 35
04	238 45.3	30.6	339 32.6	9.7	2 28.9	11.1	59.4	0	18 09	18 31	18 57	09 53	10 45	11 37	12 29
05	253 45.2	30.4	354 01.3	9.7	2 40.0	11.1	59.3	S 10	17 52	18 14	18 41	09 56	10 46	11 34	12 23
06	268 45.1	N22 30.1	8 30.0	9.7	N 2 51.1	11.1	59.3	20	17 34	17 58	18 25	10 01	10 46	11 31	12 17
W 07	283 45.0	29.8	22 58.7	9.7	3 02.2	11.0	59.3	30	17 14	17 40	18 10	10 05	10 47	11 28	12 09
E 08	298 44.9	29.5	37 27.4	9.7	3 13.2	11.0	59.3	35	17 02	17 30	18 01	10 08	10 47	11 26	12 05
D 09	313 44.8 ..	29.2	51 56.1	9.7	3 24.2	11.0	59.3	40	16 48	17 19	17 52	10 11	10 48	11 24	12 00
N 10	328 44.7	29.0	66 24.8	9.8	3 35.2	11.0	59.3	45	16 32	17 06	17 43	10 14	10 48	11 21	11 55
E 11	343 44.6	28.7	80 53.6	9.7	3 46.2	10.9	59.3	S 50	16 13	16 50	17 32	10 18	10 48	11 18	11 48
S 12	358 44.5	N22 28.4	95 22.3	9.7	N 3 57.1	10.9	59.3	52	16 03	16 43	17 27	10 20	10 49	11 16	11 45
D 13	13 44.4	28.1	109 51.0	9.7	4 08.0	10.9	59.2	54	15 53	16 36	17 21	10 22	10 49	11 15	11 42
A 14	28 44.3	27.8	124 19.7	9.8	4 18.9	10.9	59.2	56	15 41	16 27	17 16	10 25	10 49	11 13	11 38
Y 15	43 44.2 ..	27.5	138 48.5	9.7	4 29.8	10.8	59.2	58	15 27	16 18	17 09	10 27	10 49	11 11	11 34
16	58 44.1	27.2	153 17.2	9.7	4 40.6	10.8	59.2	S 60	15 11	16 07	17 02	10 30	10 50	11 09	11 30
17	73 44.0	27.0	167 45.9	9.7	4 51.4	10.7	59.2			SUN			MOON			
18	88 44.0	N22 26.7	182 14.6	9.7	N 5 02.1	10.7	59.2								
19	103 43.9	26.4	196 43.3	9.7	5 12.8	10.7	59.2	Day	Eqn. of Time 00h	Eqn. of Time 12h	Mer. Pass.	Mer. Pass. Upper	Mer. Pass. Lower	Age	Phase
20	118 43.8	26.1	211 12.0	9.7	5 23.5	10.7	59.1								
21	133 43.7 ..	25.8	225 40.7	9.7	5 34.2	10.6	59.1	d	m s	m s	h m	h m	h m	d %	
22	148 43.6	25.5	240 09.4	9.7	5 44.8	10.6	59.1	6	04 37	04 42	12 05	03 40	16 06	20 76	
23	163 43.5	25.2	254 38.1	9.7	N 5 55.4	10.5	59.1	7	04 47	04 52	12 05	04 33	16 59	21 65	🌓
	SD 15.8	d 0.3	SD 16.3		16.2		16.1	8	04 57	05 02	12 05	05 25	17 51	22 54	

UT	ARIES GHA	VENUS −4.7 GHA	Dec	MARS +1.6 GHA	Dec	JUPITER −1.8 GHA	Dec	SATURN +0.3 GHA	Dec	STARS Name	SHA	Dec
9 00	286 37.1	138 22.4	N12 14.9	186 02.1	N23 53.3	140 54.3	N14 37.8	49 37.4	S17 51.2	Acamar	315 17.5	S40 14.5
01	301 39.5	153 23.8	14.1	201 02.7	53.2	155 56.3	37.7	64 40.0	51.2	Achernar	335 25.9	S57 09.3
02	316 42.0	168 25.2	13.3	216 03.4	53.1	170 58.3	37.5	79 42.5	51.2	Acrux	173 07.6	S63 11.4
03	331 44.4	183 26.5	.. 12.5	231 04.0	.. 53.0	186 00.3	.. 37.3	94 45.1	.. 51.2	Adhara	255 11.8	S28 59.8
04	346 46.9	198 27.9	11.7	246 04.7	52.9	201 02.3	37.2	109 47.7	51.2	Aldebaran	290 48.0	N16 32.2
05	1 49.4	213 29.3	10.9	261 05.3	52.8	216 04.3	37.0	124 50.2	51.2			
T 06	16 51.8	228 30.7	N12 10.1	276 06.0	N23 52.7	231 06.3	N14 36.9	139 52.8	S17 51.1	Alioth	166 19.6	N55 52.9
H 07	31 54.3	243 32.0	09.3	291 06.6	52.6	246 08.3	36.7	154 55.3	51.1	Alkaid	152 57.8	N49 14.5
U 08	46 56.8	258 33.4	08.5	306 07.3	52.5	261 10.2	36.5	169 57.9	51.1	Al Na'ir	27 41.7	S46 52.8
R 09	61 59.2	273 34.8	.. 07.7	321 07.9	.. 52.4	276 12.2	.. 36.4	185 00.5	.. 51.1	Alnilam	275 45.2	S 1 11.7
S 10	77 01.7	288 36.2	06.9	336 08.6	52.3	291 14.2	36.2	200 03.0	51.1	Alphard	217 55.0	S 8 43.7
D 11	92 04.2	303 37.6	06.1	351 09.2	52.2	306 16.2	36.1	215 05.6	51.1			
A 12	107 06.6	318 39.0	N12 05.3	6 09.9	N23 52.0	321 18.2	N14 35.9	230 08.1	S17 51.1	Alphecca	126 09.6	N26 40.1
Y 13	122 09.1	333 40.4	04.4	21 10.5	51.9	336 20.2	35.7	245 10.7	51.1	Alpheratz	357 41.9	N29 10.5
14	137 11.6	348 41.8	03.6	36 11.2	51.8	351 22.2	35.6	260 13.3	51.1	Altair	62 06.5	N 8 54.8
15	152 14.0	3 43.2	.. 02.8	51 11.8	.. 51.7	6 24.2	.. 35.4	275 15.8	.. 51.0	Ankaa	353 14.3	S42 13.1
16	167 16.5	18 44.6	02.0	66 12.5	51.6	21 26.2	35.3	290 18.4	51.0	Antares	112 24.2	S26 27.8
17	182 18.9	33 46.0	01.2	81 13.1	51.5	36 28.1	35.1	305 20.9	51.0			
18	197 21.4	48 47.4	N12 00.4	96 13.8	N23 51.4	51 30.1	N14 34.9	320 23.5	S17 51.0	Arcturus	145 54.4	N19 06.4
19	212 23.9	63 48.8	11 59.6	111 14.4	51.3	66 32.1	34.8	335 26.1	51.0	Atria	107 24.2	S69 03.3
20	227 26.3	78 50.2	58.8	126 15.1	51.2	81 34.1	34.6	350 28.6	51.0	Avior	234 18.0	S59 33.8
21	242 28.8	93 51.7	.. 58.0	141 15.7	.. 51.1	96 36.1	.. 34.5	5 31.2	.. 51.0	Bellatrix	278 30.8	N 6 21.6
22	257 31.3	108 53.1	57.2	156 16.4	51.0	111 38.1	34.3	20 33.7	51.0	Betelgeuse	271 00.1	N 7 24.4
23	272 33.7	123 54.5	56.4	171 17.0	50.8	126 40.1	34.1	35 36.3	51.0			
10 00	287 36.2	138 55.9	N11 55.7	186 17.7	N23 50.7	141 42.1	N14 34.0	50 38.9	S17 51.0	Canopus	263 56.1	S52 42.4
01	302 38.7	153 57.4	54.9	201 18.3	50.6	156 44.1	33.8	65 41.4	50.9	Capella	280 32.8	N46 00.5
02	317 41.1	168 58.8	54.1	216 19.0	50.5	171 46.0	33.6	80 44.0	50.9	Deneb	49 30.0	N45 20.2
03	332 43.6	184 00.2	.. 53.3	231 19.6	.. 50.4	186 48.0	.. 33.5	95 46.5	.. 50.9	Denebola	182 32.4	N14 29.2
04	347 46.1	199 01.7	52.5	246 20.3	50.3	201 50.0	33.3	110 49.1	50.9	Diphda	348 54.5	S17 54.0
05	2 48.5	214 03.1	51.7	261 20.9	50.2	216 52.0	33.2	125 51.6	50.9			
F 06	17 51.0	229 04.5	N11 50.9	276 21.6	N23 50.1	231 54.0	N14 33.0	140 54.2	S17 50.9	Dubhe	193 50.5	N61 40.2
R 07	32 53.4	244 06.0	50.1	291 22.2	49.9	246 56.0	32.8	155 56.8	50.9	Elnath	278 11.2	N28 37.0
I 08	47 55.9	259 07.4	49.3	306 22.9	49.8	261 58.0	32.7	170 59.3	50.9	Eltanin	90 45.0	N51 29.5
D 09	62 58.4	274 08.9	.. 48.5	321 23.5	.. 49.7	277 00.0	.. 32.5	186 01.9	.. 50.9	Enif	33 45.5	N 9 56.9
A 10	78 00.8	289 10.3	47.7	336 24.2	49.6	292 01.9	32.4	201 04.4	50.8	Fomalhaut	15 22.3	S29 32.1
Y 11	93 03.3	304 11.8	46.9	351 24.9	49.5	307 03.9	32.2	216 07.0	50.8			
12	108 05.8	319 13.3	N11 46.1	6 25.5	N23 49.4	322 05.9	N14 32.0	231 09.5	S17 50.8	Gacrux	171 59.3	S57 12.2
13	123 08.2	334 14.7	45.3	21 26.2	49.3	337 07.9	31.9	246 12.1	50.8	Gienah	175 50.9	S17 37.7
14	138 10.7	349 16.2	44.5	36 26.8	49.1	352 09.9	31.7	261 14.7	50.8	Hadar	148 45.6	S60 27.0
15	153 13.2	4 17.6	.. 43.7	51 27.5	.. 49.0	7 11.9	.. 31.5	276 17.2	.. 50.8	Hamal	327 59.2	N23 31.9
16	168 15.6	19 19.1	42.9	66 28.1	48.9	22 13.9	31.4	291 19.8	50.8	Kaus Aust.	83 41.5	S34 22.4
17	183 18.1	34 20.6	42.1	81 28.8	48.8	37 15.9	31.2	306 22.3	50.8			
18	198 20.5	49 22.1	N11 41.3	96 29.4	N23 48.7	52 17.8	N14 31.1	321 24.9	S17 50.8	Kochab	137 19.8	N74 05.9
19	213 23.0	64 23.5	40.6	111 30.1	48.5	67 19.8	30.9	336 27.4	50.8	Markab	13 36.7	N15 17.4
20	228 25.5	79 25.0	39.8	126 30.7	48.4	82 21.8	30.7	351 30.0	50.7	Menkar	314 13.7	N 4 08.9
21	243 27.9	94 26.5	.. 39.0	141 31.4	.. 48.3	97 23.8	.. 30.6	6 32.6	.. 50.7	Menkent	148 05.7	S36 26.8
22	258 30.4	109 28.0	38.2	156 32.0	48.2	112 25.8	30.4	21 35.1	50.7	Miaplacidus	221 40.0	S69 47.1
23	273 32.9	124 29.5	37.4	171 32.7	48.1	127 27.8	30.2	36 37.7	50.7			
11 00	288 35.3	139 31.0	N11 36.6	186 33.3	N23 48.0	142 29.8	N14 30.1	51 40.2	S17 50.7	Mirfak	308 38.5	N49 54.6
01	303 37.8	154 32.5	35.8	201 34.0	47.8	157 31.8	29.9	66 42.8	50.7	Nunki	75 56.2	S26 16.4
02	318 40.3	169 34.0	35.0	216 34.7	47.7	172 33.7	29.8	81 45.3	50.7	Peacock	53 16.5	S56 40.8
03	333 42.7	184 35.5	.. 34.2	231 35.3	.. 47.6	187 35.7	.. 29.6	96 47.9	.. 50.7	Pollux	243 26.4	N27 59.2
04	348 45.2	199 37.0	33.5	246 36.0	47.5	202 37.7	29.4	111 50.4	50.7	Procyon	244 58.6	N 5 10.9
05	3 47.7	214 38.5	32.7	261 36.6	47.3	217 39.7	29.3	126 53.0	50.7			
S 06	18 50.1	229 40.0	N11 31.9	276 37.3	N23 47.2	232 41.7	N14 29.1	141 55.5	S17 50.6	Rasalhague	96 04.8	N12 33.2
A 07	33 52.6	244 41.5	31.1	291 37.9	47.1	247 43.7	28.9	156 58.1	50.6	Regulus	207 42.3	N11 53.5
T 08	48 55.0	259 43.0	30.3	306 38.6	47.0	262 45.7	28.8	172 00.7	50.6	Rigel	281 11.0	S 8 11.2
U 09	63 57.5	274 44.5	.. 29.5	321 39.2	.. 46.9	277 47.6	.. 28.6	187 03.2	.. 50.6	Rigil Kent.	139 49.4	S60 54.0
R 10	79 00.0	289 46.1	28.7	336 39.9	46.7	292 49.6	28.5	202 05.8	50.6	Sabik	102 10.6	S15 44.4
D 11	94 02.4	304 47.6	28.0	351 40.6	46.6	307 51.6	28.3	217 08.3	50.6			
A 12	109 04.9	319 49.1	N11 27.2	6 41.2	N23 46.5	322 53.6	N14 28.1	232 10.9	S17 50.6	Schedar	349 38.7	N56 37.1
Y 13	124 07.4	334 50.6	26.4	21 41.9	46.4	337 55.6	28.0	247 13.4	50.6	Shaula	96 19.6	S37 06.7
14	139 09.8	349 52.2	25.6	36 42.5	46.2	352 57.6	27.8	262 16.0	50.6	Sirius	258 32.8	S16 44.4
15	154 12.3	4 53.7	.. 24.8	51 43.2	.. 46.1	7 59.6	.. 27.6	277 18.5	.. 50.6	Spica	158 29.7	S11 14.5
16	169 14.8	19 55.2	24.0	66 43.8	46.0	23 01.5	27.5	292 21.1	50.6	Suhail	222 51.7	S43 30.0
17	184 17.2	34 56.8	23.3	81 44.5	45.9	38 03.5	27.3	307 23.6	50.5			
18	199 19.7	49 58.3	N11 22.5	96 45.1	N23 45.7	53 05.5	N14 27.2	322 26.2	S17 50.5	Vega	80 37.6	N38 48.2
19	214 22.2	64 59.9	21.7	111 45.8	45.6	68 07.5	27.0	337 28.7	50.5	Zuben'ubi	137 03.7	S16 06.3
20	229 24.6	80 01.4	20.9	126 46.5	45.5	83 09.5	26.8	352 31.3	50.5		SHA	Mer. Pass.
21	244 27.1	95 03.0	.. 20.1	141 47.1	.. 45.4	98 11.5	.. 26.7	7 33.8	.. 50.5			h m
22	259 29.5	110 04.5	19.4	156 47.8	45.2	113 13.4	26.5	22 36.4	50.5	Venus	211 19.7	14 43
23	274 32.0	125 06.1	18.6	171 48.4	45.1	128 15.4	26.3	37 38.9	50.5	Mars	258 45.5	11 34
Mer. Pass.	h m 4 48.8	v 1.5	d 0.8	v 0.7	d 0.1	v 2.0	d 0.2	v 2.6	d 0.0	Jupiter	214 05.9	14 31
										Saturn	123 02.7	20 34

UT	SUN GHA	SUN Dec	MOON GHA	v	MOON Dec	d	HP
d h	° ′	° ′	° ′	′	° ′	′	′
9 00	178 43.4	N22 24.9	269 06.8	9.7	N 6 05.9	10.5	59.1
01	193 43.3	24.6	283 35.5	9.7	6 16.4	10.5	59.1
02	208 43.2	24.4	298 04.2	9.7	6 26.9	10.4	59.1
03	223 43.1 . .	24.1	312 32.9	9.7	6 37.3	10.4	59.0
04	238 43.0	23.8	327 01.6	9.6	6 47.7	10.3	59.0
05	253 42.9	23.5	341 30.2	9.7	6 58.0	10.3	59.0
06	268 42.8	N22 23.2	355 58.9	9.6	N 7 08.3	10.2	59.0
07	283 42.7	22.9	10 27.5	9.6	7 18.5	10.2	59.0
T 08	298 42.6	22.6	24 56.1	9.7	7 28.7	10.1	59.0
H 09	313 42.5 . .	22.3	39 24.8	9.6	7 38.8	10.1	59.0
U 10	328 42.4	22.0	53 53.4	9.6	7 48.9	10.1	58.9
R 11	343 42.3	21.7	68 22.0	9.6	7 59.0	10.0	58.9
S 12	358 42.3	N22 21.4	82 50.6	9.6	N 8 09.0	9.9	58.9
D 13	13 42.2	21.1	97 19.2	9.5	8 18.9	9.9	58.9
A 14	28 42.1	20.8	111 47.7	9.6	8 28.8	9.8	58.9
Y 15	43 42.0 . .	20.5	126 16.3	9.6	8 38.6	9.8	58.9
16	58 41.9	20.2	140 44.9	9.5	8 48.4	9.7	58.8
17	73 41.8	19.9	155 13.4	9.5	8 58.1	9.7	58.8
18	88 41.7	N22 19.6	169 41.9	9.5	N 9 07.8	9.6	58.8
19	103 41.6	19.3	184 10.4	9.5	9 17.4	9.5	58.8
20	118 41.5	19.0	198 38.9	9.5	9 26.9	9.5	58.8
21	133 41.4 . .	18.7	213 07.4	9.5	9 36.4	9.5	58.8
22	148 41.3	18.4	227 35.9	9.5	9 45.9	9.3	58.7
23	163 41.2	18.1	242 04.4	9.4	9 55.2	9.3	58.7
10 00	178 41.2	N22 17.8	256 32.8	9.4	N10 04.5	9.3	58.7
01	193 41.1	17.4	271 01.2	9.4	10 13.8	9.2	58.7
02	208 41.0	17.1	285 29.6	9.4	10 23.0	9.1	58.7
03	223 40.9 . .	16.8	299 58.0	9.4	10 32.1	9.0	58.7
04	238 40.8	16.5	314 26.4	9.4	10 41.1	9.0	58.6
05	253 40.7	16.2	328 54.8	9.4	10 50.1	8.9	58.6
06	268 40.6	N22 15.9	343 23.2	9.3	N10 59.0	8.9	58.6
07	283 40.5	15.6	357 51.5	9.3	11 07.9	8.8	58.6
F 08	298 40.4	15.3	12 19.8	9.3	11 16.7	8.7	58.6
R 09	313 40.3 . .	15.0	26 48.1	9.3	11 25.4	8.6	58.6
I 10	328 40.3	14.6	41 16.4	9.3	11 34.0	8.6	58.5
D 11	343 40.2	14.3	55 44.7	9.2	11 42.6	8.5	58.5
A 12	358 40.1	N22 14.0	70 12.9	9.3	N11 51.1	8.4	58.5
Y 13	13 40.0	13.7	84 41.2	9.2	11 59.5	8.3	58.5
14	28 39.9	13.4	99 09.4	9.2	12 07.8	8.3	58.5
15	43 39.8 . .	13.1	113 37.6	9.2	12 16.1	8.2	58.5
16	58 39.7	12.7	128 05.8	9.2	12 24.3	8.1	58.4
17	73 39.6	12.4	142 34.0	9.1	12 32.4	8.1	58.4
18	88 39.5	N22 12.1	157 02.1	9.2	N12 40.5	8.0	58.4
19	103 39.5	11.8	171 30.3	9.1	12 48.5	7.9	58.4
20	118 39.4	11.5	185 58.4	9.1	12 56.4	7.8	58.4
21	133 39.3 . .	11.1	200 26.5	9.1	13 04.2	7.7	58.3
22	148 39.2	10.8	214 54.6	9.1	13 11.9	7.6	58.3
23	163 39.1	10.5	229 22.7	9.0	13 19.5	7.6	58.3
11 00	178 39.0	N22 10.2	243 50.7	9.1	N13 27.1	7.5	58.3
01	193 38.9	09.9	258 18.8	9.0	13 34.6	7.4	58.3
02	208 38.8	09.5	272 46.8	9.0	13 42.0	7.3	58.3
03	223 38.8 . .	09.2	287 14.8	9.0	13 49.3	7.3	58.2
04	238 38.7	08.9	301 42.8	9.0	13 56.6	7.1	58.2
05	253 38.6	08.6	316 10.8	8.9	14 03.7	7.1	58.2
06	268 38.5	N22 08.2	330 38.7	9.0	N14 10.8	7.0	58.2
07	283 38.4	07.9	345 06.7	8.9	14 17.8	6.9	58.2
S 08	298 38.3	07.6	359 34.6	8.9	14 24.7	6.8	58.1
A 09	313 38.2 . .	07.2	14 02.5	8.9	14 31.5	6.7	58.1
T 10	328 38.2	06.9	28 30.4	8.9	14 38.2	6.6	58.1
U 11	343 38.1	06.6	42 58.3	8.9	14 44.8	6.6	58.1
R 12	358 38.0	N22 06.3	57 26.2	8.8	N14 51.4	6.4	58.1
D 13	13 37.9	05.9	71 54.0	8.9	14 57.8	6.4	58.1
A 14	28 37.8	05.6	86 21.9	8.8	15 04.2	6.3	58.0
Y 15	43 37.7 . .	05.3	100 49.7	8.8	15 10.5	6.1	58.0
16	58 37.7	04.9	115 17.5	8.8	15 16.6	6.1	58.0
17	73 37.6	04.6	129 45.3	8.8	15 22.7	6.0	58.0
18	88 37.5	N22 04.3	144 13.1	8.8	N15 28.7	5.9	58.0
19	103 37.4	03.9	158 40.9	8.7	15 34.6	5.8	57.9
20	118 37.3	03.6	173 08.6	8.8	15 40.4	5.7	57.9
21	133 37.2 . .	03.2	187 36.4	8.7	15 46.1	5.6	57.9
22	148 37.2	02.9	202 04.1	8.7	15 51.7	5.6	57.9
23	163 37.1	02.6	216 31.8	8.8	N15 57.3	5.4	57.9
	SD 15.8	d 0.3	SD 16.1		15.9		15.8

Lat.	Twilight Naut.	Twilight Civil	Sunrise	Moonrise 9	Moonrise 10	Moonrise 11	Moonrise 12
°	h m	h m	h m	h m	h m	h m	h m
N 72	☐	☐	☐	22 44	22 38	22 31	22 20
N 70	☐	☐	☐	22 59	23 02	23 10	23 25
68	☐	☐	☐	23 11	23 21	23 36	24 01
66	////	////	01 11	23 21	23 36	23 57	24 27
64	////	////	02 01	23 29	23 48	24 13	00 13
62	////	////	02 31	23 37	23 59	24 27	00 27
60	////	01 28	02 54	23 43	24 08	00 08	00 39
N 58	////	02 04	03 12	23 49	24 16	00 16	00 49
56	////	02 29	03 27	23 54	24 23	00 23	00 58
54	01 21	02 49	03 40	23 58	24 29	00 29	01 06
52	01 54	03 05	03 52	24 02	00 02	00 35	01 13
50	02 18	03 19	04 02	24 06	00 06	00 40	01 19
45	02 59	03 46	04 23	24 14	00 14	00 51	01 33
N 40	03 27	04 08	04 40	24 21	00 21	01 01	01 44
35	03 49	04 25	04 54	24 27	00 27	01 09	01 54
30	04 06	04 39	05 06	24 32	00 32	01 16	02 02
20	04 34	05 03	05 27	24 41	00 41	01 28	02 17
N 10	04 55	05 22	05 45	00 00	00 49	01 39	02 30
0	05 13	05 39	06 02	00 04	00 56	01 49	02 42
S 10	05 29	05 56	06 18	00 09	01 04	01 59	02 55
20	05 45	06 12	06 36	00 14	01 12	02 10	03 08
30	06 00	06 30	06 56	00 19	01 21	02 23	03 23
35	06 08	06 40	07 07	00 22	01 27	02 30	03 32
40	06 17	06 51	07 21	00 26	01 33	02 39	03 42
45	06 26	07 03	07 36	00 30	01 40	02 48	03 54
S 50	06 37	07 18	07 56	00 35	01 49	03 00	04 08
52	06 42	07 25	08 05	00 38	01 53	03 06	04 15
54	06 47	07 32	08 15	00 40	01 57	03 12	04 22
56	06 53	07 41	08 27	00 43	02 02	03 19	04 31
58	06 59	07 50	08 40	00 47	02 08	03 26	04 40
S 60	07 05	08 01	08 56	00 50	02 14	03 35	04 51

Lat.	Sunset	Twilight Civil	Twilight Naut.	Moonset 9	Moonset 10	Moonset 11	Moonset 12
°	h m	h m	h m	h m	h m	h m	h m
N 72	☐	☐	☐	14 21	16 17	18 15	20 18
N 70	☐	☐	☐	14 08	15 54	17 37	19 14
68	☐	☐	☐	13 58	15 36	17 11	18 38
66	22 56	////	////	13 49	15 22	16 51	18 12
64	22 08	////	////	13 41	15 11	16 35	17 53
62	21 38	////	////	13 35	15 01	16 22	17 37
60	21 16	22 40	////	13 30	14 52	16 11	17 23
N 58	20 57	22 05	////	13 25	14 45	16 01	17 12
56	20 42	21 40	////	13 21	14 39	15 53	17 02
54	20 29	21 21	22 48	13 17	14 33	15 45	16 53
52	20 18	21 05	22 15	13 14	14 28	15 39	16 45
50	20 08	20 51	21 52	13 10	14 23	15 33	16 38
45	19 47	20 24	21 11	13 04	14 13	15 20	16 23
N 40	19 30	20 03	20 43	12 58	14 04	15 09	16 11
35	19 16	19 46	20 22	12 53	13 57	15 00	16 00
30	19 04	19 31	20 04	12 49	13 51	14 52	15 51
20	18 43	19 08	19 37	12 42	13 40	14 38	15 35
N 10	18 26	18 48	19 15	12 35	13 30	14 26	15 21
0	18 09	18 31	18 57	12 29	13 21	14 14	15 08
S 10	17 53	18 15	18 41	12 23	13 12	14 03	14 55
20	17 35	17 59	18 26	12 17	13 03	13 51	14 41
30	17 15	17 41	18 11	12 09	12 52	13 37	14 25
35	17 03	17 31	18 03	12 05	12 46	13 29	14 16
40	16 50	17 20	17 54	12 00	12 39	13 20	14 06
45	16 35	17 08	17 45	11 55	12 31	13 10	13 53
S 50	16 15	16 53	17 34	11 48	12 21	12 57	13 38
52	16 06	16 46	17 29	11 45	12 16	12 51	13 31
54	15 56	16 39	17 24	11 42	12 11	12 45	13 24
56	15 44	16 30	17 18	11 38	12 06	12 37	13 15
58	15 31	16 21	17 12	11 34	11 59	12 29	13 05
S 60	15 15	16 11	17 06	11 30	11 53	12 20	12 54

Day	SUN Eqn. of Time 00h	SUN Eqn. of Time 12h	SUN Mer. Pass.	MOON Mer. Pass. Upper	MOON Mer. Pass. Lower	Age	Phase
d	m s	m s	h m	h m	h m	d	%
9	05 06	05 11	12 05	06 17	18 43	23	43
10	05 15	05 20	12 05	07 09	19 35	24	32
11	05 24	05 28	12 05	08 02	20 28	25	22

UT	ARIES	VENUS −4.7		MARS +1.6		JUPITER −1.8		SATURN +0.3		STARS		
	GHA	GHA	Dec	GHA	Dec	GHA	Dec	GHA	Dec	Name	SHA	Dec
d h	° ′	° ′	° ′	° ′	° ′	° ′	° ′	° ′	° ′		° ′	° ′
12 00	289 34.5	140 07.6	N11 17.8	186 49.1	N23 45.0	143 17.4	N14 26.2	52 41.5	S17 50.5	Acamar	315 17.5	S40 14.5
01	304 36.9	155 09.2	17.0	201 49.7	44.8	158 19.4	26.0	67 44.0	50.5	Achernar	335 25.9	S57 09.2
02	319 39.4	170 10.8	16.2	216 50.4	44.7	173 21.4	25.8	82 46.6	50.5	Acrux	173 07.7	S63 11.4
03	334 41.9	185 12.3	.. 15.5	231 51.1	.. 44.6	188 23.4	.. 25.7	97 49.1	.. 50.5	Adhara	255 11.8	S28 59.8
04	349 44.3	200 13.9	14.7	246 51.7	44.5	203 25.4	25.5	112 51.7	50.4	Aldebaran	290 48.0	N16 32.2
05	4 46.8	215 15.5	13.9	261 52.4	44.3	218 27.3	25.4	127 54.2	50.4			
06	19 49.3	230 17.1	N11 13.1	276 53.0	N23 44.2	233 29.3	N14 25.2	142 56.8	S17 50.4	Alioth	166 19.6	N55 52.9
07	34 51.7	245 18.6	12.4	291 53.7	44.1	248 31.3	25.0	157 59.3	50.4	Alkaid	152 57.8	N49 14.5
08	49 54.2	260 20.2	11.6	306 54.4	43.9	263 33.3	24.9	173 01.9	50.4	Al Na'ir	27 41.7	S46 52.8
S 09	64 56.7	275 21.8	.. 10.8	321 55.0	.. 43.8	278 35.3	.. 24.7	188 04.4	.. 50.4	Alnilam	275 45.2	S 1 11.7
U 10	79 59.1	290 23.4	10.0	336 55.7	43.7	293 37.3	24.5	203 07.0	50.4	Alphard	217 55.0	S 8 43.7
N 11	95 01.6	305 25.0	09.3	351 56.3	43.5	308 39.2	24.4	218 09.5	50.4			
D 12	110 04.0	320 26.6	N11 08.5	6 57.0	N23 43.4	323 41.2	N14 24.2	233 12.1	S17 50.4	Alphecca	126 09.6	N26 40.1
A 13	125 06.5	335 28.2	07.7	21 57.6	43.3	338 43.2	24.0	248 14.6	50.4	Alpheratz	357 41.9	N29 10.5
Y 14	140 09.0	350 29.8	06.9	36 58.3	43.2	353 45.2	23.9	263 17.2	50.4	Altair	62 06.5	N 8 54.8
15	155 11.4	5 31.4	.. 06.2	51 59.0	.. 43.0	8 47.2	.. 23.7	278 19.7	.. 50.3	Ankaa	353 14.3	S42 13.0
16	170 13.9	20 33.0	05.4	66 59.6	42.9	23 49.2	23.6	293 22.3	50.3	Antares	112 24.2	S26 27.8
17	185 16.4	35 34.6	04.6	82 00.3	42.8	38 51.1	23.4	308 24.8	50.3			
18	200 18.8	50 36.2	N11 03.9	97 00.9	N23 42.6	53 53.1	N14 23.2	323 27.4	S17 50.3	Arcturus	145 54.4	N19 06.4
19	215 21.3	65 37.8	03.1	112 01.6	42.5	68 55.1	23.1	338 29.9	50.3	Atria	107 24.2	S69 03.3
20	230 23.8	80 39.4	02.3	127 02.3	42.3	83 57.1	22.9	353 32.5	50.3	Avior	234 18.0	S59 33.8
21	245 26.2	95 41.1	.. 01.5	142 02.9	.. 42.2	98 59.1	.. 22.7	8 35.0	.. 50.3	Bellatrix	278 30.8	N 6 21.6
22	260 28.7	110 42.7	00.8	157 03.6	42.1	114 01.0	22.6	23 37.6	50.3	Betelgeuse	271 00.1	N 7 24.4
23	275 31.1	125 44.3	11 00.0	172 04.2	41.9	129 03.0	22.4	38 40.1	50.3			
13 00	290 33.6	140 45.9	N10 59.2	187 04.9	N23 41.8	144 05.0	N14 22.2	53 42.7	S17 50.3	Canopus	263 56.0	S52 42.4
01	305 36.1	155 47.6	58.5	202 05.6	41.7	159 07.0	22.1	68 45.2	50.3	Capella	280 32.7	N46 00.5
02	320 38.5	170 49.2	57.7	217 06.2	41.5	174 09.0	21.9	83 47.8	50.3	Deneb	49 30.0	N45 20.3
03	335 41.0	185 50.9	.. 56.9	232 06.9	.. 41.4	189 11.0	.. 21.7	98 50.3	.. 50.3	Denebola	182 32.4	N14 29.2
04	350 43.5	200 52.5	56.2	247 07.5	41.3	204 12.9	21.6	113 52.9	50.2	Diphda	348 54.4	S17 54.0
05	5 45.9	215 54.1	55.4	262 08.2	41.1	219 14.9	21.4	128 55.4	50.2			
06	20 48.4	230 55.8	N10 54.6	277 08.9	N23 41.0	234 16.9	N14 21.2	143 58.0	S17 50.2	Dubhe	193 50.5	N61 40.2
07	35 50.9	245 57.4	53.9	292 09.5	40.8	249 18.9	21.1	159 00.5	50.2	Elnath	278 11.2	N28 37.0
08	50 53.3	260 59.1	53.1	307 10.2	40.7	264 20.9	20.9	174 03.1	50.2	Eltanin	90 45.0	N51 29.5
M 09	65 55.8	276 00.7	.. 52.4	322 10.8	.. 40.6	279 22.9	.. 20.8	189 05.6	.. 50.2	Enif	33 45.4	N 9 56.9
O 10	80 58.3	291 02.4	51.6	337 11.5	40.4	294 24.8	20.6	204 08.1	50.2	Fomalhaut	15 22.2	S29 32.1
N 11	96 00.7	306 04.0	50.8	352 12.2	40.3	309 26.8	20.4	219 10.7	50.2			
D 12	111 03.2	321 05.7	N10 50.1	7 12.8	N23 40.1	324 28.8	N14 20.3	234 13.2	S17 50.2	Gacrux	171 59.3	S57 12.2
A 13	126 05.6	336 07.4	49.3	22 13.5	40.0	339 30.8	20.1	249 15.8	50.2	Gienah	175 50.9	S17 37.7
Y 14	141 08.1	351 09.1	48.5	37 14.2	39.9	354 32.8	19.9	264 18.3	50.2	Hadar	148 45.6	S60 27.0
15	156 10.6	6 10.7	.. 47.8	52 14.8	.. 39.7	9 34.7	.. 19.8	279 20.9	.. 50.2	Hamal	327 59.2	N23 32.0
16	171 13.0	21 12.4	47.0	67 15.5	39.6	24 36.7	19.6	294 23.4	50.1	Kaus Aust.	83 41.5	S34 22.4
17	186 15.5	36 14.1	46.3	82 16.1	39.4	39 38.7	19.4	309 26.0	50.1			
18	201 18.0	51 15.8	N10 45.5	97 16.8	N23 39.3	54 40.7	N14 19.3	324 28.5	S17 50.1	Kochab	137 19.8	N74 05.9
19	216 20.4	66 17.5	44.8	112 17.5	39.2	69 42.7	19.1	339 31.1	50.1	Markab	13 36.7	N15 17.4
20	231 22.9	81 19.2	44.0	127 18.1	39.0	84 44.6	18.9	354 33.6	50.1	Menkar	314 13.7	N 4 08.9
21	246 25.4	96 20.9	.. 43.2	142 18.8	.. 38.9	99 46.6	.. 18.8	9 36.1	.. 50.1	Menkent	148 05.7	S36 26.8
22	261 27.8	111 22.6	42.5	157 19.5	38.7	114 48.6	18.6	24 38.7	50.1	Miaplacidus	221 40.0	S69 47.1
23	276 30.3	126 24.3	41.7	172 20.1	38.6	129 50.6	18.4	39 41.2	50.1			
14 00	291 32.8	141 26.0	N10 41.0	187 20.8	N23 38.4	144 52.6	N14 18.3	54 43.8	S17 50.1	Mirfak	308 38.5	N49 54.6
01	306 35.2	156 27.7	40.2	202 21.5	38.3	159 54.5	18.1	69 46.3	50.1	Nunki	75 56.2	S26 16.4
02	321 37.7	171 29.4	39.5	217 22.1	38.2	174 56.5	17.9	84 48.9	50.1	Peacock	53 16.5	S56 40.8
03	336 40.1	186 31.1	.. 38.7	232 22.8	.. 38.0	189 58.5	.. 17.8	99 51.4	.. 50.1	Pollux	243 26.4	N27 59.2
04	351 42.6	201 32.8	38.0	247 23.4	37.9	205 00.5	17.6	114 53.9	50.1	Procyon	244 58.6	N 5 10.9
05	6 45.1	216 34.5	37.2	262 24.1	37.7	220 02.5	17.4	129 56.5	50.1			
06	21 47.5	231 36.2	N10 36.5	277 24.8	N23 37.6	235 04.4	N14 17.3	144 59.0	S17 50.0	Rasalhague	96 04.8	N12 33.2
07	36 50.0	246 37.9	35.7	292 25.4	37.4	250 06.4	17.1	160 01.6	50.0	Regulus	207 42.3	N11 53.5
08	51 52.5	261 39.7	35.0	307 26.1	37.3	265 08.4	16.9	175 04.1	50.0	Rigel	281 11.0	S 8 11.2
T 09	66 54.9	276 41.4	.. 34.2	322 26.8	.. 37.1	280 10.4	.. 16.8	190 06.7	.. 50.0	Rigil Kent.	139 49.4	S60 54.0
U 10	81 57.4	291 43.1	33.5	337 27.4	37.0	295 12.4	16.6	205 09.2	50.0	Sabik	102 10.6	S15 44.4
E 11	96 59.9	306 44.9	32.7	352 28.1	36.8	310 14.3	16.5	220 11.7	50.0			
S 12	112 02.3	321 46.6	N10 32.0	7 28.8	N23 36.7	325 16.3	N14 16.3	235 14.3	S17 50.0	Schedar	349 38.7	N56 37.1
D 13	127 04.8	336 48.3	31.2	22 29.4	36.5	340 18.3	16.1	250 16.8	50.0	Shaula	96 19.6	S37 06.7
A 14	142 07.3	351 50.1	30.5	37 30.1	36.4	355 20.3	16.0	265 19.4	50.0	Sirius	258 32.8	S16 44.4
Y 15	157 09.7	6 51.8	.. 29.7	52 30.8	.. 36.2	10 22.3	.. 15.8	280 21.9	.. 50.0	Spica	158 29.7	S11 14.5
16	172 12.2	21 53.6	29.0	67 31.4	36.1	25 24.2	15.6	295 24.4	50.0	Suhail	222 51.7	S43 29.9
17	187 14.6	36 55.3	28.2	82 32.1	35.9	40 26.2	15.5	310 27.0	50.0			
18	202 17.1	51 57.1	N10 27.5	97 32.8	N23 35.8	55 28.2	N14 15.3	325 29.5	S17 50.0	Vega	80 37.6	N38 48.2
19	217 19.6	66 58.9	26.7	112 33.4	35.6	70 30.2	15.1	340 32.1	50.0	Zuben'ubi	137 03.7	S16 06.3
20	232 22.0	82 00.6	26.0	127 34.1	35.5	85 32.2	15.0	355 34.6	50.0			
21	247 24.5	97 02.4	.. 25.2	142 34.7	.. 35.3	100 34.1	.. 14.8	10 37.2	.. 49.9		SHA	Mer.Pass.
22	262 27.0	112 04.2	24.5	157 35.4	35.2	115 36.1	14.6	25 39.7	49.9	Venus	210 12.3	14 35
23	277 29.4	127 05.9	23.8	172 36.1	35.0	130 38.1	14.5	40 42.2	49.9	Mars	256 31.3	11 31
	h m									Jupiter	213 31.4	14 22
Mer. Pass. 4 37.0		v 1.7	d 0.8	v 0.7	d 0.1	v 2.0	d 0.2	v 2.5	d 0.0	Saturn	123 09.1	20 22

UT	SUN GHA	SUN Dec	MOON GHA	v	MOON Dec	d	HP
d h	° ′	° ′	° ′	′	° ′	′	′
12 00	178 37.0	N22 02.2	230 59.6	8.7	N16 02.7	5.3	57.8
01	193 36.9	01.9	245 27.3	8.7	16 08.0	5.3	57.8
02	208 36.8	01.5	259 55.0	8.6	16 13.3	5.1	57.8
03	223 36.7 ..	01.2	274 22.6	8.7	16 18.4	5.0	57.8
04	238 36.7	00.9	288 50.3	8.6	16 23.4	5.0	57.8
05	253 36.6	00.5	303 18.0	8.6	16 28.4	4.8	57.7
06	268 36.5	N22 00.2	317 45.6	8.7	N16 33.2	4.8	57.7
07	283 36.4	21 59.8	332 13.3	8.6	16 38.0	4.6	57.7
08	298 36.3	59.5	346 40.9	8.7	16 42.6	4.6	57.7
S 09	313 36.3 ..	59.1	1 08.6	8.6	16 47.2	4.4	57.7
U 10	328 36.2	58.8	15 36.2	8.6	16 51.6	4.3	57.6
N 11	343 36.1	58.5	30 03.8	8.7	16 55.9	4.3	57.6
D 12	358 36.0	N21 58.1	44 31.5	8.6	N17 00.2	4.1	57.6
A 13	13 35.9	57.8	58 59.1	8.6	17 04.3	4.1	57.6
Y 14	28 35.9	57.4	73 26.7	8.6	17 08.4	3.9	57.6
15	43 35.8 ..	57.1	87 54.3	8.6	17 12.3	3.8	57.5
16	58 35.7	56.7	102 21.9	8.6	17 16.1	3.8	57.5
17	73 35.6	56.4	116 49.5	8.6	17 19.9	3.6	57.5
18	88 35.5	N21 56.0	131 17.1	8.6	N17 23.5	3.5	57.5
19	103 35.5	55.7	145 44.7	8.6	17 27.0	3.5	57.5
20	118 35.4	55.3	160 12.3	8.6	17 30.5	3.3	57.4
21	133 35.3 ..	55.0	174 39.9	8.6	17 33.8	3.2	57.4
22	148 35.2	54.6	189 07.5	8.6	17 37.0	3.1	57.4
23	163 35.2	54.3	203 35.1	8.6	17 40.1	3.0	57.4
13 00	178 35.1	N21 53.9	218 02.7	8.6	N17 43.1	2.9	57.4
01	193 35.0	53.5	232 30.3	8.7	17 46.0	2.9	57.3
02	208 34.9	53.2	246 58.0	8.6	17 48.9	2.7	57.3
03	223 34.8 ..	52.8	261 25.6	8.6	17 51.6	2.5	57.3
04	238 34.8	52.5	275 53.2	8.6	17 54.1	2.5	57.3
05	253 34.7	52.1	290 20.8	8.7	17 56.6	2.4	57.3
06	268 34.6	N21 51.8	304 48.5	8.6	N17 59.0	2.3	57.2
07	283 34.5	51.4	319 16.1	8.7	18 01.3	2.2	57.2
08	298 34.5	51.0	333 43.8	8.6	18 03.5	2.1	57.2
M 09	313 34.4 ..	50.7	348 11.4	8.7	18 05.6	1.9	57.2
O 10	328 34.3	50.3	2 39.1	8.7	18 07.5	1.9	57.2
N 11	343 34.2	50.0	17 06.8	8.7	18 09.4	1.7	57.1
D 12	358 34.2	N21 49.6	31 34.5	8.7	N18 11.1	1.7	57.1
A 13	13 34.1	49.2	46 02.2	8.7	18 12.8	1.5	57.1
Y 14	28 34.0	48.9	60 29.9	8.7	18 14.3	1.5	57.1
15	43 33.9 ..	48.5	74 57.6	8.7	18 15.8	1.3	57.1
16	58 33.9	48.1	89 25.3	8.8	18 17.1	1.3	57.0
17	73 33.8	47.8	103 53.1	8.8	18 18.4	1.1	57.0
18	88 33.7	N21 47.4	118 20.9	8.8	N18 19.5	1.0	57.0
19	103 33.6	47.0	132 48.7	8.8	18 20.5	0.9	57.0
20	118 33.6	46.7	147 16.5	8.8	18 21.4	0.8	57.0
21	133 33.5 ..	46.3	161 44.3	8.8	18 22.2	0.7	56.9
22	148 33.4	45.9	176 12.1	8.9	18 22.9	0.6	56.9
23	163 33.4	45.6	190 40.0	8.9	18 23.5	0.5	56.9
14 00	178 33.3	N21 45.2	205 07.9	8.9	N18 24.0	0.4	56.9
01	193 33.2	44.8	219 35.8	8.9	18 24.4	0.3	56.8
02	208 33.1	44.4	234 03.7	8.9	18 24.7	0.2	56.8
03	223 33.1 ..	44.1	248 31.6	9.0	18 24.9	0.1	56.8
04	238 33.0	43.7	262 59.6	9.0	18 25.0	0.0	56.8
05	253 32.9	43.3	277 27.6	9.0	18 25.0	0.1	56.8
06	268 32.8	N21 43.0	291 55.6	9.0	N18 24.9	0.3	56.7
07	283 32.8	42.6	306 23.6	9.1	18 24.6	0.3	56.7
T 08	298 32.7	42.2	320 51.7	9.1	18 24.3	0.4	56.7
U 09	313 32.6 ..	41.8	335 19.8	9.1	18 23.9	0.5	56.7
E 10	328 32.6	41.5	349 47.9	9.1	18 23.4	0.7	56.7
S 11	343 32.5	41.1	4 16.0	9.2	18 22.7	0.7	56.6
D 12	358 32.4	N21 40.7	18 44.2	9.2	N18 22.0	0.9	56.6
A 13	13 32.4	40.3	33 12.4	9.2	18 21.1	0.9	56.6
Y 14	28 32.3	39.9	47 40.6	9.3	18 20.2	1.0	56.6
15	43 32.2 ..	39.6	62 08.9	9.3	18 19.2	1.2	56.6
16	58 32.1	39.2	76 37.2	9.3	18 18.0	1.2	56.5
17	73 32.1	38.8	91 05.5	9.4	18 16.8	1.3	56.5
18	88 32.0	N21 38.4	105 33.9	9.4	N18 15.5	1.5	56.5
19	103 31.9	38.0	120 02.3	9.4	18 14.0	1.5	56.5
20	118 31.9	37.7	134 30.7	9.5	18 12.5	1.6	56.4
21	133 31.8 ..	37.3	148 59.2	9.5	18 10.9	1.8	56.4
22	148 31.7	36.9	163 27.7	9.5	18 09.1	1.8	56.4
23	163 31.7	36.5	177 56.2	9.6	N18 07.3	1.9	56.4
	SD 15.8	d 0.4	SD 15.7		15.6		15.4

Lat.	Naut.	Civil	Sunrise	Moonrise 12	13	14	15
°	h m	h m	h m	h m	h m	h m	h m
N 72	☐	☐	☐	22 20	☐	23 12	25 36
N 70	☐	☐	☐	23 25	23 59	25 01	01 01
68	☐	☐	☐	24 01	00 01	00 42	01 41
66	////	////	01 25	24 27	00 27	01 10	02 09
64	////	////	02 09	00 13	00 47	01 32	02 30
62	////	00 27	02 37	00 27	01 03	01 50	02 47
60	////	01 37	02 59	00 39	01 17	02 04	03 01
N 58	////	02 10	03 17	00 49	01 29	02 17	03 13
56	00 25	02 34	03 31	00 58	01 39	02 27	03 23
54	01 29	02 53	03 44	01 06	01 48	02 37	03 33
52	02 00	03 09	03 55	01 13	01 56	02 45	03 41
50	02 22	03 22	04 05	01 19	02 03	02 53	03 48
45	03 02	03 49	04 25	01 33	02 19	03 09	04 04
N 40	03 30	04 10	04 42	01 44	02 31	03 23	04 17
35	03 51	04 27	04 56	01 54	02 42	03 34	04 28
30	04 08	04 41	05 08	02 02	02 52	03 44	04 38
20	04 35	05 04	05 28	02 17	03 08	04 01	04 54
N 10	04 56	05 23	05 46	02 30	03 23	04 16	05 09
0	05 14	05 40	06 02	02 42	03 36	04 30	05 22
S 10	05 30	05 56	06 18	02 55	03 50	04 44	05 36
20	05 44	06 12	06 35	03 08	04 04	04 59	05 50
30	05 59	06 29	06 55	03 23	04 21	05 16	06 07
35	06 07	06 39	07 06	03 32	04 31	05 26	06 16
40	06 16	06 49	07 19	03 42	04 42	05 37	06 27
45	06 25	07 02	07 35	03 54	04 55	05 51	06 40
S 50	06 35	07 16	07 54	04 08	05 11	06 07	06 56
52	06 40	07 23	08 02	04 15	05 18	06 15	07 03
54	06 45	07 30	08 12	04 22	05 27	06 23	07 11
56	06 50	07 38	08 24	04 31	05 36	06 33	07 20
58	06 56	07 47	08 37	04 40	05 47	06 44	07 31
S 60	07 03	07 58	08 52	04 51	05 59	06 56	07 43

Lat.	Sunset	Twilight Civil	Naut.	Moonset 12	13	14	15
°	h m	h m	h m	h m	h m	h m	h m
N 72	☐	☐	☐	20 18	☐	23 09	22 32
N 70	☐	☐	☐	19 14	20 32	21 19	21 41
68	☐	☐	☐	18 38	19 49	20 39	21 10
66	22 43	////	////	18 12	19 20	20 11	20 46
64	22 01	////	////	17 53	18 58	19 50	20 28
62	21 32	23 34	////	17 37	18 41	19 33	20 12
60	21 11	22 31	////	17 23	18 26	19 18	20 00
N 58	20 54	21 59	////	17 12	18 14	19 06	19 49
56	20 39	21 36	23 37	17 02	18 03	18 56	19 39
54	20 27	21 17	22 40	16 53	17 54	18 46	19 30
52	20 16	21 02	22 10	16 45	17 45	18 38	19 23
50	20 06	20 48	21 48	16 38	17 38	18 31	19 16
45	19 46	20 22	21 09	16 23	17 22	18 15	19 01
N 40	19 29	20 01	20 41	16 11	17 09	18 01	18 49
35	19 15	19 44	20 20	16 00	16 57	17 50	18 38
30	19 03	19 30	20 03	15 51	16 47	17 40	18 29
20	18 43	19 07	19 36	15 35	16 30	17 24	18 13
N 10	18 26	18 48	19 15	15 21	16 16	17 09	18 00
0	18 09	18 32	18 58	15 08	16 02	16 55	17 47
S 10	17 53	18 16	18 42	14 55	15 48	16 41	17 34
20	17 36	18 00	18 27	14 41	15 33	16 26	17 20
30	17 17	17 43	18 12	14 25	15 16	16 09	17 04
35	17 05	17 33	18 04	14 16	15 06	15 59	16 54
40	16 52	17 22	17 56	14 06	14 55	15 48	16 44
45	16 37	17 10	17 47	13 53	14 42	15 35	16 31
S 50	16 18	16 56	17 36	13 38	14 25	15 18	16 16
52	16 09	16 49	17 32	13 31	14 18	15 11	16 09
54	15 59	16 42	17 27	13 24	14 09	15 02	16 01
56	15 48	16 34	17 21	13 15	14 00	14 52	15 52
58	15 35	16 24	17 16	13 05	13 49	14 42	15 42
S 60	15 20	16 14	17 09	12 54	13 37	14 29	15 30

Day	Eqn. of Time 00h	12h	Mer. Pass.	Mer. Pass. Upper	Lower	Age	Phase
d	m s	m s	h m	h m	h m	d	%
12	05 32	05 36	12 06	08 55	21 22	26	14
13	05 40	05 43	12 06	09 49	22 16	27	7
14	05 47	05 50	12 06	10 42	23 09	28	3

UT	ARIES	VENUS −4.7		MARS +1.6		JUPITER −1.7		SATURN +0.3		STARS		
	GHA	GHA	Dec	GHA	Dec	GHA	Dec	GHA	Dec	Name	SHA	Dec
15 00	292 31.9	142 07.7 N10 23.0		187 36.7 N23 34.9		145 40.1 N14 14.3		55 44.8 S17 49.9		Acamar	315 17.5	S40 14.4
01	307 34.4	157 09.5	22.3	202 37.4	34.7	160 42.1	14.1	70 47.3	49.9	Achernar	335 25.9	S57 09.2
02	322 36.8	172 11.3	21.5	217 38.1	34.6	175 44.0	14.0	85 49.9	49.9	Acrux	173 07.7	S63 11.4
03	337 39.3	187 13.0 ..	20.8	232 38.8 ..	34.4	190 46.0 ..	13.8	100 52.4 ..	49.9	Adhara	255 11.8	S28 59.7
04	352 41.8	202 14.8	20.1	247 39.4	34.3	205 48.0	13.6	115 54.9	49.9	Aldebaran	290 48.0	N16 32.2
05	7 44.2	217 16.6	19.3	262 40.1	34.1	220 50.0	13.5	130 57.5	49.9			
06	22 46.7	232 18.4 N10 18.6		277 40.8 N23 34.0		235 51.9 N14 13.3		146 00.0 S17 49.9		Alioth	166 19.7	N55 52.9
W 07	37 49.1	247 20.2	17.9	292 41.4	33.8	250 53.9	13.1	161 02.5	49.9	Alkaid	152 57.8	N49 14.5
E 08	52 51.6	262 22.0	17.1	307 42.1	33.7	265 55.9	13.0	176 05.1	49.9	Al Na'ir	27 41.7	S46 52.8
D 09	67 54.1	277 23.8 ..	16.4	322 42.8 ..	33.5	280 57.9 ..	12.8	191 07.6 ..	49.9	Alnilam	275 45.2	S 1 11.7
N 10	82 56.5	292 25.6	15.6	337 43.4	33.4	295 59.9	12.6	206 10.2	49.9	Alphard	217 55.0	S 8 43.7
E 11	97 59.0	307 27.4	14.9	352 44.1	33.2	311 01.8	12.5	221 12.7	49.9			
S 12	113 01.5	322 29.3 N10 14.2		7 44.8 N23 33.0		326 03.8 N14 12.3		236 15.2 S17 49.9		Alphecca	126 09.6	N26 40.1
D 13	128 03.9	337 31.1	13.4	22 45.4	32.9	341 05.8	12.1	251 17.8	49.8	Alpheratz	357 41.8	N29 10.5
A 14	143 06.4	352 32.9	12.7	37 46.1	32.7	356 07.8	12.0	266 20.3	49.8	Altair	62 06.5	N 8 54.8
Y 15	158 08.9	7 34.7 ..	12.0	52 46.8 ..	32.6	11 09.7 ..	11.8	281 22.9 ..	49.8	Ankaa	353 14.2	S42 13.0
16	173 11.3	22 36.5	11.2	67 47.4	32.4	26 11.7	11.6	296 25.4	49.8	Antares	112 24.2	S26 27.8
17	188 13.8	37 38.4	10.5	82 48.1	32.3	41 13.7	11.5	311 27.9	49.8			
18	203 16.2	52 40.2 N10 09.8		97 48.8 N23 32.1		56 15.7 N14 11.3		326 30.5 S17 49.8		Arcturus	145 54.4	N19 06.4
19	218 18.7	67 42.0	09.1	112 49.4	31.9	71 17.7	11.1	341 33.0	49.8	Atria	107 24.2	S69 03.3
20	233 21.2	82 43.9	08.3	127 50.1	31.8	86 19.6	10.9	356 35.5	49.8	Avior	234 18.0	S59 33.8
21	248 23.6	97 45.7 ..	07.6	142 50.8 ..	31.6	101 21.6 ..	10.8	11 38.1 ..	49.8	Bellatrix	278 30.8	N 6 21.6
22	263 26.1	112 47.6	06.9	157 51.5	31.5	116 23.6	10.6	26 40.6	49.8	Betelgeuse	271 00.1	N 7 24.4
23	278 28.6	127 49.4	06.1	172 52.1	31.3	131 25.6	10.4	41 43.1	49.8			
16 00	293 31.0	142 51.3 N10 05.4		187 52.8 N23 31.1		146 27.5 N14 10.3		56 45.7 S17 49.8		Canopus	263 56.0	S52 42.3
01	308 33.5	157 53.1	04.7	202 53.5	31.0	161 29.5	10.1	71 48.2	49.8	Capella	280 32.7	N46 00.5
02	323 36.0	172 55.0	04.0	217 54.1	30.8	176 31.5	09.9	86 50.8	49.8	Deneb	49 30.0	N45 20.3
03	338 38.4	187 56.8 ..	03.2	232 54.8 ..	30.7	191 33.5 ..	09.8	101 53.3 ..	49.8	Denebola	182 32.4	N14 29.2
04	353 40.9	202 58.7	02.5	247 55.5	30.5	206 35.4	09.6	116 55.8	49.8	Diphda	348 54.4	S17 54.0
05	8 43.4	218 00.6	01.8	262 56.1	30.3	221 37.4	09.4	131 58.4	49.8			
06	23 45.8	233 02.4 N10 01.1		277 56.8 N23 30.2		236 39.4 N14 09.3		147 00.9 S17 49.8		Dubhe	193 50.5	N61 40.2
T 07	38 48.3	248 04.3 10 00.3		292 57.5	30.0	251 41.4	09.1	162 03.4	49.7	Elnath	278 11.1	N28 37.0
H 08	53 50.7	263 06.2 9 59.6		307 58.2	29.9	266 43.3	08.9	177 06.0	49.7	Eltanin	90 45.0	N51 29.6
U 09	68 53.2	278 08.1 .. 58.9		322 58.8 ..	29.7	281 45.3 ..	08.8	192 08.5 ..	49.7	Enif	33 45.4	N 9 56.9
R 10	83 55.7	293 09.9 58.2		337 59.5	29.5	296 47.3	08.6	207 11.0	49.7	Fomalhaut	15 22.2	S29 32.1
S 11	98 58.1	308 11.8 57.5		353 00.2	29.4	311 49.3	08.4	222 13.6	49.7			
D 12	114 00.6	323 13.7 N 9 56.8		8 00.8 N23 29.2		326 51.3 N14 08.2		237 16.1 S17 49.7		Gacrux	171 59.3	S57 12.2
A 13	129 03.1	338 15.6 56.0		23 01.5	29.0	341 53.2	08.1	252 18.6	49.7	Gienah	175 50.9	S17 37.7
Y 14	144 05.5	353 17.5 55.3		38 02.2	28.9	356 55.2	07.9	267 21.2	49.7	Hadar	148 45.6	S60 27.0
15	159 08.0	8 19.4 .. 54.6		53 02.9 ..	28.7	11 57.2 ..	07.8	282 23.7 ..	49.7	Hamal	327 59.2	N23 32.0
16	174 10.5	23 21.3 53.9		68 03.5	28.5	26 59.2	07.6	297 26.2	49.7	Kaus Aust.	83 41.5	S34 22.4
17	189 12.9	38 23.2 53.2		83 04.2	28.4	42 01.1	07.4	312 28.8	49.7			
18	204 15.4	53 25.1 N 9 52.5		98 04.9 N23 28.2		57 03.1 N14 07.3		327 31.3 S17 49.7		Kochab	137 19.9	N74 05.9
19	219 17.9	68 27.0 51.7		113 05.5	28.0	72 05.1	07.1	342 33.8	49.7	Markab	13 36.7	N15 17.4
20	234 20.3	83 29.0 51.0		128 06.2	27.9	87 07.1	06.9	357 36.4	49.7	Menkar	314 13.7	N 4 08.9
21	249 22.8	98 30.9 .. 50.3		143 06.9 ..	27.7	102 09.0 ..	06.8	12 38.9 ..	49.7	Menkent	148 05.8	S36 26.8
22	264 25.2	113 32.8 49.6		158 07.6	27.5	117 11.0	06.6	27 41.4	49.7	Miaplacidus	221 40.1	S69 47.1
23	279 27.7	128 34.7 48.9		173 08.2	27.4	132 13.0	06.4	42 44.0	49.7			
17 00	294 30.2	143 36.6 N 9 48.2		188 08.9 N23 27.2		147 15.0 N14 06.2		57 46.5 S17 49.7		Mirfak	308 38.5	N49 54.6
01	309 32.6	158 38.6 47.5		203 09.6	27.0	162 16.9	06.1	72 49.0	49.7	Nunki	75 56.2	S26 16.4
02	324 35.1	173 40.5 46.8		218 10.3	26.9	177 18.9	05.9	87 51.6	49.7	Peacock	53 16.5	S56 40.8
03	339 37.6	188 42.5 .. 46.1		233 10.9 ..	26.7	192 20.9 ..	05.7	102 54.1 ..	49.7	Pollux	243 26.4	N27 59.2
04	354 40.0	203 44.4 45.3		248 11.6	26.5	207 22.9	05.6	117 56.6	49.6	Procyon	244 58.6	N 5 10.9
05	9 42.5	218 46.3 44.6		263 12.3	26.4	222 24.8	05.4	132 59.2	49.6			
06	24 45.0	233 48.3 N 9 43.9		278 13.0 N23 26.2		237 26.8 N14 05.2		148 01.7 S17 49.6		Rasalhague	96 04.8	N12 33.2
07	39 47.4	248 50.2 43.2		293 13.6	26.0	252 28.8	05.1	163 04.2	49.6	Regulus	207 42.3	N11 53.5
08	54 49.9	263 52.2 42.5		308 14.3	25.9	267 30.8	04.9	178 06.8	49.6	Rigel	281 11.0	S 8 11.2
F 09	69 52.4	278 54.2 .. 41.8		323 15.0 ..	25.7	282 32.7 ..	04.7	193 09.3 ..	49.6	Rigil Kent.	139 49.5	S60 54.0
R 10	84 54.8	293 56.1 41.1		338 15.7	25.5	297 34.7	04.6	208 11.8	49.6	Sabik	102 10.6	S15 44.4
I 11	99 57.3	308 58.1 40.4		353 16.3	25.3	312 36.7	04.4	223 14.3	49.6			
D 12	114 59.7	324 00.1 N 9 39.7		8 17.0 N23 25.2		327 38.7 N14 04.2		238 16.9 S17 49.6		Schedar	349 38.6	N56 37.1
A 13	130 02.2	339 02.0 39.0		23 17.7	25.0	342 40.6	04.0	253 19.4	49.6	Shaula	96 19.6	S37 06.7
Y 14	145 04.7	354 04.0 38.3		38 18.4	24.8	357 42.6	03.9	268 21.9	49.6	Sirius	258 32.8	S16 44.4
15	160 07.1	9 06.0 .. 37.6		53 19.0 ..	24.7	12 44.6 ..	03.7	283 24.5 ..	49.6	Spica	158 29.7	S11 14.5
16	175 09.6	24 08.0 36.9		68 19.7	24.5	27 46.6	03.5	298 27.0	49.6	Suhail	222 51.7	S43 29.9
17	190 12.1	39 09.9 36.2		83 20.4	24.3	42 48.5	03.4	313 29.5	49.6			
18	205 14.5	54 11.9 N 9 35.5		98 21.1 N23 24.1		57 50.5 N14 03.2		328 32.1 S17 49.6		Vega	80 37.6	N38 48.2
19	220 17.0	69 13.9 34.8		113 21.7	24.0	72 52.5	03.0	343 34.6	49.6	Zuben'ubi	137 03.7	S16 06.3
20	235 19.5	84 15.9 34.1		128 22.4	23.8	87 54.4	02.9	358 37.1	49.6		SHA	Mer. Pass.
21	250 21.9	99 17.9 .. 33.4		143 23.1 ..	23.6	102 56.4 ..	02.7	13 39.6 ..	49.6		° ′	h m
22	265 24.4	114 19.9 32.7		158 23.8	23.4	117 58.4	02.5	28 42.2	49.6	Venus	209 20.2	14 27
23	280 26.8	129 21.9 32.0		173 24.4	23.3	133 00.4	02.4	43 44.7	49.6	Mars	254 21.8	11 28
	h m									Jupiter	212 56.5	14 12
Mer. Pass. 4 25.2		v 1.9 d 0.7		v 0.7 d 0.2		v 2.0 d 0.2		v 2.5 d 0.0		Saturn	123 14.7	20 10

UT	SUN GHA	SUN Dec	MOON GHA	v	MOON Dec	d	HP
d h	° ′	° ′	° ′	′	° ′	′	′
15 00	178 31.6	N21 36.1	192 24.8	9.6	N18 05.4	2.1	56.4
01	193 31.5	35.7	206 53.4	9.6	18 03.3	2.1	56.3
02	208 31.5	35.3	221 22.0	9.7	18 01.2	2.2	56.3
03	223 31.4 ..	35.0	235 50.7	9.7	17 59.0	2.3	56.3
04	238 31.3	34.6	250 19.4	9.8	17 56.7	2.4	56.3
05	253 31.3	34.2	264 48.2	9.8	17 54.3	2.5	56.3
W 06	268 31.2	N21 33.8	279 17.0	9.8	N17 51.8	2.6	56.2
E 07	283 31.1	33.4	293 45.8	9.9	17 49.2	2.7	56.2
D 08	298 31.1	33.0	308 14.7	9.9	17 46.5	2.8	56.2
N 09	313 31.0 ..	32.6	322 43.6	10.0	17 43.7	2.8	56.2
E 10	328 30.9	32.2	337 12.6	10.0	17 40.9	3.0	56.1
S 11	343 30.9	31.8	351 41.6	10.0	17 37.9	3.1	56.1
D 12	358 30.8	N21 31.4	6 10.6	10.1	N17 34.8	3.1	56.1
A 13	13 30.7	31.0	20 39.7	10.1	17 31.7	3.3	56.1
Y 14	28 30.7	30.6	35 08.8	10.2	17 28.4	3.3	56.1
15	43 30.6 ..	30.3	49 38.0	10.2	17 25.1	3.4	56.0
16	58 30.5	29.9	64 07.2	10.3	17 21.7	3.5	56.0
17	73 30.5	29.5	78 36.5	10.3	17 18.2	3.6	56.0
18	88 30.4	N21 29.1	93 05.8	10.4	N17 14.6	3.7	56.0
19	103 30.3	28.7	107 35.2	10.4	17 10.9	3.7	56.0
20	118 30.3	28.3	122 04.6	10.5	17 07.2	3.9	55.9
21	133 30.2 ..	27.9	136 34.1	10.5	17 03.3	3.9	55.9
22	148 30.2	27.5	151 03.6	10.5	16 59.4	4.0	55.9
23	163 30.1	27.1	165 33.1	10.6	16 55.4	4.2	55.9
16 00	178 30.0	N21 26.7	180 02.7	10.6	N16 51.2	4.1	55.9
01	193 30.0	26.3	194 32.3	10.7	16 47.1	4.3	55.8
02	208 29.9	25.9	209 02.0	10.8	16 42.8	4.4	55.8
03	223 29.8 ..	25.5	223 31.8	10.8	16 38.4	4.4	55.8
04	238 29.8	25.1	238 01.6	10.8	16 34.0	4.5	55.8
05	253 29.7	24.7	252 31.4	10.9	16 29.5	4.6	55.8
T 06	268 29.7	N21 24.2	267 01.3	10.9	N16 24.9	4.7	55.7
H 07	283 29.6	23.8	281 31.2	11.0	16 20.2	4.8	55.7
U 08	298 29.6	23.4	296 01.2	11.1	16 15.4	4.8	55.7
R 09	313 29.5 ..	23.0	310 31.3	11.1	16 10.6	4.9	55.7
S 10	328 29.4	22.6	325 01.4	11.1	16 05.7	5.0	55.7
D 11	343 29.4	22.2	339 31.5	11.2	16 00.7	5.1	55.6
A 12	358 29.3	N21 21.8	354 01.7	11.2	N15 55.6	5.1	55.6
Y 13	13 29.2	21.4	8 31.9	11.3	15 50.5	5.2	55.6
14	28 29.2	21.0	23 02.2	11.4	15 45.3	5.3	55.6
15	43 29.1 ..	20.6	37 32.6	11.4	15 40.0	5.4	55.6
16	58 29.1	20.2	52 03.0	11.4	15 34.6	5.4	55.5
17	73 29.0	19.8	66 33.4	11.5	15 29.2	5.5	55.5
18	88 28.9	N21 19.3	81 03.9	11.6	N15 23.7	5.6	55.5
19	103 28.9	18.9	95 34.5	11.6	15 18.1	5.7	55.5
20	118 28.8	18.5	110 05.1	11.6	15 12.4	5.7	55.5
21	133 28.8 ..	18.1	124 35.7	11.7	15 06.7	5.8	55.4
22	148 28.7	17.7	139 06.4	11.8	15 00.9	5.8	55.4
23	163 28.7	17.3	153 37.2	11.8	14 55.1	6.0	55.4
17 00	178 28.6	N21 16.9	168 08.0	11.9	N14 49.1	6.0	55.4
01	193 28.5	16.4	182 38.9	11.9	14 43.1	6.0	55.4
02	208 28.5	16.0	197 09.8	12.0	14 37.1	6.1	55.3
03	223 28.4 ..	15.6	211 40.8	12.0	14 31.0	6.2	55.3
04	238 28.4	15.2	226 11.8	12.0	14 24.8	6.3	55.3
05	253 28.3	14.8	240 42.8	12.2	14 18.5	6.3	55.3
F 06	268 28.3	N21 14.3	255 14.0	12.1	N14 12.2	6.4	55.2
R 07	283 28.2	13.9	269 45.1	12.3	14 05.8	6.4	55.2
I 08	298 28.2	13.5	284 16.4	12.2	13 59.4	6.5	55.2
D 09	313 28.1 ..	13.1	298 47.6	12.4	13 52.9	6.6	55.2
A 10	328 28.0	12.7	313 19.0	12.3	13 46.3	6.6	55.2
Y 11	343 28.0	12.2	327 50.3	12.5	13 39.7	6.7	55.2
12	358 27.9	N21 11.8	342 21.8	12.5	N13 33.0	6.8	55.2
13	13 27.9	11.4	356 53.3	12.5	13 26.2	6.8	55.1
14	28 27.8	11.0	11 24.8	12.6	13 19.4	6.8	55.1
15	43 27.8 ..	10.5	25 56.4	12.6	13 12.6	7.0	55.1
16	58 27.7	10.1	40 28.0	12.7	13 05.6	6.9	55.1
17	73 27.7	09.7	54 59.7	12.7	12 58.7	7.1	55.1
18	88 27.6	N21 09.3	69 31.4	12.8	N12 51.6	7.0	55.0
19	103 27.6	08.8	84 03.2	12.8	12 44.6	7.2	55.0
20	118 27.5	08.4	98 35.0	12.9	12 37.4	7.2	55.0
21	133 27.5 ..	08.0	113 06.9	12.9	12 30.2	7.2	55.0
22	148 27.4	07.5	127 38.8	13.0	12 23.0	7.3	55.0
23	163 27.4	07.1	142 10.8	13.1	N12 15.7	7.3	55.0
	SD 15.8	d 0.4	SD 15.3		15.2		15.0

Twilight / Moonrise

Lat.	Naut.	Civil	Sunrise	15	16	17	18
°	h m	h m	h m	h m	h m	h m	h m
N 72	□	□	□	25 36	01 36	03 26	05 09
N 70	□	□	□	01 01	02 25	03 57	05 29
68	□	□	□	01 41	02 57	04 20	05 45
66	////	////	01 38	02 09	03 20	04 37	05 58
64	////	////	02 17	02 30	03 38	04 52	06 08
62	////	00 54	02 44	02 47	03 53	05 04	06 17
60	////	01 47	03 05	03 01	04 05	05 14	06 25
N 58	////	02 17	03 22	03 13	04 16	05 23	06 31
56	00 50	02 40	03 36	03 23	04 25	05 30	06 37
54	01 38	02 58	03 48	03 33	04 33	05 37	06 42
52	02 06	03 13	03 59	03 41	04 41	05 44	06 47
50	02 28	03 26	04 08	03 48	04 48	05 49	06 51
45	03 06	03 52	04 28	04 04	05 02	06 01	07 01
N 40	03 33	04 12	04 44	04 17	05 14	06 11	07 08
35	03 53	04 29	04 58	04 28	05 24	06 19	07 15
30	04 10	04 43	05 09	04 38	05 32	06 27	07 21
20	04 37	05 05	05 29	04 54	05 47	06 40	07 31
N 10	04 57	05 24	05 47	05 09	06 00	06 51	07 40
0	05 14	05 40	06 02	05 22	06 13	07 01	07 48
S 10	05 30	05 56	06 18	05 36	06 25	07 12	07 56
20	05 44	06 11	06 35	05 50	06 38	07 23	08 05
30	05 59	06 28	06 54	06 07	06 53	07 36	08 15
35	06 06	06 38	07 05	06 16	07 02	07 43	08 21
40	06 15	06 48	07 18	06 27	07 12	07 52	08 27
45	06 23	07 00	07 33	06 40	07 23	08 01	08 35
S 50	06 34	07 14	07 51	06 56	07 37	08 13	08 44
52	06 38	07 20	08 00	07 03	07 44	08 18	08 48
54	06 43	07 28	08 09	07 11	07 51	08 24	08 52
56	06 48	07 35	08 20	07 20	07 59	08 31	08 57
58	06 54	07 44	08 33	07 31	08 08	08 38	09 03
S 60	07 00	07 54	08 47	07 43	08 19	08 47	09 09

Sunset / Twilight / Moonset

Lat.	Sunset	Civil	Naut.	15	16	17	18
°	h m	h m	h m	h m	h m	h m	h m
N 72	□	□	□	22 32	22 24	22 18	22 12
N 70	□	□	□	21 41	21 52	21 56	21 59
68	□	□	□	21 10	21 28	21 40	21 47
66	22 30	////	////	20 46	21 10	21 26	21 38
64	21 52	////	////	20 28	20 55	21 15	21 30
62	21 26	23 11	////	20 12	20 42	21 05	21 24
60	21 06	22 22	////	20 00	20 32	20 57	21 18
N 58	20 49	21 53	////	19 49	20 22	20 50	21 12
56	20 35	21 31	23 16	19 39	20 14	20 43	21 08
54	20 23	21 13	22 31	19 30	20 07	20 37	21 04
52	20 13	20 58	22 04	19 23	20 00	20 32	21 00
50	20 03	20 45	21 43	19 16	19 54	20 28	20 56
45	19 43	20 19	21 06	19 01	19 42	20 17	20 49
N 40	19 27	19 59	20 39	18 49	19 31	20 09	20 43
35	19 14	19 43	20 18	18 38	19 22	20 01	20 37
30	19 02	19 29	20 02	18 29	19 14	19 55	20 32
20	18 43	19 07	19 35	18 13	19 00	19 43	20 24
N 10	18 25	18 48	19 15	18 00	18 48	19 34	20 17
0	18 10	18 32	18 58	17 47	18 36	19 24	20 10
S 10	17 54	18 16	18 42	17 34	18 25	19 15	20 03
20	17 37	18 01	18 28	17 20	18 13	19 05	19 55
30	17 18	17 44	18 13	17 04	17 59	18 53	19 47
35	17 07	17 35	18 06	16 54	17 50	18 46	19 42
40	16 54	17 24	17 58	16 44	17 41	18 39	19 36
45	16 40	17 12	17 49	16 31	17 30	18 30	19 29
S 50	16 21	16 58	17 39	16 16	17 17	18 19	19 21
52	16 13	16 52	17 35	16 09	17 10	18 14	19 18
54	16 03	16 45	17 30	16 01	17 03	18 08	19 14
56	15 52	16 37	17 25	15 52	16 56	18 02	19 09
58	15 40	16 28	17 19	15 42	16 47	17 55	19 04
S 60	15 25	16 19	17 13	15 30	16 37	17 47	18 58

SUN / MOON

Day	Eqn. of Time 00h	Eqn. of Time 12h	Mer. Pass.	Mer. Pass. Upper	Mer. Pass. Lower	Age	Phase
d	m s	m s	h m	h m	h m	d	%
15	05 53	05 57	12 06	11 34	24 00	29	1
16	06 00	06 03	12 06	12 25	00 00	00	0
17	06 05	06 08	12 06	13 13	00 49	01	2

(Phase symbol: ●)

UT	ARIES GHA	VENUS −4.7 GHA	Dec	MARS +1.7 GHA	Dec	JUPITER −1.7 GHA	Dec	SATURN +0.4 GHA	Dec	STARS Name	SHA	Dec
18 00	295 29.3	144 23.9	N 9 31.4	188 25.1	N23 23.1	148 02.3	N14 02.2	58 47.2	S17 49.6	Acamar	315 17.5	S40 14.4
01	310 31.8	159 25.9	30.7	203 25.8	22.9	163 04.3	02.0	73 49.8	49.6	Achernar	335 25.8	S57 09.2
02	325 34.2	174 28.0	30.0	218 26.5	22.7	178 06.3	01.8	88 52.3	49.6	Acrux	173 07.7	S63 11.4
03	340 36.7	189 30.0	.. 29.3	233 27.1	.. 22.6	193 08.3	.. 01.7	103 54.8	.. 49.6	Adhara	255 11.8	S28 59.7
04	355 39.2	204 32.0	28.6	248 27.8	22.4	208 10.2	01.5	118 57.3	49.6	Aldebaran	290 48.0	N16 32.2
05	10 41.6	219 34.0	27.9	263 28.5	22.2	223 12.2	01.3	133 59.9	49.5			
06	25 44.1	234 36.1	N 9 27.2	278 29.2	N23 22.0	238 14.2	N14 01.2	149 02.4	S17 49.5	Alioth	166 19.7	N55 52.9
07	40 46.6	249 38.1	26.5	293 29.9	21.9	253 16.2	01.0	164 04.9	49.5	Alkaid	152 57.8	N49 14.5
S 08	55 49.0	264 40.1	25.8	308 30.5	21.7	268 18.1	00.8	179 07.4	49.5	Al Na'ir	27 41.6	S46 52.8
A 09	70 51.5	279 42.2	.. 25.2	323 31.2	.. 21.5	283 20.1	.. 00.7	194 10.0	.. 49.5	Alnilam	275 45.2	S 1 11.7
T 10	85 54.0	294 44.2	24.5	338 31.9	21.3	298 22.1	00.5	209 12.5	49.5	Alphard	217 55.0	S 8 43.7
U 11	100 56.4	309 46.3	23.8	353 32.6	21.1	313 24.0	00.3	224 15.0	49.5			
R 12	115 58.9	324 48.3	N 9 23.1	8 33.2	N23 21.0	328 26.0	N14 00.1	239 17.6	S17 49.5	Alphecca	126 09.6	N26 40.1
D 13	131 01.3	339 50.4	22.4	23 33.9	20.8	343 28.0	14 00.0	254 20.1	49.5	Alpheratz	357 41.8	N29 10.5
A 14	146 03.8	354 52.4	21.7	38 34.6	20.6	358 30.0	13 59.8	269 22.6	49.5	Altair	62 06.5	N 8 54.8
Y 15	161 06.3	9 54.5	.. 21.1	53 35.3	.. 20.4	13 31.9	.. 59.6	284 25.1	.. 49.5	Ankaa	353 14.2	S42 13.0
16	176 08.7	24 56.5	20.4	68 36.0	20.2	28 33.9	59.5	299 27.7	49.5	Antares	112 24.2	S26 27.8
17	191 11.2	39 58.6	19.7	83 36.6	20.1	43 35.9	59.3	314 30.2	49.5			
18	206 13.7	55 00.7	N 9 19.0	98 37.3	N23 19.9	58 37.8	N13 59.1	329 32.7	S17 49.5	Arcturus	145 54.4	N19 06.4
19	221 16.1	70 02.8	18.3	113 38.0	19.7	73 39.8	59.0	344 35.2	49.5	Atria	107 24.3	S69 03.3
20	236 18.6	85 04.8	17.7	128 38.7	19.5	88 41.8	58.8	359 37.8	49.5	Avior	234 18.0	S59 33.8
21	251 21.1	100 06.9	.. 17.0	143 39.4	.. 19.3	103 43.8	.. 58.6	14 40.3	.. 49.5	Bellatrix	278 30.7	N 6 21.6
22	266 23.5	115 09.0	16.3	158 40.0	19.1	118 45.7	58.5	29 42.8	49.5	Betelgeuse	271 00.1	N 7 24.4
23	281 26.0	130 11.1	15.6	173 40.7	19.0	133 47.7	58.3	44 45.3	49.5			
19 00	296 28.5	145 13.2	N 9 15.0	188 41.4	N23 18.8	148 49.7	N13 58.1	59 47.9	S17 49.5	Canopus	263 56.0	S52 42.3
01	311 30.9	160 15.3	14.3	203 42.1	18.6	163 51.7	57.9	74 50.4	49.5	Capella	280 32.7	N46 00.5
02	326 33.4	175 17.4	13.6	218 42.8	18.4	178 53.6	57.8	89 52.9	49.5	Deneb	49 30.0	N45 20.3
03	341 35.8	190 19.5	.. 13.0	233 43.4	.. 18.2	193 55.6	.. 57.6	104 55.4	.. 49.5	Denebola	182 32.4	N14 29.2
04	356 38.3	205 21.6	12.3	248 44.1	18.0	208 57.6	57.4	119 58.0	49.5	Diphda	348 54.4	S17 53.9
05	11 40.8	220 23.7	11.6	263 44.8	17.9	223 59.5	57.3	135 00.5	49.5			
06	26 43.2	235 25.8	N 9 10.9	278 45.5	N23 17.7	239 01.5	N13 57.1	150 03.0	S17 49.5	Dubhe	193 50.6	N61 40.2
07	41 45.7	250 27.9	10.3	293 46.2	17.5	254 03.5	56.9	165 05.5	49.5	Elnath	278 11.1	N28 37.0
S 08	56 48.2	265 30.0	09.6	308 46.9	17.3	269 05.5	56.7	180 08.0	49.5	Eltanin	90 45.0	N51 29.6
U 09	71 50.6	280 32.1	.. 08.9	323 47.5	.. 17.1	284 07.4	.. 56.6	195 10.6	.. 49.5	Enif	33 45.4	N 9 56.9
N 10	86 53.1	295 34.3	08.3	338 48.2	16.9	299 09.4	56.4	210 13.1	49.5	Fomalhaut	15 22.2	S29 32.1
D 11	101 55.6	310 36.4	07.6	353 48.9	16.7	314 11.4	56.2	225 15.6	49.5			
A 12	116 58.0	325 38.5	N 9 06.9	8 49.6	N23 16.6	329 13.3	N13 56.1	240 18.1	S17 49.5	Gacrux	171 59.3	S57 12.2
Y 13	132 00.5	340 40.7	06.3	23 50.3	16.4	344 15.3	55.9	255 20.7	49.5	Gienah	175 50.9	S17 37.7
14	147 02.9	355 42.8	05.6	38 50.9	16.2	359 17.3	55.7	270 23.2	49.5	Hadar	148 45.6	S60 27.0
15	162 05.4	10 45.0	.. 05.0	53 51.6	.. 16.0	14 19.2	.. 55.5	285 25.7	.. 49.4	Hamal	327 59.1	N23 32.0
16	177 07.9	25 47.1	04.3	68 52.3	15.8	29 21.2	55.4	300 28.2	49.4	Kaus Aust.	83 41.5	S34 22.4
17	192 10.3	40 49.3	03.6	83 53.0	15.6	44 23.2	55.2	315 30.7	49.4			
18	207 12.8	55 51.4	N 9 03.0	98 53.7	N23 15.4	59 25.2	N13 55.0	330 33.3	S17 49.4	Kochab	137 19.9	N74 05.9
19	222 15.3	70 53.6	02.3	113 54.4	15.2	74 27.1	54.9	345 35.8	49.4	Markab	13 36.7	N15 17.4
20	237 17.7	85 55.7	01.7	128 55.0	15.1	89 29.1	54.7	0 38.3	49.4	Menkar	314 13.7	N 4 08.9
21	252 20.2	100 57.9	.. 01.0	143 55.7	.. 14.9	104 31.1	.. 54.5	15 40.8	.. 49.4	Menkent	148 05.8	S36 26.8
22	267 22.7	116 00.1	9 00.4	158 56.4	14.7	119 33.0	54.3	30 43.4	49.4	Miaplacidus	221 40.1	S69 47.1
23	282 25.1	131 02.2	8 59.7	173 57.1	14.5	134 35.0	54.2	45 45.9	49.4			
20 00	297 27.6	146 04.4	N 8 59.0	188 57.8	N23 14.3	149 37.0	N13 54.0	60 48.4	S17 49.4	Mirfak	308 38.5	N49 54.6
01	312 30.1	161 06.6	58.4	203 58.5	14.1	164 39.0	53.8	75 50.9	49.4	Nunki	75 56.2	S26 16.4
02	327 32.5	176 08.8	57.7	218 59.1	13.9	179 40.9	53.7	90 53.4	49.4	Peacock	53 16.5	S56 40.8
03	342 35.0	191 10.9	.. 57.1	233 59.8	.. 13.7	194 42.9	.. 53.5	105 56.0	.. 49.4	Pollux	243 26.4	N27 59.2
04	357 37.4	206 13.1	56.4	249 00.5	13.5	209 44.9	53.3	120 58.5	49.4	Procyon	244 58.6	N 5 11.0
05	12 39.9	221 15.3	55.8	264 01.2	13.3	224 46.8	53.1	136 01.0	49.4			
06	27 42.4	236 17.5	N 8 55.1	279 01.9	N23 13.1	239 48.8	N13 53.0	151 03.5	S17 49.4	Rasalhague	96 04.8	N12 33.2
07	42 44.8	251 19.7	54.5	294 02.6	12.9	254 50.8	52.8	166 06.0	49.4	Regulus	207 42.3	N11 53.5
M 08	57 47.3	266 21.9	53.9	309 03.3	12.8	269 52.7	52.6	181 08.6	49.4	Rigel	281 11.0	S 8 11.1
O 09	72 49.8	281 24.1	.. 53.2	324 03.9	.. 12.6	284 54.7	.. 52.5	196 11.1	.. 49.4	Rigil Kent.	139 49.5	S60 54.0
N 10	87 52.2	296 26.3	52.6	339 04.6	12.4	299 56.7	52.3	211 13.6	49.4	Sabik	102 10.6	S15 44.4
D 11	102 54.7	311 28.6	51.9	354 05.3	12.2	314 58.7	52.1	226 16.1	49.4			
A 12	117 57.2	326 30.8	N 8 51.3	9 06.0	N23 12.0	330 00.6	N13 51.9	241 18.6	S17 49.4	Schedar	349 38.6	N56 37.1
Y 13	132 59.6	341 33.0	50.6	24 06.7	11.8	345 02.6	51.8	256 21.1	49.4	Shaula	96 19.6	S37 06.7
14	148 02.1	356 35.2	50.0	39 07.4	11.6	0 04.6	51.6	271 23.7	49.4	Sirius	258 32.8	S16 44.4
15	163 04.6	11 37.5	.. 49.4	54 08.1	.. 11.4	15 06.5	.. 51.4	286 26.2	.. 49.4	Spica	158 29.7	S11 14.5
16	178 07.0	26 39.7	48.7	69 08.7	11.2	30 08.5	51.3	301 28.7	49.4	Suhail	222 51.8	S43 29.9
17	193 09.5	41 41.9	48.1	84 09.4	11.0	45 10.5	51.1	316 31.2	49.4			
18	208 11.9	56 44.2	N 8 47.4	99 10.1	N23 10.8	60 12.4	N13 50.9	331 33.7	S17 49.4	Vega	80 37.6	N38 48.2
19	223 14.4	71 46.4	46.8	114 10.8	10.6	75 14.4	50.7	346 36.3	49.4	Zuben'ubi	137 03.7	S16 06.3
20	238 16.9	86 48.7	46.2	129 11.5	10.4	90 16.4	50.6	1 38.8	49.4			
21	253 19.3	101 50.9	.. 45.5	144 12.2	.. 10.2	105 18.3	.. 50.4	16 41.3	.. 49.4			
22	268 21.8	116 53.2	44.9	159 12.9	10.0	120 20.3	50.2	31 43.8	49.4			
23	283 24.3	131 55.4	44.3	174 13.5	09.8	135 22.3	50.0	46 46.3	49.4			
Mer. Pass.	h m 4 13.4	v 2.1	d 0.7	v 0.7	d 0.2	v 2.0	d 0.2	v 2.5	d 0.0			

	SHA	Mer. Pass.
	° '	h m
Venus	208 44.7	14 17
Mars	252 13.0	11 25
Jupiter	212 21.2	14 03
Saturn	123 19.4	19 57

UT	SUN GHA	SUN Dec	MOON GHA	v	Dec	d	HP
d h	° ′	° ′	° ′	′	° ′	′	′
18 00	178 27.3	N21 06.7	156 42.9	13.0	N12 08.4	7.4	54.9
01	193 27.2	06.3	171 14.9	13.2	12 01.0	7.5	54.9
02	208 27.2	05.8	185 47.1	13.1	11 53.5	7.5	54.9
03	223 27.1	.. 05.4	200 19.2	13.2	11 46.0	7.5	54.9
04	238 27.1	05.0	214 51.4	13.3	11 38.5	7.6	54.9
05	253 27.0	04.5	229 23.7	13.3	11 30.9	7.6	54.9
06	268 27.0	N21 04.1	243 56.0	13.4	N11 23.3	7.7	54.8
07	283 26.9	03.7	258 28.4	13.4	11 15.6	7.7	54.8
S 08	298 26.9	03.2	273 00.8	13.4	11 07.9	7.8	54.8
A 09	313 26.8	.. 02.8	287 33.2	13.5	11 00.1	7.8	54.8
T 10	328 26.8	02.3	302 05.7	13.6	10 52.3	7.9	54.8
U 11	343 26.7	01.9	316 38.3	13.6	10 44.4	7.9	54.8
R 12	358 26.7	N21 01.5	331 10.9	13.6	N10 36.5	7.9	54.8
D 13	13 26.7	01.0	345 43.5	13.7	10 28.6	8.0	54.7
A 14	28 26.6	00.6	0 16.2	13.7	10 20.6	8.0	54.7
Y 15	43 26.6	21 00.2	14 48.9	13.7	10 12.6	8.1	54.7
16	58 26.5	20 59.7	29 21.6	13.8	10 04.5	8.1	54.7
17	73 26.5	59.3	43 54.4	13.9	9 56.4	8.1	54.7
18	88 26.4	N20 58.8	58 27.3	13.9	N 9 48.3	8.2	54.7
19	103 26.4	58.4	73 00.2	13.9	9 40.1	8.2	54.6
20	118 26.3	57.9	87 33.1	14.0	9 31.9	8.2	54.6
21	133 26.3	.. 57.5	102 06.1	14.0	9 23.7	8.3	54.6
22	148 26.2	57.1	116 39.1	14.0	9 15.4	8.3	54.6
23	163 26.2	56.6	131 12.1	14.1	9 07.1	8.4	54.6
19 00	178 26.1	N20 56.2	145 45.2	14.1	N 8 58.7	8.4	54.6
01	193 26.1	55.7	160 18.3	14.2	8 50.3	8.4	54.6
02	208 26.0	55.3	174 51.5	14.2	8 41.9	8.4	54.6
03	223 26.0	.. 54.8	189 24.7	14.2	8 33.5	8.5	54.5
04	238 26.0	54.4	203 57.9	14.3	8 25.0	8.5	54.5
05	253 25.9	53.9	218 31.2	14.3	8 16.5	8.6	54.5
06	268 25.9	N20 53.5	233 04.5	14.4	N 8 07.9	8.6	54.5
07	283 25.8	53.0	247 37.9	14.4	7 59.3	8.6	54.5
S 08	298 25.8	52.6	262 11.3	14.4	7 50.7	8.6	54.5
U 09	313 25.7	.. 52.1	276 44.7	14.4	7 42.1	8.7	54.5
N 10	328 25.7	51.7	291 18.1	14.5	7 33.4	8.6	54.4
D 11	343 25.6	51.2	305 51.6	14.6	7 24.8	8.8	54.4
A 12	358 25.6	N20 50.8	320 25.2	14.5	N 7 16.0	8.7	54.4
Y 13	13 25.6	50.3	334 58.7	14.6	7 07.3	8.8	54.4
14	28 25.5	49.9	349 32.3	14.6	6 58.5	8.8	54.4
15	43 25.5	.. 49.4	4 05.9	14.7	6 49.7	8.8	54.4
16	58 25.4	48.9	18 39.6	14.6	6 40.9	8.8	54.4
17	73 25.4	48.5	33 13.2	14.8	6 32.1	8.9	54.4
18	88 25.4	N20 48.0	47 47.0	14.7	N 6 23.2	8.9	54.4
19	103 25.3	47.6	62 20.7	14.8	6 14.3	8.9	54.4
20	118 25.3	47.1	76 54.5	14.8	6 05.4	8.9	54.4
21	133 25.2	.. 46.7	91 28.3	14.8	5 56.5	8.9	54.3
22	148 25.2	46.2	106 02.1	14.8	5 47.6	9.0	54.3
23	163 25.1	45.7	120 35.9	14.9	5 38.6	9.0	54.3
20 00	178 25.1	N20 45.3	135 09.8	14.9	N 5 29.6	9.0	54.3
01	193 25.1	44.8	149 43.7	14.9	5 20.6	9.0	54.3
02	208 25.0	44.4	164 17.6	15.0	5 11.6	9.0	54.3
03	223 25.0	.. 43.9	178 51.6	15.0	5 02.6	9.1	54.3
04	238 24.9	43.4	193 25.6	15.0	4 53.5	9.1	54.3
05	253 24.9	43.0	207 59.6	15.0	4 44.4	9.1	54.3
06	268 24.9	N20 42.5	222 33.6	15.0	N 4 35.3	9.1	54.3
07	283 24.8	42.0	237 07.6	15.1	4 26.2	9.1	54.3
M 08	298 24.8	41.6	251 41.7	15.1	4 17.1	9.1	54.3
O 09	313 24.8	.. 41.1	266 15.8	15.1	4 08.0	9.2	54.3
N 10	328 24.7	40.6	280 49.9	15.1	3 58.8	9.1	54.2
D 11	343 24.7	40.2	295 24.0	15.1	3 49.7	9.2	54.2
A 12	358 24.6	N20 39.7	309 58.1	15.2	N 3 40.5	9.2	54.2
Y 13	13 24.6	39.2	324 32.3	15.2	3 31.3	9.2	54.2
14	28 24.6	38.8	339 06.5	15.2	3 22.1	9.2	54.2
15	43 24.5	.. 38.3	353 40.7	15.2	3 12.9	9.2	54.2
16	58 24.5	37.8	8 14.9	15.2	3 03.7	9.2	54.2
17	73 24.5	37.4	22 49.1	15.2	2 54.5	9.3	54.2
18	88 24.4	N20 36.9	37 23.3	15.3	N 2 45.2	9.2	54.2
19	103 24.4	36.4	51 57.6	15.3	2 36.0	9.3	54.2
20	118 24.4	35.9	66 31.9	15.3	2 26.7	9.2	54.2
21	133 24.3	.. 35.5	81 06.2	15.3	2 17.5	9.3	54.2
22	148 24.3	35.0	95 40.4	15.3	2 08.2	9.3	54.2
23	163 24.3	34.5	110 14.7	15.4	N 1 58.9	9.3	54.2
SD	15.8	d 0.5	SD 14.9		14.8		14.8

Twilight / Sunrise / Moonrise

Lat.	Naut.	Civil	Sunrise	Moonrise 18	19	20	21
°	h m	h m	h m	h m	h m	h m	h m
N 72	☐	☐	☐	05 09	06 48	08 22	09 55
N 70	☐	☐	☐	05 29	07 00	08 28	09 56
68	////	////	00 41	05 45	07 10	08 33	09 56
66	////	////	01 51	05 58	07 18	08 37	09 56
64	////	////	02 26	06 08	07 25	08 41	09 56
62	////	01 13	02 51	06 17	07 31	08 44	09 56
60	////	01 57	03 11	06 25	07 36	08 46	09 56
N 58	////	02 25	03 27	06 31	07 40	08 49	09 57
56	01 07	02 46	03 40	06 37	07 44	08 51	09 57
54	01 47	03 03	03 52	06 42	07 48	08 52	09 57
52	02 13	03 18	04 02	06 47	07 51	08 54	09 57
50	02 33	03 30	04 12	06 51	07 54	08 56	09 57
45	03 10	03 55	04 31	07 01	08 00	08 59	09 57
N 40	03 36	04 15	04 47	07 08	08 05	09 02	09 57
35	03 56	04 31	05 00	07 15	08 10	09 04	09 57
30	04 12	04 44	05 11	07 21	08 14	09 06	09 58
20	04 38	05 06	05 30	07 31	08 21	09 10	09 58
N 10	04 58	05 25	05 47	07 40	08 27	09 13	09 58
0	05 15	05 41	06 03	07 48	08 33	09 16	09 58
S 10	05 30	05 56	06 18	07 56	08 38	09 19	09 58
20	05 44	06 11	06 34	08 05	08 44	09 22	09 59
30	05 58	06 27	06 53	08 15	08 51	09 26	09 59
35	06 05	06 36	07 04	08 21	08 55	09 28	09 59
40	06 12	06 46	07 16	08 27	09 00	09 30	09 59
45	06 22	06 58	07 31	08 35	09 05	09 33	09 59
S 50	06 31	07 11	07 48	08 44	09 11	09 36	10 00
52	06 35	07 18	07 57	08 48	09 14	09 37	10 00
54	06 40	07 25	08 06	08 52	09 17	09 39	10 00
56	06 45	07 32	08 16	08 58	09 20	09 41	10 00
58	06 50	07 40	08 28	09 03	09 24	09 43	10 00
S 60	06 56	07 50	08 42	09 09	09 28	09 45	10 00

Sunset / Twilight / Moonset

Lat.	Sunset	Civil	Naut.	Moonset 18	19	20	21
°	h m	h m	h m	h m	h m	h m	h m
N 72	☐	☐	☐	22 12	22 07	22 03	21 58
N 70	☐	☐	☐	21 59	21 59	22 00	22 00
68	23 20	////	////	21 47	21 53	21 58	22 02
66	22 18	////	////	21 38	21 48	21 56	22 03
64	21 44	////	////	21 30	21 43	21 54	22 05
62	21 20	22 54	////	21 24	21 39	21 53	22 06
60	21 00	22 13	////	21 18	21 35	21 51	22 07
N 58	20 44	21 46	////	21 12	21 32	21 50	22 08
56	20 31	21 25	23 01	21 08	21 29	21 49	22 08
54	20 19	21 08	22 23	21 04	21 27	21 48	22 09
52	20 09	20 54	21 58	21 01	21 25	21 47	22 10
50	20 00	20 41	21 38	20 56	21 22	21 47	22 10
45	19 41	20 16	21 02	20 49	21 18	21 45	22 12
N 40	19 26	19 57	20 36	20 43	21 14	21 44	22 13
35	19 13	19 41	20 16	20 37	21 11	21 42	22 14
30	19 01	19 28	20 00	20 32	21 08	21 41	22 15
20	18 42	19 06	19 34	20 24	21 02	21 40	22 16
N 10	18 25	18 48	19 14	20 17	20 58	21 38	22 17
0	18 10	18 32	18 58	20 10	20 54	21 36	22 18
S 10	17 55	18 17	18 43	20 03	20 49	21 35	22 20
20	17 38	18 02	18 29	19 55	20 45	21 33	22 21
30	17 20	17 46	18 15	19 47	20 39	21 31	22 22
35	17 09	17 37	18 08	19 42	20 36	21 30	22 23
40	16 57	17 26	18 00	19 36	20 33	21 28	22 24
45	16 42	17 15	17 51	19 29	20 28	21 27	22 25
S 50	16 25	17 02	17 42	19 21	20 24	21 25	22 26
52	16 16	16 55	17 38	19 18	20 21	21 24	22 27
54	16 07	16 49	17 33	19 14	20 19	21 23	22 28
56	15 57	16 41	17 28	19 09	20 16	21 22	22 28
58	15 45	16 33	17 23	19 04	20 13	21 21	22 29
S 60	15 31	16 23	17 17	18 58	20 09	21 20	22 30

SUN / MOON

Day	Eqn. of Time 00ʰ	12ʰ	Mer. Pass.	Mer. Pass. Upper	Lower	Age	Phase
d	m s	m s	h m	h m	h m	d	%
18	06 11	06 13	12 06	13 59	01 36	02	6
19	06 15	06 18	12 06	14 43	02 21	03	11
20	06 19	06 21	12 06	15 26	03 05	04	18

UT	ARIES GHA	VENUS −4.6 GHA	Dec	MARS +1.7 GHA	Dec	JUPITER −1.7 GHA	Dec	SATURN +0.4 GHA	Dec	Star Name	SHA	Dec
d h	° ′	° ′	° ′	° ′	° ′	° ′	° ′	° ′	° ′		° ′	° ′
21 00	298 26.7	146 57.7	N 8 43.6	189 14.2	N23 09.6	150 24.2	N13 49.9	61 48.8	S17 49.4	Acamar	315 17.4	S40 14.4
01	313 29.2	161 59.9	43.0	204 14.9	09.4	165 26.2	49.7	76 51.4	49.4	Achernar	335 25.8	S57 09.2
02	328 31.7	177 02.2	42.4	219 15.6	09.2	180 28.2	49.5	91 53.9	49.4	Acrux	173 07.7	S63 11.4
03	343 34.1	192 04.5	.. 41.7	234 16.3	.. 09.0	195 30.2	.. 49.4	106 56.4	.. 49.4	Adhara	255 11.8	S28 59.7
04	358 36.6	207 06.8	41.1	249 17.0	08.8	210 32.1	49.2	121 58.9	49.4	Aldebaran	290 47.9	N16 32.2
05	13 39.0	222 09.0	40.5	264 17.7	08.6	225 34.1	49.0	137 01.4	49.4			
06	28 41.5	237 11.3	N 8 39.9	279 18.4	N23 08.4	240 36.1	N13 48.8	152 03.9	S17 49.4	Alioth	166 19.7	N55 52.9
07	43 44.0	252 13.6	39.2	294 19.1	08.2	255 38.0	48.7	167 06.4	49.4	Alkaid	152 57.9	N49 14.5
08	58 46.4	267 15.9	38.6	309 19.7	08.0	270 40.0	48.5	182 09.0	49.4	Al Na'ir	27 41.6	S46 52.8
09	73 48.9	282 18.2	.. 38.0	324 20.4	.. 07.8	285 42.0	.. 48.3	197 11.5	.. 49.4	Alnilam	275 45.2	S 1 11.7
10	88 51.4	297 20.5	37.4	339 21.1	07.6	300 43.9	48.1	212 14.0	49.4	Alphard	217 55.0	S 8 43.7
11	103 53.8	312 22.8	36.7	354 21.8	07.4	315 45.9	48.0	227 16.5	49.4			
12	118 56.3	327 25.1	N 8 36.1	9 22.5	N23 07.2	330 47.9	N13 47.8	242 19.0	S17 49.4	Alphecca	126 09.7	N26 40.1
13	133 58.8	342 27.4	35.5	24 23.2	07.0	345 49.8	47.6	257 21.5	49.4	Alpheratz	357 41.8	N29 10.5
14	149 01.2	357 29.7	34.9	39 23.9	06.8	0 51.8	47.5	272 24.0	49.4	Altair	62 06.5	N 8 54.8
15	164 03.7	12 32.0	.. 34.3	54 24.6	.. 06.6	15 53.8	.. 47.3	287 26.6	.. 49.4	Ankaa	353 14.2	S42 13.0
16	179 06.2	27 34.3	33.7	69 25.3	06.4	30 55.7	47.1	302 29.1	49.4	Antares	112 24.2	S26 27.8
17	194 08.6	42 36.7	33.0	84 25.9	06.2	45 57.7	46.9	317 31.6	49.4			
18	209 11.1	57 39.0	N 8 32.4	99 26.6	N23 06.0	60 59.7	N13 46.8	332 34.1	S17 49.4	Arcturus	145 54.4	N19 06.4
19	224 13.5	72 41.3	31.8	114 27.3	05.8	76 01.6	46.6	347 36.6	49.4	Atria	107 24.3	S69 03.3
20	239 16.0	87 43.7	31.2	129 28.0	05.6	91 03.6	46.4	2 39.1	49.4	Avior	234 18.0	S59 33.7
21	254 18.5	102 46.0	.. 30.6	144 28.7	.. 05.4	106 05.6	.. 46.2	17 41.6	.. 49.4	Bellatrix	278 30.7	N 6 21.6
22	269 20.9	117 48.3	30.0	159 29.4	05.2	121 07.5	46.1	32 44.2	49.4	Betelgeuse	271 00.0	N 7 24.4
23	284 23.4	132 50.7	29.4	174 30.1	05.0	136 09.5	45.9	47 46.7	49.4			
22 00	299 25.9	147 53.0	N 8 28.8	189 30.8	N23 04.8	151 11.5	N13 45.7	62 49.2	S17 49.4	Canopus	263 56.0	S52 42.3
01	314 28.3	162 55.4	28.1	204 31.5	04.6	166 13.4	45.6	77 51.7	49.4	Capella	280 32.7	N46 00.5
02	329 30.8	177 57.7	27.5	219 32.2	04.3	181 15.4	45.4	92 54.2	49.4	Deneb	49 30.0	N45 20.3
03	344 33.3	193 00.1	.. 26.9	234 32.9	.. 04.1	196 17.4	.. 45.2	107 56.7	.. 49.4	Denebola	182 32.4	N14 29.2
04	359 35.7	208 02.5	26.3	249 33.6	03.9	211 19.3	45.0	122 59.2	49.4	Diphda	348 54.4	S17 53.9
05	14 38.2	223 04.8	25.7	264 34.2	03.7	226 21.3	44.9	138 01.7	49.4			
06	29 40.6	238 07.2	N 8 25.1	279 34.9	N23 03.5	241 23.3	N13 44.7	153 04.3	S17 49.4	Dubhe	193 50.6	N61 40.2
07	44 43.1	253 09.6	24.5	294 35.6	03.3	256 25.2	44.5	168 06.8	49.4	Elnath	278 11.1	N28 37.0
08	59 45.6	268 12.0	23.9	309 36.3	03.1	271 27.2	44.3	183 09.3	49.4	Eltanin	90 45.0	N51 29.6
09	74 48.0	283 14.3	.. 23.3	324 37.0	.. 02.9	286 29.2	.. 44.2	198 11.8	.. 49.4	Enif	33 45.4	N 9 57.0
10	89 50.5	298 16.7	22.7	339 37.7	02.7	301 31.1	44.0	213 14.3	49.4	Fomalhaut	15 22.2	S29 32.1
11	104 53.0	313 19.1	22.1	354 38.4	02.5	316 33.1	43.8	228 16.8	49.4			
12	119 55.4	328 21.5	N 8 21.5	9 39.1	N23 02.3	331 35.1	N13 43.6	243 19.3	S17 49.4	Gacrux	171 59.4	S57 12.2
13	134 57.9	343 23.9	20.9	24 39.8	02.1	346 37.0	43.5	258 21.8	49.4	Gienah	175 50.9	S17 37.7
14	150 00.4	358 26.3	20.3	39 40.5	01.8	1 39.0	43.3	273 24.3	49.4	Hadar	148 45.7	S60 27.0
15	165 02.8	13 28.7	.. 19.7	54 41.2	.. 01.6	16 41.0	.. 43.1	288 26.8	.. 49.4	Hamal	327 59.1	N23 32.0
16	180 05.3	28 31.1	19.2	69 41.9	01.4	31 42.9	42.9	303 29.4	49.4	Kaus Aust.	83 41.5	S34 22.4
17	195 07.8	43 33.5	18.6	84 42.6	01.2	46 44.9	42.8	318 31.9	49.4			
18	210 10.2	58 35.9	N 8 18.0	99 43.3	N23 01.0	61 46.9	N13 42.6	333 34.4	S17 49.4	Kochab	137 20.0	N74 05.9
19	225 12.7	73 38.4	17.4	114 44.0	00.8	76 48.8	42.4	348 36.9	49.4	Markab	13 36.6	N15 17.4
20	240 15.1	88 40.8	16.8	129 44.6	00.6	91 50.8	42.3	3 39.4	49.4	Menkar	314 13.6	N 4 08.9
21	255 17.6	103 43.2	.. 16.2	144 45.3	.. 00.4	106 52.8	.. 42.1	18 41.9	.. 49.4	Menkent	148 05.8	S36 26.8
22	270 20.1	118 45.6	15.6	159 46.0	23 00.1	121 54.7	41.9	33 44.4	49.4	Miaplacidus	221 40.1	S69 47.1
23	285 22.5	133 48.1	15.0	174 46.7	22 59.9	136 56.7	41.7	48 46.9	49.4			
23 00	300 25.0	148 50.5	N 8 14.4	189 47.4	N22 59.7	151 58.7	N13 41.6	63 49.4	S17 49.4	Mirfak	308 38.4	N49 54.6
01	315 27.5	163 53.0	13.9	204 48.1	59.5	167 00.6	41.4	78 51.9	49.4	Nunki	75 56.2	S26 16.4
02	330 29.9	178 55.4	13.3	219 48.8	59.3	182 02.6	41.2	93 54.4	49.4	Peacock	53 16.5	S56 40.8
03	345 32.4	193 57.9	.. 12.7	234 49.5	.. 59.1	197 04.6	.. 41.0	108 57.0	.. 49.4	Pollux	243 26.4	N27 59.2
04	0 34.9	209 00.3	12.1	249 50.2	58.9	212 06.5	40.9	123 59.5	49.4	Procyon	244 58.6	N 5 11.0
05	15 37.3	224 02.8	11.5	264 50.9	58.6	227 08.5	40.7	139 02.0	49.4			
06	30 39.8	239 05.2	N 8 11.0	279 51.6	N22 58.4	242 10.5	N13 40.5	154 04.5	S17 49.4	Rasalhague	96 04.8	N12 33.2
07	45 42.3	254 07.7	10.4	294 52.3	58.2	257 12.4	40.3	169 07.0	49.4	Regulus	207 42.3	N11 53.5
08	60 44.7	269 10.2	09.8	309 53.0	58.0	272 14.4	40.2	184 09.5	49.4	Rigel	281 10.9	S 8 11.1
09	75 47.2	284 12.6	.. 09.2	324 53.7	.. 57.8	287 16.4	.. 40.0	199 12.0	.. 49.4	Rigil Kent.	139 49.5	S60 54.0
10	90 49.6	299 15.1	08.7	339 54.4	57.6	302 18.3	39.8	214 14.5	49.4	Sabik	102 10.6	S15 44.4
11	105 52.1	314 17.6	08.1	354 55.1	57.4	317 20.3	39.6	229 17.0	49.4			
12	120 54.6	329 20.1	N 8 07.5	9 55.8	N22 57.1	332 22.3	N13 39.5	244 19.5	S17 49.4	Schedar	349 38.6	N56 37.1
13	135 57.0	344 22.6	07.0	24 56.5	56.9	347 24.2	39.3	259 22.0	49.4	Shaula	96 19.6	S37 06.7
14	150 59.5	359 25.1	06.4	39 57.2	56.7	2 26.2	39.1	274 24.5	49.4	Sirius	258 32.8	S16 44.4
15	166 02.0	14 27.5	.. 05.8	54 57.9	.. 56.5	17 28.2	.. 38.9	289 27.0	.. 49.4	Spica	158 29.8	S11 14.5
16	181 04.4	29 30.0	05.2	69 58.6	56.3	32 30.1	38.8	304 29.5	49.4	Suhail	222 51.8	S43 29.9
17	196 06.9	44 32.5	04.7	84 59.3	56.0	47 32.1	38.6	319 32.0	49.4			
18	211 09.4	59 35.1	N 8 04.1	100 00.0	N22 55.8	62 34.1	N13 38.4	334 34.6	S17 49.4	Vega	80 37.6	N38 48.2
19	226 11.8	74 37.6	03.6	115 00.7	55.6	77 36.0	38.2	349 37.1	49.4	Zuben'ubi	137 03.7	S16 06.3
20	241 14.3	89 40.1	03.0	130 01.4	55.4	92 38.0	38.1	4 39.6	49.4			
21	256 16.7	104 42.6	.. 02.4	145 02.1	.. 55.2	107 39.9	.. 37.9	19 42.1	.. 49.4			
22	271 19.2	119 45.1	01.9	160 02.8	54.9	122 41.9	37.7	34 44.6	49.4			
23	286 21.7	134 47.6	01.3	175 03.5	54.7	137 43.9	37.5	49 47.1	49.4			
Mer. Pass.	h m 4 01.6	v 2.4	d 0.6	v 0.7	d 0.2	v 2.0	d 0.2	v 2.5	d 0.0			

	SHA	Mer. Pass.
	° ′	h m
Venus	208 27.2	14 06
Mars	250 04.9	11 21
Jupiter	211 45.6	13 53
Saturn	123 23.3	19 45

UT	SUN GHA	SUN Dec	MOON GHA	v	MOON Dec	d	HP
d h	° ′	° ′	° ′	′	° ′	′	′
21 00	178 24.2	N20 34.1	124 49.1	15.3	N 1 49.6	9.2	54.2
01	193 24.2	33.6	139 23.4	15.3	1 40.4	9.3	54.2
02	208 24.2	33.1	153 57.7	15.4	1 31.1	9.3	54.2
03	223 24.1 ..	32.6	168 32.1	15.3	1 21.8	9.3	54.2
04	238 24.1	32.1	183 06.4	15.4	1 12.5	9.3	54.2
05	253 24.1	31.7	197 40.8	15.3	1 03.2	9.3	54.2
06	268 24.0	N20 31.2	212 15.1	15.4	N 0 53.9	9.3	54.2
07	283 24.0	30.7	226 49.5	15.4	0 44.6	9.3	54.2
08	298 24.0	30.2	241 23.9	15.4	0 35.3	9.4	54.2
09	313 23.9 ..	29.8	255 58.3	15.3	0 25.9	9.3	54.2
10	328 23.9	29.3	270 32.6	15.4	0 16.6	9.3	54.2
11	343 23.9	28.8	285 07.0	15.4	N 0 07.3	9.3	54.2
12	358 23.8	N20 28.3	299 41.4	15.4	S 0 02.0	9.3	54.2
13	13 23.8	27.8	314 15.8	15.4	0 11.3	9.3	54.2
14	28 23.8	27.3	328 50.2	15.4	0 20.6	9.3	54.2
15	43 23.7 ..	26.9	343 24.6	15.4	0 29.9	9.3	54.2
16	58 23.7	26.4	357 59.0	15.4	0 39.2	9.3	54.2
17	73 23.7	25.9	12 33.4	15.4	0 48.5	9.3	54.2
18	88 23.7	N20 25.4	27 07.8	15.4	S 0 57.8	9.3	54.2
19	103 23.6	24.9	41 42.2	15.3	1 07.1	9.3	54.2
20	118 23.6	24.4	56 16.5	15.4	1 16.4	9.3	54.2
21	133 23.6 ..	23.9	70 50.9	15.4	1 25.7	9.3	54.2
22	148 23.5	23.5	85 25.3	15.4	1 35.0	9.2	54.2
23	163 23.5	23.0	99 59.7	15.3	1 44.2	9.3	54.2
22 00	178 23.5	N20 22.5	114 34.0	15.4	S 1 53.5	9.2	54.2
01	193 23.5	22.0	129 08.4	15.3	2 02.7	9.3	54.2
02	208 23.4	21.5	143 42.7	15.4	2 12.0	9.2	54.2
03	223 23.4 ..	21.0	158 17.1	15.3	2 21.2	9.3	54.2
04	238 23.4	20.5	172 51.4	15.3	2 30.5	9.2	54.2
05	253 23.3	20.0	187 25.7	15.3	2 39.7	9.2	54.2
06	268 23.3	N20 19.5	202 00.0	15.3	S 2 48.9	9.2	54.2
07	283 23.3	19.0	216 34.3	15.3	2 58.1	9.2	54.2
08	298 23.3	18.5	231 08.6	15.3	3 07.3	9.2	54.2
09	313 23.2 ..	18.0	245 42.9	15.2	3 16.5	9.2	54.2
10	328 23.2	17.6	260 17.1	15.3	3 25.7	9.1	54.2
11	343 23.2	17.1	274 51.4	15.2	3 34.8	9.2	54.2
12	358 23.2	N20 16.6	289 25.6	15.2	S 3 44.0	9.1	54.2
13	13 23.1	16.1	303 59.8	15.2	3 53.1	9.1	54.3
14	28 23.1	15.6	318 34.0	15.2	4 02.2	9.1	54.3
15	43 23.1 ..	15.1	333 08.2	15.2	4 11.3	9.1	54.3
16	58 23.1	14.6	347 42.4	15.1	4 20.4	9.1	54.3
17	73 23.0	14.1	2 16.5	15.1	4 29.5	9.0	54.3
18	88 23.0	N20 13.6	16 50.6	15.1	S 4 38.5	9.1	54.3
19	103 23.0	13.1	31 24.7	15.1	4 47.6	9.0	54.3
20	118 23.0	12.6	45 58.8	15.1	4 56.6	9.0	54.3
21	133 23.0 ..	12.1	60 32.9	15.0	5 05.6	9.0	54.3
22	148 22.9	11.6	75 06.9	15.0	5 14.6	9.0	54.3
23	163 22.9	11.1	89 40.9	15.0	5 23.6	8.9	54.3
23 00	178 22.9	N20 10.6	104 14.9	15.0	S 5 32.5	9.0	54.4
01	193 22.9	10.1	118 48.9	15.0	5 41.5	8.9	54.4
02	208 22.8	09.6	133 22.9	14.9	5 50.4	8.9	54.4
03	223 22.8 ..	09.1	147 56.8	14.9	5 59.3	8.8	54.4
04	238 22.8	08.5	162 30.7	14.8	6 08.1	8.9	54.4
05	253 22.8	08.0	177 04.5	14.9	6 17.0	8.8	54.4
06	268 22.8	N20 07.5	191 38.4	14.8	S 6 25.8	8.8	54.4
07	283 22.7	07.0	206 12.2	14.8	6 34.6	8.8	54.4
08	298 22.7	06.5	220 46.0	14.7	6 43.4	8.7	54.4
09	313 22.7 ..	06.0	235 19.7	14.7	6 52.1	8.8	54.5
10	328 22.7	05.5	249 53.4	14.7	7 00.9	8.7	54.5
11	343 22.7	05.0	264 27.1	14.7	7 09.6	8.7	54.5
12	358 22.6	N20 04.5	279 00.8	14.6	S 7 18.3	8.6	54.5
13	13 22.6	04.0	293 34.4	14.6	7 26.9	8.6	54.5
14	28 22.6	03.5	308 08.0	14.5	7 35.5	8.6	54.5
15	43 22.6 ..	02.9	322 41.5	14.6	7 44.1	8.6	54.5
16	58 22.6	02.4	337 15.1	14.5	7 52.7	8.5	54.6
17	73 22.6	01.9	351 48.6	14.4	8 01.2	8.6	54.6
18	88 22.5	N20 01.4	6 22.0	14.4	S 8 09.8	8.5	54.6
19	103 22.5	00.9	20 55.4	14.4	8 18.2	8.5	54.6
20	118 22.5	20 00.4	35 28.8	14.3	8 26.7	8.4	54.6
21	133 22.5	19 59.9	50 02.1	14.3	8 35.1	8.4	54.6
22	148 22.5	59.3	64 35.4	14.3	8 43.5	8.4	54.7
23	163 22.5	58.8	79 08.7	14.2	S 8 51.9	8.3	54.7
SD	15.8	d 0.5	SD 14.8		14.8		14.8

Twilight / Sunrise / Moonrise

Lat.	Naut.	Civil	Sunrise	Moonrise 21	22	23	24
°	h m	h m	h m	h m	h m	h m	h m
N 72	▢	▢	▢	09 55	11 28	13 02	14 40
N 70	▢	▢	▢	09 56	11 23	12 51	14 21
68	////	////	01 11	09 56	11 18	12 41	14 06
66	////	////	02 04	09 56	11 15	12 34	13 54
64	////	////	02 35	09 56	11 11	12 27	13 44
62	////	01 29	02 59	09 56	11 09	12 22	13 35
60	////	02 07	03 17	09 56	11 07	12 17	13 28
N 58	////	02 32	03 32	09 57	11 04	12 13	13 21
56	01 21	02 52	03 45	09 57	11 03	12 09	13 16
54	01 56	03 09	03 57	09 57	11 01	12 05	13 10
52	02 20	03 23	04 07	09 57	11 00	12 02	13 06
50	02 39	03 35	04 15	09 57	10 58	12 00	13 02
45	03 14	03 59	04 34	09 57	10 55	11 54	12 53
N 40	03 39	04 18	04 49	09 57	10 53	11 49	12 45
35	03 58	04 33	05 02	09 57	10 51	11 44	12 39
30	04 14	04 46	05 13	09 58	10 49	11 41	12 33
20	04 39	05 08	05 32	09 58	10 46	11 34	12 24
N 10	04 59	05 25	05 48	09 58	10 43	11 29	12 15
0	05 15	05 41	06 03	09 58	10 40	11 23	12 07
S 10	05 30	05 55	06 18	09 58	10 38	11 18	12 00
20	05 43	06 10	06 34	09 59	10 35	11 12	11 51
30	05 57	06 26	06 52	09 59	10 32	11 06	11 42
35	06 04	06 35	07 02	09 59	10 30	11 03	11 37
40	06 11	06 44	07 14	09 59	10 28	10 58	11 31
45	06 19	06 56	07 28	09 59	10 26	10 54	11 23
S 50	06 29	07 09	07 45	10 00	10 23	10 48	11 15
52	06 33	07 15	07 53	10 00	10 22	10 46	11 11
54	06 37	07 21	08 02	10 00	10 21	10 43	11 07
56	06 42	07 28	08 12	10 00	10 19	10 40	11 02
58	06 47	07 36	08 23	10 00	10 17	10 36	10 57
S 60	06 52	07 45	08 37	10 00	10 16	10 32	10 51

Sunset / Twilight / Moonset

Lat.	Sunset	Civil	Naut.	Moonset 21	22	23	24
°	h m	h m	h m	h m	h m	h m	h m
N 72	▢	▢	▢	21 58	21 53	21 48	21 42
N 70	▢	▢	▢	22 00	22 00	22 01	22 02
68	22 55	////	////	22 02	22 06	22 11	22 18
66	22 06	////	////	22 03	22 11	22 20	22 31
64	21 35	////	////	22 05	22 15	22 28	22 42
62	21 12	22 39	////	22 06	22 19	22 34	22 52
60	20 54	22 04	////	22 07	22 22	22 40	23 00
N 58	20 39	21 39	////	22 08	22 25	22 45	23 07
56	20 26	21 19	22 47	22 08	22 28	22 49	23 13
54	20 15	21 03	22 15	22 09	22 30	22 53	23 19
52	20 05	20 49	21 51	22 10	22 32	22 57	23 24
50	19 57	20 37	21 33	22 10	22 34	23 00	23 28
45	19 38	20 13	20 58	22 12	22 39	23 07	23 38
N 40	19 23	19 55	20 33	22 13	22 42	23 13	23 46
35	19 11	19 39	20 14	22 14	22 45	23 18	23 54
30	19 00	19 26	19 58	22 15	22 48	23 23	24 00
20	18 41	19 05	19 33	22 16	22 53	23 31	24 11
N 10	18 25	18 47	19 14	22 17	22 57	23 38	24 20
0	18 10	18 32	18 58	22 18	23 01	23 44	24 29
S 10	17 55	18 18	18 43	22 20	23 05	23 51	24 38
20	17 39	18 03	18 30	22 21	23 09	23 58	24 48
30	17 22	17 47	18 16	22 22	23 14	24 06	00 06
35	17 11	17 38	18 09	22 23	23 17	24 11	00 11
40	16 59	17 29	18 02	22 24	23 20	24 16	00 16
45	16 45	17 18	17 54	22 25	23 23	24 22	00 22
S 50	16 28	17 05	17 45	22 26	23 28	24 29	00 29
52	16 20	16 59	17 41	22 27	23 30	24 33	00 33
54	16 11	16 52	17 37	22 28	23 32	24 36	00 36
56	16 01	16 45	17 32	22 28	23 34	24 41	00 41
58	15 50	16 37	17 27	22 29	23 37	24 45	00 45
S 60	15 37	16 28	17 21	22 30	23 40	24 50	00 50

SUN / MOON

Day	SUN Eqn. of Time 00h	12h	Mer. Pass.	MOON Mer. Pass. Upper	Lower	Age	Phase
d	m s	m s	h m	h m	h m	d	%
21	06 23	06 25	12 06	16 08	03 47	05	26
22	06 26	06 27	12 06	16 51	04 29	06	34
23	06 28	06 29	12 06	17 34	05 12	07	44

UT	ARIES	VENUS −4.6		MARS +1.7		JUPITER −1.7		SATURN +0.4		STARS		
	GHA	GHA	Dec	GHA	Dec	GHA	Dec	GHA	Dec	Name	SHA	Dec
d h	° ′	° ′	° ′	° ′	° ′	° ′	° ′	° ′	° ′		° ′	° ′
24 00	301 24.1	149 50.2 N 8 00.8		190 04.2 N22 54.5		152 45.8 N13 37.4		64 49.6 S17 49.4		Acamar	315 17.4	S40 14.4
01	316 26.6	164 52.7	8 00.2	205 04.9	54.3	167 47.8	37.2	79 52.1	49.4	Achernar	335 25.8	S57 09.2
02	331 29.1	179 55.2	7 59.6	220 05.6	54.1	182 49.8	37.0	94 54.6	49.4	Acrux	173 07.8	S63 11.4
03	346 31.5	194 57.8 . .	59.1	235 06.3 . .	53.8	197 51.7 . .	36.8	109 57.1 . .	49.4	Adhara	255 11.7	S28 59.7
04	1 34.0	210 00.3	58.5	250 07.0	53.6	212 53.7	36.7	124 59.6	49.4	Aldebaran	290 47.9	N16 32.2
05	16 36.5	225 02.9	58.0	265 07.7	53.4	227 55.7	36.5	140 02.1	49.4			
06	31 38.9	240 05.4 N 7 57.4		280 08.4 N22 53.2		242 57.6 N13 36.3		155 04.6 S17 49.4		Alioth	166 19.7	N55 52.9
07	46 41.4	255 08.0	56.9	295 09.1	52.9	257 59.6	36.1	170 07.1	49.4	Alkaid	152 57.9	N49 14.5
08	61 43.9	270 10.5	56.3	310 09.8	52.7	273 01.6	36.0	185 09.6	49.4	Al Na'ir	27 41.6	S46 52.8
F 09	76 46.3	285 13.1 . .	55.8	325 10.5 . .	52.5	288 03.5 . .	35.8	200 12.1 . .	49.4	Alnilam	275 45.2	S 1 11.7
R 10	91 48.8	300 15.7	55.2	340 11.2	52.3	303 05.5	35.6	215 14.6	49.4	Alphard	217 55.0	S 8 43.7
I 11	106 51.2	315 18.2	54.7	355 11.9	52.1	318 07.4	35.4	230 17.1	49.4			
D 12	121 53.7	330 20.8 N 7 54.1		10 12.6 N22 51.8		333 09.4 N13 35.3		245 19.6 S17 49.4		Alphecca	126 09.7	N26 40.1
A 13	136 56.2	345 23.4	53.6	25 13.3	51.6	348 11.4	35.1	260 22.1	49.4	Alpheratz	357 41.8	N29 10.5
Y 14	151 58.6	0 26.0	53.1	40 14.0	51.4	3 13.3	34.9	275 24.6	49.4	Altair	62 06.5	N 8 54.8
15	167 01.1	15 28.6 . .	52.5	55 14.7 . .	51.2	18 15.3 . .	34.7	290 27.1 . .	49.4	Ankaa	353 14.2	S42 13.0
16	182 03.6	30 31.2	52.0	70 15.4	50.9	33 17.3	34.6	305 29.6	49.4	Antares	112 24.2	S26 27.8
17	197 06.0	45 33.8	51.4	85 16.1	50.7	48 19.2	34.4	320 32.1	49.4			
18	212 08.5	60 36.4 N 7 50.9		100 16.8 N22 50.5		63 21.2 N13 34.2		335 34.6 S17 49.4		Arcturus	145 54.4	N19 06.4
19	227 11.0	75 39.0	50.4	115 17.5	50.2	78 23.2	34.0	350 37.1	49.4	Atria	107 24.3	S69 03.3
20	242 13.4	90 41.6	49.8	130 18.2	50.0	93 25.1	33.9	5 39.6	49.5	Avior	234 18.0	S59 33.7
21	257 15.9	105 44.2 . .	49.3	145 18.9 . .	49.8	108 27.1 . .	33.7	20 42.1 . .	49.5	Bellatrix	278 30.7	N 6 21.7
22	272 18.4	120 46.8	48.8	160 19.6	49.6	123 29.0	33.5	35 44.6	49.5	Betelgeuse	271 00.0	N 7 24.4
23	287 20.8	135 49.4	48.2	175 20.3	49.3	138 31.0	33.3	50 47.1	49.5			
25 00	302 23.3	150 52.0 N 7 47.7		190 21.0 N22 49.1		153 33.0 N13 33.2		65 49.6 S17 49.5		Canopus	263 56.0	S52 42.3
01	317 25.7	165 54.7	47.2	205 21.7	48.9	168 34.9	33.0	80 52.1	49.5	Capella	280 32.7	N46 00.5
02	332 28.2	180 57.3	46.6	220 22.4	48.6	183 36.9	32.8	95 54.6	49.5	Deneb	49 30.0	N45 20.3
03	347 30.7	195 59.9 . .	46.1	235 23.1 . .	48.4	198 38.9 . .	32.6	110 57.1 . .	49.5	Denebola	182 32.4	N14 29.2
04	2 33.1	211 02.6	45.6	250 23.8	48.2	213 40.8	32.4	125 59.6	49.5	Diphda	348 54.4	S17 53.9
05	17 35.6	226 05.2	45.1	265 24.5	48.0	228 42.8	32.3	141 02.1	49.5			
06	32 38.1	241 07.8 N 7 44.5		280 25.2 N22 47.7		243 44.7 N13 32.1		156 04.6 S17 49.5		Dubhe	193 50.6	N61 40.2
07	47 40.5	256 10.5	44.0	295 25.9	47.5	258 46.7	31.9	171 07.1	49.5	Elnath	278 11.1	N28 37.0
S 08	62 43.0	271 13.1	43.5	310 26.6	47.3	273 48.7	31.7	186 09.6	49.5	Eltanin	90 45.0	N51 29.6
A 09	77 45.5	286 15.8 . .	43.0	325 27.3 . .	47.0	288 50.6 . .	31.6	201 12.1 . .	49.5	Enif	33 45.4	N 9 57.0
T 10	92 47.9	301 18.5	42.5	340 28.0	46.8	303 52.6	31.4	216 14.6	49.5	Fomalhaut	15 22.2	S29 32.1
U 11	107 50.4	316 21.1	41.9	355 28.7	46.6	318 54.6	31.2	231 17.1	49.5			
R 12	122 52.8	331 23.8 N 7 41.4		10 29.4 N22 46.3		333 56.5 N13 31.0		246 19.6 S17 49.5		Gacrux	171 59.4	S57 12.2
D 13	137 55.3	346 26.5	40.9	25 30.1	46.1	348 58.5	30.9	261 22.1	49.5	Gienah	175 50.9	S17 37.7
A 14	152 57.8	1 29.1	40.4	40 30.8	45.9	4 00.4	30.7	276 24.6	49.5	Hadar	148 45.7	S60 27.0
Y 15	168 00.2	16 31.8 . .	39.9	55 31.5 . .	45.6	19 02.4 . .	30.5	291 27.1 . .	49.5	Hamal	327 59.1	N23 32.0
16	183 02.7	31 34.5	39.4	70 32.3	45.4	34 04.4	30.3	306 29.6	49.5	Kaus Aust.	83 41.5	S34 22.4
17	198 05.2	46 37.2	38.9	85 33.0	45.2	49 06.3	30.2	321 32.1	49.5			
18	213 07.6	61 39.9 N 7 38.3		100 33.7 N22 44.9		64 08.3 N13 30.0		336 34.6 S17 49.5		Kochab	137 20.0	N74 05.9
19	228 10.1	76 42.6	37.8	115 34.4	44.7	79 10.3	29.8	351 37.1	49.5	Markab	13 36.6	N15 17.4
20	243 12.6	91 45.3	37.3	130 35.1	44.5	94 12.2	29.6	6 39.6	49.5	Menkar	314 13.6	N 4 08.9
21	258 15.0	106 48.0 . .	36.8	145 35.8 . .	44.2	109 14.2 . .	29.4	21 42.1 . .	49.5	Menkent	148 05.8	S36 26.8
22	273 17.5	121 50.7	36.3	160 36.5	44.0	124 16.1	29.3	36 44.6	49.5	Miaplacidus	221 40.1	S69 47.1
23	288 20.0	136 53.4	35.8	175 37.2	43.8	139 18.1	29.1	51 47.1	49.5			
26 00	303 22.4	151 56.1 N 7 35.3		190 37.9 N22 43.5		154 20.1 N13 28.9		66 49.6 S17 49.5		Mirfak	308 38.4	N49 54.6
01	318 24.9	166 58.8	34.8	205 38.6	43.3	169 22.0	28.7	81 52.1	49.5	Nunki	75 56.2	S26 16.4
02	333 27.3	182 01.6	34.3	220 39.3	43.1	184 24.0	28.6	96 54.6	49.5	Peacock	53 16.5	S56 40.8
03	348 29.8	197 04.3 . .	33.8	235 40.0 . .	42.8	199 26.0 . .	28.4	111 57.1 . .	49.5	Pollux	243 26.4	N27 59.2
04	3 32.3	212 07.0	33.3	250 40.7	42.6	214 27.9	28.2	126 59.6	49.5	Procyon	244 58.6	N 5 11.0
05	18 34.7	227 09.7	32.8	265 41.4	42.4	229 29.9	28.0	142 02.1	49.6			
06	33 37.2	242 12.5 N 7 32.3		280 42.1 N22 42.1		244 31.8 N13 27.9		157 04.6 S17 49.6		Rasalhague	96 04.8	N12 33.3
07	48 39.7	257 15.2	31.8	295 42.9	41.9	259 33.8	27.7	172 07.1	49.6	Regulus	207 42.3	N11 53.5
08	63 42.1	272 18.0	31.3	310 43.6	41.6	274 35.8	27.5	187 09.6	49.6	Rigel	281 10.9	S 8 11.1
S 09	78 44.6	287 20.7 . .	30.9	325 44.3 . .	41.4	289 37.7 . .	27.3	202 12.0 . .	49.6	Rigil Kent.	139 49.5	S60 54.0
U 10	93 47.1	302 23.5	30.4	340 45.0	41.2	304 39.7	27.1	217 14.5	49.6	Sabik	102 10.6	S15 44.4
N 11	108 49.5	317 26.2	29.9	355 45.7	40.9	319 41.7	27.0	232 17.0	49.6			
D 12	123 52.0	332 29.0 N 7 29.4		10 46.4 N22 40.7		334 43.6 N13 26.8		247 19.5 S17 49.6		Schedar	349 38.5	N56 37.1
A 13	138 54.5	347 31.8	28.9	25 47.1	40.4	349 45.6	26.6	262 22.0	49.6	Shaula	96 19.6	S37 06.7
Y 14	153 56.9	2 34.5	28.4	40 47.8	40.2	4 47.5	26.4	277 24.5	49.6	Sirius	258 32.8	S16 44.4
15	168 59.4	17 37.3 . .	27.9	55 48.5 . .	40.0	19 49.5 . .	26.3	292 27.0 . .	49.6	Spica	158 29.8	S11 14.5
16	184 01.8	32 40.1	27.5	70 49.2	39.7	34 51.5	26.1	307 29.5	49.6	Suhail	222 51.8	S43 29.9
17	199 04.3	47 42.9	27.0	85 49.9	39.5	49 53.4	25.9	322 32.0	49.6			
18	214 06.8	62 45.6 N 7 26.5		100 50.7 N22 39.2		64 55.4 N13 25.7		337 34.5 S17 49.6		Vega	80 37.6	N38 48.2
19	229 09.2	77 48.4	26.0	115 51.4	39.0	79 57.3	25.6	352 37.0	49.6	Zuben'ubi	137 03.7	S16 06.3
20	244 11.7	92 51.2	25.5	130 52.1	38.8	94 59.3	25.4	7 39.5	49.6		SHA	Mer. Pass.
21	259 14.2	107 54.0 . .	25.1	145 52.8 . .	38.5	110 01.3 . .	25.2	22 42.0 . .	49.6		° ′	h m
22	274 16.6	122 56.8	24.6	160 53.5	38.3	125 03.2	25.0	37 44.5	49.6	Venus	208 28.8	13 54
23	289 19.1	137 59.6	24.1	175 54.2	38.0	140 05.2	24.8	52 47.0	49.6	Mars	247 57.7	11 18
	h m									Jupiter	211 09.7	13 44
Mer. Pass.	3 49.8	v 2.7	d 0.5	v 0.7	d 0.2	v 2.0	d 0.2	v 2.5	d 0.0	Saturn	123 26.4	19 33

UT	SUN GHA	SUN Dec	MOON GHA	v	MOON Dec	d	HP
d h	° ′	° ′	° ′	′	° ′	′	′
24 00	178 22.4	N19 58.3	93 41.9	14.2	S 9 00.2	8.3	54.7
01	193 22.4	57.8	108 15.1	14.1	9 08.5	8.2	54.7
02	208 22.4	57.3	122 48.2	14.1	9 16.7	8.3	54.7
03	223 22.4 ..	56.8	137 21.3	14.1	9 25.0	8.2	54.7
04	238 22.4	56.2	151 54.4	14.0	9 33.2	8.1	54.8
05	253 22.4	55.7	166 27.4	13.9	9 41.3	8.1	54.8
06	268 22.4	N19 55.2	181 00.3	13.9	S 9 49.4	8.1	54.8
07	283 22.3	54.7	195 33.2	13.9	9 57.5	8.1	54.8
08	298 22.3	54.2	210 06.1	13.8	10 05.6	8.0	54.8
F 09	313 22.3 ..	53.6	224 38.9	13.8	10 13.6	7.9	54.9
R 10	328 22.3	53.1	239 11.7	13.8	10 21.5	7.9	54.9
I 11	343 22.3	52.6	253 44.5	13.6	10 29.4	7.9	54.9
D 12	358 22.3	N19 52.1	268 17.1	13.7	S10 37.3	7.9	54.9
A 13	13 22.3	51.5	282 49.8	13.6	10 45.2	7.8	54.9
Y 14	28 22.3	51.0	297 22.4	13.5	10 53.0	7.7	55.0
15	43 22.2 ..	50.5	311 54.9	13.5	11 00.7	7.8	55.0
16	58 22.2	50.0	326 27.4	13.4	11 08.5	7.6	55.0
17	73 22.2	49.4	340 59.8	13.4	11 16.1	7.7	55.0
18	88 22.2	N19 48.9	355 32.2	13.3	S11 23.8	7.6	55.0
19	103 22.2	48.4	10 04.5	13.3	11 31.4	7.5	55.1
20	118 22.2	47.8	24 36.8	13.2	11 38.9	7.5	55.1
21	133 22.2 ..	47.3	39 09.0	13.2	11 46.4	7.4	55.1
22	148 22.2	46.8	53 41.2	13.1	11 53.8	7.4	55.1
23	163 22.2	46.3	68 13.3	13.1	12 01.2	7.4	55.2
25 00	178 22.1	N19 45.7	82 45.4	13.0	S12 08.6	7.3	55.2
01	193 22.1	45.2	97 17.4	13.0	12 15.9	7.3	55.2
02	208 22.1	44.7	111 49.4	12.9	12 23.2	7.2	55.2
03	223 22.1 ..	44.1	126 21.3	12.8	12 30.4	7.1	55.3
04	238 22.1	43.6	140 53.1	12.8	12 37.5	7.1	55.3
05	253 22.1	43.1	155 24.9	12.7	12 44.6	7.1	55.3
06	268 22.1	N19 42.5	169 56.6	12.7	S12 51.7	7.0	55.3
07	283 22.1	42.0	184 28.3	12.6	12 58.7	6.9	55.4
S 08	298 22.1	41.5	198 59.9	12.5	13 05.6	6.9	55.4
A 09	313 22.1 ..	40.9	213 31.4	12.5	13 12.5	6.8	55.4
T 10	328 22.1	40.4	228 02.9	12.4	13 19.3	6.8	55.4
U 11	343 22.1	39.9	242 34.3	12.4	13 26.1	6.7	55.5
R 12	358 22.1	N19 39.3	257 05.7	12.3	S13 32.8	6.7	55.5
D 13	13 22.0	38.8	271 37.0	12.3	13 39.5	6.6	55.5
A 14	28 22.0	38.2	286 08.3	12.2	13 46.1	6.6	55.5
Y 15	43 22.0 ..	37.7	300 39.5	12.1	13 52.7	6.5	55.6
16	58 22.0	37.2	315 10.6	12.0	13 59.2	6.4	55.6
17	73 22.0	36.6	329 41.6	12.0	14 05.6	6.4	55.6
18	88 22.0	N19 36.1	344 12.6	12.0	S14 12.0	6.3	55.7
19	103 22.0	35.5	358 43.6	11.8	14 18.3	6.2	55.7
20	118 22.0	35.0	13 14.4	11.8	14 24.5	6.2	55.7
21	133 22.0 ..	34.4	27 45.2	11.8	14 30.7	6.1	55.7
22	148 22.0	33.9	42 16.0	11.7	14 36.8	6.1	55.8
23	163 22.0	33.4	56 46.7	11.6	14 42.9	5.9	55.8
26 00	178 22.0	N19 32.8	71 17.3	11.5	S14 48.8	6.0	55.8
01	193 22.0	32.3	85 47.8	11.5	14 54.8	5.8	55.9
02	208 22.0	31.7	100 18.3	11.4	15 00.6	5.8	55.9
03	223 22.0 ..	31.2	114 48.7	11.4	15 06.4	5.7	55.9
04	238 22.0	30.6	129 19.1	11.3	15 12.1	5.7	56.0
05	253 22.0	30.1	143 49.4	11.2	15 17.8	5.5	56.0
06	268 22.0	N19 29.5	158 19.6	11.1	S15 23.3	5.5	56.0
07	283 22.0	29.0	172 49.7	11.1	15 28.8	5.5	56.1
08	298 22.0	28.4	187 19.8	11.0	15 34.3	5.3	56.1
S 09	313 22.0 ..	27.9	201 49.8	11.0	15 39.6	5.3	56.1
U 10	328 22.0	27.3	216 19.8	10.9	15 44.9	5.2	56.1
N 11	343 22.0	26.8	230 49.7	10.8	15 50.1	5.2	56.2
D 12	358 22.0	N19 26.2	245 19.5	10.8	S15 55.3	5.1	56.2
A 13	13 22.0	25.7	259 49.3	10.6	16 00.4	4.9	56.2
Y 14	28 22.0	25.1	274 18.9	10.7	16 05.3	4.8	56.3
15	43 22.0 ..	24.6	288 48.6	10.5	16 10.1	4.8	56.3
16	58 22.0	24.0	303 18.1	10.5	16 15.1	4.7	56.3
17	73 22.0	23.5	317 47.6	10.4	16 19.8	4.6	56.4
18	88 22.0	N19 22.9	332 17.0	10.3	S16 24.5	4.6	56.4
19	103 22.0	22.4	346 46.3	10.3	16 29.1	4.5	56.4
20	118 22.0	21.8	1 15.6	10.2	16 33.6	4.5	56.5
21	133 22.0 ..	21.3	15 44.8	10.2	16 38.1	4.3	56.5
22	148 22.0	20.7	30 14.0	10.1	16 42.4	4.3	56.5
23	163 22.0	20.1	44 43.1	10.0	S16 46.7	4.2	56.6
	SD 15.8	d 0.5	SD 15.0		15.1		15.3

Lat.	Twilight Naut.	Twilight Civil	Sunrise	Moonrise 24	25	26	27
°	h m	h m	h m	h m	h m	h m	h m
N 72	▨	▨	▨	14 40	16 23	18 16	■
N 70	▨	▨	▨	14 21	15 53	17 27	18 56
68	////	////	01 33	14 06	15 31	16 56	18 16
66	////	////	02 16	13 54	15 14	16 34	17 48
64	////	00 39	02 45	13 44	15 00	16 16	17 27
62	////	01 44	03 06	13 35	14 49	16 01	17 09
60	////	02 16	03 24	13 28	14 39	15 49	16 55
N 58	00 36	02 40	03 38	13 21	14 30	15 38	16 43
56	01 34	02 59	03 51	13 16	14 23	15 29	16 33
54	02 05	03 14	04 01	13 10	14 16	15 21	16 23
52	02 27	03 28	04 11	13 06	14 10	15 13	16 15
50	02 45	03 39	04 19	13 02	14 04	15 07	16 08
45	03 18	04 02	04 37	12 53	13 53	14 53	15 52
N 40	03 42	04 21	04 52	12 45	13 43	14 41	15 39
35	04 01	04 36	05 04	12 39	13 35	14 31	15 28
30	04 16	04 48	05 15	12 33	13 27	14 22	15 19
20	04 41	05 09	05 33	12 24	13 15	14 08	15 02
N 10	05 00	05 26	05 48	12 15	13 04	13 55	14 48
0	05 15	05 41	06 03	12 07	12 54	13 43	14 34
S 10	05 29	05 55	06 17	12 00	12 44	13 31	14 21
20	05 43	06 09	06 33	11 51	12 33	13 18	14 07
30	05 55	06 25	06 50	11 42	12 21	13 03	13 50
35	06 02	06 33	07 00	11 37	12 14	12 55	13 41
40	06 09	06 42	07 12	11 31	12 06	12 45	13 30
45	06 17	06 53	07 25	11 23	11 56	12 34	13 18
S 50	06 26	07 05	07 41	11 15	11 45	12 21	13 02
52	06 29	07 11	07 49	11 11	11 40	12 14	12 55
54	06 33	07 17	07 58	11 07	11 34	12 07	12 47
56	06 38	07 24	08 07	11 02	11 28	12 00	12 39
58	06 43	07 32	08 18	10 57	11 21	11 51	12 29
S 60	06 48	07 40	08 31	10 51	11 13	11 41	12 17

Lat.	Sunset	Twilight Civil	Twilight Naut.	Moonset 24	25	26	27
°	h m	h m	h m	h m	h m	h m	h m
N 72	▨	▨	▨	21 42	21 35	21 25	■
N 70	▨	▨	▨	22 02	22 06	22 14	22 34
68	22 35	////	////	22 18	22 29	22 46	23 15
66	21 54	////	////	22 31	22 47	23 09	23 43
64	21 26	23 22	////	22 42	23 01	23 28	24 05
62	21 05	22 26	////	22 52	23 14	23 43	24 22
60	20 48	21 54	////	23 00	23 24	23 55	24 36
N 58	20 34	21 31	23 26	23 07	23 33	24 06	00 06
56	20 21	21 13	22 35	23 13	23 41	24 16	00 16
54	20 11	20 57	22 06	23 19	23 48	24 24	00 24
52	20 01	20 44	21 44	23 24	23 55	24 32	00 32
50	19 53	20 33	21 27	23 28	24 01	00 01	00 39
45	19 35	20 10	20 54	23 38	24 13	00 13	00 54
N 40	19 21	19 52	20 30	23 46	24 24	00 24	01 06
35	19 09	19 37	20 12	23 54	24 32	00 32	01 16
30	18 58	19 24	19 56	24 00	00 00	00 40	01 25
20	18 40	19 04	19 32	24 11	00 11	00 54	01 41
N 10	18 25	18 47	19 13	24 20	00 20	01 06	01 54
0	18 10	18 32	18 58	24 29	00 29	01 17	02 07
S 10	17 56	18 18	18 44	24 38	00 38	01 28	02 20
20	17 41	18 04	18 31	24 48	00 48	01 40	02 34
30	17 23	17 49	18 18	00 06	00 59	01 54	02 49
35	17 13	17 40	18 11	00 11	01 06	02 02	02 58
40	17 02	17 31	18 04	00 16	01 13	02 11	03 09
45	16 48	17 21	17 56	00 22	01 21	02 21	03 21
S 50	16 32	17 08	17 48	00 29	01 32	02 34	03 36
52	16 24	17 02	17 44	00 33	01 36	02 40	03 43
54	16 16	16 56	17 40	00 36	01 42	02 47	03 50
56	16 06	16 49	17 36	00 41	01 47	02 54	03 59
58	15 55	16 42	17 31	00 45	01 54	03 02	04 09
S 60	15 43	16 33	17 26	00 50	02 01	03 12	04 20

Day	SUN Eqn. of Time 00h	12h	Mer. Pass.	MOON Mer. Pass. Upper	Lower	Age	Phase
d	m s	m s	h m	h m	h m	d	%
24	06 30	06 31	12 07	18 18	05 56	08	53
25	06 31	06 32	12 07	19 05	06 42	09	63
26	06 32	06 32	12 07	19 55	07 30	10	72

UT	ARIES	VENUS −4.5		MARS +1.7		JUPITER −1.7		SATURN +0.4		STARS		
	GHA	GHA	Dec	GHA	Dec	GHA	Dec	GHA	Dec	Name	SHA	Dec
d h	° ′	° ′	° ′	° ′	° ′	° ′	° ′	° ′	° ′		° ′	° ′
27 00	304 21.6	153 02.4	N 7 23.6	190 54.9	N22 37.8	155 07.1	N13 24.7	67 49.4	S17 49.6	Acamar	315 17.4	S40 14.4
01	319 24.0	168 05.3	23.2	205 55.6	37.5	170 09.1	24.5	82 51.9	49.6	Achernar	335 25.7	S57 09.2
02	334 26.5	183 08.1	22.7	220 56.3	37.3	185 11.1	24.3	97 54.4	49.6	Acrux	173 07.8	S63 11.3
03	349 28.9	198 10.9	. . 22.2	235 57.0	. . 37.1	200 13.0	. . 24.1	112 56.9	. . 49.6	Adhara	255 11.7	S28 59.7
04	4 31.4	213 13.7	21.8	250 57.8	36.8	215 15.0	24.0	127 59.4	49.6	Aldebaran	290 47.9	N16 32.2
05	19 33.9	228 16.5	21.3	265 58.5	36.6	230 16.9	23.8	143 01.9	49.6			
06	34 36.3	243 19.4	N 7 20.8	280 59.2	N22 36.3	245 18.9	N13 23.6	158 04.4	S17 49.7	Alioth	166 19.7	N55 52.9
07	49 38.8	258 22.2	20.4	295 59.9	36.1	260 20.9	23.4	173 06.9	49.7	Alkaid	152 57.9	N49 14.5
08	64 41.3	273 25.1	19.9	311 00.6	35.8	275 22.8	23.2	188 09.4	49.7	Al Na'ir	27 41.6	S46 52.8
M 09	79 43.7	288 27.9	. . 19.5	326 01.3	. . 35.6	290 24.8	. . 23.1	203 11.9	. . 49.7	Alnilam	275 45.2	S 1 11.7
O 10	94 46.2	303 30.7	19.0	341 02.0	35.3	305 26.8	22.9	218 14.4	49.7	Alphard	217 55.0	S 8 43.7
N 11	109 48.7	318 33.6	18.5	356 02.7	35.1	320 28.7	22.7	233 16.8	49.7			
D 12	124 51.1	333 36.5	N 7 18.1	11 03.5	N22 34.9	335 30.7	N13 22.5	248 19.3	S17 49.7	Alphecca	126 09.7	N26 40.1
A 13	139 53.6	348 39.3	17.6	26 04.2	34.6	350 32.6	22.4	263 21.8	49.7	Alpheratz	357 41.7	N29 10.5
Y 14	154 56.1	3 42.2	17.2	41 04.9	34.4	5 34.6	22.2	278 24.3	49.7	Altair	62 06.5	N 8 54.9
15	169 58.5	18 45.0	. . 16.7	56 05.6	. . 34.1	20 36.6	. . 22.0	293 26.8	. . 49.7	Ankaa	353 14.1	S42 13.0
16	185 01.0	33 47.9	16.3	71 06.3	33.9	35 38.5	21.8	308 29.3	49.7	Antares	112 24.3	S26 27.8
17	200 03.4	48 50.8	15.8	86 07.0	33.6	50 40.5	21.6	323 31.8	49.7			
18	215 05.9	63 53.7	N 7 15.4	101 07.7	N22 33.4	65 42.4	N13 21.5	338 34.3	S17 49.7	Arcturus	145 54.4	N19 06.4
19	230 08.4	78 56.6	14.9	116 08.5	33.1	80 44.4	21.3	353 36.8	49.7	Atria	107 24.3	S69 03.3
20	245 10.8	93 59.4	14.5	131 09.2	32.9	95 46.4	21.1	8 39.3	49.7	Avior	234 18.0	S59 33.7
21	260 13.3	109 02.3	. . 14.0	146 09.9	. . 32.6	110 48.3	. . 20.9	23 41.7	. . 49.7	Bellatrix	278 30.7	N 6 21.7
22	275 15.8	124 05.2	13.6	161 10.6	32.4	125 50.3	20.7	38 44.2	49.7	Betelgeuse	271 00.0	N 7 24.4
23	290 18.2	139 08.1	13.2	176 11.3	32.1	140 52.2	20.6	53 46.7	49.7			
28 00	305 20.7	154 11.0	N 7 12.7	191 12.0	N22 31.9	155 54.2	N13 20.4	68 49.2	S17 49.7	Canopus	263 56.0	S52 42.3
01	320 23.2	169 13.9	12.3	206 12.7	31.6	170 56.2	20.2	83 51.7	49.7	Capella	280 32.6	N46 00.5
02	335 25.6	184 16.8	11.8	221 13.5	31.4	185 58.1	20.0	98 54.2	49.8	Deneb	49 30.0	N45 20.3
03	350 28.1	199 19.8	. . 11.4	236 14.2	. . 31.1	201 00.1	. . 19.9	113 56.7	. . 49.8	Denebola	182 32.4	N14 29.2
04	5 30.6	214 22.7	11.0	251 14.9	30.9	216 02.0	19.7	128 59.2	49.8	Diphda	348 54.3	S17 53.9
05	20 33.0	229 25.6	10.5	266 15.6	30.6	231 04.0	19.5	144 01.6	49.8			
06	35 35.5	244 28.5	N 7 10.1	281 16.3	N22 30.4	246 05.9	N13 19.3	159 04.1	S17 49.8	Dubhe	193 50.6	N61 40.2
07	50 37.9	259 31.5	09.7	296 17.0	30.1	261 07.9	19.1	174 06.6	49.8	Elnath	278 11.1	N28 37.0
08	65 40.4	274 34.4	09.3	311 17.7	29.9	276 09.9	19.0	189 09.1	49.8	Eltanin	90 45.0	N51 29.6
T 09	80 42.9	289 37.3	. . 08.8	326 18.5	. . 29.6	291 11.8	. . 18.8	204 11.6	. . 49.8	Enif	33 45.4	N 9 57.0
U 10	95 45.3	304 40.3	08.4	341 19.2	29.4	306 13.8	18.6	219 14.1	49.8	Fomalhaut	15 22.1	S29 32.1
E 11	110 47.8	319 43.2	08.0	356 19.9	29.1	321 15.7	18.4	234 16.6	49.8			
S 12	125 50.3	334 46.2	N 7 07.5	11 20.6	N22 28.8	336 17.7	N13 18.3	249 19.1	S17 49.8	Gacrux	171 59.4	S57 12.2
D 13	140 52.7	349 49.1	07.1	26 21.3	28.6	351 19.7	18.1	264 21.5	49.8	Gienah	175 50.9	S17 37.7
A 14	155 55.2	4 52.1	06.7	41 22.0	28.3	6 21.6	17.9	279 24.0	49.8	Hadar	148 45.7	S60 27.0
Y 15	170 57.7	19 55.0	. . 06.3	56 22.8	. . 28.1	21 23.6	. . 17.7	294 26.5	. . 49.8	Hamal	327 59.1	N23 32.0
16	186 00.1	34 58.0	05.9	71 23.5	27.8	36 25.5	17.5	309 29.0	49.8	Kaus Aust.	83 41.5	S34 22.4
17	201 02.6	50 01.0	05.5	86 24.2	27.6	51 27.5	17.3	324 31.5	49.8			
18	216 05.1	65 04.0	N 7 05.0	101 24.9	N22 27.3	66 29.5	N13 17.2	339 34.0	S17 49.8	Kochab	137 20.1	N74 05.9
19	231 07.5	80 06.9	04.6	116 25.6	27.1	81 31.4	17.0	354 36.4	49.8	Markab	13 36.6	N15 17.4
20	246 10.0	95 09.9	04.2	131 26.4	26.8	96 33.4	16.8	9 38.9	49.9	Menkar	314 13.6	N 4 08.9
21	261 12.4	110 12.9	. . 03.8	146 27.1	. . 26.6	111 35.3	. . 16.6	24 41.4	. . 49.9	Menkent	148 05.8	S36 26.8
22	276 14.9	125 15.9	03.4	161 27.8	26.3	126 37.3	16.5	39 43.9	49.9	Miaplacidus	221 40.1	S69 47.1
23	291 17.4	140 18.9	03.0	176 28.5	26.0	141 39.3	16.3	54 46.4	49.9			
29 00	306 19.8	155 21.9	N 7 02.6	191 29.2	N22 25.8	156 41.2	N13 16.1	69 48.9	S17 49.9	Mirfak	308 38.4	N49 54.6
01	321 22.3	170 24.9	02.2	206 29.9	25.5	171 43.2	15.9	84 51.4	49.9	Nunki	75 56.2	S26 16.4
02	336 24.8	185 27.9	01.8	221 30.7	25.3	186 45.1	15.7	99 53.8	49.9	Peacock	53 16.4	S56 40.8
03	351 27.2	200 30.9	. . 01.4	236 31.4	. . 25.0	201 47.1	. . 15.6	114 56.3	. . 49.9	Pollux	243 26.4	N27 59.1
04	6 29.7	215 33.9	01.0	251 32.1	24.7	216 49.0	15.4	129 58.8	49.9	Procyon	244 58.6	N 5 11.0
05	21 32.2	230 36.9	00.6	266 32.8	24.5	231 51.0	15.2	145 01.3	49.9			
06	36 34.6	245 39.9	N 7 00.2	281 33.5	N22 24.2	246 53.0	N13 15.0	160 03.8	S17 49.9	Rasalhague	96 04.8	N12 33.3
W 07	51 37.1	260 43.0	6 59.8	296 34.3	24.0	261 54.9	14.8	175 06.3	49.9	Regulus	207 42.3	N11 53.5
E 08	66 39.6	275 46.0	59.4	311 35.0	23.7	276 56.9	14.7	190 08.7	49.9	Rigel	281 10.9	S 8 11.1
D 09	81 42.0	290 49.0	. . 59.0	326 35.7	. . 23.5	291 58.8	. . 14.5	205 11.2	. . 49.9	Rigil Kent.	139 49.6	S60 54.0
N 10	96 44.5	305 52.1	58.6	341 36.4	23.2	307 00.8	14.3	220 13.7	49.9	Sabik	102 10.6	S15 44.4
E 11	111 46.9	320 55.1	58.2	356 37.1	22.9	322 02.8	14.1	235 16.2	49.9			
S 12	126 49.4	335 58.2	N 6 57.8	11 37.9	N22 22.7	337 04.7	N13 13.9	250 18.7	S17 50.0	Schedar	349 38.5	N56 37.1
D 13	141 51.9	351 01.2	57.4	26 38.6	22.4	352 06.7	13.8	265 21.1	50.0	Shaula	96 19.6	S37 06.7
A 14	156 54.3	6 04.3	57.0	41 39.3	22.2	7 08.6	13.6	280 23.6	50.0	Sirius	258 32.8	S16 44.4
Y 15	171 56.8	21 07.3	. . 56.6	56 40.0	. . 21.9	22 10.6	. . 13.4	295 26.1	. . 50.0	Spica	158 29.8	S11 14.5
16	186 59.3	36 10.4	56.3	71 40.8	21.6	37 12.5	13.2	310 28.6	50.0	Suhail	222 51.8	S43 29.9
17	202 01.7	51 13.4	55.9	86 41.5	21.4	52 14.5	13.0	325 31.1	50.0			
18	217 04.2	66 16.5	N 6 55.5	101 42.2	N22 21.1	67 16.5	N13 12.9	340 33.6	S17 50.0	Vega	80 37.6	N38 48.2
19	232 06.7	81 19.6	55.1	116 42.9	20.8	82 18.4	12.7	355 36.0	50.0	Zuben'ubi	137 03.7	S16 06.3
20	247 09.1	96 22.7	54.7	131 43.6	20.6	97 20.4	12.5	10 38.5	50.0		SHA	Mer. Pass.
21	262 11.6	111 25.7	. . 54.4	146 44.4	. . 20.3	112 22.3	. . 12.3	25 41.0	. . 50.0		° ′	h m
22	277 14.0	126 28.8	54.0	161 45.1	20.0	127 24.3	12.1	40 43.5	50.0	Venus	208 50.3	13 41
23	292 16.5	141 31.9	53.6	176 45.8	19.8	142 26.2	12.0	55 46.0	50.0	Mars	245 51.3	11 15
	h m									Jupiter	210 33.5	13 35
Mer. Pass. 3 38.0		v 3.0	d 0.4	v 0.7	d 0.3	v 2.0	d 0.2	v 2.5	d 0.0	Saturn	123 28.5	19 22

UT	SUN GHA	SUN Dec	MOON GHA	v	MOON Dec	d	HP
d h	° ′	° ′	° ′	′	° ′	′	′
27 00	178 22.0	N19 19.6	59 12.1	9.9	S16 50.9	4.0	56.6
01	193 22.0	19.0	73 41.0	9.9	16 54.9	4.1	56.6
02	208 22.0	18.5	88 09.9	9.8	16 59.0	3.9	56.7
03	223 22.0	.. 17.9	102 38.7	9.7	17 02.9	3.8	56.7
04	238 22.0	17.3	117 07.4	9.7	17 06.7	3.8	56.7
05	253 22.0	16.8	131 36.1	9.6	17 10.5	3.6	56.8
06	268 22.0	N19 16.2	146 04.7	9.6	S17 14.1	3.6	56.8
07	283 22.0	15.7	160 33.3	9.4	17 17.7	3.5	56.9
M 08	298 22.1	15.1	175 01.7	9.5	17 21.2	3.4	56.9
O 09	313 22.1	.. 14.5	189 30.2	9.3	17 24.6	3.3	56.9
N 10	328 22.1	14.0	203 58.5	9.3	17 27.9	3.2	57.0
D 11	343 22.1	13.4	218 26.8	9.2	17 31.1	3.1	57.0
A 12	358 22.1	N19 12.8	232 55.0	9.1	S17 34.2	3.0	57.0
Y 13	13 22.1	12.3	247 23.1	9.1	17 37.2	2.9	57.1
14	28 22.1	11.7	261 51.2	9.1	17 40.1	2.8	57.1
15	43 22.1	.. 11.1	276 19.3	8.9	17 42.9	2.8	57.1
16	58 22.1	10.6	290 47.2	8.9	17 45.7	2.6	57.2
17	73 22.1	10.0	305 15.1	8.8	17 48.3	2.5	57.2
18	88 22.1	N19 09.4	319 42.9	8.8	S17 50.8	2.5	57.2
19	103 22.1	08.9	334 10.7	8.7	17 53.3	2.3	57.3
20	118 22.1	08.3	348 38.4	8.7	17 55.6	2.3	57.3
21	133 22.1	.. 07.7	3 06.1	8.6	17 57.9	2.1	57.4
22	148 22.2	07.2	17 33.7	8.5	18 00.0	2.0	57.4
23	163 22.2	06.6	32 01.2	8.5	18 02.0	2.0	57.4
28 00	178 22.2	N19 06.0	46 28.7	8.4	S18 04.0	1.8	57.5
01	193 22.2	05.5	60 56.1	8.3	18 05.8	1.7	57.5
02	208 22.2	04.9	75 23.4	8.3	18 07.5	1.7	57.5
03	223 22.2	.. 04.3	89 50.7	8.2	18 09.2	1.5	57.6
04	238 22.2	03.7	104 17.9	8.2	18 10.7	1.4	57.6
05	253 22.2	03.2	118 45.1	8.1	18 12.1	1.3	57.6
06	268 22.2	N19 02.6	133 12.2	8.1	S18 13.4	1.2	57.7
07	283 22.3	02.0	147 39.3	8.0	18 14.6	1.1	57.7
T 08	298 22.3	01.4	162 06.3	8.0	18 15.7	1.0	57.8
U 09	313 22.3	.. 00.9	176 33.3	7.9	18 16.7	0.9	57.8
E 10	328 22.3	19 00.3	191 00.2	7.8	18 17.6	0.7	57.8
S 11	343 22.3	18 59.7	205 27.0	7.8	18 18.3	0.7	57.9
D 12	358 22.3	N18 59.1	219 53.8	7.8	S18 19.0	0.6	57.9
A 13	13 22.3	58.6	234 20.6	7.6	18 19.6	0.4	57.9
Y 14	28 22.3	58.0	248 47.2	7.7	18 20.0	0.4	58.0
15	43 22.4	.. 57.4	263 13.9	7.6	18 20.4	0.2	58.0
16	58 22.4	56.8	277 40.5	7.5	18 20.6	0.1	58.0
17	73 22.4	56.2	292 07.0	7.5	18 20.7	0.0	58.1
18	88 22.4	N18 55.7	306 33.5	7.5	S18 20.7	0.1	58.1
19	103 22.4	55.1	321 00.0	7.4	18 20.6	0.2	58.1
20	118 22.4	54.5	335 26.4	7.4	18 20.4	0.4	58.2
21	133 22.4	.. 53.9	349 52.8	7.3	18 20.0	0.6	58.2
22	148 22.5	53.3	4 19.1	7.2	18 19.6	0.6	58.3
23	163 22.5	52.7	18 45.3	7.3	18 19.0	0.7	58.3
29 00	178 22.5	N18 52.2	33 11.6	7.2	S18 18.3	0.8	58.3
01	193 22.5	51.6	47 37.8	7.1	18 17.5	0.9	58.4
02	208 22.5	51.0	62 03.9	7.1	18 16.6	1.0	58.4
03	223 22.5	.. 50.4	76 30.0	7.1	18 15.6	1.1	58.4
04	238 22.6	49.8	90 56.1	7.0	18 14.5	1.3	58.5
05	253 22.6	49.2	105 22.1	7.0	18 13.2	1.4	58.5
06	268 22.6	N18 48.6	119 48.1	7.0	S18 11.8	1.5	58.5
W 07	283 22.6	48.1	134 14.1	6.9	18 10.3	1.6	58.6
E 08	298 22.6	47.5	148 40.0	6.9	18 08.7	1.7	58.6
D 09	313 22.7	.. 46.9	163 05.9	6.9	18 07.0	1.8	58.6
N 10	328 22.7	46.3	177 31.8	6.8	18 05.2	2.0	58.7
E 11	343 22.7	45.7	191 57.6	6.8	18 03.2	2.0	58.7
S 12	358 22.7	N18 45.1	206 23.4	6.8	S18 01.2	2.2	58.7
D 13	13 22.7	44.5	220 49.2	6.7	17 59.0	2.3	58.8
A 14	28 22.8	43.9	235 14.9	6.7	17 56.7	2.5	58.8
Y 15	43 22.8	.. 43.3	249 40.6	6.7	17 54.2	2.5	58.8
16	58 22.8	42.7	264 06.3	6.7	17 51.7	2.7	58.9
17	73 22.8	42.1	278 32.0	6.6	17 49.0	2.7	58.9
18	88 22.8	N18 41.6	292 57.6	6.6	S17 46.3	2.9	58.9
19	103 22.9	41.0	307 23.2	6.6	17 43.4	3.1	59.0
20	118 22.9	40.4	321 48.8	6.6	17 40.3	3.1	59.0
21	133 22.9	.. 39.8	336 14.4	6.5	17 37.2	3.2	59.0
22	148 22.9	39.2	350 39.9	6.6	17 34.0	3.4	59.1
23	163 22.9	38.6	5 05.5	6.5	S17 30.6	3.5	59.1
	SD 15.8	d 0.6	SD 15.5		15.8		16.0

Lat.	Twilight Naut.	Twilight Civil	Sunrise	Moonrise 27	28	29	30
°	h m	h m	h m	h m	h m	h m	h m
N 72	□	□	□	■	■	21 55	21 36
N 70	////	////	00 27	18 56	20 05	20 42	20 57
68	////	////	01 51	18 16	19 20	20 04	20 30
66	////	////	02 28	17 48	18 50	19 37	20 09
64	////	01 10	02 54	17 27	18 28	19 17	19 53
62	////	01 57	03 14	17 09	18 10	19 00	19 39
60	////	02 26	03 30	16 55	17 55	18 46	19 27
N 58	01 04	02 48	03 44	16 43	17 43	18 34	19 17
56	01 47	03 05	03 56	16 33	17 32	18 24	19 08
54	02 14	03 20	04 06	16 23	17 22	18 15	19 00
52	02 34	03 33	04 15	16 15	17 14	18 06	18 53
50	02 51	03 44	04 23	16 08	17 06	17 59	18 46
45	03 22	04 06	04 40	15 52	16 49	17 43	18 32
N 40	03 46	04 24	04 54	15 39	16 36	17 30	18 21
35	04 04	04 38	05 06	15 28	16 25	17 19	18 11
30	04 19	04 50	05 16	15 19	16 15	17 10	18 03
20	04 42	05 10	05 34	15 02	15 58	16 53	17 48
N 10	05 00	05 27	05 49	14 48	15 43	16 39	17 35
0	05 16	05 41	06 03	14 34	15 29	16 25	17 23
S 10	05 29	05 55	06 17	14 21	15 15	16 12	17 10
20	05 42	06 08	06 32	14 07	15 00	15 57	16 57
30	05 54	06 23	06 48	13 50	14 43	15 41	16 43
35	06 00	06 31	06 58	13 41	14 33	15 31	16 34
40	06 07	06 40	07 09	13 30	14 22	15 20	16 24
45	06 14	06 50	07 22	13 18	14 09	15 07	16 13
S 50	06 22	07 02	07 38	13 02	13 53	14 51	15 58
52	06 26	07 07	07 45	12 55	13 45	14 44	15 52
54	06 30	07 13	07 53	12 47	13 37	14 36	15 45
56	06 34	07 20	08 02	12 39	13 27	14 27	15 36
58	06 38	07 27	08 13	12 29	13 16	14 16	15 27
S 60	06 43	07 35	08 24	12 17	13 04	14 04	15 17

Lat.	Sunset	Twilight Civil	Twilight Naut.	Moonset 27	28	29	30
°	h m	h m	h m	h m	h m	h m	h m
N 72	□	□	□	■	■	23 29	25 48
N 70	23 26	////	////	22 34	23 20	24 42	00 42
68	22 17	////	////	23 15	24 05	00 05	01 19
66	21 41	////	////	23 43	24 34	00 34	01 46
64	21 16	22 56	////	24 05	00 05	00 57	02 06
62	20 57	22 12	////	24 22	00 22	01 15	02 22
60	20 41	21 44	////	24 36	00 36	01 29	02 36
N 58	20 27	21 23	23 03	00 06	00 49	01 42	02 48
56	20 16	21 06	22 23	00 16	00 59	01 53	02 58
54	20 04	20 51	21 57	00 24	01 09	02 03	03 07
52	19 57	20 39	21 37	00 32	01 17	02 11	03 15
50	19 49	20 28	21 21	00 39	01 24	02 19	03 22
45	19 32	20 06	20 50	00 54	01 41	02 35	03 37
N 40	19 18	19 49	20 27	01 06	01 54	02 48	03 50
35	19 06	19 35	20 09	01 16	02 05	03 00	04 00
30	18 56	19 22	19 54	01 25	02 15	03 10	04 10
20	18 39	19 03	19 31	01 41	02 32	03 27	04 26
N 10	18 24	18 46	19 12	01 54	02 46	03 42	04 40
0	18 10	18 32	18 57	02 07	03 00	03 55	04 53
S 10	17 56	18 18	18 44	02 20	03 14	04 09	05 05
20	17 42	18 05	18 32	02 34	03 29	04 24	05 19
30	17 25	17 50	18 19	02 49	03 45	04 41	05 35
35	17 15	17 42	18 13	02 58	03 55	04 51	05 44
40	17 04	17 33	18 06	03 09	04 06	05 02	05 54
45	16 52	17 23	17 59	03 21	04 19	05 15	06 07
S 50	16 36	17 12	17 51	03 36	04 35	05 31	06 21
52	16 29	17 06	17 48	03 43	04 43	05 38	06 28
54	16 20	17 00	17 44	03 50	04 51	05 47	06 36
56	16 11	16 54	17 40	03 59	05 01	05 56	06 44
58	16 01	16 47	17 36	04 09	05 11	06 07	06 54
S 60	15 49	16 39	17 31	04 20	05 23	06 19	07 04

Day	SUN Eqn. of Time 00h	SUN Eqn. of Time 12h	SUN Mer. Pass.	MOON Mer. Pass. Upper	MOON Mer. Pass. Lower	Age	Phase
d	m s	m s	h m	h m	h m	d	%
27	06 32	06 32	12 07	20 47	08 21	11	81
28	06 31	06 31	12 07	21 42	09 14	12	89
29	06 30	06 29	12 06	22 39	10 10	13	95

UT	ARIES	VENUS −4.4		MARS +1.7		JUPITER −1.7		SATURN +0.4		STARS		
	GHA	GHA	Dec	GHA	Dec	GHA	Dec	GHA	Dec	Name	SHA	Dec
d h	° ′	° ′	° ′	° ′	° ′	° ′	° ′	° ′	° ′		° ′	° ′
30 00	307 19.0	156 35.0	N 6 53.2	191 46.5	N22 19.5	157 28.2	N13 11.8	70 48.4	S17 50.0	Acamar	315 17.4	S40 14.4
01	322 21.4	171 38.1	52.9	206 47.3	19.3	172 30.2	11.6	85 50.9	50.0	Achernar	335 25.7	S57 09.2
02	337 23.9	186 41.2	52.5	221 48.0	19.0	187 32.1	11.4	100 53.4	50.1	Acrux	173 07.8	S63 11.3
03	352 26.4	201 44.3	.. 52.1	236 48.7	.. 18.7	202 34.1	.. 11.2	115 55.9	.. 50.1	Adhara	255 11.7	S28 59.7
04	7 28.8	216 47.4	51.8	251 49.4	18.5	217 36.0	11.1	130 58.4	50.1	Aldebaran	290 47.9	N16 32.2
05	22 31.3	231 50.5	51.4	266 50.1	18.2	232 38.0	10.9	146 00.8	50.1			
06	37 33.8	246 53.6	N 6 51.0	281 50.9	N22 17.9	247 39.9	N13 10.7	161 03.3	S17 50.1	Alioth	166 19.8	N55 52.8
T 07	52 36.2	261 56.7	50.7	296 51.6	17.7	262 41.9	10.5	176 05.8	50.1	Alkaid	152 57.9	N49 14.5
H 08	67 38.7	276 59.9	50.3	311 52.3	17.4	277 43.9	10.3	191 08.3	50.1	Al Na'ir	27 41.6	S46 52.8
U 09	82 41.2	292 03.0	.. 50.0	326 53.0	.. 17.1	292 45.8	.. 10.2	206 10.7	.. 50.1	Alnilam	275 45.1	S 1 11.7
R 10	97 43.6	307 06.1	49.6	341 53.8	16.9	307 47.8	10.0	221 13.2	50.1	Alphard	217 55.0	S 8 43.6
S 11	112 46.1	322 09.2	49.2	356 54.5	16.6	322 49.7	09.8	236 15.7	50.1			
D 12	127 48.5	337 12.4	N 6 48.9	11 55.2	N22 16.3	337 51.7	N13 09.6	251 18.2	S17 50.1	Alphecca	126 09.7	N26 40.1
A 13	142 51.0	352 15.5	48.5	26 55.9	16.1	352 53.6	09.4	266 20.7	50.1	Alpheratz	357 41.7	N29 10.5
Y 14	157 53.5	7 18.7	48.2	41 56.7	15.8	7 55.6	09.3	281 23.1	50.1	Altair	62 06.5	N 8 54.9
15	172 55.9	22 21.8	.. 47.8	56 57.4	.. 15.5	22 57.6	.. 09.1	296 25.6	.. 50.1	Ankaa	353 14.1	S42 13.0
16	187 58.4	37 25.0	47.5	71 58.1	15.3	37 59.5	08.9	311 28.1	50.2	Antares	112 24.3	S26 27.8
17	203 00.9	52 28.1	47.1	86 58.8	15.0	53 01.5	08.7	326 30.6	50.2			
18	218 03.3	67 31.3	N 6 46.8	101 59.6	N22 14.7	68 03.4	N13 08.5	341 33.0	S17 50.2	Arcturus	145 54.4	N19 06.4
19	233 05.8	82 34.5	46.4	117 00.3	14.4	83 05.4	08.3	356 35.5	50.2	Atria	107 24.3	S69 03.3
20	248 08.3	97 37.6	46.1	132 01.0	14.2	98 07.3	08.2	11 38.0	50.2	Avior	234 18.0	S59 33.7
21	263 10.7	112 40.8	.. 45.8	147 01.7	.. 13.9	113 09.3	.. 08.0	26 40.5	.. 50.2	Bellatrix	278 30.7	N 6 21.7
22	278 13.2	127 44.0	45.4	162 02.5	13.6	128 11.3	07.8	41 42.9	50.2	Betelgeuse	271 00.0	N 7 24.4
23	293 15.7	142 47.1	45.1	177 03.2	13.4	143 13.2	07.6	56 45.4	50.2			
31 00	308 18.1	157 50.3	N 6 44.8	192 03.9	N22 13.1	158 15.2	N13 07.5	71 47.9	S17 50.2	Canopus	263 56.0	S52 42.3
01	323 20.6	172 53.5	44.4	207 04.7	12.8	173 17.1	07.3	86 50.4	50.2	Capella	280 32.6	N46 00.5
02	338 23.0	187 56.7	44.1	222 05.4	12.6	188 19.1	07.1	101 52.8	50.3	Deneb	49 30.0	N45 20.4
03	353 25.5	202 59.9	.. 43.7	237 06.1	.. 12.3	203 21.0	.. 06.9	116 55.3	.. 50.3	Denebola	182 32.4	N14 29.2
04	8 28.0	218 03.1	43.4	252 06.8	12.0	218 23.0	06.7	131 57.8	50.3	Diphda	348 54.3	S17 53.9
05	23 30.4	233 06.3	43.1	267 07.6	11.7	233 25.0	06.5	147 00.3	50.3			
06	38 32.9	248 09.5	N 6 42.8	282 08.3	N22 11.5	248 26.9	N13 06.4	162 02.7	S17 50.3	Dubhe	193 50.6	N61 40.2
07	53 35.4	263 12.7	42.4	297 09.0	11.2	263 28.9	06.2	177 05.2	50.3	Elnath	278 11.0	N28 37.0
F 08	68 37.8	278 15.9	42.1	312 09.8	10.9	278 30.8	06.0	192 07.7	50.3	Eltanin	90 45.0	N51 29.6
R 09	83 40.3	293 19.2	.. 41.8	327 10.5	.. 10.6	293 32.8	.. 05.8	207 10.2	.. 50.3	Enif	33 45.4	N 9 57.0
I 10	98 42.8	308 22.4	41.5	342 11.2	10.4	308 34.7	05.6	222 12.6	50.3	Fomalhaut	15 22.1	S29 32.1
D 11	113 45.2	323 25.6	41.1	357 11.9	10.1	323 36.7	05.5	237 15.1	50.3			
A 12	128 47.7	338 28.8	N 6 40.8	12 12.7	N22 09.8	338 38.6	N13 05.3	252 17.6	S17 50.3	Gacrux	171 59.4	S57 12.2
Y 13	143 50.2	353 32.1	40.5	27 13.4	09.5	353 40.6	05.1	267 20.1	50.3	Gienah	175 51.0	S17 37.7
14	158 52.6	8 35.3	40.2	42 14.1	09.3	8 42.6	04.9	282 22.5	50.3	Hadar	148 45.7	S60 27.0
15	173 55.1	23 38.5	.. 39.9	57 14.9	.. 09.0	23 44.5	.. 04.7	297 25.0	.. 50.3	Hamal	327 59.0	N23 32.0
16	188 57.5	38 41.8	39.6	72 15.6	08.7	38 46.5	04.6	312 27.5	50.4	Kaus Aust.	83 41.5	S34 22.4
17	204 00.0	53 45.0	39.3	87 16.3	08.4	53 48.4	04.4	327 30.0	50.4			
18	219 02.5	68 48.3	N 6 38.9	102 17.0	N22 08.2	68 50.4	N13 04.2	342 32.4	S17 50.4	Kochab	137 20.1	N74 05.9
19	234 04.9	83 51.5	38.6	117 17.8	07.9	83 52.3	04.0	357 34.9	50.4	Markab	13 36.6	N15 17.4
20	249 07.4	98 54.8	38.3	132 18.5	07.6	98 54.3	03.8	12 37.4	50.4	Menkar	314 13.6	N 4 09.0
21	264 09.9	113 58.1	.. 38.0	147 19.2	.. 07.3	113 56.3	.. 03.6	27 39.8	.. 50.4	Menkent	148 05.8	S36 26.8
22	279 12.3	129 01.3	37.7	162 20.0	07.1	128 58.2	03.5	42 42.3	50.4	Miaplacidus	221 40.1	S69 47.0
23	294 14.8	144 04.6	37.4	177 20.7	06.8	144 00.2	03.3	57 44.8	50.4			
1 00	309 17.3	157 07.9	N 6 37.1	192 21.4	N22 06.5	159 02.1	N13 03.1	72 47.3	S17 50.4	Mirfak	308 38.3	N49 54.6
01	324 19.7	174 11.1	36.8	207 22.2	06.2	174 04.1	02.9	87 49.7	50.4	Nunki	75 56.2	S26 16.4
02	339 22.2	189 14.4	36.5	222 22.9	05.9	189 06.0	02.7	102 52.2	50.4	Peacock	53 16.4	S56 40.8
03	354 24.6	204 17.7	.. 36.2	237 23.6	.. 05.7	204 08.0	.. 02.6	117 54.7	.. 50.4	Pollux	243 26.3	N27 59.1
04	9 27.1	219 21.0	35.9	252 24.4	05.4	219 09.9	02.4	132 57.1	50.5	Procyon	244 58.5	N 5 11.0
05	24 29.6	234 24.3	35.6	267 25.1	05.1	234 11.9	02.2	147 59.6	50.5			
06	39 32.0	249 27.6	N 6 35.4	282 25.8	N22 04.8	249 13.9	N13 02.0	163 02.1	S17 50.5	Rasalhague	96 04.9	N12 33.3
07	54 34.5	264 30.9	35.1	297 26.5	04.5	264 15.8	01.8	178 04.6	50.5	Regulus	207 42.3	N11 53.5
S 08	69 37.0	279 34.2	34.8	312 27.3	04.3	279 17.8	01.7	193 07.0	50.5	Rigel	281 10.9	S 8 11.1
A 09	84 39.4	294 37.5	.. 34.5	327 28.0	.. 04.0	294 19.7	.. 01.5	208 09.5	.. 50.5	Rigil Kent.	139 49.6	S60 54.0
T 10	99 41.9	309 40.8	34.2	342 28.7	03.7	309 21.7	01.3	223 12.0	50.5	Sabik	102 10.6	S15 44.4
U 11	114 44.4	324 44.1	33.9	357 29.5	03.4	324 23.6	01.1	238 14.4	50.5			
R 12	129 46.8	339 47.5	N 6 33.6	12 30.2	N22 03.1	339 25.6	N13 00.9	253 16.9	S17 50.5	Schedar	349 38.5	N56 37.1
D 13	144 49.3	354 50.8	33.4	27 30.9	02.9	354 27.5	00.7	268 19.4	50.5	Shaula	96 19.6	S37 06.7
A 14	159 51.8	9 54.1	33.1	42 31.7	02.6	9 29.5	00.6	283 21.9	50.6	Sirius	258 32.7	S16 44.3
Y 15	174 54.2	24 57.4	.. 32.8	57 32.4	.. 02.3	24 31.4	.. 00.4	298 24.3	.. 50.6	Spica	158 29.8	S11 14.5
16	189 56.7	40 00.8	32.5	72 33.1	02.0	39 33.4	00.2	313 26.8	50.6	Suhail	222 51.8	S43 29.9
17	204 59.1	55 04.1	32.3	87 33.9	01.7	54 35.4	13 00.0	328 29.3	50.6			
18	220 01.6	70 07.4	N 6 32.0	102 34.6	N22 01.4	69 37.3	N12 59.8	343 31.7	S17 50.6	Vega	80 37.6	N38 48.3
19	235 04.1	85 10.8	31.7	117 35.3	01.2	84 39.3	59.7	358 34.2	50.6	Zuben'ubi	137 03.7	S16 06.3
20	250 06.5	100 14.1	31.5	132 36.1	00.9	99 41.2	59.5	13 36.7	50.6		SHA	Mer.Pass.
21	265 09.0	115 17.5	.. 31.2	147 36.8	.. 00.6	114 43.2	.. 59.3	28 39.1	.. 50.6		° ′	h m
22	280 11.5	130 20.8	30.9	162 37.6	00.3	129 45.1	59.1	43 41.6	50.6	Venus	209 32.2	13 26
23	295 13.9	145 24.2	30.7	177 38.3	00.0	144 47.1	58.9	58 44.1	50.6	Mars	243 45.8	11 11
	h m									Jupiter	209 57.1	13 25
Mer.Pass. 3 26.2		v 3.2	d 0.3	v 0.7	d 0.3	v 2.0	d 0.2	v 2.5	d 0.0	Saturn	123 29.8	19 10

UT	SUN GHA	SUN Dec	MOON GHA	v	MOON Dec	d	HP
d h	° '	° '	° '	'	° '	'	'
30 00	178 23.0	N18 38.0	19 31.0	6.5	S17 27.1	3.6	59.1
01	193 23.0	37.4	33 56.5	6.5	17 23.5	3.7	59.2
02	208 23.0	36.8	48 22.0	6.4	17 19.8	3.8	59.2
03	223 23.0	.. 36.2	62 47.4	6.5	17 16.0	4.0	59.2
04	238 23.1	35.6	77 12.9	6.4	17 12.0	4.0	59.3
05	253 23.1	35.0	91 38.3	6.4	17 08.0	4.2	59.3
06	268 23.1	N18 34.4	106 03.7	6.4	S17 03.8	4.3	59.3
T 07	283 23.1	33.8	120 29.1	6.4	16 59.5	4.4	59.4
H 08	298 23.2	33.2	134 54.5	6.4	16 55.1	4.6	59.4
U 09	313 23.2	.. 32.6	149 19.9	6.4	16 50.5	4.6	59.4
R 10	328 23.2	32.0	163 45.3	6.4	16 45.9	4.8	59.4
S 11	343 23.2	31.4	178 10.7	6.4	16 41.1	4.9	59.5
D 12	358 23.3	N18 30.8	192 36.1	6.4	S16 36.2	5.0	59.5
A 13	13 23.3	30.2	207 01.5	6.3	16 31.2	5.1	59.5
Y 14	28 23.3	29.6	221 26.8	6.4	16 26.1	5.2	59.5
15	43 23.3	.. 29.0	235 52.2	6.3	16 20.9	5.3	59.6
16	58 23.4	28.4	250 17.5	6.4	16 15.6	5.4	59.6
17	73 23.4	27.8	264 42.9	6.4	16 10.2	5.6	59.6
18	88 23.4	N18 27.1	279 08.3	6.3	S16 04.6	5.7	59.7
19	103 23.5	26.5	293 33.6	6.4	15 58.9	5.7	59.7
20	118 23.5	25.9	307 59.0	6.4	15 53.2	5.9	59.7
21	133 23.5	.. 25.3	322 24.4	6.3	15 47.3	6.0	59.7
22	148 23.5	24.7	336 49.7	6.4	15 41.3	6.1	59.8
23	163 23.6	24.1	351 15.1	6.4	15 35.2	6.2	59.8
31 00	178 23.6	N18 23.5	5 40.5	6.4	S15 29.0	6.4	59.8
01	193 23.6	22.9	20 05.9	6.4	15 22.6	6.4	59.8
02	208 23.7	22.3	34 31.3	6.4	15 16.2	6.5	59.9
03	223 23.7	.. 21.7	48 56.7	6.4	15 09.7	6.7	59.9
04	238 23.7	21.1	63 22.1	6.4	15 03.0	6.7	59.9
05	253 23.7	20.4	77 47.5	6.4	14 56.3	6.9	59.9
06	268 23.8	N18 19.8	92 12.9	6.5	S14 49.4	6.9	60.0
F 07	283 23.8	19.2	106 38.4	6.4	14 42.5	7.1	60.0
R 08	298 23.8	18.6	121 03.8	6.5	14 35.4	7.1	60.0
I 09	313 23.9	.. 18.0	135 29.3	6.5	14 28.3	7.3	60.0
D 10	328 23.9	17.4	149 54.8	6.5	14 21.0	7.3	60.0
A 11	343 23.9	16.8	164 20.3	6.5	14 13.7	7.5	60.1
Y 12	358 24.0	N18 16.1	178 45.8	6.5	S14 06.2	7.6	60.1
13	13 24.0	15.5	193 11.3	6.6	13 58.6	7.6	60.1
14	28 24.0	14.9	207 36.9	6.5	13 51.0	7.8	60.1
15	43 24.1	.. 14.3	222 02.4	6.6	13 43.2	7.8	60.1
16	58 24.1	13.7	236 28.0	6.6	13 35.4	8.0	60.2
17	73 24.1	13.1	250 53.6	6.6	13 27.4	8.0	60.2
18	88 24.2	N18 12.4	265 19.2	6.7	S13 19.4	8.1	60.2
19	103 24.2	11.8	279 44.9	6.6	13 11.3	8.2	60.2
20	118 24.2	11.2	294 10.5	6.7	13 03.1	8.3	60.2
21	133 24.3	.. 10.6	308 36.2	6.7	12 54.8	8.4	60.2
22	148 24.3	10.0	323 01.9	6.7	12 46.4	8.5	60.3
23	163 24.3	09.3	337 27.6	6.8	12 37.9	8.6	60.3
1 00	178 24.4	N18 08.7	351 53.4	6.7	S12 29.3	8.7	60.3
01	193 24.4	08.1	6 19.1	6.8	12 20.6	8.7	60.3
02	208 24.4	07.5	20 44.9	6.8	12 11.9	8.9	60.3
03	223 24.5	.. 06.8	35 10.7	6.9	12 03.0	8.9	60.3
04	238 24.5	06.2	49 36.6	6.8	11 54.1	9.0	60.3
05	253 24.6	05.6	64 02.4	6.9	11 45.1	9.0	60.4
06	268 24.6	N18 05.0	78 28.3	6.9	S11 36.1	9.2	60.4
S 07	283 24.6	04.3	92 54.2	7.0	11 26.9	9.2	60.4
A 08	298 24.7	03.7	107 20.2	7.0	11 17.7	9.4	60.4
T 09	313 24.7	.. 03.1	121 46.2	6.9	11 08.3	9.3	60.4
U 10	328 24.7	02.5	136 12.1	7.1	10 59.0	9.5	60.4
R 11	343 24.8	01.8	150 38.2	7.0	10 49.5	9.6	60.4
D 12	358 24.8	N18 01.2	165 04.2	7.1	S10 39.9	9.6	60.4
A 13	13 24.9	00.6	179 30.3	7.1	10 30.3	9.6	60.5
Y 14	28 24.9	18 00.0	193 56.4	7.1	10 20.7	9.8	60.5
15	43 24.9	17 59.3	208 22.5	7.2	10 10.9	9.8	60.5
16	58 25.0	58.7	222 48.7	7.2	10 01.1	9.9	60.5
17	73 25.0	58.1	237 14.9	7.2	9 51.2	10.0	60.5
18	88 25.1	N17 57.4	251 41.1	7.2	S 9 41.2	10.0	60.5
19	103 25.1	56.8	266 07.3	7.3	9 31.2	10.1	60.5
20	118 25.1	56.2	280 33.6	7.3	9 21.1	10.1	60.5
21	133 25.2	.. 55.5	294 59.9	7.3	9 11.0	10.2	60.5
22	148 25.2	54.9	309 26.2	7.4	9 00.8	10.3	60.5
23	163 25.3	54.3	323 52.6	7.4	S 8 50.5	10.3	60.5
	SD 15.8	d 0.6	SD 16.2		16.4		16.5

Moonrise

Lat.	Twilight Naut.	Twilight Civil	Sunrise	Moonrise 30	31	1	2
°	h m	h m	h m	h m	h m	h m	h m
N 72	☐	☐	☐	21 36	21 28	21 22	21 16
N 70	////	////	01 13	20 57	21 04	21 08	21 10
68	////	////	02 08	20 30	20 46	20 56	21 04
66	////	////	02 40	20 09	20 31	20 47	20 59
64	////	01 31	03 04	19 53	20 19	20 39	20 55
62	////	02 10	03 22	19 39	20 08	20 32	20 52
60	////	02 36	03 37	19 27	19 59	20 26	20 48
N 58	01 23	02 56	03 50	19 17	19 52	20 21	20 46
56	01 58	03 12	04 01	19 08	19 45	20 16	20 43
54	02 22	03 26	04 11	19 00	19 38	20 12	20 41
52	02 41	03 38	04 20	18 53	19 33	20 08	20 39
50	02 57	03 48	04 27	18 46	19 28	20 04	20 37
45	03 27	04 10	04 44	18 32	19 17	19 57	20 33
N 40	03 49	04 27	04 57	18 21	19 07	19 50	20 30
35	04 07	04 40	05 08	18 11	19 00	19 45	20 27
30	04 21	04 52	05 18	18 03	18 53	19 40	20 24
20	04 44	05 11	05 35	17 48	18 41	19 31	20 20
N 10	05 01	05 27	05 49	17 35	18 30	19 24	20 16
0	05 16	05 41	06 03	17 23	18 20	19 17	20 12
S 10	05 29	05 54	06 16	17 10	18 10	19 10	20 09
20	05 41	06 07	06 30	16 57	18 00	19 02	20 05
30	05 52	06 21	06 46	16 43	17 48	18 54	20 00
35	05 58	06 29	06 56	16 34	17 40	18 49	19 58
40	06 05	06 37	07 06	16 24	17 32	18 43	19 55
45	06 11	06 47	07 19	16 13	17 23	18 37	19 51
S 50	06 19	06 58	07 33	15 58	17 12	18 29	19 47
52	06 22	07 03	07 40	15 52	17 07	18 25	19 45
54	06 26	07 09	07 48	15 45	17 01	18 21	19 43
56	06 29	07 15	07 57	15 36	16 54	18 17	19 41
58	06 33	07 22	08 07	15 27	16 47	18 12	19 39
S 60	06 38	07 29	08 18	15 17	16 39	18 06	19 36

Moonset

Lat.	Sunset	Twilight Civil	Twilight Naut.	Moonset 30	31	1	2
°	h m	h m	h m	h m	h m	h m	h m
N 72	☐	☐	☐	25 48	01 48	03 57	06 01
N 70	22 51	////	////	00 42	02 26	04 19	06 13
68	22 01	////	////	01 19	02 53	04 36	06 22
66	21 30	////	////	01 46	03 13	04 50	06 30
64	21 07	22 36	////	02 06	03 29	05 01	06 37
62	20 49	22 00	////	02 22	03 42	05 11	06 43
60	20 34	21 35	////	02 36	03 54	05 19	06 48
N 58	20 21	21 15	22 45	02 48	04 03	05 26	06 52
56	20 10	20 59	22 12	02 58	04 12	05 32	06 56
54	20 01	20 45	21 48	03 07	04 19	05 38	07 00
52	19 52	20 34	21 30	03 15	04 26	05 43	07 03
50	19 45	20 23	21 14	03 22	04 32	05 48	07 06
45	19 28	20 02	20 45	03 37	04 45	05 58	07 12
N 40	19 15	19 46	20 23	03 50	04 56	06 06	07 17
35	19 04	19 32	20 06	04 00	05 05	06 13	07 22
30	18 54	19 20	19 51	04 10	05 13	06 19	07 25
20	18 38	19 01	19 29	04 26	05 27	06 29	07 32
N 10	18 23	18 45	19 11	04 40	05 39	06 39	07 38
0	18 10	18 32	18 57	04 53	05 50	06 47	07 43
S 10	17 57	18 19	18 44	05 05	06 01	06 56	07 49
20	17 43	18 06	18 32	05 19	06 13	07 05	07 54
30	17 27	17 52	18 21	05 35	06 26	07 15	08 01
35	17 17	17 44	18 15	05 44	06 34	07 21	08 04
40	17 07	17 36	18 09	05 54	06 43	07 27	08 08
45	16 55	17 26	18 02	06 07	06 53	07 35	08 13
S 50	16 40	17 15	17 55	06 21	07 05	07 44	08 19
52	16 33	17 10	17 51	06 28	07 11	07 48	08 21
54	16 25	17 05	17 48	06 36	07 17	07 53	08 24
56	16 17	16 59	17 44	06 44	07 24	07 58	08 27
58	16 07	16 52	17 40	06 54	07 32	08 04	08 31
S 60	15 56	16 44	17 36	07 04	07 41	08 10	08 35

	SUN Eqn. of Time 00h	SUN Eqn. of Time 12h	SUN Mer. Pass.	MOON Mer. Pass. Upper	MOON Mer. Pass. Lower	Age	Phase
Day	m s	m s	h m	h m	h m	d	%
30	06 28	06 27	12 06	23 36	11 08	14	99
31	06 26	06 24	12 06	24 34	12 05	15	100
1	06 23	06 21	12 06	00 34	13 02	16	98

UT	ARIES	VENUS −4.3		MARS +1.7		JUPITER −1.7		SATURN +0.4		STARS		
	GHA	GHA	Dec	GHA	Dec	GHA	Dec	GHA	Dec	Name	SHA	Dec
d h	° ′	° ′	° ′	° ′	° ′	° ′	° ′	° ′	° ′		° ′	° ′
2 00	310 16.4	160 27.6	N 6 30.4	192 39.0	N21 59.7	159 49.0	N12 58.7	73 46.5	S17 50.6	Acamar	315 17.3	S40 14.4
01	325 18.9	175 30.9	30.1	207 39.8	59.5	174 51.0	58.6	88 49.0	50.7	Achernar	335 25.7	S57 09.2
02	340 21.3	190 34.3	29.9	222 40.5	59.2	189 53.0	58.4	103 51.5	50.7	Acrux	173 07.8	S63 11.3
03	355 23.8	205 37.7	. . 29.6	237 41.2	. . 58.9	204 54.9	. . 58.2	118 53.9	. . 50.7	Adhara	255 11.7	S28 59.7
04	10 26.3	220 41.0	29.4	252 42.0	58.6	219 56.9	58.0	133 56.4	50.7	Aldebaran	290 47.9	N16 32.2
05	25 28.7	235 44.4	29.1	267 42.7	58.3	234 58.8	57.8	148 58.9	50.7			
06	40 31.2	250 47.8	N 6 28.9	282 43.4	N21 58.0	250 00.8	N12 57.6	164 01.3	S17 50.7	Alioth	166 19.8	N55 52.8
07	55 33.6	265 51.2	28.6	297 44.2	57.7	265 02.7	57.5	179 03.8	50.7	Alkaid	152 57.9	N49 14.5
08	70 36.1	280 54.6	28.4	312 44.9	57.5	280 04.7	57.3	194 06.3	50.7	Al Na'ir	27 41.5	S46 52.9
S 09	85 38.6	295 58.0	. . 28.1	327 45.6	. . 57.2	295 06.6	. . 57.1	209 08.7	. . 50.7	Alnilam	275 45.1	S 1 11.6
U 10	100 41.0	311 01.4	27.9	342 46.4	56.9	310 08.6	56.9	224 11.2	50.7	Alphard	217 55.0	S 8 43.6
N 11	115 43.5	326 04.8	27.6	357 47.1	56.6	325 10.5	56.7	239 13.7	50.8			
D 12	130 46.0	341 08.2	N 6 27.4	12 47.9	N21 56.3	340 12.5	N12 56.6	254 16.1	S17 50.8	Alphecca	126 09.7	N26 40.1
A 13	145 48.4	356 11.6	27.1	27 48.6	56.0	355 14.4	56.4	269 18.6	50.8	Alpheratz	357 41.7	N29 10.5
Y 14	160 50.9	11 15.0	26.9	42 49.3	55.7	10 16.4	56.2	284 21.1	50.8	Altair	62 06.5	N 8 54.9
15	175 53.4	26 18.4	. . 26.7	57 50.1	. . 55.4	25 18.4	. . 56.0	299 23.5	. . 50.8	Ankaa	353 14.1	S42 13.0
16	190 55.8	41 21.9	26.4	72 50.8	55.1	40 20.3	55.8	314 26.0	50.8	Antares	112 24.3	S26 27.8
17	205 58.3	56 25.3	26.2	87 51.5	54.9	55 22.3	55.6	329 28.5	50.8			
18	221 00.7	71 28.7	N 6 25.9	102 52.3	N21 54.6	70 24.2	N12 55.5	344 30.9	S17 50.8	Arcturus	145 54.5	N19 06.4
19	236 03.2	86 32.1	25.7	117 53.0	54.3	85 26.2	55.3	359 33.4	50.8	Atria	107 24.4	S69 03.3
20	251 05.7	101 35.6	25.5	132 53.8	54.0	100 28.1	55.1	14 35.8	50.8	Avior	234 18.0	S59 33.7
21	266 08.1	116 39.0	. . 25.3	147 54.5	. . 53.7	115 30.1	. . 54.9	29 38.3	. . 50.9	Bellatrix	278 30.7	N 6 21.7
22	281 10.6	131 42.4	25.0	162 55.2	53.4	130 32.0	54.7	44 40.8	50.9	Betelgeuse	271 00.0	N 7 24.4
23	296 13.1	146 45.9	24.8	177 56.0	53.1	145 34.0	54.5	59 43.2	50.9			
3 00	311 15.5	161 49.3	N 6 24.6	192 56.7	N21 52.8	160 35.9	N12 54.4	74 45.7	S17 50.9	Canopus	263 55.9	S52 42.2
01	326 18.0	176 52.8	24.4	207 57.5	52.5	175 37.9	54.2	89 48.2	50.9	Capella	280 32.6	N46 00.5
02	341 20.5	191 56.2	24.1	222 58.2	52.2	190 39.9	54.0	104 50.6	50.9	Deneb	49 30.0	N45 20.4
03	356 22.9	206 59.7	. . 23.9	237 58.9	. . 51.9	205 41.8	. . 53.8	119 53.1	. . 50.9	Denebola	182 32.4	N14 29.2
04	11 25.4	222 03.2	23.7	252 59.7	51.7	220 43.8	53.6	134 55.6	50.9	Diphda	348 54.3	S17 53.9
05	26 27.9	237 06.6	23.5	268 00.4	51.4	235 45.7	53.4	149 58.0	50.9			
06	41 30.3	252 10.1	N 6 23.3	283 01.2	N21 51.1	250 47.7	N12 53.3	165 00.5	S17 51.0	Dubhe	193 50.6	N61 40.2
07	56 32.8	267 13.6	23.1	298 01.9	50.8	265 49.6	53.1	180 02.9	51.0	Elnath	278 11.0	N28 37.0
08	71 35.2	282 17.0	22.8	313 02.6	50.5	280 51.6	52.9	195 05.4	51.0	Eltanin	90 45.1	N51 29.6
M 09	86 37.7	297 20.5	. . 22.6	328 03.4	. . 50.2	295 53.5	. . 52.7	210 07.9	. . 51.0	Enif	33 45.4	N 9 57.0
O 10	101 40.2	312 24.0	22.4	343 04.1	49.9	310 55.5	52.5	225 10.3	51.0	Fomalhaut	15 22.1	S29 32.1
N 11	116 42.6	327 27.5	22.2	358 04.9	49.6	325 57.4	52.3	240 12.8	51.0			
D 12	131 45.1	342 31.0	N 6 22.0	13 05.6	N21 49.3	340 59.4	N12 52.2	255 15.3	S17 51.0	Gacrux	171 59.4	S57 12.2
A 13	146 47.6	357 34.5	21.8	28 06.3	49.0	356 01.3	52.0	270 17.7	51.0	Gienah	175 51.0	S17 37.7
Y 14	161 50.0	12 38.0	21.6	43 07.1	48.7	11 03.3	51.8	285 20.2	51.0	Hadar	148 45.8	S60 27.0
15	176 52.5	27 41.5	. . 21.4	58 07.8	. . 48.4	26 05.2	. . 51.6	300 22.6	. . 51.1	Hamal	327 59.0	N23 32.0
16	191 55.0	42 45.0	21.2	73 08.6	48.1	41 07.2	51.4	315 25.1	51.1	Kaus Aust.	83 41.5	S34 22.4
17	206 57.4	57 48.5	21.0	88 09.3	47.8	56 09.2	51.2	330 27.6	51.1			
18	221 59.9	72 52.0	N 6 20.8	103 10.1	N21 47.5	71 11.1	N12 51.1	345 30.0	S17 51.1	Kochab	137 20.2	N74 05.9
19	237 02.3	87 55.5	20.6	118 10.8	47.2	86 13.1	50.9	0 32.5	51.1	Markab	13 36.6	N15 17.4
20	252 04.8	102 59.0	20.4	133 11.5	46.9	101 15.0	50.7	15 34.9	51.1	Menkar	314 13.6	N 4 09.0
21	267 07.3	118 02.5	. . 20.3	148 12.3	. . 46.6	116 17.0	. . 50.5	30 37.4	. . 51.1	Menkent	148 05.8	S36 26.8
22	282 09.7	133 06.1	20.1	163 13.0	46.3	131 18.9	50.3	45 39.9	51.1	Miaplacidus	221 40.1	S69 47.0
23	297 12.2	148 09.6	19.9	178 13.8	46.0	146 20.9	50.1	60 42.3	51.1			
4 00	312 14.7	163 13.1	N 6 19.7	193 14.5	N21 45.7	161 22.8	N12 50.0	75 44.8	S17 51.2	Mirfak	308 38.3	N49 54.6
01	327 17.1	178 16.7	19.5	208 15.3	45.4	176 24.8	49.8	90 47.2	51.2	Nunki	75 56.2	S26 16.4
02	342 19.6	193 20.2	19.3	223 16.0	45.1	191 26.7	49.6	105 49.7	51.2	Peacock	53 16.4	S56 40.9
03	357 22.1	208 23.7	. . 19.2	238 16.7	. . 44.8	206 28.7	. . 49.4	120 52.2	. . 51.2	Pollux	243 26.3	N27 59.1
04	12 24.5	223 27.3	19.0	253 17.5	44.5	221 30.6	49.2	135 54.6	51.2	Procyon	244 58.5	N 5 11.0
05	27 27.0	238 30.8	18.8	268 18.2	44.2	236 32.6	49.0	150 57.1	51.2			
06	42 29.5	253 34.4	N 6 18.6	283 19.0	N21 43.9	251 34.5	N12 48.9	165 59.5	S17 51.2	Rasalhague	96 04.9	N12 33.3
07	57 31.9	268 37.9	18.5	298 19.7	43.6	266 36.5	48.7	181 02.0	51.2	Regulus	207 42.3	N11 53.5
T 08	72 34.4	283 41.5	18.3	313 20.5	43.3	281 38.4	48.5	196 04.4	51.3	Rigel	281 10.9	S 8 11.1
U 09	87 36.8	298 45.0	. . 18.1	328 21.2	. . 43.0	296 40.4	. . 48.3	211 06.9	. . 51.3	Rigil Kent.	139 49.6	S60 54.0
E 10	102 39.3	313 48.6	17.9	343 22.0	42.7	311 42.4	48.1	226 09.4	51.3	Sabik	102 10.6	S15 44.4
S 11	117 41.8	328 52.2	17.8	358 22.7	42.4	326 44.3	47.9	241 11.8	51.3			
D 12	132 44.2	343 55.7	N 6 17.6	13 23.4	N21 42.1	341 46.3	N12 47.7	256 14.3	S17 51.3	Schedar	349 38.4	N56 37.2
A 13	147 46.7	358 59.3	17.4	28 24.2	41.8	356 48.2	47.6	271 16.7	51.3	Shaula	96 19.6	S37 06.7
Y 14	162 49.2	14 02.9	17.3	43 24.9	41.5	11 50.2	47.4	286 19.2	51.3	Sirius	258 32.7	S16 44.3
15	177 51.6	29 06.5	. . 17.1	58 25.7	. . 41.2	26 52.1	. . 47.2	301 21.6	. . 51.3	Spica	158 29.8	S11 14.5
16	192 54.1	44 10.0	17.0	73 26.4	40.9	41 54.1	47.0	316 24.1	51.3	Suhail	222 51.8	S43 29.8
17	207 56.6	59 13.6	16.8	88 27.2	40.6	56 56.0	46.8	331 26.6	51.4			
18	222 59.0	74 17.2	N 6 16.7	103 27.9	N21 40.3	71 58.0	N12 46.6	346 29.0	S17 51.4	Vega	80 37.6	N38 48.3
19	238 01.5	89 20.8	16.5	118 28.7	40.0	86 59.9	46.5	1 31.5	51.4	Zuben'ubi	137 03.8	S16 06.3
20	253 04.0	104 24.4	16.4	133 29.4	39.7	102 01.9	46.3	16 33.9	51.4		SHA	Mer. Pass.
21	268 06.4	119 28.0	. . 16.2	148 30.2	. . 39.4	117 03.8	. . 46.1	31 36.4	. . 51.4		° ′	h m
22	283 08.9	134 31.6	16.1	163 30.9	39.1	132 05.8	45.9	46 38.8	51.4	Venus	210 33.8	13 10
23	298 11.3	149 35.2	15.9	178 31.7	38.8	147 07.7	45.7	61 41.3	51.4	Mars	241 41.2	11 08
	h m									Jupiter	209 20.4	13 16
Mer. Pass. 3 14.4		v 3.5	d 0.2	v 0.7	d 0.3	v 2.0	d 0.2	v 2.5	d 0.0	Saturn	123 30.2	18 58

SUN and MOON — GHA, Dec, v, d, HP

UT (d h)	SUN GHA	SUN Dec	MOON GHA	v	MOON Dec	d	HP
	° ′	° ′	° ′	′	° ′	′	′
2 00	178 25.3	N17 53.6	338 19.0	7.4	S 8 40.2	10.4	60.5
01	193 25.3	53.0	352 45.4	7.5	8 29.8	10.5	60.5
02	208 25.4	52.4	7 11.9	7.4	8 19.3	10.4	60.5
03	223 25.4	.. 51.7	21 38.3	7.6	8 08.9	10.6	60.5
04	238 25.5	51.1	36 04.9	7.5	7 58.3	10.6	60.5
05	253 25.5	50.5	50 31.4	7.6	7 47.7	10.6	60.5
06	268 25.6	N17 49.8	64 58.0	7.6	S 7 37.1	10.7	60.5
07	283 25.6	49.2	79 24.6	7.6	7 26.4	10.8	60.5
08	298 25.6	48.5	93 51.2	7.6	7 15.6	10.8	60.5
S 09	313 25.7	.. 47.9	108 17.8	7.7	7 04.8	10.8	60.5
U 10	328 25.7	47.3	122 44.5	7.7	6 54.0	10.9	60.6
N 11	343 25.8	46.6	137 11.2	7.8	6 43.1	10.9	60.5
D 12	358 25.8	N17 46.0	151 38.0	7.7	S 6 32.2	11.0	60.5
A 13	13 25.9	45.3	166 04.7	7.8	6 21.2	11.0	60.5
Y 14	28 25.9	44.7	180 31.5	7.9	6 10.2	11.0	60.5
15	43 26.0	.. 44.1	194 58.4	7.8	5 59.2	11.1	60.5
16	58 26.0	43.4	209 25.2	7.9	5 48.1	11.1	60.5
17	73 26.1	42.8	223 52.1	7.9	5 37.0	11.2	60.5
18	88 26.1	N17 42.1	238 19.0	8.0	S 5 25.8	11.1	60.5
19	103 26.1	41.5	252 46.0	7.9	5 14.7	11.2	60.5
20	118 26.2	40.8	267 12.9	8.0	5 03.5	11.3	60.5
21	133 26.2	.. 40.2	281 39.9	8.1	4 52.2	11.3	60.5
22	148 26.3	39.6	296 07.0	8.0	4 40.9	11.2	60.5
23	163 26.3	38.9	310 34.0	8.1	4 29.7	11.4	60.5
3 00	178 26.4	N17 38.3	325 01.1	8.1	S 4 18.3	11.3	60.5
01	193 26.4	37.6	339 28.2	8.1	4 07.0	11.4	60.5
02	208 26.5	37.0	353 55.3	8.2	3 55.6	11.4	60.5
03	223 26.5	.. 36.3	8 22.5	8.2	3 44.2	11.4	60.5
04	238 26.6	35.7	22 49.7	8.2	3 32.8	11.4	60.5
05	253 26.6	35.0	37 16.9	8.2	3 21.4	11.4	60.5
06	268 26.7	N17 34.4	51 44.1	8.3	S 3 10.0	11.5	60.5
07	283 26.7	33.7	66 11.4	8.3	2 58.5	11.5	60.5
08	298 26.8	33.1	80 38.7	8.3	2 47.0	11.5	60.4
M 09	313 26.8	.. 32.4	95 06.0	8.3	2 35.5	11.5	60.4
O 10	328 26.9	31.8	109 33.3	8.4	2 24.0	11.5	60.4
N 11	343 26.9	31.1	124 00.7	8.3	2 12.5	11.5	60.4
D 12	358 27.0	N17 30.5	138 28.0	8.4	S 2 01.0	11.5	60.4
A 13	13 27.0	29.8	152 55.4	8.5	1 49.5	11.5	60.4
Y 14	28 27.1	29.2	167 22.9	8.4	1 38.0	11.6	60.4
15	43 27.1	.. 28.5	181 50.3	8.5	1 26.4	11.5	60.4
16	58 27.2	27.9	196 17.8	8.5	1 14.9	11.5	60.4
17	73 27.2	27.2	210 45.3	8.5	1 03.4	11.6	60.4
18	88 27.3	N17 26.5	225 12.8	8.5	S 0 51.8	11.5	60.3
19	103 27.3	25.9	239 40.3	8.6	0 40.3	11.6	60.3
20	118 27.4	25.2	254 07.9	8.5	0 28.7	11.5	60.3
21	133 27.5	.. 24.6	268 35.4	8.6	S 0 17.2	11.5	60.3
22	148 27.5	23.9	283 03.0	8.6	S 0 05.7	11.6	60.3
23	163 27.6	23.3	297 30.6	8.7	N 0 05.9	11.5	60.3
4 00	178 27.6	N17 22.6	311 58.3	8.6	N 0 17.4	11.5	60.3
01	193 27.7	21.9	326 25.9	8.7	0 28.9	11.5	60.2
02	208 27.7	21.3	340 53.6	8.7	0 40.4	11.5	60.2
03	223 27.8	.. 20.6	355 21.3	8.7	0 51.9	11.5	60.2
04	238 27.8	20.0	9 49.0	8.7	1 03.4	11.4	60.2
05	253 27.9	19.3	24 16.7	8.7	1 14.8	11.5	60.2
06	268 27.9	N17 18.6	38 44.4	8.7	N 1 26.3	11.4	60.2
07	283 28.0	18.0	53 12.1	8.8	1 37.7	11.4	60.1
08	298 28.1	17.3	67 39.9	8.8	1 49.1	11.4	60.1
T 09	313 28.1	.. 16.7	82 07.7	8.8	2 00.5	11.4	60.1
U 10	328 28.2	16.0	96 35.5	8.8	2 11.9	11.3	60.1
E 11	343 28.2	15.3	111 03.3	8.8	2 23.2	11.4	60.1
S 12	358 28.3	N17 14.7	125 31.1	8.8	N 2 34.6	11.3	60.1
D 13	13 28.3	14.0	139 58.9	8.9	2 45.9	11.3	60.0
A 14	28 28.4	13.3	154 26.8	8.8	2 57.2	11.2	60.0
Y 15	43 28.5	.. 12.7	168 54.6	8.9	3 08.4	11.3	60.0
16	58 28.5	12.0	183 22.5	8.9	3 19.7	11.2	60.0
17	73 28.6	11.3	197 50.4	8.9	3 30.9	11.1	60.0
18	88 28.6	N17 10.7	212 18.3	8.9	N 3 42.0	11.2	59.9
19	103 28.7	10.0	226 46.2	8.9	3 53.2	11.1	59.9
20	118 28.7	09.3	241 14.1	8.9	4 04.3	11.1	59.9
21	133 28.8	.. 08.7	255 42.0	8.9	4 15.4	11.0	59.9
22	148 28.9	08.0	270 09.9	9.0	4 26.4	11.0	59.9
23	163 28.9	07.3	284 37.9	8.9	N 4 37.4	11.0	59.8
	SD 15.8 d 0.7		SD 16.5	16.5			16.4

Twilight, Sunrise and Moonrise

Lat.	Naut.	Civil	Sunrise	Moonrise 2	3	4	5
°	h m	h m	h m	h m	h m	h m	h m
N 72	□	□	□	21 16	21 11	21 06	21 01
N 70	////	////	01 40	21 10	21 11	21 12	21 14
68	////	////	02 23	21 04	21 10	21 17	21 24
66	////	00 48	02 52	20 59	21 10	21 20	21 32
64	////	01 49	03 13	20 55	21 10	21 24	21 39
62	////	02 22	03 30	20 52	21 09	21 27	21 45
60	00 44	02 45	03 44	20 48	21 09	21 29	21 51
N 58	01 39	03 04	03 57	20 46	21 09	21 32	21 55
56	02 09	03 19	04 07	20 43	21 09	21 34	22 00
54	02 31	03 32	04 16	20 41	21 09	21 35	22 03
52	02 48	03 43	04 24	20 39	21 08	21 37	22 07
50	03 03	03 53	04 32	20 37	21 08	21 39	22 10
45	03 31	04 14	04 47	20 33	21 08	21 42	22 17
N 40	03 53	04 30	05 00	20 30	21 08	21 45	22 23
35	04 09	04 43	05 11	20 27	21 07	21 47	22 28
30	04 23	04 54	05 20	20 24	21 07	21 50	22 32
20	04 45	05 13	05 36	20 20	21 07	21 53	22 40
N 10	05 02	05 28	05 50	20 16	21 07	21 57	22 47
0	05 16	05 41	06 03	20 12	21 07	22 00	22 53
S 10	05 28	05 53	06 15	20 09	21 06	22 03	23 00
20	05 39	06 06	06 29	20 05	21 06	22 07	23 07
30	05 50	06 19	06 44	20 00	21 06	22 11	23 15
35	05 56	06 26	06 53	19 58	21 06	22 13	23 19
40	06 02	06 34	07 03	19 55	21 06	22 16	23 24
45	06 08	06 43	07 15	19 51	21 06	22 19	23 31
S 50	06 15	06 54	07 29	19 47	21 06	22 23	23 38
52	06 18	06 59	07 36	19 45	21 06	22 24	23 42
54	06 21	07 04	07 43	19 43	21 05	22 26	23 45
56	06 24	07 10	07 51	19 41	21 05	22 28	23 50
58	06 28	07 16	08 00	19 39	21 05	22 31	23 54
S 60	06 32	07 23	08 11	19 36	21 05	22 33	24 00

Sunset, Twilight and Moonset

Lat.	Sunset	Civil	Naut.	Moonset 2	3	4	5
°	h m	h m	h m	h m	h m	h m	h m
N 72	□	□	□	06 01	08 01	09 59	11 55
N 70	22 26	////	////	06 13	08 05	09 56	11 44
68	21 45	////	////	06 22	08 09	09 53	11 36
66	21 18	23 12	////	06 30	08 11	09 51	11 29
64	20 57	22 19	////	06 37	08 14	09 50	11 23
62	20 40	21 48	////	06 43	08 16	09 48	11 18
60	20 26	21 25	23 18	06 48	08 18	09 47	11 14
N 58	20 14	21 07	22 30	06 52	08 19	09 46	11 10
56	20 04	20 52	22 01	06 56	08 21	09 45	11 07
54	19 55	20 39	21 39	07 00	08 22	09 44	11 04
52	19 47	20 28	21 22	07 03	08 23	09 43	11 01
50	19 40	20 18	21 08	07 06	08 24	09 42	10 59
45	19 25	19 58	20 40	07 12	08 27	09 41	10 53
N 40	19 12	19 42	20 19	07 17	08 29	09 39	10 49
35	19 01	19 29	20 02	07 22	08 30	09 38	10 45
30	18 52	19 18	19 49	07 25	08 32	09 37	10 41
20	18 36	19 00	19 27	07 32	08 34	09 35	10 35
N 10	18 22	18 45	19 10	07 38	08 36	09 34	10 30
0	18 10	18 31	18 57	07 43	08 38	09 32	10 25
S 10	17 57	18 19	18 44	07 49	08 40	09 30	10 20
20	17 44	18 07	18 33	07 54	08 42	09 29	10 15
30	17 28	17 54	18 22	08 01	08 44	09 27	10 09
35	17 20	17 46	18 17	08 04	08 46	09 26	10 06
40	17 10	17 38	18 11	08 08	08 47	09 25	10 02
45	16 58	17 30	18 05	08 13	08 49	09 23	09 57
S 50	16 44	17 19	17 58	08 19	08 51	09 21	09 52
52	16 37	17 14	17 55	08 21	08 52	09 21	09 50
54	16 30	17 09	17 52	08 24	08 53	09 20	09 47
56	16 22	17 03	17 49	08 27	08 54	09 19	09 44
58	16 13	16 57	17 45	08 31	08 55	09 18	09 41
S 60	16 02	16 50	17 41	08 35	08 56	09 16	09 37

SUN and MOON — Equation of Time, Meridian Passage, Age, Phase

Day	Eqn. of Time 00h	Eqn. of Time 12h	Mer. Pass.	Mer. Pass. Upper	Mer. Pass. Lower	Age	Phase %
d	m s	m s	h m	h m	h m	d	%
2	06 19	06 17	12 06	01 30	13 58	17	94
3	06 15	06 12	12 06	02 25	14 52	18	87
4	06 10	06 07	12 06	03 19	15 46	19	78

2015 AUGUST 5, 6, 7 (WED., THURS., FRI.)

UT	ARIES GHA	VENUS −4.2 GHA	Dec	MARS +1.7 GHA	Dec	JUPITER −1.7 GHA	Dec	SATURN +0.4 GHA	Dec	STARS Name	SHA	Dec
5 00	313 13.8	164 38.8	N 6 15.8	193 32.4	N21 38.5	162 09.7	N12 45.5	76 43.7	S17 51.4	Acamar	315 17.3	S40 14.4
01	328 16.3	179 42.4	15.6	208 33.2	38.2	177 11.6	45.4	91 46.2	51.5	Achernar	335 25.6	S57 09.2
02	343 18.7	194 46.0	15.5	223 33.9	37.9	192 13.6	45.2	106 48.7	51.5	Acrux	173 07.9	S63 11.3
03	358 21.2	209 49.7 ..	15.3	238 34.6 ..	37.6	207 15.5 ..	45.0	121 51.1 ..	51.5	Adhara	255 11.7	S28 59.6
04	13 23.7	224 53.3	15.2	253 35.4	37.3	222 17.5	44.8	136 53.6	51.5	Aldebaran	290 47.8	N16 32.2
05	28 26.1	239 56.9	15.1	268 36.1	37.0	237 19.4	44.6	151 56.0	51.5			
W 06	43 28.6	255 00.5	N 6 14.9	283 36.9	N21 36.7	252 21.4	N12 44.4	166 58.5	S17 51.5	Alioth	166 19.8	N55 52.8
E 07	58 31.1	270 04.2	14.8	298 37.6	36.3	267 23.4	44.2	182 00.9	51.5	Alkaid	152 58.0	N49 14.5
D 08	73 33.5	285 07.8	14.7	313 38.4	36.0	282 25.3	44.1	197 03.4	51.5	Al Na'ir	27 41.5	S46 52.9
N 09	88 36.0	300 11.4 ..	14.5	328 39.1 ..	35.7	297 27.3 ..	43.9	212 05.8 ..	51.6	Alnilam	275 45.1	S 1 11.6
E 10	103 38.4	315 15.1	14.4	343 39.9	35.4	312 29.2	43.7	227 08.3	51.6	Alphard	217 55.0	S 8 43.6
S 11	118 40.9	330 18.7	14.3	358 40.6	35.1	327 31.2	43.5	242 10.7	51.6			
D 12	133 43.4	345 22.3	N 6 14.2	13 41.4	N21 34.8	342 33.1	N12 43.3	257 13.2	S17 51.6	Alphecca	126 09.7	N26 40.1
A 13	148 45.8	0 26.0	14.0	28 42.1	34.5	357 35.1	43.1	272 15.6	51.6	Alpheratz	357 41.7	N29 10.6
Y 14	163 48.3	15 29.6	13.9	43 42.9	34.2	12 37.0	43.0	287 18.1	51.6	Altair	62 06.5	N 8 54.9
15	178 50.8	30 33.3 ..	13.8	58 43.6 ..	33.9	27 39.0 ..	42.8	302 20.6 ..	51.6	Ankaa	353 14.1	S42 13.0
16	193 53.2	45 37.0	13.7	73 44.4	33.6	42 40.9	42.6	317 23.0	51.7	Antares	112 24.3	S26 27.8
17	208 55.7	60 40.6	13.6	88 45.1	33.3	57 42.9	42.4	332 25.5	51.7			
18	223 58.2	75 44.3	N 6 13.4	103 45.9	N21 33.0	72 44.8	N12 42.2	347 27.9	S17 51.7	Arcturus	145 54.5	N19 06.4
19	239 00.6	90 47.9	13.3	118 46.6	32.6	87 46.8	42.0	2 30.4	51.7	Atria	107 24.4	S69 03.3
20	254 03.1	105 51.6	13.2	133 47.4	32.3	102 48.7	41.8	17 32.8	51.7	Avior	234 18.0	S59 33.7
21	269 05.6	120 55.3 ..	13.1	148 48.1 ..	32.0	117 50.7 ..	41.7	32 35.3 ..	51.7	Bellatrix	278 30.6	N 6 21.7
22	284 08.0	135 59.0	13.0	163 48.9	31.7	132 52.6	41.5	47 37.7	51.7	Betelgeuse	271 00.0	N 7 24.4
23	299 10.5	151 02.6	12.9	178 49.6	31.4	147 54.6	41.3	62 40.2	51.7			
6 00	314 12.9	166 06.3	N 6 12.8	193 50.4	N21 31.1	162 56.5	N12 41.1	77 42.6	S17 51.8	Canopus	263 55.9	S52 42.2
01	329 15.4	181 10.0	12.7	208 51.1	30.8	177 58.5	40.9	92 45.1	51.8	Capella	280 32.5	N46 00.5
02	344 17.9	196 13.7	12.6	223 51.9	30.5	193 00.4	40.7	107 47.5	51.8	Deneb	49 30.0	N45 20.4
03	359 20.3	211 17.4 ..	12.5	238 52.6 ..	30.2	208 02.4 ..	40.5	122 50.0 ..	51.8	Denebola	182 32.4	N14 29.2
04	14 22.8	226 21.1	12.4	253 53.4	29.8	223 04.3	40.4	137 52.4	51.8	Diphda	348 54.3	S17 53.9
05	29 25.3	241 24.8	12.3	268 54.2	29.5	238 06.3	40.2	152 54.9	51.8			
T 06	44 27.7	256 28.4	N 6 12.2	283 54.9	N21 29.2	253 08.2	N12 40.0	167 57.3	S17 51.8	Dubhe	193 50.6	N61 40.2
H 07	59 30.2	271 32.1	12.1	298 55.7	28.9	268 10.2	39.8	182 59.8	51.9	Elnath	278 11.0	N28 37.0
U 08	74 32.7	286 35.8	12.0	313 56.4	28.6	283 12.1	39.6	198 02.2	51.9	Eltanin	90 45.1	N51 29.6
R 09	89 35.1	301 39.6 ..	11.9	328 57.2 ..	28.3	298 14.1 ..	39.4	213 04.7 ..	51.9	Enif	33 45.3	N 9 57.0
S 10	104 37.6	316 43.3	11.8	343 57.9	28.0	313 16.0	39.3	228 07.1	51.9	Fomalhaut	15 22.1	S29 32.1
D 11	119 40.0	331 47.0	11.7	358 58.7	27.6	328 18.0	39.1	243 09.6	51.9			
A 12	134 42.5	346 50.7	N 6 11.7	13 59.4	N21 27.3	343 19.9	N12 38.9	258 12.0	S17 51.9	Gacrux	171 59.5	S57 12.2
Y 13	149 45.0	1 54.4	11.6	29 00.2	27.0	358 21.9	38.7	273 14.5	51.9	Gienah	175 51.0	S17 37.7
14	164 47.4	16 58.1	11.5	44 00.9	26.7	13 23.8	38.5	288 16.9	51.9	Hadar	148 45.8	S60 27.0
15	179 49.9	32 01.8 ..	11.4	59 01.7 ..	26.4	28 25.8 ..	38.3	303 19.4 ..	52.0	Hamal	327 59.0	N23 32.0
16	194 52.4	47 05.6	11.3	74 02.4	26.1	43 27.7	38.1	318 21.8	52.0	Kaus Aust.	83 41.6	S34 22.4
17	209 54.8	62 09.3	11.3	89 03.2	25.7	58 29.7	38.0	333 24.3	52.0			
18	224 57.3	77 13.0	N 6 11.2	104 04.0	N21 25.4	73 31.7	N12 37.8	348 26.7	S17 52.0	Kochab	137 20.3	N74 05.9
19	239 59.8	92 16.8	11.1	119 04.7	25.1	88 33.6	37.6	3 29.2	52.0	Markab	13 36.6	N15 17.5
20	255 02.2	107 20.5	11.0	134 05.5	24.8	103 35.6	37.4	18 31.6	52.0	Menkar	314 13.5	N 4 09.0
21	270 04.7	122 24.2 ..	11.0	149 06.2 ..	24.5	118 37.5 ..	37.2	33 34.0 ..	52.0	Menkent	148 05.9	S36 26.8
22	285 07.2	137 28.0	10.9	164 07.0	24.2	133 39.5	37.0	48 36.5	52.1	Miaplacidus	221 40.1	S69 47.0
23	300 09.6	152 31.7	10.8	179 07.7	23.8	148 41.4	36.8	63 38.9	52.1			
7 00	315 12.1	167 35.5	N 6 10.8	194 08.5	N21 23.5	163 43.4	N12 36.7	78 41.4	S17 52.1	Mirfak	308 38.3	N49 54.6
01	330 14.5	182 39.2	10.7	209 09.2	23.2	178 45.3	36.5	93 43.8	52.1	Nunki	75 56.2	S26 16.4
02	345 17.0	197 43.0	10.6	224 10.0	22.9	193 47.3	36.3	108 46.3	52.1	Peacock	53 16.4	S56 40.9
03	0 19.5	212 46.7 ..	10.6	239 10.8 ..	22.6	208 49.2 ..	36.1	123 48.7 ..	52.1	Pollux	243 26.3	N27 59.1
04	15 21.9	227 50.5	10.5	254 11.5	22.3	223 51.2	35.9	138 51.2	52.1	Procyon	244 58.5	N 5 11.0
05	30 24.4	242 54.2	10.5	269 12.3	21.9	238 53.1	35.7	153 53.6	52.2			
F 06	45 26.9	257 58.0	N 6 10.4	284 13.0	N21 21.6	253 55.1	N12 35.5	168 56.1	S17 52.2	Rasalhague	96 04.9	N12 33.3
R 07	60 29.3	273 01.8	10.4	299 13.8	21.3	268 57.0	35.4	183 58.5	52.2	Regulus	207 42.3	N11 53.5
I 08	75 31.8	288 05.5	10.3	314 14.5	21.0	283 59.0	35.2	199 01.0	52.2	Rigel	281 10.8	S 8 11.1
D 09	90 34.3	303 09.3 ..	10.3	329 15.3 ..	20.7	299 00.9 ..	35.0	214 03.4 ..	52.2	Rigil Kent.	139 49.6	S60 54.0
A 10	105 36.7	318 13.1	10.2	344 16.1	20.3	314 02.9	34.8	229 05.8	52.2	Sabik	102 10.7	S15 44.4
Y 11	120 39.2	333 16.9	10.2	359 16.8	20.0	329 04.8	34.6	244 08.3	52.2			
12	135 41.7	348 20.6	N 6 10.1	14 17.6	N21 19.7	344 06.8	N12 34.4	259 10.7	S17 52.3	Schedar	349 38.4	N56 37.2
13	150 44.1	3 24.4	10.1	29 18.3	19.4	359 08.7	34.2	274 13.2	52.3	Shaula	96 19.6	S37 06.7
14	165 46.6	18 28.2	10.0	44 19.1	19.0	14 10.7	34.0	289 15.6	52.3	Sirius	258 32.7	S16 44.3
15	180 49.0	33 32.0 ..	10.0	59 19.8 ..	18.7	29 12.6 ..	33.9	304 18.1 ..	52.3	Spica	158 29.8	S11 14.5
16	195 51.5	48 35.8	10.0	74 20.6	18.4	44 14.6	33.7	319 20.5	52.3	Suhail	222 51.8	S43 29.8
17	210 54.0	63 39.6	09.9	89 21.4	18.1	59 16.5	33.5	334 23.0	52.3			
18	225 56.4	78 43.4	N 6 09.9	104 22.1	N21 17.8	74 18.5	N12 33.3	349 25.4	S17 52.3	Vega	80 37.6	N38 48.3
19	240 58.9	93 47.2	09.9	119 22.9	17.4	89 20.4	33.1	4 27.8	52.4	Zuben'ubi	137 03.8	S16 06.2
20	256 01.4	108 50.9	09.8	134 23.6	17.1	104 22.4	32.9	19 30.3	52.4			
21	271 03.8	123 54.7 ..	09.8	149 24.4 ..	16.8	119 24.3 ..	32.7	34 32.7 ..	52.4			
22	286 06.3	138 58.6	09.8	164 25.2	16.5	134 26.3	32.6	49 35.2	52.4			
23	301 08.8	154 02.4	09.7	179 25.9	16.1	149 28.2	32.4	64 37.6	52.4			
Mer. Pass.	h m 3 02.6	v 3.7	d 0.1	v 0.8	d 0.3	v 2.0	d 0.2	v 2.4	d 0.0			

	SHA	Mer. Pass.
	° ′	h m
Venus	211 53.4	12 52
Mars	239 37.4	11 04
Jupiter	208 43.6	13 07
Saturn	123 29.7	18 46

UT	SUN GHA	Dec	MOON GHA	v	Dec	d	HP
d h	° ′	° ′	° ′	′	° ′	′	′
5 00	178 29.0	N17 06.7	299 05.8	9.0	N 4 48.4	11.0	59.8
01	193 29.0	06.0	313 33.8	8.9	4 59.4	10.8	59.8
02	208 29.1	05.3	328 01.7	9.0	5 10.2	10.9	59.8
03	223 29.2	.. 04.6	342 29.7	9.0	5 21.1	10.8	59.8
04	238 29.2	04.0	356 57.7	8.9	5 31.9	10.8	59.7
05	253 29.3	03.3	11 25.6	9.0	5 42.7	10.7	59.7
06	268 29.4	N17 02.6	25 53.6	9.0	N 5 53.4	10.7	59.7
W 07	283 29.4	02.0	40 21.6	9.0	6 04.1	10.7	59.7
E 08	298 29.5	01.3	54 49.6	9.0	6 14.8	10.6	59.6
D 09	313 29.5	17 00.6	69 17.6	9.0	6 25.4	10.5	59.6
N 10	328 29.6	16 59.9	83 45.6	9.0	6 35.9	10.5	59.6
E 11	343 29.7	59.3	98 13.6	9.0	6 46.4	10.5	59.6
S 12	358 29.7	N16 58.6	112 41.6	9.1	N 6 56.9	10.4	59.6
D 13	13 29.8	57.9	127 09.7	9.0	7 07.3	10.3	59.5
A 14	28 29.9	57.2	141 37.7	9.0	7 17.6	10.3	59.5
Y 15	43 29.9	.. 56.6	156 05.7	9.0	7 27.9	10.3	59.5
16	58 30.0	55.9	170 33.7	9.1	7 38.2	10.1	59.5
17	73 30.0	55.2	185 01.8	9.0	7 48.3	10.2	59.4
18	88 30.1	N16 54.5	199 29.8	9.0	N 7 58.5	10.1	59.4
19	103 30.2	53.8	213 57.8	9.1	8 08.6	10.0	59.4
20	118 30.2	53.2	228 25.9	9.0	8 18.6	10.0	59.4
21	133 30.3	.. 52.5	242 53.9	9.0	8 28.6	9.9	59.3
22	148 30.4	51.8	257 21.9	9.1	8 38.5	9.8	59.3
23	163 30.4	51.1	271 50.0	9.0	8 48.3	9.8	59.3
6 00	178 30.5	N16 50.4	286 18.0	9.0	N 8 58.1	9.7	59.3
01	193 30.6	49.8	300 46.0	9.0	9 07.8	9.7	59.2
02	208 30.6	49.1	315 14.0	9.1	9 17.5	9.6	59.2
03	223 30.7	.. 48.4	329 42.1	9.0	9 27.1	9.5	59.2
04	238 30.8	47.7	344 10.1	9.0	9 36.6	9.5	59.2
05	253 30.8	47.0	358 38.1	9.1	9 46.1	9.4	59.1
06	268 30.9	N16 46.3	13 06.2	9.0	N 9 55.5	9.3	59.1
T 07	283 31.0	45.7	27 34.2	9.0	10 04.8	9.3	59.1
H 08	298 31.0	45.0	42 02.2	9.0	10 14.1	9.2	59.1
U 09	313 31.1	.. 44.3	56 30.2	9.0	10 23.3	9.1	59.0
R 10	328 31.2	43.6	70 58.2	9.1	10 32.4	9.0	59.0
S 11	343 31.3	42.9	85 26.3	9.0	10 41.4	9.0	59.0
D 12	358 31.3	N16 42.2	99 54.3	9.0	N10 50.4	8.9	58.9
A 13	13 31.4	41.5	114 22.3	9.0	10 59.3	8.9	58.9
Y 14	28 31.5	40.8	128 50.3	9.0	11 08.2	8.7	58.9
15	43 31.5	.. 40.2	143 18.3	9.0	11 16.9	8.7	58.9
16	58 31.6	39.5	157 46.3	9.0	11 25.6	8.7	58.8
17	73 31.7	38.8	172 14.3	9.0	11 34.3	8.5	58.8
18	88 31.7	N16 38.1	186 42.3	9.0	N11 42.8	8.5	58.8
19	103 31.8	37.4	201 10.3	9.0	11 51.3	8.3	58.8
20	118 31.9	36.7	215 38.3	8.9	11 59.6	8.4	58.7
21	133 32.0	.. 36.0	230 06.2	9.0	12 08.0	8.2	58.7
22	148 32.0	35.3	244 34.2	9.0	12 16.2	8.1	58.7
23	163 32.1	34.6	259 02.2	9.0	12 24.3	8.1	58.7
7 00	178 32.2	N16 33.9	273 30.2	8.9	N12 32.4	8.0	58.6
01	193 32.3	33.2	287 58.1	9.0	12 40.4	7.9	58.6
02	208 32.3	32.6	302 26.1	8.9	12 48.3	7.8	58.6
03	223 32.4	.. 31.9	316 54.0	9.0	12 56.1	7.8	58.5
04	238 32.5	31.2	331 22.0	8.9	13 03.9	7.6	58.5
05	253 32.5	30.5	345 49.9	9.0	13 11.5	7.6	58.5
06	268 32.6	N16 29.8	0 17.9	8.9	N13 19.1	7.5	58.5
F 07	283 32.7	29.1	14 45.8	9.0	13 26.6	7.4	58.4
R 08	298 32.8	28.4	29 13.8	8.9	13 34.0	7.3	58.4
I 09	313 32.8	.. 27.7	43 41.7	8.9	13 41.3	7.3	58.4
D 10	328 32.9	27.0	58 09.6	9.0	13 48.6	7.1	58.4
A 11	343 33.0	26.3	72 37.6	8.9	13 55.7	7.1	58.3
Y 12	358 33.1	N16 25.6	87 05.5	8.9	N14 02.8	7.0	58.3
13	13 33.1	24.9	101 33.4	8.9	14 09.8	6.8	58.3
14	28 33.2	24.2	116 01.3	8.9	14 16.6	6.8	58.3
15	43 33.3	.. 23.5	130 29.2	8.9	14 23.4	6.7	58.2
16	58 33.4	22.8	144 57.1	8.9	14 30.1	6.7	58.2
17	73 33.4	22.1	159 25.0	8.9	14 36.8	6.5	58.2
18	88 33.5	N16 21.4	173 52.9	8.9	N14 43.3	6.4	58.1
19	103 33.6	20.7	188 20.8	8.9	14 49.7	6.4	58.1
20	118 33.7	20.0	202 48.7	8.9	14 56.1	6.2	58.1
21	133 33.7	.. 19.3	217 16.6	8.9	15 02.3	6.2	58.1
22	148 33.8	18.6	231 44.5	8.9	15 08.5	6.0	58.0
23	163 33.9	17.9	246 12.4	8.9	N15 14.5	6.0	58.0
	SD 15.8	d 0.7	SD 16.2	16.1			15.9

Lat.	Twilight Naut.	Civil	Sunrise	Moonrise 5	6	7	8
°	h m	h m	h m	h m	h m	h m	h m
N 72	////	////	00 52	21 01	20 56	20 51	20 44
N 70	////	////	02 02	21 14	21 17	21 23	21 36
68	////	////	02 38	21 24	21 33	21 47	22 08
66	////	01 20	03 03	21 32	21 46	22 05	22 32
64	////	02 05	03 25	21 39	21 57	22 20	22 50
62	////	02 33	03 38	21 45	22 07	22 33	23 06
60	01 12	02 54	03 52	21 51	22 15	22 43	23 19
N 58	01 53	03 12	04 03	21 55	22 22	22 53	23 30
56	02 19	03 26	04 13	22 00	22 28	23 01	23 40
54	02 39	03 38	04 21	22 03	22 34	23 08	23 48
52	02 55	03 49	04 29	22 07	22 39	23 15	23 56
50	03 09	03 58	04 36	22 10	22 44	23 21	24 03
45	03 36	04 17	04 51	22 17	22 54	23 34	24 18
N 40	03 56	04 33	05 03	22 23	23 02	23 44	24 30
35	04 12	04 45	05 13	22 28	23 09	23 54	24 40
30	04 25	04 56	05 22	22 32	23 16	24 02	00 02
20	04 46	05 14	05 37	22 40	23 27	24 16	00 16
N 10	05 02	05 28	05 50	22 47	23 37	24 28	00 28
0	05 16	05 41	06 02	22 53	23 46	24 39	00 39
S 10	05 27	05 53	06 15	23 00	23 55	24 51	00 51
20	05 38	06 04	06 27	23 07	24 05	00 05	01 03
30	05 48	06 17	06 42	23 15	24 17	00 17	01 18
35	05 54	06 24	06 50	23 19	24 24	00 24	01 26
40	05 59	06 31	07 00	23 24	24 31	00 31	01 35
45	06 05	06 40	07 11	23 31	24 40	00 40	01 46
S 50	06 11	06 50	07 24	23 38	24 51	00 51	02 00
52	06 14	06 54	07 31	23 42	24 56	00 56	02 06
54	06 16	06 59	07 37	23 45	25 01	01 01	02 13
56	06 19	07 04	07 45	23 49	25 08	01 08	02 21
58	06 23	07 10	07 54	23 54	25 14	01 14	02 30
S 60	06 26	07 17	08 04	24 00	00 00	01 22	02 40

Lat.	Sunset	Twilight Civil	Naut.	Moonset 5	6	7	8
°	h m	h m	h m	h m	h m	h m	h m
N 72	23 05	////	////	11 55	13 51	15 47	17 45
N 70	22 04	////	////	11 44	13 32	15 16	16 54
68	21 30	////	////	11 36	13 17	14 53	16 23
66	21 06	22 44	////	11 29	13 05	14 36	15 59
64	20 47	22 03	////	11 23	12 55	14 21	15 41
62	20 31	21 36	////	11 18	12 46	14 09	15 26
60	20 19	21 15	22 53	11 14	12 39	13 59	15 13
N 58	20 07	20 58	22 15	11 10	12 32	13 50	15 03
56	19 58	20 44	21 50	11 07	12 27	13 43	14 53
54	19 49	20 32	21 31	11 04	12 22	13 36	14 45
52	19 42	20 22	21 15	11 01	12 17	13 30	14 37
50	19 35	20 13	21 01	10 59	12 13	13 24	14 31
45	19 21	19 54	20 35	10 53	12 04	13 12	14 16
N 40	19 09	19 38	20 15	10 49	11 56	13 02	14 05
35	18 59	19 26	19 59	10 45	11 50	12 53	13 54
30	18 50	19 15	19 46	10 41	11 44	12 46	13 46
20	18 35	18 58	19 25	10 35	11 35	12 33	13 30
N 10	18 21	18 44	19 09	10 30	11 26	12 22	13 17
0	18 09	18 31	18 56	10 25	11 18	12 11	13 05
S 10	17 57	18 19	18 44	10 20	11 10	12 01	12 52
20	17 45	18 08	18 34	10 15	11 02	11 50	12 39
30	17 30	17 55	18 24	10 09	10 52	11 37	12 24
35	17 22	17 48	18 19	10 06	10 47	11 30	12 15
40	17 12	17 41	18 13	10 02	10 40	11 21	12 05
45	17 01	17 33	18 08	09 57	10 33	11 12	11 53
S 50	16 48	17 23	18 02	09 52	10 24	11 00	11 39
52	16 42	17 18	17 59	09 50	10 20	10 54	11 33
54	16 35	17 14	17 56	09 47	10 16	10 48	11 25
56	16 27	17 08	17 53	09 44	10 11	10 42	11 17
58	16 19	17 03	17 50	09 41	10 06	10 34	11 08
S 60	16 09	16 56	17 47	09 37	10 00	10 26	10 58

	SUN			MOON			
Day	Eqn. of Time 00ʰ	12ʰ	Mer. Pass.	Mer. Pass. Upper	Lower	Age	Phase
d	m s	m s	h m	h m	h m	d	%
5	06 04	06 01	12 06	04 13	16 39	20	68
6	05 58	05 55	12 06	05 06	17 32	21	57
7	05 51	05 48	12 06	05 59	18 25	22	46

UT	ARIES GHA	VENUS −4.0 GHA	Dec	MARS +1.7 GHA	Dec	JUPITER −1.7 GHA	Dec	SATURN +0.5 GHA	Dec	STARS Name	SHA	Dec
d h	° ′	° ′	° ′	° ′	° ′	° ′	° ′	° ′	° ′		° ′	° ′
8 00	316 11.2	169 06.2 N 6	09.7	194 26.7 N21	15.8	164 30.2 N12	32.2	79 40.1 S17	52.4	Acamar	315 17.3	S40 14.4
01	331 13.7	184 10.0	09.7	209 27.4	15.5	179 32.1	32.0	94 42.5	52.5	Achernar	335 25.6	S57 09.2
02	346 16.2	199 13.8	09.7	224 28.2	15.2	194 34.1	31.8	109 44.9	52.5	Acrux	173 07.9	S63 11.3
03	1 18.6	214 17.6 ..	09.6	239 29.0 ..	14.8	209 36.0 ..	31.6	124 47.4 ..	52.5	Adhara	255 11.7	S28 59.6
04	16 21.1	229 21.4	09.6	254 29.7	14.5	224 38.0	31.4	139 49.8	52.5	Aldebaran	290 47.8	N16 32.2
05	31 23.5	244 25.2	09.6	269 30.5	14.2	239 39.9	31.3	154 52.3	52.5			
S 06	46 26.0	259 29.1 N 6	09.6	284 31.2 N21	13.9	254 41.9 N12	31.1	169 54.7 S17	52.5	Alioth	166 19.8	N55 52.8
A 07	61 28.5	274 32.9	09.6	299 32.0	13.5	269 43.8	30.9	184 57.2	52.5	Alkaid	152 58.0	N49 14.5
T 08	76 30.9	289 36.7	09.6	314 32.8	13.2	284 45.8	30.7	199 59.6	52.6	Al Na'ir	27 41.5	S46 52.9
U 09	91 33.4	304 40.5 ..	09.6	329 33.5 ..	12.9	299 47.7 ..	30.5	215 02.0 ..	52.6	Alnilam	275 45.1	S 1 11.6
R 10	106 35.9	319 44.4	09.6	344 34.3	12.6	314 49.7	30.3	230 04.5	52.6	Alphard	217 55.0	S 8 43.6
D 11	121 38.3	334 48.2	09.5	359 35.0	12.2	329 51.6	30.1	245 06.9	52.6			
A 12	136 40.8	349 52.0 N 6	09.5	14 35.8 N21	11.9	344 53.6 N12	29.9	260 09.4 S17	52.6	Alphecca	126 09.7	N26 40.1
Y 13	151 43.3	4 55.9	09.5	29 36.6	11.6	359 55.5	29.8	275 11.8	52.6	Alpheratz	357 41.7	N29 10.6
14	166 45.7	19 59.7	09.5	44 37.3	11.2	14 57.5	29.6	290 14.2	52.7	Altair	62 06.5	N 8 54.9
15	181 48.2	35 03.6 ..	09.5	59 38.1 ..	10.9	29 59.4 ..	29.4	305 16.7 ..	52.7	Ankaa	353 14.1	S42 13.0
16	196 50.6	50 07.4	09.5	74 38.9	10.6	45 01.4	29.2	320 19.1	52.7	Antares	112 24.3	S26 27.8
17	211 53.1	65 11.2	09.5	89 39.6	10.3	60 03.3	29.0	335 21.6	52.7			
18	226 55.6	80 15.1 N 6	09.5	104 40.4 N21	09.9	75 05.3 N12	28.8	350 24.0 S17	52.7	Arcturus	145 54.5	N19 06.4
19	241 58.0	95 18.9	09.6	119 41.2	09.6	90 07.2	28.6	5 26.4	52.7	Atria	107 24.4	S69 03.3
20	257 00.5	110 22.8	09.6	134 41.9	09.3	105 09.2	28.5	20 28.9	52.7	Avior	234 18.0	S59 33.6
21	272 03.0	125 26.6 ..	09.6	149 42.7 ..	08.9	120 11.1 ..	28.3	35 31.3 ..	52.8	Bellatrix	278 30.6	N 6 21.7
22	287 05.4	140 30.5	09.6	164 43.4	08.6	135 13.1	28.1	50 33.8	52.8	Betelgeuse	270 59.9	N 7 24.4
23	302 07.9	155 34.4	09.6	179 44.2	08.3	150 15.0	27.9	65 36.2	52.8			
9 00	317 10.4	170 38.2 N 6	09.6	194 45.0 N21	07.9	165 17.0 N12	27.7	80 38.6 S17	52.8	Canopus	263 55.9	S52 42.2
01	332 12.8	185 42.1	09.6	209 45.7	07.6	180 18.9	27.5	95 41.1	52.8	Capella	280 32.5	N46 00.5
02	347 15.3	200 46.0	09.6	224 46.5	07.3	195 20.9	27.3	110 43.5	52.8	Deneb	49 30.0	N45 20.4
03	2 17.8	215 49.8 ..	09.7	239 47.3 ..	07.0	210 22.8 ..	27.1	125 46.0 ..	52.9	Denebola	182 32.4	N14 29.2
04	17 20.2	230 53.7	09.7	254 48.0	06.6	225 24.8	27.0	140 48.4	52.9	Diphda	348 54.2	S17 53.9
05	32 22.7	245 57.6	09.7	269 48.8	06.3	240 26.7	26.8	155 50.8	52.9			
S 06	47 25.1	261 01.4 N 6	09.7	284 49.6 N21	06.0	255 28.7 N12	26.6	170 53.3 S17	52.9	Dubhe	193 50.6	N61 40.1
U 07	62 27.6	276 05.3	09.8	299 50.3	05.6	270 30.6	26.4	185 55.7	52.9	Elnath	278 11.0	N28 37.0
N 08	77 30.1	291 09.2	09.8	314 51.1	05.3	285 32.6	26.2	200 58.1	52.9	Eltanin	90 45.1	N51 29.7
D 09	92 32.5	306 13.1 ..	09.8	329 51.9 ..	05.0	300 34.5 ..	26.0	216 00.6 ..	53.0	Enif	33 45.3	N 9 57.0
A 10	107 35.0	321 17.0	09.8	344 52.6	04.6	315 36.4	25.8	231 03.0	53.0	Fomalhaut	15 22.1	S29 32.1
Y 11	122 37.5	336 20.8	09.9	359 53.4	04.3	330 38.4	25.6	246 05.4	53.0			
12	137 39.9	351 24.7 N 6	09.9	14 54.2 N21	03.9	345 40.3 N12	25.4	261 07.9 S17	53.0	Gacrux	171 59.5	S57 12.2
13	152 42.4	6 28.6	09.9	29 54.9	03.6	0 42.3	25.3	276 10.3	53.0	Gienah	175 51.0	S17 37.7
14	167 44.9	21 32.5	10.0	44 55.7	03.3	15 44.2	25.1	291 12.8	53.0	Hadar	148 45.8	S60 27.0
15	182 47.3	36 36.4 ..	10.0	59 56.5 ..	03.0	30 46.2 ..	24.9	306 15.2 ..	53.1	Hamal	327 59.0	N23 32.0
16	197 49.8	51 40.3	10.1	74 57.2	02.6	45 48.1	24.7	321 17.6	53.1	Kaus Aust.	83 41.6	S34 22.4
17	212 52.3	66 44.2	10.1	89 58.0	02.3	60 50.1	24.5	336 20.1	53.1			
18	227 54.7	81 48.1 N 6	10.2	104 58.8 N21	01.9	75 52.0 N12	24.3	351 22.5 S17	53.1	Kochab	137 20.3	N74 05.9
19	242 57.2	96 52.0	10.2	119 59.5	01.6	90 54.0	24.1	6 24.9	53.1	Markab	13 36.6	N15 17.5
20	257 59.6	111 55.9	10.2	135 00.3	01.3	105 55.9	24.0	21 27.4	53.1	Menkar	314 13.5	N 4 09.0
21	273 02.1	126 59.8 ..	10.3	150 01.1 ..	00.9	120 57.9 ..	23.8	36 29.8 ..	53.2	Menkent	148 05.9	S36 26.8
22	288 04.6	142 03.7	10.3	165 01.8	00.6	135 59.8	23.6	51 32.2	53.2	Miaplacidus	221 40.1	S69 47.0
23	303 07.0	157 07.6	10.4	180 02.6 21	00.3	151 01.8	23.4	66 34.7	53.2			
10 00	318 09.5	172 11.5 N 6	10.5	195 03.4 N20	59.9	166 03.7 N12	23.2	81 37.1 S17	53.2	Mirfak	308 38.2	N49 54.6
01	333 12.0	187 15.4	10.5	210 04.1	59.6	181 05.7	23.0	96 39.5	53.2	Nunki	75 56.2	S26 16.4
02	348 14.4	202 19.3	10.6	225 04.9	59.3	196 07.6	22.8	111 42.0	53.2	Peacock	53 16.4	S56 40.9
03	3 16.9	217 23.2 ..	10.6	240 05.7 ..	58.9	211 09.6 ..	22.6	126 44.4 ..	53.3	Pollux	243 26.3	N27 59.1
04	18 19.4	232 27.1	10.7	255 06.4	58.6	226 11.5	22.5	141 46.8	53.3	Procyon	244 58.5	N 5 11.0
05	33 21.8	247 31.1	10.7	270 07.2	58.2	241 13.5	22.3	156 49.3	53.3			
M 06	48 24.3	262 35.0 N 6	10.8	285 08.0 N20	57.9	256 15.4 N12	22.1	171 51.7 S17	53.3	Rasalhague	96 04.9	N12 33.3
O 07	63 26.8	277 38.9	10.9	300 08.7	57.6	271 17.4	21.9	186 54.1	53.3	Regulus	207 42.3	N11 53.5
N 08	78 29.2	292 42.8	10.9	315 09.5	57.2	286 19.3	21.7	201 56.6	53.3	Rigel	281 10.8	S 8 11.1
09	93 31.7	307 46.7 ..	11.0	330 10.3 ..	56.9	301 21.3 ..	21.5	216 59.0 ..	53.4	Rigil Kent.	139 49.7	S60 54.0
D 10	108 34.1	322 50.7	11.1	345 11.1	56.5	316 23.2	21.3	232 01.4	53.4	Sabik	102 10.7	S15 44.4
A 11	123 36.6	337 54.6	11.1	0 11.8	56.2	331 25.2	21.1	247 03.9	53.4			
Y 12	138 39.1	352 58.5 N 6	11.2	15 12.6 N20	55.9	346 27.1 N12	21.0	262 06.3 S17	53.4	Schedar	349 38.4	N56 37.2
13	153 41.5	8 02.4	11.3	30 13.4	55.5	1 29.1	20.8	277 08.7	53.4	Shaula	96 19.6	S37 06.7
14	168 44.0	23 06.4	11.4	45 14.1	55.2	16 31.0	20.6	292 11.2	53.4	Sirius	258 32.7	S16 44.3
15	183 46.5	38 10.3 ..	11.4	60 14.9 ..	54.8	31 33.0 ..	20.4	307 13.6 ..	53.5	Spica	158 29.8	S11 14.5
16	198 48.9	53 14.2	11.5	75 15.7	54.5	46 34.9	20.2	322 16.0	53.5	Suhail	222 51.7	S43 29.8
17	213 51.4	68 18.2	11.6	90 16.5	54.2	61 36.9	20.0	337 18.5	53.5			
18	228 53.9	83 22.1 N 6	11.7	105 17.2 N20	53.8	76 38.8 N12	19.8	352 20.9 S17	53.5	Vega	80 37.6	N38 48.3
19	243 56.3	98 26.0	11.8	120 18.0	53.5	91 40.8	19.6	7 23.3	53.5	Zuben'ubi	137 03.8	S16 06.2
20	258 58.8	113 30.0	11.9	135 18.8	53.1	106 42.7	19.4	22 25.8	53.6		SHA	Mer. Pass.
21	274 01.2	128 33.9 ..	11.9	150 19.5 ..	52.8	121 44.7 ..	19.3	37 28.2 ..	53.6		° ′	h m
22	289 03.7	143 37.9	12.0	165 20.3	52.4	136 46.6	19.1	52 30.6	53.6	Venus	213 27.9	12 34
23	304 06.2	158 41.8	12.1	180 21.1	52.1	151 48.6	18.9	67 33.1	53.6	Mars	237 34.6	11 00
	h m									Jupiter	208 06.6	12 57
Mer. Pass.	2 50.8	*v* 3.9 *d* 0.0		*v* 0.8 *d* 0.3		*v* 1.9 *d* 0.2		*v* 2.4 *d* 0.0		Saturn	123 28.3	18 34

UT	SUN GHA	SUN Dec	MOON GHA	v	MOON Dec	d	HP
d h	° ′	° ′	° ′	′	° ′	′	′
8 00	178 34.0	N16 17.2	260 40.3	8.9	N15 20.5	5.9	58.0
01	193 34.1	16.5	275 08.2	8.9	15 26.4	5.7	58.0
02	208 34.1	15.8	289 36.1	8.8	15 32.1	5.7	57.9
03	223 34.2	.. 15.1	304 03.9	8.9	15 37.8	5.6	57.9
04	238 34.3	14.4	318 31.8	8.9	15 43.4	5.5	57.9
05	253 34.4	13.7	332 59.7	8.9	15 48.9	5.4	57.8
06	268 34.5	N16 12.9	347 27.6	8.9	N15 54.3	5.3	57.8
S 07	283 34.5	12.2	1 55.5	8.8	15 59.6	5.2	57.8
A 08	298 34.6	11.5	16 23.3	8.9	16 04.8	5.1	57.8
T 09	313 34.7	.. 10.8	30 51.2	8.9	16 09.9	5.0	57.7
U 10	328 34.8	10.1	45 19.1	8.9	16 14.9	5.0	57.7
R 11	343 34.9	09.4	59 47.0	8.9	16 19.9	4.8	57.7
D 12	358 34.9	N16 08.7	74 14.9	8.9	N16 24.7	4.7	57.7
A 13	13 35.0	08.0	88 42.8	8.9	16 29.4	4.6	57.6
Y 14	28 35.1	07.3	103 10.7	8.8	16 34.0	4.5	57.6
15	43 35.2	.. 06.6	117 38.5	8.9	16 38.5	4.5	57.6
16	58 35.3	05.9	132 06.4	8.9	16 43.0	4.3	57.6
17	73 35.3	05.1	146 34.3	8.9	16 47.3	4.2	57.5
18	88 35.4	N16 04.4	161 02.2	9.0	N16 51.5	4.1	57.5
19	103 35.5	03.7	175 30.2	8.9	16 55.6	4.0	57.5
20	118 35.6	03.0	189 58.1	8.9	16 59.6	4.0	57.5
21	133 35.7	.. 02.3	204 26.0	8.9	17 03.6	3.8	57.4
22	148 35.8	01.6	218 53.9	8.9	17 07.4	3.7	57.4
23	163 35.8	00.9	233 21.8	9.0	17 11.1	3.6	57.4
9 00	178 35.9	N16 00.2	247 49.8	8.9	N17 14.7	3.5	57.3
01	193 36.0	15 59.4	262 17.7	9.0	17 18.2	3.5	57.3
02	208 36.1	58.7	276 45.7	8.9	17 21.7	3.3	57.3
03	223 36.2	.. 58.0	291 13.6	9.0	17 25.0	3.2	57.3
04	238 36.3	57.3	305 41.6	9.0	17 28.2	3.1	57.2
05	253 36.4	56.6	320 09.6	8.9	17 31.3	3.0	57.2
06	268 36.4	N15 55.9	334 37.5	9.0	N17 34.3	2.9	57.2
S 07	283 36.5	55.1	349 05.5	9.0	17 37.2	2.8	57.2
U 08	298 36.6	54.4	3 33.5	9.0	17 40.0	2.7	57.1
N 09	313 36.7	.. 53.7	18 01.5	9.1	17 42.7	2.6	57.1
D 10	328 36.8	53.0	32 29.6	9.0	17 45.3	2.5	57.1
A 11	343 36.9	52.3	46 57.6	9.1	17 47.8	2.4	57.1
Y 12	358 37.0	N15 51.5	61 25.6	9.1	N17 50.2	2.3	57.0
13	13 37.0	50.8	75 53.7	9.1	17 52.5	2.2	57.0
14	28 37.1	50.1	90 21.8	9.1	17 54.7	2.1	57.0
15	43 37.2	.. 49.4	104 49.9	9.1	17 56.8	2.0	57.0
16	58 37.3	48.7	119 18.0	9.1	17 58.8	1.9	56.9
17	73 37.4	47.9	133 46.1	9.1	18 00.7	1.8	56.9
18	88 37.5	N15 47.2	148 14.2	9.2	N18 02.5	1.7	56.9
19	103 37.6	46.5	162 42.4	9.1	18 04.2	1.6	56.9
20	118 37.7	45.8	177 10.5	9.2	18 05.8	1.4	56.8
21	133 37.8	.. 45.0	191 38.7	9.2	18 07.2	1.4	56.8
22	148 37.8	44.3	206 06.9	9.2	18 08.6	1.3	56.8
23	163 37.9	43.6	220 35.1	9.2	18 09.9	1.2	56.8
10 00	178 38.0	N15 42.9	235 03.3	9.3	N18 11.1	1.0	56.7
01	193 38.1	42.1	249 31.6	9.3	18 12.1	1.0	56.7
02	208 38.2	41.4	263 59.9	9.3	18 13.1	0.9	56.7
03	223 38.3	.. 40.7	278 28.2	9.3	18 14.0	0.8	56.7
04	238 38.4	40.0	292 56.5	9.3	18 14.8	0.6	56.7
05	253 38.5	39.2	307 24.8	9.4	18 15.4	0.5	56.6
06	268 38.6	N15 38.5	321 53.2	9.3	N18 16.0	0.4	56.6
07	283 38.7	37.8	336 21.5	9.4	18 16.4	0.4	56.6
M 08	298 38.7	37.1	350 49.9	9.5	18 16.8	0.3	56.6
O 09	313 38.8	.. 36.3	5 18.4	9.4	18 17.1	0.1	56.5
N 10	328 38.9	35.6	19 46.8	9.5	18 17.2	0.0	56.5
D 11	343 39.0	34.9	34 15.3	9.5	18 17.3	0.0	56.5
A 12	358 39.1	N15 34.1	48 43.8	9.5	N18 17.3	0.2	56.5
Y 13	13 39.2	33.4	63 12.3	9.6	18 17.1	0.2	56.4
14	28 39.3	32.7	77 40.9	9.5	18 16.9	0.3	56.4
15	43 39.4	.. 31.9	92 09.4	9.6	18 16.6	0.5	56.4
16	58 39.5	31.2	106 38.0	9.7	18 16.1	0.5	56.4
17	73 39.6	30.5	121 06.7	9.6	18 15.6	0.6	56.4
18	88 39.7	N15 29.7	135 35.3	9.7	N18 15.0	0.8	56.3
19	103 39.8	29.0	150 04.0	9.7	18 14.2	0.8	56.3
20	118 39.9	28.3	164 32.7	9.8	18 13.4	0.9	56.3
21	133 40.0	.. 27.5	179 01.5	9.8	18 12.5	1.0	56.3
22	148 40.1	26.8	193 30.3	9.8	18 11.5	1.1	56.2
23	163 40.2	26.1	207 59.1	9.8	N18 10.4	1.3	56.2
	SD 15.8	d 0.7	SD 15.7		15.5		15.4

Moonrise

Lat.	Twilight Naut.	Twilight Civil	Sunrise	Moonrise 8	9	10	11
°	h m	h m	h m	h m	h m	h m	h m
N 72	////	////	01 32	20 44	20 22	▭	23 11
N 70	////	////	02 21	21 36	22 02	22 53	24 09
68	////	////	02 52	22 08	22 42	23 34	24 43
66	////	01 43	03 14	22 32	23 10	24 02	00 02
64	////	02 19	03 32	22 50	23 31	24 24	00 24
62	////	02 44	03 47	23 06	23 48	24 41	00 41
60	01 33	03 04	03 59	23 19	24 02	00 02	00 55
N 58	02 05	03 19	04 09	23 30	24 15	00 15	01 07
56	02 29	03 33	04 18	23 40	24 25	00 25	01 18
54	02 47	03 44	04 26	23 48	24 34	00 34	01 27
52	03 02	03 54	04 34	23 56	24 43	00 43	01 35
50	03 15	04 03	04 40	24 03	00 03	00 50	01 43
45	03 40	04 21	04 54	24 18	00 18	01 06	01 59
N 40	04 00	04 36	05 05	24 30	00 30	01 19	02 12
35	04 15	04 48	05 15	24 40	00 40	01 30	02 23
30	04 28	04 58	05 24	00 02	00 50	01 40	02 32
20	04 48	05 15	05 38	00 16	01 06	01 57	02 49
N 10	05 03	05 29	05 51	00 28	01 19	02 12	03 04
0	05 16	05 41	06 02	00 39	01 33	02 25	03 17
S 10	05 27	05 52	06 14	00 51	01 46	02 39	03 31
20	05 37	06 03	06 26	01 03	02 00	02 54	03 46
30	05 46	06 15	06 39	01 18	02 16	03 11	04 02
35	05 51	06 21	06 47	01 26	02 25	03 21	04 12
40	05 56	06 28	06 56	01 35	02 36	03 32	04 23
45	06 01	06 36	07 07	01 46	02 49	03 45	04 36
S 50	06 06	06 45	07 19	02 00	03 04	04 02	04 52
52	06 09	06 49	07 25	02 06	03 11	04 09	05 00
54	06 11	06 54	07 32	02 13	03 19	04 18	05 08
56	06 14	06 58	07 39	02 21	03 28	04 27	05 17
58	06 17	07 04	07 47	02 30	03 38	04 38	05 28
S 60	06 20	07 10	07 56	02 40	03 50	04 51	05 40

Moonset

Lat.	Sunset	Twilight Civil	Twilight Naut.	Moonset 8	9	10	11
°	h m	h m	h m	h m	h m	h m	h m
N 72	22 31	////	////	17 45	19 58	▭	20 45
N 70	21 45	////	////	16 54	18 19	19 16	19 47
68	21 16	23 28	////	16 23	17 39	18 35	19 12
66	20 54	22 22	////	15 59	17 11	18 07	18 47
64	20 37	21 48	////	15 41	16 50	17 46	18 28
62	20 23	21 24	23 32	15 26	16 33	17 29	18 12
60	20 11	21 05	22 33	15 13	16 19	17 14	17 59
N 58	20 00	20 50	22 02	15 03	16 07	17 02	17 47
56	19 51	20 37	21 40	14 53	15 57	16 51	17 37
54	19 43	20 25	21 22	14 45	15 47	16 42	17 28
52	19 36	20 16	21 07	14 37	15 39	16 34	17 21
50	19 30	20 07	20 54	14 31	15 32	16 26	17 13
45	19 16	19 49	20 29	14 16	15 16	16 10	16 58
N 40	19 05	19 35	20 11	14 05	15 03	15 57	16 46
35	18 55	19 23	19 55	13 54	14 52	15 46	16 35
30	18 47	19 13	19 43	13 46	14 43	15 36	16 26
20	18 33	18 56	19 23	13 30	14 26	15 19	16 09
N 10	18 20	18 42	19 08	13 17	14 11	15 04	15 55
0	18 09	18 30	18 55	13 05	13 58	14 51	15 42
S 10	17 58	18 19	18 45	12 52	13 44	14 37	15 29
20	17 46	18 08	18 35	12 39	13 30	14 22	15 14
30	17 32	17 57	18 25	12 24	13 13	14 05	14 58
35	17 24	17 51	18 21	12 15	13 04	13 55	14 49
40	17 15	17 44	18 16	12 05	12 53	13 44	14 38
45	17 05	17 36	18 11	11 53	12 40	13 30	14 25
S 50	16 52	17 27	18 05	11 39	12 24	13 14	14 09
52	16 47	17 23	18 03	11 33	12 17	13 06	14 02
54	16 40	17 18	18 01	11 25	12 08	12 58	13 54
56	16 33	17 13	17 58	11 17	11 59	12 48	13 44
58	16 25	17 08	17 55	11 08	11 49	12 38	13 34
S 60	16 16	17 02	17 52	10 58	11 37	12 25	13 22

Day	SUN Eqn. of Time 00h	SUN Eqn. of Time 12h	SUN Mer. Pass.	MOON Mer. Pass. Upper	MOON Mer. Pass. Lower	Age	Phase
d	m s	m s	h m	h m	h m	d	%
8	05 44	05 40	12 06	06 52	19 19	23	35
9	05 36	05 32	12 06	07 45	20 12	24	25
10	05 28	05 24	12 05	08 38	21 04	25	17

UT	ARIES GHA	VENUS −4.1 GHA	Dec	MARS +1.7 GHA	Dec	JUPITER −1.7 GHA	Dec	SATURN +0.5 GHA	Dec	STARS Name	SHA	Dec
d h	° ′	° ′	° ′	° ′	° ′	° ′	° ′	° ′	° ′		° ′	° ′
11 00	319 08.6	173 45.8	N 6 12.2	195 21.9	N20 51.8	166 50.5	N12 18.7	82 35.5	S17 53.6	Acamar	315 17.2	S40 14.4
01	334 11.1	188 49.7	12.3	210 22.6	51.4	181 52.4	18.5	97 37.9	53.6	Achernar	335 25.6	S57 09.2
02	349 13.6	203 53.7	12.4	225 23.4	51.1	196 54.4	18.3	112 40.3	53.7	Acrux	173 07.9	S63 11.3
03	4 16.0	218 57.6	.. 12.5	240 24.2	.. 50.7	211 56.3	.. 18.1	127 42.8	.. 53.7	Adhara	255 11.7	S28 59.6
04	19 18.5	234 01.6	12.6	255 25.0	50.4	226 58.3	17.9	142 45.2	53.7	Aldebaran	290 47.8	N16 32.2
05	34 21.0	249 05.5	12.7	270 25.7	50.0	242 00.2	17.8	157 47.6	53.7			
06	49 23.4	264 09.5	N 6 12.8	285 26.5	N20 49.7	257 02.2	N12 17.6	172 50.1	S17 53.7	Alioth	166 19.8	N55 52.8
07	64 25.9	279 13.4	12.9	300 27.3	49.3	272 04.1	17.4	187 52.5	53.7	Alkaid	152 58.0	N49 14.5
08	79 28.4	294 17.4	13.0	315 28.1	49.0	287 06.1	17.2	202 54.9	53.8	Al Na'ir	27 41.5	S46 52.9
09	94 30.8	309 21.3	.. 13.1	330 28.8	.. 48.7	302 08.0	.. 17.0	217 57.3	.. 53.8	Alnilam	275 45.1	S 1 11.6
10	109 33.3	324 25.3	13.2	345 29.6	48.3	317 10.0	16.8	232 59.8	53.8	Alphard	217 55.0	S 8 43.6
11	124 35.7	339 29.3	13.3	0 30.4	48.0	332 11.9	16.6	248 02.2	53.8			
12	139 38.2	354 33.2	N 6 13.4	15 31.1	N20 47.6	347 13.9	N12 16.4	263 04.6	S17 53.8	Alphecca	126 09.7	N26 40.1
13	154 40.7	9 37.2	13.6	30 31.9	47.3	2 15.8	16.2	278 07.1	53.9	Alpheratz	357 41.6	N29 10.6
14	169 43.1	24 41.1	13.7	45 32.7	46.9	17 17.8	16.1	293 09.5	53.9	Altair	62 06.5	N 8 54.9
15	184 45.6	39 45.1	.. 13.8	60 33.5	.. 46.6	32 19.7	.. 15.9	308 11.9	.. 53.9	Ankaa	353 14.0	S42 13.0
16	199 48.1	54 49.1	13.9	75 34.3	46.2	47 21.7	15.7	323 14.3	53.9	Antares	112 24.3	S26 27.8
17	214 50.5	69 53.0	14.0	90 35.0	45.9	62 23.6	15.5	338 16.8	53.9			
18	229 53.0	84 57.0	N 6 14.1	105 35.8	N20 45.5	77 25.6	N12 15.3	353 19.2	S17 53.9	Arcturus	145 54.5	N19 06.4
19	244 55.5	100 01.0	14.3	120 36.6	45.2	92 27.5	15.1	8 21.6	54.0	Atria	107 24.5	S69 03.3
20	259 57.9	115 05.0	14.4	135 37.4	44.8	107 29.5	14.9	23 24.1	54.0	Avior	234 18.0	S59 33.6
21	275 00.4	130 08.9	.. 14.5	150 38.1	.. 44.5	122 31.4	.. 14.7	38 26.5	.. 54.0	Bellatrix	278 30.6	N 6 21.7
22	290 02.9	145 12.9	14.6	165 38.9	44.1	137 33.4	14.5	53 28.9	54.0	Betelgeuse	270 59.9	N 7 24.4
23	305 05.3	160 16.9	14.8	180 39.7	43.8	152 35.3	14.4	68 31.3	54.0			
12 00	320 07.8	175 20.9	N 6 14.9	195 40.5	N20 43.4	167 37.3	N12 14.2	83 33.8	S17 54.1	Canopus	263 55.9	S52 42.2
01	335 10.2	190 24.8	15.0	210 41.2	43.1	182 39.2	14.0	98 36.2	54.1	Capella	280 32.5	N46 00.5
02	350 12.7	205 28.8	15.2	225 42.0	42.7	197 41.1	13.8	113 38.6	54.1	Deneb	49 30.0	N45 20.4
03	5 15.2	220 32.8	.. 15.3	240 42.8	.. 42.4	212 43.1	.. 13.6	128 41.0	.. 54.1	Denebola	182 32.4	N14 29.2
04	20 17.6	235 36.8	15.4	255 43.6	42.0	227 45.0	13.4	143 43.5	54.1	Diphda	348 54.2	S17 53.9
05	35 20.1	250 40.7	15.6	270 44.4	41.7	242 47.0	13.2	158 45.9	54.2			
06	50 22.6	265 44.7	N 6 15.7	285 45.1	N20 41.3	257 48.9	N12 13.0	173 48.3	S17 54.2	Dubhe	193 50.7	N61 40.1
07	65 25.0	280 48.7	15.8	300 45.9	41.0	272 50.9	12.9	188 50.7	54.2	Elnath	278 10.9	N28 37.0
08	80 27.5	295 52.7	16.0	315 46.7	40.6	287 52.8	12.7	203 53.2	54.2	Eltanin	90 45.1	N51 29.7
09	95 30.0	310 56.7	.. 16.1	330 47.5	.. 40.3	302 54.8	.. 12.5	218 55.6	.. 54.2	Enif	33 45.3	N 9 57.0
10	110 32.4	326 00.7	16.3	345 48.2	39.9	317 56.7	12.3	233 58.0	54.2	Fomalhaut	15 22.1	S29 32.1
11	125 34.9	341 04.6	16.4	0 49.0	39.6	332 58.7	12.1	249 00.4	54.3			
12	140 37.3	356 08.6	N 6 16.6	15 49.8	N20 39.2	348 00.6	N12 11.9	264 02.9	S17 54.3	Gacrux	171 59.5	S57 12.2
13	155 39.8	11 12.6	16.7	30 50.6	38.9	3 02.6	11.7	279 05.3	54.3	Gienah	175 51.0	S17 37.7
14	170 42.3	26 16.6	16.9	45 51.4	38.5	18 04.5	11.5	294 07.7	54.3	Hadar	148 45.8	S60 27.0
15	185 44.7	41 20.6	.. 17.0	60 52.1	.. 38.2	33 06.5	.. 11.3	309 10.1	.. 54.3	Hamal	327 59.0	N23 32.0
16	200 47.2	56 24.6	17.2	75 52.9	37.8	48 08.4	11.1	324 12.6	54.4	Kaus Aust.	83 41.6	S34 22.4
17	215 49.7	71 28.6	17.3	90 53.7	37.5	63 10.4	11.0	339 15.0	54.4			
18	230 52.1	86 32.6	N 6 17.5	105 54.5	N20 37.1	78 12.3	N12 10.8	354 17.4	S17 54.4	Kochab	137 20.4	N74 05.9
19	245 54.6	101 36.6	17.6	120 55.3	36.8	93 14.3	10.6	9 19.8	54.4	Markab	13 36.5	N15 17.5
20	260 57.1	116 40.6	17.8	135 56.0	36.4	108 16.2	10.4	24 22.2	54.4	Menkar	314 13.5	N 4 09.0
21	275 59.5	131 44.6	.. 17.9	150 56.8	.. 36.0	123 18.2	.. 10.2	39 24.7	.. 54.5	Menkent	148 05.9	S36 26.8
22	291 02.0	146 48.6	18.1	165 57.6	35.7	138 20.1	10.0	54 27.1	54.5	Miaplacidus	221 40.1	S69 47.0
23	306 04.5	161 52.6	18.3	180 58.4	35.3	153 22.0	09.8	69 29.5	54.5			
13 00	321 06.9	176 56.5	N 6 18.4	195 59.2	N20 35.0	168 24.0	N12 09.6	84 31.9	S17 54.5	Mirfak	308 38.2	N49 54.6
01	336 09.4	192 00.5	18.6	211 00.0	34.6	183 25.9	09.4	99 34.4	54.5	Nunki	75 56.2	S26 16.4
02	351 11.8	207 04.5	18.8	226 00.7	34.3	198 27.9	09.3	114 36.8	54.6	Peacock	53 16.4	S56 40.9
03	6 14.3	222 08.5	.. 18.9	241 01.5	.. 33.9	213 29.8	.. 09.1	129 39.2	.. 54.6	Pollux	243 26.3	N27 59.1
04	21 16.8	237 12.5	19.1	256 02.3	33.6	228 31.8	08.9	144 41.6	54.6	Procyon	244 58.5	N 5 11.0
05	36 19.2	252 16.5	19.3	271 03.1	33.2	243 33.7	08.7	159 44.0	54.6			
06	51 21.7	267 20.5	N 6 19.4	286 03.9	N20 32.8	258 35.7	N12 08.5	174 46.5	S17 54.6	Rasalhague	96 04.9	N12 33.3
07	66 24.2	282 24.5	19.6	301 04.6	32.5	273 37.6	08.3	189 48.9	54.7	Regulus	207 42.3	N11 53.5
08	81 26.6	297 28.5	19.8	316 05.4	32.1	288 39.6	08.1	204 51.3	54.7	Rigel	281 10.8	S 8 11.1
09	96 29.1	312 32.5	.. 20.0	331 06.2	.. 31.8	303 41.5	.. 07.9	219 53.7	.. 54.7	Rigil Kent.	139 49.7	S60 54.0
10	111 31.6	327 36.5	20.1	346 07.0	31.4	318 43.5	07.7	234 56.1	54.7	Sabik	102 10.7	S15 44.4
11	126 34.0	342 40.6	20.3	1 07.8	31.1	333 45.4	07.6	249 58.6	54.7			
12	141 36.5	357 44.6	N 6 20.5	16 08.6	N20 30.7	348 47.4	N12 07.4	265 01.0	S17 54.8	Schedar	349 38.3	N56 37.2
13	156 39.0	12 48.6	20.7	31 09.3	30.3	3 49.3	07.2	280 03.4	54.8	Shaula	96 19.7	S37 06.7
14	171 41.4	27 52.6	20.9	46 10.1	30.0	18 51.3	07.0	295 05.8	54.8	Sirius	258 32.7	S16 44.3
15	186 43.9	42 56.6	.. 21.1	61 10.9	.. 29.6	33 53.2	.. 06.8	310 08.2	.. 54.8	Spica	158 29.8	S11 14.5
16	201 46.3	58 00.6	21.2	76 11.7	29.3	48 55.2	06.6	325 10.7	54.8	Suhail	222 51.7	S43 29.8
17	216 48.8	73 04.6	21.4	91 12.5	28.9	63 57.1	06.4	340 13.1	54.9			
18	231 51.3	88 08.6	N 6 21.6	106 13.3	N20 28.5	78 59.0	N12 06.2	355 15.5	S17 54.9	Vega	80 37.6	N38 48.3
19	246 53.7	103 12.6	21.8	121 14.1	28.2	94 01.0	06.0	10 17.9	54.9	Zuben'ubi	137 03.8	S16 06.2
20	261 56.2	118 16.6	22.0	136 14.8	27.8	109 02.9	05.8	25 20.3	54.9		SHA	Mer. Pass.
21	276 58.7	133 20.6	.. 22.2	151 15.6	.. 27.5	124 04.9	.. 05.7	40 22.8	.. 54.9		° ′	h m
22	292 01.1	148 24.6	22.4	166 16.4	27.1	139 06.8	05.5	55 25.2	55.0	Venus	215 13.1	12 15
23	307 03.6	163 28.6	22.6	181 17.2	26.7	154 08.8	05.3	70 27.6	55.0	Mars	235 32.7	10 57
										Jupiter	207 29.5	12 48
Mer. Pass. 2 39.0		v 4.0	d 0.1	v 0.8	d 0.4	v 1.9	d 0.2	v 2.4	d 0.0	Saturn	123 26.0	18 23

UT	SUN GHA	SUN Dec	MOON GHA	v	Dec	d	HP
d h	° ′	° ′	° ′	′	° ′	′	′
11 00	178 40.3	N15 25.3	222 27.9	9.9	N18 09.1	1.3	56.2
01	193 40.3	24.6	236 56.8	9.9	18 07.8	1.4	56.2
02	208 40.4	23.9	251 25.7	9.9	18 06.4	1.5	56.2
03	223 40.5 ..	23.1	265 54.6	10.0	18 04.9	1.6	56.1
04	238 40.6	22.4	280 23.6	10.0	18 03.3	1.7	56.1
05	253 40.7	21.7	294 52.6	10.0	18 01.6	1.7	56.1
06	268 40.8	N15 20.9	309 21.6	10.1	N17 59.9	1.9	56.1
T 07	283 40.9	20.2	323 50.7	10.1	17 58.0	2.0	56.0
U 08	298 41.0	19.4	338 19.8	10.1	17 56.0	2.1	56.0
E 09	313 41.1 ..	18.7	352 48.9	10.2	17 53.9	2.1	56.0
S 10	328 41.2	18.0	7 18.1	10.2	17 51.8	2.3	56.0
D 11	343 41.3	17.2	21 47.3	10.3	17 49.5	2.3	56.0
A 12	358 41.4	N15 16.5	36 16.6	10.2	N17 47.2	2.5	55.9
Y 13	13 41.5	15.7	50 45.8	10.4	17 44.7	2.5	55.9
14	28 41.6	15.0	65 15.2	10.3	17 42.2	2.6	55.9
15	43 41.7 ..	14.2	79 44.5	10.4	17 39.6	2.7	55.9
16	58 41.8	13.5	94 13.9	10.5	17 36.9	2.8	55.9
17	73 41.9	12.8	108 43.4	10.4	17 34.1	2.9	55.8
18	88 42.0	N15 12.0	123 12.8	10.5	N17 31.2	3.0	55.8
19	103 42.1	11.3	137 42.3	10.6	17 28.2	3.0	55.8
20	118 42.2	10.5	152 11.9	10.6	17 25.2	3.2	55.8
21	133 42.3 ..	09.8	166 41.5	10.6	17 22.0	3.2	55.8
22	148 42.4	09.0	181 11.1	10.7	17 18.8	3.3	55.7
23	163 42.5	08.3	195 40.8	10.7	17 15.5	3.4	55.7
12 00	178 42.6	N15 07.6	210 10.5	10.8	N17 12.1	3.5	55.7
01	193 42.7	06.8	224 40.3	10.8	17 08.6	3.6	55.7
02	208 42.8	06.1	239 10.1	10.8	17 05.0	3.7	55.7
03	223 42.9 ..	05.3	253 39.9	10.9	17 01.3	3.7	55.6
04	238 43.0	04.6	268 09.8	10.9	16 57.6	3.8	55.6
05	253 43.1	03.8	282 39.7	11.0	16 53.8	4.0	55.6
06	268 43.2	N15 03.1	297 09.7	11.0	N16 49.8	4.0	55.6
W 07	283 43.3	02.3	311 39.7	11.0	16 45.8	4.0	55.6
E 08	298 43.4	01.5	326 09.7	11.1	16 41.8	4.2	55.5
D 09	313 43.5 ..	00.8	340 39.8	11.2	16 37.6	4.2	55.5
N 10	328 43.7	15 00.1	355 10.0	11.2	16 33.4	4.3	55.5
E 11	343 43.8	14 59.3	9 40.2	11.2	16 29.1	4.4	55.5
S 12	358 43.9	N14 58.6	24 10.4	11.3	N16 24.7	4.5	55.5
D 13	13 44.0	57.8	38 40.7	11.3	16 20.2	4.6	55.5
A 14	28 44.1	57.1	53 11.0	11.3	16 15.6	4.6	55.4
Y 15	43 44.2 ..	56.3	67 41.3	11.4	16 11.0	4.7	55.4
16	58 44.3	55.6	82 11.7	11.5	16 06.3	4.8	55.4
17	73 44.4	54.8	96 42.2	11.5	16 01.5	4.9	55.4
18	88 44.5	N14 54.1	111 12.7	11.5	N15 56.6	4.9	55.4
19	103 44.6	53.3	125 43.2	11.6	15 51.7	5.0	55.3
20	118 44.7	52.5	140 13.8	11.6	15 46.7	5.1	55.3
21	133 44.8 ..	51.8	154 44.4	11.7	15 41.6	5.2	55.3
22	148 44.9	51.0	169 15.1	11.7	15 36.4	5.2	55.3
23	163 45.0	50.3	183 45.8	11.8	15 31.2	5.3	55.3
13 00	178 45.1	N14 49.5	198 16.6	11.8	N15 25.9	5.4	55.3
01	193 45.2	48.8	212 47.4	11.9	15 20.5	5.4	55.2
02	208 45.3	48.0	227 18.3	11.9	15 15.1	5.5	55.2
03	223 45.5 ..	47.3	241 49.2	11.9	15 09.6	5.6	55.2
04	238 45.6	46.5	256 20.1	12.0	15 04.0	5.7	55.2
05	253 45.7	45.7	270 51.1	12.1	14 58.3	5.7	55.2
06	268 45.8	N14 45.0	285 22.2	12.1	N14 52.6	5.8	55.1
T 07	283 45.9	44.2	299 53.3	12.1	14 46.8	5.9	55.1
H 08	298 46.0	43.5	314 24.4	12.2	14 40.9	5.9	55.1
U 09	313 46.1 ..	42.7	328 55.6	12.2	14 35.0	6.0	55.1
R 10	328 46.2	41.9	343 26.8	12.3	14 29.0	6.0	55.1
S 11	343 46.3	41.2	357 58.1	12.3	14 23.0	6.2	55.1
D 12	358 46.4	N14 40.4	12 29.4	12.3	N14 16.8	6.1	55.0
A 13	13 46.6	39.7	27 00.7	12.5	14 10.7	6.3	55.0
Y 14	28 46.7	38.9	41 32.2	12.4	14 04.4	6.3	55.0
15	43 46.8 ..	38.1	56 03.6	12.5	13 58.1	6.4	55.0
16	58 46.9	37.4	70 35.1	12.5	13 51.7	6.4	55.0
17	73 47.0	36.6	85 06.6	12.6	13 45.3	6.5	55.0
18	88 47.1	N14 35.9	99 38.2	12.7	N13 38.8	6.5	55.0
19	103 47.2	35.1	114 09.9	12.6	13 32.3	6.6	54.9
20	118 47.3	34.3	128 41.5	12.8	13 25.7	6.7	54.9
21	133 47.4 ..	33.6	143 13.3	12.7	13 19.0	6.7	54.9
22	148 47.6	32.8	157 45.0	12.8	13 12.3	6.8	54.9
23	163 47.7	32.0	172 16.8	12.9	N13 05.5	6.9	54.9
	SD 15.8 d 0.8		SD 15.2		15.1		15.0

Lat.	Twilight Naut.	Civil	Sunrise	Moonrise 11	12	13	14
°	h m	h m	h m	h m	h m	h m	h m
N 72	////	////	01 59	23 11	25 01	01 01	02 45
N 70	////	////	02 38	24 09	00 09	01 37	03 08
68	////	01 12	03 05	24 43	00 43	02 03	03 26
66	////	02 02	03 25	00 02	01 08	02 22	03 41
64	////	02 33	03 41	00 24	01 27	02 38	03 53
62	01 05	02 55	03 55	00 41	01 43	02 51	04 03
60	01 49	03 13	04 06	00 55	01 56	03 02	04 11
N 58	02 17	03 27	04 16	01 07	02 07	03 11	04 19
56	02 38	03 40	04 24	01 18	02 16	03 20	04 25
54	02 55	03 50	04 32	01 27	02 25	03 27	04 31
52	03 09	04 00	04 39	01 35	02 33	03 34	04 36
50	03 21	04 08	04 45	01 43	02 40	03 40	04 41
45	03 45	04 25	04 58	01 59	02 54	03 53	04 52
N 40	04 03	04 39	05 08	02 12	03 07	04 03	05 00
35	04 18	04 50	05 17	02 23	03 17	04 12	05 07
30	04 30	05 00	05 25	02 32	03 26	04 20	05 14
20	04 49	05 16	05 39	02 49	03 42	04 34	05 25
N 10	05 03	05 29	05 51	03 04	03 55	04 46	05 35
0	05 15	05 40	06 02	03 17	04 08	04 57	05 44
S 10	05 26	05 51	06 12	03 31	04 21	05 08	05 53
20	05 35	06 01	06 24	03 46	04 34	05 20	06 03
30	05 44	06 12	06 37	04 02	04 50	05 34	06 14
35	05 48	06 18	06 44	04 12	04 59	05 41	06 20
40	05 52	06 24	06 53	04 23	05 09	05 50	06 27
45	05 57	06 32	07 02	04 36	05 21	06 01	06 36
S 50	06 02	06 40	07 14	04 52	05 36	06 13	06 46
52	06 04	06 44	07 20	05 00	05 43	06 19	06 50
54	06 06	06 48	07 26	05 08	05 50	06 26	06 55
56	06 08	06 52	07 32	05 17	05 59	06 33	07 01
58	06 11	06 57	07 40	05 28	06 08	06 41	07 07
S 60	06 13	07 03	07 48	05 40	06 19	06 50	07 14

Lat.	Sunset	Twilight Civil	Naut.	Moonset 11	12	13	14
°	h m	h m	h m	h m	h m	h m	h m
N 72	22 04	////	////	20 45	20 38	20 32	20 27
N 70	21 27	////	////	19 47	20 01	20 08	20 11
68	21 02	22 48	////	19 12	19 35	19 49	19 58
66	20 42	22 03	////	18 47	19 15	19 33	19 47
64	20 26	21 34	////	18 28	18 58	19 21	19 38
62	20 13	21 12	22 57	18 12	18 45	19 10	19 30
60	20 02	20 55	22 16	17 59	18 33	19 01	19 23
N 58	19 53	20 41	21 50	17 47	18 24	18 53	19 17
56	19 45	20 29	21 29	17 37	18 15	18 46	19 12
54	19 37	20 18	21 13	17 28	18 07	18 40	19 07
52	19 31	20 09	20 59	17 21	18 00	18 34	19 03
50	19 25	20 01	20 47	17 13	17 54	18 29	18 59
45	19 12	19 44	20 24	16 58	17 40	18 17	18 50
N 40	19 01	19 30	20 06	16 46	17 29	18 08	18 43
35	18 52	19 19	19 52	16 35	17 20	18 00	18 37
30	18 44	19 10	19 40	16 26	17 11	17 53	18 32
20	18 31	18 54	19 21	16 09	16 57	17 41	18 22
N 10	18 19	18 41	19 07	15 55	16 44	17 30	18 14
0	18 08	18 30	18 55	15 42	16 32	17 20	18 06
S 10	17 58	18 19	18 45	15 29	16 20	17 10	17 58
20	17 46	18 09	18 35	15 14	16 07	16 59	17 49
30	17 34	17 58	18 27	14 58	15 52	16 46	17 40
35	17 26	17 53	18 23	14 49	15 43	16 39	17 34
40	17 18	17 46	18 18	14 38	15 34	16 30	17 28
45	17 08	17 39	18 14	14 25	15 22	16 21	17 20
S 50	16 57	17 31	18 09	14 09	15 08	16 09	17 11
52	16 51	17 27	18 07	14 02	15 01	16 03	17 07
54	16 45	17 23	18 05	13 54	14 54	15 57	17 02
56	16 39	17 19	18 03	13 44	14 46	15 51	16 57
58	16 31	17 14	18 00	13 34	14 37	15 43	16 51
S 60	16 23	17 08	17 58	13 22	14 26	15 34	16 45

Day	SUN Eqn. of Time 00h	12h	Mer. Pass.	MOON Mer. Pass. Upper	Lower	Age	Phase
d	m s	m s	h m	h m	h m	d	%
11	05 19	05 15	12 05	09 30	21 55	26	10
12	05 10	05 05	12 05	10 20	22 44	27	5
13	05 00	04 54	12 05	11 08	23 32	28	1

UT	ARIES GHA	VENUS −4.1 GHA	Dec	MARS +1.7 GHA	Dec	JUPITER −1.7 GHA	Dec	SATURN +0.5 GHA	Dec	STARS Name	SHA	Dec
d h 14 00	322 06.1	178 32.6 N 6	22.8	196 18.0 N20	26.4	169 10.7 N12	05.1	85 30.0 S17	55.0	Acamar	315 17.2	S40 14.4
01	337 08.5	193 36.6	23.0	211 18.8	26.0	184 12.7	04.9	100 32.4	55.0	Achernar	335 25.5	S57 09.2
02	352 11.0	208 40.7	23.2	226 19.6	25.7	199 14.6	04.7	115 34.8	55.0	Acrux	173 07.9	S63 11.3
03	7 13.5	223 44.7 ..	23.4	241 20.3 ..	25.3	214 16.6 ..	04.5	130 37.3 ..	55.1	Adhara	255 11.6	S28 59.6
04	22 15.9	238 48.7	23.6	256 21.1	24.9	229 18.5	04.3	145 39.7	55.1	Aldebaran	290 47.8	N16 32.3
05	37 18.4	253 52.7	23.8	271 21.9	24.6	244 20.5	04.1	160 42.1	55.1			
06	52 20.8	268 56.7 N 6	24.0	286 22.7 N20	24.2	259 22.4 N12	03.9	175 44.5 S17	55.1	Alioth	166 19.8	N55 52.8
07	67 23.3	284 00.7	24.2	301 23.5	23.8	274 24.4	03.8	190 46.9	55.1	Alkaid	152 58.0	N49 14.5
08	82 25.8	299 04.7	24.4	316 24.3	23.5	289 26.3	03.6	205 49.3	55.2	Al Na'ir	27 41.5	S46 52.9
F 09	97 28.2	314 08.7 ..	24.6	331 25.1 ..	23.1	304 28.3 ..	03.4	220 51.8 ..	55.2	Alnilam	275 45.0	S 1 11.6
R 10	112 30.7	329 12.7	24.8	346 25.8	22.8	319 30.2	03.2	235 54.2	55.2	Alphard	217 54.9	S 8 43.6
I 11	127 33.2	344 16.8	25.1	1 26.6	22.4	334 32.1	03.0	250 56.6	55.2			
D 12	142 35.6	359 20.8 N 6	25.3	16 27.4 N20	22.0	349 34.1 N12	02.8	265 59.0 S17	55.2	Alphecca	126 09.8	N26 40.1
A 13	157 38.1	14 24.8	25.5	31 28.2	21.7	4 36.0	02.6	281 01.4	55.3	Alpheratz	357 41.6	N29 10.6
Y 14	172 40.6	29 28.8	25.7	46 29.0	21.3	19 38.0	02.4	296 03.8	55.3	Altair	62 06.5	N 8 54.9
15	187 43.0	44 32.8 ..	25.9	61 29.8 ..	20.9	34 39.9 ..	02.2	311 06.3 ..	55.3	Ankaa	353 14.0	S42 13.0
16	202 45.5	59 36.8	26.1	76 30.6	20.6	49 41.9	02.0	326 08.7	55.3	Antares	112 24.3	S26 27.8
17	217 47.9	74 40.8	26.4	91 31.4	20.2	64 43.8	01.9	341 11.1	55.4			
18	232 50.4	89 44.8 N 6	26.6	106 32.2 N20	19.8	79 45.8 N12	01.7	356 13.5 S17	55.4	Arcturus	145 54.5	N19 06.4
19	247 52.9	104 48.8	26.8	121 32.9	19.5	94 47.7	01.5	11 15.9	55.4	Atria	107 24.5	S69 03.3
20	262 55.3	119 52.9	27.0	136 33.7	19.1	109 49.7	01.3	26 18.3	55.4	Avior	234 17.9	S59 33.6
21	277 57.8	134 56.9 ..	27.3	151 34.5 ..	18.7	124 51.6 ..	01.1	41 20.7 ..	55.4	Bellatrix	278 30.6	N 6 21.7
22	293 00.3	150 00.9	27.5	166 35.3	18.4	139 53.6	00.9	56 23.2	55.5	Betelgeuse	270 59.9	N 7 24.4
23	308 02.7	165 04.9	27.7	181 36.1	18.0	154 55.5	00.7	71 25.6	55.5			
15 00	323 05.2	180 08.9 N 6	27.9	196 36.9 N20	17.6	169 57.5 N12	00.5	86 28.0 S17	55.5	Canopus	263 55.9	S52 42.2
01	338 07.7	195 12.9	28.2	211 37.7	17.3	184 59.4	00.3	101 30.4	55.5	Capella	280 32.5	N46 00.5
02	353 10.1	210 16.9	28.4	226 38.5	16.9	200 01.3	00.1	116 32.8	55.5	Deneb	49 30.0	N45 20.4
03	8 12.6	225 20.9 ..	28.6	241 39.3 ..	16.5	215 03.3 12 00.0		131 35.2 ..	55.6	Denebola	182 32.4	N14 29.2
04	23 15.1	240 25.0	28.9	256 40.1	16.2	230 05.2 11 59.8		146 37.6	55.6	Diphda	348 54.2	S17 53.9
05	38 17.5	255 29.0	29.1	271 40.8	15.8	245 07.2	59.6	161 40.0	55.6			
06	53 20.0	270 33.0 N 6	29.3	286 41.6 N20	15.4	260 09.1 N11	59.4	176 42.5 S17	55.6	Dubhe	193 50.7	N61 40.1
07	68 22.4	285 37.0	29.6	301 42.4	15.1	275 11.1	59.2	191 44.9	55.6	Elnath	278 10.9	N28 37.0
S 08	83 24.9	300 41.0	29.8	316 43.2	14.7	290 13.0	59.0	206 47.3	55.7	Eltanin	90 45.1	N51 29.7
A 09	98 27.4	315 45.0 ..	30.1	331 44.0 ..	14.3	305 15.0 ..	58.8	221 49.7 ..	55.7	Enif	33 45.3	N 9 57.0
T 10	113 29.8	330 49.0	30.3	346 44.8	13.9	320 16.9	58.6	236 52.1	55.7	Fomalhaut	15 22.1	S29 32.1
U 11	128 32.3	345 53.0	30.5	1 45.6	13.6	335 18.9	58.4	251 54.5	55.7			
R 12	143 34.8	0 57.0 N 6	30.8	16 46.4 N20	13.2	350 20.8 N11	58.2	266 56.9 S17	55.8	Gacrux	171 59.5	S57 12.2
D 13	158 37.2	16 01.0	31.0	31 47.2	12.8	5 22.8	58.0	281 59.3	55.8	Gienah	175 51.0	S17 37.7
A 14	173 39.7	31 05.1	31.3	46 48.0	12.5	20 24.7	57.9	297 01.8	55.8	Hadar	148 45.9	S60 27.0
Y 15	188 42.2	46 09.1 ..	31.5	61 48.8 ..	12.1	35 26.7 ..	57.7	312 04.2 ..	55.8	Hamal	327 58.9	N23 32.0
16	203 44.6	61 13.1	31.8	76 49.6	11.7	50 28.6	57.5	327 06.6	55.8	Kaus Aust.	83 41.6	S34 22.4
17	218 47.1	76 17.1	32.0	91 50.4	11.4	65 30.5	57.3	342 09.0	55.9			
18	233 49.5	91 21.1 N 6	32.3	106 51.2 N20	11.0	80 32.5 N11	57.1	357 11.4 S17	55.9	Kochab	137 20.4	N74 05.9
19	248 52.0	106 25.1	32.5	121 51.9	10.6	95 34.4	56.9	12 13.8	55.9	Markab	13 36.5	N15 17.5
20	263 54.5	121 29.1	32.8	136 52.7	10.2	110 36.4	56.7	27 16.2	55.9	Menkar	314 13.5	N 4 09.0
21	278 56.9	136 33.1 ..	33.0	151 53.5 ..	09.9	125 38.3 ..	56.5	42 18.6 ..	56.0	Menkent	148 05.9	S36 26.8
22	293 59.4	151 37.1	33.3	166 54.3	09.5	140 40.3	56.3	57 21.0	56.0	Miaplacidus	221 40.1	S69 47.0
23	309 01.9	166 41.1	33.6	181 55.1	09.1	155 42.2	56.1	72 23.4	56.0			
16 00	324 04.3	181 45.1 N 6	33.8	196 55.9 N20	08.7	170 44.2 N11	55.9	87 25.9 S17	56.0	Mirfak	308 38.2	N49 54.6
01	339 06.8	196 49.1	34.1	211 56.7	08.4	185 46.1	55.8	102 28.3	56.0	Nunki	75 56.2	S26 16.4
02	354 09.3	211 53.1	34.3	226 57.5	08.0	200 48.1	55.6	117 30.7	56.1	Peacock	53 16.4	S56 40.9
03	9 11.7	226 57.1 ..	34.6	241 58.3 ..	07.6	215 50.0 ..	55.4	132 33.1 ..	56.1	Pollux	243 26.3	N27 59.1
04	24 14.2	242 01.2	34.9	256 59.1	07.3	230 52.0	55.2	147 35.5	56.1	Procyon	244 58.5	N 5 11.0
05	39 16.7	257 05.2	35.1	271 59.9	06.9	245 53.9	55.0	162 37.9	56.1			
06	54 19.1	272 09.2 N 6	35.4	287 00.7 N20	06.5	260 55.8 N11	54.8	177 40.3 S17	56.2	Rasalhague	96 04.9	N12 33.3
07	69 21.6	287 13.2	35.7	302 01.5	06.1	275 57.8	54.6	192 42.7	56.2	Regulus	207 42.3	N11 53.5
08	84 24.0	302 17.2	35.9	317 02.3	05.8	290 59.7	54.4	207 45.1	56.2	Rigel	281 10.8	S 8 11.1
S 09	99 26.5	317 21.2 ..	36.2	332 03.1 ..	05.4	306 01.7 ..	54.2	222 47.5 ..	56.2	Rigil Kent.	139 49.7	S60 54.0
U 10	114 29.0	332 25.2	36.5	347 03.9	05.0	321 03.6	54.0	237 49.9	56.2	Sabik	102 10.7	S15 44.4
N 11	129 31.4	347 29.2	36.7	2 04.7	04.6	336 05.6	53.8	252 52.4	56.3			
D 12	144 33.9	2 33.2 N 6	37.0	17 05.5 N20	04.3	351 07.5 N11	53.7	267 54.8 S17	56.3	Schedar	349 38.3	N56 37.2
A 13	159 36.4	17 37.2	37.3	32 06.3	03.9	6 09.5	53.5	282 57.2	56.3	Shaula	96 19.7	S37 06.8
Y 14	174 38.8	32 41.2	37.6	47 07.1	03.5	21 11.4	53.3	297 59.6	56.3	Sirius	258 32.7	S16 44.3
15	189 41.3	47 45.2 ..	37.8	62 07.9 ..	03.1	36 13.4 ..	53.1	313 02.0 ..	56.4	Spica	158 29.8	S11 14.5
16	204 43.8	62 49.2	38.1	77 08.7	02.7	51 15.3	52.9	328 04.4	56.4	Suhail	222 51.7	S43 29.8
17	219 46.2	77 53.2	38.4	92 09.5	02.3	66 17.3	52.7	343 06.8	56.4			
18	234 48.7	92 57.2 N 6	38.7	107 10.3 N20	02.0	81 19.2 N11	52.5	358 09.2 S17	56.4	Vega	80 37.6	N38 48.3
19	249 51.2	108 01.1	39.0	122 11.1	01.6	96 21.2	52.3	13 11.6	56.4	Zuben'ubi	137 03.8	S16 06.2
20	264 53.6	123 05.1	39.2	137 11.9	01.2	111 23.1	52.1	28 14.0	56.5			
21	279 56.1	138 09.1 ..	39.5	152 12.7 ..	00.9	126 25.0 ..	51.9	43 16.4 ..	56.5		SHA	Mer. Pass.
22	294 58.5	153 13.1	39.8	167 13.4	00.5	141 27.0	51.7	58 18.8	56.5	Venus	217 03.7	11 56
23	310 01.0	168 17.1	40.1	182 14.2	00.1	156 28.9	51.6	73 21.2	56.5	Mars	233 31.7	10 53
Mer. Pass.	h m 2 27.3	v 4.0 d 0.2		v 0.8 d 0.4		v 1.9 d 0.2		v 2.4 d 0.0		Jupiter	206 52.3	12 39
										Saturn	123 22.8	18 11

UT	SUN GHA	SUN Dec	MOON GHA	MOON v	MOON Dec	MOON d	MOON HP
d h	° ′	° ′	° ′	′	° ′	′	′
14 00	178 47.8	N14 31.3	186 48.7	12.9	N12 58.6	6.9	54.9
01	193 47.9	30.5	201 20.6	13.0	12 51.7	6.9	54.8
02	208 48.0	29.7	215 52.6	12.9	12 44.8	7.0	54.8
03	223 48.1 ..	29.0	230 24.5	13.1	12 37.8	7.1	54.8
04	238 48.2	28.2	244 56.6	13.1	12 30.7	7.1	54.8
05	253 48.3	27.4	259 28.7	13.1	12 23.6	7.1	54.8
06	268 48.5	N14 26.7	274 00.8	13.1	N12 16.5	7.3	54.8
07	283 48.6	25.9	288 32.9	13.2	12 09.2	7.2	54.8
08	298 48.7	25.1	303 05.1	13.3	12 02.0	7.3	54.7
F 09	313 48.8 ..	24.4	317 37.4	13.3	11 54.7	7.4	54.7
R 10	328 48.9	23.6	332 09.7	13.3	11 47.3	7.4	54.7
I 11	343 49.0	22.8	346 42.0	13.4	11 39.9	7.5	54.7
D 12	358 49.2	N14 22.1	1 14.4	13.4	N11 32.4	7.5	54.7
A 13	13 49.3	21.3	15 46.8	13.5	11 24.9	7.5	54.7
Y 14	28 49.4	20.5	30 19.3	13.5	11 17.4	7.6	54.7
15	43 49.5 ..	19.7	44 51.8	13.5	11 09.8	7.7	54.6
16	58 49.6	19.0	59 24.3	13.6	11 02.1	7.7	54.6
17	73 49.7	18.2	73 56.9	13.6	10 54.4	7.7	54.6
18	88 49.9	N14 17.4	88 29.5	13.7	N10 46.7	7.8	54.6
19	103 50.0	16.6	103 02.2	13.7	10 38.9	7.8	54.6
20	118 50.1	15.9	117 34.9	13.7	10 31.1	7.9	54.6
21	133 50.2 ..	15.1	132 07.6	13.8	10 23.2	7.9	54.6
22	148 50.3	14.3	146 40.4	13.8	10 15.3	7.9	54.6
23	163 50.4	13.6	161 13.2	13.9	10 07.4	8.0	54.5
15 00	178 50.6	N14 12.8	175 46.1	13.9	N 9 59.4	8.1	54.5
01	193 50.7	12.0	190 19.0	13.9	9 51.3	8.0	54.5
02	208 50.8	11.2	204 51.9	14.0	9 43.3	8.1	54.5
03	223 50.9 ..	10.4	219 24.9	14.0	9 35.2	8.2	54.5
04	238 51.0	09.7	233 57.9	14.0	9 27.0	8.2	54.5
05	253 51.2	08.9	248 30.9	14.1	9 18.8	8.2	54.5
06	268 51.3	N14 08.1	263 04.0	14.1	N 9 10.6	8.2	54.5
07	283 51.4	07.3	277 37.1	14.2	9 02.4	8.3	54.4
S 08	298 51.5	06.6	292 10.3	14.1	8 54.1	8.3	54.4
A 09	313 51.6 ..	05.8	306 43.4	14.3	8 45.8	8.4	54.4
T 10	328 51.8	05.0	321 16.7	14.2	8 37.4	8.4	54.4
U 11	343 51.9	04.2	335 49.9	14.3	8 29.0	8.4	54.4
R 12	358 52.0	N14 03.4	350 23.2	14.3	N 8 20.6	8.4	54.4
D 13	13 52.1	02.7	4 56.5	14.4	8 12.2	8.5	54.4
A 14	28 52.2	01.9	19 29.9	14.4	8 03.7	8.5	54.4
Y 15	43 52.4 ..	01.1	34 03.3	14.4	7 55.2	8.6	54.4
16	58 52.5	14 00.3	48 36.7	14.4	7 46.6	8.5	54.3
17	73 52.6	13 59.5	63 10.1	14.5	7 38.1	8.6	54.3
18	88 52.7	N13 58.8	77 43.6	14.5	N 7 29.5	8.7	54.3
19	103 52.9	58.0	92 17.1	14.6	7 20.8	8.6	54.3
20	118 53.0	57.2	106 50.7	14.5	7 12.2	8.7	54.3
21	133 53.1 ..	56.4	121 24.2	14.6	7 03.5	8.7	54.3
22	148 53.2	55.6	135 57.8	14.7	6 54.8	8.7	54.3
23	163 53.4	54.8	150 31.5	14.6	6 46.1	8.8	54.3
16 00	178 53.5	N13 54.1	165 05.1	14.7	N 6 37.3	8.8	54.3
01	193 53.6	53.3	179 38.8	14.7	6 28.5	8.8	54.3
02	208 53.7	52.5	194 12.5	14.7	6 19.7	8.8	54.3
03	223 53.9 ..	51.7	208 46.2	14.8	6 10.9	8.9	54.2
04	238 54.0	50.9	223 20.0	14.8	6 02.0	8.8	54.2
05	253 54.1	50.1	237 53.8	14.8	5 53.2	8.9	54.2
06	268 54.2	N13 49.3	252 27.6	14.9	N 5 44.3	8.9	54.2
07	283 54.4	48.6	267 01.5	14.8	5 35.4	9.0	54.2
08	298 54.5	47.8	281 35.3	14.9	5 26.4	8.9	54.2
S 09	313 54.6 ..	47.0	296 09.2	14.9	5 17.5	9.0	54.2
U 10	328 54.7	46.2	310 43.1	15.0	5 08.5	9.0	54.2
N 11	343 54.9	45.4	325 17.1	14.9	4 59.5	9.0	54.2
D 12	358 55.0	N13 44.6	339 51.0	15.0	N 4 50.5	9.0	54.2
A 13	13 55.1	43.8	354 25.0	15.0	4 41.5	9.0	54.2
Y 14	28 55.2	43.0	8 59.0	15.0	4 32.5	9.1	54.2
15	43 55.4 ..	42.2	23 33.0	15.1	4 23.4	9.1	54.2
16	58 55.5	41.5	38 07.1	15.0	4 14.3	9.0	54.1
17	73 55.6	40.7	52 41.1	15.1	4 05.3	9.1	54.1
18	88 55.8	N13 39.9	67 15.2	15.1	N 3 56.2	9.1	54.1
19	103 55.9	39.1	81 49.3	15.1	3 47.1	9.2	54.1
20	118 56.0	38.3	96 23.4	15.2	3 37.9	9.1	54.1
21	133 56.1 ..	37.5	110 57.6	15.1	3 28.8	9.1	54.1
22	148 56.3	36.7	125 31.7	15.2	3 19.7	9.2	54.1
23	163 56.4	35.9	140 05.9	15.2	N 3 10.5	9.2	54.1
	SD 15.8	d 0.8	SD 14.9		14.8		14.8

Lat.	Twilight Naut.	Twilight Civil	Sunrise	Moonrise 14	Moonrise 15	Moonrise 16	Moonrise 17
°	h m	h m	h m	h m	h m	h m	h m
N 72	////	////	02 22	02 45	04 24	05 59	07 32
N 70	////	////	02 54	03 08	04 39	06 08	07 35
68	////	01 41	03 18	03 26	04 51	06 14	07 37
66	////	02 19	03 36	03 41	05 01	06 20	07 39
64	////	02 45	03 51	03 53	05 09	06 25	07 40
62	01 29	03 05	04 03	04 03	05 16	06 29	07 41
60	02 04	03 22	04 13	04 11	05 22	06 32	07 43
N 58	02 29	03 35	04 22	04 19	05 27	06 35	07 43
56	02 47	03 46	04 30	04 25	05 32	06 38	07 44
54	03 03	03 56	04 37	04 31	05 36	06 41	07 45
52	03 16	04 05	04 43	04 36	05 40	06 43	07 46
50	03 27	04 13	04 49	04 41	05 43	06 45	07 47
45	03 50	04 29	05 01	04 52	05 51	06 50	07 48
N 40	04 07	04 42	05 11	05 00	05 57	06 53	07 49
35	04 21	04 53	05 20	05 07	06 02	06 57	07 50
30	04 32	05 02	05 27	05 14	06 07	06 59	07 51
20	04 50	05 17	05 40	05 25	06 15	07 04	07 53
N 10	05 04	05 29	05 51	05 35	06 22	07 09	07 54
0	05 15	05 40	06 01	05 44	06 29	07 13	07 55
S 10	05 25	05 50	06 11	05 53	06 36	07 17	07 57
20	05 33	05 59	06 22	06 03	06 43	07 21	07 58
30	05 41	06 09	06 34	06 14	06 51	07 26	08 00
35	05 45	06 15	06 41	06 20	06 55	07 29	08 01
40	05 49	06 21	06 49	06 27	07 01	07 32	08 02
45	05 53	06 27	06 58	06 36	07 07	07 36	08 03
S 50	05 57	06 35	07 09	06 46	07 14	07 40	08 04
52	05 59	06 38	07 14	06 50	07 17	07 42	08 05
54	06 00	06 42	07 19	06 55	07 21	07 44	08 06
56	06 02	06 46	07 26	07 01	07 25	07 47	08 06
58	06 04	06 51	07 32	07 07	07 30	07 49	08 07
S 60	06 06	06 55	07 40	07 14	07 35	07 52	08 08

Lat.	Sunset	Twilight Civil	Twilight Naut.	Moonset 14	Moonset 15	Moonset 16	Moonset 17
°	h m	h m	h m	h m	h m	h m	h m
N 72	21 42	////	////	20 27	20 23	20 18	20 14
N 70	21 11	23 42	////	20 11	20 13	20 14	20 14
68	20 48	22 22	////	19 58	20 05	20 10	20 14
66	20 30	21 46	////	19 47	19 58	20 06	20 14
64	20 16	21 20	23 44	19 38	19 52	20 04	20 14
62	20 04	21 01	22 34	19 30	19 47	20 01	20 15
60	19 54	20 45	22 01	19 23	19 42	19 59	20 15
N 58	19 45	20 32	21 37	19 17	19 38	19 57	20 15
56	19 38	20 21	21 19	19 12	19 35	19 55	20 15
54	19 31	20 11	21 04	19 07	19 32	19 54	20 15
52	19 25	20 03	20 51	19 03	19 29	19 52	20 15
50	19 19	19 55	20 40	18 59	19 26	19 51	20 15
45	19 07	19 39	20 18	18 50	19 20	19 48	20 15
N 40	18 57	19 26	20 01	18 43	19 16	19 46	20 15
35	18 49	19 16	19 48	18 37	19 11	19 44	20 15
30	18 42	19 07	19 37	18 32	19 08	19 42	20 16
20	18 29	18 52	19 19	18 22	19 01	19 39	20 16
N 10	18 18	18 40	19 05	18 14	18 56	19 36	20 16
0	18 08	18 29	18 54	18 06	18 51	19 33	20 16
S 10	17 58	18 20	18 44	17 58	18 45	19 31	20 16
20	17 47	18 10	18 36	17 49	18 39	19 28	20 16
30	17 35	18 00	18 28	17 40	18 32	19 24	20 16
35	17 29	17 55	18 25	17 34	18 29	19 22	20 16
40	17 21	17 49	18 21	17 28	18 24	19 20	20 16
45	17 12	17 42	18 17	17 20	18 19	19 18	20 16
S 50	17 01	17 35	18 13	17 11	18 13	19 15	20 16
52	16 56	17 31	18 11	17 07	18 10	19 13	20 16
54	16 50	17 28	18 10	17 02	18 07	19 12	20 16
56	16 44	17 24	18 08	16 57	18 04	19 10	20 16
58	16 37	17 19	18 06	16 51	18 00	19 08	20 16
S 60	16 30	17 15	18 04	16 45	17 55	19 06	20 16

Day	SUN Eqn. of Time 00h	SUN Eqn. of Time 12h	SUN Mer. Pass.	MOON Mer. Pass. Upper	MOON Mer. Pass. Lower	MOON Age	MOON Phase
d	m s	m s	h m	h m	h m	d	%
14	04 49	04 44	12 05	11 55	24 17	29	0
15	04 38	04 32	12 05	12 40	00 17	01	1
16	04 26	04 20	12 04	13 23	01 01	02	3

UT	ARIES GHA	VENUS −4.1 GHA	Dec	MARS +1.7 GHA	Dec	JUPITER −1.7 GHA	Dec	SATURN +0.5 GHA	Dec	Star Name	SHA	Dec
17 00	325 03.5	183 21.1	N 6 40.4	197 15.0	N19 59.7	171 30.9	N11 51.4	88 23.6	S17 56.6	Acamar	315 17.2	S40 14.4
01	340 05.9	198 25.1	40.7	212 15.8	59.3	186 32.8	51.2	103 26.0	56.6	Achernar	335 25.5	S57 09.2
02	355 08.4	213 29.1	41.0	227 16.6	59.0	201 34.8	51.0	118 28.4	56.6	Acrux	173 08.0	S63 11.3
03	10 10.9	228 33.1 ..	41.3	242 17.4 ..	58.6	216 36.7 ..	50.8	133 30.9 ..	56.6	Adhara	255 11.6	S28 59.6
04	25 13.3	243 37.1	41.5	257 18.2	58.2	231 38.7	50.6	148 33.3	56.7	Aldebaran	290 47.8	N16 32.3
05	40 15.8	258 41.1	41.8	272 19.0	57.8	246 40.6	50.4	163 35.7	56.7			
06	55 18.3	273 45.0	N 6 42.1	287 19.8	N19 57.4	261 42.6	N11 50.2	178 38.1	S17 56.7	Alioth	166 19.9	N55 52.8
07	70 20.7	288 49.0	42.4	302 20.6	57.1	276 44.5	50.0	193 40.5	56.7	Alkaid	152 58.0	N49 14.5
M 08	85 23.2	303 53.0	42.7	317 21.4	56.7	291 46.5	49.8	208 42.9	56.7	Al Na'ir	27 41.5	S46 52.9
O 09	100 25.6	318 57.0 ..	43.0	332 22.2 ..	56.3	306 48.4 ..	49.6	223 45.3 ..	56.8	Alnilam	275 45.0	S 1 11.6
N 10	115 28.1	334 01.0	43.3	347 23.0	55.9	321 50.3	49.4	238 47.7	56.8	Alphard	217 54.9	S 8 43.6
D 11	130 30.6	349 05.0	43.6	2 23.9	55.5	336 52.3	49.3	253 50.1	56.8			
A 12	145 33.0	4 08.9	N 6 43.9	17 24.7	N19 55.2	351 54.2	N11 49.1	268 52.5	S17 56.8	Alphecca	126 09.8	N26 40.1
Y 13	160 35.5	19 12.9	44.2	32 25.5	54.8	6 56.2	48.9	283 54.9	56.9	Alpheratz	357 41.6	N29 10.6
14	175 38.0	34 16.9	44.5	47 26.3	54.4	21 58.1	48.7	298 57.3	56.9	Altair	62 06.5	N 8 54.9
15	190 40.4	49 20.9 ..	44.8	62 27.1 ..	54.0	37 00.1 ..	48.5	313 59.7 ..	56.9	Ankaa	353 14.0	S42 13.0
16	205 42.9	64 24.8	45.1	77 27.9	53.6	52 02.0	48.3	329 02.1	56.9	Antares	112 24.3	S26 27.8
17	220 45.4	79 28.8	45.4	92 28.7	53.3	67 04.0	48.1	344 04.5	57.0			
18	235 47.8	94 32.8	N 6 45.7	107 29.5	N19 52.9	82 05.9	N11 47.9	359 06.9	S17 57.0	Arcturus	145 54.5	N19 06.4
19	250 50.3	109 36.8	46.0	122 30.3	52.5	97 07.9	47.7	14 09.3	57.0	Atria	107 24.5	S69 03.4
20	265 52.8	124 40.7	46.3	137 31.1	52.1	112 09.8	47.5	29 11.7	57.0	Avior	234 17.9	S59 33.6
21	280 55.2	139 44.7 ..	46.7	152 31.9 ..	51.7	127 11.8 ..	47.3	44 14.1 ..	57.0	Bellatrix	278 30.6	N 6 21.7
22	295 57.7	154 48.7	47.0	167 32.7	51.3	142 13.7	47.1	59 16.5	57.1	Betelgeuse	270 59.9	N 7 24.5
23	311 00.1	169 52.6	47.3	182 33.5	51.0	157 15.6	47.0	74 18.9	57.1			
18 00	326 02.6	184 56.6	N 6 47.6	197 34.3	N19 50.6	172 17.6	N11 46.8	89 21.3	S17 57.1	Canopus	263 55.8	S52 42.2
01	341 05.1	200 00.6	47.9	212 35.1	50.2	187 19.5	46.6	104 23.7	57.1	Capella	280 32.4	N46 00.5
02	356 07.5	215 04.5	48.2	227 35.9	49.8	202 21.5	46.4	119 26.1	57.2	Deneb	49 30.0	N45 20.5
03	11 10.0	230 08.5 ..	48.5	242 36.7 ..	49.4	217 23.4 ..	46.2	134 28.5 ..	57.2	Denebola	182 32.4	N14 29.2
04	26 12.5	245 12.5	48.8	257 37.5	49.0	232 25.4	46.0	149 30.9	57.2	Diphda	348 54.2	S17 53.9
05	41 14.9	260 16.4	49.2	272 38.3	48.6	247 27.3	45.8	164 33.3	57.2			
06	56 17.4	275 20.4	N 6 49.5	287 39.1	N19 48.3	262 29.3	N11 45.6	179 35.7	S17 57.3	Dubhe	193 50.7	N61 40.1
07	71 19.9	290 24.4	49.8	302 39.9	47.9	277 31.2	45.4	194 38.1	57.3	Elnath	278 10.9	N28 37.0
T 08	86 22.3	305 28.3	50.1	317 40.7	47.5	292 33.2	45.2	209 40.5	57.3	Eltanin	90 45.1	N51 29.7
U 09	101 24.8	320 32.3 ..	50.4	332 41.5 ..	47.1	307 35.1 ..	45.0	224 42.9 ..	57.3	Enif	33 45.3	N 9 57.0
E 10	116 27.2	335 36.2	50.8	347 42.3	46.7	322 37.0	44.8	239 45.3	57.4	Fomalhaut	15 22.0	S29 32.1
S 11	131 29.7	350 40.2	51.1	2 43.1	46.3	337 39.0	44.7	254 47.7	57.4			
D 12	146 32.2	5 44.1	N 6 51.4	17 43.9	N19 45.9	352 40.9	N11 44.5	269 50.1	S17 57.4	Gacrux	171 59.5	S57 12.2
A 13	161 34.6	20 48.1	51.7	32 44.7	45.5	7 42.9	44.3	284 52.5	57.4	Gienah	175 51.0	S17 37.7
Y 14	176 37.1	35 52.0	52.1	47 45.6	45.2	22 44.8	44.1	299 54.9	57.5	Hadar	148 45.9	S60 27.0
15	191 39.6	50 56.0 ..	52.4	62 46.4 ..	44.8	37 46.8 ..	43.9	314 57.3 ..	57.5	Hamal	327 58.9	N23 32.1
16	206 42.0	65 59.9	52.7	77 47.2	44.4	52 48.7	43.7	329 59.7	57.5	Kaus Aust.	83 41.6	S34 22.4
17	221 44.5	81 03.9	53.0	92 48.0	44.0	67 50.7	43.5	345 02.1	57.5			
18	236 47.0	96 07.8	N 6 53.4	107 48.8	N19 43.6	82 52.6	N11 43.3	0 04.5	S17 57.6	Kochab	137 20.5	N74 05.9
19	251 49.4	111 11.7	53.7	122 49.6	43.2	97 54.6	43.1	15 06.9	57.6	Markab	13 36.5	N15 17.5
20	266 51.9	126 15.7	54.0	137 50.4	42.8	112 56.5	42.9	30 09.3	57.6	Menkar	314 13.4	N 4 09.0
21	281 54.4	141 19.6 ..	54.4	152 51.2 ..	42.4	127 58.5 ..	42.7	45 11.7 ..	57.6	Menkent	148 05.9	S36 26.8
22	296 56.8	156 23.6	54.7	167 52.0	42.1	143 00.4	42.5	60 14.1	57.7	Miaplacidus	221 40.1	S69 46.9
23	311 59.3	171 27.5	55.0	182 52.8	41.7	158 02.3	42.4	75 16.5	57.7			
19 00	327 01.7	186 31.4	N 6 55.4	197 53.6	N19 41.3	173 04.3	N11 42.2	90 18.9	S17 57.7	Mirfak	308 38.1	N49 54.7
01	342 04.2	201 35.4	55.7	212 54.4	40.9	188 06.2	42.0	105 21.3	57.7	Nunki	75 56.2	S26 16.4
02	357 06.7	216 39.3	56.0	227 55.2	40.5	203 08.2	41.8	120 23.7	57.7	Peacock	53 16.4	S56 40.9
03	12 09.1	231 43.2 ..	56.4	242 56.1 ..	40.1	218 10.1 ..	41.6	135 26.1 ..	57.8	Pollux	243 26.3	N27 59.1
04	27 11.6	246 47.2	56.7	257 56.9	39.7	233 12.1	41.4	150 28.5	57.8	Procyon	244 58.5	N 5 11.0
05	42 14.1	261 51.1	57.1	272 57.7	39.3	248 14.0	41.2	165 30.9	57.8			
06	57 16.5	276 55.0	N 6 57.4	287 58.5	N19 38.9	263 16.0	N11 41.0	180 33.3	S17 57.8	Rasalhague	96 04.9	N12 33.3
W 07	72 19.0	291 58.9	57.7	302 59.3	38.5	278 17.9	40.8	195 35.7	57.9	Regulus	207 42.3	N11 53.5
E 08	87 21.5	307 02.8	58.1	318 00.1	38.1	293 19.9	40.6	210 38.1	57.9	Rigel	281 10.8	S 8 11.1
D 09	102 23.9	322 06.8 ..	58.4	333 00.9 ..	37.8	308 21.8 ..	40.4	225 40.5 ..	57.9	Rigil Kent.	139 49.8	S60 54.0
N 10	117 26.4	337 10.7	58.8	348 01.7	37.4	323 23.8	40.2	240 42.9	57.9	Sabik	102 10.7	S15 44.4
E 11	132 28.8	352 14.6	59.1	3 02.5	37.0	338 25.7	40.0	255 45.3	58.0			
S 12	147 31.3	7 18.5	N 6 59.5	18 03.3	N19 36.6	353 27.6	N11 39.9	270 47.6	S17 58.0	Schedar	349 38.3	N56 37.2
D 13	162 33.8	22 22.4	6 59.8	33 04.1	36.2	8 29.6	39.7	285 50.0	58.0	Shaula	96 19.7	S37 06.8
A 14	177 36.2	37 26.3	7 00.2	48 05.0	35.8	23 31.5	39.5	300 52.4	58.0	Sirius	258 32.7	S16 44.3
Y 15	192 38.7	52 30.2 ..	00.5	63 05.8 ..	35.4	38 33.5 ..	39.3	315 54.8 ..	58.1	Spica	158 29.8	S11 14.4
16	207 41.2	67 34.2	00.9	78 06.6	35.0	53 35.4	39.1	330 57.2	58.1	Suhail	222 51.7	S43 29.8
17	222 43.6	82 38.1	01.2	93 07.4	34.6	68 37.4	38.9	345 59.6	58.1			
18	237 46.1	97 42.0	N 7 01.6	108 08.2	N19 34.2	83 39.3	N11 38.7	1 02.0	S17 58.1	Vega	80 37.6	N38 48.3
19	252 48.6	112 45.9	01.9	123 09.0	33.8	98 41.3	38.5	16 04.4	58.2	Zuben'ubi	137 03.8	S16 06.2
20	267 51.0	127 49.8	02.3	138 09.8	33.4	113 43.2	38.3	31 06.8	58.2			
21	282 53.5	142 53.7 ..	02.6	153 10.6 ..	33.0	128 45.2 ..	38.1	46 09.2 ..	58.2			
22	297 56.0	157 57.6	03.0	168 11.5	32.6	143 47.1	37.9	61 11.6	58.2			
23	312 58.4	173 01.5	03.3	183 12.3	32.2	158 49.0	37.7	76 14.0	58.3			
Mer. Pass. 2 15.5		v 4.0 d 0.3		v 0.8 d 0.4		v 1.9 d 0.2		v 2.4 d 0.0				

	SHA	Mer. Pass.
Venus	218 54.0	11 37
Mars	231 31.7	10 49
Jupiter	206 15.0	12 29
Saturn	123 18.7	18 00

UT	SUN GHA	SUN Dec	MOON GHA	MOON v	MOON Dec	MOON d	MOON HP	Lat.	Twilight Naut.	Twilight Civil	Sunrise	Moonrise 17	Moonrise 18	Moonrise 19	Moonrise 20
d h	° ′	° ′	° ′	′	° ′	′	′	°	h m	h m	h m	h m	h m	h m	h m
17 00	178 56.5	N13 35.1	154 40.1	15.2	N 3 01.3	9.1	54.1	N 72	////	////	02 42	07 32	09 05	10 37	12 12
01	193 56.7	34.3	169 14.3	15.2	2 52.2	9.2	54.1	N 70	////	01 08	03 10	07 35	09 02	10 28	11 56
02	208 56.8	33.5	183 48.5	15.2	2 43.0	9.2	54.1	68	////	02 03	03 30	07 37	08 59	10 21	11 44
03	223 56.9 ..	32.7	198 22.7	15.3	2 33.8	9.2	54.1	66	////	02 34	03 47	07 39	08 57	10 15	11 34
04	238 57.1	31.9	212 57.0	15.2	2 24.6	9.2	54.1	64	01 00	02 58	04 00	07 40	08 55	10 10	11 25
05	253 57.2	31.2	227 31.2	15.3	2 15.4	9.2	54.1	62	01 49	03 16	04 11	07 41	08 54	10 06	11 18
06	268 57.3	N13 30.4	242 05.5	15.3	N 2 06.2	9.3	54.1	60	02 18	03 30	04 20	07 43	08 52	10 02	11 12
07	283 57.4	29.6	256 39.8	15.2	1 56.9	9.2	54.1	N 58	02 39	03 43	04 29	07 43	08 51	09 59	11 06
M 08	298 57.6	28.8	271 14.0	15.3	1 47.7	9.2	54.1	56	02 56	03 53	04 36	07 44	08 50	09 56	11 02
O 09	313 57.7 ..	28.0	285 48.3	15.4	1 38.5	9.2	54.1	54	03 10	04 02	04 42	07 45	08 49	09 53	10 57
N 10	328 57.8	27.2	300 22.7	15.3	1 29.3	9.3	54.1	52	03 23	04 11	04 48	07 46	08 48	09 51	10 53
D 11	343 58.0	26.4	314 57.0	15.3	1 20.0	9.2	54.1	50	03 33	04 18	04 53	07 47	08 48	09 49	10 50
A 12	358 58.1	N13 25.6	329 31.3	15.3	N 1 10.8	9.3	54.1	45	03 54	04 33	05 05	07 48	08 46	09 44	10 42
Y 13	13 58.2	24.8	344 05.6	15.4	1 01.5	9.2	54.0	N 40	04 10	04 45	05 14	07 49	08 45	09 40	10 36
14	28 58.4	24.0	358 40.0	15.3	0 52.3	9.3	54.0	35	04 23	04 55	05 22	07 50	08 43	09 37	10 30
15	43 58.5 ..	23.2	13 14.3	15.4	0 43.0	9.2	54.0	30	04 34	05 04	05 29	07 51	08 42	09 34	10 25
16	58 58.6	22.4	27 48.7	15.4	0 33.8	9.3	54.0	20	04 51	05 18	05 41	07 53	08 41	09 29	10 17
17	73 58.8	21.6	42 23.1	15.3	0 24.5	9.2	54.0	N 10	05 04	05 29	05 51	07 54	08 39	09 24	10 10
18	88 58.9	N13 20.8	56 57.4	15.4	N 0 15.3	9.3	54.0	0	05 15	05 39	06 01	07 55	08 37	09 20	10 03
19	103 59.0	20.0	71 31.8	15.4	N 0 06.0	9.2	54.0	S 10	05 24	05 48	06 10	07 57	08 36	09 16	09 56
20	118 59.2	19.2	86 06.2	15.4	S 0 03.2	9.3	54.0	20	05 31	05 57	06 20	07 58	08 35	09 11	09 49
21	133 59.3 ..	18.4	100 40.6	15.3	0 12.5	9.2	54.0	30	05 38	06 07	06 31	08 00	08 33	09 06	09 41
22	148 59.4	17.6	115 14.9	15.4	0 21.7	9.3	54.0	35	05 42	06 12	06 37	08 01	08 32	09 04	09 37
23	163 59.6	16.8	129 49.3	15.4	0 31.0	9.2	54.0	40	05 45	06 17	06 45	08 02	08 31	09 00	09 31
18 00	178 59.7	N13 16.0	144 23.7	15.4	S 0 40.2	9.2	54.0	45	05 48	06 23	06 53	08 03	08 30	08 57	09 25
01	193 59.8	15.2	158 58.1	15.4	0 49.4	9.3	54.0	S 50	05 52	06 30	07 03	08 04	08 28	08 52	09 18
02	209 00.0	14.4	173 32.5	15.4	0 58.7	9.2	54.0	52	05 53	06 33	07 08	08 05	08 27	08 50	09 15
03	224 00.1 ..	13.6	188 06.9	15.4	1 07.9	9.2	54.0	54	05 55	06 36	07 13	08 06	08 27	08 48	09 11
04	239 00.3	12.8	202 41.3	15.4	1 17.1	9.2	54.0	56	05 56	06 40	07 19	08 06	08 26	08 46	09 07
05	254 00.4	12.0	217 15.7	15.4	1 26.3	9.3	54.0	58	05 58	06 44	07 25	08 07	08 25	08 43	09 02
06	269 00.5	N13 11.2	231 50.1	15.3	S 1 35.6	9.2	54.0	S 60	05 59	06 48	07 32	08 08	08 24	08 40	08 57

Lat.	Sunset	Twilight Civil	Twilight Naut.	Moonset 17	Moonset 18	Moonset 19	Moonset 20
07	284 00.7	10.3	246 24.4	15.4	1 44.8	9.1	54.0
08	299 00.8	09.5	260 58.8	15.4	1 53.9	9.2	54.0
09	314 00.9 ..	08.7	275 33.2	15.4	2 03.1	9.2	54.0
10	329 01.1	07.9	290 07.6	15.3	2 12.3	9.2	54.0
11	344 01.2	07.1	304 41.9	15.4	2 21.5	9.1	54.0

Lat.	Sunset	Civil	Naut.	17	18	19	20
°	h m	h m	h m	h m	h m	h m	h m
N 72	21 21	////	////	20 14	20 09	20 05	20 00
N 70	20 54	22 48	////	20 14	20 14	20 15	20 17
68	20 34	21 59	////	20 14	20 19	20 24	20 30
66	20 19	21 29	////	20 14	20 22	20 31	20 41
64	20 06	21 07	22 57	20 14	20 25	20 37	20 51
62	19 55	20 50	22 14	20 15	20 28	20 42	20 59
60	19 46	20 35	21 46	20 15	20 30	20 47	21 06
N 58	19 38	20 23	21 26	20 15	20 32	20 51	21 12
56	19 30	20 13	21 09	20 15	20 34	20 55	21 17
54	19 24	20 04	20 55	20 15	20 36	20 58	21 22
52	19 18	19 56	20 44	20 15	20 37	21 01	21 26
50	19 13	19 49	20 33	20 15	20 39	21 04	21 31
45	19 02	19 34	20 13	20 15	20 42	21 10	21 39
N 40	18 53	19 22	19 57	20 15	20 45	21 15	21 47
35	18 45	19 12	19 44	20 15	20 47	21 19	21 53
30	18 39	19 03	19 33	20 15	20 49	21 23	21 58
20	18 27	18 50	19 16	20 16	20 52	21 29	22 08
N 10	18 17	18 38	19 04	20 16	20 55	21 35	22 17
0	18 07	18 28	18 53	20 16	20 58	21 41	22 24
S 10	17 58	18 19	18 44	20 16	21 01	21 46	22 32
20	17 48	18 11	18 37	20 16	21 04	21 52	22 41
30	17 37	18 02	18 30	20 16	21 07	21 59	22 51
35	17 31	17 57	18 26	20 16	21 09	22 02	22 56
40	17 24	17 51	18 23	20 16	21 11	22 07	23 03
45	17 15	17 46	18 20	20 16	21 14	22 12	23 10
S 50	17 05	17 39	18 17	20 16	21 17	22 18	23 19
52	17 01	17 36	18 15	20 16	21 18	22 21	23 23
54	16 56	17 33	18 14	20 16	21 20	22 24	23 28
56	16 50	17 29	18 13	20 16	21 22	22 27	23 33
58	16 44	17 25	18 11	20 16	21 24	22 31	23 39
S 60	16 37	17 21	18 10	20 16	21 26	22 35	23 45

UT (Tues/Wed)	SUN GHA	SUN Dec	MOON GHA	MOON v	MOON Dec	MOON d	MOON HP
T 12	359 01.4	N13 06.3	319 16.3	15.3	S 2 30.6	9.2	54.0
U 13	14 01.5	05.5	333 50.6	15.4	2 39.8	9.1	54.0
E 14	29 01.6	04.7	348 25.0	15.3	2 48.9	9.1	54.0
S 15	44 01.8 ..	03.9	2 59.3	15.4	2 58.0	9.2	54.0
D 16	59 01.9	03.1	17 33.7	15.3	3 07.2	9.1	54.0
A 17	74 02.0	02.3	32 08.0	15.3	3 16.3	9.1	54.1
Y 18	89 02.2	N13 01.5	46 42.3	15.3	S 3 25.4	9.0	54.1
19	104 02.3	13 00.7	61 16.6	15.3	3 34.4	9.1	54.1
20	119 02.5	12 59.9	75 50.9	15.3	3 43.5	9.0	54.1
21	134 02.6 ..	59.0	90 25.2	15.2	3 52.5	9.1	54.1
22	149 02.7	58.2	104 59.4	15.3	4 01.6	9.0	54.1
23	164 02.9	57.4	119 33.7	15.2	4 10.6	9.0	54.1
19 00	179 03.0	N12 56.6	134 07.9	15.3	S 4 19.6	9.0	54.1
01	194 03.2	55.8	148 42.2	15.2	4 28.6	8.9	54.1
02	209 03.3	55.0	163 16.4	15.2	4 37.5	8.9	54.1
03	224 03.4 ..	54.2	177 50.6	15.2	4 46.5	8.9	54.1
04	239 03.6	53.4	192 24.8	15.1	4 55.4	8.9	54.1
05	254 03.7	52.6	206 58.9	15.2	5 04.3	8.9	54.1
06	269 03.9	N12 51.7	221 33.1	15.1	S 5 13.2	8.9	54.1
W 07	284 04.0	50.9	236 07.2	15.1	5 22.1	8.8	54.1
E 08	299 04.2	50.1	250 41.3	15.1	5 30.9	8.8	54.1
D 09	314 04.3 ..	49.3	265 15.4	15.1	5 39.7	8.9	54.1
N 10	329 04.4	48.5	279 49.5	15.1	5 48.6	8.7	54.1
E 11	344 04.6	47.7	294 23.6	15.0	5 57.3	8.8	54.1
S 12	359 04.7	N12 46.9	308 57.6	15.0	S 6 06.1	8.7	54.2
D 13	14 04.9	46.0	323 31.6	15.0	6 14.8	8.8	54.2
A 14	29 05.0	45.2	338 05.6	15.0	6 23.6	8.6	54.2
Y 15	44 05.2 ..	44.4	352 39.6	14.9	6 32.2	8.7	54.2
16	59 05.3	43.6	7 13.5	15.0	6 40.9	8.7	54.2
17	74 05.4	42.8	21 47.5	14.9	6 49.6	8.6	54.2
18	89 05.6	N12 42.0	36 21.4	14.8	S 6 58.2	8.6	54.2
19	104 05.7	41.1	50 55.2	14.9	7 06.8	8.5	54.2
20	119 05.9	40.3	65 29.1	14.8	7 15.3	8.5	54.2
21	134 06.0 ..	39.5	80 02.9	14.8	7 23.8	8.6	54.2
22	149 06.2	38.7	94 36.7	14.8	7 32.4	8.4	54.2
23	164 06.3	37.9	109 10.5	14.7	S 7 40.8	8.5	54.3
	SD 15.8	d 0.8	SD 14.7	14.7			14.8

	SUN		MOON			
Day	Eqn. of Time 00h	Eqn. of Time 12h	Mer. Pass.	Mer. Pass. Upper	Mer. Pass. Lower	Age	Phase
d	m s	m s	h m	h m	h m	d	%
17	04 14	04 08	12 04	14 05	01 44	03	7
18	04 01	03 55	12 04	14 48	02 27	04	13
19	03 48	03 41	12 04	15 30	03 09	05	20

UT	ARIES GHA	VENUS −4.1 GHA / Dec	MARS +1.8 GHA / Dec	JUPITER −1.7 GHA / Dec	SATURN +0.5 GHA / Dec	Star Name	SHA	Dec
20 THURSDAY								
00	328 00.9	188 05.3 N 7 03.7	198 13.1 N19 31.8	173 51.0 N11 37.5	91 16.4 S17 58.3	Acamar	315 17.2	S40 14.4
01	343 03.3	203 09.2 04.0	213 13.9 31.5	188 52.9 37.3	106 18.8 58.3	Achernar	335 25.5	S57 09.2
02	358 05.8	218 13.1 04.4	228 14.7 31.1	203 54.9 37.2	121 21.2 58.4	Acrux	173 08.0	S63 11.3
03	13 08.3	233 17.0 .. 04.8	243 15.5 .. 30.7	218 56.8 .. 37.0	136 23.6 .. 58.4	Adhara	255 11.6	S28 59.6
04	28 10.7	248 20.9 05.1	258 16.3 30.3	233 58.8 36.8	151 25.9 58.4	Aldebaran	290 47.7	N16 32.3
05	43 13.2	263 24.8 05.5	273 17.1 29.9	249 00.7 36.6	166 28.3 58.4			
06	58 15.7	278 28.7 N 7 05.8	288 18.0 N19 29.5	264 02.7 N11 36.4	181 30.7 S17 58.5	Alioth	166 19.9	N55 52.8
07	73 18.1	293 32.5 06.2	303 18.8 29.1	279 04.6 36.2	196 33.1 58.5	Alkaid	152 58.0	N49 14.5
08	88 20.6	308 36.4 06.6	318 19.6 28.7	294 06.6 36.0	211 35.5 58.5	Al Na'ir	27 41.5	S46 52.9
09	103 23.1	323 40.3 .. 06.9	333 20.4 .. 28.3	309 08.5 .. 35.8	226 37.9 .. 58.5	Alnilam	275 45.0	S 1 11.6
10	118 25.5	338 44.2 07.3	348 21.2 27.9	324 10.5 35.6	241 40.3 58.6	Alphard	217 54.9	S 8 43.6
11	133 28.0	353 48.0 07.6	3 22.0 27.5	339 12.4 35.4	256 42.7 58.6			
12	148 30.5	8 51.9 N 7 08.0	18 22.8 N19 27.1	354 14.3 N11 35.2	271 45.1 S17 58.6	Alphecca	126 09.8	N26 40.1
13	163 32.9	23 55.8 08.4	33 23.7 26.7	9 16.3 35.0	286 47.5 58.6	Alpheratz	357 41.6	N29 10.6
14	178 35.4	38 59.6 08.7	48 24.5 26.3	24 18.2 34.8	301 49.9 58.7	Altair	62 06.5	N 8 54.9
15	193 37.8	54 03.5 .. 09.1	63 25.3 .. 25.9	39 20.2 .. 34.7	316 52.3 .. 58.7	Ankaa	353 14.0	S42 13.0
16	208 40.3	69 07.3 09.5	78 26.1 25.5	54 22.1 34.5	331 54.6 58.7	Antares	112 24.3	S26 27.8
17	223 42.8	84 11.2 09.9	93 26.9 25.1	69 24.1 34.3	346 57.0 58.7			
18	238 45.2	99 15.1 N 7 10.2	108 27.7 N19 24.7	84 26.0 N11 34.1	1 59.4 S17 58.8	Arcturus	145 54.5	N19 06.4
19	253 47.7	114 18.9 10.6	123 28.6 24.3	99 28.0 33.9	17 01.8 58.8	Atria	107 24.6	S69 03.4
20	268 50.2	129 22.8 11.0	138 29.4 23.9	114 29.9 33.7	32 04.2 58.8	Avior	234 17.9	S59 33.6
21	283 52.6	144 26.6 .. 11.3	153 30.2 .. 23.5	129 31.9 .. 33.5	47 06.6 .. 58.8	Bellatrix	278 30.5	N 6 21.7
22	298 55.1	159 30.5 11.7	168 31.0 23.1	144 33.8 33.3	62 09.0 58.9	Betelgeuse	270 59.9	N 7 24.5
23	313 57.6	174 34.3 12.1	183 31.8 22.7	159 35.7 33.1	77 11.4 58.9			
21 FRIDAY								
00	329 00.0	189 38.1 N 7 12.5	198 32.6 N19 22.3	174 37.7 N11 32.9	92 13.8 S17 58.9	Canopus	263 55.8	S52 42.2
01	344 02.5	204 42.0 12.8	213 33.5 21.9	189 39.6 32.7	107 16.2 58.9	Capella	280 32.4	N46 00.5
02	359 04.9	219 45.8 13.2	228 34.3 21.5	204 41.6 32.5	122 18.5 59.0	Deneb	49 30.0	N45 20.5
03	14 07.4	234 49.7 .. 13.6	243 35.1 .. 21.1	219 43.5 .. 32.3	137 20.9 .. 59.0	Denebola	182 32.5	N14 29.2
04	29 09.9	249 53.5 14.0	258 35.9 20.7	234 45.5 32.1	152 23.3 59.0	Diphda	348 54.2	S17 53.9
05	44 12.3	264 57.3 14.3	273 36.7 20.3	249 47.4 31.9	167 25.7 59.1			
06	59 14.8	280 01.2 N 7 14.7	288 37.5 N19 19.9	264 49.4 N11 31.8	182 28.1 S17 59.1	Dubhe	193 50.7	N61 40.1
07	74 17.3	295 05.0 15.1	303 38.4 19.5	279 51.3 31.6	197 30.5 59.1	Elnath	278 10.9	N28 37.0
08	89 19.7	310 08.8 15.5	318 39.2 19.1	294 53.3 31.4	212 32.9 59.1	Eltanin	90 45.2	N51 29.7
09	104 22.2	325 12.6 .. 15.9	333 40.0 .. 18.7	309 55.2 .. 31.2	227 35.3 .. 59.2	Enif	33 45.3	N 9 57.0
10	119 24.7	340 16.4 16.2	348 40.8 18.3	324 57.2 31.0	242 37.6 59.2	Fomalhaut	15 22.0	S29 32.1
11	134 27.1	355 20.3 16.6	3 41.6 17.9	339 59.1 30.8	257 40.0 59.2			
12	149 29.6	10 24.1 N 7 17.0	18 42.5 N19 17.5	355 01.0 N11 30.6	272 42.4 S17 59.2	Gacrux	171 59.5	S57 12.1
13	164 32.1	25 27.9 17.4	33 43.3 17.1	10 03.0 30.4	287 44.8 59.3	Gienah	175 51.0	S17 37.7
14	179 34.5	40 31.7 17.8	48 44.1 16.7	25 04.9 30.2	302 47.2 59.3	Hadar	148 45.9	S60 27.0
15	194 37.0	55 35.5 .. 18.1	63 44.9 .. 16.2	40 06.9 .. 30.0	317 49.6 .. 59.3	Hamal	327 58.9	N23 32.1
16	209 39.4	70 39.3 18.5	78 45.7 15.8	55 08.8 29.8	332 52.0 59.3	Kaus Aust.	83 41.6	S34 22.4
17	224 41.9	85 43.1 18.9	93 46.6 15.4	70 10.8 29.6	347 54.4 59.4			
18	239 44.4	100 46.9 N 7 19.3	108 47.4 N19 15.0	85 12.7 N11 29.4	2 56.7 S17 59.4	Kochab	137 20.5	N74 05.9
19	254 46.8	115 50.7 19.7	123 48.2 14.6	100 14.7 29.2	17 59.1 59.4	Markab	13 36.5	N15 17.5
20	269 49.3	130 54.5 20.1	138 49.0 14.2	115 16.6 29.1	33 01.5 59.5	Menkar	314 13.4	N 4 09.0
21	284 51.8	145 58.3 .. 20.5	153 49.8 .. 13.8	130 18.6 .. 28.9	48 03.9 .. 59.5	Menkent	148 05.9	S36 26.8
22	299 54.2	161 02.1 20.8	168 50.7 13.4	145 20.5 28.7	63 06.3 59.5	Miaplacidus	221 40.1	S69 46.9
23	314 56.7	176 05.9 21.2	183 51.5 13.0	160 22.4 28.5	78 08.7 59.5			
22 SATURDAY								
00	329 59.2	191 09.6 N 7 21.6	198 52.3 N19 12.6	175 24.4 N11 28.3	93 11.1 S17 59.6	Mirfak	308 38.1	N49 54.7
01	345 01.6	206 13.4 22.0	213 53.1 12.2	190 26.3 28.1	108 13.4 59.6	Nunki	75 56.2	S26 16.4
02	0 04.1	221 17.2 22.4	228 53.9 11.8	205 28.3 27.9	123 15.8 59.6	Peacock	53 16.4	S56 40.9
03	15 06.6	236 21.0 .. 22.8	243 54.8 .. 11.4	220 30.2 .. 27.7	138 18.2 .. 59.6	Pollux	243 26.3	N27 59.1
04	30 09.0	251 24.8 23.2	258 55.6 11.0	235 32.2 27.5	153 20.6 59.7	Procyon	244 58.5	N 5 11.0
05	45 11.5	266 28.5 23.6	273 56.4 10.6	250 34.1 27.3	168 23.0 59.7			
06	60 13.9	281 32.3 N 7 24.0	288 57.2 N19 10.2	265 36.1 N11 27.1	183 25.4 S17 59.7	Rasalhague	96 04.9	N12 33.3
07	75 16.4	296 36.1 24.4	303 58.1 09.8	280 38.0 26.9	198 27.7 59.7	Regulus	207 42.3	N11 53.5
08	90 18.9	311 39.8 24.8	318 58.9 09.3	295 40.0 26.7	213 30.1 59.8	Rigel	281 10.8	S 8 11.1
09	105 21.3	326 43.6 .. 25.2	333 59.7 .. 08.9	310 41.9 .. 26.5	228 32.5 .. 59.8	Rigil Kent.	139 49.8	S60 54.0
10	120 23.8	341 47.3 25.6	349 00.5 08.5	325 43.9 26.3	243 34.9 59.8	Sabik	102 10.7	S15 44.4
11	135 26.3	356 51.1 25.9	4 01.3 08.1	340 45.8 26.2	258 37.3 59.9			
12	150 28.7	11 54.8 N 7 26.3	19 02.2 N19 07.7	355 47.7 N11 26.0	273 39.7 S17 59.9	Schedar	349 38.3	N56 37.2
13	165 31.2	26 58.6 26.7	34 03.0 07.3	10 49.7 25.8	288 42.0 59.9	Shaula	96 19.7	S37 06.8
14	180 33.6	42 02.3 27.1	49 03.8 06.9	25 51.6 25.6	303 44.4 17 59.9	Sirius	258 32.6	S16 44.3
15	195 36.1	57 06.1 .. 27.5	64 04.6 .. 06.5	40 53.6 .. 25.4	318 46.8 18 00.0	Spica	158 29.9	S11 14.4
16	210 38.6	72 09.8 27.9	79 05.5 06.1	55 55.5 25.2	333 49.2 00.0	Suhail	222 51.7	S43 29.8
17	225 41.0	87 13.6 28.3	94 06.3 05.7	70 57.5 25.0	348 51.6 00.0			
18	240 43.5	102 17.3 N 7 28.7	109 07.1 N19 05.3	85 59.4 N11 24.8	3 54.0 S18 00.1	Vega	80 37.7	N38 48.3
19	255 46.0	117 21.0 29.1	124 07.9 04.8	101 01.4 24.6	18 56.3 00.1	Zuben'ubi	137 03.8	S16 06.2
20	270 48.4	132 24.8 29.5	139 08.8 04.4	116 03.3 24.4	33 58.7 00.1			
21	285 50.9	147 28.5 .. 29.9	154 09.6 .. 04.0	131 05.3 .. 24.2	49 01.1 .. 00.1			
22	300 53.4	162 32.2 30.3	169 10.4 03.6	146 07.2 24.0	64 03.5 00.2			
23	315 55.8	177 35.9 30.7	184 11.2 03.2	161 09.1 23.8	79 05.9 00.2			

	SHA	Mer. Pass.
	° ′	h m
Venus	220 38.1	11 19
Mars	229 32.6	10 45
Jupiter	205 37.7	12 20
Saturn	123 13.7	17 48

	Mer. Pass.	v	d
Aries	2 03.7		
Venus		3.8	0.4
Mars		0.8	0.4
Jupiter		1.9	0.2
Saturn		2.4	0.0

UT	SUN GHA	SUN Dec	MOON GHA	MOON v	MOON Dec	MOON d	MOON HP
d h	° ′	° ′	° ′	′	° ′	′	′
20 00	179 06.5	N12 37.0	123 44.2	14.7	S 7 49.3	8.4	54.3
01	194 06.6	36.2	138 17.9	14.7	7 57.7	8.4	54.3
02	209 06.8	35.4	152 51.6	14.6	8 06.1	8.3	54.3
03	224 06.9 ..	34.6	167 25.2	14.7	8 14.4	8.4	54.3
04	239 07.0	33.8	181 58.9	14.5	8 22.8	8.3	54.3
05	254 07.2	32.9	196 32.4	14.6	8 31.1	8.2	54.3
THURSDAY 06	269 07.3	N12 32.1	211 06.0	14.5	S 8 39.3	8.2	54.3
07	284 07.5	31.3	225 39.5	14.5	8 47.5	8.2	54.3
08	299 07.6	30.5	240 13.0	14.5	8 55.7	8.2	54.4
09	314 07.8 ..	29.7	254 46.5	14.4	9 03.9	8.1	54.4
10	329 07.9	28.8	269 19.9	14.4	9 12.0	8.1	54.4
11	344 08.1	28.0	283 53.3	14.3	9 20.1	8.1	54.4
12	359 08.2	N12 27.2	298 26.6	14.4	S 9 28.2	8.0	54.4
13	14 08.4	26.4	313 00.0	14.2	9 36.2	8.0	54.4
14	29 08.5	25.5	327 33.2	14.3	9 44.2	7.9	54.4
15	44 08.7 ..	24.7	342 06.5	14.2	9 52.1	7.9	54.5
16	59 08.8	23.9	356 39.7	14.2	10 00.0	7.9	54.5
17	74 09.0	23.1	11 12.9	14.1	10 07.9	7.8	54.5
18	89 09.1	N12 22.2	25 46.0	14.1	S10 15.7	7.8	54.5
19	104 09.3	21.4	40 19.1	14.0	10 23.5	7.7	54.5
20	119 09.4	20.6	54 52.1	14.1	10 31.2	7.7	54.5
21	134 09.6 ..	19.8	69 25.2	13.9	10 38.9	7.7	54.6
22	149 09.7	18.9	83 58.1	14.0	10 46.6	7.6	54.6
23	164 09.9	18.1	98 31.1	13.8	10 54.2	7.6	54.6
21 00	179 10.0	N12 17.3	113 03.9	13.9	S11 01.8	7.5	54.6
01	194 10.2	16.5	127 36.8	13.8	11 09.3	7.5	54.6
02	209 10.3	15.6	142 09.6	13.7	11 16.8	7.4	54.6
03	224 10.5 ..	14.8	156 42.3	13.8	11 24.2	7.4	54.7
04	239 10.6	14.0	171 15.1	13.6	11 31.6	7.4	54.7
05	254 10.8	13.1	185 47.7	13.7	11 39.0	7.3	54.7
FRIDAY 06	269 10.9	N12 12.3	200 20.4	13.5	S11 46.3	7.3	54.7
07	284 11.1	11.5	214 52.9	13.6	11 53.6	7.2	54.7
08	299 11.2	10.6	229 25.5	13.4	12 00.8	7.1	54.8
09	314 11.4 ..	09.8	243 57.9	13.5	12 07.9	7.2	54.8
10	329 11.5	09.0	258 30.4	13.4	12 15.1	7.0	54.8
11	344 11.7	08.2	273 02.8	13.3	12 22.1	7.0	54.8
12	359 11.8	N12 07.3	287 35.1	13.3	S12 29.1	7.0	54.8
13	14 12.0	06.5	302 07.4	13.3	12 36.1	6.9	54.9
14	29 12.2	05.7	316 39.7	13.2	12 43.0	6.9	54.9
15	44 12.3 ..	04.8	331 11.9	13.1	12 49.9	6.8	54.9
16	59 12.5	04.0	345 44.0	13.1	12 56.7	6.7	54.9
17	74 12.6	03.2	0 16.1	13.0	13 03.4	6.7	54.9
18	89 12.8	N12 02.3	14 48.1	13.0	S13 10.1	6.7	55.0
19	104 12.9	01.5	29 20.1	13.0	13 16.8	6.6	55.0
20	119 13.1	12 00.7	43 52.1	12.9	13 23.4	6.5	55.0
21	134 13.2	11 59.8	58 24.0	12.8	13 29.9	6.5	55.0
22	149 13.4	59.0	72 55.8	12.8	13 36.4	6.4	55.1
23	164 13.5	58.2	87 27.6	12.7	13 42.8	6.3	55.1
22 00	179 13.7	N11 57.3	101 59.3	12.7	S13 49.1	6.3	55.1
01	194 13.9	56.5	116 31.0	12.6	13 55.4	6.3	55.1
02	209 14.0	55.7	131 02.6	12.6	14 01.7	6.2	55.1
03	224 14.2 ..	54.8	145 34.2	12.5	14 07.9	6.1	55.2
04	239 14.3	54.0	160 05.7	12.4	14 14.0	6.1	55.2
05	254 14.5	53.1	174 37.1	12.4	14 20.1	6.0	55.2
SATURDAY 06	269 14.6	N11 52.3	189 08.5	12.4	S14 26.1	5.9	55.2
07	284 14.8	51.5	203 39.9	12.3	14 32.0	5.9	55.3
08	299 15.0	50.6	218 11.2	12.2	14 37.9	5.8	55.3
09	314 15.1 ..	49.8	232 42.4	12.2	14 43.7	5.7	55.3
10	329 15.3	49.0	247 13.6	12.1	14 49.4	5.7	55.4
11	344 15.4	48.1	261 44.7	12.1	14 55.1	5.6	55.4
12	359 15.6	N11 47.3	276 15.8	12.0	S15 00.7	5.6	55.4
13	14 15.8	46.4	290 46.8	11.9	15 06.3	5.4	55.4
14	29 15.9	45.6	305 17.7	11.9	15 11.7	5.5	55.5
15	44 16.1 ..	44.8	319 48.6	11.8	15 17.2	5.3	55.5
16	59 16.2	43.9	334 19.4	11.8	15 22.5	5.3	55.5
17	74 16.4	43.1	348 50.2	11.7	15 27.8	5.2	55.5
18	89 16.5	N11 42.2	3 20.9	11.6	S15 33.0	5.1	55.6
19	104 16.7	41.4	17 51.5	11.6	15 38.1	5.1	55.6
20	119 16.9	40.5	32 22.1	11.6	15 43.2	5.0	55.6
21	134 17.0 ..	39.7	46 52.7	11.4	15 48.2	4.9	55.7
22	149 17.2	38.9	61 23.1	11.4	15 53.1	4.8	55.7
23	164 17.3	38.0	75 53.5	11.4	S15 57.9	4.8	55.7
	SD 15.8	d 0.8	SD 14.8		14.9		15.1

Twilight / Sunrise / Moonrise

Lat.	Naut.	Civil	Sunrise	Moonrise 20	21	22	23
°	h m	h m	h m	h m	h m	h m	h m
N 72	////	////	03 00	12 12	13 51	15 35	17 29
N 70	////	01 41	03 24	11 56	13 26	14 57	16 26
68	////	02 22	03 42	11 44	13 08	14 31	15 51
66	////	02 49	03 57	11 34	12 53	14 11	15 26
64	01 29	03 09	04 09	11 25	12 41	13 55	15 06
62	02 05	03 25	04 19	11 18	12 31	13 42	14 51
60	02 30	03 39	04 28	11 12	12 22	13 31	14 37
N 58	02 49	03 50	04 35	11 06	12 14	13 21	14 26
56	03 05	04 00	04 42	11 02	12 07	13 13	14 16
54	03 18	04 08	04 48	10 57	12 01	13 05	14 07
52	03 29	04 16	04 53	10 53	11 56	12 58	14 00
50	03 39	04 23	04 58	10 50	11 51	12 52	13 53
45	03 59	04 37	05 08	10 42	11 41	12 39	13 38
N 40	04 14	04 48	05 17	10 36	11 32	12 29	13 25
35	04 26	04 58	05 24	10 30	11 25	12 20	13 15
30	04 36	05 06	05 31	10 25	11 18	12 12	13 06
20	04 52	05 19	05 42	10 17	11 07	11 58	12 50
N 10	05 04	05 30	05 51	10 10	10 57	11 46	12 36
0	05 14	05 39	06 00	10 03	10 48	11 35	12 24
S 10	05 22	05 47	06 09	09 56	10 39	11 23	12 11
20	05 29	05 55	06 18	09 49	10 29	11 12	11 57
30	05 36	06 04	06 28	09 41	10 18	10 58	11 42
35	05 38	06 08	06 34	09 37	10 12	10 50	11 33
40	05 41	06 13	06 41	09 31	10 05	10 41	11 23
45	05 44	06 18	06 48	09 25	09 56	10 31	11 11
S 50	05 47	06 24	06 57	09 18	09 46	10 19	10 57
52	05 48	06 27	07 02	09 15	09 42	10 13	10 50
54	05 49	06 30	07 06	09 11	09 37	10 07	10 42
56	05 50	06 33	07 12	09 07	09 31	10 00	10 34
58	05 51	06 36	07 17	09 02	09 25	09 52	10 25
S 60	05 52	06 40	07 24	08 57	09 18	09 43	10 14

Sunset / Twilight / Moonset

Lat.	Sunset	Civil	Naut.	Moonset 20	21	22	23
°	h m	h m	h m	h m	h m	h m	h m
N 72	21 02	23 47	////	20 00	19 54	19 48	19 36
N 70	20 39	22 17	////	20 17	20 20	20 26	20 40
68	20 21	21 40	////	20 30	20 39	20 53	21 15
66	20 07	21 14	23 49	20 41	20 55	21 13	21 41
64	19 55	20 54	22 31	20 51	21 07	21 30	22 01
62	19 45	20 39	21 57	20 59	21 18	21 44	22 17
60	19 37	20 26	21 33	21 06	21 28	21 55	22 31
N 58	19 30	20 14	21 14	21 12	21 36	22 05	22 42
56	19 23	20 05	20 59	21 17	21 43	22 14	22 52
54	19 17	19 56	20 47	21 22	21 49	22 22	23 01
52	19 12	19 49	20 36	21 26	21 55	22 29	23 09
50	19 07	19 42	20 26	21 31	22 01	22 35	23 16
45	18 57	19 29	20 07	21 39	22 12	22 49	23 32
N 40	18 49	19 17	19 52	21 47	22 21	23 00	23 44
35	18 42	19 08	19 40	21 53	22 30	23 10	23 55
30	18 35	19 00	19 30	21 58	22 37	23 18	24 05
20	18 25	18 47	19 14	22 08	22 49	23 33	24 21
N 10	18 15	18 37	19 02	22 17	23 00	23 46	24 35
0	18 07	18 28	18 52	22 24	23 10	23 58	24 48
S 10	17 58	18 19	18 44	22 32	23 20	24 10	00 10
20	17 49	18 11	18 37	22 41	23 31	24 23	00 23
30	17 39	18 03	18 31	22 51	23 44	24 37	00 37
35	17 33	17 59	18 28	22 56	23 51	24 46	00 46
40	17 26	17 54	18 26	23 03	23 59	24 56	00 56
45	17 19	17 49	18 23	23 10	24 09	00 09	01 07
S 50	17 10	17 43	18 21	23 19	24 20	00 20	01 21
52	17 05	17 40	18 20	23 23	24 26	00 26	01 28
54	17 01	17 37	18 19	23 28	24 32	00 32	01 35
56	16 56	17 34	18 18	23 33	24 38	00 38	01 43
58	16 50	17 31	18 17	23 39	24 46	00 46	01 52
S 60	16 44	17 28	18 16	23 45	24 54	00 54	02 02

SUN / MOON

Day	Eqn. of Time 00h	Eqn. of Time 12h	Mer. Pass.	Mer. Pass. Upper	Mer. Pass. Lower	Age	Phase
d	m s	m s	h m	h m	h m	d	%
20	03 34	03 27	12 03	16 14	03 52	06	28
21	03 20	03 13	12 03	16 59	04 36	07	37
22	03 05	02 58	12 03	17 46	05 22	08	47

UT	ARIES GHA	VENUS −4.2 GHA	Dec	MARS +1.8 GHA	Dec	JUPITER −1.7 GHA	Dec	SATURN +0.5 GHA	Dec	STARS Name	SHA	Dec
23 00	330 58.3	192 39.6	N 7 31.1	199 12.1	N19 02.8	176 11.1	N11 23.6	94 08.2	S18 00.2	Acamar	315 17.1	S40 14.4
01	346 00.8	207 43.4	. . 31.5	214 12.9	. . 02.4	191 13.0	. . 23.4	109 10.6	. . 00.2	Achernar	335 25.4	S57 09.2
02	1 03.2	222 47.1	31.9	229 13.7	02.0	206 15.0	23.2	124 13.0	00.3	Acrux	173 08.0	S63 11.3
03	16 05.7	237 50.8	. . 32.3	244 14.6	. . 01.6	221 16.9	. . 23.1	139 15.4	. . 00.3	Adhara	255 11.6	S28 59.6
04	31 08.2	252 54.5	32.7	259 15.4	01.1	236 18.9	22.9	154 17.8	00.3	Aldebaran	290 47.7	N16 32.3
05	46 10.6	267 58.2	33.2	274 16.2	00.7	251 20.8	22.7	169 20.1	00.4			
06	61 13.1	283 01.9	N 7 33.6	289 17.0	N19 00.3	266 22.8	N11 22.5	184 22.5	S18 00.4	Alioth	166 19.9	N55 52.8
07	76 15.5	298 05.6	34.0	304 17.9	18 59.9	281 24.7	22.3	199 24.9	00.4	Alkaid	152 58.1	N49 14.5
08	91 18.0	313 09.3	34.4	319 18.7	59.5	296 26.7	22.1	214 27.3	00.4	Al Na'ir	27 41.5	S46 52.9
S 09	106 20.5	328 13.0	. . 34.8	334 19.5	. . 59.1	311 28.6	. . 21.9	229 29.7	. . 00.5	Alnilam	275 45.0	S 1 11.6
U 10	121 22.9	343 16.7	35.2	349 20.3	58.7	326 30.6	21.7	244 32.0	00.5	Alphard	217 54.9	S 8 43.6
N 11	136 25.4	358 20.4	35.6	4 21.2	58.2	341 32.5	21.5	259 34.4	00.5			
D 12	151 27.9	13 24.0	N 7 36.0	19 22.0	N18 57.8	356 34.4	N11 21.3	274 36.8	S18 00.6	Alphecca	126 09.8	N26 40.1
A 13	166 30.3	28 27.7	36.4	34 22.8	57.4	11 36.4	21.1	289 39.2	00.6	Alpheratz	357 41.6	N29 10.6
Y 14	181 32.8	43 31.4	36.8	49 23.7	57.0	26 38.3	20.9	304 41.6	00.6	Altair	62 06.5	N 8 54.9
15	196 35.3	58 35.1	. . 37.2	64 24.5	. . 56.6	41 40.3	. . 20.7	319 43.9	. . 00.6	Ankaa	353 14.0	S42 13.1
16	211 37.7	73 38.7	37.6	79 25.3	56.2	56 42.2	20.5	334 46.3	00.7	Antares	112 24.4	S26 27.8
17	226 40.2	88 42.4	38.0	94 26.1	55.8	71 44.2	20.3	349 48.7	00.7			
18	241 42.7	103 46.1	N 7 38.4	109 27.0	N18 55.3	86 46.1	N11 20.1	4 51.1	S18 00.7	Arcturus	145 54.5	N19 06.4
19	256 45.1	118 49.7	38.9	124 27.8	54.9	101 48.1	20.0	19 53.5	00.8	Atria	107 24.6	S69 03.4
20	271 47.6	133 53.4	39.3	139 28.6	54.5	116 50.0	19.8	34 55.8	00.8	Avior	234 17.9	S59 33.6
21	286 50.0	148 57.0	. . 39.7	154 29.5	. . 54.1	131 52.0	. . 19.6	49 58.2	. . 00.8	Bellatrix	278 30.5	N 6 21.7
22	301 52.5	164 00.7	40.1	169 30.3	53.7	146 53.9	19.4	65 00.6	00.8	Betelgeuse	270 59.8	N 7 24.5
23	316 55.0	179 04.4	40.5	184 31.1	53.3	161 55.9	19.2	80 03.0	00.9			
24 00	331 57.4	194 08.0	N 7 40.9	199 32.0	N18 52.8	176 57.8	N11 19.0	95 05.3	S18 00.9	Canopus	263 55.8	S52 42.2
01	346 59.9	209 11.6	41.3	214 32.8	52.4	191 59.7	18.8	110 07.7	00.9	Capella	280 32.4	N46 00.5
02	2 02.4	224 15.3	41.7	229 33.6	52.0	207 01.7	18.6	125 10.1	01.0	Deneb	49 30.0	N45 20.5
03	17 04.8	239 18.9	. . 42.1	244 34.4	. . 51.6	222 03.6	. . 18.4	140 12.5	. . 01.0	Denebola	182 32.5	N14 29.2
04	32 07.3	254 22.6	42.6	259 35.3	51.2	237 05.6	18.2	155 14.8	01.0	Diphda	348 54.2	S17 53.9
05	47 09.8	269 26.2	43.0	274 36.1	50.8	252 07.5	18.0	170 17.2	01.0			
06	62 12.2	284 29.8	N 7 43.4	289 36.9	N18 50.3	267 09.5	N11 17.8	185 19.6	S18 01.1	Dubhe	193 50.7	N61 40.1
07	77 14.7	299 33.4	43.8	304 37.8	49.9	282 11.4	17.6	200 22.0	01.1	Elnath	278 10.9	N28 37.0
08	92 17.1	314 37.1	44.2	319 38.6	49.5	297 13.4	17.4	215 24.3	01.1	Eltanin	90 45.2	N51 29.7
M 09	107 19.6	329 40.7	. . 44.6	334 39.4	. . 49.1	312 15.3	. . 17.2	230 26.7	. . 01.2	Enif	33 45.3	N 9 57.1
O 10	122 22.1	344 44.3	45.0	349 40.3	48.7	327 17.3	17.0	245 29.1	01.2	Fomalhaut	15 22.0	S29 32.1
N 11	137 24.5	359 47.9	45.5	4 41.1	48.2	342 19.2	16.8	260 31.5	01.2			
D 12	152 27.0	14 51.5	N 7 45.9	19 41.9	N18 47.8	357 21.2	N11 16.7	275 33.9	S18 01.2	Gacrux	171 59.6	S57 12.1
A 13	167 29.5	29 55.1	46.3	34 42.8	47.4	12 23.1	16.5	290 36.2	01.3	Gienah	175 51.0	S17 37.7
Y 14	182 31.9	44 58.7	46.7	49 43.6	47.0	27 25.0	16.3	305 38.6	01.3	Hadar	148 45.9	S60 27.0
15	197 34.4	60 02.3	. . 47.1	64 44.4	. . 46.6	42 27.0	. . 16.1	320 41.0	. . 01.3	Hamal	327 58.9	N23 32.1
16	212 36.9	75 05.9	47.5	79 45.3	46.2	57 28.9	15.9	335 43.3	01.4	Kaus Aust.	83 41.6	S34 22.4
17	227 39.3	90 09.5	48.0	94 46.1	45.7	72 30.9	15.7	350 45.7	01.4			
18	242 41.8	105 13.1	N 7 48.4	109 46.9	N18 45.3	87 32.8	N11 15.5	5 48.1	S18 01.4	Kochab	137 20.6	N74 05.9
19	257 44.3	120 16.7	48.8	124 47.8	44.9	102 34.8	15.3	20 50.5	01.4	Markab	13 36.5	N15 17.5
20	272 46.7	135 20.2	49.2	139 48.6	44.5	117 36.7	15.1	35 52.8	01.5	Menkar	314 13.4	N 4 09.0
21	287 49.2	150 23.8	. . 49.6	154 49.4	. . 44.1	132 38.7	. . 14.9	50 55.2	. . 01.5	Menkent	148 05.9	S36 26.8
22	302 51.6	165 27.4	50.1	169 50.3	43.6	147 40.6	14.7	65 57.6	01.5	Miaplacidus	221 40.1	S69 46.9
23	317 54.1	180 31.0	50.5	184 51.1	43.2	162 42.6	14.5	81 00.0	01.6			
25 00	332 56.6	195 34.5	N 7 50.9	199 51.9	N18 42.8	177 44.5	N11 14.3	96 02.3	S18 01.6	Mirfak	308 38.1	N49 54.7
01	347 59.0	210 38.1	51.3	214 52.8	42.4	192 46.5	14.1	111 04.7	01.6	Nunki	75 56.2	S26 16.4
02	3 01.5	225 41.7	51.7	229 53.6	41.9	207 48.4	13.9	126 07.1	01.7	Peacock	53 16.4	S56 40.9
03	18 04.0	240 45.2	. . 52.1	244 54.4	. . 41.5	222 50.3	. . 13.7	141 09.5	. . 01.7	Pollux	243 26.2	N27 59.1
04	33 06.4	255 48.8	52.6	259 55.3	41.1	237 52.3	13.5	156 11.8	01.7	Procyon	244 58.4	N 5 11.0
05	48 08.9	270 52.3	53.0	274 56.1	40.7	252 54.2	13.4	171 14.2	01.7			
06	63 11.4	285 55.9	N 7 53.4	289 57.0	N18 40.3	267 56.2	N11 13.2	186 16.6	S18 01.8	Rasalhague	96 04.9	N12 33.3
07	78 13.8	300 59.4	53.8	304 57.8	39.8	282 58.1	13.0	201 18.9	01.8	Regulus	207 42.3	N11 53.5
T 08	93 16.3	316 03.0	54.3	319 58.6	39.4	298 00.1	12.8	216 21.3	01.8	Rigel	281 10.7	S 8 11.1
U 09	108 18.8	331 06.5	. . 54.7	334 59.5	. . 39.0	313 02.0	. . 12.6	231 23.7	. . 01.9	Rigil Kent.	139 49.8	S60 54.0
E 10	123 21.2	346 10.0	55.1	350 00.3	38.6	328 04.0	12.4	246 26.1	01.9	Sabik	102 10.7	S15 44.4
S 11	138 23.7	1 13.6	55.5	5 01.1	38.1	343 05.9	12.2	261 28.4	01.9			
D 12	153 26.1	16 17.1	N 7 55.9	20 02.0	N18 37.7	358 07.9	N11 12.0	276 30.8	S18 01.9	Schedar	349 38.2	N56 37.2
A 13	168 28.6	31 20.6	56.4	35 02.8	37.3	13 09.8	11.8	291 33.2	02.0	Shaula	96 19.7	S37 06.8
Y 14	183 31.1	46 24.1	56.8	50 03.6	36.9	28 11.8	11.6	306 35.5	02.0	Sirius	258 32.6	S16 44.3
15	198 33.5	61 27.6	. . 57.2	65 04.5	. . 36.4	43 13.7	. . 11.4	321 37.9	. . 02.0	Spica	158 29.9	S11 14.4
16	213 36.0	76 31.2	57.6	80 05.3	36.0	58 15.6	11.2	336 40.3	02.1	Suhail	222 51.7	S43 29.8
17	228 38.5	91 34.7	58.0	95 06.2	35.6	73 17.6	11.0	351 42.7	02.1			
18	243 40.9	106 38.2	N 7 58.5	110 07.0	N18 35.2	88 19.5	N11 10.8	6 45.0	S18 02.1	Vega	80 37.7	N38 48.3
19	258 43.4	121 41.7	58.9	125 07.8	34.7	103 21.5	10.6	21 47.4	02.2	Zuben'ubi	137 03.8	S16 06.2
20	273 45.9	136 45.2	59.3	140 08.7	34.3	118 23.4	10.4	36 49.8	02.2		SHA	Mer.Pass.
21	288 48.3	151 48.7	7 59.7	155 09.5	. . 33.9	133 25.4	. . 10.2	51 52.1	. . 02.2	Venus	222 10.6	11 01
22	301 50.8	166 52.2	8 00.2	170 10.4	33.5	148 27.3	10.0	66 54.5	02.2	Mars	227 34.5	10 41
23	318 53.3	181 55.6	N 8 00.6	185 11.2	33.0	163 29.3	09.9	81 56.9	02.3	Jupiter	205 00.4	12 11
Mer.Pass. 1 51.9		v 3.6 d 0.4		v 0.8 d 0.4		v 1.9 d 0.2		v 2.4 d 0.0		Saturn	123 07.9	17 37

UT	SUN GHA	SUN Dec	MOON GHA	v	MOON Dec	d	HP
23 00	179 17.5	N11 37.2	90 23.9	11.3	S16 02.7	4.7	55.8
01	194 17.7	36.3	104 54.2	11.2	16 07.4	4.6	55.8
02	209 17.8	35.5	119 24.4	11.2	16 12.0	4.6	55.8
03	224 18.0	.. 34.6	133 54.6	11.1	16 16.6	4.5	55.8
04	239 18.2	33.8	148 24.7	11.0	16 21.1	4.3	55.9
05	254 18.3	33.0	162 54.7	11.0	16 25.4	4.4	55.9
06	269 18.5	N11 32.1	177 24.7	10.9	S16 29.8	4.2	55.9
07	284 18.6	31.3	191 54.6	10.9	16 34.0	4.1	56.0
S 08	299 18.8	30.4	206 24.5	10.8	16 38.1	4.1	56.0
U 09	314 19.0	.. 29.6	220 54.3	10.7	16 42.2	4.0	56.0
N 10	329 19.1	28.7	235 24.0	10.7	16 46.2	3.9	56.1
D 11	344 19.3	27.9	249 53.7	10.6	16 50.1	3.9	56.1
A 12	359 19.5	N11 27.0	264 23.3	10.6	S16 54.0	3.7	56.1
Y 13	14 19.6	26.2	278 52.9	10.5	16 57.7	3.7	56.2
14	29 19.8	25.3	293 22.4	10.4	17 01.4	3.6	56.2
15	44 19.9	.. 24.5	307 51.8	10.4	17 05.0	3.5	56.2
16	59 20.1	23.6	322 21.2	10.3	17 08.5	3.4	56.3
17	74 20.3	22.8	336 50.5	10.3	17 11.9	3.3	56.3
18	89 20.4	N11 21.9	351 19.8	10.2	S17 15.2	3.2	56.3
19	104 20.6	21.1	5 49.0	10.1	17 18.4	3.2	56.4
20	119 20.8	20.3	20 18.1	10.0	17 21.6	3.0	56.4
21	134 20.9	.. 19.4	34 47.1	10.1	17 24.6	3.0	56.4
22	149 21.1	18.6	49 16.2	9.9	17 27.6	2.9	56.5
23	164 21.3	17.7	63 45.1	9.9	17 30.5	2.8	56.5
24 00	179 21.4	N11 16.9	78 14.0	9.8	S17 33.3	2.7	56.5
01	194 21.6	16.0	92 42.8	9.7	17 36.0	2.6	56.6
02	209 21.8	15.1	107 11.6	9.7	17 38.6	2.5	56.6
03	224 21.9	.. 14.3	121 40.3	9.6	17 41.1	2.4	56.6
04	239 22.1	13.4	136 08.9	9.6	17 43.5	2.4	56.7
05	254 22.3	12.6	150 37.5	9.5	17 45.9	2.2	56.7
06	269 22.4	N11 11.7	165 06.0	9.5	S17 48.1	2.1	56.8
07	284 22.6	10.9	179 34.5	9.4	17 50.2	2.1	56.8
M 08	299 22.8	10.0	194 02.9	9.4	17 52.3	1.9	56.8
O 09	314 22.9	.. 09.2	208 31.3	9.2	17 54.2	1.9	56.9
N 10	329 23.1	08.3	222 59.5	9.3	17 56.1	1.7	56.9
D 11	344 23.3	07.5	237 27.8	9.1	17 57.8	1.7	56.9
A 12	359 23.4	N11 06.6	251 55.9	9.2	S17 59.5	1.6	57.0
Y 13	14 23.6	05.8	266 24.1	9.0	18 01.1	1.4	57.0
14	29 23.8	04.9	280 52.1	9.0	18 02.5	1.4	57.1
15	44 23.9	.. 04.1	295 20.1	9.0	18 03.9	1.3	57.1
16	59 24.1	03.2	309 48.1	8.9	18 05.2	1.1	57.1
17	74 24.3	02.3	324 16.0	8.8	18 06.3	1.1	57.2
18	89 24.4	N11 01.5	338 43.8	8.8	S18 07.4	0.9	57.2
19	104 24.6	11 00.6	353 11.6	8.7	18 08.3	0.9	57.2
20	119 24.8	10 59.8	7 39.3	8.7	18 09.2	0.7	57.3
21	134 25.0	.. 58.9	22 07.0	8.6	18 09.9	0.7	57.3
22	149 25.1	58.1	36 34.6	8.6	18 10.6	0.5	57.4
23	164 25.3	57.2	51 02.2	8.5	18 11.1	0.5	57.4
25 00	179 25.5	N10 56.3	65 29.7	8.5	S18 11.6	0.3	57.4
01	194 25.6	55.5	79 57.2	8.4	18 11.9	0.3	57.5
02	209 25.8	54.6	94 24.6	8.3	18 12.2	0.1	57.5
03	224 26.0	.. 53.8	108 51.9	8.3	18 12.3	0.0	57.6
04	239 26.1	52.9	123 19.2	8.3	18 12.3	0.1	57.6
05	254 26.3	52.1	137 46.5	8.2	18 12.2	0.2	57.6
06	269 26.5	N10 51.2	152 13.7	8.2	S18 12.0	0.3	57.7
07	284 26.7	50.3	166 40.9	8.1	18 11.7	0.4	57.7
T 08	299 26.8	49.5	181 08.0	8.0	18 11.3	0.5	57.8
U 09	314 27.0	.. 48.6	195 35.0	8.1	18 10.8	0.6	57.8
E 10	329 27.2	47.7	210 02.1	7.9	18 10.2	0.8	57.8
S 11	344 27.3	46.9	224 29.0	8.0	18 09.4	0.8	57.9
D 12	359 27.5	N10 46.0	238 56.0	7.8	S18 08.6	1.0	57.9
A 13	14 27.7	45.2	253 22.8	7.9	18 07.6	1.1	58.0
Y 14	29 27.9	44.3	267 49.7	7.8	18 06.5	1.1	58.0
15	44 28.0	.. 43.4	282 16.5	7.7	18 05.4	1.3	58.0
16	59 28.2	42.6	296 43.2	7.7	18 04.1	1.4	58.1
17	74 28.4	41.7	311 09.9	7.7	18 02.7	1.5	58.1
18	89 28.5	N10 40.9	325 36.6	7.6	S18 01.2	1.7	58.2
19	104 28.7	40.0	340 03.2	7.6	17 59.5	1.7	58.2
20	119 28.9	39.1	354 29.8	7.5	17 57.8	1.8	58.2
21	134 29.1	.. 38.3	8 56.3	7.5	17 56.0	2.0	58.3
22	149 29.2	37.4	23 22.8	7.5	17 54.0	2.1	58.3
23	164 29.4	36.5	37 49.3	7.4	S17 51.9	2.2	58.3
SD	15.8	d 0.9	SD 15.3		15.5		15.8

Twilight / Moonrise

Lat.	Naut.	Civil	Sunrise	23	24	25	26
N 72	////	01 09	03 18	17 29	■■■	■■■	19 51
N 70	////	02 06	03 38	16 26	17 44	18 36	19 01
68	////	02 39	03 54	15 51	17 02	17 55	18 29
66	01 00	03 02	04 07	15 26	16 33	17 26	18 05
64	01 50	03 20	04 18	15 06	16 11	17 05	17 47
62	02 20	03 35	04 27	14 51	15 54	16 48	17 31
60	02 42	03 47	04 35	14 37	15 39	16 33	17 18
N 58	02 59	03 58	04 42	14 26	15 27	16 21	17 07
56	03 13	04 07	04 48	14 16	15 16	16 10	16 58
54	03 25	04 14	04 53	14 07	15 07	16 01	16 49
52	03 36	04 21	04 58	14 00	14 58	15 53	16 42
50	03 45	04 28	05 02	13 53	14 51	15 45	16 35
45	04 03	04 41	05 12	13 38	14 35	15 29	16 20
N 40	04 17	04 51	05 20	13 25	14 21	15 16	16 08
35	04 29	05 00	05 26	13 15	14 10	15 05	15 57
30	04 38	05 08	05 32	13 06	14 01	14 55	15 48
20	04 53	05 20	05 42	12 50	13 44	14 38	15 32
N 10	05 05	05 30	05 51	12 36	13 29	14 23	15 19
0	05 14	05 38	05 59	12 24	13 15	14 10	15 06
S 10	05 21	05 46	06 07	12 11	13 02	13 56	14 53
20	05 27	05 53	06 15	11 57	12 47	13 41	14 39
30	05 33	06 01	06 25	11 42	12 31	13 24	14 23
35	05 35	06 04	06 30	11 33	12 21	13 15	14 14
40	05 37	06 09	06 36	11 23	12 10	13 04	14 04
45	05 39	06 13	06 43	11 11	11 57	12 51	13 51
S 50	05 41	06 19	06 52	10 57	11 41	12 35	13 36
52	05 42	06 21	06 55	10 50	11 34	12 27	13 29
54	05 42	06 23	07 00	10 42	11 26	12 19	13 22
56	05 43	06 26	07 04	10 34	11 17	12 10	13 13
58	05 43	06 29	07 10	10 25	11 06	11 59	13 03
S 60	05 44	06 32	07 15	10 14	10 55	11 47	12 52

Twilight / Moonset

Lat.	Sunset	Civil	Naut.	23	24	25	26
N 72	20 43	22 43	////	19 36	■■■	■■■	22 56
N 70	20 23	21 53	////	20 40	21 11	22 13	23 46
68	20 08	21 22	////	21 15	21 54	22 54	24 17
66	19 55	20 59	22 54	21 41	22 22	23 22	24 40
64	19 45	20 42	22 09	22 01	22 44	23 43	24 58
62	19 36	20 28	21 41	22 17	23 02	24 00	00 00
60	19 28	20 16	21 20	22 31	23 16	24 15	00 15
N 58	19 22	20 06	21 03	22 42	23 29	24 27	00 27
56	19 16	19 57	20 50	22 52	23 40	24 37	00 37
54	19 11	19 49	20 38	23 01	23 49	24 47	00 47
52	19 06	19 42	20 28	23 09	23 57	24 55	00 55
50	19 01	19 36	20 19	23 16	24 05	00 05	01 02
45	18 52	19 23	20 01	23 32	24 21	00 21	01 18
N 40	18 44	19 13	19 47	23 44	24 34	00 34	01 31
35	18 38	19 04	19 35	23 55	24 46	00 46	01 42
30	18 32	18 57	19 26	24 05	00 05	00 56	01 52
20	18 22	18 45	19 11	24 21	00 21	01 13	02 08
N 10	18 14	18 35	19 00	24 35	00 35	01 27	02 23
0	18 06	18 27	18 51	24 48	00 48	01 41	02 36
S 10	17 58	18 19	18 44	00 10	01 02	01 55	02 50
20	17 50	18 12	18 38	00 23	01 16	02 10	03 04
30	17 40	18 05	18 33	00 37	01 32	02 26	03 20
35	17 35	18 01	18 30	00 46	01 41	02 36	03 30
40	17 29	17 57	18 28	00 56	01 52	02 47	03 40
45	17 22	17 52	18 26	01 07	02 05	03 01	03 53
S 50	17 14	17 47	18 25	01 21	02 20	03 17	04 08
52	17 10	17 45	18 24	01 28	02 28	03 24	04 16
54	17 06	17 42	18 24	01 35	02 36	03 32	04 24
56	17 01	17 40	18 23	01 43	02 45	03 42	04 32
58	16 56	17 37	18 23	01 52	02 55	03 52	04 43
S 60	16 51	17 34	18 22	02 02	03 06	04 04	04 54

SUN / MOON

Day	Eqn. of Time 00h	Eqn. of Time 12h	Mer. Pass.	Mer. Pass. Upper	Mer. Pass. Lower	Age	Phase
d	m s	m s	h m	h m	h m	d	%
23	02 50	02 43	12 03	18 36	06 11	09	57
24	02 35	02 27	12 02	19 28	07 02	10	67
25	02 19	02 10	12 02	20 23	07 55	11	77

UT	ARIES GHA	VENUS −4.4 GHA	Dec	MARS +1.8 GHA	Dec	JUPITER −1.7 GHA	Dec	SATURN +0.5 GHA	Dec	STARS Name	SHA	Dec
d h	° ′	° ′	° ′	° ′	° ′	° ′	° ′	° ′	° ′		° ′	° ′
26 00	333 55.7	196 59.1	N 8 01.0	200 12.0	N18 32.6	178 31.2	N11 09.7	96 59.2	S18 02.3	Acamar	315 17.1	S40 14.4
01	348 58.2	212 02.6	01.4	215 12.9	32.2	193 33.2	09.5	112 01.6	02.3	Achernar	335 25.4	S57 09.2
02	4 00.6	227 06.1	01.9	230 13.7	31.8	208 35.1	09.3	127 04.0	02.4	Acrux	173 08.0	S63 11.2
03	19 03.1	242 09.6 ..	02.3	245 14.6 ..	31.3	223 37.1 ..	09.1	142 06.4 ..	02.4	Adhara	255 11.6	S28 59.6
04	34 05.6	257 13.0	02.7	260 15.4	30.9	238 39.0	08.9	157 08.7	02.4	Aldebaran	290 47.7	N16 32.3
05	49 08.0	272 16.5	03.1	275 16.2	30.5	253 40.9	08.7	172 11.1	02.5			
06	64 10.5	287 20.0	N 8 03.6	290 17.1	N18 30.0	268 42.9	N11 08.5	187 13.5	S18 02.5	Alioth	166 19.9	N55 52.8
W 07	79 13.0	302 23.4	04.0	305 17.9	29.6	283 44.8	08.3	202 15.8	02.5	Alkaid	152 58.1	N49 14.5
E 08	94 15.4	317 26.9	04.4	320 18.8	29.2	298 46.8	08.1	217 18.2	02.6	Al Na'ir	27 41.5	S46 52.9
D 09	109 17.9	332 30.3 ..	04.8	335 19.6 ..	28.8	313 48.7 ..	07.9	232 20.6 ..	02.6	Alnilam	275 45.0	S 1 11.6
N 10	124 20.4	347 33.8	05.3	350 20.4	28.3	328 50.7	07.7	247 22.9	02.6	Alphard	217 54.9	S 8 43.6
E 11	139 22.8	2 37.2	05.7	5 21.3	27.9	343 52.6	07.5	262 25.3	02.6			
S 12	154 25.3	17 40.7	N 8 06.1	20 22.1	N18 27.5	358 54.6	N11 07.3	277 27.7	S18 02.7	Alphecca	126 09.8	N26 40.1
D 13	169 27.7	32 44.1	06.5	35 23.0	27.0	13 56.5	07.1	292 30.0	02.7	Alpheratz	357 41.6	N29 10.6
A 14	184 30.2	47 47.5	07.0	50 23.8	26.6	28 58.5	06.9	307 32.4	02.7	Altair	62 06.5	N 8 54.9
Y 15	199 32.7	62 51.0 ..	07.4	65 24.6 ..	26.2	44 00.4 ..	06.7	322 34.8 ..	02.8	Ankaa	353 13.9	S42 13.1
16	214 35.1	77 54.4	07.8	80 25.5	25.7	59 02.4	06.5	337 37.1	02.8	Antares	112 24.4	S26 27.8
17	229 37.6	92 57.8	08.2	95 26.3	25.3	74 04.3	06.4	352 39.5	02.8			
18	244 40.1	108 01.2	N 8 08.7	110 27.2	N18 24.9	89 06.3	N11 06.2	7 41.9	S18 02.9	Arcturus	145 54.5	N19 06.4
19	259 42.5	123 04.6	09.1	125 28.0	24.5	104 08.2	06.0	22 44.2	02.9	Atria	107 24.6	S69 03.4
20	274 45.0	138 08.1	09.5	140 28.9	24.0	119 10.1	05.8	37 46.6	02.9	Avior	234 17.9	S59 33.6
21	289 47.5	153 11.5 ..	09.9	155 29.7 ..	23.6	134 12.1 ..	05.6	52 49.0 ..	03.0	Bellatrix	278 30.5	N 6 21.7
22	304 49.9	168 14.9	10.4	170 30.5	23.2	149 14.0	05.4	67 51.3	03.0	Betelgeuse	270 59.8	N 7 24.5
23	319 52.4	183 18.3	10.8	185 31.4	22.7	164 16.0	05.2	82 53.7	03.0			
27 00	334 54.9	198 21.7	N 8 11.2	200 32.2	N18 22.3	179 17.9	N11 05.0	97 56.1	S18 03.0	Canopus	263 55.8	S52 42.1
01	349 57.3	213 25.1	11.6	215 33.1	21.9	194 19.9	04.8	112 58.4	03.1	Capella	280 32.3	N46 00.5
02	4 59.8	228 28.4	12.1	230 33.9	21.4	209 21.8	04.6	128 00.8	03.1	Deneb	49 30.0	N45 20.5
03	20 02.2	243 31.8 ..	12.5	245 34.8 ..	21.0	224 23.8 ..	04.4	143 03.2 ..	03.1	Denebola	182 32.5	N14 29.2
04	35 04.7	258 35.2	12.9	260 35.6	20.6	239 25.7	04.2	158 05.5	03.2	Diphda	348 54.1	S17 53.9
05	50 07.2	273 38.6	13.3	275 36.5	20.1	254 27.7	04.0	173 07.9	03.2			
06	65 09.6	288 42.0	N 8 13.8	290 37.3	N18 19.7	269 29.6	N11 03.8	188 10.2	S18 03.2	Dubhe	193 50.7	N61 40.1
T 07	80 12.1	303 45.3	14.2	305 38.1	19.3	284 31.6	03.6	203 12.6	03.3	Elnath	278 10.8	N28 37.0
H 08	95 14.6	318 48.7	14.6	320 39.0	18.8	299 33.5	03.4	218 15.0	03.3	Eltanin	90 45.2	N51 29.7
U 09	110 17.0	333 52.1 ..	15.0	335 39.8 ..	18.4	314 35.5 ..	03.2	233 17.3 ..	03.3	Enif	33 45.3	N 9 57.1
R 10	125 19.5	348 55.4	15.5	350 40.7	18.0	329 37.4	03.0	248 19.7	03.4	Fomalhaut	15 22.0	S29 32.2
S 11	140 22.0	3 58.8	15.9	5 41.5	17.5	344 39.4	02.8	263 22.1	03.4			
D 12	155 24.4	19 02.1	N 8 16.3	20 42.4	N18 17.1	359 41.3	N11 02.6	278 24.4	S18 03.4	Gacrux	171 59.6	S57 12.1
A 13	170 26.9	34 05.5	16.7	35 43.2	16.7	14 43.2	02.5	293 26.8	03.4	Gienah	175 51.0	S17 37.7
Y 14	185 29.4	49 08.8	17.2	50 44.1	16.2	29 45.2	02.3	308 29.2	03.5	Hadar	148 46.0	S60 27.0
15	200 31.8	64 12.2 ..	17.6	65 44.9 ..	15.8	44 47.1 ..	02.1	323 31.5 ..	03.5	Hamal	327 58.8	N23 32.1
16	215 34.3	79 15.5	18.0	80 45.8	15.4	59 49.1	01.9	338 33.9	03.5	Kaus Aust.	83 41.6	S34 22.4
17	230 36.7	94 18.8	18.4	95 46.6	14.9	74 51.0	01.7	353 36.2	03.6			
18	245 39.2	109 22.1	N 8 18.9	110 47.5	N18 14.5	89 53.0	N11 01.5	8 38.6	S18 03.6	Kochab	137 20.7	N74 05.9
19	260 41.7	124 25.5	19.3	125 48.3	14.1	104 54.9	01.3	23 41.0	03.6	Markab	13 36.5	N15 17.5
20	275 44.1	139 28.8	19.7	140 49.1	13.6	119 56.9	01.1	38 43.3	03.7	Menkar	314 13.4	N 4 09.0
21	290 46.6	154 32.1 ..	20.2	155 50.0 ..	13.2	134 58.8 ..	00.9	53 45.7 ..	03.7	Menkent	148 05.9	S36 26.8
22	305 49.1	169 35.4	20.6	170 50.8	12.8	150 00.8	00.7	68 48.1	03.7	Miaplacidus	221 40.1	S69 46.9
23	320 51.5	184 38.7	21.0	185 51.7	12.3	165 02.7	00.5	83 50.4	03.8			
28 00	335 54.0	199 42.0	N 8 21.4	200 52.5	N18 11.9	180 04.7	N11 00.3	98 52.8	S18 03.8	Mirfak	308 38.0	N49 54.7
01	350 56.5	214 45.3	21.9	215 53.4	11.4	195 06.6	11 00.1	113 55.1	03.8	Nunki	75 56.2	S26 16.4
02	5 58.9	229 48.6	22.3	230 54.2	11.0	210 08.6	10 59.9	128 57.5	03.9	Peacock	53 16.4	S56 40.9
03	21 01.4	244 51.9 ..	22.7	245 55.1 ..	10.6	225 10.5 ..	59.7	143 59.9 ..	03.9	Pollux	243 26.2	N27 59.1
04	36 03.8	259 55.2	23.1	260 55.9	10.1	240 12.5	59.5	159 02.2	03.9	Procyon	244 58.4	N 5 11.0
05	51 06.3	274 58.5	23.6	275 56.8	09.7	255 14.4	59.3	174 04.6	04.0			
06	66 08.8	290 01.8	N 8 24.0	290 57.6	N18 09.3	270 16.3	N10 59.1	189 06.9	S18 04.0	Rasalhague	96 04.9	N12 33.3
F 07	81 11.2	305 05.0	24.4	305 58.5	08.8	285 18.3	58.9	204 09.3	04.0	Regulus	207 42.3	N11 53.4
R 08	96 13.7	320 08.3	24.8	320 59.3	08.4	300 20.2	58.7	219 11.7	04.1	Rigel	281 10.7	S 8 11.1
I 09	111 16.2	335 11.6 ..	25.3	336 00.2 ..	07.9	315 22.2 ..	58.6	234 14.0 ..	04.1	Rigil Kent.	139 49.8	S60 54.0
D 10	126 18.6	350 14.9	25.7	351 01.0	07.5	330 24.1	58.4	249 16.4	04.1	Sabik	102 10.7	S15 44.4
A 11	141 21.1	5 18.1	26.1	6 01.9	07.1	345 26.1	58.2	264 18.7	04.1			
Y 12	156 23.6	20 21.4	N 8 26.5	21 02.7	N18 06.6	0 28.0	N10 58.0	279 21.1	S18 04.2	Schedar	349 38.2	N56 37.3
13	171 26.0	35 24.6	27.0	36 03.6	06.2	15 30.0	57.8	294 23.5	04.2	Shaula	96 19.7	S37 06.8
14	186 28.5	50 27.9	27.4	51 04.4	05.7	30 31.9	57.6	309 25.8	04.2	Sirius	258 32.6	S16 44.3
15	201 31.0	65 31.1 ..	27.8	66 05.3 ..	05.3	45 33.9 ..	57.4	324 28.2 ..	04.3	Spica	158 29.9	S11 14.4
16	216 33.4	80 34.4	28.2	81 06.1	04.9	60 35.8	57.2	339 30.5	04.3	Suhail	222 51.7	S43 29.7
17	231 35.9	95 37.6	28.6	96 07.0	04.4	75 37.8	57.0	354 32.9	04.3			
18	246 38.3	110 40.8	N 8 29.1	111 07.8	N18 04.0	90 39.7	N10 56.8	9 35.3	S18 04.4	Vega	80 37.7	N38 48.3
19	261 40.8	125 44.1	29.5	126 08.7	03.5	105 41.7	56.6	24 37.6	04.4	Zuben'ubi	137 03.8	S16 06.2
20	276 43.3	140 47.3	29.9	141 09.5	03.1	120 43.6	56.4	39 40.0	04.4		SHA	Mer. Pass.
21	291 45.7	155 50.5 ..	30.3	156 10.4 ..	02.7	135 45.6 ..	56.2	54 42.3 ..	04.5		° ′	h m
22	306 48.2	170 53.7	30.8	171 11.2	02.2	150 47.5	56.0	69 44.7	04.5	Venus	223 26.8	10 44
23	321 50.7	185 56.9	31.2	186 12.1	01.8	165 49.4	55.8	84 47.0	04.5	Mars	225 37.4	10 37
	h m									Jupiter	204 23.1	12 01
Mer. Pass. 1 40.1	v 3.3	d 0.4		v 0.8	d 0.4	v 1.9	d 0.2	v 2.4	d 0.0	Saturn	123 01.2	17 26

UT	SUN GHA	Dec	MOON GHA	v	Dec	d	HP
d h	° ′	° ′	° ′	′	° ′	′	′
26 00	179 29.6	N10 35.7	52 15.7	7.4	S17 49.7	2.3	58.4
01	194 29.8	34.8	66 42.1	7.4	17 47.4	2.4	58.4
02	209 29.9	33.9	81 08.5	7.3	17 45.0	2.5	58.5
03	224 30.1	.. 33.1	95 34.8	7.3	17 42.5	2.6	58.5
04	239 30.3	32.2	110 01.1	7.2	17 39.9	2.8	58.5
05	254 30.5	31.3	124 27.3	7.3	17 37.1	2.9	58.6
W 06	269 30.6	N10 30.5	138 53.6	7.1	S17 34.2	3.0	58.6
E 07	284 30.8	29.6	153 19.7	7.2	17 31.2	3.0	58.7
D 08	299 31.0	28.7	167 45.9	7.1	17 28.2	3.3	58.7
N 09	314 31.2	.. 27.9	182 12.0	7.1	17 24.9	3.3	58.7
E 10	329 31.3	27.0	196 38.1	7.1	17 21.6	3.4	58.8
S 11	344 31.5	26.1	211 04.2	7.0	17 18.2	3.6	58.8
D 12	359 31.7	N10 25.3	225 30.2	7.1	S17 14.6	3.6	58.9
A 13	14 31.9	24.4	239 56.3	6.9	17 11.0	3.8	58.9
Y 14	29 32.1	23.5	254 22.2	7.0	17 07.2	3.9	58.9
15	44 32.2	.. 22.7	268 48.2	6.9	17 03.3	4.0	59.0
16	59 32.4	21.8	283 14.1	6.9	16 59.3	4.2	59.0
17	74 32.6	20.9	297 40.0	6.9	16 55.1	4.2	59.1
18	89 32.8	N10 20.1	312 05.9	6.9	S16 50.9	4.4	59.1
19	104 32.9	19.2	326 31.8	6.9	16 46.5	4.4	59.1
20	119 33.1	18.3	340 57.7	6.8	16 42.1	4.6	59.2
21	134 33.3	.. 17.4	355 23.5	6.8	16 37.5	4.7	59.2
22	149 33.5	16.6	9 49.3	6.8	16 32.8	4.8	59.2
23	164 33.7	15.7	24 15.1	6.7	16 28.0	4.9	59.3
27 00	179 33.8	N10 14.8	38 40.8	6.8	S16 23.1	5.0	59.3
01	194 34.0	14.0	53 06.6	6.7	16 18.1	5.2	59.3
02	209 34.2	13.1	67 32.3	6.7	16 12.9	5.2	59.4
03	224 34.4	.. 12.2	81 58.0	6.7	16 07.7	5.4	59.4
04	239 34.6	11.3	96 23.7	6.7	16 02.3	5.5	59.5
05	254 34.7	10.5	110 49.4	6.7	15 56.8	5.6	59.5
T 06	269 34.9	N10 09.6	125 15.1	6.7	S15 51.2	5.7	59.5
H 07	284 35.1	08.7	139 40.8	6.6	15 45.5	5.8	59.6
U 08	299 35.3	07.8	154 06.4	6.7	15 39.7	5.9	59.6
R 09	314 35.5	.. 07.0	168 32.1	6.6	15 33.8	6.0	59.6
S 10	329 35.6	06.1	182 57.7	6.6	15 27.8	6.2	59.7
D 11	344 35.8	05.2	197 23.3	6.6	15 21.6	6.2	59.7
A 12	359 36.0	N10 04.3	211 48.9	6.6	S15 15.4	6.4	59.8
Y 13	14 36.2	03.5	226 14.5	6.6	15 09.0	6.4	59.8
14	29 36.4	02.6	240 40.1	6.6	15 02.6	6.6	59.8
15	44 36.5	.. 01.7	255 05.7	6.6	14 56.0	6.7	59.9
16	59 36.7	00.8	269 31.3	6.6	14 49.3	6.8	59.9
17	74 36.9	10 00.0	283 56.9	6.5	14 42.5	6.8	59.9
18	89 37.1	N 9 59.1	298 22.4	6.6	S14 35.7	7.0	60.0
19	104 37.3	58.2	312 48.0	6.6	14 28.7	7.1	60.0
20	119 37.4	57.3	327 13.6	6.5	14 21.6	7.2	60.0
21	134 37.6	.. 56.5	341 39.1	6.6	14 14.4	7.3	60.1
22	149 37.8	55.6	356 04.7	6.5	14 07.1	7.4	60.1
23	164 38.0	54.7	10 30.2	6.6	13 59.7	7.5	60.1
28 00	179 38.2	N 9 53.8	24 55.8	6.6	S13 52.2	7.6	60.1
01	194 38.4	52.9	39 21.4	6.5	13 44.6	7.7	60.2
02	209 38.5	52.1	53 46.9	6.6	13 36.9	7.8	60.2
03	224 38.7	.. 51.2	68 12.5	6.5	13 29.1	7.9	60.2
04	239 38.9	50.3	82 38.0	6.6	13 21.2	8.0	60.3
05	254 39.1	49.4	97 03.6	6.6	13 13.2	8.1	60.3
F 06	269 39.3	N 9 48.5	111 29.2	6.5	S13 05.1	8.2	60.3
R 07	284 39.5	47.7	125 54.7	6.6	12 56.9	8.3	60.4
I 08	299 39.6	46.8	140 20.3	6.6	12 48.6	8.3	60.4
D 09	314 39.8	.. 45.9	154 45.9	6.6	12 40.3	8.5	60.4
A 10	329 40.0	45.0	169 11.5	6.6	12 31.8	8.5	60.4
Y 11	344 40.2	44.1	183 37.1	6.6	12 23.3	8.7	60.5
12	359 40.4	N 9 43.3	198 02.7	6.6	S12 14.6	8.7	60.5
13	14 40.6	42.4	212 28.3	6.6	12 05.9	8.9	60.5
14	29 40.8	41.5	226 53.9	6.6	11 57.0	8.9	60.6
15	44 40.9	.. 40.6	241 19.5	6.6	11 48.1	9.0	60.6
16	59 41.1	39.7	255 45.1	6.7	11 39.1	9.1	60.6
17	74 41.3	38.8	270 10.8	6.6	11 30.0	9.1	60.6
18	89 41.5	N 9 38.0	284 36.4	6.7	S11 20.9	9.3	60.6
19	104 41.7	37.1	299 02.1	6.6	11 11.6	9.3	60.7
20	119 41.9	36.2	313 27.7	6.7	11 02.3	9.4	60.7
21	134 42.1	.. 35.3	327 53.4	6.7	10 52.9	9.5	60.7
22	149 42.2	34.4	342 19.1	6.7	10 43.4	9.6	60.7
23	164 42.4	33.5	356 44.8	6.7	S10 33.8	9.7	60.8
	SD 15.9	d 0.9	SD 16.0		16.3		16.5

Twilight / Sunrise / Moonrise

Lat.	Naut.	Civil	Sunrise	Moonrise 26	27	28	29
°	h m	h m	h m	h m	h m	h m	h m
N 72	////	01 46	03 34	19 51	19 43	19 37	19 31
N 70	////	02 27	03 52	19 01	19 12	19 18	19 21
68	////	02 54	04 06	18 29	18 50	19 03	19 13
66	01 31	03 15	04 17	18 05	18 32	18 51	19 06
64	02 08	03 31	04 27	17 47	18 18	18 41	19 00
62	02 33	03 44	04 35	17 31	18 06	18 32	18 54
60	02 53	03 55	04 42	17 18	17 55	18 25	18 50
N 58	03 08	04 05	04 48	17 07	17 46	18 18	18 46
56	03 21	04 13	04 54	16 58	17 38	18 12	18 42
54	03 32	04 20	04 59	16 49	17 31	18 07	18 39
52	03 42	04 27	05 03	16 42	17 25	18 02	18 36
50	03 50	04 33	05 07	16 35	17 19	17 58	18 33
45	04 07	04 45	05 15	16 20	17 06	17 49	18 27
N 40	04 21	04 54	05 23	16 08	16 56	17 41	18 23
35	04 31	05 03	05 29	15 57	16 47	17 34	18 18
30	04 40	05 09	05 34	15 48	16 39	17 28	18 15
20	04 54	05 21	05 43	15 32	16 26	17 18	18 08
N 10	05 05	05 30	05 51	15 19	16 14	17 09	18 02
0	05 13	05 37	05 58	15 06	16 03	17 00	17 57
S 10	05 20	05 44	06 05	14 53	15 52	16 51	17 51
20	05 25	05 51	06 13	14 39	15 40	16 42	17 46
30	05 29	05 57	06 21	14 23	15 26	16 32	17 39
35	05 31	06 01	06 26	14 14	15 18	16 26	17 35
40	05 33	06 04	06 32	14 04	15 09	16 19	17 31
45	05 34	06 07	06 38	13 51	14 59	16 11	17 26
S 50	05 35	06 13	06 46	13 36	14 46	16 01	17 20
52	05 36	06 15	06 49	13 29	14 40	15 57	17 17
54	05 36	06 17	06 53	13 22	14 33	15 52	17 14
56	05 36	06 19	06 57	13 13	14 26	15 46	17 11
58	05 36	06 21	07 02	13 03	14 18	15 40	17 07
S 60	05 36	06 24	07 07	12 52	14 08	15 33	17 03

Sunset / Twilight / Moonset

Lat.	Sunset	Civil	Naut.	Moonset 26	27	28	29
°	h m	h m	h m	h m	h m	h m	h m
N 72	20 25	22 09	////	22 56	25 04	01 04	03 10
N 70	20 08	21 31	////	23 46	25 33	01 33	03 27
68	19 55	21 05	23 40	24 17	00 17	01 55	03 40
66	19 44	20 45	22 24	24 40	00 40	02 12	03 51
64	19 34	20 29	21 50	24 58	00 58	02 26	04 00
62	19 26	20 17	21 26	00 00	01 13	02 37	04 08
60	19 20	20 06	21 08	00 15	01 26	02 47	04 15
N 58	19 14	19 57	20 53	00 27	01 36	02 55	04 20
56	19 08	19 49	20 40	00 37	01 46	03 03	04 26
54	19 03	19 41	20 29	00 47	01 54	03 09	04 30
52	18 59	19 34	20 20	00 55	02 01	03 15	04 34
50	18 55	19 29	20 12	01 02	02 08	03 21	04 38
45	18 47	19 18	19 55	01 18	02 22	03 32	04 46
N 40	18 40	19 08	19 42	01 31	02 34	03 42	04 53
35	18 34	19 00	19 31	01 42	02 44	03 50	04 59
30	18 29	18 53	19 22	01 52	02 53	03 57	05 04
20	18 20	18 42	19 09	02 08	03 08	04 09	05 12
N 10	18 12	18 33	18 58	02 23	03 21	04 20	05 20
0	18 05	18 26	18 50	02 36	03 33	04 30	05 27
S 10	17 58	18 19	18 44	02 50	03 45	04 40	05 34
20	17 50	18 13	18 39	03 04	03 58	04 50	05 41
30	17 42	18 06	18 34	03 20	04 12	05 02	05 50
35	17 37	18 03	18 32	03 30	04 21	05 09	05 55
40	17 32	17 59	18 31	03 40	04 30	05 17	06 00
45	17 26	17 56	18 30	03 53	04 42	05 26	06 06
S 50	17 18	17 51	18 29	04 08	04 55	05 37	06 14
52	17 15	17 49	18 29	04 16	05 01	05 42	06 17
54	17 11	17 47	18 28	04 24	05 08	05 47	06 21
56	17 07	17 45	18 28	04 32	05 16	05 53	06 25
58	17 03	17 43	18 28	04 43	05 25	06 00	06 30
S 60	16 57	17 40	18 29	04 54	05 35	06 08	06 35

SUN / MOON

Day	Eqn. of Time 00ʰ	12ʰ	Mer. Pass.	Mer. Pass. Upper	Lower	Age	Phase
d	m s	m s	h m	h m	h m	d	%
26	02 02	01 54	12 02	21 19	08 51	12	85
27	01 45	01 36	12 02	22 16	09 48	13	93
28	01 28	01 19	12 01	23 14	10 45	14	98

UT	ARIES GHA	VENUS −4.5 GHA	Dec	MARS +1.8 GHA	Dec	JUPITER −1.7 GHA	Dec	SATURN +0.5 GHA	Dec	STARS Name	SHA	Dec
d h	° ′	° ′	° ′	° ′	° ′	° ′	° ′	° ′	° ′		° ′	° ′
29 00	336 53.1	201 00.1 N 8 31.6		201 12.9 N18 01.3		180 51.4 N10 55.6		99 49.4 S18 04.6		Acamar	315 17.1	S40 14.4
01	351 55.6	216 03.3	32.0	216 13.8	00.9	195 53.3	55.4	114 51.8	04.6	Achernar	335 25.4	S57 09.2
02	6 58.1	231 06.5	32.5	231 14.6	00.5	210 55.3	55.2	129 54.1	04.6	Acrux	173 08.0	S63 11.2
03	22 00.5	246 09.7 ..	32.9	246 15.5	18 00.0	225 57.2 ..	55.0	144 56.5 ..	04.7	Adhara	255 11.6	S28 59.6
04	37 03.0	261 12.9	33.3	261 16.4	17 59.6	240 59.2	54.8	159 58.8	04.7	Aldebaran	290 47.7	N16 32.3
05	52 05.5	276 16.1	33.7	276 17.2	59.1	256 01.1	54.6	175 01.2	04.7			
06	67 07.9	291 19.3 N 8 34.1		291 18.1 N17 58.7		271 03.1 N10 54.4		190 03.5 S18 04.8		Alioth	166 19.9	N55 52.8
S 07	82 10.4	306 22.5	34.6	306 18.9	58.3	286 05.0	54.3	205 05.9	04.8	Alkaid	152 58.1	N49 14.5
A 08	97 12.8	321 25.7	35.0	321 19.8	57.8	301 07.0	54.1	220 08.3	04.8	Al Na'ir	27 41.5	S46 52.9
T 09	112 15.3	336 28.8 ..	35.4	336 20.6 ..	57.4	316 08.9 ..	53.9	235 10.6 ..	04.9	Alnilam	275 44.9	S 1 11.6
U 10	127 17.8	351 32.0	35.8	351 21.5	56.9	331 10.9	53.7	250 13.0	04.9	Alphard	217 54.9	S 8 43.6
R 11	142 20.2	6 35.2	36.3	6 22.3	56.5	346 12.8	53.5	265 15.3	04.9			
D 12	157 22.7	21 38.3 N 8 36.7		21 23.2 N17 56.0		1 14.8 N10 53.3		280 17.7 S18 05.0		Alphecca	126 09.8	N26 40.1
A 13	172 25.2	36 41.5	37.1	36 24.0	55.6	16 16.7	53.1	295 20.0	05.0	Alpheratz	357 41.6	N29 10.7
Y 14	187 27.6	51 44.6	37.5	51 24.9	55.1	31 18.7	52.9	310 22.4	05.0	Altair	62 06.5	N 8 54.9
15	202 30.1	66 47.8 ..	37.9	66 25.8 ..	54.7	46 20.6 ..	52.7	325 24.7 ..	05.1	Ankaa	353 13.9	S42 13.1
16	217 32.6	81 50.9	38.4	81 26.6	54.3	61 22.6	52.5	340 27.1	05.1	Antares	112 24.4	S26 27.8
17	232 35.0	96 54.1	38.8	96 27.5	53.8	76 24.5	52.3	355 29.5	05.1			
18	247 37.5	111 57.2 N 8 39.2		111 28.3 N17 53.4		91 26.5 N10 52.1		10 31.8 S18 05.2		Arcturus	145 54.6	N19 06.4
19	262 39.9	127 00.3	39.6	126 29.2	52.9	106 28.4	51.9	25 34.2	05.2	Atria	107 24.7	S69 03.4
20	277 42.4	142 03.5	40.0	141 30.0	52.5	121 30.3	51.7	40 36.5	05.2	Avior	234 17.9	S59 33.5
21	292 44.9	157 06.6 ..	40.4	156 30.9 ..	52.0	136 32.3 ..	51.5	55 38.9 ..	05.3	Bellatrix	278 30.5	N 6 21.7
22	307 47.3	172 09.7	40.9	171 31.7	51.6	151 34.2	51.3	70 41.2	05.3	Betelgeuse	270 59.8	N 7 24.5
23	322 49.8	187 12.8	41.3	186 32.6	51.1	166 36.2	51.1	85 43.6	05.3			
30 00	337 52.3	202 15.9 N 8 41.7		201 33.5 N17 50.7		181 38.1 N10 50.9		100 45.9 S18 05.4		Canopus	263 55.7	S52 42.1
01	352 54.7	217 19.0	42.1	216 34.3	50.2	196 40.1	50.7	115 48.3	05.4	Capella	280 32.3	N46 00.5
02	7 57.2	232 22.1	42.5	231 35.2	49.8	211 42.0	50.5	130 50.6	05.4	Deneb	49 30.0	N45 20.5
03	22 59.7	247 25.2 ..	43.0	246 36.0 ..	49.4	226 44.0 ..	50.3	145 53.0 ..	05.5	Denebola	182 32.5	N14 29.2
04	38 02.1	262 28.3	43.4	261 36.9	48.9	241 45.9	50.1	160 55.3	05.5	Diphda	348 54.1	S17 53.9
05	53 04.6	277 31.4	43.8	276 37.7	48.5	256 47.9	50.0	175 57.7	05.5			
06	68 07.1	292 34.5 N 8 44.2		291 38.6 N17 48.0		271 49.8 N10 49.8		191 00.0 S18 05.6		Dubhe	193 50.7	N61 40.0
07	83 09.5	307 37.6	44.6	306 39.5	47.6	286 51.8	49.6	206 02.4	05.6	Elnath	278 10.8	N28 37.0
S 08	98 12.0	322 40.7	45.0	321 40.3	47.1	301 53.7	49.4	221 04.8	05.6	Eltanin	90 45.2	N51 29.7
U 09	113 14.4	337 43.7 ..	45.5	336 41.2 ..	46.7	316 55.7 ..	49.2	236 07.1 ..	05.7	Enif	33 45.3	N 9 57.1
N 10	128 16.9	352 46.8	45.9	351 42.0	46.2	331 57.6	49.0	251 09.5	05.7	Fomalhaut	15 22.0	S29 32.2
D 11	143 19.4	7 49.9	46.3	6 42.9	45.8	346 59.6	48.8	266 11.8	05.7			
A 12	158 21.8	22 52.9 N 8 46.7		21 43.8 N17 45.3		2 01.5 N10 48.6		281 14.2 S18 05.8		Gacrux	171 59.6	S57 12.1
Y 13	173 24.3	37 56.0	47.1	36 44.6	44.9	17 03.5	48.4	296 16.5	05.8	Gienah	175 51.0	S17 37.7
14	188 26.8	52 59.0	47.5	51 45.5	44.4	32 05.4	48.2	311 18.9	05.8	Hadar	148 46.0	S60 27.0
15	203 29.2	68 02.1 ..	47.9	66 46.3 ..	44.0	47 07.4 ..	48.0	326 21.2 ..	05.9	Hamal	327 58.8	N23 32.1
16	218 31.7	83 05.1	48.4	81 47.2	43.5	62 09.3	47.8	341 23.6	05.9	Kaus Aust.	83 41.6	S34 22.5
17	233 34.2	98 08.2	48.8	96 48.0	43.1	77 11.2	47.6	356 25.9	05.9			
18	248 36.6	113 11.2 N 8 49.2		111 48.9 N17 42.6		92 13.2 N10 47.4		11 28.3 S18 06.0		Kochab	137 20.7	N74 05.9
19	263 39.1	128 14.2	49.6	126 49.8	42.2	107 15.1	47.2	26 30.6	06.0	Markab	13 36.5	N15 17.5
20	278 41.5	143 17.3	50.0	141 50.6	41.7	122 17.1	47.0	41 33.0	06.0	Menkar	314 13.4	N 4 09.0
21	293 44.0	158 20.3 ..	50.4	156 51.5 ..	41.3	137 19.0 ..	46.8	56 35.3 ..	06.1	Menkent	148 06.0	S36 26.8
22	308 46.5	173 23.3	50.8	171 52.3	40.8	152 21.0	46.6	71 37.7	06.1	Miaplacidus	221 40.1	S69 46.9
23	323 48.9	188 26.3	51.2	186 53.2	40.4	167 22.9	46.4	86 40.0	06.1			
31 00	338 51.4	203 29.3 N 8 51.7		201 54.1 N17 39.9		182 24.9 N10 46.2		101 42.4 S18 06.2		Mirfak	308 38.0	N49 54.7
01	353 53.9	218 32.3	52.1	216 54.9	39.5	197 26.8	46.0	116 44.7	06.2	Nunki	75 56.2	S26 16.4
02	8 56.3	233 35.3	52.5	231 55.8	39.0	212 28.8	45.8	131 47.1	06.2	Peacock	53 16.4	S56 40.9
03	23 58.8	248 38.3 ..	52.9	246 56.7 ..	38.6	227 30.7 ..	45.6	146 49.4 ..	06.3	Pollux	243 26.2	N27 59.1
04	39 01.3	263 41.3	53.3	261 57.5	38.1	242 32.7	45.5	161 51.8	06.3	Procyon	244 58.4	N 5 11.0
05	54 03.7	278 44.3	53.7	276 58.4	37.7	257 34.6	45.3	176 54.1	06.3			
06	69 06.2	293 47.3 N 8 54.1		291 59.2 N17 37.2		272 36.6 N10 45.1		191 56.5 S18 06.4		Rasalhague	96 05.0	N12 33.3
07	84 08.7	308 50.3	54.5	307 00.1	36.8	287 38.5	44.9	206 58.8	06.4	Regulus	207 42.3	N11 53.4
08	99 11.1	323 53.3	54.9	322 01.0	36.3	302 40.5	44.7	222 01.2	06.4	Rigel	281 10.7	S 8 11.1
M 09	114 13.6	338 56.2 ..	55.3	337 01.8 ..	35.9	317 42.4 ..	44.5	237 03.5 ..	06.5	Rigil Kent.	139 49.9	S60 54.0
O 10	129 16.0	353 59.2	55.8	352 02.7	35.4	332 44.4	44.3	252 05.9	06.5	Sabik	102 10.7	S15 44.4
N 11	144 18.5	9 02.2	56.2	7 03.6	35.0	347 46.3	44.1	267 08.2	06.5			
D 12	159 21.0	24 05.1 N 8 56.6		22 04.4 N17 34.5		2 48.3 N10 43.9		282 10.6 S18 06.6		Schedar	349 38.2	N56 37.3
A 13	174 23.4	39 08.1	57.0	37 05.3	34.1	17 50.2	43.7	297 12.9	06.6	Shaula	96 19.7	S37 06.8
Y 14	189 25.9	54 11.0	57.4	52 06.1	33.6	32 52.2	43.5	312 15.3	06.6	Sirius	258 32.6	S16 44.3
15	204 28.4	69 14.0 ..	57.8	67 07.0 ..	33.1	47 54.1 ..	43.3	327 17.6 ..	06.7	Spica	158 29.9	S11 14.4
16	219 30.8	84 16.9	58.2	82 07.9	32.7	62 56.1	43.1	342 19.9	06.7	Suhail	222 51.7	S43 29.7
17	234 33.3	99 19.9	58.6	97 08.7	32.2	77 58.0	42.9	357 22.3	06.7			
18	249 35.8	114 22.8 N 8 59.0		112 09.6 N17 31.8		93 00.0 N10 42.7		12 24.6 S18 06.8		Vega	80 37.7	N38 48.4
19	264 38.2	129 25.7	59.4	127 10.5	31.3	108 01.9	42.5	27 27.0	06.8	Zuben'ubi	137 03.9	S16 06.2
20	279 40.7	144 28.6	8 59.8	142 11.3	30.9	123 03.8	42.3	42 29.3	06.8		SHA	Mer. Pass.
21	294 43.2	159 31.6	9 00.2	157 12.2 ..	30.4	138 05.8 ..	42.1	57 31.7 ..	06.9		° ′	h m
22	309 45.6	174 34.5	00.6	172 13.1	30.0	153 07.7	41.9	72 34.0	06.9	Venus	224 23.7	10 29
23	324 48.1	189 37.4	01.0	187 13.9	29.5	168 09.7	41.7	87 36.4	06.9	Mars	223 41.2	10 33
	h m									Jupiter	203 45.9	11 52
Mer. Pass.	1 28.3	v 3.1	d 0.4	v 0.9	d 0.4	v 1.9	d 0.2	v 2.4	d 0.0	Saturn	122 53.7	17 14

UT	SUN GHA	SUN Dec	MOON GHA	v	Dec	d	HP
d h	° ′	° ′	° ′	′	° ′	′	′
29 00	179 42.6	N 9 32.7	11 10.5	6.7	S10 24.1	9.7	60.8
01	194 42.8	31.8	25 36.2	6.8	10 14.4	9.8	60.8
02	209 43.0	30.9	40 02.0	6.7	10 04.6	9.9	60.8
03	224 43.2 . .	30.0	54 27.7	6.8	9 54.7	9.9	60.8
04	239 43.4	29.1	68 53.5	6.7	9 44.8	10.0	60.9
05	254 43.5	28.2	83 19.2	6.8	9 34.8	10.1	60.9
06	269 43.7	N 9 27.3	97 45.0	6.8	S 9 24.7	10.2	60.9
07	284 43.9	26.5	112 10.8	6.8	9 14.5	10.2	60.9
S 08	299 44.1	25.6	126 36.6	6.8	9 04.3	10.3	60.9
A 09	314 44.3 . .	24.7	141 02.4	6.9	8 54.0	10.4	60.9
T 10	329 44.5	23.8	155 28.3	6.8	8 43.6	10.4	61.0
U 11	344 44.7	22.9	169 54.1	6.9	8 33.2	10.5	61.0
R 12	359 44.9	N 9 22.0	184 20.0	6.9	S 8 22.7	10.6	61.0
D 13	14 45.1	21.1	198 45.9	6.9	8 12.1	10.6	61.0
A 14	29 45.2	20.2	213 11.8	6.9	8 01.5	10.6	61.0
Y 15	44 45.4 . .	19.4	227 37.7	6.9	7 50.9	10.8	61.0
16	59 45.6	18.5	242 03.6	6.9	7 40.1	10.8	61.0
17	74 45.8	17.6	256 29.5	7.0	7 29.3	10.8	61.1
18	89 46.0	N 9 16.7	270 55.5	7.0	S 7 18.5	10.9	61.1
19	104 46.2	15.8	285 21.5	7.0	7 07.6	10.9	61.1
20	119 46.4	14.9	299 47.5	7.0	6 56.7	11.0	61.1
21	134 46.6 . .	14.0	314 13.5	7.0	6 45.7	11.0	61.1
22	149 46.8	13.1	328 39.5	7.0	6 34.7	11.1	61.1
23	164 47.0	12.2	343 05.5	7.1	6 23.6	11.2	61.1
30 00	179 47.1	N 9 11.3	357 31.6	7.0	S 6 12.4	11.1	61.1
01	194 47.3	10.5	11 57.6	7.1	6 01.3	11.3	61.1
02	209 47.5	09.6	26 23.7	7.1	5 50.0	11.2	61.2
03	224 47.7 . .	08.7	40 49.8	7.1	5 38.8	11.3	61.2
04	239 47.9	07.8	55 15.9	7.1	5 27.5	11.4	61.2
05	254 48.1	06.9	69 42.0	7.2	5 16.1	11.3	61.2
06	269 48.3	N 9 06.0	84 08.2	7.1	S 5 04.8	11.4	61.2
07	284 48.5	05.1	98 34.3	7.2	4 53.4	11.5	61.2
08	299 48.7	04.2	113 00.5	7.2	4 41.9	11.5	61.2
S 09	314 48.9 . .	03.3	127 26.7	7.2	4 30.4	11.5	61.2
U 10	329 49.1	02.4	141 52.9	7.2	4 18.9	11.5	61.2
N 11	344 49.2	01.5	156 19.1	7.3	4 07.4	11.6	61.2
D 12	359 49.4	N 9 00.6	170 45.4	7.2	S 3 55.8	11.6	61.2
A 13	14 49.6	8 59.7	185 11.6	7.3	3 44.2	11.6	61.2
Y 14	29 49.8	58.8	199 37.9	7.3	3 32.6	11.6	61.2
15	44 50.0 . .	57.9	214 04.2	7.3	3 21.0	11.7	61.2
16	59 50.2	57.1	228 30.5	7.3	3 09.3	11.7	61.2
17	74 50.4	56.2	242 56.8	7.3	2 57.6	11.7	61.2
18	89 50.6	N 8 55.3	257 23.1	7.4	S 2 45.9	11.7	61.2
19	104 50.8	54.4	271 49.5	7.3	2 34.2	11.7	61.2
20	119 51.0	53.5	286 15.8	7.4	2 22.5	11.8	61.2
21	134 51.2 . .	52.6	300 42.2	7.4	2 10.7	11.7	61.2
22	149 51.4	51.7	315 08.6	7.4	1 59.0	11.8	61.2
23	164 51.6	50.8	329 35.0	7.4	1 47.2	11.8	61.2
31 00	179 51.8	N 8 49.9	344 01.4	7.4	S 1 35.4	11.8	61.2
01	194 51.9	49.0	358 27.8	7.5	1 23.6	11.8	61.2
02	209 52.1	48.1	12 54.3	7.4	1 11.8	11.8	61.2
03	224 52.3 . .	47.2	27 20.7	7.5	1 00.0	11.8	61.2
04	239 52.5	46.3	41 47.2	7.5	0 48.2	11.8	61.2
05	254 52.7	45.4	56 13.7	7.5	0 36.4	11.8	61.1
06	269 52.9	N 8 44.5	70 40.2	7.5	S 0 24.6	11.8	61.1
07	284 53.1	43.6	85 06.7	7.5	0 12.8	11.8	61.1
08	299 53.3	42.7	99 33.2	7.5	S 0 01.0	11.8	61.1
M 09	314 53.5 . .	41.8	113 59.7	7.5	N 0 10.8	11.8	61.1
O 10	329 53.7	40.9	128 26.3	7.5	0 22.6	11.8	61.1
N 11	344 53.9	40.0	142 52.8	7.6	0 34.4	11.8	61.1
D 12	359 54.1	N 8 39.1	157 19.4	7.6	N 0 46.2	11.7	61.1
A 13	14 54.3	38.2	171 46.0	7.6	0 57.9	11.8	61.1
Y 14	29 54.5	37.3	186 12.6	7.6	1 09.7	11.7	61.1
15	44 54.7 . .	36.4	200 39.2	7.6	1 21.4	11.7	61.0
16	59 54.9	35.5	215 05.8	7.6	1 33.1	11.8	61.0
17	74 55.1	34.6	229 32.4	7.6	1 44.9	11.7	61.0
18	89 55.3	N 8 33.7	243 59.0	7.7	N 1 56.6	11.6	61.0
19	104 55.5	32.8	258 25.7	7.6	2 08.2	11.7	61.0
20	119 55.7	31.9	272 52.3	7.7	2 19.9	11.6	61.0
21	134 55.9 . .	31.0	287 19.0	7.7	2 31.5	11.6	60.9
22	149 56.1	30.1	301 45.7	7.6	2 43.1	11.6	60.9
23	164 56.2	29.2	316 12.3	7.7	N 2 54.7	11.6	60.9
	SD 15.9	d 0.9	SD 16.6		16.7		16.6

Lat.	Twilight Naut.	Twilight Civil	Sunrise	Moonrise 29	30	31	1
°	h m	h m	h m	h m	h m	h m	h m
N 72	////	02 13	03 49	19 31	19 27	19 22	19 18
N 70	////	02 46	04 05	19 21	19 23	19 25	19 27
68	01 04	03 09	04 17	19 13	19 20	19 27	19 34
66	01 54	03 27	04 27	19 06	19 18	19 29	19 41
64	02 24	03 41	04 36	19 00	19 16	19 31	19 46
62	02 46	03 53	04 43	18 54	19 14	19 32	19 51
60	03 03	04 03	04 49	18 50	19 12	19 33	19 55
N 58	03 17	04 12	04 55	18 46	19 11	19 34	19 59
56	03 29	04 20	05 00	18 42	19 09	19 35	20 02
54	03 39	04 26	05 04	18 39	19 08	19 36	20 05
52	03 48	04 32	05 08	18 36	19 07	19 37	20 08
50	03 56	04 37	05 11	18 33	19 06	19 38	20 10
45	04 12	04 49	05 19	18 27	19 04	19 40	20 16
N 40	04 24	04 57	05 25	18 23	19 02	19 41	20 20
35	04 34	05 05	05 31	18 18	19 01	19 42	20 24
30	04 42	05 11	05 36	18 15	18 59	19 43	20 27
20	04 55	05 21	05 44	18 08	18 57	19 45	20 34
N 10	05 05	05 30	05 51	18 02	18 55	19 47	20 39
0	05 12	05 36	05 57	17 57	18 53	19 49	20 44
S 10	05 18	05 43	06 04	17 51	18 51	19 50	20 49
20	05 23	05 48	06 11	17 46	18 49	19 52	20 55
30	05 26	05 54	06 18	17 39	18 47	19 54	21 01
35	05 27	05 57	06 22	17 35	18 46	19 56	21 05
40	05 29	06 00	06 27	17 31	18 44	19 57	21 09
45	05 29	06 03	06 33	17 26	18 43	19 59	21 14
S 50	05 29	06 07	06 39	17 20	18 40	20 01	21 20
52	05 29	06 08	06 42	17 17	18 40	20 02	21 22
54	05 29	06 10	06 46	17 14	18 39	20 03	21 25
56	05 29	06 12	06 49	17 11	18 37	20 04	21 29
58	05 28	06 14	06 54	17 07	18 36	20 05	21 32
S 60	05 28	06 16	06 58	17 03	18 35	20 06	21 37

Lat.	Sunset	Twilight Civil	Twilight Naut.	Moonset 29	30	31	1
°	h m	h m	h m	h m	h m	h m	h m
N 72	20 08	21 42	////	03 10	05 14	07 16	09 16
N 70	19 54	21 11	////	03 27	05 22	07 16	09 10
68	19 42	20 49	22 46	03 40	05 29	07 17	09 04
66	19 32	20 31	22 01	03 51	05 34	07 17	08 59
64	19 24	20 17	21 33	04 00	05 38	07 17	08 55
62	19 17	20 06	21 12	04 08	05 42	07 18	08 52
60	19 11	19 56	20 56	04 15	05 46	07 18	08 49
N 58	19 05	19 48	20 42	04 20	05 49	07 18	08 46
56	19 01	19 40	20 30	04 26	05 51	07 18	08 44
54	18 56	19 34	20 21	04 30	05 54	07 18	08 42
52	18 53	19 28	20 12	04 34	05 56	07 18	08 40
50	18 49	19 23	20 04	04 38	05 58	07 18	08 38
45	18 42	19 12	19 49	04 46	06 02	07 19	08 34
N 40	18 35	19 03	19 36	04 53	06 06	07 19	08 31
35	18 30	18 56	19 27	04 59	06 09	07 19	08 29
30	18 25	18 50	19 19	05 04	06 11	07 19	08 26
20	18 17	18 40	19 06	05 12	06 16	07 19	08 22
N 10	18 10	18 32	18 56	05 20	06 20	07 19	08 18
0	18 04	18 25	18 49	05 27	06 24	07 20	08 15
S 10	17 58	18 19	18 44	05 34	06 27	07 20	08 12
20	17 51	18 13	18 39	05 41	06 31	07 20	08 08
30	17 44	18 08	18 36	05 50	06 35	07 20	08 04
35	17 40	18 05	18 34	05 55	06 38	07 20	08 01
40	17 35	18 02	18 34	06 00	06 41	07 20	07 59
45	17 29	17 59	18 33	06 06	06 44	07 20	07 55
S 50	17 23	17 55	18 33	06 14	06 48	07 20	07 52
52	17 20	17 54	18 33	06 17	06 49	07 20	07 50
54	17 17	17 52	18 33	06 21	06 51	07 20	07 48
56	17 13	17 51	18 34	06 25	06 53	07 20	07 46
58	17 09	17 49	18 34	06 30	06 56	07 20	07 44
S 60	17 04	17 47	18 35	06 35	06 58	07 20	07 41

	SUN			MOON			
Day	Eqn. of Time 00h	Eqn. of Time 12h	Mer. Pass.	Mer. Pass. Upper	Mer. Pass. Lower	Age	Phase
d	m s	m s	h m	h m	h m	d	%
29	01 10	01 01	12 01	24 10	11 42	15	100
30	00 52	00 43	12 01	00 10	12 38	16	99
31	00 33	00 24	12 00	01 06	13 34	17	96

UT	ARIES	VENUS −4.6		MARS +1.8		JUPITER −1.7		SATURN +0.5		STARS		
	GHA	GHA	Dec	GHA	Dec	GHA	Dec	GHA	Dec	Name	SHA	Dec
d h	° ′	° ′	° ′	° ′	° ′	° ′	° ′	° ′	° ′		° ′	° ′
1 00	339 50.5	204 40.3 N 9 01.4		202 14.8 N17 29.1		183 11.6 N10 41.5		102 38.7 S18 07.0		Acamar	315 17.1	S40 14.4
01	354 53.0	219 43.2	01.8	217 15.7	28.6	198 13.6	41.3	117 41.1	07.0	Achernar	335 25.4	S57 09.3
02	9 55.5	234 46.1	02.2	232 16.5	28.1	213 15.5	41.1	132 43.4	07.1	Acrux	173 08.0	S63 11.2
03	24 57.9	249 49.0 ..	02.6	247 17.4 ..	27.7	228 17.5 ..	40.9	147 45.8 ..	07.1	Adhara	255 11.5	S28 59.6
04	40 00.4	264 51.9	03.0	262 18.2	27.2	243 19.4	40.8	162 48.1	07.1	Aldebaran	290 47.6	N16 32.3
05	55 02.9	279 54.8	03.4	277 19.1	26.8	258 21.4	40.6	177 50.4	07.2			
06	70 05.3	294 57.7 N 9 03.8		292 20.0 N17 26.3		273 23.3 N10 40.4		192 52.8 S18 07.2		Alioth	166 19.9	N55 52.7
07	85 07.8	310 00.6	04.2	307 20.8	25.9	288 25.3	40.2	207 55.1	07.2	Alkaid	152 58.1	N49 14.4
T 08	100 10.3	325 03.4	04.6	322 21.7	25.4	303 27.2	40.0	222 57.5	07.3	Al Na'ir	27 41.5	S46 52.9
U 09	115 12.7	340 06.3 ..	05.0	337 22.6 ..	24.9	318 29.2 ..	39.8	237 59.8 ..	07.3	Alnilam	275 44.9	S 1 11.6
E 10	130 15.2	355 09.2	05.4	352 23.4	24.5	333 31.1	39.6	253 02.2	07.3	Alphard	217 54.9	S 8 43.6
S 11	145 17.6	10 12.0	05.8	7 24.3	24.0	348 33.1	39.4	268 04.5	07.4			
D 12	160 20.1	25 14.9 N 9 06.2		22 25.2 N17 23.6		3 35.0 N10 39.2		283 06.9 S18 07.4		Alphecca	126 09.8	N26 40.1
A 13	175 22.6	40 17.7	06.6	37 26.0	23.1	18 37.0	39.0	298 09.2	07.4	Alpheratz	357 41.6	N29 10.7
Y 14	190 25.0	55 20.6	07.0	52 26.9	22.7	33 38.9	38.8	313 11.5	07.5	Altair	62 06.5	N 8 54.9
15	205 27.5	70 23.4 ..	07.4	67 27.8 ..	22.2	48 40.9 ..	38.6	328 13.9 ..	07.5	Ankaa	353 13.9	S42 13.1
16	220 30.0	85 26.3	07.8	82 28.7	21.7	63 42.8	38.4	343 16.2	07.5	Antares	112 24.4	S26 27.8
17	235 32.4	100 29.1	08.2	97 29.5	21.3	78 44.8	38.2	358 18.6	07.6			
18	250 34.9	115 31.9 N 9 08.6		112 30.4 N17 20.8		93 46.7 N10 38.0		13 20.9 S18 07.6		Arcturus	145 54.6	N19 06.4
19	265 37.4	130 34.8	09.0	127 31.3	20.4	108 48.7	37.8	28 23.3	07.6	Atria	107 24.7	S69 03.4
20	280 39.8	145 37.6	09.4	142 32.1	19.9	123 50.6	37.6	43 25.6	07.7	Avior	234 17.9	S59 33.5
21	295 42.3	160 40.4 ..	09.8	157 33.0 ..	19.4	138 52.6 ..	37.4	58 28.0 ..	07.7	Bellatrix	278 30.5	N 6 21.7
22	310 44.8	175 43.2	10.2	172 33.9	19.0	153 54.5	37.2	73 30.3	07.8	Betelgeuse	270 59.8	N 7 24.5
23	325 47.2	190 46.0	10.6	187 34.7	18.5	168 56.5	37.0	88 32.6	07.8			
2 00	340 49.7	205 48.9 N 9 11.0		202 35.6 N17 18.1		183 58.4 N10 36.8		103 35.0 S18 07.8		Canopus	263 55.7	S52 42.1
01	355 52.1	220 51.7	11.3	217 36.5	17.6	199 00.4	36.6	118 37.3	07.9	Capella	280 32.3	N46 00.5
02	10 54.6	235 54.5	11.7	232 37.3	17.2	214 02.3	36.4	133 39.7	07.9	Deneb	49 30.0	N45 20.5
03	25 57.1	250 57.2 ..	12.1	247 38.2 ..	16.7	229 04.3 ..	36.2	148 42.0 ..	07.9	Denebola	182 32.5	N14 29.2
04	40 59.5	266 00.0	12.5	262 39.1	16.2	244 06.2	36.1	163 44.3	08.0	Diphda	348 54.1	S17 53.9
05	56 02.0	281 02.8	12.9	277 39.9	15.8	259 08.2	35.9	178 46.7	08.0			
06	71 04.5	296 05.6 N 9 13.3		292 40.8 N17 15.3		274 10.1 N10 35.7		193 49.0 S18 08.0		Dubhe	193 50.7	N61 40.0
W 07	86 06.9	311 08.4	13.7	307 41.7	14.8	289 12.1	35.5	208 51.4	08.1	Elnath	278 10.8	N28 37.0
E 08	101 09.4	326 11.2	14.1	322 42.6	14.4	304 14.0	35.3	223 53.7	08.1	Eltanin	90 45.3	N51 29.7
D 09	116 11.9	341 13.9 ..	14.5	337 43.4 ..	13.9	319 16.0 ..	35.1	238 56.1 ..	08.1	Enif	33 45.3	N 9 57.1
N 10	131 14.3	356 16.7	14.9	352 44.3	13.5	334 17.9	34.9	253 58.4	08.2	Fomalhaut	15 22.0	S29 32.2
E 11	146 16.8	11 19.4	15.2	7 45.2	13.0	349 19.9	34.7	269 00.7	08.2			
S 12	161 19.2	26 22.2 N 9 15.6		22 46.0 N17 12.5		4 21.8 N10 34.5		284 03.1 S18 08.2		Gacrux	171 59.6	S57 12.1
D 13	176 21.7	41 25.0	16.0	37 46.9	12.1	19 23.8	34.3	299 05.4	08.3	Gienah	175 51.0	S17 37.6
A 14	191 24.2	56 27.7	16.4	52 47.8	11.6	34 25.7	34.1	314 07.8	08.3	Hadar	148 46.0	S60 27.0
Y 15	206 26.6	71 30.4 ..	16.8	67 48.7 ..	11.2	49 27.6 ..	33.9	329 10.1 ..	08.4	Hamal	327 58.8	N23 32.1
16	221 29.1	86 33.2	17.2	82 49.5	10.7	64 29.6	33.7	344 12.4	08.4	Kaus Aust.	83 41.6	S34 22.5
17	236 31.6	101 35.9	17.5	97 50.4	10.2	79 31.5	33.5	359 14.8	08.4			
18	251 34.0	116 38.7 N 9 17.9		112 51.3 N17 09.8		94 33.5 N10 33.3		14 17.1 S18 08.5		Kochab	137 20.8	N74 05.9
19	266 36.5	131 41.4	18.3	127 52.2	09.3	109 35.4	33.1	29 19.5	08.5	Markab	13 36.5	N15 17.5
20	281 39.0	146 44.1	18.7	142 53.0	08.8	124 37.4	32.9	44 21.8	08.5	Menkar	314 13.3	N 4 09.0
21	296 41.4	161 46.8 ..	19.1	157 53.9 ..	08.4	139 39.3 ..	32.7	59 24.1 ..	08.6	Menkent	148 06.0	S36 26.8
22	311 43.9	176 49.5	19.5	172 54.8	07.9	154 41.3	32.5	74 26.5	08.6	Miaplacidus	221 40.1	S69 46.9
23	326 46.4	191 52.2	19.8	187 55.6	07.4	169 43.2	32.3	89 28.8	08.6			
3 00	341 48.8	206 54.9 N 9 20.2		202 56.5 N17 07.0		184 45.2 N10 32.1		104 31.1 S18 08.7		Mirfak	308 38.0	N49 54.7
01	356 51.3	221 57.6	20.6	217 57.4	06.5	199 47.1	31.9	119 33.5	08.7	Nunki	75 56.3	S26 16.4
02	11 53.7	237 00.3	21.0	232 58.3	06.0	214 49.1	31.7	134 35.8	08.8	Peacock	53 16.5	S56 41.0
03	26 56.2	252 03.0 ..	21.4	247 59.1 ..	05.6	229 51.0 ..	31.5	149 38.2 ..	08.8	Pollux	243 26.2	N27 59.1
04	41 58.7	267 05.7	21.7	263 00.0	05.1	244 53.0	31.3	164 40.5	08.8	Procyon	244 58.4	N 5 11.0
05	57 01.1	282 08.4	22.1	278 00.9	04.7	259 54.9	31.1	179 42.8	08.9			
06	72 03.6	297 11.1 N 9 22.5		293 01.8 N17 04.2		274 56.9 N10 31.0		194 45.2 S18 08.9		Rasalhague	96 05.0	N12 33.3
07	87 06.1	312 13.8	22.9	308 02.6	03.7	289 58.8	30.8	209 47.5	08.9	Regulus	207 42.3	N11 53.4
T 08	102 08.5	327 16.4	23.2	323 03.5	03.3	305 00.8	30.6	224 49.8	09.0	Rigel	281 10.7	S 8 11.0
H 09	117 11.0	342 19.1 ..	23.6	338 04.4 ..	02.8	320 02.7 ..	30.4	239 52.2 ..	09.0	Rigil Kent.	139 49.9	S60 54.0
U 10	132 13.5	357 21.8	24.0	353 05.3	02.3	335 04.7	30.2	254 54.5	09.0	Sabik	102 10.8	S15 44.4
R 11	147 15.9	12 24.4	24.4	8 06.1	01.9	350 06.6	30.0	269 56.9	09.1			
S 12	162 18.4	27 27.1 N 9 24.7		23 07.0 N17 01.4		5 08.6 N10 29.8		284 59.2 S18 09.1		Schedar	349 38.2	N56 37.3
D 13	177 20.9	42 29.7	25.1	38 07.9	00.9	20 10.5	29.6	300 01.5	09.1	Shaula	96 19.8	S37 06.8
A 14	192 23.3	57 32.4	25.5	53 08.8	00.5	35 12.5	29.4	315 03.9	09.2	Sirius	258 32.6	S16 44.3
Y 15	207 25.8	72 35.0 ..	25.9	68 09.6 17 00.0		50 14.4 ..	29.2	330 06.2 ..	09.2	Spica	158 29.9	S11 14.4
16	222 28.2	87 37.6	26.2	83 10.5 16 59.5		65 16.4	29.0	345 08.5	09.3	Suhail	222 51.7	S43 29.7
17	237 30.7	102 40.3	26.6	98 11.4	59.1	80 18.3	28.8	0 10.9	09.3			
18	252 33.2	117 42.9 N 9 27.0		113 12.3 N16 58.6		95 20.3 N10 28.6		15 13.2 S18 09.3		Vega	80 37.7	N38 48.4
19	267 35.6	132 45.5	27.3	128 13.1	58.1	110 22.2	28.4	30 15.5	09.4	Zuben'ubi	137 03.9	S16 06.2
20	282 38.1	147 48.2	27.7	143 14.0	57.7	125 24.2	28.2	45 17.9	09.4		SHA	Mer. Pass.
21	297 40.6	162 50.8 ..	28.1	158 14.9 ..	57.2	140 26.1 ..	28.0	60 20.2 ..	09.4		° ′	h m
22	312 43.0	177 53.4	28.4	173 15.8	56.7	155 28.1	27.8	75 22.6	09.5	Venus	224 59.2	10 15
23	327 45.5	192 56.0	28.8	188 16.7	56.2	170 30.0	27.6	90 24.9	09.5	Mars	221 45.9	10 29
	h m									Jupiter	203 08.7	11 43
Mer. Pass.	1 16.5	v 2.8	d 0.4	v 0.9	d 0.5	v 1.9	d 0.2	v 2.3	d 0.0	Saturn	122 45.3	17 03

UT	SUN		MOON				Lat.	Twilight		Sunrise	Moonrise			
								Naut.	Civil		1	2	3	4
	GHA	Dec	GHA	v	Dec	d	HP							
	° ′	° ′	° ′	′	° ′	′	′	°	h m	h m	h m	h m	h m	h m	h m
d h								N 72	////	02 36	04 04	19 18	19 13	19 09	19 04
1 00	179 56.4	N 8 28.3	330 39.0	7.7	N 3 06.3	11.5	60.9	N 70	////	03 03	04 18	19 27	19 30	19 36	19 46
01	194 56.6	27.4	345 05.7	7.7	3 17.8	11.5	60.9	68	01 37	03 23	04 28	19 34	19 44	19 56	20 15
02	209 56.8	26.5	359 32.4	7.8	3 29.3	11.5	60.9	66	02 13	03 39	04 37	19 41	19 55	20 12	20 37
03	224 57.0	.. 25.6	13 59.2	7.7	3 40.8	11.4	60.8	64	02 39	03 52	04 44	19 46	20 04	20 26	20 54
04	239 57.2	24.7	28 25.9	7.7	3 52.2	11.4	60.8	62	02 58	04 02	04 51	19 51	20 12	20 37	21 08
05	254 57.4	23.8	42 52.6	7.8	4 03.6	11.4	60.8	60	03 13	04 11	04 56	19 55	20 19	20 47	21 21
06	269 57.6	N 8 22.9	57 19.4	7.7	N 4 15.0	11.4	60.8	N 58	03 26	04 19	05 01	19 59	20 25	20 55	21 31
07	284 57.8	22.0	71 46.1	7.8	4 26.4	11.3	60.8	56	03 37	04 26	05 05	20 02	20 31	21 03	21 40
T 08	299 58.0	21.1	86 12.9	7.7	4 37.7	11.2	60.8	54	03 46	04 32	05 09	20 05	20 36	21 10	21 48
U 09	314 58.2	.. 20.1	100 39.6	7.8	4 48.9	11.3	60.7	52	03 54	04 37	05 13	20 08	20 40	21 16	21 56
E 10	329 58.4	19.2	115 06.4	7.8	5 00.2	11.1	60.7	50	04 01	04 42	05 16	20 10	20 44	21 21	22 02
S 11	344 58.6	18.3	129 33.2	7.8	5 11.3	11.2	60.7	45	04 16	04 52	05 23	20 16	20 53	21 33	22 16
D 12	359 58.8	N 8 17.4	144 00.0	7.7	N 5 22.5	11.1	60.7	N 40	04 27	05 00	05 28	20 20	21 00	21 43	22 28
A 13	14 59.0	16.5	158 26.7	7.8	5 33.6	11.0	60.7	35	04 37	05 07	05 33	20 24	21 07	21 51	22 38
Y 14	29 59.2	15.6	172 53.5	7.9	5 44.6	11.0	60.6	30	04 44	05 13	05 37	20 27	21 12	21 59	22 47
15	44 59.4	.. 14.7	187 20.4	7.8	5 55.6	11.0	60.6	20	04 56	05 22	05 44	20 34	21 22	22 12	23 02
16	59 59.6	13.8	201 47.2	7.8	6 06.6	10.9	60.6	N 10	05 05	05 29	05 51	20 39	21 31	22 23	23 16
17	74 59.8	12.9	216 14.0	7.8	6 17.5	10.9	60.6	0	05 11	05 36	05 56	20 44	21 39	22 34	23 28
18	90 00.0	N 8 12.0	230 40.8	7.8	N 6 28.4	10.8	60.5	S 10	05 16	05 41	06 02	20 49	21 47	22 45	23 41
19	105 00.2	11.1	245 07.6	7.9	6 39.2	10.7	60.5	20	05 20	05 46	06 08	20 55	21 56	22 56	23 54
20	120 00.4	10.2	259 34.5	7.8	6 49.9	10.8	60.5	30	05 23	05 51	06 15	21 01	22 06	23 09	24 10
21	135 00.6	.. 09.3	274 01.3	7.8	7 00.7	10.6	60.5	35	05 24	05 53	06 18	21 05	22 12	23 17	24 19
22	150 00.8	08.4	288 28.1	7.9	7 11.3	10.6	60.4	40	05 24	05 55	06 23	21 09	22 19	23 26	24 29
23	165 01.0	07.5	302 55.0	7.8	7 21.9	10.5	60.4	45	05 24	05 58	06 27	21 14	22 27	23 36	24 41
2 00	180 01.2	N 8 06.5	317 21.8	7.9	N 7 32.4	10.5	60.4	S 50	05 23	06 01	06 33	21 20	22 36	23 49	24 56
01	195 01.4	05.6	331 48.7	7.9	7 42.9	10.4	60.4	52	05 23	06 02	06 36	21 22	22 41	23 55	25 03
02	210 01.6	04.7	346 15.6	7.8	7 53.3	10.4	60.3	54	05 22	06 03	06 39	21 25	22 45	24 01	00 01
03	225 01.8	.. 03.8	0 42.4	7.9	8 03.7	10.3	60.3	56	05 22	06 04	06 42	21 29	22 51	24 08	00 08
04	240 02.0	02.9	15 09.3	7.9	8 14.0	10.2	60.3	58	05 21	06 06	06 45	21 32	22 57	24 16	00 16
05	255 02.2	02.0	29 36.2	7.8	8 24.2	10.2	60.3	S 60	05 19	06 07	06 49	21 37	23 04	24 26	00 26

UT	SUN		MOON				Lat.	Sunset	Twilight		Moonset			
	GHA	Dec	GHA	v	Dec	d	HP		Civil	Naut.	1	2	3	4
	° ′	° ′	° ′	′	° ′	′	′	°	h m	h m	h m	h m	h m	h m	h m
06	270 02.4	N 8 01.1	44 03.0	7.9	N 8 34.4	10.1	60.2	N 72	19 52	21 18	////	09 16	11 16	13 16	15 14
W 07	285 02.6	8 00.2	58 29.9	7.9	8 44.5	10.1	60.2	N 70	19 39	20 52	23 23	09 10	11 01	12 50	14 33
E 08	300 02.8	7 59.3	72 56.8	7.9	8 54.6	9.9	60.2	68	19 29	20 33	22 15	09 04	10 49	12 30	14 05
D 09	315 03.0	.. 58.4	87 23.7	7.9	9 04.5	9.9	60.1	66	19 20	20 18	21 41	08 59	10 39	12 15	13 44
N 10	330 03.2	57.5	101 50.6	7.9	9 14.4	9.9	60.1	64	19 13	20 05	21 17	08 55	10 31	12 02	13 27
E 11	345 03.4	56.5	116 17.5	7.9	9 24.3	9.8	60.1	62	19 07	19 55	20 59	08 52	10 24	11 52	13 13
S 12	0 03.6	N 7 55.6	130 44.4	7.9	N 9 34.1	9.7	60.1	60	19 02	19 46	20 44	08 49	10 18	11 43	13 01
D 13	15 03.8	54.7	145 11.3	7.9	9 43.8	9.6	60.0	N 58	18 57	19 39	20 32	08 46	10 12	11 35	12 51
A 14	30 04.0	53.8	159 38.2	7.9	9 53.4	9.5	60.0	56	18 53	19 32	20 21	08 44	10 08	11 28	12 42
Y 15	45 04.2	.. 52.9	174 05.1	8.0	10 02.9	9.5	60.0	54	18 49	19 26	20 12	08 42	10 03	11 22	12 34
16	60 04.4	52.0	188 32.1	7.9	10 12.4	9.4	59.9	52	18 46	19 21	20 04	08 40	10 00	11 16	12 27
17	75 04.6	51.1	202 59.0	7.9	10 21.8	9.4	59.9	50	18 43	19 16	19 57	08 38	09 56	11 11	12 21
18	90 04.8	N 7 50.2	217 25.9	7.9	N 10 31.2	9.2	59.9	45	18 36	19 06	19 43	08 34	09 49	11 00	12 08
19	105 05.0	49.2	231 52.8	8.0	10 40.4	9.2	59.8	N 40	18 31	18 58	19 31	08 31	09 42	10 51	11 56
20	120 05.2	48.3	246 19.8	7.9	10 49.6	9.1	59.8	35	18 26	18 52	19 22	08 29	09 37	10 43	11 47
21	135 05.4	.. 47.4	260 46.7	8.0	10 58.7	9.0	59.8	30	18 22	18 46	19 15	08 26	09 32	10 37	11 38
22	150 05.6	46.5	275 13.7	7.9	11 07.7	9.0	59.7	20	18 15	18 37	19 03	08 22	09 24	10 25	11 24
23	165 05.8	45.6	289 40.6	8.0	11 16.7	8.8	59.7	N 10	18 09	18 30	18 55	08 18	09 17	10 15	11 12
3 00	180 06.0	N 7 44.7	304 07.6	7.9	N 11 25.5	8.8	59.7	0	18 03	18 24	18 48	08 15	09 10	10 05	11 00
01	195 06.2	43.8	318 34.5	8.0	11 34.3	8.7	59.6	S 10	17 58	18 19	18 43	08 12	09 03	09 56	10 48
02	210 06.4	42.8	333 01.5	7.9	11 43.0	8.6	59.6	20	17 52	18 14	18 40	08 08	08 56	09 45	10 35
03	225 06.7	.. 41.9	347 28.4	8.0	11 51.6	8.5	59.6	30	17 45	18 09	18 37	08 04	08 48	09 34	10 21
04	240 06.9	41.0	1 55.4	8.0	12 00.1	8.5	59.5	35	17 42	18 07	18 36	08 01	08 43	09 27	10 13
05	255 07.1	40.1	16 22.4	7.9	12 08.6	8.3	59.5	40	17 38	18 05	18 36	07 59	08 38	09 19	10 03
06	270 07.3	N 7 39.2	30 49.3	8.0	N 12 16.9	8.3	59.5	45	17 33	18 02	18 36	07 55	08 32	09 11	09 52
T 07	285 07.5	38.3	45 16.3	8.0	12 25.2	8.2	59.4	S 50	17 27	18 00	18 37	07 52	08 25	09 00	09 39
H 08	300 07.7	37.4	59 43.3	8.0	12 33.4	8.1	59.4	52	17 25	17 59	18 38	07 50	08 21	08 55	09 33
U 09	315 07.9	.. 36.4	74 10.3	8.0	12 41.5	8.0	59.4	54	17 22	17 57	18 38	07 48	08 18	08 50	09 26
R 10	330 08.1	35.5	88 37.3	8.0	12 49.5	7.9	59.3	56	17 19	17 56	18 39	07 46	08 13	08 44	09 18
S 11	345 08.3	34.6	103 04.3	8.0	12 57.4	7.9	59.3	58	17 15	17 55	18 40	07 44	08 09	08 37	09 10
D 12	0 08.5	N 7 33.7	117 31.3	8.0	N 13 05.3	7.7	59.3	S 60	17 11	17 53	18 42	07 41	08 04	08 30	09 00
A 13	15 08.7	32.8	131 58.3	8.0	13 13.0	7.7	59.2								
Y 14	30 08.9	31.9	146 25.3	8.1	13 20.7	7.5	59.2								
15	45 09.1	.. 30.9	160 52.3	8.1	13 28.2	7.5	59.2								
16	60 09.3	30.0	175 19.4	8.0	13 35.7	7.4	59.1								
17	75 09.5	29.1	189 46.4	8.0	13 43.1	7.3	59.1								

	SUN		MOON			
18	90 09.7	N 7 28.2	204 13.4	8.1	N 13 50.4	7.1	59.1
19	105 09.9	27.3	218 40.5	8.0	13 57.5	7.1	59.0
20	120 10.1	26.4	233 07.5	8.1	14 04.6	7.0	59.0
21	135 10.3	.. 25.4	247 34.6	8.1	14 11.6	6.9	59.0
22	150 10.5	24.5	262 01.7	8.0	14 18.5	6.9	58.9
23	165 10.7	23.6	276 28.7	8.1	N 14 25.4	6.7	58.9

	SUN			MOON			
Day	Eqn. of Time		Mer. Pass.	Mer. Pass.		Age	Phase
	00ʰ	12ʰ		Upper	Lower		
d	m s	m s	h m	h m	h m	d %	
1	00 15	00 05	12 00	02 02	14 30	18 89	
2	00 04	00 14	12 00	02 57	15 25	19 81	
3	00 24	00 34	11 59	03 52	16 19	20 71	

SD 15.9   d 0.9 (SUN)

SD 16.5   16.4   16.2 (MOON)

UT	ARIES GHA	VENUS −4.6 GHA	Dec	MARS +1.8 GHA	Dec	JUPITER −1.7 GHA	Dec	SATURN +0.5 GHA	Dec	STARS Name	SHA	Dec
d h	° ′	° ′	° ′	° ′	° ′	° ′	° ′	° ′	° ′		° ′	° ′
4 00	342 48.0	207 58.6	N 9 29.2	203 17.5	N16 55.8	185 32.0	N10 27.4	105 27.2	S18 09.6	Acamar	315 17.1	S40 14.4
01	357 50.4	223 01.2	29.5	218 18.4	55.3	200 33.9	27.2	120 29.6	09.6	Achernar	335 25.3	S57 09.3
02	12 52.9	238 03.8	29.9	233 19.3	54.8	215 35.9	27.0	135 31.9	09.6	Acrux	173 08.0	S63 11.2
03	27 55.3	253 06.4 ..	30.3	248 20.2 ..	54.4	230 37.8 ..	26.8	150 34.2 ..	09.7	Adhara	255 11.5	S28 59.6
04	42 57.8	268 09.0	30.6	263 21.0	53.9	245 39.8	26.6	165 36.6	09.7	Aldebaran	290 47.6	N16 32.3
05	58 00.3	283 11.5	31.0	278 21.9	53.4	260 41.7	26.4	180 38.9	09.7			
06	73 02.7	298 14.1	N 9 31.4	293 22.8	N16 53.0	275 43.7	N10 26.2	195 41.2	S18 09.8	Alioth	166 20.0	N55 52.7
07	88 05.2	313 16.7	31.7	308 23.7	52.5	290 45.6	26.0	210 43.6	09.8	Alkaid	152 58.1	N49 14.4
08	103 07.7	328 19.3	32.1	323 24.6	52.0	305 47.6	25.8	225 45.9	09.8	Al Na'ir	27 41.5	S46 52.9
F 09	118 10.1	343 21.8 ..	32.5	338 25.4 ..	51.6	320 49.5 ..	25.7	240 48.2 ..	09.9	Alnilam	275 44.9	S 1 11.6
R 10	133 12.6	358 24.4	32.8	353 26.3	51.1	335 51.5	25.5	255 50.6	09.9	Alphard	217 54.9	S 8 43.6
I 11	148 15.1	13 26.9	33.2	8 27.2	50.6	350 53.4	25.3	270 52.9	10.0			
D 12	163 17.5	28 29.5	N 9 33.5	23 28.1	N16 50.1	5 55.4	N10 25.1	285 55.2	S18 10.0	Alphecca	126 09.9	N26 40.1
A 13	178 20.0	43 32.1	33.9	38 29.0	49.7	20 57.3	24.9	300 57.6	10.0	Alpheratz	357 41.5	N29 10.7
Y 14	193 22.5	58 34.6	34.2	53 29.8	49.2	35 59.3	24.7	315 59.9	10.1	Altair	62 06.5	N 8 54.9
15	208 24.9	73 37.1 ..	34.6	68 30.7 ..	48.7	51 01.2 ..	24.5	331 02.2 ..	10.1	Ankaa	353 13.9	S42 13.1
16	223 27.4	88 39.7	35.0	83 31.6	48.3	66 03.2	24.3	346 04.6	10.1	Antares	112 24.4	S26 27.8
17	238 29.8	103 42.2	35.3	98 32.5	47.8	81 05.1	24.1	1 06.9	10.2			
18	253 32.3	118 44.7	N 9 35.7	113 33.4	N16 47.3	96 07.1	N10 23.9	16 09.2	S18 10.2	Arcturus	145 54.6	N19 06.4
19	268 34.8	133 47.3	36.0	128 34.2	46.8	111 09.0	23.7	31 11.6	10.3	Atria	107 24.8	S69 03.4
20	283 37.2	148 49.8	36.4	143 35.1	46.4	126 11.0	23.5	46 13.9	10.3	Avior	234 17.8	S59 33.5
21	298 39.7	163 52.3 ..	36.7	158 36.0 ..	45.9	141 12.9 ..	23.3	61 16.2 ..	10.3	Bellatrix	278 30.4	N 6 21.7
22	313 42.2	178 54.8	37.1	173 36.9	45.4	156 14.9	23.1	76 18.5	10.4	Betelgeuse	270 59.8	N 7 24.5
23	328 44.6	193 57.3	37.4	188 37.8	45.0	171 16.8	22.9	91 20.9	10.4			
5 00	343 47.1	208 59.8	N 9 37.8	203 38.6	N16 44.5	186 18.8	N10 22.7	106 23.2	S18 10.4	Canopus	263 55.7	S52 42.1
01	358 49.6	224 02.3	38.2	218 39.5	44.0	201 20.7	22.5	121 25.5	10.5	Capella	280 32.3	N46 00.5
02	13 52.0	239 04.8	38.5	233 40.4	43.5	216 22.7	22.3	136 27.9	10.5	Deneb	49 30.0	N45 20.5
03	28 54.5	254 07.3 ..	38.9	248 41.3 ..	43.1	231 24.6 ..	22.1	151 30.2 ..	10.6	Denebola	182 32.5	N14 29.2
04	43 57.0	269 09.8	39.2	263 42.2	42.6	246 26.6	21.9	166 32.5	10.6	Diphda	348 54.1	S17 53.9
05	58 59.4	284 12.3	39.5	278 43.1	42.1	261 28.5	21.7	181 34.9	10.6			
06	74 01.9	299 14.7	N 9 39.9	293 43.9	N16 41.6	276 30.5	N10 21.5	196 37.2	S18 10.7	Dubhe	193 50.7	N61 40.0
07	89 04.3	314 17.2	40.2	308 44.8	41.2	291 32.4	21.3	211 39.5	10.7	Elnath	278 10.8	N28 37.0
08	104 06.8	329 19.7	40.6	323 45.7	40.7	306 34.4	21.1	226 41.9	10.7	Eltanin	90 45.3	N51 29.7
S 09	119 09.3	344 22.1 ..	40.9	338 46.6 ..	40.2	321 36.3 ..	20.9	241 44.2 ..	10.8	Enif	33 45.3	N 9 57.1
A 10	134 11.7	359 24.6	41.3	353 47.5	39.7	336 38.3	20.7	256 46.5	10.8	Fomalhaut	15 22.0	S29 32.2
T 11	149 14.2	14 27.1	41.6	8 48.4	39.3	351 40.3	20.5	271 48.8	10.9			
U 12	164 16.7	29 29.5	N 9 42.0	23 49.2	N16 38.8	6 42.2	N10 20.3	286 51.2	S18 10.9	Gacrux	171 59.6	S57 12.1
R 13	179 19.1	44 32.0	42.3	38 50.1	38.3	21 44.2	20.2	301 53.5	10.9	Gienah	175 51.0	S17 37.6
D 14	194 21.6	59 34.4	42.7	53 51.0	37.8	36 46.1	20.0	316 55.8	11.0	Hadar	148 46.0	S60 26.9
A 15	209 24.1	74 36.8 ..	43.0	68 51.9 ..	37.4	51 48.1 ..	19.8	331 58.2 ..	11.0	Hamal	327 58.8	N23 32.1
Y 16	224 26.5	89 39.3	43.3	83 52.8	36.9	66 50.0	19.6	347 00.5	11.0	Kaus Aust.	83 41.7	S34 22.5
17	239 29.0	104 41.7	43.7	98 53.7	36.4	81 52.0	19.4	2 02.8	11.1			
18	254 31.4	119 44.1	N 9 44.0	113 54.5	N16 35.9	96 53.9	N10 19.2	17 05.1	S18 11.1	Kochab	137 20.8	N74 05.9
19	269 33.9	134 46.6	44.4	128 55.4	35.5	111 55.9	19.0	32 07.5	11.2	Markab	13 36.5	N15 17.6
20	284 36.4	149 49.0	44.7	143 56.3	35.0	126 57.8	18.8	47 09.8	11.2	Menkar	314 13.3	N 4 09.0
21	299 38.8	164 51.4 ..	45.0	158 57.2 ..	34.5	141 59.8 ..	18.6	62 12.1 ..	11.2	Menkent	148 06.0	S36 26.7
22	314 41.3	179 53.8	45.4	173 58.1	34.0	157 01.7	18.4	77 14.5	11.3	Miaplacidus	221 40.0	S69 46.9
23	329 43.8	194 56.2	45.7	188 59.0	33.6	172 03.7	18.2	92 16.8	11.3			
6 00	344 46.2	209 58.6	N 9 46.1	203 59.9	N16 33.1	187 05.6	N10 18.0	107 19.1	S18 11.3	Mirfak	308 37.9	N49 54.7
01	359 48.7	225 01.0	46.4	219 00.7	32.6	202 07.6	17.8	122 21.4	11.4	Nunki	75 56.3	S26 16.4
02	14 51.2	240 03.4	46.7	234 01.6	32.1	217 09.5	17.6	137 23.8	11.4	Peacock	53 16.5	S56 41.0
03	29 53.6	255 05.8 ..	47.1	249 02.5 ..	31.6	232 11.5 ..	17.4	152 26.1 ..	11.5	Pollux	243 26.2	N27 59.1
04	44 56.1	270 08.2	47.4	264 03.4	31.2	247 13.4	17.2	167 28.4	11.5	Procyon	244 58.4	N 5 11.0
05	59 58.6	285 10.6	47.7	279 04.3	30.7	262 15.4	17.0	182 30.7	11.5			
06	75 01.0	300 12.9	N 9 48.1	294 05.2	N16 30.2	277 17.3	N10 16.8	197 33.1	S18 11.6	Rasalhague	96 05.0	N12 33.3
07	90 03.5	315 15.3	48.4	309 06.1	29.7	292 19.3	16.6	212 35.4	11.6	Regulus	207 42.2	N11 53.4
08	105 05.9	330 17.7	48.7	324 06.9	29.3	307 21.2	16.4	227 37.7	11.7	Rigel	281 10.6	S 8 11.0
S 09	120 08.4	345 20.1 ..	49.0	339 07.8 ..	28.8	322 23.2 ..	16.2	242 40.0 ..	11.7	Rigil Kent.	139 49.9	S60 54.0
U 10	135 10.9	0 22.4	49.4	354 08.7	28.3	337 25.1	16.0	257 42.4	11.7	Sabik	102 10.8	S15 44.4
N 11	150 13.3	15 24.8	49.7	9 09.6	27.8	352 27.1	15.8	272 44.7	11.8			
D 12	165 15.8	30 27.1	N 9 50.0	24 10.5	N16 27.3	7 29.0	N10 15.6	287 47.0	S18 11.8	Schedar	349 38.2	N56 37.3
A 13	180 18.3	45 29.5	50.4	39 11.4	26.9	22 31.0	15.4	302 49.3	11.8	Shaula	96 19.8	S37 06.8
Y 14	195 20.7	60 31.8	50.7	54 12.3	26.4	37 32.9	15.2	317 51.7	11.9	Sirius	258 32.5	S16 44.3
15	210 23.2	75 34.2 ..	51.0	69 13.2 ..	25.9	52 34.9 ..	15.0	332 54.0 ..	11.9	Spica	158 29.9	S11 14.4
16	225 25.7	90 36.5	51.3	84 14.0	25.4	67 36.8	14.8	347 56.3	12.0	Suhail	222 51.7	S43 29.7
17	240 28.1	105 38.8	51.7	99 14.9	24.9	82 38.8	14.7	2 58.6	12.0			
18	255 30.6	120 41.2	N 9 52.0	114 15.8	N16 24.5	97 40.7	N10 14.5	18 01.0	S18 12.0	Vega	80 37.7	N38 48.4
19	270 33.1	135 43.5	52.3	129 16.7	24.0	112 42.7	14.3	33 03.3	12.1	Zuben'ubi	137 03.9	S16 06.2
20	285 35.5	150 45.8	52.6	144 17.6	23.5	127 44.6	14.1	48 05.6	12.1		SHA	Mer.Pass.
21	300 38.0	165 48.1 ..	53.0	159 18.5 ..	23.0	142 46.6 ..	13.9	63 07.9 ..	12.2		° ′	h m
22	315 40.4	180 50.4	53.3	174 19.4	22.5	157 48.5	13.7	78 10.3	12.2	Venus	225 12.7	10 02
23	330 42.9	195 52.7	53.6	189 20.3	22.1	172 50.5	13.5	93 12.6	12.2	Mars	219 51.5	10 25
	h m									Jupiter	202 31.7	11 33
Mer. Pass.	1 04.7	v 2.5	d 0.3	v 0.9	d 0.5	v 2.0	d 0.2	v 2.3	d 0.0	Saturn	122 36.1	16 52

UT	SUN GHA	SUN Dec	MOON GHA	v	Dec	d	HP
d h	° '	° '	° '	'	° '	'	'
4 00	180 10.9	N 7 22.7	290 55.8	8.1	N14 32.1	6.6	58.9
01	195 11.1	21.8	305 22.9	8.1	14 38.7	6.5	58.8
02	210 11.4	20.8	319 50.0	8.1	14 45.2	6.4	58.8
03	225 11.6	.. 19.9	334 17.1	8.1	14 51.6	6.4	58.8
04	240 11.8	19.0	348 44.2	8.2	14 58.0	6.2	58.7
05	255 12.0	18.1	3 11.4	8.1	15 04.2	6.1	58.7
06	270 12.2	N 7 17.2	17 38.5	8.2	N15 10.3	6.0	58.6
07	285 12.4	16.2	32 05.7	8.1	15 16.3	6.0	58.6
08	300 12.6	15.3	46 32.8	8.2	15 22.3	5.8	58.6
F 09	315 12.8	.. 14.4	61 00.0	8.2	15 28.1	5.7	58.5
R 10	330 13.0	13.5	75 27.2	8.2	15 33.8	5.6	58.5
I 11	345 13.2	12.6	89 54.4	8.2	15 39.4	5.6	58.5
D 12	0 13.4	N 7 11.6	104 21.6	8.2	N15 45.0	5.4	58.4
A 13	15 13.6	10.7	118 48.8	8.2	15 50.4	5.3	58.4
Y 14	30 13.8	09.8	133 16.0	8.2	15 55.7	5.2	58.4
15	45 14.0	.. 08.9	147 43.2	8.3	16 00.9	5.2	58.3
16	60 14.2	07.9	162 10.5	8.3	16 06.1	5.0	58.3
17	75 14.4	07.0	176 37.8	8.2	16 11.1	4.9	58.3
18	90 14.7	N 7 06.1	191 05.0	8.3	N16 16.0	4.8	58.2
19	105 14.9	05.2	205 32.3	8.3	16 20.8	4.7	58.2
20	120 15.1	04.3	219 59.6	8.4	16 25.5	4.6	58.2
21	135 15.3	.. 03.3	234 27.0	8.3	16 30.1	4.5	58.1
22	150 15.5	02.4	248 54.3	8.3	16 34.6	4.4	58.1
23	165 15.7	01.5	263 21.6	8.4	16 39.0	4.3	58.0
5 00	180 15.9	N 7 00.6	277 49.0	8.4	N16 43.3	4.2	58.0
01	195 16.1	6 59.6	292 16.4	8.4	16 47.5	4.1	58.0
02	210 16.3	58.7	306 43.8	8.4	16 51.6	4.0	57.9
03	225 16.5	.. 57.8	321 11.2	8.5	16 55.6	3.8	57.9
04	240 16.7	56.9	335 38.7	8.4	16 59.4	3.8	57.9
05	255 16.9	55.9	350 06.1	8.5	17 03.2	3.7	57.8
06	270 17.1	N 6 55.0	4 33.6	8.5	N17 06.9	3.6	57.8
S 07	285 17.4	54.1	19 01.1	8.5	17 10.5	3.4	57.8
A 08	300 17.6	53.2	33 28.6	8.6	17 13.9	3.4	57.7
T 09	315 17.8	.. 52.2	47 56.2	8.5	17 17.3	3.2	57.7
U 10	330 18.0	51.3	62 23.7	8.6	17 20.5	3.2	57.7
R 11	345 18.2	50.4	76 51.3	8.6	17 23.7	3.0	57.6
D 12	0 18.4	N 6 49.5	91 18.9	8.6	N17 26.7	2.9	57.6
A 13	15 18.6	48.5	105 46.5	8.6	17 29.6	2.9	57.6
Y 14	30 18.8	47.6	120 14.1	8.7	17 32.5	2.7	57.5
15	45 19.0	.. 46.7	134 41.8	8.7	17 35.2	2.6	57.5
16	60 19.2	45.8	149 09.5	8.7	17 37.8	2.6	57.5
17	75 19.4	44.8	163 37.2	8.8	17 40.4	2.4	57.4
18	90 19.7	N 6 43.9	178 05.0	8.7	N17 42.8	2.3	57.4
19	105 19.9	43.0	192 32.7	8.8	17 45.1	2.2	57.4
20	120 20.1	42.0	207 00.5	8.8	17 47.3	2.1	57.3
21	135 20.3	.. 41.1	221 28.3	8.9	17 49.4	2.0	57.3
22	150 20.5	40.2	235 56.2	8.8	17 51.4	1.9	57.3
23	165 20.7	39.3	250 24.0	8.9	17 53.3	1.8	57.2
6 00	180 20.9	N 6 38.3	264 51.9	8.9	N17 55.1	1.7	57.2
01	195 21.1	37.4	279 19.8	9.0	17 56.8	1.5	57.2
02	210 21.3	36.5	293 47.8	9.0	17 58.3	1.5	57.1
03	225 21.5	.. 35.5	308 15.8	9.0	17 59.8	1.4	57.1
04	240 21.7	34.6	322 43.8	9.0	18 01.2	1.3	57.1
05	255 22.0	33.7	337 11.8	9.1	18 02.5	1.1	57.0
06	270 22.2	N 6 32.8	351 39.9	9.1	N18 03.6	1.1	57.0
07	285 22.4	31.8	6 08.0	9.1	18 04.7	1.0	57.0
08	300 22.6	30.9	20 36.1	9.1	18 05.7	0.9	56.9
S 09	315 22.8	.. 30.0	35 04.2	9.2	18 06.6	0.7	56.9
U 10	330 23.0	29.0	49 32.4	9.2	18 07.3	0.7	56.9
N 11	345 23.2	28.1	64 00.6	9.3	18 08.0	0.5	56.9
D 12	0 23.4	N 6 27.2	78 28.9	9.3	N18 08.5	0.5	56.8
A 13	15 23.6	26.2	92 57.2	9.3	18 09.0	0.4	56.8
Y 14	30 23.9	25.3	107 25.5	9.3	18 09.4	0.2	56.8
15	45 24.1	.. 24.4	121 53.8	9.4	18 09.6	0.0	56.7
16	60 24.3	23.4	136 22.2	9.4	18 09.8	0.0	56.7
17	75 24.5	22.5	150 50.6	9.5	18 09.8	0.2	56.7
18	90 24.7	N 6 21.6	165 19.1	9.5	N18 09.8	0.2	56.6
19	105 24.9	20.7	179 47.6	9.5	18 09.6	0.2	56.6
20	120 25.1	19.7	194 16.1	9.6	18 09.4	0.3	56.6
21	135 25.3	.. 18.8	208 44.7	9.6	18 09.1	0.5	56.5
22	150 25.5	17.9	223 13.3	9.6	18 08.6	0.5	56.5
23	165 25.8	16.9	237 41.9	9.7	N18 08.1	0.7	56.5
	SD 15.9	d 0.9	SD 15.9		15.7		15.5

Lat.	Twilight Naut.	Twilight Civil	Sunrise	Moonrise 4	5	6	7
°	h m	h m	h m	h m	h m	h m	h m
N 72	////	02 56	04 19	19 04	18 58	☐	20 54
N 70	01 12	03 19	04 30	19 46	20 08	20 51	21 59
68	02 01	03 36	04 39	20 15	20 45	21 32	22 35
66	02 30	03 50	04 47	20 37	21 11	21 59	23 01
64	02 52	04 02	04 53	20 54	21 32	22 21	23 20
62	03 09	04 11	04 59	21 08	21 48	22 38	23 36
60	03 23	04 19	05 03	21 21	22 02	22 52	23 50
N 58	03 34	04 26	05 08	21 31	22 14	23 04	24 01
56	03 44	04 32	05 11	21 40	22 24	23 15	24 11
54	03 53	04 38	05 15	21 48	22 33	23 24	24 20
52	04 00	04 43	05 18	21 56	22 41	23 32	24 28
50	04 06	04 47	05 20	22 02	22 48	23 40	24 35
45	04 20	04 56	05 26	22 16	23 04	23 55	24 50
N 40	04 31	05 03	05 31	22 28	23 17	24 09	00 09
35	04 39	05 10	05 35	22 38	23 28	24 20	00 20
30	04 46	05 15	05 39	22 47	23 37	24 29	00 29
20	04 57	05 23	05 45	23 02	23 54	24 46	00 46
N 10	05 05	05 29	05 51	23 16	24 08	00 08	01 01
0	05 11	05 35	05 56	23 28	24 22	00 22	01 14
S 10	05 15	05 39	06 00	23 41	24 35	00 35	01 28
20	05 18	05 43	06 05	23 54	24 50	00 50	01 43
30	05 19	05 47	06 11	24 10	00 10	01 07	02 00
35	05 20	05 49	06 14	24 19	00 19	01 16	02 09
40	05 19	05 51	06 18	24 29	00 29	01 28	02 20
45	05 19	05 53	06 22	24 41	00 41	01 41	02 34
S 50	05 17	05 54	06 27	24 56	00 56	01 57	02 50
52	05 16	05 55	06 29	25 03	01 03	02 04	02 57
54	05 15	05 56	06 31	00 01	01 11	02 12	03 05
56	05 14	05 57	06 34	00 08	01 19	02 22	03 15
58	05 13	05 58	06 37	00 16	01 29	02 32	03 25
S 60	05 11	05 59	06 40	00 26	01 40	02 45	03 38

Lat.	Sunset	Twilight Civil	Twilight Naut.	Moonset 4	5	6	7
°	h m	h m	h m	h m	h m	h m	h m
N 72	19 35	20 57	////	15 14	17 13	☐	18 55
N 70	19 25	20 35	22 34	14 33	16 04	17 11	17 50
68	19 16	20 18	21 51	14 05	15 27	16 30	17 13
66	19 09	20 05	21 23	13 44	15 01	16 03	16 48
64	19 02	19 54	21 02	13 27	14 41	15 41	16 28
62	18 57	19 44	20 46	13 13	14 25	15 24	16 11
60	18 53	19 37	20 32	13 01	14 11	15 10	15 58
N 58	18 49	19 30	20 21	12 51	13 59	14 58	15 46
56	18 45	19 24	20 12	12 42	13 49	14 47	15 36
54	18 42	19 18	20 03	12 34	13 40	14 38	15 27
52	18 39	19 14	19 56	12 27	13 32	14 30	15 19
50	18 36	19 09	19 50	12 21	13 25	14 22	15 12
45	18 31	19 01	19 36	12 08	13 10	14 06	14 56
N 40	18 26	18 53	19 26	11 56	12 57	13 53	14 44
35	18 22	18 47	19 18	11 47	12 47	13 42	14 33
30	18 18	18 42	19 11	11 38	12 37	13 32	14 23
20	18 12	18 34	19 00	11 24	12 21	13 16	14 07
N 10	18 07	18 28	18 53	11 12	12 07	13 01	13 53
0	18 02	18 23	18 47	11 00	11 54	12 47	13 39
S 10	17 57	18 18	18 43	10 48	11 41	12 33	13 26
20	17 52	18 15	18 40	10 35	11 27	12 19	13 11
30	17 47	18 11	18 39	10 21	11 11	12 02	12 55
35	17 44	18 09	18 39	10 13	11 01	11 52	12 45
40	17 40	18 07	18 39	10 03	10 51	11 41	12 34
45	17 36	18 06	18 40	09 52	10 38	11 28	12 21
S 50	17 32	18 04	18 41	09 39	10 23	11 12	12 05
52	17 29	18 03	18 42	09 33	10 16	11 04	11 58
54	17 27	18 03	18 43	09 26	10 08	10 56	11 49
56	17 24	18 02	18 45	09 18	09 59	10 46	11 40
58	17 22	18 01	18 46	09 10	09 49	10 36	11 30
S 60	17 18	18 00	18 48	09 00	09 37	10 23	11 18

Day	SUN Eqn. of Time 00h	12h	Mer. Pass.	MOON Mer. Pass. Upper	Lower	Age	Phase
d	m s	m s	h m	h m	h m	d	%
4	00 43	00 53	11 59	04 47	17 14	21	60
5	01 03	01 13	11 59	05 41	18 08	22	49
6	01 23	01 33	11 58	06 35	19 01	23	39

UT (d h)	ARIES GHA	VENUS −4.7 GHA	VENUS Dec	MARS +1.8 GHA	MARS Dec	JUPITER −1.7 GHA	JUPITER Dec	SATURN +0.6 GHA	SATURN Dec	STARS Name	SHA	Dec
7 00	345 45.4	210 55.1	N 9 53.9	204 21.2	N16 21.6	187 52.5	N10 13.3	108 14.9	S18 12.3	Acamar	315 17.0	S40 14.4
01	0 47.8	225 57.4	54.2	219 22.1	21.1	202 54.4	13.1	123 17.2	12.3	Achernar	335 25.3	S57 09.3
02	15 50.3	240 59.7	54.5	234 22.9	20.6	217 56.4	12.9	138 19.6	12.3	Acrux	173 08.1	S63 11.2
03	30 52.8	256 01.9 ..	54.9	249 23.8 ..	20.1	232 58.3 ..	12.7	153 21.9 ..	12.4	Adhara	255 11.5	S28 59.6
04	45 55.2	271 04.2	55.2	264 24.7	19.6	248 00.3	12.5	168 24.2	12.4	Aldebaran	290 47.6	N16 32.3
05	60 57.7	286 06.5	55.5	279 25.6	19.2	263 02.2	12.3	183 26.5	12.5			
06	76 00.2	301 08.8	N 9 55.8	294 26.5	N16 18.7	278 04.2	N10 12.1	198 28.9	S18 12.5	Alioth	166 20.0	N55 52.7
07	91 02.6	316 11.1	56.1	309 27.4	18.2	293 06.1	11.9	213 31.2	12.5	Alkaid	152 58.1	N49 14.4
08	106 05.1	331 13.3	56.4	324 28.3	17.7	308 08.1	11.7	228 33.5	12.6	Al Na'ir	27 41.5	S46 52.9
09	121 07.5	346 15.6 ..	56.8	339 29.2 ..	17.2	323 10.0 ..	11.5	243 35.8 ..	12.6	Alnilam	275 44.9	S 1 11.6
10	136 10.0	1 17.9	57.1	354 30.1	16.7	338 12.0	11.3	258 38.1	12.7	Alphard	217 54.9	S 8 43.6
11	151 12.5	16 20.1	57.4	9 31.0	16.3	353 13.9	11.1	273 40.5	12.7			
12	166 14.9	31 22.4	N 9 57.7	24 31.9	N16 15.8	8 15.9	N10 10.9	288 42.8	S18 12.7	Alphecca	126 09.9	N26 40.1
13	181 17.4	46 24.6	58.0	39 32.7	15.3	23 17.8	10.7	303 45.1	12.8	Alpheratz	357 41.5	N29 10.7
14	196 19.9	61 26.9	58.3	54 33.6	14.8	38 19.8	10.5	318 47.4	12.8	Altair	62 06.5	N 8 54.9
15	211 22.3	76 29.1 ..	58.6	69 34.5 ..	14.3	53 21.7 ..	10.3	333 49.8 ..	12.9	Ankaa	353 13.9	S42 13.1
16	226 24.8	91 31.4	58.9	84 35.4	13.8	68 23.7	10.1	348 52.1	12.9	Antares	112 24.4	S26 27.8
17	241 27.3	106 33.6	59.2	99 36.3	13.4	83 25.6	09.9	3 54.4	12.9			
18	256 29.7	121 35.8	N 9 59.5	114 37.2	N16 12.9	98 27.6	N10 09.7	18 56.7	S18 13.0	Arcturus	145 54.6	N19 06.4
19	271 32.2	136 38.1	9 59.8	129 38.1	12.4	113 29.5	09.5	33 59.0	13.0	Atria	107 24.8	S69 03.4
20	286 34.7	151 40.3	10 00.1	144 39.0	11.9	128 31.5	09.3	49 01.4	13.0	Avior	234 17.8	S59 33.5
21	301 37.1	166 42.5 ..	00.4	159 39.9 ..	11.4	143 33.4 ..	09.1	64 03.7 ..	13.1	Bellatrix	278 30.4	N 6 21.7
22	316 39.6	181 44.7	00.7	174 40.8	10.9	158 35.4	09.0	79 06.0	13.1	Betelgeuse	270 59.7	N 7 24.5
23	331 42.0	196 47.0	01.1	189 41.7	10.5	173 37.4	08.8	94 08.3	13.2			
8 00	346 44.5	211 49.2	N10 01.4	204 42.6	N16 10.0	188 39.3	N10 08.6	109 10.6	S18 13.2	Canopus	263 55.7	S52 42.1
01	1 47.0	226 51.4	01.7	219 43.5	09.5	203 41.3	08.4	124 13.0	13.2	Capella	280 32.2	N46 00.5
02	16 49.4	241 53.6	02.0	234 44.4	09.0	218 43.2	08.2	139 15.3	13.3	Deneb	49 30.0	N45 20.6
03	31 51.9	256 55.8 ..	02.3	249 45.3 ..	08.5	233 45.2 ..	08.0	154 17.6 ..	13.3	Denebola	182 32.5	N14 29.2
04	46 54.4	271 58.0	02.6	264 46.1	08.0	248 47.1	07.8	169 19.9	13.4	Diphda	348 54.1	S17 53.9
05	61 56.8	287 00.1	02.8	279 47.0	07.5	263 49.1	07.6	184 22.2	13.4			
06	76 59.3	302 02.3	N10 03.1	294 47.9	N16 07.1	278 51.0	N10 07.4	199 24.6	S18 13.4	Dubhe	193 50.7	N61 40.0
07	92 01.8	317 04.5	03.4	309 48.8	06.6	293 53.0	07.2	214 26.9	13.5	Elnath	278 10.7	N28 37.0
08	107 04.2	332 06.7	03.7	324 49.7	06.1	308 54.9	07.0	229 29.2	13.5	Eltanin	90 45.3	N51 29.7
09	122 06.7	347 08.9 ..	04.0	339 50.6 ..	05.6	323 56.9 ..	06.8	244 31.5 ..	13.6	Enif	33 45.3	N 9 57.1
10	137 09.2	2 11.0	04.3	354 51.5	05.1	338 58.8	06.6	259 33.8	13.6	Fomalhaut	15 22.0	S29 32.2
11	152 11.6	17 13.2	04.6	9 52.4	04.6	354 00.8	06.4	274 36.2	13.6			
12	167 14.1	32 15.4	N10 04.9	24 53.3	N16 04.1	9 02.7	N10 06.2	289 38.5	S18 13.7	Gacrux	171 59.6	S57 12.1
13	182 16.5	47 17.5	05.2	39 54.2	03.6	24 04.7	06.0	304 40.8	13.7	Gienah	175 51.0	S17 37.6
14	197 19.0	62 19.7	05.5	54 55.1	03.2	39 06.6	05.8	319 43.1	13.8	Hadar	148 46.0	S60 26.9
15	212 21.5	77 21.8 ..	05.8	69 56.0 ..	02.7	54 08.6 ..	05.6	334 45.4 ..	13.8	Hamal	327 58.8	N23 32.1
16	227 23.9	92 24.0	06.1	84 56.9	02.2	69 10.6	05.4	349 47.7	13.8	Kaus Aust.	83 41.7	S34 22.5
17	242 26.4	107 26.1	06.4	99 57.8	01.7	84 12.5	05.2	4 50.1	13.9			
18	257 28.9	122 28.2	N10 06.6	114 58.7	N16 01.2	99 14.5	N10 05.0	19 52.4	S18 13.9	Kochab	137 20.9	N74 05.9
19	272 31.3	137 30.4	06.9	129 59.6	00.7	114 16.4	04.8	34 54.7	14.0	Markab	13 36.5	N15 17.6
20	287 33.8	152 32.5	07.2	145 00.5	16 00.2	129 18.4	04.6	49 57.0	14.0	Menkar	314 13.3	N 4 09.0
21	302 36.3	167 34.6 ..	07.5	160 01.4	15 59.7	144 20.3 ..	04.4	64 59.3 ..	14.0	Menkent	148 06.0	S36 26.7
22	317 38.7	182 36.8	07.8	175 02.3	59.3	159 22.3	04.2	80 01.6	14.1	Miaplacidus	221 40.0	S69 46.8
23	332 41.2	197 38.9	08.1	190 03.2	58.8	174 24.2	04.0	95 04.0	14.1			
9 00	347 43.7	212 41.0	N10 08.4	205 04.1	N15 58.3	189 26.2	N10 03.8	110 06.3	S18 14.2	Mirfak	308 37.9	N49 54.7
01	2 46.1	227 43.1	08.6	220 05.0	57.8	204 28.1	03.6	125 08.6	14.2	Nunki	75 56.3	S26 16.4
02	17 48.6	242 45.2	08.9	235 05.9	57.3	219 30.1	03.5	140 10.9	14.2	Peacock	53 16.5	S56 41.0
03	32 51.0	257 47.3 ..	09.2	250 06.8 ..	56.8	234 32.0 ..	03.3	155 13.2 ..	14.3	Pollux	243 26.1	N27 59.1
04	47 53.5	272 49.4	09.5	265 07.7	56.3	249 34.0	03.1	170 15.5	14.3	Procyon	244 58.4	N 5 11.0
05	62 56.0	287 51.5	09.8	280 08.6	55.8	264 35.9	02.9	185 17.9	14.4			
06	77 58.4	302 53.6	N10 10.0	295 09.5	N15 55.3	279 37.9	N10 02.7	200 20.2	S18 14.4	Rasalhague	96 05.0	N12 33.3
07	93 00.9	317 55.7	10.3	310 10.4	54.8	294 39.9	02.5	215 22.5	14.4	Regulus	207 42.2	N11 53.4
08	108 03.4	332 57.8	10.6	325 11.3	54.4	309 41.8	02.3	230 24.8	14.5	Rigel	281 10.6	S 8 11.0
09	123 05.8	347 59.8 ..	10.9	340 12.2 ..	53.9	324 43.8 ..	02.1	245 27.1 ..	14.5	Rigil Kent.	139 49.9	S60 54.0
10	138 08.3	3 01.9	11.1	355 13.1	53.4	339 45.7	01.9	260 29.4	14.6	Sabik	102 10.8	S15 44.4
11	153 10.8	18 04.0	11.4	10 14.0	52.9	354 47.7	01.7	275 31.7	14.6			
12	168 13.2	33 06.1	N10 11.7	25 14.9	N15 52.4	9 49.6	N10 01.5	290 34.1	S18 14.6	Schedar	349 38.1	N56 37.3
13	183 15.7	48 08.1	12.0	40 15.8	51.9	24 51.6	01.3	305 36.4	14.7	Shaula	96 19.8	S37 06.8
14	198 18.1	63 10.2	12.2	55 16.7	51.4	39 53.5	01.1	320 38.7	14.7	Sirius	258 32.5	S16 44.3
15	213 20.6	78 12.2 ..	12.5	70 17.6 ..	50.9	54 55.5 ..	00.9	335 41.0 ..	14.8	Spica	158 29.9	S11 14.4
16	228 23.1	93 14.3	12.8	85 18.5	50.4	69 57.4	00.7	350 43.3	14.8	Suhail	222 51.7	S43 29.7
17	243 25.5	108 16.3	13.0	100 19.4	49.9	84 59.4	00.5	5 45.6	14.8			
18	258 28.0	123 18.4	N10 13.3	115 20.3	N15 49.4	100 01.3	N10 00.3	20 47.9	S18 14.9	Vega	80 37.8	N38 48.4
19	273 30.5	138 20.4	13.6	130 21.2	48.9	115 03.3	10 00.1	35 50.3	14.9	Zuben'ubi	137 03.9	S16 06.2
20	288 32.9	153 22.5	13.8	145 22.1	48.5	130 05.3	9 59.9	50 52.6	15.0			
21	303 35.4	168 24.5 ..	14.1	160 23.0 ..	48.0	145 07.2 ..	59.7	65 54.9 ..	15.0		SHA	Mer.Pass.
22	318 37.9	183 26.5	14.4	175 23.9	47.5	160 09.2	59.5	80 57.2	15.0	Venus	225 04.6	9 51
23	333 40.3	198 28.6	14.6	190 24.8	47.0	175 11.1	59.3	95 59.5	15.1	Mars	217 58.1	10 21
	h m									Jupiter	201 54.8	11 24
Mer. Pass. 0 52.9	v 2.2	d 0.3		v 0.9	d 0.5	v 2.0	d 0.2	v 2.3	d 0.0	Saturn	122 26.1	16 41

UT	SUN GHA	SUN Dec	MOON GHA	v	Dec	d	HP
d h	° '	° '	° '	'	° '	'	'
7 00	180 26.0	N 6 16.0	252 10.6	9.7	N18 07.4	0.7	56.5
01	195 26.2	15.1	266 39.3	9.7	18 06.7	0.8	56.4
02	210 26.4	14.1	281 08.0	9.8	18 05.9	0.9	56.4
03	225 26.6	.. 13.2	295 36.8	9.8	18 05.0	1.1	56.4
04	240 26.8	12.3	310 05.6	9.9	18 03.9	1.1	56.3
05	255 27.0	11.3	324 34.5	9.9	18 02.8	1.2	56.3
06	270 27.2	N 6 10.4	339 03.4	9.9	N18 01.6	1.3	56.3
07	285 27.5	09.5	353 32.3	10.0	18 00.3	1.4	56.3
08	300 27.7	08.5	8 01.3	10.0	17 58.9	1.5	56.2
M 09	315 27.9	.. 07.6	22 30.3	10.1	17 57.4	1.6	56.2
O 10	330 28.1	06.6	36 59.4	10.1	17 55.8	1.7	56.2
N 11	345 28.3	05.7	51 28.5	10.1	17 54.1	1.8	56.2
D 12	0 28.5	N 6 04.8	65 57.6	10.2	N17 52.3	1.8	56.1
A 13	15 28.7	03.8	80 26.8	10.2	17 50.5	2.0	56.1
Y 14	30 28.9	02.9	94 56.0	10.3	17 48.5	2.0	56.1
15	45 29.2	.. 02.0	109 25.3	10.3	17 46.5	2.2	56.0
16	60 29.4	01.0	123 54.6	10.3	17 44.3	2.2	56.0
17	75 29.6	6 00.1	138 23.9	10.4	17 42.1	2.4	56.0
18	90 29.8	N 5 59.2	152 53.3	10.5	N17 39.7	2.4	56.0
19	105 30.0	58.2	167 22.8	10.5	17 37.3	2.5	55.9
20	120 30.2	57.3	181 52.3	10.5	17 34.8	2.6	55.9
21	135 30.4	.. 56.4	196 21.8	10.5	17 32.2	2.6	55.9
22	150 30.7	55.4	210 51.3	10.7	17 29.6	2.8	55.9
23	165 30.9	54.5	225 21.0	10.6	17 26.8	2.9	55.8
8 00	180 31.1	N 5 53.5	239 50.6	10.7	N17 23.9	2.9	55.8
01	195 31.3	52.6	254 20.3	10.8	17 21.0	3.0	55.8
02	210 31.5	51.7	268 50.1	10.7	17 18.0	3.2	55.8
03	225 31.7	.. 50.7	283 19.8	10.9	17 14.8	3.2	55.7
04	240 31.9	49.8	297 49.7	10.8	17 11.6	3.3	55.7
05	255 32.1	48.9	312 19.5	11.0	17 08.3	3.3	55.7
06	270 32.4	N 5 47.9	326 49.5	10.9	N17 05.0	3.5	55.7
07	285 32.6	47.0	341 19.4	11.1	17 01.5	3.5	55.6
T 08	300 32.8	46.0	355 49.5	11.0	16 58.0	3.6	55.6
U 09	315 33.0	.. 45.1	10 19.5	11.1	16 54.4	3.7	55.6
E 10	330 33.2	44.2	24 49.6	11.2	16 50.7	3.8	55.6
S 11	345 33.4	43.2	39 19.8	11.2	16 46.9	3.9	55.5
D 12	0 33.6	N 5 42.3	53 50.0	11.2	N16 43.0	3.9	55.5
A 13	15 33.9	41.3	68 20.2	11.3	16 39.1	4.0	55.5
Y 14	30 34.1	40.4	82 50.5	11.3	16 35.1	4.1	55.5
15	45 34.3	.. 39.5	97 20.8	11.4	16 31.0	4.2	55.5
16	60 34.5	38.5	111 51.2	11.4	16 26.8	4.3	55.4
17	75 34.7	37.6	126 21.6	11.5	16 22.5	4.3	55.4
18	90 34.9	N 5 36.6	140 52.1	11.5	N16 18.2	4.4	55.4
19	105 35.2	35.7	155 22.6	11.6	16 13.8	4.5	55.4
20	120 35.4	34.8	169 53.2	11.6	16 09.3	4.6	55.4
21	135 35.6	.. 33.8	184 23.8	11.6	16 04.7	4.6	55.3
22	150 35.8	32.9	198 54.4	11.7	16 00.1	4.8	55.3
23	165 36.0	31.9	213 25.1	11.8	15 55.3	4.8	55.3
9 00	180 36.2	N 5 31.0	227 55.9	11.8	N15 50.5	4.8	55.3
01	195 36.4	30.1	242 26.7	11.8	15 45.7	5.0	55.2
02	210 36.7	29.1	256 57.5	11.9	15 40.7	5.0	55.2
03	225 36.9	.. 28.2	271 28.4	11.9	15 35.7	5.0	55.2
04	240 37.1	27.2	285 59.3	12.0	15 30.7	5.2	55.2
05	255 37.3	26.3	300 30.3	12.0	15 25.5	5.2	55.2
06	270 37.5	N 5 25.3	315 01.3	12.1	N15 20.3	5.3	55.1
07	285 37.7	24.4	329 32.4	12.1	15 15.0	5.4	55.1
W 08	300 38.0	23.5	344 03.5	12.2	15 09.6	5.4	55.1
E 09	315 38.2	.. 22.5	358 34.7	12.2	15 04.2	5.5	55.1
D 10	330 38.4	21.6	13 05.9	12.3	14 58.7	5.6	55.1
N 11	345 38.6	20.6	27 37.2	12.3	14 53.1	5.6	55.1
E 12	0 38.8	N 5 19.7	42 08.5	12.3	N14 47.5	5.7	55.0
S 13	15 39.0	18.7	56 39.8	12.4	14 41.8	5.8	55.0
D 14	30 39.2	17.8	71 11.2	12.4	14 36.0	5.8	55.0
A 15	45 39.5	.. 16.9	85 42.6	12.5	14 30.2	5.9	55.0
Y 16	60 39.7	15.9	100 14.1	12.5	14 24.3	5.9	55.0
17	75 39.9	15.0	114 45.6	12.6	14 18.4	6.1	54.9
18	90 40.1	N 5 14.0	129 17.2	12.6	N14 12.3	6.0	54.9
19	105 40.3	13.1	143 48.8	12.7	14 06.3	6.2	54.9
20	120 40.5	12.1	158 20.5	12.7	14 00.1	6.2	54.9
21	135 40.8	.. 11.2	172 52.2	12.7	13 53.9	6.3	54.9
22	150 41.0	10.2	187 23.9	12.8	13 47.6	6.3	54.9
23	165 41.2	09.3	201 55.7	12.8	N13 41.3	6.4	54.8
	SD 15.9	d 0.9	SD 15.3		15.1		15.0

Lat.	Twilight Naut.	Twilight Civil	Sunrise	Moonrise 7	8	9	10
°	h m	h m	h m	h m	h m	h m	h m
N 72	00 24	03 14	04 33	20 54	22 42	24 26	00 26
N 70	01 45	03 34	04 43	21 59	23 23	24 52	00 52
68	02 21	03 49	04 50	22 35	23 51	25 13	01 13
66	02 46	04 01	04 56	23 01	24 12	00 12	01 28
64	03 04	04 11	05 02	23 20	24 29	00 29	01 41
62	03 19	04 20	05 06	23 36	24 42	00 42	01 52
60	03 32	04 27	05 10	23 50	24 54	00 54	02 02
N 58	03 42	04 33	05 14	24 01	00 01	01 04	02 10
56	03 51	04 39	05 17	24 11	00 11	01 13	02 17
54	03 59	04 43	05 20	24 20	00 20	01 20	02 23
52	04 06	04 48	05 22	24 28	00 28	01 27	02 29
50	04 12	04 52	05 25	24 35	00 35	01 34	02 34
45	04 24	05 00	05 30	24 50	00 50	01 47	02 45
N 40	04 34	05 06	05 34	00 09	01 03	01 58	02 55
35	04 42	05 12	05 37	00 20	01 13	02 08	03 02
30	04 48	05 16	05 41	00 29	01 22	02 16	03 09
20	04 58	05 24	05 46	00 46	01 38	02 30	03 21
N 10	05 05	05 29	05 50	01 01	01 52	02 43	03 32
0	05 10	05 34	05 55	01 14	02 05	02 54	03 41
S 10	05 13	05 37	05 59	01 28	02 18	03 06	03 51
20	05 15	05 41	06 03	01 43	02 32	03 18	04 02
30	05 16	05 43	06 07	02 00	02 48	03 33	04 13
35	05 15	05 45	06 10	02 09	02 57	03 41	04 20
40	05 15	05 46	06 13	02 20	03 08	03 50	04 28
45	05 13	05 47	06 16	02 34	03 20	04 01	04 37
S 50	05 11	05 48	06 20	02 50	03 35	04 14	04 48
52	05 10	05 49	06 22	02 57	03 42	04 20	04 53
54	05 08	05 49	06 24	03 05	03 50	04 27	04 59
56	05 06	05 49	06 26	03 15	03 59	04 35	05 05
58	05 04	05 50	06 29	03 25	04 09	04 43	05 11
S 60	05 02	05 50	06 32	03 38	04 20	04 53	05 19

Lat.	Sunset	Twilight Civil	Twilight Naut.	Moonset 7	8	9	10
°	h m	h m	h m	h m	h m	h m	h m
N 72	19 19	20 37	23 05	18 55	18 50	18 45	18 41
N 70	19 10	20 18	22 03	17 50	18 08	18 18	18 22
68	19 03	20 04	21 30	17 13	17 40	17 57	18 07
66	18 57	19 52	21 06	16 48	17 19	17 40	17 55
64	18 52	19 42	20 48	16 28	17 02	17 26	17 45
62	18 47	19 34	20 33	16 11	16 47	17 15	17 36
60	18 44	19 27	20 21	15 58	16 35	17 05	17 29
N 58	18 40	19 21	20 11	15 46	16 25	16 56	17 22
56	18 37	19 15	20 03	15 36	16 16	16 49	17 16
54	18 34	19 11	19 55	15 27	16 08	16 42	17 11
52	18 32	19 07	19 48	15 19	16 01	16 36	17 06
50	18 30	19 03	19 42	15 12	15 54	16 30	17 02
45	18 25	18 55	19 30	14 56	15 40	16 18	16 52
N 40	18 21	18 48	19 21	14 44	15 28	16 09	16 45
35	18 18	18 43	19 13	14 33	15 19	16 00	16 38
30	18 15	18 39	19 07	14 23	15 10	15 52	16 32
20	18 09	18 32	18 57	14 07	14 55	15 39	16 21
N 10	18 05	18 26	18 51	13 53	14 42	15 28	16 12
0	18 01	18 22	18 46	13 39	14 29	15 17	16 04
S 10	17 57	18 18	18 43	13 26	14 17	15 06	15 55
20	17 53	18 15	18 41	13 11	14 03	14 55	15 46
30	17 49	18 12	18 40	12 55	13 48	14 42	15 35
35	17 46	18 11	18 41	12 45	13 39	14 34	15 29
40	17 43	18 10	18 42	12 34	13 29	14 25	15 22
45	17 40	18 09	18 43	12 21	13 17	14 15	15 13
S 50	17 36	18 08	18 46	12 05	13 02	14 02	15 03
52	17 34	18 08	18 47	11 58	12 56	13 56	14 59
54	17 32	18 08	18 49	11 49	12 48	13 50	14 54
56	17 30	18 07	18 50	11 40	12 40	13 43	14 48
58	17 28	18 07	18 53	11 30	12 30	13 35	14 42
S 60	17 25	18 07	18 55	11 18	12 19	13 25	14 35

Day	SUN Eqn. of Time 00h	SUN Eqn. of Time 12h	SUN Mer. Pass.	MOON Mer. Pass. Upper	MOON Mer. Pass. Lower	Age	Phase
d	m s	m s	h m	h m	h m	d	%
7	01 43	01 54	11 58	07 27	19 52	24	29
8	02 04	02 14	11 58	08 17	20 42	25	20
9	02 24	02 35	11 57	09 06	21 29	26	13

UT	ARIES GHA	VENUS −4.7 GHA	Dec	MARS +1.8 GHA	Dec	JUPITER −1.7 GHA	Dec	SATURN +0.6 GHA	Dec	STARS Name	SHA	Dec
d h	° ′	° ′	° ′	° ′	° ′	° ′	° ′	° ′	° ′		° ′	° ′
10 00	348 42.8	213 30.6	N10 14.9	205 25.7	N15 46.5	190 13.1	N 9 59.1	111 01.8	S18 15.1	Acamar	315 17.0	S40 14.4
01	3 45.3	228 32.6	15.2	220 26.6	46.0	205 15.0	58.9	126 04.1	15.2	Achernar	335 25.3	S57 09.3
02	18 47.7	243 34.6	15.4	235 27.5	45.5	220 17.0	58.7	141 06.4	15.2	Acrux	173 08.1	S63 11.2
03	33 50.2	258 36.6 ..	15.7	250 28.4 ..	45.0	235 18.9 ..	58.5	156 08.8 ..	15.2	Adhara	255 11.5	S28 59.5
04	48 52.6	273 38.6	15.9	265 29.3	44.5	250 20.9	58.3	171 11.1	15.3	Aldebaran	290 47.6	N16 32.3
05	63 55.1	288 40.6	16.2	280 30.2	44.0	265 22.8	58.1	186 13.4	15.3			
06	78 57.6	303 42.6	N10 16.5	295 31.1	N15 43.5	280 24.8	N 9 58.0	201 15.7	S18 15.4	Alioth	166 20.0	N55 52.7
07	94 00.0	318 44.6	16.7	310 32.0	43.0	295 26.7	57.8	216 18.0	15.4	Alkaid	152 58.1	N49 14.4
T 08	109 02.5	333 46.6	17.0	325 32.9	42.5	310 28.7	57.6	231 20.3	15.5	Al Na'ir	27 41.5	S46 53.0
H 09	124 05.0	348 48.6 ..	17.2	340 33.8 ..	42.0	325 30.7 ..	57.4	246 22.6 ..	15.5	Alnilam	275 44.9	S 1 11.6
U 10	139 07.4	3 50.6	17.5	355 34.7	41.5	340 32.6	57.2	261 24.9	15.5	Alphard	217 54.9	S 8 43.6
R 11	154 09.9	18 52.6	17.7	10 35.6	41.0	355 34.6	57.0	276 27.3	15.6			
S 12	169 12.4	33 54.6	N10 18.0	25 36.5	N15 40.6	10 36.5	N 9 56.8	291 29.6	S18 15.6	Alphecca	126 09.9	N26 40.1
D 13	184 14.8	48 56.5	18.3	40 37.4	40.1	25 38.5	56.6	306 31.9	15.7	Alpheratz	357 41.5	N29 10.7
A 14	199 17.3	63 58.5	18.5	55 38.3	39.6	40 40.4	56.4	321 34.2	15.7	Altair	62 06.5	N 8 54.9
Y 15	214 19.7	79 00.5 ..	18.8	70 39.2 ..	39.1	55 42.4 ..	56.2	336 36.5 ..	15.7	Ankaa	353 13.9	S42 13.1
16	229 22.2	94 02.4	19.0	85 40.1	38.6	70 44.3	56.0	351 38.8	15.8	Antares	112 24.4	S26 27.8
17	244 24.7	109 04.4	19.3	100 41.0	38.1	85 46.3	55.8	6 41.1	15.8			
18	259 27.1	124 06.3	N10 19.5	115 41.9	N15 37.6	100 48.3	N 9 55.6	21 43.4	S18 15.9	Arcturus	145 54.6	N19 06.4
19	274 29.6	139 08.3	19.7	130 42.8	37.1	115 50.2	55.4	36 45.7	15.9	Atria	107 24.8	S69 03.4
20	289 32.1	154 10.2	20.0	145 43.7	36.6	130 52.2	55.2	51 48.0	15.9	Avior	234 17.8	S59 33.5
21	304 34.5	169 12.2 ..	20.2	160 44.7 ..	36.1	145 54.1 ..	55.0	66 50.4 ..	16.0	Bellatrix	278 30.4	N 6 21.7
22	319 37.0	184 14.1	20.5	175 45.6	35.6	160 56.1	54.8	81 52.7	16.0	Betelgeuse	270 59.7	N 7 24.5
23	334 39.5	199 16.1	20.7	190 46.5	35.1	175 58.0	54.6	96 55.0	16.1			
11 00	349 41.9	214 18.0	N10 21.0	205 47.4	N15 34.6	191 00.0	N 9 54.4	111 57.3	S18 16.1	Canopus	263 55.6	S52 42.1
01	4 44.4	229 19.9	21.2	220 48.3	34.1	206 01.9	54.2	126 59.6	16.1	Capella	280 32.2	N46 00.5
02	19 46.9	244 21.9	21.5	235 49.2	33.6	221 03.9	54.0	142 01.9	16.2	Deneb	49 30.0	N45 20.6
03	34 49.3	259 23.8 ..	21.7	250 50.1 ..	33.1	236 05.8 ..	53.8	157 04.2 ..	16.2	Denebola	182 32.5	N14 29.2
04	49 51.8	274 25.7	21.9	265 51.0	32.6	251 07.8	53.6	172 06.5	16.3	Diphda	348 54.1	S17 53.9
05	64 54.2	289 27.6	22.2	280 51.9	32.1	266 09.8	53.4	187 08.8	16.3			
06	79 56.7	304 29.5	N10 22.4	295 52.8	N15 31.6	281 11.7	N 9 53.2	202 11.1	S18 16.4	Dubhe	193 50.6	N61 40.0
07	94 59.2	319 31.4	22.7	310 53.7	31.1	296 13.7	53.0	217 13.4	16.4	Elnath	278 10.7	N28 37.0
08	110 01.6	334 33.3	22.9	325 54.6	30.6	311 15.6	52.8	232 15.8	16.4	Eltanin	90 45.3	N51 29.7
F 09	125 04.1	349 35.2 ..	23.1	340 55.5 ..	30.1	326 17.6 ..	52.6	247 18.1 ..	16.5	Enif	33 45.3	N 9 57.1
R 10	140 06.6	4 37.1	23.4	355 56.4	29.6	341 19.5	52.5	262 20.4	16.5	Fomalhaut	15 22.0	S29 32.2
I 11	155 09.0	19 39.0	23.6	10 57.3	29.1	356 21.5	52.3	277 22.7	16.6			
D 12	170 11.5	34 40.9	N10 23.8	25 58.3	N15 28.6	11 23.4	N 9 52.1	292 25.0	S18 16.6	Gacrux	171 59.6	S57 12.1
A 13	185 14.0	49 42.8	24.1	40 59.2	28.1	26 25.4	51.9	307 27.3	16.6	Gienah	175 51.0	S17 37.6
Y 14	200 16.4	64 44.7	24.3	56 00.1	27.6	41 27.4	51.7	322 29.6	16.7	Hadar	148 46.1	S60 26.9
15	215 18.9	79 46.6 ..	24.5	71 01.0 ..	27.1	56 29.3 ..	51.5	337 31.9 ..	16.7	Hamal	327 58.8	N23 32.1
16	230 21.4	94 48.4	24.8	86 01.9	26.6	71 31.3	51.3	352 34.2	16.8	Kaus Aust.	83 41.7	S34 22.5
17	245 23.8	109 50.3	25.0	101 02.8	26.1	86 33.2	51.1	7 36.5	16.8			
18	260 26.3	124 52.2	N10 25.2	116 03.7	N15 25.6	101 35.2	N 9 50.9	22 38.8	S18 16.9	Kochab	137 20.9	N74 05.9
19	275 28.7	139 54.0	25.4	131 04.6	25.1	116 37.1	50.7	37 41.1	16.9	Markab	13 36.5	N15 17.6
20	290 31.2	154 55.9	25.7	146 05.5	24.6	131 39.1	50.5	52 43.4	16.9	Menkar	314 13.3	N 4 09.0
21	305 33.7	169 57.7 ..	25.9	161 06.4 ..	24.1	146 41.0 ..	50.3	67 45.7 ..	17.0	Menkent	148 06.0	S36 26.7
22	320 36.1	184 59.6	26.1	176 07.3	23.6	161 43.0	50.1	82 48.1	17.0	Miaplacidus	221 40.0	S69 46.8
23	335 38.6	200 01.5	26.3	191 08.3	23.1	176 45.0	49.9	97 50.4	17.1			
12 00	350 41.1	215 03.3	N10 26.6	206 09.2	N15 22.6	191 46.9	N 9 49.7	112 52.7	S18 17.1	Mirfak	308 37.9	N49 54.7
01	5 43.5	230 05.1	26.8	221 10.1	22.1	206 48.9	49.5	127 55.0	17.1	Nunki	75 56.3	S26 16.4
02	20 46.0	245 07.0	27.0	236 11.0	21.6	221 50.8	49.3	142 57.3	17.2	Peacock	53 16.5	S56 41.0
03	35 48.5	260 08.8 ..	27.2	251 11.9 ..	21.1	236 52.8 ..	49.1	157 59.6 ..	17.2	Pollux	243 26.1	N27 59.1
04	50 50.9	275 10.6	27.4	266 12.8	20.6	251 54.7	48.9	173 01.9	17.3	Procyon	244 58.3	N 5 11.0
05	65 53.4	290 12.5	27.7	281 13.7	20.1	266 56.7	48.7	188 04.2	17.3			
06	80 55.8	305 14.3	N10 27.9	296 14.6	N15 19.6	281 58.7	N 9 48.5	203 06.5	S18 17.4	Rasalhague	96 05.0	N12 33.3
07	95 58.3	320 16.1	28.1	311 15.5	19.1	297 00.6	48.3	218 08.8	17.4	Regulus	207 42.2	N11 53.4
S 08	111 00.8	335 17.9	28.3	326 16.4	18.6	312 02.6	48.1	233 11.1	17.4	Rigel	281 10.6	S 8 11.0
A 09	126 03.2	350 19.8 ..	28.5	341 17.4 ..	18.1	327 04.5 ..	47.9	248 13.4 ..	17.5	Rigil Kent.	139 50.0	S60 54.0
T 10	141 05.7	5 21.6	28.7	356 18.3	17.6	342 06.5	47.7	263 15.7	17.5	Sabik	102 10.8	S15 44.4
U 11	156 08.2	20 23.4	28.9	11 19.2	17.1	357 08.4	47.5	278 18.0	17.6			
R 12	171 10.6	35 25.2	N10 29.2	26 20.1	N15 16.6	12 10.4	N 9 47.3	293 20.3	S18 17.6	Schedar	349 38.1	N56 37.3
D 13	186 13.1	50 27.0	29.4	41 21.0	16.1	27 12.3	47.2	308 22.6	17.7	Shaula	96 19.8	S37 06.8
A 14	201 15.6	65 28.8	29.6	56 21.9	15.6	42 14.3	47.0	323 24.9	17.7	Sirius	258 32.5	S16 44.3
Y 15	216 18.0	80 30.6 ..	29.8	71 22.8 ..	15.1	57 16.3 ..	46.8	338 27.2 ..	17.7	Spica	158 29.9	S11 14.4
16	231 20.5	95 32.4	30.0	86 23.7	14.6	72 18.2	46.6	353 29.5	17.8	Suhail	222 51.6	S43 29.7
17	246 23.0	110 34.1	30.2	101 24.7	14.1	87 20.2	46.4	8 31.8	17.8			
18	261 25.4	125 35.9	N10 30.4	116 25.6	N15 13.6	102 22.1	N 9 46.2	23 34.1	S18 17.9	Vega	80 37.8	N38 48.4
19	276 27.9	140 37.7	30.6	131 26.5	13.1	117 24.1	46.0	38 36.4	17.9	Zuben'ubi	137 03.9	S16 06.2
20	291 30.3	155 39.5	30.8	146 27.4	12.6	132 26.0	45.8	53 38.7	17.9		SHA	Mer. Pass.
21	306 32.8	170 41.2 ..	31.0	161 28.3 ..	12.1	147 28.0 ..	45.6	68 41.0 ..	18.0		° ′	h m
22	321 35.3	185 43.0	31.2	176 29.2	11.6	162 30.0	45.4	83 43.4	18.0	Venus	224 36.1	9 42
23	336 37.7	200 44.8	31.4	191 30.1	11.1	177 31.9	45.2	98 45.7	18.1	Mars	216 05.4	10 16
	h m									Jupiter	201 18.1	11 15
Mer. Pass.	0 41.1	v 1.9	d 0.2	v 0.9	d 0.5	v 2.0	d 0.2	v 2.3	d 0.0	Saturn	122 15.4	16 30

UT	SUN GHA	SUN Dec	MOON GHA	MOON v	MOON Dec	MOON d	MOON HP
d h	° ′	° ′	° ′	′	° ′	′	′
10 00	180 41.4	N 5 08.4	216 27.5	12.9	N13 34.9	6.4	54.8
01	195 41.6	07.4	230 59.4	12.9	13 28.5	6.5	54.8
02	210 41.8	06.5	245 31.3	13.0	13 22.0	6.6	54.8
03	225 42.1	.. 05.5	260 03.3	13.0	13 15.4	6.6	54.8
04	240 42.3	04.6	274 35.3	13.1	13 08.8	6.7	54.8
05	255 42.5	03.6	289 07.4	13.1	13 02.1	6.7	54.7
06	270 42.7	N 5 02.7	303 39.5	13.1	N12 55.4	6.8	54.7
T 07	285 42.9	01.7	318 11.6	13.2	12 48.6	6.8	54.7
H 08	300 43.1	5 00.8	332 43.8	13.2	12 41.8	6.9	54.7
U 09	315 43.4	4 59.8	347 16.0	13.3	12 34.9	7.0	54.7
R 10	330 43.6	58.9	1 48.3	13.3	12 27.9	7.0	54.7
S 11	345 43.8	57.9	16 20.6	13.3	12 20.9	7.0	54.7
D 12	0 44.0	N 4 57.0	30 52.9	13.4	N12 13.9	7.1	54.6
A 13	15 44.2	56.1	45 25.3	13.4	12 06.8	7.2	54.6
Y 14	30 44.5	55.1	59 57.7	13.5	11 59.6	7.2	54.6
15	45 44.7	.. 54.2	74 30.2	13.5	11 52.4	7.2	54.6
16	60 44.9	53.2	89 02.7	13.5	11 45.2	7.3	54.6
17	75 45.1	52.3	103 35.2	13.6	11 37.9	7.4	54.6
18	90 45.3	N 4 51.3	118 07.8	13.6	N11 30.5	7.4	54.6
19	105 45.5	50.4	132 40.4	13.7	11 23.1	7.4	54.5
20	120 45.8	49.4	147 13.1	13.7	11 15.7	7.5	54.5
21	135 46.0	.. 48.5	161 45.8	13.7	11 08.2	7.5	54.5
22	150 46.2	47.5	176 18.5	13.8	11 00.7	7.6	54.5
23	165 46.4	46.6	190 51.3	13.8	10 53.1	7.6	54.5
11 00	180 46.6	N 4 45.6	205 24.1	13.8	N10 45.5	7.7	54.5
01	195 46.9	44.7	219 56.9	13.9	10 37.8	7.7	54.5
02	210 47.1	43.7	234 29.8	13.9	10 30.1	7.8	54.4
03	225 47.3	.. 42.8	249 02.7	14.0	10 22.3	7.8	54.4
04	240 47.5	41.8	263 35.7	13.9	10 14.5	7.8	54.4
05	255 47.7	40.9	278 08.6	14.1	10 06.7	7.9	54.4
06	270 47.9	N 4 39.9	292 41.7	14.0	N 9 58.8	7.9	54.4
07	285 48.2	39.0	307 14.7	14.1	9 50.9	8.0	54.4
F 08	300 48.4	38.0	321 47.8	14.1	9 42.9	8.0	54.4
R 09	315 48.6	.. 37.1	336 20.9	14.2	9 34.9	8.0	54.4
I 10	330 48.8	36.1	350 54.1	14.2	9 26.9	8.1	54.4
D 11	345 49.0	35.2	5 27.3	14.2	9 18.8	8.1	54.3
A 12	0 49.3	N 4 34.2	20 00.5	14.3	N 9 10.7	8.1	54.3
Y 13	15 49.5	33.3	34 33.8	14.3	9 02.6	8.2	54.3
14	30 49.7	32.3	49 07.1	14.3	8 54.4	8.2	54.3
15	45 49.9	.. 31.4	63 40.4	14.3	8 46.2	8.2	54.3
16	60 50.1	30.4	78 13.7	14.4	8 38.0	8.3	54.3
17	75 50.3	29.5	92 47.1	14.4	8 29.7	8.3	54.3
18	90 50.6	N 4 28.5	107 20.5	14.5	N 8 21.4	8.4	54.3
19	105 50.8	27.6	121 54.0	14.4	8 13.0	8.4	54.3
20	120 51.0	26.6	136 27.4	14.5	8 04.6	8.4	54.3
21	135 51.2	.. 25.7	151 00.9	14.6	7 56.2	8.4	54.2
22	150 51.4	24.7	165 34.5	14.5	7 47.8	8.5	54.2
23	165 51.7	23.8	180 08.0	14.6	7 39.3	8.5	54.2
12 00	180 51.9	N 4 22.8	194 41.6	14.6	N 7 30.8	8.5	54.2
01	195 52.1	21.9	209 15.2	14.7	7 22.3	8.6	54.2
02	210 52.3	20.9	223 48.9	14.6	7 13.7	8.6	54.2
03	225 52.5	.. 20.0	238 22.5	14.7	7 05.1	8.6	54.2
04	240 52.8	19.0	252 56.2	14.7	6 56.5	8.6	54.2
05	255 53.0	18.1	267 29.9	14.8	6 47.9	8.7	54.2
06	270 53.2	N 4 17.1	282 03.7	14.7	N 6 39.2	8.7	54.2
S 07	285 53.4	16.1	296 37.4	14.8	6 30.5	8.7	54.2
A 08	300 53.6	15.2	311 11.2	14.8	6 21.8	8.8	54.1
T 09	315 53.9	.. 14.2	325 45.0	14.9	6 13.0	8.7	54.1
U 10	330 54.1	13.3	340 18.9	14.8	6 04.3	8.8	54.1
R 11	345 54.3	12.3	354 52.7	14.9	5 55.5	8.8	54.1
D 12	0 54.5	N 4 11.4	9 26.6	14.9	N 5 46.7	8.8	54.1
A 13	15 54.7	10.4	24 00.5	14.9	5 37.9	8.9	54.1
Y 14	30 55.0	09.5	38 34.4	15.0	5 29.0	8.9	54.1
15	45 55.2	.. 08.5	53 08.4	14.9	5 20.1	8.9	54.1
16	60 55.4	07.6	67 42.3	15.0	5 11.2	8.9	54.1
17	75 55.6	06.6	82 16.3	15.0	5 02.3	8.9	54.1
18	90 55.8	N 4 05.7	96 50.3	15.1	N 4 53.4	8.9	54.1
19	105 56.1	04.7	111 24.4	15.0	4 44.5	9.0	54.1
20	120 56.3	03.8	125 58.4	15.1	4 35.5	9.0	54.1
21	135 56.5	.. 02.8	140 32.5	15.1	4 26.5	9.0	54.1
22	150 56.7	01.8	155 06.5	15.1	4 17.5	9.0	54.1
23	165 56.9	00.9	169 40.6	15.1	N 4 08.5	9.0	54.0
	SD 15.9	d 1.0	SD 14.9		14.8		14.7

Twilight / Sunrise / Moonrise

Lat.	Twilight Naut.	Twilight Civil	Sunrise	Moonrise 10	11	12	13
°	h m	h m	h m	h m	h m	h m	h m
N 72	01 23	03 31	04 47	00 26	02 05	03 40	05 14
N 70	02 10	03 48	04 55	00 52	02 22	03 51	05 18
68	02 39	04 01	05 01	01 13	02 36	03 59	05 22
66	03 00	04 12	05 06	01 28	02 47	04 06	05 25
64	03 16	04 21	05 10	01 41	02 56	04 12	05 27
62	03 30	04 28	05 14	01 52	03 04	04 17	05 29
60	03 41	04 34	05 17	02 02	03 11	04 21	05 31
N 58	03 50	04 40	05 20	02 10	03 17	04 25	05 33
56	03 58	04 45	05 23	02 17	03 23	04 29	05 35
54	04 05	04 49	05 25	02 23	03 27	04 32	05 36
52	04 11	04 53	05 27	02 29	03 32	04 34	05 37
50	04 17	04 56	05 29	02 34	03 35	04 37	05 38
45	04 28	05 04	05 33	02 45	03 44	04 42	05 41
N 40	04 37	05 09	05 37	02 55	03 51	04 47	05 43
35	04 44	05 14	05 40	03 02	03 57	04 51	05 45
30	04 50	05 18	05 42	03 09	04 02	04 54	05 46
20	04 58	05 24	05 46	03 21	04 11	05 00	05 49
N 10	05 05	05 29	05 50	03 32	04 19	05 06	05 51
0	05 09	05 33	05 53	03 41	04 27	05 11	05 54
S 10	05 11	05 36	05 57	03 51	04 34	05 16	05 56
20	05 12	05 38	06 00	04 02	04 42	05 21	05 58
30	05 12	05 40	06 04	04 13	04 51	05 27	06 01
35	05 11	05 41	06 06	04 20	04 56	05 30	06 02
40	05 10	05 41	06 08	04 28	05 02	05 34	06 04
45	05 08	05 42	06 11	04 37	05 09	05 39	06 06
S 50	05 04	05 42	06 14	04 48	05 17	05 44	06 09
52	05 03	05 42	06 15	04 53	05 21	05 46	06 10
54	05 01	05 42	06 17	04 59	05 25	05 49	06 11
56	04 59	05 42	06 18	05 05	05 30	05 52	06 12
58	04 56	05 41	06 20	05 11	05 35	05 55	06 14
S 60	04 53	05 41	06 23	05 19	05 41	05 59	06 16

Sunset / Twilight / Moonset

Lat.	Sunset	Twilight Civil	Twilight Naut.	Moonset 10	11	12	13
°	h m	h m	h m	h m	h m	h m	h m
N 72	19 03	20 18	22 20	18 41	18 37	18 32	18 28
N 70	18 56	20 02	21 38	18 22	18 25	18 26	18 27
68	18 50	19 49	21 05	18 07	18 15	18 21	18 25
66	18 45	19 39	20 50	17 55	18 07	18 16	18 24
64	18 41	19 31	20 34	17 45	18 00	18 12	18 24
62	18 38	19 23	20 21	17 36	17 54	18 09	18 23
60	18 34	19 17	20 11	17 29	17 49	18 06	18 22
N 58	18 32	19 12	20 01	17 22	17 44	18 03	18 22
56	18 29	19 07	19 53	17 16	17 40	18 01	18 21
54	18 27	19 03	19 47	17 11	17 36	17 59	18 21
52	18 25	18 59	19 41	17 06	17 33	17 57	18 20
50	18 23	18 56	19 35	17 02	17 30	17 55	18 20
45	18 19	18 49	19 24	16 52	17 23	17 52	18 19
N 40	18 16	18 43	19 16	16 45	17 18	17 48	18 18
35	18 13	18 39	19 09	16 38	17 13	17 46	18 17
30	18 11	18 35	19 03	16 32	17 08	17 43	18 17
20	18 07	18 29	18 55	16 21	17 01	17 39	18 16
N 10	18 03	18 24	18 49	16 12	16 54	17 35	18 15
0	18 00	18 21	18 45	16 04	16 48	17 31	18 14
S 10	17 57	18 18	18 42	15 55	16 42	17 28	18 13
20	17 54	18 16	18 41	15 46	16 35	17 24	18 12
30	17 50	18 14	18 42	15 35	16 28	17 20	18 11
35	17 48	18 13	18 43	15 29	16 23	17 17	18 10
40	17 46	18 13	18 44	15 22	16 18	17 14	18 10
45	17 43	18 13	18 47	15 13	16 12	17 11	18 09
S 50	17 40	18 13	18 50	15 03	16 05	17 06	18 08
52	17 39	18 13	18 52	14 59	16 02	17 05	18 07
54	17 38	18 13	18 54	14 54	15 58	17 03	18 07
56	17 36	18 13	18 56	14 48	15 54	17 00	18 06
58	17 34	18 13	18 59	14 42	15 50	16 58	18 06
S 60	17 32	18 14	19 02	14 35	15 45	16 55	18 05

SUN / MOON

Day	SUN Eqn. of Time 00ʰ	SUN Eqn. of Time 12ʰ	SUN Mer. Pass.	MOON Mer. Pass. Upper	MOON Mer. Pass. Lower	Age	Phase
d	m s	m s	h m	h m	h m	d	%
10	02 45	02 56	11 57	09 53	22 15	27	7
11	03 06	03 17	11 57	10 38	22 59	28	3
12	03 27	03 38	11 56	11 21	23 43	29	1

UT	ARIES GHA	VENUS −4.7 GHA	Dec	MARS +1.8 GHA	Dec	JUPITER −1.7 GHA	Dec	SATURN +0.6 GHA	Dec
13 00	351 40.2	215 46.5	N10 31.6	206 31.1	N15 10.6	192 33.9	N 9 45.0	113 48.0	S18 18.1
01	6 42.7	230 48.3	31.8	221 32.0	10.1	207 35.8	44.8	128 50.3	18.2
02	21 45.1	245 50.1	32.0	236 32.9	09.6	222 37.8	44.6	143 52.6	18.2
03	36 47.6	260 51.8 ..	32.2	251 33.8 ..	09.1	237 39.7 ..	44.4	158 54.9 ..	18.2
04	51 50.1	275 53.6	32.4	266 34.7	08.5	252 41.7	44.2	173 57.2	18.3
05	66 52.5	290 55.3	32.6	281 35.6	08.0	267 43.7	44.0	188 59.5	18.3
S 06	81 55.0	305 57.0	N10 32.8	296 36.5	N15 07.5	282 45.6	N 9 43.8	204 01.8	S18 18.4
U 07	96 57.4	320 58.8	33.0	311 37.5	07.0	297 47.6	43.6	219 04.1	18.4
N 08	111 59.9	336 00.5	33.2	326 38.4	06.5	312 49.5	43.4	234 06.4	18.5
D 09	127 02.4	351 02.2 ..	33.4	341 39.3 ..	06.0	327 51.5 ..	43.2	249 08.7 ..	18.5
A 10	142 04.8	6 04.0	33.6	356 40.2	05.5	342 53.4	43.0	264 11.0	18.5
Y 11	157 07.3	21 05.7	33.8	11 41.1	05.0	357 55.4	42.8	279 13.3	18.6
12	172 09.8	36 07.4	N10 34.0	26 42.0	N15 04.5	12 57.4	N 9 42.6	294 15.6	S18 18.6
13	187 12.2	51 09.1	34.2	41 42.9	04.0	27 59.3	42.4	309 17.9	18.7
14	202 14.7	66 10.8	34.4	56 43.9	03.5	43 01.3	42.2	324 20.2	18.7
15	217 17.2	81 12.6 ..	34.6	71 44.8 ..	03.0	58 03.2 ..	42.0	339 22.5 ..	18.8
16	232 19.6	96 14.3	34.7	86 45.7	02.5	73 05.2	41.9	354 24.8	18.8
17	247 22.1	111 16.0	34.9	101 46.6	02.0	88 07.1	41.7	9 27.1	18.8
18	262 24.6	126 17.7	N10 35.1	116 47.5	N15 01.5	103 09.1	N 9 41.5	24 29.4	S18 18.9
19	277 27.0	141 19.4	35.3	131 48.4	01.0	118 11.1	41.3	39 31.7	18.9
20	292 29.5	156 21.1	35.5	146 49.4	15 00.4	133 13.0	41.1	54 34.0	19.0
21	307 31.9	171 22.7 ..	35.7	161 50.3	14 59.9	148 15.0 ..	40.9	69 36.3 ..	19.0
22	322 34.4	186 24.4	35.8	176 51.2	59.4	163 16.9	40.7	84 38.6	19.1
23	337 36.9	201 26.1	36.0	191 52.1	58.9	178 18.9	40.5	99 40.9	19.1
14 00	352 39.3	216 27.8	N10 36.2	206 53.0	N14 58.4	193 20.9	N 9 40.3	114 43.2	S18 19.1
01	7 41.8	231 29.5	36.4	221 54.0	57.9	208 22.8	40.1	129 45.5	19.2
02	22 44.3	246 31.1	36.6	236 54.9	57.4	223 24.8	39.9	144 47.8	19.2
03	37 46.7	261 32.8 ..	36.7	251 55.8 ..	56.9	238 26.7 ..	39.7	159 50.1 ..	19.3
04	52 49.2	276 34.5	36.9	266 56.7	56.4	253 28.7	39.5	174 52.4	19.3
05	67 51.7	291 36.1	37.1	281 57.6	55.9	268 30.6	39.3	189 54.7	19.4
M 06	82 54.1	306 37.8	N10 37.3	296 58.5	N14 55.4	283 32.6	N 9 39.1	204 57.0	S18 19.4
O 07	97 56.6	321 39.5	37.4	311 59.5	54.9	298 34.6	38.9	219 59.2	19.4
N 08	112 59.0	336 41.1	37.6	327 00.4	54.4	313 36.5	38.7	235 01.5	19.5
D 09	128 01.5	351 42.8 ..	37.8	342 01.3 ..	53.8	328 38.5 ..	38.5	250 03.8 ..	19.5
A 10	143 04.0	6 44.4	38.0	357 02.2	53.3	343 40.4	38.3	265 06.1	19.6
Y 11	158 06.4	21 46.1	38.1	12 03.1	52.8	358 42.4	38.1	280 08.4	19.6
12	173 08.9	36 47.7	N10 38.3	27 04.1	N14 52.3	13 44.4	N 9 37.9	295 10.7	S18 19.7
13	188 11.4	51 49.3	38.5	42 05.0	51.8	28 46.3	37.7	310 13.0	19.7
14	203 13.8	66 51.0	38.6	57 05.9	51.3	43 48.3	37.5	325 15.3	19.7
15	218 16.3	81 52.6 ..	38.8	72 06.8 ..	50.8	58 50.2 ..	37.3	340 17.6 ..	19.8
16	233 18.8	96 54.2	39.0	87 07.7	50.3	73 52.2	37.1	355 19.9	19.8
17	248 21.2	111 55.8	39.1	102 08.7	49.8	88 54.1	37.0	10 22.2	19.9
18	263 23.7	126 57.5	N10 39.3	117 09.6	N14 49.3	103 56.1	N 9 36.8	25 24.5	S18 19.9
19	278 26.2	141 59.1	39.4	132 10.5	48.7	118 58.1	36.6	40 26.8	20.0
20	293 28.6	157 00.7	39.6	147 11.4	48.2	134 00.0	36.4	55 29.1	20.0
21	308 31.1	172 02.3 ..	39.8	162 12.4	47.7	149 02.0 ..	36.2	70 31.4 ..	20.0
22	323 33.5	187 03.9	39.9	177 13.3	47.2	164 03.9	36.0	85 33.7	20.1
23	338 36.0	202 05.5	40.1	192 14.2	46.7	179 05.9	35.8	100 36.0	20.1
15 00	353 38.5	217 07.1	N10 40.2	207 15.1	N14 46.2	194 07.9	N 9 35.6	115 38.3	S18 20.2
01	8 40.9	232 08.7	40.4	222 16.0	45.7	209 09.8	35.4	130 40.6	20.2
02	23 43.4	247 10.3	40.6	237 17.0	45.2	224 11.8	35.2	145 42.9	20.3
03	38 45.9	262 11.9 ..	40.7	252 17.9 ..	44.7	239 13.7 ..	35.0	160 45.2 ..	20.3
04	53 48.3	277 13.5	40.9	267 18.8	44.1	254 15.7	34.8	175 47.5	20.4
05	68 50.8	292 15.1	41.0	282 19.7	43.6	269 17.7	34.6	190 49.8	20.4
T 06	83 53.3	307 16.7	N10 41.2	297 20.7	N14 43.1	284 19.6	N 9 34.4	205 52.1	S18 20.4
U 07	98 55.7	322 18.2	41.3	312 21.6	42.6	299 21.6	34.2	220 54.4	20.5
E 08	113 58.2	337 19.8	41.5	327 22.5	42.1	314 23.5	34.0	235 56.6	20.5
S 09	129 00.6	352 21.4 ..	41.6	342 23.4 ..	41.6	329 25.5 ..	33.8	250 58.9 ..	20.6
D 10	144 03.1	7 23.0	41.8	357 24.3	41.1	344 27.5	33.6	266 01.2	20.6
A 11	159 05.6	22 24.5	41.9	12 25.3	40.6	359 29.4	33.4	281 03.5	20.7
Y 12	174 08.0	37 26.1	N10 42.1	27 26.2	N14 40.0	14 31.4	N 9 33.2	296 05.8	S18 20.7
13	189 10.5	52 27.6	42.2	42 27.1	39.5	29 33.3	33.0	311 08.1	20.7
14	204 13.0	67 29.2	42.4	57 28.0	39.0	44 35.3	32.8	326 10.4	20.8
15	219 15.4	82 30.7 ..	42.5	72 29.0 ..	38.5	59 37.3 ..	32.6	341 12.7 ..	20.8
16	234 17.9	97 32.3	42.6	87 29.9	38.0	74 39.2	32.4	356 15.0	20.9
17	249 20.4	112 33.8	42.8	102 30.8	37.5	89 41.2	32.3	11 17.3	20.9
18	264 22.8	127 35.4	N10 42.9	117 31.7	N14 37.0	104 43.1	N 9 32.1	26 19.6	S18 21.0
19	279 25.3	142 36.9	43.1	132 32.7	36.4	119 45.1	31.9	41 21.9	21.0
20	294 27.8	157 38.5	43.2	147 33.6	35.9	134 47.1	31.7	56 24.2	21.1
21	309 30.2	172 40.0 ..	43.3	162 34.5 ..	35.4	149 49.0 ..	31.5	71 26.5 ..	21.1
22	324 32.7	187 41.5	43.5	177 35.4	34.9	164 51.0	31.3	86 28.7	21.1
23	339 35.1	202 43.1	43.6	192 36.4	34.4	179 52.9	31.1	101 31.0	21.2
Mer. Pass.	h m 0 29.3	v 1.6 d 0.2		v 0.9 d 0.5		v 2.0 d 0.2		v 2.3 d 0.0	

STARS

Name	SHA	Dec
Acamar	315 17.0	S40 14.4
Achernar	335 25.3	S57 09.3
Acrux	173 08.1	S63 11.2
Adhara	255 11.5	S28 59.5
Aldebaran	290 47.6	N16 32.3
Alioth	166 20.0	N55 52.7
Alkaid	152 58.2	N49 14.4
Al Na'ir	27 41.5	S46 53.0
Alnilam	275 44.8	S 1 11.6
Alphard	217 54.9	S 8 43.6
Alphecca	126 09.9	N26 40.1
Alpheratz	357 41.5	N29 10.7
Altair	62 06.6	N 8 54.9
Ankaa	353 13.9	S42 13.1
Antares	112 24.5	S26 27.8
Arcturus	145 54.6	N19 06.3
Atria	107 24.9	S69 03.4
Avior	234 17.8	S59 33.5
Bellatrix	278 30.4	N 6 21.7
Betelgeuse	270 59.7	N 7 24.5
Canopus	263 55.6	S52 42.1
Capella	280 32.2	N46 00.5
Deneb	49 30.0	N45 20.6
Denebola	182 32.5	N14 29.2
Diphda	348 54.1	S17 53.9
Dubhe	193 50.6	N61 40.0
Elnath	278 10.7	N28 37.0
Eltanin	90 45.4	N51 29.7
Enif	33 45.3	N 9 57.1
Fomalhaut	15 22.0	S29 32.2
Gacrux	171 59.6	S57 12.0
Gienah	175 51.0	S17 37.6
Hadar	148 46.1	S60 26.9
Hamal	327 58.7	N23 32.1
Kaus Aust.	83 41.7	S34 22.5
Kochab	137 21.0	N74 05.8
Markab	13 36.5	N15 17.6
Menkar	314 13.3	N 4 09.0
Menkent	148 06.0	S36 26.7
Miaplacidus	221 40.0	S69 46.8
Mirfak	308 37.9	N49 54.7
Nunki	75 56.3	S26 16.4
Peacock	53 16.5	S56 41.0
Pollux	243 26.1	N27 59.1
Procyon	244 58.3	N 5 11.0
Rasalhague	96 05.0	N12 33.3
Regulus	207 42.2	N11 53.4
Rigel	281 10.6	S 8 11.0
Rigil Kent.	139 50.0	S60 54.0
Sabik	102 10.8	S15 44.4
Schedar	349 38.1	N56 37.4
Shaula	96 19.8	S37 06.8
Sirius	258 32.5	S16 44.2
Spica	158 29.9	S11 14.4
Suhail	222 51.6	S43 29.7
Vega	80 37.8	N38 48.4
Zuben'ubi	137 03.9	S16 06.2

	SHA	Mer. Pass.
	° '	h m
Venus	223 48.5	9 33
Mars	214 13.7	10 12
Jupiter	200 41.5	11 05
Saturn	122 03.8	16 19

SUN and MOON

UT	SUN GHA	SUN Dec	MOON GHA	v	MOON Dec	d	HP
d h	° ′	° ′	° ′	′	° ′	′	′
13 00	180 57.2	N 3 59.9	184 14.7	15.2	N 3 59.5	9.1	54.0
01	195 57.4	59.0	198 48.9	15.1	3 50.4	9.0	54.0
02	210 57.6	58.0	213 23.0	15.1	3 41.4	9.1	54.0
03	225 57.8	.. 57.1	227 57.1	15.2	3 32.3	9.1	54.0
04	240 58.0	56.1	242 31.3	15.2	3 23.2	9.1	54.0
05	255 58.3	55.2	257 05.5	15.2	N 3 14.1	9.1	54.0
06	270 58.5	N 3 54.2					
07	285 58.7	53.2					
S 08	300 58.9	52.3	A partial eclipse of				
U 09	315 59.1	.. 51.3	the Sun occurs on this				
N 10	330 59.4	50.4	date. See page 5.				
D 11	345 59.6	49.4					
A 12	0 59.8	N 3 48.5	359 05.1	15.3	N 2 10.2	9.2	54.0
Y 13	16 00.0	47.5	13 39.4	15.3	2 01.0	9.2	54.0
14	31 00.2	46.5	28 13.7	15.3	1 51.8	9.1	54.0
15	46 00.5	.. 45.6	42 48.0	15.3	1 42.7	9.2	54.0
16	61 00.7	44.6	57 22.3	15.3	1 33.5	9.2	54.0
17	76 00.9	43.7	71 56.6	15.3	1 24.3	9.2	54.0
18	91 01.1	N 3 42.7	86 30.9	15.3	N 1 15.1	9.2	54.0
19	106 01.4	41.8	101 05.2	15.3	1 05.9	9.2	54.0
20	121 01.6	40.8	115 39.5	15.4	0 56.7	9.2	54.0
21	136 01.8	.. 39.8	130 13.9	15.3	0 47.5	9.2	54.0
22	151 02.0	38.9	144 48.2	15.4	0 38.3	9.3	54.0
23	166 02.2	37.9	159 22.5	15.4	N 0 29.0	9.2	54.0
14 00	181 02.5	N 3 37.0	173 56.9	15.3	N 0 19.8	9.2	54.0
01	196 02.7	36.0	188 31.2	15.4	0 10.6	9.2	54.0
02	211 02.9	35.1	203 05.6	15.3	N 0 01.4	9.2	54.0
03	226 03.1	.. 34.1	217 39.9	15.4	S 0 07.8	9.2	54.0
04	241 03.3	33.1	232 14.3	15.3	0 17.0	9.2	54.0
05	256 03.6	32.2	246 48.6	15.4	0 26.2	9.2	53.9
06	271 03.8	N 3 31.2	261 23.0	15.4	S 0 35.4	9.2	53.9
07	286 04.0	30.3	275 57.4	15.3	0 44.6	9.2	53.9
M 08	301 04.2	29.3	290 31.7	15.4	0 53.8	9.2	53.9
O 09	316 04.4	.. 28.3	305 06.1	15.3	1 03.0	9.2	53.9
N 10	331 04.7	27.4	319 40.4	15.4	1 12.2	9.2	53.9
D 11	346 04.9	26.4	334 14.8	15.3	1 21.4	9.2	53.9
A 12	1 05.1	N 3 25.5	348 49.1	15.4	S 1 30.6	9.2	53.9
Y 13	16 05.3	24.5	3 23.5	15.3	1 39.8	9.1	53.9
14	31 05.6	23.6	17 57.8	15.4	1 48.9	9.2	53.9
15	46 05.8	.. 22.6	32 32.2	15.3	1 58.1	9.1	53.9
16	61 06.0	21.6	47 06.5	15.3	2 07.2	9.2	53.9
17	76 06.2	20.7	61 40.8	15.4	2 16.4	9.1	54.0
18	91 06.4	N 3 19.7	76 15.2	15.3	S 2 25.5	9.1	54.0
19	106 06.7	18.8	90 49.5	15.3	2 34.6	9.1	54.0
20	121 06.9	17.8	105 23.8	15.3	2 43.7	9.1	54.0
21	136 07.1	.. 16.8	119 58.1	15.3	2 52.8	9.1	54.0
22	151 07.3	15.9	134 32.4	15.3	3 01.9	9.1	54.0
23	166 07.6	14.9	149 06.7	15.3	3 11.0	9.1	54.0
15 00	181 07.8	N 3 14.0	163 41.0	15.2	S 3 20.1	9.0	54.0
01	196 08.0	13.0	178 15.2	15.3	3 29.1	9.1	54.0
02	211 08.2	12.0	192 49.5	15.2	3 38.2	9.0	54.0
03	226 08.4	.. 11.1	207 23.7	15.3	3 47.2	9.0	54.0
04	241 08.7	10.1	221 58.0	15.2	3 56.2	9.0	54.0
05	256 08.9	09.2	236 32.2	15.2	4 05.2	8.9	54.0
06	271 09.1	N 3 08.2	251 06.4	15.2	S 4 14.1	9.0	54.0
07	286 09.3	07.2	265 40.6	15.2	4 23.1	8.9	54.0
T 08	301 09.5	06.3	280 14.8	15.2	4 32.0	9.0	54.0
U 09	316 09.8	.. 05.3	294 49.0	15.2	4 41.0	8.9	54.0
E 10	331 10.0	04.3	309 23.2	15.1	4 49.9	8.9	54.0
S 11	346 10.2	03.4	323 57.3	15.2	4 58.8	8.8	54.0
D 12	1 10.4	N 3 02.4	338 31.5	15.1	S 5 07.6	8.9	54.0
A 13	16 10.7	01.5	353 05.6	15.1	5 16.5	8.8	54.0
Y 14	31 10.9	3 00.5	7 39.7	15.1	5 25.3	8.8	54.0
15	46 11.1	2 59.5	22 13.8	15.0	5 34.1	8.8	54.0
16	61 11.3	58.6	36 47.8	15.1	5 42.9	8.8	54.0
17	76 11.5	57.6	51 21.9	15.0	5 51.7	8.7	54.0
18	91 11.8	N 2 56.6	65 55.9	15.0	S 6 00.4	8.7	54.0
19	106 12.0	55.7	80 29.9	15.0	6 09.1	8.7	54.0
20	121 12.2	54.7	95 03.9	15.0	6 17.8	8.7	54.0
21	136 12.4	.. 53.8	109 37.9	14.9	6 26.5	8.6	54.0
22	151 12.7	52.8	124 11.8	15.0	6 35.1	8.6	54.0
23	166 12.9	51.8	138 45.8	14.9	S 6 43.7	8.6	54.1
	SD 15.9	d 1.0	SD 14.7		14.7		14.7

Twilight and Moonrise

Lat.	Naut.	Civil	Sunrise	Moonrise 13	14	15	16
°	h m	h m	h m	h m	h m	h m	h m
N 72	01 55	03 48	05 01	05 14	06 46	08 18	09 51
N 70	02 30	04 02	05 07	05 18	06 45	08 11	09 38
68	02 55	04 13	05 12	05 22	06 44	08 06	09 28
66	03 13	04 22	05 16	05 25	06 43	08 01	09 19
64	03 28	04 30	05 19	05 27	06 42	07 57	09 12
62	03 39	04 36	05 22	05 29	06 42	07 54	09 06
60	03 49	04 42	05 25	05 31	06 41	07 51	09 01
N 58	03 58	04 47	05 27	05 33	06 41	07 48	08 56
56	04 05	04 51	05 29	05 35	06 40	07 46	08 52
54	04 11	04 55	05 31	05 36	06 40	07 44	08 48
52	04 17	04 58	05 32	05 37	06 40	07 42	08 45
50	04 22	05 01	05 34	05 38	06 39	07 40	08 41
45	04 32	05 07	05 37	05 41	06 39	07 37	08 35
N 40	04 40	05 12	05 40	05 43	06 38	07 34	08 29
35	04 47	05 16	05 42	05 45	06 38	07 31	08 25
30	04 52	05 20	05 44	05 46	06 38	07 29	08 20
20	04 59	05 25	05 47	05 49	06 37	07 25	08 13
N 10	05 04	05 29	05 50	05 51	06 36	07 21	08 07
0	05 08	05 32	05 52	05 54	06 36	07 18	08 01
S 10	05 09	05 34	05 55	05 56	06 35	07 15	07 55
20	05 10	05 35	05 57	05 58	06 35	07 12	07 49
30	05 08	05 36	06 00	06 01	06 34	07 08	07 42
35	05 07	05 36	06 02	06 02	06 34	07 06	07 38
40	05 05	05 36	06 03	06 04	06 34	07 03	07 33
45	05 02	05 36	06 05	06 06	06 33	07 00	07 28
S 50	04 58	05 35	06 07	06 09	06 33	06 57	07 22
52	04 56	05 35	06 08	06 10	06 33	06 55	07 19
54	04 53	05 34	06 09	06 11	06 32	06 54	07 16
56	04 51	05 34	06 11	06 12	06 32	06 52	07 12
58	04 47	05 33	06 12	06 14	06 32	06 50	07 09
S 60	04 44	05 32	06 13	06 16	06 31	06 47	07 04

Sunset, Twilight and Moonset

Lat.	Sunset	Civil	Naut.	Moonset 13	14	15	16
°	h m	h m	h m	h m	h m	h m	h m
N 72	18 48	20 00	21 48	18 28	18 24	18 19	18 15
N 70	18 42	19 46	21 16	18 27	18 27	18 28	18 29
68	18 38	19 35	20 53	18 25	18 30	18 35	18 41
66	18 34	19 27	20 35	18 24	18 32	18 41	18 51
64	18 31	19 19	20 21	18 24	18 35	18 46	18 59
62	18 28	19 13	20 10	18 23	18 36	18 50	19 06
60	18 25	19 08	20 00	18 22	18 38	18 54	19 12
N 58	18 23	19 03	19 52	18 22	18 39	18 58	19 17
56	18 21	18 59	19 45	18 21	18 41	19 01	19 22
54	18 20	18 55	19 38	18 21	18 42	19 03	19 27
52	18 18	18 52	19 33	18 20	18 43	19 06	19 31
50	18 17	18 49	19 28	18 20	18 44	19 08	19 34
45	18 14	18 43	19 18	18 19	18 46	19 13	19 42
N 40	18 11	18 38	19 10	18 18	18 47	19 17	19 48
35	18 09	18 34	19 04	18 17	18 49	19 21	19 54
30	18 07	18 31	18 59	18 17	18 50	19 24	19 59
20	18 04	18 26	18 52	18 16	18 52	19 29	20 07
N 10	18 01	18 22	18 47	18 15	18 54	19 34	20 15
0	17 59	18 20	18 44	18 14	18 56	19 39	20 22
S 10	17 57	18 18	18 42	18 13	18 58	19 43	20 29
20	17 54	18 16	18 42	18 12	19 00	19 48	20 37
30	17 52	18 16	18 43	18 11	19 02	19 54	20 45
35	17 50	18 16	18 45	18 10	19 04	19 57	20 50
40	17 49	18 16	18 47	18 10	19 05	20 01	20 56
45	17 47	18 16	18 50	18 09	19 07	20 05	21 03
S 50	17 45	18 17	18 55	18 08	19 09	20 10	21 11
52	17 44	18 18	18 57	18 07	19 10	20 12	21 14
54	17 43	18 18	18 59	18 07	19 11	20 15	21 19
56	17 42	18 19	19 02	18 06	19 12	20 18	21 23
58	17 41	18 20	19 05	18 06	19 13	20 21	21 28
S 60	17 39	18 21	19 09	18 05	19 15	20 24	21 34

SUN and MOON

Day	Eqn. of Time 00ʰ	12ʰ	Mer. Pass.	Mer. Pass. Upper	Lower	Age	Phase %
d	m s	m s	h m	h m	h m	d	%
13	03 48	03 59	11 56	12 04	24 25	00	0
14	04 09	04 20	11 56	12 46	00 25	01	1
15	04 31	04 41	11 55	13 28	01 07	02	4

UT	ARIES GHA	VENUS −4.8 GHA	Dec	MARS +1.8 GHA	Dec	JUPITER −1.7 GHA	Dec	SATURN +0.6 GHA	Dec	STARS Name	SHA	Dec
16 00	354 37.6	217 44.6	N10 43.8	207 37.3	N14 33.9	194 54.9	N 9 30.9	116 33.3	S18 21.2	Acamar	315 17.0	S40 14.4
01	9 40.1	232 46.1	43.9	222 38.2	33.4	209 56.9	30.7	131 35.6	21.3	Achernar	335 25.2	S57 09.3
02	24 42.5	247 47.6	44.0	237 39.1	32.8	224 58.8	30.5	146 37.9	21.3	Acrux	173 08.1	S63 11.2
03	39 45.0	262 49.1 ..	44.2	252 40.1 ..	32.3	240 00.8 ..	30.3	161 40.2 ..	21.4	Adhara	255 11.4	S28 59.5
04	54 47.5	277 50.6	44.3	267 41.0	31.8	255 02.7	30.1	176 42.5	21.4	Aldebaran	290 47.5	N16 32.3
05	69 49.9	292 52.2	44.4	282 41.9	31.3	270 04.7	29.9	191 44.8	21.5			
W 06	84 52.4	307 53.7	N10 44.6	297 42.8	N14 30.8	285 06.7	N 9 29.7	206 47.1	S18 21.5	Alioth	166 20.0	N55 52.7
E 07	99 54.9	322 55.2	44.7	312 43.8	30.3	300 08.6	29.5	221 49.4	21.5	Alkaid	152 58.2	N49 14.4
D 08	114 57.3	337 56.7	44.8	327 44.7	29.7	315 10.6	29.3	236 51.7	21.6	Al Na'ir	27 41.5	S46 53.0
N 09	129 59.8	352 58.2 ..	44.9	342 45.6 ..	29.2	330 12.5 ..	29.1	251 54.0 ..	21.6	Alnilam	275 44.8	S 1 11.6
E 10	145 02.3	7 59.7	45.1	357 46.6	28.7	345 14.5	28.9	266 56.2	21.7	Alphard	217 54.9	S 8 43.6
S 11	160 04.7	23 01.1	45.2	12 47.5	28.2	0 16.5	28.7	281 58.5	21.7			
D 12	175 07.2	38 02.6	N10 45.3	27 48.4	N14 27.7	15 18.4	N 9 28.5	297 00.8	S18 21.8	Alphecca	126 09.9	N26 40.1
A 13	190 09.6	53 04.1	45.4	42 49.3	27.2	30 20.4	28.3	312 03.1	21.8	Alpheratz	357 41.5	N29 10.7
Y 14	205 12.1	68 05.6	45.6	57 50.3	26.6	45 22.3	28.1	327 05.4	21.9	Altair	62 06.6	N 8 55.0
15	220 14.6	83 07.1 ..	45.7	72 51.2 ..	26.1	60 24.3 ..	27.9	342 07.7 ..	21.9	Ankaa	353 13.8	S42 13.1
16	235 17.0	98 08.5	45.8	87 52.1	25.6	75 26.3	27.8	357 10.0	21.9	Antares	112 24.5	S26 27.8
17	250 19.5	113 10.0	45.9	102 53.1	25.1	90 28.2	27.6	12 12.3	22.0			
18	265 22.0	128 11.5	N10 46.0	117 54.0	N14 24.6	105 30.2	N 9 27.4	27 14.6	S18 22.0	Arcturus	145 54.6	N19 06.3
19	280 24.4	143 13.0	46.2	132 54.9	24.1	120 32.1	27.2	42 16.8	22.1	Atria	107 24.9	S69 03.4
20	295 26.9	158 14.4	46.3	147 55.8	23.5	135 34.1	27.0	57 19.1	22.1	Avior	234 17.7	S59 33.5
21	310 29.4	173 15.9 ..	46.4	162 56.8 ..	23.0	150 36.1 ..	26.8	72 21.4 ..	22.2	Bellatrix	278 30.4	N 6 21.7
22	325 31.8	188 17.3	46.5	177 57.7	22.5	165 38.0	26.6	87 23.7	22.2	Betelgeuse	270 59.7	N 7 24.5
23	340 34.3	203 18.8	46.6	192 58.6	22.0	180 40.0	26.4	102 26.0	22.3			
17 00	355 36.7	218 20.2	N10 46.7	207 59.6	N14 21.5	195 42.0	N 9 26.2	117 28.3	S18 22.3	Canopus	263 55.6	S52 42.1
01	10 39.2	233 21.7	46.8	223 00.5	21.0	210 43.9	26.0	132 30.6	22.3	Capella	280 32.1	N46 00.5
02	25 41.7	248 23.1	46.9	238 01.4	20.4	225 45.9	25.8	147 32.9	22.4	Deneb	49 30.1	N45 20.6
03	40 44.1	263 24.6 ..	47.1	253 02.3 ..	19.9	240 47.8 ..	25.6	162 35.2 ..	22.4	Denebola	182 32.5	N14 29.2
04	55 46.6	278 26.0	47.2	268 03.3	19.4	255 49.8	25.4	177 37.4	22.5	Diphda	348 54.1	S17 53.9
05	70 49.1	293 27.4	47.3	283 04.2	18.9	270 51.8	25.2	192 39.7	22.5			
T 06	85 51.5	308 28.9	N10 47.4	298 05.1	N14 18.4	285 53.7	N 9 25.0	207 42.0	S18 22.6	Dubhe	193 50.6	N61 39.9
H 07	100 54.0	323 30.3	47.5	313 06.1	17.8	300 55.7	24.8	222 44.3	22.6	Elnath	278 10.7	N28 37.0
U 08	115 56.5	338 31.7	47.6	328 07.0	17.3	315 57.6	24.6	237 46.6	22.7	Eltanin	90 45.4	N51 29.7
R 09	130 58.9	353 33.2 ..	47.7	343 07.9 ..	16.8	330 59.6 ..	24.4	252 48.9 ..	22.7	Enif	33 45.3	N 9 57.1
S 10	146 01.4	8 34.6	47.8	358 08.9	16.3	346 01.6	24.2	267 51.2	22.7	Fomalhaut	15 22.0	S29 32.2
D 11	161 03.9	23 36.0	47.9	13 09.8	15.8	1 03.5	24.0	282 53.5	22.8			
A 12	176 06.3	38 37.4	N10 48.0	28 10.7	N14 15.2	16 05.5	N 9 23.8	297 55.7	S18 22.8	Gacrux	171 59.6	S57 12.0
Y 13	191 08.8	53 38.8	48.1	43 11.7	14.7	31 07.5	23.6	312 58.0	22.9	Gienah	175 51.0	S17 37.4
14	206 11.2	68 40.2	48.2	58 12.6	14.2	46 09.4	23.4	328 00.3	22.9	Hadar	148 46.1	S60 26.9
15	221 13.7	83 41.6 ..	48.3	73 13.5 ..	13.7	61 11.4 ..	23.3	343 02.6 ..	23.0	Hamal	327 58.7	N23 32.1
16	236 16.2	98 43.0	48.4	88 14.5	13.2	76 13.3	23.1	358 04.9	23.0	Kaus Aust.	83 41.7	S34 22.5
17	251 18.6	113 44.4	48.5	103 15.4	12.6	91 15.3	22.9	13 07.2	23.1			
18	266 21.1	128 45.8	N10 48.6	118 16.3	N14 12.1	106 17.3	N 9 22.7	28 09.5	S18 23.1	Kochab	137 21.0	N74 05.8
19	281 23.6	143 47.2	48.7	133 17.3	11.6	121 19.2	22.5	43 11.7	23.1	Markab	13 36.5	N15 17.6
20	296 26.0	158 48.6	48.8	148 18.2	11.1	136 21.2	22.3	58 14.0	23.2	Menkar	314 13.3	N 4 09.0
21	311 28.5	173 50.0 ..	48.9	163 19.1 ..	10.6	151 23.2 ..	22.1	73 16.3 ..	23.2	Menkent	148 06.0	S36 26.7
22	326 31.0	188 51.4	49.0	178 20.1	10.0	166 25.1	21.9	88 18.6	23.3	Miaplacidus	221 39.9	S69 46.8
23	341 33.4	203 52.8	49.1	193 21.0	09.5	181 27.1	21.7	103 20.9	23.3			
18 00	356 35.9	218 54.1	N10 49.1	208 21.9	N14 09.0	196 29.0	N 9 21.5	118 23.2	S18 23.4	Mirfak	308 37.8	N49 54.7
01	11 38.3	233 55.5	49.2	223 22.9	08.5	211 31.0	21.3	133 25.5	23.4	Nunki	75 56.3	S26 16.4
02	26 40.8	248 56.9	49.3	238 23.8	08.0	226 33.0	21.1	148 27.7	23.5	Peacock	53 16.5	S56 41.0
03	41 43.3	263 58.3 ..	49.4	253 24.7 ..	07.4	241 34.9 ..	20.9	163 30.0 ..	23.5	Pollux	243 26.1	N27 59.1
04	56 45.7	278 59.6	49.5	268 25.7	06.9	256 36.9	20.7	178 32.3	23.6	Procyon	244 58.3	N 5 11.0
05	71 48.2	294 01.0	49.6	283 26.6	06.4	271 38.9	20.5	193 34.6	23.6			
F 06	86 50.7	309 02.4	N10 49.7	298 27.5	N14 05.9	286 40.8	N 9 20.3	208 36.9	S18 23.6	Rasalhague	96 05.0	N12 33.3
R 07	101 53.1	324 03.7	49.7	313 28.5	05.3	301 42.8	20.1	223 39.2	23.7	Regulus	207 42.2	N11 53.4
I 08	116 55.6	339 05.1	49.8	328 29.4	04.8	316 44.7	19.9	238 41.4	23.7	Rigel	281 10.6	S 8 11.0
D 09	131 58.1	354 06.4 ..	49.9	343 30.3 ..	04.3	331 46.7 ..	19.7	253 43.7 ..	23.8	Rigil Kent.	139 50.0	S60 54.0
A 10	147 00.5	9 07.8	50.0	358 31.3	03.8	346 48.7	19.5	268 46.0	23.8	Sabik	102 10.8	S15 44.4
Y 11	162 03.0	24 09.1	50.1	13 32.2	03.3	1 50.6	19.3	283 48.3	23.9			
12	177 05.5	39 10.5	N10 50.1	28 33.1	N14 02.7	16 52.6	N 9 19.2	298 50.6	S18 23.9	Schedar	349 38.1	N56 37.4
13	192 07.9	54 11.8	50.2	43 34.1	02.2	31 54.6	19.0	313 52.9	24.0	Shaula	96 19.8	S37 06.8
14	207 10.4	69 13.2	50.3	58 35.0	01.7	46 56.5	18.8	328 55.2	24.0	Sirius	258 32.5	S16 44.2
15	222 12.8	84 14.5 ..	50.4	73 35.9 ..	01.2	61 58.5 ..	18.6	343 57.4 ..	24.1	Spica	158 29.9	S11 14.4
16	237 15.3	99 15.8	50.4	88 36.9	00.6	77 00.5	18.4	358 59.7	24.1	Suhail	222 51.6	S43 29.7
17	252 17.8	114 17.2	50.5	103 37.8	14 00.1	92 02.4	18.2	14 02.0	24.1			
18	267 20.2	129 18.5	N10 50.6	118 38.8	N13 59.6	107 04.4	N 9 18.0	29 04.3	S18 24.2	Vega	80 37.8	N38 48.4
19	282 22.7	144 19.8	50.7	133 39.7	59.1	122 06.3	17.8	44 06.6	24.2	Zuben'ubi	137 03.9	S16 06.2
20	297 25.2	159 21.1	50.7	148 40.6	58.5	137 08.3	17.6	59 08.8	24.3			
21	312 27.6	174 22.4 ..	50.8	163 41.6 ..	58.0	152 10.3 ..	17.4	74 11.1 ..	24.3		SHA	Mer. Pass.
22	327 30.1	189 23.8	50.9	178 42.5	57.5	167 12.2	17.2	89 13.4	24.4	Venus	222 43.5	9 26
23	342 32.6	204 25.1	50.9	193 43.4	57.0	182 14.2	17.0	104 15.7	24.4	Mars	212 22.8	10 07
Mer. Pass.	h m 0 17.5	v 1.4	d 0.1	v 0.9	d 0.5	v 2.0	d 0.2	v 2.3	d 0.0	Jupiter Saturn	200 05.2 121 51.5	10 56 16 08

SUN and MOON

UT	SUN GHA	SUN Dec	MOON GHA	v	MOON Dec	d	HP
d h	° ′	° ′	° ′	′	° ′	′	′
16 00	181 13.1	N 2 50.9	153 19.7	14.9	S 6 52.3	8.6	54.1
01	196 13.3	49.9	167 53.6	14.9	7 00.9	8.5	54.1
02	211 13.5	48.9	182 27.5	14.8	7 09.4	8.5	54.1
03	226 13.8	.. 48.0	197 01.3	14.8	7 17.9	8.5	54.1
04	241 14.0	47.0	211 35.1	14.8	7 26.4	8.4	54.1
05	256 14.2	46.1	226 08.9	14.8	7 34.8	8.5	54.1
W 06	271 14.4	N 2 45.1	240 42.7	14.7	S 7 43.3	8.4	54.1
E 07	286 14.7	44.1	255 16.4	14.8	7 51.7	8.3	54.1
D 08	301 14.9	43.2	269 50.2	14.7	8 00.0	8.3	54.1
N 09	316 15.1	.. 42.2	284 23.9	14.6	8 08.3	8.3	54.1
E 10	331 15.3	41.2	298 57.5	14.7	8 16.6	8.3	54.1
S 11	346 15.5	40.3	313 31.2	14.6	8 24.9	8.2	54.1
D 12	1 15.8	N 2 39.3	328 04.8	14.6	S 8 33.1	8.2	54.1
A 13	16 16.0	38.3	342 38.4	14.6	8 41.3	8.2	54.2
Y 14	31 16.2	37.4	357 12.0	14.5	8 49.5	8.1	54.2
15	46 16.4	.. 36.4	11 45.5	14.5	8 57.6	8.1	54.2
16	61 16.7	35.5	26 19.0	14.5	9 05.7	8.0	54.2
17	76 16.9	34.5	40 52.5	14.4	9 13.7	8.1	54.2
18	91 17.1	N 2 33.5	55 25.9	14.4	S 9 21.8	7.9	54.2
19	106 17.3	32.6	69 59.3	14.4	9 29.7	8.0	54.2
20	121 17.5	31.6	84 32.7	14.4	9 37.7	7.9	54.2
21	136 17.8	.. 30.6	99 06.1	14.3	9 45.6	7.9	54.2
22	151 18.0	29.7	113 39.4	14.3	9 53.5	7.8	54.2
23	166 18.2	28.7	128 12.7	14.3	10 01.3	7.8	54.3
17 00	181 18.4	N 2 27.7	142 46.0	14.2	S10 09.1	7.7	54.3
01	196 18.7	26.8	157 19.2	14.2	10 16.8	7.7	54.3
02	211 18.9	25.8	171 52.4	14.1	10 24.5	7.7	54.3
03	226 19.1	.. 24.8	186 25.5	14.2	10 32.2	7.6	54.3
04	241 19.3	23.9	200 58.7	14.0	10 39.8	7.6	54.3
05	256 19.6	22.9	215 31.7	14.1	10 47.4	7.5	54.3
T 06	271 19.8	N 2 21.9	230 04.8	14.0	S10 54.9	7.5	54.3
H 07	286 20.0	21.0	244 37.8	14.0	11 02.4	7.5	54.4
U 08	301 20.2	20.0	259 10.8	13.9	11 09.9	7.4	54.4
R 09	316 20.4	.. 19.1	273 43.7	13.9	11 17.3	7.3	54.4
S 10	331 20.7	18.1	288 16.6	13.9	11 24.6	7.3	54.4
D 11	346 20.9	17.1	302 49.5	13.8	11 31.9	7.3	54.4
A 12	1 21.1	N 2 16.2	317 22.3	13.8	S11 39.2	7.2	54.4
Y 13	16 21.3	15.2	331 55.1	13.8	11 46.4	7.1	54.4
14	31 21.6	14.2	346 27.9	13.7	11 53.5	7.2	54.4
15	46 21.8	.. 13.3	1 00.6	13.7	12 00.7	7.0	54.5
16	61 22.0	12.3	15 33.3	13.6	12 07.7	7.0	54.5
17	76 22.2	11.3	30 05.9	13.6	12 14.7	7.0	54.5
18	91 22.4	N 2 10.4	44 38.5	13.6	S12 21.7	6.9	54.5
19	106 22.7	09.4	59 11.1	13.5	12 28.6	6.9	54.5
20	121 22.9	08.4	73 43.6	13.5	12 35.5	6.8	54.5
21	136 23.1	.. 07.5	88 16.1	13.4	12 42.3	6.8	54.5
22	151 23.3	06.5	102 48.5	13.4	12 49.1	6.7	54.6
23	166 23.6	05.5	117 20.9	13.4	12 55.8	6.6	54.6
18 00	181 23.8	N 2 04.6	131 53.3	13.3	S13 02.4	6.6	54.6
01	196 24.0	03.6	146 25.6	13.3	13 09.0	6.5	54.6
02	211 24.2	02.6	160 57.8	13.3	13 15.5	6.5	54.6
03	226 24.4	.. 01.7	175 30.1	13.1	13 22.0	6.5	54.6
04	241 24.7	2 00.7	190 02.2	13.2	13 28.5	6.3	54.7
05	256 24.9	1 59.7	204 34.4	13.1	13 34.8	6.3	54.7
F 06	271 25.1	N 1 58.8	219 06.5	13.0	S13 41.1	6.3	54.7
R 07	286 25.3	57.8	233 38.5	13.0	13 47.4	6.2	54.7
I 08	301 25.6	56.8	248 10.5	13.0	13 53.6	6.1	54.7
D 09	316 25.8	.. 55.9	262 42.5	12.9	13 59.7	6.1	54.8
A 10	331 26.0	54.9	277 14.4	12.9	14 05.8	6.0	54.8
Y 11	346 26.2	53.9	291 46.3	12.8	14 11.8	6.0	54.8
12	1 26.5	N 1 52.9	306 18.1	12.7	S14 17.8	5.9	54.8
13	16 26.7	52.0	320 49.8	12.8	14 23.7	5.8	54.8
14	31 26.9	51.0	335 21.6	12.7	14 29.5	5.8	54.8
15	46 27.1	.. 50.0	349 53.3	12.6	14 35.3	5.7	54.9
16	61 27.3	49.1	4 24.9	12.6	14 41.0	5.6	54.9
17	76 27.6	48.1	18 56.5	12.5	14 46.6	5.6	54.9
18	91 27.8	N 1 47.1	33 28.0	12.5	S14 52.2	5.5	54.9
19	106 28.0	46.2	47 59.5	12.5	14 57.7	5.4	54.9
20	121 28.2	45.2	62 31.0	12.4	15 03.1	5.4	55.0
21	136 28.5	.. 44.2	77 02.4	12.3	15 08.5	5.3	55.0
22	151 28.7	43.3	91 33.7	12.3	15 13.8	5.3	55.0
23	166 28.9	42.3	106 05.0	12.3	S15 19.1	5.1	55.0
	SD 15.9	d 1.0	SD 14.8	14.8			14.9

Twilight, Sunrise and Moonrise

Lat.	Twilight Naut.	Civil	Sunrise	Moonrise 16	17	18	19
°	h m	h m	h m	h m	h m	h m	h m
N 72	02 21	04 03	05 14	09 51	11 28	13 08	14 55
N 70	02 49	04 15	05 19	09 38	11 07	12 36	14 05
68	03 10	04 25	05 22	09 28	10 51	12 13	13 34
66	03 26	04 33	05 25	09 19	10 38	11 55	13 10
64	03 38	04 39	05 28	09 12	10 27	11 41	12 52
62	03 49	04 45	05 30	09 06	10 18	11 29	12 38
60	03 58	04 49	05 32	09 01	10 10	11 19	12 25
N 58	04 05	04 53	05 33	08 56	10 03	11 10	12 14
56	04 12	04 57	05 35	08 52	09 57	11 02	12 05
54	04 18	05 00	05 36	08 48	09 52	10 55	11 57
52	04 23	05 03	05 37	08 45	09 47	10 49	11 49
50	04 27	05 06	05 38	08 41	09 42	10 43	11 43
45	04 36	05 11	05 40	08 35	09 33	10 31	11 29
N 40	04 43	05 15	05 42	08 29	09 25	10 21	11 17
35	04 49	05 19	05 44	08 25	09 18	10 13	11 07
30	04 53	05 21	05 45	08 20	09 12	10 05	10 58
20	05 00	05 26	05 48	08 13	09 02	09 52	10 43
N 10	05 04	05 29	05 50	08 07	08 53	09 41	10 30
0	05 07	05 31	05 51	08 01	08 45	09 31	10 18
S 10	05 08	05 32	05 53	07 55	08 37	09 20	10 06
20	05 07	05 33	05 55	07 49	08 28	09 09	09 53
30	05 05	05 32	05 56	07 42	08 18	08 56	09 38
35	05 03	05 32	05 57	07 38	08 12	08 49	09 30
40	05 00	05 31	05 58	07 33	08 06	08 41	09 20
45	04 56	05 30	05 59	07 28	07 58	08 31	09 09
S 50	04 51	05 29	06 01	07 22	07 49	08 20	08 55
52	04 49	05 28	06 01	07 19	07 45	08 14	08 49
54	04 46	05 27	06 02	07 16	07 41	08 09	08 42
56	04 42	05 26	06 03	07 12	07 36	08 02	08 34
58	04 39	05 25	06 04	07 09	07 30	07 55	08 25
S 60	04 34	05 23	06 04	07 04	07 24	07 46	08 15

Sunset, Twilight and Moonset

Lat.	Sunset	Twilight Civil	Naut.	Moonset 16	17	18	19
°	h m	h m	h m	h m	h m	h m	h m
N 72	18 32	19 42	21 22	18 15	18 10	18 05	17 57
N 70	18 28	19 31	20 55	18 29	18 32	18 37	18 48
68	18 25	19 22	20 36	18 41	18 49	19 01	19 20
66	18 22	19 14	20 21	18 51	19 03	19 19	19 43
64	18 20	19 08	20 08	18 59	19 15	19 35	20 02
62	18 18	19 03	19 58	19 06	19 24	19 47	20 17
60	18 16	18 58	19 49	19 12	19 33	19 58	20 29
N 58	18 15	18 54	19 42	19 17	19 40	20 07	20 40
56	18 13	18 51	19 36	19 22	19 47	20 15	20 50
54	18 12	18 48	19 30	19 27	19 53	20 23	20 59
52	18 11	18 45	19 25	19 31	19 58	20 29	21 06
50	18 10	18 42	19 21	19 34	20 03	20 35	21 13
45	18 08	18 37	19 12	19 42	20 13	20 48	21 28
N 40	18 06	18 33	19 05	19 48	20 22	20 59	21 40
35	18 05	18 30	19 00	19 54	20 29	21 08	21 50
30	18 03	18 27	18 55	19 59	20 36	21 16	21 59
20	18 01	18 23	18 49	20 07	20 47	21 30	22 15
N 10	17 59	18 20	18 45	20 15	20 57	21 42	22 29
0	17 58	18 19	18 43	20 22	21 07	21 53	22 41
S 10	17 56	18 17	18 42	20 29	21 16	22 04	22 54
20	17 55	18 17	18 42	20 37	21 26	22 17	23 08
30	17 53	18 17	18 45	20 45	21 38	22 31	23 24
35	17 52	18 18	18 47	20 50	21 44	22 39	23 33
40	17 52	18 19	18 50	20 56	21 52	22 48	23 43
45	17 51	18 20	18 54	21 03	22 01	22 59	23 55
S 50	17 49	18 22	18 59	21 11	22 12	23 12	24 10
52	17 49	18 22	19 02	21 14	22 17	23 18	24 17
54	17 48	18 23	19 05	21 19	22 22	23 24	24 25
56	17 48	18 25	19 08	21 23	22 28	23 32	24 34
58	17 47	18 26	19 12	21 28	22 35	23 41	24 43
S 60	17 46	18 28	19 17	21 34	22 43	23 50	24 55

SUN and MOON data

Day	SUN Eqn. of Time 00h	12h	Mer. Pass.	MOON Mer. Pass. Upper	Lower	Age	Phase
d	m s	m s	h m	h m	h m	d	%
16	04 52	05 03	11 55	14 12	01 50	03	9
17	05 13	05 24	11 55	14 56	02 34	04	15
18	05 35	05 45	11 54	15 42	03 19	05	23

UT	ARIES GHA	VENUS −4.8 GHA	Dec	MARS +1.8 GHA	Dec	JUPITER −1.7 GHA	Dec	SATURN +0.6 GHA	Dec	STARS Name	SHA	Dec
d h	° ′	° ′	° ′	° ′	° ′	° ′	° ′	° ′	° ′		° ′	° ′
19 00	357 35.0	219 26.4	N10 51.0	208 44.4	N13 56.4	197 16.2	N 9 16.8	119 18.0	S18 24.5	Acamar	315 16.9	S40 14.4
01	12 37.5	234 27.7	51.1	223 45.3	55.9	212 18.1	16.6	134 20.3	24.5	Achernar	335 25.2	S57 09.3
02	27 40.0	249 29.0	51.1	238 46.2	55.4	227 20.1	16.4	149 22.5	24.6	Acrux	173 08.1	S63 11.1
03	42 42.4	264 30.3 . .	51.2	253 47.2 . .	54.9	242 22.1 . .	16.2	164 24.8 . .	24.6	Adhara	255 11.4	S28 59.5
04	57 44.9	279 31.6	51.3	268 48.1	54.3	257 24.0	16.0	179 27.1	24.6	Aldebaran	290 47.5	N16 32.3
05	72 47.3	294 32.9	51.3	283 49.1	53.8	272 26.0	15.8	194 29.4	24.7			
06	87 49.8	309 34.2	N10 51.4	298 50.0	N13 53.3	287 27.9	N 9 15.6	209 31.7	S18 24.7	Alioth	166 20.0	N55 52.7
07	102 52.3	324 35.5	51.4	313 50.9	52.8	302 29.9	15.4	224 33.9	24.8	Alkaid	152 58.2	N49 14.4
S 08	117 54.7	339 36.8	51.5	328 51.9	52.2	317 31.9	15.2	239 36.2	24.8	Al Na'ir	27 41.5	S46 53.0
A 09	132 57.2	354 38.1 . .	51.6	343 52.8 . .	51.7	332 33.8 . .	15.1	254 38.5 . .	24.9	Alnilam	275 44.8	S 1 11.6
T 10	147 59.7	9 39.3	51.6	358 53.8	51.2	347 35.8	14.9	269 40.8	24.9	Alphard	217 54.8	S 8 43.6
U 11	163 02.1	24 40.6	51.7	13 54.7	50.7	2 37.8	14.7	284 43.1	25.0			
R 12	178 04.6	39 41.9	N10 51.7	28 55.6	N13 50.1	17 39.7	N 9 14.5	299 45.3	S18 25.0	Alphecca	126 09.9	N26 40.1
D 13	193 07.1	54 43.2	51.8	43 56.6	49.6	32 41.7	14.3	314 47.6	25.1	Alpheratz	357 41.5	N29 10.7
A 14	208 09.5	69 44.4	51.8	58 57.5	49.1	47 43.7	14.1	329 49.9	25.1	Altair	62 06.6	N 8 55.0
Y 15	223 12.0	84 45.7 . .	51.9	73 58.5 . .	48.6	62 45.6 . .	13.9	344 52.2 . .	25.2	Ankaa	353 13.8	S42 13.1
16	238 14.4	99 47.0	51.9	88 59.4	48.0	77 47.6	13.7	359 54.5	25.2	Antares	112 24.5	S26 27.8
17	253 16.9	114 48.2	52.0	104 00.3	47.5	92 49.6	13.5	14 56.7	25.2			
18	268 19.4	129 49.5	N10 52.0	119 01.3	N13 47.0	107 51.5	N 9 13.3	29 59.0	S18 25.3	Arcturus	145 54.6	N19 06.3
19	283 21.8	144 50.8	52.1	134 02.2	46.5	122 53.5	13.1	45 01.3	25.3	Atria	107 25.0	S69 03.4
20	298 24.3	159 52.0	52.1	149 03.2	45.9	137 55.5	12.9	60 03.6	25.4	Avior	234 17.7	S59 33.5
21	313 26.8	174 53.3 . .	52.2	164 04.1 . .	45.4	152 57.4 . .	12.7	75 05.9 . .	25.4	Bellatrix	278 30.3	N 6 21.7
22	328 29.2	189 54.5	52.2	179 05.0	44.9	167 59.4	12.5	90 08.1	25.5	Betelgeuse	270 59.7	N 7 24.5
23	343 31.7	204 55.8	52.3	194 06.0	44.3	183 01.4	12.3	105 10.4	25.5			
20 00	358 34.2	219 57.0	N10 52.3	209 06.9	N13 43.8	198 03.3	N 9 12.1	120 12.7	S18 25.6	Canopus	263 55.5	S52 42.1
01	13 36.6	234 58.3	52.4	224 07.9	43.3	213 05.3	11.9	135 15.0	25.6	Capella	280 32.1	N46 00.5
02	28 39.1	249 59.5	52.4	239 08.8	42.8	228 07.2	11.7	150 17.3	25.7	Deneb	49 30.1	N45 20.6
03	43 41.6	265 00.7 . .	52.4	254 09.7 . .	42.2	243 09.2 . .	11.5	165 19.5 . .	25.7	Denebola	182 32.5	N14 29.2
04	58 44.0	280 02.0	52.5	269 10.7	41.7	258 11.2	11.4	180 21.8	25.8	Diphda	348 54.1	S17 53.9
05	73 46.5	295 03.2	52.5	284 11.6	41.2	273 13.1	11.2	195 24.1	25.8			
06	88 48.9	310 04.4	N10 52.6	299 12.6	N13 40.6	288 15.1	N 9 11.0	210 26.4	S18 25.8	Dubhe	193 50.6	N61 39.9
07	103 51.4	325 05.7	52.6	314 13.5	40.1	303 17.1	10.8	225 28.6	25.9	Elnath	278 10.6	N28 37.0
S 08	118 53.9	340 06.9	52.6	329 14.5	39.6	318 19.0	10.6	240 30.9	25.9	Eltanin	90 45.4	N51 29.7
U 09	133 56.3	355 08.1 . .	52.7	344 15.4 . .	39.1	333 21.0 . .	10.4	255 33.2 . .	26.0	Enif	33 45.3	N 9 57.1
N 10	148 58.8	10 09.3	52.7	359 16.3	38.5	348 23.0	10.2	270 35.5	26.0	Fomalhaut	15 22.0	S29 32.2
D 11	164 01.3	25 10.5	52.7	14 17.3	38.0	3 24.9	10.0	285 37.8	26.1			
A 12	179 03.7	40 11.7	N10 52.8	29 18.2	N13 37.5	18 26.9	N 9 09.8	300 40.0	S18 26.1	Gacrux	171 59.6	S57 12.0
Y 13	194 06.2	55 12.9	52.8	44 19.2	36.9	33 28.9	09.6	315 42.3	26.2	Gienah	175 51.0	S17 37.6
14	209 08.7	70 14.2	52.8	59 20.1	36.4	48 30.8	09.4	330 44.6	26.2	Hadar	148 46.1	S60 26.9
15	224 11.1	85 15.4 . .	52.8	74 21.1 . .	35.9	63 32.8 . .	09.2	345 46.9 . .	26.3	Hamal	327 58.7	N23 32.1
16	239 13.6	100 16.6	52.9	89 22.0	35.4	78 34.8	09.0	0 49.1	26.3	Kaus Aust.	83 41.7	S34 22.5
17	254 16.1	115 17.8	52.9	104 22.9	34.8	93 36.7	08.8	15 51.4	26.4			
18	269 18.5	130 19.0	N10 52.9	119 23.9	N13 34.3	108 38.7	N 9 08.6	30 53.7	S18 26.4	Kochab	137 21.1	N74 05.8
19	284 21.0	145 20.2	52.9	134 24.8	33.8	123 40.7	08.4	45 56.0	26.4	Markab	13 36.5	N15 17.6
20	299 23.4	160 21.3	53.0	149 25.8	33.2	138 42.6	08.2	60 58.2	26.5	Menkar	314 13.2	N 4 09.0
21	314 25.9	175 22.5 . .	53.0	164 26.7 . .	32.7	153 44.6 . .	08.0	76 00.5 . .	26.5	Menkent	148 06.0	S36 26.7
22	329 28.4	190 23.7	53.0	179 27.7	32.2	168 46.6	07.8	91 02.8	26.6	Miaplacidus	221 39.9	S69 46.8
23	344 30.8	205 24.9	53.0	194 28.6	31.6	183 48.5	07.7	106 05.1	26.6			
21 00	359 33.3	220 26.1	N10 53.1	209 29.6	N13 31.1	198 50.5	N 9 07.5	121 07.3	S18 26.7	Mirfak	308 37.8	N49 54.7
01	14 35.8	235 27.3	53.1	224 30.5	30.6	213 52.5	07.3	136 09.6	26.7	Nunki	75 56.3	S26 16.4
02	29 38.2	250 28.4	53.1	239 31.4	30.1	228 54.4	07.1	151 11.9	26.8	Peacock	53 16.6	S56 41.0
03	44 40.7	265 29.6 . .	53.1	254 32.4 . .	29.5	243 56.4 . .	06.9	166 14.2 . .	26.8	Pollux	243 26.1	N27 59.1
04	59 43.2	280 30.8	53.1	269 33.3	29.0	258 58.4	06.7	181 16.4	26.9	Procyon	244 58.3	N 5 11.0
05	74 45.6	295 31.9	53.1	284 34.3	28.5	274 00.3	06.5	196 18.7	26.9			
06	89 48.1	310 33.1	N10 53.2	299 35.2	N13 27.9	289 02.3	N 9 06.3	211 21.0	S18 27.0	Rasalhague	96 05.1	N12 33.3
07	104 50.5	325 34.3	53.2	314 36.2	27.4	304 04.3	06.1	226 23.3	27.0	Regulus	207 42.2	N11 53.4
08	119 53.0	340 35.4	53.2	329 37.1	26.9	319 06.2	05.9	241 25.5	27.1	Rigel	281 10.5	S 8 11.0
M 09	134 55.5	355 36.6 . .	53.2	344 38.1 . .	26.3	334 08.2 . .	05.7	256 27.8 . .	27.1	Rigil Kent.	139 50.0	S60 53.9
O 10	149 57.9	10 37.8	53.2	359 39.0	25.8	349 10.2	05.5	271 30.1	27.1	Sabik	102 10.8	S15 44.4
N 11	165 00.4	25 38.9	53.2	14 40.0	25.3	4 12.1	05.3	286 32.4	27.2			
D 12	180 02.9	40 40.1	N10 53.2	29 40.9	N13 24.7	19 14.1	N 9 05.1	301 34.6	S18 27.2	Schedar	349 38.1	N56 37.4
A 13	195 05.3	55 41.2	53.2	44 41.9	24.2	34 16.1	04.9	316 36.9	27.3	Shaula	96 19.9	S37 06.8
Y 14	210 07.8	70 42.3	53.2	59 42.8	23.7	49 18.0	04.7	331 39.2	27.3	Sirius	258 32.4	S16 44.2
15	225 10.3	85 43.5 . .	53.2	74 43.7 . .	23.1	64 20.0 . .	04.5	346 41.5 . .	27.4	Spica	158 29.9	S11 14.4
16	240 12.7	100 44.6	53.2	89 44.7	22.6	79 22.0	04.3	1 43.7	27.4	Suhail	222 51.6	S43 29.7
17	255 15.2	115 45.8	53.2	104 45.6	22.1	94 23.9	04.2	16 46.0	27.5			
18	270 17.7	130 46.9	N10 53.2	119 46.6	N13 21.5	109 25.9	N 9 04.0	31 48.3	S18 27.5	Vega	80 37.8	N38 48.4
19	285 20.1	145 48.0	53.2	134 47.5	21.0	124 27.9	03.8	46 50.5	27.6	Zuben'ubi	137 03.9	S16 06.2
20	300 22.6	160 49.2	53.2	149 48.5	20.5	139 29.8	03.6	61 52.8	27.6			
21	315 25.0	175 50.3 . .	53.2	164 49.4 . .	19.9	154 31.8 . .	03.4	76 55.1 . .	27.7		SHA	Mer.Pass.
22	330 27.5	190 51.4	53.2	179 50.4	19.4	169 33.8	03.2	91 57.4	27.7	Venus	221 22.9	9 19
23	345 30.0	205 52.5	53.2	194 51.3	18.9	184 35.8	03.0	106 59.6	27.8	Mars	210 32.8	10 03
Mer. Pass.	h m 0 05.7	v 1.2	d 0.0	v 0.9	d 0.5	v 2.0	d 0.2	v 2.3	d 0.0	Jupiter	199 29.2	10 46
										Saturn	121 38.5	15 57

SUN / MOON

UT	SUN GHA	SUN Dec	MOON GHA	v	MOON Dec	d	HP
d h	° ′	° ′	° ′	′	° ′	′	′
19 00	181 29.1	N 1 41.3	120 36.3	12.2	S15 24.2	5.1	55.1
01	196 29.3	40.4	135 07.5	12.1	15 29.3	5.1	55.1
02	211 29.6	39.4	149 38.6	12.2	15 34.4	4.9	55.1
03	226 29.8	.. 38.4	164 09.8	12.0	15 39.3	4.9	55.1
04	241 30.0	37.5	178 40.8	12.0	15 44.2	4.9	55.1
05	256 30.2	36.5	193 11.8	12.0	15 49.1	4.7	55.2
06	271 30.5	N 1 35.5	207 42.8	11.9	S15 53.8	4.7	55.2
S 07	286 30.7	34.6	222 13.7	11.9	15 58.5	4.6	55.2
A 08	301 30.9	33.6	236 44.6	11.8	16 03.1	4.5	55.2
T 09	316 31.1	.. 32.6	251 15.4	11.7	16 07.6	4.5	55.3
U 10	331 31.3	31.6	265 46.1	11.8	16 12.1	4.4	55.3
R 11	346 31.6	30.7	280 16.9	11.6	16 16.5	4.3	55.3
D 12	1 31.8	N 1 29.7	294 47.5	11.6	S16 20.8	4.2	55.3
A 13	16 32.0	28.7	309 18.1	11.6	16 25.0	4.2	55.4
Y 14	31 32.2	27.8	323 48.7	11.5	16 29.2	4.0	55.4
15	46 32.5	.. 26.8	338 19.2	11.5	16 33.2	4.0	55.4
16	61 32.7	25.8	352 49.7	11.4	16 37.2	4.0	55.4
17	76 32.9	24.9	7 20.1	11.3	16 41.2	3.8	55.5
18	91 33.1	N 1 23.9	21 50.4	11.4	S16 45.0	3.8	55.5
19	106 33.3	22.9	36 20.8	11.2	16 48.8	3.7	55.5
20	121 33.6	22.0	50 51.0	11.2	16 52.5	3.6	55.5
21	136 33.8	.. 21.0	65 21.2	11.2	16 56.1	3.5	55.6
22	151 34.0	20.0	79 51.4	11.1	16 59.6	3.4	55.6
23	166 34.2	19.0	94 21.5	11.1	17 03.0	3.4	55.6
20 00	181 34.5	N 1 18.1	108 51.6	11.0	S17 06.4	3.3	55.7
01	196 34.7	17.1	123 21.6	11.0	17 09.7	3.1	55.7
02	211 34.9	16.1	137 51.6	10.9	17 12.8	3.2	55.7
03	226 35.1	.. 15.2	152 21.5	10.8	17 16.0	3.0	55.7
04	241 35.4	14.2	166 51.3	10.8	17 19.0	2.9	55.8
05	256 35.6	13.2	181 21.1	10.8	17 21.9	2.9	55.8
06	271 35.8	N 1 12.3	195 50.9	10.7	S17 24.8	2.7	55.8
07	286 36.0	11.3	210 20.6	10.7	17 27.5	2.7	55.9
S 08	301 36.2	10.3	224 50.3	10.6	17 30.2	2.6	55.9
U 09	316 36.5	.. 09.3	239 19.9	10.6	17 32.8	2.5	55.9
N 10	331 36.7	08.4	253 49.5	10.5	17 35.3	2.4	55.9
D 11	346 36.9	07.4	268 19.0	10.4	17 37.7	2.4	56.0
A 12	1 37.1	N 1 06.4	282 48.4	10.5	S17 40.1	2.2	56.0
Y 13	16 37.3	05.5	297 17.9	10.3	17 42.3	2.1	56.0
14	31 37.6	04.5	311 47.2	10.3	17 44.4	2.1	56.1
15	46 37.8	.. 03.5	326 16.5	10.3	17 46.5	2.0	56.1
16	61 38.0	02.5	340 45.8	10.2	17 48.5	1.8	56.1
17	76 38.2	01.6	355 15.0	10.2	17 50.3	1.8	56.2
18	91 38.5	N 1 00.6	9 44.2	10.2	S17 52.1	1.7	56.2
19	106 38.7	0 59.6	24 13.4	10.0	17 53.8	1.6	56.2
20	121 38.9	58.7	38 42.4	10.1	17 55.4	1.5	56.3
21	136 39.1	.. 57.7	53 11.5	10.0	17 56.9	1.4	56.3
22	151 39.3	56.7	67 40.5	9.9	17 58.3	1.3	56.3
23	166 39.6	55.8	82 09.4	9.9	17 59.6	1.3	56.4
21 00	181 39.8	N 0 54.8	96 38.3	9.8	S18 00.9	1.1	56.4
01	196 40.0	53.8	111 07.1	9.8	18 02.0	1.0	56.4
02	211 40.2	52.8	125 35.9	9.8	18 03.0	1.0	56.4
03	226 40.5	.. 51.9	140 04.7	9.7	18 04.0	0.8	56.5
04	241 40.7	50.9	154 33.4	9.7	18 04.8	0.7	56.5
05	256 40.9	49.9	169 02.1	9.6	18 05.5	0.7	56.6
06	271 41.1	N 0 49.0	183 30.7	9.5	S18 06.2	0.5	56.6
07	286 41.3	48.0	197 59.2	9.6	18 06.7	0.5	56.6
08	301 41.6	47.0	212 27.8	9.5	18 07.2	0.3	56.7
M 09	316 41.8	.. 46.0	226 56.3	9.4	18 07.5	0.3	56.7
O 10	331 42.0	45.1	241 24.7	9.4	18 07.8	0.1	56.7
N 11	346 42.2	44.1	255 53.1	9.4	18 07.9	0.1	56.8
D 12	1 42.5	N 0 43.1	270 21.5	9.3	S18 08.0	0.1	56.8
A 13	16 42.7	42.2	284 49.8	9.2	18 07.9	0.1	56.8
Y 14	31 42.9	41.2	299 18.0	9.3	18 07.8	0.3	56.9
15	46 43.1	.. 40.2	313 46.3	9.2	18 07.5	0.3	56.9
16	61 43.3	39.2	328 14.5	9.1	18 07.2	0.5	56.9
17	76 43.6	38.3	342 42.6	9.1	18 06.7	0.5	57.0
18	91 43.8	N 0 37.3	357 10.7	9.1	S18 06.2	0.7	57.0
19	106 44.0	36.3	11 38.8	9.0	18 05.5	0.7	57.0
20	121 44.2	35.4	26 06.8	9.0	18 04.8	0.9	57.1
21	136 44.4	.. 34.4	40 34.8	8.9	18 03.9	1.0	57.1
22	151 44.7	33.4	55 02.7	9.0	18 02.9	1.0	57.2
23	166 44.9	32.4	69 30.7	8.8	S18 01.9	1.2	57.2
	SD 16.0	d 1.0	SD 15.1		15.3		15.5

Twilight / Sunrise / Moonrise

Lat.	Twilight Naut.	Twilight Civil	Sunrise	Moonrise 19	20	21	22
°	h m	h m	h m	h m	h m	h m	h m
N 72	02 43	04 18	05 28	14 55	17 02	■■	18 07
N 70	03 06	04 28	05 31	14 05	15 26	16 28	17 02
68	03 24	04 36	05 33	13 34	14 46	15 45	16 26
66	03 37	04 43	05 35	13 10	14 19	15 17	16 00
64	03 49	04 48	05 36	12 52	13 58	14 55	15 40
62	03 58	04 53	05 37	12 38	13 41	14 38	15 24
60	04 06	04 57	05 39	12 25	13 27	14 23	15 11
N 58	04 13	05 00	05 40	12 14	13 15	14 11	14 59
56	04 18	05 03	05 40	12 05	13 05	14 00	14 49
54	04 23	05 06	05 41	11 57	12 56	13 51	14 40
52	04 28	05 08	05 42	11 49	12 48	13 42	14 32
50	04 32	05 10	05 43	11 43	12 40	13 34	14 25
45	04 40	05 15	05 44	11 29	12 25	13 19	14 09
N 40	04 46	05 18	05 45	11 17	12 12	13 05	13 57
35	04 51	05 21	05 46	11 07	12 01	12 54	13 46
30	04 55	05 23	05 47	10 58	11 51	12 44	13 36
20	05 01	05 26	05 48	10 43	11 35	12 27	13 20
N 10	05 04	05 28	05 49	10 30	11 21	12 13	13 06
0	05 06	05 30	05 50	10 18	11 07	11 59	12 52
S 10	05 06	05 30	05 51	10 06	10 54	11 45	12 39
20	05 04	05 30	05 52	09 53	10 40	11 31	12 25
30	05 01	05 29	05 53	09 38	10 24	11 14	12 09
35	04 58	05 28	05 53	09 30	10 14	11 04	11 59
40	04 55	05 26	05 53	09 20	10 04	10 53	11 48
45	04 50	05 25	05 54	09 09	09 51	10 41	11 36
S 50	04 44	05 22	05 54	08 55	09 36	10 24	11 20
52	04 41	05 21	05 54	08 49	09 29	10 17	11 13
54	04 38	05 19	05 55	08 42	09 21	10 08	11 05
56	04 34	05 18	05 55	08 34	09 12	09 59	10 56
58	04 30	05 16	05 55	08 25	09 02	09 49	10 46
S 60	04 25	05 14	05 55	08 15	08 51	09 37	10 34

Sunset / Twilight / Moonset

Lat.	Sunset	Twilight Civil	Twilight Naut.	Moonset 19	20	21	22
°	h m	h m	h m	h m	h m	h m	h m
N 72	18 17	19 26	20 59	17 57	17 34	■■	20 10
N 70	18 14	19 16	20 37	18 48	19 10	19 57	21 14
68	18 12	19 09	20 20	19 20	19 50	20 39	21 50
66	18 11	19 02	20 07	19 43	20 18	21 08	22 15
64	18 09	18 57	19 56	20 02	20 39	21 29	22 35
62	18 08	18 53	19 47	20 17	20 56	21 47	22 51
60	18 07	18 49	19 39	20 29	21 10	22 01	23 04
N 58	18 06	18 45	19 33	20 40	21 22	22 13	23 16
56	18 05	18 43	19 27	20 50	21 32	22 24	23 26
54	18 05	18 40	19 22	20 59	21 42	22 33	23 34
52	18 04	18 38	19 18	21 06	21 50	22 42	23 42
50	18 03	18 36	19 14	21 13	21 57	22 49	23 49
45	18 02	18 32	19 06	21 28	22 13	23 05	24 04
N 40	18 01	18 28	19 00	21 40	22 26	23 19	24 17
35	18 00	18 26	18 55	21 50	22 37	23 30	24 27
30	18 00	18 24	18 51	21 59	22 47	23 39	24 36
20	17 58	18 20	18 46	22 15	23 04	23 56	24 52
N 10	17 58	18 19	18 43	22 29	23 18	24 11	00 11
0	17 57	18 17	18 41	22 41	23 32	24 24	00 24
S 10	17 56	18 17	18 41	22 54	23 46	24 38	00 38
20	17 56	18 18	18 43	23 08	24 00	00 00	00 53
30	17 55	18 19	18 47	23 24	24 17	00 17	01 09
35	17 55	18 20	18 49	23 33	24 26	00 26	01 19
40	17 54	18 21	18 53	23 43	24 37	00 37	01 30
45	17 54	18 23	18 58	23 55	24 50	00 50	01 43
S 50	17 54	18 26	19 04	24 10	00 10	01 06	01 58
52	17 54	18 27	19 07	24 17	00 17	01 14	02 06
54	17 54	18 29	19 10	24 25	00 25	01 22	02 14
56	17 53	18 31	19 14	24 34	00 34	01 31	02 23
58	17 53	18 32	19 19	24 43	00 43	01 42	02 33
S 60	17 53	18 35	19 24	24 55	00 55	01 54	02 45

SUN / MOON

Day	SUN Eqn. of Time 00h	SUN Eqn. of Time 12h	SUN Mer. Pass.	MOON Mer. Pass. Upper	MOON Mer. Pass. Lower	Age	Phase
d	m s	m s	h m	h m	h m	d	%
19	05 56	06 07	11 54	16 30	04 05	06	32
20	06 17	06 28	11 54	17 20	04 54	07	41
21	06 39	06 49	11 53	18 12	05 45	08	51

2015 SEPTEMBER 22, 23, 24 (TUES., WED., THURS.)

UT (d h)	ARIES GHA	VENUS −4.8 GHA	Dec	MARS +1.8 GHA	Dec	JUPITER −1.7 GHA	Dec	SATURN +0.6 GHA	Dec	Name	SHA	Dec
22 00	0 32.4	220 53.7	N10 53.2	209 52.3	N13 18.3	199 37.7	N 9 02.8	122 01.9	S18 27.8	Acamar	315 16.9	S40 14.4
01	15 34.9	235 54.8	53.2	224 53.2	17.8	214 39.7	02.6	137 04.2	27.9	Achernar	335 25.2	S57 09.3
02	30 37.4	250 55.9	53.2	239 54.2	17.3	229 41.7	02.4	152 06.5	27.9	Acrux	173 08.1	S63 11.1
03	45 39.8	265 57.0 ..	53.2	254 55.1 ..	16.7	244 43.6 ..	02.2	167 08.7 ..	27.9	Adhara	255 11.4	S28 59.5
04	60 42.3	280 58.1	53.2	269 56.1	16.2	259 45.6	02.0	182 11.0	28.0	Aldebaran	290 47.5	N16 32.3
05	75 44.8	295 59.2	53.2	284 57.0	15.7	274 47.6	01.8	197 13.3	28.0			
06	90 47.2	311 00.3	N10 53.2	299 58.0	N13 15.1	289 49.5	N 9 01.6	212 15.5	S18 28.1	Alioth	166 20.0	N55 52.6
07	105 49.7	326 01.4	53.2	314 58.9	14.6	304 51.5	01.4	227 17.8	28.1	Alkaid	152 58.2	N49 14.4
08	120 52.2	341 02.5	53.2	329 59.9	14.1	319 53.5	01.2	242 20.1	28.2	Al Na'ir	27 41.5	S46 53.0
09	135 54.6	356 03.6 ..	53.2	345 00.8 ..	13.5	334 55.4 ..	01.0	257 22.4 ..	28.2	Alnilam	275 44.8	S 1 11.6
10	150 57.1	11 04.7	53.1	0 01.8	13.0	349 57.4	00.9	272 24.6	28.3	Alphard	217 54.8	S 8 43.6
11	165 59.5	26 05.8	53.1	15 02.7	12.5	4 59.4	00.7	287 26.9	28.3			
12	181 02.0	41 06.9	N10 53.1	30 03.7	N13 11.9	20 01.3	N 9 00.5	302 29.2	S18 28.4	Alphecca	126 09.9	N26 40.1
13	196 04.5	56 08.0	53.1	45 04.6	11.4	35 03.3	00.3	317 31.4	28.4	Alpheratz	357 41.5	N29 10.7
14	211 06.9	71 09.1	53.1	60 05.6	10.9	50 05.3	9 00.1	332 33.7	28.5	Altair	62 06.6	N 8 55.0
15	226 09.4	86 10.2 ..	53.1	75 06.5 ..	10.3	65 07.2	8 59.9	347 36.0 ..	28.5	Ankaa	353 13.8	S42 13.1
16	241 11.9	101 11.2	53.0	90 07.5	09.8	80 09.2	59.7	2 38.2	28.6	Antares	112 24.5	S26 27.8
17	256 14.3	116 12.3	53.0	105 08.4	09.3	95 11.2	59.5	17 40.5	28.6			
18	271 16.8	131 13.4	N10 53.0	120 09.4	N13 08.7	110 13.2	N 8 59.3	32 42.8	S18 28.7	Arcturus	145 54.6	N19 06.3
19	286 19.3	146 14.5	53.0	135 10.3	08.2	125 15.1	59.1	47 45.1	28.7	Atria	107 25.0	S69 03.4
20	301 21.7	161 15.5	52.9	150 11.3	07.6	140 17.1	58.9	62 47.3	28.8	Avior	234 17.7	S59 33.5
21	316 24.2	176 16.6 ..	52.9	165 12.2 ..	07.1	155 19.1 ..	58.7	77 49.6 ..	28.8	Bellatrix	278 30.3	N 6 21.7
22	331 26.7	191 17.7	52.9	180 13.2	06.6	170 21.0	58.5	92 51.9	28.8	Betelgeuse	270 59.6	N 7 24.5
23	346 29.1	206 18.7	52.9	195 14.1	06.0	185 23.0	58.3	107 54.1	28.9			
23 00	1 31.6	221 19.8	N10 52.8	210 15.1	N13 05.5	200 25.0	N 8 58.1	122 56.4	S18 28.9	Canopus	263 55.5	S52 42.1
01	16 34.0	236 20.8	52.8	225 16.0	05.0	215 26.9	57.9	137 58.7	29.0	Capella	280 32.1	N46 00.5
02	31 36.5	251 21.9	52.8	240 17.0	04.4	230 28.9	57.8	153 00.9	29.0	Deneb	49 30.1	N45 20.6
03	46 39.0	266 23.0 ..	52.7	255 18.0 ..	03.9	245 30.9 ..	57.6	168 03.2 ..	29.1	Denebola	182 32.4	N14 29.2
04	61 41.4	281 24.0	52.7	270 18.9	03.4	260 32.9	57.4	183 05.5	29.1	Diphda	348 54.0	S17 53.9
05	76 43.9	296 25.1	52.7	285 19.9	02.8	275 34.8	57.2	198 07.7	29.2			
06	91 46.4	311 26.1	N10 52.6	300 20.8	N13 02.3	290 36.8	N 8 57.0	213 10.0	S18 29.2	Dubhe	193 50.6	N61 39.9
07	106 48.8	326 27.2	52.6	315 21.8	01.7	305 38.8	56.8	228 12.3	29.3	Elnath	278 10.6	N28 37.0
08	121 51.3	341 28.2	52.6	330 22.7	01.2	320 40.7	56.6	243 14.6	29.3	Eltanin	90 45.4	N51 29.7
09	136 53.8	356 29.2 ..	52.5	345 23.7 ..	00.7	335 42.7 ..	56.4	258 16.8 ..	29.4	Enif	33 45.3	N 9 57.1
10	151 56.2	11 30.3	52.5	0 24.6	13 00.1	350 44.7	56.2	273 19.1	29.4	Fomalhaut	15 22.0	S29 32.2
11	166 58.7	26 31.3	52.5	15 25.6	12 59.6	5 46.6	56.0	288 21.4	29.5			
12	182 01.1	41 32.3	N10 52.4	30 26.5	N12 59.1	20 48.6	N 8 55.8	303 23.6	S18 29.5	Gacrux	171 59.6	S57 12.0
13	197 03.6	56 33.4	52.4	45 27.5	58.5	35 50.6	55.6	318 25.9	29.6	Gienah	175 51.0	S17 37.6
14	212 06.1	71 34.4	52.3	60 28.4	58.0	50 52.6	55.4	333 28.2	29.6	Hadar	148 46.1	S60 26.9
15	227 08.5	86 35.4 ..	52.3	75 29.4 ..	57.4	65 54.5 ..	55.2	348 30.4 ..	29.7	Hamal	327 58.7	N23 32.2
16	242 11.0	101 36.4	52.3	90 30.4	56.9	80 56.5	55.0	3 32.7	29.7	Kaus Aust.	83 41.7	S34 22.5
17	257 13.5	116 37.5	52.2	105 31.3	56.4	95 58.5	54.8	18 35.0	29.8			
18	272 15.9	131 38.5	N10 52.2	120 32.3	N12 55.8	111 00.4	N 8 54.7	33 37.2	S18 29.8	Kochab	137 21.1	N74 05.8
19	287 18.4	146 39.5	52.1	135 33.2	55.3	126 02.4	54.5	48 39.5	29.9	Markab	13 36.5	N15 17.6
20	302 20.9	161 40.5	52.1	150 34.2	54.7	141 04.4	54.3	63 41.8	29.9	Menkar	314 13.2	N 4 09.0
21	317 23.3	176 41.5 ..	52.0	165 35.1 ..	54.2	156 06.4 ..	54.1	78 44.0 ..	29.9	Menkent	148 06.0	S36 26.7
22	332 25.8	191 42.5	52.0	180 36.1	53.7	171 08.3	53.9	93 46.3	30.0	Miaplacidus	221 39.9	S69 46.8
23	347 28.3	206 43.5	51.9	195 37.0	53.1	186 10.3	53.7	108 48.6	30.0			
24 00	2 30.7	221 44.5	N10 51.9	210 38.0	N12 52.6	201 12.3	N 8 53.5	123 50.8	S18 30.1	Mirfak	308 37.8	N49 54.7
01	17 33.2	236 45.5	51.8	225 39.0	52.0	216 14.2	53.3	138 53.1	30.1	Nunki	75 56.3	S26 16.4
02	32 35.6	251 46.5	51.8	240 39.9	51.5	231 16.2	53.1	153 55.4	30.2	Peacock	53 16.6	S56 41.0
03	47 38.1	266 47.5 ..	51.7	255 40.9 ..	51.0	246 18.2 ..	52.9	168 57.6 ..	30.2	Pollux	243 26.0	N27 59.1
04	62 40.6	281 48.5	51.7	270 41.8	50.4	261 20.1	52.7	183 59.9	30.3	Procyon	244 58.3	N 5 11.0
05	77 43.0	296 49.5	51.6	285 42.8	49.9	276 22.1	52.5	199 02.1	30.3			
06	92 45.5	311 50.5	N10 51.5	300 43.7	N12 49.3	291 24.1	N 8 52.3	214 04.4	S18 30.4	Rasalhague	96 05.1	N12 33.3
07	107 48.0	326 51.5	51.5	315 44.7	48.8	306 26.1	52.1	229 06.7	30.4	Regulus	207 42.2	N11 53.4
08	122 50.4	341 52.5	51.4	330 45.7	48.3	321 28.0	51.9	244 08.9	30.5	Rigel	281 10.5	S 8 11.0
09	137 52.9	356 53.5 ..	51.4	345 46.6 ..	47.7	336 30.0 ..	51.8	259 11.2 ..	30.5	Rigil Kent.	139 50.0	S60 53.9
10	152 55.4	11 54.5	51.3	0 47.6	47.2	351 32.0	51.6	274 13.5	30.6	Sabik	102 10.8	S15 44.4
11	167 57.8	26 55.4	51.2	15 48.5	46.6	6 34.0	51.4	289 15.7	30.6			
12	183 00.3	41 56.4	N10 51.2	30 49.5	N12 46.1	21 35.9	N 8 51.2	304 18.0	S18 30.7	Schedar	349 38.1	N56 37.4
13	198 02.8	56 57.4	51.1	45 50.4	45.6	36 37.9	51.0	319 20.3	30.7	Shaula	96 19.9	S37 06.8
14	213 05.2	71 58.4	51.0	60 51.4	45.0	51 39.9	50.8	334 22.5	30.8	Sirius	258 32.4	S16 44.2
15	228 07.7	86 59.3 ..	51.0	75 52.4 ..	44.5	66 41.8 ..	50.6	349 24.8 ..	30.8	Spica	158 29.9	S11 14.4
16	243 10.1	102 00.3	50.9	90 53.3	43.9	81 43.8	50.4	4 27.1	30.9	Suhail	222 51.6	S43 29.7
17	258 12.6	117 01.3	50.8	105 54.3	43.4	96 45.8	50.2	19 29.3	30.9			
18	273 15.1	132 02.2	N10 50.8	120 55.2	N12 42.9	111 47.8	N 8 50.0	34 31.6	S18 31.0	Vega	80 37.9	N38 48.4
19	288 17.5	147 03.2	50.7	135 56.2	42.3	126 49.7	49.8	49 33.8	31.0	Zuben'ubi	137 03.9	S16 06.2
20	303 20.0	162 04.2	50.6	150 57.2	41.8	141 51.7	49.6	64 36.1	31.1			
21	318 22.5	177 05.1 ..	50.6	165 58.1 ..	41.2	156 53.7 ..	49.4	79 38.4 ..	31.1			
22	333 24.9	192 06.1	50.5	180 59.1	40.7	171 55.6	49.2	94 40.6	31.2			
23	348 27.4	207 07.0	50.4	196 00.0	40.2	186 57.6	49.0	109 42.9	31.2			
Mer. Pass. h m 23 50.0		v 1.0 d 0.0		v 1.0 d 0.5		v 2.0 d 0.2		v 2.3 d 0.0				

	SHA	Mer. Pass.
Venus	219 48.2	9 14
Mars	208 43.5	9 58
Jupiter	198 53.4	10 37
Saturn	121 24.8	15 46

SUN and MOON

UT	SUN GHA	SUN Dec	MOON GHA	v	MOON Dec	d	HP
d h	° ′	° ′	° ′	′	° ′	′	′
22 00	181 45.1	N 0 31.5	83 58.5	8.9	S18 00.7	1.3	57.2
01	196 45.3	30.5	98 26.4	8.8	17 59.4	1.4	57.3
02	211 45.5	29.5	112 54.2	8.7	17 58.0	1.5	57.3
03	226 45.8	.. 28.5	127 21.9	8.7	17 56.5	1.5	57.3
04	241 46.0	27.6	141 49.6	8.7	17 55.0	1.7	57.4
05	256 46.2	26.6	156 17.3	8.7	17 53.3	1.8	57.4
06	271 46.4	N 0 25.6	170 45.0	8.6	S17 51.5	1.9	57.5
07	286 46.7	24.7	185 12.6	8.6	17 49.6	2.1	57.5
T 08	301 46.9	23.7	199 40.2	8.5	17 47.5	2.1	57.5
U 09	316 47.1	.. 22.7	214 07.7	8.5	17 45.4	2.2	57.6
E 10	331 47.3	21.7	228 35.2	8.5	17 43.2	2.3	57.6
S 11	346 47.5	20.8	243 02.7	8.5	17 40.9	2.5	57.6
D 12	1 47.8	N 0 19.8	257 30.2	8.4	S17 38.4	2.5	57.7
A 13	16 48.0	18.8	271 57.6	8.4	17 35.9	2.7	57.7
Y 14	31 48.2	17.9	286 25.0	8.3	17 33.2	2.7	57.8
15	46 48.4	.. 16.9	300 52.3	8.3	17 30.5	2.9	57.8
16	61 48.6	15.9	315 19.6	8.3	17 27.6	3.0	57.8
17	76 48.9	14.9	329 46.9	8.3	17 24.6	3.0	57.9
18	91 49.1	N 0 14.0	344 14.2	8.2	S17 21.6	3.2	57.9
19	106 49.3	13.0	358 41.4	8.2	17 18.4	3.3	58.0
20	121 49.5	12.0	13 08.6	8.2	17 15.1	3.4	58.0
21	136 49.7	.. 11.0	27 35.8	8.2	17 11.7	3.5	58.0
22	151 50.0	10.1	42 03.0	8.1	17 08.2	3.6	58.1
23	166 50.2	09.1	56 30.1	8.1	17 04.6	3.8	58.1
23 00	181 50.4	N 0 08.1	70 57.2	8.1	S17 00.8	3.8	58.2
01	196 50.6	07.2	85 24.3	8.0	16 57.0	3.9	58.2
02	211 50.8	06.2	99 51.3	8.0	16 53.1	4.1	58.2
03	226 51.1	.. 05.2	114 18.3	8.0	16 49.0	4.1	58.3
04	241 51.3	04.2	128 45.3	8.0	16 44.9	4.3	58.3
05	256 51.5	03.3	143 12.3	7.9	16 40.6	4.3	58.4
06	271 51.7	N 0 02.3	157 39.2	8.0	S16 36.3	4.5	58.4
W 07	286 51.9	01.3	172 06.2	7.9	16 31.8	4.6	58.4
E 08	301 52.2	N 00.3	186 33.1	7.9	16 27.2	4.7	58.5
D 09	316 52.4	S 00.6	201 00.0	7.8	16 22.5	4.8	58.5
N 10	331 52.6	01.6	215 26.8	7.9	16 17.7	4.9	58.6
E 11	346 52.8	02.6	229 53.7	7.8	16 12.8	5.0	58.6
S 12	1 53.0	S 0 03.5	244 20.5	7.8	S16 07.8	5.1	58.6
D 13	16 53.3	04.5	258 47.3	7.7	16 02.7	5.2	58.7
A 14	31 53.5	05.5	273 14.0	7.7	15 57.5	5.3	58.7
Y 15	46 53.7	.. 06.5	287 40.8	7.7	15 52.2	5.4	58.7
16	61 53.9	07.4	302 07.5	7.8	15 46.8	5.6	58.8
17	76 54.1	08.4	316 34.3	7.7	15 41.2	5.6	58.8
18	91 54.4	S 0 09.4	331 01.0	7.7	S15 35.6	5.7	58.9
19	106 54.6	10.4	345 27.7	7.6	15 29.9	5.9	58.9
20	121 54.8	11.3	359 54.3	7.7	15 24.0	5.9	58.9
21	136 55.0	.. 12.3	14 21.0	7.6	15 18.1	6.1	59.0
22	151 55.2	13.3	28 47.6	7.6	15 12.0	6.1	59.0
23	166 55.5	14.2	43 14.2	7.6	15 05.9	6.3	59.1
24 00	181 55.7	S 0 15.2	57 40.8	7.6	S14 59.6	6.3	59.1
01	196 55.9	16.2	72 07.4	7.6	14 53.3	6.5	59.1
02	211 56.1	17.2	86 34.0	7.6	14 46.8	6.5	59.2
03	226 56.3	.. 18.1	101 00.6	7.5	14 40.3	6.7	59.2
04	241 56.6	19.1	115 27.1	7.6	14 33.6	6.8	59.3
05	256 56.8	20.1	129 53.7	7.5	14 26.8	6.8	59.3
06	271 57.0	S 0 21.1	144 20.2	7.5	S14 20.0	7.0	59.3
07	286 57.2	22.0	158 46.7	7.5	14 13.0	7.1	59.4
T 08	301 57.4	23.0	173 13.2	7.5	14 05.9	7.1	59.4
H 09	316 57.6	.. 24.0	187 39.7	7.5	13 58.8	7.3	59.4
U 10	331 57.9	25.0	202 06.2	7.5	13 51.5	7.3	59.5
R 11	346 58.1	25.9	216 32.7	7.4	13 44.2	7.5	59.5
S 12	1 58.3	S 0 26.9	230 59.1	7.5	S13 36.7	7.5	59.6
D 13	16 58.5	27.9	245 25.6	7.4	13 29.2	7.7	59.6
A 14	31 58.7	28.8	259 52.0	7.5	13 21.5	7.7	59.6
Y 15	46 59.0	.. 29.8	274 18.5	7.4	13 13.8	7.8	59.7
16	61 59.2	30.8	288 44.9	7.4	13 06.0	8.0	59.7
17	76 59.4	31.8	303 11.3	7.4	12 58.0	8.0	59.7
18	91 59.6	S 0 32.7	317 37.7	7.4	S12 50.0	8.1	59.8
19	106 59.8	33.7	332 04.1	7.4	12 41.9	8.2	59.8
20	122 00.0	34.7	346 30.5	7.4	12 33.7	8.3	59.9
21	137 00.3	.. 35.7	0 56.9	7.4	12 25.4	8.4	59.9
22	152 00.5	36.6	15 23.3	7.3	12 17.0	8.4	59.9
23	167 00.7	37.6	29 49.6	7.4	S12 08.6	8.6	60.0
	SD 16.0	d 1.0	SD 15.7		16.0		16.2

Twilight / Sunrise / Moonrise

Lat.	Naut.	Civil	Sunrise	Moonrise 22	23	24	25
°	h m	h m	h m	h m	h m	h m	h m
N 72	03 02	04 33	05 41	18 07	17 57	17 51	17 46
N 70	03 22	04 41	05 42	17 02	17 19	17 27	17 31
68	03 37	04 47	05 43	16 26	16 52	17 08	17 20
66	03 49	04 52	05 44	16 00	16 32	16 54	17 10
64	03 59	04 57	05 44	15 40	16 15	16 41	17 02
62	04 07	05 01	05 45	15 24	16 01	16 31	16 55
60	04 14	05 04	05 46	15 11	15 50	16 22	16 49
N 58	04 20	05 07	05 46	14 59	15 40	16 14	16 43
56	04 25	05 09	05 46	14 49	15 31	16 07	16 39
54	04 29	05 11	05 47	14 40	15 23	16 01	16 34
52	04 33	05 13	05 47	14 32	15 16	15 55	16 30
50	04 37	05 15	05 47	14 25	15 10	15 50	16 27
45	04 44	05 18	05 48	14 09	14 56	15 39	16 19
N 40	04 49	05 21	05 48	13 57	14 45	15 30	16 12
35	04 54	05 23	05 48	13 46	14 35	15 22	16 07
30	04 57	05 25	05 49	13 36	14 27	15 15	16 02
20	05 01	05 27	05 49	13 20	14 12	15 03	15 53
N 10	05 04	05 28	05 49	13 06	13 59	14 53	15 46
0	05 05	05 29	05 49	12 52	13 47	14 43	15 39
S 10	05 04	05 28	05 49	12 39	13 35	14 33	15 32
20	05 02	05 27	05 49	12 25	13 22	14 22	15 24
30	04 57	05 25	05 49	12 09	13 08	14 10	15 15
35	04 54	05 23	05 49	11 59	12 59	14 03	15 10
40	04 50	05 21	05 48	11 48	12 49	13 55	15 05
45	04 44	05 19	05 48	11 36	12 38	13 46	14 58
S 50	04 37	05 15	05 48	11 20	12 24	13 35	14 50
52	04 34	05 14	05 47	11 13	12 18	13 29	14 47
54	04 30	05 12	05 47	11 05	12 10	13 24	14 42
56	04 26	05 10	05 47	10 56	12 02	13 17	14 38
58	04 21	05 07	05 47	10 46	11 53	13 10	14 33
S 60	04 15	05 05	05 46	10 34	11 43	13 02	14 27

Sunset / Twilight / Moonset

Lat.	Sunset	Civil	Naut.	Moonset 22	23	24	25
°	h m	h m	h m	h m	h m	h m	h m
N 72	18 01	19 09	20 38	20 10	22 15	24 18	00 18
N 70	18 00	19 02	20 19	21 14	22 52	24 41	00 41
68	18 00	18 55	20 05	21 50	23 18	24 58	00 58
66	17 59	18 50	19 53	22 15	23 38	25 12	01 12
64	17 59	18 46	19 44	22 35	23 54	25 23	01 23
62	17 58	18 43	19 36	22 51	24 07	00 07	01 33
60	17 58	18 39	19 29	23 04	24 18	00 18	01 41
N 58	17 58	18 37	19 24	23 16	24 28	00 28	01 48
56	17 57	18 34	19 19	23 26	24 36	00 36	01 54
54	17 57	18 32	19 14	23 34	24 44	00 44	02 00
52	17 57	18 31	19 10	23 42	24 50	00 50	02 05
50	17 57	18 29	19 07	23 49	24 56	00 56	02 10
45	17 56	18 26	19 00	24 04	00 04	01 09	02 20
N 40	17 56	18 23	18 55	24 17	00 17	01 20	02 28
35	17 56	18 21	18 51	24 27	00 27	01 29	02 35
30	17 56	18 20	18 48	24 36	00 36	01 37	02 41
20	17 56	18 18	18 43	24 52	00 52	01 51	02 52
N 10	17 56	18 17	18 41	00 11	01 06	02 03	03 01
0	17 56	18 16	18 40	00 24	01 18	02 14	03 09
S 10	17 56	18 17	18 41	00 38	01 31	02 25	03 18
20	17 56	18 18	18 44	00 53	01 45	02 36	03 27
30	17 57	18 20	18 48	01 09	02 00	02 50	03 37
35	17 57	18 22	18 52	01 19	02 09	02 57	03 43
40	17 57	18 24	18 56	01 30	02 19	03 06	03 50
45	17 58	18 27	19 01	01 43	02 31	03 16	03 57
S 50	17 58	18 31	19 09	01 58	02 46	03 28	04 07
52	17 59	18 32	19 13	02 06	02 53	03 34	04 11
54	17 59	18 34	19 16	02 14	03 00	03 40	04 16
56	17 59	18 36	19 21	02 23	03 08	03 47	04 21
58	18 00	18 39	19 26	02 33	03 18	03 55	04 27
S 60	18 00	18 42	19 32	02 45	03 28	04 04	04 33

SUN and MOON

Day	Eqn. of Time 00ʰ	Eqn. of Time 12ʰ	Mer. Pass.	Mer. Pass. Upper	Mer. Pass. Lower	Age	Phase
d	m s	m s	h m	h m	h m	d	%
22	07 00	07 11	11 53	19 05	06 38	09	62
23	07 21	07 32	11 52	20 00	07 33	10	72
24	07 42	07 53	11 52	20 56	08 28	11	82

UT	ARIES	VENUS −4.7		MARS +1.8		JUPITER −1.7		SATURN +0.6		STARS		
	GHA	GHA	Dec	GHA	Dec	GHA	Dec	GHA	Dec	Name	SHA	Dec
d h	° ′	° ′	° ′	° ′	° ′	° ′	° ′	° ′	° ′		° ′	° ′
25 00	3 29.9	222 08.0	N10 50.3	211 01.0	N12 39.6	201 59.6	N 8 48.9	124 45.2	S18 31.3	Acamar	315 16.9	S40 14.4
01	18 32.3	237 08.9	50.3	226 01.9	39.1	217 01.6	48.7	139 47.4	31.3	Achernar	335 25.2	S57 09.3
02	33 34.8	252 09.9	50.2	241 02.9	38.5	232 03.5	48.5	154 49.7	31.4	Acrux	173 08.1	S63 11.1
03	48 37.2	267 10.8 . .	50.1	256 03.9 . .	38.0	247 05.5 . .	48.3	169 52.0 . .	31.4	Adhara	255 11.4	S28 59.5
04	63 39.7	282 11.7	50.0	271 04.8	37.4	262 07.5	48.1	184 54.2	31.4	Aldebaran	290 47.5	N16 32.3
05	78 42.2	297 12.7	49.9	286 05.8	36.9	277 09.5	47.9	199 56.5	31.5			
06	93 44.6	312 13.6	N10 49.9	301 06.7	N12 36.4	292 11.4	N 8 47.7	214 58.7	S18 31.5	Alioth	166 20.0	N55 52.6
07	108 47.1	327 14.6	49.8	316 07.7	35.8	307 13.4	47.5	230 01.0	31.6	Alkaid	152 58.2	N49 14.4
08	123 49.6	342 15.5	49.7	331 08.7	35.3	322 15.4	47.3	245 03.3	31.6	Al Na'ir	27 41.5	S46 53.0
F 09	138 52.0	357 16.4 . .	49.6	346 09.6 . .	34.7	337 17.3 . .	47.1	260 05.5 . .	31.7	Alnilam	275 44.8	S 1 11.6
R 10	153 54.5	12 17.3	49.5	1 10.6	34.2	352 19.3	46.9	275 07.8	31.7	Alphard	217 54.8	S 8 43.6
I 11	168 57.0	27 18.3	49.4	16 11.6	33.6	7 21.3	46.7	290 10.0	31.8			
D 12	183 59.4	42 19.2	N10 49.3	31 12.5	N12 33.1	22 23.3	N 8 46.5	305 12.3	S18 31.8	Alphecca	126 10.0	N26 40.1
A 13	199 01.9	57 20.1	49.3	46 13.5	32.6	37 25.2	46.3	320 14.6	31.9	Alpheratz	357 41.5	N29 10.8
Y 14	214 04.4	72 21.0	49.2	61 14.4	32.0	52 27.2	46.2	335 16.8	31.9	Altair	62 06.6	N 8 55.0
15	229 06.8	87 22.0	49.1	76 15.4 . .	31.5	67 29.2 . .	46.0	350 19.1 . .	32.0	Ankaa	353 13.8	S42 13.1
16	244 09.3	102 22.9	49.0	91 16.4	30.9	82 31.2	45.8	5 21.4	32.0	Antares	112 24.5	S26 27.8
17	259 11.7	117 23.8	48.9	106 17.3	30.4	97 33.1	45.6	20 23.6	32.1			
18	274 14.2	132 24.7	N10 48.8	121 18.3	N12 29.8	112 35.1	N 8 45.4	35 25.9	S18 32.1	Arcturus	145 54.6	N19 06.3
19	289 16.7	147 25.6	48.7	136 19.2	29.3	127 37.1	45.2	50 28.1	32.2	Atria	107 25.1	S69 03.3
20	304 19.1	162 26.5	48.6	151 20.2	28.7	142 39.1	45.0	65 30.4	32.2	Avior	234 17.6	S59 33.4
21	319 21.6	177 27.4 . .	48.5	166 21.2 . .	28.2	157 41.0 . .	44.8	80 32.7 . .	32.3	Bellatrix	278 30.3	N 6 21.7
22	334 24.1	192 28.3	48.4	181 22.1	27.7	172 43.0	44.6	95 34.9	32.3	Betelgeuse	270 59.6	N 7 24.5
23	349 26.5	207 29.2	48.3	196 23.1	27.1	187 45.0	44.4	110 37.2	32.4			
26 00	4 29.0	222 30.1	N10 48.2	211 24.1	N12 26.6	202 47.0	N 8 44.2	125 39.4	S18 32.4	Canopus	263 55.5	S52 42.1
01	19 31.5	237 31.0	48.1	226 25.0	26.0	217 48.9	44.0	140 41.7	32.5	Capella	280 32.0	N46 00.5
02	34 33.9	252 31.9	48.0	241 26.0	25.5	232 50.9	43.8	155 44.0	32.5	Deneb	49 30.1	N45 20.6
03	49 36.4	267 32.8 . .	47.9	256 27.0 . .	24.9	247 52.9 . .	43.7	170 46.2 . .	32.6	Denebola	182 32.4	N14 29.2
04	64 38.8	282 33.7	47.8	271 27.9	24.4	262 54.9	43.5	185 48.5	32.6	Diphda	348 54.0	S17 53.9
05	79 41.3	297 34.6	47.7	286 28.9	23.8	277 56.8	43.3	200 50.7	32.7			
06	94 43.8	312 35.5	N10 47.6	301 29.8	N12 23.3	292 58.8	N 8 43.1	215 53.0	S18 32.7	Dubhe	193 50.6	N61 39.9
07	109 46.2	327 36.3	47.5	316 30.8	22.7	308 00.8	42.9	230 55.3	32.8	Elnath	278 10.6	N28 37.0
S 08	124 48.7	342 37.2	47.4	331 31.8	22.2	323 02.8	42.7	245 57.5	32.8	Eltanin	90 45.5	N51 29.7
A 09	139 51.2	357 38.1 . .	47.3	346 32.7 . .	21.7	338 04.7 . .	42.5	260 59.8 . .	32.9	Enif	33 45.3	N 9 57.1
T 10	154 53.6	12 39.0	47.2	1 33.7	21.1	353 06.7	42.3	276 02.0	32.9	Fomalhaut	15 22.0	S29 32.2
U 11	169 56.1	27 39.8	47.1	16 34.7	20.6	8 08.7	42.1	291 04.3	33.0			
R 12	184 58.6	42 40.7	N10 46.9	31 35.6	N12 20.0	23 10.7	N 8 41.9	306 06.5	S18 33.0	Gacrux	171 59.6	S57 12.0
D 13	200 01.0	57 41.6	46.8	46 36.6	19.5	38 12.6	41.7	321 08.8	33.1	Gienah	175 51.0	S17 37.6
A 14	215 03.5	72 42.5	46.7	61 37.6	18.9	53 14.6	41.5	336 11.1	33.1	Hadar	148 46.1	S60 26.9
Y 15	230 06.0	87 43.3 . .	46.6	76 38.5 . .	18.4	68 16.6 . .	41.3	351 13.3 . .	33.2	Hamal	327 58.7	N23 32.2
16	245 08.4	102 44.2	46.5	91 39.5	17.8	83 18.6	41.1	6 15.6	33.2	Kaus Aust.	83 41.8	S34 22.5
17	260 10.9	117 45.1	46.4	106 40.5	17.3	98 20.5	41.0	21 17.8	33.3			
18	275 13.3	132 45.9	N10 46.3	121 41.4	N12 16.7	113 22.5	N 8 40.8	36 20.1	S18 33.3	Kochab	137 21.1	N74 05.8
19	290 15.8	147 46.8	46.1	136 42.4	16.2	128 24.5	40.6	51 22.4	33.4	Markab	13 36.5	N15 17.6
20	305 18.3	162 47.6	46.0	151 43.4	15.6	143 26.5	40.4	66 24.6	33.4	Menkar	314 13.2	N 4 09.1
21	320 20.7	177 48.5 . .	45.9	166 44.3 . .	15.1	158 28.4 . .	40.2	81 26.9 . .	33.5	Menkent	148 06.0	S36 26.7
22	335 23.2	192 49.3	45.8	181 45.3	14.6	173 30.4	40.0	96 29.1	33.5	Miaplacidus	221 39.8	S69 46.8
23	350 25.7	207 50.2	45.6	196 46.3	14.0	188 32.4	39.8	111 31.4	33.6			
27 00	5 28.1	222 51.0	N10 45.5	211 47.2	N12 13.5	203 34.4	N 8 39.6	126 33.6	S18 33.6	Mirfak	308 37.7	N49 54.8
01	20 30.6	237 51.9	45.4	226 48.2	12.9	218 36.3	39.4	141 35.9	33.7	Nunki	75 56.4	S26 16.4
02	35 33.1	252 52.7	45.3	241 49.2	12.4	233 38.3	39.2	156 38.1	33.7	Peacock	53 16.6	S56 41.0
03	50 35.5	267 53.6 . .	45.1	256 50.1 . .	11.8	248 40.3 . .	39.0	171 40.4 . .	33.7	Pollux	243 26.0	N27 59.1
04	65 38.0	282 54.4	45.0	271 51.1	11.3	263 42.3	38.8	186 42.7	33.8	Procyon	244 58.2	N 5 11.0
05	80 40.5	297 55.2	44.9	286 52.1	10.7	278 44.2	38.7	201 44.9	33.8			
06	95 42.9	312 56.1	N10 44.8	301 53.0	N12 10.2	293 46.2	N 8 38.5	216 47.2	S18 33.9	Rasalhague	96 05.1	N12 33.3
07	110 45.4	327 56.9	44.6	316 54.0	09.6	308 48.2	38.3	231 49.4	33.9	Regulus	207 42.2	N11 53.4
08	125 47.8	342 57.7	44.5	331 55.0	09.1	323 50.2	38.1	246 51.7	34.0	Rigel	281 10.5	S 8 11.0
S 09	140 50.3	357 58.6 . .	44.4	346 55.9 . .	08.5	338 52.1 . .	37.9	261 53.9 . .	34.0	Rigil Kent.	139 50.1	S60 53.9
U 10	155 52.8	12 59.4	44.2	1 56.9	08.0	353 54.1	37.7	276 56.2	34.1	Sabik	102 10.9	S15 44.4
N 11	170 55.2	28 00.2	44.1	16 57.9	07.4	8 56.1	37.5	291 58.5	34.1			
D 12	185 57.7	43 01.0	N10 44.0	31 58.8	N12 06.9	23 58.1	N 8 37.3	307 00.7	S18 34.2	Schedar	349 38.1	N56 37.4
A 13	201 00.2	58 01.9	43.8	46 59.8	06.3	39 00.1	37.1	322 03.0	34.2	Shaula	96 19.9	S37 06.8
Y 14	216 02.6	73 02.7	43.7	62 00.8	05.8	54 02.0	36.9	337 05.2	34.3	Sirius	258 32.4	S16 44.2
15	231 05.1	88 03.5 . .	43.6	77 01.7 . .	05.2	69 04.0 . .	36.7	352 07.5 . .	34.3	Spica	158 29.9	S11 14.4
16	246 07.6	103 04.3	43.4	92 02.7	04.7	84 06.0	36.5	7 09.7	34.4	Suhail	222 51.6	S43 29.6
17	261 10.0	118 05.1	43.3	107 03.7	04.1	99 08.0	36.3	22 12.0	34.4			
18	276 12.5	133 05.9	N10 43.1	122 04.6	N12 03.6	114 09.9	N 8 36.2	37 14.2	S18 34.5	Vega	80 37.9	N38 48.4
19	291 14.9	148 06.8	43.0	137 05.6	03.0	129 11.9	36.0	52 16.5	34.5	Zuben'ubi	137 03.9	S16 06.2
20	306 17.4	163 07.6	42.8	152 06.6	02.5	144 13.9	35.8	67 18.7	34.6		SHA	Mer. Pass.
21	321 19.9	178 08.4 . .	42.7	167 07.5 . .	01.9	159 15.9 . .	35.6	82 21.0 . .	34.6		° ′	h m
22	336 22.3	193 09.2	42.6	182 08.5	01.4	174 17.8	35.4	97 23.3	34.7	Venus	218 01.1	9 09
23	351 24.8	208 10.0	42.4	197 09.5	00.8	189 19.8	35.2	112 25.5	34.7	Mars	206 55.1	9 54
	h m									Jupiter	198 18.0	10 27
Mer. Pass. 23 38.2		v 0.9	d 0.1	v 1.0	d 0.5	v 2.0	d 0.2	v 2.3	d 0.0	Saturn	121 10.4	15 35

UT	SUN GHA	SUN Dec	MOON GHA	v	MOON Dec	d	HP
d h	° ′	° ′	° ′	′	° ′	′	′
25 00	182 00.9	S 0 38.6	44 16.0	7.4	S12 00.0	8.7	60.0
01	197 01.1	39.6	58 42.4	7.3	11 51.3	8.7	60.0
02	212 01.4	40.5	73 08.7	7.4	11 42.6	8.8	60.1
03	227 01.6	.. 41.5	87 35.1	7.3	11 33.8	8.9	60.1
04	242 01.8	42.5	102 01.4	7.3	11 24.9	9.0	60.1
05	257 02.0	43.4	116 27.7	7.4	11 15.9	9.1	60.2
06	272 02.2	S 0 44.4	130 54.1	7.3	S11 06.8	9.1	60.2
07	287 02.4	45.4	145 20.4	7.3	10 57.7	9.3	60.2
08	302 02.7	46.4	159 46.7	7.3	10 48.4	9.3	60.3
F 09	317 02.9	.. 47.3	174 13.0	7.3	10 39.1	9.4	60.3
R 10	332 03.1	48.3	188 39.3	7.4	10 29.7	9.5	60.3
I 11	347 03.3	49.3	203 05.7	7.3	10 20.2	9.5	60.4
D 12	2 03.5	S 0 50.3	217 32.0	7.3	S10 10.7	9.7	60.4
A 13	17 03.7	51.2	231 58.3	7.3	10 01.0	9.7	60.4
Y 14	32 04.0	52.2	246 24.6	7.3	9 51.3	9.8	60.5
15	47 04.2	.. 53.2	260 50.9	7.3	9 41.5	9.8	60.5
16	62 04.4	54.2	275 17.2	7.2	9 31.7	10.0	60.5
17	77 04.6	55.1	289 43.4	7.3	9 21.7	10.0	60.5
18	92 04.8	S 0 56.1	304 09.7	7.3	S 9 11.7	10.0	60.6
19	107 05.0	57.1	318 36.0	7.3	9 01.7	10.2	60.6
20	122 05.3	58.0	333 02.3	7.3	8 51.5	10.2	60.6
21	137 05.5	0 59.0	347 28.6	7.3	8 41.3	10.3	60.7
22	152 05.7	1 00.0	1 54.9	7.2	8 31.0	10.3	60.7
23	167 05.9	01.0	16 21.1	7.3	8 20.7	10.4	60.7
26 00	182 06.1	S 1 01.9	30 47.4	7.3	S 8 10.3	10.5	60.7
01	197 06.3	02.9	45 13.7	7.2	7 59.8	10.5	60.8
02	212 06.6	03.9	59 39.9	7.3	7 49.3	10.6	60.8
03	227 06.8	.. 04.9	74 06.2	7.3	7 38.7	10.6	60.8
04	242 07.0	05.8	88 32.5	7.2	7 28.1	10.8	60.8
05	257 07.2	06.8	102 58.7	7.3	7 17.3	10.7	60.9
06	272 07.4	S 1 07.8	117 25.0	7.2	S 7 06.6	10.8	60.9
S 07	287 07.6	08.7	131 51.2	7.3	6 55.8	10.9	60.9
A 08	302 07.9	09.7	146 17.5	7.2	6 44.9	11.0	60.9
T 09	317 08.1	.. 10.7	160 43.7	7.3	6 33.9	10.9	61.0
U 10	332 08.3	11.7	175 10.0	7.2	6 23.0	11.1	61.0
R 11	347 08.5	12.6	189 36.2	7.3	6 11.9	11.1	61.0
D 12	2 08.7	S 1 13.6	204 02.5	7.2	S 6 00.8	11.1	61.0
A 13	17 08.9	14.6	218 28.7	7.2	5 49.7	11.2	61.1
Y 14	32 09.2	15.6	232 55.0	7.2	5 38.5	11.2	61.1
15	47 09.4	.. 16.5	247 21.2	7.2	5 27.3	11.3	61.1
16	62 09.6	17.5	261 47.4	7.2	5 16.0	11.3	61.1
17	77 09.8	18.5	276 13.7	7.2	5 04.7	11.3	61.1
18	92 10.0	S 1 19.5	290 39.9	7.2	S 4 53.4	11.4	61.1
19	107 10.2	20.4	305 06.1	7.2	4 42.0	11.5	61.2
20	122 10.4	21.4	319 32.3	7.3	4 30.5	11.4	61.2
21	137 10.7	.. 22.4	333 58.6	7.2	4 19.1	11.5	61.2
22	152 10.9	23.3	348 24.8	7.2	4 07.6	11.6	61.2
23	167 11.1	24.3	2 51.0	7.2	3 56.0	11.5	61.2
27 00	182 11.3	S 1 25.3	17 17.2	7.2	S 3 44.5	11.6	61.2
01	197 11.5	26.3	31 43.4	7.2	3 32.9	11.7	61.3
02	212 11.7	27.2	46 09.6	7.2	3 21.2	11.6	61.3
03	227 11.9	.. 28.2	60 35.8	7.2	3 09.6	11.7	61.3
04	242 12.2	29.2	75 02.0	7.2	2 57.9	11.7	61.3
05	257 12.4	30.2	89 28.2	7.2	2 46.2	11.7	61.3
06	272 12.6	S 1 31.1	103 54.4	7.2	S 2 34.5	11.8	61.3
07	287 12.8	32.1	118 20.6	7.2	2 22.7	11.8	61.3
08	302 13.0	33.1	132 46.8	7.2	2 10.9	11.8	61.3
S 09	317 13.2	.. 34.0	147 13.0	7.2	1 59.1	11.8	61.4
U 10	332 13.4	35.0	161 39.2	7.1	1 47.3	11.8	61.4
N 11	347 13.7	36.0	176 05.3	7.2	1 35.5	11.8	61.4
D 12	2 13.9	S 1 37.0	190 31.5	7.2	S 1 23.7	11.9	61.4
A 13	17 14.1	37.9	204 54.7	7.1	1 11.8	11.9	61.4
Y 14	32 14.3	38.9	219 23.8	7.2	0 59.9	11.8	61.4
15	47 14.5	.. 39.9	233 50.0	7.1	0 48.1	11.9	61.4
16	62 14.7	40.9	248 16.1	7.2	0 36.2	11.9	61.4
17	77 14.9	41.8	262 42.3	7.1	S 0 24.3	11.9	61.4
18	92 15.1	S 1 42.8	277 08.4	7.2	S 0 12.4	11.9	61.4
19	107 15.4	43.8	291 34.6	7.1	S 0 00.5	11.9	61.4
20	122 15.6	44.7	306 00.7	7.1	N 0 11.4	11.9	61.4
21	137 15.8	.. 45.7	320 26.8	7.2	0 23.3	11.9	61.4
22	152 16.0	46.7	334 53.0	7.1	0 35.2	11.9	61.4
23	167 16.2	47.7	349 19.1	7.1	N 0 47.1	11.9	61.4
	SD 16.0	d 1.0	SD 16.5		16.6		16.7

Lat.	Twilight Naut.	Civil	Sunrise	Moonrise 25	26	27	28
°	h m	h m	h m	h m	h m	h m	h m
N 72	03 20	04 47	05 55	17 46	17 41	17 36	17 32
N 70	03 37	04 53	05 54	17 31	17 34	17 36	17 38
68	03 49	04 58	05 54	17 20	17 28	17 35	17 43
66	04 00	05 02	05 53	17 10	17 23	17 35	17 47
64	04 08	05 06	05 53	17 02	17 19	17 35	17 50
62	04 16	05 09	05 53	16 55	17 15	17 34	17 53
60	04 22	05 11	05 53	16 49	17 12	17 34	17 56
N 58	04 27	05 13	05 52	16 43	17 09	17 34	17 58
56	04 31	05 15	05 52	16 39	17 07	17 33	18 00
54	04 35	05 17	05 52	16 34	17 04	17 33	18 02
52	04 39	05 18	05 52	16 30	17 02	17 33	18 04
50	04 42	05 19	05 52	16 27	17 01	17 33	18 05
45	04 48	05 22	05 51	16 19	16 56	17 33	18 09
N 40	04 52	05 24	05 51	16 12	16 53	17 32	18 12
35	04 56	05 25	05 51	16 07	16 50	17 32	18 14
30	04 59	05 26	05 50	16 02	16 47	17 32	18 17
20	05 02	05 28	05 50	15 53	16 43	17 32	18 21
N 10	05 04	05 28	05 49	15 46	16 39	17 31	18 24
0	05 04	05 28	05 48	15 39	16 35	17 31	18 27
S 10	05 02	05 26	05 47	15 32	16 31	17 31	18 31
20	04 59	05 24	05 46	15 24	16 27	17 31	18 35
30	04 53	05 21	05 45	15 15	16 22	17 30	18 39
35	04 49	05 19	05 44	15 10	16 20	17 30	18 41
40	04 45	05 16	05 43	15 05	16 17	17 30	18 44
45	04 38	05 13	05 42	14 58	16 13	17 30	18 47
S 50	04 30	05 09	05 41	14 50	16 09	17 30	18 51
52	04 27	05 07	05 40	14 47	16 07	17 30	18 53
54	04 22	05 04	05 40	14 42	16 05	17 30	18 55
56	04 17	05 02	05 39	14 38	16 03	17 30	18 57
58	04 11	04 59	05 38	14 33	16 00	17 30	19 00
S 60	04 05	04 55	05 37	14 27	15 57	17 30	19 02

Lat.	Sunset	Twilight Civil	Naut.	Moonset 25	26	27	28
°	h m	h m	h m	h m	h m	h m	h m
N 72	17 46	18 53	20 19	00 18	02 20	04 23	06 25
N 70	17 47	18 47	20 03	00 41	02 33	04 27	06 22
68	17 47	18 42	19 50	00 58	02 43	04 31	06 20
66	17 48	18 39	19 40	01 12	02 51	04 34	06 18
64	17 48	18 35	19 32	01 23	02 58	04 36	06 16
62	17 49	18 33	19 25	01 33	03 04	04 38	06 14
60	17 49	18 30	19 19	01 41	03 09	04 40	06 13
N 58	17 49	18 28	19 14	01 48	03 13	04 42	06 12
56	17 49	18 26	19 10	01 54	03 17	04 43	06 11
54	17 50	18 25	19 06	02 00	03 21	04 45	06 10
52	17 50	18 24	19 03	02 05	03 24	04 46	06 09
50	17 50	18 22	19 00	02 10	03 27	04 47	06 08
45	17 51	18 20	18 54	02 20	03 33	04 50	06 07
N 40	17 51	18 18	18 50	02 28	03 39	04 51	06 05
35	17 52	18 17	18 46	02 35	03 43	04 53	06 04
30	17 52	18 16	18 44	02 41	03 47	04 55	06 03
20	17 53	18 15	18 40	02 52	03 54	04 57	06 01
N 10	17 54	18 15	18 39	03 01	04 00	04 59	05 59
0	17 55	18 15	18 39	03 09	04 05	05 01	05 58
S 10	17 56	18 17	18 41	03 18	04 11	05 03	05 56
20	17 57	18 19	18 44	03 27	04 17	05 06	05 54
30	17 58	18 22	18 50	03 37	04 23	05 08	05 52
35	17 59	18 24	18 54	03 43	04 27	05 09	05 51
40	18 00	18 27	18 59	03 50	04 31	05 11	05 50
45	18 01	18 31	19 05	03 57	04 36	05 13	05 49
S 50	18 03	18 35	19 14	04 07	04 42	05 15	05 47
52	18 04	18 37	19 18	04 11	04 44	05 15	05 46
54	18 04	18 40	19 22	04 16	04 47	05 16	05 45
56	18 05	18 43	19 27	04 21	04 50	05 18	05 44
58	18 06	18 46	19 33	04 27	04 54	05 19	05 43
S 60	18 07	18 49	19 40	04 33	04 58	05 20	05 42

Day	SUN Eqn. of Time 00h	12h	Mer. Pass.	MOON Mer. Pass. Upper	Lower	Age	Phase
d	m s	m s	h m	h m	h m	d	%
25	08 03	08 14	11 52	21 52	09 24	12	90
26	08 24	08 34	11 51	22 48	10 20	13	96
27	08 45	08 55	11 51	23 44	11 16	14	99

UT	ARIES	VENUS −4.7		MARS +1.8		JUPITER −1.7		SATURN +0.6		STARS		
	GHA	GHA	Dec	GHA	Dec	GHA	Dec	GHA	Dec	Name	SHA	Dec
d h	° ′	° ′	° ′	° ′	° ′	° ′	° ′	° ′	° ′		° ′	° ′
28 00	6 27.3	223 10.8	N10 42.3	212 10.5	N12 00.3	204 21.8	N 8 35.0	127 27.8	S18 34.8	Acamar	315 16.9	S40 14.4
01	21 29.7	238 11.6	42.1	227 11.4	11 59.7	219 23.8	34.8	142 30.0	34.8	Achernar	335 25.2	S57 09.3
02	36 32.2	253 12.4	42.0	242 12.4	59.2	234 25.8	34.6	157 32.3	34.9	Acrux	173 08.1	S63 11.1
03	51 34.7	268 13.2 . .	41.8	257 13.4 . .	58.6	249 27.7 . .	34.4	172 34.5 . .	34.9	Adhara	255 11.4	S28 59.5
04	66 37.1	283 13.9	41.7	272 14.3	58.1	264 29.7	34.2	187 36.8	35.0	Aldebaran	290 47.4	N16 32.3
05	81 39.6	298 14.7	41.5	287 15.3	57.5	279 31.7	34.0	202 39.0	35.0			
06	96 42.1	313 15.5	N10 41.4	302 16.3	N11 57.0	294 33.7	N 8 33.9	217 41.3	S18 35.1	Alioth	166 20.0	N55 52.6
07	111 44.5	328 16.3	41.2	317 17.3	56.4	309 35.6	33.7	232 43.5	35.1	Alkaid	152 58.2	N49 14.3
08	126 47.0	343 17.1	41.0	332 18.2	55.9	324 37.6	33.5	247 45.8	35.2	Al Na'ir	27 41.5	S46 53.0
M 09	141 49.4	358 17.9 . .	40.9	347 19.2 . .	55.3	339 39.6 . .	33.3	262 48.0 . .	35.2	Alnilam	275 44.7	S 1 11.6
O 10	156 51.9	13 18.7	40.7	2 20.2	54.8	354 41.6	33.1	277 50.3	35.3	Alphard	217 54.8	S 8 43.6
N 11	171 54.4	28 19.4	40.6	17 21.1	54.2	9 43.6	32.9	292 52.5	35.3			
D 12	186 56.8	43 20.2	N10 40.4	32 22.1	N11 53.7	24 45.5	N 8 32.7	307 54.8	S18 35.4	Alphecca	126 10.0	N26 40.1
A 13	201 59.3	58 21.0	40.2	47 23.1	53.1	39 47.5	32.5	322 57.1	35.4	Alpheratz	357 41.5	N29 10.8
Y 14	217 01.8	73 21.8	40.1	62 24.1	52.6	54 49.5	32.3	337 59.3	35.5	Altair	62 06.6	N 8 55.0
15	232 04.2	88 22.5 . .	39.9	77 25.0 . .	52.0	69 51.5 . .	32.1	353 01.6 . .	35.5	Ankaa	353 13.8	S42 13.2
16	247 06.7	103 23.3	39.8	92 26.0	51.5	84 53.5	31.9	8 03.8	35.6	Antares	112 24.5	S26 27.8
17	262 09.2	118 24.1	39.6	107 27.0	50.9	99 55.4	31.8	23 06.1	35.6			
18	277 11.6	133 24.8	N10 39.4	122 27.9	N11 50.4	114 57.4	N 8 31.6	38 08.3	S18 35.7	Arcturus	145 54.6	N19 06.3
19	292 14.1	148 25.6	39.3	137 28.9	49.8	129 59.4	31.4	53 10.6	35.7	Atria	107 25.1	S69 03.3
20	307 16.5	163 26.4	39.1	152 29.9	49.3	145 01.4	31.2	68 12.8	35.8	Avior	234 17.6	S59 33.4
21	322 19.0	178 27.1 . .	38.9	167 30.9 . .	48.7	160 03.3 . .	31.0	83 15.1 . .	35.8	Bellatrix	278 30.3	N 6 21.7
22	337 21.5	193 27.9	38.8	182 31.8	48.2	175 05.3	30.8	98 17.3	35.9	Betelgeuse	270 59.6	N 7 24.5
23	352 23.9	208 28.6	38.6	197 32.8	47.6	190 07.3	30.6	113 19.6	35.9			
29 00	7 26.4	223 29.4	N10 38.4	212 33.8	N11 47.1	205 09.3	N 8 30.4	128 21.8	S18 36.0	Canopus	263 55.4	S52 42.1
01	22 28.9	238 30.1	38.2	227 34.7	46.5	220 11.3	30.2	143 24.1	36.0	Capella	280 32.0	N46 00.5
02	37 31.3	253 30.9	38.1	242 35.7	46.0	235 13.2	30.0	158 26.3	36.1	Deneb	49 30.1	N45 20.6
03	52 33.8	268 31.6 . .	37.9	257 36.7 . .	45.4	250 15.2 . .	29.8	173 28.6 . .	36.1	Denebola	182 32.4	N14 29.2
04	67 36.3	283 32.4	37.7	272 37.7	44.8	265 17.2	29.6	188 30.8	36.2	Diphda	348 54.0	S17 53.9
05	82 38.7	298 33.1	37.5	287 38.6	44.3	280 19.2	29.5	203 33.1	36.2			
06	97 41.2	313 33.9	N10 37.4	302 39.6	N11 43.7	295 21.2	N 8 29.3	218 35.3	S18 36.3	Dubhe	193 50.6	N61 39.9
07	112 43.7	328 34.6	37.2	317 40.6	43.2	310 23.1	29.1	233 37.6	36.3	Elnath	278 10.6	N28 37.0
08	127 46.1	343 35.3	37.0	332 41.6	42.6	325 25.1	28.9	248 39.8	36.4	Eltanin	90 45.5	N51 29.7
T 09	142 48.6	358 36.1 . .	36.8	347 42.5 . .	42.1	340 27.1 . .	28.7	263 42.1 . .	36.4	Enif	33 45.4	N 9 57.1
U 10	157 51.0	13 36.8	36.6	2 43.5	41.5	355 29.1	28.5	278 44.3	36.5	Fomalhaut	15 22.0	S29 32.2
E 11	172 53.5	28 37.5	36.5	17 44.5	41.0	10 31.1	28.3	293 46.6	36.5			
S 12	187 56.0	43 38.3	N10 36.3	32 45.5	N11 40.4	25 33.0	N 8 28.1	308 48.8	S18 36.6	Gacrux	171 59.6	S57 12.0
D 13	202 58.4	58 39.0	36.1	47 46.4	39.9	40 35.0	27.9	323 51.1	36.6	Gienah	175 51.0	S17 37.6
A 14	218 00.9	73 39.7	35.9	62 47.4	39.3	55 37.0	27.7	338 53.3	36.7	Hadar	148 46.2	S60 26.9
Y 15	233 03.4	88 40.5 . .	35.7	77 48.4 . .	38.8	70 39.0 . .	27.5	353 55.6 . .	36.7	Hamal	327 58.7	N23 32.2
16	248 05.8	103 41.2	35.5	92 49.4	38.2	85 41.0	27.4	8 57.8	36.8	Kaus Aust.	83 41.8	S34 22.5
17	263 08.3	118 41.9	35.3	107 50.3	37.7	100 42.9	27.2	24 00.1	36.8			
18	278 10.8	133 42.6	N10 35.2	122 51.3	N11 37.1	115 44.9	N 8 27.0	39 02.3	S18 36.9	Kochab	137 21.2	N74 05.8
19	293 13.2	148 43.3	35.0	137 52.3	36.5	130 46.9	26.8	54 04.6	36.9	Markab	13 36.5	N15 17.6
20	308 15.7	163 44.1	34.8	152 53.3	36.0	145 48.9	26.6	69 06.8	37.0	Menkar	314 13.2	N 4 09.1
21	323 18.1	178 44.8 . .	34.6	167 54.2 . .	35.4	160 50.9 . .	26.4	84 09.1 . .	37.0	Menkent	148 06.1	S36 26.7
22	338 20.6	193 45.5	34.4	182 55.2	34.9	175 52.9	26.2	99 11.3	37.1	Miaplacidus	221 39.8	S69 46.8
23	353 23.1	208 46.2	34.2	197 56.2	34.3	190 54.8	26.0	114 13.6	37.1			
30 00	8 25.5	223 46.9	N10 34.0	212 57.2	N11 33.8	205 56.8	N 8 25.8	129 15.8	S18 37.2	Mirfak	308 37.7	N49 54.8
01	23 28.0	238 47.6	33.8	227 58.2	33.2	220 58.8	25.6	144 18.1	37.2	Nunki	75 56.4	S26 16.4
02	38 30.5	253 48.3	33.6	242 59.1	32.7	236 00.8	25.4	159 20.3	37.3	Peacock	53 16.6	S56 41.0
03	53 32.9	268 49.0 . .	33.4	258 00.1 . .	32.1	251 02.8 . .	25.3	174 22.6 . .	37.3	Pollux	243 26.0	N27 59.1
04	68 35.4	283 49.7	33.2	273 01.1	31.5	266 04.7	25.1	189 24.8	37.4	Procyon	244 58.2	N 5 11.0
05	83 37.9	298 50.4	33.0	288 02.1	31.0	281 06.7	24.9	204 27.0	37.4			
06	98 40.3	313 51.1	N10 32.8	303 03.0	N11 30.4	296 08.7	N 8 24.7	219 29.3	S18 37.5	Rasalhague	96 05.1	N12 33.3
07	113 42.8	328 51.8	32.6	318 04.0	29.9	311 10.7	24.5	234 31.5	37.5	Regulus	207 42.2	N11 53.4
08	128 45.3	343 52.5	32.4	333 05.0	29.3	326 12.7	24.3	249 33.8	37.6	Rigel	281 10.5	S 8 11.0
W 09	143 47.7	358 53.2 . .	32.2	348 06.0 . .	28.8	341 14.6 . .	24.1	264 36.0 . .	37.6	Rigil Kent.	139 50.1	S60 53.9
E 10	158 50.2	13 53.9	32.0	3 06.9	28.2	356 16.6	23.9	279 38.3	37.7	Sabik	102 10.9	S15 44.4
D 11	173 52.6	28 54.6	31.8	18 07.9	27.7	11 18.6	23.7	294 40.5	37.7			
N 12	188 55.1	43 55.3	N10 31.6	33 08.9	N11 27.1	26 20.6	N 8 23.5	309 42.8	S18 37.8	Schedar	349 38.1	N56 37.4
E 13	203 57.6	58 56.0	31.4	48 09.9	26.5	41 22.6	23.4	324 45.0	37.9	Shaula	96 19.9	S37 06.8
S 14	219 00.0	73 56.7	31.2	63 10.9	26.0	56 24.6	23.2	339 47.3	37.9	Sirius	258 32.4	S16 44.2
D 15	234 02.5	88 57.3 . .	30.9	78 11.8 . .	25.4	71 26.5 . .	23.0	354 49.5 . .	38.0	Spica	158 29.9	S11 14.4
A 16	249 05.0	103 58.0	30.7	93 12.8	24.9	86 28.5	22.8	9 51.8	38.0	Suhail	222 51.5	S43 29.6
Y 17	264 07.4	118 58.7	30.5	108 13.8	24.3	101 30.5	22.6	24 54.0	38.1			
18	279 09.9	133 59.4	N10 30.3	123 14.8	N11 23.8	116 32.5	N 8 22.4	39 56.3	S18 38.1	Vega	80 37.9	N38 48.4
19	294 12.4	149 00.0	30.1	138 15.8	23.2	131 34.5	22.2	54 58.5	38.2	Zuben'ubi	137 04.0	S16 06.2
20	309 14.8	164 00.7	29.9	153 16.7	22.7	146 36.5	22.0	70 00.7	38.2		SHA	Mer.Pass.
21	324 17.3	179 01.4 . .	29.7	168 17.7 . .	22.1	161 38.4 . .	21.8	85 03.0 . .	38.3		° ′	h m
22	339 19.8	194 02.1	29.4	183 18.7	21.5	176 40.4	21.6	100 05.2	38.3	Venus	216 03.0	9 06
23	354 22.2	209 02.7	29.2	198 19.7	21.0	191 42.4	21.5	115 07.5	38.4	Mars	205 07.4	9 49
	h m									Jupiter	197 42.9	10 18
Mer. Pass. 23 26.4		v 0.7	d 0.2	v 1.0	d 0.6	v 2.0	d 0.2	v 2.2	d 0.1	Saturn	120 55.4	15 24

UT	SUN GHA	SUN Dec	MOON GHA	v	MOON Dec	d	HP
d h	° ′	° ′	° ′	′	° ′	′	′
28 00	182 16.4	S 1 48.6	3 45.2	7.1	N 0 59.0	11.9	61.4
01	197 16.6	49.6	18 11.3	7.1	1 10.9	11.8	61.4
02	212 16.8	50.6	32 37.4	7.1	1 22.7	11.7	61.4
03	227 17.1	. . 51.6	47 03.5	7.1	1 34.6	11.9	61.4
04	242 17.3	52.5	61 29.6	7.0	1 46.5	11.8	61.4
05	257 17.5	53.5	75 55.6	7.1	1 58.3	11.8	61.4
06	272 17.7	S 1 54.5	90 21.7	7.1	N 2 10.1	11.8	61.4
07	287 17.9	55.4	104 47.8	7.1	2 21.9	11.8	61.4
08	302 18.1	56.4	119 13.9	7.0	2 33.7	11.8	61.4
M 09	317 18.3	. . 57.4	133 39.9	7.1	2 45.5	11.8	61.4
O 10	332 18.5	58.4	148 06.0	7.0	2 57.3	11.7	61.4
N 11	347 18.7	1 59.3	162 32.0	7.0	3 09.0	11.7	61.4
D 12	2 19.0	S 2 00.3	176 58.0	7.1	N 3 20.7	11.7	61.4
A 13	17 19.2	01.3	191 24.1	7.0	3 32.4	11.7	61.4
Y 14	32 19.4	02.3	205 50.1	7.0	3 44.1	11.6	61.4
15	47 19.6	. . 03.2	220 16.1	7.0	3 55.7	11.6	61.4
16	62 19.8	04.2	234 42.1	7.0	4 07.3	11.6	61.4
17	77 20.0	05.2	249 08.1	7.0	4 18.9	11.5	61.4
18	92 20.2	S 2 06.1	263 34.1	7.0	N 4 30.4	11.5	61.4
19	107 20.4	07.1	278 00.1	7.0	4 41.9	11.5	61.4
20	122 20.6	08.1	292 26.1	6.9	4 53.4	11.4	61.3
21	137 20.9	. . 09.1	306 52.0	7.0	5 04.8	11.4	61.3
22	152 21.1	10.0	321 18.0	7.0	5 16.2	11.4	61.3
23	167 21.3	11.0	335 44.0	6.9	5 27.6	11.3	61.3
29 00	182 21.5	S 2 12.0	350 09.9	7.0	N 5 38.9	11.3	61.3
01	197 21.7	12.9	4 35.9	6.9	5 50.2	11.2	61.3
02	212 21.9	13.9	19 01.8	6.9	6 01.4	11.2	61.3
03	227 22.1	. . 14.9	33 27.7	6.9	6 12.6	11.1	61.3
04	242 22.3	15.9	47 53.7	6.9	6 23.7	11.1	61.2
05	257 22.5	16.8	62 19.6	6.9	6 34.8	11.0	61.2
06	272 22.7	S 2 17.8	76 45.5	6.9	N 6 45.8	11.0	61.2
07	287 23.0	18.8	91 11.4	6.9	6 56.8	10.9	61.2
T 08	302 23.2	19.7	105 37.3	6.9	7 07.7	10.9	61.2
U 09	317 23.4	. . 20.7	120 03.2	6.9	7 18.6	10.8	61.2
E 10	332 23.6	21.7	134 29.1	6.8	7 29.4	10.8	61.1
S 11	347 23.8	22.7	148 54.9	6.9	7 40.2	10.7	61.1
D 12	2 24.0	S 2 23.6	163 20.8	6.9	N 7 50.9	10.6	61.1
A 13	17 24.2	24.6	177 46.7	6.8	8 01.5	10.6	61.1
Y 14	32 24.4	25.6	192 12.5	6.9	8 12.1	10.5	61.1
15	47 24.6	. . 26.5	206 38.4	6.8	8 22.6	10.5	61.0
16	62 24.8	27.5	221 04.2	6.9	8 33.1	10.4	61.0
17	77 25.0	28.5	235 30.1	6.8	8 43.5	10.3	61.0
18	92 25.2	S 2 29.5	249 55.9	6.8	N 8 53.8	10.3	61.0
19	107 25.5	30.4	264 21.7	6.8	9 04.1	10.1	61.0
20	122 25.7	31.4	278 47.5	6.9	9 14.2	10.2	60.9
21	137 25.9	. . 32.4	293 13.4	6.8	9 24.4	10.0	60.9
22	152 26.1	33.3	307 39.2	6.8	9 34.4	10.0	60.9
23	167 26.3	34.3	322 05.0	6.8	9 44.4	9.9	60.9
30 00	182 26.5	S 2 35.3	336 30.8	6.8	N 9 54.3	9.8	60.8
01	197 26.7	36.3	350 56.6	6.8	10 04.1	9.7	60.8
02	212 26.9	37.2	5 22.4	6.8	10 13.8	9.7	60.8
03	227 27.1	. . 38.2	19 48.2	6.8	10 23.5	9.6	60.8
04	242 27.3	39.2	34 14.0	6.7	10 33.1	9.5	60.7
05	257 27.5	40.1	48 39.7	6.8	10 42.6	9.4	60.7
06	272 27.7	S 2 41.1	63 05.5	6.8	N10 52.0	9.4	60.7
W 07	287 27.9	42.1	77 31.3	6.8	11 01.4	9.3	60.6
E 08	302 28.1	43.1	91 57.1	6.7	11 10.7	9.1	60.6
D 09	317 28.4	. . 44.0	106 22.8	6.8	11 19.8	9.1	60.6
N 10	332 28.6	45.0	120 48.6	6.8	11 28.9	9.1	60.6
E 11	347 28.8	46.0	135 14.4	6.8	11 38.0	8.9	60.5
S 12	2 29.0	S 2 46.9	149 40.2	6.7	N11 46.9	8.8	60.5
D 13	17 29.2	47.9	164 05.9	6.8	11 55.7	8.8	60.5
A 14	32 29.4	48.9	178 31.7	6.8	12 04.5	8.6	60.4
Y 15	47 29.6	. . 49.8	192 57.5	6.7	12 13.1	8.6	60.4
16	62 29.8	50.8	207 23.2	6.8	12 21.7	8.5	60.4
17	77 30.0	51.8	221 49.0	6.8	12 30.2	8.4	60.3
18	92 30.2	S 2 52.8	236 14.8	6.8	N12 38.6	8.3	60.3
19	107 30.4	53.7	250 40.6	6.7	12 46.9	8.2	60.3
20	122 30.6	54.7	265 06.3	6.8	12 55.1	8.1	60.2
21	137 30.8	. . 55.7	279 32.1	6.8	13 03.2	8.0	60.2
22	152 31.0	56.6	293 57.9	6.8	13 11.2	7.9	60.2
23	167 31.2	57.6	308 23.7	6.8	N13 19.1	7.8	60.1
	SD 16.0	d 1.0	SD 16.7		16.6		16.5

Lat.	Twilight Naut.	Twilight Civil	Sunrise	Moonrise 28	Moonrise 29	Moonrise 30	Moonrise 1
°	h m	h m	h m	h m	h m	h m	h m
N 72	03 37	05 01	06 08	17 32	17 28	17 24	17 19
N 70	03 51	05 05	06 06	17 38	17 41	17 45	17 54
68	04 02	05 09	06 04	17 43	17 51	18 02	18 19
66	04 11	05 12	06 03	17 47	18 00	18 16	18 38
64	04 18	05 14	06 02	17 50	18 07	18 28	18 54
62	04 24	05 17	06 01	17 53	18 14	18 37	19 07
60	04 29	05 18	06 00	17 56	18 19	18 46	19 18
N 58	04 34	05 20	05 59	17 58	18 24	18 53	19 28
56	04 37	05 21	05 58	18 00	18 28	19 00	19 36
54	04 41	05 22	05 57	18 02	18 32	19 06	19 44
52	04 44	05 23	05 57	18 04	18 36	19 11	19 51
50	04 46	05 24	05 56	18 05	18 39	19 16	19 57
45	04 52	05 26	05 55	18 09	18 46	19 27	20 10
N 40	04 55	05 27	05 54	18 12	18 52	19 35	20 21
35	04 58	05 28	05 53	18 14	18 58	19 43	20 31
30	05 00	05 28	05 52	18 17	19 02	19 50	20 39
20	05 03	05 28	05 50	18 21	19 10	20 01	20 53
N 10	05 03	05 28	05 49	18 24	19 17	20 11	21 06
0	05 02	05 26	05 47	18 27	19 24	20 21	21 18
S 10	05 00	05 24	05 45	18 31	19 31	20 31	21 30
20	04 56	05 22	05 44	18 35	19 38	20 41	21 42
30	04 49	05 17	05 41	18 39	19 47	20 53	21 57
35	04 45	05 15	05 40	18 41	19 51	21 00	22 06
40	04 39	05 11	05 38	18 44	19 57	21 08	22 16
45	04 32	05 07	05 37	18 47	20 03	21 17	22 27
S 50	04 23	05 02	05 34	18 51	20 11	21 29	22 41
52	04 19	04 59	05 33	18 53	20 15	21 34	22 47
54	04 14	04 57	05 32	18 55	20 19	21 40	22 55
56	04 08	04 54	05 31	18 57	20 23	21 46	23 03
58	04 02	04 50	05 30	19 00	20 28	21 53	23 12
S 60	03 55	04 46	05 28	19 02	20 34	22 01	23 22

Lat.	Sunset	Twilight Civil	Twilight Naut.	Moonset 28	Moonset 29	Moonset 30	Moonset 1
°	h m	h m	h m	h m	h m	h m	h m
N 72	17 31	18 37	20 00	06 25	08 28	10 31	12 35
N 70	17 33	18 33	19 47	06 22	08 17	10 11	12 01
68	17 35	18 30	19 36	06 20	08 08	09 55	11 37
66	17 36	18 27	19 28	06 18	08 01	09 42	11 18
64	17 38	18 25	19 21	06 16	07 55	09 32	11 03
62	17 39	18 23	19 15	06 14	07 50	09 23	10 51
60	17 40	18 21	19 10	06 13	07 45	09 15	10 40
N 58	17 41	18 20	19 06	06 12	07 41	09 08	10 31
56	17 42	18 18	19 02	06 11	07 38	09 02	10 23
54	17 42	18 17	18 59	06 10	07 35	08 57	10 15
52	17 43	18 17	18 56	06 09	07 32	08 52	10 09
50	17 44	18 16	18 53	06 08	07 29	08 48	10 03
45	17 45	18 14	18 48	06 07	07 23	08 39	09 51
N 40	17 46	18 13	18 45	06 05	07 19	08 31	09 40
35	17 47	18 13	18 42	06 04	07 15	08 24	09 32
30	17 48	18 12	18 40	06 03	07 11	08 18	09 24
20	17 50	18 12	18 38	06 01	07 05	08 08	09 11
N 10	17 52	18 13	18 37	05 59	06 59	07 59	08 59
0	17 54	18 14	18 38	05 58	06 54	07 51	08 48
S 10	17 55	18 16	18 41	05 56	06 49	07 43	08 37
20	17 58	18 20	18 45	05 54	06 44	07 34	08 26
30	18 00	18 24	18 52	05 52	06 38	07 24	08 12
35	18 01	18 27	18 56	05 51	06 34	07 18	08 05
40	18 03	18 30	19 02	05 50	06 30	07 12	07 56
45	18 05	18 35	19 09	05 49	06 25	07 04	07 46
S 50	18 07	18 40	19 19	05 47	06 20	06 55	07 34
52	18 09	18 43	19 23	05 46	06 17	06 51	07 28
54	18 10	18 45	19 28	05 45	06 14	06 46	07 22
56	18 11	18 49	19 34	05 44	06 11	06 41	07 15
58	18 13	18 52	19 41	05 43	06 08	06 35	07 07
S 60	18 14	18 57	19 48	05 42	06 04	06 29	06 58

	SUN			MOON			
Day	Eqn. of Time 00h	Eqn. of Time 12h	Mer. Pass.	Mer. Pass. Upper	Mer. Pass. Lower	Age	Phase
d	m s	m s	h m	h m	h m	d %	
28	09 05	09 15	11 51	24 41	12 13	15 100	
29	09 26	09 36	11 50	00 41	13 09	16 97	◯
30	09 46	09 55	11 50	01 38	14 06	17 92	

2015 OCTOBER 1, 2, 3 (THURS., FRI., SAT.)

UT	ARIES GHA	VENUS −4.7 GHA	Dec	MARS +1.8 GHA	Dec	JUPITER −1.7 GHA	Dec	SATURN +0.6 GHA	Dec	STARS Name	SHA	Dec
1 00	9 24.7	224 03.4 N10	29.0	213 20.6 N11	20.4	206 44.4 N 8	21.3	130 09.7 S18	38.4	Acamar	315 16.9	S40 14.4
01	24 27.1	239 04.1	28.8	228 21.6	19.9	221 46.4	21.1	145 12.0	38.5	Achernar	335 25.2	S57 09.4
02	39 29.6	254 04.7	28.6	243 22.6	19.3	236 48.3	20.9	160 14.2	38.5	Acrux	173 08.1	S63 11.1
03	54 32.1	269 05.4 ..	28.3	258 23.6 ..	18.8	251 50.3 ..	20.7	175 16.5 ..	38.6	Adhara	255 11.3	S28 59.5
04	69 34.5	284 06.1	28.1	273 24.6	18.2	266 52.3	20.5	190 18.7	38.6	Aldebaran	290 47.4	N16 32.3
05	84 37.0	299 06.7	27.9	288 25.5	17.6	281 54.3	20.3	205 21.0	38.7			
06	99 39.5	314 07.4 N10	27.7	303 26.5 N11	17.1	296 56.3 N 8	20.1	220 23.2 S18	38.7	Alioth	166 20.0	N55 52.6
T 07	114 41.9	329 08.0	27.4	318 27.5	16.5	311 58.3	19.9	235 25.4	38.8	Alkaid	152 58.2	N49 14.3
H 08	129 44.4	344 08.7	27.2	333 28.5	16.0	327 00.3	19.7	250 27.7	38.8	Al Na'ir	27 41.5	S46 53.0
U 09	144 46.9	359 09.3 ..	27.0	348 29.5 ..	15.4	342 02.2 ..	19.5	265 29.9 ..	38.9	Alnilam	275 44.7	S 1 11.6
R 10	159 49.3	14 10.0	26.8	3 30.5	14.8	357 04.2	19.4	280 32.2	38.9	Alphard	217 54.8	S 8 43.6
S 11	174 51.8	29 10.6	26.5	18 31.4	14.3	12 06.2	19.2	295 34.4	39.0			
D 12	189 54.2	44 11.3 N10	26.3	33 32.4 N11	13.7	27 08.2 N 8	19.0	310 36.7 S18	39.0	Alphecca	126 10.0	N26 40.1
A 13	204 56.7	59 11.9	26.1	48 33.4	13.2	42 10.2	18.8	325 38.9	39.1	Alpheratz	357 41.5	N29 10.8
Y 14	219 59.2	74 12.6	25.8	63 34.4	12.6	57 12.2	18.6	340 41.1	39.1	Altair	62 06.6	N 8 55.0
15	235 01.6	89 13.2 ..	25.6	78 35.4 ..	12.1	72 14.1 ..	18.4	355 43.4 ..	39.2	Ankaa	353 13.8	S42 13.2
16	250 04.1	104 13.8	25.4	93 36.3	11.5	87 16.1	18.2	10 45.6	39.2	Antares	112 24.5	S26 27.8
17	265 06.6	119 14.5	25.1	108 37.3	10.9	102 18.1	18.0	25 47.9	39.3			
18	280 09.0	134 15.1 N10	24.9	123 38.3 N11	10.4	117 20.1 N 8	17.8	40 50.1 S18	39.3	Arcturus	145 54.7	N19 06.3
19	295 11.5	149 15.8	24.7	138 39.3	09.8	132 22.1	17.7	55 52.4	39.4	Atria	107 25.1	S69 03.3
20	310 14.0	164 16.4	24.4	153 40.3	09.3	147 24.1	17.5	70 54.6	39.4	Avior	234 17.6	S59 33.4
21	325 16.4	179 17.0 ..	24.2	168 41.3 ..	08.7	162 26.0 ..	17.3	85 56.9 ..	39.5	Bellatrix	278 30.3	N 6 21.7
22	340 18.9	194 17.6	23.9	183 42.2	08.1	177 28.0	17.1	100 59.1	39.5	Betelgeuse	270 59.6	N 7 24.5
23	355 21.4	209 18.3	23.7	198 43.2	07.6	192 30.0	16.9	116 01.3	39.6			
2 00	10 23.8	224 18.9 N10	23.5	213 44.2 N11	07.0	207 32.0 N 8	16.7	131 03.6 S18	39.6	Canopus	263 55.4	S52 42.1
01	25 26.3	239 19.5	23.2	228 45.2	06.5	222 34.0	16.5	146 05.8	39.7	Capella	280 32.0	N46 00.5
02	40 28.7	254 20.1	23.0	243 46.2	05.9	237 36.0	16.3	161 08.1	39.7	Deneb	49 30.1	N45 20.6
03	55 31.2	269 20.8 ..	22.7	258 47.1 ..	05.3	252 38.0 ..	16.1	176 10.3 ..	39.8	Denebola	182 32.4	N14 29.1
04	70 33.7	284 21.4	22.5	273 48.1	04.8	267 39.9	15.9	191 12.5	39.8	Diphda	348 54.0	S17 53.9
05	85 36.1	299 22.0	22.2	288 49.1	04.2	282 41.9	15.8	206 14.8	39.9			
06	100 38.6	314 22.6 N10	22.0	303 50.1 N11	03.7	297 43.9 N 8	15.6	221 17.0 S18	39.9	Dubhe	193 50.6	N61 39.9
07	115 41.1	329 23.2	21.7	318 51.1	03.1	312 45.9	15.4	236 19.3	40.0	Elnath	278 10.5	N28 37.0
08	130 43.5	344 23.9	21.5	333 52.1	02.5	327 47.9	15.2	251 21.5	40.0	Eltanin	90 45.5	N51 29.7
F 09	145 46.0	359 24.5 ..	21.2	348 53.1 ..	02.0	342 49.9 ..	15.0	266 23.8 ..	40.1	Enif	33 45.4	N 9 57.1
R 10	160 48.5	14 25.1	21.0	3 54.0	01.4	357 51.8	14.8	281 26.0	40.1	Fomalhaut	15 22.0	S29 32.2
I 11	175 50.9	29 25.7	20.7	18 55.0	00.9	12 53.8	14.6	296 28.2	40.2			
D 12	190 53.4	44 26.3 N10	20.5	33 56.0 N11	00.3	27 55.8 N 8	14.4	311 30.5 S18	40.2	Gacrux	171 59.6	S57 12.0
A 13	205 55.9	59 26.9	20.2	48 57.0 10	59.7	42 57.8	14.2	326 32.7	40.3	Gienah	175 51.0	S17 37.6
Y 14	220 58.3	74 27.5	19.9	63 58.0	59.2	57 59.8	14.1	341 35.0	40.3	Hadar	148 46.2	S60 26.8
15	236 00.8	89 28.1 ..	19.7	78 59.0 ..	58.6	73 01.8 ..	13.9	356 37.2 ..	40.4	Hamal	327 58.7	N23 32.2
16	251 03.2	104 28.7	19.4	93 59.9	58.1	88 03.8	13.7	11 39.4	40.5	Kaus Aust.	83 41.8	S34 22.5
17	266 05.7	119 29.3	19.2	109 00.9	57.5	103 05.8	13.5	26 41.7	40.5			
18	281 08.2	134 29.9 N10	18.9	124 01.9 N10	56.9	118 07.7 N 8	13.3	41 43.9 S18	40.6	Kochab	137 21.2	N74 05.8
19	296 10.6	149 30.5	18.6	139 02.9	56.4	133 09.7	13.1	56 46.2	40.6	Markab	13 36.5	N15 17.6
20	311 13.1	164 31.1	18.4	154 03.9	55.8	148 11.7	12.9	71 48.4	40.7	Menkar	314 13.2	N 4 09.1
21	326 15.6	179 31.7 ..	18.1	169 04.9 ..	55.2	163 13.7 ..	12.7	86 50.6 ..	40.7	Menkent	148 06.1	S36 26.7
22	341 18.0	194 32.3	17.9	184 05.9	54.7	178 15.7	12.5	101 52.9	40.8	Miaplacidus	221 39.8	S69 46.7
23	356 20.5	209 32.9	17.6	199 06.8	54.1	193 17.7	12.3	116 55.1	40.8			
3 00	11 23.0	224 33.5 N10	17.3	214 07.8 N10	53.6	208 19.7 N 8	12.2	131 57.4 S18	40.9	Mirfak	308 37.7	N49 54.8
01	26 25.4	239 34.0	17.1	229 08.8	53.0	223 21.6	12.0	146 59.6	40.9	Nunki	75 56.4	S26 16.4
02	41 27.9	254 34.6	16.8	244 09.8	52.4	238 23.6	11.8	162 01.8	41.0	Peacock	53 16.6	S56 41.0
03	56 30.3	269 35.2 ..	16.5	259 10.8 ..	51.9	253 25.6 ..	11.6	177 04.1 ..	41.0	Pollux	243 26.0	N27 59.1
04	71 32.8	284 35.8	16.2	274 11.8	51.3	268 27.6	11.4	192 06.3	41.1	Procyon	244 58.2	N 5 11.0
05	86 35.3	299 36.4	16.0	289 12.8	50.8	283 29.6	11.2	207 08.6	41.1			
06	101 37.7	314 36.9 N10	15.7	304 13.7 N10	50.2	298 31.6 N 8	11.0	222 10.8 S18	41.2	Rasalhague	96 05.1	N12 33.3
S 07	116 40.2	329 37.5	15.4	319 14.7	49.6	313 33.6	10.8	237 13.0	41.2	Regulus	207 42.1	N11 53.4
A 08	131 42.7	344 38.1	15.2	334 15.7	49.1	328 35.6	10.6	252 15.3	41.3	Rigel	281 10.5	S 8 11.0
T 09	146 45.1	359 38.7 ..	14.9	349 16.7 ..	48.5	343 37.5 ..	10.5	267 17.5 ..	41.3	Rigil Kent.	139 50.1	S60 53.9
U 10	161 47.6	14 39.2	14.6	4 17.7	47.9	358 39.5	10.3	282 19.8	41.4	Sabik	102 10.9	S15 44.4
R 11	176 50.1	29 39.8	14.3	19 18.7	47.4	13 41.5	10.1	297 22.0	41.4			
D 12	191 52.5	44 40.4 N10	14.1	34 19.7 N10	46.8	28 43.5 N 8	09.9	312 24.2 S18	41.5	Schedar	349 38.1	N56 37.5
A 13	206 55.0	59 41.0	13.8	49 20.7	46.3	43 45.5	09.7	327 26.5	41.5	Shaula	96 19.9	S37 06.8
Y 14	221 57.5	74 41.5	13.5	64 21.6	45.7	58 47.5	09.5	342 28.7	41.6	Sirius	258 32.4	S16 44.3
15	236 59.9	89 42.1 ..	13.2	79 22.6 ..	45.1	73 49.5 ..	09.3	357 30.9 ..	41.6	Spica	158 29.9	S11 14.4
16	252 02.4	104 42.7	12.9	94 23.6	44.6	88 51.5	09.1	12 33.2	41.7	Suhail	222 51.5	S43 29.6
17	267 04.8	119 43.2	12.6	109 24.6	44.0	103 53.4	09.0	27 35.4	41.7			
18	282 07.3	134 43.8 N10	12.4	124 25.6 N10	43.4	118 55.4 N 8	08.8	42 37.7 S18	41.8	Vega	80 37.9	N38 48.4
19	297 09.8	149 44.3	12.1	139 26.6	42.9	133 57.4	08.6	57 39.9	41.8	Zuben'ubi	137 04.0	S16 06.2
20	312 12.2	164 44.9	11.8	154 27.6	42.3	148 59.4	08.4	72 42.1	41.9		SHA	Mer.Pass.
21	327 14.7	179 45.4 ..	11.5	169 28.6 ..	41.7	164 01.4 ..	08.2	87 44.4 ..	41.9		° ′	h m
22	342 17.2	194 46.0	11.2	184 29.5	41.2	179 03.4	08.0	102 46.6	42.0	Venus	213 55.1	9 02
23	357 19.6	209 46.6	10.9	199 30.5	40.6	194 05.4	07.8	117 48.8	42.1	Mars	203 20.4	9 44
	h m									Jupiter	197 08.2	10 09
Mer.Pass.	23 14.6	v 0.6	d 0.3	v 1.0	d 0.6	v 2.0	d 0.2	v 2.2	d 0.1	Saturn	120 39.8	15 13

UT	SUN GHA	SUN Dec	MOON GHA	v	MOON Dec	d	HP
d h	° ′	° ′	° ′	′	° ′	′	′
1 00	182 31.4	S 2 58.6	322 49.5	6.8	N13 26.9	7.7	60.1
01	197 31.6	2 59.5	337 15.3	6.8	13 34.6	7.6	60.1
02	212 31.8	3 00.5	351 41.1	6.8	13 42.2	7.6	60.0
03	227 32.0	.. 01.5	6 06.9	6.8	13 49.8	7.4	60.0
04	242 32.2	02.5	20 32.7	6.8	13 57.2	7.3	60.0
05	257 32.5	03.4	34 58.5	6.8	14 04.5	7.2	59.9
06	272 32.7	S 3 04.4	49 24.3	6.9	N14 11.7	7.1	59.9
07	287 32.9	05.4	63 50.2	6.8	14 18.8	7.1	59.9
08	302 33.1	06.3	78 16.0	6.9	14 25.9	6.9	59.8
09	317 33.3	.. 07.3	92 41.9	6.8	14 32.8	6.8	59.8
10	332 33.5	08.3	107 07.7	6.9	14 39.6	6.7	59.8
11	347 33.7	09.2	121 33.6	6.9	14 46.3	6.6	59.7
12	2 33.9	S 3 10.2	135 59.5	6.8	N14 52.9	6.5	59.7
13	17 34.1	11.2	150 25.3	6.9	14 59.4	6.4	59.6
14	32 34.3	12.2	164 51.2	7.0	15 05.8	6.2	59.6
15	47 34.5	.. 13.1	179 17.2	6.9	15 12.0	6.2	59.6
16	62 34.7	14.1	193 43.1	6.9	15 18.2	6.1	59.5
17	77 34.9	15.1	208 09.0	7.0	15 24.3	5.9	59.5
18	92 35.1	S 3 16.0	222 35.0	6.9	N15 30.2	5.9	59.5
19	107 35.3	17.0	237 00.9	7.0	15 36.1	5.7	59.4
20	122 35.5	18.0	251 26.9	7.0	15 41.8	5.7	59.4
21	137 35.7	.. 18.9	265 52.9	7.0	15 47.5	5.5	59.3
22	152 35.9	19.9	280 18.9	7.1	15 53.0	5.4	59.3
23	167 36.1	20.9	294 45.0	7.0	15 58.4	5.3	59.3
2 00	182 36.3	S 3 21.8	309 11.0	7.1	N16 03.7	5.2	59.2
01	197 36.5	22.8	323 37.1	7.1	16 08.9	5.1	59.2
02	212 36.7	23.8	338 03.2	7.1	16 14.0	5.0	59.2
03	227 36.9	.. 24.7	352 29.3	7.1	16 19.0	4.9	59.1
04	242 37.1	25.7	6 55.4	7.2	16 23.9	4.7	59.1
05	257 37.3	26.7	21 21.6	7.1	16 28.6	4.7	59.0
06	272 37.5	S 3 27.6	35 47.7	7.2	N16 33.3	4.5	59.0
07	287 37.7	28.6	50 13.9	7.2	16 37.8	4.4	59.0
08	302 37.9	29.6	64 40.1	7.3	16 42.2	4.4	58.9
09	317 38.1	.. 30.6	79 06.4	7.2	16 46.6	4.2	58.9
10	332 38.3	31.5	93 32.6	7.3	16 50.8	4.0	58.8
11	347 38.5	32.5	107 58.9	7.3	16 54.8	4.0	58.8
12	2 38.7	S 3 33.5	122 25.2	7.4	N16 58.8	3.9	58.8
13	17 38.9	34.4	136 51.6	7.3	17 02.7	3.8	58.7
14	32 39.1	35.4	151 17.9	7.4	17 06.5	3.6	58.7
15	47 39.3	.. 36.4	165 44.3	7.4	17 10.1	3.5	58.6
16	62 39.5	37.3	180 10.7	7.5	17 13.6	3.5	58.6
17	77 39.7	38.3	194 37.2	7.5	17 17.1	3.3	58.6
18	92 39.9	S 3 39.3	209 03.7	7.5	N17 20.4	3.2	58.5
19	107 40.1	40.2	223 30.2	7.5	17 23.6	3.0	58.5
20	122 40.3	41.2	237 56.7	7.6	17 26.6	3.0	58.4
21	137 40.5	.. 42.2	252 23.3	7.6	17 29.6	2.9	58.4
22	152 40.7	43.1	266 49.9	7.6	17 32.5	2.7	58.4
23	167 40.9	44.1	281 16.5	7.7	17 35.2	2.7	58.3
3 00	182 41.1	S 3 45.1	295 43.2	7.7	N17 37.9	2.5	58.3
01	197 41.3	46.0	310 09.9	7.7	17 40.4	2.4	58.2
02	212 41.5	47.0	324 36.6	7.8	17 42.8	2.3	58.2
03	227 41.7	.. 48.0	339 03.4	7.8	17 45.1	2.2	58.2
04	242 41.9	48.9	353 30.2	7.8	17 47.3	2.1	58.1
05	257 42.1	49.9	7 57.0	7.9	17 49.4	2.0	58.1
06	272 42.3	S 3 50.9	22 23.9	7.9	N17 51.4	1.9	58.0
07	287 42.5	51.8	36 50.8	8.0	17 53.3	1.7	58.0
08	302 42.7	52.8	51 17.8	8.0	17 55.0	1.7	58.0
09	317 42.9	.. 53.8	65 44.8	8.0	17 56.7	1.5	57.9
10	332 43.1	54.7	80 11.8	8.1	17 58.2	1.4	57.9
11	347 43.3	55.7	94 38.9	8.1	17 59.6	1.3	57.8
12	2 43.5	S 3 56.7	109 06.0	8.2	N18 00.9	1.2	57.8
13	17 43.6	57.6	123 33.2	8.2	18 02.1	1.2	57.8
14	32 43.8	58.6	138 00.4	8.2	18 03.3	0.9	57.7
15	47 44.0	3 59.6	152 27.6	8.3	18 04.2	0.9	57.7
16	62 44.2	4 00.5	166 54.9	8.3	18 05.1	0.8	57.6
17	77 44.4	01.5	181 22.2	8.4	18 05.9	0.7	57.6
18	92 44.6	S 4 02.5	195 49.6	8.4	N18 06.6	0.5	57.6
19	107 44.8	03.4	210 17.0	8.5	18 07.1	0.5	57.5
20	122 45.0	04.4	224 44.5	8.5	18 07.6	0.4	57.5
21	137 45.2	.. 05.4	239 12.0	8.5	18 08.0	0.2	57.5
22	152 45.4	06.3	253 39.5	8.6	18 08.2	0.2	57.4
23	167 45.6	07.3	268 07.1	8.6	N18 08.4	0.0	57.4
	SD 16.0	d 1.0	SD 16.3		16.0		15.7

Thursday / Friday / Saturday row labels correspond to the three day blocks above (THURSDAY for day 1, FRIDAY for day 2, SATURDAY for day 3).

Lat.	Twilight Naut.	Twilight Civil	Sunrise	Moonrise 1	Moonrise 2	Moonrise 3	Moonrise 4
°	h m	h m	h m	h m	h m	h m	h m
N 72	03 52	05 14	06 22	17 19	17 15	17 09	18 30
N 70	04 04	05 17	06 18	17 54	18 11	18 46	19 47
68	04 13	05 20	06 15	18 19	18 45	19 26	20 25
66	04 21	05 21	06 12	18 38	19 09	19 53	20 52
64	04 27	05 23	06 10	18 54	19 29	20 15	21 12
62	04 32	05 24	06 08	19 07	19 44	20 32	21 28
60	04 37	05 25	06 07	19 18	19 58	20 46	21 42
N 58	04 40	05 26	06 05	19 28	20 09	20 58	21 54
56	04 44	05 27	06 04	19 36	20 19	21 08	22 04
54	04 46	05 28	06 03	19 44	20 28	21 18	22 13
52	04 49	05 28	06 02	19 51	20 36	21 26	22 21
50	04 51	05 29	06 01	19 57	20 43	21 33	22 29
45	04 55	05 29	05 59	20 10	20 58	21 49	22 44
N 40	04 58	05 30	05 57	20 21	21 10	22 02	22 57
35	05 01	05 30	05 55	20 31	21 21	22 13	23 08
30	05 02	05 30	05 54	20 39	21 30	22 23	23 17
20	05 03	05 29	05 51	20 53	21 46	22 40	23 33
N 10	05 03	05 28	05 49	21 06	22 01	22 55	23 48
0	05 01	05 25	05 46	21 18	22 14	23 08	24 01
S 10	04 58	05 23	05 44	21 30	22 27	23 22	24 14
20	04 53	05 19	05 41	21 42	22 41	23 37	24 29
30	04 46	05 14	05 38	21 57	22 58	23 54	24 45
35	04 41	05 10	05 36	22 06	23 07	24 04	00 04
40	04 34	05 06	05 34	22 16	23 18	24 15	00 15
45	04 26	05 01	05 31	22 27	23 31	24 28	00 28
S 50	04 16	04 55	05 28	22 41	23 47	24 44	00 44
52	04 11	04 52	05 26	22 47	23 54	24 52	00 52
54	04 06	04 49	05 25	22 55	24 02	00 02	01 00
56	04 00	04 45	05 23	23 03	24 11	00 11	01 10
58	03 52	04 41	05 21	23 12	24 22	00 22	01 20
S 60	03 44	04 36	05 19	23 22	24 34	00 34	01 33

Lat.	Sunset	Twilight Civil	Twilight Naut.	Moonset 1	Moonset 2	Moonset 3	Moonset 4
°	h m	h m	h m	h m	h m	h m	h m
N 72	17 15	18 22	19 43	12 35	14 37	16 38	17 08
N 70	17 19	18 19	19 32	12 01	13 41	15 01	15 51
68	17 22	18 17	19 23	11 37	13 08	14 21	15 13
66	17 25	18 16	19 16	11 18	12 44	13 54	14 46
64	17 27	18 14	19 10	11 03	12 25	13 33	14 25
62	17 29	18 13	19 05	10 51	12 09	13 16	14 09
60	17 31	18 12	19 01	10 40	11 56	13 02	13 55
N 58	17 32	18 11	18 57	10 31	11 45	12 50	13 43
56	17 34	18 11	18 54	10 23	11 36	12 39	13 33
54	17 35	18 10	18 51	10 15	11 27	12 30	13 23
52	17 36	18 10	18 49	10 09	11 19	12 22	13 15
50	17 37	18 09	18 47	10 03	11 13	12 14	13 08
45	17 39	18 09	18 43	09 51	10 58	11 59	12 52
N 40	17 41	18 08	18 40	09 40	10 46	11 46	12 39
35	17 43	18 08	18 38	09 32	10 35	11 35	12 28
30	17 45	18 09	18 36	09 24	10 26	11 25	12 19
20	17 48	18 10	18 35	09 11	10 11	11 08	12 02
N 10	17 50	18 11	18 36	08 59	09 57	10 54	11 48
0	17 53	18 13	18 37	08 48	09 45	10 40	11 34
S 10	17 55	18 16	18 41	08 37	09 32	10 26	11 20
20	17 58	18 20	18 46	08 26	09 18	10 12	11 06
30	18 02	18 26	18 54	08 12	09 03	09 55	10 49
35	18 04	18 29	18 58	08 05	08 54	09 45	10 39
40	18 06	18 33	19 05	07 56	08 44	09 34	10 28
45	18 09	18 38	19 13	07 46	08 32	09 21	10 15
S 50	18 12	18 45	19 24	07 34	08 17	09 05	09 59
52	18 14	18 48	19 29	07 28	08 10	08 58	09 51
54	18 15	18 51	19 34	07 22	08 03	08 50	09 43
56	18 17	18 55	19 41	07 15	07 54	08 40	09 33
58	18 19	18 59	19 48	07 07	07 45	08 30	09 23
S 60	18 22	19 04	19 57	06 58	07 34	08 18	09 10

Day	SUN Eqn. of Time 00h	SUN Eqn. of Time 12h	SUN Mer. Pass.	MOON Mer. Pass. Upper	MOON Mer. Pass. Lower	Age	Phase
d	m s	m s	h m	h m	h m	d %	
1	10 05	10 15	11 50	02 35	15 03	18 84	
2	10 25	10 34	11 49	03 31	15 59	19 75	
3	10 44	10 53	11 49	04 27	16 54	20 65	

UT	ARIES	VENUS −4.7		MARS +1.8		JUPITER −1.7		SATURN +0.6		STARS		
	GHA	GHA	Dec	GHA	Dec	GHA	Dec	GHA	Dec	Name	SHA	Dec
d h	° ′	° ′	° ′	° ′	° ′	° ′	° ′	° ′	° ′		° ′	° ′
4 00	12 22.1	224 47.1	N10 10.6	214 31.5	N10 40.1	209 07.4	N 8 07.6	132 51.1	S18 42.1	Acamar	315 16.9	S40 14.4
01	27 24.6	239 47.7	10.3	229 32.5	39.5	224 09.3	07.4	147 53.3	42.2	Achernar	335 25.2	S57 09.4
02	42 27.0	254 48.2	10.1	244 33.5	38.9	239 11.3	07.3	162 55.6	42.2	Acrux	173 08.1	S63 11.1
03	57 29.5	269 48.7 ..	09.8	259 34.5 ..	38.4	254 13.3 ..	07.1	177 57.8 ..	42.3	Adhara	255 11.3	S28 59.5
04	72 32.0	284 49.3	09.5	274 35.5	37.8	269 15.3	06.9	193 00.0	42.3	Aldebaran	290 47.4	N16 32.3
05	87 34.4	299 49.8	09.2	289 36.5	37.2	284 17.3	06.7	208 02.3	42.4			
06	102 36.9	314 50.4	N10 08.9	304 37.5	N10 36.7	299 19.3	N 8 06.5	223 04.5	S18 42.4	Alioth	166 20.0	N55 52.6
07	117 39.3	329 50.9	08.6	319 38.5	36.1	314 21.3	06.3	238 06.7	42.5	Alkaid	152 58.2	N49 14.3
08	132 41.8	344 51.5	08.3	334 39.4	35.5	329 23.3	06.1	253 09.0	42.5	Al Na'ir	27 41.5	S46 53.0
S 09	147 44.3	359 52.0 ..	08.0	349 40.4 ..	35.0	344 25.3 ..	05.9	268 11.2 ..	42.6	Alnilam	275 44.7	S 1 11.6
U 10	162 46.7	14 52.5	07.7	4 41.4	34.4	359 27.3	05.7	283 13.4	42.6	Alphard	217 54.8	S 8 43.6
N 11	177 49.2	29 53.1	07.4	19 42.4	33.8	14 29.2	05.6	298 15.7	42.7			
D 12	192 51.7	44 53.6	N10 07.1	34 43.4	N10 33.3	29 31.2	N 8 05.4	313 17.9	S18 42.7	Alphecca	126 10.0	N26 40.1
A 13	207 54.1	59 54.1	06.8	49 44.4	32.7	44 33.2	05.2	328 20.2	42.8	Alpheratz	357 41.5	N29 10.8
Y 14	222 56.6	74 54.7	06.5	64 45.4	32.2	59 35.2	05.0	343 22.4	42.8	Altair	62 06.6	N 8 55.0
15	237 59.1	89 55.2 ..	06.2	79 46.4 ..	31.6	74 37.2 ..	04.8	358 24.6 ..	42.9	Ankaa	353 13.8	S42 13.2
16	253 01.5	104 55.7	05.9	94 47.4	31.0	89 39.2	04.6	13 26.9	42.9	Antares	112 24.5	S26 27.8
17	268 04.0	119 56.3	05.6	109 48.4	30.5	104 41.2	04.4	28 29.1	43.0			
18	283 06.5	134 56.8	N10 05.3	124 49.4	N10 29.9	119 43.2	N 8 04.2	43 31.3	S18 43.0	Arcturus	145 54.7	N19 06.3
19	298 08.9	149 57.3	04.9	139 50.3	29.3	134 45.2	04.1	58 33.6	43.1	Atria	107 25.2	S69 03.3
20	313 11.4	164 57.8	04.6	154 51.3	28.8	149 47.2	03.9	73 35.8	43.1	Avior	234 17.5	S59 33.4
21	328 13.8	179 58.3 ..	04.3	169 52.3 ..	28.2	164 49.1 ..	03.7	88 38.0 ..	43.2	Bellatrix	278 30.2	N 6 21.7
22	343 16.3	194 58.9	04.0	184 53.3	27.6	179 51.1	03.5	103 40.3	43.2	Betelgeuse	270 59.5	N 7 24.5
23	358 18.8	209 59.4	03.7	199 54.3	27.1	194 53.1	03.3	118 42.5	43.3			
5 00	13 21.2	224 59.9	N10 03.4	214 55.3	N10 26.5	209 55.1	N 8 03.1	133 44.7	S18 43.4	Canopus	263 55.4	S52 42.1
01	28 23.7	240 00.4	03.1	229 56.3	25.9	224 57.1	02.9	148 47.0	43.4	Capella	280 32.0	N46 00.5
02	43 26.2	255 00.9	02.8	244 57.3	25.4	239 59.1	02.7	163 49.2	43.5	Deneb	49 30.2	N45 20.6
03	58 28.6	270 01.4 ..	02.4	259 58.3 ..	24.8	255 01.1 ..	02.6	178 51.4 ..	43.5	Denebola	182 32.4	N14 29.1
04	73 31.1	285 01.9	02.1	274 59.3	24.2	270 03.1	02.4	193 53.7	43.6	Diphda	348 54.0	S17 53.9
05	88 33.6	300 02.5	01.8	290 00.3	23.7	285 05.1	02.2	208 55.9	43.6			
06	103 36.0	315 03.0	N10 01.5	305 01.3	N10 23.1	300 07.1	N 8 02.0	223 58.1	S18 43.7	Dubhe	193 50.5	N61 39.8
07	118 38.5	330 03.5	01.2	320 02.2	22.5	315 09.0	01.8	239 00.4	43.7	Elnath	278 10.5	N28 37.0
08	133 40.9	345 04.0	00.9	335 03.2	22.0	330 11.0	01.6	254 02.6	43.8	Eltanin	90 45.5	N51 29.7
M 09	148 43.4	0 04.5 ..	00.5	350 04.2 ..	21.4	345 13.0 ..	01.4	269 04.8 ..	43.8	Enif	33 45.4	N 9 57.1
O 10	163 45.9	15 05.0	10 00.2	5 05.2	20.8	0 15.0	01.2	284 07.1	43.9	Fomalhaut	15 22.0	S29 32.2
N 11	178 48.3	30 05.5	9 59.9	20 06.2	20.3	15 17.0	01.1	299 09.3	43.9			
D 12	193 50.8	45 06.0	N 9 59.6	35 07.2	N10 19.7	30 19.0	N 8 00.9	314 11.5	S18 44.0	Gacrux	171 59.6	S57 12.0
A 13	208 53.3	60 06.5	59.2	50 08.2	19.1	45 21.0	00.7	329 13.8	44.0	Gienah	175 51.0	S17 37.6
Y 14	223 55.7	75 07.0	58.9	65 09.2	18.6	60 23.0	00.5	344 16.0	44.1	Hadar	148 46.2	S60 26.8
15	238 58.2	90 07.5 ..	58.6	80 10.2 ..	18.0	75 25.0 ..	00.3	359 18.2 ..	44.1	Hamal	327 58.6	N23 32.2
16	254 00.7	105 08.0	58.3	95 11.2	17.4	90 27.0	8 00.1	14 20.5	44.2	Kaus Aust.	83 41.8	S34 22.5
17	269 03.1	120 08.5	57.9	110 12.2	16.9	105 29.0	7 59.9	29 22.7	44.2			
18	284 05.6	135 08.9	N 9 57.6	125 13.2	N10 16.3	120 31.0	N 7 59.7	44 24.9	S18 44.3	Kochab	137 21.3	N74 05.7
19	299 08.1	150 09.4	57.3	140 14.2	15.7	135 33.0	59.6	59 27.2	44.3	Markab	13 36.5	N15 17.6
20	314 10.5	165 09.9	56.9	155 15.2	15.2	150 34.9	59.4	74 29.4	44.4	Menkar	314 13.2	N 4 09.1
21	329 13.0	180 10.4 ..	56.6	170 16.2 ..	14.6	165 36.9 ..	59.2	89 31.6 ..	44.5	Menkent	148 06.1	S36 26.7
22	344 15.4	195 10.9	56.3	185 17.2	14.0	180 38.9	59.0	104 33.9	44.5	Miaplacidus	221 39.7	S69 46.7
23	359 17.9	210 11.4	55.9	200 18.2	13.5	195 40.9	58.8	119 36.1	44.6			
6 00	14 20.4	225 11.9	N 9 55.6	215 19.1	N10 12.9	210 42.9	N 7 58.6	134 38.3	S18 44.6	Mirfak	308 37.7	N49 54.8
01	29 22.8	240 12.3	55.3	230 20.1	12.3	225 44.9	58.4	149 40.6	44.7	Nunki	75 56.4	S26 16.4
02	44 25.3	255 12.8	54.9	245 21.1	11.8	240 46.9	58.2	164 42.8	44.7	Peacock	53 16.7	S56 41.0
03	59 27.8	270 13.3 ..	54.6	260 22.1 ..	11.2	255 48.9 ..	58.1	179 45.0 ..	44.8	Pollux	243 25.9	N27 59.1
04	74 30.2	285 13.8	54.2	275 23.1	10.6	270 50.9	57.9	194 47.2	44.8	Procyon	244 58.2	N 5 11.0
05	89 32.7	300 14.3	53.9	290 24.1	10.1	285 52.9	57.7	209 49.5	44.9			
06	104 35.2	315 14.7	N 9 53.6	305 25.1	N10 09.5	300 54.9	N 7 57.5	224 51.7	S18 44.9	Rasalhague	96 05.1	N12 33.3
07	119 37.6	330 15.2	53.2	320 26.1	08.9	315 56.9	57.3	239 53.9	45.0	Regulus	207 42.1	N11 53.4
08	134 40.1	345 15.7	52.9	335 27.1	08.3	330 58.9	57.1	254 56.2	45.0	Rigel	281 10.4	S 8 11.0
T 09	149 42.6	0 16.1 ..	52.5	350 28.1 ..	07.8	346 00.9 ..	56.9	269 58.4 ..	45.1	Rigil Kent.	139 50.1	S60 53.9
U 10	164 45.0	15 16.6	52.2	5 29.1	07.2	1 02.8	56.8	285 00.6	45.1	Sabik	102 10.9	S15 44.4
E 11	179 47.5	30 17.1	51.8	20 30.1	06.6	16 04.8	56.6	300 02.9	45.2			
S 12	194 49.9	45 17.6	N 9 51.5	35 31.1	N10 06.1	31 06.8	N 7 56.4	315 05.1	S18 45.2	Schedar	349 38.0	N56 37.5
D 13	209 52.4	60 18.0	51.1	50 32.1	05.5	46 08.8	56.2	330 07.3	45.3	Shaula	96 19.9	S37 06.8
A 14	224 54.9	75 18.5	50.8	65 33.1	04.9	61 10.8	56.0	345 09.5	45.3	Sirius	258 32.3	S16 44.3
Y 15	239 57.3	90 18.9 ..	50.4	80 34.1 ..	04.4	76 12.8 ..	55.8	0 11.8 ..	45.4	Spica	158 29.9	S11 14.4
16	254 59.8	105 19.4	50.1	95 35.1	03.8	91 14.8	55.6	15 14.0	45.4	Suhail	222 51.5	S43 29.6
17	270 02.3	120 19.9	49.7	110 36.1	03.2	106 16.8	55.4	30 16.2	45.5			
18	285 04.7	135 20.3	N 9 49.4	125 37.1	N10 02.7	121 18.8	N 7 55.3	45 18.5	S18 45.6	Vega	80 37.9	N38 48.4
19	300 07.2	150 20.8	49.0	140 38.1	02.1	136 20.8	55.1	60 20.7	45.6	Zuben'ubi	137 04.0	S16 06.2
20	315 09.7	165 21.2	48.7	155 39.1	01.5	151 22.8	54.9	75 22.9	45.7		SHA	Mer. Pass.
21	330 12.1	180 21.7 ..	48.3	170 40.1 ..	00.9	166 24.8 ..	54.7	90 25.2 ..	45.7		° ′	h m
22	345 14.6	195 22.1	48.0	185 41.1	10 00.4	181 26.8	54.5	105 27.4	45.8	Venus	211 38.7	9 00
23	0 17.0	210 22.6	47.6	200 42.1	N 9 59.8	196 28.8	54.3	120 29.6	45.8	Mars	201 34.1	9 40
	h m									Jupiter	196 33.9	9 59
Mer. Pass. 23 02.8		v 0.5	d 0.3	v 1.0	d 0.6	v 2.0	d 0.2	v 2.2	d 0.1	Saturn	120 23.5	15 03

UT	SUN GHA	SUN Dec	MOON GHA	v	MOON Dec	d	HP
d h	° ′	° ′	° ′	′	° ′	′	′
4 00	182 45.8	S 4 08.2	282 34.7	8.7	N18 08.4	0.1	57.3
01	197 46.0	09.2	297 02.4	8.8	18 08.3	0.1	57.3
02	212 46.2	10.2	311 30.2	8.8	18 08.2	0.3	57.3
03	227 46.4	.. 11.1	325 58.0	8.8	18 07.9	0.4	57.2
04	242 46.6	12.1	340 25.8	8.9	18 07.5	0.5	57.2
05	257 46.8	13.1	354 53.7	8.9	18 07.0	0.5	57.2
S 06	272 47.0	S 4 14.0	9 21.6	9.0	N18 06.5	0.7	57.1
U 07	287 47.2	15.0	23 49.6	9.0	18 05.8	0.8	57.1
N 08	302 47.3	16.0	38 17.6	9.1	18 05.0	0.9	57.0
D 09	317 47.5	.. 16.9	52 45.7	9.1	18 04.1	1.0	57.0
A 10	332 47.7	17.9	67 13.8	9.2	18 03.1	1.1	57.0
Y 11	347 47.9	18.9	81 42.0	9.2	18 02.0	1.1	56.9
12	2 48.1	S 4 19.8	96 10.2	9.3	N18 00.9	1.3	56.9
13	17 48.3	20.8	110 38.5	9.4	17 59.6	1.4	56.9
14	32 48.5	21.8	125 06.9	9.3	17 58.2	1.5	56.9
15	47 48.7	.. 22.7	139 35.2	9.5	17 56.7	1.5	56.8
16	62 48.9	23.7	154 03.7	9.5	17 55.2	1.7	56.8
17	77 49.1	24.6	168 32.2	9.5	17 53.5	1.8	56.7
18	92 49.3	S 4 25.6	183 00.7	9.6	N17 51.7	1.8	56.7
19	107 49.5	26.6	197 29.3	9.7	17 49.9	2.0	56.6
20	122 49.6	27.5	211 58.0	9.7	17 47.9	2.0	56.6
21	137 49.8	.. 28.5	226 26.7	9.8	17 45.9	2.2	56.6
22	152 50.0	29.5	240 55.5	9.8	17 43.7	2.2	56.5
23	167 50.2	30.4	255 24.3	9.9	17 41.5	2.3	56.5
5 00	182 50.4	S 4 31.4	269 53.2	9.9	N17 39.2	2.5	56.5
01	197 50.6	32.3	284 22.1	10.0	17 36.7	2.5	56.4
02	212 50.8	33.3	298 51.1	10.0	17 34.2	2.6	56.4
03	227 51.0	.. 34.3	313 20.1	10.1	17 31.6	2.7	56.4
04	242 51.2	35.2	327 49.2	10.2	17 28.9	2.7	56.3
05	257 51.4	36.2	342 18.4	10.2	17 26.2	2.9	56.3
M 06	272 51.5	S 4 37.2	356 47.6	10.2	N17 23.3	3.0	56.3
O 07	287 51.7	38.1	11 16.8	10.3	17 20.3	3.0	56.2
N 08	302 51.9	39.1	25 46.1	10.4	17 17.3	3.1	56.2
D 09	317 52.1	.. 40.0	40 15.5	10.4	17 14.2	3.3	56.2
A 10	332 52.3	41.0	54 44.9	10.5	17 10.9	3.3	56.1
Y 11	347 52.5	42.0	69 14.4	10.6	17 07.6	3.4	56.1
12	2 52.7	S 4 42.9	83 44.0	10.6	N17 04.2	3.4	56.1
13	17 52.9	43.9	98 13.6	10.6	17 00.8	3.6	56.1
14	32 53.1	44.9	112 43.2	10.7	16 57.2	3.6	56.0
15	47 53.2	.. 45.8	127 12.9	10.8	16 53.6	3.8	56.0
16	62 53.4	46.8	141 42.7	10.8	16 49.8	3.8	56.0
17	77 53.6	47.7	156 12.5	10.9	16 46.0	3.9	55.9
18	92 53.8	S 4 48.7	170 42.4	10.9	N16 42.1	3.9	55.9
19	107 54.0	49.7	185 12.3	11.0	16 38.2	4.1	55.9
20	122 54.2	50.6	199 42.3	11.1	16 34.1	4.1	55.8
21	137 54.4	.. 51.6	214 12.4	11.1	16 30.0	4.2	55.8
22	152 54.6	52.5	228 42.5	11.1	16 25.8	4.3	55.8
23	167 54.7	53.5	243 12.6	11.2	16 21.5	4.4	55.8
6 00	182 54.9	S 4 54.5	257 42.8	11.3	N16 17.1	4.4	55.7
01	197 55.1	55.4	272 13.1	11.3	16 12.7	4.5	55.7
02	212 55.3	56.4	286 43.4	11.4	16 08.2	4.6	55.7
03	227 55.5	.. 57.3	301 13.8	11.5	16 03.6	4.7	55.6
04	242 55.7	58.3	315 44.3	11.4	15 58.9	4.7	55.6
05	257 55.9	4 59.3	330 14.7	11.6	15 54.2	4.8	55.6
T 06	272 56.0	S 5 00.2	344 45.3	11.6	N15 49.4	4.9	55.6
U 07	287 56.2	01.2	359 15.9	11.7	15 44.5	5.0	55.5
E 08	302 56.4	02.1	13 46.6	11.7	15 39.5	5.0	55.5
S 09	317 56.6	.. 03.1	28 17.3	11.7	15 34.5	5.1	55.5
D 10	332 56.8	04.1	42 48.0	11.9	15 29.4	5.2	55.5
A 11	347 57.0	05.0	57 18.9	11.8	15 24.2	5.2	55.4
Y 12	2 57.2	S 5 06.0	71 49.7	12.0	N15 19.0	5.4	55.4
13	17 57.3	06.9	86 20.7	12.0	15 13.6	5.3	55.4
14	32 57.5	07.9	100 51.7	12.0	15 08.3	5.5	55.3
15	47 57.7	.. 08.9	115 22.7	12.1	15 02.8	5.5	55.3
16	62 57.9	09.8	129 53.8	12.1	14 57.3	5.6	55.3
17	77 58.1	10.8	144 24.9	12.2	14 51.7	5.6	55.3
18	92 58.3	S 5 11.7	158 56.1	12.3	N14 46.1	5.8	55.3
19	107 58.4	12.7	173 27.4	12.3	14 40.3	5.7	55.2
20	122 58.6	13.7	187 58.7	12.4	14 34.6	5.9	55.2
21	137 58.8	.. 14.6	202 30.1	12.4	14 28.7	5.9	55.2
22	152 59.0	15.6	217 01.5	12.4	14 22.8	6.0	55.2
23	167 59.2	16.5	231 32.9	12.5	N14 16.8	6.0	55.1
	SD 16.0	d 1.0	SD 15.5		15.3		15.1

Lat.	Twilight Naut.	Twilight Civil	Sunrise	Moonrise 4	5	6	7
°	h m	h m	h m	h m	h m	h m	h m
N 72	04 07	05 28	06 35	18 30	20 21	22 06	23 46
N 70	04 17	05 29	06 30	19 47	21 08	22 37	24 06
68	04 25	05 30	06 26	20 25	21 38	22 59	24 22
66	04 31	05 31	06 22	20 52	22 01	23 16	24 35
64	04 36	05 32	06 19	21 12	22 19	23 31	24 45
62	04 40	05 32	06 16	21 28	22 33	23 42	24 54
60	04 44	05 33	06 14	21 42	22 45	23 52	25 02
N 58	04 47	05 33	06 12	21 54	22 56	24 01	00 01
56	04 50	05 33	06 10	22 04	23 05	24 09	00 09
54	04 52	05 33	06 08	22 13	23 13	24 16	00 16
52	04 54	05 33	06 07	22 21	23 21	24 22	00 22
50	04 56	05 33	06 05	22 29	23 27	24 27	00 27
45	04 59	05 33	06 02	22 44	23 41	24 39	00 39
N 40	05 01	05 33	06 00	22 57	23 53	24 49	00 49
35	05 03	05 32	05 57	23 08	24 03	00 03	00 58
30	05 04	05 31	05 55	23 17	24 11	00 11	01 05
20	05 04	05 30	05 52	23 33	24 26	00 26	01 18
N 10	05 03	05 27	05 48	23 48	24 39	00 39	01 29
0	05 00	05 24	05 45	24 01	00 01	00 51	01 39
S 10	04 56	05 21	05 42	24 14	00 14	01 03	01 50
20	04 50	05 16	05 38	24 29	00 29	01 16	02 01
30	04 42	05 10	05 34	24 45	00 45	01 31	02 13
35	04 36	05 06	05 32	00 04	00 54	01 40	02 21
40	04 29	05 01	05 29	00 15	01 05	01 50	02 29
45	04 20	04 56	05 25	00 28	01 18	02 01	02 39
S 50	04 09	04 49	05 21	00 44	01 33	02 15	02 50
52	04 04	04 45	05 19	00 52	01 41	02 21	02 56
54	03 58	04 41	05 17	01 00	01 49	02 29	03 02
56	03 51	04 37	05 15	01 10	01 58	02 36	03 08
58	03 43	04 32	05 13	01 20	02 08	02 45	03 16
S 60	03 34	04 27	05 10	01 33	02 19	02 56	03 24

Lat.	Sunset	Twilight Civil	Twilight Naut.	Moonset 4	5	6	7
°	h m	h m	h m	h m	h m	h m	h m
N 72	17 00	18 07	19 26	17 08	17 03	16 59	16 55
N 70	17 05	18 06	19 17	15 51	16 16	16 28	16 34
68	17 10	18 05	19 10	15 13	15 45	16 04	16 17
66	17 13	18 04	19 04	14 46	15 22	15 46	16 03
64	17 16	18 04	18 59	14 25	15 04	15 32	15 52
62	17 19	18 03	18 55	14 09	14 49	15 19	15 43
60	17 22	18 03	18 51	13 55	14 36	15 09	15 34
N 58	17 24	18 03	18 48	13 43	14 26	15 00	15 27
56	17 26	18 03	18 46	13 33	14 16	14 51	15 21
54	17 28	18 03	18 44	13 23	14 08	14 44	15 15
52	17 29	18 03	18 42	13 15	14 00	14 38	15 10
50	17 31	18 03	18 40	13 08	13 53	14 32	15 05
45	17 34	18 03	18 37	12 52	13 39	14 19	14 55
N 40	17 37	18 04	18 35	12 39	13 28	14 09	14 46
35	17 39	18 04	18 34	12 28	13 16	14 00	14 39
30	17 41	18 05	18 33	12 19	13 07	13 52	14 32
20	17 45	18 07	18 33	12 02	12 52	13 38	14 21
N 10	17 48	18 09	18 34	11 48	12 38	13 26	14 11
0	17 52	18 13	18 37	11 34	12 25	13 15	14 02
S 10	17 55	18 16	18 41	11 20	12 13	13 03	13 52
20	17 59	18 21	18 47	11 06	11 59	12 51	13 42
30	18 03	18 28	18 56	10 49	11 43	12 37	13 31
35	18 06	18 32	19 02	10 39	11 34	12 29	13 24
40	18 09	18 36	19 09	10 28	11 23	12 20	13 16
45	18 12	18 42	19 18	10 15	11 11	12 09	13 07
S 50	18 17	18 50	19 29	09 59	10 56	11 56	12 57
52	18 19	18 53	19 35	09 51	10 49	11 49	12 52
54	18 21	18 57	19 41	09 43	10 41	11 43	12 46
56	18 23	19 01	19 48	09 33	10 32	11 35	12 40
58	18 26	19 06	19 56	09 23	10 22	11 26	12 33
S 60	18 29	19 12	20 06	09 10	10 11	11 16	12 25

Day	SUN Eqn. of Time 00h	SUN Eqn. of Time 12h	SUN Mer. Pass.	MOON Mer. Pass. Upper	MOON Mer. Pass. Lower	Age	Phase
d	m s	m s	h m	h m	h m	d	%
4	11 03	11 12	11 49	05 21	17 48	21	54
5	11 21	11 30	11 48	06 13	18 38	22	44
6	11 39	11 48	11 48	07 03	19 27	23	34

UT	ARIES GHA	VENUS −4.7 GHA	VENUS Dec	MARS +1.8 GHA	MARS Dec	JUPITER −1.7 GHA	JUPITER Dec	SATURN +0.6 GHA	SATURN Dec	STARS Name	SHA	Dec
7 00	15 19.5	225 23.0	N 9 47.3	215 43.1	N 9 59.2	211 30.8	N 7 54.1	135 31.8	S18 45.9	Acamar	315 16.8	S40 14.4
01	30 22.0	240 23.5	46.9	230 44.1	58.7	226 32.8	54.0	150 34.1	45.9	Achernar	335 25.1	S57 09.4
02	45 24.4	255 23.9	46.5	245 45.1	58.1	241 34.8	53.8	165 36.3	46.0	Acrux	173 08.1	S63 11.1
03	60 26.9	270 24.4	.. 46.2	260 46.1	.. 57.5	256 36.7	.. 53.6	180 38.5	.. 46.0	Adhara	255 11.3	S28 59.5
04	75 29.4	285 24.8	45.8	275 47.1	57.0	271 38.7	53.4	195 40.8	46.1	Aldebaran	290 47.4	N16 32.3
05	90 31.8	300 25.3	45.4	290 48.1	56.4	286 40.7	53.2	210 43.0	46.1			
W 06	105 34.3	315 25.7	N 9 45.1	305 49.1	N 9 55.8	301 42.7	N 7 53.0	225 45.2	S18 46.2	Alioth	166 20.0	N55 52.6
E 07	120 36.8	330 26.2	44.7	320 50.1	55.2	316 44.7	52.8	240 47.4	46.2	Alkaid	152 58.2	N49 14.3
D 08	135 39.2	345 26.6	44.3	335 51.1	54.7	331 46.7	52.7	255 49.7	46.3	Al Na'ir	27 41.5	S46 53.0
N 09	150 41.7	0 27.1	.. 44.0	350 52.1	.. 54.1	346 48.7	.. 52.5	270 51.9	.. 46.3	Alnilam	275 44.7	S 1 11.6
E 10	165 44.2	15 27.5	43.6	5 53.1	53.5	1 50.7	52.3	285 54.1	46.4	Alphard	217 54.7	S 8 43.6
S 11	180 46.6	30 27.9	43.2	20 54.1	53.0	16 52.7	52.1	300 56.4	46.5			
D 12	195 49.1	45 28.4	N 9 42.9	35 55.1	N 9 52.4	31 54.7	N 7 51.9	315 58.6	S18 46.5	Alphecca	126 10.0	N26 40.1
A 13	210 51.5	60 28.8	42.5	50 56.1	51.8	46 56.7	51.7	331 00.8	46.6	Alpheratz	357 41.5	N29 10.8
Y 14	225 54.0	75 29.2	42.1	65 57.0	51.3	61 58.7	51.5	346 03.0	46.6	Altair	62 06.7	N 8 55.0
15	240 56.5	90 29.7	.. 41.8	80 58.0	.. 50.7	77 00.7	.. 51.3	1 05.3	.. 46.7	Ankaa	353 13.8	S42 13.2
16	255 58.9	105 30.1	41.4	95 59.0	50.1	92 02.7	51.2	16 07.5	46.7	Antares	112 24.6	S26 27.8
17	271 01.4	120 30.5	41.0	111 00.0	49.5	107 04.7	51.0	31 09.7	46.8			
18	286 03.9	135 30.9	N 9 40.6	126 01.1	N 9 49.0	122 06.7	N 7 50.8	46 11.9	S18 46.8	Arcturus	145 54.7	N19 06.3
19	301 06.3	150 31.4	40.3	141 02.1	48.4	137 08.7	50.6	61 14.2	46.9	Atria	107 25.2	S69 03.3
20	316 08.8	165 31.8	39.9	156 03.1	47.8	152 10.7	50.4	76 16.4	46.9	Avior	234 17.5	S59 33.4
21	331 11.3	180 32.2	.. 39.5	171 04.1	.. 47.3	167 12.7	.. 50.2	91 18.6	.. 47.0	Bellatrix	278 30.2	N 6 21.7
22	346 13.7	195 32.6	39.1	186 05.1	46.7	182 14.7	50.0	106 20.9	47.0	Betelgeuse	270 59.5	N 7 24.5
23	1 16.2	210 33.1	38.7	201 06.1	46.1	197 16.7	49.9	121 23.1	47.1			
8 00	16 18.7	225 33.5	N 9 38.4	216 07.1	N 9 45.5	212 18.7	N 7 49.7	136 25.3	S18 47.1	Canopus	263 55.4	S52 42.1
01	31 21.1	240 33.9	38.0	231 08.1	45.0	227 20.7	49.5	151 27.5	47.2	Capella	280 31.9	N46 00.5
02	46 23.6	255 34.3	37.6	246 09.1	44.4	242 22.7	49.3	166 29.8	47.2	Deneb	49 30.2	N45 20.6
03	61 26.0	270 34.7	.. 37.2	261 10.1	.. 43.8	257 24.7	.. 49.1	181 32.0	.. 47.3	Denebola	182 32.4	N14 29.1
04	76 28.5	285 35.2	36.8	276 11.1	43.3	272 26.7	48.9	196 34.2	47.4	Diphda	348 54.0	S17 53.9
05	91 31.0	300 35.6	36.4	291 12.1	42.7	287 28.7	48.7	211 36.4	47.4			
T 06	106 33.4	315 36.0	N 9 36.1	306 13.1	N 9 42.1	302 30.7	N 7 48.6	226 38.7	S18 47.5	Dubhe	193 50.5	N61 39.8
H 07	121 35.9	330 36.4	35.7	321 14.1	41.5	317 32.6	48.4	241 40.9	47.5	Elnath	278 10.5	N28 37.0
U 08	136 38.4	345 36.8	35.3	336 15.1	41.0	332 34.6	48.2	256 43.1	47.6	Eltanin	90 45.6	N51 29.7
R 09	151 40.8	0 37.2	.. 34.9	351 16.1	.. 40.4	347 36.6	.. 48.0	271 45.3	.. 47.6	Enif	33 45.4	N 9 57.1
S 10	166 43.3	15 37.6	34.5	6 17.1	39.8	2 38.6	47.8	286 47.6	47.7	Fomalhaut	15 22.0	S29 32.2
D 11	181 45.8	30 38.0	34.1	21 18.1	39.2	17 40.6	47.6	301 49.8	47.7			
A 12	196 48.2	45 38.4	N 9 33.7	36 19.1	N 9 38.7	32 42.6	N 7 47.5	316 52.0	S18 47.8	Gacrux	171 59.6	S57 11.9
Y 13	211 50.7	60 38.8	33.3	51 20.1	38.1	47 44.6	47.3	331 54.2	47.8	Gienah	175 51.0	S17 37.6
14	226 53.1	75 39.3	32.9	66 21.1	37.5	62 46.6	47.1	346 56.5	47.9	Hadar	148 46.2	S60 26.8
15	241 55.6	90 39.7	.. 32.5	81 22.1	.. 37.0	77 48.6	.. 46.9	1 58.7	.. 47.9	Hamal	327 58.6	N23 32.2
16	256 58.1	105 40.1	32.1	96 23.1	36.4	92 50.6	46.7	17 00.9	48.0	Kaus Aust.	83 41.8	S34 22.5
17	272 00.5	120 40.5	31.7	111 24.1	35.8	107 52.6	46.5	32 03.1	48.0			
18	287 03.0	135 40.9	N 9 31.3	126 25.1	N 9 35.2	122 54.6	N 7 46.3	47 05.4	S18 48.1	Kochab	137 21.3	N74 05.7
19	302 05.5	150 41.3	30.9	141 26.1	34.7	137 56.6	46.2	62 07.6	48.1	Markab	13 36.5	N15 17.6
20	317 07.9	165 41.7	30.5	156 27.1	34.1	152 58.6	46.0	77 09.8	48.2	Menkar	314 13.1	N 4 09.1
21	332 10.4	180 42.0	.. 30.1	171 28.1	.. 33.5	168 00.6	.. 45.8	92 12.0	.. 48.3	Menkent	148 06.1	S36 26.7
22	347 12.9	195 42.4	29.7	186 29.1	32.9	183 02.6	45.6	107 14.3	48.3	Miaplacidus	221 39.7	S69 46.7
23	2 15.3	210 42.8	29.3	201 30.1	32.4	198 04.6	45.4	122 16.5	48.4			
9 00	17 17.8	225 43.2	N 9 28.9	216 31.1	N 9 31.8	213 06.6	N 7 45.2	137 18.7	S18 48.4	Mirfak	308 37.7	N49 54.8
01	32 20.3	240 43.6	28.5	231 32.1	31.2	228 08.6	45.0	152 20.9	48.5	Nunki	75 56.4	S26 16.4
02	47 22.7	255 44.0	28.1	246 33.1	30.7	243 10.6	44.9	167 23.2	48.5	Peacock	53 16.7	S56 41.1
03	62 25.2	270 44.4	.. 27.7	261 34.1	.. 30.1	258 12.6	.. 44.7	182 25.4	.. 48.6	Pollux	243 25.9	N27 59.1
04	77 27.6	285 44.8	27.3	276 35.1	29.5	273 14.6	44.5	197 27.6	48.6	Procyon	244 58.2	N 5 11.0
05	92 30.1	300 45.2	26.9	291 36.1	28.9	288 16.6	44.3	212 29.8	48.7			
F 06	107 32.6	315 45.6	N 9 26.5	306 37.1	N 9 28.4	303 18.6	N 7 44.1	227 32.0	S18 48.7	Rasalhague	96 05.1	N12 33.3
R 07	122 35.0	330 45.9	26.1	321 38.1	27.8	318 20.6	43.9	242 34.3	48.8	Regulus	207 42.1	N11 53.4
I 08	137 37.5	345 46.3	25.7	336 39.1	27.2	333 22.6	43.8	257 36.5	48.8	Rigel	281 10.4	S 8 11.0
D 09	152 40.0	0 46.7	.. 25.3	351 40.2	.. 26.6	348 24.6	.. 43.6	272 38.7	.. 48.9	Rigil Kent.	139 50.1	S60 53.9
A 10	167 42.4	15 47.1	24.9	6 41.2	26.1	3 26.6	43.4	287 40.9	48.9	Sabik	102 10.9	S15 44.4
Y 11	182 44.9	30 47.5	24.4	21 42.2	25.5	18 28.6	43.2	302 43.2	49.0			
12	197 47.4	45 47.8	N 9 24.0	36 43.2	N 9 24.9	33 30.6	N 7 43.0	317 45.4	S18 49.1	Schedar	349 38.0	N56 37.5
13	212 49.8	60 48.2	23.6	51 44.2	24.3	48 32.6	42.8	332 47.6	49.1	Shaula	96 20.0	S37 06.8
14	227 52.3	75 48.6	23.2	66 45.2	23.8	63 34.6	42.6	347 49.8	49.2	Sirius	258 32.3	S16 44.3
15	242 54.7	90 49.0	.. 22.8	81 46.2	.. 23.2	78 36.6	.. 42.5	2 52.0	.. 49.2	Spica	158 29.9	S11 14.4
16	257 57.2	105 49.3	22.4	96 47.2	22.6	93 38.6	42.3	17 54.3	49.3	Suhail	222 51.5	S43 29.6
17	272 59.7	120 49.7	21.9	111 48.2	22.0	108 40.6	42.1	32 56.5	49.3			
18	288 02.1	135 50.1	N 9 21.5	126 49.2	N 9 21.5	123 42.6	N 7 41.9	47 58.7	S18 49.4	Vega	80 37.9	N38 48.4
19	303 04.6	150 50.5	21.1	141 50.2	20.9	138 44.6	41.7	63 00.9	49.4	Zuben'ubi	137 04.0	S16 06.2
20	318 07.1	165 50.8	20.7	156 51.2	20.3	153 46.6	41.5	78 03.2	49.5		SHA	Mer. Pass.
21	333 09.5	180 51.2	.. 20.3	171 52.2	.. 19.7	168 48.6	.. 41.4	93 05.4	.. 49.5	Venus	209 14.8	8 58
22	348 12.0	195 51.6	19.8	186 53.2	19.2	183 50.6	41.2	108 07.6	49.6	Mars	199 48.4	9 35
23	3 14.5	210 51.9	19.4	201 54.2	18.6	198 52.6	41.0	123 09.8	49.6	Jupiter	196 00.0	9 49
Mer. Pass. 22 51.0		v 0.4 d 0.4		v 1.0 d 0.6		v 2.0 d 0.2		v 2.2 d 0.1		Saturn	120 06.7	14 52

UT	SUN GHA	SUN Dec	MOON GHA	v	MOON Dec	d	HP
d h	° ′	° ′	° ′	′	° ′	′	′
7 00	182 59.4	S 5 17.5	246 04.4	12.6	N14 10.8	6.1	55.1
01	197 59.5	18.4	260 36.0	12.6	14 04.7	6.1	55.1
02	212 59.7	19.4	275 07.6	12.7	13 58.6	6.3	55.1
03	227 59.9	.. 20.4	289 39.3	12.7	13 52.3	6.2	55.0
04	243 00.1	21.3	304 11.0	12.8	13 46.1	6.4	55.0
05	258 00.3	22.3	318 42.8	12.8	13 39.7	6.4	55.0
W 06	273 00.4	S 5 23.2	333 14.6	12.8	N13 33.3	6.4	55.0
E 07	288 00.6	24.2	347 46.4	12.9	13 26.9	6.5	55.0
D 08	303 00.8	25.2	2 18.3	13.0	13 20.4	6.6	54.9
N 09	318 01.0	.. 26.1	16 50.3	13.0	13 13.8	6.6	54.9
E 10	333 01.2	27.1	31 22.3	13.1	13 07.2	6.7	54.9
S 11	348 01.3	28.0	45 54.4	13.1	13 00.5	6.7	54.9
D 12	3 01.5	S 5 29.0	60 26.5	13.1	N12 53.8	6.8	54.9
A 13	18 01.7	29.9	74 58.6	13.2	12 47.0	6.8	54.8
Y 14	33 01.9	30.9	89 30.8	13.3	12 40.2	6.9	54.8
15	48 02.1	.. 31.8	104 03.1	13.3	12 33.3	7.0	54.8
16	63 02.2	32.8	118 35.4	13.3	12 26.3	6.9	54.8
17	78 02.4	33.8	133 07.7	13.4	12 19.4	7.1	54.8
18	93 02.6	S 5 34.7	147 40.1	13.4	N12 12.3	7.1	54.7
19	108 02.8	35.7	162 12.5	13.5	12 05.2	7.1	54.7
20	123 03.0	36.6	176 45.0	13.5	11 58.1	7.2	54.7
21	138 03.1	.. 37.6	191 17.5	13.5	11 50.9	7.3	54.7
22	153 03.3	38.5	205 50.0	13.6	11 43.6	7.2	54.7
23	168 03.5	39.5	220 22.6	13.7	11 36.4	7.4	54.7
8 00	183 03.7	S 5 40.4	234 55.3	13.6	N11 29.0	7.4	54.6
01	198 03.9	41.4	249 27.9	13.8	11 21.6	7.4	54.6
02	213 04.0	42.4	264 00.7	13.7	11 14.2	7.5	54.6
03	228 04.2	.. 43.3	278 33.4	13.8	11 06.7	7.5	54.6
04	243 04.4	44.3	293 06.2	13.9	10 59.2	7.5	54.6
05	258 04.6	45.2	307 39.1	13.9	10 51.7	7.6	54.6
06	273 04.7	S 5 46.2	322 12.0	13.9	N10 44.1	7.7	54.5
T 07	288 04.9	47.1	336 44.9	14.0	10 36.4	7.7	54.5
H 08	303 05.1	48.1	351 17.9	14.0	10 28.7	7.7	54.5
U 09	318 05.3	.. 49.0	5 50.9	14.0	10 21.0	7.8	54.5
R 10	333 05.4	50.0	20 23.9	14.1	10 13.2	7.8	54.5
S 11	348 05.6	50.9	34 57.0	14.1	10 05.4	7.9	54.5
D 12	3 05.8	S 5 51.9	49 30.1	14.1	N 9 57.5	7.8	54.4
A 13	18 06.0	52.9	64 03.2	14.2	9 49.7	8.0	54.4
Y 14	33 06.1	53.8	78 36.4	14.2	9 41.7	8.0	54.4
15	48 06.3	.. 54.8	93 09.6	14.3	9 33.7	8.0	54.4
16	63 06.5	55.7	107 42.9	14.3	9 25.7	8.0	54.4
17	78 06.7	56.7	122 16.2	14.3	9 17.7	8.1	54.4
18	93 06.8	S 5 57.6	136 49.5	14.4	N 9 09.6	8.1	54.4
19	108 07.0	58.6	151 22.9	14.4	9 01.5	8.1	54.4
20	123 07.2	5 59.5	165 56.3	14.4	8 53.4	8.2	54.3
21	138 07.4	6 00.5	180 29.7	14.4	8 45.2	8.3	54.3
22	153 07.5	01.4	195 03.1	14.5	8 36.9	8.2	54.3
23	168 07.7	02.4	209 36.6	14.5	8 28.7	8.3	54.3
9 00	183 07.9	S 6 03.3	224 10.1	14.6	N 8 20.4	8.3	54.3
01	198 08.1	04.3	238 43.7	14.6	8 12.1	8.4	54.3
02	213 08.2	05.2	253 17.3	14.6	8 03.7	8.4	54.3
03	228 08.4	.. 06.2	267 50.9	14.6	7 55.4	8.5	54.3
04	243 08.6	07.1	282 24.5	14.7	7 46.9	8.4	54.2
05	258 08.7	08.1	296 58.2	14.6	7 38.5	8.5	54.2
06	273 08.9	S 6 09.0	311 31.8	14.8	N 7 30.0	8.5	54.2
F 07	288 09.1	10.0	326 05.6	14.7	7 21.5	8.5	54.2
R 08	303 09.3	10.9	340 39.3	14.8	7 13.0	8.6	54.2
I 09	318 09.4	.. 11.9	355 13.1	14.8	7 04.4	8.5	54.2
D 10	333 09.6	12.8	9 46.9	14.8	6 55.9	8.6	54.2
A 11	348 09.8	13.8	24 20.7	14.8	6 47.3	8.7	54.2
Y 12	3 09.9	S 6 14.7	38 54.5	14.9	N 6 38.6	8.6	54.2
13	18 10.1	15.7	53 28.4	14.9	6 30.0	8.7	54.2
14	33 10.3	16.6	68 02.3	14.9	6 21.3	8.7	54.2
15	48 10.5	.. 17.6	82 36.2	14.9	6 12.6	8.8	54.1
16	63 10.6	18.5	97 10.1	15.0	6 03.8	8.7	54.1
17	78 10.8	19.5	111 44.1	15.0	5 55.1	8.8	54.1
18	93 11.0	S 6 20.4	126 18.1	15.0	N 5 46.3	8.8	54.1
19	108 11.1	21.4	140 52.1	15.0	5 37.5	8.8	54.1
20	123 11.3	22.3	155 26.1	15.0	5 28.7	8.9	54.1
21	138 11.5	.. 23.3	170 00.1	15.1	5 19.8	8.8	54.1
22	153 11.6	24.2	184 34.2	15.1	5 11.0	8.9	54.1
23	168 11.8	25.2	199 08.3	15.1	N 5 02.1	8.9	54.1
	SD 16.0	d 1.0	SD 14.9		14.8		14.8

Twilight / Moonrise

Lat.	Naut.	Civil	Sunrise	Moonrise 7	8	9	10
°	h m	h m	h m	h m	h m	h m	h m
N 72	04 22	05 41	06 49	23 46	25 22	01 22	02 56
N 70	04 30	05 41	06 42	24 06	00 06	01 35	03 02
68	04 36	05 41	06 37	24 22	00 22	01 45	03 07
66	04 41	05 40	06 32	24 35	00 35	01 53	03 12
64	04 45	05 40	06 28	24 45	00 45	02 00	03 15
62	04 48	05 40	06 24	24 54	00 54	02 06	03 18
60	04 51	05 40	06 21	25 02	01 02	02 11	03 21
N 58	04 54	05 39	06 19	00 01	01 08	02 16	03 24
56	04 56	05 39	06 16	00 09	01 14	02 20	03 26
54	04 58	05 39	06 14	00 16	01 19	02 24	03 28
52	04 59	05 38	06 12	00 22	01 24	02 27	03 29
50	05 00	05 38	06 10	00 27	01 29	02 30	03 31
45	05 03	05 37	06 06	00 39	01 38	02 36	03 34
N 40	05 04	05 36	06 03	00 49	01 46	02 42	03 37
35	05 05	05 34	06 00	00 58	01 52	02 46	03 40
30	05 05	05 33	05 57	01 05	01 58	02 50	03 43
20	05 05	05 30	05 53	01 18	02 08	02 57	03 46
N 10	05 03	05 27	05 48	01 29	02 17	03 03	03 49
0	04 59	05 24	05 44	01 39	02 25	03 09	03 52
S 10	04 55	05 19	05 40	01 50	02 33	03 15	03 55
20	04 48	05 14	05 36	02 01	02 42	03 21	03 59
30	04 38	05 06	05 30	02 13	02 52	03 28	04 02
35	04 32	05 02	05 27	02 21	02 58	03 32	04 05
40	04 24	04 56	05 24	02 29	03 04	03 37	04 07
45	04 14	04 50	05 20	02 39	03 12	03 42	04 10
S 50	04 02	04 42	05 15	02 50	03 21	03 48	04 13
52	03 56	04 38	05 13	02 56	03 25	03 51	04 15
54	03 49	04 34	05 10	03 02	03 30	03 54	04 17
56	03 42	04 29	05 07	03 08	03 35	03 58	04 19
58	03 33	04 23	05 04	03 16	03 40	04 02	04 21
S 60	03 23	04 17	05 01	03 24	03 47	04 06	04 23

Sunset / Twilight / Moonset

Lat.	Sunset	Civil	Naut.	Moonset 7	8	9	10
°	h m	h m	h m	h m	h m	h m	h m
N 72	16 44	17 52	19 11	16 55	16 51	16 46	16 42
N 70	16 51	17 52	19 03	16 34	16 37	16 38	16 39
68	16 57	17 53	18 57	16 17	16 25	16 31	16 36
66	17 02	17 53	18 52	16 03	16 16	16 26	16 34
64	17 06	17 53	18 48	15 52	16 08	16 21	16 32
62	17 10	17 54	18 45	15 43	16 01	16 17	16 31
60	17 13	17 54	18 42	15 34	15 55	16 13	16 29
N 58	17 16	17 55	18 40	15 27	15 50	16 10	16 28
56	17 18	17 55	18 38	15 21	15 45	16 07	16 27
54	17 20	17 56	18 36	15 15	15 41	16 04	16 26
52	17 22	17 56	18 35	15 10	15 37	16 02	16 25
50	17 24	17 57	18 34	15 05	15 34	16 00	16 24
45	17 28	17 58	18 32	14 55	15 26	15 55	16 23
N 40	17 32	17 59	18 30	14 46	15 20	15 51	16 21
35	17 35	18 00	18 29	14 39	15 14	15 48	16 20
30	17 38	18 02	18 29	14 32	15 09	15 45	16 18
20	17 42	18 04	18 30	14 21	15 01	15 39	16 16
N 10	17 47	18 08	18 32	14 11	14 54	15 35	16 14
0	17 51	18 12	18 36	14 02	14 47	15 30	16 13
S 10	17 55	18 16	18 41	13 52	14 40	15 26	16 11
20	18 00	18 22	18 48	13 42	14 32	15 21	16 09
30	18 05	18 29	18 58	13 31	14 23	15 15	16 07
35	18 08	18 34	19 04	13 24	14 18	15 12	16 06
40	18 12	18 40	19 12	13 16	14 13	15 08	16 04
45	18 16	18 46	19 22	13 07	14 06	15 04	16 02
S 50	18 21	18 55	19 35	12 57	13 58	14 59	16 00
52	18 24	18 58	19 41	12 52	13 54	14 57	15 59
54	18 26	19 03	19 48	12 46	13 50	14 54	15 58
56	18 29	19 08	19 55	12 40	13 46	14 51	15 57
58	18 33	19 13	20 04	12 33	13 40	14 48	15 56
S 60	18 36	19 20	20 15	12 25	13 35	14 45	15 55

	SUN Eqn. of Time 00h	12h	Mer. Pass.	MOON Mer. Pass. Upper	Lower	Age	Phase
Day	m s	m s	h m	h m	h m	d	%
7	11 57	12 06	11 48	07 50	20 13	24	25
8	12 14	12 23	11 48	08 36	20 58	25	17
9	12 31	12 39	11 47	09 20	21 41	26	11

2015 OCTOBER 10, 11, 12 (SAT., SUN., MON.)

UT	ARIES	VENUS −4.6		MARS +1.8		JUPITER −1.8		SATURN +0.6		STARS		
	GHA	GHA	Dec	GHA	Dec	GHA	Dec	GHA	Dec	Name	SHA	Dec
d h	° ′	° ′	° ′	° ′	° ′	° ′	° ′	° ′	° ′		° ′	° ′
10 00	18 16.9	225 52.3 N 9 19.0		216 55.2 N 9 18.0		213 54.6 N 7 40.8		138 12.0 S18 49.7		Acamar	315 16.8	S40 14.4
01	33 19.4	240 52.6	18.6	231 56.3	17.4	228 56.6	40.6	153 14.3	49.7	Achernar	335 25.1	S57 09.4
02	48 21.9	255 53.0	18.1	246 57.3	16.9	243 58.6	40.4	168 16.5	49.8	Acrux	173 08.1	S63 11.0
03	63 24.3	270 53.4 . .	17.7	261 58.3 . .	16.3	259 00.6 . .	40.3	183 18.7 . .	49.9	Adhara	255 11.3	S28 59.5
04	78 26.8	285 53.7	17.3	276 59.3	15.7	274 02.6	40.1	198 20.9	49.9	Aldebaran	290 47.4	N16 32.3
05	93 29.2	300 54.1	16.8	292 00.3	15.1	289 04.6	39.9	213 23.1	50.0			
06	108 31.7	315 54.4 N 9 16.4		307 01.3 N 9 14.6		304 06.6 N 7 39.7		228 25.4 S18 50.0		Alioth	166 20.0	N55 52.5
07	123 34.2	330 54.8	16.0	322 02.3	14.0	319 08.6	39.5	243 27.6	50.1	Alkaid	152 58.2	N49 14.3
S 08	138 36.6	345 55.2	15.6	337 03.3	13.4	334 10.6	39.3	258 29.8	50.1	Al Na'ir	27 41.5	S46 53.1
A 09	153 39.1	0 55.5 . .	15.1	352 04.3 . .	12.8	349 12.7 . .	39.2	273 32.0 . .	50.2	Alnilam	275 44.7	S 1 11.6
T 10	168 41.6	15 55.9	14.7	7 05.3	12.3	4 14.7	39.0	288 34.2	50.2	Alphard	217 54.7	S 8 43.6
U 11	183 44.0	30 56.2	14.3	22 06.3	11.7	19 16.7	38.8	303 36.5	50.3			
R 12	198 46.5	45 56.6 N 9 13.8		37 07.3 N 9 11.1		34 18.7 N 7 38.6		318 38.7 S18 50.3		Alphecca	126 10.0	N26 40.1
D 13	213 49.0	60 56.9	13.4	52 08.3	10.5	49 20.7	38.4	333 40.9	50.4	Alpheratz	357 41.5	N29 10.8
A 14	228 51.4	75 57.3	12.9	67 09.4	10.0	64 22.7	38.2	348 43.1	50.4	Altair	62 06.7	N 8 55.0
Y 15	243 53.9	90 57.6 . .	12.5	82 10.4 . .	09.4	79 24.7 . .	38.1	3 45.3 . .	50.5	Ankaa	353 13.8	S42 13.2
16	258 56.3	105 58.0	12.1	97 11.4	08.8	94 26.7	37.9	18 47.6	50.6	Antares	112 24.6	S26 27.8
17	273 58.8	120 58.3	11.6	112 12.4	08.2	109 28.7	37.7	33 49.8	50.6			
18	289 01.3	135 58.7 N 9 11.2		127 13.4 N 9 07.7		124 30.7 N 7 37.5		48 52.0 S18 50.7		Arcturus	145 54.7	N19 06.3
19	304 03.7	150 59.0	10.7	142 14.4	07.1	139 32.7	37.3	63 54.2	50.7	Atria	107 25.2	S69 03.3
20	319 06.2	165 59.3	10.3	157 15.4	06.5	154 34.7	37.1	78 56.4	50.8	Avior	234 17.5	S59 33.4
21	334 08.7	180 59.7 . .	09.9	172 16.4 . .	05.9	169 36.7 . .	37.0	93 58.7 . .	50.8	Bellatrix	278 30.2	N 6 21.7
22	349 11.1	196 00.0	09.4	187 17.4	05.4	184 38.7	36.8	109 00.9	50.9	Betelgeuse	270 59.5	N 7 24.5
23	4 13.6	211 00.4	09.0	202 18.4	04.8	199 40.7	36.6	124 03.1	50.9			
11 00	19 16.1	226 00.7 N 9 08.5		217 19.4 N 9 04.2		214 42.7 N 7 36.4		139 05.3 S18 51.0		Canopus	263 55.3	S52 42.1
01	34 18.5	241 01.0	08.1	232 20.5	03.6	229 44.7	36.2	154 07.5	51.0	Capella	280 31.9	N46 00.5
02	49 21.0	256 01.4	07.6	247 21.5	03.0	244 46.7	36.0	169 09.8	51.1	Deneb	49 30.2	N45 20.6
03	64 23.5	271 01.7 . .	07.2	262 22.5 . .	02.5	259 48.7 . .	35.9	184 12.0 . .	51.1	Denebola	182 32.4	N14 29.1
04	79 25.9	286 02.0	06.7	277 23.5	01.9	274 50.7	35.7	199 14.2	51.2	Diphda	348 54.0	S17 53.9
05	94 28.4	301 02.4	06.3	292 24.5	01.3	289 52.7	35.5	214 16.4	51.2			
06	109 30.8	316 02.7 N 9 05.8		307 25.5 N 9 00.7		304 54.7 N 7 35.3		229 18.6 S18 51.3		Dubhe	193 50.5	N61 39.8
07	124 33.3	331 03.0	05.4	322 26.5	9 00.2	319 56.7	35.1	244 20.8	51.4	Elnath	278 10.5	N28 37.0
08	139 35.8	346 03.4	04.9	337 27.5	8 59.6	334 58.7	34.9	259 23.1	51.4	Eltanin	90 45.6	N51 29.7
S 09	154 38.2	1 03.7 . .	04.5	352 28.5 . .	59.0	350 00.7 . .	34.8	274 25.3 . .	51.5	Enif	33 45.4	N 9 57.1
U 10	169 40.7	16 04.0	04.0	7 29.5	58.4	5 02.7	34.6	289 27.5	51.5	Fomalhaut	15 22.0	S29 32.2
N 11	184 43.2	31 04.4	03.5	22 30.6	57.9	20 04.7	34.4	304 29.7	51.6			
D 12	199 45.6	46 04.7 N 9 03.1		37 31.6 N 8 57.3		35 06.8 N 7 34.2		319 31.9 S18 51.6		Gacrux	171 59.6	S57 11.9
A 13	214 48.1	61 05.0	02.6	52 32.6	56.7	50 08.8	34.0	334 34.2	51.7	Gienah	175 51.0	S17 37.6
Y 14	229 50.6	76 05.3	02.2	67 33.6	56.1	65 10.8	33.8	349 36.4	51.7	Hadar	148 46.2	S60 26.8
15	244 53.0	91 05.7 . .	01.7	82 34.6 . .	55.5	80 12.8 . .	33.7	4 38.6 . .	51.8	Hamal	327 58.6	N23 32.2
16	259 55.5	106 06.0	01.2	97 35.6	55.0	95 14.8	33.5	19 40.8	51.8	Kaus Aust.	83 41.8	S34 22.5
17	274 57.9	121 06.3	00.8	112 36.6	54.4	110 16.8	33.3	34 43.0	51.9			
18	290 00.4	136 06.6 N 9 00.3		127 37.6 N 8 53.8		125 18.8 N 7 33.1		49 45.2 S18 51.9		Kochab	137 21.3	N74 05.7
19	305 02.9	151 06.9	8 59.9	142 38.6	53.2	140 20.8	32.9	64 47.5	52.0	Markab	13 36.5	N15 17.6
20	320 05.3	166 07.3	59.4	157 39.7	52.7	155 22.8	32.7	79 49.7	52.1	Menkar	314 13.1	N 4 09.1
21	335 07.8	181 07.6 . .	58.9	172 40.7 . .	52.1	170 24.8 . .	32.6	94 51.9 . .	52.1	Menkent	148 06.1	S36 26.7
22	350 10.3	196 07.9	58.5	187 41.7	51.5	185 26.8	32.4	109 54.1	52.2	Miaplacidus	221 39.6	S69 46.7
23	5 12.7	211 08.2	58.0	202 42.7	50.9	200 28.8	32.2	124 56.3	52.2			
12 00	20 15.2	226 08.5 N 8 57.5		217 43.7 N 8 50.3		215 30.8 N 7 32.0		139 58.5 S18 52.3		Mirfak	308 37.6	N49 54.8
01	35 17.7	241 08.8	57.1	232 44.7	49.8	230 32.8	31.8	155 00.8	52.3	Nunki	75 56.4	S26 16.4
02	50 20.1	256 09.1	56.6	247 45.7	49.2	245 34.8	31.7	170 03.0	52.4	Peacock	53 16.7	S56 41.1
03	65 22.6	271 09.4 . .	56.1	262 46.7 . .	48.6	260 36.8 . .	31.5	185 05.2 . .	52.4	Pollux	243 25.9	N27 59.1
04	80 25.1	286 09.8	55.6	277 47.8	48.0	275 38.8	31.3	200 07.4	52.5	Procyon	244 58.1	N 5 11.0
05	95 27.5	301 10.1	55.2	292 48.8	47.4	290 40.9	31.1	215 09.6	52.5			
06	110 30.0	316 10.4 N 8 54.7		307 49.8 N 8 46.9		305 42.9 N 7 30.9		230 11.8 S18 52.6		Rasalhague	96 05.2	N12 33.3
07	125 32.4	331 10.7	54.2	322 50.8	46.3	320 44.9	30.7	245 14.0	52.7	Regulus	207 42.1	N11 53.4
08	140 34.9	346 11.0	53.7	337 51.8	45.7	335 46.9	30.6	260 16.3	52.7	Rigel	281 10.4	S 8 11.0
M 09	155 37.4	1 11.3 . .	53.3	352 52.8 . .	45.1	350 48.9 . .	30.4	275 18.5 . .	52.8	Rigil Kent.	139 50.1	S60 53.9
O 10	170 39.8	16 11.6	52.8	7 53.8	44.6	5 50.9	30.2	290 20.7	52.8	Sabik	102 10.9	S15 44.4
N 11	185 42.3	31 11.9	52.3	22 54.9	44.0	20 52.9	30.0	305 22.9	52.9			
D 12	200 44.8	46 12.2 N 8 51.8		37 55.9 N 8 43.4		35 54.9 N 7 29.8		320 25.1 S18 52.9		Schedar	349 38.0	N56 37.5
A 13	215 47.2	61 12.5	51.4	52 56.9	42.8	50 56.9	29.6	335 27.3	53.0	Shaula	96 20.0	S37 06.8
Y 14	230 49.7	76 12.8	50.9	67 57.9	42.2	65 58.9	29.5	350 29.6	53.0	Sirius	258 32.3	S16 44.3
15	245 52.2	91 13.1 . .	50.4	82 58.9 . .	41.7	81 00.9 . .	29.3	5 31.8 . .	53.1	Spica	158 29.9	S11 14.4
16	260 54.6	106 13.4	49.9	97 59.9	41.1	96 02.9	29.1	20 34.0	53.1	Suhail	222 51.4	S43 29.6
17	275 57.1	121 13.7	49.4	113 00.9	40.5	111 04.9	28.9	35 36.2	53.2			
18	290 59.6	136 14.0 N 8 48.9		128 02.0 N 8 39.9		126 07.0 N 7 28.7		50 38.4 S18 53.2		Vega	80 38.0	N38 48.4
19	306 02.0	151 14.3	48.5	143 03.0	39.3	141 09.0	28.6	65 40.6	53.3	Zuben'ubi	137 04.0	S16 06.2
20	321 04.5	166 14.6	48.0	158 04.0	38.8	156 11.0	28.4	80 42.8	53.4		SHA	Mer. Pass.
21	336 06.9	181 14.9 . .	47.5	173 05.0 . .	38.2	171 13.0 . .	28.2	95 45.1 . .	53.4		° ′	h m
22	351 09.4	196 15.2	47.0	188 06.0	37.6	186 15.0	28.0	110 47.3	53.5	Venus	206 44.6	8 56
23	6 11.9	211 15.4	46.5	203 07.0	37.0	201 17.0	27.8	125 49.5	53.5	Mars	198 03.4	9 30
	h m									Jupiter	195 26.6	9 40
Mer. Pass. 22 39.2		v 0.3 d 0.5		v 1.0 d 0.6		v 2.0 d 0.2		v 2.2 d 0.1		Saturn	119 49.3	14 41

UT	SUN GHA	SUN Dec	MOON GHA	v	MOON Dec	d	HP
d h	° ′	° ′	° ′	′	° ′	′	′
10 00	183 12.0	S 6 26.1	213 42.4	15.1	N 4 53.2	8.9	54.1
01	198 12.2	27.1	228 16.5	15.1	4 44.3	9.0	54.1
02	213 12.3	28.0	242 50.6	15.1	4 35.3	8.9	54.1
03	228 12.5	.. 29.0	257 24.7	15.2	4 26.4	9.0	54.1
04	243 12.7	29.9	271 58.9	15.2	4 17.4	9.0	54.1
05	258 12.8	30.9	286 33.1	15.2	4 08.4	9.0	54.0
06	273 13.0	S 6 31.8	301 07.3	15.2	N 3 59.4	9.0	54.0
07	288 13.2	32.8	315 41.5	15.2	3 50.4	9.0	54.0
S 08	303 13.3	33.7	330 15.7	15.2	3 41.4	9.1	54.0
A 09	318 13.5	.. 34.7	344 49.9	15.2	3 32.3	9.0	54.0
T 10	333 13.7	35.6	359 24.1	15.3	3 23.3	9.1	54.0
U 11	348 13.8	36.6	13 58.4	15.3	3 14.2	9.1	54.0
R 12	3 14.0	S 6 37.5	28 32.7	15.2	N 3 05.1	9.1	54.0
D 13	18 14.2	38.5	43 06.9	15.3	2 56.0	9.1	54.0
A 14	33 14.3	39.4	57 41.2	15.3	2 46.9	9.1	54.0
Y 15	48 14.5	.. 40.4	72 15.5	15.3	2 37.8	9.2	54.0
16	63 14.7	41.3	86 49.8	15.3	2 28.6	9.1	54.0
17	78 14.8	42.2	101 24.1	15.3	2 19.5	9.2	54.0
18	93 15.0	S 6 43.2	115 58.4	15.4	N 2 10.3	9.1	54.0
19	108 15.1	44.1	130 32.8	15.3	2 01.2	9.2	54.0
20	123 15.3	45.1	145 07.1	15.3	1 52.0	9.1	54.0
21	138 15.5	.. 46.0	159 41.4	15.4	1 42.9	9.2	54.0
22	153 15.6	47.0	174 15.8	15.3	1 33.7	9.2	54.0
23	168 15.8	47.9	188 50.1	15.4	1 24.5	9.2	54.0
11 00	183 16.0	S 6 48.9	203 24.5	15.3	N 1 15.3	9.2	54.0
01	198 16.1	49.8	217 58.8	15.4	1 06.1	9.2	54.0
02	213 16.3	50.8	232 33.2	15.3	0 56.9	9.2	54.0
03	228 16.5	.. 51.7	247 07.5	15.4	0 47.7	9.2	54.0
04	243 16.6	52.6	261 41.9	15.4	0 38.5	9.2	54.0
05	258 16.8	53.6	276 16.3	15.3	0 29.3	9.2	54.0
06	273 16.9	S 6 54.5	290 50.6	15.4	N 0 20.1	9.2	54.0
07	288 17.1	55.5	305 25.0	15.4	0 10.9	9.2	54.0
08	303 17.3	56.4	319 59.4	15.4	N 0 01.7	9.3	54.0
S 09	318 17.4	.. 57.4	334 33.8	15.3	S 0 07.6	9.2	54.0
U 10	333 17.6	58.3	349 08.1	15.4	0 16.8	9.2	54.0
N 11	348 17.8	6 59.2	3 42.5	15.4	0 26.0	9.2	54.0
D 12	3 17.9	S 7 00.2	18 16.9	15.3	S 0 35.2	9.2	54.0
A 13	18 18.1	01.1	32 51.2	15.4	0 44.4	9.2	54.0
Y 14	33 18.2	02.1	47 25.6	15.3	0 53.6	9.2	54.0
15	48 18.4	.. 03.0	61 59.9	15.4	1 02.8	9.2	54.0
16	63 18.6	04.0	76 34.3	15.3	1 12.0	9.2	54.0
17	78 18.7	04.9	91 08.6	15.4	1 21.2	9.2	54.0
18	93 18.9	S 7 05.8	105 43.0	15.3	S 1 30.4	9.2	54.0
19	108 19.0	06.8	120 17.3	15.3	1 39.6	9.2	54.0
20	123 19.2	07.7	134 51.6	15.3	1 48.8	9.2	54.0
21	138 19.4	.. 08.7	149 25.9	15.4	1 58.0	9.1	54.0
22	153 19.5	09.6	164 00.3	15.3	2 07.1	9.2	54.0
23	168 19.7	10.6	178 34.6	15.3	2 16.3	9.1	54.0
12 00	183 19.9	S 7 11.5	193 08.9	15.2	S 2 25.4	9.1	54.0
01	198 20.0	12.4	207 43.1	15.3	2 34.6	9.1	54.0
02	213 20.1	13.4	222 17.4	15.3	2 43.7	9.1	54.0
03	228 20.3	.. 14.3	236 51.7	15.2	2 52.8	9.2	54.0
04	243 20.5	15.3	251 25.9	15.3	3 02.0	9.1	54.0
05	258 20.6	16.2	266 00.2	15.2	3 11.1	9.0	54.0
06	273 20.8	S 7 17.1	280 34.4	15.2	S 3 20.1	9.1	54.0
07	288 20.9	18.1	295 08.6	15.3	3 29.2	9.1	54.0
08	303 21.1	19.0	309 42.9	15.2	3 38.3	9.0	54.0
M 09	318 21.2	.. 20.0	324 17.1	15.1	3 47.3	9.1	54.0
O 10	333 21.4	20.9	338 51.2	15.2	3 56.4	9.0	54.0
N 11	348 21.6	21.8	353 25.4	15.2	4 05.4	9.0	54.0
D 12	3 21.7	S 7 22.8	7 59.6	15.1	S 4 14.4	9.0	54.0
A 13	18 21.9	23.7	22 33.7	15.1	4 23.4	9.0	54.0
Y 14	33 22.0	24.7	37 07.8	15.1	4 32.4	8.9	54.0
15	48 22.2	.. 25.6	51 41.9	15.1	4 41.3	9.0	54.0
16	63 22.4	26.5	66 16.0	15.1	4 50.3	8.9	54.0
17	78 22.5	27.5	80 50.1	15.1	4 59.2	8.9	54.0
18	93 22.6	S 7 28.4	95 24.2	15.0	S 5 08.1	8.9	54.0
19	108 22.8	29.3	109 58.2	15.0	5 17.0	8.9	54.0
20	123 23.0	30.3	124 32.2	15.0	5 25.9	8.8	54.0
21	138 23.1	.. 31.2	139 06.2	15.0	5 34.7	8.8	54.0
22	153 23.3	32.2	153 40.2	15.0	5 43.5	8.8	54.0
23	168 23.4	33.1	168 14.2	14.9	5 52.3	8.8	54.0
	SD 16.0	d 0.9	SD 14.7		14.7		14.7

Twilight / Moonrise

Lat.	Naut.	Civil	Sunrise	Moonrise 10	11	12	13
°	h m	h m	h m	h m	h m	h m	h m
N 72	04 36	05 54	07 03	02 56	04 28	06 00	07 34
N 70	04 42	05 53	06 54	03 02	04 29	05 55	07 23
68	04 47	05 51	06 47	03 07	04 29	05 51	07 14
66	04 51	05 50	06 42	03 12	04 30	05 48	07 07
64	04 54	05 49	06 37	03 15	04 30	05 45	07 00
62	04 56	05 48	06 32	03 18	04 31	05 43	06 55
60	04 59	05 47	06 29	03 21	04 31	05 41	06 51
N 58	05 00	05 46	06 25	03 24	04 31	05 39	06 47
56	05 02	05 45	06 22	03 26	04 31	05 37	06 43
54	05 03	05 44	06 20	03 28	04 32	05 36	06 40
52	05 04	05 43	06 17	03 29	04 32	05 34	06 37
50	05 05	05 42	06 15	03 31	04 32	05 33	06 34
45	05 07	05 41	06 10	03 34	04 32	05 30	06 29
N 40	05 07	05 39	06 06	03 37	04 33	05 28	06 24
35	05 08	05 37	06 02	03 40	04 33	05 26	06 20
30	05 07	05 35	05 59	03 42	04 33	05 25	06 16
20	05 06	05 31	05 53	03 46	04 34	05 22	06 10
N 10	05 03	05 27	05 48	03 49	04 34	05 19	06 05
0	04 59	05 23	05 44	03 52	04 35	05 17	06 00
S 10	04 53	05 17	05 39	03 55	04 35	05 14	05 55
20	04 45	05 11	05 33	03 59	04 35	05 12	05 49
30	04 34	05 03	05 27	04 02	04 36	05 09	05 43
35	04 27	04 58	05 23	04 05	04 36	05 08	05 40
40	04 19	04 52	05 19	04 07	04 37	05 06	05 36
45	04 08	04 44	05 14	04 10	04 37	05 04	05 31
S 50	03 55	04 35	05 08	04 13	04 37	05 01	05 26
52	03 48	04 31	05 06	04 15	04 38	05 00	05 24
54	03 41	04 26	05 03	04 17	04 38	04 59	05 21
56	03 33	04 21	04 59	04 19	04 38	04 58	05 18
58	03 23	04 15	04 56	04 21	04 38	04 56	05 15
S 60	03 11	04 08	04 52	04 23	04 39	04 55	05 11

Twilight / Moonset

Lat.	Sunset	Civil	Naut.	Moonset 10	11	12	13
°	h m	h m	h m	h m	h m	h m	h m
N 72	16 29	17 37	18 55	16 42	16 38	16 33	16 29
N 70	16 37	17 39	18 49	16 39	16 40	16 40	16 41
68	16 45	17 41	18 45	16 36	16 41	16 46	16 51
66	16 51	17 42	18 41	16 34	16 42	16 51	17 00
64	16 56	17 43	18 38	16 32	16 43	16 55	17 07
62	17 00	17 45	18 36	16 31	16 44	16 58	17 13
60	17 04	17 46	18 34	16 29	16 45	17 01	17 18
N 58	17 07	17 47	18 32	16 28	16 46	17 04	17 23
56	17 10	17 48	18 31	16 27	16 47	17 06	17 27
54	17 13	17 49	18 29	16 26	16 47	17 09	17 31
52	17 16	17 49	18 28	16 25	16 48	17 11	17 35
50	17 18	17 50	18 28	16 24	16 48	17 12	17 38
45	17 23	17 52	18 26	16 23	16 49	17 16	17 45
N 40	17 27	17 54	18 26	16 21	16 50	17 20	17 51
35	17 31	17 56	18 26	16 20	16 51	17 23	17 56
30	17 34	17 58	18 26	16 18	16 52	17 25	18 00
20	17 40	18 02	18 28	16 16	16 53	17 30	18 08
N 10	17 45	18 06	18 31	16 14	16 54	17 34	18 14
0	17 50	18 11	18 35	16 13	16 55	17 37	18 21
S 10	17 55	18 16	18 41	16 11	16 56	17 41	18 27
20	18 01	18 23	18 49	16 09	16 57	17 45	18 34
30	18 07	18 31	19 00	16 07	16 58	17 50	18 41
35	18 11	18 37	19 07	16 06	16 59	17 52	18 46
40	18 15	18 43	19 16	16 04	16 59	17 55	18 51
45	18 20	18 50	19 26	16 02	17 00	17 58	18 57
S 50	18 26	19 00	19 40	16 00	17 01	18 03	19 04
52	18 29	19 04	19 47	15 59	17 02	18 04	19 07
54	18 32	19 09	19 54	15 58	17 02	18 06	19 11
56	18 35	19 14	20 03	15 57	17 03	18 09	19 15
58	18 39	19 21	20 13	15 56	17 04	18 11	19 19
S 60	18 44	19 28	20 25	15 55	17 04	18 14	19 24

SUN / MOON

Day	Eqn. of Time 00h	12h	Mer. Pass.	Mer. Pass. Upper	Lower	Age	Phase
d	m s	m s	h m	h m	h m	d	%
10	12 48	12 56	11 47	10 02	22 24	27	6
11	13 04	13 11	11 47	10 45	23 06	28	2
12	13 19	13 27	11 47	11 27	23 48	29	0

UT	ARIES GHA	VENUS −4.6 GHA	Dec	MARS +1.8 GHA	Dec	JUPITER −1.8 GHA	Dec	SATURN +0.6 GHA	Dec	STARS Name	SHA	Dec
13 00	21 14.3	226 15.7	N 8 46.0	218 08.0	N 8 36.4	216 19.0	N 7 27.7	140 51.7	S18 53.6	Acamar	315 16.8	S40 14.5
01	36 16.8	241 16.0	45.5	233 09.1	35.9	231 21.0	27.5	155 53.9	53.6	Achernar	335 25.1	S57 09.4
02	51 19.3	256 16.3	45.0	248 10.1	35.3	246 23.0	27.3	170 56.1	53.7	Acrux	173 08.0	S63 11.0
03	66 21.7	271 16.6 ..	44.5	263 11.1 ..*	34.7	261 25.0 ..	27.1	185 58.3 ..	53.7	Adhara	255 11.2	S28 59.5
04	81 24.2	286 16.9	44.1	278 12.1	34.1	276 27.0	26.9	201 00.6	53.8	Aldebaran	290 47.4	N16 32.3
05	96 26.7	301 17.2	43.6	293 13.1	33.5	291 29.1	26.7	216 02.8	53.8			
06	111 29.1	316 17.5	N 8 43.1	308 14.1	N 8 33.0	306 31.1	N 7 26.6	231 05.0	S18 53.9	Alioth	166 20.0	N55 52.5
07	126 31.6	331 17.7	42.6	323 15.2	32.4	321 33.1	26.4	246 07.2	53.9	Alkaid	152 58.2	N49 14.3
T 08	141 34.0	346 18.0	42.1	338 16.2	31.8	336 35.1	26.2	261 09.4	54.0	Al Na'ir	27 41.6	S46 53.1
U 09	156 36.5	1 18.3 ..	41.6	353 17.2 ..	31.2	351 37.1 ..	26.0	276 11.6 ..	54.1	Alnilam	275 44.6	S 1 11.6
E 10	171 39.0	16 18.6	41.1	8 18.2	30.6	6 39.1	25.8	291 13.8	54.1	Alphard	217 54.7	S 8 43.6
S 11	186 41.4	31 18.9	40.6	23 19.2	30.1	21 41.1	25.7	306 16.0	54.2			
D 12	201 43.9	46 19.1	N 8 40.1	38 20.2	N 8 29.5	36 43.1	N 7 25.5	321 18.3	S18 54.2	Alphecca	126 10.0	N26 40.1
A 13	216 46.4	61 19.4	39.6	53 21.3	28.9	51 45.1	25.3	336 20.5	54.3	Alpheratz	357 45.5	N29 10.8
Y 14	231 48.8	76 19.7	39.1	68 22.3	28.3	66 47.1	25.1	351 22.7	54.3	Altair	62 06.7	N 8 55.0
15	246 51.3	91 20.0 ..	38.6	83 23.3 ..	27.7	81 49.1 ..	24.9	6 24.9 ..	54.4	Ankaa	353 13.8	S42 13.2
16	261 53.8	106 20.2	38.1	98 24.3	27.2	96 51.2	24.8	21 27.1	54.4	Antares	112 24.6	S26 27.8
17	276 56.2	121 20.5	37.6	113 25.3	26.6	111 53.2	24.6	36 29.3	54.5			
18	291 58.7	136 20.8	N 8 37.1	128 26.3	N 8 26.0	126 55.2	N 7 24.4	51 31.5	S18 54.5	Arcturus	145 54.7	N19 06.3
19	307 01.2	151 21.1	36.6	143 27.4	25.4	141 57.2	24.2	66 33.7	54.6	Atria	107 25.3	S69 03.3
20	322 03.6	166 21.3	36.1	158 28.4	24.8	156 59.2	24.0	81 36.0	54.7	Avior	234 17.4	S59 33.4
21	337 06.1	181 21.6 ..	35.5	173 29.4 ..	24.3	172 01.2 ..	23.8	96 38.2 ..	54.7	Bellatrix	278 30.2	N 6 21.7
22	352 08.5	196 21.9	35.0	188 30.4	23.7	187 03.2	23.7	111 40.4	54.8	Betelgeuse	270 59.5	N 7 24.5
23	7 11.0	211 22.1	34.5	203 31.4	23.1	202 05.2	23.5	126 42.6	54.8			
14 00	22 13.5	226 22.4	N 8 34.0	218 32.4	N 8 22.5	217 07.2	N 7 23.3	141 44.8	S18 54.9	Canopus	263 55.3	S52 42.1
01	37 15.9	241 22.7	33.5	233 33.5	21.9	232 09.3	23.1	156 47.0	54.9	Capella	280 31.9	N46 00.5
02	52 18.4	256 22.9	33.0	248 34.5	21.4	247 11.3	22.9	171 49.2	55.0	Deneb	49 30.2	N45 20.7
03	67 20.9	271 23.2 ..	32.5	263 35.5 ..	20.8	262 13.3 ..	22.8	186 51.4 ..	55.0	Denebola	182 32.4	N14 29.1
04	82 23.3	286 23.5	32.0	278 36.5	20.2	277 15.3	22.6	201 53.6	55.1	Diphda	348 54.0	S17 54.0
05	97 25.8	301 23.7	31.5	293 37.5	19.6	292 17.3	22.4	216 55.9	55.1			
06	112 28.3	316 24.0	N 8 30.9	308 38.6	N 8 19.0	307 19.3	N 7 22.2	231 58.1	S18 55.2	Dubhe	193 50.5	N61 39.8
W 07	127 30.7	331 24.3	30.4	323 39.6	18.4	322 21.3	22.0	247 00.3	55.3	Elnath	278 10.5	N28 37.0
E 08	142 33.2	346 24.5	29.9	338 40.6	17.9	337 23.3	21.9	262 02.5	55.3	Eltanin	90 45.6	N51 29.7
D 09	157 35.6	1 24.8 ..	29.4	353 41.6 ..	17.3	352 25.4 ..	21.7	277 04.7 ..	55.4	Enif	33 45.4	N 9 57.1
N 10	172 38.1	16 25.0	28.9	8 42.6	16.7	7 27.4	21.5	292 06.9	55.4	Fomalhaut	15 22.0	S29 32.3
E 11	187 40.6	31 25.3	28.3	23 43.7	16.1	22 29.4	21.3	307 09.1	55.5			
S 12	202 43.0	46 25.6	N 8 27.8	38 44.7	N 8 15.5	37 31.4	N 7 21.1	322 11.3	S18 55.5	Gacrux	171 59.6	S57 11.9
D 13	217 45.5	61 25.8	27.3	53 45.7	15.0	52 33.4	21.0	337 13.5	55.6	Gienah	175 51.0	S17 37.6
A 14	232 48.0	76 26.1	26.8	68 46.7	14.4	67 35.4	20.8	352 15.8	55.6	Hadar	148 46.2	S60 26.8
Y 15	247 50.4	91 26.3 ..	26.3	83 47.7 ..	13.8	82 37.4 ..	20.6	7 18.0 ..	55.7	Hamal	327 58.6	N23 32.2
16	262 52.9	106 26.6	25.7	98 48.8	13.2	97 39.4	20.4	22 20.2	55.7	Kaus Aust.	83 41.9	S34 22.5
17	277 55.4	121 26.8	25.2	113 49.8	12.6	112 41.5	20.2	37 22.4	55.8			
18	292 57.8	136 27.1	N 8 24.7	128 50.8	N 8 12.0	127 43.5	N 7 20.1	52 24.6	S18 55.8	Kochab	137 21.4	N74 05.7
19	308 00.3	151 27.3	24.2	143 51.8	11.5	142 45.5	19.9	67 26.8	55.9	Markab	13 36.5	N15 17.6
20	323 02.8	166 27.6	23.6	158 52.8	10.9	157 47.5	19.7	82 29.0	56.0	Menkar	314 13.1	N 4 09.1
21	338 05.2	181 27.8 ..	23.1	173 53.9 ..	10.3	172 49.5 ..	19.5	97 31.2 ..	56.0	Menkent	148 06.1	S36 26.7
22	353 07.7	196 28.1	22.6	188 54.9	09.7	187 51.5	19.3	112 33.4	56.1	Miaplacidus	221 39.6	S69 46.7
23	8 10.1	211 28.3	22.0	203 55.9	09.1	202 53.5	19.2	127 35.6	56.1			
15 00	23 12.6	226 28.6	N 8 21.5	218 56.9	N 8 08.6	217 55.6	N 7 19.0	142 37.9	S18 56.2	Mirfak	308 37.6	N49 54.8
01	38 15.1	241 28.8	21.0	233 57.9	08.0	232 57.6	18.8	157 40.1	56.2	Nunki	75 56.5	S26 16.4
02	53 17.5	256 29.1	20.5	248 59.0	07.4	247 59.6	18.6	172 42.3	56.3	Peacock	53 16.7	S56 41.1
03	68 20.0	271 29.3 ..	19.9	264 00.0 ..	06.8	263 01.6 ..	18.4	187 44.5 ..	56.3	Pollux	243 25.9	N27 59.0
04	83 22.5	286 29.6	19.4	279 01.0	06.2	278 03.6	18.3	202 46.7	56.4	Procyon	244 58.1	N 5 11.0
05	98 24.9	301 29.8	18.9	294 02.0	05.6	293 05.6	18.1	217 48.9	56.4			
06	113 27.4	316 30.0	N 8 18.3	309 03.0	N 8 05.1	308 07.6	N 7 17.9	232 51.1	S18 56.5	Rasalhague	96 05.2	N12 33.3
07	128 29.9	331 30.3	17.8	324 04.1	04.5	323 09.7	17.7	247 53.3	56.6	Regulus	207 42.1	N11 53.4
T 08	143 32.3	346 30.5	17.2	339 05.1	03.9	338 11.7	17.5	262 55.5	56.6	Rigel	281 10.4	S 8 11.1
H 09	158 34.8	1 30.7 ..	16.7	354 06.1 ..	03.3	353 13.7 ..	17.4	277 57.7 ..	56.7	Rigil Kent.	139 50.1	S60 53.8
U 10	173 37.3	16 31.0	16.2	9 07.1	02.7	8 15.7	17.2	292 59.9	56.7	Sabik	102 10.9	S15 44.4
R 11	188 39.7	31 31.2	15.6	24 08.2	02.1	23 17.7	17.0	308 02.1	56.8			
S 12	203 42.2	46 31.4	N 8 15.1	39 09.2	N 8 01.6	38 19.7	N 7 16.8	323 04.4	S18 56.8	Schedar	349 38.1	N56 37.5
D 13	218 44.6	61 31.7	14.5	54 10.2	01.0	53 21.7	16.7	338 06.6	56.9	Shaula	96 20.0	S37 06.7
A 14	233 47.1	76 31.9	14.0	69 11.2	8 00.4	68 23.8	16.5	353 08.8	56.9	Sirius	258 32.3	S16 44.3
Y 15	248 49.6	91 32.1 ..	13.5	84 12.2	7 59.8	83 25.8 ..	16.3	8 11.0 ..	57.0	Spica	158 29.9	S11 14.4
16	263 52.0	106 32.4	12.9	99 13.3	59.2	98 27.8	16.1	23 13.2	57.0	Suhail	222 51.4	S43 29.6
17	278 54.5	121 32.6	12.4	114 14.3	58.6	113 29.8	15.9	38 15.4	57.1			
18	293 57.0	136 32.8	N 8 11.8	129 15.3	N 7 58.1	128 31.8	N 7 15.8	53 17.6	S18 57.2	Vega	80 38.0	N38 48.4
19	308 59.4	151 33.1	11.3	144 16.3	57.5	143 33.8	15.6	68 19.8	57.2	Zuben'ubi	137 04.0	S16 06.2
20	324 01.9	166 33.3	10.7	159 17.4	56.9	158 35.9	15.4	83 22.0	57.3		SHA	Mer.Pass.
21	339 04.4	181 33.5 ..	10.2	174 18.4 ..	56.3	173 37.9 ..	15.2	98 24.2 ..	57.3		° ′	h m
22	354 06.8	196 33.8	09.6	189 19.4	55.7	188 39.9	15.0	113 26.4	57.4	Venus	204 08.9	8 54
23	9 09.3	211 34.0	09.1	204 20.4	55.1	203 41.9	14.9	128 28.6	57.4	Mars	196 19.0	9 25
	h m									Jupiter	194 53.8	9 30
Mer.Pass.	22 27.4	v 0.3	d 0.5	v 1.0	d 0.6	v 2.0	d 0.2	v 2.2	d 0.1	Saturn	119 31.3	14 31

SUN and MOON

UT	SUN GHA	SUN Dec	MOON GHA	v	MOON Dec	d	HP
d h	° ′	° ′	° ′	′	° ′	′	′
13 00	183 23.6	S 7 34.0	182 48.1	14.9	S 6 01.1	8.8	54.0
01	198 23.7	35.0	197 22.0	14.9	6 09.9	8.7	54.1
02	213 23.9	35.9	211 55.9	14.9	6 18.6	8.7	54.1
03	228 24.0 . .	36.8	226 29.8	14.9	6 27.3	8.7	54.1
04	243 24.2	37.8	241 03.7	14.8	6 36.0	8.7	54.1
05	258 24.3	38.7	255 37.5	14.8	6 44.7	8.6	54.1
06	273 24.5	S 7 39.6	270 11.3	14.8	S 6 53.3	8.6	54.1
07	288 24.6	40.6	284 45.1	14.8	7 01.9	8.6	54.1
08	303 24.8	41.5	299 18.9	14.7	7 10.5	8.6	54.1
09	318 24.9 . .	42.5	313 52.6	14.7	7 19.1	8.5	54.1
10	333 25.1	43.4	328 26.3	14.7	7 27.6	8.5	54.1
11	348 25.2	44.3	343 00.0	14.7	7 36.1	8.4	54.1
12	3 25.4	S 7 45.3	357 33.7	14.6	S 7 44.5	8.5	54.1
13	18 25.5	46.2	12 07.3	14.6	7 53.0	8.4	54.1
14	33 25.7	47.1	26 40.9	14.6	8 01.4	8.4	54.1
15	48 25.8 . .	48.1	41 14.5	14.5	8 09.8	8.3	54.1
16	63 26.0	49.0	55 48.0	14.6	8 18.1	8.3	54.2
17	78 26.1	49.9	70 21.6	14.5	8 26.4	8.3	54.2
18	93 26.3	S 7 50.9	84 55.1	14.4	S 8 34.7	8.2	54.2
19	108 26.4	51.8	99 28.5	14.5	8 42.9	8.3	54.2
20	123 26.6	52.7	114 02.0	14.4	8 51.2	8.1	54.2
21	138 26.7 . .	53.7	128 35.4	14.4	8 59.3	8.2	54.2
22	153 26.9	54.6	143 08.8	14.3	9 07.5	8.1	54.2
23	168 27.0	55.5	157 42.1	14.3	9 15.6	8.0	54.2
14 00	183 27.2	S 7 56.5	172 15.4	14.3	S 9 23.6	8.1	54.2
01	198 27.3	57.4	186 48.7	14.3	9 31.7	8.0	54.2
02	213 27.5	58.3	201 22.0	14.2	9 39.7	7.9	54.2
03	228 27.6	7 59.3	215 55.2	14.2	9 47.6	7.9	54.2
04	243 27.8	8 00.2	230 28.4	14.2	9 55.5	7.9	54.3
05	258 27.9	01.1	245 01.6	14.1	10 03.4	7.8	54.3
06	273 28.1	S 8 02.0	259 34.7	14.1	S10 11.2	7.8	54.3
07	288 28.2	03.0	274 07.8	14.1	10 19.0	7.8	54.3
08	303 28.4	03.9	288 40.9	14.0	10 26.8	7.7	54.3
09	318 28.5 . .	04.8	303 13.9	14.0	10 34.5	7.6	54.3
10	333 28.6	05.8	317 46.9	14.0	10 42.1	7.7	54.3
11	348 28.8	06.7	332 19.9	13.9	10 49.8	7.5	54.3
12	3 28.9	S 8 07.6	346 52.8	13.9	S10 57.3	7.6	54.3
13	18 29.1	08.6	1 25.7	13.8	11 04.9	7.5	54.3
14	33 29.2	09.5	15 58.5	13.9	11 12.4	7.4	54.4
15	48 29.4 . .	10.4	30 31.4	13.7	11 19.8	7.4	54.4
16	63 29.5	11.4	45 04.1	13.8	11 27.2	7.3	54.4
17	78 29.7	12.3	59 36.9	13.7	11 34.5	7.3	54.4
18	93 29.8	S 8 13.2	74 09.6	13.7	S11 41.8	7.3	54.4
19	108 29.9	14.1	88 42.3	13.6	11 49.1	7.2	54.4
20	123 30.1	15.1	103 14.9	13.6	11 56.3	7.2	54.4
21	138 30.2 . .	16.0	117 47.5	13.6	12 03.5	7.1	54.4
22	153 30.4	16.9	132 20.1	13.5	12 10.6	7.0	54.4
23	168 30.5	17.9	146 52.6	13.5	12 17.6	7.0	54.5
15 00	183 30.7	S 8 18.8	161 25.1	13.5	S12 24.6	7.0	54.5
01	198 30.8	19.7	175 57.6	13.4	12 31.6	6.9	54.5
02	213 30.9	20.6	190 30.0	13.3	12 38.5	6.8	54.5
03	228 31.1 . .	21.6	205 02.3	13.4	12 45.3	6.8	54.5
04	243 31.2	22.5	219 34.7	13.3	12 52.1	6.7	54.5
05	258 31.4	23.4	234 07.0	13.2	12 58.8	6.7	54.5
06	273 31.5	S 8 24.3	248 39.2	13.3	S13 05.5	6.6	54.5
07	288 31.6	25.3	263 11.5	13.1	13 12.1	6.6	54.6
08	303 31.8	26.2	277 43.6	13.2	13 18.7	6.5	54.6
09	318 31.9 . .	27.1	292 15.8	13.1	13 25.2	6.4	54.6
10	333 32.1	28.0	306 47.9	13.0	13 31.6	6.4	54.6
11	348 32.2	29.0	321 19.9	13.0	13 38.0	6.4	54.6
12	3 32.3	S 8 29.9	335 51.9	13.0	S13 44.4	6.3	54.6
13	18 32.5	30.8	350 23.9	13.0	13 50.7	6.2	54.6
14	33 32.6	31.7	4 55.9	12.8	13 56.9	6.1	54.7
15	48 32.8 . .	32.7	19 27.7	12.9	14 03.0	6.1	54.7
16	63 32.9	33.6	33 59.6	12.8	14 09.1	6.0	54.7
17	78 33.0	34.5	48 31.4	12.8	14 15.1	6.0	54.7
18	93 33.2	S 8 35.4	63 03.2	12.7	S14 21.1	5.9	54.7
19	108 33.3	36.4	77 34.9	12.7	14 27.0	5.9	54.7
20	123 33.5	37.3	92 06.6	12.6	14 32.9	5.7	54.7
21	138 33.6 . .	38.2	106 38.2	12.7	14 38.6	5.8	54.8
22	153 33.7	39.1	121 09.9	12.5	14 44.4	5.6	54.8
23	168 33.9	40.1	135 41.4	12.5	S14 50.0	5.6	54.8
	SD 16.1	d 0.9	SD 14.7		14.8		14.9

Day of week labels: 13 TUESDAY, 14 WEDNESDAY, 15 THURSDAY

Twilight, Sunrise and Moonrise

Lat.	Naut.	Civil	Sunrise	Moonrise 13	Moonrise 14	Moonrise 15	Moonrise 16
°	h m	h m	h m	h m	h m	h m	h m
N 72	04 49	06 07	07 17	07 34	09 09	10 49	12 34
N 70	04 54	06 04	07 07	07 23	08 51	10 21	11 51
68	04 57	06 02	06 59	07 14	08 37	10 00	11 22
66	05 00	05 59	06 52	07 07	08 25	09 44	11 00
64	05 02	05 57	06 46	07 00	08 16	09 31	10 43
62	05 04	05 55	06 40	06 55	08 08	09 19	10 29
60	05 06	05 54	06 36	06 51	08 01	09 10	10 17
N 58	05 07	05 52	06 32	06 47	07 54	09 02	10 07
56	05 08	05 51	06 28	06 43	07 49	08 54	09 58
54	05 09	05 49	06 25	06 40	07 44	08 48	09 50
52	05 09	05 48	06 22	06 37	07 40	08 42	09 43
50	05 10	05 47	06 20	06 34	07 36	08 37	09 37
45	05 10	05 44	06 14	06 29	07 27	08 25	09 23
N 40	05 10	05 42	06 09	06 24	07 20	08 16	09 12
35	05 10	05 39	06 05	06 20	07 14	08 08	09 02
30	05 09	05 37	06 01	06 16	07 08	08 01	08 54
20	05 06	05 32	05 54	06 10	06 59	07 49	08 40
N 10	05 03	05 27	05 48	06 05	06 51	07 38	08 27
0	04 58	05 22	05 43	06 00	06 43	07 29	08 15
S 10	04 51	05 16	05 37	05 55	06 36	07 19	08 04
20	04 42	05 08	05 31	05 49	06 28	07 08	07 51
30	04 31	04 59	05 24	05 43	06 19	06 56	07 37
35	04 23	04 54	05 19	05 40	06 14	06 50	07 29
40	04 14	04 47	05 15	05 36	06 08	06 42	07 20
45	04 02	04 39	05 09	05 31	06 01	06 33	07 09
S 50	03 48	04 29	05 02	05 26	05 53	06 22	06 56
52	03 41	04 24	04 59	05 24	05 49	06 17	06 50
54	03 33	04 18	04 56	05 21	05 45	06 12	06 43
56	03 23	04 13	04 52	05 18	05 40	06 06	06 35
58	03 13	04 06	04 48	05 15	05 35	05 59	06 27
S 60	03 00	03 58	04 43	05 11	05 30	05 51	06 17

Sunset, Twilight and Moonset

Lat.	Sunset	Civil	Naut.	Moonset 13	Moonset 14	Moonset 15	Moonset 16
°	h m	h m	h m	h m	h m	h m	h m
N 72	16 13	17 23	18 40	16 29	16 24	16 18	16 11
N 70	16 23	17 26	18 36	16 41	16 43	16 47	16 55
68	16 32	17 29	18 33	16 51	16 59	17 09	17 25
66	16 39	17 31	18 30	17 00	17 11	17 26	17 47
64	16 45	17 33	18 28	17 07	17 22	17 40	18 04
62	16 51	17 35	18 26	17 13	17 30	17 52	18 19
60	16 55	17 37	18 25	17 18	17 38	18 02	18 31
N 58	16 59	17 39	18 24	17 23	17 45	18 10	18 41
56	17 03	17 40	18 23	17 27	17 51	18 18	18 51
54	17 06	17 42	18 22	17 31	17 56	18 25	18 59
52	17 09	17 43	18 22	17 35	18 01	18 31	19 06
50	17 12	17 44	18 22	17 38	18 06	18 37	19 13
45	17 18	17 47	18 21	17 45	18 15	18 49	19 27
N 40	17 23	17 50	18 21	17 51	18 23	18 59	19 39
35	17 27	17 52	18 22	17 56	18 30	19 08	19 49
30	17 31	17 55	18 23	18 00	18 36	19 15	19 58
20	17 38	18 00	18 25	18 08	18 47	19 29	20 13
N 10	17 44	18 05	18 29	18 14	18 56	19 40	20 26
0	17 49	18 10	18 35	18 21	19 05	19 51	20 39
S 10	17 55	18 17	18 41	18 27	19 14	20 02	20 51
20	18 02	18 24	18 50	18 34	19 23	20 13	21 04
30	18 09	18 33	19 02	18 41	19 34	20 26	21 20
35	18 13	18 39	19 10	18 46	19 40	20 34	21 28
40	18 18	18 46	19 19	18 51	19 47	20 43	21 38
45	18 24	18 54	19 31	18 57	19 55	20 53	21 50
S 50	18 31	19 05	19 46	19 04	20 05	21 06	22 05
52	18 34	19 10	19 53	19 07	20 10	21 11	22 11
54	18 38	19 15	20 01	19 11	20 15	21 18	22 19
56	18 42	19 21	20 11	19 15	20 20	21 25	22 27
58	18 46	19 28	20 22	19 19	20 27	21 33	22 37
S 60	18 51	19 36	20 35	19 24	20 34	21 42	22 48

SUN and MOON

	SUN			MOON			
Day	Eqn. of Time 00h	Eqn. of Time 12h	Mer. Pass.	Mer. Pass. Upper	Mer. Pass. Lower	Age	Phase
d	m s	m s	h m	h m	h m	d	%
13	13 34	13 41	11 46	12 10	24 32	00	0
14	13 48	13 55	11 46	12 54	00 32	01	2
15	14 02	14 09	11 46	13 40	01 17	02	6

2015 OCTOBER 16, 17, 18 (FRI., SAT., SUN.)

UT	ARIES	VENUS −4.6		MARS +1.7		JUPITER −1.8		SATURN +0.6		STARS		
	GHA	GHA	Dec	GHA	Dec	GHA	Dec	GHA	Dec	Name	SHA	Dec
d h	° ′	° ′	° ′	° ′	° ′	° ′	° ′	° ′	° ′		° ′	° ′
16 00	24 11.7	226 34.2 N 8 08.5		219 21.5 N 7 54.6		218 43.9 N 7 14.7		143 30.8 S18 57.5		Acamar	315 16.8	S40 14.5
01	39 14.2	241 34.4	08.0	234 22.5	54.0	233 45.9	14.5	158 33.1	57.5	Achernar	335 25.1	S57 09.4
02	54 16.7	256 34.7	07.4	249 23.5	53.4	248 48.0	14.3	173 35.3	57.6	Acrux	173 08.0	S63 11.0
03	69 19.1	271 34.9 ..	06.9	264 24.5 ..	52.8	263 50.0 ..	14.2	188 37.5 ..	57.7	Adhara	255 11.2	S28 59.5
04	84 21.6	286 35.1	06.3	279 25.5	52.2	278 52.0	14.0	203 39.7	57.7	Aldebaran	290 47.3	N16 32.3
05	99 24.1	301 35.3	05.8	294 26.6	51.6	293 54.0	13.8	218 41.9	57.8			
06	114 26.5	316 35.5 N 8 05.2		309 27.6 N 7 51.1		308 56.0 N 7 13.6		233 44.1 S18 57.8		Alioth	166 20.0	N55 52.5
07	129 29.0	331 35.8	04.7	324 28.6	50.5	323 58.0	13.4	248 46.3	57.9	Alkaid	152 58.2	N49 14.2
08	144 31.5	346 36.0	04.1	339 29.6	49.9	339 00.1	13.3	263 48.5	57.9	Al Na'ir	27 41.6	S46 53.1
F 09	159 33.9	1 36.2 ..	03.5	354 30.7 ..	49.3	354 02.1 ..	13.1	278 50.7 ..	58.0	Alnilam	275 44.6	S 1 11.6
R 10	174 36.4	16 36.4	03.0	9 31.7	48.7	9 04.1	12.9	293 52.9	58.0	Alphard	217 54.7	S 8 43.6
I 11	189 38.9	31 36.6	02.4	24 32.7	48.1	24 06.1	12.7	308 55.1	58.1			
D 12	204 41.3	46 36.8 N 8 01.9		39 33.7 N 7 47.6		39 08.1 N 7 12.5		323 57.3 S18 58.1		Alphecca	126 10.0	N26 40.0
A 13	219 43.8	61 37.1	01.3	54 34.8	47.0	54 10.1	12.4	338 59.5	58.2	Alpheratz	357 41.5	N29 10.8
Y 14	234 46.2	76 37.3	00.7	69 35.8	46.4	69 12.2	12.2	354 01.7	58.3	Altair	62 06.7	N 8 55.0
15	249 48.7	91 37.5 8 00.2		84 36.8 ..	45.8	84 14.2 ..	12.0	9 03.9 ..	58.3	Ankaa	353 13.8	S42 13.2
16	264 51.2	106 37.7 7 59.6		99 37.8	45.2	99 16.2	11.8	24 06.1	58.4	Antares	112 24.6	S26 27.8
17	279 53.6	121 37.9	59.0	114 38.9	44.6	114 18.2	11.7	39 08.4	58.4			
18	294 56.1	136 38.1 N 7 58.5		129 39.9 N 7 44.1		129 20.2 N 7 11.5		54 10.6 S18 58.5		Arcturus	145 54.7	N19 06.3
19	309 58.6	151 38.3	57.9	144 40.9	43.5	144 22.3	11.3	69 12.8	58.5	Atria	107 25.3	S69 03.3
20	325 01.0	166 38.5	57.3	159 41.9	42.9	159 24.3	11.1	84 15.0	58.6	Avior	234 17.4	S59 33.4
21	340 03.5	181 38.8 ..	56.8	174 43.0 ..	42.3	174 26.3 ..	10.9	99 17.2 ..	58.6	Bellatrix	278 30.2	N 6 21.7
22	355 06.0	196 39.0	56.2	189 44.0	41.7	189 28.3	10.8	114 19.4	58.7	Betelgeuse	270 59.5	N 7 24.5
23	10 08.4	211 39.2	55.6	204 45.0	41.1	204 30.3	10.6	129 21.6	58.7			
17 00	25 10.9	226 39.4 N 7 55.1		219 46.1 N 7 40.5		219 32.4 N 7 10.4		144 23.8 S18 58.8		Canopus	263 55.3	S52 42.1
01	40 13.4	241 39.6	54.5	234 47.1	40.0	234 34.4	10.2	159 26.0	58.9	Capella	280 31.8	N46 00.5
02	55 15.8	256 39.8	53.9	249 48.1	39.4	249 36.4	10.1	174 28.2	58.9	Deneb	49 30.2	N45 20.7
03	70 18.3	271 40.0 ..	53.4	264 49.1 ..	38.8	264 38.4 ..	09.9	189 30.4 ..	59.0	Denebola	182 32.4	N14 29.1
04	85 20.7	286 40.2	52.8	279 50.2	38.2	279 40.4	09.7	204 32.6	59.0	Diphda	348 54.0	S17 54.0
05	100 23.2	301 40.4	52.2	294 51.2	37.6	294 42.4	09.5	219 34.8	59.1			
06	115 25.7	316 40.6 N 7 51.6		309 52.2 N 7 37.0		309 44.5 N 7 09.3		234 37.0 S18 59.1		Dubhe	193 50.5	N61 39.8
07	130 28.1	331 40.8	51.1	324 53.2	36.4	324 46.5	09.2	249 39.2	59.2	Elnath	278 10.4	N28 37.0
S 08	145 30.6	346 41.0	50.5	339 54.3	35.9	339 48.5	09.0	264 41.4	59.2	Eltanin	90 45.6	N51 29.7
A 09	160 33.1	1 41.2 ..	49.9	354 55.3 ..	35.3	354 50.5 ..	08.8	279 43.6 ..	59.3	Enif	33 45.4	N 9 57.1
T 10	175 35.5	16 41.4	49.3	9 56.3	34.7	9 52.6	08.6	294 45.8	59.3	Fomalhaut	15 22.0	S29 32.3
U 11	190 38.0	31 41.6	48.7	24 57.4	34.1	24 54.6	08.5	309 48.0	59.4			
R 12	205 40.5	46 41.8 N 7 48.2		39 58.4 N 7 33.5		39 56.6 N 7 08.3		324 50.2 S18 59.5		Gacrux	171 59.6	S57 11.9
D 13	220 42.9	61 42.0	47.6	54 59.4	32.9	54 58.6	08.1	339 52.4	59.5	Gienah	175 51.0	S17 37.6
A 14	235 45.4	76 42.2	47.0	70 00.4	32.4	70 00.6	07.9	354 54.6	59.6	Hadar	148 46.2	S60 26.8
Y 15	250 47.8	91 42.4 ..	46.4	85 01.5 ..	31.8	85 02.7 ..	07.8	9 56.8 ..	59.6	Hamal	327 58.6	N23 32.2
16	265 50.3	106 42.6	45.8	100 02.5	31.2	100 04.7	07.6	24 59.1	59.7	Kaus Aust.	83 41.9	S34 22.5
17	280 52.8	121 42.8	45.2	115 03.5	30.6	115 06.7	07.4	40 01.3	59.7			
18	295 55.2	136 43.0 N 7 44.7		130 04.5 N 7 30.0		130 08.7 N 7 07.2		55 03.5 S18 59.8		Kochab	137 21.4	N74 05.7
19	310 57.7	151 43.1	44.1	145 05.6	29.4	145 10.7	07.0	70 05.7	59.8	Markab	13 36.5	N15 17.6
20	326 00.2	166 43.3	43.5	160 06.6	28.8	160 12.8	06.9	85 07.9 18 59.9		Menkar	314 13.1	N 4 09.1
21	341 02.6	181 43.5 ..	42.9	175 07.6 ..	28.3	175 14.8 ..	06.7	100 10.1 19 00.0		Menkent	148 06.1	S36 26.6
22	356 05.1	196 43.7	42.3	190 08.7	27.7	190 16.8	06.5	115 12.3	00.0	Miaplacidus	221 39.5	S69 46.7
23	11 07.6	211 43.9	41.7	205 09.7	27.1	205 18.8	06.3	130 14.5	00.1			
18 00	26 10.0	226 44.1 N 7 41.1		220 10.7 N 7 26.5		220 20.8 N 7 06.2		145 16.7 S19 00.1		Mirfak	308 37.6	N49 54.8
01	41 12.5	241 44.3	40.5	235 11.7	25.9	235 22.9	06.0	160 18.9	00.2	Nunki	75 56.5	S26 16.4
02	56 15.0	256 44.5	40.0	250 12.8	25.3	250 24.9	05.8	175 21.1	00.2	Peacock	53 16.8	S56 41.1
03	71 17.4	271 44.6 ..	39.4	265 13.8 ..	24.7	265 26.9 ..	05.6	190 23.3 ..	00.3	Pollux	243 25.9	N27 59.0
04	86 19.9	286 44.8	38.8	280 14.8	24.2	280 28.9	05.5	205 25.5	00.3	Procyon	244 58.1	N 5 11.0
05	101 22.3	301 45.0	38.2	295 15.9	23.6	295 31.0	05.3	220 27.7	00.4			
06	116 24.8	316 45.2 N 7 37.6		310 16.9 N 7 23.0		310 33.0 N 7 05.1		235 29.9 S19 00.4		Rasalhague	96 05.2	N12 33.3
07	131 27.3	331 45.4	37.0	325 17.9	22.4	325 35.0	04.9	250 32.1	00.5	Regulus	207 42.1	N11 53.4
08	146 29.7	346 45.6	36.4	340 19.0	21.8	340 37.0	04.8	265 34.3	00.6	Rigel	281 10.4	S 8 11.1
S 09	161 32.2	1 45.7 ..	35.8	355 20.0 ..	21.2	355 39.1 ..	04.6	280 36.5 ..	00.6	Rigil Kent.	139 50.1	S60 53.8
U 10	176 34.7	16 45.9	35.2	10 21.0	20.6	10 41.1	04.4	295 38.7	00.7	Sabik	102 10.9	S15 44.4
N 11	191 37.1	31 46.1	34.6	25 22.0	20.0	25 43.1	04.2	310 40.9	00.7			
D 12	206 39.6	46 46.3 N 7 34.0		40 23.1 N 7 19.5		40 45.1 N 7 04.0		325 43.1 S19 00.8		Schedar	349 38.0	N56 37.5
A 13	221 42.1	61 46.5	33.4	55 24.1	18.9	55 47.1	03.9	340 45.3	00.8	Shaula	96 20.0	S37 06.7
Y 14	236 44.5	76 46.6	32.8	70 25.1	18.3	70 49.2	03.7	355 47.5	00.9	Sirius	258 32.3	S16 44.3
15	251 47.0	91 46.8 ..	32.2	85 26.2 ..	17.7	85 51.2 ..	03.5	10 49.7 ..	00.9	Spica	158 29.9	S11 14.4
16	266 49.5	106 47.0	31.6	100 27.2	17.1	100 53.2	03.3	25 51.9	01.0	Suhail	222 51.4	S43 29.6
17	281 51.9	121 47.2	31.0	115 28.2	16.5	115 55.2	03.2	40 54.1	01.1			
18	296 54.4	136 47.3 N 7 30.4		130 29.3 N 7 15.9		130 57.3 N 7 03.0		55 56.3 S19 01.1		Vega	80 38.0	N38 48.4
19	311 56.8	151 47.5	29.8	145 30.3	15.4	145 59.3	02.8	70 58.5	01.2	Zuben'ubi	137 04.0	S16 06.2
20	326 59.3	166 47.7	29.2	160 31.3	14.8	161 01.3	02.6	86 00.7	01.2		SHA	Mer. Pass.
21	342 01.8	181 47.9 ..	28.6	175 32.4 ..	14.2	176 03.3 ..	02.5	101 02.9 ..	01.3		° ′	h m
22	357 04.2	196 48.0	28.0	190 33.4	13.6	191 05.4	02.3	116 05.1	01.3	Venus	201 28.5	8 53
23	12 06.7	211 48.2	27.4	205 34.4	13.0	206 07.4	02.1	131 07.3	01.4	Mars	194 35.2	9 20
	h m									Jupiter	194 21.5	9 21
Mer. Pass. 22 15.6		v 0.2 d 0.6		v 1.0 d 0.6		v 2.0 d 0.2		v 2.2 d 0.1		Saturn	119 12.9	14 20

UT	SUN GHA	SUN Dec	MOON GHA	v	MOON Dec	d	HP
	° ′	° ′	° ′	′	° ′	′	′
16 00	183 34.0	S 8 41.0	150 12.9	12.5	S14 55.6	5.5	54.8
01	198 34.1	41.9	164 44.4	12.5	15 01.1	5.5	54.8
02	213 34.3	42.8	179 15.9	12.3	15 06.6	5.3	54.8
03	228 34.4	.. 43.7	193 47.2	12.4	15 11.9	5.3	54.8
04	243 34.5	44.7	208 18.6	12.3	15 17.2	5.3	54.9
05	258 34.7	45.6	222 49.9	12.3	15 22.5	5.2	54.9
06	273 34.8	S 8 46.5	237 21.2	12.2	S15 27.7	5.1	54.9
07	288 35.0	47.4	251 52.4	12.2	15 32.8	5.0	54.9
08	303 35.1	48.4	266 23.6	12.1	15 37.8	5.0	54.9
F 09	318 35.2	.. 49.3	280 54.7	12.1	15 42.8	4.9	54.9
R 10	333 35.4	50.2	295 25.8	12.1	15 47.7	4.8	55.0
I 11	348 35.5	51.1	309 56.9	12.0	15 52.5	4.7	55.0
D 12	3 35.6	S 8 52.0	324 27.9	12.0	S15 57.2	4.7	55.0
A 13	18 35.8	53.0	338 58.9	11.9	16 01.9	4.6	55.0
Y 14	33 35.9	53.9	353 29.8	11.9	16 06.5	4.5	55.0
15	48 36.0	.. 54.8	8 00.7	11.8	16 11.0	4.5	55.1
16	63 36.2	55.7	22 31.5	11.8	16 15.5	4.3	55.1
17	78 36.3	56.6	37 02.3	11.8	16 19.8	4.3	55.1
18	93 36.4	S 8 57.6	51 33.1	11.7	S16 24.1	4.3	55.1
19	108 36.6	58.5	66 03.8	11.7	16 28.4	4.1	55.1
20	123 36.7	8 59.4	80 34.5	11.6	16 32.5	4.1	55.1
21	138 36.8	9 00.3	95 05.1	11.6	16 36.6	4.0	55.2
22	153 36.9	01.2	109 35.7	11.6	16 40.6	3.9	55.2
23	168 37.1	02.1	124 06.3	11.5	16 44.5	3.8	55.2
17 00	183 37.2	S 9 03.1	138 36.8	11.5	S16 48.3	3.8	55.2
01	198 37.3	04.0	153 07.3	11.4	16 52.1	3.6	55.2
02	213 37.5	04.9	167 37.7	11.4	16 55.7	3.6	55.3
03	228 37.6	.. 05.8	182 08.1	11.3	16 59.3	3.5	55.3
04	243 37.7	06.7	196 38.4	11.4	17 02.8	3.5	55.3
05	258 37.9	07.6	211 08.8	11.2	17 06.3	3.3	55.3
06	273 38.0	S 9 08.6	225 39.0	11.2	S17 09.6	3.3	55.3
S 07	288 38.1	09.5	240 09.2	11.2	17 12.9	3.1	55.4
A 08	303 38.2	10.4	254 39.4	11.2	17 16.0	3.1	55.4
T 09	318 38.4	.. 11.3	269 09.6	11.1	17 19.1	3.0	55.4
U 10	333 38.5	12.2	283 39.7	11.1	17 22.1	3.0	55.4
R 11	348 38.6	13.1	298 09.8	11.0	17 25.1	2.8	55.5
D 12	3 38.8	S 9 14.1	312 39.8	11.0	S17 27.9	2.8	55.5
A 13	18 38.9	15.0	327 09.8	10.9	17 30.7	2.6	55.5
Y 14	33 39.0	15.9	341 39.7	10.9	17 33.3	2.6	55.5
15	48 39.1	.. 16.8	356 09.6	10.9	17 35.9	2.5	55.5
16	63 39.3	17.7	10 39.5	10.8	17 38.4	2.4	55.6
17	78 39.4	18.6	25 09.3	10.8	17 40.8	2.3	55.6
18	93 39.5	S 9 19.5	39 39.1	10.8	S17 43.1	2.3	55.6
19	108 39.6	20.5	54 08.9	10.7	17 45.4	2.1	55.6
20	123 39.8	21.4	68 38.6	10.7	17 47.5	2.1	55.7
21	138 39.9	.. 22.3	83 08.3	10.6	17 49.6	1.9	55.7
22	153 40.0	23.2	97 37.9	10.6	17 51.5	1.9	55.7
23	168 40.1	24.1	112 07.5	10.6	17 53.4	1.8	55.7
18 00	183 40.3	S 9 25.0	126 37.1	10.5	S17 55.2	1.7	55.7
01	198 40.4	25.9	141 06.6	10.5	17 56.9	1.6	55.8
02	213 40.5	26.8	155 36.1	10.5	17 58.5	1.5	55.8
03	228 40.6	.. 27.7	170 05.6	10.4	18 00.0	1.4	55.8
04	243 40.8	28.7	184 35.0	10.4	18 01.4	1.3	55.8
05	258 40.9	29.6	199 04.4	10.4	18 02.7	1.3	55.9
06	273 41.0	S 9 30.5	213 33.8	10.3	S18 04.0	1.1	55.9
07	288 41.1	31.4	228 03.1	10.3	18 05.1	1.0	55.9
08	303 41.3	32.3	242 32.4	10.3	18 06.1	1.0	55.9
S 09	318 41.4	.. 33.2	257 01.7	10.2	18 07.1	0.8	55.9
U 10	333 41.5	34.1	271 30.9	10.2	18 07.9	0.8	56.0
N 11	348 41.6	35.0	286 00.1	10.1	18 08.7	0.7	56.0
D 12	3 41.7	S 9 35.9	300 29.2	10.2	S18 09.4	0.6	56.0
A 13	18 41.9	36.8	314 58.4	10.1	18 10.0	0.4	56.1
Y 14	33 42.0	37.8	329 27.5	10.0	18 10.4	0.4	56.1
15	48 42.1	.. 38.7	343 56.5	10.0	18 10.8	0.3	56.1
16	63 42.2	39.6	358 25.5	10.0	18 11.1	0.2	56.1
17	78 42.3	40.5	12 54.5	10.0	18 11.3	0.1	56.2
18	93 42.5	S 9 41.4	27 23.5	10.0	S18 11.4	0.1	56.2
19	108 42.6	42.3	41 52.5	9.9	18 11.4	0.1	56.2
20	123 42.7	43.2	56 21.4	9.8	18 11.3	0.2	56.3
21	138 42.8	.. 44.1	70 50.2	9.9	18 11.1	0.3	56.3
22	153 42.9	45.0	85 19.1	9.8	18 10.8	0.4	56.3
23	168 43.1	45.9	99 47.9	9.8	S18 10.4	0.5	56.3
	SD 16.1	d 0.9	SD 15.0		15.1		15.3

Lat.	Twilight Naut.	Twilight Civil	Sunrise	Moonrise 16	17	18	19
°	h m	h m	h m	h m	h m	h m	h m
N 72	05 02	06 21	07 32	12 34	14 30	■■	16 34
N 70	05 05	06 16	07 20	11 51	13 15	14 24	15 06
68	05 08	06 12	07 10	11 22	12 38	13 41	14 27
66	05 09	06 09	07 02	11 00	12 11	13 12	14 00
64	05 11	06 06	06 55	10 43	11 51	12 50	13 39
62	05 12	06 03	06 49	10 29	11 35	12 33	13 22
60	05 13	06 01	06 43	10 17	11 21	12 18	13 08
N 58	05 13	05 59	06 39	10 07	11 09	12 06	12 56
56	05 14	05 57	06 35	09 58	10 59	11 55	12 45
54	05 14	05 55	06 31	09 50	10 50	11 46	12 36
52	05 14	05 53	06 27	09 43	10 42	11 37	12 28
50	05 14	05 52	06 24	09 37	10 35	11 30	12 20
45	05 14	05 48	06 18	09 23	10 20	11 14	12 04
N 40	05 13	05 45	06 12	09 12	10 07	11 01	11 51
35	05 12	05 42	06 07	09 02	09 56	10 49	11 40
30	05 11	05 39	06 03	08 54	09 47	10 39	11 31
20	05 07	05 33	05 55	08 40	09 31	10 23	11 14
N 10	05 03	05 27	05 49	08 27	09 17	10 08	10 59
0	04 57	05 21	05 42	08 15	09 04	09 54	10 46
S 10	04 49	05 14	05 36	08 04	08 51	09 41	10 32
20	04 40	05 06	05 28	07 51	08 37	09 26	10 18
30	04 27	04 56	05 20	07 37	08 21	09 09	10 01
35	04 19	04 50	05 15	07 29	08 12	08 59	09 52
40	04 09	04 42	05 10	07 20	08 02	08 48	09 41
45	03 56	04 33	05 04	07 09	07 49	08 35	09 28
S 50	03 41	04 22	04 56	06 56	07 34	08 20	09 12
52	03 33	04 17	04 52	06 50	07 27	08 12	09 04
54	03 24	04 11	04 48	06 43	07 20	08 04	08 56
56	03 14	04 04	04 44	06 35	07 11	07 55	08 47
58	03 02	03 57	04 39	06 27	07 01	07 44	08 36
S 60	02 48	03 48	04 34	06 17	06 50	07 32	08 24

Lat.	Sunset	Twilight Civil	Twilight Naut.	Moonset 16	17	18	19
°	h m	h m	h m	h m	h m	h m	h m
N 72	15 57	17 08	18 26	16 11	15 57	■■	17 27
N 70	16 09	17 13	18 23	16 55	17 12	17 49	18 54
68	16 20	17 17	18 21	17 25	17 50	18 32	19 33
66	16 28	17 21	18 20	17 47	18 17	19 00	20 01
64	16 35	17 24	18 18	18 04	18 37	19 22	20 21
62	16 41	17 26	18 18	18 19	18 54	19 40	20 38
60	16 46	17 29	18 17	18 31	19 08	19 54	20 52
N 58	16 51	17 31	18 16	18 41	19 20	20 07	21 04
56	16 55	17 33	18 16	18 51	19 30	20 18	21 14
54	16 59	17 35	18 16	18 59	19 39	20 27	21 23
52	17 03	17 37	18 16	19 06	19 47	20 35	21 31
50	17 06	17 38	18 16	19 13	19 55	20 43	21 39
45	17 12	17 42	18 16	19 27	20 10	20 59	21 54
N 40	17 17	17 45	18 17	19 39	20 23	21 12	22 07
35	17 23	17 49	18 18	19 49	20 34	21 24	22 18
30	17 28	17 52	18 20	19 58	20 44	21 34	22 27
20	17 35	17 58	18 23	20 13	21 00	21 50	22 44
N 10	17 42	18 03	18 28	20 26	21 14	22 05	22 58
0	17 49	18 10	18 34	20 39	21 28	22 19	23 11
S 10	17 55	18 17	18 42	20 51	21 41	22 33	23 24
20	18 03	18 25	18 51	21 04	21 56	22 47	23 38
30	18 11	18 36	19 04	21 20	22 12	23 04	23 54
35	18 16	18 42	19 13	21 28	22 22	23 14	24 04
40	18 22	18 50	19 23	21 38	22 33	23 25	24 14
45	18 28	18 59	19 36	21 50	22 46	23 38	24 27
S 50	18 36	19 10	19 52	22 05	23 01	23 54	24 42
52	18 40	19 15	20 00	22 11	23 09	24 01	00 01
54	18 44	19 21	20 09	22 19	23 17	24 10	00 10
56	18 48	19 28	20 19	22 27	23 26	24 19	00 19
58	18 53	19 36	20 31	22 37	23 36	24 29	00 29
S 60	18 59	19 45	20 45	22 48	23 48	24 42	00 42

Day	SUN Eqn. of Time 00h	12h	Mer. Pass.	MOON Mer. Pass. Upper	Lower	Age	Phase
d	m s	m s	h m	h m	h m	d	%
16	14 16	14 22	11 46	14 27	02 03	03	11
17	14 29	14 35	11 45	15 16	02 51	04	18
18	14 41	14 47	11 45	16 07	03 41	05	26

UT	ARIES	VENUS −4.6		MARS +1.7		JUPITER −1.8		SATURN +0.6		STARS		
	GHA	GHA	Dec	GHA	Dec	GHA	Dec	GHA	Dec	Name	SHA	Dec
d h	° ′	° ′	° ′	° ′	° ′	° ′	° ′	° ′	° ′		° ′	° ′
19 00	27 09.2	226 48.4	N 7 26.7	220 35.4	N 7 12.4	221 09.4	N 7 01.9	146 09.5	S19 01.4	Acamar	315 16.8	S40 14.5
01	42 11.6	241 48.5	.. 26.1	235 36.5	.. 11.8	236 11.4	.. 01.8	161 11.7	.. 01.5	Achernar	335 25.1	S57 09.4
02	57 14.1	256 48.7	25.5	250 37.5	11.2	251 13.5	01.6	176 13.9	01.5	Acrux	173 08.0	S63 11.0
03	72 16.6	271 48.9	.. 24.9	265 38.5	.. 10.7	266 15.5	.. 01.4	191 16.1	.. 01.6	Adhara	255 11.2	S28 59.6
04	87 19.0	286 49.0	24.3	280 39.6	10.1	281 17.5	01.2	206 18.3	01.7	Aldebaran	290 47.3	N16 32.3
05	102 21.5	301 49.2	23.7	295 40.6	09.5	296 19.5	01.1	221 20.5	01.7			
06	117 23.9	316 49.4	N 7 23.1	310 41.6	N 7 08.9	311 21.6	N 7 00.9	236 22.7	S19 01.8	Alioth	166 20.0	N55 52.5
07	132 26.4	331 49.5	22.5	325 42.7	08.3	326 23.6	00.7	251 24.9	01.8	Alkaid	152 58.2	N49 14.2
M 08	147 28.9	346 49.7	21.8	340 43.7	07.7	341 25.6	00.5	266 27.1	01.9	Al Na'ir	27 41.6	S46 53.1
O 09	162 31.3	1 49.9	.. 21.2	355 44.7	.. 07.1	356 27.6	.. 00.4	281 29.3	.. 01.9	Alnilam	275 44.6	S 1 11.6
N 10	177 33.8	16 50.0	20.6	10 45.8	06.5	11 29.7	00.2	296 31.5	02.0	Alphard	217 54.7	S 8 43.6
D 11	192 36.3	31 50.2	20.0	25 46.8	06.0	26 31.7	7 00.0	311 33.7	02.0			
A 12	207 38.7	46 50.3	N 7 19.4	40 47.8	N 7 05.4	41 33.7	N 6 59.8	326 35.9	S19 02.1	Alphecca	126 10.0	N26 40.0
Y 13	222 41.2	61 50.5	18.8	55 48.9	04.8	56 35.7	59.7	341 38.1	02.2	Alpheratz	357 41.5	N29 10.8
14	237 43.7	76 50.7	18.1	70 49.9	04.2	71 37.8	59.5	356 40.3	02.2	Altair	62 06.7	N 8 55.0
15	252 46.1	91 50.8	.. 17.5	85 50.9	.. 03.6	86 39.8	.. 59.3	11 42.5	.. 02.3	Ankaa	353 13.8	S42 13.2
16	267 48.6	106 51.0	16.9	100 52.0	03.0	101 41.8	59.1	26 44.7	02.3	Antares	112 24.6	S26 27.8
17	282 51.1	121 51.1	16.3	115 53.0	02.4	116 43.9	59.0	41 46.9	02.4			
18	297 53.5	136 51.3	N 7 15.6	130 54.0	N 7 01.8	131 45.9	N 6 58.8	56 49.1	S19 02.4	Arcturus	145 54.7	N19 06.3
19	312 56.0	151 51.5	15.0	145 55.1	01.3	146 47.9	58.6	71 51.3	02.5	Atria	107 25.3	S69 03.3
20	327 58.4	166 51.6	14.4	160 56.1	00.7	161 49.9	58.4	86 53.5	02.5	Avior	234 17.4	S59 33.4
21	343 00.9	181 51.8	.. 13.8	175 57.1	7 00.1	176 52.0	.. 58.3	101 55.7	.. 02.6	Bellatrix	278 30.1	N 6 21.7
22	358 03.4	196 51.9	13.1	190 58.2	6 59.5	191 54.0	58.1	116 57.9	02.7	Betelgeuse	270 59.4	N 7 24.5
23	13 05.8	211 52.1	12.5	205 59.2	58.9	206 56.0	57.9	132 00.1	02.7			
20 00	28 08.3	226 52.2	N 7 11.9	221 00.2	N 6 58.3	221 58.0	N 6 57.7	147 02.3	S19 02.8	Canopus	263 55.2	S52 42.1
01	43 10.8	241 52.4	11.3	236 01.3	57.7	237 00.1	57.6	162 04.5	02.8	Capella	280 31.8	N46 00.5
02	58 13.2	256 52.5	10.6	251 02.3	57.1	252 02.1	57.4	177 06.7	02.9	Deneb	49 30.3	N45 20.7
03	73 15.7	271 52.7	.. 10.0	266 03.3	.. 56.6	267 04.1	.. 57.2	192 08.9	.. 02.9	Denebola	182 32.4	N14 29.1
04	88 18.2	286 52.8	09.4	281 04.4	56.0	282 06.2	57.0	207 11.1	03.0	Diphda	348 54.0	S17 54.0
05	103 20.6	301 53.0	08.7	296 05.4	55.4	297 08.2	56.9	222 13.3	03.0			
06	118 23.1	316 53.1	N 7 08.1	311 06.4	N 6 54.8	312 10.2	N 6 56.7	237 15.5	S19 03.1	Dubhe	193 50.4	N61 39.8
07	133 25.6	331 53.3	07.5	326 07.5	54.2	327 12.2	56.5	252 17.7	03.2	Elnath	278 10.4	N28 37.0
T 08	148 28.0	346 53.4	06.8	341 08.5	53.6	342 14.3	56.3	267 19.9	03.2	Eltanin	90 45.7	N51 29.7
U 09	163 30.5	1 53.6	.. 06.2	356 09.5	.. 53.0	357 16.3	.. 56.2	282 22.1	.. 03.3	Enif	33 45.4	N 9 57.1
E 10	178 32.9	16 53.7	05.6	11 10.6	52.4	12 18.3	56.0	297 24.3	03.3	Fomalhaut	15 22.0	S29 32.3
S 11	193 35.4	31 53.9	04.9	26 11.6	51.9	27 20.4	55.8	312 26.5	03.4			
D 12	208 37.9	46 54.0	N 7 04.3	41 12.7	N 6 51.3	42 22.4	N 6 55.6	327 28.7	S19 03.4	Gacrux	171 59.6	S57 11.9
A 13	223 40.3	61 54.2	03.7	56 13.7	50.7	57 24.4	55.5	342 30.9	03.5	Gienah	175 51.0	S17 37.6
Y 14	238 42.8	76 54.3	03.0	71 14.7	50.1	72 26.4	55.3	357 33.1	03.5	Hadar	148 46.2	S60 26.8
15	253 45.3	91 54.4	.. 02.4	86 15.8	.. 49.5	87 28.5	.. 55.1	12 35.3	.. 03.6	Hamal	327 58.6	N23 32.2
16	268 47.7	106 54.6	01.7	101 16.8	48.9	102 30.5	55.0	27 37.5	03.6	Kaus Aust.	83 41.9	S34 22.5
17	283 50.2	121 54.7	01.1	116 17.8	48.3	117 32.5	54.8	42 39.7	03.7			
18	298 52.7	136 54.9	N 7 00.5	131 18.9	N 6 47.7	132 34.6	N 6 54.6	57 41.9	S19 03.8	Kochab	137 21.4	N74 05.7
19	313 55.1	151 55.0	6 59.8	146 19.9	47.1	147 36.6	54.4	72 44.1	03.8	Markab	13 36.5	N15 17.6
20	328 57.6	166 55.1	59.2	161 20.9	46.6	162 38.6	54.3	87 46.2	03.9	Menkar	314 13.1	N 4 09.1
21	344 00.1	181 55.3	.. 58.5	176 22.0	.. 46.0	177 40.7	.. 54.1	102 48.4	.. 03.9	Menkent	148 06.1	S36 26.6
22	359 02.5	196 55.4	57.9	191 23.0	45.4	192 42.7	53.9	117 50.6	04.0	Miaplacidus	221 39.5	S69 46.7
23	14 05.0	211 55.6	57.2	206 24.0	44.8	207 44.7	53.7	132 52.8	04.0			
21 00	29 07.4	226 55.7	N 6 56.6	221 25.1	N 6 44.2	222 46.8	N 6 53.5	147 55.0	S19 04.1	Mirfak	308 37.6	N49 54.8
01	44 09.9	241 55.8	56.0	236 26.1	43.6	237 48.8	53.4	162 57.2	04.1	Nunki	75 56.5	S26 16.4
02	59 12.4	256 56.0	55.3	251 27.2	43.0	252 50.8	53.2	177 59.4	04.2	Peacock	53 16.8	S56 41.1
03	74 14.8	271 56.1	.. 54.7	266 28.2	.. 42.4	267 52.8	.. 53.0	193 01.6	.. 04.3	Pollux	243 25.8	N27 59.0
04	89 17.3	286 56.2	54.0	281 29.2	41.8	282 54.9	52.9	208 03.8	04.3	Procyon	244 58.1	N 5 11.0
05	104 19.8	301 56.4	53.4	296 30.3	41.3	297 56.9	52.7	223 06.0	04.4			
06	119 22.2	316 56.5	N 6 52.7	311 31.3	N 6 40.7	312 58.9	N 6 52.5	238 08.2	S19 04.4	Rasalhague	96 05.2	N12 33.3
W 07	134 24.7	331 56.6	52.1	326 32.3	40.1	328 01.0	52.4	253 10.4	04.5	Regulus	207 42.0	N11 53.4
E 08	149 27.2	346 56.8	51.4	341 33.4	39.5	343 03.0	52.2	268 12.6	04.5	Rigel	281 10.3	S 8 11.1
D 09	164 29.6	1 56.9	.. 50.8	356 34.4	.. 38.9	358 05.0	.. 52.0	283 14.8	.. 04.6	Rigil Kent.	139 50.1	S60 53.8
N 10	179 32.1	16 57.0	50.1	11 35.5	38.3	13 07.1	51.8	298 17.0	04.6	Sabik	102 11.0	S15 44.4
E 11	194 34.5	31 57.2	49.4	26 36.5	37.7	28 09.1	51.7	313 19.2	04.7			
S 12	209 37.0	46 57.3	N 6 48.8	41 37.5	N 6 37.1	43 11.1	N 6 51.5	328 21.4	S19 04.8	Schedar	349 38.0	N56 37.5
D 13	224 39.5	61 57.4	48.1	56 38.6	36.5	58 13.2	51.3	343 23.6	04.8	Shaula	96 20.0	S37 06.7
A 14	239 41.9	76 57.5	47.5	71 39.6	36.0	73 15.2	51.1	358 25.8	04.9	Sirius	258 32.2	S16 44.3
Y 15	254 44.4	91 57.7	.. 46.8	86 40.6	.. 35.4	88 17.2	.. 51.0	13 28.0	.. 04.9	Spica	158 29.9	S11 14.4
16	269 46.9	106 57.8	46.2	101 41.7	34.8	103 19.3	50.8	28 30.2	05.0	Suhail	222 51.4	S43 29.6
17	284 49.3	121 57.9	45.5	116 42.7	34.2	118 21.3	50.6	43 32.4	05.0			
18	299 51.8	136 58.0	N 6 44.8	131 43.8	N 6 33.6	133 23.3	N 6 50.5	58 34.6	S19 05.1	Vega	80 38.0	N38 48.4
19	314 54.3	151 58.2	44.2	146 44.8	33.0	148 25.4	50.3	73 36.8	05.1	Zuben'ubi	137 04.0	S16 06.2
20	329 56.7	166 58.3	43.5	161 45.8	32.4	163 27.4	50.1	88 38.9	05.2			
21	344 59.2	181 58.4	.. 42.9	176 46.9	.. 31.8	178 29.4	.. 49.9	103 41.1	.. 05.3			
22	0 01.7	196 58.5	42.2	191 47.9	31.2	193 31.5	49.8	118 43.3	05.3			
23	15 04.1	211 58.7	41.5	206 49.0	30.6	208 33.5	49.6	133 45.5	05.4			

							SHA	Mer. Pass.
							° ′	h m
Venus							198 43.9	8 52
Mars							192 51.9	9 15
Jupiter							193 49.7	9 11
Saturn							118 54.0	14 10

	h m					
Mer. Pass.	22 03.8	v 0.1 d 0.6	v 1.0 d 0.6	v 2.0 d 0.2	v 2.2 d 0.1

UT	SUN GHA	SUN Dec	MOON GHA	v	Dec	d	HP
d h	° ′	° ′	° ′	′	° ′	′	′
19 00	183 43.2	S 9 46.8	114 16.7	9.8	S18 09.9	0.6	56.4
01	198 43.3	47.7	128 45.5	9.7	18 09.3	0.7	56.4
02	213 43.4	48.6	143 14.2	9.7	18 08.6	0.7	56.4
03	228 43.5	.. 49.5	157 42.9	9.7	18 07.9	0.9	56.5
04	243 43.7	50.4	172 11.6	9.7	18 07.0	1.0	56.5
05	258 43.8	51.4	186 40.3	9.6	18 06.0	1.1	56.5
06	273 43.9	S 9 52.3	201 08.9	9.6	S18 04.9	1.2	56.5
M 07	288 44.0	53.2	215 37.5	9.6	18 03.7	1.2	56.6
O 08	303 44.1	54.1	230 06.1	9.5	18 02.5	1.4	56.6
N 09	318 44.2	.. 55.0	244 34.6	9.6	18 01.1	1.5	56.6
D 10	333 44.4	55.9	259 03.2	9.5	17 59.6	1.6	56.7
A 11	348 44.5	56.8	273 31.7	9.5	17 58.0	1.7	56.7
Y 12	3 44.6	S 9 57.7	288 00.2	9.4	S17 56.3	1.7	56.7
13	18 44.7	58.6	302 28.6	9.5	17 54.6	1.9	56.7
14	33 44.8	9 59.5	316 57.1	9.4	17 52.7	2.0	56.8
15	48 44.9	10 00.4	331 25.5	9.4	17 50.7	2.1	56.8
16	63 45.0	01.3	345 53.9	9.4	17 48.6	2.2	56.8
17	78 45.2	02.2	0 22.3	9.3	17 46.4	2.2	56.9
18	93 45.3	S10 03.1	14 50.6	9.4	S17 44.2	2.4	56.9
19	108 45.4	04.0	29 19.0	9.3	17 41.8	2.5	56.9
20	123 45.5	04.9	43 47.3	9.3	17 39.3	2.6	57.0
21	138 45.6	.. 05.8	58 15.6	9.2	17 36.7	2.7	57.0
22	153 45.7	06.7	72 43.8	9.3	17 34.0	2.8	57.0
23	168 45.8	07.6	87 12.1	9.2	17 31.2	2.9	57.0
20 00	183 45.9	S10 08.5	101 40.3	9.2	S17 28.3	2.9	57.1
01	198 46.1	09.4	116 08.5	9.2	17 25.4	3.1	57.1
02	213 46.2	10.3	130 36.7	9.2	17 22.3	3.2	57.1
03	228 46.3	.. 11.2	145 04.9	9.2	17 19.1	3.3	57.2
04	243 46.4	12.1	159 33.1	9.1	17 15.8	3.4	57.2
05	258 46.5	13.0	174 01.2	9.2	17 12.4	3.5	57.2
06	273 46.6	S10 13.9	188 29.4	9.1	S17 08.9	3.6	57.3
T 07	288 46.7	14.8	202 57.5	9.1	17 05.3	3.7	57.3
U 08	303 46.8	15.7	217 25.6	9.0	17 01.6	3.8	57.3
E 09	318 46.9	.. 16.6	231 53.6	9.1	16 57.8	3.9	57.4
S 10	333 47.1	17.5	246 21.7	9.1	16 53.9	3.9	57.4
D 11	348 47.2	18.4	260 49.8	9.0	16 50.0	4.1	57.4
A 12	3 47.3	S10 19.3	275 17.8	9.0	S16 45.9	4.2	57.5
Y 13	18 47.4	20.2	289 45.8	9.0	16 41.7	4.3	57.5
14	33 47.5	21.1	304 13.8	9.0	16 37.4	4.4	57.5
15	48 47.6	.. 22.0	318 41.8	9.0	16 33.0	4.5	57.6
16	63 47.7	22.9	333 09.8	9.0	16 28.5	4.6	57.6
17	78 47.8	23.8	347 37.8	9.0	16 23.9	4.7	57.6
18	93 47.9	S10 24.7	2 05.8	8.9	S16 19.2	4.8	57.7
19	108 48.0	25.5	16 33.7	8.9	16 14.4	4.9	57.7
20	123 48.1	26.4	31 01.6	9.0	16 09.5	5.0	57.7
21	138 48.2	.. 27.3	45 29.6	8.9	16 04.5	5.0	57.8
22	153 48.3	28.2	59 57.5	8.9	15 59.5	5.2	57.8
23	168 48.4	29.1	74 25.4	8.9	15 54.3	5.3	57.8
21 00	183 48.6	S10 30.0	88 53.3	8.8	S15 49.0	5.4	57.9
01	198 48.7	30.9	103 21.1	8.9	15 43.6	5.5	57.9
02	213 48.8	31.8	117 49.0	8.9	15 38.1	5.5	57.9
03	228 48.9	.. 32.7	132 16.9	8.8	15 32.6	5.7	58.0
04	243 49.0	33.6	146 44.7	8.9	15 26.9	5.8	58.0
05	258 49.1	34.5	161 12.6	8.8	15 21.1	5.8	58.0
06	273 49.2	S10 35.4	175 40.4	8.8	S15 15.3	6.0	58.1
W 07	288 49.3	36.3	190 08.2	8.8	15 09.3	6.0	58.1
E 08	303 49.4	37.2	204 36.0	8.8	15 03.3	6.2	58.1
D 09	318 49.5	.. 38.1	219 03.8	8.8	14 57.1	6.2	58.2
N 10	333 49.6	38.9	233 31.6	8.8	14 50.9	6.4	58.2
E 11	348 49.7	39.8	247 59.4	8.8	14 44.5	6.4	58.2
S 12	3 49.8	S10 40.7	262 27.2	8.8	S14 38.1	6.5	58.3
D 13	18 49.9	41.6	276 55.0	8.7	14 31.6	6.5	58.3
A 14	33 50.0	42.5	291 22.7	8.8	14 25.0	6.7	58.4
Y 15	48 50.1	.. 43.4	305 50.5	8.7	14 18.3	6.8	58.4
16	63 50.2	44.3	320 18.2	8.8	14 11.5	6.9	58.4
17	78 50.3	45.2	334 46.0	8.7	14 04.6	7.0	58.5
18	93 50.4	S10 46.1	349 13.7	8.7	S13 57.6	7.1	58.5
19	108 50.5	46.9	3 41.4	8.7	13 50.5	7.1	58.5
20	123 50.6	47.8	18 09.1	8.8	13 43.4	7.3	58.6
21	138 50.7	.. 48.7	32 36.9	8.7	13 36.1	7.3	58.6
22	153 50.8	49.6	47 04.6	8.7	13 28.8	7.5	58.6
23	168 50.9	50.5	61 32.3	8.7	S13 21.3	7.5	58.7
	SD 16.1	d 0.9	SD 15.5		15.7		15.9

Lat.	Twilight Naut.	Twilight Civil	Sunrise	Moonrise 19	20	21	22
°	h m	h m	h m	h m	h m	h m	h m
N 72	05 15	06 34	07 47	16 34	16 14	16 06	16 01
N 70	05 17	06 28	07 33	15 06	15 27	15 37	15 42
68	05 18	06 23	07 21	14 27	14 57	15 15	15 28
66	05 19	06 18	07 12	14 00	14 34	14 58	15 16
64	05 19	06 14	07 04	13 39	14 16	14 44	15 06
62	05 19	06 11	06 57	13 22	14 01	14 32	14 57
60	05 20	06 08	06 51	13 08	13 49	14 22	14 50
N 58	05 20	06 05	06 45	12 56	13 38	14 13	14 43
56	05 20	06 03	06 41	12 45	13 28	14 05	14 37
54	05 19	06 00	06 37	12 36	13 20	13 58	14 32
52	05 19	05 58	06 33	12 28	13 13	13 52	14 27
50	05 19	05 56	06 29	12 20	13 06	13 46	14 23
45	05 18	05 52	06 22	12 04	12 51	13 34	14 14
N 40	05 16	05 48	06 15	11 51	12 39	13 24	14 06
35	05 15	05 44	06 10	11 40	12 29	13 15	13 59
30	05 13	05 41	06 05	11 31	12 20	13 08	13 53
20	05 08	05 34	05 56	11 14	12 05	12 54	13 43
N 10	05 03	05 27	05 49	10 59	11 51	12 43	13 34
0	04 56	05 21	05 42	10 46	11 39	12 32	13 26
S 10	04 48	05 13	05 34	10 32	11 26	12 21	13 17
20	04 37	05 04	05 26	10 18	11 12	12 09	13 08
30	04 23	04 52	05 17	10 01	10 57	11 56	12 58
35	04 15	04 46	05 12	09 52	10 48	11 48	12 52
40	04 04	04 38	05 06	09 41	10 38	11 39	12 45
45	03 51	04 28	04 58	09 28	10 26	11 29	12 37
S 50	03 33	04 16	04 50	09 12	10 11	11 17	12 27
52	03 25	04 10	04 46	09 04	10 04	11 11	12 23
54	03 15	04 03	04 42	08 56	09 57	11 04	12 18
56	03 04	03 56	04 37	08 47	09 48	10 57	12 13
58	02 52	03 48	04 31	08 36	09 38	10 49	12 07
S 60	02 36	03 39	04 25	08 24	09 27	10 40	12 00

Lat.	Sunset	Twilight Civil	Twilight Naut.	Moonset 19	20	21	22
°	h m	h m	h m	h m	h m	h m	h m
N 72	15 41	16 54	18 12	17 27	19 38	21 37	23 35
N 70	15 55	17 00	18 11	18 54	20 24	22 05	23 52
68	16 07	17 06	18 10	19 33	20 54	22 26	24 05
66	16 17	17 10	18 09	20 01	21 16	22 42	24 16
64	16 25	17 14	18 09	20 21	21 33	22 56	24 25
62	16 32	17 18	18 09	20 38	21 48	23 07	24 32
60	16 38	17 21	18 09	20 52	22 00	23 16	24 39
N 58	16 43	17 23	18 09	21 04	22 10	23 25	24 45
56	16 48	17 26	18 09	21 14	22 19	23 32	24 50
54	16 52	17 28	18 09	21 23	22 27	23 38	24 54
52	16 56	17 31	18 10	21 31	22 35	23 44	24 59
50	17 00	17 33	18 10	21 39	22 41	23 49	25 02
45	17 07	17 37	18 11	21 54	22 55	24 01	00 01
N 40	17 14	17 41	18 13	22 07	23 06	24 10	00 10
35	17 19	17 45	18 15	22 18	23 16	24 18	00 18
30	17 24	17 49	18 17	22 27	23 25	24 25	00 25
20	17 33	17 55	18 21	22 44	23 39	24 37	00 37
N 10	17 41	18 02	18 27	22 58	23 52	24 48	00 48
0	17 48	18 09	18 34	23 11	24 04	00 04	00 57
S 10	17 56	18 17	18 42	23 24	24 16	00 16	01 07
20	18 04	18 26	18 53	23 38	24 28	00 28	01 18
30	18 13	18 38	19 07	23 54	24 43	00 43	01 29
35	18 19	18 45	19 16	24 04	00 04	00 51	01 36
40	18 25	18 53	19 27	24 14	00 14	01 01	01 44
45	18 32	19 03	19 40	24 27	00 27	01 12	01 53
S 50	18 41	19 15	19 58	24 42	00 42	01 25	02 03
52	18 45	19 21	20 06	00 01	00 49	01 31	02 08
54	18 49	19 28	20 16	00 10	00 57	01 38	02 13
56	18 54	19 35	20 27	00 19	01 05	01 45	02 19
58	19 00	19 44	20 41	00 29	01 15	01 54	02 26
S 60	19 06	19 53	20 57	00 42	01 27	02 04	02 34

Day	SUN Eqn. of Time 00h	SUN Eqn. of Time 12h	SUN Mer. Pass.	MOON Mer. Pass. Upper	MOON Mer. Pass. Lower	Age	Phase
d	m s	m s	h m	h m	h m	d	%
19	14 52	14 58	11 45	16 58	04 32	06	36
20	15 04	15 09	11 45	17 51	05 25	07	46
21	15 14	15 19	11 45	18 45	06 18	08	57

UT	ARIES GHA	VENUS −4.5 GHA	VENUS Dec	MARS +1.7 GHA	MARS Dec	JUPITER −1.8 GHA	JUPITER Dec	SATURN +0.6 GHA	SATURN Dec	STARS Name	SHA	Dec
22 00	30 06.6	226 58.8	N 6 40.9	221 50.0	N 6 30.1	223 35.5	N 6 49.4	148 47.7	S19 05.4	Acamar	315 16.8	S40 14.5
01	45 09.0	241 58.9	40.2	236 51.0	29.5	238 37.6	49.2	163 49.9	05.5	Achernar	335 25.1	S57 09.5
02	60 11.5	256 59.0	39.5	251 52.1	28.9	253 39.6	49.1	178 52.1	05.5	Acrux	173 08.0	S63 11.0
03	75 14.0	271 59.1 ..	38.9	266 53.1 ..	28.3	268 41.6 ..	48.9	193 54.3 ..	05.6	Adhara	255 11.2	S28 59.6
04	90 16.4	286 59.3	38.2	281 54.2	27.7	283 43.7	48.7	208 56.5	05.6	Aldebaran	290 47.3	N16 32.3
05	105 18.9	301 59.4	37.5	296 55.2	27.1	298 45.7	48.6	223 58.7	05.7			
06	120 21.4	316 59.5	N 6 36.9	311 56.2	N 6 26.5	313 47.7	N 6 48.4	239 00.9	S19 05.8	Alioth	166 20.0	N55 52.5
07	135 23.8	331 59.6	36.2	326 57.3	25.9	328 49.8	48.2	254 03.1	05.8	Alkaid	152 58.2	N49 14.2
T 08	150 26.3	346 59.7	35.5	341 58.3	25.3	343 51.8	48.0	269 05.3	05.9	Al Na'ir	27 41.6	S46 53.1
H 09	165 28.8	1 59.8 ..	34.9	356 59.3 ..	24.8	358 53.8 ..	47.9	284 07.5 ..	05.9	Alnilam	275 44.6	S 1 11.6
U 10	180 31.2	17 00.0	34.2	12 00.4	24.2	13 55.9	47.7	299 09.7	06.0	Alphard	217 54.6	S 8 43.6
R 11	195 33.7	32 00.1	33.5	27 01.4	23.6	28 57.9	47.5	314 11.9	06.0			
S 12	210 36.2	47 00.2	N 6 32.8	42 02.5	N 6 23.0	43 59.9	N 6 47.4	329 14.1	S19 06.1	Alphecca	126 10.0	N26 40.0
D 13	225 38.6	62 00.3	32.2	57 03.5	22.4	59 02.0	47.2	344 16.2	06.1	Alpheratz	357 41.5	N29 10.8
A 14	240 41.1	77 00.4	31.5	72 04.6	21.8	74 04.0	47.0	359 18.4	06.2	Altair	62 06.7	N 8 55.0
Y 15	255 43.5	92 00.5 ..	30.8	87 05.6 ..	21.2	89 06.0 ..	46.8	14 20.6 ..	06.3	Ankaa	353 13.8	S42 13.2
16	270 46.0	107 00.6	30.1	102 06.6	20.6	104 08.1	46.7	29 22.8	06.3	Antares	112 24.6	S26 27.8
17	285 48.5	122 00.7	29.5	117 07.7	20.0	119 10.1	46.5	44 25.0	06.4			
18	300 50.9	137 00.9	N 6 28.8	132 08.7	N 6 19.4	134 12.2	N 6 46.3	59 27.2	S19 06.4	Arcturus	145 54.7	N19 06.2
19	315 53.4	152 01.0	28.1	147 09.8	18.9	149 14.2	46.2	74 29.4	06.5	Atria	107 25.3	S69 03.3
20	330 55.9	167 01.1	27.4	162 10.8	18.3	164 16.2	46.0	89 31.6	06.5	Avior	234 17.3	S59 33.4
21	345 58.3	182 01.2 ..	26.8	177 11.8 ..	17.7	179 18.3 ..	45.8	104 33.8 ..	06.6	Bellatrix	278 30.1	N 6 21.7
22	1 00.8	197 01.3	26.1	192 12.9	17.1	194 20.3	45.6	119 36.0	06.6	Betelgeuse	270 59.4	N 7 24.5
23	16 03.3	212 01.4	25.4	207 13.9	16.5	209 22.3	45.5	134 38.2	06.7			
23 00	31 05.7	227 01.5	N 6 24.7	222 15.0	N 6 15.9	224 24.4	N 6 45.3	149 40.4	S19 06.8	Canopus	263 55.2	S52 42.1
01	46 08.2	242 01.6	24.0	237 16.0	15.3	239 26.4	45.1	164 42.6	06.8	Capella	280 31.8	N46 00.5
02	61 10.6	257 01.7	23.4	252 17.0	14.7	254 28.4	45.0	179 44.8	06.9	Deneb	49 30.3	N45 20.7
03	76 13.1	272 01.8 ..	22.7	267 18.1 ..	14.1	269 30.5 ..	44.8	194 46.9 ..	06.9	Denebola	182 32.4	N14 29.1
04	91 15.6	287 01.9	22.0	282 19.1	13.5	284 32.5	44.6	209 49.1	07.0	Diphda	348 54.0	S17 54.0
05	106 18.0	302 02.0	21.3	297 20.2	12.9	299 34.6	44.5	224 51.3	07.0			
06	121 20.5	317 02.1	N 6 20.6	312 21.2	N 6 12.4	314 36.6	N 6 44.3	239 53.5	S19 07.1	Dubhe	193 50.4	N61 39.8
07	136 23.0	332 02.2	19.9	327 22.3	11.8	329 38.6	44.1	254 55.7	07.1	Elnath	278 10.4	N28 37.0
F 08	151 25.4	347 02.3	19.2	342 23.3	11.2	344 40.7	43.9	269 57.9	07.2	Eltanin	90 45.7	N51 29.7
R 09	166 27.9	2 02.4 ..	18.5	357 24.3 ..	10.6	359 42.7 ..	43.8	285 00.1 ..	07.3	Enif	33 45.4	N 9 57.1
I 10	181 30.4	17 02.5	17.9	12 25.4	10.0	14 44.7	43.6	300 02.3	07.3	Fomalhaut	15 22.0	S29 32.3
11	196 32.8	32 02.6	17.2	27 26.4	09.4	29 46.8	43.4	315 04.5	07.4			
D 12	211 35.3	47 02.7	N 6 16.5	42 27.5	N 6 08.8	44 48.8	N 6 43.3	330 06.7	S19 07.4	Gacrux	171 59.6	S57 11.9
A 13	226 37.8	62 02.8	15.8	57 28.5	08.2	59 50.9	43.1	345 08.9	07.5	Gienah	175 51.0	S17 37.6
Y 14	241 40.2	77 02.9	15.1	72 29.6	07.6	74 52.9	42.9	0 11.1	07.5	Hadar	148 46.2	S60 26.8
15	256 42.7	92 03.0 ..	14.4	87 30.6 ..	07.0	89 54.9 ..	42.7	15 13.2 ..	07.6	Hamal	327 58.6	N23 32.2
16	271 45.1	107 03.1	13.7	102 31.6	06.4	104 57.0	42.6	30 15.4	07.6	Kaus Aust.	83 41.9	S34 22.5
17	286 47.6	122 03.2	13.0	117 32.7	05.9	119 59.0	42.4	45 17.6	07.7			
18	301 50.1	137 03.3	N 6 12.3	132 33.7	N 6 05.3	135 01.1	N 6 42.2	60 19.8	S19 07.8	Kochab	137 21.4	N74 05.6
19	316 52.5	152 03.4	11.6	147 34.8	04.7	150 03.1	42.1	75 22.0	07.8	Markab	13 36.5	N15 17.6
20	331 55.0	167 03.5	10.9	162 35.8	04.1	165 05.1	41.9	90 24.2	07.9	Menkar	314 13.1	N 4 09.1
21	346 57.5	182 03.6 ..	10.2	177 36.9 ..	03.5	180 07.2 ..	41.7	105 26.4 ..	07.9	Menkent	148 06.1	S36 26.6
22	1 59.9	197 03.7	09.5	192 37.9	02.9	195 09.2	41.6	120 28.6	08.0	Miaplacidus	221 39.4	S69 46.7
23	17 02.4	212 03.8	08.8	207 38.9	02.3	210 11.3	41.4	135 30.8	08.0			
24 00	32 04.9	227 03.9	N 6 08.1	222 40.0	N 6 01.7	225 13.3	N 6 41.2	150 33.0	S19 08.1	Mirfak	308 37.6	N49 54.8
01	47 07.3	242 04.0	07.4	237 41.0	01.1	240 15.3	41.0	165 35.2	08.1	Nunki	75 56.5	S26 16.4
02	62 09.8	257 04.0	06.7	252 42.1	6 00.5	255 17.4	40.9	180 37.3	08.2	Peacock	53 16.8	S56 41.1
03	77 12.2	272 04.1 ..	06.0	267 43.1	5 59.9	270 19.4 ..	40.7	195 39.5 ..	08.3	Pollux	243 25.8	N27 59.0
04	92 14.7	287 04.2	05.3	282 44.2	59.4	285 21.5	40.5	210 41.7	08.3	Procyon	244 58.1	N 5 11.0
05	107 17.2	302 04.3	04.6	297 45.2	58.8	300 23.5	40.4	225 43.9	08.4			
06	122 19.6	317 04.4	N 6 03.9	312 46.3	N 5 58.2	315 25.5	N 6 40.2	240 46.1	S19 08.4	Rasalhague	96 05.2	N12 33.3
07	137 22.1	332 04.5	03.2	327 47.3	57.6	330 27.6	40.0	255 48.3	08.5	Regulus	207 42.0	N11 53.4
S 08	152 24.6	347 04.6	02.5	342 48.3	57.0	345 29.6	39.9	270 50.5	08.5	Rigel	281 10.3	S 8 11.1
A 09	167 27.0	2 04.7 ..	01.8	357 49.4 ..	56.4	0 31.7 ..	39.7	285 52.7 ..	08.6	Rigil Kent.	139 50.1	S60 53.8
T 10	182 29.5	17 04.8	01.1	12 50.4	55.8	15 33.7	39.5	300 54.9	08.6	Sabik	102 11.0	S15 44.4
U 11	197 32.0	32 04.8	6 00.4	27 51.5	55.2	30 35.7	39.4	315 57.1	08.7			
R 12	212 34.4	47 04.9	N 5 59.7	42 52.5	N 5 54.6	45 37.8	N 6 39.2	330 59.3	S19 08.8	Schedar	349 38.1	N56 37.6
D 13	227 36.9	62 05.0	59.0	57 53.6	54.0	60 39.8	39.0	346 01.4	08.8	Shaula	96 20.0	S37 06.7
A 14	242 39.4	77 05.1	58.3	72 54.6	53.4	75 41.9	38.8	1 03.6	08.9	Sirius	258 32.2	S16 44.3
Y 15	257 41.8	92 05.2 ..	57.6	87 55.7 ..	52.9	90 43.9 ..	38.7	16 05.8 ..	08.9	Spica	158 29.9	S11 14.4
16	272 44.3	107 05.3	56.9	102 56.7	52.3	105 45.9	38.5	31 08.0	09.0	Suhail	222 51.3	S43 29.6
17	287 46.7	122 05.3	56.2	117 57.7	51.7	120 48.0	38.3	46 10.2	09.0			
18	302 49.2	137 05.4	N 5 55.4	132 58.8	N 5 51.1	135 50.0	N 6 38.2	61 12.4	S19 09.1	Vega	80 38.0	N38 48.4
19	317 51.7	152 05.5	54.7	147 59.8	50.5	150 52.1	38.0	76 14.6	09.1	Zuben'ubi	137 04.0	S16 06.2
20	332 54.1	167 05.6	54.0	163 00.9	49.9	165 54.1	37.8	91 16.8	09.2		SHA	Mer.Pass.
21	347 56.6	182 05.7 ..	53.3	178 01.9 ..	49.3	180 56.2 ..	37.7	106 19.0 ..	09.3			
22	2 59.1	197 05.7	52.6	193 03.0	48.7	195 58.2	37.5	121 21.1	09.3	Venus	195 55.8	8 52
23	18 01.5	212 05.8	51.9	208 04.0	48.1	211 00.2	37.3	136 23.3	09.4	Mars	191 09.2	9 10
Mer.Pass. 21 52.0		v 0.1	d 0.7	v 1.0	d 0.6	v 2.0	d 0.2	v 2.2	d 0.1	Jupiter	193 18.7	9 01
										Saturn	118 34.6	13 59

SUN and MOON

UT	SUN GHA	SUN Dec	MOON GHA	v	MOON Dec	d	HP
d h	° ′	° ′	° ′	′	° ′	′	′
22 00	183 51.0	S10 51.4	76 00.0	8.6	S13 13.8	7.6	58.7
01	198 51.1	52.3	90 27.6	8.7	13 06.2	7.7	58.7
02	213 51.2	53.2	104 55.3	8.7	12 58.5	7.8	58.8
03	228 51.3	.. 54.0	119 23.0	8.7	12 50.7	7.9	58.8
04	243 51.4	54.9	133 50.7	8.6	12 42.8	7.9	58.8
05	258 51.5	55.8	148 18.3	8.7	12 34.9	8.0	58.9
06	273 51.6	S10 56.7	162 46.0	8.6	S12 26.9	8.2	58.9
07	288 51.7	57.6	177 13.6	8.7	12 18.7	8.2	58.9
T 08	303 51.8	58.5	191 41.3	8.6	12 10.5	8.3	59.0
H 09	318 51.9	10 59.4	206 08.9	8.6	12 02.2	8.3	59.0
U 10	333 52.0	11 00.2	220 36.5	8.7	11 53.9	8.5	59.0
R 11	348 52.1	01.1	235 04.2	8.6	11 45.4	8.5	59.1
S 12	3 52.2	S11 02.0	249 31.8	8.6	S11 36.9	8.6	59.1
D 13	18 52.3	02.9	263 59.4	8.6	11 28.3	8.7	59.1
A 14	33 52.4	03.8	278 27.0	8.6	11 19.6	8.8	59.2
Y 15	48 52.5	.. 04.7	292 54.6	8.6	11 10.8	8.8	59.2
16	63 52.6	05.5	307 22.2	8.6	11 02.0	9.0	59.3
17	78 52.6	06.4	321 49.8	8.6	10 53.0	9.0	59.3
18	93 52.7	S11 07.3	336 17.4	8.5	S10 44.0	9.1	59.3
19	108 52.8	08.2	350 44.9	8.6	10 34.9	9.1	59.4
20	123 52.9	09.1	5 12.5	8.5	10 25.8	9.2	59.4
21	138 53.0	.. 09.9	19 40.0	8.6	10 16.6	9.3	59.4
22	153 53.1	10.8	34 07.6	8.5	10 07.3	9.4	59.5
23	168 53.2	11.7	48 35.1	8.6	9 57.9	9.5	59.5
23 00	183 53.3	S11 12.6	63 02.7	8.5	S 9 48.4	9.5	59.5
01	198 53.4	13.5	77 30.2	8.5	9 38.9	9.6	59.6
02	213 53.5	14.3	91 57.7	8.5	9 29.3	9.6	59.6
03	228 53.6	.. 15.2	106 25.2	8.6	9 19.7	9.7	59.6
04	243 53.7	16.1	120 52.8	8.5	9 10.0	9.8	59.6
05	258 53.8	17.0	135 20.3	8.4	9 00.2	9.9	59.7
06	273 53.8	S11 17.9	149 47.7	8.5	S 8 50.3	9.9	59.7
07	288 53.9	18.7	164 15.2	8.5	8 40.4	10.0	59.7
08	303 54.0	19.6	178 42.7	8.5	8 30.4	10.0	59.8
F 09	318 54.1	.. 20.5	193 10.2	8.4	8 20.4	10.1	59.8
R 10	333 54.2	21.4	207 37.6	8.5	8 10.3	10.2	59.8
I 11	348 54.3	22.2	222 05.1	8.4	8 00.1	10.2	59.9
D 12	3 54.4	S11 23.1	236 32.5	8.4	S 7 49.9	10.3	59.9
A 13	18 54.5	24.0	250 59.9	8.5	7 39.6	10.4	59.9
Y 14	33 54.6	24.9	265 27.4	8.4	7 29.2	10.4	60.0
15	48 54.6	.. 25.8	279 54.8	8.4	7 18.8	10.5	60.0
16	63 54.7	26.6	294 22.2	8.4	7 08.3	10.5	60.0
17	78 54.8	27.5	308 49.6	8.3	6 57.8	10.6	60.0
18	93 54.9	S11 28.4	323 16.9	8.4	S 6 47.2	10.6	60.1
19	108 55.0	29.3	337 44.3	8.4	6 36.6	10.7	60.1
20	123 55.1	30.1	352 11.7	8.3	6 25.9	10.7	60.1
21	138 55.2	.. 31.0	6 39.0	8.4	6 15.2	10.8	60.2
22	153 55.3	31.9	21 06.4	8.3	6 04.4	10.8	60.2
23	168 55.3	32.7	35 33.7	8.3	5 53.6	10.9	60.2
24 00	183 55.4	S11 33.6	50 01.0	8.3	S 5 42.7	10.9	60.2
01	198 55.5	34.5	64 28.3	8.3	5 31.8	11.0	60.3
02	213 55.6	35.4	78 55.6	8.2	5 20.8	11.0	60.3
03	228 55.7	.. 36.2	93 22.8	8.3	5 09.8	11.0	60.3
04	243 55.8	37.1	107 50.1	8.3	4 58.8	11.1	60.4
05	258 55.8	38.0	122 17.4	8.2	4 47.7	11.2	60.4
06	273 55.9	S11 38.8	136 44.6	8.2	S 4 36.5	11.2	60.4
07	288 56.0	39.7	151 11.8	8.2	4 25.3	11.2	60.4
S 08	303 56.1	40.6	165 39.0	8.2	4 14.1	11.2	60.5
A 09	318 56.2	.. 41.5	180 06.2	8.2	4 02.9	11.3	60.5
T 10	333 56.3	42.3	194 33.4	8.1	3 51.6	11.3	60.5
U 11	348 56.3	43.2	209 00.5	8.2	3 40.3	11.4	60.5
R 12	3 56.4	S11 44.1	223 27.7	8.1	S 3 28.9	11.4	60.6
D 13	18 56.5	44.9	237 54.8	8.1	3 17.5	11.4	60.6
A 14	33 56.6	45.8	252 21.9	8.1	3 06.1	11.5	60.6
Y 15	48 56.7	.. 46.7	266 49.0	8.1	2 54.6	11.4	60.6
16	63 56.7	47.5	281 16.1	8.1	2 43.2	11.5	60.6
17	78 56.8	48.4	295 43.2	8.0	2 31.7	11.6	60.7
18	93 56.9	S11 49.3	310 10.2	8.0	S 2 20.1	11.5	60.7
19	108 57.0	50.1	324 37.2	8.0	2 08.6	11.6	60.7
20	123 57.1	51.0	339 04.2	8.0	1 57.0	11.6	60.7
21	138 57.1	.. 51.9	353 31.2	8.0	1 45.4	11.6	60.8
22	153 57.2	52.7	7 58.2	7.9	1 33.8	11.6	60.8
23	168 57.3	53.6	22 25.2	7.9	S 1 22.2	11.7	60.8
	SD 16.1	d 0.9	SD 16.1		16.3		16.5

Twilight / Sunrise / Moonrise

Lat.	Naut.	Civil	Sunrise	Moonrise 22	23	24	25
°	h m	h m	h m	h m	h m	h m	h m
N 72	05 28	06 47	08 03	16 01	15 56	15 51	15 46
N 70	05 28	06 39	07 46	15 42	15 45	15 47	15 49
68	05 28	06 33	07 33	15 28	15 36	15 44	15 50
66	05 28	06 27	07 22	15 16	15 29	15 41	15 52
64	05 27	06 23	07 13	15 06	15 23	15 39	15 53
62	05 27	06 19	07 05	14 57	15 18	15 37	15 55
60	05 26	06 15	06 58	14 50	15 13	15 35	15 56
N 58	05 26	06 12	06 52	14 43	15 09	15 33	15 57
56	05 25	06 09	06 47	14 37	15 06	15 32	15 58
54	05 25	06 06	06 42	14 32	15 02	15 31	15 58
52	05 24	06 03	06 38	14 27	14 59	15 29	15 59
50	05 23	06 01	06 34	14 23	14 56	15 28	16 00
45	05 21	05 56	06 26	14 14	14 51	15 26	16 01
N 40	05 19	05 51	06 19	14 06	14 46	15 24	16 02
35	05 17	05 47	06 12	13 59	14 41	15 22	16 03
30	05 15	05 43	06 07	13 53	14 37	15 21	16 04
20	05 09	05 35	05 57	13 43	14 31	15 18	16 06
N 10	05 03	05 28	05 49	13 34	14 25	15 16	16 08
0	04 55	05 20	05 41	13 26	14 20	15 14	16 09
S 10	04 46	05 11	05 33	13 17	14 14	15 12	16 10
20	04 35	05 02	05 24	13 08	14 08	15 10	16 12
30	04 20	04 49	05 14	12 58	14 02	15 07	16 14
35	04 11	04 42	05 08	12 52	13 58	15 06	16 15
40	03 59	04 33	05 01	12 45	13 53	15 04	16 16
45	03 45	04 22	04 53	12 37	13 48	15 02	16 18
S 50	03 26	04 09	04 44	12 27	13 42	15 00	16 19
52	03 17	04 03	04 40	12 23	13 39	14 59	16 20
54	03 07	03 56	04 35	12 18	13 36	14 58	16 21
56	02 55	03 48	04 29	12 13	13 33	14 56	16 22
58	02 41	03 39	04 23	12 07	13 29	14 55	16 23
S 60	02 24	03 29	04 16	12 00	13 25	14 53	16 24

Sunset / Twilight / Moonset

Lat.	Sunset	Civil	Naut.	Moonset 22	23	24	25
°	h m	h m	h m	h m	h m	h m	h m
N 72	15 24	16 40	17 59	23 35	25 33	01 33	03 32
N 70	15 41	16 48	17 59	23 52	25 41	01 41	03 33
68	15 54	16 54	17 59	24 05	00 05	01 48	03 34
66	16 05	17 00	17 59	24 16	00 16	01 54	03 34
64	16 15	17 05	18 00	24 25	00 25	01 58	03 35
62	16 23	17 09	18 00	24 32	00 32	02 02	03 35
60	16 29	17 13	18 01	24 39	00 39	02 06	03 36
N 58	16 35	17 16	18 02	24 45	00 45	02 09	03 36
56	16 41	17 19	18 02	24 50	00 50	02 12	03 36
54	16 46	17 22	18 03	24 54	00 54	02 14	03 37
52	16 50	17 25	18 04	24 59	00 59	02 17	03 37
50	16 54	17 27	18 05	25 02	01 02	02 19	03 37
45	17 02	17 32	18 07	00 01	01 10	02 23	03 38
N 40	17 10	17 37	18 09	00 10	01 17	02 27	03 38
35	17 16	17 42	18 11	00 18	01 23	02 30	03 38
30	17 21	17 46	18 14	00 25	01 28	02 33	03 39
20	17 31	17 53	18 19	00 37	01 37	02 37	03 39
N 10	17 40	18 01	18 26	00 48	01 44	02 41	03 40
0	17 48	18 09	18 33	00 57	01 51	02 45	03 40
S 10	17 56	18 17	18 43	01 07	01 58	02 49	03 40
20	18 05	18 28	18 54	01 18	02 06	02 53	03 41
30	18 15	18 40	19 09	01 29	02 14	02 58	03 41
35	18 21	18 48	19 19	01 36	02 19	03 00	03 41
40	18 28	18 57	19 31	01 44	02 24	03 03	03 41
45	18 36	19 07	19 45	01 53	02 30	03 06	03 42
S 50	18 46	19 21	20 04	02 03	02 38	03 10	03 42
52	18 50	19 27	20 13	02 08	02 41	03 12	03 42
54	18 55	19 34	20 24	02 13	02 45	03 14	03 42
56	19 01	19 42	20 36	02 19	02 49	03 16	03 42
58	19 07	19 52	20 51	02 26	02 54	03 19	03 42
S 60	19 14	20 02	21 08	02 34	02 59	03 21	03 42

SUN and MOON

Day	SUN Eqn. of Time 00h	12h	Mer. Pass.	MOON Mer. Pass. Upper	Lower	Age	Phase
d	m s	m s	h m	h m	h m	d	%
22	15 24	15 28	11 45	19 38	07 12	09	68
23	15 33	15 37	11 44	20 32	08 05	10	78
24	15 42	15 46	11 44	21 27	09 00	11	87

UT	ARIES GHA	VENUS −4.5 GHA	Dec	MARS +1.7 GHA	Dec	JUPITER −1.8 GHA	Dec	SATURN +0.5 GHA	Dec	STARS Name	SHA	Dec
25 00	33 04.0	227 05.9	N 5 51.2	223 05.1	N 5 47.5	226 02.3	N 6 37.2	151 25.5	S19 09.4	Acamar	315 16.8	S40 14.5
01	48 06.5	242 06.0	50.4	238 06.1	46.9	241 04.3	37.0	166 27.7	09.5	Achernar	335 25.1	S57 09.5
02	63 08.9	257 06.0	49.7	253 07.2	46.3	256 06.4	36.8	181 29.9	09.5	Acrux	173 08.0	S63 11.0
03	78 11.4	272 06.1 ..	49.0	268 08.2 ..	45.7	271 08.4 ..	36.7	196 32.1 ..	09.6	Adhara	255 11.1	S28 59.6
04	93 13.9	287 06.2	48.3	283 09.3	45.2	286 10.5	36.5	211 34.3	09.6	Aldebaran	290 47.3	N16 32.3
05	108 16.3	302 06.3	47.6	298 10.3	44.6	301 12.5	36.3	226 36.5	09.7			
S 06	123 18.8	317 06.3	N 5 46.9	313 11.3	N 5 44.0	316 14.5	N 6 36.2	241 38.7	S19 09.8	Alioth	166 20.0	N55 52.5
U 07	138 21.2	332 06.4	46.1	328 12.4	43.4	331 16.6	36.0	256 40.8	09.8	Alkaid	152 58.2	N49 14.2
N 08	153 23.7	347 06.5	45.4	343 13.4	42.8	346 18.6	35.8	271 43.0	09.9	Al Na'ir	27 41.6	S46 53.1
D 09	168 26.2	2 06.6 ..	44.7	358 14.5 ..	42.2	1 20.7 ..	35.6	286 45.2 ..	09.9	Alnilam	275 44.6	S 1 11.6
A 10	183 28.6	17 06.6	44.0	13 15.5	41.6	16 22.7	35.5	301 47.4	10.0	Alphard	217 54.6	S 8 43.6
Y 11	198 31.1	32 06.7	43.2	28 16.6	41.0	31 24.8	35.3	316 49.6	10.0			
12	213 33.6	47 06.8	N 5 42.5	43 17.6	N 5 40.4	46 26.8	N 6 35.1	331 51.8	S19 10.1	Alphecca	126 10.0	N26 40.0
13	228 36.0	62 06.9	41.8	58 18.7	39.8	61 28.9	35.0	346 54.0	10.1	Alpheratz	357 41.5	N29 10.8
14	243 38.5	77 06.9	41.1	73 19.7	39.2	76 30.9	34.8	1 56.2	10.2	Altair	62 06.7	N 8 55.0
15	258 41.0	92 07.0 ..	40.3	88 20.8 ..	38.6	91 32.9 ..	34.6	16 58.3 ..	10.3	Ankaa	353 13.8	S42 13.3
16	273 43.4	107 07.1	39.6	103 21.8	38.1	106 35.0	34.5	32 00.5	10.3	Antares	112 24.6	S26 27.8
17	288 45.9	122 07.1	38.9	118 22.9	37.5	121 37.0	34.3	47 02.7	10.4			
18	303 48.3	137 07.2	N 5 38.2	133 23.9	N 5 36.9	136 39.1	N 6 34.1	62 04.9	S19 10.4	Arcturus	145 54.7	N19 06.2
19	318 50.8	152 07.3	37.4	148 25.0	36.3	151 41.1	34.0	77 07.1	10.5	Atria	107 25.4	S69 03.3
20	333 53.3	167 07.3	36.7	163 26.0	35.7	166 43.2	33.8	92 09.3	10.5	Avior	234 17.3	S59 33.4
21	348 55.7	182 07.4 ..	36.0	178 27.1 ..	35.1	181 45.2 ..	33.6	107 11.5 ..	10.6	Bellatrix	278 30.1	N 6 21.7
22	3 58.2	197 07.5	35.2	193 28.1	34.5	196 47.3	33.5	122 13.7	10.6	Betelgeuse	270 59.4	N 7 24.5
23	19 00.7	212 07.5	34.5	208 29.2	33.9	211 49.3	33.3	137 15.8	10.7			
26 00	34 03.1	227 07.6	N 5 33.8	223 30.2	N 5 33.3	226 51.4	N 6 33.1	152 18.0	S19 10.8	Canopus	263 55.2	S52 42.1
01	49 05.6	242 07.7	33.0	238 31.2	32.7	241 53.4	33.0	167 20.2	10.8	Capella	280 31.8	N46 00.5
02	64 08.1	257 07.7	32.3	253 32.3	32.1	256 55.5	32.8	182 22.4	10.9	Deneb	49 30.3	N45 20.7
03	79 10.5	272 07.8 ..	31.6	268 33.3 ..	31.5	271 57.5 ..	32.6	197 24.6 ..	10.9	Denebola	182 32.3	N14 29.1
04	94 13.0	287 07.8	30.8	283 34.4	30.9	286 59.5	32.5	212 26.8	11.0	Diphda	348 54.0	S17 54.0
05	109 15.5	302 07.9	30.1	298 35.4	30.4	302 01.6	32.3	227 29.0	11.0			
M 06	124 17.9	317 08.0	N 5 29.4	313 36.5	N 5 29.8	317 03.6	N 6 32.1	242 31.2	S19 11.1	Dubhe	193 50.4	N61 39.7
O 07	139 20.4	332 08.0	28.6	328 37.5	29.2	332 05.7	32.0	257 33.3	11.1	Elnath	278 10.4	N28 37.0
N 08	154 22.8	347 08.1	27.9	343 38.6	28.6	347 07.7	31.8	272 35.5	11.2	Eltanin	90 45.7	N51 29.7
D 09	169 25.3	2 08.2 ..	27.2	358 39.6 ..	28.0	2 09.8 ..	31.6	287 37.7 ..	11.3	Enif	33 45.4	N 9 57.1
A 10	184 27.8	17 08.2	26.4	13 40.7	27.4	17 11.8	31.5	302 39.9	11.3	Fomalhaut	15 22.1	S29 32.3
Y 11	199 30.2	32 08.3	25.7	28 41.7	26.8	32 13.9	31.3	317 42.1	11.4			
12	214 32.7	47 08.3	N 5 24.9	43 42.8	N 5 26.2	47 15.9	N 6 31.1	332 44.3	S19 11.4	Gacrux	171 59.5	S57 11.9
13	229 35.2	62 08.4	24.2	58 43.8	25.6	62 18.0	31.0	347 46.5	11.5	Gienah	175 50.9	S17 37.6
14	244 37.6	77 08.4	23.5	73 44.9	25.0	77 20.0	30.8	2 48.6	11.5	Hadar	148 46.2	S60 26.7
15	259 40.1	92 08.5 ..	22.7	88 45.9 ..	24.4	92 22.1 ..	30.6	17 50.8 ..	11.6	Hamal	327 58.6	N23 32.2
16	274 42.6	107 08.6	22.0	103 47.0	23.8	107 24.1	30.5	32 53.0	11.6	Kaus Aust.	83 41.9	S34 22.5
17	289 45.0	122 08.6	21.2	118 48.0	23.2	122 26.2	30.3	47 55.2	11.7			
18	304 47.5	137 08.7	N 5 20.5	133 49.1	N 5 22.6	137 28.2	N 6 30.1	62 57.4	S19 11.8	Kochab	137 21.4	N74 05.6
19	319 49.9	152 08.7	19.7	148 50.1	22.1	152 30.3	30.0	77 59.6	11.8	Markab	13 36.5	N15 17.6
20	334 52.4	167 08.8	19.0	163 51.2	21.5	167 32.3	29.8	93 01.8	11.9	Menkar	314 13.1	N 4 09.0
21	349 54.9	182 08.8 ..	18.2	178 52.2 ..	20.9	182 34.4 ..	29.6	108 03.9 ..	11.9	Menkent	148 06.1	S36 26.6
22	4 57.3	197 08.9	17.5	193 53.3	20.3	197 36.4	29.5	123 06.1	12.0	Miaplacidus	221 39.4	S69 46.7
23	19 59.8	212 08.9	16.8	208 54.3	19.7	212 38.5	29.3	138 08.3	12.0			
27 00	35 02.3	227 09.0	N 5 16.0	223 55.4	N 5 19.1	227 40.5	N 6 29.1	153 10.5	S19 12.1	Mirfak	308 37.5	N49 54.9
01	50 04.7	242 09.0	15.3	238 56.4	18.5	242 42.6	29.0	168 12.7	12.1	Nunki	75 56.5	S26 16.4
02	65 07.2	257 09.1	14.5	253 57.5	17.9	257 44.6	28.8	183 14.9	12.2	Peacock	53 16.8	S56 41.1
03	80 09.7	272 09.1 ..	13.8	268 58.5 ..	17.3	272 46.7 ..	28.6	198 17.1 ..	12.3	Pollux	243 25.8	N27 59.0
04	95 12.1	287 09.2	13.0	283 59.6	16.7	287 48.7	28.5	213 19.2	12.3	Procyon	244 58.0	N 5 11.0
05	110 14.6	302 09.2	12.3	299 00.6	16.1	302 50.8	28.3	228 21.4	12.4			
T 06	125 17.1	317 09.3	N 5 11.5	314 01.7	N 5 15.5	317 52.8	N 6 28.1	243 23.6	S19 12.4	Rasalhague	96 05.2	N12 33.3
U 07	140 19.5	332 09.3	10.8	329 02.7	14.9	332 54.9	28.0	258 25.8	12.5	Regulus	207 42.0	N11 53.4
E 08	155 22.0	347 09.4	10.0	344 03.8	14.3	347 57.0	27.8	273 28.0	12.5	Rigel	281 10.3	S 8 11.1
S 09	170 24.4	2 09.4 ..	09.2	359 04.8 ..	13.8	2 59.0 ..	27.6	288 30.2 ..	12.6	Rigil Kent.	139 50.1	S60 53.8
D 10	185 26.9	17 09.5	08.5	14 05.9	13.2	18 01.0	27.5	303 32.3	12.6	Sabik	102 11.0	S15 44.4
A 11	200 29.4	32 09.5	07.7	29 06.9	12.6	33 03.1	27.3	318 34.5	12.7			
Y 12	215 31.8	47 09.6	N 5 07.0	44 08.0	N 5 12.0	48 05.1	N 6 27.1	333 36.7	S19 12.8	Schedar	349 38.1	N56 37.6
13	230 34.3	62 09.6	06.2	59 09.1	11.4	63 07.2	27.0	348 38.9	12.8	Shaula	96 20.0	S37 06.7
14	245 36.8	77 09.6	05.5	74 10.1	10.8	78 09.2	26.8	3 41.1	12.9	Sirius	258 32.2	S16 44.3
15	260 39.2	92 09.7 ..	04.7	89 11.2 ..	10.2	93 11.3 ..	26.7	18 43.3 ..	12.9	Spica	158 29.9	S11 14.4
16	275 41.7	107 09.7	03.9	104 12.2	09.6	108 13.3	26.5	33 45.5	13.0	Suhail	222 51.3	S43 29.6
17	290 44.2	122 09.8	03.2	119 13.3	09.0	123 15.4	26.3	48 47.6	13.0			
18	305 46.6	137 09.8	N 5 02.4	134 14.3	N 5 08.4	138 17.4	N 6 26.2	63 49.8	S19 13.1	Vega	80 38.1	N38 48.4
19	320 49.1	152 09.9	01.7	149 15.4	07.8	153 19.5	26.0	78 52.0	13.1	Zuben'ubi	137 04.0	S16 06.2
20	335 51.6	167 09.9	00.9	164 16.4	07.2	168 21.5	25.8	93 54.2	13.2		SHA	Mer.Pass.
21	350 54.0	182 09.9	5 00.1	179 17.5 ..	06.6	183 23.6 ..	25.7	108 56.4 ..	13.3			h m
22	5 56.5	197 10.0	4 59.4	194 18.5	06.0	198 25.6	25.5	123 58.6	13.3	Venus	193 04.5	8 51
23	20 58.9	212 10.0	N 4 58.6	209 19.6	05.4	213 27.7	25.3	139 00.7	13.4	Mars	189 27.1	9 05
	h m									Jupiter	192 48.2	8 51
Mer.Pass.	21 40.2	v 0.1	d 0.7	v 1.0	d 0.6	v 2.0	d 0.2	v 2.2	d 0.1	Saturn	118 14.9	13 49

SUN and MOON

UT	SUN GHA	SUN Dec	MOON GHA	v	MOON Dec	d	HP
25 00	183 57.4	S11 54.5	36 52.1	7.9	S 1 10.5	11.7	60.8
01	198 57.5	55.3	51 19.0	7.9	0 58.8	11.6	60.8
02	213 57.5	56.2	65 45.9	7.9	0 47.2	11.7	60.8
03	228 57.6 ..	57.1	80 12.8	7.9	0 35.5	11.7	60.9
04	243 57.7	57.9	94 39.7	7.8	0 23.8	11.7	60.9
05	258 57.8	58.8	109 06.5	7.8	0 12.1	11.8	60.9
06	273 57.8	S11 59.7	123 33.3	7.8	S 0 00.3	11.7	60.9
07	288 57.9	12 00.5	138 00.1	7.8	N 0 11.4	11.7	60.9
S 08	303 58.0	01.4	152 26.9	7.8	0 23.1	11.8	60.9
U 09	318 58.1 ..	02.2	166 53.6	7.8	0 34.9	11.7	61.0
N 10	333 58.1	03.1	181 20.4	7.7	0 46.6	11.8	61.0
11	348 58.2	04.0	195 47.1	7.7	0 58.4	11.7	61.0
D 12	3 58.3	S12 04.8	210 13.8	7.6	N 1 10.1	11.8	61.0
A 13	18 58.4	05.7	224 40.4	7.7	1 21.9	11.7	61.0
Y 14	33 58.4	06.6	239 07.1	7.6	1 33.6	11.7	61.0
15	48 58.5 ..	07.4	253 33.7	7.6	1 45.3	11.8	61.0
16	63 58.6	08.3	268 00.3	7.5	1 57.1	11.7	61.1
17	78 58.7	09.1	282 26.8	7.6	2 08.8	11.7	61.1
18	93 58.7	S12 10.0	296 53.4	7.5	N 2 20.5	11.7	61.1
19	108 58.8	10.9	311 19.9	7.5	2 32.2	11.7	61.1
20	123 58.9	11.7	325 46.4	7.5	2 43.9	11.7	61.1
21	138 58.9 ..	12.6	340 12.9	7.4	2 55.6	11.6	61.1
22	153 59.0	13.4	354 39.3	7.5	3 07.2	11.7	61.1
23	168 59.1	14.3	9 05.8	7.4	3 18.9	11.6	61.1
26 00	183 59.2	S12 15.1	23 32.2	7.4	N 3 30.5	11.6	61.1
01	198 59.2	16.0	37 58.6	7.3	3 42.1	11.6	61.1
02	213 59.3	16.9	52 24.9	7.3	3 53.7	11.6	61.1
03	228 59.4 ..	17.7	66 51.2	7.3	4 05.3	11.5	61.1
04	243 59.4	18.6	81 17.5	7.3	4 16.8	11.5	61.1
05	258 59.5	19.4	95 43.8	7.3	4 28.3	11.5	61.2
06	273 59.6	S12 20.3	110 10.1	7.2	N 4 39.8	11.5	61.2
07	288 59.6	21.1	124 36.3	7.2	4 51.3	11.4	61.2
M 08	303 59.7	22.0	139 02.5	7.2	5 02.7	11.4	61.2
O 09	318 59.8 ..	22.9	153 28.7	7.1	5 14.1	11.3	61.2
N 10	333 59.8	23.7	167 54.8	7.1	5 25.4	11.4	61.2
11	348 59.9	24.6	182 20.9	7.1	5 36.8	11.3	61.2
D 12	4 00.0	S12 25.4	196 47.0	7.1	N 5 48.1	11.2	61.2
A 13	19 00.0	26.3	211 13.1	7.0	5 59.3	11.2	61.2
Y 14	34 00.1	27.1	225 39.1	7.0	6 10.5	11.2	61.2
15	49 00.2 ..	28.0	240 05.1	7.0	6 21.7	11.1	61.2
16	64 00.2	28.8	254 31.1	7.0	6 32.8	11.1	61.2
17	79 00.3	29.7	268 57.1	6.9	6 43.9	11.1	61.2
18	94 00.4	S12 30.5	283 23.0	7.0	N 6 55.0	10.9	61.2
19	109 00.4	31.4	297 49.0	6.8	7 05.9	11.0	61.2
20	124 00.5	32.2	312 14.8	6.9	7 16.9	10.9	61.2
21	139 00.6 ..	33.1	326 40.7	6.8	7 27.8	10.8	61.2
22	154 00.6	33.9	341 06.5	6.8	7 38.6	10.8	61.1
23	169 00.7	34.8	355 32.3	6.8	7 49.4	10.8	61.1
27 00	184 00.8	S12 35.6	9 58.1	6.8	N 8 00.2	10.6	61.1
01	199 00.8	36.5	24 23.9	6.7	8 10.8	10.7	61.1
02	214 00.9	37.3	38 49.6	6.7	8 21.5	10.5	61.1
03	229 00.9 ..	38.2	53 15.3	6.7	8 32.0	10.5	61.1
04	244 01.0	39.0	67 41.0	6.7	8 42.5	10.5	61.1
05	259 01.1	39.9	82 06.7	6.6	8 53.0	10.4	61.1
06	274 01.1	S12 40.7	96 32.3	6.6	N 9 03.4	10.3	61.1
07	289 01.2	41.6	110 57.9	6.6	9 13.7	10.2	61.1
T 08	304 01.3	42.4	125 23.5	6.6	9 23.9	10.2	61.1
U 09	319 01.3 ..	43.3	139 49.1	6.5	9 34.1	10.1	61.1
E 10	334 01.4	44.1	154 14.6	6.5	9 44.2	10.1	61.0
S 11	349 01.4	45.0	168 40.1	6.5	9 54.3	10.0	61.0
D 12	4 01.5	S12 45.8	183 05.6	6.5	N10 04.3	9.9	61.0
A 13	19 01.6	46.6	197 31.1	6.4	10 14.2	9.8	61.0
Y 14	34 01.6	47.5	211 56.5	6.4	10 24.0	9.7	61.0
15	49 01.7 ..	48.3	226 22.0	6.4	10 33.7	9.7	61.0
16	64 01.7	49.2	240 47.4	6.4	10 43.4	9.6	61.0
17	79 01.8	50.0	255 12.8	6.3	10 53.0	9.5	61.0
18	94 01.8	S12 50.9	269 38.1	6.4	N11 02.5	9.5	60.9
19	109 01.9	51.7	284 03.5	6.3	11 12.0	9.4	60.9
20	124 02.0	52.6	298 28.8	6.3	11 21.4	9.2	60.9
21	139 02.0 ..	53.4	312 54.1	6.3	11 30.6	9.2	60.9
22	154 02.1	54.2	327 19.4	6.2	11 39.8	9.1	60.9
23	169 02.1	55.1	341 44.6	6.3	N11 48.9	9.1	60.9
SD	16.1	d 0.9	16.6		16.7		16.6

Twilight and Moonrise

Lat.	Naut.	Civil	Sunrise	Moonrise 25	26	27	28
N 72	05 40	07 01	08 19	15 46	15 42	15 37	15 32
N 70	05 39	06 51	08 00	15 49	15 51	15 54	16 00
68	05 38	06 43	07 45	15 50	15 58	16 07	16 21
66	05 37	06 37	07 32	15 52	16 04	16 18	16 37
64	05 35	06 31	07 22	15 53	16 09	16 28	16 51
62	05 34	06 26	07 13	15 55	16 14	16 36	17 02
60	05 33	06 22	07 06	15 56	16 18	16 43	17 12
N 58	05 32	06 18	06 59	15 57	16 21	16 49	17 21
56	05 31	06 15	06 53	15 58	16 24	16 54	17 28
54	05 30	06 11	06 48	15 58	16 27	16 59	17 35
52	05 29	06 08	06 43	15 59	16 30	17 03	17 41
50	05 28	06 06	06 39	16 00	16 32	17 07	17 47
45	05 25	05 59	06 30	16 01	16 38	17 16	17 59
N 40	05 22	05 54	06 22	16 02	16 42	17 24	18 09
35	05 20	05 49	06 15	16 03	16 46	17 30	18 17
30	05 17	05 45	06 09	16 04	16 49	17 36	18 25
20	05 10	05 36	05 59	16 06	16 55	17 45	18 38
N 10	05 03	05 28	05 49	16 08	17 00	17 54	18 49
0	04 55	05 19	05 41	16 09	17 05	18 02	19 00
S 10	04 45	05 10	05 32	16 10	17 10	18 10	19 11
20	04 33	04 59	05 22	16 12	17 15	18 19	19 23
30	04 17	04 46	05 11	16 14	17 22	18 29	19 36
35	04 07	04 38	05 05	16 15	17 25	18 35	19 44
40	03 54	04 29	04 57	16 16	17 29	18 42	19 53
45	03 39	04 17	04 49	16 18	17 34	18 50	20 04
S 50	03 19	04 03	04 38	16 19	17 40	18 59	20 16
52	03 09	03 56	04 33	16 20	17 42	19 04	20 22
54	02 58	03 49	04 28	16 21	17 45	19 09	20 29
56	02 45	03 40	04 22	16 22	17 49	19 14	20 36
58	02 30	03 30	04 15	16 23	17 52	19 20	20 45
S 60	02 10	03 19	04 08	16 24	17 56	19 27	20 54

Sunset, Twilight and Moonset

Lat.	Sunset	Civil	Naut.	Moonset 25	26	27	28
N 72	15 07	16 26	17 45	03 32	05 33	07 36	09 42
N 70	15 27	16 35	17 47	03 33	05 27	07 22	09 16
68	15 42	16 43	17 48	03 34	05 21	07 10	08 56
66	15 54	16 50	17 50	03 34	05 17	07 00	08 41
64	16 05	16 55	17 51	03 35	05 13	06 52	08 28
62	16 13	17 00	17 52	03 35	05 10	06 45	08 17
60	16 21	17 05	17 54	03 36	05 07	06 39	08 08
N 58	16 28	17 09	17 55	03 36	05 05	06 34	08 00
56	16 34	17 12	17 56	03 37	05 03	06 29	07 53
54	16 39	17 16	17 57	03 37	05 01	06 25	07 47
52	16 44	17 19	17 58	03 37	04 59	06 21	07 41
50	16 48	17 22	17 59	03 37	04 57	06 17	07 36
45	16 58	17 28	18 02	03 38	04 54	06 10	07 25
N 40	17 06	17 33	18 05	03 38	04 51	06 04	07 16
35	17 12	17 38	18 08	03 38	04 48	05 59	07 08
30	17 19	17 43	18 11	03 39	04 46	05 54	07 01
20	17 29	17 52	18 18	03 39	04 42	05 46	06 50
N 10	17 38	18 00	18 25	03 40	04 39	05 39	06 39
0	17 47	18 09	18 33	03 40	04 35	05 32	06 30
S 10	17 56	18 18	18 43	03 40	04 32	05 25	06 20
20	18 06	18 29	18 56	03 41	04 29	05 18	06 10
30	18 17	18 42	19 12	03 41	04 25	05 10	05 58
35	18 24	18 50	19 22	03 41	04 23	05 05	05 51
40	18 31	19 00	19 35	03 41	04 20	05 00	05 44
45	18 40	19 12	19 50	03 42	04 17	04 54	05 35
S 50	18 51	19 26	20 10	03 42	04 14	04 47	05 24
52	18 56	19 33	20 20	03 42	04 12	04 44	05 19
54	19 01	19 41	20 32	03 42	04 10	04 40	05 14
56	19 07	19 50	20 45	03 42	04 08	04 36	05 08
58	19 14	20 00	21 01	03 42	04 06	04 32	05 01
S 60	19 22	20 14	21 21	03 42	04 04	04 27	04 53

SUN / MOON

Day	Eqn. of Time 00h	Eqn. of Time 12h	Mer. Pass.	Mer. Pass. Upper	Mer. Pass. Lower	Age	Phase
	m s	m s	h m	h m	h m	d	%
25	15 49	15 53	11 44	22 22	09 54	12	94
26	15 56	16 00	11 44	23 19	10 50	13	98
27	16 03	16 06	11 44	24 16	11 47	14	100

UT	ARIES GHA	VENUS −4.5 GHA	Dec	MARS +1.7 GHA	Dec	JUPITER −1.8 GHA	Dec	SATURN +0.5 GHA	Dec	STARS Name	SHA	Dec
28 00	36 01.4	227 10.1	N 4 57.9	224 20.6	N 5 04.9	228 29.7	N 6 25.2	154 02.9	S19 13.4	Acamar	315 16.8	S40 14.5
01	51 03.9	242 10.1	57.1	239 21.7	04.3	243 31.8	25.0	169 05.1	13.5	Achernar	335 25.1	S57 09.5
02	66 06.3	257 10.1	56.3	254 22.7	03.7	258 33.8	24.8	184 07.3	13.5	Acrux	173 07.9	S63 11.0
03	81 08.8	272 10.2 ..	55.6	269 23.8 ..	03.1	273 35.9 ..	24.7	199 09.5 ..	13.6	Adhara	255 11.1	S28 59.6
04	96 11.3	287 10.2	54.8	284 24.8	02.5	288 37.9	24.5	214 11.7	13.6	Aldebaran	290 47.3	N16 32.3
05	111 13.7	302 10.3	54.0	299 25.9	01.9	303 40.0	24.3	229 13.8	13.7			
W 06	126 16.2	317 10.3	N 4 53.3	314 26.9	N 5 01.3	318 42.1	N 6 24.2	244 16.0	S19 13.8	Alioth	166 19.9	N55 52.4
E 07	141 18.7	332 10.3	52.5	329 28.0	00.7	333 44.1	24.0	259 18.2	13.8	Alkaid	152 58.2	N49 14.2
D 08	156 21.1	347 10.4	51.7	344 29.0	5 00.1	348 46.2	23.9	274 20.4	13.9	Al Na'ir	27 41.6	S46 53.1
N 09	171 23.6	2 10.4 ..	51.0	359 30.1	4 59.5	3 48.2 ..	23.7	289 22.6 ..	13.9	Alnilam	275 44.5	S 1 11.6
E 10	186 26.0	17 10.4	50.2	14 31.2	58.9	18 50.3	23.5	304 24.8	14.0	Alphard	217 54.6	S 8 43.6
S 11	201 28.5	32 10.5	49.4	29 32.2	58.3	33 52.3	23.4	319 26.9	14.0			
D 12	216 31.0	47 10.5	N 4 48.6	44 33.3	N 4 57.7	48 54.4	N 6 23.2	334 29.1	S19 14.1	Alphecca	126 10.0	N26 40.0
A 13	231 33.4	62 10.5	47.9	59 34.3	57.1	63 56.4	23.0	349 31.3	14.1	Alpheratz	357 41.5	N29 10.8
Y 14	246 35.9	77 10.6	47.1	74 35.4	56.5	78 58.5	22.9	4 33.5	14.2	Altair	62 06.8	N 8 55.0
15	261 38.4	92 10.6 ..	46.3	89 36.4 ..	56.0	94 00.5 ..	22.7	19 35.7 ..	14.3	Ankaa	353 13.8	S42 13.3
16	276 40.8	107 10.6	45.5	104 37.5	55.4	109 02.6	22.5	34 37.9	14.3	Antares	112 24.6	S26 27.8
17	291 43.3	122 10.7	44.8	119 38.5	54.8	124 04.7	22.4	49 40.0	14.4			
18	306 45.8	137 10.7	N 4 44.0	134 39.6	N 4 54.2	139 06.7	N 6 22.2	64 42.2	S19 14.4	Arcturus	145 54.7	N19 06.2
19	321 48.2	152 10.7	43.2	149 40.6	53.6	154 08.8	22.1	79 44.4	14.5	Atria	107 25.4	S69 03.3
20	336 50.7	167 10.7	42.4	164 41.7	53.0	169 10.8	21.9	94 46.6	14.5	Avior	234 17.3	S59 33.4
21	351 53.2	182 10.8 ..	41.7	179 42.7 ..	52.4	184 12.9 ..	21.7	109 48.8 ..	14.6	Bellatrix	278 30.1	N 6 21.7
22	6 55.6	197 10.8	40.9	194 43.8	51.8	199 14.9	21.6	124 50.9	14.6	Betelgeuse	270 59.4	N 7 24.5
23	21 58.1	212 10.8	40.1	209 44.9	51.2	214 17.0	21.4	139 53.1	14.7			
29 00	37 00.5	227 10.8	N 4 39.3	224 45.9	N 4 50.6	229 19.0	N 6 21.2	154 55.3	S19 14.8	Canopus	263 55.1	S52 42.2
01	52 03.0	242 10.9	38.6	239 47.0	50.0	244 21.1	21.1	169 57.5	14.8	Capella	280 31.7	N46 00.5
02	67 05.5	257 10.9	37.8	254 48.0	49.4	259 23.2	20.9	184 59.7	14.9	Deneb	49 30.3	N45 20.7
03	82 07.9	272 10.9 ..	37.0	269 49.1 ..	48.8	274 25.2 ..	20.7	200 01.9 ..	14.9	Denebola	182 32.3	N14 29.1
04	97 10.4	287 11.0	36.2	284 50.1	48.2	289 27.3	20.6	215 04.0	15.0	Diphda	348 54.0	S17 54.0
05	112 12.9	302 11.0	35.4	299 51.2	47.6	304 29.3	20.4	230 06.2	15.0			
T 06	127 15.3	317 11.0	N 4 34.6	314 52.2	N 4 47.0	319 31.4	N 6 20.3	245 08.4	S19 15.1	Dubhe	193 50.3	N61 39.7
H 07	142 17.8	332 11.0	33.9	329 53.3	46.4	334 33.4	20.1	260 10.6	15.1	Elnath	278 10.3	N28 37.0
U 08	157 20.3	347 11.0	33.1	344 54.4	45.9	349 35.5	19.9	275 12.8	15.2	Eltanin	90 45.7	N51 29.7
R 09	172 22.7	2 11.1 ..	32.3	359 55.4 ..	45.3	4 37.6 ..	19.8	290 14.9 ..	15.3	Enif	33 45.5	N 9 57.1
S 10	187 25.2	17 11.1	31.5	14 56.5	44.7	19 39.6	19.6	305 17.1	15.3	Fomalhaut	15 22.1	S29 32.3
D 11	202 27.7	32 11.1	30.7	29 57.5	44.1	34 41.7	19.4	320 19.3	15.4			
A 12	217 30.1	47 11.1	N 4 29.9	44 58.6	N 4 43.5	49 43.7	N 6 19.3	335 21.5	S19 15.4	Gacrux	171 59.5	S57 11.9
Y 13	232 32.6	62 11.2	29.1	59 59.6	42.9	64 45.8	19.1	350 23.7	15.5	Gienah	175 50.9	S17 37.6
14	247 35.0	77 11.2	28.4	75 00.7	42.3	79 47.8	19.0	5 25.9	15.5	Hadar	148 46.2	S60 26.7
15	262 37.5	92 11.2 ..	27.6	90 01.7 ..	41.7	94 49.9 ..	18.8	20 28.0 ..	15.6	Hamal	327 58.6	N23 32.2
16	277 40.0	107 11.2	26.8	105 02.8	41.1	109 52.0	18.6	35 30.2	15.6	Kaus Aust.	83 41.9	S34 22.5
17	292 42.4	122 11.2	26.0	120 03.9	40.5	124 54.0	18.5	50 32.4	15.7			
18	307 44.9	137 11.3	N 4 25.2	135 04.9	N 4 39.9	139 56.1	N 6 18.3	65 34.6	S19 15.8	Kochab	137 21.5	N74 05.6
19	322 47.4	152 11.3	24.4	150 06.0	39.3	154 58.1	18.1	80 36.8	15.8	Markab	13 36.5	N15 17.6
20	337 49.8	167 11.3	23.6	165 07.0	38.7	170 00.2	18.0	95 38.9	15.9	Menkar	314 13.1	N 4 09.0
21	352 52.3	182 11.3 ..	22.8	180 08.1 ..	38.1	185 02.3 ..	17.8	110 41.1 ..	15.9	Menkent	148 06.1	S36 26.6
22	7 54.8	197 11.3	22.0	195 09.1	37.5	200 04.3	17.7	125 43.3	16.0	Miaplacidus	221 39.3	S69 46.7
23	22 57.2	212 11.3	21.2	210 10.2	36.9	215 06.4	17.5	140 45.5	16.0			
30 00	37 59.7	227 11.3	N 4 20.4	225 11.2	N 4 36.3	230 08.4	N 6 17.3	155 47.7	S19 16.1	Mirfak	308 37.5	N49 54.9
01	53 02.1	242 11.4	19.7	240 12.3	35.8	245 10.5	17.2	170 49.8	16.1	Nunki	75 56.5	S26 12.4
02	68 04.6	257 11.4	18.9	255 13.4	35.2	260 12.5	17.0	185 52.0	16.2	Peacock	53 16.9	S56 41.1
03	83 07.1	272 11.4 ..	18.1	270 14.4 ..	34.6	275 14.6 ..	16.8	200 54.2 ..	16.3	Pollux	243 25.8	N27 59.0
04	98 09.5	287 11.4	17.3	285 15.5	34.0	290 16.7	16.7	215 56.4	16.3	Procyon	244 58.0	N 5 10.9
05	113 12.0	302 11.4	16.5	300 16.5	33.4	305 18.7	16.5	230 58.6	16.4			
F 06	128 14.5	317 11.4	N 4 15.7	315 17.6	N 4 32.8	320 20.8	N 6 16.4	246 00.7	S19 16.4	Rasalhague	96 05.2	N12 33.3
R 07	143 16.9	332 11.4	14.9	330 18.6	32.2	335 22.9	16.2	261 02.9	16.5	Regulus	207 42.0	N11 53.3
I 08	158 19.4	347 11.5	14.1	345 19.7	31.6	350 24.9	16.0	276 05.1	16.5	Rigel	281 10.3	S 8 11.1
D 09	173 21.9	2 11.5 ..	13.3	0 20.8 ..	31.0	5 27.0 ..	15.9	291 07.3 ..	16.6	Rigil Kent.	139 50.1	S60 53.8
A 10	188 24.3	17 11.5	12.5	15 21.8	30.4	20 29.0	15.7	306 09.5	16.6	Sabik	102 11.0	S15 44.4
Y 11	203 26.8	32 11.5	11.7	30 22.9	29.8	35 31.1	15.6	321 11.6	16.7			
12	218 29.3	47 11.5	N 4 10.9	45 23.9	N 4 29.2	50 33.2	N 6 15.4	336 13.8	S19 16.8	Schedar	349 38.1	N56 37.6
13	233 31.7	62 11.5	10.1	60 25.0	28.6	65 35.2	15.2	351 16.0	16.8	Shaula	96 20.0	S37 06.7
14	248 34.2	77 11.5	09.3	75 26.0	28.0	80 37.3	15.1	6 18.2	16.9	Sirius	258 32.2	S16 44.3
15	263 36.6	92 11.5 ..	08.5	90 27.1 ..	27.4	95 39.3 ..	14.9	21 20.4 ..	16.9	Spica	158 29.9	S11 14.4
16	278 39.1	107 11.5	07.7	105 28.2	26.8	110 41.4	14.7	36 22.5	17.0	Suhail	222 51.3	S43 29.6
17	293 41.6	122 11.5	06.9	120 29.2	26.2	125 43.5	14.6	51 24.7	17.0			
18	308 44.0	137 11.5	N 4 06.1	135 30.3	N 4 25.7	140 45.5	N 6 14.4	66 26.9	S19 17.1	Vega	80 38.1	N38 48.4
19	323 46.5	152 11.5	05.3	150 31.3	25.1	155 47.6	14.3	81 29.1	17.1	Zuben'ubi	137 04.0	S16 06.2
20	338 49.0	167 11.6	04.4	165 32.4	24.5	170 49.6	14.1	96 31.3	17.2			
21	353 51.4	182 11.6 ..	03.6	180 33.5 ..	23.9	185 51.7 ..	13.9	111 33.4 ..	17.3		SHA	Mer.Pass.
22	8 53.9	197 11.6	02.8	195 34.5	23.3	200 53.8	13.8	126 35.6	17.3	Venus	190 10.3	8 51
23	23 56.4	212 11.6	02.0	210 35.6	22.7	215 55.8	13.6	141 37.8	17.4	Mars	187 45.4	9 00
Mer. Pass.	h m 21 28.4	v 0.0	d 0.8	v 1.1	d 0.6	v 2.1	d 0.2	v 2.2	d 0.1	Jupiter	192 18.5	8 42
										Saturn	117 54.8	13 38

UT	SUN GHA	SUN Dec	MOON GHA	v	MOON Dec	d	HP
d h	° ′	° ′	° ′	′	° ′	′	′
28 00	184 02.2	S12 55.9	356 09.9	6.2	N11 58.0	8.9	60.8
01	199 02.2	56.8	10 35.1	6.2	12 06.9	8.8	60.8
02	214 02.3	57.6	25 00.3	6.2	12 15.7	8.8	60.8
03	229 02.3	.. 58.4	39 25.5	6.2	12 24.5	8.7	60.8
04	244 02.4	12 59.3	53 50.7	6.2	12 33.2	8.5	60.8
05	259 02.5	13 00.1	68 15.9	6.1	12 41.7	8.5	60.7
06	274 02.5	S13 01.0	82 41.0	6.2	N12 50.2	8.4	60.7
W 07	289 02.6	01.8	97 06.2	6.1	12 58.6	8.3	60.7
E 08	304 02.6	02.6	111 31.3	6.1	13 06.9	8.2	60.7
D 09	319 02.7	.. 03.5	125 56.4	6.1	13 15.1	8.1	60.6
N 10	334 02.7	04.3	140 21.5	6.1	13 23.2	8.0	60.6
E 11	349 02.8	05.2	154 46.6	6.1	13 31.2	7.9	60.6
S 12	4 02.8	S13 06.0	169 11.7	6.1	N13 39.1	7.8	60.5
D 13	19 02.9	06.8	183 36.8	6.0	13 46.9	7.7	60.5
A 14	34 02.9	07.7	198 01.8	6.1	13 54.6	7.6	60.5
Y 15	49 03.0	.. 08.5	212 26.9	6.0	14 02.2	7.5	60.5
16	64 03.0	09.3	226 51.9	6.1	14 09.7	7.4	60.5
17	79 03.1	10.2	241 16.9	6.1	14 17.1	7.3	60.4
18	94 03.1	S13 11.0	255 42.0	6.0	N14 24.4	7.2	60.4
19	109 03.2	11.8	270 07.0	6.0	14 31.6	7.1	60.4
20	124 03.2	12.7	284 32.0	6.0	14 38.7	7.0	60.4
21	139 03.3	.. 13.5	298 57.0	6.1	14 45.7	6.9	60.3
22	154 03.3	14.3	313 22.1	6.0	14 52.6	6.7	60.3
23	169 03.4	15.2	327 47.1	6.0	14 59.3	6.7	60.3
29 00	184 03.4	S13 16.0	342 12.1	6.0	N15 06.0	6.5	60.2
01	199 03.5	16.8	356 37.1	6.0	15 12.5	6.5	60.2
02	214 03.5	17.7	11 02.1	6.0	15 19.0	6.3	60.2
03	229 03.5	.. 18.5	25 27.1	6.0	15 25.3	6.2	60.2
04	244 03.6	19.3	39 52.1	6.0	15 31.5	6.1	60.1
05	259 03.6	20.2	54 17.1	6.1	15 37.6	6.0	60.1
06	274 03.7	S13 21.0	68 42.2	6.0	N15 43.6	5.9	60.1
T 07	289 03.7	21.8	83 07.2	6.0	15 49.5	5.7	60.0
H 08	304 03.8	22.7	97 32.2	6.1	15 55.2	5.7	60.0
U 09	319 03.8	.. 23.5	111 57.3	6.0	16 00.9	5.5	60.0
R 10	334 03.9	24.3	126 22.3	6.1	16 06.4	5.4	59.9
11	349 03.9	25.1	140 47.4	6.0	16 11.8	5.4	59.9
S 12	4 04.0	S13 26.0	155 12.4	6.1	N16 17.2	5.1	59.9
D 13	19 04.0	26.8	169 37.5	6.1	16 22.3	5.1	59.8
A 14	34 04.0	27.6	184 02.6	6.1	16 27.4	5.0	59.8
Y 15	49 04.1	.. 28.5	198 27.7	6.1	16 32.4	4.8	59.8
16	64 04.1	29.3	212 52.8	6.2	16 37.2	4.7	59.7
17	79 04.2	30.1	227 18.0	6.1	16 41.9	4.7	59.7
18	94 04.2	S13 30.9	241 43.1	6.2	N16 46.6	4.5	59.7
19	109 04.2	31.8	256 08.3	6.2	16 51.1	4.3	59.6
20	124 04.3	32.6	270 33.5	6.2	16 55.4	4.3	59.6
21	139 04.3	.. 33.4	284 58.7	6.2	16 59.7	4.1	59.6
22	154 04.4	34.2	299 23.9	6.2	17 03.8	4.0	59.5
23	169 04.4	35.1	313 49.1	6.3	17 07.8	3.9	59.5
30 00	184 04.4	S13 35.9	328 14.4	6.3	N17 11.7	3.8	59.4
01	199 04.5	36.7	342 39.7	6.3	17 15.5	3.7	59.4
02	214 04.5	37.5	357 05.0	6.3	17 19.2	3.5	59.4
03	229 04.6	.. 38.4	11 30.3	6.4	17 22.7	3.5	59.3
04	244 04.6	39.2	25 55.7	6.3	17 26.2	3.3	59.3
05	259 04.6	40.0	40 21.0	6.5	17 29.5	3.2	59.3
06	274 04.7	S13 40.8	54 46.5	6.4	N17 32.7	3.0	59.2
07	289 04.7	41.6	69 11.9	6.5	17 35.7	3.0	59.2
08	304 04.7	42.5	83 37.4	6.5	17 38.7	2.8	59.2
F 09	319 04.8	.. 43.3	98 02.9	6.5	17 41.5	2.7	59.1
R 10	334 04.8	44.1	112 28.4	6.6	17 44.2	2.6	59.1
I 11	349 04.9	44.9	126 54.0	6.6	17 46.8	2.5	59.0
D 12	4 04.9	S13 45.8	141 19.6	6.6	N17 49.3	2.4	59.0
A 13	19 04.9	46.6	155 45.2	6.7	17 51.7	2.2	59.0
Y 14	34 05.0	47.4	170 10.9	6.7	17 53.9	2.2	58.9
15	49 05.0	.. 48.2	184 36.6	6.7	17 56.1	2.0	58.9
16	64 05.0	49.0	199 02.3	6.8	17 58.1	1.9	58.8
17	79 05.1	49.8	213 28.1	6.8	18 00.0	1.7	58.8
18	94 05.1	S13 50.7	227 53.9	6.9	N18 01.7	1.7	58.8
19	109 05.1	51.5	242 19.8	6.9	18 03.4	1.5	58.7
20	124 05.2	52.3	256 45.7	6.9	18 04.9	1.4	58.7
21	139 05.2	.. 53.1	271 11.6	7.0	18 06.3	1.4	58.6
22	154 05.2	53.9	285 37.6	7.0	18 07.7	1.1	58.6
23	169 05.3	54.7	300 03.6	7.1	N18 08.8	1.1	58.6
	SD 16.1	d 0.8	SD 16.5		16.3		16.1

Moonrise

Lat.	Twilight Naut.	Twilight Civil	Sunrise	28	29	30	31
°	h m	h m	h m	h m	h m	h m	h m
N 72	05 53	07 14	08 36	15 32	15 27	15 18	▭
N 70	05 50	07 03	08 14	16 00	16 12	16 37	17 27
68	05 48	06 54	07 57	16 21	16 41	17 15	18 08
66	05 45	06 46	07 43	16 37	17 04	17 42	18 36
64	05 44	06 40	07 32	16 51	17 21	18 03	18 57
62	05 42	06 34	07 22	17 02	17 36	18 20	19 14
60	05 40	06 29	07 14	17 12	17 48	18 34	19 28
N 58	05 38	06 25	07 06	17 21	17 59	18 46	19 41
56	05 37	06 21	07 00	17 28	18 08	18 56	19 51
54	05 35	06 17	06 54	17 35	18 17	19 05	20 00
52	05 34	06 13	06 49	17 41	18 24	19 14	20 09
50	05 32	06 10	06 44	17 47	18 31	19 21	20 16
45	05 29	06 03	06 34	17 59	18 45	19 37	20 32
N 40	05 25	05 57	06 25	18 09	18 57	19 50	20 45
35	05 22	05 52	06 18	18 17	19 08	20 01	20 56
30	05 19	05 47	06 11	18 25	19 17	20 11	21 06
20	05 11	05 37	06 00	18 38	19 32	20 27	21 23
N 10	05 03	05 28	05 50	18 49	19 46	20 42	21 37
0	04 54	05 19	05 40	19 00	19 58	20 56	21 51
S 10	04 44	05 09	05 31	19 11	20 11	21 09	22 05
20	04 31	04 57	05 20	19 23	20 25	21 24	22 20
30	04 14	04 43	05 08	19 36	20 41	21 41	22 36
35	04 03	04 35	05 01	19 44	20 50	21 51	22 46
40	03 50	04 24	04 53	19 53	21 00	22 02	22 57
45	03 33	04 12	04 44	20 04	21 13	22 15	23 10
S 50	03 12	03 57	04 33	20 16	21 28	22 32	23 26
52	03 02	03 51	04 27	20 22	21 35	22 39	23 34
54	02 50	03 41	04 21	20 29	21 43	22 48	23 42
56	02 35	03 32	04 15	20 36	21 52	22 57	23 52
58	02 18	03 22	04 08	20 45	22 02	23 08	24 02
S 60	01 57	03 09	03 59	20 54	22 13	23 20	24 14

Moonset

Lat.	Sunset	Twilight Civil	Twilight Naut.	28	29	30	31
°	h m	h m	h m	h m	h m	h m	h m
N 72	14 50	16 12	17 33	09 42	11 50	14 00	▭
N 70	15 12	16 23	17 36	09 16	11 06	12 41	13 48
68	15 29	16 32	17 38	08 56	10 37	12 03	13 07
66	15 43	16 40	17 41	08 41	10 15	11 36	12 39
64	15 55	16 47	17 43	08 28	09 58	11 16	12 18
62	16 05	16 52	17 45	08 17	09 44	10 59	12 00
60	16 13	16 57	17 46	08 08	09 32	10 45	11 46
N 58	16 20	17 02	17 48	08 00	09 21	10 33	11 34
56	16 27	17 06	17 50	07 53	09 12	10 23	11 23
54	16 33	17 10	17 51	07 47	09 04	10 14	11 14
52	16 38	17 13	17 53	07 41	08 57	10 06	11 06
50	16 43	17 16	17 54	07 36	08 51	09 59	10 58
45	16 53	17 23	17 58	07 25	08 37	09 43	10 42
N 40	17 02	17 30	18 01	07 16	08 25	09 30	10 29
35	17 09	17 35	18 05	07 08	08 16	09 19	10 18
30	17 16	17 40	18 09	07 01	08 07	09 10	10 08
20	17 27	17 50	18 16	06 50	07 53	08 54	09 51
N 10	17 37	17 59	18 24	06 39	07 40	08 39	09 36
0	17 47	18 08	18 33	06 30	07 28	08 26	09 22
S 10	17 57	18 19	18 44	06 20	07 16	08 12	09 09
20	18 07	18 30	18 57	06 10	07 03	07 58	08 54
30	18 20	18 45	19 15	05 58	06 49	07 42	08 37
35	18 27	18 53	19 25	05 51	06 40	07 32	08 27
40	18 35	19 04	19 39	05 44	06 31	07 21	08 16
45	18 44	19 16	19 55	05 35	06 19	07 09	08 02
S 50	18 56	19 32	20 17	05 24	06 06	06 53	07 46
52	19 01	19 39	20 28	05 19	06 00	06 46	07 38
54	19 07	19 48	20 40	05 14	05 53	06 38	07 30
56	19 14	19 57	20 55	05 08	05 45	06 29	07 20
58	19 21	20 08	21 12	05 01	05 36	06 19	07 10
S 60	19 30	20 21	21 35	04 53	05 26	06 07	06 57

Day	SUN Eqn. of Time 00h	SUN Eqn. of Time 12h	Mer. Pass.	MOON Mer. Pass. Upper	MOON Mer. Pass. Lower	Age	Phase
d	m s	m s	h m	h m	h m	d	%
28	16 09	16 11	11 44	00 16	12 45	15	98
29	16 14	16 16	11 44	01 14	13 43	16	94
30	16 18	16 19	11 44	02 12	14 41	17	88

UT	ARIES GHA	VENUS −4.5 GHA	Dec	MARS +1.7 GHA	Dec	JUPITER −1.8 GHA	Dec	SATURN +0.5 GHA	Dec
31 00	38 58.8	227 11.6 N 4 01.2		225 36.6 N 4 22.1		230 57.9 N 6 13.5		156 40.0 S19 17.4	
01	54 01.3	242 11.6 4 00.4		240 37.7	21.5	246 00.0	13.3	171 42.1	17.5
02	69 03.8	257 11.6 3 59.6		255 38.7	20.9	261 02.0	13.1	186 44.3	17.5
03	84 06.2	272 11.6 .. 58.8		270 39.8 .. 20.3		276 04.1 .. 13.0		201 46.5 .. 17.6	
04	99 08.7	287 11.6 58.0		285 40.9	19.7	291 06.2	12.8	216 48.7	17.7
05	114 11.1	302 11.6 57.2		300 41.9	19.1	306 08.2	12.7	231 50.9	17.7
06	129 13.6	317 11.6 N 3 56.4		315 43.0 N 4 18.5		321 10.3 N 6 12.5		246 53.0 S19 17.8	
07	144 16.1	332 11.6 55.5		330 44.0	17.9	336 12.3	12.3	261 55.2	17.8
S 08	159 18.5	347 11.6 54.7		345 45.1	17.3	351 14.4	12.2	276 57.4	17.9
A 09	174 21.0	2 11.6 .. 53.9		0 46.2 .. 16.7		6 16.5 .. 12.0		291 59.6 .. 17.9	
T 10	189 23.5	17 11.6 53.1		15 47.2	16.1	21 18.5	11.9	307 01.7	18.0
U 11	204 25.9	32 11.6 52.3		30 48.3	15.5	36 20.6	11.7	322 03.9	18.0
R 12	219 28.4	47 11.6 N 3 51.5		45 49.3 N 4 14.9		51 22.7 N 6 11.5		337 06.1 S19 18.1	
D 13	234 30.9	62 11.6 50.7		60 50.4	14.4	66 24.7	11.4	352 08.3	18.2
A 14	249 33.3	77 11.6 49.8		75 51.5	13.8	81 26.8	11.2	7 10.5	18.2
Y 15	264 35.8	92 11.6 .. 49.0		90 52.5 .. 13.2		96 28.9 .. 11.1		22 12.6 .. 18.3	
16	279 38.3	107 11.6 48.2		105 53.6	12.6	111 30.9	10.9	37 14.8	18.3
17	294 40.7	122 11.6 47.4		120 54.6	12.0	126 33.0	10.7	52 17.0	18.4
18	309 43.2	137 11.6 N 3 46.6		135 55.7 N 4 11.4		141 35.1 N 6 10.6		67 19.2 S19 18.4	
19	324 45.6	152 11.6 45.8		150 56.8	10.8	156 37.1	10.4	82 21.3	18.5
20	339 48.1	167 11.6 44.9		165 57.8	10.2	171 39.2	10.3	97 23.5	18.5
21	354 50.6	182 11.6 .. 44.1		180 58.9 .. 09.6		186 41.3 .. 10.1		112 25.7 .. 18.6	
22	9 53.0	197 11.5 43.3		195 59.9	09.0	201 43.3	09.9	127 27.9	18.7
23	24 55.5	212 11.5 42.5		211 01.0	08.4	216 45.4	09.8	142 30.1	18.7
1 00	39 58.0	227 11.5 N 3 41.6		226 02.1 N 4 07.8		231 47.5 N 6 09.6		157 32.2 S19 18.8	
01	55 00.4	242 11.5 40.8		241 03.1	07.2	246 49.5	09.5	172 34.4	18.8
02	70 02.9	257 11.5 40.0		256 04.2	06.6	261 51.6	09.3	187 36.6	18.9
03	85 05.4	272 11.5 .. 39.2		271 05.2 .. 06.0		276 53.7 .. 09.2		202 38.8 .. 18.9	
04	100 07.8	287 11.5 38.4		286 06.3	05.4	291 55.7	09.0	217 40.9	19.0
05	115 10.3	302 11.5 37.5		301 07.4	04.8	306 57.8	08.8	232 43.1	19.0
06	130 12.8	317 11.5 N 3 36.7		316 08.4 N 4 04.2		321 59.9 N 6 08.7		247 45.3 S19 19.1	
07	145 15.2	332 11.5 35.9		331 09.5	03.6	337 01.9	08.5	262 47.5	19.2
S 08	160 17.7	347 11.5 35.1		346 10.5	03.1	352 04.0	08.4	277 49.7	19.2
U 09	175 20.1	2 11.4 .. 34.2		1 11.6 .. 02.5		7 06.1 .. 08.2		292 51.8 .. 19.3	
N 10	190 22.6	17 11.4 33.4		16 12.7	01.9	22 08.1	08.0	307 54.0	19.3
D 11	205 25.1	32 11.4 32.6		31 13.7	01.3	37 10.2	07.9	322 56.2	19.4
A 12	220 27.5	47 11.4 N 3 31.7		46 14.8 N 4 00.7		52 12.3 N 6 07.7		337 58.4 S19 19.4	
Y 13	235 30.0	62 11.4 30.9		61 15.8 4 00.1		67 14.3	07.6	353 00.5	19.5
14	250 32.5	77 11.4 30.1		76 16.9 3 59.5		82 16.4	07.4	8 02.7	19.5
15	265 34.9	92 11.4 .. 29.3		91 18.0 .. 58.9		97 18.5 .. 07.3		23 04.9 .. 19.6	
16	280 37.4	107 11.4 28.4		106 19.0	58.3	112 20.5	07.1	38 07.1	19.7
17	295 39.9	122 11.3 27.6		121 20.1	57.7	127 22.6	06.9	53 09.2	19.7
18	310 42.3	137 11.3 N 3 26.8		136 21.2 N 3 57.1		142 24.7 N 6 06.8		68 11.4 S19 19.8	
19	325 44.8	152 11.3 25.9		151 22.2	56.5	157 26.7	06.6	83 13.6	19.8
20	340 47.2	167 11.3 25.1		166 23.3	55.9	172 28.8	06.5	98 15.8	19.9
21	355 49.7	182 11.3 .. 24.3		181 24.3 .. 55.3		187 30.9 .. 06.3		113 17.9 .. 19.9	
22	10 52.2	197 11.3 23.4		196 25.4	54.7	202 33.0	06.1	128 20.1	20.0
23	25 54.6	212 11.2 22.6		211 26.5	54.1	217 35.0	06.0	143 22.3	20.0
2 00	40 57.1	227 11.2 N 3 21.8		226 27.5 N 3 53.5		232 37.1 N 6 05.8		158 24.5 S19 20.1	
01	55 59.6	242 11.2 20.9		241 28.6	52.9	247 39.2	05.7	173 26.6	20.2
02	71 02.0	257 11.2 20.1		256 29.7	52.3	262 41.2	05.5	188 28.8	20.2
03	86 04.5	272 11.2 .. 19.2		271 30.7 .. 51.8		277 43.3 .. 05.4		203 31.0 .. 20.3	
04	101 07.0	287 11.2 18.4		286 31.8	51.2	292 45.4	05.2	218 33.2	20.3
05	116 09.4	302 11.1 17.6		301 32.8	50.6	307 47.4	05.0	233 35.3	20.4
06	131 11.9	317 11.1 N 3 16.7		316 33.9 N 3 50.0		322 49.5 N 6 04.9		248 37.5 S19 20.4	
07	146 14.4	332 11.1 15.9		331 35.0	49.4	337 51.6	04.7	263 39.7	20.5
M 08	161 16.8	347 11.1 15.0		346 36.0	48.8	352 53.7	04.6	278 41.9	20.5
O 09	176 19.3	2 11.1 .. 14.2		1 37.1 .. 48.2		7 55.7 .. 04.4		293 44.0 .. 20.6	
N 10	191 21.7	17 11.0 13.4		16 38.2	47.6	22 57.8	04.3	308 46.2	20.7
D 11	206 24.2	32 11.0 12.5		31 39.2	47.0	37 59.9	04.1	323 48.4	20.7
A 12	221 26.7	47 11.0 N 3 11.7		46 40.3 N 3 46.4		53 01.9 N 6 03.9		338 50.6 S19 20.8	
Y 13	236 29.1	62 11.0 10.8		61 41.3	45.8	68 04.0	03.8	353 52.7	20.8
14	251 31.6	77 10.9 10.0		76 42.4	45.2	83 06.1	03.6	8 54.9	20.9
15	266 34.1	92 10.9 .. 09.2		91 43.5 .. 44.6		98 08.2 .. 03.5		23 57.1 .. 20.9	
16	281 36.5	107 10.9 08.3		106 44.5	44.0	113 10.2	03.3	38 59.3	21.0
17	296 39.0	122 10.9 07.5		121 45.6	43.4	128 12.3	03.2	54 01.4	21.0
18	311 41.5	137 10.8 N 3 06.6		136 46.7 N 3 42.8		143 14.4 N 6 03.0		69 03.6 S19 21.1	
19	326 43.9	152 10.8 05.8		151 47.7	42.2	158 16.5	02.8	84 05.8	21.2
20	341 46.4	167 10.8 04.9		166 48.8	41.6	173 18.5	02.7	99 08.0	21.2
21	356 48.9	182 10.8 .. 04.1		181 49.9 .. 41.0		188 20.6 .. 02.5		114 10.1 .. 21.3	
22	11 51.3	197 10.7 03.2		196 50.9	40.4	203 22.7	02.4	129 12.3	21.3
23	26 53.8	212 10.7 02.4		211 52.0	39.9	218 24.7	02.2	144 14.5	21.4
Mer. Pass. 21 16.6		v 0.0 d 0.8		v 1.1 d 0.6		v 2.1 d 0.2		v 2.2 d 0.1	

STARS

Name	SHA	Dec
Acamar	315 16.8	S40 14.5
Achernar	335 25.1	S57 09.5
Acrux	173 07.9	S63 11.0
Adhara	255 11.1	S28 59.6
Aldebaran	290 47.2	N16 32.3
Alioth	166 19.9	N55 52.4
Alkaid	152 58.2	N49 14.2
Al Na'ir	27 41.7	S46 53.1
Alnilam	275 44.5	S 1 11.6
Alphard	217 54.6	S 8 43.6
Alphecca	126 10.0	N26 40.0
Alpheratz	357 41.5	N29 10.8
Altair	62 06.8	N 8 55.0
Ankaa	353 13.8	S42 13.3
Antares	112 24.6	S26 27.8
Arcturus	145 54.7	N19 06.2
Atria	107 25.4	S69 03.2
Avior	234 17.2	S59 33.4
Bellatrix	278 30.1	N 6 21.7
Betelgeuse	270 59.4	N 7 24.4
Canopus	263 55.1	S52 42.2
Capella	280 31.7	N46 00.5
Deneb	49 30.3	N45 20.7
Denebola	182 32.3	N14 29.1
Diphda	348 54.0	S17 54.0
Dubhe	193 50.3	N61 39.7
Elnath	278 10.3	N28 37.0
Eltanin	90 45.8	N51 29.7
Enif	33 45.5	N 9 57.1
Fomalhaut	15 22.1	S29 32.3
Gacrux	171 59.5	S57 11.9
Gienah	175 50.9	S17 37.6
Hadar	148 46.1	S60 26.7
Hamal	327 58.6	N23 32.2
Kaus Aust.	83 41.9	S34 22.5
Kochab	137 21.5	N74 05.6
Markab	13 36.5	N15 17.6
Menkar	314 13.1	N 4 09.0
Menkent	148 06.0	S36 26.6
Miaplacidus	221 39.3	S69 46.7
Mirfak	308 37.5	N49 54.9
Nunki	75 56.5	S26 16.4
Peacock	53 16.9	S56 41.1
Pollux	243 25.7	N27 59.0
Procyon	244 58.0	N 5 10.9
Rasalhague	96 05.2	N12 33.3
Regulus	207 42.0	N11 53.3
Rigel	281 10.3	S 8 11.1
Rigil Kent.	139 50.1	S60 53.8
Sabik	102 11.0	S15 44.4
Schedar	349 38.1	N56 37.6
Shaula	96 20.1	S37 06.7
Sirius	258 32.1	S16 44.3
Spica	158 29.9	S11 14.4
Suhail	222 51.3	S43 29.6
Vega	80 38.1	N38 48.4
Zuben'ubi	137 04.0	S16 06.2

	SHA	Mer. Pass.
Venus	187 13.6	8 51
Mars	186 04.1	8 55
Jupiter	191 49.5	8 32
Saturn	117 34.3	13 28

UT	SUN GHA	SUN Dec	MOON GHA	v	Dec	d	HP
d h	° ′	° ′	° ′	′	° ′	′	′
31 00	184 05.3	S13 55.6	314 29.7	7.1	N18 09.9	1.0	58.5
01	199 05.3	56.4	328 55.8	7.2	18 10.9	0.8	58.5
02	214 05.3	57.2	343 22.0	7.2	18 11.7	0.8	58.4
03	229 05.4 ..	58.0	357 48.2	7.2	18 12.5	0.6	58.4
04	244 05.4	58.8	12 14.4	7.4	18 13.1	0.5	58.4
05	259 05.4	13 59.6	26 40.8	7.3	18 13.6	0.4	58.3
S 06	274 05.5	S14 00.4	41 07.1	7.4	N18 14.0	0.2	58.3
A 07	289 05.5	01.3	55 33.5	7.5	18 14.2	0.2	58.2
T 08	304 05.5	02.1	70 00.0	7.5	18 14.4	0.1	58.2
U 09	319 05.6 ..	02.9	84 26.5	7.5	18 14.5	0.1	58.2
R 10	334 05.6	03.7	98 53.0	7.7	18 14.4	0.2	58.1
D 11	349 05.6	04.5	113 19.7	7.6	18 14.2	0.3	58.1
A 12	4 05.6	S14 05.3	127 46.3	7.7	N18 13.9	0.3	58.0
Y 13	19 05.7	06.1	142 13.0	7.8	18 13.6	0.5	58.0
14	34 05.7	06.9	156 39.8	7.8	18 13.1	0.7	58.0
15	49 05.7 ..	07.7	171 06.6	7.9	18 12.4	0.7	57.9
16	64 05.7	08.5	185 33.5	8.0	18 11.7	0.8	57.9
17	79 05.8	09.4	200 00.5	8.0	18 10.9	0.9	57.8
18	94 05.8	S14 10.2	214 27.5	8.0	N18 10.0	1.1	57.8
19	109 05.8	11.0	228 54.5	8.2	18 08.9	1.1	57.8
20	124 05.8	11.8	243 21.7	8.1	18 07.8	1.3	57.7
21	139 05.9 ..	12.6	257 48.8	8.3	18 06.5	1.3	57.7
22	154 05.9	13.4	272 16.1	8.3	18 05.2	1.5	57.6
23	169 05.9	14.2	286 43.4	8.3	18 03.7	1.5	57.6
1 00	184 05.9	S14 15.0	301 10.7	8.5	N18 02.2	1.7	57.6
01	199 06.0	15.8	315 38.2	8.4	18 00.5	1.8	57.5
02	214 06.0	16.6	330 05.6	8.6	17 58.7	1.8	57.5
03	229 06.0 ..	17.4	344 33.2	8.6	17 56.9	2.0	57.4
04	244 06.0	18.2	359 00.8	8.7	17 54.9	2.1	57.4
05	259 06.0	19.0	13 28.5	8.7	17 52.8	2.2	57.4
S 06	274 06.1	S14 19.8	27 56.2	8.8	N17 50.6	2.2	57.3
U 07	289 06.1	20.6	42 24.0	8.9	17 48.4	2.4	57.3
N 08	304 06.1	21.4	56 51.9	8.9	17 46.0	2.5	57.3
D 09	319 06.1 ..	22.2	71 19.8	9.0	17 43.5	2.5	57.2
A 10	334 06.1	23.0	85 47.8	9.0	17 41.0	2.7	57.2
Y 11	349 06.2	23.8	100 15.8	9.2	17 38.3	2.7	57.1
12	4 06.2	S14 24.6	114 44.0	9.1	N17 35.6	2.9	57.1
13	19 06.2	25.4	129 12.1	9.3	17 32.7	2.9	57.1
14	34 06.2	26.2	143 40.4	9.3	17 29.8	3.0	57.0
15	49 06.2 ..	27.0	158 08.7	9.4	17 26.8	3.2	57.0
16	64 06.2	27.8	172 37.1	9.5	17 23.6	3.2	56.9
17	79 06.3	28.6	187 05.6	9.5	17 20.4	3.3	56.9
18	94 06.3	S14 29.4	201 34.1	9.6	N17 17.1	3.4	56.9
19	109 06.3	30.2	216 02.7	9.6	17 13.7	3.5	56.8
20	124 06.3	31.0	230 31.3	9.7	17 10.2	3.6	56.8
21	139 06.3 ..	31.8	245 00.0	9.8	17 06.6	3.6	56.8
22	154 06.3	32.6	259 28.8	9.9	17 03.0	3.8	56.7
23	169 06.4	33.4	273 57.7	9.9	16 59.2	3.8	56.7
2 00	184 06.4	S14 34.2	288 26.6	10.0	N16 55.4	4.0	56.7
01	199 06.4	35.0	302 55.6	10.0	16 51.4	4.0	56.6
02	214 06.4	35.8	317 24.6	10.2	16 47.4	4.1	56.6
03	229 06.4 ..	36.6	331 53.8	10.2	16 43.3	4.1	56.5
04	244 06.4	37.4	346 23.0	10.2	16 39.2	4.3	56.5
05	259 06.4	38.2	0 52.2	10.3	16 34.9	4.3	56.5
M 06	274 06.4	S14 39.0	15 21.5	10.4	N16 30.6	4.5	56.4
O 07	289 06.5	39.8	29 50.9	10.5	16 26.1	4.5	56.4
N 08	304 06.5	40.6	44 20.4	10.5	16 21.6	4.5	56.4
D 09	319 06.5 ..	41.4	58 49.9	10.6	16 17.1	4.7	56.3
A 10	334 06.5	42.2	73 19.5	10.7	16 12.4	4.8	56.3
Y 11	349 06.5	43.0	87 49.2	10.7	16 07.6	4.8	56.3
12	4 06.5	S14 43.7	102 18.9	10.8	N16 02.8	4.9	56.2
13	19 06.5	44.5	116 48.7	10.9	15 57.9	4.9	56.2
14	34 06.5	45.3	131 18.6	10.9	15 53.0	5.1	56.2
15	49 06.5 ..	46.1	145 48.5	11.0	15 47.9	5.1	56.1
16	64 06.6	46.9	160 18.5	11.1	15 42.8	5.2	56.1
17	79 06.6	47.7	174 48.6	11.1	15 37.6	5.3	56.1
18	94 06.6	S14 48.5	189 18.7	11.2	N15 32.3	5.3	56.0
19	109 06.6	49.3	203 48.9	11.3	15 27.0	5.4	56.0
20	124 06.6	50.1	218 19.2	11.3	15 21.6	5.5	56.0
21	139 06.6 ..	50.9	232 49.5	11.4	15 16.1	5.5	55.9
22	154 06.6	51.6	247 19.9	11.5	15 10.6	5.6	55.9
23	169 06.6	52.4	261 50.4	11.5	N15 05.0	5.7	55.9
SD	16.1	d 0.8	SD 15.8		15.6		15.3

Twilight / Sunrise / Moonrise

Lat.	Naut.	Civil	Sunrise	Moonrise 31	1	2	3
°	h m	h m	h m	h m	h m	h m	h m
N 72	06 05	07 28	08 54	▭	17 45	19 37	21 22
N 70	06 01	07 15	08 29	17 27	18 44	20 14	21 45
68	05 57	07 04	08 09	18 08	19 18	20 39	22 03
66	05 54	06 56	07 54	18 36	19 43	20 59	22 18
64	05 51	06 48	07 41	18 57	20 02	21 15	22 30
62	05 49	06 42	07 30	19 14	20 18	21 28	22 40
60	05 47	06 36	07 21	19 28	20 31	21 39	22 49
N 58	05 44	06 31	07 13	19 41	20 42	21 48	22 56
56	05 42	06 26	07 06	19 51	20 52	21 57	23 03
54	05 40	06 22	07 00	20 00	21 01	22 04	23 09
52	05 39	06 19	06 54	20 09	21 08	22 11	23 14
50	05 37	06 15	06 49	20 16	21 15	22 17	23 19
45	05 33	06 07	06 38	20 32	21 30	22 30	23 29
N 40	05 28	06 00	06 29	20 45	21 42	22 40	23 38
35	05 25	05 54	06 21	20 56	21 53	22 49	23 45
30	05 21	05 49	06 14	21 06	22 02	22 57	23 52
20	05 12	05 39	06 01	21 23	22 18	23 11	24 03
N 10	05 04	05 29	05 50	21 37	22 31	23 23	24 12
0	04 54	05 19	05 40	21 51	22 44	23 34	24 22
S 10	04 43	05 08	05 30	22 05	22 57	23 45	24 31
20	04 29	04 56	05 19	22 20	23 11	23 57	24 40
30	04 11	04 40	05 06	22 36	23 26	24 11	00 11
35	03 59	04 31	04 58	22 46	23 35	24 19	00 19
40	03 45	04 20	04 50	22 57	23 46	24 28	00 28
45	03 28	04 07	04 39	23 10	23 58	24 38	00 38
S 50	03 05	03 51	04 27	23 26	24 12	00 12	00 51
52	02 54	03 43	04 21	23 34	24 19	00 19	00 57
54	02 41	03 34	04 15	23 42	24 27	00 27	01 03
56	02 25	03 24	04 08	23 52	24 36	00 35	01 11
58	02 06	03 13	04 00	24 02	00 02	00 45	01 19
S 60	01 42	02 59	03 51	24 14	00 14	00 56	01 28

Twilight / Sunset / Moonset

Lat.	Sunset	Civil	Naut.	Moonset 31	1	2	3
°	h m	h m	h m	h m	h m	h m	h m
N 72	14 31	15 58	17 21	▭	15 22	15 16	15 11
N 70	14 57	16 11	17 25	13 48	14 23	14 39	14 46
68	15 17	16 22	17 28	13 07	13 48	14 12	14 27
66	15 32	16 30	17 32	12 39	13 23	13 52	14 12
64	15 45	16 38	17 34	12 18	13 03	13 36	13 59
62	15 56	16 44	17 37	12 00	12 47	13 22	13 48
60	16 05	16 50	17 39	11 46	12 34	13 11	13 39
N 58	16 13	16 55	17 42	11 34	12 23	13 01	13 31
56	16 20	17 00	17 44	11 23	12 13	12 52	13 24
54	16 27	17 04	17 46	11 14	12 04	12 44	13 18
52	16 32	17 08	17 48	11 06	11 56	12 37	13 12
50	16 38	17 11	17 50	10 58	11 49	12 31	13 07
45	16 49	17 19	17 54	10 42	11 33	12 17	12 55
N 40	16 58	17 26	17 58	10 29	11 21	12 06	12 46
35	17 06	17 32	18 02	10 18	11 10	11 57	12 38
30	17 13	17 38	18 06	10 08	11 01	11 48	12 31
20	17 26	17 48	18 14	09 51	10 44	11 33	12 18
N 10	17 37	17 58	18 23	09 36	10 30	11 21	12 08
0	17 47	18 08	18 33	09 22	10 17	11 09	11 57
S 10	17 58	18 19	18 45	09 09	10 04	10 56	11 47
20	18 09	18 32	18 59	08 54	09 49	10 43	11 36
30	18 22	18 47	19 17	08 37	09 33	10 29	11 23
35	18 30	18 57	19 29	08 27	09 23	10 20	11 16
40	18 38	19 08	19 43	08 16	09 12	10 10	11 08
45	18 49	19 21	20 01	08 02	08 59	09 58	10 58
S 50	19 01	19 37	20 24	07 46	08 44	09 44	10 46
52	19 07	19 45	20 35	07 38	08 36	09 38	10 41
54	19 13	19 54	20 48	07 30	08 28	09 30	10 35
56	19 21	20 05	21 04	07 20	08 19	09 22	10 28
58	19 29	20 16	21 24	07 10	08 08	09 13	10 20
S 60	19 38	20 30	21 50	06 57	07 56	09 02	10 11

SUN / MOON

Day	Eqn. of Time 00h	12h	Mer. Pass.	Mer. Pass. Upper	Lower	Age	Phase
d	m s	m s	h m	h m	h m	d	%
31	16 21	16 22	11 44	03 09	15 37	18	79
1	16 24	16 25	11 44	04 04	16 31	19	70
2	16 25	16 26	11 44	04 56	17 21	20	60

UT	ARIES GHA	VENUS −4.4 GHA	VENUS Dec	MARS +1.7 GHA	MARS Dec	JUPITER −1.8 GHA	JUPITER Dec	SATURN +0.5 GHA	SATURN Dec	STARS Name	SHA	Dec
3 00	41 56.2	227 10.7	N 3 01.5	226 53.0	N 3 39.3	233 26.8	N 6 02.1	159 16.7	S19 21.4	Acamar	315 16.8	S40 14.5
01	56 58.7	242 10.6	3 00.7	241 54.1	38.7	248 28.9	01.9	174 18.8	21.5	Achernar	335 25.1	S57 09.5
02	72 01.2	257 10.6	2 59.8	256 55.2	38.1	263 31.0	01.8	189 21.0	21.5	Acrux	173 07.9	S63 11.0
03	87 03.6	272 10.6	.. 59.0	271 56.2	.. 37.5	278 33.0	.. 01.6	204 23.2	.. 21.6	Adhara	255 11.1	S28 59.6
04	102 06.1	287 10.6	58.1	286 57.3	36.9	293 35.1	01.4	219 25.4	21.7	Aldebaran	290 47.2	N16 32.3
05	117 08.6	302 10.5	57.3	301 58.4	36.3	308 37.2	01.3	234 27.5	21.7			
06	132 11.0	317 10.5	N 2 56.4	316 59.4	N 3 35.7	323 39.3	N 6 01.1	249 29.7	S19 21.8	Alioth	166 19.9	N55 52.4
07	147 13.5	332 10.5	55.6	332 00.5	35.1	338 41.3	01.0	264 31.9	21.8	Alkaid	152 58.2	N49 14.1
08	162 16.0	347 10.4	54.7	347 01.6	34.5	353 43.4	00.8	279 34.1	21.9	Al Na'ir	27 41.7	S46 53.1
09	177 18.4	2 10.4	.. 53.9	2 02.6	.. 33.9	8 45.5	.. 00.7	294 36.2	.. 21.9	Alnilam	275 44.5	S 1 11.6
10	192 20.9	17 10.4	53.0	17 03.7	33.3	23 47.6	00.5	309 38.4	22.0	Alphard	217 54.6	S 8 43.6
11	207 23.3	32 10.3	52.2	32 04.8	32.7	38 49.6	00.4	324 40.6	22.0			
12	222 25.8	47 10.3	N 2 51.3	47 05.8	N 3 32.1	53 51.7	N 6 00.2	339 42.8	S19 22.1	Alphecca	126 10.0	N26 40.0
13	237 28.3	62 10.3	50.5	62 06.9	31.5	68 53.8	6 00.0	354 44.9	22.2	Alpheratz	357 41.5	N29 10.8
14	252 30.7	77 10.2	49.6	77 08.0	30.9	83 55.9	5 59.9	9 47.1	22.2	Altair	62 06.8	N 8 54.9
15	267 33.2	92 10.2	.. 48.8	92 09.0	.. 30.3	98 57.9	.. 59.7	24 49.3	.. 22.3	Ankaa	353 13.8	S42 13.3
16	282 35.7	107 10.2	47.9	107 10.1	29.7	114 00.0	59.6	39 51.4	22.3	Antares	112 24.6	S26 27.8
17	297 38.1	122 10.1	47.0	122 11.1	29.1	129 02.1	59.4	54 53.6	22.4			
18	312 40.6	137 10.1	N 2 46.2	137 12.2	N 3 28.5	144 04.2	N 5 59.3	69 55.8	S19 22.4	Arcturus	145 54.6	N19 06.2
19	327 43.1	152 10.1	45.3	152 13.3	28.0	159 06.3	59.1	84 58.0	22.5	Atria	107 25.4	S69 03.2
20	342 45.5	167 10.0	44.5	167 14.3	27.4	174 08.3	59.0	100 00.1	22.5	Avior	234 17.2	S59 33.4
21	357 48.0	182 10.0	.. 43.6	182 15.4	.. 26.8	189 10.4	.. 58.8	115 02.3	.. 22.6	Bellatrix	278 30.0	N 6 21.7
22	12 50.5	197 10.0	42.7	197 16.5	26.2	204 12.5	58.7	130 04.5	22.7	Betelgeuse	270 59.3	N 7 24.4
23	27 52.9	212 09.9	41.9	212 17.5	25.6	219 14.6	58.5	145 06.7	22.7			
4 00	42 55.4	227 09.9	N 2 41.0	227 18.6	N 3 25.0	234 16.6	N 5 58.3	160 08.8	S19 22.8	Canopus	263 55.1	S52 42.2
01	57 57.8	242 09.8	40.2	242 19.7	24.4	249 18.7	58.2	175 11.0	22.8	Capella	280 31.7	N46 00.5
02	73 00.3	257 09.8	39.3	257 20.7	23.8	264 20.8	58.0	190 13.2	22.9	Deneb	49 30.4	N45 20.7
03	88 02.8	272 09.8	.. 38.4	272 21.8	.. 23.2	279 22.9	.. 57.9	205 15.3	.. 22.9	Denebola	182 32.3	N14 29.0
04	103 05.2	287 09.7	37.6	287 22.9	22.6	294 24.9	57.7	220 17.5	23.0	Diphda	348 54.0	S17 54.0
05	118 07.7	302 09.7	36.7	302 23.9	22.0	309 27.0	57.6	235 19.7	23.0			
06	133 10.2	317 09.6	N 2 35.9	317 25.0	N 3 21.4	324 29.1	N 5 57.4	250 21.9	S19 23.1	Dubhe	193 50.3	N61 39.7
07	148 12.6	332 09.6	35.0	332 26.1	20.8	339 31.2	57.3	265 24.0	23.2	Elnath	278 10.3	N28 37.0
08	163 15.1	347 09.6	34.1	347 27.1	20.2	354 33.3	57.1	280 26.2	23.2	Eltanin	90 45.8	N51 29.6
09	178 17.6	2 09.5	.. 33.3	2 28.2	.. 19.6	9 35.3	.. 57.0	295 28.4	.. 23.3	Enif	33 45.5	N 9 57.1
10	193 20.0	17 09.5	32.4	17 29.3	19.0	24 37.4	56.8	310 30.6	23.3	Fomalhaut	15 22.1	S29 32.3
11	208 22.5	32 09.4	31.5	32 30.3	18.4	39 39.5	56.6	325 32.7	23.4			
12	223 25.0	47 09.4	N 2 30.7	47 31.4	N 3 17.8	54 41.6	N 5 56.5	340 34.9	S19 23.4	Gacrux	171 59.5	S57 11.8
13	238 27.4	62 09.4	29.8	62 32.5	17.2	69 43.7	56.3	355 37.1	23.5	Gienah	175 50.9	S17 37.6
14	253 29.9	77 09.3	28.9	77 33.5	16.6	84 45.7	56.2	10 39.2	23.5	Hadar	148 46.1	S60 26.7
15	268 32.3	92 09.3	.. 28.1	92 34.6	.. 16.1	99 47.8	.. 56.0	25 41.4	.. 23.6	Hamal	327 58.6	N23 32.2
16	283 34.8	107 09.2	27.2	107 35.7	15.5	114 49.9	55.9	40 43.6	23.6	Kaus Aust.	83 42.0	S34 22.5
17	298 37.3	122 09.2	26.3	122 36.7	14.9	129 52.0	55.7	55 45.8	23.7			
18	313 39.7	137 09.1	N 2 25.4	137 37.8	N 3 14.3	144 54.1	N 5 55.6	70 47.9	S19 23.8	Kochab	137 21.5	N74 05.6
19	328 42.2	152 09.1	24.6	152 38.9	13.7	159 56.1	55.4	85 50.1	23.8	Markab	13 36.5	N15 17.6
20	343 44.7	167 09.0	23.7	167 39.9	13.1	174 58.2	55.3	100 52.3	23.9	Menkar	314 13.0	N 4 09.0
21	358 47.1	182 09.0	.. 22.8	182 41.0	.. 12.5	190 00.3	.. 55.1	115 54.4	.. 23.9	Menkent	148 06.0	S36 26.6
22	13 49.6	197 08.9	22.0	197 42.1	11.9	205 02.4	55.0	130 56.6	24.0	Miaplacidus	221 39.2	S69 46.7
23	28 52.1	212 08.9	21.1	212 43.1	11.3	220 04.5	54.8	145 58.8	24.0			
5 00	43 54.5	227 08.9	N 2 20.2	227 44.2	N 3 10.7	235 06.5	N 5 54.7	161 01.0	S19 24.1	Mirfak	308 37.5	N49 54.9
01	58 57.0	242 08.8	19.3	242 45.3	10.1	250 08.6	54.5	176 03.1	24.1	Nunki	75 56.5	S26 16.4
02	73 59.4	257 08.8	18.5	257 46.3	09.5	265 10.7	54.3	191 05.3	24.2	Peacock	53 16.9	S56 41.1
03	89 01.9	272 08.7	.. 17.6	272 47.4	.. 08.9	280 12.8	.. 54.2	206 07.5	.. 24.3	Pollux	243 25.7	N27 59.0
04	104 04.4	287 08.7	16.7	287 48.5	08.3	295 14.9	54.0	221 09.6	24.3	Procyon	244 58.0	N 5 10.9
05	119 06.8	302 08.6	15.9	302 49.6	07.7	310 17.0	53.9	236 11.8	24.4			
06	134 09.3	317 08.6	N 2 15.0	317 50.6	N 3 07.1	325 19.0	N 5 53.7	251 14.0	S19 24.4	Rasalhague	96 05.2	N12 33.3
07	149 11.8	332 08.5	14.1	332 51.7	06.5	340 21.1	53.6	266 16.2	24.5	Regulus	207 41.9	N11 53.3
08	164 14.2	347 08.5	13.2	347 52.8	05.9	355 23.2	53.4	281 18.3	24.5	Rigel	281 10.3	S 8 11.1
09	179 16.7	2 08.4	.. 12.3	2 53.8	.. 05.3	10 25.3	.. 53.3	296 20.5	.. 24.6	Rigil Kent.	139 50.1	S60 53.8
10	194 19.2	17 08.4	11.5	17 54.9	04.8	25 27.4	53.1	311 22.7	24.6	Sabik	102 11.0	S15 44.4
11	209 21.6	32 08.3	10.6	32 56.0	04.2	40 29.4	53.0	326 24.8	24.7			
12	224 24.1	47 08.2	N 2 09.7	47 57.0	N 3 03.6	55 31.5	N 5 52.8	341 27.0	S19 24.8	Schedar	349 38.1	N56 37.6
13	239 26.6	62 08.2	08.8	62 58.1	03.0	70 33.6	52.7	356 29.2	24.8	Shaula	96 20.1	S37 06.7
14	254 29.0	77 08.1	08.0	77 59.2	02.4	85 35.7	52.5	11 31.4	24.9	Sirius	258 32.1	S16 44.3
15	269 31.5	92 08.1	.. 07.1	93 00.2	.. 01.8	100 37.8	.. 52.4	26 33.5	.. 24.9	Spica	158 29.9	S11 14.4
16	284 33.9	107 08.0	06.2	108 01.3	01.2	115 39.9	52.2	41 35.7	25.0	Suhail	222 51.2	S43 29.6
17	299 36.4	122 08.0	05.3	123 02.4	00.6	130 41.9	52.1	56 37.9	25.0			
18	314 38.9	137 07.9	N 2 04.4	138 03.4	N 3 00.0	145 44.0	N 5 51.9	71 40.0	S19 25.1	Vega	80 38.1	N38 48.3
19	329 41.3	152 07.9	03.6	153 04.5	2 59.4	160 46.1	51.8	86 42.2	25.1	Zuben'ubi	137 04.0	S16 06.2
20	344 43.8	167 07.8	02.7	168 05.6	58.8	175 48.2	51.6	101 44.4	25.2			
21	359 46.3	182 07.8	.. 01.8	183 06.7	.. 58.2	190 50.3	.. 51.5	116 46.5	.. 25.3			
22	14 48.7	197 07.7	00.9	198 07.7	57.6	205 52.4	51.3	131 48.7	25.3			
23	29 51.2	212 07.6	00.0	213 08.8	57.0	220 54.5	51.2	146 50.9	25.4			

	SHA	Mer. Pass.
Venus	184 14.5	8 51
Mars	184 23.2	8 50
Jupiter	191 21.3	8 22
Saturn	117 13.4	13 17

Mer. Pass. 21 04.8   v 0.0   d 0.9   v 1.1   d 0.6   v 2.1   d 0.2   v 2.2   d 0.1

UT	SUN GHA	SUN Dec	MOON GHA	MOON v	MOON Dec	MOON d	MOON HP
d h	° ′	° ′	° ′	′	° ′	′	′
3 00	184 06.6	S14 53.2	276 20.9	11.6	N14 59.3	5.8	55.8
01	199 06.6	54.0	290 51.5	11.7	14 53.5	5.8	55.8
02	214 06.6	54.8	305 22.2	11.7	14 47.7	5.9	55.8
03	229 06.6	.. 55.6	319 52.9	11.8	14 41.8	5.9	55.7
04	244 06.6	56.4	334 23.7	11.8	14 35.9	6.1	55.7
05	259 06.6	57.1	348 54.5	11.9	14 29.8	6.0	55.7
06	274 06.6	S14 57.9	3 25.4	12.0	N14 23.8	6.2	55.7
07	289 06.6	58.7	17 56.4	12.0	14 17.6	6.2	55.6
08	304 06.6	14 59.5	32 27.4	12.1	14 11.4	6.3	55.6
09	319 06.6	15 00.3	46 58.5	12.2	14 05.1	6.3	55.6
10	334 06.6	01.1	61 29.7	12.2	13 58.8	6.4	55.5
11	349 06.6	01.8	76 00.9	12.3	13 52.4	6.4	55.5
12	4 06.6	S15 02.6	90 32.2	12.3	N13 46.0	6.5	55.5
13	19 06.6	03.4	105 03.5	12.4	13 39.5	6.6	55.5
14	34 06.6	04.2	119 34.9	12.5	13 32.9	6.6	55.4
15	49 06.6	.. 05.0	134 06.4	12.5	13 26.3	6.7	55.4
16	64 06.6	05.7	148 37.9	12.6	13 19.6	6.7	55.4
17	79 06.6	06.5	163 09.5	12.6	13 12.9	6.8	55.3
18	94 06.6	S15 07.3	177 41.1	12.7	N13 06.1	6.8	55.3
19	109 06.6	08.1	192 12.8	12.7	12 59.3	6.9	55.3
20	124 06.6	08.8	206 44.5	12.9	12 52.4	7.0	55.3
21	139 06.6	.. 09.6	221 16.4	12.8	12 45.4	7.0	55.2
22	154 06.6	10.4	235 48.2	12.9	12 38.4	7.0	55.2
23	169 06.6	11.2	250 20.1	13.0	12 31.4	7.1	55.2
4 00	184 06.6	S15 12.0	264 52.1	13.0	N12 24.3	7.2	55.2
01	199 06.6	12.7	279 24.1	13.1	12 17.1	7.2	55.1
02	214 06.6	13.5	293 56.2	13.2	12 09.9	7.3	55.1
03	229 06.6	.. 14.3	308 28.4	13.1	12 02.6	7.3	55.1
04	244 06.6	15.1	323 00.5	13.3	11 55.3	7.3	55.1
05	259 06.6	15.8	337 32.8	13.3	11 48.0	7.4	55.0
06	274 06.6	S15 16.6	352 05.1	13.3	N11 40.6	7.5	55.0
07	289 06.6	17.4	6 37.4	13.4	11 33.1	7.4	55.0
08	304 06.6	18.1	21 09.8	13.5	11 25.7	7.6	55.0
09	319 06.6	.. 18.9	35 42.3	13.5	11 18.1	7.6	55.0
10	334 06.6	19.7	50 14.8	13.5	11 10.5	7.6	54.9
11	349 06.6	20.5	64 47.3	13.6	11 02.9	7.6	54.9
12	4 06.6	S15 21.2	79 19.9	13.7	N10 55.3	7.7	54.9
13	19 06.6	22.0	93 52.6	13.7	10 47.6	7.8	54.9
14	34 06.6	22.8	108 25.3	13.7	10 39.8	7.8	54.8
15	49 06.5	.. 23.5	122 58.0	13.8	10 32.0	7.8	54.8
16	64 06.5	24.3	137 30.8	13.8	10 24.2	7.9	54.8
17	79 06.5	25.1	152 03.6	13.9	10 16.3	7.9	54.8
18	94 06.5	S15 25.9	166 36.5	13.9	N10 08.4	8.0	54.8
19	109 06.5	26.6	181 09.4	14.0	10 00.4	7.9	54.7
20	124 06.5	27.4	195 42.4	14.0	9 52.5	8.1	54.7
21	139 06.5	.. 28.2	210 15.4	14.0	9 44.4	8.0	54.7
22	154 06.5	28.9	224 48.4	14.1	9 36.4	8.1	54.7
23	169 06.5	29.7	239 21.5	14.1	9 28.3	8.2	54.7
5 00	184 06.5	S15 30.5	253 54.6	14.2	N 9 20.1	8.1	54.7
01	199 06.4	31.2	268 27.8	14.2	9 12.0	8.2	54.6
02	214 06.4	32.0	283 01.0	14.3	9 03.8	8.3	54.6
03	229 06.4	.. 32.7	297 34.3	14.3	8 55.5	8.2	54.6
04	244 06.4	33.5	312 07.6	14.3	8 47.3	8.3	54.6
05	259 06.4	34.3	326 40.9	14.4	8 39.0	8.4	54.6
06	274 06.4	S15 35.0	341 14.3	14.4	N 8 30.6	8.3	54.5
07	289 06.4	35.8	355 47.7	14.4	8 22.3	8.4	54.5
08	304 06.3	36.6	10 21.1	14.5	8 13.9	8.5	54.5
09	319 06.3	.. 37.3	24 54.6	14.5	8 05.4	8.4	54.5
10	334 06.3	38.1	39 28.1	14.6	7 57.0	8.5	54.5
11	349 06.3	38.8	54 01.7	14.6	7 48.5	8.5	54.4
12	4 06.3	S15 39.6	68 35.3	14.6	N 7 40.0	8.6	54.5
13	19 06.3	40.4	83 08.9	14.6	7 31.4	8.5	54.4
14	34 06.2	41.1	97 42.5	14.7	7 22.9	8.6	54.4
15	49 06.2	.. 41.9	112 16.2	14.7	7 14.3	8.7	54.4
16	64 06.2	42.6	126 49.9	14.8	7 05.6	8.6	54.4
17	79 06.2	43.4	141 23.7	14.7	6 57.0	8.7	54.4
18	94 06.2	S15 44.2	155 57.4	14.8	N 6 48.3	8.7	54.4
19	109 06.2	44.9	170 31.2	14.9	6 39.6	8.7	54.4
20	124 06.1	45.7	185 05.1	14.8	6 30.9	8.8	54.3
21	139 06.1	.. 46.4	199 38.9	14.9	6 22.1	8.7	54.3
22	154 06.1	47.2	214 12.8	14.9	6 13.4	8.8	54.3
23	169 06.1	47.9	228 46.7	14.9	N 6 04.6	8.9	54.3
SD	16.2	d 0.8	SD 15.1		15.0		14.8

Left-margin day labels: TUESDAY (rows 3 00–3 23), WEDNESDAY (rows 4 00–4 23), THURSDAY (rows 5 00–5 23).

Lat.	Twilight Naut.	Civil	Sunrise	Moonrise 3	4	5	6
°	h m	h m	h m	h m	h m	h m	h m
N 72	06 17	07 41	09 14	21 22	23 00	24 35	00 35
N 70	06 11	07 27	08 44	21 45	23 16	24 44	00 44
68	06 07	07 15	08 22	22 03	23 28	24 51	00 51
66	06 03	07 05	08 05	22 18	23 38	24 57	00 57
64	05 59	06 57	07 51	22 30	23 46	25 01	01 01
62	05 56	06 49	07 39	22 40	23 53	25 06	01 06
60	05 53	06 43	07 29	22 49	23 59	25 09	01 09
N 58	05 51	06 37	07 20	22 56	24 04	00 04	01 12
56	05 48	06 32	07 12	23 03	24 09	00 09	01 15
54	05 46	06 28	07 06	23 09	24 13	00 13	01 18
52	05 43	06 24	07 00	23 14	24 17	00 17	01 20
50	05 41	06 20	06 54	23 19	24 21	00 21	01 22
45	05 36	06 11	06 42	23 29	24 28	00 28	01 27
N 40	05 32	06 06	06 32	23 38	24 34	00 34	01 30
35	05 27	05 57	06 23	23 45	24 40	00 40	01 34
30	05 23	05 51	06 16	23 52	24 45	00 45	01 37
20	05 14	05 40	06 03	24 03	00 03	00 53	01 42
N 10	05 04	05 29	05 51	24 12	00 12	01 00	01 46
0	04 54	05 19	05 40	24 22	00 22	01 07	01 50
S 10	04 42	05 07	05 29	24 31	00 31	01 13	01 54
20	04 27	04 54	05 17	24 40	00 40	01 21	01 59
30	04 08	04 38	05 03	00 11	00 52	01 29	02 04
35	03 56	04 28	04 55	00 19	00 58	01 33	02 07
40	03 41	04 17	04 46	00 28	01 05	01 39	02 10
45	03 23	04 03	04 35	00 38	01 14	01 45	02 14
S 50	02 58	03 45	04 22	00 51	01 24	01 52	02 18
52	02 46	03 37	04 16	00 57	01 28	01 56	02 20
54	02 32	03 27	04 09	01 03	01 34	01 59	02 22
56	02 15	03 17	04 01	01 11	01 39	02 03	02 25
58	01 54	03 04	03 53	01 19	01 46	02 08	02 27
S 60	01 26	02 50	03 43	01 28	01 53	02 13	02 31

Lat.	Sunset	Twilight Civil	Naut.	Moonset 3	4	5	6
°	h m	h m	h m	h m	h m	h m	h m
N 72	14 12	15 44	17 09	15 11	15 06	15 02	14 57
N 70	14 42	15 59	17 14	14 46	14 50	14 51	14 52
68	15 04	16 11	17 19	14 27	14 36	14 43	14 48
66	15 21	16 21	17 23	14 12	14 26	14 36	14 45
64	15 35	16 29	17 27	13 59	14 16	14 30	14 42
62	15 47	16 37	17 30	13 48	14 08	14 25	14 39
60	15 57	16 43	17 33	13 39	14 02	14 21	14 37
N 58	16 06	16 49	17 36	13 31	13 56	14 17	14 35
56	16 14	16 54	17 38	13 24	13 50	14 13	14 33
54	16 21	16 59	17 41	13 18	13 45	14 10	14 32
52	16 27	17 03	17 43	13 12	13 41	14 07	14 30
50	16 33	17 07	17 45	13 07	13 37	14 04	14 29
45	16 45	17 15	17 50	12 55	13 28	13 58	14 26
N 40	16 55	17 23	17 55	12 46	13 21	13 53	14 24
35	17 03	17 30	18 00	12 38	13 15	13 49	14 22
30	17 11	17 36	18 04	12 31	13 10	13 46	14 20
20	17 24	17 47	18 13	12 18	13 00	13 39	14 16
N 10	17 36	17 58	18 23	12 08	12 52	13 33	14 14
0	17 47	18 08	18 33	11 57	12 44	13 28	14 11
S 10	17 58	18 20	18 46	11 47	12 36	13 22	14 08
20	18 10	18 33	19 01	11 36	12 27	13 17	14 05
30	18 24	18 50	19 20	11 23	12 17	13 10	14 02
35	18 32	19 00	19 32	11 16	12 12	13 06	14 00
40	18 42	19 11	19 47	11 08	12 05	13 02	13 57
45	18 53	19 25	20 06	10 58	11 57	12 56	13 55
S 50	19 06	19 43	20 30	10 46	11 48	12 50	13 52
52	19 12	19 52	20 43	10 41	11 44	12 47	13 50
54	19 19	20 01	20 57	10 35	11 39	12 44	13 48
56	19 27	20 12	21 15	10 28	11 34	12 41	13 47
58	19 36	20 25	21 37	10 20	11 28	12 37	13 45
S 60	19 46	20 40	22 06	10 11	11 22	12 32	13 43

Day	SUN Eqn. of Time 00h	12h	Mer. Pass.	MOON Mer. Pass. Upper	Lower	Age	Phase
d	m s	m s	h m	h m	h m	d	%
3	16 26	16 26	11 44	05 46	18 10	21	50
4	16 27	16 26	11 44	06 33	18 55	22	41
5	16 26	16 25	11 44	07 17	19 39	23	31

UT	ARIES GHA	VENUS −4.4 GHA	Dec	MARS +1.7 GHA	Dec	JUPITER −1.8 GHA	Dec	SATURN +0.5 GHA	Dec	STARS Name	SHA	Dec
d h	° ′	° ′	° ′	° ′	° ′	° ′	° ′	° ′	° ′		° ′	° ′
6 00	44 53.7	227 07.6	N 1 59.1	228 09.9	N 2 56.4	235 56.5	N 5 51.0	161 53.1	S19 25.4	Acamar	315 16.7	S40 14.6
01	59 56.1	242 07.5	58.3	243 10.9	55.8	250 58.6	50.9	176 55.2	25.5	Achernar	335 25.1	S57 09.5
02	74 58.6	257 07.5	57.4	258 12.0	55.2	266 00.7	50.7	191 57.4	25.5	Acrux	173 07.9	S63 10.9
03	90 01.1	272 07.4 ..	56.5	273 13.1 ..	54.6	281 02.8 ..	50.5	206 59.6 ..	25.6	Adhara	255 11.1	S28 59.6
04	105 03.5	287 07.4	55.6	288 14.1	54.0	296 04.9	50.4	222 01.7	25.6	Aldebaran	290 47.2	N16 32.3
05	120 06.0	302 07.3	54.7	303 15.2	53.4	311 07.0	50.2	237 03.9	25.7			
06	135 08.4	317 07.2	N 1 53.8	318 16.3	N 2 52.9	326 09.1	N 5 50.1	252 06.1	S19 25.8	Alioth	166 19.9	N55 52.4
07	150 10.9	332 07.2	52.9	333 17.4	52.3	341 11.1	49.9	267 08.2	25.8	Alkaid	152 58.2	N49 14.1
08	165 13.4	347 07.1	52.0	348 18.4	51.7	356 13.2	49.8	282 10.4	25.9	Al Na'ir	27 41.7	S46 53.1
09	180 15.8	2 07.1 ..	51.2	3 19.5 ..	51.1	11 15.3 ..	49.6	297 12.6 ..	25.9	Alnilam	275 44.5	S 1 11.6
10	195 18.3	17 07.0	50.3	18 20.6	50.5	26 17.4	49.5	312 14.8	26.0	Alphard	217 54.5	S 8 43.6
11	210 20.8	32 06.9	49.4	33 21.6	49.9	41 19.5	49.3	327 16.9	26.0			
12	225 23.2	47 06.9	N 1 48.5	48 22.7	N 2 49.3	56 21.6	N 5 49.2	342 19.1	S19 26.1	Alphecca	126 10.0	N26 40.0
13	240 25.7	62 06.8	47.6	63 23.8	48.7	71 23.7	49.0	357 21.3	26.1	Alpheratz	357 41.5	N29 10.9
14	255 28.2	77 06.8	46.7	78 24.8	48.1	86 25.8	48.9	12 23.4	26.2	Altair	62 06.8	N 8 54.9
15	270 30.6	92 06.7 ..	45.8	93 25.9 ..	47.5	101 27.8 ..	48.7	27 25.6 ..	26.2	Ankaa	353 13.9	S42 13.3
16	285 33.1	107 06.6	44.9	108 27.0	46.9	116 29.9	48.6	42 27.8	26.3	Antares	112 24.6	S26 27.8
17	300 35.5	122 06.6	44.0	123 28.1	46.3	131 32.0	48.4	57 29.9	26.4			
18	315 38.0	137 06.5	N 1 43.1	138 29.1	N 2 45.7	146 34.1	N 5 48.3	72 32.1	S19 26.4	Arcturus	145 54.6	N19 06.2
19	330 40.5	152 06.4	42.3	153 30.2	45.1	161 36.2	48.1	87 34.3	26.5	Atria	107 25.4	S69 03.2
20	345 42.9	167 06.4	41.4	168 31.3	44.5	176 38.3	48.0	102 36.5	26.5	Avior	234 17.2	S59 33.4
21	0 45.4	182 06.3 ..	40.5	183 32.3 ..	43.9	191 40.4 ..	47.8	117 38.6 ..	26.6	Bellatrix	278 30.0	N 6 21.7
22	15 47.9	197 06.2	39.6	198 33.4	43.3	206 42.5	47.7	132 40.8	26.6	Betelgeuse	270 59.3	N 7 24.4
23	30 50.3	212 06.2	38.7	213 34.5	42.7	221 44.5	47.5	147 43.0	26.7			
7 00	45 52.8	227 06.1	N 1 37.8	228 35.6	N 2 42.1	236 46.6	N 5 47.4	162 45.1	S19 26.7	Canopus	263 55.1	S52 42.2
01	60 55.3	242 06.0	36.9	243 36.6	41.6	251 48.7	47.2	177 47.3	26.8	Capella	280 31.7	N46 00.5
02	75 57.7	257 06.0	36.0	258 37.7	41.0	266 50.8	47.1	192 49.5	26.9	Deneb	49 30.4	N45 20.7
03	91 00.2	272 05.9 ..	35.1	273 38.8 ..	40.4	281 52.9 ..	46.9	207 51.6 ..	26.9	Denebola	182 32.3	N14 29.0
04	106 02.7	287 05.8	34.2	288 39.8	39.8	296 55.0	46.8	222 53.8	27.0	Diphda	348 54.0	S17 54.0
05	121 05.1	302 05.8	33.3	303 40.9	39.2	311 57.1	46.6	237 56.0	27.0			
06	136 07.6	317 05.7	N 1 32.4	318 42.0	N 2 38.6	326 59.2	N 5 46.5	252 58.1	S19 27.1	Dubhe	193 50.2	N61 39.7
07	151 10.0	332 05.6	31.5	333 43.1	38.0	342 01.3	46.3	268 00.3	27.1	Elnath	278 10.3	N28 37.0
08	166 12.5	347 05.6	30.6	348 44.1	37.4	357 03.4	46.2	283 02.5	27.2	Eltanin	90 45.8	N51 29.6
09	181 15.0	2 05.5 ..	29.7	3 45.2 ..	36.8	12 05.4 ..	46.0	298 04.6 ..	27.2	Enif	33 45.5	N 9 57.1
10	196 17.4	17 05.4	28.8	18 46.3	36.2	27 07.5	45.9	313 06.8	27.3	Fomalhaut	15 22.1	S29 32.3
11	211 19.9	32 05.3	27.9	33 47.3	35.6	42 09.6	45.8	328 09.0	27.4			
12	226 22.4	47 05.3	N 1 27.0	48 48.4	N 2 35.0	57 11.7	N 5 45.6	343 11.1	S19 27.4	Gacrux	171 59.4	S57 11.8
13	241 24.8	62 05.2	26.1	63 49.5	34.4	72 13.8	45.5	358 13.3	27.5	Gienah	175 50.9	S17 37.6
14	256 27.3	77 05.1	25.2	78 50.6	33.8	87 15.9	45.3	13 15.5	27.5	Hadar	148 46.1	S60 26.7
15	271 29.8	92 05.1 ..	24.3	93 51.6 ..	33.2	102 18.0 ..	45.2	28 17.7 ..	27.6	Hamal	327 58.6	N23 32.2
16	286 32.2	107 05.0	23.4	108 52.7	32.6	117 20.1	45.0	43 19.8	27.6	Kaus Aust.	83 42.0	S34 22.4
17	301 34.7	122 04.9	22.5	123 53.8	32.0	132 22.2	44.9	58 22.0	27.7			
18	316 37.1	137 04.8	N 1 21.6	138 54.8	N 2 31.4	147 24.3	N 5 44.7	73 24.2	S19 27.7	Kochab	137 21.5	N74 05.6
19	331 39.6	152 04.8	20.7	153 55.9	30.9	162 26.4	44.6	88 26.3	27.8	Markab	13 36.6	N15 17.6
20	346 42.1	167 04.7	19.8	168 57.0	30.3	177 28.5	44.4	103 28.5	27.8	Menkar	314 13.0	N 4 09.0
21	1 44.5	182 04.6 ..	18.9	183 58.1 ..	29.7	192 30.5 ..	44.3	118 30.7 ..	27.9	Menkent	148 06.0	S36 26.6
22	16 47.0	197 04.5	18.0	198 59.1	29.1	207 32.6	44.1	133 32.8	28.0	Miaplacidus	221 39.2	S69 46.7
23	31 49.5	212 04.5	17.1	214 00.2	28.5	222 34.7	44.0	148 35.0	28.0			
8 00	46 51.9	227 04.4	N 1 16.2	229 01.3	N 2 27.9	237 36.8	N 5 43.8	163 37.2	S19 28.1	Mirfak	308 37.5	N49 54.9
01	61 54.4	242 04.3	15.3	244 02.4	27.3	252 38.9	43.7	178 39.3	28.1	Nunki	75 56.6	S26 16.4
02	76 56.9	257 04.2	14.4	259 03.4	26.7	267 41.0	43.5	193 41.5	28.2	Peacock	53 16.9	S56 41.1
03	91 59.3	272 04.2 ..	13.5	274 04.5 ..	26.1	282 43.1 ..	43.4	208 43.7 ..	28.2	Pollux	243 25.7	N27 59.0
04	107 01.8	287 04.1	12.5	289 05.6	25.5	297 45.2	43.2	223 45.8	28.3	Procyon	244 57.9	N 5 10.9
05	122 04.3	302 04.0	11.6	304 06.7	24.9	312 47.3	43.1	238 48.0	28.3			
06	137 06.7	317 03.9	N 1 10.7	319 07.7	N 2 24.3	327 49.4	N 5 42.9	253 50.2	S19 28.4	Rasalhague	96 05.2	N12 33.3
07	152 09.2	332 03.9	09.8	334 08.8	23.7	342 51.5	42.8	268 52.3	28.5	Regulus	207 41.9	N11 53.3
08	167 11.6	347 03.8	08.9	349 09.9	23.1	357 53.6	42.6	283 54.5	28.5	Rigel	281 10.2	S 8 11.1
09	182 14.1	2 03.7 ..	08.0	4 10.9 ..	22.5	12 55.7 ..	42.5	298 56.7 ..	28.6	Rigil Kent.	139 50.1	S60 53.8
10	197 16.6	17 03.6	07.1	19 12.0	21.9	27 57.8	42.3	313 58.8	28.6	Sabik	102 11.0	S15 44.4
11	212 19.0	32 03.5	06.2	34 13.1	21.3	42 59.9	42.2	329 01.0	28.7			
12	227 21.5	47 03.5	N 1 05.3	49 14.2	N 2 20.8	58 02.0	N 5 42.1	344 03.2	S19 28.7	Schedar	349 38.1	N56 37.6
13	242 24.0	62 03.4	04.4	64 15.2	20.2	73 04.0	41.9	359 05.3	28.8	Shaula	96 20.1	S37 06.7
14	257 26.4	77 03.3	03.5	79 16.3	19.6	88 06.1	41.8	14 07.5	28.8	Sirius	258 32.1	S16 44.3
15	272 28.9	92 03.2 ..	02.5	94 17.4 ..	19.0	103 08.2 ..	41.6	29 09.7 ..	28.9	Spica	158 29.9	S11 14.4
16	287 31.4	107 03.1	01.6	109 18.5	18.4	118 10.3	41.5	44 11.8	28.9	Suhail	222 51.2	S43 29.6
17	302 33.8	122 03.1	1 00.7	124 19.5	17.8	133 12.4	41.3	59 14.0	29.0			
18	317 36.3	137 03.0	N 0 59.8	139 20.6	N 2 17.2	148 14.5	N 5 41.2	74 16.2	S19 29.1	Vega	80 38.1	N38 48.3
19	332 38.7	152 02.9	58.9	154 21.7	16.6	163 16.6	41.0	89 18.3	29.1	Zuben'ubi	137 04.0	S16 06.2
20	347 41.2	167 02.8	58.0	169 22.8	16.0	178 18.7	40.9	104 20.5	29.2		SHA	Mer. Pass.
21	2 43.7	182 02.7 ..	57.1	184 23.8 ..	15.4	193 20.8 ..	40.7	119 22.7 ..	29.2		° ′	h m
22	17 46.1	197 02.6	56.2	199 24.9	14.8	208 22.9	40.6	134 24.8	29.3	Venus	181 13.3	8 52
23	32 48.6	212 02.6	55.2	214 26.0	14.2	223 25.0	40.4	149 27.0	29.3	Mars	182 42.8	8 45
	h m									Jupiter	190 53.8	8 12
Mer. Pass. 20 53.0		v −0.1	d 0.9	v 1.1	d 0.6	v 2.1	d 0.1	v 2.2	d 0.1	Saturn	116 52.3	13 07

UT	SUN GHA	SUN Dec	MOON GHA	v	MOON Dec	d	HP
d h	° ′	° ′	° ′	′	° ′	′	′
6 00	184 06.1	S15 48.7	243 20.6	15.0	N 5 55.7	8.8	54.3
01	199 06.0	49.5	257 54.6	15.0	5 46.9	8.8	54.3
02	214 06.0	50.2	272 28.6	15.0	5 38.1	8.9	54.3
03	229 06.0 ..	51.0	287 02.6	15.0	5 29.2	8.9	54.3
04	244 06.0	51.7	301 36.6	15.1	5 20.3	8.9	54.3
05	259 06.0	52.5	316 10.7	15.1	5 11.4	9.0	54.2
06	274 05.9	S15 53.2	330 44.8	15.1	N 5 02.4	8.9	54.2
07	289 05.9	54.0	345 18.9	15.1	4 53.5	9.0	54.2
F 08	304 05.9	54.7	359 53.0	15.1	4 44.5	9.0	54.2
R 09	319 05.9 ..	55.5	14 27.1	15.2	4 35.5	9.0	54.2
I 10	334 05.8	56.2	29 01.3	15.1	4 26.5	9.0	54.2
D 11	349 05.8	57.0	43 35.4	15.2	4 17.5	9.1	54.2
A 12	4 05.8	S15 57.7	58 09.6	15.2	N 4 08.4	9.0	54.2
Y 13	19 05.8	58.5	72 43.8	15.3	3 59.4	9.1	54.2
14	34 05.7	15 59.2	87 18.1	15.2	3 50.3	9.1	54.2
15	49 05.7	16 00.0	101 52.3	15.3	3 41.2	9.1	54.2
16	64 05.7	00.7	116 26.6	15.2	3 32.1	9.1	54.1
17	79 05.7	01.5	131 00.8	15.3	3 23.0	9.1	54.1
18	94 05.6	S16 02.2	145 35.1	15.3	N 3 13.9	9.1	54.1
19	109 05.6	03.0	160 09.4	15.3	3 04.8	9.1	54.1
20	124 05.6	03.7	174 43.7	15.3	2 55.7	9.2	54.1
21	139 05.5 ..	04.4	189 18.0	15.4	2 46.5	9.1	54.1
22	154 05.5	05.2	203 52.4	15.3	2 37.3	9.1	54.1
23	169 05.5	05.9	218 26.7	15.4	2 28.2	9.1	54.1
7 00	184 05.5	S16 06.7	233 01.1	15.3	N 2 19.0	9.2	54.1
01	199 05.4	07.4	247 35.4	15.4	2 09.8	9.2	54.1
02	214 05.4	08.2	262 09.8	15.4	2 00.6	9.2	54.1
03	229 05.4 ..	08.9	276 44.2	15.4	1 51.4	9.2	54.1
04	244 05.3	09.6	291 18.6	15.4	1 42.2	9.2	54.1
05	259 05.3	10.4	305 53.0	15.4	1 33.0	9.3	54.1
06	274 05.3	S16 11.1	320 27.4	15.4	N 1 23.7	9.2	54.1
S 07	289 05.2	11.9	335 01.8	15.4	1 14.5	9.2	54.1
A 08	304 05.2	12.6	349 36.2	15.4	1 05.3	9.3	54.1
T 09	319 05.2 ..	13.4	4 10.6	15.4	0 56.0	9.2	54.1
U 10	334 05.1	14.1	18 45.0	15.4	0 46.8	9.3	54.1
R 11	349 05.1	14.8	33 19.4	15.4	0 37.5	9.2	54.1
D 12	4 05.1	S16 15.6	47 53.8	15.4	N 0 28.3	9.3	54.1
A 13	19 05.0	16.3	62 28.2	15.4	0 19.0	9.2	54.1
Y 14	34 05.0	17.0	77 02.6	15.5	0 09.8	9.3	54.1
15	49 05.0 ..	17.8	91 37.1	15.4	N 0 00.5	9.2	54.1
16	64 04.9	18.5	106 11.5	15.4	S 0 08.7	9.3	54.0
17	79 04.9	19.3	120 45.9	15.4	0 18.0	9.2	54.0
18	94 04.9	S16 20.0	135 20.3	15.4	S 0 27.2	9.3	54.0
19	109 04.8	20.7	149 54.7	15.4	0 36.5	9.2	54.0
20	124 04.8	21.5	164 29.1	15.4	0 45.7	9.3	54.0
21	139 04.8 ..	22.2	179 03.5	15.4	0 55.0	9.2	54.0
22	154 04.7	22.9	193 37.9	15.4	1 04.2	9.3	54.0
23	169 04.7	23.7	208 12.3	15.4	1 13.5	9.2	54.0
8 00	184 04.6	S16 24.4	222 46.7	15.4	S 1 22.7	9.2	54.0
01	199 04.6	25.1	237 21.1	15.4	1 31.9	9.3	54.0
02	214 04.6	25.9	251 55.5	15.3	1 41.2	9.2	54.0
03	229 04.5 ..	26.6	266 29.8	15.4	1 50.4	9.2	54.0
04	244 04.5	27.3	281 04.2	15.3	1 59.6	9.2	54.0
05	259 04.4	28.0	295 38.5	15.4	2 08.8	9.2	54.1
06	274 04.4	S16 28.8	310 12.9	15.3	S 2 18.0	9.2	54.1
07	289 04.4	29.5	324 47.2	15.3	2 27.2	9.2	54.1
S 08	304 04.3	30.2	339 21.5	15.3	2 36.4	9.2	54.1
U 09	319 04.3 ..	31.0	353 55.8	15.3	2 45.6	9.2	54.1
N 10	334 04.2	31.7	8 30.1	15.3	2 54.8	9.1	54.1
D 11	349 04.2	32.4	23 04.4	15.2	3 03.9	9.2	54.1
A 12	4 04.2	S16 33.1	37 38.6	15.3	S 3 13.1	9.1	54.1
Y 13	19 04.1	33.9	52 12.9	15.2	3 22.2	9.2	54.1
14	34 04.1	34.6	66 47.1	15.3	3 31.4	9.1	54.1
15	49 04.0 ..	35.3	81 21.4	15.2	3 40.5	9.1	54.1
16	64 04.0	36.0	95 55.6	15.2	3 49.6	9.1	54.1
17	79 03.9	36.8	110 29.8	15.1	3 58.7	9.1	54.1
18	94 03.9	S16 37.5	125 03.9	15.2	S 4 07.8	9.0	54.1
19	109 03.8	38.2	139 38.1	15.1	4 16.8	9.1	54.1
20	124 03.8	38.9	154 12.2	15.1	4 25.9	9.0	54.1
21	139 03.7 ..	39.7	168 46.3	15.1	4 34.9	9.0	54.1
22	154 03.7	40.4	183 20.4	15.1	4 43.9	9.0	54.1
23	169 03.7	41.1	197 54.5	15.1	S 4 52.9	9.0	54.1
	SD 16.2	d 0.7	SD 14.8		14.7		14.7

Lat.	Twilight Naut.	Twilight Civil	Sunrise	Moonrise 6	7	8	9
°	h m	h m	h m	h m	h m	h m	h m
N 72	06 28	07 55	09 35	00 35	02 08	03 40	05 13
N 70	06 22	07 38	09 00	00 44	02 11	03 37	05 05
68	06 16	07 25	08 35	00 51	02 13	03 35	04 58
66	06 11	07 14	08 16	00 57	02 15	03 33	04 52
64	06 07	07 05	08 00	01 01	02 16	03 31	04 47
62	06 03	06 57	07 47	01 06	02 18	03 30	04 43
60	06 00	06 50	07 37	01 09	02 19	03 29	04 39
N 58	05 56	06 44	07 27	01 12	02 20	03 28	04 36
56	05 54	06 38	07 19	01 15	02 21	03 27	04 33
54	05 51	06 33	07 12	01 18	02 22	03 26	04 30
52	05 48	06 29	07 05	01 20	02 23	03 25	04 28
50	05 46	06 24	06 59	01 22	02 23	03 24	04 26
45	05 40	06 14	06 46	01 27	02 25	03 23	04 21
N 40	05 35	06 07	06 35	01 30	02 26	03 21	04 17
35	05 30	06 00	06 26	01 34	02 27	03 20	04 14
30	05 25	05 53	06 18	01 37	02 28	03 19	04 11
20	05 15	05 41	06 04	01 42	02 30	03 18	04 06
N 10	05 05	05 30	05 52	01 46	02 31	03 16	04 01
0	04 54	05 19	05 40	01 50	02 33	03 15	03 57
S 10	04 41	05 06	05 28	01 54	02 34	03 13	03 53
20	04 25	04 52	05 16	01 59	02 36	03 12	03 49
30	04 05	04 35	05 01	02 04	02 37	03 10	03 44
35	03 52	04 25	04 52	02 07	02 38	03 09	03 41
40	03 37	04 13	04 43	02 10	02 39	03 08	03 38
45	03 17	03 58	04 31	02 14	02 41	03 07	03 34
S 50	02 52	03 40	04 17	02 18	02 42	03 06	03 30
52	02 39	03 31	04 10	02 20	02 43	03 05	03 28
54	02 23	03 21	04 03	02 22	02 44	03 05	03 26
56	02 05	03 09	03 55	02 25	02 44	03 04	03 24
58	01 41	02 56	03 46	02 27	02 45	03 03	03 21
S 60	01 08	02 40	03 35	02 31	02 46	03 02	03 18

Lat.	Sunset	Twilight Civil	Twilight Naut.	Moonset 6	7	8	9
°	h m	h m	h m	h m	h m	h m	h m
N 72	13 51	15 31	16 58	14 57	14 53	14 48	14 43
N 70	14 26	15 48	17 04	14 52	14 53	14 53	14 53
68	14 51	16 01	17 10	14 48	14 53	14 57	15 02
66	15 11	16 12	17 15	14 45	14 53	15 01	15 09
64	15 26	16 21	17 19	14 42	14 53	15 04	15 15
62	15 39	16 29	17 23	14 39	14 53	15 06	15 20
60	15 50	16 36	17 27	14 37	14 53	15 08	15 25
N 58	15 59	16 43	17 30	14 35	14 53	15 10	15 29
56	16 08	16 48	17 33	14 33	14 53	15 12	15 33
54	16 15	16 53	17 36	14 32	14 53	15 14	15 36
52	16 22	16 58	17 38	14 30	14 53	15 15	15 39
50	16 28	17 02	17 41	14 29	14 53	15 17	15 42
45	16 41	17 12	17 47	14 26	14 53	15 20	15 47
N 40	16 51	17 20	17 52	14 24	14 53	15 22	15 52
35	17 01	17 27	17 57	14 22	14 53	15 24	15 57
30	17 09	17 34	18 02	14 20	14 53	15 26	16 00
20	17 23	17 46	18 12	14 16	14 53	15 30	16 07
N 10	17 35	17 57	18 22	14 14	14 53	15 32	16 13
0	17 47	18 09	18 34	14 11	14 53	15 35	16 18
S 10	17 59	18 21	18 47	14 08	14 53	15 38	16 24
20	18 12	18 35	19 03	14 05	14 53	15 41	16 29
30	18 27	18 52	19 23	14 02	14 53	15 44	16 36
35	18 35	19 03	19 36	14 00	14 53	15 46	16 40
40	18 45	19 19	19 51	13 57	14 53	15 48	16 44
45	18 57	19 30	20 11	13 55	14 53	15 51	16 49
S 50	19 11	19 49	20 37	13 52	14 53	15 54	16 55
52	19 18	19 58	20 51	13 50	14 53	15 55	16 58
54	19 25	20 08	21 06	13 48	14 53	15 57	17 01
56	19 34	20 20	21 25	13 47	14 53	15 58	17 04
58	19 43	20 34	21 50	13 45	14 52	16 00	17 08
S 60	19 54	20 50	22 26	13 43	14 52	16 02	17 12

Day	SUN Eqn. of Time 00h	SUN Eqn. of Time 12h	SUN Mer. Pass.	MOON Mer. Pass. Upper	MOON Mer. Pass. Lower	Age	Phase
d	m s	m s	h m	h m	h m	d	%
6	16 24	16 23	11 44	08 00	20 22	24	23
7	16 22	16 20	11 44	08 43	21 04	25	16
8	16 19	16 17	11 44	09 25	21 46	26	9

UT	ARIES GHA	VENUS −4.4 GHA	Dec	MARS +1.7 GHA	Dec	JUPITER −1.9 GHA	Dec	SATURN +0.5 GHA	Dec	STARS Name	SHA	Dec
d h	° ′	° ′	° ′	° ′	° ′	° ′	° ′	° ′	° ′		° ′	° ′
9 00	47 51.1	227 02.5 N 0	54.3	229 27.1 N 2	13.6	238 27.1 N 5	40.3	164 29.2 S19	29.4	Acamar	315 16.7	S40 14.6
01	62 53.5	242 02.4	53.4	244 28.1	13.0	253 29.2	40.1	179 31.3	29.4	Achernar	335 25.2	S57 09.5
02	77 56.0	257 02.3	52.5	259 29.2	12.4	268 31.3	40.0	194 33.5	29.5	Acrux	173 07.8	S63 10.9
03	92 58.5	272 02.2 . .	51.6	274 30.3 . .	11.8	283 33.4 . .	39.9	209 35.7 . .	29.6	Adhara	255 11.0	S28 59.6
04	108 00.9	287 02.1	50.7	289 31.4	11.2	298 35.5	39.7	224 37.8	29.6	Aldebaran	290 47.2	N16 32.3
05	123 03.4	302 02.1	49.7	304 32.4	10.7	313 37.6	39.6	239 40.0	29.7			
06	138 05.9	317 02.0 N 0	48.8	319 33.5 N 2	10.1	328 39.7 N 5	39.4	254 42.2 S19	29.7	Alioth	166 19.9	N55 52.4
07	153 08.3	332 01.9	47.9	334 34.6	09.5	343 41.8	39.3	269 44.3	29.8	Alkaid	152 58.2	N49 14.1
08	168 10.8	347 01.8	47.0	349 35.7	08.9	358 43.9	39.1	284 46.5	29.8	Al Na'ir	27 41.7	S46 53.1
M 09	183 13.2	2 01.7 . .	46.1	4 36.7 . .	08.3	13 46.0 . .	39.0	299 48.7 . .	29.9	Alnilam	275 44.5	S 1 11.6
O 10	198 15.7	17 01.6	45.1	19 37.8	07.7	28 48.1	38.8	314 50.8	29.9	Alphard	217 54.5	S 8 43.6
N 11	213 18.2	32 01.5	44.2	34 38.9	07.1	43 50.2	38.7	329 53.0	30.0			
D 12	228 20.6	47 01.4 N 0	43.3	49 40.0 N 2	06.5	58 52.3 N 5	38.5	344 55.2 S19	30.0	Alphecca	126 10.0	N26 39.9
A 13	243 23.1	62 01.3	42.4	64 41.0	05.9	73 54.4	38.4	359 57.3	30.1	Alpheratz	357 41.5	N29 10.9
Y 14	258 25.6	77 01.3	41.5	79 42.1	05.3	88 56.5	38.3	14 59.5	30.2	Altair	62 06.8	N 8 54.9
15	273 28.0	92 01.2 . .	40.5	94 43.2 . .	04.7	103 58.6 . .	38.1	30 01.7 . .	30.2	Ankaa	353 13.9	S42 13.3
16	288 30.5	107 01.1	39.6	109 44.3	04.1	119 00.7	38.0	45 03.8	30.3	Antares	112 24.6	S26 27.8
17	303 33.0	122 01.0	38.7	124 45.3	03.5	134 02.8	37.8	60 06.0	30.3			
18	318 35.4	137 00.9 N 0	37.8	139 46.4 N 2	02.9	149 04.9 N 5	37.7	75 08.2 S19	30.4	Arcturus	145 54.6	N19 06.2
19	333 37.9	152 00.8	36.9	154 47.5	02.3	164 07.0	37.5	90 10.3	30.4	Atria	107 25.5	S69 03.2
20	348 40.4	167 00.7	35.9	169 48.6	01.7	179 09.1	37.4	105 12.5	30.5	Avior	234 17.1	S59 33.4
21	3 42.8	182 00.6 . .	35.0	184 49.6 . .	01.2	194 11.2 . .	37.2	120 14.7 . .	30.5	Bellatrix	278 30.0	N 6 21.7
22	18 45.3	197 00.5	34.1	199 50.7	00.6	209 13.3	37.1	135 16.8	30.6	Betelgeuse	270 59.3	N 7 24.4
23	33 47.7	212 00.4	33.2	214 51.8	2 00.0	224 15.4	36.9	150 19.0	30.7			
10 00	48 50.2	227 00.3 N 0	32.2	229 52.9 N 1	59.4	239 17.5 N 5	36.8	165 21.1 S19	30.7	Canopus	263 55.0	S52 42.2
01	63 52.7	242 00.3	31.3	244 54.0	58.8	254 19.6	36.7	180 23.3	30.8	Capella	280 31.6	N46 00.5
02	78 55.1	257 00.2	30.4	259 55.0	58.2	269 21.7	36.5	195 25.5	30.8	Deneb	49 30.4	N45 20.7
03	93 57.6	272 00.1 . .	29.5	274 56.1 . .	57.6	284 23.8 . .	36.4	210 27.6 . .	30.9	Denebola	182 32.3	N14 29.0
04	109 00.1	287 00.0	28.5	289 57.2	57.0	299 25.9	36.2	225 29.8	30.9	Diphda	348 54.0	S17 54.0
05	124 02.5	301 59.9	27.6	304 58.3	56.4	314 28.0	36.1	240 32.0	31.0			
06	139 05.0	316 59.8 N 0	26.7	319 59.3 N 1	55.8	329 30.1 N 5	35.9	255 34.1 S19	31.0	Dubhe	193 50.2	N61 39.7
07	154 07.5	331 59.7	25.8	335 00.4	55.2	344 32.2	35.8	270 36.3	31.1	Elnath	278 10.3	N28 37.0
08	169 09.9	346 59.6	24.8	350 01.5	54.6	359 34.3	35.7	285 38.5	31.1	Eltanin	90 45.8	N51 29.6
T 09	184 12.4	1 59.5 . .	23.9	5 02.6 . .	54.0	14 36.4 . .	35.5	300 40.6 . .	31.2	Enif	33 45.5	N 9 57.1
U 10	199 14.8	16 59.4	23.0	20 03.6	53.4	29 38.5	35.4	315 42.8	31.3	Fomalhaut	15 22.1	S29 32.3
E 11	214 17.3	31 59.3	22.0	35 04.7	52.8	44 40.6	35.2	330 45.0	31.3			
S 12	229 19.8	46 59.2 N 0	21.1	50 05.8 N 1	52.2	59 42.7 N 5	35.1	345 47.1 S19	31.4	Gacrux	171 59.4	S57 11.8
D 13	244 22.2	61 59.1	20.2	65 06.9	51.7	74 44.8	34.9	0 49.3	31.4	Gienah	175 50.9	S17 37.6
A 14	259 24.7	76 59.0	19.3	80 08.0	51.1	89 46.9	34.8	15 51.5	31.5	Hadar	148 46.1	S60 26.7
Y 15	274 27.2	91 58.9 . .	18.3	95 09.0 . .	50.5	104 49.0 . .	34.6	30 53.6 . .	31.5	Hamal	327 58.6	N23 32.2
16	289 29.6	106 58.8	17.4	110 10.1	49.9	119 51.1	34.5	45 55.8	31.6	Kaus Aust.	83 42.0	S34 22.4
17	304 32.1	121 58.7	16.5	125 11.2	49.3	134 53.2	34.4	60 58.0	31.6			
18	319 34.6	136 58.6 N 0	15.5	140 12.3 N 1	48.7	149 55.3 N 5	34.2	76 00.1 S19	31.7	Kochab	137 21.5	N74 05.5
19	334 37.0	151 58.5	14.6	155 13.3	48.1	164 57.4	34.1	91 02.3	31.7	Markab	13 36.6	N15 17.6
20	349 39.5	166 58.4	13.7	170 14.4	47.5	179 59.6	33.9	106 04.4	31.8	Menkar	314 13.0	N 4 09.0
21	4 42.0	181 58.3 . .	12.7	185 15.5 . .	46.9	195 01.7 . .	33.8	121 06.6 . .	31.9	Menkent	148 06.0	S36 26.6
22	19 44.4	196 58.2	11.8	200 16.6	46.3	210 03.8	33.6	136 08.8	31.9	Miaplacidus	221 39.1	S69 46.7
23	34 46.9	211 58.1	10.9	215 17.7	45.7	225 05.9	33.5	151 10.9	32.0			
11 00	49 49.3	226 58.0 N 0	09.9	230 18.7 N 1	45.1	240 08.0 N 5	33.4	166 13.1 S19	32.0	Mirfak	308 37.5	N49 54.9
01	64 51.8	241 57.9	09.0	245 19.8	44.5	255 10.1	33.2	181 15.3	32.1	Nunki	75 56.6	S26 16.4
02	79 54.3	256 57.8	08.1	260 20.9	43.9	270 12.2	33.1	196 17.4	32.1	Peacock	53 17.0	S56 41.1
03	94 56.7	271 57.7 . .	07.1	275 22.0 . .	43.3	285 14.3 . .	32.9	211 19.6 . .	32.2	Pollux	243 25.7	N27 59.0
04	109 59.2	286 57.6	06.2	290 23.0	42.8	300 16.4	32.8	226 21.8	32.2	Procyon	244 57.9	N 5 10.9
05	125 01.7	301 57.5	05.3	305 24.1	42.2	315 18.5	32.6	241 23.9	32.3			
06	140 04.1	316 57.4 N 0	04.3	320 25.2 N 1	41.6	330 20.6 N 5	32.5	256 26.1 S19	32.3	Rasalhague	96 05.3	N12 33.3
W 07	155 06.6	331 57.3	03.4	335 26.3	41.0	345 22.7	32.4	271 28.3	32.4	Regulus	207 41.9	N11 53.3
E 08	170 09.1	346 57.2	02.5	350 27.4	40.4	0 24.8	32.2	286 30.4	32.5	Rigel	281 10.2	S 8 11.1
D 09	185 11.5	1 57.1 . .	01.5	5 28.4 . .	39.8	15 26.9 . .	32.1	301 32.6 . .	32.5	Rigil Kent.	139 50.1	S60 53.7
N 10	200 14.0	16 57.0 N	00.6	20 29.5	39.2	30 29.0	31.9	316 34.7	32.6	Sabik	102 11.0	S15 44.4
E 11	215 16.5	31 56.9 S	00.4	35 30.6	38.6	45 31.1	31.8	331 36.9	32.6			
S 12	230 18.9	46 56.8 S 0	01.3	50 31.7 N 1	38.0	60 33.3 N 5	31.7	346 39.1 S19	32.7	Schedar	349 38.1	N56 37.6
D 13	245 21.4	61 56.7	02.2	65 32.8	37.4	75 35.4	31.5	1 41.2	32.7	Shaula	96 20.1	S37 06.7
A 14	260 23.8	76 56.5	03.2	80 33.8	36.8	90 37.5	31.4	16 43.4	32.8	Sirius	258 32.1	S16 44.3
Y 15	275 26.3	91 56.4 . .	04.1	95 34.9 . .	36.2	105 39.6 . .	31.2	31 45.6 . .	32.8	Spica	158 29.8	S11 14.4
16	290 28.8	106 56.3	05.1	110 36.0	35.6	120 41.7	31.1	46 47.7	32.9	Suhail	222 51.2	S43 29.6
17	305 31.2	121 56.2	06.0	125 37.1	35.0	135 43.8	30.9	61 49.9	32.9			
18	320 33.7	136 56.1 S 0	06.9	140 38.2 N 1	34.5	150 45.9 N 5	30.8	76 52.1 S19	33.0	Vega	80 38.1	N38 48.3
19	335 36.2	151 56.0	07.9	155 39.2	33.9	165 48.0	30.7	91 54.2	33.1	Zuben'ubi	137 04.0	S16 06.2
20	350 38.6	166 55.9	08.8	170 40.3	33.3	180 50.1	30.5	106 56.4	33.1		SHA	Mer. Pass.
21	5 41.1	181 55.8 . .	09.8	185 41.4 . .	32.7	195 52.2 . .	30.4	121 58.5 . .	33.2		° ′	h m
22	20 43.6	196 55.7	10.7	200 42.5	32.1	210 54.3	30.2	137 00.7	33.2	Venus	178 10.1	8 52
23	35 46.0	211 55.6	11.6	215 43.6	31.5	225 56.5	30.1	152 02.9	33.3	Mars	181 02.7	8 40
	h m									Jupiter	190 27.3	8 02
Mer. Pass. 20 41.3		v −0.1 d 0.9		v 1.1 d 0.6		v 2.1 d 0.1		v 2.2 d 0.1		Saturn	116 30.9	12 57

UT	SUN GHA	SUN Dec	MOON GHA	v	MOON Dec	d	HP
d h	° ′	° ′	° ′	′	° ′	′	′
9 00	184 03.6	S16 41.8	212 28.6	15.0	S 5 01.9	9.0	54.1
01	199 03.6	42.6	227 02.6	15.0	5 10.9	8.9	54.1
02	214 03.5	43.3	241 36.6	15.0	5 19.8	9.0	54.1
03	229 03.5	.. 44.0	256 10.6	15.0	5 28.8	8.9	54.1
04	244 03.4	44.7	270 44.6	15.0	5 37.7	8.9	54.1
05	259 03.4	45.4	285 18.6	14.9	5 46.6	8.8	54.1
06	274 03.3	S16 46.1	299 52.5	14.9	S 5 55.4	8.9	54.2
M 07	289 03.3	46.9	314 26.4	14.9	6 04.3	8.8	54.2
O 08	304 03.2	47.6	329 00.3	14.8	6 13.1	8.8	54.2
N 09	319 03.2	.. 48.3	343 34.1	14.9	6 21.9	8.8	54.2
D 10	334 03.1	49.0	358 08.0	14.8	6 30.7	8.7	54.2
A 11	349 03.1	49.7	12 41.8	14.7	6 39.4	8.8	54.2
Y 12	4 03.0	S16 50.4	27 15.5	14.8	S 6 48.2	8.7	54.2
13	19 03.0	51.2	41 49.3	14.7	6 56.9	8.7	54.2
14	34 02.9	51.9	56 23.0	14.7	7 05.6	8.6	54.2
15	49 02.9	.. 52.6	70 56.7	14.7	7 14.2	8.6	54.2
16	64 02.8	53.3	85 30.4	14.6	7 22.8	8.6	54.2
17	79 02.8	54.0	100 04.0	14.6	7 31.4	8.6	54.2
18	94 02.7	S16 54.7	114 37.6	14.6	S 7 40.0	8.6	54.2
19	109 02.6	55.4	129 11.2	14.5	7 48.6	8.5	54.2
20	124 02.6	56.1	143 44.7	14.6	7 57.1	8.5	54.3
21	139 02.5	.. 56.9	158 18.3	14.4	8 05.6	8.4	54.3
22	154 02.5	57.6	172 51.7	14.5	8 14.0	8.4	54.3
23	169 02.4	58.3	187 25.2	14.4	8 22.4	8.4	54.3
10 00	184 02.4	S16 59.0	201 58.6	14.4	S 8 30.8	8.4	54.3
01	199 02.3	16 59.7	216 32.0	14.4	8 39.2	8.3	54.3
02	214 02.3	17 00.4	231 05.4	14.3	8 47.5	8.3	54.3
03	229 02.2	.. 01.1	245 38.7	14.3	8 55.8	8.3	54.3
04	244 02.1	01.8	260 12.0	14.2	9 04.1	8.2	54.3
05	259 02.1	02.5	274 45.2	14.2	9 12.3	8.2	54.3
06	274 02.0	S17 03.2	289 18.4	14.2	S 9 20.5	8.1	54.4
T 07	289 02.0	03.9	303 51.6	14.2	9 28.6	8.2	54.4
U 08	304 01.9	04.6	318 24.8	14.1	9 36.8	8.0	54.4
E 09	319 01.8	.. 05.3	332 57.9	14.1	9 44.8	8.1	54.4
S 10	334 01.8	06.1	347 31.0	14.0	9 52.9	8.0	54.4
D 11	349 01.7	06.8	2 04.0	14.0	10 00.9	7.9	54.4
A 12	4 01.7	S17 07.5	16 37.0	14.0	S10 08.8	8.0	54.4
Y 13	19 01.6	08.2	31 10.0	13.9	10 16.8	7.9	54.4
14	34 01.5	08.9	45 42.9	13.9	10 24.7	7.8	54.4
15	49 01.5	.. 09.6	60 15.8	13.8	10 32.5	7.8	54.4
16	64 01.4	10.3	74 48.6	13.9	10 40.3	7.7	54.5
17	79 01.4	11.0	89 21.5	13.7	10 48.0	7.8	54.5
18	94 01.3	S17 11.7	103 54.2	13.8	S10 55.8	7.6	54.5
19	109 01.2	12.4	118 27.0	13.7	11 03.4	7.7	54.5
20	124 01.2	13.1	132 59.7	13.6	11 11.1	7.5	54.5
21	139 01.1	.. 13.8	147 32.3	13.6	11 18.6	7.6	54.5
22	154 01.0	14.5	162 04.9	13.6	11 26.2	7.5	54.5
23	169 01.0	15.2	176 37.5	13.5	11 33.7	7.4	54.5
11 00	184 00.9	S17 15.9	191 10.0	13.5	S11 41.1	7.4	54.6
01	199 00.8	16.6	205 42.5	13.5	11 48.5	7.3	54.6
02	214 00.8	17.2	220 15.0	13.4	11 55.8	7.3	54.6
03	229 00.7	.. 17.9	234 47.4	13.3	12 03.1	7.3	54.6
04	244 00.6	18.6	249 19.7	13.4	12 10.4	7.2	54.6
05	259 00.6	19.3	263 52.1	13.3	12 17.6	7.1	54.6
06	274 00.5	S17 20.0	278 24.4	13.2	S12 24.7	7.1	54.6
W 07	289 00.4	20.7	292 56.6	13.2	12 31.8	7.0	54.6
E 08	304 00.4	21.4	307 28.8	13.1	12 38.8	7.0	54.7
D 09	319 00.3	.. 22.1	322 00.9	13.2	12 45.8	7.0	54.7
N 10	334 00.2	22.8	336 33.1	13.0	12 52.8	6.8	54.7
E 11	349 00.2	23.5	351 05.1	13.1	12 59.6	6.9	54.7
S 12	4 00.1	S17 24.2	5 37.2	12.9	S13 06.5	6.7	54.7
D 13	19 00.0	24.9	20 09.1	13.0	13 13.2	6.7	54.7
A 14	34 00.0	25.6	34 41.1	12.9	13 19.9	6.7	54.7
Y 15	48 59.9	.. 26.3	49 13.0	12.8	13 26.6	6.6	54.8
16	63 59.8	26.9	63 44.8	12.8	13 33.2	6.5	54.8
17	78 59.7	27.6	78 16.6	12.8	13 39.7	6.5	54.8
18	93 59.7	S17 28.3	92 48.4	12.7	S13 46.2	6.4	54.8
19	108 59.6	29.0	107 20.1	12.7	13 52.6	6.4	54.8
20	123 59.5	29.7	121 51.8	12.6	13 59.0	6.3	54.8
21	138 59.5	.. 30.4	136 23.4	12.6	14 05.3	6.2	54.8
22	153 59.4	31.1	150 55.0	12.5	14 11.5	6.2	54.9
23	168 59.3	31.7	165 26.5	12.5	S14 17.7	6.1	54.9
	SD 16.2	d 0.7	SD 14.8		14.8		14.9

Moonrise

Lat.	Twilight Naut.	Civil	Sunrise	9	10	11	12
°	h m	h m	h m	h m	h m	h m	h m
N 72	06 40	08 09	09 59	05 13	06 49	08 28	10 14
N 70	06 32	07 50	09 17	05 05	06 33	08 04	09 36
68	06 25	07 36	08 48	04 58	06 21	07 46	09 09
66	06 19	07 23	08 27	04 52	06 11	07 31	08 49
64	06 14	07 13	08 10	04 47	06 03	07 19	08 33
62	06 10	07 04	07 56	04 43	05 55	07 08	08 20
60	06 06	06 57	07 44	04 39	05 49	07 00	08 09
N 58	06 02	06 50	07 34	04 36	05 44	06 52	07 59
56	05 59	06 44	07 25	04 33	05 39	06 45	07 51
54	05 56	06 39	07 17	04 30	05 35	06 39	07 43
52	05 53	06 34	07 10	04 28	05 31	06 34	07 36
50	05 50	06 29	07 04	04 26	05 27	06 29	07 30
45	05 44	06 19	06 50	04 21	05 20	06 19	07 17
N 40	05 38	06 10	06 39	04 17	05 13	06 10	07 07
35	05 32	06 03	06 29	04 14	05 08	06 02	06 57
30	05 27	05 56	06 21	04 11	05 03	05 56	06 49
20	05 16	05 43	06 06	04 06	04 55	05 45	06 36
N 10	05 05	05 31	05 53	04 01	04 48	05 35	06 24
0	04 54	05 19	05 40	03 57	04 41	05 26	06 12
S 10	04 40	05 06	05 28	03 53	04 34	05 17	06 01
20	04 24	04 51	05 14	03 49	04 27	05 07	05 49
30	04 03	04 33	04 59	03 44	04 19	04 56	05 36
35	03 49	04 22	04 50	03 41	04 14	04 50	05 28
40	03 33	04 10	04 40	03 38	04 09	04 42	05 19
45	03 12	03 54	04 27	03 34	04 03	04 34	05 09
S 50	02 45	03 34	04 12	03 30	03 56	04 24	04 56
52	02 31	03 25	04 05	03 28	03 53	04 20	04 51
54	02 15	03 14	03 58	03 26	03 49	04 15	04 44
56	01 54	03 02	03 49	03 24	03 45	04 09	04 37
58	01 27	02 47	03 39	03 21	03 40	04 03	04 29
S 60	00 45	02 30	03 27	03 18	03 35	03 56	04 20

Moonset

Lat.	Sunset	Twilight Civil	Naut.	9	10	11	12
°	h m	h m	h m	h m	h m	h m	h m
N 72	13 27	15 17	16 47	14 43	14 38	14 32	14 24
N 70	14 10	15 36	16 55	14 53	14 55	14 57	15 03
68	14 39	15 51	17 01	15 02	15 08	15 17	15 30
66	15 00	16 03	17 07	15 09	15 19	15 32	15 51
64	15 17	16 14	17 12	15 15	15 29	15 45	16 07
62	15 31	16 22	17 17	15 20	15 37	15 56	16 21
60	15 43	16 30	17 21	15 25	15 44	16 06	16 33
N 58	15 53	16 37	17 25	15 29	15 50	16 14	16 43
56	16 02	16 43	17 28	15 33	15 55	16 21	16 52
54	16 11	16 48	17 31	15 36	16 00	16 27	16 59
52	16 17	16 54	17 34	15 39	16 04	16 33	17 06
50	16 23	16 58	17 37	15 42	16 08	16 38	17 13
45	16 37	17 08	17 44	15 47	16 17	16 50	17 27
N 40	16 48	17 17	17 50	15 52	16 24	16 59	17 38
35	16 58	17 25	17 55	15 57	16 31	17 07	17 48
30	17 07	17 32	18 01	16 00	16 36	17 15	17 56
20	17 22	17 45	18 11	16 07	16 46	17 27	18 11
N 10	17 35	17 57	18 22	16 13	16 54	17 38	18 24
0	17 47	18 09	18 34	16 18	17 02	17 48	18 36
S 10	18 00	18 22	18 48	16 24	17 10	17 58	18 48
20	18 14	18 37	19 04	16 29	17 19	18 09	19 01
30	18 29	18 55	19 26	16 36	17 28	18 22	19 15
35	18 38	19 06	19 39	16 40	17 34	18 29	19 24
40	18 49	19 19	19 56	16 44	17 40	18 37	19 34
45	19 01	19 35	20 17	16 49	17 48	18 47	19 45
S 50	19 16	19 55	20 44	16 55	17 57	18 58	19 59
52	19 24	20 04	20 58	16 58	18 01	19 04	20 06
54	19 31	20 15	21 15	17 01	18 06	19 10	20 13
56	19 40	20 28	21 36	17 04	18 11	19 17	20 21
58	19 50	20 42	22 05	17 08	18 16	19 24	20 30
S 60	20 02	21 00	22 51	17 12	18 23	19 33	20 40

SUN / MOON

Day	Eqn. of Time 00h	12h	Mer. Pass.	Mer. Pass. Upper	Lower	Age	Phase
d	m s	m s	h m	h m	h m	d	%
9	16 15	16 12	11 44	10 08	22 29	27	5
10	16 10	16 07	11 44	10 51	23 14	28	2
11	16 04	16 01	11 44	11 37	24 00	29	0

UT	ARIES GHA	VENUS −4.4 GHA	Dec	MARS +1.6 GHA	Dec	JUPITER −1.9 GHA	Dec	SATURN +0.5 GHA	Dec	STARS Name	SHA	Dec
12 00	50 48.5	226 55.5	S 0 12.6	230 44.6	N 1 30.9	240 58.6	N 5 30.0	167 05.0	S19 33.3	Acamar	315 16.7	S40 14.6
01	65 50.9	241 55.3	13.5	245 45.7	30.3	256 00.7	29.8	182 07.2	33.4	Achernar	335 25.2	S57 09.6
02	80 53.4	256 55.2	14.5	260 46.8	29.7	271 02.8	29.7	197 09.4	33.4	Acrux	173 07.8	S63 10.9
03	95 55.9	271 55.1	.. 15.4	275 47.9	.. 29.1	286 04.9	.. 29.5	212 11.5	.. 33.5	Adhara	255 11.0	S28 59.6
04	110 58.3	286 55.0	16.3	290 49.0	28.5	301 07.0	29.4	227 13.7	33.5	Aldebaran	290 47.2	N16 32.3
05	126 00.8	301 54.9	17.3	305 50.0	27.9	316 09.1	29.3	242 15.8	33.6			
06	141 03.3	316 54.8	S 0 18.2	320 51.1	N 1 27.3	331 11.2	N 5 29.1	257 18.0	S19 33.7	Alioth	166 19.9	N55 52.4
07	156 05.7	331 54.7	19.2	335 52.2	26.8	346 13.3	29.0	272 20.2	33.7	Alkaid	152 58.2	N49 14.1
T 08	171 08.2	346 54.6	20.1	350 53.3	26.2	1 15.4	28.8	287 22.3	33.8	Al Na'ir	27 41.7	S46 53.1
H 09	186 10.7	1 54.5	.. 21.1	5 54.4	.. 25.6	16 17.6	.. 28.7	302 24.5	.. 33.8	Alnilam	275 44.5	S 1 11.6
U 10	201 13.1	16 54.3	22.0	20 55.4	25.0	31 19.7	28.6	317 26.7	33.9	Alphard	217 54.5	S 8 43.6
R 11	216 15.6	31 54.2	23.0	35 56.5	24.4	46 21.8	28.4	332 28.8	33.9			
S 12	231 18.1	46 54.1	S 0 23.9	50 57.6	N 1 23.8	61 23.9	N 5 28.3	347 31.0	S19 34.0	Alphecca	126 10.0	N26 39.9
D 13	246 20.5	61 54.0	24.9	65 58.7	23.2	76 26.0	28.1	2 33.1	34.0	Alpheratz	357 41.5	N29 10.9
A 14	261 23.0	76 53.9	25.8	80 59.8	22.6	91 28.1	28.0	17 35.3	34.1	Altair	62 06.8	N 8 54.9
Y 15	276 25.4	91 53.8	.. 26.7	96 00.8	.. 22.0	106 30.2	.. 27.9	32 37.5	.. 34.1	Ankaa	353 13.9	S42 13.3
16	291 27.9	106 53.6	27.7	111 01.9	21.4	121 32.3	27.7	47 39.6	34.2	Antares	112 24.6	S26 27.8
17	306 30.4	121 53.5	28.6	126 03.0	20.8	136 34.5	27.6	62 41.8	34.3			
18	321 32.8	136 53.4	S 0 29.6	141 04.1	N 1 20.2	151 36.6	N 5 27.4	77 44.0	S19 34.3	Arcturus	145 54.6	N19 06.2
19	336 35.3	151 53.3	30.5	156 05.2	19.6	166 38.7	27.3	92 46.1	34.4	Atria	107 25.5	S69 03.2
20	351 37.8	166 53.2	31.5	171 06.2	19.1	181 40.8	27.2	107 48.3	34.4	Avior	234 17.1	S59 33.5
21	6 40.2	181 53.1	.. 32.4	186 07.3	.. 18.5	196 42.9	.. 27.0	122 50.4	.. 34.5	Bellatrix	278 30.0	N 6 21.7
22	21 42.7	196 52.9	33.4	201 08.4	17.9	211 45.0	26.9	137 52.6	34.5	Betelgeuse	270 59.3	N 7 24.4
23	36 45.2	211 52.8	34.3	216 09.5	17.3	226 47.1	26.7	152 54.8	34.6			
13 00	51 47.6	226 52.7	S 0 35.3	231 10.6	N 1 16.7	241 49.3	N 5 26.6	167 56.9	S19 34.6	Canopus	263 55.0	S52 42.2
01	66 50.1	241 52.6	36.2	246 11.7	16.1	256 51.4	26.5	182 59.1	34.7	Capella	280 31.6	N46 00.5
02	81 52.6	256 52.5	37.2	261 12.7	15.5	271 53.5	26.3	198 01.3	34.7	Deneb	49 30.4	N45 20.7
03	96 55.0	271 52.4	.. 38.1	276 13.8	.. 14.9	286 55.6	.. 26.2	213 03.4	.. 34.8	Denebola	182 32.2	N14 29.0
04	111 57.5	286 52.2	39.1	291 14.9	14.3	301 57.7	26.0	228 05.6	34.9	Diphda	348 54.0	S17 54.0
05	126 59.9	301 52.1	40.0	306 16.0	13.7	316 59.8	25.9	243 07.7	34.9			
06	142 02.4	316 52.0	S 0 41.0	321 17.1	N 1 13.1	332 01.9	N 5 25.8	258 09.9	S19 35.0	Dubhe	193 50.2	N61 39.7
07	157 04.9	331 51.9	41.9	336 18.1	12.5	347 04.1	25.6	273 12.1	35.0	Elnath	278 10.2	N28 37.0
08	172 07.3	346 51.7	42.9	351 19.2	11.9	2 06.2	25.5	288 14.2	35.1	Eltanin	90 45.8	N51 29.6
F 09	187 09.8	1 51.6	.. 43.8	6 20.3	.. 11.4	17 08.3	.. 25.3	303 16.4	.. 35.1	Enif	33 45.5	N 9 57.1
R 10	202 12.3	16 51.5	44.8	21 21.4	10.8	32 10.4	25.2	318 18.6	35.2	Fomalhaut	15 22.1	S29 32.3
I 11	217 14.7	31 51.4	45.7	36 22.5	10.2	47 12.5	25.1	333 20.7	35.2			
D 12	232 17.2	46 51.3	S 0 46.7	51 23.6	N 1 09.6	62 14.6	N 5 24.9	348 22.9	S19 35.3	Gacrux	171 59.4	S57 11.8
A 13	247 19.7	61 51.1	47.7	66 24.6	09.0	77 16.8	24.8	3 25.0	35.3	Gienah	175 50.8	S17 37.6
Y 14	262 22.1	76 51.0	48.6	81 25.7	08.4	92 18.9	24.7	18 27.2	35.4	Hadar	148 46.1	S60 26.7
15	277 24.6	91 50.9	.. 49.6	96 26.8	.. 07.8	107 21.0	.. 24.5	33 29.4	.. 35.4	Hamal	327 58.6	N23 32.2
16	292 27.1	106 50.8	50.5	111 27.9	07.2	122 23.1	24.4	48 31.5	35.5	Kaus Aust.	83 42.0	S34 22.4
17	307 29.5	121 50.6	51.5	126 29.0	06.6	137 25.2	24.2	63 33.7	35.6			
18	322 32.0	136 50.5	S 0 52.4	141 30.1	N 1 06.0	152 27.3	N 5 24.1	78 35.8	S19 35.6	Kochab	137 21.5	N74 05.5
19	337 34.4	151 50.4	53.4	156 31.1	05.4	167 29.5	24.0	93 38.0	35.7	Markab	13 36.6	N15 17.6
20	352 36.9	166 50.3	54.3	171 32.2	04.8	182 31.6	23.8	108 40.2	35.7	Menkar	314 13.0	N 4 09.0
21	7 39.4	181 50.1	.. 55.3	186 33.3	.. 04.3	197 33.7	.. 23.7	123 42.3	.. 35.8	Menkent	148 06.0	S36 26.6
22	22 41.8	196 50.0	56.3	201 34.4	03.7	212 35.8	23.6	138 44.5	35.8	Miaplacidus	221 39.1	S69 46.7
23	37 44.3	211 49.9	57.2	216 35.5	03.1	227 37.9	23.4	153 46.7	35.9			
14 00	52 46.8	226 49.8	S 0 58.2	231 36.6	N 1 02.5	242 40.1	N 5 23.3	168 48.8	S19 35.9	Mirfak	308 37.5	N49 54.9
01	67 49.2	241 49.6	0 59.1	246 37.6	01.9	257 42.2	23.1	183 51.0	36.0	Nunki	75 56.6	S26 16.4
02	82 51.7	256 49.5	1 00.1	261 38.7	01.3	272 44.3	23.0	198 53.1	36.0	Peacock	53 17.0	S56 41.1
03	97 54.2	271 49.4	.. 01.0	276 39.8	.. 00.7	287 46.4	.. 22.9	213 55.3	.. 36.1	Pollux	243 25.6	N27 59.0
04	112 56.6	286 49.2	02.0	291 40.9	1 00.1	302 48.5	22.7	228 57.5	36.2	Procyon	244 57.9	N 5 10.9
05	127 59.1	301 49.1	03.0	306 42.0	0 59.5	317 50.6	22.6	243 59.6	36.2			
06	143 01.5	316 49.0	S 1 03.9	321 43.1	N 0 58.9	332 52.8	N 5 22.5	259 01.8	S19 36.3	Rasalhague	96 05.3	N12 33.3
07	158 04.0	331 48.9	04.9	336 44.1	58.3	347 54.9	22.3	274 03.9	36.3	Regulus	207 41.9	N11 53.3
S 08	173 06.5	346 48.7	05.8	351 45.2	57.8	2 57.0	22.2	289 06.1	36.4	Rigel	281 10.2	S 8 11.1
A 09	188 08.9	1 48.6	.. 06.8	6 46.3	.. 57.2	17 59.1	.. 22.1	304 08.3	.. 36.4	Rigil Kent.	139 50.1	S60 53.7
T 10	203 11.4	16 48.5	07.8	21 47.4	56.6	33 01.2	21.9	319 10.4	36.5	Sabik	102 11.0	S15 44.4
U 11	218 13.9	31 48.3	08.7	36 48.5	56.0	48 03.4	21.8	334 12.6	36.5			
R 12	233 16.3	46 48.2	S 1 09.7	51 49.6	N 0 55.4	63 05.5	N 5 21.6	349 14.7	S19 36.6	Schedar	349 38.1	N56 37.6
D 13	248 18.8	61 48.1	10.6	66 50.6	54.8	78 07.6	21.5	4 16.9	36.6	Shaula	96 20.1	S37 06.7
A 14	263 21.3	76 47.9	11.6	81 51.7	54.2	93 09.7	21.4	19 19.1	36.7	Sirius	258 32.1	S16 44.3
Y 15	278 23.7	91 47.8	.. 12.6	96 52.8	.. 53.6	108 11.9	.. 21.2	34 21.2	.. 36.7	Spica	158 29.8	S11 14.4
16	293 26.2	106 47.7	13.5	111 53.9	53.0	123 14.0	21.1	49 23.4	36.8	Suhail	222 51.2	S43 29.6
17	308 28.7	121 47.5	14.5	126 55.0	52.4	138 16.1	21.0	64 25.6	36.9			
18	323 31.1	136 47.4	S 1 15.4	141 56.1	N 0 51.8	153 18.2	N 5 20.8	79 27.7	S19 36.9	Vega	80 38.2	N38 48.3
19	338 33.6	151 47.3	16.4	156 57.1	51.3	168 20.3	20.7	94 29.9	37.0	Zuben'ubi	137 04.0	S16 06.2
20	353 36.0	166 47.1	17.4	171 58.2	50.7	183 22.5	20.6	109 32.0	37.0		SHA	Mer. Pass.
21	8 38.5	181 47.0	.. 18.3	186 59.3	.. 50.1	198 24.6	.. 20.4	124 34.2	.. 37.1		° '	h m
22	23 41.0	196 46.9	19.3	202 00.4	49.5	213 26.7	20.3	139 36.4	37.1	Venus	175 05.1	8 53
23	38 43.4	211 46.7	20.3	217 01.5	48.9	228 28.8	20.1	154 38.5	37.2	Mars	179 22.9	8 35
Mer. Pass. 20 29.5		v −0.1	d 1.0	v 1.1	d 0.6	v 2.1	d 0.1	v 2.2	d 0.1	Jupiter	190 01.6	7 52
										Saturn	116 09.3	12 46

UT	SUN GHA	SUN Dec	MOON GHA	v	MOON Dec	d	HP
d h	° ′	° ′	° ′	′	° ′	′	′
12 00	183 59.2	S17 32.4	179 58.0	12.5	S14 23.8	6.0	54.9
01	198 59.2	33.1	194 29.5	12.4	14 29.8	6.0	54.9
02	213 59.1	33.8	209 00.9	12.4	14 35.8	5.9	54.9
03	228 59.0	.. 34.5	223 32.3	12.3	14 41.7	5.9	54.9
04	243 58.9	35.2	238 03.6	12.2	14 47.6	5.8	54.9
05	258 58.9	35.8	252 34.8	12.3	14 53.4	5.7	55.0
06	273 58.8	S17 36.5	267 06.1	12.2	S14 59.1	5.6	55.0
T 07	288 58.7	37.2	281 37.3	12.1	15 04.7	5.6	55.0
H 08	303 58.6	37.9	296 08.4	12.1	15 10.3	5.5	55.0
U 09	318 58.6	.. 38.6	310 39.5	12.0	15 15.8	5.5	55.0
R 10	333 58.5	39.2	325 10.5	12.0	15 21.3	5.3	55.0
S 11	348 58.4	39.9	339 41.5	12.0	15 26.6	5.3	55.1
D 12	3 58.3	S17 40.6	354 12.5	11.9	S15 31.9	5.3	55.1
A 13	18 58.2	41.3	8 43.4	11.9	15 37.2	5.1	55.1
Y 14	33 58.2	42.0	23 14.3	11.8	15 42.3	5.1	55.1
15	48 58.1	.. 42.6	37 45.1	11.8	15 47.4	5.0	55.1
16	63 58.0	43.3	52 15.9	11.7	15 52.4	5.0	55.1
17	78 57.9	44.0	66 46.6	11.7	15 57.4	4.8	55.2
18	93 57.8	S17 44.7	81 17.3	11.7	S16 02.2	4.8	55.2
19	108 57.8	45.3	95 48.0	11.6	16 07.0	4.7	55.2
20	123 57.7	46.0	110 18.6	11.6	16 11.7	4.7	55.2
21	138 57.6	.. 46.7	124 49.2	11.5	16 16.4	4.5	55.2
22	153 57.5	47.4	139 19.7	11.5	16 20.9	4.5	55.2
23	168 57.4	48.0	153 50.2	11.4	16 25.4	4.4	55.3
13 00	183 57.4	S17 48.7	168 20.6	11.4	S16 29.8	4.4	55.3
01	198 57.3	49.4	182 51.0	11.4	16 34.2	4.2	55.3
02	213 57.2	50.0	197 21.4	11.3	16 38.4	4.2	55.3
03	228 57.1	.. 50.7	211 51.7	11.2	16 42.6	4.1	55.3
04	243 57.0	51.4	226 21.9	11.3	16 46.7	4.0	55.3
05	258 56.9	52.1	240 52.2	11.1	16 50.7	3.9	55.4
06	273 56.9	S17 52.7	255 22.3	11.2	S16 54.6	3.9	55.4
07	288 56.8	53.4	269 52.5	11.1	16 58.5	3.7	55.4
F 08	303 56.8	54.1	284 22.6	11.1	17 02.2	3.7	55.4
R 09	318 56.6	.. 54.7	298 52.7	11.0	17 05.9	3.6	55.4
I 10	333 56.5	55.4	313 22.7	11.0	17 09.5	3.5	55.4
D 11	348 56.4	56.1	327 52.7	10.9	17 13.0	3.4	55.5
A 12	3 56.3	S17 56.7	342 22.6	10.9	S17 16.4	3.4	55.5
Y 13	18 56.2	57.4	356 52.5	10.9	17 19.8	3.3	55.5
14	33 56.2	58.1	11 22.4	10.8	17 23.1	3.1	55.5
15	48 56.1	.. 58.7	25 52.2	10.8	17 26.2	3.1	55.5
16	63 56.0	17 59.4	40 22.0	10.8	17 29.3	3.0	55.6
17	78 55.9	18 00.0	54 51.8	10.7	17 32.3	2.9	55.6
18	93 55.8	S18 00.7	69 21.5	10.6	S17 35.2	2.8	55.6
19	108 55.7	01.4	83 51.1	10.7	17 38.0	2.8	55.6
20	123 55.6	02.0	98 20.8	10.6	17 40.8	2.6	55.6
21	138 55.5	.. 02.7	112 50.4	10.6	17 43.4	2.6	55.6
22	153 55.4	03.3	127 20.0	10.5	17 46.0	2.5	55.7
23	168 55.4	04.0	141 49.5	10.5	17 48.5	2.3	55.7
14 00	183 55.3	S18 04.7	156 19.0	10.5	S17 50.8	2.3	55.7
01	198 55.2	05.3	170 48.5	10.4	17 53.1	2.2	55.7
02	213 55.1	06.0	185 17.9	10.4	17 55.3	2.1	55.7
03	228 55.0	.. 06.6	199 47.3	10.3	17 57.4	2.0	55.8
04	243 54.9	07.3	214 16.6	10.4	17 59.4	2.0	55.8
05	258 54.8	08.0	228 46.0	10.3	18 01.4	1.8	55.8
06	273 54.7	S18 08.6	243 15.3	10.2	S18 03.2	1.7	55.8
S 07	288 54.6	09.3	257 44.5	10.3	18 04.9	1.7	55.8
A 08	303 54.5	09.9	272 13.8	10.2	18 06.6	1.5	55.9
T 09	318 54.4	.. 10.6	286 43.0	10.2	18 08.1	1.5	55.9
U 10	333 54.3	11.2	301 12.2	10.1	18 09.6	1.3	55.9
R 11	348 54.2	11.9	315 41.3	10.1	18 10.9	1.3	55.9
D 12	3 54.1	S18 12.5	330 10.4	10.1	S18 12.2	1.2	55.9
A 13	18 54.0	13.2	344 39.5	10.1	18 13.4	1.0	56.0
Y 14	33 53.9	13.8	359 08.6	10.0	18 14.4	1.0	56.0
15	48 53.8	.. 14.5	13 37.6	10.0	18 15.4	0.9	56.0
16	63 53.8	15.1	28 06.6	10.0	18 16.3	0.8	56.0
17	78 53.7	15.8	42 35.6	9.9	18 17.1	0.7	56.0
18	93 53.6	S18 16.4	57 04.5	10.0	S18 17.8	0.6	56.1
19	108 53.5	17.1	71 33.5	9.9	18 18.4	0.5	56.1
20	123 53.4	17.7	86 02.4	9.8	18 18.9	0.4	56.1
21	138 53.3	.. 18.4	100 31.2	9.9	18 19.3	0.3	56.1
22	153 53.2	19.0	115 00.1	9.8	18 19.6	0.2	56.1
23	168 53.1	19.7	129 28.9	9.8	S18 19.8	0.1	56.2
SD	16.2	d 0.7	SD 15.0		15.1		15.2

Twilight / Moonrise table:

Lat.	Naut.	Civil	Sunrise	Moonrise 12	13	14	15
°	h m	h m	h m	h m	h m	h m	h m
N 72	06 51	08 23	10 29	10 14	12 09	■■	■■
N 70	06 42	08 02	09 34	09 36	11 05	12 22	13 14
68	06 34	07 46	09 02	09 09	10 29	11 39	12 31
66	06 27	07 33	08 38	08 49	10 04	11 09	12 02
64	06 22	07 21	08 20	08 33	09 44	10 48	11 40
62	06 17	07 12	08 05	08 20	09 28	10 30	11 22
60	06 12	07 04	07 52	08 09	09 15	10 15	11 08
N 58	06 08	06 56	07 41	07 59	09 04	10 03	10 55
56	06 04	06 50	07 32	07 51	08 54	09 52	10 45
54	06 01	06 44	07 23	07 43	08 45	09 43	10 35
52	05 58	06 38	07 16	07 36	08 37	09 34	10 27
50	05 54	06 34	07 09	07 30	08 30	09 27	10 19
45	05 47	06 23	06 54	07 17	08 15	09 11	10 03
N 40	05 41	06 13	06 42	07 07	08 03	08 57	09 50
35	05 35	06 05	06 32	06 57	07 52	08 46	09 38
30	05 29	05 58	06 23	06 49	07 43	08 36	09 28
20	05 18	05 44	06 07	06 36	07 27	08 20	09 11
N 10	05 06	05 32	05 54	06 24	07 14	08 05	08 57
0	04 54	05 19	05 41	06 12	07 01	07 51	08 43
S 10	04 39	05 05	05 28	06 01	06 48	07 38	08 29
20	04 22	04 50	05 13	05 49	06 35	07 23	08 14
30	04 00	04 31	04 57	05 36	06 19	07 06	07 57
35	03 46	04 20	04 48	05 28	06 10	06 57	07 48
40	03 29	04 06	04 37	05 19	06 00	06 46	07 36
45	03 08	03 50	04 24	05 09	05 48	06 33	07 23
S 50	02 39	03 29	04 08	04 56	05 34	06 17	07 07
52	02 24	03 19	04 01	04 51	05 27	06 09	06 59
54	02 06	03 08	03 52	04 44	05 19	06 01	06 51
56	01 44	02 55	03 43	04 37	05 11	05 52	06 42
58	01 12	02 39	03 32	04 29	05 02	05 42	06 31
S 60	00 11	02 20	03 20	04 20	04 51	05 30	06 19

Sunset / Twilight / Moonset table:

Lat.	Sunset	Civil	Naut.	Moonset 12	13	14	15
°	h m	h m	h m	h m	h m	h m	h m
N 72	12 59	15 04	16 36	14 24	14 11	■■	■■
N 70	13 53	15 25	16 46	15 03	15 16	15 43	16 39
68	14 26	15 42	16 53	15 30	15 51	16 27	17 22
66	14 49	15 55	17 00	15 51	16 17	16 56	17 51
64	15 08	16 06	17 06	16 07	16 37	17 18	18 13
62	15 23	16 16	17 11	16 21	16 53	17 36	18 30
60	15 36	16 24	17 15	16 33	17 07	17 50	18 45
N 58	15 47	16 31	17 20	16 43	17 19	18 03	18 57
56	15 56	16 38	17 23	16 52	17 29	18 14	19 08
54	16 05	16 44	17 27	16 59	17 38	18 23	19 17
52	16 12	16 49	17 30	17 06	17 46	18 32	19 25
50	16 19	16 54	17 33	17 13	17 53	18 39	19 33
45	16 34	17 05	17 41	17 27	18 08	18 56	19 49
N 40	16 46	17 15	17 47	17 38	18 21	19 09	20 02
35	16 56	17 23	17 53	17 48	18 32	19 20	20 13
30	17 05	17 30	17 59	17 56	18 41	19 30	20 23
20	17 21	17 44	18 11	18 11	18 57	19 47	20 40
N 10	17 35	17 57	18 22	18 24	19 12	20 02	20 54
0	17 48	18 10	18 35	18 36	19 25	20 16	21 08
S 10	18 01	18 23	18 49	18 48	19 38	20 30	21 21
20	18 15	18 39	19 07	19 01	19 53	20 45	21 36
30	18 32	18 58	19 29	19 15	20 09	21 01	21 52
35	18 41	19 09	19 43	19 24	20 18	21 11	22 02
40	18 52	19 23	20 00	19 34	20 29	21 23	22 13
45	19 06	19 39	20 22	19 45	20 42	21 36	22 26
S 50	19 22	20 00	20 51	19 59	20 57	21 52	22 42
52	19 29	20 10	21 06	20 06	21 05	21 59	22 49
54	19 37	20 22	21 25	20 13	21 13	22 08	22 57
56	19 47	20 35	21 48	20 21	21 22	22 17	23 06
58	19 58	20 51	22 21	20 30	21 32	22 28	23 16
S 60	20 10	21 11	////	20 40	21 44	22 40	23 28

SUN / MOON:

Day	Eqn. of Time 00h	Eqn. of Time 12h	Mer. Pass.	Mer. Pass. Upper	Mer. Pass. Lower	Age	Phase
d	m s	m s	h m	h m	h m	d	%
12	15 57	15 53	11 44	12 24	00 00	01	1
13	15 50	15 46	11 44	13 13	00 48	02	3
14	15 41	15 37	11 44	14 04	01 38	03	8

UT	ARIES GHA	VENUS −4.3 GHA	VENUS Dec	MARS +1.6 GHA	MARS Dec	JUPITER −1.9 GHA	JUPITER Dec	SATURN +0.5 GHA	SATURN Dec	STARS Name	SHA	Dec
d h	° ′	° ′	° ′	° ′	° ′	° ′	° ′	° ′	° ′		° ′	° ′
15 00	53 45.9	226 46.6	S 1 21.2	232 02.6	N 0 48.3	243 31.0	N 5 20.0	169 40.7	S19 37.2	Acamar	315 16.7	S40 14.6
01	68 48.4	241 46.5	22.2	247 03.7	47.7	258 33.1	19.9	184 42.8	37.3	Achernar	335 25.2	S57 09.6
02	83 50.8	256 46.3	23.2	262 04.7	47.1	273 35.2	19.7	199 45.0	37.3	Acrux	173 07.8	S63 10.9
03	98 53.3	271 46.2	.. 24.1	277 05.8	.. 46.5	288 37.3	.. 19.6	214 47.2	.. 37.4	Adhara	255 11.0	S28 59.6
04	113 55.8	286 46.1	25.1	292 06.9	45.9	303 39.4	19.5	229 49.3	37.5	Aldebaran	290 47.2	N16 32.3
05	128 58.2	301 45.9	26.0	307 08.0	45.3	318 41.6	19.3	244 51.5	37.5			
06	144 00.7	316 45.8	S 1 27.0	322 09.1	N 0 44.8	333 43.7	N 5 19.2	259 53.6	S19 37.6	Alioth	166 19.8	N55 52.3
07	159 03.2	331 45.6	28.0	337 10.2	44.2	348 45.8	19.1	274 55.8	37.6	Alkaid	152 58.2	N49 14.1
08	174 05.6	346 45.5	28.9	352 11.2	43.6	3 47.9	18.9	289 58.0	37.7	Al Na'ir	27 41.7	S46 53.1
S 09	189 08.1	1 45.4	.. 29.9	7 12.3	.. 43.0	18 50.1	.. 18.8	305 00.1	.. 37.7	Alnilam	275 44.4	S 1 11.7
U 10	204 10.5	16 45.2	30.9	22 13.4	42.4	33 52.2	18.7	320 02.3	37.8	Alphard	217 54.5	S 8 43.6
N 11	219 13.0	31 45.1	31.8	37 14.5	41.8	48 54.3	18.5	335 04.4	37.8			
D 12	234 15.5	46 44.9	S 1 32.8	52 15.6	N 0 41.2	63 56.4	N 5 18.4	350 06.6	S19 37.9	Alphecca	126 10.0	N26 39.9
A 13	249 17.9	61 44.8	33.8	67 16.7	40.6	78 58.6	18.3	5 08.8	37.9	Alpheratz	357 41.5	N29 10.9
Y 14	264 20.4	76 44.7	34.7	82 17.8	40.0	94 00.7	18.1	20 10.9	38.0	Altair	62 06.8	N 8 54.9
15	279 22.9	91 44.5	.. 35.7	97 18.8	.. 39.4	109 02.8	.. 18.0	35 13.1	.. 38.0	Ankaa	353 13.9	S42 13.3
16	294 25.3	106 44.4	36.7	112 19.9	38.9	124 05.0	17.9	50 15.2	38.1	Antares	112 24.6	S26 27.8
17	309 27.8	121 44.2	37.7	127 21.0	38.3	139 07.1	17.7	65 17.4	38.2			
18	324 30.3	136 44.1	S 1 38.6	142 22.1	N 0 37.7	154 09.2	N 5 17.6	80 19.6	S19 38.2	Arcturus	145 54.6	N19 06.2
19	339 32.7	151 44.0	39.6	157 23.2	37.1	169 11.3	17.5	95 21.7	38.3	Atria	107 25.5	S69 03.2
20	354 35.2	166 43.8	40.6	172 24.3	36.5	184 13.5	17.3	110 23.9	38.3	Avior	234 17.0	S59 33.5
21	9 37.7	181 43.7	.. 41.5	187 25.4	.. 35.9	199 15.6	.. 17.2	125 26.0	.. 38.4	Bellatrix	278 30.0	N 6 21.7
22	24 40.1	196 43.5	42.5	202 26.5	35.3	214 17.7	17.1	140 28.2	38.4	Betelgeuse	270 59.3	N 7 24.4
23	39 42.6	211 43.4	43.5	217 27.5	34.7	229 19.8	16.9	155 30.4	38.5			
16 00	54 45.0	226 43.2	S 1 44.4	232 28.6	N 0 34.1	244 22.0	N 5 16.8	170 32.5	S19 38.5	Canopus	263 55.0	S52 42.2
01	69 47.5	241 43.1	45.4	247 29.7	33.5	259 24.1	16.7	185 34.7	38.6	Capella	280 31.6	N46 00.6
02	84 50.0	256 43.0	46.4	262 30.8	33.0	274 26.2	16.5	200 36.8	38.6	Deneb	49 30.4	N45 20.7
03	99 52.4	271 42.8	.. 47.3	277 31.9	.. 32.4	289 28.4	.. 16.4	215 39.0	.. 38.7	Denebola	182 32.2	N14 29.0
04	114 54.9	286 42.7	48.3	292 33.0	31.8	304 30.5	16.3	230 41.2	38.7	Diphda	348 54.0	S17 54.0
05	129 57.4	301 42.5	49.3	307 34.1	31.2	319 32.6	16.1	245 43.3	38.8			
06	144 59.8	316 42.4	S 1 50.3	322 35.1	N 0 30.6	334 34.7	N 5 16.0	260 45.5	S19 38.9	Dubhe	193 50.1	N61 39.6
07	160 02.3	331 42.2	51.2	337 36.2	30.0	349 36.9	15.9	275 47.6	38.9	Elnath	278 10.2	N28 37.0
08	175 04.8	346 42.1	52.2	352 37.3	29.4	4 39.0	15.7	290 49.8	39.0	Eltanin	90 45.8	N51 29.6
M 09	190 07.2	1 41.9	.. 53.2	7 38.4	.. 28.8	19 41.1	.. 15.6	305 52.0	.. 39.0	Enif	33 45.5	N 9 57.1
O 10	205 09.7	16 41.8	54.2	22 39.5	28.2	34 43.3	15.5	320 54.1	39.1	Fomalhaut	15 22.1	S29 32.3
N 11	220 12.1	31 41.6	55.1	37 40.6	27.6	49 45.4	15.3	335 56.3	39.1			
D 12	235 14.6	46 41.5	S 1 56.1	52 41.7	N 0 27.1	64 47.5	N 5 15.2	350 58.4	S19 39.2	Gacrux	171 59.4	S57 11.8
A 13	250 17.1	61 41.3	57.1	67 42.8	26.5	79 49.6	15.1	6 00.6	39.2	Gienah	175 50.8	S17 37.6
Y 14	265 19.5	76 41.2	58.0	82 43.8	25.9	94 51.8	14.9	21 02.7	39.3	Hadar	148 46.1	S60 26.7
15	280 22.0	91 41.0	1 59.0	97 44.9	.. 25.3	109 53.9	.. 14.8	36 04.9	.. 39.3	Hamal	327 58.6	N23 32.2
16	295 24.5	106 40.9	2 00.0	112 46.0	24.7	124 56.0	14.7	51 07.1	39.4	Kaus Aust.	83 42.0	S34 22.4
17	310 26.9	121 40.7	01.0	127 47.1	24.1	139 58.2	14.5	66 09.2	39.4			
18	325 29.4	136 40.6	S 2 01.9	142 48.2	N 0 23.5	155 00.3	N 5 14.4	81 11.4	S19 39.5	Kochab	137 21.5	N74 05.5
19	340 31.9	151 40.4	02.9	157 49.3	22.9	170 02.4	14.3	96 13.5	39.6	Markab	13 36.6	N15 17.6
20	355 34.3	166 40.3	03.9	172 50.4	22.3	185 04.6	14.1	111 15.7	39.6	Menkar	314 13.0	N 4 09.0
21	10 36.8	181 40.1	.. 04.9	187 51.5	.. 21.8	200 06.7	.. 14.0	126 17.9	.. 39.7	Menkent	148 06.0	S36 26.6
22	25 39.3	196 40.0	05.8	202 52.5	21.2	215 08.8	13.9	141 20.0	39.7	Miaplacidus	221 39.0	S69 46.7
23	40 41.7	211 39.8	06.8	217 53.6	20.6	230 11.0	13.7	156 22.2	39.8			
17 00	55 44.2	226 39.7	S 2 07.8	232 54.7	N 0 20.0	245 13.1	N 5 13.6	171 24.3	S19 39.8	Mirfak	308 37.4	N49 54.9
01	70 46.6	241 39.5	08.7	247 55.8	19.4	260 15.2	13.5	186 26.5	39.9	Nunki	75 56.6	S26 16.4
02	85 49.1	256 39.4	09.7	262 56.9	18.8	275 17.4	13.4	201 28.7	39.9	Peacock	53 17.0	S56 41.1
03	100 51.6	271 39.2	.. 10.7	277 58.0	.. 18.2	290 19.5	.. 13.2	216 30.8	.. 40.0	Pollux	243 25.6	N27 59.0
04	115 54.0	286 39.1	11.7	292 59.1	17.6	305 21.6	13.1	231 33.0	40.0	Procyon	244 57.9	N 5 10.9
05	130 56.5	301 38.9	12.7	308 00.2	17.0	320 23.8	13.0	246 35.1	40.1			
06	145 59.0	316 38.8	S 2 13.7	323 01.2	N 0 16.5	335 25.9	N 5 12.8	261 37.3	S19 40.1	Rasalhague	96 05.3	N12 33.2
07	161 01.4	331 38.6	14.6	338 02.3	15.9	350 28.0	12.7	276 39.4	40.2	Regulus	207 41.9	N11 53.3
08	176 03.9	346 38.5	15.6	353 03.4	15.3	5 30.2	12.6	291 41.6	40.2	Rigel	281 10.2	S 8 11.1
T 09	191 06.4	1 38.3	.. 16.6	8 04.5	.. 14.7	20 32.3	.. 12.4	306 43.8	.. 40.3	Rigil Kent.	139 50.1	S60 53.7
U 10	206 08.8	16 38.1	17.6	23 05.6	14.1	35 34.4	12.3	321 45.9	40.4	Sabik	102 11.0	S15 44.4
E 11	221 11.3	31 38.0	18.5	38 06.7	13.5	50 36.6	12.2	336 48.1	40.4			
S 12	236 13.8	46 37.8	S 2 19.5	53 07.8	N 0 12.9	65 38.7	N 5 12.0	351 50.2	S19 40.5	Schedar	349 38.1	N56 37.7
D 13	251 16.2	61 37.7	20.5	68 08.9	12.3	80 40.8	11.9	6 52.4	40.5	Shaula	96 20.1	S37 06.7
A 14	266 18.7	76 37.5	21.5	83 10.0	11.7	95 43.0	11.8	21 54.6	40.6	Sirius	258 32.0	S16 44.3
Y 15	281 21.1	91 37.4	.. 22.5	98 11.0	.. 11.2	110 45.1	.. 11.7	36 56.7	.. 40.6	Spica	158 29.8	S11 14.4
16	296 23.6	106 37.2	23.4	113 12.1	10.6	125 47.2	11.5	51 58.9	40.7	Suhail	222 51.1	S43 29.6
17	311 26.1	121 37.0	24.4	128 13.2	10.0	140 49.4	11.4	67 01.0	40.7			
18	326 28.5	136 36.9	S 2 25.4	143 14.3	N 0 09.4	155 51.5	N 5 11.3	82 03.2	S19 40.8	Vega	80 38.2	N38 48.3
19	341 31.0	151 36.7	26.4	158 15.4	08.8	170 53.6	11.1	97 05.3	40.8	Zuben'ubi	137 03.9	S16 06.2
20	356 33.5	166 36.6	27.4	173 16.5	08.2	185 55.8	11.0	112 07.5	40.9			
21	11 35.9	181 36.4	.. 28.3	188 17.6	.. 07.6	200 57.9	.. 10.9	127 09.7	.. 40.9		SHA	Mer. Pass.
22	26 38.4	196 36.3	29.3	203 18.7	07.0	216 00.1	10.7	142 11.8	41.0		° ′	h m
23	41 40.9	211 36.1	30.3	218 19.8	06.4	231 02.2	10.6	157 14.0	41.1	Venus	171 58.2	8 53
	h m									Mars	177 43.6	8 29
Mer. Pass. 20 17.7		v −0.1 d 1.0		v 1.1 d 0.6		v 2.1 d 0.1		v 2.2 d 0.1		Jupiter	189 36.9	7 41
										Saturn	115 47.5	12 36

UT	SUN GHA	SUN Dec	MOON GHA	v	MOON Dec	d	HP
d h	° ′	° ′	° ′	′	° ′	′	′
15 00	183 53.0	S18 20.3	143 57.7	9.8	S18 19.9	0.0	56.2
01	198 52.9	21.0	158 26.5	9.8	18 19.9	0.1	56.2
02	213 52.8	21.6	172 55.3	9.7	18 19.8	0.2	56.2
03	228 52.7	.. 22.2	187 24.0	9.7	18 19.6	0.3	56.2
04	243 52.6	22.9	201 52.7	9.7	18 19.3	0.4	56.3
05	258 52.5	23.5	216 21.4	9.7	18 18.9	0.4	56.3
06	273 52.4	S18 24.2	230 50.1	9.7	S18 18.5	0.6	56.3
07	288 52.3	24.8	245 18.8	9.6	18 17.9	0.7	56.3
08	303 52.1	25.5	259 47.4	9.6	18 17.2	0.8	56.3
S 09	318 52.0	.. 26.1	274 16.0	9.6	18 16.4	0.9	56.4
U 10	333 51.9	26.7	288 44.6	9.6	18 15.5	1.0	56.4
N 11	348 51.8	27.4	303 13.2	9.6	18 14.5	1.0	56.4
D 12	3 51.7	S18 28.0	317 41.8	9.5	S18 13.5	1.2	56.4
A 13	18 51.6	28.7	332 10.3	9.6	18 12.3	1.3	56.4
Y 14	33 51.5	29.3	346 38.9	9.5	18 11.0	1.4	56.5
15	48 51.4	.. 29.9	1 07.4	9.5	18 09.6	1.5	56.5
16	63 51.3	30.6	15 35.9	9.5	18 08.1	1.5	56.5
17	78 51.2	31.2	30 04.4	9.5	18 06.6	1.7	56.5
18	93 51.1	S18 31.8	44 32.9	9.5	S18 04.9	1.8	56.6
19	108 51.0	32.5	59 01.4	9.5	18 03.1	1.9	56.6
20	123 50.9	33.1	73 29.9	9.4	18 01.2	2.0	56.6
21	138 50.8	.. 33.7	87 58.3	9.5	17 59.2	2.0	56.6
22	153 50.7	34.4	102 26.8	9.4	17 57.2	2.2	56.6
23	168 50.6	35.0	116 55.2	9.4	17 55.0	2.3	56.7
16 00	183 50.5	S18 35.6	131 23.6	9.4	S17 52.7	2.4	56.7
01	198 50.3	36.3	145 52.0	9.4	17 50.3	2.5	56.7
02	213 50.2	36.9	160 20.4	9.4	17 47.8	2.5	56.7
03	228 50.1	.. 37.5	174 48.8	9.4	17 45.3	2.7	56.8
04	243 50.0	38.2	189 17.2	9.4	17 42.6	2.8	56.8
05	258 49.9	38.8	203 45.6	9.4	17 39.8	2.9	56.8
06	273 49.8	S18 39.4	218 14.0	9.3	S17 36.9	3.0	56.8
07	288 49.7	40.0	232 42.3	9.4	17 33.9	3.0	56.8
08	303 49.6	40.7	247 10.7	9.4	17 30.9	3.2	56.9
M 09	318 49.5	.. 41.3	261 39.1	9.3	17 27.7	3.3	56.9
O 10	333 49.3	41.9	276 07.4	9.4	17 24.4	3.4	56.9
N 11	348 49.2	42.6	290 35.8	9.3	17 21.0	3.4	56.9
D 12	3 49.1	S18 43.2	305 04.1	9.3	S17 17.6	3.6	57.0
A 13	18 49.0	43.8	319 32.4	9.4	17 14.0	3.7	57.0
Y 14	33 48.9	44.4	334 00.8	9.3	17 10.3	3.7	57.0
15	48 48.8	.. 45.1	348 29.1	9.4	17 06.6	3.9	57.0
16	63 48.7	45.7	2 57.5	9.3	17 02.7	4.0	57.1
17	78 48.5	46.3	17 25.8	9.3	16 58.7	4.0	57.1
18	93 48.4	S18 46.9	31 54.1	9.3	S16 54.7	4.2	57.1
19	108 48.3	47.5	46 22.4	9.4	16 50.5	4.3	57.1
20	123 48.2	48.2	60 50.8	9.3	16 46.2	4.3	57.2
21	138 48.1	.. 48.8	75 19.1	9.3	16 41.9	4.5	57.2
22	153 48.0	49.4	89 47.4	9.4	16 37.4	4.5	57.2
23	168 47.8	50.0	104 15.8	9.3	16 32.9	4.6	57.2
17 00	183 47.7	S18 50.6	118 44.1	9.3	S16 28.3	4.8	57.2
01	198 47.6	51.3	133 12.4	9.4	16 23.5	4.8	57.3
02	213 47.5	51.9	147 40.8	9.3	16 18.7	4.9	57.3
03	228 47.4	.. 52.5	162 09.1	9.3	16 13.8	5.0	57.3
04	243 47.3	53.1	176 37.4	9.4	16 08.8	5.2	57.3
05	258 47.1	53.7	191 05.8	9.3	16 03.6	5.2	57.4
06	273 47.0	S18 54.3	205 34.1	9.4	S15 58.4	5.3	57.4
07	288 46.9	54.9	220 02.5	9.3	15 53.1	5.4	57.4
08	303 46.8	55.6	234 30.8	9.4	15 47.7	5.5	57.4
T 09	318 46.7	.. 56.2	248 59.2	9.3	15 42.2	5.5	57.5
U 10	333 46.5	56.8	263 27.5	9.4	15 36.7	5.7	57.5
E 11	348 46.4	57.4	277 55.9	9.3	15 31.0	5.8	57.5
S 12	3 46.3	S18 58.0	292 24.2	9.4	S15 25.2	5.8	57.5
D 13	18 46.2	58.6	306 52.6	9.4	15 19.4	6.0	57.6
A 14	33 46.1	59.2	321 21.0	9.4	15 13.4	6.0	57.6
Y 15	48 45.9	18 59.8	335 49.4	9.4	15 07.4	6.1	57.6
16	63 45.8	19 00.4	350 17.8	9.3	15 01.3	6.3	57.6
17	78 45.7	01.1	4 46.1	9.4	14 55.0	6.3	57.7
18	93 45.6	S19 01.7	19 14.5	9.4	S14 48.7	6.4	57.7
19	108 45.4	02.3	33 42.9	9.4	14 42.3	6.4	57.7
20	123 45.3	02.9	48 11.3	9.5	14 35.9	6.6	57.7
21	138 45.2	.. 03.5	62 39.8	9.4	14 29.3	6.7	57.8
22	153 45.1	04.1	77 08.2	9.4	14 22.6	6.7	57.8
23	168 44.9	04.7	91 36.6	9.4	S14 15.9	6.8	57.8
	SD 16.2	d 0.6	SD 15.4		15.5		15.7

Lat.	Twilight Naut.	Twilight Civil	Sunrise	Moonrise 15	Moonrise 16	Moonrise 17	Moonrise 18
°	h m	h m	h m	h m	h m	h m	h m
N 72	07 02	08 37	11 17	■■■	14 37	14 25	14 18
N 70	06 51	08 14	09 54	13 14	13 39	13 51	13 56
68	06 43	07 56	09 16	12 31	13 05	13 26	13 39
66	06 35	07 41	08 50	12 02	12 40	13 06	13 25
64	06 29	07 29	08 29	11 40	12 20	12 51	13 13
62	06 23	07 19	08 13	11 22	12 05	12 37	13 03
60	06 18	07 10	07 59	11 08	11 51	12 26	12 55
N 58	06 14	07 02	07 48	10 55	11 40	12 17	12 47
56	06 10	06 55	07 38	10 45	11 30	12 08	12 41
54	06 06	06 49	07 29	10 35	11 21	12 01	12 35
52	06 02	06 43	07 21	10 27	11 13	11 54	12 29
50	05 59	06 38	07 14	10 19	11 06	11 48	12 25
45	05 51	06 27	06 58	10 03	10 51	11 35	12 14
N 40	05 44	06 17	06 46	09 50	10 38	11 24	12 05
35	05 37	06 08	06 35	09 38	10 28	11 14	11 58
30	05 31	06 00	06 26	09 28	10 18	11 06	11 51
20	05 19	05 46	06 09	09 11	10 02	10 52	11 40
N 10	05 07	05 33	05 55	08 57	09 48	10 39	11 30
0	04 54	05 19	05 41	08 43	09 35	10 28	11 20
S 10	04 39	05 05	05 27	08 29	09 22	10 16	11 11
20	04 21	04 49	05 13	08 14	09 08	10 04	11 00
30	03 58	04 29	04 56	07 57	08 52	09 49	10 49
35	03 44	04 18	04 46	07 48	08 42	09 41	10 42
40	03 26	04 04	04 34	07 36	08 32	09 31	10 34
45	03 03	03 46	04 21	07 23	08 19	09 20	10 26
S 50	02 33	03 25	04 04	07 07	08 04	09 07	10 15
52	02 17	03 14	03 56	06 59	07 57	09 01	10 10
54	01 57	03 02	03 47	06 51	07 49	08 54	10 04
56	01 32	02 48	03 37	06 42	07 40	08 46	09 58
58	00 55	02 31	03 26	06 31	07 30	08 37	09 51
S 60	////	02 11	03 13	06 19	07 18	08 27	09 43

Lat.	Sunset	Twilight Civil	Twilight Naut.	Moonset 15	Moonset 16	Moonset 17	Moonset 18
°	h m	h m	h m	h m	h m	h m	h m
N 72	12 11	14 51	16 26	■■■	17 06	19 07	21 03
N 70	13 35	15 14	16 37	16 39	18 03	19 41	21 24
68	14 13	15 32	16 46	17 22	18 37	20 05	21 40
66	14 39	15 47	16 53	17 51	19 01	20 24	21 53
64	14 59	15 59	17 00	18 13	19 20	20 39	22 04
62	15 16	16 10	17 05	18 30	19 36	20 51	22 13
60	15 29	16 18	17 10	18 45	19 49	21 02	22 21
N 58	15 41	16 26	17 15	18 57	20 00	21 11	22 28
56	15 51	16 33	17 19	19 08	20 10	21 19	22 34
54	16 00	16 40	17 23	19 17	20 18	21 26	22 39
52	16 08	16 46	17 27	19 25	20 26	21 33	22 44
50	16 16	16 51	17 30	19 33	20 33	21 38	22 48
45	16 31	17 02	17 38	19 49	20 48	21 51	22 58
N 40	16 43	17 12	17 45	20 02	21 00	22 01	23 05
35	16 54	17 21	17 52	20 13	21 10	22 10	23 12
30	17 04	17 29	17 58	20 23	21 19	22 17	23 18
20	17 20	17 43	18 10	20 40	21 34	22 31	23 28
N 10	17 35	17 57	18 22	20 54	21 48	22 42	23 37
0	17 48	18 10	18 36	21 08	22 00	22 53	23 45
S 10	18 02	18 24	18 51	21 21	22 13	23 03	23 53
20	18 17	18 41	19 09	21 36	22 26	23 15	24 02
30	18 34	19 00	19 32	21 52	22 41	23 28	24 12
35	18 44	19 12	19 47	22 02	22 50	23 35	24 17
40	18 56	19 27	20 04	22 13	23 00	23 43	24 24
45	19 10	19 44	20 27	22 26	23 12	23 53	24 31
S 50	19 27	20 06	20 58	22 42	23 26	24 05	00 05
52	19 34	20 17	21 15	22 49	23 32	24 10	00 10
54	19 43	20 29	21 35	22 57	23 40	24 16	00 16
56	19 53	20 43	22 00	23 06	23 48	24 23	00 23
58	20 05	21 00	22 40	23 16	23 57	24 30	00 30
S 60	20 18	21 22	////	23 28	24 07	00 07	00 39

	SUN Eqn. of Time 00h	SUN Eqn. of Time 12h	SUN Mer. Pass.	MOON Mer. Pass. Upper	MOON Mer. Pass. Lower	Age	Phase
Day							
d	m s	m s	h m	h m	h m	d	%
15	15 32	15 27	11 45	14 55	02 29	04	14
16	15 22	15 17	11 45	15 48	03 22	05	22
17	15 11	15 05	11 45	16 40	04 14	06	31

UT	ARIES GHA	VENUS −4.3 GHA	VENUS Dec	MARS +1.6 GHA	MARS Dec	JUPITER −1.9 GHA	JUPITER Dec	SATURN +0.5 GHA	SATURN Dec	STARS Name	SHA	Dec
d h	° ′	° ′	° ′	° ′	° ′	° ′	° ′	° ′	° ′		° ′	° ′
18 00	56 43.3	226 35.9	S 2 31.3	233 20.9	N 0 05.9	246 04.3	N 5 10.5	172 16.1	S19 41.1	Acamar	315 16.7	S40 14.6
01	71 45.8	241 35.8	32.3	248 21.9	05.3	261 06.5	10.4	187 18.3	41.2	Achernar	335 25.2	S57 09.6
02	86 48.3	256 35.6	33.2	263 23.0	04.7	276 08.6	10.2	202 20.5	41.2	Acrux	173 07.7	S63 10.9
03	101 50.7	271 35.4	.. 34.2	278 24.1	.. 04.1	291 10.7	.. 10.1	217 22.6	.. 41.3	Adhara	255 11.0	S28 59.6
04	116 53.2	286 35.3	35.2	293 25.2	03.5	306 12.9	10.0	232 24.8	41.3	Aldebaran	290 47.2	N16 32.3
05	131 55.6	301 35.1	36.2	308 26.3	02.9	321 15.0	09.8	247 26.9	41.4			
06	146 58.1	316 35.0	S 2 37.2	323 27.4	N 0 02.3	336 17.2	N 5 09.7	262 29.1	S19 41.4	Alioth	166 19.8	N55 52.3
W 07	162 00.6	331 34.8	38.2	338 28.5	01.7	351 19.3	09.6	277 31.2	41.5	Alkaid	152 58.1	N49 14.1
E 08	177 03.0	346 34.6	39.1	353 29.6	01.2	6 21.4	09.5	292 33.4	41.5	Al Na'ir	27 41.8	S46 53.1
D 09	192 05.5	1 34.5	.. 40.1	8 30.7	N 00.6	21 23.6	.. 09.3	307 35.6	.. 41.6	Alnilam	275 44.4	S 1 11.7
N 10	207 08.0	16 34.3	41.1	23 31.8	00.0	36 25.7	09.2	322 37.7	41.6	Alphard	217 54.4	S 8 43.7
E 11	222 10.4	31 34.1	42.1	38 32.8	S 00.6	51 27.9	09.1	337 39.9	41.7			
S 12	237 12.9	46 34.0	S 2 43.1	53 33.9	S 0 01.2	66 30.0	N 5 08.9	352 42.0	S19 41.7	Alphecca	126 10.0	N26 39.9
D 13	252 15.4	61 33.8	44.1	68 35.0	01.8	81 32.1	08.8	7 44.2	41.8	Alpheratz	357 41.6	N29 10.9
A 14	267 17.8	76 33.6	45.0	83 36.1	02.4	96 34.3	08.7	22 46.4	41.9	Altair	62 06.8	N 8 54.9
Y 15	282 20.3	91 33.5	.. 46.0	98 37.2	.. 03.0	111 36.4	.. 08.6	37 48.5	.. 41.9	Ankaa	353 13.9	S42 13.3
16	297 22.7	106 33.3	47.0	113 38.3	03.5	126 38.5	08.4	52 50.7	42.0	Antares	112 24.6	S26 27.8
17	312 25.2	121 33.1	48.0	128 39.4	04.1	141 40.7	08.3	67 52.8	42.0			
18	327 27.7	136 33.0	S 2 49.0	143 40.5	S 0 04.7	156 42.8	N 5 08.2	82 55.0	S19 42.1	Arcturus	145 54.6	N19 06.1
19	342 30.1	151 32.8	50.0	158 41.6	05.3	171 45.0	08.0	97 57.1	42.1	Atria	107 25.5	S69 03.2
20	357 32.6	166 32.6	51.0	173 42.7	05.9	186 47.1	07.9	112 59.3	42.2	Avior	234 17.0	S59 33.5
21	12 35.1	181 32.5	.. 51.9	188 43.7	.. 06.5	201 49.3	.. 07.8	128 01.5	.. 42.2	Bellatrix	278 30.0	N 6 21.7
22	27 37.5	196 32.3	52.9	203 44.8	07.1	216 51.4	07.7	143 03.6	42.3	Betelgeuse	270 59.3	N 7 24.4
23	42 40.0	211 32.1	53.9	218 45.9	07.7	231 53.5	07.5	158 05.8	42.3			
19 00	57 42.5	226 32.0	S 2 54.9	233 47.0	S 0 08.2	246 55.7	N 5 07.4	173 07.9	S19 42.4	Canopus	263 55.0	S52 42.2
01	72 44.9	241 31.8	55.9	248 48.1	08.8	261 57.8	07.3	188 10.1	42.4	Capella	280 31.6	N46 00.6
02	87 47.4	256 31.6	56.9	263 49.2	09.4	277 00.0	07.2	203 12.2	42.5	Deneb	49 30.5	N45 20.7
03	102 49.9	271 31.5	.. 57.9	278 50.3	.. 10.0	292 02.1	.. 07.0	218 14.4	.. 42.5	Denebola	182 32.2	N14 29.0
04	117 52.3	286 31.3	58.8	293 51.4	10.6	307 04.2	06.9	233 16.6	42.6	Diphda	348 54.1	S17 54.0
05	132 54.8	301 31.1	2 59.8	308 52.5	11.2	322 06.4	06.8	248 18.7	42.6			
06	147 57.2	316 30.9	S 3 00.8	323 53.6	S 0 11.8	337 08.5	N 5 06.7	263 20.9	S19 42.7	Dubhe	193 50.1	N61 39.6
07	162 59.7	331 30.8	01.8	338 54.7	12.4	352 10.7	06.5	278 23.0	42.8	Elnath	278 10.2	N28 37.0
T 08	178 02.2	346 30.6	02.8	353 55.8	12.9	7 12.8	06.4	293 25.2	42.8	Eltanin	90 45.9	N51 29.6
H 09	193 04.6	1 30.4	.. 03.8	8 56.8	.. 13.5	22 15.0	.. 06.3	308 27.3	.. 42.9	Enif	33 45.5	N 9 57.1
U 10	208 07.1	16 30.3	04.8	23 57.9	14.1	37 17.1	06.1	323 29.5	42.9	Fomalhaut	15 22.1	S29 32.3
R 11	223 09.6	31 30.1	05.8	38 59.0	14.7	52 19.3	06.0	338 31.7	43.0			
S 12	238 12.0	46 29.9	S 3 06.7	54 00.1	S 0 15.3	67 21.4	N 5 05.9	353 33.8	S19 43.0	Gacrux	171 59.3	S57 11.8
D 13	253 14.5	61 29.7	07.7	69 01.2	15.9	82 23.5	05.8	8 36.0	43.1	Gienah	175 50.8	S17 37.6
A 14	268 17.0	76 29.6	08.7	84 02.3	16.5	97 25.7	05.6	23 38.1	43.1	Hadar	148 46.0	S60 26.7
Y 15	283 19.4	91 29.4	.. 09.7	99 03.4	.. 17.0	112 27.8	.. 05.5	38 40.3	.. 43.2	Hamal	327 58.6	N23 32.2
16	298 21.9	106 29.2	10.7	114 04.5	17.6	127 30.0	05.4	53 42.4	43.2	Kaus Aust.	83 42.0	S34 22.4
17	313 24.4	121 29.0	11.7	129 05.6	18.2	142 32.1	05.3	68 44.6	43.3			
18	328 26.8	136 28.9	S 3 12.7	144 06.7	S 0 18.8	157 34.3	N 5 05.1	83 46.8	S19 43.3	Kochab	137 21.5	N74 05.5
19	343 29.3	151 28.7	13.7	159 07.8	19.4	172 36.4	05.0	98 48.9	43.4	Markab	13 36.6	N15 17.6
20	358 31.7	166 28.5	14.7	174 08.9	20.0	187 38.6	04.9	113 51.1	43.4	Menkar	314 13.0	N 4 09.0
21	13 34.2	181 28.3	.. 15.6	189 09.9	.. 20.6	202 40.7	.. 04.8	128 53.2	.. 43.5	Menkent	148 06.0	S36 26.6
22	28 36.7	196 28.2	16.6	204 11.0	21.1	217 42.9	04.6	143 55.4	43.6	Miaplacidus	221 39.0	S69 46.7
23	43 39.1	211 28.0	17.6	219 12.1	21.7	232 45.0	04.5	158 57.5	43.6			
20 00	58 41.6	226 27.8	S 3 18.6	234 13.2	S 0 22.3	247 47.1	N 5 04.4	173 59.7	S19 43.7	Mirfak	308 37.4	N49 54.9
01	73 44.1	241 27.6	19.6	249 14.3	22.9	262 49.3	04.3	189 01.9	43.7	Nunki	75 56.6	S26 16.4
02	88 46.5	256 27.4	20.6	264 15.4	23.5	277 51.4	04.1	204 04.0	43.8	Peacock	53 17.0	S56 41.1
03	103 49.0	271 27.3	.. 21.6	279 16.5	.. 24.1	292 53.6	.. 04.0	219 06.2	.. 43.8	Pollux	243 25.6	N27 59.0
04	118 51.5	286 27.1	22.6	294 17.6	24.7	307 55.7	03.9	234 08.3	43.9	Procyon	244 57.9	N 5 10.9
05	133 53.9	301 26.9	23.6	309 18.7	25.2	322 57.9	03.8	249 10.5	43.9			
06	148 56.4	316 26.7	S 3 24.6	324 19.8	S 0 25.8	338 00.0	N 5 03.6	264 12.6	S19 44.0	Rasalhague	96 05.3	N12 33.2
07	163 58.8	331 26.5	25.5	339 20.9	26.4	353 02.2	03.5	279 14.8	44.0	Regulus	207 41.8	N11 53.3
08	179 01.3	346 26.4	26.5	354 22.0	27.0	8 04.3	03.4	294 17.0	44.1	Rigel	281 10.2	S 8 11.1
F 09	194 03.8	1 26.2	.. 27.5	9 23.1	.. 27.6	23 06.5	.. 03.3	309 19.1	.. 44.1	Rigil Kent.	139 50.0	S60 53.7
R 10	209 06.2	16 26.0	28.5	24 24.2	28.2	38 08.6	03.1	324 21.3	44.2	Sabik	102 11.0	S15 44.4
I 11	224 08.7	31 25.8	29.5	39 25.2	28.8	53 10.8	03.0	339 23.4	44.2			
D 12	239 11.2	46 25.6	S 3 30.5	54 26.3	S 0 29.3	68 12.9	N 5 02.9	354 25.6	S19 44.3	Schedar	349 38.1	N56 37.7
A 13	254 13.6	61 25.4	31.5	69 27.4	29.9	83 15.1	02.8	9 27.7	44.3	Shaula	96 20.1	S37 06.7
Y 14	269 16.1	76 25.3	32.5	84 28.5	30.5	98 17.2	02.6	24 29.9	44.4	Sirius	258 32.0	S16 44.4
15	284 18.6	91 25.1	.. 33.5	99 29.6	.. 31.1	113 19.4	.. 02.5	39 32.0	.. 44.4	Spica	158 29.8	S11 14.4
16	299 21.0	106 24.9	34.5	114 30.7	31.7	128 21.5	02.4	54 34.2	44.5	Suhail	222 51.1	S43 29.7
17	314 23.5	121 24.7	35.5	129 31.8	32.3	143 23.7	02.3	69 36.4	44.6			
18	329 26.0	136 24.5	S 3 36.5	144 32.9	S 0 32.9	158 25.8	N 5 02.1	84 38.5	S19 44.6	Vega	80 38.2	N38 48.3
19	344 28.4	151 24.3	37.5	159 34.0	33.4	173 28.0	02.0	99 40.7	44.7	Zuben'ubi	137 03.9	S16 06.2
20	359 30.9	166 24.2	38.4	174 35.1	34.0	188 30.1	01.9	114 42.8	44.7		SHA	Mer. Pass.
21	14 33.3	181 24.0	.. 39.4	189 36.2	.. 34.6	203 32.3	.. 01.8	129 45.0	.. 44.8		° ′	h m
22	29 35.8	196 23.8	40.4	204 37.3	35.2	218 34.4	01.7	144 47.1	44.8	Venus	168 49.5	8 54
23	44 38.3	211 23.6	41.4	219 38.4	35.8	233 36.6	01.5	159 49.3	44.9	Mars	176 04.6	8 24
	h m									Jupiter	189 13.2	7 31
Mer. Pass. 20 05.9	v −0.2	d 1.0		v 1.1	d 0.6	v 2.1	d 0.1	v 2.2	d 0.1	Saturn	115 25.5	12 26

UT	SUN GHA	SUN Dec	MOON GHA	v	Dec	d	HP
d h	° ′	° ′	° ′	′	° ′	′	′
18 00	183 44.8	S19 05.3	106 05.0	9.5	S14 09.1	6.9	57.8
01	198 44.7	05.9	120 33.5	9.4	14 02.2	7.0	57.9
02	213 44.6	06.5	135 01.9	9.4	13 55.2	7.1	57.9
03	228 44.4	.. 07.1	149 30.3	9.5	13 48.1	7.2	57.9
04	243 44.3	07.7	163 58.8	9.5	13 40.9	7.2	57.9
05	258 44.2	08.3	178 27.3	9.4	13 33.7	7.4	58.0
06	273 44.0	S19 08.9	192 55.7	9.5	S13 26.3	7.4	58.0
W 07	288 43.9	09.5	207 24.2	9.5	13 18.9	7.5	58.0
E 08	303 43.8	10.1	221 52.7	9.5	13 11.4	7.6	58.0
D 09	318 43.7	.. 10.7	236 21.2	9.5	13 03.8	7.6	58.1
N 10	333 43.5	11.3	250 49.7	9.5	12 56.2	7.8	58.1
E 11	348 43.4	11.9	265 18.2	9.5	12 48.4	7.8	58.1
S 12	3 43.3	S19 12.5	279 46.7	9.5	S12 40.6	7.9	58.1
D 13	18 43.1	13.1	294 15.2	9.5	12 32.7	7.9	58.2
A 14	33 43.0	13.7	308 43.7	9.5	12 24.8	8.1	58.2
Y 15	48 42.9	.. 14.3	323 12.2	9.5	12 16.7	8.1	58.2
16	63 42.7	14.9	337 40.7	9.6	12 08.6	8.2	58.2
17	78 42.6	15.5	352 09.3	9.5	12 00.4	8.3	58.3
18	93 42.5	S19 16.1	6 37.8	9.6	S11 52.1	8.4	58.3
19	108 42.4	16.7	21 06.4	9.5	11 43.7	8.4	58.3
20	123 42.2	17.3	35 34.9	9.6	11 35.3	8.5	58.3
21	138 42.1	.. 17.8	50 03.5	9.5	11 26.8	8.5	58.4
22	153 42.0	18.4	64 32.0	9.6	11 18.3	8.7	58.4
23	168 41.8	19.0	79 00.6	9.5	11 09.6	8.7	58.4
19 00	183 41.7	S19 19.6	93 29.1	9.6	S11 00.9	8.8	58.4
01	198 41.5	20.2	107 57.7	9.6	10 52.1	8.8	58.5
02	213 41.4	20.8	122 26.3	9.6	10 43.3	9.0	58.5
03	228 41.3	.. 21.4	136 54.9	9.6	10 34.3	9.0	58.5
04	243 41.1	22.0	151 23.5	9.5	10 25.3	9.0	58.6
05	258 41.0	22.6	165 52.0	9.6	10 16.3	9.1	58.6
06	273 40.9	S19 23.1	180 20.6	9.6	S10 07.2	9.2	58.6
T 07	288 40.7	23.7	194 49.2	9.6	9 58.0	9.3	58.6
H 08	303 40.6	24.3	209 17.8	9.6	9 48.7	9.3	58.7
U 09	318 40.5	.. 24.9	223 46.4	9.6	9 39.4	9.4	58.7
R 10	333 40.3	25.5	238 15.0	9.6	9 30.0	9.4	58.7
S 11	348 40.2	26.1	252 43.6	9.6	9 20.6	9.5	58.7
D 12	3 40.0	S19 26.6	267 12.2	9.6	S 9 11.1	9.6	58.8
A 13	18 39.9	27.2	281 40.8	9.6	9 01.5	9.6	58.8
Y 14	33 39.8	27.8	296 09.4	9.6	8 51.9	9.7	58.8
15	48 39.6	.. 28.4	310 38.0	9.6	8 42.2	9.8	58.8
16	63 39.5	29.0	325 06.6	9.6	8 32.4	9.8	58.9
17	78 39.3	29.5	339 35.2	9.6	8 22.6	9.8	58.9
18	93 39.2	S19 30.1	354 03.8	9.6	S 8 12.8	9.9	58.9
19	108 39.1	30.7	8 32.4	9.6	8 02.9	10.0	58.9
20	123 38.9	31.3	23 01.0	9.6	7 52.9	10.0	59.0
21	138 38.8	.. 31.9	37 29.6	9.6	7 42.9	10.1	59.0
22	153 38.6	32.4	51 58.2	9.6	7 32.8	10.1	59.0
23	168 38.5	33.0	66 26.8	9.6	7 22.7	10.2	59.0
20 00	183 38.4	S19 33.6	80 55.4	9.6	S 7 12.5	10.2	59.1
01	198 38.2	34.2	95 24.0	9.6	7 02.3	10.3	59.1
02	213 38.1	34.7	109 52.6	9.6	6 52.0	10.3	59.1
03	228 37.9	.. 35.3	124 21.2	9.6	6 41.7	10.4	59.1
04	243 37.8	35.9	138 49.8	9.5	6 31.3	10.4	59.2
05	258 37.6	36.5	153 18.3	9.6	6 20.9	10.5	59.2
06	273 37.5	S19 37.0	167 46.9	9.5	S 6 10.4	10.5	59.2
07	288 37.3	37.6	182 15.4	9.6	5 59.9	10.6	59.2
08	303 37.2	38.2	196 44.0	9.6	5 49.3	10.6	59.2
F 09	318 37.1	.. 38.7	211 12.5	9.6	5 38.7	10.6	59.3
R 10	333 36.9	39.3	225 41.1	9.5	5 28.1	10.7	59.3
I 11	348 36.8	39.9	240 09.6	9.5	5 17.4	10.7	59.3
D 12	3 36.6	S19 40.4	254 38.1	9.5	S 5 06.7	10.8	59.3
A 13	18 36.5	41.0	269 06.6	9.5	4 55.9	10.8	59.4
Y 14	33 36.3	41.6	283 35.1	9.5	4 45.1	10.8	59.4
15	48 36.2	.. 42.1	298 03.6	9.5	4 34.3	10.9	59.4
16	63 36.0	42.7	312 32.1	9.5	4 23.4	10.9	59.4
17	78 35.9	43.3	327 00.6	9.4	4 12.5	10.9	59.5
18	93 35.7	S19 43.8	341 29.0	9.5	S 4 01.6	11.0	59.5
19	108 35.6	44.4	355 57.5	9.4	3 50.6	11.0	59.5
20	123 35.4	45.0	10 25.9	9.4	3 39.6	11.0	59.5
21	138 35.3	.. 45.5	24 54.3	9.5	3 28.6	11.1	59.5
22	153 35.1	46.1	39 22.8	9.3	3 17.5	11.1	59.6
23	168 35.0	46.6	53 51.1	9.4	S 3 06.4	11.1	59.6
	SD 16.2	d 0.6	SD 15.8		16.0		16.2

Lat.	Twilight Naut.	Twilight Civil	Sunrise	Moonrise 18	19	20	21
°	h m	h m	h m	h m	h m	h m	h m
N 72	07 12	08 52	▪	14 18	14 12	14 07	14 02
N 70	07 01	08 26	10 15	13 56	13 59	14 00	14 01
68	06 51	08 06	09 30	13 39	13 48	13 55	14 01
66	06 43	07 50	09 01	13 25	13 39	13 50	14 01
64	06 36	07 37	08 39	13 13	13 31	13 46	14 00
62	06 30	07 26	08 21	13 03	13 24	13 43	14 00
60	06 24	07 17	08 07	12 55	13 19	13 40	14 00
N 58	06 19	07 08	07 55	12 47	13 14	13 37	13 59
56	06 15	07 01	07 44	12 41	13 09	13 35	13 59
54	06 10	06 54	07 34	12 35	13 05	13 32	13 59
52	06 06	06 48	07 26	12 29	13 01	13 31	13 59
50	06 03	06 43	07 19	12 25	12 58	13 29	13 59
45	05 54	06 30	07 02	12 14	12 50	13 25	13 58
N 40	05 47	06 20	06 49	12 05	12 44	13 22	13 58
35	05 40	06 11	06 38	11 58	12 39	13 19	13 58
30	05 33	06 03	06 28	11 51	12 34	13 16	13 58
20	05 21	05 48	06 11	11 40	12 26	13 12	13 57
N 10	05 08	05 34	05 56	11 30	12 19	13 08	13 57
0	04 54	05 20	05 42	11 20	12 12	13 04	13 57
S 10	04 39	05 05	05 27	11 11	12 05	13 01	13 57
20	04 20	04 48	05 12	11 00	11 58	12 57	13 56
30	03 56	04 28	04 54	10 49	11 50	12 53	13 56
35	03 41	04 16	04 44	10 42	11 45	12 50	13 56
40	03 23	04 01	04 32	10 34	11 40	12 47	13 56
45	02 59	03 43	04 18	10 26	11 34	12 44	13 56
S 50	02 27	03 20	04 00	10 15	11 26	12 40	13 56
52	02 10	03 09	03 52	10 10	11 23	12 38	13 56
54	01 49	02 56	03 43	10 04	11 19	12 36	13 55
56	01 21	02 41	03 32	09 58	11 14	12 34	13 55
58	00 34	02 23	03 20	09 51	11 10	12 31	13 55
S 60	////	02 01	03 06	09 43	11 04	12 29	13 55

Lat.	Sunset	Twilight Civil	Naut.	Moonset 18	19	20	21
°	h m	h m	h m	h m	h m	h m	h m
N 72	▪	14 38	16 17	21 03	22 58	24 52	00 52
N 70	13 14	15 04	16 29	21 24	23 10	24 57	00 57
68	13 59	15 24	16 39	21 40	23 19	25 00	01 00
66	14 29	15 40	16 47	21 53	23 27	25 03	01 03
64	14 51	15 53	16 54	22 04	23 33	25 05	01 05
62	15 09	16 04	17 00	22 13	23 39	25 07	01 07
60	15 23	16 13	17 06	22 21	23 44	25 09	01 09
N 58	15 35	16 22	17 11	22 28	23 48	25 11	01 11
56	15 46	16 29	17 15	22 34	23 52	25 12	01 12
54	15 56	16 36	17 20	22 39	23 55	25 13	01 13
52	16 04	16 42	17 24	22 44	23 58	25 15	01 15
50	16 12	16 48	17 27	22 48	24 01	00 01	01 16
45	16 28	17 00	17 36	22 58	24 07	00 07	01 18
N 40	16 41	17 10	17 43	23 05	24 12	00 12	01 20
35	16 52	17 20	17 50	23 12	24 16	00 16	01 21
30	17 02	17 28	17 57	23 18	24 20	00 20	01 23
20	17 20	17 43	18 10	23 28	24 26	00 26	01 25
N 10	17 35	17 57	18 23	23 37	24 32	00 32	01 27
0	17 49	18 11	18 36	23 45	24 37	00 37	01 29
S 10	18 03	18 26	18 52	23 53	24 42	00 42	01 31
20	18 19	18 43	19 11	24 02	00 02	00 48	01 33
30	18 37	19 03	19 35	24 12	00 12	00 54	01 35
35	18 47	19 16	19 50	24 17	00 17	00 57	01 37
40	18 59	19 30	20 09	24 24	00 24	01 01	01 38
45	19 14	19 48	20 33	24 31	00 31	01 06	01 40
S 50	19 31	20 11	21 05	00 05	00 40	01 12	01 42
52	19 40	20 23	21 23	00 10	00 44	01 14	01 43
54	19 49	20 36	21 44	00 16	00 48	01 17	01 44
56	20 00	20 52	22 14	00 23	00 53	01 20	01 45
58	20 12	21 09	23 05	00 30	00 59	01 23	01 46
S 60	20 26	21 32	////	00 39	01 05	01 27	01 47

Day	SUN Eqn. of Time 00h	12h	Mer. Pass.	MOON Mer. Pass. Upper	Lower	Age	Phase
d	m s	m s	h m	h m	h m	d	%
18	14 59	14 53	11 45	17 33	05 06	07	42
19	14 47	14 40	11 45	18 25	05 59	08	53
20	14 34	14 27	11 46	19 17	06 51	09	64

UT	ARIES GHA	VENUS −4.3 GHA	Dec	MARS +1.6 GHA	Dec	JUPITER −1.9 GHA	Dec	SATURN +0.5 GHA	Dec	STARS Name	SHA	Dec
d h	° ′	° ′	° ′	° ′	° ′	° ′	° ′	° ′	° ′		° ′	° ′
21 00	59 40.7	226 23.4	S 3 42.4	234 39.5	S 0 36.4	248 38.7	N 5 01.4	174 51.5	S19 44.9	Acamar	315 16.7	S40 14.6
01	74 43.2	241 23.2	43.4	249 40.6	37.0	263 40.9	01.3	189 53.6	45.0	Achernar	335 25.2	S57 09.6
02	89 45.7	256 23.0	44.4	264 41.7	37.5	278 43.0	01.2	204 55.8	45.0	Acrux	173 07.7	S63 10.9
03	104 48.1	271 22.9 ..	45.4	279 42.7 ..	38.1	293 45.2 ..	01.0	219 57.9 ..	45.1	Adhara	255 11.0	S28 59.7
04	119 50.6	286 22.7	46.4	294 43.8	38.7	308 47.3	00.9	235 00.1	45.1	Aldebaran	290 47.2	N16 32.3
05	134 53.1	301 22.5	47.4	309 44.9	39.3	323 49.5	00.8	250 02.2	45.2			
06	149 55.5	316 22.3	S 3 48.4	324 46.0	S 0 39.9	338 51.6	N 5 00.7	265 04.4	S19 45.2	Alioth	166 19.8	N55 52.3
S 07	164 58.0	331 22.1	49.4	339 47.1	40.5	353 53.8	00.5	280 06.6	45.3	Alkaid	152 58.1	N49 14.0
A 08	180 00.5	346 21.9	50.4	354 48.2	41.0	8 55.9	00.4	295 08.7	45.3	Al Na'ir	27 41.8	S46 53.1
T 09	195 02.9	1 21.7 ..	51.4	9 49.3 ..	41.6	23 58.1 ..	00.3	310 10.9 ..	45.4	Alnilam	275 44.4	S 1 11.7
U 10	210 05.4	16 21.5	52.4	24 50.4	42.2	39 00.3	00.2	325 13.0	45.4	Alphard	217 54.4	S 8 43.7
R 11	225 07.8	31 21.3	53.4	39 51.5	42.8	54 02.4	5 00.1	340 15.2	45.5			
D 12	240 10.3	46 21.1	S 3 54.4	54 52.6	S 0 43.4	69 04.6	N 4 59.9	355 17.3	S19 45.6	Alphecca	126 10.0	N26 39.9
A 13	255 12.8	61 21.0	55.4	69 53.7	44.0	84 06.7	59.8	10 19.5	45.6	Alpheratz	357 41.6	N29 10.9
Y 14	270 15.2	76 20.8	56.3	84 54.8	44.6	99 08.9	59.7	25 21.6	45.7	Altair	62 06.8	N 8 54.9
15	285 17.7	91 20.6 ..	57.3	99 55.9 ..	45.1	114 11.0 ..	59.6	40 23.8 ..	45.7	Ankaa	353 13.9	S42 13.4
16	300 20.2	106 20.4	58.3	114 57.0	45.7	129 13.2	59.4	55 26.0	45.8	Antares	112 24.6	S26 27.8
17	315 22.6	121 20.2	3 59.3	129 58.1	46.3	144 15.3	59.3	70 28.1	45.8			
18	330 25.1	136 20.0	S 4 00.3	144 59.2	S 0 46.9	159 17.5	N 4 59.2	85 30.3	S19 45.9	Arcturus	145 54.6	N19 06.1
19	345 27.6	151 19.8	01.3	160 00.3	47.5	174 19.6	59.1	100 32.4	45.9	Atria	107 25.5	S69 03.2
20	0 30.0	166 19.6	02.3	175 01.4	48.1	189 21.8	59.0	115 34.6	46.0	Avior	234 17.0	S59 33.5
21	15 32.5	181 19.4 ..	03.3	190 02.5 ..	48.6	204 24.0 ..	58.8	130 36.7 ..	46.0	Bellatrix	278 29.9	N 6 21.7
22	30 34.9	196 19.2	04.3	205 03.5	49.2	219 26.1	58.7	145 38.9	46.1	Betelgeuse	270 59.2	N 7 24.4
23	45 37.4	211 19.0	05.3	220 04.6	49.8	234 28.3	58.6	160 41.0	46.1			
22 00	60 39.9	226 18.8	S 4 06.3	235 05.7	S 0 50.4	249 30.4	N 4 58.5	175 43.2	S19 46.2	Canopus	263 55.0	S52 42.3
01	75 42.3	241 18.6	07.3	250 06.8	51.0	264 32.6	58.4	190 45.4	46.2	Capella	280 31.6	N46 00.6
02	90 44.8	256 18.4	08.3	265 07.9	51.6	279 34.7	58.2	205 47.5	46.3	Deneb	49 30.5	N45 20.6
03	105 47.3	271 18.2 ..	09.3	280 09.0 ..	52.1	294 36.9 ..	58.1	220 49.7 ..	46.3	Denebola	182 32.2	N14 29.0
04	120 49.7	286 18.0	10.3	295 10.1	52.7	309 39.1	58.0	235 51.8	46.4	Diphda	348 54.1	S17 54.0
05	135 52.2	301 17.8	11.3	310 11.2	53.3	324 41.2	57.9	250 54.0	46.4			
06	150 54.7	316 17.6	S 4 12.3	325 12.3	S 0 53.9	339 43.4	N 4 57.8	265 56.1	S19 46.5	Dubhe	193 50.1	N61 39.6
07	165 57.1	331 17.4	13.3	340 13.4	54.5	354 45.5	57.6	280 58.3	46.6	Elnath	278 10.2	N28 37.0
08	180 59.6	346 17.2	14.3	355 14.5	55.1	9 47.7	57.5	296 00.4	46.6	Eltanin	90 45.9	N51 29.6
S 09	196 02.1	1 17.0 ..	15.3	10 15.6 ..	55.6	24 49.8 ..	57.4	311 02.6 ..	46.7	Enif	33 45.5	N 9 57.1
U 10	211 04.5	16 16.8	16.3	25 16.7	56.2	39 52.0	57.3	326 04.8	46.7	Fomalhaut	15 22.2	S29 32.3
N 11	226 07.0	31 16.7	17.3	40 17.8	56.8	54 54.2	57.2	341 06.9	46.8			
D 12	241 09.4	46 16.5	S 4 18.3	55 18.9	S 0 57.4	69 56.3	N 4 57.0	356 09.1	S19 46.8	Gacrux	171 59.3	S57 11.8
A 13	256 11.9	61 16.2	19.3	70 20.0	58.0	84 58.5	56.9	11 11.2	46.9	Gienah	175 50.8	S17 37.6
Y 14	271 14.4	76 16.0	20.3	85 21.1	58.6	100 00.6	56.8	26 13.4	46.9	Hadar	148 46.0	S60 26.7
15	286 16.8	91 15.8 ..	21.3	100 22.2 ..	59.1	115 02.8 ..	56.7	41 15.5 ..	47.0	Hamal	327 58.6	N23 32.2
16	301 19.3	106 15.6	22.3	115 23.3	0 59.7	130 05.0	56.6	56 17.7	47.0	Kaus Aust.	83 42.0	S34 22.4
17	316 21.8	121 15.4	23.3	130 24.4	1 00.3	145 07.1	56.4	71 19.8	47.1			
18	331 24.2	136 15.2	S 4 24.3	145 25.5	S 1 00.9	160 09.3	N 4 56.3	86 22.0	S19 47.1	Kochab	137 21.5	N74 05.5
19	346 26.7	151 15.0	25.3	160 26.6	01.5	175 11.4	56.2	101 24.2	47.2	Markab	13 36.6	N15 17.6
20	1 29.2	166 14.8	26.3	175 27.7	02.1	190 13.6	56.1	116 26.3	47.2	Menkar	314 13.0	N 4 09.0
21	16 31.6	181 14.6 ..	27.3	190 28.8 ..	02.6	205 15.8 ..	56.0	131 28.5 ..	47.3	Menkent	148 06.0	S36 26.6
22	31 34.1	196 14.4	28.3	205 29.9	03.2	220 17.9	55.8	146 30.6	47.3	Miaplacidus	221 38.9	S69 46.7
23	46 36.5	211 14.2	29.3	220 31.0	03.8	235 20.1	55.7	161 32.8	47.4			
23 00	61 39.0	226 14.0	S 4 30.3	235 32.0	S 1 04.4	250 22.2	N 4 55.6	176 34.9	S19 47.4	Mirfak	308 37.4	N49 54.9
01	76 41.5	241 13.8	31.3	250 33.1	05.0	265 24.4	55.5	191 37.1	47.5	Nunki	75 56.6	S26 16.4
02	91 43.9	256 13.6	32.3	265 34.2	05.6	280 26.6	55.4	206 39.2	47.5	Peacock	53 17.0	S56 41.1
03	106 46.4	271 13.4 ..	33.3	280 35.3 ..	06.1	295 28.7 ..	55.2	221 41.4 ..	47.6	Pollux	243 25.6	N27 59.0
04	121 48.9	286 13.2	34.3	295 36.4	06.7	310 30.9	55.1	236 43.6	47.6	Procyon	244 57.8	N 5 10.9
05	136 51.3	301 13.0	35.3	310 37.5	07.3	325 33.1	55.0	251 45.7	47.7			
06	151 53.8	316 12.8	S 4 36.3	325 38.6	S 1 07.9	340 35.2	N 4 54.9	266 47.9	S19 47.8	Rasalhague	96 05.3	N12 33.2
07	166 56.3	331 12.6	37.3	340 39.7	08.5	355 37.4	54.8	281 50.0	47.8	Regulus	207 41.8	N11 53.3
08	181 58.7	346 12.4	38.3	355 40.8	09.1	10 39.5	54.7	296 52.2	47.9	Rigel	281 10.2	S 8 11.1
M 09	197 01.2	1 12.2 ..	39.3	10 41.9 ..	09.6	25 41.7 ..	54.5	311 54.3 ..	47.9	Rigil Kent.	139 50.0	S60 53.7
O 10	212 03.7	16 12.0	40.3	25 43.0	10.2	40 43.9	54.4	326 56.5	48.0	Sabik	102 11.0	S15 44.4
N 11	227 06.1	31 11.7	41.3	40 44.1	10.8	55 46.0	54.3	341 58.6	48.0			
D 12	242 08.6	46 11.5	S 4 42.3	55 45.2	S 1 11.4	70 48.2	N 4 54.2	357 00.8	S19 48.1	Schedar	349 38.1	N56 37.7
A 13	257 11.0	61 11.3	43.3	70 46.3	12.0	85 50.4	54.1	12 03.0	48.1	Shaula	96 20.1	S37 06.7
Y 14	272 13.5	76 11.1	44.3	85 47.4	12.5	100 52.5	54.0	27 05.1	48.2	Sirius	258 32.0	S16 44.4
15	287 16.0	91 10.9 ..	45.3	100 48.5 ..	13.1	115 54.7 ..	53.8	42 07.3 ..	48.2	Spica	158 29.8	S11 14.4
16	302 18.4	106 10.7	46.3	115 49.6	13.7	130 56.9	53.7	57 09.4	48.3	Suhail	222 51.1	S43 29.7
17	317 20.9	121 10.5	47.3	130 50.7	14.3	145 59.0	53.6	72 11.6	48.3			
18	332 23.4	136 10.3	S 4 48.3	145 51.8	S 1 14.9	161 01.2	N 4 53.5	87 13.7	S19 48.4	Vega	80 38.2	N38 48.3
19	347 25.8	151 10.1	49.3	160 52.9	15.5	176 03.4	53.4	102 15.9	48.4	Zuben'ubi	137 03.9	S16 06.2
20	2 28.3	166 09.8	50.3	175 54.0	16.0	191 05.5	53.2	117 18.0	48.5		SHA	Mer.Pass.
21	17 30.8	181 09.6 ..	51.3	190 55.1 ..	16.6	206 07.7 ..	53.1	132 20.2 ..	48.5		° ′	h m
22	32 33.2	196 09.4	52.3	205 56.2	17.2	221 09.9	53.0	147 22.3	48.6	Venus	165 39.0	8 55
23	47 35.7	211 09.2	53.3	220 57.3	17.8	236 12.0	52.9	162 24.5	48.6	Mars	174 25.9	8 19
	h m									Jupiter	188 50.5	7 21
Mer.Pass. 19 54.1		v −0.2	d 1.0	v 1.1	d 0.6	v 2.2	d 0.1	v 2.2	d 0.1	Saturn	115 03.3	12 15

UT	SUN GHA	Dec	MOON GHA	v	Dec	d	HP
d h	° ′	° ′	° ′	′	° ′	′	′
21 00	183 34.8	S19 47.2	68 19.5	9.4	S 2 55.3	11.1	59.6
01	198 34.7	47.8	82 47.9	9.3	2 44.2	11.1	59.6
02	213 34.5	48.3	97 16.2	9.4	2 33.0	11.2	59.7
03	228 34.4	48.9	111 44.6	9.3	2 21.8	11.2	59.7
04	243 34.2	49.4	126 12.9	9.3	2 10.6	11.2	59.7
05	258 34.1	50.0	140 41.2	9.3	1 59.4	11.3	59.7
06	273 33.9	S19 50.6	155 09.5	9.2	S 1 48.1	11.2	59.7
07	288 33.8	51.1	169 37.7	9.3	1 36.9	11.3	59.8
S 08	303 33.6	51.7	184 06.0	9.2	1 25.6	11.3	59.8
A 09	318 33.5	52.2	198 34.2	9.2	1 14.3	11.4	59.8
T 10	333 33.3	52.8	213 02.4	9.2	1 02.9	11.3	59.8
U 11	348 33.1	53.3	227 30.6	9.2	0 51.6	11.4	59.8
R 12	3 33.0	S19 53.9	241 58.8	9.1	S 0 40.2	11.3	59.9
D 13	18 32.8	54.4	256 26.9	9.1	0 28.9	11.4	59.9
A 14	33 32.7	55.0	270 55.0	9.1	0 17.5	11.4	59.9
Y 15	48 32.5	55.6	285 23.1	9.1	S 0 06.1	11.4	59.9
16	63 32.4	56.1	299 51.2	9.1	N 0 05.3	11.4	59.9
17	78 32.2	56.6	314 19.3	9.0	0 16.7	11.4	59.9
18	93 32.1	S19 57.2	328 47.3	9.0	N 0 28.1	11.4	60.0
19	108 31.9	57.7	343 15.3	9.0	0 39.5	11.4	60.0
20	123 31.7	58.3	357 43.3	8.9	0 50.9	11.4	60.0
21	138 31.6	58.8	12 11.2	9.0	1 02.3	11.4	60.0
22	153 31.4	59.4	26 39.2	8.9	1 13.7	11.5	60.0
23	168 31.3	19 59.9	41 07.1	8.8	1 25.2	11.4	60.0
22 00	183 31.1	S20 00.5	55 34.9	8.9	N 1 36.6	11.4	60.1
01	198 30.9	01.0	70 02.8	8.8	1 48.0	11.4	60.1
02	213 30.8	01.5	84 30.6	8.8	1 59.4	11.4	60.1
03	228 30.6	02.1	98 58.4	8.8	2 10.8	11.4	60.1
04	243 30.5	02.6	113 26.2	8.7	2 22.2	11.4	60.1
05	258 30.3	03.2	127 53.9	8.7	2 33.6	11.4	60.1
06	273 30.1	S20 03.7	142 21.6	8.7	N 2 45.0	11.4	60.2
07	288 30.0	04.3	156 49.3	8.6	2 56.4	11.3	60.2
S 08	303 29.8	04.8	171 16.9	8.7	3 07.7	11.4	60.2
U 09	318 29.7	05.3	185 44.6	8.5	3 19.1	11.3	60.2
N 10	333 29.5	05.9	200 12.1	8.6	3 30.4	11.3	60.2
11	348 29.3	06.4	214 39.7	8.5	3 41.7	11.3	60.2
D 12	3 29.2	S20 06.9	229 07.2	8.5	N 3 53.0	11.3	60.2
A 13	18 29.0	07.5	243 34.7	8.5	4 04.3	11.3	60.2
Y 14	33 28.8	08.0	258 02.2	8.4	4 15.6	11.2	60.3
15	48 28.7	08.6	272 29.6	8.4	4 26.8	11.2	60.3
16	63 28.5	09.1	286 57.0	8.3	4 38.0	11.2	60.3
17	78 28.4	09.6	301 24.3	8.4	4 49.2	11.2	60.3
18	93 28.2	S20 10.2	315 51.7	8.2	N 5 00.4	11.1	60.3
19	108 28.0	10.7	330 18.9	8.3	5 11.5	11.1	60.3
20	123 27.9	11.2	344 46.2	8.2	5 22.6	11.1	60.3
21	138 27.7	11.8	359 13.4	8.2	5 33.7	11.1	60.3
22	153 27.5	12.3	13 40.6	8.1	5 44.8	11.0	60.3
23	168 27.4	12.8	28 07.7	8.1	5 55.8	11.0	60.3
23 00	183 27.2	S20 13.3	42 34.8	8.1	N 6 06.8	11.0	60.4
01	198 27.0	13.9	57 01.9	8.1	6 17.8	10.9	60.4
02	213 26.9	14.4	71 29.0	7.9	6 28.7	10.9	60.4
03	228 26.7	14.9	85 56.0	7.9	6 39.6	10.8	60.4
04	243 26.5	15.5	100 22.9	8.0	6 50.4	10.8	60.4
05	258 26.4	16.0	114 49.9	7.8	7 01.2	10.8	60.4
06	273 26.2	S20 16.5	129 16.7	7.9	N 7 12.0	10.7	60.4
07	288 26.0	17.0	143 43.6	7.8	7 22.7	10.7	60.4
M 08	303 25.8	17.6	158 10.4	7.8	7 33.4	10.6	60.4
O 09	318 25.7	18.1	172 37.2	7.7	7 44.0	10.6	60.4
N 10	333 25.5	18.6	187 03.9	7.7	7 54.6	10.5	60.4
D 11	348 25.3	19.1	201 30.6	7.7	8 05.1	10.5	60.4
A 12	3 25.2	S20 19.7	215 57.3	7.6	N 8 15.6	10.5	60.4
Y 13	18 25.0	20.2	230 23.9	7.6	8 26.1	10.3	60.4
14	33 24.8	20.7	244 50.5	7.6	8 36.4	10.4	60.4
15	48 24.6	21.2	259 17.1	7.5	8 46.8	10.3	60.4
16	63 24.5	21.7	273 43.6	7.5	8 57.1	10.2	60.4
17	78 24.3	22.3	288 10.1	7.4	9 07.3	10.1	60.4
18	93 24.1	S20 22.8	302 36.5	7.4	N 9 17.4	10.1	60.4
19	108 24.0	23.3	317 02.9	7.4	9 27.5	10.1	60.4
20	123 23.8	23.8	331 29.3	7.3	9 37.6	10.0	60.4
21	138 23.6	24.3	345 55.6	7.3	9 47.6	9.9	60.4
22	153 23.4	24.8	0 21.9	7.2	9 57.5	9.8	60.4
23	168 23.3	25.3	14 48.1	7.2	N10 07.3	9.8	60.4
SD	16.2	d 0.5	SD 16.3		16.4		16.5

Twilight / Sunrise / Moonrise

Lat.	Twilight Naut.	Twilight Civil	Sunrise	Moonrise 21	Moonrise 22	Moonrise 23	Moonrise 24
°	h m	h m	h m	h m	h m	h m	h m
N 72	07 22	09 06	■	14 02	13 57	13 52	13 47
N 70	07 10	08 37	10 41	14 01	14 03	14 05	14 08
68	06 59	08 16	09 45	14 01	14 07	14 15	14 25
66	06 50	07 59	09 12	14 01	14 11	14 23	14 38
64	06 43	07 45	08 48	14 00	14 14	14 30	14 50
62	06 36	07 33	08 30	14 00	14 17	14 36	14 59
60	06 30	07 23	08 14	14 00	14 20	14 42	15 08
N 58	06 24	07 14	08 01	13 59	14 22	14 47	15 15
56	06 19	07 06	07 50	13 59	14 24	14 51	15 22
54	06 15	06 59	07 40	13 59	14 26	14 55	15 27
52	06 11	06 53	07 31	13 59	14 28	14 58	15 33
50	06 07	06 47	07 23	13 59	14 29	15 02	15 37
45	05 58	06 34	07 06	13 58	14 32	15 09	15 48
N 40	05 50	06 23	06 53	13 58	14 35	15 14	15 57
35	05 43	06 14	06 41	13 58	14 38	15 19	16 04
30	05 36	06 05	06 31	13 58	14 40	15 24	16 11
20	05 22	05 49	06 13	13 57	14 44	15 32	16 22
N 10	05 09	05 35	05 57	13 57	14 47	15 39	16 32
0	04 55	05 20	05 42	13 57	14 50	15 45	16 42
S 10	04 39	05 05	05 28	13 57	14 54	15 52	16 51
20	04 20	04 48	05 12	13 56	14 57	15 59	17 02
30	03 55	04 27	04 53	13 56	15 01	16 07	17 13
35	03 39	04 14	04 42	13 56	15 03	16 12	17 20
40	03 20	03 59	04 30	13 56	15 06	16 17	17 28
45	02 55	03 40	04 15	13 56	15 09	16 23	17 37
S 50	02 21	03 16	03 57	13 56	15 13	16 31	17 48
52	02 03	03 05	03 48	13 56	15 15	16 35	17 54
54	01 40	02 51	03 38	13 56	15 17	16 38	17 59
56	01 08	02 35	03 27	13 55	15 19	16 43	18 06
58	////	02 15	03 16	13 55	15 21	16 47	18 13
S 60	////	01 51	03 00	13 55	15 24	16 53	18 21

Sunset / Twilight / Moonset

Lat.	Sunset	Twilight Civil	Twilight Naut.	Moonset 21	Moonset 22	Moonset 23	Moonset 24
°	h m	h m	h m	h m	h m	h m	h m
N 72	■	14 25	16 09	00 52	02 48	04 46	06 49
N 70	12 50	14 54	16 21	00 57	02 45	04 36	06 29
68	13 46	15 16	16 32	01 00	02 43	04 28	06 13
66	14 19	15 33	16 41	01 03	02 41	04 21	06 01
64	14 43	15 47	16 49	01 05	02 39	04 15	05 51
62	15 02	15 58	16 56	01 07	02 38	04 10	05 42
60	15 17	16 09	17 02	01 09	02 37	04 05	05 34
N 58	15 30	16 17	17 07	01 11	02 35	04 02	05 28
56	15 42	16 25	17 12	01 12	02 35	03 58	05 22
54	15 52	16 32	17 17	01 13	02 34	03 55	05 17
52	16 01	16 39	17 21	01 15	02 33	03 52	05 12
50	16 08	16 45	17 25	01 16	02 32	03 50	05 08
45	16 25	16 58	17 34	01 18	02 30	03 44	04 59
N 40	16 39	17 09	17 42	01 20	02 29	03 40	04 51
35	16 51	17 18	17 49	01 21	02 28	03 36	04 44
30	17 01	17 27	17 56	01 23	02 27	03 32	04 39
20	17 19	17 43	18 10	01 25	02 25	03 26	04 29
N 10	17 35	17 57	18 23	01 27	02 24	03 21	04 20
0	17 50	18 12	18 37	01 29	02 22	03 16	04 12
S 10	18 05	18 27	18 53	01 31	02 21	03 11	04 04
20	18 21	18 45	19 13	01 33	02 19	03 06	03 55
30	18 39	19 06	19 38	01 35	02 17	03 00	03 45
35	18 50	19 19	19 54	01 37	02 16	02 57	03 40
40	19 03	19 34	20 13	01 38	02 15	02 53	03 33
45	19 18	19 53	20 38	01 40	02 13	02 48	03 26
S 50	19 36	20 17	21 12	01 42	02 12	02 43	03 17
52	19 45	20 29	21 31	01 43	02 11	02 40	03 13
54	19 55	20 42	21 54	01 44	02 10	02 38	03 08
56	20 06	20 59	22 28	01 45	02 09	02 35	03 03
58	20 19	21 18	////	01 46	02 08	02 31	02 58
S 60	20 34	21 43	////	01 47	02 07	02 28	02 51

SUN / MOON

Day	Eqn. of Time 00h	Eqn. of Time 12h	Mer. Pass.	Mer. Pass. Upper	Mer. Pass. Lower	Age	Phase
d	m s	m s	h m	h m	h m	d	%
21	14 20	14 12	11 46	20 09	07 43	10	75
22	14 05	13 57	11 46	21 03	08 36	11	84
23	13 49	13 41	11 46	21 58	09 31	12	92

2015 NOVEMBER 24, 25, 26 (TUES., WED., THURS.)

UT	ARIES GHA	VENUS −4.3 GHA	Dec	MARS +1.6 GHA	Dec	JUPITER −1.9 GHA	Dec	SATURN +0.5 GHA	Dec	STARS Name	SHA	Dec
d h	° ′	° ′	° ′	° ′	° ′	° ′	° ′	° ′	° ′		° ′	° ′
24 00	62 38.2	226 09.0	S 4 54.3	235 58.4	S 1 18.4	251 14.2	N 4 52.8	177 26.7	S19 48.7	Acamar	315 16.7	S40 14.6
01	77 40.6	241 08.8	55.3	250 59.5	18.9	266 16.4	52.7	192 28.8	48.7	Achernar	335 25.2	S57 09.6
02	92 43.1	256 08.6	56.3	266 00.6	19.5	281 18.5	52.5	207 31.0	48.8	Acrux	173 07.7	S63 10.9
03	107 45.5	271 08.4	.. 57.3	281 01.7	.. 20.1	296 20.7	.. 52.4	222 33.1	.. 48.8	Adhara	255 10.9	S28 59.7
04	122 48.0	286 08.1	58.3	296 02.8	20.7	311 22.9	52.3	237 35.3	48.9	Aldebaran	290 47.1	N16 32.3
05	137 50.5	301 07.9	4 59.3	311 03.9	21.3	326 25.0	52.2	252 37.4	48.9			
T 06	152 52.9	316 07.7	S 5 00.3	326 05.0	S 1 21.8	341 27.2	N 4 52.1	267 39.6	S19 49.0	Alioth	166 19.8	N55 52.3
U 07	167 55.4	331 07.5	01.3	341 06.1	22.4	356 29.4	52.0	282 41.7	49.0	Alkaid	152 58.1	N49 14.0
E 08	182 57.9	346 07.3	02.3	356 07.2	23.0	11 31.5	51.9	297 43.9	49.1	Al Na'ir	27 41.8	S46 53.1
S 09	198 00.3	1 07.1	.. 03.3	11 08.3	.. 23.6	26 33.7	.. 51.7	312 46.1	.. 49.2	Alnilam	275 44.4	S 1 11.7
D 10	213 02.8	16 06.8	04.3	26 09.4	24.2	41 35.9	51.6	327 48.2	49.2	Alphard	217 54.4	S 8 43.7
A 11	228 05.3	31 06.6	05.3	41 10.5	24.8	56 38.0	51.5	342 50.4	49.3			
Y 12	243 07.7	46 06.4	S 5 06.3	56 11.6	S 1 25.3	71 40.2	N 4 51.4	357 52.5	S19 49.3	Alphecca	126 10.0	N26 39.9
13	258 10.2	61 06.2	07.3	71 12.7	25.9	86 42.4	51.3	12 54.7	49.4	Alpheratz	357 41.6	N29 10.9
14	273 12.6	76 06.0	08.3	86 13.8	26.5	101 44.5	51.2	27 56.8	49.4	Altair	62 06.8	N 8 54.9
15	288 15.1	91 05.7	.. 09.3	101 14.9	.. 27.1	116 46.7	.. 51.0	42 59.0	.. 49.5	Ankaa	353 13.9	S42 13.4
16	303 17.6	106 05.5	10.3	116 16.0	27.7	131 48.9	50.9	58 01.1	49.5	Antares	112 24.6	S26 27.8
17	318 20.0	121 05.3	11.3	131 17.1	28.2	146 51.0	50.8	73 03.3	49.6			
18	333 22.5	136 05.1	S 5 12.3	146 18.2	S 1 28.8	161 53.2	N 4 50.7	88 05.4	S19 49.6	Arcturus	145 54.6	N19 06.1
19	348 25.0	151 04.9	13.3	161 19.3	29.4	176 55.4	50.6	103 07.6	49.7	Atria	107 25.5	S69 03.1
20	3 27.4	166 04.6	14.3	176 20.4	30.0	191 57.6	50.5	118 09.8	49.7	Avior	234 16.9	S59 33.5
21	18 29.9	181 04.4	.. 15.3	191 21.5	.. 30.6	206 59.7	.. 50.4	133 11.9	.. 49.8	Bellatrix	278 29.9	N 6 21.7
22	33 32.4	196 04.2	16.3	206 22.6	31.1	222 01.9	50.2	148 14.1	49.8	Betelgeuse	270 59.2	N 7 24.4
23	48 34.8	211 04.0	17.3	221 23.7	31.7	237 04.1	50.1	163 16.2	49.9			
25 00	63 37.3	226 03.7	S 5 18.4	236 24.8	S 1 32.3	252 06.2	N 4 50.0	178 18.4	S19 49.9	Canopus	263 54.9	S52 42.3
01	78 39.8	241 03.5	19.4	251 25.9	32.9	267 08.4	49.9	193 20.5	50.0	Capella	280 31.5	N46 00.6
02	93 42.2	256 03.3	20.4	266 27.0	33.5	282 10.6	49.8	208 22.7	50.0	Deneb	49 30.5	N45 20.6
03	108 44.7	271 03.1	.. 21.4	281 28.1	.. 34.0	297 12.8	.. 49.7	223 24.8	.. 50.1	Denebola	182 32.2	N14 29.0
04	123 47.1	286 02.8	22.4	296 29.2	34.6	312 14.9	49.6	238 27.0	50.1	Diphda	348 54.1	S17 54.0
05	138 49.6	301 02.6	23.4	311 30.3	35.2	327 17.1	49.4	253 29.1	50.2			
W 06	153 52.1	316 02.4	S 5 24.4	326 31.4	S 1 35.8	342 19.3	N 4 49.3	268 31.3	S19 50.2	Dubhe	193 50.0	N61 39.6
E 07	168 54.5	331 02.2	25.4	341 32.4	36.4	357 21.5	49.2	283 33.5	50.3	Elnath	278 10.2	N28 37.0
D 08	183 57.0	346 01.9	26.4	356 33.5	36.9	12 23.6	49.1	298 35.6	50.3	Eltanin	90 45.9	N51 29.6
N 09	198 59.5	1 01.7	.. 27.4	11 34.6	.. 37.5	27 25.8	.. 49.0	313 37.8	.. 50.4	Enif	33 45.6	N 9 57.1
E 10	214 01.9	16 01.5	28.4	26 35.7	38.1	42 28.0	48.9	328 39.9	50.4	Fomalhaut	15 22.2	S29 32.3
S 11	229 04.4	31 01.3	29.4	41 36.8	38.7	57 30.1	48.8	343 42.1	50.5			
D 12	244 06.9	46 01.0	S 5 30.4	56 37.9	S 1 39.3	72 32.3	N 4 48.6	358 44.2	S19 50.5	Gacrux	171 59.3	S57 11.8
A 13	259 09.3	61 00.8	31.4	71 39.0	39.8	87 34.5	48.5	13 46.4	50.6	Gienah	175 50.8	S17 37.6
Y 14	274 11.8	76 00.6	32.4	86 40.1	40.4	102 36.7	48.4	28 48.5	50.6	Hadar	148 46.0	S60 26.6
15	289 14.3	91 00.3	.. 33.4	101 41.2	.. 41.0	117 38.8	.. 48.3	43 50.7	.. 50.7	Hamal	327 58.6	N23 32.2
16	304 16.7	106 00.1	34.4	116 42.3	41.6	132 41.0	48.2	58 52.8	50.8	Kaus Aust.	83 42.0	S34 22.4
17	319 19.2	120 59.9	35.4	131 43.4	42.2	147 43.2	48.1	73 55.0	50.8			
18	334 21.6	135 59.7	S 5 36.4	146 44.5	S 1 42.7	162 45.4	N 4 48.0	88 57.1	S19 50.9	Kochab	137 21.4	N74 05.4
19	349 24.1	150 59.4	37.4	161 45.6	43.3	177 47.5	47.9	103 59.3	50.9	Markab	13 36.6	N15 17.6
20	4 26.6	165 59.2	38.4	176 46.7	43.9	192 49.7	47.7	119 01.5	51.0	Menkar	314 13.0	N 4 09.0
21	19 29.0	180 59.0	.. 39.4	191 47.9	.. 44.5	207 51.9	.. 47.6	134 03.6	.. 51.0	Menkent	148 05.9	S36 26.6
22	34 31.5	195 58.7	40.4	206 49.0	45.0	222 54.1	47.5	149 05.8	51.1	Miaplacidus	221 38.9	S69 46.7
23	49 34.0	210 58.5	41.4	221 50.1	45.6	237 56.3	47.4	164 07.9	51.1			
26 00	64 36.4	225 58.3	S 5 42.4	236 51.2	S 1 46.2	252 58.4	N 4 47.3	179 10.1	S19 51.2	Mirfak	308 37.4	N49 55.0
01	79 38.9	240 58.0	43.5	251 52.3	46.8	268 00.6	47.2	194 12.2	51.2	Nunki	75 56.6	S26 16.4
02	94 41.4	255 57.8	44.5	266 53.4	47.4	283 02.8	47.1	209 14.4	51.3	Peacock	53 17.1	S56 41.1
03	109 43.8	270 57.6	.. 45.5	281 54.5	.. 47.9	298 05.0	.. 47.0	224 16.5	.. 51.3	Pollux	243 25.5	N27 59.0
04	124 46.3	285 57.3	46.5	296 55.6	48.5	313 07.1	46.8	239 18.7	51.4	Procyon	244 57.8	N 5 10.9
05	139 48.8	300 57.1	47.5	311 56.7	49.1	328 09.3	46.7	254 20.8	51.4			
T 06	154 51.2	315 56.9	S 5 48.5	326 57.8	S 1 49.7	343 11.5	N 4 46.6	269 23.0	S19 51.5	Rasalhague	96 05.3	N12 33.2
H 07	169 53.7	330 56.6	49.5	341 58.9	50.3	358 13.7	46.5	284 25.2	51.5	Regulus	207 41.8	N11 53.3
U 08	184 56.1	345 56.4	50.5	357 00.0	50.8	13 15.9	46.4	299 27.3	51.6	Rigel	281 10.2	S 8 11.1
R 09	199 58.6	0 56.2	.. 51.5	12 01.1	.. 51.4	28 18.0	.. 46.3	314 29.5	.. 51.6	Rigil Kent.	139 50.0	S60 53.7
S 10	215 01.1	15 55.9	52.5	27 02.2	52.0	43 20.2	46.2	329 31.6	51.7	Sabik	102 11.0	S15 44.4
D 11	230 03.5	30 55.7	53.5	42 03.3	52.6	58 22.4	46.1	344 33.8	51.7			
A 12	245 06.0	45 55.4	S 5 54.5	57 04.4	S 1 53.1	73 24.6	N 4 46.0	359 35.9	S19 51.8	Schedar	349 38.2	N56 37.7
Y 13	260 08.5	60 55.2	55.5	72 05.5	53.7	88 26.8	45.8	14 38.1	51.8	Shaula	96 20.1	S37 06.7
14	275 10.9	75 55.0	56.5	87 06.6	54.3	103 28.9	45.7	29 40.2	51.9	Sirius	258 32.0	S16 44.4
15	290 13.4	90 54.7	.. 57.5	102 07.7	.. 54.9	118 31.1	.. 45.6	44 42.4	.. 51.9	Spica	158 29.8	S11 14.5
16	305 15.9	105 54.5	58.5	117 08.8	55.5	133 33.3	45.5	59 44.5	52.0	Suhail	222 51.0	S43 29.7
17	320 18.3	120 54.3	5 59.5	132 09.9	56.0	148 35.5	45.4	74 46.7	52.0			
18	335 20.8	135 54.0	S 6 00.5	147 11.0	S 1 56.6	163 37.7	N 4 45.3	89 48.8	S19 52.1	Vega	80 38.2	N38 48.3
19	350 23.2	150 53.8	01.5	162 12.1	57.2	178 39.8	45.2	104 51.0	52.1	Zuben'ubi	137 03.9	S16 06.2
20	5 25.7	165 53.5	02.5	177 13.2	57.8	193 42.0	45.1	119 53.2	52.2		SHA	Mer. Pass.
21	20 28.2	180 53.3	.. 03.5	192 14.3	.. 58.3	208 44.2	.. 45.0	134 55.3	.. 52.2		° ′	h m
22	35 30.6	195 53.0	04.6	207 15.4	58.9	223 46.4	44.8	149 57.5	52.3	Venus	162 26.5	8 56
23	50 33.1	210 52.8	05.6	222 16.5	59.5	238 48.6	44.7	164 59.6	52.3	Mars	172 47.5	8 14
Mer. Pass.	h m 19 42.3	v −0.2	d 1.0	v 1.1	d 0.6	v 2.2	d 0.1	v 2.2	d 0.1	Jupiter	188 29.0	7 11
										Saturn	114 41.1	12 05

UT	SUN GHA	SUN Dec	MOON GHA	v	Dec	d	HP
d h	° ′	° ′	° ′	′	° ′	′	′
24 00	183 23.1	S20 25.9	29 14.3	7.2	N10 17.1	9.7	60.4
01	198 22.9	26.4	43 40.5	7.1	10 26.8	9.7	60.4
02	213 22.7	26.9	58 06.6	7.1	10 36.5	9.6	60.4
03	228 22.6 ..	27.4	72 32.7	7.1	10 46.1	9.5	60.4
04	243 22.4	27.9	86 58.8	7.0	10 55.6	9.4	60.4
05	258 22.2	28.4	101 24.8	7.0	11 05.0	9.4	60.4
06	273 22.0	S20 28.9	115 50.8	7.0	N11 14.4	9.3	60.4
T 07	288 21.8	29.4	130 16.8	6.9	11 23.7	9.2	60.4
U 08	303 21.7	30.0	144 42.7	6.8	11 32.9	9.2	60.4
E 09	318 21.5 ..	30.5	159 08.5	6.9	11 42.1	9.0	60.4
S 10	333 21.3	31.0	173 34.4	6.8	11 51.1	9.0	60.4
D 11	348 21.1	31.5	188 00.2	6.8	12 00.1	8.9	60.4
A 12	3 21.0	S20 32.0	202 26.0	6.7	N12 09.0	8.8	60.4
Y 13	18 20.8	32.5	216 51.7	6.7	12 17.8	8.8	60.4
14	33 20.6	33.0	231 17.4	6.7	12 26.6	8.6	60.4
15	48 20.4 ..	33.5	245 43.1	6.7	12 35.2	8.6	60.4
16	63 20.2	34.0	260 08.8	6.6	12 43.8	8.5	60.4
17	78 20.1	34.5	274 34.4	6.5	12 52.3	8.4	60.3
18	93 19.9	S20 35.0	288 59.9	6.6	N13 00.7	8.3	60.3
19	108 19.7	35.5	303 25.5	6.5	13 09.0	8.2	60.3
20	123 19.5	36.0	317 51.0	6.5	13 17.2	8.1	60.3
21	138 19.3 ..	36.5	332 16.5	6.5	13 25.3	8.0	60.3
22	153 19.1	37.0	346 42.0	6.4	13 33.3	8.0	60.3
23	168 19.0	37.5	1 07.4	6.4	13 41.3	7.8	60.3
25 00	183 18.8	S20 38.0	15 32.8	6.4	N13 49.1	7.8	60.3
01	198 18.6	38.5	29 58.2	6.3	13 56.9	7.6	60.3
02	213 18.4	39.0	44 23.5	6.3	14 04.5	7.6	60.2
03	228 18.2 ..	39.5	58 48.8	6.3	14 12.1	7.5	60.2
04	243 18.0	40.0	73 14.1	6.3	14 19.6	7.3	60.2
05	258 17.9	40.5	87 39.4	6.2	14 26.9	7.3	60.2
06	273 17.7	S20 41.0	102 04.6	6.3	N14 34.2	7.1	60.2
W 07	288 17.5	41.5	116 29.9	6.2	14 41.3	7.1	60.2
E 08	303 17.3	42.0	130 55.1	6.1	14 48.4	6.9	60.2
D 09	318 17.1 ..	42.5	145 20.2	6.2	14 55.3	6.9	60.1
N 10	333 16.9	42.9	159 45.4	6.1	15 02.2	6.7	60.1
E 11	348 16.7	43.4	174 10.5	6.2	15 08.9	6.7	60.1
S 12	3 16.6	S20 43.9	188 35.7	6.1	N15 15.6	6.5	60.1
D 13	18 16.4	44.4	203 00.8	6.0	15 22.1	6.4	60.1
A 14	33 16.2	44.9	217 25.8	6.1	15 28.5	6.4	60.1
Y 15	48 16.0 ..	45.4	231 50.9	6.1	15 34.9	6.2	60.0
16	63 15.8	45.9	246 16.0	6.0	15 41.1	6.1	60.0
17	78 15.6	46.4	260 41.0	6.0	15 47.2	5.9	60.0
18	93 15.4	S20 46.9	275 06.0	6.0	N15 53.1	5.9	60.0
19	108 15.2	47.3	289 31.0	6.0	15 59.0	5.8	60.0
20	123 15.0	47.8	303 56.0	6.0	16 04.8	5.7	59.9
21	138 14.9 ..	48.3	318 21.0	6.0	16 10.5	5.5	59.9
22	153 14.7	48.8	332 46.0	6.0	16 16.0	5.4	59.9
23	168 14.5	49.3	347 11.0	5.9	16 21.4	5.3	59.9
26 00	183 14.3	S20 49.8	1 35.9	6.0	N16 26.7	5.2	59.9
01	198 14.1	50.2	16 00.9	5.9	16 31.9	5.1	59.8
02	213 13.9	50.7	30 25.8	6.0	16 37.0	5.0	59.8
03	228 13.7 ..	51.2	44 50.8	5.9	16 42.0	4.9	59.8
04	243 13.5	51.7	59 15.7	6.0	16 46.9	4.7	59.8
05	258 13.3	52.2	73 40.7	5.9	16 51.6	4.6	59.7
06	273 13.1	S20 52.6	88 05.6	5.9	N16 56.2	4.5	59.7
T 07	288 12.9	53.1	102 30.5	6.0	17 00.7	4.4	59.7
H 08	303 12.7	53.6	116 55.5	5.9	17 05.1	4.3	59.7
U 09	318 12.6 ..	54.1	131 20.4	6.0	17 09.4	4.1	59.6
R 10	333 12.4	54.5	145 45.4	5.9	17 13.5	4.0	59.6
S 11	348 12.2	55.0	160 10.3	6.0	17 17.5	4.0	59.6
D 12	3 12.0	S20 55.5	174 35.3	6.0	N17 21.5	3.7	59.6
A 13	18 11.8	56.0	189 00.3	5.9	17 25.2	3.7	59.5
Y 14	33 11.6	56.4	203 25.2	6.0	17 28.9	3.6	59.5
15	48 11.4 ..	56.9	217 50.2	6.0	17 32.5	3.4	59.5
16	63 11.2	57.4	232 15.2	6.0	17 35.9	3.3	59.5
17	78 11.0	57.9	246 40.2	6.1	17 39.2	3.2	59.4
18	93 10.8	S20 58.3	261 05.3	6.0	N17 42.4	3.1	59.4
19	108 10.6	58.8	275 30.3	6.1	17 45.5	2.9	59.4
20	123 10.4	59.3	289 55.4	6.1	17 48.4	2.8	59.4
21	138 10.2	20 59.7	304 20.5	6.1	17 51.2	2.8	59.3
22	153 10.0	21 00.2	318 45.5	6.1	17 54.0	2.5	59.3
23	168 09.8	S21 00.7	333 10.6	6.1	N17 56.5	2.5	59.3
	SD 16.2	d 0.5	SD 16.5		16.4		16.2

Twilight / Sunrise / Moonrise

Lat.	Naut.	Civil	Sunrise	24	25	26	27
°	h m	h m	h m	h m	h m	h m	h m
N 72	07 32	09 20	■■■	13 47	13 41	13 32	▭
N 70	07 18	08 48	11 22	14 08	14 15	14 31	15 06
68	07 07	08 25	10 01	14 25	14 40	15 06	15 48
66	06 57	08 07	09 24	14 38	15 00	15 31	16 17
64	06 49	07 52	08 58	14 50	15 15	15 50	16 38
62	06 42	07 40	08 38	14 59	15 28	16 06	16 56
60	06 35	07 29	08 21	15 08	15 40	16 20	17 10
N 58	06 29	07 20	08 07	15 15	15 49	16 31	17 23
56	06 24	07 11	07 56	15 22	15 58	16 41	17 33
54	06 19	07 04	07 45	15 27	16 05	16 50	17 43
52	06 15	06 57	07 36	15 33	16 12	16 58	17 51
50	06 11	06 51	07 28	15 37	16 18	17 05	17 59
45	06 01	06 38	07 10	15 48	16 32	17 21	18 15
N 40	05 53	06 26	06 56	15 57	16 43	17 33	18 28
35	05 45	06 16	06 44	16 04	16 52	17 44	18 40
30	05 38	06 07	06 33	16 11	17 00	17 54	18 49
20	05 24	05 51	06 15	16 22	17 15	18 10	19 07
N 10	05 10	05 36	05 58	16 32	17 28	18 24	19 21
0	04 55	05 21	05 43	16 42	17 39	18 38	19 35
S 10	04 39	05 05	05 28	16 51	17 51	18 51	19 49
20	04 19	04 47	05 11	17 02	18 04	19 06	20 04
30	03 54	04 26	04 52	17 13	18 19	19 22	20 21
35	03 37	04 12	04 41	17 20	18 28	19 32	20 31
40	03 17	03 57	04 28	17 28	18 37	19 43	20 43
45	02 52	03 37	04 13	17 37	18 49	19 56	20 56
S 50	02 16	03 13	03 54	17 48	19 03	20 12	21 13
52	01 57	03 00	03 45	17 54	19 10	20 19	21 21
54	01 32	02 46	03 35	17 59	19 17	20 28	21 29
56	00 55	02 29	03 23	18 06	19 25	20 37	21 39
58	////	02 09	03 10	18 13	19 34	20 48	21 50
S 60	////	01 42	02 54	18 21	19 45	21 00	22 02

Sunset / Twilight / Moonset

Lat.	Sunset	Civil	Naut.	24	25	26	27
°	h m	h m	h m	h m	h m	h m	h m
N 72	■■■	14 13	16 01	06 49	08 55	11 06	▭
N 70	12 11	14 45	16 15	06 29	08 21	10 08	11 34
68	13 32	15 08	16 26	06 13	07 57	09 33	10 52
66	14 09	15 26	16 36	06 01	07 39	09 08	10 23
64	14 36	15 41	16 44	05 51	07 24	08 49	10 01
62	14 56	15 54	16 51	05 42	07 11	08 34	09 44
60	15 12	16 04	16 58	05 34	07 01	08 20	09 30
N 58	15 26	16 14	17 04	05 28	06 51	08 09	09 17
56	15 38	16 22	17 09	05 22	06 43	07 59	09 07
54	15 48	16 29	17 14	05 17	06 36	07 51	08 57
52	15 57	16 36	17 18	05 12	06 30	07 43	08 49
50	16 06	16 42	17 23	05 08	06 24	07 36	08 41
45	16 23	16 56	17 32	04 59	06 12	07 21	08 25
N 40	16 38	17 07	17 41	04 51	06 01	07 09	08 12
35	16 50	17 17	17 48	04 44	05 52	06 59	08 01
30	17 01	17 26	17 56	04 39	05 45	06 49	07 51
20	17 19	17 43	18 10	04 29	05 32	06 34	07 34
N 10	17 35	17 58	18 24	04 20	05 20	06 20	07 19
0	17 51	18 13	18 38	04 12	05 09	06 07	07 05
S 10	18 06	18 29	18 55	04 04	04 58	05 54	06 52
20	18 23	18 47	19 15	03 55	04 47	05 41	06 37
30	18 42	19 09	19 41	03 45	04 33	05 25	06 20
35	18 53	19 22	19 57	03 40	04 26	05 16	06 10
40	19 06	19 38	20 17	03 33	04 17	05 06	05 59
45	19 22	19 57	20 43	03 26	04 07	04 54	05 45
S 50	19 41	20 22	21 19	03 17	03 55	04 39	05 29
52	19 50	20 35	21 39	03 13	03 49	04 32	05 22
54	20 00	20 49	22 05	03 08	03 43	04 24	05 13
56	20 12	21 06	22 43	03 03	03 36	04 16	05 04
58	20 25	21 27	////	02 58	03 28	04 06	04 53
S 60	20 41	21 55	////	02 51	03 20	03 55	04 41

SUN / MOON

Day	Eqn. of Time 00h	Eqn. of Time 12h	Mer. Pass.	Mer. Pass. Upper	Mer. Pass. Lower	Age	Phase
d	m s	m s	h m	h m	h m	d	%
24	13 33	13 24	11 47	22 55	10 27	13	97
25	13 15	13 07	11 47	23 53	11 24	14	100
26	12 58	12 48	11 47	24 52	12 23	15	99

UT	ARIES GHA	VENUS −4.2 GHA	Dec	MARS +1.6 GHA	Dec	JUPITER −2.0 GHA	Dec	SATURN +0.4 GHA	Dec	STARS Name	SHA	Dec
27 00	65 35.6	225 52.6	S 6 06.6	237 17.6	S 2 00.1	253 50.7	N 4 44.6	180 01.8	S19 52.4	Acamar	315 16.7	S40 14.7
01	80 38.0	240 52.3	07.6	252 18.7	00.7	268 52.9	44.5	195 03.9	52.4	Achernar	335 25.2	S57 09.6
02	95 40.5	255 52.1	08.6	267 19.8	01.2	283 55.1	44.4	210 06.1	52.5	Acrux	173 07.6	S63 10.9
03	110 43.0	270 51.8	.. 09.6	282 20.9	.. 01.8	298 57.3	.. 44.3	225 08.2	.. 52.5	Adhara	255 10.9	S28 59.7
04	125 45.4	285 51.6	10.6	297 22.0	02.4	313 59.5	44.2	240 10.4	52.6	Aldebaran	290 47.1	N16 32.3
05	140 47.9	300 51.3	11.6	312 23.1	03.0	329 01.7	44.1	255 12.5	52.6			
06	155 50.4	315 51.1	S 6 12.6	327 24.2	S 2 03.5	344 03.8	N 4 44.0	270 14.7	S19 52.7	Alioth	166 19.7	N55 52.3
07	170 52.8	330 50.9	13.6	342 25.3	04.1	359 06.0	43.9	285 16.8	52.7	Alkaid	152 58.1	N49 14.0
08	185 55.3	345 50.6	14.6	357 26.4	04.7	14 08.2	43.8	300 19.0	52.8	Al Na'ir	27 41.8	S46 53.1
F 09	200 57.7	0 50.4	.. 15.6	12 27.5	.. 05.3	29 10.4	.. 43.6	315 21.2	.. 52.8	Alnilam	275 44.4	S 1 11.7
R 10	216 00.2	15 50.1	16.6	27 28.6	05.8	44 12.6	43.5	330 23.3	52.9	Alphard	217 54.4	S 8 43.7
I 11	231 02.7	30 49.9	17.6	42 29.7	06.4	59 14.8	43.4	345 25.5	52.9			
D 12	246 05.1	45 49.6	S 6 18.6	57 30.8	S 2 07.0	74 16.9	N 4 43.3	0 27.6	S19 53.0	Alphecca	126 10.0	N26 39.9
A 13	261 07.6	60 49.4	19.6	72 31.9	07.6	89 19.1	43.2	15 29.8	53.1	Alpheratz	357 41.6	N29 10.9
Y 14	276 10.1	75 49.1	20.6	87 33.0	08.2	104 21.3	43.1	30 31.9	53.1	Altair	62 06.9	N 8 54.9
15	291 12.5	90 48.9	.. 21.6	102 34.1	.. 08.7	119 23.5	.. 43.0	45 34.1	.. 53.2	Ankaa	353 13.9	S42 13.4
16	306 15.0	105 48.6	22.6	117 35.2	09.3	134 25.7	42.9	60 36.2	53.2	Antares	112 24.6	S26 27.8
17	321 17.5	120 48.4	23.6	132 36.3	09.9	149 27.9	42.8	75 38.4	53.3			
18	336 19.9	135 48.1	S 6 24.6	147 37.4	S 2 10.5	164 30.1	N 4 42.7	90 40.5	S19 53.3	Arcturus	145 54.6	N19 06.1
19	351 22.4	150 47.9	25.7	162 38.5	11.0	179 32.2	42.6	105 42.7	53.4	Atria	107 25.4	S69 03.1
20	6 24.9	165 47.6	26.7	177 39.6	11.6	194 34.4	42.5	120 44.8	53.4	Avior	234 16.9	S59 33.5
21	21 27.3	180 47.4	.. 27.7	192 40.7	.. 12.2	209 36.6	.. 42.3	135 47.0	.. 53.5	Bellatrix	278 29.9	N 6 21.7
22	36 29.8	195 47.1	28.7	207 41.8	12.8	224 38.8	42.2	150 49.2	53.5	Betelgeuse	270 59.2	N 7 24.4
23	51 32.2	210 46.9	29.7	222 42.9	13.3	239 41.0	42.1	165 51.3	53.6			
28 00	66 34.7	225 46.6	S 6 30.7	237 44.0	S 2 13.9	254 43.2	N 4 42.0	180 53.5	S19 53.6	Canopus	263 54.9	S52 42.3
01	81 37.2	240 46.4	31.7	252 45.1	14.5	269 45.4	41.9	195 55.6	53.7	Capella	280 31.5	N46 00.6
02	96 39.6	255 46.1	32.7	267 46.2	15.1	284 47.6	41.8	210 57.8	53.7	Deneb	49 30.5	N45 20.6
03	111 42.1	270 45.9	.. 33.7	282 47.3	.. 15.6	299 49.7	.. 41.7	225 59.9	.. 53.8	Denebola	182 32.1	N14 29.0
04	126 44.6	285 45.6	34.7	297 48.4	16.2	314 51.9	41.6	241 02.1	53.8	Diphda	348 54.1	S17 54.1
05	141 47.0	300 45.4	35.7	312 49.5	16.8	329 54.1	41.5	256 04.2	53.9			
06	156 49.5	315 45.1	S 6 36.7	327 50.7	S 2 17.4	344 56.3	N 4 41.4	271 06.4	S19 53.9	Dubhe	193 50.0	N61 39.6
07	171 52.0	330 44.8	37.7	342 51.8	17.9	359 58.5	41.3	286 08.5	54.0	Elnath	278 10.2	N28 37.0
S 08	186 54.4	345 44.6	38.7	357 52.9	18.5	15 00.7	41.2	301 10.7	54.0	Eltanin	90 45.9	N51 29.5
A 09	201 56.9	0 44.3	.. 39.7	12 54.0	.. 19.1	30 02.9	.. 41.1	316 12.8	.. 54.1	Enif	33 45.6	N 9 57.1
T 10	216 59.4	15 44.1	40.7	27 55.1	19.7	45 05.1	41.0	331 15.0	54.1	Fomalhaut	15 22.2	S29 32.3
U 11	232 01.8	30 43.8	41.7	42 56.2	20.2	60 07.3	40.8	346 17.2	54.2			
R 12	247 04.3	45 43.6	S 6 42.7	57 57.3	S 2 20.8	75 09.4	N 4 40.7	1 19.3	S19 54.2	Gacrux	171 59.2	S57 11.8
D 13	262 06.7	60 43.3	43.7	72 58.4	21.4	90 11.6	40.6	16 21.5	54.3	Gienah	175 50.7	S17 37.6
A 14	277 09.2	75 43.0	44.7	87 59.5	22.0	105 13.8	40.5	31 23.6	54.3	Hadar	148 46.0	S60 26.6
Y 15	292 11.7	90 42.8	.. 45.8	103 00.6	.. 22.5	120 16.0	.. 40.4	46 25.8	.. 54.4	Hamal	327 58.6	N23 32.3
16	307 14.1	105 42.5	46.8	118 01.7	23.1	135 18.2	40.3	61 27.9	54.4	Kaus Aust.	83 42.0	S34 22.4
17	322 16.6	120 42.3	47.8	133 02.8	23.7	150 20.4	40.2	76 30.1	54.5			
18	337 19.1	135 42.0	S 6 48.8	148 03.9	S 2 24.3	165 22.6	N 4 40.1	91 32.2	S19 54.5	Kochab	137 21.4	N74 05.4
19	352 21.5	150 41.7	49.8	163 05.0	24.8	180 24.8	40.0	106 34.4	54.6	Markab	13 36.6	N15 17.6
20	7 24.0	165 41.5	50.8	178 06.1	25.4	195 27.0	39.9	121 36.5	54.6	Menkar	314 13.0	N 4 09.0
21	22 26.5	180 41.2	.. 51.8	193 07.2	.. 26.0	210 29.2	.. 39.8	136 38.7	.. 54.7	Menkent	148 05.9	S36 26.6
22	37 28.9	195 41.0	52.8	208 08.3	26.6	225 31.4	39.7	151 40.8	54.7	Miaplacidus	221 38.8	S69 46.8
23	52 31.4	210 40.7	53.8	223 09.4	27.1	240 33.6	39.6	166 43.0	54.8			
29 00	67 33.9	225 40.4	S 6 54.8	238 10.5	S 2 27.7	255 35.7	N 4 39.5	181 45.1	S19 54.8	Mirfak	308 37.4	N49 55.0
01	82 36.3	240 40.2	55.8	253 11.6	28.3	270 37.9	39.4	196 47.3	54.9	Nunki	75 56.6	S26 16.4
02	97 38.8	255 39.9	56.8	268 12.7	28.9	285 40.1	39.3	211 49.5	54.9	Peacock	53 17.1	S56 41.1
03	112 41.2	270 39.6	.. 57.8	283 13.8	.. 29.4	300 42.3	.. 39.2	226 51.6	.. 55.0	Pollux	243 25.5	N27 59.0
04	127 43.7	285 39.4	58.8	298 14.9	30.0	315 44.5	39.0	241 53.8	55.0	Procyon	244 57.8	N 5 10.9
05	142 46.2	300 39.1	6 59.8	313 16.0	30.6	330 46.7	38.9	256 55.9	55.1			
06	157 48.6	315 38.9	S 7 00.8	328 17.1	S 2 31.2	345 48.9	N 4 38.8	271 58.1	S19 55.1	Rasalhague	96 05.3	N12 33.2
07	172 51.1	330 38.6	01.8	343 18.2	31.7	0 51.1	38.7	287 00.2	55.2	Regulus	207 41.8	N11 53.3
08	187 53.6	345 38.3	02.8	358 19.3	32.3	15 53.3	38.6	302 02.4	55.2	Rigel	281 10.1	S 8 11.2
S 09	202 56.0	0 38.1	.. 03.8	13 20.5	.. 32.9	30 55.5	.. 38.5	317 04.5	.. 55.3	Rigil Kent.	139 50.0	S60 53.7
U 10	217 58.5	15 37.8	04.8	28 21.6	33.5	45 57.7	38.4	332 06.7	55.3	Sabik	102 11.0	S15 44.4
N 11	233 01.0	30 37.5	05.8	43 22.7	34.0	60 59.9	38.3	347 08.8	55.4			
D 12	248 03.4	45 37.3	S 7 06.8	58 23.8	S 2 34.6	76 02.1	N 4 38.2	2 11.0	S19 55.4	Schedar	349 38.2	N56 37.7
A 13	263 05.9	60 37.0	07.8	73 24.9	35.2	91 04.3	38.1	17 13.1	55.5	Shaula	96 20.1	S37 06.7
Y 14	278 08.4	75 36.7	08.8	88 26.0	35.8	106 06.5	38.0	32 15.3	55.5	Sirius	258 32.0	S16 44.4
15	293 10.8	90 36.4	.. 09.8	103 27.1	.. 36.3	121 08.7	.. 37.9	47 17.5	.. 55.6	Spica	158 29.7	S11 14.5
16	308 13.3	105 36.2	10.9	118 28.2	36.9	136 10.9	37.8	62 19.6	55.6	Suhail	222 51.0	S43 29.7
17	323 15.7	120 35.9	11.9	133 29.3	37.5	151 13.1	37.7	77 21.8	55.7			
18	338 18.2	135 35.6	S 7 12.9	148 30.4	S 2 38.0	166 15.3	N 4 37.6	92 23.9	S19 55.7	Vega	80 38.2	N38 48.3
19	353 20.7	150 35.4	13.9	163 31.5	38.6	181 17.5	37.5	107 26.1	55.8	Zuben'ubi	137 03.9	S16 06.2
20	8 23.1	165 35.1	14.9	178 32.6	39.2	196 19.6	37.4	122 28.2	55.8			
21	23 25.6	180 34.8	.. 15.9	193 33.7	.. 39.8	211 21.8	.. 37.3	137 30.4	.. 55.9		SHA	Mer. Pass.
22	38 28.1	195 34.6	16.9	208 34.8	40.3	226 24.0	37.2	152 32.5	55.9	Venus	159 11.9	8 57
23	53 30.5	210 34.3	17.9	223 35.9	40.9	241 26.2	37.1	167 34.7	56.0	Mars	171 09.3	8 08
										Jupiter	188 08.5	7 00
Mer. Pass. 19 30.5		v −0.3	d 1.0	v 1.1	d 0.6	v 2.2	d 0.1	v 2.2	d 0.1	Saturn	114 18.8	11 55

UT	SUN GHA	SUN Dec	MOON GHA	v	MOON Dec	d	HP
27 d h	° '	° '	° '	'	° '	'	'
00	183 09.6	S21 01.1	347 35.7	6.2	N17 59.0	2.3	59.2
01	198 09.4	01.6	2 00.9	6.2	18 01.3	2.3	59.2
02	213 09.2	02.1	16 26.1	6.2	18 03.6	2.1	59.2
03	228 09.0	.. 02.5	30 51.3	6.2	18 05.7	2.0	59.1
04	243 08.8	03.0	45 16.5	6.2	18 07.7	1.8	59.1
05	258 08.6	03.4	59 41.7	6.3	18 09.5	1.8	59.1
06	273 08.4	S21 03.9	74 07.0	6.3	N18 11.3	1.6	59.1
07	288 08.2	04.4	88 32.3	6.3	18 12.9	1.5	59.0
F 08	303 08.0	04.8	102 57.6	6.4	18 14.4	1.3	59.0
R 09	318 07.8	.. 05.3	117 23.0	6.4	18 15.7	1.3	59.0
I 10	333 07.6	05.7	131 48.4	6.4	18 17.0	1.1	58.9
D 11	348 07.4	06.2	146 13.8	6.5	18 18.1	1.1	58.9
A 12	3 07.2	S21 06.7	160 39.3	6.5	N18 19.2	0.9	58.9
Y 13	18 07.0	07.1	175 04.8	6.6	18 20.1	0.7	58.8
14	33 06.8	07.6	189 30.4	6.5	18 20.8	0.7	58.8
15	48 06.6	.. 08.0	203 55.9	6.6	18 21.5	0.5	58.8
16	63 06.4	08.5	218 21.5	6.7	18 22.0	0.5	58.7
17	78 06.2	08.9	232 47.2	6.7	18 22.5	0.3	58.7
18	93 06.0	S21 09.4	247 12.9	6.7	N18 22.8	0.2	58.7
19	108 05.8	09.8	261 38.6	6.8	18 23.0	0.0	58.6
20	123 05.6	10.3	276 04.4	6.9	18 23.0	0.0	58.6
21	138 05.4	.. 10.7	290 30.3	6.8	18 23.0	0.2	58.6
22	153 05.2	11.2	304 56.1	6.9	18 22.8	0.3	58.5
23	168 05.0	11.7	319 22.0	7.0	18 22.5	0.3	58.5
28 00	183 04.7	S21 12.1	333 48.0	7.0	N18 22.2	0.6	58.5
01	198 04.5	12.5	348 14.0	7.1	18 21.6	0.6	58.4
02	213 04.3	13.0	2 40.1	7.1	18 21.0	0.7	58.4
03	228 04.1	.. 13.4	17 06.2	7.2	18 20.3	0.9	58.4
04	243 03.9	13.9	31 32.4	7.2	18 19.4	0.9	58.3
05	258 03.7	14.3	45 58.6	7.3	18 18.5	1.1	58.3
06	273 03.5	S21 14.8	60 24.9	7.3	N18 17.4	1.2	58.3
S 07	288 03.3	15.2	74 51.2	7.4	18 16.2	1.3	58.2
A 08	303 03.1	15.7	89 17.6	7.4	18 14.9	1.4	58.2
T 09	318 02.9	.. 16.1	103 44.0	7.5	18 13.5	1.5	58.1
U 10	333 02.7	16.6	118 10.5	7.6	18 12.0	1.6	58.1
R 11	348 02.5	17.0	132 37.1	7.6	18 10.4	1.7	58.1
D 12	3 02.2	S21 17.4	147 03.7	7.6	N18 08.7	1.9	58.0
A 13	18 02.0	17.9	161 30.3	7.8	18 06.8	1.9	58.0
Y 14	33 01.8	18.3	175 57.1	7.8	18 04.9	2.1	58.0
15	48 01.6	.. 18.8	190 23.9	7.8	18 02.8	2.1	57.9
16	63 01.4	19.2	204 50.7	7.9	18 00.7	2.3	57.9
17	78 01.2	19.6	219 17.6	8.0	17 58.4	2.4	57.9
18	93 01.0	S21 20.1	233 44.6	8.0	N17 56.0	2.5	57.8
19	108 00.8	20.5	248 11.6	8.1	17 53.5	2.5	57.8
20	123 00.6	20.9	262 38.7	8.2	17 51.0	2.7	57.8
21	138 00.3	.. 21.4	277 05.9	8.2	17 48.3	2.8	57.7
22	153 00.1	21.8	291 33.1	8.3	17 45.5	2.9	57.7
23	167 59.9	22.2	306 00.4	8.4	17 42.6	2.9	57.6
29 00	182 59.7	S21 22.7	320 27.8	8.4	N17 39.7	3.1	57.6
01	197 59.5	23.1	334 55.2	8.5	17 36.6	3.2	57.6
02	212 59.3	23.5	349 22.7	8.6	17 33.4	3.3	57.5
03	227 59.1	.. 24.0	3 50.3	8.6	17 30.1	3.3	57.5
04	242 58.8	24.4	18 17.9	8.7	17 26.8	3.5	57.5
05	257 58.6	24.8	32 45.6	8.7	17 23.3	3.6	57.4
06	272 58.4	S21 25.3	47 13.3	8.9	N17 19.7	3.6	57.4
07	287 58.2	25.7	61 41.2	8.9	17 16.1	3.8	57.4
08	302 58.0	26.1	76 09.1	9.0	17 12.3	3.8	57.3
S 09	317 57.8	.. 26.5	90 37.1	9.0	17 08.5	4.0	57.3
U 10	332 57.5	27.0	105 05.1	9.1	17 04.5	4.0	57.2
N 11	347 57.3	27.4	119 33.2	9.2	17 00.5	4.1	57.2
D 12	2 57.1	S21 27.8	134 01.4	9.3	N16 56.4	4.2	57.2
A 13	17 56.9	28.2	148 29.7	9.3	16 52.2	4.3	57.1
Y 14	32 56.7	28.7	162 58.0	9.4	16 47.9	4.4	57.1
15	47 56.5	.. 29.1	177 26.4	9.4	16 43.5	4.4	57.1
16	62 56.2	29.5	191 54.8	9.6	16 39.1	4.6	57.0
17	77 56.0	29.9	206 23.4	9.6	16 34.5	4.6	57.0
18	92 55.8	S21 30.3	220 52.0	9.7	N16 29.9	4.8	57.0
19	107 55.6	30.8	235 20.7	9.7	16 25.1	4.8	56.9
20	122 55.4	31.2	249 49.4	9.9	16 20.3	4.8	56.9
21	137 55.1	.. 31.6	264 18.3	9.9	16 15.5	5.0	56.9
22	152 54.9	32.0	278 47.2	9.9	16 10.5	5.1	56.8
23	167 54.7	32.4	293 16.1	10.1	N16 05.4	5.1	56.8
	SD 16.2	d 0.4	SD 16.0		15.8		15.6

Twilight / Sunrise / Moonrise

Lat.	Twilight Naut.	Twilight Civil	Sunrise	Moonrise 27	28	29	30
°	h m	h m	h m	h m	h m	h m	h m
N 72	07 41	09 34	■■	□	14 40	16 53	18 45
N 70	07 26	08 59	■■	15 06	16 12	17 40	19 15
68	07 14	08 34	10 17	15 48	16 51	18 11	19 37
66	07 04	08 15	09 35	16 17	17 19	18 33	19 54
64	06 55	07 59	09 07	16 38	17 40	18 51	20 08
62	06 47	07 46	08 45	16 56	17 56	19 06	20 19
60	06 40	07 35	08 28	17 10	18 10	19 18	20 29
N 58	06 34	07 25	08 13	17 23	18 22	19 28	20 38
56	06 29	07 16	08 01	17 33	18 33	19 38	20 45
54	06 24	07 08	07 50	17 43	18 42	19 46	20 52
52	06 19	07 01	07 41	17 51	18 50	19 53	20 58
50	06 14	06 55	07 32	17 59	18 58	20 00	21 03
45	06 05	06 41	07 14	18 15	19 13	20 14	21 15
N 40	05 56	06 29	06 59	18 28	19 26	20 25	21 25
35	05 48	06 19	06 46	18 40	19 37	20 35	21 33
30	05 40	06 10	06 35	18 49	19 47	20 44	21 40
20	05 26	05 53	06 16	19 07	20 03	20 59	21 53
N 10	05 11	05 37	06 00	19 21	20 18	21 12	22 04
0	04 56	05 22	05 44	19 35	20 31	21 24	22 14
S 10	04 39	05 06	05 28	19 49	20 45	21 36	22 24
20	04 19	04 47	05 11	20 04	20 59	21 49	22 35
30	03 53	04 25	04 52	20 21	21 16	22 04	22 48
35	03 36	04 11	04 40	20 31	21 25	22 13	22 55
40	03 15	03 55	04 27	20 43	21 36	22 23	23 03
45	02 49	03 35	04 11	20 56	21 49	22 34	23 13
S 50	02 11	03 09	03 51	21 13	22 05	22 48	23 24
52	01 51	02 57	03 42	21 21	22 12	22 54	23 29
54	01 24	02 42	03 31	21 29	22 20	23 01	23 35
56	00 40	02 24	03 19	21 39	22 29	23 09	23 42
58	////	02 02	03 05	21 50	22 40	23 18	23 49
S 60	////	01 33	02 49	22 02	22 51	23 29	23 57

Sunset / Twilight / Moonset

Lat.	Sunset	Twilight Civil	Twilight Naut.	Moonset 27	28	29	30
°	h m	h m	h m	h m	h m	h m	h m
N 72	■■	14 00	15 53	□	13 58	13 37	13 30
N 70	■■	14 36	16 09	11 34	12 25	12 49	12 59
68	13 18	15 01	16 21	10 52	11 46	12 18	12 37
66	14 00	15 20	16 31	10 23	11 18	11 55	12 19
64	14 29	15 36	16 40	10 01	10 57	11 36	12 04
62	14 50	15 49	16 48	09 44	10 40	11 21	11 52
60	15 07	16 01	16 55	09 30	10 26	11 09	11 42
N 58	15 22	16 10	17 01	09 17	10 13	10 58	11 32
56	15 34	16 19	17 07	09 07	10 03	10 48	11 24
54	15 45	16 27	17 12	08 57	09 54	10 40	11 17
52	15 55	16 34	17 16	08 49	09 45	10 32	11 11
50	16 03	16 40	17 21	08 41	09 38	10 25	11 05
45	16 21	16 54	17 31	08 25	09 22	10 11	10 53
N 40	16 36	17 06	17 40	08 12	09 09	09 59	10 42
35	16 49	17 17	17 48	08 01	08 58	09 48	10 33
30	17 00	17 26	17 57	07 51	08 48	09 39	10 25
20	17 19	17 43	18 10	07 34	08 31	09 24	10 12
N 10	17 36	17 58	18 24	07 19	08 16	09 10	10 00
0	17 52	18 14	18 40	07 05	08 02	08 57	09 48
S 10	18 07	18 30	18 57	06 52	07 48	08 44	09 37
20	18 24	18 49	19 17	06 37	07 34	08 30	09 25
30	18 44	19 11	19 44	06 20	07 17	08 14	09 11
35	18 56	19 25	20 00	06 10	07 07	08 05	09 03
40	19 09	19 41	20 21	05 59	06 55	07 54	08 54
45	19 25	20 01	20 48	05 45	06 42	07 42	08 43
S 50	19 45	20 27	21 26	05 29	06 26	07 26	08 30
52	19 55	20 40	21 47	05 22	06 18	07 19	08 24
54	20 05	20 55	22 15	05 13	06 09	07 11	08 17
56	20 18	21 13	23 01	05 04	06 00	07 03	08 09
58	20 32	21 36	////	04 53	05 49	06 52	08 01
S 60	20 48	22 06	////	04 41	05 36	06 41	07 51

SUN / MOON

Day	SUN Eqn. of Time 00h	SUN Eqn. of Time 12h	SUN Mer. Pass.	MOON Mer. Pass. Upper	MOON Mer. Pass. Lower	Age	Phase
d	m s	m s	h m	h m	h m	d	%
27	12 39	12 29	11 48	00 52	13 20	16	97
28	12 19	12 09	11 48	01 49	14 17	17	92
29	11 59	11 49	11 48	02 44	15 11	18	85

UT	ARIES GHA	VENUS −4.2 GHA	Dec	MARS +1.5 GHA	Dec	JUPITER −2.0 GHA	Dec	SATURN +0.4 GHA	Dec	Star Name	SHA	Dec
30 00	68 33.0	225 34.0	S 7 18.9	238 37.0	S 2 41.5	256 28.4	N 4 37.0	182 36.8	S19 56.0	Acamar	315 16.7	S40 14.7
01	83 35.5	240 33.7	19.9	253 38.1	42.1	271 30.6	36.9	197 39.0	56.1	Achernar	335 25.2	S57 09.6
02	98 37.9	255 33.5	20.9	268 39.2	42.6	286 32.8	36.8	212 41.1	56.1	Acrux	173 07.6	S63 10.9
03	113 40.4	270 33.2	.. 21.9	283 40.3	.. 43.2	301 35.0	.. 36.7	227 43.3	.. 56.2	Adhara	255 10.9	S28 59.7
04	128 42.8	285 32.9	22.9	298 41.4	43.8	316 37.2	36.6	242 45.4	56.2	Aldebaran	290 47.1	N16 32.3
05	143 45.3	300 32.6	23.9	313 42.5	44.3	331 39.4	36.5	257 47.6	56.3			
M 06	158 47.8	315 32.4	S 7 24.9	328 43.7	S 2 44.9	346 41.6	N 4 36.4	272 49.8	S19 56.3	Alioth	166 19.7	N55 52.3
O 07	173 50.2	330 32.1	25.9	343 44.8	45.5	1 43.8	36.3	287 51.9	56.4	Alkaid	152 58.1	N49 14.0
N 08	188 52.7	345 31.8	26.9	358 45.9	46.1	16 46.0	36.2	302 54.1	56.4	Al Na'ir	27 41.8	S46 53.1
D 09	203 55.2	0 31.5	.. 27.9	13 47.0	.. 46.6	31 48.2	.. 36.1	317 56.2	.. 56.5	Alnilam	275 44.4	S 1 11.7
A 10	218 57.6	15 31.3	28.9	28 48.1	47.2	46 50.4	36.0	332 58.4	56.5	Alphard	217 54.3	S 8 43.7
Y 11	234 00.1	30 31.0	29.9	43 49.2	47.8	61 52.6	35.8	348 00.5	56.6			
12	249 02.6	45 30.7	S 7 30.9	58 50.3	S 2 48.4	76 54.8	N 4 35.7	3 02.7	S19 56.6	Alphecca	126 10.0	N26 39.8
13	264 05.0	60 30.4	31.9	73 51.4	48.9	91 57.0	35.6	18 04.8	56.7	Alpheratz	357 41.6	N29 10.9
14	279 07.5	75 30.1	32.9	88 52.5	49.5	106 59.2	35.5	33 07.0	56.7	Altair	62 06.9	N 8 54.9
15	294 10.0	90 29.9	.. 33.9	103 53.6	.. 50.1	122 01.4	.. 35.4	48 09.1	.. 56.8	Ankaa	353 13.9	S42 13.4
16	309 12.4	105 29.6	34.9	118 54.7	50.6	137 03.6	35.3	63 11.3	56.8	Antares	112 24.6	S26 27.8
17	324 14.9	120 29.3	35.9	133 55.8	51.2	152 05.8	35.2	78 13.4	56.9			
18	339 17.3	135 29.0	S 7 36.9	148 56.9	S 2 51.8	167 08.0	N 4 35.1	93 15.6	S19 56.9	Arcturus	145 54.5	N19 06.1
19	354 19.8	150 28.8	37.9	163 58.0	52.4	182 10.3	35.0	108 17.7	57.0	Atria	107 25.4	S69 03.1
20	9 22.3	165 28.5	38.9	178 59.1	52.9	197 12.5	34.9	123 19.9	57.0	Avior	234 16.9	S59 33.5
21	24 24.7	180 28.2	.. 39.9	194 00.2	.. 53.5	212 14.7	.. 34.8	138 22.1	.. 57.1	Bellatrix	278 29.9	N 6 21.7
22	39 27.2	195 27.9	40.9	209 01.3	54.1	227 16.9	34.7	153 24.2	57.1	Betelgeuse	270 59.2	N 7 24.4
23	54 29.7	210 27.6	41.9	224 02.5	54.6	242 19.1	34.6	168 26.4	57.2			
1 00	69 32.1	225 27.3	S 7 42.9	239 03.6	S 2 55.2	257 21.3	N 4 34.5	183 28.5	S19 57.2	Canopus	263 54.9	S52 42.3
01	84 34.6	240 27.1	43.9	254 04.7	55.8	272 23.5	34.4	198 30.7	57.3	Capella	280 31.5	N46 00.6
02	99 37.1	255 26.8	44.9	269 05.8	56.4	287 25.7	34.3	213 32.8	57.3	Deneb	49 30.5	N45 20.6
03	114 39.5	270 26.5	.. 45.9	284 06.9	.. 56.9	302 27.9	.. 34.2	228 35.0	.. 57.4	Denebola	182 32.1	N14 29.0
04	129 42.0	285 26.2	46.9	299 08.0	57.5	317 30.1	34.1	243 37.1	57.4	Diphda	348 54.1	S17 54.1
05	144 44.5	300 25.9	47.9	314 09.1	58.1	332 32.3	34.0	258 39.3	57.5			
T 06	159 46.9	315 25.6	S 7 48.9	329 10.2	S 2 58.6	347 34.5	N 4 33.9	273 41.4	S19 57.5	Dubhe	193 49.9	N61 39.6
U 07	174 49.4	330 25.3	49.9	344 11.3	59.2	2 36.7	33.8	288 43.6	57.6	Elnath	278 10.1	N28 37.0
E 08	189 51.8	345 25.1	50.9	359 12.4	2 59.8	17 38.9	33.7	303 45.7	57.6	Eltanin	90 45.9	N51 29.5
S 09	204 54.3	0 24.8	.. 51.9	14 13.5	3 00.3	32 41.1	.. 33.6	318 47.9	.. 57.7	Enif	33 45.6	N 9 57.1
D 10	219 56.8	15 24.5	52.9	29 14.6	00.9	47 43.3	33.5	333 50.0	57.7	Fomalhaut	15 22.2	S29 32.3
A 11	234 59.2	30 24.2	53.9	44 15.7	01.5	62 45.5	33.4	348 52.2	57.8			
Y 12	250 01.7	45 23.9	S 7 54.9	59 16.8	S 3 02.1	77 47.7	N 4 33.3	3 54.4	S19 57.8	Gacrux	171 59.2	S57 11.8
13	265 04.2	60 23.6	55.9	74 17.9	02.6	92 49.9	33.2	18 56.5	57.9	Gienah	175 50.7	S17 37.6
14	280 06.6	75 23.3	56.9	89 19.1	03.2	107 52.1	33.1	33 58.7	57.9	Hadar	148 45.9	S60 26.6
15	295 09.1	90 23.0	.. 57.9	104 20.2	.. 03.8	122 54.4	.. 33.0	49 00.8	.. 58.0	Hamal	327 58.6	N23 32.3
16	310 11.6	105 22.8	58.9	119 21.3	04.3	137 56.6	32.9	64 03.0	58.0	Kaus Aust.	83 42.0	S34 22.4
17	325 14.0	120 22.5	7 59.9	134 22.4	04.9	152 58.8	32.8	79 05.1	58.1			
18	340 16.5	135 22.2	S 8 00.9	149 23.5	S 3 05.5	168 01.0	N 4·32.7	94 07.3	S19 58.1	Kochab	137 21.4	N74 05.4
19	355 18.9	150 21.9	01.9	164 24.6	06.0	183 03.2	32.6	109 09.4	58.2	Markab	13 36.6	N15 17.6
20	10 21.4	165 21.6	02.9	179 25.7	06.6	198 05.4	32.5	124 11.6	58.2	Menkar	314 13.0	N 4 09.0
21	25 23.9	180 21.3	.. 03.9	194 26.8	.. 07.2	213 07.6	.. 32.5	139 13.7	.. 58.3	Menkent	148 05.9	S36 26.6
22	40 26.3	195 21.0	04.9	209 27.9	07.8	228 09.8	32.4	154 15.9	58.3	Miaplacidus	221 38.8	S69 46.8
23	55 28.8	210 20.7	05.9	224 29.0	08.3	243 12.0	32.3	169 18.0	58.4			
2 00	70 31.3	225 20.4	S 8 06.9	239 30.1	S 3 08.9	258 14.2	N 4 32.2	184 20.2	S19 58.4	Mirfak	308 37.4	N49 55.0
01	85 33.7	240 20.1	07.9	254 31.2	09.5	273 16.4	32.1	199 22.3	58.5	Nunki	75 56.6	S26 16.4
02	100 36.2	255 19.8	08.9	269 32.3	10.0	288 18.6	32.0	214 24.5	58.5	Peacock	53 17.1	S56 41.0
03	115 38.7	270 19.5	.. 09.9	284 33.4	.. 10.6	303 20.9	.. 31.9	229 26.7	.. 58.6	Pollux	243 25.5	N27 59.0
04	130 41.1	285 19.2	10.9	299 34.6	11.2	318 23.1	31.8	244 28.8	58.6	Procyon	244 57.8	N 5 10.9
05	145 43.6	300 18.9	11.9	314 35.7	11.7	333 25.3	31.7	259 31.0	58.7			
W 06	160 46.1	315 18.6	S 8 12.9	329 36.8	S 3 12.3	348 27.5	N 4 31.6	274 33.1	S19 58.7	Rasalhague	96 05.3	N12 33.2
E 07	175 48.5	330 18.4	13.9	344 37.9	12.9	3 29.7	31.5	289 35.3	58.8	Regulus	207 41.7	N11 53.2
D 08	190 51.0	345 18.1	14.9	359 39.0	13.4	18 31.9	31.4	304 37.4	58.8	Rigel	281 10.1	S 8 11.2
N 09	205 53.4	0 17.8	.. 15.9	14 40.1	.. 14.0	33 34.1	.. 31.3	319 39.6	.. 58.9	Rigil Kent.	139 49.9	S60 53.7
E 10	220 55.9	15 17.5	16.9	29 41.2	14.6	48 36.3	31.2	334 41.7	58.9	Sabik	102 11.0	S15 44.4
S 11	235 58.4	30 17.2	17.9	44 42.3	15.2	63 38.5	31.1	349 43.9	59.0			
D 12	251 00.8	45 16.9	S 8 18.9	59 43.4	S 3 15.7	78 40.8	N 4 31.0	4 46.0	S19 59.0	Schedar	349 38.2	N56 37.7
A 13	266 03.3	60 16.6	19.9	74 44.5	16.3	93 43.0	30.9	19 48.2	59.1	Shaula	96 20.1	S37 06.7
Y 14	281 05.8	75 16.3	20.9	89 45.6	16.9	108 45.2	30.8	34 50.3	59.1	Sirius	258 32.0	S16 44.4
15	296 08.2	90 16.0	.. 21.9	104 46.7	.. 17.4	123 47.4	.. 30.7	49 52.5	.. 59.2	Spica	158 29.7	S11 14.5
16	311 10.7	105 15.7	22.9	119 47.8	18.0	138 49.6	30.6	64 54.6	59.2	Suhail	222 51.0	S43 29.7
17	326 13.2	120 15.4	23.9	134 49.0	18.6	153 51.8	30.5	79 56.8	59.3			
18	341 15.6	135 15.1	S 8 24.9	149 50.1	S 3 19.1	168 54.0	N 4 30.4	94 59.0	S19 59.3	Vega	80 38.2	N38 48.3
19	356 18.1	150 14.8	25.9	164 51.2	19.7	183 56.3	30.3	110 01.1	59.4	Zuben'ubi	137 03.9	S16 06.2
20	11 20.6	165 14.5	26.9	179 52.3	20.3	198 58.5	30.2	125 03.3	59.4		SHA	Mer. Pass.
21	26 23.0	180 14.2	.. 27.9	194 53.4	.. 20.8	214 00.7	.. 30.1	140 05.4	.. 59.5			h m
22	41 25.5	195 13.9	28.9	209 54.5	21.4	229 02.9	30.0	155 07.6	59.5	Venus	155 55.2	8 58
23	56 27.9	210 13.5	29.9	224 55.6	22.0	244 05.1	29.9	170 09.7	59.5	Mars	169 31.4	8 03
	h m									Jupiter	187 49.1	6 50
Mer. Pass. 19 18.7		*v* −0.3	*d* 1.0	*v* 1.1	*d* 0.6	*v* 2.2	*d* 0.1	*v* 2.2	*d* 0.0	Saturn	113 56.4	11 44

SUN and MOON

UT	SUN GHA	SUN Dec	MOON GHA	v	MOON Dec	d	HP
d h	° ′	° ′	° ′	′	° ′	′	′
30 00	182 54.5	S21 32.8	307 45.2	10.1	N16 00.3	5.2	56.8
01	197 54.3	33.3	322 14.3	10.2	15 55.1	5.3	56.7
02	212 54.0	33.7	336 43.5	10.3	15 49.8	5.3	56.7
03	227 53.8	34.1	351 12.8	10.3	15 44.5	5.5	56.6
04	242 53.6	34.5	5 42.1	10.4	15 39.0	5.5	56.6
05	257 53.4	34.9	20 11.5	10.5	15 33.5	5.6	56.6
06	272 53.1	S21 35.3	34 41.0	10.5	N15 27.9	5.7	56.5
M 07	287 52.9	35.7	49 10.5	10.7	15 22.2	5.7	56.5
O 08	302 52.7	36.1	63 40.2	10.6	15 16.5	5.8	56.5
N 09	317 52.5	36.6	78 09.8	10.8	15 10.7	5.9	56.4
D 10	332 52.3	37.0	92 39.6	10.9	15 04.8	5.9	56.4
A 11	347 52.0	37.4	107 09.5	10.9	14 58.9	6.0	56.4
Y 12	2 51.8	S21 37.8	121 39.4	10.9	N14 52.9	6.1	56.3
13	17 51.6	38.2	136 09.3	11.1	14 46.8	6.2	56.3
14	32 51.4	38.6	150 39.4	11.1	14 40.6	6.2	56.3
15	47 51.1	39.0	165 09.5	11.2	14 34.4	6.3	56.2
16	62 50.9	39.4	179 39.7	11.3	14 28.1	6.4	56.2
17	77 50.7	39.8	194 10.0	11.3	14 21.7	6.4	56.2
18	92 50.4	S21 40.2	208 40.3	11.4	N14 15.3	6.4	56.2
19	107 50.2	40.6	223 10.7	11.5	14 08.9	6.5	56.1
20	122 50.0	41.0	237 41.2	11.5	14 02.3	6.6	56.1
21	137 49.8	41.4	252 11.7	11.6	13 55.7	6.7	56.1
22	152 49.5	41.8	266 42.3	11.7	13 49.0	6.7	56.0
23	167 49.3	42.2	281 13.0	11.7	13 42.3	6.8	56.0
1 00	182 49.1	S21 42.6	295 43.7	11.9	N13 35.5	6.8	56.0
01	197 48.9	43.0	310 14.6	11.8	13 28.7	6.9	55.9
02	212 48.6	43.4	324 45.4	12.0	13 21.8	7.0	55.9
03	227 48.4	43.8	339 16.4	12.0	13 14.8	7.0	55.9
04	242 48.2	44.2	353 47.4	12.1	13 07.8	7.1	55.8
05	257 47.9	44.6	8 18.5	12.1	13 00.7	7.1	55.8
06	272 47.7	S21 45.0	22 49.6	12.2	N12 53.6	7.2	55.8
T 07	287 47.5	45.4	37 20.8	12.3	12 46.4	7.2	55.7
U 08	302 47.2	45.8	51 52.1	12.3	12 39.2	7.3	55.7
E 09	317 47.0	46.2	66 23.4	12.4	12 31.9	7.3	55.7
S 10	332 46.8	46.6	80 54.8	12.5	12 24.6	7.4	55.7
D 11	347 46.6	46.9	95 26.3	12.5	12 17.2	7.4	55.6
A 12	2 46.3	S21 47.3	109 57.8	12.6	N12 09.8	7.5	55.6
Y 13	17 46.1	47.7	124 29.4	12.7	12 02.3	7.5	55.6
14	32 45.9	48.1	139 01.1	12.7	11 54.8	7.6	55.5
15	47 45.6	48.5	153 32.8	12.8	11 47.2	7.7	55.5
16	62 45.4	48.9	168 04.6	12.8	11 39.5	7.6	55.5
17	77 45.2	49.3	182 36.4	12.9	11 31.9	7.7	55.5
18	92 44.9	S21 49.7	197 08.3	12.9	N11 24.2	7.8	55.4
19	107 44.7	50.0	211 40.2	13.0	11 16.4	7.8	55.4
20	122 44.5	50.4	226 12.2	13.1	11 08.6	7.9	55.4
21	137 44.2	50.8	240 44.3	13.1	11 00.7	7.9	55.4
22	152 44.0	51.2	255 16.4	13.2	10 52.8	7.9	55.3
23	167 43.8	51.6	269 48.6	13.3	10 44.9	8.0	55.3
2 00	182 43.5	S21 52.0	284 20.9	13.2	N10 36.9	8.0	55.3
01	197 43.3	52.3	298 53.1	13.4	10 28.9	8.0	55.3
02	212 43.0	52.7	313 25.5	13.4	10 20.9	8.1	55.2
03	227 42.8	53.1	327 57.9	13.5	10 12.8	8.2	55.2
04	242 42.6	53.5	342 30.4	13.5	10 04.6	8.1	55.2
05	257 42.3	53.8	357 02.9	13.5	9 56.5	8.2	55.2
06	272 42.1	S21 54.2	11 35.4	13.6	N 9 48.3	8.3	55.1
W 07	287 41.9	54.6	26 08.0	13.7	9 40.0	8.2	55.1
E 08	302 41.6	55.0	40 40.7	13.7	9 31.8	8.4	55.1
D 09	317 41.4	55.4	55 13.4	13.8	9 23.4	8.3	55.1
N 10	332 41.2	55.7	69 46.2	13.8	9 15.1	8.4	55.0
E 11	347 40.9	56.1	84 19.0	13.8	9 06.7	8.4	55.0
S 12	2 40.7	S21 56.5	98 51.8	13.9	N 8 58.3	8.4	55.0
D 13	17 40.4	56.8	113 24.7	14.0	8 49.9	8.5	55.0
A 14	32 40.2	57.2	127 57.7	14.0	8 41.4	8.6	54.9
Y 15	47 40.0	57.6	142 30.7	14.0	8 32.9	8.6	54.9
16	62 39.7	58.0	157 03.7	14.1	8 24.3	8.5	54.9
17	77 39.5	58.3	171 36.8	14.2	8 15.8	8.6	54.9
18	92 39.2	S21 58.7	186 10.0	14.1	N 8 07.2	8.6	54.9
19	107 39.0	59.1	200 43.1	14.3	7 58.6	8.7	54.8
20	122 38.8	59.4	215 16.4	14.2	7 49.9	8.7	54.8
21	137 38.5	21 59.8	229 49.6	14.3	7 41.2	8.7	54.8
22	152 38.3	22 00.2	244 22.9	14.4	7 32.5	8.7	54.8
23	167 38.0	S22 00.5	258 56.3	14.3	N 7 23.8	8.8	54.8
	SD 16.2	d 0.4	SD 15.4		15.2		15.0

Twilight, Sunrise and Moonrise

Lat.	Twilight Naut.	Twilight Civil	Sunrise	Moonrise 30	Moonrise 1	Moonrise 2	Moonrise 3
°	h m	h m	h m	h m	h m	h m	h m
N 72	07 50	09 48	■■■	18 45	20 30	22 08	23 43
N 70	07 34	09 10	■■■	19 15	20 49	22 20	23 48
68	07 21	08 43	10 34	19 37	21 03	22 29	23 52
66	07 10	08 22	09 46	19 54	21 15	22 36	23 56
64	07 00	08 06	09 15	20 08	21 25	22 43	23 59
62	06 52	07 52	08 52	20 19	21 34	22 48	24 01
60	06 45	07 40	08 34	20 29	21 41	22 53	24 04
N 58	06 39	07 30	08 19	20 38	21 48	22 57	24 05
56	06 33	07 21	08 06	20 45	21 53	23 01	24 07
54	06 28	07 13	07 55	20 52	21 58	23 04	24 09
52	06 23	07 05	07 45	20 58	22 03	23 07	24 10
50	06 18	06 59	07 36	21 03	22 07	23 10	24 12
45	06 08	06 44	07 17	21 15	22 16	23 16	24 14
N 40	05 59	06 32	07 02	21 25	22 23	23 21	24 17
35	05 50	06 21	06 49	21 33	22 30	23 25	24 19
30	05 42	06 12	06 38	21 40	22 35	23 29	24 21
20	05 27	05 55	06 18	21 53	22 45	23 35	24 24
N 10	05 13	05 39	06 01	22 04	22 53	23 41	24 27
0	04 57	05 23	05 45	22 14	23 01	23 46	24 29
S 10	04 40	05 06	05 29	22 24	23 09	23 51	24 32
20	04 19	04 47	05 12	22 35	23 18	23 57	24 35
30	03 52	04 24	04 51	22 48	23 27	24 03	00 03
35	03 35	04 10	04 39	22 55	23 33	24 07	00 07
40	03 14	03 54	04 26	23 03	23 39	24 11	00 11
45	02 46	03 33	04 09	23 13	23 46	24 16	00 16
S 50	02 07	03 07	03 49	23 24	23 55	24 22	00 22
52	01 45	02 53	03 39	23 29	23 59	24 25	00 25
54	01 16	02 38	03 28	23 35	24 03	00 03	00 27
56	00 20	02 19	03 16	23 42	24 08	00 08	00 31
58	////	01 56	03 01	23 49	24 13	00 13	00 34
S 60	////	01 24	02 44	23 57	24 20	00 20	00 38

Sunset, Twilight and Moonset

Lat.	Sunset	Twilight Civil	Twilight Naut.	Moonset 30	Moonset 1	Moonset 2	Moonset 3
°	h m	h m	h m	h m	h m	h m	h m
N 72	■■■	13 49	15 47	13 30	13 24	13 19	13 14
N 70	■■■	14 28	16 03	12 59	13 04	13 06	13 07
68	13 03	14 54	16 16	12 37	12 48	12 56	13 01
66	13 52	15 15	16 27	12 19	12 35	12 47	12 56
64	14 22	15 32	16 37	12 04	12 24	12 39	12 52
62	14 45	15 46	16 45	11 52	12 15	12 33	12 48
60	15 03	15 57	16 52	11 42	12 07	12 28	12 45
N 58	15 18	16 08	16 59	11 32	12 00	12 23	12 42
56	15 31	16 17	17 04	11 24	11 54	12 18	12 40
54	15 42	16 25	17 10	11 17	11 48	12 14	12 37
52	15 52	16 32	17 15	11 11	11 43	12 11	12 35
50	16 01	16 39	17 19	11 05	11 39	12 07	12 33
45	16 20	16 53	17 30	10 53	11 29	12 00	12 29
N 40	16 35	17 05	17 39	10 42	11 20	11 54	12 26
35	16 48	17 16	17 47	10 33	11 13	11 49	12 23
30	17 00	17 26	17 55	10 25	11 07	11 45	12 20
20	17 19	17 43	18 10	10 12	10 56	11 37	12 15
N 10	17 36	17 59	18 25	10 00	10 46	11 30	12 11
0	17 53	18 15	18 41	09 48	10 37	11 23	12 07
S 10	18 09	18 32	18 58	09 37	10 28	11 16	12 03
20	18 26	18 51	19 19	09 25	10 18	11 09	11 59
30	18 47	19 14	19 46	09 11	10 07	11 01	11 54
35	18 59	19 28	20 04	09 03	10 00	10 56	11 51
40	19 13	19 45	20 25	08 54	09 53	10 51	11 48
45	19 29	20 05	20 52	08 43	09 44	10 45	11 44
S 50	19 50	20 32	21 32	08 30	09 34	10 37	11 39
52	19 59	20 45	21 54	08 24	09 29	10 34	11 37
54	20 10	21 01	22 25	08 17	09 23	10 30	11 35
56	20 23	21 20	23 27	08 09	09 17	10 25	11 33
58	20 38	21 44	////	08 01	09 11	10 21	11 30
S 60	20 55	22 17	////	07 51	09 03	10 15	11 27

SUN and MOON

Day	SUN Eqn. of Time 00h	SUN Eqn. of Time 12h	SUN Mer. Pass.	MOON Mer. Pass. Upper	MOON Mer. Pass. Lower	Age	Phase
d	m s	m s	h m	h m	h m	d	%
30	11 38	11 28	11 49	03 36	16 01	19	76
1	11 17	11 06	11 49	04 26	16 49	20	67
2	10 55	10 43	11 49	05 12	17 35	21	58

2015 DECEMBER 3, 4, 5 (THURS., FRI., SAT.)

UT	ARIES	VENUS −4.2		MARS +1.5		JUPITER −2.0		SATURN +0.5		STARS		
	GHA	GHA	Dec	GHA	Dec	GHA	Dec	GHA	Dec	Name	SHA	Dec
d h	° ′	° ′	° ′	° ′	° ′	° ′	° ′	° ′	° ′		° ′	° ′
3 00	71 30.4	225 13.2	S 8 30.9	239 56.7	S 3 22.5	259 07.3	N 4 29.8	185 11.9	S19 59.6	Acamar	315 16.7	S40 14.7
01	86 32.9	240 12.9	31.9	254 57.8	23.1	274 09.5	29.7	200 14.0	59.6	Achernar	335 25.3	S57 09.7
02	101 35.3	255 12.6	32.9	269 58.9	23.7	289 11.8	29.6	215 16.2	59.7	Acrux	173 07.5	S63 10.9
03	116 37.8	270 12.3	.. 33.9	285 00.0	.. 24.2	304 14.0	.. 29.6	230 18.3	.. 59.7	Adhara	255 10.9	S28 59.7
04	131 40.3	285 12.0	34.9	300 01.1	24.8	319 16.2	29.5	245 20.5	59.8	Aldebaran	290 47.1	N16 32.3
05	146 42.7	300 11.7	35.9	315 02.3	25.4	334 18.4	29.4	260 22.6	59.8			
06	161 45.2	315 11.4	S 8 36.9	330 03.4	S 3 25.9	349 20.6	N 4 29.3	275 24.8	S19 59.9	Alioth	166 19.7	N55 52.2
07	176 47.7	330 11.1	37.9	345 04.5	26.5	4 22.8	29.2	290 26.9	19 59.9	Alkaid	152 58.0	N49 14.0
T 08	191 50.1	345 10.8	38.9	0 05.6	27.1	19 25.1	29.1	305 29.1	20 00.0	Al Na'ir	27 41.8	S46 53.1
H 09	206 52.6	0 10.5	.. 39.8	15 06.7	.. 27.6	34 27.3	.. 29.0	320 31.2	.. 00.0	Alnilam	275 44.4	S 1 11.7
U 10	221 55.0	15 10.2	40.8	30 07.8	28.2	49 29.5	28.9	335 33.4	00.1	Alphard	217 54.3	S 8 43.7
R 11	236 57.5	30 09.9	41.8	45 08.9	28.8	64 31.7	28.8	350 35.6	00.1			
S 12	252 00.0	45 09.6	S 8 42.8	60 10.0	S 3 29.3	79 33.9	N 4 28.7	5 37.7	S20 00.2	Alphecca	126 10.0	N26 39.8
D 13	267 02.4	60 09.3	43.8	75 11.1	29.9	94 36.1	28.6	20 39.9	00.2	Alpheratz	357 41.6	N29 10.9
A 14	282 04.9	75 08.9	44.8	90 12.2	30.5	109 38.4	28.5	35 42.0	00.3	Altair	62 06.9	N 8 54.9
Y 15	297 07.4	90 08.6	.. 45.8	105 13.3	.. 31.0	124 40.6	.. 28.4	50 44.2	.. 00.3	Ankaa	353 14.0	S42 13.4
16	312 09.8	105 08.3	46.8	120 14.5	31.6	139 42.8	28.3	65 46.3	00.4	Antares	112 24.6	S26 27.8
17	327 12.3	120 08.0	47.8	135 15.6	32.2	154 45.0	28.2	80 48.5	00.4			
18	342 14.8	135 07.7	S 8 48.8	150 16.7	S 3 32.7	169 47.2	N 4 28.1	95 50.6	S20 00.5	Arcturus	145 54.5	N19 06.1
19	357 17.2	150 07.4	49.8	165 17.8	33.3	184 49.5	28.0	110 52.8	00.5	Atria	107 25.4	S69 03.1
20	12 19.7	165 07.1	50.8	180 18.9	33.9	199 51.7	28.0	125 54.9	00.6	Avior	234 16.8	S59 33.5
21	27 22.2	180 06.8	.. 51.8	195 20.0	.. 34.4	214 53.9	.. 27.9	140 57.1	.. 00.6	Bellatrix	278 29.9	N 6 21.6
22	42 24.6	195 06.4	52.8	210 21.1	35.0	229 56.1	27.8	155 59.2	00.7	Betelgeuse	270 59.2	N 7 24.4
23	57 27.1	210 06.1	53.8	225 22.2	35.6	244 58.3	27.7	171 01.4	00.7			
4 00	72 29.5	225 05.8	S 8 54.8	240 23.3	S 3 36.1	260 00.6	N 4 27.6	186 03.5	S20 00.8	Canopus	263 54.9	S52 42.3
01	87 32.0	240 05.5	55.7	255 24.4	36.7	275 02.8	27.5	201 05.7	00.8	Capella	280 31.5	N46 00.6
02	102 34.5	255 05.2	56.7	270 25.6	37.3	290 05.0	27.4	216 07.9	00.9	Deneb	49 30.6	N45 20.6
03	117 36.9	270 04.9	.. 57.7	285 26.7	.. 37.8	305 07.2	.. 27.3	231 10.0	.. 00.9	Denebola	182 32.1	N14 28.9
04	132 39.4	285 04.6	58.7	300 27.8	38.4	320 09.4	27.2	246 12.2	01.0	Diphda	348 54.1	S17 54.1
05	147 41.9	300 04.2	8 59.7	315 28.9	39.0	335 11.7	27.1	261 14.3	01.0			
06	162 44.3	315 03.9	S 9 00.7	330 30.0	S 3 39.5	350 13.9	N 4 27.0	276 16.5	S20 01.1	Dubhe	193 49.9	N61 39.6
07	177 46.8	330 03.6	01.7	345 31.1	40.1	5 16.1	26.9	291 18.6	01.1	Elnath	278 10.1	N28 37.0
08	192 49.3	345 03.3	02.7	0 32.2	40.7	20 18.3	26.8	306 20.8	01.2	Eltanin	90 45.9	N51 29.5
F 09	207 51.7	0 03.0	.. 03.7	15 33.3	.. 41.2	35 20.6	.. 26.7	321 22.9	.. 01.2	Enif	33 45.6	N 9 57.1
R 10	222 54.2	15 02.6	04.7	30 34.4	41.8	50 22.8	26.7	336 25.1	01.3	Fomalhaut	15 22.2	S29 32.4
I 11	237 56.7	30 02.3	05.7	45 35.5	42.4	65 25.0	26.6	351 27.2	01.3			
D 12	252 59.1	45 02.0	S 9 06.7	60 36.7	S 3 42.9	80 27.2	N 4 26.5	6 29.4	S20 01.4	Gacrux	171 59.2	S57 11.8
A 13	268 01.6	60 01.7	07.7	75 37.8	43.5	95 29.5	26.4	21 31.5	01.4	Gienah	175 50.7	S17 37.7
Y 14	283 04.0	75 01.4	08.6	90 38.9	44.1	110 31.7	26.3	36 33.7	01.5	Hadar	148 45.9	S60 26.6
15	298 06.5	90 01.0	.. 09.6	105 40.0	.. 44.6	125 33.9	.. 26.2	51 35.8	.. 01.5	Hamal	327 58.6	N23 32.3
16	313 09.0	105 00.7	10.6	120 41.1	45.2	140 36.1	26.1	66 38.0	01.5	Kaus Aust.	83 42.0	S34 22.4
17	328 11.4	120 00.4	11.6	135 42.2	45.7	155 38.4	26.0	81 40.2	01.6			
18	343 13.9	135 00.1	S 9 12.6	150 43.3	S 3 46.3	170 40.6	N 4 25.9	96 42.3	S20 01.6	Kochab	137 21.4	N74 05.4
19	358 16.4	149 59.8	13.6	165 44.4	46.9	185 42.8	25.8	111 44.5	01.7	Markab	13 36.6	N15 17.6
20	13 18.8	164 59.4	14.6	180 45.5	47.4	200 45.0	25.7	126 46.6	01.7	Menkar	314 13.0	N 4 09.0
21	28 21.3	179 59.1	.. 15.6	195 46.6	.. 48.0	215 47.3	.. 25.7	141 48.8	.. 01.8	Menkent	148 05.9	S36 26.6
22	43 23.8	194 58.8	16.6	210 47.8	48.6	230 49.5	25.6	156 50.9	01.8	Miaplacidus	221 38.7	S69 46.8
23	58 26.2	209 58.5	17.5	225 48.9	49.1	245 51.7	25.5	171 53.1	01.9			
5 00	73 28.7	224 58.1	S 9 18.5	240 50.0	S 3 49.7	260 53.9	N 4 25.4	186 55.2	S20 01.9	Mirfak	308 37.4	N49 55.0
01	88 31.1	239 57.8	19.5	255 51.1	50.3	275 56.2	25.3	201 57.4	02.0	Nunki	75 56.6	S26 16.4
02	103 33.6	254 57.5	20.5	270 52.2	50.8	290 58.4	25.2	216 59.5	02.0	Peacock	53 17.1	S56 41.0
03	118 36.1	269 57.1	.. 21.5	285 53.3	.. 51.4	306 00.6	.. 25.1	232 01.7	.. 02.1	Pollux	243 25.5	N27 59.0
04	133 38.5	284 56.8	22.5	300 54.4	51.9	321 02.8	25.0	247 03.8	02.1	Procyon	244 57.8	N 5 10.9
05	148 41.0	299 56.5	23.5	315 55.5	52.5	336 05.1	24.9	262 06.0	02.2			
06	163 43.5	314 56.2	S 9 24.5	330 56.6	S 3 53.1	351 07.3	N 4 24.8	277 08.1	S20 02.2	Rasalhague	96 05.3	N12 33.2
07	178 45.9	329 55.8	25.5	345 57.8	53.6	6 09.5	24.7	292 10.3	02.3	Regulus	207 41.7	N11 53.2
S 08	193 48.4	344 55.5	26.4	0 58.9	54.2	21 11.8	24.7	307 12.5	02.3	Rigel	281 10.1	S 8 11.2
A 09	208 50.9	359 55.2	.. 27.4	16 00.0	.. 54.8	36 14.0	.. 24.6	322 14.6	.. 02.4	Rigil Kent.	139 49.9	S60 53.7
T 10	223 53.3	14 54.8	28.4	31 01.1	55.3	51 16.2	24.5	337 16.8	02.4	Sabik	102 11.0	S15 44.4
U 11	238 55.8	29 54.5	29.4	46 02.2	55.9	66 18.4	24.4	352 18.9	02.5			
R 12	253 58.3	44 54.2	S 9 30.4	61 03.3	S 3 56.5	81 20.7	N 4 24.3	7 21.1	S20 02.5	Schedar	349 38.2	N56 37.7
D 13	269 00.7	59 53.9	31.4	76 04.4	57.0	96 22.9	24.2	22 23.2	02.6	Shaula	96 20.1	S37 06.7
A 14	284 03.2	74 53.5	32.4	91 05.5	57.6	111 25.1	24.1	37 25.4	02.6	Sirius	258 31.9	S16 44.4
Y 15	299 05.6	89 53.2	.. 33.3	106 06.6	.. 58.1	126 27.4	.. 24.0	52 27.5	.. 02.7	Spica	158 29.7	S11 14.5
16	314 08.1	104 52.9	34.3	121 07.8	58.7	141 29.6	23.9	67 29.7	02.7	Suhail	222 51.0	S43 29.7
17	329 10.6	119 52.5	35.3	136 08.9	59.3	156 31.8	23.9	82 31.8	02.8			
18	344 13.0	134 52.2	S 9 36.3	151 10.0	S 3 59.8	171 34.1	N 4 23.8	97 34.0	S20 02.8	Vega	80 38.2	N38 48.2
19	359 15.5	149 51.9	37.3	166 11.1	4 00.4	186 36.3	23.7	112 36.1	02.9	Zuben'ubi	137 03.9	S16 06.2
20	14 18.0	164 51.5	38.3	181 12.2	01.0	201 38.5	23.6	127 38.3	02.9		SHA	Mer. Pass.
21	29 20.4	179 51.2	.. 39.3	196 13.3	.. 01.5	216 40.7	.. 23.5	142 40.4	.. 02.9		° ′	h m
22	44 22.9	194 50.8	40.2	211 14.4	02.1	231 43.0	23.4	157 42.6	03.0	Venus	152 36.3	9 00
23	59 25.4	209 50.5	41.2	226 15.5	02.6	246 45.2	23.3	172 44.8	03.0	Mars	167 53.8	7 58
	h m									Jupiter	187 31.0	6 39
Mer. Pass. 19 06.9		v −0.3	d 1.0	v 1.1	d 0.6	v 2.2	d 0.1	v 2.2	d 0.0	Saturn	113 34.0	11 34

UT	SUN GHA	SUN Dec	MOON GHA	v	MOON Dec	d	HP
d h	° ′	° ′	° ′	′	° ′	′	′
3 00	182 37.8	S22 00.9	273 29.6	14.5	N 7 15.0	8.7	54.8
01	197 37.6	01.2	288 03.1	14.4	7 06.3	8.8	54.7
02	212 37.3	01.6	302 36.5	14.5	6 57.5	8.9	54.7
03	227 37.1 ..	02.0	317 10.0	14.6	6 48.6	8.8	54.7
04	242 36.8	02.3	331 43.6	14.5	6 39.8	8.9	54.7
05	257 36.6	02.7	346 17.1	14.6	6 30.9	8.9	54.7
06	272 36.3	S22 03.0	0 50.7	14.7	N 6 22.0	8.9	54.6
07	287 36.1	03.4	15 24.4	14.6	6 13.1	8.9	54.6
08	302 35.8	03.8	29 58.0	14.8	6 04.2	9.0	54.6
09	317 35.6 ..	04.1	44 31.8	14.7	5 55.2	9.0	54.6
10	332 35.4	04.5	59 05.5	14.8	5 46.2	9.0	54.6
11	347 35.1	04.8	73 39.3	14.8	5 37.2	9.0	54.6
12	2 34.9	S22 05.2	88 13.1	14.8	N 5 28.2	9.0	54.5
13	17 34.6	05.5	102 46.9	14.9	5 19.2	9.1	54.5
14	32 34.4	05.9	117 20.8	14.9	5 10.1	9.0	54.5
15	47 34.1 ..	06.2	131 54.7	14.9	5 01.1	9.1	54.5
16	62 33.9	06.6	146 28.6	14.9	4 52.0	9.1	54.5
17	77 33.6	07.0	161 02.5	15.0	4 42.9	9.1	54.5
18	92 33.4	S22 07.3	175 36.5	15.0	N 4 33.8	9.1	54.5
19	107 33.1	07.7	190 10.5	15.0	4 24.7	9.2	54.5
20	122 32.9	08.0	204 44.5	15.1	4 15.5	9.1	54.4
21	137 32.7 ..	08.3	219 18.6	15.0	4 06.4	9.2	54.4
22	152 32.4	08.7	233 52.6	15.1	3 57.2	9.2	54.4
23	167 32.2	09.0	248 26.7	15.1	3 48.0	9.2	54.4
4 00	182 31.9	S22 09.4	263 00.8	15.2	N 3 38.8	9.2	54.4
01	197 31.7	09.7	277 35.0	15.1	3 29.6	9.2	54.4
02	212 31.4	10.1	292 09.1	15.2	3 20.4	9.2	54.4
03	227 31.2 ..	10.4	306 43.3	15.2	3 11.2	9.2	54.4
04	242 30.9	10.8	321 17.5	15.2	3 02.0	9.3	54.3
05	257 30.7	11.1	335 51.7	15.2	2 52.7	9.2	54.3
06	272 30.4	S22 11.4	350 25.9	15.3	N 2 43.5	9.3	54.3
07	287 30.2	11.8	5 00.2	15.2	2 34.2	9.2	54.3
08	302 29.9	12.1	19 34.4	15.3	2 25.0	9.3	54.3
09	317 29.7 ..	12.5	34 08.7	15.3	2 15.7	9.3	54.3
10	332 29.4	12.8	48 43.0	15.3	2 06.4	9.3	54.3
11	347 29.2	13.1	63 17.3	15.3	1 57.1	9.2	54.3
12	2 28.9	S22 13.5	77 51.6	15.3	N 1 47.9	9.3	54.3
13	17 28.7	13.8	92 25.9	15.4	1 38.6	9.3	54.3
14	32 28.4	14.2	107 00.3	15.3	1 29.3	9.3	54.3
15	47 28.2 ..	14.5	121 34.6	15.4	1 20.0	9.3	54.2
16	62 27.9	14.8	136 09.0	15.4	1 10.7	9.4	54.2
17	77 27.6	15.2	150 43.4	15.3	1 01.3	9.3	54.2
18	92 27.4	S22 15.5	165 17.7	15.4	N 0 52.0	9.3	54.2
19	107 27.1	15.8	179 52.1	15.4	0 42.7	9.3	54.2
20	122 26.9	16.2	194 26.5	15.4	0 33.4	9.3	54.2
21	137 26.6 ..	16.5	209 00.9	15.4	0 24.1	9.3	54.2
22	152 26.4	16.8	223 35.3	15.4	0 14.8	9.3	54.2
23	167 26.1	17.1	238 09.7	15.4	N 0 05.5	9.4	54.2
5 00	182 25.9	S22 17.5	252 44.1	15.4	S 0 03.9	9.3	54.2
01	197 25.6	17.8	267 18.5	15.4	0 13.2	9.3	54.2
02	212 25.4	18.1	281 52.9	15.4	0 22.5	9.3	54.2
03	227 25.1 ..	18.4	296 27.3	15.5	0 31.8	9.3	54.2
04	242 24.8	18.8	311 01.8	15.4	0 41.1	9.3	54.2
05	257 24.6	19.1	325 36.2	15.4	0 50.4	9.3	54.2
06	272 24.3	S22 19.4	340 10.6	15.4	S 0 59.7	9.3	54.2
07	287 24.1	19.7	354 45.0	15.4	1 09.0	9.3	54.2
08	302 23.8	20.1	9 19.4	15.4	1 18.3	9.3	54.2
09	317 23.6 ..	20.4	23 53.8	15.4	1 27.6	9.3	54.2
10	332 23.3	20.7	38 28.2	15.4	1 36.9	9.3	54.2
11	347 23.1	21.0	53 02.6	15.4	1 46.2	9.2	54.2
12	2 22.8	S22 21.3	67 37.0	15.4	S 1 55.4	9.3	54.2
13	17 22.5	21.7	82 11.4	15.4	2 04.7	9.2	54.2
14	32 22.3	22.0	96 45.8	15.3	2 13.9	9.3	54.2
15	47 22.0 ..	22.3	111 20.1	15.4	2 23.2	9.2	54.2
16	62 21.8	22.6	125 54.5	15.4	2 32.4	9.2	54.2
17	77 21.5	22.9	140 28.9	15.3	2 41.6	9.3	54.2
18	92 21.2	S22 23.2	155 03.2	15.3	S 2 50.9	9.2	54.2
19	107 21.0	23.6	169 37.5	15.4	3 00.1	9.2	54.2
20	122 20.7	23.9	184 11.9	15.3	3 09.3	9.2	54.2
21	137 20.5 ..	24.2	198 46.2	15.3	3 18.5	9.1	54.2
22	152 20.2	24.5	213 20.5	15.3	3 27.6	9.2	54.2
23	167 19.9	24.8	227 54.8	15.2	S 3 36.8	9.1	54.2
	SD 16.3	d 0.3	SD 14.9		14.8		14.8

THURSDAY / FRIDAY / SATURDAY

Lat.	Twilight Naut.	Twilight Civil	Sunrise	Moonrise 3	4	5	6
°	h m	h m	h m	h m	h m	h m	h m
N 72	07 58	10 02	■■	23 43	25 16	01 16	02 48
N 70	07 41	09 19	■■	23 48	25 15	01 15	02 42
68	07 27	08 51	10 53	23 52	25 15	01 15	02 37
66	07 15	08 29	09 56	23 56	25 14	01 14	02 33
64	07 06	08 12	09 23	23 59	25 14	01 14	02 29
62	06 57	07 57	08 59	24 01	00 01	01 14	02 26
60	06 50	07 45	08 40	24 04	00 04	01 14	02 24
N 58	06 43	07 34	08 24	24 05	00 05	01 13	02 21
56	06 37	07 25	08 11	24 07	00 07	01 13	02 19
54	06 31	07 17	07 59	24 09	00 09	01 13	02 17
52	06 26	07 09	07 49	24 10	00 10	01 13	02 16
50	06 21	07 02	07 40	24 12	00 12	01 13	02 14
45	06 11	06 47	07 21	24 14	00 14	01 13	02 11
N 40	06 01	06 35	07 05	24 17	00 17	01 12	02 08
35	05 53	06 24	06 52	24 19	00 19	01 12	02 06
30	05 45	06 14	06 40	24 21	00 21	01 12	02 03
20	05 29	05 56	06 20	24 24	00 24	01 12	02 00
N 10	05 14	05 40	06 03	24 27	00 27	01 12	01 57
0	04 58	05 24	05 46	24 29	00 29	01 11	01 54
S 10	04 40	05 07	05 30	24 32	00 32	01 11	01 51
20	04 19	04 48	05 12	24 35	00 35	01 11	01 48
30	03 51	04 24	04 51	00 03	00 38	01 11	01 44
35	03 34	04 10	04 39	00 07	00 39	01 11	01 42
40	03 12	03 53	04 25	00 11	00 42	01 11	01 40
45	02 44	03 32	04 08	00 16	00 44	01 11	01 37
S 50	02 03	03 04	03 47	00 22	00 47	01 10	01 34
52	01 40	02 51	03 37	00 25	00 48	01 10	01 33
54	01 08	02 35	03 26	00 27	00 49	01 10	01 31
56	////	02 15	03 13	00 31	00 51	01 10	01 30
58	////	01 50	02 58	00 34	00 53	01 10	01 28
S 60	////	01 15	02 40	00 38	00 55	01 10	01 26

Lat.	Sunset	Twilight Civil	Twilight Naut.	Moonset 3	4	5	6
°	h m	h m	h m	h m	h m	h m	h m
N 72	■■	13 37	15 42	13 14	13 09	13 04	12 59
N 70	■■	14 20	15 59	13 07	13 07	13 07	13 07
68	12 47	14 49	16 13	13 01	13 06	13 10	13 14
66	13 44	15 11	16 24	12 56	13 04	13 12	13 20
64	14 17	15 28	16 34	12 52	13 03	13 13	13 24
62	14 41	15 42	16 42	12 48	13 02	13 15	13 28
60	15 00	15 55	16 50	12 45	13 01	13 16	13 32
N 58	15 15	16 05	16 57	12 42	13 00	13 17	13 35
56	15 29	16 15	17 03	12 40	12 59	13 19	13 38
54	15 40	16 23	17 08	12 37	12 59	13 19	13 41
52	15 51	16 31	17 14	12 35	12 58	13 20	13 43
50	16 00	16 37	17 18	12 33	12 57	13 21	13 45
45	16 19	16 52	17 29	12 29	12 56	13 23	13 50
N 40	16 35	17 05	17 39	12 26	12 55	13 24	13 54
35	16 48	17 16	17 47	12 23	12 54	13 26	13 57
30	17 00	17 26	17 55	12 20	12 53	13 27	14 00
20	17 20	17 44	18 11	12 15	12 52	13 29	14 05
N 10	17 37	18 00	18 26	12 11	12 51	13 30	14 10
0	17 54	18 16	18 42	12 07	12 50	13 32	14 14
S 10	18 10	18 33	19 00	12 03	12 48	13 33	14 19
20	18 28	18 53	19 22	11 59	12 47	13 35	14 23
30	18 49	19 16	19 49	11 54	12 46	13 37	14 28
35	19 01	19 31	20 07	11 51	12 45	13 38	14 31
40	19 16	19 48	20 28	11 48	12 44	13 39	14 35
45	19 32	20 09	20 57	11 44	12 42	13 41	14 39
S 50	19 54	20 37	21 38	11 39	12 41	13 42	14 44
52	20 04	20 50	22 01	11 37	12 40	13 43	14 46
54	20 15	21 07	22 35	11 35	12 40	13 44	14 48
56	20 28	21 28	////	11 33	12 39	13 45	14 51
58	20 43	21 52	////	11 30	12 38	13 46	14 54
S 60	21 01	22 28	////	11 27	12 37	13 47	14 57

Day	SUN Eqn. of Time 00ʰ	SUN Eqn. of Time 12ʰ	SUN Mer. Pass.	MOON Mer. Pass. Upper	MOON Mer. Pass. Lower	Age	Phase
d	m s	m s	h m	h m	h m	d	%
3	10 32	10 20	11 50	05 57	18 18	22	48
4	10 08	09 56	11 50	06 39	19 01	23	39
5	09 44	09 32	11 50	07 22	19 43	24	30

2015 DECEMBER 6, 7, 8 (SUN., MON., TUES.)

UT	ARIES GHA	VENUS −4.2 GHA	Dec	MARS +1.5 GHA	Dec	JUPITER −2.0 GHA	Dec	SATURN +0.5 GHA	Dec	STARS Name	SHA	Dec
6 00	74 27.8	224 50.2	S 9 42.2	241 16.6	S 4 03.2	261 47.4	N 4 23.2	187 46.9	S20 03.1	Acamar	315 16.8	S40 14.7
01	89 30.3	239 49.8	43.2	256 17.8	03.8	276 49.7	23.2	202 49.1	03.1	Achernar	335 25.3	S57 09.7
02	104 32.8	254 49.5	44.2	271 18.9	04.3	291 51.9	23.1	217 51.2	03.2	Acrux	173 07.5	S63 10.9
03	119 35.2	269 49.2	.. 45.2	286 20.0	.. 04.9	306 54.1	.. 23.0	232 53.4	.. 03.2	Adhara	255 10.9	S28 59.7
04	134 37.7	284 48.8	46.2	301 21.1	05.4	321 56.4	22.9	247 55.5	03.3	Aldebaran	290 47.1	N16 32.3
05	149 40.1	299 48.5	47.1	316 22.2	06.0	336 58.6	22.8	262 57.7	03.3			
06	164 42.6	314 48.1	S 9 48.1	331 23.3	S 4 06.6	352 00.8	N 4 22.7	277 59.8	S20 03.4	Alioth	166 19.6	N55 52.2
07	179 45.1	329 47.8	49.1	346 24.4	07.1	7 03.1	22.6	293 02.0	03.4	Alkaid	152 58.0	N49 14.0
08	194 47.5	344 47.5	50.1	1 25.5	07.7	22 05.3	22.5	308 04.1	03.5	Al Na'ir	27 41.9	S46 53.1
S 09	209 50.0	359 47.1	.. 51.1	16 26.7	.. 08.3	37 07.6	.. 22.5	323 06.3	.. 03.5	Alnilam	275 44.3	S 1 11.7
U 10	224 52.5	14 46.8	52.0	31 27.8	08.8	52 09.8	22.4	338 08.4	03.6	Alphard	217 54.3	S 8 43.7
N 11	239 54.9	29 46.4	53.0	46 28.9	09.4	67 12.0	22.3	353 10.6	03.6			
D 12	254 57.4	44 46.1	S 9 54.0	61 30.0	S 4 09.9	82 14.3	N 4 22.2	8 12.8	S20 03.7	Alphecca	126 10.0	N26 39.8
A 13	269 59.9	59 45.8	55.0	76 31.1	10.5	97 16.5	22.1	23 14.9	03.7	Alpheratz	357 41.6	N29 10.9
Y 14	285 02.3	74 45.4	56.0	91 32.2	11.1	112 18.7	22.0	38 17.1	03.8	Altair	62 06.9	N 8 54.9
15	300 04.8	89 45.1	.. 57.0	106 33.3	.. 11.6	127 21.0	.. 21.9	53 19.2	.. 03.8	Ankaa	353 14.0	S42 13.4
16	315 07.2	104 44.7	57.9	121 34.4	12.2	142 23.2	21.9	68 21.4	03.9	Antares	112 24.6	S26 27.8
17	330 09.7	119 44.4	58.9	136 35.6	12.7	157 25.4	21.8	83 23.5	03.9			
18	345 12.2	134 44.0	S 9 59.9	151 36.7	S 4 13.3	172 27.7	N 4 21.7	98 25.7	S20 04.0	Arcturus	145 54.5	N19 06.1
19	0 14.6	149 43.7	10 00.9	166 37.8	13.9	187 29.9	21.6	113 27.8	04.0	Atria	107 25.4	S69 03.1
20	15 17.1	164 43.3	01.9	181 38.9	14.4	202 32.2	21.5	128 30.0	04.0	Avior	234 16.8	S59 33.5
21	30 19.6	179 43.0	.. 02.8	196 40.0	.. 15.0	217 34.4	.. 21.4	143 32.1	.. 04.1	Bellatrix	278 29.9	N 6 21.6
22	45 22.0	194 42.7	03.8	211 41.1	15.5	232 36.6	21.3	158 34.3	04.1	Betelgeuse	270 59.2	N 7 24.4
23	60 24.5	209 42.3	04.8	226 42.2	16.1	247 38.9	21.3	173 36.4	04.2			
7 00	75 27.0	224 42.0	S10 05.8	241 43.4	S 4 16.7	262 41.1	N 4 21.2	188 38.6	S20 04.2	Canopus	263 54.9	S52 42.3
01	90 29.4	239 41.6	06.8	256 44.5	17.2	277 43.3	21.1	203 40.8	04.3	Capella	280 31.5	N46 00.6
02	105 31.9	254 41.3	07.7	271 45.6	17.8	292 45.6	21.0	218 42.9	04.3	Deneb	49 30.6	N45 20.6
03	120 34.4	269 40.9	.. 08.7	286 46.7	.. 18.3	307 47.8	.. 20.9	233 45.1	.. 04.4	Denebola	182 32.1	N14 28.9
04	135 36.8	284 40.6	09.7	301 47.8	18.9	322 50.1	20.8	248 47.2	04.4	Diphda	348 54.1	S17 54.1
05	150 39.3	299 40.2	10.7	316 48.9	19.5	337 52.3	20.7	263 49.4	04.5			
06	165 41.7	314 39.9	S10 11.6	331 50.0	S 4 20.0	352 54.5	N 4 20.7	278 51.5	S20 04.5	Dubhe	193 49.8	N61 39.6
07	180 44.2	329 39.5	12.6	346 51.1	20.6	7 56.8	20.6	293 53.7	04.6	Elnath	278 10.1	N28 37.0
08	195 46.7	344 39.2	13.6	1 52.3	21.1	22 59.0	20.5	308 55.8	04.6	Eltanin	90 45.9	N51 29.5
M 09	210 49.1	359 38.8	.. 14.6	16 53.4	.. 21.7	38 01.3	.. 20.4	323 58.0	.. 04.7	Enif	33 45.6	N 9 57.1
O 10	225 51.6	14 38.5	15.6	31 54.5	22.3	53 03.5	20.3	339 00.1	04.7	Fomalhaut	15 22.2	S29 32.4
N 11	240 54.1	29 38.1	16.5	46 55.6	22.8	68 05.7	20.2	354 02.3	04.8			
D 12	255 56.5	44 37.7	S10 17.5	61 56.7	S 4 23.4	83 08.0	N 4 20.2	9 04.4	S20 04.8	Gacrux	171 59.1	S57 11.8
A 13	270 59.0	59 37.4	18.5	76 57.8	23.9	98 10.2	20.1	24 06.6	04.9	Gienah	175 50.7	S17 37.7
Y 14	286 01.5	74 37.0	19.5	91 58.9	24.5	113 12.5	20.0	39 08.8	04.9	Hadar	148 45.9	S60 26.6
15	301 03.9	89 36.7	.. 20.4	107 00.1	.. 25.0	128 14.7	.. 19.9	54 10.9	.. 05.0	Hamal	327 58.6	N23 32.3
16	316 06.4	104 36.3	21.4	122 01.2	25.6	143 17.0	19.8	69 13.1	05.0	Kaus Aust.	83 42.0	S34 22.4
17	331 08.9	119 36.0	22.4	137 02.3	26.2	158 19.2	19.7	84 15.2	05.0			
18	346 11.3	134 35.6	S10 23.4	152 03.4	S 4 26.7	173 21.4	N 4 19.7	99 17.4	S20 05.1	Kochab	137 21.3	N74 05.4
19	1 13.8	149 35.3	24.3	167 04.5	27.3	188 23.7	19.6	114 19.5	05.1	Markab	13 36.7	N15 17.6
20	16 16.2	164 34.9	25.3	182 05.6	27.8	203 25.9	19.5	129 21.7	05.2	Menkar	314 13.0	N 4 09.0
21	31 18.7	179 34.5	.. 26.3	197 06.7	.. 28.4	218 28.2	.. 19.4	144 23.8	.. 05.2	Menkent	148 05.9	S36 26.6
22	46 21.2	194 34.2	27.3	212 07.9	29.0	233 30.4	19.3	159 26.0	05.3	Miaplacidus	221 38.7	S69 46.8
23	61 23.6	209 33.8	28.2	227 09.0	29.5	248 32.7	19.2	174 28.1	05.3			
8 00	76 26.1	224 33.5	S10 29.2	242 10.1	S 4 30.1	263 34.9	N 4 19.2	189 30.3	S20 05.4	Mirfak	308 37.4	N49 55.0
01	91 28.6	239 33.1	30.2	257 11.2	30.6	278 37.1	19.1	204 32.4	05.4	Nunki	75 56.6	S26 16.4
02	106 31.0	254 32.8	31.2	272 12.3	31.2	293 39.4	19.0	219 34.6	05.5	Peacock	53 17.1	S56 41.0
03	121 33.5	269 32.4	.. 32.1	287 13.4	.. 31.7	308 41.6	.. 18.9	234 36.8	.. 05.5	Pollux	243 25.4	N27 59.0
04	136 36.0	284 32.0	33.1	302 14.5	32.3	323 43.9	18.8	249 38.9	05.6	Procyon	244 57.7	N 5 10.9
05	151 38.4	299 31.7	34.1	317 15.7	32.9	338 46.1	18.7	264 41.1	05.6			
06	166 40.9	314 31.3	S10 35.0	332 16.8	S 4 33.4	353 48.4	N 4 18.7	279 43.2	S20 05.7	Rasalhague	96 05.3	N12 33.2
07	181 43.3	329 30.9	36.0	347 17.9	34.0	8 50.6	18.6	294 45.4	05.7	Regulus	207 41.7	N11 53.2
08	196 45.8	344 30.6	37.0	2 19.0	34.5	23 52.9	18.5	309 47.5	05.8	Rigel	281 10.1	S 8 11.2
T 09	211 48.3	359 30.2	.. 38.0	17 20.1	.. 35.1	38 55.1	.. 18.4	324 49.7	.. 05.8	Rigil Kent.	139 49.9	S60 53.7
U 10	226 50.7	14 29.9	38.9	32 21.2	35.6	53 57.4	18.3	339 51.8	05.8	Sabik	102 11.0	S15 44.4
E 11	241 53.2	29 29.5	39.9	47 22.3	36.2	68 59.6	18.3	354 54.0	05.9			
S 12	256 55.7	44 29.1	S10 40.9	62 23.5	S 4 36.8	84 01.9	N 4 18.2	9 56.1	S20 05.9	Schedar	349 38.2	N56 37.7
D 13	271 58.1	59 28.8	41.8	77 24.6	37.3	99 04.1	18.1	24 58.3	06.0	Shaula	96 20.1	S37 06.7
A 14	287 00.6	74 28.4	42.8	92 25.7	37.9	114 06.4	18.0	40 00.4	06.0	Sirius	258 31.9	S16 44.4
Y 15	302 03.1	89 28.0	.. 43.8	107 26.8	.. 38.4	129 08.6	.. 17.9	55 02.6	.. 06.1	Spica	158 29.7	S11 14.5
16	317 05.5	104 27.7	44.7	122 27.9	39.0	144 10.9	17.8	70 04.8	06.1	Suhail	222 50.9	S43 29.7
17	332 08.0	119 27.3	45.7	137 29.0	39.5	159 13.1	17.8	85 06.9	06.2			
18	347 10.5	134 26.9	S10 46.7	152 30.1	S 4 40.1	174 15.3	N 4 17.7	100 09.1	S20 06.2	Vega	80 38.2	N38 48.2
19	2 12.9	149 26.6	47.7	167 31.3	40.7	189 17.6	17.6	115 11.2	06.3	Zuben'ubi	137 03.9	S16 06.2
20	17 15.4	164 26.2	48.6	182 32.4	41.2	204 19.8	17.5	130 13.4	06.3		SHA	Mer. Pass.
21	32 17.8	179 25.8	.. 49.6	197 33.5	.. 41.8	219 22.1	.. 17.4	145 15.5	.. 06.4	Venus	149 15.0	9 01
22	47 20.3	194 25.5	50.6	212 34.6	42.3	234 24.3	17.4	160 17.7	06.4	Mars	166 16.4	7 53
23	62 22.8	209 25.1	51.5	227 35.7	42.9	249 26.6	17.3	175 19.8	06.5	Jupiter	187 14.1	6 28
Mer. Pass. 18 55.1		v −0.4	d 1.0	v 1.1	d 0.6	v 2.2	d 0.1	v 2.2	d 0.0	Saturn	113 11.6	11 24

UT	SUN GHA	Dec	MOON GHA	v	Dec	d	HP
d h	° '	° '	° '	'	° '	'	'
6 00	182 19.7	S22 25.1	242 29.0	15.3	S 3 45.9	9.2	54.2
01	197 19.4	25.4	257 03.3	15.2	3 55.1	9.1	54.2
02	212 19.2	25.7	271 37.5	15.2	4 04.2	9.1	54.2
03	227 18.9 ..	26.0	286 11.7	15.3	4 13.3	9.1	54.2
04	242 18.6	26.3	300 46.0	15.1	4 22.4	9.1	54.2
05	257 18.4	26.7	315 20.1	15.2	4 31.5	9.0	54.2
06	272 18.1	S22 27.0	329 54.3	15.2	S 4 40.5	9.1	54.2
07	287 17.9	27.3	344 28.5	15.1	4 49.6	9.0	54.2
08	302 17.6	27.6	359 02.6	15.1	4 58.6	9.0	54.2
09	317 17.3 ..	27.9	13 36.7	15.1	5 07.6	9.0	54.2
10	332 17.1	28.2	28 10.8	15.1	5 16.6	9.0	54.2
11	347 16.8	28.5	42 44.9	15.0	5 25.6	8.9	54.2
12	2 16.5	S22 28.8	57 18.9	15.1	S 5 34.5	9.0	54.2
13	17 16.3	29.1	71 53.0	15.0	5 43.5	8.9	54.2
14	32 16.0	29.4	86 27.0	15.0	5 52.4	8.9	54.2
15	47 15.7 ..	29.7	101 01.0	14.9	6 01.3	8.9	54.2
16	62 15.5	30.0	115 34.9	14.9	6 10.2	8.8	54.3
17	77 15.2	30.3	130 08.8	14.9	6 19.0	8.8	54.3
18	92 15.0	S22 30.6	144 42.7	14.9	S 6 27.8	8.8	54.3
19	107 14.7	30.9	159 16.6	14.9	6 36.6	8.8	54.3
20	122 14.4	31.2	173 50.5	14.8	6 45.4	8.8	54.3
21	137 14.2 ..	31.4	188 24.3	14.8	6 54.2	8.7	54.3
22	152 13.9	31.7	202 58.1	14.8	7 02.9	8.7	54.3
23	167 13.6	32.0	217 31.9	14.7	7 11.6	8.7	54.3
7 00	182 13.4	S22 32.3	232 05.6	14.7	S 7 20.3	8.6	54.3
01	197 13.1	32.6	246 39.3	14.7	7 28.9	8.7	54.3
02	212 12.8	32.9	261 13.0	14.6	7 37.6	8.6	54.3
03	227 12.6 ..	33.2	275 46.6	14.6	7 46.2	8.5	54.3
04	242 12.3	33.5	290 20.2	14.6	7 54.7	8.6	54.4
05	257 12.0	33.8	304 53.8	14.6	8 03.3	8.5	54.4
06	272 11.8	S22 34.1	319 27.4	14.5	S 8 11.8	8.5	54.4
07	287 11.5	34.3	334 00.9	14.5	8 20.3	8.4	54.4
08	302 11.2	34.6	348 34.4	14.4	8 28.7	8.4	54.4
09	317 11.0 ..	34.9	3 07.8	14.4	8 37.1	8.4	54.4
10	332 10.7	35.2	17 41.2	14.4	8 45.5	8.4	54.4
11	347 10.4	35.5	32 14.6	14.3	8 53.9	8.3	54.4
12	2 10.1	S22 35.8	46 47.9	14.3	S 9 02.2	8.3	54.4
13	17 09.9	36.0	61 21.2	14.3	9 10.5	8.2	54.4
14	32 09.6	36.3	75 54.5	14.2	9 18.7	8.2	54.5
15	47 09.3 ..	36.6	90 27.7	14.2	9 26.9	8.2	54.5
16	62 09.1	36.9	105 00.9	14.1	9 35.1	8.2	54.5
17	77 08.8	37.2	119 34.0	14.1	9 43.3	8.1	54.5
18	92 08.5	S22 37.4	134 07.1	14.1	S 9 51.4	8.1	54.5
19	107 08.3	37.7	148 40.2	14.0	9 59.4	8.1	54.5
20	122 08.0	38.0	163 13.2	14.0	10 07.5	8.0	54.5
21	137 07.7 ..	38.3	177 46.2	13.9	10 15.5	7.9	54.5
22	152 07.4	38.5	192 19.1	13.9	10 23.4	7.9	54.6
23	167 07.2	38.8	206 52.0	13.9	10 31.3	7.9	54.6
8 00	182 06.9	S22 39.1	221 24.9	13.8	S10 39.2	7.8	54.6
01	197 06.6	39.4	235 57.7	13.8	10 47.0	7.8	54.6
02	212 06.4	39.6	250 30.5	13.7	10 54.8	7.8	54.6
03	227 06.1 ..	39.9	265 03.2	13.7	11 02.6	7.7	54.6
04	242 05.8	40.2	279 35.9	13.6	11 10.3	7.6	54.6
05	257 05.5	40.4	294 08.5	13.6	11 17.9	7.6	54.7
06	272 05.3	S22 40.7	308 41.1	13.6	S11 25.5	7.6	54.7
07	287 05.0	41.0	323 13.7	13.5	11 33.1	7.5	54.7
08	302 04.7	41.3	337 46.2	13.5	11 40.6	7.5	54.7
09	317 04.4 ..	41.5	352 18.7	13.4	11 48.1	7.4	54.7
10	332 04.2	41.8	6 51.1	13.3	11 55.5	7.4	54.7
11	347 03.9	42.0	21 23.4	13.4	12 02.9	7.4	54.7
12	2 03.6	S22 42.3	35 55.8	13.2	S12 10.3	7.2	54.8
13	17 03.4	42.6	50 28.0	13.3	12 17.5	7.3	54.8
14	32 03.1	42.8	65 00.3	13.1	12 24.8	7.1	54.8
15	47 02.8 ..	43.1	79 32.4	13.2	12 31.9	7.2	54.8
16	62 02.5	43.4	94 04.6	13.0	12 39.1	7.1	54.8
17	77 02.3	43.6	108 36.6	13.1	12 46.2	7.0	54.8
18	92 02.0	S22 43.9	123 08.7	12.9	S12 53.2	7.0	54.9
19	107 01.7	44.1	137 40.6	13.0	13 00.2	6.9	54.9
20	122 01.4	44.4	152 12.6	12.9	13 07.1	6.8	54.9
21	137 01.2 ..	44.7	166 44.5	12.8	13 13.9	6.8	54.9
22	152 00.9	44.9	181 16.3	12.8	13 20.7	6.8	54.9
23	167 00.6	45.2	195 48.1	12.7	S13 27.5	6.7	54.9
	SD 16.3	d 0.3	SD 14.8		14.8		14.9

Day labels: SUNDAY (06h block), MONDAY (7 00h block), TUESDAY (8 00h block).

Lat.	Twilight Naut.	Twilight Civil	Sunrise	Moonrise 6	7	8	9
°	h m	h m	h m	h m	h m	h m	h m
N 72	08 05	10 16	■■■	02 48	04 23	06 01	07 44
N 70	07 47	09 28	■■■	02 42	04 10	05 40	07 13
68	07 33	08 58	11 16	02 37	04 00	05 25	06 50
66	07 21	08 35	10 06	02 33	03 52	05 12	06 32
64	07 10	08 17	09 30	02 29	03 45	05 01	06 17
62	07 02	08 02	09 05	02 26	03 39	04 52	06 05
60	06 54	07 50	08 45	02 24	03 34	04 45	05 55
N 58	06 47	07 39	08 29	02 21	03 29	04 38	05 46
56	06 41	07 29	08 15	02 19	03 25	04 32	05 38
54	06 35	07 20	08 03	02 17	03 22	04 27	05 31
52	06 30	07 13	07 53	02 16	03 19	04 22	05 25
50	06 25	07 06	07 44	02 14	03 16	04 17	05 19
45	06 14	06 50	07 24	02 11	03 09	04 08	05 07
N 40	06 04	06 38	07 08	02 08	03 04	04 00	04 57
35	05 55	06 26	06 54	02 06	02 59	03 54	04 49
30	05 47	06 16	06 42	02 03	02 55	03 48	04 41
20	05 31	05 58	06 22	02 00	02 48	03 38	04 29
N 10	05 15	05 42	06 05	01 57	02 42	03 29	04 17
0	04 59	05 25	05 48	01 54	02 37	03 21	04 07
S 10	04 41	05 08	05 31	01 51	02 31	03 13	03 56
20	04 19	04 48	05 13	01 48	02 25	03 04	03 45
30	03 51	04 24	04 51	01 44	02 18	02 54	03 33
35	03 33	04 10	04 39	01 42	02 14	02 49	03 26
40	03 11	03 52	04 25	01 40	02 10	02 42	03 17
45	02 42	03 31	04 07	01 37	02 05	02 35	03 08
S 50	02 00	03 03	03 46	01 34	01 59	02 26	02 56
52	01 36	02 48	03 36	01 33	01 56	02 22	02 51
54	01 01	02 32	03 24	01 31	01 53	02 17	02 45
56	////	02 12	03 11	01 30	01 50	02 12	02 39
58	////	01 46	02 55	01 28	01 46	02 07	02 31
S 60	////	01 07	02 37	01 26	01 42	02 01	02 23

Lat.	Sunset	Twilight Civil	Twilight Naut.	Moonset 6	7	8	9
°	h m	h m	h m	h m	h m	h m	h m
N 72	■■■	13 27	15 37	12 59	12 54	12 48	12 41
N 70	■■■	14 14	15 55	13 07	13 08	13 10	13 13
68	12 27	14 44	16 10	13 14	13 19	13 26	13 37
66	13 37	15 07	16 22	13 20	13 29	13 40	13 56
64	14 12	15 25	16 32	13 24	13 37	13 52	14 11
62	14 37	15 40	16 41	13 28	13 43	14 01	14 23
60	14 57	15 53	16 48	13 32	13 49	14 10	14 34
N 58	15 13	16 04	16 55	13 35	13 55	14 17	14 44
56	15 27	16 13	17 02	13 38	13 59	14 23	14 52
54	15 39	16 22	17 08	13 41	14 04	14 29	14 59
52	15 49	16 30	17 13	13 43	14 07	14 35	15 06
50	15 59	16 37	17 18	13 45	14 11	14 39	15 12
45	16 18	16 52	17 29	13 50	14 18	14 50	15 25
N 40	16 35	17 05	17 39	13 54	14 25	14 58	15 35
35	16 48	17 16	17 48	13 57	14 30	15 06	15 44
30	17 00	17 26	17 56	14 00	14 35	15 12	15 52
20	17 20	17 44	18 12	14 05	14 43	15 24	16 06
N 10	17 38	18 01	18 27	14 10	14 51	15 33	16 18
0	17 55	18 17	18 44	14 14	14 58	15 43	16 30
S 10	18 12	18 35	19 02	14 19	15 05	15 52	16 41
20	18 30	18 55	19 24	14 23	15 12	16 02	16 53
30	18 51	19 19	19 52	14 28	15 20	16 13	17 07
35	19 04	19 33	20 10	14 31	15 25	16 20	17 15
40	19 18	19 51	20 32	14 35	15 31	16 28	17 25
45	19 36	20 12	21 01	14 39	15 37	16 36	17 36
S 50	19 57	20 41	21 43	14 44	15 45	16 47	17 49
52	20 07	20 55	22 08	14 46	15 49	16 52	17 55
54	20 19	21 12	22 44	14 49	15 53	16 58	18 02
56	20 33	21 32	////	14 51	15 57	17 03	18 09
58	20 48	21 59	////	14 54	16 02	17 10	18 18
S 60	21 07	22 38	////	14 57	16 08	17 18	18 27

Day	SUN Eqn. of Time 00h	12h	Mer. Pass.	MOON Mer. Pass. Upper	Lower	Age	Phase
d	m s	m s	h m	h m	h m	d	%
6	09 19	09 07	11 51	08 04	20 25	25	22
7	08 54	08 41	11 51	08 47	21 09	26	15
8	08 28	08 15	11 52	09 32	21 55	27	9

UT	ARIES	VENUS −4.2		MARS +1.5		JUPITER −2.0		SATURN +0.5		STARS		
	GHA	GHA	Dec	GHA	Dec	GHA	Dec	GHA	Dec	Name	SHA	Dec
d h	° ′	° ′	° ′	° ′	° ′	° ′	° ′	° ′	° ′		° ′	° ′
9 00	77 25.2	224 24.7	S10 52.5	242 36.8	S 4 43.4	264 28.9	N 4 17.2	190 22.0	S20 06.5	Acamar	315 16.8	S40 14.7
01	92 27.7	239 24.3	53.5	257 38.0	44.0	279 31.1	17.1	205 24.1	06.6	Achernar	335 25.3	S57 09.7
02	107 30.2	254 24.0	54.4	272 39.1	44.5	294 33.4	17.0	220 26.3	06.6	Acrux	173 07.4	S63 10.9
03	122 32.6	269 23.6	.. 55.4	287 40.2	.. 45.1	309 35.6	.. 17.0	235 28.5	.. 06.6	Adhara	255 10.9	S28 59.7
04	137 35.1	284 23.2	56.4	302 41.3	45.7	324 37.9	16.9	250 30.6	06.7	Aldebaran	290 47.1	N16 32.3
05	152 37.6	299 22.9	57.3	317 42.4	46.2	339 40.1	16.8	265 32.8	06.7			
W 06	167 40.0	314 22.5	S10 58.3	332 43.5	S 4 46.8	354 42.4	N 4 16.7	280 34.9	S20 06.8	Alioth	166 19.6	N55 52.2
E 07	182 42.5	329 22.1	10 59.3	347 44.6	47.3	9 44.6	16.6	295 37.1	06.8	Alkaid	152 58.0	N49 13.9
D 08	197 45.0	344 21.7	11 00.2	2 45.8	47.9	24 46.9	16.6	310 39.2	06.9	Al Na'ir	27 41.9	S46 53.1
N 09	212 47.4	359 21.4	.. 01.2	17 46.9	.. 48.4	39 49.1	.. 16.5	325 41.4	.. 06.9	Alnilam	275 44.3	S 1 11.7
E 10	227 49.9	14 21.0	02.2	32 48.0	49.0	54 51.4	16.4	340 43.5	07.0	Alphard	217 54.3	S 8 43.7
S 11	242 52.3	29 20.6	03.1	47 49.1	49.5	69 53.6	16.3	355 45.7	07.0			
D 12	257 54.8	44 20.2	S11 04.1	62 50.2	S 4 50.1	84 55.9	N 4 16.3	10 47.8	S20 07.1	Alphecca	126 10.0	N26 39.8
A 13	272 57.3	59 19.9	05.0	77 51.3	50.6	99 58.1	16.2	25 50.0	07.1	Alpheratz	357 41.6	N29 10.9
Y 14	287 59.7	74 19.5	06.0	92 52.5	51.2	115 00.4	16.1	40 52.2	07.2	Altair	62 06.9	N 8 54.9
15	303 02.2	89 19.1	.. 07.0	107 53.6	.. 51.8	130 02.6	.. 16.0	55 54.3	.. 07.2	Ankaa	353 14.0	S42 13.4
16	318 04.7	104 18.7	07.9	122 54.7	52.3	145 04.9	15.9	70 56.5	07.3	Antares	112 24.6	S26 27.8
17	333 07.1	119 18.3	08.9	137 55.8	52.9	160 07.2	15.9	85 58.6	07.3			
18	348 09.6	134 18.0	S11 09.9	152 56.9	S 4 53.4	175 09.4	N 4 15.8	101 00.8	S20 07.3	Arcturus	145 54.5	N19 06.0
19	3 12.1	149 17.6	10.8	167 58.0	54.0	190 11.7	15.7	116 02.9	07.4	Atria	107 25.4	S69 03.1
20	18 14.5	164 17.2	11.8	182 59.2	54.5	205 13.9	15.6	131 05.1	07.4	Avior	234 16.8	S59 33.6
21	33 17.0	179 16.8	.. 12.7	198 00.3	.. 55.1	220 16.2	.. 15.6	146 07.2	.. 07.5	Bellatrix	278 29.9	N 6 21.6
22	48 19.4	194 16.4	13.7	213 01.4	55.6	235 18.4	15.5	161 09.4	07.5	Betelgeuse	270 59.2	N 7 24.4
23	63 21.9	209 16.1	14.7	228 02.5	56.2	250 20.7	15.4	176 11.5	07.6			
10 00	78 24.4	224 15.7	S11 15.6	243 03.6	S 4 56.7	265 22.9	N 4 15.3	191 13.7	S20 07.6	Canopus	263 54.9	S52 42.4
01	93 26.8	239 15.3	16.6	258 04.7	57.3	280 25.2	15.2	206 15.9	07.7	Capella	280 31.5	N46 00.6
02	108 29.3	254 14.9	17.5	273 05.9	57.8	295 27.5	15.2	221 18.0	07.7	Deneb	49 30.6	N45 20.6
03	123 31.8	269 14.5	.. 18.5	288 07.0	.. 58.4	310 29.7	.. 15.1	236 20.2	.. 07.8	Denebola	182 32.0	N14 28.9
04	138 34.2	284 14.1	19.5	303 08.1	58.9	325 32.0	15.0	251 22.3	07.8	Diphda	348 54.1	S17 54.1
05	153 36.7	299 13.8	20.4	318 09.2	4 59.5	340 34.2	14.9	266 24.5	07.9			
T 06	168 39.2	314 13.4	S11 21.4	333 10.3	S 5 00.1	355 36.5	N 4 14.9	281 26.6	S20 07.9	Dubhe	193 49.8	N61 39.6
H 07	183 41.6	329 13.0	22.3	348 11.4	00.6	10 38.8	14.8	296 28.8	07.9	Elnath	278 10.1	N28 37.0
U 08	198 44.1	344 12.6	23.3	3 12.6	01.2	25 41.0	14.7	311 30.9	08.0	Eltanin	90 45.9	N51 29.5
R 09	213 46.6	359 12.2	.. 24.3	18 13.7	.. 01.7	40 43.3	.. 14.6	326 33.1	.. 08.0	Enif	33 45.6	N 9 57.1
S 10	228 49.0	14 11.8	25.2	33 14.8	02.3	55 45.5	14.6	341 35.2	08.1	Fomalhaut	15 22.2	S29 32.4
D 11	243 51.5	29 11.4	26.2	48 15.9	02.8	70 47.8	14.5	356 37.4	08.1			
A 12	258 53.9	44 11.1	S11 27.1	63 17.0	S 5 03.4	85 50.0	N 4 14.4	11 39.6	S20 08.2	Gacrux	171 59.1	S57 11.8
Y 13	273 56.4	59 10.7	28.1	78 18.2	03.9	100 52.3	14.3	26 41.7	08.2	Gienah	175 50.6	S17 37.7
14	288 58.9	74 10.3	29.0	93 19.3	04.5	115 54.6	14.3	41 43.9	08.3	Hadar	148 45.8	S60 26.6
15	304 01.3	89 09.9	.. 30.0	108 20.4	.. 05.0	130 56.8	.. 14.2	56 46.0	.. 08.3	Hamal	327 58.6	N23 32.3
16	319 03.8	104 09.5	30.9	123 21.5	05.6	145 59.1	14.1	71 48.2	08.4	Kaus Aust.	83 42.0	S34 22.4
17	334 06.3	119 09.1	31.9	138 22.6	06.1	161 01.4	14.0	86 50.3	08.4			
18	349 08.7	134 08.7	S11 32.9	153 23.7	S 5 06.7	176 03.6	N 4 14.0	101 52.5	S20 08.5	Kochab	137 21.3	N74 05.3
19	4 11.2	149 08.3	33.8	168 24.9	07.2	191 05.9	13.9	116 54.6	08.5	Markab	13 36.7	N15 17.6
20	19 13.7	164 07.9	34.8	183 26.0	07.8	206 08.1	13.8	131 56.8	08.5	Menkar	314 13.0	N 4 09.0
21	34 16.1	179 07.5	.. 35.7	198 27.1	.. 08.3	221 10.4	.. 13.7	146 59.0	.. 08.6	Menkent	148 05.8	S36 26.6
22	49 18.6	194 07.2	36.7	213 28.2	08.9	236 12.7	13.7	162 01.1	08.6	Miaplacidus	221 38.6	S69 46.8
23	64 21.1	209 06.8	37.6	228 29.3	09.4	251 14.9	13.6	177 03.3	08.7			
11 00	79 23.5	224 06.4	S11 38.6	243 30.4	S 5 10.0	266 17.2	N 4 13.5	192 05.4	S20 08.7	Mirfak	308 37.4	N49 55.0
01	94 26.0	239 06.0	39.5	258 31.6	10.5	281 19.5	13.4	207 07.6	08.8	Nunki	75 56.6	S26 16.4
02	109 28.4	254 05.6	40.5	273 32.7	11.1	296 21.7	13.4	222 09.7	08.8	Peacock	53 17.1	S56 41.0
03	124 30.9	269 05.2	.. 41.4	288 33.8	.. 11.6	311 24.0	.. 13.3	237 11.9	.. 08.9	Pollux	243 25.4	N27 59.0
04	139 33.4	284 04.8	42.4	303 34.9	12.2	326 26.2	13.2	252 14.0	08.9	Procyon	244 57.7	N 5 10.8
05	154 35.8	299 04.4	43.3	318 36.0	12.7	341 28.5	13.1	267 16.2	09.0			
F 06	169 38.3	314 04.0	S11 44.3	333 37.2	S 5 13.3	356 30.8	N 4 13.1	282 18.3	S20 09.0	Rasalhague	96 05.3	N12 33.2
R 07	184 40.8	329 03.6	45.2	348 38.3	13.8	11 33.0	13.0	297 20.5	09.1	Regulus	207 41.7	N11 53.2
I 08	199 43.2	344 03.2	46.2	3 39.4	14.4	26 35.3	12.9	312 22.7	09.1	Rigel	281 10.1	S 8 11.2
D 09	214 45.7	359 02.8	.. 47.1	18 40.5	.. 14.9	41 37.6	.. 12.8	327 24.8	.. 09.1	Rigil Kent.	139 49.9	S60 53.7
A 10	229 48.2	14 02.4	48.1	33 41.6	15.5	56 39.8	12.8	342 27.0	09.2	Sabik	102 11.0	S15 44.4
Y 11	244 50.6	29 02.0	49.0	48 42.7	16.0	71 42.1	12.7	357 29.1	09.2			
12	259 53.1	44 01.6	S11 50.0	63 43.9	S 5 16.6	86 44.4	N 4 12.6	12 31.3	S20 09.3	Schedar	349 38.2	N56 37.7
13	274 55.6	59 01.2	50.9	78 45.0	17.1	101 46.6	12.5	27 33.4	09.3	Shaula	96 20.1	S37 06.7
14	289 58.0	74 00.8	51.9	93 46.1	17.7	116 48.9	12.5	42 35.6	09.4	Sirius	258 31.9	S16 44.4
15	305 00.5	89 00.4	.. 52.8	108 47.2	.. 18.2	131 51.2	.. 12.4	57 37.7	.. 09.4	Spica	158 29.7	S11 14.5
16	320 02.9	104 00.0	53.8	123 48.3	18.8	146 53.4	12.3	72 39.9	09.5	Suhail	222 50.9	S43 29.7
17	335 05.4	118 59.6	54.7	138 49.5	19.3	161 55.7	12.3	87 42.1	09.5			
18	350 07.9	133 59.2	S11 55.7	153 50.6	S 5 19.9	176 58.0	N 4 12.2	102 44.2	S20 09.6	Vega	80 38.2	N38 48.2
19	5 10.3	148 58.8	56.6	168 51.7	20.4	192 00.2	12.1	117 46.4	09.6	Zuben'ubi	137 03.8	S16 06.2
20	20 12.8	163 58.4	57.6	183 52.8	21.0	207 02.5	12.0	132 48.5	09.7		SHA	Mer.Pass.
21	35 15.3	178 58.0	.. 58.5	198 53.9	.. 21.5	222 04.8	.. 12.0	147 50.7	.. 09.7		° ′	h m
22	50 17.7	193 57.6	11 59.5	213 55.1	22.1	237 07.0	11.9	162 52.8	09.7	Venus	145 51.3	9 03
23	65 20.2	208 57.2	S12 00.4	228 56.2	22.6	252 09.3	11.8	177 55.0	09.8	Mars	164 39.2	7 47
	h m									Jupiter	186 58.6	6 18
Mer.Pass. 18 43.3		v −0.4 d 1.0		v 1.1 d 0.6		v 2.3 d 0.1		v 2.2 d 0.0		Saturn	112 49.3	11 13

UT	SUN GHA	SUN Dec	MOON GHA	v	MOON Dec	d	HP
d h	° ′	° ′	° ′	′	° ′	′	′
9 00	182 00.3	S22 45.4	210 19.8	12.7	S13 34.2	6.6	55.0
01	197 00.0	45.7	224 51.5	12.6	13 40.8	6.6	55.0
02	211 59.8	45.9	239 23.1	12.6	13 47.4	6.5	55.0
03	226 59.5 ..	46.2	253 54.7	12.5	13 53.9	6.5	55.0
04	241 59.2	46.4	268 26.2	12.5	14 00.4	6.4	55.0
05	256 58.9	46.7	282 57.7	12.4	14 06.8	6.3	55.0
06	271 58.7	S22 46.9	297 29.1	12.4	S14 13.1	6.3	55.1
W 07	286 58.4	47.2	312 00.5	12.3	14 19.4	6.2	55.1
E 08	301 58.1	47.4	326 31.8	12.3	14 25.6	6.2	55.1
D 09	316 57.8 ..	47.7	341 03.1	12.2	14 31.8	6.0	55.1
N 10	331 57.5	47.9	355 34.3	12.2	14 37.8	6.1	55.1
E 11	346 57.3	48.2	10 05.5	12.1	14 43.9	5.9	55.2
S 12	1 57.0	S22 48.4	24 36.6	12.1	S14 49.8	5.9	55.2
D 13	16 56.7	48.7	39 07.7	12.0	14 55.7	5.8	55.2
A 14	31 56.4	48.9	53 38.7	11.9	15 01.5	5.8	55.2
Y 15	46 56.1 ..	49.1	68 09.6	11.9	15 07.3	5.7	55.2
16	61 55.9	49.4	82 40.5	11.9	15 13.0	5.6	55.3
17	76 55.6	49.6	97 11.4	11.8	15 18.6	5.6	55.3
18	91 55.3	S22 49.9	111 42.2	11.8	S15 24.2	5.4	55.3
19	106 55.0	50.1	126 13.0	11.7	15 29.6	5.4	55.3
20	121 54.7	50.4	140 43.7	11.6	15 35.0	5.4	55.3
21	136 54.5 ..	50.6	155 14.3	11.6	15 40.4	5.2	55.3
22	151 54.2	50.8	169 44.9	11.5	15 45.6	5.2	55.4
23	166 53.9	51.1	184 15.4	11.5	15 50.8	5.2	55.4
10 00	181 53.6	S22 51.3	198 45.9	11.5	S15 56.0	5.0	55.4
01	196 53.3	51.5	213 16.4	11.4	16 01.0	5.0	55.4
02	211 53.1	51.8	227 46.8	11.3	16 06.0	4.9	55.4
03	226 52.8 ..	52.0	242 17.1	11.3	16 10.9	4.8	55.5
04	241 52.5	52.2	256 47.4	11.2	16 15.7	4.7	55.5
05	256 52.2	52.5	271 17.6	11.2	16 20.4	4.7	55.5
06	271 51.9	S22 52.7	285 47.8	11.2	S16 25.1	4.6	55.5
T 07	286 51.6	52.9	300 18.0	11.0	16 29.7	4.5	55.5
H 08	301 51.4	53.2	314 48.0	11.1	16 34.2	4.4	55.6
U 09	316 51.1 ..	53.4	329 18.1	11.0	16 38.6	4.4	55.6
R 10	331 50.8	53.6	343 48.1	10.9	16 43.0	4.2	55.6
S 11	346 50.5	53.8	358 18.0	10.9	16 47.2	4.2	55.6
D 12	1 50.2	S22 54.1	12 47.9	10.8	S16 51.4	4.1	55.7
A 13	16 49.9	54.3	27 17.7	10.8	16 55.5	4.0	55.7
Y 14	31 49.7	54.5	41 47.5	10.7	16 59.5	4.0	55.7
15	46 49.4 ..	54.7	56 17.2	10.7	17 03.5	3.8	55.7
16	61 49.1	55.0	70 46.9	10.7	17 07.3	3.8	55.7
17	76 48.8	55.2	85 16.6	10.6	17 11.1	3.7	55.8
18	91 48.5	S22 55.4	99 46.2	10.5	S17 14.8	3.6	55.8
19	106 48.2	55.6	114 15.7	10.5	17 18.4	3.5	55.8
20	121 48.0	55.9	128 45.2	10.5	17 21.9	3.4	55.8
21	136 47.7 ..	56.1	143 14.7	10.4	17 25.3	3.3	55.8
22	151 47.4	56.3	157 44.1	10.4	17 28.6	3.3	55.9
23	166 47.1	56.5	172 13.5	10.3	17 31.9	3.1	55.9
11 00	181 46.8	S22 56.7	186 42.8	10.2	S17 35.0	3.1	55.9
01	196 46.5	56.9	201 12.0	10.3	17 38.1	3.0	55.9
02	211 46.2	57.2	215 41.3	10.2	17 41.1	2.9	55.9
03	226 46.0 ..	57.4	230 10.5	10.1	17 44.0	2.8	56.0
04	241 45.7	57.6	244 39.6	10.1	17 46.8	2.7	56.0
05	256 45.4	57.8	259 08.7	10.1	17 49.5	2.6	56.0
06	271 45.1	S22 58.0	273 37.8	10.0	S17 52.1	2.5	56.0
07	286 44.8	58.2	288 06.8	10.0	17 54.6	2.5	56.1
08	301 44.5	58.4	302 35.8	9.9	17 57.1	2.3	56.1
F 09	316 44.2 ..	58.7	317 04.7	9.9	17 59.4	2.2	56.1
R 10	331 43.9	58.9	331 33.6	9.8	18 01.6	2.2	56.1
I 11	346 43.7	59.1	346 02.4	9.9	18 03.8	2.0	56.1
D 12	1 43.4	S22 59.3	0 31.3	9.7	S18 05.8	2.0	56.2
A 13	16 43.1	59.5	15 00.0	9.8	18 07.8	1.8	56.2
Y 14	31 42.8	59.7	29 28.8	9.7	18 09.6	1.8	56.2
15	46 42.5	22 59.9	43 57.5	9.6	18 11.4	1.7	56.2
16	61 42.2	23 00.1	58 26.1	9.7	18 13.1	1.6	56.2
17	76 41.9	00.3	72 54.8	9.6	18 14.7	1.4	56.3
18	91 41.6	S23 00.5	87 23.4	9.5	S18 16.1	1.4	56.3
19	106 41.4	00.7	101 51.9	9.5	18 17.5	1.3	56.3
20	121 41.1	00.9	116 20.4	9.5	18 18.8	1.2	56.3
21	136 40.8 ..	01.1	130 48.9	9.5	18 20.0	1.0	56.4
22	151 40.5	01.3	145 17.4	9.4	18 21.0	1.0	56.4
23	166 40.2	01.5	159 45.8	9.4	S18 22.0	0.9	56.4
	SD 16.3	d 0.2	SD 15.0		15.2		15.3

Twilight / Moonrise

Lat.	Naut.	Civil	Sunrise	Moonrise 9	10	11	12
°	h m	h m	h m	h m	h m	h m	h m
N 72	08 11	10 28	■	07 44	09 37	■	■
N 70	07 53	09 36	■	07 13	08 45	10 11	11 16
68	07 38	09 04	■	06 50	08 13	09 29	10 30
66	07 25	08 41	10 14	06 32	07 50	09 01	10 00
64	07 15	08 22	09 37	06 17	07 31	08 39	09 37
62	07 06	08 07	09 11	06 05	07 16	08 22	09 20
60	06 58	07 54	08 50	05 55	07 03	08 08	09 05
N 58	06 50	07 42	08 33	05 46	06 53	07 55	08 52
56	06 44	07 33	08 19	05 38	06 43	07 45	08 41
54	06 38	07 24	08 07	05 31	06 35	07 36	08 31
52	06 33	07 16	07 56	05 25	06 27	07 27	08 23
50	06 27	07 09	07 47	05 19	06 21	07 20	08 15
45	06 16	06 53	07 27	05 07	06 06	07 04	07 59
N 40	06 06	06 40	07 10	04 57	05 54	06 51	07 45
35	05 57	06 29	06 57	04 49	05 44	06 40	07 34
30	05 49	06 18	06 45	04 41	05 36	06 30	07 24
20	05 33	06 00	06 24	04 29	05 21	06 13	07 07
N 10	05 17	05 43	06 06	04 17	05 07	05 59	06 52
0	05 00	05 26	05 49	04 07	04 55	05 45	06 38
S 10	04 42	05 09	05 32	03 56	04 43	05 32	06 24
20	04 20	04 49	05 13	03 45	04 30	05 18	06 09
30	03 51	04 25	04 52	03 33	04 15	05 01	05 52
35	03 33	04 10	04 39	03 26	04 06	04 52	05 42
40	03 11	03 52	04 25	03 17	03 57	04 41	05 30
45	02 41	03 30	04 07	03 08	03 45	04 28	05 17
S 50	01 58	03 01	03 45	02 56	03 31	04 13	05 01
52	01 33	02 47	03 35	02 51	03 25	04 05	04 53
54	00 54	02 30	03 23	02 45	03 18	03 57	04 45
56	////	02 09	03 09	02 39	03 10	03 48	04 35
58	////	01 42	02 53	02 31	03 01	03 38	04 25
S 60	////	01 00	02 34	02 23	02 51	03 27	04 12

Twilight / Moonset

Lat.	Sunset	Civil	Naut.	Moonset 9	10	11	12
°	h m	h m	h m	h m	h m	h m	h m
N 72	■	13 17	15 34	12 41	12 29	■	■
N 70	■	14 09	15 52	13 13	13 22	13 41	14 25
68	■	14 41	16 07	13 37	13 54	14 23	15 11
66	13 31	15 04	16 20	13 56	14 18	14 52	15 41
64	14 08	15 23	16 30	14 11	14 37	15 14	16 04
62	14 34	15 38	16 39	14 24	14 53	15 31	16 22
60	14 55	15 51	16 47	14 34	15 05	15 46	16 37
N 58	15 12	16 03	16 55	14 44	15 17	15 58	16 49
56	15 26	16 12	17 01	14 52	15 26	16 09	17 00
54	15 38	16 21	17 07	14 59	15 35	16 18	17 10
52	15 49	16 29	17 13	15 06	15 43	16 27	17 18
50	15 58	16 36	17 18	15 12	15 50	16 34	17 26
45	16 18	16 52	17 29	15 25	16 05	16 50	17 42
N 40	16 35	17 05	17 39	15 35	16 17	17 04	17 56
35	16 48	17 16	17 48	15 44	16 27	17 15	18 07
30	17 01	17 27	17 57	15 52	16 36	17 25	18 17
20	17 21	17 45	18 13	16 06	16 52	17 42	18 34
N 10	17 39	18 02	18 28	16 18	17 06	17 56	18 49
0	17 56	18 19	18 45	16 30	17 19	18 10	19 03
S 10	18 14	18 37	19 04	16 41	17 32	18 24	19 17
20	18 32	18 57	19 26	16 53	17 46	18 39	19 32
30	18 54	19 21	19 54	17 07	18 02	18 56	19 49
35	19 06	19 36	20 12	17 15	18 11	19 06	19 58
40	19 21	19 54	20 35	17 25	18 21	19 17	20 10
45	19 39	20 16	21 05	17 36	18 34	19 30	20 23
S 50	20 00	20 44	21 48	17 49	18 49	19 46	20 39
52	20 11	20 59	22 14	17 55	18 56	19 54	20 46
54	20 23	21 16	22 54	18 02	19 04	20 02	20 55
56	20 37	21 37	////	18 09	19 13	20 12	21 04
58	20 53	22 05	////	18 18	19 23	20 22	21 15
S 60	21 12	22 48	////	18 27	19 34	20 35	21 27

SUN / MOON

Day	Eqn. of Time 00ʰ	Eqn. of Time 12ʰ	Mer. Pass.	Mer. Pass. Upper	Mer. Pass. Lower	Age	Phase
d	m s	m s	h m	h m	h m	d	%
9	08 02	07 49	11 52	10 18	22 42	28	4
10	07 35	07 21	11 53	11 07	23 32	29	1
11	07 08	06 54	11 53	11 58	24 24	00	0

2015 DECEMBER 12, 13, 14 (SAT., SUN., MON.)

UT	ARIES	VENUS −4.1		MARS +1.4		JUPITER −2.0		SATURN +0.5		STARS		
	GHA	GHA	Dec	GHA	Dec	GHA	Dec	GHA	Dec	Name	SHA	Dec
d h	° ′	° ′	° ′	° ′	° ′	° ′	° ′	° ′	° ′		° ′	° ′
12 00	80 22.7	223 56.8	S12 01.4	243 57.3	S 5 23.2	267 11.6	N 4 11.7	192 57.1	S20 09.8	Acamar	315 16.8	S40 14.7
01	95 25.1	238 58.4	02.3	258 58.4	23.7	282 13.9	11.7	207 59.3	09.9	Achernar	335 25.3	S57 09.7
02	110 27.6	253 56.0	03.2	273 59.5	24.3	297 16.1	11.6	223 01.5	09.9	Acrux	173 07.4	S63 10.9
03	125 30.1	268 55.6 ..	04.2	289 00.7 ..	24.8	312 18.4 ..	11.5	238 03.6 ..	10.0	Adhara	255 10.8	S28 59.8
04	140 32.5	283 55.1	05.1	304 01.8	25.4	327 20.7	11.5	253 05.8	10.0	Aldebaran	290 47.1	N16 32.3
05	155 35.0	298 54.7	06.1	319 02.9	25.9	342 22.9	11.4	268 07.9	10.1			
06	170 37.4	313 54.3	S12 07.0	334 04.0	S 5 26.5	357 25.2	N 4 11.3	283 10.1	S20 10.1	Alioth	166 19.6	N55 52.2
07	185 39.9	328 53.9	08.0	349 05.1	27.0	12 27.5	11.2	298 12.2	10.2	Alkaid	152 58.0	N49 13.9
S 08	200 42.4	343 53.5	08.9	4 06.3	27.6	27 29.7	11.2	313 14.4	10.2	Al Na'ir	27 41.9	S46 53.1
A 09	215 44.8	358 53.1 ..	09.8	19 07.4 ..	28.1	42 32.0 ..	11.1	328 16.5 ..	10.2	Alnilam	275 44.3	S 1 11.7
T 10	230 47.3	13 52.7	10.8	34 08.5	28.7	57 34.3	11.0	343 18.7	10.3	Alphard	217 54.3	S 8 43.7
U 11	245 49.8	28 52.3	11.7	49 09.6	29.2	72 36.6	11.0	358 20.9	10.3			
R 12	260 52.2	43 51.9	S12 12.7	64 10.7	S 5 29.8	87 38.8	N 4 10.9	13 23.0	S20 10.4	Alphecca	126 10.0	N26 39.8
D 13	275 54.7	58 51.5	13.6	79 11.9	30.3	102 41.1	10.8	28 25.2	10.4	Alpheratz	357 41.6	N29 10.9
A 14	290 57.2	73 51.0	14.5	94 13.0	30.9	117 43.4	10.8	43 27.3	10.5	Altair	62 06.9	N 8 54.9
Y 15	305 59.6	88 50.6 ..	15.5	109 14.1 ..	31.4	132 45.7 ..	10.7	58 29.5 ..	10.5	Ankaa	353 14.0	S42 13.4
16	321 02.1	103 50.2	16.4	124 15.2	32.0	147 47.9	10.6	73 31.6	10.5	Antares	112 24.6	S26 27.8
17	336 04.5	118 49.8	17.4	139 16.3	32.5	162 50.2	10.5	88 33.8	10.6			
18	351 07.0	133 49.4	S12 18.3	154 17.5	S 5 33.0	177 52.5	N 4 10.5	103 35.9	S20 10.7	Arcturus	145 54.5	N19 06.0
19	6 09.5	148 49.0	19.2	169 18.6	33.6	192 54.8	10.4	118 38.1	10.7	Atria	107 25.4	S69 03.1
20	21 11.9	163 48.6	20.2	184 19.7	34.1	207 57.0	10.3	133 40.3	10.7	Avior	234 16.8	S59 33.6
21	36 14.4	178 48.1 ..	21.1	199 20.8 ..	34.7	222 59.3 ..	10.3	148 42.4 ..	10.8	Bellatrix	278 29.9	N 6 21.6
22	51 16.9	193 47.7	22.1	214 21.9	35.2	238 01.6	10.2	163 44.6	10.8	Betelgeuse	270 59.1	N 7 24.4
23	66 19.3	208 47.3	23.0	229 23.1	35.8	253 03.9	10.1	178 46.7	10.9			
13 00	81 21.8	223 46.9	S12 23.9	244 24.2	S 5 36.3	268 06.1	N 4 10.1	193 48.9	S20 10.9	Canopus	263 54.8	S52 42.4
01	96 24.3	238 46.5	24.9	259 25.3	36.9	283 08.4	10.0	208 51.0	11.0	Capella	280 31.5	N46 00.6
02	111 26.7	253 46.1	25.8	274 26.4	37.4	298 10.7	09.9	223 53.2	11.0	Deneb	49 30.6	N45 20.6
03	126 29.2	268 45.6 ..	26.7	289 27.5 ..	38.0	313 13.0 ..	09.9	238 55.4 ..	11.1	Denebola	182 32.0	N14 28.9
04	141 31.7	283 45.2	27.7	304 28.7	38.5	328 15.2	09.8	253 57.5	11.1	Diphda	348 54.1	S17 54.1
05	156 34.1	298 44.8	28.6	319 29.8	39.1	343 17.5	09.7	268 59.7	11.2			
06	171 36.6	313 44.4	S12 29.5	334 30.9	S 5 39.6	358 19.8	N 4 09.6	284 01.8	S20 11.2	Dubhe	193 49.8	N61 39.6
07	186 39.0	328 44.0	30.5	349 32.0	40.2	13 22.1	09.6	299 04.0	11.2	Elnath	278 10.1	N28 37.0
08	201 41.5	343 43.5	31.4	4 33.1	40.7	28 24.3	09.5	314 06.1	11.3	Eltanin	90 45.9	N51 29.5
S 09	216 44.0	358 43.1 ..	32.3	19 34.3 ..	41.2	43 26.6 ..	09.4	329 08.3 ..	11.3	Enif	33 45.6	N 9 57.1
U 10	231 46.4	13 42.7	33.3	34 35.4	41.8	58 28.9	09.4	344 10.4	11.4	Fomalhaut	15 22.2	S29 32.4
N 11	246 48.9	28 42.3	34.2	49 36.5	42.3	73 31.2	09.3	359 12.6	11.4			
D 12	261 51.4	43 41.8	S12 35.1	64 37.6	S 5 42.9	88 33.5	N 4 09.2	14 14.8	S20 11.5	Gacrux	171 59.0	S57 11.8
A 13	276 53.8	58 41.4	36.1	79 38.7	43.4	103 35.7	09.2	29 16.9	11.5	Gienah	175 50.6	S17 37.7
Y 14	291 56.3	73 41.0	37.0	94 39.9	44.0	118 38.0	09.1	44 19.1	11.6	Hadar	148 45.8	S60 26.6
15	306 58.8	88 40.6 ..	37.9	109 41.0 ..	44.5	133 40.3 ..	09.0	59 21.2 ..	11.6	Hamal	327 58.6	N23 32.3
16	322 01.2	103 40.2	38.9	124 42.1	45.1	148 42.6	09.0	74 23.4	11.6	Kaus Aust.	83 42.0	S34 22.4
17	337 03.7	118 39.7	39.8	139 43.2	45.6	163 44.9	08.9	89 25.5	11.7			
18	352 06.2	133 39.3	S12 40.7	154 44.4	S 5 46.1	178 47.1	N 4 08.8	104 27.7	S20 11.7	Kochab	137 21.3	N74 05.3
19	7 08.6	148 38.9	41.6	169 45.5	46.7	193 49.4	08.8	119 29.9	11.8	Markab	13 36.7	N15 17.6
20	22 11.1	163 38.4	42.6	184 46.6	47.2	208 51.7	08.7	134 32.0	11.8	Menkar	314 13.0	N 4 09.0
21	37 13.5	178 38.0 ..	43.5	199 47.7 ..	47.8	223 54.0 ..	08.6	149 34.2 ..	11.9	Menkent	148 05.8	S36 26.6
22	52 16.0	193 37.6	44.4	214 48.8	48.3	238 56.3	08.6	164 36.3	11.9	Miaplacidus	221 38.6	S69 46.8
23	67 18.5	208 37.2	45.4	229 50.0	48.9	253 58.5	08.5	179 38.5	12.0			
14 00	82 20.9	223 36.7	S12 46.3	244 51.1	S 5 49.4	269 00.8	N 4 08.4	194 40.6	S20 12.0	Mirfak	308 37.4	N49 55.0
01	97 23.4	238 36.3	47.2	259 52.2	50.0	284 03.1	08.4	209 42.8	12.1	Nunki	75 56.6	S26 16.4
02	112 25.9	253 35.9	48.1	274 53.3	50.5	299 05.4	08.3	224 45.0	12.1	Peacock	53 17.1	S56 41.0
03	127 28.3	268 35.4 ..	49.1	289 54.5 ..	51.0	314 07.7 ..	08.2	239 47.1 ..	12.1	Pollux	243 25.4	N27 59.0
04	142 30.8	283 35.0	50.0	304 55.6	51.6	329 10.0	08.2	254 49.3	12.2	Procyon	244 57.7	N 5 10.8
05	157 33.3	298 34.6	50.9	319 56.7	52.1	344 12.2	08.1	269 51.4	12.2			
06	172 35.7	313 34.1	S12 51.8	334 57.8	S 5 52.7	359 14.5	N 4 08.0	284 53.6	S20 12.3	Rasalhague	96 05.3	N12 33.2
07	187 38.2	328 33.7	52.8	349 58.9	53.2	14 16.8	08.0	299 55.7	12.3	Regulus	207 41.6	N11 53.2
08	202 40.7	343 33.3	53.7	5 00.1	53.8	29 19.1	07.9	314 57.9	12.4	Rigel	281 10.1	S 8 11.2
M 09	217 43.1	358 32.8 ..	54.6	20 01.2 ..	54.3	44 21.4 ..	07.9	330 00.1 ..	12.4	Rigil Kent.	139 49.8	S60 53.7
O 10	232 45.6	13 32.4	55.5	35 02.3	54.8	59 23.7	07.8	345 02.2	12.5	Sabik	102 11.0	S15 44.4
N 11	247 48.0	28 32.0	56.5	50 03.4	55.4	74 26.0	07.7	0 04.4	12.5			
D 12	262 50.5	43 31.5	S12 57.4	65 04.6	S 5 55.9	89 28.2	N 4 07.7	15 06.5	S20 12.5	Schedar	349 38.3	N56 37.7
A 13	277 53.0	58 31.1	58.3	80 05.7	56.5	104 30.5	07.6	30 08.7	12.6	Shaula	96 20.1	S37 06.7
Y 14	292 55.4	73 30.7	12 59.2	95 06.8	57.0	119 32.8	07.5	45 10.8	12.6	Sirius	258 31.9	S16 44.5
15	307 57.9	88 30.2	13 00.1	110 07.9 ..	57.6	134 35.1 ..	07.5	60 13.0 ..	12.7	Spica	158 29.6	S11 14.5
16	323 00.4	103 29.8	01.1	125 09.0	58.1	149 37.4	07.4	75 15.2	12.7	Suhail	222 50.9	S43 29.7
17	338 02.8	118 29.4	02.0	140 10.2	58.6	164 39.7	07.3	90 17.3	12.8			
18	353 05.3	133 28.9	S13 02.9	155 11.3	S 5 59.2	179 42.0	N 4 07.3	105 19.5	S20 12.8	Vega	80 38.2	N38 48.2
19	8 07.8	148 28.5	03.8	170 12.4	5 59.7	194 44.2	07.2	120 21.6	12.9	Zuben'ubi	137 03.8	S16 06.2
20	23 10.2	163 28.0	04.7	185 13.5	6 00.3	209 46.5	07.1	135 23.8	12.9		SHA	Mer. Pass.
21	38 12.7	178 27.6 ..	05.7	200 14.7 ..	00.8	224 48.8 ..	07.1	150 25.9 ..	12.9		° ′	h m
22	53 15.2	193 27.2	06.6	215 15.8	01.4	239 51.1	07.0	165 28.1	13.0	Venus	142 25.1	9 05
23	68 17.6	208 26.7	07.5	230 16.9	01.9	254 53.4	07.0	180 30.3	13.0	Mars	163 02.4	7 42
	h m									Jupiter	186 44.3	6 07
Mer. Pass. 18 31.5		v −0.4	d 0.9	v 1.1	d 0.5	v 2.3	d 0.1	v 2.2	d 0.0	Saturn	112 27.1	11 03

UT	SUN GHA	SUN Dec	MOON GHA	v	Dec	d	HP
d h	° ′	° ′	° ′	′	° ′	′	′
12 00	181 39.9	S23 01.7	174 14.2	9.4	S18 22.9	0.8	56.4
01	196 39.6	01.9	188 42.6	9.3	18 23.7	0.7	56.4
02	211 39.3	02.1	203 10.9	9.3	18 24.4	0.5	56.5
03	226 39.0	.. 02.3	217 39.2	9.3	18 24.9	0.5	56.5
04	241 38.7	02.5	232 07.5	9.3	18 25.4	0.4	56.5
05	256 38.5	02.7	246 35.8	9.2	18 25.8	0.3	56.5
06	271 38.2	S23 02.9	261 04.0	9.2	S18 26.1	0.2	56.5
S 07	286 37.9	03.1	275 32.2	9.2	18 26.3	0.0	56.6
A 08	301 37.6	03.3	290 00.4	9.1	18 26.3	0.0	56.6
T 09	316 37.3	.. 03.5	304 28.5	9.1	18 26.3	0.1	56.6
U 10	331 37.0	03.6	318 56.6	9.1	18 26.2	0.3	56.6
R 11	346 36.7	03.8	333 24.7	9.1	18 25.9	0.3	56.7
D 12	1 36.4	S23 04.0	347 52.8	9.1	S18 25.6	0.4	56.7
A 13	16 36.1	04.2	2 20.9	9.0	18 25.2	0.6	56.7
Y 14	31 35.8	04.4	16 48.9	9.0	18 24.6	0.6	56.7
15	46 35.5	.. 04.6	31 16.9	9.0	18 24.0	0.8	56.7
16	61 35.2	04.8	45 44.9	9.0	18 23.2	0.8	56.8
17	76 35.0	05.0	60 12.9	8.9	18 22.4	1.0	56.8
18	91 34.7	S23 05.1	74 40.9	8.9	S18 21.4	1.1	56.8
19	106 34.4	05.3	89 08.8	8.9	18 20.3	1.1	56.8
20	121 34.1	05.5	103 36.7	8.9	18 19.2	1.3	56.8
21	136 33.8	.. 05.7	118 04.6	8.9	18 17.9	1.4	56.9
22	151 33.5	05.9	132 32.5	8.9	18 16.5	1.4	56.9
23	166 33.2	06.1	147 00.4	8.9	18 15.1	1.6	56.9
13 00	181 32.9	S23 06.2	161 28.3	8.8	S18 13.5	1.7	56.9
01	196 32.6	06.4	175 56.1	8.9	18 11.8	1.8	56.9
02	211 32.3	06.6	190 24.0	8.8	18 10.0	1.9	57.0
03	226 32.0	.. 06.8	204 51.8	8.8	18 08.1	2.0	57.0
04	241 31.7	06.9	219 19.6	8.8	18 06.1	2.1	57.0
05	256 31.4	07.1	233 47.4	8.8	18 04.0	2.2	57.0
06	271 31.1	S23 07.3	248 15.2	8.8	S18 01.8	2.3	57.0
S 07	286 30.8	07.5	262 43.0	8.8	17 59.5	2.4	57.1
U 08	301 30.6	07.6	277 10.8	8.8	17 57.1	2.5	57.1
N 09	316 30.3	.. 07.8	291 38.6	8.8	17 54.6	2.7	57.1
D 10	331 30.0	08.0	306 06.4	8.8	17 51.9	2.7	57.1
A 11	346 29.7	08.2	320 34.2	8.7	17 49.2	2.8	57.1
Y 12	1 29.4	S23 08.3	335 01.9	8.8	S17 46.4	2.9	57.2
13	16 29.1	08.5	349 29.7	8.8	17 43.5	3.1	57.2
14	31 28.8	08.7	3 57.5	8.7	17 40.4	3.1	57.2
15	46 28.5	.. 08.8	18 25.2	8.8	17 37.3	3.3	57.2
16	61 28.2	09.0	32 53.0	8.7	17 34.0	3.3	57.2
17	76 27.9	09.2	47 20.7	8.8	17 30.7	3.4	57.3
18	91 27.6	S23 09.3	61 48.5	8.8	S17 27.3	3.6	57.3
19	106 27.3	09.5	76 16.3	8.7	17 23.7	3.6	57.3
20	121 27.0	09.7	90 44.0	8.8	17 20.1	3.8	57.3
21	136 26.7	.. 09.8	105 11.8	8.8	17 16.3	3.8	57.3
22	151 26.4	10.0	119 39.6	8.7	17 12.5	4.0	57.4
23	166 26.1	10.1	134 07.3	8.8	17 08.5	4.0	57.4
14 00	181 25.8	S23 10.3	148 35.1	8.8	S17 04.5	4.2	57.4
01	196 25.5	10.5	163 02.9	8.8	17 00.3	4.2	57.4
02	211 25.2	10.6	177 30.7	8.7	16 56.1	4.4	57.4
03	226 24.9	.. 10.8	191 58.4	8.8	16 51.7	4.4	57.5
04	241 24.6	10.9	206 26.2	8.8	16 47.3	4.6	57.5
05	256 24.3	11.1	220 54.0	8.8	16 42.7	4.6	57.5
06	271 24.0	S23 11.2	235 21.8	8.9	S16 38.1	4.8	57.5
07	286 23.7	11.4	249 49.7	8.8	16 33.3	4.8	57.5
M 08	301 23.4	11.5	264 17.5	8.8	16 28.5	5.0	57.6
O 09	316 23.1	.. 11.7	278 45.3	8.9	16 23.5	5.0	57.6
N 10	331 22.8	11.9	293 13.2	8.8	16 18.5	5.1	57.6
D 11	346 22.5	12.0	307 41.0	8.9	16 13.4	5.3	57.6
A 12	1 22.2	S23 12.2	322 08.9	8.9	S16 08.1	5.3	57.6
Y 13	16 21.9	12.3	336 36.8	8.9	16 02.8	5.4	57.6
14	31 21.7	12.5	351 04.7	8.9	15 57.4	5.5	57.7
15	46 21.4	.. 12.6	5 32.6	8.9	15 51.9	5.7	57.7
16	61 21.1	12.7	20 00.5	8.9	15 46.2	5.7	57.7
17	76 20.8	12.9	34 28.4	8.9	15 40.5	5.8	57.7
18	91 20.5	S23 13.0	48 56.3	9.0	S15 34.7	5.8	57.7
19	106 20.2	13.2	63 24.3	9.0	15 28.9	6.0	57.8
20	121 19.9	13.3	77 52.3	8.9	15 22.9	6.1	57.8
21	136 19.6	.. 13.5	92 20.2	9.0	15 16.8	6.2	57.8
22	151 19.3	13.6	106 48.2	9.0	15 10.6	6.2	57.8
23	166 19.0	13.8	121 16.2	9.1	S15 04.4	6.4	57.8
	SD 16.3	d 0.2	SD 15.4		15.6		15.7

Twilight / Sunrise / Moonrise

Lat.	Naut.	Civil	Sunrise	12	13	14	15
°	h m	h m	h m	h m	h m	h m	h m
N 72	08 17	10 39	■■	■■	13 11	12 47	12 37
N 70	07 57	09 43	■■	11 16	11 50	12 05	12 11
68	07 42	09 10	■■	10 30	11 11	11 36	11 51
66	07 29	08 45	10 22	10 00	10 44	11 15	11 35
64	07 18	08 26	09 42	09 37	10 23	10 57	11 22
62	07 09	08 11	09 15	09 20	10 06	10 43	11 11
60	07 01	07 57	08 54	09 05	09 52	10 31	11 02
N 58	06 53	07 46	08 37	08 52	09 40	10 20	10 53
56	06 47	07 36	08 23	08 41	09 30	10 11	10 46
54	06 41	07 27	08 10	08 31	09 21	10 03	10 39
52	06 35	07 19	08 00	08 23	09 12	09 56	10 34
50	06 30	07 12	07 50	08 15	09 05	09 49	10 28
45	06 19	06 56	07 29	07 59	08 49	09 35	10 17
N 40	06 08	06 42	07 13	07 45	08 36	09 24	10 07
35	05 59	06 31	06 59	07 34	08 25	09 14	09 59
30	05 51	06 20	06 47	07 24	08 16	09 05	09 51
20	05 34	06 02	06 26	07 07	07 59	08 50	09 39
N 10	05 18	05 45	06 07	06 52	07 44	08 37	09 28
0	05 02	05 28	05 50	06 38	07 31	08 24	09 17
S 10	04 43	05 10	05 33	06 24	07 17	08 12	09 07
20	04 21	04 50	05 14	06 09	07 03	07 59	08 56
30	03 52	04 25	04 52	05 52	06 46	07 44	08 43
35	03 34	04 10	04 40	05 42	06 36	07 35	08 36
40	03 11	03 52	04 25	05 30	06 25	07 25	08 27
45	02 41	03 30	04 07	05 17	06 12	07 13	08 18
S 50	01 56	03 01	03 45	05 01	05 56	06 59	08 06
52	01 30	02 46	03 34	04 53	05 49	06 52	08 00
54	00 48	02 29	03 22	04 45	05 41	06 44	07 54
56	////	02 07	03 08	04 35	05 31	06 36	07 47
58	////	01 39	02 52	04 25	05 21	06 27	07 40
S 60	////	00 53	02 32	04 12	05 09	06 16	07 31

Sunset / Twilight / Moonset

Lat.	Sunset	Civil	Naut.	12	13	14	15
°	h m	h m	h m	h m	h m	h m	h m
N 72	■■	13 09	15 31	■■	14 22	16 38	18 38
N 70	■■	14 05	15 50	14 25	15 42	17 19	19 02
68	■■	14 38	16 06	15 11	16 21	17 47	19 21
66	13 26	15 02	16 19	15 41	16 48	18 08	19 36
64	14 05	15 22	16 30	16 04	17 08	18 25	19 49
62	14 33	15 37	16 39	16 22	17 25	18 38	19 59
60	14 54	15 51	16 47	16 37	17 39	18 50	20 08
N 58	15 11	16 02	16 54	16 49	17 50	19 00	20 16
56	15 25	16 12	17 01	17 00	18 01	19 09	20 22
54	15 37	16 21	17 07	17 10	18 10	19 16	20 28
52	15 48	16 29	17 13	17 18	18 18	19 23	20 34
50	15 58	16 36	17 18	17 26	18 25	19 30	20 39
45	16 18	16 52	17 29	17 42	18 40	19 43	20 49
N 40	16 35	17 06	17 40	17 56	18 53	19 54	20 58
35	16 49	17 17	17 49	18 07	19 04	20 04	21 06
30	17 01	17 28	17 57	18 17	19 13	20 12	21 12
20	17 22	17 46	18 14	18 34	19 29	20 26	21 23
N 10	17 41	18 03	18 30	18 49	19 43	20 38	21 33
0	17 58	18 20	18 46	19 03	19 56	20 50	21 42
S 10	18 15	18 38	19 05	19 17	20 09	21 01	21 52
20	18 34	18 58	19 28	19 32	20 23	21 13	22 01
30	18 56	19 23	19 56	19 49	20 39	21 27	22 12
35	19 09	19 38	20 15	19 58	20 48	21 35	22 19
40	19 23	19 56	20 38	20 10	20 59	21 44	22 26
45	19 41	20 18	21 08	20 23	21 11	21 55	22 34
S 50	20 03	20 48	21 52	20 39	21 26	22 08	22 44
52	20 14	21 03	22 19	20 46	21 33	22 13	22 49
54	20 26	21 20	23 02	20 55	21 41	22 20	22 54
56	20 40	21 42	////	21 04	21 49	22 27	22 59
58	20 57	22 11	////	21 15	21 59	22 35	23 05
S 60	21 17	22 57	////	21 27	22 10	22 45	23 12

Day	SUN Eqn. of Time 00h	12h	Mer. Pass.	MOON Mer. Pass. Upper	Lower	Age	Phase
d	m s	m s	h m	h m	h m	d	%
12	06 40	06 26	11 54	12 50	00 24	01	1
13	06 12	05 58	11 54	13 44	01 17	02	5
14	05 44	05 30	11 55	14 37	02 10	03	10

UT	ARIES GHA	VENUS −4.1 GHA	Dec	MARS +1.4 GHA	Dec	JUPITER −2.1 GHA	Dec	SATURN +0.5 GHA	Dec	Star Name	SHA	Dec
15 00	83 20.1	223 26.3	S13 08.4	245 18.0	S 6 02.4	269 55.7	N 4 06.9	195 32.4	S20 13.1	Acamar	315 16.8	S40 14.7
01	98 22.5	238 25.8	09.3	260 19.2	03.0	284 58.0	06.8	210 34.6	13.1	Achernar	335 25.3	S57 09.7
02	113 25.0	253 25.4	10.3	275 20.3	03.5	300 00.3	06.8	225 36.7	13.2	Acrux	173 07.4	S63 10.9
03	128 27.5	268 25.0 ..	11.2	290 21.4 ..	04.1	315 02.6 ..	06.7	240 38.9 ..	13.2	Adhara	255 10.8	S28 59.8
04	143 29.9	283 24.5	12.1	305 22.5	04.6	330 04.8	06.6	255 41.0	13.3	Aldebaran	290 47.1	N16 32.3
05	158 32.4	298 24.1	13.0	320 23.6	05.1	345 07.1	06.6	270 43.2	13.3			
06	173 34.9	313 23.6	S13 13.9	335 24.8	S 6 05.7	0 09.4	N 4 06.5	285 45.4	S20 13.3	Alioth	166 19.5	N55 52.2
07	188 37.3	328 23.2	14.8	350 25.9	06.2	15 11.7	06.4	300 47.5	13.4	Alkaid	152 57.9	N49 13.9
08	203 39.8	343 22.7	15.7	5 27.0	06.8	30 14.0	06.4	315 49.7	13.4	Al Na'ir	27 41.9	S46 53.1
09	218 42.3	358 22.3 ..	16.7	20 28.1 ..	07.3	45 16.3 ..	06.3	330 51.8 ..	13.5	Alnilam	275 44.3	S 1 11.7
10	233 44.7	13 21.8	17.6	35 29.3	07.8	60 18.6	06.3	345 54.0	13.5	Alphard	217 54.2	S 8 43.7
11	248 47.2	28 21.4	18.5	50 30.4	08.4	75 20.9	06.2	0 56.1	13.6			
T 12	263 49.6	43 20.9	S13 19.4	65 31.5	S 6 08.9	90 23.2	N 4 06.1	15 58.3	S20 13.6	Alphecca	126 09.9	N26 39.8
U 13	278 52.1	58 20.5	20.3	80 32.6	09.5	105 25.5	06.1	31 00.5	13.7	Alpheratz	357 41.6	N29 10.9
E 14	293 54.6	73 20.0	21.2	95 33.8	10.0	120 27.8	06.0	46 02.6	13.7	Altair	62 06.9	N 8 54.9
S 15	308 57.0	88 19.6 ..	22.1	110 34.9 ..	10.5	135 30.1 ..	06.0	61 04.8 ..	13.7	Ankaa	353 14.0	S42 13.4
D 16	323 59.5	103 19.1	23.0	125 36.0	11.1	150 32.3	05.9	76 06.9	13.8	Antares	112 24.5	S26 27.8
A 17	339 02.0	118 18.7	23.9	140 37.1	11.6	165 34.6	05.8	91 09.1	13.8			
Y 18	354 04.4	133 18.2	S13 24.9	155 38.3	S 6 12.2	180 36.9	N 4 05.8	106 11.2	S20 13.9	Arcturus	145 54.5	N19 06.0
19	9 06.9	148 17.8	25.8	170 39.4	12.7	195 39.2	05.7	121 13.4	13.9	Atria	107 25.3	S69 03.1
20	24 09.4	163 17.3	26.7	185 40.5	13.2	210 41.5	05.6	136 15.6	14.0	Avior	234 16.7	S59 33.6
21	39 11.8	178 16.9 ..	27.6	200 41.6 ..	13.8	225 43.8 ..	05.6	151 17.7 ..	14.0	Bellatrix	278 29.9	N 6 21.6
22	54 14.3	193 16.4	28.5	215 42.8	14.3	240 46.1	05.5	166 19.9	14.0	Betelgeuse	270 59.1	N 7 24.4
23	69 16.8	208 16.0	29.4	230 43.9	14.9	255 48.4	05.5	181 22.0	14.1			
16 00	84 19.2	223 15.5	S13 30.3	245 45.0	S 6 15.4	270 50.7	N 4 05.4	196 24.2	S20 14.1	Canopus	263 54.8	S52 42.4
01	99 21.7	238 15.1	31.2	260 46.1	15.9	285 53.0	05.3	211 26.4	14.2	Capella	280 31.4	N46 00.6
02	114 24.1	253 14.6	32.1	275 47.3	16.5	300 55.3	05.3	226 28.5	14.2	Deneb	49 30.6	N45 20.6
03	129 26.6	268 14.2 ..	33.0	290 48.4 ..	17.0	315 57.6 ..	05.2	241 30.7 ..	14.3	Denebola	182 32.0	N14 28.9
04	144 29.1	283 13.7	33.9	305 49.5	17.5	330 59.9	05.2	256 32.8	14.3	Diphda	348 54.1	S17 54.1
05	159 31.5	298 13.3	34.8	320 50.6	18.1	346 02.2	05.1	271 35.0	14.4			
06	174 34.0	313 12.8	S13 35.7	335 51.8	S 6 18.6	1 04.5	N 4 05.0	286 37.1	S20 14.4	Dubhe	193 49.7	N61 39.6
W 07	189 36.5	328 12.3	36.6	350 52.9	19.2	16 06.8	05.0	301 39.3	14.4	Elnath	278 10.1	N28 37.0
E 08	204 38.9	343 11.9	37.6	5 54.0	19.7	31 09.1	04.9	316 41.5	14.5	Eltanin	90 45.9	N51 29.4
D 09	219 41.4	358 11.4 ..	38.5	20 55.1 ..	20.2	46 11.4 ..	04.9	331 43.6 ..	14.5	Enif	33 45.6	N 9 57.1
N 10	234 43.9	13 11.0	39.4	35 56.3	20.8	61 13.7	04.8	346 45.8	14.6	Fomalhaut	15 22.2	S29 32.4
E 11	249 46.3	28 10.5	40.3	50 57.4	21.3	76 16.0	04.7	1 47.9	14.6			
S 12	264 48.8	43 10.1	S13 41.2	65 58.5	S 6 21.9	91 18.3	N 4 04.7	16 50.1	S20 14.7	Gacrux	171 59.0	S57 11.8
D 13	279 51.3	58 09.6	42.1	80 59.6	22.4	106 20.6	04.6	31 52.3	14.7	Gienah	175 50.6	S17 37.7
A 14	294 53.7	73 09.1	43.0	96 00.8	22.9	121 22.9	04.6	46 54.4	14.8	Hadar	148 45.7	S60 26.6
Y 15	309 56.2	88 08.7 ..	43.9	111 01.9 ..	23.5	136 25.2 ..	04.5	61 56.6 ..	14.8	Hamal	327 58.6	N23 32.3
16	324 58.6	103 08.2	44.8	126 03.0	24.0	151 27.5	04.5	76 58.7	14.8	Kaus Aust.	83 42.0	S34 22.4
17	340 01.1	118 07.7	45.7	141 04.1	24.5	166 29.8	04.4	92 00.9	14.9			
18	355 03.6	133 07.3	S13 46.6	156 05.3	S 6 25.1	181 32.1	N 4 04.3	107 03.0	S20 14.9	Kochab	137 21.2	N74 05.3
19	10 06.0	148 06.8	47.5	171 06.4	25.6	196 34.4	04.3	122 05.2	15.0	Markab	13 36.7	N15 17.6
20	25 08.5	163 06.4	48.4	186 07.5	26.1	211 36.7	04.2	137 07.4	15.0	Menkar	314 13.0	N 4 09.0
21	40 11.0	178 05.9 ..	49.3	201 08.6 ..	26.7	226 39.0 ..	04.2	152 09.5 ..	15.1	Menkent	148 05.8	S36 26.6
22	55 13.4	193 05.4	50.2	216 09.8	27.2	241 41.3	04.1	167 11.7	15.1	Miaplacidus	221 38.5	S69 46.8
23	70 15.9	208 05.0	51.0	231 10.9	27.8	256 43.6	04.0	182 13.8	15.1			
17 00	85 18.4	223 04.5	S13 51.9	246 12.0	S 6 28.3	271 45.9	N 4 04.0	197 16.0	S20 15.2	Mirfak	308 37.4	N49 55.0
01	100 20.8	238 04.0	52.8	261 13.1	28.8	286 48.2	03.9	212 18.2	15.2	Nunki	75 56.6	S26 16.4
02	115 23.3	253 03.6	53.7	276 14.3	29.4	301 50.5	03.9	227 20.3	15.3	Peacock	53 17.1	S56 41.0
03	130 25.8	268 03.1 ..	54.6	291 15.4 ..	29.9	316 52.8 ..	03.8	242 22.5 ..	15.3	Pollux	243 25.4	N27 59.0
04	145 28.2	283 02.6	55.5	306 16.5	30.4	331 55.1	03.8	257 24.6	15.4	Procyon	244 57.7	N 5 10.8
05	160 30.7	298 02.2	56.4	321 17.6	31.0	346 57.4	03.7	272 26.8	15.4			
06	175 33.1	313 01.7	S13 57.3	336 18.8	S 6 31.5	1 59.7	N 4 03.6	287 29.0	S20 15.5	Rasalhague	96 05.2	N12 33.1
07	190 35.6	328 01.2	58.2	351 19.9	32.0	17 02.0	03.6	302 31.1	15.5	Regulus	207 41.6	N11 53.2
T 08	205 38.1	343 00.8	13 59.1	6 21.0	32.6	32 04.3	03.5	317 33.3	15.5	Rigel	281 10.1	S 8 11.2
H 09	220 40.5	358 00.3	14 00.0	21 22.1 ..	33.1	47 06.6 ..	03.5	332 35.4 ..	15.6	Rigil Kent.	139 49.8	S60 53.6
U 10	235 43.0	12 59.8	00.9	36 23.3	33.6	62 08.9	03.4	347 37.6	15.6	Sabik	102 11.0	S15 44.4
R 11	250 45.5	27 59.3	01.8	51 24.4	34.2	77 11.2	03.4	2 39.8	15.7			
S 12	265 47.9	42 58.9	S14 02.7	66 25.5	S 6 34.7	92 13.5	N 4 03.3	17 41.9	S20 15.7	Schedar	349 38.3	N56 37.7
D 13	280 50.4	57 58.4	03.6	81 26.7	35.3	107 15.8	03.3	32 44.1	15.8	Shaula	96 20.0	S37 06.7
A 14	295 52.9	72 57.9	04.4	96 27.8	35.8	122 18.1	03.2	47 46.2	15.8	Sirius	258 31.9	S16 44.5
Y 15	310 55.3	87 57.4 ..	05.3	111 28.9 ..	36.3	137 20.4 ..	03.1	62 48.4 ..	15.8	Spica	158 29.6	S11 14.5
16	325 57.8	102 57.0	06.2	126 30.0	36.9	152 22.7	03.1	77 50.5	15.9	Suhail	222 50.8	S43 29.8
17	341 00.2	117 56.5	07.1	141 31.2	37.4	167 25.0	03.0	92 52.7	15.9			
18	356 02.7	132 56.0	S14 08.0	156 32.3	S 6 37.9	182 27.4	N 4 03.0	107 54.9	S20 16.0	Vega	80 38.2	N38 48.2
19	11 05.2	147 55.5	08.9	171 33.4	38.5	197 29.7	02.9	122 57.0	16.0	Zuben'ubi	137 03.8	S16 06.2
20	26 07.6	162 55.1	09.8	186 34.5	39.0	212 32.0	02.9	137 59.2	16.1		SHA	Mer. Pass.
21	41 10.1	177 54.6 ..	10.7	201 35.7 ..	39.5	227 34.3 ..	02.8	153 01.3 ..	16.1	Venus	138 56.3	9 07
22	56 12.6	192 54.1	11.5	216 36.8	40.1	242 36.6	02.8	168 03.5	16.1	Mars	161 25.8	7 36
23	71 15.9	207 53.6	12.4	231 37.9	40.6	257 38.9	02.7	183 05.7	16.2	Jupiter	186 31.5	5 56
Mer. Pass. 18 19.7		v −0.5	d 0.9	v 1.1	d 0.5	v 2.3	d 0.1	v 2.2	d 0.0	Saturn	112 05.0	10 53

SUN and MOON

UT	SUN GHA	SUN Dec	MOON GHA	v	MOON Dec	d	HP
d h	° ′	° ′	° ′	′	° ′	′	′
15 00	181 18.7	S23 13.9	135 44.3	9.0	S14 58.0	6.4	57.8
01	196 18.4	14.0	150 12.3	9.1	14 51.6	6.5	57.9
02	211 18.1	14.2	164 40.4	9.1	14 45.1	6.6	57.9
03	226 17.8	.. 14.3	179 08.5	9.0	14 38.5	6.7	57.9
04	241 17.5	14.5	193 36.5	9.2	14 31.8	6.8	57.9
05	256 17.2	14.6	208 04.7	9.1	14 25.0	6.9	57.9
06	271 16.9	S23 14.7	222 32.8	9.1	S14 18.1	6.9	58.0
T 07	286 16.6	14.9	237 00.9	9.2	14 11.2	7.1	58.0
U 08	301 16.3	15.0	251 29.1	9.2	14 04.1	7.1	58.0
E 09	316 16.0	.. 15.1	265 57.3	9.2	13 57.0	7.2	58.0
S 10	331 15.7	15.3	280 25.5	9.2	13 49.8	7.3	58.0
D 11	346 15.4	15.4	294 53.7	9.2	13 42.5	7.3	58.0
A 12	1 15.1	S23 15.5	309 21.9	9.3	S13 35.2	7.5	58.1
Y 13	16 14.8	15.7	323 50.2	9.2	13 27.7	7.5	58.1
14	31 14.5	15.8	338 18.4	9.3	13 20.2	7.6	58.1
15	46 14.2	.. 15.9	352 46.7	9.3	13 12.6	7.7	58.1
16	61 13.8	16.0	7 15.0	9.4	13 04.9	7.8	58.1
17	76 13.5	16.2	21 43.4	9.3	12 57.1	7.8	58.1
18	91 13.2	S23 16.3	36 11.7	9.4	S12 49.3	8.0	58.2
19	106 12.9	16.4	50 40.1	9.4	12 41.3	8.0	58.2
20	121 12.6	16.5	65 08.5	9.4	12 33.3	8.0	58.2
21	136 12.3	.. 16.7	79 36.9	9.4	12 25.3	8.2	58.2
22	151 12.0	16.8	94 05.3	9.4	12 17.1	8.2	58.2
23	166 11.7	16.9	108 33.7	9.5	12 08.9	8.3	58.2
16 00	181 11.4	S23 17.0	123 02.2	9.5	S12 00.6	8.4	58.3
01	196 11.1	17.2	137 30.7	9.5	11 52.2	8.4	58.3
02	211 10.8	17.3	151 59.2	9.5	11 43.8	8.5	58.3
03	226 10.5	.. 17.4	166 27.7	9.5	11 35.3	8.6	58.3
04	241 10.2	17.5	180 56.2	9.6	11 26.7	8.7	58.3
05	256 09.9	17.6	195 24.8	9.5	11 18.0	8.7	58.3
06	271 09.6	S23 17.8	209 53.3	9.6	S11 09.3	8.8	58.3
W 07	286 09.3	17.9	224 21.9	9.6	11 00.5	8.8	58.4
E 08	301 09.0	18.0	238 50.5	9.6	10 51.7	8.9	58.4
D 09	316 08.7	.. 18.1	253 19.1	9.7	10 42.8	9.0	58.4
N 10	331 08.4	18.2	267 47.8	9.6	10 33.8	9.0	58.4
E 11	346 08.1	18.3	282 16.4	9.7	10 24.8	9.1	58.4
S 12	1 07.8	S23 18.4	296 45.1	9.7	S10 15.7	9.2	58.4
D 13	16 07.5	18.5	311 13.8	9.7	10 06.5	9.2	58.5
A 14	31 07.2	18.7	325 42.5	9.7	9 57.3	9.3	58.5
Y 15	46 06.9	.. 18.8	340 11.2	9.8	9 48.0	9.4	58.5
16	61 06.6	18.9	354 40.0	9.8	9 38.6	9.4	58.5
17	76 06.3	19.0	9 08.8	9.7	9 29.2	9.5	58.5
18	91 06.0	S23 19.1	23 37.5	9.8	S 9 19.7	9.5	58.5
19	106 05.7	19.2	38 06.3	9.8	9 10.2	9.6	58.5
20	121 05.4	19.3	52 35.1	9.8	9 00.6	9.6	58.6
21	136 05.1	.. 19.4	67 03.9	9.9	8 51.0	9.7	58.6
22	151 04.8	19.5	81 32.8	9.8	8 41.3	9.7	58.6
23	166 04.5	19.6	96 01.6	9.9	8 31.6	9.8	58.6
17 00	181 04.2	S23 19.7	110 30.5	9.9	S 8 21.8	9.9	58.6
01	196 03.8	19.8	124 59.4	9.9	8 11.9	9.9	58.6
02	211 03.5	19.9	139 28.3	9.9	8 02.0	9.9	58.6
03	226 03.2	.. 20.0	153 57.2	9.9	7 52.1	10.0	58.7
04	241 02.9	20.1	168 26.1	9.9	7 42.1	10.1	58.7
05	256 02.6	20.2	182 55.0	9.9	7 32.0	10.0	58.7
06	271 02.3	S23 20.3	197 23.9	10.0	S 7 22.0	10.2	58.7
T 07	286 02.0	20.4	211 52.9	10.0	7 11.8	10.2	58.7
H 08	301 01.7	20.5	226 21.9	9.9	7 01.6	10.2	58.7
U 09	316 01.4	.. 20.6	240 50.8	10.0	6 51.4	10.2	58.7
R 10	331 01.1	20.7	255 19.8	10.0	6 41.2	10.3	58.8
S 11	346 00.8	20.8	269 48.8	10.0	6 30.9	10.4	58.8
D 12	1 00.5	S23 20.9	284 17.8	10.0	S 6 20.5	10.4	58.8
A 13	16 00.2	21.0	298 46.8	10.0	6 10.1	10.4	58.8
Y 14	30 59.9	21.1	313 15.8	10.0	5 59.7	10.5	58.8
15	45 59.6	.. 21.1	327 44.8	10.1	5 49.2	10.5	58.8
16	60 59.3	21.2	342 13.9	10.0	5 38.7	10.5	58.8
17	75 59.0	21.3	356 42.9	10.0	5 28.2	10.6	58.8
18	90 58.7	S23 21.4	11 11.9	10.1	S 5 17.6	10.6	58.9
19	105 58.4	21.5	25 41.0	10.1	5 07.0	10.6	58.9
20	120 58.0	21.6	40 10.0	10.1	4 56.4	10.7	58.9
21	135 57.7	.. 21.7	54 39.1	10.1	4 45.7	10.7	58.9
22	150 57.4	21.8	69 08.2	10.0	4 35.0	10.7	58.9
23	165 57.1	21.8	83 37.2	10.1	S 4 24.3	10.8	58.9
	SD 16.3	d 0.1	SD 15.8		15.9		16.0

Twilight / Sunrise / Moonrise

Lat.	Naut.	Civil	Sunrise	Moonrise 15	16	17	18
°	h m	h m	h m	h m	h m	h m	h m
N 72	08 21	10 48	■■	12 37	12 31	12 25	12 19
N 70	08 01	09 49	■■	12 11	12 14	12 16	12 17
68	07 45	09 14	■■	11 51	12 01	12 08	12 14
66	07 32	08 49	10 28	11 35	11 50	12 02	12 12
64	07 21	08 30	09 47	11 22	11 41	11 57	12 11
62	07 12	08 14	09 19	11 11	11 34	11 52	12 11
60	07 04	08 00	08 58	11 02	11 27	11 48	12 08
N 58	06 56	07 49	08 40	10 53	11 21	11 45	12 07
56	06 49	07 39	08 26	10 46	11 16	11 42	12 06
54	06 43	07 29	08 13	10 39	11 11	11 39	12 05
52	06 38	07 21	08 02	10 34	11 06	11 36	12 04
50	06 32	07 14	07 52	10 28	11 02	11 34	12 03
45	06 21	06 58	07 32	10 17	10 54	11 28	12 01
N 40	06 10	06 45	07 15	10 07	10 47	11 24	12 00
35	06 01	06 33	07 01	09 59	10 41	11 20	11 59
30	05 52	06 22	06 49	09 51	10 35	11 17	11 58
20	05 36	06 04	06 28	09 39	10 26	11 11	11 56
N 10	05 20	05 46	06 09	09 28	10 18	11 06	11 54
0	05 03	05 29	05 52	09 17	10 10	11 01	11 53
S 10	04 44	05 11	05 34	09 07	10 02	10 57	11 51
20	04 22	04 51	05 15	08 56	09 54	10 52	11 50
30	03 53	04 26	04 53	08 43	09 44	10 46	11 48
35	03 34	04 11	04 40	08 36	09 39	10 42	11 47
40	03 11	03 53	04 26	08 27	09 32	10 39	11 46
45	02 41	03 30	04 08	08 18	09 25	10 34	11 44
S 50	01 56	03 01	03 45	08 06	09 16	10 29	11 43
52	01 28	02 46	03 34	08 00	09 12	10 26	11 42
54	00 44	02 28	03 22	07 54	09 08	10 24	11 41
56	////	02 06	03 08	07 47	09 03	10 21	11 40
58	////	01 37	02 51	07 40	08 57	10 17	11 39
S 60	////	00 49	02 31	07 31	08 51	10 14	11 38

Sunset / Twilight / Moonset

Lat.	Sunset	Civil	Naut.	Moonset 15	16	17	18
°	h m	h m	h m	h m	h m	h m	h m
N 72	■■	13 02	15 30	18 38	20 33	22 26	24 19
N 70	■■	14 02	15 50	19 02	20 48	22 33	24 19
68	■■	14 37	16 05	19 21	20 59	22 39	24 19
66	13 22	15 02	16 18	19 36	21 09	22 43	24 18
64	14 04	15 21	16 29	19 49	21 17	22 47	24 18
62	14 32	15 37	16 39	19 59	21 24	22 50	24 18
60	14 53	15 51	16 47	20 08	21 30	22 53	24 18
N 58	15 10	16 02	16 55	20 16	21 35	22 56	24 18
56	15 25	16 12	17 01	20 22	21 39	22 58	24 18
54	15 38	16 21	17 08	20 28	21 43	23 00	24 18
52	15 49	16 29	17 13	20 34	21 47	23 02	24 18
50	15 58	16 37	17 18	20 39	21 50	23 04	24 18
45	16 19	16 53	17 30	20 49	21 58	23 07	24 18
N 40	16 36	17 06	17 40	20 58	22 04	23 10	24 18
35	16 50	17 18	17 50	21 06	22 09	23 13	24 18
30	17 02	17 29	17 58	21 12	22 13	23 15	24 18
20	17 23	17 47	18 15	21 23	22 21	23 19	24 17
N 10	17 42	18 05	18 31	21 33	22 28	23 23	24 17
0	17 59	18 22	18 48	21 42	22 34	23 26	24 17
S 10	18 17	18 40	19 07	21 52	22 41	23 29	24 17
20	18 36	19 00	19 29	22 01	22 47	23 32	24 17
30	18 58	19 25	19 58	22 12	22 55	23 36	24 16
35	19 11	19 40	20 17	22 19	22 59	23 38	24 16
40	19 26	19 58	20 40	22 26	23 04	23 41	24 16
45	19 44	20 21	21 10	22 34	23 10	23 43	24 16
S 50	20 06	20 50	21 56	22 44	23 16	23 47	24 16
52	20 17	21 05	22 23	22 49	23 20	23 48	24 15
54	20 29	21 23	23 08	22 54	23 23	23 50	24 15
56	20 43	21 45	////	22 59	23 27	23 52	24 15
58	21 00	22 15	////	23 05	23 31	23 54	24 15
S 60	21 20	23 04	////	23 12	23 35	23 56	24 15

SUN and MOON (daily data)

Day	Eqn. of Time 00h	Eqn. of Time 12h	Mer. Pass.	Mer. Pass. Upper	Mer. Pass. Lower	Age	Phase
d	m s	m s	h m	h m	h m	d	%
15	05 15	05 01	11 55	15 30	03 04	04	18
16	04 46	04 32	11 55	16 22	03 56	05	27
17	04 17	04 03	11 56	17 14	04 48	06	37

UT	ARIES GHA	VENUS −4.1 GHA	Dec	MARS +1.4 GHA	Dec	JUPITER −2.1 GHA	Dec	SATURN +0.5 GHA	Dec	STARS Name	SHA	Dec
18 00	86 17.5	222 53.2	S14 13.3	246 39.0	S 6 41.1	272 41.2	N 4 02.6	198 07.8	S20 16.2	Acamar	315 16.8	S40 14.7
01	101 20.0	237 52.7	14.2	261 40.2	41.7	287 43.5	02.6	213 10.0	16.3	Achernar	335 25.4	S57 09.7
02	116 22.4	252 52.2	15.1	276 41.3	42.2	302 45.8	02.5	228 12.1	16.3	Acrux	173 07.3	S63 10.9
03	131 24.9	267 51.7	.. 16.0	291 42.4	.. 42.7	317 48.1	.. 02.5	243 14.3	.. 16.4	Adhara	255 10.8	S28 59.8
04	146 27.4	282 51.2	16.8	306 43.6	43.3	332 50.4	02.4	258 16.5	16.4	Aldebaran	290 47.1	N16 32.3
05	161 29.8	297 50.8	17.7	321 44.7	43.8	347 52.7	02.4	273 18.6	16.4			
06	176 32.3	312 50.3	S14 18.6	336 45.8	S 6 44.3	2 55.1	N 4 02.3	288 20.8	S20 16.5	Alioth	166 19.5	N55 52.2
07	191 34.7	327 49.8	19.5	351 46.9	44.9	17 57.4	02.3	303 22.9	16.5	Alkaid	152 57.9	N49 13.9
F 08	206 37.2	342 49.3	20.4	6 48.1	45.4	32 59.7	02.2	318 25.1	16.6	Al Na'ir	27 41.9	S46 53.1
R 09	221 39.7	357 48.8	.. 21.3	21 49.2	.. 45.9	48 02.0	.. 02.2	333 27.3	.. 16.6	Alnilam	275 44.3	S 1 11.7
I 10	236 42.1	12 48.4	22.1	36 50.3	46.5	63 04.3	02.1	348 29.4	16.7	Alphard	217 54.2	S 8 43.8
D 11	251 44.6	27 47.9	23.0	51 51.5	47.0	78 06.6	02.1	3 31.6	16.7			
A 12	266 47.1	42 47.4	S14 23.9	66 52.6	S 6 47.5	93 08.9	N 4 02.0	18 33.7	S20 16.7	Alphecca	126 09.9	N26 39.8
Y 13	281 49.5	57 46.9	24.8	81 53.7	48.1	108 11.2	01.9	33 35.9	16.8	Alpheratz	357 41.7	N29 10.9
14	296 52.0	72 46.4	25.7	96 54.8	48.6	123 13.5	01.9	48 38.1	16.8	Altair	62 06.9	N 8 54.9
15	311 54.5	87 45.9	.. 26.5	111 56.0	.. 49.1	138 15.9	.. 01.8	63 40.2	.. 16.9	Ankaa	353 14.0	S42 13.4
16	326 56.9	102 45.4	27.4	126 57.1	49.6	153 18.2	01.8	78 42.4	16.9	Antares	112 24.5	S26 27.8
17	341 59.4	117 45.0	28.3	141 58.2	50.2	168 20.5	01.7	93 44.5	17.0			
18	357 01.9	132 44.5	S14 29.2	156 59.3	S 6 50.7	183 22.8	N 4 01.7	108 46.7	S20 17.0	Arcturus	145 54.4	N19 06.0
19	12 04.3	147 44.0	30.0	172 00.5	51.2	198 25.1	01.6	123 48.9	17.0	Atria	107 25.3	S69 03.0
20	27 06.8	162 43.5	30.9	187 01.6	51.8	213 27.4	01.6	138 51.0	17.1	Avior	234 16.7	S59 33.6
21	42 09.2	177 43.0	.. 31.8	202 02.7	.. 52.3	228 29.7	.. 01.5	153 53.2	.. 17.1	Bellatrix	278 29.8	N 6 21.6
22	57 11.7	192 42.5	32.7	217 03.9	52.8	243 32.1	01.5	168 55.3	17.2	Betelgeuse	270 59.1	N 7 24.4
23	72 14.2	207 42.0	33.5	232 05.0	53.4	258 34.4	01.4	183 57.5	17.2			
19 00	87 16.6	222 41.5	S14 34.4	247 06.1	S 6 53.9	273 36.7	N 4 01.4	198 59.7	S20 17.3	Canopus	263 54.8	S52 42.4
01	102 19.1	237 41.0	35.3	262 07.2	54.4	288 39.0	01.3	214 01.8	17.3	Capella	280 31.4	N46 00.6
02	117 21.6	252 40.5	36.1	277 08.4	55.0	303 41.3	01.3	229 04.0	17.3	Deneb	49 30.6	N45 20.6
03	132 24.0	267 40.1	.. 37.0	292 09.5	.. 55.5	318 43.6	.. 01.2	244 06.2	.. 17.4	Denebola	182 32.0	N14 28.9
04	147 26.5	282 39.6	37.9	307 10.6	56.0	333 46.0	01.2	259 08.3	17.4	Diphda	348 54.1	S17 54.1
05	162 29.0	297 39.1	38.8	322 11.8	56.6	348 48.3	01.1	274 10.5	17.5			
06	177 31.4	312 38.6	S14 39.6	337 12.9	S 6 57.1	3 50.6	N 4 01.1	289 12.6	S20 17.5	Dubhe	193 49.7	N61 39.6
07	192 33.9	327 38.1	40.5	352 14.0	57.6	18 52.9	01.0	304 14.8	17.6	Elnath	278 10.1	N28 37.0
S 08	207 36.3	342 37.6	41.4	7 15.1	58.1	33 55.2	01.0	319 17.0	17.6	Eltanin	90 45.9	N51 29.4
A 09	222 38.8	357 37.1	.. 42.2	22 16.3	.. 58.7	48 57.5	.. 00.9	334 19.1	.. 17.6	Enif	33 45.6	N 9 57.1
T 10	237 41.3	12 36.6	43.1	37 17.4	59.2	63 59.9	00.9	349 21.3	17.7	Fomalhaut	15 22.3	S29 32.4
U 11	252 43.7	27 36.1	44.0	52 18.5	6 59.7	79 02.2	00.8	4 23.4	17.7			
R 12	267 46.2	42 35.6	S14 44.8	67 19.7	S 7 00.3	94 04.5	N 4 00.8	19 25.6	S20 17.8	Gacrux	171 59.0	S57 11.8
D 13	282 48.7	57 35.1	45.7	82 20.8	00.8	109 06.8	00.7	34 27.8	17.8	Gienah	175 50.6	S17 37.7
A 14	297 51.1	72 34.6	46.6	97 21.9	01.3	124 09.1	00.7	49 29.9	17.8	Hadar	148 45.7	S60 26.6
Y 15	312 53.6	87 34.1	.. 47.4	112 23.1	.. 01.8	139 11.5	.. 00.6	64 32.1	.. 17.9	Hamal	327 58.6	N23 32.3
16	327 56.1	102 33.6	48.3	127 24.2	02.4	154 13.8	00.6	79 34.2	17.9	Kaus Aust.	83 42.0	S34 22.4
17	342 58.5	117 33.1	49.2	142 25.3	02.9	169 16.1	00.5	94 36.4	18.0			
18	358 01.0	132 32.6	S14 50.0	157 26.4	S 7 03.4	184 18.4	N 4 00.5	109 38.6	S20 18.0	Kochab	137 21.2	N74 05.3
19	13 03.5	147 32.1	50.9	172 27.6	04.0	199 20.7	00.4	124 40.7	18.1	Markab	13 36.7	N15 17.6
20	28 05.9	162 31.6	51.8	187 28.7	04.5	214 23.1	00.4	139 42.9	18.1	Menkar	314 13.0	N 4 09.0
21	43 08.4	177 31.1	.. 52.6	202 29.8	.. 05.0	229 25.4	.. 00.3	154 45.1	.. 18.1	Menkent	148 05.8	S36 26.6
22	58 10.8	192 30.6	53.5	217 31.0	05.5	244 27.7	00.3	169 47.2	18.2	Miaplacidus	221 38.5	S69 46.8
23	73 13.3	207 30.1	54.3	232 32.1	06.1	259 30.0	00.2	184 49.4	18.2			
20 00	88 15.8	222 29.6	S14 55.2	247 33.2	S 7 06.6	274 32.3	N 4 00.2	199 51.5	S20 18.3	Mirfak	308 37.4	N49 55.0
01	103 18.2	237 29.1	56.1	262 34.3	07.1	289 34.7	00.1	214 53.7	18.3	Nunki	75 56.6	S26 16.4
02	118 20.7	252 28.6	56.9	277 35.5	07.7	304 37.0	00.1	229 55.9	18.4	Peacock	53 17.2	S56 41.0
03	133 23.2	267 28.1	.. 57.8	292 36.6	.. 08.2	319 39.3	.. 00.0	244 58.0	.. 18.4	Pollux	243 25.4	N27 59.0
04	148 25.6	282 27.6	58.6	307 37.7	08.7	334 41.6	4 00.0	260 00.2	18.4	Procyon	244 57.7	N 5 10.8
05	163 28.1	297 27.1	14 59.5	322 38.9	09.2	349 44.0	3 59.9	275 02.3	18.5			
06	178 30.6	312 26.6	S15 00.3	337 40.0	S 7 09.8	4 46.3	N 3 59.9	290 04.5	S20 18.5	Rasalhague	96 05.2	N12 33.1
07	193 33.0	327 26.1	01.2	352 41.1	10.3	19 48.6	59.8	305 06.7	18.6	Regulus	207 41.6	N11 53.2
S 08	208 35.5	342 25.5	02.1	7 42.3	10.8	34 50.9	59.8	320 08.8	18.6	Rigel	281 10.1	S 8 11.2
U 09	223 37.9	357 25.0	.. 02.9	22 43.4	.. 11.3	49 53.3	.. 59.7	335 11.0	.. 18.6	Rigil Kent.	139 49.8	S60 53.6
N 10	238 40.4	12 24.5	03.8	37 44.5	11.9	64 55.6	59.7	350 13.2	18.7	Sabik	102 10.9	S15 44.4
D 11	253 42.9	27 24.0	04.6	52 45.7	12.4	79 57.9	59.6	5 15.3	18.7			
A 12	268 45.3	42 23.5	S15 05.5	67 46.8	S 7 12.9	95 00.2	N 3 59.6	20 17.5	S20 18.8	Schedar	349 38.3	N56 37.7
Y 13	283 47.8	57 23.0	06.3	82 47.9	13.5	110 02.6	59.5	35 19.6	18.8	Shaula	96 20.0	S37 06.7
14	298 50.3	72 22.5	07.2	97 49.0	14.0	125 04.9	59.5	50 21.8	18.9	Sirius	258 31.9	S16 44.5
15	313 52.7	87 22.0	.. 08.0	112 50.2	.. 14.5	140 07.2	.. 59.4	65 24.0	.. 18.9	Spica	158 29.6	S11 14.5
16	328 55.2	102 21.5	08.9	127 51.3	15.0	155 09.5	59.4	80 26.1	18.9	Suhail	222 50.8	S43 29.8
17	343 57.7	117 21.0	09.7	142 52.4	15.6	170 11.9	59.4	95 28.3	19.0			
18	359 00.1	132 20.4	S15 10.6	157 53.6	S 7 16.1	185 14.2	N 3 59.3	110 30.5	S20 19.0	Vega	80 38.2	N38 48.2
19	14 02.6	147 19.9	11.4	172 54.7	16.6	200 16.5	59.3	125 32.6	19.1	Zuben'ubi	137 03.8	S16 06.2
20	29 05.1	162 19.4	12.3	187 55.8	17.1	215 18.8	59.2	140 34.8	19.1		SHA	Mer. Pass.
21	44 07.5	177 18.9	.. 13.1	202 57.0	.. 17.7	230 21.2	.. 59.2	155 36.9	.. 19.2	Venus	135 24.9	9 10
22	59 10.0	192 18.4	14.0	217 58.1	18.2	245 23.5	59.1	170 39.1	19.2	Mars	159 49.5	7 31
23	74 12.4	207 17.9	14.8	232 59.2	18.7	260 25.8	59.1	185 41.3	19.2	Jupiter	186 20.1	5 45
Mer. Pass. 18 07.9		v −0.5	d 0.9	v 1.1	d 0.5	v 2.3	d 0.1	v 2.2	d 0.0	Saturn	111 43.0	10 42

UT	SUN GHA	SUN Dec	MOON GHA	v	Dec	d	HP
d h	° ′	° ′	° ′	′	° ′	′	′
18 00	180 56.8	S23 21.9	98 06.3	10.1	S 4 13.5	10.8	58.9
01	195 56.5	22.0	112 35.4	10.0	4 02.7	10.8	59.0
02	210 56.2	22.1	127 04.4	10.1	3 51.9	10.9	59.0
03	225 55.9 ..	22.2	141 33.5	10.1	3 41.0	10.8	59.0
04	240 55.6	22.2	156 02.6	10.0	3 30.2	10.9	59.0
05	255 55.3	22.3	170 31.6	10.1	3 19.3	10.9	59.0
06	270 55.0	S23 22.4	185 00.7	10.1	S 3 08.4	11.0	59.0
07	285 54.7	22.5	199 29.8	10.1	2 57.4	10.9	59.0
08	300 54.4	22.6	213 58.9	10.1	2 46.5	11.0	59.0
F 09	315 54.1 ..	22.6	228 27.9	10.1	2 35.5	11.0	59.0
R 10	330 53.8	22.7	242 57.0	10.0	2 24.5	11.0	59.1
I 11	345 53.5	22.8	257 26.0	10.1	2 13.5	11.1	59.1
D 12	0 53.1	S23 22.9	271 55.1	10.0	S 2 02.4	11.0	59.1
A 13	15 52.8	22.9	286 24.1	10.1	1 51.4	11.1	59.1
Y 14	30 52.5	23.0	300 53.2	10.1	1 40.3	11.0	59.1
15	45 52.2 ..	23.1	315 22.2	10.1	1 29.3	11.1	59.1
16	60 51.9	23.1	329 51.3	10.0	1 18.2	11.1	59.1
17	75 51.6	23.2	344 20.3	10.1	1 07.1	11.1	59.1
18	90 51.3	S23 23.3	358 49.3	10.0	S 0 56.0	11.2	59.1
19	105 51.0	23.3	13 18.3	10.0	0 44.8	11.1	59.2
20	120 50.7	23.4	27 47.3	10.0	0 33.7	11.1	59.2
21	135 50.4 ..	23.5	42 16.3	10.0	0 22.6	11.2	59.2
22	150 50.1	23.5	56 45.3	9.9	0 11.4	11.1	59.2
23	165 49.8	23.6	71 14.2	10.0	S 0 00.3	11.2	59.2
19 00	180 49.5	S23 23.7	85 43.2	9.9	N 0 10.9	11.1	59.2
01	195 49.2	23.7	100 12.1	10.0	0 22.0	11.2	59.2
02	210 48.8	23.8	114 41.1	9.9	0 33.2	11.1	59.2
03	225 48.5 ..	23.8	129 10.0	9.9	0 44.3	11.2	59.2
04	240 48.2	23.9	143 38.9	9.9	0 55.5	11.1	59.2
05	255 47.9	24.0	158 07.8	9.8	1 06.6	11.2	59.3
06	270 47.6	S23 24.0	172 36.6	9.9	N 1 17.8	11.1	59.3
07	285 47.3	24.1	187 05.5	9.8	1 28.9	11.2	59.3
S 08	300 47.0	24.1	201 34.3	9.9	1 40.1	11.1	59.3
A 09	315 46.7 ..	24.2	216 03.2	9.8	1 51.2	11.1	59.3
T 10	330 46.4	24.3	230 32.0	9.8	2 02.3	11.2	59.3
U 11	345 46.1	24.3	245 00.8	9.7	2 13.5	11.1	59.3
R 12	0 45.8	S23 24.4	259 29.5	9.8	N 2 24.6	11.1	59.3
D 13	15 45.5	24.4	273 58.3	9.7	2 35.7	11.1	59.3
A 14	30 45.1	24.5	288 27.0	9.7	2 46.8	11.0	59.3
Y 15	45 44.8 ..	24.5	302 55.7	9.7	2 57.8	11.1	59.3
16	60 44.5	24.6	317 24.4	9.7	3 08.9	11.1	59.3
17	75 44.2	24.6	331 53.1	9.6	3 20.0	11.0	59.4
18	90 43.9	S23 24.7	346 21.7	9.6	N 3 31.0	11.0	59.4
19	105 43.6	24.7	0 50.3	9.6	3 42.0	11.0	59.4
20	120 43.3	24.8	15 18.9	9.6	3 53.0	11.0	59.4
21	135 43.0 ..	24.8	29 47.5	9.5	4 04.0	10.9	59.4
22	150 42.7	24.8	44 16.0	9.5	4 14.9	11.0	59.4
23	165 42.4	24.9	58 44.5	9.5	4 25.9	10.9	59.4
20 00	180 42.1	S23 24.9	73 13.0	9.5	N 4 36.8	10.9	59.4
01	195 41.8	25.0	87 41.5	9.4	4 47.7	10.8	59.4
02	210 41.4	25.0	102 09.9	9.5	4 58.5	10.9	59.4
03	225 41.1 ..	25.1	116 38.4	9.3	5 09.4	10.8	59.4
04	240 40.8	25.1	131 06.7	9.4	5 20.2	10.8	59.4
05	255 40.5	25.1	145 35.1	9.3	5 31.0	10.7	59.4
06	270 40.2	S23 25.2	160 03.4	9.3	N 5 41.7	10.8	59.4
07	285 39.9	25.2	174 31.7	9.3	5 52.5	10.6	59.4
08	300 39.6	25.3	189 00.0	9.2	6 03.1	10.7	59.5
S 09	315 39.3 ..	25.3	203 28.2	9.2	6 13.8	10.6	59.5
U 10	330 39.0	25.3	217 56.4	9.2	6 24.4	10.6	59.5
N 11	345 38.7	25.4	232 24.6	9.2	6 35.0	10.6	59.5
D 12	0 38.4	S23 25.4	246 52.8	9.1	N 6 45.6	10.5	59.5
A 13	15 38.0	25.4	261 20.9	9.1	6 56.1	10.5	59.5
Y 14	30 37.7	25.5	275 49.0	9.0	7 06.6	10.4	59.5
15	45 37.4 ..	25.5	290 17.0	9.0	7 17.0	10.4	59.5
16	60 37.1	25.5	304 45.0	9.0	7 27.4	10.3	59.5
17	75 36.8	25.6	319 13.0	9.0	7 37.7	10.3	59.5
18	90 36.5	S23 25.6	333 41.0	8.9	N 7 48.0	10.3	59.5
19	105 36.2	25.6	348 08.9	8.9	7 58.3	10.2	59.5
20	120 35.9	25.6	2 36.8	8.8	8 08.5	10.2	59.5
21	135 35.6 ..	25.7	17 04.6	8.8	8 18.7	10.1	59.5
22	150 35.3	25.7	31 32.4	8.8	8 28.8	10.1	59.5
23	165 35.0	25.7	46 00.2	8.7	N 8 38.9	10.0	59.5
	SD 16.3	d 0.1	SD 16.1		16.2		16.2

Twilight / Moonrise

Lat.	Naut.	Civil	Sunrise	18	19	20	21
°	h m	h m	h m	h m	h m	h m	h m
N 72	08 24	10 55	■	12 19	12 14	12 09	12 04
N 70	08 04	09 52	■	12 17	12 17	12 18	12 21
68	07 48	09 17	■	12 14	12 20	12 26	12 34
66	07 35	08 52	10 33	12 12	12 22	12 33	12 45
64	07 24	08 32	09 50	12 11	12 24	12 38	12 55
62	07 14	08 16	09 22	12 09	12 25	12 43	13 03
60	07 06	08 03	09 00	12 08	12 27	12 47	13 10
N 58	06 58	07 51	08 43	12 07	12 28	12 51	13 16
56	06 52	07 41	08 28	12 06	12 29	12 54	13 22
54	06 45	07 32	08 16	12 05	12 30	12 57	13 27
52	06 40	07 23	08 04	12 04	12 31	13 00	13 31
50	06 34	07 16	07 55	12 03	12 32	13 02	13 35
45	06 23	07 00	07 34	12 01	12 34	13 08	13 44
N 40	06 12	06 46	07 17	12 00	12 36	13 12	13 51
35	06 03	06 35	07 03	11 59	12 37	13 16	13 58
30	05 54	06 24	06 50	11 58	12 38	13 20	14 03
20	05 38	06 05	06 29	11 56	12 40	13 26	14 13
N 10	05 21	05 48	06 11	11 54	12 42	13 31	14 22
0	05 04	05 31	05 53	11 53	12 44	13 37	14 30
S 10	04 45	05 13	05 36	11 51	12 46	13 42	14 39
20	04 23	04 52	05 17	11 50	12 48	13 47	14 47
30	03 54	04 27	04 55	11 48	12 50	13 54	14 58
35	03 35	04 12	04 42	11 47	12 52	13 57	15 04
40	03 12	03 54	04 27	11 46	12 53	14 02	15 10
45	02 42	03 31	04 08	11 44	12 55	14 07	15 18
S 50	01 56	03 01	03 46	11 43	12 57	14 13	15 28
52	01 28	02 46	03 35	11 42	12 58	14 15	15 32
54	00 42	02 28	03 23	11 41	12 59	14 18	15 37
56	////	02 06	03 09	11 40	13 01	14 22	15 42
58	////	01 36	02 52	11 39	13 02	14 25	15 49
S 60	////	00 46	02 31	11 38	13 04	14 30	15 55

Sunset / Twilight / Moonset

Lat.	Sunset	Civil	Naut.	18	19	20	21
°	h m	h m	h m	h m	h m	h m	h m
N 72	■	12 59	15 30	24 19	00 19	02 12	04 09
N 70	■	14 01	15 50	24 19	00 19	02 05	03 53
68	■	14 36	16 06	24 19	00 19	01 59	03 41
66	13 21	15 02	16 19	24 18	00 18	01 55	03 31
64	14 04	15 21	16 30	24 18	00 18	01 50	03 23
62	14 32	15 38	16 40	24 18	00 18	01 47	03 16
60	14 53	15 51	16 48	24 18	00 18	01 44	03 10
N 58	15 11	16 03	16 55	24 18	00 18	01 41	03 04
56	15 26	16 13	17 02	24 18	00 18	01 39	03 00
54	15 38	16 22	17 08	24 18	00 18	01 37	02 55
52	15 49	16 30	17 14	24 18	00 18	01 35	02 52
50	15 59	16 38	17 19	24 18	00 18	01 33	02 48
45	16 20	16 54	17 31	24 18	00 18	01 29	02 41
N 40	16 37	17 07	17 42	24 18	00 18	01 26	02 34
35	16 51	17 19	17 51	24 18	00 18	01 23	02 29
30	17 03	17 30	18 00	24 18	00 18	01 20	02 24
20	17 25	17 49	18 16	24 17	00 17	01 16	02 16
N 10	17 43	18 06	18 32	24 17	00 17	01 12	02 09
0	18 01	18 23	18 49	24 17	00 17	01 09	02 02
S 10	18 18	18 41	19 08	24 17	00 17	01 05	01 55
20	18 37	19 02	19 31	24 17	00 17	01 02	01 48
30	18 59	19 27	20 00	24 16	00 16	00 57	01 40
35	19 12	19 42	20 19	24 16	00 16	00 55	01 35
40	19 27	20 00	20 42	24 16	00 16	00 52	01 30
45	19 45	20 23	21 13	24 16	00 16	00 49	01 24
S 50	20 08	20 53	21 58	24 16	00 15	00 45	01 16
52	20 19	21 08	22 26	24 15	00 15	00 43	01 13
54	20 31	21 26	23 13	24 15	00 15	00 41	01 09
56	20 45	21 48	////	24 15	00 15	00 39	01 05
58	21 02	22 18	////	24 15	00 15	00 37	01 00
S 60	21 23	23 09	////	24 15	00 15	00 34	00 55

SUN / MOON

Day	Eqn. of Time 00h	Eqn. of Time 12h	Mer. Pass.	Mer. Pass. Upper	Mer. Pass. Lower	Age	Phase
d	m s	m s	h m	h m	h m	d	%
18	03 48	03 33	11 56	18 05	05 39	07	49
19	03 18	03 04	11 57	18 57	06 31	08	60
20	02 49	02 34	11 57	19 49	07 23	09	71

UT	ARIES	VENUS −4.1		MARS +1.4		JUPITER −2.1		SATURN +0.5		STARS		
	GHA	GHA	Dec	GHA	Dec	GHA	Dec	GHA	Dec	Name	SHA	Dec
d h	° ′	° ′	° ′	° ′	° ′	° ′	° ′	° ′	° ′		° ′	° ′
21 00	89 14.9	222 17.4	S15 15.7	248 00.4	S 7 19.2	275 28.2	N 3 59.0	200 43.4	S20 19.3	Acamar	315 16.8	S40 14.8
01	104 17.4	237 16.8	16.5	263 01.5	19.8	290 30.5	59.0	215 45.6	19.3	Achernar	335 25.4	S57 09.7
02	119 19.8	252 16.3	17.4	278 02.6	20.3	305 32.8	58.9	230 47.7	19.4	Acrux	173 07.3	S63 10.9
03	134 22.3	267 15.8	. . 18.2	293 03.7	. . 20.8	320 35.1	. . 58.9	245 49.9	. . 19.4	Adhara	255 10.8	S28 59.8
04	149 24.8	282 15.3	19.1	308 04.9	21.3	335 37.5	58.8	260 52.1	19.4	Aldebaran	290 47.1	N16 32.3
05	164 27.2	297 14.8	19.9	323 06.0	21.9	350 39.8	58.8	275 54.2	19.5			
06	179 29.7	312 14.2	S15 20.8	338 07.1	S 7 22.4	5 42.1	N 3 58.8	290 56.4	S20 19.5	Alioth	166 19.5	N55 52.2
07	194 32.2	327 13.7	21.6	353 08.3	22.9	20 44.5	58.7	305 58.6	19.6	Alkaid	152 57.9	N49 13.9
08	209 34.6	342 13.2	22.4	8 09.4	23.4	35 46.8	58.7	321 00.7	19.6	Al Na'ir	27 41.9	S46 53.1
M 09	224 37.1	357 12.7	. . 23.3	23 10.5	. . 24.0	50 49.1	. . 58.6	336 02.9	. . 19.7	Alnilam	275 44.3	S 1 11.7
O 10	239 39.6	12 12.2	24.1	38 11.7	24.5	65 51.5	58.6	351 05.1	19.7	Alphard	217 54.2	S 8 43.8
N 11	254 42.0	27 11.6	25.0	53 12.8	25.0	80 53.8	58.5	6 07.2	19.7			
D 12	269 44.5	42 11.1	S15 25.8	68 13.9	S 7 25.5	95 56.1	N 3 58.5	21 09.4	S20 19.8	Alphecca	126 09.9	N26 39.7
A 13	284 46.9	57 10.6	26.6	83 15.1	26.1	110 58.5	58.4	36 11.5	19.8	Alpheratz	357 41.7	N29 10.9
Y 14	299 49.4	72 10.1	27.5	98 16.2	26.6	126 00.8	58.4	51 13.7	19.9	Altair	62 06.9	N 8 54.9
15	314 51.9	87 09.5	. . 28.3	113 17.3	. . 27.1	141 03.1	. . 58.4	66 15.9	. . 19.9	Ankaa	353 14.1	S42 13.4
16	329 54.3	102 09.0	29.2	128 18.5	27.6	156 05.5	58.3	81 18.0	19.9	Antares	112 24.5	S26 27.8
17	344 56.8	117 08.5	30.0	143 19.6	28.1	171 07.8	58.3	96 20.2	20.0			
18	359 59.3	132 08.0	S15 30.8	158 20.7	S 7 28.7	186 10.1	N 3 58.2	111 22.4	S20 20.0	Arcturus	145 54.4	N19 06.0
19	15 01.7	147 07.4	31.7	173 21.9	29.2	201 12.5	58.2	126 24.5	20.1	Atria	107 25.3	S69 03.0
20	30 04.2	162 06.9	32.5	188 23.0	29.7	216 14.8	58.1	141 26.7	20.1	Avior	234 16.7	S59 33.6
21	45 06.7	177 06.4	. . 33.3	203 24.1	. . 30.2	231 17.1	. . 58.1	156 28.8	. . 20.1	Bellatrix	278 29.8	N 6 21.6
22	60 09.1	192 05.9	34.2	218 25.3	30.8	246 19.5	58.1	171 31.0	20.2	Betelgeuse	270 59.1	N 7 24.4
23	75 11.6	207 05.3	35.0	233 26.4	31.3	261 21.8	58.0	186 33.2	20.2			
22 00	90 14.1	222 04.8	S15 35.8	248 27.5	S 7 31.8	276 24.1	N 3 58.0	201 35.3	S20 20.3	Canopus	263 54.8	S52 42.4
01	105 16.5	237 04.3	36.7	263 28.6	32.3	291 26.5	57.9	216 37.5	20.3	Capella	280 31.4	N46 00.6
02	120 19.0	252 03.7	37.5	278 29.8	32.9	306 28.8	57.9	231 39.7	20.4	Deneb	49 30.6	N45 20.6
03	135 21.4	267 03.2	. . 38.3	293 30.9	. . 33.4	321 31.1	. . 57.8	246 41.8	. . 20.4	Denebola	182 31.9	N14 28.9
04	150 23.9	282 02.7	39.2	308 32.0	33.9	336 33.5	57.8	261 44.0	20.4	Diphda	348 54.1	S17 54.1
05	165 26.4	297 02.2	40.0	323 33.2	34.4	351 35.8	57.8	276 46.2	20.5			
06	180 28.8	312 01.6	S15 40.8	338 34.3	S 7 34.9	6 38.1	N 3 57.7	291 48.3	S20 20.5	Dubhe	193 49.6	N61 39.5
07	195 31.3	327 01.1	41.7	353 35.4	35.5	21 40.5	57.7	306 50.5	20.6	Elnath	278 10.1	N28 37.0
08	210 33.8	342 00.6	42.5	8 36.6	36.0	36 42.8	57.6	321 52.6	20.6	Eltanin	90 45.9	N51 29.4
T 09	225 36.2	357 00.0	. . 43.3	23 37.7	. . 36.5	51 45.2	. . 57.6	336 54.8	. . 20.6	Enif	33 45.6	N 9 57.1
U 10	240 38.7	11 59.5	44.1	38 38.8	37.0	66 47.5	57.5	351 57.0	20.7	Fomalhaut	15 22.3	S29 32.4
E 11	255 41.2	26 58.9	45.0	53 40.0	37.5	81 49.8	57.5	6 59.1	20.7			
S 12	270 43.6	41 58.4	S15 45.8	68 41.1	S 7 38.1	96 52.2	N 3 57.5	22 01.3	S20 20.8	Gacrux	171 58.9	S57 11.8
D 13	285 46.1	56 57.9	46.6	83 42.2	38.6	111 54.5	57.4	37 03.5	20.8	Gienah	175 50.5	S17 37.7
A 14	300 48.5	71 57.3	47.5	98 43.4	39.1	126 56.9	57.4	52 05.6	20.8	Hadar	148 45.7	S60 26.6
Y 15	315 51.0	86 56.8	. . 48.3	113 44.5	. . 39.6	141 59.2	. . 57.3	67 07.8	. . 20.9	Hamal	327 58.6	N23 32.3
16	330 53.5	101 56.3	49.1	128 45.6	40.2	157 01.5	57.3	82 10.0	20.9	Kaus Aust.	83 42.0	S34 22.4
17	345 55.9	116 55.7	49.9	143 46.8	40.7	172 03.9	57.3	97 12.1	21.0			
18	0 58.4	131 55.2	S15 50.7	158 47.9	S 7 41.2	187 06.2	N 3 57.2	112 14.3	S20 21.0	Kochab	137 21.2	N74 05.3
19	16 00.9	146 54.7	51.6	173 49.0	41.7	202 08.6	57.2	127 16.5	21.0	Markab	13 36.7	N15 17.6
20	31 03.3	161 54.1	52.4	188 50.2	42.2	217 10.9	57.1	142 18.6	21.1	Menkar	314 13.0	N 4 09.0
21	46 05.8	176 53.6	. . 53.2	203 51.3	. . 42.8	232 13.2	. . 57.1	157 20.8	. . 21.1	Menkent	148 05.7	S36 26.6
22	61 08.3	191 53.0	54.0	218 52.4	43.3	247 15.6	57.1	172 22.9	21.2	Miaplacidus	221 38.5	S69 46.8
23	76 10.7	206 52.5	54.9	233 53.6	43.8	262 17.9	57.0	187 25.1	21.2			
23 00	91 13.2	221 51.9	S15 55.7	248 54.7	S 7 44.3	277 20.3	N 3 57.0	202 27.3	S20 21.3	Mirfak	308 37.4	N49 55.0
01	106 15.7	236 51.4	56.5	263 55.8	44.8	292 22.6	56.9	217 29.4	21.3	Nunki	75 56.6	S26 16.4
02	121 18.1	251 50.9	57.3	278 57.0	45.3	307 25.0	56.9	232 31.6	21.3	Peacock	53 17.2	S56 41.0
03	136 20.6	266 50.3	. . 58.1	293 58.1	. . 45.9	322 27.3	. . 56.9	247 33.8	. . 21.4	Pollux	243 25.3	N27 59.0
04	151 23.0	281 49.8	58.9	308 59.2	46.4	337 29.6	56.8	262 35.9	21.4	Procyon	244 57.7	N 5 10.8
05	166 25.5	296 49.2	15 59.8	324 00.4	46.9	352 32.0	56.8	277 38.1	21.5			
06	181 28.0	311 48.7	S16 00.6	339 01.5	S 7 47.4	7 34.3	N 3 56.7	292 40.3	S20 21.5	Rasalhague	96 05.2	N12 33.1
W 07	196 30.4	326 48.1	01.4	354 02.7	47.9	22 36.7	56.7	307 42.4	21.5	Regulus	207 41.6	N11 53.2
E 08	211 32.9	341 47.6	02.2	9 03.8	48.5	37 39.0	56.7	322 44.6	21.6	Rigel	281 10.1	S 8 11.2
D 09	226 35.4	356 47.0	. . 03.0	24 04.9	. . 49.0	52 41.4	. . 56.6	337 46.8	. . 21.6	Rigil Kent.	139 49.7	S60 53.6
N 10	241 37.8	11 46.5	03.8	39 06.1	49.5	67 43.7	56.6	352 48.9	21.7	Sabik	102 10.9	S15 44.4
E 11	256 40.3	26 46.0	04.6	54 07.2	50.0	82 46.1	56.5	7 51.1	21.7			
S 12	271 42.8	41 45.4	S16 05.5	69 08.3	S 7 50.5	97 48.4	N 3 56.5	22 53.3	S20 21.7	Schedar	349 38.3	N56 37.7
D 13	286 45.2	56 44.9	06.3	84 09.5	51.1	112 50.7	56.5	37 55.4	21.8	Shaula	96 20.0	S37 06.6
A 14	301 47.7	71 44.3	07.1	99 10.6	51.6	127 53.1	56.4	52 57.6	21.8	Sirius	258 31.9	S16 44.5
Y 15	316 50.2	86 43.8	. . 07.9	114 11.7	. . 52.1	142 55.4	. . 56.4	67 59.7	. . 21.9	Spica	158 29.6	S11 14.5
16	331 52.6	101 43.2	08.7	129 12.9	52.6	157 57.8	56.4	83 01.9	21.9	Suhail	222 50.8	S43 29.8
17	346 55.1	116 42.7	09.5	144 14.0	53.1	173 00.1	56.3	98 04.1	21.9			
18	1 57.5	131 42.1	S16 10.3	159 15.1	S 7 53.6	188 02.5	N 3 56.3	113 06.2	S20 22.0	Vega	80 38.2	N38 48.2
19	17 00.0	146 41.5	11.1	174 16.3	54.2	203 04.8	56.2	128 08.4	22.0	Zuben'ubi	137 03.8	S16 06.2
20	32 02.5	161 41.0	11.9	189 17.4	54.7	218 07.2	56.2	143 10.6	22.1		SHA	Mer. Pass.
21	47 04.9	176 40.4	. . 12.7	204 18.5	. . 55.2	233 09.5	. . 56.2	158 12.7	. . 22.1		° ′	h m
22	62 07.4	191 39.9	13.5	219 19.7	55.7	248 11.9	56.1	173 14.9	22.1	Venus	131 50.8	9 12
23	77 09.9	206 39.3	14.3	234 20.8	56.2	263 14.2	56.1	188 17.1	22.2	Mars	158 13.5	7 26
	h m									Jupiter	186 10.1	5 34
Mer. Pass. 17 56.1		v −0.5	d 0.8	v 1.1	d 0.5	v 2.3	d 0.0	v 2.2	d 0.0	Saturn	111 21.3	10 32

UT	SUN GHA	SUN Dec	MOON GHA	v	Dec	d	HP	Lat.	Twilight Naut.	Twilight Civil	Sunrise	Moonrise 21	Moonrise 22	Moonrise 23	Moonrise 24
d h	° ′	° ′	° ′	′	° ′	′	′	°	h m	h m	h m	h m	h m	h m	h m
21 00	180 34.6	S23 25.7	60 27.9	8.7	N 8 48.9	10.0	59.5	N 72	08 26	10 58	■■■	12 04	11 58	11 50	11 29
01	195 34.3	25.8	74 55.6	8.7	8 58.9	9.9	59.5	N 70	08 06	09 55	■■■	12 21	12 25	12 35	12 57
02	210 34.0	25.8	89 23.3	8.6	9 08.8	9.9	59.5	68	07 50	09 19	■■■	12 34	12 46	13 05	13 36
03	225 33.7 ..	25.8	103 50.9	8.6	9 18.7	9.8	59.5	66	07 37	08 54	10 35	12 45	13 02	13 27	14 04
04	240 33.4	25.8	118 18.5	8.6	9 28.5	9.7	59.5	64	07 26	08 34	09 52	12 55	13 16	13 45	14 25
05	255 33.1	25.8	132 46.1	8.5	9 38.2	9.7	59.5	62	07 16	08 18	09 24	13 03	13 28	14 00	14 42
06	270 32.8	S23 25.9	147 13.6	8.5	N 9 47.9	9.6	59.5	60	07 08	08 04	09 02	13 10	13 37	14 12	14 56
07	285 32.5	25.9	161 41.1	8.4	9 57.5	9.6	59.5	N 58	07 00	07 53	08 45	13 16	13 46	14 23	15 08
08	300 32.2	25.9	176 08.5	8.4	10 07.1	9.5	59.5	56	06 53	07 42	08 30	13 22	13 54	14 32	15 19
M 09	315 31.9 ..	25.9	190 35.9	8.4	10 16.6	9.5	59.5	54	06 47	07 33	08 17	13 27	14 00	14 40	15 28
O 10	330 31.5	25.9	205 03.3	8.3	10 26.1	9.4	59.5	52	06 41	07 25	08 06	13 31	14 06	14 48	15 36
N 11	345 31.2	25.9	219 30.6	8.3	10 35.5	9.3	59.5	50	06 36	07 18	07 56	13 35	14 12	14 55	15 44
D 12	0 30.9	S23 26.0	233 57.9	8.3	N10 44.8	9.3	59.5	45	06 24	07 02	07 35	13 44	14 24	15 09	16 00
A 13	15 30.6	26.0	248 25.2	8.2	10 54.1	9.2	59.5	N 40	06 14	06 48	07 19	13 51	14 34	15 21	16 13
Y 14	30 30.3	26.0	262 52.4	8.2	11 03.3	9.1	59.5	35	06 04	06 36	07 04	13 58	14 43	15 31	16 24
15	45 30.0 ..	26.0	277 19.6	8.1	11 12.4	9.1	59.5	30	05 56	06 26	06 52	14 03	14 50	15 40	16 34
16	60 29.7	26.0	291 46.7	8.1	11 21.5	9.0	59.5	20	05 39	06 06	06 31	14 13	15 03	15 56	16 51
17	75 29.4	26.0	306 13.8	8.1	11 30.5	8.9	59.5	N 10	05 23	05 49	06 12	14 22	15 15	16 09	17 05
18	90 29.1	S23 26.0	320 40.9	8.0	N11 39.4	8.8	59.5	0	05 06	05 32	05 55	14 30	15 26	16 22	17 19
19	105 28.8	26.0	335 07.9	8.0	11 48.2	8.8	59.5	S 10	04 47	05 14	05 37	14 39	15 36	16 35	17 33
20	120 28.4	26.0	349 34.9	8.0	11 57.0	8.7	59.5	20	04 24	04 53	05 18	14 47	15 48	16 49	17 48
21	135 28.1 ..	26.1	4 01.9	7.9	12 05.7	8.6	59.5	30	03 55	04 28	04 56	14 58	16 02	17 05	18 05
22	150 27.8	26.1	18 28.8	7.9	12 14.3	8.6	59.5	35	03 36	04 13	04 43	15 04	16 09	17 14	18 15
23	165 27.5	26.1	32 55.7	7.8	12 22.9	8.4	59.5	40	03 13	03 55	04 28	15 10	16 18	17 24	18 26
22 00	180 27.2	S23 26.1	47 22.5	7.8	N12 31.3	8.4	59.5	45	02 43	03 32	04 10	15 18	16 29	17 37	18 40
01	195 26.9	26.1	61 49.3	7.8	12 39.7	8.4	59.5	S 50	01 57	03 03	03 47	15 28	16 42	17 52	18 56
02	210 26.6	26.1	76 16.1	7.7	12 48.1	8.2	59.5	52	01 29	02 47	03 36	15 32	16 47	17 59	19 04
03	225 26.3 ..	26.1	90 42.8	7.7	12 56.3	8.1	59.5	54	00 42	02 29	03 24	15 37	16 54	18 07	19 12
04	240 26.0	26.1	105 09.5	7.7	13 04.4	8.1	59.5	56	////	02 07	03 10	15 42	17 01	18 16	19 22
05	255 25.7	26.1	119 36.2	7.6	13 12.5	8.0	59.5	58	////	01 37	02 53	15 49	17 10	18 26	19 33
06	270 25.3	S23 26.1	134 02.8	7.6	N13 20.5	7.9	59.5	S 60	////	00 46	02 32	15 55	17 19	18 37	19 46

UT	SUN GHA	SUN Dec	MOON GHA	v	Dec	d	HP	Lat.	Sunset	Twilight Civil	Twilight Naut.	Moonset 21	Moonset 22	Moonset 23	Moonset 24
07	285 25.0	26.1	148 29.4	7.5	13 28.4	7.8	59.5	°	h m	h m	h m	h m	h m	h m	h m
08	300 24.7	26.1	162 55.9	7.6	13 36.2	7.8	59.5	N 72	■■■	12 59	15 31	04 09	06 09	08 15	10 35
T 09	315 24.4 ..	26.1	177 22.5	7.4	13 44.0	7.6	59.4	N 70	■■■	14 02	15 51	03 53	05 43	07 30	09 08
U 10	330 24.1	26.1	191 48.9	7.5	13 51.6	7.6	59.4	68	■■■	14 38	16 07	03 41	05 23	07 01	08 29
E 11	345 23.8	26.1	206 15.4	7.4	13 59.2	7.4	59.4	66	13 22	15 03	16 20	03 31	05 07	06 40	08 01
S 12	0 23.5	S23 26.0	220 41.8	7.4	N14 06.6	7.4	59.4	64	14 05	15 23	16 31	03 23	04 55	06 22	07 41
D 13	15 23.2	26.0	235 08.2	7.3	14 14.0	7.3	59.4	62	14 33	15 39	16 41	03 16	04 44	06 08	07 24
A 14	30 22.9	26.0	249 34.5	7.3	14 21.3	7.2	59.4	60	14 55	15 52	16 49	03 10	04 35	05 56	07 10
Y 15	45 22.6 ..	26.0	264 00.8	7.3	14 28.5	7.1	59.4	N 58	15 12	16 04	16 57	03 04	04 27	05 46	06 58
16	60 22.2	26.0	278 27.1	7.3	14 35.6	7.0	59.4	56	15 27	16 14	17 04	03 00	04 20	05 37	06 47
17	75 21.9	26.0	292 53.4	7.2	14 42.6	6.9	59.4	54	15 40	16 24	17 10	02 55	04 13	05 29	06 38
18	90 21.6	S23 26.0	307 19.6	7.2	N14 49.5	6.8	59.4	52	15 51	16 32	17 15	02 52	04 08	05 22	06 30
19	105 21.3	26.0	321 45.8	7.1	14 56.3	6.7	59.4	50	16 01	16 39	17 21	02 48	04 03	05 15	06 23
20	120 21.0	26.0	336 11.9	7.2	15 03.0	6.6	59.4	45	16 21	16 55	17 33	02 41	03 52	05 01	06 07
21	135 20.7 ..	26.0	350 38.1	7.1	15 09.6	6.6	59.4	N 40	16 38	17 09	17 43	02 34	03 43	04 50	05 54
22	150 20.4	26.0	5 04.2	7.0	15 16.2	6.4	59.3	35	16 52	17 21	17 52	02 29	03 35	04 40	05 43
23	165 20.1	25.9	19 30.2	7.1	15 22.6	6.3	59.3	30	17 05	17 31	18 01	02 24	03 28	04 32	05 34
23 00	180 19.8	S23 25.9	33 56.3	7.0	N15 28.9	6.2	59.3	20	17 26	17 50	18 18	02 16	03 16	04 17	05 17
01	195 19.5	25.9	48 22.3	7.0	15 35.1	6.2	59.3	N 10	17 45	18 08	18 34	02 09	03 06	04 04	05 03
02	210 19.1	25.9	62 48.3	6.9	15 41.3	6.0	59.3	0	18 02	18 25	18 51	02 02	02 56	03 52	04 49
03	225 18.8 ..	25.9	77 14.2	7.0	15 47.3	5.9	59.3	S 10	18 20	18 43	19 10	01 55	02 47	03 40	04 36
04	240 18.5	25.9	91 40.2	6.9	15 53.2	5.8	59.3	20	18 39	19 03	19 33	01 48	02 36	03 28	04 22
05	255 18.2	25.8	106 06.1	6.9	15 59.0	5.7	59.3	30	19 01	19 28	20 02	01 40	02 25	03 13	04 05
06	270 17.9	S23 25.8	120 32.0	6.8	N16 04.7	5.6	59.3	35	19 14	19 44	20 20	01 35	02 18	03 05	03 56
W 07	285 17.6	25.8	134 57.8	6.9	16 10.3	5.5	59.3	40	19 29	20 02	20 44	01 30	02 10	02 55	03 45
E 08	300 17.3	25.8	149 23.7	6.8	16 15.8	5.4	59.2	45	19 47	20 25	21 14	01 24	02 02	02 44	03 32
D 09	315 17.0 ..	25.8	163 49.5	6.8	16 21.2	5.3	59.2	S 50	20 10	20 54	22 00	01 16	01 51	02 30	03 16
N 10	330 16.7	25.7	178 15.3	6.8	16 26.5	5.2	59.2	52	20 21	21 09	22 28	01 13	01 46	02 24	03 09
E 11	345 16.4	25.7	192 41.1	6.8	16 31.7	5.0	59.2	54	20 33	21 27	23 15	01 09	01 40	02 17	03 01
S 12	0 16.0	S23 25.7	207 06.9	6.7	N16 36.7	5.0	59.2	56	20 47	21 50	////	01 05	01 34	02 09	02 52
D 13	15 15.7	25.7	221 32.6	6.8	16 41.7	4.9	59.2	58	21 04	22 20	////	01 00	01 28	02 01	02 41
A 14	30 15.4	25.6	235 58.4	6.7	16 46.6	4.7	59.2	S 60	21 25	23 11	////	00 55	01 20	01 51	02 30
Y 15	45 15.1 ..	25.6	250 24.1	6.7	16 51.3	4.6	59.1								
16	60 14.8	25.6	264 49.8	6.7	16 55.9	4.5	59.1			SUN			MOON		
17	75 14.5	25.5	279 15.5	6.7	17 00.4	4.5	59.1								
18	90 14.2	S23 25.5	293 41.2	6.6	N17 04.9	4.3	59.1	Day	Eqn. of Time 00ʰ	12ʰ	Mer. Pass.	Mer. Pass. Upper	Mer. Pass. Lower	Age	Phase
19	105 13.9	25.5	308 06.8	6.7	17 09.2	4.1	59.1	d	m s	m s	h m	h m	h m	d %	
20	120 13.6	25.4	322 32.5	6.6	17 13.3	4.1	59.1	21	02 19	02 04	11 58	20 43	08 16	10 81	
21	135 13.3 ..	25.4	336 58.1	6.6	17 17.4	4.0	59.1	22	01 49	01 35	11 58	21 39	09 11	11 89	
22	150 12.9	25.4	351 23.7	6.7	17 21.4	3.8	59.0	23	01 20	01 05	11 59	22 36	10 07	12 95	
23	165 12.6	25.3	5 49.4	6.6	N17 25.2	3.7	59.0								
	SD 16.3	d 0.0	SD 16.2		16.2		16.1									

UT	ARIES	VENUS −4.1		MARS +1.3		JUPITER −2.1		SATURN +0.5		STARS		
	GHA	GHA	Dec	GHA	Dec	GHA	Dec	GHA	Dec	Name	SHA	Dec
d h	° ′	° ′	° ′	° ′	° ′	° ′	° ′	° ′	° ′		° ′	° ′
24 00	92 12.3	221 38.8	S16 15.2	249 21.9	S 7 56.7	278 16.6	N 3 56.1	203 19.2	S20 22.2	Acamar	315 16.8	S40 14.8
01	107 14.8	236 38.2	16.0	264 23.1	57.3	293 18.9	56.0	218 21.4	22.3	Achernar	335 25.4	S57 09.7
02	122 17.3	251 37.7	16.8	279 24.2	57.8	308 21.3	56.0	233 23.6	22.3	Acrux	173 07.2	S63 10.9
03	137 19.7	266 37.1	. . 17.6	294 25.3	. . 58.3	323 23.6	. . 55.9	248 25.7	. . 22.3	Adhara	255 10.8	S28 59.8
04	152 22.2	281 36.6	18.4	309 26.5	58.8	338 26.0	55.9	263 27.9	22.4	Aldebaran	290 47.1	N16 32.3
05	167 24.7	296 36.0	19.2	324 27.6	59.3	353 28.3	55.9	278 30.1	22.4			
06	182 27.1	311 35.4	S16 20.0	339 28.8	S 7 59.8	8 30.7	N 3 55.8	293 32.2	S20 22.5	Alioth	166 19.4	N55 52.2
07	197 29.6	326 34.9	20.8	354 29.9	8 00.4	23 33.0	55.8	308 34.4	22.5	Alkaid	152 57.9	N49 13.9
T 08	212 32.0	341 34.3	21.6	9 31.0	00.9	38 35.4	55.8	323 36.6	22.5	Al Na'ir	27 41.9	S46 53.1
H 09	227 34.5	356 33.8	. . 22.4	24 32.2	. . 01.4	53 37.7	. . 55.7	338 38.7	. . 22.6	Alnilam	275 44.3	S 1 11.7
U 10	242 37.0	11 33.2	23.2	39 33.3	01.9	68 40.1	55.7	353 40.9	22.6	Alphard	217 54.2	S 8 43.8
R 11	257 39.4	26 32.6	24.0	54 34.4	02.4	83 42.4	55.7	8 43.1	22.7			
S 12	272 41.9	41 32.1	S16 24.8	69 35.6	S 8 02.9	98 44.8	N 3 55.6	23 45.2	S20 22.7	Alphecca	126 09.9	N26 39.7
D 13	287 44.4	56 31.5	25.6	84 36.7	03.4	113 47.1	55.6	38 47.4	22.7	Alpheratz	357 41.7	N29 10.9
A 14	302 46.8	71 31.0	26.4	99 37.8	04.0	128 49.5	55.6	53 49.6	22.8	Altair	62 06.9	N 8 54.8
Y 15	317 49.3	86 30.4	. . 27.1	114 39.0	. . 04.5	143 51.9	. . 55.5	68 51.7	. . 22.8	Ankaa	353 14.1	S42 13.4
16	332 51.8	101 29.8	27.9	129 40.1	05.0	158 54.2	55.5	83 53.9	22.9	Antares	112 24.5	S26 27.8
17	347 54.2	116 29.3	28.7	144 41.2	05.5	173 56.6	55.4	98 56.1	22.9			
18	2 56.7	131 28.7	S16 29.5	159 42.4	S 8 06.0	188 58.9	N 3 55.4	113 58.2	S20 22.9	Arcturus	145 54.4	N19 06.0
19	17 59.2	146 28.1	30.3	174 43.5	06.5	204 01.3	55.4	129 00.4	23.0	Atria	107 25.3	S69 03.0
20	33 01.6	161 27.6	31.1	189 44.7	07.0	219 03.6	55.3	144 02.6	23.0	Avior	234 16.7	S59 33.6
21	48 04.1	176 27.0	. . 31.9	204 45.8	. . 07.6	234 06.0	. . 55.3	159 04.7	. . 23.1	Bellatrix	278 29.8	N 6 21.6
22	63 06.5	191 26.4	32.7	219 46.9	08.1	249 08.3	55.3	174 06.9	23.1	Betelgeuse	270 59.1	N 7 24.4
23	78 09.0	206 25.9	33.5	234 48.1	08.6	264 10.7	55.2	189 09.1	23.1			
25 00	93 11.5	221 25.3	S16 34.3	249 49.2	S 8 09.1	279 13.0	N 3 55.2	204 11.2	S20 23.2	Canopus	263 54.8	S52 42.4
01	108 13.9	236 24.7	35.1	264 50.3	09.6	294 15.4	55.2	219 13.4	23.2	Capella	280 31.4	N46 00.6
02	123 16.4	251 24.2	35.8	279 51.5	10.1	309 17.8	55.1	234 15.6	23.3	Deneb	49 30.6	N45 20.5
03	138 18.9	266 23.6	. . 36.6	294 52.6	. . 10.6	324 20.1	. . 55.1	249 17.7	. . 23.3	Denebola	182 31.9	N14 28.9
04	153 21.3	281 23.0	37.4	309 53.7	11.2	339 22.5	55.1	264 19.9	23.3	Diphda	348 54.2	S17 54.1
05	168 23.8	296 22.5	38.2	324 54.9	11.7	354 24.8	55.0	279 22.1	23.4			
06	183 26.3	311 21.9	S16 39.0	339 56.0	S 8 12.2	9 27.2	N 3 55.0	294 24.2	S20 23.4	Dubhe	193 49.6	N61 39.5
07	198 28.7	326 21.3	39.8	354 57.2	12.7	24 29.6	55.0	309 26.4	23.5	Elnath	278 10.1	N28 37.0
08	213 31.2	341 20.7	40.6	9 58.3	13.2	39 31.9	54.9	324 28.6	23.5	Eltanin	90 45.9	N51 29.4
F 09	228 33.6	356 20.2	. . 41.3	24 59.4	. . 13.7	54 34.3	. . 54.9	339 30.7	. . 23.5	Enif	33 45.6	N 9 57.1
R 10	243 36.1	11 19.6	42.1	40 00.6	14.2	69 36.6	54.9	354 32.9	23.6	Fomalhaut	15 22.3	S29 32.4
I 11	258 38.6	26 19.0	42.9	55 01.7	14.7	84 39.0	54.8	9 35.1	23.6			
D 12	273 41.0	41 18.4	S16 43.7	70 02.8	S 8 15.3	99 41.3	N 3 54.8	24 37.2	S20 23.7	Gacrux	171 58.9	S57 11.8
A 13	288 43.5	56 17.9	44.5	85 04.0	15.8	114 43.7	54.8	39 39.4	23.7	Gienah	175 50.5	S17 37.7
Y 14	303 46.0	71 17.3	45.3	100 05.1	16.3	129 46.1	54.7	54 41.6	23.7	Hadar	148 45.6	S60 26.6
15	318 48.4	86 16.7	. . 46.0	115 06.3	. . 16.8	144 48.4	. . 54.7	69 43.7	. . 23.8	Hamal	327 58.6	N23 32.3
16	333 50.9	101 16.1	46.8	130 07.4	17.3	159 50.8	54.7	84 45.9	23.8	Kaus Aust.	83 42.0	S34 22.4
17	348 53.4	116 15.6	47.6	145 08.5	17.8	174 53.2	54.7	99 48.1	23.9			
18	3 55.8	131 15.0	S16 48.4	160 09.7	S 8 18.3	189 55.5	N 3 54.6	114 50.2	S20 23.9	Kochab	137 21.1	N74 05.3
19	18 58.3	146 14.4	49.1	175 10.8	18.8	204 57.9	54.6	129 52.4	23.9	Markab	13 36.7	N15 17.6
20	34 00.8	161 13.8	49.9	190 11.9	19.3	220 00.2	54.6	144 54.6	24.0	Menkar	314 13.0	N 4 09.0
21	49 03.2	176 13.3	. . 50.7	205 13.1	. . 19.9	235 02.6	. . 54.5	159 56.7	. . 24.0	Menkent	148 05.7	S36 26.6
22	64 05.7	191 12.7	51.5	220 14.2	20.4	250 05.0	54.5	174 58.9	24.1	Miaplacidus	221 38.4	S69 46.9
23	79 08.1	206 12.1	52.2	235 15.4	20.9	265 07.3	54.5	190 01.1	24.1			
26 00	94 10.6	221 11.5	S16 53.0	250 16.5	S 8 21.4	280 09.7	N 3 54.4	205 03.2	S20 24.1	Mirfak	308 37.4	N49 55.0
01	109 13.1	236 10.9	53.8	265 17.6	21.9	295 12.1	54.4	220 05.4	24.2	Nunki	75 56.6	S26 16.4
02	124 15.5	251 10.3	54.6	280 18.8	22.4	310 14.4	54.4	235 07.6	24.2	Peacock	53 17.2	S56 41.0
03	139 18.0	266 09.8	. . 55.3	295 19.9	. . 22.9	325 16.8	. . 54.3	250 09.8	. . 24.3	Pollux	243 25.3	N27 59.0
04	154 20.5	281 09.2	56.1	310 21.0	23.4	340 19.1	54.3	265 11.9	24.3	Procyon	244 57.6	N 5 10.8
05	169 22.9	296 08.6	56.9	325 22.2	23.9	355 21.5	54.3	280 14.1	24.3			
06	184 25.4	311 08.0	S16 57.6	340 23.3	S 8 24.4	10 23.9	N 3 54.3	295 16.3	S20 24.4	Rasalhague	96 05.2	N12 33.1
07	199 27.9	326 07.4	58.4	355 24.5	25.0	25 26.2	54.2	310 18.4	24.4	Regulus	207 41.5	N11 53.2
S 08	214 30.3	341 06.8	16 59.2	10 25.6	25.5	40 28.6	54.2	325 20.6	24.5	Rigel	281 10.1	S 8 11.2
A 09	229 32.8	356 06.3	17 00.0	25 26.7	. . 26.0	55 31.0	. . 54.2	340 22.8	. . 24.5	Rigil Kent.	139 49.7	S60 53.6
T 10	244 35.3	11 05.7	00.7	40 27.9	26.5	70 33.3	54.1	355 24.9	24.5	Sabik	102 10.9	S15 44.4
U 11	259 37.7	26 05.1	01.5	55 29.0	27.0	85 35.7	54.1	10 27.1	24.6			
R 12	274 40.2	41 04.5	S17 02.3	70 30.1	S 8 27.5	100 38.1	N 3 54.1	25 29.3	S20 24.6	Schedar	349 38.3	N56 37.7
D 13	289 42.6	56 03.9	03.0	85 31.3	28.0	115 40.4	54.0	40 31.4	24.6	Shaula	96 20.0	S37 06.6
A 14	304 45.1	71 03.3	03.8	100 32.4	28.5	130 42.8	54.0	55 33.6	24.7	Sirius	258 31.9	S16 44.5
Y 15	319 47.6	86 02.7	. . 04.5	115 33.6	. . 29.0	145 45.2	. . 54.0	70 35.8	. . 24.7	Spica	158 29.5	S11 14.5
16	334 50.0	101 02.1	05.3	130 34.7	29.5	160 47.5	54.0	85 37.9	24.8	Suhail	222 50.8	S43 29.8
17	349 52.5	116 01.6	06.1	145 35.8	30.0	175 49.9	53.9	100 40.1	24.8			
18	4 55.0	131 01.0	S17 06.8	160 37.0	S 8 30.6	190 52.3	N 3 53.9	115 42.3	S20 24.8	Vega	80 38.2	N38 48.1
19	19 57.4	146 00.4	07.6	175 38.1	31.1	205 54.6	53.9	130 44.4	24.9	Zuben'ubi	137 03.7	S16 06.3
20	34 59.9	160 59.8	08.3	190 39.3	31.6	220 57.0	53.8	145 46.6	24.9		SHA	Mer. Pass.
21	50 02.4	175 59.2	. . 09.1	205 40.4	. . 32.1	235 59.4	. . 53.8	160 48.8	. . 25.0		° ′	h m
22	65 04.8	190 58.6	09.9	220 41.5	32.6	251 01.8	53.8	175 51.0	25.0	Venus	128 13.8	9 15
23	80 07.3	205 58.0	10.6	235 42.7	33.1	266 04.1	53.8	190 53.1	25.0	Mars	156 37.7	7 20
	h m									Jupiter	186 01.6	5 22
Mer. Pass. 17 44.3		*v* −0.6	*d* 0.8	*v* 1.1	*d* 0.5	*v* 2.4	*d* 0.0	*v* 2.2	*d* 0.0	Saturn	110 59.8	10 22

SUN and MOON

UT	SUN GHA	SUN Dec	MOON GHA	v	MOON Dec	d	HP
d h	° ′	° ′	° ′	′	° ′	′	′
24 00	180 12.3	S23 25.3	20 15.0	6.6	N17 28.9	3.6	59.0
01	195 12.0	25.3	34 40.6	6.6	17 32.5	3.5	59.0
02	210 11.7	25.2	49 06.2	6.6	17 36.0	3.4	59.0
03	225 11.4	.. 25.2	63 31.8	6.6	17 39.4	3.3	59.0
04	240 11.1	25.2	77 57.4	6.6	17 42.7	3.1	58.9
05	255 10.8	25.1	92 23.0	6.6	17 45.8	3.1	58.9
06	270 10.5	S23 25.1	106 48.6	6.6	N17 48.9	2.9	58.9
07	285 10.2	25.0	121 14.2	6.6	17 51.8	2.8	58.9
T 08	300 09.9	25.0	135 39.8	6.6	17 54.6	2.7	58.9
H 09	315 09.5	.. 25.0	150 05.4	6.6	17 57.3	2.6	58.9
U 10	330 09.2	24.9	164 31.0	6.7	17 59.9	2.4	58.8
R 11	345 08.9	24.9	178 56.7	6.6	18 02.3	2.3	58.8
S 12	0 08.6	S23 24.8	193 22.3	6.6	N18 04.6	2.3	58.8
D 13	15 08.3	24.8	207 47.9	6.6	18 06.9	2.1	58.8
A 14	30 08.0	24.7	222 13.5	6.7	18 09.0	1.9	58.8
Y 15	45 07.7	.. 24.7	236 39.2	6.6	18 10.9	1.9	58.7
16	60 07.4	24.6	251 04.8	6.7	18 12.8	1.8	58.7
17	75 07.1	24.6	265 30.5	6.7	18 14.6	1.6	58.7
18	90 06.8	S23 24.5	279 56.2	6.7	N18 16.2	1.5	58.7
19	105 06.4	24.5	294 21.9	6.7	18 17.7	1.4	58.6
20	120 06.1	24.4	308 47.6	6.7	18 19.1	1.3	58.6
21	135 05.8	.. 24.4	323 13.3	6.8	18 20.4	1.1	58.6
22	150 05.5	24.3	337 39.1	6.8	18 21.5	1.1	58.6
23	165 05.2	24.3	352 04.9	6.7	18 22.6	0.9	58.6
25 00	180 04.9	S23 24.2	6 30.6	6.9	N18 23.5	0.8	58.5
01	195 04.6	24.2	20 56.5	6.8	18 24.3	0.7	58.5
02	210 04.3	24.1	35 22.3	6.8	18 25.0	0.6	58.5
03	225 04.0	.. 24.1	49 48.1	6.9	18 25.6	0.4	58.5
04	240 03.7	24.0	64 14.0	6.9	18 26.0	0.4	58.4
05	255 03.4	23.9	78 39.9	7.0	18 26.4	0.2	58.4
06	270 03.0	S23 23.9	93 05.9	6.9	N18 26.6	0.1	58.4
07	285 02.7	23.8	107 31.8	7.0	18 26.7	0.0	58.4
08	300 02.4	23.8	121 57.8	7.0	18 26.7	0.1	58.4
F 09	315 02.1	.. 23.7	136 23.8	7.1	18 26.6	0.3	58.3
R 10	330 01.8	23.6	150 49.9	7.1	18 26.3	0.3	58.3
I 11	345 01.5	23.6	165 16.0	7.1	18 26.0	0.5	58.3
D 12	0 01.2	S23 23.5	179 42.1	7.1	N18 25.5	0.6	58.2
A 13	15 00.9	23.5	194 08.2	7.2	18 24.9	0.7	58.2
Y 14	30 00.6	23.4	208 34.4	7.2	18 24.2	0.8	58.2
15	45 00.3	.. 23.3	223 00.6	7.3	18 23.4	0.9	58.2
16	60 00.0	23.3	237 26.9	7.3	18 22.5	1.1	58.2
17	74 59.6	23.2	251 53.2	7.3	18 21.4	1.3	58.1
18	89 59.3	S23 23.1	266 19.5	7.4	N18 20.3	1.3	58.1
19	104 59.0	23.0	280 45.9	7.5	18 19.0	1.3	58.1
20	119 58.7	23.0	295 12.4	7.4	18 17.7	1.5	58.1
21	134 58.4	.. 22.9	309 38.8	7.5	18 16.2	1.6	58.0
22	149 58.1	22.8	324 05.3	7.6	18 14.6	1.7	58.0
23	164 57.8	22.8	338 31.9	7.6	18 12.9	1.8	58.0
26 00	179 57.5	S23 22.7	352 58.5	7.6	N18 11.1	2.0	57.9
01	194 57.2	22.6	7 25.1	7.7	18 09.1	2.0	57.9
02	209 56.9	22.5	21 51.8	7.8	18 07.1	2.1	57.9
03	224 56.6	.. 22.5	36 18.6	7.8	18 05.0	2.3	57.9
04	239 56.3	22.4	50 45.4	7.8	18 02.7	2.3	57.8
05	254 55.9	22.3	65 12.2	7.9	18 00.4	2.5	57.8
06	269 55.6	S23 22.2	79 39.1	8.0	N17 57.9	2.5	57.8
07	284 55.3	22.1	94 06.1	8.0	17 55.4	2.7	57.8
S 08	299 55.0	22.1	108 33.1	8.0	17 52.7	2.7	57.7
A 09	314 54.7	.. 22.0	123 00.1	8.1	17 50.0	2.9	57.7
T 10	329 54.4	21.9	137 27.2	8.2	17 47.1	2.9	57.7
U 11	344 54.1	21.8	151 54.4	8.2	17 44.1	3.1	57.6
R 12	359 53.8	S23 21.7	166 21.6	8.3	N17 41.0	3.1	57.6
D 13	14 53.5	21.6	180 48.9	8.3	17 37.9	3.3	57.6
A 14	29 53.2	21.6	195 16.2	8.4	17 34.6	3.4	57.6
Y 15	44 52.9	.. 21.5	209 43.6	8.4	17 31.2	3.5	57.5
16	59 52.6	21.4	224 11.0	8.5	17 27.7	3.5	57.5
17	74 52.2	21.3	238 38.5	8.6	17 24.2	3.7	57.5
18	89 51.9	S23 21.2	253 06.1	8.6	N17 20.5	3.7	57.4
19	104 51.6	21.1	267 33.7	8.7	17 16.8	3.9	57.4
20	119 51.3	21.0	282 01.4	8.7	17 12.9	4.0	57.4
21	134 51.0	.. 20.9	296 29.1	8.8	17 08.9	4.0	57.4
22	149 50.7	20.8	310 56.9	8.9	17 04.9	4.1	57.3
23	164 50.4	20.8	325 24.8	8.9	N17 00.8	4.3	57.3
SD	16.3	d 0.1	SD 16.0		15.9		15.7

Twilight, Sunrise and Moonrise

Lat.	Twilight Naut.	Twilight Civil	Sunrise	Moonrise 24	25	26	27
°	h m	h m	h m	h m	h m	h m	h m
N 72	08 27	10 57	■■■■	11 29	▭	13 58	16 00
N 70	08 07	09 55	■■■■	12 57	13 45	15 04	16 38
68	07 51	09 20	■■■■	13 36	14 28	15 40	17 05
66	07 38	08 55	10 35	14 04	14 57	16 06	17 25
64	07 27	08 35	09 53	14 25	15 19	16 25	17 41
62	07 17	08 19	09 25	14 42	15 36	16 42	17 54
60	07 09	08 06	09 03	14 56	15 51	16 55	18 05
N 58	07 01	07 54	08 46	15 08	16 03	17 06	18 15
56	06 54	07 44	08 31	15 19	16 14	17 16	18 24
54	06 48	07 35	08 18	15 28	16 23	17 25	18 31
52	06 43	07 26	08 07	15 36	16 32	17 33	18 38
50	06 37	07 19	07 57	15 44	16 39	17 40	18 44
45	06 26	07 03	07 37	16 00	16 56	17 55	18 57
N 40	06 15	06 49	07 20	16 13	17 09	18 08	19 08
35	06 06	06 38	07 06	16 24	17 20	18 18	19 17
30	05 57	06 27	06 53	16 34	17 30	18 28	19 25
20	05 41	06 08	06 32	16 51	17 47	18 44	19 39
N 10	05 24	05 51	06 14	17 05	18 02	18 58	19 52
0	05 07	05 34	05 56	17 19	18 16	19 11	20 03
S 10	04 48	05 16	05 39	17 33	18 30	19 24	20 14
20	04 26	04 55	05 20	17 48	18 45	19 38	20 26
30	03 57	04 30	04 58	18 05	19 02	19 54	20 40
35	03 38	04 15	04 45	18 15	19 12	20 03	20 48
40	03 15	03 57	04 29	18 26	19 23	20 13	20 57
45	02 44	03 34	04 11	18 40	19 36	20 26	21 08
S 50	01 59	03 04	03 49	18 56	19 53	20 41	21 21
52	01 31	02 49	03 38	19 04	20 00	20 48	21 27
54	00 44	02 31	03 26	19 12	20 09	20 55	21 33
56	////	02 09	03 13	19 22	20 18	21 04	21 41
58	////	01 39	02 55	19 33	20 29	21 14	21 49
S 60	////	00 48	02 34	19 46	20 42	21 25	21 58

Sunset, Twilight and Moonset

Lat.	Sunset	Twilight Civil	Twilight Naut.	Moonset 24	25	26	27
°	h m	h m	h m	h m	h m	h m	h m
N 72	■■■■	13 03	15 33	10 35	▭	12 02	11 50
N 70	■■■■	14 05	15 53	09 08	10 19	10 55	11 11
68	■■■■	14 40	16 09	08 29	09 35	10 18	10 43
66	13 25	15 05	16 22	08 01	09 06	09 52	10 23
64	14 07	15 25	16 33	07 41	08 45	09 32	10 06
62	14 35	15 41	16 43	07 24	08 27	09 16	09 52
60	14 57	15 54	16 51	07 10	08 12	09 02	09 40
N 58	15 14	16 06	16 59	06 58	08 00	08 50	09 30
56	15 29	16 16	17 05	06 47	07 49	08 40	09 21
54	15 41	16 25	17 12	06 38	07 40	08 31	09 13
52	15 53	16 33	17 17	06 30	07 31	08 23	09 06
50	16 02	16 41	17 23	06 23	07 23	08 16	09 00
45	16 23	16 57	17 34	06 07	07 07	08 00	08 46
N 40	16 40	17 11	17 45	05 54	06 54	07 47	08 35
35	16 54	17 22	17 54	05 43	06 42	07 37	08 25
30	17 07	17 33	18 03	05 34	06 33	07 27	08 16
20	17 28	17 52	18 19	05 17	06 15	07 10	08 01
N 10	17 46	18 09	18 35	05 03	06 01	06 56	07 48
0	18 04	18 26	18 52	04 49	05 47	06 42	07 36
S 10	18 21	18 44	19 11	04 36	05 32	06 29	07 24
20	18 40	19 05	19 34	04 22	05 17	06 14	07 11
30	19 02	19 30	20 03	04 05	05 00	05 57	06 55
35	19 15	19 45	20 22	03 56	04 50	05 48	06 47
40	19 30	20 03	20 45	03 45	04 39	05 37	06 36
45	19 48	20 26	21 15	03 32	04 25	05 23	06 25
S 50	20 11	20 55	22 01	03 16	04 09	05 07	06 10
52	20 22	21 10	22 26	03 09	04 01	05 00	06 03
54	20 34	21 28	23 15	03 01	03 52	04 51	05 56
56	20 48	21 51	////	02 52	03 43	04 42	05 48
58	21 05	22 20	////	02 41	03 32	04 31	05 38
S 60	21 25	22 58	////	02 30	03 19	04 19	05 27

SUN and MOON data

Day	SUN Eqn. of Time 00h	SUN Eqn. of Time 12h	SUN Mer. Pass.	MOON Mer. Pass. Upper	MOON Mer. Pass. Lower	Age	Phase
d	m s	m s	h m	h m	h m	d	%
24	00 50	00 35	11 59	23 33	11 04	13	99
25	00 20	00 05	12 00	24 29	12 01	14	100
26	00 09	00 24	12 00	00 29	12 57	15	99

UT	ARIES	VENUS −4.1		MARS +1.3		JUPITER −2.1		SATURN +0.5		STARS		
	GHA	GHA	Dec	GHA	Dec	GHA	Dec	GHA	Dec	Name	SHA	Dec
d h	° ′	° ′	° ′	° ′	° ′	° ′	° ′	° ′	° ′		° ′	° ′
27 00	95 09.8	220 57.4	S17 11.4	250 43.8	S 8 33.6	281 06.5	N 3 53.7	205 55.3	S20 25.1	Acamar	315 16.8	S40 14.8
01	110 12.2	235 56.8	12.1	265 44.9	34.1	296 08.9	53.7	220 57.5	25.1	Achernar	335 25.4	S57 09.7
02	125 14.7	250 56.2	12.9	280 46.1	34.6	311 11.2	53.7	235 59.6	25.2	Acrux	173 07.2	S63 10.9
03	140 17.1	265 55.6	.. 13.6	295 47.2	.. 35.1	326 13.6	.. 53.6	251 01.8	.. 25.2	Adhara	255 10.8	S28 59.8
04	155 19.6	280 55.0	14.4	310 48.4	35.6	341 16.0	53.6	266 04.0	25.2	Aldebaran	290 47.1	N16 32.3
05	170 22.1	295 54.4	15.2	325 49.5	36.1	356 18.4	53.6	281 06.1	25.3			
06	185 24.5	310 53.8	S17 15.9	340 50.6	S 8 36.6	11 20.7	N 3 53.6	296 08.3	S20 25.3	Alioth	166 19.4	N55 52.1
07	200 27.0	325 53.2	16.7	355 51.8	37.2	26 23.1	53.5	311 10.5	25.3	Alkaid	152 57.8	N49 13.9
08	215 29.5	340 52.6	17.4	10 52.9	37.7	41 25.5	53.5	326 12.7	25.4	Al Na'ir	27 41.9	S46 53.1
S 09	230 31.9	355 52.0	.. 18.2	25 54.1	.. 38.2	56 27.8	.. 53.5	341 14.8	.. 25.4	Alnilam	275 44.3	S 1 11.8
U 10	245 34.4	10 51.4	18.9	40 55.2	38.7	71 30.2	53.5	356 17.0	25.5	Alphard	217 54.2	S 8 43.8
N 11	260 36.9	25 50.8	19.7	55 56.3	39.2	86 32.6	53.4	11 19.2	25.5			
D 12	275 39.3	40 50.2	S17 20.4	70 57.5	S 8 39.7	101 35.0	N 3 53.4	26 21.3	S20 25.5	Alphecca	126 09.9	N26 39.7
A 13	290 41.8	55 49.6	21.2	85 58.6	40.2	116 37.3	53.4	41 23.5	25.6	Alpheratz	357 41.7	N29 10.9
Y 14	305 44.3	70 49.0	21.9	100 59.8	40.7	131 39.7	53.4	56 25.7	25.6	Altair	62 06.9	N 8 54.8
15	320 46.7	85 48.4	.. 22.7	116 00.9	.. 41.2	146 42.1	.. 53.3	71 27.8	.. 25.7	Ankaa	353 14.1	S42 13.4
16	335 49.2	100 47.8	23.4	131 02.0	41.7	161 44.5	53.3	86 30.0	25.7	Antares	112 24.5	S26 27.8
17	350 51.6	115 47.2	24.1	146 03.2	42.2	176 46.8	53.3	101 32.2	25.7			
18	5 54.1	130 46.6	S17 24.9	161 04.3	S 8 42.7	191 49.2	N 3 53.3	116 34.4	S20 25.8	Arcturus	145 54.4	N19 06.0
19	20 56.6	145 46.0	25.6	176 05.5	43.2	206 51.6	53.2	131 36.5	25.8	Atria	107 25.2	S69 03.0
20	35 59.0	160 45.4	26.4	191 06.6	43.7	221 54.0	53.2	146 38.7	25.8	Avior	234 16.6	S59 33.7
21	51 01.5	175 44.8	.. 27.1	206 07.7	.. 44.2	236 56.3	.. 53.2	161 40.9	.. 25.9	Bellatrix	278 29.8	N 6 21.6
22	66 04.0	190 44.2	27.9	221 08.9	44.7	251 58.7	53.2	176 43.0	25.9	Betelgeuse	270 59.1	N 7 24.4
23	81 06.4	205 43.6	28.6	236 10.0	45.2	267 01.1	53.1	191 45.2	26.0			
28 00	96 08.9	220 43.0	S17 29.3	251 11.2	S 8 45.7	282 03.5	N 3 53.1	206 47.4	S20 26.0	Canopus	263 54.8	S52 42.5
01	111 11.4	235 42.4	30.1	266 12.3	46.2	297 05.9	53.1	221 49.5	26.0	Capella	280 31.4	N46 00.7
02	126 13.8	250 41.8	30.8	281 13.4	46.8	312 08.2	53.1	236 51.7	26.1	Deneb	49 30.6	N45 20.5
03	141 16.3	265 41.2	.. 31.6	296 14.6	.. 47.3	327 10.6	.. 53.0	251 53.9	.. 26.1	Denebola	182 31.9	N14 28.9
04	156 18.7	280 40.6	32.3	311 15.7	47.8	342 13.0	53.0	266 56.1	26.2	Diphda	348 54.2	S17 54.1
05	171 21.2	295 39.9	33.0	326 16.9	48.3	357 15.4	53.0	281 58.2	26.2			
06	186 23.7	310 39.3	S17 33.8	341 18.0	S 8 48.8	12 17.7	N 3 53.0	297 00.4	S20 26.2	Dubhe	193 49.5	N61 39.5
07	201 26.1	325 38.7	34.5	356 19.2	49.3	27 20.1	52.9	312 02.6	26.3	Elnath	278 10.1	N28 37.0
08	216 28.6	340 38.1	35.2	11 20.3	49.8	42 22.5	52.9	327 04.7	26.3	Eltanin	90 45.9	N51 29.4
M 09	231 31.1	355 37.5	.. 36.0	26 21.4	.. 50.3	57 24.9	.. 52.9	342 06.9	.. 26.3	Enif	33 45.6	N 9 57.1
O 10	246 33.5	10 36.9	36.7	41 22.6	50.8	72 27.3	52.9	357 09.1	26.4	Fomalhaut	15 22.3	S29 32.4
N 11	261 36.0	25 36.3	37.4	56 23.7	51.3	87 29.6	52.8	12 11.3	26.4			
D 12	276 38.5	40 35.7	S17 38.2	71 24.9	S 8 51.8	102 32.0	N 3 52.8	27 13.4	S20 26.5	Gacrux	171 58.8	S57 11.8
A 13	291 40.9	55 35.1	38.9	86 26.0	52.3	117 34.4	52.8	42 15.6	26.5	Gienah	175 50.5	S17 37.7
Y 14	306 43.4	70 34.4	39.6	101 27.1	52.8	132 36.8	52.8	57 17.8	26.5	Hadar	148 45.6	S60 26.6
15	321 45.9	85 33.8	.. 40.4	116 28.3	.. 53.3	147 39.2	.. 52.7	72 19.9	.. 26.6	Hamal	327 58.6	N23 32.3
16	336 48.3	100 33.2	41.1	131 29.4	53.8	162 41.6	52.7	87 22.1	26.6	Kaus Aust.	83 42.0	S34 22.4
17	351 50.8	115 32.6	41.8	146 30.6	54.3	177 43.9	52.7	102 24.3	26.7			
18	6 53.2	130 32.0	S17 42.5	161 31.7	S 8 54.8	192 46.3	N 3 52.7	117 26.5	S20 26.7	Kochab	137 21.1	N74 05.3
19	21 55.7	145 31.4	43.3	176 32.8	55.3	207 48.7	52.7	132 28.6	26.7	Markab	13 36.7	N15 17.6
20	36 58.2	160 30.7	44.0	191 34.0	55.8	222 51.1	52.6	147 30.8	26.8	Menkar	314 13.0	N 4 09.0
21	52 00.6	175 30.1	.. 44.7	206 35.1	.. 56.3	237 53.5	.. 52.6	162 33.0	.. 26.8	Menkent	148 05.7	S36 26.6
22	67 03.1	190 29.5	45.4	221 36.3	56.8	252 55.9	52.6	177 35.1	26.8	Miaplacidus	221 38.4	S69 46.9
23	82 05.6	205 28.9	46.2	236 37.4	57.3	267 58.2	52.6	192 37.3	26.9			
29 00	97 08.0	220 28.3	S17 46.9	251 38.6	S 8 57.8	283 00.6	N 3 52.6	207 39.5	S20 26.9	Mirfak	308 37.4	N49 55.1
01	112 10.5	235 27.6	47.6	266 39.7	58.3	298 03.0	52.5	222 41.7	27.0	Nunki	75 56.6	S26 16.4
02	127 13.0	250 27.0	48.3	281 40.8	58.8	313 05.4	52.5	237 43.8	27.0	Peacock	53 17.2	S56 41.0
03	142 15.4	265 26.4	.. 49.1	296 42.0	.. 59.3	328 07.8	.. 52.5	252 46.0	.. 27.0	Pollux	243 25.3	N27 59.0
04	157 17.9	280 25.8	49.8	311 43.1	8 59.8	343 10.2	52.5	267 48.2	27.1	Procyon	244 57.6	N 5 10.8
05	172 20.4	295 25.2	50.5	326 44.3	9 00.3	358 12.5	52.4	282 50.3	27.1			
06	187 22.8	310 24.5	S17 51.2	341 45.4	S 9 00.8	13 14.9	N 3 52.4	297 52.5	S20 27.1	Rasalhague	96 05.2	N12 33.1
07	202 25.3	325 23.9	51.9	356 46.5	01.3	28 17.3	52.4	312 54.7	27.2	Regulus	207 41.5	N11 53.2
08	217 27.7	340 23.3	52.6	11 47.7	01.8	43 19.7	52.4	327 56.9	27.2	Rigel	281 10.1	S 8 11.2
T 09	232 30.2	355 22.7	.. 53.4	26 48.8	.. 02.3	58 22.1	.. 52.4	342 59.0	.. 27.3	Rigil Kent.	139 49.6	S60 53.6
U 10	247 32.7	10 22.0	54.1	41 50.0	02.8	73 24.5	52.3	358 01.2	27.3	Sabik	102 10.9	S15 44.4
E 11	262 35.1	25 21.4	54.8	56 51.1	03.3	88 26.9	52.3	13 03.4	27.3			
S 12	277 37.6	40 20.8	S17 55.5	71 52.3	S 9 03.8	103 29.3	N 3 52.3	28 05.6	S20 27.4	Schedar	349 38.4	N56 37.7
D 13	292 40.1	55 20.2	56.2	86 53.4	04.3	118 31.6	52.3	43 07.7	27.4	Shaula	96 20.0	S37 06.6
A 14	307 42.5	70 19.5	56.9	101 54.5	04.8	133 34.0	52.3	58 09.9	27.4	Sirius	258 31.8	S16 44.5
Y 15	322 45.0	85 18.9	.. 57.6	116 55.7	.. 05.3	148 36.4	.. 52.2	73 12.1	.. 27.5	Spica	158 29.5	S11 14.5
16	337 47.5	100 18.3	58.4	131 56.8	05.8	163 38.8	52.2	88 14.2	27.5	Suhail	222 50.8	S43 29.8
17	352 49.9	115 17.6	59.1	146 58.0	06.3	178 41.2	52.2	103 16.4	27.6			
18	7 52.4	130 17.0	S17 59.8	161 59.1	S 9 06.8	193 43.6	N 3 52.2	118 18.6	S20 27.6	Vega	80 38.2	N38 48.1
19	22 54.9	145 16.4	18 00.5	177 00.3	07.3	208 46.0	52.2	133 20.8	27.6	Zuben'ubi	137 03.7	S16 06.3
20	37 57.3	160 15.8	01.2	192 01.4	07.8	223 48.4	52.1	148 22.9	27.7		SHA	Mer. Pass.
21	52 59.8	175 15.1	.. 01.9	207 02.5	.. 08.3	238 50.8	.. 52.1	163 25.1	.. 27.7		° ′	h m
22	68 02.2	190 14.5	02.6	222 03.7	08.8	253 53.2	52.1	178 27.3	27.7	Venus	124 34.1	9 18
23	83 04.7	205 13.9	03.3	237 04.8	09.3	268 55.5	52.1	193 29.5	27.8	Mars	155 02.3	7 15
	h m									Jupiter	185 54.6	5 11
Mer. Pass. 17 32.5		v −0.6	d 0.7	v 1.1	d 0.5	v 2.4	d 0.0	v 2.2	d 0.0	Saturn	110 38.5	10 11

UT	SUN GHA	SUN Dec	MOON GHA	v	MOON Dec	d	HP
d h	° ′	° ′	° ′	′	° ′	′	′
27 00	179 50.1	S23 20.7	339 52.7	9.0	N16 56.5	4.3	57.3
01	194 49.8	20.6	354 20.7	9.1	16 52.2	4.4	57.2
02	209 49.5	20.5	8 48.8	9.1	16 47.8	4.5	57.2
03	224 49.2	.. 20.4	23 16.9	9.2	16 43.3	4.6	57.2
04	239 48.9	20.3	37 45.1	9.3	16 38.7	4.7	57.2
05	254 48.6	20.2	52 13.4	9.3	16 34.0	4.8	57.1
06	269 48.3	S23 20.1	66 41.7	9.4	N16 29.2	4.8	57.1
07	284 47.9	20.0	81 10.1	9.4	16 24.4	5.0	57.1
S 08	299 47.6	19.9	95 38.5	9.5	16 19.4	5.0	57.0
U 09	314 47.3	.. 19.8	110 07.0	9.6	16 14.4	5.1	57.0
N 10	329 47.0	19.7	124 35.6	9.6	16 09.3	5.2	57.0
D 11	344 46.7	19.6	139 04.2	9.8	16 04.1	5.3	56.9
A 12	359 46.4	S23 19.5	153 33.0	9.7	N15 58.8	5.3	56.9
Y 13	14 46.1	19.4	168 01.7	9.9	15 53.5	5.5	56.9
14	29 45.8	19.3	182 30.6	9.9	15 48.0	5.5	56.9
15	44 45.5	.. 19.2	196 59.5	10.0	15 42.5	5.6	56.8
16	59 45.2	19.1	211 28.5	10.0	15 36.9	5.6	56.8
17	74 44.9	18.9	225 57.5	10.1	15 31.3	5.8	56.8
18	89 44.6	S23 18.8	240 26.6	10.2	N15 25.5	5.8	56.7
19	104 44.3	18.7	254 55.8	10.3	15 19.7	5.9	56.7
20	119 44.0	18.6	269 25.1	10.3	15 13.8	6.0	56.7
21	134 43.7	.. 18.5	283 54.4	10.4	15 07.8	6.0	56.6
22	149 43.3	18.4	298 23.8	10.5	15 01.8	6.1	56.6
23	164 43.0	18.3	312 53.3	10.5	14 55.7	6.2	56.6
28 00	179 42.7	S23 18.2	327 22.8	10.6	N14 49.5	6.3	56.6
01	194 42.4	18.1	341 52.4	10.7	14 43.2	6.3	56.5
02	209 42.1	17.9	356 22.0	10.8	14 36.9	6.4	56.5
03	224 41.8	.. 17.8	10 51.8	10.8	14 30.5	6.5	56.5
04	239 41.5	17.7	25 21.6	10.8	14 24.0	6.5	56.4
05	254 41.2	17.6	39 51.4	11.0	14 17.5	6.6	56.4
06	269 40.9	S23 17.5	54 21.4	11.0	N14 10.9	6.7	56.4
07	284 40.6	17.4	68 51.4	11.0	14 04.2	6.7	56.4
08	299 40.3	17.2	83 21.4	11.2	13 57.5	6.8	56.3
M 09	314 40.0	.. 17.1	97 51.6	11.2	13 50.7	6.9	56.3
O 10	329 39.7	17.0	112 21.8	11.2	13 43.8	6.9	56.3
N 11	344 39.4	16.9	126 52.0	11.4	13 36.9	7.0	56.2
D 12	359 39.1	S23 16.7	141 22.4	11.4	N13 29.9	7.0	56.2
A 13	14 38.8	16.6	155 52.8	11.4	13 22.9	7.1	56.2
Y 14	29 38.5	16.5	170 23.2	11.6	13 15.8	7.2	56.2
15	44 38.2	.. 16.4	184 53.8	11.6	13 08.6	7.2	56.1
16	59 37.8	16.2	199 24.4	11.6	13 01.4	7.3	56.1
17	74 37.5	16.1	213 55.0	11.8	12 54.1	7.3	56.1
18	89 37.2	S23 16.0	228 25.8	11.8	N12 46.8	7.4	56.0
19	104 36.9	15.9	242 56.6	11.8	12 39.4	7.4	56.0
20	119 36.6	15.7	257 27.4	12.0	12 32.0	7.5	56.0
21	134 36.3	.. 15.5	271 58.4	12.0	12 24.5	7.5	56.0
22	149 36.0	15.5	286 29.4	12.0	12 17.0	7.6	55.9
23	164 35.7	15.3	301 00.4	12.1	12 09.4	7.7	55.9
29 00	179 35.4	S23 15.2	315 31.5	12.2	N12 01.7	7.6	55.9
01	194 35.1	15.1	330 02.7	12.2	11 54.1	7.8	55.9
02	209 34.8	14.9	344 33.9	12.4	11 46.3	7.8	55.8
03	224 34.5	.. 14.8	359 05.3	12.3	11 38.5	7.8	55.8
04	239 34.2	14.7	13 36.6	12.4	11 30.7	7.9	55.8
05	254 33.9	14.5	28 08.0	12.5	11 22.8	7.9	55.7
06	269 33.6	S23 14.4	42 39.5	12.6	N11 14.9	8.0	55.7
07	284 33.3	14.3	57 11.1	12.6	11 06.9	8.0	55.7
T 08	299 33.0	14.1	71 42.7	12.7	10 58.9	8.1	55.7
U 09	314 32.7	.. 14.0	86 14.4	12.7	10 50.8	8.1	55.6
E 10	329 32.4	13.8	100 46.1	12.8	10 42.7	8.1	55.6
S 11	344 32.1	13.7	115 17.9	12.8	10 34.6	8.2	55.6
D 12	359 31.8	S23 13.6	129 49.7	12.9	N10 26.4	8.2	55.6
A 13	14 31.5	13.4	144 21.6	13.0	10 18.2	8.3	55.5
Y 14	29 31.2	13.3	158 53.6	13.0	10 09.9	8.3	55.5
15	44 30.9	.. 13.1	173 25.6	13.1	10 01.6	8.3	55.5
16	59 30.6	13.0	187 57.7	13.1	9 53.3	8.4	55.5
17	74 30.3	12.8	202 29.8	13.2	9 44.9	8.4	55.4
18	89 29.9	S23 12.7	217 02.0	13.2	N 9 36.5	8.5	55.4
19	104 29.6	12.5	231 34.2	13.3	9 28.0	8.4	55.4
20	119 29.3	12.4	246 06.5	13.3	9 19.6	8.5	55.3
21	134 29.0	.. 12.2	260 38.8	13.4	9 11.1	8.6	55.3
22	149 28.7	12.1	275 11.2	13.5	9 02.5	8.6	55.3
23	164 28.4	11.9	289 43.7	13.5	N 8 53.9	8.6	55.3
	SD 16.3	d 0.1	SD 15.5		15.3		15.1

Twilight / Moonrise

Lat.	Twilight Naut.	Twilight Civil	Sunrise	Moonrise 27	28	29	30
°	h m	h m	h m	h m	h m	h m	h m
N 72	08 27	10 53	■	16 00	17 51	19 34	21 12
N 70	08 07	09 54	■	16 38	18 15	19 49	21 20
68	07 51	09 20		17 05	18 33	20 01	21 27
66	07 38	08 55	10 34	17 25	18 48	20 11	21 32
64	07 27	08 35	09 53	17 41	19 00	20 19	21 37
62	07 18	08 19	09 25	17 54	19 10	20 26	21 41
60	07 09	08 06	09 03	18 05	19 19	20 32	21 44
N 58	07 02	07 54	08 46	18 15	19 26	20 37	21 47
56	06 55	07 44	08 32	18 24	19 33	20 42	21 50
54	06 49	07 35	08 19	18 31	19 39	20 46	21 52
52	06 44	07 27	08 08	18 38	19 44	20 50	21 55
50	06 38	07 20	07 58	18 44	19 49	20 53	21 57
45	06 27	07 04	07 38	18 57	19 59	21 01	22 01
N 40	06 16	06 50	07 21	19 08	20 08	21 07	22 05
35	06 07	06 39	07 07	19 17	20 16	21 12	22 08
30	05 58	06 28	06 55	19 25	20 22	21 17	22 11
20	05 42	06 09	06 33	19 39	20 33	21 25	22 15
N 10	05 26	05 52	06 15	19 52	20 43	21 32	22 20
0	05 09	05 35	05 58	20 03	20 52	21 39	22 24
S 10	04 50	05 17	05 40	20 14	21 02	21 46	22 28
20	04 28	04 57	05 21	20 26	21 11	21 53	22 32
30	03 59	04 32	04 59	20 40	21 22	22 01	22 37
35	03 40	04 17	04 46	20 48	21 29	22 05	22 39
40	03 17	03 59	04 31	20 57	21 36	22 11	22 42
45	02 47	03 36	04 13	21 08	21 45	22 17	22 46
S 50	02 01	03 07	03 51	21 21	21 55	22 24	22 50
52	01 34	02 52	03 40	21 27	22 00	22 27	22 52
54	00 49	02 34	03 28	21 33	22 05	22 31	22 54
56	////	02 12	03 14	21 41	22 10	22 35	22 57
58	////	01 42	02 57	21 49	22 17	22 40	22 59
S 60	////	00 54	02 37	21 58	22 24	22 45	23 02

Sunset / Twilight / Moonset

Lat.	Sunset	Twilight Civil	Twilight Naut.	Moonset 27	28	29	30
°	h m	h m	h m	h m	h m	h m	h m
N 72	■	13 10	15 36	11 50	11 43	11 37	11 32
N 70	■	14 09	15 56	11 11	11 18	11 21	11 22
68	■	14 43	16 12	10 43	10 58	11 08	11 14
66	13 29	15 08	16 25	10 23	10 43	10 57	11 07
64	14 10	15 28	16 36	10 06	10 30	10 48	11 01
62	14 38	15 43	16 45	09 52	10 19	10 40	10 56
60	14 59	15 57	16 54	09 40	10 10	10 33	10 52
N 58	15 17	16 08	17 01	09 30	10 02	10 27	10 48
56	15 31	16 19	17 08	09 21	09 54	10 22	10 45
54	15 44	16 28	17 14	09 13	09 48	10 17	10 42
52	15 55	16 36	17 19	09 06	09 42	10 12	10 39
50	16 05	16 43	17 25	09 00	09 37	10 09	10 36
45	16 25	16 59	17 36	08 46	09 26	10 00	10 31
N 40	16 42	17 12	17 47	08 35	09 16	09 53	10 26
35	16 56	17 24	17 59	08 25	09 08	09 46	10 22
30	17 08	17 35	18 05	08 16	09 01	09 41	10 18
20	17 29	17 53	18 21	08 01	08 48	09 31	10 12
N 10	17 48	18 11	18 37	07 48	08 37	09 23	10 06
0	18 05	18 28	18 54	07 36	08 27	09 15	10 01
S 10	18 23	18 46	19 13	07 24	08 17	09 07	09 55
20	18 41	19 06	19 35	07 11	08 05	08 59	09 50
30	19 03	19 31	20 04	06 55	07 53	08 49	09 43
35	19 16	19 46	20 23	06 47	07 45	08 43	09 39
40	19 31	20 04	20 46	06 36	07 37	08 37	09 35
45	19 49	20 26	21 16	06 25	07 27	08 29	09 30
S 50	20 11	20 56	22 01	06 10	07 15	08 20	09 24
52	20 23	21 11	22 28	06 03	07 09	08 16	09 21
54	20 34	21 29	23 12	05 56	07 03	08 11	09 18
56	20 48	21 50	////	05 48	06 56	08 06	09 15
58	21 05	22 20	////	05 38	06 48	08 00	09 11
S 60	21 25	23 07	////	05 27	06 40	07 53	09 06

SUN and MOON

Day	Eqn. of Time 00h	12h	Mer. Pass.	Mer. Pass. Upper	Lower	Age	Phase
d	m s	m s	h m	h m	h m	d	%
27	00 39	00 54	12 01	01 23	13 50	16	95
28	01 08	01 23	12 01	02 15	14 40	17	90
29	01 38	01 52	12 02	03 04	15 27	18	83

UT	ARIES	VENUS −4.1		MARS +1.3		JUPITER −2.2		SATURN +0.5		STARS		
	GHA	GHA	Dec	GHA	Dec	GHA	Dec	GHA	Dec	Name	SHA	Dec
d h	° ′	° ′	° ′	° ′	° ′	° ′	° ′	° ′	° ′		° ′	° ′
30 00	98 07.2	220 13.2	S18 04.0	252 06.0	S 9 09.8	283 57.9	N 3 52.1	208 31.6	S20 27.8	Acamar	315 16.8	S40 14.8
01	113 09.6	235 12.6	04.7	267 07.1	10.3	299 00.3	52.1	223 33.8	27.9	Achernar	335 25.4	S57 09.7
02	128 12.1	250 12.0	05.4	282 08.3	10.8	314 02.7	52.0	238 36.0	27.9	Acrux	173 07.1	S63 10.9
03	143 14.6	265 11.3	.. 06.1	297 09.4	.. 11.3	329 05.1	.. 52.0	253 38.2	.. 27.9	Adhara	255 10.8	S28 59.8
04	158 17.0	280 10.7	06.8	312 10.6	11.8	344 07.5	52.0	268 40.3	28.0	Aldebaran	290 47.1	N16 32.3
05	173 19.5	295 10.1	07.5	327 11.7	12.3	359 09.9	52.0	283 42.5	28.0			
06	188 22.0	310 09.4	S18 08.2	342 12.8	S 9 12.8	14 12.3	N 3 52.0	298 44.7	S20 28.0	Alioth	166 19.4	N55 52.1
W 07	203 24.4	325 08.8	08.9	357 14.0	13.3	29 14.7	51.9	313 46.8	28.1	Alkaid	152 57.8	N49 13.8
E 08	218 26.9	340 08.1	09.6	12 15.1	13.8	44 17.1	51.9	328 49.0	28.1	Al Na'ir	27 42.0	S46 53.1
D 09	233 29.3	355 07.5	.. 10.3	27 16.3	.. 14.3	59 19.5	.. 51.9	343 51.2	.. 28.2	Alnilam	275 44.3	S 1 11.8
N 10	248 31.8	10 06.9	11.0	42 17.4	14.8	74 21.9	51.9	358 53.4	28.2	Alphard	217 54.1	S 8 43.8
E 11	263 34.3	25 06.2	11.7	57 18.6	15.3	89 24.3	51.9	13 55.5	28.2			
S 12	278 36.7	40 05.6	S18 12.4	72 19.7	S 9 15.8	104 26.7	N 3 51.9	28 57.7	S20 28.3	Alphecca	126 09.8	N26 39.7
D 13	293 39.2	55 05.0	13.1	87 20.8	16.3	119 29.1	51.8	43 59.9	28.3	Alpheratz	357 41.7	N29 10.9
A 14	308 41.7	70 04.3	13.8	102 22.0	16.8	134 31.5	51.8	59 02.1	28.3	Altair	62 06.9	N 8 54.8
Y 15	323 44.1	85 03.7	.. 14.5	117 23.1	.. 17.2	149 33.9	.. 51.8	74 04.2	.. 28.4	Ankaa	353 14.1	S42 13.4
16	338 46.6	100 03.0	15.2	132 24.3	17.7	164 36.2	51.8	89 06.4	28.4	Antares	112 24.5	S26 27.8
17	353 49.1	115 02.4	15.9	147 25.4	18.2	179 38.6	51.8	104 08.6	28.5			
18	8 51.5	130 01.8	S18 16.6	162 26.6	S 9 18.7	194 41.0	N 3 51.8	119 10.8	S20 28.5	Arcturus	145 54.3	N19 06.0
19	23 54.0	145 01.1	17.3	177 27.7	19.2	209 43.4	51.7	134 12.9	28.5	Atria	107 25.2	S69 03.0
20	38 56.5	160 00.5	18.0	192 28.9	19.7	224 45.8	51.7	149 15.1	28.6	Avior	234 16.6	S59 33.7
21	53 58.9	174 59.8	.. 18.6	207 30.0	.. 20.2	239 48.2	.. 51.7	164 17.3	.. 28.6	Bellatrix	278 29.8	N 6 21.6
22	69 01.4	189 59.2	19.3	222 31.1	20.7	254 50.6	51.7	179 19.5	28.6	Betelgeuse	270 59.1	N 7 24.4
23	84 03.8	204 58.5	20.0	237 32.3	21.2	269 53.0	51.7	194 21.6	28.7			
31 00	99 06.3	219 57.9	S18 20.7	252 33.4	S 9 21.7	284 55.4	N 3 51.7	209 23.8	S20 28.7	Canopus	263 54.8	S52 42.5
01	114 08.8	234 57.2	21.4	267 34.6	22.2	299 57.8	51.7	224 26.0	28.8	Capella	280 31.4	N46 00.7
02	129 11.2	249 56.6	22.1	282 35.7	22.7	315 00.2	51.6	239 28.2	28.8	Deneb	49 30.7	N45 20.5
03	144 13.7	264 55.9	.. 22.8	297 36.9	.. 23.2	330 02.6	.. 51.6	254 30.3	.. 28.8	Denebola	182 31.9	N14 28.8
04	159 16.2	279 55.3	23.4	312 38.0	23.7	345 05.0	51.6	269 32.5	28.9	Diphda	348 54.2	S17 54.1
05	174 18.6	294 54.7	24.1	327 39.2	24.2	0 07.4	51.6	284 34.7	28.9			
06	189 21.1	309 54.0	S18 24.8	342 40.3	S 9 24.7	15 09.8	N 3 51.6	299 36.9	S20 28.9	Dubhe	193 49.5	N61 39.5
07	204 23.6	324 53.4	25.5	357 41.5	25.2	30 12.2	51.6	314 39.0	29.0	Elnath	278 10.1	N28 37.0
T 08	219 26.0	339 52.7	26.2	12 42.6	25.7	45 14.6	51.6	329 41.2	29.0	Eltanin	90 45.9	N51 29.4
H 09	234 28.5	354 52.1	.. 26.8	27 43.7	.. 26.1	60 17.0	.. 51.5	344 43.4	.. 29.0	Enif	33 45.7	N 9 57.0
U 10	249 31.0	9 51.4	27.5	42 44.9	26.6	75 19.4	51.5	359 45.6	29.1	Fomalhaut	15 22.3	S29 32.4
R 11	264 33.4	24 50.8	28.2	57 46.0	27.1	90 21.8	51.5	14 47.7	29.1			
S 12	279 35.9	39 50.1	S18 28.9	72 47.2	S 9 27.6	105 24.2	N 3 51.5	29 49.9	S20 29.2	Gacrux	171 58.8	S57 11.8
D 13	294 38.3	54 49.5	29.6	87 48.3	28.1	120 26.6	51.5	44 52.1	29.2	Gienah	175 50.5	S17 37.7
A 14	309 40.8	69 48.8	30.2	102 49.5	28.6	135 29.1	51.5	59 54.3	29.2	Hadar	148 45.6	S60 26.6
Y 15	324 43.3	84 48.1	.. 30.9	117 50.6	.. 29.1	150 31.5	.. 51.5	74 56.4	.. 29.3	Hamal	327 58.6	N23 32.3
16	339 45.7	99 47.5	31.6	132 51.8	29.6	165 33.9	51.4	89 58.6	29.3	Kaus Aust.	83 41.9	S34 22.4
17	354 48.2	114 46.8	32.3	147 52.9	30.1	180 36.3	51.4	105 00.8	29.3			
18	9 50.7	129 46.2	S18 32.9	162 54.1	S 9 30.6	195 38.7	N 3 51.4	120 03.0	S20 29.4	Kochab	137 21.0	N74 05.2
19	24 53.1	144 45.5	33.6	177 55.2	31.1	210 41.1	51.4	135 05.1	29.4	Markab	13 36.7	N15 17.6
20	39 55.6	159 44.9	34.3	192 56.3	31.6	225 43.5	51.4	150 07.3	29.4	Menkar	314 13.0	N 4 09.0
21	54 58.1	174 44.2	.. 34.9	207 57.5	.. 32.1	240 45.9	.. 51.4	165 09.5	.. 29.5	Menkent	148 05.6	S36 26.6
22	70 00.5	189 43.6	35.6	222 58.6	32.5	255 48.3	51.4	180 11.7	29.5	Miaplacidus	221 38.4	S69 46.9
23	85 03.0	204 42.9	36.3	237 59.8	33.0	270 50.7	51.4	195 13.8	29.6			
1 00	100 05.4	219 42.2	S18 36.9	253 00.9	S 9 33.5	285 53.1	N 3 51.3	210 16.0	S20 29.6	Mirfak	308 37.4	N49 55.1
01	115 07.9	234 41.6	37.6	268 02.1	34.0	300 55.5	51.3	225 18.2	29.6	Nunki	75 56.6	S26 16.4
02	130 10.4	249 40.9	38.3	283 03.2	34.5	315 57.9	51.3	240 20.4	29.7	Peacock	53 17.2	S56 41.0
03	145 12.8	264 40.3	.. 38.9	298 04.4	.. 35.0	331 00.3	.. 51.3	255 22.6	.. 29.7	Pollux	243 25.3	N27 59.0
04	160 15.3	279 39.6	39.6	313 05.5	35.5	346 02.7	51.3	270 24.7	29.7	Procyon	244 57.6	N 5 10.8
05	175 17.8	294 38.9	40.3	328 06.7	36.0	1 05.1	51.3	285 26.9	29.8			
06	190 20.2	309 38.3	S18 40.9	343 07.8	S 9 36.5	16 07.5	N 3 51.3	300 29.1	S20 29.8	Rasalhague	96 05.2	N12 33.1
07	205 22.7	324 37.6	41.6	358 09.0	37.0	31 10.0	51.2	315 31.3	29.8	Regulus	207 41.5	N11 53.2
F 08	220 25.2	339 37.0	42.2	13 10.1	37.5	46 12.4	51.2	330 33.4	29.9	Rigel	281 10.1	S 8 11.3
R 09	235 27.6	354 36.3	.. 42.9	28 11.3	.. 37.9	61 14.8	.. 51.2	345 35.6	.. 29.9	Rigil Kent.	139 49.6	S60 53.6
I 10	250 30.1	9 35.6	43.6	43 12.4	38.4	76 17.2	51.2	0 37.8	30.0	Sabik	102 10.9	S15 44.4
D 11	265 32.6	24 35.0	44.2	58 13.6	38.9	91 19.6	51.2	15 40.0	30.0			
A 12	280 35.0	39 34.3	S18 44.9	73 14.7	S 9 39.4	106 22.0	N 3 51.2	30 42.1	S20 30.0	Schedar	349 38.4	N56 37.7
Y 13	295 37.5	54 33.6	45.5	88 15.8	39.9	121 24.4	51.2	45 44.3	30.1	Shaula	96 20.0	S37 06.6
14	310 39.9	69 33.0	46.2	103 17.0	40.4	136 26.8	51.2	60 46.5	30.1	Sirius	258 31.8	S16 44.5
15	325 42.4	84 32.3	.. 46.9	118 18.1	.. 40.9	151 29.2	.. 51.2	75 48.7	.. 30.1	Spica	158 29.5	S11 14.6
16	340 44.9	99 31.6	47.5	133 19.3	41.4	166 31.6	51.2	90 50.9	30.2	Suhail	222 50.7	S43 29.8
17	355 47.3	114 31.0	48.2	148 20.4	41.9	181 34.1	51.2	105 53.0	30.2			
18	10 49.8	129 30.3	S18 48.8	163 21.6	S 9 42.4	196 36.5	N 3 51.1	120 55.2	S20 30.2	Vega	80 38.2	N38 48.1
19	25 52.3	144 29.6	49.5	178 22.7	42.8	211 38.9	51.1	135 57.4	30.3	Zuben'ubi	137 03.7	S16 06.3
20	40 54.7	159 29.0	50.1	193 23.9	43.3	226 41.3	51.1	150 59.6	30.3		SHA	Mer.Pass.
21	55 57.2	174 28.3	.. 50.8	208 25.0	.. 43.8	241 43.7	.. 51.1	166 01.7	.. 30.4		° ′	h m
22	70 59.7	189 27.6	51.4	223 26.2	44.3	256 46.1	51.1	181 03.9	30.4	Venus	120 51.6	9 21
23	86 02.1	204 27.0	52.1	238 27.3	44.8	271 48.5	51.1	196 06.1	30.4	Mars	153 27.1	7 09
	h m									Jupiter	185 49.1	5 00
Mer.Pass. 17 20.7	v −0.7 d 0.7			v 1.1 d 0.5		v 2.4 d 0.0		v 2.2 d 0.0		Saturn	110 17.5	10 01

SUN / MOON

UT	SUN GHA	SUN Dec	MOON GHA	v	MOON Dec	d	HP
d h	° ′	° ′	° ′	′	° ′	′	′
30 00	179 28.1	S23 11.8	304 16.2	13.5	N 8 45.3	8.6	55.3
01	194 27.8	11.6	318 48.7	13.6	8 36.7	8.7	55.2
02	209 27.5	11.5	333 21.3	13.7	8 28.0	8.7	55.2
03	224 27.2	.. 11.3	347 54.0	13.7	8 19.3	8.7	55.2
04	239 26.9	11.2	2 26.7	13.7	8 10.6	8.8	55.2
05	254 26.6	11.0	16 59.4	13.8	8 01.8	8.8	55.2
06	269 26.3	S23 10.9	31 32.2	13.8	N 7 53.0	8.8	55.1
W 07	284 26.0	10.7	46 05.0	13.9	7 44.2	8.9	55.1
E 08	299 25.7	10.5	60 37.9	14.0	7 35.3	8.8	55.1
D 09	314 25.4	.. 10.4	75 10.9	13.9	7 26.5	8.9	55.1
N 10	329 25.1	10.2	89 43.8	14.1	7 17.6	8.9	55.0
E 11	344 24.8	10.1	104 16.9	14.0	7 08.7	9.0	55.0
S 12	359 24.5	S23 09.9	118 49.9	14.1	N 6 59.7	8.9	55.0
D 13	14 24.2	09.7	133 23.0	14.2	6 50.8	9.0	55.0
A 14	29 23.9	09.6	147 56.2	14.2	6 41.8	9.0	55.0
Y 15	44 23.6	.. 09.4	162 29.4	14.2	6 32.8	9.0	54.9
16	59 23.3	09.2	177 02.6	14.3	6 23.8	9.1	54.9
17	74 23.0	09.1	191 35.9	14.3	6 14.7	9.1	54.9
18	89 22.7	S23 08.9	206 09.2	14.3	N 6 05.6	9.0	54.9
19	104 22.4	08.7	220 42.5	14.4	5 56.6	9.1	54.9
20	119 22.1	08.6	235 15.9	14.4	5 47.5	9.2	54.9
21	134 21.8	.. 08.4	249 49.3	14.5	5 38.3	9.1	54.8
22	149 21.5	08.2	264 22.8	14.5	5 29.2	9.2	54.8
23	164 21.2	08.1	278 56.3	14.5	5 20.0	9.1	54.8
31 00	179 20.9	S23 07.9	293 29.8	14.6	N 5 10.9	9.2	54.8
01	194 20.6	07.7	308 03.4	14.6	5 01.7	9.2	54.8
02	209 20.3	07.6	322 37.0	14.6	4 52.5	9.2	54.7
03	224 20.0	.. 07.4	337 10.6	14.7	4 43.3	9.3	54.7
04	239 19.7	07.2	351 44.3	14.7	4 34.0	9.2	54.7
05	254 19.4	07.0	6 18.0	14.7	4 24.8	9.2	54.7
06	269 19.1	S23 06.9	20 51.7	14.8	N 4 15.6	9.3	54.7
T 07	284 18.8	06.7	35 25.5	14.8	4 06.3	9.3	54.7
H 08	299 18.5	06.5	49 59.3	14.8	3 57.0	9.3	54.6
U 09	314 18.2	06.3	64 33.1	14.8	3 47.7	9.3	54.6
R 10	329 17.9	06.1	79 06.9	14.9	3 38.4	9.3	54.6
S 11	344 17.6	06.0	93 40.8	14.9	3 29.1	9.3	54.6
D 12	359 17.3	S23 05.8	108 14.7	14.9	N 3 19.8	9.4	54.6
A 13	14 17.0	05.6	122 48.6	15.0	3 10.5	9.3	54.6
Y 14	29 16.7	05.4	137 22.6	15.0	3 01.2	9.4	54.6
15	44 16.4	.. 05.2	151 56.6	14.9	2 51.8	9.3	54.5
16	59 16.1	05.0	166 30.5	15.1	2 42.5	9.4	54.5
17	74 15.8	04.9	181 04.6	15.1	2 33.1	9.3	54.5
18	89 15.5	S23 04.7	195 38.6	15.1	N 2 23.8	9.4	54.5
19	104 15.2	04.5	210 12.7	15.0	2 14.4	9.3	54.5
20	119 14.9	04.3	224 46.7	15.1	2 05.1	9.4	54.5
21	134 14.6	.. 04.1	239 20.8	15.2	1 55.7	9.4	54.5
22	149 14.3	03.9	253 55.0	15.1	1 46.3	9.3	54.5
23	164 14.0	03.7	268 29.1	15.2	1 37.0	9.4	54.4
1 00	179 13.7	S23 03.5	283 03.3	15.1	N 1 27.6	9.4	54.4
01	194 13.4	03.4	297 37.4	15.2	1 18.2	9.4	54.4
02	209 13.2	03.2	312 11.6	15.2	1 08.8	9.3	54.4
03	224 12.9	.. 03.0	326 45.8	15.2	0 59.5	9.4	54.4
04	239 12.6	02.8	341 20.0	15.3	0 50.1	9.4	54.4
05	254 12.3	02.6	355 54.3	15.2	0 40.7	9.4	54.4
06	269 12.0	S23 02.4	10 28.5	15.3	N 0 31.3	9.4	54.4
07	284 11.7	02.2	25 02.8	15.2	0 21.9	9.3	54.4
08	299 11.4	02.0	39 37.0	15.3	0 12.6	9.4	54.4
F 09	314 11.1	.. 01.8	54 11.3	15.3	N 0 03.2	9.4	54.3
R 10	329 10.8	01.6	68 45.6	15.3	S 0 06.2	9.3	54.3
I 11	344 10.5	01.4	83 19.9	15.3	0 15.5	9.4	54.3
D 12	359 10.2	S23 01.2	97 54.2	15.3	S 0 24.9	9.4	54.3
A 13	14 09.9	01.0	112 28.5	15.3	0 34.3	9.3	54.3
Y 14	29 09.6	00.8	127 02.8	15.3	0 43.6	9.3	54.3
15	44 09.3	.. 00.6	141 37.1	15.3	0 52.9	9.4	54.3
16	59 09.0	00.4	156 11.4	15.4	1 02.3	9.3	54.3
17	74 08.7	00.2	170 45.8	15.3	1 11.6	9.3	54.3
18	89 08.4	S23 00.0	185 20.1	15.3	S 1 20.9	9.3	54.3
19	104 08.1	22 59.8	199 54.4	15.4	1 30.3	9.3	54.3
20	119 07.8	59.6	214 28.8	15.3	1 39.6	9.3	54.3
21	134 07.5	.. 59.4	229 03.1	15.4	1 48.9	9.3	54.3
22	149 07.2	59.2	243 37.5	15.3	1 58.2	9.3	54.3
23	164 06.9	58.9	258 11.8	15.3	S 2 07.5	9.2	54.3
	SD 16.3	d 0.2	SD 15.0		14.9		14.8

Twilight / Sunrise / Moonrise

Lat.	Naut.	Civil	Sunrise	Moonrise 30	31	1	2
°	h m	h m	h m	h m	h m	h m	h m
N 72	08 25	10 46	■■	21 12	22 47	24 19	00 19
N 70	08 06	09 51	■■	21 20	22 49	24 16	00 16
68	07 50	09 18	■■	21 27	22 51	24 13	00 13
66	07 38	08 54	10 30	21 32	22 52	24 11	00 11
64	07 27	08 35	09 51	21 37	22 53	24 09	00 09
62	07 18	08 19	09 24	21 41	22 54	24 07	00 07
60	07 09	08 06	09 03	21 44	22 55	24 06	00 06
N 58	07 02	07 54	08 46	21 47	22 56	24 04	00 04
56	06 56	07 44	08 31	21 50	22 57	24 03	00 03
54	06 50	07 36	08 19	21 52	22 58	24 02	00 02
52	06 44	07 28	08 08	21 55	22 58	24 01	00 01
50	06 39	07 20	07 59	21 57	22 59	24 00	00 00
45	06 27	07 04	07 38	22 01	23 00	23 59	24 57
N 40	06 17	06 51	07 22	22 05	23 01	23 57	24 53
35	06 08	06 40	07 08	22 08	23 02	23 56	24 49
30	05 59	06 29	06 55	22 11	23 03	23 54	24 46
20	05 43	06 11	06 35	22 15	23 04	23 52	24 40
N 10	05 27	05 54	06 16	22 20	23 05	23 51	24 36
0	05 10	05 37	05 59	22 24	23 07	23 49	24 31
S 10	04 52	05 19	05 42	22 28	23 08	23 47	24 27
20	04 29	04 59	05 23	22 32	23 09	23 46	24 22
30	04 01	04 34	05 01	22 37	23 10	23 44	24 17
35	03 42	04 19	04 48	22 39	23 11	23 43	24 14
40	03 19	04 01	04 34	22 42	23 12	23 41	24 11
45	02 49	03 39	04 16	22 46	23 13	23 40	24 07
S 50	02 05	03 09	03 54	22 50	23 15	23 38	24 02
52	01 38	02 55	03 43	22 52	23 15	23 37	24 00
54	00 56	02 37	03 31	22 54	23 16	23 37	23 58
56	////	02 16	03 17	22 57	23 17	23 36	23 55
58	////	01 47	03 01	22 59	23 17	23 35	23 53
S 60	////	01 02	02 41	23 02	23 18	23 34	23 49

Sunset / Twilight / Moonset

Lat.	Sunset	Civil	Naut.	Moonset 30	31	1	2
°	h m	h m	h m	h m	h m	h m	h m
N 72	■■	13 20	15 41	11 32	11 27	11 22	11 17
N 70	■■	14 15	16 00	11 22	11 23	11 23	11 23
68	■■	14 48	16 16	11 14	11 19	11 23	11 27
66	13 36	15 12	16 28	11 07	11 16	11 24	11 31
64	14 15	15 31	16 39	11 01	11 13	11 24	11 34
62	14 42	15 47	16 48	10 56	11 11	11 24	11 37
60	15 03	16 00	16 56	10 52	11 09	11 24	11 40
N 58	15 20	16 11	17 04	10 48	11 07	11 25	11 42
56	15 34	16 21	17 10	10 45	11 05	11 25	11 44
54	15 47	16 30	17 16	10 42	11 04	11 25	11 46
52	15 58	16 38	17 22	10 39	11 03	11 25	11 48
50	16 07	16 46	17 27	10 36	11 01	11 25	11 49
45	16 28	17 01	17 38	10 31	10 59	11 26	11 52
N 40	16 44	17 15	17 49	10 26	10 57	11 26	11 55
35	16 58	17 26	17 58	10 22	10 54	11 26	11 57
30	17 10	17 37	18 06	10 18	10 53	11 26	12 00
20	17 31	17 55	18 23	10 12	10 50	11 27	12 03
N 10	17 49	18 12	18 38	10 06	10 47	11 27	12 06
0	18 07	18 29	18 55	10 01	10 44	11 27	12 09
S 10	18 24	18 47	19 14	09 55	10 42	11 27	12 12
20	18 43	19 07	19 36	09 50	10 39	11 28	12 16
30	19 04	19 32	20 05	09 43	10 36	11 28	12 19
35	19 16	19 47	20 23	09 39	10 34	11 28	12 21
40	19 32	20 05	20 46	09 35	10 32	11 28	12 24
45	19 50	20 27	21 16	09 30	10 30	11 28	12 27
S 50	20 12	20 56	22 00	09 24	10 27	11 29	12 30
52	20 22	21 10	22 26	09 21	10 25	11 29	12 31
54	20 34	21 28	23 07	09 18	10 24	11 29	12 33
56	20 48	21 49	////	09 15	10 22	11 29	12 35
58	21 04	22 17	////	09 11	10 20	11 29	12 37
S 60	21 24	23 02	////	09 06	10 18	11 29	12 39

SUN / MOON

Day	SUN Eqn. of Time 00h	12h	Mer. Pass.	MOON Mer. Pass. Upper	Lower	Age	Phase
d	m s	m s	h m	h m	h m	d	%
30	02 07	02 21	12 02	03 50	16 12	19	75
31	02 36	02 50	12 03	04 34	16 56	20	66
1	03 04	03 19	12 03	05 17	17 38	21	57

EXPLANATION

PRINCIPLE AND ARRANGEMENT

1. *Object.*   The object of this Almanac is to provide, in a convenient form, the data required for the practice of astronomical navigation at sea.

2. *Principle.*   The main contents of the Almanac consist of data from which the *Greenwich Hour Angle* (GHA) and the *Declination* (Dec) of all the bodies used for navigation can be obtained for any instant of *Universal Time* (UT, specifically UT1, or previously Greenwich Mean Time (GMT)).

The *Local Hour Angle* (LHA) can then be obtained by means of the formula:

$$\text{LHA} = \text{GHA} \; {- \text{ west} \atop + \text{ east}} \; \text{longitude}$$

The remaining data consist of: times of rising and setting of the Sun and Moon, and times of twilight; miscellaneous calendarial and planning data and auxiliary tables, including a list of Standard Times; corrections to be applied to observed altitude.

For the Sun, Moon, and planets the GHA and Dec are tabulated directly for each hour of UT throughout the year. For the stars the *Sidereal Hour Angle* (SHA) is given, and the GHA is obtained from:

$$\text{GHA Star} = \text{GHA Aries} + \text{SHA Star}$$

The SHA and Dec of the stars change slowly and may be regarded as constant over periods of several days. GHA Aries, or the Greenwich Hour Angle of the first point of Aries (the Vernal Equinox), is tabulated for each hour. Permanent tables give the appropriate increments and corrections to the tabulated hourly values of GHA and Dec for the minutes and seconds of UT.

The six-volume series of *Sight Reduction Tables for Marine Navigation* (published in U.S.A. as Pub. No. 229) has been designed for the solution of the navigational triangle and is intended for use with *The Nautical Almanac*.

Two alternative procedures for sight reduction are described on pages 277–318. The first requires the use of programmable calculators or computers, while the second uses a set of concise tables that is given on pages 286–317.

The tabular accuracy is $0\!'\!.1$ throughout. The time argument on the daily pages of this Almanac is UT1 denoted throughout by UT. This scale may differ from the broadcast time signals (UTC) by an amount which, if ignored, will introduce an error of up to $0\!'\!.2$ in longitude determined from astronomical observations. The difference arises because the time argument depends on the variable rate of rotation of the Earth while the broadcast time signals are based on an atomic time-scale. Step adjustments of exactly one second are made to the time signals as required (normally at 24^h on December 31 and June 30) so that the difference between the time signals and UT, as used in this Almanac, may not exceed $0^s\!.9$. Those who require to reduce observations to a precision of better than 1^s must therefore obtain the correction (DUT1) to the time signals from coding in the signal, or from other sources; the required time is given by UT1=UTC+DUT1 to a precision of $0^s\!.1$. Alternatively, the longitude, when determined from astronomical observations, may be corrected by the corresponding amount shown in the following table:

Correction to time signals	Correction to longitude
$-0^s\!.9$ to $-0^s\!.7$	$0\!'\!.2$ to east
$-0^s\!.6$ to $-0^s\!.3$	$0\!'\!.1$ to east
$-0^s\!.2$ to $+0^s\!.2$	no correction
$+0^s\!.3$ to $+0^s\!.6$	$0\!'\!.1$ to west
$+0^s\!.7$ to $+0^s\!.9$	$0\!'\!.2$ to west

3. *Lay-out.* The ephemeral data for three days are presented on an opening of two pages: the left-hand page contains the data for the planets and stars; the right-hand page contains the data for the Sun and Moon, together with times of twilight, sunrise, sunset, moonrise and moonset.

The remaining contents are arranged as follows: for ease of reference the altitude-correction tables are given on pages A2, A3, A4, xxxiv and xxxv; calendar, Moon's phases, eclipses, and planet notes (i.e. data of general interest) precede the main tabulations. The Explanation is followed by information on standard times, star charts and list of star positions, sight reduction procedures and concise sight reduction tables, tables of increments and corrections and other auxiliary tables that are frequently used.

MAIN DATA

4. *Daily pages.* The daily pages give the GHA of Aries, the GHA and Dec of the Sun, Moon, and the four navigational planets, for each hour of UT. For the Moon, values of v and d are also tabulated for each hour to facilitate the correction of GHA and Dec to intermediate times; v and d for the Sun and planets change so slowly that they are given, at the foot of the appropriate columns, once only on the page; v is zero for Aries and negligible for the Sun, and is omitted. The SHA and Dec of the 57 selected stars, arranged in alphabetical order of proper name, are also given.

5. *Stars.* The SHA and Dec of 173 stars, including the 57 selected stars, are tabulated for each month on pages 268–273; no interpolation is required and the data can be used in precisely the same way as those for the selected stars on the daily pages. The stars are arranged in order of SHA.

The list of 173 includes all stars down to magnitude 3·0, together with a few fainter ones to fill the larger gaps. The 57 selected stars have been chosen from amongst these on account of brightness and distribution in the sky; they will suffice for the majority of observations.

The 57 selected stars are known by their proper names, but they are also numbered in descending order of SHA. In the list of 173 stars, the constellation names are always given on the left-hand page; on the facing page proper names are given where well-known names exist. Numbers for the selected stars are given in both columns.

An index to the selected stars, containing lists in both alphabetical and numerical order, is given on page xxxiii and is also reprinted on the bookmark.

6. *Increments and corrections.* The tables printed on tinted paper (pages ii–xxxi) at the back of the Almanac provide the increments and corrections for minutes and seconds to be applied to the hourly values of GHA and Dec. They consist of sixty tables, one for each minute, separated into two parts: increments to GHA for Sun and planets, Aries, and Moon for every minute and second; and, for each minute, corrections to be applied to GHA and Dec corresponding to the values of v and d given on the daily pages.

The increments are based on the following adopted hourly rates of increase of the GHA: Sun and planets, 15° precisely; Aries, 15° 02'.46; Moon, 14° 19'.0. The values of v on the daily pages are the excesses of the actual hourly motions over the adopted values; they are generally positive, except for Venus. The tabulated hourly values of the Sun's GHA have been adjusted to reduce to a minimum the error caused by treating v as negligible. The values of d on the daily pages are the hourly differences of the Dec. For the Moon, the true values of v and d are given for each hour; otherwise mean values are given for the three days on the page.

7. *Method of entry.* The UT of an observation is expressed as a day and hour, followed by a number of minutes and seconds. The tabular values of GHA and Dec, and, where necessary, the corresponding values of v and d, are taken directly from the daily pages for the day and hour of UT; this hour is always *before* the time of observation. SHA and Dec of the selected stars are also taken from the daily pages.

The table of Increments and Corrections for the minute of UT is then selected. For the GHA, the increment for minutes and seconds is taken from the appropriate column opposite the seconds of UT; the v-correction is taken from the second part of the same table opposite the value of v as given on the daily pages. Both increment and v-correction are to be added to the GHA, except for Venus when v is prefixed by a minus sign and the v-correction is to be subtracted. For the Dec there is no increment, but a d-correction is applied in the same way as the v-correction; d is given without sign on the daily pages and the sign of the correction is to be supplied by inspection of the Dec column. In many cases the correction may be applied mentally.

8. *Examples.* (a) Sun and Moon. Required the GHA and Dec of the Sun and Moon on 2015 January 26 at 15^h 47^m 13^s UT.

		SUN			MOON			
		GHA	Dec	d	GHA	v	Dec	d
		° ′	° ′	′	° ′	′	° ′	′
Daily page, January 26^d 15^h		41 52·6	S 18 41·2	0·6	323 02·2	9·9	N 9 46·8	9·4
Increments for	47^m 13^s	11 48·3			11 16·0			
v or d corrections for	47^m		−0·5		+7·8		+7·4	
Sum for January 26^d 15^h 47^m 13^s		53 40·9	S 18 40·7		334 26·0		N 9 54·2	

(b) Planets. Required the LHA and Dec of (i) Venus on 2015 January 26 at 12^h 42^m 56^s UT in longitude E 93° 49′; (ii) Saturn on 2015 January 26 at 8^h 43^m 46^s UT in longitude W 39° 52′.

		VENUS					SATURN			
		GHA	v	Dec	d		GHA	v	Dec	d
		° ′	′	° ′	′		° ′	′	° ′	′
Daily page, Jan. 26^d	(12^h)	334 09·5	−0·5	S 13 25·8	1·1	(8^h)	3 50·0	2·3	S 18 50·3	0·0
Increments (planets)	(42^m 56^s)	10 44·0				(43^m 46^s)	10 56·5			
v or d corrections	(42^m)	−0·4		−0·8		(43^m)	+1·7		+0·0	
Sum = GHA and Dec.		344 53·1		S 13 25·0			14 48·2		S 18 50·3	
Longitude	(east)	+ 93 49·0				(west)	− 39 52·0			
Multiples of 360°		−360					+360			
LHA planet		78 42·1					334 56·2			

(c) Stars. Required the GHA and Dec of (i) *Aldebaran* on 2015 January 26 at 14^h 48^m 56^s UT; (ii) *Vega* on 2015 January 26 at 2^h 08^m 10^s UT.

		Aldebaran				Vega	
		GHA	Dec			GHA	Dec
		° ′	° ′			° ′	° ′
Daily page (SHA and Dec)		290 47·9	N 16 32.2			80 38·6	N 38 47.9
Daily page (GHA Aries)	(14^h)	335 32·8		(2^h)		155 03·3	
Increments (Aries)	(48^m 56^s)	12 16·0		(08^m 10^s)		2 02·8	
Sum = GHA star		638 36·7				237 44·7	
Multiples of 360°		−360					
GHA star		278 36·7				237 44·7	

9. *Polaris (Pole Star) tables.* The tables on pages 274–276 provide means by which the latitude can be deduced from an observed altitude of *Polaris*, and they also give its azimuth; their use is explained and illustrated on those pages. They are based on the following formula:

$$\text{Latitude} - H_O = -p \cos h + \tfrac{1}{2} p \sin p \sin^2 h \tan(\text{latitude})$$

where

H_O = Apparent altitude (corrected for refraction)

p = polar distance of *Polaris* = 90° − Dec

h = local hour angle of *Polaris* = LHA Aries + SHA

a_0, which is a function of LHA Aries only, is the value of both terms of the above formula calculated for mean values of the SHA (317° 05′) and Dec (N 89° 19′.7) of *Polaris*, for a mean latitude of 50°, and adjusted by the addition of a constant (58′.8).

a_1, which is a function of LHA Aries and latitude, is the excess of the value of the second term over its mean value for latitude 50°, increased by a constant (0.6) to make it always positive. a_2, which is a function of LHA Aries and date, is the correction to the first term for the variation of *Polaris* from its adopted mean position; it is increased by a constant (0.6) to make it positive. The sum of the added constants is 1°, so that:

$$\text{Latitude} = \text{Apparent altitude (corrected for refraction)} - 1° + a_0 + a_1 + a_2$$

RISING AND SETTING PHENOMENA

10. *General.* On the right-hand daily pages are given the times of sunrise and sunset, of the beginning and end of civil and nautical twilights, and of moonrise and moonset for a range of latitudes from N 72° to S 60°. These times, which are given to the nearest minute, are strictly the UT of the phenomena on the Greenwich meridian; they are given for every day for moonrise and moonset, but only for the middle day of the three on each page for the solar phenomena.

They are approximately the Local Mean Times (LMT) of the corresponding phenomena on other meridians; they can be formally interpolated if desired. The UT of a phenomenon is obtained from the LMT by:

$$\text{UT} = \text{LMT} \begin{array}{c} + \text{ west} \\ - \text{ east} \end{array} \text{longitude}$$

in which the longitude must first be converted to time by the table on page i or otherwise.

Interpolation for latitude can be done mentally or with the aid of Table I on page xxxii.

The following symbols are used to indicate the conditions under which, in high latitudes, some of the phenomena do not occur:

☐ Sun or Moon remains continuously above the horizon;

■ Sun or Moon remains continuously below the horizon;

//// twilight lasts all night.

Basis of the tabulations. At sunrise and sunset 16′ is allowed for semi-diameter and 34′ for horizontal refraction, so that at the times given the Sun's upper limb is on the visible horizon; all times refer to phenomena as seen from sea level with a clear horizon.

At the times given for the beginning and end of twilight, the Sun's zenith distance is 96° for civil, and 102° for nautical twilight. The degree of illumination at the times given for civil twilight (in good conditions and in the absence of other illumination) is such that the brightest stars are visible and the horizon is clearly defined. At the times given for nautical twilight the horizon is in general not visible, and it is too dark for observation with a marine sextant.

Times corresponding to other depressions of the Sun may be obtained by interpolation or, for depressions of more than 12°, less reliably, by extrapolation; times so obtained will be subject to considerable uncertainty near extreme conditions.

At moonrise and moonset allowance is made for semi-diameter, parallax, and refraction (34′), so that at the times given the Moon's upper limb is on the visible horizon as seen from sea level.

11. *Sunrise, sunset, twilight.* The tabulated times may be regarded, without serious error, as the LMT of the phenomena on any of the three days on the page and in any longitude. Precise times may normally be obtained by interpolating the tabular values for latitude and to the correct day and longitude, the latter being expressed as a fraction of a day by dividing it by 360°, positive for west and negative for east longitudes. In the extreme conditions near ☐, ■ or //// interpolation may not be possible in one direction, but accurate times are of little value in these circumstances.

Examples. Required the UT of (a) the beginning of morning twilights and sunrise on 2015 January 13 for latitude S 48° 55′, longitude E 75° 18′; (b) sunset and the end of evening twilights on 2015 January 15 for latitude N 67° 10′, longitude W 168° 05′.

(a)	Twilight Nautical	Civil	Sunrise	(b)	Sunset	Twilight Civil	Nautical
	d h m	d h m	d h m		d h m	d h m	d h m
From p. 19							
LMT for Lat S 45°	13 03 09	13 03 55	13 04 31	N 66°	15 14 22	15 15 42	15 16 53
Corr. to S 48° 55′	−30	−20	−16	N 67° 10′	−24	−12	−6
(p. xxxii, Table I)							
Long (p. i) E 75° 18′	−5 01	−5 01	−5 01	W 168° 05′	+11 12	+11 12	+11 12
UT	12 21 38	12 22 34	12 23 14		16 01 10	16 02 42	16 03 59

The LMT are strictly for January 14 (middle date on page) and 0° longitude; for more precise times it is necessary to interpolate, but rounding errors may accumulate to about 2^{m}.

(a) to January $13^{\text{d}} − 75°/360° = $ Jan. $12^{\text{d}}8$, i.e. $\frac{1}{3}(1·2) = 0·4$ backwards towards the data for the same latitude interpolated similarly from page 17; the corrections are $−2^{\text{m}}$ to nautical twilight, $−2^{\text{m}}$ to civil twilight and $−1^{\text{m}}$ to sunrise.

(b) to January $15^{\text{d}} + 168°/360° = $ Jan. $15^{\text{d}}5$, i.e. $\frac{1}{3}(1·5) = 0·5$ forwards towards the data for the same latitude interpolated similarly from page 21; the corrections are $+8^{\text{m}}$ to sunset, $+4^{\text{m}}$ to civil twilight, and $+4^{\text{m}}$ to nautical twilight.

12. *Moonrise, moonset.*   Precise times of moonrise and moonset are rarely needed; a glance at the tables will generally give sufficient indication of whether the Moon is available for observation and of the hours of rising and setting. If needed, precise times may be obtained as follows. Interpolate for latitude, using Table I on page xxxii, on the day wanted and also on the preceding day in east longitudes or the following day in west longitudes; take the difference between these times and interpolate for longitude by applying to the time for the day wanted the correction from Table II on page xxxii, so that the resulting time is between the two times used. In extreme conditions near ☐ or ■ interpolation for latitude or longitude may be possible only in one direction; accurate times are of little value in these circumstances.

To facilitate this interpolation the times of moonrise and moonset are given for four days on each page; where no phenomenon occurs during a particular day (as happens once a month) the time of the phenomenon on the following day, increased by 24^{h}, is given; extra care must be taken when interpolating between two values, when one of those values exceeds 24^{h}. In practice it suffices to use the daily difference between the times for the nearest tabular latitude, and generally, to enter Table II with the nearest tabular arguments as in the examples below.

Examples. Required the UT of moonrise and moonset in latitude S 47° 10′, longitudes E 124° 00′ and W 78° 31′ on 2015 January 5.

	Longitude E 124° 00′ Moonrise	Moonset	Longitude W 78° 31′ Moonrise	Moonset
	d h m	d h m	d h m	d h m
LMT for Lat. S 45°	5 19 43	5 04 48	5 19 43	5 04 48
Lat correction (p. xxxii, Table I)	+07	−07	+07	−07
Long correction (p. xxxii, Table II)	−13	−20	+07	+13
Correct LMT	5 19 37	5 04 21	5 19 57	5 04 54
Longitude (p. i)	−8 16	−8 16	+5 14	+5 14
UT	5 11 21	4 20 05	6 01 11	5 10 08

ALTITUDE CORRECTION TABLES

13. *General.* In general two corrections are given for application to altitudes observed with a marine sextant; additional corrections are required for Venus and Mars and also for very low altitudes.

Tables of the correction for dip of the horizon, due to height of eye above sea level, are given on pages A2 and xxxiv. Strictly this correction should be applied first and subtracted from the sextant altitude to give apparent altitude, which is the correct argument for the other tables.

Separate tables are given of the second correction for the Sun, for stars and planets (on pages A2 and A3), and for the Moon (on pages xxxiv and xxxv). For the Sun, values are given for both lower and upper limbs, for two periods of the year. The star tables are used for the planets, but additional corrections for parallax (page A2) are required for Venus and Mars. The Moon tables are in two parts: the main correction is a function of apparent altitude only and is tabulated for the lower limb (30′ must be subtracted to obtain the correction for the upper limb); the other, which is given for both lower and upper limbs, depends also on the horizontal parallax, which has to be taken from the daily pages.

An additional correction, given on page A4, is required for the change in the refraction, due to variations of pressure and temperature from the adopted standard conditions; it may generally be ignored for altitudes greater than 10°, except possibly in extreme conditions. The correction tables for the Sun, stars, and planets are in two parts; only those for altitudes greater than 10° are reprinted on the bookmark.

14. *Critical tables.* Some of the altitude correction tables are arranged as critical tables. In these an interval of apparent altitude (or height of eye) corresponds to a single value of the correction; no interpolation is required. At a "critical" entry the upper of the two possible values of the correction is to be taken. For example, in the table of dip, a correction of −4′1 corresponds to all values of the height of eye from 5·3 to 5·5 metres (17·5 to 18·3 feet) inclusive.

15. *Examples.* The following examples illustrate the use of the altitude correction tables; the sextant altitudes given are assumed to be taken on 2015 August 9 with a marine sextant at height 5·4 metres (18 feet), temperature −3°C and pressure 982 mb, the Moon sights being taken at about 10^h UT.

	SUN lower limb	SUN upper limb	MOON lower limb	MOON upper limb	VENUS	*Polaris*
	° ′	° ′	° ′	° ′	° ′	° ′
Sextant altitude	21 19·7	3 20·2	33 27·6	26 06·7	4 32·6	49 36·5
Dip, height 5·4 metres (18 feet)	−4·1	−4·1	−4·1	−4·1	−4·1	−4·1
Main correction	+13·6	−29·3	+57·4	+60·5	−10·8	−0·8
−30′ for upper limb (Moon)	—	—	—	−30·0	—	—
L, U correction for Moon	—	—	+4·3	+3·3	—	—
Additional correction for Venus	—	—	—	—	+0·5	—
Additional refraction correction	−0·1	−0·6	−0·1	−0·1	−0·5	0·0
Corrected sextant altitude	21 29·1	2 46·2	34 25·1	26 36·3	4 17·7	49 31·6

The main corrections have been taken out with apparent altitude (sextant altitude corrected for index error and dip) as argument, interpolating where possible. These refinements are rarely necessary.

16. *Composition of the Corrections.* The table for the dip of the sea horizon is based on the formula:

Correction for dip $= -1\!\cdot\!76\sqrt{(\text{height of eye in metres})} = -0\!\cdot\!97\sqrt{(\text{height of eye in feet})}$

The correction table for the Sun includes the effects of semi-diameter, parallax and mean refraction.

The correction tables for the stars and planets allow for the effect of mean refraction.

The phase correction for Venus has been incorporated in the tabulations for GHA and Dec, and no correction for phase is required. The additional corrections for Venus and Mars allow for parallax. Alternatively, the correction for parallax may be calculated from $p\cos H$, where p is the parallax and H is the altitude. In 2015 the values for p are:

	Jan. 1	May 3	June 22	July 14	July 30	Sept. 1	Sept. 18	Oct. 12	Dec. 3	Dec. 31
Venus	0′1	0′2	0′3	0′4	0′5	0′4	0′3	0′2	0′1	

	Jan. 1	Dec. 31
Mars	0′1	

The correction table for the Moon includes the effect of semi-diameter, parallax, augmentation and mean refraction.

Mean refraction is calculated for a temperature of 10°C (50°F), a pressure of 1010 mb (29·83 inches), humidity of 80% and wavelength 0·50169 μm.

17. *Bubble sextant observations.* When observing with a bubble sextant no correction is necessary for dip, semi-diameter, or augmentation. The altitude corrections for the stars and planets on page A2 and on the bookmark should be used for the Sun as well as for the stars and planets; for the Moon it is easiest to take the mean of the corrections for lower and upper limbs and subtract 15′ from the altitude; the correction for dip must not be applied.

AUXILIARY AND PLANNING DATA

18. *Sun and Moon.* On the daily pages are given: hourly values of the horizontal parallax of the Moon; the semi-diameters and the times of meridian passage of both Sun and Moon over the Greenwich meridian; the equation of time; the age of the Moon, the percent (%) illuminated and a symbol indicating the phase. The times of the phases of the Moon are given in UT on page 4. For the Moon, the semi-diameters for each of the three days are given at the foot of the column; for the Sun a single value is sufficient. Table II on page xxxii may be used for interpolating the time of the Moon's meridian passage for longitude. The equation of time is given daily at 00^h and 12^h UT. The sign is *positive* for unshaded values and *negative* for shaded values. To obtain apparent time add the equation of time to mean time when the sign is *positive*. Subtract the equation of time from mean time when the sign is *negative*. At 12^h UT, when the sign is *positive*, meridian passage of the Sun occurs *before* 12^h UT, otherwise it occurs *after* 12^h UT.

19. *Planets.* The magnitudes of the planets are given immediately following their names in the headings on the daily pages; also given, for the middle day of the three on the page, are their SHA at 00^h UT and their times of meridian passage.

The planet notes and diagram on pages 8 and 9 provide descriptive information as to the suitability of the planets for observation during the year, and of their positions and movements.

20. *Stars.* The time of meridian passage of the first point of Aries over the Greenwich meridian is given on the daily pages, for the middle day of the three on the page, to $0^m\!.1$. The interval between successive meridian passages is $23^h\,56^m\!.1$ (24^h less $3^m\!.9$) so that times for intermediate days and other meridians can readily be derived. If a precise time is required it may be obtained by finding the UT at which LHA Aries is zero.

The meridian passage of a star occurs when its LHA is zero, that is when LHA Aries + SHA = 360°. An approximate time can be obtained from the planet diagram on page 9.

The star charts on pages 266 and 267 are intended to assist identification. They show the relative positions of the stars in the sky as seen from the Earth and include all 173 stars used in the Almanac, together with a few others to complete the main constellation configurations. The local meridian at any time may be located on the chart by means of its SHA which is 360° − LHA Aries, or west longitude − GHA Aries.

21. *Star globe.* To set a star globe on which is printed a scale of LHA Aries, first set the globe for latitude and then rotate about the polar axis until the scale under the edge of the meridian circle reads LHA Aries.

To mark the positions of the Sun, Moon, and planets on the star globe, take the difference GHA Aries − GHA body and use this along the LHA Aries scale, in conjunction with the declination, to plot the position. GHA Aries − GHA body is most conveniently found by taking the difference when the GHA of the body is small (less than 15°), which happens once a day.

22. *Calendar.* On page 4 are given lists of ecclesiastical festivals, and of the principal anniversaries and holidays in the United Kingdom and the United States of America. The calendar on page 5 includes the day of the year as well as the day of the week.

Brief particulars are given, at the foot of page 5, of the solar and lunar eclipses occurring during the year; the times given are in UT. The principal features of the more important solar eclipses are shown on the maps on pages 6 and 7.

23. *Standard times.* The lists on pages 262–265 give the standard times used in most countries. In general no attempt is made to give details of the beginning and end of summer time, since they are liable to frequent changes at short notice. For the latest information consult Admiralty List of Radio Signals Volume 2 (NP 282) corrected by Section VI of the weekly edition of Admiralty Notices to Mariners.

The Date or Calendar Line is an arbitrary line, on either side of which the date differs by one day; when crossing this line on a westerly course, the date must be advanced one day; when crossing it on an easterly course, the date must be put back one day. The line is a modification of the line of the 180th meridian, and is drawn so as to include, as far as possible, islands of any one group, etc., on the same side of the line. It may be traced by starting at the South Pole and joining up to the following positions:

Lat	S 51·0	S 45·0	S 15·0	S 5·0	N 48·0	N 53·0	N 65·5
Long	180·0	W 172·5	W 172·5	180·0	180·0	E 170·0	W 169·0

thence through the middle of the Diomede Islands to Lat N 68°·0, Long W 169°·0, passing east of Ostrov Vrangelya (Wrangel Island) to Lat N 75°·0, Long 180°·0, and thence to the North Pole.

ACCURACY

24. *Main data.* The quantities tabulated in this Almanac are generally correct to the nearest $0\!\cdot\!1$; the exception is the Sun's GHA which is deliberately adjusted by up to $0\!\cdot\!15$ to reduce the error due to ignoring the v-correction. The GHA and Dec at intermediate times cannot be obtained to this precision, since at least two quantities must be added; moreover, the v- and d-corrections are based on mean values of v and d and are taken from tables for the whole minute only. The largest error that can occur in the GHA or Dec of any body other than the Sun or Moon is less than $0\!\cdot\!2$; it may reach $0\!\cdot\!25$ for the GHA of the Sun and $0\!\cdot\!3$ for that of the Moon.

In practice it may be expected that only one third of the values of GHA and Dec taken out will have errors larger than $0\!\cdot\!05$ and less than one tenth will have errors larger than $0\!\cdot\!1$.

25. *Altitude corrections.* The errors in the altitude corrections are nominally of the same order as those in GHA and Dec, as they result from the addition of several quantities each correctly rounded off to $0\!\cdot\!1$. But the actual values of the dip and of the refraction at low altitudes may, in extreme atmospheric conditions, differ considerably from the mean values used in the tables.

USE OF THIS ALMANAC IN 2016

This Almanac may be used for the Sun and stars in 2016 in the following manner.

For the Sun, take out the GHA and Dec for the same date but, for January and February (for February 29 use March 1), for a time $5^h\ 48^m\ 00^s$ *earlier* and, for March to December, for a time $18^h\ 12^m\ 00^s$ *later* than the UT of observation; in both cases *add* 87° 00′ to the GHA so obtained. The error, mainly due to planetary perturbations of the Earth, is unlikely to exceed $0\!\cdot\!4$.

For the stars, calculate the GHA and Dec for the same date and the same time, but for January and February (for February 29 use March 1) *subtract* $15\!\cdot\!1$ and for March to December *add* $44\!\cdot\!0$ to the GHA so found. The error, due to incomplete correction for precession and nutation, is unlikely to exceed $0\!\cdot\!4$. If preferred, the same result can be obtained by using a time $5^h\ 48^m\ 00^s$ earlier for January and February (for February 29 use March 1) and $18^h\ 12^m\ 00^s$ later for March to December, than the UT of observation (as for the Sun) and adding 86° $59\!\cdot\!2$ to the GHA (or adding 87° as for the Sun and subtracting $0\!\cdot\!8$, for precession, from the SHA of the star).

The Almanac cannot be so used for the Moon or planets.

LIST I — PLACES FAST ON UTC (mainly those EAST OF GREENWICH)

The times given } *added* to UTC to give Standard Time
below should be } *subtracted* from Standard Time to give UTC.

	h m		h m
Admiralty Islands	10	Denmark*†	01
Afghanistan	04 30	Djibouti	03
Albania*	01		
Algeria	01	Egypt, Arab Republic of	02
Amirante Islands	04	Equatorial Guinea, Republic of	01
Andaman Islands	05 30	Eritrea	03
Angola	01	Estonia*†	02
Armenia	04	Ethiopia	03
Australia			
Australian Capital Territory*	10	Fiji*	12
New South Wales*¹	10	Finland*†	02
Northern Territory	09 30	France*†	01
Queensland	10		
South Australia*	09 30	Gabon	01
Tasmania*	10	Georgia	04
Victoria*	10	Germany*†	01
Western Australia	08	Gibraltar*	01
Whitsunday Islands	10	Greece*†	02
Austria*†	01	Guam	10
Azerbaijan*	04		
		Hong Kong	08
Bahrain	03	Hungary*†	01
Balearic Islands*†	01		
Bangladesh	06	India	05 30
Belarus	03	Indonesia, Republic of	
Belgium*†	01	Bangka, Billiton, Java, West and	
Benin	01	Central Kalimantan, Madura, Sumatra	07
Bosnia and Herzegovina*	01	Bali, Flores, South and East	
Botswana, Republic of	02	Kalimantan, Lombok, Sulawesi,	
Brunei	08	Sumba, Sumbawa, West Timor ...	08
Bulgaria*†	02	Aru, Irian Jaya, Kai, Moluccas	
Burma (Myanmar)	06 30	Tanimbar	09
Burundi	02	Iran*	03 30
		Iraq	03
Cambodia	07	Israel*	02
Cameroon Republic	01	Italy*†	01
Caroline Islands²	10		
Central African Republic	01	Jan Mayen Island*	01
Chad	01	Japan	09
Chagos Archipelago & Diego Garcia	06	Jordan	03
Chatham Islands*	12 45		
China, People's Republic of	08	Kazakhstan	
Christmas Island, Indian Ocean ...	07	Western: Aktau, Uralsk, Atyrau ...	05
Cocos (Keeling) Islands	06 30	Eastern & Central: Kzyl-Orda, Astana	06
Comoro Islands (Comoros)	03	Kenya	03
Congo, Democratic Republic		Kerguelen Islands	05
West: Kinshasa, Equateur	01	Kiribati Republic	
East: Orientale, Kasai, Kivu, Shaba	02	Gilbert Islands	12
Congo Republic	01	Phoenix Islands³	13
Corsica*†	01	Line Islands³	14
Crete*†	02	Korea, North	09
Croatia*†	01	Korea, South	09
Cyprus†: Ercan*, Larnaca*	02	Kuwait	03
Czech Republic*†	01	Kyrgyzstan	06
		Laccadive Islands	05 30
		Laos	07
		Latvia*†	02

* Daylight-saving time may be kept in these places.   † For Summer time dates see List II footnotes.
¹ Except Broken Hill Area* which keeps 09ʰ 30ᵐ.
² Except Pohnpei, Pingelap and Kosrae which keep 11ʰ and Palau which keeps 09ʰ.
³ The Line and Phoenix Is. not part of the Kiribati Republic keep 10ʰ and 11ʰ, respectively, slow on UTC.

	h	m		h	m
Lebanon*	02		Irkutsk, Bratsk, Ulan-Ude	09	
Lesotho	02		Tiksi, Yakutsk, Chita	10	
Libya	02		Vladivostok, Khabarovsk, Okhotsk		
Liechtenstein*	01		Sakhalin Island	11	
Lithuania*†	02		Petropavlovsk-K., Magadan, Anadyr		
Lord Howe Island*	10	30	Kuril Islands	12	
Luxembourg*†	01		Rwanda	02	
Macau	08		Ryukyu Islands	09	
Macedonia*, former Yugoslav Republic	01		Samoa*	13	
Macias Nguema (Fernando Póo)	01		Santa Cruz Islands	11	
Madagascar, Democratic Republic of	03		Sardinia*†	01	
Malawi	02		Saudi Arabia	03	
Malaysia, Malaya, Sabah, Sarawak	08		Schouten Islands	09	
Maldives, Republic of The	05		Serbia*	01	
Malta*†	01		Seychelles	04	
Mariana Islands	10		Sicily*†	01	
Marshall Islands	12		Singapore	08	
Mauritius	04		Slovakia*†	01	
Moldova*	02		Slovenia*†	01	
Monaco*	01		Socotra	03	
Mongolia	08		Solomon Islands	11	
Montenegro*	01		Somalia Republic	03	
Mozambique	02		South Africa, Republic of	02	
Namibia*	01		Spain*†	01	
Nauru	12		Spanish Possessions in North Africa*	01	
Nepal	05	45	Spitsbergen (Svalbard)*	01	
Netherlands, The*†	01		Sri Lanka	05	30
New Caledonia	11		Sudan, Republic of	03	
New Zealand*	12		Swaziland	02	
Nicobar Islands	05	30	Sweden*†	01	
Niger	01		Switzerland*	01	
Nigeria, Republic of	01		Syria (Syrian Arab Republic)*	02	
Norfolk Island	11	30	Taiwan	08	
Norway*	01		Tajikistan	05	
Novaya Zemlya	04		Tanzania	03	
Okinawa	09		Thailand	07	
Oman	04		Timor-Leste	09	
Pagalu (Annobon Islands)	01		Tonga	13	
Pakistan	05		Tunisia	01	
Palau Islands	09		Turkey*	02	
Papua New Guinea	10		Turkmenistan	05	
Pescadores Islands	08		Tuvalu	12	
Philippine Republic	08		Uganda	03	
Poland*†	01		Ukraine*	02	
Qatar	03		United Arab Emirates	04	
Reunion	04		Uzbekistan	05	
Romania*†	02		Vanuatu, Republic of	11	
Russia [1]			Vietnam, Socialist Republic of	07	
Kaliningrad	03		Yemen	03	
Moscow, St. Petersburg, Volgograd					
Arkhangelsk, Astrakhan, Samara	04		Zambia, Republic of	02	
Ekaterinburg, Ufa, Perm, Novyy Port	06		Zimbabwe	02	
Omsk, Novosibirsk, Tomsk	07				
Norilsk, Krasnoyarsk, Dikson	08				

* Daylight-saving time may be kept in these places.   † For Summer time dates see List II footnotes.
[1] The boundaries between the zones are irregular; listed are chief towns in each zone.

LIST II — PLACES NORMALLY KEEPING UTC

Ascension Island	Ghana	Irish Republic*†	Morocco*	Sierra Leone
Burkina-Faso	Great Britain†	Ivory Coast	Portugal*†	Togo Republic
Canary Islands*†	Guinea-Bissau	Liberia	Principe	Tristan da Cunha
Channel Islands†	Guinea Republic	Madeira*†	St. Helena	
Faeroes*, The	Iceland	Mali	São Tomé	
Gambia, The	Ireland, Northern†	Mauritania	Senegal	

* Daylight-saving time may be kept in these places.

† Summer time (daylight-saving time), one hour in advance of UTC, will be kept from 2015 March 29^d 01^h to October 25^d 01^h UTC (Ninth Summer Time Directive of the European Union). Ratification by member countries has not been verified.

LIST III — PLACES SLOW ON UTC (WEST OF GREENWICH)

The times given ⎱ subtracted from UTC to give Standard Time
below should be ⎰ added to Standard Time to give UTC.

	h	m		h	m
American Samoa	11		Canada (continued)		
Argentina	03		Prince Edward Island*	04	
Austral (Tubuai) Islands[1]	10		Quebec, east of long. W. 63°	04	
Azores*†	01		west of long. W. 63°* ...	05	
			Saskatchewan	06	
Bahamas*	05		Yukon*	08	
Barbados	04		Cape Verde Islands	01	
Belize	06		Cayman Islands	05	
Bermuda*	04		Chile*	04	
Bolivia	04		Colombia	05	
Brazil			Cook Islands	10	
Fernando de Noronha I., Trindade I.,			Costa Rica	06	
Oceanic Is.	02		Cuba*	05	
N and NE coastal states, Bahia,			Curaçao Island	04	
Tocantins*, Goiás*, Brasilia*,					
Minas Gerais*, Espirito Santo*,			Dominican Republic	04	
S and E coastal states*	03				
Mato Grosso do Sul*, Mato Grosso*,			Easter Island (I. de Pascua)*	06	
Rondônia, Amazonas, Roraima, Acre	04		Ecuador	05	
British Antarctic Territory[2,3]	03		El Salvador	06	
Canada[3]‡			Falkland Islands	03	
Alberta*	07		Fernando de Noronha Island	02	
British Columbia*	08		French Guiana	03	
Labrador*	04				
Manitoba*	06		Galápagos Islands	06	
New Brunswick*	04		Greenland		
Newfoundland*	03	30	Danmarkshavn, Mesters Vig	00	
Nunavut*			General*	03	
east of long. W. 85°	05		Scoresby Sound*	01	
long. W. 85° to W. 102°	06		Thule*, Pituffik*	04	
west of long. W. 102°	07		Grenada	04	
Northwest Territories*	07		Guadeloupe	04	
Nova Scotia*	04		Guatemala	06	
Ontario, east of long. W. 90°*	05		Guyana, Republic of	04	
Ontario, west of long. W. 90°* ...	06				

* Daylight-saving time may be kept in these places.   ‡ Dates for DST are given at the end of List III.

[1] This is the legal standard time, but local mean time is generally used.

[2] Stations may use UTC.

[3] Some areas may keep another time zone.

LIST III — (continued)

	h	m		h	m
Haiti*	05		United States of America‡(continued)		
Honduras	06		Idaho, southern part	07	
			northern part	08	
Jamaica	05		Illinois	06	
Johnston Island	10		Indiana[2]	05	
Juan Fernandez Islands*	04		Iowa	06	
			Kansas[2]	06	
Leeward Islands	04		Kentucky, eastern part	05	
			western part	06	
Marquesas Islands	09	30	Louisiana	06	
Martinique	04		Maine	05	
Mexico			Maryland	05	
General*	06		Massachusetts	05	
Sonora, Sinaloa*, Nayarit*,			Michigan[2]	05	
Chihuahua*, Southern District			Minnesota	06	
of Lower California*	07		Mississippi	06	
Northern District of Lower California*	08		Missouri	06	
Midway Islands	11		Montana	07	
			Nebraska, eastern part	06	
Nicaragua	06		western part	07	
Niue	11		Nevada	08	
			New Hampshire	05	
Panama, Republic of	05		New Jersey	05	
Paraguay*	04		New Mexico	07	
Peru	05		New York	05	
Pitcairn Island	08		North Carolina	05	
Puerto Rico	04		North Dakota, eastern part	06	
			western part	07	
St. Pierre and Miquelon*	03		Ohio	05	
Society Islands	10		Oklahoma	06	
South Georgia	02		Oregon[2]	08	
Suriname	03		Pennsylvania	05	
			Rhode Island	05	
Trindade Island, South Atlantic ...	02		South Carolina	05	
Trinidad and Tobago	04		South Dakota, eastern part	06	
Tuamotu Archipelago	10		western part	07	
Tubuai (Austral) Islands	10		Tennessee, eastern part	05	
Turks and Caicos Islands*	05		western part	06	
			Texas[2]	06	
United States of America‡			Utah	07	
Alabama	06		Vermont	05	
Alaska	09		Virginia	05	
Aleutian Islands, east of W. 169° 30′	09		Washington D.C.	05	
Aleutian Islands, west of W. 169° 30′	10		Washington	08	
Arizona[1]	07		West Virginia	05	
Arkansas	06		Wisconsin	06	
California	08		Wyoming	07	
Colorado	07		Uruguay*	03	
Connecticut	05				
Delaware	05		Venezuela	04	30
District of Columbia	05		Virgin Islands	04	
Florida[2]	05				
Georgia	05		Windward Islands	04	
Hawaii[1]	10				

* Daylight-saving time may be kept in these places.
‡ Daylight-saving (Summer) time, one hour fast on the time given, is kept during 2015 from March 8 (second Sunday) to November 1 (first Sunday), changing at $02^h\ 00^m$ local clock time.
[1] Exempt from keeping daylight-saving time, except for a portion of Arizona.
[2] A small portion of the state is in another time zone.

NORTHERN STARS

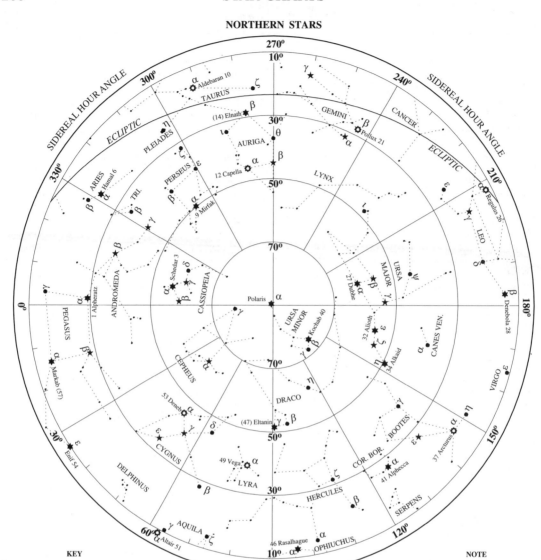

KEY

✿ Selected stars of magnitude 1.5 and brighter
★ Selected stars of magnitude 1.6 and fainter
★ Other tabulated stars of magnitude 2.5 and brighter
● Other tabulated stars of magnitude 2.6 and fainter
· Untabulated stars

NOTE

The numbers enclosed in brackets refer to those stars of the selected list which are not used in Sight Reduction Tables A.P. 3270, N.P. 303.

EQUATORIAL STARS (SHA 0° to 180°)

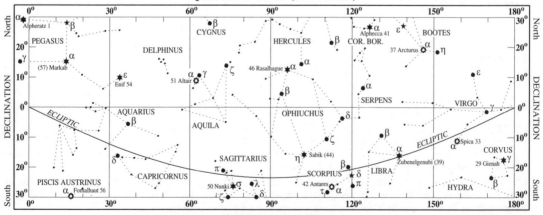

SIDEREAL HOUR ANGLE

SOUTHERN STARS

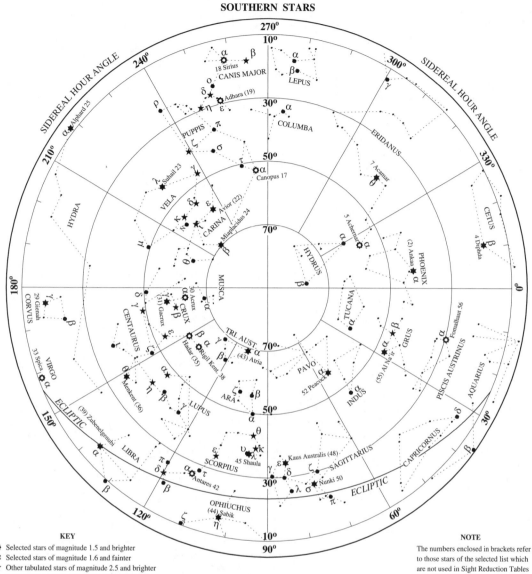

KEY

- ✿ Selected stars of magnitude 1.5 and brighter
- ★ Selected stars of magnitude 1.6 and fainter
- ★ Other tabulated stars of magnitude 2.5 and brighter
- ● Other tabulated stars of magnitude 2.6 and fainter
- · Untabulated stars

NOTE

The numbers enclosed in brackets refer to those stars of the selected list which are not used in Sight Reduction Tables A.P. 3270, N.P. 303.

EQUATORIAL STARS (SHA 180° to 360°)

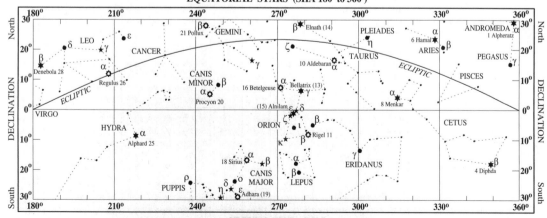

SIDEREAL HOUR ANGLE

			SHA							Declination						
Mag.	Name and Number			JAN.	FEB.	MAR.	APR.	MAY	JUNE		JAN.	FEB.	MAR.	APR.	MAY	JUNE
			°	′	′	′	′	′	′	°	′	′	′	′	′	′
3·2	γ Cephei		4	60·3	60·8	61·0	60·8	60·1	59·3	N 77	43·3	43·2	43·0	42·9	42·8	42·8
2·5	α Pegasi	57	13	37·4	37·5	37·4	37·3	37·2	36·9	N 15	17·3	17·2	17·2	17·1	17·2	17·3
2·4	β Pegasi		13	52·5	52·5	52·5	52·4	52·2	52·0	N 28	10·0	09·9	09·9	09·8	09·8	09·9
1·2	α Piscis Aust.	56	15	23·1	23·1	23·1	22·9	22·7	22·5	S 29	32·6	32·6	32·5	32·4	32·3	32·2
2·1	β Gruis		19	07·0	07·1	07·0	06·8	06·6	06·3	S 46	48·5	48·4	48·3	48·1	48·0	47·9
2·9	α Tucanæ		25	07·9	07·9	07·8	07·5	07·2	06·8	S 60	11·2	11·0	10·9	10·7	10·6	10·6
1·7	α Gruis	55	27	42·8	42·8	42·7	42·5	42·3	41·9	S 46	53·3	53·2	53·1	53·0	52·9	52·8
2·9	δ Capricorni		33	02·2	02·2	02·1	01·9	01·7	01·5	S 16	03·5	03·5	03·5	03·4	03·3	03·2
2·4	ε Pegasi	54	33	46·3	46·3	46·2	46·1	45·9	45·6	N 9	56·8	56·7	56·7	56·7	56·7	56·8
2·9	β Aquarii		36	55·0	55·0	54·9	54·7	54·5	54·2	S 5	30·2	30·2	30·2	30·2	30·1	30·0
2·4	α Cephei		40	16·3	16·4	16·2	15·9	15·5	15·1	N 62	39·2	39·1	38·9	38·8	38·8	38·9
2·5	ε Cygni		48	18·0	17·9	17·8	17·6	17·3	17·1	N 34	01·8	01·7	01·6	01·5	01·6	01·7
1·3	α Cygni	53	49	31·1	31·1	30·9	30·7	30·4	30·2	N 45	20·3	20·1	20·0	19·9	20·0	20·1
3·1	α Indi		50	21·2	21·1	20·9	20·6	20·3	20·0	S 47	14·2	14·1	14·0	14·0	13·9	13·9
1·9	α Pavonis	52	53	18·2	18·1	17·8	17·5	17·1	16·8	S 56	41·1	41·0	40·9	40·8	40·7	40·7
2·2	γ Cygni		54	18·8	18·7	18·6	18·3	18·1	17·8	N 40	18·5	18·3	18·2	18·2	18·3	18·4
0·8	α Aquilæ	51	62	07·5	07·4	07·2	07·0	06·8	06·6	N 8	54·6	54·6	54·5	54·5	54·6	54·7
2·7	γ Aquilæ		63	15·6	15·5	15·4	15·2	15·0	14·8	N 10	39·2	39·1	39·0	39·0	39·1	39·2
2·9	δ Cygni		63	38·7	38·6	38·4	38·1	37·9	37·6	N 45	10·2	10·1	10·0	09·9	10·0	10·2
3·1	β Cygni		67	10·4	10·3	10·1	09·9	09·6	09·4	N 27	59·6	59·5	59·4	59·4	59·5	59·6
2·9	π Sagittarii		72	20·4	20·3	20·1	19·9	19·6	19·4	S 20	59·8	59·8	59·8	59·7	59·7	59·7
3·0	ζ Aquilæ		73	28·7	28·6	28·4	28·2	28·0	27·8	N 13	53·3	53·2	53·2	53·2	53·2	53·4
2·6	ζ Sagittarii		74	06·8	06·6	06·4	06·2	05·9	05·7	S 29	51·3	51·3	51·3	51·2	51·2	51·2
2·0	σ Sagittarii	50	75	57·3	57·2	57·0	56·7	56·5	56·3	S 26	16·5	16·5	16·4	16·4	16·4	16·4
0·0	α Lyræ	49	80	38·6	38·5	38·3	38·0	37·8	37·6	N 38	48·0	47·8	47·8	47·8	47·9	48·0
2·8	λ Sagittarii		82	46·8	46·6	46·4	46·2	45·9	45·8	S 25	24·6	24·6	24·6	24·6	24·5	24·5
1·9	ε Sagittarii	48	83	42·8	42·6	42·3	42·1	41·8	41·6	S 34	22·4	22·4	22·4	22·3	22·3	22·4
2·7	δ Sagittarii		84	30·9	30·7	30·5	30·3	30·0	29·9	S 29	49·1	49·0	49·0	49·0	49·0	49·0
3·0	γ Sagittarii		88	18·7	18·5	18·2	18·0	17·7	17·6	S 30	25·2	25·2	25·2	25·2	25·2	25·2
2·2	γ Draconis	47	90	46·1	45·9	45·6	45·3	45·1	45·0	N 51	29·3	29·1	29·1	29·1	29·2	29·4
2·8	β Ophiuchi		93	57·0	56·8	56·6	56·4	56·2	56·1	N 4	33·8	33·7	33·7	33·7	33·8	33·9
2·4	κ Scorpii		94	07·3	07·1	06·8	06·6	06·3	06·2	S 39	02·0	01·9	01·9	02·0	02·0	02·0
1·9	θ Scorpii		95	24·3	24·0	23·7	23·4	23·2	23·0	S 43	00·1	00·1	00·1	00·1	00·2	00·2
2·1	α Ophiuchi	46	96	05·7	05·6	05·4	05·1	05·0	04·9	N 12	33·1	33·0	32·9	33·0	33·0	33·1
1·6	λ Scorpii	45	96	20·8	20·6	20·3	20·0	19·8	19·6	S 37	06·6	06·6	06·6	06·6	06·6	06·7
3·0	α Aræ		96	45·2	44·9	44·6	44·3	44·0	43·9	S 49	52·9	52·9	52·9	52·9	53·0	53·1
2·7	υ Scorpii		97	03·4	03·2	02·9	02·7	02·4	02·3	S 37	18·2	18·2	18·2	18·2	18·2	18·3
2·8	β Draconis		97	18·9	18·6	18·3	18·0	17·8	17·7	N 52	17·4	17·3	17·2	17·3	17·4	17·6
2·8	β Aræ		98	22·1	21·7	21·4	21·0	20·7	20·5	S 55	32·3	32·2	32·2	32·3	32·3	32·4
Var.‡	α Herculis		101	10·2	10·0	09·8	09·6	09·4	09·3	N 14	22·5	22·4	22·4	22·4	22·5	22·6
2·4	η Ophiuchi	44	102	11·6	11·4	11·1	10·9	10·7	10·6	S 15	44·4	44·4	44·5	44·5	44·5	44·4
3·1	ζ Aræ		105	02·3	01·9	01·5	01·2	00·9	00·7	S 56	00·4	00·4	00·4	00·5	00·6	00·7
2·3	ε Scorpii		107	13·1	12·8	12·6	12·3	12·1	12·0	S 34	18·9	19·0	19·0	19·0	19·1	19·1
1·9	α Triang. Aust.	43	107	26·4	25·9	25·3	24·8	24·4	24·2	S 69	02·9	02·8	02·8	02·9	03·0	03·1
2·8	ζ Herculis		109	32·5	32·2	32·0	31·8	31·7	31·6	N 31	34·5	34·4	34·4	34·4	34·6	34·7
2·6	ζ Ophiuchi		110	30·3	30·1	29·9	29·7	29·5	29·5	S 10	35·7	35·7	35·8	35·8	35·7	35·7
2·8	τ Scorpii		110	47·8	47·6	47·4	47·1	47·0	46·9	S 28	14·6	14·6	14·6	14·7	14·7	14·7
2·8	β Herculis		112	17·2	17·0	16·8	16·6	16·4	16·4	N 21	27·5	27·4	27·3	27·4	27·5	27·6
1·0	α Scorpii	42	112	25·2	24·9	24·7	24·5	24·3	24·2	S 26	27·7	27·7	27·7	27·8	27·8	27·8
2·7	η Draconis		113	57·6	57·3	56·9	56·6	56·4	56·4	N 61	28·7	28·6	28·6	28·7	28·8	29·0
2·7	δ Ophiuchi		116	13·1	12·9	12·7	12·5	12·4	12·3	S 3	43·8	43·9	43·9	43·9	43·9	43·9
2·6	β Scorpii		118	25·4	25·2	24·9	24·7	24·6	24·5	S 19	50·6	50·6	50·7	50·7	50·7	50·7
2·3	δ Scorpii		119	41·7	41·5	41·3	41·1	40·9	40·9	S 22	39·6	39·7	39·7	39·8	39·8	39·8
2·9	π Scorpii		120	03·6	03·4	03·1	02·9	02·8	02·7	S 26	09·2	09·2	09·3	09·3	09·4	09·4
2·8	β Trianguli Aust.		120	52·9	52·5	52·0	51·7	51·4	51·3	S 63	28·2	28·2	28·3	28·4	28·5	28·6
2·6	α Serpentis		123	45·0	44·8	44·5	44·4	44·3	44·2	N 6	22·8	22·7	22·7	22·7	22·7	22·8
2·8	γ Lupi		125	57·9	57·6	57·3	57·1	56·9	56·9	S 41	12·7	12·8	12·8	12·9	13·0	13·0
2·2	α Coronæ Bor.	41	126	10·3	10·1	09·8	09·7	09·6	09·6	N 26	39·8	39·7	39·7	39·8	39·9	40·0

‡ 2·9 — 3·6

Mag.	Name and Number		SHA							Declination					
			JULY	AUG.	SEPT.	OCT.	NOV.	DEC.		JULY	AUG.	SEPT.	OCT.	NOV.	DEC.
		°	′	′	′	′	′	′	°	′	′	′	′	′	′
3·2	γ Cephei	4	58·6	58·0	57·8	57·9	58·3	59·0	N 77	42·9	43·0	43·2	43·4	43·6	43·6
2·5	Markab 57	13	36·7	36·5	36·5	36·5	36·6	36·7	N 15	17·4	17·5	17·6	17·6	17·6	17·6
2·4	Scheat	13	51·7	51·6	51·5	51·5	51·6	51·7	N 28	10·0	10·1	10·3	10·4	10·4	10·4
1·2	Fomalhaut 56	15	22·2	22·1	22·0	22·0	22·1	22·2	S 29	32·1	32·1	32·2	32·3	32·3	32·4
2·1	β Gruis	19	06·0	05·8	05·7	05·8	05·9	06·1	S 46	47·9	47·9	48·0	48·1	48·2	48·2
2·9	α Tucanæ	25	06·4	06·2	06·2	06·3	06·5	06·8	S 60	10·6	10·7	10·8	10·9	11·0	11·0
1·7	Al Na'ir 55	27	41·7	41·5	41·5	41·6	41·7	41·9	S 46	52·8	52·9	53·0	53·1	53·1	53·1
2·9	δ Capricorni	33	01·3	01·2	01·2	01·2	01·3	01·4	S 16	03·2	03·1	03·1	03·2	03·2	03·2
2·4	Enif 54	33	45·4	45·3	45·3	45·4	45·5	45·6	N 9	56·9	57·0	57·1	57·1	57·1	57·1
2·9	β Aquarii	36	54·1	54·0	54·0	54·0	54·2	54·2	S 5	30·0	29·9	29·9	29·9	29·9	29·9
2·4	Alderamin	40	14·9	14·8	14·9	15·2	15·5	15·8	N 62	39·1	39·3	39·5	39·6	39·6	39·6
2·5	ε Cygni	48	16·9	16·9	16·9	17·1	17·2	17·4	N 34	01·9	02·0	02·1	02·2	02·2	02·1
1·3	Deneb 53	49	30·0	30·0	30·1	30·2	30·4	30·6	N 45	20·3	20·4	20·6	20·7	20·7	20·6
3·1	α Indi	50	19·8	19·7	19·8	19·9	20·1	20·3	S 47	13·9	14·0	14·1	14·1	14·2	14·1
1·9	Peacock 52	53	16·5	16·4	16·5	16·7	17·0	17·1	S 56	40·8	40·9	41·0	41·1	41·1	41·0
2·2	γ Cygni	54	17·7	17·7	17·8	17·9	18·1	18·3	N 40	18·5	18·7	18·8	18·9	18·9	18·8
0·8	Altair 51	62	06·5	06·5	06·6	06·7	06·8	06·9	N 8	54·8	54·9	54·9	55·0	54·9	54·9
2·7	γ Aquilæ	63	14·6	14·6	14·7	14·8	15·0	15·0	N 10	39·3	39·4	39·5	39·5	39·4	39·4
2·9	δ Cygni	63	37·5	37·6	37·7	37·9	38·1	38·3	N 45	10·3	10·5	10·6	10·6	10·6	10·5
3·1	Albireo	67	09·3	09·3	09·5	09·6	09·8	09·9	N 27	59·8	59·9	60·0	60·0	60·0	59·9
2·9	π Sagittarii	72	19·3	19·3	19·4	19·6	19·7	19·7	S 20	59·7	59·7	59·7	59·7	59·7	59·7
3·0	ζ Aquilæ	73	27·8	27·8	27·9	28·0	28·1	28·2	N 13	53·5	53·6	53·6	53·6	53·6	53·5
2·6	ζ Sagittarii	74	05·6	05·6	05·7	05·9	06·0	06·0	S 29	51·2	51·2	51·3	51·3	51·3	51·3
2·0	Nunki 50	75	56·2	56·2	56·3	56·5	56·6	56·6	S 26	16·4	16·4	16·4	16·4	16·4	16·4
0·0	Vega 49	80	37·6	37·6	37·8	38·0	38·2	38·2	N 38	48·2	48·3	48·4	48·4	48·3	48·2
2·8	λ Sagittarii	82	45·7	45·7	45·8	46·0	46·1	46·1	S 25	24·5	24·5	24·6	24·6	24·6	24·5
1·9	Kaus Australis 48	83	41·5	41·6	41·7	41·9	42·0	42·0	S 34	22·4	22·4	22·5	22·5	22·4	22·4
2·7	δ Sagittarii	84	29·8	29·8	29·9	30·1	30·2	30·2	S 29	49·0	49·1	49·1	49·1	49·1	49·1
3·0	γ Sagittarii	88	17·5	17·5	17·7	17·8	17·9	17·9	S 30	25·2	25·2	25·2	25·2	25·2	25·2
2·2	Eltanin 47	90	45·0	45·1	45·4	45·6	45·8	45·9	N 51	29·5	29·7	29·7	29·7	29·6	29·5
2·8	β Ophiuchi	93	56·1	56·1	56·2	56·4	56·5	56·5	N 4	33·9	34·0	34·0	34·0	34·0	33·9
2·4	κ Scorpii	94	06·1	06·2	06·3	06·5	06·6	06·6	S 39	02·1	02·1	02·1	02·1	02·1	02·0
1·9	θ Scorpii	95	23·0	23·1	23·2	23·4	23·5	23·5	S 43	00·3	00·3	00·3	00·3	00·3	00·2
2·1	Rasalhague 46	96	04·8	04·9	05·0	05·2	05·3	05·2	N 12	33·2	33·3	33·3	33·3	33·2	33·2
1·6	Shaula 45	96	19·6	19·7	19·8	20·0	20·1	20·1	S 37	06·7	06·8	06·8	06·7	06·7	06·7
3·0	α Aræ	96	43·8	43·9	44·1	44·3	44·4	44·4	S 49	53·1	53·2	53·2	53·2	53·1	53·0
2·7	υ Scorpii	97	02·2	02·3	02·5	02·6	02·7	02·7	S 37	18·3	18·3	18·4	18·3	18·3	18·2
2·8	β Draconis	97	17·8	17·9	18·2	18·5	18·6	18·7	N 52	17·7	17·8	17·9	17·9	17·7	17·6
2·8	β Aræ	98	20·5	20·6	20·8	21·1	21·2	21·2	S 55	32·5	32·6	32·6	32·6	32·5	32·4
Var.‡	α Herculis	101	09·3	09·4	09·6	09·7	09·8	09·7	N 14	22·7	22·7	22·8	22·7	22·7	22·6
2·4	Sabik 44	102	10·6	10·7	10·8	10·9	11·0	11·0	S 15	44·4	44·4	44·4	44·4	44·4	44·4
3·1	ζ Aræ	105	00·7	00·9	01·1	01·4	01·5	01·4	S 56	00·8	00·8	00·8	00·8	00·7	00·6
2·3	ε Scorpii	107	12·0	12·1	12·3	12·4	12·5	12·4	S 34	19·1	19·2	19·1	19·1	19·1	19·0
1·9	Atria 43	107	24·2	24·5	24·9	25·3	25·5	25·4	S 69	03·3	03·3	03·4	03·3	03·2	03·1
2·8	ζ Herculis	109	31·6	31·7	31·9	32·1	32·2	32·1	N 31	34·8	34·9	34·9	34·9	34·7	34·6
2·6	ζ Ophiuchi	110	29·5	29·5	29·7	29·8	29·8	29·8	S 10	35·7	35·7	35·7	35·6	35·7	35·7
2·8	τ Scorpii	110	46·9	47·0	47·1	47·2	47·3	47·2	S 28	14·7	14·7	14·7	14·7	14·7	14·7
2·8	β Herculis	112	16·4	16·5	16·7	16·8	16·9	16·8	N 21	27·7	27·7	27·7	27·7	27·6	27·5
1·0	Antares 42	112	24·2	24·3	24·5	24·6	24·6	24·5	S 26	27·8	27·8	27·8	27·8	27·8	27·8
2·7	η Draconis	113	56·5	56·8	57·2	57·5	57·7	57·7	N 61	29·1	29·2	29·2	29·1	29·0	28·8
2·7	δ Ophiuchi	116	12·3	12·4	12·5	12·6	12·7	12·6	S 3	43·8	43·8	43·8	43·8	43·8	43·9
2·6	β Scorpii	118	24·6	24·7	24·8	24·9	24·9	24·8	S 19	50·7	50·7	50·7	50·7	50·7	50·7
2·3	Dschubba	119	40·9	41·0	41·1	41·2	41·2	41·1	S 22	39·8	39·8	39·8	39·8	39·7	39·7
2·9	π Scorpii	120	02·8	02·9	03·0	03·1	03·1	03·0	S 26	09·4	09·4	09·4	09·3	09·3	09·3
2·8	β Trianguli Aust.	120	51·4	51·7	52·0	52·3	52·3	52·1	S 63	28·7	28·8	28·7	28·6	28·5	28·4
2·6	α Serpentis	123	44·3	44·4	44·5	44·6	44·6	44·5	N 6	22·9	22·9	22·9	22·9	22·8	22·7
2·8	γ Lupi	125	56·9	57·1	57·2	57·4	57·4	57·2	S 41	13·1	13·1	13·1	13·0	12·9	12·9
2·2	Alphecca 41	126	09·6	09·8	09·9	10·0	10·0	09·9	N 26	40·1	40·1	40·1	40·0	39·9	39·8

‡ 2·9 — 3·6

Mag.	Name and Number		SHA							Declination					
			JAN.	FEB.	MAR.	APR.	MAY	JUNE		JAN.	FEB.	MAR.	APR.	MAY	JUNE
		°	′	′	′	′	′	′	°	′	′	′	′	′	′
3·1	γ Ursæ Minoris	129	50·1	49·5	49·0	48·6	48·5	48·7	N 71	46·6	46·6	46·6	46·7	46·9	47·0
2·9	γ Trianguli Aust.	129	55·0	54·4	53·9	53·5	53·3	53·3	S 68	43·7	43·7	43·8	43·9	44·0	44·2
2·6	β Libræ	130	32·8	32·5	32·3	32·2	32·1	32·1	S 9	26·2	26·2	26·3	26·3	26·3	26·3
2·7	β Lupi	135	07·1	06·8	06·6	06·4	06·3	06·2	S 43	11·4	11·4	11·5	11·6	11·7	11·8
2·8	α Libræ 39	137	04·3	04·1	03·9	03·7	03·6	03·6	S 16	06·1	06·2	06·2	06·3	06·3	06·3
2·1	β Ursæ Minoris 40	137	20·7	20·1	19·5	19·1	19·1	19·4	N 74	05·4	05·4	05·4	05·5	05·7	05·9
2·4	ε Bootis	138	35·5	35·2	35·0	34·9	34·8	34·9	N 27	00·6	00·5	00·5	00·6	00·7	00·8
2·3	α Lupi	139	15·9	15·5	15·3	15·1	15·0	15·0	S 47	26·8	26·9	27·0	27·1	27·2	27·3
−0·3	α Centauri 38	139	50·3	49·9	49·5	49·3	49·2	49·3	S 60	53·4	53·5	53·6	53·7	53·9	54·0
2·3	η Centauri	140	52·9	52·6	52·4	52·2	52·1	52·1	S 42	13·1	13·2	13·3	13·4	13·5	13·6
3·0	γ Bootis	141	49·9	49·6	49·4	49·3	49·2	49·3	N 38	14·4	14·3	14·4	14·5	14·6	14·7
0·0	α Bootis 37	145	54·8	54·6	54·4	54·3	54·3	54·3	N 19	06·2	06·1	06·1	06·1	06·2	06·3
2·1	θ Centauri 36	148	06·3	06·0	05·8	05·7	05·6	05·7	S 36	26·4	26·5	26·6	26·7	26·8	26·8
0·6	β Centauri 35	148	46·3	45·9	45·6	45·4	45·3	45·4	S 60	26·4	26·5	26·6	26·7	26·9	27·0
2·6	ζ Centauri	150	52·5	52·2	52·0	51·8	51·8	51·9	S 47	21·4	21·5	21·7	21·8	21·9	22·0
2·7	η Bootis	151	09·0	08·8	08·6	08·5	08·5	08·5	N 18	19·3	19·2	19·2	19·2	19·3	19·4
1·9	η Ursæ Majoris 34	152	58·2	57·9	57·6	57·5	57·5	57·6	N 49	14·1	14·0	14·1	14·2	14·3	14·5
2·3	ε Centauri	154	47·0	46·6	46·4	46·3	46·2	46·3	S 53	32·3	32·4	32·5	32·6	32·8	32·8
1·0	α Virginis 33	158	30·1	29·9	29·7	29·6	29·6	29·7	S 11	14·3	14·4	14·5	14·5	14·5	14·5
2·3	ζ Ursæ Majoris	158	52·2	51·9	51·6	51·5	51·6	51·8	N 54	50·5	50·5	50·6	50·7	50·9	51·0
2·8	ι Centauri	159	38·1	37·8	37·6	37·6	37·6	37·6	S 36	47·3	47·4	47·5	47·6	47·7	47·7
2·8	ε Virginis	164	16·0	15·8	15·7	15·6	15·6	15·7	N 10	52·6	52·5	52·5	52·6	52·6	52·7
2·9	α Canum Venat.	165	49·0	48·8	48·6	48·6	48·6	48·7	N 38	14·0	14·0	14·0	14·1	14·2	14·3
1·8	ε Ursæ Majoris 32	166	19·8	19·4	19·2	19·2	19·3	19·4	N 55	52·4	52·4	52·5	52·6	52·8	52·9
1·3	β Crucis	167	50·4	50·0	49·8	49·7	49·8	50·0	S 59	46·0	46·1	46·3	46·4	46·6	46·6
2·9	γ Virginis	169	23·5	23·3	23·2	23·1	23·2	23·2	S 1	32·0	32·1	32·1	32·1	32·1	32·1
2·2	γ Centauri	169	24·3	24·0	23·9	23·8	23·9	24·0	S 49	02·3	02·5	02·6	02·7	02·8	02·9
2·7	α Muscæ	170	27·8	27·4	27·1	27·1	27·2	27·5	S 69	12·8	12·9	13·1	13·3	13·4	13·5
2·7	β Corvi	171	12·1	11·8	11·7	11·7	11·7	11·8	S 23	28·7	28·8	28·9	29·0	29·0	29·0
1·6	γ Crucis 31	171	59·4	59·1	58·9	58·8	58·9	59·1	S 57	11·6	11·7	11·9	12·1	12·2	12·2
1·3	α Crucis 30	173	07·7	07·3	07·1	07·1	07·2	07·4	S 63	10·7	10·8	11·0	11·2	11·3	11·4
2·6	γ Corvi 29	175	51·0	50·8	50·7	50·7	50·7	50·8	S 17	37·5	37·6	37·7	37·8	37·8	37·8
2·6	δ Centauri	177	42·4	42·1	42·0	42·0	42·1	42·2	S 50	48·2	48·3	48·5	48·6	48·7	48·8
2·4	γ Ursæ Majoris	181	20·7	20·4	20·2	20·3	20·4	20·6	N 53	36·3	36·4	36·5	36·6	36·7	36·8
2·1	β Leonis 28	182	32·4	32·2	32·1	32·1	32·2	32·3	N 14	29·1	29·1	29·1	29·1	29·1	29·2
2·6	δ Leonis	191	16·2	16·0	15·9	16·0	16·0	16·1	N 20	26·2	26·2	26·2	26·3	26·4	26·4
3·0	ψ Ursæ Majoris	192	22·2	22·0	21·9	22·0	22·1	22·3	N 44	24·7	24·7	24·8	24·9	25·0	25·0
1·8	α Ursæ Majoris 27	193	50·1	49·8	49·7	49·8	50·1	50·3	N 61	39·8	39·9	40·0	40·2	40·3	40·3
2·4	β Ursæ Majoris	194	18·7	18·4	18·3	18·4	18·6	18·8	N 56	17·8	17·8	17·9	18·1	18·1	18·2
2·7	μ Velorum	198	08·1	07·9	07·9	08·0	08·2	08·3	S 49	29·9	30·1	30·3	30·4	30·5	30·5
2·8	θ Carinæ	199	06·7	06·4	06·4	06·6	06·9	07·2	S 64	28·3	28·5	28·6	28·8	28·9	28·9
2·3	γ Leonis	204	47·7	47·6	47·5	47·6	47·7	47·8	N 19	45·7	45·6	45·7	45·7	45·8	45·8
1·4	α Leonis 26	207	42·1	42·0	42·0	42·0	42·1	42·2	N 11	53·4	53·3	53·3	53·4	53·4	53·4
3·0	ε Leonis	213	19·1	19·0	19·0	19·1	19·2	19·3	N 23	42·0	42·0	42·0	42·1	42·1	42·2
3·1	N Velorum	217	04·0	03·9	04·0	04·2	04·5	04·7	S 57	06·1	06·3	06·4	06·5	06·6	06·5
2·0	α Hydræ 25	217	54·7	54·6	54·6	54·7	54·8	54·9	S 8	43·6	43·7	43·8	43·8	43·8	43·7
2·5	κ Velorum	219	20·6	20·5	20·6	20·8	21·0	21·2	S 55	04·5	04·7	04·9	05·0	05·0	05·0
2·2	ι Carinæ	220	36·8	36·7	36·8	37·1	37·3	37·6	S 59	20·3	20·5	20·7	20·8	20·8	20·8
1·7	β Carinæ 24	221	38·4	38·3	38·5	38·9	39·4	39·8	S 69	46·8	47·0	47·1	47·2	47·3	47·2
2·2	λ Velorum 23	222	51·2	51·1	51·2	51·3	51·5	51·7	S 43	29·7	29·9	30·0	30·1	30·1	30·0
3·1	ι Ursæ Majoris	224	56·1	56·0	56·0	56·2	56·4	56·5	N 47	58·6	58·7	58·8	58·9	58·9	58·9
2·0	δ Velorum	228	42·5	42·4	42·6	42·8	43·1	43·3	S 54	45·9	46·1	46·3	46·4	46·4	46·3
1·9	ε Carinæ 22	234	16·8	16·9	17·0	17·3	17·6	17·9	S 59	33·6	33·8	33·9	34·0	34·0	33·9
1·8	γ Velorum	237	29·4	29·4	29·6	29·8	30·0	30·1	S 47	23·0	23·2	23·3	23·4	23·4	23·3
2·8	ρ Puppis	237	56·8	56·7	56·8	57·0	57·1	57·2	S 24	21·1	21·2	21·3	21·3	21·3	21·2
2·3	ζ Puppis	238	57·7	57·7	57·9	58·1	58·2	58·3	S 40	02·9	03·1	03·2	03·2	03·2	03·1
1·1	β Geminorum 21	243	26·0	26·0	26·1	26·3	26·4	26·4	N 27	59·1	59·1	59·2	59·2	59·2	59·2
0·4	α Canis Minoris 20	244	58·3	58·2	58·3	58·5	58·6	58·6	N 5	10·9	10·9	10·8	10·9	10·9	10·9

Mag.	Name and Number		SHA °	JULY	AUG.	SEPT.	OCT.	NOV.	DEC.	Declination °	JULY	AUG.	SEPT.	OCT.	NOV.	DEC.
3·1	γ Ursæ Minoris		129	49·1	49·6	50·1	50·5	50·6	50·5	N 71	47·1	47·1	47·1	47·0	46·8	46·6
2·9	γ Trianguli Aust.		129	53·5	53·8	54·2	54·5	54·5	54·2	S 68	44·3	44·3	44·2	44·1	44·0	43·9
2·6	β Libræ		130	32·1	32·2	32·3	32·4	32·4	32·3	S 9	26·2	26·2	26·2	26·2	26·2	26·3
2·7	β Lupi		135	06·3	06·5	06·6	06·8	06·7	06·5	S 43	11·8	11·8	11·7	11·7	11·6	11·5
2·8	Zubenelgenubi	39	137	03·7	03·8	03·9	04·0	04·0	03·8	S 16	06·3	06·2	06·2	06·2	06·2	06·2
2·1	Kochab	40	137	19·8	20·4	21·0	21·4	21·5	21·3	N 74	05·9	05·9	05·8	05·7	05·5	05·3
2·4	ε Bootis		138	34·9	35·1	35·2	35·3	35·3	35·1	N 27	00·9	00·9	00·9	00·8	00·7	00·5
2·3	α Lupi		139	15·1	15·3	15·5	15·6	15·5	15·3	S 47	27·3	27·3	27·3	27·2	27·1	27·0
−0·3	Rigil Kent.	38	139	49·4	49·7	50·0	50·1	50·1	49·8	S 60	54·0	54·0	54·0	53·8	53·7	53·6
2·3	η Centauri		140	52·2	52·4	52·5	52·6	52·5	52·3	S 42	13·6	13·6	13·5	13·4	13·4	13·3
3·0	γ Bootis		141	49·4	49·6	49·7	49·8	49·8	49·6	N 38	14·8	14·8	14·7	14·6	14·5	14·3
0·0	Arcturus	37	145	54·4	54·5	54·6	54·7	54·6	54·5	N 19	06·4	06·4	06·3	06·3	06·2	06·0
2·1	Menkent	36	148	05·7	05·9	06·0	06·1	06·0	05·8	S 36	26·8	26·8	26·7	26·7	26·6	26·6
0·6	Hadar	35	148	45·6	45·8	46·1	46·2	46·1	45·8	S 60	27·0	27·0	26·9	26·8	26·7	26·6
2·6	ζ Centauri		150	52·0	52·2	52·3	52·4	52·3	52·0	S 47	22·0	22·0	21·9	21·8	21·7	21·7
2·7	η Bootis		151	08·6	08·7	08·8	08·9	08·8	08·6	N 18	19·4	19·5	19·4	19·4	19·2	19·1
1·9	Alkaid	34	152	57·8	58·0	58·2	58·2	58·2	58·0	N 49	14·5	14·5	14·4	14·3	14·1	13·9
2·3	ε Centauri		154	46·5	46·7	46·9	46·9	46·8	46·5	S 53	32·9	32·8	32·7	32·6	32·5	32·5
1·0	Spica	33	158	29·7	29·8	29·9	29·9	29·8	29·6	S 11	14·5	14·5	14·4	14·4	14·4	14·5
2·3	Mizar		158	52·0	52·2	52·3	52·4	52·3	52·0	N 54	51·0	51·0	50·9	50·7	50·5	50·4
2·8	ι Centauri		159	37·7	37·9	38·0	38·0	37·9	37·6	S 36	47·7	47·7	47·6	47·5	47·5	47·5
2·8	ε Virginis		164	15·8	15·9	15·9	15·9	15·8	15·6	N 10	52·7	52·7	52·7	52·6	52·5	52·4
2·9	Cor Caroli		165	48·9	49·0	49·1	49·1	49·0	48·7	N 38	14·4	14·3	14·2	14·1	14·0	13·8
1·8	Alioth	32	166	19·6	19·8	20·0	20·0	19·9	19·6	N 55	52·9	52·8	52·7	52·5	52·3	52·2
1·3	Mimosa		167	50·2	50·4	50·6	50·6	50·4	50·0	S 59	46·6	46·6	46·5	46·3	46·2	46·2
2·9	γ Virginis		169	23·3	23·4	23·4	23·4	23·3	23·1	S 1	32·0	32·0	32·0	32·0	32·1	32·2
2·2	Muhlifain		169	24·2	24·3	24·4	24·4	24·2	23·9	S 49	02·9	02·8	02·7	02·6	02·5	02·5
2·7	α Muscæ		170	27·8	28·2	28·4	28·4	28·1	27·6	S 69	13·5	13·5	13·3	13·2	13·1	13·0
2·7	β Corvi		171	11·9	12·0	12·0	12·0	11·9	11·6	S 23	29·0	29·0	28·9	28·9	28·8	28·9
1·6	Gacrux	31	171	59·3	59·5	59·6	59·6	59·4	59·0	S 57	12·2	12·2	12·0	11·9	11·8	11·8
1·3	Acrux	30	173	07·7	07·9	08·1	08·0	07·8	07·4	S 63	11·4	11·3	11·2	11·0	10·9	10·9
2·6	Gienah	29	175	50·9	51·0	51·0	51·0	50·8	50·6	S 17	37·7	37·7	37·6	37·6	37·6	37·7
2·6	δ Centauri		177	42·4	42·5	42·6	42·6	42·4	42·0	S 50	48·8	48·7	48·5	48·4	48·4	48·4
2·4	Phecda		181	20·8	20·9	21·0	20·9	20·7	20·3	N 53	36·8	36·7	36·5	36·4	36·2	36·1
2·1	Denebola	28	182	32·4	32·4	32·5	32·4	32·2	32·0	N 14	29·2	29·2	29·2	29·1	29·0	28·9
2·6	δ Leonis		191	16·2	16·3	16·3	16·2	16·0	15·7	N 20	26·4	26·4	26·3	26·3	26·1	26·0
3·0	ψ Ursæ Majoris		192	22·4	22·5	22·5	22·3	22·1	21·8	N 44	25·0	24·9	24·8	24·7	24·5	24·4
1·8	Dubhe	27	193	50·5	50·7	50·6	50·5	50·2	49·7	N 61	40·2	40·1	40·0	39·8	39·6	39·6
2·4	Merak		194	19·0	19·1	19·1	18·9	18·6	18·3	N 56	18·1	18·0	17·9	17·7	17·6	17·5
2·7	μ Velorum		198	08·5	08·6	08·6	08·4	08·2	07·8	S 49	30·4	30·3	30·1	30·0	30·0	30·1
2·8	θ Carinæ		199	07·4	07·6	07·6	07·4	07·0	06·6	S 64	28·8	28·7	28·6	28·4	28·4	28·4
2·3	Algeiba		204	47·9	47·9	47·8	47·7	47·5	47·2	N 19	45·8	45·8	45·7	45·7	45·6	45·5
1·4	Regulus	26	207	42·3	42·3	42·2	42·1	41·9	41·6	N 11	53·5	53·5	53·4	53·4	53·3	53·2
3·0	ε Leonis		213	19·4	19·3	19·3	19·1	18·9	18·6	N 23	42·1	42·1	42·1	42·0	41·9	41·8
3·1	N Velorum		217	04·9	04·9	04·8	04·6	04·2	03·9	S 57	06·4	06·3	06·1	06·0	06·0	06·1
2·0	Alphard	25	217	55·0	54·9	54·9	54·7	54·5	54·2	S 8	43·7	43·6	43·6	43·6	43·6	43·7
2·5	κ Velorum		219	21·4	21·4	21·3	21·1	20·7	20·4	S 55	04·9	04·7	04·6	04·5	04·5	04·6
2·2	ι Carinæ		220	37·8	37·8	37·7	37·4	37·0	36·7	S 59	20·7	20·5	20·4	20·3	20·3	20·4
1·7	Miaplacidus	24	221	40·0	40·1	40·0	39·6	39·0	38·6	S 69	47·1	47·0	46·8	46·7	46·7	46·8
2·2	Suhail	23	222	51·7	51·7	51·6	51·4	51·1	50·9	S 43	29·9	29·8	29·7	29·6	29·6	29·8
3·1	ι Ursæ Majoris		224	56·6	56·5	56·3	56·1	55·8	55·4	N 47	58·8	58·7	58·6	58·5	58·4	58·4
2·0	δ Velorum		228	43·4	43·4	43·2	42·9	42·6	42·3	S 54	46·2	46·0	45·9	45·8	45·8	46·0
1·9	Avior	22	234	18·0	17·9	17·8	17·4	17·1	16·7	S 59	33·8	33·6	33·5	33·4	33·5	33·6
1·8	γ Velorum		237	30·2	30·1	30·0	29·7	29·4	29·2	S 47	23·1	23·0	22·9	22·8	22·9	23·0
2·8	ρ Puppis		237	57·2	57·1	57·0	56·8	56·5	56·3	S 24	21·1	21·0	20·9	20·9	21·0	21·1
2·3	ζ Puppis		238	58·4	58·3	58·1	57·9	57·6	57·4	S 40	03·0	02·9	02·7	02·7	02·8	02·9
1·1	Pollux	21	243	26·4	26·3	26·1	25·9	25·6	25·4	N 27	59·2	59·1	59·1	59·0	59·0	59·0
0·4	Procyon	20	244	58·6	58·5	58·3	58·1	57·9	57·7	N 5	10·9	11·0	11·0	11·0	10·9	10·8

Mag.	Name and Number		SHA	JAN.	FEB.	MAR.	APR.	MAY	JUNE	Declination	JAN.	FEB.	MAR.	APR.	MAY	JUNE
			°	′	′	′	′	′	′	°	′	′	′	′	′	′
1·6	α Geminorum		**246**	06·2	06·2	06·3	06·4	06·6	06·6	N 31	51·0	51·1	51·1	51·1	51·1	51·1
3·3	σ Puppis		**247**	33·8	33·8	34·0	34·2	34·4	34·5	S 43	20·1	20·3	20·4	20·4	20·4	20·3
2·9	β Canis Minoris		**248**	00·1	00·1	00·2	00·3	00·4	00·5	N 8	15·3	15·2	15·2	15·2	15·2	15·3
2·4	η Canis Majoris		**248**	49·2	49·2	49·3	49·5	49·6	49·7	S 29	20·2	20·3	20·4	20·4	20·4	20·3
2·7	π Puppis		**250**	34·4	34·4	34·5	34·7	34·9	35·0	S 37	07·7	07·9	08·0	08·0	07·9	07·8
1·8	δ Canis Majoris		**252**	44·5	44·5	44·6	44·8	44·9	45·0	S 26	25·3	25·4	25·5	25·5	25·4	25·3
3·0	o Canis Majoris		**254**	04·8	04·8	04·9	05·1	05·2	05·3	S 23	51·6	51·7	51·8	51·8	51·7	51·6
1·5	ε Canis Majoris	19	**255**	11·3	11·3	11·4	11·6	11·8	11·8	S 28	59·8	60·0	60·0	60·0	60·0	59·9
2·9	τ Puppis		**257**	24·7	24·9	25·1	25·3	25·5	25·7	S 50	38·2	38·4	38·5	38·5	38·4	38·3
−1·5	α Canis Majoris	18	**258**	32·4	32·4	32·6	32·7	32·8	32·9	S 16	44·5	44·6	44·6	44·6	44·6	44·5
1·9	γ Geminorum		**260**	20·9	20·9	21·0	21·2	21·3	21·3	N 16	22·9	22·9	22·9	22·9	22·9	22·9
−0·7	α Carinæ	17	**263**	55·1	55·3	55·5	55·8	56·0	56·1	S 52	42·5	42·7	42·7	42·7	42·6	42·5
2·0	β Canis Majoris		**264**	09·1	09·2	09·3	09·5	09·6	09·6	S 17	58·1	58·2	58·2	58·2	58·2	58·1
2·6	θ Aurigæ		**269**	48·3	48·4	48·5	48·7	48·8	48·8	N 37	12·6	12·6	12·7	12·7	12·6	12·6
1·9	β Aurigæ		**269**	50·0	50·0	50·2	50·4	50·5	50·5	N 44	56·7	56·8	56·8	56·8	56·8	56·7
Var.‡	α Orionis	16	**270**	59·8	59·9	60·0	60·1	60·2	60·2	N 7	24·3	24·3	24·3	24·3	24·3	24·3
2·1	κ Orionis		**272**	52·6	52·6	52·8	52·9	53·0	53·0	S 9	40·2	40·2	40·2	40·2	40·2	40·1
1·9	ζ Orionis		**274**	36·8	36·9	37·0	37·2	37·2	37·2	S 1	56·4	56·4	56·4	56·4	56·4	56·3
2·6	α Columbæ		**274**	56·7	56·8	57·0	57·1	57·3	57·3	S 34	04·3	04·4	04·4	04·4	04·3	04·2
3·0	ζ Tauri		**275**	21·4	21·5	21·6	21·7	21·8	21·8	N 21	08·9	08·9	08·9	08·9	08·9	08·9
1·7	ε Orionis	15	**275**	45·0	45·0	45·2	45·3	45·4	45·3	S 1	11·8	11·9	11·9	11·9	11·8	11·8
2·8	ι Orionis		**275**	57·1	57·2	57·3	57·4	57·5	57·5	S 5	54·3	54·3	54·4	54·4	54·3	54·2
2·6	α Leporis		**276**	38·7	38·8	38·9	39·1	39·2	39·2	S 17	49·0	49·1	49·1	49·1	49·0	48·9
2·2	δ Orionis		**276**	48·0	48·1	48·2	48·3	48·4	48·4	S 0	17·6	17·6	17·6	17·6	17·6	17·5
2·8	β Leporis		**277**	46·3	46·4	46·5	46·7	46·7	46·7	S 20	45·2	45·2	45·3	45·2	45·2	45·1
1·7	β Tauri	14	**278**	10·9	11·0	11·1	11·3	11·3	11·3	N 28	37·0	37·0	37·0	37·0	37·0	37·0
1·6	γ Orionis	13	**278**	30·5	30·6	30·7	30·9	30·9	30·9	N 6	21·5	21·5	21·5	21·5	21·5	21·6
0·1	α Aurigæ	12	**280**	32·4	32·5	32·7	32·9	33·0	32·9	N 46	00·7	00·7	00·7	00·7	00·6	00·5
0·1	β Orionis	11	**281**	10·7	10·8	10·9	11·1	11·1	11·1	S 8	11·3	11·4	11·4	11·4	11·3	11·3
2·8	β Eridani		**282**	50·8	50·9	51·0	51·1	51·2	51·2	S 5	04·3	04·3	04·4	04·3	04·3	04·2
2·7	ι Aurigæ		**285**	29·9	30·0	30·2	30·3	30·4	30·3	N 33	11·2	11·3	11·3	11·2	11·2	11·2
0·9	α Tauri	10	**290**	47·9	47·9	48·1	48·2	48·2	48·2	N 16	32·2	32·2	32·2	32·1	32·1	32·2
2·9	ε Persei		**300**	16·5	16·7	16·8	17·0	17·0	16·9	N 40	03·2	03·2	03·1	03·1	03·0	03·0
3·0	γ Eridani		**300**	18·8	18·9	19·0	19·1	19·1	19·0	S 13	28·2	28·3	28·3	28·2	28·2	28·0
2·9	ζ Persei		**301**	13·4	13·5	13·7	13·8	13·8	13·7	N 31	55·6	55·6	55·6	55·5	55·5	55·5
2·9	η Tauri		**302**	53·9	54·0	54·2	54·3	54·3	54·2	N 24	09·0	09·0	08·9	08·9	08·9	08·9
1·8	α Persei	9	**308**	38·5	38·6	38·8	39·0	39·0	38·8	N 49	54·9	54·9	54·9	54·8	54·7	54·6
Var.§	β Persei		**312**	42·3	42·5	42·6	42·7	42·7	42·5	N 41	00·8	00·8	00·8	00·7	00·6	00·6
2·5	α Ceti	8	**314**	13·8	13·9	14·0	14·1	14·0	13·9	N 4	08·8	08·7	08·7	08·7	08·8	08·8
3·2	θ Eridani	7	**315**	17·4	17·6	17·7	17·8	17·8	17·7	S 40	15·0	15·1	15·0	14·9	14·7	14·6
2·0	α Ursæ Minoris		**317**	05·0	17·7	29·3	36·1	35·2	27·4	N 89	19·9	19·9	19·9	19·7	19·6	19·5
3·0	β Trianguli		**327**	23·1	23·2	23·3	23·4	23·3	23·1	N 35	03·6	03·5	03·5	03·4	03·3	03·3
2·0	α Arietis	6	**327**	59·4	59·5	59·6	59·7	59·6	59·4	N 23	32·0	32·0	31·9	31·9	31·9	31·9
2·3	γ Andromedæ		**328**	47·3	47·4	47·6	47·6	47·5	47·3	N 42	24·2	24·2	24·1	24·0	23·9	23·9
2·9	α Hydri		**330**	11·5	11·8	12·0	12·1	12·1	11·8	S 61	30·2	30·2	30·1	29·9	29·7	29·5
2·6	β Arietis		**331**	07·7	07·8	07·9	07·9	07·9	07·7	N 20	52·9	52·8	52·8	52·8	52·8	52·8
0·5	α Eridani	5	**335**	26·1	26·3	26·5	26·5	26·5	26·2	S 57	10·0	10·0	09·8	09·7	09·5	09·3
2·7	δ Cassiopeiæ		**338**	17·5	17·7	17·9	17·9	17·8	17·4	N 60	19·0	19·0	18·9	18·7	18·6	18·6
2·1	β Andromedæ		**342**	21·2	21·3	21·4	21·4	21·2	21·0	N 35	42·1	42·1	42·0	41·9	41·9	41·9
Var.‖	γ Cassiopeiæ		**345**	35·3	35·6	35·7	35·7	35·5	35·1	N 60	48·1	48·1	47·9	47·8	47·7	47·7
2·0	β Ceti	4	**348**	54·9	55·0	55·0	55·0	54·9	54·7	S 17	54·4	54·4	54·4	54·3	54·2	54·1
2·2	α Cassiopeiæ	3	**349**	39·3	39·5	39·6	39·5	39·3	39·0	N 56	37·4	37·4	37·2	37·1	37·0	37·0
2·4	α Phœnicis	2	**353**	14·8	14·9	15·0	15·0	14·8	14·5	S 42	13·7	13·7	13·6	13·4	13·3	13·1
2·8	β Hydri		**353**	23·2	23·8	24·0	23·9	23·6	22·9	S 77	10·5	10·4	10·2	10·0	09·9	09·7
2·8	γ Pegasi		**356**	29·8	29·9	29·9	29·9	29·7	29·5	N 15	16·1	16·0	16·0	16·0	16·0	16·1
2·3	β Cassiopeiæ		**357**	30·0	30·3	30·3	30·3	30·0	29·6	N 59	14·2	14·1	14·0	13·9	13·8	13·8
2·1	α Andromedæ	1	**357**	42·4	42·5	42·6	42·5	42·3	42·1	N 29	10·5	10·5	10·4	10·3	10·3	10·4

‡ 0·1 — 1·2   § 2·1 — 3·4   ‖ Irregular variable; 2013 mag. 2·1

Mag.	Name and Number		SHA °	JULY	AUG.	SEPT.	OCT.	NOV.	DEC.	Dec.	JULY	AUG.	SEPT.	OCT.	NOV.	DEC.
1·6	*Castor*		246	06·6	06·5	06·3	06·0	05·8	05·5	N 31	51·1	51·0	51·0	50·9	50·9	50·9
3·3	σ *Puppis*		247	34·5	34·4	34·2	34·0	33·7	33·5	S 43	20·1	20·0	19·9	19·9	19·9	20·1
2·9	β *Canis Minoris*		247	60·4	60·3	60·1	59·9	59·7	59·5	N 8	15·3	15·3	15·4	15·3	15·3	15·2
2·4	η *Canis Majoris*		248	49·7	49·6	49·4	49·2	48·9	48·7	S 29	20·2	20·0	20·0	20·0	20·0	20·2
2·7	π *Puppis*		250	35·0	34·9	34·7	34·4	34·2	34·0	S 37	07·7	07·5	07·4	07·4	07·5	07·7
1·8	*Wezen*		252	45·0	44·8	44·7	44·4	44·2	44·0	S 26	25·2	25·1	25·0	25·0	25·1	25·2
3·0	o *Canis Majoris*		254	05·2	05·1	04·9	04·7	04·5	04·3	S 23	51·5	51·4	51·3	51·3	51·4	51·5
1·5	*Adhara*	19	255	11·8	11·7	11·5	11·2	11·0	10·8	S 28	59·7	59·6	59·5	59·5	59·6	59·8
2·9	τ *Puppis*		257	25·6	25·5	25·2	25·0	24·7	24·5	S 50	38·1	38·0	37·9	37·9	38·0	38·1
−1·5	*Sirius*	18	258	32·8	32·7	32·5	32·3	32·1	31·9	S 16	44·4	44·3	44·2	44·3	44·3	44·5
1·9	*Alhena*		260	21·2	21·0	20·8	20·6	20·4	20·2	N 16	22·9	23·0	23·0	23·0	22·9	22·9
−0·7	*Canopus*	17	263	56·0	55·9	55·6	55·3	55·0	54·8	S 52	42·3	42·2	42·1	42·1	42·2	42·4
2·0	*Mirzam*		264	09·5	09·4	09·2	09·0	08·8	08·6	S 17	58·0	57·9	57·8	57·8	57·9	58·0
2·6	θ *Aurigæ*		269	48·6	48·4	48·2	47·9	47·6	47·5	N 37	12·5	12·5	12·5	12·5	12·5	12·6
1·9	*Menkalinan*		269	50·4	50·1	49·8	49·5	49·3	49·1	N 44	56·6	56·6	56·6	56·6	56·6	56·7
Var.‡	*Betelgeuse*	16	270	60·1	59·9	59·7	59·5	59·3	59·1	N 7	24·4	24·4	24·5	24·5	24·4	24·4
2·1	κ *Orionis*		272	52·9	52·7	52·5	52·3	52·1	52·0	S 9	40·0	39·9	39·9	39·9	40·0	40·0
1·9	*Alnitak*		274	37·1	36·9	36·7	36·5	36·3	36·2	S 1	56·2	56·2	56·1	56·1	56·2	56·3
2·6	*Phact*		274	57·2	57·0	56·7	56·5	56·3	56·2	S 34	04·0	03·9	03·9	03·9	04·0	04·1
3·0	ζ *Tauri*		275	21·7	21·5	21·2	21·0	20·8	20·7	N 21	08·9	08·9	08·9	08·9	08·9	08·9
1·7	*Alnilam*	15	275	45·2	45·0	44·8	44·6	44·4	44·3	S 1	11·7	11·6	11·6	11·6	11·6	11·7
2·8	ι *Orionis*		275	57·4	57·2	57·0	56·8	56·6	56·5	S 5	54·1	54·1	54·0	54·0	54·1	54·2
2·6	α *Leporis*		276	39·0	38·9	38·7	38·4	38·3	38·1	S 17	48·8	48·7	48·6	48·7	48·7	48·9
2·2	δ *Orionis*		276	48·2	48·1	47·9	47·6	47·5	47·3	S 0	17·4	17·4	17·3	17·3	17·4	17·5
2·8	β *Leporis*		277	46·6	46·4	46·2	46·0	45·8	45·7	S 20	44·9	44·8	44·8	44·8	44·9	45·0
1·7	*Elnath*	14	278	11·1	10·9	10·7	10·5	10·2	10·1	N 28	37·0	37·0	37·0	37·0	37·0	37·0
1·6	*Bellatrix*	13	278	30·8	30·6	30·4	30·2	30·0	29·9	N 6	21·6	21·7	21·7	21·7	21·7	21·6
0·1	*Capella*	12	280	32·7	32·5	32·2	31·9	31·6	31·4	N 46	00·5	00·5	00·5	00·5	00·5	00·6
0·1	*Rigel*	11	281	11·0	10·8	10·6	10·4	10·2	10·1	S 8	11·2	11·1	11·0	11·1	11·1	11·2
2·8	β *Eridani*		282	51·0	50·8	50·6	50·4	50·3	50·2	S 5	04·1	04·1	04·0	04·0	04·1	04·2
2·7	ι *Aurigæ*		285	30·1	29·9	29·6	29·4	29·2	29·1	N 33	11·1	11·2	11·2	11·2	11·2	11·3
0·9	*Aldebaran*	10	290	48·0	47·8	47·5	47·3	47·2	47·1	N 16	32·2	32·2	32·3	32·3	32·3	32·3
2·9	ε *Persei*		300	16·6	16·4	16·1	15·9	15·7	15·6	N 40	03·0	03·0	03·1	03·1	03·2	03·3
3·0	γ *Eridani*		300	18·9	18·7	18·4	18·3	18·1	18·1	S 13	27·9	27·8	27·8	27·8	27·9	28·0
2·9	ζ *Persei*		301	13·5	13·2	13·0	12·7	12·6	12·5	N 31	55·5	55·5	55·6	55·6	55·7	55·7
2·9	*Alcyone*		302	54·0	53·7	53·5	53·3	53·2	53·1	N 24	08·9	09·0	09·0	09·1	09·1	09·1
1·8	*Mirfak*	9	308	38·5	38·2	37·9	37·6	37·4	37·4	N 49	54·6	54·6	54·7	54·8	54·9	55·0
Var.§	*Algol*		312	42·3	42·0	41·7	41·5	41·4	41·4	N 41	00·6	00·7	00·7	00·8	00·9	01·0
2·5	*Menkar*	8	314	13·7	13·5	13·3	13·1	13·0	13·0	N 4	08·9	09·0	09·0	09·1	09·0	09·0
3·2	*Acamar*	7	315	17·5	17·2	17·0	16·8	16·7	16·8	S 40	14·4	14·4	14·4	14·5	14·6	14·7
2·0	*Polaris*		316	74·6	60·0	46·6	36·9	32·6	36·5	N 89	19·4	19·4	19·5	19·7	19·8	20·0
3·0	β *Trianguli*		327	22·8	22·6	22·4	22·2	22·2	22·2	N 35	03·4	03·5	03·6	03·7	03·7	03·8
2·0	*Hamal*	6	327	59·2	58·9	58·7	58·6	58·6	58·6	N 23	32·0	32·0	32·1	32·2	32·2	32·3
2·3	*Almak*		328	47·0	46·7	46·5	46·4	46·3	46·3	N 42	24·0	24·0	24·2	24·3	24·4	24·4
2·9	α *Hydri*		330	11·5	11·1	10·7	10·6	10·6	10·8	S 61	29·4	29·4	29·5	29·6	29·8	29·9
2·6	*Sheratan*		331	07·4	07·2	07·0	06·9	06·9	06·9	N 20	52·9	53·0	53·0	53·1	53·1	53·2
0·5	*Achernar*	5	335	25·9	25·5	25·3	25·1	25·2	25·3	S 57	09·2	09·2	09·3	09·4	09·6	09·7
2·7	*Ruchbah*		338	17·0	16·6	16·4	16·2	16·2	16·3	N 60	18·6	18·7	18·9	19·0	19·2	19·3
2·1	*Mirach*		342	20·7	20·5	20·3	20·2	20·2	20·3	N 35	42·0	42·1	42·2	42·3	42·4	42·4
Var.||	γ *Cassiopeiæ*		345	34·7	34·4	34·1	34·0	34·1	34·2	N 60	47·7	47·9	48·0	48·2	48·3	48·4
2·0	*Diphda*	4	348	54·4	54·2	54·1	54·0	54·0	54·1	S 17	54·0	53·9	53·9	54·0	54·0	54·1
2·2	*Schedar*	3	349	38·6	38·3	38·1	38·1	38·1	38·3	N 56	37·1	37·2	37·4	37·5	37·6	37·7
2·4	*Ankaa*	2	353	14·3	14·0	13·9	13·8	13·9	14·0	S 42	13·0	13·0	13·1	13·2	13·3	13·4
2·8	β *Hydri*		353	22·1	21·4	20·9	20·9	21·3	21·9	S 77	09·7	09·7	09·9	10·0	10·2	10·2
2·8	*Algenib*		356	29·3	29·1	28·9	28·9	28·9	29·0	N 15	16·2	16·3	16·4	16·4	16·4	16·4
2·3	*Caph*		357	29·2	28·9	28·8	28·7	28·9	29·1	N 59	13·9	14·0	14·2	14·4	14·5	14·5
2·1	*Alpheratz*	1	357	41·8	41·6	41·5	41·5	41·5	41·6	N 29	10·5	10·6	10·7	10·8	10·9	10·9

‡ 0·1 — 1·2   § 2·1 — 3·4 || Irregular variable; 2013 mag. 2·1

POLARIS (POLE STAR) TABLES, 2015
FOR DETERMINING LATITUDE FROM SEXTANT ALTITUDE AND FOR AZIMUTH

LHA ARIES	0° – 9°	10° – 19°	20° – 29°	30° – 39°	40° – 49°	50° – 59°	60° – 69°	70° – 79°	80° – 89°	90° – 99°	100° – 109°	110° – 119°
°	a_0	a_0	a_0	a_0	a_0	a_0	a_0	a_0	a_0	a_0	a_0	a_0
0	0 29·4	0 25·1	0 21·7	0 19·5	0 18·6	0 18·8	0 20·3	0 23·0	0 26·8	0 31·5	0 37·1	0 43·3
1	28·9	24·7	21·5	19·4	18·5	18·9	20·5	23·3	27·2	32·0	37·7	44·0
2	28·5	24·3	21·2	19·2	18·5	19·0	20·7	23·6	27·6	32·6	38·3	44·7
3	28·0	23·9	20·9	19·1	18·5	19·1	21·0	24·0	28·1	33·1	38·9	45·3
4	27·6	23·6	20·7	19·0	18·5	19·3	21·2	24·4	28·5	33·7	39·5	46·0
5	0 27·1	0 23·3	0 20·5	0 18·9	0 18·5	0 19·4	0 21·5	0 24·7	0 29·0	0 34·2	0 40·2	0 46·7
6	26·7	22·9	20·3	18·8	18·6	19·6	21·8	25·1	29·5	34·8	40·8	47·3
7	26·3	22·6	20·1	18·7	18·6	19·7	22·1	25·5	30·0	35·3	41·4	48·0
8	25·8	22·3	19·9	18·7	18·7	19·9	22·4	25·9	30·5	35·9	42·1	48·7
9	25·4	22·0	19·7	18·6	18·7	20·1	22·7	26·3	31·0	36·5	42·7	49·4
10	0 25·1	0 21·7	0 19·5	0 18·6	0 18·8	0 20·3	0 23·0	0 26·8	0 31·5	0 37·1	0 43·3	0 50·1

Lat.	a_1	a_1	a_1	a_1	a_1	a_1	a_1	a_1	a_1	a_1	a_1	a_1
°	′	′	′	′	′	′	′	′	′	′	′	′
0	0·5	0·5	0·6	0·6	0·6	0·6	0·6	0·5	0·5	0·4	0·4	0·3
10	·5	·5	·6	·6	·6	·6	·6	·5	·5	·5	·4	·4
20	·5	·6	·6	·6	·6	·6	·6	·5	·5	·5	·4	·4
30	·5	·6	·6	·6	·6	·6	·6	·6	·5	·5	·5	·5
40	0·6	0·6	0·6	0·6	0·6	0·6	0·6	0·6	0·6	0·5	0·5	0·5
45	·6	·6	·6	·6	·6	·6	·6	·6	·6	·6	·6	·6
50	·6	·6	·6	·6	·6	·6	·6	·6	·6	·6	·6	·6
55	·6	·6	·6	·6	·6	·6	·6	·6	·6	·6	·6	·7
60	·6	·6	·6	·6	·6	·6	·6	·6	·7	·7	·7	·7
62	0·7	0·6	0·6	0·6	0·6	0·6	0·6	0·6	0·7	0·7	0·7	0·7
64	·7	·6	·6	·6	·6	·6	·6	·7	·7	·7	·8	·8
66	·7	·7	·6	·6	·6	·6	·6	·7	·7	·8	·8	·8
68	0·7	0·7	0·6	0·6	0·6	0·6	0·6	0·7	0·7	0·8	0·8	0·9

Month	a_2	a_2	a_2	a_2	a_2	a_2	a_2	a_2	a_2	a_2	a_2	a_2
	′	′	′	′	′	′	′	′	′	′	′	′
Jan.	0·8	0·8	0·8	0·8	0·8	0·8	0·8	0·8	0·8	0·7	0·7	0·7
Feb.	·7	·7	·8	·8	·8	·9	·9	·9	·9	·9	·8	·8
Mar.	·6	·6	·7	·7	·8	·8	·9	·9	·9	·9	·9	0·9
Apr.	0·4	0·5	0·5	0·6	0·6	0·7	0·8	0·8	0·9	0·9	0·9	1·0
May	·3	·3	·4	·4	·5	·6	·6	·7	·8	·8	·9	0·9
June	·2	·3	·3	·3	·4	·4	·5	·5	·6	·7	·7	·8
July	0·3	0·3	0·3	0·3	0·3	0·3	0·4	0·4	0·5	0·5	0·6	0·6
Aug.	·4	·4	·4	·3	·3	·3	·3	·3	·4	·4	·4	·5
Sept.	·6	·5	·5	·4	·4	·4	·3	·3	·3	·3	·3	·3
Oct.	0·8	0·7	0·7	0·6	0·6	0·5	0·4	0·4	0·4	0·3	0·3	0·3
Nov.	0·9	0·9	0·9	0·8	·7	·7	·6	·5	·5	·4	·3	·3
Dec.	1·1	1·0	1·0	1·0	0·9	0·8	0·8	0·7	0·6	0·5	0·4	0·4

Lat.	AZIMUTH											
°	°	°	°	°	°	°	°	°	°	°	°	°
0	0·4	0·3	0·2	0·1	0·0	359·9	359·7	359·6	359·5	359·5	359·4	359·4
20	0·4	0·3	0·2	0·1	0·0	359·8	359·7	359·6	359·5	359·4	359·4	359·3
40	0·5	0·4	0·3	0·1	0·0	359·8	359·7	359·5	359·4	359·3	359·2	359·2
50	0·6	0·5	0·3	0·1	0·0	359·8	359·6	359·4	359·3	359·2	359·1	359·0
55	0·7	0·6	0·4	0·2	0·0	359·8	359·6	359·4	359·2	359·1	359·0	358·9
60	0·8	0·6	0·4	0·2	0·0	359·7	359·5	359·3	359·1	358·9	358·8	358·7
65	1·0	0·8	0·5	0·2	359·9	359·7	359·4	359·1	358·9	358·7	358·6	358·5

Latitude = Apparent altitude (corrected for refraction) $-1° + a_0 + a_1 + a_2$

The table is entered with LHA Aries to determine the column to be used; each column refers to a range of 10°. a_0 is taken, with mental interpolation, from the upper table with the units of LHA Aries in degrees as argument; a_1, a_2 are taken, without interpolation, from the second and third tables with arguments latitude and month respectively. a_0, a_1, a_2, are always positive. The final table gives the azimuth of *Polaris*.

LHA ARIES	120°–129°	130°–139°	140°–149°	150°–159°	160°–169°	170°–179°	180°–189°	190°–199°	200°–209°	210°–219°	220°–229°	230°–239°
°	a_0	a_0	a_0	a_0	a_0	a_0	a_0	a_0	a_0	a_0	a_0	a_0
0	0 50·1	0 57·0	1 04·0	1 10·9	1 17·4	1 23·3	1 28·4	1 32·7	1 36·0	1 38·1	1 39·0	1 38·8
1	50·7	57·7	04·7	11·6	18·0	23·8	28·9	33·1	36·2	38·2	39·1	38·7
2	51·4	58·4	05·4	12·2	18·6	24·4	29·4	33·4	36·5	38·4	39·1	38·6
3	52·1	59·1	06·1	12·9	19·2	24·9	29·8	33·8	36·7	38·5	39·1	38·5
4	52·8	0 59·8	06·8	13·5	19·8	25·4	30·3	34·1	37·0	38·6	39·1	38·4
5	0 53·5	1 00·5	1 07·5	1 14·2	1 20·4	1 26·0	1 30·7	1 34·5	1 37·2	1 38·7	1 39·1	1 38·2
6	54·2	01·2	08·2	14·8	21·0	26·5	31·1	34·8	37·4	38·8	39·0	38·1
7	54·9	01·9	08·9	15·5	21·6	27·0	31·5	35·1	37·6	38·9	39·0	37·9
8	55·6	02·7	09·5	16·1	22·2	27·5	31·9	35·4	37·8	39·0	38·9	37·7
9	56·3	03·3	10·2	16·7	22·7	28·0	32·3	35·7	37·9	39·0	38·9	37·5
10	0 57·0	1 04·0	1 10·9	1 17·4	1 23·3	1 28·4	1 32·7	1 36·0	1 38·1	1 39·0	1 38·8	1 37·3

Lat.	a_1	a_1	a_1	a_1	a_1	a_1	a_1	a_1	a_1	a_1	a_1	a_1
°	′	′	′	′	′	′	′	′	′	′	′	′
0	0·3	0·3	0·3	0·4	0·4	0·4	0·5	0·5	0·6	0·6	0·6	0·6
10	·4	·4	·4	·4	·4	·5	·5	·5	·6	·6	·6	·6
20	·4	·4	·4	·4	·5	·5	·5	·6	·6	·6	·6	·6
30	·5	·5	·5	·5	·5	·5	·5	·6	·6	·6	·6	·6
40	0·5	0·5	0·5	0·5	0·5	0·6	0·6	0·6	0·6	0·6	0·6	0·6
45	·6	·6	·6	·6	·6	·6	·6	·6	·6	·6	·6	·6
50	·6	·6	·6	·6	·6	·6	·6	·6	·6	·6	·6	·6
55	·7	·7	·7	·6	·6	·6	·6	·6	·6	·6	·6	·6
60	·7	·7	·7	·7	·7	·7	·6	·6	·6	·6	·6	·6
62	0·8	0·8	0·8	0·7	0·7	0·7	0·7	0·6	0·6	0·6	0·6	0·6
64	·8	·8	·8	·8	·7	·7	·7	·6	·6	·6	·6	·6
66	·8	·8	·8	·8	·8	·7	·7	·7	·6	·6	·6	·6
68	0·9	0·9	0·9	0·9	0·8	0·8	0·7	0·7	0·6	0·6	0·6	0·6

Month	a_2	a_2	a_2	a_2	a_2	a_2	a_2	a_2	a_2	a_2	a_2	a_2
	′	′	′	′	′	′	′	′	′	′	′	′
Jan.	0·6	0·6	0·6	0·5	0·5	0·5	0·4	0·4	0·4	0·4	0·4	0·4
Feb.	·8	·7	·7	·7	·6	·6	·5	·5	·4	·4	·4	·3
Mar.	0·9	0·9	·8	·8	·8	·7	·6	·6	·5	·5	·4	·4
Apr.	1·0	1·0	0·9	0·9	0·9	0·8	0·8	0·7	0·7	0·6	0·6	0·5
May	0·9	1·0	1·0	1·0	1·0	0·9	0·9	·9	·8	·8	·7	·6
June	·8	0·9	0·9	0·9	0·9	1·0	1·0	·9	·9	·9	·8	·8
July	0·7	0·7	0·8	0·8	0·9	0·9	0·9	0·9	0·9	0·9	0·9	0·9
Aug.	·5	·6	·6	·6	·7	·7	·8	·8	·8	·9	·9	·9
Sept.	·4	·4	·4	·5	·5	·6	·6	·7	·7	·8	·8	·8
Oct.	0·3	0·3	0·3	0·3	0·3	0·4	0·4	0·5	0·5	0·6	0·6	0·7
Nov.	·2	·2	·2	·2	·2	·2	·3	·3	·3	·4	·5	·5
Dec.	0·3	0·3	0·2	0·2	0·2	0·1	0·1	0·2	0·2	0·2	0·3	0·4

Lat.	AZIMUTH											
°	°	°	°	°	°	°	°	°	°	°	°	°
0	359·3	359·3	359·3	359·4	359·4	359·5	359·6	359·7	359·8	359·9	0·0	0·1
20	359·3	359·3	359·3	359·3	359·4	359·5	359·6	359·7	359·8	359·9	0·0	0·1
40	359·1	359·1	359·1	359·2	359·3	359·4	359·5	359·6	359·7	359·9	0·0	0·2
50	359·0	359·0	359·0	359·0	359·1	359·2	359·4	359·5	359·7	359·9	0·0	0·2
55	358·8	358·8	358·9	358·9	359·0	359·1	359·3	359·5	359·6	359·8	0·0	0·2
60	358·7	358·7	358·7	358·8	358·9	359·0	359·2	359·4	359·6	359·8	0·0	0·3
65	358·4	358·4	358·5	358·5	358·7	358·8	359·0	359·3	359·5	359·8	0·1	0·3

ILLUSTRATION

On 2015 April 21 at 23^h 18^m 56^s UT in longitude W 37° 14′ the apparent altitude (corrected for refraction), H_O, of *Polaris* was 49° 31′·6

From the daily pages:	°	′
GHA Aries (23^h)	194	41·8
Increment (18^m 56^s)	4	44·8
Longitude (west)	−37	14
LHA Aries	162	13

	°	′
H_O	49	31·6
a_0 (argument 162° 13′)	1	18·7
a_1 (Lat 50° approx.)		0·6
a_2 (April)		0·9
Sum − 1° = Lat =	49	51·8

POLARIS (POLE STAR) TABLES, 2015
FOR DETERMINING LATITUDE FROM SEXTANT ALTITUDE AND FOR AZIMUTH

LHA ARIES	240° – 249°	250° – 259°	260° – 269°	270° – 279°	280° – 289°	290° – 299°	300° – 309°	310° – 319°	320° – 329°	330° – 339°	340° – 349°	350° – 359°
°	a_0	a_0	a_0	a_0	a_0	a_0	a_0	a_0	a_0	a_0	a_0	a_0
0	I 37·3	I 34·7	I 31·1	I 26·4	I 20·9	I 14·7	I 08·1	I 01·1	0 54·1	0 47·2	0 40·7	0 34·7
I	37·1	34·4	30·6	25·9	20·3	14·1	07·4	I 00·4	53·4	46·5	40·0	34·1
2	36·9	34·1	30·2	25·4	19·7	13·4	06·7	0 59·7	52·7	45·9	39·4	33·6
3	36·7	33·7	29·8	24·8	19·1	12·8	06·0	59·0	52·0	45·2	38·8	33·0
4	36·4	33·4	29·3	24·3	18·5	12·1	05·3	58·3	51·3	44·5	38·2	32·5
5	I 36·2	I 33·0	I 28·8	I 23·7	I 17·9	I 11·5	I 04·6	0 57·6	0 50·6	0 43·9	0 37·6	0 31·9
6	35·9	32·7	28·4	23·2	17·3	10·8	03·9	56·9	49·9	43·2	37·0	31·4
7	35·6	32·3	27·9	22·6	16·6	10·1	03·2	56·2	49·3	42·6	36·4	30·9
8	35·3	31·9	27·4	22·1	16·0	09·4	02·5	55·5	48·6	41·9	35·8	30·4
9	35·1	31·5	26·9	21·5	15·4	08·8	01·8	54·8	47·9	41·3	35·2	29·9
10	I 34·7	I 31·1	I 26·4	I 20·9	I 14·7	I 08·1	I 01·1	0 54·1	0 47·2	0 40·7	0 34·7	0 29·4

Lat.	a_1	a_1	a_1	a_1	a_1	a_1	a_1	a_1	a_1	a_1	a_1	a_1
0	0·6	0·5	0·5	0·4	0·4	0·3	0·3	0·3	0·3	0·4	0·4	0·4
10	·6	·5	·5	·5	·4	·4	·4	·4	·4	·4	·4	·5
20	·6	·5	·5	·5	·4	·4	·4	·4	·4	·4	·5	·5
30	·6	·6	·5	·5	·5	·5	·5	·5	·5	·5	·5	·5
40	0·6	0·6	0·6	0·5	0·5	0·5	0·5	0·5	0·5	0·5	0·5	0·6
45	·6	·6	·6	·6	·6	·6	·6	·6	·6	·6	·6	·6
50	·6	·6	·6	·6	·6	·6	·6	·6	·6	·6	·6	·6
55	·6	·6	·6	·6	·6	·7	·7	·7	·7	·6	·6	·6
60	·6	·6	·7	·7	·7	·7	·7	·7	·7	·7	·7	·7
62	0·6	0·6	0·7	0·7	0·7	0·7	0·8	0·8	0·8	0·7	0·7	0·7
64	·6	·7	·7	·7	·8	·8	·8	·8	·8	·8	·7	·7
66	·6	·7	·7	·8	·8	·8	·8	·8	·8	·8	·8	·7
68	0·6	0·7	0·7	0·8	0·8	0·9	0·9	0·9	0·9	0·9	0·8	0·8

Month	a_2	a_2	a_2	a_2	a_2	a_2	a_2	a_2	a_2	a_2	a_2	a_2
Jan.	0·4	0·4	0·4	0·5	0·5	0·5	0·6	0·6	0·6	0·7	0·7	0·7
Feb.	·3	·3	·3	·3	·4	·4	·4	·5	·5	·5	·6	·6
Mar.	·3	·3	·3	·3	·3	·3	·3	·3	·4	·4	·4	·5
Apr.	0·4	0·4	0·3	0·3	0·3	0·2	0·2	0·2	0·3	0·3	0·3	0·4
May	·6	·5	·4	·4	·3	·3	·3	·2	·2	·2	·2	·3
June	·7	·7	·6	·5	·5	·4	·4	·3	·3	·3	·3	·2
July	0·8	0·8	0·7	0·7	0·6	0·6	0·5	0·5	0·4	0·4	0·3	0·3
Aug.	·9	·9	·8	·8	·8	·7	·7	·6	·6	·6	·5	·5
Sept.	·9	·9	·9	·9	·9	·9	·8	·8	·8	·7	·7	·6
Oct.	0·8	0·8	0·8	0·9	0·9	0·9	0·9	0·9	0·9	0·9	0·9	0·8
Nov.	·6	·7	·7	·8	·9	·9	1·0	1·0	1·0	1·0	1·0	1·0
Dec.	0·4	0·5	0·6	0·7	0·8	0·8	0·9	0·9	1·0	1·0	1·0	1·1

Lat.	AZIMUTH											
°	°	°	°	°	°	°	°	°	°	°	°	°
0	0·3	0·4	0·5	0·5	0·6	0·6	0·7	0·7	0·7	0·6	0·6	0·5
20	0·3	0·4	0·5	0·6	0·6	0·7	0·7	0·7	0·7	0·7	0·6	0·5
40	0·3	0·5	0·6	0·7	0·8	0·8	0·9	0·9	0·9	0·8	0·7	0·7
50	0·4	0·5	0·7	0·8	0·9	1·0	1·0	1·0	1·0	1·0	0·9	0·8
55	0·4	0·6	0·8	0·9	1·0	1·1	1·2	1·2	1·1	1·1	1·0	0·9
60	0·5	0·7	0·9	1·0	1·2	1·3	1·3	1·3	1·3	1·3	1·2	1·0
65	0·6	0·8	1·0	1·2	1·4	1·5	1·6	1·6	1·6	1·5	1·4	1·2

Latitude = Apparent altitude (corrected for refraction) $-1° + a_0 + a_1 + a_2$

The table is entered with LHA Aries to determine the column to be used; each column refers to a range of 10°. a_0 is taken, with mental interpolation, from the upper table with the units of LHA Aries in degrees as argument; a_1, a_2 are taken, without interpolation, from the second and third tables with arguments latitude and month respectively. a_0, a_1, a_2, are always positive. The final table gives the azimuth of *Polaris*.

SIGHT REDUCTION PROCEDURES
METHODS AND FORMULAE FOR DIRECT COMPUTATION

1. *Introduction.* In this section formulae and methods are provided for *calculating* position at sea from observed altitudes taken with a marine sextant using a computer or programmable calculator.

The method uses analogous concepts and similar terminology as that used in *manual* methods of astro-navigation, where position is found by plotting position lines from their intercept and azimuth on a marine chart.

The algorithms are presented in standard algebra suitable for translating into the programming language of the user's computer. The basic ephemeris data may be taken directly from the main tabular pages of a current version of *The Nautical Almanac*. Formulae are given for calculating altitude and azimuth from the *GHA* and *Dec* of a body, and the estimated position of the observer. Formulae are also given for reducing sextant observations to observed altitudes by applying the corrections for dip, refraction, parallax and semi-diameter.

The intercept and azimuth obtained from each observation determine a position line, and the observer should lie on or close to each position line. The method of least squares is used to calculate the fix by finding the position where the sum of the squares of the distances from the position lines is a minimum. The use of least squares has other advantages. For example it is possible to improve the estimated position at the time of fix by repeating the calculation. It is also possible to include more observations in the solution and to reject doubtful ones.

2. *Notation.*

GHA = Greenwich hour angle. The range of GHA is from $0°$ to $360°$ starting at $0°$ on the Greenwich meridian increasing to the west, back to $360°$ on the Greenwich meridian.

SHA = sidereal hour angle. The range is $0°$ to $360°$.

Dec = declination. The sign convention for declination is north is positive, south is negative. The range is from $-90°$ at the south celestial pole to $+90°$ at the north celestial pole.

$Long$ = longitude. The sign convention is east is positive, west is negative. The range is $-180°$ to $+180°$.

Lat = latitude. The sign convention is north is positive, south is negative. The range is from $-90°$ to $+90°$.

LHA = $GHA + Long$ = local hour angle. The LHA increases to the west from $0°$ on the local meridian to $360°$.

H_C = calculated altitude. Above the horizon is positive, below the horizon is negative. The range is from $-90°$ in the nadir to $+90°$ in the zenith.

H_S = sextant altitude.

H = apparent altitude = sextant altitude corrected for instrumental error and dip.

H_O = observed altitude = apparent altitude corrected for refraction and, in appropriate cases, corrected for parallax and semi-diameter.

Z = Z_n = true azimuth. Z is measured from true north through east, south, west and back to north. The range is from $0°$ to $360°$.

I = sextant index error.

D = dip of horizon.

R = atmospheric refraction.

HP = horizontal parallax of the Sun, Moon, Venus or Mars.
PA = parallax in altitude of the Sun, Moon, Venus or Mars.
SD = semi-diameter of the Sun or Moon.
p = intercept = $H_O - H_C$. Towards is positive, away is negative.
T = course or track, measured as for azimuth from the north.
V = speed in knots.

3. *Entering Basic Data.*　When quantities such as *GHA* are entered, which in *The Nautical Almanac* are given in degrees and minutes, convert them to degrees and decimals of a degree by dividing the minutes by 60 and adding to the degrees; for example, if $GHA = 123° 45'\!6$, enter the two numbers 123 and 45·6 into the memory and set $GHA = 123 + 45·6/60 = 123°\!7600$. Although four decimal places of a degree are shown in the examples, it is assumed that full precision is maintained in the calculations.

When using a computer or programmable calculator, write a subroutine to convert degrees and minutes to degrees and decimals. Scientific calculators usually have a special key for this purpose. For quantities like *Dec* which require a minus sign for southern declination, change the sign from plus to minus after the value has been converted to degrees and decimals, e.g. $Dec = S\,0° 12'\!3 = S\,0°\!2050 = -0°\!2050$. Other quantities which require conversion are semi-diameter, horizontal parallax, longitude and latitude.

4. *Interpolation of GHA and Dec*　The *GHA* and *Dec* of the Sun, Moon and planets are interpolated to the time of observation by direct calculation as follows: If the universal time is $a^h\ b^m\ c^s$, form the interpolation factor $x = b/60 + c/3600$. Enter the tabular value GHA_0 for the preceding hour (a) and the tabular value GHA_1 for the following hour ($a+1$) then the interpolated value *GHA* is given by

$$GHA = GHA_0 + x(GHA_1 - GHA_0)$$

If the *GHA* passes through 360° between tabular values add 360° to GHA_1 before interpolation. If the interpolated value exceeds 360°, subtract 360° from *GHA*.

Similarly for declination, enter the tabular value Dec_0 for the preceding hour (a) and the tabular value Dec_1 for the following hour ($a+1$), then the interpolated value *Dec* is given by

$$Dec = Dec_0 + x(Dec_1 - Dec_0)$$

5. *Example.*　(a) Find the *GHA* and *Dec* of the Sun on 2015 November 16 at $20^h\ 47^m\ 13^s$ UT.

The interpolation factor　$x = 47/60 + 13/3600 = 0^h\!7869$

page 223　　$20^h\ GHA_0 = 123°\ 48'\!2 = 123°\!8033$

$21^h\ GHA_1 = 138°\ 48'\!1 = 138°\!8017$

$20^h\!7869\ GHA = 123·8033 + 0·7869(138·8017 - 123·8033) = 135°\!6062$

$20^h\ Dec_0 = S\,18°\ 48'\!2 = -18°\!8033$

$21^h\ Dec_1 = S\,18°\ 48'\!8 = -18°\!8133$

$20^h\!7869\ Dec = -18·8033 + 0·7869(-18·8133 + 18·8033) = -18°\!8112$

GHA Aries is interpolated in the same way as *GHA* of a body. For a star the *SHA* and *Dec* are taken from the tabular page and do not require interpolation, then

$$GHA = GHA\ Aries + SHA$$

where *GHA* Aries is interpolated to the time of observation.

(b) Find the *GHA* and *Dec* of *Vega* on 2015 November 16 at $20^h \ 47^m \ 13^s$ UT.

The interpolation factor $x = 0^h7869$ as in the previous example

$$\text{page 222} \qquad 20^h \ GHA \ \text{Aries}_0 = 355° \ 34'\!3 = 355°\!5717$$

$$21^h \ GHA \ \text{Aries}_1 = 10° \ 36'\!8 = 370°\!6133 \quad (360° \ \text{added})$$

$$20^h7869 \ GHA \ \text{Aries} = 355\!\cdot\!5717 + 0\!\cdot\!7869(370\!\cdot\!6133 - 355\!\cdot\!5717) = 367°\!4086$$

$$SHA = 80° \ 38'\!2 = 80°\!6367$$

$$GHA = GHA \ \text{Aries} + SHA = 88°\!0453 \quad (\text{multiple of } 360° \ \text{removed})$$

$$Dec = N \, 38° \ 48'\!3 = +38°\!8050$$

6. *The calculated altitude and azimuth.* The calculated altitude H_C and true azimuth Z are determined from the *GHA* and *Dec* interpolated to the time of observation and from the *Long* and *Lat* estimated at the time of observation as follows:

Step 1. Calculate the local hour angle

$$LHA = GHA + Long$$

Add or subtract multiples of 360° to set *LHA* in the range 0° to 360°.

Step 2. Calculate S, C and the altitude H_C from

$$S = \sin Dec$$
$$C = \cos Dec \, \cos LHA$$
$$H_C = \sin^{-1}(S \, \sin Lat + C \, \cos Lat)$$

where $\sin^{-1}$ is the inverse function of sine.

Step 3. Calculate X and A from

$$X = (S \, \cos Lat - C \, \sin Lat)/\cos H_C$$
$$\text{If} \ \ X > +1 \quad \text{set} \quad X = +1$$
$$\text{If} \ \ X < -1 \quad \text{set} \quad X = -1$$
$$A = \cos^{-1} X$$

where $\cos^{-1}$ is the inverse function of cosine.

Step 4. Determine the azimuth Z

$$\text{If} \ \ LHA > 180° \quad \text{then} \quad Z = A$$
$$\text{Otherwise} \quad Z = 360° - A$$

7. *Example.* Find the calculated altitude H_C and azimuth Z when

$$GHA = 53° \quad Dec = S \, 15° \quad Lat = N \, 32° \quad Long = W \, 16°$$

For the calculation

$$GHA = 53°\!0000 \quad Dec = -15°\!0000 \quad Lat = +32°\!0000 \quad Long = -16°\!0000$$

Step 1. $\qquad\qquad\qquad LHA = 53\!\cdot\!0000 - 16\!\cdot\!0000 = 37\!\cdot\!0000$

Step 2. $\qquad\qquad\qquad\quad S = -0\!\cdot\!2588$

$$C = +0\!\cdot\!9659 \times 0\!\cdot\!7986 = 0\!\cdot\!7714$$

$$\sin H_C = -0\!\cdot\!2588 \times 0\!\cdot\!5299 + 0\!\cdot\!7714 \times 0\!\cdot\!8480 = 0\!\cdot\!5171$$

$$H_C = 31°\!1346$$

Step 3. $X = (-0{\cdot}2588 \times 0{\cdot}8480 - 0{\cdot}7714 \times 0{\cdot}5299)/0{\cdot}8560 = -0{\cdot}7340$

$A = 137{\cdot}^\circ 2239$

Step 4.   Since $LHA \leq 180^\circ$ then $Z = 360^\circ - A = 222{\cdot}^\circ 7761$

8. *Reduction from sextant altitude to observed altitude.*   The sextant altitude H_S is corrected for both dip and index error to produce the apparent altitude. The observed altitude H_O is calculated by applying a correction for refraction. For the Sun, Moon, Venus and Mars a correction for parallax is also applied to H, and for the Sun and Moon a further correction for semi-diameter is required. The corrections are calculated as follows:

Step 1.   Calculate dip

$$D = 0{\cdot}^\circ 0293 \sqrt{h}$$

where h is the height of eye above the horizon in metres.

Step 2.   Calculate apparent altitude

$$H = H_S + I - D$$

where I is the sextant index error.

Step 3.   Calculate refraction (R) at a standard temperature of 10° Celsius (C) and pressure of 1010 millibars (mb)

$$R_0 = 0{\cdot}^\circ 0167/\tan(H + 7{\cdot}32/(H + 4{\cdot}32))$$

If the temperature T° C and pressure P mb are known calculate the refraction from

$$R = fR_0 \qquad \text{where} \qquad f = 0{\cdot}28P/(T + 273)$$

otherwise set $R = R_0$

Step 4.   Calculate the parallax in altitude (PA) from the horizontal parallax (HP) and the apparent altitude (H) for the Sun, Moon, Venus and Mars as follows:

$$PA = HP \cos H$$

For the Sun $HP = 0{\cdot}^\circ 0024$. This correction is very small and could be ignored.

For the Moon HP is taken for the nearest hour from the main tabular page and converted to degrees.

For Venus and Mars the HP is taken from the critical table at the bottom of page 259 and converted to degrees.

For the navigational stars and the remaining planets, Jupiter and Saturn set $PA = 0$.

If an error of $0{\cdot}2$ is significant the expression for the parallax in altitude for the Moon should include a small correction OB for the oblateness of the Earth as follows:

$$PA = HP \cos H + OB$$
where $OB = -0{\cdot}^\circ 0032 \sin^2 Lat \cos H + 0{\cdot}^\circ 0032 \sin(2Lat) \cos Z \sin H$

At mid-latitudes and for altitudes of the Moon below 60° a simple approximation to OB is

$$OB = -0{\cdot}^\circ 0017 \cos H$$

Step 5.   Calculate the semi-diameter for the Sun and Moon as follows:

Sun: *SD* is taken from the main tabular page and converted to degrees.

Moon: $SD = 0°2724 HP$ where *HP* is taken for the nearest hour from the main tabular page and converted to degrees.

Step 6.   Calculate the observed altitude

$$H_O = H - R + PA \pm SD$$

where the plus sign is used if the lower limb of the Sun or Moon was observed and the minus sign if the upper limb was observed.

9. *Example*.   The following example illustrates how to use a calculator to reduce the sextant altitude (H_S) to observed altitude (H_O); the sextant altitudes given are assumed to be taken on 2015 August 9 with a marine sextant, zero index error, at height 5·4 m, temperature $-3°$ C and pressure 982 mb, the Moon sights are assumed to be taken at 10^h UT.

Body limb	Sun lower	Sun upper	Moon lower	Moon upper	Venus —	*Polaris* —
Sextant altitude: H_S	21·3283	3·3367	33·4600	26·1117	4·5433	49·6083
Step 1. Dip: $D = 0·0293\sqrt{h}$	0·0681	0·0681	0·0681	0·0681	0·0681	0·0681
Step 2. Apparent altitude: $H = H_S + I - D$	21·2602	3·2686	33·3919	26·0436	4·4752	49·5402
Step 3. Refraction: R_0	0·0423	0·2256	0·0251	0·0338	0·1798	0·0142
f	1·0184	1·0184	1·0184	1·0184	1·0184	1·0184
$R = f R_0$	0·0431	0·2298	0·0256	0·0344	0·1831	0·0144
Step 4. Parallax:			(57′·1)	(57′·1)	(0′·5)	
HP	0·0024	0·0024	0·9517	0·9517	0·0083	—
Parallax in altitude: $PA = HP \cos H$	0·0022	0·0024	0·7946	0·8550	0·0083	—
Step 5. Semi-diameter: Sun : $SD = 15·8/60$	0·2633	0·2633	—	—	—	—
Moon : $SD = 0·2724 HP$	—	—	0·2592	0·2592	—	—
Step 6. Observed altitude: $H_O = H - R + PA \pm SD$	21·4827	2·7779	34·4201	26·6050	4·3005	49·5258

Note that for the Moon the correction for the oblateness of the Earth of about $-0°0017 \cos H$, which equals $-0°0014$ for the lower limb and $-0°0015$ for the upper limb, has been ignored in the above calculation.

10. *Position from intercept and azimuth using a chart.*   An estimate is made of the position at the adopted time of fix. The position at the time of observation is then calculated by dead reckoning from the time of fix. For example if the course (track) *T* and the speed *V* (in knots) of the observer are constant then *Long* and *Lat* at the time of observation are calculated from

$$Long = L_F + t\,(V/60)\sin T / \cos B_F$$
$$Lat = B_F + t\,(V/60)\cos T$$

where L_F and B_F are the estimated longitude and latitude at the time of fix and t is the time interval in hours from the time of fix to the time of observation, t is positive if the time of observation is after the time of fix and negative if it was before.

The position line of an observation is plotted on a chart using the intercept

$$p = H_O - H_C$$

and azimuth Z with origin at the calculated position (*Long, Lat*) at the time of observation, where H_C and Z are calculated using the method in section 6, page 279. Starting from this calculated position a line is drawn on the chart along the direction of the azimuth to the body. Convert p to nautical miles by multiplying by 60. The position line is drawn at right angles to the azimuth line, distance p from (*Long, Lat*) towards the body if p is positive and distance p away from the body if p is negative. Provided there are no gross errors the navigator should be somewhere on or near the position line at the time of observation. Two or more position lines are required to determine a fix.

11. *Position from intercept and azimuth by calculation.* The position of the fix may be calculated from two or more sextant observations as follows.

If p_1, Z_1, are the intercept and azimuth of the first observation, p_2, Z_2, of the second observation and so on, form the summations

$$A = \cos^2 Z_1 + \cos^2 Z_2 + \cdots$$
$$B = \cos Z_1 \sin Z_1 + \cos Z_2 \sin Z_2 + \cdots$$
$$C = \sin^2 Z_1 + \sin^2 Z_2 + \cdots$$
$$D = p_1 \cos Z_1 + p_2 \cos Z_2 + \cdots$$
$$E = p_1 \sin Z_1 + p_2 \sin Z_2 + \cdots$$

where the number of terms in each summation is equal to the number of observations.

With $G = AC - B^2$, an improved estimate of the position at the time of fix (L_I, B_I) is given by

$$L_I = L_F + (AE - BD)/(G\cos B_F), \qquad B_I = B_F + (CD - BE)/G$$

Calculate the distance d between the initial estimated position (L_F, B_F) at the time of fix and the improved estimated position (L_I, B_I) in nautical miles from

$$d = 60\sqrt{((L_I - L_F)^2 \cos^2 B_F + (B_I - B_F)^2)}$$

If d exceeds about 20 nautical miles set $L_F = L_I$, $B_F = B_I$ and repeat the calculation until d, the distance between the position at the previous estimate and the improved estimate, is less than about 20 nautical miles.

12. *Example of direct computation.* Using the method described above, calculate the position of a ship on 2015 July 4 at $21^h\,00^m\,00^s$ UT from the marine sextant observations of the three stars *Regulus* (No. 26) at $20^h\,39^m\,23^s$ UT, *Antares* (No. 42) at $20^h\,45^m\,47^s$ UT and *Kochab* (No. 40) at $21^h\,10^m\,34^s$ UT, where the observed altitudes of the three stars corrected for the effects of refraction, dip and instrumental error, are $27°\!.2674$, $25°\!.8742$ and $47°\!.5309$ respectively. The ship was travelling at a constant speed of 20 knots on a course of 325° during the period of observation, and the position of the ship at the time of fix $21^h\,00^m\,00^s$ UT is only known to the nearest whole degree W 15°, N 32°.

Intermediate values for the first iteration are shown in the table. *GHA* Aries was interpolated from the nearest tabular values on page 132. For the first iteration set $L_F = -15°0000$, $B_F = +32°0000$ at the time of fix at 21^h 00^m 00^s UT.

First Iteration

Body	Regulus	Antares	Kochab
No.	26	42	40
time of observation	20^h 39^m 23^s	20^h 45^m 47^s	21^h 10^m 34^s
H_O	27·2674	25·8742	47·5309
interpolation factor	0·6564	0·7631	0·1761
GHA Aries	232·3832	233·9876	240·2007
SHA (page 132)	207·7050	112·4033	137·3283
GHA	80·0882	346·3910	17·5290
Dec (page 132)	+11·8900	−26·4633	+74·0983
t	−0·3436	−0·2369	+0·1761
Long	−14·9225	−14·9466	−15·0397
Lat	+31·9062	+31·9353	+32·0481
Z	267·2721	151·6809	358·9823
H_C	27·2443	25·5684	47·9310
p	+0·0231	+0·3058	−0·4001

$A = 1·7769$ $B = -0·3878$ $C = 1·2231$ $D = -0·6703$ $E = 0·1291$ $G = 2·0229$

$(AE - BD)/(G\cos B_F) = -0·0178,$ $(CD - BE)/G = -0·3805$

An improved estimate of the position at the time of fix is

$L_I = L_F - 0·0178 = -15·0178$ and $B_I = B_F - 0·3805 = +31·6195$

Since the distance between the previous estimated position and the improved estimate $d = 22·9$ nautical miles set $L_F = -15·0178$, and $B_F = +31·6195$ and repeat the calculation. The table shows the intermediate values of the calculation for the second iteration. In each iteration the quantities H_O, *GHA*, *Dec* and t do not change.

Second Iteration

Body	Regulus	Antares	Kochab
No.	26	42	40
Long	−14·9407	−14·9646	−15·0574
Lat	+31·5256	+31·5548	+31·6675
Z	267·4581	151·5778	358·9969
H_C	27·2773	25·8960	47·5508
p	−0·0098	−0·0218	−0·0199

$A = 1·7751$ $B = -0·3918$ $C = 1·2249$ $D = -0·0003$ $E = -0·0002$ $G = 2·0208$

$(AE - BD)/(G\cos B_F) = -0·0003,$ $(CD - BE)/G = -0·0002$

An improved estimate of the position at the time of fix is

$L_I = L_F - 0·0003 = -15·0181$ and $B_I = B_F - 0·0002 = +31·6192$

The distance between the previous estimated position and the improved estimated position $d = 0·02$ nautical miles is so small that a third iteration would produce a negligible improvement to the estimate of the position.

USE OF CONCISE SIGHT REDUCTION TABLES

1. *Introduction.*   The concise sight reduction tables given on pages 286 to 317 are intended for use when neither more extensive tables nor electronic computing aids are available. These "NAO sight reduction tables" provide for the reduction of the local hour angle and declination of a celestial object to azimuth and altitude, referred to an assumed position on the Earth, for use in the intercept method of celestial navigation which is now standard practice.

2. *Form of tables.*   Entries in the reduction table are at a fixed interval of one degree for all latitudes and hour angles. A compact arrangement results from division of the navigational triangle into two right spherical triangles, so that the table has to be entered twice. Assumed latitude and local hour angle are the arguments for the first entry. The reduction table responds with the intermediate arguments A, B, and Z_1, where A is used as one of the arguments for the second entry to the table, B has to be incremented by the declination to produce the quantity F, and Z_1 is a component of the azimuth angle. The reduction table is then reentered with A and F and yields H, P, and Z_2 where H is the altitude, P is the complement of the parallactic angle, and Z_2 is the second component of the azimuth angle. It is usually necessary to adjust the tabular altitude for the fractional parts of the intermediate entering arguments to derive computed altitude, and an auxiliary table is provided for the purpose. Rules governing signs of the quantities which must be added or subtracted are given in the instructions and summarized on each tabular page. Azimuth angle is the sum of two components and is converted to true azimuth by familiar rules, repeated at the bottom of the tabular pages.

Tabular altitude and intermediate quantities are given to the nearest minute of arc, although errors of $2'$ in computed altitude may accrue during adjustment for the minutes parts of entering arguments. Components of azimuth angle are stated to $0°.1$; for derived true azimuth, only whole degrees are warranted. Since objects near the zenith are difficult to observe with a marine sextant, they should be avoided; altitudes greater than about $80°$ are not suited to reduction by this method.

In many circumstances the accuracy provided by these tables is sufficient. However, to maintain the full accuracy ($0'.1$) of the ephemeral data in the almanac throughout their reduction to altitude and azimuth, more extensive tables or a calculator should be used.

3. *Use of Tables.*

Step 1.   Determine the Greenwich hour angle (*GHA*) and Declination (*Dec*) of the body from the almanac. Select an assumed latitude (*Lat*) of integral degrees nearest to the estimated latitude. Choose an assumed longitude nearest to the estimated longitude such that the local hour angle

$$LHA = GHA \begin{matrix} - \text{ west} \\ + \text{ east} \end{matrix} \text{ longitude}$$

has integral degrees.

Step 2.   Enter the reduction table with *Lat* and *LHA* as arguments. Record the quantities A, B and Z_1. Apply the rules for the sign of B and Z_1: B is minus if $90° < LHA < 270°$: Z_1 has the same sign as B. Set $A° =$ nearest whole degree of A and $A' =$ minutes part of A. This step may be repeated for all reductions before leaving the latitude opening of the table.

Step 3.   Record the declination *Dec*. Apply the rules for the sign of *Dec*: *Dec* is minus if the name of *Dec* (*i.e.* N or S) is contrary to latitude. Add B and *Dec* algebraically to produce F. If F is negative, the object is below the horizon (in sight reduction, this can occur when the objects are close to the horizon). Regard F as positive until step 7. Set $F° =$ nearest whole degree of F and $F' =$ minutes part of F.

Step 4.   Enter the reduction table a second time with $A°$ and $F°$ as arguments and record H, P, and Z_2. Set $P° =$ nearest whole degree of P and $Z_2° =$ nearest whole degree of Z_2.

Step 5.   Enter the auxiliary table with F' and $P°$ as arguments to obtain $corr_1$ to H for F'. Apply the rule for the sign of $corr_1$: $corr_1$ is minus if $F < 90°$ and $F' > 29'$ or if $F > 90°$ and $F' < 30'$, otherwise $corr_1$ is plus.

Step 6.   Enter the auxiliary table with A' and $Z_2°$ as arguments to obtain $corr_2$ to H for A'. Apply the rule for the sign of $corr_2$: $corr_2$ is minus if $A' < 30'$, otherwise $corr_2$ is plus.

Step 7.   Calculate the computed altitude H_C as the sum of H, $corr_1$ and $corr_2$. Apply the rule for the sign of H_C: H_C is minus if F is negative.

Step 8.   Apply the rule for the sign of Z_2: Z_2 is minus if $F > 90°$. If F is negative, replace Z_2 by $180° - Z_2$. Set the azimuth angle Z equal to the algebraic sum of Z_1 and Z_2 and ignore the resulting sign. Obtain the true azimuth Z_n from the rules

For N latitude, if	$LHA > 180°$	$Z_n = Z$
if	$LHA < 180°$	$Z_n = 360° - Z$
For S latitude, if	$LHA > 180°$	$Z_n = 180° - Z$
if	$LHA < 180°$	$Z_n = 180° + Z$

Observed altitude H_O is compared with H_C to obtain the altitude difference, which, with Z_n, is used to plot the position line.

4. *Example.*   (a) Required the altitude and azimuth of *Schedar* on 2015 February 4 at UT 06^h 32^m from the estimated position 5° east, 53° north.

1. Assumed latitude $Lat =$ 53° N
    From the almanac $GHA =$ 221° 46'
    Assumed longitude   5° 14' E
    Local hour angle $LHA =$ 227

2. Reduction table, 1st entry
    $(Lat, LHA) = (53, 227)$ $A =$ 26   07 $A° = 26, A' = 7$
                                    $B = -27$ 12 $Z_1 = -49.4$, $90° < LHA < 270°$
3. From the almanac $Dec = +56$ 37   *Lat* and *Dec* same
    Sum $= B + Dec$ $F = +29$ 25 $F° = 29, F' = 25$

4. Reduction table, 2nd entry
    $(A°, F°) = (26, 29)$ $H =$ 25   50 $P° = 61$
                                            $Z_2 = 76.3, Z_2° = 76$

5. Auxiliary table, 1st entry
    $(F', P°) = (25, 61)$ $corr_1 =$ ___ +22 $F < 90°, F' < 29'$
    Sum   26   12
6. Auxiliary table, 2nd entry
    $(A', Z_2°) = (7, 76)$ $corr_2 =$ ___ -2 $A' < 30'$
7. Sum = computed altitude $H_C = +26°$ 10' $F > 0°$

8. Azimuth, first component $Z_1 = -49.4$ same sign as B
                second component $Z_2 = +76.3$ $F < 90°, F > 0°$
    Sum = azimuth angle $Z =$ 26.9

    True azimuth $Z_n =$ 027°   N *Lat*, $LHA > 180°$

continued on page 318

SIGHT REDUCTION TABLE

B: (−) for 90° < LHA < 270°
Dec:(−) for Lat. contrary name

Z₁: same sign as B
Z₂: (−) for F > 90°

Lat./A		0°			1°			2°			3°			4°			5°			Lat./A	
LHA/F	F	A/H	B/P	Z_1/Z_2	A/H	B/P	Z_1/Z_2	A/H	B/P	Z_1/Z_2	A/H	B/P	Z_1/Z_2	A/H	B/P	Z_1/Z_2	A/H	B/P	Z_1/Z_2	LHA	
0	180	0 00	90 00	90·0	0 00	89 00	90·0	0 00	88 00	90·0	0 00	87 00	90·0	0 00	86 00	90·0	0 00	85 00	90·0	180	360
1	179	1 00	90 00	90·0	1 00	89 00	90·0	1 00	88 00	90·0	1 00	87 00	89·9	1 00	86 00	89·9	1 00	85 00	89·9	181	359
2	178	2 00	90 00	90·0	2 00	89 00	90·0	2 00	88 00	89·9	2 00	87 00	89·9	2 00	86 00	89·9	2 00	85 00	89·8	182	358
3	177	3 00	90 00	90·0	3 00	89 00	89·9	3 00	88 00	89·9	3 00	87 00	89·8	3 00	86 00	89·8	2 59	85 00	89·7	183	357
4	176	4 00	90 00	90·0	4 00	89 00	89·9	4 00	88 00	89·9	4 00	87 00	89·8	3 59	85 59	89·7	3 59	84 59	89·7	184	356
5	175	5 00	90 00	90·0	5 00	89 00	89·9	5 00	88 00	89·8	5 00	86 59	89·7	4 59	85 59	89·7	4 59	84 59	89·6	185	355
6	174	6 00	90 00	90·0	6 00	89 00	89·9	6 00	87 59	89·8	6 00	86 59	89·6	5 59	85 59	89·6	5 59	84 58	89·5	186	354
7	173	7 00	90 00	90·0	7 00	89 00	89·9	7 00	87 59	89·7	6 59	86 59	89·6	6 59	85 59	89·5	6 58	84 58	89·4	187	353
8	172	8 00	90 00	90·0	8 00	88 59	89·9	8 00	87 59	89·7	7 59	86 58	89·6	7 59	85 58	89·4	7 58	84 57	89·3	188	352
9	171	9 00	90 00	90·0	9 00	88 59	89·8	9 00	87 59	89·7	8 59	86 58	89·5	8 59	85 58	89·4	8 58	84 56	89·3	189	351
10	170	10 00	90 00	90·0	10 00	88 59	89·8	10 00	87 59	89·6	9 59	86 57	89·5	9 59	85 56	89·3	9 58	84 56	89·2	190	350
11	169	11 00	90 00	90·0	11 00	88 59	89·8	11 00	87 58	89·6	10 59	86 57	89·4	10 58	85 56	89·2	10 57	84 54	89·0	191	349
12	168	12 00	90 00	90·0	12 00	88 59	89·8	12 00	87 57	89·6	11 59	86 56	89·4	11 58	85 55	89·2	11 57	84 53	88·9	192	348
13	167	13 00	90 00	90·0	13 00	88 58	89·8	13 00	87 57	89·5	12 59	86 55	89·3	12 58	85 54	89·1	12 57	84 52	88·8	193	347
14	166	14 00	90 00	90·0	14 00	88 58	89·7	13 59	87 56	89·5	13 59	86 55	89·3	13 58	85 53	89·0	13 57	84 51	88·7	194	346
15	165	15 00	90 00	90·0	15 00	88 58	89·7	14 59	87 56	89·4	14 59	86 54	89·3	14 58	85 52	88·9	14 56	84 49	88·7	195	345
16	164	16 00	90 00	90·0	16 00	88 58	89·7	15 59	87 55	89·4	15 59	86 53	89·3	15 58	85 50	88·9	15 56	84 48	88·6	196	344
17	163	17 00	90 00	90·0	17 00	88 57	89·7	16 59	87 55	89·4	16 59	86 52	89·2	16 57	85 49	88·8	16 56	84 46	88·5	197	343
18	162	18 00	90 00	90·0	18 00	88 57	89·7	17 59	87 54	89·4	17 58	86 51	89·0	17 57	85 48	88·7	17 56	84 45	88·4	198	342
19	161	19 00	90 00	90·0	19 00	88 57	89·7	18 59	87 53	89·3	18 58	86 50	89·0	18 57	85 46	88·6	18 55	84 43	88·3	199	341
20	160	20 00	90 00	90·0	20 00	88 56	89·6	19 59	87 52	89·3	19 58	86 48	89·0	19 57	85 45	88·5	19 55	84 41	88·2	200	340
21	159	21 00	90 00	90·0	21 00	88 56	89·6	20 59	87 51	89·2	20 58	86 47	88·9	20 57	85 43	88·5	20 55	84 39	88·1	201	339
22	158	22 00	90 00	90·0	22 00	88 55	89·6	21 59	87 51	89·2	21 58	86 46	88·8	21 57	85 41	88·4	21 55	84 37	88·0	202	338
23	157	23 00	90 00	90·0	23 00	88 55	89·6	22 59	87 50	89·2	22 58	86 44	88·7	22 56	85 39	88·3	22 54	84 34	87·9	203	337
24	156	24 00	90 00	90·0	24 00	88 54	89·6	23 59	87 49	89·1	23 58	86 43	88·7	23 56	85 37	88·2	23 54	84 32	87·8	204	336
25	155	25 00	90 00	90·0	25 00	88 54	89·5	24 59	87 48	89·1	24 58	86 41	88·6	24 56	85 35	88·1	24 56	84 29	87·7	205	335
26	154	26 00	90 00	90·0	26 00	88 53	89·5	25 59	87 47	89·0	25 58	86 40	88·5	25 56	85 33	88·0	25 54	84 26	87·6	206	334
27	153	27 00	90 00	90·0	27 00	88 53	89·5	26 59	87 45	89·0	26 57	86 38	88·5	26 56	85 31	87·9	26 53	84 24	87·5	207	333
28	152	28 00	90 00	90·0	28 00	88 52	89·5	27 59	87 44	89·0	27 57	86 36	88·4	27 56	85 28	87·9	27 53	84 20	87·3	208	332
29	151	29 00	90 00	90·0	29 00	88 51	89·4	28 59	87 43	88·9	28 57	86 34	88·3	28 55	85 26	87·8	28 53	84 17	87·2	209	331
30	150	30 00	90 00	90·0	30 00	88 51	89·4	29 59	87 41	88·8	29 57	86 32	88·3	29 55	85 23	87·7	29 52	84 14	87·1	210	330
31	149	31 00	90 00	90·0	31 00	88 50	89·4	30 59	87 40	88·8	30 57	86 30	88·2	30 55	85 20	87·6	30 52	84 10	87·0	211	329
32	148	32 00	90 00	90·0	32 00	88 49	89·4	31 59	87 39	88·7	31 57	86 28	88·1	31 55	85 17	87·5	31 52	84 07	86·9	212	328
33	147	33 00	90 00	90·0	33 00	88 48	89·4	32 59	87 37	88·7	32 57	86 25	88·1	32 54	85 14	87·4	32 52	84 03	86·8	213	327
34	146	34 00	90 00	90·0	34 00	88 48	89·3	33 59	87 35	88·7	33 57	86 23	88·0	33 54	85 11	87·3	33 51	83 59	86·6	214	326
35	145	35 00	90 00	90·0	35 00	88 47	89·3	34 59	87 34	88·6	34 57	86 20	87·9	34 54	85 07	87·2	34 51	83 54	86·5	215	325
36	144	36 00	90 00	90·0	36 00	88 46	89·3	35 58	87 32	88·5	35 57	86 18	87·8	35 54	85 04	87·1	35 51	83 50	86·4	216	324
37	143	37 00	90 00	90·0	37 00	88 45	89·2	36 58	87 30	88·5	36 56	86 15	87·7	36 54	85 00	87·0	36 50	83 45	86·2	217	323
38	142	38 00	90 00	90·0	38 00	88 44	89·2	37 58	87 28	88·4	37 56	86 12	87·7	37 53	84 56	86·9	37 49	83 40	86·1	218	322
39	141	39 00	90 00	90·0	39 00	88 43	89·2	38 58	87 26	88·4	38 56	86 09	87·6	38 53	84 52	86·8	38 49	83 35	86·0	219	321
40	140	40 00	90 00	90·0	40 00	88 42	89·2	39 58	87 23	88·3	39 56	86 05	87·5	39 53	84 47	86·7	39 49	83 29	85·8	220	320
41	139	41 00	90 00	90·0	41 00	88 41	89·1	40 58	87 21	88·3	40 56	86 02	87·4	40 53	84 42	86·5	40 49	83 23	85·7	221	319
42	138	42 00	90 00	90·0	42 00	88 39	89·1	41 58	87 19	88·2	41 56	85 58	87·3	41 52	84 37	86·4	41 48	83 17	85·5	222	318
43	137	43 00	90 00	90·0	43 00	88 38	89·1	42 58	87 16	88·1	42 56	85 54	87·2	42 52	84 32	86·3	42 48	83 11	85·4	223	317
44	136	43 59	90 00	90·0	43 59	88 37	89·0	43 58	87 13	88·1	43 55	85 50	87·1	43 52	84 27	86·1	43 47	83 04	85·2	224	316
45	135	44 59	90 00	90·0	44 59	88 35	89·0	44 58	87 10	88·0	44 55	85 46	87·0	44 52	84 21	86·0	44 47	82 57	85·0	225	315

Lat./A	LHA/F	0° A/H	0° B/P	0° Z_1/Z_2	1° A/H	1° B/P	1° Z_1/Z_2	2° A/H	2° B/P	2° Z_1/Z_2	3° A/H	3° B/P	3° Z_1/Z_2	4° A/H	4° B/P	4° Z_1/Z_2	5° A/H	5° B/P	5° Z_1/Z_2	LHA	LHA
45	135	45 00	90 00	90·0	44 59	88 35	89·0	44 58	87 10	88·0	44 55	85 46	87·0	44 52	84 21	86·0	44 47	82 57	85·0	225	315
46	134	46 00	90 00	90·0	45 59	88 34	89·0	45 58	87 07	87·9	45 55	85 41	86·9	45 51	84 15	85·9	45 46	82 49	84·8	226	314
47	133	47 00	90 00	90·0	46 59	88 32	88·9	46 58	87 04	87·9	46 55	85 36	86·9	46 51	84 09	85·8	46 46	82 41	84·7	227	313
48	132	48 00	90 00	90·0	47 59	88 30	88·9	47 58	87 01	87·9	47 55	85 31	86·8	47 51	84 02	85·7	47 46	82 33	84·5	228	312
49	131	49 00	90 00	90·0	48 59	88 29	88·8	48 58	86 57	87·8	48 55	85 26	86·7	48 50	83 55	85·6	48 45	82 24	84·3	229	311
50	130	50 00	90 00	90·0	49 59	88 27	88·8	49 58	86 53	87·7	49 54	85 20	86·6	49 50	83 47	85·2	49 44	82 15	84·1	230	310
51	129	51 00	90 00	90·0	50 59	88 25	88·7	50 57	86 49	87·6	50 54	85 14	86·3	50 50	83 40	85·1	50 44	82 05	83·9	231	309
52	128	52 00	90 00	90·0	51 59	88 23	88·7	51 57	86 45	87·5	51 54	85 08	86·2	51 49	83 31	84·9	51 43	81 55	83·6	232	308
53	127	53 00	90 00	90·0	52 59	88 20	88·7	52 57	86 41	87·4	52 54	85 01	86·0	52 49	83 22	84·7	52 43	81 44	83·4	233	307
54	126	54 00	90 00	90·0	53 59	88 18	88·6	53 57	86 36	87·3	53 54	84 54	85·9	53 49	83 13	84·5	53 42	81 32	83·2	234	306
55	125	55 00	90 00	90·0	54 59	88 15	88·6	54 57	86 31	87·2	54 53	84 47	85·7	54 48	83 03	84·3	54 41	81 20	82·9	235	305
56	124	56 00	90 00	90·0	55 59	88 13	88·5	55 57	86 26	87·1	55 53	84 39	85·6	55 48	82 52	84·1	55 41	81 06	82·6	236	304
57	123	57 00	90 00	90·0	56 59	88 10	88·5	56 57	86 20	87·0	56 53	84 30	85·4	56 47	82 41	83·9	56 40	80 52	82·4	237	303
58	122	58 00	90 00	90·0	57 59	88 07	88·4	57 57	86 14	86·9	57 52	84 21	85·2	57 47	82 29	83·6	57 39	80 38	82·1	238	302
59	121	59 00	90 00	90·0	58 59	88 04	88·4	58 57	86 07	86·8	58 52	84 11	85·0	58 46	82 16	83·4	58 38	80 22	81·7	239	301
60	120	60 00	90 00	90·0	59 59	88 00	88·3	59 57	86 00	86·7	59 52	84 01	84·8	59 46	82 02	83·1	59 37	80 05	81·4	240	300
61	119	61 00	90 00	90·0	60 59	87 56	88·2	60 56	85 53	86·6	60 52	83 50	84·6	60 45	81 48	82·8	60 37	79 46	81·1	241	299
62	118	62 00	90 00	90·0	61 59	87 52	88·1	61 56	85 45	86·5	61 51	83 38	84·4	61 44	81 32	82·5	61 36	79 27	80·7	242	298
63	117	63 00	90 00	90·0	62 59	87 48	88·0	62 56	85 36	86·4	62 51	83 25	84·1	62 44	81 15	82·2	62 35	79 06	80·3	243	297
64	116	64 00	90 00	90·0	63 59	87 43	88·0	63 56	85 27	86·2	63 50	83 11	83·9	63 43	80 56	81·9	63 33	78 43	79·9	244	296
65	115	65 00	90 00	90·0	64 59	87 38	87·9	64 56	85 17	86·1	64 50	82 56	83·6	64 42	80 36	81·5	64 32	78 18	79·4	245	295
66	114	66 00	90 00	90·0	65 59	87 33	87·8	65 55	85 06	85·9	65 49	82 39	83·3	65 41	80 15	81·1	65 31	77 52	78·9	246	294
67	113	67 00	90 00	90·0	66 59	87 27	87·6	66 55	84 54	85·7	66 49	82 22	83·0	66 40	79 51	80·7	66 29	77 23	78·4	247	293
68	112	68 00	90 00	90·0	67 59	87 20	87·5	67 55	84 40	85·5	67 48	82 02	82·6	67 39	79 26	80·2	67 28	76 51	77·8	248	292
69	111	69 00	90 00	90·0	68 59	87 13	87·4	68 55	84 26	85·3	68 48	81 41	82·2	68 38	78 58	79·7	68 26	76 17	77·2	249	291
70	110	70 00	90 00	90·0	69 59	87 05	87·3	69 54	84 10	85·1	69 47	81 17	81·8	69 37	78 27	79·2	69 25	75 39	76·5	250	290
71	109	71 00	90 00	90·0	70 58	86 56	87·1	70 54	83 53	84·8	70 46	80 51	81·4	70 36	77 53	78·5	70 23	74 58	75·8	251	289
72	108	72 00	90 00	90·0	71 58	86 46	86·9	71 54	83 33	84·5	71 46	80 22	80·8	71 35	77 15	77·9	71 20	74 12	75·0	252	288
73	107	73 00	90 00	90·0	72 58	86 35	86·7	72 53	83 11	84·2	72 45	79 50	80·3	72 33	76 33	77·1	72 18	73 20	74·1	253	287
74	106	74 00	90 00	90·0	73 58	86 23	86·5	73 53	82 47	83·9	73 44	79 14	79·7	73 31	75 46	76·3	73 15	72 23	73·1	254	286
75	105	75 00	90 00	90·0	74 58	86 09	86·3	74 52	82 19	83·5	74 43	78 33	78·9	74 29	74 53	75·4	74 12	71 19	72·0	255	285
76	104	76 00	90 00	90·0	75 58	85 52	86·0	75 52	81 47	83·1	75 41	77 47	78·1	75 27	73 53	74·4	75 09	70 07	70·7	256	284
77	103	77 00	90 00	90·0	76 58	85 34	85·7	76 51	81 11	82·6	76 40	76 53	77·2	76 25	72 44	73·2	76 05	68 45	69·3	257	283
78	102	78 00	90 00	90·0	77 58	85 12	85·3	77 50	80 28	82·0	77 38	75 51	76·2	77 22	71 25	71·8	77 01	67 11	67·7	258	282
79	101	79 00	90 00	90·0	78 57	84 46	84·9	78 49	79 38	81·4	78 36	74 39	74·9	78 18	69 52	70·3	77 56	65 22	65·8	259	281
80	100	80 00	90 00	90·0	79 57	84 16	84·3	79 48	78 38	80·7	79 34	73 12	73·5	79 14	68 04	68·4	78 50	63 16	63·7	260	280
81	99	81 00	90 00	90·0	80 57	83 38	83·7	80 47	77 25	79·8	80 31	71 29	71·7	80 09	65 55	66·2	79 43	60 47	61·2	261	279
82	98	82 00	90 00	90·0	81 56	82 51	82·9	81 45	75 55	78·8	81 28	69 22	69·6	81 04	63 19	63·6	80 34	57 51	57·9	262	278
83	97	83 00	90 00	90·0	82 56	81 51	81·9	82 43	74 01	77·6	82 23	66 44	66·9	81 57	60 09	60·4	81 24	54 20	54·6	263	277
84	96	84 00	90 00	90·0	83 55	80 31	80·6	83 41	71 32	76·1	83 18	63 22	63·5	82 48	56 13	56·4	82 12	50 04	50·3	264	276
85	95	85 00	90 00	90·0	84 54	78 40	78·7	84 37	68 10	74·1	84 10	58 59	59·1	83 36	51 56	51·4	82 56	44 53	45·1	265	275
86	94	86 00	90 00	90·0	85 53	75 57	76·0	85 32	63 24	63·5	85 00	53 05	53·2	84 21	45 41	45·1	83 36	38 34	38·7	266	274
87	93	87 00	90 00	90·0	86 50	71 33	71·6	86 24	56 17	56·3	85 45	44 58	45·0	85 00	36 49	36·9	84 10	30 53	31·0	267	273
88	92	88 00	90 00	90·0	87 46	63 26	63·4	87 10	44 59	45·0	86 24	33 40	33·7	85 32	26 31	26·6	84 37	21 45	21·8	268	272
89	91	89 00	90 00	90·0	88 35	45 00	45·0	87 46	26 33	26·6	86 50	18 25	18·4	85 53	14 01	14·0	84 54	11 17	11·3	269	271
90	90	90 00	0 00	0·0	89 00	0 00	0·0	88 00	0 00	0·0	87 00	0 00	0·0	86 00	0 00	0·0	85 00	0 00	0·0	270	270

N. Lat: for LHA > 180° ... $Z_n = Z$
for LHA < 180° ... $Z_n = 360° - Z$

S. Lat.: for LHA > 180° ... $Z_n = 180° - Z$
for LHA < 180° ... $Z_n = 180° + Z$

SIGHT REDUCTION TABLE

B: (−) for 90° < LHA < 270°
Dec:(−) for Lat. contrary name

Z₁: same sign as B
Z₂: (−) for F > 90°

LHA/F	6° A/H	6° B/P	6° Z_1/Z_2	7° A/H	7° B/P	7° Z_1/Z_2	8° A/H	8° B/P	8° Z_1/Z_2	9° A/H	9° B/P	9° Z_1/Z_2	10° A/H	10° B/P	10° Z_1/Z_2	11° A/H	11° B/P	11° Z_1/Z_2	LHA
0 180	0 00	84 00	90·0	0 00	83 00	90·0	0 00	82 00	90·0	0 00	81 00	90·0	0 00	80 00	90·0	0 00	79 00	90·0	180 360
1 179	1 00	84 00	89·9	1 00	83 00	89·9	0 59	82 00	89·9	0 59	81 00	89·8	0 59	80 00	89·8	0 59	79 00	89·8	181 359
2 178	1 59	84 00	89·7	1 59	83 00	89·7	1 59	82 00	89·7	1 59	81 00	89·7	1 58	80 00	89·7	1 58	79 00	89·6	182 358
3 177	2 59	84 00	89·6	2 59	82 59	89·6	2 58	81 59	89·6	2 58	80 59	89·6	2 57	79 59	89·5	2 57	78 59	89·4	183 357
4 176	3 59	83 59	89·5	3 58	82 59	89·5	3 58	81 59	89·4	3 57	80 59	89·4	3 56	79 59	89·3	3 56	78 58	89·2	184 356
5 175	4 58	83 59	89·4	4 58	82 58	89·4	4 57	81 58	89·3	4 56	80 58	89·2	4 55	79 58	89·1	4 54	78 58	89·0	185 355
6 174	5 58	83 58	89·4	5 57	82 58	89·3	5 56	81 57	89·2	5 56	80 57	89·1	5 55	79 57	89·0	5 53	78 56	88·9	186 354
7 173	6 58	83 57	89·3	6 57	82 57	89·1	6 56	81 56	89·0	6 55	80 56	88·9	6 54	79 56	88·8	6 52	78 55	88·7	187 353
8 172	7 57	83 56	89·2	7 56	82 56	89·0	7 55	81 55	89·0	7 54	80 55	88·8	7 53	79 54	88·6	7 51	78 54	88·5	188 352
9 171	8 57	83 56	89·1	8 56	82 55	88·9	8 55	81 54	88·9	8 53	80 53	88·7	8 52	79 53	88·4	8 50	78 52	88·3	189 351
10 170	9 57	83 54	89·0	9 55	82 54	88·8	9 54	81 53	88·7	9 53	80 52	88·6	9 51	79 51	88·2	9 49	78 50	88·1	190 350
11 169	10 56	83 53	88·8	10 55	82 52	88·6	10 53	81 51	88·6	10 52	80 50	88·5	10 50	79 49	88·1	10 48	78 48	87·9	191 349
12 168	11 56	83 52	88·7	11 55	82 51	88·5	11 53	81 49	88·5	11 51	80 48	88·1	11 49	79 47	87·9	11 47	78 46	87·7	192 348
13 167	12 56	83 51	88·6	12 54	82 49	88·4	12 52	81 48	88·4	12 50	80 46	87·9	12 48	79 45	87·7	12 45	78 43	87·5	193 347
14 166	13 55	83 49	88·5	13 54	82 47	88·3	13 52	81 46	88·0	13 49	80 44	87·8	13 47	79 42	87·5	13 44	78 40	87·3	194 346
15 165	14 55	83 47	88·4	14 53	82 45	88·1	14 51	81 43	87·9	14 49	80 41	87·6	14 46	79 39	87·3	14 43	78 37	87·1	195 345
16 164	15 55	83 46	88·3	15 53	82 43	88·0	15 50	81 41	87·7	15 48	80 39	87·4	15 45	79 36	87·1	15 42	78 34	86·9	196 344
17 163	16 54	83 44	88·2	16 52	82 41	87·9	16 50	81 38	87·6	16 47	80 36	87·3	16 44	79 33	87·0	16 41	78 31	86·7	197 343
18 162	17 54	83 42	88·1	17 52	82 39	87·7	17 49	81 36	87·4	17 46	80 33	87·1	17 43	79 30	86·8	17 39	78 27	86·5	198 342
19 161	18 54	83 39	87·9	18 51	82 36	87·6	18 48	81 33	87·3	18 45	80 29	86·9	18 42	79 26	86·6	18 38	78 23	86·2	199 341
20 160	19 53	83 37	87·8	19 51	82 33	87·5	19 48	81 30	87·1	19 45	80 26	86·7	19 41	79 22	86·4	19 37	78 19	86·0	200 340
21 159	20 53	83 35	87·7	20 50	82 30	87·3	20 47	81 26	86·9	20 44	80 22	86·6	20 40	79 18	86·2	20 36	78 14	85·8	201 339
22 158	21 52	83 32	87·6	21 50	82 27	87·2	21 46	81 23	86·8	21 43	80 18	86·4	21 39	79 14	86·0	21 35	78 10	85·6	202 338
23 157	22 52	83 29	87·5	22 49	82 24	87·0	22 46	81 19	86·6	22 42	80 14	86·2	22 38	79 09	85·8	22 33	78 05	85·4	203 337
24 156	23 52	83 26	87·3	23 49	82 21	86·9	23 45	81 15	86·5	23 41	80 10	86·0	23 37	79 05	85·6	23 32	77 59	85·1	204 336
25 155	24 51	83 23	87·2	24 48	82 17	86·7	24 44	81 11	86·3	24 40	80 05	85·8	24 36	78 59	85·4	24 31	77 54	84·9	205 335
26 154	25 51	83 20	87·1	25 48	82 13	86·6	25 44	81 07	86·1	25 39	80 00	85·6	25 35	78 54	85·2	25 29	77 48	84·7	206 334
27 153	26 50	83 16	87·0	26 47	82 09	86·4	26 43	81 02	85·9	26 38	79 55	85·4	26 34	78 48	84·9	26 28	77 42	84·4	207 333
28 152	27 50	83 13	86·8	27 46	82 05	86·3	27 42	80 57	85·8	27 38	79 50	85·2	27 32	78 42	84·7	27 27	77 35	84·2	208 332
29 151	28 50	83 09	86·7	28 46	82 01	86·1	28 41	80 52	85·6	28 37	79 44	85·0	28 31	78 36	84·5	28 25	77 28	84·0	209 331
30 150	29 49	83 05	86·5	29 45	81 56	86·0	29 41	80 47	85·4	29 36	79 38	84·8	29 30	78 29	84·3	29 24	77 21	83·7	210 330
31 149	30 49	83 01	86·4	30 45	81 51	85·8	30 40	80 41	85·2	30 35	79 32	84·6	30 29	78 23	84·0	30 22	77 13	83·5	211 329
32 148	31 48	82 56	86·3	31 44	81 46	85·5	31 39	80 35	85·0	31 34	79 25	84·4	31 27	78 15	83·8	31 21	77 05	83·2	212 328
33 147	32 48	82 51	86·1	32 43	81 40	85·5	32 38	80 29	84·8	32 33	79 18	84·2	32 26	78 08	83·6	32 19	76 57	82·9	213 327
34 146	33 47	82 46	86·0	33 43	81 35	85·3	33 37	80 23	84·6	33 32	79 11	84·0	33 25	78 00	83·3	33 18	76 48	82·7	214 326
35 145	34 47	82 41	85·8	34 42	81 29	85·1	34 37	80 16	84·4	34 30	79 03	83·7	34 24	77 51	83·1	34 16	76 39	82·4	215 325
36 144	35 46	82 36	85·7	35 41	81 22	84·9	35 36	80 09	84·2	35 29	78 55	83·5	35 22	77 42	82·8	35 14	76 29	82·1	216 324
37 143	36 46	82 30	85·5	36 41	81 16	84·8	36 35	80 01	84·0	36 28	78 47	83·3	36 21	77 33	82·5	36 13	76 19	81·8	217 323
38 142	37 45	82 24	85·3	37 40	81 09	84·6	37 34	79 53	83·8	37 27	78 38	83·0	37 19	77 23	82·3	37 11	76 09	81·5	218 322
39 141	38 45	82 18	85·2	38 39	81 01	84·4	38 33	79 45	83·6	38 26	78 29	82·8	38 18	77 13	82·0	38 09	75 57	81·2	219 321
40 140	39 44	82 11	85·0	39 39	80 54	84·2	39 32	79 36	83·3	39 25	78 19	82·5	39 16	77 02	81·7	39 07	75 46	80·9	220 320
41 139	40 44	82 04	84·8	40 38	80 46	84·0	40 31	79 27	83·1	40 23	78 09	82·3	40 15	76 51	81·4	40 05	75 33	80·6	221 319
42 138	41 43	81 57	84·6	41 37	80 37	83·7	41 30	79 17	82·9	41 22	77 58	82·0	41 13	76 39	81·1	41 04	75 21	80·3	222 318
43 137	42 42	81 49	84·4	42 36	80 28	83·5	42 29	79 07	82·6	42 21	77 47	81·7	42 12	76 27	80·8	42 02	75 07	79·9	223 317
44 136	43 42	81 41	84·2	43 35	80 19	83·3	43 28	78 57	82·3	43 19	77 35	81·4	43 10	76 14	80·5	43 00	74 53	79·6	224 316
45 135	44 41	81 33	84·0	44 34	80 09	83·1	44 27	78 46	82·1	44 18	77 22	81·1	44 08	76 00	80·1	43 57	74 38	79·2	225 315

Lat. / A — LHA (right); LHA / F — Lat. / A (left)

Lat. / A	6°			7°			8°			9°			10°			11°			Lat. / A
LHA/F	A/H	B/P	Z_1/Z_2	A/H	B/P	Z_1/Z_2	A/H	B/P	Z_1/Z_2	A/H	B/P	Z_1/Z_2	A/H	B/P	Z_1/Z_2	A/H	B/P	Z_1/Z_2	LHA
45 135	44 41	81 33	84·0	44 34	80 09	83·1	44 27	78 46	82·1	44 18	77 22	81·1	44 08	76 00	80·1	43 57	74 38	79·2	225 315
46 134	45 41	81 24	83·8	45 34	79 59	82·8	45 26	78 34	81·8	45 16	77 09	80·8	45 06	75 45	79·8	44 55	74 22	78·8	226 314
47 133	46 40	81 14	83·6	46 33	79 48	82·6	46 24	78 21	81·5	46 15	76 56	80·5	46 04	75 30	79·5	45 53	74 05	78·4	227 313
48 132	47 39	81 04	83·4	47 31	79 36	82·3	47 23	78 08	81·2	47 13	76 41	80·1	47 01	75 14	79·1	46 51	73 48	78·0	228 312
49 131	48 38	80 54	83·1	48 30	79 24	82·0	48 22	77 55	80·9	48 12	76 26	79·8	47 59	74 57	78·7	47 48	73 30	77·6	229 311
50 130	49 38	80 43	82·9	49 30	79 11	81·7	49 20	77 40	80·6	49 10	76 09	79·4	48 58	74 40	78·3	48 46	73 10	77·2	230 310
51 129	50 37	80 31	82·6	50 29	78 58	81·4	50 19	77 25	80·2	50 08	75 52	79·1	49 56	74 21	77·9	49 43	72 50	76·7	231 309
52 128	51 36	80 19	82·4	51 27	78 43	81·1	51 18	77 08	79·9	51 06	75 34	78·7	50 54	74 01	77·5	50 40	72 29	76·3	232 308
53 127	52 35	80 06	82·1	52 25	78 28	80·8	52 16	76 51	79·5	52 04	75 15	78·3	51 51	73 40	77·0	51 37	72 06	75·8	233 307
54 126	53 34	79 52	81·8	53 25	78 12	80·5	53 14	76 33	79·2	53 02	74 55	77·8	52 49	73 18	76·6	52 35	71 42	75·3	234 306
55 125	54 33	79 37	81·5	54 24	77 55	80·1	54 13	76 14	78·8	54 00	74 34	77·4	53 47	72 55	76·1	53 31	71 17	74·8	235 305
56 124	55 32	79 21	81·2	55 22	77 37	79·8	55 11	75 54	78·3	54 58	74 11	76·9	54 44	72 30	75·6	54 28	70 50	74·2	236 304
57 123	56 31	79 05	80·9	56 21	77 18	79·4	56 09	75 32	77·9	55 56	73 47	76·5	55 41	72 04	75·0	55 25	70 22	73·6	237 303
58 122	57 30	78 47	80·5	57 19	76 57	79·0	57 07	75 09	77·4	56 53	73 22	76·0	56 38	71 36	74·5	56 21	69 51	73·0	238 302
59 121	58 29	78 28	80·1	58 18	76 35	78·5	58 05	74 44	77·0	57 51	72 54	75·4	57 35	71 06	73·9	57 17	69 19	72·4	239 301
60 120	59 28	78 08	79·7	59 16	76 12	78·1	59 03	74 18	76·4	58 48	72 25	74·8	58 32	70 34	73·3	58 13	68 45	71·7	240 300
61 119	60 26	77 46	79·3	60 14	75 47	77·6	60 01	73 50	75·9	59 45	71 54	74·2	59 28	70 01	72·6	59 09	68 09	71·0	241 299
62 118	61 25	77 23	78·9	61 12	75 21	77·1	60 58	73 20	75·3	60 42	71 21	73·6	60 24	69 25	71·9	60 05	67 31	70·3	242 298
63 117	62 23	76 58	78·4	62 10	74 52	76·5	61 56	72 48	74·7	61 39	70 46	72·9	61 20	68 46	71·2	61 00	66 49	69·5	243 297
64 116	63 22	76 31	77·9	63 08	74 21	76·0	62 53	72 13	74·1	62 35	70 08	72·2	62 16	68 05	70·4	61 55	66 05	68·6	244 296
65 115	64 20	76 02	77·4	64 06	73 48	75·4	63 50	71 36	73·4	63 32	69 27	71·5	63 12	67 21	69·6	62 50	65 18	67·7	245 295
66 114	65 18	75 31	76·8	65 03	73 12	74·7	64 47	70 56	72·6	64 28	68 43	70·6	64 07	66 34	68·7	63 44	64 27	66·8	246 294
67 113	66 16	74 57	76·2	66 01	72 33	74·0	65 43	70 13	71·8	65 23	67 56	69·8	65 02	65 43	67·8	64 38	63 33	65·8	247 293
68 112	67 14	74 20	75·5	66 58	71 51	73·2	66 40	69 26	71·0	66 19	67 05	68·8	65 56	64 48	66·7	65 32	62 35	64·7	248 292
69 111	68 12	73 39	74·8	67 55	71 05	72·4	67 36	68 35	70·1	67 14	66 09	67·8	66 50	63 48	65·7	66 25	61 31	63·6	249 291
70 110	69 09	72 55	74·0	68 51	70 15	71·5	68 31	67 40	69·1	68 09	65 09	66·7	67 44	62 44	64·5	67 17	60 23	62·3	250 290
71 109	70 07	72 06	73·1	69 48	69 20	70·5	69 27	66 39	68·0	69 03	64 03	65·6	68 37	61 34	63·2	68 09	59 10	61·0	251 289
72 108	71 03	71 13	72·2	70 44	68 20	69·4	70 21	65 33	66·8	69 57	62 52	64·3	69 29	60 17	61·9	69 00	57 50	59·6	252 288
73 107	72 00	70 14	71·1	71 39	67 13	68·3	71 16	64 20	65·5	70 50	61 33	62·9	70 21	58 54	60·4	69 50	56 23	58·0	253 287
74 106	72 56	69 08	70·0	72 34	65 59	67·0	72 09	62 59	64·1	71 42	60 07	61·4	71 12	57 24	58·8	70 40	54 49	56·4	254 286
75 105	73 52	67 54	68·7	73 28	64 52	65·5	73 03	61 30	62·6	72 34	58 32	59·7	72 02	55 44	57·1	71 28	53 06	54·5	255 285
76 104	74 48	66 31	67·3	74 23	63 05	64·0	73 55	59 51	60·8	73 25	56 47	57·9	72 51	53 55	55·1	72 16	51 13	52·6	256 284
77 103	75 42	64 57	65·6	75 16	61 22	62·2	74 46	58 00	58·9	74 14	54 51	55·9	73 39	51 55	53·1	73 02	49 10	50·4	257 283
78 102	76 36	63 11	63·8	76 08	59 26	60·2	75 37	55 57	56·8	75 02	52 42	53·6	74 26	49 42	50·8	73 47	46 56	48·1	258 282
79 101	77 29	61 09	61·7	76 59	57 14	57·9	76 26	53 38	54·4	75 49	50 18	51·2	75 11	47 16	48·2	74 30	44 27	45·5	259 281
80 100	78 21	58 49	59·3	77 49	54 44	55·3	77 13	51 01	51·7	76 35	47 38	48·4	75 54	44 34	45·4	75 11	41 47	42·7	260 280
81 99	79 12	56 06	56·6	78 37	51 52	52·4	77 59	48 04	48·7	77 18	44 39	45·4	76 35	41 35	42·4	75 49	38 50	39·7	261 279
82 98	80 01	52 56	53·4	79 23	48 35	49·1	78 42	44 43	45·3	77 59	41 18	41·9	77 13	38 17	39·0	76 26	35 36	36·4	262 278
83 97	80 47	49 13	49·6	80 07	44 47	45·2	79 23	40 56	41·4	78 37	37 35	38·1	77 49	34 39	35·3	76 59	32 06	32·8	263 277
84 96	81 31	44 51	45·2	80 47	40 24	40·8	80 01	36 38	37·1	79 12	33 25	33·9	78 21	30 39	31·2	77 29	28 16	28·8	264 276
85 95	82 12	39 40	39·9	81 24	35 22	35·7	80 34	31 48	32·2	79 43	28 49	29·2	78 50	26 18	26·7	77 56	24 09	24·6	265 275
86 94	82 48	33 34	33·8	81 57	29 36	29·8	81 04	26 24	26·7	80 09	23 46	24·1	79 14	21 35	21·9	78 18	19 44	20·1	266 274
87 93	83 18	26 28	26·6	82 23	23 05	23·3	81 28	20 25	20·6	80 31	18 17	18·5	79 34	16 32	16·8	78 36	15 04	15·4	267 273
88 92	83 41	18 22	18·5	82 43	15 52	16·0	81 45	13 57	14·1	80 47	12 26	12·6	79 48	11 12	11·4	78 49	10 11	10·4	268 272
89 91	83 55	9 26	9·5	82 56	8 05	8·2	81 56	7 05	7·1	80 57	6 17	6·4	79 57	5 39	5·7	78 57	5 08	5·2	269 271
90 90	84 00	0 00	0·0	83 00	0 00	0·0	82 00	0 00	0·0	81 00	0 00	0·0	80 00	0 00	0·0	79 00	0 00	0·0	270 270

N. Lat: for LHA > 180° ... $Z_n = Z$
for LHA < 180° ... $Z_n = 360° - Z$

S. Lat: for LHA > 180° ... $Z_n = 180° - Z$
for LHA < 180° ... $Z_n = 180° + Z$

SIGHT REDUCTION TABLE

B: (−) for 90° < LHA < 270°
Dec:(−) for Lat. contrary name

Z_1: same sign as B
Z_2: (−) for F > 90°

Lat./A →	12° A/H	12° B/P	12° Z_1/Z_2	13° A/H	13° B/P	13° Z_1/Z_2	14° A/H	14° B/P	14° Z_1/Z_2	15° A/H	15° B/P	15° Z_1/Z_2	16° A/H	16° B/P	16° Z_1/Z_2	17° A/H	17° B/P	17° Z_1/Z_2	Lat./A LHA
0 / 180	0 00	78 00	90·0	0 00	77 00	90·0	0 00	76 00	90·0	0 00	75 00	90·0	0 00	74 00	90·0	0 00	73 00	90·0	180 / 360
1 / 179	0 59	78 00	89·8	0 58	77 00	89·8	0 58	76 00	89·8	0 58	75 00	89·7	0 58	74 00	89·7	0 57	73 00	89·7	181 / 359
2 / 178	1 57	77 59	89·6	1 57	77 00	89·5	1 56	76 00	89·5	1 56	74 59	89·5	1 55	73 59	89·4	1 55	72 59	89·4	182 / 358
3 / 177	2 56	77 59	89·4	2 55	76 59	89·3	2 55	75 59	89·3	2 54	74 59	89·2	2 53	73 59	89·2	2 52	72 59	89·1	183 / 357
4 / 176	3 55	77 58	89·2	3 54	76 58	89·1	3 53	75 58	89·0	3 52	74 58	89·0	3 51	73 58	88·9	3 49	72 58	88·8	184 / 356
5 / 175	4 53	77 57	89·0	4 52	76 57	88·9	4 51	75 57	88·7	4 50	74 57	88·7	4 48	73 57	88·6	4 47	72 56	88·5	185 / 355
6 / 174	5 52	77 56	88·7	5 51	76 56	88·6	5 49	75 56	88·4	5 48	74 55	88·4	5 46	73 55	88·3	5 44	72 55	88·2	186 / 354
7 / 173	6 51	77 55	88·5	6 49	76 54	88·4	6 47	75 54	88·2	6 46	74 54	88·2	6 44	73 53	88·1	6 42	72 53	87·9	187 / 353
8 / 172	7 49	77 53	88·3	7 48	76 53	88·2	7 46	75 52	87·9	7 44	74 52	87·9	7 41	73 51	87·8	7 39	72 51	87·6	188 / 352
9 / 171	8 48	77 51	88·1	8 46	76 51	88·0	8 44	75 50	87·7	8 41	74 49	87·7	8 39	73 49	87·5	8 36	72 48	87·3	189 / 351
10 / 170	9 47	77 49	87·9	9 44	76 48	87·7	9 42	75 48	87·4	9 39	74 47	87·4	9 37	73 46	87·2	9 34	72 45	87·0	190 / 350
11 / 169	10 45	77 47	87·7	10 43	76 46	87·5	10 40	75 45	87·1	10 37	74 44	87·1	10 34	73 43	86·9	10 31	72 42	86·7	191 / 349
12 / 168	11 44	77 44	87·5	11 41	76 43	87·3	11 38	75 42	86·9	11 35	74 41	86·9	11 32	73 40	86·6	11 28	72 39	86·4	192 / 348
13 / 167	12 43	77 42	87·3	12 40	76 40	87·0	12 36	75 39	86·6	12 33	74 37	86·6	12 29	73 36	86·4	12 25	72 35	86·1	193 / 347
14 / 166	13 41	77 39	87·0	13 38	76 37	86·8	13 35	75 35	86·3	13 31	74 34	86·3	13 27	73 32	86·1	13 23	72 31	85·8	194 / 346
15 / 165	14 40	77 35	86·8	14 36	76 33	86·6	14 33	75 32	86·0	14 29	74 30	86·0	14 24	73 28	85·8	14 20	72 26	85·5	195 / 345
16 / 164	15 38	77 32	86·6	15 35	76 30	86·3	15 31	75 28	85·8	15 26	74 25	85·8	15 22	73 23	85·5	15 17	72 21	85·2	196 / 344
17 / 163	16 37	77 28	86·4	16 33	76 26	86·1	16 29	75 23	85·5	16 24	74 21	85·5	16 19	73 19	85·2	16 14	72 16	84·9	197 / 343
18 / 162	17 36	77 24	86·1	17 31	76 21	85·8	17 27	75 19	85·2	17 22	74 16	85·2	17 17	73 13	84·9	17 11	72 11	84·6	198 / 342
19 / 161	18 34	77 20	85·9	18 30	76 17	85·6	18 25	75 14	84·9	18 20	74 11	84·9	18 14	73 08	84·6	18 08	72 05	84·3	199 / 341
20 / 160	19 33	77 15	85·7	19 28	76 12	85·3	19 23	75 08	84·6	19 17	74 05	84·6	19 12	73 02	84·3	19 05	71 59	83·9	200 / 340
21 / 159	20 31	77 10	85·4	20 26	76 07	85·1	20 21	75 03	84·3	20 15	73 59	84·3	20 09	72 56	84·0	20 03	71 52	83·6	201 / 339
22 / 158	21 30	77 05	85·2	21 24	76 01	84·8	21 19	74 57	84·0	21 13	73 53	84·0	21 06	72 49	83·6	21 00	71 45	83·3	202 / 338
23 / 157	22 28	77 00	85·0	22 23	75 55	84·5	22 17	74 51	83·7	22 10	73 46	83·7	22 04	72 42	83·3	21 56	71 38	82·9	203 / 337
24 / 156	23 27	76 54	84·7	23 21	75 49	84·3	23 15	74 44	83·9	23 08	73 39	83·4	23 01	72 34	83·0	22 53	71 30	82·6	204 / 336
25 / 155	24 25	76 48	84·5	24 19	75 43	84·0	24 13	74 37	83·6	24 06	73 32	83·1	23 58	72 27	82·7	23 50	71 22	82·2	205 / 335
26 / 154	25 23	76 42	84·2	25 17	75 36	83·7	25 10	74 30	83·3	25 03	73 24	82·8	24 55	72 18	82·3	24 47	71 13	81·9	206 / 334
27 / 153	26 22	76 35	84·0	26 15	75 28	83·5	26 08	74 22	83·0	26 01	73 16	82·5	25 52	72 10	82·0	25 44	71 04	81·5	207 / 333
28 / 152	27 20	76 28	83·7	27 13	75 21	83·2	27 06	74 14	82·7	26 58	73 07	82·2	26 50	72 00	81·7	26 41	70 54	81·2	208 / 332
29 / 151	28 18	76 20	83·4	28 11	75 13	82·9	28 04	74 05	82·4	27 55	72 58	81·8	27 47	71 51	81·3	27 37	70 44	80·8	209 / 331
30 / 150	29 17	76 13	83·2	29 09	75 04	82·6	29 01	73 56	82·0	28 53	72 48	81·5	28 44	71 41	81·0	28 34	70 33	80·4	210 / 330
31 / 149	30 15	76 04	82·9	30 07	74 56	82·3	29 59	73 47	81·7	29 50	72 38	81·2	29 41	71 30	80·6	29 30	70 22	80·0	211 / 329
32 / 148	31 13	75 56	82·6	31 05	74 46	82·0	30 57	73 37	81·4	30 47	72 28	80·8	30 38	71 19	80·2	30 27	70 11	79·6	212 / 328
33 / 147	32 11	75 47	82·3	32 03	74 37	81·7	31 54	73 27	81·1	31 44	72 17	80·5	31 34	71 07	79·9	31 23	69 58	79·2	213 / 327
34 / 146	33 10	75 37	82·0	33 01	74 26	81·4	32 52	73 16	80·7	32 42	72 05	80·1	32 31	70 55	79·5	32 20	69 45	78·8	214 / 326
35 / 145	34 08	75 27	81·7	33 59	74 16	81·0	33 49	73 04	80·4	33 39	71 53	79·7	33 28	70 42	79·1	33 16	69 32	78·4	215 / 325
36 / 144	35 06	75 17	81·4	34 56	74 04	80·7	34 46	72 52	80·0	34 36	71 40	79·4	34 24	70 29	78·7	34 12	69 18	78·0	216 / 324
37 / 143	36 04	75 06	81·1	35 54	73 53	80·4	35 44	72 40	79·7	35 33	71 27	79·0	35 21	70 15	78·3	35 08	69 03	77·6	217 / 323
38 / 142	37 02	74 54	80·8	36 52	73 40	80·0	36 41	72 27	79·3	36 29	71 13	78·6	36 17	70 00	77·8	36 04	68 48	77·1	218 / 322
39 / 141	38 00	74 42	80·4	37 49	73 27	79·7	37 38	72 13	78·9	37 26	70 59	78·2	37 13	69 45	77·4	37 00	68 32	76·7	219 / 321
40 / 140	38 57	74 30	80·1	38 47	73 14	79·3	38 35	71 58	78·5	38 23	70 43	77·7	38 10	69 29	77·0	37 56	68 15	76·2	220 / 320
41 / 139	39 55	74 16	79·8	39 44	72 59	78·9	39 32	71 43	78·1	39 19	70 27	77·3	39 06	69 12	76·5	38 51	67 57	75·7	221 / 319
42 / 138	40 53	74 02	79·4	40 41	72 45	78·5	40 29	71 27	77·7	40 16	70 10	76·9	40 02	68 54	76·1	39 47	67 38	75·3	222 / 318
43 / 137	41 51	73 48	79·0	41 39	72 29	78·2	41 26	71 11	77·3	41 12	69 53	76·4	40 58	68 35	75·6	40 42	67 19	74·7	223 / 317
44 / 136	42 48	73 32	78·6	42 36	72 12	77·7	42 23	70 53	76·9	42 09	69 34	76·0	41 54	68 16	75·1	41 38	66 58	74·2	224 / 316
45 / 135	43 46	73 16	78·3	43 33	71 55	77·3	43 19	70 35	76·4	43 05	69 15	75·5	42 49	67 56	74·6	42 33	66 37	73·7	225 / 315

Lat. / A		12°			13°			14°			15°			16°			17°			Lat. / A	
LHA/F		A/H	B/P	Z_1/Z_2	A/H	B/P	Z_1/Z_2	A/H	B/P	Z_1/Z_2	A/H	B/P	Z_1/Z_2	A/H	B/P	Z_1/Z_2	A/H	B/P	Z_1/Z_2	LHA	
45	135	43 46	73 16	78·3	43 33	71 55	77·3	43 19	70 35	76·4	43 05	69 15	75·5	42 49	67 56	74·6	42 33	66 37	73·7	225	315
46	134	44 43	72 59	77·9	44 30	71 37	76·9	44 16	70 15	75·9	44 01	68 54	75·0	43 45	67 34	74·1	43 28	66 15	73·2	226	314
47	133	45 40	72 41	77·4	45 27	71 18	76·4	45 12	69 55	75·5	44 57	68 33	74·5	44 40	67 12	73·5	44 23	65 51	72·6	227	313
48	132	46 38	72 23	77·0	46 24	70 58	76·0	46 09	69 34	75·0	45 53	68 11	74·0	45 35	66 48	73·0	45 17	65 27	72·0	228	312
49	131	47 35	72 03	76·5	47 20	70 37	75·5	47 05	69 11	74·4	46 48	67 47	73·4	46 30	66 23	72·4	46 12	65 01	71·4	229	311
50	130	48 32	71 42	76·1	48 17	70 15	75·0	48 01	68 48	73·9	47 44	67 22	72·9	47 25	65 58	71·8	47 06	64 34	70·8	230	310
51	129	49 29	71 20	75·6	49 13	69 51	74·5	48 57	68 23	73·4	48 39	66 56	72·3	48 20	65 30	71·2	48 00	64 05	70·1	231	309
52	128	50 25	70 57	75·1	50 09	69 27	73·9	49 52	67 57	72·8	49 34	66 29	71·7	49 15	65 02	70·6	48 54	63 35	69·5	232	308
53	127	51 22	70 33	74·6	51 06	69 01	73·4	50 48	67 30	72·2	50 29	66 00	71·0	50 09	64 31	69·9	49 48	63 04	68·8	233	307
54	126	52 19	70 07	74·0	52 02	68 33	72·8	51 43	67 01	71·6	51 24	65 30	70·4	51 03	64 00	69·2	50 41	62 31	68·1	234	306
55	125	53 15	69 40	73·5	52 57	68 04	72·2	52 38	66 31	70·9	52 18	64 58	69·7	51 57	63 26	68·5	51 34	61 56	67·3	235	305
56	124	54 11	69 11	72·9	53 53	67 34	71·6	53 33	65 58	70·3	53 12	64 24	69·0	52 50	62 51	67·8	52 27	61 20	66·6	236	304
57	123	55 07	68 41	72·2	54 48	67 02	70·9	54 28	65 24	69·6	54 06	63 48	68·3	53 43	62 14	67·0	53 19	60 42	65·8	237	303
58	122	56 03	68 09	71·6	55 43	66 28	70·2	55 22	64 48	68·8	55 00	63 11	67·5	54 36	61 35	66·2	54 12	60 01	64·9	238	302
59	121	56 59	67 34	70·9	56 38	65 51	69·5	56 16	64 10	68·1	55 53	62 31	66·7	55 29	60 54	65·4	55 03	59 18	64·1	239	301
60	120	57 54	66 58	70·2	57 33	65 13	68·7	57 10	63 30	67·3	56 46	61 49	65·9	56 21	60 10	64·5	55 54	58 33	63·1	240	300
61	119	58 49	66 20	69·4	58 27	64 32	67·9	58 04	62 47	66·4	57 39	61 04	65·0	57 13	59 24	63·6	56 46	57 46	62·2	241	299
62	118	59 44	65 38	68·6	59 21	63 49	67·1	58 57	62 02	65·5	58 31	60 17	64·0	58 05	58 35	62·6	57 36	56 56	61·2	242	298
63	117	60 38	64 55	67·8	60 15	63 03	66·2	59 50	61 13	64·6	59 23	59 27	63·1	58 55	57 43	61·6	58 26	56 03	60·2	243	297
64	116	61 32	64 08	66·9	61 08	62 14	65·2	60 42	60 22	63·6	60 15	58 34	62·0	59 46	56 49	60·5	59 16	55 06	59·1	244	296
65	115	62 26	63 18	66·0	62 01	61 21	64·2	61 34	59 28	62·6	61 06	57 37	61·0	60 36	55 51	59·4	60 05	54 07	57·9	245	295
66	114	63 20	62 25	65·0	62 53	60 25	63·2	62 26	58 30	61·5	61 56	56 37	59·8	61 25	54 49	58·2	60 53	53 04	56·7	246	294
67	113	64 13	61 27	63·9	63 45	59 25	62·1	63 16	57 27	60·3	62 46	55 34	58·6	62 14	53 44	57·0	61 41	51 57	55·4	247	293
68	112	65 05	60 26	62·8	64 37	58 21	60·9	64 07	56 21	59·1	63 35	54 25	57·4	63 02	52 34	55·7	62 27	50 47	54·1	248	292
69	111	65 57	59 20	61·6	65 27	57 13	59·6	64 56	55 10	57·8	64 23	53 13	56·0	63 49	51 20	54·3	63 14	49 32	52·7	249	291
70	110	66 48	58 08	60·3	66 18	55 59	58·3	65 45	53 55	56·4	65 11	51 55	54·6	64 36	50 01	52·9	63 59	48 12	51·2	250	290
71	109	67 39	56 52	58·9	67 07	54 40	56·8	66 33	52 33	54·9	65 58	50 34	53·1	65 21	48 38	51·3	64 43	46 48	49·7	251	289
72	108	68 29	55 29	57·4	67 55	53 16	55·3	67 20	51 06	53·3	66 44	49 04	51·5	66 06	47 08	49·7	65 26	45 18	48·0	252	288
73	107	69 18	53 59	55·8	68 43	51 42	53·7	68 07	49 33	51·6	67 29	47 30	49·8	66 49	45 33	48·0	66 08	43 43	46·3	253	287
74	106	70 06	52 22	54·1	69 30	50 03	51·9	68 52	47 52	49·8	68 12	45 49	47·9	67 31	43 52	46·1	66 49	42 02	44·4	254	286
75	105	70 53	50 36	52·2	70 15	48 16	50·0	69 36	46 04	47·9	68 55	44 00	46·0	68 12	42 04	44·2	67 29	40 15	42·5	255	285
76	104	71 38	48 42	50·2	70 59	46 20	47·9	70 19	44 08	45·9	69 36	42 05	43·9	68 52	40 09	42·1	68 07	38 21	40·5	256	284
77	103	72 23	46 37	48·0	71 42	44 15	45·7	70 59	42 03	43·7	70 15	40 01	41·7	69 30	38 07	39·9	68 43	36 21	38·3	257	283
78	102	73 06	44 22	45·6	72 23	42 00	43·4	71 38	39 49	41·3	70 53	37 49	39·4	70 06	35 57	37·6	69 18	34 13	36·0	258	282
79	101	73 47	41 55	43·1	73 02	39 34	40·8	72 16	37 26	38·8	71 28	35 27	36·9	70 40	33 38	35·2	69 50	31 58	33·6	259	281
80	100	74 26	39 15	40·3	73 39	36 57	38·1	72 51	34 51	36·1	72 02	32 57	34·3	71 12	31 12	32·6	70 21	29 36	31·1	260	280
81	99	75 02	36 21	37·3	74 14	34 07	35·1	73 24	32 06	33·2	72 34	30 17	31·5	71 42	28 37	29·9	70 50	27 06	28·4	261	279
82	98	75 37	33 13	34·1	74 46	31 05	32·0	73 55	29 10	30·2	73 03	27 27	28·5	72 10	25 53	27·0	71 16	24 29	25·7	262	278
83	97	76 08	29 50	30·6	75 16	27 50	28·6	74 23	26 03	26·9	73 29	24 27	25·4	72 34	23 02	24·0	71 39	21 44	22·8	263	277
84	96	76 36	26 11	26·8	75 42	24 22	25·0	74 48	22 45	23·5	73 52	21 19	22·1	72 56	20 02	20·9	72 00	18 53	19·8	264	276
85	95	77 01	22 11	22·8	76 05	20 41	21·3	75 09	19 16	19·9	74 12	18 01	18·7	73 15	16 54	17·6	72 18	15 55	16·7	265	275
86	94	77 22	18 10	18·6	76 25	16 49	17·3	75 27	15 38	16·1	74 29	14 36	15·1	73 31	13 40	14·2	72 33	12 51	13·5	266	274
87	93	77 38	13 50	14·1	76 40	12 46	13·1	75 41	11 51	12·2	74 43	11 03	11·4	73 44	10 21	10·8	72 45	9 43	10·2	267	273
88	92	77 50	9 19	9·5	76 51	8 36	8·8	75 52	7 58	8·2	74 52	7 25	7·7	73 53	6 56	7·2	72 53	6 31	6·8	268	272
89	91	77 58	4 42	4·8	76 58	4 19	4·4	75 58	4 00	4·1	74 58	3 44	3·9	73 58	3 29	3·6	72 58	3 16	3·4	269	271
90	90	78 00	0 00	0·0	77 00	0 00	0·0	76 00	0 00	0·0	75 00	0 00	0·0	74 00	0 00	0·0	73 00	0 00	0·0	270	270

N. Lat: for LHA > 180°... $Z_n = Z$
for LHA < 180°... $Z_n = 360° - Z$

S. Lat.: for LHA > 180°... $Z_n = 180° - Z$
for LHA < 180°... $Z_n = 180° + Z$

SIGHT REDUCTION TABLE

B: (—) for 90° < LHA < 270°
Dec:(—) for Lat. contrary name

Z₁: same sign as B
Z₂: (—) for F > 90°

Lat./A LHA/F	18° A/H	18° B/P	18° Z₁/Z₂	19° A/H	19° B/P	19° Z₁/Z₂	20° A/H	20° B/P	20° Z₁/Z₂	21° A/H	21° B/P	21° Z₁/Z₂	22° A/H	22° B/P	22° Z₁/Z₂	23° A/H	23° B/P	23° Z₁/Z₂	Lat./A LHA
0	0 00	72 00	90·0	0 00	71 00	90·0	0 00	70 00	90·0	0 00	69 00	90·0	0 00	68 00	90·0	0 00	67 00	90·0	180
1	0 57	72 00	89·7	0 57	71 00	89·7	0 56	70 00	89·7	0 56	69 00	89·6	0 56	68 00	89·6	0 55	67 00	89·6	181
2	1 54	71 59	89·4	1 53	70 59	89·3	1 53	69 59	89·3	1 52	68 59	89·3	1 51	67 59	89·3	1 50	66 59	89·2	182
3	2 51	71 59	89·1	2 50	70 59	89·0	2 49	69 58	89·0	2 48	68 58	88·9	2 47	67 58	88·9	2 46	66 58	88·8	183
4	3 48	71 58	88·8	3 47	70 57	88·7	3 46	69 57	88·6	3 44	68 57	88·6	3 42	67 57	88·5	3 41	66 57	88·4	184
5	4 45	71 56	88·5	4 44	70 56	88·4	4 42	69 56	88·3	4 40	68 56	88·2	4 38	67 55	88·1	4 36	66 55	88·0	185
6	5 42	71 54	88·1	5 40	70 54	88·0	5 38	69 54	87·9	5 36	68 54	87·8	5 34	67 53	87·7	5 31	66 53	87·6	186
7	6 39	71 52	87·8	6 37	70 52	87·7	6 35	69 52	87·6	6 32	68 51	87·5	6 29	67 51	87·4	6 26	66 51	87·3	187
8	7 36	71 50	87·5	7 34	70 50	87·4	7 31	69 49	87·2	7 28	68 49	87·1	7 25	67 48	87·0	7 22	66 48	86·9	188
9	8 33	71 47	87·2	8 30	70 47	87·0	8 27	69 46	86·9	8 24	68 46	86·8	8 20	67 45	86·6	8 17	66 45	86·5	189
10	9 30	71 44	86·9	9 27	70 44	86·7	9 23	69 43	86·5	9 20	68 42	86·4	9 16	67 42	86·2	9 12	66 41	86·1	190
11	10 27	71 41	86·6	10 24	70 40	86·4	10 20	69 39	86·2	10 16	68 39	86·0	10 11	67 38	85·8	10 07	66 37	85·7	191
12	11 24	71 37	86·2	11 20	70 36	86·0	11 16	69 35	85·8	11 12	68 34	85·6	11 07	67 33	85·4	11 02	66 32	85·3	192
13	12 21	71 33	85·9	12 17	70 32	85·7	12 12	69 31	85·5	12 07	68 30	85·3	12 02	67 29	85·1	11 57	66 28	84·8	193
14	13 18	71 29	85·6	13 13	70 28	85·4	13 08	69 26	85·1	13 03	68 25	84·9	12 58	67 24	84·7	12 52	66 22	84·4	194
15	14 15	71 24	85·3	14 10	70 23	85·0	14 05	69 21	84·8	13 59	68 20	84·5	13 53	67 18	84·3	13 47	66 17	84·0	195
16	15 12	71 19	84·9	15 06	70 18	84·7	15 01	69 16	84·4	14 55	68 14	84·1	14 48	67 12	83·9	14 42	66 10	83·6	196
17	16 09	71 14	84·6	16 03	70 12	84·3	15 57	69 10	84·0	15 50	68 08	83·7	15 44	67 06	83·5	15 37	66 04	83·2	197
18	17 05	71 08	84·3	16 59	70 06	84·0	16 53	69 03	83·7	16 46	68 01	83·4	16 39	66 59	83·1	16 32	65 57	82·8	198
19	18 02	71 02	83·9	17 56	69 59	83·6	17 49	68 57	83·3	17 42	67 54	83·0	17 34	66 52	82·7	17 26	65 49	82·3	199
20	18 59	70 56	83·6	18 52	69 53	83·3	18 45	68 50	82·9	18 37	67 47	82·6	18 29	66 44	82·2	18 21	65 41	81·9	200
21	19 56	70 49	83·2	19 48	69 45	82·9	19 41	68 42	82·5	19 33	67 39	82·2	19 24	66 36	81·8	19 16	65 33	81·5	201
22	20 52	70 41	82·9	20 45	69 38	82·5	20 37	68 34	82·1	20 28	67 31	81·8	20 19	66 27	81·4	20 10	65 24	81·0	202
23	21 49	70 33	82·5	21 41	69 29	82·1	21 32	68 26	81·7	21 24	67 22	81·4	21 14	66 18	81·0	21 05	65 15	80·6	203
24	22 45	70 25	82·2	22 37	69 21	81·8	22 28	68 17	81·3	22 19	67 12	80·9	22 09	66 09	80·5	21 59	65 05	80·1	204
25	23 42	70 17	81·8	23 33	69 12	81·4	23 24	68 07	80·9	23 14	67 03	80·5	23 04	65 58	80·1	22 54	64 54	79·7	205
26	24 38	70 07	81·4	24 29	69 02	81·0	24 20	67 57	80·5	24 09	66 52	80·1	23 59	65 48	79·6	23 48	64 43	79·2	206
27	25 35	69 58	81·1	25 25	68 52	80·6	25 15	67 47	80·1	25 05	66 42	79·7	24 54	65 36	79·2	24 42	64 32	78·7	207
28	26 31	69 48	80·7	26 21	68 42	80·2	26 11	67 36	79·7	26 00	66 30	79·2	25 49	65 24	78·7	25 36	64 19	78·3	208
29	27 27	69 37	80·3	27 17	68 31	79·8	27 06	67 24	79·3	26 55	66 18	78·8	26 43	65 12	78·3	26 30	64 07	77·8	209
30	28 24	69 26	79·9	28 13	68 19	79·4	28 01	67 12	78·9	27 50	66 06	78·3	27 37	64 59	77·8	27 24	63 53	77·3	210
31	29 20	69 14	79·5	29 09	68 07	78·9	28 57	67 00	78·4	28 44	65 53	77·8	28 31	64 46	77·3	28 18	63 39	76·8	211
32	30 16	69 02	79·1	30 04	67 54	78·5	29 52	66 46	77·9	29 39	65 39	77·4	29 26	64 32	76·8	29 12	63 25	76·3	212
33	31 12	68 49	78·7	31 00	67 41	78·1	30 47	66 32	77·5	30 34	65 24	76·9	30 20	64 17	76·3	30 05	63 09	75·8	213
34	32 08	68 36	78·2	31 55	67 27	77·6	31 42	66 18	77·0	31 28	65 09	76·4	31 14	64 01	75·8	30 59	62 53	75·2	214
35	33 04	68 22	77·8	32 51	67 12	77·2	32 37	66 03	76·5	32 23	64 54	75·9	32 08	63 45	75·3	31 52	62 36	74·7	215
36	33 59	68 07	77·3	33 46	66 57	76·7	33 32	65 47	76·0	33 17	64 37	75·4	33 01	63 28	74·8	32 45	62 19	74·2	216
37	34 55	67 52	76·9	34 41	66 41	76·2	34 26	65 30	75·5	34 11	64 20	74·9	33 55	63 10	74·2	33 38	62 01	73·6	217
38	35 50	67 36	76·4	35 36	66 24	75·7	35 21	65 13	75·0	35 05	64 02	74·4	34 48	62 51	73·7	34 31	61 41	73·0	218
39	36 46	67 19	76·0	36 31	66 06	75·2	36 15	64 54	74·5	35 59	63 43	73·8	35 42	62 32	73·1	35 24	61 21	72·4	219
40	37 41	67 01	75·5	37 26	65 48	74·7	37 10	64 35	74·0	36 53	63 23	73·3	36 35	62 12	72·6	36 17	61 01	71·8	220
41	38 36	66 42	75·0	38 20	65 29	74·2	38 04	64 15	73·4	37 46	63 02	72·7	37 28	61 50	72·0	37 09	60 39	71·2	221
42	39 31	66 23	74·5	39 15	65 08	73·7	38 58	63 54	72·9	38 40	62 41	72·1	38 21	61 28	71·4	38 01	60 16	70·6	222
43	40 26	66 03	73·9	40 09	64 47	73·1	39 51	63 33	72·3	39 33	62 18	71·5	39 13	61 05	70·7	38 53	59 52	70·0	223
44	41 21	65 42	73·4	41 03	64 25	72·5	40 45	63 10	71·7	40 26	61 55	70·9	40 06	60 41	70·1	39 45	59 27	69·3	224
45	42 16	65 19	72·8	41 57	64 02	72·0	41 38	62 46	71·1	41 19	61 30	70·3	40 58	60 15	69·5	40 37	59 01	68·7	225

Lat./A (°)	LHA/F	18° A/H	18° B/P	18° Z₁/Z₂	19° A/H	19° B/P	19° Z₁/Z₂	20° A/H	20° B/P	20° Z₁/Z₂	21° A/H	21° B/P	21° Z₁/Z₂	22° A/H	22° B/P	22° Z₁/Z₂	23° A/H	23° B/P	23° Z₁/Z₂	Lat./A (°)	LHA
135	45	42 16	65 19	72.8	41 57	64 02	72.0	41 38	62 46	71.1	41 19	61 30	70.3	40 58	60 15	69.5	40 37	59 01	68.7	315	225
134	46	43 10	64 56	72.3	42 51	63 38	71.4	42 32	62 21	70.5	42 11	61 05	69.6	41 50	59 49	68.8	41 28	58 34	68.0	314	226
133	47	44 04	64 32	71.7	43 45	63 13	70.8	43 25	61 55	69.9	43 04	60 38	69.0	42 42	59 21	68.1	42 19	58 06	67.3	313	227
132	48	44 58	64 06	71.1	44 38	62 46	70.1	44 18	61 27	69.2	43 56	60 09	68.3	43 33	58 53	67.4	43 10	57 37	66.5	312	228
131	49	45 52	63 39	70.4	45 32	62 18	69.5	45 10	60 59	68.5	44 48	59 40	67.6	44 24	58 22	66.7	44 00	57 06	65.8	311	229
130	50	46 46	63 11	69.8	46 25	61 49	68.8	46 03	60 29	67.8	45 39	59 09	66.9	45 15	57 51	65.9	44 50	56 34	65.0	310	230
129	51	47 39	62 42	69.1	47 17	61 19	68.1	46 55	59 57	67.1	46 31	58 37	66.1	46 06	57 18	65.2	45 40	56 00	64.2	309	231
128	52	48 33	62 11	68.4	48 10	60 47	67.4	47 46	59 25	66.4	47 22	58 03	65.4	46 56	56 44	64.4	46 30	55 25	63.4	308	232
127	53	49 25	61 38	67.7	49 02	60 13	66.6	48 38	58 50	65.6	48 13	57 28	64.6	47 46	56 07	63.6	47 19	54 48	62.6	307	233
126	54	50 18	61 04	67.0	49 54	59 38	65.9	49 29	58 14	64.8	49 03	56 51	63.7	48 36	55 30	62.7	48 08	54 10	61.7	306	234
125	55	51 10	60 28	66.2	50 46	59 01	65.1	50 20	57 36	64.0	49 53	56 12	62.9	49 25	54 50	61.9	48 56	53 30	60.8	305	235
124	56	52 03	59 50	65.4	51 37	58 23	64.2	51 10	56 56	63.1	50 43	55 32	62.0	50 14	54 09	61.0	49 44	52 48	59.9	304	236
123	57	52 54	59 11	64.6	52 28	57 42	63.4	52 00	56 15	62.2	51 32	54 49	61.1	51 02	53 26	60.0	50 32	52 04	59.0	303	237
122	58	53 46	58 29	63.7	53 18	56 59	62.5	52 50	55 31	61.3	52 21	54 05	60.2	51 50	52 41	59.1	51 19	51 18	58.0	302	238
121	59	54 37	57 45	62.8	54 08	56 14	61.5	53 39	54 44	60.4	53 09	53 18	59.2	52 37	51 54	58.1	52 06	50 30	57.0	301	239
120	60	55 27	56 59	61.8	54 58	55 27	60.6	54 28	53 57	59.4	53 57	52 29	58.2	53 25	51 04	57.0	52 52	49 40	55.9	300	240
119	61	56 17	56 10	60.9	55 47	54 37	59.6	55 16	53 06	58.3	54 44	51 38	57.1	54 11	50 12	55.9	53 37	48 48	54.8	299	241
118	62	57 07	55 19	59.8	56 36	53 45	58.5	56 04	52 13	57.2	55 31	50 44	56.0	54 57	49 17	54.8	54 22	47 53	53.7	298	242
117	63	57 56	54 25	58.8	57 24	52 49	57.4	56 51	51 17	56.1	56 17	49 47	54.9	55 42	48 20	53.7	55 06	46 55	52.5	297	243
116	64	58 44	53 27	57.6	58 12	51 51	56.3	57 37	50 18	55.0	57 03	48 48	53.7	56 27	47 20	52.5	55 50	45 55	51.3	296	244
115	65	59 32	52 27	56.5	58 58	50 50	55.1	58 24	49 16	53.7	57 47	47 45	52.5	57 10	46 17	51.2	56 32	44 52	50.0	295	245
114	66	60 19	51 23	55.2	59 45	49 45	53.8	59 09	48 11	52.5	58 32	46 39	51.2	57 53	45 11	49.9	57 14	43 47	48.7	294	246
113	67	61 06	50 15	53.9	60 30	48 37	52.5	59 53	47 02	51.1	59 15	45 30	49.8	58 35	44 02	48.6	57 55	42 38	47.4	293	247
112	68	61 52	49 04	52.6	61 15	47 25	51.1	60 36	45 50	49.8	59 57	44 18	48.4	59 17	42 50	47.2	58 36	41 26	46.0	292	248
111	69	62 37	47 48	51.2	61 58	46 09	49.7	61 19	44 33	48.3	60 39	43 02	47.0	59 57	41 34	45.7	59 15	40 10	44.5	291	249
110	70	63 21	46 28	49.7	62 41	44 48	48.2	62 01	43 13	46.8	61 19	41 42	45.4	60 36	40 15	44.2	59 53	38 52	43.0	290	250
109	71	64 04	45 03	48.1	63 23	43 24	46.6	62 41	41 49	45.2	61 58	40 18	43.9	61 15	38 52	42.6	60 30	37 29	41.4	289	251
108	72	64 45	43 34	46.4	64 04	41 54	44.9	63 21	40 22	43.5	62 37	38 50	42.2	61 52	37 29	40.9	61 06	36 03	39.7	288	252
107	73	65 26	41 59	44.7	64 43	40 20	43.2	63 59	38 46	41.8	63 14	37 18	40.5	62 27	35 53	39.2	61 41	34 34	38.0	287	253
106	74	66 06	40 19	42.9	65 21	38 41	41.4	64 36	37 08	40.0	63 49	35 41	38.7	63 02	34 18	37.4	62 14	33 00	36.3	286	254
105	75	66 44	38 32	40.9	65 58	36 56	39.5	65 11	35 25	38.1	64 23	33 59	36.8	63 35	32 39	35.6	62 46	31 22	34.4	285	255
104	76	67 20	36 40	38.9	66 33	35 05	37.4	65 45	33 37	36.1	64 56	32 13	34.8	64 07	30 55	33.6	63 16	29 41	32.5	284	256
103	77	67 55	34 42	36.8	67 07	33 09	35.3	66 18	31 44	34.0	65 27	30 22	32.8	64 37	29 09	31.6	63 45	27 55	30.6	283	257
102	78	68 29	32 37	34.5	67 39	31 07	33.1	66 48	29 44	31.9	65 57	28 26	30.7	65 05	27 14	29.6	64 13	26 06	28.5	282	258
101	79	69 00	30 25	32.2	68 09	29 00	30.8	67 17	27 40	29.6	66 25	26 26	28.5	65 32	25 17	27.4	64 38	24 12	26.4	281	259
100	80	69 29	28 07	29.7	68 37	26 46	28.4	67 44	25 30	27.3	66 50	24 20	26.2	65 57	23 15	25.2	65 02	22 15	24.3	280	260
99	81	69 57	25 43	27.1	69 03	24 26	25.9	68 09	23 15	24.8	67 14	22 10	23.8	66 19	21 10	22.9	65 23	20 14	22.1	279	261
98	82	70 21	23 11	24.5	69 27	22 00	23.3	68 31	20 56	22.3	67 36	19 56	21.4	66 40	19 00	20.6	65 43	18 09	19.8	278	262
97	83	70 44	20 34	21.7	69 48	19 29	20.7	68 51	18 31	19.7	67 55	17 37	18.9	66 58	16 47	18.1	66 01	16 01	17.4	277	263
96	84	71 03	17 50	18.8	70 07	16 53	17.9	69 09	16 01	17.1	68 12	15 14	16.3	67 14	14 30	15.7	66 16	13 50	15.1	276	264
95	85	71 20	15 01	15.8	70 23	14 12	15.0	69 25	13 25	14.3	68 26	12 48	13.7	67 28	12 10	13.1	66 29	11 36	12.6	275	265
94	86	71 35	12 07	12.8	70 36	11 27	12.1	69 37	10 51	11.6	68 38	10 18	11.0	67 39	9 48	10.6	66 40	9 20	10.1	274	266
93	87	71 46	9 09	9.6	70 46	8 39	9.1	69 47	8 11	8.7	68 48	7 46	8.3	67 48	7 23	8.0	66 49	7 02	7.6	273	267
92	88	71 54	6 08	6.4	70 54	5 47	6.1	69 54	5 29	5.8	68 55	5 12	5.6	67 55	4 56	5.3	66 55	4 42	5.1	272	268
91	89	71 58	3 04	3.2	70 58	2 54	3.1	69 59	2 45	2.9	68 59	2 36	2.8	67 59	2 28	2.7	66 59	2 21	2.6	271	269
90	90	72 00	0 00	0.0	71 00	0 00	0.0	70 00	0 00	0.0	69 00	0 00	0.0	68 00	0 00	0.0	67 00	0 00	0.0	270	270

N. Lat: for LHA > 180° ... $Z_n = Z$
   for LHA < 180° ... $Z_n = 360° - Z$

S. Lat: for LHA > 180° ... $Z_n = 180° - Z$
   for LHA < 180° ... $Z_n = 180° + Z$

SIGHT REDUCTION TABLE

B: (−) for 90° < LHA < 270°
Dec:(−) for Lat. contrary name

Z1: same sign as B
Z2: (−) for F > 90°

Lat. / A → degrees 24°–29°; Lat. / A and LHA at right.

LHA/F	F	24° A/H	24° B/P	24° Z1/Z2	25° A/H	25° B/P	25° Z1/Z2	26° A/H	26° B/P	26° Z1/Z2	27° A/H	27° B/P	27° Z1/Z2	28° A/H	28° B/P	28° Z1/Z2	29° A/H	29° B/P	29° Z1/Z2	Lat./A	LHA
0	180	0 00	66 00	90·0	0 00	65 00	90·0	0 00	64 00	90·0	0 00	63 00	90·0	0 00	62 00	90·0	0 00	61 00	90·0	180	360
1	179	0 55	66 00	89·6	0 54	65 00	89·6	0 54	64 00	89·6	0 53	63 00	89·5	0 53	62 00	89·5	0 52	61 00	89·5	181	359
2	178	1 50	65 59	89·2	1 49	64 59	89·2	1 48	63 59	89·1	1 47	62 59	89·1	1 46	61 59	89·1	1 45	60 59	89·0	182	358
3	177	2 44	65 58	88·8	2 43	64 58	88·7	2 42	63 58	88·7	2 40	62 58	88·6	2 39	61 58	88·6	2 37	60 58	88·5	183	357
4	176	3 39	65 57	88·4	3 37	64 57	88·3	3 36	63 57	88·2	3 34	62 57	88·2	3 32	61 57	88·1	3 30	60 56	88·1	184	356
5	175	4 34	65 55	88·0	4 32	64 55	87·9	4 30	63 55	87·8	4 27	62 55	87·7	4 25	61 55	87·7	4 22	60 54	87·6	185	355
6	174	5 29	65 53	87·6	5 26	64 53	87·5	5 23	63 53	87·4	5 21	62 52	87·3	5 18	61 52	87·2	5 15	60 52	87·1	186	354
7	173	6 24	65 50	87·1	6 20	64 50	87·0	6 17	63 50	86·9	6 14	62 50	86·8	6 11	61 49	86·7	6 07	60 49	86·6	187	353
8	172	7 18	65 47	86·7	7 15	64 47	86·7	7 11	63 47	86·5	7 07	62 46	86·3	7 04	61 46	86·2	6 59	60 46	86·1	188	352
9	171	8 13	65 44	86·3	8 09	64 44	86·2	8 05	63 43	86·0	8 01	62 43	85·9	7 56	61 42	85·7	7 52	60 42	85·6	189	351
10	170	9 08	65 40	85·9	9 03	64 40	85·7	8 59	63 39	85·6	8 54	62 39	85·4	8 49	61 38	85·3	8 44	60 38	85·1	190	350
11	169	10 02	65 36	85·5	9 57	64 35	85·3	9 52	63 35	85·1	9 47	62 34	85·0	9 42	61 33	84·8	9 36	60 33	84·6	191	349
12	168	10 57	65 32	85·1	10 52	64 31	84·9	10 46	63 30	84·7	10 41	62 29	84·5	10 35	61 28	84·3	10 29	60 28	84·1	192	348
13	167	11 52	65 27	84·6	11 46	64 26	84·4	11 40	63 25	84·2	11 34	62 24	84·0	11 27	61 23	83·8	11 21	60 22	83·6	193	347
14	166	12 46	65 21	84·2	12 40	64 20	84·0	12 34	63 19	83·8	12 27	62 18	83·5	12 20	61 17	83·3	12 13	60 16	83·1	194	346
15	165	13 41	65 15	83·8	13 34	64 14	83·5	13 27	63 13	83·3	13 20	62 11	83·1	13 13	61 10	82·8	13 05	60 09	82·6	195	345
16	164	14 35	65 09	83·3	14 28	64 07	83·1	14 21	63 06	82·8	14 13	62 04	82·6	14 05	61 03	82·3	13 57	60 02	82·1	196	344
17	163	15 29	65 02	82·9	15 22	64 00	82·6	15 14	62 59	82·4	15 06	61 57	82·1	14 58	60 56	81·8	14 49	59 54	81·6	197	343
18	162	16 24	64 55	82·5	16 16	63 53	82·2	16 08	62 51	81·9	15 59	61 49	81·6	15 50	60 47	81·3	15 41	59 46	81·0	198	342
19	161	17 18	64 47	82·0	17 10	63 45	81·7	17 01	62 43	81·4	16 52	61 41	81·1	16 42	60 39	80·8	16 33	59 37	80·5	199	341
20	160	18 12	64 39	81·6	18 03	63 36	81·3	17 54	62 34	80·9	17 45	61 32	80·6	17 34	60 30	80·3	17 24	59 28	80·0	200	340
21	159	19 07	64 30	81·1	18 57	63 28	80·8	18 47	62 25	80·4	18 37	61 23	80·1	18 26	60 20	79·9	18 16	59 18	79·5	201	339
22	158	20 01	64 21	80·7	19 51	63 18	80·3	19 41	62 15	80·0	19 30	61 13	79·6	19 19	60 10	79·3	19 08	59 08	78·9	202	338
23	157	20 55	64 11	80·2	20 44	63 08	79·8	20 34	62 05	79·5	20 22	61 02	79·1	20 11	59 59	78·7	19 59	58 57	78·4	203	337
24	156	21 49	64 01	79·7	21 38	62 58	79·3	21 27	61 54	79·0	21 15	60 51	78·6	21 03	59 48	78·2	20 50	58 45	77·8	204	336
25	155	22 43	63 50	79·3	22 31	62 46	78·8	22 19	61 43	78·4	22 07	60 39	78·0	21 55	59 36	77·7	21 42	58 33	77·3	205	335
26	154	23 36	63 39	78·8	23 25	62 35	78·4	23 12	61 31	77·9	22 59	60 27	77·5	22 46	59 24	77·1	22 33	58 20	76·7	206	334
27	153	24 30	63 27	78·3	24 18	62 22	77·8	24 05	61 18	77·4	23 52	60 14	77·0	23 38	59 10	76·5	23 24	58 07	76·1	207	333
28	152	25 24	63 14	77·8	25 11	62 10	77·3	24 57	61 05	76·9	24 44	60 01	76·4	24 29	58 57	76·0	24 15	57 53	75·5	208	332
29	151	26 17	63 01	77·3	26 04	61 56	76·8	25 50	60 51	76·3	25 36	59 47	75·9	25 21	58 42	75·4	25 05	57 38	75·0	209	331
30	150	27 11	62 48	76·8	26 57	61 42	76·3	26 42	60 37	75·8	26 27	59 32	75·3	26 12	58 27	74·8	25 56	57 23	74·4	210	330
31	149	28 04	62 33	76·3	27 50	61 27	75·8	27 35	60 22	75·2	27 19	59 16	74·7	27 03	58 11	74·2	26 46	57 07	73·8	211	329
32	148	28 57	62 18	75·7	28 42	61 12	75·2	28 27	60 06	74·7	28 10	59 00	74·2	27 54	57 55	73·7	27 37	56 50	73·1	212	328
33	147	29 50	62 02	75·2	29 35	60 56	74·7	29 19	59 49	74·1	29 02	58 43	73·6	28 45	57 38	73·0	28 27	56 32	72·5	213	327
34	146	30 43	61 46	74·7	30 27	60 39	74·1	30 10	59 32	73·5	29 53	58 26	73·0	29 35	57 20	72·4	29 17	56 14	71·9	214	326
35	145	31 36	61 28	74·1	31 19	60 21	73·5	31 02	59 14	72·9	30 44	58 07	72·4	30 26	57 01	71·8	30 07	55 55	71·2	215	325
36	144	32 29	61 10	73·5	32 11	60 02	72·9	31 53	58 55	72·3	31 35	57 48	71·7	31 16	56 41	71·2	30 56	55 35	70·6	216	324
37	143	33 21	60 52	73·0	33 03	59 43	72·3	32 45	58 35	71·7	32 26	57 28	71·1	32 06	56 21	70·5	31 46	55 14	69·9	217	323
38	142	34 13	60 32	72·4	33 55	59 23	71·8	33 36	58 15	71·1	33 16	57 07	70·5	32 56	55 59	69·9	32 35	54 53	69·3	218	322
39	141	35 06	60 11	71·8	34 47	59 02	71·1	34 27	57 53	70·5	34 06	56 45	69·8	33 45	55 37	69·2	33 24	54 30	68·6	219	321
40	140	35 58	59 50	71·2	35 38	58 40	70·5	35 17	57 31	69·8	34 56	56 22	69·1	34 35	55 14	68·5	34 12	54 07	67·9	220	320
41	139	36 49	59 28	70·5	36 29	58 17	69·8	36 08	57 08	69·1	35 46	55 59	68·5	35 24	54 50	67·8	35 01	53 42	67·1	221	319
42	138	37 41	59 04	69·9	37 20	57 54	69·2	36 58	56 43	68·5	36 36	55 34	67·8	36 13	54 25	67·1	35 49	53 17	66·4	222	318
43	137	38 32	58 40	69·2	38 11	57 29	68·5	37 48	56 18	67·8	37 25	55 08	67·1	37 02	53 59	66·4	36 37	52 50	65·7	223	317
44	136	39 23	58 15	68·6	39 01	57 03	67·8	38 38	55 52	67·1	38 14	54 41	66·3	37 50	53 32	65·6	37 25	52 23	64·9	224	316
45	135	40 14	57 48	67·9	39 51	56 36	67·1	39 28	55 24	66·3	39 03	54 13	65·6	38 38	53 04	64·9	38 12	51 54	64·1	225	315

Lat./A LHA/F	°	24° A/H	24° B/P	24° Z_1/Z_2	25° A/H	25° B/P	25° Z_1/Z_2	26° A/H	26° B/P	26° Z_1/Z_2	27° A/H	27° B/P	27° Z_1/Z_2	28° A/H	28° B/P	28° Z_1/Z_2	29° A/H	29° B/P	29° Z_1/Z_2	Lat./A LHA	°
45	135	40 14	57 48	67·9	39 51	56 36	67·1	39 28	55 24	66·3	39 03	54 13	65·6	38 38	53 04	64·9	38 12	51 54	64·1	225	315
46	134	41 05	57 21	67·2	40 41	56 08	66·4	40 17	54 56	65·6	39 52	53 44	64·8	39 26	52 34	64·1	38 59	51 25	63·3	226	314
47	133	41 55	56 52	66·4	41 31	55 38	65·6	41 06	54 26	64·8	40 41	53 13	64·0	40 13	52 04	63·3	39 46	50 54	62·5	227	313
48	132	42 45	56 22	65·7	42 22	55 08	64·9	41 54	53 55	64·0	41 28	52 43	63·2	41 00	51 33	62·5	40 32	50 22	61·7	228	312
49	131	43 35	55 50	64·9	43 09	54 36	64·1	42 43	53 22	63·2	42 15	52 10	62·4	41 47	50 59	61·6	41 18	49 48	60·9	229	311
50	130	44 25	55 17	64·1	43 58	54 02	63·3	43 31	52 49	62·4	43 03	51 36	61·6	42 34	50 24	60·8	42 04	49 14	60·0	230	310
51	129	45 14	54 43	63·3	44 47	53 28	62·4	44 18	52 13	61·6	43 49	51 00	60·7	43 20	49 48	59·9	42 49	48 38	59·1	231	309
52	128	46 03	54 08	62·5	45 35	52 52	61·6	45 06	51 37	60·7	44 36	50 23	59·9	44 05	49 11	59·0	43 34	48 00	58·2	232	308
53	127	46 51	53 30	61·6	46 22	52 14	60·7	45 53	50 59	59·8	45 22	49 45	58·9	44 51	48 32	58·1	44 18	47 21	57·2	233	307
54	126	47 39	52 51	60·8	47 09	51 34	59·8	46 39	50 19	58·9	46 07	49 05	58·0	45 35	47 52	57·1	45 02	46 41	56·3	234	306
55	125	48 27	52 11	59·8	47 56	50 53	58·9	47 25	49 37	58·0	46 53	48 23	57·1	46 20	47 10	56·2	45 46	45 59	55·3	235	305
56	124	49 14	51 28	58·9	48 43	50 10	57·9	48 10	48 54	57·0	47 37	47 40	56·1	47 03	46 27	55·2	46 29	45 15	54·3	236	304
57	123	50 01	50 44	57·9	49 28	49 26	56·9	48 55	48 09	56·0	48 21	46 54	55·0	47 46	45 41	54·1	47 11	44 30	53·3	237	303
58	122	50 47	49 58	56·9	50 14	48 39	55·9	49 40	47 22	54·9	49 05	46 07	54·0	48 29	44 54	53·1	47 53	43 43	52·2	238	302
59	121	51 33	49 09	55·9	50 58	47 51	54·9	50 23	46 34	53·9	49 48	45 18	52·9	49 11	44 05	52·0	48 34	42 54	51·1	239	301
60	120	52 18	48 19	54·8	51 43	47 01	53·8	51 07	45 43	52·8	50 30	44 28	51·8	49 53	43 14	50·9	49 14	42 03	50·0	240	300
61	119	53 02	47 26	53·7	52 26	46 07	52·7	51 49	44 50	51·7	51 12	43 35	50·7	50 33	42 22	49·7	49 54	41 10	48·8	241	299
62	118	53 46	46 31	52·6	53 09	45 12	51·5	52 31	43 54	50·5	51 53	42 39	49·5	51 13	41 27	48·6	50 33	40 16	47·6	242	298
63	117	54 29	45 33	51·4	53 51	44 14	50·3	53 13	42 57	49·3	52 33	41 42	48·3	51 53	40 30	47·3	51 12	39 19	46·4	243	297
64	116	55 12	44 30	50·2	54 33	43 14	49·1	53 53	41 57	48·1	53 13	40 40	47·1	52 31	39 30	46·1	51 49	38 20	45·2	244	296
65	115	55 53	43 30	48·9	55 13	42 11	47·8	54 33	40 55	46·8	53 51	39 40	45·8	53 09	38 30	44·8	52 26	37 19	43·9	245	295
66	114	56 34	42 25	47·6	55 53	41 06	46·5	55 12	39 50	45·4	54 29	38 36	44·4	53 46	37 25	43·5	53 02	36 16	42·6	246	294
67	113	57 14	41 16	46·2	56 32	39 58	45·1	55 50	38 42	44·1	55 06	37 29	43·1	54 22	36 19	42·1	53 37	35 11	41·2	247	293
68	112	57 53	40 05	44·8	57 10	38 47	43·7	56 27	37 32	42·7	55 42	36 19	41·7	54 57	35 10	40·7	54 11	34 03	39·8	248	292
69	111	58 32	38 50	43·3	57 47	37 33	42·2	57 03	36 18	41·2	56 17	35 07	40·2	55 31	33 59	39·3	54 44	32 53	38·4	249	291
70	110	59 09	37 32	41·8	58 24	36 16	40·7	57 38	35 02	39·7	56 51	33 52	38·7	56 04	32 45	37·8	55 16	31 41	36·9	250	290
71	109	59 45	36 11	40·2	58 58	34 55	39·2	58 12	33 43	38·1	57 24	32 35	37·2	56 36	31 29	36·3	55 47	30 26	35·4	251	289
72	108	60 19	34 46	38·6	59 32	33 32	37·6	58 44	32 21	36·5	57 56	31 14	35·6	57 07	30 10	34·7	56 17	29 08	33·8	252	288
73	107	60 53	33 18	36·9	60 05	32 05	35·9	59 16	30 56	34·9	58 26	29 51	34·0	57 37	28 49	33·1	56 46	27 49	32·2	253	287
74	106	61 25	31 46	35·2	60 36	30 35	34·2	59 46	29 28	33·2	58 55	28 25	32·3	58 05	27 24	31·4	57 13	26 26	30·6	254	286
75	105	61 56	30 10	33·4	61 06	29 02	32·4	60 15	27 57	31·4	59 23	26 56	30·5	58 31	25 57	29·7	57 39	25 02	28·9	255	285
76	104	62 26	28 31	31·5	61 34	27 25	30·5	60 42	26 23	29·6	59 50	25 24	28·8	58 57	24 28	28·0	58 04	23 35	27·2	256	284
77	103	62 53	26 48	29·6	62 01	25 45	28·6	61 08	24 46	27·8	60 15	23 49	27·0	59 21	22 56	26·2	58 27	22 05	25·5	257	283
78	102	63 20	25 02	27·6	62 26	24 02	26·7	61 32	23 05	25·9	60 38	22 12	25·1	59 44	21 22	24·4	58 49	20 34	23·7	258	282
79	101	63 44	23 12	25·5	62 50	22 15	24·7	61 55	21 22	23·9	61 00	20 32	23·2	60 05	19 44	22·5	59 09	19 00	21·8	259	281
80	100	64 07	21 18	23·4	63 12	20 25	22·6	62 16	19 36	21·9	61 20	18 49	21·2	60 24	18 05	20·6	59 28	17 24	20·0	260	280
81	99	64 28	19 22	21·3	63 32	18 33	20·5	62 35	17 47	19·9	61 39	17 04	19·2	60 42	16 24	18·6	59 45	15 46	18·1	261	279
82	98	64 47	17 22	19·1	63 50	16 37	18·4	62 53	15 56	17·8	61 56	15 17	17·2	60 58	14 40	16·7	60 01	14 06	16·2	262	278
83	97	65 03	15 18	16·8	64 06	14 39	16·2	63 08	14 02	15·6	62 10	13 27	15·1	61 12	12 55	14·7	60 14	12 24	14·2	263	277
84	96	65 18	13 13	14·5	64 20	12 38	14·0	63 22	12 06	13·5	62 23	11 36	13·0	61 25	11 07	12·6	60 26	10 41	12·2	264	276
85	95	65 31	11 05	12·1	64 32	10 35	11·7	63 33	10 08	11·3	62 35	9 42	10·9	61 36	9 19	10·6	60 37	8 56	10·2	265	275
86	94	65 41	8 54	9·8	64 44	8 30	9·4	63 43	8 08	9·1	62 44	7 48	8·8	61 44	7 29	8·5	60 45	7 10	8·2	266	274
87	93	65 49	6 42	7·3	64 50	6 24	7·1	63 50	6 07	6·8	62 51	5 52	6·6	61 51	5 37	6·4	60 52	5 24	6·2	267	273
88	92	65 55	4 29	4·9	64 56	4 17	4·7	63 56	4 06	4·6	62 56	3 55	4·4	61 56	3 45	4·3	60 56	3 36	4·1	268	272
89	91	65 59	2 15	2·5	64 59	2 09	2·4	63 59	2 03	2·3	62 59	1 58	2·2	61 59	1 53	2·1	60 59	1 48	2·1	269	271
90	90	66 00	0 00	0·0	65 00	0 00	0·0	64 00	0 00	0·0	63 00	0 00	0·0	62 00	0 00	0·0	61 00	0 00	0·0	270	270

N. Lat.: for LHA > 180° ... $Z_n = Z$
for LHA < 180° ... $Z_n = 360° − Z$

S. Lat.: for LHA > 180° ... $Z_n = 180° − Z$
for LHA < 180° ... $Z_n = 180° + Z$

SIGHT REDUCTION TABLE

B: (−) for 90° < LHA < 270°
Dec:(−) for Lat. contrary name

Z₁: same sign as B
Z₂: (−) for F > 90°

Lat./A LHA/F	30° A/H	30° B/P	30° Z₁/Z₂	31° A/H	31° B/P	31° Z₁/Z₂	32° A/H	32° B/P	32° Z₁/Z₂	33° A/H	33° B/P	33° Z₁/Z₂	34° A/H	34° B/P	34° Z₁/Z₂	35° A/H	35° B/P	35° Z₁/Z₂	Lat./A LHA
0	0 00	60 00	90·0	0 00	59 00	90·0	0 00	58 00	90·0	0 00	57 00	90·0	0 00	56 00	90·0	0 00	55 00	90·0	180/360
1	0 52	60 00	89·5	0 51	59 00	89·5	0 51	58 00	89·5	0 50	57 00	89·5	0 50	56 00	89·4	0 49	55 00	89·4	181/359
2	1 44	59 59	89·0	1 43	58 59	89·0	1 42	57 59	88·9	1 41	56 59	88·9	1 39	55 59	88·9	1 38	54 59	88·9	182/358
3	2 36	59 58	88·5	2 34	58 58	88·5	2 33	57 58	88·4	2 31	56 58	88·4	2 29	55 58	88·3	2 27	54 58	88·3	183/357
4	3 28	59 56	88·0	3 26	58 56	88·0	3 23	57 56	87·9	3 21	56 56	87·8	3 19	55 56	87·8	3 17	54 56	87·7	184/356
5	4 20	59 54	87·5	4 17	58 54	87·4	4 14	57 54	87·3	4 12	56 54	87·3	4 09	55 54	87·2	4 06	54 54	87·1	185/355
6	5 12	59 52	87·0	5 08	58 52	86·9	5 05	57 52	86·8	5 02	56 51	86·7	4 58	55 51	86·6	4 55	54 51	86·6	186/354
7	6 04	59 49	86·5	6 00	58 49	86·4	5 56	57 48	86·3	5 52	56 48	86·2	5 48	55 48	86·1	5 44	54 48	86·0	187/353
8	6 55	59 45	86·0	6 51	58 45	85·9	6 47	57 45	85·7	6 42	56 45	85·6	6 38	55 44	85·5	6 33	54 44	85·4	188/352
9	7 47	59 42	85·5	7 42	58 41	85·3	7 37	57 41	85·2	7 32	56 41	85·1	7 27	55 40	84·9	7 22	54 40	84·8	189/351
10	8 39	59 37	85·0	8 34	58 37	84·8	8 28	57 36	84·6	8 22	56 36	84·5	8 17	55 36	84·4	8 11	54 35	84·2	190/350
11	9 31	59 32	84·4	9 25	58 32	84·3	9 19	57 31	84·1	9 13	56 31	84·0	9 06	55 30	83·8	9 00	54 30	83·6	191/349
12	10 22	59 27	83·9	10 16	58 26	83·8	10 09	57 26	83·6	10 03	56 25	83·4	9 56	55 25	83·2	9 48	54 24	83·0	192/348
13	11 14	59 21	83·4	11 07	58 20	83·2	11 00	57 20	83·0	10 52	56 19	82·8	10 45	55 18	82·6	10 37	54 18	82·5	193/347
14	12 06	59 15	82·9	11 58	58 14	82·7	11 50	57 13	82·5	11 42	56 12	82·3	11 34	55 12	82·1	11 26	54 11	81·9	194/346
15	12 57	59 08	82·4	12 49	58 07	82·1	12 41	57 06	81·9	12 32	56 05	81·7	12 23	55 04	81·5	12 14	54 04	81·3	195/345
16	13 49	59 01	81·8	13 40	57 59	81·6	13 31	56 58	81·4	13 22	55 57	81·1	13 13	54 57	80·9	13 03	53 56	80·7	196/344
17	14 40	58 53	81·3	14 31	57 51	81·1	14 21	56 50	80·8	14 12	55 49	80·5	14 02	54 48	80·3	13 51	53 47	80·1	197/343
18	15 31	58 44	80·8	15 22	57 43	80·5	15 12	56 42	80·2	15 01	55 40	79·9	14 51	54 39	79·7	14 40	53 38	79·4	198/342
19	16 23	58 35	80·2	16 12	57 34	79·9	16 02	56 32	79·7	15 51	55 31	79·3	15 40	54 30	79·1	15 28	53 29	78·8	199/341
20	17 14	58 26	79·7	17 03	57 24	79·4	16 52	56 23	79·1	16 40	55 21	78·8	16 28	54 20	78·5	16 16	53 19	78·2	200/340
21	18 05	58 16	79·1	17 53	57 14	78·8	17 42	56 12	78·5	17 29	55 11	78·2	17 17	54 09	77·9	17 04	53 08	77·6	201/339
22	18 56	58 05	78·6	18 44	57 03	78·2	18 31	56 01	77·9	18 19	55 00	77·6	18 05	53 58	77·3	17 52	52 56	77·0	202/338
23	19 47	57 54	78·0	19 34	56 52	77·7	19 21	55 50	77·3	19 08	54 48	76·9	18 54	53 46	76·6	18 40	52 44	76·3	203/337
24	20 37	57 42	77·4	20 24	56 40	77·1	20 11	55 38	76·7	19 57	54 36	76·3	19 42	53 34	76·0	19 28	52 32	75·7	204/336
25	21 28	57 30	76·9	21 14	56 27	76·5	21 00	55 25	76·1	20 46	54 23	75·7	20 31	53 21	75·4	20 15	52 19	75·0	205/335
26	22 19	57 17	76·3	22 04	56 14	75·9	21 49	55 12	75·5	21 34	54 09	75·1	21 19	53 07	74·7	21 03	52 05	74·4	206/334
27	23 09	57 03	75·7	22 54	56 00	75·3	22 39	54 57	74·9	22 23	53 55	74·4	22 07	52 52	74·1	21 50	51 50	73·7	207/333
28	23 59	56 49	75·1	23 44	55 46	74·7	23 28	54 43	74·3	23 11	53 40	73·8	22 54	52 37	73·4	22 37	51 35	73·0	208/332
29	24 50	56 34	74·5	24 33	55 31	74·1	24 17	54 27	73·6	23 59	53 24	73·2	23 42	52 22	72·8	23 24	51 19	72·4	209/331
30	25 40	56 19	73·9	25 23	55 15	73·4	25 05	54 11	73·0	24 48	53 08	72·5	24 29	52 05	72·1	24 11	51 03	71·7	210/330
31	26 29	56 02	73·3	26 12	54 58	72·8	25 54	53 54	72·3	25 35	52 51	71·9	25 17	51 48	71·4	24 57	50 45	71·0	211/329
32	27 19	55 45	72·6	27 01	54 41	72·2	26 42	53 37	71·7	26 23	52 33	71·2	26 04	51 30	70·7	25 44	50 27	70·3	212/328
33	28 09	55 27	72·0	27 50	54 23	71·5	27 31	53 19	71·0	27 11	52 15	70·5	26 50	51 12	70·0	26 30	50 08	69·6	213/327
34	28 58	55 09	71·4	28 38	54 04	70·8	28 19	53 00	70·3	27 58	51 56	69·8	27 37	50 52	69·3	27 16	49 49	68·8	214/326
35	29 47	54 49	70·7	29 27	53 44	70·2	29 06	52 40	69·6	28 45	51 36	69·1	28 24	50 32	68·6	28 01	49 29	68·1	215/325
36	30 36	54 29	70·0	30 15	53 24	69·5	29 54	52 19	68·9	29 32	51 15	68·4	29 10	50 11	67·9	28 47	49 07	67·4	216/324
37	31 25	54 08	69·4	31 03	53 03	68·8	30 41	51 58	68·2	30 19	50 53	67·7	29 56	49 49	67·2	29 32	48 45	66·6	217/323
38	32 13	53 46	68·7	31 51	52 40	68·1	31 28	51 35	67·5	31 05	50 30	66·9	30 41	49 26	66·4	30 17	48 23	65·9	218/322
39	33 02	53 23	68·0	32 39	52 17	67·4	32 15	51 12	66·8	31 51	50 07	66·2	31 27	49 03	65·6	31 02	47 59	65·1	219/321
40	33 50	53 00	67·2	33 26	51 53	66·6	33 02	50 48	66·0	32 37	49 43	65·4	32 12	48 39	64·9	31 46	47 34	64·3	220/320
41	34 37	52 35	66·5	34 13	51 29	65·9	33 48	50 23	65·3	33 23	49 17	64·7	32 57	48 13	64·1	32 30	47 09	63·5	221/319
42	35 25	52 09	65·8	35 00	51 03	65·1	34 34	49 56	64·5	34 08	48 51	63·9	33 42	47 46	63·3	33 14	46 42	62·7	222/318
43	36 12	51 43	65·1	35 46	50 36	64·3	35 20	49 29	63·7	34 53	48 24	63·1	34 26	47 19	62·5	33 58	46 15	61·9	223/317
44	36 59	51 15	64·2	36 33	50 08	63·6	36 06	49 01	62·9	35 38	47 55	62·3	35 10	46 51	61·6	34 41	45 46	61·0	224/316
45	37 46	50 46	63·4	37 19	49 39	62·7	36 51	48 32	62·1	36 22	47 26	61·4	35 53	46 21	60·8	35 24	45 17	60·2	225/315

Lat./A LHA/F	30° A/H	30° B/P	30° Z₁/Z₂	31° A/H	31° B/P	31° Z₁/Z₂	32° A/H	32° B/P	32° Z₁/Z₂	33° A/H	33° B/P	33° Z₁/Z₂	34° A/H	34° B/P	34° Z₁/Z₂	35° A/H	35° B/P	35° Z₁/Z₂	Lat./A LHA
45 135	37 46	50 46	63·4	37 19	49 39	62·7	36 51	48 32	62·1	36 22	47 26	61·4	35 53	46 21	60·8	35 24	45 17	60·2	225 315
46 134	38 32	50 16	62·6	38 04	49 08	61·9	37 36	48 02	61·2	37 06	46 56	60·6	36 37	45 51	59·9	36 06	44 46	59·3	226 314
47 133	39 18	49 45	61·8	38 49	48 37	61·1	38 20	47 30	60·4	37 50	46 24	59·7	37 19	45 19	59·1	36 48	44 15	58·4	227 313
48 132	40 04	49 13	61·0	39 34	48 05	60·2	39 04	46 58	59·5	38 33	45 51	58·8	38 02	44 47	58·2	37 30	43 42	57·5	228 312
49 131	40 49	48 39	60·1	40 19	47 31	59·4	39 48	46 24	58·6	39 16	45 18	57·9	38 44	44 12	57·2	38 11	43 08	56·6	229 311
50 130	41 34	48 04	59·2	41 03	46 56	58·5	40 31	45 49	57·7	39 59	44 42	57·0	39 26	43 37	56·3	38 52	42 33	55·6	230 310
51 129	42 18	47 28	58·3	41 46	46 20	57·5	41 14	45 12	56·8	40 41	44 06	56·1	40 07	43 01	55·4	39 32	41 57	54·7	231 309
52 128	43 02	46 50	57·4	42 29	45 42	56·6	41 56	44 34	55·9	41 22	43 28	55·1	40 47	42 23	54·4	40 12	41 19	53·7	232 308
53 127	43 46	46 11	56·4	43 12	45 03	55·6	42 38	43 55	54·9	42 03	42 49	54·1	41 28	41 44	53·4	40 52	40 41	52·7	233 307
54 126	44 29	45 31	55·5	43 54	44 22	54·7	43 19	43 15	53·9	42 44	42 09	53·1	42 07	41 04	52·4	41 30	40 01	51·7	234 306
55 125	45 11	44 49	54·5	44 36	43 40	53·7	44 00	42 33	52·9	43 24	41 27	52·1	42 46	40 23	51·4	42 09	39 19	50·7	235 305
56 124	45 53	44 05	53·5	45 17	42 57	52·6	44 40	41 50	51·8	44 03	40 44	51·1	43 25	39 40	50·3	42 46	38 37	49·6	236 304
57 123	46 35	43 20	52·4	45 58	42 11	51·6	45 20	41 05	50·8	44 42	39 59	50·0	44 03	38 55	49·3	43 24	37 53	48·5	237 303
58 122	47 16	42 33	51·3	46 38	41 25	50·5	45 59	40 19	49·7	45 20	39 13	48·9	44 40	38 09	48·2	44 00	37 07	47·5	238 302
59 121	47 56	41 44	50·2	47 17	40 36	49·4	46 38	39 30	48·6	45 58	38 25	47·8	45 17	37 22	47·1	44 36	36 20	46·3	239 301
60 120	48 35	40 54	49·1	47 56	39 46	48·3	47 16	38 40	47·5	46 35	37 36	46·7	45 53	36 33	45·9	45 11	35 32	45·2	240 300
61 119	49 14	40 01	47·9	48 34	38 54	47·1	47 53	37 48	46·3	47 11	36 45	45·5	46 29	35 42	44·7	45 46	34 42	44·0	241 299
62 118	49 53	39 07	46·8	49 11	38 00	45·9	48 29	36 55	45·1	47 46	35 52	44·3	47 03	34 50	43·6	46 19	33 50	42·8	242 298
63 117	50 30	38 11	45·5	49 48	37 04	44·7	49 05	36 00	43·9	48 21	34 57	43·1	47 37	33 57	42·3	46 53	32 57	41·6	243 297
64 116	51 07	37 13	44·3	50 23	36 07	43·4	49 40	35 03	42·6	48 55	34 01	41·8	48 10	33 01	41·1	47 25	32 03	40·4	244 296
65 115	51 43	36 12	43·1	50 58	35 07	42·2	50 14	34 04	41·3	49 28	33 03	40·6	48 43	32 04	39·8	47 56	31 07	39·1	245 295
66 114	52 18	35 10	41·7	51 33	34 06	40·8	50 47	33 04	40·0	50 01	32 04	39·3	49 14	31 05	38·5	48 27	30 09	37·8	246 294
67 113	52 52	34 05	40·3	52 06	33 02	39·5	51 19	32 01	38·7	50 32	31 02	37·9	49 44	30 05	37·2	48 56	29 10	36·5	247 293
68 112	53 25	32 59	38·9	52 38	31 56	38·1	51 50	30 57	37·3	51 02	29 59	36·6	50 14	29 03	35·8	49 25	28 09	35·2	248 292
69 111	53 57	31 50	37·5	53 09	30 49	36·7	52 21	29 50	35·9	51 32	28 53	35·2	50 43	27 59	34·5	49 53	27 06	33·8	249 291
70 110	54 28	30 39	36·1	53 39	29 39	35·2	52 50	28 42	34·5	52 00	27 46	33·8	51 10	26 53	33·1	50 20	26 02	32·4	250 290
71 109	54 58	29 25	34·6	54 08	28 27	33·8	53 18	27 31	33·0	52 28	26 38	32·3	51 37	25 46	31·6	50 46	24 56	31·0	251 289
72 108	55 27	28 09	33·0	54 37	27 13	32·2	53 46	26 19	31·5	52 54	25 27	30·8	52 03	24 37	30·2	51 10	23 49	29·5	252 288
73 107	55 55	26 51	31·4	55 03	25 57	30·7	54 12	25 04	30·0	53 19	24 14	29·3	52 27	23 26	28·7	51 34	22 40	28·1	253 287
74 106	56 21	25 31	29·8	55 29	24 39	29·1	54 36	23 48	28·4	53 43	23 00	27·8	52 50	22 14	27·1	51 57	21 29	26·6	254 286
75 105	56 46	24 09	28·2	55 53	23 18	27·5	55 00	22 30	26·8	54 06	21 44	26·2	53 12	21 00	25·6	52 18	20 17	25·0	255 285
76 104	57 10	22 44	26·5	56 16	21 56	25·8	55 22	21 10	25·2	54 28	20 26	24·6	53 33	19 44	24·0	52 38	19 04	23·5	256 284
77 103	57 33	21 17	24·8	56 38	20 31	24·1	55 43	19 48	23·5	54 48	19 06	23·0	53 53	18 27	22·4	52 57	17 49	21·9	257 283
78 102	57 54	19 48	23·0	56 59	19 05	22·4	56 03	18 24	21·9	55 07	17 45	21·3	54 11	17 08	20·8	53 15	16 32	20·3	258 282
79 101	58 13	18 17	21·2	57 17	17 37	20·7	56 22	16 59	20·1	55 25	16 22	19·6	54 28	15 48	19·2	53 31	15 13	18·7	259 281
80 100	58 32	16 44	19·4	57 35	16 07	18·9	56 38	15 32	18·4	55 41	14 58	17·9	54 44	14 26	17·5	53 47	13 56	17·1	260 280
81 99	58 48	15 10	17·6	57 51	14 36	17·1	56 53	14 03	16·6	55 56	13 33	16·2	54 58	13 03	15·8	54 00	12 36	15·4	261 279
82 98	59 03	13 33	15·7	58 05	13 02	15·3	57 07	12 33	14·9	56 09	12 06	14·5	55 11	11 40	14·1	54 13	11 14	13·8	262 278
83 97	59 16	11 55	13·8	58 18	11 28	13·4	57 19	11 02	13·0	56 21	10 38	12·7	55 22	10 16	12·4	54 24	9 52	12·1	263 277
84 96	59 28	10 16	11·9	58 29	9 52	11·5	57 30	9 30	11·2	56 31	9 09	10·9	55 32	8 49	10·6	54 33	8 29	10·4	264 276
85 95	59 37	8 35	9·9	58 38	8 15	9·6	57 39	7 56	9·4	56 40	7 39	9·1	55 41	7 22	8·9	54 41	7 06	8·7	265 275
86 94	59 46	6 53	8·0	58 46	6 37	7·7	57 47	6 22	7·5	56 47	6 08	7·3	55 48	5 54	7·1	54 48	5 41	7·0	266 274
87 93	59 52	5 11	6·0	58 52	4 59	5·8	57 52	4 47	5·6	56 53	4 36	5·5	55 53	4 26	5·4	54 53	4 16	5·2	267 273
88 92	59 56	3 28	4·0	58 57	3 19	3·9	57 57	3 12	3·8	56 57	3 05	3·7	55 57	2 58	3·6	54 57	2 51	3·5	268 272
89 91	59 59	1 44	2·0	58 59	1 40	1·9	57 59	1 36	1·9	56 59	1 32	1·8	55 59	1 29	1·8	54 59	1 26	1·7	269 271
90 90	60 00	0 00	0·0	59 00	0 00	0·0	58 00	0 00	0·0	57 00	0 00	0·0	56 00	0 00	0·0	55 00	0 00	0·0	270 270

N. Lat.: for LHA > 180° ... $Z_n = Z$
for LHA < 180° ... $Z_n = 360° - Z$

S. Lat.: for LHA > 180° ... $Z_n = 180° - Z$
for LHA < 180° ... $Z_n = 180° + Z$

SIGHT REDUCTION TABLE

B: (−) for 90° < LHA < 270°
Dec:(−) for Lat. contrary name

Z₁: same sign as B
Z₂: (−) for F > 90°

LHA/F	Lat./A	36° A/H	36° B/P	36° Z₁/Z₂	37° A/H	37° B/P	37° Z₁/Z₂	38° A/H	38° B/P	38° Z₁/Z₂	39° A/H	39° B/P	39° Z₁/Z₂	40° A/H	40° B/P	40° Z₁/Z₂	41° A/H	41° B/P	41° Z₁/Z₂	Lat./A	LHA
0°	180	0 00	54 00	90·0	0 00	53 00	90·0	0 00	52 00	90·0	0 00	51 00	90·0	0 00	50 00	90·0	0 00	49 00	90·0	360	180
1	179	0 49	54 00	89·4	0 48	53 00	89·4	0 47	52 00	89·4	0 47	51 00	89·4	0 46	50 00	89·4	0 45	49 00	89·3	359	181
2	178	1 37	53 59	88·8	1 36	52 59	88·8	1 35	51 59	88·8	1 33	50 59	88·7	1 32	49 59	88·7	1 31	48 59	88·7	358	182
3	177	2 26	53 58	88·2	2 24	52 58	88·2	2 22	51 58	88·2	2 20	50 58	88·1	2 18	49 58	88·1	2 16	48 58	88·0	357	183
4	176	3 14	53 56	87·6	3 12	52 56	87·6	3 09	51 56	87·5	3 06	50 56	87·5	3 04	49 56	87·4	3 01	48 56	87·4	356	184
5	175	4 03	53 54	87·1	3 59	52 54	87·0	3 56	51 54	86·9	3 53	50 54	86·8	3 50	49 54	86·8	3 46	48 54	86·7	355	185
6	174	4 51	53 51	86·5	4 47	52 51	86·4	4 43	51 51	86·3	4 40	50 51	86·2	4 36	49 51	86·1	4 31	48 51	86·1	354	186
7	173	5 39	53 48	85·9	5 35	52 48	85·8	5 31	51 48	85·7	5 26	50 47	85·6	5 21	49 47	85·5	5 17	48 48	85·4	353	187
8	172	6 28	53 44	85·3	6 23	52 44	85·2	6 18	51 44	85·1	6 13	50 44	84·9	6 07	49 43	84·8	6 02	48 43	84·7	352	188
9	171	7 16	53 40	84·7	7 11	52 39	84·6	7 05	51 39	84·4	6 59	50 39	84·3	6 53	49 39	84·2	6 47	48 39	84·1	351	189
10	170	8 05	53 35	84·1	7 58	52 35	83·9	7 52	51 34	83·8	7 45	50 34	83·7	7 39	49 34	83·5	7 32	48 34	83·4	350	190
11	169	8 53	53 30	83·5	8 46	52 29	83·3	8 39	51 29	83·2	8 32	50 29	83·0	8 24	49 29	82·9	8 17	48 28	82·7	349	191
12	168	9 41	53 24	82·9	9 33	52 23	82·7	9 26	51 23	82·5	9 18	50 23	82·4	9 10	49 23	82·2	9 02	48 22	82·1	348	192
13	167	10 29	53 17	82·3	10 21	52 17	82·1	10 13	51 17	81·9	10 04	50 16	81·7	9 55	49 16	81·6	9 46	48 16	81·4	347	193
14	166	11 17	53 10	81·7	11 08	52 10	81·5	10 59	51 10	81·3	10 50	50 09	81·1	10 41	49 09	80·9	10 31	48 09	80·7	346	194
15	165	12 05	53 03	81·0	11 56	52 02	80·8	11 46	51 02	80·6	11 36	50 02	80·4	11 26	49 03	80·2	11 16	48 01	80·0	345	195
16	164	12 53	52 55	80·4	12 43	51 54	80·2	12 33	50 54	80·0	12 22	49 53	79·8	12 11	48 53	79·6	12 00	47 53	79·3	344	196
17	163	13 41	52 46	79·8	13 30	51 46	79·6	13 19	50 45	79·3	13 08	49 45	79·1	12 57	48 44	78·9	12 45	47 44	78·7	343	197
18	162	14 29	52 37	79·2	14 17	51 37	78·9	14 06	50 36	78·7	13 54	49 35	78·4	13 42	48 35	78·2	13 29	47 34	78·0	342	198
19	161	15 16	52 28	78·6	15 04	51 27	78·3	14 52	50 26	78·0	14 39	49 25	77·8	14 27	48 25	77·5	14 13	47 24	77·3	341	199
20	160	16 04	52 17	77·9	15 51	51 16	77·6	15 38	50 16	77·4	15 25	49 15	77·1	15 12	48 14	76·8	14 58	47 14	76·6	340	200
21	159	16 51	52 07	77·3	16 38	51 05	77·0	16 24	50 05	76·7	16 10	49 04	76·4	15 56	48 03	76·1	15 42	47 03	75·9	339	201
22	158	17 39	51 55	76·6	17 24	50 54	76·3	17 10	49 53	76·0	16 56	48 52	75·7	16 41	47 51	75·4	16 25	46 51	75·2	338	202
23	157	18 26	51 43	76·0	18 11	50 42	75·7	17 56	49 41	75·4	17 41	48 40	75·0	17 25	47 39	74·7	17 09	46 38	74·4	337	203
24	156	19 13	51 30	75·3	18 57	50 29	75·0	18 42	49 28	74·7	18 26	48 27	74·3	18 09	47 26	74·0	17 53	46 25	73·7	336	204
25	155	20 00	51 17	74·7	19 44	50 15	74·3	19 27	49 14	74·0	19 10	48 13	73·6	18 53	47 12	73·3	18 36	46 12	73·0	335	205
26	154	20 46	51 03	74·0	20 30	50 01	73·6	20 13	49 00	73·3	19 55	47 59	72·9	19 37	46 58	72·6	19 19	45 57	72·3	334	206
27	153	21 33	50 48	73·3	21 15	49 47	73·0	20 58	48 45	72·6	20 40	47 44	72·2	20 21	46 43	71·9	20 02	45 43	71·5	333	207
28	152	22 19	50 33	72·6	22 01	49 31	72·3	21 43	48 30	71·9	21 24	47 28	71·5	21 05	46 28	71·1	20 45	45 27	70·8	332	208
29	151	23 06	50 17	72·0	22 47	49 15	71·6	22 28	48 14	71·2	22 08	47 12	70·8	21 48	46 11	70·4	21 28	45 11	70·0	331	209
30	150	23 52	50 00	71·3	23 32	48 58	70·8	23 12	47 57	70·4	22 52	46 55	70·0	22 31	45 54	69·6	22 10	44 54	69·3	330	210
31	149	24 37	49 43	70·5	24 17	48 41	70·1	23 57	47 39	69·7	23 36	46 38	69·3	23 14	45 37	68·9	22 52	44 36	68·5	329	211
32	148	25 23	49 25	69·8	25 02	48 23	69·4	24 41	47 21	69·0	24 19	46 19	68·5	23 57	45 18	68·1	23 34	44 17	67·7	328	212
33	147	26 08	49 06	69·1	25 47	48 04	68·7	25 25	47 02	68·2	25 02	46 00	67·8	24 40	44 59	67·3	24 16	43 58	66·9	327	213
34	146	26 54	48 46	68·4	26 32	47 44	67·9	26 09	46 42	67·4	25 45	45 40	67·0	25 22	44 39	66·6	24 58	43 38	66·1	326	214
35	145	27 39	48 26	67·6	27 16	47 23	67·1	26 52	46 21	66·7	26 28	45 20	66·2	26 04	44 19	65·8	25 39	43 18	65·3	325	215
36	144	28 24	48 04	66·9	28 00	47 02	66·4	27 36	46 00	65·9	27 11	44 58	65·4	26 46	43 57	65·0	26 20	42 57	64·5	324	216
37	143	29 08	47 42	66·1	28 44	46 40	65·6	28 19	45 38	65·1	27 53	44 36	64·6	27 27	43 35	64·2	27 01	42 34	63·7	323	217
38	142	29 52	47 19	65·3	29 27	46 17	64·8	29 01	45 15	64·3	28 35	44 13	63·8	28 08	43 12	63·3	27 41	42 12	62·9	322	218
39	141	30 36	46 56	64·5	30 10	45 53	64·0	29 44	44 51	63·5	29 17	43 49	63·0	28 48	42 48	62·5	28 21	41 48	62·0	321	219
40	140	31 20	46 31	63·7	30 53	45 28	63·2	30 26	44 26	62·7	29 58	43 25	62·2	29 30	42 24	61·7	29 01	41 23	61·2	320	220
41	139	32 03	46 05	62·9	31 36	45 03	62·4	31 08	44 01	61·8	30 39	42 59	61·3	30 10	41 58	60·8	29 41	40 58	60·3	319	221
42	138	32 46	45 39	62·1	32 18	44 36	61·5	31 49	43 34	61·0	31 20	42 33	60·5	30 50	41 32	59·9	30 20	40 32	59·4	318	222
43	137	33 29	45 11	61·3	33 00	44 09	60·7	32 30	43 07	60·1	32 00	42 05	59·7	31 30	41 05	59·1	30 59	40 04	58·5	317	223
44	136	34 12	44 43	60·4	33 42	43 40	59·8	33 11	42 38	59·3	32 40	41 37	58·8	32 09	40 36	58·2	31 37	39 36	57·6	316	224
45	135	34 54	44 13	59·6	34 23	43 11	59·0	33 52	42 09	58·4	33 20	41 08	57·9	32 48	40 07	57·3	32 15	39 08	56·7	315	225

Lat./A LHA/F	36° A/H	36° B/P	36° Z_1/Z_2	37° A/H	37° B/P	37° Z_1/Z_2	38° A/H	38° B/P	38° Z_1/Z_2	39° A/H	39° B/P	39° Z_1/Z_2	40° A/H	40° B/P	40° Z_1/Z_2	41° A/H	41° B/P	41° Z_1/Z_2	Lat./A LHA	A
45	34 54	44 13	59.6	34 23	43 11	59.0	33 52	42 09	58.4	33 20	41 08	57.8	32 48	40 07	57.3	32 15	39 08	56.7	225	315
46	35 35	43 43	58.7	35 04	42 40	58.1	34 32	41 38	57.5	33 59	40 37	56.9	33 26	39 37	56.4	32 53	38 38	55.8	226	314
47	36 17	43 11	57.8	35 44	42 09	57.2	35 12	41 07	56.6	34 38	40 06	56.0	34 04	39 06	55.4	33 30	38 07	54.9	227	313
48	36 57	42 39	56.9	36 24	41 36	56.2	35 51	40 35	55.6	35 17	39 34	55.0	34 42	38 34	54.5	34 07	37 35	53.9	228	312
49	37 38	42 05	56.0	37 04	41 03	55.3	36 30	40 01	54.7	35 55	39 01	54.1	35 19	38 01	53.5	34 43	37 03	53.0	229	311
50	38 18	41 30	55.0	37 43	40 28	54.4	37 08	39 27	53.7	36 32	38 27	53.1	35 56	37 27	52.5	35 19	36 29	52.0	230	310
51	38 57	40 54	54.0	38 22	39 52	53.4	37 46	38 51	52.8	37 09	37 51	52.1	36 32	36 52	51.6	35 55	35 54	51.0	231	309
52	39 36	40 17	53.0	39 00	39 15	52.4	38 23	38 14	51.8	37 46	37 15	51.1	37 08	36 16	50.6	36 30	35 18	50.0	232	308
53	40 15	39 38	52.0	39 38	38 37	51.4	39 00	37 36	50.8	38 22	36 37	50.1	37 43	35 39	49.5	37 04	34 42	49.0	233	307
54	40 53	38 58	51.0	40 15	37 57	50.4	39 36	36 57	49.7	38 57	35 58	49.1	38 18	35 01	48.5	37 38	34 04	47.9	234	306
55	41 30	38 17	50.0	40 52	37 17	49.3	40 12	36 17	48.7	39 32	35 19	48.1	38 52	34 21	47.4	38 11	33 25	46.9	235	305
56	42 07	37 35	48.9	41 28	36 35	48.3	40 47	35 36	47.6	40 07	34 38	47.0	39 26	33 41	46.4	38 44	32 45	45.8	236	304
57	42 44	36 51	47.9	42 03	35 51	47.2	41 22	34 53	46.5	40 41	33 55	45.9	39 59	32 59	45.3	39 16	32 04	44.7	237	303
58	43 19	36 06	46.8	42 38	35 07	46.1	41 56	34 09	45.4	41 14	33 12	44.8	40 31	32 16	44.2	39 48	31 22	43.6	238	302
59	43 54	35 20	45.8	43 12	34 21	45.0	42 29	33 24	44.3	41 46	32 27	43.7	41 03	31 32	43.1	40 19	30 39	42.5	239	301
60	44 29	34 32	44.5	43 46	33 34	43.8	43 02	32 37	43.2	42 18	31 42	42.5	41 34	30 47	41.9	40 49	29 54	41.3	240	300
61	45 02	33 43	43.3	44 18	32 45	42.6	43 34	31 49	42.0	42 49	30 55	41.4	42 04	30 01	40.8	41 18	29 09	40.2	241	299
62	45 35	32 52	42.1	44 51	31 55	41.5	44 05	31 00	40.8	43 20	30 06	40.2	42 34	29 14	39.6	41 47	28 22	39.0	242	298
63	46 07	32 00	40.9	45 22	31 04	40.3	44 36	30 10	39.6	43 49	29 17	39.0	43 03	28 25	38.4	42 15	27 35	37.8	243	297
64	46 39	31 06	39.7	45 52	30 11	39.0	45 06	29 18	38.4	44 18	28 26	37.8	43 31	27 35	37.2	42 43	26 46	36.6	244	296
65	47 09	30 11	38.4	46 22	29 17	37.8	45 35	28 25	37.1	44 47	27 34	36.5	43 58	26 44	36.0	43 09	25 56	35.4	245	295
66	47 39	29 14	37.1	46 51	28 21	36.5	46 03	27 30	35.9	45 14	26 40	35.3	44 25	25 52	34.7	43 35	25 04	34.2	246	294
67	48 08	28 16	35.8	47 19	27 24	35.2	46 30	26 34	34.6	45 41	25 45	34.0	44 50	24 58	33.4	44 00	24 12	32.9	247	293
68	48 36	27 17	34.5	47 46	26 26	33.9	46 56	25 37	33.3	46 06	24 50	32.7	45 15	24 03	32.2	44 24	23 19	31.6	248	292
69	49 03	26 15	33.1	48 13	25 26	32.5	47 22	24 38	31.9	46 31	23 52	31.4	45 39	23 08	30.8	44 48	22 24	30.3	249	291
70	49 29	25 13	31.8	48 38	24 25	31.2	47 46	23 39	30.6	46 55	22 54	30.0	46 03	22 11	29.5	45 10	21 29	29.0	250	290
71	49 54	24 08	30.4	49 02	23 22	29.8	48 10	22 37	29.2	47 17	21 54	28.7	46 25	21 13	28.2	45 32	20 32	27.7	251	289
72	50 18	23 02	28.9	49 25	22 18	28.4	48 33	21 35	27.8	47 39	20 53	27.3	46 46	20 13	26.8	45 52	19 34	26.3	252	288
73	50 41	21 55	27.5	49 48	21 12	26.9	48 54	20 31	26.4	48 00	19 51	25.9	47 06	19 13	25.4	46 12	18 35	25.0	253	287
74	51 03	20 47	26.0	50 09	20 06	25.5	49 15	19 26	25.0	48 20	18 48	24.5	47 25	18 11	24.0	46 30	17 36	23.6	254	286
75	51 24	19 36	24.5	50 29	18 57	24.0	49 34	18 20	23.5	48 39	17 43	23.1	47 44	17 09	22.6	46 48	16 35	22.2	255	285
76	51 43	18 25	23.0	50 48	17 48	22.5	49 52	17 12	22.0	48 57	16 38	21.6	48 01	16 05	21.2	47 05	15 33	20.8	256	284
77	52 02	17 12	21.4	51 06	16 37	21.0	50 09	16 04	20.6	49 13	15 31	20.1	48 17	15 00	19.8	47 20	14 31	19.4	257	283
78	52 19	15 58	19.9	51 22	15 25	19.5	50 25	14 54	19.0	49 29	14 24	18.7	48 32	13 55	18.3	47 35	13 27	18.0	258	282
79	52 35	14 43	18.3	51 37	14 13	17.9	50 40	13 43	17.5	49 43	13 16	17.2	48 46	12 49	16.8	47 48	12 23	16.5	259	281
80	52 49	13 27	16.7	51 52	12 59	16.3	50 54	12 32	16.0	49 56	12 06	15.7	48 58	11 42	15.3	48 01	11 18	15.0	260	280
81	53 02	12 09	15.1	52 04	11 44	14.7	51 06	11 19	14.4	50 08	10 56	14.1	49 10	10 34	13.8	48 12	10 12	13.6	261	279
82	53 14	10 51	13.4	52 16	10 28	13.1	51 18	10 06	12.9	50 19	9 45	12.6	49 20	9 25	12.3	48 22	9 06	12.1	262	278
83	53 25	9 31	11.8	52 26	9 11	11.5	51 27	8 52	11.3	50 29	8 34	11.0	49 30	8 16	10.8	48 31	7 59	10.6	263	277
84	53 34	8 11	10.1	52 35	7 54	9.9	51 36	7 37	9.7	50 37	7 21	9.5	49 38	7 06	9.3	48 38	6 51	9.1	264	276
85	53 42	6 50	8.5	52 43	6 36	8.3	51 43	6 22	8.1	50 44	6 09	7.9	49 44	5 56	7.8	48 45	5 44	7.6	265	275
86	53 49	5 29	6.8	52 49	5 17	6.6	51 49	5 06	6.5	50 50	4 55	6.3	49 50	4 45	6.2	48 50	4 35	6.1	266	274
87	53 54	4 07	5.1	52 54	3 58	5.0	51 54	3 50	4.9	50 54	3 42	4.8	49 54	3 34	4.7	48 55	3 27	4.6	267	273
88	53 57	2 45	3.4	52 57	2 39	3.3	51 57	2 33	3.2	50 57	2 28	3.2	49 58	2 23	3.1	48 58	2 18	3.0	268	272
89	53 59	1 23	1.7	52 59	1 20	1.7	51 59	1 17	1.6	50 59	1 14	1.6	49 59	1 11	1.6	48 59	1 09	1.5	269	271
90	54 00	0 00	0.0	53 00	0 00	0.0	52 00	0 00	0.0	51 00	0 00	0.0	50 00	0 00	0.0	49 00	0 00	0.0	270	270

N. Lat.: for LHA > 180° ... $Z_n = Z$
for LHA < 180° ... $Z_n = 360° - Z$

S. Lat.: for LHA > 180° ... $Z_n = 180° - Z$
for LHA < 180° ... $Z_n = 180° + Z$

SIGHT REDUCTION TABLE

B: (–) for 90° < LHA < 270°
Dec:(–) for Lat. contrary name

Z₁: same sign as B
Z₂: (–) for F > 90°

Lat./A		42°			43°			44°			45°			46°			47°			Lat./A	
LHA/F		A/H	B/P	Z_1/Z_2	A/H	B/P	Z_1/Z_2	A/H	B/P	Z_1/Z_2	A/H	B/P	Z_1/Z_2	A/H	B/P	Z_1/Z_2	A/H	B/P	Z_1/Z_2	LHA	
0	180	0 00	48 00	90.0	0 00	47 00	90.0	0 00	46 00	90.0	0 00	45 00	90.0	0 00	44 00	90.0	0 00	43 00	90.0	180	360
1	179	0 45	48 00	89.3	0 44	47 00	89.3	0 43	46 00	89.3	0 42	45 00	89.3	0 42	44 00	89.3	0 41	43 00	89.3	181	359
2	178	1 29	47 59	88.7	1 28	46 59	88.6	1 26	45 59	88.6	1 25	44 59	88.6	1 23	43 59	88.6	1 22	42 59	88.5	182	358
3	177	2 14	47 58	88.0	2 12	46 58	88.0	2 09	45 58	87.9	2 07	44 58	87.9	2 05	43 58	87.8	2 03	42 58	87.8	183	357
4	176	2 58	47 56	87.3	2 55	46 56	87.3	2 53	45 56	87.2	2 50	44 56	87.2	2 47	43 56	87.1	2 44	42 56	87.1	184	356
5	175	3 43	47 53	86.6	3 39	46 53	86.6	3 36	45 53	86.5	3 32	44 53	86.5	3 28	43 53	86.4	3 24	42 53	86.3	185	355
6	174	4 27	47 51	86.0	4 23	46 51	85.9	4 19	45 51	85.8	4 14	44 51	85.7	4 10	43 51	85.7	4 05	42 51	85.6	186	354
7	173	5 12	47 47	85.3	5 07	46 47	85.2	5 02	45 47	85.1	4 57	44 47	85.0	4 51	43 47	85.0	4 46	42 47	84.9	187	353
8	172	5 56	47 43	84.6	5 51	46 43	84.5	5 45	45 43	84.4	5 39	44 43	84.2	5 33	43 43	84.2	5 27	42 43	84.1	188	352
9	171	6 41	47 39	84.0	6 34	46 39	83.8	6 28	45 39	83.7	6 21	44 39	83.6	6 14	43 39	83.5	6 07	42 39	83.4	189	351
10	170	7 25	47 34	83.3	7 18	46 34	83.1	7 11	45 34	83.0	7 03	44 34	82.9	6 56	43 34	82.8	6 48	42 34	82.7	190	350
11	169	8 09	47 28	82.6	8 01	46 28	82.4	7 53	45 28	82.3	7 45	44 28	82.2	7 37	43 28	82.0	7 29	42 28	81.9	191	349
12	168	8 53	47 22	81.9	8 45	46 22	81.8	8 36	45 22	81.6	8 27	44 22	81.5	8 18	43 22	81.3	8 09	42 22	81.2	192	348
13	167	9 37	47 16	81.2	9 28	46 15	81.1	9 19	45 15	80.9	9 09	44 15	80.7	8 59	43 15	80.6	8 49	42 16	80.4	193	347
14	166	10 21	47 08	80.5	10 11	46 08	80.3	10 01	45 08	80.2	9 51	44 08	80.0	9 40	43 08	79.8	9 30	42 08	79.7	194	346
15	165	11 05	47 01	79.8	10 55	46 00	79.6	10 44	45 00	79.5	10 33	44 00	79.3	10 21	43 00	79.1	10 10	42 01	78.9	195	345
16	164	11 49	46 52	79.1	11 38	45 52	78.9	11 26	44 52	78.8	11 14	43 52	78.5	11 02	42 52	78.3	10 50	41 52	78.2	196	344
17	163	12 33	46 43	78.4	12 21	45 43	78.2	12 08	44 43	78.0	11 56	43 43	77.8	11 43	42 43	77.6	11 30	41 44	77.4	197	343
18	162	13 17	46 34	77.7	13 04	45 34	77.5	12 51	44 34	77.3	12 37	43 34	77.1	12 24	42 34	76.8	12 10	41 34	76.6	198	342
19	161	14 00	46 24	77.0	13 46	45 24	76.8	13 33	44 24	76.5	13 19	43 24	76.3	13 04	42 24	76.1	12 50	41 24	75.9	199	341
20	160	14 43	46 13	76.3	14 29	45 13	76.1	14 15	44 13	75.8	14 00	43 13	75.6	13 45	42 13	75.3	13 29	41 14	75.1	200	340
21	159	15 27	46 02	75.6	15 12	45 02	75.3	14 56	44 02	75.1	14 41	43 02	74.8	14 25	42 02	74.6	14 09	41 03	74.3	201	339
22	158	16 10	45 50	74.9	15 54	44 50	74.6	15 38	43 50	74.3	15 22	42 50	74.1	15 05	41 50	73.8	14 48	40 51	73.5	202	338
23	157	16 53	45 38	74.1	16 36	44 38	73.9	16 19	43 38	73.6	16 02	42 38	73.3	15 45	41 38	73.0	15 27	40 39	72.8	203	337
24	156	17 36	45 25	73.4	17 18	44 25	73.1	17 01	43 25	72.8	16 43	42 25	72.5	16 25	41 25	72.2	16 06	40 26	72.0	204	336
25	155	18 18	45 11	72.6	18 00	44 11	72.4	17 42	43 11	72.1	17 23	42 11	71.8	17 04	41 11	71.5	16 45	40 12	71.2	205	335
26	154	19 01	44 57	71.9	18 42	43 57	71.6	18 23	42 57	71.3	18 03	41 57	71.0	17 44	40 57	70.7	17 24	39 58	70.4	206	334
27	153	19 43	44 42	71.2	19 24	43 42	70.8	19 04	42 42	70.5	18 43	41 42	70.2	18 23	40 43	69.9	18 02	39 43	69.6	207	333
28	152	20 25	44 26	70.4	20 05	43 26	70.1	19 44	42 26	69.7	19 23	41 27	69.4	19 02	40 27	69.1	18 40	39 28	68.8	208	332
29	151	21 07	44 10	69.6	20 46	43 10	69.3	20 25	42 10	68.9	20 03	41 11	68.6	19 41	40 11	68.3	19 18	39 12	67.9	209	331
30	150	21 49	43 53	68.9	21 27	42 53	68.5	21 05	41 53	68.1	20 42	40 54	67.8	20 19	39 54	67.4	19 56	38 55	67.1	210	330
31	149	22 30	43 35	68.1	22 08	42 35	67.7	21 45	41 36	67.3	21 21	40 36	67.0	20 58	39 37	66.6	20 34	38 38	66.3	211	329
32	148	23 11	43 17	67.3	22 48	42 17	66.9	22 24	41 17	66.5	22 00	40 18	66.2	21 36	39 19	65.8	21 11	38 20	65.4	212	328
33	147	23 53	42 58	66.5	23 28	41 58	66.1	23 04	40 58	65.7	22 39	39 59	65.3	22 14	39 00	65.0	21 48	38 02	64.6	213	327
34	146	24 33	42 38	65.7	24 08	41 38	65.3	23 43	40 39	64.9	23 17	39 40	64.5	22 51	38 41	64.1	22 25	37 42	63.7	214	326
35	145	25 14	42 18	64.9	24 48	41 18	64.5	24 22	40 18	64.1	23 56	39 19	63.7	23 29	38 21	63.3	23 02	37 23	62.9	215	325
36	144	25 54	41 56	64.1	25 28	40 57	63.6	25 01	39 57	63.2	24 34	38 58	62.8	24 06	38 00	62.4	23 38	37 02	62.0	216	324
37	143	26 34	41 34	63.2	26 07	40 35	62.8	25 39	39 35	62.4	25 11	38 37	61.9	24 43	37 38	61.5	24 14	36 41	61.1	217	323
38	142	27 13	41 11	62.4	26 46	40 12	61.9	26 17	39 13	61.5	25 48	38 14	61.1	25 20	37 16	60.7	24 50	36 19	60.3	218	322
39	141	27 53	40 48	61.5	27 24	39 48	61.1	26 55	38 50	60.6	26 25	37 51	60.2	25 55	36 53	59.8	25 25	35 56	59.4	219	321
40	140	28 32	40 23	60.7	28 02	39 24	60.2	27 33	38 25	59.8	27 02	37 27	59.3	26 31	36 30	58.9	26 00	35 32	58.5	220	320
41	139	29 11	39 58	59.8	28 40	38 59	59.3	28 10	38 01	58.9	27 38	37 03	58.4	27 07	36 05	58.0	26 35	35 08	57.6	221	319
42	138	29 49	39 32	58.9	29 18	38 33	58.4	28 46	37 35	58.0	28 14	36 37	57.5	27 42	35 40	57.1	27 09	34 43	56.6	222	318
43	137	30 27	39 05	58.0	29 55	38 06	57.5	29 23	37 08	57.1	28 50	36 11	56.6	28 17	35 14	56.1	27 43	34 18	55.7	223	317
44	136	31 05	38 37	57.1	30 32	37 39	56.6	29 59	36 41	56.1	29 25	35 44	55.7	28 51	34 47	55.2	28 17	33 51	54.8	224	316
45	135	31 42	38 09	56.2	31 08	37 10	55.7	30 34	36 13	55.2	30 00	35 16	54.7	29 25	34 20	54.3	28 50	33 24	53.8	225	315

LHA	F	42° A/H	42° B/P	42° Z_1/Z_2	43° A/H	43° B/P	43° Z_1/Z_2	44° A/H	44° B/P	44° Z_1/Z_2	45° A/H	45° B/P	45° Z_1/Z_2	46° A/H	46° B/P	46° Z_1/Z_2	47° A/H	47° B/P	47° Z_1/Z_2	A	LHA
45	135	31 42	38 09	56·2	31 08	37 10	55·7	30 34	36 13	55·2	30 00	35 16	54·7	29 25	34 20	54·3	28 50	33 24	53·8	225	315
46	134	32 19	37 39	55·3	31 45	36 41	54·8	31 10	35 44	54·3	30 34	34 47	53·8	29 59	33 51	53·3	29 23	32 56	52·9	226	314
47	133	32 55	37 08	54·3	32 22	36 11	53·8	31 45	35 14	53·3	31 08	34 18	52·8	30 33	33 22	52·4	29 55	32 27	51·9	227	313
48	132	33 31	36 37	53·4	32 55	35 40	52·9	32 19	34 43	52·3	31 42	33 47	51·9	31 05	32 52	51·4	30 27	31 58	50·9	228	312
49	131	34 07	36 05	52·4	33 30	35 08	51·9	32 53	34 11	51·4	32 15	33 16	50·9	31 37	32 21	50·4	30 59	31 27	49·9	229	311
50	130	34 42	35 31	51·4	34 04	34 35	50·9	33 26	33 39	50·4	32 48	32 44	49·9	32 09	31 50	49·4	31 30	30 56	48·9	230	310
51	129	35 17	34 57	50·4	34 38	34 01	49·9	33 59	33 05	49·4	33 20	32 11	48·9	32 40	31 17	48·4	32 00	30 24	47·9	231	309
52	128	35 51	34 22	49·4	35 12	33 26	48·9	34 32	32 31	48·4	33 52	31 37	47·9	33 11	30 44	47·4	32 30	29 52	46·9	232	308
53	127	36 24	33 45	48·4	35 44	32 50	47·9	35 04	31 56	47·3	34 23	31 02	46·8	33 42	30 10	46·3	33 00	29 18	45·9	233	307
54	126	36 57	33 08	47·4	36 17	32 13	46·8	35 35	31 20	46·3	34 54	30 27	45·8	34 12	29 35	45·3	33 29	28 44	44·8	234	306
55	125	37 30	32 30	46·3	36 48	31 36	45·8	36 06	30 43	45·2	35 24	29 50	44·7	34 41	28 58	44·2	33 58	28 08	43·8	235	305
56	124	38 02	31 51	45·2	37 19	30 57	44·7	36 37	30 04	44·2	35 53	29 13	43·6	35 10	28 22	43·2	34 26	27 32	42·7	236	304
57	123	38 33	31 10	44·1	37 50	30 17	43·6	37 06	29 25	43·1	36 22	28 34	42·6	35 38	27 45	42·1	34 53	26 56	41·6	237	303
58	122	39 04	30 29	43·0	38 20	29 36	42·5	37 36	28 45	42·0	36 51	27 55	41·5	36 06	27 06	41·0	35 20	26 18	40·5	238	302
59	121	39 34	29 46	41·9	38 49	28 55	41·4	38 04	28 04	40·9	37 19	27 15	40·4	36 33	26 27	39·9	35 46	25 39	39·4	239	301
60	120	40 04	29 03	40·8	39 18	28 18	40·2	38 32	27 22	39·7	37 46	26 34	39·2	36 59	25 47	38·8	36 12	25 00	38·3	240	300
61	119	40 32	28 18	39·6	39 46	27 28	39·1	38 59	26 39	38·6	38 12	25 52	38·1	37 25	25 05	37·6	36 37	24 20	37·2	241	299
62	118	41 00	27 32	38·5	40 13	26 43	37·9	39 26	25 56	37·4	38 38	25 09	36·9	37 50	24 23	36·5	37 02	23 39	36·0	242	298
63	117	41 28	26 45	37·3	40 40	25 58	36·8	39 52	25 11	36·3	39 03	24 25	35·8	38 14	23 40	35·3	37 25	22 57	34·9	243	297
64	116	41 54	25 58	36·1	41 06	25 11	35·6	40 17	24 25	35·1	39 28	23 40	34·6	38 38	22 57	34·1	37 48	22 14	33·7	244	296
65	115	42 20	25 09	34·9	41 31	24 24	34·4	40 41	23 38	33·9	39 51	22 55	33·4	39 01	22 14	33·0	38 11	21 31	32·5	245	295
66	114	42 45	24 19	33·6	41 55	23 34	33·1	41 05	22 50	32·7	40 14	22 08	32·2	39 23	21 27	31·8	38 32	20 46	31·3	246	294
67	113	43 09	23 28	32·4	42 19	22 44	31·9	41 28	22 02	31·4	40 37	21 20	31·0	39 45	20 40	30·5	38 53	20 01	30·1	247	293
68	112	43 33	22 35	31·1	42 42	21 53	30·6	41 50	21 12	30·2	40 58	20 32	29·7	40 06	19 53	29·3	39 13	19 15	28·9	248	292
69	111	43 56	21 42	29·8	43 04	21 01	29·4	42 11	20 22	28·9	41 19	19 43	28·5	40 26	19 05	28·1	39 33	18 29	27·7	249	291
70	110	44 18	20 48	28·5	43 25	20 08	28·1	42 32	19 30	27·7	41 38	18 53	27·2	40 45	18 17	26·8	39 51	17 41	26·5	250	290
71	109	44 38	19 53	27·2	43 45	19 15	26·8	42 51	18 38	26·4	41 57	18 02	26·0	41 03	17 27	25·6	40 09	16 53	25·2	251	289
72	108	44 58	18 57	25·9	44 04	18 24	25·5	43 10	17 45	25·1	42 16	17 10	24·7	41 21	16 37	24·3	40 26	16 05	24·0	252	288
73	107	45 17	17 59	24·6	44 23	17 24	24·1	43 28	16 51	23·8	42 33	16 18	23·4	41 38	15 45	23·0	40 42	15 15	22·7	253	287
74	106	45 35	17 01	23·2	44 40	16 28	22·8	43 45	15 56	22·4	42 49	15 25	22·1	41 54	14 54	21·7	40 58	14 25	21·4	254	286
75	105	45 53	16 02	21·8	44 57	15 31	21·4	44 01	15 00	21·1	43 05	14 31	20·8	42 09	14 02	20·4	41 12	13 34	20·1	255	285
76	104	46 09	15 02	20·4	45 12	14 33	20·1	44 16	14 04	19·7	43 19	13 36	19·4	42 23	13 09	19·1	41 26	12 43	18·8	256	284
77	103	46 24	14 00	19·0	45 27	13 34	18·7	44 30	13 07	18·4	43 33	12 41	18·1	42 36	12 15	17·8	41 39	11 51	17·5	257	283
78	102	46 38	13 00	17·6	45 40	12 34	17·3	44 43	12 09	17·0	43 46	11 45	16·7	42 48	11 21	16·5	41 51	10 58	16·2	258	282
79	101	46 51	11 58	16·2	45 53	11 34	15·9	44 55	11 11	15·6	43 57	10 48	15·4	43 00	10 26	15·1	42 02	10 05	14·9	259	281
80	100	47 03	10 55	14·8	46 04	10 33	14·5	45 06	10 12	14·2	44 08	9 51	14·0	43 10	9 31	13·8	42 12	9 12	13·6	260	280
81	99	47 13	9 51	13·3	46 15	9 31	13·1	45 16	9 12	12·8	44 18	8 53	12·6	43 19	8 35	12·4	42 21	8 18	12·2	261	279
82	98	47 23	8 47	11·9	46 24	8 29	11·6	45 25	8 12	11·4	44 27	7 55	11·2	43 28	7 39	11·1	42 29	7 24	10·9	262	278
83	97	47 32	7 42	10·4	46 33	7 27	10·2	45 33	7 12	10·0	44 34	6 57	9·9	43 35	6 43	9·7	42 36	6 29	9·5	263	277
84	96	47 39	6 37	8·9	46 40	6 24	8·8	45 40	6 11	8·6	44 41	5 58	8·5	43 42	5 46	8·3	42 42	5 34	8·2	264	276
85	95	47 46	5 32	7·4	46 46	5 20	7·3	45 46	5 09	7·2	44 47	4 59	7·1	43 47	4 49	6·9	42 48	4 39	6·8	265	275
86	94	47 51	4 26	6·0	46 51	4 17	5·9	45 51	4 08	5·7	44 52	3 59	5·7	43 52	3 51	5·6	42 52	3 43	5·5	266	274
87	93	47 55	3 20	4·5	46 55	3 13	4·4	45 55	3 06	4·3	44 55	3 00	4·2	43 55	2 54	4·2	42 56	2 48	4·1	267	273
88	92	47 58	2 13	3·0	46 58	2 09	2·9	45 58	2 04	2·9	44 58	2 00	2·8	43 58	1 56	2·8	42 58	1 52	2·7	268	272
89	91	47 59	1 07	1·5	46 59	1 04	1·5	45 59	1 02	1·4	44 59	1 00	1·4	43 59	0 58	1·4	42 59	0 56	1·4	269	271
90	90	48 00	0 00	0·0	47 00	0 00	0·0	46 00	0 00	0·0	45 00	0 00	0·0	44 00	0 00	0·0	43 00	0 00	0·0	270	270

N. Lat: for LHA > 180° ... $Z_n = Z$
for LHA < 180° ... $Z_n = 360° - Z$

S. Lat.: for LHA > 180° ... $Z_n = 180° - Z$
for LHA < 180° ... $Z_n = 180° + Z$

SIGHT REDUCTION TABLE

B: (−) for 90° < LHA < 270°
Dec:(−) for Lat. contrary name

Z₁: same sign as B → Z_1: same sign as B
Z₂: (−) for F > 90° → Z_2: (−) for F > 90°

Lat./A LHA/F	48° A/H	48° B/P	48° Z_1/Z_2	49° A/H	49° B/P	49° Z_1/Z_2	50° A/H	50° B/P	50° Z_1/Z_2	51° A/H	51° B/P	51° Z_1/Z_2	52° A/H	52° B/P	52° Z_1/Z_2	53° A/H	53° B/P	53° Z_1/Z_2	Lat./A LHA
0 180	0 00	42 00	90·0	0 00	41 00	90·0	0 00	40 00	90·0	0 00	39 00	90·0	0 00	38 00	90·0	0 00	37 00	90·0	180 360
1 179	0 40	42 00	89·3	0 39	41 00	89·2	0 39	40 00	89·2	0 38	39 00	89·2	0 37	38 00	89·2	0 36	37 00	89·2	181 359
2 178	1 20	41 59	88·5	1 19	40 59	88·5	1 17	39 59	88·5	1 16	38 59	88·4	1 14	37 59	88·4	1 12	36 59	88·4	182 358
3 177	2 00	41 58	87·8	1 58	40 58	87·7	1 56	39 58	87·7	1 53	38 58	87·7	1 51	37 58	87·6	1 48	36 58	87·6	183 357
4 176	2 41	41 56	87·0	2 37	40 56	87·0	2 34	39 56	86·9	2 31	38 56	86·9	2 28	37 56	86·8	2 24	36 56	86·8	184 356
5 175	3 21	41 53	86·3	3 17	40 54	86·2	3 13	39 54	86·2	3 09	38 54	86·1	3 05	37 54	86·1	3 00	36 54	86·0	185 355
6 174	4 01	41 51	85·5	3 56	40 51	85·5	3 51	39 51	85·4	3 46	38 51	85·3	3 41	37 51	85·3	3 36	36 51	85·2	186 354
7 173	4 41	41 47	84·8	4 35	40 47	84·7	4 30	39 47	84·6	4 24	38 48	84·5	4 18	37 48	84·5	4 12	36 48	84·4	187 353
8 172	5 21	41 43	84·0	5 14	40 43	83·9	5 08	39 43	83·9	5 01	38 44	83·8	4 55	37 44	83·7	4 48	36 44	83·6	188 352
9 171	6 01	41 39	83·3	5 53	40 39	83·2	5 46	39 39	83·1	5 39	38 39	83·0	5 32	37 39	82·9	5 24	36 40	82·8	189 351
10 170	6 40	41 34	82·5	6 32	40 34	82·4	6 25	39 34	82·3	6 16	38 34	82·2	6 08	37 35	82·1	6 00	36 35	82·0	190 350
11 169	7 20	41 28	81·8	7 11	40 28	81·7	7 03	39 29	81·5	6 54	38 29	81·4	6 45	37 29	81·3	6 36	36 29	81·2	191 349
12 168	8 00	41 22	81·0	7 50	40 22	80·9	7 41	39 23	80·8	7 31	38 23	80·6	7 21	37 23	80·5	7 11	36 24	80·4	192 348
13 167	8 39	41 16	80·3	8 29	40 16	80·1	8 19	39 16	80·0	8 08	38 16	79·8	7 58	37 17	79·7	7 47	36 17	79·6	193 347
14 166	9 19	41 09	79·5	9 08	40 09	79·3	8 57	39 09	79·2	8 45	38 09	79·0	8 34	37 10	78·9	8 22	36 10	78·7	194 346
15 165	9 58	41 01	78·7	9 47	40 01	78·6	9 35	39 02	78·4	9 22	38 02	78·2	9 10	37 02	78·1	8 57	36 03	77·9	195 345
16 164	10 38	40 53	78·0	10 25	39 53	77·8	10 12	38 53	77·6	9 59	37 54	77·4	9 46	36 54	77·3	9 33	35 55	77·1	196 344
17 163	11 17	40 44	77·2	11 04	39 44	77·0	10 50	38 45	76·8	10 36	37 45	76·6	10 22	36 46	76·5	10 08	35 47	76·3	197 343
18 162	11 56	40 34	76·4	11 42	39 35	76·2	11 27	38 35	76·0	11 13	37 36	75·8	10 58	36 37	75·6	10 43	35 38	75·5	198 342
19 161	12 35	40 25	75·6	12 20	39 25	75·4	12 05	38 26	75·2	11 49	37 27	75·0	11 34	36 27	74·8	11 18	35 28	74·6	199 341
20 160	13 14	40 14	74·9	12 58	39 15	74·6	12 42	38 15	74·4	12 26	37 16	74·2	12 09	36 17	74·0	11 53	35 18	73·8	200 340
21 159	13 52	40 03	74·1	13 36	39 04	73·8	13 19	38 04	73·6	13 02	37 05	73·4	12 45	36 06	73·2	12 27	35 08	73·0	201 339
22 158	14 31	39 51	73·3	14 14	38 52	73·0	13 56	37 53	72·8	13 38	36 54	72·6	13 20	35 55	72·3	13 02	34 56	72·1	202 338
23 157	15 09	39 39	72·5	14 51	38 40	72·2	14 33	37 41	72·0	14 14	36 42	71·7	13 55	35 43	71·5	13 36	34 45	71·3	203 337
24 156	15 48	39 26	71·7	15 29	38 27	71·4	15 09	37 28	71·2	14 50	36 30	70·9	14 30	35 31	70·7	14 10	34 33	70·4	204 336
25 155	16 26	39 13	70·9	16 06	38 14	70·6	15 46	37 15	70·3	15 25	36 17	70·1	15 05	35 18	69·8	14 44	34 20	69·6	205 335
26 154	17 03	38 59	70·1	16 43	38 00	69·8	16 22	37 01	69·5	16 01	36 03	69·2	15 39	35 05	69·0	15 18	34 07	68·7	206 334
27 153	17 41	38 44	69·3	17 20	37 46	69·0	16 58	36 47	68·7	16 36	35 49	68·4	16 14	34 51	68·1	15 51	33 53	67·9	207 333
28 152	18 19	38 29	68·4	17 56	37 30	68·1	17 34	36 32	67·8	17 11	35 34	67·5	16 48	34 36	67·3	16 25	33 38	67·0	208 332
29 151	18 56	38 13	67·6	18 33	37 15	67·3	18 09	36 16	67·0	17 46	35 18	66·7	17 22	34 21	66·4	16 58	33 23	66·1	209 331
30 150	19 33	37 57	66·8	19 09	36 58	66·5	18 45	36 00	66·1	18 20	35 03	65·8	17 56	34 05	65·5	17 31	33 08	65·2	210 330
31 149	20 10	37 40	65·9	19 45	36 41	65·6	19 20	35 44	65·3	18 55	34 46	65·0	18 29	33 49	64·7	18 03	32 52	64·4	211 329
32 148	20 46	37 22	65·1	20 21	36 24	64·8	19 55	35 26	64·4	19 29	34 29	64·1	19 02	33 32	63·8	18 36	32 35	63·5	212 328
33 147	21 22	37 03	64·2	20 56	36 06	63·9	20 30	35 08	63·6	20 03	34 11	63·2	19 35	33 14	62·9	19 08	32 18	62·6	213 327
34 146	21 58	36 44	63·4	21 31	35 47	63·0	21 04	34 49	62·7	20 36	33 53	62·3	20 08	32 56	62·0	19 40	32 00	61·7	214 326
35 145	22 34	36 25	62·5	22 06	35 27	62·1	21 38	34 30	61·8	21 10	33 33	61·4	20 41	32 37	61·1	20 12	31 41	60·8	215 325
36 144	23 10	36 04	61·6	22 41	35 07	61·3	22 12	34 10	60·9	21 43	33 14	60·5	21 13	32 18	60·2	20 43	31 22	59·9	216 324
37 143	23 45	35 43	60·8	23 15	34 46	60·4	22 45	33 50	60·0	22 15	32 53	59·6	21 45	31 57	59·3	21 14	31 02	59·0	217 323
38 142	24 20	35 21	59·9	23 49	34 25	59·5	23 19	33 28	59·1	22 48	32 33	58·7	22 16	31 37	58·4	21 45	30 42	58·0	218 322
39 141	24 54	34 59	59·0	24 23	34 02	58·6	23 52	33 07	58·2	23 20	32 11	57·8	22 48	31 16	57·5	22 15	30 21	57·1	219 321
40 140	25 28	34 36	58·1	24 57	33 40	57·7	24 24	32 44	57·2	23 52	31 49	56·9	23 19	30 54	56·5	22 45	30 00	56·2	220 320
41 139	26 02	34 12	57·1	25 30	33 16	56·7	24 57	32 21	56·3	24 24	31 26	56·0	23 49	30 32	55·6	23 15	29 38	55·2	221 319
42 138	26 36	33 47	56·2	26 02	32 52	55·8	25 28	31 57	55·4	24 54	31 02	55·0	24 20	30 08	54·6	23 45	29 15	54·3	222 318
43 137	27 09	33 22	55·3	26 35	32 27	54·9	26 00	31 32	54·5	25 25	30 38	54·1	24 50	29 45	53·7	24 14	28 52	53·3	223 317
44 136	27 42	32 56	54·3	27 07	32 01	53·9	26 31	31 07	53·5	25 55	30 13	53·1	25 19	29 20	52·7	24 43	28 28	52·4	224 316
45 135	28 14	32 29	53·4	27 38	31 35	53·0	27 02	30 41	52·5	26 25	29 48	52·1	25 48	28 55	51·8	25 11	28 03	51·4	225 315

Lat./A A	LHA/F	48° A/H	48° B/P	48° Z₁/Z₂	49° A/H	49° B/P	49° Z₁/Z₂	50° A/H	50° B/P	50° Z₁/Z₂	51° A/H	51° B/P	51° Z₁/Z₂	52° A/H	52° B/P	52° Z₁/Z₂	53° A/H	53° B/P	53° Z₁/Z₂	LHA	A
135	45	28 14	32 29	53·4	27 38	31 35	53·0	27 02	30 41	52·5	26 25	29 48	52·1	25 48	28 55	51·8	25 11	28 03	51·4	225	315
134	46	28 46	32 01	52·4	28 10	31 08	52·0	27 32	30 14	51·6	26 55	29 22	51·2	26 17	28 29	50·8	25 39	27 38	50·4	226	314
133	47	29 18	31 33	51·5	28 40	30 40	51·0	28 02	29 47	50·6	27 24	28 55	50·2	26 46	28 03	49·8	26 07	27 12	49·4	227	313
132	48	29 49	31 04	50·5	29 11	30 11	50·0	28 32	29 19	49·6	27 53	28 27	49·2	27 14	27 36	48·8	26 34	26 46	48·4	228	312
131	49	30 20	30 34	49·5	29 41	29 42	49·0	29 01	28 50	48·6	28 21	27 59	48·2	27 41	27 08	47·8	27 01	26 18	47·4	229	311
130	50	30 50	30 04	48·5	30 10	29 12	48·0	29 30	28 20	47·6	28 49	27 30	47·2	28 08	26 40	46·8	27 27	25 51	46·4	230	310
129	51	31 20	29 32	47·5	30 39	28 41	47·0	29 58	27 50	46·6	29 17	27 00	46·2	28 35	26 11	45·8	27 53	25 22	45·4	231	309
128	52	31 49	29 00	46·4	31 08	28 09	46·0	30 26	27 19	45·6	29 44	26 30	45·2	29 01	25 41	44·8	28 19	24 53	44·4	232	308
127	53	32 18	28 27	45·4	31 36	27 37	45·0	30 53	26 48	44·5	30 10	25 59	44·1	29 27	25 11	43·7	28 44	24 24	43·3	233	307
126	54	32 46	27 53	44·4	32 03	27 04	44·0	31 20	26 15	43·5	30 36	25 27	43·1	29 52	24 40	42·7	29 08	23 53	42·3	234	306
125	55	33 14	27 19	43·3	32 30	26 30	42·9	31 46	25 42	42·4	31 02	24 55	42·0	30 17	24 08	41·6	29 32	23 23	41·2	235	305
124	56	33 42	26 44	42·2	32 57	25 55	41·8	32 12	25 08	41·4	31 27	24 22	41·0	30 41	23 36	40·6	29 56	22 51	40·2	236	304
123	57	34 08	26 07	41·1	33 23	25 20	40·7	32 37	24 34	40·3	31 51	23 48	39·9	31 05	23 03	39·5	30 19	22 19	39·1	237	303
122	58	34 34	25 30	40·1	33 48	24 44	39·6	33 02	23 58	39·2	32 15	23 14	38·8	31 28	22 29	38·4	30 41	21 46	38·0	238	302
121	59	35 00	24 53	39·0	34 13	24 07	38·5	33 26	23 22	38·1	32 39	22 38	37·7	31 51	21 55	37·3	31 03	21 13	37·0	239	301
120	60	35 25	24 14	37·8	34 37	23 30	37·4	33 50	22 46	37·0	33 02	22 02	36·6	32 13	21 20	36·2	31 25	20 39	35·9	240	300
119	61	35 49	23 35	36·7	35 01	22 51	36·3	34 12	22 08	35·9	33 24	21 26	35·5	32 35	20 45	35·1	31 46	20 04	34·8	241	299
118	62	36 13	22 55	35·6	35 24	22 12	35·2	34 35	21 30	34·8	33 45	20 49	34·4	32 56	20 09	34·0	32 06	19 29	33·7	242	298
117	63	36 36	22 14	34·4	35 46	21 32	34·0	34 56	20 51	33·6	34 06	20 11	33·3	33 16	19 32	32·9	32 26	18 53	32·5	243	297
116	64	36 58	21 32	33·3	36 08	20 52	32·9	35 17	20 12	32·5	34 27	19 33	32·1	33 36	18 54	31·8	32 45	18 17	31·4	244	296
115	65	37 20	20 50	32·2	36 29	20 10	31·7	35 38	19 32	31·3	34 47	18 54	31·0	33 55	18 16	30·6	33 03	17 40	30·3	245	295
114	66	37 41	20 07	31·0	36 49	19 28	30·5	35 58	18 51	30·2	35 06	18 14	29·8	34 13	17 38	29·5	33 21	17 02	29·1	246	294
113	67	38 01	19 23	29·7	37 09	18 46	29·4	36 17	18 09	29·0	35 24	17 33	28·6	34 31	16 59	28·3	33 38	16 24	28·0	247	293
112	68	38 21	18 38	28·5	37 28	18 02	28·2	36 35	17 27	27·8	35 42	16 53	27·5	34 48	16 19	27·1	33 55	15 46	26·8	248	292
111	69	38 40	17 53	27·3	37 46	17 18	27·0	36 53	16 44	26·6	35 59	16 11	26·3	35 05	15 38	26·0	34 11	15 07	25·7	249	291
110	70	38 58	17 07	26·1	38 04	16 33	25·7	37 10	16 01	25·4	36 15	15 29	25·1	35 21	14 58	24·8	34 26	14 27	24·5	250	290
109	71	39 15	16 20	24·9	38 21	15 48	24·5	37 26	15 17	24·2	36 31	14 46	23·9	35 36	14 16	23·6	34 41	13 47	23·3	251	289
108	72	39 31	15 33	23·6	38 36	15 02	23·3	37 41	14 32	23·0	36 46	14 03	22·7	35 50	13 34	22·4	34 55	13 07	22·1	252	288
107	73	39 47	14 45	22·4	38 51	14 16	22·1	37 56	13 47	21·8	37 00	13 19	21·5	36 04	12 52	21·2	35 08	12 25	20·9	253	287
106	74	40 02	13 56	21·1	39 06	13 28	20·8	38 10	13 01	20·5	37 13	12 35	20·3	36 17	12 09	20·0	35 21	11 44	19·8	254	286
105	75	40 16	13 07	19·8	39 19	12 41	19·5	38 23	12 15	19·3	37 26	11 50	19·0	36 29	11 26	18·8	35 33	11 02	18·5	255	285
104	76	40 29	12 17	18·5	39 32	11 53	18·3	38 35	11 28	18·0	37 38	11 05	17·8	36 41	10 42	17·6	35 44	10 20	17·3	256	284
103	77	40 41	11 27	17·3	39 44	11 04	17·0	38 47	10 41	16·8	37 49	10 19	16·5	36 52	9 58	16·3	35 54	9 37	16·1	257	283
102	78	40 53	10 36	16·0	39 55	10 15	15·7	38 57	9 54	15·5	38 00	9 33	15·3	37 02	9 14	15·1	36 04	8 54	14·9	258	282
101	79	41 04	9 45	14·7	40 07	9 25	14·4	39 07	9 06	14·2	38 09	8 47	14·0	37 11	8 29	13·9	36 13	8 11	13·7	259	281
100	80	41 13	8 53	13·3	40 15	8 35	13·2	39 16	8 17	13·0	38 18	8 00	12·8	37 19	7 44	12·6	36 21	7 27	12·5	260	280
99	81	41 22	8 01	12·0	40 23	7 45	11·9	39 25	7 29	11·7	38 26	7 13	11·5	37 27	6 58	11·4	36 28	6 43	11·2	261	279
98	82	41 30	7 09	10·7	40 31	6 54	10·5	39 32	6 40	10·4	38 33	6 26	10·3	37 34	6 12	10·1	36 35	5 59	10·1	262	278
97	83	41 37	6 16	9·4	40 38	6 03	9·4	39 39	5 50	9·1	38 39	5 38	9·0	37 40	5 26	8·9	36 41	5 15	8·7	263	277
96	84	41 43	5 23	8·1	40 44	5 12	8·1	39 44	5 01	7·9	38 45	4 50	7·8	37 45	4 40	7·6	36 46	4 30	7·5	264	276
95	85	41 48	4 29	6·7	40 49	4 20	6·7	39 49	4 11	6·6	38 49	4 02	6·4	37 50	3 54	6·3	36 50	3 45	6·3	265	275
94	86	41 52	3 36	5·4	40 53	3 28	5·4	39 53	3 21	5·3	38 53	3 14	5·2	37 53	3 07	5·1	36 54	3 01	5·0	266	274
93	87	41 56	2 42	4·0	40 56	2 36	4·0	39 56	2 31	3·9	38 56	2 26	3·8	37 56	2 20	3·8	36 56	2 16	3·8	267	273
92	88	41 58	1 48	2·7	40 58	1 44	2·7	39 58	1 41	2·6	38 58	1 37	2·6	37 58	1 34	2·5	36 58	1 30	2·5	268	272
91	89	42 00	0 54	1·3	41 00	0 52	1·3	40 00	0 50	1·3	39 00	0 49	1·3	38 00	0 47	1·3	37 00	0 45	1·3	269	271
90	90	42 00	0 00	0·0	41 00	0 00	0·0	40 00	0 00	0·0	39 00	0 00	0·0	38 00	0 00	0·0	37 00	0 00	0·0	270	270

N. Lat: for LHA > 180° ... Zₙ = Z
for LHA < 180° ... Zₙ = 360° − Z

S. Lat: for LHA > 180° ... Zₙ = 180° − Z
for LHA < 180° ... Zₙ = 180° + Z

SIGHT REDUCTION TABLE

B: (−) for 90° < LHA < 270°
Dec:(−) for Lat. contrary name

Z₁: same sign as B
Z₂: (−) for F > 90°

Lat. / A (data columns are "A")

LHA/F	54° A/H	54° B/P	54° Z₁/Z₂	55° A/H	55° B/P	55° Z₁/Z₂	56° A/H	56° B/P	56° Z₁/Z₂	57° A/H	57° B/P	57° Z₁/Z₂	58° A/H	58° B/P	58° Z₁/Z₂	59° A/H	59° B/P	59° Z₁/Z₂	Lat./A – LHA
0 180	0 00	36 00	90.0	0 00	35 00	90.0	0 00	34 00	90.0	0 00	33 00	90.0	0 00	32 00	90.0	0 00	31 00	90.0	180 360
1 179	0 35	36 00	89.2	0 34	35 00	89.2	0 34	34 00	89.2	0 33	33 00	89.2	0 32	32 00	89.2	0 31	31 00	89.1	181 359
2 178	1 11	35 59	88.4	1 09	34 59	88.4	1 07	33 59	88.3	1 05	32 59	88.3	1 04	31 59	88.3	1 02	30 59	88.3	182 358
3 177	1 46	35 58	87.6	1 43	34 58	87.6	1 41	33 58	87.5	1 38	32 58	87.5	1 35	31 58	87.5	1 33	30 58	87.4	183 357
4 176	2 21	35 56	86.8	2 18	34 56	86.7	2 14	33 56	86.7	2 11	32 56	86.7	2 07	31 56	86.6	2 04	30 56	86.6	184 356
5 175	2 56	35 54	86.0	2 52	34 54	85.9	2 48	33 54	85.9	2 43	32 54	85.8	2 39	31 54	85.8	2 34	30 54	85.7	185 355
6 174	3 31	35 51	85.1	3 26	34 51	85.1	3 21	33 51	85.0	3 16	32 51	85.0	3 11	31 52	84.9	3 05	30 52	84.9	186 354
7 173	4 06	35 48	84.3	4 00	34 48	84.3	3 54	33 48	84.2	3 48	32 48	84.1	3 42	31 48	84.1	3 36	30 49	84.0	187 353
8 172	4 42	35 44	83.5	4 34	34 44	83.4	4 28	33 44	83.4	4 21	32 45	83.3	4 14	31 45	83.2	4 07	30 45	83.1	188 352
9 171	5 17	35 40	82.7	5 09	34 40	82.6	5 01	33 40	82.5	4 53	32 41	82.4	4 45	31 41	82.3	4 37	30 41	82.3	189 351
10 170	5 51	35 35	81.9	5 43	34 35	81.8	5 34	33 36	81.7	5 26	32 36	81.6	5 17	31 36	81.5	5 08	30 37	81.4	190 350
11 169	6 26	35 30	81.1	6 17	34 30	81.0	6 08	33 31	80.8	5 58	32 31	80.7	5 48	31 31	80.6	5 38	30 32	80.5	191 349
12 168	7 01	35 24	80.2	6 51	34 24	80.1	6 41	33 25	80.0	6 30	32 25	79.9	6 20	31 26	79.8	6 09	30 27	79.7	192 348
13 167	7 36	35 18	79.4	7 25	34 18	79.3	7 14	33 19	79.2	7 02	32 19	79.0	6 51	31 20	78.9	6 39	30 21	78.8	193 347
14 166	8 11	35 11	78.6	7 59	34 12	78.5	7 46	33 12	78.3	7 34	32 13	78.2	7 22	31 14	78.1	7 09	30 15	77.9	194 346
15 165	8 45	35 04	77.8	8 32	34 04	77.6	8 19	33 05	77.5	8 06	32 06	77.3	7 53	31 07	77.2	7 40	30 08	77.1	195 345
16 164	9 19	34 56	76.9	9 06	33 57	76.8	8 52	32 58	76.6	8 38	31 58	76.5	8 24	31 00	76.3	8 10	30 01	76.2	196 344
17 163	9 54	34 47	76.1	9 39	33 48	75.9	9 25	32 49	75.8	9 10	31 50	75.6	8 55	30 52	75.5	8 40	29 53	75.3	197 343
18 162	10 28	34 39	75.3	10 13	33 40	75.1	9 57	32 41	74.9	9 41	31 42	74.8	9 25	30 43	74.6	9 09	29 45	74.4	198 342
19 161	11 02	34 29	74.4	10 46	33 30	74.2	10 29	32 32	74.1	10 13	31 33	73.9	9 56	30 35	73.7	9 39	29 36	73.6	199 341
20 160	11 36	34 19	73.6	11 19	33 20	73.4	11 02	32 22	73.2	10 44	31 24	73.0	10 27	30 25	72.8	10 09	29 27	72.7	200 340
21 159	12 10	34 09	72.7	11 52	33 10	72.5	11 34	32 12	72.3	11 15	31 14	72.2	10 57	30 16	72.0	10 38	29 17	71.8	201 339
22 158	12 43	33 58	71.9	12 24	33 00	71.7	12 06	32 01	71.5	11 46	31 03	71.3	11 27	30 05	71.1	11 07	29 07	70.9	202 338
23 157	13 17	33 46	71.0	12 57	32 48	70.8	12 37	31 50	70.6	12 17	30 52	70.4	11 57	29 54	70.2	11 37	28 57	70.0	203 337
24 156	13 50	33 34	70.2	13 29	32 36	70.0	13 09	31 38	69.7	12 48	30 41	69.5	12 27	29 43	69.3	12 06	28 46	69.1	204 336
25 155	14 23	33 22	69.3	14 02	32 24	69.1	13 40	31 26	68.9	13 18	30 29	68.6	12 56	29 31	68.4	12 34	28 34	68.2	205 335
26 154	14 56	33 09	68.5	14 34	32 11	68.2	14 11	31 14	68.0	13 49	30 16	67.8	13 26	29 19	67.5	13 03	28 22	67.3	206 334
27 153	15 29	32 55	67.6	15 06	31 58	67.3	14 42	31 00	67.1	14 19	30 03	66.9	13 55	29 06	66.6	13 31	28 10	66.4	207 333
28 152	16 01	32 41	66.7	15 37	31 44	66.5	15 13	30 47	66.2	14 49	29 50	66.0	14 24	28 53	65.7	14 00	27 57	65.5	208 332
29 151	16 33	32 26	65.8	16 09	31 29	65.6	15 44	30 32	65.3	15 19	29 36	65.1	14 53	28 39	64.8	14 28	27 43	64.6	209 331
30 150	17 05	32 11	65.0	16 40	31 14	64.7	16 14	30 17	64.4	15 48	29 21	64.2	15 22	28 25	63.9	14 55	27 29	63.7	210 330
31 149	17 37	31 55	64.1	17 11	30 58	63.8	16 44	30 02	63.5	16 17	29 06	63.3	15 50	28 10	63.0	15 23	27 15	62.7	211 329
32 148	18 09	31 38	63.2	17 42	30 42	62.9	17 14	29 46	62.6	16 47	28 51	62.3	16 19	27 55	62.1	15 50	27 00	61.8	212 328
33 147	18 40	31 21	62.3	18 12	30 25	62.0	17 44	29 30	61.7	17 15	28 34	61.4	16 47	27 39	61.2	16 17	26 45	60.9	213 327
34 146	19 11	31 04	61.4	18 42	30 08	61.1	18 13	29 13	60.8	17 44	28 18	60.5	17 14	27 23	60.2	16 44	26 29	60.0	214 326
35 145	19 42	30 46	60.5	19 12	29 50	60.2	18 42	28 55	59.9	18 12	28 01	59.6	17 42	27 06	59.3	17 11	26 12	59.0	215 325
36 144	20 13	30 27	59.6	19 42	29 32	59.2	19 11	28 37	58.9	18 40	27 43	58.6	18 09	26 49	58.4	17 37	25 55	58.1	216 324
37 143	20 43	30 07	58.6	20 12	29 13	58.3	19 40	28 19	58.0	19 08	27 25	57.7	18 36	26 31	57.4	18 03	25 38	57.1	217 323
38 142	21 13	29 48	57.7	20 41	28 53	57.4	20 08	27 59	57.1	19 35	27 06	56.8	19 02	26 13	56.5	18 29	25 20	56.2	218 322
39 141	21 43	29 27	56.8	21 10	28 33	56.4	20 36	27 40	56.1	20 03	26 47	55.8	19 29	25 54	55.5	18 55	25 02	55.2	219 321
40 140	22 12	29 06	55.8	21 38	28 13	55.5	21 04	27 20	55.2	20 30	26 27	54.9	19 55	25 35	54.6	19 20	24 43	54.3	220 320
41 139	22 41	28 44	54.9	22 06	27 51	54.5	21 31	26 59	54.2	20 56	26 07	53.9	20 21	25 15	53.6	19 45	24 24	53.3	221 319
42 138	23 10	28 22	53.9	22 34	27 29	53.6	21 58	26 37	53.3	21 22	25 46	52.9	20 46	24 55	52.6	20 10	24 04	52.3	222 318
43 137	23 38	27 59	53.0	23 02	27 07	52.6	22 25	26 15	52.3	21 48	25 24	52.0	21 11	24 34	51.7	20 34	23 43	51.4	223 317
44 136	24 06	27 36	52.0	23 29	26 44	51.7	22 51	25 53	51.3	22 14	25 02	51.0	21 36	24 12	50.7	20 58	23 23	50.4	224 316
45 135	24 34	27 11	51.0	23 56	26 20	50.7	23 17	25 30	50.3	22 39	24 40	50.0	22 00	23 50	49.7	21 21	23 01	49.4	225 315

S. Lat.: for LHA > 180° ... $Z_n = 180° - Z$
for LHA < 180° ... $Z_n = 180° + Z$

Lat./A LHA/F	F	54° A/H	54° B/P	54° Z₁/Z₂	55° A/H	55° B/P	55° Z₁/Z₂	56° A/H	56° B/P	56° Z₁/Z₂	57° A/H	57° B/P	57° Z₁/Z₂	58° A/H	58° B/P	58° Z₁/Z₂	59° A/H	59° B/P	59° Z₁/Z₂	Lat./A LHA	LHA2
45	135	24 34	27 11	51·0	23 56	26 20	50·7	23 17	25 30	50·3	22 39	24 40	50·0	22 00	23 50	49·7	21 21	23 01	49·4	225	315
46	134	25 01	26 47	50·0	24 22	25 56	49·7	23 43	25 06	49·4	23 04	24 17	49·0	22 24	23 28	48·7	21 45	22 39	48·4	226	314
47	133	25 28	26 22	49·0	24 48	25 32	48·7	24 08	24 42	48·4	23 28	23 53	48·0	22 48	23 05	47·7	22 08	22 17	47·4	227	313
48	132	25 54	25 56	48·1	25 14	25 06	47·7	24 33	24 17	47·4	23 53	23 29	47·0	23 11	22 41	46·7	22 30	21 54	46·4	228	312
49	131	26 20	25 29	47·1	25 39	24 40	46·7	24 58	23 52	46·4	24 16	23 05	46·0	23 34	22 17	45·7	22 52	21 31	45·4	229	311
50	130	26 46	25 02	46·0	26 04	24 14	45·7	25 22	23 26	45·3	24 40	22 39	45·0	23 57	21 53	44·7	23 14	21 07	44·4	230	310
51	129	27 11	24 34	45·0	26 28	23 47	44·7	25 45	23 00	44·3	25 02	22 14	44·0	24 19	21 28	43·7	23 36	20 43	43·4	231	309
52	128	27 36	24 06	44·0	26 52	23 19	43·6	26 09	22 33	43·3	25 25	21 48	43·0	24 41	21 03	42·7	23 57	20 18	42·3	232	308
53	127	28 00	23 37	43·0	27 16	22 51	42·6	26 32	22 06	42·3	25 47	21 21	41·9	25 02	20 37	41·6	24 17	19 53	41·3	233	307
54	126	28 24	23 07	41·9	27 39	22 22	41·6	26 54	21 38	41·2	26 09	20 54	40·9	25 23	20 10	40·6	24 37	19 27	40·3	234	306
55	125	28 47	22 37	40·9	28 01	21 53	40·5	27 16	21 09	40·2	26 30	20 26	39·9	25 43	19 43	39·5	24 57	19 01	39·2	235	305
56	124	29 10	22 07	39·8	28 24	21 23	39·5	27 37	20 40	39·1	26 50	19 57	38·8	26 04	19 16	38·5	25 17	18 34	38·2	236	304
57	123	29 32	21 35	38·8	28 45	20 52	38·4	27 58	20 10	38·1	27 11	19 29	37·8	26 23	18 48	37·4	25 35	18 07	37·1	237	303
58	122	29 54	21 03	37·7	29 06	20 21	37·3	28 19	19 40	37·0	27 31	18 59	36·7	26 42	18 19	36·4	25 54	17 40	36·1	238	302
59	121	30 15	20 31	36·6	29 27	19 50	36·3	28 38	19 09	35·9	27 50	18 30	35·6	27 01	17 50	35·3	26 12	17 12	35·0	239	301
60	120	30 36	19 58	35·5	29 47	19 18	35·2	28 58	18 38	34·8	28 09	18 00	34·5	27 19	17 21	34·2	26 29	16 43	34·0	240	300
61	119	30 56	19 24	34·4	30 07	18 45	34·1	29 17	18 06	33·8	28 27	17 29	33·5	27 37	16 51	33·2	26 46	16 14	32·9	241	299
62	118	31 16	18 50	33·3	30 26	18 12	33·0	29 35	17 34	32·7	28 45	16 57	32·4	27 54	16 21	32·1	27 03	15 45	31·8	242	298
63	117	31 35	18 15	32·2	30 44	17 38	31·9	29 53	17 02	31·6	29 02	16 26	31·3	28 10	15 50	31·0	27 19	15 15	30·7	243	297
64	116	31 53	17 40	31·1	31 02	17 04	30·8	30 10	16 28	30·5	29 19	15 53	30·2	28 27	15 19	29·9	27 35	14 45	29·6	244	296
65	115	32 11	17 04	30·0	31 19	16 29	29·7	30 27	15 55	29·4	29 35	15 20	29·1	28 42	14 48	28·8	27 50	14 15	28·5	245	295
66	114	32 29	16 28	28·8	31 36	15 54	28·5	30 43	15 20	28·2	29 50	14 48	28·0	28 57	14 16	27·7	28 04	13 44	27·4	246	294
67	113	32 45	15 51	27·7	31 52	15 18	27·4	30 59	14 46	27·1	30 05	14 14	26·8	29 12	13 43	26·6	28 18	13 13	26·3	247	293
68	112	33 01	15 14	26·5	32 08	14 42	26·3	31 14	14 11	26·0	30 20	13 40	25·7	29 26	13 10	25·5	28 31	12 41	25·2	248	292
69	111	33 17	14 36	25·4	32 23	14 05	25·1	31 28	13 35	24·8	30 34	13 06	24·6	29 39	12 37	24·4	28 44	12 09	24·1	249	291
70	110	33 33	13 57	24·2	32 37	13 28	24·0	31 42	12 59	23·7	30 47	12 31	23·5	29 52	12 04	23·2	28 57	11 37	23·0	250	290
71	109	33 46	13 18	23·1	32 51	12 51	22·8	31 55	12 23	22·6	31 00	11 56	22·3	30 04	11 30	22·1	29 09	11 04	21·9	251	289
72	108	33 59	12 39	21·9	33 04	12 13	21·6	32 08	11 46	21·4	31 12	11 21	21·2	30 16	10 56	21·0	29 20	10 31	20·8	252	288
73	107	34 12	12 00	20·7	33 16	11 34	20·5	32 20	11 09	20·2	31 23	10 45	20·0	30 27	10 21	19·8	29 30	9 58	19·6	253	287
74	106	34 24	11 19	19·5	33 28	10 55	19·3	32 31	10 32	19·1	31 34	10 09	18·9	30 37	9 46	18·7	29 41	9 24	18·5	254	286
75	105	34 36	10 39	18·3	33 39	10 16	18·1	32 42	9 54	17·9	31 44	9 32	17·7	30 47	9 11	17·5	29 50	8 50	17·4	255	285
76	104	34 46	9 58	17·1	33 49	9 37	16·9	32 52	9 16	16·7	31 54	8 56	16·6	30 57	8 36	16·4	29 59	8 16	16·2	256	284
77	103	34 56	9 17	15·9	33 59	8 57	15·7	33 01	8 38	15·6	32 03	8 19	15·4	31 05	8 00	15·2	30 07	7 42	15·1	257	283
78	102	35 06	8 35	14·7	34 08	8 17	14·5	33 10	7 59	14·4	32 11	7 41	14·2	31 13	7 24	14·1	30 15	7 07	13·9	258	282
79	101	35 14	7 54	13·5	34 16	7 37	13·3	33 18	7 20	13·2	32 19	7 04	13·0	31 21	6 48	12·9	30 22	6 32	12·8	259	281
80	100	35 22	7 11	12·3	34 24	6 56	12·1	33 25	6 41	12·0	32 26	6 26	11·9	31 27	6 12	11·7	30 29	5 57	11·6	260	280
81	99	35 29	6 29	11·1	34 30	6 15	10·9	33 32	6 01	10·8	32 33	5 48	10·7	31 34	5 35	10·6	30 35	5 22	10·5	261	279
82	98	35 36	5 46	9·9	34 37	5 34	9·7	33 37	5 22	9·6	32 38	5 10	9·5	31 38	4 58	9·4	30 40	4 47	9·3	262	278
83	97	35 41	5 04	8·6	34 42	4 53	8·5	33 43	4 42	8·4	32 43	4 32	8·3	31 44	4 21	8·2	30 45	4 11	8·2	263	277
84	96	35 46	4 21	7·4	34 47	4 11	7·3	33 47	4 02	7·2	32 48	3 53	7·1	31 48	3 44	7·1	30 49	3 36	7·0	264	276
85	95	35 51	3 37	6·2	34 51	3 30	6·1	33 51	3 22	6·0	32 51	3 14	5·9	31 52	3 07	5·9	30 52	3 00	5·8	265	275
86	94	35 54	2 54	4·9	34 54	2 48	4·9	33 54	2 42	4·8	32 55	2 36	4·8	31 55	2 30	4·7	30 55	2 24	4·7	266	274
87	93	35 57	2 11	3·7	34 57	2 06	3·7	33 57	2 01	3·6	32 57	1 57	3·6	31 57	1 52	3·5	30 57	1 48	3·5	267	273
88	92	35 58	1 27	2·5	34 59	1 24	2·4	33 59	1 21	2·4	32 59	1 18	2·4	31 59	1 15	2·4	30 59	1 12	2·3	268	272
89	91	36 00	0 44	1·2	35 00	0 42	1·2	34 00	0 40	1·2	33 00	0 39	1·2	32 00	0 37	1·2	31 00	0 36	1·2	269	271
90	90	36 00	0 00	0·0	35 00	0 00	0·0	34 00	0 00	0·0	33 00	0 00	0·0	32 00	0 00	0·0	31 00	0 00	0·0	270	270

N. Lat.: for LHA > 180° ... $Z_n = Z$
for LHA < 180° ... $Z_n = 360° - Z$

SIGHT REDUCTION TABLE

B: (−) for 90° < LHA < 270°
Dec:(−) for Lat. contrary name

Z₁: same sign as B
Z₂:(−) for F > 90°

Lat./A →	60° A/H	60° B/P	60° Z₁/Z₂	61° A/H	61° B/P	61° Z₁/Z₂	62° A/H	62° B/P	62° Z₁/Z₂	63° A/H	63° B/P	63° Z₁/Z₂	64° A/H	64° B/P	64° Z₁/Z₂	65° A/H	65° B/P	65° Z₁/Z₂	Lat./A LHA
0 / 180	0 00	30 00	90·0	0 00	29 00	90·0	0 00	28 00	90·0	0 00	27 00	90·0	0 00	26 00	90·0	0 00	25 00	90·0	180 / 360
1 / 179	0 30	30 00	89·1	0 29	29 00	89·1	0 28	28 00	89·1	0 27	27 00	89·1	0 26	26 00	89·1	0 25	25 00	89·1	181 / 359
2 / 178	1 00	29 59	88·3	0 58	28 59	88·3	0 56	27 59	88·2	0 54	26 59	88·2	0 53	25 59	88·2	0 51	24 59	88·2	182 / 358
3 / 177	1 30	29 58	87·4	1 27	28 58	87·4	1 24	27 58	87·4	1 22	26 58	87·3	1 19	25 58	87·3	1 16	24 58	87·3	183 / 357
4 / 176	2 00	29 56	86·5	1 56	28 56	86·5	1 53	27 57	86·5	1 49	26 57	86·4	1 45	25 57	86·4	1 41	24 57	86·4	184 / 356
5 / 175	2 30	29 54	85·7	2 25	28 54	85·6	2 21	27 55	85·6	2 16	26 55	85·5	2 11	25 55	85·5	2 07	24 55	85·5	185 / 355
6 / 174	3 00	29 52	84·8	2 54	28 52	84·7	2 49	27 52	84·7	2 43	26 52	84·6	2 38	25 53	84·6	2 32	24 53	84·6	186 / 354
7 / 173	3 30	29 49	83·9	3 23	28 49	83·9	3 17	27 49	83·8	3 10	26 50	83·8	3 04	25 50	83·7	2 57	24 50	83·7	187 / 353
8 / 172	3 59	29 45	83·1	3 52	28 46	83·0	3 45	27 46	82·9	3 37	26 46	82·9	3 30	25 47	82·8	3 22	24 47	82·7	188 / 352
9 / 171	4 29	29 42	82·2	4 21	28 42	82·1	4 13	27 42	82·0	4 04	26 43	82·0	3 56	25 43	81·9	3 47	24 44	81·8	189 / 351
10 / 170	4 59	29 37	81·3	4 50	28 38	81·2	4 41	27 38	81·2	4 31	26 39	81·1	4 22	25 39	81·0	4 13	24 40	80·9	190 / 350
11 / 169	5 28	29 33	80·4	5 18	28 33	80·4	5 08	27 34	80·3	4 58	26 34	80·2	4 48	25 35	80·1	4 38	24 36	80·0	191 / 349
12 / 168	5 58	29 27	79·6	5 47	28 28	79·5	5 36	27 29	79·4	5 25	26 29	79·3	5 14	25 30	79·2	5 02	24 31	79·1	192 / 348
13 / 167	6 27	29 22	78·7	6 16	28 22	78·6	6 04	27 23	78·5	5 52	26 24	78·4	5 40	25 25	78·3	5 27	24 26	78·2	193 / 347
14 / 166	6 57	29 15	77·8	6 44	28 16	77·7	6 31	27 17	77·6	6 18	26 18	77·5	6 05	25 20	77·4	5 52	24 21	77·3	194 / 346
15 / 165	7 26	29 09	76·9	7 13	28 10	76·8	6 59	27 11	76·7	6 45	26 12	76·6	6 31	25 14	76·5	6 17	24 15	76·4	195 / 345
16 / 164	7 55	29 02	76·1	7 41	28 03	75·9	7 26	27 04	75·8	7 11	26 06	75·7	6 56	25 07	75·5	6 41	24 09	75·4	196 / 344
17 / 163	8 24	28 54	75·2	8 09	27 56	75·0	7 53	26 57	74·9	7 38	25 59	74·8	7 22	25 00	74·6	7 06	24 02	74·5	197 / 343
18 / 162	8 53	28 46	74·3	8 37	27 48	74·1	8 20	26 50	74·0	8 04	25 51	73·9	7 47	24 53	73·7	7 30	23 55	73·6	198 / 342
19 / 161	9 22	28 38	73·4	9 05	27 40	73·2	8 48	26 41	73·1	8 30	25 43	72·9	8 12	24 45	72·8	7 55	23 48	72·7	199 / 341
20 / 160	9 51	28 29	72·5	9 33	27 31	72·3	9 14	26 33	72·2	8 56	25 35	72·0	8 37	24 37	71·9	8 19	23 40	71·7	200 / 340
21 / 159	10 19	28 19	71·6	10 00	27 22	71·4	9 41	26 24	71·3	9 22	25 26	71·1	9 02	24 29	71·0	8 43	23 32	70·8	201 / 339
22 / 158	10 48	28 10	70·7	10 28	27 12	70·5	10 08	26 15	70·4	9 48	25 17	70·2	9 27	24 20	70·0	9 07	23 23	69·9	202 / 338
23 / 157	11 16	27 59	69·8	10 55	27 02	69·6	10 34	26 05	69·5	10 13	25 08	69·3	9 52	24 11	69·1	9 30	23 14	69·0	203 / 337
24 / 156	11 44	27 49	68·9	11 22	26 51	68·7	11 00	25 54	68·5	10 38	24 58	68·4	10 16	24 01	68·2	9 54	23 04	68·0	204 / 336
25 / 155	12 12	27 37	68·0	11 49	26 40	67·8	11 27	25 44	67·6	11 04	24 47	67·4	10 41	23 51	67·3	10 17	22 55	67·1	205 / 335
26 / 154	12 40	27 26	67·1	12 16	26 29	66·9	11 53	25 33	66·7	11 29	24 36	66·5	11 05	23 40	66·3	10 41	22 44	66·2	206 / 334
27 / 153	13 07	27 13	66·2	12 43	26 17	66·0	12 18	25 21	65·8	11 54	24 25	65·6	11 29	23 29	65·4	11 04	22 34	65·2	207 / 333
28 / 152	13 35	27 01	65·3	13 09	26 05	65·1	12 44	25 09	64·9	12 18	24 13	64·7	11 53	23 18	64·5	11 27	22 23	64·3	208 / 332
29 / 151	14 02	26 48	64·4	13 36	25 52	64·1	13 09	24 56	63·9	12 43	24 01	63·7	12 16	23 06	63·5	11 49	22 11	63·3	209 / 331
30 / 150	14 29	26 34	63·4	14 02	25 39	63·2	13 35	24 43	63·0	13 07	23 49	62·8	12 40	22 54	62·6	12 12	21 59	62·4	210 / 330
31 / 149	14 55	26 20	62·5	14 28	25 25	62·3	14 00	24 30	62·1	13 31	23 36	61·8	13 03	22 41	61·6	12 34	21 47	61·4	211 / 329
32 / 148	15 22	26 05	61·6	14 53	25 11	61·3	14 24	24 16	61·1	13 55	23 22	60·9	13 26	22 28	60·7	12 56	21 35	60·5	212 / 328
33 / 147	15 48	25 50	60·6	15 18	24 56	60·4	14 49	24 02	60·2	14 19	23 08	59·9	13 49	22 15	59·7	13 18	21 22	59·5	213 / 327
34 / 146	16 14	25 35	59·7	15 44	24 41	59·5	15 13	23 47	59·2	14 42	22 54	59·0	14 11	22 01	58·8	13 40	21 08	58·6	214 / 326
35 / 145	16 40	25 19	58·8	16 09	24 25	58·5	15 37	23 32	58·3	15 06	22 39	58·0	14 34	21 47	57·8	14 02	20 54	57·6	215 / 325
36 / 144	17 05	25 02	57·8	16 33	24 09	57·6	16 01	23 17	57·3	15 29	22 24	57·1	14 56	21 32	56·9	14 23	20 40	56·6	216 / 324
37 / 143	17 31	24 45	56·9	16 58	23 53	56·6	16 25	23 00	56·4	15 51	22 09	56·1	15 18	21 17	55·9	14 44	20 26	55·7	217 / 323
38 / 142	17 56	24 28	55·9	17 22	23 36	55·7	16 48	22 44	55·4	16 14	21 53	55·2	15 39	21 01	54·9	15 05	20 11	54·7	218 / 322
39 / 141	18 20	24 10	55·0	17 46	23 18	54·7	17 11	22 27	54·4	16 36	21 37	54·2	16 01	20 46	54·0	15 25	19 55	53·7	219 / 321
40 / 140	18 45	23 52	54·0	18 09	23 00	53·7	17 34	22 10	53·5	16 58	21 19	53·2	16 22	20 29	53·0	15 46	19 39	52·7	220 / 320
41 / 139	19 09	23 33	53·0	18 33	22 42	52·8	17 56	21 52	52·5	17 20	21 02	52·2	16 43	20 13	52·0	16 06	19 23	51·8	221 / 319
42 / 138	19 33	23 13	52·1	18 56	22 23	51·8	18 19	21 34	51·5	17 41	20 44	51·3	17 03	19 55	51·0	16 26	19 07	50·8	222 / 318
43 / 137	19 56	22 54	51·1	19 18	22 04	50·8	18 40	21 15	50·5	18 02	20 26	50·3	17 24	19 38	50·0	16 45	18 50	49·8	223 / 317
44 / 136	20 19	22 33	50·1	19 41	21 44	49·8	19 02	20 56	49·5	18 23	20 08	49·3	17 44	19 20	49·0	17 04	18 33	48·8	224 / 316
45 / 135	20 42	22 12	49·1	20 03	21 24	48·8	19 23	20 36	48·6	18 43	19 49	48·3	18 03	19 02	48·1	17 23	18 15	47·8	225 / 315

Lat./A — LHA/F (left index)

Lat./A		60°			61°			62°			63°			64°			65°			Lat./A	
LHA/F		A/H	B/P	Z1/Z2	A/H	B/P	Z1/Z2	A/H	B/P	Z1/Z2	A/H	B/P	Z1/Z2	A/H	B/P	Z1/Z2	A/H	B/P	Z1/Z2	LHA	
45	135	20 42	22 12	49·1	20 03	21 24	48·8	19 23	20 36	48·6	18 43	19 49	48·3	18 03	19 02	48·1	17 23	18 15	47·8	225	315
46	134	21 05	21 51	48·1	20 25	21 04	47·8	19 44	20 16	47·6	19 04	19 29	47·3	18 23	18 43	47·1	17 42	17 57	46·8	226	314
47	133	21 27	21 30	47·1	20 46	20 43	46·8	20 05	19 56	46·6	19 24	19 10	46·3	18 42	18 24	46·1	18 00	17 39	45·8	227	313
48	132	21 49	21 07	46·1	21 07	20 21	45·8	20 25	19 35	45·6	19 43	18 50	45·3	19 01	18 04	45·1	18 18	17 20	44·8	228	312
49	131	22 10	20 45	45·1	21 28	19 59	44·8	20 45	19 14	44·6	20 02	18 29	44·3	19 19	17 45	44·0	18 36	17 01	43·8	229	311
50	130	22 31	20 22	44·1	21 48	19 37	43·8	21 05	18 52	43·5	20 21	18 08	43·3	19 37	17 24	43·0	18 53	16 41	42·8	230	310
51	129	22 52	19 58	43·1	22 08	19 14	42·8	21 24	18 30	42·5	20 40	17 47	42·3	19 55	17 04	42·0	19 10	16 21	41·8	231	309
52	128	23 12	19 34	42·1	22 28	18 51	41·8	21 43	18 08	41·5	20 58	17 25	41·2	20 13	16 43	41·0	19 27	16 01	40·8	232	308
53	127	23 32	19 09	41·0	22 47	18 27	40·7	22 01	17 45	40·5	21 15	17 03	40·2	20 30	16 21	40·0	19 44	15 41	39·7	233	307
54	126	23 52	18 45	40·0	23 06	18 03	39·7	22 19	17 21	39·4	21 33	16 40	39·2	20 46	16 00	39·0	20 00	15 20	38·7	234	306
55	125	24 11	18 19	39·0	23 24	17 38	38·7	22 37	16 58	38·4	21 50	16 17	38·2	21 03	15 38	37·9	20 15	14 58	37·7	235	305
56	124	24 29	17 54	37·9	23 42	17 13	37·6	22 54	16 34	37·4	22 07	15 54	37·1	21 19	15 15	36·9	20 31	14 37	36·7	236	304
57	123	24 48	17 27	36·9	23 59	16 48	36·6	23 11	16 09	36·3	22 23	15 31	36·1	21 34	14 53	35·8	20 46	14 15	35·6	237	303
58	122	25 05	17 01	35·8	24 17	16 22	35·5	23 28	15 44	35·3	22 39	15 07	35·0	21 49	14 30	34·8	21 00	13 53	34·6	238	302
59	121	25 23	16 34	34·8	24 33	15 56	34·5	23 44	15 19	34·2	22 54	14 42	34·0	22 04	14 06	33·8	21 14	13 30	33·5	239	301
60	120	25 40	16 06	33·7	24 50	15 29	33·4	23 59	14 53	33·2	23 09	14 18	32·9	22 19	13 42	32·7	21 28	13 07	32·5	240	300
61	119	25 56	15 38	32·6	25 05	15 03	32·4	24 15	14 27	32·1	23 24	13 53	31·9	22 33	13 18	31·7	21 42	12 44	31·5	241	299
62	118	26 12	15 10	31·5	25 21	14 35	31·3	24 29	14 01	31·1	23 38	13 27	30·8	22 46	12 54	30·6	21 55	12 21	30·4	242	298
63	117	26 27	14 41	30·5	25 36	14 08	30·2	24 44	13 34	30·0	23 52	13 01	29·8	22 59	12 29	29·5	22 07	11 57	29·3	243	297
64	116	26 42	14 12	29·4	25 50	13 39	29·1	24 57	13 07	28·9	24 05	12 35	28·7	23 12	12 04	28·5	22 19	11 33	28·3	244	296
65	115	26 57	13 43	28·3	26 04	13 11	28·1	25 11	12 40	27·8	24 18	12 09	27·6	23 25	11 39	27·4	22 31	11 09	27·2	245	295
66	114	27 11	13 13	27·2	26 17	12 42	27·0	25 24	12 12	26·8	24 30	11 43	26·6	23 36	11 13	26·4	22 43	10 44	26·2	246	294
67	113	27 24	12 43	26·1	26 30	12 13	25·9	25 36	11 44	25·7	24 42	11 16	25·5	23 48	10 47	25·3	22 54	10 20	25·1	247	293
68	112	27 37	12 12	25·0	26 43	11 44	24·8	25 48	11 16	24·6	24 54	10 48	24·4	23 59	10 21	24·2	23 04	9 55	24·0	248	292
69	111	27 50	11 41	23·9	26 55	11 14	23·7	26 00	10 47	23·5	25 05	10 21	23·3	24 09	9 55	23·1	23 14	9 29	23·0	249	291
70	110	28 01	11 10	22·8	27 06	10 44	22·6	26 11	10 18	22·4	25 15	9 53	22·2	24 20	9 28	22·0	23 24	9 04	21·9	250	290
71	109	28 13	10 39	21·7	27 17	10 14	21·5	26 21	9 49	21·3	25 25	9 25	21·0	24 30	9 01	21·0	23 33	8 38	20·8	251	289
72	108	28 24	10 07	20·6	27 27	9 43	20·4	26 31	9 20	20·2	25 35	8 57	20·0	24 38	8 34	19·9	23 42	8 12	19·7	252	288
73	107	28 34	9 35	19·4	27 37	9 12	19·3	26 41	8 50	19·1	25 44	8 28	18·9	24 47	8 07	18·8	23 50	7 46	18·6	253	287
74	106	28 44	9 03	18·3	27 47	8 41	18·2	26 50	8 20	18·0	25 52	8 00	17·8	24 55	7 39	17·7	23 58	7 19	17·6	254	286
75	105	28 53	8 30	17·2	27 55	8 10	17·0	26 58	7 50	16·9	26 01	7 31	16·7	25 03	7 12	16·6	24 06	6 53	16·5	255	285
76	104	29 01	7 57	16·1	28 04	7 38	15·9	27 06	7 20	15·8	26 08	7 02	15·6	25 10	6 44	15·5	24 13	6 26	15·4	256	284
77	103	29 09	7 24	14·9	28 11	7 06	14·8	27 13	6 49	14·7	26 15	6 32	14·5	25 17	6 16	14·4	24 19	5 59	14·3	257	283
78	102	29 17	6 51	13·8	28 18	6 34	13·7	27 20	6 19	13·5	26 22	6 03	13·4	25 23	5 47	13·3	24 25	5 32	13·2	258	282
79	101	29 24	6 17	12·7	28 25	6 02	12·5	27 27	5 48	12·4	26 28	5 33	12·3	25 29	5 19	12·2	24 31	5 05	12·1	259	281
80	100	29 30	5 44	11·5	28 31	5 30	11·4	27 32	5 17	11·3	26 33	5 03	11·2	25 35	4 50	11·1	24 36	4 38	11·0	260	280
81	99	29 36	5 10	10·4	28 37	4 57	10·3	27 38	4 45	10·2	26 38	4 33	10·1	25 39	4 22	10·0	24 40	4 10	9·9	261	279
82	98	29 41	4 36	9·2	28 41	4 25	9·1	27 42	4 14	9·0	26 43	4 03	9·0	25 44	3 53	8·9	24 44	3 43	8·8	262	278
83	97	29 45	4 01	8·1	28 46	3 52	8·0	27 46	3 42	7·9	26 47	3 33	7·8	25 48	3 24	7·8	24 48	3 15	7·7	263	277
84	96	29 49	3 27	6·9	28 50	3 19	6·9	27 50	3 11	6·8	26 50	3 03	6·7	25 51	2 55	6·7	24 51	2 47	6·6	264	276
85	95	29 52	2 53	5·8	28 53	2 46	5·7	27 53	2 39	5·7	26 53	2 33	5·6	25 54	2 26	5·6	24 54	2 20	5·5	265	275
86	94	29 55	2 18	4·6	28 55	2 13	4·6	27 56	2 07	4·5	26 56	2 02	4·5	25 56	1 57	4·4	24 56	1 52	4·4	266	274
87	93	29 57	1 44	3·5	28 57	1 40	3·4	27 57	1 36	3·4	26 58	1 32	3·4	25 58	1 28	3·3	24 58	1 24	3·3	267	273
88	92	29 59	1 09	2·3	28 59	1 06	2·3	27 59	1 04	2·3	26 59	1 01	2·2	25 59	0 59	2·2	24 59	0 56	2·2	268	272
89	91	30 00	0 35	1·2	29 00	0 33	1·1	28 00	0 32	1·1	27 00	0 31	1·1	26 00	0 29	1·1	25 00	0 28	1·1	269	271
90	90	30 00	0 00	0·0	29 00	0 00	0·0	28 00	0 00	0·0	27 00	0 00	0·0	26 00	0 00	0·0	25 00	0 00	0·0	270	270

N. Lat: for LHA > 180° ... Zn = Z
for LHA < 180° ... Zn = 360° − Z

S. Lat.: for LHA > 180° ... Zn = 180° − Z
for LHA < 180° ... Zn = 180° + Z

LATITUDE / A: 66° – 71°

SIGHT REDUCTION TABLE

B: (−) for 90° < LHA < 270°
Dec:(−) for Lat. contrary name

Z₁: same sign as B
Z₂: (−) for F > 90°

Lat./A LHA/F	F	66° A/H	66° B/P	66° Z₁/Z₂	67° A/H	67° B/P	67° Z₁/Z₂	68° A/H	68° B/P	68° Z₁/Z₂	69° A/H	69° B/P	69° Z₁/Z₂	70° A/H	70° B/P	70° Z₁/Z₂	71° A/H	71° B/P	71° Z₁/Z₂	Lat./A LHA	(LHA)
0	180	0 00	24 00	90·0	0 00	23 00	90·0	0 00	22 00	90·0	0 00	21 00	90·0	0 00	20 00	90·0	0 00	19 00	90·0	180	360
1	179	0 24	24 00	89·1	0 23	23 00	89·1	0 22	22 00	89·1	0 22	21 00	89·1	0 21	20 00	89·1	0 20	19 00	89·1	181	359
2	178	0 49	23 59	88·2	0 47	22 59	88·2	0 45	21 59	88·1	0 43	20 59	88·1	0 41	19 59	88·1	0 39	18 59	88·1	182	358
3	177	1 13	23 58	87·3	1 10	22 58	87·2	1 07	21 58	87·2	1 04	20 58	87·2	1 02	19 58	87·2	0 59	18 59	87·2	183	357
4	176	1 38	23 57	86·3	1 34	22 57	86·3	1 30	21 57	86·3	1 26	20 57	86·3	1 22	19 57	86·2	1 18	18 57	86·2	184	356
5	175	2 02	23 55	85·4	1 57	22 55	85·4	1 52	21 55	85·4	1 47	20 56	85·3	1 42	19 56	85·3	1 38	18 56	85·3	185	355
6	174	2 26	23 53	84·5	2 20	22 53	84·5	2 15	21 53	84·4	2 09	20 54	84·4	2 03	19 54	84·4	1 57	18 54	84·3	186	354
7	173	2 50	23 50	83·6	2 44	22 51	83·6	2 37	21 51	83·5	2 30	20 52	83·5	2 23	19 52	83·4	2 16	18 52	83·4	187	353
8	172	3 15	23 48	82·7	3 07	22 48	82·6	2 59	21 48	82·6	2 52	20 49	82·5	2 44	19 49	82·5	2 36	18 50	82·4	188	352
9	171	3 39	23 44	81·8	3 30	22 45	81·7	3 22	21 45	81·6	3 13	20 46	81·6	3 04	19 46	81·5	2 55	18 47	81·5	189	351
10	170	4 03	23 41	80·8	3 53	22 41	80·8	3 44	21 42	80·7	3 34	20 42	80·6	3 24	19 43	80·6	3 14	18 44	80·5	190	350
11	169	4 27	23 36	79·9	4 17	22 37	79·9	4 06	21 38	79·8	3 55	20 39	79·7	3 45	19 40	79·6	3 34	18 41	79·6	191	349
12	168	4 51	23 32	79·0	4 40	22 33	78·9	4 28	21 34	78·9	4 16	20 35	78·8	4 05	19 36	78·7	3 53	18 37	78·6	192	348
13	167	5 15	23 27	78·1	5 03	22 28	78·0	4 50	21 29	77·9	4 37	20 30	77·8	4 25	19 32	77·8	4 12	18 33	77·7	193	347
14	166	5 39	23 22	77·2	5 25	22 23	77·1	5 12	21 24	77·0	4 58	20 26	76·9	4 45	19 27	76·8	4 31	18 28	76·7	194	346
15	165	6 03	23 16	76·2	5 48	22 18	76·1	5 34	21 19	76·0	5 19	20 21	76·0	5 05	19 22	75·9	4 50	18 24	75·8	195	345
16	164	6 26	23 10	75·3	6 11	22 12	75·2	5 56	21 13	75·1	5 40	20 15	75·0	5 25	19 17	74·9	5 09	18 19	74·8	196	344
17	163	6 50	23 04	74·4	6 34	22 06	74·3	6 17	21 08	74·2	6 01	20 09	74·1	5 44	19 11	74·0	5 28	18 14	73·9	197	343
18	162	7 13	22 57	73·5	6 56	21 59	73·3	6 39	21 01	73·2	6 21	20 03	73·1	6 04	19 06	73·0	5 46	18 08	72·9	198	342
19	161	7 37	22 50	72·5	7 19	21 51	72·4	7 00	20 54	72·3	6 42	19 57	72·2	6 24	18 59	72·1	6 05	18 02	72·0	199	341
20	160	8 00	22 42	71·6	7 41	21 45	71·5	7 22	20 47	71·4	7 02	19 50	71·2	6 43	18 53	71·1	6 24	17 56	71·0	200	340
21	159	8 23	22 34	70·7	8 03	21 37	70·5	7 43	20 40	70·4	7 23	19 43	70·3	7 02	18 46	70·2	6 42	17 49	70·1	201	339
22	158	8 46	22 26	69·7	8 25	21 29	69·6	8 04	20 32	69·5	7 43	19 35	69·3	7 22	18 39	69·2	7 00	17 42	69·1	202	338
23	157	9 09	22 17	68·8	8 47	21 21	68·7	8 25	20 24	68·5	8 03	19 28	68·4	7 41	18 31	68·3	7 19	17 35	68·1	203	337
24	156	9 31	22 08	67·9	9 09	21 12	67·7	8 46	20 16	67·6	8 23	19 19	67·4	8 00	18 24	67·3	7 37	17 28	67·2	204	336
25	155	9 54	21 58	66·9	9 30	21 03	66·8	9 07	20 07	66·6	8 43	19 11	66·5	8 19	18 15	66·3	7 55	17 20	66·2	205	335
26	154	10 16	21 49	66·0	9 52	20 53	65·8	9 27	19 57	65·7	9 02	19 02	65·5	8 37	18 07	65·4	8 12	17 12	65·2	206	334
27	153	10 38	21 38	65·0	10 13	20 43	64·9	9 48	19 48	64·7	9 22	18 53	64·6	8 56	17 58	64·4	8 30	17 03	64·3	207	333
28	152	11 00	21 28	64·1	10 34	20 33	63·9	10 08	19 38	63·8	9 41	18 43	63·6	9 14	17 49	63·5	8 48	16 55	63·3	208	332
29	151	11 22	21 17	63·1	10 55	20 22	63·0	10 28	19 28	62·8	10 00	18 34	62·6	9 33	17 39	62·5	9 05	16 46	62·3	209	331
30	150	11 44	21 05	62·2	11 16	20 11	62·0	10 48	19 17	61·8	10 19	18 23	61·7	9 51	17 30	61·5	9 22	16 36	61·4	210	330
31	149	12 06	20 53	61·2	11 37	20 00	61·1	11 07	19 06	60·9	10 38	18 13	60·7	10 09	17 20	60·5	9 39	16 27	60·4	211	329
32	148	12 27	20 41	60·3	11 57	19 48	60·1	11 27	18 55	59·9	10 57	18 02	59·7	10 27	17 09	59·6	9 56	16 17	59·4	212	328
33	147	12 48	20 29	59·3	12 17	19 36	59·1	11 46	18 43	58·9	11 15	17 51	58·8	10 44	16 58	58·6	10 13	16 06	58·4	213	327
34	146	13 09	20 16	58·4	12 37	19 23	58·2	12 06	18 31	58·0	11 34	17 39	57·8	11 02	16 47	57·7	10 29	15 56	57·5	214	326
35	145	13 29	20 02	57·4	12 57	19 10	57·2	12 24	18 19	57·0	11 52	17 27	56·8	11 19	16 36	56·7	10 46	15 45	56·5	215	325
36	144	13 50	19 49	56·4	13 17	18 57	56·2	12 43	18 06	56·0	12 10	17 15	55·9	11 36	16 24	55·7	11 02	15 34	55·5	216	324
37	143	14 10	19 34	55·5	13 36	18 44	55·3	13 02	17 53	55·1	12 27	17 03	54·9	11 53	16 12	54·7	11 18	15 23	54·5	217	323
38	142	14 30	19 20	54·5	13 55	18 30	54·3	13 20	17 40	54·1	12 45	16 50	53·9	12 09	16 00	53·7	11 34	15 11	53·5	218	322
39	141	14 50	19 05	53·5	14 14	18 15	53·3	13 38	17 26	53·1	13 02	16 37	52·9	12 26	15 48	52·7	11 49	14 59	52·6	219	321
40	140	15 09	18 50	52·5	14 33	18 01	52·3	13 56	17 12	52·1	13 19	16 23	51·9	12 42	15 35	51·7	12 05	14 47	51·6	220	320
41	139	15 29	18 34	51·5	14 51	17 46	51·3	14 14	16 57	51·1	13 36	16 09	50·9	12 58	15 22	50·8	12 20	14 34	50·6	221	319
42	138	15 48	18 18	50·6	15 09	17 30	50·3	14 31	16 43	50·1	13 52	15 55	49·9	13 14	15 08	49·8	12 35	14 21	49·6	222	318
43	137	16 06	18 02	49·6	15 27	17 15	49·4	14 48	16 28	49·2	14 09	15 41	49·0	13 29	14 54	48·8	12 50	14 08	48·6	223	317
44	136	16 25	17 46	48·6	15 45	16 59	48·4	15 05	16 12	48·2	14 25	15 26	48·0	13 45	14 40	47·8	13 04	13 55	47·6	224	316
45	135	16 43	17 29	47·6	16 02	16 42	47·4	15 22	15 57	47·2	14 41	15 11	47·0	14 00	14 26	46·8	13 19	13 41	46·6	225	315

Lat./A LHA/F	A	66° A/H	66° B/P	66° Z_1/Z_2	67° A/H	67° B/P	67° Z_1/Z_2	68° A/H	68° B/P	68° Z_1/Z_2	69° A/H	69° B/P	69° Z_1/Z_2	70° A/H	70° B/P	70° Z_1/Z_2	71° A/H	71° B/P	71° Z_1/Z_2	LHA	LHA
45	135	16 43	17 29	47·6	16 02	16 42	47·4	15 22	15 57	47·2	14 41	15 11	47·0	14 00	14 26	46·8	13 19	13 41	46·6	225	315
46	134	17 01	17 11	46·6	16 19	16 26	46·4	15 38	15 41	46·2	14 56	14 56	46·0	14 15	14 11	45·8	13 33	13 27	45·6	226	314
47	133	17 18	16 53	45·6	16 36	16 09	45·4	15 54	15 24	45·2	15 12	14 40	45·0	14 29	13 56	44·8	13 46	13 13	44·6	227	313
48	132	17 36	16 35	44·6	16 53	15 51	44·4	16 10	15 08	44·2	15 27	14 24	44·0	14 43	13 41	43·8	14 00	12 58	43·6	228	312
49	131	17 53	16 17	43·6	17 09	15 34	43·4	16 25	14 51	43·2	15 42	14 08	43·0	14 58	13 26	42·8	14 13	12 44	42·6	229	311
50	130	18 09	15 58	42·6	17 25	15 16	42·4	16 41	14 33	42·1	15 56	13 52	41·9	15 11	13 10	41·8	14 27	12 29	41·6	230	310
51	129	18 26	15 39	41·6	17 41	14 57	41·3	16 56	14 16	41·1	16 10	13 35	40·9	15 25	12 54	40·8	14 39	12 14	40·6	231	309
52	128	18 42	15 20	40·5	17 56	14 37	40·3	17 10	13 58	40·1	16 24	13 18	39·9	15 38	12 38	39·7	14 52	11 58	39·6	232	308
53	127	18 57	15 00	39·5	18 11	14 20	39·3	17 24	13 40	39·1	16 38	13 00	38·9	15 51	12 21	38·7	15 04	11 42	38·6	233	307
54	126	19 13	14 40	38·5	18 26	14 01	38·3	17 39	13 22	38·1	16 51	12 43	37·9	16 04	12 05	37·7	15 16	11 26	37·5	234	306
55	125	19 28	14 20	37·5	18 40	13 41	37·3	17 52	13 03	37·1	17 04	12 25	36·9	16 16	11 48	36·7	15 28	11 10	36·5	235	305
56	124	19 42	13 59	36·4	18 54	13 21	36·2	18 06	12 44	36·0	17 17	12 07	35·8	16 28	11 30	35·7	15 40	10 54	35·5	236	304
57	123	19 57	13 38	35·4	19 08	13 01	35·2	18 19	12 25	35·0	17 29	11 49	34·8	16 40	11 13	34·6	15 51	10 37	34·5	237	303
58	122	20 11	13 17	34·4	19 21	12 41	34·2	18 31	12 05	34·0	17 42	11 30	33·8	16 52	10 55	33·6	16 02	10 20	33·5	238	302
59	121	20 24	12 55	33·3	19 34	12 20	33·1	18 44	11 45	32·9	17 53	11 11	32·7	17 03	10 37	32·6	16 12	10 03	32·4	239	301
60	120	20 37	12 33	32·3	19 47	11 59	32·1	18 56	11 25	31·9	18 05	10 52	31·7	17 14	10 19	31·6	16 23	9 46	31·4	240	300
61	119	20 50	12 11	31·2	19 59	11 38	31·1	19 08	11 05	30·9	18 16	10 33	30·7	17 24	10 00	30·5	16 33	9 29	30·4	241	299
62	118	21 03	11 48	30·2	20 11	11 16	30·0	19 19	10 44	29·8	18 27	10 13	29·7	17 35	9 42	29·5	16 42	9 11	29·4	242	298
63	117	21 15	11 26	29·2	20 22	10 54	29·0	19 30	10 24	28·8	18 37	9 53	28·6	17 45	9 23	28·5	16 52	8 53	28·3	243	297
64	116	21 27	11 03	28·1	20 34	10 32	27·9	19 41	10 03	27·7	18 47	9 33	27·6	17 54	9 04	27·4	17 01	8 35	27·3	244	296
65	115	21 38	10 39	27·0	20 44	10 10	26·9	19 51	9 41	26·7	18 57	9 13	26·5	18 03	8 45	26·4	17 10	8 17	26·3	245	295
66	114	21 49	10 16	26·0	20 55	9 48	25·8	20 01	9 20	25·7	19 07	8 52	25·5	18 12	8 25	25·4	17 18	7 58	25·2	246	294
67	113	21 59	9 52	24·9	21 05	9 25	24·8	20 10	8 58	24·6	19 16	8 32	24·5	18 21	8 06	24·3	17 26	7 40	24·2	247	293
68	112	22 09	9 28	23·9	21 14	9 02	23·7	20 19	8 36	23·5	19 24	8 11	23·4	18 29	7 46	23·3	17 34	7 21	23·1	248	292
69	111	22 19	9 04	22·8	21 24	8 39	22·6	20 28	8 14	22·5	19 33	7 50	22·4	18 37	7 26	22·2	17 42	7 02	22·1	249	291
70	110	22 28	8 39	21·7	21 32	8 16	21·6	20 37	7 52	21·4	19 41	7 29	21·3	18 45	7 06	21·2	17 49	6 43	21·1	250	290
71	109	22 37	8 15	20·7	21 41	7 52	20·5	20 45	7 30	20·4	19 48	7 07	20·2	18 52	6 45	20·1	17 56	6 24	20·0	251	289
72	108	22 45	7 50	19·6	21 49	7 28	19·4	20 52	7 07	19·3	19 56	6 46	19·2	18 59	6 25	19·1	18 02	6 04	19·0	252	288
73	107	22 53	7 25	18·5	21 56	7 04	18·4	21 00	6 44	18·2	20 03	6 24	18·1	19 05	6 04	18·0	18 08	5 45	17·9	253	287
74	106	23 01	7 00	17·4	22 04	6 40	17·3	21 06	6 21	17·2	20 09	6 02	17·1	19 12	5 44	17·0	18 14	5 25	16·9	254	286
75	105	23 08	6 34	16·3	22 10	6 16	16·2	21 13	5 58	16·1	20 15	5 40	16·0	19 17	5 23	15·9	18 20	5 06	15·8	255	285
76	104	23 15	6 09	15·3	22 17	5 52	15·2	21 19	5 35	15·1	20 21	5 18	15·0	19 23	5 02	14·9	18 25	4 46	14·8	256	284
77	103	23 21	5 43	14·2	22 23	5 27	14·1	21 24	5 12	14·0	20 26	4 56	13·9	19 28	4 41	13·8	18 30	4 26	13·7	257	283
78	102	23 27	5 17	13·1	22 28	5 03	13·0	21 30	4 48	12·9	20 31	4 34	12·8	19 33	4 20	12·7	18 34	4 06	12·7	258	282
79	101	23 32	4 51	12·0	22 33	4 38	11·9	21 35	4 24	11·8	20 36	4 11	11·8	19 37	3 58	11·7	18 38	3 46	11·6	259	281
80	100	23 37	4 25	10·9	22 38	4 13	10·8	21 39	4 01	10·8	20 40	3 49	10·7	19 41	3 37	10·6	18 42	3 25	10·6	260	280
81	99	23 41	3 59	9·8	22 42	3 48	9·8	21 43	3 37	9·7	20 44	3 26	9·6	19 45	3 16	9·6	18 45	3 05	9·5	261	279
82	98	23 45	3 33	8·7	22 46	3 23	8·7	21 46	3 13	8·6	20 47	3 03	8·6	19 48	2 54	8·5	18 48	2 45	8·5	262	278
83	97	23 49	3 06	7·7	22 49	2 58	7·6	21 50	2 49	7·5	20 50	2 41	7·5	19 51	2 32	7·4	18 51	2 24	7·4	263	277
84	96	23 52	2 40	6·6	22 52	2 32	6·5	21 52	2 25	6·5	20 53	2 18	6·4	19 53	2 11	6·4	18 54	2 04	6·3	264	276
85	95	23 54	2 13	5·5	22 54	2 07	5·4	21 55	2 01	5·4	20 55	1 55	5·4	19 55	1 49	5·3	18 55	1 43	5·3	265	275
86	94	23 56	1 47	4·4	22 56	1 42	4·3	21 57	1 37	4·3	20 57	1 32	4·3	19 57	1 27	4·3	18 57	1 23	4·2	266	274
87	93	23 58	1 20	3·3	22 58	1 16	3·3	21 58	1 13	3·2	20 58	1 09	3·2	19 58	1 05	3·2	18 58	1 02	3·2	267	273
88	92	23 59	0 53	2·2	22 59	0 51	2·2	21 59	0 48	2·2	20 59	0 46	2·1	19 59	0 44	2·1	18 59	0 41	2·1	268	272
89	91	24 00	0 27	1·1	23 00	0 25	1·1	22 00	0 24	1·1	21 00	0 23	1·1	20 00	0 22	1·1	19 00	0 21	1·1	269	271
90	90	24 00	0 00	0·0	23 00	0 00	0·0	22 00	0 00	0·0	21 00	0 00	0·0	20 00	0 00	0·0	19 00	0 00	0·0	270	270

N. Lat.: for LHA > 180°... $Z_n = Z$, for LHA < 180°... $Z_n = 360° - Z$

S. Lat.: for LHA > 180°... $Z_n = 180° - Z$, for LHA < 180°... $Z_n = 180° + Z$

SIGHT REDUCTION TABLE

B: (−) for 90° < LHA < 270°
Dec:(−) for Lat. contrary name

Z₁: same sign as B
Z₂:(−) for F > 90°

Lat./A LHA	F	72° A/H	72° B/P	72° Z₁/Z₂	73° A/H	73° B/P	73° Z₁/Z₂	74° A/H	74° B/P	74° Z₁/Z₂	75° A/H	75° B/P	75° Z₁/Z₂	76° A/H	76° B/P	76° Z₁/Z₂	77° A/H	77° B/P	77° Z₁/Z₂	Lat./A LHA	A
0	180	0 00	18 00	90.0	0 00	17 00	90.0	0 00	16 00	90.0	0 00	15 00	90.0	0 00	14 00	90.0	0 00	13 00	90.0	180	360
1	179	0 19	18 00	89.0	0 18	17 00	89.0	0 17	16 00	89.0	0 16	15 00	89.0	0 15	14 00	89.0	0 13	13 00	89.0	181	359
2	178	0 37	17 59	88.1	0 35	16 59	88.1	0 33	15 59	88.1	0 31	14 59	88.1	0 29	13 59	88.1	0 27	13 00	88.1	182	358
3	177	0 56	17 59	87.1	0 53	16 59	87.1	0 50	15 59	87.1	0 47	14 59	87.1	0 44	13 59	87.1	0 40	12 59	87.1	183	357
4	176	1 14	17 58	86.2	1 10	16 58	86.2	1 06	15 59	86.2	1 02	14 58	86.1	0 58	13 58	86.1	0 54	12 58	86.1	184	356
5	175	1 33	17 56	85.2	1 28	16 56	85.2	1 23	15 57	85.2	1 18	14 57	85.2	1 12	13 57	85.1	1 07	12 57	85.1	185	355
6	174	1 51	17 54	84.3	1 45	16 55	84.3	1 39	15 55	84.2	1 33	14 55	84.2	1 27	13 56	84.2	1 21	12 56	84.2	186	354
7	173	2 09	17 52	83.3	2 03	16 53	83.3	1 56	15 53	83.3	1 48	14 54	83.2	1 41	13 54	83.2	1 34	12 54	83.2	187	353
8	172	2 28	17 50	82.4	2 20	16 51	82.3	2 12	15 51	82.3	2 04	14 52	82.3	1 56	13 52	82.2	1 48	12 53	82.2	188	352
9	171	2 46	17 48	81.4	2 37	16 48	81.4	2 28	15 49	81.3	2 19	14 49	81.3	2 10	13 50	81.3	2 01	12 51	81.2	189	351
10	170	3 05	17 45	80.5	2 55	16 45	80.4	2 45	15 46	80.4	2 35	14 47	80.3	2 24	13 48	80.3	2 14	12 49	80.3	190	350
11	169	3 23	17 41	79.5	3 12	16 42	79.5	3 01	15 43	79.4	2 50	14 44	79.4	2 39	13 45	79.3	2 28	12 46	79.3	191	349
12	168	3 41	17 38	78.6	3 29	16 39	78.5	3 17	15 40	78.5	3 05	14 41	78.4	2 53	13 42	78.3	2 41	12 44	78.3	192	348
13	167	3 59	17 34	77.6	3 46	16 35	77.5	3 33	15 37	77.5	3 20	14 38	77.4	3 07	13 39	77.4	2 54	12 41	77.3	193	347
14	166	4 17	17 30	76.7	4 03	16 31	76.6	3 49	15 33	76.5	3 35	14 34	76.5	3 21	13 36	76.4	3 07	12 38	76.3	194	346
15	165	4 35	17 25	75.7	4 20	16 27	75.6	4 05	15 29	75.6	3 50	14 31	75.5	3 35	13 32	75.4	3 20	12 34	75.4	195	345
16	164	4 53	17 21	74.7	4 37	16 23	74.7	4 21	15 25	74.6	4 05	14 27	74.5	3 49	13 29	74.5	3 33	12 31	74.4	196	344
17	163	5 11	17 16	73.8	4 54	16 18	73.7	4 37	15 20	73.6	4 20	14 22	73.5	4 03	13 25	73.5	3 46	12 27	73.4	197	343
18	162	5 29	17 10	72.8	5 11	16 13	72.7	4 53	15 15	72.7	4 35	14 18	72.6	4 17	13 20	72.5	3 59	12 23	72.4	198	342
19	161	5 46	17 05	71.9	5 28	16 07	71.8	5 09	15 10	71.7	4 50	14 13	71.6	4 31	13 16	71.5	4 12	12 19	71.5	199	341
20	160	6 04	16 59	70.9	5 44	16 02	70.8	5 25	15 05	70.7	5 05	14 08	70.6	4 45	13 11	70.5	4 25	12 14	70.5	200	340
21	159	6 21	16 52	69.9	6 01	15 56	69.8	5 40	14 59	69.7	5 19	14 03	69.7	4 58	13 06	69.6	4 37	12 10	69.5	201	339
22	158	6 39	16 46	69.0	6 17	15 50	68.9	5 56	14 53	68.8	5 34	13 57	68.7	5 12	13 01	68.6	4 50	12 05	68.5	202	338
23	157	6 56	16 39	68.0	6 34	15 43	67.9	6 11	14 47	67.8	5 48	13 51	67.7	5 25	12 56	67.6	5 03	12 00	67.5	203	337
24	156	7 13	16 32	67.1	6 50	15 36	66.9	6 26	14 41	66.8	6 03	13 45	66.7	5 39	12 50	66.6	5 15	11 55	66.5	204	336
25	155	7 30	16 25	66.1	7 06	15 29	66.0	6 41	14 34	65.9	6 17	13 39	65.8	5 52	12 44	65.7	5 27	11 49	65.6	205	335
26	154	7 47	16 17	65.1	7 22	15 22	65.0	6 56	14 27	64.9	6 31	13 32	64.8	6 05	12 38	64.7	5 40	11 43	64.6	206	334
27	153	8 04	16 09	64.1	7 38	15 14	64.0	7 11	14 20	63.9	6 45	13 26	63.8	6 18	12 32	63.7	5 52	11 37	63.6	207	333
28	152	8 20	16 00	63.2	7 53	15 06	63.0	7 26	14 12	62.9	6 59	13 19	62.8	6 31	12 25	62.7	6 04	11 31	62.6	208	332
29	151	8 37	15 52	62.2	8 09	14 58	62.1	7 41	14 05	61.9	7 13	13 11	61.8	6 44	12 18	61.7	6 16	11 25	61.6	209	331
30	150	8 53	15 43	61.2	8 24	14 50	61.1	7 55	13 57	61.0	7 26	13 04	60.9	6 57	12 11	60.7	6 27	11 18	60.6	210	330
31	149	9 09	15 34	60.3	8 40	14 41	60.1	8 10	13 49	60.0	7 40	12 56	59.9	7 09	12 04	59.8	6 39	11 12	59.7	211	329
32	148	9 25	15 24	59.3	8 55	14 32	59.1	8 24	13 40	59.0	7 53	12 48	58.9	7 22	11 56	58.8	6 51	11 05	58.7	212	328
33	147	9 41	15 15	58.3	9 10	14 23	58.2	8 38	13 31	58.0	8 06	12 40	57.9	7 34	11 49	57.8	7 02	10 57	57.7	213	327
34	146	9 57	15 05	57.3	9 25	14 13	57.2	8 52	13 22	57.0	8 19	12 31	56.9	7 46	11 41	56.8	7 14	10 50	56.7	214	326
35	145	10 13	14 54	56.3	9 39	14 04	56.2	9 06	13 13	56.1	8 32	12 23	55.9	7 59	11 33	55.8	7 25	10 43	55.7	215	325
36	144	10 28	14 44	55.4	9 54	13 54	55.2	9 19	13 04	55.1	8 45	12 14	54.9	8 11	11 24	54.8	7 36	10 35	54.7	216	324
37	143	10 43	14 33	54.4	10 08	13 43	54.2	9 33	12 54	54.1	8 58	12 05	53.9	8 22	11 16	53.8	7 47	10 27	53.7	217	323
38	142	10 58	14 22	53.4	10 22	13 33	53.2	9 46	12 44	53.1	9 10	11 55	53.0	8 34	11 07	52.8	7 58	10 19	52.7	218	322
39	141	11 13	14 10	52.4	10 36	13 22	52.2	9 59	12 34	52.1	9 22	11 46	52.0	8 45	10 58	51.8	8 08	10 10	51.7	219	321
40	140	11 27	13 59	51.4	10 50	13 11	51.3	10 12	12 23	51.1	9 35	11 36	51.0	8 57	10 49	50.8	8 19	10 02	50.7	220	320
41	139	11 42	13 47	50.4	11 04	13 00	50.3	10 25	12 13	50.1	9 47	11 26	50.0	9 08	10 39	49.9	8 29	9 53	49.7	221	319
42	138	11 56	13 34	49.4	11 17	12 48	49.3	10 38	12 02	49.1	9 58	11 16	49.0	9 19	10 30	48.9	8 39	9 44	48.7	222	318
43	137	12 10	13 22	48.4	11 30	12 36	48.3	10 50	11 51	48.1	10 10	11 05	48.0	9 30	10 20	47.9	8 49	9 35	47.7	223	317
44	136	12 24	13 09	47.4	11 43	12 24	47.3	11 02	11 39	47.1	10 21	10 55	47.0	9 40	10 10	46.9	8 59	9 26	46.7	224	316
45	135	12 37	12 56	46.4	11 56	12 12	46.3	11 14	11 28	46.1	10 33	10 44	46.0	9 51	10 00	45.9	9 09	9 16	45.7	225	315

Latitude columns 77°–72°. Left index (top labels): ° (315→270), LHA (225→270). Same columns at bottom are labelled LHA/F (135→90) and (45→90).

° (315)	LHA (225)	77° A/H	77° B/P	77° Z_1/Z_2	76° A/H	76° B/P	76° Z_1/Z_2	75° A/H	75° B/P	75° Z_1/Z_2	74° A/H	74° B/P	74° Z_1/Z_2	73° A/H	73° B/P	73° Z_1/Z_2	72° A/H	72° B/P	72° Z_1/Z_2	LHA/F (135)	(45)
315	225	9 09	9 16	45·7	9 51	10 00	45·9	10 33	10 44	46·0	11 14	11 28	46·1	11 56	12 12	46·3	12 37	12 56	46·4	135	45
314	226	9 19	9 07	44·7	10 01	9 50	44·9	10 44	10 33	45·0	11 26	11 16	45·1	12 08	11 59	45·3	12 51	12 43	45·4	134	46
313	227	9 28	8 57	43·7	10 11	9 39	43·9	10 55	10 21	44·0	11 38	11 04	44·1	12 21	11 47	44·3	13 04	12 30	44·4	133	47
312	228	9 37	8 47	42·7	10 21	9 28	42·9	11 05	10 10	43·0	11 49	10 52	43·1	12 33	11 34	43·3	13 17	12 16	43·4	132	48
311	229	9 46	8 37	41·7	10 31	9 17	41·9	11 16	9 58	42·0	12 00	10 39	42·1	12 45	11 21	42·3	13 29	12 02	42·4	131	49
310	230	9 55	8 26	40·7	10 41	9 06	40·9	11 26	9 46	41·0	12 11	10 27	41·1	12 57	11 07	41·3	13 42	11 48	41·4	130	50
309	231	10 04	8 16	39·7	10 50	8 55	39·8	11 36	9 34	40·0	12 22	10 14	40·1	13 08	10 53	40·3	13 54	11 33	40·4	129	51
308	232	10 13	8 05	38·7	10 59	8 44	38·8	11 46	9 21	39·0	12 33	10 01	39·1	13 19	10 40	39·2	14 06	11 19	39·4	128	52
307	233	10 21	7 55	37·7	11 08	8 32	37·8	11 56	9 10	38·0	12 43	9 47	38·1	13 30	10 26	38·2	14 17	11 04	38·4	127	53
306	234	10 29	7 44	36·7	11 17	8 20	36·8	12 05	8 57	36·9	12 53	9 34	37·1	13 41	10 11	37·2	14 29	10 49	37·4	126	54
305	235	10 37	7 33	35·7	11 26	8 08	35·8	12 14	8 44	35·9	13 03	9 20	36·1	13 51	9 57	36·2	14 40	10 33	36·4	125	55
304	236	10 45	7 21	34·7	11 34	7 56	34·8	12 23	8 31	34·9	13 13	9 07	35·1	14 02	9 42	35·2	14 51	10 18	35·3	124	56
303	237	10 52	7 10	33·7	11 42	7 44	33·8	12 32	8 18	33·9	13 22	8 53	34·0	14 12	9 27	34·2	15 01	10 02	34·3	123	57
302	238	11 00	6 58	32·7	11 50	7 32	32·8	12 41	8 05	32·9	13 31	8 38	33·0	14 21	9 12	33·2	15 12	9 46	33·3	122	58
301	239	11 07	6 47	31·7	11 58	7 19	31·8	12 49	7 51	31·9	13 40	8 24	32·0	14 31	8 57	32·1	15 22	9 30	32·3	121	59
300	240	11 14	6 35	30·6	12 06	7 06	30·8	12 57	7 38	30·9	13 49	8 10	31·0	14 40	8 41	31·1	15 31	9 14	31·3	120	60
299	241	11 21	6 23	29·6	12 13	6 54	29·7	13 05	7 24	29·8	13 57	7 55	30·0	14 49	8 26	30·1	15 41	8 57	30·2	119	61
298	242	11 27	6 11	28·6	12 20	6 41	28·7	13 13	7 10	28·8	14 05	7 40	28·9	14 58	8 10	29·1	15 50	8 40	29·2	118	62
297	243	11 34	5 59	27·6	12 27	6 27	27·7	13 20	6 56	27·8	14 13	7 25	27·9	15 06	7 54	28·0	15 59	8 23	28·2	117	63
296	244	11 40	5 47	26·6	12 34	6 14	26·7	13 27	6 42	26·8	14 21	7 10	26·9	15 14	7 38	27·0	16 08	8 06	27·2	116	64
295	245	11 46	5 34	25·6	12 40	6 01	25·7	13 34	6 28	25·8	14 28	6 55	25·9	15 23	7 22	26·0	16 16	7 49	26·2	115	65
294	246	11 52	5 22	24·6	12 46	5 47	24·6	13 41	6 13	24·7	14 35	6 39	24·9	15 29	7 05	25·0	16 24	7 32	25·1	114	66
293	247	11 57	5 09	23·5	12 52	5 34	23·6	13 47	5 59	23·7	14 42	6 24	23·8	15 37	6 49	23·9	16 32	7 14	24·1	113	67
292	248	12 02	4 57	22·5	12 58	5 20	22·6	13 53	5 44	22·7	14 48	6 08	22·8	15 44	6 32	22·9	16 39	6 56	23·0	112	68
291	249	12 07	4 44	21·5	13 03	5 06	21·6	13 59	5 29	21·7	14 55	5 52	21·8	15 50	6 15	21·9	16 46	6 38	22·0	111	69
290	250	12 12	4 31	20·5	13 08	4 52	20·6	14 05	5 14	20·6	15 01	5 36	20·6	15 57	5 58	20·8	16 53	6 20	20·9	110	70
289	251	12 17	4 18	19·5	13 13	4 38	19·5	14 10	4 59	19·6	15 06	5 20	19·7	16 03	5 41	19·8	16 59	6 02	19·9	109	71
288	252	12 21	4 05	18·4	13 18	4 24	18·5	14 15	4 44	18·6	15 12	5 04	18·7	16 09	5 24	18·8	17 05	5 44	18·9	108	72
287	253	12 25	3 52	17·4	13 23	4 10	17·5	14 20	4 29	17·6	15 17	4 48	17·6	16 14	5 06	17·7	17 11	5 26	17·8	107	73
286	254	12 29	3 38	16·4	13 27	3 56	16·5	14 24	4 13	16·5	15 22	4 31	16·6	16 19	4 49	16·7	17 17	5 07	16·8	106	74
285	255	12 33	3 25	15·4	13 31	3 42	15·4	14 29	3 58	15·5	15 26	4 15	15·6	16 24	4 31	15·7	17 22	4 48	15·7	105	75
284	256	12 36	3 12	14·4	13 35	3 27	14·4	14 33	3 43	14·5	15 31	3 58	14·5	16 29	4 14	14·6	17 27	4 30	14·7	104	76
283	257	12 40	2 58	13·3	13 38	3 13	13·4	14 36	3 27	13·4	15 35	3 41	13·5	16 33	3 56	13·6	17 31	4 11	13·6	103	77
282	258	12 43	2 45	12·3	13 41	2 58	12·4	14 40	3 11	12·4	15 38	3 25	12·5	16 37	3 38	12·5	17 36	3 52	12·6	102	78
281	259	12 45	2 31	11·3	13 44	2 43	11·3	14 43	2 56	11·4	15 42	3 08	11·4	16 41	3 20	11·5	17 39	3 33	11·6	101	79
280	260	12 48	2 18	10·3	13 47	2 29	10·3	14 46	2 40	10·3	15 45	2 51	10·4	16 44	3 02	10·4	17 43	3 14	10·5	100	80
279	261	12 50	2 04	9·2	13 49	2 14	9·3	14 49	2 24	9·3	15 48	2 34	9·4	16 47	2 44	9·4	17 46	2 55	9·5	99	81
278	262	12 52	1 50	8·2	13 52	1 59	8·2	14 51	2 08	8·3	15 50	2 17	8·3	16 50	2 26	8·4	17 49	2 35	8·4	98	82
277	263	12 54	1 37	7·2	13 54	1 44	7·2	14 53	1 52	7·2	15 53	2 00	7·3	16 52	2 08	7·3	17 52	2 16	7·4	97	83
276	264	12 56	1 23	6·2	13 55	1 30	6·2	14 55	1 36	6·2	15 55	1 43	6·2	16 54	1 50	6·3	17 54	1 57	6·3	96	84
275	265	12 57	1 09	5·1	13 57	1 15	5·2	14 56	1 20	5·2	15 56	1 26	5·2	16 56	1 32	5·2	17 56	1 37	5·3	95	85
274	266	12 58	0 55	4·1	13 58	1 00	4·1	14 58	1 04	4·1	15 58	1 09	4·2	16 57	1 13	4·2	17 57	1 18	4·2	94	86
273	267	12 59	0 42	3·1	13 59	0 45	3·1	14 59	0 48	3·1	15 59	0 52	3·1	16 59	0 55	3·1	17 58	0 58	3·2	93	87
272	268	13 00	0 28	2·1	13 59	0 30	2·1	14 59	0 32	2·1	15 59	0 34	2·1	16 59	0 37	2·1	17 59	0 39	2·1	92	88
271	269	13 00	0 14	1·0	14 00	0 15	1·0	15 00	0 16	1·0	16 00	0 17	1·0	17 00	0 18	1·0	18 00	0 19	1·1	91	89
270	270	13 00	0 00	0·0	14 00	0 00	0·0	15 00	0 00	0·0	16 00	0 00	0·0	17 00	0 00	0·0	18 00	0 00	0·0	90	90

N. Lat.: for LHA > 180° ... $Z_n = Z$
for LHA < 180° ... $Z_n = 360° − Z$

S. Lat.: for LHA > 180° ... $Z_n = 180° − Z$
for LHA < 180° ... $Z_n = 180° + Z$

SIGHT REDUCTION TABLE

B: (−) for 90° < LHA < 270°
Dec:(−) for Lat. contrary name

Z₁: same sign as B → Z_1: same sign as B
Z₂: (−) for F > 90° → Z_2: (−) for F > 90°

Lat./A LHA	F	78° A/H	78° B/P	78° Z_1/Z_2	79° A/H	79° B/P	79° Z_1/Z_2	80° A/H	80° B/P	80° Z_1/Z_2	81° A/H	81° B/P	81° Z_1/Z_2	82° A/H	82° B/P	82° Z_1/Z_2	83° A/H	83° B/P	83° Z_1/Z_2	Lat./A A	LHA
0	180	0 00	12 00	90.0	0 00	11 00	90.0	0 00	10 00	90.0	0 00	9 00	90.0	0 00	8 00	90.0	0 00	7 00	90.0	360	180
1	179	0 12	12 00	89.0	0 11	11 00	89.0	0 10	10 00	89.0	0 09	9 00	89.0	0 08	8 00	89.0	0 07	7 00	89.0	359	181
2	178	0 25	11 59	88.0	0 23	11 00	88.0	0 21	10 00	88.0	0 19	9 00	88.0	0 17	8 00	88.0	0 15	7 00	88.0	358	182
3	177	0 37	11 59	87.1	0 34	10 59	87.1	0 31	9 59	87.0	0 28	8 59	87.0	0 25	7 59	87.0	0 22	6 59	87.0	357	183
4	176	0 50	11 58	86.1	0 46	10 58	86.1	0 42	9 59	86.1	0 38	8 59	86.0	0 33	7 59	86.0	0 29	6 59	86.0	356	184
5	175	1 02	11 57	85.1	0 57	10 58	85.1	0 52	9 58	85.1	0 47	8 58	85.1	0 42	7 58	85.0	0 37	6 58	85.0	355	185
6	174	1 15	11 56	84.1	1 09	10 56	84.1	1 02	9 57	84.1	0 56	8 57	84.1	0 50	7 57	84.1	0 44	6 58	84.0	354	186
7	173	1 27	11 55	83.1	1 20	10 55	83.1	1 13	9 56	83.1	1 06	8 56	83.1	0 58	7 56	83.1	0 51	6 57	83.1	353	187
8	172	1 39	11 53	82.2	1 31	10 54	82.1	1 23	9 54	82.1	1 15	8 55	82.1	1 07	7 55	82.1	0 58	6 56	82.1	352	188
9	171	1 52	11 51	81.2	1 43	10 52	81.2	1 33	9 53	81.1	1 24	8 53	81.1	1 15	7 54	81.1	1 06	6 55	81.1	351	189
10	170	2 04	11 49	80.2	1 54	10 50	80.2	1 44	9 51	80.1	1 33	8 52	80.1	1 23	7 53	80.1	1 13	6 54	80.1	350	190
11	169	2 16	11 47	79.2	2 05	10 48	79.2	1 54	9 49	79.2	1 43	8 50	79.1	1 31	7 51	79.1	1 20	6 52	79.1	349	191
12	168	2 29	11 45	78.3	2 16	10 46	78.2	2 04	9 47	78.2	1 52	8 48	78.1	1 39	7 50	78.1	1 27	6 51	78.1	348	192
13	167	2 41	11 42	77.3	2 28	10 43	77.2	2 14	9 45	77.2	2 01	8 46	77.2	1 48	7 48	77.1	1 34	6 49	77.1	347	193
14	166	2 53	11 39	76.3	2 39	10 41	76.2	2 24	9 43	76.2	2 10	8 44	76.2	1 56	7 46	76.1	1 41	6 48	76.1	346	194
15	165	3 05	11 36	75.3	2 50	10 38	75.3	2 35	9 40	75.2	2 19	8 42	75.2	2 04	7 44	75.1	1 48	6 46	75.1	345	195
16	164	3 17	11 33	74.3	3 01	10 35	74.3	2 45	9 37	74.2	2 28	8 39	74.2	2 12	7 42	74.1	1 56	6 44	74.1	344	196
17	163	3 29	11 29	73.4	3 12	10 32	73.3	2 55	9 34	73.3	2 37	8 37	73.2	2 20	7 39	73.2	2 03	6 42	73.1	343	197
18	162	3 41	11 26	72.4	3 23	10 28	72.3	3 05	9 31	72.3	2 46	8 34	72.2	2 28	7 37	72.2	2 09	6 40	72.1	342	198
19	161	3 53	11 22	71.4	3 34	10 25	71.3	3 14	9 28	71.3	2 55	8 31	71.2	2 36	7 34	71.2	2 16	6 37	71.1	341	199
20	160	4 05	11 18	70.4	3 45	10 21	70.3	3 24	9 24	70.3	3 04	8 28	70.3	2 44	7 31	70.2	2 23	6 35	70.1	340	200
21	159	4 16	11 13	69.4	3 55	10 17	69.4	3 34	9 21	69.3	3 13	8 25	69.3	2 52	7 28	69.2	2 30	6 32	69.1	339	201
22	158	4 28	11 09	68.4	4 06	10 13	68.4	3 44	9 17	68.3	3 22	8 21	68.3	2 59	7 25	68.2	2 37	6 30	68.1	338	202
23	157	4 40	11 04	67.5	4 17	10 09	67.4	3 53	9 13	67.3	3 30	8 18	67.3	3 07	7 22	67.2	2 44	6 27	67.2	337	203
24	156	4 51	10 59	66.5	4 27	10 04	66.4	4 03	9 09	66.3	3 39	8 14	66.3	3 15	7 19	66.2	2 50	6 24	66.2	336	204
25	155	5 02	10 54	65.5	4 38	9 59	65.4	4 13	9 05	65.3	3 47	8 10	65.3	3 22	7 16	65.2	2 57	6 21	65.2	335	205
26	154	5 14	10 49	64.5	4 48	9 55	64.4	4 22	9 00	64.3	3 56	8 06	64.3	3 30	7 12	64.2	3 04	6 18	64.2	334	206
27	153	5 25	10 43	63.5	4 58	9 50	63.4	4 31	8 56	63.4	4 04	8 02	63.3	3 37	7 08	63.2	3 10	6 15	63.2	333	207
28	152	5 36	10 38	62.5	5 08	9 44	62.4	4 41	8 51	62.4	4 13	7 58	62.3	3 45	7 04	62.2	3 17	6 11	62.2	332	208
29	151	5 47	10 32	61.5	5 18	9 39	61.4	4 50	8 46	61.4	4 21	7 53	61.3	3 52	7 00	61.2	3 23	6 08	61.2	331	209
30	150	5 58	10 26	60.5	5 28	9 33	60.5	4 59	8 41	60.4	4 29	7 49	60.3	3 59	6 56	60.2	3 30	6 04	60.2	330	210
31	149	6 09	10 20	59.6	5 38	9 28	59.5	5 08	8 36	59.4	4 37	7 44	59.3	4 07	6 52	59.2	3 36	6 00	59.2	329	211
32	148	6 20	10 13	58.6	5 48	9 22	58.5	5 17	8 30	58.4	4 45	7 39	58.3	4 14	6 48	58.3	3 42	5 57	58.2	328	212
33	147	6 30	10 06	57.6	5 58	9 16	57.5	5 26	8 25	57.4	4 53	7 34	57.3	4 21	6 43	57.3	3 48	5 53	57.2	327	213
34	146	6 41	10 00	56.6	6 08	9 09	56.5	5 34	8 19	56.4	5 01	7 29	56.3	4 28	6 39	56.3	3 54	5 49	56.2	326	214
35	145	6 51	9 53	55.6	6 17	9 03	55.5	5 43	8 13	55.4	5 09	7 24	55.3	4 35	6 34	55.3	4 00	5 45	55.2	325	215
36	144	7 01	9 45	54.6	6 26	8 56	54.5	5 51	8 07	54.4	5 17	7 18	54.3	4 42	6 29	54.3	4 06	5 40	54.2	324	216
37	143	7 11	9 38	53.6	6 36	8 49	53.5	6 00	8 01	53.4	5 24	7 13	53.3	4 48	6 24	53.3	4 12	5 36	53.2	323	217
38	142	7 21	9 31	52.6	6 45	8 43	52.5	6 08	7 55	52.4	5 32	7 07	52.3	4 55	6 19	52.3	4 18	5 32	52.2	322	218
39	141	7 31	9 23	51.6	6 54	8 35	51.5	6 16	7 48	51.4	5 39	7 01	51.3	5 01	6 14	51.3	4 24	5 27	51.2	321	219
40	140	7 41	9 15	50.6	7 03	8 28	50.5	6 25	7 42	50.4	5 46	6 55	50.3	5 08	6 09	50.3	4 30	5 22	50.2	320	220
41	139	7 50	9 07	49.6	7 11	8 21	49.5	6 32	7 35	49.4	5 53	6 49	49.4	5 14	6 03	49.3	4 35	5 18	49.2	319	221
42	138	8 00	8 59	48.6	7 20	8 13	48.5	6 40	7 28	48.4	6 01	6 43	48.4	5 21	5 58	48.3	4 41	5 13	48.2	318	222
43	137	8 09	8 50	47.6	7 29	8 05	47.5	6 48	7 21	47.4	6 07	6 36	47.4	5 27	5 52	47.3	4 46	5 08	47.2	317	223
44	136	8 18	8 42	46.6	7 37	7 58	46.5	6 56	7 14	46.4	6 14	6 30	46.4	5 33	5 46	46.3	4 51	5 03	46.2	316	224
45	135	8 27	8 33	45.6	7 45	7 50	45.5	7 03	7 06	45.4	6 21	6 23	45.4	5 39	5 41	45.3	4 57	4 58	45.2	315	225

Lat. / A	LHA/F	78° A/H	78° B/P	78° Z₁/Z₂	79° A/H	79° B/P	79° Z₁/Z₂	80° A/H	80° B/P	80° Z₁/Z₂	81° A/H	81° B/P	81° Z₁/Z₂	82° A/H	82° B/P	82° Z₁/Z₂	83° A/H	83° B/P	83° Z₁/Z₂	Lat. / A	LHA
45	135	8 27	8 33	45·6	7 45	7 50	45·5	7 03	7 06	45·4	6 21	6 23	45·4	5 39	5 41	45·3	4 57	4 58	45·2	225	315
46	134	8 36	8 24	44·6	7 53	7 41	44·5	7 11	6 59	44·4	6 28	6 17	44·4	5 45	5 35	44·3	5 02	4 53	44·2	226	314
47	133	8 45	8 15	43·6	8 01	7 33	43·5	7 18	6 51	43·4	6 34	6 10	43·4	5 51	5 28	43·3	5 07	4 47	43·2	227	313
48	132	8 53	8 06	42·6	8 09	7 25	42·5	7 25	6 44	42·4	6 41	6 03	42·4	5 56	5 22	42·3	5 12	4 42	42·2	228	312
49	131	9 02	7 56	41·6	8 17	7 16	41·5	7 32	6 36	41·4	6 47	5 56	41·4	6 02	5 16	41·3	5 17	4 36	41·2	229	311
50	130	9 10	7 47	40·6	8 24	7 07	40·5	7 39	6 28	40·4	6 53	5 49	40·3	6 07	5 10	40·3	5 21	4 31	40·2	230	310
51	129	9 18	7 37	39·6	8 32	6 58	39·5	7 45	6 20	39·4	6 59	5 42	39·3	6 13	5 03	39·3	5 26	4 25	39·2	231	309
52	128	9 26	7 27	38·6	8 39	6 49	38·5	7 52	6 12	38·4	7 05	5 34	38·3	6 18	4 57	38·3	5 31	4 19	38·2	232	308
53	127	9 33	7 17	37·6	8 46	6 40	37·5	7 58	6 03	37·4	7 11	5 27	37·3	6 23	4 50	37·3	5 35	4 14	37·2	233	307
54	126	9 41	7 07	36·6	8 53	6 31	36·5	8 05	5 55	36·4	7 16	5 19	36·3	6 28	4 43	36·3	5 39	4 08	36·2	234	306
55	125	9 48	6 57	35·6	9 00	6 22	35·5	8 11	5 47	35·4	7 22	5 11	35·3	6 33	4 37	35·3	5 44	4 02	35·2	235	305
56	124	9 56	6 47	34·6	9 06	6 12	34·5	8 17	5 38	34·4	7 27	5 04	34·3	6 38	4 30	34·3	5 48	3 56	34·2	236	304
57	123	10 03	6 36	33·6	9 13	6 03	33·5	8 22	5 29	33·4	7 32	4 56	33·3	6 42	4 23	33·3	5 52	3 50	33·2	237	303
58	122	10 09	6 26	32·6	9 19	5 53	32·5	8 28	5 20	32·4	7 37	4 48	32·3	6 47	4 16	32·3	5 56	3 43	32·2	238	302
59	121	10 16	6 15	31·6	9 25	5 43	31·5	8 34	5 11	31·4	7 42	4 40	31·3	6 51	4 08	31·2	6 00	3 37	31·2	239	301
60	120	10 22	6 04	30·6	9 31	5 33	30·5	8 39	5 02	30·4	7 47	4 32	30·3	6 55	4 01	30·2	6 04	3 31	30·2	240	300
61	119	10 29	5 53	29·5	9 36	5 23	29·5	8 44	4 53	29·4	7 52	4 23	29·3	6 59	3 54	29·2	6 07	3 24	29·2	241	299
62	118	10 35	5 42	28·5	9 42	5 13	28·4	8 49	4 44	28·4	7 56	4 15	28·3	7 04	3 46	28·2	6 11	3 18	28·2	242	298
63	117	10 41	5 31	27·5	9 47	5 03	27·4	8 54	4 35	27·4	8 01	4 07	27·3	7 07	3 39	27·2	6 14	3 11	27·2	243	297
64	116	10 46	5 19	26·5	9 52	4 52	26·4	8 59	4 25	26·3	8 05	3 58	26·3	7 11	3 32	26·2	6 17	3 05	26·2	244	296
65	115	10 52	5 08	25·5	9 57	4 42	25·4	9 03	4 16	25·3	8 09	3 50	25·3	7 15	3 24	25·2	6 20	2 58	25·2	245	295
66	114	10 57	4 56	24·5	10 02	4 31	24·4	9 08	4 06	24·3	8 13	3 41	24·3	7 18	3 16	24·2	6 24	2 52	24·2	246	294
67	113	11 02	4 45	23·5	10 07	4 21	23·4	9 12	3 56	23·3	8 17	3 32	23·3	7 22	3 09	23·2	6 26	2 45	23·2	247	293
68	112	11 07	4 33	22·4	10 11	4 10	22·4	9 16	3 47	22·3	8 20	3 24	22·3	7 25	3 01	22·2	6 29	2 38	22·1	248	292
69	111	11 12	4 21	21·4	10 16	3 59	21·4	9 20	3 37	21·3	8 24	3 15	21·3	7 28	2 53	21·2	6 32	2 31	21·1	249	291
70	110	11 16	4 09	20·4	10 20	3 48	20·3	9 23	3 27	20·3	8 27	3 06	20·2	7 31	2 45	20·2	6 35	2 24	20·1	250	290
71	109	11 20	3 58	19·4	10 24	3 37	19·3	9 27	3 17	19·3	8 30	2 57	19·2	7 34	2 37	19·2	6 37	2 17	19·1	251	289
72	108	11 24	3 45	18·4	10 27	3 26	18·3	9 30	3 07	18·3	8 33	2 48	18·2	7 36	2 29	18·2	6 39	2 10	18·1	252	288
73	107	11 28	3 33	17·4	10 31	3 15	17·3	9 34	2 57	17·2	8 36	2 39	17·2	7 39	2 21	17·2	6 42	2 03	17·1	253	287
74	106	11 32	3 21	16·3	10 34	3 04	16·3	9 37	2 47	16·2	8 39	2 30	16·2	7 41	2 13	16·1	6 44	1 56	16·1	254	286
75	105	11 35	3 09	15·3	10 37	2 53	15·3	9 39	2 37	15·2	8 41	2 21	15·2	7 44	2 05	15·1	6 46	1 49	15·1	255	285
76	104	11 38	2 57	14·3	10 40	2 42	14·3	9 42	2 27	14·2	8 44	2 12	14·2	7 46	1 57	14·1	6 47	1 42	14·1	256	284
77	103	11 41	2 44	13·3	10 43	2 30	13·2	9 44	2 16	13·2	8 46	2 02	13·2	7 48	1 49	13·1	6 49	1 35	13·1	257	283
78	102	11 44	2 32	12·3	10 45	2 19	12·2	9 47	2 06	12·2	8 48	1 53	12·1	7 49	1 40	12·1	6 51	1 28	12·1	258	282
79	101	11 47	2 19	11·2	10 48	2 07	11·2	9 49	1 56	11·2	8 50	1 44	11·1	7 51	1 32	11·1	6 52	1 21	11·1	259	281
80	100	11 49	2 07	10·2	10 50	1 56	10·2	9 51	1 45	10·2	8 52	1 35	10·1	7 53	1 24	10·1	6 54	1 13	10·1	260	280
81	99	11 51	1 54	9·2	10 52	1 45	9·2	9 53	1 35	9·1	8 53	1 25	9·1	7 54	1 16	9·1	6 55	1 06	9·1	261	279
82	98	11 53	1 42	8·2	10 53	1 33	8·1	9 54	1 24	8·1	8 55	1 16	8·1	7 55	1 07	8·1	6 56	0 59	8·1	262	278
83	97	11 55	1 29	7·1	10 55	1 21	7·1	9 55	1 14	7·1	8 56	1 06	7·1	7 56	0 59	7·1	6 57	0 51	7·1	263	277
84	96	11 56	1 16	6·1	10 56	1 10	6·1	9 57	1 03	6·1	8 57	0 57	6·1	7 57	0 50	6·1	6 58	0 44	6·0	264	276
85	95	11 57	1 04	5·1	10 57	0 58	5·1	9 58	0 53	5·1	8 58	0 47	5·1	7 58	0 42	5·0	6 58	0 37	5·0	265	275
86	94	11 58	0 51	4·1	10 58	0 47	4·1	9 59	0 42	4·1	8 59	0 38	4·0	7 59	0 34	4·0	6 59	0 29	4·0	266	274
87	93	11 59	0 38	3·1	10 59	0 35	3·1	9 59	0 32	3·0	8 59	0 28	3·0	7 59	0 25	3·0	6 59	0 22	3·0	267	273
88	92	12 00	0 26	2·0	11 00	0 23	2·0	10 00	0 21	2·0	9 00	0 19	2·0	8 00	0 17	2·0	7 00	0 15	2·0	268	272
89	91	12 00	0 13	1·0	11 00	0 12	1·0	10 00	0 11	1·0	9 00	0 10	1·0	8 00	0 08	1·0	7 00	0 07	1·0	269	271
90	90	12 00	0 00	0·0	11 00	0 00	0·0	10 00	0 00	0·0	9 00	0 00	0·0	8 00	0 00	0·0	7 00	0 00	0·0	270	270

N. Lat: for LHA > 180° ... $Z_n = Z$
for LHA < 180° ... $Z_n = 360° - Z$

S. Lat.: for LHA > 180° ... $Z_n = 180° - Z$
for LHA < 180° ... $Z_n = 180° + Z$

SIGHT REDUCTION TABLE

B: (−) for 90° < LHA < 270°
Dec:(−) for Lat. contrary name

Z₁: same sign as B
Z₂: (−) for F > 90°

Lat. / A	84°			85°			86°			87°			88°			89°			Lat. / A
LHA/F	A/H	B/P	Z_1/Z_2	A/H	B/P	Z_1/Z_2	A/H	B/P	Z_1/Z_2	A/H	B/P	Z_1/Z_2	A/H	B/P	Z_1/Z_2	A/H	B/P	Z_1/Z_2	LHA
0	0 00	6 00	90·0	0 00	5 00	90·0	0 00	4 00	90·0	0 00	3 00	90·0	0 00	2 00	90·0	0 00	1 00	90·0	180
1	0 06	6 00	89·0	0 05	5 00	89·0	0 04	4 00	89·0	0 03	3 00	89·0	0 02	2 00	89·0	0 01	1 00	89·0	179
2	0 13	6 00	88·0	0 10	5 00	88·0	0 08	4 00	88·0	0 06	3 00	88·0	0 04	2 00	88·0	0 02	1 00	88·0	178
3	0 19	6 00	87·0	0 16	5 00	87·0	0 13	4 00	87·0	0 09	3 00	87·0	0 06	2 00	87·0	0 03	1 00	87·0	177
4	0 25	5 59	86·0	0 21	4 59	86·0	0 17	3 59	86·0	0 13	3 00	86·0	0 08	2 00	86·0	0 04	1 00	86·0	176
5	0 31	5 59	85·0	0 26	4 59	85·0	0 21	3 59	85·0	0 16	2 59	85·0	0 10	2 00	85·0	0 05	1 00	85·0	175
6	0 38	5 58	84·0	0 31	4 58	84·0	0 25	3 59	84·0	0 19	2 59	84·0	0 13	1 59	84·0	0 06	1 00	84·0	174
7	0 44	5 57	83·0	0 37	4 58	83·0	0 29	3 58	83·0	0 22	2 59	83·0	0 15	1 59	83·0	0 07	1 00	83·0	173
8	0 50	5 57	82·0	0 42	4 57	82·0	0 33	3 58	82·0	0 25	2 58	82·0	0 17	1 59	82·0	0 08	0 59	82·0	172
9	0 56	5 56	81·0	0 47	4 56	81·0	0 38	3 57	81·0	0 28	2 58	81·0	0 19	1 59	81·0	0 09	0 59	81·0	171
10	1 02	5 55	80·1	0 52	4 55	80·0	0 42	3 56	80·0	0 31	2 57	80·0	0 21	1 58	80·0	0 10	0 59	80·0	170
11	1 09	5 53	79·1	0 57	4 55	79·1	0 46	3 56	79·0	0 34	2 57	79·0	0 23	1 58	79·0	0 11	0 59	79·0	169
12	1 15	5 52	78·1	1 02	4 53	78·0	0 50	3 55	78·0	0 37	2 56	78·0	0 25	1 57	78·0	0 12	0 59	78·0	168
13	1 21	5 51	77·1	1 07	4 52	77·0	0 54	3 54	77·0	0 40	2 55	77·0	0 27	1 57	77·0	0 13	0 58	77·0	167
14	1 27	5 49	76·1	1 12	4 51	76·1	0 58	3 53	76·0	0 44	2 55	76·0	0 29	1 56	76·0	0 15	0 58	76·0	166
15	1 33	5 47	75·1	1 18	4 50	75·1	1 02	3 52	75·0	0 47	2 54	75·0	0 31	1 56	75·0	0 16	0 58	75·0	165
16	1 39	5 46	74·1	1 23	4 48	74·1	1 06	3 51	74·1	0 50	2 53	74·0	0 33	1 55	74·0	0 17	0 58	74·0	164
17	1 45	5 44	73·1	1 28	4 47	73·1	1 10	3 50	73·1	0 53	2 52	73·0	0 35	1 55	73·0	0 18	0 57	73·0	163
18	1 51	5 42	72·1	1 33	4 45	72·1	1 14	3 48	72·1	0 56	2 51	72·0	0 37	1 54	72·0	0 19	0 57	72·0	162
19	1 57	5 41	71·1	1 38	4 44	71·1	1 18	3 47	71·1	0 59	2 50	71·0	0 39	1 53	71·0	0 20	0 57	71·0	161
20	2 03	5 38	70·1	1 42	4 42	70·1	1 22	3 46	70·1	1 02	2 49	70·0	0 41	1 53	70·0	0 21	0 56	70·0	160
21	2 09	5 36	69·1	1 47	4 40	69·1	1 26	3 44	69·1	1 04	2 48	69·0	0 43	1 52	69·0	0 22	0 56	69·0	159
22	2 15	5 34	68·1	1 52	4 38	68·1	1 30	3 43	68·1	1 07	2 47	68·0	0 45	1 51	68·0	0 22	0 56	68·0	158
23	2 20	5 32	67·1	1 57	4 36	67·1	1 34	3 41	67·1	1 10	2 46	67·0	0 47	1 50	67·0	0 23	0 55	67·0	157
24	2 26	5 29	66·1	2 02	4 34	66·1	1 38	3 39	66·1	1 13	2 44	66·0	0 49	1 50	66·0	0 24	0 55	66·0	156
25	2 32	5 26	65·1	2 07	4 32	65·1	1 41	3 38	65·1	1 16	2 43	65·0	0 51	1 49	65·0	0 25	0 54	65·0	155
26	2 38	5 24	64·1	2 11	4 30	64·1	1 45	3 36	64·1	1 19	2 42	64·0	0 53	1 48	64·0	0 26	0 54	64·0	154
27	2 43	5 21	63·1	2 16	4 27	63·1	1 49	3 34	63·1	1 22	2 40	63·0	0 54	1 47	63·0	0 27	0 53	63·0	153
28	2 49	5 18	62·1	2 21	4 25	62·1	1 53	3 32	62·1	1 24	2 39	62·0	0 56	1 46	62·0	0 28	0 53	62·0	152
29	2 54	5 15	61·1	2 25	4 23	61·1	1 56	3 30	61·1	1 27	2 37	61·0	0 58	1 45	61·0	0 29	0 52	61·0	151
30	3 00	5 12	60·1	2 30	4 20	60·1	2 00	3 28	60·1	1 30	2 36	60·0	1 00	1 44	60·0	0 30	0 52	60·0	150
31	3 05	5 09	59·1	2 34	4 17	59·1	2 04	3 26	59·1	1 33	2 34	59·0	1 02	1 43	59·0	0 31	0 51	59·0	149
32	3 11	5 06	58·1	2 39	4 15	58·1	2 07	3 24	58·1	1 35	2 33	58·0	1 04	1 42	58·0	0 32	0 51	58·0	148
33	3 16	5 02	57·1	2 43	4 12	57·1	2 11	3 21	57·1	1 38	2 31	57·0	1 05	1 41	57·0	0 33	0 50	57·0	147
34	3 21	4 59	56·1	2 48	4 09	56·1	2 14	3 19	56·1	1 41	2 29	56·0	1 07	1 39	56·0	0 33	0 50	56·0	146
35	3 26	4 55	55·1	2 52	4 06	55·1	2 18	3 17	55·1	1 43	2 27	55·0	1 09	1 38	55·0	0 34	0 49	55·0	145
36	3 31	4 52	54·1	2 56	4 03	54·1	2 21	3 14	54·1	1 46	2 26	54·0	1 11	1 37	54·0	0 35	0 49	54·0	144
37	3 36	4 48	53·2	3 00	4 00	53·2	2 24	3 12	53·1	1 48	2 24	53·0	1 12	1 36	53·0	0 36	0 48	53·0	143
38	3 41	4 44	52·2	3 05	3 57	52·2	2 28	3 09	52·1	1 51	2 22	52·0	1 14	1 35	52·0	0 37	0 47	52·0	142
39	3 46	4 40	51·2	3 09	3 53	51·2	2 31	3 07	51·1	1 53	2 20	51·0	1 16	1 33	51·0	0 38	0 47	51·0	141
40	3 51	4 36	50·2	3 13	3 50	50·2	2 34	3 04	50·1	1 56	2 18	50·0	1 17	1 32	50·0	0 39	0 46	50·0	140
41	3 56	4 32	49·2	3 17	3 47	49·2	2 37	3 01	49·1	1 58	2 16	49·0	1 19	1 31	49·0	0 39	0 45	49·0	139
42	4 01	4 28	48·2	3 21	3 43	48·2	2 41	2 58	48·1	2 00	2 14	48·0	1 20	1 29	48·0	0 40	0 45	48·0	138
43	4 05	4 24	47·2	3 24	3 40	47·2	2 44	2 56	47·1	2 03	2 12	47·0	1 22	1 28	47·0	0 41	0 44	47·0	137
44	4 10	4 19	46·2	3 28	3 36	46·2	2 47	2 53	46·1	2 05	2 10	46·0	1 23	1 26	46·0	0 42	0 43	46·0	136
45	4 14	4 15	45·2	3 32	3 32	45·2	2 50	2 50	45·1	2 07	2 07	45·0	1 25	1 25	45·0	0 42	0 42	45·0	135

Lat. / A	84°			85°			86°			87°			88°			89°			Lat. / A
LHA/F	A/H	B/P	Z₁/Z₂	A/H	B/P	Z₁/Z₂	A/H	B/P	Z₁/Z₂	A/H	B/P	Z₁/Z₂	A/H	B/P	Z₁/Z₂	A/H	B/P	Z₁/Z₂	LHA
45	4 14	4 15	45.2	3 32	3 32	45.1	2 50	2 50	45.1	2 07	2 07	45.0	1 25	1 25	45.0	0 42	0 42	45.0	225
46	4 19	4 11	44.2	3 36	3 29	44.1	2 53	2 47	44.1	2 09	2 05	44.0	1 26	1 23	44.0	0 43	0 42	44.0	226
47	4 23	4 06	43.2	3 39	3 25	43.1	2 55	2 44	43.1	2 12	2 03	43.0	1 28	1 22	43.0	0 44	0 41	43.0	227
48	4 27	4 01	42.2	3 43	3 21	42.1	2 58	2 41	42.1	2 14	2 01	42.0	1 29	1 20	42.0	0 45	0 40	42.0	228
49	4 31	3 57	41.2	3 46	3 17	41.1	3 01	2 38	41.1	2 16	1 58	41.0	1 31	1 19	41.0	0 45	0 39	41.0	229
50	4 36	3 52	40.2	3 50	3 13	40.1	3 04	2 34	40.1	2 18	1 56	40.0	1 32	1 17	40.0	0 46	0 39	40.0	230
51	4 40	3 47	39.2	3 53	3 09	39.1	3 06	2 31	39.1	2 20	1 53	39.0	1 33	1 16	39.0	0 47	0 38	39.0	231
52	4 43	3 42	38.2	3 56	3 05	38.1	3 09	2 28	38.1	2 22	1 51	38.0	1 35	1 14	38.0	0 47	0 37	38.0	232
53	4 47	3 37	37.2	3 59	3 01	37.1	3 12	2 25	37.1	2 24	1 48	37.0	1 36	1 12	37.0	0 48	0 36	37.0	233
54	4 51	3 32	36.1	4 03	2 57	36.1	3 14	2 21	36.1	2 26	1 46	36.0	1 37	1 11	36.0	0 49	0 35	36.0	234
55	4 55	3 27	35.1	4 06	2 52	35.1	3 17	2 18	35.1	2 27	1 43	35.0	1 38	1 09	35.0	0 49	0 34	35.0	235
56	4 58	3 22	34.1	4 09	2 48	34.1	3 19	2 14	34.1	2 29	1 41	34.0	1 39	1 07	34.0	0 50	0 34	34.0	236
57	5 02	3 17	33.1	4 12	2 44	33.1	3 21	2 11	33.1	2 31	1 38	33.0	1 41	1 05	33.0	0 50	0 33	33.0	237
58	5 05	3 11	32.1	4 14	2 39	32.1	3 23	2 07	32.1	2 33	1 35	32.0	1 42	1 04	32.0	0 51	0 32	32.0	238
59	5 08	3 06	31.1	4 17	2 35	31.1	3 26	2 04	31.1	2 34	1 32	31.0	1 43	1 02	31.0	0 51	0 31	31.0	239
60	5 12	3 00	30.1	4 20	2 30	30.1	3 28	2 00	30.1	2 36	1 30	30.0	1 44	1 00	30.0	0 52	0 30	30.0	240
61	5 15	2 55	29.1	4 22	2 26	29.1	3 30	1 56	29.1	2 37	1 27	29.0	1 45	0 58	29.0	0 52	0 29	29.0	241
62	5 18	2 49	28.1	4 25	2 21	28.1	3 32	1 53	28.1	2 39	1 25	28.0	1 46	0 56	28.0	0 53	0 28	28.0	242
63	5 21	2 44	27.1	4 27	2 16	27.1	3 34	1 49	27.1	2 40	1 22	27.0	1 47	0 54	27.0	0 53	0 27	27.0	243
64	5 23	2 38	26.1	4 30	2 12	26.1	3 36	1 45	26.1	2 42	1 19	26.0	1 48	0 53	26.0	0 54	0 26	26.0	244
65	5 26	2 33	25.1	4 32	2 07	25.1	3 37	1 42	25.1	2 43	1 16	25.0	1 49	0 51	25.0	0 54	0 25	25.0	245
66	5 29	2 27	24.1	4 34	2 02	24.1	3 39	1 38	24.1	2 44	1 13	24.0	1 50	0 49	24.0	0 55	0 24	24.0	246
67	5 31	2 21	23.1	4 36	1 57	23.1	3 41	1 34	23.1	2 46	1 10	23.0	1 50	0 47	23.0	0 55	0 23	23.0	247
68	5 34	2 15	22.1	4 38	1 53	22.1	3 42	1 30	22.0	2 47	1 07	22.0	1 51	0 45	22.0	0 56	0 22	22.0	248
69	5 36	2 09	21.1	4 40	1 48	21.1	3 44	1 26	21.1	2 48	1 05	21.0	1 52	0 43	21.0	0 56	0 22	21.0	249
70	5 38	2 04	20.1	4 42	1 43	20.1	3 46	1 22	20.1	2 49	1 02	20.0	1 53	0 41	20.0	0 56	0 21	20.0	250
71	5 40	1 58	19.1	4 44	1 38	19.1	3 47	1 18	19.1	2 50	0 59	19.0	1 53	0 39	19.0	0 57	0 20	19.0	251
72	5 42	1 52	18.1	4 45	1 33	18.1	3 48	1 14	18.1	2 51	0 56	18.0	1 54	0 37	18.0	0 57	0 19	18.0	252
73	5 44	1 46	17.1	4 47	1 28	17.1	3 49	1 10	17.1	2 52	0 53	17.0	1 55	0 35	17.0	0 58	0 18	17.0	253
74	5 46	1 40	16.1	4 48	1 23	16.1	3 51	1 06	16.1	2 53	0 50	16.0	1 55	0 33	16.0	0 58	0 17	16.0	254
75	5 48	1 33	15.1	4 50	1 18	15.1	3 52	1 02	15.1	2 54	0 47	15.0	1 56	0 31	15.0	0 58	0 16	15.0	255
76	5 49	1 27	14.1	4 51	1 13	14.1	3 53	0 58	14.1	2 55	0 44	14.0	1 56	0 29	14.0	0 58	0 15	14.0	256
77	5 51	1 21	13.1	4 52	1 08	13.0	3 54	0 54	13.1	2 55	0 41	13.0	1 57	0 27	13.0	0 59	0 13	13.0	257
78	5 52	1 15	12.1	4 53	1 03	12.0	3 55	0 50	12.1	2 56	0 37	12.0	1 57	0 25	12.0	0 59	0 12	12.0	258
79	5 53	1 09	11.1	4 54	0 57	11.0	3 56	0 46	11.1	2 56	0 34	11.0	1 58	0 23	11.0	0 59	0 11	11.0	259
80	5 55	1 03	10.1	4 55	0 52	10.0	3 56	0 42	10.0	2 57	0 31	10.0	1 58	0 21	10.0	0 59	0 10	10.0	260
81	5 56	0 57	9.0	4 56	0 47	9.0	3 57	0 38	9.0	2 58	0 28	9.0	1 59	0 19	9.0	0 59	0 09	9.0	261
82	5 56	0 50	8.0	4 57	0 42	8.0	3 58	0 33	8.0	2 58	0 25	8.0	1 59	0 17	8.0	0 59	0 08	8.0	262
83	5 57	0 44	7.0	4 58	0 37	7.0	3 58	0 29	7.0	2 59	0 22	7.0	1 59	0 15	7.0	1 00	0 07	7.0	263
84	5 58	0 38	6.0	4 58	0 31	6.0	3 59	0 25	6.0	2 59	0 19	6.0	1 59	0 13	6.0	1 00	0 06	6.0	264
85	5 59	0 31	5.0	4 59	0 26	5.0	3 59	0 21	5.0	2 59	0 16	5.0	2 00	0 10	5.0	1 00	0 05	5.0	265
86	5 59	0 25	4.0	4 59	0 21	4.0	3 59	0 17	4.0	2 59	0 13	4.0	2 00	0 08	4.0	1 00	0 04	4.0	266
87	6 00	0 19	3.0	5 00	0 16	3.0	4 00	0 13	3.0	3 00	0 09	3.0	2 00	0 06	3.0	1 00	0 03	3.0	267
88	6 00	0 13	2.0	5 00	0 10	2.0	4 00	0 08	2.0	3 00	0 06	2.0	2 00	0 04	2.0	1 00	0 02	2.0	268
89	6 00	0 06	1.0	5 00	0 05	1.0	4 00	0 04	1.0	3 00	0 03	1.0	2 00	0 02	1.0	1 00	0 01	1.0	269
90	6 00	0 00	0.0	5 00	0 00	0.0	4 00	0 00	0.0	3 00	0 00	0.0	2 00	0 00	0.0	1 00	0 00	0.0	270

N. Lat.: for LHA > 180° ... $Z_n = Z$; for LHA < 180° ... $Z_n = 360° - Z$

S. Lat.: for LHA > 180° ... $Z_n = 180° - Z$; for LHA < 180° ... $Z_n = 180° + Z$

AUXILIARY TABLE

Sign for corr₂ for A'. →

Sign of corr₁ for F'. *Reverse* sign if F > 90°.

F' +/−	P°	Z°:	30 / □	29 / 31	28 / 32	27 / 33	26 / 34	25 / 35	24 / 36	23 / 37	22 / 38	21 / 39	20 / 40	19 / 41	18 / 42	17 / 43	16 / 44	15 / 45	14 / 46	13 / 47	12 / 48	11 / 49	10 / 50	9 / 51	8 / 52	7 / 53	6 / 54	5 / 55	4 / 56	3 / 57	2 / 58	1 / 59 (−A'/+)
1 / 59	1	89	1	1	0	0	0	0	0	0	0	0	0	0	0	0	0	0	0	0	0	0	0	0	0	0	0	0	0	0	0	0
2 / 58	2	88	1	1	1	1	1	1	1	1	1	1	1	1	1	1	0	0	0	0	0	0	0	0	0	0	0	0	0	0	0	0
3 / 57	3	87	2	2	1	1	1	1	1	1	1	1	1	1	1	1	1	1	1	1	1	1	1	0	0	0	0	0	1	0	0	0
4 / 56	4	86	2	2	2	2	2	2	2	2	2	1	1	1	1	1	1	1	1	1	1	1	1	1	1	1	1	1	1	1	0	0
5 / 55	5	85	3	3	2	2	2	2	2	2	2	2	2	2	2	1	1	1	1	1	1	1	1	1	1	1	1	0	1	1	1	0
6 / 54	6	84	3	3	3	3	3	3	3	2	2	2	2	2	2	2	2	2	1	1	1	1	1	1	2	1	2	1	1	1	1	1
7 / 53	7	83	4	4	3	3	3	3	3	3	3	3	2	2	2	2	2	2	2	2	2	2	2	2	2	2	2	2	1	1	1	1
8 / 52	8	82	4	4	4	4	4	3	3	3	3	3	3	3	3	3	3	2	2	2	2	2	2	2	2	2	2	2	2	1	1	1
9 / 51	9	81	5	5	4	4	4	4	4	4	3	3	3	3	3	3	3	3	3	2	2	2	2	2	2	2	2	2	2	2	1	1
10 / 50	10	80	5	5	5	5	5	4	4	4	4	4	3	3	3	3	3	3	3	3	2	2	3	2	2	2	2	2	2	2	2	1
11 / 49	11	79	6	6	5	5	5	5	5	4	5	4	4	4	4	4	4	3	3	3	3	3	3	3	2	2	2	2	2	2	2	1
12 / 48	12	78	6	6	6	6	5	5	5	5	5	5	4	4	4	4	4	4	3	3	3	3	3	3	3	3	2	3	2	2	2	1
13 / 47	13	77	7	7	6	6	6	6	5	6	5	5	5	5	5	4	4	4	4	4	4	3	3	3	3	3	3	3	2	2	2	1
14 / 46	14	76	7	7	7	7	6	6	6	6	6	5	5	5	5	5	4	4	4	4	4	4	3	3	3	3	3	3	3	3	2	2
15 / 45	15	75	8	8	7	7	7	7	6	6	6	6	6	6	5	5	5	5	5	4	4	4	3	3	3	3	3	3	3	3	2	2
16 / 44	16	74	8	8	8	7	7	7	7	6	6	6	6	6	5	5	5	5	5	5	4	4	4	4	4	4	3	3	3	3	3	2
17 / 43	17	73	9	8	8	8	8	7	7	7	7	6	6	6	6	6	6	5	5	5	5	4	4	4	4	4	3	3	3	3	3	2
18 / 42	18	72	9	9	9	8	8	8	7	7	7	7	7	6	6	6	6	6	5	5	5	5	4	4	4	4	4	3	3	3	3	2
19 / 41	19	71	10	9	9	9	8	8	8	8	8	7	7	7	7	7	6	6	6	5	5	5	5	4	4	4	4	4	3	3	3	2
20 / 40	20	70	10	10	10	9	9	9	8	8	8	8	7	8	7	7	7	6	6	6	6	5	5	5	5	4	4	4	4	3	3	2
21 / 39	21	69	11	10	10	10	10	9	9	9	8	9	8	8	8	7	7	7	6	6	6	6	5	5	5	4	4	4	4	3	3	2
22 / 38	22	68	11	11	11	10	10	10	9	9	9	9	9	9	8	8	7	7	7	6	6	6	5	5	5	4	4	4	4	4	3	3
23 / 37	23	67	12	11	11	11	11	10	10	10	10	9	9	9	8	8	8	7	7	7	6	6	5	5	5	5	4	4	4	4	3	3
24 / 36	24	66	12	12	12	11	11	11	10	10	10	10	9	9	9	9	8	7	7	7	7	6	6	5	5	5	4	4	4	4	3	3
25 / 35	25	65	13	12	12	12	11	11	11	10	10	10	10	9	9	9	8	8	8	7	7	6	6	6	5	5	5	4	4	4	4	3
26 / 34	26	64	13	13	13	12	12	12	11	11	11	11	10	10	10	9	9	8	8	8	7	7	6	6	6	5	5	5	4	4	4	3
27 / 33	27	63	14	13	13	13	13	12	12	12	11	11	11	11	10	10	9	9	8	8	8	7	7	6	6	6	5	5	4	4	4	3
28 / 32	28	62	14	14	14	13	13	13	12	12	12	12	11	11	11	10	10	9	9	9	8	8	7	7	6	6	5	5	5	4	4	3
29 / 31	29	61	15	14	14	14	14	13	13	13	12	12	12	11	11	11	10	10	9	9	8	8	8	7	7	6	6	5	5	4	4	4
30 / □	30	60	15	15	15	14	14	13	13	13	13	12	12	12	12	11	10	10	10	9	9	8	8	7	7	6	6	5	5	5	4	4
31 / 29	31	59	15	15	14	14	15	14	14	14	13	13	12	12	11	11	10	9	8	8	7	6	5	5	5	4	3	3	2	2	1	1
32 / 28	32	58	16	15	15	15	15	15	14	14	13	13	12	11	11	11	10	9	8	8	7	7	6	5	5	4	4	3	3	2	1	1
33 / 27	33	57	16	16	15	16	16	15	14	14	14	14	12	12	11	11	10	9	9	8	7	7	6	6	5	4	4	3	3	2	1	1
34 / 26	34	56	17	16	16	16	16	16	15	15	15	14	13	12	12	11	10	9	9	8	7	7	6	6	5	4	4	3	3	2	1	1
35 / 25	35	55	17	17	16	17	17	16	15	15	15	14	13	13	12	11	10	9	9	8	7	7	6	6	5	4	4	3	3	2	1	1
36 / 24	36	54	18	17	16	17	17	16	16	16	15	14	14	13	12	12	11	10	9	8	7	7	6	6	5	4	4	3	3	2	1	1
37 / 23	37	53	18	17	17	17	17	17	16	16	15	15	14	13	12	12	11	10	9	8	7	7	6	6	5	4	4	3	3	2	1	1
38 / 22	38	52	18	18	17	17	17	17	16	16	16	15	14	13	13	12	11	10	9	8	7	7	6	6	5	5	4	3	3	2	2	1
39 / 21	39	51	19	18	18	17	18	17	16	16	16	15	14	13	13	12	11	10	9	8	7	7	6	6	5	5	4	4	3	2	2	1
40 / 20	40	50	19	19	18	18	18	17	17	16	16	15	14	14	13	12	11	10	9	8	8	7	6	6	5	5	4	4	3	2	2	1

For $Z_2 < 10°$, use $10°$

For $P > 80°$, use $80°$

$-A'$ / $+A'$ $Z_2°$	□30 / 30	29 / 31	28 / 32	27 / 33	26 / 34	25 / 35	24 / 36	23 / 37	22 / 38	21 / 39	20 / 40	19 / 41	18 / 42	17 / 43	16 / 44	15 / 45	14 / 46	13 / 47	12 / 48	11 / 49	10 / 50	9 / 51	8 / 52	7 / 53	6 / 54	5 / 55	4 / 56	3 / 57	2 / 58	1 / 59	F' +/− $P°$
49			18	18	17	16	16	15	14	14	13	12	12	11	10	10	9	9	8	7	~7	6	5	~5	4	3	3	~2	~1	~1	41
48		19	19	18	17	17	16	15	15	14	13	13	12	11	11	10	9	9	8	7	7	6	5	5	4	3	3	2	1	1	42
47		19	19	18	18	17	16	16	15	14	14	13	12	12	11	10	10	9	8	8	7	6	5	5	4	3	3	2	1	1	43
46		20	19	19	18	17	17	16	15	15	14	13	13	12	11	10	10	9	8	8	7	6	6	5	4	3	3	2	2	1	44
45		21	20	19	19	18	17	16	16	15	14	13	13	12	11	11	10	9	8	8	7	6	6	5	4	4	3	2	2	1	45
44	20	21	20	19	19	18	17	17	16	15	14	14	13	12	12	11	10	9	9	8	7	6	6	5	4	4	3	2	2	1	46
43	20	22	20	19	19	18	18	17	16	15	15	14	13	12	12	11	10	10	9	8	7	7	6	5	4	4	3	2	2	1	47
42	20	22	21	20	19	19	18	17	17	16	15	14	13	13	12	11	11	10	9	8	8	7	6	5	5	4	3	3	2	1	48
41	21	22	21	20	20	19	18	18	17	16	15	15	14	13	12	12	11	10	9	9	8	7	6	6	5	4	3	3	2	1	49
40	21	22	21	21	20	19	18	18	17	16	16	15	14	13	13	12	11	10	9	9	8	7	6	6	5	4	4	3	2	1	50
39	22	23	22	21	20	19	19	18	17	17	16	15	14	14	13	12	11	10	10	9	8	7	7	6	5	4	4	3	2	1	51
38	22	23	22	21	21	20	19	18	18	17	16	15	15	14	13	12	11	11	10	9	8	8	7	6	5	4	4	3	2	1	52
37	22	23	22	22	21	20	19	18	18	17	16	16	15	14	13	12	12	11	10	9	8	8	7	6	5	5	4	3	2	1	53
36	23	24	23	22	21	20	20	19	18	17	17	16	15	14	14	13	12	11	10	10	9	8	7	6	6	5	4	3	2	1	54
35	23	24	23	22	22	21	20	19	18	18	17	16	15	15	14	13	12	11	11	10	9	8	7	6	6	5	4	3	2	1	55
34	23	25	23	22	22	21	20	20	19	18	17	17	16	15	14	13	12	11	11	10	9	8	7	6	6	5	4	3	2	1	56
33	24	25	24	23	22	22	21	20	19	18	18	17	16	15	14	13	13	12	11	10	9	8	8	7	6	5	4	3	2	1	57
32	24	25	24	24	22	22	21	20	19	19	18	17	16	16	15	14	13	12	11	10	9	8	8	7	6	5	4	3	2	1	58
31	24	25	24	24	23	22	21	21	20	19	18	18	17	16	15	14	13	12	11	11	9	8	8	7	6	5	4	3	2	1	59
30	25	26	25	24	23	22	22	21	20	19	19	18	17	16	15	14	13	12	11	11	9	8	8	7	6	5	4	3	2	1	60
29	25	26	25	25	24	23	22	21	20	20	19	18	17	16	15	14	13	12	11	11	9	8	8	7	6	5	4	3	2	1	61
28	25	26	26	25	24	23	22	22	21	20	19	18	18	17	16	14	13	12	12	11	9	8	8	7	6	5	4	3	2	1	62
27	25	27	26	25	24	23	22	22	21	20	19	18	18	17	16	14	13	12	12	11	9	8	8	7	6	5	4	3	2	1	63
26	26	27	26	26	25	23	22	22	21	20	20	19	18	17	16	15	14	13	12	11	9	8	8	7	6	5	4	3	2	1	64
25	26	27	26	26	25	24	23	22	22	21	20	19	18	17	16	15	14	13	12	11	9	8	8	7	6	5	4	3	2	1	65
24	26	27	26	26	25	24	23	22	21	20	20	19	18	17	16	15	14	13	12	11	9	8	8	7	6	5	4	3	2	1	66
23	27	27	27	26	25	24	23	22	22	21	20	19	18	17	16	15	14	13	12	11	10	9	8	7	6	5	4	3	2	1	67
22	27	28	27	26	26	24	23	22	22	21	21	20	18	17	16	15	14	13	12	11	10	9	8	7	6	5	4	3	2	1	68
21	27	28	27	27	26	24	23	23	22	21	21	20	18	17	16	15	14	13	12	11	10	9	8	7	6	5	4	3	2	1	69
20	27	28	27	27	26	25	24	23	22	21	21	20	18	17	16	15	14	13	12	11	10	9	8	7	6	5	4	3	2	1	70
19	28	28	27	27	26	25	24	23	22	21	21	20	18	17	16	15	14	13	12	11	10	9	8	7	6	5	4	3	2	1	71
18	29	28	27	28	26	25	24	23	22	22	21	20	18	17	16	15	14	13	12	11	10	9	8	7	6	5	4	3	2	1	72
17	29	28	27	28	26	25	24	23	22	22	22	20	18	17	16	15	14	13	12	11	10	9	8	7	6	5	4	3	2	1	73
16	29	28	27	28	26	26	24	24	23	22	22	20	18	17	16	15	14	13	12	11	10	9	8	7	6	5	4	3	2	1	74
15	29	28	28	28	26	26	24	24	23	22	22	21	18	17	16	15	14	13	12	11	10	9	8	7	6	5	4	3	2	1	75
14	29	28	27	28	26	25	24	23	22	22	21	20	18	17	16	15	14	13	12	11	10	9	8	7	6	5	4	3	2	1	76
13	29	28	28	28	26	25	24	23	22	22	22	21	18	18	16	15	14	13	12	11	10	9	8	7	6	5	4	3	2	1	77
12	29	28	28	28	26	25	24	23	23	22	22	21	18	18	16	15	14	13	12	11	10	9	8	7	6	5	4	3	2	1	78
11	29	28	28	27	27	26	24	23	23	22	22	21	18	18	16	15	14	13	12	11	10	9	8	7	6	5	4	3	2	1	79
10	30	29	28	27	27	25	24	23	22	22	21	20	18	18	16	15	14	13	12	10	10	9	8	7	6	6	4	3	2	1	80

USE OF CONCISE SIGHT REDUCTION TABLES (continued)

4. *Example.* (b) Required the altitude and azimuth of *Vega* on 2015 July 29 at UT 04^h 50^m from the estimated position 152° west, 15° south.

1. Assumed latitude　　　　　$Lat =$　15° S
   From the almanac　　　　　$GHA =$　99° 39′
   Assumed longitude　　　　　　　151° 39′ W
   Local hour angle　　　　　$LHA =$ 308

2. Reduction table, 1st entry
   $(Lat, LHA) = (15, 308)$　　$A =$　49　34　　$A° = 50, A' = 34$
   　　　　　　　　　　　　$B = +66$　29　　$Z_1 = +71.7,$　　　　　　　　$LHA > 270°$
3. From the almanac　　　$Dec = -38$　48　　　　　　　　　*Lat* and *Dec* contrary
   Sum $= B + Dec$　　　　$F = +27$　41　　$F° = 28, F' = 41$

4. Reduction table, 2nd entry
   $(A°, F°) = (50, 28)$　　　　$H =$　17　34　　$P° = 37$
   　　　　　　　　　　　　　　　　　　　　$Z_2 = 67.8, Z_2° = 68$

5. Auxiliary table, 1st entry
   $(F', P°) = (41, 37)$　　　$corr_1 =$　　-11　　　　　　　　$F < 90°, F' > 29'$
   Sum　　　　　　　　　　　　　　17　23
6. Auxiliary table, 2nd entry
   $(A', Z_2°) = (34, 68)$　　$corr_2 =$　　$+10$　　　　　　　　　　$A' > 30'$
7. Sum $=$ computed altitude　$H_C = +17°$ 33′　　　　　　　　　　　$F > 0°$

8. Azimuth, first component　$Z_1 = +71.7$　　　　　　　same sign as B
   　　　　second component　$Z_2 = +67.8$　　　　　　$F < 90°, F > 0°$
   Sum $=$ azimuth angle　　$Z =$　139.5

   True azimuth　　　　　　$Z_n =$　040°　　　　　　　S *Lat, LHA* > 180°

5. *Form for use with the Concise Sight Reduction Tables.* The form on the following page lays out the procedure explained on pages 284-285. Each step is shown, with notes and rules to ensure accuracy, rather than speed, throughout the calculation. The form is mainly intended for the calculation of star positions. It therefore includes the formation of the Greenwich hour of Aries (*GHA* Aries), and thus the Greenwich hour angle of the star (*GHA*) from its tabular sidereal hour angle (*SHA*). These calculations, included in step 1 of the form, can easily be replaced by the interpolation of *GHA* and *Dec* for the Sun, Moon or planets.

The form may be freely copied, however, acknowledgement of the source is requested.

Date & UT of observation h m s		Body	Estimated Latitude & Longitude ° ′ ° ′

Step	Calculate Altitude & Azimuth		Summary of Rules & Notes
Assumed latitude	$Lat =$ °		Nearest estimated latitude, integral number of degrees.
Assumed longitude	$Long =$ ° ′		Choose $Long$ so that LHA has integral number of degrees.
1. From the almanac:	$Dec =$ ° ′		Record the Dec for use in Step 3.
GHA Aries h	$=$ ° !		Needed if using SHA. Tabular value.
Increment m s	$=$ ° !		for minutes and seconds of time.
SHA	$SHA =$ ° !		
$GHA = GHA\ Aries + SHA$	$GHA =$ ° ′		Remove multiples of 360°.
Assumed longitude	$Long =$ ° ′		West longitudes are negative.
$LHA = GHA + Long$	$LHA =$ °		Remove multiples of 360°.
2. Reduction table, 1st entry $(Lat, LHA) = ($ °, °$)$ record A, B and Z_1.	$A =$ ° ′	$A° =$ °	nearest whole degree of A.
		$A' =$ ′	minutes part of A.
	$B =$ ° ′		B is minus if $90° < LHA < 270°$.
		$Z_1 =$ °	Z_1 has the same sign as B.
3. From step 1	$Dec =$ ° ′		Dec is minus if contrary to Lat.
$F = B + Dec$	$F =$ ° ′		Regard F as positive until step 7.
		$F° =$ °	nearest whole degree of F.
		$F' =$ ′	minutes part of F.
4. Reduction table, 2nd entry $(A°, F°) = ($ °, °$)$ record H, P and Z_2.	$H =$ ° ′	$P° =$ °	nearest whole degree of P.
		$Z_2 =$ °	
5. Auxiliary table, 1st entry $(F', P°) = ($ ′, °$)$ record $corr_1$	$corr_1 =$ ′		$corr_1$ is minus if $F < 90°$ & $F' > 29'$, or if $F > 90°$ & $F' < 30'$.
6. Auxiliary table, 2nd entry $(A', Z_2°) = ($ ′, °$)$ record $corr_2$	$corr_2 =$ ′		$Z_2°$ nearest whole degree of Z_2. $corr_2$ is minus if $A' < 30'$.
7. Calculated altitude $=$ $H_c = H + corr_1 + corr_2$	$H_c =$ ° ′		H_c is minus if F is negative, and object is below the horizon.
8. Azimuth, 1st component	$Z_1 =$ °		Z_1 has the same sign as B.
2nd component	$Z_2 =$ °		Z_2 is minus if $F > 90°$. If F is negative, $Z_2 = 180° - Z_2$
$Z = Z_1 + Z_2$	$Z =$ °		Ignore the sign of Z.
			N Lat: If $LHA > 180°$, $Z_n = Z$, or if $LHA < 180°$, $Z_n = 360° - Z$,
			S Lat: If $LHA > 180°$, $Z_n = 180° - Z$, or if $LHA < 180°$, $Z_n = 180° + Z$.
True azimuth	$Z_n =$ °		©HMNAO

For use with *The Nautical Almanac's* Concise Sight Reduction Tables pages 284-318.

CONVERSION OF ARC TO TIME

0°–59°		60°–119°		120°–179°		180°–239°		240°–299°		300°–359°			0′.00	0′.25	0′.50	0′.75
o	h m	o	h m	o	h m	o	h m	o	h m	o	h m	′	m s	m s	m s	m s
0	0 00	60	4 00	120	8 00	180	12 00	240	16 00	300	20 00	0	0 00	0 01	0 02	0 03
1	0 04	61	4 04	121	8 04	181	12 04	241	16 04	301	20 04	1	0 04	0 05	0 06	0 07
2	0 08	62	4 08	122	8 08	182	12 08	242	16 08	302	20 08	2	0 08	0 09	0 10	0 11
3	0 12	63	4 12	123	8 12	183	12 12	243	16 12	303	20 12	3	0 12	0 13	0 14	0 15
4	0 16	64	4 16	124	8 16	184	12 16	244	16 16	304	20 16	4	0 16	0 17	0 18	0 19
5	0 20	65	4 20	125	8 20	185	12 20	245	16 20	305	20 20	5	0 20	0 21	0 22	0 23
6	0 24	66	4 24	126	8 24	186	12 24	246	16 24	306	20 24	6	0 24	0 25	0 26	0 27
7	0 28	67	4 28	127	8 28	187	12 28	247	16 28	307	20 28	7	0 28	0 29	0 30	0 31
8	0 32	68	4 32	128	8 32	188	12 32	248	16 32	308	20 32	8	0 32	0 33	0 34	0 35
9	0 36	69	4 36	129	8 36	189	12 36	249	16 36	309	20 36	9	0 36	0 37	0 38	0 39
10	0 40	70	4 40	130	8 40	190	12 40	250	16 40	310	20 40	10	0 40	0 41	0 42	0 43
11	0 44	71	4 44	131	8 44	191	12 44	251	16 44	311	20 44	11	0 44	0 45	0 46	0 47
12	0 48	72	4 48	132	8 48	192	12 48	252	16 48	312	20 48	12	0 48	0 49	0 50	0 51
13	0 52	73	4 52	133	8 52	193	12 52	253	16 52	313	20 52	13	0 52	0 53	0 54	0 55
14	0 56	74	4 56	134	8 56	194	12 56	254	16 56	314	20 56	14	0 56	0 57	0 58	0 59
15	1 00	75	5 00	135	9 00	195	13 00	255	17 00	315	21 00	15	1 00	1 01	1 02	1 03
16	1 04	76	5 04	136	9 04	196	13 04	256	17 04	316	21 04	16	1 04	1 05	1 06	1 07
17	1 08	77	5 08	137	9 08	197	13 08	257	17 08	317	21 08	17	1 08	1 09	1 10	1 11
18	1 12	78	5 12	138	9 12	198	13 12	258	17 12	318	21 12	18	1 12	1 13	1 14	1 15
19	1 16	79	5 16	139	9 16	199	13 16	259	17 16	319	21 16	19	1 16	1 17	1 18	1 19
20	1 20	80	5 20	140	9 20	200	13 20	260	17 20	320	21 20	20	1 20	1 21	1 22	1 23
21	1 24	81	5 24	141	9 24	201	13 24	261	17 24	321	21 24	21	1 24	1 25	1 26	1 27
22	1 28	82	5 28	142	9 28	202	13 28	262	17 28	322	21 28	22	1 28	1 29	1 30	1 31
23	1 32	83	5 32	143	9 32	203	13 32	263	17 32	323	21 32	23	1 32	1 33	1 34	1 35
24	1 36	84	5 36	144	9 36	204	13 36	264	17 36	324	21 36	24	1 36	1 37	1 38	1 39
25	1 40	85	5 40	145	9 40	205	13 40	265	17 40	325	21 40	25	1 40	1 41	1 42	1 43
26	1 44	86	5 44	146	9 44	206	13 44	266	17 44	326	21 44	26	1 44	1 45	1 46	1 47
27	1 48	87	5 48	147	9 48	207	13 48	267	17 48	327	21 48	27	1 48	1 49	1 50	1 51
28	1 52	88	5 52	148	9 52	208	13 52	268	17 52	328	21 52	28	1 52	1 53	1 54	1 55
29	1 56	89	5 56	149	9 56	209	13 56	269	17 56	329	21 56	29	1 56	1 57	1 58	1 59
30	2 00	90	6 00	150	10 00	210	14 00	270	18 00	330	22 00	30	2 00	2 01	2 02	2 03
31	2 04	91	6 04	151	10 04	211	14 04	271	18 04	331	22 04	31	2 04	2 05	2 06	2 07
32	2 08	92	6 08	152	10 08	212	14 08	272	18 08	332	22 08	32	2 08	2 09	2 10	2 11
33	2 12	93	6 12	153	10 12	213	14 12	273	18 12	333	22 12	33	2 12	2 13	2 14	2 15
34	2 16	94	6 16	154	10 16	214	14 16	274	18 16	334	22 16	34	2 16	2 17	2 18	2 19
35	2 20	95	6 20	155	10 20	215	14 20	275	18 20	335	22 20	35	2 20	2 21	2 22	2 23
36	2 24	96	6 24	156	10 24	216	14 24	276	18 24	336	22 24	36	2 24	2 25	2 26	2 27
37	2 28	97	6 28	157	10 28	217	14 28	277	18 28	337	22 28	37	2 28	2 29	2 30	2 31
38	2 32	98	6 32	158	10 32	218	14 32	278	18 32	338	22 32	38	2 32	2 33	2 34	2 35
39	2 36	99	6 36	159	10 36	219	14 36	279	18 36	339	22 36	39	2 36	2 37	2 38	2 39
40	2 40	100	6 40	160	10 40	220	14 40	280	18 40	340	22 40	40	2 40	2 41	2 42	2 43
41	2 44	101	6 44	161	10 44	221	14 44	281	18 44	341	22 44	41	2 44	2 45	2 46	2 47
42	2 48	102	6 48	162	10 48	222	14 48	282	18 48	342	22 48	42	2 48	2 49	2 50	2 51
43	2 52	103	6 52	163	10 52	223	14 52	283	18 52	343	22 52	43	2 52	2 53	2 54	2 55
44	2 56	104	6 56	164	10 56	224	14 56	284	18 56	344	22 56	44	2 56	2 57	2 58	2 59
45	3 00	105	7 00	165	11 00	225	15 00	285	19 00	345	23 00	45	3 00	3 01	3 02	3 03
46	3 04	106	7 04	166	11 04	226	15 04	286	19 04	346	23 04	46	3 04	3 05	3 06	3 07
47	3 08	107	7 08	167	11 08	227	15 08	287	19 08	347	23 08	47	3 08	3 09	3 10	3 11
48	3 12	108	7 12	168	11 12	228	15 12	288	19 12	348	23 12	48	3 12	3 13	3 14	3 15
49	3 16	109	7 16	169	11 16	229	15 16	289	19 16	349	23 16	49	3 16	3 17	3 18	3 19
50	3 20	110	7 20	170	11 20	230	15 20	290	19 20	350	23 20	50	3 20	3 21	3 22	3 23
51	3 24	111	7 24	171	11 24	231	15 24	291	19 24	351	23 24	51	3 24	3 25	3 26	3 27
52	3 28	112	7 28	172	11 28	232	15 28	292	19 28	352	23 28	52	3 28	3 29	3 30	3 31
53	3 32	113	7 32	173	11 32	233	15 32	293	19 32	353	23 32	53	3 32	3 33	3 34	3 35
54	3 36	114	7 36	174	11 36	234	15 36	294	19 36	354	23 36	54	3 36	3 37	3 38	3 39
55	3 40	115	7 40	175	11 40	235	15 40	295	19 40	355	23 40	55	3 40	3 41	3 42	3 43
56	3 44	116	7 44	176	11 44	236	15 44	296	19 44	356	23 44	56	3 44	3 45	3 46	3 47
57	3 48	117	7 48	177	11 48	237	15 48	297	19 48	357	23 48	57	3 48	3 49	3 50	3 51
58	3 52	118	7 52	178	11 52	238	15 52	298	19 52	358	23 52	58	3 52	3 53	3 54	3 55
59	3 56	119	7 56	179	11 56	239	15 56	299	19 56	359	23 56	59	3 56	3 57	3 58	3 59

The above table is for converting expressions in arc to their equivalent in time; its main use in this Almanac is for the conversion of longitude for application to LMT (*added* if *west*, *subtracted* if *east*) to give UT or vice versa, particularly in the case of sunrise, sunset, etc.

i

0ᵐ / 1ᵐ — INCREMENTS AND CORRECTIONS

m 0 s	SUN PLANETS ° ′	ARIES ° ′	MOON ° ′	v or d ′	Corrⁿ ′	v or d ′	Corrⁿ ′	v or d ′	Corrⁿ ′	m 1 s	SUN PLANETS ° ′	ARIES ° ′	MOON ° ′	v or d ′	Corrⁿ ′	v or d ′	Corrⁿ ′	v or d ′	Corrⁿ ′
00	0 00·0	0 00·0	0 00·0	0·0	0·0	6·0	0·1	12·0	0·1	00	0 15·0	0 15·0	0 14·3	0·0	0·0	6·0	0·2	12·0	0·3
01	0 00·3	0 00·3	0 00·2	0·1	0·0	6·1	0·1	12·1	0·1	01	0 15·3	0 15·3	0 14·6	0·1	0·0	6·1	0·2	12·1	0·3
02	0 00·5	0 00·5	0 00·5	0·2	0·0	6·2	0·1	12·2	0·1	02	0 15·5	0 15·5	0 14·8	0·2	0·0	6·2	0·2	12·2	0·3
03	0 00·8	0 00·8	0 00·7	0·3	0·0	6·3	0·1	12·3	0·1	03	0 15·8	0 15·8	0 15·0	0·3	0·0	6·3	0·2	12·3	0·3
04	0 01·0	0 01·0	0 01·0	0·4	0·0	6·4	0·1	12·4	0·1	04	0 16·0	0 16·0	0 15·3	0·4	0·0	6·4	0·2	12·4	0·3
05	0 01·3	0 01·3	0 01·2	0·5	0·0	6·5	0·1	12·5	0·1	05	0 16·3	0 16·3	0 15·5	0·5	0·0	6·5	0·2	12·5	0·3
06	0 01·5	0 01·5	0 01·4	0·6	0·0	6·6	0·1	12·6	0·1	06	0 16·5	0 16·5	0 15·7	0·6	0·0	6·6	0·2	12·6	0·3
07	0 01·8	0 01·8	0 01·7	0·7	0·0	6·7	0·1	12·7	0·1	07	0 16·8	0 16·8	0 16·0	0·7	0·0	6·7	0·2	12·7	0·3
08	0 02·0	0 02·0	0 01·9	0·8	0·0	6·8	0·1	12·8	0·1	08	0 17·0	0 17·0	0 16·2	0·8	0·0	6·8	0·2	12·8	0·3
09	0 02·3	0 02·3	0 02·1	0·9	0·0	6·9	0·1	12·9	0·1	09	0 17·3	0 17·3	0 16·5	0·9	0·0	6·9	0·2	12·9	0·3
10	0 02·5	0 02·5	0 02·4	1·0	0·0	7·0	0·1	13·0	0·1	10	0 17·5	0 17·5	0 16·7	1·0	0·0	7·0	0·2	13·0	0·3
11	0 02·8	0 02·8	0 02·6	1·1	0·0	7·1	0·1	13·1	0·1	11	0 17·8	0 17·8	0 16·9	1·1	0·0	7·1	0·2	13·1	0·3
12	0 03·0	0 03·0	0 02·9	1·2	0·0	7·2	0·1	13·2	0·1	12	0 18·0	0 18·0	0 17·2	1·2	0·0	7·2	0·2	13·2	0·3
13	0 03·3	0 03·3	0 03·1	1·3	0·0	7·3	0·1	13·3	0·1	13	0 18·3	0 18·3	0 17·4	1·3	0·0	7·3	0·2	13·3	0·3
14	0 03·5	0 03·5	0 03·3	1·4	0·0	7·4	0·1	13·4	0·1	14	0 18·5	0 18·6	0 17·7	1·4	0·0	7·4	0·2	13·4	0·3
15	0 03·8	0 03·8	0 03·6	1·5	0·0	7·5	0·1	13·5	0·1	15	0 18·8	0 18·8	0 17·9	1·5	0·0	7·5	0·2	13·5	0·3
16	0 04·0	0 04·0	0 03·8	1·6	0·0	7·6	0·1	13·6	0·1	16	0 19·0	0 19·1	0 18·1	1·6	0·0	7·6	0·2	13·6	0·3
17	0 04·3	0 04·3	0 04·1	1·7	0·0	7·7	0·1	13·7	0·1	17	0 19·3	0 19·3	0 18·4	1·7	0·0	7·7	0·2	13·7	0·3
18	0 04·5	0 04·5	0 04·3	1·8	0·0	7·8	0·1	13·8	0·1	18	0 19·5	0 19·6	0 18·6	1·8	0·0	7·8	0·2	13·8	0·3
19	0 04·8	0 04·8	0 04·5	1·9	0·0	7·9	0·1	13·9	0·1	19	0 19·8	0 19·8	0 18·9	1·9	0·0	7·9	0·2	13·9	0·3
20	0 05·0	0 05·0	0 04·8	2·0	0·0	8·0	0·1	14·0	0·1	20	0 20·0	0 20·1	0 19·1	2·0	0·1	8·0	0·2	14·0	0·4
21	0 05·3	0 05·3	0 05·0	2·1	0·0	8·1	0·1	14·1	0·1	21	0 20·3	0 20·3	0 19·3	2·1	0·1	8·1	0·2	14·1	0·4
22	0 05·5	0 05·5	0 05·2	2·2	0·0	8·2	0·1	14·2	0·1	22	0 20·5	0 20·6	0 19·6	2·2	0·1	8·2	0·2	14·2	0·4
23	0 05·8	0 05·8	0 05·5	2·3	0·0	8·3	0·1	14·3	0·1	23	0 20·8	0 20·8	0 19·8	2·3	0·1	8·3	0·2	14·3	0·4
24	0 06·0	0 06·0	0 05·7	2·4	0·0	8·4	0·1	14·4	0·1	24	0 21·0	0 21·1	0 20·0	2·4	0·1	8·4	0·2	14·4	0·4
25	0 06·3	0 06·3	0 06·0	2·5	0·0	8·5	0·1	14·5	0·1	25	0 21·3	0 21·3	0 20·3	2·5	0·1	8·5	0·2	14·5	0·4
26	0 06·5	0 06·5	0 06·2	2·6	0·0	8·6	0·1	14·6	0·1	26	0 21·5	0 21·6	0 20·5	2·6	0·1	8·6	0·2	14·6	0·4
27	0 06·8	0 06·8	0 06·4	2·7	0·0	8·7	0·1	14·7	0·1	27	0 21·8	0 21·8	0 20·8	2·7	0·1	8·7	0·2	14·7	0·4
28	0 07·0	0 07·0	0 06·7	2·8	0·0	8·8	0·1	14·8	0·1	28	0 22·0	0 22·1	0 21·0	2·8	0·1	8·8	0·2	14·8	0·4
29	0 07·3	0 07·3	0 06·9	2·9	0·0	8·9	0·1	14·9	0·1	29	0 22·3	0 22·3	0 21·2	2·9	0·1	8·9	0·2	14·9	0·4
30	0 07·5	0 07·5	0 07·2	3·0	0·0	9·0	0·1	15·0	0·1	30	0 22·5	0 22·6	0 21·5	3·0	0·1	9·0	0·2	15·0	0·4
31	0 07·8	0 07·8	0 07·4	3·1	0·0	9·1	0·1	15·1	0·1	31	0 22·8	0 22·8	0 21·7	3·1	0·1	9·1	0·2	15·1	0·4
32	0 08·0	0 08·0	0 07·6	3·2	0·0	9·2	0·1	15·2	0·1	32	0 23·0	0 23·1	0 22·0	3·2	0·1	9·2	0·2	15·2	0·4
33	0 08·3	0 08·3	0 07·9	3·3	0·0	9·3	0·1	15·3	0·1	33	0 23·3	0 23·3	0 22·2	3·3	0·1	9·3	0·2	15·3	0·4
34	0 08·5	0 08·5	0 08·1	3·4	0·0	9·4	0·1	15·4	0·1	34	0 23·5	0 23·6	0 22·4	3·4	0·1	9·4	0·2	15·4	0·4
35	0 08·8	0 08·8	0 08·4	3·5	0·0	9·5	0·1	15·5	0·1	35	0 23·8	0 23·8	0 22·7	3·5	0·1	9·5	0·2	15·5	0·4
36	0 09·0	0 09·0	0 08·6	3·6	0·0	9·6	0·1	15·6	0·1	36	0 24·0	0 24·1	0 22·9	3·6	0·1	9·6	0·2	15·6	0·4
37	0 09·3	0 09·3	0 08·8	3·7	0·0	9·7	0·1	15·7	0·1	37	0 24·3	0 24·3	0 23·1	3·7	0·1	9·7	0·2	15·7	0·4
38	0 09·5	0 09·5	0 09·1	3·8	0·0	9·8	0·1	15·8	0·1	38	0 24·5	0 24·6	0 23·4	3·8	0·1	9·8	0·2	15·8	0·4
39	0 09·8	0 09·8	0 09·3	3·9	0·0	9·9	0·1	15·9	0·1	39	0 24·8	0 24·8	0 23·6	3·9	0·1	9·9	0·2	15·9	0·4
40	0 10·0	0 10·0	0 09·5	4·0	0·0	10·0	0·1	16·0	0·1	40	0 25·0	0 25·1	0 23·9	4·0	0·1	10·0	0·3	16·0	0·4
41	0 10·3	0 10·3	0 09·8	4·1	0·0	10·1	0·1	16·1	0·1	41	0 25·3	0 25·3	0 24·1	4·1	0·1	10·1	0·3	16·1	0·4
42	0 10·5	0 10·5	0 10·0	4·2	0·0	10·2	0·1	16·2	0·1	42	0 25·5	0 25·6	0 24·3	4·2	0·1	10·2	0·3	16·2	0·4
43	0 10·8	0 10·8	0 10·3	4·3	0·0	10·3	0·1	16·3	0·1	43	0 25·8	0 25·8	0 24·6	4·3	0·1	10·3	0·3	16·3	0·4
44	0 11·0	0 11·0	0 10·5	4·4	0·0	10·4	0·1	16·4	0·1	44	0 26·0	0 26·1	0 24·8	4·4	0·1	10·4	0·3	16·4	0·4
45	0 11·3	0 11·3	0 10·7	4·5	0·0	10·5	0·1	16·5	0·1	45	0 26·3	0 26·3	0 25·1	4·5	0·1	10·5	0·3	16·5	0·4
46	0 11·5	0 11·5	0 11·0	4·6	0·0	10·6	0·1	16·6	0·1	46	0 26·5	0 26·6	0 25·3	4·6	0·1	10·6	0·3	16·6	0·4
47	0 11·8	0 11·8	0 11·2	4·7	0·0	10·7	0·1	16·7	0·1	47	0 26·8	0 26·8	0 25·5	4·7	0·1	10·7	0·3	16·7	0·4
48	0 12·0	0 12·0	0 11·5	4·8	0·0	10·8	0·1	16·8	0·1	48	0 27·0	0 27·1	0 25·8	4·8	0·1	10·8	0·3	16·8	0·4
49	0 12·3	0 12·3	0 11·7	4·9	0·0	10·9	0·1	16·9	0·1	49	0 27·3	0 27·3	0 26·0	4·9	0·1	10·9	0·3	16·9	0·4
50	0 12·5	0 12·5	0 11·9	5·0	0·0	11·0	0·1	17·0	0·1	50	0 27·5	0 27·6	0 26·2	5·0	0·1	11·0	0·3	17·0	0·4
51	0 12·8	0 12·8	0 12·2	5·1	0·0	11·1	0·1	17·1	0·1	51	0 27·8	0 27·8	0 26·5	5·1	0·1	11·1	0·3	17·1	0·4
52	0 13·0	0 13·0	0 12·4	5·2	0·0	11·2	0·1	17·2	0·1	52	0 28·0	0 28·1	0 26·7	5·2	0·1	11·2	0·3	17·2	0·4
53	0 13·3	0 13·3	0 12·6	5·3	0·0	11·3	0·1	17·3	0·1	53	0 28·3	0 28·3	0 27·0	5·3	0·1	11·3	0·3	17·3	0·4
54	0 13·5	0 13·5	0 12·9	5·4	0·0	11·4	0·1	17·4	0·1	54	0 28·5	0 28·6	0 27·2	5·4	0·1	11·4	0·3	17·4	0·4
55	0 13·8	0 13·8	0 13·1	5·5	0·0	11·5	0·1	17·5	0·1	55	0 28·8	0 28·8	0 27·4	5·5	0·1	11·5	0·3	17·5	0·4
56	0 14·0	0 14·0	0 13·4	5·6	0·0	11·6	0·1	17·6	0·1	56	0 29·0	0 29·1	0 27·7	5·6	0·1	11·6	0·3	17·6	0·4
57	0 14·3	0 14·3	0 13·6	5·7	0·0	11·7	0·1	17·7	0·1	57	0 29·3	0 29·3	0 27·9	5·7	0·1	11·7	0·3	17·7	0·4
58	0 14·5	0 14·5	0 13·8	5·8	0·0	11·8	0·1	17·8	0·1	58	0 29·5	0 29·6	0 28·2	5·8	0·1	11·8	0·3	17·8	0·4
59	0 14·8	0 14·8	0 14·1	5·9	0·0	11·9	0·1	17·9	0·1	59	0 29·8	0 29·8	0 28·4	5·9	0·1	11·9	0·3	17·9	0·4
60	0 15·0	0 15·0	0 14·3	6·0	0·1	12·0	0·1	18·0	0·2	60	0 30·0	0 30·1	0 28·6	6·0	0·2	12·0	0·3	18·0	0·5

$\begin{smallmatrix}m\\2\end{smallmatrix}$	SUN PLANETS	ARIES	MOON	v or Corr^n d		v or Corr^n d		v or Corr^n d	
s	° ′	° ′	° ′	′	′	′	′	′	′
00	0 30.0	0 30.1	0 28.6	0.0	0.0	6.0	0.3	12.0	0.5
01	0 30.3	0 30.3	0 28.9	0.1	0.0	6.1	0.3	12.1	0.5
02	0 30.5	0 30.6	0 29.1	0.2	0.0	6.2	0.3	12.2	0.5
03	0 30.8	0 30.8	0 29.3	0.3	0.0	6.3	0.3	12.3	0.5
04	0 31.0	0 31.1	0 29.6	0.4	0.0	6.4	0.3	12.4	0.5
05	0 31.3	0 31.3	0 29.8	0.5	0.0	6.5	0.3	12.5	0.5
06	0 31.5	0 31.6	0 30.1	0.6	0.0	6.6	0.3	12.6	0.5
07	0 31.8	0 31.8	0 30.3	0.7	0.0	6.7	0.3	12.7	0.5
08	0 32.0	0 32.1	0 30.5	0.8	0.0	6.8	0.3	12.8	0.5
09	0 32.3	0 32.3	0 30.8	0.9	0.0	6.9	0.3	12.9	0.5
10	0 32.5	0 32.6	0 31.0	1.0	0.0	7.0	0.3	13.0	0.5
11	0 32.8	0 32.8	0 31.3	1.1	0.0	7.1	0.3	13.1	0.5
12	0 33.0	0 33.1	0 31.5	1.2	0.1	7.2	0.3	13.2	0.6
13	0 33.3	0 33.3	0 31.7	1.3	0.1	7.3	0.3	13.3	0.6
14	0 33.5	0 33.6	0 32.0	1.4	0.1	7.4	0.3	13.4	0.6
15	0 33.8	0 33.8	0 32.2	1.5	0.1	7.5	0.3	13.5	0.6
16	0 34.0	0 34.1	0 32.5	1.6	0.1	7.6	0.3	13.6	0.6
17	0 34.3	0 34.3	0 32.7	1.7	0.1	7.7	0.3	13.7	0.6
18	0 34.5	0 34.6	0 32.9	1.8	0.1	7.8	0.3	13.8	0.6
19	0 34.8	0 34.8	0 33.2	1.9	0.1	7.9	0.3	13.9	0.6
20	0 35.0	0 35.1	0 33.4	2.0	0.1	8.0	0.3	14.0	0.6
21	0 35.3	0 35.3	0 33.6	2.1	0.1	8.1	0.3	14.1	0.6
22	0 35.5	0 35.6	0 33.9	2.2	0.1	8.2	0.3	14.2	0.6
23	0 35.8	0 35.8	0 34.1	2.3	0.1	8.3	0.3	14.3	0.6
24	0 36.0	0 36.1	0 34.4	2.4	0.1	8.4	0.4	14.4	0.6
25	0 36.3	0 36.3	0 34.6	2.5	0.1	8.5	0.4	14.5	0.6
26	0 36.5	0 36.6	0 34.8	2.6	0.1	8.6	0.4	14.6	0.6
27	0 36.8	0 36.9	0 35.1	2.7	0.1	8.7	0.4	14.7	0.6
28	0 37.0	0 37.1	0 35.3	2.8	0.1	8.8	0.4	14.8	0.6
29	0 37.3	0 37.4	0 35.6	2.9	0.1	8.9	0.4	14.9	0.6
30	0 37.5	0 37.6	0 35.8	3.0	0.1	9.0	0.4	15.0	0.6
31	0 37.8	0 37.9	0 36.0	3.1	0.1	9.1	0.4	15.1	0.6
32	0 38.0	0 38.1	0 36.3	3.2	0.1	9.2	0.4	15.2	0.6
33	0 38.3	0 38.4	0 36.5	3.3	0.1	9.3	0.4	15.3	0.6
34	0 38.5	0 38.6	0 36.7	3.4	0.1	9.4	0.4	15.4	0.6
35	0 38.8	0 38.9	0 37.0	3.5	0.1	9.5	0.4	15.5	0.6
36	0 39.0	0 39.1	0 37.2	3.6	0.2	9.6	0.4	15.6	0.7
37	0 39.3	0 39.4	0 37.5	3.7	0.2	9.7	0.4	15.7	0.7
38	0 39.5	0 39.6	0 37.7	3.8	0.2	9.8	0.4	15.8	0.7
39	0 39.8	0 39.9	0 37.9	3.9	0.2	9.9	0.4	15.9	0.7
40	0 40.0	0 40.1	0 38.2	4.0	0.2	10.0	0.4	16.0	0.7
41	0 40.3	0 40.4	0 38.4	4.1	0.2	10.1	0.4	16.1	0.7
42	0 40.5	0 40.6	0 38.7	4.2	0.2	10.2	0.4	16.2	0.7
43	0 40.8	0 40.9	0 38.9	4.3	0.2	10.3	0.4	16.3	0.7
44	0 41.0	0 41.1	0 39.1	4.4	0.2	10.4	0.4	16.4	0.7
45	0 41.3	0 41.4	0 39.4	4.5	0.2	10.5	0.4	16.5	0.7
46	0 41.5	0 41.6	0 39.6	4.6	0.2	10.6	0.4	16.6	0.7
47	0 41.8	0 41.9	0 39.8	4.7	0.2	10.7	0.4	16.7	0.7
48	0 42.0	0 42.1	0 40.1	4.8	0.2	10.8	0.5	16.8	0.7
49	0 42.3	0 42.4	0 40.3	4.9	0.2	10.9	0.5	16.9	0.7
50	0 42.5	0 42.6	0 40.6	5.0	0.2	11.0	0.5	17.0	0.7
51	0 42.8	0 42.9	0 40.8	5.1	0.2	11.1	0.5	17.1	0.7
52	0 43.0	0 43.1	0 41.0	5.2	0.2	11.2	0.5	17.2	0.7
53	0 43.3	0 43.4	0 41.3	5.3	0.2	11.3	0.5	17.3	0.7
54	0 43.5	0 43.6	0 41.5	5.4	0.2	11.4	0.5	17.4	0.7
55	0 43.8	0 43.9	0 41.8	5.5	0.2	11.5	0.5	17.5	0.7
56	0 44.0	0 44.1	0 42.0	5.6	0.2	11.6	0.5	17.6	0.7
57	0 44.3	0 44.4	0 42.2	5.7	0.2	11.7	0.5	17.7	0.7
58	0 44.5	0 44.6	0 42.5	5.8	0.2	11.8	0.5	17.8	0.7
59	0 44.8	0 44.9	0 42.7	5.9	0.2	11.9	0.5	17.9	0.7
60	0 45.0	0 45.1	0 43.0	6.0	0.3	12.0	0.5	18.0	0.8

$\begin{smallmatrix}m\\3\end{smallmatrix}$	SUN PLANETS	ARIES	MOON	v or Corr^n d		v or Corr^n d		v or Corr^n d	
s	° ′	° ′	° ′	′	′	′	′	′	′
00	0 45.0	0 45.1	0 43.0	0.0	0.0	6.0	0.4	12.0	0.7
01	0 45.3	0 45.4	0 43.2	0.1	0.0	6.1	0.4	12.1	0.7
02	0 45.5	0 45.6	0 43.4	0.2	0.0	6.2	0.4	12.2	0.7
03	0 45.8	0 45.9	0 43.7	0.3	0.0	6.3	0.4	12.3	0.7
04	0 46.0	0 46.1	0 43.9	0.4	0.0	6.4	0.4	12.4	0.7
05	0 46.3	0 46.4	0 44.1	0.5	0.0	6.5	0.4	12.5	0.7
06	0 46.5	0 46.6	0 44.4	0.6	0.0	6.6	0.4	12.6	0.7
07	0 46.8	0 46.9	0 44.6	0.7	0.0	6.7	0.4	12.7	0.7
08	0 47.0	0 47.1	0 44.9	0.8	0.0	6.8	0.4	12.8	0.7
09	0 47.3	0 47.4	0 45.1	0.9	0.1	6.9	0.4	12.9	0.8
10	0 47.5	0 47.6	0 45.3	1.0	0.1	7.0	0.4	13.0	0.8
11	0 47.8	0 47.9	0 45.6	1.1	0.1	7.1	0.4	13.1	0.8
12	0 48.0	0 48.1	0 45.8	1.2	0.1	7.2	0.4	13.2	0.8
13	0 48.3	0 48.4	0 46.1	1.3	0.1	7.3	0.4	13.3	0.8
14	0 48.5	0 48.6	0 46.3	1.4	0.1	7.4	0.4	13.4	0.8
15	0 48.8	0 48.9	0 46.5	1.5	0.1	7.5	0.4	13.5	0.8
16	0 49.0	0 49.1	0 46.8	1.6	0.1	7.6	0.4	13.6	0.8
17	0 49.3	0 49.4	0 47.0	1.7	0.1	7.7	0.4	13.7	0.8
18	0 49.5	0 49.6	0 47.2	1.8	0.1	7.8	0.5	13.8	0.8
19	0 49.8	0 49.9	0 47.5	1.9	0.1	7.9	0.5	13.9	0.8
20	0 50.0	0 50.1	0 47.7	2.0	0.1	8.0	0.5	14.0	0.8
21	0 50.3	0 50.4	0 48.0	2.1	0.1	8.1	0.5	14.1	0.8
22	0 50.5	0 50.6	0 48.2	2.2	0.1	8.2	0.5	14.2	0.8
23	0 50.8	0 50.9	0 48.4	2.3	0.1	8.3	0.5	14.3	0.8
24	0 51.0	0 51.1	0 48.7	2.4	0.1	8.4	0.5	14.4	0.8
25	0 51.3	0 51.4	0 48.9	2.5	0.1	8.5	0.5	14.5	0.8
26	0 51.5	0 51.6	0 49.2	2.6	0.2	8.6	0.5	14.6	0.9
27	0 51.8	0 51.9	0 49.4	2.7	0.2	8.7	0.5	14.7	0.9
28	0 52.0	0 52.1	0 49.6	2.8	0.2	8.8	0.5	14.8	0.9
29	0 52.3	0 52.4	0 49.9	2.9	0.2	8.9	0.5	14.9	0.9
30	0 52.5	0 52.6	0 50.1	3.0	0.2	9.0	0.5	15.0	0.9
31	0 52.8	0 52.9	0 50.3	3.1	0.2	9.1	0.5	15.1	0.9
32	0 53.0	0 53.1	0 50.6	3.2	0.2	9.2	0.5	15.2	0.9
33	0 53.3	0 53.4	0 50.8	3.3	0.2	9.3	0.5	15.3	0.9
34	0 53.5	0 53.6	0 51.1	3.4	0.2	9.4	0.5	15.4	0.9
35	0 53.8	0 53.9	0 51.3	3.5	0.2	9.5	0.6	15.5	0.9
36	0 54.0	0 54.1	0 51.5	3.6	0.2	9.6	0.6	15.6	0.9
37	0 54.3	0 54.4	0 51.8	3.7	0.2	9.7	0.6	15.7	0.9
38	0 54.5	0 54.6	0 52.0	3.8	0.2	9.8	0.6	15.8	0.9
39	0 54.8	0 54.9	0 52.3	3.9	0.2	9.9	0.6	15.9	0.9
40	0 55.0	0 55.2	0 52.5	4.0	0.2	10.0	0.6	16.0	0.9
41	0 55.3	0 55.4	0 52.7	4.1	0.2	10.1	0.6	16.1	0.9
42	0 55.5	0 55.7	0 53.0	4.2	0.2	10.2	0.6	16.2	0.9
43	0 55.8	0 55.9	0 53.2	4.3	0.3	10.3	0.6	16.3	1.0
44	0 56.0	0 56.2	0 53.4	4.4	0.3	10.4	0.6	16.4	1.0
45	0 56.3	0 56.4	0 53.7	4.5	0.3	10.5	0.6	16.5	1.0
46	0 56.5	0 56.7	0 53.9	4.6	0.3	10.6	0.6	16.6	1.0
47	0 56.8	0 56.9	0 54.2	4.7	0.3	10.7	0.6	16.7	1.0
48	0 57.0	0 57.2	0 54.4	4.8	0.3	10.8	0.6	16.8	1.0
49	0 57.3	0 57.4	0 54.6	4.9	0.3	10.9	0.6	16.9	1.0
50	0 57.5	0 57.7	0 54.9	5.0	0.3	11.0	0.6	17.0	1.0
51	0 57.8	0 57.9	0 55.1	5.1	0.3	11.1	0.6	17.1	1.0
52	0 58.0	0 58.2	0 55.4	5.2	0.3	11.2	0.7	17.2	1.0
53	0 58.3	0 58.4	0 55.6	5.3	0.3	11.3	0.7	17.3	1.0
54	0 58.5	0 58.7	0 55.8	5.4	0.3	11.4	0.7	17.4	1.0
55	0 58.8	0 58.9	0 56.1	5.5	0.3	11.5	0.7	17.5	1.0
56	0 59.0	0 59.2	0 56.3	5.6	0.3	11.6	0.7	17.6	1.0
57	0 59.3	0 59.4	0 56.6	5.7	0.3	11.7	0.7	17.7	1.0
58	0 59.5	0 59.7	0 56.8	5.8	0.3	11.8	0.7	17.8	1.0
59	0 59.8	0 59.9	0 57.0	5.9	0.3	11.9	0.7	17.9	1.0
60	1 00.0	1 00.2	0 57.3	6.0	0.4	12.0	0.7	18.0	1.1

4ᵐ

4 s	SUN PLANETS	ARIES	MOON	v or d / Corrⁿ	v or d / Corrⁿ	v or d / Corrⁿ
00	1 00·0	1 00·2	0 57·3	0·0 0·0	6·0 0·5	12·0 0·9
01	1 00·3	1 00·4	0 57·5	0·1 0·0	6·1 0·5	12·1 0·9
02	1 00·5	1 00·7	0 57·7	0·2 0·0	6·2 0·5	12·2 0·9
03	1 00·8	1 00·9	0 58·0	0·3 0·0	6·3 0·5	12·3 0·9
04	1 01·0	1 01·2	0 58·2	0·4 0·0	6·4 0·5	12·4 0·9
05	1 01·3	1 01·4	0 58·5	0·5 0·0	6·5 0·5	12·5 0·9
06	1 01·5	1 01·7	0 58·7	0·6 0·0	6·6 0·5	12·6 0·9
07	1 01·8	1 01·9	0 58·9	0·7 0·1	6·7 0·5	12·7 1·0
08	1 02·0	1 02·2	0 59·2	0·8 0·1	6·8 0·5	12·8 1·0
09	1 02·3	1 02·4	0 59·4	0·9 0·1	6·9 0·5	12·9 1·0
10	1 02·5	1 02·7	0 59·7	1·0 0·1	7·0 0·5	13·0 1·0
11	1 02·8	1 02·9	0 59·9	1·1 0·1	7·1 0·5	13·1 1·0
12	1 03·0	1 03·2	1 00·1	1·2 0·1	7·2 0·5	13·2 1·0
13	1 03·3	1 03·4	1 00·4	1·3 0·1	7·3 0·5	13·3 1·0
14	1 03·5	1 03·7	1 00·6	1·4 0·1	7·4 0·6	13·4 1·0
15	1 03·8	1 03·9	1 00·8	1·5 0·1	7·5 0·6	13·5 1·0
16	1 04·0	1 04·2	1 01·1	1·6 0·1	7·6 0·6	13·6 1·0
17	1 04·3	1 04·4	1 01·3	1·7 0·1	7·7 0·6	13·7 1·0
18	1 04·5	1 04·7	1 01·6	1·8 0·1	7·8 0·6	13·8 1·0
19	1 04·8	1 04·9	1 01·8	1·9 0·1	7·9 0·6	13·9 1·0
20	1 05·0	1 05·2	1 02·0	2·0 0·2	8·0 0·6	14·0 1·1
21	1 05·3	1 05·4	1 02·3	2·1 0·2	8·1 0·6	14·1 1·1
22	1 05·5	1 05·7	1 02·5	2·2 0·2	8·2 0·6	14·2 1·1
23	1 05·8	1 05·9	1 02·8	2·3 0·2	8·3 0·6	14·3 1·1
24	1 06·0	1 06·2	1 03·0	2·4 0·2	8·4 0·6	14·4 1·1
25	1 06·3	1 06·4	1 03·2	2·5 0·2	8·5 0·6	14·5 1·1
26	1 06·5	1 06·7	1 03·5	2·6 0·2	8·6 0·6	14·6 1·1
27	1 06·8	1 06·9	1 03·7	2·7 0·2	8·7 0·7	14·7 1·1
28	1 07·0	1 07·2	1 03·9	2·8 0·2	8·8 0·7	14·8 1·1
29	1 07·3	1 07·4	1 04·2	2·9 0·2	8·9 0·7	14·9 1·1
30	1 07·5	1 07·7	1 04·4	3·0 0·2	9·0 0·7	15·0 1·1
31	1 07·8	1 07·9	1 04·7	3·1 0·2	9·1 0·7	15·1 1·1
32	1 08·0	1 08·2	1 04·9	3·2 0·2	9·2 0·7	15·2 1·1
33	1 08·3	1 08·4	1 05·1	3·3 0·2	9·3 0·7	15·3 1·1
34	1 08·5	1 08·7	1 05·4	3·4 0·3	9·4 0·7	15·4 1·2
35	1 08·8	1 08·9	1 05·6	3·5 0·3	9·5 0·7	15·5 1·2
36	1 09·0	1 09·2	1 05·9	3·6 0·3	9·6 0·7	15·6 1·2
37	1 09·3	1 09·4	1 06·1	3·7 0·3	9·7 0·7	15·7 1·2
38	1 09·5	1 09·7	1 06·3	3·8 0·3	9·8 0·7	15·8 1·2
39	1 09·8	1 09·9	1 06·6	3·9 0·3	9·9 0·7	15·9 1·2
40	1 10·0	1 10·2	1 06·8	4·0 0·3	10·0 0·8	16·0 1·2
41	1 10·3	1 10·4	1 07·0	4·1 0·3	10·1 0·8	16·1 1·2
42	1 10·5	1 10·7	1 07·3	4·2 0·3	10·2 0·8	16·2 1·2
43	1 10·8	1 10·9	1 07·5	4·3 0·3	10·3 0·8	16·3 1·2
44	1 11·0	1 11·2	1 07·8	4·4 0·3	10·4 0·8	16·4 1·2
45	1 11·3	1 11·4	1 08·0	4·5 0·3	10·5 0·8	16·5 1·2
46	1 11·5	1 11·7	1 08·2	4·6 0·3	10·6 0·8	16·6 1·2
47	1 11·8	1 11·9	1 08·5	4·7 0·4	10·7 0·8	16·7 1·3
48	1 12·0	1 12·2	1 08·7	4·8 0·4	10·8 0·8	16·8 1·3
49	1 12·3	1 12·4	1 09·0	4·9 0·4	10·9 0·8	16·9 1·3
50	1 12·5	1 12·7	1 09·2	5·0 0·4	11·0 0·8	17·0 1·3
51	1 12·8	1 12·9	1 09·4	5·1 0·4	11·1 0·8	17·1 1·3
52	1 13·0	1 13·2	1 09·7	5·2 0·4	11·2 0·8	17·2 1·3
53	1 13·3	1 13·5	1 09·9	5·3 0·4	11·3 0·8	17·3 1·3
54	1 13·5	1 13·7	1 10·2	5·4 0·4	11·4 0·9	17·4 1·3
55	1 13·8	1 14·0	1 10·4	5·5 0·4	11·5 0·9	17·5 1·3
56	1 14·0	1 14·2	1 10·6	5·6 0·4	11·6 0·9	17·6 1·3
57	1 14·3	1 14·5	1 10·9	5·7 0·4	11·7 0·9	17·7 1·3
58	1 14·5	1 14·7	1 11·1	5·8 0·4	11·8 0·9	17·8 1·3
59	1 14·8	1 15·0	1 11·3	5·9 0·4	11·9 0·9	17·9 1·3
60	1 15·0	1 15·2	1 11·6	6·0 0·5	12·0 0·9	18·0 1·4

5ᵐ

5 s	SUN PLANETS	ARIES	MOON	v or d / Corrⁿ	v or d / Corrⁿ	v or d / Corrⁿ
00	1 15·0	1 15·2	1 11·6	0·0 0·0	6·0 0·6	12·0 1·1
01	1 15·3	1 15·5	1 11·8	0·1 0·0	6·1 0·6	12·1 1·1
02	1 15·5	1 15·7	1 12·1	0·2 0·0	6·2 0·6	12·2 1·1
03	1 15·8	1 16·0	1 12·3	0·3 0·0	6·3 0·6	12·3 1·1
04	1 16·0	1 16·2	1 12·5	0·4 0·0	6·4 0·6	12·4 1·1
05	1 16·3	1 16·5	1 12·8	0·5 0·0	6·5 0·6	12·5 1·1
06	1 16·5	1 16·7	1 13·0	0·6 0·1	6·6 0·6	12·6 1·2
07	1 16·8	1 17·0	1 13·3	0·7 0·1	6·7 0·6	12·7 1·2
08	1 17·0	1 17·2	1 13·5	0·8 0·1	6·8 0·6	12·8 1·2
09	1 17·3	1 17·5	1 13·7	0·9 0·1	6·9 0·6	12·9 1·2
10	1 17·5	1 17·7	1 14·0	1·0 0·1	7·0 0·6	13·0 1·2
11	1 17·8	1 18·0	1 14·2	1·1 0·1	7·1 0·7	13·1 1·2
12	1 18·0	1 18·2	1 14·4	1·2 0·1	7·2 0·7	13·2 1·2
13	1 18·3	1 18·5	1 14·7	1·3 0·1	7·3 0·7	13·3 1·2
14	1 18·5	1 18·7	1 14·9	1·4 0·1	7·4 0·7	13·4 1·2
15	1 18·8	1 19·0	1 15·2	1·5 0·1	7·5 0·7	13·5 1·2
16	1 19·0	1 19·2	1 15·4	1·6 0·1	7·6 0·7	13·6 1·2
17	1 19·3	1 19·5	1 15·6	1·7 0·2	7·7 0·7	13·7 1·3
18	1 19·5	1 19·7	1 15·9	1·8 0·2	7·8 0·7	13·8 1·3
19	1 19·8	1 20·0	1 16·1	1·9 0·2	7·9 0·7	13·9 1·3
20	1 20·0	1 20·2	1 16·4	2·0 0·2	8·0 0·7	14·0 1·3
21	1 20·3	1 20·5	1 16·6	2·1 0·2	8·1 0·7	14·1 1·3
22	1 20·5	1 20·7	1 16·8	2·2 0·2	8·2 0·8	14·2 1·3
23	1 20·8	1 21·0	1 17·1	2·3 0·2	8·3 0·8	14·3 1·3
24	1 21·0	1 21·2	1 17·3	2·4 0·2	8·4 0·8	14·4 1·3
25	1 21·3	1 21·5	1 17·5	2·5 0·2	8·5 0·8	14·5 1·3
26	1 21·5	1 21·7	1 17·8	2·6 0·2	8·6 0·8	14·6 1·3
27	1 21·8	1 22·0	1 18·0	2·7 0·2	8·7 0·8	14·7 1·3
28	1 22·0	1 22·2	1 18·3	2·8 0·3	8·8 0·8	14·8 1·4
29	1 22·3	1 22·5	1 18·5	2·9 0·3	8·9 0·8	14·9 1·4
30	1 22·5	1 22·7	1 18·7	3·0 0·3	9·0 0·8	15·0 1·4
31	1 22·8	1 23·0	1 19·0	3·1 0·3	9·1 0·8	15·1 1·4
32	1 23·0	1 23·2	1 19·2	3·2 0·3	9·2 0·8	15·2 1·4
33	1 23·3	1 23·5	1 19·5	3·3 0·3	9·3 0·9	15·3 1·4
34	1 23·5	1 23·7	1 19·7	3·4 0·3	9·4 0·9	15·4 1·4
35	1 23·8	1 24·0	1 19·9	3·5 0·3	9·5 0·9	15·5 1·4
36	1 24·0	1 24·2	1 20·2	3·6 0·3	9·6 0·9	15·6 1·4
37	1 24·3	1 24·5	1 20·4	3·7 0·3	9·7 0·9	15·7 1·4
38	1 24·5	1 24·7	1 20·7	3·8 0·3	9·8 0·9	15·8 1·4
39	1 24·8	1 25·0	1 20·9	3·9 0·4	9·9 0·9	15·9 1·5
40	1 25·0	1 25·2	1 21·1	4·0 0·4	10·0 0·9	16·0 1·5
41	1 25·3	1 25·5	1 21·4	4·1 0·4	10·1 0·9	16·1 1·5
42	1 25·5	1 25·7	1 21·6	4·2 0·4	10·2 0·9	16·2 1·5
43	1 25·8	1 26·0	1 21·8	4·3 0·4	10·3 0·9	16·3 1·5
44	1 26·0	1 26·2	1 22·1	4·4 0·4	10·4 1·0	16·4 1·5
45	1 26·3	1 26·5	1 22·3	4·5 0·4	10·5 1·0	16·5 1·5
46	1 26·5	1 26·7	1 22·6	4·6 0·4	10·6 1·0	16·6 1·5
47	1 26·8	1 27·0	1 22·8	4·7 0·4	10·7 1·0	16·7 1·5
48	1 27·0	1 27·2	1 23·0	4·8 0·4	10·8 1·0	16·8 1·5
49	1 27·3	1 27·5	1 23·3	4·9 0·4	10·9 1·0	16·9 1·5
50	1 27·5	1 27·7	1 23·5	5·0 0·5	11·0 1·0	17·0 1·6
51	1 27·8	1 28·0	1 23·8	5·1 0·5	11·1 1·0	17·1 1·6
52	1 28·0	1 28·2	1 24·0	5·2 0·5	11·2 1·0	17·2 1·6
53	1 28·3	1 28·5	1 24·2	5·3 0·5	11·3 1·0	17·3 1·6
54	1 28·5	1 28·7	1 24·5	5·4 0·5	11·4 1·0	17·4 1·6
55	1 28·8	1 29·0	1 24·7	5·5 0·5	11·5 1·1	17·5 1·6
56	1 29·0	1 29·2	1 24·9	5·6 0·5	11·6 1·1	17·6 1·6
57	1 29·3	1 29·5	1 25·2	5·7 0·5	11·7 1·1	17·7 1·6
58	1 29·5	1 29·7	1 25·4	5·8 0·5	11·8 1·1	17·8 1·6
59	1 29·8	1 30·0	1 25·7	5·9 0·5	11·9 1·1	17·9 1·6
60	1 30·0	1 30·2	1 25·9	6·0 0·6	12·0 1·1	18·0 1·7

iv

m 6	SUN PLANETS	ARIES	MOON	v or d Corrⁿ		v or d Corrⁿ		v or d Corrⁿ	
s	° ′	° ′	° ′	′	′	′	′	′	′
00	1 30·0	1 30·2	1 25·9	0·0	0·0	6·0	0·7	12·0	1·3
01	1 30·3	1 30·5	1 26·1	0·1	0·0	6·1	0·7	12·1	1·3
02	1 30·5	1 30·7	1 26·4	0·2	0·0	6·2	0·7	12·2	1·3
03	1 30·8	1 31·0	1 26·6	0·3	0·0	6·3	0·7	12·3	1·3
04	1 31·0	1 31·2	1 26·9	0·4	0·0	6·4	0·7	12·4	1·3
05	1 31·3	1 31·5	1 27·1	0·5	0·1	6·5	0·7	12·5	1·4
06	1 31·5	1 31·8	1 27·3	0·6	0·1	6·6	0·7	12·6	1·4
07	1 31·8	1 32·0	1 27·6	0·7	0·1	6·7	0·7	12·7	1·4
08	1 32·0	1 32·3	1 27·8	0·8	0·1	6·8	0·7	12·8	1·4
09	1 32·3	1 32·5	1 28·0	0·9	0·1	6·9	0·7	12·9	1·4
10	1 32·5	1 32·8	1 28·3	1·0	0·1	7·0	0·8	13·0	1·4
11	1 32·8	1 33·0	1 28·5	1·1	0·1	7·1	0·8	13·1	1·4
12	1 33·0	1 33·3	1 28·8	1·2	0·1	7·2	0·8	13·2	1·4
13	1 33·3	1 33·5	1 29·0	1·3	0·1	7·3	0·8	13·3	1·4
14	1 33·5	1 33·8	1 29·2	1·4	0·2	7·4	0·8	13·4	1·5
15	1 33·8	1 34·0	1 29·5	1·5	0·2	7·5	0·8	13·5	1·5
16	1 34·0	1 34·3	1 29·7	1·6	0·2	7·6	0·8	13·6	1·5
17	1 34·3	1 34·5	1 30·0	1·7	0·2	7·7	0·8	13·7	1·5
18	1 34·5	1 34·8	1 30·2	1·8	0·2	7·8	0·8	13·8	1·5
19	1 34·8	1 35·0	1 30·4	1·9	0·2	7·9	0·9	13·9	1·5
20	1 35·0	1 35·3	1 30·7	2·0	0·2	8·0	0·9	14·0	1·5
21	1 35·3	1 35·5	1 30·9	2·1	0·2	8·1	0·9	14·1	1·5
22	1 35·5	1 35·8	1 31·1	2·2	0·2	8·2	0·9	14·2	1·5
23	1 35·8	1 36·0	1 31·4	2·3	0·2	8·3	0·9	14·3	1·5
24	1 36·0	1 36·3	1 31·6	2·4	0·3	8·4	0·9	14·4	1·6
25	1 36·3	1 36·5	1 31·9	2·5	0·3	8·5	0·9	14·5	1·6
26	1 36·5	1 36·8	1 32·1	2·6	0·3	8·6	0·9	14·6	1·6
27	1 36·8	1 37·0	1 32·3	2·7	0·3	8·7	0·9	14·7	1·6
28	1 37·0	1 37·3	1 32·6	2·8	0·3	8·8	1·0	14·8	1·6
29	1 37·3	1 37·5	1 32·8	2·9	0·3	8·9	1·0	14·9	1·6
30	1 37·5	1 37·8	1 33·1	3·0	0·3	9·0	1·0	15·0	1·6
31	1 37·8	1 38·0	1 33·3	3·1	0·3	9·1	1·0	15·1	1·6
32	1 38·0	1 38·3	1 33·5	3·2	0·3	9·2	1·0	15·2	1·6
33	1 38·3	1 38·5	1 33·8	3·3	0·4	9·3	1·0	15·3	1·7
34	1 38·5	1 38·8	1 34·0	3·4	0·4	9·4	1·0	15·4	1·7
35	1 38·8	1 39·0	1 34·3	3·5	0·4	9·5	1·0	15·5	1·7
36	1 39·0	1 39·3	1 34·5	3·6	0·4	9·6	1·0	15·6	1·7
37	1 39·3	1 39·5	1 34·7	3·7	0·4	9·7	1·1	15·7	1·7
38	1 39·5	1 39·8	1 35·0	3·8	0·4	9·8	1·1	15·8	1·7
39	1 39·8	1 40·0	1 35·2	3·9	0·4	9·9	1·1	15·9	1·7
40	1 40·0	1 40·3	1 35·4	4·0	0·4	10·0	1·1	16·0	1·7
41	1 40·3	1 40·5	1 35·7	4·1	0·4	10·1	1·1	16·1	1·7
42	1 40·5	1 40·8	1 35·9	4·2	0·5	10·2	1·1	16·2	1·8
43	1 40·8	1 41·0	1 36·2	4·3	0·5	10·3	1·1	16·3	1·8
44	1 41·0	1 41·3	1 36·4	4·4	0·5	10·4	1·1	16·4	1·8
45	1 41·3	1 41·5	1 36·6	4·5	0·5	10·5	1·1	16·5	1·8
46	1 41·5	1 41·8	1 36·9	4·6	0·5	10·6	1·1	16·6	1·8
47	1 41·8	1 42·0	1 37·1	4·7	0·5	10·7	1·2	16·7	1·8
48	1 42·0	1 42·3	1 37·4	4·8	0·5	10·8	1·2	16·8	1·8
49	1 42·3	1 42·5	1 37·6	4·9	0·5	10·9	1·2	16·9	1·8
50	1 42·5	1 42·8	1 37·8	5·0	0·5	11·0	1·2	17·0	1·8
51	1 42·8	1 43·0	1 38·1	5·1	0·6	11·1	1·2	17·1	1·9
52	1 43·0	1 43·3	1 38·3	5·2	0·6	11·2	1·2	17·2	1·9
53	1 43·3	1 43·5	1 38·5	5·3	0·6	11·3	1·2	17·3	1·9
54	1 43·5	1 43·8	1 38·8	5·4	0·6	11·4	1·2	17·4	1·9
55	1 43·8	1 44·0	1 39·0	5·5	0·6	11·5	1·2	17·5	1·9
56	1 44·0	1 44·3	1 39·3	5·6	0·6	11·6	1·3	17·6	1·9
57	1 44·3	1 44·5	1 39·5	5·7	0·6	11·7	1·3	17·7	1·9
58	1 44·5	1 44·8	1 39·7	5·8	0·6	11·8	1·3	17·8	1·9
59	1 44·8	1 45·0	1 40·0	5·9	0·6	11·9	1·3	17·9	1·9
60	1 45·0	1 45·3	1 40·2	6·0	0·7	12·0	1·3	18·0	2·0

m 7	SUN PLANETS	ARIES	MOON	v or d Corrⁿ		v or d Corrⁿ		v or d Corrⁿ	
s	° ′	° ′	° ′	′	′	′	′	′	′
00	1 45·0	1 45·3	1 40·2	0·0	0·0	6·0	0·8	12·0	1·5
01	1 45·3	1 45·5	1 40·5	0·1	0·0	6·1	0·8	12·1	1·5
02	1 45·5	1 45·8	1 40·7	0·2	0·0	6·2	0·8	12·2	1·5
03	1 45·8	1 46·0	1 40·9	0·3	0·0	6·3	0·8	12·3	1·5
04	1 46·0	1 46·3	1 41·2	0·4	0·1	6·4	0·8	12·4	1·6
05	1 46·3	1 46·5	1 41·4	0·5	0·1	6·5	0·8	12·5	1·6
06	1 46·5	1 46·8	1 41·6	0·6	0·1	6·6	0·8	12·6	1·6
07	1 46·8	1 47·0	1 41·9	0·7	0·1	6·7	0·8	12·7	1·6
08	1 47·0	1 47·3	1 42·1	0·8	0·1	6·8	0·9	12·8	1·6
09	1 47·3	1 47·5	1 42·4	0·9	0·1	6·9	0·9	12·9	1·6
10	1 47·5	1 47·8	1 42·6	1·0	0·1	7·0	0·9	13·0	1·6
11	1 47·8	1 48·0	1 42·8	1·1	0·1	7·1	0·9	13·1	1·6
12	1 48·0	1 48·3	1 43·1	1·2	0·2	7·2	0·9	13·2	1·7
13	1 48·3	1 48·5	1 43·3	1·3	0·2	7·3	0·9	13·3	1·7
14	1 48·5	1 48·8	1 43·6	1·4	0·2	7·4	0·9	13·4	1·7
15	1 48·8	1 49·0	1 43·8	1·5	0·2	7·5	0·9	13·5	1·7
16	1 49·0	1 49·3	1 44·0	1·6	0·2	7·6	1·0	13·6	1·7
17	1 49·3	1 49·5	1 44·3	1·7	0·2	7·7	1·0	13·7	1·7
18	1 49·5	1 49·8	1 44·5	1·8	0·2	7·8	1·0	13·8	1·7
19	1 49·8	1 50·1	1 44·8	1·9	0·2	7·9	1·0	13·9	1·7
20	1 50·0	1 50·3	1 45·0	2·0	0·3	8·0	1·0	14·0	1·8
21	1 50·3	1 50·6	1 45·2	2·1	0·3	8·1	1·0	14·1	1·8
22	1 50·5	1 50·8	1 45·5	2·2	0·3	8·2	1·0	14·2	1·8
23	1 50·8	1 51·1	1 45·7	2·3	0·3	8·3	1·0	14·3	1·8
24	1 51·0	1 51·3	1 45·9	2·4	0·3	8·4	1·1	14·4	1·8
25	1 51·3	1 51·6	1 46·2	2·5	0·3	8·5	1·1	14·5	1·8
26	1 51·5	1 51·8	1 46·4	2·6	0·3	8·6	1·1	14·6	1·8
27	1 51·8	1 52·1	1 46·7	2·7	0·3	8·7	1·1	14·7	1·8
28	1 52·0	1 52·3	1 46·9	2·8	0·4	8·8	1·1	14·8	1·9
29	1 52·3	1 52·6	1 47·1	2·9	0·4	8·9	1·1	14·9	1·9
30	1 52·5	1 52·8	1 47·4	3·0	0·4	9·0	1·1	15·0	1·9
31	1 52·8	1 53·1	1 47·6	3·1	0·4	9·1	1·1	15·1	1·9
32	1 53·0	1 53·3	1 47·9	3·2	0·4	9·2	1·2	15·2	1·9
33	1 53·3	1 53·6	1 48·1	3·3	0·4	9·3	1·2	15·3	1·9
34	1 53·5	1 53·8	1 48·3	3·4	0·4	9·4	1·2	15·4	1·9
35	1 53·8	1 54·1	1 48·6	3·5	0·4	9·5	1·2	15·5	1·9
36	1 54·0	1 54·3	1 48·8	3·6	0·5	9·6	1·2	15·6	2·0
37	1 54·3	1 54·6	1 49·0	3·7	0·5	9·7	1·2	15·7	2·0
38	1 54·5	1 54·8	1 49·3	3·8	0·5	9·8	1·2	15·8	2·0
39	1 54·8	1 55·1	1 49·5	3·9	0·5	9·9	1·2	15·9	2·0
40	1 55·0	1 55·3	1 49·8	4·0	0·5	10·0	1·3	16·0	2·0
41	1 55·3	1 55·6	1 50·0	4·1	0·5	10·1	1·3	16·1	2·0
42	1 55·5	1 55·8	1 50·2	4·2	0·5	10·2	1·3	16·2	2·0
43	1 55·8	1 56·1	1 50·5	4·3	0·5	10·3	1·3	16·3	2·0
44	1 56·0	1 56·3	1 50·7	4·4	0·6	10·4	1·3	16·4	2·1
45	1 56·3	1 56·6	1 51·0	4·5	0·6	10·5	1·3	16·5	2·1
46	1 56·5	1 56·8	1 51·2	4·6	0·6	10·6	1·3	16·6	2·1
47	1 56·8	1 57·1	1 51·4	4·7	0·6	10·7	1·3	16·7	2·1
48	1 57·0	1 57·3	1 51·7	4·8	0·6	10·8	1·4	16·8	2·1
49	1 57·3	1 57·6	1 51·9	4·9	0·6	10·9	1·4	16·9	2·1
50	1 57·5	1 57·8	1 52·1	5·0	0·6	11·0	1·4	17·0	2·1
51	1 57·8	1 58·1	1 52·4	5·1	0·6	11·1	1·4	17·1	2·1
52	1 58·0	1 58·3	1 52·6	5·2	0·7	11·2	1·4	17·2	2·2
53	1 58·3	1 58·6	1 52·9	5·3	0·7	11·3	1·4	17·3	2·2
54	1 58·5	1 58·8	1 53·1	5·4	0·7	11·4	1·4	17·4	2·2
55	1 58·8	1 59·1	1 53·3	5·5	0·7	11·5	1·4	17·5	2·2
56	1 59·0	1 59·3	1 53·6	5·6	0·7	11·6	1·5	17·6	2·2
57	1 59·3	1 59·6	1 53·8	5·7	0·7	11·7	1·5	17·7	2·2
58	1 59·5	1 59·8	1 54·1	5·8	0·7	11·8	1·5	17·8	2·2
59	1 59·8	2 00·1	1 54·3	5·9	0·7	11·9	1·5	17·9	2·2
60	2 00·0	2 00·3	1 54·5	6·0	0·8	12·0	1·5	18·0	2·3

v

m 8	SUN PLANETS	ARIES	MOON	v or d	Corrⁿ	v or d	Corrⁿ	v or d	Corrⁿ
s	° ′	° ′	° ′	′	′	′	′	′	′
00	2 00·0	2 00·3	1 54·5	0·0	0·0	6·0	0·9	12·0	1·7
01	2 00·3	2 00·6	1 54·8	0·1	0·0	6·1	0·9	12·1	1·7
02	2 00·5	2 00·8	1 55·0	0·2	0·0	6·2	0·9	12·2	1·7
03	2 00·8	2 01·1	1 55·2	0·3	0·0	6·3	0·9	12·3	1·7
04	2 01·0	2 01·3	1 55·5	0·4	0·1	6·4	0·9	12·4	1·8
05	2 01·3	2 01·6	1 55·7	0·5	0·1	6·5	0·9	12·5	1·8
06	2 01·5	2 01·8	1 56·0	0·6	0·1	6·6	0·9	12·6	1·8
07	2 01·8	2 02·1	1 56·2	0·7	0·1	6·7	0·9	12·7	1·8
08	2 02·0	2 02·3	1 56·4	0·8	0·1	6·8	1·0	12·8	1·8
09	2 02·3	2 02·6	1 56·7	0·9	0·1	6·9	1·0	12·9	1·8
10	2 02·5	2 02·8	1 56·9	1·0	0·1	7·0	1·0	13·0	1·8
11	2 02·8	2 03·1	1 57·2	1·1	0·2	7·1	1·0	13·1	1·9
12	2 03·0	2 03·3	1 57·4	1·2	0·2	7·2	1·0	13·2	1·9
13	2 03·3	2 03·6	1 57·6	1·3	0·2	7·3	1·0	13·3	1·9
14	2 03·5	2 03·8	1 57·9	1·4	0·2	7·4	1·0	13·4	1·9
15	2 03·8	2 04·1	1 58·1	1·5	0·2	7·5	1·1	13·5	1·9
16	2 04·0	2 04·3	1 58·4	1·6	0·2	7·6	1·1	13·6	1·9
17	2 04·3	2 04·6	1 58·6	1·7	0·2	7·7	1·1	13·7	1·9
18	2 04·5	2 04·8	1 58·8	1·8	0·3	7·8	1·1	13·8	2·0
19	2 04·8	2 05·1	1 59·1	1·9	0·3	7·9	1·1	13·9	2·0
20	2 05·0	2 05·3	1 59·3	2·0	0·3	8·0	1·1	14·0	2·0
21	2 05·3	2 05·6	1 59·5	2·1	0·3	8·1	1·1	14·1	2·0
22	2 05·5	2 05·8	1 59·8	2·2	0·3	8·2	1·2	14·2	2·0
23	2 05·8	2 06·1	2 00·0	2·3	0·3	8·3	1·2	14·3	2·0
24	2 06·0	2 06·3	2 00·3	2·4	0·3	8·4	1·2	14·4	2·0
25	2 06·3	2 06·6	2 00·5	2·5	0·4	8·5	1·2	14·5	2·1
26	2 06·5	2 06·8	2 00·7	2·6	0·4	8·6	1·2	14·6	2·1
27	2 06·8	2 07·1	2 01·0	2·7	0·4	8·7	1·2	14·7	2·1
28	2 07·0	2 07·3	2 01·2	2·8	0·4	8·8	1·2	14·8	2·1
29	2 07·3	2 07·6	2 01·5	2·9	0·4	8·9	1·3	14·9	2·1
30	2 07·5	2 07·8	2 01·7	3·0	0·4	9·0	1·3	15·0	2·1
31	2 07·8	2 08·1	2 01·9	3·1	0·4	9·1	1·3	15·1	2·1
32	2 08·0	2 08·4	2 02·2	3·2	0·5	9·2	1·3	15·2	2·2
33	2 08·3	2 08·6	2 02·4	3·3	0·5	9·3	1·3	15·3	2·2
34	2 08·5	2 08·9	2 02·6	3·4	0·5	9·4	1·3	15·4	2·2
35	2 08·8	2 09·1	2 02·9	3·5	0·5	9·5	1·3	15·5	2·2
36	2 09·0	2 09·4	2 03·1	3·6	0·5	9·6	1·4	15·6	2·2
37	2 09·3	2 09·6	2 03·4	3·7	0·5	9·7	1·4	15·7	2·2
38	2 09·5	2 09·9	2 03·6	3·8	0·5	9·8	1·4	15·8	2·2
39	2 09·8	2 10·1	2 03·8	3·9	0·6	9·9	1·4	15·9	2·3
40	2 10·0	2 10·4	2 04·1	4·0	0·6	10·0	1·4	16·0	2·3
41	2 10·3	2 10·6	2 04·3	4·1	0·6	10·1	1·4	16·1	2·3
42	2 10·5	2 10·9	2 04·6	4·2	0·6	10·2	1·4	16·2	2·3
43	2 10·8	2 11·1	2 04·8	4·3	0·6	10·3	1·5	16·3	2·3
44	2 11·0	2 11·4	2 05·0	4·4	0·6	10·4	1·5	16·4	2·3
45	2 11·3	2 11·6	2 05·3	4·5	0·6	10·5	1·5	16·5	2·3
46	2 11·5	2 11·9	2 05·5	4·6	0·7	10·6	1·5	16·6	2·4
47	2 11·8	2 12·1	2 05·7	4·7	0·7	10·7	1·5	16·7	2·4
48	2 12·0	2 12·4	2 06·0	4·8	0·7	10·8	1·5	16·8	2·4
49	2 12·3	2 12·6	2 06·2	4·9	0·7	10·9	1·5	16·9	2·4
50	2 12·5	2 12·9	2 06·5	5·0	0·7	11·0	1·6	17·0	2·4
51	2 12·8	2 13·1	2 06·7	5·1	0·7	11·1	1·6	17·1	2·4
52	2 13·0	2 13·4	2 06·9	5·2	0·7	11·2	1·6	17·2	2·4
53	2 13·3	2 13·6	2 07·2	5·3	0·8	11·3	1·6	17·3	2·5
54	2 13·5	2 13·9	2 07·4	5·4	0·8	11·4	1·6	17·4	2·5
55	2 13·8	2 14·1	2 07·7	5·5	0·8	11·5	1·6	17·5	2·5
56	2 14·0	2 14·4	2 07·9	5·6	0·8	11·6	1·6	17·6	2·5
57	2 14·3	2 14·6	2 08·1	5·7	0·8	11·7	1·7	17·7	2·5
58	2 14·5	2 14·9	2 08·4	5·8	0·8	11·8	1·7	17·8	2·5
59	2 14·8	2 15·1	2 08·6	5·9	0·8	11·9	1·7	17·9	2·5
60	2 15·0	2 15·4	2 08·9	6·0	0·9	12·0	1·7	18·0	2·6

m 9	SUN PLANETS	ARIES	MOON	v or d	Corrⁿ	v or d	Corrⁿ	v or d	Corrⁿ
s	° ′	° ′	° ′	′	′	′	′	′	′
00	2 15·0	2 15·4	2 08·9	0·0	0·0	6·0	1·0	12·0	1·9
01	2 15·3	2 15·6	2 09·1	0·1	0·0	6·1	1·0	12·1	1·9
02	2 15·5	2 15·9	2 09·3	0·2	0·0	6·2	1·0	12·2	1·9
03	2 15·8	2 16·1	2 09·6	0·3	0·0	6·3	1·0	12·3	1·9
04	2 16·0	2 16·4	2 09·8	0·4	0·1	6·4	1·0	12·4	2·0
05	2 16·3	2 16·6	2 10·0	0·5	0·1	6·5	1·0	12·5	2·0
06	2 16·5	2 16·9	2 10·3	0·6	0·1	6·6	1·0	12·6	2·0
07	2 16·8	2 17·1	2 10·5	0·7	0·1	6·7	1·1	12·7	2·0
08	2 17·0	2 17·4	2 10·8	0·8	0·1	6·8	1·1	12·8	2·0
09	2 17·3	2 17·6	2 11·0	0·9	0·1	6·9	1·1	12·9	2·0
10	2 17·5	2 17·9	2 11·2	1·0	0·2	7·0	1·1	13·0	2·1
11	2 17·8	2 18·1	2 11·5	1·1	0·2	7·1	1·1	13·1	2·1
12	2 18·0	2 18·4	2 11·7	1·2	0·2	7·2	1·1	13·2	2·1
13	2 18·3	2 18·6	2 12·0	1·3	0·2	7·3	1·2	13·3	2·1
14	2 18·5	2 18·9	2 12·2	1·4	0·2	7·4	1·2	13·4	2·1
15	2 18·8	2 19·1	2 12·4	1·5	0·2	7·5	1·2	13·5	2·1
16	2 19·0	2 19·4	2 12·7	1·6	0·3	7·6	1·2	13·6	2·2
17	2 19·3	2 19·6	2 12·9	1·7	0·3	7·7	1·2	13·7	2·2
18	2 19·5	2 19·9	2 13·1	1·8	0·3	7·8	1·2	13·8	2·2
19	2 19·8	2 20·1	2 13·4	1·9	0·3	7·9	1·3	13·9	2·2
20	2 20·0	2 20·4	2 13·6	2·0	0·3	8·0	1·3	14·0	2·2
21	2 20·3	2 20·6	2 13·9	2·1	0·3	8·1	1·3	14·1	2·2
22	2 20·5	2 20·9	2 14·1	2·2	0·3	8·2	1·3	14·2	2·2
23	2 20·8	2 21·1	2 14·3	2·3	0·4	8·3	1·3	14·3	2·3
24	2 21·0	2 21·4	2 14·6	2·4	0·4	8·4	1·3	14·4	2·3
25	2 21·3	2 21·6	2 14·8	2·5	0·4	8·5	1·3	14·5	2·3
26	2 21·5	2 21·9	2 15·1	2·6	0·4	8·6	1·4	14·6	2·3
27	2 21·8	2 22·1	2 15·3	2·7	0·4	8·7	1·4	14·7	2·3
28	2 22·0	2 22·4	2 15·5	2·8	0·4	8·8	1·4	14·8	2·3
29	2 22·3	2 22·6	2 15·8	2·9	0·5	8·9	1·4	14·9	2·4
30	2 22·5	2 22·9	2 16·0	3·0	0·5	9·0	1·4	15·0	2·4
31	2 22·8	2 23·1	2 16·2	3·1	0·5	9·1	1·4	15·1	2·4
32	2 23·0	2 23·4	2 16·5	3·2	0·5	9·2	1·5	15·2	2·4
33	2 23·3	2 23·6	2 16·7	3·3	0·5	9·3	1·5	15·3	2·4
34	2 23·5	2 23·9	2 17·0	3·4	0·5	9·4	1·5	15·4	2·4
35	2 23·8	2 24·1	2 17·2	3·5	0·6	9·5	1·5	15·5	2·5
36	2 24·0	2 24·4	2 17·4	3·6	0·6	9·6	1·5	15·6	2·5
37	2 24·3	2 24·6	2 17·7	3·7	0·6	9·7	1·5	15·7	2·5
38	2 24·5	2 24·9	2 17·9	3·8	0·6	9·8	1·6	15·8	2·5
39	2 24·8	2 25·1	2 18·2	3·9	0·6	9·9	1·6	15·9	2·5
40	2 25·0	2 25·4	2 18·4	4·0	0·6	10·0	1·6	16·0	2·5
41	2 25·3	2 25·6	2 18·6	4·1	0·6	10·1	1·6	16·1	2·5
42	2 25·5	2 25·9	2 18·9	4·2	0·7	10·2	1·6	16·2	2·6
43	2 25·8	2 26·1	2 19·1	4·3	0·7	10·3	1·6	16·3	2·6
44	2 26·0	2 26·4	2 19·3	4·4	0·7	10·4	1·6	16·4	2·6
45	2 26·3	2 26·7	2 19·6	4·5	0·7	10·5	1·7	16·5	2·6
46	2 26·5	2 26·9	2 19·8	4·6	0·7	10·6	1·7	16·6	2·6
47	2 26·8	2 27·2	2 20·1	4·7	0·7	10·7	1·7	16·7	2·6
48	2 27·0	2 27·4	2 20·3	4·8	0·8	10·8	1·7	16·8	2·7
49	2 27·3	2 27·7	2 20·5	4·9	0·8	10·9	1·7	16·9	2·7
50	2 27·5	2 27·9	2 20·8	5·0	0·8	11·0	1·7	17·0	2·7
51	2 27·8	2 28·2	2 21·0	5·1	0·8	11·1	1·8	17·1	2·7
52	2 28·0	2 28·4	2 21·3	5·2	0·8	11·2	1·8	17·2	2·7
53	2 28·3	2 28·7	2 21·5	5·3	0·8	11·3	1·8	17·3	2·7
54	2 28·5	2 28·9	2 21·7	5·4	0·9	11·4	1·8	17·4	2·8
55	2 28·8	2 29·2	2 22·0	5·5	0·9	11·5	1·8	17·5	2·8
56	2 29·0	2 29·4	2 22·2	5·6	0·9	11·6	1·8	17·6	2·8
57	2 29·3	2 29·7	2 22·5	5·7	0·9	11·7	1·9	17·7	2·8
58	2 29·5	2 29·9	2 22·7	5·8	0·9	11·8	1·9	17·8	2·8
59	2 29·8	2 30·2	2 22·9	5·9	0·9	11·9	1·9	17·9	2·8
60	2 30·0	2 30·4	2 23·2	6·0	1·0	12·0	1·9	18·0	2·9

10ᵐ

10 s	SUN PLANETS	ARIES	MOON	v or d	Corrⁿ	v or d	Corrⁿ	v or d	Corrⁿ
00	2 30.0	2 30.4	2 23.2	0.0	0.0	6.0	1.1	12.0	2.1
01	2 30.3	2 30.7	2 23.4	0.1	0.0	6.1	1.1	12.1	2.1
02	2 30.5	2 30.9	2 23.6	0.2	0.0	6.2	1.1	12.2	2.1
03	2 30.8	2 31.2	2 23.9	0.3	0.1	6.3	1.1	12.3	2.2
04	2 31.0	2 31.4	2 24.1	0.4	0.1	6.4	1.1	12.4	2.2
05	2 31.3	2 31.7	2 24.4	0.5	0.1	6.5	1.1	12.5	2.2
06	2 31.5	2 31.9	2 24.6	0.6	0.1	6.6	1.2	12.6	2.2
07	2 31.8	2 32.2	2 24.8	0.7	0.1	6.7	1.2	12.7	2.2
08	2 32.0	2 32.4	2 25.1	0.8	0.1	6.8	1.2	12.8	2.2
09	2 32.3	2 32.7	2 25.3	0.9	0.2	6.9	1.2	12.9	2.3
10	2 32.5	2 32.9	2 25.6	1.0	0.2	7.0	1.2	13.0	2.3
11	2 32.8	2 33.2	2 25.8	1.1	0.2	7.1	1.2	13.1	2.3
12	2 33.0	2 33.4	2 26.0	1.2	0.2	7.2	1.3	13.2	2.3
13	2 33.3	2 33.7	2 26.3	1.3	0.2	7.3	1.3	13.3	2.3
14	2 33.5	2 33.9	2 26.5	1.4	0.2	7.4	1.3	13.4	2.3
15	2 33.8	2 34.2	2 26.7	1.5	0.3	7.5	1.3	13.5	2.4
16	2 34.0	2 34.4	2 27.0	1.6	0.3	7.6	1.3	13.6	2.4
17	2 34.3	2 34.7	2 27.2	1.7	0.3	7.7	1.3	13.7	2.4
18	2 34.5	2 34.9	2 27.5	1.8	0.3	7.8	1.4	13.8	2.4
19	2 34.8	2 35.2	2 27.7	1.9	0.3	7.9	1.4	13.9	2.4
20	2 35.0	2 35.4	2 27.9	2.0	0.4	8.0	1.4	14.0	2.5
21	2 35.3	2 35.7	2 28.2	2.1	0.4	8.1	1.4	14.1	2.5
22	2 35.5	2 35.9	2 28.4	2.2	0.4	8.2	1.4	14.2	2.5
23	2 35.8	2 36.2	2 28.7	2.3	0.4	8.3	1.5	14.3	2.5
24	2 36.0	2 36.4	2 28.9	2.4	0.4	8.4	1.5	14.4	2.5
25	2 36.3	2 36.7	2 29.1	2.5	0.4	8.5	1.5	14.5	2.5
26	2 36.5	2 36.9	2 29.4	2.6	0.5	8.6	1.5	14.6	2.6
27	2 36.8	2 37.2	2 29.6	2.7	0.5	8.7	1.5	14.7	2.6
28	2 37.0	2 37.4	2 29.8	2.8	0.5	8.8	1.5	14.8	2.6
29	2 37.3	2 37.7	2 30.1	2.9	0.5	8.9	1.6	14.9	2.6
30	2 37.5	2 37.9	2 30.3	3.0	0.5	9.0	1.6	15.0	2.6
31	2 37.8	2 38.2	2 30.6	3.1	0.5	9.1	1.6	15.1	2.6
32	2 38.0	2 38.4	2 30.8	3.2	0.6	9.2	1.6	15.2	2.7
33	2 38.3	2 38.7	2 31.0	3.3	0.6	9.3	1.6	15.3	2.7
34	2 38.5	2 38.9	2 31.3	3.4	0.6	9.4	1.6	15.4	2.7
35	2 38.8	2 39.2	2 31.5	3.5	0.6	9.5	1.7	15.5	2.7
36	2 39.0	2 39.4	2 31.8	3.6	0.6	9.6	1.7	15.6	2.7
37	2 39.3	2 39.7	2 32.0	3.7	0.6	9.7	1.7	15.7	2.7
38	2 39.5	2 39.9	2 32.2	3.8	0.7	9.8	1.7	15.8	2.8
39	2 39.8	2 40.2	2 32.5	3.9	0.7	9.9	1.7	15.9	2.8
40	2 40.0	2 40.4	2 32.7	4.0	0.7	10.0	1.8	16.0	2.8
41	2 40.3	2 40.7	2 32.9	4.1	0.7	10.1	1.8	16.1	2.8
42	2 40.5	2 40.9	2 33.2	4.2	0.7	10.2	1.8	16.2	2.8
43	2 40.8	2 41.2	2 33.4	4.3	0.8	10.3	1.8	16.3	2.9
44	2 41.0	2 41.4	2 33.7	4.4	0.8	10.4	1.8	16.4	2.9
45	2 41.3	2 41.7	2 33.9	4.5	0.8	10.5	1.8	16.5	2.9
46	2 41.5	2 41.9	2 34.1	4.6	0.8	10.6	1.9	16.6	2.9
47	2 41.8	2 42.2	2 34.4	4.7	0.8	10.7	1.9	16.7	2.9
48	2 42.0	2 42.4	2 34.6	4.8	0.8	10.8	1.9	16.8	2.9
49	2 42.3	2 42.7	2 34.9	4.9	0.9	10.9	1.9	16.9	3.0
50	2 42.5	2 42.9	2 35.1	5.0	0.9	11.0	1.9	17.0	3.0
51	2 42.8	2 43.2	2 35.3	5.1	0.9	11.1	1.9	17.1	3.0
52	2 43.0	2 43.4	2 35.6	5.2	0.9	11.2	2.0	17.2	3.0
53	2 43.3	2 43.7	2 35.8	5.3	0.9	11.3	2.0	17.3	3.0
54	2 43.5	2 43.9	2 36.1	5.4	0.9	11.4	2.0	17.4	3.0
55	2 43.8	2 44.2	2 36.3	5.5	1.0	11.5	2.0	17.5	3.1
56	2 44.0	2 44.4	2 36.5	5.6	1.0	11.6	2.0	17.6	3.1
57	2 44.3	2 44.7	2 36.8	5.7	1.0	11.7	2.0	17.7	3.1
58	2 44.5	2 45.0	2 37.0	5.8	1.0	11.8	2.1	17.8	3.1
59	2 44.8	2 45.2	2 37.2	5.9	1.0	11.9	2.1	17.9	3.1
60	2 45.0	2 45.5	2 37.5	6.0	1.1	12.0	2.1	18.0	3.2

11ᵐ

11 s	SUN PLANETS	ARIES	MOON	v or d	Corrⁿ	v or d	Corrⁿ	v or d	Corrⁿ
00	2 45.0	2 45.5	2 37.5	0.0	0.0	6.0	1.2	12.0	2.3
01	2 45.3	2 45.7	2 37.7	0.1	0.0	6.1	1.2	12.1	2.3
02	2 45.5	2 46.0	2 38.0	0.2	0.0	6.2	1.2	12.2	2.3
03	2 45.8	2 46.2	2 38.2	0.3	0.1	6.3	1.2	12.3	2.4
04	2 46.0	2 46.5	2 38.4	0.4	0.1	6.4	1.2	12.4	2.4
05	2 46.3	2 46.7	2 38.7	0.5	0.1	6.5	1.2	12.5	2.4
06	2 46.5	2 47.0	2 38.9	0.6	0.1	6.6	1.3	12.6	2.4
07	2 46.8	2 47.2	2 39.2	0.7	0.1	6.7	1.3	12.7	2.4
08	2 47.0	2 47.5	2 39.4	0.8	0.2	6.8	1.3	12.8	2.5
09	2 47.3	2 47.7	2 39.6	0.9	0.2	6.9	1.3	12.9	2.5
10	2 47.5	2 48.0	2 39.9	1.0	0.2	7.0	1.3	13.0	2.5
11	2 47.8	2 48.2	2 40.1	1.1	0.2	7.1	1.4	13.1	2.5
12	2 48.0	2 48.5	2 40.3	1.2	0.2	7.2	1.4	13.2	2.5
13	2 48.3	2 48.7	2 40.6	1.3	0.2	7.3	1.4	13.3	2.5
14	2 48.5	2 49.0	2 40.8	1.4	0.3	7.4	1.4	13.4	2.6
15	2 48.8	2 49.2	2 41.1	1.5	0.3	7.5	1.4	13.5	2.6
16	2 49.0	2 49.5	2 41.3	1.6	0.3	7.6	1.5	13.6	2.6
17	2 49.3	2 49.7	2 41.5	1.7	0.3	7.7	1.5	13.7	2.6
18	2 49.5	2 50.0	2 41.8	1.8	0.3	7.8	1.5	13.8	2.6
19	2 49.8	2 50.2	2 42.0	1.9	0.4	7.9	1.5	13.9	2.7
20	2 50.0	2 50.5	2 42.3	2.0	0.4	8.0	1.5	14.0	2.7
21	2 50.3	2 50.7	2 42.5	2.1	0.4	8.1	1.6	14.1	2.7
22	2 50.5	2 51.0	2 42.7	2.2	0.4	8.2	1.6	14.2	2.7
23	2 50.8	2 51.2	2 43.0	2.3	0.4	8.3	1.6	14.3	2.7
24	2 51.0	2 51.5	2 43.2	2.4	0.5	8.4	1.6	14.4	2.8
25	2 51.3	2 51.7	2 43.4	2.5	0.5	8.5	1.6	14.5	2.8
26	2 51.5	2 52.0	2 43.7	2.6	0.5	8.6	1.6	14.6	2.8
27	2 51.8	2 52.2	2 43.9	2.7	0.5	8.7	1.7	14.7	2.8
28	2 52.0	2 52.5	2 44.2	2.8	0.5	8.8	1.7	14.8	2.8
29	2 52.3	2 52.7	2 44.4	2.9	0.6	8.9	1.7	14.9	2.9
30	2 52.5	2 53.0	2 44.6	3.0	0.6	9.0	1.7	15.0	2.9
31	2 52.8	2 53.2	2 44.9	3.1	0.6	9.1	1.7	15.1	2.9
32	2 53.0	2 53.5	2 45.1	3.2	0.6	9.2	1.8	15.2	2.9
33	2 53.3	2 53.7	2 45.4	3.3	0.6	9.3	1.8	15.3	2.9
34	2 53.5	2 54.0	2 45.6	3.4	0.7	9.4	1.8	15.4	3.0
35	2 53.8	2 54.2	2 45.8	3.5	0.7	9.5	1.8	15.5	3.0
36	2 54.0	2 54.5	2 46.1	3.6	0.7	9.6	1.8	15.6	3.0
37	2 54.3	2 54.7	2 46.3	3.7	0.7	9.7	1.9	15.7	3.0
38	2 54.5	2 55.0	2 46.6	3.8	0.7	9.8	1.9	15.8	3.0
39	2 54.8	2 55.2	2 46.8	3.9	0.7	9.9	1.9	15.9	3.0
40	2 55.0	2 55.5	2 47.0	4.0	0.8	10.0	1.9	16.0	3.1
41	2 55.3	2 55.7	2 47.3	4.1	0.8	10.1	1.9	16.1	3.1
42	2 55.5	2 56.0	2 47.5	4.2	0.8	10.2	2.0	16.2	3.1
43	2 55.8	2 56.2	2 47.7	4.3	0.8	10.3	2.0	16.3	3.1
44	2 56.0	2 56.5	2 48.0	4.4	0.8	10.4	2.0	16.4	3.1
45	2 56.3	2 56.7	2 48.2	4.5	0.9	10.5	2.0	16.5	3.2
46	2 56.5	2 57.0	2 48.5	4.6	0.9	10.6	2.0	16.6	3.2
47	2 56.8	2 57.2	2 48.7	4.7	0.9	10.7	2.1	16.7	3.2
48	2 57.0	2 57.5	2 48.9	4.8	0.9	10.8	2.1	16.8	3.2
49	2 57.3	2 57.7	2 49.2	4.9	0.9	10.9	2.1	16.9	3.2
50	2 57.5	2 58.0	2 49.4	5.0	1.0	11.0	2.1	17.0	3.3
51	2 57.8	2 58.2	2 49.7	5.1	1.0	11.1	2.1	17.1	3.3
52	2 58.0	2 58.5	2 49.9	5.2	1.0	11.2	2.1	17.2	3.3
53	2 58.3	2 58.7	2 50.1	5.3	1.0	11.3	2.2	17.3	3.3
54	2 58.5	2 59.0	2 50.4	5.4	1.0	11.4	2.2	17.4	3.3
55	2 58.8	2 59.2	2 50.6	5.5	1.1	11.5	2.2	17.5	3.4
56	2 59.0	2 59.5	2 50.8	5.6	1.1	11.6	2.2	17.6	3.4
57	2 59.3	2 59.7	2 51.1	5.7	1.1	11.7	2.2	17.7	3.4
58	2 59.5	3 00.0	2 51.3	5.8	1.1	11.8	2.3	17.8	3.4
59	2 59.8	3 00.2	2 51.6	5.9	1.1	11.9	2.3	17.9	3.4
60	3 00.0	3 00.5	2 51.8	6.0	1.2	12.0	2.3	18.0	3.5

vii

12ᵐ

12 s	SUN PLANETS	ARIES	MOON	v or Corrⁿ d	v or Corrⁿ d	v or Corrⁿ d
	° ′	° ′	° ′	′ ′	′ ′	′ ′
00	3 00·0	3 00·5	2 51·8	0·0 0·0	6·0 1·3	12·0 2·5
01	3 00·3	3 00·7	2 52·0	0·1 0·0	6·1 1·3	12·1 2·5
02	3 00·5	3 01·0	2 52·3	0·2 0·0	6·2 1·3	12·2 2·5
03	3 00·8	3 01·2	2 52·5	0·3 0·1	6·3 1·3	12·3 2·6
04	3 01·0	3 01·5	2 52·8	0·4 0·1	6·4 1·3	12·4 2·6
05	3 01·3	3 01·7	2 53·0	0·5 0·1	6·5 1·4	12·5 2·6
06	3 01·5	3 02·0	2 53·2	0·6 0·1	6·6 1·4	12·6 2·6
07	3 01·8	3 02·2	2 53·5	0·7 0·1	6·7 1·4	12·7 2·6
08	3 02·0	3 02·5	2 53·7	0·8 0·2	6·8 1·4	12·8 2·7
09	3 02·3	3 02·7	2 53·9	0·9 0·2	6·9 1·4	12·9 2·7
10	3 02·5	3 03·0	2 54·2	1·0 0·2	7·0 1·5	13·0 2·7
11	3 02·8	3 03·3	2 54·4	1·1 0·2	7·1 1·5	13·1 2·7
12	3 03·0	3 03·5	2 54·7	1·2 0·3	7·2 1·5	13·2 2·8
13	3 03·3	3 03·8	2 54·9	1·3 0·3	7·3 1·5	13·3 2·8
14	3 03·5	3 04·0	2 55·1	1·4 0·3	7·4 1·5	13·4 2·8
15	3 03·8	3 04·3	2 55·4	1·5 0·3	7·5 1·6	13·5 2·8
16	3 04·0	3 04·5	2 55·6	1·6 0·3	7·6 1·6	13·6 2·8
17	3 04·3	3 04·8	2 55·9	1·7 0·4	7·7 1·6	13·7 2·9
18	3 04·5	3 05·0	2 56·1	1·8 0·4	7·8 1·6	13·8 2·9
19	3 04·8	3 05·3	2 56·3	1·9 0·4	7·9 1·6	13·9 2·9
20	3 05·0	3 05·5	2 56·6	2·0 0·4	8·0 1·7	14·0 2·9
21	3 05·3	3 05·8	2 56·8	2·1 0·4	8·1 1·7	14·1 2·9
22	3 05·5	3 06·0	2 57·0	2·2 0·5	8·2 1·7	14·2 3·0
23	3 05·8	3 06·3	2 57·3	2·3 0·5	8·3 1·7	14·3 3·0
24	3 06·0	3 06·5	2 57·5	2·4 0·5	8·4 1·8	14·4 3·0
25	3 06·3	3 06·8	2 57·8	2·5 0·5	8·5 1·8	14·5 3·0
26	3 06·5	3 07·0	2 58·0	2·6 0·5	8·6 1·8	14·6 3·0
27	3 06·8	3 07·3	2 58·2	2·7 0·6	8·7 1·8	14·7 3·1
28	3 07·0	3 07·5	2 58·5	2·8 0·6	8·8 1·8	14·8 3·1
29	3 07·3	3 07·8	2 58·7	2·9 0·6	8·9 1·9	14·9 3·1
30	3 07·5	3 08·0	2 59·0	3·0 0·6	9·0 1·9	15·0 3·1
31	3 07·8	3 08·3	2 59·2	3·1 0·6	9·1 1·9	15·1 3·1
32	3 08·0	3 08·5	2 59·4	3·2 0·7	9·2 1·9	15·2 3·2
33	3 08·3	3 08·8	2 59·7	3·3 0·7	9·3 1·9	15·3 3·2
34	3 08·5	3 09·0	2 59·9	3·4 0·7	9·4 2·0	15·4 3·2
35	3 08·8	3 09·3	3 00·2	3·5 0·7	9·5 2·0	15·5 3·2
36	3 09·0	3 09·5	3 00·4	3·6 0·8	9·6 2·0	15·6 3·3
37	3 09·3	3 09·8	3 00·6	3·7 0·8	9·7 2·0	15·7 3·3
38	3 09·5	3 10·0	3 00·9	3·8 0·8	9·8 2·0	15·8 3·3
39	3 09·8	3 10·3	3 01·1	3·9 0·8	9·9 2·1	15·9 3·3
40	3 10·0	3 10·5	3 01·3	4·0 0·8	10·0 2·1	16·0 3·3
41	3 10·3	3 10·8	3 01·6	4·1 0·9	10·1 2·1	16·1 3·4
42	3 10·5	3 11·0	3 01·8	4·2 0·9	10·2 2·1	16·2 3·4
43	3 10·8	3 11·3	3 02·1	4·3 0·9	10·3 2·1	16·3 3·4
44	3 11·0	3 11·5	3 02·3	4·4 0·9	10·4 2·2	16·4 3·4
45	3 11·3	3 11·8	3 02·5	4·5 0·9	10·5 2·2	16·5 3·4
46	3 11·5	3 12·0	3 02·8	4·6 1·0	10·6 2·2	16·6 3·5
47	3 11·8	3 12·3	3 03·0	4·7 1·0	10·7 2·2	16·7 3·5
48	3 12·0	3 12·5	3 03·3	4·8 1·0	10·8 2·3	16·8 3·5
49	3 12·3	3 12·8	3 03·5	4·9 1·0	10·9 2·3	16·9 3·5
50	3 12·5	3 13·0	3 03·7	5·0 1·0	11·0 2·3	17·0 3·5
51	3 12·8	3 13·3	3 04·0	5·1 1·1	11·1 2·3	17·1 3·6
52	3 13·0	3 13·5	3 04·2	5·2 1·1	11·2 2·3	17·2 3·6
53	3 13·3	3 13·8	3 04·4	5·3 1·1	11·3 2·4	17·3 3·6
54	3 13·5	3 14·0	3 04·7	5·4 1·1	11·4 2·4	17·4 3·6
55	3 13·8	3 14·3	3 04·9	5·5 1·1	11·5 2·4	17·5 3·6
56	3 14·0	3 14·5	3 05·2	5·6 1·2	11·6 2·4	17·6 3·7
57	3 14·3	3 14·8	3 05·4	5·7 1·2	11·7 2·4	17·7 3·7
58	3 14·5	3 15·0	3 05·6	5·8 1·2	11·8 2·5	17·8 3·7
59	3 14·8	3 15·3	3 05·9	5·9 1·2	11·9 2·5	17·9 3·7
60	3 15·0	3 15·5	3 06·1	6·0 1·3	12·0 2·5	18·0 3·8

13ᵐ

13 s	SUN PLANETS	ARIES	MOON	v or Corrⁿ d	v or Corrⁿ d	v or Corrⁿ d
	° ′	° ′	° ′	′ ′	′ ′	′ ′
00	3 15·0	3 15·5	3 06·1	0·0 0·0	6·0 1·4	12·0 2·7
01	3 15·3	3 15·8	3 06·4	0·1 0·0	6·1 1·4	12·1 2·7
02	3 15·5	3 16·0	3 06·6	0·2 0·0	6·2 1·4	12·2 2·7
03	3 15·8	3 16·3	3 06·8	0·3 0·1	6·3 1·4	12·3 2·8
04	3 16·0	3 16·5	3 07·1	0·4 0·1	6·4 1·4	12·4 2·8
05	3 16·3	3 16·8	3 07·3	0·5 0·1	6·5 1·5	12·5 2·8
06	3 16·5	3 17·0	3 07·5	0·6 0·1	6·6 1·5	12·6 2·8
07	3 16·8	3 17·3	3 07·8	0·7 0·2	6·7 1·5	12·7 2·9
08	3 17·0	3 17·5	3 08·0	0·8 0·2	6·8 1·5	12·8 2·9
09	3 17·3	3 17·8	3 08·3	0·9 0·2	6·9 1·6	12·9 2·9
10	3 17·5	3 18·0	3 08·5	1·0 0·2	7·0 1·6	13·0 2·9
11	3 17·8	3 18·3	3 08·7	1·1 0·2	7·1 1·6	13·1 2·9
12	3 18·0	3 18·5	3 09·0	1·2 0·3	7·2 1·6	13·2 3·0
13	3 18·3	3 18·8	3 09·2	1·3 0·3	7·3 1·6	13·3 3·0
14	3 18·5	3 19·0	3 09·5	1·4 0·3	7·4 1·7	13·4 3·0
15	3 18·8	3 19·3	3 09·7	1·5 0·3	7·5 1·7	13·5 3·0
16	3 19·0	3 19·5	3 09·9	1·6 0·4	7·6 1·7	13·6 3·1
17	3 19·3	3 19·8	3 10·2	1·7 0·4	7·7 1·7	13·7 3·1
18	3 19·5	3 20·0	3 10·4	1·8 0·4	7·8 1·8	13·8 3·1
19	3 19·8	3 20·3	3 10·7	1·9 0·4	7·9 1·8	13·9 3·1
20	3 20·0	3 20·5	3 10·9	2·0 0·5	8·0 1·8	14·0 3·2
21	3 20·3	3 20·8	3 11·1	2·1 0·5	8·1 1·8	14·1 3·2
22	3 20·5	3 21·0	3 11·4	2·2 0·5	8·2 1·8	14·2 3·2
23	3 20·8	3 21·3	3 11·6	2·3 0·5	8·3 1·9	14·3 3·2
24	3 21·0	3 21·6	3 11·8	2·4 0·5	8·4 1·9	14·4 3·2
25	3 21·3	3 21·8	3 12·1	2·5 0·6	8·5 1·9	14·5 3·3
26	3 21·5	3 22·1	3 12·3	2·6 0·6	8·6 1·9	14·6 3·3
27	3 21·8	3 22·3	3 12·6	2·7 0·6	8·7 2·0	14·7 3·3
28	3 22·0	3 22·6	3 12·8	2·8 0·6	8·8 2·0	14·8 3·3
29	3 22·3	3 22·8	3 13·0	2·9 0·7	8·9 2·0	14·9 3·4
30	3 22·5	3 23·1	3 13·3	3·0 0·7	9·0 2·0	15·0 3·4
31	3 22·8	3 23·3	3 13·5	3·1 0·7	9·1 2·0	15·1 3·4
32	3 23·0	3 23·6	3 13·8	3·2 0·7	9·2 2·1	15·2 3·4
33	3 23·3	3 23·8	3 14·0	3·3 0·7	9·3 2·1	15·3 3·4
34	3 23·5	3 24·1	3 14·2	3·4 0·8	9·4 2·1	15·4 3·5
35	3 23·8	3 24·3	3 14·5	3·5 0·8	9·5 2·1	15·5 3·5
36	3 24·0	3 24·6	3 14·7	3·6 0·8	9·6 2·2	15·6 3·5
37	3 24·3	3 24·8	3 14·9	3·7 0·8	9·7 2·2	15·7 3·5
38	3 24·5	3 25·1	3 15·2	3·8 0·9	9·8 2·2	15·8 3·6
39	3 24·8	3 25·3	3 15·4	3·9 0·9	9·9 2·2	15·9 3·6
40	3 25·0	3 25·6	3 15·7	4·0 0·9	10·0 2·3	16·0 3·6
41	3 25·3	3 25·8	3 15·9	4·1 0·9	10·1 2·3	16·1 3·6
42	3 25·5	3 26·1	3 16·1	4·2 0·9	10·2 2·3	16·2 3·6
43	3 25·8	3 26·3	3 16·4	4·3 1·0	10·3 2·3	16·3 3·7
44	3 26·0	3 26·6	3 16·6	4·4 1·0	10·4 2·3	16·4 3·7
45	3 26·3	3 26·8	3 16·9	4·5 1·0	10·5 2·4	16·5 3·7
46	3 26·5	3 27·1	3 17·1	4·6 1·0	10·6 2·4	16·6 3·7
47	3 26·8	3 27·3	3 17·3	4·7 1·1	10·7 2·4	16·7 3·8
48	3 27·0	3 27·6	3 17·6	4·8 1·1	10·8 2·4	16·8 3·8
49	3 27·3	3 27·8	3 17·8	4·9 1·1	10·9 2·5	16·9 3·8
50	3 27·5	3 28·1	3 18·0	5·0 1·1	11·0 2·5	17·0 3·8
51	3 27·8	3 28·3	3 18·3	5·1 1·1	11·1 2·5	17·1 3·8
52	3 28·0	3 28·6	3 18·5	5·2 1·2	11·2 2·5	17·2 3·9
53	3 28·3	3 28·8	3 18·8	5·3 1·2	11·3 2·5	17·3 3·9
54	3 28·5	3 29·1	3 19·0	5·4 1·2	11·4 2·6	17·4 3·9
55	3 28·8	3 29·3	3 19·2	5·5 1·2	11·5 2·6	17·5 3·9
56	3 29·0	3 29·6	3 19·5	5·6 1·3	11·6 2·6	17·6 4·0
57	3 29·3	3 29·8	3 19·7	5·7 1·3	11·7 2·6	17·7 4·0
58	3 29·5	3 30·1	3 20·0	5·8 1·3	11·8 2·7	17·8 4·0
59	3 29·8	3 30·3	3 20·2	5·9 1·3	11·9 2·7	17·9 4·0
60	3 30·0	3 30·6	3 20·4	6·0 1·4	12·0 2·7	18·0 4·1

14ᵐ s	SUN PLANETS ° ′	ARIES ° ′	MOON ° ′	v or d ′	Corrⁿ ′	v or d ′	Corrⁿ ′	v or d ′	Corrⁿ ′	15ᵐ s	SUN PLANETS ° ′	ARIES ° ′	MOON ° ′	v or d ′	Corrⁿ ′	v or d ′	Corrⁿ ′	v or d ′	Corrⁿ ′
00	3 30·0	3 30·6	3 20·4	0·0	0·0	6·0	1·5	12·0	2·9	00	3 45·0	3 45·6	3 34·8	0·0	0·0	6·0	1·6	12·0	3·1
01	3 30·3	3 30·8	3 20·7	0·1	0·0	6·1	1·5	12·1	2·9	01	3 45·3	3 45·9	3 35·0	0·1	0·0	6·1	1·6	12·1	3·1
02	3 30·5	3 31·1	3 20·9	0·2	0·0	6·2	1·5	12·2	2·9	02	3 45·5	3 46·1	3 35·2	0·2	0·1	6·2	1·6	12·2	3·2
03	3 30·8	3 31·3	3 21·1	0·3	0·1	6·3	1·5	12·3	3·0	03	3 45·8	3 46·4	3 35·5	0·3	0·1	6·3	1·6	12·3	3·2
04	3 31·0	3 31·6	3 21·4	0·4	0·1	6·4	1·5	12·4	3·0	04	3 46·0	3 46·6	3 35·7	0·4	0·1	6·4	1·7	12·4	3·2
05	3 31·3	3 31·8	3 21·6	0·5	0·1	6·5	1·6	12·5	3·0	05	3 46·3	3 46·9	3 35·9	0·5	0·1	6·5	1·7	12·5	3·2
06	3 31·5	3 32·1	3 21·9	0·6	0·1	6·6	1·6	12·6	3·0	06	3 46·5	3 47·1	3 36·2	0·6	0·2	6·6	1·7	12·6	3·3
07	3 31·8	3 32·3	3 22·1	0·7	0·2	6·7	1·6	12·7	3·1	07	3 46·8	3 47·4	3 36·4	0·7	0·2	6·7	1·7	12·7	3·3
08	3 32·0	3 32·6	3 22·3	0·8	0·2	6·8	1·6	12·8	3·1	08	3 47·0	3 47·6	3 36·7	0·8	0·2	6·8	1·8	12·8	3·3
09	3 32·3	3 32·8	3 22·6	0·9	0·2	6·9	1·7	12·9	3·1	09	3 47·3	3 47·9	3 36·9	0·9	0·2	6·9	1·8	12·9	3·3
10	3 32·5	3 33·1	3 22·8	1·0	0·2	7·0	1·7	13·0	3·1	10	3 47·5	3 48·1	3 37·1	1·0	0·3	7·0	1·8	13·0	3·4
11	3 32·8	3 33·3	3 23·1	1·1	0·3	7·1	1·7	13·1	3·2	11	3 47·8	3 48·4	3 37·4	1·1	0·3	7·1	1·8	13·1	3·4
12	3 33·0	3 33·6	3 23·3	1·2	0·3	7·2	1·7	13·2	3·2	12	3 48·0	3 48·6	3 37·6	1·2	0·3	7·2	1·9	13·2	3·4
13	3 33·3	3 33·8	3 23·5	1·3	0·3	7·3	1·8	13·3	3·2	13	3 48·3	3 48·9	3 37·9	1·3	0·3	7·3	1·9	13·3	3·4
14	3 33·5	3 34·1	3 23·8	1·4	0·3	7·4	1·8	13·4	3·2	14	3 48·5	3 49·1	3 38·1	1·4	0·4	7·4	1·9	13·4	3·5
15	3 33·8	3 34·3	3 24·0	1·5	0·4	7·5	1·8	13·5	3·3	15	3 48·8	3 49·4	3 38·3	1·5	0·4	7·5	1·9	13·5	3·5
16	3 34·0	3 34·6	3 24·3	1·6	0·4	7·6	1·8	13·6	3·3	16	3 49·0	3 49·6	3 38·6	1·6	0·4	7·6	2·0	13·6	3·5
17	3 34·3	3 34·8	3 24·5	1·7	0·4	7·7	1·9	13·7	3·3	17	3 49·3	3 49·9	3 38·8	1·7	0·4	7·7	2·0	13·7	3·5
18	3 34·5	3 35·1	3 24·7	1·8	0·4	7·8	1·9	13·8	3·3	18	3 49·5	3 50·1	3 39·0	1·8	0·5	7·8	2·0	13·8	3·6
19	3 34·8	3 35·3	3 25·0	1·9	0·5	7·9	1·9	13·9	3·4	19	3 49·8	3 50·4	3 39·3	1·9	0·5	7·9	2·0	13·9	3·6
20	3 35·0	3 35·6	3 25·2	2·0	0·5	8·0	1·9	14·0	3·4	20	3 50·0	3 50·6	3 39·5	2·0	0·5	8·0	2·1	14·0	3·6
21	3 35·3	3 35·8	3 25·4	2·1	0·5	8·1	2·0	14·1	3·4	21	3 50·3	3 50·9	3 39·8	2·1	0·5	8·1	2·1	14·1	3·6
22	3 35·5	3 36·1	3 25·7	2·2	0·5	8·2	2·0	14·2	3·4	22	3 50·5	3 51·1	3 40·0	2·2	0·6	8·2	2·1	14·2	3·7
23	3 35·8	3 36·3	3 25·9	2·3	0·6	8·3	2·0	14·3	3·5	23	3 50·8	3 51·4	3 40·2	2·3	0·6	8·3	2·1	14·3	3·7
24	3 36·0	3 36·6	3 26·2	2·4	0·6	8·4	2·0	14·4	3·5	24	3 51·0	3 51·6	3 40·5	2·4	0·6	8·4	2·2	14·4	3·7
25	3 36·3	3 36·8	3 26·4	2·5	0·6	8·5	2·1	14·5	3·5	25	3 51·3	3 51·9	3 40·7	2·5	0·6	8·5	2·2	14·5	3·7
26	3 36·5	3 37·1	3 26·6	2·6	0·6	8·6	2·1	14·6	3·5	26	3 51·5	3 52·1	3 41·0	2·6	0·7	8·6	2·2	14·6	3·8
27	3 36·8	3 37·3	3 26·9	2·7	0·7	8·7	2·1	14·7	3·6	27	3 51·8	3 52·4	3 41·2	2·7	0·7	8·7	2·2	14·7	3·8
28	3 37·0	3 37·6	3 27·1	2·8	0·7	8·8	2·1	14·8	3·6	28	3 52·0	3 52·6	3 41·4	2·8	0·7	8·8	2·3	14·8	3·8
29	3 37·3	3 37·8	3 27·4	2·9	0·7	8·9	2·2	14·9	3·6	29	3 52·3	3 52·9	3 41·7	2·9	0·7	8·9	2·3	14·9	3·8
30	3 37·5	3 38·1	3 27·6	3·0	0·7	9·0	2·2	15·0	3·6	30	3 52·5	3 53·1	3 41·9	3·0	0·8	9·0	2·3	15·0	3·9
31	3 37·8	3 38·3	3 27·8	3·1	0·7	9·1	2·2	15·1	3·6	31	3 52·8	3 53·4	3 42·1	3·1	0·8	9·1	2·4	15·1	3·9
32	3 38·0	3 38·6	3 28·1	3·2	0·8	9·2	2·2	15·2	3·7	32	3 53·0	3 53·6	3 42·4	3·2	0·8	9·2	2·4	15·2	3·9
33	3 38·3	3 38·8	3 28·3	3·3	0·8	9·3	2·2	15·3	3·7	33	3 53·3	3 53·9	3 42·6	3·3	0·9	9·3	2·4	15·3	4·0
34	3 38·5	3 39·1	3 28·5	3·4	0·8	9·4	2·3	15·4	3·7	34	3 53·5	3 54·1	3 42·9	3·4	0·9	9·4	2·4	15·4	4·0
35	3 38·8	3 39·3	3 28·8	3·5	0·8	9·5	2·3	15·5	3·7	35	3 53·8	3 54·4	3 43·1	3·5	0·9	9·5	2·5	15·5	4·0
36	3 39·0	3 39·6	3 29·0	3·6	0·9	9·6	2·3	15·6	3·8	36	3 54·0	3 54·6	3 43·3	3·6	0·9	9·6	2·5	15·6	4·0
37	3 39·3	3 39·9	3 29·3	3·7	0·9	9·7	2·3	15·7	3·8	37	3 54·3	3 54·9	3 43·6	3·7	1·0	9·7	2·5	15·7	4·1
38	3 39·5	3 40·1	3 29·5	3·8	0·9	9·8	2·4	15·8	3·8	38	3 54·5	3 55·1	3 43·8	3·8	1·0	9·8	2·5	15·8	4·1
39	3 39·8	3 40·4	3 29·7	3·9	0·9	9·9	2·4	15·9	3·8	39	3 54·8	3 55·4	3 44·1	3·9	1·0	9·9	2·6	15·9	4·1
40	3 40·0	3 40·6	3 30·0	4·0	1·0	10·0	2·4	16·0	3·9	40	3 55·0	3 55·6	3 44·3	4·0	1·0	10·0	2·6	16·0	4·1
41	3 40·3	3 40·9	3 30·2	4·1	1·0	10·1	2·4	16·1	3·9	41	3 55·3	3 55·9	3 44·5	4·1	1·1	10·1	2·6	16·1	4·2
42	3 40·5	3 41·1	3 30·5	4·2	1·0	10·2	2·5	16·2	3·9	42	3 55·5	3 56·1	3 44·8	4·2	1·1	10·2	2·6	16·2	4·2
43	3 40·8	3 41·4	3 30·7	4·3	1·0	10·3	2·5	16·3	3·9	43	3 55·8	3 56·4	3 45·0	4·3	1·1	10·3	2·7	16·3	4·2
44	3 41·0	3 41·6	3 30·9	4·4	1·1	10·4	2·5	16·4	4·0	44	3 56·0	3 56·6	3 45·2	4·4	1·1	10·4	2·7	16·4	4·2
45	3 41·3	3 41·9	3 31·2	4·5	1·1	10·5	2·5	16·5	4·0	45	3 56·3	3 56·9	3 45·5	4·5	1·2	10·5	2·7	16·5	4·3
46	3 41·5	3 42·1	3 31·4	4·6	1·1	10·6	2·6	16·6	4·0	46	3 56·5	3 57·1	3 45·7	4·6	1·2	10·6	2·7	16·6	4·3
47	3 41·8	3 42·4	3 31·6	4·7	1·1	10·7	2·6	16·7	4·0	47	3 56·8	3 57·4	3 46·0	4·7	1·2	10·7	2·8	16·7	4·3
48	3 42·0	3 42·6	3 31·9	4·8	1·2	10·8	2·6	16·8	4·1	48	3 57·0	3 57·6	3 46·2	4·8	1·2	10·8	2·8	16·8	4·3
49	3 42·3	3 42·9	3 32·1	4·9	1·2	10·9	2·6	16·9	4·1	49	3 57·3	3 57·9	3 46·4	4·9	1·3	10·9	2·8	16·9	4·4
50	3 42·5	3 43·1	3 32·4	5·0	1·2	11·0	2·7	17·0	4·1	50	3 57·5	3 58·2	3 46·7	5·0	1·3	11·0	2·8	17·0	4·4
51	3 42·8	3 43·4	3 32·6	5·1	1·2	11·1	2·7	17·1	4·1	51	3 57·8	3 58·4	3 46·9	5·1	1·3	11·1	2·9	17·1	4·4
52	3 43·0	3 43·6	3 32·8	5·2	1·3	11·2	2·7	17·2	4·2	52	3 58·0	3 58·7	3 47·2	5·2	1·3	11·2	2·9	17·2	4·4
53	3 43·3	3 43·9	3 33·1	5·3	1·3	11·3	2·7	17·3	4·2	53	3 58·3	3 58·9	3 47·4	5·3	1·4	11·3	2·9	17·3	4·5
54	3 43·5	3 44·1	3 33·3	5·4	1·3	11·4	2·8	17·4	4·2	54	3 58·5	3 59·2	3 47·6	5·4	1·4	11·4	2·9	17·4	4·5
55	3 43·8	3 44·4	3 33·6	5·5	1·3	11·5	2·8	17·5	4·2	55	3 58·8	3 59·4	3 47·9	5·5	1·4	11·5	3·0	17·5	4·5
56	3 44·0	3 44·6	3 33·8	5·6	1·4	11·6	2·8	17·6	4·3	56	3 59·0	3 59·7	3 48·1	5·6	1·4	11·6	3·0	17·6	4·5
57	3 44·3	3 44·9	3 34·0	5·7	1·4	11·7	2·8	17·7	4·3	57	3 59·3	3 59·9	3 48·4	5·7	1·5	11·7	3·0	17·7	4·6
58	3 44·5	3 45·1	3 34·3	5·8	1·4	11·8	2·9	17·8	4·3	58	3 59·5	4 00·2	3 48·6	5·8	1·5	11·8	3·0	17·8	4·6
59	3 44·8	3 45·4	3 34·5	5·9	1·4	11·9	2·9	17·9	4·3	59	3 59·8	4 00·4	3 48·8	5·9	1·5	11·9	3·1	17·9	4·6
60	3 45·0	3 45·6	3 34·8	6·0	1·5	12·0	2·9	18·0	4·4	60	4 00·0	4 00·7	3 49·1	6·0	1·6	12·0	3·1	18·0	4·7

16ᵐ

16 s	SUN PLANETS ° ′	ARIES ° ′	MOON ° ′	v or d ′	Corrⁿ ′	v or d ′	Corrⁿ ′	v or d ′	Corrⁿ ′
00	4 00·0	4 00·7	3 49·1	0·0	0·0	6·0	1·7	12·0	3·3
01	4 00·3	4 00·9	3 49·3	0·1	0·0	6·1	1·7	12·1	3·3
02	4 00·5	4 01·2	3 49·5	0·2	0·1	6·2	1·7	12·2	3·4
03	4 00·8	4 01·4	3 49·8	0·3	0·1	6·3	1·7	12·3	3·4
04	4 01·0	4 01·7	3 50·0	0·4	0·1	6·4	1·8	12·4	3·4
05	4 01·3	4 01·9	3 50·3	0·5	0·1	6·5	1·8	12·5	3·4
06	4 01·5	4 02·2	3 50·5	0·6	0·2	6·6	1·8	12·6	3·5
07	4 01·8	4 02·4	3 50·7	0·7	0·2	6·7	1·8	12·7	3·5
08	4 02·0	4 02·7	3 51·0	0·8	0·2	6·8	1·9	12·8	3·5
09	4 02·3	4 02·9	3 51·2	0·9	0·2	6·9	1·9	12·9	3·5
10	4 02·5	4 03·2	3 51·5	1·0	0·3	7·0	1·9	13·0	3·6
11	4 02·8	4 03·4	3 51·7	1·1	0·3	7·1	2·0	13·1	3·6
12	4 03·0	4 03·7	3 51·9	1·2	0·3	7·2	2·0	13·2	3·6
13	4 03·3	4 03·9	3 52·2	1·3	0·4	7·3	2·0	13·3	3·7
14	4 03·5	4 04·2	3 52·4	1·4	0·4	7·4	2·0	13·4	3·7
15	4 03·8	4 04·4	3 52·6	1·5	0·4	7·5	2·1	13·5	3·7
16	4 04·0	4 04·7	3 52·9	1·6	0·4	7·6	2·1	13·6	3·7
17	4 04·3	4 04·9	3 53·1	1·7	0·5	7·7	2·1	13·7	3·8
18	4 04·5	4 05·2	3 53·4	1·8	0·5	7·8	2·1	13·8	3·8
19	4 04·8	4 05·4	3 53·6	1·9	0·5	7·9	2·2	13·9	3·8
20	4 05·0	4 05·7	3 53·8	2·0	0·6	8·0	2·2	14·0	3·9
21	4 05·3	4 05·9	3 54·1	2·1	0·6	8·1	2·2	14·1	3·9
22	4 05·5	4 06·2	3 54·3	2·2	0·6	8·2	2·3	14·2	3·9
23	4 05·8	4 06·4	3 54·6	2·3	0·6	8·3	2·3	14·3	3·9
24	4 06·0	4 06·7	3 54·8	2·4	0·7	8·4	2·3	14·4	4·0
25	4 06·3	4 06·9	3 55·0	2·5	0·7	8·5	2·3	14·5	4·0
26	4 06·5	4 07·2	3 55·3	2·6	0·7	8·6	2·4	14·6	4·0
27	4 06·8	4 07·4	3 55·5	2·7	0·7	8·7	2·4	14·7	4·0
28	4 07·0	4 07·7	3 55·7	2·8	0·8	8·8	2·4	14·8	4·1
29	4 07·3	4 07·9	3 56·0	2·9	0·8	8·9	2·4	14·9	4·1
30	4 07·5	4 08·2	3 56·2	3·0	0·8	9·0	2·5	15·0	4·1
31	4 07·8	4 08·4	3 56·5	3·1	0·9	9·1	2·5	15·1	4·2
32	4 08·0	4 08·7	3 56·7	3·2	0·9	9·2	2·5	15·2	4·2
33	4 08·3	4 08·9	3 56·9	3·3	0·9	9·3	2·6	15·3	4·2
34	4 08·5	4 09·2	3 57·2	3·4	0·9	9·4	2·6	15·4	4·2
35	4 08·8	4 09·4	3 57·4	3·5	1·0	9·5	2·6	15·5	4·3
36	4 09·0	4 09·7	3 57·7	3·6	1·0	9·6	2·6	15·6	4·3
37	4 09·3	4 09·9	3 57·9	3·7	1·0	9·7	2·7	15·7	4·3
38	4 09·5	4 10·2	3 58·1	3·8	1·0	9·8	2·7	15·8	4·3
39	4 09·8	4 10·4	3 58·4	3·9	1·1	9·9	2·7	15·9	4·4
40	4 10·0	4 10·7	3 58·6	4·0	1·1	10·0	2·8	16·0	4·4
41	4 10·3	4 10·9	3 58·8	4·1	1·1	10·1	2·8	16·1	4·4
42	4 10·5	4 11·2	3 59·1	4·2	1·2	10·2	2·8	16·2	4·5
43	4 10·8	4 11·4	3 59·3	4·3	1·2	10·3	2·8	16·3	4·5
44	4 11·0	4 11·7	3 59·6	4·4	1·2	10·4	2·9	16·4	4·5
45	4 11·3	4 11·9	3 59·8	4·5	1·2	10·5	2·9	16·5	4·5
46	4 11·5	4 12·2	4 00·0	4·6	1·3	10·6	2·9	16·6	4·6
47	4 11·8	4 12·4	4 00·3	4·7	1·3	10·7	2·9	16·7	4·6
48	4 12·0	4 12·7	4 00·5	4·8	1·3	10·8	3·0	16·8	4·6
49	4 12·3	4 12·9	4 00·8	4·9	1·3	10·9	3·0	16·9	4·6
50	4 12·5	4 13·2	4 01·0	5·0	1·4	11·0	3·0	17·0	4·7
51	4 12·8	4 13·4	4 01·2	5·1	1·4	11·1	3·1	17·1	4·7
52	4 13·0	4 13·7	4 01·5	5·2	1·4	11·2	3·1	17·2	4·7
53	4 13·3	4 13·9	4 01·7	5·3	1·5	11·3	3·1	17·3	4·8
54	4 13·5	4 14·2	4 02·0	5·4	1·5	11·4	3·1	17·4	4·8
55	4 13·8	4 14·4	4 02·2	5·5	1·5	11·5	3·2	17·5	4·8
56	4 14·0	4 14·7	4 02·4	5·6	1·5	11·6	3·2	17·6	4·8
57	4 14·3	4 14·9	4 02·7	5·7	1·6	11·7	3·2	17·7	4·9
58	4 14·5	4 15·2	4 02·9	5·8	1·6	11·8	3·2	17·8	4·9
59	4 14·8	4 15·4	4 03·1	5·9	1·6	11·9	3·3	17·9	4·9
60	4 15·0	4 15·7	4 03·4	6·0	1·7	12·0	3·3	18·0	5·0

17ᵐ

17 s	SUN PLANETS ° ′	ARIES ° ′	MOON ° ′	v or d ′	Corrⁿ ′	v or d ′	Corrⁿ ′	v or d ′	Corrⁿ ′
00	4 15·0	4 15·7	4 03·4	0·0	0·0	6·0	1·8	12·0	3·5
01	4 15·3	4 15·9	4 03·6	0·1	0·0	6·1	1·8	12·1	3·5
02	4 15·5	4 16·2	4 03·9	0·2	0·1	6·2	1·8	12·2	3·6
03	4 15·8	4 16·5	4 04·1	0·3	0·1	6·3	1·8	12·3	3·6
04	4 16·0	4 16·7	4 04·3	0·4	0·1	6·4	1·9	12·4	3·6
05	4 16·3	4 17·0	4 04·6	0·5	0·1	6·5	1·9	12·5	3·6
06	4 16·5	4 17·2	4 04·8	0·6	0·2	6·6	1·9	12·6	3·7
07	4 16·8	4 17·5	4 05·1	0·7	0·2	6·7	2·0	12·7	3·7
08	4 17·0	4 17·7	4 05·3	0·8	0·2	6·8	2·0	12·8	3·7
09	4 17·3	4 18·0	4 05·5	0·9	0·3	6·9	2·0	12·9	3·8
10	4 17·5	4 18·2	4 05·8	1·0	0·3	7·0	2·0	13·0	3·8
11	4 17·8	4 18·5	4 06·0	1·1	0·3	7·1	2·1	13·1	3·8
12	4 18·0	4 18·7	4 06·2	1·2	0·4	7·2	2·1	13·2	3·9
13	4 18·3	4 19·0	4 06·5	1·3	0·4	7·3	2·1	13·3	3·9
14	4 18·5	4 19·2	4 06·7	1·4	0·4	7·4	2·2	13·4	3·9
15	4 18·8	4 19·5	4 07·0	1·5	0·4	7·5	2·2	13·5	3·9
16	4 19·0	4 19·7	4 07·2	1·6	0·5	7·6	2·2	13·6	4·0
17	4 19·3	4 20·0	4 07·4	1·7	0·5	7·7	2·2	13·7	4·0
18	4 19·5	4 20·2	4 07·7	1·8	0·5	7·8	2·3	13·8	4·0
19	4 19·8	4 20·5	4 07·9	1·9	0·6	7·9	2·3	13·9	4·1
20	4 20·0	4 20·7	4 08·2	2·0	0·6	8·0	2·3	14·0	4·1
21	4 20·3	4 21·0	4 08·4	2·1	0·6	8·1	2·4	14·1	4·1
22	4 20·5	4 21·2	4 08·6	2·2	0·6	8·2	2·4	14·2	4·1
23	4 20·8	4 21·5	4 08·9	2·3	0·7	8·3	2·4	14·3	4·2
24	4 21·0	4 21·7	4 09·1	2·4	0·7	8·4	2·5	14·4	4·2
25	4 21·3	4 22·0	4 09·3	2·5	0·7	8·5	2·5	14·5	4·2
26	4 21·5	4 22·2	4 09·6	2·6	0·8	8·6	2·5	14·6	4·3
27	4 21·8	4 22·5	4 09·8	2·7	0·8	8·7	2·5	14·7	4·3
28	4 22·0	4 22·7	4 10·1	2·8	0·8	8·8	2·6	14·8	4·3
29	4 22·3	4 23·0	4 10·3	2·9	0·8	8·9	2·6	14·9	4·3
30	4 22·5	4 23·2	4 10·5	3·0	0·9	9·0	2·6	15·0	4·4
31	4 22·8	4 23·5	4 10·8	3·1	0·9	9·1	2·7	15·1	4·4
32	4 23·0	4 23·7	4 11·0	3·2	0·9	9·2	2·7	15·2	4·4
33	4 23·3	4 24·0	4 11·3	3·3	1·0	9·3	2·7	15·3	4·5
34	4 23·5	4 24·2	4 11·5	3·4	1·0	9·4	2·7	15·4	4·5
35	4 23·8	4 24·5	4 11·7	3·5	1·0	9·5	2·8	15·5	4·5
36	4 24·0	4 24·7	4 12·0	3·6	1·1	9·6	2·8	15·6	4·6
37	4 24·3	4 25·0	4 12·2	3·7	1·1	9·7	2·8	15·7	4·6
38	4 24·5	4 25·2	4 12·5	3·8	1·1	9·8	2·9	15·8	4·6
39	4 24·8	4 25·5	4 12·7	3·9	1·1	9·9	2·9	15·9	4·6
40	4 25·0	4 25·7	4 12·9	4·0	1·2	10·0	2·9	16·0	4·7
41	4 25·3	4 26·0	4 13·2	4·1	1·2	10·1	2·9	16·1	4·7
42	4 25·5	4 26·2	4 13·4	4·2	1·2	10·2	3·0	16·2	4·7
43	4 25·8	4 26·5	4 13·6	4·3	1·3	10·3	3·0	16·3	4·8
44	4 26·0	4 26·7	4 13·9	4·4	1·3	10·4	3·0	16·4	4·8
45	4 26·3	4 27·0	4 14·1	4·5	1·3	10·5	3·1	16·5	4·8
46	4 26·5	4 27·2	4 14·4	4·6	1·3	10·6	3·1	16·6	4·8
47	4 26·8	4 27·5	4 14·6	4·7	1·4	10·7	3·1	16·7	4·9
48	4 27·0	4 27·7	4 14·8	4·8	1·4	10·8	3·2	16·8	4·9
49	4 27·3	4 28·0	4 15·1	4·9	1·4	10·9	3·2	16·9	4·9
50	4 27·5	4 28·2	4 15·3	5·0	1·5	11·0	3·2	17·0	5·0
51	4 27·8	4 28·5	4 15·6	5·1	1·5	11·1	3·3	17·1	5·0
52	4 28·0	4 28·7	4 15·8	5·2	1·5	11·2	3·3	17·2	5·0
53	4 28·3	4 29·0	4 16·0	5·3	1·5	11·3	3·3	17·3	5·0
54	4 28·5	4 29·2	4 16·3	5·4	1·6	11·4	3·3	17·4	5·1
55	4 28·8	4 29·5	4 16·5	5·5	1·6	11·5	3·4	17·5	5·1
56	4 29·0	4 29·7	4 16·7	5·6	1·6	11·6	3·4	17·6	5·1
57	4 29·3	4 30·0	4 17·0	5·7	1·7	11·7	3·4	17·7	5·2
58	4 29·5	4 30·2	4 17·2	5·8	1·7	11·8	3·4	17·8	5·2
59	4 29·8	4 30·5	4 17·5	5·9	1·7	11·9	3·5	17·9	5·2
60	4 30·0	4 30·7	4 17·7	6·0	1·8	12·0	3·5	18·0	5·3

x

18ᵐ

s	SUN PLANETS	ARIES	MOON	v or d	Corrⁿ	v or d	Corrⁿ	v or d	Corrⁿ
	° ′	° ′	° ′	′	′	′	′	′	′
00	4 30·0	4 30·7	4 17·7	0·0	0·0	6·0	1·9	12·0	3·7
01	4 30·3	4 31·0	4 17·9	0·1	0·0	6·1	1·9	12·1	3·7
02	4 30·5	4 31·2	4 18·2	0·2	0·1	6·2	1·9	12·2	3·8
03	4 30·8	4 31·5	4 18·4	0·3	0·1	6·3	1·9	12·3	3·8
04	4 31·0	4 31·7	4 18·7	0·4	0·1	6·4	2·0	12·4	3·8
05	4 31·3	4 32·0	4 18·9	0·5	0·2	6·5	2·0	12·5	3·9
06	4 31·5	4 32·2	4 19·1	0·6	0·2	6·6	2·0	12·6	3·9
07	4 31·8	4 32·5	4 19·4	0·7	0·2	6·7	2·1	12·7	3·9
08	4 32·0	4 32·7	4 19·6	0·8	0·2	6·8	2·1	12·8	3·9
09	4 32·3	4 33·0	4 19·8	0·9	0·3	6·9	2·1	12·9	4·0
10	4 32·5	4 33·2	4 20·1	1·0	0·3	7·0	2·2	13·0	4·0
11	4 32·8	4 33·5	4 20·3	1·1	0·3	7·1	2·2	13·1	4·0
12	4 33·0	4 33·7	4 20·6	1·2	0·4	7·2	2·2	13·2	4·1
13	4 33·3	4 34·0	4 20·8	1·3	0·4	7·3	2·3	13·3	4·1
14	4 33·5	4 34·2	4 21·0	1·4	0·4	7·4	2·3	13·4	4·1
15	4 33·8	4 34·5	4 21·3	1·5	0·5	7·5	2·3	13·5	4·2
16	4 34·0	4 34·8	4 21·5	1·6	0·5	7·6	2·3	13·6	4·2
17	4 34·3	4 35·0	4 21·8	1·7	0·5	7·7	2·4	13·7	4·2
18	4 34·5	4 35·3	4 22·0	1·8	0·6	7·8	2·4	13·8	4·3
19	4 34·8	4 35·5	4 22·2	1·9	0·6	7·9	2·4	13·9	4·3
20	4 35·0	4 35·8	4 22·5	2·0	0·6	8·0	2·5	14·0	4·3
21	4 35·3	4 36·0	4 22·7	2·1	0·6	8·1	2·5	14·1	4·3
22	4 35·5	4 36·3	4 22·9	2·2	0·7	8·2	2·5	14·2	4·4
23	4 35·8	4 36·5	4 23·2	2·3	0·7	8·3	2·6	14·3	4·4
24	4 36·0	4 36·8	4 23·4	2·4	0·7	8·4	2·6	14·4	4·4
25	4 36·3	4 37·0	4 23·7	2·5	0·8	8·5	2·6	14·5	4·5
26	4 36·5	4 37·3	4 23·9	2·6	0·8	8·6	2·7	14·6	4·5
27	4 36·8	4 37·5	4 24·1	2·7	0·8	8·7	2·7	14·7	4·5
28	4 37·0	4 37·8	4 24·4	2·8	0·9	8·8	2·7	14·8	4·6
29	4 37·3	4 38·0	4 24·6	2·9	0·9	8·9	2·7	14·9	4·6
30	4 37·5	4 38·3	4 24·9	3·0	0·9	9·0	2·8	15·0	4·6
31	4 37·8	4 38·5	4 25·1	3·1	1·0	9·1	2·8	15·1	4·7
32	4 38·0	4 38·8	4 25·3	3·2	1·0	9·2	2·8	15·2	4·7
33	4 38·3	4 39·0	4 25·6	3·3	1·0	9·3	2·9	15·3	4·7
34	4 38·5	4 39·3	4 25·8	3·4	1·0	9·4	2·9	15·4	4·7
35	4 38·8	4 39·5	4 26·1	3·5	1·1	9·5	2·9	15·5	4·8
36	4 39·0	4 39·8	4 26·3	3·6	1·1	9·6	3·0	15·6	4·8
37	4 39·3	4 40·0	4 26·5	3·7	1·1	9·7	3·0	15·7	4·8
38	4 39·5	4 40·3	4 26·8	3·8	1·2	9·8	3·0	15·8	4·9
39	4 39·8	4 40·5	4 27·0	3·9	1·2	9·9	3·1	15·9	4·9
40	4 40·0	4 40·8	4 27·2	4·0	1·2	10·0	3·1	16·0	4·9
41	4 40·3	4 41·0	4 27·5	4·1	1·3	10·1	3·1	16·1	5·0
42	4 40·5	4 41·3	4 27·7	4·2	1·3	10·2	3·1	16·2	5·0
43	4 40·8	4 41·5	4 28·0	4·3	1·3	10·3	3·2	16·3	5·0
44	4 41·0	4 41·8	4 28·2	4·4	1·4	10·4	3·2	16·4	5·1
45	4 41·3	4 42·0	4 28·4	4·5	1·4	10·5	3·2	16·5	5·1
46	4 41·5	4 42·3	4 28·7	4·6	1·4	10·6	3·3	16·6	5·1
47	4 41·8	4 42·5	4 28·9	4·7	1·4	10·7	3·3	16·7	5·1
48	4 42·0	4 42·8	4 29·2	4·8	1·5	10·8	3·3	16·8	5·2
49	4 42·3	4 43·0	4 29·4	4·9	1·5	10·9	3·4	16·9	5·2
50	4 42·5	4 43·3	4 29·6	5·0	1·5	11·0	3·4	17·0	5·2
51	4 42·8	4 43·5	4 29·9	5·1	1·6	11·1	3·4	17·1	5·3
52	4 43·0	4 43·8	4 30·1	5·2	1·6	11·2	3·5	17·2	5·3
53	4 43·3	4 44·0	4 30·3	5·3	1·6	11·3	3·5	17·3	5·3
54	4 43·5	4 44·3	4 30·6	5·4	1·7	11·4	3·5	17·4	5·4
55	4 43·8	4 44·5	4 30·8	5·5	1·7	11·5	3·5	17·5	5·4
56	4 44·0	4 44·8	4 31·1	5·6	1·7	11·6	3·6	17·6	5·4
57	4 44·3	4 45·0	4 31·3	5·7	1·8	11·7	3·6	17·7	5·5
58	4 44·5	4 45·3	4 31·5	5·8	1·8	11·8	3·6	17·8	5·5
59	4 44·8	4 45·5	4 31·8	5·9	1·8	11·9	3·7	17·9	5·5
60	4 45·0	4 45·8	4 32·0	6·0	1·9	12·0	3·7	18·0	5·6

19ᵐ

s	SUN PLANETS	ARIES	MOON	v or d	Corrⁿ	v or d	Corrⁿ	v or d	Corrⁿ
	° ′	° ′	° ′	′	′	′	′	′	′
00	4 45·0	4 45·8	4 32·0	0·0	0·0	6·0	2·0	12·0	3·9
01	4 45·3	4 46·0	4 32·3	0·1	0·0	6·1	2·0	12·1	3·9
02	4 45·5	4 46·3	4 32·5	0·2	0·1	6·2	2·0	12·2	4·0
03	4 45·8	4 46·5	4 32·7	0·3	0·1	6·3	2·0	12·3	4·0
04	4 46·0	4 46·8	4 33·0	0·4	0·1	6·4	2·1	12·4	4·0
05	4 46·3	4 47·0	4 33·2	0·5	0·2	6·5	2·1	12·5	4·1
06	4 46·5	4 47·3	4 33·4	0·6	0·2	6·6	2·1	12·6	4·1
07	4 46·8	4 47·5	4 33·7	0·7	0·2	6·7	2·2	12·7	4·1
08	4 47·0	4 47·8	4 33·9	0·8	0·3	6·8	2·2	12·8	4·2
09	4 47·3	4 48·0	4 34·2	0·9	0·3	6·9	2·2	12·9	4·2
10	4 47·5	4 48·3	4 34·4	1·0	0·3	7·0	2·3	13·0	4·2
11	4 47·8	4 48·5	4 34·6	1·1	0·4	7·1	2·3	13·1	4·3
12	4 48·0	4 48·8	4 34·9	1·2	0·4	7·2	2·3	13·2	4·3
13	4 48·3	4 49·0	4 35·1	1·3	0·4	7·3	2·4	13·3	4·3
14	4 48·5	4 49·3	4 35·4	1·4	0·5	7·4	2·4	13·4	4·4
15	4 48·8	4 49·5	4 35·6	1·5	0·5	7·5	2·4	13·5	4·4
16	4 49·0	4 49·8	4 35·8	1·6	0·5	7·6	2·5	13·6	4·4
17	4 49·3	4 50·0	4 36·1	1·7	0·6	7·7	2·5	13·7	4·5
18	4 49·5	4 50·3	4 36·3	1·8	0·6	7·8	2·5	13·8	4·5
19	4 49·8	4 50·5	4 36·6	1·9	0·6	7·9	2·6	13·9	4·5
20	4 50·0	4 50·8	4 36·8	2·0	0·7	8·0	2·6	14·0	4·6
21	4 50·3	4 51·0	4 37·0	2·1	0·7	8·1	2·6	14·1	4·6
22	4 50·5	4 51·3	4 37·3	2·2	0·7	8·2	2·7	14·2	4·6
23	4 50·8	4 51·5	4 37·5	2·3	0·7	8·3	2·7	14·3	4·6
24	4 51·0	4 51·8	4 37·7	2·4	0·8	8·4	2·7	14·4	4·7
25	4 51·3	4 52·0	4 38·0	2·5	0·8	8·5	2·8	14·5	4·7
26	4 51·5	4 52·3	4 38·2	2·6	0·8	8·6	2·8	14·6	4·7
27	4 51·8	4 52·5	4 38·5	2·7	0·9	8·7	2·8	14·7	4·8
28	4 52·0	4 52·8	4 38·7	2·8	0·9	8·8	2·9	14·8	4·8
29	4 52·3	4 53·1	4 38·9	2·9	0·9	8·9	2·9	14·9	4·8
30	4 52·5	4 53·3	4 39·2	3·0	1·0	9·0	2·9	15·0	4·9
31	4 52·8	4 53·6	4 39·4	3·1	1·0	9·1	3·0	15·1	4·9
32	4 53·0	4 53·8	4 39·7	3·2	1·0	9·2	3·0	15·2	4·9
33	4 53·3	4 54·1	4 39·9	3·3	1·1	9·3	3·0	15·3	5·0
34	4 53·5	4 54·3	4 40·1	3·4	1·1	9·4	3·1	15·4	5·0
35	4 53·8	4 54·6	4 40·4	3·5	1·1	9·5	3·1	15·5	5·0
36	4 54·0	4 54·8	4 40·6	3·6	1·2	9·6	3·1	15·6	5·1
37	4 54·3	4 55·1	4 40·8	3·7	1·2	9·7	3·2	15·7	5·1
38	4 54·5	4 55·3	4 41·1	3·8	1·2	9·8	3·2	15·8	5·1
39	4 54·8	4 55·6	4 41·3	3·9	1·3	9·9	3·2	15·9	5·2
40	4 55·0	4 55·8	4 41·6	4·0	1·3	10·0	3·3	16·0	5·2
41	4 55·3	4 56·1	4 41·8	4·1	1·3	10·1	3·3	16·1	5·2
42	4 55·5	4 56·3	4 42·0	4·2	1·4	10·2	3·3	16·2	5·3
43	4 55·8	4 56·6	4 42·3	4·3	1·4	10·3	3·3	16·3	5·3
44	4 56·0	4 56·8	4 42·5	4·4	1·4	10·4	3·4	16·4	5·3
45	4 56·3	4 57·1	4 42·8	4·5	1·5	10·5	3·4	16·5	5·4
46	4 56·5	4 57·3	4 43·0	4·6	1·5	10·6	3·4	16·6	5·4
47	4 56·8	4 57·6	4 43·2	4·7	1·5	10·7	3·5	16·7	5·4
48	4 57·0	4 57·8	4 43·5	4·8	1·6	10·8	3·5	16·8	5·5
49	4 57·3	4 58·1	4 43·7	4·9	1·6	10·9	3·5	16·9	5·5
50	4 57·5	4 58·3	4 43·9	5·0	1·6	11·0	3·6	17·0	5·5
51	4 57·8	4 58·6	4 44·2	5·1	1·7	11·1	3·6	17·1	5·6
52	4 58·0	4 58·8	4 44·4	5·2	1·7	11·2	3·6	17·2	5·6
53	4 58·3	4 59·1	4 44·7	5·3	1·7	11·3	3·7	17·3	5·6
54	4 58·5	4 59·3	4 44·9	5·4	1·8	11·4	3·7	17·4	5·7
55	4 58·8	4 59·6	4 45·1	5·5	1·8	11·5	3·7	17·5	5·7
56	4 59·0	4 59·8	4 45·4	5·6	1·8	11·6	3·8	17·6	5·7
57	4 59·3	5 00·1	4 45·6	5·7	1·9	11·7	3·8	17·7	5·8
58	4 59·5	5 00·3	4 45·9	5·8	1·9	11·8	3·8	17·8	5·8
59	4 59·8	5 00·6	4 46·1	5·9	2·0	11·9	3·9	17·9	5·8
60	5 00·0	5 00·8	4 46·3	6·0	2·0	12·0	3·9	18·0	5·9

20 m	SUN PLANETS	ARIES	MOON	v or Corrⁿ d		v or Corrⁿ d		v or Corrⁿ d	
s	° ′	° ′	° ′	′	′	′	′	′	′
00	5 00·0	5 00·8	4 46·3	0·0	0·0	6·0	2·1	12·0	4·1
01	5 00·3	5 01·1	4 46·6	0·1	0·0	6·1	2·1	12·1	4·1
02	5 00·5	5 01·3	4 46·8	0·2	0·1	6·2	2·1	12·2	4·2
03	5 00·8	5 01·6	4 47·0	0·3	0·1	6·3	2·2	12·3	4·2
04	5 01·0	5 01·8	4 47·3	0·4	0·1	6·4	2·2	12·4	4·2
05	5 01·3	5 02·1	4 47·5	0·5	0·2	6·5	2·2	12·5	4·3
06	5 01·5	5 02·3	4 47·8	0·6	0·2	6·6	2·3	12·6	4·3
07	5 01·8	5 02·6	4 48·0	0·7	0·2	6·7	2·3	12·7	4·3
08	5 02·0	5 02·8	4 48·2	0·8	0·3	6·8	2·3	12·8	4·4
09	5 02·3	5 03·1	4 48·5	0·9	0·3	6·9	2·4	12·9	4·4
10	5 02·5	5 03·3	4 48·7	1·0	0·3	7·0	2·4	13·0	4·4
11	5 02·8	5 03·6	4 49·0	1·1	0·4	7·1	2·4	13·1	4·5
12	5 03·0	5 03·8	4 49·2	1·2	0·4	7·2	2·5	13·2	4·5
13	5 03·3	5 04·1	4 49·4	1·3	0·4	7·3	2·5	13·3	4·5
14	5 03·5	5 04·3	4 49·7	1·4	0·5	7·4	2·5	13·4	4·6
15	5 03·8	5 04·6	4 49·9	1·5	0·5	7·5	2·6	13·5	4·6
16	5 04·0	5 04·8	4 50·2	1·6	0·5	7·6	2·6	13·6	4·6
17	5 04·3	5 05·1	4 50·4	1·7	0·6	7·7	2·6	13·7	4·7
18	5 04·5	5 05·3	4 50·6	1·8	0·6	7·8	2·7	13·8	4·7
19	5 04·8	5 05·6	4 50·9	1·9	0·6	7·9	2·7	13·9	4·7
20	5 05·0	5 05·8	4 51·1	2·0	0·7	8·0	2·7	14·0	4·8
21	5 05·3	5 06·1	4 51·3	2·1	0·7	8·1	2·8	14·1	4·8
22	5 05·5	5 06·3	4 51·6	2·2	0·8	8·2	2·8	14·2	4·9
23	5 05·8	5 06·6	4 51·8	2·3	0·8	8·3	2·8	14·3	4·9
24	5 06·0	5 06·8	4 52·1	2·4	0·8	8·4	2·9	14·4	4·9
25	5 06·3	5 07·1	4 52·3	2·5	0·9	8·5	2·9	14·5	5·0
26	5 06·5	5 07·3	4 52·5	2·6	0·9	8·6	2·9	14·6	5·0
27	5 06·8	5 07·6	4 52·8	2·7	0·9	8·7	3·0	14·7	5·0
28	5 07·0	5 07·8	4 53·0	2·8	1·0	8·8	3·0	14·8	5·1
29	5 07·3	5 08·1	4 53·3	2·9	1·0	8·9	3·0	14·9	5·1
30	5 07·5	5 08·3	4 53·5	3·0	1·0	9·0	3·1	15·0	5·1
31	5 07·8	5 08·6	4 53·7	3·1	1·1	9·1	3·1	15·1	5·2
32	5 08·0	5 08·8	4 54·0	3·2	1·1	9·2	3·1	15·2	5·2
33	5 08·3	5 09·1	4 54·2	3·3	1·1	9·3	3·2	15·3	5·2
34	5 08·5	5 09·3	4 54·4	3·4	1·2	9·4	3·2	15·4	5·3
35	5 08·8	5 09·6	4 54·7	3·5	1·2	9·5	3·2	15·5	5·3
36	5 09·0	5 09·8	4 54·9	3·6	1·2	9·6	3·3	15·6	5·3
37	5 09·3	5 10·1	4 55·2	3·7	1·3	9·7	3·3	15·7	5·4
38	5 09·5	5 10·3	4 55·4	3·8	1·3	9·8	3·3	15·8	5·4
39	5 09·8	5 10·6	4 55·6	3·9	1·3	9·9	3·4	15·9	5·4
40	5 10·0	5 10·8	4 55·9	4·0	1·4	10·0	3·4	16·0	5·5
41	5 10·3	5 11·1	4 56·1	4·1	1·4	10·1	3·5	16·1	5·5
42	5 10·5	5 11·4	4 56·4	4·2	1·4	10·2	3·5	16·2	5·5
43	5 10·8	5 11·6	4 56·6	4·3	1·5	10·3	3·5	16·3	5·6
44	5 11·0	5 11·9	4 56·8	4·4	1·5	10·4	3·6	16·4	5·6
45	5 11·3	5 12·1	4 57·1	4·5	1·5	10·5	3·6	16·5	5·6
46	5 11·5	5 12·4	4 57·3	4·6	1·6	10·6	3·6	16·6	5·7
47	5 11·8	5 12·6	4 57·5	4·7	1·6	10·7	3·7	16·7	5·7
48	5 12·0	5 12·9	4 57·8	4·8	1·6	10·8	3·7	16·8	5·7
49	5 12·3	5 13·1	4 58·0	4·9	1·7	10·9	3·7	16·9	5·8
50	5 12·5	5 13·4	4 58·3	5·0	1·7	11·0	3·8	17·0	5·8
51	5 12·8	5 13·6	4 58·5	5·1	1·7	11·1	3·8	17·1	5·8
52	5 13·0	5 13·9	4 58·7	5·2	1·8	11·2	3·8	17·2	5·9
53	5 13·3	5 14·1	4 59·0	5·3	1·8	11·3	3·9	17·3	5·9
54	5 13·5	5 14·4	4 59·2	5·4	1·8	11·4	3·9	17·4	5·9
55	5 13·8	5 14·6	4 59·5	5·5	1·9	11·5	3·9	17·5	6·0
56	5 14·0	5 14·9	4 59·7	5·6	1·9	11·6	4·0	17·6	6·0
57	5 14·3	5 15·1	4 59·9	5·7	1·9	11·7	4·0	17·7	6·0
58	5 14·5	5 15·4	5 00·2	5·8	2·0	11·8	4·0	17·8	6·1
59	5 14·8	5 15·6	5 00·4	5·9	2·0	11·9	4·1	17·9	6·1
60	5 15·0	5 15·9	5 00·7	6·0	2·1	12·0	4·1	18·0	6·2

21 m	SUN PLANETS	ARIES	MOON	v or Corrⁿ d		v or Corrⁿ d		v or Corrⁿ d	
s	° ′	° ′	° ′	′	′	′	′	′	′
00	5 15·0	5 15·9	5 00·7	0·0	0·0	6·0	2·2	12·0	4·3
01	5 15·3	5 16·1	5 00·9	0·1	0·0	6·1	2·2	12·1	4·3
02	5 15·5	5 16·4	5 01·1	0·2	0·1	6·2	2·2	12·2	4·4
03	5 15·8	5 16·6	5 01·4	0·3	0·1	6·3	2·3	12·3	4·4
04	5 16·0	5 16·9	5 01·6	0·4	0·1	6·4	2·3	12·4	4·4
05	5 16·3	5 17·1	5 01·8	0·5	0·2	6·5	2·3	12·5	4·5
06	5 16·5	5 17·4	5 02·1	0·6	0·2	6·6	2·4	12·6	4·5
07	5 16·8	5 17·6	5 02·3	0·7	0·3	6·7	2·4	12·7	4·6
08	5 17·0	5 17·9	5 02·6	0·8	0·3	6·8	2·4	12·8	4·6
09	5 17·3	5 18·1	5 02·8	0·9	0·3	6·9	2·5	12·9	4·6
10	5 17·5	5 18·4	5 03·0	1·0	0·4	7·0	2·5	13·0	4·7
11	5 17·8	5 18·6	5 03·3	1·1	0·4	7·1	2·5	13·1	4·7
12	5 18·0	5 18·9	5 03·5	1·2	0·4	7·2	2·6	13·2	4·7
13	5 18·3	5 19·1	5 03·8	1·3	0·5	7·3	2·6	13·3	4·8
14	5 18·5	5 19·4	5 04·0	1·4	0·5	7·4	2·7	13·4	4·8
15	5 18·8	5 19·6	5 04·2	1·5	0·5	7·5	2·7	13·5	4·8
16	5 19·0	5 19·9	5 04·5	1·6	0·6	7·6	2·7	13·6	4·9
17	5 19·3	5 20·1	5 04·7	1·7	0·6	7·7	2·8	13·7	4·9
18	5 19·5	5 20·4	5 04·9	1·8	0·6	7·8	2·8	13·8	4·9
19	5 19·8	5 20·6	5 05·2	1·9	0·7	7·9	2·8	13·9	5·0
20	5 20·0	5 20·9	5 05·4	2·0	0·7	8·0	2·9	14·0	5·0
21	5 20·3	5 21·1	5 05·7	2·1	0·8	8·1	2·9	14·1	5·1
22	5 20·5	5 21·4	5 05·9	2·2	0·8	8·2	2·9	14·2	5·1
23	5 20·8	5 21·6	5 06·1	2·3	0·8	8·3	3·0	14·3	5·1
24	5 21·0	5 21·9	5 06·4	2·4	0·9	8·4	3·0	14·4	5·2
25	5 21·3	5 22·1	5 06·6	2·5	0·9	8·5	3·0	14·5	5·2
26	5 21·5	5 22·4	5 06·9	2·6	0·9	8·6	3·1	14·6	5·2
27	5 21·8	5 22·6	5 07·1	2·7	1·0	8·7	3·1	14·7	5·3
28	5 22·0	5 22·9	5 07·3	2·8	1·0	8·8	3·2	14·8	5·3
29	5 22·3	5 23·1	5 07·6	2·9	1·0	8·9	3·2	14·9	5·3
30	5 22·5	5 23·4	5 07·8	3·0	1·1	9·0	3·2	15·0	5·4
31	5 22·8	5 23·6	5 08·0	3·1	1·1	9·1	3·3	15·1	5·4
32	5 23·0	5 23·9	5 08·3	3·2	1·1	9·2	3·3	15·2	5·4
33	5 23·3	5 24·1	5 08·5	3·3	1·2	9·3	3·3	15·3	5·5
34	5 23·5	5 24·4	5 08·8	3·4	1·2	9·4	3·4	15·4	5·5
35	5 23·8	5 24·6	5 09·0	3·5	1·3	9·5	3·4	15·5	5·6
36	5 24·0	5 24·9	5 09·2	3·6	1·3	9·6	3·4	15·6	5·6
37	5 24·3	5 25·1	5 09·5	3·7	1·3	9·7	3·5	15·7	5·6
38	5 24·5	5 25·4	5 09·7	3·8	1·4	9·8	3·5	15·8	5·7
39	5 24·8	5 25·6	5 10·0	3·9	1·4	9·9	3·5	15·9	5·7
40	5 25·0	5 25·9	5 10·2	4·0	1·4	10·0	3·6	16·0	5·7
41	5 25·3	5 26·1	5 10·4	4·1	1·5	10·1	3·6	16·1	5·8
42	5 25·5	5 26·4	5 10·7	4·2	1·5	10·2	3·7	16·2	5·8
43	5 25·8	5 26·6	5 10·9	4·3	1·5	10·3	3·7	16·3	5·8
44	5 26·0	5 26·9	5 11·1	4·4	1·6	10·4	3·7	16·4	5·9
45	5 26·3	5 27·1	5 11·4	4·5	1·6	10·5	3·8	16·5	5·9
46	5 26·5	5 27·4	5 11·6	4·6	1·6	10·6	3·8	16·6	5·9
47	5 26·8	5 27·6	5 11·9	4·7	1·7	10·7	3·8	16·7	6·0
48	5 27·0	5 27·9	5 12·1	4·8	1·7	10·8	3·9	16·8	6·0
49	5 27·3	5 28·1	5 12·3	4·9	1·8	10·9	3·9	16·9	6·1
50	5 27·5	5 28·4	5 12·6	5·0	1·8	11·0	3·9	17·0	6·1
51	5 27·8	5 28·6	5 12·8	5·1	1·8	11·1	4·0	17·1	6·1
52	5 28·0	5 28·9	5 13·1	5·2	1·9	11·2	4·0	17·2	6·2
53	5 28·3	5 29·1	5 13·3	5·3	1·9	11·3	4·0	17·3	6·2
54	5 28·5	5 29·4	5 13·5	5·4	1·9	11·4	4·1	17·4	6·2
55	5 28·8	5 29·7	5 13·8	5·5	2·0	11·5	4·1	17·5	6·3
56	5 29·0	5 29·9	5 14·0	5·6	2·0	11·6	4·2	17·6	6·3
57	5 29·3	5 30·2	5 14·3	5·7	2·0	11·7	4·2	17·7	6·3
58	5 29·5	5 30·4	5 14·5	5·8	2·1	11·8	4·2	17·8	6·4
59	5 29·8	5 30·7	5 14·7	5·9	2·1	11·9	4·3	17·9	6·4
60	5 30·0	5 30·9	5 15·0	6·0	2·2	12·0	4·3	18·0	6·5

22ᵐ

s	SUN PLANETS	ARIES	MOON	v or d	Corrⁿ	v or d	Corrⁿ	v or d	Corrⁿ
00	5 30.0	5 30.9	5 15.0	0.0	0.0	6.0	2.3	12.0	4.5
01	5 30.3	5 31.2	5 15.2	0.1	0.0	6.1	2.3	12.1	4.5
02	5 30.5	5 31.4	5 15.4	0.2	0.1	6.2	2.3	12.2	4.6
03	5 30.8	5 31.7	5 15.7	0.3	0.1	6.3	2.4	12.3	4.6
04	5 31.0	5 31.9	5 15.9	0.4	0.2	6.4	2.4	12.4	4.7
05	5 31.3	5 32.2	5 16.2	0.5	0.2	6.5	2.4	12.5	4.7
06	5 31.5	5 32.4	5 16.4	0.6	0.2	6.6	2.5	12.6	4.7
07	5 31.8	5 32.7	5 16.6	0.7	0.3	6.7	2.5	12.7	4.8
08	5 32.0	5 32.9	5 16.9	0.8	0.3	6.8	2.6	12.8	4.8
09	5 32.3	5 33.2	5 17.1	0.9	0.3	6.9	2.6	12.9	4.8
10	5 32.5	5 33.4	5 17.4	1.0	0.4	7.0	2.6	13.0	4.9
11	5 32.8	5 33.7	5 17.6	1.1	0.4	7.1	2.7	13.1	4.9
12	5 33.0	5 33.9	5 17.8	1.2	0.5	7.2	2.7	13.2	5.0
13	5 33.3	5 34.2	5 18.1	1.3	0.5	7.3	2.7	13.3	5.0
14	5 33.5	5 34.4	5 18.3	1.4	0.5	7.4	2.8	13.4	5.0
15	5 33.8	5 34.7	5 18.5	1.5	0.6	7.5	2.8	13.5	5.1
16	5 34.0	5 34.9	5 18.8	1.6	0.6	7.6	2.9	13.6	5.1
17	5 34.3	5 35.2	5 19.0	1.7	0.6	7.7	2.9	13.7	5.1
18	5 34.5	5 35.4	5 19.3	1.8	0.7	7.8	2.9	13.8	5.2
19	5 34.8	5 35.7	5 19.5	1.9	0.7	7.9	3.0	13.9	5.2
20	5 35.0	5 35.9	5 19.7	2.0	0.8	8.0	3.0	14.0	5.3
21	5 35.3	5 36.2	5 20.0	2.1	0.8	8.1	3.0	14.1	5.3
22	5 35.5	5 36.4	5 20.2	2.2	0.8	8.2	3.1	14.2	5.3
23	5 35.8	5 36.7	5 20.5	2.3	0.9	8.3	3.1	14.3	5.4
24	5 36.0	5 36.9	5 20.7	2.4	0.9	8.4	3.2	14.4	5.4
25	5 36.3	5 37.2	5 20.9	2.5	0.9	8.5	3.2	14.5	5.4
26	5 36.5	5 37.4	5 21.2	2.6	1.0	8.6	3.2	14.6	5.5
27	5 36.8	5 37.7	5 21.4	2.7	1.0	8.7	3.3	14.7	5.5
28	5 37.0	5 37.9	5 21.6	2.8	1.0	8.8	3.3	14.8	5.6
29	5 37.3	5 38.2	5 21.9	2.9	1.1	8.9	3.3	14.9	5.6
30	5 37.5	5 38.4	5 22.1	3.0	1.1	9.0	3.4	15.0	5.6
31	5 37.8	5 38.7	5 22.4	3.1	1.2	9.1	3.4	15.1	5.7
32	5 38.0	5 38.9	5 22.6	3.2	1.2	9.2	3.5	15.2	5.7
33	5 38.3	5 39.2	5 22.8	3.3	1.2	9.3	3.5	15.3	5.7
34	5 38.5	5 39.4	5 23.1	3.4	1.3	9.4	3.5	15.4	5.8
35	5 38.8	5 39.7	5 23.3	3.5	1.3	9.5	3.6	15.5	5.8
36	5 39.0	5 39.9	5 23.6	3.6	1.4	9.6	3.6	15.6	5.9
37	5 39.3	5 40.2	5 23.8	3.7	1.4	9.7	3.6	15.7	5.9
38	5 39.5	5 40.4	5 24.0	3.8	1.4	9.8	3.7	15.8	5.9
39	5 39.8	5 40.7	5 24.3	3.9	1.5	9.9	3.7	15.9	6.0
40	5 40.0	5 40.9	5 24.5	4.0	1.5	10.0	3.8	16.0	6.0
41	5 40.3	5 41.2	5 24.7	4.1	1.5	10.1	3.8	16.1	6.0
42	5 40.5	5 41.4	5 25.0	4.2	1.6	10.2	3.8	16.2	6.1
43	5 40.8	5 41.7	5 25.2	4.3	1.6	10.3	3.9	16.3	6.1
44	5 41.0	5 41.9	5 25.5	4.4	1.7	10.4	3.9	16.4	6.1
45	5 41.3	5 42.2	5 25.7	4.5	1.7	10.5	3.9	16.5	6.2
46	5 41.5	5 42.4	5 25.9	4.6	1.7	10.6	4.0	16.6	6.2
47	5 41.8	5 42.7	5 26.2	4.7	1.8	10.7	4.0	16.7	6.3
48	5 42.0	5 42.9	5 26.4	4.8	1.8	10.8	4.1	16.8	6.3
49	5 42.3	5 43.2	5 26.7	4.9	1.8	10.9	4.1	16.9	6.3
50	5 42.5	5 43.4	5 26.9	5.0	1.9	11.0	4.1	17.0	6.4
51	5 42.8	5 43.7	5 27.1	5.1	1.9	11.1	4.2	17.1	6.4
52	5 43.0	5 43.9	5 27.4	5.2	2.0	11.2	4.2	17.2	6.5
53	5 43.3	5 44.2	5 27.6	5.3	2.0	11.3	4.2	17.3	6.5
54	5 43.5	5 44.4	5 27.9	5.4	2.0	11.4	4.3	17.4	6.5
55	5 43.8	5 44.7	5 28.1	5.5	2.1	11.5	4.3	17.5	6.6
56	5 44.0	5 44.9	5 28.3	5.6	2.1	11.6	4.4	17.6	6.6
57	5 44.3	5 45.2	5 28.6	5.7	2.1	11.7	4.4	17.7	6.6
58	5 44.5	5 45.4	5 28.8	5.8	2.2	11.8	4.4	17.8	6.7
59	5 44.8	5 45.7	5 29.0	5.9	2.2	11.9	4.5	17.9	6.7
60	5 45.0	5 45.9	5 29.3	6.0	2.3	12.0	4.5	18.0	6.8

23ᵐ

s	SUN PLANETS	ARIES	MOON	v or d	Corrⁿ	v or d	Corrⁿ	v or d	Corrⁿ
00	5 45.0	5 45.9	5 29.3	0.0	0.0	6.0	2.4	12.0	4.7
01	5 45.3	5 46.2	5 29.5	0.1	0.0	6.1	2.4	12.1	4.7
02	5 45.5	5 46.4	5 29.8	0.2	0.1	6.2	2.4	12.2	4.8
03	5 45.8	5 46.7	5 30.0	0.3	0.1	6.3	2.5	12.3	4.8
04	5 46.0	5 46.9	5 30.2	0.4	0.2	6.4	2.5	12.4	4.9
05	5 46.3	5 47.2	5 30.5	0.5	0.2	6.5	2.5	12.5	4.9
06	5 46.5	5 47.4	5 30.7	0.6	0.2	6.6	2.6	12.6	4.9
07	5 46.8	5 47.7	5 31.0	0.7	0.3	6.7	2.6	12.7	5.0
08	5 47.0	5 48.0	5 31.2	0.8	0.3	6.8	2.7	12.8	5.0
09	5 47.3	5 48.2	5 31.4	0.9	0.4	6.9	2.7	12.9	5.1
10	5 47.5	5 48.5	5 31.7	1.0	0.4	7.0	2.7	13.0	5.1
11	5 47.8	5 48.7	5 31.9	1.1	0.4	7.1	2.8	13.1	5.1
12	5 48.0	5 49.0	5 32.1	1.2	0.5	7.2	2.8	13.2	5.2
13	5 48.3	5 49.2	5 32.4	1.3	0.5	7.3	2.9	13.3	5.2
14	5 48.5	5 49.5	5 32.6	1.4	0.5	7.4	2.9	13.4	5.2
15	5 48.8	5 49.7	5 32.9	1.5	0.6	7.5	2.9	13.5	5.3
16	5 49.0	5 50.0	5 33.1	1.6	0.6	7.6	3.0	13.6	5.3
17	5 49.3	5 50.2	5 33.3	1.7	0.7	7.7	3.0	13.7	5.4
18	5 49.5	5 50.5	5 33.6	1.8	0.7	7.8	3.1	13.8	5.4
19	5 49.8	5 50.7	5 33.8	1.9	0.7	7.9	3.1	13.9	5.4
20	5 50.0	5 51.0	5 34.1	2.0	0.8	8.0	3.1	14.0	5.5
21	5 50.3	5 51.2	5 34.3	2.1	0.8	8.1	3.2	14.1	5.5
22	5 50.5	5 51.5	5 34.5	2.2	0.9	8.2	3.2	14.2	5.6
23	5 50.8	5 51.7	5 34.8	2.3	0.9	8.3	3.3	14.3	5.6
24	5 51.0	5 52.0	5 35.0	2.4	0.9	8.4	3.3	14.4	5.6
25	5 51.3	5 52.2	5 35.2	2.5	1.0	8.5	3.3	14.5	5.7
26	5 51.5	5 52.5	5 35.5	2.6	1.0	8.6	3.4	14.6	5.7
27	5 51.8	5 52.7	5 35.7	2.7	1.1	8.7	3.4	14.7	5.8
28	5 52.0	5 53.0	5 36.0	2.8	1.1	8.8	3.4	14.8	5.8
29	5 52.3	5 53.2	5 36.2	2.9	1.1	8.9	3.5	14.9	5.8
30	5 52.5	5 53.5	5 36.4	3.0	1.2	9.0	3.5	15.0	5.9
31	5 52.8	5 53.7	5 36.7	3.1	1.2	9.1	3.6	15.1	5.9
32	5 53.0	5 54.0	5 36.9	3.2	1.3	9.2	3.6	15.2	6.0
33	5 53.3	5 54.2	5 37.2	3.3	1.3	9.3	3.6	15.3	6.0
34	5 53.5	5 54.5	5 37.4	3.4	1.3	9.4	3.7	15.4	6.0
35	5 53.8	5 54.7	5 37.6	3.5	1.4	9.5	3.7	15.5	6.1
36	5 54.0	5 55.0	5 37.9	3.6	1.4	9.6	3.8	15.6	6.1
37	5 54.3	5 55.2	5 38.1	3.7	1.4	9.7	3.8	15.7	6.1
38	5 54.5	5 55.5	5 38.4	3.8	1.5	9.8	3.8	15.8	6.2
39	5 54.8	5 55.7	5 38.6	3.9	1.5	9.9	3.9	15.9	6.2
40	5 55.0	5 56.0	5 38.8	4.0	1.6	10.0	3.9	16.0	6.3
41	5 55.3	5 56.2	5 39.1	4.1	1.6	10.1	4.0	16.1	6.3
42	5 55.5	5 56.5	5 39.3	4.2	1.6	10.2	4.0	16.2	6.3
43	5 55.8	5 56.7	5 39.5	4.3	1.7	10.3	4.0	16.3	6.4
44	5 56.0	5 57.0	5 39.8	4.4	1.7	10.4	4.1	16.4	6.4
45	5 56.3	5 57.2	5 40.0	4.5	1.8	10.5	4.1	16.5	6.4
46	5 56.5	5 57.5	5 40.3	4.6	1.8	10.6	4.2	16.6	6.5
47	5 56.8	5 57.7	5 40.5	4.7	1.8	10.7	4.2	16.7	6.5
48	5 57.0	5 58.0	5 40.7	4.8	1.9	10.8	4.2	16.8	6.6
49	5 57.3	5 58.2	5 41.0	4.9	1.9	10.9	4.3	16.9	6.6
50	5 57.5	5 58.5	5 41.2	5.0	2.0	11.0	4.3	17.0	6.7
51	5 57.8	5 58.7	5 41.5	5.1	2.0	11.1	4.3	17.1	6.7
52	5 58.0	5 59.0	5 41.7	5.2	2.0	11.2	4.4	17.2	6.7
53	5 58.3	5 59.2	5 41.9	5.3	2.1	11.3	4.4	17.3	6.8
54	5 58.5	5 59.5	5 42.2	5.4	2.1	11.4	4.5	17.4	6.8
55	5 58.8	5 59.7	5 42.4	5.5	2.2	11.5	4.5	17.5	6.9
56	5 59.0	6 00.0	5 42.6	5.6	2.2	11.6	4.5	17.6	6.9
57	5 59.3	6 00.2	5 42.9	5.7	2.2	11.7	4.6	17.7	6.9
58	5 59.5	6 00.5	5 43.1	5.8	2.3	11.8	4.6	17.8	7.0
59	5 59.8	6 00.7	5 43.4	5.9	2.3	11.9	4.7	17.9	7.0
60	6 00.0	6 01.0	5 43.6	6.0	2.4	12.0	4.7	18.0	7.1

24ᵐ s	SUN PLANETS	ARIES	MOON	v or Corrⁿ d	v or Corrⁿ d	v or Corrⁿ d
00	6 00·0	6 01·0	5 43·6	0·0 0·0	6·0 2·5	12·0 4·9
01	6 00·3	6 01·2	5 43·8	0·1 0·0	6·1 2·5	12·1 4·9
02	6 00·5	6 01·5	5 44·1	0·2 0·1	6·2 2·5	12·2 5·0
03	6 00·8	6 01·7	5 44·3	0·3 0·1	6·3 2·6	12·3 5·0
04	6 01·0	6 02·0	5 44·6	0·4 0·2	6·4 2·6	12·4 5·1
05	6 01·3	6 02·2	5 44·8	0·5 0·2	6·5 2·7	12·5 5·1
06	6 01·5	6 02·5	5 45·0	0·6 0·2	6·6 2·7	12·6 5·1
07	6 01·8	6 02·7	5 45·3	0·7 0·3	6·7 2·7	12·7 5·2
08	6 02·0	6 03·0	5 45·5	0·8 0·3	6·8 2·8	12·8 5·2
09	6 02·3	6 03·2	5 45·7	0·9 0·4	6·9 2·8	12·9 5·3
10	6 02·5	6 03·5	5 46·0	1·0 0·4	7·0 2·9	13·0 5·3
11	6 02·8	6 03·7	5 46·2	1·1 0·4	7·1 2·9	13·1 5·3
12	6 03·0	6 04·0	5 46·5	1·2 0·5	7·2 2·9	13·2 5·4
13	6 03·3	6 04·2	5 46·7	1·3 0·5	7·3 3·0	13·3 5·4
14	6 03·5	6 04·5	5 46·9	1·4 0·6	7·4 3·0	13·4 5·5
15	6 03·8	6 04·7	5 47·2	1·5 0·6	7·5 3·1	13·5 5·5
16	6 04·0	6 05·0	5 47·4	1·6 0·7	7·6 3·1	13·6 5·6
17	6 04·3	6 05·2	5 47·7	1·7 0·7	7·7 3·1	13·7 5·6
18	6 04·5	6 05·5	5 47·9	1·8 0·7	7·8 3·2	13·8 5·6
19	6 04·8	6 05·7	5 48·1	1·9 0·8	7·9 3·2	13·9 5·7
20	6 05·0	6 06·0	5 48·4	2·0 0·8	8·0 3·3	14·0 5·7
21	6 05·3	6 06·3	5 48·6	2·1 0·9	8·1 3·3	14·1 5·8
22	6 05·5	6 06·5	5 48·8	2·2 0·9	8·2 3·3	14·2 5·8
23	6 05·8	6 06·8	5 49·1	2·3 0·9	8·3 3·4	14·3 5·8
24	6 06·0	6 07·0	5 49·3	2·4 1·0	8·4 3·4	14·4 5·9
25	6 06·3	6 07·3	5 49·6	2·5 1·0	8·5 3·5	14·5 5·9
26	6 06·5	6 07·5	5 49·8	2·6 1·1	8·6 3·5	14·6 6·0
27	6 06·8	6 07·8	5 50·0	2·7 1·1	8·7 3·6	14·7 6·0
28	6 07·0	6 08·0	5 50·3	2·8 1·1	8·8 3·6	14·8 6·0
29	6 07·3	6 08·3	5 50·5	2·9 1·2	8·9 3·6	14·9 6·1
30	6 07·5	6 08·5	5 50·8	3·0 1·2	9·0 3·7	15·0 6·1
31	6 07·8	6 08·8	5 51·0	3·1 1·3	9·1 3·7	15·1 6·2
32	6 08·0	6 09·0	5 51·2	3·2 1·3	9·2 3·8	15·2 6·2
33	6 08·3	6 09·3	5 51·5	3·3 1·3	9·3 3·8	15·3 6·2
34	6 08·5	6 09·5	5 51·7	3·4 1·4	9·4 3·8	15·4 6·3
35	6 08·8	6 09·8	5 52·0	3·5 1·4	9·5 3·9	15·5 6·3
36	6 09·0	6 10·0	5 52·2	3·6 1·5	9·6 3·9	15·6 6·4
37	6 09·3	6 10·3	5 52·4	3·7 1·5	9·7 4·0	15·7 6·4
38	6 09·5	6 10·5	5 52·7	3·8 1·6	9·8 4·0	15·8 6·5
39	6 09·8	6 10·8	5 52·9	3·9 1·6	9·9 4·0	15·9 6·5
40	6 10·0	6 11·0	5 53·1	4·0 1·6	10·0 4·1	16·0 6·5
41	6 10·3	6 11·3	5 53·4	4·1 1·7	10·1 4·1	16·1 6·6
42	6 10·5	6 11·5	5 53·6	4·2 1·7	10·2 4·2	16·2 6·6
43	6 10·8	6 11·8	5 53·9	4·3 1·8	10·3 4·2	16·3 6·7
44	6 11·0	6 12·0	5 54·1	4·4 1·8	10·4 4·2	16·4 6·7
45	6 11·3	6 12·3	5 54·3	4·5 1·8	10·5 4·3	16·5 6·7
46	6 11·5	6 12·5	5 54·6	4·6 1·9	10·6 4·3	16·6 6·8
47	6 11·8	6 12·8	5 54·8	4·7 1·9	10·7 4·4	16·7 6·8
48	6 12·0	6 13·0	5 55·1	4·8 2·0	10·8 4·4	16·8 6·9
49	6 12·3	6 13·3	5 55·3	4·9 2·0	10·9 4·5	16·9 6·9
50	6 12·5	6 13·5	5 55·5	5·0 2·0	11·0 4·5	17·0 6·9
51	6 12·8	6 13·8	5 55·8	5·1 2·1	11·1 4·5	17·1 7·0
52	6 13·0	6 14·0	5 56·0	5·2 2·1	11·2 4·6	17·2 7·0
53	6 13·3	6 14·3	5 56·2	5·3 2·2	11·3 4·6	17·3 7·1
54	6 13·5	6 14·5	5 56·5	5·4 2·2	11·4 4·7	17·4 7·1
55	6 13·8	6 14·8	5 56·7	5·5 2·2	11·5 4·7	17·5 7·1
56	6 14·0	6 15·0	5 57·0	5·6 2·3	11·6 4·7	17·6 7·2
57	6 14·3	6 15·3	5 57·2	5·7 2·3	11·7 4·8	17·7 7·2
58	6 14·5	6 15·5	5 57·4	5·8 2·4	11·8 4·8	17·8 7·3
59	6 14·8	6 15·8	5 57·7	5·9 2·4	11·9 4·9	17·9 7·3
60	6 15·0	6 16·0	5 57·9	6·0 2·5	12·0 4·9	18·0 7·4

25ᵐ s	SUN PLANETS	ARIES	MOON	v or Corrⁿ d	v or Corrⁿ d	v or Corrⁿ d
00	6 15·0	6 16·0	5 57·9	0·0 0·0	6·0 2·6	12·0 5·1
01	6 15·3	6 16·3	5 58·2	0·1 0·0	6·1 2·6	12·1 5·1
02	6 15·5	6 16·5	5 58·4	0·2 0·1	6·2 2·6	12·2 5·2
03	6 15·8	6 16·8	5 58·6	0·3 0·1	6·3 2·7	12·3 5·2
04	6 16·0	6 17·0	5 58·9	0·4 0·2	6·4 2·7	12·4 5·3
05	6 16·3	6 17·3	5 59·1	0·5 0·2	6·5 2·8	12·5 5·3
06	6 16·5	6 17·5	5 59·3	0·6 0·3	6·6 2·8	12·6 5·4
07	6 16·8	6 17·8	5 59·6	0·7 0·3	6·7 2·8	12·7 5·4
08	6 17·0	6 18·0	5 59·8	0·8 0·3	6·8 2·9	12·8 5·4
09	6 17·3	6 18·3	6 00·1	0·9 0·4	6·9 2·9	12·9 5·5
10	6 17·5	6 18·5	6 00·3	1·0 0·4	7·0 3·0	13·0 5·5
11	6 17·8	6 18·8	6 00·5	1·1 0·5	7·1 3·0	13·1 5·6
12	6 18·0	6 19·0	6 00·8	1·2 0·5	7·2 3·1	13·2 5·6
13	6 18·3	6 19·3	6 01·0	1·3 0·6	7·3 3·1	13·3 5·7
14	6 18·5	6 19·5	6 01·3	1·4 0·6	7·4 3·1	13·4 5·7
15	6 18·8	6 19·8	6 01·5	1·5 0·6	7·5 3·2	13·5 5·7
16	6 19·0	6 20·0	6 01·7	1·6 0·7	7·6 3·2	13·6 5·8
17	6 19·3	6 20·3	6 02·0	1·7 0·7	7·7 3·3	13·7 5·8
18	6 19·5	6 20·5	6 02·2	1·8 0·8	7·8 3·3	13·8 5·9
19	6 19·8	6 20·8	6 02·5	1·9 0·8	7·9 3·4	13·9 5·9
20	6 20·0	6 21·0	6 02·7	2·0 0·9	8·0 3·4	14·0 6·0
21	6 20·3	6 21·3	6 02·9	2·1 0·9	8·1 3·4	14·1 6·0
22	6 20·5	6 21·5	6 03·2	2·2 0·9	8·2 3·5	14·2 6·0
23	6 20·8	6 21·8	6 03·4	2·3 1·0	8·3 3·5	14·3 6·1
24	6 21·0	6 22·0	6 03·6	2·4 1·0	8·4 3·6	14·4 6·1
25	6 21·3	6 22·3	6 03·9	2·5 1·1	8·5 3·6	14·5 6·2
26	6 21·5	6 22·5	6 04·1	2·6 1·1	8·6 3·7	14·6 6·2
27	6 21·8	6 22·8	6 04·4	2·7 1·1	8·7 3·7	14·7 6·2
28	6 22·0	6 23·0	6 04·6	2·8 1·2	8·8 3·7	14·8 6·3
29	6 22·3	6 23·3	6 04·8	2·9 1·2	8·9 3·8	14·9 6·3
30	6 22·5	6 23·5	6 05·1	3·0 1·3	9·0 3·8	15·0 6·4
31	6 22·8	6 23·8	6 05·3	3·1 1·3	9·1 3·9	15·1 6·4
32	6 23·0	6 24·0	6 05·6	3·2 1·4	9·2 3·9	15·2 6·5
33	6 23·3	6 24·3	6 05·8	3·3 1·4	9·3 4·0	15·3 6·5
34	6 23·5	6 24·5	6 06·0	3·4 1·4	9·4 4·0	15·4 6·5
35	6 23·8	6 24·8	6 06·3	3·5 1·5	9·5 4·0	15·5 6·6
36	6 24·0	6 25·1	6 06·5	3·6 1·5	9·6 4·1	15·6 6·6
37	6 24·3	6 25·3	6 06·7	3·7 1·6	9·7 4·1	15·7 6·7
38	6 24·5	6 25·6	6 07·0	3·8 1·6	9·8 4·2	15·8 6·7
39	6 24·8	6 25·8	6 07·2	3·9 1·7	9·9 4·2	15·9 6·8
40	6 25·0	6 26·1	6 07·5	4·0 1·7	10·0 4·3	16·0 6·8
41	6 25·3	6 26·3	6 07·7	4·1 1·7	10·1 4·3	16·1 6·8
42	6 25·5	6 26·6	6 07·9	4·2 1·8	10·2 4·3	16·2 6·9
43	6 25·8	6 26·8	6 08·2	4·3 1·8	10·3 4·4	16·3 6·9
44	6 26·0	6 27·1	6 08·4	4·4 1·9	10·4 4·4	16·4 7·0
45	6 26·3	6 27·3	6 08·7	4·5 1·9	10·5 4·5	16·5 7·0
46	6 26·5	6 27·6	6 08·9	4·6 2·0	10·6 4·5	16·6 7·1
47	6 26·8	6 27·8	6 09·1	4·7 2·0	10·7 4·5	16·7 7·1
48	6 27·0	6 28·1	6 09·4	4·8 2·0	10·8 4·6	16·8 7·1
49	6 27·3	6 28·3	6 09·6	4·9 2·1	10·9 4·6	16·9 7·2
50	6 27·5	6 28·6	6 09·8	5·0 2·1	11·0 4·7	17·0 7·2
51	6 27·8	6 28·8	6 10·1	5·1 2·2	11·1 4·7	17·1 7·3
52	6 28·0	6 29·1	6 10·3	5·2 2·2	11·2 4·8	17·2 7·3
53	6 28·3	6 29·3	6 10·6	5·3 2·3	11·3 4·8	17·3 7·4
54	6 28·5	6 29·6	6 10·8	5·4 2·3	11·4 4·8	17·4 7·4
55	6 28·8	6 29·8	6 11·0	5·5 2·3	11·5 4·9	17·5 7·4
56	6 29·0	6 30·1	6 11·3	5·6 2·4	11·6 4·9	17·6 7·5
57	6 29·3	6 30·3	6 11·5	5·7 2·4	11·7 5·0	17·7 7·5
58	6 29·5	6 30·6	6 11·8	5·8 2·5	11·8 5·0	17·8 7·6
59	6 29·8	6 30·8	6 12·0	5·9 2·5	11·9 5·1	17·9 7·6
60	6 30·0	6 31·1	6 12·2	6·0 2·6	12·0 5·1	18·0 7·7

26ᵐ

s	SUN PLANETS	ARIES	MOON	v or Corrⁿ d		v or Corrⁿ d		v or Corrⁿ d	
00	6 30.0	6 31.1	6 12.2	0.0	0.0	6.0	2.7	12.0	5.3
01	6 30.3	6 31.3	6 12.5	0.1	0.0	6.1	2.7	12.1	5.3
02	6 30.5	6 31.6	6 12.7	0.2	0.1	6.2	2.7	12.2	5.4
03	6 30.8	6 31.8	6 12.9	0.3	0.1	6.3	2.8	12.3	5.4
04	6 31.0	6 32.1	6 13.2	0.4	0.2	6.4	2.8	12.4	5.5
05	6 31.3	6 32.3	6 13.4	0.5	0.2	6.5	2.9	12.5	5.5
06	6 31.5	6 32.6	6 13.7	0.6	0.3	6.6	2.9	12.6	5.6
07	6 31.8	6 32.8	6 13.9	0.7	0.3	6.7	3.0	12.7	5.6
08	6 32.0	6 33.1	6 14.1	0.8	0.4	6.8	3.0	12.8	5.7
09	6 32.3	6 33.3	6 14.4	0.9	0.4	6.9	3.0	12.9	5.7
10	6 32.5	6 33.6	6 14.6	1.0	0.4	7.0	3.1	13.0	5.7
11	6 32.8	6 33.8	6 14.9	1.1	0.5	7.1	3.1	13.1	5.8
12	6 33.0	6 34.1	6 15.1	1.2	0.5	7.2	3.2	13.2	5.8
13	6 33.3	6 34.3	6 15.3	1.3	0.6	7.3	3.2	13.3	5.9
14	6 33.5	6 34.6	6 15.6	1.4	0.6	7.4	3.3	13.4	5.9
15	6 33.8	6 34.8	6 15.8	1.5	0.7	7.5	3.3	13.5	6.0
16	6 34.0	6 35.1	6 16.1	1.6	0.7	7.6	3.4	13.6	6.0
17	6 34.3	6 35.3	6 16.3	1.7	0.8	7.7	3.4	13.7	6.1
18	6 34.5	6 35.6	6 16.5	1.8	0.8	7.8	3.4	13.8	6.1
19	6 34.8	6 35.8	6 16.8	1.9	0.8	7.9	3.5	13.9	6.1
20	6 35.0	6 36.1	6 17.0	2.0	0.9	8.0	3.5	14.0	6.2
21	6 35.3	6 36.3	6 17.2	2.1	0.9	8.1	3.6	14.1	6.2
22	6 35.5	6 36.6	6 17.5	2.2	1.0	8.2	3.6	14.2	6.3
23	6 35.8	6 36.8	6 17.7	2.3	1.0	8.3	3.7	14.3	6.3
24	6 36.0	6 37.1	6 18.0	2.4	1.1	8.4	3.7	14.4	6.4
25	6 36.3	6 37.3	6 18.2	2.5	1.1	8.5	3.8	14.5	6.4
26	6 36.5	6 37.6	6 18.4	2.6	1.1	8.6	3.8	14.6	6.4
27	6 36.8	6 37.8	6 18.7	2.7	1.2	8.7	3.8	14.7	6.5
28	6 37.0	6 38.1	6 18.9	2.8	1.2	8.8	3.9	14.8	6.5
29	6 37.3	6 38.3	6 19.2	2.9	1.3	8.9	3.9	14.9	6.6
30	6 37.5	6 38.6	6 19.4	3.0	1.3	9.0	4.0	15.0	6.6
31	6 37.8	6 38.8	6 19.6	3.1	1.4	9.1	4.0	15.1	6.7
32	6 38.0	6 39.1	6 19.9	3.2	1.4	9.2	4.1	15.2	6.7
33	6 38.3	6 39.3	6 20.1	3.3	1.5	9.3	4.1	15.3	6.8
34	6 38.5	6 39.6	6 20.3	3.4	1.5	9.4	4.2	15.4	6.8
35	6 38.8	6 39.8	6 20.6	3.5	1.5	9.5	4.2	15.5	6.8
36	6 39.0	6 40.1	6 20.8	3.6	1.6	9.6	4.2	15.6	6.9
37	6 39.3	6 40.3	6 21.1	3.7	1.6	9.7	4.3	15.7	6.9
38	6 39.5	6 40.6	6 21.3	3.8	1.7	9.8	4.3	15.8	7.0
39	6 39.8	6 40.8	6 21.5	3.9	1.7	9.9	4.4	15.9	7.0
40	6 40.0	6 41.1	6 21.8	4.0	1.8	10.0	4.4	16.0	7.1
41	6 40.3	6 41.3	6 22.0	4.1	1.8	10.1	4.5	16.1	7.1
42	6 40.5	6 41.6	6 22.3	4.2	1.9	10.2	4.5	16.2	7.2
43	6 40.8	6 41.8	6 22.5	4.3	1.9	10.3	4.5	16.3	7.2
44	6 41.0	6 42.1	6 22.7	4.4	1.9	10.4	4.6	16.4	7.2
45	6 41.3	6 42.3	6 23.0	4.5	2.0	10.5	4.6	16.5	7.3
46	6 41.5	6 42.6	6 23.2	4.6	2.0	10.6	4.7	16.6	7.3
47	6 41.8	6 42.8	6 23.4	4.7	2.1	10.7	4.7	16.7	7.4
48	6 42.0	6 43.1	6 23.7	4.8	2.1	10.8	4.8	16.8	7.4
49	6 42.3	6 43.4	6 23.9	4.9	2.2	10.9	4.8	16.9	7.5
50	6 42.5	6 43.6	6 24.2	5.0	2.2	11.0	4.9	17.0	7.5
51	6 42.8	6 43.9	6 24.4	5.1	2.3	11.1	4.9	17.1	7.6
52	6 43.0	6 44.1	6 24.6	5.2	2.3	11.2	4.9	17.2	7.6
53	6 43.3	6 44.4	6 24.9	5.3	2.3	11.3	5.0	17.3	7.6
54	6 43.5	6 44.6	6 25.1	5.4	2.4	11.4	5.0	17.4	7.7
55	6 43.8	6 44.9	6 25.4	5.5	2.4	11.5	5.1	17.5	7.7
56	6 44.0	6 45.1	6 25.6	5.6	2.5	11.6	5.1	17.6	7.8
57	6 44.3	6 45.4	6 25.8	5.7	2.5	11.7	5.2	17.7	7.8
58	6 44.5	6 45.6	6 26.1	5.8	2.6	11.8	5.2	17.8	7.9
59	6 44.8	6 45.9	6 26.3	5.9	2.6	11.9	5.3	17.9	7.9
60	6 45.0	6 46.1	6 26.6	6.0	2.7	12.0	5.3	18.0	8.0

27ᵐ

s	SUN PLANETS	ARIES	MOON	v or Corrⁿ d		v or Corrⁿ d		v or Corrⁿ d	
00	6 45.0	6 46.1	6 26.6	0.0	0.0	6.0	2.8	12.0	5.5
01	6 45.3	6 46.4	6 26.8	0.1	0.0	6.1	2.8	12.1	5.5
02	6 45.5	6 46.6	6 27.0	0.2	0.1	6.2	2.8	12.2	5.6
03	6 45.8	6 46.9	6 27.3	0.3	0.1	6.3	2.9	12.3	5.6
04	6 46.0	6 47.1	6 27.5	0.4	0.2	6.4	2.9	12.4	5.7
05	6 46.3	6 47.4	6 27.7	0.5	0.2	6.5	3.0	12.5	5.7
06	6 46.5	6 47.6	6 28.0	0.6	0.3	6.6	3.0	12.6	5.8
07	6 46.8	6 47.9	6 28.2	0.7	0.3	6.7	3.1	12.7	5.8
08	6 47.0	6 48.1	6 28.5	0.8	0.4	6.8	3.1	12.8	5.9
09	6 47.3	6 48.4	6 28.7	0.9	0.4	6.9	3.2	12.9	5.9
10	6 47.5	6 48.6	6 28.9	1.0	0.5	7.0	3.2	13.0	6.0
11	6 47.8	6 48.9	6 29.2	1.1	0.5	7.1	3.3	13.1	6.0
12	6 48.0	6 49.1	6 29.4	1.2	0.6	7.2	3.3	13.2	6.1
13	6 48.3	6 49.4	6 29.7	1.3	0.6	7.3	3.3	13.3	6.1
14	6 48.5	6 49.6	6 29.9	1.4	0.6	7.4	3.4	13.4	6.1
15	6 48.8	6 49.9	6 30.1	1.5	0.7	7.5	3.4	13.5	6.2
16	6 49.0	6 50.1	6 30.4	1.6	0.7	7.6	3.5	13.6	6.2
17	6 49.3	6 50.4	6 30.6	1.7	0.8	7.7	3.5	13.7	6.3
18	6 49.5	6 50.6	6 30.8	1.8	0.8	7.8	3.6	13.8	6.3
19	6 49.8	6 50.9	6 31.1	1.9	0.9	7.9	3.6	13.9	6.4
20	6 50.0	6 51.1	6 31.3	2.0	0.9	8.0	3.7	14.0	6.4
21	6 50.3	6 51.4	6 31.6	2.1	1.0	8.1	3.7	14.1	6.5
22	6 50.5	6 51.6	6 31.8	2.2	1.0	8.2	3.8	14.2	6.5
23	6 50.8	6 51.9	6 32.0	2.3	1.1	8.3	3.8	14.3	6.6
24	6 51.0	6 52.1	6 32.3	2.4	1.1	8.4	3.9	14.4	6.6
25	6 51.3	6 52.4	6 32.5	2.5	1.1	8.5	3.9	14.5	6.6
26	6 51.5	6 52.6	6 32.8	2.6	1.2	8.6	3.9	14.6	6.7
27	6 51.8	6 52.9	6 33.0	2.7	1.2	8.7	4.0	14.7	6.7
28	6 52.0	6 53.1	6 33.2	2.8	1.3	8.8	4.0	14.8	6.8
29	6 52.3	6 53.4	6 33.5	2.9	1.3	8.9	4.1	14.9	6.8
30	6 52.5	6 53.6	6 33.7	3.0	1.4	9.0	4.1	15.0	6.9
31	6 52.8	6 53.9	6 33.9	3.1	1.4	9.1	4.2	15.1	6.9
32	6 53.0	6 54.1	6 34.2	3.2	1.5	9.2	4.2	15.2	7.0
33	6 53.3	6 54.4	6 34.4	3.3	1.5	9.3	4.3	15.3	7.0
34	6 53.5	6 54.6	6 34.7	3.4	1.6	9.4	4.3	15.4	7.1
35	6 53.8	6 54.9	6 34.9	3.5	1.6	9.5	4.4	15.5	7.1
36	6 54.0	6 55.1	6 35.1	3.6	1.7	9.6	4.4	15.6	7.2
37	6 54.3	6 55.4	6 35.4	3.7	1.7	9.7	4.5	15.7	7.2
38	6 54.5	6 55.6	6 35.6	3.8	1.7	9.8	4.5	15.8	7.2
39	6 54.8	6 55.9	6 35.9	3.9	1.8	9.9	4.5	15.9	7.3
40	6 55.0	6 56.1	6 36.1	4.0	1.8	10.0	4.6	16.0	7.3
41	6 55.3	6 56.4	6 36.3	4.1	1.9	10.1	4.6	16.1	7.4
42	6 55.5	6 56.6	6 36.6	4.2	1.9	10.2	4.7	16.2	7.4
43	6 55.8	6 56.9	6 36.8	4.3	2.0	10.3	4.7	16.3	7.5
44	6 56.0	6 57.1	6 37.0	4.4	2.0	10.4	4.8	16.4	7.5
45	6 56.3	6 57.4	6 37.3	4.5	2.1	10.5	4.8	16.5	7.6
46	6 56.5	6 57.6	6 37.5	4.6	2.1	10.6	4.9	16.6	7.6
47	6 56.8	6 57.9	6 37.8	4.7	2.2	10.7	4.9	16.7	7.7
48	6 57.0	6 58.1	6 38.0	4.8	2.2	10.8	5.0	16.8	7.7
49	6 57.3	6 58.4	6 38.2	4.9	2.2	10.9	5.0	16.9	7.7
50	6 57.5	6 58.6	6 38.5	5.0	2.3	11.0	5.0	17.0	7.8
51	6 57.8	6 58.9	6 38.7	5.1	2.3	11.1	5.1	17.1	7.8
52	6 58.0	6 59.1	6 39.0	5.2	2.4	11.2	5.1	17.2	7.9
53	6 58.3	6 59.4	6 39.2	5.3	2.4	11.3	5.2	17.3	7.9
54	6 58.5	6 59.6	6 39.4	5.4	2.5	11.4	5.2	17.4	8.0
55	6 58.8	6 59.9	6 39.7	5.5	2.5	11.5	5.3	17.5	8.0
56	6 59.0	7 00.1	6 39.9	5.6	2.6	11.6	5.3	17.6	8.1
57	6 59.3	7 00.4	6 40.2	5.7	2.6	11.7	5.4	17.7	8.1
58	6 59.5	7 00.6	6 40.4	5.8	2.7	11.8	5.4	17.8	8.2
59	6 59.8	7 00.9	6 40.6	5.9	2.7	11.9	5.5	17.9	8.2
60	7 00.0	7 01.1	6 40.9	6.0	2.8	12.0	5.5	18.0	8.3

28ᵐ	SUN PLANETS	ARIES	MOON	v or d Corrⁿ		v or d Corrⁿ		v or d Corrⁿ	
s	° ′	° ′	° ′	′	′	′	′	′	′
00	7 00·0	7 01·1	6 40·9	0·0	0·0	6·0	2·9	12·0	5·7
01	7 00·3	7 01·4	6 41·1	0·1	0·0	6·1	2·9	12·1	5·7
02	7 00·5	7 01·7	6 41·3	0·2	0·1	6·2	2·9	12·2	5·8
03	7 00·8	7 01·9	6 41·6	0·3	0·1	6·3	3·0	12·3	5·8
04	7 01·0	7 02·2	6 41·8	0·4	0·2	6·4	3·0	12·4	5·9
05	7 01·3	7 02·4	6 42·1	0·5	0·2	6·5	3·1	12·5	5·9
06	7 01·5	7 02·7	6 42·3	0·6	0·3	6·6	3·1	12·6	6·0
07	7 01·8	7 02·9	6 42·5	0·7	0·3	6·7	3·2	12·7	6·0
08	7 02·0	7 03·2	6 42·8	0·8	0·4	6·8	3·2	12·8	6·1
09	7 02·3	7 03·4	6 43·0	0·9	0·4	6·9	3·3	12·9	6·1
10	7 02·5	7 03·7	6 43·3	1·0	0·5	7·0	3·3	13·0	6·2
11	7 02·8	7 03·9	6 43·5	1·1	0·5	7·1	3·4	13·1	6·2
12	7 03·0	7 04·2	6 43·7	1·2	0·6	7·2	3·4	13·2	6·3
13	7 03·3	7 04·4	6 44·0	1·3	0·6	7·3	3·5	13·3	6·3
14	7 03·5	7 04·7	6 44·2	1·4	0·7	7·4	3·5	13·4	6·4
15	7 03·8	7 04·9	6 44·4	1·5	0·7	7·5	3·6	13·5	6·4
16	7 04·0	7 05·2	6 44·7	1·6	0·8	7·6	3·6	13·6	6·5
17	7 04·3	7 05·4	6 44·9	1·7	0·8	7·7	3·7	13·7	6·5
18	7 04·5	7 05·7	6 45·2	1·8	0·9	7·8	3·7	13·8	6·6
19	7 04·8	7 05·9	6 45·4	1·9	0·9	7·9	3·8	13·9	6·6
20	7 05·0	7 06·2	6 45·6	2·0	1·0	8·0	3·8	14·0	6·7
21	7 05·3	7 06·4	6 45·9	2·1	1·0	8·1	3·8	14·1	6·7
22	7 05·5	7 06·7	6 46·1	2·2	1·0	8·2	3·9	14·2	6·7
23	7 05·8	7 06·9	6 46·4	2·3	1·1	8·3	3·9	14·3	6·8
24	7 06·0	7 07·2	6 46·6	2·4	1·1	8·4	4·0	14·4	6·8
25	7 06·3	7 07·4	6 46·8	2·5	1·2	8·5	4·0	14·5	6·9
26	7 06·5	7 07·7	6 47·1	2·6	1·2	8·6	4·1	14·6	6·9
27	7 06·8	7 07·9	6 47·3	2·7	1·3	8·7	4·1	14·7	7·0
28	7 07·0	7 08·2	6 47·5	2·8	1·3	8·8	4·2	14·8	7·0
29	7 07·3	7 08·4	6 47·8	2·9	1·4	8·9	4·2	14·9	7·1
30	7 07·5	7 08·7	6 48·0	3·0	1·4	9·0	4·3	15·0	7·1
31	7 07·8	7 08·9	6 48·3	3·1	1·5	9·1	4·3	15·1	7·2
32	7 08·0	7 09·2	6 48·5	3·2	1·5	9·2	4·4	15·2	7·2
33	7 08·3	7 09·4	6 48·7	3·3	1·6	9·3	4·4	15·3	7·3
34	7 08·5	7 09·7	6 49·0	3·4	1·6	9·4	4·5	15·4	7·3
35	7 08·8	7 09·9	6 49·2	3·5	1·7	9·5	4·5	15·5	7·4
36	7 09·0	7 10·2	6 49·5	3·6	1·7	9·6	4·6	15·6	7·4
37	7 09·3	7 10·4	6 49·7	3·7	1·8	9·7	4·6	15·7	7·5
38	7 09·5	7 10·7	6 49·9	3·8	1·8	9·8	4·7	15·8	7·5
39	7 09·8	7 10·9	6 50·2	3·9	1·9	9·9	4·7	15·9	7·6
40	7 10·0	7 11·2	6 50·4	4·0	1·9	10·0	4·8	16·0	7·6
41	7 10·3	7 11·4	6 50·6	4·1	1·9	10·1	4·8	16·1	7·6
42	7 10·5	7 11·7	6 50·9	4·2	2·0	10·2	4·8	16·2	7·7
43	7 10·8	7 11·9	6 51·1	4·3	2·0	10·3	4·9	16·3	7·7
44	7 11·0	7 12·2	6 51·4	4·4	2·1	10·4	4·9	16·4	7·8
45	7 11·3	7 12·4	6 51·6	4·5	2·1	10·5	5·0	16·5	7·8
46	7 11·5	7 12·7	6 51·8	4·6	2·2	10·6	5·0	16·6	7·9
47	7 11·8	7 12·9	6 52·1	4·7	2·2	10·7	5·1	16·7	7·9
48	7 12·0	7 13·2	6 52·3	4·8	2·3	10·8	5·1	16·8	8·0
49	7 12·3	7 13·4	6 52·6	4·9	2·3	10·9	5·2	16·9	8·0
50	7 12·5	7 13·7	6 52·8	5·0	2·4	11·0	5·2	17·0	8·1
51	7 12·8	7 13·9	6 53·0	5·1	2·4	11·1	5·3	17·1	8·1
52	7 13·0	7 14·2	6 53·3	5·2	2·5	11·2	5·3	17·2	8·2
53	7 13·3	7 14·4	6 53·5	5·3	2·5	11·3	5·4	17·3	8·2
54	7 13·5	7 14·7	6 53·8	5·4	2·6	11·4	5·4	17·4	8·3
55	7 13·8	7 14·9	6 54·0	5·5	2·6	11·5	5·5	17·5	8·3
56	7 14·0	7 15·2	6 54·2	5·6	2·7	11·6	5·5	17·6	8·4
57	7 14·3	7 15·4	6 54·5	5·7	2·7	11·7	5·6	17·7	8·4
58	7 14·5	7 15·7	6 54·7	5·8	2·8	11·8	5·6	17·8	8·5
59	7 14·8	7 15·9	6 54·9	5·9	2·8	11·9	5·7	17·9	8·5
60	7 15·0	7 16·2	6 55·2	6·0	2·9	12·0	5·7	18·0	8·6

29ᵐ	SUN PLANETS	ARIES	MOON	v or d Corrⁿ		v or d Corrⁿ		v or d Corrⁿ	
s	° ′	° ′	° ′	′	′	′	′	′	′
00	7 15·0	7 16·2	6 55·2	0·0	0·0	6·0	3·0	12·0	5·9
01	7 15·3	7 16·4	6 55·4	0·1	0·0	6·1	3·0	12·1	5·9
02	7 15·5	7 16·7	6 55·7	0·2	0·1	6·2	3·0	12·2	6·0
03	7 15·8	7 16·9	6 55·9	0·3	0·1	6·3	3·1	12·3	6·0
04	7 16·0	7 17·2	6 56·1	0·4	0·2	6·4	3·1	12·4	6·1
05	7 16·3	7 17·4	6 56·4	0·5	0·2	6·5	3·2	12·5	6·1
06	7 16·5	7 17·7	6 56·6	0·6	0·3	6·6	3·2	12·6	6·2
07	7 16·8	7 17·9	6 56·9	0·7	0·3	6·7	3·3	12·7	6·2
08	7 17·0	7 18·2	6 57·1	0·8	0·4	6·8	3·3	12·8	6·3
09	7 17·3	7 18·4	6 57·3	0·9	0·4	6·9	3·4	12·9	6·3
10	7 17·5	7 18·7	6 57·6	1·0	0·5	7·0	3·4	13·0	6·4
11	7 17·8	7 18·9	6 57·8	1·1	0·5	7·1	3·5	13·1	6·4
12	7 18·0	7 19·2	6 58·0	1·2	0·6	7·2	3·5	13·2	6·5
13	7 18·3	7 19·4	6 58·3	1·3	0·6	7·3	3·6	13·3	6·5
14	7 18·5	7 19·7	6 58·5	1·4	0·7	7·4	3·6	13·4	6·6
15	7 18·8	7 20·0	6 58·8	1·5	0·7	7·5	3·7	13·5	6·6
16	7 19·0	7 20·2	6 59·0	1·6	0·8	7·6	3·7	13·6	6·7
17	7 19·3	7 20·5	6 59·2	1·7	0·8	7·7	3·8	13·7	6·7
18	7 19·5	7 20·7	6 59·5	1·8	0·9	7·8	3·8	13·8	6·8
19	7 19·8	7 21·0	6 59·7	1·9	0·9	7·9	3·9	13·9	6·8
20	7 20·0	7 21·2	7 00·0	2·0	1·0	8·0	3·9	14·0	6·9
21	7 20·3	7 21·5	7 00·2	2·1	1·0	8·1	4·0	14·1	6·9
22	7 20·5	7 21·7	7 00·4	2·2	1·1	8·2	4·0	14·2	7·0
23	7 20·8	7 22·0	7 00·7	2·3	1·1	8·3	4·1	14·3	7·0
24	7 21·0	7 22·2	7 00·9	2·4	1·2	8·4	4·1	14·4	7·1
25	7 21·3	7 22·5	7 01·1	2·5	1·2	8·5	4·2	14·5	7·1
26	7 21·5	7 22·7	7 01·4	2·6	1·3	8·6	4·2	14·6	7·2
27	7 21·8	7 23·0	7 01·6	2·7	1·3	8·7	4·3	14·7	7·2
28	7 22·0	7 23·2	7 01·9	2·8	1·4	8·8	4·3	14·8	7·3
29	7 22·3	7 23·5	7 02·1	2·9	1·4	8·9	4·4	14·9	7·3
30	7 22·5	7 23·7	7 02·3	3·0	1·5	9·0	4·4	15·0	7·4
31	7 22·8	7 24·0	7 02·6	3·1	1·5	9·1	4·5	15·1	7·4
32	7 23·0	7 24·2	7 02·8	3·2	1·6	9·2	4·5	15·2	7·5
33	7 23·3	7 24·5	7 03·1	3·3	1·6	9·3	4·6	15·3	7·5
34	7 23·5	7 24·7	7 03·3	3·4	1·7	9·4	4·6	15·4	7·6
35	7 23·8	7 25·0	7 03·5	3·5	1·7	9·5	4·7	15·5	7·6
36	7 24·0	7 25·2	7 03·8	3·6	1·8	9·6	4·7	15·6	7·7
37	7 24·3	7 25·5	7 04·0	3·7	1·8	9·7	4·8	15·7	7·7
38	7 24·5	7 25·7	7 04·3	3·8	1·9	9·8	4·8	15·8	7·8
39	7 24·8	7 26·0	7 04·5	3·9	1·9	9·9	4·9	15·9	7·8
40	7 25·0	7 26·2	7 04·7	4·0	2·0	10·0	4·9	16·0	7·9
41	7 25·3	7 26·5	7 05·0	4·1	2·0	10·1	5·0	16·1	7·9
42	7 25·5	7 26·7	7 05·2	4·2	2·1	10·2	5·0	16·2	8·0
43	7 25·8	7 27·0	7 05·4	4·3	2·1	10·3	5·1	16·3	8·0
44	7 26·0	7 27·2	7 05·7	4·4	2·2	10·4	5·1	16·4	8·1
45	7 26·3	7 27·5	7 05·9	4·5	2·2	10·5	5·2	16·5	8·1
46	7 26·5	7 27·7	7 06·2	4·6	2·3	10·6	5·2	16·6	8·2
47	7 26·8	7 28·0	7 06·4	4·7	2·3	10·7	5·3	16·7	8·2
48	7 27·0	7 28·2	7 06·6	4·8	2·4	10·8	5·3	16·8	8·3
49	7 27·3	7 28·5	7 06·9	4·9	2·4	10·9	5·4	16·9	8·3
50	7 27·5	7 28·7	7 07·1	5·0	2·5	11·0	5·4	17·0	8·4
51	7 27·8	7 29·0	7 07·4	5·1	2·5	11·1	5·5	17·1	8·4
52	7 28·0	7 29·2	7 07·6	5·2	2·6	11·2	5·5	17·2	8·5
53	7 28·3	7 29·5	7 07·8	5·3	2·6	11·3	5·6	17·3	8·5
54	7 28·5	7 29·7	7 08·1	5·4	2·7	11·4	5·6	17·4	8·6
55	7 28·8	7 30·0	7 08·3	5·5	2·7	11·5	5·7	17·5	8·6
56	7 29·0	7 30·2	7 08·5	5·6	2·8	11·6	5·7	17·6	8·7
57	7 29·3	7 30·5	7 08·8	5·7	2·8	11·7	5·8	17·7	8·7
58	7 29·5	7 30·7	7 09·0	5·8	2·9	11·8	5·8	17·8	8·8
59	7 29·8	7 31·0	7 09·3	5·9	2·9	11·9	5·9	17·9	8·8
60	7 30·0	7 31·2	7 09·5	6·0	3·0	12·0	5·9	18·0	8·9

30ᵐ

30ᵐ (s)	SUN PLANETS	ARIES	MOON	v or Corrⁿ d	v or Corrⁿ d	v or Corrⁿ d
	° ′	° ′	° ′	′ ′	′ ′	′ ′
00	7 30.0	7 31.2	7 09.5	0.0 0.0	6.0 3.1	12.0 6.1
01	7 30.3	7 31.5	7 09.7	0.1 0.1	6.1 3.1	12.1 6.2
02	7 30.5	7 31.7	7 10.0	0.2 0.1	6.2 3.2	12.2 6.2
03	7 30.8	7 32.0	7 10.2	0.3 0.2	6.3 3.2	12.3 6.3
04	7 31.0	7 32.2	7 10.5	0.4 0.2	6.4 3.3	12.4 6.3
05	7 31.3	7 32.5	7 10.7	0.5 0.3	6.5 3.3	12.5 6.4
06	7 31.5	7 32.7	7 10.9	0.6 0.3	6.6 3.4	12.6 6.4
07	7 31.8	7 33.0	7 11.2	0.7 0.4	6.7 3.4	12.7 6.5
08	7 32.0	7 33.2	7 11.4	0.8 0.4	6.8 3.5	12.8 6.5
09	7 32.3	7 33.5	7 11.6	0.9 0.5	6.9 3.5	12.9 6.6
10	7 32.5	7 33.7	7 11.9	1.0 0.5	7.0 3.6	13.0 6.6
11	7 32.8	7 34.0	7 12.1	1.1 0.6	7.1 3.6	13.1 6.7
12	7 33.0	7 34.2	7 12.4	1.2 0.6	7.2 3.7	13.2 6.7
13	7 33.3	7 34.5	7 12.6	1.3 0.7	7.3 3.7	13.3 6.8
14	7 33.5	7 34.7	7 12.8	1.4 0.7	7.4 3.8	13.4 6.8
15	7 33.8	7 35.0	7 13.1	1.5 0.8	7.5 3.8	13.5 6.9
16	7 34.0	7 35.2	7 13.3	1.6 0.8	7.6 3.9	13.6 6.9
17	7 34.3	7 35.5	7 13.6	1.7 0.9	7.7 3.9	13.7 7.0
18	7 34.5	7 35.7	7 13.8	1.8 0.9	7.8 4.0	13.8 7.0
19	7 34.8	7 36.0	7 14.0	1.9 1.0	7.9 4.0	13.9 7.1
20	7 35.0	7 36.2	7 14.3	2.0 1.0	8.0 4.1	14.0 7.1
21	7 35.3	7 36.5	7 14.5	2.1 1.1	8.1 4.1	14.1 7.2
22	7 35.5	7 36.7	7 14.7	2.2 1.1	8.2 4.2	14.2 7.2
23	7 35.8	7 37.0	7 15.0	2.3 1.2	8.3 4.2	14.3 7.3
24	7 36.0	7 37.2	7 15.2	2.4 1.2	8.4 4.3	14.4 7.3
25	7 36.3	7 37.5	7 15.5	2.5 1.3	8.5 4.3	14.5 7.4
26	7 36.5	7 37.7	7 15.7	2.6 1.3	8.6 4.4	14.6 7.4
27	7 36.8	7 38.0	7 15.9	2.7 1.4	8.7 4.4	14.7 7.5
28	7 37.0	7 38.3	7 16.2	2.8 1.4	8.8 4.5	14.8 7.5
29	7 37.3	7 38.5	7 16.4	2.9 1.5	8.9 4.5	14.9 7.6
30	7 37.5	7 38.8	7 16.7	3.0 1.5	9.0 4.6	15.0 7.6
31	7 37.8	7 39.0	7 16.9	3.1 1.6	9.1 4.6	15.1 7.7
32	7 38.0	7 39.3	7 17.1	3.2 1.6	9.2 4.7	15.2 7.7
33	7 38.3	7 39.5	7 17.4	3.3 1.7	9.3 4.7	15.3 7.8
34	7 38.5	7 39.8	7 17.6	3.4 1.7	9.4 4.8	15.4 7.8
35	7 38.8	7 40.0	7 17.9	3.5 1.8	9.5 4.8	15.5 7.9
36	7 39.0	7 40.3	7 18.1	3.6 1.8	9.6 4.9	15.6 7.9
37	7 39.3	7 40.5	7 18.3	3.7 1.9	9.7 4.9	15.7 8.0
38	7 39.5	7 40.8	7 18.6	3.8 1.9	9.8 5.0	15.8 8.0
39	7 39.8	7 41.0	7 18.8	3.9 2.0	9.9 5.0	15.9 8.1
40	7 40.0	7 41.3	7 19.0	4.0 2.0	10.0 5.1	16.0 8.1
41	7 40.3	7 41.5	7 19.3	4.1 2.1	10.1 5.1	16.1 8.2
42	7 40.5	7 41.8	7 19.5	4.2 2.1	10.2 5.2	16.2 8.2
43	7 40.8	7 42.0	7 19.8	4.3 2.2	10.3 5.2	16.3 8.3
44	7 41.0	7 42.3	7 20.0	4.4 2.2	10.4 5.3	16.4 8.3
45	7 41.3	7 42.5	7 20.2	4.5 2.3	10.5 5.3	16.5 8.4
46	7 41.5	7 42.8	7 20.5	4.6 2.3	10.6 5.4	16.6 8.4
47	7 41.8	7 43.0	7 20.7	4.7 2.4	10.7 5.4	16.7 8.5
48	7 42.0	7 43.3	7 21.0	4.8 2.4	10.8 5.5	16.8 8.5
49	7 42.3	7 43.5	7 21.2	4.9 2.5	10.9 5.5	16.9 8.6
50	7 42.5	7 43.8	7 21.4	5.0 2.5	11.0 5.6	17.0 8.6
51	7 42.8	7 44.0	7 21.7	5.1 2.6	11.1 5.6	17.1 8.7
52	7 43.0	7 44.3	7 21.9	5.2 2.6	11.2 5.7	17.2 8.7
53	7 43.3	7 44.5	7 22.1	5.3 2.7	11.3 5.7	17.3 8.8
54	7 43.5	7 44.8	7 22.4	5.4 2.7	11.4 5.8	17.4 8.8
55	7 43.8	7 45.0	7 22.6	5.5 2.8	11.5 5.8	17.5 8.9
56	7 44.0	7 45.3	7 22.9	5.6 2.8	11.6 5.9	17.6 8.9
57	7 44.3	7 45.5	7 23.1	5.7 2.9	11.7 5.9	17.7 9.0
58	7 44.5	7 45.8	7 23.3	5.8 2.9	11.8 6.0	17.8 9.0
59	7 44.8	7 46.0	7 23.6	5.9 3.0	11.9 6.0	17.9 9.1
60	7 45.0	7 46.3	7 23.8	6.0 3.1	12.0 6.1	18.0 9.2

31ᵐ

31ᵐ (s)	SUN PLANETS	ARIES	MOON	v or Corrⁿ d	v or Corrⁿ d	v or Corrⁿ d
	° ′	° ′	° ′	′ ′	′ ′	′ ′
00	7 45.0	7 46.3	7 23.8	0.0 0.0	6.0 3.2	12.0 6.3
01	7 45.3	7 46.5	7 24.1	0.1 0.1	6.1 3.2	12.1 6.4
02	7 45.5	7 46.8	7 24.3	0.2 0.1	6.2 3.3	12.2 6.4
03	7 45.8	7 47.0	7 24.5	0.3 0.2	6.3 3.3	12.3 6.5
04	7 46.0	7 47.3	7 24.8	0.4 0.2	6.4 3.4	12.4 6.5
05	7 46.3	7 47.5	7 25.0	0.5 0.3	6.5 3.4	12.5 6.6
06	7 46.5	7 47.8	7 25.2	0.6 0.3	6.6 3.5	12.6 6.6
07	7 46.8	7 48.0	7 25.5	0.7 0.4	6.7 3.5	12.7 6.7
08	7 47.0	7 48.3	7 25.7	0.8 0.4	6.8 3.6	12.8 6.7
09	7 47.3	7 48.5	7 26.0	0.9 0.5	6.9 3.6	12.9 6.8
10	7 47.5	7 48.8	7 26.2	1.0 0.5	7.0 3.7	13.0 6.8
11	7 47.8	7 49.0	7 26.4	1.1 0.6	7.1 3.7	13.1 6.9
12	7 48.0	7 49.3	7 26.7	1.2 0.6	7.2 3.8	13.2 6.9
13	7 48.3	7 49.5	7 26.9	1.3 0.7	7.3 3.8	13.3 7.0
14	7 48.5	7 49.8	7 27.2	1.4 0.7	7.4 3.9	13.4 7.0
15	7 48.8	7 50.0	7 27.4	1.5 0.8	7.5 3.9	13.5 7.1
16	7 49.0	7 50.3	7 27.6	1.6 0.8	7.6 4.0	13.6 7.1
17	7 49.3	7 50.5	7 27.9	1.7 0.9	7.7 4.0	13.7 7.2
18	7 49.5	7 50.8	7 28.1	1.8 0.9	7.8 4.1	13.8 7.2
19	7 49.8	7 51.0	7 28.4	1.9 1.0	7.9 4.1	13.9 7.3
20	7 50.0	7 51.3	7 28.6	2.0 1.1	8.0 4.2	14.0 7.4
21	7 50.3	7 51.5	7 28.8	2.1 1.1	8.1 4.3	14.1 7.4
22	7 50.5	7 51.8	7 29.1	2.2 1.2	8.2 4.3	14.2 7.5
23	7 50.8	7 52.0	7 29.3	2.3 1.2	8.3 4.4	14.3 7.5
24	7 51.0	7 52.3	7 29.5	2.4 1.3	8.4 4.4	14.4 7.6
25	7 51.3	7 52.5	7 29.8	2.5 1.3	8.5 4.5	14.5 7.6
26	7 51.5	7 52.8	7 30.0	2.6 1.4	8.6 4.5	14.6 7.7
27	7 51.8	7 53.0	7 30.3	2.7 1.4	8.7 4.6	14.7 7.7
28	7 52.0	7 53.3	7 30.5	2.8 1.5	8.8 4.6	14.8 7.8
29	7 52.3	7 53.5	7 30.7	2.9 1.5	8.9 4.7	14.9 7.8
30	7 52.5	7 53.8	7 31.0	3.0 1.6	9.0 4.7	15.0 7.9
31	7 52.8	7 54.0	7 31.2	3.1 1.6	9.1 4.8	15.1 7.9
32	7 53.0	7 54.3	7 31.5	3.2 1.7	9.2 4.8	15.2 8.0
33	7 53.3	7 54.5	7 31.7	3.3 1.7	9.3 4.9	15.3 8.0
34	7 53.5	7 54.8	7 31.9	3.4 1.8	9.4 4.9	15.4 8.1
35	7 53.8	7 55.0	7 32.2	3.5 1.8	9.5 5.0	15.5 8.1
36	7 54.0	7 55.3	7 32.4	3.6 1.9	9.6 5.0	15.6 8.2
37	7 54.3	7 55.5	7 32.6	3.7 1.9	9.7 5.1	15.7 8.2
38	7 54.5	7 55.8	7 32.9	3.8 2.0	9.8 5.1	15.8 8.3
39	7 54.8	7 56.0	7 33.1	3.9 2.0	9.9 5.2	15.9 8.3
40	7 55.0	7 56.3	7 33.4	4.0 2.1	10.0 5.3	16.0 8.4
41	7 55.3	7 56.6	7 33.6	4.1 2.2	10.1 5.3	16.1 8.5
42	7 55.5	7 56.8	7 33.8	4.2 2.2	10.2 5.4	16.2 8.5
43	7 55.8	7 57.1	7 34.1	4.3 2.3	10.3 5.4	16.3 8.6
44	7 56.0	7 57.3	7 34.3	4.4 2.3	10.4 5.5	16.4 8.6
45	7 56.3	7 57.6	7 34.6	4.5 2.4	10.5 5.5	16.5 8.7
46	7 56.5	7 57.8	7 34.8	4.6 2.4	10.6 5.6	16.6 8.7
47	7 56.8	7 58.1	7 35.0	4.7 2.5	10.7 5.6	16.7 8.8
48	7 57.0	7 58.3	7 35.3	4.8 2.5	10.8 5.7	16.8 8.8
49	7 57.3	7 58.6	7 35.5	4.9 2.6	10.9 5.7	16.9 8.9
50	7 57.5	7 58.8	7 35.7	5.0 2.6	11.0 5.8	17.0 8.9
51	7 57.8	7 59.1	7 36.0	5.1 2.7	11.1 5.8	17.1 9.0
52	7 58.0	7 59.3	7 36.2	5.2 2.7	11.2 5.9	17.2 9.0
53	7 58.3	7 59.6	7 36.5	5.3 2.8	11.3 5.9	17.3 9.1
54	7 58.5	7 59.8	7 36.7	5.4 2.8	11.4 6.0	17.4 9.1
55	7 58.8	8 00.1	7 36.9	5.5 2.9	11.5 6.0	17.5 9.2
56	7 59.0	8 00.3	7 37.2	5.6 2.9	11.6 6.1	17.6 9.2
57	7 59.3	8 00.6	7 37.4	5.7 3.0	11.7 6.1	17.7 9.3
58	7 59.5	8 00.8	7 37.7	5.8 3.0	11.8 6.2	17.8 9.3
59	7 59.8	8 01.1	7 37.9	5.9 3.1	11.9 6.2	17.9 9.4
60	8 00.0	8 01.3	7 38.1	6.0 3.2	12.0 6.3	18.0 9.5

32m

32^m s	SUN PLANETS	ARIES	MOON	v or d	Corrⁿ	v or d	Corrⁿ	v or d	Corrⁿ
00	8 00·0	8 01·3	7 38·1	0·0	0·0	6·0	3·3	12·0	6·5
01	8 00·3	8 01·6	7 38·4	0·1	0·1	6·1	3·3	12·1	6·6
02	8 00·5	8 01·8	7 38·6	0·2	0·1	6·2	3·4	12·2	6·6
03	8 00·8	8 02·1	7 38·8	0·3	0·2	6·3	3·4	12·3	6·7
04	8 01·0	8 02·3	7 39·1	0·4	0·2	6·4	3·5	12·4	6·7
05	8 01·3	8 02·6	7 39·3	0·5	0·3	6·5	3·5	12·5	6·8
06	8 01·5	8 02·8	7 39·6	0·6	0·3	6·6	3·6	12·6	6·8
07	8 01·8	8 03·1	7 39·8	0·7	0·4	6·7	3·6	12·7	6·9
08	8 02·0	8 03·3	7 40·0	0·8	0·4	6·8	3·7	12·8	6·9
09	8 02·3	8 03·6	7 40·3	0·9	0·5	6·9	3·7	12·9	7·0
10	8 02·5	8 03·8	7 40·5	1·0	0·5	7·0	3·8	13·0	7·0
11	8 02·8	8 04·1	7 40·8	1·1	0·6	7·1	3·8	13·1	7·1
12	8 03·0	8 04·3	7 41·0	1·2	0·7	7·2	3·9	13·2	7·2
13	8 03·3	8 04·6	7 41·2	1·3	0·7	7·3	4·0	13·3	7·2
14	8 03·5	8 04·8	7 41·5	1·4	0·8	7·4	4·0	13·4	7·3
15	8 03·8	8 05·1	7 41·7	1·5	0·8	7·5	4·1	13·5	7·3
16	8 04·0	8 05·3	7 42·0	1·6	0·9	7·6	4·1	13·6	7·4
17	8 04·3	8 05·6	7 42·2	1·7	0·9	7·7	4·2	13·7	7·4
18	8 04·5	8 05·8	7 42·4	1·8	1·0	7·8	4·2	13·8	7·5
19	8 04·8	8 06·1	7 42·7	1·9	1·0	7·9	4·3	13·9	7·5
20	8 05·0	8 06·3	7 42·9	2·0	1·1	8·0	4·3	14·0	7·6
21	8 05·3	8 06·6	7 43·1	2·1	1·1	8·1	4·4	14·1	7·6
22	8 05·5	8 06·8	7 43·4	2·2	1·2	8·2	4·4	14·2	7·7
23	8 05·8	8 07·1	7 43·6	2·3	1·2	8·3	4·5	14·3	7·7
24	8 06·0	8 07·3	7 43·9	2·4	1·3	8·4	4·6	14·4	7·8
25	8 06·3	8 07·6	7 44·1	2·5	1·4	8·5	4·6	14·5	7·9
26	8 06·5	8 07·8	7 44·3	2·6	1·4	8·6	4·7	14·6	7·9
27	8 06·8	8 08·1	7 44·6	2·7	1·5	8·7	4·7	14·7	8·0
28	8 07·0	8 08·3	7 44·8	2·8	1·5	8·8	4·8	14·8	8·0
29	8 07·3	8 08·6	7 45·1	2·9	1·6	8·9	4·8	14·9	8·1
30	8 07·5	8 08·8	7 45·3	3·0	1·6	9·0	4·9	15·0	8·1
31	8 07·8	8 09·1	7 45·5	3·1	1·7	9·1	4·9	15·1	8·2
32	8 08·0	8 09·3	7 45·8	3·2	1·7	9·2	5·0	15·2	8·2
33	8 08·3	8 09·6	7 46·0	3·3	1·8	9·3	5·0	15·3	8·3
34	8 08·5	8 09·8	7 46·2	3·4	1·8	9·4	5·1	15·4	8·3
35	8 08·8	8 10·1	7 46·5	3·5	1·9	9·5	5·1	15·5	8·4
36	8 09·0	8 10·3	7 46·7	3·6	2·0	9·6	5·2	15·6	8·5
37	8 09·3	8 10·6	7 47·0	3·7	2·0	9·7	5·3	15·7	8·5
38	8 09·5	8 10·8	7 47·2	3·8	2·1	9·8	5·3	15·8	8·6
39	8 09·8	8 11·1	7 47·4	3·9	2·1	9·9	5·4	15·9	8·6
40	8 10·0	8 11·3	7 47·7	4·0	2·2	10·0	5·4	16·0	8·7
41	8 10·3	8 11·6	7 47·9	4·1	2·2	10·1	5·5	16·1	8·7
42	8 10·5	8 11·8	7 48·2	4·2	2·3	10·2	5·5	16·2	8·8
43	8 10·8	8 12·1	7 48·4	4·3	2·3	10·3	5·6	16·3	8·8
44	8 11·0	8 12·3	7 48·6	4·4	2·4	10·4	5·6	16·4	8·9
45	8 11·3	8 12·6	7 48·9	4·5	2·4	10·5	5·7	16·5	8·9
46	8 11·5	8 12·8	7 49·1	4·6	2·5	10·6	5·7	16·6	9·0
47	8 11·8	8 13·1	7 49·3	4·7	2·5	10·7	5·8	16·7	9·0
48	8 12·0	8 13·3	7 49·6	4·8	2·6	10·8	5·9	16·8	9·1
49	8 12·3	8 13·6	7 49·8	4·9	2·7	10·9	5·9	16·9	9·2
50	8 12·5	8 13·8	7 50·1	5·0	2·7	11·0	6·0	17·0	9·2
51	8 12·8	8 14·1	7 50·3	5·1	2·8	11·1	6·0	17·1	9·3
52	8 13·0	8 14·3	7 50·5	5·2	2·8	11·2	6·1	17·2	9·3
53	8 13·3	8 14·6	7 50·8	5·3	2·9	11·3	6·1	17·3	9·4
54	8 13·5	8 14·9	7 51·0	5·4	2·9	11·4	6·2	17·4	9·4
55	8 13·8	8 15·1	7 51·3	5·5	3·0	11·5	6·2	17·5	9·5
56	8 14·0	8 15·4	7 51·5	5·6	3·0	11·6	6·3	17·6	9·5
57	8 14·3	8 15·6	7 51·7	5·7	3·1	11·7	6·3	17·7	9·6
58	8 14·5	8 15·9	7 52·0	5·8	3·1	11·8	6·4	17·8	9·6
59	8 14·8	8 16·1	7 52·2	5·9	3·2	11·9	6·4	17·9	9·7
60	8 15·0	8 16·4	7 52·5	6·0	3·3	12·0	6·5	18·0	9·8

33m

33^m s	SUN PLANETS	ARIES	MOON	v or d	Corrⁿ	v or d	Corrⁿ	v or d	Corrⁿ
00	8 15·0	8 16·4	7 52·5	0·0	0·0	6·0	3·4	12·0	6·7
01	8 15·3	8 16·6	7 52·7	0·1	0·1	6·1	3·4	12·1	6·8
02	8 15·5	8 16·9	7 52·9	0·2	0·1	6·2	3·5	12·2	6·8
03	8 15·8	8 17·1	7 53·2	0·3	0·2	6·3	3·5	12·3	6·9
04	8 16·0	8 17·4	7 53·4	0·4	0·2	6·4	3·6	12·4	6·9
05	8 16·3	8 17·6	7 53·6	0·5	0·3	6·5	3·6	12·5	7·0
06	8 16·5	8 17·9	7 53·9	0·6	0·3	6·6	3·7	12·6	7·0
07	8 16·8	8 18·1	7 54·1	0·7	0·4	6·7	3·7	12·7	7·1
08	8 17·0	8 18·4	7 54·4	0·8	0·4	6·8	3·8	12·8	7·1
09	8 17·3	8 18·6	7 54·6	0·9	0·5	6·9	3·9	12·9	7·2
10	8 17·5	8 18·9	7 54·8	1·0	0·6	7·0	3·9	13·0	7·3
11	8 17·8	8 19·1	7 55·1	1·1	0·6	7·1	4·0	13·1	7·3
12	8 18·0	8 19·4	7 55·3	1·2	0·7	7·2	4·0	13·2	7·4
13	8 18·3	8 19·6	7 55·6	1·3	0·7	7·3	4·1	13·3	7·4
14	8 18·5	8 19·9	7 55·8	1·4	0·8	7·4	4·1	13·4	7·5
15	8 18·8	8 20·1	7 56·0	1·5	0·8	7·5	4·2	13·5	7·5
16	8 19·0	8 20·4	7 56·3	1·6	0·9	7·6	4·2	13·6	7·6
17	8 19·3	8 20·6	7 56·5	1·7	0·9	7·7	4·3	13·7	7·6
18	8 19·5	8 20·9	7 56·7	1·8	1·0	7·8	4·4	13·8	7·7
19	8 19·8	8 21·1	7 57·0	1·9	1·1	7·9	4·4	13·9	7·8
20	8 20·0	8 21·4	7 57·2	2·0	1·1	8·0	4·5	14·0	7·8
21	8 20·3	8 21·6	7 57·5	2·1	1·2	8·1	4·5	14·1	7·9
22	8 20·5	8 21·9	7 57·7	2·2	1·2	8·2	4·6	14·2	7·9
23	8 20·8	8 22·1	7 57·9	2·3	1·3	8·3	4·6	14·3	8·0
24	8 21·0	8 22·4	7 58·2	2·4	1·3	8·4	4·7	14·4	8·0
25	8 21·3	8 22·6	7 58·4	2·5	1·4	8·5	4·7	14·5	8·1
26	8 21·5	8 22·9	7 58·7	2·6	1·5	8·6	4·8	14·6	8·2
27	8 21·8	8 23·1	7 58·9	2·7	1·5	8·7	4·9	14·7	8·2
28	8 22·0	8 23·4	7 59·1	2·8	1·6	8·8	4·9	14·8	8·3
29	8 22·3	8 23·6	7 59·4	2·9	1·6	8·9	5·0	14·9	8·3
30	8 22·5	8 23·9	7 59·6	3·0	1·7	9·0	5·0	15·0	8·4
31	8 22·8	8 24·1	7 59·8	3·1	1·7	9·1	5·1	15·1	8·4
32	8 23·0	8 24·4	8 00·1	3·2	1·8	9·2	5·1	15·2	8·5
33	8 23·3	8 24·6	8 00·3	3·3	1·8	9·3	5·2	15·3	8·5
34	8 23·5	8 24·9	8 00·6	3·4	1·9	9·4	5·2	15·4	8·6
35	8 23·8	8 25·1	8 00·8	3·5	2·0	9·5	5·3	15·5	8·7
36	8 24·0	8 25·4	8 01·0	3·6	2·0	9·6	5·4	15·6	8·7
37	8 24·3	8 25·6	8 01·3	3·7	2·1	9·7	5·4	15·7	8·8
38	8 24·5	8 25·9	8 01·5	3·8	2·1	9·8	5·5	15·8	8·8
39	8 24·8	8 26·1	8 01·8	3·9	2·2	9·9	5·5	15·9	8·9
40	8 25·0	8 26·4	8 02·0	4·0	2·2	10·0	5·6	16·0	8·9
41	8 25·3	8 26·6	8 02·2	4·1	2·3	10·1	5·6	16·1	9·0
42	8 25·5	8 26·9	8 02·5	4·2	2·3	10·2	5·7	16·2	9·0
43	8 25·8	8 27·1	8 02·7	4·3	2·4	10·3	5·8	16·3	9·1
44	8 26·0	8 27·4	8 02·9	4·4	2·5	10·4	5·8	16·4	9·2
45	8 26·3	8 27·6	8 03·2	4·5	2·5	10·5	5·9	16·5	9·2
46	8 26·5	8 27·9	8 03·4	4·6	2·6	10·6	5·9	16·6	9·3
47	8 26·8	8 28·1	8 03·7	4·7	2·6	10·7	6·0	16·7	9·3
48	8 27·0	8 28·4	8 03·9	4·8	2·7	10·8	6·0	16·8	9·4
49	8 27·3	8 28·6	8 04·1	4·9	2·7	10·9	6·1	16·9	9·4
50	8 27·5	8 28·9	8 04·4	5·0	2·8	11·0	6·1	17·0	9·5
51	8 27·8	8 29·1	8 04·6	5·1	2·8	11·1	6·2	17·1	9·5
52	8 28·0	8 29·4	8 04·9	5·2	2·9	11·2	6·3	17·2	9·6
53	8 28·3	8 29·6	8 05·1	5·3	3·0	11·3	6·3	17·3	9·7
54	8 28·5	8 29·9	8 05·3	5·4	3·0	11·4	6·4	17·4	9·7
55	8 28·8	8 30·1	8 05·6	5·5	3·1	11·5	6·4	17·5	9·8
56	8 29·0	8 30·4	8 05·8	5·6	3·1	11·6	6·5	17·6	9·8
57	8 29·3	8 30·6	8 06·1	5·7	3·2	11·7	6·5	17·7	9·9
58	8 29·5	8 30·9	8 06·3	5·8	3·2	11·8	6·6	17·8	9·9
59	8 29·8	8 31·1	8 06·5	5·9	3·3	11·9	6·6	17·9	10·0
60	8 30·0	8 31·4	8 06·8	6·0	3·4	12·0	6·7	18·0	10·1

34 s	SUN PLANETS	ARIES	MOON	v or Corrn d		v or Corrn d		v or Corrn d	
00	8 30.0	8 31.4	8 06.8	0.0	0.0	6.0	3.5	12.0	6.9
01	8 30.3	8 31.6	8 07.0	0.1	0.1	6.1	3.5	12.1	7.0
02	8 30.5	8 31.9	8 07.2	0.2	0.1	6.2	3.6	12.2	7.0
03	8 30.8	8 32.1	8 07.5	0.3	0.2	6.3	3.6	12.3	7.1
04	8 31.0	8 32.4	8 07.7	0.4	0.2	6.4	3.7	12.4	7.1
05	8 31.3	8 32.6	8 08.0	0.5	0.3	6.5	3.7	12.5	7.2
06	8 31.5	8 32.9	8 08.2	0.6	0.3	6.6	3.8	12.6	7.2
07	8 31.8	8 33.2	8 08.4	0.7	0.4	6.7	3.9	12.7	7.3
08	8 32.0	8 33.4	8 08.7	0.8	0.5	6.8	3.9	12.8	7.4
09	8 32.3	8 33.7	8 08.9	0.9	0.5	6.9	4.0	12.9	7.4
10	8 32.5	8 33.9	8 09.2	1.0	0.6	7.0	4.0	13.0	7.5
11	8 32.8	8 34.2	8 09.4	1.1	0.6	7.1	4.1	13.1	7.5
12	8 33.0	8 34.4	8 09.6	1.2	0.7	7.2	4.1	13.2	7.6
13	8 33.3	8 34.7	8 09.9	1.3	0.7	7.3	4.2	13.3	7.6
14	8 33.5	8 34.9	8 10.1	1.4	0.8	7.4	4.3	13.4	7.7
15	8 33.8	8 35.2	8 10.3	1.5	0.9	7.5	4.3	13.5	7.8
16	8 34.0	8 35.4	8 10.6	1.6	0.9	7.6	4.4	13.6	7.8
17	8 34.3	8 35.7	8 10.8	1.7	1.0	7.7	4.4	13.7	7.9
18	8 34.5	8 35.9	8 11.1	1.8	1.0	7.8	4.5	13.8	7.9
19	8 34.8	8 36.2	8 11.3	1.9	1.1	7.9	4.5	13.9	8.0
20	8 35.0	8 36.4	8 11.5	2.0	1.2	8.0	4.6	14.0	8.1
21	8 35.3	8 36.7	8 11.8	2.1	1.2	8.1	4.7	14.1	8.1
22	8 35.5	8 36.9	8 12.0	2.2	1.3	8.2	4.7	14.2	8.2
23	8 35.8	8 37.2	8 12.3	2.3	1.3	8.3	4.8	14.3	8.2
24	8 36.0	8 37.4	8 12.5	2.4	1.4	8.4	4.8	14.4	8.3
25	8 36.3	8 37.7	8 12.7	2.5	1.4	8.5	4.9	14.5	8.3
26	8 36.5	8 37.9	8 13.0	2.6	1.5	8.6	4.9	14.6	8.4
27	8 36.8	8 38.2	8 13.2	2.7	1.6	8.7	5.0	14.7	8.5
28	8 37.0	8 38.4	8 13.4	2.8	1.6	8.8	5.1	14.8	8.5
29	8 37.3	8 38.7	8 13.7	2.9	1.7	8.9	5.1	14.9	8.6
30	8 37.5	8 38.9	8 13.9	3.0	1.7	9.0	5.2	15.0	8.6
31	8 37.8	8 39.2	8 14.2	3.1	1.8	9.1	5.2	15.1	8.7
32	8 38.0	8 39.4	8 14.4	3.2	1.8	9.2	5.3	15.2	8.7
33	8 38.3	8 39.7	8 14.6	3.3	1.9	9.3	5.3	15.3	8.8
34	8 38.5	8 39.9	8 14.9	3.4	2.0	9.4	5.4	15.4	8.9
35	8 38.8	8 40.2	8 15.1	3.5	2.0	9.5	5.5	15.5	8.9
36	8 39.0	8 40.4	8 15.4	3.6	2.1	9.6	5.5	15.6	9.0
37	8 39.3	8 40.7	8 15.6	3.7	2.1	9.7	5.6	15.7	9.0
38	8 39.5	8 40.9	8 15.8	3.8	2.2	9.8	5.6	15.8	9.1
39	8 39.8	8 41.2	8 16.1	3.9	2.2	9.9	5.7	15.9	9.1
40	8 40.0	8 41.4	8 16.3	4.0	2.3	10.0	5.8	16.0	9.2
41	8 40.3	8 41.7	8 16.5	4.1	2.4	10.1	5.8	16.1	9.3
42	8 40.5	8 41.9	8 16.8	4.2	2.4	10.2	5.9	16.2	9.3
43	8 40.8	8 42.2	8 17.0	4.3	2.5	10.3	5.9	16.3	9.4
44	8 41.0	8 42.4	8 17.3	4.4	2.5	10.4	6.0	16.4	9.4
45	8 41.3	8 42.7	8 17.5	4.5	2.6	10.5	6.0	16.5	9.5
46	8 41.5	8 42.9	8 17.7	4.6	2.6	10.6	6.1	16.6	9.5
47	8 41.8	8 43.2	8 18.0	4.7	2.7	10.7	6.2	16.7	9.6
48	8 42.0	8 43.4	8 18.2	4.8	2.8	10.8	6.2	16.8	9.7
49	8 42.3	8 43.7	8 18.5	4.9	2.8	10.9	6.3	16.9	9.7
50	8 42.5	8 43.9	8 18.7	5.0	2.9	11.0	6.3	17.0	9.8
51	8 42.8	8 44.2	8 18.9	5.1	2.9	11.1	6.4	17.1	9.8
52	8 43.0	8 44.4	8 19.2	5.2	3.0	11.2	6.4	17.2	9.9
53	8 43.3	8 44.7	8 19.4	5.3	3.0	11.3	6.5	17.3	9.9
54	8 43.5	8 44.9	8 19.7	5.4	3.1	11.4	6.6	17.4	10.0
55	8 43.8	8 45.2	8 19.9	5.5	3.2	11.5	6.6	17.5	10.1
56	8 44.0	8 45.4	8 20.1	5.6	3.2	11.6	6.7	17.6	10.1
57	8 44.3	8 45.7	8 20.4	5.7	3.3	11.7	6.7	17.7	10.2
58	8 44.5	8 45.9	8 20.6	5.8	3.3	11.8	6.8	17.8	10.2
59	8 44.8	8 46.2	8 20.8	5.9	3.4	11.9	6.8	17.9	10.3
60	8 45.0	8 46.4	8 21.1	6.0	3.5	12.0	6.9	18.0	10.4

35 s	SUN PLANETS	ARIES	MOON	v or Corrn d		v or Corrn d		v or Corrn d	
00	8 45.0	8 46.4	8 21.1	0.0	0.0	6.0	3.6	12.0	7.1
01	8 45.3	8 46.7	8 21.3	0.1	0.1	6.1	3.6	12.1	7.1
02	8 45.5	8 46.9	8 21.6	0.2	0.1	6.2	3.7	12.2	7.2
03	8 45.8	8 47.2	8 21.8	0.3	0.2	6.3	3.7	12.3	7.3
04	8 46.0	8 47.4	8 22.0	0.4	0.2	6.4	3.8	12.4	7.3
05	8 46.3	8 47.7	8 22.3	0.5	0.3	6.5	3.8	12.5	7.4
06	8 46.5	8 47.9	8 22.5	0.6	0.4	6.6	3.9	12.6	7.5
07	8 46.8	8 48.2	8 22.8	0.7	0.4	6.7	4.0	12.7	7.5
08	8 47.0	8 48.4	8 23.0	0.8	0.5	6.8	4.0	12.8	7.6
09	8 47.3	8 48.7	8 23.2	0.9	0.5	6.9	4.1	12.9	7.6
10	8 47.5	8 48.9	8 23.5	1.0	0.6	7.0	4.1	13.0	7.7
11	8 47.8	8 49.2	8 23.7	1.1	0.7	7.1	4.2	13.1	7.8
12	8 48.0	8 49.4	8 23.9	1.2	0.7	7.2	4.3	13.2	7.8
13	8 48.3	8 49.7	8 24.2	1.3	0.8	7.3	4.3	13.3	7.9
14	8 48.5	8 49.9	8 24.4	1.4	0.8	7.4	4.4	13.4	7.9
15	8 48.8	8 50.2	8 24.7	1.5	0.9	7.5	4.4	13.5	8.0
16	8 49.0	8 50.4	8 24.9	1.6	0.9	7.6	4.5	13.6	8.0
17	8 49.3	8 50.7	8 25.1	1.7	1.0	7.7	4.6	13.7	8.1
18	8 49.5	8 50.9	8 25.4	1.8	1.1	7.8	4.6	13.8	8.2
19	8 49.8	8 51.2	8 25.6	1.9	1.1	7.9	4.7	13.9	8.2
20	8 50.0	8 51.5	8 25.9	2.0	1.2	8.0	4.7	14.0	8.3
21	8 50.3	8 51.7	8 26.1	2.1	1.2	8.1	4.8	14.1	8.3
22	8 50.5	8 52.0	8 26.3	2.2	1.3	8.2	4.9	14.2	8.4
23	8 50.8	8 52.2	8 26.6	2.3	1.4	8.3	4.9	14.3	8.5
24	8 51.0	8 52.5	8 26.8	2.4	1.4	8.4	5.0	14.4	8.5
25	8 51.3	8 52.7	8 27.0	2.5	1.5	8.5	5.0	14.5	8.6
26	8 51.5	8 53.0	8 27.3	2.6	1.5	8.6	5.1	14.6	8.6
27	8 51.8	8 53.2	8 27.5	2.7	1.6	8.7	5.1	14.7	8.7
28	8 52.0	8 53.5	8 27.8	2.8	1.7	8.8	5.2	14.8	8.8
29	8 52.3	8 53.7	8 28.0	2.9	1.7	8.9	5.3	14.9	8.8
30	8 52.5	8 54.0	8 28.2	3.0	1.8	9.0	5.3	15.0	8.9
31	8 52.8	8 54.2	8 28.5	3.1	1.8	9.1	5.4	15.1	8.9
32	8 53.0	8 54.5	8 28.7	3.2	1.9	9.2	5.4	15.2	9.0
33	8 53.3	8 54.7	8 29.0	3.3	2.0	9.3	5.5	15.3	9.1
34	8 53.5	8 55.0	8 29.2	3.4	2.0	9.4	5.6	15.4	9.1
35	8 53.8	8 55.2	8 29.4	3.5	2.1	9.5	5.6	15.5	9.2
36	8 54.0	8 55.5	8 29.7	3.6	2.1	9.6	5.7	15.6	9.2
37	8 54.3	8 55.7	8 29.9	3.7	2.2	9.7	5.7	15.7	9.3
38	8 54.5	8 56.0	8 30.2	3.8	2.2	9.8	5.8	15.8	9.3
39	8 54.8	8 56.2	8 30.4	3.9	2.3	9.9	5.9	15.9	9.4
40	8 55.0	8 56.5	8 30.6	4.0	2.4	10.0	5.9	16.0	9.5
41	8 55.3	8 56.7	8 30.9	4.1	2.4	10.1	6.0	16.1	9.5
42	8 55.5	8 57.0	8 31.1	4.2	2.5	10.2	6.0	16.2	9.6
43	8 55.8	8 57.2	8 31.3	4.3	2.5	10.3	6.1	16.3	9.6
44	8 56.0	8 57.5	8 31.6	4.4	2.6	10.4	6.2	16.4	9.7
45	8 56.3	8 57.7	8 31.8	4.5	2.7	10.5	6.2	16.5	9.8
46	8 56.5	8 58.0	8 32.1	4.6	2.7	10.6	6.3	16.6	9.8
47	8 56.8	8 58.2	8 32.3	4.7	2.8	10.7	6.3	16.7	9.9
48	8 57.0	8 58.5	8 32.5	4.8	2.8	10.8	6.4	16.8	9.9
49	8 57.3	8 58.7	8 32.8	4.9	2.9	10.9	6.4	16.9	10.0
50	8 57.5	8 59.0	8 33.0	5.0	3.0	11.0	6.5	17.0	10.1
51	8 57.8	8 59.2	8 33.3	5.1	3.0	11.1	6.6	17.1	10.1
52	8 58.0	8 59.5	8 33.5	5.2	3.1	11.2	6.6	17.2	10.2
53	8 58.3	8 59.7	8 33.7	5.3	3.1	11.3	6.7	17.3	10.2
54	8 58.5	9 00.0	8 34.0	5.4	3.2	11.4	6.7	17.4	10.3
55	8 58.8	9 00.2	8 34.2	5.5	3.3	11.5	6.8	17.5	10.4
56	8 59.0	9 00.5	8 34.4	5.6	3.3	11.6	6.9	17.6	10.4
57	8 59.3	9 00.7	8 34.7	5.7	3.4	11.7	6.9	17.7	10.5
58	8 59.5	9 01.0	8 34.9	5.8	3.4	11.8	7.0	17.8	10.5
59	8 59.8	9 01.2	8 35.2	5.9	3.5	11.9	7.0	17.9	10.6
60	9 00.0	9 01.5	8 35.4	6.0	3.6	12.0	7.1	18.0	10.7

36ᵐ SUN PLANETS	ARIES	MOON	v or Corrⁿ d	v or Corrⁿ d	v or Corrⁿ d	37ᵐ SUN PLANETS	ARIES	MOON	v or Corrⁿ d	v or Corrⁿ d	v or Corrⁿ d
s	° ′	° ′	° ′	′ ′	′ ′	′ ′	s	° ′	° ′	° ′	′ ′	′ ′	′ ′
00	9 00·0	9 01·5	8 35·4	0·0 0·0	6·0 3·7	12·0 7·3	00	9 15·0	9 16·5	8 49·7	0·0 0·0	6·0 3·8	12·0 7·5
01	9 00·3	9 01·7	8 35·6	0·1 0·1	6·1 3·7	12·1 7·4	01	9 15·3	9 16·8	8 50·0	0·1 0·1	6·1 3·8	12·1 7·6
02	9 00·5	9 02·0	8 35·9	0·2 0·1	6·2 3·8	12·2 7·4	02	9 15·5	9 17·0	8 50·2	0·2 0·1	6·2 3·9	12·2 7·6
03	9 00·8	9 02·2	8 36·1	0·3 0·2	6·3 3·8	12·3 7·5	03	9 15·8	9 17·3	8 50·4	0·3 0·2	6·3 3·9	12·3 7·7
04	9 01·0	9 02·5	8 36·4	0·4 0·2	6·4 3·9	12·4 7·5	04	9 16·0	9 17·5	8 50·7	0·4 0·3	6·4 4·0	12·4 7·8
05	9 01·3	9 02·7	8 36·6	0·5 0·3	6·5 4·0	12·5 7·6	05	9 16·3	9 17·8	8 50·9	0·5 0·3	6·5 4·1	12·5 7·8
06	9 01·5	9 03·0	8 36·8	0·6 0·4	6·6 4·0	12·6 7·7	06	9 16·5	9 18·0	8 51·1	0·6 0·4	6·6 4·1	12·6 7·9
07	9 01·8	9 03·2	8 37·1	0·7 0·4	6·7 4·1	12·7 7·7	07	9 16·8	9 18·3	8 51·4	0·7 0·4	6·7 4·2	12·7 7·9
08	9 02·0	9 03·5	8 37·3	0·8 0·5	6·8 4·1	12·8 7·8	08	9 17·0	9 18·5	8 51·6	0·8 0·5	6·8 4·3	12·8 8·0
09	9 02·3	9 03·7	8 37·5	0·9 0·5	6·9 4·2	12·9 7·8	09	9 17·3	9 18·8	8 51·9	0·9 0·6	6·9 4·3	12·9 8·1
10	9 02·5	9 04·0	8 37·8	1·0 0·6	7·0 4·3	13·0 7·9	10	9 17·5	9 19·0	8 52·1	1·0 0·6	7·0 4·4	13·0 8·1
11	9 02·8	9 04·2	8 38·0	1·1 0·7	7·1 4·3	13·1 8·0	11	9 17·8	9 19·3	8 52·3	1·1 0·7	7·1 4·4	13·1 8·2
12	9 03·0	9 04·5	8 38·3	1·2 0·7	7·2 4·4	13·2 8·0	12	9 18·0	9 19·5	8 52·6	1·2 0·8	7·2 4·5	13·2 8·3
13	9 03·3	9 04·7	8 38·5	1·3 0·8	7·3 4·4	13·3 8·1	13	9 18·3	9 19·8	8 52·8	1·3 0·8	7·3 4·6	13·3 8·3
14	9 03·5	9 05·0	8 38·7	1·4 0·9	7·4 4·5	13·4 8·2	14	9 18·5	9 20·0	8 53·1	1·4 0·9	7·4 4·6	13·4 8·4
15	9 03·8	9 05·2	8 39·0	1·5 0·9	7·5 4·6	13·5 8·2	15	9 18·8	9 20·3	8 53·3	1·5 0·9	7·5 4·7	13·5 8·4
16	9 04·0	9 05·5	8 39·2	1·6 1·0	7·6 4·6	13·6 8·3	16	9 19·0	9 20·5	8 53·5	1·6 1·0	7·6 4·8	13·6 8·5
17	9 04·3	9 05·7	8 39·5	1·7 1·0	7·7 4·7	13·7 8·3	17	9 19·3	9 20·8	8 53·8	1·7 1·1	7·7 4·8	13·7 8·6
18	9 04·5	9 06·0	8 39·7	1·8 1·1	7·8 4·7	13·8 8·4	18	9 19·5	9 21·0	8 54·0	1·8 1·1	7·8 4·9	13·8 8·6
19	9 04·8	9 06·2	8 39·9	1·9 1·2	7·9 4·8	13·9 8·5	19	9 19·8	9 21·3	8 54·3	1·9 1·2	7·9 4·9	13·9 8·7
20	9 05·0	9 06·5	8 40·2	2·0 1·2	8·0 4·9	14·0 8·5	20	9 20·0	9 21·5	8 54·5	2·0 1·3	8·0 5·0	14·0 8·8
21	9 05·3	9 06·7	8 40·4	2·1 1·3	8·1 4·9	14·1 8·6	21	9 20·3	9 21·8	8 54·7	2·1 1·3	8·1 5·1	14·1 8·8
22	9 05·5	9 07·0	8 40·6	2·2 1·3	8·2 5·0	14·2 8·6	22	9 20·5	9 22·0	8 55·0	2·2 1·4	8·2 5·1	14·2 8·9
23	9 05·8	9 07·2	8 40·9	2·3 1·4	8·3 5·0	14·3 8·7	23	9 20·8	9 22·3	8 55·2	2·3 1·4	8·3 5·2	14·3 8·9
24	9 06·0	9 07·5	8 41·1	2·4 1·5	8·4 5·1	14·4 8·8	24	9 21·0	9 22·5	8 55·4	2·4 1·5	8·4 5·3	14·4 9·0
25	9 06·3	9 07·7	8 41·4	2·5 1·5	8·5 5·2	14·5 8·8	25	9 21·3	9 22·8	8 55·7	2·5 1·6	8·5 5·3	14·5 9·1
26	9 06·5	9 08·0	8 41·6	2·6 1·6	8·6 5·2	14·6 8·9	26	9 21·5	9 23·0	8 55·9	2·6 1·6	8·6 5·4	14·6 9·1
27	9 06·8	9 08·2	8 41·8	2·7 1·6	8·7 5·3	14·7 8·9	27	9 21·8	9 23·3	8 56·2	2·7 1·7	8·7 5·4	14·7 9·2
28	9 07·0	9 08·5	8 42·1	2·8 1·7	8·8 5·4	14·8 9·0	28	9 22·0	9 23·5	8 56·4	2·8 1·8	8·8 5·5	14·8 9·3
29	9 07·3	9 08·7	8 42·3	2·9 1·8	8·9 5·4	14·9 9·1	29	9 22·3	9 23·8	8 56·6	2·9 1·8	8·9 5·6	14·9 9·3
30	9 07·5	9 09·0	8 42·6	3·0 1·8	9·0 5·5	15·0 9·1	30	9 22·5	9 24·0	8 56·9	3·0 1·9	9·0 5·6	15·0 9·4
31	9 07·8	9 09·2	8 42·8	3·1 1·9	9·1 5·5	15·1 9·2	31	9 22·8	9 24·3	8 57·1	3·1 1·9	9·1 5·7	15·1 9·4
32	9 08·0	9 09·5	8 43·0	3·2 1·9	9·2 5·6	15·2 9·2	32	9 23·0	9 24·5	8 57·4	3·2 2·0	9·2 5·8	15·2 9·5
33	9 08·3	9 09·8	8 43·3	3·3 2·0	9·3 5·7	15·3 9·3	33	9 23·3	9 24·8	8 57·6	3·3 2·1	9·3 5·8	15·3 9·6
34	9 08·5	9 10·0	8 43·5	3·4 2·1	9·4 5·7	15·4 9·4	34	9 23·5	9 25·0	8 57·8	3·4 2·1	9·4 5·9	15·4 9·6
35	9 08·8	9 10·3	8 43·8	3·5 2·1	9·5 5·8	15·5 9·4	35	9 23·8	9 25·3	8 58·1	3·5 2·2	9·5 5·9	15·5 9·7
36	9 09·0	9 10·5	8 44·0	3·6 2·2	9·6 5·8	15·6 9·5	36	9 24·0	9 25·5	8 58·3	3·6 2·3	9·6 6·0	15·6 9·8
37	9 09·3	9 10·8	8 44·2	3·7 2·3	9·7 5·9	15·7 9·6	37	9 24·3	9 25·8	8 58·5	3·7 2·3	9·7 6·1	15·7 9·8
38	9 09·5	9 11·0	8 44·5	3·8 2·3	9·8 6·0	15·8 9·6	38	9 24·5	9 26·0	8 58·8	3·8 2·4	9·8 6·1	15·8 9·9
39	9 09·8	9 11·3	8 44·7	3·9 2·4	9·9 6·0	15·9 9·7	39	9 24·8	9 26·3	8 59·0	3·9 2·4	9·9 6·2	15·9 9·9
40	9 10·0	9 11·5	8 44·9	4·0 2·4	10·0 6·1	16·0 9·7	40	9 25·0	9 26·5	8 59·3	4·0 2·5	10·0 6·3	16·0 10·0
41	9 10·3	9 11·8	8 45·2	4·1 2·5	10·1 6·1	16·1 9·8	41	9 25·3	9 26·8	8 59·5	4·1 2·6	10·1 6·3	16·1 10·1
42	9 10·5	9 12·0	8 45·4	4·2 2·6	10·2 6·2	16·2 9·9	42	9 25·5	9 27·0	8 59·7	4·2 2·6	10·2 6·4	16·2 10·1
43	9 10·8	9 12·3	8 45·7	4·3 2·6	10·3 6·3	16·3 9·9	43	9 25·8	9 27·3	9 00·0	4·3 2·7	10·3 6·4	16·3 10·2
44	9 11·0	9 12·5	8 45·9	4·4 2·7	10·4 6·3	16·4 10·0	44	9 26·0	9 27·5	9 00·2	4·4 2·8	10·4 6·5	16·4 10·3
45	9 11·3	9 12·8	8 46·1	4·5 2·7	10·5 6·4	16·5 10·0	45	9 26·3	9 27·8	9 00·5	4·5 2·8	10·5 6·6	16·5 10·3
46	9 11·5	9 13·0	8 46·4	4·6 2·8	10·6 6·4	16·6 10·1	46	9 26·5	9 28·1	9 00·7	4·6 2·9	10·6 6·6	16·6 10·4
47	9 11·8	9 13·3	8 46·6	4·7 2·9	10·7 6·5	16·7 10·2	47	9 26·8	9 28·3	9 00·9	4·7 2·9	10·7 6·7	16·7 10·4
48	9 12·0	9 13·5	8 46·9	4·8 2·9	10·8 6·6	16·8 10·2	48	9 27·0	9 28·6	9 01·2	4·8 3·0	10·8 6·8	16·8 10·5
49	9 12·3	9 13·8	8 47·1	4·9 3·0	10·9 6·6	16·9 10·3	49	9 27·3	9 28·8	9 01·4	4·9 3·1	10·9 6·8	16·9 10·6
50	9 12·5	9 14·0	8 47·3	5·0 3·0	11·0 6·7	17·0 10·3	50	9 27·5	9 29·1	9 01·6	5·0 3·1	11·0 6·9	17·0 10·6
51	9 12·8	9 14·3	8 47·6	5·1 3·1	11·1 6·8	17·1 10·4	51	9 27·8	9 29·3	9 01·9	5·1 3·2	11·1 6·9	17·1 10·7
52	9 13·0	9 14·5	8 47·8	5·2 3·2	11·2 6·8	17·2 10·5	52	9 28·0	9 29·6	9 02·1	5·2 3·3	11·2 7·0	17·2 10·8
53	9 13·3	9 14·8	8 48·0	5·3 3·2	11·3 6·9	17·3 10·5	53	9 28·3	9 29·8	9 02·4	5·3 3·3	11·3 7·1	17·3 10·8
54	9 13·5	9 15·0	8 48·3	5·4 3·3	11·4 6·9	17·4 10·6	54	9 28·5	9 30·1	9 02·6	5·4 3·4	11·4 7·1	17·4 10·9
55	9 13·8	9 15·3	8 48·5	5·5 3·3	11·5 7·0	17·5 10·6	55	9 28·8	9 30·3	9 02·8	5·5 3·4	11·5 7·2	17·5 10·9
56	9 14·0	9 15·5	8 48·8	5·6 3·4	11·6 7·1	17·6 10·7	56	9 29·0	9 30·6	9 03·1	5·6 3·5	11·6 7·3	17·6 11·0
57	9 14·3	9 15·8	8 49·0	5·7 3·5	11·7 7·1	17·7 10·8	57	9 29·3	9 30·8	9 03·3	5·7 3·6	11·7 7·3	17·7 11·1
58	9 14·5	9 16·0	8 49·2	5·8 3·5	11·8 7·2	17·8 10·8	58	9 29·5	9 31·1	9 03·6	5·8 3·6	11·8 7·4	17·8 11·1
59	9 14·8	9 16·3	8 49·5	5·9 3·6	11·9 7·2	17·9 10·9	59	9 29·8	9 31·3	9 03·8	5·9 3·7	11·9 7·4	17·9 11·2
60	9 15·0	9 16·5	8 49·7	6·0 3·7	12·0 7·3	18·0 11·0	60	9 30·0	9 31·6	9 04·0	6·0 3·8	12·0 7·5	18·0 11·3

xx

38ᵐ	SUN PLANETS	ARIES	MOON	v or Corrⁿ d		v or Corrⁿ d		v or Corrⁿ d	
s	° ′	° ′	° ′	′	′	′	′	′	′
00	9 30.0	9 31.6	9 04.0	0.0	0.0	6.0	3.9	12.0	7.7
01	9 30.3	9 31.8	9 04.3	0.1	0.1	6.1	3.9	12.1	7.8
02	9 30.5	9 32.1	9 04.5	0.2	0.1	6.2	4.0	12.2	7.8
03	9 30.8	9 32.3	9 04.7	0.3	0.2	6.3	4.0	12.3	7.9
04	9 31.0	9 32.6	9 05.0	0.4	0.3	6.4	4.1	12.4	8.0
05	9 31.3	9 32.8	9 05.2	0.5	0.3	6.5	4.2	12.5	8.0
06	9 31.5	9 33.1	9 05.5	0.6	0.4	6.6	4.2	12.6	8.1
07	9 31.8	9 33.3	9 05.7	0.7	0.4	6.7	4.3	12.7	8.1
08	9 32.0	9 33.6	9 05.9	0.8	0.5	6.8	4.4	12.8	8.2
09	9 32.3	9 33.8	9 06.2	0.9	0.6	6.9	4.4	12.9	8.3
10	9 32.5	9 34.1	9 06.4	1.0	0.6	7.0	4.5	13.0	8.3
11	9 32.8	9 34.3	9 06.7	1.1	0.7	7.1	4.6	13.1	8.4
12	9 33.0	9 34.6	9 06.9	1.2	0.8	7.2	4.6	13.2	8.5
13	9 33.3	9 34.8	9 07.1	1.3	0.8	7.3	4.7	13.3	8.5
14	9 33.5	9 35.1	9 07.4	1.4	0.9	7.4	4.7	13.4	8.6
15	9 33.8	9 35.3	9 07.6	1.5	1.0	7.5	4.8	13.5	8.7
16	9 34.0	9 35.6	9 07.9	1.6	1.0	7.6	4.9	13.6	8.7
17	9 34.3	9 35.8	9 08.1	1.7	1.1	7.7	4.9	13.7	8.8
18	9 34.5	9 36.1	9 08.3	1.8	1.2	7.8	5.0	13.8	8.9
19	9 34.8	9 36.3	9 08.6	1.9	1.2	7.9	5.1	13.9	8.9
20	9 35.0	9 36.6	9 08.8	2.0	1.3	8.0	5.1	14.0	9.0
21	9 35.3	9 36.8	9 09.0	2.1	1.3	8.1	5.2	14.1	9.0
22	9 35.5	9 37.1	9 09.3	2.2	1.4	8.2	5.3	14.2	9.1
23	9 35.8	9 37.3	9 09.5	2.3	1.5	8.3	5.3	14.3	9.2
24	9 36.0	9 37.6	9 09.8	2.4	1.5	8.4	5.4	14.4	9.2
25	9 36.3	9 37.8	9 10.0	2.5	1.6	8.5	5.5	14.5	9.3
26	9 36.5	9 38.1	9 10.2	2.6	1.7	8.6	5.5	14.6	9.4
27	9 36.8	9 38.3	9 10.5	2.7	1.7	8.7	5.6	14.7	9.4
28	9 37.0	9 38.6	9 10.7	2.8	1.8	8.8	5.6	14.8	9.5
29	9 37.3	9 38.8	9 11.0	2.9	1.9	8.9	5.7	14.9	9.6
30	9 37.5	9 39.1	9 11.2	3.0	1.9	9.0	5.8	15.0	9.6
31	9 37.8	9 39.3	9 11.4	3.1	2.0	9.1	5.8	15.1	9.7
32	9 38.0	9 39.6	9 11.7	3.2	2.1	9.2	5.9	15.2	9.8
33	9 38.3	9 39.8	9 11.9	3.3	2.1	9.3	6.0	15.3	9.8
34	9 38.5	9 40.1	9 12.1	3.4	2.2	9.4	6.0	15.4	9.9
35	9 38.8	9 40.3	9 12.4	3.5	2.2	9.5	6.1	15.5	9.9
36	9 39.0	9 40.6	9 12.6	3.6	2.3	9.6	6.2	15.6	10.0
37	9 39.3	9 40.8	9 12.9	3.7	2.4	9.7	6.2	15.7	10.1
38	9 39.5	9 41.1	9 13.1	3.8	2.4	9.8	6.3	15.8	10.1
39	9 39.8	9 41.3	9 13.3	3.9	2.5	9.9	6.4	15.9	10.2
40	9 40.0	9 41.6	9 13.6	4.0	2.6	10.0	6.4	16.0	10.3
41	9 40.3	9 41.8	9 13.8	4.1	2.6	10.1	6.5	16.1	10.3
42	9 40.5	9 42.1	9 14.1	4.2	2.7	10.2	6.5	16.2	10.4
43	9 40.8	9 42.3	9 14.3	4.3	2.8	10.3	6.6	16.3	10.5
44	9 41.0	9 42.6	9 14.5	4.4	2.8	10.4	6.7	16.4	10.5
45	9 41.3	9 42.8	9 14.8	4.5	2.9	10.5	6.7	16.5	10.6
46	9 41.5	9 43.1	9 15.0	4.6	3.0	10.6	6.8	16.6	10.7
47	9 41.8	9 43.3	9 15.2	4.7	3.0	10.7	6.9	16.7	10.7
48	9 42.0	9 43.6	9 15.5	4.8	3.1	10.8	6.9	16.8	10.8
49	9 42.3	9 43.8	9 15.7	4.9	3.1	10.9	7.0	16.9	10.8
50	9 42.5	9 44.1	9 16.0	5.0	3.2	11.0	7.1	17.0	10.9
51	9 42.8	9 44.3	9 16.2	5.1	3.3	11.1	7.1	17.1	11.0
52	9 43.0	9 44.6	9 16.4	5.2	3.3	11.2	7.2	17.2	11.0
53	9 43.3	9 44.8	9 16.7	5.3	3.4	11.3	7.3	17.3	11.1
54	9 43.5	9 45.1	9 16.9	5.4	3.5	11.4	7.3	17.4	11.2
55	9 43.8	9 45.3	9 17.2	5.5	3.5	11.5	7.4	17.5	11.2
56	9 44.0	9 45.6	9 17.4	5.6	3.6	11.6	7.4	17.6	11.3
57	9 44.3	9 45.8	9 17.6	5.7	3.7	11.7	7.5	17.7	11.4
58	9 44.5	9 46.1	9 17.9	5.8	3.7	11.8	7.6	17.8	11.4
59	9 44.8	9 46.4	9 18.1	5.9	3.8	11.9	7.6	17.9	11.5
60	9 45.0	9 46.6	9 18.4	6.0	3.9	12.0	7.7	18.0	11.6

39ᵐ	SUN PLANETS	ARIES	MOON	v or Corrⁿ d		v or Corrⁿ d		v or Corrⁿ d	
s	° ′	° ′	° ′	′	′	′	′	′	′
00	9 45.0	9 46.6	9 18.4	0.0	0.0	6.0	4.0	12.0	7.9
01	9 45.3	9 46.9	9 18.6	0.1	0.1	6.1	4.0	12.1	8.0
02	9 45.5	9 47.1	9 18.8	0.2	0.1	6.2	4.1	12.2	8.0
03	9 45.8	9 47.4	9 19.1	0.3	0.2	6.3	4.1	12.3	8.1
04	9 46.0	9 47.6	9 19.3	0.4	0.3	6.4	4.2	12.4	8.2
05	9 46.3	9 47.9	9 19.5	0.5	0.3	6.5	4.3	12.5	8.2
06	9 46.5	9 48.1	9 19.8	0.6	0.4	6.6	4.3	12.6	8.3
07	9 46.8	9 48.4	9 20.0	0.7	0.5	6.7	4.4	12.7	8.4
08	9 47.0	9 48.6	9 20.3	0.8	0.5	6.8	4.5	12.8	8.4
09	9 47.3	9 48.9	9 20.5	0.9	0.6	6.9	4.5	12.9	8.5
10	9 47.5	9 49.1	9 20.7	1.0	0.7	7.0	4.6	13.0	8.6
11	9 47.8	9 49.4	9 21.0	1.1	0.7	7.1	4.7	13.1	8.6
12	9 48.0	9 49.6	9 21.2	1.2	0.8	7.2	4.7	13.2	8.7
13	9 48.3	9 49.9	9 21.5	1.3	0.9	7.3	4.8	13.3	8.8
14	9 48.5	9 50.1	9 21.7	1.4	0.9	7.4	4.9	13.4	8.8
15	9 48.8	9 50.4	9 21.9	1.5	1.0	7.5	4.9	13.5	8.9
16	9 49.0	9 50.6	9 22.2	1.6	1.1	7.6	5.0	13.6	9.0
17	9 49.3	9 50.9	9 22.4	1.7	1.1	7.7	5.1	13.7	9.0
18	9 49.5	9 51.1	9 22.6	1.8	1.2	7.8	5.1	13.8	9.1
19	9 49.8	9 51.4	9 22.9	1.9	1.3	7.9	5.2	13.9	9.2
20	9 50.0	9 51.6	9 23.1	2.0	1.3	8.0	5.3	14.0	9.2
21	9 50.3	9 51.9	9 23.4	2.1	1.4	8.1	5.3	14.1	9.3
22	9 50.5	9 52.1	9 23.6	2.2	1.4	8.2	5.4	14.2	9.3
23	9 50.8	9 52.4	9 23.8	2.3	1.5	8.3	5.5	14.3	9.4
24	9 51.0	9 52.6	9 24.1	2.4	1.6	8.4	5.5	14.4	9.5
25	9 51.3	9 52.9	9 24.3	2.5	1.6	8.5	5.6	14.5	9.5
26	9 51.5	9 53.1	9 24.6	2.6	1.7	8.6	5.7	14.6	9.6
27	9 51.8	9 53.4	9 24.8	2.7	1.8	8.7	5.7	14.7	9.7
28	9 52.0	9 53.6	9 25.0	2.8	1.8	8.8	5.8	14.8	9.7
29	9 52.3	9 53.9	9 25.3	2.9	1.9	8.9	5.9	14.9	9.8
30	9 52.5	9 54.1	9 25.5	3.0	2.0	9.0	5.9	15.0	9.9
31	9 52.8	9 54.4	9 25.7	3.1	2.0	9.1	6.0	15.1	9.9
32	9 53.0	9 54.6	9 26.0	3.2	2.1	9.2	6.1	15.2	10.0
33	9 53.3	9 54.9	9 26.2	3.3	2.2	9.3	6.1	15.3	10.1
34	9 53.5	9 55.1	9 26.5	3.4	2.2	9.4	6.2	15.4	10.1
35	9 53.8	9 55.4	9 26.7	3.5	2.3	9.5	6.3	15.5	10.2
36	9 54.0	9 55.6	9 26.9	3.6	2.4	9.6	6.3	15.6	10.3
37	9 54.3	9 55.9	9 27.2	3.7	2.4	9.7	6.4	15.7	10.3
38	9 54.5	9 56.1	9 27.4	3.8	2.5	9.8	6.5	15.8	10.4
39	9 54.8	9 56.4	9 27.7	3.9	2.6	9.9	6.5	15.9	10.5
40	9 55.0	9 56.6	9 27.9	4.0	2.6	10.0	6.6	16.0	10.5
41	9 55.3	9 56.9	9 28.1	4.1	2.7	10.1	6.6	16.1	10.6
42	9 55.5	9 57.1	9 28.4	4.2	2.8	10.2	6.7	16.2	10.7
43	9 55.8	9 57.4	9 28.6	4.3	2.8	10.3	6.8	16.3	10.7
44	9 56.0	9 57.6	9 28.8	4.4	2.9	10.4	6.8	16.4	10.8
45	9 56.3	9 57.9	9 29.1	4.5	3.0	10.5	6.9	16.5	10.9
46	9 56.5	9 58.1	9 29.3	4.6	3.0	10.6	7.0	16.6	10.9
47	9 56.8	9 58.4	9 29.6	4.7	3.1	10.7	7.0	16.7	11.0
48	9 57.0	9 58.6	9 29.8	4.8	3.2	10.8	7.1	16.8	11.1
49	9 57.3	9 58.9	9 30.0	4.9	3.2	10.9	7.2	16.9	11.1
50	9 57.5	9 59.1	9 30.3	5.0	3.3	11.0	7.2	17.0	11.2
51	9 57.8	9 59.4	9 30.5	5.1	3.4	11.1	7.3	17.1	11.3
52	9 58.0	9 59.6	9 30.8	5.2	3.4	11.2	7.4	17.2	11.3
53	9 58.3	9 59.9	9 31.0	5.3	3.5	11.3	7.4	17.3	11.4
54	9 58.5	10 00.1	9 31.2	5.4	3.6	11.4	7.5	17.4	11.5
55	9 58.8	10 00.4	9 31.5	5.5	3.6	11.5	7.6	17.5	11.5
56	9 59.0	10 00.6	9 31.7	5.6	3.7	11.6	7.6	17.6	11.6
57	9 59.3	10 00.9	9 32.0	5.7	3.8	11.7	7.7	17.7	11.7
58	9 59.5	10 01.1	9 32.2	5.8	3.8	11.8	7.8	17.8	11.7
59	9 59.8	10 01.4	9 32.4	5.9	3.9	11.9	7.8	17.9	11.8
60	10 00.0	10 01.6	9 32.7	6.0	4.0	12.0	7.9	18.0	11.9

40 m	SUN PLANETS	ARIES	MOON	v or d Corr	v or d Corr	v or d Corr
s	° ′	° ′	° ′	′ ′	′ ′	′ ′
00	10 00·0	10 01·6	9 32·7	0·0 0·0	6·0 4·1	12·0 8·1
01	10 00·3	10 01·9	9 32·9	0·1 0·1	6·1 4·1	12·1 8·2
02	10 00·5	10 02·1	9 33·1	0·2 0·1	6·2 4·2	12·2 8·2
03	10 00·8	10 02·4	9 33·4	0·3 0·2	6·3 4·3	12·3 8·3
04	10 01·0	10 02·6	9 33·6	0·4 0·3	6·4 4·3	12·4 8·4
05	10 01·3	10 02·9	9 33·9	0·5 0·3	6·5 4·4	12·5 8·4
06	10 01·5	10 03·1	9 34·1	0·6 0·4	6·6 4·5	12·6 8·5
07	10 01·8	10 03·4	9 34·3	0·7 0·5	6·7 4·5	12·7 8·6
08	10 02·0	10 03·6	9 34·6	0·8 0·5	6·8 4·6	12·8 8·6
09	10 02·3	10 03·9	9 34·8	0·9 0·6	6·9 4·7	12·9 8·7
10	10 02·5	10 04·1	9 35·1	1·0 0·7	7·0 4·7	13·0 8·8
11	10 02·8	10 04·4	9 35·3	1·1 0·7	7·1 4·8	13·1 8·8
12	10 03·0	10 04·7	9 35·5	1·2 0·8	7·2 4·9	13·2 8·9
13	10 03·3	10 04·9	9 35·8	1·3 0·9	7·3 4·9	13·3 9·0
14	10 03·5	10 05·2	9 36·0	1·4 0·9	7·4 5·0	13·4 9·0
15	10 03·8	10 05·4	9 36·2	1·5 1·0	7·5 5·1	13·5 9·1
16	10 04·0	10 05·7	9 36·5	1·6 1·1	7·6 5·1	13·6 9·2
17	10 04·3	10 05·9	9 36·7	1·7 1·1	7·7 5·2	13·7 9·2
18	10 04·5	10 06·2	9 37·0	1·8 1·2	7·8 5·3	13·8 9·3
19	10 04·8	10 06·4	9 37·2	1·9 1·3	7·9 5·3	13·9 9·4
20	10 05·0	10 06·7	9 37·4	2·0 1·4	8·0 5·4	14·0 9·5
21	10 05·3	10 06·9	9 37·7	2·1 1·4	8·1 5·5	14·1 9·5
22	10 05·5	10 07·2	9 37·9	2·2 1·5	8·2 5·5	14·2 9·6
23	10 05·8	10 07·4	9 38·2	2·3 1·6	8·3 5·6	14·3 9·7
24	10 06·0	10 07·7	9 38·4	2·4 1·6	8·4 5·7	14·4 9·7
25	10 06·3	10 07·9	9 38·6	2·5 1·7	8·5 5·7	14·5 9·8
26	10 06·5	10 08·2	9 38·9	2·6 1·8	8·6 5·8	14·6 9·9
27	10 06·8	10 08·4	9 39·1	2·7 1·8	8·7 5·9	14·7 9·9
28	10 07·0	10 08·7	9 39·3	2·8 1·9	8·8 5·9	14·8 10·0
29	10 07·3	10 08·9	9 39·6	2·9 2·0	8·9 6·0	14·9 10·1
30	10 07·5	10 09·2	9 39·8	3·0 2·0	9·0 6·1	15·0 10·1
31	10 07·8	10 09·4	9 40·1	3·1 2·1	9·1 6·1	15·1 10·2
32	10 08·0	10 09·7	9 40·3	3·2 2·2	9·2 6·2	15·2 10·3
33	10 08·3	10 09·9	9 40·5	3·3 2·2	9·3 6·3	15·3 10·3
34	10 08·5	10 10·2	9 40·8	3·4 2·3	9·4 6·3	15·4 10·4
35	10 08·8	10 10·4	9 41·0	3·5 2·4	9·5 6·4	15·5 10·5
36	10 09·0	10 10·7	9 41·3	3·6 2·4	9·6 6·5	15·6 10·5
37	10 09·3	10 10·9	9 41·5	3·7 2·5	9·7 6·5	15·7 10·6
38	10 09·5	10 11·2	9 41·7	3·8 2·6	9·8 6·6	15·8 10·7
39	10 09·8	10 11·4	9 42·0	3·9 2·6	9·9 6·7	15·9 10·7
40	10 10·0	10 11·7	9 42·2	4·0 2·7	10·0 6·8	16·0 10·8
41	10 10·3	10 11·9	9 42·4	4·1 2·8	10·1 6·8	16·1 10·9
42	10 10·5	10 12·2	9 42·7	4·2 2·8	10·2 6·9	16·2 10·9
43	10 10·8	10 12·4	9 42·9	4·3 2·9	10·3 7·0	16·3 11·0
44	10 11·0	10 12·7	9 43·2	4·4 3·0	10·4 7·0	16·4 11·1
45	10 11·3	10 12·9	9 43·4	4·5 3·0	10·5 7·1	16·5 11·1
46	10 11·5	10 13·2	9 43·6	4·6 3·1	10·6 7·2	16·6 11·2
47	10 11·8	10 13·4	9 43·9	4·7 3·2	10·7 7·2	16·7 11·3
48	10 12·0	10 13·7	9 44·1	4·8 3·2	10·8 7·3	16·8 11·3
49	10 12·3	10 13·9	9 44·4	4·9 3·3	10·9 7·4	16·9 11·4
50	10 12·5	10 14·2	9 44·6	5·0 3·4	11·0 7·4	17·0 11·5
51	10 12·8	10 14·4	9 44·8	5·1 3·4	11·1 7·5	17·1 11·5
52	10 13·0	10 14·7	9 45·1	5·2 3·5	11·2 7·6	17·2 11·6
53	10 13·3	10 14·9	9 45·3	5·3 3·6	11·3 7·6	17·3 11·7
54	10 13·5	10 15·2	9 45·6	5·4 3·6	11·4 7·7	17·4 11·7
55	10 13·8	10 15·4	9 45·8	5·5 3·7	11·5 7·8	17·5 11·8
56	10 14·0	10 15·7	9 46·0	5·6 3·8	11·6 7·8	17·6 11·9
57	10 14·3	10 15·9	9 46·3	5·7 3·8	11·7 7·9	17·7 11·9
58	10 14·5	10 16·2	9 46·5	5·8 3·9	11·8 8·0	17·8 12·0
59	10 14·8	10 16·4	9 46·7	5·9 4·0	11·9 8·0	17·9 12·1
60	10 15·0	10 16·7	9 47·0	6·0 4·1	12·0 8·1	18·0 12·2

41 m	SUN PLANETS	ARIES	MOON	v or d Corr	v or d Corr	v or d Corr
s	° ′	° ′	° ′	′ ′	′ ′	′ ′
00	10 15·0	10 16·7	9 47·0	0·0 0·0	6·0 4·2	12·0 8·3
01	10 15·3	10 16·9	9 47·2	0·1 0·1	6·1 4·2	12·1 8·4
02	10 15·5	10 17·2	9 47·5	0·2 0·1	6·2 4·3	12·2 8·4
03	10 15·8	10 17·4	9 47·7	0·3 0·2	6·3 4·4	12·3 8·5
04	10 16·0	10 17·7	9 47·9	0·4 0·3	6·4 4·4	12·4 8·6
05	10 16·3	10 17·9	9 48·2	0·5 0·3	6·5 4·5	12·5 8·6
06	10 16·5	10 18·2	9 48·4	0·6 0·4	6·6 4·6	12·6 8·7
07	10 16·8	10 18·4	9 48·7	0·7 0·5	6·7 4·6	12·7 8·8
08	10 17·0	10 18·7	9 48·9	0·8 0·6	6·8 4·7	12·8 8·9
09	10 17·3	10 18·9	9 49·1	0·9 0·6	6·9 4·8	12·9 8·9
10	10 17·5	10 19·2	9 49·4	1·0 0·7	7·0 4·8	13·0 9·0
11	10 17·8	10 19·4	9 49·6	1·1 0·8	7·1 4·9	13·1 9·1
12	10 18·0	10 19·7	9 49·8	1·2 0·8	7·2 5·0	13·2 9·1
13	10 18·3	10 19·9	9 50·1	1·3 0·9	7·3 5·0	13·3 9·2
14	10 18·5	10 20·2	9 50·3	1·4 1·0	7·4 5·1	13·4 9·3
15	10 18·8	10 20·4	9 50·6	1·5 1·0	7·5 5·2	13·5 9·3
16	10 19·0	10 20·7	9 50·8	1·6 1·1	7·6 5·3	13·6 9·4
17	10 19·3	10 20·9	9 51·0	1·7 1·2	7·7 5·3	13·7 9·5
18	10 19·5	10 21·2	9 51·3	1·8 1·2	7·8 5·4	13·8 9·5
19	10 19·8	10 21·4	9 51·5	1·9 1·3	7·9 5·5	13·9 9·6
20	10 20·0	10 21·7	9 51·8	2·0 1·4	8·0 5·5	14·0 9·7
21	10 20·3	10 21·9	9 52·0	2·1 1·5	8·1 5·6	14·1 9·8
22	10 20·5	10 22·2	9 52·2	2·2 1·5	8·2 5·7	14·2 9·8
23	10 20·8	10 22·4	9 52·5	2·3 1·6	8·3 5·7	14·3 9·9
24	10 21·0	10 22·7	9 52·7	2·4 1·7	8·4 5·8	14·4 10·0
25	10 21·3	10 23·0	9 52·9	2·5 1·7	8·5 5·9	14·5 10·0
26	10 21·5	10 23·2	9 53·2	2·6 1·8	8·6 5·9	14·6 10·1
27	10 21·8	10 23·5	9 53·4	2·7 1·9	8·7 6·0	14·7 10·2
28	10 22·0	10 23·7	9 53·7	2·8 1·9	8·8 6·1	14·8 10·2
29	10 22·3	10 24·0	9 53·9	2·9 2·0	8·9 6·2	14·9 10·3
30	10 22·5	10 24·2	9 54·1	3·0 2·1	9·0 6·2	15·0 10·4
31	10 22·8	10 24·5	9 54·4	3·1 2·1	9·1 6·3	15·1 10·4
32	10 23·0	10 24·7	9 54·6	3·2 2·2	9·2 6·4	15·2 10·5
33	10 23·3	10 25·0	9 54·9	3·3 2·3	9·3 6·4	15·3 10·6
34	10 23·5	10 25·2	9 55·1	3·4 2·4	9·4 6·5	15·4 10·6
35	10 23·8	10 25·5	9 55·3	3·5 2·4	9·5 6·6	15·5 10·7
36	10 24·0	10 25·7	9 55·6	3·6 2·5	9·6 6·6	15·6 10·8
37	10 24·3	10 26·0	9 55·8	3·7 2·6	9·7 6·7	15·7 10·9
38	10 24·5	10 26·2	9 56·1	3·8 2·6	9·8 6·8	15·8 10·9
39	10 24·8	10 26·5	9 56·3	3·9 2·7	9·9 6·8	15·9 11·0
40	10 25·0	10 26·7	9 56·5	4·0 2·8	10·0 6·9	16·0 11·1
41	10 25·3	10 27·0	9 56·8	4·1 2·8	10·1 7·0	16·1 11·1
42	10 25·5	10 27·2	9 57·0	4·2 2·9	10·2 7·1	16·2 11·2
43	10 25·8	10 27·5	9 57·2	4·3 3·0	10·3 7·1	16·3 11·3
44	10 26·0	10 27·7	9 57·5	4·4 3·0	10·4 7·2	16·4 11·3
45	10 26·3	10 28·0	9 57·7	4·5 3·1	10·5 7·3	16·5 11·4
46	10 26·5	10 28·2	9 58·0	4·6 3·2	10·6 7·3	16·6 11·5
47	10 26·8	10 28·5	9 58·2	4·7 3·3	10·7 7·4	16·7 11·6
48	10 27·0	10 28·7	9 58·4	4·8 3·3	10·8 7·5	16·8 11·6
49	10 27·3	10 29·0	9 58·7	4·9 3·4	10·9 7·5	16·9 11·7
50	10 27·5	10 29·2	9 58·9	5·0 3·5	11·0 7·6	17·0 11·8
51	10 27·8	10 29·5	9 59·2	5·1 3·5	11·1 7·7	17·1 11·8
52	10 28·0	10 29·7	9 59·4	5·2 3·6	11·2 7·7	17·2 11·9
53	10 28·3	10 30·0	9 59·6	5·3 3·7	11·3 7·8	17·3 12·0
54	10 28·5	10 30·2	9 59·9	5·4 3·7	11·4 7·9	17·4 12·0
55	10 28·8	10 30·5	10 00·1	5·5 3·8	11·5 8·0	17·5 12·1
56	10 29·0	10 30·7	10 00·3	5·6 3·9	11·6 8·0	17·6 12·2
57	10 29·3	10 31·0	10 00·6	5·7 3·9	11·7 8·1	17·7 12·2
58	10 29·5	10 31·2	10 00·8	5·8 4·0	11·8 8·2	17·8 12·3
59	10 29·8	10 31·5	10 01·1	5·9 4·1	11·9 8·2	17·9 12·4
60	10 30·0	10 31·7	10 01·3	6·0 4·2	12·0 8·3	18·0 12·5

xxii

42ᵐ

m 42 / s	SUN PLANETS	ARIES	MOON	v or Corrⁿ d		v or Corrⁿ d		v or Corrⁿ d	
00	10 30·0	10 31·7	10 01·3	0·0	0·0	6·0	4·3	12·0	8·5
01	10 30·3	10 32·0	10 01·5	0·1	0·1	6·1	4·3	12·1	8·6
02	10 30·5	10 32·2	10 01·8	0·2	0·1	6·2	4·4	12·2	8·6
03	10 30·8	10 32·5	10 02·0	0·3	0·2	6·3	4·5	12·3	8·7
04	10 31·0	10 32·7	10 02·3	0·4	0·3	6·4	4·5	12·4	8·8
05	10 31·3	10 33·0	10 02·5	0·5	0·4	6·5	4·6	12·5	8·9
06	10 31·5	10 33·2	10 02·7	0·6	0·4	6·6	4·7	12·6	8·9
07	10 31·8	10 33·5	10 03·0	0·7	0·5	6·7	4·7	12·7	9·0
08	10 32·0	10 33·7	10 03·2	0·8	0·6	6·8	4·8	12·8	9·1
09	10 32·3	10 34·0	10 03·4	0·9	0·6	6·9	4·9	12·9	9·1
10	10 32·5	10 34·2	10 03·7	1·0	0·7	7·0	5·0	13·0	9·2
11	10 32·8	10 34·5	10 03·9	1·1	0·8	7·1	5·0	13·1	9·3
12	10 33·0	10 34·7	10 04·2	1·2	0·9	7·2	5·1	13·2	9·4
13	10 33·3	10 35·0	10 04·4	1·3	0·9	7·3	5·2	13·3	9·4
14	10 33·5	10 35·2	10 04·6	1·4	1·0	7·4	5·2	13·4	9·5
15	10 33·8	10 35·5	10 04·9	1·5	1·1	7·5	5·3	13·5	9·6
16	10 34·0	10 35·7	10 05·1	1·6	1·1	7·6	5·4	13·6	9·6
17	10 34·3	10 36·0	10 05·4	1·7	1·2	7·7	5·5	13·7	9·7
18	10 34·5	10 36·2	10 05·6	1·8	1·3	7·8	5·5	13·8	9·8
19	10 34·8	10 36·5	10 05·8	1·9	1·3	7·9	5·6	13·9	9·8
20	10 35·0	10 36·7	10 06·1	2·0	1·4	8·0	5·7	14·0	9·9
21	10 35·3	10 37·0	10 06·3	2·1	1·5	8·1	5·7	14·1	10·0
22	10 35·5	10 37·2	10 06·5	2·2	1·6	8·2	5·8	14·2	10·1
23	10 35·8	10 37·5	10 06·8	2·3	1·6	8·3	5·9	14·3	10·1
24	10 36·0	10 37·7	10 07·0	2·4	1·7	8·4	6·0	14·4	10·2
25	10 36·3	10 38·0	10 07·3	2·5	1·8	8·5	6·0	14·5	10·3
26	10 36·5	10 38·2	10 07·5	2·6	1·8	8·6	6·1	14·6	10·3
27	10 36·8	10 38·5	10 07·7	2·7	1·9	8·7	6·2	14·7	10·4
28	10 37·0	10 38·7	10 08·0	2·8	2·0	8·8	6·2	14·8	10·5
29	10 37·3	10 39·0	10 08·2	2·9	2·1	8·9	6·3	14·9	10·6
30	10 37·5	10 39·2	10 08·5	3·0	2·1	9·0	6·4	15·0	10·6
31	10 37·8	10 39·5	10 08·7	3·1	2·2	9·1	6·4	15·1	10·7
32	10 38·0	10 39·7	10 08·9	3·2	2·3	9·2	6·5	15·2	10·8
33	10 38·3	10 40·0	10 09·2	3·3	2·3	9·3	6·6	15·3	10·8
34	10 38·5	10 40·2	10 09·4	3·4	2·4	9·4	6·7	15·4	10·9
35	10 38·8	10 40·5	10 09·7	3·5	2·5	9·5	6·7	15·5	11·0
36	10 39·0	10 40·7	10 09·9	3·6	2·6	9·6	6·8	15·6	11·1
37	10 39·3	10 41·0	10 10·1	3·7	2·6	9·7	6·9	15·7	11·1
38	10 39·5	10 41·3	10 10·4	3·8	2·7	9·8	6·9	15·8	11·2
39	10 39·8	10 41·5	10 10·6	3·9	2·8	9·9	7·0	15·9	11·3
40	10 40·0	10 41·8	10 10·8	4·0	2·8	10·0	7·1	16·0	11·3
41	10 40·3	10 42·0	10 11·1	4·1	2·9	10·1	7·2	16·1	11·4
42	10 40·5	10 42·3	10 11·3	4·2	3·0	10·2	7·2	16·2	11·5
43	10 40·8	10 42·5	10 11·6	4·3	3·0	10·3	7·3	16·3	11·5
44	10 41·0	10 42·8	10 11·8	4·4	3·1	10·4	7·4	16·4	11·6
45	10 41·3	10 43·0	10 12·0	4·5	3·2	10·5	7·4	16·5	11·7
46	10 41·5	10 43·3	10 12·3	4·6	3·3	10·6	7·5	16·6	11·8
47	10 41·8	10 43·5	10 12·5	4·7	3·3	10·7	7·6	16·7	11·8
48	10 42·0	10 43·8	10 12·8	4·8	3·4	10·8	7·7	16·8	11·9
49	10 42·3	10 44·0	10 13·0	4·9	3·5	10·9	7·7	16·9	12·0
50	10 42·5	10 44·3	10 13·2	5·0	3·5	11·0	7·8	17·0	12·0
51	10 42·8	10 44·5	10 13·5	5·1	3·6	11·1	7·9	17·1	12·1
52	10 43·0	10 44·8	10 13·7	5·2	3·7	11·2	7·9	17·2	12·2
53	10 43·3	10 45·0	10 13·9	5·3	3·8	11·3	8·0	17·3	12·3
54	10 43·5	10 45·3	10 14·2	5·4	3·8	11·4	8·1	17·4	12·3
55	10 43·8	10 45·5	10 14·4	5·5	3·9	11·5	8·1	17·5	12·4
56	10 44·0	10 45·8	10 14·7	5·6	4·0	11·6	8·2	17·6	12·5
57	10 44·3	10 46·0	10 14·9	5·7	4·0	11·7	8·3	17·7	12·5
58	10 44·5	10 46·3	10 15·1	5·8	4·1	11·8	8·4	17·8	12·6
59	10 44·8	10 46·5	10 15·4	5·9	4·2	11·9	8·4	17·9	12·7
60	10 45·0	10 46·8	10 15·6	6·0	4·3	12·0	8·5	18·0	12·8

43ᵐ

m 43 / s	SUN PLANETS	ARIES	MOON	v or Corrⁿ d		v or Corrⁿ d		v or Corrⁿ d	
00	10 45·0	10 46·8	10 15·6	0·0	0·0	6·0	4·4	12·0	8·7
01	10 45·3	10 47·0	10 15·9	0·1	0·1	6·1	4·4	12·1	8·8
02	10 45·5	10 47·3	10 16·1	0·2	0·1	6·2	4·5	12·2	8·8
03	10 45·8	10 47·5	10 16·3	0·3	0·2	6·3	4·6	12·3	8·9
04	10 46·0	10 47·8	10 16·6	0·4	0·3	6·4	4·6	12·4	9·0
05	10 46·3	10 48·0	10 16·8	0·5	0·4	6·5	4·7	12·5	9·1
06	10 46·5	10 48·3	10 17·0	0·6	0·4	6·6	4·8	12·6	9·1
07	10 46·8	10 48·5	10 17·3	0·7	0·5	6·7	4·9	12·7	9·2
08	10 47·0	10 48·8	10 17·5	0·8	0·6	6·8	4·9	12·8	9·3
09	10 47·3	10 49·0	10 17·8	0·9	0·7	6·9	5·0	12·9	9·4
10	10 47·5	10 49·3	10 18·0	1·0	0·7	7·0	5·1	13·0	9·4
11	10 47·8	10 49·5	10 18·2	1·1	0·8	7·1	5·1	13·1	9·5
12	10 48·0	10 49·8	10 18·5	1·2	0·9	7·2	5·2	13·2	9·6
13	10 48·3	10 50·0	10 18·7	1·3	0·9	7·3	5·3	13·3	9·6
14	10 48·5	10 50·3	10 19·0	1·4	1·0	7·4	5·4	13·4	9·7
15	10 48·8	10 50·5	10 19·2	1·5	1·1	7·5	5·4	13·5	9·8
16	10 49·0	10 50·8	10 19·4	1·6	1·2	7·6	5·5	13·6	9·9
17	10 49·3	10 51·0	10 19·7	1·7	1·2	7·7	5·6	13·7	9·9
18	10 49·5	10 51·3	10 19·9	1·8	1·3	7·8	5·7	13·8	10·0
19	10 49·8	10 51·5	10 20·2	1·9	1·4	7·9	5·7	13·9	10·1
20	10 50·0	10 51·8	10 20·4	2·0	1·5	8·0	5·8	14·0	10·2
21	10 50·3	10 52·0	10 20·6	2·1	1·5	8·1	5·9	14·1	10·2
22	10 50·5	10 52·3	10 20·9	2·2	1·6	8·2	5·9	14·2	10·3
23	10 50·8	10 52·5	10 21·1	2·3	1·7	8·3	6·0	14·3	10·4
24	10 51·0	10 52·8	10 21·3	2·4	1·7	8·4	6·1	14·4	10·4
25	10 51·3	10 53·0	10 21·6	2·5	1·8	8·5	6·2	14·5	10·5
26	10 51·5	10 53·3	10 21·8	2·6	1·9	8·6	6·2	14·6	10·6
27	10 51·8	10 53·5	10 22·1	2·7	2·0	8·7	6·3	14·7	10·7
28	10 52·0	10 53·8	10 22·3	2·8	2·0	8·8	6·4	14·8	10·7
29	10 52·3	10 54·0	10 22·5	2·9	2·1	8·9	6·5	14·9	10·8
30	10 52·5	10 54·3	10 22·8	3·0	2·2	9·0	6·5	15·0	10·9
31	10 52·8	10 54·5	10 23·0	3·1	2·2	9·1	6·6	15·1	10·9
32	10 53·0	10 54·8	10 23·3	3·2	2·3	9·2	6·7	15·2	11·0
33	10 53·3	10 55·0	10 23·5	3·3	2·4	9·3	6·7	15·3	11·1
34	10 53·5	10 55·3	10 23·7	3·4	2·5	9·4	6·8	15·4	11·2
35	10 53·8	10 55·5	10 24·0	3·5	2·5	9·5	6·9	15·5	11·2
36	10 54·0	10 55·8	10 24·2	3·6	2·6	9·6	7·0	15·6	11·3
37	10 54·3	10 56·0	10 24·4	3·7	2·7	9·7	7·0	15·7	11·4
38	10 54·5	10 56·3	10 24·7	3·8	2·8	9·8	7·1	15·8	11·5
39	10 54·8	10 56·5	10 24·9	3·9	2·8	9·9	7·2	15·9	11·5
40	10 55·0	10 56·8	10 25·2	4·0	2·9	10·0	7·3	16·0	11·6
41	10 55·3	10 57·0	10 25·4	4·1	3·0	10·1	7·3	16·1	11·7
42	10 55·5	10 57·3	10 25·6	4·2	3·0	10·2	7·4	16·2	11·7
43	10 55·8	10 57·5	10 25·9	4·3	3·1	10·3	7·5	16·3	11·8
44	10 56·0	10 57·8	10 26·1	4·4	3·2	10·4	7·5	16·4	11·9
45	10 56·3	10 58·0	10 26·4	4·5	3·3	10·5	7·6	16·5	12·0
46	10 56·5	10 58·3	10 26·6	4·6	3·3	10·6	7·7	16·6	12·0
47	10 56·8	10 58·5	10 26·8	4·7	3·4	10·7	7·8	16·7	12·1
48	10 57·0	10 58·8	10 27·1	4·8	3·5	10·8	7·8	16·8	12·2
49	10 57·3	10 59·0	10 27·3	4·9	3·6	10·9	7·9	16·9	12·3
50	10 57·5	10 59·3	10 27·5	5·0	3·6	11·0	8·0	17·0	12·3
51	10 57·8	10 59·6	10 27·8	5·1	3·7	11·1	8·0	17·1	12·4
52	10 58·0	10 59·8	10 28·0	5·2	3·8	11·2	8·1	17·2	12·5
53	10 58·3	11 00·1	10 28·3	5·3	3·8	11·3	8·2	17·3	12·5
54	10 58·5	11 00·3	10 28·5	5·4	3·9	11·4	8·3	17·4	12·6
55	10 58·8	11 00·6	10 28·7	5·5	4·0	11·5	8·3	17·5	12·7
56	10 59·0	11 00·8	10 29·0	5·6	4·1	11·6	8·4	17·6	12·8
57	10 59·3	11 01·1	10 29·2	5·7	4·1	11·7	8·5	17·7	12·8
58	10 59·5	11 01·3	10 29·5	5·8	4·2	11·8	8·6	17·8	12·9
59	10 59·8	11 01·6	10 29·7	5·9	4·3	11·9	8·6	17·9	13·0
60	11 00·0	11 01·8	10 29·9	6·0	4·4	12·0	8·7	18·0	13·1

44ᵐ

s	SUN PLANETS	ARIES	MOON	v or Corrⁿ d	v or Corrⁿ d	v or Corrⁿ d
00	11 00·0	11 01·8	10 29·9	0·0 0·0	6·0 4·5	12·0 8·9
01	11 00·3	11 02·1	10 30·2	0·1 0·1	6·1 4·5	12·1 9·0
02	11 00·5	11 02·3	10 30·4	0·2 0·1	6·2 4·6	12·2 9·0
03	11 00·8	11 02·6	10 30·6	0·3 0·2	6·3 4·7	12·3 9·1
04	11 01·0	11 02·8	10 30·9	0·4 0·3	6·4 4·7	12·4 9·2
05	11 01·3	11 03·1	10 31·1	0·5 0·4	6·5 4·8	12·5 9·3
06	11 01·5	11 03·3	10 31·4	0·6 0·4	6·6 4·9	12·6 9·3
07	11 01·8	11 03·6	10 31·6	0·7 0·5	6·7 5·0	12·7 9·4
08	11 02·0	11 03·8	10 31·8	0·8 0·6	6·8 5·0	12·8 9·5
09	11 02·3	11 04·1	10 32·1	0·9 0·7	6·9 5·1	12·9 9·6
10	11 02·5	11 04·3	10 32·3	1·0 0·7	7·0 5·2	13·0 9·6
11	11 02·8	11 04·6	10 32·6	1·1 0·8	7·1 5·3	13·1 9·7
12	11 03·0	11 04·8	10 32·8	1·2 0·9	7·2 5·3	13·2 9·8
13	11 03·3	11 05·1	10 33·0	1·3 1·0	7·3 5·4	13·3 9·9
14	11 03·5	11 05·3	10 33·3	1·4 1·0	7·4 5·5	13·4 9·9
15	11 03·8	11 05·6	10 33·5	1·5 1·1	7·5 5·6	13·5 10·0
16	11 04·0	11 05·8	10 33·8	1·6 1·2	7·6 5·6	13·6 10·1
17	11 04·3	11 06·1	10 34·0	1·7 1·3	7·7 5·7	13·7 10·2
18	11 04·5	11 06·3	10 34·2	1·8 1·3	7·8 5·8	13·8 10·2
19	11 04·8	11 06·6	10 34·5	1·9 1·4	7·9 5·9	13·9 10·3
20	11 05·0	11 06·8	10 34·7	2·0 1·5	8·0 5·9	14·0 10·4
21	11 05·3	11 07·1	10 34·9	2·1 1·6	8·1 6·0	14·1 10·5
22	11 05·5	11 07·3	10 35·2	2·2 1·6	8·2 6·1	14·2 10·5
23	11 05·8	11 07·6	10 35·4	2·3 1·7	8·3 6·2	14·3 10·6
24	11 06·0	11 07·8	10 35·7	2·4 1·8	8·4 6·2	14·4 10·7
25	11 06·3	11 08·1	10 35·9	2·5 1·9	8·5 6·3	14·5 10·8
26	11 06·5	11 08·3	10 36·1	2·6 1·9	8·6 6·4	14·6 10·8
27	11 06·8	11 08·6	10 36·4	2·7 2·0	8·7 6·5	14·7 10·9
28	11 07·0	11 08·8	10 36·6	2·8 2·1	8·8 6·5	14·8 11·0
29	11 07·3	11 09·1	10 36·9	2·9 2·2	8·9 6·6	14·9 11·1
30	11 07·5	11 09·3	10 37·1	3·0 2·2	9·0 6·7	15·0 11·1
31	11 07·8	11 09·6	10 37·3	3·1 2·3	9·1 6·7	15·1 11·2
32	11 08·0	11 09·8	10 37·6	3·2 2·4	9·2 6·8	15·2 11·3
33	11 08·3	11 10·1	10 37·8	3·3 2·4	9·3 6·9	15·3 11·3
34	11 08·5	11 10·3	10 38·0	3·4 2·5	9·4 7·0	15·4 11·4
35	11 08·8	11 10·6	10 38·3	3·5 2·6	9·5 7·0	15·5 11·5
36	11 09·0	11 10·8	10 38·5	3·6 2·7	9·6 7·1	15·6 11·6
37	11 09·3	11 11·1	10 38·8	3·7 2·7	9·7 7·2	15·7 11·6
38	11 09·5	11 11·3	10 39·0	3·8 2·8	9·8 7·3	15·8 11·7
39	11 09·8	11 11·6	10 39·2	3·9 2·9	9·9 7·3	15·9 11·8
40	11 10·0	11 11·8	10 39·5	4·0 3·0	10·0 7·4	16·0 11·9
41	11 10·3	11 12·1	10 39·7	4·1 3·0	10·1 7·5	16·1 11·9
42	11 10·5	11 12·3	10 40·0	4·2 3·1	10·2 7·6	16·2 12·0
43	11 10·8	11 12·6	10 40·2	4·3 3·2	10·3 7·6	16·3 12·1
44	11 11·0	11 12·8	10 40·4	4·4 3·3	10·4 7·7	16·4 12·2
45	11 11·3	11 13·1	10 40·7	4·5 3·3	10·5 7·8	16·5 12·2
46	11 11·5	11 13·3	10 40·9	4·6 3·4	10·6 7·9	16·6 12·3
47	11 11·8	11 13·6	10 41·1	4·7 3·5	10·7 7·9	16·7 12·4
48	11 12·0	11 13·8	10 41·4	4·8 3·6	10·8 8·0	16·8 12·5
49	11 12·3	11 14·1	10 41·6	4·9 3·6	10·9 8·1	16·9 12·5
50	11 12·5	11 14·3	10 41·9	5·0 3·7	11·0 8·2	17·0 12·6
51	11 12·8	11 14·6	10 42·1	5·1 3·8	11·1 8·2	17·1 12·7
52	11 13·0	11 14·8	10 42·3	5·2 3·9	11·2 8·3	17·2 12·8
53	11 13·3	11 15·1	10 42·6	5·3 3·9	11·3 8·4	17·3 12·8
54	11 13·5	11 15·3	10 42·8	5·4 4·0	11·4 8·5	17·4 12·9
55	11 13·8	11 15·6	10 43·1	5·5 4·1	11·5 8·5	17·5 13·0
56	11 14·0	11 15·8	10 43·3	5·6 4·2	11·6 8·6	17·6 13·1
57	11 14·3	11 16·1	10 43·5	5·7 4·2	11·7 8·7	17·7 13·1
58	11 14·5	11 16·3	10 43·8	5·8 4·3	11·8 8·8	17·8 13·2
59	11 14·8	11 16·6	10 44·0	5·9 4·4	11·9 8·8	17·9 13·3
60	11 15·0	11 16·8	10 44·3	6·0 4·5	12·0 8·9	18·0 13·4

45ᵐ

s	SUN PLANETS	ARIES	MOON	v or Corrⁿ d	v or Corrⁿ d	v or Corrⁿ d
00	11 15·0	11 16·8	10 44·3	0·0 0·0	6·0 4·6	12·0 9·1
01	11 15·3	11 17·1	10 44·5	0·1 0·1	6·1 4·6	12·1 9·2
02	11 15·5	11 17·3	10 44·7	0·2 0·2	6·2 4·7	12·2 9·3
03	11 15·8	11 17·6	10 45·0	0·3 0·2	6·3 4·8	12·3 9·3
04	11 16·0	11 17·9	10 45·2	0·4 0·3	6·4 4·9	12·4 9·4
05	11 16·3	11 18·1	10 45·4	0·5 0·4	6·5 4·9	12·5 9·5
06	11 16·5	11 18·4	10 45·7	0·6 0·5	6·6 5·0	12·6 9·6
07	11 16·8	11 18·6	10 45·9	0·7 0·5	6·7 5·1	12·7 9·6
08	11 17·0	11 18·9	10 46·2	0·8 0·6	6·8 5·2	12·8 9·7
09	11 17·3	11 19·1	10 46·4	0·9 0·7	6·9 5·2	12·9 9·8
10	11 17·5	11 19·4	10 46·6	1·0 0·8	7·0 5·3	13·0 9·9
11	11 17·8	11 19·6	10 46·9	1·1 0·8	7·1 5·4	13·1 9·9
12	11 18·0	11 19·9	10 47·1	1·2 0·9	7·2 5·5	13·2 10·0
13	11 18·3	11 20·1	10 47·4	1·3 1·0	7·3 5·5	13·3 10·1
14	11 18·5	11 20·4	10 47·6	1·4 1·1	7·4 5·6	13·4 10·2
15	11 18·8	11 20·6	10 47·8	1·5 1·1	7·5 5·7	13·5 10·2
16	11 19·0	11 20·9	10 48·1	1·6 1·2	7·6 5·8	13·6 10·3
17	11 19·3	11 21·1	10 48·3	1·7 1·3	7·7 5·8	13·7 10·4
18	11 19·5	11 21·4	10 48·5	1·8 1·4	7·8 5·9	13·8 10·5
19	11 19·8	11 21·6	10 48·8	1·9 1·4	7·9 6·0	13·9 10·5
20	11 20·0	11 21·9	10 49·0	2·0 1·5	8·0 6·1	14·0 10·6
21	11 20·3	11 22·1	10 49·3	2·1 1·6	8·1 6·1	14·1 10·7
22	11 20·5	11 22·4	10 49·5	2·2 1·7	8·2 6·2	14·2 10·8
23	11 20·8	11 22·6	10 49·7	2·3 1·7	8·3 6·3	14·3 10·8
24	11 21·0	11 22·9	10 50·0	2·4 1·8	8·4 6·4	14·4 10·9
25	11 21·3	11 23·1	10 50·2	2·5 1·9	8·5 6·4	14·5 11·0
26	11 21·5	11 23·4	10 50·5	2·6 2·0	8·6 6·5	14·6 11·1
27	11 21·8	11 23·6	10 50·7	2·7 2·0	8·7 6·6	14·7 11·1
28	11 22·0	11 23·9	10 50·9	2·8 2·1	8·8 6·7	14·8 11·2
29	11 22·3	11 24·1	10 51·2	2·9 2·2	8·9 6·7	14·9 11·3
30	11 22·5	11 24·4	10 51·4	3·0 2·3	9·0 6·8	15·0 11·4
31	11 22·8	11 24·6	10 51·6	3·1 2·4	9·1 6·9	15·1 11·5
32	11 23·0	11 24·9	10 51·9	3·2 2·4	9·2 7·0	15·2 11·5
33	11 23·3	11 25·1	10 52·1	3·3 2·5	9·3 7·1	15·3 11·6
34	11 23·5	11 25·4	10 52·4	3·4 2·6	9·4 7·1	15·4 11·7
35	11 23·8	11 25·6	10 52·6	3·5 2·7	9·5 7·2	15·5 11·8
36	11 24·0	11 25·9	10 52·8	3·6 2·7	9·6 7·3	15·6 11·8
37	11 24·3	11 26·1	10 53·1	3·7 2·8	9·7 7·4	15·7 11·9
38	11 24·5	11 26·4	10 53·3	3·8 2·9	9·8 7·4	15·8 12·0
39	11 24·8	11 26·6	10 53·6	3·9 3·0	9·9 7·5	15·9 12·1
40	11 25·0	11 26·9	10 53·8	4·0 3·0	10·0 7·6	16·0 12·1
41	11 25·3	11 27·1	10 54·0	4·1 3·1	10·1 7·7	16·1 12·2
42	11 25·5	11 27·4	10 54·3	4·2 3·2	10·2 7·7	16·2 12·3
43	11 25·8	11 27·6	10 54·5	4·3 3·3	10·3 7·8	16·3 12·4
44	11 26·0	11 27·9	10 54·7	4·4 3·3	10·4 7·9	16·4 12·4
45	11 26·3	11 28·1	10 55·0	4·5 3·4	10·5 8·0	16·5 12·5
46	11 26·5	11 28·4	10 55·2	4·6 3·5	10·6 8·0	16·6 12·6
47	11 26·8	11 28·6	10 55·5	4·7 3·6	10·7 8·1	16·7 12·7
48	11 27·0	11 28·9	10 55·7	4·8 3·6	10·8 8·2	16·8 12·7
49	11 27·3	11 29·1	10 55·9	4·9 3·7	10·9 8·3	16·9 12·8
50	11 27·5	11 29·4	10 56·2	5·0 3·8	11·0 8·3	17·0 12·9
51	11 27·8	11 29·6	10 56·4	5·1 3·9	11·1 8·4	17·1 13·0
52	11 28·0	11 29·9	10 56·7	5·2 3·9	11·2 8·5	17·2 13·0
53	11 28·3	11 30·1	10 56·9	5·3 4·0	11·3 8·6	17·3 13·1
54	11 28·5	11 30·4	10 57·1	5·4 4·1	11·4 8·6	17·4 13·2
55	11 28·8	11 30·6	10 57·4	5·5 4·2	11·5 8·7	17·5 13·3
56	11 29·0	11 30·9	10 57·6	5·6 4·2	11·6 8·8	17·6 13·3
57	11 29·3	11 31·1	10 57·9	5·7 4·3	11·7 8·9	17·7 13·4
58	11 29·5	11 31·4	10 58·1	5·8 4·4	11·8 8·9	17·8 13·5
59	11 29·8	11 31·6	10 58·3	5·9 4·5	11·9 9·0	17·9 13·6
60	11 30·0	11 31·9	10 58·6	6·0 4·6	12·0 9·1	18·0 13·7

46ᵐ

46 s	SUN PLANETS	ARIES	MOON	v or d	Corrⁿ	v or d	Corrⁿ	v or d	Corrⁿ
00	11 30·0	11 31·9	10 58·6	0·0	0·0	6·0	4·7	12·0	9·3
01	11 30·3	11 32·1	10 58·8	0·1	0·1	6·1	4·7	12·1	9·4
02	11 30·5	11 32·4	10 59·0	0·2	0·2	6·2	4·8	12·2	9·5
03	11 30·8	11 32·6	10 59·3	0·3	0·2	6·3	4·9	12·3	9·5
04	11 31·0	11 32·9	10 59·5	0·4	0·3	6·4	5·0	12·4	9·6
05	11 31·3	11 33·1	10 59·8	0·5	0·4	6·5	5·0	12·5	9·7
06	11 31·5	11 33·4	11 00·0	0·6	0·5	6·6	5·1	12·6	9·8
07	11 31·8	11 33·6	11 00·2	0·7	0·5	6·7	5·2	12·7	9·8
08	11 32·0	11 33·9	11 00·5	0·8	0·6	6·8	5·3	12·8	9·9
09	11 32·3	11 34·1	11 00·7	0·9	0·7	6·9	5·3	12·9	10·0
10	11 32·5	11 34·4	11 01·0	1·0	0·8	7·0	5·4	13·0	10·1
11	11 32·8	11 34·6	11 01·2	1·1	0·9	7·1	5·5	13·1	10·2
12	11 33·0	11 34·9	11 01·4	1·2	0·9	7·2	5·6	13·2	10·2
13	11 33·3	11 35·1	11 01·7	1·3	1·0	7·3	5·7	13·3	10·3
14	11 33·5	11 35·4	11 01·9	1·4	1·1	7·4	5·7	13·4	10·4
15	11 33·8	11 35·6	11 02·1	1·5	1·2	7·5	5·8	13·5	10·5
16	11 34·0	11 35·9	11 02·4	1·6	1·2	7·6	5·9	13·6	10·5
17	11 34·3	11 36·2	11 02·6	1·7	1·3	7·7	6·0	13·7	10·6
18	11 34·5	11 36·4	11 02·9	1·8	1·4	7·8	6·0	13·8	10·7
19	11 34·8	11 36·7	11 03·1	1·9	1·5	7·9	6·1	13·9	10·8
20	11 35·0	11 36·9	11 03·3	2·0	1·6	8·0	6·2	14·0	10·9
21	11 35·3	11 37·2	11 03·6	2·1	1·6	8·1	6·3	14·1	10·9
22	11 35·5	11 37·4	11 03·8	2·2	1·7	8·2	6·4	14·2	11·0
23	11 35·8	11 37·7	11 04·1	2·3	1·8	8·3	6·4	14·3	11·1
24	11 36·0	11 37·9	11 04·3	2·4	1·9	8·4	6·5	14·4	11·2
25	11 36·3	11 38·2	11 04·5	2·5	1·9	8·5	6·6	14·5	11·2
26	11 36·5	11 38·4	11 04·8	2·6	2·0	8·6	6·7	14·6	11·3
27	11 36·8	11 38·7	11 05·0	2·7	2·1	8·7	6·7	14·7	11·4
28	11 37·0	11 38·9	11 05·2	2·8	2·2	8·8	6·8	14·8	11·5
29	11 37·3	11 39·2	11 05·5	2·9	2·2	8·9	6·9	14·9	11·5
30	11 37·5	11 39·4	11 05·7	3·0	2·3	9·0	7·0	15·0	11·6
31	11 37·8	11 39·7	11 06·0	3·1	2·4	9·1	7·1	15·1	11·7
32	11 38·0	11 39·9	11 06·2	3·2	2·5	9·2	7·1	15·2	11·8
33	11 38·3	11 40·2	11 06·4	3·3	2·6	9·3	7·2	15·3	11·9
34	11 38·5	11 40·4	11 06·7	3·4	2·6	9·4	7·3	15·4	11·9
35	11 38·8	11 40·7	11 06·9	3·5	2·7	9·5	7·4	15·5	12·0
36	11 39·0	11 40·9	11 07·2	3·6	2·8	9·6	7·4	15·6	12·1
37	11 39·3	11 41·2	11 07·4	3·7	2·9	9·7	7·5	15·7	12·2
38	11 39·5	11 41·4	11 07·6	3·8	2·9	9·8	7·6	15·8	12·2
39	11 39·8	11 41·7	11 07·9	3·9	3·0	9·9	7·7	15·9	12·3
40	11 40·0	11 41·9	11 08·1	4·0	3·1	10·0	7·8	16·0	12·4
41	11 40·3	11 42·2	11 08·3	4·1	3·2	10·1	7·8	16·1	12·5
42	11 40·5	11 42·4	11 08·6	4·2	3·3	10·2	7·9	16·2	12·6
43	11 40·8	11 42·7	11 08·8	4·3	3·3	10·3	8·0	16·3	12·6
44	11 41·0	11 42·9	11 09·1	4·4	3·4	10·4	8·1	16·4	12·7
45	11 41·3	11 43·2	11 09·3	4·5	3·5	10·5	8·1	16·5	12·8
46	11 41·5	11 43·4	11 09·5	4·6	3·6	10·6	8·2	16·6	12·9
47	11 41·8	11 43·7	11 09·8	4·7	3·6	10·7	8·3	16·7	12·9
48	11 42·0	11 43·9	11 10·0	4·8	3·7	10·8	8·4	16·8	13·0
49	11 42·3	11 44·2	11 10·3	4·9	3·8	10·9	8·4	16·9	13·1
50	11 42·5	11 44·4	11 10·5	5·0	3·9	11·0	8·5	17·0	13·2
51	11 42·8	11 44·7	11 10·7	5·1	4·0	11·1	8·6	17·1	13·3
52	11 43·0	11 44·9	11 11·0	5·2	4·0	11·2	8·7	17·2	13·3
53	11 43·3	11 45·2	11 11·2	5·3	4·1	11·3	8·8	17·3	13·4
54	11 43·5	11 45·4	11 11·5	5·4	4·2	11·4	8·8	17·4	13·5
55	11 43·8	11 45·7	11 11·7	5·5	4·3	11·5	8·9	17·5	13·6
56	11 44·0	11 45·9	11 11·9	5·6	4·3	11·6	9·0	17·6	13·6
57	11 44·3	11 46·2	11 12·2	5·7	4·4	11·7	9·1	17·7	13·7
58	11 44·5	11 46·4	11 12·4	5·8	4·5	11·8	9·1	17·8	13·8
59	11 44·8	11 46·7	11 12·6	5·9	4·6	11·9	9·2	17·9	13·9
60	11 45·0	11 46·9	11 12·9	6·0	4·7	12·0	9·3	18·0	14·0

47ᵐ

47 s	SUN PLANETS	ARIES	MOON	v or d	Corrⁿ	v or d	Corrⁿ	v or d	Corrⁿ
00	11 45·0	11 46·9	11 12·9	0·0	0·0	6·0	4·8	12·0	9·5
01	11 45·3	11 47·2	11 13·1	0·1	0·1	6·1	4·8	12·1	9·6
02	11 45·5	11 47·4	11 13·4	0·2	0·2	6·2	4·9	12·2	9·7
03	11 45·8	11 47·7	11 13·6	0·3	0·2	6·3	5·0	12·3	9·7
04	11 46·0	11 47·9	11 13·8	0·4	0·3	6·4	5·1	12·4	9·8
05	11 46·3	11 48·2	11 14·1	0·5	0·4	6·5	5·1	12·5	9·9
06	11 46·5	11 48·4	11 14·3	0·6	0·5	6·6	5·2	12·6	10·0
07	11 46·8	11 48·7	11 14·6	0·7	0·6	6·7	5·3	12·7	10·1
08	11 47·0	11 48·9	11 14·8	0·8	0·6	6·8	5·4	12·8	10·1
09	11 47·3	11 49·2	11 15·0	0·9	0·7	6·9	5·5	12·9	10·2
10	11 47·5	11 49·4	11 15·3	1·0	0·8	7·0	5·5	13·0	10·3
11	11 47·8	11 49·7	11 15·5	1·1	0·9	7·1	5·6	13·1	10·4
12	11 48·0	11 49·9	11 15·7	1·2	1·0	7·2	5·7	13·2	10·5
13	11 48·3	11 50·2	11 16·0	1·3	1·0	7·3	5·8	13·3	10·5
14	11 48·5	11 50·4	11 16·2	1·4	1·1	7·4	5·9	13·4	10·6
15	11 48·8	11 50·7	11 16·5	1·5	1·2	7·5	5·9	13·5	10·7
16	11 49·0	11 50·9	11 16·7	1·6	1·3	7·6	6·0	13·6	10·8
17	11 49·3	11 51·2	11 16·9	1·7	1·3	7·7	6·1	13·7	10·8
18	11 49·5	11 51·4	11 17·2	1·8	1·4	7·8	6·2	13·8	10·9
19	11 49·8	11 51·7	11 17·4	1·9	1·5	7·9	6·3	13·9	11·0
20	11 50·0	11 51·9	11 17·7	2·0	1·6	8·0	6·3	14·0	11·1
21	11 50·3	11 52·2	11 17·9	2·1	1·7	8·1	6·4	14·1	11·2
22	11 50·5	11 52·4	11 18·1	2·2	1·7	8·2	6·5	14·2	11·2
23	11 50·8	11 52·7	11 18·4	2·3	1·8	8·3	6·6	14·3	11·3
24	11 51·0	11 52·9	11 18·6	2·4	1·9	8·4	6·7	14·4	11·4
25	11 51·3	11 53·2	11 18·8	2·5	2·0	8·5	6·7	14·5	11·5
26	11 51·5	11 53·4	11 19·1	2·6	2·1	8·6	6·8	14·6	11·6
27	11 51·8	11 53·7	11 19·3	2·7	2·1	8·7	6·9	14·7	11·6
28	11 52·0	11 53·9	11 19·6	2·8	2·2	8·8	7·0	14·8	11·7
29	11 52·3	11 54·2	11 19·8	2·9	2·3	8·9	7·0	14·9	11·8
30	11 52·5	11 54·5	11 20·0	3·0	2·4	9·0	7·1	15·0	11·9
31	11 52·8	11 54·7	11 20·3	3·1	2·5	9·1	7·2	15·1	12·0
32	11 53·0	11 55·0	11 20·5	3·2	2·5	9·2	7·3	15·2	12·0
33	11 53·3	11 55·2	11 20·8	3·3	2·6	9·3	7·4	15·3	12·1
34	11 53·5	11 55·5	11 21·0	3·4	2·7	9·4	7·4	15·4	12·2
35	11 53·8	11 55·7	11 21·2	3·5	2·8	9·5	7·5	15·5	12·3
36	11 54·0	11 56·0	11 21·5	3·6	2·9	9·6	7·6	15·6	12·4
37	11 54·3	11 56·2	11 21·7	3·7	2·9	9·7	7·7	15·7	12·4
38	11 54·5	11 56·5	11 22·0	3·8	3·0	9·8	7·8	15·8	12·5
39	11 54·8	11 56·7	11 22·2	3·9	3·1	9·9	7·8	15·9	12·6
40	11 55·0	11 57·0	11 22·4	4·0	3·2	10·0	7·9	16·0	12·7
41	11 55·3	11 57·2	11 22·7	4·1	3·2	10·1	8·0	16·1	12·7
42	11 55·5	11 57·5	11 22·9	4·2	3·3	10·2	8·1	16·2	12·8
43	11 55·8	11 57·7	11 23·1	4·3	3·4	10·3	8·2	16·3	12·9
44	11 56·0	11 58·0	11 23·4	4·4	3·5	10·4	8·2	16·4	13·0
45	11 56·3	11 58·2	11 23·6	4·5	3·6	10·5	8·3	16·5	13·1
46	11 56·5	11 58·5	11 23·9	4·6	3·6	10·6	8·4	16·6	13·1
47	11 56·8	11 58·7	11 24·1	4·7	3·7	10·7	8·5	16·7	13·2
48	11 57·0	11 59·0	11 24·3	4·8	3·8	10·8	8·5	16·8	13·3
49	11 57·3	11 59·2	11 24·6	4·9	3·9	10·9	8·6	16·9	13·3
50	11 57·5	11 59·5	11 24·8	5·0	4·0	11·0	8·7	17·0	13·5
51	11 57·8	11 59·7	11 25·1	5·1	4·0	11·1	8·8	17·1	13·5
52	11 58·0	12 00·0	11 25·3	5·2	4·1	11·2	8·9	17·2	13·6
53	11 58·3	12 00·2	11 25·5	5·3	4·2	11·3	8·9	17·3	13·7
54	11 58·5	12 00·5	11 25·8	5·4	4·3	11·4	9·0	17·4	13·8
55	11 58·8	12 00·7	11 26·0	5·5	4·4	11·5	9·1	17·5	13·9
56	11 59·0	12 01·0	11 26·2	5·6	4·4	11·6	9·2	17·6	13·9
57	11 59·3	12 01·2	11 26·5	5·7	4·5	11·7	9·3	17·7	14·0
58	11 59·5	12 01·5	11 26·7	5·8	4·6	11·8	9·3	17·8	14·1
59	11 59·8	12 01·7	11 27·0	5·9	4·7	11·9	9·4	17·9	14·2
60	12 00·0	12 02·0	11 27·2	6·0	4·8	12·0	9·5	18·0	14·3

xxv

48ᵐ

48	SUN PLANETS	ARIES	MOON	v or d Corrⁿ	v or d Corrⁿ	v or d Corrⁿ
s	° ′	° ′	° ′	′ ′	′ ′	′ ′
00	12 00·0	12 02·0	11 27·2	0·0 0·0	6·0 4·9	12·0 9·7
01	12 00·3	12 02·2	11 27·4	0·1 0·1	6·1 4·9	12·1 9·8
02	12 00·5	12 02·5	11 27·7	0·2 0·2	6·2 5·0	12·2 9·9
03	12 00·8	12 02·7	11 27·9	0·3 0·2	6·3 5·1	12·3 9·9
04	12 01·0	12 03·0	11 28·2	0·4 0·3	6·4 5·2	12·4 10·0
05	12 01·3	12 03·2	11 28·4	0·5 0·4	6·5 5·3	12·5 10·1
06	12 01·5	12 03·5	11 28·6	0·6 0·5	6·6 5·3	12·6 10·2
07	12 01·8	12 03·7	11 28·9	0·7 0·6	6·7 5·4	12·7 10·3
08	12 02·0	12 04·0	11 29·1	0·8 0·6	6·8 5·5	12·8 10·3
09	12 02·3	12 04·2	11 29·3	0·9 0·7	6·9 5·6	12·9 10·4
10	12 02·5	12 04·5	11 29·6	1·0 0·8	7·0 5·7	13·0 10·5
11	12 02·8	12 04·7	11 29·8	1·1 0·9	7·1 5·7	13·1 10·6
12	12 03·0	12 05·0	11 30·1	1·2 1·0	7·2 5·8	13·2 10·7
13	12 03·3	12 05·2	11 30·3	1·3 1·1	7·3 5·9	13·3 10·8
14	12 03·5	12 05·5	11 30·5	1·4 1·1	7·4 6·0	13·4 10·8
15	12 03·8	12 05·7	11 30·8	1·5 1·2	7·5 6·1	13·5 10·9
16	12 04·0	12 06·0	11 31·0	1·6 1·3	7·6 6·1	13·6 11·0
17	12 04·3	12 06·2	11 31·3	1·7 1·4	7·7 6·2	13·7 11·1
18	12 04·5	12 06·5	11 31·5	1·8 1·5	7·8 6·3	13·8 11·2
19	12 04·8	12 06·7	11 31·7	1·9 1·5	7·9 6·4	13·9 11·2
20	12 05·0	12 07·0	11 32·0	2·0 1·6	8·0 6·5	14·0 11·3
21	12 05·3	12 07·2	11 32·2	2·1 1·7	8·1 6·5	14·1 11·4
22	12 05·5	12 07·5	11 32·4	2·2 1·8	8·2 6·6	14·2 11·5
23	12 05·8	12 07·7	11 32·7	2·3 1·9	8·3 6·7	14·3 11·6
24	12 06·0	12 08·0	11 32·9	2·4 1·9	8·4 6·8	14·4 11·6
25	12 06·3	12 08·2	11 33·2	2·5 2·0	8·5 6·9	14·5 11·7
26	12 06·5	12 08·5	11 33·4	2·6 2·1	8·6 7·0	14·6 11·8
27	12 06·8	12 08·7	11 33·6	2·7 2·2	8·7 7·0	14·7 11·9
28	12 07·0	12 09·0	11 33·9	2·8 2·3	8·8 7·1	14·8 12·0
29	12 07·3	12 09·2	11 34·1	2·9 2·3	8·9 7·2	14·9 12·0
30	12 07·5	12 09·5	11 34·4	3·0 2·4	9·0 7·3	15·0 12·1
31	12 07·8	12 09·7	11 34·6	3·1 2·5	9·1 7·4	15·1 12·2
32	12 08·0	12 10·0	11 34·8	3·2 2·6	9·2 7·4	15·2 12·3
33	12 08·3	12 10·2	11 35·1	3·3 2·7	9·3 7·5	15·3 12·4
34	12 08·5	12 10·5	11 35·3	3·4 2·7	9·4 7·6	15·4 12·4
35	12 08·8	12 10·7	11 35·6	3·5 2·8	9·5 7·7	15·5 12·5
36	12 09·0	12 11·0	11 35·8	3·6 2·9	9·6 7·8	15·6 12·6
37	12 09·3	12 11·2	11 36·0	3·7 3·0	9·7 7·8	15·7 12·7
38	12 09·5	12 11·5	11 36·3	3·8 3·1	9·8 7·9	15·8 12·8
39	12 09·8	12 11·7	11 36·5	3·9 3·2	9·9 8·0	15·9 12·9
40	12 10·0	12 12·0	11 36·7	4·0 3·2	10·0 8·1	16·0 12·9
41	12 10·3	12 12·2	11 37·0	4·1 3·3	10·1 8·2	16·1 13·0
42	12 10·5	12 12·5	11 37·2	4·2 3·4	10·2 8·2	16·2 13·1
43	12 10·8	12 12·8	11 37·5	4·3 3·5	10·3 8·3	16·3 13·2
44	12 11·0	12 13·0	11 37·7	4·4 3·6	10·4 8·4	16·4 13·3
45	12 11·3	12 13·3	11 37·9	4·5 3·6	10·5 8·5	16·5 13·3
46	12 11·5	12 13·5	11 38·2	4·6 3·7	10·6 8·6	16·6 13·4
47	12 11·8	12 13·8	11 38·4	4·7 3·8	10·7 8·6	16·7 13·5
48	12 12·0	12 14·0	11 38·7	4·8 3·9	10·8 8·7	16·8 13·6
49	12 12·3	12 14·3	11 38·9	4·9 4·0	10·9 8·8	16·9 13·7
50	12 12·5	12 14·5	11 39·1	5·0 4·0	11·0 8·9	17·0 13·7
51	12 12·8	12 14·8	11 39·4	5·1 4·1	11·1 9·0	17·1 13·8
52	12 13·0	12 15·0	11 39·6	5·2 4·2	11·2 9·1	17·2 13·9
53	12 13·3	12 15·3	11 39·8	5·3 4·3	11·3 9·1	17·3 14·0
54	12 13·5	12 15·5	11 40·1	5·4 4·4	11·4 9·2	17·4 14·1
55	12 13·8	12 15·8	11 40·3	5·5 4·4	11·5 9·3	17·5 14·1
56	12 14·0	12 16·0	11 40·6	5·6 4·5	11·6 9·4	17·6 14·2
57	12 14·3	12 16·3	11 40·8	5·7 4·6	11·7 9·5	17·7 14·3
58	12 14·5	12 16·5	11 41·0	5·8 4·7	11·8 9·5	17·8 14·4
59	12 14·8	12 16·8	11 41·3	5·9 4·8	11·9 9·6	17·9 14·5
60	12 15·0	12 17·0	11 41·5	6·0 4·9	12·0 9·7	18·0 14·6

49ᵐ

49	SUN PLANETS	ARIES	MOON	v or d Corrⁿ	v or d Corrⁿ	v or d Corrⁿ
s	° ′	° ′	° ′	′ ′	′ ′	′ ′
00	12 15·0	12 17·0	11 41·5	0·0 0·0	6·0 5·0	12·0 9·9
01	12 15·3	12 17·3	11 41·8	0·1 0·1	6·1 5·0	12·1 10·0
02	12 15·5	12 17·5	11 42·0	0·2 0·2	6·2 5·1	12·2 10·1
03	12 15·8	12 17·8	11 42·2	0·3 0·2	6·3 5·2	12·3 10·1
04	12 16·0	12 18·0	11 42·5	0·4 0·3	6·4 5·3	12·4 10·2
05	12 16·3	12 18·3	11 42·7	0·5 0·4	6·5 5·4	12·5 10·3
06	12 16·5	12 18·5	11 42·9	0·6 0·5	6·6 5·4	12·6 10·4
07	12 16·8	12 18·8	11 43·2	0·7 0·6	6·7 5·5	12·7 10·5
08	12 17·0	12 19·0	11 43·4	0·8 0·7	6·8 5·6	12·8 10·6
09	12 17·3	12 19·3	11 43·7	0·9 0·7	6·9 5·7	12·9 10·6
10	12 17·5	12 19·5	11 43·9	1·0 0·8	7·0 5·8	13·0 10·7
11	12 17·8	12 19·8	11 44·1	1·1 0·9	7·1 5·9	13·1 10·8
12	12 18·0	12 20·0	11 44·4	1·2 1·0	7·2 5·9	13·2 10·9
13	12 18·3	12 20·3	11 44·6	1·3 1·1	7·3 6·0	13·3 11·0
14	12 18·5	12 20·5	11 44·9	1·4 1·2	7·4 6·1	13·4 11·1
15	12 18·8	12 20·8	11 45·1	1·5 1·2	7·5 6·2	13·5 11·1
16	12 19·0	12 21·0	11 45·3	1·6 1·3	7·6 6·3	13·6 11·2
17	12 19·3	12 21·3	11 45·6	1·7 1·4	7·7 6·4	13·7 11·3
18	12 19·5	12 21·5	11 45·8	1·8 1·5	7·8 6·4	13·8 11·4
19	12 19·8	12 21·8	11 46·1	1·9 1·6	7·9 6·5	13·9 11·5
20	12 20·0	12 22·0	11 46·3	2·0 1·7	8·0 6·6	14·0 11·6
21	12 20·3	12 22·3	11 46·5	2·1 1·7	8·1 6·7	14·1 11·6
22	12 20·5	12 22·5	11 46·8	2·2 1·8	8·2 6·8	14·2 11·7
23	12 20·8	12 22·8	11 47·0	2·3 1·9	8·3 6·8	14·3 11·8
24	12 21·0	12 23·0	11 47·2	2·4 2·0	8·4 6·9	14·4 11·9
25	12 21·3	12 23·3	11 47·5	2·5 2·1	8·5 7·0	14·5 12·0
26	12 21·5	12 23·5	11 47·7	2·6 2·1	8·6 7·1	14·6 12·0
27	12 21·8	12 23·8	11 48·0	2·7 2·2	8·7 7·2	14·7 12·1
28	12 22·0	12 24·0	11 48·2	2·8 2·3	8·8 7·3	14·8 12·2
29	12 22·3	12 24·3	11 48·4	2·9 2·4	8·9 7·3	14·9 12·3
30	12 22·5	12 24·5	11 48·7	3·0 2·5	9·0 7·4	15·0 12·4
31	12 22·8	12 24·8	11 48·9	3·1 2·6	9·1 7·5	15·1 12·5
32	12 23·0	12 25·0	11 49·2	3·2 2·6	9·2 7·6	15·2 12·5
33	12 23·3	12 25·3	11 49·4	3·3 2·7	9·3 7·7	15·3 12·6
34	12 23·5	12 25·5	11 49·6	3·4 2·8	9·4 7·8	15·4 12·7
35	12 23·8	12 25·8	11 49·9	3·5 2·9	9·5 7·8	15·5 12·8
36	12 24·0	12 26·0	11 50·1	3·6 3·0	9·6 7·9	15·6 12·9
37	12 24·3	12 26·3	11 50·3	3·7 3·1	9·7 8·0	15·7 13·0
38	12 24·5	12 26·5	11 50·6	3·8 3·1	9·8 8·1	15·8 13·0
39	12 24·8	12 26·8	11 50·8	3·9 3·2	9·9 8·2	15·9 13·1
40	12 25·0	12 27·0	11 51·1	4·0 3·3	10·0 8·3	16·0 13·2
41	12 25·3	12 27·3	11 51·3	4·1 3·4	10·1 8·3	16·1 13·3
42	12 25·5	12 27·5	11 51·5	4·2 3·5	10·2 8·4	16·2 13·4
43	12 25·8	12 27·8	11 51·8	4·3 3·5	10·3 8·5	16·3 13·4
44	12 26·0	12 28·0	11 52·0	4·4 3·6	10·4 8·6	16·4 13·5
45	12 26·3	12 28·3	11 52·3	4·5 3·7	10·5 8·7	16·5 13·6
46	12 26·5	12 28·5	11 52·5	4·6 3·8	10·6 8·7	16·6 13·7
47	12 26·8	12 28·8	11 52·7	4·7 3·9	10·7 8·8	16·7 13·8
48	12 27·0	12 29·0	11 53·0	4·8 4·0	10·8 8·9	16·8 13·9
49	12 27·3	12 29·3	11 53·2	4·9 4·0	10·9 9·0	16·9 13·9
50	12 27·5	12 29·5	11 53·4	5·0 4·1	11·0 9·1	17·0 14·0
51	12 27·8	12 29·8	11 53·7	5·1 4·2	11·1 9·2	17·1 14·1
52	12 28·0	12 30·0	11 53·9	5·2 4·3	11·2 9·2	17·2 14·2
53	12 28·3	12 30·3	11 54·2	5·3 4·4	11·3 9·3	17·3 14·3
54	12 28·5	12 30·5	11 54·4	5·4 4·5	11·4 9·4	17·4 14·4
55	12 28·8	12 30·8	11 54·6	5·5 4·5	11·5 9·5	17·5 14·4
56	12 29·0	12 31·1	11 54·9	5·6 4·6	11·6 9·6	17·6 14·5
57	12 29·3	12 31·3	11 55·1	5·7 4·7	11·7 9·7	17·7 14·6
58	12 29·5	12 31·6	11 55·4	5·8 4·8	11·8 9·7	17·8 14·7
59	12 29·8	12 31·8	11 55·6	5·9 4·9	11·9 9·8	17·9 14·8
60	12 30·0	12 32·1	11 55·8	6·0 5·0	12·0 9·9	18·0 14·9

50	SUN PLANETS	ARIES	MOON	v or d	Corrⁿ	v or d	Corrⁿ	v or d	Corrⁿ
s	° ′	° ′	° ′	′	′	′	′	′	′
00	12 30·0	12 32·1	11 55·8	0·0	0·0	6·0	5·1	12·0	10·1
01	12 30·3	12 32·3	11 56·1	0·1	0·1	6·1	5·1	12·1	10·2
02	12 30·5	12 32·6	11 56·3	0·2	0·2	6·2	5·2	12·2	10·3
03	12 30·8	12 32·8	11 56·5	0·3	0·3	6·3	5·3	12·3	10·4
04	12 31·0	12 33·1	11 56·8	0·4	0·3	6·4	5·4	12·4	10·4
05	12 31·3	12 33·3	11 57·0	0·5	0·4	6·5	5·5	12·5	10·5
06	12 31·5	12 33·6	11 57·3	0·6	0·5	6·6	5·6	12·6	10·6
07	12 31·8	12 33·8	11 57·5	0·7	0·6	6·7	5·6	12·7	10·7
08	12 32·0	12 34·1	11 57·7	0·8	0·7	6·8	5·7	12·8	10·8
09	12 32·3	12 34·3	11 58·0	0·9	0·8	6·9	5·8	12·9	10·9
10	12 32·5	12 34·6	11 58·2	1·0	0·8	7·0	5·9	13·0	10·9
11	12 32·8	12 34·8	11 58·5	1·1	0·9	7·1	6·0	13·1	11·0
12	12 33·0	12 35·1	11 58·7	1·2	1·0	7·2	6·1	13·2	11·1
13	12 33·3	12 35·3	11 58·9	1·3	1·1	7·3	6·1	13·3	11·2
14	12 33·5	12 35·6	11 59·2	1·4	1·2	7·4	6·2	13·4	11·3
15	12 33·8	12 35·8	11 59·4	1·5	1·3	7·5	6·3	13·5	11·4
16	12 34·0	12 36·1	11 59·7	1·6	1·3	7·6	6·4	13·6	11·4
17	12 34·3	12 36·3	11 59·9	1·7	1·4	7·7	6·5	13·7	11·5
18	12 34·5	12 36·6	12 00·1	1·8	1·5	7·8	6·6	13·8	11·6
19	12 34·8	12 36·8	12 00·4	1·9	1·6	7·9	6·6	13·9	11·7
20	12 35·0	12 37·1	12 00·6	2·0	1·7	8·0	6·7	14·0	11·8
21	12 35·3	12 37·3	12 00·8	2·1	1·8	8·1	6·8	14·1	11·9
22	12 35·5	12 37·6	12 01·1	2·2	1·9	8·2	6·9	14·2	12·0
23	12 35·8	12 37·8	12 01·3	2·3	1·9	8·3	7·0	14·3	12·0
24	12 36·0	12 38·1	12 01·6	2·4	2·0	8·4	7·1	14·4	12·1
25	12 36·3	12 38·3	12 01·8	2·5	2·1	8·5	7·2	14·5	12·2
26	12 36·5	12 38·6	12 02·0	2·6	2·2	8·6	7·2	14·6	12·3
27	12 36·8	12 38·8	12 02·3	2·7	2·3	8·7	7·3	14·7	12·4
28	12 37·0	12 39·1	12 02·5	2·8	2·4	8·8	7·4	14·8	12·5
29	12 37·3	12 39·3	12 02·8	2·9	2·4	8·9	7·5	14·9	12·5
30	12 37·5	12 39·6	12 03·0	3·0	2·5	9·0	7·6	15·0	12·6
31	12 37·8	12 39·8	12 03·2	3·1	2·6	9·1	7·7	15·1	12·7
32	12 38·0	12 40·1	12 03·5	3·2	2·7	9·2	7·7	15·2	12·8
33	12 38·3	12 40·3	12 03·7	3·3	2·8	9·3	7·8	15·3	12·9
34	12 38·5	12 40·6	12 03·9	3·4	2·9	9·4	7·9	15·4	13·0
35	12 38·8	12 40·8	12 04·2	3·5	2·9	9·5	8·0	15·5	13·0
36	12 39·0	12 41·1	12 04·4	3·6	3·0	9·6	8·1	15·6	13·1
37	12 39·3	12 41·3	12 04·7	3·7	3·1	9·7	8·2	15·7	13·2
38	12 39·5	12 41·6	12 04·9	3·8	3·2	9·8	8·2	15·8	13·3
39	12 39·8	12 41·8	12 05·1	3·9	3·3	9·9	8·3	15·9	13·4
40	12 40·0	12 42·1	12 05·4	4·0	3·4	10·0	8·4	16·0	13·5
41	12 40·3	12 42·3	12 05·6	4·1	3·5	10·1	8·5	16·1	13·6
42	12 40·5	12 42·6	12 05·9	4·2	3·5	10·2	8·6	16·2	13·6
43	12 40·8	12 42·8	12 06·1	4·3	3·6	10·3	8·7	16·3	13·7
44	12 41·0	12 43·1	12 06·3	4·4	3·7	10·4	8·8	16·4	13·8
45	12 41·3	12 43·3	12 06·6	4·5	3·8	10·5	8·8	16·5	13·9
46	12 41·5	12 43·6	12 06·8	4·6	3·9	10·6	8·9	16·6	14·0
47	12 41·8	12 43·8	12 07·0	4·7	4·0	10·7	9·0	16·7	14·1
48	12 42·0	12 44·1	12 07·3	4·8	4·0	10·8	9·1	16·8	14·1
49	12 42·3	12 44·3	12 07·5	4·9	4·1	10·9	9·2	16·9	14·2
50	12 42·5	12 44·6	12 07·8	5·0	4·2	11·0	9·3	17·0	14·3
51	12 42·8	12 44·8	12 08·0	5·1	4·3	11·1	9·3	17·1	14·4
52	12 43·0	12 45·1	12 08·2	5·2	4·4	11·2	9·4	17·2	14·5
53	12 43·3	12 45·3	12 08·5	5·3	4·5	11·3	9·5	17·3	14·6
54	12 43·5	12 45·6	12 08·7	5·4	4·5	11·4	9·6	17·4	14·6
55	12 43·8	12 45·8	12 09·0	5·5	4·6	11·5	9·7	17·5	14·7
56	12 44·0	12 46·1	12 09·2	5·6	4·7	11·6	9·8	17·6	14·8
57	12 44·3	12 46·3	12 09·4	5·7	4·8	11·7	9·8	17·7	14·9
58	12 44·5	12 46·6	12 09·7	5·8	4·9	11·8	9·9	17·8	15·0
59	12 44·8	12 46·8	12 09·9	5·9	5·0	11·9	10·0	17·9	15·1
60	12 45·0	12 47·1	12 10·2	6·0	5·1	12·0	10·1	18·0	15·2

51	SUN PLANETS	ARIES	MOON	v or d	Corrⁿ	v or d	Corrⁿ	v or d	Corrⁿ
s	° ′	° ′	° ′	′	′	′	′	′	′
00	12 45·0	12 47·1	12 10·2	0·0	0·0	6·0	5·2	12·0	10·3
01	12 45·3	12 47·3	12 10·4	0·1	0·1	6·1	5·2	12·1	10·4
02	12 45·5	12 47·6	12 10·6	0·2	0·2	6·2	5·3	12·2	10·5
03	12 45·8	12 47·8	12 10·9	0·3	0·3	6·3	5·4	12·3	10·6
04	12 46·0	12 48·1	12 11·1	0·4	0·4	6·4	5·5	12·4	10·6
05	12 46·3	12 48·3	12 11·3	0·5	0·4	6·5	5·6	12·5	10·7
06	12 46·5	12 48·6	12 11·6	0·6	0·5	6·6	5·7	12·6	10·8
07	12 46·8	12 48·8	12 11·8	0·7	0·6	6·7	5·8	12·7	10·9
08	12 47·0	12 49·1	12 12·1	0·8	0·7	6·8	5·8	12·8	11·0
09	12 47·3	12 49·4	12 12·3	0·9	0·8	6·9	5·9	12·9	11·1
10	12 47·5	12 49·6	12 12·5	1·0	0·9	7·0	6·0	13·0	11·2
11	12 47·8	12 49·9	12 12·8	1·1	0·9	7·1	6·1	13·1	11·2
12	12 48·0	12 50·1	12 13·0	1·2	1·0	7·2	6·2	13·2	11·3
13	12 48·3	12 50·4	12 13·3	1·3	1·1	7·3	6·3	13·3	11·4
14	12 48·5	12 50·6	12 13·5	1·4	1·2	7·4	6·4	13·4	11·5
15	12 48·8	12 50·9	12 13·7	1·5	1·3	7·5	6·4	13·5	11·6
16	12 49·0	12 51·1	12 14·0	1·6	1·4	7·6	6·5	13·6	11·7
17	12 49·3	12 51·4	12 14·2	1·7	1·5	7·7	6·6	13·7	11·8
18	12 49·5	12 51·6	12 14·4	1·8	1·5	7·8	6·7	13·8	11·8
19	12 49·8	12 51·9	12 14·7	1·9	1·6	7·9	6·8	13·9	11·9
20	12 50·0	12 52·1	12 14·9	2·0	1·7	8·0	6·9	14·0	12·0
21	12 50·3	12 52·4	12 15·2	2·1	1·8	8·1	7·0	14·1	12·1
22	12 50·5	12 52·6	12 15·4	2·2	1·9	8·2	7·0	14·2	12·2
23	12 50·8	12 52·9	12 15·6	2·3	2·0	8·3	7·1	14·3	12·3
24	12 51·0	12 53·1	12 15·9	2·4	2·1	8·4	7·2	14·4	12·4
25	12 51·3	12 53·4	12 16·1	2·5	2·1	8·5	7·3	14·5	12·4
26	12 51·5	12 53·6	12 16·4	2·6	2·2	8·6	7·4	14·6	12·5
27	12 51·8	12 53·9	12 16·6	2·7	2·3	8·7	7·5	14·7	12·6
28	12 52·0	12 54·1	12 16·8	2·8	2·4	8·8	7·6	14·8	12·7
29	12 52·3	12 54·4	12 17·1	2·9	2·5	8·9	7·6	14·9	12·8
30	12 52·5	12 54·6	12 17·3	3·0	2·6	9·0	7·7	15·0	12·9
31	12 52·8	12 54·9	12 17·5	3·1	2·7	9·1	7·8	15·1	13·0
32	12 53·0	12 55·1	12 17·8	3·2	2·7	9·2	7·9	15·2	13·0
33	12 53·3	12 55·4	12 18·0	3·3	2·8	9·3	8·0	15·3	13·1
34	12 53·5	12 55·6	12 18·3	3·4	2·9	9·4	8·1	15·4	13·2
35	12 53·8	12 55·9	12 18·5	3·5	3·0	9·5	8·2	15·5	13·3
36	12 54·0	12 56·1	12 18·7	3·6	3·1	9·6	8·2	15·6	13·4
37	12 54·3	12 56·4	12 19·0	3·7	3·2	9·7	8·3	15·7	13·5
38	12 54·5	12 56·6	12 19·2	3·8	3·3	9·8	8·4	15·8	13·6
39	12 54·8	12 56·9	12 19·5	3·9	3·3	9·9	8·5	15·9	13·6
40	12 55·0	12 57·1	12 19·7	4·0	3·4	10·0	8·6	16·0	13·7
41	12 55·3	12 57·4	12 19·9	4·1	3·5	10·1	8·7	16·1	13·8
42	12 55·5	12 57·6	12 20·2	4·2	3·6	10·2	8·8	16·2	13·9
43	12 55·8	12 57·9	12 20·4	4·3	3·7	10·3	8·8	16·3	14·0
44	12 56·0	12 58·1	12 20·6	4·4	3·8	10·4	8·9	16·4	14·1
45	12 56·3	12 58·4	12 20·9	4·5	3·9	10·5	9·0	16·5	14·2
46	12 56·5	12 58·6	12 21·1	4·6	3·9	10·6	9·1	16·6	14·2
47	12 56·8	12 58·9	12 21·4	4·7	4·0	10·7	9·2	16·7	14·3
48	12 57·0	12 59·1	12 21·6	4·8	4·1	10·8	9·3	16·8	14·4
49	12 57·3	12 59·4	12 21·8	4·9	4·2	10·9	9·4	16·9	14·5
50	12 57·5	12 59·6	12 22·1	5·0	4·3	11·0	9·4	17·0	14·6
51	12 57·8	12 59·9	12 22·3	5·1	4·4	11·1	9·5	17·1	14·7
52	12 58·0	13 00·1	12 22·6	5·2	4·5	11·2	9·6	17·2	14·8
53	12 58·3	13 00·4	12 22·8	5·3	4·5	11·3	9·7	17·3	14·8
54	12 58·5	13 00·6	12 23·0	5·4	4·6	11·4	9·8	17·4	14·9
55	12 58·8	13 00·9	12 23·3	5·5	4·7	11·5	9·9	17·5	15·0
56	12 59·0	13 01·1	12 23·5	5·6	4·8	11·6	10·0	17·6	15·1
57	12 59·3	13 01·4	12 23·8	5·7	4·9	11·7	10·0	17·7	15·2
58	12 59·5	13 01·6	12 24·0	5·8	5·0	11·8	10·1	17·8	15·3
59	12 59·8	13 01·9	12 24·2	5·9	5·1	11·9	10·2	17·9	15·4
60	13 00·0	13 02·1	12 24·5	6·0	5·2	12·0	10·3	18·0	15·5

52^m	SUN PLANETS	ARIES	MOON	v or Corrⁿ d		v or Corrⁿ d		v or Corrⁿ d	
s	° ′	° ′	° ′	′	′	′	′	′	′
00	13 00·0	13 02·1	12 24·5	0·0	0·0	6·0	5·3	12·0	10·5
01	13 00·3	13 02·4	12 24·7	0·1	0·1	6·1	5·3	12·1	10·6
02	13 00·5	13 02·6	12 24·9	0·2	0·2	6·2	5·4	12·2	10·7
03	13 00·8	13 02·9	12 25·2	0·3	0·3	6·3	5·5	12·3	10·8
04	13 01·0	13 03·1	12 25·4	0·4	0·4	6·4	5·6	12·4	10·9
05	13 01·3	13 03·4	12 25·7	0·5	0·4	6·5	5·7	12·5	10·9
06	13 01·5	13 03·6	12 25·9	0·6	0·5	6·6	5·8	12·6	11·0
07	13 01·8	13 03·9	12 26·1	0·7	0·6	6·7	5·9	12·7	11·1
08	13 02·0	13 04·1	12 26·4	0·8	0·7	6·8	6·0	12·8	11·2
09	13 02·3	13 04·4	12 26·6	0·9	0·8	6·9	6·0	12·9	11·3
10	13 02·5	13 04·6	12 26·9	1·0	0·9	7·0	6·1	13·0	11·4
11	13 02·8	13 04·9	12 27·1	1·1	1·0	7·1	6·2	13·1	11·5
12	13 03·0	13 05·1	12 27·3	1·2	1·1	7·2	6·3	13·2	11·6
13	13 03·3	13 05·4	12 27·6	1·3	1·1	7·3	6·4	13·3	11·6
14	13 03·5	13 05·6	12 27·8	1·4	1·2	7·4	6·5	13·4	11·7
15	13 03·8	13 05·9	12 28·0	1·5	1·3	7·5	6·6	13·5	11·8
16	13 04·0	13 06·1	12 28·3	1·6	1·4	7·6	6·7	13·6	11·9
17	13 04·3	13 06·4	12 28·5	1·7	1·5	7·7	6·7	13·7	12·0
18	13 04·5	13 06·6	12 28·8	1·8	1·6	7·8	6·8	13·8	12·1
19	13 04·8	13 06·9	12 29·0	1·9	1·7	7·9	6·9	13·9	12·2
20	13 05·0	13 07·1	12 29·2	2·0	1·8	8·0	7·0	14·0	12·3
21	13 05·3	13 07·4	12 29·5	2·1	1·8	8·1	7·1	14·1	12·3
22	13 05·5	13 07·7	12 29·7	2·2	1·9	8·2	7·2	14·2	12·4
23	13 05·8	13 07·9	12 30·0	2·3	2·0	8·3	7·3	14·3	12·5
24	13 06·0	13 08·2	12 30·2	2·4	2·1	8·4	7·4	14·4	12·6
25	13 06·3	13 08·4	12 30·4	2·5	2·2	8·5	7·4	14·5	12·7
26	13 06·5	13 08·7	12 30·7	2·6	2·3	8·6	7·5	14·6	12·8
27	13 06·8	13 08·9	12 30·9	2·7	2·4	8·7	7·6	14·7	12·9
28	13 07·0	13 09·2	12 31·1	2·8	2·5	8·8	7·7	14·8	13·0
29	13 07·3	13 09·4	12 31·4	2·9	2·5	8·9	7·8	14·9	13·0
30	13 07·5	13 09·7	12 31·6	3·0	2·6	9·0	7·9	15·0	13·1
31	13 07·8	13 09·9	12 31·9	3·1	2·7	9·1	8·0	15·1	13·2
32	13 08·0	13 10·2	12 32·1	3·2	2·8	9·2	8·0	15·2	13·3
33	13 08·3	13 10·4	12 32·3	3·3	2·9	9·3	8·1	15·3	13·4
34	13 08·5	13 10·7	12 32·6	3·4	3·0	9·4	8·2	15·4	13·5
35	13 08·8	13 10·9	12 32·8	3·5	3·1	9·5	8·3	15·5	13·6
36	13 09·0	13 11·2	12 33·1	3·6	3·2	9·6	8·4	15·6	13·7
37	13 09·3	13 11·4	12 33·3	3·7	3·2	9·7	8·5	15·7	13·7
38	13 09·5	13 11·7	12 33·5	3·8	3·3	9·8	8·6	15·8	13·8
39	13 09·8	13 11·9	12 33·8	3·9	3·4	9·9	8·7	15·9	13·9
40	13 10·0	13 12·2	12 34·0	4·0	3·5	10·0	8·8	16·0	14·0
41	13 10·3	13 12·4	12 34·2	4·1	3·6	10·1	8·8	16·1	14·1
42	13 10·5	13 12·7	12 34·5	4·2	3·7	10·2	8·9	16·2	14·2
43	13 10·8	13 12·9	12 34·7	4·3	3·8	10·3	9·0	16·3	14·3
44	13 11·0	13 13·2	12 35·0	4·4	3·9	10·4	9·1	16·4	14·3
45	13 11·3	13 13·4	12 35·2	4·5	3·9	10·5	9·2	16·5	14·4
46	13 11·5	13 13·7	12 35·4	4·6	4·0	10·6	9·3	16·6	14·5
47	13 11·8	13 13·9	12 35·7	4·7	4·1	10·7	9·4	16·7	14·6
48	13 12·0	13 14·2	12 35·9	4·8	4·2	10·8	9·5	16·8	14·7
49	13 12·3	13 14·4	12 36·2	4·9	4·3	10·9	9·5	16·9	14·8
50	13 12·5	13 14·7	12 36·4	5·0	4·4	11·0	9·6	17·0	14·9
51	13 12·8	13 14·9	12 36·6	5·1	4·5	11·1	9·7	17·1	15·0
52	13 13·0	13 15·2	12 36·9	5·2	4·6	11·2	9·8	17·2	15·1
53	13 13·3	13 15·4	12 37·1	5·3	4·6	11·3	9·9	17·3	15·1
54	13 13·5	13 15·7	12 37·4	5·4	4·7	11·4	10·0	17·4	15·2
55	13 13·8	13 15·9	12 37·6	5·5	4·8	11·5	10·1	17·5	15·3
56	13 14·0	13 16·2	12 37·8	5·6	4·9	11·6	10·2	17·6	15·4
57	13 14·3	13 16·4	12 38·1	5·7	5·0	11·7	10·2	17·7	15·5
58	13 14·5	13 16·7	12 38·3	5·8	5·1	11·8	10·3	17·8	15·6
59	13 14·8	13 16·9	12 38·5	5·9	5·2	11·9	10·4	17·9	15·7
60	13 15·0	13 17·2	12 38·8	6·0	5·3	12·0	10·5	18·0	15·8

53^m	SUN PLANETS	ARIES	MOON	v or Corrⁿ d		v or Corrⁿ d		v or Corrⁿ d	
s	° ′	° ′	° ′	′	′	′	′	′	′
00	13 15·0	13 17·2	12 38·8	0·0	0·0	6·0	5·4	12·0	10·7
01	13 15·3	13 17·4	12 39·0	0·1	0·1	6·1	5·4	12·1	10·8
02	13 15·5	13 17·7	12 39·3	0·2	0·2	6·2	5·5	12·2	10·9
03	13 15·8	13 17·9	12 39·5	0·3	0·3	6·3	5·6	12·3	11·0
04	13 16·0	13 18·2	12 39·7	0·4	0·4	6·4	5·7	12·4	11·1
05	13 16·3	13 18·4	12 40·0	0·5	0·4	6·5	5·8	12·5	11·1
06	13 16·5	13 18·7	12 40·2	0·6	0·5	6·6	5·9	12·6	11·2
07	13 16·8	13 18·9	12 40·5	0·7	0·6	6·7	6·0	12·7	11·3
08	13 17·0	13 19·2	12 40·7	0·8	0·7	6·8	6·1	12·8	11·4
09	13 17·3	13 19·4	12 40·9	0·9	0·8	6·9	6·2	12·9	11·5
10	13 17·5	13 19·7	12 41·2	1·0	0·9	7·0	6·2	13·0	11·6
11	13 17·8	13 19·9	12 41·4	1·1	1·0	7·1	6·3	13·1	11·7
12	13 18·0	13 20·2	12 41·6	1·2	1·1	7·2	6·4	13·2	11·8
13	13 18·3	13 20·4	12 41·9	1·3	1·2	7·3	6·5	13·3	11·9
14	13 18·5	13 20·7	12 42·1	1·4	1·2	7·4	6·6	13·4	11·9
15	13 18·8	13 20·9	12 42·4	1·5	1·3	7·5	6·7	13·5	12·0
16	13 19·0	13 21·2	12 42·6	1·6	1·4	7·6	6·8	13·6	12·1
17	13 19·3	13 21·4	12 42·8	1·7	1·5	7·7	6·9	13·7	12·2
18	13 19·5	13 21·7	12 43·1	1·8	1·6	7·8	7·0	13·8	12·3
19	13 19·8	13 21·9	12 43·3	1·9	1·7	7·9	7·0	13·9	12·4
20	13 20·0	13 22·2	12 43·6	2·0	1·8	8·0	7·1	14·0	12·5
21	13 20·3	13 22·4	12 43·8	2·1	1·9	8·1	7·2	14·1	12·6
22	13 20·5	13 22·7	12 44·0	2·2	2·0	8·2	7·3	14·2	12·7
23	13 20·8	13 22·9	12 44·3	2·3	2·1	8·3	7·4	14·3	12·8
24	13 21·0	13 23·2	12 44·5	2·4	2·1	8·4	7·5	14·4	12·8
25	13 21·3	13 23·4	12 44·7	2·5	2·2	8·5	7·6	14·5	12·9
26	13 21·5	13 23·7	12 45·0	2·6	2·3	8·6	7·7	14·6	13·0
27	13 21·8	13 23·9	12 45·2	2·7	2·4	8·7	7·8	14·7	13·1
28	13 22·0	13 24·2	12 45·5	2·8	2·5	8·8	7·8	14·8	13·2
29	13 22·3	13 24·4	12 45·7	2·9	2·6	8·9	7·9	14·9	13·3
30	13 22·5	13 24·7	12 45·9	3·0	2·7	9·0	8·0	15·0	13·4
31	13 22·8	13 24·9	12 46·2	3·1	2·8	9·1	8·1	15·1	13·5
32	13 23·0	13 25·2	12 46·4	3·2	2·9	9·2	8·2	15·2	13·6
33	13 23·3	13 25·4	12 46·7	3·3	2·9	9·3	8·3	15·3	13·6
34	13 23·5	13 25·7	12 46·9	3·4	3·0	9·4	8·4	15·4	13·7
35	13 23·8	13 26·0	12 47·1	3·5	3·1	9·5	8·5	15·5	13·8
36	13 24·0	13 26·2	12 47·4	3·6	3·2	9·6	8·6	15·6	13·9
37	13 24·3	13 26·5	12 47·6	3·7	3·3	9·7	8·6	15·7	14·0
38	13 24·5	13 26·7	12 47·9	3·8	3·4	9·8	8·7	15·8	14·1
39	13 24·8	13 27·0	12 48·1	3·9	3·5	9·9	8·8	15·9	14·2
40	13 25·0	13 27·2	12 48·3	4·0	3·6	10·0	8·9	16·0	14·3
41	13 25·3	13 27·5	12 48·6	4·1	3·7	10·1	9·0	16·1	14·4
42	13 25·5	13 27·7	12 48·8	4·2	3·7	10·2	9·1	16·2	14·4
43	13 25·8	13 28·0	12 49·0	4·3	3·8	10·3	9·2	16·3	14·5
44	13 26·0	13 28·2	12 49·3	4·4	3·9	10·4	9·3	16·4	14·6
45	13 26·3	13 28·5	12 49·5	4·5	4·0	10·5	9·4	16·5	14·7
46	13 26·5	13 28·7	12 49·8	4·6	4·1	10·6	9·5	16·6	14·8
47	13 26·8	13 29·0	12 50·0	4·7	4·2	10·7	9·5	16·7	14·9
48	13 27·0	13 29·2	12 50·2	4·8	4·3	10·8	9·6	16·8	15·0
49	13 27·3	13 29·5	12 50·5	4·9	4·4	10·9	9·7	16·9	15·1
50	13 27·5	13 29·7	12 50·7	5·0	4·5	11·0	9·8	17·0	15·2
51	13 27·8	13 30·0	12 51·0	5·1	4·5	11·1	9·9	17·1	15·2
52	13 28·0	13 30·2	12 51·2	5·2	4·6	11·2	10·0	17·2	15·3
53	13 28·3	13 30·5	12 51·4	5·3	4·7	11·3	10·1	17·3	15·4
54	13 28·5	13 30·7	12 51·7	5·4	4·8	11·4	10·2	17·4	15·5
55	13 28·8	13 31·0	12 51·9	5·5	4·9	11·5	10·3	17·5	15·6
56	13 29·0	13 31·2	12 52·1	5·6	5·0	11·6	10·3	17·6	15·7
57	13 29·3	13 31·5	12 52·4	5·7	5·1	11·7	10·4	17·7	15·8
58	13 29·5	13 31·7	12 52·6	5·8	5·2	11·8	10·5	17·8	15·9
59	13 29·8	13 32·0	12 52·9	5·9	5·3	11·9	10·6	17·9	16·0
60	13 30·0	13 32·2	12 53·1	6·0	5·4	12·0	10·7	18·0	16·1

54ᵐ / 55ᵐ INCREMENTS AND CORRECTIONS

54 m / s	SUN PLANETS	ARIES	MOON	v or d Corrⁿ	v or d Corrⁿ	v or d Corrⁿ
00	13 30·0	13 32·2	12 53·1	0·0 0·0	6·0 5·5	12·0 10·9
01	13 30·3	13 32·5	12 53·3	0·1 0·1	6·1 5·5	12·1 11·0
02	13 30·5	13 32·7	12 53·6	0·2 0·2	6·2 5·6	12·2 11·1
03	13 30·8	13 33·0	12 53·8	0·3 0·3	6·3 5·7	12·3 11·2
04	13 31·0	13 33·2	12 54·1	0·4 0·4	6·4 5·8	12·4 11·3
05	13 31·3	13 33·5	12 54·3	0·5 0·5	6·5 5·9	12·5 11·4
06	13 31·5	13 33·7	12 54·5	0·6 0·5	6·6 6·0	12·6 11·4
07	13 31·8	13 34·0	12 54·8	0·7 0·6	6·7 6·1	12·7 11·5
08	13 32·0	13 34·2	12 55·0	0·8 0·7	6·8 6·2	12·8 11·6
09	13 32·3	13 34·5	12 55·2	0·9 0·8	6·9 6·3	12·9 11·7
10	13 32·5	13 34·7	12 55·5	1·0 0·9	7·0 6·4	13·0 11·8
11	13 32·8	13 35·0	12 55·7	1·1 1·0	7·1 6·4	13·1 11·9
12	13 33·0	13 35·2	12 56·0	1·2 1·1	7·2 6·5	13·2 12·0
13	13 33·3	13 35·5	12 56·2	1·3 1·2	7·3 6·6	13·3 12·1
14	13 33·5	13 35·7	12 56·4	1·4 1·3	7·4 6·7	13·4 12·2
15	13 33·8	13 36·0	12 56·7	1·5 1·4	7·5 6·8	13·5 12·3
16	13 34·0	13 36·2	12 56·9	1·6 1·5	7·6 6·9	13·6 12·4
17	13 34·3	13 36·5	12 57·2	1·7 1·5	7·7 7·0	13·7 12·4
18	13 34·5	13 36·7	12 57·4	1·8 1·6	7·8 7·1	13·8 12·5
19	13 34·8	13 37·0	12 57·6	1·9 1·7	7·9 7·2	13·9 12·6
20	13 35·0	13 37·2	12 57·9	2·0 1·8	8·0 7·3	14·0 12·7
21	13 35·3	13 37·5	12 58·1	2·1 1·9	8·1 7·4	14·1 12·8
22	13 35·5	13 37·7	12 58·3	2·2 2·0	8·2 7·4	14·2 12·9
23	13 35·8	13 38·0	12 58·6	2·3 2·1	8·3 7·5	14·3 13·0
24	13 36·0	13 38·2	12 58·8	2·4 2·2	8·4 7·6	14·4 13·1
25	13 36·3	13 38·5	12 59·1	2·5 2·3	8·5 7·7	14·5 13·2
26	13 36·5	13 38·7	12 59·3	2·6 2·4	8·6 7·8	14·6 13·3
27	13 36·8	13 39·0	12 59·5	2·7 2·5	8·7 7·9	14·7 13·4
28	13 37·0	13 39·2	12 59·8	2·8 2·5	8·8 8·0	14·8 13·4
29	13 37·3	13 39·5	13 00·0	2·9 2·6	8·9 8·1	14·9 13·5
30	13 37·5	13 39·7	13 00·3	3·0 2·7	9·0 8·2	15·0 13·6
31	13 37·8	13 40·0	13 00·5	3·1 2·8	9·1 8·3	15·1 13·7
32	13 38·0	13 40·2	13 00·7	3·2 2·9	9·2 8·4	15·2 13·8
33	13 38·3	13 40·5	13 01·0	3·3 3·0	9·3 8·4	15·3 13·9
34	13 38·5	13 40·7	13 01·2	3·4 3·1	9·4 8·5	15·4 14·0
35	13 38·8	13 41·0	13 01·5	3·5 3·2	9·5 8·6	15·5 14·1
36	13 39·0	13 41·2	13 01·7	3·6 3·3	9·6 8·7	15·6 14·2
37	13 39·3	13 41·5	13 01·9	3·7 3·4	9·7 8·8	15·7 14·3
38	13 39·5	13 41·7	13 02·2	3·8 3·5	9·8 8·9	15·8 14·4
39	13 39·8	13 42·0	13 02·4	3·9 3·5	9·9 9·0	15·9 14·4
40	13 40·0	13 42·2	13 02·6	4·0 3·6	10·0 9·1	16·0 14·5
41	13 40·3	13 42·5	13 02·9	4·1 3·7	10·1 9·2	16·1 14·6
42	13 40·5	13 42·7	13 03·1	4·2 3·8	10·2 9·3	16·2 14·7
43	13 40·8	13 43·0	13 03·4	4·3 3·9	10·3 9·4	16·3 14·8
44	13 41·0	13 43·2	13 03·6	4·4 4·0	10·4 9·4	16·4 14·9
45	13 41·3	13 43·5	13 03·8	4·5 4·1	10·5 9·5	16·5 15·0
46	13 41·5	13 43·7	13 04·1	4·6 4·2	10·6 9·6	16·6 15·1
47	13 41·8	13 44·0	13 04·3	4·7 4·3	10·7 9·7	16·7 15·2
48	13 42·0	13 44·3	13 04·6	4·8 4·4	10·8 9·8	16·8 15·3
49	13 42·3	13 44·5	13 04·8	4·9 4·5	10·9 9·9	16·9 15·4
50	13 42·5	13 44·8	13 05·0	5·0 4·5	11·0 10·0	17·0 15·4
51	13 42·8	13 45·0	13 05·3	5·1 4·6	11·1 10·1	17·1 15·5
52	13 43·0	13 45·3	13 05·5	5·2 4·7	11·2 10·2	17·2 15·6
53	13 43·3	13 45·5	13 05·7	5·3 4·8	11·3 10·3	17·3 15·7
54	13 43·5	13 45·8	13 06·0	5·4 4·9	11·4 10·4	17·4 15·8
55	13 43·8	13 46·0	13 06·2	5·5 5·0	11·5 10·4	17·5 15·9
56	13 44·0	13 46·3	13 06·5	5·6 5·1	11·6 10·5	17·6 16·0
57	13 44·3	13 46·5	13 06·7	5·7 5·2	11·7 10·6	17·7 16·1
58	13 44·5	13 46·8	13 06·9	5·8 5·3	11·8 10·7	17·8 16·2
59	13 44·8	13 47·0	13 07·2	5·9 5·4	11·9 10·8	17·9 16·3
60	13 45·0	13 47·3	13 07·4	6·0 5·5	12·0 10·9	18·0 16·4

55 m / s	SUN PLANETS	ARIES	MOON	v or d Corrⁿ	v or d Corrⁿ	v or d Corrⁿ
00	13 45·0	13 47·3	13 07·4	0·0 0·0	6·0 5·6	12·0 11·1
01	13 45·3	13 47·5	13 07·7	0·1 0·1	6·1 5·6	12·1 11·2
02	13 45·5	13 47·8	13 07·9	0·2 0·2	6·2 5·7	12·2 11·3
03	13 45·8	13 48·0	13 08·1	0·3 0·3	6·3 5·8	12·3 11·4
04	13 46·0	13 48·3	13 08·4	0·4 0·4	6·4 5·9	12·4 11·5
05	13 46·3	13 48·5	13 08·6	0·5 0·5	6·5 6·0	12·5 11·6
06	13 46·5	13 48·8	13 08·8	0·6 0·6	6·6 6·1	12·6 11·7
07	13 46·8	13 49·0	13 09·1	0·7 0·6	6·7 6·2	12·7 11·7
08	13 47·0	13 49·3	13 09·3	0·8 0·7	6·8 6·3	12·8 11·8
09	13 47·3	13 49·5	13 09·6	0·9 0·8	6·9 6·4	12·9 11·9
10	13 47·5	13 49·8	13 09·8	1·0 0·9	7·0 6·5	13·0 12·0
11	13 47·8	13 50·0	13 10·0	1·1 1·0	7·1 6·6	13·1 12·1
12	13 48·0	13 50·3	13 10·3	1·2 1·1	7·2 6·7	13·2 12·2
13	13 48·3	13 50·5	13 10·5	1·3 1·2	7·3 6·8	13·3 12·3
14	13 48·5	13 50·8	13 10·8	1·4 1·3	7·4 6·8	13·4 12·4
15	13 48·8	13 51·0	13 11·0	1·5 1·4	7·5 6·9	13·5 12·5
16	13 49·0	13 51·3	13 11·2	1·6 1·5	7·6 7·0	13·6 12·6
17	13 49·3	13 51·5	13 11·5	1·7 1·6	7·7 7·1	13·7 12·7
18	13 49·5	13 51·8	13 11·7	1·8 1·7	7·8 7·2	13·8 12·8
19	13 49·8	13 52·0	13 12·0	1·9 1·8	7·9 7·3	13·9 12·9
20	13 50·0	13 52·3	13 12·2	2·0 1·9	8·0 7·4	14·0 13·0
21	13 50·3	13 52·5	13 12·4	2·1 1·9	8·1 7·5	14·1 13·0
22	13 50·5	13 52·8	13 12·7	2·2 2·0	8·2 7·6	14·2 13·1
23	13 50·8	13 53·0	13 12·9	2·3 2·1	8·3 7·7	14·3 13·2
24	13 51·0	13 53·3	13 13·1	2·4 2·2	8·4 7·8	14·4 13·3
25	13 51·3	13 53·5	13 13·4	2·5 2·3	8·5 7·9	14·5 13·4
26	13 51·5	13 53·8	13 13·6	2·6 2·4	8·6 8·0	14·6 13·5
27	13 51·8	13 54·0	13 13·9	2·7 2·5	8·7 8·0	14·7 13·6
28	13 52·0	13 54·3	13 14·1	2·8 2·6	8·8 8·1	14·8 13·7
29	13 52·3	13 54·5	13 14·3	2·9 2·7	8·9 8·2	14·9 13·8
30	13 52·5	13 54·8	13 14·6	3·0 2·8	9·0 8·3	15·0 13·9
31	13 52·8	13 55·0	13 14·8	3·1 2·9	9·1 8·4	15·1 14·0
32	13 53·0	13 55·3	13 15·1	3·2 3·0	9·2 8·5	15·2 14·1
33	13 53·3	13 55·5	13 15·3	3·3 3·1	9·3 8·6	15·3 14·2
34	13 53·5	13 55·8	13 15·5	3·4 3·1	9·4 8·7	15·4 14·2
35	13 53·8	13 56·0	13 15·8	3·5 3·2	9·5 8·8	15·5 14·3
36	13 54·0	13 56·3	13 16·0	3·6 3·3	9·6 8·9	15·6 14·4
37	13 54·3	13 56·5	13 16·2	3·7 3·4	9·7 9·0	15·7 14·5
38	13 54·5	13 56·8	13 16·5	3·8 3·5	9·8 9·1	15·8 14·6
39	13 54·8	13 57·0	13 16·7	3·9 3·6	9·9 9·2	15·9 14·7
40	13 55·0	13 57·3	13 17·0	4·0 3·7	10·0 9·3	16·0 14·8
41	13 55·3	13 57·5	13 17·2	4·1 3·8	10·1 9·3	16·1 14·9
42	13 55·5	13 57·8	13 17·4	4·2 3·9	10·2 9·4	16·2 15·0
43	13 55·8	13 58·0	13 17·7	4·3 4·0	10·3 9·5	16·3 15·1
44	13 56·0	13 58·3	13 17·9	4·4 4·1	10·4 9·6	16·4 15·2
45	13 56·3	13 58·5	13 18·2	4·5 4·2	10·5 9·7	16·5 15·3
46	13 56·5	13 58·8	13 18·4	4·6 4·3	10·6 9·8	16·6 15·4
47	13 56·8	13 59·0	13 18·6	4·7 4·3	10·7 9·9	16·7 15·4
48	13 57·0	13 59·3	13 18·9	4·8 4·4	10·8 10·0	16·8 15·5
49	13 57·3	13 59·5	13 19·1	4·9 4·5	10·9 10·1	16·9 15·6
50	13 57·5	13 59·8	13 19·3	5·0 4·6	11·0 10·2	17·0 15·7
51	13 57·8	14 00·0	13 19·6	5·1 4·7	11·1 10·3	17·1 15·8
52	13 58·0	14 00·3	13 19·8	5·2 4·8	11·2 10·4	17·2 15·9
53	13 58·3	14 00·5	13 20·1	5·3 4·9	11·3 10·5	17·3 16·0
54	13 58·5	14 00·8	13 20·3	5·4 5·0	11·4 10·5	17·4 16·1
55	13 58·8	14 01·0	13 20·5	5·5 5·1	11·5 10·6	17·5 16·2
56	13 59·0	14 01·3	13 20·8	5·6 5·2	11·6 10·7	17·6 16·3
57	13 59·3	14 01·5	13 21·0	5·7 5·3	11·7 10·8	17·7 16·4
58	13 59·5	14 01·8	13 21·3	5·8 5·4	11·8 10·9	17·8 16·5
59	13 59·8	14 02·0	13 21·5	5·9 5·5	11·9 11·0	17·9 16·6
60	14 00·0	14 02·3	13 21·7	6·0 5·6	12·0 11·1	18·0 16·7

56^m	SUN PLANETS	ARIES	MOON	v or Corr^n d		v or Corr^n d		v or Corr^n d	
s	° ′	° ′	° ′	′	′	′	′	′	′
00	14 00·0	14 02·3	13 21·7	0·0	0·0	6·0	5·7	12·0	11·3
01	14 00·3	14 02·6	13 22·0	0·1	0·1	6·1	5·7	12·1	11·4
02	14 00·5	14 02·8	13 22·2	0·2	0·2	6·2	5·8	12·2	11·5
03	14 00·8	14 03·1	13 22·4	0·3	0·3	6·3	5·9	12·3	11·6
04	14 01·0	14 03·3	13 22·7	0·4	0·4	6·4	6·0	12·4	11·7
05	14 01·3	14 03·6	13 22·9	0·5	0·5	6·5	6·1	12·5	11·8
06	14 01·5	14 03·8	13 23·2	0·6	0·6	6·6	6·2	12·6	11·9
07	14 01·8	14 04·1	13 23·4	0·7	0·7	6·7	6·3	12·7	12·0
08	14 02·0	14 04·3	13 23·6	0·8	0·8	6·8	6·4	12·8	12·1
09	14 02·3	14 04·6	13 23·9	0·9	0·8	6·9	6·5	12·9	12·1
10	14 02·5	14 04·8	13 24·1	1·0	0·9	7·0	6·6	13·0	12·2
11	14 02·8	14 05·1	13 24·4	1·1	1·0	7·1	6·7	13·1	12·3
12	14 03·0	14 05·3	13 24·6	1·2	1·1	7·2	6·8	13·2	12·4
13	14 03·3	14 05·8	13 24·8	1·3	1·2	7·3	6·9	13·3	12·5
14	14 03·5	14 05·8	13 25·1	1·4	1·3	7·4	7·0	13·4	12·6
15	14 03·8	14 06·1	13 25·3	1·5	1·4	7·5	7·1	13·5	12·7
16	14 04·0	14 06·3	13 25·6	1·6	1·5	7·6	7·2	13·6	12·8
17	14 04·3	14 06·6	13 25·8	1·7	1·6	7·7	7·3	13·7	12·9
18	14 04·5	14 06·8	13 26·0	1·8	1·7	7·8	7·3	13·8	13·0
19	14 04·8	14 07·1	13 26·3	1·9	1·8	7·9	7·4	13·9	13·1
20	14 05·0	14 07·3	13 26·5	2·0	1·9	8·0	7·5	14·0	13·2
21	14 05·3	14 07·6	13 26·7	2·1	2·0	8·1	7·6	14·1	13·3
22	14 05·5	14 07·8	13 27·0	2·2	2·1	8·2	7·7	14·2	13·4
23	14 05·8	14 08·1	13 27·2	2·3	2·2	8·3	7·8	14·3	13·5
24	14 06·0	14 08·3	13 27·5	2·4	2·3	8·4	7·9	14·4	13·6
25	14 06·3	14 08·6	13 27·7	2·5	2·4	8·5	8·0	14·5	13·7
26	14 06·5	14 08·8	13 27·9	2·6	2·4	8·6	8·1	14·6	13·7
27	14 06·8	14 09·1	13 28·2	2·7	2·5	8·7	8·2	14·7	13·8
28	14 07·0	14 09·3	13 28·4	2·8	2·6	8·8	8·3	14·8	13·9
29	14 07·3	14 09·6	13 28·7	2·9	2·7	8·9	8·4	14·9	14·0
30	14 07·5	14 09·8	13 28·9	3·0	2·8	9·0	8·5	15·0	14·1
31	14 07·8	14 10·1	13 29·1	3·1	2·9	9·1	8·6	15·1	14·2
32	14 08·0	14 10·3	13 29·4	3·2	3·0	9·2	8·7	15·2	14·3
33	14 08·3	14 10·6	13 29·6	3·3	3·1	9·3	8·8	15·3	14·4
34	14 08·5	14 10·8	13 29·8	3·4	3·2	9·4	8·9	15·4	14·5
35	14 08·8	14 11·1	13 30·1	3·5	3·3	9·5	8·9	15·5	14·6
36	14 09·0	14 11·3	13 30·3	3·6	3·4	9·6	9·0	15·6	14·7
37	14 09·3	14 11·6	13 30·6	3·7	3·5	9·7	9·1	15·7	14·8
38	14 09·5	14 11·8	13 30·8	3·8	3·6	9·8	9·2	15·8	14·9
39	14 09·8	14 12·1	13 31·0	3·9	3·7	9·9	9·3	15·9	15·0
40	14 10·0	14 12·3	13 31·3	4·0	3·8	10·0	9·4	16·0	15·1
41	14 10·3	14 12·6	13 31·5	4·1	3·9	10·1	9·5	16·1	15·2
42	14 10·5	14 12·8	13 31·8	4·2	4·0	10·2	9·6	16·2	15·3
43	14 10·8	14 13·1	13 32·0	4·3	4·0	10·3	9·7	16·3	15·3
44	14 11·0	14 13·3	13 32·2	4·4	4·1	10·4	9·8	16·4	15·4
45	14 11·3	14 13·6	13 32·5	4·5	4·2	10·5	9·9	16·5	15·5
46	14 11·5	14 13·8	13 32·7	4·6	4·3	10·6	10·0	16·6	15·6
47	14 11·8	14 14·1	13 32·9	4·7	4·4	10·7	10·1	16·7	15·7
48	14 12·0	14 14·3	13 33·2	4·8	4·5	10·8	10·2	16·8	15·8
49	14 12·3	14 14·6	13 33·4	4·9	4·6	10·9	10·3	16·9	15·9
50	14 12·5	14 14·8	13 33·7	5·0	4·7	11·0	10·4	17·0	16·0
51	14 12·8	14 15·1	13 33·9	5·1	4·8	11·1	10·5	17·1	16·1
52	14 13·0	14 15·3	13 34·1	5·2	4·9	11·2	10·5	17·2	16·2
53	14 13·3	14 15·6	13 34·4	5·3	5·0	11·3	10·6	17·3	16·3
54	14 13·5	14 15·8	13 34·6	5·4	5·1	11·4	10·7	17·4	16·4
55	14 13·8	14 16·1	13 34·9	5·5	5·2	11·5	10·8	17·5	16·5
56	14 14·0	14 16·3	13 35·1	5·6	5·3	11·6	10·9	17·6	16·6
57	14 14·3	14 16·6	13 35·3	5·7	5·4	11·7	11·0	17·7	16·7
58	14 14·5	14 16·8	13 35·6	5·8	5·5	11·8	11·1	17·8	16·8
59	14 14·8	14 17·1	13 35·8	5·9	5·6	11·9	11·2	17·9	16·9
60	14 15·0	14 17·3	13 36·1	6·0	5·7	12·0	11·3	18·0	17·0

57^m	SUN PLANETS	ARIES	MOON	v or Corr^n d		v or Corr^n d		v or Corr^n d	
s	° ′	° ′	° ′	′	′	′	′	′	′
00	14 15·0	14 17·3	13 36·1	0·0	0·0	6·0	5·8	12·0	11·5
01	14 15·3	14 17·6	13 36·3	0·1	0·1	6·1	5·8	12·1	11·6
02	14 15·5	14 17·8	13 36·5	0·2	0·2	6·2	5·9	12·2	11·7
03	14 15·8	14 18·1	13 36·8	0·3	0·3	6·3	6·0	12·3	11·8
04	14 16·0	14 18·3	13 37·0	0·4	0·4	6·4	6·1	12·4	11·9
05	14 16·3	14 18·6	13 37·2	0·5	0·5	6·5	6·2	12·5	12·0
06	14 16·5	14 18·8	13 37·5	0·6	0·6	6·6	6·3	12·6	12·1
07	14 16·8	14 19·1	13 37·7	0·7	0·7	6·7	6·4	12·7	12·2
08	14 17·0	14 19·3	13 38·0	0·8	0·8	6·8	6·5	12·8	12·3
09	14 17·3	14 19·6	13 38·2	0·9	0·9	6·9	6·6	12·9	12·4
10	14 17·5	14 19·8	13 38·4	1·0	1·0	7·0	6·7	13·0	12·5
11	14 17·8	14 20·1	13 38·7	1·1	1·1	7·1	6·8	13·1	12·6
12	14 18·0	14 20·3	13 38·9	1·2	1·2	7·2	6·9	13·2	12·7
13	14 18·3	14 20·6	13 39·2	1·3	1·2	7·3	7·0	13·3	12·7
14	14 18·5	14 20·9	13 39·4	1·4	1·3	7·4	7·1	13·4	12·8
15	14 18·8	14 21·1	13 39·6	1·5	1·4	7·5	7·2	13·5	12·9
16	14 19·0	14 21·4	13 39·9	1·6	1·5	7·6	7·3	13·6	13·0
17	14 19·3	14 21·6	13 40·1	1·7	1·6	7·7	7·4	13·7	13·1
18	14 19·5	14 21·9	13 40·3	1·8	1·7	7·8	7·5	13·8	13·2
19	14 19·8	14 22·1	13 40·6	1·9	1·8	7·9	7·6	13·9	13·3
20	14 20·0	14 22·4	13 40·8	2·0	1·9	8·0	7·7	14·0	13·4
21	14 20·3	14 22·6	13 41·1	2·1	2·0	8·1	7·8	14·1	13·5
22	14 20·5	14 22·9	13 41·3	2·2	2·1	8·2	7·9	14·2	13·6
23	14 20·8	14 23·1	13 41·5	2·3	2·2	8·3	8·0	14·3	13·7
24	14 21·0	14 23·4	13 41·8	2·4	2·3	8·4	8·1	14·4	13·8
25	14 21·3	14 23·6	13 42·0	2·5	2·4	8·5	8·1	14·5	13·9
26	14 21·5	14 23·9	13 42·3	2·6	2·5	8·6	8·2	14·6	14·0
27	14 21·8	14 24·1	13 42·5	2·7	2·6	8·7	8·3	14·7	14·1
28	14 22·0	14 24·4	13 42·7	2·8	2·7	8·8	8·4	14·8	14·2
29	14 22·3	14 24·6	13 43·0	2·9	2·8	8·9	8·5	14·9	14·3
30	14 22·5	14 24·9	13 43·2	3·0	2·9	9·0	8·6	15·0	14·4
31	14 22·8	14 25·1	13 43·4	3·1	3·0	9·1	8·7	15·1	14·5
32	14 23·0	14 25·4	13 43·7	3·2	3·1	9·2	8·8	15·2	14·6
33	14 23·3	14 25·6	13 43·9	3·3	3·2	9·3	8·9	15·3	14·7
34	14 23·5	14 25·9	13 44·2	3·4	3·3	9·4	9·0	15·4	14·8
35	14 23·8	14 26·1	13 44·4	3·5	3·4	9·5	9·1	15·5	14·9
36	14 24·0	14 26·4	13 44·6	3·6	3·5	9·6	9·2	15·6	15·0
37	14 24·3	14 26·6	13 44·9	3·7	3·5	9·7	9·3	15·7	15·0
38	14 24·5	14 26·9	13 45·1	3·8	3·6	9·8	9·4	15·8	15·1
39	14 24·8	14 27·1	13 45·4	3·9	3·7	9·9	9·5	15·9	15·2
40	14 25·0	14 27·4	13 45·6	4·0	3·8	10·0	9·6	16·0	15·3
41	14 25·3	14 27·6	13 45·8	4·1	3·9	10·1	9·7	16·1	15·4
42	14 25·5	14 27·9	13 46·1	4·2	4·0	10·2	9·8	16·2	15·5
43	14 25·8	14 28·1	13 46·3	4·3	4·1	10·3	9·9	16·3	15·6
44	14 26·0	14 28·4	13 46·5	4·4	4·2	10·4	10·0	16·4	15·7
45	14 26·3	14 28·6	13 46·8	4·5	4·3	10·5	10·1	16·5	15·8
46	14 26·5	14 28·9	13 47·0	4·6	4·4	10·6	10·2	16·6	15·9
47	14 26·8	14 29·1	13 47·3	4·7	4·5	10·7	10·3	16·7	16·0
48	14 27·0	14 29·4	13 47·5	4·8	4·6	10·8	10·4	16·8	16·1
49	14 27·3	14 29·6	13 47·7	4·9	4·7	10·9	10·4	16·9	16·2
50	14 27·5	14 29·9	13 48·0	5·0	4·8	11·0	10·5	17·0	16·3
51	14 27·8	14 30·1	13 48·2	5·1	4·9	11·1	10·6	17·1	16·4
52	14 28·0	14 30·4	13 48·5	5·2	5·0	11·2	10·7	17·2	16·5
53	14 28·3	14 30·6	13 48·7	5·3	5·1	11·3	10·8	17·3	16·6
54	14 28·5	14 30·9	13 48·9	5·4	5·2	11·4	10·9	17·4	16·7
55	14 28·8	14 31·1	13 49·2	5·5	5·3	11·5	11·0	17·5	16·8
56	14 29·0	14 31·4	13 49·4	5·6	5·4	11·6	11·1	17·6	16·9
57	14 29·3	14 31·6	13 49·7	5·7	5·5	11·7	11·2	17·7	17·0
58	14 29·5	14 31·9	13 49·9	5·8	5·6	11·8	11·3	17·8	17·1
59	14 29·8	14 32·1	13 50·1	5·9	5·7	11·9	11·4	17·9	17·2
60	14 30·0	14 32·4	13 50·4	6·0	5·8	12·0	11·5	18·0	17·3

58ᵐ

s	SUN PLANETS	ARIES	MOON	v or d	Corrⁿ	v or d	Corrⁿ	v or d	Corrⁿ
00	14 30·0	14 32·4	13 50·4	0·0	0·0	6·0	5·9	12·0	11·7
01	14 30·3	14 32·6	13 50·6	0·1	0·1	6·1	5·9	12·1	11·8
02	14 30·5	14 32·9	13 50·8	0·2	0·2	6·2	6·0	12·2	11·9
03	14 30·8	14 33·1	13 51·1	0·3	0·3	6·3	6·1	12·3	12·0
04	14 31·0	14 33·4	13 51·3	0·4	0·4	6·4	6·2	12·4	12·1
05	14 31·3	14 33·6	13 51·6	0·5	0·5	6·5	6·3	12·5	12·2
06	14 31·5	14 33·9	13 51·8	0·6	0·6	6·6	6·4	12·6	12·3
07	14 31·8	14 34·1	13 52·0	0·7	0·7	6·7	6·5	12·7	12·4
08	14 32·0	14 34·4	13 52·3	0·8	0·8	6·8	6·6	12·8	12·5
09	14 32·3	14 34·6	13 52·5	0·9	0·9	6·9	6·7	12·9	12·6
10	14 32·5	14 34·9	13 52·8	1·0	1·0	7·0	6·8	13·0	12·7
11	14 32·8	14 35·1	13 53·0	1·1	1·1	7·1	6·9	13·1	12·8
12	14 33·0	14 35·4	13 53·2	1·2	1·2	7·2	7·0	13·2	12·9
13	14 33·3	14 35·6	13 53·5	1·3	1·3	7·3	7·1	13·3	13·0
14	14 33·5	14 35·9	13 53·7	1·4	1·4	7·4	7·2	13·4	13·1
15	14 33·8	14 36·1	13 53·9	1·5	1·5	7·5	7·3	13·5	13·2
16	14 34·0	14 36·4	13 54·2	1·6	1·6	7·6	7·4	13·6	13·3
17	14 34·3	14 36·6	13 54·4	1·7	1·7	7·7	7·5	13·7	13·4
18	14 34·5	14 36·9	13 54·7	1·8	1·8	7·8	7·6	13·8	13·5
19	14 34·8	14 37·1	13 54·9	1·9	1·9	7·9	7·7	13·9	13·6
20	14 35·0	14 37·4	13 55·1	2·0	2·0	8·0	7·8	14·0	13·7
21	14 35·3	14 37·6	13 55·4	2·1	2·0	8·1	7·9	14·1	13·7
22	14 35·5	14 37·9	13 55·6	2·2	2·1	8·2	8·0	14·2	13·8
23	14 35·8	14 38·1	13 55·9	2·3	2·2	8·3	8·1	14·3	13·9
24	14 36·0	14 38·4	13 56·1	2·4	2·3	8·4	8·2	14·4	14·0
25	14 36·3	14 38·6	13 56·3	2·5	2·4	8·5	8·3	14·5	14·1
26	14 36·5	14 38·9	13 56·6	2·6	2·5	8·6	8·4	14·6	14·2
27	14 36·8	14 39·2	13 56·8	2·7	2·6	8·7	8·5	14·7	14·3
28	14 37·0	14 39·4	13 57·0	2·8	2·7	8·8	8·6	14·8	14·4
29	14 37·3	14 39·7	13 57·3	2·9	2·8	8·9	8·7	14·9	14·5
30	14 37·5	14 39·9	13 57·5	3·0	2·9	9·0	8·8	15·0	14·6
31	14 37·8	14 40·2	13 57·8	3·1	3·0	9·1	8·9	15·1	14·7
32	14 38·0	14 40·4	13 58·0	3·2	3·1	9·2	9·0	15·2	14·8
33	14 38·3	14 40·7	13 58·2	3·3	3·2	9·3	9·1	15·3	14·9
34	14 38·5	14 40·9	13 58·5	3·4	3·3	9·4	9·2	15·4	15·0
35	14 38·8	14 41·2	13 58·7	3·5	3·4	9·5	9·3	15·5	15·1
36	14 39·0	14 41·4	13 59·0	3·6	3·5	9·6	9·4	15·6	15·2
37	14 39·3	14 41·7	13 59·2	3·7	3·6	9·7	9·5	15·7	15·3
38	14 39·5	14 41·9	13 59·4	3·8	3·7	9·8	9·6	15·8	15·4
39	14 39·8	14 42·2	13 59·7	3·9	3·8	9·9	9·7	15·9	15·5
40	14 40·0	14 42·4	13 59·9	4·0	3·9	10·0	9·8	16·0	15·6
41	14 40·3	14 42·7	14 00·1	4·1	4·0	10·1	9·8	16·1	15·7
42	14 40·5	14 42·9	14 00·4	4·2	4·1	10·2	9·9	16·2	15·8
43	14 40·8	14 43·2	14 00·6	4·3	4·2	10·3	10·0	16·3	15·9
44	14 41·0	14 43·4	14 00·9	4·4	4·3	10·4	10·1	16·4	16·0
45	14 41·3	14 43·7	14 01·1	4·5	4·4	10·5	10·2	16·5	16·1
46	14 41·5	14 43·9	14 01·3	4·6	4·5	10·6	10·3	16·6	16·2
47	14 41·8	14 44·2	14 01·6	4·7	4·6	10·7	10·4	16·7	16·3
48	14 42·0	14 44·4	14 01·8	4·8	4·7	10·8	10·5	16·8	16·4
49	14 42·3	14 44·7	14 02·1	4·9	4·8	10·9	10·6	16·9	16·5
50	14 42·5	14 44·9	14 02·3	5·0	4·9	11·0	10·7	17·0	16·6
51	14 42·8	14 45·2	14 02·5	5·1	5·0	11·1	10·8	17·1	16·7
52	14 43·0	14 45·4	14 02·8	5·2	5·1	11·2	10·9	17·2	16·8
53	14 43·3	14 45·7	14 03·0	5·3	5·2	11·3	11·0	17·3	16·9
54	14 43·5	14 45·9	14 03·3	5·4	5·3	11·4	11·1	17·4	17·0
55	14 43·8	14 46·2	14 03·5	5·5	5·4	11·5	11·2	17·5	17·1
56	14 44·0	14 46·4	14 03·7	5·6	5·5	11·6	11·3	17·6	17·2
57	14 44·3	14 46·6	14 04·0	5·7	5·6	11·7	11·4	17·7	17·3
58	14 44·5	14 46·9	14 04·2	5·8	5·7	11·8	11·5	17·8	17·4
59	14 44·8	14 47·2	14 04·4	5·9	5·8	11·9	11·6	17·9	17·5
60	14 45·0	14 47·4	14 04·7	6·0	5·9	12·0	11·7	18·0	17·6

59ᵐ

s	SUN PLANETS	ARIES	MOON	v or d	Corrⁿ	v or d	Corrⁿ	v or d	Corrⁿ
00	14 45·0	14 47·4	14 04·7	0·0	0·0	6·0	6·0	12·0	11·9
01	14 45·3	14 47·7	14 04·9	0·1	0·1	6·1	6·0	12·1	12·0
02	14 45·5	14 47·9	14 05·2	0·2	0·2	6·2	6·1	12·2	12·1
03	14 45·8	14 48·2	14 05·4	0·3	0·3	6·3	6·2	12·3	12·2
04	14 46·0	14 48·4	14 05·6	0·4	0·4	6·4	6·3	12·4	12·3
05	14 46·3	14 48·7	14 05·9	0·5	0·5	6·5	6·4	12·5	12·4
06	14 46·5	14 48·9	14 06·1	0·6	0·6	6·6	6·5	12·6	12·5
07	14 46·8	14 49·2	14 06·4	0·7	0·7	6·7	6·6	12·7	12·6
08	14 47·0	14 49·4	14 06·6	0·8	0·8	6·8	6·7	12·8	12·7
09	14 47·3	14 49·7	14 06·8	0·9	0·9	6·9	6·8	12·9	12·8
10	14 47·5	14 49·9	14 07·1	1·0	1·0	7·0	6·9	13·0	12·9
11	14 47·8	14 50·2	14 07·3	1·1	1·1	7·1	7·0	13·1	13·0
12	14 48·0	14 50·4	14 07·5	1·2	1·2	7·2	7·1	13·2	13·1
13	14 48·3	14 50·7	14 07·8	1·3	1·3	7·3	7·2	13·3	13·2
14	14 48·5	14 50·9	14 08·0	1·4	1·4	7·4	7·3	13·4	13·3
15	14 48·8	14 51·2	14 08·3	1·5	1·5	7·5	7·4	13·5	13·4
16	14 49·0	14 51·4	14 08·5	1·6	1·6	7·6	7·5	13·6	13·5
17	14 49·3	14 51·7	14 08·7	1·7	1·7	7·7	7·6	13·7	13·6
18	14 49·5	14 51·9	14 09·0	1·8	1·8	7·8	7·7	13·8	13·7
19	14 49·8	14 52·2	14 09·2	1·9	1·9	7·9	7·8	13·9	13·8
20	14 50·0	14 52·4	14 09·5	2·0	2·0	8·0	7·9	14·0	13·9
21	14 50·3	14 52·7	14 09·7	2·1	2·1	8·1	8·0	14·1	14·0
22	14 50·5	14 52·9	14 09·9	2·2	2·2	8·2	8·1	14·2	14·1
23	14 50·8	14 53·2	14 10·2	2·3	2·3	8·3	8·2	14·3	14·2
24	14 51·0	14 53·4	14 10·4	2·4	2·4	8·4	8·3	14·4	14·3
25	14 51·3	14 53·7	14 10·6	2·5	2·5	8·5	8·4	14·5	14·4
26	14 51·5	14 53·9	14 10·9	2·6	2·6	8·6	8·5	14·6	14·5
27	14 51·8	14 54·2	14 11·1	2·7	2·7	8·7	8·6	14·7	14·6
28	14 52·0	14 54·4	14 11·4	2·8	2·8	8·8	8·7	14·8	14·7
29	14 52·3	14 54·7	14 11·6	2·9	2·9	8·9	8·8	14·9	14·8
30	14 52·5	14 54·9	14 11·8	3·0	3·0	9·0	8·9	15·0	14·9
31	14 52·8	14 55·2	14 12·1	3·1	3·1	9·1	9·0	15·1	15·0
32	14 53·0	14 55·4	14 12·3	3·2	3·2	9·2	9·1	15·2	15·1
33	14 53·3	14 55·7	14 12·6	3·3	3·3	9·3	9·2	15·3	15·2
34	14 53·5	14 55·9	14 12·8	3·4	3·4	9·4	9·3	15·4	15·3
35	14 53·8	14 56·2	14 13·0	3·5	3·5	9·5	9·4	15·5	15·4
36	14 54·0	14 56·4	14 13·3	3·6	3·6	9·6	9·5	15·6	15·5
37	14 54·3	14 56·7	14 13·5	3·7	3·7	9·7	9·6	15·7	15·6
38	14 54·5	14 56·9	14 13·8	3·8	3·8	9·8	9·7	15·8	15·7
39	14 54·8	14 57·2	14 14·0	3·9	3·9	9·9	9·8	15·9	15·8
40	14 55·0	14 57·5	14 14·2	4·0	4·0	10·0	9·9	16·0	15·9
41	14 55·3	14 57·7	14 14·5	4·1	4·1	10·1	10·0	16·1	16·0
42	14 55·5	14 58·0	14 14·7	4·2	4·2	10·2	10·1	16·2	16·1
43	14 55·8	14 58·2	14 14·9	4·3	4·3	10·3	10·2	16·3	16·2
44	14 56·0	14 58·5	14 15·2	4·4	4·4	10·4	10·3	16·4	16·3
45	14 56·3	14 58·7	14 15·4	4·5	4·5	10·5	10·4	16·5	16·4
46	14 56·5	14 59·0	14 15·7	4·6	4·6	10·6	10·5	16·6	16·5
47	14 56·8	14 59·2	14 15·9	4·7	4·7	10·7	10·6	16·7	16·6
48	14 57·0	14 59·5	14 16·1	4·8	4·8	10·8	10·7	16·8	16·7
49	14 57·3	14 59·7	14 16·4	4·9	4·9	10·9	10·8	16·9	16·8
50	14 57·5	15 00·0	14 16·6	5·0	5·0	11·0	10·9	17·0	16·9
51	14 57·8	15 00·2	14 16·9	5·1	5·1	11·1	11·0	17·1	17·0
52	14 58·0	15 00·5	14 17·1	5·2	5·2	11·2	11·1	17·2	17·1
53	14 58·3	15 00·7	14 17·3	5·3	5·3	11·3	11·2	17·3	17·2
54	14 58·5	15 01·0	14 17·6	5·4	5·4	11·4	11·3	17·4	17·3
55	14 58·8	15 01·2	14 17·8	5·5	5·5	11·5	11·4	17·5	17·4
56	14 59·0	15 01·5	14 18·0	5·6	5·6	11·6	11·5	17·6	17·5
57	14 59·3	15 01·7	14 18·3	5·7	5·7	11·7	11·6	17·7	17·6
58	14 59·5	15 02·0	14 18·5	5·8	5·8	11·8	11·7	17·8	17·7
59	14 59·8	15 02·2	14 18·8	5·9	5·9	11·9	11·8	17·9	17·8
60	15 00·0	15 02·5	14 19·0	6·0	6·0	12·0	11·9	18·0	17·9

TABLES FOR INTERPOLATING SUNRISE, MOONRISE, ETC.

TABLE I—FOR LATITUDE

Tabular Interval			Difference between the times for consecutive latitudes																
10°	5°	2°	5^m	10^m	15^m	20^m	25^m	30^m	35^m	40^m	45^m	50^m	55^m	60^m	1^{h}05^m	1^{h}10^m	1^{h}15^m	1^{h}20^m
0 30	0 15	0 06	0	0	1	1	1	1	1	2	2	2	2	2	0 02	0 02	0 02	0 02
1 00	0 30	0 12	0	1	1	2	2	3	3	3	4	4	4	5	05	05	05	05
1 30	0 45	0 18	1	1	2	3	3	4	4	5	5	6	7	7	07	07	07	07
2 00	1 00	0 24	1	2	3	4	5	5	6	7	7	8	9	10	10	10	10	10
2 30	1 15	0 30	1	2	4	5	6	7	8	9	9	10	11	12	12	13	13	13
3 00	1 30	0 36	1	3	4	6	7	8	9	10	11	12	13	14	0 15	0 15	0 16	0 16
3 30	1 45	0 42	2	3	5	7	8	10	11	12	13	14	16	17	18	18	19	19
4 00	2 00	0 48	2	4	6	8	9	11	13	14	15	16	18	19	20	21	22	22
4 30	2 15	0 54	2	4	7	9	11	13	15	16	18	19	21	22	23	24	25	26
5 00	2 30	1 00	2	5	7	10	12	14	16	18	20	22	23	25	26	27	28	29
5 30	2 45	1 06	3	5	8	11	13	16	18	20	22	24	26	28	0 29	0 30	0 31	0 32
6 00	3 00	1 12	3	6	9	12	14	17	20	22	24	26	29	31	32	33	34	36
6 30	3 15	1 18	3	6	10	13	16	19	22	24	26	29	31	34	36	37	38	40
7 00	3 30	1 24	3	7	10	14	17	20	23	26	29	31	34	37	39	41	42	44
7 30	3 45	1 30	4	7	11	15	18	22	25	28	31	34	37	40	43	44	46	48
8 00	4 00	1 36	4	8	12	16	20	23	27	30	34	37	41	44	0 47	0 48	0 51	0 53
8 30	4 15	1 42	4	8	13	17	21	25	29	33	36	40	44	48	0 51	0 53	0 56	0 58
9 00	4 30	1 48	4	9	13	18	22	27	31	35	39	43	47	52	0 55	0 58	1 01	1 04
9 30	4 45	1 54	5	9	14	19	24	28	33	38	42	47	51	56	1 00	1 04	1 08	1 12
10 00	5 00	2 00	5	10	15	20	25	30	35	40	45	50	55	60	1 05	1 10	1 15	1 20

Table I is for interpolating the LMT of sunrise, twilight, moonrise, etc., for latitude. It is to be entered, in the appropriate column on the left, with the difference between true latitude and the nearest tabular latitude which is *less* than the true latitude; and with the argument at the top which is the nearest value of the difference between the times for the tabular latitude and the next higher one; the correction so obtained is applied to the time for the tabular latitude; the sign of the correction can be seen by inspection. It is to be noted that the interpolation is not linear, so that when using this table it is essential to take out the tabular phenomenon for the latitude *less* than the true latitude.

TABLE II—FOR LONGITUDE

Long. East or West	Difference between the times for given date and preceding date (for east longitude) or for given date and following date (for west longitude)																		
	10^m	20^m	30^m	40^m	50^m	60^m	1^h+ 10^m	20^m	30^m	1^h+ 40^m	50^m	60^m	2^{h}10^m	2^{h}20^m	2^{h}30^m	2^{h}40^m	2^{h}50^m	3^{h}00^m
0	0	0	0	0	0	0	0	0	0	0	0	0	0 00	0 00	0 00	0 00	0 00	0 00
10	0	1	1	1	1	2	2	2	2	3	3	3	04	04	04	04	05	05
20	1	1	2	2	3	3	4	4	5	6	6	7	07	08	08	09	09	10
30	1	2	2	3	4	5	6	7	7	8	9	10	11	12	12	13	14	15
40	1	2	3	4	6	7	8	9	10	11	12	13	14	16	17	18	19	20
50	1	3	4	6	7	8	10	11	12	14	15	17	0 18	0 19	0 21	0 22	0 24	0 25
60	2	3	5	7	8	10	12	13	15	17	18	20	22	23	25	27	28	30
70	2	4	6	8	10	12	14	16	17	19	21	23	25	27	29	31	33	35
80	2	4	7	9	11	13	16	18	20	22	24	27	29	31	33	36	38	40
90	2	5	7	10	12	15	17	20	22	25	27	30	32	35	37	40	42	45
100	3	6	8	11	14	17	19	22	25	28	31	33	0 36	0 39	0 42	0 44	0 47	0 50
110	3	6	9	12	15	18	21	24	27	31	34	37	40	43	46	49	0 52	0 55
120	3	7	10	13	17	20	23	27	30	33	37	40	43	47	50	53	0 57	1 00
130	4	7	11	14	18	22	25	29	32	36	40	43	47	51	54	0 58	1 01	1 05
140	4	8	12	16	19	23	27	31	35	39	43	47	51	54	0 58	1 02	1 06	1 10
150	4	8	13	17	21	25	29	33	38	42	46	50	0 54	0 58	1 03	1 07	1 11	1 15
160	4	9	13	18	22	27	31	36	40	44	49	53	0 58	1 02	1 07	1 11	1 16	1 20
170	5	9	14	19	24	28	33	38	42	47	52	57	1 01	1 06	1 11	1 16	1 20	1 25
180	5	10	15	20	25	30	35	40	45	50	55	60	1 05	1 10	1 15	1 20	1 25	1 30

Table II is for interpolating the LMT of moonrise, moonset and the Moon's meridian passage for longitude. It is entered with longitude and with the difference between the times for the given date and for the preceding date (in east longitudes) or following date (in west longitudes). The correction is normally *added* for west longitudes and *subtracted* for east longitudes, but if, as occasionally happens, the times become earlier each day instead of later, the signs of the corrections must be reversed.

INDEX TO SELECTED STARS, 2015

Name	No	Mag	SHA	Dec	No	Name	Mag	SHA	Dec
			°	°				°	°
Acamar	7	3·2	315	S 40	1	Alpheratz	2·1	358	N 29
Achernar	5	0·5	335	S 57	2	Ankaa	2·4	353	S 42
Acrux	30	1·3	173	S 63	3	Schedar	2·2	350	N 57
Adhara	19	1·5	255	S 29	4	Diphda	2·0	349	S 18
Aldebaran	10	0·9	291	N 17	5	Achernar	0·5	335	S 57
Alioth	32	1·8	166	N 56	6	Hamal	2·0	328	N 24
Alkaid	34	1·9	153	N 49	7	Acamar	3·2	315	S 40
Al Na'ir	55	1·7	28	S 47	8	Menkar	2·5	314	N 4
Alnilam	15	1·7	276	S 1	9	Mirfak	1·8	309	N 50
Alphard	25	2·0	218	S 9	10	Aldebaran	0·9	291	N 17
Alphecca	41	2·2	126	N 27	11	Rigel	0·1	281	S 8
Alpheratz	1	2·1	358	N 29	12	Capella	0·1	281	N 46
Altair	51	0·8	62	N 9	13	Bellatrix	1·6	279	N 6
Ankaa	2	2·4	353	S 42	14	Elnath	1·7	278	N 29
Antares	42	1·0	112	S 26	15	Alnilam	1·7	276	S 1
Arcturus	37	0·0	146	N 19	16	Betelgeuse	Var.*	271	N 7
Atria	43	1·9	107	S 69	17	Canopus	−0·7	264	S 53
Avior	22	1·9	234	S 60	18	Sirius	−1·5	259	S 17
Bellatrix	13	1·6	279	N 6	19	Adhara	1·5	255	S 29
Betelgeuse	16	Var.*	271	N 7	20	Procyon	0·4	245	N 5
Canopus	17	−0·7	264	S 53	21	Pollux	1·1	243	N 28
Capella	12	0·1	281	N 46	22	Avior	1·9	234	S 60
Deneb	53	1·3	50	N 45	23	Suhail	2·2	223	S 43
Denebola	28	2·1	183	N 14	24	Miaplacidus	1·7	222	S 70
Diphda	4	2·0	349	S 18	25	Alphard	2·0	218	S 9
Dubhe	27	1·8	194	N 62	26	Regulus	1·4	208	N 12
Elnath	14	1·7	278	N 29	27	Dubhe	1·8	194	N 62
Eltanin	47	2·2	91	N 51	28	Denebola	2·1	183	N 14
Enif	54	2·4	34	N 10	29	Gienah	2·6	176	S 18
Fomalhaut	56	1·2	15	S 30	30	Acrux	1·3	173	S 63
Gacrux	31	1·6	172	S 57	31	Gacrux	1·6	172	S 57
Gienah	29	2·6	176	S 18	32	Alioth	1·8	166	N 56
Hadar	35	0·6	149	S 60	33	Spica	1·0	158	S 11
Hamal	6	2·0	328	N 24	34	Alkaid	1·9	153	N 49
Kaus Australis	48	1·9	84	S 34	35	Hadar	0·6	149	S 60
Kochab	40	2·1	137	N 74	36	Menkent	2·1	148	S 36
Markab	57	2·5	14	N 15	37	Arcturus	0·0	146	N 19
Menkar	8	2·5	314	N 4	38	Rigil Kentaurus	−0·3	140	S 61
Menkent	36	2·1	148	S 36	39	Zubenelgenubi	2·8	137	S 16
Miaplacidus	24	1·7	222	S 70	40	Kochab	2·1	137	N 74
Mirfak	9	1·8	309	N 50	41	Alphecca	2·2	126	N 27
Nunki	50	2·0	76	S 26	42	Antares	1·0	112	S 26
Peacock	52	1·9	53	S 57	43	Atria	1·9	107	S 69
Pollux	21	1·1	243	N 28	44	Sabik	2·4	102	S 16
Procyon	20	0·4	245	N 5	45	Shaula	1·6	96	S 37
Rasalhague	46	2·1	96	N 13	46	Rasalhague	2·1	96	N 13
Regulus	26	1·4	208	N 12	47	Eltanin	2·2	91	N 51
Rigel	11	0·1	281	S 8	48	Kaus Australis	1·9	84	S 34
Rigil Kentaurus	38	−0·3	140	S 61	49	Vega	0·0	81	N 39
Sabik	44	2·4	102	S 16	50	Nunki	2·0	76	S 26
Schedar	3	2·2	350	N 57	51	Altair	0·8	62	N 9
Shaula	45	1·6	96	S 37	52	Peacock	1·9	53	S 57
Sirius	18	−1·5	259	S 17	53	Deneb	1·3	50	N 45
Spica	33	1·0	158	S 11	54	Enif	2·4	34	N 10
Suhail	23	2·2	223	S 43	55	Al Na'ir	1·7	28	S 47
Vega	49	0·0	81	N 39	56	Fomalhaut	1·2	15	S 30
Zubenelgenubi	39	2·8	137	S 16	57	Markab	2·5	14	N 15

*0·1 — 1·2

xxxiii

ALTITUDE CORRECTION TABLES 0°–35°— MOON

App. Alt.	0°–4° Corrⁿ	5°–9° Corrⁿ	10°–14° Corrⁿ	15°–19° Corrⁿ	20°–24° Corrⁿ	25°–29° Corrⁿ	30°–34° Corrⁿ	App. Alt.
00	0° 34·5	5° 58·2	10° 62·1	15° 62·8	20° 62·2	25° 60·8	30° 58·9	00
10	36·5	58·5	62·2	62·8	62·2	60·8	58·8	10
20	38·3	58·7	62·2	62·8	62·1	60·7	58·8	20
30	40·0	58·9	62·3	62·8	62·1	60·7	58·7	30
40	41·5	59·1	62·3	62·8	62·0	60·6	58·6	40
50	42·9	59·3	62·4	62·7	62·0	60·6	58·5	50
00	1° 44·2	6° 59·5	11° 62·4	16° 62·7	21° 62·0	26° 60·5	31° 58·5	00
10	45·4	59·7	62·4	62·7	61·9	60·4	58·4	10
20	46·5	59·9	62·5	62·7	61·9	60·4	58·3	20
30	47·5	60·0	62·5	62·7	61·9	60·3	58·2	30
40	48·4	60·2	62·5	62·7	61·8	60·3	58·2	40
50	49·3	60·3	62·6	62·7	61·8	60·2	58·1	50
00	2° 50·1	7° 60·5	12° 62·6	17° 62·7	22° 61·7	27° 60·1	32° 58·0	00
10	50·8	60·6	62·6	62·6	61·7	60·1	57·9	10
20	51·5	60·7	62·6	62·6	61·6	60·0	57·8	20
30	52·2	60·9	62·7	62·6	61·6	59·9	57·8	30
40	52·8	61·0	62·7	62·6	61·6	59·9	57·7	40
50	53·4	61·1	62·7	62·6	61·5	59·8	57·6	50
00	3° 53·9	8° 61·2	13° 62·7	18° 62·5	23° 61·5	28° 59·7	33° 57·5	00
10	54·4	61·3	62·7	62·5	61·4	59·7	57·4	10
20	54·9	61·4	62·7	62·5	61·4	59·6	57·4	20
30	55·3	61·5	62·8	62·5	61·3	59·5	57·3	30
40	55·7	61·6	62·8	62·4	61·3	59·5	57·2	40
50	56·1	61·6	62·8	62·4	61·2	59·4	57·1	50
00	4° 56·4	9° 61·7	14° 62·8	19° 62·4	24° 61·2	29° 59·3	34° 57·0	00
10	56·8	61·8	62·8	62·4	61·1	59·3	56·9	10
20	57·1	61·9	62·8	62·3	61·1	59·2	56·9	20
30	57·4	61·9	62·8	62·3	61·0	59·1	56·8	30
40	57·7	62·0	62·8	62·3	61·0	59·1	56·7	40
50	58·0	62·1	62·8	62·2	60·9	59·0	56·6	50

HP	L U	L U	L U	L U	L U	L U	L U	HP
54·0	0·3 0·9	0·3 0·9	0·4 1·0	0·5 1·1	0·6 1·2	0·7 1·3	0·9 1·5	54·0
54·3	0·7 1·1	0·7 1·2	0·8 1·2	0·8 1·3	0·9 1·4	1·1 1·5	1·2 1·7	54·3
54·6	1·1 1·4	1·1 1·4	1·1 1·4	1·2 1·5	1·3 1·6	1·4 1·7	1·5 1·8	54·6
54·9	1·4 1·6	1·5 1·6	1·5 1·6	1·6 1·7	1·6 1·8	1·8 1·9	1·9 2·0	54·9
55·2	1·8 1·8	1·8 1·8	1·9 1·8	1·9 1·9	2·0 2·0	2·1 2·1	2·2 2·2	55·2
55·5	2·2 2·0	2·2 2·0	2·3 2·1	2·3 2·1	2·4 2·2	2·4 2·3	2·5 2·4	55·5
55·8	2·6 2·2	2·6 2·2	2·6 2·3	2·7 2·3	2·7 2·4	2·8 2·4	2·9 2·5	55·8
56·1	3·0 2·4	3·0 2·5	3·0 2·5	3·0 2·5	3·1 2·6	3·1 2·6	3·2 2·7	56·1
56·4	3·3 2·7	3·4 2·7	3·4 2·7	3·4 2·7	3·4 2·8	3·5 2·8	3·5 2·9	56·4
56·7	3·7 2·9	3·7 2·9	3·8 2·9	3·8 2·9	3·8 3·0	3·8 3·0	3·9 3·0	56·7
57·0	4·1 3·1	4·1 3·1	4·1 3·1	4·1 3·1	4·2 3·2	4·2 3·2	4·2 3·2	57·0
57·3	4·5 3·3	4·5 3·3	4·5 3·3	4·5 3·3	4·5 3·3	4·5 3·4	4·6 3·4	57·3
57·6	4·9 3·5	4·9 3·5	4·9 3·5	4·9 3·5	4·9 3·5	4·9 3·5	4·9 3·6	57·6
57·9	5·3 3·8	5·3 3·8	5·2 3·8	5·2 3·7	5·2 3·7	5·2 3·7	5·2 3·7	57·9
58·2	5·6 4·0	5·6 4·0	5·6 4·0	5·6 4·0	5·6 3·9	5·6 3·9	5·6 3·9	58·2
58·5	6·0 4·2	6·0 4·2	6·0 4·2	6·0 4·2	6·0 4·1	5·9 4·1	5·9 4·1	58·5
58·8	6·4 4·4	6·4 4·4	6·4 4·4	6·3 4·4	6·3 4·3	6·3 4·3	6·2 4·2	58·8
59·1	6·8 4·6	6·8 4·6	6·7 4·6	6·7 4·6	6·7 4·5	6·6 4·5	6·6 4·4	59·1
59·4	7·2 4·8	7·1 4·8	7·1 4·8	7·1 4·8	7·0 4·7	7·0 4·7	6·9 4·6	59·4
59·7	7·5 5·1	7·5 5·0	7·5 5·0	7·5 5·0	7·4 4·9	7·3 4·8	7·2 4·8	59·7
60·0	7·9 5·3	7·9 5·3	7·9 5·2	7·8 5·2	7·8 5·1	7·7 5·0	7·6 4·9	60·0
60·3	8·3 5·5	8·3 5·5	8·2 5·4	8·2 5·4	8·1 5·3	8·0 5·2	7·9 5·1	60·3
60·6	8·7 5·7	8·7 5·7	8·6 5·7	8·6 5·6	8·5 5·5	8·4 5·4	8·2 5·3	60·6
60·9	9·1 5·9	9·0 5·9	9·0 5·9	8·9 5·8	8·8 5·7	8·7 5·6	8·6 5·4	60·9
61·2	9·5 6·2	9·4 6·1	9·4 6·1	9·3 6·0	9·2 5·9	9·1 5·8	8·9 5·6	61·2
61·5	9·8 6·4	9·8 6·3	9·7 6·3	9·7 6·2	9·5 6·1	9·4 5·9	9·2 5·8	61·5

DIP

Ht. of Eye (m)	Corrⁿ	Ht. of Eye (ft.)	Ht. of Eye (m)	Corrⁿ	Ht. of Eye (ft.)
2·4	−2·8	8·0	9·5	−5·5	31·5
2·6	−2·9	8·6	9·9	−5·6	32·7
2·8	−3·0	9·2	10·3	−5·7	33·9
3·0	−3·1	9·8	10·6	−5·8	35·1
3·2	−3·2	10·5	11·0	−5·9	36·3
3·4	−3·3	11·2	11·4	−6·0	37·6
3·6	−3·4	11·9	11·8	−6·1	38·9
3·8	−3·5	12·6	12·2	−6·2	40·1
4·0	−3·6	13·3	12·6	−6·3	41·5
4·3	−3·7	14·1	13·0	−6·4	42·8
4·5	−3·8	14·9	13·4	−6·5	44·2
4·7	−3·9	15·7	13·8	−6·6	45·5
5·0	−4·0	16·5	14·2	−6·7	46·9
5·2	−4·1	17·4	14·7	−6·8	48·4
5·5	−4·2	18·3	15·1	−6·9	49·8
5·8	−4·3	19·1	15·5	−7·0	51·3
6·1	−4·4	20·1	16·0	−7·1	52·8
6·3	−4·5	21·0	16·5	−7·2	54·3
6·6	−4·6	22·0	16·9	−7·3	55·8
6·9	−4·7	22·9	17·4	−7·4	57·4
7·2	−4·8	23·9	17·9	−7·5	58·9
7·5	−4·9	24·9	18·4	−7·6	60·5
7·9	−5·0	26·0	18·8	−7·7	62·1
8·2	−5·1	27·1	19·3	−7·8	63·8
8·5	−5·2	28·1	19·8	−7·9	65·4
8·8	−5·3	29·2	20·4	−8·0	67·1
9·2	−5·4	30·4	20·9	−8·1	68·8
9·5		31·5	21·4		70·5

MOON CORRECTION TABLE

The correction is in two parts; the first correction is taken from the upper part of the table with argument apparent altitude, and the second from the lower part, with argument HP, in the same column as that from which the first correction was taken. Separate corrections are given in the lower part for lower (L) and upper(U) limbs. All corrections are to be **added** to apparent altitude, *but 30′ is to be subtracted from the altitude of the upper limb.*

For corrections for pressure and temperature see page A4.

For bubble sextant observations ignore dip, take the mean of upper and lower limb corrections and subtract 15′ from the altitude.

App. Alt. = Apparent altitude = Sextant altitude corrected for index error and dip.

ALTITUDE CORRECTION TABLES 35°–90°— MOON

App. Alt.	35°–39° Corrⁿ	40°–44° Corrⁿ	45°–49° Corrⁿ	50°–54° Corrⁿ	55°–59° Corrⁿ	60°–64° Corrⁿ	65°–69° Corrⁿ	70°–74° Corrⁿ	75°–79° Corrⁿ	80°–84° Corrⁿ	85°–89° Corrⁿ	App. Alt.
00	35 56·5	40 53·7	45 50·5	50 46·9	55 43·1	60 38·9	65 34·6	70 30·0	75 25·3	80 20·5	85 15·6	00
10	56·4	53·6	50·4	46·8	42·9	38·8	34·4	29·9	25·2	20·4	15·5	10
20	56·3	53·5	50·2	46·7	42·8	38·7	34·3	29·7	25·0	20·2	15·3	20
30	56·2	53·4	50·1	46·5	42·7	38·5	34·1	29·6	24·9	20·0	15·1	30
40	56·2	53·3	50·0	46·4	42·5	38·4	34·0	29·4	24·7	19·9	15·0	40
50	56·1	53·2	49·9	46·3	42·4	38·2	33·8	29·3	24·5	19·7	14·8	50
00	36 56·0	41 53·1	46 49·8	51 46·2	56 42·3	61 38·1	66 33·7	71 29·1	76 24·4	81 19·6	86 14·6	00
10	55·9	53·0	49·7	46·0	42·1	37·9	33·5	29·0	24·2	19·4	14·5	10
20	55·8	52·9	49·5	45·9	42·0	37·8	33·4	28·8	24·1	19·2	14·3	20
30	55·7	52·8	49·4	45·8	41·9	37·7	33·2	28·7	23·9	19·1	14·2	30
40	55·6	52·6	49·3	45·7	41·7	37·5	33·1	28·5	23·8	18·9	14·0	40
50	55·5	52·5	49·2	45·5	41·6	37·4	32·9	28·3	23·6	18·7	13·8	50
00	37 55·4	42 52·4	47 49·1	52 45·4	57 41·4	62 37·2	67 32·8	72 28·2	77 23·4	82 18·6	87 13·7	00
10	55·3	52·3	49·0	45·3	41·3	37·1	32·6	28·0	23·3	18·4	13·5	10
20	55·2	52·2	48·8	45·2	41·2	36·9	32·5	27·9	23·1	18·2	13·3	20
30	55·1	52·1	48·7	45·0	41·0	36·8	32·3	27·7	22·9	18·1	13·2	30
40	55·0	52·0	48·6	44·9	40·9	36·6	32·2	27·6	22·8	17·9	13·0	40
50	55·0	51·9	48·5	44·8	40·8	36·5	32·0	27·4	22·6	17·8	12·8	50
00	38 54·9	43 51·8	48 48·4	53 44·6	58 40·6	63 36·4	68 31·9	73 27·2	78 22·5	83 17·6	88 12·7	00
10	54·8	51·7	48·3	44·5	40·5	36·2	31·7	27·1	22·3	17·4	12·5	10
20	54·7	51·6	48·1	44·4	40·3	36·1	31·6	26·9	22·1	17·3	12·3	20
30	54·6	51·5	48·0	44·2	40·2	35·9	31·4	26·8	22·0	17·1	12·2	30
40	54·5	51·4	47·9	44·1	40·1	35·8	31·3	26·6	21·8	16·9	12·0	40
50	54·4	51·2	47·8	44·0	39·9	35·6	31·1	26·5	21·7	16·8	11·8	50
00	39 54·3	44 51·1	49 47·7	54 43·9	59 39·8	64 35·5	69 31·0	74 26·3	79 21·5	84 16·6	89 11·7	00
10	54·2	51·0	47·5	43·7	39·6	35·3	30·8	26·1	21·3	16·4	11·5	10
20	54·1	50·9	47·4	43·6	39·5	35·2	30·7	26·0	21·2	16·3	11·4	20
30	54·0	50·8	47·3	43·5	39·4	35·0	30·5	25·8	21·0	16·1	11·2	30
40	53·9	50·7	47·2	43·3	39·2	34·9	30·4	25·7	20·9	16·0	11·0	40
50	53·8	50·6	47·0	43·2	39·1	34·7	30·2	25·5	20·7	15·8	10·9	50

HP	L	U	L	U	L	U	L	U	L	U	L	U	L	U	L	U	L	U	L	U	L	U	HP
54·0	1·1	1·7	1·3	1·9	1·5	2·1	1·7	2·4	2·0	2·6	2·3	2·9	2·6	3·2	2·9	3·5	3·2	3·8	3·5	4·1	3·8	4·5	54·0
54·3	1·4	1·8	1·6	2·0	1·8	2·2	2·0	2·5	2·2	2·7	2·5	3·0	2·8	3·2	3·1	3·5	3·3	3·8	3·6	4·1	3·9	4·4	54·3
54·6	1·7	2·0	1·9	2·2	2·1	2·4	2·3	2·6	2·5	2·8	2·7	3·0	3·0	3·3	3·2	3·5	3·5	3·8	3·8	4·0	4·0	4·3	54·6
54·9	2·0	2·2	2·2	2·3	2·3	2·5	2·5	2·7	2·7	2·9	2·9	3·1	3·2	3·3	3·4	3·5	3·6	3·8	3·9	4·0	4·1	4·3	54·9
55·2	2·3	2·3	2·5	2·4	2·6	2·6	2·8	2·8	3·0	2·9	3·2	3·1	3·4	3·3	3·6	3·5	3·8	3·7	4·0	4·0	4·2	4·2	55·2
55·5	2·7	2·5	2·8	2·6	2·9	2·7	3·1	2·9	3·2	3·0	3·4	3·2	3·6	3·4	3·7	3·5	3·9	3·7	4·1	3·9	4·3	4·1	55·5
55·8	3·0	2·6	3·1	2·7	3·2	2·8	3·3	3·0	3·5	3·1	3·6	3·3	3·8	3·4	3·9	3·6	4·1	3·7	4·2	3·9	4·4	4·0	55·8
56·1	3·3	2·8	3·4	2·9	3·5	3·0	3·6	3·1	3·7	3·2	3·8	3·3	4·0	3·4	4·1	3·6	4·2	3·7	4·3	3·8	4·5	4·0	56·1
56·4	3·6	2·9	3·7	3·0	3·8	3·1	3·9	3·2	3·9	3·3	4·0	3·4	4·1	3·5	4·3	3·6	4·4	3·7	4·5	3·8	4·6	3·9	56·4
56·7	3·9	3·1	4·0	3·1	4·1	3·2	4·1	3·3	4·2	3·3	4·3	3·4	4·3	3·5	4·4	3·6	4·5	3·7	4·6	3·8	4·7	3·8	56·7
57·0	4·3	3·2	4·3	3·3	4·3	3·3	4·4	3·4	4·4	3·4	4·5	3·5	4·5	3·5	4·6	3·6	4·7	3·6	4·7	3·7	4·8	3·8	57·0
57·3	4·6	3·4	4·6	3·4	4·6	3·4	4·6	3·5	4·7	3·5	4·7	3·5	4·7	3·6	4·8	3·6	4·8	3·6	4·8	3·7	4·9	3·7	57·3
57·6	4·9	3·6	4·9	3·6	4·9	3·6	4·9	3·6	4·9	3·6	4·9	3·6	4·9	3·6	5·0	3·6	5·0	3·6	5·0	3·6	5·0	3·6	57·6
57·9	5·2	3·7	5·2	3·7	5·2	3·7	5·2	3·7	5·2	3·7	5·1	3·6	5·1	3·6	5·1	3·6	5·1	3·6	5·1	3·6	5·1	3·6	57·9
58·2	5·5	3·9	5·5	3·8	5·5	3·8	5·4	3·8	5·4	3·7	5·4	3·7	5·3	3·7	5·3	3·6	5·2	3·6	5·2	3·5	5·2	3·5	58·2
58·5	5·9	4·0	5·8	4·0	5·8	3·9	5·7	3·9	5·6	3·8	5·6	3·8	5·5	3·7	5·5	3·6	5·4	3·6	5·3	3·5	5·3	3·4	58·5
58·8	6·2	4·2	6·1	4·1	6·0	4·1	6·0	4·0	5·9	3·9	5·8	3·8	5·7	3·7	5·6	3·6	5·5	3·5	5·4	3·5	5·3	3·4	58·8
59·1	6·5	4·3	6·4	4·3	6·3	4·2	6·2	4·1	6·1	4·0	6·0	3·9	5·9	3·8	5·8	3·6	5·7	3·5	5·6	3·4	5·4	3·3	59·1
59·4	6·8	4·5	6·7	4·4	6·6	4·3	6·5	4·2	6·4	4·1	6·2	3·9	6·1	3·8	6·0	3·7	5·8	3·5	5·7	3·4	5·5	3·2	59·4
59·7	7·1	4·7	7·0	4·5	6·9	4·4	6·8	4·3	6·6	4·1	6·5	4·0	6·3	3·8	6·1	3·7	6·0	3·5	5·8	3·3	5·6	3·2	59·7
60·0	7·5	4·8	7·3	4·7	7·2	4·5	7·0	4·4	6·9	4·2	6·7	4·0	6·5	3·9	6·3	3·7	6·1	3·5	5·9	3·3	5·7	3·1	60·0
60·3	7·8	5·0	7·6	4·8	7·5	4·7	7·3	4·5	7·1	4·3	6·9	4·1	6·7	3·9	6·5	3·7	6·3	3·5	6·0	3·2	5·8	3·0	60·3
60·6	8·1	5·1	7·9	5·0	7·7	4·8	7·6	4·6	7·3	4·4	7·1	4·2	6·9	3·9	6·7	3·7	6·4	3·4	6·2	3·2	5·9	2·9	60·6
60·9	8·4	5·3	8·2	5·1	8·0	4·9	7·8	4·7	7·6	4·5	7·3	4·2	7·1	4·0	6·8	3·7	6·6	3·4	6·3	3·2	6·0	2·9	60·9
61·2	8·7	5·4	8·5	5·2	8·3	5·0	8·1	4·8	7·8	4·5	7·6	4·3	7·3	4·0	7·0	3·7	6·7	3·4	6·4	3·1	6·1	2·8	61·2
61·5	9·1	5·6	8·8	5·4	8·6	5·1	8·3	4·9	8·1	4·6	7·8	4·3	7·5	4·0	7·2	3·7	6·9	3·4	6·5	3·1	6·2	2·7	61·5

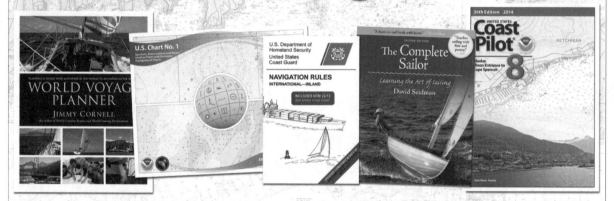

Celestial Navigation
at your fingertips

Complete package for celestial navigation on your iPad, iPhone, iPod Touch or Android device. Performs celestial sight reductions, calculates fixes, presents them visually, manages sights on multiple trips and assists in sight planning. Includes Almanac of the Sun, Moon, planets and stars for the years 1980-2099. All this for less than the price of the Nautical Almanac for a single year!

navimatics.com

bogerd martin
CHARTS & NAUTICAL SUPPLIES

➤ **Nautical charts:** We hold a large stock of nautical charts covering all areas of the World, corrected up to date and ready for dispatch to your vessel in any part of the world.

➤ **Nautical publications:** covering all aspects of navigation, maritime legislation and training.

➤ **Folio management services:** we offer tailor made solutions for your vessel's inventory of charts and publications, following up new editions and ensuring that you receive the new editions on time and according to your specific trading requirements.

➤ **Chart Track:** Integrated with a folio management programme on board the ship, Chart Track also enables the user to receive weekly Notices to Mariners and Tracings via e-mail.

➤ **Digital products:** ENC's , ARCS , digital publications all available from one source. New licences or additions to existing licences can be processed at very short notice. We offer an advisory service for the selection of ENC's , tailored to your vessel's particularly requirements.

➤ **Global distribution:** same -day dispatch to your vessel from our bases in Antwerp, Tianjin and Hong Kong to ensure swift delivery on time wherever your vessel may be going.

www.martin.be

ANTWERP:	TIANJIN:	HONG KONG:
Bogerd Martin	**Bogerd Martin**	**Bogerd Martin**
Antwerp	**Tianjin**	**Hong Kong**
Oude leeuwenrui 37	N°3. 6 Mi Xingang	2501B Ever Gain Plaza
2000 Antwerp - Belgium	Binhai New Area Tanggu	88 Container port road
Tel: + 32 (0)3 213 41 70	Tianjin 300456 - China	Kwai Chung -Hong Kong
Fax: +32 (0)3 232 61 67	Tel: +86 (22) 25762721	Tel: +852 3565 4410
sales@martin.be	charts-tj@martincn.com	sales@martinhk.com.hk

Nautical Books

Navigation, Seamanship

Towing & Salvage

Ship Design & Naval Architecture

Yachting & Leisure

Marine Engineering

Cargo Work

Log Books

Maritime Business, Maritime Law

Publications

Almanacs & Sight Reduction Tables

ITU - Call Signs, Ship Stations,
Coastal Stations, MMS

Shipping Guides - Atlas, Guide to Port Entry

IMO - Solas, Marpol, STCW95
(Wide Range of Stock)

Plotting Instrument

Binoculars & Magnifying Glasses

Sextants

Weather Instruments

Clocks & Chronometers

Global Positioning Systems (GPS)

Iridium Satellite Telephones

Brands

C. Plath

B. Cooke & Sons

Blundell Harley

ACR

Admiralty

Oceangrafix

Maui Jim

Reactor Watches

Davis Instruments

and more.

Software For:

Electronic Chart Viewers and ECDIS
Software/Hardware

Interactive Diesel Engine Training

Tide Tables & Tidal Current Tables

Electronic Charts

Port Guides

Vessel Traffic Services

Superyacht operations

Fleet Tracking

Nautical Surveys

Because of our strategic location, we are able to provide fast delivery of charts and other important products to ships calling on ports throughout Latin America and the Caribbean Basin.

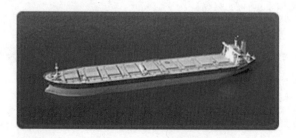